THE URANTIA BOOK

THE URANTIA BOOK

URANTIA FOUNDATION
533 WEST DIVERSEY PARKWAY
CHICAGO, ILLINOIS 60614
U.S.A.

THE URANTIA BOOK

2023

Text Identification Number: **UF-ENG-001-1955-21**

This is the 10th printing of the 4th (6.25" x 9.25") edition.

ISBN: 978-0-911560-51-0 (paperback)
ISBN: 978-0-911560-07-7 (hard cover)
ISBN: 978-0-911560-13-8 (gift edition—blue and white)
ISBN: 978-0-911560-18-3 (gift edition—Cambridge)

The Urantia Book was first published in 1955 by Urantia Foundation.

URANTIA FOUNDATION

533 W. Diversey Parkway / Chicago / Illinois / 60614 / United States

(773) 525-3319

urantia.org / urantia@urantia.org

The Standard Reference Text of *The Urantia Book* corrects the small number of errors found in the early editions of the book. All corrections were approved by Urantia Foundation's Board of Trustees.

Urantia Foundation offers no official interpretation of the teachings in *The Urantia Book.* Interpretation of the text is left to the individual reader.

The Concentric Circles Symbol identifies the inviolate text of *The Urantia Book*.
Urantia Foundation certifies that this edition is accurate and complete.

Library of Congress Catalog Card Information
The Urantia Book, Chicago, 1955 lxvi, 2097 pages
Catalog Card Number: BP605. U74 U7 1955
Library of Congress Classification Revised 1975

TRANSLATIONS OF *THE URANTIA BOOK*

Arabic— كِتاب يورانشيا
Bulgarian—*КНИГАТА УРАНТИЯ*
Czech—*Kniha Urantia*
Danish—*Urantia Bogen*
Dutch—*Het Urantia Boek*
Estonian—*Urantia raamat*
Finnish—*Urantia-kirja*
French—*Le Livre d'Urantia*
German – *Das Urantia Buch*
Greek—*Το Βιβλίο της Ουράντια*
Hebrew—הספר של אורנטיה
Hungarian—*Az Urantia könyv*
Indonesian—*Buku Urantia*
Italian—*Il Libro di Urantia*
Japanese—ウランティア ブック
Korean—유란시아 서
Lithuanian—*Urantijos Knyga*
Polish—*Księga Urantii*
Portuguese—*O Livro de Urântia*
Romanian—*Cartea Urantia*
Russian—*КНИГА УРАНТИИ*
Spanish—*El libro de Urantia*
Swedish—*Urantiaboken*
Turkish—*Urantia'nın Kitabı*

THE URANTIA BOOK AND TRANSLATIONS IN DIGITAL FORMAT

Readers: Amazon Kindle, Apple Book, Kobo eReader.
Tablets and Smartphones: downloads of *The Urantia Book* and translations for ipad and iphone at: **appstore.com/theurantiabook** and Android at: **urantia.org/urantia-book/buy**

SERVICES

Download a free audio recording of *The Urantia Book* at **urantia.org/audio**
Free online courses at: **ubis.urantia.org**

Find study groups of *The Urantia Book* at: **urantiastudygroup.org**

The Parts of the Book

PART I

THE CENTRAL AND SUPERUNIVERSES

Sponsored by a Uversa Corps of Superuniverse Personalities
acting by authority of the Orvonton
Ancients of Days

PART II

THE LOCAL UNIVERSE

Sponsored by a Nebadon Corps of Local Universe
Personalities acting by authority of
Gabriel of Salvington

PART III

THE HISTORY OF URANTIA

These papers were sponsored by a Corps of Local Universe
Personalities acting by authority of
Gabriel of Salvington

PART IV

THE LIFE AND TEACHINGS OF JESUS

This group of papers was sponsored by a commission of twelve
Urantia Midwayers acting under the supervision of
a Melchizedek revelatory director.
The basis of this narrative was supplied by a secondary
midwayer who was onetime assigned to the superhuman
watchcare of the Apostle Andrew.

The formatting and pagination of this printing corresponds to that of the first printing in 1955.

The numbers at the top of each page identify the location in the book of a given page, section, and paragraph. For example: 25:3.4 shows the reader that he or she is in Paper 25, in section 3, and at paragraph 4. Paragraph 4 is the fourth paragraph of the section and the first complete paragraph on the given page. The reader may count forward from that point to identify the numbers of the succeeding paragraphs in the section.

The Titles of the Papers

PART II. THE LOCAL UNIVERSE

PART III. THE HISTORY OF URANTIA

PART IV. THE LIFE AND TEACHINGS OF JESUS

Contents of the Book

PART III. THE HISTORY OF URANTIA

PART IV. THE LIFE AND TEACHINGS OF JESUS

FOREWORD

IN THE MINDS of the mortals of Urantia—that being the name of your world—there exists great confusion respecting the meaning of such terms as God, divinity, and deity. Human beings are still more confused and uncertain about the relationships of the divine personalities designated by these numerous appellations. Because of this conceptual poverty associated with so much ideational confusion, I have been directed to formulate this introductory statement in explanation of the meanings which should be attached to certain word symbols as they may be hereinafter used in those papers which the Orvonton corps of truth revealers have been authorized to translate into the English language of Urantia.

It is exceedingly difficult to present enlarged concepts and advanced truth, in our endeavor to expand cosmic consciousness and enhance spiritual perception, when we are restricted to the use of a circumscribed language of the realm. But our mandate admonishes us to make every effort to convey our meanings by using the word symbols of the English tongue. We have been instructed to introduce new terms only when the concept to be portrayed finds no terminology in English which can be employed to convey such a new concept partially or even with more or less distortion of meaning.

In the hope of facilitating comprehension and of preventing confusion on the part of every mortal who may peruse these papers, we deem it wise to present in this initial statement an outline of the meanings to be attached to numerous English words which are to be employed in designation of Deity and certain associated concepts of the things, meanings, and values of universal reality.

But in order to formulate this Foreword of definitions and limitations of terminology, it is necessary to anticipate the usage of these terms in the subsequent presentations. This Foreword is not, therefore, a finished statement within itself; it is only a definitive guide designed to assist those who shall read the accompanying papers dealing with Deity and the universe of universes which have been formulated by an Orvonton commission sent to Urantia for this purpose.

Your world, Urantia, is one of many similar inhabited planets which comprise the local universe of *Nebadon.* This universe, together with similar creations, makes up the superuniverse of *Orvonton,* from whose capital, Uversa, our commission hails. Orvonton is one of the seven evolutionary superuniverses of time and space which circle the never-beginning, never-ending creation of divine perfection—the central universe of *Havona.* At the heart of this eternal and central universe is the stationary Isle of Paradise, the geographic center of infinity and the dwelling place of the eternal God.

The seven evolving superuniverses in association with the central and divine universe, we commonly refer to as the *grand universe;* these are the now organized and inhabited creations. They are all a part of the *master universe,* which also embraces the uninhabited but mobilizing universes of outer space.

I. DEITY AND DIVINITY

The universe of universes presents phenomena of deity activities on diverse levels of cosmic realities, mind meanings, and spirit values, but all of these ministrations—personal or otherwise—are divinely co-ordinated.

DEITY is personalizable as God, is prepersonal and superpersonal in ways not altogether comprehensible by man. Deity is characterized by the quality of unity—actual or potential—on all supermaterial levels of reality; and this unifying quality is best comprehended by creatures as divinity.

Deity functions on personal, prepersonal, and superpersonal levels. Total Deity is functional on the following seven levels:

1. *Static*—self-contained and self-existent Deity.
2. *Potential*—self-willed and self-purposive Deity.
3. *Associative*—self-personalized and divinely fraternal Deity.
4. *Creative*—self-distributive and divinely revealed Deity.
5. *Evolutional*—self-expansive and creature-identified Deity.
6. *Supreme*—self-experiential and creature-Creator-unifying Deity. Deity functioning on the first creature-identificational level as time-space overcontrollers of the grand universe, sometimes designated the Supremacy of Deity.
7. *Ultimate*—self-projected and time-space-transcending Deity. Deity omnipotent, omniscient, and omnipresent. Deity functioning on the second level of unifying divinity expression as effective overcontrollers and absonite upholders of the master universe. As compared with the ministry of the Deities to the grand universe, this absonite function in the master universe is tantamount to universal overcontrol and supersustenance, sometimes called the Ultimacy of Deity.

The finite level of reality is characterized by creature life and time-space limitations. Finite realities may not have endings, but they always have beginnings—they are created. The Deity level of Supremacy may be conceived as a function in relation to finite existences.

The absonite level of reality is characterized by things and beings without beginnings or endings and by the transcendence of time and space. Absoniters are not created; they are eventuated—they simply are. The Deity level of Ultimacy connotes a function in relation to absonite realities. No matter in what part of the master universe, whenever time and space are transcended, such an absonite phenomenon is an act of the Ultimacy of Deity.

The absolute level is beginningless, endless, timeless, and spaceless. For example: On Paradise, time and space are nonexistent; the time-space status of Paradise is absolute. This level is Trinity attained, existentially, by the Paradise Deities, but this third level of unifying Deity expression is not fully unified experientially. Whenever, wherever, and however the absolute level of Deity functions, Paradise-absolute values and meanings are manifest.

Deity may be existential, as in the Eternal Son; experiential, as in the Supreme Being; associative, as in God the Sevenfold; undivided, as in the Paradise Trinity.

Deity is the source of all that which is divine. Deity is characteristically and invariably divine, but all that which is divine is not necessarily Deity, though it will be co-ordinated with Deity and will tend towards some phase of unity with Deity—spiritual, mindal, or personal.

DIVINITY is the characteristic, unifying, and co-ordinating quality of Deity.

Divinity is creature comprehensible as truth, beauty, and goodness; correlated in personality as love, mercy, and ministry; disclosed on impersonal levels as justice, power, and sovereignty.

Divinity may be perfect—complete—as on existential and creator levels of Paradise perfection; it may be imperfect, as on experiential and creature levels of time-space evolution; or it may be relative, neither perfect nor imperfect, as on certain Havona levels of existential-experiential relationships.

When we attempt to conceive of perfection in all phases and forms of relativity, we encounter seven conceivable types:

1. Absolute perfection in all aspects.

2. Absolute perfection in some phases and relative perfection in all other aspects.

3. Absolute, relative, and imperfect aspects in varied association.

4. Absolute perfection in some respects, imperfection in all others.

5. Absolute perfection in no direction, relative perfection in all manifestations.

6. Absolute perfection in no phase, relative in some, imperfect in others.

7. Absolute perfection in no attribute, imperfection in all.

II. GOD

Evolving mortal creatures experience an irresistible urge to symbolize their finite concepts of God. Man's consciousness of moral duty and his spiritual idealism represent a value level—an experiential reality—which is difficult of symbolization.

Cosmic consciousness implies the recognition of a First Cause, the one and only uncaused reality. God, the Universal Father, functions on three Deity-personality levels of subinfinite value and relative divinity expression:

1. *Prepersonal*—as in the ministry of the Father fragments, such as the Thought Adjusters.

2. *Personal*—as in the evolutionary experience of created and procreated beings.

3. *Superpersonal*—as in the eventuated existences of certain absonite and associated beings.

GOD is a word symbol designating all personalizations of Deity. The term requires a different definition on each personal level of Deity function and must be still further redefined within each of these levels, as this term may be used to designate the diverse co-ordinate and subordinate personalizations of Deity; for example: the Paradise Creator Sons—the local universe fathers.

The term God, as we make use of it, may be understood:

By designation—as God the Father.

By context—as when used in the discussion of some one deity level or association. When in doubt as to the exact interpretation of the word God, it would be advisable to refer it to the person of the Universal Father.

The term God always denotes *personality.* Deity may, or may not, refer to divinity personalities.

The word GOD is used, in these papers, with the following meanings:

1. *God the Father*—Creator, Controller, and Upholder. The Universal Father, the First Person of Deity.

2. *God the Son*—Co-ordinate Creator, Spirit Controller, and Spiritual Administrator. The Eternal Son, the Second Person of Deity.

3. *God the Spirit*—Conjoint Actor, Universal Integrator, and Mind Bestower. The Infinite Spirit, the Third Person of Deity.

4. *God the Supreme*—the actualizing or evolving God of time and space. Personal Deity associatively realizing the time-space experiential achievement of creature-Creator identity. The Supreme Being is personally experiencing the achievement of Deity unity as the evolving and experiential God of the evolutionary creatures of time and space.

5. *God the Sevenfold*—Deity personality anywhere actually functioning in time and space. The personal Paradise Deities and their creative associates functioning in and beyond the borders of the central universe and power-personalizing as the Supreme Being on the first creature level of unifying Deity revelation in time and space. This level, the grand universe, is the sphere of the time-space descension of Paradise personalities in reciprocal association with the time-space ascension of evolutionary creatures.

6. *God the Ultimate*—the eventuating God of supertime and transcended space. The second experiential level of unifying Deity manifestation. God the Ultimate implies the attained realization of the synthesized absonite-superpersonal, time-space-transcended, and eventuated-experiential values, co-ordinated on final creative levels of Deity reality.

7. *God the Absolute*—the experientializing God of transcended superpersonal values and divinity meanings, now existential as the *Deity Absolute.* This is the third level of unifying Deity expression and expansion. On this supercreative level, Deity experiences exhaustion of personalizable potential, encounters completion of divinity, and undergoes depletion of capacity for self-revelation to successive and progressive levels of other-personalization. Deity now encounters, impinges upon, and experiences identity with, the *Unqualified Absolute.*

III. THE FIRST SOURCE AND CENTER

Total, infinite reality is existential in seven phases and as seven co-ordinate Absolutes:

1. The First Source and Center.
2. The Second Source and Center.
3. The Third Source and Center.
4. The Isle of Paradise.
5. The Deity Absolute.
6. The Universal Absolute.
7. The Unqualified Absolute.

God, as the First Source and Center, is primal in relation to total reality—unqualifiedly. The First Source and Center is infinite as well as eternal and is therefore limited or conditioned only by volition.

God—the Universal Father—is the personality of the First Source and Center and as such maintains personal relations of infinite control over all co-ordinate and subordinate sources and centers. Such control is personal and infinite in *potential,* even though it may never actually function owing to the perfection of the function of such co-ordinate and subordinate sources and centers and personalities.

The First Source and Center is, therefore, primal in all domains: deified or undeified, personal or impersonal, actual or potential, finite or infinite. No thing or being, no relativity or finality, exists except in direct or indirect relation to, and dependence on, the primacy of the First Source and Center.

The First Source and Center is related to the universe as:

1. The gravity forces of the material universes are convergent in the gravity center of nether Paradise. That is just why the geographic location of his person is eternally fixed in absolute relation to the force-energy center of the nether or material plane of Paradise. But the absolute personality of Deity exists on the upper or spiritual plane of Paradise.

2. The mind forces are convergent in the Infinite Spirit; the differential and divergent cosmic mind in the Seven Master Spirits; the factualizing mind of the Supreme as a time-space experience in Majeston.

3. The universe spirit forces are convergent in the Eternal Son.

4. The unlimited capacity for deity action resides in the Deity Absolute.

5. The unlimited capacity for infinity response exists in the Unqualified Absolute.

6. The two Absolutes—Qualified and Unqualified—are co-ordinated and unified in and by the Universal Absolute.

7. The potential personality of an evolutionary moral being or of any other moral being is centered in the personality of the Universal Father.

REALITY, as comprehended by finite beings, is partial, relative, and shadowy. The maximum Deity reality fully comprehensible by evolutionary finite creatures is embraced within the Supreme Being. Nevertheless there are antecedent and eternal realities, superfinite realities, which are ancestral to this Supreme Deity of evolutionary time-space creatures. In attempting to portray the origin and nature of universal reality, we are forced to employ the technique of time-space reasoning in order to reach the level of the finite mind. Therefore

must many of the simultaneous events of eternity be presented as sequential transactions.

As a time-space creature would view the origin and differentiation of Reality, the eternal and infinite I AM achieved Deity liberation from the fetters of unqualified infinity through the exercise of inherent and eternal free will, and this divorcement from unqualified infinity produced the first *absolute divinity-tension.* This tension of infinity differential is resolved by the Universal Absolute, which functions to unify and co-ordinate the dynamic infinity of Total Deity and the static infinity of the Unqualified Absolute.

In this original transaction the theoretical I AM achieved the realization of personality by becoming the Eternal Father of the Original Son simultaneously with becoming the Eternal Source of the Isle of Paradise. Coexistent with the differentiation of the Son from the Father, and in the presence of Paradise, there appeared the person of the Infinite Spirit and the central universe of Havona. With the appearance of coexistent personal Deity, the Eternal Son and the Infinite Spirit, the Father escaped, as a personality, from otherwise inevitable diffusion throughout the potential of Total Deity. Thenceforth it is only in Trinity association with his two Deity equals that the Father fills all Deity potential, while increasingly experiential Deity is being actualized on the divinity levels of Supremacy, Ultimacy, and Absoluteness.

The concept of the I AM is a philosophic concession which we make to the time-bound, space-fettered, finite mind of man, to the impossibility of creature comprehension of eternity existences—nonbeginning, nonending realities and relationships. To the time-space creature, all things must have a beginning save only the ONE UNCAUSED—the primeval cause of causes. Therefore do we conceptualize this philosophic value-level as the I AM, at the same time instructing all creatures that the Eternal Son and the Infinite Spirit are coeternal with the I AM; in other words, that there never was a time when the I AM was not the *Father* of the Son and, with him, of the Spirit.

The Infinite is used to denote the fullness—the finality—implied by the primacy of the First Source and Center. The *theoretical* I AM is a creature-philosophic extension of the "infinity of will," but the Infinite is an *actual* value-level representing the eternity-intension of the true infinity of the absolute and unfettered free will of the Universal Father. This concept is sometimes designated the Father-Infinite.

Much of the confusion of all orders of beings, high and low, in their efforts to discover the Father-Infinite, is inherent in their limitations of comprehension. The absolute primacy of the Universal Father is not apparent on subinfinite levels; therefore is it probable that only the Eternal Son and the Infinite Spirit truly know the Father as an infinity; to all other personalities such a concept represents the exercise of faith.

IV. UNIVERSE REALITY

Reality differentially actualizes on diverse universe levels; reality originates in and by the infinite volition of the Universal Father and is realizable in three primal phases on many different levels of universe actualization:

1. *Undeified reality* ranges from the energy domains of the nonpersonal to the reality realms of the nonpersonalizable values of universal existence, even to the presence of the Unqualified Absolute.

2. *Deified reality* embraces all infinite Deity potentials ranging upward through all realms of personality from the lowest finite to the highest infinite, thus encompassing the domain of all that which is personalizable and more—even to the presence of the Deity Absolute.

3. *Interassociated reality.* Universe reality is supposedly either deified or undeified, but to subdeified beings there exists a vast domain of interassociated reality, potential and actualizing, which is difficult of identification. Much of this co-ordinate reality is embraced within the realms of the Universal Absolute.

This is the primal concept of original reality: The Father initiates and maintains Reality. The primal *differentials* of reality are the deified and the undeified—the Deity Absolute and the Unqualified Absolute. The primal *relationship* is the tension between them. This Father-initiated divinity-tension is perfectly resolved by, and eternalizes as, the Universal Absolute.

From the viewpoint of time and space, reality is further divisible as:

1. *Actual and Potential.* Realities existing in fullness of expression in contrast to those which carry undisclosed capacity for growth. The Eternal Son is an absolute spiritual actuality; mortal man is very largely an unrealized spiritual potentiality.

2. *Absolute and Subabsolute.* Absolute realities are eternity existences. Subabsolute realities are projected on two levels: Absonites—realities which are relative with respect to both time and eternity. Finites—realities which are projected in space and are actualized in time.

3. *Existential and Experiential.* Paradise Deity is existential, but the emerging Supreme and Ultimate are experiential.

4. *Personal and Impersonal.* Deity expansion, personality expression, and universe evolution are forever conditioned by the Father's freewill act which forever separated the mind-spirit-personal meanings and values of actuality and potentiality centering in the Eternal Son from those things which center and inhere in the eternal Isle of Paradise.

PARADISE is a term inclusive of the personal and the nonpersonal focal Absolutes of all phases of universe reality. Paradise, properly qualified, may connote any and all forms of reality, Deity, divinity, personality, and energy—spiritual, mindal, or material. All share Paradise as the place of origin, function, and destiny, as regards values, meanings, and factual existence.

The Isle of Paradise—Paradise not otherwise qualified—is the Absolute of the material-gravity control of the First Source and Center. Paradise is motionless, being the only stationary thing in the universe of universes. The Isle of Paradise has a universe location but no position in space. This eternal Isle is the actual source of the physical universes—past, present, and future. The nuclear Isle of Light is a Deity derivative, but it is hardly Deity; neither are the material creations a part of Deity; they are a consequence.

Paradise is not a creator; it is a unique controller of many universe activities, far more of a controller than a reactor. Throughout the material universes Paradise influences the reactions and conduct of all beings having to do with force, energy, and power, but Paradise itself is unique, exclusive, and isolated in the universes. Paradise represents nothing and nothing represents Paradise. It is neither a force nor a presence; it is just *Paradise.*

V. PERSONALITY REALITIES

Personality is a level of deified reality and ranges from the mortal and midwayer level of the higher mind activation of worship and wisdom up through the morontial and spiritual to the attainment of finality of personality status. That is the evolutionary ascent of mortal- and kindred-creature personality, but there are numerous other orders of universe personalities.

Reality is subject to universal expansion, personality to infinite diversification, and both are capable of well-nigh unlimited Deity co-ordination and eternal stabilization. While the metamorphic range of nonpersonal reality is definitely limited, we know of no limitations to the progressive evolution of personality realities.

On attained experiential levels all personality orders or values are associable and even cocreational. Even God and man can coexist in a unified personality, as is so exquisitely demonstrated in the present status of Christ Michael—Son of Man and Son of God.

All subinfinite orders and phases of personality are associative attainables and are potentially cocreational. The prepersonal, the personal, and the superpersonal are all linked together by mutual potential of co-ordinate attainment, progressive achievement, and cocreational capacity. But never does the impersonal directly transmute to the personal. Personality is never spontaneous; it is the gift of the Paradise Father. Personality is superimposed upon energy, and it is associated only with living energy systems; identity can be associated with nonliving energy patterns.

The Universal Father is the secret of the reality of personality, the bestowal of personality, and the destiny of personality. The Eternal Son is the absolute personality, the secret of spiritual energy, morontia spirits, and perfected spirits. The Conjoint Actor is the spirit-mind personality, the source of intelligence, reason, and the universal mind. But the Isle of Paradise is nonpersonal and extraspiritual, being the essence of the universal body, the source and center of physical matter, and the absolute master pattern of universal material reality.

These qualities of universal reality are manifest in Urantian human experience on the following levels:

1. *Body.* The material or physical organism of man. The living electrochemical mechanism of animal nature and origin.

2. *Mind.* The thinking, perceiving, and feeling mechanism of the human organism. The total conscious and unconscious experience. The intelligence associated with the emotional life reaching upward through worship and wisdom to the spirit level.

3. *Spirit.* The divine spirit that indwells the mind of man—the Thought Adjuster. This immortal spirit is prepersonal—not a personality, though destined to become a part of the personality of the surviving mortal creature.

4. *Soul.* The soul of man is an experiential acquirement. As a mortal creature chooses to "do the will of the Father in heaven," so the indwelling spirit becomes the father of a *new reality* in human experience. The mortal and material mind is the mother of this same emerging reality. The substance of this new reality is neither material nor spiritual—it is *morontial.* This is the emerging

and immortal soul which is destined to survive mortal death and begin the Paradise ascension.

Personality. The personality of mortal man is neither body, mind, nor spirit; neither is it the soul. Personality is the one changeless reality in an otherwise ever-changing creature experience; and it unifies all other associated factors of individuality. The personality is the unique bestowal which the Universal Father makes upon the living and associated energies of matter, mind, and spirit, and which survives with the survival of the morontial soul.

Morontia is a term designating a vast level intervening between the material and the spiritual. It may designate personal or impersonal realities, living or nonliving energies. The warp of morontia is spiritual; its woof is physical.

VI. ENERGY AND PATTERN

Any and all things responding to the personality circuit of the Father, we call personal. Any and all things responding to the spirit circuit of the Son, we call spirit. Any and all that responds to the mind circuit of the Conjoint Actor, we call mind, mind as an attribute of the Infinite Spirit—mind in all its phases. Any and all that responds to the material-gravity circuit centering in nether Paradise, we call matter—energy-matter in all its metamorphic states.

ENERGY we use as an all-inclusive term applied to spiritual, mindal, and material realms. *Force* is also thus broadly used. *Power* is ordinarily limited to the designation of the electronic level of material or linear-gravity-responsive matter in the grand universe. Power is also employed to designate sovereignty. We cannot follow your generally accepted definitions of force, energy, and power. There is such paucity of language that we must assign multiple meanings to these terms.

Physical energy is a term denoting all phases and forms of phenomenal motion, action, and potential.

In discussing physical-energy manifestations, we generally use the terms cosmic force, emergent energy, and universe power. These are often employed as follows:

1. *Cosmic force* embraces all energies deriving from the Unqualified Absolute but which are as yet unresponsive to Paradise gravity.

2. *Emergent energy* embraces those energies which are responsive to Paradise gravity but are as yet unresponsive to local or linear gravity. This is the pre-electronic level of energy-matter.

3. *Universe power* includes all forms of energy which, while still responding to Paradise gravity, are directly responsive to linear gravity. This is the electronic level of energy-matter and all subsequent evolutions thereof.

Mind is a phenomenon connoting the presence-activity of *living ministry* in addition to varied energy systems; and this is true on all levels of intelligence. In personality, mind ever intervenes between spirit and matter; therefore is the universe illuminated by three kinds of light: material light, intellectual insight, and spirit luminosity.

Light—spirit luminosity—is a word symbol, a figure of speech, which connotes the personality manifestation characteristic of spirit beings of diverse orders. This luminous emanation is in no respect related either to intellectual insight or to physical-light manifestations.

PATTERN can be projected as material, spiritual, or mindal, or any combination of these energies. It can pervade personalities, identities, entities, or nonliving matter. But pattern is pattern and remains pattern; only *copies* are multiplied.

Pattern may configure energy, but it does not control it. Gravity is the sole control of energy-matter. Neither space nor pattern are gravity responsive, but there is no relationship between space and pattern; space is neither pattern nor potential pattern. Pattern is a configuration of reality which has already paid all gravity debt; the *reality* of any pattern consists of its energies, its mind, spirit, or material components.

In contrast to the aspect of the *total,* pattern discloses the *individual* aspect of energy and of personality. Personality or identity forms are patterns resultant from energy (physical, spiritual, or mindal) but are not inherent therein. That quality of energy or of personality by virtue of which pattern is caused to appear may be attributed to God—Deity—to Paradise force endowment, to the coexistence of personality and power.

Pattern is a master design from which copies are made. Eternal Paradise is the absolute of patterns; the Eternal Son is the pattern personality; the Universal Father is the direct ancestor-source of both. But Paradise does not bestow pattern, and the Son cannot bestow personality.

VII. THE SUPREME BEING

The Deity mechanism of the master universe is twofold as concerns eternity relationships. God the Father, God the Son, and God the Spirit are eternal—are existential beings—while God the Supreme, God the Ultimate, and God the Absolute are *actualizing* Deity personalities of the post-Havona epochs in the time-space and the time-space-transcended spheres of master universe evolutionary expansion. These actualizing Deity personalities are future eternals from the time when, and as, they power-personalize in the growing universes by the technique of the experiential actualization of the associative-creative potentials of the eternal Paradise Deities.

Deity is, therefore, dual in presence:

1. *Existential*—beings of eternal existence, past, present, and future.
2. *Experiential*—beings actualizing in the post-Havona present but of unending existence throughout all future eternity.

The Father, Son, and Spirit are existential—existential in actuality (though all potentials are supposedly experiential). The Supreme and the Ultimate are wholly experiential. The Deity Absolute is experiential in actualization but existential in potentiality. The essence of Deity is eternal, but only the three original persons of Deity are unqualifiedly eternal. All other Deity personalities have an origin, but they are eternal in destiny.

Having achieved existential Deity expression of himself in the Son and the Spirit, the Father is now achieving experiential expression on hitherto impersonal and unrevealed deity levels as God the Supreme, God the Ultimate, and God the Absolute; but these experiential Deities are not now fully existent; they are in process of actualization.

God the Supreme in Havona is the personal spirit reflection of the triune Paradise Deity. This associative Deity relationship is now creatively expanding outward in God the Sevenfold and is synthesizing in the experiential power of the Almighty Supreme in the grand universe. Paradise Deity, existential as three persons, is thus experientially evolving in two phases of Supremacy, while these dual phases are power-personality unifying as one Lord, the Supreme Being.

The Universal Father achieves freewill liberation from the bonds of infinity and the fetters of eternity by the technique of trinitization, threefold Deity personalization. The Supreme Being is even now evolving as a subeternal personality unification of the sevenfold manifestation of Deity in the time-space segments of the grand universe.

The Supreme Being is not a direct creator, except that he is the father of Majeston, but he is a synthetic co-ordinator of all creature-Creator universe activities. The Supreme Being, now actualizing in the evolutionary universes, is the Deity correlator and synthesizer of time-space divinity, of triune Paradise Deity in experiential association with the Supreme Creators of time and space. When finally actualized, this evolutionary Deity will constitute the eternal fusion of the finite and the infinite—the everlasting and indissoluble union of experiential power and spirit personality.

All time-space finite reality, under the directive urge of the evolving Supreme Being, is engaged in an ever-ascending mobilization and perfecting unification (power-personality synthesis) of all phases and values of finite reality, in association with varied phases of Paradise reality, to the end and for the purpose of subsequently embarking upon the attempt to reach absonite levels of supercreature attainment.

VIII. GOD THE SEVENFOLD

To atone for finity of status and to compensate for creature limitations of concept, the Universal Father has established the evolutionary creature's sevenfold approach to Deity:

1. The Paradise Creator Sons.
2. The Ancients of Days.
3. The Seven Master Spirits.
4. The Supreme Being.
5. God the Spirit.
6. God the Son.
7. God the Father.

This sevenfold Deity personalization in time and space and to the seven superuniverses enables mortal man to attain the presence of God, who is spirit. This sevenfold Deity, to finite time-space creatures sometime power-personalizing in the Supreme Being, is the functional Deity of the mortal evolutionary creatures of the Paradise-ascension career. Such an experiential discovery-career of the realization of God begins with the recognition of the divinity of the Creator

Son of the local universe and ascends through the superuniverse Ancients of Days and by way of the person of one of the Seven Master Spirits to the attainment of the discovery and recognition of the divine personality of the Universal Father on Paradise.

The grand universe is the threefold Deity domain of the Trinity of Supremacy, God the Sevenfold, and the Supreme Being. God the Supreme is potential in the Paradise Trinity, from whom he derives his personality and spirit attributes; but he is now actualizing in the Creator Sons, Ancients of Days, and the Master Spirits, from whom he derives his power as Almighty to the superuniverses of time and space. This power manifestation of the immediate God of evolutionary creatures actually time-space evolves concomitantly with them. The Almighty Supreme, evolving on the value-level of nonpersonal activities, and the spirit person of God the Supreme are *one reality*—the Supreme Being.

The Creator Sons in the Deity association of God the Sevenfold provide the mechanism whereby the mortal becomes immortal and the finite attains the embrace of the infinite. The Supreme Being provides the technique for the power-personality mobilization, the divine synthesis, of *all* these manifold transactions, thus enabling the finite to attain the absonite and, through other possible future actualizations, to attempt the attainment of the Ultimate. The Creator Sons and their associated Divine Ministers are participants in this supreme mobilization, but the Ancients of Days and the Seven Master Spirits are probably eternally fixed as permanent administrators in the grand universe.

The function of God the Sevenfold dates from the organization of the seven superuniverses, and it will probably expand in connection with the future evolution of the creations of outer space. The organization of these future universes of the primary, secondary, tertiary, and quartan space levels of progressive evolution will undoubtedly witness the inauguration of the transcendent and absonite approach to Deity.

IX. GOD THE ULTIMATE

Just as the Supreme Being progressively evolves from the antecedent divinity endowment of the encompassed grand universe potential of energy and personality, so does God the Ultimate eventuate from the potentials of divinity residing in the transcended time-space domains of the master universe. The actualization of Ultimate Deity signalizes absonite unification of the first experiential Trinity and signifies unifying Deity expansion on the second level of creative self-realization. This constitutes the personality-power equivalent of the universe experiential-Deity actualization of Paradise absonite realities on the eventuating levels of transcended time-space values. The completion of such an experiential unfoldment is designed to afford ultimate service-destiny for all time-space creatures who have attained absonite levels through the completed realization of the Supreme Being and by the ministry of God the Sevenfold.

God the Ultimate is designative of personal Deity functioning on the divinity levels of the absonite and on the universe spheres of supertime and transcended space. The Ultimate is a supersupreme eventuation of Deity. The Supreme is the Trinity unification comprehended by finite beings; the Ultimate is the unification of the Paradise Trinity comprehended by absonite beings.

The Universal Father, through the mechanism of evolutionary Deity, is actually engaged in the stupendous and amazing *act* of personality focalization and power mobilization, on their respective universe meaning-levels, of the divine reality values of the finite, the absonite, and even of the absolute.

The first three and past-eternal Deities of Paradise—the Universal Father, the Eternal Son, and the Infinite Spirit—are, in the eternal future, to be personality-complemented by the experiential actualization of associate evolutionary Deities—God the Supreme, God the Ultimate, and possibly God the Absolute.

God the Supreme and God the Ultimate, now evolving in the experiential universes, are not existential—not past eternals, only future eternals, time-space-conditioned and transcendental-conditioned eternals. They are Deities of supreme, ultimate, and possibly supreme-ultimate endowments, but they have experienced historic universe origins. They will never have an end, but they do have personality beginnings. They are indeed actualizations of eternal and infinite Deity potentials, but they themselves are neither unqualifiedly eternal nor infinite.

X. GOD THE ABSOLUTE

There are many features of the eternal reality of the *Deity Absolute* which cannot be fully explained to the time-space finite mind, but the actualization of *God the Absolute* would be in consequence of the unification of the second experiential Trinity, the Absolute Trinity. This would constitute the experiential realization of absolute divinity, the unification of absolute meanings on absolute levels; but we are not certain regarding the encompassment of all absolute values since we have at no time been informed that the Qualified Absolute is the equivalent of the Infinite. Superultimate destinies are involved in absolute meanings and infinite spirituality, and without both of these unachieved realities we cannot establish absolute values.

God the Absolute is the realization-attainment goal of all superabsonite beings, but the power and personality potential of the Deity Absolute transcends our concept, and we hesitate to discuss those realities which are so far removed from experiential actualization.

XI. THE THREE ABSOLUTES

When the combined thought of the Universal Father and the Eternal Son, functioning in the God of Action, constituted the creation of the divine and central universe, the Father followed the expression of his thought into the word of his Son and the act of their Conjoint Executive by differentiating his Havona presence from the potentials of infinity. And these undisclosed infinity potentials remain space concealed in the Unqualified Absolute and divinely enshrouded in the Deity Absolute, while these two become one in the functioning of the Universal Absolute, the unrevealed infinity-unity of the Paradise Father.

Both potency of cosmic force and potency of spirit force are in process of progressive revelation-realization as the enrichment of all reality is effected by experiential growth and through the correlation of the experiential with the existential by the Universal Absolute. By virtue of the equipoising presence of the Universal Absolute, the First Source and Center realizes extension of experiential power, enjoys identification with his evolutionary creatures, and achieves expansion of experiential Deity on the levels of Supremacy, Ultimacy, and Absoluteness.

When it is not possible fully to distinguish the Deity Absolute from the Unqualified Absolute, their supposedly combined function or co-ordinated presence is designated the action of the Universal Absolute.

1. *The Deity Absolute* seems to be the all-powerful activator, while the Unqualified Absolute appears to be the all-efficient mechanizer of the supremely unified and ultimately co-ordinated universe of universes, even universes upon universes, made, making, and yet to be made.

The Deity Absolute cannot, or at least does not, react to any universe situation in a subabsolute manner. Every response of this Absolute to any given situation appears to be made in terms of the welfare of the whole creation of things and beings, not only in its present state of existence, but also in view of the infinite possibilities of all future eternity.

The Deity Absolute is that potential which was segregated from total, infinite reality by the freewill choice of the Universal Father, and within which all divinity activities—existential and experiential—take place. This is the *Qualified* Absolute in contradistinction to the *Unqualified* Absolute; but the Universal Absolute is superadditive to both in the encompassment of all absolute potential.

2. *The Unqualified Absolute* is nonpersonal, extradivine, and undeified. The Unqualified Absolute is therefore devoid of personality, divinity, and all creator prerogatives. Neither fact nor truth, experience nor revelation, philosophy nor absonity are able to penetrate the nature and character of this Absolute without universe qualification.

Let it be made clear that the Unqualified Absolute is a *positive reality* pervading the grand universe and, apparently, extending with equal space presence on out into the force activities and prematerial evolutions of the staggering stretches of the space regions beyond the seven superuniverses. The Unqualified Absolute is not a mere negativism of philosophic concept predicated on the assumptions of metaphysical sophistries concerning the universality, dominance, and primacy of the unconditioned and the unqualified. The Unqualified Absolute is a positive universe overcontrol in infinity; this overcontrol is space-force unlimited but is definitely conditioned by the presence of life, mind, spirit, and personality, and is further conditioned by the will-reactions and purposeful mandates of the Paradise Trinity.

We are convinced that the Unqualified Absolute is not an undifferentiated and all-pervading influence comparable either to the pantheistic concepts of metaphysics or to the sometime ether hypothesis of science. The Unqualified Absolute is force unlimited and Deity conditioned, but we do not fully perceive the relation of this Absolute to the spirit realities of the universes.

3. *The Universal Absolute,* we logically deduce, was inevitable in the Universal Father's absolute freewill act of differentiating universe realities into deified and undeified—personalizable and nonpersonalizable—values. The Universal Absolute is the Deity phenomenon indicative of the resolution of the tension created by the freewill act of thus differentiating universe reality, and functions as the associative co-ordinator of these sum totals of existential potentialities.

The tension-presence of the Universal Absolute signifies the adjustment of differential between deity reality and undeified reality inherent in the separation of the dynamics of freewill divinity from the statics of unqualified infinity.

Always remember: Potential infinity is absolute and inseparable from eternity. Actual infinity in time can never be anything but partial and must therefore be nonabsolute; neither can infinity of actual personality be absolute except in unqualified Deity. And it is the differential of infinity potential in the Unqualified Absolute and the Deity Absolute that eternalizes the Universal Absolute, thereby making it cosmically possible to have material universes in space and spiritually possible to have finite personalities in time.

The finite can coexist in the cosmos along with the Infinite only because the associative presence of the Universal Absolute so perfectly equalizes the tensions between time and eternity, finity and infinity, reality potential and reality actuality, Paradise and space, man and God. Associatively the Universal Absolute constitutes the identification of the zone of progressing evolutional reality existent in the time-space, and in the transcended time-space, universes of subinfinite Deity manifestation.

The Universal Absolute is the potential of the static-dynamic Deity functionally realizable on time-eternity levels as finite-absolute values and as possible of experiential-existential approach. This incomprehensible aspect of Deity may be static, potential, and associative but is not experientially creative or evolutional as concerns the intelligent personalities now functioning in the master universe.

The Absolute. The two Absolutes—qualified and unqualified—while so apparently divergent in function as they may be observed by mind creatures, are perfectly and divinely unified in and by the Universal Absolute. In the last analysis and in the final comprehension all three are one Absolute. On subinfinite levels they are functionally differentiated, but in infinity they are ONE.

We never use the term the Absolute as a negation of aught or as a denial of anything. Neither do we regard the Universal Absolute as self-determinative, a sort of pantheistic and impersonal Deity. The Absolute, in all that pertains to universe personality, is strictly Trinity limited and Deity dominated.

XII. THE TRINITIES

The original and eternal Paradise Trinity is existential and was inevitable. This never-beginning Trinity was inherent in the fact of the differentiation of the personal and the nonpersonal by the Father's unfettered will and factualized when his personal will co-ordinated these dual realities by mind. The post-Havona Trinities are experiential—are inherent in the creation of two subabsolute and evolutional levels of power-personality manifestation in the master universe.

The Paradise Trinity—the eternal Deity union of the Universal Father, the Eternal Son, and the Infinite Spirit—is existential in actuality, but all potentials are experiential. Therefore does this Trinity constitute the only Deity reality embracing infinity, and therefore do there occur the universe phenomena of the actualization of God the Supreme, God the Ultimate, and God the Absolute.

The first and second experiential Trinities, the post-Havona Trinities, cannot be infinite because they embrace *derived Deities,* Deities evolved by the experiential actualization of realities created or eventuated by the existential

Paradise Trinity. Infinity of divinity is being ever enriched, if not enlarged, by finity and absonity of creature and Creator experience.

Trinities are truths of relationship and facts of co-ordinate Deity manifestation. Trinity functions encompass Deity realities, and Deity realities always seek realization and manifestation in personalization. God the Supreme, God the Ultimate, and even God the Absolute are therefore divine inevitabilities. These three experiential Deities were potential in the existential Trinity, the Paradise Trinity, but their universe emergence as personalities of power is dependent in part on their own experiential functioning in the universes of power and personality and in part on the experiential achievements of the post-Havona Creators and Trinities.

The two post-Havona Trinities, the Ultimate and the Absolute experiential Trinities, are not now fully manifest; they are in process of universe realization. These Deity associations may be described as follows:

1. *The Ultimate Trinity,* now evolving, will eventually consist of the Supreme Being, the Supreme Creator Personalities, and the absonite Architects of the Master Universe, those unique universe planners who are neither creators nor creatures. God the Ultimate will eventually and inevitably powerize and personalize as the Deity consequence of the unification of this experiential Ultimate Trinity in the expanding arena of the well-nigh limitless master universe.

2. *The Absolute Trinity*—the second experiential Trinity—now in process of actualization, will consist of God the Supreme, God the Ultimate, and the unrevealed Consummator of Universe Destiny. This Trinity functions on both personal and superpersonal levels, even to the borders of the nonpersonal, and its unification in universality would experientialize Absolute Deity.

The Ultimate Trinity is experientially unifying in completion, but we truly doubt the possibility of such full unification of the Absolute Trinity. Our concept, however, of the eternal Paradise Trinity is an ever-present reminder that Deity trinitization may accomplish what is otherwise nonattainable; hence do we postulate the sometime appearance of the *Supreme-Ultimate* and the possible trinitization-factualization of God the Absolute.

The philosophers of the universes postulate a *Trinity of Trinities,* an existential-experiential Trinity Infinite, but they are not able to envisage its personalization; possibly it would equivalate to the person of the Universal Father on the conceptual level of the I AM. But irrespective of all this, the original Paradise Trinity is potentially infinite since the Universal Father actually is infinite.

ACKNOWLEDGMENT

In formulating the succeeding presentations having to do with the portrayal of the character of the Universal Father and the nature of his Paradise associates, together with an attempted description of the perfect central universe and the encircling seven superuniverses, we are to be guided by the mandate of the superuniverse rulers which directs that we shall, in all our efforts to reveal truth and co-ordinate essential knowledge, give preference to the highest existing human concepts pertaining to the subjects to be presented. We may resort to pure revelation only when the concept of presentation has had no adequate previous expression by the human mind.

Successive planetary revelations of divine truth invariably embrace the highest existing concepts of spiritual values as a part of the new and enhanced co-ordination of planetary knowledge. Accordingly, in making these presentations about God and his universe associates, we have selected as the basis of these papers more than one thousand human concepts representing the highest and most advanced planetary knowledge of spiritual values and universe meanings. Wherein these human concepts, assembled from the God-knowing mortals of the past and the present, are inadequate to portray the truth as we are directed to reveal it, we will unhesitatingly supplement them, for this purpose drawing upon our own superior knowledge of the reality and divinity of the Paradise Deities and their transcendent residential universe.

We are fully cognizant of the difficulties of our assignment; we recognize the impossibility of fully translating the language of the concepts of divinity and eternity into the symbols of the language of the finite concepts of the mortal mind. But we know that there dwells within the human mind a fragment of God, and that there sojourns with the human soul the Spirit of Truth; and we further know that these spirit forces conspire to enable material man to grasp the reality of spiritual values and to comprehend the philosophy of universe meanings. But even more certainly we know that these spirits of the Divine Presence are able to assist man in the spiritual appropriation of all truth contributory to the enhancement of the ever-progressing reality of personal religious experience—God-consciousness.

[Indited by an Orvonton Divine Counselor, Chief of the Corps of Superuniverse Personalities assigned to portray on Urantia the truth concerning the Paradise Deities and the universe of universes.]

PART I

THE CENTRAL AND SUPERUNIVERSES

Sponsored by a Uversa Corps of Superuniverse Personalities
acting by authority of the Orvonton
Ancients of Days.

PART I
The Central and Superuniverses

PAPER 1
THE UNIVERSAL FATHER

THE Universal Father is the God of all creation, the First Source and Center of all things and beings. First think of God as a creator, then as a controller, and lastly as an infinite upholder. The truth about the Universal Father had begun to dawn upon mankind when the prophet said: "You, God, are alone; there is none beside you. You have created the heaven and the heaven of heavens, with all their hosts; you preserve and control them. By the Sons of God were the universes made. The Creator covers himself with light as with a garment and stretches out the heavens as a curtain." Only the concept of the Universal Father—one God in the place of many gods—enabled mortal man to comprehend the Father as divine creator and infinite controller.

The myriads of planetary systems were all made to be eventually inhabited by many different types of intelligent creatures, beings who could know God, receive the divine affection, and love him in return. The universe of universes is the work of God and the dwelling place of his diverse creatures. "God created the heavens and formed the earth; he established the universe and created this world not in vain; he formed it to be inhabited."

The enlightened worlds all recognize and worship the Universal Father, the eternal maker and infinite upholder of all creation. The will creatures of universe upon universe have embarked upon the long, long Paradise journey, the fascinating struggle of the eternal adventure of attaining God the Father. The transcendent goal of the children of time is to find the eternal God, to comprehend the divine nature, to recognize the Universal Father. God-knowing creatures have only one supreme ambition, just one consuming desire, and that is to become, as they are in their spheres, like him as he is in his Paradise perfection of personality and in his universal sphere of righteous supremacy. From the Universal Father who inhabits eternity there has gone forth the supreme mandate, "Be you perfect, even as I am perfect." In love and mercy the messengers of Paradise have carried this divine exhortation down through the ages and out through the universes, even to such lowly animal-origin creatures as the human races of Urantia.

This magnificent and universal injunction to strive for the attainment of the perfection of divinity is the first duty, and should be the highest ambition, of all the struggling creature creation of the God of perfection. This possibility of the attainment of divine perfection is the final and certain destiny of all man's eternal spiritual progress.

Urantia mortals can hardly hope to be perfect in the infinite sense, but it is entirely possible for human beings, starting out as they do on this planet, to attain the supernal and divine goal which the infinite God has set for mortal man; and when they do achieve this destiny, they will, in all that pertains to self-realization and mind attainment, be just as replete in their sphere of divine perfection as God himself is in his sphere of infinity and eternity. Such perfection may not be universal in the material sense, unlimited in intellectual grasp, or final in spiritual experience, but it is final and complete in all finite aspects of divinity of will, perfection of personality motivation, and God-consciousness.

This is the true meaning of that divine command, "Be you perfect, even as I am perfect," which ever urges mortal man onward and beckons him inward in that long and fascinating struggle for the attainment of higher and higher levels of spiritual values and true universe meanings. This sublime search for the God of universes is the supreme adventure of the inhabitants of all the worlds of time and space.

1. THE FATHER'S NAME

Of all the names by which God the Father is known throughout the universes, those which designate him as the First Source and the Universe Center are most often encountered. The First Father is known by various names in different universes and in different sectors of the same universe. The names which the creature assigns to the Creator are much dependent on the creature's concept of the Creator. The First Source and Universe Center has never revealed himself by name, only by nature. If we believe that we are the children of this Creator, it is only natural that we should eventually call him Father. But this is the name of our own choosing, and it grows out of the recognition of our personal relationship with the First Source and Center.

The Universal Father never imposes any form of arbitrary recognition, formal worship, or slavish service upon the intelligent will creatures of the universes. The evolutionary inhabitants of the worlds of time and space must of themselves—in their own hearts—recognize, love, and voluntarily worship him. The Creator refuses to coerce or compel the submission of the spiritual free wills of his material creatures. The affectionate dedication of the human will to the doing of the Father's will is man's choicest gift to God; in fact, such a consecration of creature will constitutes man's only possible gift of true value to the Paradise Father. In God, man lives, moves, and has his being; there is nothing which man can give to God except this choosing to abide by the Father's will, and such decisions, effected by the intelligent will creatures of the universes, constitute the reality of that true worship which is so satisfying to the love-dominated nature of the Creator Father.

When you have once become truly God-conscious, after you really discover the majestic Creator and begin to experience the realization of the indwelling presence of the divine controller, then, in accordance with your enlightenment and in accordance with the manner and method by which the divine Sons reveal

God, you will find a name for the Universal Father which will be adequately expressive of your concept of the First Great Source and Center. And so, on different worlds and in various universes, the Creator becomes known by numerous appellations, in spirit of relationship all meaning the same but, in words and symbols, each name standing for the degree, the depth, of his enthronement in the hearts of his creatures of any given realm.

Near the center of the universe of universes, the Universal Father is generally known by names which may be regarded as meaning the First Source. Farther out in the universes of space, the terms employed to designate the Universal Father more often mean the Universal Center. Still farther out in the starry creation, he is known, as on the headquarters world of your local universe, as the First Creative Source and Divine Center. In one near-by constellation God is called the Father of Universes. In another, the Infinite Upholder, and to the east, the Divine Controller. He has also been designated the Father of Lights, the Gift of Life, and the All-powerful One.

On those worlds where a Paradise Son has lived a bestowal life, God is generally known by some name indicative of personal relationship, tender affection, and fatherly devotion. On your constellation headquarters God is referred to as the Universal Father, and on different planets in your local system of inhabited worlds he is variously known as the Father of Fathers, the Paradise Father, the Havona Father, and the Spirit Father. Those who know God through the revelations of the bestowals of the Paradise Sons, eventually yield to the sentimental appeal of the touching relationship of the creature-Creator association and refer to God as "our Father."

On a planet of sex creatures, in a world where the impulses of parental emotion are inherent in the hearts of its intelligent beings, the term Father becomes a very expressive and appropriate name for the eternal God. He is best known, most universally acknowledged, on your planet, Urantia, by the name *God.* The name he is given is of little importance; the significant thing is that you should know him and aspire to be like him. Your prophets of old truly called him "the everlasting God" and referred to him as the one who "inhabits eternity."

2. THE REALITY OF GOD

God is primal reality in the spirit world; God is the source of truth in the mind spheres; God overshadows all throughout the material realms. To all created intelligences God is a personality, and to the universe of universes he is the First Source and Center of eternal reality. God is neither manlike nor machinelike. The First Father is universal spirit, eternal truth, infinite reality, and father personality.

The eternal God is infinitely more than reality idealized or the universe personalized. God is not simply the supreme desire of man, the mortal quest objectified. Neither is God merely a concept, the power-potential of righteousness. The Universal Father is not a synonym for nature, neither is he natural law personified. God is a transcendent reality, not merely man's traditional concept of supreme values. God is not a psychological focalization of spiritual meanings, neither is he "the noblest work of man." God may be any or all of these concepts in the minds of men, but he is more. He is a saving person and a loving Father to all who enjoy spiritual peace on earth, and who crave to experience personality survival in death.

The actuality of the existence of God is demonstrated in human experience by the indwelling of the divine presence, the spirit Monitor sent from Paradise to live in the mortal mind of man and there to assist in evolving the immortal soul of eternal survival. The presence of this divine Adjuster in the human mind is disclosed by three experiential phenomena:

1. The intellectual capacity for knowing God—God-consciousness.

2. The spiritual urge to find God—God-seeking.

3. The personality craving to be like God—the wholehearted desire to do the Father's will.

The existence of God can never be proved by scientific experiment or by the pure reason of logical deduction. God can be realized only in the realms of human experience; nevertheless, the true concept of the reality of God is reasonable to logic, plausible to philosophy, essential to religion, and indispensable to any hope of personality survival.

Those who know God have experienced the fact of his presence; such God-knowing mortals hold in their personal experience the only positive proof of the existence of the living God which one human being can offer to another. The existence of God is utterly beyond all possibility of demonstration except for the contact between the God-consciousness of the human mind and the God-presence of the Thought Adjuster that indwells the mortal intellect and is bestowed upon man as the free gift of the Universal Father.

In theory you may think of God as the Creator, and he is the personal creator of Paradise and the central universe of perfection, but the universes of time and space are all created and organized by the Paradise corps of the Creator Sons. The Universal Father is not the personal creator of the local universe of Nebadon; the universe in which you live is the creation of his Son Michael. Though the Father does not personally create the evolutionary universes, he does control them in many of their universal relationships and in certain of their manifestations of physical, mindal, and spiritual energies. God the Father is the personal creator of the Paradise universe and, in association with the Eternal Son, the creator of all other personal universe Creators.

As a physical controller in the material universe of universes, the First Source and Center functions in the patterns of the eternal Isle of Paradise, and through this absolute gravity center the eternal God exercises cosmic over-control of the physical level equally in the central universe and throughout the universe of universes. As mind, God functions in the Deity of the Infinite Spirit; as spirit, God is manifest in the person of the Eternal Son and in the persons of the divine children of the Eternal Son. This interrelation of the First Source and Center with the co-ordinate Persons and Absolutes of Paradise does not in the least preclude the *direct* personal action of the Universal Father throughout all creation and on all levels thereof. Through the presence of his fragmentized spirit the Creator Father maintains immediate contact with his creature children and his created universes.

3. GOD IS A UNIVERSAL SPIRIT

"God is spirit." He is a universal spiritual presence. The Universal Father is an infinite spiritual reality; he is "the sovereign, eternal, immortal, invisible, and only true God." Even though you are "the offspring of God," you ought not to think that the Father is like yourselves in form and physique because you are said to be created "in his image"—indwelt by Mystery Monitors dispatched from the central abode of his eternal presence. Spirit beings are real, notwithstanding they are invisible to human eyes; even though they have not flesh and blood.

Said the seer of old: "Lo, he goes by me, and I see him not; he passes on also, but I perceive him not." We may constantly observe the works of God, we may be highly conscious of the material evidences of his majestic conduct, but rarely may we gaze upon the visible manifestation of his divinity, not even to behold the presence of his delegated spirit of human indwelling.

The Universal Father is not invisible because he is hiding himself away from the lowly creatures of materialistic handicaps and limited spiritual endowments. The situation rather is: "You cannot see my face, for no mortal can see me and live." No material man could behold the spirit God and preserve his mortal existence. The glory and the spiritual brilliance of the divine personality presence is impossible of approach by the lower groups of spirit beings or by any order of material personalities. The spiritual luminosity of the Father's personal presence is a "light which no mortal man can approach; which no material creature has seen or can see." But it is not necessary to see God with the eyes of the flesh in order to discern him by the faith-vision of the spiritualized mind.

The spirit nature of the Universal Father is shared fully with his coexistent self, the Eternal Son of Paradise. Both the Father and the Son in like manner share the universal and eternal spirit fully and unreservedly with their conjoint personality co-ordinate, the Infinite Spirit. God's spirit is, in and of himself, absolute; in the Son it is unqualified, in the Spirit, universal, and in and by all of them, infinite.

God is a universal spirit; God is the universal person. The supreme personal reality of the finite creation is spirit; the ultimate reality of the personal cosmos is absonite spirit. Only the levels of infinity are absolute, and only on such levels is there finality of oneness between matter, mind, and spirit.

In the universes God the Father is, in potential, the overcontroller of matter, mind, and spirit. Only by means of his far-flung personality circuit does God deal directly with the personalities of his vast creation of will creatures, but he is contactable (outside of Paradise) only in the presences of his fragmented entities, the will of God abroad in the universes. This Paradise spirit that indwells the minds of the mortals of time and there fosters the evolution of the immortal soul of the surviving creature is of the nature and divinity of the Universal Father. But the minds of such evolutionary creatures originate in the local universes and must gain divine perfection by achieving those experiential transformations of spiritual attainment which are the inevitable result of a creature's choosing to do the will of the Father in heaven.

In the inner experience of man, mind is joined to matter. Such material-linked minds cannot survive mortal death. The technique of survival is embraced in those adjustments of the human will and those transformations in the mortal mind whereby such a God-conscious intellect gradually becomes spirit taught and eventually spirit led. This evolution of the human mind from matter association to spirit union results in the transmutation of the potentially spirit phases of the mortal mind into the morontia realities of the immortal soul. Mortal mind subservient to matter is destined to become increasingly material and consequently to suffer eventual personality extinction; mind yielded to spirit is destined to become increasingly spiritual and ultimately to achieve oneness with the surviving and guiding divine spirit and in this way to attain survival and eternity of personality existence.

I come forth from the Eternal, and I have repeatedly returned to the presence of the Universal Father. I know of the actuality and personality of the First Source and Center, the Eternal and Universal Father. I know that, while the great God is absolute, eternal, and infinite, he is also good, divine, and gracious. I know the truth of the great declarations: "God is spirit" and "God is love," and these two attributes are most completely revealed to the universe in the Eternal Son.

4. THE MYSTERY OF GOD

The infinity of the perfection of God is such that it eternally constitutes him mystery. And the greatest of all the unfathomable mysteries of God is the phenomenon of the divine indwelling of mortal minds. The manner in which the Universal Father sojourns with the creatures of time is the most profound of all universe mysteries; the divine presence in the mind of man is the mystery of mysteries.

The physical bodies of mortals are "the temples of God." Notwithstanding that the Sovereign Creator Sons come near the creatures of their inhabited worlds and "draw all men to themselves"; though they "stand at the door" of consciousness "and knock" and delight to come in to all who will "open the doors of their hearts"; although there does exist this intimate personal communion between the Creator Sons and their mortal creatures, nevertheless, mortal men have something from God himself which actually dwells within them; their bodies are the temples thereof.

When you are through down here, when your course has been run in temporary form on earth, when your trial trip in the flesh is finished, when the dust that composes the mortal tabernacle "returns to the earth whence it came"; then, it is revealed, the indwelling "Spirit shall return to God who gave it." There sojourns within each moral being of this planet a fragment of God, a part and parcel of divinity. It is not yet yours by right of possession, but it is designedly intended to be one with you if you survive the mortal existence.

We are constantly confronted with this mystery of God; we are nonplused by the increasing unfolding of the endless panorama of the truth of his infinite goodness, endless mercy, matchless wisdom, and superb character.

The divine mystery consists in the inherent difference which exists between the finite and the infinite, the temporal and the eternal, the time-space creature and the Universal Creator, the material and the spiritual, the imperfection of man and the perfection of Paradise Deity. The God of universal love unfailingly manifests himself to every one of his creatures up to the fullness of that creature's capacity to spiritually grasp the qualities of divine truth, beauty, and goodness.

To every spirit being and to every mortal creature in every sphere and on every world of the universe of universes, the Universal Father reveals all of his gracious and divine self that can be discerned or comprehended by such spirit beings and by such mortal creatures. God is no respecter of persons, either spiritual or material. The divine presence which any child of the universe enjoys at any given moment is limited only by the capacity of such a creature to receive and to discern the spirit actualities of the supermaterial world.

As a reality in human spiritual experience God is not a mystery. But when an attempt is made to make plain the realities of the spirit world to the physical minds of the material order, mystery appears: mysteries so subtle and so profound that only the faith-grasp of the God-knowing mortal can achieve the philosophic miracle of the recognition of the Infinite by the finite, the discernment of the eternal God by the evolving mortals of the material worlds of time and space.

5. PERSONALITY OF THE UNIVERSAL FATHER

Do not permit the magnitude of God, his infinity, either to obscure or eclipse his personality. "He who planned the ear, shall he not hear? He who formed the eye, shall he not see?" The Universal Father is the acme of divine personality; he is the origin and destiny of personality throughout all creation. God is both infinite and personal; he is an infinite personality. The Father is truly a personality, notwithstanding that the infinity of his person places him forever beyond the full comprehension of material and finite beings.

God is much more than a personality as personality is understood by the human mind; he is even far more than any possible concept of a superpersonality. But it is utterly futile to discuss such incomprehensible concepts of divine personality with the minds of material creatures whose maximum concept of the reality of being consists in the idea and ideal of personality. The material creature's highest possible concept of the Universal Creator is embraced within the spiritual ideals of the exalted idea of divine personality. Therefore, although you may know that God must be much more than the human conception of personality, you equally well know that the Universal Father cannot possibly be anything less than an eternal, infinite, true, good, and beautiful personality.

God is not hiding from any of his creatures. He is unapproachable to so many orders of beings only because he "dwells in a light which no material creature can approach." The immensity and grandeur of the divine personality is beyond the grasp of the unperfected mind of evolutionary mortals. He "measures the waters in the hollow of his hand, measures a universe with the span of his hand. It is he who sits on the circle of the earth, who stretches out the heavens as a curtain and spreads them out as a universe to dwell in." "Lift up your eyes on high and behold who has created all these things, who brings out their worlds by number and calls them all by their names"; and so it is true that "the invisible things of God are partially understood by the things which are made." Today, and as you are, you must discern the invisible Maker through his manifold and diverse creation, as well as through the revelation and ministration of his Sons and their numerous subordinates.

Even though material mortals cannot see the person of God, they should rejoice in the assurance that he is a person; by faith accept the truth which portrays that the Universal Father so loved the world as to provide for the eternal spiritual progression of its lowly inhabitants; that he "delights in his children." God is lacking in none of those superhuman and divine attributes which constitute a perfect, eternal, loving, and infinite Creator personality.

In the local creations (excepting the personnel of the superuniverses) God has no personal or residential manifestation aside from the Paradise Creator Sons who are the fathers of the inhabited worlds and the sovereigns of the local universes. If the faith of the creature were perfect, he would assuredly know that when he had seen a Creator Son he had seen the Universal Father; in seeking for the Father, he would not ask nor expect to see other than the Son. Mortal man simply cannot see God until he achieves completed spirit transformation and actually attains Paradise.

The natures of the Paradise Creator Sons do not encompass all the unqualified potentials of the universal absoluteness of the infinite nature of the First Great Source and Center, but the Universal Father is in every way *divinely* present in the Creator Sons. The Father and his Sons are one. These Paradise Sons of the order of Michael are perfect personalities, even the pattern for all local universe personality from that of the Bright and Morning Star down to the lowest human creature of progressing animal evolution.

Without God and except for his great and central person, there would be no personality throughout all the vast universe of universes. *God is personality.*

Notwithstanding that God is an eternal power, a majestic presence, a transcendent ideal, and a glorious spirit, though he is all these and infinitely more, nonetheless, he is truly and everlastingly a perfect Creator personality, a person who can "know and be known," who can "love and be loved," and one who can befriend us; while you can be known, as other humans have been known, as the friend of God. He is a real spirit and a spiritual reality.

As we see the Universal Father revealed throughout his universe; as we discern him indwelling his myriads of creatures; as we behold him in the persons of his Sovereign Sons; as we continue to sense his divine presence here and there, near and afar, let us not doubt nor question his personality primacy. Notwithstanding all these far-flung distributions, he remains a true person and everlastingly maintains personal connection with the countless hosts of his creatures scattered throughout the universe of universes.

The idea of the personality of the Universal Father is an enlarged and truer concept of God which has come to mankind chiefly through revelation. Reason, wisdom, and religious experience all infer and imply the personality of God, but they do not altogether validate it. Even the indwelling Thought Adjuster is prepersonal. The truth and maturity of any religion is directly proportional to its concept of the infinite personality of God and to its grasp of the absolute unity of Deity. The idea of a personal Deity becomes, then, the measure of religious maturity after religion has first formulated the concept of the unity of God.

Primitive religion had many personal gods, and they were fashioned in the image of man. Revelation affirms the validity of the personality concept of God which is merely possible in the scientific postulate of a First Cause and is only provisionally suggested in the philosophic idea of Universal Unity. Only by personality approach can any person begin to comprehend the unity of God. To deny the personality of the First Source and Center leaves one only the choice of two philosophic dilemmas: materialism or pantheism.

In the contemplation of Deity, the concept of personality must be divested of the idea of corporeality. A material body is not indispensable to personality in either man or God. The corporeality error is shown in both extremes of human philosophy. In materialism, since man loses his body at death, he ceases to exist as a personality; in pantheism, since God has no body, he is not, therefore, a person. The superhuman type of progressing personality functions in a union of mind and spirit.

Personality is not simply an attribute of God; it rather stands for the totality of the co-ordinated infinite nature and the unified divine will which is exhibited in eternity and universality of perfect expression. Personality, in the supreme sense, is the revelation of God to the universe of universes.

God, being eternal, universal, absolute, and infinite, does not grow in knowledge nor increase in wisdom. God does not acquire experience, as finite man might conjecture or comprehend, but he does, within the realms of his own eternal personality, enjoy those continuous expansions of self-realization which are in certain ways comparable to, and analogous with, the acquirement of new experience by the finite creatures of the evolutionary worlds.

The absolute perfection of the infinite God would cause him to suffer the awful limitations of unqualified finality of perfectness were it not a fact that the Universal Father directly participates in the personality struggle of every imperfect soul in the wide universe who seeks, by divine aid, to ascend to the spiritually perfect worlds on high. This progressive experience of every spirit being and every mortal creature throughout the universe of universes is a part of the Father's ever-expanding Deity-consciousness of the never-ending divine circle of ceaseless self-realization.

It is literally true: "In all your afflictions he is afflicted." "In all your triumphs he triumphs in and with you." His prepersonal divine spirit is a real part of you. The Isle of Paradise responds to all the physical metamorphoses of the universe of universes; the Eternal Son includes all the spirit impulses of all creation; the Conjoint Actor encompasses all the mind expression of the expanding cosmos. The Universal Father realizes in the fullness of the divine consciousness all the individual experience of the progressive struggles of the expanding minds and the ascending spirits of every entity, being, and personality of the whole evolutionary creation of time and space. And all this is literally true, for "in Him we all live and move and have our being."

6. PERSONALITY IN THE UNIVERSE

Human personality is the time-space image-shadow cast by the divine Creator personality. And no actuality can ever be adequately comprehended by an examination of its shadow. Shadows should be interpreted in terms of the true substance.

God is to science a cause, to philosophy an idea, to religion a person, even the loving heavenly Father. God is to the scientist a primal force, to the philosopher a hypothesis of unity, to the religionist a living spiritual experience. Man's inadequate concept of the personality of the Universal Father can be improved only by man's spiritual progress in the universe and will become truly adequate only when the pilgrims of time and space finally attain the divine embrace of the living God on Paradise.

Never lose sight of the antipodal viewpoints of personality as it is conceived by God and man. Man views and comprehends personality, looking from the finite to the infinite; God looks from the infinite to the finite. Man possesses the lowest type of personality; God, the highest, even supreme, ultimate, and absolute. Therefore did the better concepts of the divine personality have patiently to await the appearance of improved ideas of human personality, especially the enhanced revelation of both human and divine personality in the Urantian bestowal life of Michael, the Creator Son.

The prepersonal divine spirit which indwells the mortal mind carries, in its very presence, the valid proof of its actual existence, but the concept of the divine personality can be grasped only by the spiritual insight of genuine personal religious experience. Any person, human or divine, may be known and comprehended quite apart from the external reactions or the material presence of that person.

Some degree of moral affinity and spiritual harmony is essential to friendship between two persons; a loving personality can hardly reveal himself to a loveless person. Even to approach the knowing of a divine personality, all of man's personality endowments must be wholly consecrated to the effort; half-hearted, partial devotion will be unavailing.

The more completely man understands himself and appreciates the personality values of his fellows, the more he will crave to know the Original Personality, and the more earnestly such a God-knowing human will strive to become like the Original Personality. You can argue over opinions about God, but experience with him and in him exists above and beyond all human controversy and mere intellectual logic. The God-knowing man describes his spiritual experiences, not to convince unbelievers, but for the edification and mutual satisfaction of believers.

To assume that the universe can be known, that it is intelligible, is to assume that the universe is mind made and personality managed. Man's mind can only perceive the mind phenomena of other minds, be they human or superhuman. If man's personality can experience the universe, there is a divine mind and an actual personality somewhere concealed in that universe.

God is spirit—spirit personality; man is also a spirit—potential spirit personality. Jesus of Nazareth attained the full realization of this potential of spirit personality in human experience; therefore his life of achieving the Father's will becomes man's most real and ideal revelation of the personality of God. Even though the personality of the Universal Father can be grasped only in actual religious experience, in Jesus' earth life we are inspired by the perfect demonstration of such a realization and revelation of the personality of God in a truly human experience.

7. SPIRITUAL VALUE OF THE PERSONALITY CONCEPT

When Jesus talked about "the living God," he referred to a personal Deity—the Father in heaven. The concept of the personality of Deity facilitates fellowship; it favors intelligent worship; it promotes refreshing trustfulness. Interactions can be had between nonpersonal things, but not fellowship. The fellowship relation of father and son, as between God and man, cannot be enjoyed unless both are persons. Only personalities can commune with each other, albeit this personal communion may be greatly facilitated by the presence of just such an impersonal entity as the Thought Adjuster.

Man does not achieve union with God as a drop of water might find unity with the ocean. Man attains divine union by progressive reciprocal spiritual communion, by personality intercourse with the personal God, by increasingly attaining the divine nature through wholehearted and intelligent conformity to the divine will. Such a sublime relationship can exist only between personalities.

The concept of truth might possibly be entertained apart from personality, the concept of beauty may exist without personality, but the concept of divine goodness is understandable only in relation to personality. Only a *person* can love and be loved. Even beauty and truth would be divorced from survival hope if they were not attributes of a personal God, a loving Father.

We cannot fully understand how God can be primal, changeless, all-powerful, and perfect, and at the same time be surrounded by an ever-changing and apparently law-limited universe, an evolving universe of relative imperfections. But we can *know* such a truth in our own personal experience since we all maintain identity of personality and unity of will in spite of the constant changing of both ourselves and our environment.

Ultimate universe reality cannot be grasped by mathematics, logic, or philosophy, only by personal experience in progressive conformity to the divine will of a personal God. Neither science, philosophy, nor theology can validate the personality of God. Only the personal experience of the faith sons of the heavenly Father can effect the actual spiritual realization of the personality of God.

The higher concepts of universe personality imply: identity, self-consciousness, self-will, and possibility for self-revelation. And these characteristics further imply fellowship with other and equal personalities, such as exists in the personality associations of the Paradise Deities. And the absolute unity of these associations is so perfect that divinity becomes known by indivisibility, by oneness. "The Lord God is *one.*" Indivisibility of personality does not interfere with God's bestowing his spirit to live in the hearts of mortal men. Indivisibility of a human father's personality does not prevent the reproduction of mortal sons and daughters.

This concept of indivisibility in association with the concept of unity implies transcendence of both time and space by the Ultimacy of Deity; therefore neither space nor time can be absolute or infinite. The First Source and Center is that infinity who unqualifiedly transcends all mind, all matter, and all spirit.

The fact of the Paradise Trinity in no manner violates the truth of the divine unity. The three personalities of Paradise Deity are, in all universe reality reactions and in all creature relations, as one. Neither does the existence of these three eternal persons violate the truth of the indivisibility of Deity. I am fully aware that I have at my command no language adequate to make clear to the mortal mind how these universe problems appear to us. But you should not become discouraged; not all of these things are wholly clear to even the high personalities belonging to my group of Paradise beings. Ever bear in mind that these profound truths pertaining to Deity will increasingly clarify as your minds become progressively spiritualized during the successive epochs of the long mortal ascent to Paradise.

[Presented by a Divine Counselor, a member of a group of celestial personalities assigned by the Ancients of Days on Uversa, the headquarters of the seventh superuniverse, to supervise those portions of this forthcoming revelation which have to do with affairs beyond the borders of the local universe of Nebadon. I am commissioned to sponsor those papers portraying the nature and attributes of God because I represent the highest source of information available for such a purpose on any inhabited world. I have served as a Divine Counselor in all seven of the superuniverses and have long resided at the Paradise center of all things. Many times have I enjoyed the supreme pleasure of a sojourn in the immediate personal presence of the Universal Father. I portray the reality and truth of the Father's nature and attributes with unchallengeable authority; I know whereof I speak.]

PAPER 2

THE NATURE OF GOD

INASMUCH as man's highest possible concept of God is embraced within the human idea and ideal of a primal and infinite personality, it is permissible, and may prove helpful, to study certain characteristics of the divine nature which constitute the character of Deity. The nature of God can best be understood by the revelation of the Father which Michael of Nebadon unfolded in his manifold teachings and in his superb mortal life in the flesh. The divine nature can also be better understood by man if he regards himself as a child of God and looks up to the Paradise Creator as a true spiritual Father.

The nature of God can be studied in a revelation of supreme ideas, the divine character can be envisaged as a portrayal of supernal ideals, but the most enlightening and spiritually edifying of all revelations of the divine nature is to be found in the comprehension of the religious life of Jesus of Nazareth, both before and after his attainment of full consciousness of divinity. If the incarnated life of Michael is taken as the background of the revelation of God to man, we may attempt to put in human word symbols certain ideas and ideals concerning the divine nature which may possibly contribute to a further illumination and unification of the human concept of the nature and the character of the personality of the Universal Father.

In all our efforts to enlarge and spiritualize the human concept of God, we are tremendously handicapped by the limited capacity of the mortal mind. We are also seriously handicapped in the execution of our assignment by the limitations of language and by the poverty of material which can be utilized for purposes of illustration or comparison in our efforts to portray divine values and to present spiritual meanings to the finite, mortal mind of man. All our efforts to enlarge the human concept of God would be well-nigh futile except for the fact that the mortal mind is indwelt by the bestowed Adjuster of the Universal Father and is pervaded by the Truth Spirit of the Creator Son. Depending, therefore, on the presence of these divine spirits within the heart of man for assistance in the enlargement of the concept of God, I cheerfully undertake the execution of my mandate to attempt the further portrayal of the nature of God to the mind of man.

1. THE INFINITY OF GOD

"Touching the Infinite, we cannot find him out. The divine footsteps are not known." "His understanding is infinite and his greatness is unsearchable." The blinding light of the Father's presence is such that to his lowly creatures he apparently "dwells in the thick darkness." Not only are his thoughts and plans unsearchable, but "he does great and marvelous things without number." "God is great; we comprehend him not, neither can the number of his years be searched out." "Will God indeed dwell on the earth? Behold, the heaven (universe) and the heaven of heavens (universe of universes) cannot contain him." "How unsearchable are his judgments and his ways past finding out!"

"There is but one God, the infinite Father, who is also a faithful Creator." "The divine Creator is also the Universal Disposer, the source and destiny of souls. He is the Supreme Soul, the Primal Mind, and the Unlimited Spirit of all creation." "The great Controller makes no mistakes. He is resplendent in majesty and glory." "The Creator God is wholly devoid of fear and enmity. He is immortal, eternal, self-existent, divine, and bountiful." "How pure and beautiful, how deep and unfathomable is the supernal Ancestor of all things!" "The Infinite is most excellent in that he imparts himself to men. He is the beginning and the end, the Father of every good and perfect purpose." "With God all things are possible; the eternal Creator is the cause of causes."

Notwithstanding the infinity of the stupendous manifestations of the Father's eternal and universal personality, he is unqualifiedly self-conscious of both his infinity and eternity; likewise he knows fully his perfection and power. He is the only being in the universe, aside from his divine co-ordinates, who experiences a perfect, proper, and complete appraisal of himself.

The Father constantly and unfailingly meets the need of the differential of demand for himself as it changes from time to time in various sections of his master universe. The great God knows and understands himself; he is infinitely self-conscious of all his primal attributes of perfection. God is not a cosmic accident; neither is he a universe experimenter. The Universe Sovereigns may engage in adventure; the Constellation Fathers may experiment; the system heads may practice; but the Universal Father sees the end from the beginning, and his divine plan and eternal purpose actually embrace and comprehend all the experiments and all the adventures of all his subordinates in every world, system, and constellation in every universe of his vast domains.

No thing is new to God, and no cosmic event ever comes as a surprise; he inhabits the circle of eternity. He is without beginning or end of days. To God there is no past, present, or future; all time is present at any given moment. He is the great and only I AM.

The Universal Father is absolutely and without qualification infinite in all his attributes; and this fact, in and of itself, automatically shuts him off from all direct personal communication with finite material beings and other lowly created intelligences.

And all this necessitates such arrangements for contact and communication with his manifold creatures as have been ordained, first, in the personalities of the Paradise Sons of God, who, although perfect in divinity, also often partake of the nature of the very flesh and blood of the planetary races, becoming one of you and one with you; thus, as it were, God becomes man, as occurred in the bestowal of Michael, who was called interchangeably the Son of God and the Son of Man. And second, there are the personalities of the Infinite Spirit, the various orders of the seraphic hosts and other celestial intelligences who draw near to the material beings of lowly origin and in so many ways minister to them and serve them. And third, there are the impersonal Mystery Monitors, Thought Adjusters, the actual gift of the great God himself sent to indwell such as the humans of Urantia, sent without announcement and without explanation. In endless profusion they descend from the heights of glory to grace and indwell the humble minds of those mortals who possess the capacity for God-consciousness or the potential therefor.

In these ways and in many others, in ways unknown to you and utterly beyond finite comprehension, does the Paradise Father lovingly and willingly downstep and otherwise modify, dilute, and attenuate his infinity in order that he may be able to draw nearer the finite minds of his creature children. And so, through a series of personality distributions which are diminishingly absolute, the infinite Father is enabled to enjoy close contact with the diverse intelligences of the many realms of his far-flung universe.

All this he has done and now does, and evermore will continue to do, without in the least detracting from the fact and reality of his infinity, eternity, and primacy. And these things are absolutely true, notwithstanding the difficulty of their comprehension, the mystery in which they are enshrouded, or the impossibility of their being fully understood by creatures such as dwell on Urantia.

Because the First Father is infinite in his plans and eternal in his purposes, it is inherently impossible for any finite being ever to grasp or comprehend these divine plans and purposes in their fullness. Mortal man can glimpse the Father's purposes only now and then, here and there, as they are revealed in relation to the outworking of the plan of creature ascension on its successive levels of universe progression. Though man cannot encompass the significance of infinity, the infinite Father does most certainly fully comprehend and lovingly embrace all the finity of all his children in all universes.

Divinity and eternity the Father shares with large numbers of the higher Paradise beings, but we question whether infinity and consequent universal primacy is fully shared with any save his co-ordinate associates of the Paradise Trinity. Infinity of personality must, perforce, embrace all finitude of personality; hence the truth—literal truth—of the teaching which declares that "In Him we live and move and have our being." That fragment of the pure Deity of the Universal Father which indwells mortal man *is* a part of the infinity of the First Great Source and Center, the Father of Fathers.

2. THE FATHER'S ETERNAL PERFECTION

Even your olden prophets understood the eternal, never-beginning, never-ending, circular nature of the Universal Father. God is literally and eternally present in his universe of universes. He inhabits the present moment with all his absolute majesty and eternal greatness. "The Father has life in himself, and this life is eternal life." Throughout the eternal ages it has been the Father who "gives to all life." There is infinite perfection in the divine integrity. "I am the Lord; I change not." Our knowledge of the universe of universes discloses not only that he is the Father of lights, but also that in his conduct of interplanetary affairs there "is no variableness neither shadow of changing." He "declares the end from the beginning." He says: "My counsel shall stand; I will do all my pleasures" "according to the eternal purpose which I purposed in my Son." Thus are the plans and purposes of the First Source and Center like himself: eternal, perfect, and forever changeless.

There is finality of completeness and perfection of repleteness in the mandates of the Father. "Whatsoever God does, it shall be forever; nothing can be added to it nor anything taken from it." The Universal Father does not repent of his original purposes of wisdom and perfection. His plans are steadfast, his counsel immutable, while his acts are divine and infallible. "A thousand years in his sight are but as yesterday when it is past and as a watch in the night." The perfection of divinity and the magnitude of eternity are forever beyond the full grasp of the circumscribed mind of mortal man.

The reactions of a changeless God, in the execution of his eternal purpose, may seem to vary in accordance with the changing attitude and the shifting minds of his created intelligences; that is, they may apparently and superficially vary; but underneath the surface and beneath all outward manifestations, there is still present the changeless purpose, the everlasting plan, of the eternal God.

Out in the universes, perfection must necessarily be a relative term, but in the central universe and especially on Paradise, perfection is undiluted; in certain phases it is even absolute. Trinity manifestations vary the exhibition of the divine perfection but do not attenuate it.

God's primal perfection consists not in an assumed righteousness but rather in the inherent perfection of the goodness of his divine nature. He is final, complete, and perfect. There is no thing lacking in the beauty and perfection of his righteous character. And the whole scheme of living existences on the worlds of space is centered in the divine purpose of elevating all will creatures to the high destiny of the experience of sharing the Father's Paradise perfection. God is neither self-centered nor self-contained; he never ceases to bestow himself upon all self-conscious creatures of the vast universe of universes.

God is eternally and infinitely perfect, he cannot personally know imperfection as his own experience, but he does share the consciousness of all the experience of imperfectness of all the struggling creatures of the evolutionary universes of all the Paradise Creator Sons. The personal and liberating touch of the God of perfection overshadows the hearts and encircuits the natures of all those mortal creatures who have ascended to the universe level of moral discernment. In this manner, as well as through the contacts of the divine presence, the Universal Father actually participates in the experience *with* immaturity and imperfection in the evolving career of every moral being of the entire universe.

Human limitations, potential evil, are not a part of the divine nature, but mortal experience *with* evil and all man's relations thereto are most certainly a part of God's ever-expanding self-realization in the children of time—creatures of moral responsibility who have been created or evolved by every Creator Son going out from Paradise.

3. JUSTICE AND RIGHTEOUSNESS

God is righteous; therefore is he just. "The Lord is righteous in all his ways." "'I have not done without cause all that I have done,' says the Lord." "The judgments of the Lord are true and righteous altogether." The justice of the Universal Father cannot be influenced by the acts and performances of his creatures, "for there is no iniquity with the Lord our God, no respect of persons, no taking of gifts."

How futile to make puerile appeals to such a God to modify his changeless decrees so that we can avoid the just consequences of the operation of his wise natural laws and righteous spiritual mandates! "Be not deceived; God is not mocked, for whatsoever a man sows that shall he also reap." True, even in the justice of reaping the harvest of wrongdoing, this divine justice is always tempered with mercy. Infinite wisdom is the eternal arbiter which determines the proportions of justice and mercy which shall be meted out in any given circumstance. The greatest punishment (in reality an inevitable consequence) for wrongdoing and deliberate rebellion against the government of God is loss of existence as an individual subject of that government. The final result of wholehearted sin is annihilation. In the last analysis, such sin-identified individuals have destroyed themselves by becoming wholly unreal through their embrace of iniquity. The factual disappearance of such a creature is, however, always delayed until the ordained order of justice current in that universe has been fully complied with.

Cessation of existence is usually decreed at the dispensational or epochal adjudication of the realm or realms. On a world such as Urantia it comes at the end of a planetary dispensation. Cessation of existence can be decreed at such times by co-ordinate action of all tribunals of jurisdiction, extending from the planetary council up through the courts of the Creator Son to the judgment tribunals of the Ancients of Days. The mandate of dissolution originates in the higher courts of the superuniverse following an unbroken confirmation of the indictment originating on the sphere of the wrongdoer's residence; and then, when sentence of extinction has been confirmed on high, the execution is by the direct act of those judges residential on, and operating from, the headquarters of the superuniverse.

When this sentence is finally confirmed, the sin-identified being instantly becomes as though he had not been. There is no resurrection from such a fate; it is everlasting and eternal. The living energy factors of identity are resolved by the transformations of time and the metamorphoses of space into the cosmic potentials whence they once emerged. As for the personality of the iniquitous one, it is deprived of a continuing life vehicle by the creature's failure to make those choices and final decisions which would have assured eternal life. When the continued embrace of sin by the associated mind culminates in complete self-identification with iniquity, then upon the cessation of life, upon cosmic dissolution, such an isolated personality is absorbed into the oversoul of creation, becoming a part of the evolving experience of the Supreme Being. Never again does it appear as a personality; its identity becomes as though it had never been. In the case of an Adjuster-indwelt personality, the experiential spirit values survive in the reality of the continuing Adjuster.

In any universe contest between actual levels of reality, the personality of the higher level will ultimately triumph over the personality of the lower level. This inevitable outcome of universe controversy is inherent in the fact that divinity of quality equals the degree of reality or actuality of any will creature. Undiluted evil, complete error, willful sin, and unmitigated iniquity are inherently and automatically suicidal. Such attitudes of cosmic unreality can survive in the universe only because of transient mercy-tolerance pending the action of the justice-determining and fairness-finding mechanisms of the universe tribunals of righteous adjudication.

The rule of the Creator Sons in the local universes is one of creation and spiritualization. These Sons devote themselves to the effective execution of the

Paradise plan of progressive mortal ascension, to the rehabilitation of rebels and wrong thinkers, but when all such loving efforts are finally and forever rejected, the final decree of dissolution is executed by forces acting under the jurisdiction of the Ancients of Days.

4. THE DIVINE MERCY

Mercy is simply justice tempered by that wisdom which grows out of perfection of knowledge and the full recognition of the natural weaknesses and environmental handicaps of finite creatures. "Our God is full of compassion, gracious, long-suffering, and plenteous in mercy." Therefore "whosoever calls upon the Lord shall be saved," "for he will abundantly pardon." "The mercy of the Lord is from everlasting to everlasting"; yes, "his mercy endures forever." "I am the Lord who executes loving-kindness, judgment, and righteousness in the earth, for in these things I delight." "I do not afflict willingly nor grieve the children of men," for I am "the Father of mercies and the God of all comfort."

God is inherently kind, naturally compassionate, and everlastingly merciful. And never is it necessary that any influence be brought to bear upon the Father to call forth his loving-kindness. The creature's need is wholly sufficient to insure the full flow of the Father's tender mercies and his saving grace. Since God knows all about his children, it is easy for him to forgive. The better man understands his neighbor, the easier it will be to forgive him, even to love him.

Only the discernment of infinite wisdom enables a righteous God to minister justice and mercy at the same time and in any given universe situation. The heavenly Father is never torn by conflicting attitudes towards his universe children; God is never a victim of attitudinal antagonisms. God's all-knowingness unfailingly directs his free will in the choosing of that universe conduct which perfectly, simultaneously, and equally satisfies the demands of all his divine attributes and the infinite qualities of his eternal nature.

Mercy is the natural and inevitable offspring of goodness and love. The good nature of a loving Father could not possibly withhold the wise ministry of mercy to each member of every group of his universe children. Eternal justice and divine mercy together constitute what in human experience would be called *fairness.*

Divine mercy represents a fairness technique of adjustment between the universe levels of perfection and imperfection. Mercy is the justice of Supremacy adapted to the situations of the evolving finite, the righteousness of eternity modified to meet the highest interests and universe welfare of the children of time. Mercy is not a contravention of justice but rather an understanding interpretation of the demands of supreme justice as it is fairly applied to the subordinate spiritual beings and to the material creatures of the evolving universes. Mercy is the justice of the Paradise Trinity wisely and lovingly visited upon the manifold intelligences of the creations of time and space as it is formulated by divine wisdom and determined by the all-knowing mind and the sovereign free will of the Universal Father and all his associated Creators.

5. THE LOVE OF GOD

"God is love"; therefore his only personal attitude towards the affairs of the universe is always a reaction of divine affection. The Father loves us sufficiently to bestow his life upon us. "He makes his sun to rise on the evil and on the good and sends rain on the just and on the unjust."

It is wrong to think of God as being coaxed into loving his children because of the sacrifices of his Sons or the intercession of his subordinate creatures, "for the Father himself loves you." It is in response to this paternal affection that God sends the marvelous Adjusters to indwell the minds of men. God's love is universal; "whosoever will may come." He would "have all men be saved by coming into the knowledge of the truth." He is "not willing that any should perish."

The Creators are the very first to attempt to save man from the disastrous results of his foolish transgression of the divine laws. God's love is by nature a fatherly affection; therefore does he sometimes "chasten us for our own profit, that we may be partakers of his holiness." Even during your fiery trials remember that "in all our afflictions he is afflicted with us."

God is divinely kind to sinners. When rebels return to righteousness, they are mercifully received, "for our God will abundantly pardon." "I am he who blots out your transgressions for my own sake, and I will not remember your sins." "Behold what manner of love the Father has bestowed upon us that we should be called the sons of God."

After all, the greatest evidence of the goodness of God and the supreme reason for loving him is the indwelling gift of the Father—the Adjuster who so patiently awaits the hour when you both shall be eternally made one. Though you cannot find God by searching, if you will submit to the leading of the indwelling spirit, you will be unerringly guided, step by step, life by life, through universe upon universe, and age by age, until you finally stand in the presence of the Paradise personality of the Universal Father.

How unreasonable that you should not worship God because the limitations of human nature and the handicaps of your material creation make it impossible for you to see him. Between you and God there is a tremendous distance (physical space) to be traversed. There likewise exists a great gulf of spiritual differential which must be bridged; but notwithstanding all that physically and spiritually separates you from the Paradise personal presence of God, stop and ponder the solemn fact that God lives within you; he has in his own way already bridged the gulf. He has sent of himself, his spirit, to live in you and to toil with you as you pursue your eternal universe career.

I find it easy and pleasant to worship one who is so great and at the same time so affectionately devoted to the uplifting ministry of his lowly creatures. I naturally love one who is so powerful in creation and in the control thereof, and yet who is so perfect in goodness and so faithful in the loving-kindness which constantly overshadows us. I think I would love God just as much if he were not so great and powerful, as long as he is so good and merciful. We all love the Father more because of his nature than in recognition of his amazing attributes.

When I observe the Creator Sons and their subordinate administrators struggling so valiantly with the manifold difficulties of time inherent in the evolution of the universes of space, I discover that I bear these lesser rulers of the universes a great and profound affection. After all, I think we all, including the mortals of the realms, love the Universal Father and all other beings, divine or human, because we discern that these personalities truly love us. The experience of loving is very much a direct response to the experience of being loved. Knowing that God loves me, I should continue to love him supremely, even though he were divested of all his attributes of supremacy, ultimacy, and absoluteness.

The Father's love follows us now and throughout the endless circle of the eternal ages. As you ponder the loving nature of God, there is only one reasonable and natural personality reaction thereto: You will increasingly love your Maker; you will yield to God an affection analogous to that given by a child to an earthly parent; for, as a father, a real father, a true father, loves his children, so the Universal Father loves and forever seeks the welfare of his created sons and daughters.

But the love of God is an intelligent and farseeing parental affection. The divine love functions in unified association with divine wisdom and all other infinite characteristics of the perfect nature of the Universal Father. God is love, but love is not God. The greatest manifestation of the divine love for mortal beings is observed in the bestowal of the Thought Adjusters, but your greatest revelation of the Father's love is seen in the bestowal life of his Son Michael as he lived on earth the ideal spiritual life. It is the indwelling Adjuster who individualizes the love of God to each human soul.

At times I am almost pained to be compelled to portray the divine affection of the heavenly Father for his universe children by the employment of the human word symbol *love.* This term, even though it does connote man's highest concept of the mortal relations of respect and devotion, is so frequently designative of so much of human relationship that is wholly ignoble and utterly unfit to be known by any word which is also used to indicate the matchless affection of the living God for his universe creatures! How unfortunate that I cannot make use of some supernal and exclusive term which would convey to the mind of man the true nature and exquisitely beautiful significance of the divine affection of the Paradise Father.

When man loses sight of the love of a personal God, the kingdom of God becomes merely the kingdom of good. Notwithstanding the infinite unity of the divine nature, love is the dominant characteristic of all God's personal dealings with his creatures.

6. THE GOODNESS OF GOD

In the physical universe we may see the divine beauty, in the intellectual world we may discern eternal truth, but the goodness of God is found only in the spiritual world of personal religious experience. In its true essence, religion is a faith-trust in the goodness of God. God could be great and absolute, somehow even intelligent and personal, in philosophy, but in religion God must also be moral; he must be good. Man might fear a great God, but he trusts and loves only a good God. This goodness of God is a part of the personality of God, and its full revelation appears only in the personal religious experience of the believing sons of God.

Religion implies that the superworld of spirit nature is cognizant of, and responsive to, the fundamental needs of the human world. Evolutionary religion may become ethical, but only revealed religion becomes truly and spiritually moral. The olden concept that God is a Deity dominated by kingly morality was upstepped by Jesus to that affectionately touching level of intimate family morality of the parent-child relationship, than which there is none more tender and beautiful in mortal experience.

The "richness of the goodness of God leads erring man to repentance." "Every good gift and every perfect gift comes down from the Father of lights." "God is good; he is the eternal refuge of the souls of men." "The Lord God is merciful and gracious. He is long-suffering and abundant in goodness and truth." "Taste and see that the Lord is good! Blessed is the man who trusts him." "The Lord is gracious and full of compassion. He is the God of salvation." "He heals the brokenhearted and binds up the wounds of the soul. He is man's all-powerful benefactor."

The concept of God as a king-judge, although it fostered a high moral standard and created a law-respecting people as a group, left the individual believer in a sad position of insecurity respecting his status in time and in eternity. The later Hebrew prophets proclaimed God to be a Father to Israel; Jesus revealed God as the Father of each human being. The entire mortal concept of God is transcendently illuminated by the life of Jesus. Selflessness is inherent in parental love. God loves not *like* a father, but *as* a father. He is the Paradise Father of every universe personality.

Righteousness implies that God is the source of the moral law of the universe. Truth exhibits God as a revealer, as a teacher. But love gives and craves affection, seeks understanding fellowship such as exists between parent and child. Righteousness may be the divine thought, but love is a father's attitude. The erroneous supposition that the righteousness of God was irreconcilable with the selfless love of the heavenly Father, presupposed absence of unity in the nature of Deity and led directly to the elaboration of the atonement doctrine, which is a philosophic assault upon both the unity and the free-willness of God.

The affectionate heavenly Father, whose spirit indwells his children on earth, is not a divided personality—one of justice and one of mercy—neither does it require a mediator to secure the Father's favor or forgiveness. Divine righteousness is not dominated by strict retributive justice; God as a father transcends God as a judge.

God is never wrathful, vengeful, or angry. It is true that wisdom does often restrain his love, while justice conditions his rejected mercy. His love of righteousness cannot help being exhibited as equal hatred for sin. The Father is not an inconsistent personality; the divine unity is perfect. In the Paradise Trinity there is absolute unity despite the eternal identities of the co-ordinates of God.

God loves the sinner and *hates* the sin: such a statement is true philosophically, but God is a transcendent personality, and persons can only love and hate other persons. Sin is not a person. God loves the sinner because he is a personality reality (potentially eternal), while towards sin God strikes no personal attitude, for sin is not a spiritual reality; it is not personal; therefore does only the justice of God take cognizance of its existence. The love of God saves the sinner; the law of God destroys the sin. This attitude of the divine nature would apparently change if the sinner finally identified himself wholly with sin just as the same mortal mind may also fully identify itself with the indwelling spirit Adjuster. Such a sin-identified mortal would then become wholly unspiritual in nature (and therefore personally unreal) and would experience eventual extinction of being. Unreality, even incompleteness of creature nature, cannot exist forever in a progressingly real and increasingly spiritual universe.

Facing the world of personality, God is discovered to be a loving person; facing the spiritual world, he is a personal love; in religious experience he is both. Love identifies the volitional will of God. The goodness of God rests at the bottom of the divine free-willness—the universal tendency to love, show mercy, manifest patience, and minister forgiveness.

7. DIVINE TRUTH AND BEAUTY

All finite knowledge and creature understanding are *relative.* Information and intelligence, gleaned from even high sources, is only relatively complete, locally accurate, and personally true.

Physical facts are fairly uniform, but truth is a living and flexible factor in the philosophy of the universe. Evolving personalities are only partially wise and relatively true in their communications. They can be certain only as far as their personal experience extends. That which apparently may be wholly true in one place may be only relatively true in another segment of creation.

Divine truth, final truth, is uniform and universal, but the story of things spiritual, as it is told by numerous individuals hailing from various spheres, may sometimes vary in details owing to this relativity in the completeness of knowledge and in the repleteness of personal experience as well as in the length and extent of that experience. While the laws and decrees, the thoughts and attitudes, of the First Great Source and Center are eternally, infinitely, and universally true; at the same time, their application to, and adjustment for, every universe, system, world, and created intelligence, are in accordance with the plans and technique of the Creator Sons as they function in their respective universes, as well as in harmony with the local plans and procedures of the Infinite Spirit and of all other associated celestial personalities.

The false science of materialism would sentence mortal man to become an outcast in the universe. Such partial knowledge is potentially evil; it is knowledge composed of both good and evil. Truth is beautiful because it is both replete and symmetrical. When man searches for truth, he pursues the divinely real.

Philosophers commit their gravest error when they are misled into the fallacy of abstraction, the practice of focusing the attention upon one aspect of reality and then of pronouncing such an isolated aspect to be the whole truth. The wise philosopher will always look for the creative design which is behind, and pre-existent to, all universe phenomena. The creator thought invariably precedes creative action.

Intellectual self-consciousness can discover the beauty of truth, its spiritual quality, not only by the philosophic consistency of its concepts, but more certainly and surely by the unerring response of the ever-present Spirit of Truth. Happiness ensues from the recognition of truth because it can be *acted out;* it can be lived. Disappointment and sorrow attend upon error because, not being a reality, it cannot be realized in experience. Divine truth is best known by its *spiritual flavor.*

The eternal quest is for unification, for divine coherence. The far-flung physical universe coheres in the Isle of Paradise; the intellectual universe coheres in the God of mind, the Conjoint Actor; the spiritual universe is coherent in the personality of the Eternal Son. But the isolated mortal of time and space coheres in God the Father through the direct relationship between the indwelling Thought Adjuster and the Universal Father. Man's Adjuster is a fragment of God and everlastingly seeks for divine unification; it coheres with, and in, the Paradise Deity of the First Source and Center.

The discernment of supreme beauty is the discovery and integration of reality: The discernment of the divine goodness in the eternal truth, that is ultimate beauty. Even the charm of human art consists in the harmony of its unity.

The great mistake of the Hebrew religion was its failure to associate the goodness of God with the factual truths of science and the appealing beauty of art. As civilization progressed, and since religion continued to pursue the same unwise course of overemphasizing the goodness of God to the relative exclusion of truth and neglect of beauty, there developed an increasing tendency for certain types of men to turn away from the abstract and dissociated concept of isolated goodness. The overstressed and isolated morality of modern religion, which fails to hold the devotion and loyalty of many twentieth-century men, would rehabilitate itself if, in addition to its moral mandates, it would give equal consideration to the truths of science, philosophy, and spiritual experience, and to the beauties of the physical creation, the charm of intellectual art, and the grandeur of genuine character achievement.

The religious challenge of this age is to those farseeing and forward-looking men and women of spiritual insight who will dare to construct a new and appealing philosophy of living out of the enlarged and exquisitely integrated modern concepts of cosmic truth, universe beauty, and divine goodness. Such a new and righteous vision of morality will attract all that is good in the mind of man and challenge that which is best in the human soul. Truth, beauty, and goodness are divine realities, and as man ascends the scale of spiritual living, these supreme qualities of the Eternal become increasingly co-ordinated and unified in God, who is love.

All truth—material, philosophic, or spiritual—is both beautiful and good. All real beauty—material art or spiritual symmetry—is both true and good. All genuine goodness—whether personal morality, social equity, or divine ministry—is equally true and beautiful. Health, sanity, and happiness are integrations of truth, beauty, and goodness as they are blended in human experience. Such levels of efficient living come about through the unification of energy systems, idea systems, and spirit systems.

Truth is coherent, beauty attractive, goodness stabilizing. And when these values of that which is real are co-ordinated in personality experience, the result is a high order of love conditioned by wisdom and qualified by loyalty. The real purpose of all universe education is to effect the better co-ordination of the isolated child of the worlds with the larger realities of his expanding experience. Reality is finite on the human level, infinite and eternal on the higher and divine levels.

[Presented by a Divine Counselor acting by authority of the Ancients of Days on Uversa.]

PAPER 3

THE ATTRIBUTES OF GOD

GOD is everywhere present; the Universal Father rules the circle of eternity. But he rules in the local universes in the persons of his Paradise Creator Sons, even as he bestows life through these Sons. "God has given us eternal life, and this life is in his Sons." These Creator Sons of God are the personal expression of himself in the sectors of time and to the children of the whirling planets of the evolving universes of space.

The highly personalized Sons of God are clearly discernible by the lower orders of created intelligences, and so do they compensate for the invisibility of the infinite and therefore less discernible Father. The Paradise Creator Sons of the Universal Father are a revelation of an otherwise invisible being, invisible because of the absoluteness and infinity inherent in the circle of eternity and in the personalities of the Paradise Deities.

Creatorship is hardly an attribute of God; it is rather the aggregate of his acting nature. And this universal function of creatorship is eternally manifested as it is conditioned and controlled by all the co-ordinated attributes of the infinite and divine reality of the First Source and Center. We sincerely doubt whether any one characteristic of the divine nature can be regarded as being antecedent to the others, but if such were the case, then the creatorship nature of Deity would take precedence over all other natures, activities, and attributes. And the creatorship of Deity culminates in the universal truth of the Fatherhood of God.

1. GOD'S EVERYWHERENESS

The ability of the Universal Father to be everywhere present, and at the same time, constitutes his omnipresence. God alone can be in two places, in numberless places, at the same time. God is simultaneously present "in heaven above and on the earth beneath"; as the Psalmist exclaimed: "Whither shall I go from your spirit? or whither shall I flee from your presence?"

"'I am a God at hand as well as afar off,' says the Lord. 'Do not I fill heaven and earth?'" The Universal Father is all the time present in all parts and in all hearts of his far-flung creation. He is "the fullness of him who fills all and in all," and "who works all in all," and further, the concept of his personality is such that "the heaven (universe) and heaven of heavens (universe of universes) cannot contain him." It is literally true that God is all and in all. But even that is not *all* of God. The Infinite can be finally revealed only in infinity; the cause can never be fully comprehended by an analysis of effects; the living God is immeasurably greater than the sum total of creation that has come into being as a result of the creative acts of his unfettered free will. God is revealed throughout the cosmos, but the cosmos can never contain or encompass the entirety of the infinity of God.

The Father's presence unceasingly patrols the master universe. "His going forth is from the end of the heaven, and his circuit to the ends of it; and there is nothing hidden from the light thereof."

The creature not only exists in God, but God also lives in the creature. "We know we dwell in him because he lives in us; he has given us his spirit. This gift from the Paradise Father is man's inseparable companion." "He is the ever-present and all-pervading God." "The spirit of the everlasting Father is concealed in the mind of every mortal child." "Man goes forth searching for a friend while that very friend lives within his own heart." "The true God is not afar off; he is a part of us; his spirit speaks from within us." "The Father lives in the child. God is always with us. He is the guiding spirit of eternal destiny."

Truly of the human race has it been said, "You are of God" because "he who dwells in love dwells in God, and God in him." Even in wrongdoing you torment the indwelling gift of God, for the Thought Adjuster must needs go through the consequences of evil thinking with the human mind of its incarceration.

The omnipresence of God is in reality a part of his infinite nature; space constitutes no barrier to Deity. God is, in perfection and without limitation, discernibly present only on Paradise and in the central universe. He is not thus observably present in the creations encircling Havona, for God has limited his direct and actual presence in recognition of the sovereignty and the divine prerogatives of the co-ordinate creators and rulers of the universes of time and space. Hence must the concept of the divine presence allow for a wide range of both mode and channel of manifestation embracing the presence circuits of the Eternal Son, the Infinite Spirit, and the Isle of Paradise. Nor is it always possible to distinguish between the presence of the Universal Father and the actions of his eternal co-ordinates and agencies, so perfectly do they fulfill all the infinite requirements of his unchanging purpose. But not so with the personality circuit and the Adjusters; here God acts uniquely, directly, and exclusively.

The Universal Controller is potentially present in the gravity circuits of the Isle of Paradise in all parts of the universe at all times and in the same degree, in accordance with the mass, in response to the physical demands for this presence, and because of the inherent nature of all creation which causes all things to adhere and consist in him. Likewise is the First Source and Center potentially present in the Unqualified Absolute, the repository of the uncreated universes of the eternal future. God thus potentially pervades the physical universes of the past, present, and future. He is the primordial foundation of the coherence of the so-called material creation. This nonspiritual Deity potential becomes actual here and there throughout the level of physical existences by the inexplicable intrusion of some one of his exclusive agencies upon the stage of universe action.

The mind presence of God is correlated with the absolute mind of the Conjoint Actor, the Infinite Spirit, but in the finite creations it is better discerned in the everywhere functioning of the cosmic mind of the Paradise Master Spirits. Just as the First Source and Center is potentially present in the mind circuits of the Conjoint Actor, so is he potentially present in the tensions of the Universal Absolute. But mind of the human order is a bestowal of the Daughters of the Conjoint Actor, the Divine Ministers of the evolving universes.

The everywhere-present spirit of the Universal Father is co-ordinated with the function of the universal spirit presence of the Eternal Son and the everlasting divine potential of the Deity Absolute. But neither the spiritual activity of the Eternal Son and his Paradise Sons nor the mind bestowals of the Infinite Spirit seem to exclude the direct action of the Thought Adjusters, the indwelling fragments of God, in the hearts of his creature children.

Concerning God's presence in a planet, system, constellation, or a universe, the degree of such presence in any creational unit is a measure of the degree of the evolving presence of the Supreme Being: It is determined by the en masse recognition of God and loyalty to him on the part of the vast universe organization, running down to the systems and planets themselves. Therefore it is sometimes with the hope of conserving and safeguarding these phases of God's precious presence that, when some planets (or even systems) have plunged far into spiritual darkness, they are in a certain sense quarantined, or partially isolated from intercourse with the larger units of creation. And all this, as it operates on Urantia, is a spiritually defensive reaction of the majority of the worlds to save themselves, as far as possible, from suffering the isolating consequences of the alienating acts of a headstrong, wicked, and rebellious minority.

While the Father parentally encircuits all his sons—all personalities—his influence in them is limited by the remoteness of their origin from the Second and the Third Persons of Deity and augmented as their destiny attainment nears such levels. The *fact* of God's presence in creature minds is determined by whether or not they are indwelt by Father fragments, such as the Mystery Monitors, but his *effective* presence is determined by the degree of co-operation accorded these indwelling Adjusters by the minds of their sojourn.

The fluctuations of the Father's presence are not due to the changeableness of God. The Father does not retire in seclusion because he has been slighted; his affections are not alienated because of the creature's wrongdoing. Rather, having been endowed with the power of choice (concerning Himself), his children, in the exercise of that choice, directly determine the degree and limitations of the Father's divine influence in their own hearts and souls. The Father has freely bestowed himself upon us without limit and without favor. He is no respecter of persons, planets, systems, or universes. In the sectors of time he confers differential honor only on the Paradise personalities of God the Sevenfold, the co-ordinate creators of the finite universes.

2. GOD'S INFINITE POWER

All the universes know that "the Lord God omnipotent reigns." The affairs of this world and other worlds are divinely supervised. "He does according to his will in the army of heaven and among the inhabitants of the earth." It is eternally true, "there is no power but of God."

Within the bounds of that which is consistent with the divine nature, it is literally true that "with God all things are possible." The long-drawn-out evolutionary processes of peoples, planets, and universes are under the perfect control of the universe creators and administrators and unfold in accordance with the eternal purpose of the Universal Father, proceeding in harmony and order and in keeping with the all-wise plan of God. There is only one lawgiver. He upholds the worlds in space and swings the universes around the endless circle of the eternal circuit.

Of all the divine attributes, his omnipotence, especially as it prevails in the material universe, is the best understood. Viewed as an unspiritual phenomenon, God is energy. This declaration of physical fact is predicated on the incomprehensible truth that the First Source and Center is the primal cause of the universal physical phenomena of all space. From this divine activity all physical energy and other material manifestations are derived. Light, that is, light without heat, is another of the nonspiritual manifestations of the Deities. And there is still another form of nonspiritual energy which is virtually unknown on Urantia; it is as yet unrecognized.

God controls all power; he has made "a way for the lightning"; he has ordained the circuits of all energy. He has decreed the time and manner of the manifestation of all forms of energy-matter. And all these things are held forever in his everlasting grasp—in the gravitational control centering on nether Paradise. The light and energy of the eternal God thus swing on forever around his majestic circuit, the endless but orderly procession of the starry hosts composing the universe of universes. All creation circles eternally around the Paradise-Personality center of all things and beings.

The omnipotence of the Father pertains to the everywhere dominance of the absolute level, whereon the three energies, material, mindal, and spiritual, are indistinguishable in close proximity to him—the Source of all things. Creature mind, being neither Paradise monota nor Paradise spirit, is not directly responsive to the Universal Father. God *adjusts* with the mind of imperfection—with Urantia mortals through the Thought Adjusters.

The Universal Father is not a transient force, a shifting power, or a fluctuating energy. The power and wisdom of the Father are wholly adequate to cope with any and all universe exigencies. As the emergencies of human experience arise, he has foreseen them all, and therefore he does not react to the affairs of the universe in a detached way but rather in accordance with the dictates of eternal wisdom and in consonance with the mandates of infinite judgment. Regardless of appearances, the power of God is not functioning in the universe as a blind force.

Situations do arise in which it appears that emergency rulings have been made, that natural laws have been suspended, that misadaptations have been recognized, and that an effort is being made to rectify the situation; but such is not the case. Such concepts of God have their origin in the limited range of your viewpoint, in the finiteness of your comprehension, and in the circumscribed scope of your survey; such misunderstanding of God is due to the profound ignorance you enjoy regarding the existence of the higher laws of the realm, the magnitude of the Father's character, the infinity of his attributes, and the fact of his free-willness.

The planetary creatures of God's spirit indwelling, scattered hither and yon throughout the universes of space, are so nearly infinite in number and order, their intellects are so diverse, their minds are so limited and sometimes so gross, their vision is so curtailed and localized, that it is almost impossible to formulate generalizations of law adequately expressive of the Father's infinite attributes and at the same time to any degree comprehensible to these created intelligences. Therefore, to you the creature, many of the acts of the all-powerful Creator seem to be arbitrary, detached, and not infrequently heartless and cruel. But again I assure you that this is not true. God's doings are all purposeful, intelligent, wise, kind, and eternally considerate of the best good, not always of an individual being, an individual race, an individual planet, or even an individual universe; but they are for the welfare and best good of all concerned, from the lowest to the highest. In the epochs of time the welfare of the part may sometimes appear to differ from the welfare of the whole; in the circle of eternity such apparent differences are nonexistent.

We are all a part of the family of God, and we must therefore sometimes share in the family discipline. Many of the acts of God which so disturb and confuse us are the result of the decisions and final rulings of all-wisdom, empowering the Conjoint Actor to execute the choosing of the infallible will of the infinite mind, to enforce the decisions of the personality of perfection, whose survey, vision, and solicitude embrace the highest and eternal welfare of all his vast and far-flung creation.

Thus it is that your detached, sectional, finite, gross, and highly materialistic viewpoint and the limitations inherent in the nature of your being constitute such a handicap that you are unable to see, comprehend, or know the wisdom and kindness of many of the divine acts which to you seem fraught with such crushing cruelty, and which seem to be characterized by such utter indifference to the comfort and welfare, to the planetary happiness and personal prosperity, of your fellow creatures. It is because of the limits of human vision, it is because of your circumscribed understanding and finite comprehension, that you misunderstand the motives, and pervert the purposes, of God. But many things occur on the evolutionary worlds which are not the personal doings of the Universal Father.

The divine omnipotence is perfectly co-ordinated with the other attributes of the personality of God. The power of God is, ordinarily, only limited in its universe spiritual manifestation by three conditions or situations:

1. By the nature of God, especially by his infinite love, by truth, beauty, and goodness.
2. By the will of God, by his mercy ministry and fatherly relationship with the personalities of the universe.
3. By the law of God, by the righteousness and justice of the eternal Paradise Trinity.

God is unlimited in power, divine in nature, final in will, infinite in attributes, eternal in wisdom, and absolute in reality. But all these characteristics of the Universal Father are unified in Deity and universally expressed in the Paradise Trinity and in the divine Sons of the Trinity. Otherwise, outside of Paradise and the central universe of Havona, everything pertaining to God is limited by the evolutionary presence of the Supreme, conditioned by the eventuating presence of the Ultimate, and co-ordinated by the three existential Absolutes—Deity, Universal, and Unqualified. And God's presence is thus limited because such is the will of God.

3. GOD'S UNIVERSAL KNOWLEDGE

"God knows all things." The divine mind is conscious of, and conversant with, the thought of all creation. His knowledge of events is universal and perfect. The divine entities going out from him are a part of him; he who "balances the clouds" is also "perfect in knowledge." "The eyes of the Lord are in every place." Said your great teacher of the insignificant sparrow, "One of them shall not fall to the ground without my Father's knowledge," and also, "The very hairs of your head are numbered." "He tells the number of the stars; he calls them all by their names."

The Universal Father is the only personality in all the universe who does actually know the number of the stars and planets of space. All the worlds of every universe are constantly within the consciousness of God. He also says: "I have surely seen the affliction of my people, I have heard their cry, and I know their sorrows." For "the Lord looks from heaven; he beholds all the sons of men; from the place of his habitation he looks upon all the inhabitants of the earth." Every creature child may truly say: "He knows the way I take, and when he has tried me, I shall come forth as gold." "God knows our downsittings and our uprisings; he understands our thoughts afar off and is acquainted with all our ways." "All things are naked and open to the eyes of him with whom we have to do." And it should be a real comfort to every human being to understand that "he knows your frame; he remembers that you are dust." Jesus, speaking of the living God, said, "Your Father knows what you have need of even before you ask him."

God is possessed of unlimited power to know all things; his consciousness is universal. His personal circuit encompasses all personalities, and his knowledge of even the lowly creatures is supplemented indirectly through the descending series of divine Sons and directly through the indwelling Thought Adjusters. And furthermore, the Infinite Spirit is all the time everywhere present.

We are not wholly certain as to whether or not God chooses to foreknow events of sin. But even if God should foreknow the freewill acts of his children, such foreknowledge does not in the least abrogate their freedom. One thing is certain: God is never subjected to surprise.

Omnipotence does not imply the power to do the nondoable, the ungodlike act. Neither does omniscience imply the knowing of the unknowable. But such statements can hardly be made comprehensible to the finite mind. The creature can hardly understand the range and limitations of the will of the Creator.

4. GOD'S LIMITLESSNESS

The successive bestowal of himself upon the universes as they are brought into being in no wise lessens the potential of power or the store of wisdom as they continue to reside and repose in the central personality of Deity. In potential of force, wisdom, and love, the Father has never lessened aught of his possession nor become divested of any attribute of his glorious personality as the result of the unstinted bestowal of himself upon the Paradise Sons, upon his subordinate creations, and upon the manifold creatures thereof.

The creation of every new universe calls for a new adjustment of gravity; but even if creation should continue indefinitely, eternally, even to infinity, so that eventually the material creation would exist without limitations, still the power of control and co-ordination reposing in the Isle of Paradise would be found equal to, and adequate for, the mastery, control, and co-ordination of such an infinite universe. And subsequent to this bestowal of limitless force and power upon a boundless universe, the Infinite would still be surcharged with the same degree of force and energy; the Unqualified Absolute would still be undiminished; God would still possess the same infinite potential, just as if force, energy, and power had never been poured forth for the endowment of universe upon universe.

And so with wisdom: The fact that mind is so freely distributed to the thinking of the realms in no wise impoverishes the central source of divine wisdom. As the universes multiply, and beings of the realms increase in number to the limits of comprehension, if mind continues without end to be bestowed upon these beings of high and low estate, still will God's central personality continue to embrace the same eternal, infinite, and all-wise mind.

The fact that he sends forth spirit messengers from himself to indwell the men and women of your world and other worlds in no wise lessens his ability to function as a divine and all-powerful spirit personality; and there is absolutely no limit to the extent or number of such spirit Monitors which he can and may send out. This giving of himself to his creatures creates a boundless, almost inconceivable future possibility of progressive and successive existences for these divinely endowed mortals. And this prodigal distribution of himself as these ministering spirit entities in no manner diminishes the wisdom and perfection of truth and knowledge which repose in the person of the all-wise, all-knowing, and all-powerful Father.

To the mortals of time there is a future, but God inhabits eternity. Even though I hail from near the very abiding place of Deity, I cannot presume to speak with perfection of understanding concerning the infinity of many of the divine attributes. Infinity of mind alone can fully comprehend infinity of existence and eternity of action.

Mortal man cannot possibly know the infinitude of the heavenly Father. Finite mind cannot think through such an absolute truth or fact. But this same finite human being can actually *feel*—literally experience—the full and undiminished impact of such an infinite Father's LOVE. Such a love can be truly experienced, albeit while quality of experience is unlimited, quantity of such an experience is strictly limited by the human capacity for spiritual receptivity and by the associated capacity to love the Father in return.

Finite appreciation of infinite qualities far transcends the logically limited capacities of the creature because of the fact that mortal man is made in the image of God—there lives within him a fragment of infinity. Therefore man's nearest and dearest approach to God is by and through love, for God is love. And all of such a unique relationship is an actual experience in cosmic sociology, the Creator-creature relationship—the Father-child affection.

5. THE FATHER'S SUPREME RULE

In his contact with the post-Havona creations, the Universal Father does not exercise his infinite power and final authority by direct transmittal but rather through his Sons and their subordinate personalities. And God does all this of his own free will. Any and all powers delegated, if occasion should arise, if it should become the choice of the divine mind, could be exercised direct; but, as a rule, such action only takes place as a result of the failure of the delegated personality to fulfill the divine trust. At such times and in the face of such default and within the limits of the reservation of divine power and potential, the Father does act independently and in accordance with the mandates of his own choice; and that choice is always one of unfailing perfection and infinite wisdom.

The Father rules through his Sons; on down through the universe organization there is an unbroken chain of rulers ending with the Planetary Princes, who direct the destinies of the evolutionary spheres of the Father's vast domains. It is no mere poetic expression that exclaims: "The earth is the Lord's and the fullness thereof." "He removes kings and sets up kings." "The Most Highs rule in the kingdoms of men."

In the affairs of men's hearts the Universal Father may not always have his way; but in the conduct and destiny of a planet the divine plan prevails; the eternal purpose of wisdom and love triumphs.

Said Jesus: "My Father, who gave them to me, is greater than all; and no one is able to pluck them out of my Father's hand." As you glimpse the manifold workings and view the staggering immensity of God's well-nigh limitless creation, you may falter in your concept of his primacy, but you should not fail to accept him as securely and everlastingly enthroned at the Paradise center of all things and as the beneficent Father of all intelligent beings. There is but "one God and Father of all, who is above all and in all," "and he is before all things, and in him all things consist."

The uncertainties of life and the vicissitudes of existence do not in any manner contradict the concept of the universal sovereignty of God. All evolutionary creature life is beset by certain *inevitabilities.* Consider the following:

1. Is *courage*—strength of character—desirable? Then must man be reared in an environment which necessitates grappling with hardships and reacting to disappointments.

2. Is *altruism*—service of one's fellows—desirable? Then must life experience provide for encountering situations of social inequality.

3. Is *hope*—the grandeur of trust—desirable? Then human existence must constantly be confronted with insecurities and recurrent uncertainties.

4. Is *faith*—the supreme assertion of human thought—desirable? Then must the mind of man find itself in that troublesome predicament where it ever knows less than it can believe.

5. Is the *love of truth* and the willingness to go wherever it leads, desirable? Then must man grow up in a world where error is present and falsehood always possible.

6. Is *idealism*—the approaching concept of the divine—desirable? Then must man struggle in an environment of relative goodness and beauty, surroundings stimulative of the irrepressible reach for better things.

7. Is *loyalty*—devotion to highest duty—desirable? Then must man carry on amid the possibilities of betrayal and desertion. The valor of devotion to duty consists in the implied danger of default.

8. Is *unselfishness*—the spirit of self-forgetfulness—desirable? Then must mortal man live face to face with the incessant clamoring of an inescapable self for recognition and honor. Man could not dynamically choose the divine life if there were no self-life to forsake. Man could never lay saving hold on righteousness if there were no potential evil to exalt and differentiate the good by contrast.

9. Is *pleasure*—the satisfaction of happiness—desirable? Then must man live in a world where the alternative of pain and the likelihood of suffering are ever-present experiential possibilities.

Throughout the universe, every unit is regarded as a part of the whole. Survival of the part is dependent on co-operation with the plan and purpose of the whole, the wholehearted desire and perfect willingness to do the Father's divine will. The only evolutionary world without error (the possibility of unwise judgment) would be a world without *free* intelligence. In the Havona universe there are a billion perfect worlds with their perfect inhabitants, but evolving man must be fallible if he is to be free. Free and inexperienced intelligence cannot possibly at first be uniformly wise. The possibility of mistaken judgment (evil) becomes sin only when the human will consciously endorses and knowingly embraces a deliberate immoral judgment.

The full appreciation of truth, beauty, and goodness is inherent in the perfection of the divine universe. The inhabitants of the Havona worlds do not require the potential of relative value levels as a choice stimulus; such perfect beings are able to identify and choose the good in the absence of all contrastive and thought-compelling moral situations. But all such perfect beings are, in moral nature and spiritual status, what they are by virtue of the fact of existence. They have experientially earned advancement only within their inherent status. Mortal man earns even his status as an ascension candidate by his own faith and hope. Everything divine which the human mind grasps and the human soul acquires is an experiential attainment; it is a *reality* of personal experience and is therefore a unique possession in contrast to the inherent goodness and righteousness of the inerrant personalities of Havona.

The creatures of Havona are naturally brave, but they are not courageous in the human sense. They are innately kind and considerate, but hardly altruistic in the human way. They are expectant of a pleasant future, but not hopeful in the exquisite manner of the trusting mortal of the uncertain evolutionary spheres. They have faith in the stability of the universe, but they are utter strangers to that saving faith whereby mortal man climbs from the status of an animal up to the portals of Paradise. They love the truth, but they know nothing of its soul-saving qualities. They are idealists, but they were born that way; they are wholly ignorant of the ecstasy of becoming such by exhilarating choice. They are loyal, but they have never experienced the thrill of wholehearted and intelligent devotion to duty in the face of temptation to default. They are unselfish, but they never gained such levels of experience by the magnificent conquest of a belligerent self. They enjoy pleasure, but they do not comprehend the sweetness of the pleasure escape from the pain potential.

6. THE FATHER'S PRIMACY

With divine selflessness, consummate generosity, the Universal Father relinquishes authority and delegates power, but he is still primal; his hand is on the mighty lever of the circumstances of the universal realms; he has reserved all final decisions and unerringly wields the all-powerful veto scepter of his eternal purpose with unchallengeable authority over the welfare and destiny of the outstretched, whirling, and ever-circling creation.

The sovereignty of God is unlimited; it is the fundamental fact of all creation. The universe was not inevitable. The universe is not an accident, neither is it self-existent. The universe is a work of creation and is therefore wholly subject to the will of the Creator. The will of God is divine truth, living love; therefore are the perfecting creations of the evolutionary universes characterized by goodness—nearness to divinity; by potential evil—remoteness from divinity.

All religious philosophy, sooner or later, arrives at the concept of unified universe rule, of one God. Universe causes cannot be lower than universe effects. The source of the streams of universe life and of the cosmic mind must be above the levels of their manifestation. The human mind cannot be consistently explained in terms of the lower orders of existence. Man's mind can be truly comprehended only by recognizing the reality of higher orders of thought and purposive will. Man as a moral being is inexplicable unless the reality of the Universal Father is acknowledged.

The mechanistic philosopher professes to reject the idea of a universal and sovereign will, the very sovereign will whose activity in the elaboration of universe laws he so deeply reverences. What unintended homage the mechanist pays the law-Creator when he conceives such laws to be self-acting and self-explanatory!

It is a great blunder to humanize God, except in the concept of the indwelling Thought Adjuster, but even that is not so stupid as completely to *mechanize* the idea of the First Great Source and Center.

Does the Paradise Father suffer? I do not know. The Creator Sons most certainly can and sometimes do, even as do mortals. The Eternal Son and the Infinite Spirit suffer in a modified sense. I think the Universal Father does, but I cannot understand *how;* perhaps through the personality circuit or through the individuality of the Thought Adjusters and other bestowals of his eternal nature. He has said of the mortal races, "In all your afflictions I am afflicted." He unquestionably experiences a fatherly and sympathetic understanding; he may truly suffer, but I do not comprehend the nature thereof.

The infinite and eternal Ruler of the universe of universes is power, form, energy, process, pattern, principle, presence, and idealized reality. But he is more; he is personal; he exercises a sovereign will, experiences self-consciousness of divinity, executes the mandates of a creative mind, pursues the satisfaction of the realization of an eternal purpose, and manifests a Father's love and affection for his universe children. And all these more personal traits of the Father can be better understood by observing them as they were revealed in the bestowal life of Michael, your Creator Son, while he was incarnated on Urantia.

God the Father loves men; God the Son serves men; God the Spirit inspires the children of the universe to the ever-ascending adventure of finding God the Father by the ways ordained by God the Sons through the ministry of the grace of God the Spirit.

[Being the Divine Counselor assigned to the presentation of the revelation of the Universal Father, I have continued with this statement of the attributes of Deity.]

PAPER 4
GOD'S RELATION TO THE UNIVERSE

THE Universal Father has an eternal purpose pertaining to the material, intellectual, and spiritual phenomena of the universe of universes, which he is executing throughout all time. God created the universes of his own free and sovereign will, and he created them in accordance with his all-wise and eternal purpose. It is doubtful whether anyone except the Paradise Deities and their highest associates really knows very much about the eternal purpose of God. Even the exalted citizens of Paradise hold very diverse opinions about the nature of the eternal purpose of the Deities.

It is easy to deduce that the purpose in creating the perfect central universe of Havona was purely the satisfaction of the divine nature. Havona may serve as the pattern creation for all other universes and as the finishing school for the pilgrims of time on their way to Paradise; however, such a supernal creation must exist primarily for the pleasure and satisfaction of the perfect and infinite Creators.

The amazing plan for perfecting evolutionary mortals and, after their attainment of Paradise and the Corps of the Finality, providing further training for some undisclosed future work, does seem to be, at present, one of the chief concerns of the seven superuniverses and their many subdivisions; but this ascension scheme for spiritualizing and training the mortals of time and space is by no means the exclusive occupation of the universe intelligences. There are, indeed, many other fascinating pursuits which occupy the time and enlist the energies of the celestial hosts.

1. THE UNIVERSE ATTITUDE OF THE FATHER

For ages the inhabitants of Urantia have misunderstood the providence of God. There is a providence of divine outworking on your world, but it is not the childish, arbitrary, and material ministry many mortals have conceived it to be. The providence of God consists in the interlocking activities of the celestial beings and the divine spirits who, in accordance with cosmic law, unceasingly labor for the honor of God and for the spiritual advancement of his universe children.

Can you not advance in your concept of God's dealing with man to that level where you recognize that the watchword of the universe is *progress?* Through long ages the human race has struggled to reach its present position. Throughout all these millenniums Providence has been working out the plan of progressive evolution. The two thoughts are not opposed in practice, only in man's mistaken concepts. Divine providence is never arrayed in opposition to true human progress, either temporal or spiritual. Providence is always consistent with the unchanging and perfect nature of the supreme Lawmaker.

"God is faithful" and "all his commandments are just." "His faithfulness is established in the very skies." "Forever, O Lord, your word is settled in heaven. Your faithfulness is to all generations; you have established the earth and it abides." "He is a faithful Creator."

There is no limitation of the forces and personalities which the Father may use to uphold his purpose and sustain his creatures. "The eternal God is our refuge, and underneath are the everlasting arms." "He who dwells in the secret place of the Most High shall abide under the shadow of the Almighty." "Behold, he who keeps us shall neither slumber nor sleep." "We know that all things work together for good to those who love God," "for the eyes of the Lord are over the righteous, and his ears are open to their prayers."

God upholds "all things by the word of his power." And when new worlds are born, he "sends forth his Sons and they are created." God not only creates, but he "preserves them all." God constantly upholds all things material and all beings spiritual. The universes are eternally stable. There is stability in the midst of apparent instability. There is an underlying order and security in the midst of the energy upheavals and the physical cataclysms of the starry realms.

The Universal Father has not withdrawn from the management of the universes; he is not an inactive Deity. If God should retire as the present upholder of all creation, there would immediately occur a universal collapse. Except for God, there would be no such thing as *reality.* At this very moment, as during the remote ages of the past and in the eternal future, God continues to uphold. The divine reach extends around the circle of eternity. The universe is not wound up like a clock to run just so long and then cease to function; all things are constantly being renewed. The Father unceasingly pours forth energy, light, and life. The work of God is literal as well as spiritual. "He stretches out the north over the empty space and hangs the earth upon nothing."

A being of my order is able to discover ultimate harmony and to detect far-reaching and profound co-ordination in the routine affairs of universe administration. Much that seems disjointed and haphazard to the mortal mind appears orderly and constructive to my understanding. But there is very much going on in the universes that I do not fully comprehend. I have long been a student of, and am more or less conversant with, the recognized forces, energies, minds, morontias, spirits, and personalities of the local universes and the superuniverses. I have a general understanding of how these agencies and personalities operate, and I am intimately familiar with the workings of the accredited spirit intelligences of the grand universe. Notwithstanding my knowledge of the phenomena of the universes, I am constantly confronted with cosmic reactions which I cannot fully fathom. I am continually encountering apparently fortuitous conspiracies of the interassociation of forces, energies, intellects, and spirits, which I cannot satisfactorily explain.

I am entirely competent to trace out and to analyze the working of all phenomena directly resulting from the functioning of the Universal Father, the Eternal Son, the Infinite Spirit, and, to a large extent, the Isle of Paradise. My perplexity is occasioned by encountering what appears to be the performance of their mysterious co-ordinates, the three Absolutes of potentiality. These Absolutes seem to supersede matter, to transcend mind, and to supervene spirit. I am constantly confused and often perplexed by my inability to comprehend these complex transactions which I attribute to the presences and performances of the Unqualified Absolute, the Deity Absolute, and the Universal Absolute.

These Absolutes must be the not-fully-revealed presences abroad in the universe which, in the phenomena of space potency and in the function of other superultimates, render it impossible for physicists, philosophers, or even religionists to predict with certainty as to just how the primordials of force, concept, or spirit will respond to demands made in a complex reality situation involving supreme adjustments and ultimate values.

There is also an organic unity in the universes of time and space which seems to underlie the whole fabric of cosmic events. This living presence of the evolving Supreme Being, this Immanence of the Projected Incomplete, is inexplicably manifested ever and anon by what appears to be an amazingly fortuitous co-ordination of apparently unrelated universe happenings. This must be the function of Providence—the realm of the Supreme Being and the Conjoint Actor.

I am inclined to believe that it is this far-flung and generally unrecognizable control of the co-ordination and interassociation of all phases and forms of universe activity that causes such a variegated and apparently hopelessly confused medley of physical, mental, moral, and spiritual phenomena so unerringly to work out to the glory of God and for the good of men and angels.

But in the larger sense the apparent "accidents" of the cosmos are undoubtedly a part of the finite drama of the time-space adventure of the Infinite in his eternal manipulation of the Absolutes.

2. GOD AND NATURE

Nature is in a limited sense the physical habit of God. The conduct, or action, of God is qualified and provisionally modified by the experimental plans and the evolutionary patterns of a local universe, a constellation, a system, or a planet. God acts in accordance with a well-defined, unchanging, immutable law throughout the wide-spreading master universe; but he modifies the patterns of his action so as to contribute to the co-ordinate and balanced conduct of each universe, constellation, system, planet, and personality in accordance with the local objects, aims, and plans of the finite projects of evolutionary unfolding.

Therefore, nature, as mortal man understands it, presents the underlying foundation and fundamental background of a changeless Deity and his immutable laws, modified by, fluctuating because of, and experiencing upheavals through, the working of the local plans, purposes, patterns, and conditions which have been inaugurated and are being carried out by the local universe, constellation, system, and planetary forces and personalities. For example: As God's laws have been ordained in Nebadon, they are modified by the plans established by the Creator Son and Creative Spirit of this local universe; and in addition to all this the operation of these laws has been further influenced by the errors, defaults, and insurrections of certain beings resident upon your planet and belonging to your immediate planetary system of Satania.

Nature is a time-space resultant of two cosmic factors: first, the immutability, perfection, and rectitude of Paradise Deity, and second, the experimental plans, executive blunders, insurrectionary errors, incompleteness of development, and imperfection of wisdom of the extra-Paradise creatures, from the highest to the lowest. Nature therefore carries a uniform, unchanging, majestic, and marvelous thread of perfection from the circle of eternity; but in each universe, on each planet, and in each individual life, this nature is modified, qualified, and perchance marred by the acts, the mistakes, and the disloyalties of the creatures of the evolutionary systems and universes; and therefore must nature ever be of a changing mood, whimsical withal, though stable underneath, and varied in accordance with the operating procedures of a local universe.

Nature is the perfection of Paradise divided by the incompletion, evil, and sin of the unfinished universes. This quotient is thus expressive of both the perfect and the partial, of both the eternal and the temporal. Continuing evolution modifies nature by augmenting the content of Paradise perfection and by diminishing the content of the evil, error, and disharmony of relative reality.

God is not personally present in nature or in any of the forces of nature, for the phenomenon of nature is the superimposition of the imperfections of progressive evolution and, sometimes, the consequences of insurrectionary rebellion, upon the Paradise foundations of God's universal law. As it appears on such a world as Urantia, nature can never be the adequate expression, the true representation, the faithful portrayal, of an all-wise and infinite God.

Nature, on your world, is a qualification of the laws of perfection by the evolutionary plans of the local universe. What a travesty to worship nature because it is in a limited, qualified sense pervaded by God; because it is a phase of the universal and, therefore, divine power! Nature also is a manifestation of the unfinished, the incomplete, the imperfect outworkings of the development, growth, and progress of a universe experiment in cosmic evolution.

The apparent defects of the natural world are not indicative of any such corresponding defects in the character of God. Rather are such observed imperfections merely the inevitable stop-moments in the exhibition of the ever-moving reel of infinity picturization. It is these very defect-interruptions of perfection-continuity which make it possible for the finite mind of material man to catch a fleeting glimpse of divine reality in time and space. The material manifestations of divinity appear defective to the evolutionary mind of man only because mortal man persists in viewing the phenomena of nature through natural eyes, human vision unaided by morontia mota or by revelation, its compensatory substitute on the worlds of time.

And nature is marred, her beautiful face is scarred, her features are seared, by the rebellion, the misconduct, the misthinking of the myriads of creatures who are a part of nature, but who have contributed to her disfigurement in time. No, nature is not God. Nature is not an object of worship.

3. GOD'S UNCHANGING CHARACTER

All too long has man thought of God as one like himself. God is not, never was, and never will be jealous of man or any other being in the universe of universes. Knowing that the Creator Son intended man to be the masterpiece of the planetary creation, to be the ruler of all the earth, the sight of his being dominated by his own baser passions, the spectacle of his bowing down before idols of wood, stone, gold, and selfish ambition—these sordid scenes stir God and his Sons to be jealous *for* man, but never of him.

The eternal God is incapable of wrath and anger in the sense of these human emotions and as man understands such reactions. These sentiments are mean and despicable; they are hardly worthy of being called human, much less divine; and such attitudes are utterly foreign to the perfect nature and gracious character of the Universal Father.

Much, very much, of the difficulty which Urantia mortals have in understanding God is due to the far-reaching consequences of the Lucifer rebellion and the Caligastia betrayal. On worlds not segregated by sin, the evolutionary races are able to formulate far better ideas of the Universal Father; they suffer less from confusion, distortion, and perversion of concept.

God repents of nothing he has ever done, now does, or ever will do. He is all-wise as well as all-powerful. Man's wisdom grows out of the trials and errors of human experience; God's wisdom consists in the unqualified perfection of his infinite universe insight, and this divine foreknowledge effectively directs the creative free will.

The Universal Father never does anything that causes subsequent sorrow or regret, but the will creatures of the planning and making of his Creator personalities in the outlying universes, by their unfortunate choosing, sometimes occasion emotions of divine sorrow in the personalities of their Creator parents. But though the Father neither makes mistakes, harbors regrets, nor experiences sorrows, he is a being with a father's affection, and his heart is undoubtedly grieved when his children fail to attain the spiritual levels they are capable of reaching with the assistance which has been so freely provided by the spiritual-attainment plans and the mortal-ascension policies of the universes.

The infinite goodness of the Father is beyond the comprehension of the finite mind of time; hence must there always be afforded a contrast with comparative evil (not sin) for the effective exhibition of all phases of relative goodness. Perfection of divine goodness can be discerned by mortal imperfection of insight only because it stands in contrastive association with relative imperfection in the relationships of time and matter in the motions of space.

The character of God is infinitely superhuman; therefore must such a nature of divinity be personalized, as in the divine Sons, before it can even be faith-grasped by the finite mind of man.

4. THE REALIZATION OF GOD

God is the only stationary, self-contained, and changeless being in the whole universe of universes, having no outside, no beyond, no past, and no future. God is purposive energy (creative spirit) and absolute will, and these are self-existent and universal.

Since God is self-existent, he is absolutely independent. The very identity of God is inimical to change. "I, the Lord, change not." God is immutable; but not until you achieve Paradise status can you even begin to understand how God can pass from simplicity to complexity, from identity to variation, from quiescence to motion, from infinity to finitude, from the divine to the human, and from unity to duality and triunity. And God can thus modify the manifestations of his absoluteness because divine immutability does not imply immobility; God has will—he *is* will.

God is the being of absolute self-determination; there are no limits to his universe reactions save those which are self-imposed, and his freewill acts are conditioned only by those divine qualities and perfect attributes which inherently characterize his eternal nature. Therefore is God related to the universe as the being of final goodness plus a free will of creative infinity.

The Father-Absolute is the creator of the central and perfect universe and the Father of all other Creators. Personality, goodness, and numerous other characteristics, God shares with man and other beings, but infinity of will is his alone. God is limited in his creative acts only by the sentiments of his eternal nature and by the dictates of his infinite wisdom. God personally chooses only that which is infinitely perfect, hence the supernal perfection of the central universe; and while the Creator Sons fully share his divinity, even phases of his absoluteness, they are not altogether limited by that finality of wisdom which directs the Father's infinity of will. Hence, in the Michael order of sonship, creative free will becomes even more active, wholly divine and well-nigh ultimate, if not absolute. The Father is infinite and eternal, but to deny the possibility of his volitional self-limitation amounts to a denial of this very concept of his volitional absoluteness.

God's absoluteness pervades all seven levels of universe reality. And the whole of this absolute nature is subject to the relationship of the Creator to his universe creature family. Precision may characterize trinitarian justice in the universe of universes, but in all his vast family relationship with the creatures of time the God of universes is governed by *divine sentiment.* First and last—eternally—the infinite God is a *Father.* Of all the possible titles by which he might appropriately be known, I have been instructed to portray the God of all creation as the Universal Father.

In God the Father freewill performances are not ruled by power, nor are they guided by intellect alone; the divine personality is defined as consisting in spirit and manifesting himself to the universes as love. Therefore, in all his personal relations with the creature personalities of the universes, the First Source and Center is always and consistently a loving Father. God is a Father in the highest sense of the term. He is eternally motivated by the perfect idealism of divine love, and that tender nature finds its strongest expression and greatest satisfaction in loving and being loved.

In science, God is the First Cause; in religion, the universal and loving Father; in philosophy, the one being who exists by himself, not dependent on any other being for existence but beneficently conferring reality of existence on all things and upon all other beings. But it requires revelation to show that the First Cause of science and the self-existent Unity of philosophy are the God of religion, full of mercy and goodness and pledged to effect the eternal survival of his children on earth.

We crave the concept of the Infinite, but we worship the experience-idea of God, our anywhere and any-time capacity to grasp the personality and divinity factors of our highest concept of Deity.

The consciousness of a victorious human life on earth is born of that creature faith which dares to challenge each recurring episode of existence when confronted with the awful spectacle of human limitations, by the unfailing declaration: Even if I cannot do this, there lives in me one who can and will do it, a part of the Father-Absolute of the universe of universes. And that is "the victory which overcomes the world, even your faith."

5. ERRONEOUS IDEAS OF GOD

Religious tradition is the imperfectly preserved record of the experiences of the God-knowing men of past ages, but such records are untrustworthy as guides for religious living or as the source of true information about the Universal

Father. Such ancient beliefs have been invariably altered by the fact that primitive man was a mythmaker.

One of the greatest sources of confusion on Urantia concerning the nature of God grows out of the failure of your sacred books clearly to distinguish between the personalities of the Paradise Trinity and between Paradise Deity and the local universe creators and administrators. During the past dispensations of partial understanding, your priests and prophets failed clearly to differentiate between Planetary Princes, System Sovereigns, Constellation Fathers, Creator Sons, Superuniverse Rulers, the Supreme Being, and the Universal Father. Many of the messages of subordinate personalities, such as Life Carriers and various orders of angels, have been, in your records, presented as coming from God himself. Urantian religious thought still confuses the associate personalities of Deity with the Universal Father himself, so that all are included under one appellation.

The people of Urantia continue to suffer from the influence of primitive concepts of God. The gods who go on a rampage in the storm; who shake the earth in their wrath and strike down men in their anger; who inflict their judgments of displeasure in times of famine and flood—these are the gods of primitive religion; they are not the Gods who live and rule the universes. Such concepts are a relic of the times when men supposed that the universe was under the guidance and domination of the whims of such imaginary gods. But mortal man is beginning to realize that he lives in a realm of comparative law and order as far as concerns the administrative policies and conduct of the Supreme Creators and the Supreme Controllers.

The barbarous idea of appeasing an angry God, of propitiating an offended Lord, of winning the favor of Deity through sacrifices and penance and even by the shedding of blood, represents a religion wholly puerile and primitive, a philosophy unworthy of an enlightened age of science and truth. Such beliefs are utterly repulsive to the celestial beings and the divine rulers who serve and reign in the universes. It is an affront to God to believe, hold, or teach that innocent blood must be shed in order to win his favor or to divert the fictitious divine wrath.

The Hebrews believed that "without the shedding of blood there could be no remission of sin." They had not found deliverance from the old and pagan idea that the Gods could not be appeased except by the sight of blood, though Moses did make a distinct advance when he forbade human sacrifices and substituted therefor, in the primitive minds of his childlike Bedouin followers, the ceremonial sacrifice of animals.

The bestowal of a Paradise Son on your world was inherent in the situation of closing a planetary age; it was inescapable, and it was not made necessary for the purpose of winning the favor of God. This bestowal also happened to be the final personal act of a Creator Son in the long adventure of earning the experiential sovereignty of his universe. What a travesty upon the infinite character of God! this teaching that his fatherly heart in all its austere coldness and hardness was so untouched by the misfortunes and sorrows of his creatures that his tender mercies were not forthcoming until he saw his blameless Son bleeding and dying upon the cross of Calvary!

But the inhabitants of Urantia are to find deliverance from these ancient errors and pagan superstitions respecting the nature of the Universal Father. The revelation of the truth about God is appearing, and the human race is destined to know the Universal Father in all that beauty of character and loveliness of attributes so magnificently portrayed by the Creator Son who sojourned on Urantia as the Son of Man and the Son of God.

[Presented by a Divine Counselor of Uversa.]

PAPER 5

GOD'S RELATION TO THE INDIVIDUAL

IF THE finite mind of man is unable to comprehend how so great and so majestic a God as the Universal Father can descend from his eternal abode in infinite perfection to fraternize with the individual human creature, then must such a finite intellect rest assurance of divine fellowship upon the truth of the fact that an actual fragment of the living God resides within the intellect of every normal-minded and morally conscious Urantia mortal. The indwelling Thought Adjusters are a part of the eternal Deity of the Paradise Father. Man does not have to go farther than his own inner experience of the soul's contemplation of this spiritual-reality presence to find God and attempt communion with him.

God has distributed the infinity of his eternal nature throughout the existential realities of his six absolute co-ordinates, but he may, at any time, make direct personal contact with any part or phase or kind of creation through the agency of his prepersonal fragments. And the eternal God has also reserved to himself the prerogative of bestowing personality upon the divine Creators and the living creatures of the universe of universes, while he has further reserved the prerogative of maintaining direct and parental contact with all these personal beings through the personality circuit.

1. THE APPROACH TO GOD

The inability of the finite creature to approach the infinite Father is inherent, not in the Father's aloofness, but in the finiteness and material limitations of created beings. The magnitude of the spiritual difference between the highest personality of universe existence and the lower groups of created intelligences is inconceivable. Were it possible for the lower orders of intelligence to be transported instantly into the presence of the Father himself, they would not know they were there. They would there be just as oblivious of the presence of the Universal Father as where they now are. There is a long, long road ahead of mortal man before he can consistently and within the realms of possibility ask for safe conduct into the Paradise presence of the Universal Father. Spiritually, man must be translated many times before he can attain a plane that will yield the spiritual vision which will enable him to see even any one of the Seven Master Spirits.

Our Father is not in hiding; he is not in arbitrary seclusion. He has mobilized the resources of divine wisdom in a never-ending effort to reveal himself to the children of his universal domains. There is an infinite grandeur and an inexpressible generosity connected with the majesty of his love which causes him to yearn for the association of every created being who can comprehend, love, or approach him; and it is, therefore, the limitations inherent in you, inseparable from your finite personality and material existence, that determine the time and place and circumstances in which you may achieve the goal of the journey of mortal ascension and stand in the presence of the Father at the center of all things.

Although the approach to the Paradise presence of the Father must await your attainment of the highest finite levels of spirit progression, you should rejoice in the recognition of the ever-present possibility of immediate communion with the bestowal spirit of the Father so intimately associated with your inner soul and your spiritualizing self.

The mortals of the realms of time and space may differ greatly in innate abilities and intellectual endowment, they may enjoy environments exceptionally favorable to social advancement and moral progress, or they may suffer from the lack of almost every human aid to culture and supposed advancement in the arts of civilization; but the possibilities for spiritual progress in the ascension career are equal to all; increasing levels of spiritual insight and cosmic meanings are attained quite independently of all such sociomoral differentials of the diversified material environments on the evolutionary worlds.

However Urantia mortals may differ in their intellectual, social, economic, and even moral opportunities and endowments, forget not that their spiritual endowment is uniform and unique. They all enjoy the same divine presence of the gift from the Father, and they are all equally privileged to seek intimate personal communion with this indwelling spirit of divine origin, while they may all equally choose to accept the uniform spiritual leading of these Mystery Monitors.

If mortal man is wholeheartedly spiritually motivated, unreservedly consecrated to the doing of the Father's will, then, since he is so certainly and so effectively spiritually endowed by the indwelling and divine Adjuster, there cannot fail to materialize in that individual's experience the sublime consciousness of knowing God and the supernal assurance of surviving for the purpose of finding God by the progressive experience of becoming more and more like him.

Man is spiritually indwelt by a surviving Thought Adjuster. If such a human mind is sincerely and spiritually motivated, if such a human soul desires to know God and become like him, honestly wants to do the Father's will, there exists no negative influence of mortal deprivation nor positive power of possible interference which can prevent such a divinely motivated soul from securely ascending to the portals of Paradise.

The Father desires all his creatures to be in personal communion with him. He has on Paradise a place to receive all those whose survival status and spiritual nature make possible such attainment. Therefore settle in your philosophy now and forever: To each of you and to all of us, God is approachable, the Father is attainable, the way is open; the forces of divine love and the ways and means of divine administration are all interlocked in an effort to facilitate the advancement of every worthy intelligence of every universe to the Paradise presence of the Universal Father.

The fact that vast time is involved in the attainment of God makes the presence and personality of the Infinite none the less real. Your ascension is a part of the circuit of the seven superuniverses, and though you swing around it countless times, you may expect, in spirit and in status, to be ever swinging inward. You can depend upon being translated from sphere to sphere, from the outer circuits ever nearer the inner center, and some day, doubt not, you shall stand in the divine and central presence and see him, figuratively speaking, face to face. It is a question of the attainment of actual and literal spiritual levels; and these spiritual levels are attainable by any being who has been indwelt by a Mystery Monitor, and who has subsequently eternally fused with that Thought Adjuster.

The Father is not in spiritual hiding, but so many of his creatures have hidden themselves away in the mists of their own willful decisions and for the time being have separated themselves from the communion of his spirit and the spirit of his Son by the choosing of their own perverse ways and by the indulgence of the self-assertiveness of their intolerant minds and unspiritual natures.

Mortal man may draw near God and may repeatedly forsake the divine will so long as the power of choice remains. Man's final doom is not sealed until he has lost the power to choose the Father's will. There is never a closure of the Father's heart to the need and the petition of his children. Only do his offspring close their hearts forever to the Father's drawing power when they finally and forever lose the desire to do his divine will—to know him and to be like him. Likewise is man's eternal destiny assured when Adjuster fusion proclaims to the universe that such an ascender has made the final and irrevocable choice to live the Father's will.

The great God makes direct contact with mortal man and gives a part of his infinite and eternal and incomprehensible self to live and dwell within him. God has embarked upon the eternal adventure with man. If you yield to the leadings of the spiritual forces in you and around you, you cannot fail to attain the high destiny established by a loving God as the universe goal of his ascendant creatures from the evolutionary worlds of space.

2. THE PRESENCE OF GOD

The physical presence of the Infinite is the reality of the material universe. The mind presence of Deity must be determined by the depth of individual intellectual experience and by the evolutionary personality level. The spiritual presence of Divinity must of necessity be differential in the universe. It is determined by the spiritual capacity of receptivity and by the degree of the consecration of the creature's will to the doing of the divine will.

God lives in every one of his spirit-born sons. The Paradise Sons always have access to the presence of God, "the right hand of the Father," and all of his creature personalities have access to the "bosom of the Father." This refers to the personality circuit, whenever, wherever, and however contacted, or otherwise entails personal, self-conscious contact and communion with the Universal Father, whether at the central abode or at some other designated place, as on one of the seven sacred spheres of Paradise.

The divine presence cannot, however, be discovered anywhere in nature or even in the lives of God-knowing mortals so fully and so certainly as in your attempted communion with the indwelling Mystery Monitor, the Paradise Thought Adjuster. What a mistake to dream of God far off in the skies when the spirit of the Universal Father lives within your own mind!

It is because of this God fragment that indwells you that you can hope, as you progress in harmonizing with the Adjuster's spiritual leadings, more fully to discern the presence and transforming power of those other spiritual influences that surround you and impinge upon you but do not function as an integral part of you. The fact that you are not intellectually conscious of close and intimate contact with the indwelling Adjuster does not in the least disprove such an exalted experience. The proof of fraternity with the divine Adjuster consists wholly in the nature and extent of the fruits of the spirit which are yielded in the life experience of the individual believer. "By their fruits you shall know them."

It is exceedingly difficult for the meagerly spiritualized, material mind of mortal man to experience marked consciousness of the spirit activities of such divine entities as the Paradise Adjusters. As the soul of joint mind and Adjuster creation becomes increasingly existent, there also evolves a new phase of soul consciousness which is capable of experiencing the presence, and of recognizing the spirit leadings and other supermaterial activities, of the Mystery Monitors.

The entire experience of Adjuster communion is one involving moral status, mental motivation, and spiritual experience. The self-realization of such an achievement is mainly, though not exclusively, limited to the realms of soul consciousness, but the proofs are forthcoming and abundant in the manifestation of the fruits of the spirit in the lives of all such inner-spirit contactors.

3. TRUE WORSHIP

Though the Paradise Deities, from the universe standpoint, are as one, in their spiritual relations with such beings as inhabit Urantia they are also three distinct and separate persons. There is a difference between the Godheads in the matter of personal appeals, communion, and other intimate relations. In the highest sense, we worship the Universal Father and him only. True, we can and do worship the Father as he is manifested in his Creator Sons, but it is the Father, directly or indirectly, who is worshiped and adored.

Supplications of all kinds belong to the realm of the Eternal Son and the Son's spiritual organization. Prayers, all formal communications, everything except adoration and worship of the Universal Father, are matters that concern a local universe; they do not ordinarily proceed out of the realm of the jurisdiction of a Creator Son. But worship is undoubtedly encircuited and dispatched to the person of the Creator by the function of the Father's personality circuit. We further believe that such registry of the homage of an Adjuster-indwelt creature is facilitated by the Father's spirit presence. There exists a tremendous amount of evidence to substantiate such a belief, and I know that all orders of Father fragments are empowered to register the bona fide adoration of their subjects acceptably in the presence of the Universal Father. The Adjusters undoubtedly also utilize direct prepersonal channels of communication with God, and they are likewise able to utilize the spirit-gravity circuits of the Eternal Son.

Worship is for its own sake; prayer embodies a self- or creature-interest element; that is the great difference between worship and prayer. There is absolutely no self-request or other element of personal interest in true worship; we simply worship God for what we comprehend him to be. Worship asks nothing and expects nothing for the worshiper. We do not worship the Father because of anything we may derive from such veneration; we render such devotion and engage in such worship as a natural and spontaneous reaction to the recognition of the Father's matchless personality and because of his lovable nature and adorable attributes.

The moment the element of self-interest intrudes upon worship, that instant devotion translates from worship to prayer and more appropriately should be directed to the person of the Eternal Son or the Creator Son. But in practical religious experience there exists no reason why prayer should not be addressed to God the Father as a part of true worship.

When you deal with the practical affairs of your daily life, you are in the hands of the spirit personalities having origin in the Third Source and Center; you are co-operating with the agencies of the Conjoint Actor. And so it is: You worship God; pray to, and commune with, the Son; and work out the details of your earthly sojourn in connection with the intelligences of the Infinite Spirit operating on your world and throughout your universe.

The Creator or Sovereign Sons who preside over the destinies of the local universes stand in the place of both the Universal Father and the Eternal Son of Paradise. These Universe Sons receive, in the name of the Father, the adoration of worship and give ear to the pleas of their petitioning subjects throughout their respective creations. To the children of a local universe a Michael Son is, to all practical intents and purposes, God. He is the local universe personification of the Universal Father and the Eternal Son. The Infinite Spirit maintains personal contact with the children of these realms through the Universe Spirits, the administrative and creative associates of the Paradise Creator Sons.

Sincere worship connotes the mobilization of all the powers of the human personality under the dominance of the evolving soul and subject to the divine directionization of the associated Thought Adjuster. The mind of material limitations can never become highly conscious of the real significance of true worship. Man's realization of the reality of the worship experience is chiefly determined by the developmental status of his evolving immortal soul. The spiritual growth of the soul takes place wholly independently of the intellectual self-consciousness.

The worship experience consists in the sublime attempt of the betrothed Adjuster to communicate to the divine Father the inexpressible longings and the unutterable aspirations of the human soul—the conjoint creation of the God-seeking mortal mind and the God-revealing immortal Adjuster. Worship is, therefore, the act of the material mind's assenting to the attempt of its spiritualizing self, under the guidance of the associated spirit, to communicate with God as a faith son of the Universal Father. The mortal mind consents to worship; the immortal soul craves and initiates worship; the divine Adjuster presence conducts such worship in behalf of the mortal mind and the evolving immortal soul. True worship, in the last analysis, becomes an experience realized on four cosmic levels: the intellectual, the morontial, the spiritual, and the personal—the consciousness of mind, soul, and spirit, and their unification in personality.

4. GOD IN RELIGION

The morality of the religions of evolution *drives* men forward in the God quest by the motive power of fear. The religions of revelation *allure* men to seek for a God of love because they crave to become like him. But religion is not merely a passive feeling of "absolute dependence" and "surety of survival"; it is a living and dynamic experience of divinity attainment predicated on humanity service.

The great and immediate service of true religion is the establishment of an enduring unity in human experience, a lasting peace and a profound assurance.

With primitive man, even polytheism is a relative unification of the evolving concept of Deity; polytheism is monotheism in the making. Sooner or later, God is destined to be comprehended as the reality of values, the substance of meanings, and the life of truth.

God is not only the determiner of destiny; he *is* man's eternal destination. All nonreligious human activities seek to bend the universe to the distorting service of self; the truly religious individual seeks to identify the self with the universe and then to dedicate the activities of this unified self to the service of the universe family of fellow beings, human and superhuman.

The domains of philosophy and art intervene between the nonreligious and the religious activities of the human self. Through art and philosophy the material-minded man is inveigled into the contemplation of the spiritual realities and universe values of eternal meanings.

All religions teach the worship of Deity and some doctrine of human salvation. The Buddhist religion promises salvation from suffering, unending peace; the Jewish religion promises salvation from difficulties, prosperity predicated on righteousness; the Greek religion promised salvation from disharmony, ugliness, by the realization of beauty; Christianity promises salvation from sin, sanctity; Mohammedanism provides deliverance from the rigorous moral standards of Judaism and Christianity. The religion of Jesus *is* salvation from self, deliverance from the evils of creature isolation in time and in eternity.

The Hebrews based their religion on goodness; the Greeks on beauty; both religions sought truth. Jesus revealed a God of love, and love is all-embracing of truth, beauty, and goodness.

The Zoroastrians had a religion of morals; the Hindus a religion of metaphysics; the Confucianists a religion of ethics. Jesus lived a religion of *service.* All these religions are of value in that they are valid approaches to the religion of Jesus. Religion is destined to become the reality of the spiritual unification of all that is good, beautiful, and true in human experience.

The Greek religion had a watchword "Know yourself"; the Hebrews centered their teaching on "Know your God"; the Christians preach a gospel aimed at a "knowledge of the Lord Jesus Christ"; Jesus proclaimed the good news of "knowing God, and yourself as a son of God." These differing concepts of the purpose of religion determine the individual's attitude in various life situations and foreshadow the depth of worship and the nature of his personal habits of prayer. The spiritual status of any religion may be determined by the nature of its prayers.

The concept of a semihuman and jealous God is an inevitable transition between polytheism and sublime monotheism. An exalted anthropomorphism is the highest attainment level of purely evolutionary religion. Christianity has elevated the concept of anthropomorphism from the ideal of the human to the transcendent and divine concept of the person of the glorified Christ. And this is the highest anthropomorphism that man can ever conceive.

The Christian concept of God is an attempt to combine three separate teachings:

1. *The Hebrew concept*—God as a vindicator of moral values, a righteous God.

2. *The Greek concept*—God as a unifier, a God of wisdom.

3. *Jesus' concept*—God as a living friend, a loving Father, the divine presence.

It must therefore be evident that composite Christian theology encounters great difficulty in attaining consistency. This difficulty is further aggravated by the fact that the doctrines of early Christianity were generally based on the personal religious experience of three different persons: Philo of Alexandria, Jesus of Nazareth, and Paul of Tarsus.

In the study of the religious life of Jesus, view him positively. Think not so much of his sinlessness as of his righteousness, his loving service. Jesus upstepped the passive love disclosed in the Hebrew concept of the heavenly Father to the higher *active* and creature-loving affection of a God who is the Father of every individual, even of the wrongdoer.

5. THE CONSCIOUSNESS OF GOD

Morality has its origin in the reason of self-consciousness; it is superanimal but wholly evolutionary. Human evolution embraces in its unfolding all endowments antecedent to the bestowal of the Adjusters and to the pouring out of the Spirit of Truth. But the attainment of levels of morality does not deliver man from the real struggles of mortal living. Man's physical environment entails the battle for existence; the social surroundings necessitate ethical adjustments; the moral situations require the making of choices in the highest realms of reason; the spiritual experience (having realized God) demands that man find him and sincerely strive to be like him.

Religion is not grounded in the facts of science, the obligations of society, the assumptions of philosophy, or the implied duties of morality. Religion is an independent realm of human response to life situations and is unfailingly exhibited at all stages of human development which are postmoral. Religion may permeate all four levels of the realization of values and the enjoyment of universe fellowship: the physical or material level of self-preservation; the social or emotional level of fellowship; the moral or duty level of reason; the spiritual level of the consciousness of universe fellowship through divine worship.

The fact-seeking scientist conceives of God as the First Cause, a God of force. The emotional artist sees God as the ideal of beauty, a God of aesthetics. The reasoning philosopher is sometimes inclined to posit a God of universal unity, even a pantheistic Deity. The religionist of faith believes in a God who fosters survival, the Father in heaven, the God of love.

Moral conduct is always an antecedent of evolved religion and a part of even revealed religion, but never the whole of religious experience. Social service is the result of moral thinking and religious living. Morality does not biologically lead to the higher spiritual levels of religious experience. The adoration of the abstract beautiful is not the worship of God; neither is exaltation of nature nor the reverence of unity the worship of God.

Evolutionary religion is the mother of the science, art, and philosophy which elevated man to the level of receptivity to revealed religion, including the bestowal of Adjusters and the coming of the Spirit of Truth. The evolutionary picture of human existence begins and ends with religion, albeit very different qualities of religion, one evolutional and biological, the other revelational and periodical. And so, while religion is normal and natural to man, it is also optional. Man does not have to be religious against his will.

Religious experience, being essentially spiritual, can never be fully understood by the material mind; hence the function of theology, the psychology of religion. The essential doctrine of the human realization of God creates a paradox in finite comprehension. It is well-nigh impossible for human logic and finite reason to harmonize the concept of divine immanence, God within and a part of every individual, with the idea of God's transcendence, the divine domination of the universe of universes. These two essential concepts of Deity must be unified in the faith-grasp of the concept of the transcendence of a personal God and in the realization of the indwelling presence of a fragment of that God in order to justify intelligent worship and validate the hope of personality survival. The difficulties and paradoxes of religion are inherent in the fact that the realities of religion are utterly beyond the mortal capacity for intellectual comprehension.

Mortal man secures three great satisfactions from religious experience, even in the days of his temporal sojourn on earth:

1. *Intellectually* he acquires the satisfactions of a more unified human consciousness.

2. *Philosophically* he enjoys the substantiation of his ideals of moral values.

3. *Spiritually* he thrives in the experience of divine companionship, in the spiritual satisfactions of true worship.

God-consciousness, as it is experienced by an evolving mortal of the realms, must consist of three varying factors, three differential levels of reality realization. There is first the mind consciousness—the comprehension of the *idea* of God. Then follows the soul consciousness—the realization of the *ideal* of God. Last, dawns the spirit consciousness—the realization of the *spirit reality* of God. By the unification of these factors of the divine realization, no matter how incomplete, the mortal personality at all times overspreads all conscious levels with a realization of the *personality* of God. In those mortals who have attained the Corps of the Finality all this will in time lead to the realization of the *supremacy* of God and may subsequently eventuate in the realization of the *ultimacy* of God, some phase of the absonite superconsciousness of the Paradise Father.

The experience of God-consciousness remains the same from generation to generation, but with each advancing epoch in human knowledge the philosophic concept and the theologic definitions of God *must* change. God-knowingness, religious consciousness, is a universe reality, but no matter how valid (real) religious experience is, it must be willing to subject itself to intelligent criticism and reasonable philosophic interpretation; it must not seek to be a thing apart in the totality of human experience.

Eternal survival of personality is wholly dependent on the choosing of the mortal mind, whose decisions determine the survival potential of the immortal soul. When the mind believes God and the soul knows God, and when, with the fostering Adjuster, they all *desire* God, then is survival assured. Limitations of intellect, curtailment of education, deprivation of culture, impoverishment of social status, even inferiority of the human standards of morality resulting from the unfortunate lack of educational, cultural, and social advantages, cannot invalidate the presence of the divine spirit in such unfortunate and humanly handicapped but believing individuals. The indwelling of the Mystery Monitor constitutes the inception and insures the possibility of the potential of growth and survival of the immortal soul.

The ability of mortal parents to procreate is not predicated on their educational, cultural, social, or economic status. The union of the parental factors under natural conditions is quite sufficient to initiate offspring. A human mind discerning right and wrong and possessing the capacity to worship God, in union with a divine Adjuster, is all that is required in that mortal to initiate and foster the production of his immortal soul of survival qualities if such a spirit-endowed individual seeks God and sincerely desires to become like him, honestly elects to do the will of the Father in heaven.

6. THE GOD OF PERSONALITY

The Universal Father is the God of personalities. The domain of universe personality, from the lowest mortal and material creature of personality status to the highest persons of creator dignity and divine status, has its center and circumference in the Universal Father. God the Father is the bestower and the conservator of every personality. And the Paradise Father is likewise the destiny of all those finite personalities who wholeheartedly choose to do the divine will, those who love God and long to be like him.

Personality is one of the unsolved mysteries of the universes. We are able to form adequate concepts of the factors entering into the make-up of various orders and levels of personality, but we do not fully comprehend the real nature of the personality itself. We clearly perceive the numerous factors which, when put together, constitute the vehicle for human personality, but we do not fully comprehend the nature and significance of such a finite personality.

Personality is potential in all creatures who possess a mind endowment ranging from the minimum of self-consciousness to the maximum of God-consciousness. But mind endowment alone is not personality, neither is spirit nor physical energy. Personality is that quality and value in cosmic reality which is exclusively bestowed by God the Father upon these living systems of the associated and coordinated energies of matter, mind, and spirit. Neither is personality a progressive achievement. Personality may be material or spiritual, but there either is personality or there is no personality. The other-than-personal never attains the level of the personal except by the direct act of the Paradise Father.

The bestowal of personality is the exclusive function of the Universal Father, the personalization of the living energy systems which he endows with the attributes of relative creative consciousness and the freewill control thereof. There is no personality apart from God the Father, and no personality exists except for God the Father. The fundamental attributes of human selfhood, as well as the absolute Adjuster nucleus of the human personality, are the bestowals of the Universal Father, acting in his exclusively personal domain of cosmic ministry.

The Adjusters of prepersonal status indwell numerous types of mortal creatures, thus insuring that these same beings may survive mortal death to personalize as morontia creatures with the potential of ultimate spirit attainment. For, when such a creature mind of personality endowment is indwelt by a fragment of the spirit of the eternal God, the prepersonal bestowal of the personal Father, then does this finite personality possess the potential of the divine and the eternal and aspire to a destiny akin to the Ultimate, even reaching out for a realization of the Absolute.

Capacity for divine personality is inherent in the prepersonal Adjuster; capacity for human personality is potential in the cosmic-mind endowment of the human being. But the experiential personality of mortal man is not observable as an active and functional reality until after the material life vehicle of the mortal creature has been touched by the liberating divinity of the Universal Father, being thus launched upon the seas of experience as a self-conscious and a (relatively) self-determinative and self-creative personality. The material self is truly and *unqualifiedly personal.*

The material self has personality and identity, temporal identity; the prepersonal spirit Adjuster also has identity, eternal identity. This material personality and this spirit prepersonality are capable of so uniting their creative attributes as to bring into existence the surviving identity of the immortal soul.

Having thus provided for the growth of the immortal soul and having liberated man's inner self from the fetters of absolute dependence on antecedent causation, the Father stands aside. Now, man having thus been liberated from the fetters of causation response, at least as pertains to eternal destiny, and provision having been made for the growth of the immortal self, the soul, it remains for man himself to will the creation or to inhibit the creation of this surviving and eternal self which is his for the choosing. No other being, force, creator, or agency in all the wide universe of universes can interfere to any degree with the absolute sovereignty of the mortal free will, as it operates within the realms of choice, regarding the eternal destiny of the personality of the choosing mortal. As pertains to eternal survival, God has decreed the sovereignty of the material and mortal will, and that decree is absolute.

The bestowal of creature personality confers relative liberation from slavish response to antecedent causation, and the personalities of all such moral beings, evolutionary or otherwise, are centered in the personality of the Universal Father. They are ever drawn towards his Paradise presence by that kinship of being which constitutes the vast and universal family circle and fraternal circuit of the eternal God. There is a kinship of divine spontaneity in all personality.

The personality circuit of the universe of universes is centered in the person of the Universal Father, and the Paradise Father is personally conscious of, and in personal touch with, all personalities of all levels of self-conscious existence. And this personality consciousness of all creation exists independently of the mission of the Thought Adjusters.

As all gravity is circuited in the Isle of Paradise, as all mind is circuited in the Conjoint Actor and all spirit in the Eternal Son, so is all personality circuited in the personal presence of the Universal Father, and this circuit unerringly transmits the worship of all personalities to the Original and Eternal Personality.

Concerning those personalities who are not Adjuster indwelt: The attribute of choice-liberty is also bestowed by the Universal Father, and such persons are likewise embraced in the great circuit of divine love, the personality circuit of the Universal Father. God provides for the sovereign choice of all true personalities. No personal creature can be coerced into the eternal adventure; the portal of eternity opens only in response to the freewill choice of the freewill sons of the God of free will.

And this represents my efforts to present the relation of the living God to the children of time. And when all is said and done, I can do nothing more helpful than to reiterate that God is your universe Father, and that you are all his planetary children.

[This is the fifth and last of the series presenting the narrative of the Universal Father by a Divine Counselor of Uversa.]

PAPER 6

THE ETERNAL SON

THE Eternal Son is the perfect and final expression of the "first" personal and absolute concept of the Universal Father. Accordingly, whenever and however the Father personally and absolutely expresses himself, he does so through his Eternal Son, who ever has been, now is, and ever will be, the living and divine Word. And this Eternal Son is residential at the center of all things, in association with, and immediately enshrouding the personal presence of, the Eternal and Universal Father.

We speak of God's "first" thought and allude to an impossible time origin of the Eternal Son for the purpose of gaining access to the thought channels of the human intellect. Such distortions of language represent our best efforts at contact-compromise with the time-bound minds of mortal creatures. In the sequential sense the Universal Father never could have had a first thought, nor could the Eternal Son ever have had a beginning. But I was instructed to portray the realities of eternity to the time-limited minds of mortals by such symbols of thought and to designate the relationships of eternity by such time concepts of sequentiality.

The Eternal Son is the spiritual personalization of the Paradise Father's universal and infinite concept of divine reality, unqualified spirit, and absolute personality. And thereby does the Son constitute the divine revelation of the creator identity of the Universal Father. The perfect personality of the Son discloses that the Father is actually the eternal and universal source of all the meanings and values of the spiritual, the volitional, the purposeful, and the personal.

In an effort to enable the finite mind of time to form some sequential concept of the relationships of the eternal and infinite beings of the Paradise Trinity, we utilize such license of conception as to refer to the "Father's first personal, universal, and infinite concept." It is impossible for me to convey to the human mind any adequate idea of the eternal relations of the Deities; therefore do I employ such terms as will afford the finite mind something of an idea of the relationship of these eternal beings in the subsequent eras of time. We believe the Son sprang from the Father; we are taught that both are unqualifiedly eternal. It is apparent, therefore, that no time creature can ever fully comprehend this mystery of a Son who is derived from the Father, and yet who is co-ordinately eternal with the Father himself.

1. IDENTITY OF THE ETERNAL SON

The Eternal Son is the original and only-begotten Son of God. He is God the Son, the Second Person of Deity and the associate creator of all things. As the Father is the First Great Source and Center, so the Eternal Son is the Second Great Source and Center.

The Eternal Son is the spiritual center and the divine administrator of the spiritual government of the universe of universes. The Universal Father is first a creator and then a controller; the Eternal Son is first a cocreator and then a *spiritual administrator.* "God is spirit," and the Son is a personal revelation of that spirit. The First Source and Center is the Volitional Absolute; the Second Source and Center is the Personality Absolute.

The Universal Father never personally functions as a creator except in conjunction with the Son or with the co-ordinate action of the Son. Had the New Testament writer referred to the Eternal Son, he would have uttered the truth when he wrote: "In the beginning was the Word, and the Word was with God, and the Word was God. All things were made by him, and without him was not anything made that was made."

When a Son of the Eternal Son appeared on Urantia, those who fraternized with this divine being in human form alluded to him as "He who was from the beginning, whom we have heard, whom we have seen with our eyes, whom we have looked upon, and our hands have handled, even the Word of life." And this bestowal Son came forth from the Father just as truly as did the Original Son, as is suggested in one of his earthly prayers: "And now, O my Father, glorify me with your own self, with the glory which I had with you before this world was."

The Eternal Son is known by different names in various universes. In the central universe he is known as the Co-ordinate Source, the Cocreator, and the Associate Absolute. On Uversa, the headquarters of the superuniverse, we designate the Son as the Co-ordinate Spirit Center and as the Eternal Spirit Administrator. On Salvington, the headquarters of your local universe, this Son is of record as the Second Eternal Source and Center. The Melchizedeks speak of him as the Son of Sons. On your world, but not in your system of inhabited spheres, this Original Son has been confused with a co-ordinate Creator Son, Michael of Nebadon, who bestowed himself upon the mortal races of Urantia.

Although any of the Paradise Sons may fittingly be called Sons of God, we are in the habit of reserving the designation "the Eternal Son" for this Original Son, the Second Source and Center, cocreator with the Universal Father of the central universe of power and perfection and cocreator of all other divine Sons who spring from the infinite Deities.

2. NATURE OF THE ETERNAL SON

The Eternal Son is just as changeless and infinitely dependable as the Universal Father. He is also just as spiritual as the Father, just as truly an unlimited spirit. To you of lowly origin the Son would appear to be more personal since he is one step nearer you in approachability than is the Universal Father.

The Eternal Son is the eternal Word of God. He is wholly like the Father; in fact, the Eternal Son *is* God the Father personally manifest to the universe of universes. And thus it was and is and forever will be true of the Eternal Son and of all the co-ordinate Creator Sons: "He who has seen the Son has seen the Father."

In nature the Son is wholly like the spirit Father. When we worship the Universal Father, actually we at the same time worship God the Son and God the Spirit. God the Son is just as divinely real and eternal in nature as God the Father.

The Son not only possesses all the Father's infinite and transcendent righteousness, but the Son is also reflective of all the Father's holiness of character. The Son shares the Father's perfection and jointly shares the responsibility of aiding all creatures of imperfection in their spiritual efforts to attain divine perfection.

The Eternal Son possesses all the Father's character of divinity and attributes of spirituality. The Son *is* the fullness of God's absoluteness in personality and spirit, and these qualities the Son reveals in his personal management of the spiritual government of the universe of universes.

God is, indeed, a universal spirit; God is spirit; and this spirit nature of the Father is focalized and personalized in the Deity of the Eternal Son. In the Son all spiritual characteristics are apparently greatly enhanced by differentiation from the universality of the First Source and Center. And as the Father shares his spirit nature with the Son, so do they together just as fully and unreservedly share the divine spirit with the Conjoint Actor, the Infinite Spirit.

In the love of truth and in the creation of beauty the Father and the Son are equal except that the Son *appears* to devote himself more to the realization of the exclusively spiritual beauty of universal values.

In divine goodness I discern no difference between the Father and the Son. The Father loves his universe children as a father; the Eternal Son looks upon all creatures both as father and as brother.

3. MINISTRY OF THE FATHER'S LOVE

The Son shares the justice and righteousness of the Trinity but overshadows these divinity traits by the infinite personalization of the Father's love and mercy; the Son is the revelation of divine love to the universes. As God is love, so the Son is mercy. The Son cannot love more than the Father, but he can show mercy to creatures in one additional way, for he not only is a primal creator like the Father, but he is also the Eternal Son of that same Father, thereby sharing in the sonship experience of all other sons of the Universal Father.

The Eternal Son is the great mercy minister to all creation. Mercy is the essence of the Son's spiritual character. The mandates of the Eternal Son, as they go forth over the spirit circuits of the Second Source and Center, are keyed in tones of mercy.

To comprehend the love of the Eternal Son, you must first perceive its divine source, the Father, who *is* love, and then behold the unfolding of this infinite affection in the far-flung ministry of the Infinite Spirit and his almost limitless host of ministering personalities.

The ministry of the Eternal Son is devoted to the revelation of the God of love to the universe of universes. This divine Son is not engaged in the ignoble task of trying to persuade his gracious Father to love his lowly creatures and to show mercy to the wrongdoers of time. How wrong to envisage the Eternal Son as appealing to the Universal Father to show mercy to his lowly creatures on the material worlds of space! Such concepts of God are crude and grotesque. Rather should you realize that all the merciful ministrations of the Sons of God are a direct revelation of the Father's heart of universal love and infinite compassion. The Father's love is the real and eternal source of the Son's mercy.

God is love, the Son is mercy. Mercy is applied love, the Father's love in action in the person of his Eternal Son. The love of this universal Son is likewise universal. As love is comprehended on a sex planet, the love of God is more comparable to the love of a father, while the love of the Eternal Son is more like the affection of a mother. Crude, indeed, are such illustrations, but I employ them in the hope of conveying to the human mind the thought that there is a difference, not in divine content but in quality and technique of expression, between the love of the Father and the love of the Son.

4. ATTRIBUTES OF THE ETERNAL SON

The Eternal Son motivates the spirit level of cosmic reality; the spiritual power of the Son is absolute in relation to all universe actualities. He exercises perfect control over the interassociation of all undifferentiated spirit energy and over all actualized spirit reality through his absolute grasp of spirit gravity. All pure unfragmented spirit and all spiritual beings and values are responsive to the infinite drawing power of the primal Son of Paradise. And if the eternal future should witness the appearance of an unlimited universe, the spirit gravity and the spirit power of the Original Son will be found wholly adequate for the spiritual control and effective administration of such a boundless creation.

The Son is omnipotent only in the spiritual realm. In the eternal economy of universe administration, wasteful and needless repetition of function is never encountered; the Deities are not given to useless duplication of universe ministry.

The omnipresence of the Original Son constitutes the spiritual unity of the universe of universes. The spiritual cohesion of all creation rests upon the everywhere active presence of the divine spirit of the Eternal Son. When we conceive of the Father's spiritual presence, we find it difficult to differentiate it in our thinking from the spiritual presence of the Eternal Son. The spirit of the Father is eternally resident in the spirit of the Son.

The Father must be spiritually omnipresent, but such omnipresence appears to be inseparable from the everywhere spirit activities of the Eternal Son. We do, however, believe that in all situations of Father-Son presence of a dual spiritual nature the spirit of the Son is co-ordinate with the spirit of the Father.

In his contact with personality, the Father acts in the personality circuit. In his personal and detectable contact with spiritual creation, he appears in the fragments of the totality of his Deity, and these Father fragments have a solitary, unique, and exclusive function wherever and whenever they appear in the universes. In all such situations the spirit of the Son is co-ordinate with the spiritual function of the fragmented presence of the Universal Father.

Spiritually the Eternal Son is omnipresent. The spirit of the Eternal Son is most certainly with you and around you, but not within you and a part of you like the Mystery Monitor. The indwelling Father fragment adjusts the human mind to progressively divine attitudes, whereupon such an ascending mind becomes increasingly responsive to the spiritual drawing power of the all-powerful spirit-gravity circuit of the Second Source and Center.

The Original Son is universally and spiritually self-conscious. In wisdom the Son is the full equal of the Father. In the realms of knowledge, omniscience, we cannot distinguish between the First and Second Sources; like the Father, the Son knows all; he is never surprised by any universe event; he comprehends the end from the beginning.

The Father and the Son really know the number and whereabouts of all the spirits and spiritualized beings in the universe of universes. Not only does the Son know all things by virtue of his own omnipresent spirit, but the Son, equally with the Father and the Conjoint Actor, is fully cognizant of the vast reflectivity intelligence of the Supreme Being, which intelligence is at all times aware of all things that transpire on all the worlds of the seven superuniverses. And there are other ways in which the Paradise Son is omniscient.

The Eternal Son, as a loving, merciful, and ministering spiritual personality, is wholly and infinitely equal with the Universal Father, while in all those merciful and affectionate personal contacts with the ascendant beings of the lower realms the Eternal Son is just as kind and considerate, just as patient and long-suffering, as are his Paradise Sons in the local universes who so frequently bestow themselves upon the evolutionary worlds of time.

It is needless further to expatiate on the attributes of the Eternal Son. With the exceptions noted, it is only necessary to study the spiritual attributes of God the Father to understand and correctly evaluate the attributes of God the Son.

5. LIMITATIONS OF THE ETERNAL SON

The Eternal Son does not personally function in the physical domains, nor does he function, except through the Conjoint Actor, in the levels of mind ministry to creature beings. But these qualifications do not in any manner otherwise limit the Eternal Son in the full and free exercise of all the divine attributes of *spiritual* omniscience, omnipresence, and omnipotence.

The Eternal Son does not personally pervade the potentials of spirit inherent in the infinity of the Deity Absolute, but as these potentials become actual, they come within the all-powerful grasp of the spirit-gravity circuit of the Son.

Personality is the exclusive gift of the Universal Father. The Eternal Son derives personality from the Father, but he does not, without the Father, bestow personality. The Son gives origin to a vast spirit host, but such derivations are not personalities. When the Son creates personality, he does so in conjunction with the Father or with the Conjoint Creator, who may act for the Father in such relationships. The Eternal Son is thus a cocreator of personalities, but he bestows personality upon no being and of himself, alone, never creates personal beings. This limitation of action does not, however, deprive the Son of the ability to create any or all types of other-than-personal reality.

The Eternal Son is limited in transmittal of creator prerogatives. The Father, in eternalizing the Original Son, bestowed upon him the power and privilege of subsequently joining with the Father in the divine act of producing additional Sons possessing creative attributes, and this they have done and now do. But when these co-ordinate Sons have been produced, the prerogatives of creatorship are apparently not further transmissible. The Eternal Son transmits creatorship powers only to the first or direct personalization. Therefore, when the Father and the Son unite to personalize a Creator Son, they achieve their purpose; but the Creator Son thus brought into existence is never able to transmit or delegate the prerogatives of creatorship to the various orders of Sons which he may subsequently create, notwithstanding that, in the highest local universe Sons, there does appear a very limited reflection of the creative attributes of a Creator Son.

The Eternal Son, as an infinite and exclusively personal being, cannot fragmentize his nature, cannot distribute and bestow individualized portions of his selfhood upon other entities or persons as do the Universal Father and the Infinite Spirit. But the Son can and does bestow himself as an unlimited spirit to bathe all creation and unceasingly draw all spirit personalities and spiritual realities to himself.

Ever remember, the Eternal Son is the personal portrayal of the spirit Father to all creation. The Son is personal and nothing but personal in the Deity sense; such a divine and absolute personality cannot be disintegrated or fragmentized. God the Father and God the Spirit are truly personal, but they are also everything else in addition to being such Deity personalities.

Though the Eternal Son cannot personally participate in the bestowal of the Thought Adjusters, he did sit in council with the Universal Father in the eternal past, approving the plan and pledging endless co-operation, when the Father, in projecting the bestowal of the Thought Adjusters, proposed to the Son, "Let us make mortal man in our own image." And as the spirit fragment of the Father dwells within you, so does the spirit presence of the Son envelop you, while these two forever work as one for your spiritual advancement.

6. THE SPIRIT MIND

The Eternal Son is spirit and has mind, but not a mind or a spirit which mortal mind can comprehend. Mortal man perceives mind on the finite, cosmic, material, and personal levels. Man also observes mind phenomena in living organisms functioning on the subpersonal (animal) level, but it is difficult for him to grasp the nature of mind when associated with supermaterial beings and as a part of exclusive spirit personalities. Mind must, however, be differently defined when it refers to the spirit level of existence, and when it is used to denote spirit functions of intelligence. That kind of mind which is directly allied with spirit is comparable neither to that mind which co-ordinates spirit and matter nor to that mind which is allied only with matter.

Spirit is ever conscious, minded, and possessed of varied phases of identity. Without mind in some phase there would be no spiritual consciousness in the fraternity of spirit beings. The equivalent of mind, the ability to know and be known, is indigenous to Deity. Deity may be personal, prepersonal, superpersonal, or impersonal, but Deity is never mindless, that is, never without the ability at least to communicate with similar entities, beings, or personalities.

The mind of the Eternal Son is like that of the Father but unlike any other mind in the universe, and with the mind of the Father it is ancestor to the diverse and far-flung minds of the Conjoint Creator. The mind of the Father and the Son, that intellect which is ancestral to the absolute mind of the Third Source and Center, is perhaps best illustrated in the premind of a Thought Adjuster, for, though these Father fragments are entirely outside of the mind circuits of the Conjoint Actor, they have some form of premind; they know as they are known; they enjoy the equivalent of human thinking.

The Eternal Son is wholly spiritual; man is very nearly entirely material; therefore much pertaining to the spirit personality of the Eternal Son, to his seven spiritual spheres encircling Paradise and to the nature of the impersonal creations of the Paradise Son, will have to await your attainment of spirit status following your completion of the morontia ascension of the local universe of

Nebadon. And then, as you pass through the superuniverse and on to Havona, many of these spirit-concealed mysteries will clarify as you begin to be endowed with the "mind of the spirit"—spiritual insight.

7. PERSONALITY OF THE ETERNAL SON

The Eternal Son is that infinite personality from whose unqualified personality fetters the Universal Father escaped by the technique of trinitization, and by virtue of which he has ever since continued to bestow himself in endless profusion upon his ever-expanding universe of Creators and creatures. The Son is *absolute personality;* God is *father personality*—the source of personality, the bestower of personality, the cause of personality. Every personal being derives personality from the Universal Father just as the Original Son eternally derives his personality from the Paradise Father.

The personality of the Paradise Son is absolute and purely spiritual, and this absolute personality is also the divine and eternal pattern, first, of the Father's bestowal of personality upon the Conjoint Actor and, subsequently, of his bestowal of personality upon the myriads of his creatures throughout a far-flung universe.

The Eternal Son is truly a merciful minister, a divine spirit, a spiritual power, and a real personality. The Son is the spiritual and personal nature of God made manifest to the universes—the sum and substance of the First Source and Center, divested of all that which is nonpersonal, extradivine, nonspiritual, and pure potential. But it is impossible to convey to the human mind a word picture of the beauty and grandeur of the supernal personality of the Eternal Son. Everything that tends to obscure the Universal Father operates with almost equal influence to prevent the conceptual recognition of the Eternal Son. You must await your attainment of Paradise, and then you will understand why I was unable to portray the character of this absolute personality to the understanding of the finite mind.

8. REALIZATION OF THE ETERNAL SON

Concerning identity, nature, and other attributes of personality, the Eternal Son is the full equal, the perfect complement, and the eternal counterpart of the Universal Father. In the same sense that God is the Universal Father, the Son is the Universal Mother. And all of us, high and low, constitute their universal family.

To appreciate the character of the Son, you should study the revelation of the divine character of the Father; they are forever and inseparably one. As divine personalities they are virtually indistinguishable by the lower orders of intelligence. They are not so difficult of separate recognition by those whose origin is in the creative acts of the Deities themselves. Beings of nativity in the central universe and on Paradise discern the Father and the Son not only as one personal unity of universal control but also as two separate personalities functioning in definite domains of universe administration.

As persons you may conceive of the Universal Father and the Eternal Son as separate individuals, for they indeed are; but in the administration of the universes they are so intertwined and interrelated that it is not always possible to distinguish between them. When, in the affairs of the universes, the Father and the Son are encountered in confusing interassociations, it is not always profitable to attempt to segregate their operations; merely recall that God is the initiating thought and the Son is the expressionful word. In each local universe this inseparability is personalized in the divinity of the Creator Son, who stands for both Father and Son to the creatures of ten million inhabited worlds.

The Eternal Son is infinite, but he is approachable through the persons of his Paradise Sons and through the patient ministry of the Infinite Spirit. Without the bestowal service of the Paradise Sons and the loving ministry of the creatures of the Infinite Spirit, beings of material origin could hardly hope to attain the Eternal Son. And it is equally true: With the help and guidance of these celestial agencies the God-conscious mortal will certainly attain Paradise and sometime stand in the personal presence of this majestic Son of Sons.

Even though the Eternal Son is the pattern of mortal personality attainment, you find it easier to grasp the reality of both the Father and the Spirit because the Father is the actual bestower of your human personality and the Infinite Spirit is the absolute source of your mortal mind. But as you ascend in the Paradise path of spiritual progression, the personality of the Eternal Son will become increasingly real to you, and the reality of his infinitely spiritual mind will become more discernible to your progressively spiritualizing mind.

Never can the concept of the Eternal Son shine brightly in your material or subsequent morontial mind; not until you spiritize and commence your spirit ascension will the comprehension of the personality of the Eternal Son begin to equal the vividness of your concept of the personality of the Creator Son of Paradise origin who, in person and as a person, onetime incarnated and lived on Urantia as a man among men.

Throughout your local universe experience the Creator Son, whose personality is comprehensible by man, must compensate for your inability to grasp the full significance of the more exclusively spiritual, but none the less personal, Eternal Son of Paradise. As you progress through Orvonton and Havona, as you leave behind you the vivid picture and deep memories of the Creator Son of your local universe, the passing of this material and morontia experience will be compensated by ever-enlarging concepts and intensifying comprehension of the Eternal Son of Paradise, whose reality and nearness will ever augment as you progress Paradiseward.

The Eternal Son is a grand and glorious personality. Although it is beyond the powers of the mortal and material mind to grasp the actuality of the personality of such an infinite being, doubt not, he is a person. I know whereof I speak. Times almost without number I have stood in the divine presence of this Eternal Son and then journeyed forth in the universe to execute his gracious bidding.

[Indited by a Divine Counselor assigned to formulate this statement depicting the Eternal Son of Paradise.]

PAPER 7

RELATION OF THE ETERNAL SON TO THE UNIVERSE

THE Original Son is ever concerned with the execution of the spiritual aspects of the Father's eternal purpose as it progressively unfolds in the phenomena of the evolving universes with their manifold groups of living beings. We do not fully comprehend this eternal plan, but the Paradise Son undoubtedly does.

The Son is like the Father in that he seeks to bestow everything possible of himself upon his co-ordinate Sons and upon their subordinate Sons. And the Son shares the Father's self-distributive nature in the unstinted bestowal of himself upon the Infinite Spirit, their conjoint executive.

As the upholder of spirit realities, the Second Source and Center is the eternal counterpoise of the Isle of Paradise, which so magnificently upholds all things material. Thus is the First Source and Center forever revealed in the material beauty of the exquisite patterns of the central Isle and in the spiritual values of the supernal personality of the Eternal Son.

The Eternal Son is the actual upholder of the vast creation of spirit realities and spiritual beings. The spirit world is the habit, the personal conduct, of the Son, and the impersonal realities of spirit nature are always responsive to the will and purpose of the perfect personality of the Absolute Son.

The Son is not, however, personally responsible for the conduct of all spirit personalities. The will of the personal creature is relatively free and hence determines the actions of such volitional beings. Therefore the freewill spirit world is not always truly representative of the character of the Eternal Son, even as nature on Urantia is not truly revelatory of the perfection and immutability of Paradise and Deity. But no matter what may characterize the freewill action of man or angel, the Son's eternal grasp of the universal gravity control of all spirit realities continues as absolute.

1. THE SPIRIT-GRAVITY CIRCUIT

Everything taught concerning the immanence of God, his omnipresence, omnipotence, and omniscience, is equally true of the Son in the spiritual domains. The pure and universal spirit gravity of all creation, this exclusively spiritual circuit, leads directly back to the person of the Second Source and Center on Paradise. He presides over the control and operation of that ever-present and unerring spiritual grasp of all true spirit values. Thus does the Eternal Son exercise absolute spiritual sovereignty. He literally holds all spirit realities and all spiritualized values, as it were, in the hollow of his hand. The control of universal spiritual gravity *is* universal spiritual sovereignty.

This gravity control of spiritual things operates independently of time and space; therefore is spirit energy undiminished in transmission. Spirit gravity never suffers time delays, nor does it undergo space diminution. It does not decrease in accordance with the square of the distance of its transmission; the circuits of pure spirit power are not retarded by the mass of the material creation. And this transcendence of time and space by pure spirit energies is inherent in the absoluteness of the Son; it is not due to the interposition of the antigravity forces of the Third Source and Center.

Spirit realities respond to the drawing power of the center of spiritual gravity in accordance with their qualitative value, their actual degree of spirit nature. Spirit substance (quality) is just as responsive to spirit gravity as the organized energy of physical matter (quantity) is responsive to physical gravity. Spiritual values and spirit forces are *real.* From the viewpoint of personality, spirit is the soul of creation; matter is the shadowy physical body.

The reactions and fluctuations of spirit gravity are ever true to the content of spiritual values, the qualitative spiritual status of an individual or a world. This drawing power is instantly responsive to the inter- and intraspirit values of any universe situation or planetary condition. Every time a spiritual reality actualizes in the universes, this change necessitates the immediate and instantaneous readjustment of spirit gravity. Such a new spirit is actually a part of the Second Source and Center; and just as certainly as mortal man becomes a spiritized being, he will attain the spiritual Son, the center and source of spirit gravity.

The Son's spiritual drawing power is inherent to a lesser degree in many Paradise orders of sonship. For there do exist within the absolute spirit-gravity circuit those local systems of spiritual attraction that function in the lesser units of creation. Such subabsolute focalizations of spirit gravity are a part of the divinity of the Creator personalities of time and space and are correlated with the emerging experiential overcontrol of the Supreme Being.

Spirit-gravity pull and response thereto operate not only on the universe as a whole but also even between individuals and groups of individuals. There is a spiritual cohesiveness among the spiritual and spiritized personalities of any world, race, nation, or believing group of individuals. There is a direct attractiveness of a spirit nature between spiritually minded persons of like tastes and longings. The term *kindred spirits* is not wholly a figure of speech.

Like the material gravity of Paradise, the spiritual gravity of the Eternal Son is absolute. Sin and rebellion may interfere with the operation of local universe circuits, but nothing can suspend the spirit gravity of the Eternal Son. The Lucifer rebellion produced many changes in your system of inhabited worlds and on Urantia, but we do not observe that the resultant spiritual quarantine of your planet in the least affected the presence and function of either the omnipresent spirit of the Eternal Son or the associated spirit-gravity circuit.

All reactions of the spirit-gravity circuit of the grand universe are predictable. We recognize all actions and reactions of the omnipresent spirit of the Eternal Son and find them to be dependable. In accordance with well-known laws, we can and do measure spiritual gravity just as man attempts to compute the workings of finite physical gravity. There is an unvarying response of the Son's spirit to all spirit things, beings, and persons, and this response is always in accordance with the degree of actuality (the qualitative degree of reality) of all such spiritual values.

But alongside this very dependable and predictable function of the spiritual presence of the Eternal Son, there are encountered phenomena which are not so predictable in their reactions. Such phenomena probably indicate the co-ordinate action of the Deity Absolute in the realms of emerging spiritual potentials. We know that the spirit presence of the Eternal Son is the influence of a majestic and infinite personality, but we hardly regard the reactions associated with the conjectured performances of the Deity Absolute as personal.

Viewed from the personality standpoint and by persons, the Eternal Son and the Deity Absolute appear to be related in the following way: The Eternal Son dominates the realm of actual spiritual values, whereas the Deity Absolute seems to pervade the vast domain of potential spirit values. All actual value of spirit nature finds lodgment in the gravity grasp of the Eternal Son but, if potential, then apparently in the presence of the Deity Absolute.

Spirit seems to emerge from the potentials of the Deity Absolute; evolving spirit finds correlation in the experiential and incomplete grasps of the Supreme and the Ultimate; spirit eventually finds final destiny in the absolute grasp of the spiritual gravity of the Eternal Son. This appears to be the cycle of experiential spirit, but existential spirit is inherent in the infinity of the Second Source and Center.

2. THE ADMINISTRATION OF THE ETERNAL SON

On Paradise the presence and personal activity of the Original Son is profound, absolute in the spiritual sense. As we pass outward from Paradise through Havona and into the realms of the seven superuniverses, we detect less and less of the personal activity of the Eternal Son. In the post-Havona universes the presence of the Eternal Son is personalized in the Paradise Sons, conditioned by the experiential realities of the Supreme and the Ultimate, and co-ordinated with the unlimited spirit potential of the Deity Absolute.

In the central universe the personal activity of the Original Son is discernible in the exquisite spiritual harmony of the eternal creation. Havona is so marvelously perfect that the spiritual status and the energy states of this pattern universe are in perfect and perpetual balance.

In the superuniverses the Son is not personally present or resident; in these creations he maintains only a superpersonal representation. These spirit manifestations of the Son are not personal; they are not in the personality circuit of the Universal Father. We know of no better term to use than to designate them *superpersonalities;* and they are finite beings; they are neither absonite nor absolute.

The administration of the Eternal Son in the superuniverses, being exclusively spiritual and superpersonal, is not discernible by creature personalities. Nonetheless, the all-pervading spiritual urge of the Son's personal influence is encountered in every phase of the activities of all sectors of the domains of the Ancients of Days. In the local universes, however, we observe the Eternal Son personally present in the persons of the Paradise Sons. Here the infinite Son spiritually and creatively functions in the persons of the majestic corps of the co-ordinate Creator Sons.

3. RELATION OF THE ETERNAL SON TO THE INDIVIDUAL

In the local universe ascent the mortals of time look to the Creator Son as the personal representative of the Eternal Son. But when they begin the ascent of the superuniverse training regime, the pilgrims of time increasingly detect the supernal presence of the inspiring spirit of the Eternal Son, and they are able to profit by the intake of this ministry of spiritual energization. In Havona the ascenders become still more conscious of the loving embrace of the all-pervading spirit of the Original Son. At no stage of the entire mortal ascension does the spirit of the Eternal Son indwell the mind or soul of the pilgrim of time, but his beneficence is ever near and always concerned with the welfare and spiritual security of the advancing children of time.

The spiritual-gravity pull of the Eternal Son constitutes the inherent secret of the Paradise ascension of surviving human souls. All genuine spirit values and all bona fide spiritualized individuals are held within the unfailing grasp of the spiritual gravity of the Eternal Son. The mortal mind, for example, initiates its career as a material mechanism and is eventually mustered into the Corps of the Finality as a well-nigh perfected spirit existence, becoming progressively less subject to material gravity and correspondingly more responsive to the inward pulling urge of spirit gravity during this entire experience. The spirit-gravity circuit literally pulls the soul of man Paradiseward.

The spirit-gravity circuit is the basic channel for transmitting the genuine prayers of the believing human heart from the level of human consciousness to the actual consciousness of Deity. That which represents true spiritual value in your petitions will be seized by the universal circuit of spirit gravity and will pass immediately and simultaneously to all divine personalities concerned. Each will occupy himself with that which belongs to his personal province. Therefore, in your practical religious experience, it is immaterial whether, in addressing your supplications, you visualize the Creator Son of your local universe or the Eternal Son at the center of all things.

The discriminative operation of the spirit-gravity circuit might possibly be compared to the functions of the neural circuits in the material human body: Sensations travel inward over the neural paths; some are detained and responded to by the lower automatic spinal centers; others pass on to the less automatic but habit-trained centers of the lower brain, while the most important and vital incoming messages flash by these subordinate centers and are immediately registered in the highest levels of human consciousness.

But how much more perfect is the superb technique of the spiritual world! If anything originates in your consciousness that is fraught with supreme spiritual value, when once you give it expression, no power in the universe can prevent its flashing directly to the Absolute Spirit Personality of all creation.

Conversely, if your supplications are purely material and wholly self-centered, there exists no plan whereby such unworthy prayers can find lodgment in the spirit circuit of the Eternal Son. The content of any petition which is not "spirit indited" can find no place in the universal spiritual circuit; such purely selfish and material requests fall dead; they do not ascend in the circuits of true spirit values. Such words are as "sounding brass and a tinkling cymbal."

It is the motivating thought, the spiritual content, that validates the mortal supplication. Words are valueless.

4. THE DIVINE PERFECTION PLANS

The Eternal Son is in everlasting liaison with the Father in the successful prosecution of the *divine plan of progress:* the universal plan for the creation, evolution, ascension, and perfection of will creatures. And, in divine faithfulness, the Son is the eternal equal of the Father.

The Father and his Son are as one in the formulation and prosecution of this gigantic attainment plan for advancing the material beings of time to the perfection of eternity. This project for the spiritual elevation of the ascendant souls of space is a joint creation of the Father and the Son, and they are, with the co-operation of the Infinite Spirit, engaged in associative execution of their divine purpose.

This divine plan of perfection attainment embraces three unique, though marvelously correlated, enterprises of universal adventure:

1. *The Plan of Progressive Attainment.* This is the Universal Father's plan of evolutionary ascension, a program unreservedly accepted by the Eternal Son when he concurred in the Father's proposal, "Let us make mortal creatures in our own image." This provision for upstepping the creatures of time involves the Father's bestowal of the Thought Adjusters and the endowing of material creatures with the prerogatives of personality.

2. *The Bestowal Plan.* The next universal plan is the great Father-revelation enterprise of the Eternal Son and his co-ordinate Sons. This is the proposal of the Eternal Son and consists of his bestowal of the Sons of God upon the evolutionary creations, there to personalize and factualize, to incarnate and make real, the love of the Father and the mercy of the Son to the creatures of all universes. Inherent in the bestowal plan, and as a provisional feature of this ministration of love, the Paradise Sons act as rehabilitators of that which misguided creature will has placed in spiritual jeopardy. Whenever and wherever there occurs a delay in the functioning of the attainment plan, if rebellion, perchance, should mar or complicate this enterprise, then do the emergency provisions of the bestowal plan become active forthwith. The Paradise Sons stand pledged and ready to function as retrievers, to go into the very realms of rebellion and there restore the spiritual status of the spheres. And such a heroic service a co-ordinate Creator Son did perform on Urantia in connection with his experiential bestowal career of sovereignty acquirement.

3. *The Plan of Mercy Ministry.* When the attainment plan and the bestowal plan had been formulated and proclaimed, alone and of himself, the Infinite Spirit projected and put in operation the tremendous and universal enterprise of mercy ministry. This is the service so essential to the practical and effective operation of both the attainment and the bestowal undertakings, and the spiritual personalities of the Third Source and Center all partake of the spirit of mercy ministry which is so much a part of the nature of the Third Person of Deity. Not only in creation but also in administration, the Infinite Spirit functions truly and literally as the conjoint executive of the Father and the Son.

The Eternal Son is the personal trustee, the divine custodian, of the Father's universal plan of creature ascension. Having promulgated the universal mandate, "Be you perfect, even as I am perfect," the Father intrusted the execution of this tremendous undertaking to the Eternal Son; and the Eternal Son shares the fostering of this supernal enterprise with his divine co-ordinate, the Infinite Spirit. Thus do the Deities effectively co-operate in the work of creation, control, evolution, revelation, and ministration—and if required, in restoration and rehabilitation.

5. THE SPIRIT OF BESTOWAL

The Eternal Son without reservation joined with the Universal Father in broadcasting that tremendous injunction to all creation: "Be you perfect, even as your Father in Havona is perfect." And ever since, that invitation-command has motivated all the survival plans and the bestowal projects of the Eternal Son and his vast family of co-ordinate and associated Sons. And in these very bestowals the Sons of God have become to all evolutionary creatures "the way, the truth, and the life."

The Eternal Son cannot contact directly with human beings as does the Father through the gift of the prepersonal Thought Adjusters, but the Eternal Son does draw near to created personalities by a series of downstepping gradations of divine sonship until he is enabled to stand in man's presence and, at times, as man himself.

The purely personal nature of the Eternal Son is incapable of fragmentation. The Eternal Son ministers as a spiritual influence or as a person, never otherwise. The Son finds it impossible to become a part of creature experience in the sense that the Father-Adjuster participates therein, but the Eternal Son compensates this limitation by the technique of bestowal. What the experience of fragmented entities means to the Universal Father, the incarnation experiences of the Paradise Sons mean to the Eternal Son.

The Eternal Son comes not to mortal man as the divine will, the Thought Adjuster indwelling the human mind, but the Eternal Son did come to mortal man on Urantia when the divine *personality* of his Son, Michael of Nebadon, incarnated in the human nature of Jesus of Nazareth. To share the experience of created personalities, the Paradise Sons of God must assume the very natures of such creatures and incarnate their divine personalities as the actual creatures themselves. Incarnation, the secret of Sonarington, is the technique of the Son's escape from the otherwise all-encompassing fetters of personality absolutism.

Long, long ago the Eternal Son bestowed himself upon each of the circuits of the central creation for the enlightenment and advancement of all the inhabitants and pilgrims of Havona, including the ascending pilgrims of time. On none of these seven bestowals did he function as either an ascender or a Havoner. He existed as himself. His experience was unique; it was not *with* or *as* a human or other pilgrim but in some way associative in the superpersonal sense.

Neither did he pass through the rest that intervenes between the inner Havona circuit and the shores of Paradise. It is not possible for him, an absolute being, to suspend consciousness of personality, for in him center all lines of spiritual gravity. And during the times of these bestowals the central Paradise lodgment of spiritual luminosity was undimmed, and the Son's grasp of universal spirit gravity was undiminished.

The bestowals of the Eternal Son in Havona are not within the scope of human imagination; they were transcendental. He added to the experience of all Havona then and subsequently, but we do not know whether he added to the supposed experiential capacity of his existential nature. That would fall within the bestowal mystery of the Paradise Sons. We do, however, believe that whatever the Eternal Son acquired on these bestowal missions, he has ever since retained; but we do not know what it is.

Whatever our difficulty in comprehending the bestowals of the Second Person of Deity, we do comprehend the Havona bestowal of a Son of the Eternal Son, who literally passed through the circuits of the central universe and actually shared those experiences which constitute an ascender's preparation for Deity attainment. This was the original Michael, the first-born Creator Son, and he passed through the life experiences of the ascending pilgrims from circuit to circuit, personally journeying a stage of each circle with them in the days of Grandfanda, the first of all mortals to attain Havona.

Whatever else this original Michael revealed, he made the transcendent bestowal of the Original Mother Son real to the creatures of Havona. So real, that forevermore each pilgrim of time who labors in the adventure of making the Havona circuits is cheered and strengthened by the certain knowledge that the Eternal Son of God seven times abdicated the power and glory of Paradise to participate in the experiences of the time-space pilgrims on the seven circuits of progressive Havona attainment.

The Eternal Son is the exemplary inspiration for all the Sons of God in their ministrations of bestowal throughout the universes of time and space. The coordinate Creator Sons and the associate Magisterial Sons, together with other unrevealed orders of sonship, all partake of this wonderful willingness to bestow themselves upon the varied orders of creature life and as the creatures themselves. Therefore, in spirit and because of kinship of nature as well as fact of origin, it becomes true that in the bestowal of each Son of God upon the worlds of space, in and through and by these bestowals, the Eternal Son has bestowed himself upon the intelligent will creatures of the universes.

In spirit and nature, if not in all attributes, each Paradise Son is a divinely perfect portraiture of the Original Son. It is literally true, whosoever has seen a Paradise Son has seen the Eternal Son of God.

6. THE PARADISE SONS OF GOD

The lack of a knowledge of the multiple Sons of God is a source of great confusion on Urantia. And this ignorance persists in the face of such statements as the record of a conclave of these divine personalities: "When the Sons of God proclaimed joy, and all of the Morning Stars sang together." Every millennium of sector standard time the various orders of the divine Sons forgather for their periodic conclaves.

The Eternal Son is the personal source of the adorable attributes of mercy and service which so abundantly characterize all orders of the descending Sons of God as they function throughout creation. All the divine nature, if not all the infinity of attributes, the Eternal Son unfailingly transmits to the Paradise Sons who go out from the eternal Isle to reveal his divine character to the universe of universes.

The Original and Eternal Son is the offspring-person of the "first" completed and infinite thought of the Universal Father. Every time the Universal Father and the Eternal Son jointly project a new, original, identical, unique, and absolute personal thought, that very instant this creative idea is perfectly and finally personalized in the being and personality of a new and original *Creator Son.* In spirit nature, divine wisdom, and co-ordinate creative power, these Creator Sons are potentially equal with God the Father and God the Son.

The Creator Sons go out from Paradise into the universes of time and, with the co-operation of the controlling and creative agencies of the Third Source and Center, complete the organization of the local universes of progressive evolution. These Sons are not attached to, nor are they concerned with, the central and universal controls of matter, mind, and spirit. Hence are they limited in their creative acts by the pre-existence, priority, and primacy of the First Source and Center and his co-ordinate Absolutes. These Sons are able to administer only that which they bring into existence. Absolute administration is inherent in priority of existence and is inseparable from eternity of presence. The Father remains primal in the universes.

Much as the Creator Sons are personalized by the Father and the Son, so are the *Magisterial Sons* personalized by the Son and the Spirit. These are the Sons who, in the experiences of creature incarnation, earn the right to serve as the judges of survival in the creations of time and space.

The Father, Son, and Spirit also unite to personalize the versatile *Trinity Teacher Sons,* who range the grand universe as the supernal teachers of all personalities, human and divine. And there are numerous other orders of Paradise sonship that have not been brought to the attention of Urantia mortals.

Between the Original Mother Son and these hosts of Paradise Sons scattered throughout all creation, there is a direct and exclusive channel of communication, a channel whose function is inherent in the quality of spiritual kinship which unites them in bonds of near-absolute spiritual association. This intersonship circuit is entirely different from the universal circuit of spirit gravity, which also centers in the person of the Second Source and Center. All Sons of God who take origin in the persons of the Paradise Deities are in direct and constant communication with the Eternal Mother Son. And such communication is instantaneous; it is independent of time though sometimes conditioned by space.

The Eternal Son not only has at all times perfect knowledge concerning the status, thoughts, and manifold activities of all orders of Paradise sonship, but he also has perfection of knowledge at all times regarding everything of spiritual value which exists in the hearts of all creatures in the primary central creation of eternity and in the secondary time creations of the co-ordinate Creator Sons.

7. THE SUPREME REVELATION OF THE FATHER

The Eternal Son is a complete, exclusive, universal, and final revelation of the spirit and the personality of the Universal Father. All knowledge of, and information concerning, the Father must come from the Eternal Son and his Paradise Sons. The Eternal Son is from eternity and is wholly and without spiritual qualification one with the Father. In divine personality they are co-ordinate; in spiritual nature they are equal; in divinity they are identical.

The character of God could not possibly be intrinsically improved upon in the person of the Son, for the divine Father is infinitely perfect, but that character and personality are amplified, by divestment of the nonpersonal and nonspiritual, for revelation to creature beings. The First Source and Center is much more than a personality, but all of the spirit qualities of the father personality of the First Source and Center are spiritually present in the absolute personality of the Eternal Son.

The primal Son and his Sons are engaged in making a universal revelation of the spiritual and personal nature of the Father to all creation. In the central universe, the superuniverses, the local universes, or on the inhabited planets, it is a Paradise Son who reveals the Universal Father to men and angels. The Eternal Son and his Sons reveal the avenue of creature approach to the Universal Father. And even we of high origin understand the Father much more fully as we study the revelation of his character and personality in the Eternal Son and in the Sons of the Eternal Son.

The Father comes down to you as a personality only through the divine Sons of the Eternal Son. And you attain the Father by this same living way; you ascend to the Father by the guidance of this group of divine Sons. And this remains true notwithstanding that your very personality is a direct bestowal of the Universal Father.

In all these widespread activities of the far-flung spiritual administration of the Eternal Son, do not forget that the Son is a person just as truly and actually as the Father is a person. Indeed, to beings of the onetime human order the Eternal Son will be more easy to approach than the Universal Father. In the progress of the pilgrims of time through the circuits of Havona, you will be competent to attain the Son long before you are prepared to discern the Father.

More of the character and merciful nature of the Eternal Son of mercy you should comprehend as you meditate on the revelation of these divine attributes which was made in loving service by your own Creator Son, onetime Son of Man on earth, now the exalted sovereign of your local universe—the Son of Man and the Son of God.

[Indited by a Divine Counselor assigned to formulate this statement depicting the Eternal Son of Paradise.]

PAPER 8

THE INFINITE SPIRIT

BACK in eternity, when the Universal Father's "first" infinite and absolute thought finds in the Eternal Son such a perfect and adequate word for its divine expression, there ensues the supreme desire of both the Thought-God and the Word-God for a universal and infinite agent of mutual expression and combined action.

In the dawn of eternity both the Father and the Son become infinitely cognizant of their mutual interdependence, their eternal and absolute oneness; and therefore do they enter into an infinite and everlasting covenant of divine partnership. This never-ending compact is made for the execution of their united concepts throughout all of the circle of eternity; and ever since this eternity event the Father and the Son continue in this divine union.

We are now face to face with the eternity origin of the Infinite Spirit, the Third Person of Deity. The very instant that God the Father and God the Son conjointly conceive an identical and infinite action—the execution of an absolute thought-plan—that very moment, the Infinite Spirit springs full-fledgedly into existence.

In thus reciting the order of the origin of the Deities, I do so merely to enable you to think of their relationship. In reality they are all three existent from eternity; they are existential. They are without beginning or ending of days; they are co-ordinate, supreme, ultimate, absolute, and infinite. They are and always have been and ever shall be. And they are three distinctly individualized but eternally associated persons, God the Father, God the Son, and God the Spirit.

1. THE GOD OF ACTION

In the eternity of the past, upon the personalization of the Infinite Spirit the divine personality cycle becomes perfect and complete. The God of Action is existent, and the vast stage of space is set for the stupendous drama of creation—the universal adventure—the divine panorama of the eternal ages.

The first act of the Infinite Spirit is the inspection and recognition of his divine parents, the Father-Father and the Mother-Son. He, the Spirit, unqualifiedly identifies both of them. He is fully cognizant of their separate personalities and infinite attributes as well as of their combined nature and united function. Next, voluntarily, with transcendent willingness and inspiring spontaneity, the Third Person of Deity, notwithstanding his equality with the First and Second Persons, pledges eternal loyalty to God the Father and acknowledges everlasting dependence upon God the Son.

Inherent in the nature of this transaction and in mutual recognition of the personality independence of each and the executive union of all three, the cycle of eternity is established. The Paradise Trinity is existent. The stage of universal space is set for the manifold and never-ending panorama of the creative unfolding of the purpose of the Universal Father through the personality of the Eternal Son and by the execution of the God of Action, the executive agency for the reality performances of the Father-Son creator partnership.

The God of Action functions and the dead vaults of space are astir. One billion perfect spheres flash into existence. Prior to this hypothetical eternity moment the space-energies inherent in Paradise are existent and potentially operative, but they have no actuality of being; neither can physical gravity be measured except by the reaction of material realities to its incessant pull. There is no material universe at this (assumed) eternally distant moment, but the very instant that one billion worlds materialize, there is in evidence gravity sufficient and adequate to hold them in the everlasting grasp of Paradise.

There now flashes through the creation of the Gods the second form of energy, and this outflowing spirit is instantly grasped by the spiritual gravity of the Eternal Son. Thus the twofold gravity-embraced universe is touched with the energy of infinity and immersed in the spirit of divinity. In this way is the soil of life prepared for the consciousness of mind made manifest in the associated intelligence circuits of the Infinite Spirit.

Upon these seeds of potential existence, diffused throughout the central creation of the Gods, the Father acts, and creature personality appears. Then does the presence of the Paradise Deities fill all organized space and begin effectively to draw all things and beings Paradiseward.

The Infinite Spirit eternalizes concurrently with the birth of the Havona worlds, this central universe being created by him and with him and in him in obedience to the combined concepts and united wills of the Father and the Son. The Third Person deitizes by this very act of conjoint creation, and he thus forever becomes the Conjoint Creator.

These are the grand and awful times of the creative expansion of the Father and the Son by, and in, the action of their conjoint associate and exclusive executive, the Third Source and Center. There exists no record of these stirring times. We have only the meager disclosures of the Infinite Spirit to substantiate these mighty transactions, and he merely verifies the fact that the central universe and all that pertains thereto eternalized simultaneously with his attainment of personality and conscious existence.

In brief, the Infinite Spirit testifies that, since he is eternal, so also is the central universe eternal. And this is the traditional starting point of the history of the universe of universes. Absolutely nothing is known, and no records are in existence, regarding any event or transaction prior to this stupendous eruption of creative energy and administrative wisdom that crystallized the vast universe which exists, and so exquisitely functions, at the center of all things. Beyond this event lie the unsearchable transactions of eternity and the depths of infinity—absolute mystery.

And we thus portray the sequential origin of the Third Source and Center as an interpretative condescension to the time-bound and space-conditioned mind of mortal creatures. The mind of man must have a starting point for the visualization of universe history, and I have been directed to provide this technique of approach to the historic concept of eternity. In the material mind, consistency demands a First Cause; therefore do we postulate the Universal Father as the First Source and the Absolute Center of all creation, at the same time instructing all creature minds that the Son and the Spirit are coeternal with the Father in all phases of universe history and in all realms of creative activity. And we do this without in any sense being disregardful of the reality and eternity of the Isle of Paradise and of the Unqualified, Universal, and Deity Absolutes.

It is enough of a reach of the material mind of the children of time to conceive of the Father in eternity. We know that any child can best relate himself to reality by first mastering the relationships of the child-parent situation and then by enlarging this concept to embrace the family as a whole. Subsequently the growing mind of the child will be able to adjust to the concept of family relations, to relationships of the community, the race, and the world, and then to those of the universe, the superuniverse, even the universe of universes.

2. NATURE OF THE INFINITE SPIRIT

The Conjoint Creator is from eternity and is wholly and without qualification one with the Universal Father and the Eternal Son. The Infinite Spirit reflects in perfection not only the nature of the Paradise Father but also the nature of the Original Son.

The Third Source and Center is known by numerous titles: the Universal Spirit, the Supreme Guide, the Conjoint Creator, the Divine Executive, the Infinite Mind, the Spirit of Spirits, the Paradise Mother Spirit, the Conjoint Actor, the Final Co-ordinator, the Omnipresent Spirit, the Absolute Intelligence, the Divine Action; and on Urantia he is sometimes confused with the cosmic mind.

It is altogether proper to denominate the Third Person of Deity the Infinite Spirit, for God is spirit. But material creatures who tend towards the error of viewing matter as basic reality and mind, together with spirit, as postulates rooted in matter, would better comprehend the Third Source and Center if he were called the Infinite Reality, the Universal Organizer, or the Personality Co-ordinator.

The Infinite Spirit, as a universe revelation of divinity, is unsearchable and utterly beyond human comprehension. To sense the absoluteness of the Spirit, you need only contemplate the infinity of the Universal Father and stand in awe of the eternity of the Original Son.

There is mystery indeed in the person of the Infinite Spirit but not so much as in the Father and the Son. Of all aspects of the Father's nature, the Conjoint Creator most strikingly discloses his infinity. Even if the master universe eventually expands to infinity, the spirit presence, energy control, and mind potential of the Conjoint Actor will be found adequate to meet the demands of such a limitless creation.

Though in every way sharing the perfection, the righteousness, and the love of the Universal Father, the Infinite Spirit inclines towards the mercy attributes of the Eternal Son, thus becoming the mercy minister of the Paradise Deities to the grand universe. Ever and always—universally and eternally—the Spirit is a mercy minister, for, as the divine Sons reveal the love of God, so the divine Spirit depicts the mercy of God.

It is not possible that the Spirit could have more of goodness than the Father since all goodness takes origin in the Father, but in the acts of the Spirit we can the better comprehend such goodness. The Father's faithfulness and the Son's constancy are made very real to the spirit beings and the material creatures of the spheres by the loving ministry and ceaseless service of the personalities of the Infinite Spirit.

The Conjoint Creator inherits all the Father's beauty of thought and character of truth. And these sublime traits of divinity are co-ordinated in the near-supreme levels of the cosmic mind in subordination to the infinite and eternal wisdom of the unconditioned and limitless mind of the Third Source and Center.

3. RELATION OF THE SPIRIT TO THE FATHER AND THE SON

As the Eternal Son is the word expression of the "first" absolute and infinite thought of the Universal Father, so the Conjoint Actor is the perfect execution of the "first" completed creative concept or plan for combined action by the Father-Son personality partnership of absolute thought-word union. The Third Source and Center eternalizes concurrently with the central or fiat creation, and only this central creation is eternal in existence among universes.

Since the personalization of the Third Source, the First Source no more personally participates in universe creation. The Universal Father delegates everything possible to his Eternal Son; likewise does the Eternal Son bestow all possible authority and power upon the Conjoint Creator.

The Eternal Son and the Conjoint Creator have, as partners and through their co-ordinate personalities, planned and fashioned every post-Havona universe which has been brought into existence. The Spirit sustains the same personal relation to the Son in all subsequent creation that the Son sustains to the Father in the first and central creation.

A Creator Son of the Eternal Son and a Creative Spirit of the Infinite Spirit created you and your universe; and while the Father in faithfulness upholds that which they have organized, it devolves upon this Universe Son and this Universe Spirit to foster and sustain their work as well as to minister to the creatures of their own making.

The Infinite Spirit is the effective agent of the all-loving Father and the all-merciful Son for the execution of their conjoint project of drawing to themselves all truth-loving souls on all the worlds of time and space. The very instant the Eternal Son accepted his Father's plan of perfection attainment for the creatures of the universes, the moment the ascension project became a Father-Son plan, that instant the Infinite Spirit became the conjoint administrator of the Father and the Son for the execution of their united and eternal purpose. And in so doing the Infinite Spirit pledged all his resources of divine presence and of spirit personalities to the Father and the Son; he has dedicated *all* to the stupendous plan of exalting surviving will creatures to the divine heights of Paradise perfection.

The Infinite Spirit is a complete, exclusive, and universal revelation of the Universal Father and his Eternal Son. All knowledge of the Father-Son partnership must be had through the Infinite Spirit, the conjoint representative of the divine thought-word union.

The Eternal Son is the only avenue of approach to the Universal Father, and the Infinite Spirit is the only means of attaining the Eternal Son. Only by the patient ministry of the Spirit are the ascendant beings of time able to discover the Son.

At the center of all things the Infinite Spirit is the first of the Paradise Deities to be attained by the ascending pilgrims. The Third Person enshrouds the Second and the First Persons and therefore must always be first recognized by all who are candidates for presentation to the Son and his Father.

And in many other ways does the Spirit equally represent and similarly serve the Father and the Son.

4. THE SPIRIT OF DIVINE MINISTRY

Paralleling the physical universe wherein Paradise gravity holds all things together is the spiritual universe wherein the word of the Son interprets the thought of God and, when "made flesh," demonstrates the loving mercy of the combined nature of the associated Creators. But in and through all this material and spiritual creation there is a vast stage whereon the Infinite Spirit and his spirit offspring show forth the combined mercy, patience, and everlasting affection of the divine parents towards the intelligent children of their co-operative devising and making. Everlasting ministry to mind is the essence of the Spirit's divine character. And all the spirit offspring of the Conjoint Actor partake of this desire to minister, this divine urge to service.

God is love, the Son is mercy, the Spirit is ministry—the ministry of divine love and endless mercy to all intelligent creation. The Spirit is the personification of the Father's love and the Son's mercy; in him are they eternally united for universal service. The Spirit is *love applied* to the creature creation, the combined love of the Father and the Son.

On Urantia the Infinite Spirit is known as an omnipresent influence, a universal presence, but in Havona you shall know him as a personal presence of actual ministry. Here the ministry of the Paradise Spirit is the exemplary and inspiring pattern for each of his co-ordinate Spirits and subordinate personalities ministering to the created beings on the worlds of time and space. In this divine universe the Infinite Spirit fully participated in the seven transcendental appearances of the Eternal Son; likewise did he participate with the original Michael Son in the seven bestowals upon the circuits of Havona, thereby becoming the sympathetic and understanding spirit minister to every pilgrim of time traversing these perfect circles on high.

When a Creator Son of God accepts the creatorship charge of responsibility for a projected local universe, the personalities of the Infinite Spirit pledge themselves as the tireless ministers of this Michael Son when he goes forth on his mission of creative adventure. Especially in the persons of the Creative Daughters, the local universe Mother Spirits, do we find the Infinite Spirit devoted to the task of fostering the ascension of the material creatures to higher and higher levels of spiritual attainment. And all this work of creature ministry is done in perfect harmony with the purposes, and in close association with the personalities, of the Creator Sons of these local universes.

As the Sons of God are engaged in the gigantic task of revealing the Father's personality of love to a universe, so is the Infinite Spirit dedicated to the unending ministry of revealing the combined love of the Father and the Son to the individual minds of all the children of each universe. In these local creations the

Spirit does not come down to the material races in the likeness of mortal flesh as do certain of the Sons of God, but the Infinite Spirit and his co-ordinate Spirits do downstep themselves, do joyfully undergo an amazing series of divinity attenuations, until they appear as angels to stand by your side and guide you through the lowly paths of earthly existence.

By this very diminishing series the Infinite Spirit does actually, and as a person, draw very near to every being of the animal-origin spheres. And all this the Spirit does without in the least invalidating his existence as the Third Person of Deity at the center of all things.

The Conjoint Creator is truly and forever the great ministering personality, the universal mercy minister. To comprehend the ministry of the Spirit, ponder the truth that he is the combined portrayal of the Father's unending love and of the Son's eternal mercy. The Spirit's ministry is not, however, restricted solely to the representation of the Eternal Son and the Universal Father. The Infinite Spirit also possesses the power to minister to the creatures of the realm in his own name and right; the Third Person is of divine dignity and also bestows the universal ministry of mercy in his own behalf.

As man learns more of the loving and tireless ministry of the lower orders of the creature family of this Infinite Spirit, he will all the more admire and adore the transcendent nature and matchless character of this combined Action of the Universal Father and the Eternal Son. Indeed is this Spirit "the eyes of the Lord which are ever over the righteous" and "the divine ears which are ever open to their prayers."

5. THE PRESENCE OF GOD

The outstanding attribute of the Infinite Spirit is omnipresence. Throughout all the universe of universes there is everywhere present this all-pervading spirit, which is so akin to the presence of a universal and divine mind. Both the Second Person and the Third Person of Deity are represented on all worlds by their ever-present spirits.

The Father is *infinite* and is therefore limited only by volition. In the bestowal of Adjusters and in the encircuitment of personality, the Father acts alone, but in the contact of spirit forces with intelligent beings, he utilizes the spirits and personalities of the Eternal Son and the Infinite Spirit. He is at will spiritually present equally with the Son or with the Conjoint Actor; he is present *with* the Son and *in* the Spirit. The Father is most certainly everywhere present, and we discern his presence by and through any and all of these diverse but associated forces, influences, and presences.

In your sacred writings the term *Spirit of God* seems to be used interchangeably to designate both the Infinite Spirit on Paradise and the Creative Spirit of your local universe. The Holy Spirit is the spiritual circuit of this Creative Daughter of the Paradise Infinite Spirit. The Holy Spirit is a circuit indigenous to each local universe and is confined to the spiritual realm of that creation; but the Infinite Spirit is omnipresent.

There are many spiritual influences, and they are all as *one*. Even the work of the Thought Adjusters, though independent of all other influences, unvaryingly coincides with the spirit ministry of the combined influences of the Infinite Spirit and a local universe Mother Spirit. As these spiritual presences operate in the lives of Urantians, they cannot be segregated. In your minds and upon your souls they function as one spirit, notwithstanding their diverse origins. And as this united spiritual ministration is experienced, it becomes to you the influence of the Supreme, "who is ever able to keep you from failing and to present you blameless before your Father on high."

Ever remember that the Infinite Spirit is the *Conjoint* Actor; both the Father and the Son are functioning in and through him; he is present not only as himself but also as the Father and as the Son and as the Father-Son. In recognition of this and for many additional reasons the spirit presence of the Infinite Spirit is often referred to as "the spirit of God."

It would also be consistent to refer to the liaison of all spiritual ministry as the spirit of God, for such a liaison is truly the union of the spirits of God the Father, God the Son, God the Spirit, and God the Sevenfold—even the spirit of God the Supreme.

6. PERSONALITY OF THE INFINITE SPIRIT

Do not allow the widespread bestowal and the far-flung distribution of the Third Source and Center to obscure or otherwise detract from the fact of his personality. The Infinite Spirit is a universe presence, an eternal action, a cosmic power, a holy influence, and a universal mind; he is all of these and infinitely more, but he is also a true and divine personality.

The Infinite Spirit is a complete and perfect personality, the divine equal and co-ordinate of the Universal Father and the Eternal Son. The Conjoint Creator is just as real and visible to the higher intelligences of the universes as are the Father and the Son; indeed more so, for it is the Spirit whom all ascenders must attain before they may approach the Father through the Son.

The Infinite Spirit, the Third Person of Deity, is possessed of all the attributes which you associate with personality. The Spirit is endowed with absolute mind: "The Spirit searches all things, even the deep things of God." The Spirit is endowed not only with mind but also with will. In the bestowal of his gifts it is recorded: "But all these works that one and the selfsame Spirit, dividing to every man severally and as he wills."

"The love of the Spirit" is real, as also are his sorrows; therefore "Grieve not the Spirit of God." Whether we observe the Infinite Spirit as Paradise Deity or as a local universe Creative Spirit, we find that the Conjoint Creator is not only the Third Source and Center but also a divine person. This divine personality also reacts to the universe as a person. The Spirit speaks to you, "He who has an ear, let him hear what the Spirit says." "The Spirit himself makes intercession for you." The Spirit exerts a direct and personal influence upon created beings, "For as many as are led by the Spirit of God, they are the sons of God."

Even though we behold the phenomenon of the ministry of the Infinite Spirit to the remote worlds of the universe of universes, even though we envisage this same co-ordinating Deity acting in and through the untold legions of the manifold beings who take origin in the Third Source and Center, even though we recognize the omnipresence of the Spirit, nonetheless, we still affirm that this same Third Source and Center is a person, the Conjoint Creator of all things and all beings and all universes.

In the administration of universes the Father, Son, and Spirit are perfectly and eternally interassociated. Though each is engaged in a personal ministry to all creation, all three are divinely and absolutely interlocked in a service of creation and control which forever makes them *one*.

In the person of the Infinite Spirit the Father and the Son are mutually present, always and in unqualified perfection, for the Spirit is like the Father and like the Son, and also like the Father and the Son as they two are forever one.

[Presented on Urantia by a Divine Counselor of Uversa commissioned by the Ancients of Days to portray the nature and work of the Infinite Spirit.]

PAPER 9

RELATION OF THE INFINITE SPIRIT TO THE UNIVERSE

A STRANGE thing occurred when, in the presence of Paradise, the Universal Father and the Eternal Son unite to personalize themselves. Nothing in this eternity situation foreshadows that the Conjoint Actor would personalize as an unlimited spirituality co-ordinated with absolute mind and endowed with unique prerogatives of energy manipulation. His coming into being completes the Father's liberation from the bonds of centralized perfection and from the fetters of personality absolutism. And this liberation is disclosed in the amazing power of the Conjoint Creator to create beings well adapted to serve as ministering spirits even to the material creatures of the subsequently evolving universes.

The Father is infinite in love and volition, in spiritual thought and purpose; he is the universal upholder. The Son is infinite in wisdom and truth, in spiritual expression and interpretation; he is the universal revealer. Paradise is infinite in potential for force endowment and in capacity for energy dominance; it is the universal stabilizer. The Conjoint Actor possesses unique prerogatives of synthesis, infinite capacity to co-ordinate all existing universe energies, all actual universe spirits, and all real universe intellects; the Third Source and Center is the universal unifier of the manifold energies and diverse creations which have appeared in consequence of the divine plan and the eternal purpose of the Universal Father.

The Infinite Spirit, the Conjoint Creator, is a universal and divine minister. The Spirit unceasingly ministers the Son's mercy and the Father's love, even in harmony with the stable, unvarying, and righteous justice of the Paradise Trinity. His influence and personalities are ever near you; they really know and truly understand you.

Throughout the universes the agencies of the Conjoint Actor ceaselessly manipulate the forces and energies of all space. Like the First Source and Center, the Third is responsive to both the spiritual and the material. The Conjoint Actor is the revelation of the unity of God, in whom all things consist—things, meanings, and values; energies, minds, and spirits.

The Infinite Spirit pervades all space; he indwells the circle of eternity; and the Spirit, like the Father and the Son, is perfect and changeless—absolute.

1. ATTRIBUTES OF THE THIRD SOURCE AND CENTER

The Third Source and Center is known by many names, all designative of relationship and in recognition of function: As God the Spirit, he is the personality co-ordinate and divine equal of God the Son and God the Father. As the Infinite Spirit, he is an omnipresent spiritual influence. As the Universal Manipulator, he is the ancestor of the power-control creatures and the activator of the cosmic forces of space. As the Conjoint Actor, he is the joint representative and partnership executive of the Father-Son. As the Absolute Mind, he is the source of the endowment of intellect throughout the universes. As the God of Action, he is the apparent ancestor of motion, change, and relationship.

Some of the attributes of the Third Source and Center are derived from the Father, some from the Son, while still others are not observed to be actively and personally present in either the Father or the Son—attributes that can hardly be explained except by assuming that the Father-Son partnership which eternalizes the Third Source and Center consistently functions in consonance with, and in recognition of, the eternal fact of the absoluteness of Paradise. The Conjoint Creator embodies the fullness of the combined and infinite concepts of the First and Second Persons of Deity.

While you envisage the Father as an original creator and the Son as a spiritual administrator, you should think of the Third Source and Center as a universal co-ordinator, a minister of unlimited co-operation. The Conjoint Actor is the correlator of all actual reality; he is the Deity repository of the Father's thought and the Son's word and in action is eternally regardful of the material absoluteness of the central Isle. The Paradise Trinity has ordained the universal order of *progress,* and the providence of God is the domain of the Conjoint Creator and the evolving Supreme Being. No actual or actualizing reality can escape eventual relationship with the Third Source and Center.

The Universal Father presides over the realms of pre-energy, prespirit, and personality; the Eternal Son dominates the spheres of spiritual activities; the presence of the Isle of Paradise unifies the domain of physical energy and materializing power; the Conjoint Actor operates not only as an infinite spirit representing the Son but also as a universal manipulator of the forces and energies of Paradise, thus bringing into existence the universal and absolute mind. The Conjoint Actor functions throughout the grand universe as a positive and distinct personality, especially in the higher spheres of spiritual values, physical-energy relationships, and true mind meanings. He functions specifically wherever and whenever energy and spirit associate and interact; he dominates all reactions with mind, wields great power in the spiritual world, and exerts a mighty influence over energy and matter. At all times the Third Source is expressive of the nature of the First Source and Center.

The Third Source and Center perfectly and without qualification shares the omnipresence of the First Source and Center, sometimes being called the Omnipresent Spirit. In a peculiar and very personal manner the God of mind shares the omniscience of the Universal Father and his Eternal Son; the knowledge of the Spirit is profound and complete. The Conjoint Creator manifests certain phases of the omnipotence of the Universal Father but is actually omnipotent only in the domain of mind. The Third Person of Deity is the intellectual center and the universal administrator of the mind realms; herein is he absolute—his sovereignty is unqualified.

The Conjoint Actor seems to be motivated by the Father-Son partnership, but all his actions appear to recognize the Father-Paradise relationship. At times and in certain functions he seems to compensate for the incompleteness of the development of the experiential Deities—God the Supreme and God the Ultimate.

And herein is an infinite mystery: That the Infinite simultaneously revealed his infinity in the Son and as Paradise, and then there springs into existence a being equal to God in divinity, reflective of the Son's spiritual nature, and capable of activating the Paradise pattern, a being provisionally subordinate in sovereignty but in many ways apparently the most versatile in *action.* And such apparent superiority in action is disclosed in an attribute of the Third Source and Center which is superior even to physical gravity—the universal manifestation of the Isle of Paradise.

In addition to this supercontrol of energy and things physical, the Infinite Spirit is superbly endowed with those attributes of patience, mercy, and love which are so exquisitely revealed in his spiritual ministry. The Spirit is supremely competent to minister love and to overshadow justice with mercy. God the Spirit possesses all the supernal kindness and merciful affection of the Original and Eternal Son. The universe of your origin is being forged out between the anvil of justice and the hammer of suffering; but those who wield the hammer are the children of mercy, the spirit offspring of the Infinite Spirit.

2. THE OMNIPRESENT SPIRIT

God is spirit in a threefold sense: He himself is spirit; in his Son he appears as spirit without qualification; in the Conjoint Actor, as spirit allied with mind. And in addition to these spiritual realities, we think we discern levels of experiential spirit phenomena—the spirits of the Supreme Being, Ultimate Deity, and Deity Absolute.

The Infinite Spirit is just as much a complement of the Eternal Son as the Son is a complement of the Universal Father. The Eternal Son is a spiritualized personalization of the Father; the Infinite Spirit is a personalized spiritualization of the Eternal Son and the Universal Father.

There are many untrammeled lines of spiritual force and sources of supermaterial power linking the people of Urantia directly with the Deities of Paradise. There exist the connection of the Thought Adjusters direct with the Universal Father, the widespread influence of the spiritual-gravity urge of the Eternal Son, and the spiritual presence of the Conjoint Creator. There is a difference in function between the spirit of the Son and the spirit of the Spirit. The Third Person in his spiritual ministry may function as mind plus spirit or as spirit alone.

In addition to these Paradise presences, Urantians benefit by the spiritual influences and activities of the local and the superuniverse, with their almost endless array of loving personalities who ever lead the true of purpose and the honest of heart upward and inward towards the ideals of divinity and the goal of supreme perfection.

The presence of the universal spirit of the Eternal Son we *know*—we can unmistakably recognize it. The presence of the Infinite Spirit, the Third Person of Deity, even mortal man may know, for material creatures can actually experience the beneficence of this divine influence which functions as the Holy Spirit of local universe bestowal upon the races of mankind. Human beings can also in some degree become conscious of the Adjuster, the impersonal presence of the Universal Father. These divine spirits which work for man's uplifting and spiritualization all act in unison and in perfect co-operation. They are as one in the spiritual operation of the plans of mortal ascension and perfection attainment.

3. THE UNIVERSAL MANIPULATOR

The Isle of Paradise is the source and substance of physical gravity; and that should be sufficient to inform you that gravity is one of the most *real* and eternally dependable things in the whole physical universe of universes. Gravity cannot be modified or annulled except by the forces and energies conjointly sponsored by the Father and the Son, which have been intrusted to, and are functionally associated with, the person of the Third Source and Center.

The Infinite Spirit possesses a unique and amazing power—*antigravity.* This power is not functionally (observably) present in either the Father or the Son. This ability to withstand the pull of material gravity, inherent in the Third Source, is revealed in the personal reactions of the Conjoint Actor to certain phases of universe relationships. And this unique attribute is transmissible to certain of the higher personalities of the Infinite Spirit.

Antigravity can annul gravity within a local frame; it does so by the exercise of equal force presence. It operates only with reference to material gravity, and it is not the action of mind. The gravity-resistant phenomenon of a gyroscope is a fair illustration of the *effect* of antigravity but of no value to illustrate the *cause* of antigravity.

Still further does the Conjoint Actor display powers which can transcend force and neutralize energy. Such powers operate by slowing down energy to the point of materialization and by other techniques unknown to you.

The Conjoint Creator is not energy nor the source of energy nor the destiny of energy; he is the *manipulator* of energy. The Conjoint Creator is action—motion, change, modification, co-ordination, stabilization, and equilibrium. The energies subject to the direct or indirect control of Paradise are by nature responsive to the acts of the Third Source and Center and his manifold agencies.

The universe of universes is permeated by the power-control creatures of the Third Source and Center: physical controllers, power directors, power centers, and other representatives of the God of Action who have to do with the regulation and stabilization of physical energies. These unique creatures of physical function all possess varying attributes of power control, such as antigravity, which they utilize in their efforts to establish the physical equilibrium of the matter and energies of the grand universe.

All these material activities of the God of Action appear to relate his function to the Isle of Paradise, and indeed the agencies of power are all regardful of, even dependent on, the absoluteness of the eternal Isle. But the Conjoint Actor does not act for, or in response to, Paradise. He acts, personally, for the Father and the Son. Paradise is not a person. The nonpersonal, impersonal, and otherwise not personal doings of the Third Source and Center are all volitional acts of the Conjoint Actor himself; they are not reflections, derivations, or repercussions of anything or anybody.

Paradise is the pattern of infinity; the God of Action is the activator of that pattern. Paradise is the material fulcrum of infinity; the agencies of the Third Source and Center are the levers of intelligence which motivate the material level and inject spontaneity into the mechanism of the physical creation.

4. THE ABSOLUTE MIND

There is an intellectual nature of the Third Source and Center that is distinct from his physical and spiritual attributes. Such a nature is hardly contactable, but it is associable—intellectually though not personally. It is distinguishable from the physical attributes and the spiritual character of the Third Person on mind levels of function, but to the discernment of personalities this nature never functions independently of physical or spiritual manifestations.

The absolute mind is the mind of the Third Person; it is inseparable from the personality of God the Spirit. Mind, in functioning beings, is not separated from energy or spirit, or both. Mind is not inherent in energy; energy is receptive and responsive to mind; mind can be superimposed upon energy, but consciousness is not inherent in the purely material level. Mind does not have to be added to pure spirit, for spirit is innately conscious and identifying. Spirit is always intelligent, *minded* in some way. It may be this mind or that mind, it may be premind or supermind, even spirit mind, but it does the equivalent of thinking and knowing. The insight of spirit transcends, supervenes, and theoretically antedates the consciousness of mind.

The Conjoint Creator is absolute only in the domain of mind, in the realms of universal intelligence. The mind of the Third Source and Center is infinite; it utterly transcends the active and functioning mind circuits of the universe of universes. The mind endowment of the seven superuniverses is derived from the Seven Master Spirits, the primary personalities of the Conjoint Creator. These Master Spirits distribute mind to the grand universe as the cosmic mind, and your local universe is pervaded by the Nebadon variant of the Orvonton type of cosmic mind.

Infinite mind ignores time, ultimate mind transcends time, cosmic mind is conditioned by time. And so with space: The Infinite Mind is independent of space, but as descent is made from the infinite to the adjutant levels of mind, intellect must increasingly reckon with the fact and limitations of space.

Cosmic force responds to mind even as cosmic mind responds to spirit. Spirit is divine purpose, and spirit mind is divine purpose in action. Energy is thing, mind is meaning, spirit is value. Even in time and space, mind establishes those relative relationships between energy and spirit which are suggestive of mutual kinship in eternity.

Mind transmutes the values of spirit into the meanings of intellect; volition has power to bring the meanings of mind to fruit in both the material and spiritual domains. The Paradise ascent involves a relative and differential growth in spirit, mind, and energy. The personality is the unifier of these components of experiential individuality.

5. THE MINISTRY OF MIND

The Third Source and Center is infinite in mind. If the universe should grow to infinity, still his mind potential would be adequate to endow limitless numbers of creatures with suitable minds and other prerequisites of intellect.

In the domain of *created mind* the Third Person, with his co-ordinate and subordinate associates, rules supreme. The realms of creature mind are of exclusive origin in the Third Source and Center; he is the bestower of mind. Even the Father fragments find it impossible to indwell the minds of men until the way has been properly prepared for them by the mind action and spiritual function of the Infinite Spirit.

The unique feature of mind is that it can be bestowed upon such a wide range of life. Through his creative and creature associates the Third Source and Center ministers to all minds on all spheres. He ministers to human and subhuman intellect through the adjutants of the local universes and, through the agency of the physical controllers, ministers even to the lowest nonexperiencing entities of the most primitive types of living things. And always is the direction of mind a ministry of mind-spirit or mind-energy personalities.

Since the Third Person of Deity is the source of mind, it is quite natural that the evolutionary will creatures find it easier to form comprehensible concepts of the Infinite Spirit than they do of either the Eternal Son or the Universal Father. The reality of the Conjoint Creator is disclosed imperfectly in the very existence of human mind. The Conjoint Creator is the ancestor of the cosmic mind, and the mind of man is an individualized circuit, an impersonal portion, of that cosmic mind as it is bestowed in a local universe by a Creative Daughter of the Third Source and Center.

Because the Third Person is the source of mind, do not presume to reckon that all phenomena of mind are divine. Human intellect is rooted in the material origin of the animal races. Universe intelligence is no more a true revelation of God who is mind than is physical nature a true revelation of the beauty and harmony of Paradise. Perfection is in nature, but nature is not perfect. The Conjoint Creator is the source of mind, but mind is not the Conjoint Creator.

Mind, on Urantia, is a compromise between the essence of thought perfection and the evolving mentality of your immature human nature. The plan for your intellectual evolution is, indeed, one of sublime perfection, but you are far short of that divine goal as you function in the tabernacles of the flesh. Mind is truly of divine origin, and it does have a divine destiny, but your mortal minds are not yet of divine dignity.

Too often, all too often, you mar your minds by insincerity and sear them with unrighteousness; you subject them to animal fear and distort them by useless anxiety. Therefore, though the source of mind is divine, mind as you know it on your world of ascension can hardly become the object of great admiration, much less of adoration or worship. The contemplation of the immature and inactive human intellect should lead only to reactions of humility.

6. THE MIND-GRAVITY CIRCUIT

The Third Source and Center, the universal intelligence, is personally conscious of every *mind,* every intellect, in all creation, and he maintains a personal and perfect contact with all these physical, morontial, and spiritual creatures of mind endowment in the far-flung universes. All these activities of mind are grasped in the absolute mind-gravity circuit which focalizes in the Third Source and Center and is a part of the personal consciousness of the Infinite Spirit.

Much as the Father draws all personality to himself, and as the Son attracts all spiritual reality, so does the Conjoint Actor exercise a drawing power on all minds; he unqualifiedly dominates and controls the universal mind circuit. All true and genuine intellectual values, all divine thoughts and perfect ideas, are unerringly drawn into this absolute circuit of mind.

Mind gravity can operate independently of material and spiritual gravity, but wherever and whenever the latter two impinge, mind gravity always functions. When all three are associated, personality gravity may embrace the material creature—physical or morontial, finite or absonite. But irrespective of this, the endowment of mind even in impersonal beings qualifies them to think and endows them with consciousness despite the total absence of personality.

Selfhood of personality dignity, human or divine, immortal or potentially immortal, does not however originate in either spirit, mind, or matter; it is the bestowal of the Universal Father. Neither is the interaction of spirit, mind, and material gravity a prerequisite to the appearance of personality gravity. The Father's circuit may embrace a mind-material being who is unresponsive to spirit gravity, or it may include a mind-spirit being who is unresponsive to material gravity. The operation of personality gravity is always a volitional act of the Universal Father.

While mind is energy associated in purely material beings and spirit associated in purely spiritual personalities, innumerable orders of personality, including the human, possess minds that are associated with both energy and spirit. The spiritual aspects of creature mind unfailingly respond to the spirit-gravity pull of the Eternal Son; the material features respond to the gravity urge of the material universe.

Cosmic mind, when not associated with either energy or spirit, is subject to the gravity demands of neither material nor spiritual circuits. Pure mind is subject only to the universal gravity grasp of the Conjoint Actor. Pure mind is close of kin to infinite mind, and infinite mind (the theoretical co-ordinate of the absolutes of spirit and energy) is apparently a law in itself.

The greater the spirit-energy divergence, the greater the observable function of mind; the lesser the diversity of energy and spirit, the lesser the observable function of mind. Apparently, the maximum function of the cosmic mind is in the time universes of space. Here mind seems to function in a mid-zone between energy and spirit, but this is not true of the higher levels of mind; on Paradise, energy and spirit are essentially one.

The mind-gravity circuit is dependable; it emanates from the Third Person of Deity on Paradise, but not all the observable function of mind is predictable. Throughout all known creation there parallels this circuit of mind some little-understood presence whose function is not predictable. We believe that this unpredictability is partly attributable to the function of the Universal Absolute. What this function is, we do not know; what actuates it, we can only conjecture; concerning its relation to creatures, we can only speculate.

Certain phases of the unpredictability of finite mind may be due to the incompleteness of the Supreme Being, and there is a vast zone of activities wherein the Conjoint Actor and the Universal Absolute may possibly be tangent. There is much about mind that is unknown, but of this we are sure: The Infinite Spirit is the perfect expression of the mind of the Creator to all creatures; the Supreme Being is the evolving expression of the minds of all creatures to their Creator.

7. UNIVERSE REFLECTIVITY

The Conjoint Actor is able to co-ordinate all levels of universe actuality in such manner as to make possible the simultaneous recognition of the mental, the material, and the spiritual. This is the phenomenon of *universe reflectivity,* that unique and inexplicable power to see, hear, sense, and know all things as they transpire throughout a superuniverse, and to focalize, by reflectivity, all this information and knowledge at any desired point. The action of reflectivity is shown in perfection on each of the headquarters worlds of the seven superuniverses. It is also operative throughout all sectors of the superuniverses and within the boundaries of the local universes. Reflectivity finally focalizes on Paradise.

The phenomenon of reflectivity, as it is disclosed on the superuniverse headquarters worlds in the amazing performances of the reflective personalities there stationed, represents the most complex interassociation of all phases of existence to be found in all creation. Lines of spirit can be traced back to the Son, physical energy to Paradise, and mind to the Third Source; but in the extraordinary phenomenon of universe reflectivity there is a unique and exceptional unification of all three, so associated as to enable the universe rulers to know about remote conditions instantaneously, simultaneously with their occurrence.

Much of the technique of reflectivity we comprehend, but there are many phases which truly baffle us. We know that the Conjoint Actor is the universe center of the mind circuit, that he is the ancestor of the cosmic mind, and that cosmic mind operates under the dominance of the absolute mind gravity of the Third Source and Center. We know further that the circuits of the cosmic mind influence the intellectual levels of all known existence; they contain the universal space reports, and just as certainly they focus in the Seven Master Spirits and converge in the Third Source and Center.

The relationship between the finite cosmic mind and the divine absolute mind appears to be evolving in the experiential mind of the Supreme. We are taught that, in the dawn of time, this experiential mind was bestowed upon the Supreme by the Infinite Spirit, and we conjecture that certain features of the phenomenon of reflectivity can be accounted for only by postulating the activity of the Supreme Mind. If the Supreme is not concerned in reflectivity, we are at a loss to explain the intricate transactions and unerring operations of this consciousness of the cosmos.

Reflectivity appears to be omniscience within the limits of the experiential finite and may represent the emergence of the presence-consciousness of the Supreme Being. If this assumption is true, then the utilization of reflectivity in any of its phases is equivalent to partial contact with the consciousness of the Supreme.

8. PERSONALITIES OF THE INFINITE SPIRIT

The Infinite Spirit possesses full power to transmit many of his powers and prerogatives to his co-ordinate and subordinate personalities and agencies.

The first Deity-creating act of the Infinite Spirit, functioning apart from the Trinity but in some unrevealed association with the Father and the Son, personalized in the existence of the Seven Master Spirits of Paradise, the distributors of the Infinite Spirit to the universes.

There is no direct representative of the Third Source and Center on the headquarters of a superuniverse. Each of these seven creations is dependent on one of the Master Spirits of Paradise, who acts through the seven Reflective Spirits situated at the capital of the superuniverse.

The next and continuing creative act of the Infinite Spirit is disclosed, from time to time, in the production of the Creative Spirits. Every time the Universal Father and the Eternal Son become parent to a Creator Son, the Infinite Spirit becomes ancestor to a local universe Creative Spirit who becomes the close associate of that Creator Son in all subsequent universe experience.

Just as it is necessary to distinguish between the Eternal Son and the Creator Sons, so it is necessary to differentiate between the Infinite Spirit and the Creative Spirits, the local universe co-ordinates of the Creator Sons. What the Infinite Spirit is to the total creation, a Creative Spirit is to a local universe.

The Third Source and Center is represented in the grand universe by a vast array of ministering spirits, messengers, teachers, adjudicators, helpers, and advisers, together with supervisors of certain circuits of physical, morontial, and spiritual nature. Not all of these beings are personalities in the strict meaning of the term. Personality of the finite-creature variety is characterized by:

1. Subjective self-consciousness.
2. Objective response to the Father's personality circuit.

There are creator personalities and creature personalities, and in addition to these two fundamental types there are *personalities of the Third Source and Center,* beings who are personal to the Infinite Spirit, but who are not unqualifiedly personal to creature beings. These Third Source personalities are not a part of the Father's personality circuit. First Source personality and Third Source personality are mutually contactable; all personality is contactable.

The Father bestows personality by his personal free will. Why he does so we can only conjecture; how he does so we do not know. Neither do we know why the Third Source bestows non-Father personality, but this the Infinite Spirit does in his own behalf, in creative conjunction with the Eternal Son and in numerous ways unknown to you. The Infinite Spirit can also act for the Father in the bestowal of First Source personality.

There are numerous types of Third Source personalities. The Infinite Spirit bestows Third Source personality upon numerous groups who are not included in the Father's personality circuit, such as certain of the power directors. Likewise does the Infinite Spirit treat as personalities numerous groups of beings, such as the Creative Spirits, who are in a class by themselves in their relations to encircuited creatures of the Father.

Both First Source and Third Source personalities are endowed with all and more than man associates with the concept of personality; they have minds embracing memory, reason, judgment, creative imagination, idea association, decision, choice, and numerous additional powers of intellect wholly unknown to mortals. With few exceptions the orders revealed to you possess form and distinct individuality; they are real beings. A majority of them are visible to all orders of spirit existence.

Even you will be able to see your spiritual associates of the lower orders as soon as you are delivered from the limited vision of your present material eyes and have been endowed with a morontia form with its enlarged sensitivity to the reality of spiritual things.

The functional family of the Third Source and Center, as it is revealed in these narratives, falls into three great groups:

I. *The Supreme Spirits.* A group of composite origin that embraces, among others, the following orders:

1. The Seven Master Spirits of Paradise.
2. The Reflective Spirits of the Superuniverses.
3. The Creative Spirits of the Local Universes.

II. *The Power Directors.* A group of control creatures and agencies that function throughout all organized space.

III. *The Personalities of the Infinite Spirit.* This designation does not necessarily imply that these beings are Third Source personalities though some of them are unique as will creatures. They are usually grouped in three major classifications:

1. The Higher Personalities of the Infinite Spirit.
2. The Messenger Hosts of Space.
3. The Ministering Spirits of Time.

These groups serve on Paradise, in the central or residential universe, in the superuniverses, and they embrace orders that function in the local universes, even to the constellations, systems, and planets.

The spirit personalities of the vast family of the Divine and Infinite Spirit are forever dedicated to the service of the ministry of the love of God and the mercy of the Son to all the intelligent creatures of the evolutionary worlds of time and space. These spirit beings constitute the living ladder whereby mortal man climbs from chaos to glory.

[Revealed on Urantia by a Divine Counselor of Uversa commissioned by the Ancients of Days to portray the nature and work of the Infinite Spirit.]

PAPER 10

THE PARADISE TRINITY

THE Paradise Trinity of eternal Deities facilitates the Father's escape from personality absolutism. The Trinity perfectly associates the limitless expression of God's infinite personal will with the absoluteness of Deity. The Eternal Son and the various Sons of divine origin, together with the Conjoint Actor and his universe children, effectively provide for the Father's liberation from the limitations otherwise inherent in primacy, perfection, changelessness, eternity, universality, absoluteness, and infinity.

The Paradise Trinity effectively provides for the full expression and perfect revelation of the eternal nature of Deity. The Stationary Sons of the Trinity likewise afford a full and perfect revelation of divine justice. The Trinity is Deity unity, and this unity rests eternally upon the absolute foundations of the divine oneness of the three original and co-ordinate and coexistent personalities, God the Father, God the Son, and God the Spirit.

From the present situation on the circle of eternity, looking backward into the endless past, we can discover only one inescapable inevitability in universe affairs, and that is the Paradise Trinity. I deem the Trinity to have been inevitable. As I view the past, present, and future of time, I consider nothing else in all the universe of universes to have been inevitable. The present master universe, viewed in retrospect or in prospect, is unthinkable without the Trinity. Given the Paradise Trinity, we can postulate alternate or even multiple ways of doing all things, but without the Trinity of Father, Son, and Spirit we are unable to conceive how the Infinite could achieve threefold and co-ordinate personalization in the face of the absolute oneness of Deity. No other concept of creation measures up to the Trinity standards of the completeness of the absoluteness inherent in Deity unity coupled with the repleteness of volitional liberation inherent in the threefold personalization of Deity.

1. SELF-DISTRIBUTION OF THE FIRST SOURCE AND CENTER

It would seem that the Father, back in eternity, inaugurated a policy of profound self-distribution. There is inherent in the selfless, loving, and lovable nature of the Universal Father something which causes him to reserve to himself the exercise of only those powers and that authority which he apparently finds it impossible to delegate or to bestow.

The Universal Father all along has divested himself of every part of himself that was bestowable on any other Creator or creature. He has delegated to his divine Sons and their associated intelligences every power and all authority that could be delegated. He has actually transferred to his Sovereign Sons, in their respective universes, every prerogative of administrative authority that was transferable. In the affairs of a local universe, he has made each Sovereign Creator Son just as perfect, competent, and authoritative as is the Eternal Son in the original and central universe. He has given away, actually bestowed, with the dignity and sanctity of personality possession, all of himself and all of his attributes, everything he possibly could divest himself of, in every way, in every age, in every place, and to every person, and in every universe except that of his central indwelling.

Divine personality is not self-centered; self-distribution and sharing of personality characterize divine freewill selfhood. Creatures crave association with other personal creatures; Creators are moved to share divinity with their universe children; the personality of the Infinite is disclosed as the Universal Father, who shares reality of being and equality of self with two co-ordinate personalities, the Eternal Son and the Conjoint Actor.

For knowledge concerning the Father's personality and divine attributes we will always be dependent on the revelations of the Eternal Son, for when the conjoint act of creation was effected, when the Third Person of Deity sprang into personality existence and executed the combined concepts of his divine parents, the Father ceased to exist as the unqualified personality. With the coming into being of the Conjoint Actor and the materialization of the central core of creation, certain eternal changes took place. God gave himself as an absolute personality to his Eternal Son. Thus does the Father bestow the "personality of infinity" upon his only-begotten Son, while they both bestow the "conjoint personality" of their eternal union upon the Infinite Spirit.

For these and other reasons beyond the concept of the finite mind, it is exceedingly difficult for the human creature to comprehend God's infinite father-personality except as it is universally revealed in the Eternal Son and, with the Son, is universally active in the Infinite Spirit.

Since the Paradise Sons of God visit the evolutionary worlds and sometimes even there dwell in the likeness of mortal flesh, and since these bestowals make it possible for mortal man actually to know something of the nature and character of divine personality, therefore must the creatures of the planetary spheres look to the bestowals of these Paradise Sons for reliable and trustworthy information regarding the Father, the Son, and the Spirit.

2. DEITY PERSONALIZATION

By the technique of trinitization the Father divests himself of that unqualified spirit personality which is the Son, but in so doing he constitutes himself the Father of this very Son and thereby possesses himself of unlimited capacity to become the divine Father of all subsequently created, eventuated, or other personalized types of intelligent will creatures. As the *absolute and unqualified personality* the Father can function only as and with the Son, but as a *personal Father* he continues to bestow personality upon the diverse hosts of the differing levels of intelligent will creatures, and he forever maintains personal relations of loving association with this vast family of universe children.

After the Father has bestowed upon the personality of his Son the fullness of himself, and when this act of self-bestowal is complete and perfect, of the infinite power and nature which are thus existent in the Father-Son union, the eternal partners conjointly bestow those qualities and attributes which constitute still another being like themselves; and this conjoint personality, the Infinite Spirit, completes the existential personalization of Deity.

The Son is indispensable to the fatherhood of God. The Spirit is indispensable to the fraternity of the Second and Third Persons. Three persons are a minimum social group, but this is least of all the many reasons for believing in the inevitability of the Conjoint Actor.

The First Source and Center is the infinite *father-personality,* the unlimited source personality. The Eternal Son is the unqualified *personality-absolute,* that divine being who stands throughout all time and eternity as the perfect revelation of the personal nature of God. The Infinite Spirit is the *conjoint personality,* the unique personal consequence of the everlasting Father-Son union.

The personality of the First Source and Center is the personality of infinity minus the absolute personality of the Eternal Son. The personality of the Third Source and Center is the superadditive consequence of the union of the liberated Father-personality and the absolute Son-personality.

The Universal Father, the Eternal Son, and the Infinite Spirit are unique persons; none is a duplicate; each is original; all are united.

The Eternal Son alone experiences the fullness of divine personality relationship, consciousness of both sonship with the Father and paternity to the Spirit and of divine equality with both Father-ancestor and Spirit-associate. The Father knows the experience of having a Son who is his equal, but the Father knows no ancestral antecedents. The Eternal Son has the experience of sonship, recognition of personality ancestry, and at the same time the Son is conscious of being joint parent to the Infinite Spirit. The Infinite Spirit is conscious of twofold personality ancestry but is not parental to a co-ordinate Deity personality. With the Spirit the existential cycle of Deity personalization attains completion; the primary personalities of the Third Source and Center are experiential and are seven in number.

I am of origin in the Paradise Trinity. I know the Trinity as unified Deity; I also know that the Father, Son, and Spirit exist and act in their definite personal capacities. I positively know that they not only act personally and collectively, but that they also co-ordinate their performances in various groupings, so that in the end they function in seven different singular and plural capacities. And since these seven associations exhaust the possibilities for such divinity combination, it is inevitable that the realities of the universe shall appear in seven variations of values, meanings, and personality.

3. THE THREE PERSONS OF DEITY

Notwithstanding there is only one Deity, there are three positive and divine personalizations of Deity. Regarding the endowment of man with the divine Adjusters, the Father said: "Let us make mortal man in our own image." Repeatedly throughout the Urantian writings there occurs this reference to the acts and doings of plural Deity, clearly showing recognition of the existence and working of the three Sources and Centers.

We are taught that the Son and the Spirit sustain the same and equal relations to the Father in the Trinity association. In eternity and as Deities they undoubtedly do, but in time and as personalities they certainly disclose relationships of a very diverse nature. Looking from Paradise out on the universes, these relationships do seem to be very similar, but when viewed from the domains of space, they appear to be quite different.

The divine Sons are indeed the "Word of God," but the children of the Spirit are truly the "Act of God." God speaks through the Son and, with the Son, acts through the Infinite Spirit, while in all universe activities the Son and the Spirit are exquisitely fraternal, working as two equal brothers with admiration and love for an honored and divinely respected common Father.

The Father, Son, and Spirit are certainly equal in nature, co-ordinate in being, but there are unmistakable differences in their universe performances, and when acting alone, each person of Deity is apparently limited in absoluteness.

The Universal Father, prior to his self-willed divestment of the personality, powers, and attributes which constitute the Son and the Spirit, seems to have been (philosophically considered) an unqualified, absolute, and infinite Deity. But such a theoretical First Source and Center without a Son could not in any sense of the word be considered the *Universal Father;* fatherhood is not real without sonship. Furthermore, the Father, to have been absolute in a total sense, must have existed at some eternally distant moment alone. But he never had such a solitary existence; the Son and the Spirit are both coeternal with the Father. The First Source and Center has always been, and will forever be, the eternal Father of the Original Son and, with the Son, the eternal progenitor of the Infinite Spirit.

We observe that the Father has divested himself of all direct manifestations of absoluteness except absolute fatherhood and absolute volition. We do not know whether volition is an inalienable attribute of the Father; we can only observe that he did *not* divest himself of volition. Such infinity of will must have been eternally inherent in the First Source and Center.

In bestowing absoluteness of personality upon the Eternal Son, the Universal Father escapes from the fetters of personality absolutism, but in so doing he takes a step which makes it forever impossible for him to act alone as the personality-absolute. And with the final personalization of coexistent Deity—the Conjoint Actor—there ensues the critical trinitarian interdependence of the three divine personalities with regard to the totality of Deity function in absolute.

God is the Father-Absolute of all personalities in the universe of universes. The Father is personally absolute in liberty of action, but in the universes of time and space, made, in the making, and yet to be made, the Father is not discernibly absolute as total Deity except in the Paradise Trinity.

The First Source and Center functions outside of Havona in the phenomenal universes as follows:

1. As creator, through the Creator Sons, his grandsons.

2. As controller, through the gravity center of Paradise.

3. As spirit, through the Eternal Son.

4. As mind, through the Conjoint Creator.

5. As a Father, he maintains parental contact with all creatures through his personality circuit.

6. As a person, he acts *directly* throughout creation by his exclusive fragments—in mortal man by the Thought Adjusters.

7. As total Deity, he functions only in the Paradise Trinity.

All these relinquishments and delegations of jurisdiction by the Universal Father are wholly voluntary and self-imposed. The all-powerful Father purposefully assumes these limitations of universe authority.

The Eternal Son seems to function as one with the Father in all spiritual respects except in the bestowals of the God fragments and in other prepersonal activities. Neither is the Son closely identified with the intellectual activities of material creatures nor with the energy activities of the material universes. As absolute the Son functions as a person and only in the domain of the spiritual universe.

The Infinite Spirit is amazingly universal and unbelievably versatile in all his operations. He performs in the spheres of mind, matter, and spirit. The Conjoint Actor represents the Father-Son association, but he also functions as himself. He is not directly concerned with physical gravity, with spiritual gravity, or with the personality circuit, but he more or less participates in all other universe activities. While apparently dependent on three existential and absolute gravity controls, the Infinite Spirit appears to exercise three supercontrols. This threefold endowment is employed in many ways to transcend and seemingly to neutralize even the manifestations of primary forces and energies, right up to the superultimate borders of absoluteness. In certain situations these supercontrols absolutely transcend even the primal manifestations of cosmic reality.

4. THE TRINITY UNION OF DEITY

Of all absolute associations, the Paradise Trinity (the first triunity) is unique as an exclusive association of personal Deity. God functions as God only in relation to God and to those who can know God, but as absolute Deity only in the Paradise Trinity and in relation to universe totality.

Eternal Deity is perfectly unified; nevertheless there are three perfectly individualized persons of Deity. The Paradise Trinity makes possible the simultaneous expression of all the diversity of the character traits and infinite powers of the First Source and Center and his eternal co-ordinates and of all the divine unity of the universe functions of undivided Deity.

The Trinity is an association of infinite persons functioning in a nonpersonal capacity but not in contravention of personality. The illustration is crude, but a father, son, and grandson could form a corporate entity which would be nonpersonal but nonetheless subject to their personal wills.

The Paradise Trinity is *real.* It exists as the Deity union of Father, Son, and Spirit; yet the Father, the Son, or the Spirit, or any two of them, can function in relation to this selfsame Paradise Trinity. The Father, Son, and Spirit can collaborate in a non-Trinity manner, but not as three Deities. As persons they can collaborate as they choose, but that is not the Trinity.

Ever remember that what the Infinite Spirit does is the function of the Conjoint Actor. Both the Father and the Son are functioning in and through and as him. But it would be futile to attempt to elucidate the Trinity mystery: three as one and in one, and one as two and acting for two.

The Trinity is so related to total universe affairs that it must be reckoned with in our attempts to explain the totality of any isolated cosmic event or personality relationship. The Trinity functions on all levels of the cosmos, and mortal man is limited to the finite level; therefore must man be content with a finite concept of the Trinity as the Trinity.

As a mortal in the flesh you should view the Trinity in accordance with your individual enlightenment and in harmony with the reactions of your mind and soul. You can know very little of the absoluteness of the Trinity, but as you ascend Paradiseward, you will many times experience astonishment at successive revelations and unexpected discoveries of Trinity supremacy and ultimacy, if not of absoluteness.

5. FUNCTIONS OF THE TRINITY

The personal Deities have attributes, but it is hardly consistent to speak of the Trinity as having attributes. This association of divine beings may more properly be regarded as having *functions,* such as justice administration, totality attitudes, co-ordinate action, and cosmic overcontrol. These functions are actively supreme, ultimate, and (within the limits of Deity) absolute as far as all living realities of personality value are concerned.

The functions of the Paradise Trinity are not simply the sum of the Father's apparent endowment of divinity plus those specialized attributes that are unique in the personal existence of the Son and the Spirit. The Trinity association of the three Paradise Deities results in the evolution, eventuation, and deitization of new meanings, values, powers, and capacities for universal revelation, action, and administration. Living associations, human families, social groups, or the Paradise Trinity are not augmented by mere arithmetical summation. The group potential is always far in excess of the simple sum of the attributes of the component individuals.

The Trinity maintains a unique attitude as the Trinity towards the entire universe of the past, present, and future. And the functions of the Trinity can best be considered in relation to the universe attitudes of the Trinity. Such attitudes are simultaneous and may be multiple concerning any isolated situation or event:

1. *Attitude toward the Finite.* The maximum self-limitation of the Trinity is its attitude toward the finite. The Trinity is not a person, nor is the Supreme Being an exclusive personalization of the Trinity, but the Supreme is the nearest approach to a power-personality focalization of the Trinity which can be comprehended by finite creatures. Hence the Trinity in relation to the finite is sometimes spoken of as the Trinity of Supremacy.

2. *Attitude toward the Absonite.* The Paradise Trinity has regard for those levels of existence which are more than finite but less than absolute, and this relationship is sometimes denominated the Trinity of Ultimacy. Neither the Ultimate nor the Supreme are wholly representative of the Paradise Trinity, but in a qualified sense and to their respective levels, each seems to represent the Trinity during the prepersonal eras of experiential-power development.

3. *The Absolute Attitude* of the Paradise Trinity is in relation to absolute existences and culminates in the action of total Deity.

The Trinity Infinite involves the co-ordinate action of all triunity relationships of the First Source and Center—undeified as well as deified—and hence is very difficult for personalities to grasp. In the contemplation of the Trinity as infinite, do not ignore the seven triunities; thereby certain difficulties of understanding may be avoided, and certain paradoxes may be partially resolved.

But I do not command language which would enable me to convey to the limited human mind the full truth and the eternal significance of the Paradise Trinity and the nature of the never-ending interassociation of the three beings of infinite perfection.

6. THE STATIONARY SONS OF THE TRINITY

All law takes origin in the First Source and Center; *he is law.* The administration of spiritual law inheres in the Second Source and Center. The revelation of law, the promulgation and interpretation of the divine statutes, is the function of the Third Source and Center. The application of law, justice, falls within the province of the Paradise Trinity and is carried out by certain Sons of the Trinity.

Justice is inherent in the universal sovereignty of the Paradise Trinity, but goodness, mercy, and truth are the universe ministry of the divine personalities, whose Deity union constitutes the Trinity. Justice is not the attitude of the Father, the Son, or the Spirit. Justice is the Trinity attitude of these personalities of love, mercy, and ministry. No one of the Paradise Deities fosters the administration of justice. Justice is never a personal attitude; it is always a plural function.

Evidence, the basis of fairness (justice in harmony with mercy), is supplied by the personalities of the Third Source and Center, the conjoint representative of the Father and the Son to all realms and to the minds of the intelligent beings of all creation.

Judgment, the final application of justice in accordance with the evidence submitted by the personalities of the Infinite Spirit, is the work of the Stationary Sons of the Trinity, beings partaking of the Trinity nature of the united Father, Son, and Spirit.

This group of Trinity Sons embraces the following personalities:

1. Trinitized Secrets of Supremacy.
2. Eternals of Days.
3. Ancients of Days.
4. Perfections of Days.
5. Recents of Days.
6. Unions of Days.
7. Faithfuls of Days.
8. Perfectors of Wisdom.
9. Divine Counselors.
10. Universal Censors.

We are the children of the three Paradise Deities functioning as the Trinity, for I chance to belong to the tenth order of this group, the Universal Censors. These orders are not representative of the attitude of the Trinity in a universal sense; they represent this collective attitude of Deity only in the domains of executive judgment—justice. They were specifically designed by the Trinity for the precise work to which they are assigned, and they represent the Trinity only in those functions for which they were personalized.

The Ancients of Days and their Trinity-origin associates mete out the just judgment of supreme fairness to the seven superuniverses. In the central universe such functions exist in theory only; there fairness is self-evident in perfection, and Havona perfection precludes all possibility of disharmony.

Justice is the collective thought of righteousness; mercy is its personal expression. Mercy is the attitude of love; precision characterizes the operation of law; divine judgment is the soul of fairness, ever conforming to the justice of the Trinity, ever fulfilling the divine love of God. When fully perceived and completely understood, the righteous justice of the Trinity and the merciful love of the Universal Father are coincident. But man has no such full understanding of divine justice. Thus in the Trinity, as man would view it, the personalities of Father, Son, and Spirit are adjusted to co-ordinate ministry of love and law in the experiential universes of time.

7. THE OVERCONTROL OF SUPREMACY

The First, Second, and Third Persons of Deity are equal to each other, and they are one. "The Lord our God is one God." There is perfection of purpose and oneness of execution in the divine Trinity of eternal Deities. The Father, the Son, and the Conjoint Actor are truly and divinely one. Of a truth it is written: "I am the first, and I am the last, and beside me there is no God."

As things appear to the mortal on the finite level, the Paradise Trinity, like the Supreme Being, is concerned only with the total—total planet, total universe, total superuniverse, total grand universe. This totality attitude exists because the Trinity is the total of Deity and for many other reasons.

The Supreme Being is something less and something other than the Trinity functioning in the finite universes; but within certain limits and during the present era of incomplete power-personalization, this evolutionary Deity does appear to reflect the attitude of the Trinity of Supremacy. The Father, Son, and Spirit do not personally function with the Supreme Being, but during the present universe age they collaborate with him as the Trinity. We understand that they sustain a similar relationship to the Ultimate. We often conjecture as to what will be the personal relationship between the Paradise Deities and God the Supreme when he has finally evolved, but we do not really know.

We do not find the overcontrol of Supremacy to be wholly predictable. Furthermore, this unpredictability appears to be characterized by a certain developmental incompleteness, undoubtedly an earmark of the incompleteness of the Supreme and of the incompleteness of finite reaction to the Paradise Trinity.

The mortal mind can immediately think of a thousand and one things—catastrophic physical events, appalling accidents, horrific disasters, painful illnesses, and world-wide scourges—and ask whether such visitations are correlated in the unknown maneuvering of this probable functioning of the Supreme Being. Frankly, we do not know; we are not really sure. But we do observe that, as time passes, all these difficult and more or less mysterious situations *always* work out for the welfare and progress of the universes. It may be that the circumstances of existence and the inexplicable vicissitudes of living are all interwoven into a meaningful pattern of high value by the function of the Supreme and the overcontrol of the Trinity.

As a son of God you can discern the personal attitude of love in all the acts of God the Father. But you will not always be able to understand how many of the universe acts of the Paradise Trinity redound to the good of the individual mortal on the evolutionary worlds of space. In the progress of eternity the acts of the Trinity will be revealed as altogether meaningful and considerate, but they do not always so appear to the creatures of time.

8. THE TRINITY BEYOND THE FINITE

Many truths and facts pertaining to the Paradise Trinity can only be even partially comprehended by recognizing a function that transcends the finite.

It would be inadvisable to discuss the functions of the Trinity of Ultimacy, but it may be disclosed that God the Ultimate is the Trinity manifestation comprehended by the Transcendentalers. We are inclined to the belief that the unification of the master universe is the eventuating act of the Ultimate and is probably reflective of certain, but not all, phases of the absonite overcontrol of the Paradise Trinity. The Ultimate is a qualified manifestation of the Trinity in relation to the absonite only in the sense that the Supreme thus partially represents the Trinity in relation to the finite.

The Universal Father, the Eternal Son, and the Infinite Spirit are, in a certain sense, the constituent personalities of total Deity. Their union in the Paradise Trinity and the absolute function of the Trinity equivalate to the function of total Deity. And such completion of Deity transcends both the finite and the absonite.

While no single person of the Paradise Deities actually fills all Deity potential, collectively all three do. Three infinite persons seem to be the minimum number of beings required to activate the prepersonal and existential potential of total Deity—the Deity Absolute.

We know the Universal Father, the Eternal Son, and the Infinite Spirit as *persons,* but I do not personally know the Deity Absolute. I love and worship God the Father; I respect and honor the Deity Absolute.

I once sojourned in a universe where a certain group of beings taught that the finaliters, in eternity, were eventually to become the children of the Deity Absolute. But I am unwilling to accept this solution of the mystery which enshrouds the future of the finaliters.

The Corps of the Finality embrace, among others, those mortals of time and space who have attained perfection in all that pertains to the will of God. As creatures and within the limits of creature capacity they fully and truly know God. Having thus found God as the Father of all creatures, these finaliters must sometime begin the quest for the superfinite Father. But this quest involves a grasp of the absonite nature of the ultimate attributes and character of the Paradise Father. Eternity will disclose whether such an attainment is possible, but we are convinced, even if the finaliters do grasp this ultimate of divinity, they will probably be unable to attain the superultimate levels of absolute Deity.

It may be possible that the finaliters will partially attain the Deity Absolute, but even if they should, still in the eternity of eternities the problem of the Universal Absolute will continue to intrigue, mystify, baffle, and challenge the ascending and progressing finaliters, for we perceive that the unfathomability of the cosmic relationships of the Universal Absolute will tend to grow in proportions as the material universes and their spiritual administration continue to expand.

Only infinity can disclose the Father-Infinite.

[Sponsored by a Universal Censor acting by authority from the Ancients of Days resident on Uversa.]

PAPER 11

THE ETERNAL ISLE OF PARADISE

PARADISE is the eternal center of the universe of universes and the abiding place of the Universal Father, the Eternal Son, the Infinite Spirit, and their divine co-ordinates and associates. This central Isle is the most gigantic organized body of cosmic reality in all the master universe. Paradise is a material sphere as well as a spiritual abode. All of the intelligent creation of the Universal Father is domiciled on material abodes; hence must the absolute controlling center also be material, literal. And again it should be reiterated that spirit things and spiritual beings are *real.*

The material beauty of Paradise consists in the magnificence of its physical perfection; the grandeur of the Isle of God is exhibited in the superb intellectual accomplishments and mind development of its inhabitants; the glory of the central Isle is shown forth in the infinite endowment of divine spirit personality—the light of life. But the depths of the spiritual beauty and the wonders of this magnificent ensemble are utterly beyond the comprehension of the finite mind of material creatures. The glory and spiritual splendor of the divine abode are impossible of mortal comprehension. And Paradise is from eternity; there are neither records nor traditions respecting the origin of this nuclear Isle of Light and Life.

1. THE DIVINE RESIDENCE

Paradise serves many purposes in the administration of the universal realms, but to creature beings it exists primarily as the dwelling place of Deity. The personal presence of the Universal Father is resident at the very center of the upper surface of this well-nigh circular, but not spherical, abode of the Deities. This Paradise presence of the Universal Father is immediately surrounded by the personal presence of the Eternal Son, while they are both invested by the unspeakable glory of the Infinite Spirit.

God dwells, has dwelt, and everlastingly will dwell in this same central and eternal abode. We have always found him there and always will. The Universal Father is cosmically focalized, spiritually personalized, and geographically resident at this center of the universe of universes.

We all know the direct course to pursue to find the Universal Father. You are not able to comprehend much about the divine residence because of its remoteness from you and the immensity of the intervening space, but those who are able to comprehend the meaning of these enormous distances know God's location and residence just as certainly and literally as you know the location of New York, London, Rome, or Singapore, cities definitely and geographically located on Urantia. If you were an intelligent navigator, equipped with ship, maps, and compass, you could readily find these cities. Likewise, if you had the time and means of passage, were spiritually qualified, and had the necessary guidance, you could be piloted through universe upon universe and from circuit to circuit, ever journeying inward through the starry realms, until at last you would stand before the central shining of the spiritual glory of the Universal Father. Provided with all the necessities for the journey, it is just as possible to find the personal presence of God at the center of all things as to find distant cities on your own planet. That you have not visited these places in no way disproves their reality or actual existence. That so few of the universe creatures have found God on Paradise in no way disproves either the reality of his existence or the actuality of his spiritual person at the center of all things.

The Father is always to be found at this central location. Did he move, universal pandemonium would be precipitated, for there converge in him at this residential center the universal lines of gravity from the ends of creation. Whether we trace the personality circuit back through the universes or follow the ascending personalities as they journey inward to the Father; whether we trace the lines of material gravity to nether Paradise or follow the insurging cycles of cosmic force; whether we trace the lines of spiritual gravity to the Eternal Son or follow the inward processional of the Paradise Sons of God; whether we trace out the mind circuits or follow the trillions upon trillions of celestial beings who spring from the Infinite Spirit—by any of these observations or by all of them we are led directly back to the Father's presence, to his central abode. Here is God personally, literally, and actually present. And from his infinite being there flow the flood-streams of life, energy, and personality to all universes.

2. NATURE OF THE ETERNAL ISLE

Since you are beginning to glimpse the enormousness of the material universe discernible even from your astronomical location, your space position in the starry systems, it should become evident to you that such a tremendous material universe must have an adequate and worthy capital, a headquarters commensurate with the dignity and infinitude of the universal Ruler of all this vast and far-flung creation of material realms and living beings.

In form Paradise differs from the inhabited space bodies: it is not spherical. It is definitely ellipsoid, being one-sixth longer in the north-south diameter than in the east-west diameter. The central Isle is essentially flat, and the distance from the upper surface to the nether surface is one tenth that of the east-west diameter.

These differences in dimensions, taken in connection with its stationary status and the greater out-pressure of force-energy at the north end of the Isle, make it possible to establish absolute direction in the master universe.

The central Isle is geographically divided into three domains of activity:

1. Upper Paradise.
2. Peripheral Paradise.
3. Nether Paradise.

We speak of that surface of Paradise which is occupied with personality activities as the upper side, and the opposite surface as the nether side. The periphery of Paradise provides for activities that are not strictly personal or nonpersonal. The Trinity seems to dominate the personal or upper plane, the Unqualified Absolute the nether or impersonal plane. We hardly conceive of the Unqualified Absolute as a person, but we do think of the functional space presence of this Absolute as focalized on nether Paradise.

The eternal Isle is composed of a single form of materialization—stationary systems of reality. This literal substance of Paradise is a homogeneous organization of space potency not to be found elsewhere in all the wide universe of universes. It has received many names in different universes, and the Melchizedeks of Nebadon long since named it *absolutum.* This Paradise source material is neither dead nor alive; it is the original nonspiritual expression of the First Source and Center; it is *Paradise,* and Paradise is without duplicate.

It appears to us that the First Source and Center has concentrated all absolute potential for cosmic reality in Paradise as a part of his technique of self-liberation from infinity limitations, as a means of making possible subinfinite, even time-space, creation. But it does not follow that Paradise is time-space limited just because the universe of universes discloses these qualities. Paradise exists without time and has no location in space.

Roughly: space seemingly originates just below nether Paradise; time just above upper Paradise. Time, as you understand it, is not a feature of Paradise existence, though the citizens of the central Isle are fully conscious of nontime sequence of events. Motion is not inherent on Paradise; it is volitional. But the concept of distance, even absolute distance, has very much meaning as it may be applied to relative locations on Paradise. Paradise is nonspatial; hence its areas are absolute and therefore serviceable in many ways beyond the concept of mortal mind.

3. UPPER PARADISE

On upper Paradise there are three grand spheres of activity, the *Deity presence,* the *Most Holy Sphere,* and the *Holy Area.* The vast region immediately surrounding the presence of the Deities is set aside as the Most Holy Sphere and is reserved for the functions of worship, trinitization, and high spiritual attainment. There are no material structures nor purely intellectual creations in this zone; they could not exist there. It is useless for me to undertake to portray to the human mind the divine nature and the beauteous grandeur of the Most Holy Sphere of Paradise. This realm is wholly spiritual, and you are almost wholly material. A purely spiritual reality is, to a purely material being, apparently nonexistent.

While there are no physical materializations in the area of the Most Holy, there are abundant souvenirs of your material days in the Holy Land sectors and still more in the reminiscent historic areas of peripheral Paradise.

The Holy Area, the outlying or residential region, is divided into seven concentric zones. Paradise is sometimes called "the Father's House" since it is his eternal residence, and these seven zones are often designated "the Father's Paradise mansions." The inner or first zone is occupied by Paradise Citizens and the natives of Havona who may chance to be dwelling on Paradise. The next or second zone is the residential area of the natives of the seven superuniverses of time and space. This second zone is in part subdivided into seven immense divisions, the Paradise home of the spirit beings and ascendant creatures who hail from the universes of evolutionary progression. Each of these sectors is exclusively dedicated to the welfare and advancement of the personalities of a single superuniverse, but these facilities are almost infinitely beyond the requirements of the present seven superuniverses.

Each of the seven sectors of Paradise is subdivided into residential units suitable for the lodgment headquarters of one billion glorified individual working groups. One thousand of these units constitute a division. One hundred thousand divisions equal one congregation. Ten million congregations constitute an assembly. One billion assemblies make one grand unit. And this ascending series continues through the second grand unit, the third, and so on to the seventh grand unit. And seven of the grand units make up the master units, and seven of the master units constitute a superior unit; and thus by sevens the ascending series expands through the superior, supersuperior, celestial, supercelestial, to the supreme units. But even this does not utilize all the space available. This staggering number of residential designations on Paradise, a number beyond your concept, occupies considerably less than one per cent of the assigned area of the Holy Land. There is still plenty of room for those who are on their way inward, even for those who shall not start the Paradise climb until the times of the eternal future.

4. PERIPHERAL PARADISE

The central Isle ends abruptly at the periphery, but its size is so enormous that this terminal angle is relatively indiscernible within any circumscribed area. The peripheral surface of Paradise is occupied, in part, by the landing and dispatching fields for various groups of spirit personalities. Since the nonpervaded-space zones nearly impinge upon the periphery, all personality transports destined to Paradise land in these regions. Neither upper nor nether Paradise is approachable by transport supernaphim or other types of space traversers.

The Seven Master Spirits have their personal seats of power and authority on the seven spheres of the Spirit, which circle about Paradise in the space between the shining orbs of the Son and the inner circuit of the Havona worlds, but they maintain force-focal headquarters on the Paradise periphery. Here the slowly circulating presences of the Seven Supreme Power Directors indicate the location of the seven flash stations for certain Paradise energies going forth to the seven superuniverses.

Here on peripheral Paradise are the enormous historic and prophetic exhibit areas assigned to the Creator Sons, dedicated to the local universes of time and space. There are just seven trillion of these historic reservations now set up or in reserve, but these arrangements all together occupy only about four per cent of that portion of the peripheral area thus assigned. We infer that these vast reserves belong to creations sometime to be situated beyond the borders of the present known and inhabited seven superuniverses.

That portion of Paradise which has been designated for the use of the existing universes is occupied only from one to four per cent, while the area assigned to these activities is at least one million times that actually required for such purposes. Paradise is large enough to accommodate the activities of an almost infinite creation.

But a further attempt to visualize to you the glories of Paradise would be futile. You must wait, and ascend while you wait, for truly, "Eye has not seen, nor ear heard, neither has it entered into the mind of mortal man, the things which the Universal Father has prepared for those who survive the life in the flesh on the worlds of time and space."

5. NETHER PARADISE

Concerning nether Paradise, we know only that which is revealed; personalities do not sojourn there. It has nothing whatever to do with the affairs of spirit intelligences, nor does the Deity Absolute there function. We are informed that all physical-energy and cosmic-force circuits have their origin on nether Paradise, and that it is constituted as follows:

1. Directly underneath the location of the Trinity, in the central portion of nether Paradise, is the unknown and unrevealed Zone of Infinity.

2. This Zone is immediately surrounded by an unnamed area.

3. Occupying the outer margins of the under surface is a region having mainly to do with space potency and force-energy. The activities of this vast elliptical force center are not identifiable with the known functions of any triunity, but the primordial force-charge of space appears to be focalized in this area. This center consists of three concentric elliptical zones: The innermost is the focal point of the force-energy activities of Paradise itself; the outermost may possibly be identified with the functions of the Unqualified Absolute, but we are not certain concerning the space functions of the mid-zone.

The inner zone of this force center seems to act as a gigantic heart whose pulsations direct currents to the outermost borders of physical space. It directs and modifies force-energies but hardly drives them. The reality pressure-presence of this primal force is definitely greater at the north end of the Paradise center than in the southern regions; this is a uniformly registered difference. The mother force of space seems to flow in at the south and out at the north through the operation of some unknown circulatory system which is concerned with the diffusion of this basic form of force-energy. From time to time there are also noted differences in the east-west pressures. The forces emanating from this zone are not responsive to observable physical gravity but are always obedient to Paradise gravity.

The mid-zone of the force center immediately surrounds this area. This mid-zone appears to be static except that it expands and contracts through three cycles of activity. The least of these pulsations is in an east-west direction, the next in a north-south direction, while the greatest fluctuation is in every direction, a generalized expansion and contraction. The function of this mid-area has never been really identified, but it must have something to do with reciprocal adjustment between the inner and the outer zones of the force center. It is believed by many that the mid-zone is the control mechanism of the mid-space or quiet zones which separate the successive space levels of the master universe, but no evidence or revelation confirms this. This inference is derived from the knowledge that this mid-area is in some manner related to the functioning of the nonpervaded-space mechanism of the master universe.

The outer zone is the largest and most active of the three concentric and elliptical belts of unidentified space potential. This area is the site of unimagined activities, the central circuit point of emanations which proceed spaceward in every direction to the outermost borders of the seven superuniverses and on beyond to overspread the enormous and incomprehensible domains of all outer space. This space presence is entirely impersonal notwithstanding that in some undisclosed manner it seems to be indirectly responsive to the will and mandates of the infinite Deities when acting as the Trinity. This is believed to be the central focalization, the Paradise center, of the space presence of the Unqualified Absolute.

All forms of force and all phases of energy seem to be encircuited; they circulate throughout the universes and return by definite routes. But with the emanations of the activated zone of the Unqualified Absolute there appears to be either an outgoing or an incoming—never both simultaneously. This outer zone pulsates in agelong cycles of gigantic proportions. For a little more than one billion Urantia years the space-force of this center is outgoing; then for a similar length of time it will be incoming. And the space-force manifestations of this center are universal; they extend throughout all pervadable space.

All physical force, energy, and matter are one. All force-energy originally proceeded from nether Paradise and will eventually return thereto following the completion of its space circuit. But the energies and material organizations of the universe of universes did not all come from nether Paradise in their present phenomenal states; space is the womb of several forms of matter and prematter. Though the outer zone of the Paradise force center is the source of space-energies, space does not originate there. Space is not force, energy, or power. Nor do the pulsations of this zone account for the respiration of space, but the incoming and outgoing phases of this zone are synchronized with the two-billion-year expansion-contraction cycles of space.

6. SPACE RESPIRATION

We do not know the actual mechanism of space respiration; we merely observe that all space alternately contracts and expands. This respiration affects both the horizontal extension of pervaded space and the vertical extensions of unpervaded space which exist in the vast space reservoirs above and below Paradise. In attempting to imagine the volume outlines of these space reservoirs, you might think of an hourglass.

As the universes of the horizontal extension of pervaded space expand, the reservoirs of the vertical extension of unpervaded space contract and vice versa. There is a confluence of pervaded and unpervaded space just underneath nether Paradise. Both types of space there flow through the transmuting regulation channels, where changes are wrought making pervadable space nonpervadable and vice versa in the contraction and expansion cycles of the cosmos.

"Unpervaded" space means: unpervaded by those forces, energies, powers, and presences known to exist in pervaded space. We do not know whether vertical (reservoir) space is destined always to function as the equipoise of horizontal (universe) space; we do not know whether there is a creative intent concerning unpervaded space; we really know very little about the space reservoirs, merely that they exist, and that they seem to counterbalance the space-expansion-contraction cycles of the universe of universes.

The cycles of space respiration extend in each phase for a little more than one billion Urantia years. During one phase the universes expand; during the next they contract. Pervaded space is now approaching the mid-point of the expanding phase, while unpervaded space nears the mid-point of the contracting phase, and we are informed that the outermost limits of both space extensions are, theoretically, now approximately equidistant from Paradise. The unpervaded-space reservoirs now extend vertically above upper Paradise and below nether Paradise just as far as the pervaded space of the universe extends horizontally outward from peripheral Paradise to and even beyond the fourth outer space level.

For a billion years of Urantia time the space reservoirs contract while the master universe and the force activities of all horizontal space expand. It thus requires a little over two billion Urantia years to complete the entire expansion-contraction cycle.

7. SPACE FUNCTIONS OF PARADISE

Space does not exist on any of the surfaces of Paradise. If one "looked" directly up from the upper surface of Paradise, one would "see" nothing but unpervaded space going out or coming in, just now coming in. Space does not touch Paradise; only the quiescent *midspace zones* come in contact with the central Isle.

Paradise is the actually motionless nucleus of the relatively quiescent zones existing between pervaded and unpervaded space. Geographically these zones appear to be a relative extension of Paradise, but there probably is some motion in them. We know very little about them, but we observe that these zones of lessened space motion separate pervaded and unpervaded space. Similar zones once existed between the levels of pervaded space, but these are now less quiescent.

The vertical cross section of total space would slightly resemble a maltese cross, with the horizontal arms representing pervaded (universe) space and the vertical arms representing unpervaded (reservoir) space. The areas between the four arms would separate them somewhat as the midspace zones separate pervaded and unpervaded space. These quiescent midspace zones grow larger and larger at greater and greater distances from Paradise and eventually encompass the borders of all space and completely incapsulate both the space reservoirs and the entire horizontal extension of pervaded space.

Space is neither a subabsolute condition within, nor the presence of, the Unqualified Absolute, neither is it a function of the Ultimate. It is a bestowal of Paradise, and the space of the grand universe and that of all outer regions is believed to be actually pervaded by the ancestral space potency of the Unqualified Absolute. From near approach to peripheral Paradise, this pervaded space extends horizontally outward through the fourth space level and beyond the periphery of the master universe, but how far beyond we do not know.

If you imagine a finite, but inconceivably large, V-shaped plane situated at right angles to both the upper and lower surfaces of Paradise, with its point nearly tangent to peripheral Paradise, and then visualize this plane in elliptical revolution about Paradise, its revolution would roughly outline the volume of pervaded space.

There is an upper and a lower limit to horizontal space with reference to any given location in the universes. If one could move far enough at right angles to the plane of Orvonton, either up or down, eventually the upper or lower limit of pervaded space would be encountered. Within the known dimensions of the master universe these limits draw farther and farther apart at greater and greater distances from Paradise; space thickens, and it thickens somewhat faster than does the plane of creation, the universes.

The relatively quiet zones between the space levels, such as the one separating the seven superuniverses from the first outer space level, are enormous elliptical regions of quiescent space activities. These zones separate the vast galaxies which race around Paradise in orderly procession. You may visualize the first outer space level, where untold universes are now in process of formation, as a vast procession of galaxies swinging around Paradise, bounded above and below by the midspace zones of quiescence and bounded on the inner and outer margins by relatively quiet space zones.

A space level thus functions as an elliptical region of motion surrounded on all sides by relative motionlessness. Such relationships of motion and quiescence constitute a curved space path of lessened resistance to motion which is universally followed by cosmic force and emergent energy as they circle forever around the Isle of Paradise.

This alternate zoning of the master universe, in association with the alternate clockwise and counterclockwise flow of the galaxies, is a factor in the stabilization of physical gravity designed to prevent the accentuation of gravity pressure to the point of disruptive and dispersive activities. Such an arrangement exerts antigravity influence and acts as a brake upon otherwise dangerous velocities.

8. PARADISE GRAVITY

The inescapable pull of gravity effectively grips all the worlds of all the universes of all space. Gravity is the all-powerful grasp of the physical presence of Paradise. Gravity is the omnipotent strand on which are strung the gleaming stars, blazing suns, and whirling spheres which constitute the universal physical adornment of the eternal God, who is all things, fills all things, and in whom all things consist.

The center and focal point of absolute material gravity is the Isle of Paradise, complemented by the dark gravity bodies encircling Havona and equilibrated by the upper and nether space reservoirs. All known emanations of nether Paradise invariably and unerringly respond to the central gravity pull operating upon the endless circuits of the elliptical space levels of the master universe. Every known form of cosmic reality has the bend of the ages, the trend of the circle, the swing of the great ellipse.

Space is nonresponsive to gravity, but it acts as an equilibrant on gravity. Without the space cushion, explosive action would jerk surrounding space bodies. Pervaded space also exerts an antigravity influence upon physical or linear gravity; space can actually neutralize such gravity action even though it cannot delay it. Absolute gravity is Paradise gravity. Local or linear gravity pertains to the electrical stage of energy or matter; it operates within the central, super-, and outer universes, wherever suitable materialization has taken place.

The numerous forms of cosmic force, physical energy, universe power, and various materializations disclose three general, though not perfectly clear-cut, stages of response to Paradise gravity:

1. *Pregravity Stages (Force).* This is the first step in the individuation of space potency into the pre-energy forms of cosmic force. This state is analogous to the concept of the primordial force-charge of space, sometimes called *pure energy* or *segregata.*

2. *Gravity Stages (Energy).* This modification of the force-charge of space is produced by the action of the Paradise force organizers. It signalizes the appearance of energy systems responsive to the pull of Paradise gravity. This emergent energy is originally neutral but consequent upon further metamorphosis will exhibit the so-called negative and positive qualities. We designate these stages *ultimata.*

3. *Postgravity Stages (Universe Power).* In this stage, energy-matter discloses response to the control of linear gravity. In the central universe these physical systems are threefold organizations known as *triata.* They are the superpower mother systems of the creations of time and space. The physical systems of the superuniverses are mobilized by the Universe Power Directors and their associates. These material organizations are dual in constitution and are known as *gravita.* The dark gravity bodies encircling Havona are neither triata nor gravita, and their drawing power discloses both forms of physical gravity, linear and absolute.

Space potency is not subject to the interactions of any form of gravitation. This primal endowment of Paradise is not an actual level of reality, but it is ancestral to all relative functional nonspirit realities—all manifestations of force-energy and the organization of power and matter. Space potency is a term difficult to define. It does not mean that which is ancestral to space; its meaning should convey the idea of the potencies and potentials existent within space. It may be roughly conceived to include all those absolute influences and potentials which emanate from Paradise and constitute the space presence of the Unqualified Absolute.

Paradise is the absolute source and the eternal focal point of all energy-matter in the universe of universes. The Unqualified Absolute is the revealer, regulator, and repository of that which has Paradise as its source and origin. The universal presence of the Unqualified Absolute seems to be equivalent to the concept of a potential infinity of gravity extension, an elastic tension of Paradise presence. This concept aids us in grasping the fact that everything is drawn inward towards Paradise. The illustration is crude but nonetheless helpful. It also explains why gravity always acts preferentially in the plane perpendicular to the mass, a phenomenon indicative of the differential dimensions of Paradise and the surrounding creations.

9. THE UNIQUENESS OF PARADISE

Paradise is unique in that it is the realm of primal origin and the final goal of destiny for all spirit personalities. Although it is true that not all of the lower spirit beings of the local universes are immediately destined to Paradise, Paradise still remains the goal of desire for all supermaterial personalities.

Paradise is the geographic center of infinity; it is not a part of universal creation, not even a real part of the eternal Havona universe. We commonly refer to the central Isle as belonging to the divine universe, but it really does not. Paradise is an eternal and exclusive existence.

In the eternity of the past, when the Universal Father gave infinite personality expression of his spirit self in the being of the Eternal Son, simultaneously he revealed the infinity potential of his nonpersonal self as Paradise. Nonpersonal and nonspiritual Paradise appears to have been the inevitable repercussion to the Father's will and act which eternalized the Original Son. Thus did the Father project reality in two actual phases—the personal and the nonpersonal, the spiritual and the nonspiritual. The tension between them, in the face of will to action by the Father and the Son, gave existence to the Conjoint Actor and the central universe of material worlds and spiritual beings.

When reality is differentiated into the personal and the nonpersonal (Eternal Son and Paradise), it is hardly proper to call that which is nonpersonal "Deity" unless somehow qualified. The energy and material repercussions of the acts of Deity could hardly be called Deity. Deity may cause much that is not Deity, and Paradise is not Deity; neither is it conscious as mortal man could ever possibly understand such a term.

Paradise is not ancestral to any being or living entity; it is not a creator. Personality and mind-spirit relationships are *transmissible,* but pattern is not. Patterns are never reflections; they are duplications—reproductions. Paradise is the absolute of patterns; Havona is an exhibit of these potentials in actuality.

God's residence is central and eternal, glorious and ideal. His home is the beauteous pattern for all universe headquarters worlds; and the central universe of his immediate indwelling is the pattern for all universes in their ideals, organization, and ultimate destiny.

Paradise is the universal headquarters of all personality activities and the source-center of all force-space and energy manifestations. Everything which has been, now is, or is yet to be, has come, now comes, or will come forth from this central abiding place of the eternal Gods. Paradise is the center of all creation, the source of all energies, and the place of primal origin of all personalities.

After all, to mortals the most important thing about eternal Paradise is the fact that this perfect abode of the Universal Father is the real and far-distant destiny of the immortal souls of the mortal and material sons of God, the ascending creatures of the evolutionary worlds of time and space. Every God-knowing mortal who has espoused the career of doing the Father's will has already embarked upon the long, long Paradise trail of divinity pursuit and perfection attainment. And when such an animal-origin being does stand, as countless numbers now do, before the Gods on Paradise, having ascended from the lowly spheres of space, such an achievement represents the reality of a spiritual transformation bordering on the limits of supremacy.

[Presented by a Perfector of Wisdom commissioned thus to function by the Ancients of Days on Uversa.]

PAPER 12

THE UNIVERSE OF UNIVERSES

THE immensity of the far-flung creation of the Universal Father is utterly beyond the grasp of finite imagination; the enormousness of the master universe staggers the concept of even my order of being. But the mortal mind can be taught much about the plan and arrangement of the universes; you can know something of their physical organization and marvelous administration; you may learn much about the various groups of intelligent beings who inhabit the seven superuniverses of time and the central universe of eternity.

In principle, that is, in eternal potential, we conceive of material creation as being infinite because the Universal Father is actually infinite, but as we study and observe the total material creation, we know that at any given moment in time it is limited, although to your finite minds it is comparatively limitless, virtually boundless.

We are convinced, from the study of physical law and from the observation of the starry realms, that the infinite Creator is not yet manifest in finality of cosmic expression, that much of the cosmic potential of the Infinite is still self-contained and unrevealed. To created beings the master universe might appear to be almost infinite, but it is far from finished; there are still physical limits to the material creation, and the experiential revelation of the eternal purpose is still in progress.

1. SPACE LEVELS OF THE MASTER UNIVERSE

The universe of universes is not an infinite plane, a boundless cube, nor a limitless circle; it certainly has dimensions. The laws of physical organization and administration prove conclusively that the whole vast aggregation of force-energy and matter-power functions ultimately as a space unit, as an organized and co-ordinated whole. The observable behavior of the material creation constitutes evidence of a physical universe of definite limits. The final proof of both a circular and delimited universe is afforded by the, to us, well-known fact that all forms of basic energy ever swing around the curved path of the space levels of the master universe in obedience to the incessant and absolute pull of Paradise gravity.

The successive space levels of the master universe constitute the major divisions of pervaded space—total creation, organized and partially inhabited or yet to be organized and inhabited. If the master universe were not a series of elliptical space levels of lessened resistance to motion, alternating with zones of relative quiescence, we conceive that some of the cosmic energies would be observed to shoot off on an infinite range, off on a straight-line path into trackless space; but we never find force, energy, or matter thus behaving; ever they whirl, always swinging onward in the tracks of the great space circuits.

Proceeding outward from Paradise through the horizontal extension of pervaded space, the master universe is existent in six concentric ellipses, the space levels encircling the central Isle:

1. The Central Universe—Havona.
2. The Seven Superuniverses.
3. The First Outer Space Level.
4. The Second Outer Space Level.
5. The Third Outer Space Level.
6. The Fourth and Outermost Space Level.

Havona, the central universe, is not a time creation; it is an eternal existence. This never-beginning, never-ending universe consists of one billion spheres of sublime perfection and is surrounded by the enormous dark gravity bodies. At the center of Havona is the stationary and absolutely stabilized Isle of Paradise, surrounded by its twenty-one satellites. Owing to the enormous encircling masses of the dark gravity bodies about the fringe of the central universe, the mass content of this central creation is far in excess of the total known mass of all seven sectors of the grand universe.

The Paradise-Havona System, the eternal universe encircling the eternal Isle, constitutes the perfect and eternal nucleus of the master universe; all seven of the superuniverses and all regions of outer space revolve in established orbits around the gigantic central aggregation of the Paradise satellites and the Havona spheres.

The Seven Superuniverses are not primary physical organizations; nowhere do their boundaries divide a nebular family, neither do they cross a local universe, a prime creative unit. Each superuniverse is simply a geographic space clustering of approximately one seventh of the organized and partially inhabited post-Havona creation, and each is about equal in the number of local universes embraced and in the space encompassed. *Nebadon,* your local universe, is one of the newer creations in *Orvonton,* the seventh superuniverse.

The Grand Universe is the present organized and inhabited creation. It consists of the seven superuniverses, with an aggregate evolutionary potential of around seven trillion inhabited planets, not to mention the eternal spheres of the central creation. But this tentative estimate takes no account of architectural administrative spheres, neither does it include the outlying groups of unorganized universes. The present ragged edge of the grand universe, its uneven and unfinished periphery, together with the tremendously unsettled condition of the whole astronomical plot, suggests to our star students that even the seven superuniverses are, as yet, uncompleted. As we move from within, from the divine center outward in any one direction, we do, eventually, come to the outer limits of the organized and inhabited creation; we come to the outer limits of the grand universe. And it is near this outer border, in a far-off corner of such a magnificent creation, that your local universe has its eventful existence.

The Outer Space Levels. Far out in space, at an enormous distance from the seven inhabited superuniverses, there are assembling vast and unbelievably stupendous circuits of force and materializing energies. Between the energy circuits of the seven superuniverses and this gigantic outer belt of force activity, there is a space zone of comparative quiet, which varies in width but averages about four hundred thousand light-years. These space zones are free from star dust—cosmic fog. Our students of these phenomena are in doubt as to the exact status of the space-forces existing in this zone of relative quiet which encircles the seven superuniverses. But about one-half million light-years beyond the periphery of the present grand universe we observe the beginnings of a zone of an unbelievable energy action which increases in volume and intensity for over twenty-five million light-years. These tremendous wheels of energizing forces are situated in the first outer space level, a continuous belt of cosmic activity encircling the whole of the known, organized, and inhabited creation.

Still greater activities are taking place beyond these regions, for the Uversa physicists have detected early evidence of force manifestations more than fifty million light-years beyond the outermost ranges of the phenomena in the first outer space level. These activities undoubtedly presage the organization of the material creations of the second outer space level of the master universe.

The central universe is the creation of eternity; the seven superuniverses are the creations of time; the four outer space levels are undoubtedly destined to eventuate-evolve the ultimacy of creation. And there are those who maintain that the Infinite can never attain full expression short of infinity; and therefore do they postulate an additional and unrevealed creation beyond the fourth and outermost space level, a possible ever-expanding, never-ending universe of infinity. In theory we do not know how to limit either the infinity of the Creator or the potential infinity of creation, but as it exists and is administered, we regard the master universe as having limitations, as being definitely delimited and bounded on its outer margins by open space.

2. THE DOMAINS OF THE UNQUALIFIED ABSOLUTE

When Urantia astronomers peer through their increasingly powerful telescopes into the mysterious stretches of outer space and there behold the amazing evolution of almost countless physical universes, they should realize that they are gazing upon the mighty outworking of the unsearchable plans of the Architects of the Master Universe. True, we do possess evidences which are suggestive of the presence of certain Paradise personality influences here and there throughout the vast energy manifestations now characteristic of these outer regions, but from the larger viewpoint the space regions extending beyond the outer borders of the seven superuniverses are generally recognized as constituting the domains of the Unqualified Absolute.

Although the unaided human eye can see only two or three nebulae outside the borders of the superuniverse of Orvonton, your telescopes literally reveal millions upon millions of these physical universes in process of formation. Most of the starry realms visually exposed to the search of your present-day telescopes are in Orvonton, but with photographic technique the larger telescopes penetrate far beyond the borders of the grand universe into the domains of outer space, where untold universes are in process of organization. And there are yet other millions of universes beyond the range of your present instruments.

In the not-distant future, new telescopes will reveal to the wondering gaze of Urantian astronomers no less than 375 million new galaxies in the remote stretches of outer space. At the same time these more powerful telescopes will disclose that many island universes formerly believed to be in outer space are really a part of the galactic system of Orvonton. The seven superuniverses are still growing; the periphery of each is gradually expanding; new nebulae are constantly being stabilized and organized; and some of the nebulae which Urantian astronomers regard as extragalactic are actually on the fringe of Orvonton and are traveling along with us.

The Uversa star students observe that the grand universe is surrounded by the ancestors of a series of starry and planetary clusters which completely encircle the present inhabited creation as concentric rings of outer universes upon universes. The physicists of Uversa calculate that the energy and matter of these outer and uncharted regions already equal many times the total material mass and energy charge embraced in all seven superuniverses. We are informed that the metamorphosis of cosmic force in these outer space levels is a function of the Paradise force organizers. We also know that these forces are ancestral to those physical energies which at present activate the grand universe. The Orvonton power directors, however, have nothing to do with these far-distant realms, neither are the energy movements therein discernibly connected with the power circuits of the organized and inhabited creations.

We know very little of the significance of these tremendous phenomena of outer space. A greater creation of the future is in process of formation. We can observe its immensity, we can discern its extent and sense its majestic dimensions, but otherwise we know little more about these realms than do the astronomers of Urantia. As far as we know, no material beings on the order of humans, no angels or other spirit creatures, exist in this outer ring of nebulae, suns, and planets. This distant domain is beyond the jurisdiction and administration of the superuniverse governments.

Throughout Orvonton it is believed that a new type of creation is in process, an order of universes destined to become the scene of the future activities of the assembling Corps of the Finality; and if our conjectures are correct, then the endless future may hold for all of you the same enthralling spectacles that the endless past has held for your seniors and predecessors.

3. UNIVERSAL GRAVITY

All forms of force-energy—material, mindal, or spiritual—are alike subject to those grasps, those universal presences, which we call gravity. Personality also is responsive to gravity—to the Father's exclusive circuit; but though this circuit is exclusive to the Father, he is not excluded from the other circuits; the Universal Father is infinite and acts over *all* four absolute-gravity circuits in the master universe:

1. The Personality Gravity of the Universal Father.
2. The Spirit Gravity of the Eternal Son.
3. The Mind Gravity of the Conjoint Actor.
4. The Cosmic Gravity of the Isle of Paradise.

These four circuits are not related to the nether Paradise force center; they are neither force, energy, nor power circuits. They are absolute *presence* circuits and like God are independent of time and space.

In this connection it is interesting to record certain observations made on Uversa during recent millenniums by the corps of gravity researchers. This expert group of workers has arrived at the following conclusions regarding the different gravity systems of the master universe:

1. *Physical Gravity.* Having formulated an estimate of the summation of the entire physical-gravity capacity of the grand universe, they have laboriously effected a comparison of this finding with the estimated total of absolute gravity presence now operative. These calculations indicate that the total gravity action on the grand universe is a very small part of the estimated gravity pull of Paradise, computed on the basis of the gravity response of basic physical units of universe matter. These investigators reach the amazing conclusion that the central universe and the surrounding seven superuniverses are at the present time making use of only about five per cent of the active functioning of the Paradise absolute-gravity grasp. In other words: At the present moment about ninety-five per cent of the active cosmic-gravity action of the Isle of Paradise, computed on this totality theory, is engaged in controlling material systems beyond the borders of the present organized universes. These calculations all refer to absolute gravity; linear gravity is an interactive phenomenon which can be computed only by knowing the actual Paradise gravity.

2. *Spiritual Gravity.* By the same technique of comparative estimation and calculation these researchers have explored the present reaction capacity of spirit gravity and, with the co-operation of Solitary Messengers and other spirit personalities, have arrived at the summation of the active spirit gravity of the Second Source and Center. And it is most instructive to note that they find about the same value for the actual and functional presence of spirit gravity in the grand universe that they postulate for the present total of active spirit gravity. In other words: At the present time practically the entire spirit gravity of the Eternal Son, computed on this theory of totality, is observable as functioning in the grand universe. If these findings are dependable, we may conclude that the universes now evolving in outer space are at the present time wholly nonspiritual. And if this is true, it would satisfactorily explain why spirit-endowed beings are in possession of little or no information about these vast energy manifestations aside from knowing the fact of their physical existence.

3. *Mind Gravity.* By these same principles of comparative computation these experts have attacked the problem of mind-gravity presence and response. The mind unit of estimation was arrived at by averaging three material and three spiritual types of mentality, although the type of mind found in the power directors and their associates proved to be a disturbing factor in the effort to arrive at a basic unit for mind-gravity estimation. There was little to impede the estimation of the present capacity of the Third Source and Center for mind-gravity function in accordance with this theory of totality. Although the findings in this instance are not so conclusive as in the estimates of physical and spirit gravity, they are, comparatively considered, very instructive, even intriguing. These investigators deduce that about eighty-five per cent of the mind-gravity response to the intellectual drawing of the Conjoint Actor takes origin in the existing grand universe. This would suggest the possibility that mind activities are involved in connection with the observable physical activities now in progress throughout the realms of outer space. While this estimate is probably far from accurate, it accords, in principle, with our belief that intelligent force organizers

are at present directing universe evolution in the space levels beyond the present outer limits of the grand universe. Whatever the nature of this postulated intelligence, it is apparently not spirit-gravity responsive.

But all these computations are at best estimates based on assumed laws. We think they are fairly reliable. Even if a few spirit beings were located in outer space, their collective presence would not markedly influence calculations involving such enormous measurements.

Personality Gravity is noncomputable. We recognize the circuit, but we cannot measure either qualitative or quantitative realities responsive thereto.

4. SPACE AND MOTION

All units of cosmic energy are in primary revolution, are engaged in the execution of their mission, while swinging around the universal orbit. The universes of space and their component systems and worlds are all revolving spheres, moving along the endless circuits of the master universe space levels. Absolutely nothing is stationary in all the master universe except the very center of Havona, the eternal Isle of Paradise, the center of gravity.

The Unqualified Absolute is functionally limited to space, but we are not so sure about the relation of this Absolute to motion. Is motion inherent therein? We do not know. We know that motion is not inherent in space; even the motions *of* space are not innate. But we are not so sure about the relation of the Unqualified to motion. Who, or what, is really responsible for the gigantic activities of force-energy transmutations now in progress out beyond the borders of the present seven superuniverses? Concerning the origin of motion we have the following opinions:

1. We think the Conjoint Actor initiates motion *in* space.
2. If the Conjoint Actor produces the motions *of* space, we cannot prove it.
3. The Universal Absolute does not originate initial motion but does equalize and control all of the tensions originated by motion.

In outer space the force organizers are apparently responsible for the production of the gigantic universe wheels which are now in process of stellar evolution, but their ability so to function must have been made possible by some modification of the space presence of the Unqualified Absolute.

Space is, from the human viewpoint, nothing—negative; it exists only as related to something positive and nonspatial. Space is, however, real. It contains and conditions motion. It even moves. Space motions may be roughly classified as follows:

1. Primary motion—space respiration, the motion of space itself.

2. Secondary motion—the alternate directional swings of the successive space levels.

3. Relative motions—relative in the sense that they are not evaluated with Paradise as a base point. Primary and secondary motions are absolute, motion in relation to unmoving Paradise.

4. Compensatory or correlating movement designed to co-ordinate all other motions.

The present relationship of your sun and its associated planets, while disclosing many relative and absolute motions in space, tends to convey the impression to astronomic observers that you are comparatively stationary in space, and that the surrounding starry clusters and streams are engaged in outward flight at ever-increasing velocities as your calculations proceed outward in space. But such is not the case. You fail to recognize the present outward and uniform expansion of the physical creations of all pervaded space. Your own local creation (Nebadon) participates in this movement of universal outward expansion. The entire seven superuniverses participate in the two-billion-year cycles of space respiration along with the outer regions of the master universe.

When the universes expand and contract, the material masses in pervaded space alternately move against and with the pull of Paradise gravity. The work that is done in moving the material energy mass of creation is *space* work but not *power-energy* work.

Although your spectroscopic estimations of astronomic velocities are fairly reliable when applied to the starry realms belonging to your superuniverse and its associate superuniverses, such reckonings with reference to the realms of outer space are wholly unreliable. Spectral lines are displaced from the normal towards the violet by an approaching star; likewise these lines are displaced towards the red by a receding star. Many influences interpose to make it appear that the recessional velocity of the external universes increases at the rate of more than one hundred miles a second for every million light-years increase in distance. By this method of reckoning, subsequent to the perfection of more powerful telescopes, it will appear that these far-distant systems are in flight from this part of the universe at the unbelievable rate of more than thirty thousand miles a second. But this apparent speed of recession is not real; it results from numerous factors of error embracing angles of observation and other time-space distortions.

But the greatest of all such distortions arises because the vast universes of outer space, in the realms next to the domains of the seven superuniverses, seem to be revolving in a direction opposite to that of the grand universe. That is, these myriads of nebulae and their accompanying suns and spheres are at the present time revolving clockwise about the central creation. The seven superuniverses revolve about Paradise in a counterclockwise direction. It appears that the second outer universe of galaxies, like the seven superuniverses, revolves counterclockwise about Paradise. And the astronomic observers of Uversa think they detect evidence of revolutionary movements in a third outer belt of far-distant space which are beginning to exhibit directional tendencies of a clockwise nature.

It is probable that these alternate directions of successive space processions of the universes have something to do with the intramaster universe gravity technique of the Universal Absolute, which consists of a co-ordination of forces and an equalization of space tensions. Motion as well as space is a complement or equilibrant of gravity.

5. SPACE AND TIME

Like space, time is a bestowal of Paradise, but not in the same sense, only indirectly. Time comes by virtue of motion and because mind is inherently aware of sequentiality. From a practical viewpoint, motion is essential to time, but there is no universal time unit based on motion except in so far as the Paradise-Havona standard day is arbitrarily so recognized. The totality of space respiration destroys its local value as a time source.

Space is not infinite, even though it takes origin from Paradise; not absolute, for it is pervaded by the Unqualified Absolute. We do not know the absolute limits of space, but we do know that the absolute of time is eternity.

Time and space are inseparable only in the time-space creations, the seven superuniverses. Nontemporal space (space without time) theoretically exists, but the only truly nontemporal place is Paradise *area.* Nonspatial time (time without space) exists in mind of the Paradise level of function.

The relatively motionless midspace zones impinging on Paradise and separating pervaded from unpervaded space are the transition zones from time to eternity, hence the necessity of Paradise pilgrims becoming unconscious during this transit when it is to culminate in Paradise citizenship. Time-conscious *visitors* can go to Paradise without thus sleeping, but they remain creatures of time.

Relationships to time do not exist without motion in space, but consciousness of time does. Sequentiality can consciousize time even in the absence of motion. Man's mind is less time-bound than space-bound because of the inherent nature of mind. Even during the days of the earth life in the flesh, though man's mind is rigidly space-bound, the creative human imagination is comparatively time free. But time itself is not genetically a quality of mind.

There are three different levels of time cognizance:

1. Mind-perceived time—consciousness of sequence, motion, and a sense of duration.

2. Spirit-perceived time—insight into motion Godward and the awareness of the motion of ascent to levels of increasing divinity.

3. Personality *creates* a unique time sense out of insight into Reality plus a consciousness of presence and an awareness of duration.

Unspiritual animals know only the past and live in the present. Spirit-indwelt man has powers of prevision (insight); he may visualize the future. Only forward-looking and progressive attitudes are personally real. Static ethics and traditional morality are just slightly superanimal. Nor is stoicism a high order of self-realization. Ethics and morals become truly human when they are dynamic and progressive, alive with universe reality.

The human personality is not merely a concomitant of time-and-space events; the human personality can also act as the cosmic cause of such events.

6. UNIVERSAL OVERCONTROL

The universe is nonstatic. Stability is not the result of inertia but rather the product of balanced energies, co-operative minds, co-ordinated morontias, spirit overcontrol, and personality unification. Stability is wholly and always proportional to divinity.

In the physical control of the master universe the Universal Father exercises priority and primacy through the Isle of Paradise; God is absolute in the spiritual administration of the cosmos in the person of the Eternal Son. Concerning the domains of mind, the Father and the Son function co-ordinately in the Conjoint Actor.

The Third Source and Center assists in the maintenance of the equilibrium and co-ordination of the combined physical and spiritual energies and organizations by the absoluteness of his grasp of the cosmic mind and by the exercise of his inherent and universal physical- and spiritual-gravity complements. Whenever and wherever there occurs a liaison between the material and the spiritual, such a mind phenomenon is an act of the Infinite Spirit. Mind alone can interassociate the physical forces and energies of the material level with the spiritual powers and beings of the spirit level.

In all your contemplation of universal phenomena, make certain that you take into consideration the interrelation of physical, intellectual, and spiritual energies, and that due allowance is made for the unexpected phenomena attendant upon their unification by personality and for the unpredictable phenomena resulting from the actions and reactions of experiential Deity and the Absolutes.

The universe is highly predictable only in the quantitative or gravity-measurement sense; even the primal physical forces are not responsive to linear gravity, nor are the higher mind meanings and true spirit values of ultimate universe realities. Qualitatively, the universe is not highly predictable as regards new associations of forces, either physical, mindal, or spiritual, although many such combinations of energies or forces become partially predictable when subjected to critical observation. When matter, mind, and spirit are unified by creature personality, we are unable fully to predict the decisions of such a freewill being.

All phases of primordial force, nascent spirit, and other nonpersonal ultimates appear to react in accordance with certain relatively stable but unknown laws and are characterized by a latitude of performance and an elasticity of response which are often disconcerting when encountered in the phenomena of a circumscribed and isolated situation. What is the explanation of this unpredictable freedom of reaction disclosed by these emerging universe actualities? These unknown, unfathomable unpredictables—whether pertaining to the behavior of a primordial unit of force, the reaction of an unidentified level of mind, or the phenomenon of a vast preuniverse in the making in the domains of outer space—probably disclose the activities of the Ultimate and the presence-performances of the Absolutes, which antedate the function of all universe Creators.

We do not really know, but we surmise that such amazing versatility and such profound co-ordination signify the presence and performance of the Absolutes, and that such diversity of response in the face of apparently uniform causation discloses the reaction of the Absolutes, not only to the immediate and situational causation, but also to all other related causations throughout the entire master universe.

Individuals have their guardians of destiny; planets, systems, constellations, universes, and superuniverses each have their respective rulers who labor for the good of their domains. Havona and even the grand universe are watched over by those intrusted with such high responsibilities. But who fosters and cares for the fundamental needs of the master universe as a whole, from Paradise to the fourth and outermost space level? Existentially such overcare is probably attributable to the Paradise Trinity, but from an experiential viewpoint the appearance of the post-Havona universes is dependent on:

1. The Absolutes in potential.
2. The Ultimate in direction.

3. The Supreme in evolutionary co-ordination.

4. The Architects of the Master Universe in administration prior to the appearance of specific rulers.

The Unqualified Absolute pervades all space. We are not altogether clear as to the exact status of the Deity and Universal Absolutes, but we know the latter functions wherever the Deity and Unqualified Absolutes function. The Deity Absolute may be universally present but hardly space present. The Ultimate is, or sometime will be, space present to the outer margins of the fourth space level. We doubt that the Ultimate will ever have a space presence beyond the periphery of the master universe, but within this limit the Ultimate is progressively integrating the creative organization of the potentials of the three Absolutes.

7. THE PART AND THE WHOLE

There is operative throughout all time and space and with regard to all reality of whatever nature an inexorable and impersonal law which is equivalent to the function of a cosmic providence. Mercy characterizes God's attitude of love for the individual; impartiality motivates God's attitude toward the total. The will of God does not necessarily prevail in the part—the heart of any one personality—but his will does actually rule the whole, the universe of universes.

In all his dealings with all his beings it is true that the laws of God are not inherently arbitrary. To you, with your limited vision and finite viewpoint, the acts of God must often appear to be dictatorial and arbitrary. The laws of God are merely the habits of God, his way of repeatedly doing things; and he ever does all things well. You observe that God does the same thing in the same way, repeatedly, simply because that is the best way to do that particular thing in a given circumstance; and the best way is the right way, and therefore does infinite wisdom always order it done in that precise and perfect manner. You should also remember that nature is not the exclusive act of Deity; other influences are present in those phenomena which man calls nature.

It is repugnant to the divine nature to suffer any sort of deterioration or ever to permit the execution of any purely personal act in an inferior way. It should be made clear, however, that, *if,* in the divinity of any situation, in the extremity of any circumstance, in any case where the course of supreme wisdom might indicate the demand for different conduct—if the demands of perfection might for any reason dictate another method of reaction, a better one, then and there would the all-wise God function in that better and more suitable way. That would be the expression of a higher law, not the reversal of a lower law.

God is not a habit-bound slave to the chronicity of the repetition of his own voluntary acts. There is no conflict among the laws of the Infinite; they are all perfections of the infallible nature; they are all the unquestioned acts expressive of faultless decisions. Law is the unchanging reaction of an infinite, perfect, and divine mind. The acts of God are all volitional notwithstanding this apparent sameness. In God there "is no variableness neither shadow of changing." But all this which can be truly said of the Universal Father cannot be said with equal certainty of all his subordinate intelligences or of his evolutionary creatures.

Because God is changeless, therefore can you depend, in all ordinary circumstances, on his doing the same thing in the same identical and ordinary way. God is the assurance of stability for all created things and beings. He is God; therefore he changes not.

And all this steadfastness of conduct and uniformity of action is personal, conscious, and highly volitional, for the great God is not a helpless slave to his own perfection and infinity. God is not a self-acting automatic force; he is not a slavish law-bound power. God is neither a mathematical equation nor a chemical formula. He is a freewill and primal personality. He is the Universal Father, a being surcharged with personality and the universal fount of all creature personality.

The will of God does not uniformly prevail in the heart of the God-seeking material mortal, but if the time frame is enlarged beyond the moment to embrace the whole of the first life, then does God's will become increasingly discernible in the spirit fruits which are borne in the lives of the spirit-led children of God. And then, if human life is further enlarged to include the morontia experience, the divine will is observed to shine brighter and brighter in the spiritualizing acts of those creatures of time who have begun to taste the divine delights of experiencing the relationship of the personality of man with the personality of the Universal Father.

The Fatherhood of God and the brotherhood of man present the paradox of the part and the whole on the level of personality. God loves *each* individual as an individual child in the heavenly family. Yet God thus loves *every* individual; he is no respecter of persons, and the universality of his love brings into being a relationship of the whole, the universal brotherhood.

The love of the Father absolutely individualizes each personality as a unique child of the Universal Father, a child without duplicate in infinity, a will creature irreplaceable in all eternity. The Father's love glorifies each child of God, illuminating each member of the celestial family, sharply silhouetting the unique nature of each personal being against the impersonal levels that lie outside the fraternal circuit of the Father of all. The love of God strikingly portrays the transcendent value of each will creature, unmistakably reveals the high value which the Universal Father has placed upon each and every one of his children from the highest creator personality of Paradise status to the lowest personality of will dignity among the savage tribes of men in the dawn of the human species on some evolutionary world of time and space.

This very love of God for the individual brings into being the divine family of all individuals, the universal brotherhood of the freewill children of the Paradise Father. And this brotherhood, being universal, is a relationship of the whole. Brotherhood, when universal, discloses not the *each* relationship, but the *all* relationship. Brotherhood is a reality of the total and therefore discloses qualities of the whole in contradistinction to qualities of the part.

Brotherhood constitutes a fact of relationship between every personality in universal existence. No person can escape the benefits or the penalties that may come as a result of relationship to other persons. The part profits or suffers in measure with the whole. The good effort of each man benefits all men; the error or evil of each man augments the tribulation of all men. As moves the part, so moves the whole. As the progress of the whole, so the progress of the part. The relative velocities of part and whole determine whether the part is retarded by the inertia of the whole or is carried forward by the momentum of the cosmic brotherhood.

It is a mystery that God is a highly personal self-conscious being with residential headquarters, and at the same time personally present in such a vast universe and personally in contact with such a well-nigh infinite number of beings. That such a phenomenon is a mystery beyond human comprehension should not in the least lessen your faith. Do not allow the magnitude of the infinity, the immensity of the eternity, and the grandeur and glory of the matchless character of God to overawe, stagger, or discourage you; for the Father is not very far from any one of you; he dwells within you, and in him do we all literally move, actually live, and veritably have our being.

Even though the Paradise Father functions through his divine creators and his creature children, he also enjoys the most intimate inner contact with you, so sublime, so highly personal, that it is even beyond my comprehension—that mysterious communion of the Father fragment with the human soul and with the mortal mind of its actual indwelling. Knowing what you do of these gifts of God, you therefore know that the Father is in intimate touch, not only with his divine associates, but also with his evolutionary mortal children of time. The Father indeed abides on Paradise, but his divine presence also dwells in the minds of men.

Even though the spirit of a Son be poured out upon all flesh, even though a Son once dwelt with you in the likeness of mortal flesh, even though the seraphim personally guard and guide you, how can any of these divine beings of the Second and Third Centers ever hope to come as near to you or to understand you as fully as the Father, who has given a part of himself to be in you, to be your real and divine, even your eternal, self?

8. MATTER, MIND, AND SPIRIT

"God is spirit," but Paradise is not. The material universe is always the arena wherein take place all spiritual activities; spirit beings and spirit ascenders live and work on physical spheres of material reality.

The bestowal of cosmic force, the domain of cosmic gravity, is the function of the Isle of Paradise. All original force-energy proceeds from Paradise, and the matter for the making of untold universes now circulates throughout the master universe in the form of a supergravity presence which constitutes the force-charge of pervaded space.

Whatever the transformations of force in the outlying universes, having gone out from Paradise, it journeys on subject to the never-ending, ever-present, unfailing pull of the eternal Isle, obediently and inherently swinging on forever around the eternal space paths of the universes. Physical energy is the one reality which is true and steadfast in its obedience to universal law. Only in the realms of creature volition has there been deviation from the divine paths and the original plans. Power and energy are the universal evidences of the stability, constancy, and eternity of the central Isle of Paradise.

The bestowal of spirit and the spiritualization of personalities, the domain of spiritual gravity, is the realm of the Eternal Son. And this spirit gravity of the Son, ever drawing all spiritual realities to himself, is just as real and absolute as is the all-powerful material grasp of the Isle of Paradise. But material-minded man is naturally more familiar with the material manifestations of a physical nature than with the equally real and mighty operations of a spiritual nature which are discerned only by the spiritual insight of the soul.

As the mind of any personality in the universe becomes more spiritual—Godlike—it becomes less responsive to material gravity. Reality, measured by physical-gravity response, is the antithesis of reality as determined by quality of spirit content. Physical-gravity action is a quantitative determiner of non-spirit energy; spiritual-gravity action is the qualitative measure of the living energy of divinity.

What Paradise is to the physical creation, and what the Eternal Son is to the spiritual universe, the Conjoint Actor is to the realms of mind—the intelligent universe of material, morontial, and spiritual beings and personalities.

The Conjoint Actor reacts to both material and spiritual realities and therefore inherently becomes the universal minister to all intelligent beings, beings who may represent a union of both the material and spiritual phases of creation. The endowment of intelligence, the ministry to the material and the spiritual in the phenomenon of mind, is the exclusive domain of the Conjoint Actor, who thus becomes the partner of the spiritual mind, the essence of the morontia mind, and the substance of the material mind of the evolutionary creatures of time.

Mind is the technique whereby spirit realities become experiential to creature personalities. And in the last analysis the unifying possibilities of even human mind, the ability to co-ordinate things, ideas, and values, is supermaterial.

Though it is hardly possible for the mortal mind to comprehend the seven levels of relative cosmic reality, the human intellect should be able to grasp much of the meaning of three functioning levels of finite reality:

1. *Matter.* Organized energy which is subject to linear gravity except as it is modified by motion and conditioned by mind.

2. *Mind.* Organized consciousness which is not wholly subject to material gravity, and which becomes truly liberated when modified by spirit.

3. *Spirit.* The highest personal reality. True spirit is not subject to physical gravity but eventually becomes the motivating influence of all evolving energy systems of personality dignity.

The goal of existence of all personalities is spirit; material manifestations are relative, and the cosmic mind intervenes between these universal opposites. The bestowal of mind and the ministration of spirit are the work of the associate persons of Deity, the Infinite Spirit and the Eternal Son. Total Deity reality is not mind but spirit-mind—mind-spirit unified by personality. Nevertheless the absolutes of both the spirit and the thing converge in the person of the Universal Father.

On Paradise the three energies, physical, mindal, and spiritual, are co-ordinate. In the evolutionary cosmos energy-matter is dominant except in personality, where spirit, through the mediation of mind, is striving for the mastery. Spirit is the fundamental reality of the personality experience of all creatures because God is spirit. Spirit is unchanging, and therefore, in all personality relations, it transcends both mind and matter, which are experiential variables of progressive attainment.

In cosmic evolution matter becomes a philosophic shadow cast by mind in the presence of spirit luminosity of divine enlightenment, but this does not invalidate the reality of matter-energy. Mind, matter, and spirit are equally real, but they are not of equal value to personality in the attainment of divinity. Consciousness of divinity is a progressive spiritual experience.

The brighter the shining of the spiritualized personality (the Father in the universe, the fragment of potential spirit personality in the individual creature), the greater the shadow cast by the intervening mind upon its material investment. In time, man's body is just as real as mind or spirit, but in death, both mind (identity) and spirit survive while the body does not. A cosmic reality can be nonexistent in personality experience. And so your Greek figure of speech—the material as the shadow of the more real spirit substance—does have a philosophic significance.

9. PERSONAL REALITIES

Spirit is the basic personal reality in the universes, and personality is basic to all progressing experience with spiritual reality. Every phase of personality experience on every successive level of universe progression swarms with clues to the discovery of alluring personal realities. Man's true destiny consists in the creation of new and spirit goals and then in responding to the cosmic allurements of such supernal goals of nonmaterial value.

Love is the secret of beneficial association between personalities. You cannot really know a person as the result of a single contact. You cannot appreciatingly know music through mathematical deduction, even though music is a form of mathematical rhythm. The number assigned to a telephone subscriber does not in any manner identify the personality of that subscriber or signify anything concerning his character.

Mathematics, material science, is indispensable to the intelligent discussion of the material aspects of the universe, but such knowledge is not necessarily a part of the higher realization of truth or of the personal appreciation of spiritual realities. Not only in the realms of life but even in the world of physical energy, the sum of two or more things is very often something *more* than, or something *different* from, the predictable additive consequences of such unions. The entire science of mathematics, the whole domain of philosophy, the highest physics or chemistry, could not predict or know that the union of two gaseous hydrogen atoms with one gaseous oxygen atom would result in a new and qualitatively superadditive substance—liquid water. The understanding knowledge of this one physiochemical phenomenon should have prevented the development of materialistic philosophy and mechanistic cosmology.

Technical analysis does not reveal what a person or a thing can do. For example: Water is used effectively to extinguish fire. That water will put out fire is a fact of everyday experience, but no analysis of water could ever be made to disclose such a property. Analysis determines that water is composed of hydrogen and oxygen; a further study of these elements discloses that oxygen is the real supporter of combustion and that hydrogen will itself freely burn.

Your religion is becoming real because it is emerging from the slavery of fear and the bondage of superstition. Your philosophy struggles for emancipation from dogma and tradition. Your science is engaged in the agelong contest between truth and error while it fights for deliverance from the bondage of abstraction, the slavery of mathematics, and the relative blindness of mechanistic materialism.

Mortal man has a spirit nucleus. The mind is a personal-energy system existing around a divine spirit nucleus and functioning in a material environment. Such a living relationship of personal mind and spirit constitutes the universe potential of eternal personality. Real trouble, lasting disappointment, serious defeat, or inescapable death can come only after self-concepts presume fully to displace the governing power of the central spirit nucleus, thereby disrupting the cosmic scheme of personality identity.

[Presented by a Perfector of Wisdom acting by authority of the Ancients of Days.]

PAPER 13

THE SACRED SPHERES OF PARADISE

BETWEEN the central Isle of Paradise and the innermost of the Havona planetary circuits there are situated in space three lesser circuits of special spheres. The innermost circuit consists of the seven secret spheres of the Universal Father; the second group is composed of the seven luminous worlds of the Eternal Son; in the outermost are the seven immense spheres of the Infinite Spirit, the executive-headquarters worlds of the Seven Master Spirits.

These three seven-world circuits of the Father, the Son, and the Spirit are spheres of unexcelled grandeur and unimagined glory. Even their material or physical construction is of an order unrevealed to you. Each circuit is diverse in material, and each world of each circuit is different excepting the seven worlds of the Son, which are alike in physical constitution. All twenty-one are enormous spheres, and each group of seven is differently eternalized. As far as we know they have always been; like Paradise they are eternal. There exists neither record nor tradition of their origin.

The seven secret spheres of the Universal Father, circulating about Paradise in close proximity to the eternal Isle, are highly reflective of the spiritual luminosity of the central shining of the eternal Deities, shedding this light of divine glory throughout Paradise and even upon the seven circuits of Havona.

On the seven sacred worlds of the Eternal Son there appear to take origin the impersonal energies of spirit luminosity. No personal being may sojourn on any of these seven shining realms. With spiritual glory they illuminate all Paradise and Havona, and they directionize pure spirit luminosity to the seven superuniverses. These brilliant spheres of the second circuit likewise emit their light (light without heat) to Paradise and to the billion worlds of the seven-circuited central universe.

The seven worlds of the Infinite Spirit are occupied by the Seven Master Spirits, who preside over the destinies of the seven superuniverses, sending forth the spiritual illumination of the Third Person of Deity to these creations of time and space. And all Havona, but not the Isle of Paradise, is bathed in these spiritualizing influences.

Although the worlds of the Father are ultimate status spheres for all Father-endowed personalities, this is not their exclusive function. Many beings and entities other than personal sojourn on these worlds. Each world in the circuit of the Father and the circuit of the Spirit has a distinct type of permanent citizenship, but we think the Son's worlds are inhabited by uniform types of other-than-personal beings. Father fragments are among the natives of Divinington; the other orders of permanent citizenship are unrevealed to you.

The twenty-one Paradise satellites serve many purposes in both central and superuniverses not disclosed in these narratives. You are able to understand so little of the life of these spheres that you cannot hope to gain anything like a consistent view of them, either as to nature or function; thousands of activities are there going on which are unrevealed to you. These twenty-one spheres embrace the *potentials* of the function of the master universe. These papers afford only a fleeting glimpse of certain circumscribed activities pertaining to the present universe age of the grand universe—rather, one of the seven sectors of the grand universe.

1. THE SEVEN SACRED WORLDS OF THE FATHER

The Father's circuit of sacred life spheres contains the only inherent personality secrets in the universe of universes. These satellites of Paradise, the innermost of the three circuits, are the only forbidden domains concerned with personality in the central universe. Nether Paradise and the worlds of the Son are likewise closed to personalities, but neither of those realms is in any way directly concerned with personality.

The Paradise worlds of the Father are directed by the highest order of the Stationary Sons of the Trinity, the Trinitized Secrets of Supremacy. Of these worlds I can tell little; of their manifold activities I may tell less. Such information concerns only those beings who function thereon and go forth therefrom. And though I am somewhat familiar with six of these special worlds, never have I landed on Divinington; that world is wholly forbidden to me.

One of the reasons for the secrecy of these worlds is because each of these sacred spheres enjoys a specialized representation, or manifestation, of the Deities composing the Paradise Trinity; not a personality, but a unique presence of Divinity which can only be appreciated and comprehended by those particular groups of intelligences resident on, or admissible to, that particular sphere. The Trinitized Secrets of Supremacy are the personal agents of these specialized and impersonal presences of Divinity. And the Secrets of Supremacy are highly personal beings, superbly endowed and marvelously adapted to their exalted and exacting work.

1. DIVININGTON. This world is, in a unique sense, the "bosom of the Father," the personal-communion sphere of the Universal Father, and thereon is a special manifestation of his divinity. Divinington is the Paradise rendezvous of the Thought Adjusters, but it is also the home of numerous other entities, personalities, and other beings taking origin in the Universal Father. Many personalities besides the Eternal Son are of direct origin by the solitary acts of the Universal Father. Only the Father fragments and those personalities and other beings of direct and exclusive origin in the Universal Father fraternize and function on this abode.

The secrets of Divinington include the secret of the bestowal and mission of Thought Adjusters. Their nature, origin, and the technique of their contact with the lowly creatures of the evolutionary worlds is a secret of this Paradise sphere. These amazing transactions do not personally concern the rest of us, and therefore do the Deities deem it proper to withhold certain features of this great and divine ministry from our full understanding. In so far as we come in contact with this phase of divine activity, we are permitted full knowledge of these transactions, but concerning the intimate details of this great bestowal we are not fully informed.

This sphere also holds the secrets of the nature, purpose, and activities of all other forms of Father fragments, of the Gravity Messengers, and of hosts of other beings unrevealed to you. It is highly probable that those truths pertaining to Divinington which are withheld from me, if revealed, would merely confuse and handicap me in my present work, and still again, perhaps they are beyond the conceptual capacity of my order of being.

2. SONARINGTON. This sphere is the "bosom of the Son," the personal receiving world of the Eternal Son. It is the Paradise headquarters of the descending and ascending Sons of God when, and after, they are fully accredited and finally approved. This world is the Paradise home for all Sons of the Eternal Son and of his co-ordinate and associate Sons. There are numerous orders of divine sonship attached to this supernal abode which have not been revealed to mortals since they are not concerned with the plans of the ascension scheme of human spiritual progression through the universes and on to Paradise.

The secrets of Sonarington include the secret of the incarnation of the divine Sons. When a Son of God becomes a Son of Man, is literally born of woman, as occurred on your world nineteen hundred years ago, it is a universal mystery. It is occurring right along throughout the universes, and it is a Sonarington secret of divine sonship. The Adjusters are a mystery of God the Father. The incarnation of the divine Sons is a mystery of God the Son; it is a secret locked up in the seventh sector of Sonarington, a realm penetrated by none save those who have personally passed through this unique experience. Only those phases of incarnation having to do with your ascension career have been brought to your notice. There are many other phases of the mystery of the incarnation of the Paradise Sons of unrevealed types on missions of universe service which are undisclosed to you. And there are still other Sonarington mysteries.

3. SPIRITINGTON. This world is the "bosom of the Spirit," the Paradise home of the high beings that exclusively represent the Infinite Spirit. Here forgather the Seven Master Spirits and certain of their offspring from all universes. At this celestial abode may also be found numerous unrevealed orders of spirit personalities, beings assigned to the manifold activities of the universe not associated with the plans of upstepping the mortal creatures of time to the Paradise levels of eternity.

The secrets of Spiritington involve the impenetrable mysteries of reflectivity. We tell you of the vast and universal phenomenon of reflectivity, more particularly as it is operative on the headquarters worlds of the seven superuniverses, but we never fully explain this phenomenon, for we do not fully understand it. Much, very much, we do comprehend, but many basic details are still mysterious to us. Reflectivity is a secret of God the Spirit. You have been instructed concerning reflectivity functions in relation to the ascension scheme of mortal survival, and it does so operate, but reflectivity is also an indispensable feature of the normal working of numerous other phases of universe occupation. This endowment of the Infinite Spirit is also utilized in channels other than those of intelligence gathering and information dissemination. And there are other secrets of Spiritington.

4. VICEGERINGTON. This planet is the "bosom of the Father and the Son" and is the secret sphere of certain unrevealed beings who take origin by the acts of the Father and the Son. This is also the Paradise home of many

glorified beings of complex ancestry, those whose origin is complicated because of the many diverse techniques operative in the seven superuniverses. Many groups of beings forgather on this world whose identity has not been revealed to Urantia mortals.

The secrets of Vicegerington include the secrets of trinitization, and trinitization constitutes the secret of authority to represent the Trinity, to act as vicegerents of the Gods. Authority to represent the Trinity attaches only to those beings, revealed and unrevealed, who are trinitized, created, eventuated, or eternalized by any two or all three of the Paradise Trinity. Personalities brought into being by the trinitizing acts of certain types of glorified creatures represent no more than the conceptual potential mobilized in that trinitization, albeit such creatures may ascend the path of Deity embrace open to all of their kind.

Nontrinitized beings do not fully understand the technique of trinitization by either two or three Creators or by certain creatures. You will never fully understand such a phenomenon unless, in the far-distant future of your glorified career, you should essay and succeed in such an adventure, because otherwise these secrets of Vicegerington will always be forbidden you. But to me, a high Trinity-origin being, all sectors of Vicegerington are open. I fully understand, and just as fully and sacredly protect, the secret of my origin and destiny.

There are still other forms and phases of trinitization which have not been brought to the notice of the Urantia peoples, and these experiences, in their personal aspects, are duly protected in the secret sector of Vicegerington.

5. SOLITARINGTON. This world is the "bosom of the Father and the Spirit" and is the rendezvous of a magnificent host of unrevealed beings of origin in the conjoint acts of the Universal Father and the Infinite Spirit, beings who partake of the traits of the Father in addition to their Spirit inheritance.

This is also the home of the Solitary Messengers and of other personalities of the superangelic orders. You know of very few of these beings; there are vast numbers of orders unrevealed on Urantia. Because they are domiciled on the fifth world, it does not necessarily follow that the Father had aught to do with the creation of Solitary Messengers or their superangelic associates, but in this universe age he does have to do with their function. During the present universe age this is also the status sphere of the Universe Power Directors.

There are numerous additional orders of spirit personalities, beings unknown to mortal man, who look upon Solitarington as their Paradise home sphere. It should be remembered that all divisions and levels of universe activities are just as fully provided with spirit ministers as is the realm concerned with helping mortal man ascend to his divine Paradise destiny.

The secrets of Solitarington. Besides certain secrets of trinitization, this world holds the secrets of the personal relation of the Infinite Spirit with certain of the higher offspring of the Third Source and Center. On Solitarington are held the mysteries of the intimate association of numerous unrevealed orders with the spirits of the Father, of the Son, and of the Spirit, with the threefold spirit of the Trinity, and with the spirits of the Supreme, the Ultimate, and the Supreme-Ultimate.

6. SERAPHINGTON. This sphere is the "bosom of the Son and the Spirit" and is the home world of the vast hosts of unrevealed beings created by the Son and the Spirit. This is also the destiny sphere of all ministering orders of the

angelic hosts, including supernaphim, seconaphim, and seraphim. There also serve in the central and outlying universes many orders of superb spirits who are not "ministering spirits to those who shall be heirs of salvation." All these spirit workers in all levels and realms of universe activities look upon Seraphington as their Paradise home.

The secrets of Seraphington involve a threefold mystery, only one of which I may mention—the mystery of seraphic transport. The ability of various orders of seraphim and allied spirit beings to envelop within their spirit forms all orders of nonmaterial personalities and to carry them away on lengthy interplanetary journeys, is a secret locked up in the sacred sectors of Seraphington. The transport seraphim comprehend this mystery, but they do not communicate it to the rest of us, or perhaps they cannot. The other mysteries of Seraphington pertain to the personal experiences of types of spirit servers as yet not revealed to mortals. And we refrain from discussing the secrets of such closely related beings because you can almost comprehend such near orders of existence, and it would be akin to betrayal of trust to present even our partial knowledge of such phenomena.

7. ASCENDINGTON. This unique world is the "bosom of the Father, Son, and Spirit," the rendezvous of the ascendant creatures of space, the receiving sphere of the pilgrims of time who are passing through the Havona universe on their way to Paradise. Ascendington is the actual Paradise home of the ascendant souls of time and space until they attain Paradise status. You mortals will spend most of your Havona "vacations" on Ascendington. During your Havona life Ascendington will be to you what the reversion directors were during the local and superuniverse ascension. Here you will engage in thousands of activities which are beyond the grasp of mortal imagination. And as on every previous advance in the Godward ascent, your human self will here enter into new relationships with your divine self.

The secrets of Ascendington include the mystery of the gradual and certain building up in the material and mortal mind of a spiritual and potentially immortal counterpart of character and identity. This phenomenon constitutes one of the most perplexing mysteries of the universes—the evolution of an immortal soul within the mind of a mortal and material creature.

You will never fully understand this mysterious transaction until you reach Ascendington. And that is just why all Ascendington will be open to your wondering gaze. One seventh of Ascendington is forbidden to me—that sector concerned with this very secret which is (or will be) the exclusive experience and possession of your type of being. This experience belongs to your human order of existence. My order of personality is not directly concerned with such transactions. It is therefore forbidden to me and eventually revealed to you. But even after it is revealed to you, for some reason it forever remains your secret. You do not reveal it to us nor to any other order of beings. We know about the eternal fusion of a divine Adjuster and an immortal soul of human origin, but the ascendant finaliters know this very experience as an absolute reality.

2. FATHER-WORLD RELATIONSHIPS

These home worlds of the diverse orders of spiritual beings are tremendous and stupendous spheres, and they are equal to Paradise in their matchless beauty and superb glory. They are rendezvous worlds, reunion spheres, serving as permanent cosmic addresses. As finaliters you will be domiciled on Paradise, but Ascendington will be your home address at all times, even when you enter service in outer space. Through all eternity you will regard Ascendington as your home of sentimental memories and reminiscent recollections. When you become seventh-stage spirit beings, possibly you will give up your residential status on Paradise.

If outer universes are in the making, if they are to be inhabited by time creatures of ascension potential, then we infer that these children of the future will also be destined to look upon Ascendington as their Paradise home world.

Ascendington is the only sacred sphere that will be unreservedly open to your inspection as a Paradise arrival. Vicegerington is the only sacred sphere that is wholly and unreservedly open to my scrutiny. Though its secrets are concerned in my origin, in this universe age I do not regard Vicegerington as my home. Trinity-origin beings and trinitized beings are not the same.

The Trinity-origin beings do not fully share the Father's worlds; they have their sole homes on the Isle of Paradise in close proximity to the Most Holy Sphere. They often appear on Ascendington, the "bosom of the Father-Son-Spirit," where they fraternize with their brethren who have come up from the lowly worlds of space.

You might assume that Creator Sons, being of Father-Son origin, would regard Vicegerington as their home, but such is not the case in this universe age of the function of God the Sevenfold. And there are many similar problems that will perplex you, for you are sure to encounter many difficulties as you attempt to understand these things which are so near Paradise. Nor can you successfully reason out these questions; you know so little. And if you knew more about the Father's worlds, you would simply encounter more difficulties until you knew *all* about them. Status on any of these secret worlds is acquired by service as well as by nature of origin, and the successive universe ages may and do redistribute certain of these personality groupings.

The worlds of the inner circuit are really fraternal or status worlds more than actual residential spheres. Mortals will attain some status on each of the Father's worlds save one. For example: When you mortals attain Havona, you are granted clearance for Ascendington, where you are most welcome, but you are not permitted to visit the other six sacred worlds. Subsequent to your passage through the Paradise regime and after your admission to the Corps of the Finality, you are granted clearance for Sonarington since you are sons of God as well as ascenders—and you are even more. But there will always remain one seventh of Sonarington, the sector of the incarnation secrets of the divine Sons, which will not be open to your scrutiny. Never will those secrets be revealed to the ascendant sons of God.

Eventually you will have full access to Ascendington and relative access to the other spheres of the Father except Divinington. But even when you are granted permission to land on five additional secret spheres, after you have become a finaliter, you will not be allowed to visit all sectors of such worlds. Nor will you be permitted to land on the shores of Divinington, the "bosom of the Father," though you shall surely stand repeatedly at the "right hand of the Father." Never throughout all eternity will there arise any necessity for your presence on the world of the Thought Adjusters.

These rendezvous worlds of spirit life are forbidden ground to the extent that we are asked not to negotiate entrance to those phases of these spheres which are wholly outside our realms of experience. You may become creature perfect even as the Universal Father is deity perfect, but you may not know all the experiential secrets of all other orders of universe personalities. When the Creator has an experiential personality secret with his creature, the Creator preserves that secret in eternal confidence.

All these secrets are supposedly known to the collective body of the Trinitized Secrets of Supremacy. These beings are fully known only by their special world groups; they are little comprehended by other orders. After you attain Paradise, you will know and ardently love the ten Secrets of Supremacy who direct Ascendington. Excepting Divinington, you will also achieve a partial understanding of the Secrets of Supremacy on the other worlds of the Father, though not so perfectly as on Ascendington.

The Trinitized Secrets of Supremacy, as their name might suggest, are related to the Supreme; they are likewise related to the Ultimate and to the future Supreme-Ultimate. These Secrets of Supremacy are the secrets of the Supreme and also the secrets of the Ultimate, even the secrets of the Supreme-Ultimate.

3. THE SACRED WORLDS OF THE ETERNAL SON

The seven luminous spheres of the Eternal Son are the worlds of the seven phases of pure-spirit existence. These shining orbs are the source of the threefold light of Paradise and Havona, their influence being largely, but not wholly, confined to the central universe.

Personality is not present on these Paradise satellites; therefore is there little concerning these pure-spirit abodes which can be presented to the mortal and material personality. We are taught that these worlds teem with the otherwise-than-personal life of the beings of the Eternal Son. We infer that these entities are being assembled for ministry in the projected new universes of outer space. The Paradise philosophers maintain that each Paradise cycle, about two billion years of Urantia time, witnesses the creation of additional reserves of these orders on the secret worlds of the Eternal Son.

As far as I am informed, no personality has ever been on any one of these spheres of the Eternal Son. I have never been assigned to visit one of these worlds in all my long experience in and out of Paradise. Even the personalities cocreated by the Eternal Son do not go to these worlds. We infer that all types of impersonal spirits—regardless of parentage—are admitted to these spirit homes. As I am a person and have a spirit form, no doubt such a world would seem empty and deserted even if I were permitted to pay it a visit. High spirit personalities are not given to the gratification of purposeless curiosity, purely useless adventure. There is at all times altogether too much intriguing and purposeful adventure to permit the development of any great interest in those projects which are either futile or unreal.

4. THE WORLDS OF THE INFINITE SPIRIT

Between the inner circuit of Havona and the shining spheres of the Eternal Son there circle the seven orbs of the Infinite Spirit, worlds inhabited by the offspring of the Infinite Spirit, by the trinitized sons of glorified created personalities, and by other types of unrevealed beings concerned with the effective administration of the many enterprises of the various realms of universe activities.

The Seven Master Spirits are the supreme and ultimate representatives of the Infinite Spirit. They maintain their personal stations, their power focuses, on the periphery of Paradise, but all operations concerned with their management and direction of the grand universe are conducted on and from these seven special executive spheres of the Infinite Spirit. The Seven Master Spirits are, in reality, the mind-spirit balance wheel of the universe of universes, an all-embracing, all-encompassing, and all-co-ordinating power of central location.

From these seven special spheres the Master Spirits operate to equalize and stabilize the cosmic-mind circuits of the grand universe. They also have to do with the differential spiritual attitude and presence of the Deities throughout the grand universe. Physical reactions are uniform, unvarying, and always instantaneous and automatic. But experiential spiritual presence is in accordance with the underlying conditions or states of spiritual receptivity inherent in the individual minds of the realms.

Physical authority, presence, and function are unvarying in all the universes, small or great. The differing factor in spiritual presence, or reaction, is the fluctuating differential in its recognition and reception by will creatures. Whereas the spiritual presence of absolute and existential Deity is in no manner whatever influenced by attitudes of loyalty or disloyalty on the part of created beings, at the same time it is true that the functioning presence of subabsolute and experiential Deity is definitely and directly influenced by the decisions, choices, and will-attitudes of such finite creature beings—by the loyalty and devotion of the individual being, planet, system, constellation, or universe. But this spiritual presence of divinity is not whimsical nor arbitrary; its experiential variance is inherent in the freewill endowment of personal creatures.

The determiner of the differential of spiritual presence exists in your own hearts and minds and consists in the manner of your own choosing, in the decisions of your minds, and in the determination of your own wills. This differential is inherent in the freewill reactions of intelligent personal beings, beings whom the Universal Father has ordained shall exercise this liberty of choosing. And the Deities are ever true to the ebb and flow of their spirits in meeting and satisfying the conditions and demands of this differential of creature choice, now bestowing more of their presence in response to a sincere desire for the same and again withdrawing themselves from the scene as their creatures decide adversely in the exercise of their divinely bestowed freedom of choice. And thus does the spirit of divinity become humbly obedient to the choosing of the creatures of the realms.

The executive abodes of the Seven Master Spirits are, in reality, the Paradise headquarters of the seven superuniverses and their correlated segments in outer space. Each Master Spirit presides over one superuniverse, and each of these seven worlds is exclusively assigned to one of the Master Spirits. There is literally no phase of the sub-Paradise administration of the seven superuniverses which is not provided for on these executive worlds. They are not so exclusive as the spheres of the Father or those of the Son, and though residential status is limited to native beings and those who work thereon, these seven administrative planets are always open to all beings who desire to visit them, and who can command the necessary means of transit.

To me, these executive worlds are the most interesting and intriguing spots outside of Paradise. In no other place in the wide universe can one observe such varied activities, involving so many different orders of living beings, having to do with operations on so many diverse levels, occupations at once material, intellectual, and spiritual. When I am accorded a period of release from assignment, if I chance to be on Paradise or in Havona, I usually proceed to one of these busy worlds of the Seven Master Spirits, there to inspire my mind with such spectacles of enterprise, devotion, loyalty, wisdom, and effectiveness. Nowhere else can I observe such an amazing interassociation of personality performances on all seven levels of universe reality. And I am always stimulated by the activities of those who well know how to do their work, and who so thoroughly enjoy doing it.

[Presented by a Perfector of Wisdom commissioned thus to function by the Ancients of Days on Uversa.]

PAPER 14

THE CENTRAL AND DIVINE UNIVERSE

THE perfect and divine universe occupies the center of all creation; it is the eternal core around which the vast creations of time and space revolve. Paradise is the gigantic nuclear Isle of absolute stability which rests motionless at the very heart of the magnificent eternal universe. This central planetary family is called Havona and is far-distant from the local universe of Nebadon. It is of enormous dimensions and almost unbelievable mass and consists of one billion spheres of unimagined beauty and superb grandeur, but the true magnitude of this vast creation is really beyond the understanding grasp of the human mind.

This is the one and only settled, perfect, and established aggregation of worlds. This is a wholly created and perfect universe; it is not an evolutionary development. This is the eternal core of perfection, about which swirls that endless procession of universes which constitute the tremendous evolutionary experiment, the audacious adventure of the Creator Sons of God, who aspire to duplicate in time and to reproduce in space the pattern universe, the ideal of divine completeness, supreme finality, ultimate reality, and eternal perfection.

1. THE PARADISE-HAVONA SYSTEM

From the periphery of Paradise to the inner borders of the seven superuniverses there are the following seven space conditions and motions:

1. The quiescent midspace zones impinging on Paradise.

2. The clockwise processional of the three Paradise and the seven Havona circuits.

3. The semiquiet space zone separating the Havona circuits from the dark gravity bodies of the central universe.

4. The inner, counterclockwise-moving belt of the dark gravity bodies.

5. The second unique space zone dividing the two space paths of the dark gravity bodies.

6. The outer belt of dark gravity bodies, revolving clockwise around Paradise.

7. A third space zone—a semiquiet zone—separating the outer belt of dark gravity bodies from the innermost circuits of the seven superuniverses.

The billion *worlds of Havona* are arranged in seven concentric circuits immediately surrounding the three circuits of Paradise satellites. There are upwards of thirty-five million worlds in the innermost Havona circuit and over two hundred and forty-five million in the outermost, with proportionate numbers intervening. Each circuit differs, but all are perfectly balanced and exquisitely organized, and each is pervaded by a specialized representation of the Infinite Spirit, one of the Seven Spirits of the Circuits. In addition to other functions this impersonal Spirit co-ordinates the conduct of celestial affairs throughout each circuit.

The Havona planetary circuits are not superimposed; their worlds follow each other in an orderly linear procession. The central universe whirls around the stationary Isle of Paradise in one vast plane, consisting of ten concentric stabilized units—the three circuits of Paradise spheres and the seven circuits of Havona worlds. Physically regarded, the Havona and the Paradise circuits are all one and the same system; their separation is in recognition of functional and administrative segregation.

Time is not reckoned on Paradise; the sequence of successive events is inherent in the concept of those who are indigenous to the central Isle. But time is germane to the Havona circuits and to numerous beings of both celestial and terrestrial origin sojourning thereon. Each Havona world has its own local time, determined by its circuit. All worlds in a given circuit have the same length of year since they uniformly swing around Paradise, and the length of these planetary years decreases from the outermost to the innermost circuit.

Besides Havona-circuit time, there is the Paradise-Havona standard day and other time designations which are determined on, and are sent out from, the seven Paradise satellites of the Infinite Spirit. The Paradise-Havona standard day is based on the length of time required for the planetary abodes of the first or inner Havona circuit to complete one revolution around the Isle of Paradise; and though their velocity is enormous, owing to their situation between the dark gravity bodies and gigantic Paradise, it requires almost one thousand years for these spheres to complete their circuit. You have unwittingly read the truth when your eyes rested on the statement "A day is as a thousand years with God, as but a watch in the night." One Paradise-Havona day is just seven minutes, three and one-eighth seconds less than one thousand years of the present Urantia leap-year calendar.

This Paradise-Havona day is the standard time measurement for the seven superuniverses, although each maintains its own internal time standards.

On the outskirts of this vast central universe, far out beyond the seventh belt of Havona worlds, there swirl an unbelievable number of enormous dark gravity bodies. These multitudinous dark masses are quite unlike other space bodies in many particulars; even in form they are very different. These dark gravity bodies neither reflect nor absorb light; they are nonreactive to physical-energy light, and they so completely encircle and enshroud Havona as to hide it from the view of even near-by inhabited universes of time and space.

The great belt of dark gravity bodies is divided into two equal elliptical circuits by a unique space intrusion. The inner belt revolves counterclockwise; the outer revolves clockwise. These alternate directions of motion, coupled with the extraordinary mass of the dark bodies, so effectively equalize the lines of Havona gravity as to render the central universe a physically balanced and perfectly stabilized creation.

The inner procession of dark gravity bodies is tubular in arrangement, consisting of three circular groupings. A cross section of this circuit would exhibit three concentric circles of about equal density. The outer circuit of dark gravity bodies is arranged perpendicularly, being ten thousand times higher than the inner circuit. The up-and-down diameter of the outer circuit is fifty thousand times that of the transverse diameter.

The intervening space which exists between these two circuits of gravity bodies is *unique* in that nothing like it is to be found elsewhere in all the wide universe. This zone is characterized by enormous wave movements of an up-and-down nature and is permeated by tremendous energy activities of an unknown order.

In our opinion, nothing like the dark gravity bodies of the central universe will characterize the future evolution of the outer space levels; we regard these alternate processions of stupendous gravity-balancing bodies as unique in the master universe.

2. CONSTITUTION OF HAVONA

Spirit beings do not dwell in nebulous space; they do not inhabit ethereal worlds; they are domiciled on actual spheres of a material nature, worlds just as real as those on which mortals live. The Havona worlds are actual and literal, albeit their literal substance differs from the material organization of the planets of the seven superuniverses.

The physical realities of Havona represent an order of energy organization radically different from any prevailing in the evolutionary universes of space. Havona energies are threefold; superuniverse units of energy-matter contain a twofold energy charge, although one form of energy exists in negative and positive phases. The creation of the central universe is threefold (Trinity); the creation of a local universe (directly) is twofold, by a Creator Son and a Creative Spirit.

The material of Havona consists of the organization of exactly one thousand basic chemical elements and the balanced function of the seven forms of Havona energy. Each of these basic energies manifests seven phases of excitation, so that the Havona natives respond to forty-nine differing sensation stimuli. In other words, viewed from a purely physical standpoint, the natives of the central universe possess forty-nine specialized forms of sensation. The morontia senses are seventy, and the higher spiritual orders of reaction response vary in different types of beings from seventy to two hundred and ten.

None of the physical beings of the central universe would be visible to Urantians. Neither would any of the physical stimuli of those faraway worlds excite a reaction in your gross sense organs. If a Urantia mortal could be transported to Havona, he would there be deaf, blind, and utterly lacking in all other sense reactions; he could only function as a limited self-conscious being deprived of all environmental stimuli and all reactions thereto.

There are numerous physical phenomena and spiritual reactions transpiring in the central creation which are unknown on worlds such as Urantia. The basic organization of a threefold creation is wholly unlike that of the twofold constitution of the created universes of time and space.

All natural law is co-ordinated on a basis entirely different than in the dual-energy systems of the evolving creations. The entire central universe is organized in accordance with the threefold system of perfect and symmetrical control. Throughout the whole Paradise-Havona system there is maintained a perfect balance between all cosmic realities and all spiritual forces. Paradise, with an absolute grasp of material creation, perfectly regulates and maintains the physical energies of this central universe; the Eternal Son, as a part of his all-embracing spirit grasp, most perfectly sustains the spiritual status of all who indwell Havona. On Paradise nothing is experimental, and the Paradise-Havona system is a unit of creative perfection.

The universal spiritual gravity of the Eternal Son is amazingly active throughout the central universe. All spirit values and spiritual personalities are unceasingly drawn inward towards the abode of the Gods. This Godward urge is intense and inescapable. The ambition to attain God is stronger in the central universe, not because spirit gravity is stronger than in the outlying universes, but because those beings who have attained Havona are more fully spiritualized and hence more responsive to the ever-present action of the universal spirit-gravity pull of the Eternal Son.

Likewise does the Infinite Spirit draw all intellectual values Paradiseward. Throughout the central universe the mind gravity of the Infinite Spirit functions in liaison with the spirit gravity of the Eternal Son, and these together constitute the combined urge of the ascendant souls to find God, to attain Deity, to achieve Paradise, and to know the Father.

Havona is a spiritually perfect and physically stable universe. The control and balanced stability of the central universe appear to be perfect. Everything physical or spiritual is perfectly predictable, but mind phenomena and personality volition are not. We do infer that sin can be reckoned as impossible of occurrence, but we do this on the ground that the native freewill creatures of Havona have never been guilty of transgressing the will of Deity. Through all eternity these supernal beings have been consistently loyal to the Eternals of Days. Neither has sin appeared in any creature who has entered Havona as a pilgrim. There has never been an instance of misconduct by any creature of any group of personalities ever created in, or admitted to, the central Havona universe. So perfect and so divine are the methods and means of selection in the universes of time that never in the records of Havona has an error occurred; no mistakes have ever been made; no ascendant soul has ever been prematurely admitted to the central universe.

3. THE HAVONA WORLDS

Concerning the government of the central universe, there is none. Havona is so exquisitely perfect that no intellectual system of government is required. There are no regularly constituted courts, neither are there legislative assemblies; Havona requires only administrative direction. Here may be observed the height of the ideals of true *self*-government.

There is no need of government among such perfect and near-perfect intelligences. They stand in no need of regulation, for they are beings of native perfection interspersed with evolutionary creatures who have long since passed the scrutiny of the supreme tribunals of the superuniverses.

The administration of Havona is not automatic, but it is marvelously perfect and divinely efficient. It is chiefly planetary and is vested in the resident Eternal of Days, each Havona sphere being directed by one of these Trinity-origin personalities. Eternals of Days are not creators, but they are perfect administrators.

They teach with supreme skill and direct their planetary children with a perfection of wisdom bordering on absoluteness.

The billion spheres of the central universe constitute the training worlds of the high personalities native to Paradise and Havona and further serve as the final proving grounds for ascending creatures from the evolutionary worlds of time. In the execution of the Universal Father's great plan of creature ascension the pilgrims of time are landed on the receiving worlds of the outer or seventh circuit, and subsequent to increased training and enlarged experience, they are progressively advanced inward, planet by planet and circle by circle, until they finally attain the Deities and achieve residence on Paradise.

At present, although the spheres of the seven circuits are maintained in all their supernal glory, only about one per cent of all planetary capacity is utilized in the work of furthering the Father's universal plan of mortal ascension. About one tenth of one per cent of the area of these enormous worlds is dedicated to the life and activities of the Corps of the Finality, beings eternally settled in light and life who often sojourn and minister on the Havona worlds. These exalted beings have their personal residences on Paradise.

The planetary construction of the Havona spheres is entirely unlike that of the evolutionary worlds and systems of space. Nowhere else in all the grand universe is it convenient to utilize such enormous spheres as inhabited worlds. Triata physical constitution, coupled with the balancing effect of the immense dark gravity bodies, makes it possible so perfectly to equalize the physical forces and so exquisitely to balance the various attractions of this tremendous creation. Antigravity is also employed in the organization of the material functions and the spiritual activities of these enormous worlds.

The architecture, lighting, and heating, as well as the biologic and artistic embellishment, of the Havona spheres, are quite beyond the greatest possible stretch of human imagination. You cannot be told much about Havona; to understand its beauty and grandeur you must see it. But there are real rivers and lakes on these perfect worlds.

Spiritually these worlds are ideally appointed; they are fittingly adapted to their purpose of harboring the numerous orders of differing beings who function in the central universe. Manifold activities take place on these beautiful worlds which are far beyond human comprehension.

4. CREATURES OF THE CENTRAL UNIVERSE

There are seven basic forms of living things and beings on the Havona worlds, and each of these basic forms exists in three distinct phases. Each of these three phases is divided into seventy major divisions, and each major division is composed of one thousand minor divisions, with yet other subdivisions, and so on. These basic life groups might be classified as:

1. Material.
2. Morontial.
3. Spiritual.
4. Absonite.
5. Ultimate.
6. Coabsolute.
7. Absolute.

Decay and death are not a part of the cycle of life on the Havona worlds. In the central universe the lower living things undergo the transmutation of materialization. They do change form and manifestation, but they do not resolve by process of decay and cellular death.

The Havona natives are all the offspring of the Paradise Trinity. They are without creature parents, and they are nonreproducing beings. We cannot portray the creation of these citizens of the central universe, beings who never were created. The entire story of the creation of Havona is an attempt to time-space an eternity fact which has no relation to time or space as mortal man comprehends them. But we must concede human philosophy a point of origin; even personalities far above the human level require a concept of "beginnings." Nevertheless, the Paradise-Havona system is eternal.

The natives of Havona live on the billion spheres of the central universe in the same sense that other orders of permanent citizenship dwell on their respective spheres of nativity. As the material order of sonship carries on the material, intellectual, and spiritual economy of a billion local systems in a superuniverse, so, in a larger sense, do the Havona natives live and function on the billion worlds of the central universe. You might possibly regard these Havoners as material creatures in the sense that the word "material" could be expanded to describe the physical realities of the divine universe.

There is a life that is native to Havona and possesses significance in and of itself. Havoners minister in many ways to Paradise descenders and to superuniverse ascenders, but they also live lives that are unique in the central universe and have relative meaning quite apart from either Paradise or the superuniverses.

As the worship of the faith sons of the evolutionary worlds ministers to the satisfaction of the Universal Father's love, so the exalted adoration of the Havona creatures satiates the perfect ideals of divine beauty and truth. As mortal man strives to do the will of God, these beings of the central universe live to gratify the ideals of the Paradise Trinity. In their very nature they *are* the will of God. Man rejoices in the goodness of God, Havoners exult in the divine beauty, while you both enjoy the ministry of the liberty of living truth.

Havoners have both optional present and future unrevealed destinies. And there is a progression of native creatures that is peculiar to the central universe, a progression that involves neither ascent to Paradise nor penetration of the superuniverses. This progression to higher Havona status may be suggested as follows:

1. Experiential progress outward from the first to the seventh circuit.
2. Progress inward from the seventh to the first circuit.
3. Intracircuit progress—progression within the worlds of a given circuit.

In addition to the Havona natives, the inhabitants of the central universe embrace numerous classes of pattern beings for various universe groups—advisers, directors, and teachers of their kind and to their kind throughout creation. All beings in all universes are fashioned along the lines of some one order of pattern creature living on some one of the billion worlds of Havona. Even the mortals of time have their goal and ideals of creature existence on the outer circuits of these pattern spheres on high.

Then there are those beings who have attained the Universal Father, and who are entitled to go and come, who are assigned here and there in the universes on missions of special service. And on every Havona world will be found the attainment candidates, those who have physically attained the central universe, but who have not yet achieved that spiritual development which will enable them to claim Paradise residence.

The Infinite Spirit is represented on the Havona worlds by a host of personalities, beings of grace and glory, who administer the details of the intricate intellectual and spiritual affairs of the central universe. On these worlds of divine perfection they perform the work indigenous to the normal conduct of this vast creation and, in addition, carry on the manifold tasks of teaching, training, and ministering to the enormous numbers of ascendant creatures who have climbed to glory from the dark worlds of space.

There are numerous groups of beings native to the Paradise-Havona system that are in no way directly associated with the ascension scheme of creature perfection attainment; therefore are they omitted from the personality classifications presented to the mortal races. Only the major groups of superhuman beings and those orders directly connected with your survival experience are herein presented.

Havona teems with the life of all phases of intelligent beings, who there seek to advance from lower to higher circuits in their efforts to attain higher levels of divinity realization and enlarged appreciation of supreme meanings, ultimate values, and absolute reality.

5. LIFE IN HAVONA

On Urantia you pass through a short and intense test during your initial life of material existence. On the mansion worlds and up through your system, constellation, and local universe, you traverse the morontia phases of ascension. On the training worlds of the superuniverse you pass through the true spirit stages of progression and are prepared for eventual transit to Havona. On the seven circuits of Havona your attainment is intellectual, spiritual, and experiential. And there is a definite task to be achieved on each of the worlds of each of these circuits.

Life on the divine worlds of the central universe is so rich and full, so complete and replete, that it wholly transcends the human concept of anything a created being could possibly experience. The social and economic activities of this eternal creation are entirely dissimilar to the occupations of material creatures living on evolutionary worlds like Urantia. Even the technique of Havona thought is unlike the process of thinking on Urantia.

The regulations of the central universe are fittingly and inherently natural; the rules of conduct are not arbitrary. In every requirement of Havona there is disclosed the reason of righteousness and the rule of justice. And these two factors, combined, equal what on Urantia would be denominated *fairness.* When you arrive in Havona, you will naturally enjoy doing things the way they should be done.

When intelligent beings first attain the central universe, they are received and domiciled on the pilot world of the seventh Havona circuit. As the new arrivals progress spiritually, attain identity comprehension of their superuniverse Master Spirit, they are transferred to the sixth circle. (It is from these arrangements in the central universe that the circles of progress in the human mind have been designated.) After ascenders have attained a realization of Supremacy and are thereby prepared for the Deity adventure, they are taken to the fifth circuit; and after attaining the Infinite Spirit, they are transferred to the fourth. Following the attainment of the Eternal Son, they are removed to the third; and when they have recognized the Universal Father, they go to sojourn on the second circuit of worlds, where they become more familiar with the Paradise hosts. Arrival on the first circuit of Havona signifies the acceptance of the candidates of time into the service of Paradise. Indefinitely, according to the length and nature of the creature ascension, they will tarry on the inner circuit of progressive spiritual attainment. From this inner circuit the ascending pilgrims pass inward to Paradise residence and admission to the Corps of the Finality.

During your sojourn in Havona as a pilgrim of ascent, you will be allowed to visit freely among the worlds of the circuit of your assignment. You will also be permitted to go back to the planets of those circuits you have previously traversed. And all this is possible to those who sojourn on the circles of Havona without the necessity of being ensupernaphimed. The pilgrims of time are able to equip themselves to traverse "achieved" space but must depend on the ordained technique to negotiate "unachieved" space; a pilgrim cannot leave Havona nor go forward beyond his assigned circuit without the aid of a transport supernaphim.

There is a refreshing originality about this vast central creation. Aside from the physical organization of matter and the fundamental constitution of the basic orders of intelligent beings and other living things, there is nothing in common between the worlds of Havona. Every one of these planets is an original, unique, and exclusive creation; each planet is a matchless, superb, and perfect production. And this diversity of individuality extends to all features of the physical, intellectual, and spiritual aspects of planetary existence. Each of these billion perfection spheres has been developed and embellished in accordance with the plans of the resident Eternal of Days. And this is just why no two of them are alike.

Not until you traverse the last of the Havona circuits and visit the last of the Havona worlds, will the tonic of adventure and the stimulus of curiosity disappear from your career. And then will the urge, the forward impulse of eternity, replace its forerunner, the adventure lure of time.

Monotony is indicative of immaturity of the creative imagination and inactivity of intellectual co-ordination with the spiritual endowment. By the time an ascendant mortal begins the exploration of these heavenly worlds, he has already attained emotional, intellectual, and social, if not spiritual, maturity.

Not only will you find undreamed-of changes confronting you as you advance from circuit to circuit in Havona, but your astonishment will be inexpressible as you progress from planet to planet within each circuit. Each of these billion study worlds is a veritable university of surprises. Continuing astonishment, unending wonder, is the experience of those who traverse these circuits and tour these gigantic spheres. Monotony is not a part of the Havona career.

Love of adventure, curiosity, and dread of monotony—these traits inherent in evolving human nature—were not put there just to aggravate and annoy you during your short sojourn on earth, but rather to suggest to you that death is only the beginning of an endless career of adventure, an everlasting life of anticipation, an eternal voyage of discovery.

Curiosity—the spirit of investigation, the urge of discovery, the drive of exploration—is a part of the inborn and divine endowment of evolutionary space creatures. These natural impulses were not given you merely to be frustrated and repressed. True, these ambitious urges must frequently be restrained during your short life on earth, disappointment must be often experienced, but they are to be fully realized and gloriously gratified during the long ages to come.

6. THE PURPOSE OF THE CENTRAL UNIVERSE

The range of the activities of seven-circuited Havona is enormous. In general, they may be described as:

1. Havonal.
2. Paradisiacal.
3. Ascendant-finite—Supreme-Ultimate evolutional.

Many superfinite activities take place in the Havona of the present universe age, involving untold diversities of absonite and other phases of mind and spirit functions. It is possible that the central universe serves many purposes which are not revealed to me, as it functions in numerous ways beyond the comprehension of the created mind. Nevertheless, I will endeavor to depict how this perfect creation ministers to the needs and contributes to the satisfactions of seven orders of universe intelligence.

1. *The Universal Father*—the First Source and Center. God the Father derives supreme parental satisfaction from the perfection of the central creation. He enjoys the experience of love satiety on near-equality levels. The perfect Creator is divinely pleased with the adoration of the perfect creature.

Havona affords the Father supreme achievement gratification. The perfection realization in Havona compensates for the time-space delay of the eternal urge of infinite expansion.

The Father enjoys the Havona reciprocation of the divine beauty. It satisfies the divine mind to afford a perfect pattern of exquisite harmony for all evolving universes.

Our Father beholds the central universe with perfect pleasure because it is a worthy revelation of spirit reality to all personalities of the universe of universes.

The God of universes has favorable regard for Havona and Paradise as the eternal power nucleus for all subsequent universe expansion in time and space.

The eternal Father views with never-ending satisfaction the Havona creation as the worthy and alluring goal for the ascension candidates of time, his mortal grandchildren of space achieving their Creator-Father's eternal home. And God takes pleasure in the Paradise-Havona universe as the eternal home of Deity and the divine family.

2. *The Eternal Son*—the Second Source and Center. To the Eternal Son the superb central creation affords eternal proof of the partnership effectiveness of the divine family—Father, Son, and Spirit. It is the spiritual and material basis for absolute confidence in the Universal Father.

Havona affords the Eternal Son an almost unlimited base for the ever-expanding realization of spirit power. The central universe afforded the Eternal Son the arena wherein he could safely and securely demonstrate the spirit and technique of the bestowal ministry for the instruction of his associate Paradise Sons.

Havona is the reality foundation for the Eternal Son's spirit-gravity control of the universe of universes. This universe affords the Son the gratification of parental craving, spiritual reproduction.

The Havona worlds and their perfect inhabitants are the first and the eternally final demonstration that the Son is the Word of the Father. Thereby is the consciousness of the Son as an infinite complement of the Father perfectly gratified.

And this universe affords the opportunity for the realization of reciprocation of equality fraternity between the Universal Father and the Eternal Son, and this constitutes the everlasting proof of the infinite personality of each.

3. *The Infinite Spirit*—the Third Source and Center. The Havona universe affords the Infinite Spirit proof of being the Conjoint Actor, the infinite representative of the unified Father-Son. In Havona the Infinite Spirit derives the combined satisfaction of functioning as a creative activity while enjoying the satisfaction of absolute coexistence with this divine achievement.

In Havona the Infinite Spirit found an arena wherein he could demonstrate the ability and willingness to serve as a potential mercy minister. In this perfect creation the Spirit rehearsed for the adventure of ministry in the evolutionary universes.

This perfect creation afforded the Infinite Spirit opportunity to participate in universe administration with both divine parents—to administer a universe as associate-Creator offspring, thereby preparing for the joint administration of the local universes as the Creative Spirit associates of the Creator Sons.

The Havona worlds are the mind laboratory of the creators of the cosmic mind and the ministers to every creature mind in existence. Mind is different on each Havona world and serves as the pattern for all spiritual and material creature intellects.

These perfect worlds are the mind graduate schools for all beings destined for Paradise society. They afforded the Spirit abundant opportunity to test out the technique of mind ministry on safe and advisory personalities.

Havona is a compensation to the Infinite Spirit for his widespread and unselfish work in the universes of space. Havona is the perfect home and retreat for the untiring Mind Minister of time and space.

4. *The Supreme Being*—the evolutionary unification of experiential Deity. The Havona creation is the eternal and perfect proof of the spiritual reality of the Supreme Being. This perfect creation is a revelation of the perfect and symmetrical spirit nature of God the Supreme before the beginnings of the power-personality synthesis of the finite reflections of the Paradise Deities in the experiential universes of time and space.

In Havona the power potentials of the Almighty are unified with the spiritual nature of the Supreme. This central creation is an exemplification of the future-eternal unity of the Supreme.

Havona is a perfect pattern of the universality potential of the Supreme. This universe is a finished portrayal of the future perfection of the Supreme and is suggestive of the potential of the Ultimate.

Havona exhibits finality of spirit values existing as living will creatures of supreme and perfect self-control; mind existing as ultimately equivalent to spirit; reality and unity of intelligence with an unlimited potential.

5. *The Co-ordinate Creator Sons.* Havona is the educational training ground where the Paradise Michaels are prepared for their subsequent adventures in universe creation. This divine and perfect creation is a pattern for every Creator Son. He strives to make his own universe eventually attain to these Paradise-Havona levels of perfection.

A Creator Son uses the creatures of Havona as personality-pattern possibilities for his own mortal children and spirit beings. The Michael and other Paradise Sons view Paradise and Havona as the divine destiny of the children of time.

The Creator Sons know that the central creation is the real source of that indispensable universe overcontrol which stabilizes and unifies their local universes. They know that the personal presence of the ever-present influence of the Supreme and of the Ultimate is in Havona.

Havona and Paradise are the source of a Michael Son's creative power. Here dwell the beings who co-operate with him in universe creation. From Paradise come the Universe Mother Spirits, the cocreators of local universes.

The Paradise Sons regard the central creation as the home of their divine parents—their home. It is the place they enjoy returning to ever and anon.

6. *The Co-ordinate Ministering Daughters.* The Universe Mother Spirits, cocreators of the local universes, secure their prepersonal training on the worlds of Havona in close association with the Spirits of the Circuits. In the central universe the Spirit Daughters of the local universes were duly trained in the methods of co-operation with the Sons of Paradise, all the while subject to the will of the Father.

On the worlds of Havona the Spirit and the Daughters of the Spirit find the mind patterns for all their groups of spiritual and material intelligences, and this central universe is the sometime destiny of those creatures which a Universe Mother Spirit jointly sponsors with an associated Creator Son.

The Universe Mother Creator remembers Paradise and Havona as the place of her origin and the home of the Infinite Mother Spirit, the abode of the personality presence of the Infinite Mind.

From this central universe also came the bestowal of the personal prerogatives of creatorship which a Universe Divine Minister employs as complemental to a Creator Son in the work of creating living will creatures.

And lastly, since these Daughter Spirits of the Infinite Mother Spirit will not likely ever return to their Paradise home, they derive great satisfaction from the universal reflectivity phenomenon associated with the Supreme Being in Havona and personalized in Majeston on Paradise.

7. *The Evolutionary Mortals of the Ascending Career.* Havona is the home of the pattern personality of every mortal type and the home of all superhuman personalities of mortal association who are not native to the creations of time.

These worlds provide the stimulus of all human impulses towards the attainment of true spirit values on the highest conceivable reality levels. Havona is the pre-Paradise training goal of every ascending mortal. Here mortals attain pre-Paradise Deity—the Supreme Being. Havona stands before every will creature as the portal to Paradise and God attainment.

Paradise is the home, and Havona the workshop and playground, of the finaliters. And every God-knowing mortal craves to be a finaliter.

The central universe is not only man's established destiny, but it is also the starting place of the eternal career of the finaliters as they shall sometime be started out on the undisclosed and universal adventure in the experience of exploring the infinity of the Universal Father.

Havona will unquestionably continue to function with absonite significance even in future universe ages which may witness space pilgrims attempting to find God on superfinite levels. Havona has capacity to serve as a training universe for absonite beings. It will probably be the finishing school when the seven superuniverses are functioning as the intermediate school for the graduates of the primary schools of outer space. And we incline to the opinion that the potentials of eternal Havona are really unlimited, that the central universe has eternal capacity to serve as an experiential training universe for all past, present, or future types of created beings.

[Presented by a Perfector of Wisdom commissioned thus to function by the Ancients of Days on Uversa.]

PAPER 15

THE SEVEN SUPERUNIVERSES

AS FAR as the Universal Father is concerned—as a Father—the universes are virtually nonexistent; he deals with personalities; he is the Father of personalities. As far as the Eternal Son and the Infinite Spirit are concerned—as creator partners—the universes are localized and individual under the joint rule of the Creator Sons and the Creative Spirits. As far as the Paradise Trinity is concerned, outside Havona there are just seven inhabited universes, the seven superuniverses which hold jurisdiction over the circle of the first post-Havona space level. The Seven Master Spirits radiate their influence out from the central Isle, thus constituting the vast creation one gigantic wheel, the hub being the eternal Isle of Paradise, the seven spokes the radiations of the Seven Master Spirits, the rim the outer regions of the grand universe.

Early in the materialization of the universal creation the sevenfold scheme of the superuniverse organization and government was formulated. The first post-Havona creation was divided into seven stupendous segments, and the headquarters worlds of these superuniverse governments were designed and constructed. The present scheme of administration has existed from near eternity, and the rulers of these seven superuniverses are rightly called Ancients of Days.

Of the vast body of knowledge concerning the superuniverses, I can hope to tell you little, but there is operative throughout these realms a technique of intelligent control for both physical and spiritual forces, and the universal gravity presences there function in majestic power and perfect harmony. It is important first to gain an adequate idea of the physical constitution and material organization of the superuniverse domains, for then you will be the better prepared to grasp the significance of the marvelous organization provided for their spiritual government and for the intellectual advancement of the will creatures who dwell on the myriads of inhabited planets scattered hither and yon throughout these seven superuniverses.

1. THE SUPERUNIVERSE SPACE LEVEL

Within the limited range of the records, observations, and memories of the generations of a million or a billion of your short years, to all practical intents and purposes, Urantia and the universe to which it belongs are experiencing the adventure of one long and uncharted plunge into new space; but according to the records of Uversa, in accordance with older observations, in harmony with the more extensive experience and calculations of our order, and as a result of conclusions based on these and other findings, we know that the universes are engaged in an orderly, well-understood, and perfectly controlled processional, swinging in majestic grandeur around the First Great Source and Center and his residential universe.

We have long since discovered that the seven superuniverses traverse a great ellipse, a gigantic and elongated circle. Your solar system and other worlds of time are not plunging headlong, without chart and compass, into unmapped space. The local universe to which your system belongs is pursuing a definite and well-understood counterclockwise course around the vast swing that encircles the central universe. This cosmic path is well charted and is just as thoroughly known to the superuniverse star observers as the orbits of the planets constituting your solar system are known to Urantia astronomers.

Urantia is situated in a local universe and a superuniverse not fully organized, and your local universe is in immediate proximity to numerous partially completed physical creations. You belong to one of the relatively recent universes. But you are not, today, plunging on wildly into uncharted space nor swinging out blindly into unknown regions. You are following the orderly and predetermined path of the superuniverse space level. You are now passing through the very same space that your planetary system, or its predecessors, traversed ages ago; and some day in the remote future your system, or its successors, will again traverse the identical space through which you are now so swiftly plunging.

In this age and as direction is regarded on Urantia, superuniverse number one swings almost due north, approximately opposite, in an easterly direction, to the Paradise residence of the Great Sources and Centers and the central universe of Havona. This position, with the corresponding one to the west, represents the nearest physical approach of the spheres of time to the eternal Isle. Superuniverse number two is in the north, preparing for the westward swing, while number three now holds the northernmost segment of the great space path, having already turned into the bend leading to the southerly plunge. Number four is on the comparatively straightaway southerly flight, the advance regions now approaching opposition to the Great Centers. Number five has about left its position opposite the Center of Centers while continuing on the direct southerly course just preceding the eastward swing; number six occupies most of the southern curve, the segment from which your superuniverse has nearly passed.

Your local universe of Nebadon belongs to Orvonton, the seventh superuniverse, which swings on between superuniverses one and six, having not long since (as we reckon time) turned the southeastern bend of the superuniverse space level. Today, the solar system to which Urantia belongs is a few billion years past the swing around the southern curvature so that you are just now advancing beyond the southeastern bend and are moving swiftly through the long and comparatively straightaway northern path. For untold ages Orvonton will pursue this almost direct northerly course.

Urantia belongs to a system which is well out towards the borderland of your local universe; and your local universe is at present traversing the periphery of Orvonton. Beyond you there are still others, but you are far removed in space from those physical systems which swing around the great circle in comparative proximity to the Great Source and Center.

2. ORGANIZATION OF THE SUPERUNIVERSES

Only the Universal Father knows the location and actual number of inhabited worlds in space; he calls them all by name and number. I can give only the approximate number of inhabited or inhabitable planets, for some local universes have more worlds suitable for intelligent life than others. Nor have all projected local universes been organized. Therefore the estimates which I offer are solely for the purpose of affording some idea of the immensity of the material creation.

There are seven superuniverses in the grand universe, and they are constituted approximately as follows:

1. *The System.* The basic unit of the supergovernment consists of about one thousand inhabited or inhabitable worlds. Blazing suns, cold worlds, planets too near the hot suns, and other spheres not suitable for creature habitation are not included in this group. These one thousand worlds adapted to support life are called a system, but in the younger systems only a comparatively small number of these worlds may be inhabited. Each inhabited planet is presided over by a Planetary Prince, and each local system has an architectural sphere as its headquarters and is ruled by a System Sovereign.

2. *The Constellation.* One hundred systems (about 100,000 inhabitable planets) make up a constellation. Each constellation has an architectural headquarters sphere and is presided over by three Vorondadek Sons, the Most Highs. Each constellation also has a Faithful of Days in observation, an ambassador of the Paradise Trinity.

3. *The Local Universe.* One hundred constellations (about 10,000,000 inhabitable planets) constitute a local universe. Each local universe has a magnificent architectural headquarters world and is ruled by one of the co-ordinate Creator Sons of God of the order of Michael. Each universe is blessed by the presence of a Union of Days, a representative of the Paradise Trinity.

4. *The Minor Sector.* One hundred local universes (about 1,000,000,000 inhabitable planets) constitute a minor sector of the superuniverse government; it has a wonderful headquarters world, wherefrom its rulers, the Recents of Days, administer the affairs of the minor sector. There are three Recents of Days, Supreme Trinity Personalities, on each minor sector headquarters.

5. *The Major Sector.* One hundred minor sectors (about 100,000,000,000 inhabitable worlds) make one major sector. Each major sector is provided with a superb headquarters and is presided over by three Perfections of Days, Supreme Trinity Personalities.

6. *The Superuniverse.* Ten major sectors (about 1,000,000,000,000 inhabitable planets) constitute a superuniverse. Each superuniverse is provided with an enormous and glorious headquarters world and is ruled by three Ancients of Days.

7. *The Grand Universe.* Seven superuniverses make up the present organized grand universe, consisting of approximately seven trillion inhabitable worlds plus the architectural spheres and the one billion inhabited spheres of Havona. The superuniverses are ruled and administered indirectly and reflectively from Paradise by the Seven Master Spirits. The billion worlds of Havona are directly administered by the Eternals of Days, one such Supreme Trinity Personality presiding over each of these perfect spheres.

Excluding the Paradise-Havona spheres, the plan of universe organization provides for the following units:

Superuniverses	7
Major sectors	70
Minor sectors	7,000
Local universes	700,000
Constellations	70,000,000
Local systems	7,000,000,000
Inhabitable planets	7,000,000,000,000

Each of the seven superuniverses is constituted, approximately, as follows:

One system embraces, approximately	1,000 worlds
One constellation (100 systems)	100,000 worlds
One universe (100 constellations)	10,000,000 worlds
One minor sector (100 universes)	1,000,000,000 worlds
One major sector (100 minor sectors)	100,000,000,000 worlds
One superuniverse (10 major sectors)	1,000,000,000,000 worlds

All such estimates are approximations at best, for new systems are constantly evolving while other organizations are temporarily passing out of material existence.

3. THE SUPERUNIVERSE OF ORVONTON

Practically all of the starry realms visible to the naked eye on Urantia belong to the seventh section of the grand universe, the superuniverse of Orvonton. The vast Milky Way starry system represents the central nucleus of Orvonton, being largely beyond the borders of your local universe. This great aggregation of suns, dark islands of space, double stars, globular clusters, star clouds, spiral and other nebulae, together with myriads of individual planets, forms a watchlike, elongated-circular grouping of about one seventh of the inhabited evolutionary universes.

From the astronomical position of Urantia, as you look through the cross section of near-by systems to the great Milky Way, you observe that the spheres of Orvonton are traveling in a vast elongated plane, the breadth being far greater than the thickness and the length far greater than the breadth.

Observation of the so-called Milky Way discloses the comparative increase in Orvonton stellar density when the heavens are viewed in one direction, while on either side the density diminishes; the number of stars and other spheres decreases away from the chief plane of our material superuniverse. When the angle of observation is propitious, gazing through the main body of this realm of maximum density, you are looking toward the residential universe and the center of all things.

Of the ten major divisions of Orvonton, eight have been roughly identified by Urantian astronomers. The other two are difficult of separate recognition because you are obliged to view these phenomena from the inside. If you could look upon the superuniverse of Orvonton from a position far-distant in space, you would immediately recognize the ten major sectors of the seventh galaxy.

The rotational center of your minor sector is situated far away in the enormous and dense star cloud of Sagittarius, around which your local universe and its associated creations all move, and from opposite sides of the vast Sagittarius subgalactic system you may observe two great streams of star clouds emerging in stupendous stellar coils.

The nucleus of the physical system to which your sun and its associated planets belong is the center of the onetime Andronover nebula. This former spiral nebula was slightly distorted by the gravity disruptions associated with the events which were attendant upon the birth of your solar system, and which were occasioned by the near approach of a large neighboring nebula. This near collision changed Andronover into a somewhat globular aggregation but did not wholly destroy the two-way procession of the suns and their associated physical groups. Your solar system now occupies a fairly central position in one of the arms of this distorted spiral, situated about halfway from the center out towards the edge of the star stream.

The Sagittarius sector and all other sectors and divisions of Orvonton are in rotation around Uversa, and some of the confusion of Urantian star observers arises out of the illusions and relative distortions produced by the following multiple revolutionary movements:

1. The revolution of Urantia around its sun.

2. The circuit of your solar system about the nucleus of the former Andronover nebula.

3. The rotation of the Andronover stellar family and the associated clusters about the composite rotation-gravity center of the star cloud of Nebadon.

4. The swing of the local star cloud of Nebadon and its associated creations around the Sagittarius center of their minor sector.

5. The rotation of the one hundred minor sectors, including Sagittarius, about their major sector.

6. The whirl of the ten major sectors, the so-called star drifts, about the Uversa headquarters of Orvonton.

7. The movement of Orvonton and six associated superuniverses around Paradise and Havona, the counterclockwise processional of the superuniverse space level.

These multiple motions are of several orders: The space paths of your planet and your solar system are genetic, inherent in origin. The absolute counterclockwise motion of Orvonton is also genetic, inherent in the architectural plans of the master universe. But the intervening motions are of composite origin, being derived in part from the constitutive segmentation of matter-energy into the superuniverses and in part produced by the intelligent and purposeful action of the Paradise force organizers.

The local universes are in closer proximity as they approach Havona; the circuits are greater in number, and there is increased superimposition, layer upon layer. But farther out from the eternal center there are fewer and fewer systems, layers, circuits, and universes.

4. NEBULAE—THE ANCESTORS OF UNIVERSES

While creation and universe organization remain forever under the control of the infinite Creators and their associates, the whole phenomenon proceeds in accordance with an ordained technique and in conformity to the gravity laws of force, energy, and matter. But there is something of mystery associated with the universal force-charge of space; we quite understand the organization of the material creations from the ultimatonic stage forward, but we do not fully comprehend the cosmic ancestry of the ultimatons. We are confident that these ancestral forces have a Paradise origin because they forever swing through pervaded space in the exact gigantic outlines of Paradise. Though nonresponsive to Paradise gravity, this force-charge of space, the ancestor of all materialization, does always respond to the presence of nether Paradise, being apparently circuited in and out of the nether Paradise center.

The Paradise force organizers transmute space potency into primordial force and evolve this prematerial potential into the primary and secondary energy manifestations of physical reality. When this energy attains gravity-responding levels, the power directors and their associates of the superuniverse regime appear upon the scene and begin their never-ending manipulations designed to establish the manifold power circuits and energy channels of the universes of time and space. Thus does physical matter appear in space, and so is the stage set for the inauguration of universe organization.

This segmentation of energy is a phenomenon which has never been solved by the physicists of Nebadon. Their chief difficulty lies in the relative inaccessibility of the Paradise force organizers, for the living power directors, though they are competent to deal with space-energy, do not have the least conception of the origin of the energies they so skillfully and intelligently manipulate.

Paradise force organizers are nebulae originators; they are able to initiate about their space presence the tremendous cyclones of force which, when once started, can never be stopped or limited until the all-pervading forces are mobilized for the eventual appearance of the ultimatonic units of universe matter. Thus are brought into being the spiral and other nebulae, the mother wheels of the direct-origin suns and their varied systems. In outer space there may be seen ten different forms of nebulae, phases of primary universe evolution, and these vast energy wheels had the same origin as did those in the seven superuniverses.

Nebulae vary greatly in size and in the resulting number and aggregate mass of their stellar and planetary offspring. A sun-forming nebula just north of the borders of Orvonton, but within the superuniverse space level, has already given origin to approximately forty thousand suns, and the mother wheel is still throwing off suns, the majority of which are many times the size of yours. Some of the larger nebulae of outer space are giving origin to as many as one hundred million suns.

Nebulae are not directly related to any of the administrative units, such as minor sectors or local universes, although some local universes have been organized from the products of a single nebula. Each local universe embraces exactly one one-hundred-thousandth part of the total energy charge of a superuniverse irrespective of nebular relationship, for energy is not organized by nebulae—it is universally distributed.

Not all spiral nebulae are engaged in sun making. Some have retained control of many of their segregated stellar offspring, and their spiral appearance is occasioned by the fact that their suns pass out of the nebular arm in close formation but return by diverse routes, thus making it easy to observe them at one point but more difficult to see them when widely scattered on their different returning routes farther out and away from the arm of the nebula. There are not many sun-forming nebulae active in Orvonton at the present time, though Andromeda, which is outside the inhabited superuniverse, is very active. This far-distant nebula is visible to the naked eye, and when you view it, pause to consider that the light you behold left those distant suns almost one million years ago.

The Milky Way galaxy is composed of vast numbers of former spiral and other nebulae, and many still retain their original configuration. But as the result of internal catastrophes and external attraction, many have suffered such distortion and rearrangement as to cause these enormous aggregations to appear as gigantic luminous masses of blazing suns, like the Magellanic Cloud. The globular type of star clusters predominates near the outer margins of Orvonton.

The vast star clouds of Orvonton should be regarded as individual aggregations of matter comparable to the separate nebulae observable in the space regions external to the Milky Way galaxy. Many of the so-called star clouds of space, however, consist of gaseous material only. The energy potential of these stellar gas clouds is unbelievably enormous, and some of it is taken up by near-by suns and redispatched in space as solar emanations.

5. THE ORIGIN OF SPACE BODIES

The bulk of the mass contained in the suns and planets of a superuniverse originates in the nebular wheels; very little of superuniverse mass is organized by the direct action of the power directors (as in the construction of architectural spheres), although a constantly varying quantity of matter originates in open space.

As to origin, the majority of the suns, planets, and other spheres can be classified in one of the following ten groups:

1. *Concentric Contraction Rings.* Not all nebulae are spiral. Many an immense nebula, instead of splitting into a double star system or evolving as a spiral, undergoes condensation by multiple-ring formation. For long periods such a nebula appears as an enormous central sun surrounded by numerous gigantic clouds of encircling, ring-appearing formations of matter.

2. *The Whirled Stars* embrace those suns which are thrown off the great mother wheels of highly heated gases. They are not thrown off as rings but in right- and left-handed processions. Whirled stars are also of origin in other-than-spiral nebulae.

3. *Gravity-explosion Planets.* When a sun is born of a spiral or of a barred nebula, not infrequently it is thrown out a considerable distance. Such a sun is highly gaseous, and subsequently, after it has somewhat cooled and condensed, it may chance to swing near some enormous mass of matter, a gigantic sun or a dark island of space. Such an approach may not be near enough to result in collision but still near enough to allow the gravity pull of the greater body to start tidal convulsions in the lesser, thus initiating a series of tidal upheavals which occur simultaneously on opposite sides of the convulsed sun. At their height

these explosive eruptions produce a series of varying-sized aggregations of matter which may be projected beyond the gravity-reclamation zone of the erupting sun, thus becoming stabilized in orbits of their own around one of the two bodies concerned in this episode. Later on the larger collections of matter unite and gradually draw the smaller bodies to themselves. In this way many of the solid planets of the lesser systems are brought into existence. Your own solar system had just such an origin.

4. *Centrifugal Planetary Daughters.* Enormous suns, when in certain stages of development, and if their revolutionary rate greatly accelerates, begin to throw off large quantities of matter which may subsequently be assembled to form small worlds that continue to encircle the parent sun.

5. *Gravity-deficiency Spheres.* There is a critical limit to the size of individual stars. When a sun reaches this limit, unless it slows down in revolutionary rate, it is doomed to split; sun fission occurs, and a new double star of this variety is born. Numerous small planets may be subsequently formed as a by-product of this gigantic disruption.

6. *Contractural Stars.* In the smaller systems the largest outer planet sometimes draws to itself its neighboring worlds, while those planets near the sun begin their terminal plunge. With your solar system, such an end would mean that the four inner planets would be claimed by the sun, while the major planet, Jupiter, would be greatly enlarged by capturing the remaining worlds. Such an end of a solar system would result in the production of two adjacent but unequal suns, one type of double star formation. Such catastrophes are infrequent except out on the fringe of the superuniverse starry aggregations.

7. *Cumulative Spheres.* From the vast quantity of matter circulating in space, small planets may slowly accumulate. They grow by meteoric accretion and by minor collisions. In certain sectors of space, conditions favor such forms of planetary birth. Many an inhabited world has had such an origin.

Some of the dense dark islands are the direct result of the accretions of transmuting energy in space. Another group of these dark islands have come into being by the accumulation of enormous quantities of cold matter, mere fragments and meteors, circulating through space. Such aggregations of matter have never been hot and, except for density, are in composition very similar to Urantia.

8. *Burned-out Suns.* Some of the dark islands of space are burned-out isolated suns, all available space-energy having been emitted. The organized units of matter approximate full condensation, virtual complete consolidation; and it requires ages upon ages for such enormous masses of highly condensed matter to be recharged in the circuits of space and thus to be prepared for new cycles of universe function following a collision or some equally revivifying cosmic happening.

9. *Collisional Spheres.* In those regions of thicker clustering, collisions are not uncommon. Such an astronomic readjustment is accompanied by tremendous energy changes and matter transmutations. Collisions involving dead suns are peculiarly influential in creating widespread energy fluctuations. Collisional debris often constitutes the material nucleuses for the subsequent formation of planetary bodies adapted to mortal habitation.

10. *Architectural Worlds.* These are the worlds which are built according to plans and specifications for some special purpose, such as Salvington, the headquarters of your local universe, and Uversa, the seat of government of our superuniverse.

There are numerous other techniques for evolving suns and segregating planets, but the foregoing procedures suggest the methods whereby the vast majority of stellar systems and planetary families are brought into existence. To undertake to describe all the various techniques involved in stellar metamorphosis and planetary evolution would require the narration of almost one hundred different modes of sun formation and planetary origin. As your star students scan the heavens, they will observe phenomena indicative of all these modes of stellar evolution, but they will seldom detect evidence of the formation of those small, nonluminous collections of matter which serve as inhabited planets, the most important of the vast material creations.

6. THE SPHERES OF SPACE

Irrespective of origin, the various spheres of space are classifiable into the following major divisions:

1. The suns—the stars of space.
2. The dark islands of space.
3. Minor space bodies—comets, meteors, and planetesimals.
4. The planets, including the inhabited worlds.
5. Architectural spheres—worlds made to order.

With the exception of the architectural spheres, all space bodies have had an evolutionary origin, evolutionary in the sense that they have not been brought into being by fiat of Deity, evolutionary in the sense that the creative acts of God have unfolded by a time-space technique through the operation of many of the created and eventuated intelligences of Deity.

The Suns. These are the stars of space in all their various stages of existence. Some are solitary evolving space systems; others are double stars, contracting or disappearing planetary systems. The stars of space exist in no less than a thousand different states and stages. You are familiar with suns that emit light accompanied by heat; but there are also suns which shine without heat.

The trillions upon trillions of years that an ordinary sun will continue to give out heat and light well illustrates the vast store of energy which each unit of matter contains. The actual energy stored in these invisible particles of physical matter is well-nigh unimaginable. And this energy becomes almost wholly available as light when subjected to the tremendous heat pressure and the associated energy activities which prevail in the interior of the blazing suns. Still other conditions enable these suns to transform and send forth much of the energy of space which comes their way in the established space circuits. Many phases of physical energy and all forms of matter are attracted to, and subsequently distributed by, the solar dynamos. In this way the suns serve as local accelerators of energy circulation, acting as automatic power-control stations.

The superuniverse of Orvonton is illuminated and warmed by more than ten trillion blazing suns. These suns are the stars of your observable astronomic system. More than two trillion are too distant and too small ever to be seen from

Urantia. But in the master universe there are as many suns as there are glasses of water in the oceans of your world.

The Dark Islands of Space. These are the dead suns and other large aggregations of matter devoid of light and heat. The dark islands are sometimes enormous in mass and exert a powerful influence in universe equilibrium and energy manipulation. The density of some of these large masses is well-nigh unbelievable. And this great concentration of mass enables these dark islands to function as powerful balance wheels, holding large neighboring systems in effective leash. They hold the gravity balance of power in many constellations; many physical systems which would otherwise speedily dive to destruction in near-by suns are held securely in the gravity grasp of these guardian dark islands. It is because of this function that we can locate them accurately. We have measured the gravity pull of the luminous bodies, and we can therefore calculate the exact size and location of the dark islands of space which so effectively function to hold a given system steady in its course.

Minor Space Bodies. The meteors and other small particles of matter circulating and evolving in space constitute an enormous aggregate of energy and material substance.

Many comets are unestablished wild offspring of the solar mother wheels, which are being gradually brought under control of the central governing sun. Comets also have numerous other origins. A comet's tail points away from the attracting body or sun because of the electrical reaction of its highly expanded gases and because of the actual pressure of light and other energies emanating from the sun. This phenomenon constitutes one of the positive proofs of the reality of light and its associated energies; it demonstrates that light has weight. Light is a real substance, not simply waves of hypothetical ether.

The Planets. These are the larger aggregations of matter which follow an orbit around a sun or some other space body; they range in size from planetesimals to enormous gaseous, liquid, or solid spheres. The cold worlds which have been built up by the assemblage of floating space material, when they happen to be in proper relation to a near-by sun, are the more ideal planets to harbor intelligent inhabitants. The dead suns are not, as a rule, suited to life; they are usually too far away from a living, blazing sun, and further, they are altogether too massive; gravity is tremendous at the surface.

In your superuniverse not one cool planet in forty is habitable by beings of your order. And, of course, the superheated suns and the frigid outlying worlds are unfit to harbor higher life. In your solar system only three planets are at present suited to harbor life. Urantia, in size, density, and location, is in many respects ideal for human habitation.

The laws of physical-energy behavior are basically universal, but local influences have much to do with the physical conditions which prevail on individual planets and in local systems. An almost endless variety of creature life and other living manifestations characterizes the countless worlds of space. There are, however, certain points of similarity in a group of worlds associated in a given system, while there also is a universe pattern of intelligent life. There are physical relationships among those planetary systems which belong to the same physical circuit, and which closely follow each other in the endless swing around the circle of universes.

7. THE ARCHITECTURAL SPHERES

While each superuniverse government presides near the center of the evolutionary universes of its space segment, it occupies a world made to order and is peopled by accredited personalities. These headquarters worlds are architectural spheres, space bodies specifically constructed for their special purpose. While sharing the light of near-by suns, these spheres are independently lighted and heated. Each has a sun which gives forth light without heat, like the satellites of Paradise, while each is supplied with heat by the circulation of certain energy currents near the surface of the sphere. These headquarters worlds belong to one of the greater systems situated near the astronomical center of their respective superuniverses.

Time is standardized on the headquarters of the superuniverses. The standard day of the superuniverse of Orvonton is equal to almost thirty days of Urantia time, and the Orvonton year equals one hundred standard days. This Uversa year is standard in the seventh superuniverse, and it is twenty-two minutes short of three thousand days of Urantia time, about eight and one fifth of your years.

The headquarters worlds of the seven superuniverses partake of the nature and grandeur of Paradise, their central pattern of perfection. In reality, all headquarters worlds are paradisiacal. They are indeed heavenly abodes, and they increase in material size, morontia beauty, and spirit glory from Jerusem to the central Isle. And all the satellites of these headquarters worlds are also architectural spheres.

The various headquarters worlds are provided with every phase of material and spiritual creation. All kinds of material, morontial, and spiritual beings are at home on these rendezvous worlds of the universes. As mortal creatures ascend the universe, passing from the material to the spiritual realms, they never lose their appreciation for, and enjoyment of, their former levels of existence.

Jerusem, the headquarters of your local system of Satania, has its seven worlds of transition culture, each of which is encircled by seven satellites, among which are the seven mansion worlds of morontia detention, man's first postmortal residence. As the term heaven has been used on Urantia, it has sometimes meant these seven mansion worlds, the first mansion world being denominated the first heaven, and so on to the seventh.

Edentia, the headquarters of your constellation of Norlatiadek, has its seventy satellites of socializing culture and training, on which ascenders sojourn upon the completion of the Jerusem regime of personality mobilization, unification, and realization.

Salvington, the capital of Nebadon, your local universe, is surrounded by ten university clusters of forty-nine spheres each. Hereon is man spiritualized following his constellation socialization.

Uminor the third, the headquarters of your minor sector, Ensa, is surrounded by the seven spheres of the higher physical studies of the ascendant life.

Umajor the fifth, the headquarters of your major sector, Splandon, is surrounded by the seventy spheres of the advancing intellectual training of the superuniverse.

Uversa, the headquarters of Orvonton, your superuniverse, is immediately surrounded by the seven higher universities of advanced spiritual training for ascending will creatures. Each of these seven clusters of wonder spheres consists of seventy specialized worlds containing thousands upon thousands of replete institutions and organizations devoted to universe training and spirit culture wherein the pilgrims of time are re-educated and re-examined preparatory to their long flight to Havona. The arriving pilgrims of time are always received on these associated worlds, but the departing graduates are always dispatched for Havona direct from the shores of Uversa.

Uversa is the spiritual and administrative headquarters for approximately one trillion inhabited or inhabitable worlds. The glory, grandeur, and perfection of the Orvonton capital surpass any of the wonders of the time-space creations.

If all the projected local universes and their component parts were established, there would be slightly less than five hundred billion architectural worlds in the seven superuniverses.

8. ENERGY CONTROL AND REGULATION

The headquarters spheres of the superuniverses are so constructed that they are able to function as efficient power-energy regulators for their various sectors, serving as focal points for the directionization of energy to their component local universes. They exert a powerful influence over the balance and control of the physical energies circulating through organized space.

Further regulative functions are performed by the superuniverse power centers and physical controllers, living and semiliving intelligent entities constituted for this express purpose. These power centers and controllers are difficult of understanding; the lower orders are not volitional, they do not possess will, they do not choose, their functions are very intelligent but apparently automatic and inherent in their highly specialized organization. The power centers and physical controllers of the superuniverses assume direction and partial control of the thirty energy systems which comprise the gravita domain. The physical-energy circuits administered by the power centers of Uversa require a little over 968 million years to complete the encirclement of the superuniverse.

Evolving energy has substance; it has weight, although weight is always relative, depending on revolutionary velocity, mass, and antigravity. Mass in matter tends to retard velocity in energy; and the anywhere-present velocity of energy represents: the initial endowment of velocity, minus retardation by mass encountered in transit, plus the regulatory function of the living energy controllers of the superuniverse and the physical influence of near-by highly heated or heavily charged bodies.

The universal plan for the maintenance of equilibrium between matter and energy necessitates the everlasting making and unmaking of the lesser material units. The Universe Power Directors have the ability to condense and detain, or to expand and liberate, varying quantities of energy.

Given a sufficient duration of retarding influence, gravity would eventually convert all energy into matter were it not for two factors: First, because of the antigravity influences of the energy controllers, and second, because organized matter tends to disintegrate under certain conditions found in very hot stars and under certain peculiar conditions in space near highly energized cold bodies of condensed matter.

When mass becomes overaggregated and threatens to unbalance energy, to deplete the physical power circuits, the physical controllers intervene unless gravity's own further tendency to overmaterialize energy is defeated by the occurrence of a collision among the dead giants of space, thus in an instant completely dissipating the cumulative collections of gravity. In these collisional episodes enormous masses of matter are suddenly converted into the rarest form of energy, and the struggle for universal equilibrium is begun anew. Eventually the larger physical systems become stabilized, become physically settled, and are swung into the balanced and established circuits of the superuniverses. Subsequent to this event no more collisions or other devastating catastrophes will occur in such established systems.

During the times of plus energy there are power disturbances and heat fluctuations accompanied by electrical manifestations. During times of minus energy there are increased tendencies for matter to aggregate, condense, and to get out of control in the more delicately balanced circuits, with resultant tidal or collisional adjustments which quickly restore the balance between circulating energy and more literally stabilized matter. To forecast and otherwise to understand such likely behavior of the blazing suns and the dark islands of space is one of the tasks of the celestial star observers.

We are able to recognize most of the laws governing universe equilibrium and to predict much pertaining to universe stability. Practically, our forecasts are reliable, but we are always confronted by certain forces which are not wholly amenable to the laws of energy control and matter behavior known to us. The predictability of all physical phenomena becomes increasingly difficult as we proceed outward in the universes from Paradise. As we pass beyond the borders of the personal administration of the Paradise Rulers, we are confronted with increasing inability to reckon in accordance with the standards established and the experience acquired in connection with observations having exclusively to do with the physical phenomena of the near-by astronomic systems. Even in the realms of the seven superuniverses we are living in the midst of force actions and energy reactions which pervade all our domains and extend in unified equilibrium on through all regions of outer space.

The farther out we go, the more certainly we encounter those variational and unpredictable phenomena which are so unerringly characteristic of the unfathomable presence-performances of the Absolutes and the experiential Deities. And these phenomena must be indicative of some universal overcontrol of all things.

The superuniverse of Orvonton is apparently now running down; the outer universes seem to be winding up for unparalleled future activities; the central Havona universe is eternally stabilized. Gravity and absence of heat (cold) organize and hold matter together; heat and antigravity disrupt matter and dissipate energy. The living power directors and force organizers are the secret of the special control and intelligent direction of the endless metamorphoses of universe making, unmaking, and remaking. Nebulae may disperse, suns burn out, systems vanish, and planets perish, but the universes do not run down.

9. CIRCUITS OF THE SUPERUNIVERSES

The universal circuits of Paradise do actually pervade the realms of the seven superuniverses. These presence circuits are: the personality gravity of the Universal Father, the spiritual gravity of the Eternal Son, the mind gravity of the Conjoint Actor, and the material gravity of the eternal Isle.

In addition to the universal Paradise circuits and in addition to the presence-performances of the Absolutes and the experiential Deities, there function within the superuniverse space level only two energy-circuit divisions or power segregations: the superuniverse circuits and the local universe circuits.

The Superuniverse Circuits:

1. The unifying intelligence circuit of one of the Seven Master Spirits of Paradise. Such a cosmic-mind circuit is limited to a single superuniverse.

2. The reflective-service circuit of the seven Reflective Spirits in each superuniverse.

3. The secret circuits of the Mystery Monitors, in some manner inter-associated and routed by Divinington to the Universal Father on Paradise.

4. The circuit of the intercommunion of the Eternal Son with his Paradise Sons.

5. The flash presence of the Infinite Spirit.

6. The broadcasts of Paradise, the space reports of Havona.

7. The energy circuits of the power centers and the physical controllers.

The Local Universe Circuits:

1. The bestowal spirit of the Paradise Sons, the Comforter of the bestowal worlds. The Spirit of Truth, the spirit of Michael on Urantia.

2. The circuit of the Divine Ministers, the local universe Mother Spirits, the Holy Spirit of your world.

3. The intelligence-ministry circuit of a local universe, including the diversely functioning presence of the adjutant mind-spirits.

When there develops such a spiritual harmony in a local universe that its individual and combined circuits become indistinguishable from those of the superuniverse, when such identity of function and oneness of ministry actually prevail, then does the local universe immediately swing into the settled circuits of light and life, becoming at once eligible for admission into the spiritual confederation of the perfected union of the supercreation. The requisites for admission to the councils of the Ancients of Days, membership in the superuniverse confederation, are:

1. *Physical Stability.* The stars and planets of a local universe must be in equilibrium; the periods of immediate stellar metamorphosis must be over. The universe must be proceeding on a clear track; its orbit must be safely and finally settled.

2. *Spiritual Loyalty.* There must exist a state of universal recognition of, and loyalty to, the Sovereign Son of God who presides over the affairs of such a local universe. There must have come into being a state of harmonious co-operation between the individual planets, systems, and constellations of the entire local universe.

Your local universe is not even reckoned as belonging to the settled physical order of the superuniverse, much less as holding membership in the recognized spiritual family of the supergovernment. Although Nebadon does not yet have representation on Uversa, we of the superuniverse government are dispatched to its worlds on special missions from time to time, even as I have come to Urantia directly from Uversa. We lend every possible assistance to your directors and rulers in the solution of their difficult problems; we are desirous of seeing your universe qualified for full admission into the associated creations of the superuniverse family.

10. RULERS OF THE SUPERUNIVERSES

The headquarters of the superuniverses are the seats of the high spiritual government of the time-space domains. The executive branch of the supergovernment, taking origin in the Councils of the Trinity, is immediately directed by one of the Seven Master Spirits of supreme supervision, beings who sit upon seats of Paradise authority and administer the superuniverses through the Seven Supreme Executives stationed on the seven special worlds of the Infinite Spirit, the outermost satellites of Paradise.

The superuniverse headquarters are the abiding places of the Reflective Spirits and the Reflective Image Aids. From this midway position these marvelous beings conduct their tremendous reflectivity operations, thus ministering to the central universe above and to the local universes below.

Each superuniverse is presided over by three Ancients of Days, the joint chief executives of the supergovernment. In its executive branch the personnel of the superuniverse government consists of seven different groups:

1. Ancients of Days.
2. Perfectors of Wisdom.
3. Divine Counselors.
4. Universal Censors.
5. Mighty Messengers.
6. Those High in Authority.
7. Those without Name and Number.

The three Ancients of Days are immediately assisted by a corps of one billion Perfectors of Wisdom, with whom are associated three billion Divine Counselors. One billion Universal Censors are attached to each superuniverse administration. These three groups are Co-ordinate Trinity Personalities, taking origin directly and divinely in the Paradise Trinity.

The remaining three orders, Mighty Messengers, Those High in Authority, and Those without Name and Number, are glorified ascendant mortals. The first of these orders came up through the ascendant regime and passed through Havona in the days of Grandfanda. Having attained Paradise, they were mustered into the Corps of the Finality, embraced by the Paradise Trinity, and subsequently assigned to the supernal service of the Ancients of Days. As a class, these three orders are known as Trinitized Sons of Attainment, being of dual origin but now of Trinity service. Thus was the executive branch of the superuniverse government enlarged to include the glorified and perfected children of the evolutionary worlds.

The co-ordinate council of the superuniverse is composed of the seven executive groups previously named and the following sector rulers and other regional overseers:

1. Perfections of Days—the rulers of the superuniverse major sectors.

2. Recents of Days—the directors of the superuniverse minor sectors.

3. Unions of Days—the Paradise advisers to the rulers of the local universes.

4. Faithfuls of Days—the Paradise counselors to the Most High rulers of the constellation governments.

5. Trinity Teacher Sons who may chance to be on duty at superuniverse headquarters.

6. Eternals of Days who may happen to be present at superuniverse headquarters.

7. The seven Reflective Image Aids—the spokesmen of the seven Reflective Spirits and through them representatives of the Seven Master Spirits of Paradise.

The Reflective Image Aids also function as the representatives of numerous groups of beings who are influential in the superuniverse governments, but who are not, at present, for various reasons, fully active in their individual capacities. Embraced within this group are: the evolving superuniverse personality manifestation of the Supreme Being, the Unqualified Supervisors of the Supreme, the Qualified Vicegerents of the Ultimate, the unnamed liaison reflectivators of Majeston, and the superpersonal spirit representatives of the Eternal Son.

At almost all times it is possible to find representatives of all groups of created beings on the headquarters worlds of the superuniverses. The routine ministering work of the superuniverses is performed by the mighty seconaphim and by other members of the vast family of the Infinite Spirit. In the work of these marvelous centers of superuniverse administration, control, ministry, and executive judgment, the intelligences of every sphere of universal life are mingled in effective service, wise administration, loving ministry, and just judgment.

The superuniverses do not maintain any sort of ambassadorial representation; they are completely isolated from each other. They know of mutual affairs only through the Paradise clearinghouse maintained by the Seven Master Spirits. Their rulers work in the councils of divine wisdom for the welfare of their own superuniverses regardless of what may be transpiring in other sections of the universal creation. This isolation of the superuniverses will persist until such time as their co-ordination is achieved by the more complete factualization of the personality-sovereignty of the evolving experiential Supreme Being.

11. THE DELIBERATIVE ASSEMBLY

It is on such worlds as Uversa that the beings representative of the autocracy of perfection and the democracy of evolution meet face to face. The executive branch of the supergovernment originates in the realms of perfection; the legislative branch springs from the flowering of the evolutionary universes.

The deliberative assembly of the superuniverse is confined to the headquarters world. This legislative or advisory council consists of seven houses, to each of which every local universe admitted to the superuniverse councils elects a native representative. These representatives are chosen by the high councils of such local universes from among the ascending-pilgrim graduates of Orvonton who are tarrying on Uversa, accredited for transport to Havona. The average term of service is about one hundred years of superuniverse standard time.

Never have I known of a disagreement between the Orvonton executives and the Uversa assembly. Never yet, in the history of our superuniverse, has the deliberative body ever passed a recommendation that the executive division of the supergovernment has even hesitated to carry out. There always has prevailed the most perfect harmony and working agreement, all of which testifies to the fact that evolutionary beings can really attain the heights of perfected wisdom which qualifies them to consort with the personalities of perfect origin and divine nature. The presence of the deliberative assemblies on the superuniverse headquarters reveals the wisdom, and foreshadows the ultimate triumph, of the whole vast evolutionary concept of the Universal Father and his Eternal Son.

12. THE SUPREME TRIBUNALS

When we speak of executive and deliberative branches of the Uversa government, you may, from the analogy of certain forms of Urantian civil government, reason that we must have a third or judicial branch, and we do; but it does not have a separate personnel. Our courts are constituted as follows: There presides, in accordance with the nature and gravity of the case, an Ancient of Days, a Perfector of Wisdom, or a Divine Counselor. The evidence for or against an individual, a planet, system, constellation, or universe is presented and interpreted by the Censors. The defense of the children of time and the evolutionary planets is offered by the Mighty Messengers, the official observers of the superuniverse government to the local universes and systems. The attitude of the higher government is portrayed by Those High in Authority. And ordinarily the verdict is formulated by a varying-sized commission consisting equally of Those without Name and Number and a group of understanding personalities chosen from the deliberative assembly.

The courts of the Ancients of Days are the high review tribunals for the spiritual adjudication of all component universes. The Sovereign Sons of the local universes are supreme in their own domains; they are subject to the supergovernment only in so far as they voluntarily submit matters for counsel or adjudication by the Ancients of Days except in matters involving the extinction of will creatures. Mandates of judgment originate in the local universes, but sentences involving the extinction of will creatures are always formulated on, and executed from, the headquarters of the superuniverse. The Sons of the local universes can decree the survival of mortal man, but only the Ancients of Days may sit in executive judgment on the issues of eternal life and death.

In all matters not requiring trial, the submission of evidence, the Ancients of Days or their associates render decisions, and these rulings are always unanimous. We are here dealing with the councils of perfection. There are no disagreements nor minority opinions in the decrees of these supreme and superlative tribunals.

With certain few exceptions the supergovernments exercise jurisdiction over all things and all beings in their respective domains. There is no appeal from the rulings and decisions of the superuniverse authorities since they represent the concurred opinions of the Ancients of Days and that Master Spirit who, from Paradise, presides over the destiny of the superuniverse concerned.

13. THE SECTOR GOVERNMENTS

A *major sector* comprises about one tenth of a superuniverse and consists of one hundred minor sectors, ten thousand local universes, about one hundred billion inhabitable worlds. These major sectors are administered by three Perfections of Days, Supreme Trinity Personalities.

The courts of the Perfections of Days are constituted much as are those of the Ancients of Days except that they do not sit in spiritual judgment upon the realms. The work of these major sector governments has chiefly to do with the intellectual status of a far-flung creation. The major sectors detain, adjudicate, dispense, and tabulate, for reporting to the courts of the Ancients of Days, all matters of superuniverse importance of a routine and administrative nature which are not immediately concerned with the spiritual administration of the realms or with the outworking of the mortal-ascension plans of the Paradise Rulers. The personnel of a major sector government is no different from that of the superuniverse.

As the magnificent satellites of Uversa are concerned with your final spiritual preparation for Havona, so are the seventy satellites of Umajor the fifth devoted to your superuniverse intellectual training and development. From all Orvonton, here are gathered together the wise beings who labor untiringly to prepare the mortals of time for their further progress towards the career of eternity. Most of this training of ascending mortals is conducted on the seventy study worlds.

The *minor sector* governments are presided over by three Recents of Days. Their administration is concerned mainly with the physical control, unification, stabilization, and routine co-ordination of the administration of the component local universes. Each minor sector embraces as many as one hundred local universes, ten thousand constellations, one million systems, or about one billion inhabitable worlds.

Minor sector headquarters worlds are the grand rendezvous of the Master Physical Controllers. These headquarters worlds are surrounded by the seven instruction spheres which constitute the entrance schools of the superuniverse and are the centers of training for physical and administrative knowledge concerning the universe of universes.

The administrators of the minor sector governments are under the immediate jurisdiction of the major sector rulers. The Recents of Days receive all reports of observations and co-ordinate all recommendations which come up to a superuniverse from the Unions of Days who are stationed as Trinity observers and advisers on the headquarters spheres of the local universes and from the Faithfuls of Days who are similarly attached to the councils of the Most Highs at the headquarters of the constellations. All such reports are transmitted to the Perfections of Days on the major sectors, subsequently to be passed on to the courts of the Ancients of Days. Thus the Trinity regime extends from the constellations of the local universes up to the headquarters of the superuniverse. The local system headquarters do not have Trinity representatives.

14. PURPOSES OF THE SEVEN SUPERUNIVERSES

There are seven major purposes which are being unfolded in the evolution of the seven superuniverses. Each major purpose in superuniverse evolution will find fullest expression in only one of the seven superuniverses, and therefore does each superuniverse have a special function and a unique nature.

Orvonton, the seventh superuniverse, the one to which your local universe belongs, is known chiefly because of its tremendous and lavish bestowal of merciful ministry to the mortals of the realms. It is renowned for the manner in which justice prevails as tempered by mercy and power rules as conditioned by patience, while the sacrifices of time are freely made to secure the stabilization of eternity. Orvonton is a universe demonstration of love and mercy.

It is, however, very difficult to describe our conception of the true nature of the evolutionary purpose which is unfolding in Orvonton, but it may be suggested by saying that in this supercreation we feel that the six unique purposes of cosmic evolution as manifested in the six associated supercreations are here being interassociated into a meaning-of-the-whole; and it is for this reason that we have sometimes conjectured that the evolved and finished personalization of God the Supreme will in the remote future and from Uversa rule the perfected seven superuniverses in all the experiential majesty of his then attained almighty sovereign power.

As Orvonton is unique in nature and individual in destiny, so also is each of its six associated superuniverses. A great deal that is going on in Orvonton is not, however, revealed to you, and of these unrevealed features of Orvonton life, many are to find most complete expression in some other superuniverse. The seven purposes of superuniverse evolution are operative throughout all seven superuniverses, but each supercreation will give fullest expression to only one of these purposes. To understand more about these superuniverse purposes, much that you do not understand would have to be revealed, and even then you would comprehend but little. This entire narrative presents only a fleeting glimpse of the immense creation of which your world and local system are a part.

Your world is called Urantia, and it is number 606 in the planetary group, or system, of Satania. This system has at present 619 inhabited worlds, and more than two hundred additional planets are evolving favorably toward becoming inhabited worlds at some future time.

Satania has a headquarters world called Jerusem, and it is system number twenty-four in the constellation of Norlatiadek. Your constellation, Norlatiadek, consists of one hundred local systems and has a headquarters world called Edentia. Norlatiadek is number seventy in the universe of Nebadon. The local universe of Nebadon consists of one hundred constellations and has a capital known as Salvington. The universe of Nebadon is number eighty-four in the minor sector of Ensa.

The minor sector of Ensa consists of one hundred local universes and has a capital called Uminor the third. This minor sector is number three in the major sector of Splandon. Splandon consists of one hundred minor sectors and has a headquarters world called Umajor the fifth. It is the fifth major sector of the superuniverse of Orvonton, the seventh segment of the grand universe. Thus you can locate your planet in the scheme of the organization and administration of the universe of universes.

The grand universe number of your world, Urantia, is 5,342,482,337,666. That is the registry number on Uversa and on Paradise, your number in the catalogue of the inhabited worlds. I know the physical-sphere registry number, but it is of such an extraordinary size that it is of little practical significance to the mortal mind.

Your planet is a member of an enormous cosmos; you belong to a well-nigh infinite family of worlds, but your sphere is just as precisely administered and just as lovingly fostered as if it were the only inhabited world in all existence.

[Presented by a Universal Censor hailing from Uversa.]

PAPER 16

THE SEVEN MASTER SPIRITS

THE Seven Master Spirits of Paradise are the primary personalities of the Infinite Spirit. In this sevenfold creative act of self-duplication the Infinite Spirit exhausted the associative possibilities mathematically inherent in the factual existence of the three persons of Deity. Had it been possible to produce a larger number of Master Spirits, they would have been created, but there are just seven associative possibilities, and only seven, inherent in three Deities. And this explains why the universe is operated in seven grand divisions, and why the number seven is basically fundamental in its organization and administration.

The Seven Master Spirits thus have their origin in, and derive their individual characteristics from, the following seven likenesses:

1. The Universal Father.
2. The Eternal Son.
3. The Infinite Spirit.
4. The Father and the Son.
5. The Father and the Spirit.
6. The Son and the Spirit.
7. The Father, Son, and Spirit.

We know very little about the action of the Father and the Son in the creation of the Master Spirits. Apparently they were brought into existence by the personal acts of the Infinite Spirit, but we have been definitely instructed that both the Father and the Son participated in their origin.

In spirit character and nature these Seven Spirits of Paradise are as one, but in all other aspects of identity they are very unlike, and the results of their functioning in the superuniverses are such that the individual differences of each are unmistakably discernible. All the afterplans of the seven segments of the grand universe—and even the correlative segments of outer space—have been conditioned by the other-than-spiritual diversity of these Seven Master Spirits of supreme and ultimate supervision.

The Master Spirits have many functions, but at the present time their particular domain is the central supervision of the seven superuniverses. Each Master Spirit maintains an enormous force-focal headquarters, which slowly circulates around the periphery of Paradise, always maintaining a position opposite the superuniverse of immediate supervision and at the Paradise focal point of its specialized power control and segmental energy distribution. The radial boundary lines of any one of the superuniverses do actually converge at the Paradise headquarters of the supervising Master Spirit.

1. RELATION TO TRIUNE DEITY

The Conjoint Creator, the Infinite Spirit, is necessary to the completion of the triune personalization of undivided Deity. This threefold Deity personalization is inherently sevenfold in possibility of individual and associative expression; hence the subsequent plan to create universes inhabited by intelligent and potentially spiritual beings, duly expressive of the Father, Son, and Spirit, made the personalization of the Seven Master Spirits inescapable. We have come to speak of the threefold personalization of Deity as the *absolute inevitability,* while we have come to look upon the appearance of the Seven Master Spirits as the *subabsolute inevitability.*

While the Seven Master Spirits are hardly expressive of *threefold* Deity, they are the eternal portrayal of *sevenfold* Deity, the active and associative functions of the three ever-existent persons of Deity. By and in and through these Seven Spirits, the Universal Father, the Eternal Son, or the Infinite Spirit, or any dual association, is able to function as such. When the Father, the Son, and the Spirit act together, they can and do function through Master Spirit Number Seven, but not as the Trinity. The Master Spirits singly and collectively represent any and all possible Deity functions, single and several, but not collective, not the Trinity. Master Spirit Number Seven is personally nonfunctional with regard to the Paradise Trinity, and that is just why he can function *personally* for the Supreme Being.

But when the Seven Master Spirits vacate their individual seats of personal power and superuniverse authority and assemble about the Conjoint Actor in the triune presence of Paradise Deity, then and there are they collectively representative of the functional power, wisdom, and authority of undivided Deity—the Trinity—to and in the evolving universes. Such a Paradise union of the primal sevenfold expression of Deity does actually embrace, literally encompass, all of every attribute and attitude of the three eternal Deities in Supremacy and in Ultimacy. To all practical intents and purposes the Seven Master Spirits do, then and there, encompass the functional domain of the Supreme-Ultimate to and in the master universe.

As far as we can discern, these Seven Spirits are associated with the divine activities of the three eternal persons of Deity; we detect no evidence of direct association with the functioning presences of the three eternal phases of the Absolute. When associated, the Master Spirits represent the Paradise Deities in what may be roughly conceived as the finite domain of action. It might embrace much that is ultimate but *not* absolute.

2. RELATION TO THE INFINITE SPIRIT

Just as the Eternal and Original Son is revealed through the persons of the constantly increasing number of divine Sons, so is the Infinite and Divine Spirit revealed through the channels of the Seven Master Spirits and their associated spirit groups. At the center of centers the Infinite Spirit is approachable, but not all who attain Paradise are immediately able to discern his personality and differentiated presence; but all who attain the central universe can and do immediately commune with one of the Seven Master Spirits, the one presiding over the superuniverse from which the newly arrived space pilgrim hails.

To the universe of universes the Paradise Father speaks only through his Son, while he and the Son conjointly act only through the Infinite Spirit. Outside of Paradise and Havona the Infinite Spirit *speaks* only by the voices of the Seven Master Spirits.

The Infinite Spirit exerts an influence of *personal presence* within the confines of the Paradise-Havona system; elsewhere his personal spirit presence is exerted by and through one of the Seven Master Spirits. Therefore is the superuniverse spirit presence of the Third Source and Center on any world or in any individual conditioned by the unique nature of the supervisory Master Spirit of that segment of creation. Conversely, the combined lines of spirit force and intelligence pass inward to the Third Person of Deity by way of the Seven Master Spirits.

The Seven Master Spirits are collectively endowed with the supreme-ultimate attributes of the Third Source and Center. While each one individually partakes of this endowment, only collectively do they disclose the attributes of omnipotence, omniscience, and omnipresence. No one of them can so function universally; as individuals and in the exercise of these powers of supremacy and ultimacy each is personally limited to the superuniverse of immediate supervision.

All of everything which has been told you concerning the divinity and personality of the Conjoint Actor applies equally and fully to the Seven Master Spirits, who so effectively distribute the Infinite Spirit to the seven segments of the grand universe in accordance with their divine endowment and in the manner of their differing and individually unique natures. It would therefore be proper to apply to the collective group of seven any or all of the names of the Infinite Spirit. Collectively they are one with the Conjoint Creator on all subabsolute levels.

3. IDENTITY AND DIVERSITY OF THE MASTER SPIRITS

The Seven Master Spirits are indescribable beings, but they are distinctly and definitely personal. They have names, but we elect to introduce them by number. As primary personalizations of the Infinite Spirit, they are akin, but as primary expressions of the seven possible associations of triune Deity, they are essentially diverse in nature, and this diversity of nature determines their differential of superuniverse conduct. These Seven Master Spirits may be described as follows:

Master Spirit Number One. In a special manner this Spirit is the direct representation of the Paradise Father. He is a peculiar and efficient manifestation of the power, love, and wisdom of the Universal Father. He is the close associate and supernal adviser of the chief of Mystery Monitors, that being who presides over the College of Personalized Adjusters on Divinington. In all associations of the Seven Master Spirits, it is always Master Spirit Number One who speaks for the Universal Father.

This Spirit presides over the first superuniverse and, while unfailingly exhibiting the divine nature of a primary personalization of the Infinite Spirit, seems more especially to resemble the Universal Father in character. He is always in personal liaison with the seven Reflective Spirits at the headquarters of the first superuniverse.

Master Spirit Number Two. This Spirit adequately portrays the matchless nature and charming character of the Eternal Son, the first-born of all creation. He is always in close association with all orders of the Sons of God whenever they may happen to be in the residential universe as individuals or in joyous conclave. In all the assemblies of the Seven Master Spirits he always speaks for, and in behalf of, the Eternal Son.

This Spirit directs the destinies of superuniverse number two and rules this vast domain much as would the Eternal Son. He is always in liaison with the seven Reflective Spirits situated at the capital of the second superuniverse.

Master Spirit Number Three. This Spirit personality especially resembles the Infinite Spirit, and he directs the movements and work of many of the high personalities of the Infinite Spirit. He presides over their assemblies and is closely associated with all personalities who take exclusive origin in the Third Source and Center. When the Seven Master Spirits are in council, it is Master Spirit Number Three who always speaks for the Infinite Spirit.

This Spirit is in charge of superuniverse number three, and he administers the affairs of this segment much as would the Infinite Spirit. He is always in liaison with the Reflective Spirits at the headquarters of the third superuniverse.

Master Spirit Number Four. Partaking of the combined natures of the Father and the Son, this Master Spirit is the determining influence regarding Father-Son policies and procedures in the councils of the Seven Master Spirits. This Spirit is the chief director and adviser of those ascendant beings who have attained the Infinite Spirit and thus have become candidates for seeing the Son and the Father. He fosters that enormous group of personalities taking origin in the Father and the Son. When it becomes necessary to represent the Father and the Son in the association of the Seven Master Spirits, it is always Master Spirit Number Four who speaks.

This Spirit fosters the fourth segment of the grand universe in accordance with his peculiar association of the attributes of the Universal Father and the Eternal Son. He is always in personal liaison with the Reflective Spirits of the headquarters of the fourth superuniverse.

Master Spirit Number Five. This divine personality who exquisitely blends the character of the Universal Father and the Infinite Spirit is the adviser of that enormous group of beings known as the power directors, power centers, and physical controllers. This Spirit also fosters all personalities taking origin in the Father and the Conjoint Actor. In the councils of the Seven Master Spirits, when the Father-Spirit attitude is in question, it is always Master Spirit Number Five who speaks.

This Spirit directs the welfare of the fifth superuniverse in such a way as to suggest the combined action of the Universal Father and the Infinite Spirit. He is always in liaison with the Reflective Spirits at the headquarters of the fifth superuniverse.

Master Spirit Number Six. This divine being seems to portray the combined character of the Eternal Son and the Infinite Spirit. Whenever the creatures jointly created by the Son and the Spirit forgather in the central universe, it is this Master Spirit who is their adviser; and whenever, in the councils of the Seven Master Spirits, it becomes necessary to speak conjointly for the Eternal Son and the Infinite Spirit, it is Master Spirit Number Six who responds.

This Spirit directs the affairs of the sixth superuniverse much as would the Eternal Son and the Infinite Spirit. He is always in liaison with the Reflective Spirits at the headquarters of the sixth superuniverse.

Master Spirit Number Seven. The presiding Spirit of the seventh superuniverse is a uniquely equal portrayal of the Universal Father, the Eternal Son, and the Infinite Spirit. The Seventh Spirit, the fostering adviser of all triune-origin beings, is also the adviser and director of all the ascending pilgrims of Havona, those lowly beings who have attained the courts of glory through the combined ministry of the Father, the Son, and the Spirit.

The Seventh Master Spirit is not organically representative of the Paradise Trinity; but it is a known fact that his personal and spiritual nature *is* the Conjoint Actor's portraiture in equal proportions of the three infinite persons whose Deity union *is* the Paradise Trinity, and whose function as such *is* the source of the personal and spiritual nature of God the Supreme. Hence the Seventh Master Spirit discloses a personal and organic relationship to the spirit person of the evolving Supreme. Therefore in the Master Spirit councils on high, when it becomes necessary to cast the ballot for the combined personal attitude of the Father, Son, and Spirit or to depict the spiritual attitude of the Supreme Being, it is Master Spirit Number Seven who functions. He thus inherently becomes the presiding head of the Paradise council of the Seven Master Spirits.

No one of the Seven Spirits is organically representative of the Paradise Trinity, but when they unite as sevenfold Deity, this union in a deity sense—not in a personal sense—equivalates to a functional level associable with Trinity functions. In this sense the "Sevenfold Spirit" is functionally associable with the Paradise Trinity. It is also in this sense that Master Spirit Number Seven sometimes speaks in confirmation of Trinity attitudes or, rather, acts as spokesman for the attitude of the Sevenfold-Spirit-union regarding the attitude of the Threefold-Deity-union, the attitude of the Paradise Trinity.

The multiple functions of the Seventh Master Spirit thus range from a combined portraiture of the *personal natures* of the Father, Son, and Spirit, through a representation of the *personal attitude* of God the Supreme, to a disclosure of the *deity attitude* of the Paradise Trinity. And in certain respects this presiding Spirit is similarly expressive of the *attitudes* of the Ultimate and of the Supreme-Ultimate.

It is Master Spirit Number Seven who, in his multiple capacities, personally sponsors the progress of the ascension candidates from the worlds of time in their attempts to achieve comprehension of the undivided Deity of Supremacy. Such comprehension involves a grasp of the existential sovereignty of the Trinity of Supremacy so co-ordinated with a concept of the growing experiential sovereignty of the Supreme Being as to constitute the creature grasp of the unity of Supremacy. Creature realization of these three factors equals Havona comprehension of Trinity reality and endows the pilgrims of time with the ability eventually to penetrate the Trinity, to discover the three infinite persons of Deity.

The inability of the Havona pilgrims fully to find God the Supreme is compensated by the Seventh Master Spirit, whose triune nature in such a peculiar manner is revelatory of the spirit person of the Supreme. During the present universe age of the noncontactability of the person of the Supreme, Master Spirit Number Seven functions in the place of the God of ascendant creatures in the matter of personal relationships. He is the one high spirit being that all ascenders are certain to recognize and somewhat comprehend when they reach the centers of glory.

This Master Spirit is always in liaison with the Reflective Spirits of Uversa, the headquarters of the seventh superuniverse, our own segment of creation. His administration of Orvonton discloses the marvelous symmetry of the co-ordinate blending of the divine natures of Father, Son, and Spirit.

4. ATTRIBUTES AND FUNCTIONS OF THE MASTER SPIRITS

The Seven Master Spirits are the full representation of the Infinite Spirit to the evolutionary universes. They represent the Third Source and Center in the relationships of energy, mind, and spirit. While they function as the co-ordinating heads of the universal administrative control of the Conjoint Actor, do not forget that they have their origin in the creative acts of the Paradise Deities. It is literally true that these Seven Spirits are the personalized physical power, cosmic mind, and spiritual presence of the triune Deity, "the Seven Spirits of God sent forth to all the universe."

The Master Spirits are unique in that they function on all universe levels of reality excepting the absolute. They are, therefore, efficient and perfect supervisors of all phases of administrative affairs on all levels of superuniverse activities. It is difficult for the mortal mind to understand very much about the Master Spirits because their work is so highly specialized yet all-embracing, so exceptionally material and at the same time so exquisitely spiritual. These versatile creators of the cosmic mind are the ancestors of the Universe Power Directors and are, themselves, supreme directors of the vast and far-flung spirit-creature creation.

The Seven Master Spirits are the creators of the Universe Power Directors and their associates, entities who are indispensable to the organization, control, and regulation of the physical energies of the grand universe. And these same Master Spirits very materially assist the Creator Sons in the work of shaping and organizing the local universes.

We are unable to trace any personal connection between the cosmic-energy work of the Master Spirits and the force functions of the Unqualified Absolute. The energy manifestations under the jurisdiction of the Master Spirits are all directed from the periphery of Paradise; they do not appear to be in any direct manner associated with the force phenomena identified with the nether surface of Paradise.

Unquestionably, when we encounter the functional activities of the various Morontia Power Supervisors, we are face to face with certain of the unrevealed activities of the Master Spirits. Who, aside from these ancestors of both physical controllers and spirit ministers, could have contrived so to combine and associate material and spiritual energies as to produce a hitherto nonexistent phase of universe reality—morontia substance and morontia mind?

Much of the reality of the spiritual worlds is of the morontia order, a phase of universe reality wholly unknown on Urantia. The goal of personality existence is spiritual, but the morontia creations always intervene, bridging the gulf between the material realms of mortal origin and the superuniverse spheres of advancing spiritual status. It is in this realm that the Master Spirits make their great contribution to the plan of man's Paradise ascension.

The Seven Master Spirits have personal representatives who function throughout the grand universe; but since a large majority of these subordinate beings are not directly concerned with the ascendant scheme of mortal progression in the path of Paradise perfection, little or nothing has been revealed about them. Much, very much, of the activity of the Seven Master Spirits remains hidden from human understanding because in no way does it directly pertain to your problem of Paradise ascent.

It is highly probable, though we cannot offer definite proof, that the Master Spirit of Orvonton exerts a decided influence in the following spheres of activity:

1. The life-initiation procedures of the local universe Life Carriers.

2. The life activations of the adjutant mind-spirits bestowed upon the worlds by a local universe Creative Spirit.

3. The fluctuations in energy manifestations exhibited by the linear-gravity-responding units of organized matter.

4. The behavior of emergent energy when fully liberated from the grasp of the Unqualified Absolute, thus becoming responsive to the direct influence of linear gravity and to the manipulations of the Universe Power Directors and their associates.

5. The bestowal of the ministry spirit of a local universe Creative Spirit, known on Urantia as the Holy Spirit.

6. The subsequent bestowal of the spirit of the bestowal Sons, on Urantia called the Comforter or the Spirit of Truth.

7. The reflectivity mechanism of the local universes and the superuniverse. Many features connected with this extraordinary phenomenon can hardly be reasonably explained or rationally understood without postulating the activity of the Master Spirits in association with the Conjoint Actor and the Supreme Being.

Notwithstanding our failure adequately to comprehend the manifold workings of the Seven Master Spirits, we are confident there are two realms in the vast range of universe activities with which they have nothing whatever to do: the bestowal and ministry of the Thought Adjusters and the inscrutable functions of the Unqualified Absolute.

5. RELATION TO CREATURES

Each segment of the grand universe, each individual universe and world, enjoys the benefits of the united counsel and wisdom of all Seven Master Spirits but receives the personal touch and tinge of only one. And the personal nature of each Master Spirit entirely pervades and uniquely conditions his superuniverse.

Through this personal influence of the Seven Master Spirits every creature of every order of intelligent beings, outside of Paradise and Havona, must bear the characteristic stamp of individuality indicative of the ancestral nature of some one of these Seven Paradise Spirits. As concerns the seven superuniverses, each native creature, man or angel, will forever bear this badge of natal identification.

The Seven Master Spirits do not directly invade the material minds of the individual creatures on the evolutionary worlds of space. The mortals of Urantia do not experience the personal presence of the mind-spirit influence of the Master Spirit of Orvonton. If this Master Spirit does attain any sort of contact with the individual mortal mind during the earlier evolutionary ages of an inhabited world, it must occur through the ministry of the local universe Creative Spirit, the consort and associate of the Creator Son of God who presides over the destinies of each local creation. But this very Creative Mother Spirit is, in nature and character, quite like the Master Spirit of Orvonton.

The physical stamp of a Master Spirit is a part of man's material origin. The entire morontia career is lived under the continuing influence of this same Master Spirit. It is hardly strange that the subsequent spirit career of such an ascending mortal never fully eradicates the characteristic stamp of this same supervising Spirit. The impress of a Master Spirit is basic to the very existence of every pre-Havona stage of mortal ascension.

The distinctive personality trends exhibited in the life experience of evolutionary mortals, which are characteristic in each superuniverse, and which are directly expressive of the nature of the dominating Master Spirit, are never fully effaced, not even after such ascenders are subjected to the long training and unifying discipline encountered on the one billion educational spheres of Havona. Even the subsequent intense Paradise culture does not suffice to eradicate the earmarks of superuniverse origin. Throughout all eternity an ascendant mortal will exhibit traits indicative of the presiding Spirit of his superuniverse of nativity. Even in the Corps of the Finality, when it is desired to arrive at or to portray a *complete* Trinity relationship to the evolutionary creation, always a group of seven finaliters is assembled, one from each superuniverse.

6. THE COSMIC MIND

The Master Spirits are the sevenfold source of the cosmic mind, the intellectual potential of the grand universe. This cosmic mind is a subabsolute manifestation of the mind of the Third Source and Center and, in certain ways, is functionally related to the mind of the evolving Supreme Being.

On a world like Urantia we do not encounter the direct influence of the Seven Master Spirits in the affairs of the human races. You live under the immediate influence of the Creative Spirit of Nebadon. Nevertheless these same Master Spirits dominate the basic reactions of all creature mind because they are the actual sources of the intellectual and spiritual potentials which have been specialized in the local universes for function in the lives of those individuals who inhabit the evolutionary worlds of time and space.

The fact of the cosmic mind explains the kinship of various types of human and superhuman minds. Not only are kindred spirits attracted to each other, but kindred minds are also very fraternal and inclined towards co-operation the one with the other. Human minds are sometimes observed to be running in channels of astonishing similarity and inexplicable agreement.

There exists in all personality associations of the cosmic mind a quality which might be denominated the "reality response." It is this universal cosmic endowment of will creatures which saves them from becoming helpless victims of the implied a priori assumptions of science, philosophy, and religion. This reality sensitivity of the cosmic mind responds to certain phases of reality just as energy-material responds to gravity. It would be still more correct to say that these supermaterial realities so respond to the mind of the cosmos.

The cosmic mind unfailingly responds (recognizes response) on three levels of universe reality. These responses are self-evident to clear-reasoning and deep-thinking minds. These levels of reality are:

1. *Causation*—the reality domain of the physical senses, the scientific realms of logical uniformity, the differentiation of the factual and the nonfactual, reflective conclusions based on cosmic response. This is the mathematical form of the cosmic discrimination.

2. *Duty*—the reality domain of morals in the philosophic realm, the arena of reason, the recognition of relative right and wrong. This is the judicial form of the cosmic discrimination.

3. *Worship*—the spiritual domain of the reality of religious experience, the personal realization of divine fellowship, the recognition of spirit values, the assurance of eternal survival, the ascent from the status of servants of God to the joy and liberty of the sons of God. This is the highest insight of the cosmic mind, the reverential and worshipful form of the cosmic discrimination.

These scientific, moral, and spiritual insights, these cosmic responses, are innate in the cosmic mind, which endows all will creatures. The experience of living never fails to develop these three cosmic intuitions; they are constitutive in the self-consciousness of reflective thinking. But it is sad to record that so few persons on Urantia take delight in cultivating these qualities of courageous and independent cosmic thinking.

In the local universe mind bestowals, these three insights of the cosmic mind constitute the a priori assumptions which make it possible for man to function as a rational and self-conscious personality in the realms of science, philosophy, and religion. Stated otherwise, the recognition of the *reality* of these three manifestations of the Infinite is by a cosmic technique of self-revelation. Matter-energy is recognized by the mathematical logic of the senses; mind-reason intuitively knows its moral duty; spirit-faith (worship) is the religion of the reality of spiritual experience. These three basic factors in reflective thinking may be unified and co-ordinated in personality development, or they may become disproportionate and virtually unrelated in their respective functions. But when they become unified, they produce a strong character consisting in the correlation of a factual science, a moral philosophy, and a genuine religious experience. And it is these three cosmic intuitions that give objective validity, reality, to man's experience in and with things, meanings, and values.

It is the purpose of education to develop and sharpen these innate endowments of the human mind; of civilization to express them; of life experience to realize them; of religion to ennoble them; and of personality to unify them.

7. MORALS, VIRTUE, AND PERSONALITY

Intelligence alone cannot explain the moral nature. Morality, virtue, is indigenous to human personality. Moral intuition, the realization of duty, is a component of human mind endowment and is associated with the other inalienables of human nature: scientific curiosity and spiritual insight. Man's mentality far transcends that of his animal cousins, but it is his moral and religious natures that especially distinguish him from the animal world.

The selective response of an animal is limited to the motor level of behavior. The supposed insight of the higher animals is on a motor level and usually appears only after the experience of motor trial and error. Man is able to exercise scientific, moral, and spiritual insight prior to all exploration or experimentation.

Only a personality can know what it is doing before it does it; only personalities possess insight in advance of experience. A personality can look before it leaps and can therefore learn from looking as well as from leaping. A nonpersonal animal ordinarily learns only by leaping.

As a result of experience an animal becomes able to examine the different ways of attaining a goal and to select an approach based on accumulated experience. But a personality can also examine the goal itself and pass judgment on its worth-whileness, its value. Intelligence alone can discriminate as to the best means of attaining indiscriminate ends, but a moral being possesses an insight which enables him to discriminate between ends as well as between means. And a moral being in choosing virtue is nonetheless intelligent. He knows what he is doing, why he is doing it, where he is going, and how he will get there.

When man fails to discriminate the ends of his mortal striving, he finds himself functioning on the animal level of existence. He has failed to avail himself of the superior advantages of that material acumen, moral discrimination, and spiritual insight which are an integral part of his cosmic-mind endowment as a personal being.

Virtue is righteousness—conformity with the cosmos. To name virtues is not to define them, but to live them is to know them. Virtue is not mere knowledge nor yet wisdom but rather the reality of progressive experience in the attainment of ascending levels of cosmic achievement. In the day-by-day life of mortal man, virtue is realized by the consistent choosing of good rather than evil, and such choosing ability is evidence of the possession of a moral nature.

Man's choosing between good and evil is influenced, not only by the keenness of his moral nature, but also by such influences as ignorance, immaturity, and delusion. A sense of proportion is also concerned in the exercise of virtue because evil may be perpetrated when the lesser is chosen in the place of the greater as a result of distortion or deception. The art of relative estimation or comparative measurement enters into the practice of the virtues of the moral realm.

Man's moral nature would be impotent without the art of measurement, the discrimination embodied in his ability to scrutinize meanings. Likewise would moral choosing be futile without that cosmic insight which yields the consciousness of spiritual values. From the standpoint of intelligence, man ascends to the level of a moral being because he is endowed with personality.

Morality can never be advanced by law or by force. It is a personal and freewill matter and must be disseminated by the contagion of the contact of morally fragrant persons with those who are less morally responsive, but who are also in some measure desirous of doing the Father's will.

Moral acts are those human performances which are characterized by the highest intelligence, directed by selective discrimination in the choice of superior ends as well as in the selection of moral means to attain these ends. Such conduct is virtuous. Supreme virtue, then, is wholeheartedly to choose to do the will of the Father in heaven.

8. URANTIA PERSONALITY

The Universal Father bestows personality upon numerous orders of beings as they function on diverse levels of universe actuality. Urantia human beings are endowed with personality of the finite-mortal type, functioning on the level of the ascending sons of God.

Though we can hardly undertake to define personality, we may attempt to narrate our understanding of the known factors which go to make up the ensemble of material, mental, and spiritual energies whose interassociation constitutes the mechanism wherein and whereon and wherewith the Universal Father causes his bestowed personality to function.

Personality is a unique endowment of original nature whose existence is independent of, and antecedent to, the bestowal of the Thought Adjuster. Nevertheless, the presence of the Adjuster does augment the qualitative manifestation of personality. Thought Adjusters, when they come forth from the Father, are identical in nature, but personality is diverse, original, and exclusive; and the manifestation of personality is further conditioned and qualified by the nature and qualities of the associated energies of a material, mindal, and spiritual nature which constitute the organismal vehicle for personality manifestation.

Personalities may be similar, but they are never the same. Persons of a given series, type, order, or pattern may and do resemble one another, but they are never identical. Personality is that feature of an individual which we *know,* and which enables us to identify such a being at some future time regardless of the nature and extent of changes in form, mind, or spirit status. Personality is that part of any individual which enables us to recognize and positively identify that person as the one we have previously known, no matter how much he may have changed because of the modification of the vehicle of expression and manifestation of his personality.

Creature personality is distinguished by two self-manifesting and characteristic phenomena of mortal reactive behavior: self-consciousness and associated relative free will.

Self-consciousness consists in intellectual awareness of personality actuality; it includes the ability to recognize the reality of other personalities. It indicates capacity for individualized experience in and with cosmic realities, equivalating to the attainment of identity status in the personality relationships of the universe. Self-consciousness connotes recognition of the actuality of mind ministration and the realization of relative independence of creative and determinative free will.

The relative free will which characterizes the self-consciousness of human personality is involved in:

1. Moral decision, highest wisdom.
2. Spiritual choice, truth discernment.
3. Unselfish love, brotherhood service.
4. Purposeful co-operation, group loyalty.
5. Cosmic insight, the grasp of universe meanings.
6. Personality dedication, wholehearted devotion to doing the Father's will.

7. Worship, the sincere pursuit of divine values and the wholehearted love of the divine Value-Giver.

The Urantia type of human personality may be viewed as functioning in a physical mechanism consisting of the planetary modification of the Nebadon type of organism belonging to the electrochemical order of life activation and endowed with the Nebadon order of the Orvonton series of the cosmic mind of parental reproductive pattern. The bestowal of the divine gift of personality upon such a mind-endowed mortal mechanism confers the dignity of cosmic citizenship and enables such a mortal creature forthwith to become reactive to the constitutive recognition of the three basic mind realities of the cosmos:

1. The mathematical or logical recognition of the uniformity of physical causation.

2. The reasoned recognition of the obligation of moral conduct.

3. The faith-grasp of the fellowship worship of Deity, associated with the loving service of humanity.

The full function of such a personality endowment is the beginning realization of Deity kinship. Such a selfhood, indwelt by a prepersonal fragment of God the Father, is in truth and in fact a spiritual son of God. Such a creature not only discloses capacity for the reception of the gift of the divine presence but also exhibits reactive response to the personality-gravity circuit of the Paradise Father of all personalities.

9. REALITY OF HUMAN CONSCIOUSNESS

The cosmic-mind-endowed, Adjuster-indwelt, personal creature possesses innate recognition-realization of energy reality, mind reality, and spirit reality. The will creature is thus equipped to discern the fact, the law, and the love of God. Aside from these three inalienables of human consciousness, all human experience is really subjective except that intuitive realization of validity attaches to the *unification* of these three universe reality responses of cosmic recognition.

The God-discerning mortal is able to sense the unification value of these three cosmic qualities in the evolution of the surviving soul, man's supreme undertaking in the physical tabernacle where the moral mind collaborates with the indwelling divine spirit to dualize the immortal soul. From its earliest inception the soul is *real;* it has cosmic survival qualities.

If mortal man fails to survive natural death, the real spiritual values of his human experience survive as a part of the continuing experience of the Thought Adjuster. The personality values of such a nonsurvivor persist as a factor in the personality of the actualizing Supreme Being. Such persisting qualities of personality are deprived of identity but not of experiential values accumulated during the mortal life in the flesh. The survival of identity is dependent on the survival of the immortal soul of morontia status and increasingly divine value. Personality identity survives in and by the survival of the soul.

Human self-consciousness implies the recognition of the reality of selves other than the conscious self and further implies that such awareness is mutual; that the self is known as it knows. This is shown in a purely human manner in man's social life. But you cannot become so absolutely certain of a fellow being's reality as you can of the reality of the presence of God that lives within you.

The social consciousness is not inalienable like the God-consciousness; it is a cultural development and is dependent on knowledge, symbols, and the contributions of the constitutive endowments of man—science, morality, and religion. And these cosmic gifts, socialized, constitute civilization.

Civilizations are unstable because they are not cosmic; they are not innate in the individuals of the races. They must be nurtured by the combined contributions of the constitutive factors of man—science, morality, and religion. Civilizations come and go, but science, morality, and religion always survive the crash.

Jesus not only revealed God to man, but he also made a new revelation of man to himself and to other men. In the life of Jesus you see man at his best. Man thus becomes so beautifully real because Jesus had so much of God in his life, and the realization (recognition) of God is inalienable and constitutive in all men.

Unselfishness, aside from parental instinct, is not altogether natural; other persons are not naturally loved or socially served. It requires the enlightenment of reason, morality, and the urge of religion, God-knowingness, to generate an unselfish and altruistic social order. Man's own personality awareness, self-consciousness, is also directly dependent on this very fact of innate other-awareness, this innate ability to recognize and grasp the reality of other personality, ranging from the human to the divine.

Unselfish social consciousness must be, at bottom, a religious consciousness; that is, if it is objective; otherwise it is a purely subjective philosophic abstraction and therefore devoid of love. Only a God-knowing individual can love another person as he loves himself.

Self-consciousness is in essence a communal consciousness: God and man, Father and son, Creator and creature. In human self-consciousness four universe-reality realizations are latent and inherent:

1. The quest for knowledge, the logic of science.
2. The quest for moral values, the sense of duty.
3. The quest for spiritual values, the religious experience.
4. The quest for personality values, the ability to recognize the reality of God as a personality and the concurrent realization of our fraternal relationship with fellow personalities.

You become conscious of man as your creature brother because you are already conscious of God as your Creator Father. Fatherhood is the relationship out of which we reason ourselves into the recognition of brotherhood. And Fatherhood becomes, or may become, a universe reality to all moral creatures because the Father has himself bestowed personality upon all such beings and has encircuited them within the grasp of the universal personality circuit. We worship God, first, because *he is,* then, because *he is in us,* and last, because *we are in him.*

Is it strange that the cosmic mind should be self-consciously aware of its own source, the infinite mind of the Infinite Spirit, and at the same time conscious of the physical reality of the far-flung universes, the spiritual reality of the Eternal Son, and the personality reality of the Universal Father?

[Sponsored by a Universal Censor from Uversa.]

PAPER 17

THE SEVEN SUPREME SPIRIT GROUPS

THE seven Supreme Spirit groups are the universal co-ordinating directors of the seven-segmented administration of the grand universe. Although all are classed among the functional family of the Infinite Spirit, the following three groups are usually classified as children of the Paradise Trinity:

1. The Seven Master Spirits.
2. The Seven Supreme Executives.
3. The Reflective Spirits.

The remaining four groups are brought into being by the creative acts of the Infinite Spirit or by his associates of creative status:

4. The Reflective Image Aids.
5. The Seven Spirits of the Circuits.
6. The Local Universe Creative Spirits.
7. The Adjutant Mind-Spirits.

These seven orders are known on Uversa as the seven Supreme Spirit groups. Their functional domain extends from the personal presence of the Seven Master Spirits on the periphery of the eternal Isle, through the seven Paradise satellites of the Spirit, the Havona circuits, the governments of the superuniverses, and the administration and supervision of the local universes, even to the lowly service of the adjutants bestowed upon the realms of evolutionary mind on the worlds of time and space.

The Seven Master Spirits are the co-ordinating directors of this far-flung administrative realm. In some matters pertaining to the administrative regulation of organized physical power, mind energy, and impersonal spirit ministry, they act personally and directly, and in others they function through their multifarious associates. In all matters of an executive nature—rulings, regulations, adjustments, and administrative decisions—the Master Spirits act in the persons of the Seven Supreme Executives. In the central universe the Master Spirits may function through the Seven Spirits of the Havona Circuits; on the headquarters of the seven superuniverses they reveal themselves through the channel of the Reflective Spirits and act through the persons of the Ancients of Days, with whom they are in personal communication through the Reflective Image Aids.

The Seven Master Spirits do not directly and personally contact universe administration below the courts of the Ancients of Days. Your local universe is administered as a part of our superuniverse by the Master Spirit of Orvonton, but his function in relation to the native beings of Nebadon is immediately discharged and personally directed by the Creative Mother Spirit resident on Salvington, the headquarters of your local universe.

1. THE SEVEN SUPREME EXECUTIVES

The executive headquarters of the Master Spirits occupy the seven Paradise satellites of the Infinite Spirit, which swing around the central Isle between the shining spheres of the Eternal Son and the innermost Havona circuit. These executive spheres are under the direction of the Supreme Executives, a group of seven who were trinitized by the Father, Son, and Spirit in accordance with the specifications of the Seven Master Spirits for beings of a type that could function as their universal representatives.

The Master Spirits maintain contact with the various divisions of the superuniverse governments through these Supreme Executives. It is they who very largely determine the basic constitutive trends of the seven superuniverses. They are uniformly and divinely perfect, but they also possess diversity of personality. They have no presiding head; each time they meet together, they choose one of their number to preside over that joint council. Periodically they journey to Paradise to sit in council with the Seven Master Spirits.

The Seven Supreme Executives function as the administrative co-ordinators of the grand universe; they might be termed the board of managing directors of the post-Havona creation. They are not concerned with the internal affairs of Paradise, and they direct their limited spheres of Havona activity through the Seven Spirits of the Circuits. Otherwise there are few limits to the scope of their supervision; they engage in the direction of things physical, intellectual, and spiritual; they see all, hear all, feel all, even know all, that transpires in the seven superuniverses and in Havona.

These Supreme Executives do not originate policies, nor do they modify universe procedures; they are concerned with the execution of the plans of divinity promulgated by the Seven Master Spirits. Neither do they interfere with the rule of the Ancients of Days in the superuniverses nor with the sovereignty of the Creator Sons in the local universes. They are the co-ordinating executives whose function it is to carry out the combined policies of all duly constituted rulers in the grand universe.

Each of the executives and the facilities of his sphere are devoted to the efficient administration of a single superuniverse. Supreme Executive Number One, functioning on executive sphere number one, is wholly occupied with the affairs of superuniverse number one, and so on to Supreme Executive Number Seven, working from the seventh Paradise satellite of the Spirit and devoting his energies to the management of the seventh superuniverse. The name of this seventh sphere is Orvonton, for the Paradise satellites of the Spirit have the same names as their related superuniverses; in fact, the superuniverses were named after them.

On the executive sphere of the seventh superuniverse the staff engaged in keeping straight the affairs of Orvonton runs into numbers beyond human comprehension and embraces practically every order of celestial intelligence. All superuniverse services of personality dispatch (except Inspired Trinity Spirits and Thought Adjusters) pass through one of these seven executive worlds on their universe journeys to and from Paradise, and here are maintained the central registries for all personalities created by the Third Source and Center who function in the superuniverses. The system of material, morontial, and spiritual records on one of these executive worlds of the Spirit amazes even a being of my order.

The immediate subordinates of the Supreme Executives consist for the greater part of the trinitized sons of Paradise-Havona personalities and of the trinitized offspring of the glorified mortal graduates from the agelong training of the ascendant scheme of time and space. These trinitized sons are designated for service with the Supreme Executives by the chief of the Supreme Council of the Paradise Corps of the Finality.

Each Supreme Executive has two advisory cabinets: The children of the Infinite Spirit on the headquarters of each superuniverse choose representatives from their ranks to serve for one millennium in the primary advisory cabinet of their Supreme Executive. In all matters affecting the ascending mortals of time, there is a secondary cabinet, consisting of mortals of Paradise attainment and of the trinitized sons of glorified mortals; this body is chosen by the perfecting and ascending beings who transiently dwell on the seven superuniverse headquarters. All other chiefs of affairs are appointed by the Supreme Executives.

From time to time, great conclaves take place on these Paradise satellites of the Spirit. Trinitized sons assigned to these worlds, together with the ascenders who have attained Paradise, assemble with the spirit personalities of the Third Source and Center in the reunions of the struggles and triumphs of the ascendant career. The Supreme Executives always preside over such fraternal gatherings.

Once in each Paradise millennium the Seven Supreme Executives vacate their seats of authority and go to Paradise, where they hold their millennial conclave of universal greeting and well-wishing to the intelligent hosts of creation. This eventful occasion takes place in the immediate presence of Majeston, the chief of all reflective spirit groups. And they are thus able to communicate simultaneously with all their associates in the grand universe through the unique functioning of universal reflectivity.

2. MAJESTON—CHIEF OF REFLECTIVITY

The Reflective Spirits are of divine Trinity origin. There are fifty of these unique and somewhat mysterious beings. Seven of these extraordinary personalities were created at a time, and each such creative episode was effected by a liaison of the Paradise Trinity and one of the Seven Master Spirits.

This momentous transaction, occurring in the dawn of time, represents the initial effort of the Supreme Creator Personalities, represented by the Master Spirits, to function as cocreators with the Paradise Trinity. This union of the creative power of the Supreme Creators with the creative potentials of the Trinity is the very source of the actuality of the Supreme Being. Therefore, when the cycle of reflective creation had run its course, when each of the Seven Master Spirits had found perfect creative synchrony with the Paradise Trinity, when the forty-ninth Reflective Spirit had personalized, then a new and far-reaching reaction occurred in the Deity Absolute which imparted new personality prerogatives to the Supreme Being and culminated in the personalization of Majeston, the reflectivity chief and Paradise center of all the work of the forty-nine Reflective Spirits and their associates throughout the universe of universes.

Majeston is a true person, the personal and infallible center of reflectivity phenomena in all seven superuniverses of time and space. He maintains permanent Paradise headquarters near the center of all things at the rendezvous of the Seven Master Spirits. He is concerned solely with the co-ordination and maintenance of the reflectivity service in the far-flung creation; he is not otherwise involved in the administration of universe affairs.

Majeston is not included in our catalogue of Paradise personalities because he is the only existing personality of divinity created by the Supreme Being in functional liaison with the Deity Absolute. He is a person, but he is exclusively and apparently automatically concerned with this one phase of universe economy; he does not now function in any personal capacity with relation to other (nonreflective) orders of universe personalities.

The creation of Majeston signalized the first supreme creative act of the Supreme Being. This will to action was volitional in the Supreme Being, but the stupendous reaction of the Deity Absolute was not foreknown. Not since the eternity-appearance of Havona had the universe witnessed such a tremendous factualization of such a gigantic and far-flung alignment of power and co-ordination of functional spirit activities. The Deity response to the creative wills of the Supreme Being and his associates was vastly beyond their purposeful intent and greatly in excess of their conceptual forecasts.

We stand in awe of the possibility of what the future ages, wherein the Supreme and the Ultimate may attain new levels of divinity and ascend to new domains of personality function, may witness in the realms of the deitization of still other unexpected and undreamed of beings who will possess unimagined powers of enhanced universe co-ordination. There would seem to be no limit to the Deity Absolute's potential of response to such unification of relationships between experiential Deity and the existential Paradise Trinity.

3. THE REFLECTIVE SPIRITS

The forty-nine Reflective Spirits are of Trinity origin, but each of the seven creative episodes attendant upon their appearance was productive of a type of being in nature resembling the characteristics of the coancestral Master Spirit. Thus they variously reflect the natures and characters of the seven possible combinations of the association of the divinity characteristics of the Universal Father, the Eternal Son, and the Infinite Spirit. For this reason it is necessary to have seven of these Reflective Spirits on the headquarters of each superuniverse. One of each of the seven types is required in order to achieve the perfect reflection of all phases of every possible manifestation of the three Paradise Deities as such phenomena might occur in any part of the seven superuniverses. One of each type was accordingly assigned to service in each of the superuniverses. These groups of seven dissimilar Reflective Spirits maintain headquarters on the capitals of the superuniverses at the reflective focus of each realm, and this is not identical with the point of spiritual polarity.

The Reflective Spirits have names, but these designations are not revealed on the worlds of space. They pertain to the nature and character of these beings and are a part of one of the seven universal mysteries of the secret spheres of Paradise.

The attribute of reflectivity, the phenomenon of the mind levels of the Conjoint Actor, the Supreme Being, and the Master Spirits, is transmissible to all beings concerned in the working of this vast scheme of universal intelligence. And herein is a great mystery: Neither the Master Spirits nor the Paradise Deities, singly or collectively, disclose these powers of co-ordinate universal reflectivity just as they are manifested in these forty-nine liaison personalities of Majeston, and yet they are the creators of all these marvelously endowed beings. Divine heredity does sometimes disclose in the creature certain attributes which are not discernible in the Creator.

The personnel of the reflectivity service, with the exception of Majeston and the Reflective Spirits, are all the creatures of the Infinite Spirit and his immediate associates and subordinates. The Reflective Spirits of each superuniverse are the creators of their Reflective Image Aids, their personal voices to the courts of the Ancients of Days.

The Reflective Spirits are not merely transmitting agents; they are retentive personalities as well. Their offspring, the seconaphim, are also retentive or record personalities. Everything of true spiritual value is registered in duplicate, and one impression is preserved in the personal equipment of some member of one of the numerous orders of secoraphic personalities belonging to the vast staff of the Reflective Spirits.

The formal records of the universes are passed up by and through the angelic recorders, but the true spiritual records are assembled by reflectivity and are preserved in the minds of suitable and appropriate personalities belonging to the family of the Infinite Spirit. These are the *live* records in contrast with the formal and *dead* records of the universe, and they are perfectly preserved in the living minds of the recording personalities of the Infinite Spirit.

The reflectivity organization is also the news-gathering and the decree-disseminating mechanism of all creation. It is in constant operation in contrast with the periodic functioning of the various broadcast services.

Everything of import transpiring on a local universe headquarters is inherently reflected to the capital of its superuniverse. And conversely, everything of local universe significance is reflected outward to the local universe capitals from the headquarters of their superuniverse. The reflectivity service from the universes of time up to the superuniverses is apparently automatic or self-operating, but it is not. It is all very personal and intelligent; its precision results from perfection of personality co-operation and therefore can hardly be attributed to the impersonal presence-performances of the Absolutes.

While Thought Adjusters do not participate in the operation of the universal reflectivity system, we have every reason to believe that all Father fragments are fully cognizant of these transactions and are able to avail themselves of their content.

During the present universe age the space range of the extra-Paradise reflectivity service seems to be limited by the periphery of the seven superuniverses. Otherwise, the function of this service seems to be independent of time and space. It appears to be independent of all known subabsolute universe circuits.

On the headquarters of each superuniverse the reflective organization acts as a segregated unit; but on certain special occasions, under the direction of Majeston, all seven may and do act in universal unison, as in the event of the jubilee occasioned by the settling of an entire local universe in light and life and at the times of the millennial greetings of the Seven Supreme Executives.

4. THE REFLECTIVE IMAGE AIDS

The forty-nine Reflective Image Aids were created by the Reflective Spirits, and there are just seven Aids on the headquarters of each superuniverse. The first creative act of the seven Reflective Spirits of Uversa was the production of their seven Image Aids, each Reflective Spirit creating his own Aid. The Image Aids are, in certain attributes and characteristics, perfect reproductions of their Reflective Mother Spirits; they are virtual duplications minus the attribute of reflectivity. They are true images and constantly function as the channel of communication between the Reflective Spirits and the superuniverse authorities. The Image Aids are not merely assistants; they are actual representations of their respective Spirit ancestors; they are *images,* and they are true to their name.

The Reflective Spirits themselves are true personalities but of such an order as to be incomprehensible to material beings. Even on a superuniverse headquarters sphere they require the assistance of their Image Aids in all personal intercourse with the Ancients of Days and their associates. In contacts between the Image Aids and the Ancients of Days, sometimes one Aid functions acceptably, while on other occasions two, three, four, or even all seven are required for the full and proper presentation of the communication intrusted to their transmission. Likewise, the messages of the Image Aids are variously received by one, two, or all three Ancients of Days, as the content of the communication may require.

The Image Aids serve forever by the sides of their ancestral Spirits, and they have at their disposal an unbelievable host of helper seconaphim. The Image Aids do not directly function in connection with the training worlds of ascending mortals. They are closely associated with the intelligence service of the universal scheme of mortal progression, but you will not personally come in contact with them when you sojourn in the Uversa schools because these seemingly personal beings are devoid of will; they do not exercise the power of choice. They are true images, wholly reflective of the personality and mind of the individual Spirit ancestor. As a class, ascending mortals do not intimately contact with reflectivity. Always some being of the reflective nature will be interposed between you and the actual operation of the service.

5. THE SEVEN SPIRITS OF THE CIRCUITS

The Seven Spirits of the Havona Circuits are the joint impersonal representation of the Infinite Spirit and the Seven Master Spirits to the seven circuits of the central universe. They are the servants of the Master Spirits, whose collective offspring they are. The Master Spirits provide a distinct and diversified administrative individuality in the seven superuniverses. Through these uniform Spirits of the Havona Circuits they are enabled to provide a unified, uniform, and co-ordinated spiritual supervision for the central universe.

The Seven Spirits of the Circuits are each limited to the permeation of a single Havona circuit. They are not directly concerned with the regimes of the Eternals of Days, the rulers of the individual Havona worlds. But they are in liaison with the Seven Supreme Executives, and they synchronize with the central universe presence of the Supreme Being. Their work is wholly confined to Havona.

These Spirits of the Circuits make contact with those who sojourn in Havona through their personal offspring, the tertiary supernaphim. While the Circuit Spirits are coexistent with the Seven Master Spirits, their function in the creation of tertiary supernaphim did not attain major importance until the first pilgrims of time arrived on the outer circuit of Havona in the days of Grandfanda.

As you advance from circuit to circuit in Havona, you will learn of the Spirits of the Circuits, but you will not be able to hold personal communion with them, even though you may personally enjoy, and recognize the impersonal presence of, their spiritual influence.

The Circuit Spirits are related to the native inhabitants of Havona much as the Thought Adjusters are related to the mortal creatures inhabiting the worlds of the evolutionary universes. Like the Thought Adjusters, the Circuit Spirits are impersonal, and they consort with the perfect minds of Havona beings much as the impersonal spirits of the Universal Father indwell the finite minds of mortal men. But the Spirits of the Circuits never become a permanent part of Havona personalities.

6. THE LOCAL UNIVERSE CREATIVE SPIRITS

Much that pertains to the nature and function of the local universe Creative Spirits properly belongs to the narrative of their association with the Creator Sons in the organization and management of the local creations; but there are many features of the prelocal universe experiences of these marvelous beings which may be narrated as a part of this discussion of the seven Supreme Spirit groups.

We are conversant with six phases of the career of a local universe Mother Spirit, and we speculate much concerning the probability of a seventh stage of activity. These different stages of existence are:

1. *Initial Paradise Differentiation.* When a Creator Son is personalized by the joint action of the Universal Father and the Eternal Son, simultaneously there occurs in the person of the Infinite Spirit what is known as the "supreme reaction of complement." We do not comprehend the nature of this reaction, but we understand that it designates an inherent modification of those personalizable possibilities which are embraced within the creative potential of the Conjoint Creator. The birth of a co-ordinate Creator Son signalizes the birth within the person of the Infinite Spirit of the potential of the future local universe consort of this Paradise Son. We are not cognizant of this new prepersonal identification of entity, but we know that this fact finds place on the Paradise records of the career of such a Creator Son.

2. *Preliminary Creatorship Training.* During the long period of the preliminary training of a Michael Son in the organization and administration of universes, his future consort undergoes further development of entity and becomes group conscious of destiny. We do not know, but we suspect that such a group-conscious entity becomes space cognizant and begins that preliminary training requisite to the acquirement of spirit skill in her future work of collaboration with the complemental Michael in universe creation and administration.

3. *The Stage of Physical Creation.* At the time the creatorship charge is administered to a Michael Son by the Eternal Son, the Master Spirit who directs the superuniverse to which this new Creator Son is destined gives expression to the "prayer of identification" in the presence of the Infinite Spirit; and for the first time, the entity of the subsequent Creative Spirit appears as differentiated from the person of the Infinite Spirit. And proceeding directly to the person of the petitioning Master Spirit, this entity is immediately lost to our recognition, becoming apparently a part of the person of this Master Spirit. The newly identified Creative Spirit remains with the Master Spirit until the moment of the departure of the Creator Son for the adventure of space; whereupon the Master Spirit commits the new Spirit consort to the keeping of the Creator Son, at the same time administering to the Spirit consort the charge of eternal fidelity and unending loyalty. And then occurs one of the most profoundly touching episodes which ever take place on Paradise. The Universal Father speaks in acknowledgment of the eternal union of the Creator Son and the Creative Spirit and in confirmation of the bestowal of certain joint powers of administration by the Master Spirit of superuniverse jurisdiction.

The Father-united Creator Son and Creative Spirit then go forth on their adventure of universe creation. And they work together in this form of association throughout the long and arduous period of the material organization of their universe.

4. *The Life-Creation Era.* Upon the declaration of intention to create life by the Creator Son, there ensue on Paradise the "personalization ceremonies," participated in by the Seven Master Spirits and personally experienced by the supervising Master Spirit. This is a Paradise Deity contribution to the individuality of the Spirit consort of the Creator Son and becomes manifest to the universe in the phenomenon of "the primary eruption" in the person of the Infinite Spirit. Simultaneously with this phenomenon on Paradise, the heretofore impersonal Spirit consort of the Creator Son becomes, to all practical intents and purposes, a bona fide person. Henceforth and forevermore, this same local universe Mother Spirit will be regarded as a person and will maintain personal relations with all the personality hosts of the ensuing life creation.

5. *The Postbestowal Ages.* Another and great change occurs in the never-ending career of a Creative Spirit when the Creator Son returns to universe headquarters after the completion of his seventh bestowal and subsequent to his acquirement of full universe sovereignty. On that occasion, before the assembled administrators of the universe, the triumphant Creator Son elevates the Universe Mother Spirit to cosovereignty and acknowledges the Spirit consort as his equal.

6. *The Ages of Light and Life.* Upon the establishment of the era of light and life the local universe cosovereign enters upon the sixth phase of a Creative Spirit's career. But we may not portray the nature of this great experience. Such things pertain to a future stage of evolution in Nebadon.

7. *The Unrevealed Career.* We know of these six phases of the career of a local universe Mother Spirit. It is inevitable that we should ask: Is there a seventh career? We are mindful that, when finaliters attain what appears to be their final destiny of mortal ascension, they are of record as entering upon the career of sixth-stage spirits. We conjecture that there awaits the finaliters still

another and unrevealed career in universe assignment. It is only to be expected that we would likewise regard the Universe Mother Spirits as having ahead of them some undisclosed career which will constitute their seventh phase of personal experience in universe service and loyal co-operation with the order of the Creator Michaels.

7. THE ADJUTANT MIND-SPIRITS

These adjutant spirits are the sevenfold mind bestowal of a local universe Mother Spirit upon the living creatures of the conjoint creation of a Creator Son and such a Creative Spirit. This bestowal becomes possible at the time of the Spirit's elevation to the status of personality prerogatives. The narration of the nature and functioning of the seven adjutant mind-spirits belongs more appropriately to the story of your local universe of Nebadon.

8. FUNCTIONS OF THE SUPREME SPIRITS

The seven groups of Supreme Spirits constitute the nucleus of the functional family of the Third Source and Center both as the Infinite Spirit and as the Conjoint Actor. The domain of the Supreme Spirits extends from the presence of the Trinity on Paradise to the functioning of mind of the evolutionary-mortal order on the planets of space. Thus do they unify the descending administrative levels and co-ordinate the manifold functions of the personnel thereof. Whether it is a Reflective Spirit group in liaison with the Ancients of Days, a Creative Spirit acting in concert with a Michael Son, or the Seven Master Spirits encircuited around the Paradise Trinity, the activity of the Supreme Spirits is encountered everywhere in the central, super-, and local universes. They function alike with the Trinity personalities of the order of "Days" and with the Paradise personalities of the order of "Sons."

Together with their Infinite Mother Spirit, the Supreme Spirit groups are the immediate creators of the vast creature family of the Third Source and Center. All orders of the ministering spirits spring from this association. Primary supernaphim originate in the Infinite Spirit; secondary beings of this order are created by the Master Spirits; tertiary supernaphim by the Seven Spirits of the Circuits. The Reflective Spirits, collectively, are the mother-makers of a marvelous order of the angelic hosts, the mighty seconaphim of the superuniverse services. A Creative Spirit is the mother of the angelic orders of a local creation; such seraphic ministers are original in each local universe, though they are fashioned after the patterns of the central universe. All these creators of ministering spirits are only indirectly assisted by the central lodgment of the Infinite Spirit, the original and eternal mother of all the angelic ministers.

The seven Supreme Spirit groups are the co-ordinators of the inhabited creation. The association of their directing heads, the Seven Master Spirits, appears to co-ordinate the far-flung activities of God the Sevenfold:

1. Collectively the Master Spirits near-equivalate to the divinity level of the Trinity of Paradise Deities.

2. Individually they exhaust the primary associable possibilities of triune Deity.

3. As diversified representatives of the Conjoint Actor they are the repositories of that spirit-mind-power sovereignty of the Supreme Being which he does not yet personally exercise.

4. Through the Reflective Spirits they synchronize the superuniverse governments of the Ancients of Days with Majeston, the Paradise center of universal reflectivity.

5. In their participation in the individualization of the local universe Divine Ministers, the Master Spirits contribute to the last level of God the Sevenfold, the Creator Son-Creative Spirit union of the local universes.

Functional unity, inherent in the Conjoint Actor, is disclosed to the evolving universes in the Seven Master Spirits, his primary personalities. But in the perfected superuniverses of the future this unity will undoubtedly be inseparable from the experiential sovereignty of the Supreme.

[Presented by a Divine Counselor of Uversa.]

PAPER 18

THE SUPREME TRINITY PERSONALITIES

SUPREME Trinity Personalities are all created for specific service. They are designed by the divine Trinity for the fulfillment of certain specific duties, and they are qualified to serve with perfection of technique and finality of devotion. There are seven orders of the Supreme Trinity Personalities:

1. Trinitized Secrets of Supremacy.
2. Eternals of Days.
3. Ancients of Days.
4. Perfections of Days.
5. Recents of Days.
6. Unions of Days.
7. Faithfuls of Days.

These beings of administrative perfection are of definite and final numbers. Their creation is a past event; no more are being personalized.

Throughout the grand universe these Supreme Trinity Personalities represent the administrative policies of the Paradise Trinity; they represent the justice and *are* the executive judgment of the Paradise Trinity. They form an interrelated line of administrative perfection extending from the Paradise spheres of the Father to the headquarters worlds of the local universes and to the capitals of their component constellations.

All Trinity-origin beings are created in Paradise perfection in all their divine attributes. Only in the realms of experience has the passing of time added to their equipment for cosmic service. There is never any danger of default or risk of rebellion with Trinity-origin beings. They are of divinity essence, and they have never been known to depart from the divine and perfect path of personality conduct.

1. THE TRINITIZED SECRETS OF SUPREMACY

There are seven worlds in the innermost circuit of the Paradise satellites, and each of these exalted worlds is presided over by a corps of ten Trinitized Secrets of Supremacy. They are not creators, but they are supreme and ultimate administrators. The conduct of the affairs of these seven fraternal spheres is wholly committed to this corps of seventy supreme directors. Though the offspring of the Trinity supervise these seven sacred spheres nearest Paradise, this group of worlds is universally known as the personal circuit of the Universal Father.

The Trinitized Secrets of Supremacy function in groups of ten as co-ordinate and joint directors of their respective spheres, but they also function individually in particular fields of responsibility. The work of each of these special worlds is divided into seven major departments, and one of these co-ordinate rulers presides over each such division of specialized activities. The remaining three act as the personal representatives of triune Deity in relation to the other seven, one representing the Father, one the Son, and one the Spirit.

Although there is a definite class resemblance which typifies the Trinitized Secrets of Supremacy, they also disclose seven distinct group characteristics. The ten supreme directors of Divinington affairs are reflective of the personal character and nature of the Universal Father; and so it is with each of these seven spheres: Each group of ten resembles that Deity or Deity association which is characteristic of their domain. The ten directors who rule Ascendington are reflective of the combined nature of the Father, Son, and Spirit.

I can reveal very little about the work of these high personalities on the seven sacred worlds of the Father, for they are truly the *Secrets* of Supremacy. There are no arbitrary secrets associated with the approach to the Universal Father, the Eternal Son, or the Infinite Spirit. The Deities are an open book to all who attain divine perfection, but all the Secrets of Supremacy can never be fully attained. Always will we be unable fully to penetrate the realms containing the personality secrets of Deity association with the sevenfold grouping of created beings.

Since the work of these supreme directors has to do with the intimate and personal contact of the Deities with these seven basic groupings of universe beings when domiciled on these seven special worlds or while functioning throughout the grand universe, it is fitting that these very personal relations and extraordinary contacts should be held sacredly secret. The Paradise Creators respect the privacy and sanctity of personality even in their lowly creatures. And this is true both of individuals and of the various separate orders of personalities.

To beings of even high universe attainment these secret worlds ever remain a test of loyalty. It is given us fully and personally to know the eternal Gods, freely to know their characters of divinity and perfection, but it is not granted us fully to penetrate all of the personal relations of the Paradise Rulers with all of their creature beings.

2. THE ETERNALS OF DAYS

Each of the billion worlds of Havona is directed by a Supreme Trinity Personality. These rulers are known as the Eternals of Days, and they number exactly one billion, one for each of the Havona spheres. They are the offspring of the Paradise Trinity, but like the Secrets of Supremacy there are no records of their origin. Forever have these two groups of all-wise fathers ruled their exquisite worlds of the Paradise-Havona system, and they function without rotation or reassignment.

The Eternals of Days are visible to all will creatures dwelling in their domains. They preside over the regular planetary conclaves. Periodically, and by rotation, they visit the headquarters spheres of the seven superuniverses. They are close of kin to, and are the divine equals of, the Ancients of Days, who preside over the destinies of the seven supergovernments. When an Eternal of Days is absent from his sphere, his world is directed by a Trinity Teacher Son.

Except for the established orders of life, such as the Havona natives and other living creatures of the central universe, the resident Eternals of Days have developed their respective spheres entirely in accordance with their own personal ideas and ideals. They visit each other's planets, but they do not copy or imitate; they are always and wholly original.

The architecture, natural embellishment, morontia structures, and spirit creations are exclusive and unique on each sphere. Every world is a place of everlasting beauty and is wholly unlike any other world in the central universe. And you will each spend a longer or shorter time on each of these unique and thrilling spheres on your way inward through Havona to Paradise. It is natural, on your world, to speak of Paradise as *upward,* but it would be more correct to refer to the divine goal of ascension as *inward.*

3. THE ANCIENTS OF DAYS

When mortals of time graduate from the training worlds surrounding the headquarters of a local universe and are advanced to the educational spheres of their superuniverse, they have progressed in spiritual development to that point where they are able to recognize and communicate with the high spiritual rulers and directors of these advanced realms, including the Ancients of Days.

The Ancients of Days are all basically identical; they disclose the combined character and unified nature of the Trinity. They possess individuality and are in personality diverse, but they do not differ from each other as do the Seven Master Spirits. They provide the uniform directorship of the otherwise differing seven superuniverses, each of which is a distinct, segregated, and unique creation. The Seven Master Spirits are unlike in nature and attributes, but the Ancients of Days, the personal rulers of the superuniverses, are all uniform and superperfect offspring of the Paradise Trinity.

The Seven Master Spirits on high determine the *nature* of their respective superuniverses, but the Ancients of Days dictate the *administration* of these same superuniverses. They superimpose administrative uniformity on creative diversity and insure the harmony of the whole in the face of the underlying creational differences of the seven segmental groupings of the grand universe.

The Ancients of Days were all trinitized at the same time. They represent the beginning of the personality records of the universe of universes, hence their name—*Ancients* of Days. When you reach Paradise and search the written records of the beginning of things, you will find that the first entry appearing in the personality section is the recital of the trinitization of these twenty-one Ancients of Days.

These high beings always govern in groups of three. There are many phases of activity in which they work as individuals, still others in which any two can function, but in the higher spheres of their administration they must act jointly. They never personally leave their residential worlds, but then they do not have to, for these worlds are the superuniverse focal points of the far-flung reflectivity system.

The personal abodes of each trio of the Ancients of Days are located at the point of spiritual polarity on their headquarters sphere. Such a sphere is divided into seventy administrative sectors and has seventy divisional capitals in which the Ancients of Days reside from time to time.

In power, scope of authority, and extent of jurisdiction the Ancients of Days are the most powerful and mighty of any of the direct rulers of the time-space creations. In all the vast universe of universes they alone are invested with the high powers of final executive judgment concerning the eternal extinction of will creatures. And all three Ancients of Days must participate in the final decrees of the supreme tribunal of a superuniverse.

Aside from the Deities and their Paradise associates, the Ancients of Days are the most perfect, most versatile, and the most divinely endowed rulers in all time-space existence. Apparently they are the supreme rulers of the superuniverses; but they have not experientially earned this right to rule and are therefore destined sometime to be superseded by the Supreme Being, an experiential sovereign, whose vicegerents they will undoubtedly become.

The Supreme Being is achieving the sovereignty of the seven superuniverses by experiential service just as a Creator Son experientially earns the sovereignty of his local universe. But during the present age of the unfinished evolution of the Supreme, the Ancients of Days provide the co-ordinated and perfect administrative overcontrol of the evolving universes of time and space. And the wisdom of originality and the initiative of individuality characterize all the decrees and rulings of the Ancients of Days.

4. THE PERFECTIONS OF DAYS

There are just two hundred and ten Perfections of Days, and they preside over the governments of the ten major sectors of each superuniverse. They were trinitized for the special work of assisting the superuniverse directors, and they rule as the immediate and personal vicegerents of the Ancients of Days.

Three Perfections of Days are assigned to each major sector capital, but unlike the Ancients of Days, it is not necessary that all three be present at all times. From time to time one of this trio may absent himself to confer in person with the Ancients of Days concerning the welfare of his realm.

These triune rulers of the major sectors are peculiarly perfect in the mastery of administrative details, hence their name—*Perfections* of Days. In recording the names of these beings of the spiritual world, we are confronted with the problem of translating into your tongue, and very often it is exceedingly difficult to render a satisfactory translation. We dislike to use arbitrary designations which would be meaningless to you; hence we often find it difficult to choose a suitable name, one which will be clear to you and at the same time be somewhat representative of the original.

The Perfections of Days have a moderate-sized corps of Divine Counselors, Perfectors of Wisdom, and Universal Censors attached to their governments. They have still larger numbers of Mighty Messengers, Those High in Authority, and Those without Name and Number. But much of the routine work of major sector affairs is carried on by the Celestial Guardians and the High Son Assistants. These two groups are drawn from among the trinitized offspring of either Paradise-Havona personalities or glorified mortal finaliters. Certain of these two orders of creature-trinitized beings are retrinitized by the Paradise Deities and then are dispatched to assist in the administration of the superuniverse governments.

Most of the Celestial Guardians and the High Son Assistants are assigned to the service of the major and the minor sectors, but the Trinitized Custodians (Trinity-embraced seraphim and midwayers) are the officers of the courts of all three divisions, functioning in the tribunals of the Ancients of Days, the Perfections of Days, and the Recents of Days. The Trinitized Ambassadors (Trinity-embraced ascendant mortals of Son- or Spirit-fused nature) may be encountered anywhere in a superuniverse, but the majority are in the service of the minor sectors.

Before the times of the full unfolding of the governmental scheme of the seven superuniverses, practically all administrators of the various divisions of these governments, excepting the Ancients of Days, served apprenticeships of varying duration under the Eternals of Days on the various worlds of the perfect Havona universe. The later trinitized beings likewise passed through a season of training under the Eternals of Days before they were attached to the service of the Ancients of Days, the Perfections of Days, and the Recents of Days. They are all seasoned, tried, and experienced administrators.

You will early see the Perfections of Days when you advance to the headquarters of Splandon after your sojourn on the worlds of your minor sector, for these exalted rulers are closely associated with the seventy major sector worlds of higher training for the ascendant creatures of time. The Perfections of Days, in person, administer the group pledges to the ascending graduates of the major sector schools.

The work of the pilgrims of time on the worlds surrounding a major sector headquarters is chiefly of an intellectual nature in contrast with the more physical and material character of the training on the seven educational spheres of a minor sector and with the spiritual undertakings on the four hundred ninety university worlds of a superuniverse headquarters.

Although you are entered only upon the registry of the major sector of Splandon, which embraces the local universe of your origin, you will have to pass through every one of the ten major divisions of our superuniverse. You will see all thirty of the Orvonton Perfections of Days before you reach Uversa.

5. THE RECENTS OF DAYS

The Recents of Days are the youngest of the supreme directors of the superuniverses; in groups of three they preside over the affairs of the minor sectors. In nature they are co-ordinate with the Perfections of Days, but in administrative authority they are subordinate. There are just twenty-one thousand of these personally glorious and divinely efficient Trinity personalities. They were created simultaneously, and together they passed through their Havona training under the Eternals of Days.

The Recents of Days have a corps of associates and assistants similar to that of the Perfections of Days. In addition they have assigned to them enormous numbers of the various subordinate orders of celestial beings. In the administration of the minor sectors they utilize large numbers of the resident ascending mortals, the personnel of the various courtesy colonies, and the various groups originating in the Infinite Spirit.

The governments of the minor sectors are very largely, though not exclusively, concerned with the great physical problems of the superuniverses. The minor sector spheres are the headquarters of the Master Physical Controllers. On these worlds ascending mortals carry on studies and experiments having to do with an examination of the activities of the third order of the Supreme Power Centers and of all seven orders of the Master Physical Controllers.

Since the regime of a minor sector is so extensively concerned with physical problems, its three Recents of Days are seldom together on the capital sphere. Most of the time one is away in conference with the Perfections of Days of the supervising major sector or absent while representing the Ancients of Days at the Paradise conclaves of the high Trinity-origin beings. They alternate with the Perfections of Days in representing the Ancients of Days at the supreme councils on Paradise. Meanwhile, another Recent of Days may be away on a tour of inspection of the headquarters worlds of the local universes belonging to his jurisdiction. But at least one of these rulers always remains on duty at the headquarters of a minor sector.

You will all sometime know the three Recents of Days in charge of Ensa, your minor sector, since you must pass through their hands on your way inward to the training worlds of the major sectors. In ascending to Uversa, you will pass through only one group of minor sector training spheres.

6. THE UNIONS OF DAYS

The Trinity personalities of the order of "Days" do not function in an administrative capacity below the level of the superuniverse governments. In the evolving local universes they act only as counselors and advisers. The Unions of Days are a group of liaison personalities accredited by the Paradise Trinity to the dual rulers of the local universes. Each organized and inhabited local universe has assigned to it one of these Paradise counselors, who acts as the representative of the Trinity, and in some respects, of the Universal Father, to the local creation.

There are seven hundred thousand of these beings in existence, though they have not all been commissioned. The reserve corps of the Unions of Days functions on Paradise as the Supreme Council of Universe Adjustments.

In a special manner these Trinity observers co-ordinate the administrative activities of all branches of the universal government, from those of the local universes up through the sector governments to those of the superuniverse, hence their name—*Unions* of Days. They make a threefold report to their superiors: They report pertinent data of a physical and semi-intellectual nature to the Recents of Days of their minor sector; they report intellectual and quasi-spiritual happenings to the Perfections of Days of their major sector; they report spiritual and semiparadisiacal matters to the Ancients of Days at the capital of their superuniverse.

Since they are Trinity-origin beings, all of the Paradise circuits are available to them for intercommunication, and thus are they always in touch with each other and with all other required personalities up to the supreme councils of Paradise.

A Union of Days is not organically connected with the government of the local universe of his assignment. Aside from his duties as an observer, he acts only at the request of the local authorities. He is an ex officio member of all primary councils and all important conclaves of the local creation, but he does not participate in the technical consideration of administrative problems.

When a local universe is settled in light and life, its glorified beings associate freely with the Union of Days, who then functions in an enlarged capacity in such a realm of evolutionary perfection. But he is still primarily a Trinity ambassador and Paradise counselor.

A local universe is directly ruled by a divine Son of dual Deity origin, but he has constantly by his side a Paradise brother, a Trinity-origin personality. In the event of the temporary absence of a Creator Son from the headquarters of his local universe, the acting rulers are largely guided in their major decisions by the counsel of their Union of Days.

7. THE FAITHFULS OF DAYS

These high Trinity-origin personalities are the Paradise advisers to the rulers of the one hundred constellations in each local universe. There are seventy million Faithfuls of Days, and like the Unions of Days, not all are in service. Their Paradise reserve corps is the Advisory Commission of Interuniverse Ethics and Self-government. Faithfuls of Days rotate in service in accordance with the rulings of the supreme council of their reserve corps.

All that a Union of Days is to a Creator Son of a local universe, the Faithfuls of Days are to the Vorondadek Sons who rule the constellations of that local creation. They are supremely devoted and divinely faithful to the welfare of their constellations of assignment, hence the name—*Faithfuls* of Days. They act only as counselors; never do they participate in administrative activities except upon the invitation of the constellation authorities. Neither are they directly concerned in the educational ministry to the pilgrims of ascension on the architectural training spheres surrounding a constellation headquarters. All such undertakings are under the supervision of the Vorondadek Sons.

All Faithfuls of Days functioning in the constellations of a local universe are under the jurisdiction of, and report directly to, the Union of Days. They do not have a far-flung system of intercommunication, being ordinarily self-limited to an interassociation within the limits of a local universe. Any Faithful of Days on duty in Nebadon can and does communicate with all others of his order on duty in this local universe.

Like the Union of Days on a universe headquarters, the Faithfuls of Days maintain their personal residences on the constellation capitals separate from those of the administrative directors of such realms. Their abodes are indeed modest in comparison with the homes of the Vorondadek rulers of the constellations.

The Faithfuls of Days are the last link in the long administrative-advisory chain which reaches from the sacred spheres of the Universal Father near the center of all things to the primary divisions of the local universes. The Trinity-origin regime stops with the constellations; no such Paradise advisers are permanently situated on their component systems or on the inhabited worlds. These latter administrative units are wholly under the jurisdiction of beings native to the local universes.

[Presented by a Divine Counselor of Uversa.]

PAPER 19

THE CO-ORDINATE TRINITY-ORIGIN BEINGS

THIS Paradise group, designated the Co-ordinate Trinity-origin Beings, embraces the Trinity Teacher Sons, also classed among the Paradise Sons of God, three groups of high superuniverse administrators, and the somewhat impersonal category of the Inspired Trinity Spirits. Even the Havona natives may properly be included in this classification of Trinity personalities along with numerous groups of beings resident on Paradise. Those Trinity-origin beings to be considered in this discussion are:

1. Trinity Teacher Sons.
2. Perfectors of Wisdom.
3. Divine Counselors.
4. Universal Censors.
5. Inspired Trinity Spirits.
6. Havona Natives.
7. Paradise Citizens.

Excepting the Trinity Teacher Sons and possibly the Inspired Trinity Spirits, these groups are of definite numbers; their creation is a finished and past event.

1. THE TRINITY TEACHER SONS

Of all the high orders of celestial personalities revealed to you, the Trinity Teacher Sons alone act in a dual capacity. By origin of Trinity nature, in function they are almost wholly devoted to the services of divine sonship. They are the liaison beings who bridge the universe gulf between Trinity- and dual-origin personalities.

While the Stationary Sons of the Trinity are of completed numbers, the Teacher Sons are constantly increasing. What the final number of Teacher Sons will be I do not know. I can, however, state that, at the last periodic report to Uversa, the Paradise records indicated 21,001,624,821 of these Sons in service.

These beings are the only group of the Sons of God revealed to you whose origin is in the Paradise Trinity. They range the central and superuniverses, and an enormous corps is assigned to each local universe. They also serve the individual planets as do the other Paradise Sons of God. Since the scheme of the grand universe is not fully developed, large numbers of Teacher Sons are held in the reserves on Paradise, and they volunteer for emergency duty and unusual service in all divisions of the grand universe, on the lone worlds of space, in the local and superuniverses, and on the worlds of Havona. They also function on Paradise, but it will be more helpful to postpone their detailed consideration until we come to the discussion of the Paradise Sons of God.

In this connection, however, it may be noted that Teacher Sons are the supreme co-ordinating personalities of Trinity origin. In such a far-flung universe of universes there is always great danger of succumbing to the error of the circumscribed viewpoint, to the evil inherent in a segmentalized conception of reality and divinity.

For example: The human mind would ordinarily crave to approach the cosmic philosophy portrayed in these revelations by proceeding from the simple and the finite to the complex and the infinite, from human origins to divine destinies. But that path does not lead to *spiritual wisdom.* Such a procedure is the easiest path to a certain form of *genetic knowledge,* but at best it can only reveal man's origin; it reveals little or nothing about his divine destiny.

Even in the study of man's biologic evolution on Urantia, there are grave objections to the exclusive historic approach to his present-day status and his current problems. The true perspective of any reality problem—human or divine, terrestrial or cosmic—can be had only by the full and unprejudiced study and correlation of three phases of universe reality: origin, history, and destiny. The proper understanding of these three experiential realities affords the basis for a wise estimate of the current status.

When the human mind undertakes to follow the philosophic technique of starting from the lower to approach the higher, whether in biology or theology, it is always in danger of committing four errors of reasoning:

1. It may utterly fail to perceive the final and completed evolutionary goal of either personal attainment or cosmic destiny.

2. It may commit the supreme philosophical blunder by oversimplifying cosmic evolutionary (experiential) reality, thus leading to the distortion of facts, to the perversion of truth, and to the misconception of destinies.

3. The study of causation is the perusal of history. But the knowledge of *how* a being becomes does not necessarily provide an intelligent understanding of the present status and true character of such a being.

4. History alone fails adequately to reveal future development—destiny. Finite origins are helpful, but only divine causes reveal final effects. Eternal ends are not shown in time beginnings. The present can be truly interpreted only in the light of the correlated past and future.

Therefore, because of these and for still other reasons, do we employ the technique of approaching man and his planetary problems by embarkation on the time-space journey from the infinite, eternal, and divine Paradise Source and Center of all personality reality and all cosmic existence.

2. THE PERFECTORS OF WISDOM

The Perfectors of Wisdom are a specialized creation of the Paradise Trinity designed to personify the wisdom of divinity in the superuniverses. There are exactly seven billion of these beings in existence, and one billion are assigned to each of the seven superuniverses.

In common with their co-ordinates, the Divine Counselors and the Universal Censors, the Perfectors of Wisdom passed through the wisdom of Paradise, of Havona, and except for Divinington, of the Father's Paradise spheres. After these experiences the Perfectors of Wisdom were permanently assigned to the service of the Ancients of Days. They serve neither on Paradise nor on the worlds of the Paradise-Havona circuits; they are wholly occupied with the administration of the superuniverse governments.

Wherever and whenever a Perfector of Wisdom functions, there and then divine wisdom functions. There is actuality of presence and perfection of manifestation in the knowledge and wisdom represented in the doings of these mighty and majestic personalities. They do not *reflect* the wisdom of the Paradise Trinity; they *are* that wisdom. They are the sources of wisdom for all teachers in the application of universe knowledge; they are the fountains of discretion and the wellsprings of discrimination to the institutions of learning and discernment in all universes.

Wisdom is twofold in origin, being derived from the perfection of divine insight inherent in perfect beings and from the personal experience acquired by evolutionary creatures. The Perfectors of Wisdom *are* the divine wisdom of the Paradise perfection of Deity insight. Their administrative associates on Uversa, the Mighty Messengers, Those without Name and Number, and Those High in Authority, when acting together, *are* the universe wisdom of experience. A divine being can have perfection of divine knowledge. An evolutionary mortal can sometime attain perfection of ascendant knowledge, but neither of these beings alone exhausts the potentials of all possible wisdom. Accordingly, whenever in the conduct of the superuniverse it is desired to achieve the maximum of administrative wisdom, these perfectors of the wisdom of divine insight are always associated with those ascendant personalities who have come up to the high responsibilities of superuniverse authority through the experiential tribulations of evolutionary progression.

The Perfectors of Wisdom will always require this complement of experiential wisdom for the completion of their administrative sagacity. But it has been postulated that a high and hitherto unattained level of wisdom may possibly be achieved by the Paradise finaliters *after* they are sometime inducted into the seventh stage of spirit existence. If this inference is correct, then would such perfected beings of evolutionary ascent undoubtedly become the most effective universe administrators ever to be known in all creation. I believe that such is the high destiny of finaliters.

The versatility of the Perfectors of Wisdom enables them to participate in practically all of the celestial services of the ascendant creatures. The Perfectors of Wisdom and my order of personality, the Divine Counselors, together with the Universal Censors, constitute the highest orders of beings who may and do engage in the work of revealing truth to the individual planets and systems, whether in their earlier epochs or when settled in light and life. From time to time we all make contact with the service of the ascending mortals, from an initial-life planet on up through a local universe and the superuniverse, particularly the latter.

3. THE DIVINE COUNSELORS

These Trinity-origin beings are the counsel of Deity to the realms of the seven superuniverses. They are not *reflective* of the divine counsel of the Trinity; they *are* that counsel. There are twenty-one billion Counselors in service, and three billion are assigned to each superuniverse.

Divine Counselors are the associates and equals of the Universal Censors and the Perfectors of Wisdom, from one to seven Counselors being associated with each of these latter personalities. All three orders participate in the government of the Ancients of Days, including major and minor sectors, in the local universes and constellations, and in the councils of the local system sovereigns.

We act as individuals, as I do in inditing this statement, but we also function as a trio whenever the occasion requires. When we act in an executive capacity, always there are associated together a Perfector of Wisdom, a Universal Censor, and from one to seven Divine Counselors.

One Perfector of Wisdom, seven Divine Counselors, and one Universal Censor constitute a tribunal of Trinity divinity, the highest mobile advisory body in the universes of time and space. Such a group of nine is known either as a fact-finding or as a truth-revealing tribunal, and when it sits in judgment upon a problem and renders a decision, it is just as if an Ancient of Days had adjudicated the matter, for in all the annals of the superuniverses such a verdict has never been reversed by the Ancients of Days.

When the three Ancients of Days function, the Paradise Trinity functions. When the tribunal of nine arrives at a decision following its united deliberations, to all intents and purposes the Ancients of Days have spoken. And it is in this manner that the Paradise Rulers make personal contact, in administrative matters and governmental regulation, with the individual worlds, systems, and universes.

Divine Counselors are the perfection of the divine counsel of the Paradise Trinity. We represent, in fact *are,* the counsel of perfection. When we are supplemented by the experiential counsel of our associates, the perfected and Trinity-embraced beings of evolutionary ascent, our combined conclusions are not only complete but replete. When our united counsel has been associated, adjudicated, confirmed, and promulgated by a Universal Censor, it is very probable that it approaches the threshold of universal totality. Such verdicts represent the nearest possible approach to the absolute attitude of Deity within the time-space limits of the situation involved and the problem concerned.

Seven Divine Counselors in liaison with a trinitized evolutionary trio—a Mighty Messenger, One High in Authority, and One without Name and Number—represent the nearest superuniverse approach to the union of the human viewpoint and the divine attitude on near-paradisiacal levels of spiritual meanings and reality values. Such close approximation of the united cosmic attitudes of the creature and the Creator is only surpassed in the Paradise bestowal Sons, who are, in every phase of personality experience, God and man.

4. THE UNIVERSAL CENSORS

There are exactly eight billion Universal Censors in existence. These unique beings *are* the judgment of Deity. They are not merely reflective of the decisions of perfection; they *are* the judgment of the Paradise Trinity. Even the Ancients of Days do not sit in judgment except in association with the Universal Censors.

One Censor is commissioned on each of the billion worlds of the central universe, being attached to the planetary administration of the resident Eternal of Days. Neither Perfectors of Wisdom nor Divine Counselors are thus permanently attached to the Havona administrations, nor do we altogether understand why Universal Censors are stationed in the central universe. Their present activities hardly account for their assignment in Havona, and we therefore suspect that they are there in anticipation of the needs of some future universe age in which the Havona population may partially change.

One billion Censors are assigned to each of the seven superuniverses. Both in an individual capacity and in association with Perfectors of Wisdom and Divine Counselors, they operate throughout all divisions of the seven superuniverses. Thus the Censors act on all levels of the grand universe, from the perfect worlds of Havona to the councils of the System Sovereigns, and they are an organic part of all dispensational adjudications of the evolutionary worlds.

Whenever and wherever a Universal Censor is present, then and there is the judgment of Deity. And since the Censors always render their verdicts in liaison with Perfectors of Wisdom and Divine Counselors, such decisions embrace the united wisdom, counsel, and judgment of the Paradise Trinity. In this juridical trio the Perfector of Wisdom would be the "I was," the Divine Counselor the "I will be," but the Universal Censor is always "I am."

The Censors are universe totaling personalities. When a thousand witnesses have given testimony—or a million—when the voice of wisdom has spoken and the counsel of divinity has recorded, when the testimony of ascendant perfection has been added, then the Censor functions, and there is immediately revealed an unerring and divine totaling of all that has transpired; and such a disclosure represents the divine conclusion, the sum and substance of a final and perfect decision. Therefore, when a Censor has spoken, no one else may speak, for the Censor has depicted the true and unmistakable total of all that has gone before. When he speaks, there is no appeal.

Most fully do I understand the operation of the mind of a Perfector of Wisdom, but I certainly do not fully comprehend the working of the adjudicating mind of a Universal Censor. It appears to me that the Censors formulate new meanings and originate new values from the association of the facts, truths, and findings presented to them in the course of an investigation of universe affairs. It seems probable that the Universal Censors are able to bring forth original interpretations of the combination of perfect Creator insight and the perfected creature experience. This association of Paradise perfection and universe experience undoubtedly eventuates a new value in ultimates.

But this is not the end of our difficulties regarding the working of the minds of the Universal Censors. Having made due allowances for all that we know or conjecture about the functioning of a Censor in any given universe situation, we find that we are still unable to predict decisions or to forecast verdicts. We very accurately determine the probable result of the association of Creator attitude and creature experience, but such conclusions are not always accurate forecasts of Censor disclosures. It seems likely that the Censors are in some manner in liaison with the Deity Absolute; we are otherwise unable to explain many of their decisions and rulings.

Perfectors of Wisdom, Divine Counselors, and Universal Censors, together with the seven orders of Supreme Trinity Personalities, constitute those ten groups which have been sometimes designated *Stationary Sons of the Trinity.* Together they comprise the grand corps of Trinity administrators, rulers, executives, advisers, counselors, and judges. Their numbers slightly exceed thirty-seven billion. Two billion and seventy are stationed in the central universe and just over five billion in each superuniverse.

It is very difficult to portray the functional limits of the Stationary Sons of the Trinity. It would be incorrect to state that their acts are finite limited, for there are transactions of superuniverse record which indicate otherwise. They act on any level of universe administration or adjudication that may be required by time-space conditions and that pertains to the past, present, and future evolution of the master universe.

5. INSPIRED TRINITY SPIRITS

I will be able to tell you very little concerning the Inspired Trinity Spirits, for they are one of the few wholly secret orders of beings in existence, secret, no doubt, because it is impossible for them fully to reveal themselves even to those of us whose origin is so near the source of their creation. They come into being by the act of the Paradise Trinity and may be utilized by any one or two of the Deities as well as by all three. We do not know whether these Spirits are of completed numbers or are constantly increasing, but we incline to the belief that their number is not fixed.

We fully understand neither the nature nor the conduct of the Inspired Spirits. They may possibly belong to the category of superpersonal spirits. They seem to operate over all known circuits and appear to act well-nigh independently of time and space. But we know little about them except as we deduce their character from the nature of their activities, the results of which we certainly observe here and there in the universes.

Under certain conditions these Inspired Spirits can individualize themselves sufficiently for recognition by beings of Trinity origin. I have seen them; but it would never be possible for the lower orders of celestial beings to recognize one of them. Certain circumstances also arise from time to time in the conduct of the evolving universes in which any being of Trinity origin may directly employ these Spirits in the furtherance of his assignments. We therefore know that they exist, and that under certain conditions we may command and receive their assistance, sometimes recognize their presence. But they are not a part of the manifest and definitely revealed organization intrusted with the conduct of the time-space universes before such material creations are settled in light and life. They have no clearly discernible place in the present economy or administration of the evolving seven superuniverses. They are a secret of the Paradise Trinity.

The Melchizedeks of Nebadon teach that Inspired Trinity Spirits are destined, sometime in the eternal future, to function in the places of the Solitary Messengers, whose ranks are slowly but certainly being depleted by their assignment as associates of certain types of trinitized sons.

The Inspired Spirits are the solitary Spirits of the universe of universes. As Spirits they are very much like the Solitary Messengers except that the latter are distinct personalities. We obtain much of our knowledge of the Inspired Spirits from the Solitary Messengers, who detect their nearness by virtue of an inherent sensitivity to the presence of the Inspired Spirits which functions just as unfailingly as a magnetic needle points to a magnetic pole. When a Solitary Messenger is near an Inspired Trinity Spirit, he is conscious of a qualitative indication of such a divine presence and also of a very definite quantitative registration which enables him actually to know the classification or number of the Spirit presence or presences.

I may relate a further interesting fact: When a Solitary Messenger is on a planet whose inhabitants are indwelt by Thought Adjusters, as on Urantia, he is aware of a qualitative excitation in his detection-sensitivity to spirit presence. In such instances there is no quantitative excitation, only a qualitative agitation. When on a planet to which Adjusters do not come, contact with the natives does not produce any such reaction. This suggests that Thought Adjusters are in some manner related to, or are connected with, the Inspired Spirits of the Paradise Trinity. In some way they may possibly be associated in certain phases of their work; but we do not really know. They both originate near the center and source of all things, but they are not the same order of being. Thought Adjusters spring from the Father alone; Inspired Spirits are the offspring of the Paradise Trinity.

The Inspired Spirits do not apparently belong to the evolutionary scheme of the individual planets or universes, and yet they seem to be almost everywhere. Even as I am engaged in the formulation of this statement, my associated Solitary Messenger's personal sensitivity to the presence of this order of Spirit indicates that there is with us at this very moment, not over twenty-five feet away, a Spirit of the Inspired order and of the third volume of power presence. The third volume of power presence suggests to us the probability that three Inspired Spirits are functioning in liaison.

Of more than twelve orders of beings associated with me at this time, the Solitary Messenger is the only one aware of the presence of these mysterious entities of the Trinity. And further, while we are thus apprised of the nearness of these divine Spirits, we are all equally ignorant of their mission. We really do not know whether they are merely interested observers of our doings, or whether they are, in some manner unknown to us, actually contributing to the success of our undertaking.

We know that the Trinity Teacher Sons are devoted to the *conscious* enlightenment of universe creatures. I have arrived at the settled conclusion that the Inspired Trinity Spirits, by *superconscious* techniques, are also functioning as teachers of the realms. I am persuaded that there is a vast body of essential spiritual knowledge, truth indispensable to high spiritual attainment, which cannot be consciously received; self-consciousness would effectively jeopardize the certainty of reception. If we are right in this concept, and my entire order of being shares it, it may be the mission of these Inspired Spirits to overcome this difficulty, to bridge this gap in the universal scheme of moral enlightenment and spiritual advancement. We think that these two types of Trinity-origin teachers effect some kind of liaison in their activities, but we do not really know.

On the superuniverse training worlds and on the eternal circuits of Havona, I have fraternized with the perfecting mortals—spiritualized and ascendant souls from the evolutionary realms—but never have they been aware of the Inspired Spirits, which ever and anon the powers of detection resident in the Solitary Messengers would indicate were very near us. I have freely conversed with all orders of the Sons of God, high and low, and they likewise are unconscious of the admonitions of the Inspired Trinity Spirits. They can and do look back in their experiences and recount happenings which are difficult to explain if the action of such Spirits is not taken into account. But excepting Solitary Messengers, and sometimes Trinity-origin beings, none of the celestial family have ever been conscious of the nearness of the Inspired Spirits.

I do not believe the Inspired Trinity Spirits are playing hide and seek with me. They are probably trying just as hard to disclose themselves to me as I am to communicate with them; our difficulties and limitations must be mutual and inherent. I am satisfied that there are no arbitrary secrets in the universe; therefore will I never cease in my efforts to solve the mystery of the isolation of these Spirits belonging to my order of creation.

And from all this, you mortals, just now taking your first step on the eternal journey, can well see that you must advance a long way before you will progress by "sight" and "material" assurance. You will long use faith and be dependent on revelation if you hope to progress quickly and safely.

6. HAVONA NATIVES

The Havona natives are the direct creation of the Paradise Trinity, and their number is beyond the concept of your circumscribed minds. Neither is it possible for Urantians to conceive of the inherent endowments of such divinely perfect creatures as these Trinity-origin races of the eternal universe. You can never truly envisage these glorious creatures; you must await your arrival in Havona, when you can greet them as spirit comrades.

During your long sojourn on the billion worlds of Havona culture you will develop an eternal friendship for these superb beings. And how deep is that friendship which grows up between the lowest personal creature from the worlds of space and these high personal beings native to the perfect spheres of the central universe! Ascending mortals, in their long and loving association with the Havona natives, do much to compensate for the spiritual impoverishment of the earlier stages of mortal progression. At the same time, through their contacts with ascending pilgrims, the Havoners gain an experience which to no small extent overcomes the experiential handicap of having always lived a life of divine perfection. The good to both ascending mortal and Havona native is great and mutual.

Havona natives, like all other Trinity-origin personalities, are projected in divine perfection, and as with other Trinity-origin personalities, the passing of time may add to their stores of experiential endowments. But unlike the Stationary Sons of the Trinity, Havoners may evolve in status, may have an unrevealed future eternity-destiny. This is illustrated by those Havoners who service-factualize capacity for fusion with a non-Adjuster Father fragment and so qualify for membership in the Mortal Corps of the Finality. And there are other finaliter corps open to these natives of the central universe.

The status evolution of Havona natives has occasioned much speculation on Uversa. Since they are constantly filtering into the several Paradise Corps of the Finality, and since no more are being created, it is apparent that the number of natives remaining in Havona is constantly diminishing. The ultimate consequences of these transactions have never been revealed to us, but we do not believe that Havona will ever be entirely depleted of its natives. We have entertained the theory that Havoners will possibly cease entering the finaliter corps sometime during the ages of the successive creations of the outer space levels.

We have also entertained the thought that in these subsequent universe ages the central universe may be peopled by a mixed group of resident beings, a citizenship consisting only in part of the original Havona natives. We do not know what order or type of creature may be thus destined to residential status in the future Havona, but we have thought of:

1. The univitatia, who are at present the permanent citizens of the local universe constellations.

2. Future types of mortals who may be born on the inhabited spheres of the superuniverses in the flowering of the ages of light and life.

3. The incoming spiritual aristocracy of the successive outer universes.

We know that the Havona of the previous universe age was somewhat different from the Havona of the present age. We deem it no more than reasonable to assume that we are now witnessing those slow changes in the central universe that are anticipatory of the ages to come. One thing is certain: The universe is nonstatic; only God is changeless.

7. PARADISE CITIZENS

There are resident on Paradise numerous groups of superb beings, the Paradise Citizens. They are not directly concerned with the scheme of perfecting ascending will creatures and are not, therefore, fully revealed to Urantia mortals. There are more than three thousand orders of these supernal intelligences, the last group having been personalized simultaneously with the mandate of the Trinity which promulgated the creative plan of the seven superuniverses of time and space.

Paradise Citizens and Havona natives are sometimes designated collectively as *Paradise-Havona personalities.*

This completes the story of those beings who are brought into existence by the Paradise Trinity. None of them have ever gone astray. And yet, in the highest sense, they are all freewill endowed.

Trinity-origin beings possess prerogatives of transit which make them independent of transport personalities, such as seraphim. We all possess the power of moving about freely and quickly in the universe of universes. Excepting the Inspired Trinity Spirits, we cannot attain the almost unbelievable velocity of the Solitary Messengers, but we are able so to utilize the sum total of the transport facilities in space that we can reach any point in a superuniverse, from its headquarters, in less than one year of Urantia time. It required 109 days of your time for me to journey from Uversa to Urantia.

Through these same avenues we are enabled to intercommunicate instantaneously. Our entire order of creation finds itself in touch with every individual embraced within every division of the children of the Paradise Trinity save only the Inspired Spirits.

[Presented by a Divine Counselor of Uversa.]

PAPER 20

THE PARADISE SONS OF GOD

AS THEY function in the superuniverse of Orvonton, the Sons of God are classified under three general heads:

1. The Descending Sons of God.
2. The Ascending Sons of God.
3. The Trinitized Sons of God.

Descending orders of sonship include personalities who are of direct and divine creation. Ascending sons, such as mortal creatures, achieve this status by experiential participation in the creative technique known as evolution. Trinitized Sons are a group of composite origin which includes all beings embraced by the Paradise Trinity even though not of direct Trinity origin.

1. THE DESCENDING SONS OF GOD

All descending Sons of God have high and divine origins. They are dedicated to the descending ministry of service on the worlds and systems of time and space, there to facilitate the progress in the Paradise climb of the lowly creatures of evolutionary origin—the ascending sons of God. Of the numerous orders of descending Sons, seven will be depicted in these narratives. Those Sons who come forth from the Deities on the central Isle of Light and Life are called the *Paradise Sons of God* and embrace the following three orders:

1. Creator Sons—the Michaels.
2. Magisterial Sons—the Avonals.
3. Trinity Teacher Sons—the Daynals.

The remaining four orders of descending sonship are known as the *Local Universe Sons of God:*

4. Melchizedek Sons.
5. Vorondadek Sons.
6. Lanonandek Sons.
7. The Life Carriers.

Melchizedeks are the joint offspring of a local universe Creator Son, Creative Spirit, and Father Melchizedek. Both Vorondadeks and Lanonandeks are brought into being by a Creator Son and his Creative Spirit associate. Vorondadeks are best known as the Most Highs, the Constellation Fathers; Lanonandeks as System Sovereigns and as Planetary Princes. The threefold order of Life Carriers is brought into being by a Creator Son and Creative Spirit associated with one of the three Ancients of Days of the superuniverse of jurisdiction. But the natures and activities of these Local Universe Sons of God are more properly portrayed in those papers dealing with the affairs of the local creations.

The Paradise Sons of God are of threefold origin: The primary or Creator Sons are brought into being by the Universal Father and the Eternal Son; the secondary or Magisterial Sons are children of the Eternal Son and the Infinite Spirit; the Trinity Teacher Sons are the offspring of the Father, Son, and Spirit. From the standpoint of service, worship, and supplication the Paradise Sons are as one; their spirit is one, and their work is identical in quality and completeness.

As the Paradise orders of Days proved to be divine administrators, so have the orders of Paradise Sons revealed themselves as divine ministers—creators, servers, bestowers, judges, teachers, and truth revealers. They range the universe of universes from the shores of the eternal Isle to the inhabited worlds of time and space, performing manifold services in the central and superuniverses not disclosed in these narratives. They are variously organized, dependent on the nature and whereabouts of their service, but in a local universe both Magisterial and Teacher Sons serve under the direction of the Creator Son who presides over that domain.

The Creator Sons seem to possess a spiritual endowment centering in their persons, which they control and which they can bestow, as did your own Creator Son when he poured out his spirit upon all mortal flesh on Urantia. Each Creator Son is endowed with this spiritual drawing power in his own realm; he is personally conscious of every act and emotion of every descending Son of God serving in his domain. Here is a divine reflection, a local universe duplication, of that absolute spiritual drawing power of the Eternal Son which enables him to reach out to make and maintain contact with all his Paradise Sons, no matter where they may be in all the universe of universes.

The Paradise Creator Sons serve not only as Sons in their descending ministrations of service and bestowal, but when they have completed their bestowal careers, each functions as a universe Father in his own creation, while the other Sons of God continue the service of bestowal and spiritual uplifting designed to win the planets, one by one, to the willing recognition of the loving rule of the Universal Father, culminating in creature consecration to the will of the Paradise Father and in planetary loyalty to the universe sovereignty of his Creator Son.

In a sevenfold Creator Son, Creator and creature are forever blended in understanding, sympathetic, and merciful association. The entire order of Michael, the Creator Sons, is so unique that the consideration of their natures and activities will be reserved to the next paper in this series, while this narrative will be chiefly concerned with the two remaining orders of Paradise sonship: the Magisterial Sons and the Trinity Teacher Sons.

2. THE MAGISTERIAL SONS

Every time an original and absolute concept of being formulated by the Eternal Son unites with a new and divine ideal of loving service conceived by the Infinite Spirit, a new and original Son of God, a Paradise Magisterial Son, is produced. These Sons constitute the order of Avonals in contradistinction to the order of Michael, the Creator Sons. Though not creators in the personal sense, they are closely associated with the Michaels in all their work. The Avonals are planetary ministers and judges, the magistrates of the time-space realms —of all races, to all worlds, and in all universes.

We have reasons for believing that the total number of Magisterial Sons in the grand universe is about one billion. They are a self-governing order, being directed by their supreme council on Paradise, which is made up of experienced Avonals drawn from the services of all universes. But when assigned to, and commissioned in, a local universe, they serve under the direction of the Creator Son of that domain.

Avonals are the Paradise Sons of service and bestowal to the individual planets of the local universes. And since each Avonal Son has an exclusive personality, since no two are alike, their work is individually unique in the realms of their sojourn, where they are often incarnated in the likeness of mortal flesh and sometimes are born of earthly mothers on the evolutionary worlds.

In addition to their services on the higher administrative levels, the Avonals have a threefold function on the inhabited worlds:

1. *Judicial Actions.* They act at the close of the planetary dispensations. In time, scores—hundreds—of such missions may be executed on each individual world, and they may go to the same or to other worlds times without number as dispensation terminators, liberators of the sleeping survivors.

2. *Magisterial Missions.* A planetary visitation of this type usually occurs prior to the arrival of a bestowal Son. On such a mission an Avonal appears as an adult of the realm by a technique of incarnation not involving mortal birth. Subsequent to this first and usual magisterial visit, Avonals may repeatedly serve in a magisterial capacity on the same planet both before and after the appearance of the bestowal Son. On these additional magisterial missions an Avonal may or may not appear in material and visible form, but on none of them will he be born into the world as a helpless babe.

3. *Bestowal Missions.* The Avonal Sons do all, at least once, bestow themselves upon some mortal race on some evolutionary world. Judicial visits are numerous, magisterial missions may be plural, but on each planet there appears but one bestowal Son. Bestowal Avonals are born of woman as Michael of Nebadon was incarnated on Urantia.

There is no limit to the number of times the Avonal Sons may serve on magisterial and on bestowal missions, but usually, when the experience has been seven times traversed, there is suspension in favor of those who have had less of such service. These Sons of multiple bestowal experience are then assigned to the high personal council of a Creator Son, thus becoming participants in the administration of universe affairs.

In all their work for and on the inhabited worlds, the Magisterial Sons are assisted by two orders of local universe creatures, the Melchizedeks and the archangels, while on bestowal missions they are also accompanied by the Brilliant Evening Stars, likewise of origin in the local creations. In every planetary effort the secondary Paradise Sons, the Avonals, are supported by the full power and authority of a primary Paradise Son, the Creator Son of their local universe of service. To all intents and purposes their work on the inhabited spheres is just as effective and acceptable as would have been the service of a Creator Son upon such worlds of mortal habitation.

3. JUDICIAL ACTIONS

The Avonals are known as Magisterial Sons because they are the high magistrates of the realms, the adjudicators of the successive dispensations of the worlds of time. They preside over the awakening of the sleeping survivors, sit in judgment on the realm, bring to an end a dispensation of suspended justice, execute the mandates of an age of probationary mercy, reassign the space creatures of planetary ministry to the tasks of the new dispensation, and return to the headquarters of their local universe upon the completion of their mission.

When they sit in judgment on the destinies of an age, the Avonals decree the fate of the evolutionary races, but though they may render judgments extinguishing the identity of personal creatures, they do not execute such sentences. Verdicts of this nature are executed by none but the authorities of a superuniverse.

The arrival of a Paradise Avonal on an evolutionary world for the purpose of terminating a dispensation and of inaugurating a new era of planetary progression is not necessarily either a magisterial mission or a bestowal mission. Magisterial missions sometimes, and bestowal missions always, are incarnations; that is, on such assignments the Avonals serve on a planet in material form—literally. Their other visits are "technical," and in this capacity an Avonal is not incarnated for planetary service. If a Magisterial Son comes solely as a dispensational adjudicator, he arrives on a planet as a spiritual being, invisible to the material creatures of the realm. Such technical visits occur repeatedly in the long history of an inhabited world.

Avonal Sons may act as planetary judges prior to both the magisterial and bestowal experiences. On either of these missions, however, the incarnated Son will judge the passing planetary age; likewise does a Creator Son when incarnated on a mission of bestowal in the likeness of mortal flesh. When a Paradise Son visits an evolutionary world and becomes like one of its people, his presence terminates a dispensation and constitutes a judgment of the realm.

4. MAGISTERIAL MISSIONS

Prior to the planetary appearance of a bestowal Son, an inhabited world is usually visited by a Paradise Avonal on a magisterial mission. If it is an initial magisterial visitation, the Avonal is always incarnated as a material being. He appears on the planet of assignment as a full-fledged male of the mortal races, a being fully visible to, and in physical contact with, the mortal creatures of his day and generation. Throughout a magisterial incarnation the connection of the Avonal Son with the local and the universal spiritual forces is complete and unbroken.

A planet may experience many magisterial visitations both before and after the appearance of a bestowal Son. It may be visited many times by the same or other Avonals, acting as dispensational adjudicators, but such technical missions of judgment are neither bestowal nor magisterial, and the Avonals are never incarnated at such times. Even when a planet is blessed with repeated magisterial missions, the Avonals do not always submit to mortal incarnation; and when they do serve in the likeness of mortal flesh, they always appear as adult beings of the realm; they are not born of woman.

When incarnated on either bestowal or magisterial missions, the Paradise Sons have experienced Adjusters, and these Adjusters are different for each incarnation. The Adjusters that occupy the minds of the incarnated Sons of God can never hope for personality through fusion with the human-divine beings of their indwelling, but they are often personalized by fiat of the Universal Father. Such Adjusters form the supreme Divinington council of direction for the administration, identification, and dispatch of Mystery Monitors to the inhabited realms. They also receive and accredit Adjusters on their return to the "bosom of the Father" upon the mortal dissolution of their earthly tabernacles. In this way the faithful Adjusters of the world judges become the exalted chiefs of their kind.

Urantia has never been host to an Avonal Son on a magisterial mission. Had Urantia followed the general plan of inhabited worlds, it would have been blessed with a magisterial mission sometime between the days of Adam and the bestowal of Christ Michael. But the regular sequence of Paradise Sons on your planet was wholly deranged by the appearance of your Creator Son on his terminal bestowal nineteen hundred years ago.

Urantia may yet be visited by an Avonal commissioned to incarnate on a magisterial mission, but regarding the future appearance of Paradise Sons, not even "the angels in heaven know the time or manner of such visitations," for a Michael-bestowal world becomes the individual and personal ward of a Master Son and, as such, is wholly subject to his own plans and rulings. And with your world, this is further complicated by Michael's promise to return. Regardless of the misunderstandings about the Urantian sojourn of Michael of Nebadon, one thing is certainly authentic—his promise to come back to your world. In view of this prospect, only time can reveal the future order of the visitations of the Paradise Sons of God on Urantia.

5. BESTOWAL OF THE PARADISE SONS OF GOD

The Eternal Son is the eternal Word of God. The Eternal Son is the perfect expression of the "first" absolute and infinite thought of his eternal Father. When a personal duplication or divine extension of this Original Son starts on a bestowal mission of mortal incarnation, it becomes literally true that the divine "Word is made flesh," and that the Word thus dwells among the lowly beings of animal origin.

On Urantia there is a widespread belief that the purpose of a Son's bestowal is, in some manner, to influence the attitude of the Universal Father. But your enlightenment should indicate that this is not true. The bestowals of the Avonal and the Michael Sons are a necessary part of the experiential process designed to make these Sons safe and sympathetic magistrates and rulers of the peoples and planets of time and space. The career of sevenfold bestowal is the supreme goal of all Paradise Creator Sons. And all Magisterial Sons are motivated by this same spirit of service which so abundantly characterizes the primary Creator Sons and the Eternal Son of Paradise.

Some order of Paradise Son must be bestowed upon each mortal-inhabited world in order to make it possible for Thought Adjusters to indwell the minds of all normal human beings on that sphere, for the Adjusters do not come to *all* bona fide human beings until the Spirit of Truth has been poured out upon all flesh; and the sending of the Spirit of Truth is dependent upon the return to universe headquarters of a Paradise Son who has successfully executed a mission of mortal bestowal upon an evolving world.

During the course of the long history of an inhabited planet, many dispensational adjudications will take place, and more than one magisterial mission may occur, but ordinarily only once will a bestowal Son serve on the sphere. It is only required that each inhabited world have one bestowal Son come to live the full mortal life from birth to death. Sooner or later, regardless of spiritual status, every mortal-inhabited world is destined to become host to a Magisterial Son on a bestowal mission except the one planet in each local universe whereon a Creator Son elects to make his mortal bestowal.

Understanding more about the bestowal Sons, you discern why so much interest attaches to Urantia in the history of Nebadon. Your small and insignificant planet is of local universe concern simply because it is the mortal home world of Jesus of Nazareth. It was the scene of the final and triumphant bestowal of your Creator Son, the arena in which Michael won the supreme personal sovereignty of the universe of Nebadon.

At the headquarters of his local universe a Creator Son, especially after the completion of his own mortal bestowal, spends much of his time in counseling and instructing the college of associate Sons, the Magisterial Sons and others. In love and devotion, with tender mercy and affectionate consideration, these Magisterial Sons bestow themselves upon the worlds of space. And in no way are these planetary services inferior to the mortal bestowals of the Michaels. It is true that your Creator Son selected for the realm of his final adventure in creature experience one which had had unusual misfortunes. But no planet could ever be in such a condition that it would require the bestowal of a Creator Son to effect its spiritual rehabilitation. Any Son of the bestowal group would have equally sufficed, for in all their work on the worlds of a local universe the Magisterial Sons are just as divinely effective and all wise as would have been their Paradise brother, the Creator Son.

Though the possibility of disaster always attends these Paradise Sons during their bestowal incarnations, I have yet to see the record of the failure or default of either a Magisterial or a Creator Son on a mission of bestowal. Both are of origin too close to absolute perfection to fail. They indeed assume the risk, really become like the mortal creatures of flesh and blood and thereby gain the unique creature experience, but within the range of my observation they always succeed. They never fail to achieve the goal of the bestowal mission. The story of their bestowal and planetary service throughout Nebadon constitutes the most noble and fascinating chapter in the history of your local universe.

6. THE MORTAL-BESTOWAL CAREERS

The method whereby a Paradise Son becomes ready for mortal incarnation as a bestowal Son, becomes enmothered on the bestowal planet, is a universal mystery; and any effort to detect the working of this Sonarington technique is doomed to meet with certain failure. Let the sublime knowledge of the mortal life of Jesus of Nazareth sink into your souls, but waste no thought in useless speculation as to how this mysterious incarnation of Michael of Nebadon was effected. Let us all rejoice in the knowledge and assurance that such achievements are possible to the divine nature and waste no time on futile conjectures about the technique employed by divine wisdom to effect such phenomena.

On a mortal-bestowal mission a Paradise Son is always born of woman and grows up as a male child of the realm, as Jesus did on Urantia. These Sons of supreme service all pass from infancy through youth to manhood just as does a human being. In every respect they become like the mortals of the race into which they are born. They make petitions to the Father as do the children of the realms in which they serve. From a material viewpoint, these human-divine Sons live ordinary lives with just one exception: They do not beget offspring on the worlds of their sojourn; that is a universal restriction imposed on all orders of the Paradise bestowal Sons.

As Jesus worked on your world as the carpenter's son, so do other Paradise Sons labor in various capacities on their bestowal planets. You could hardly think of a vocation that has not been followed by some Paradise Son in the course of his bestowal on some one of the evolutionary planets of time.

When a bestowal Son has mastered the experience of living the mortal life, when he has achieved perfection of attunement with his indwelling Adjuster, thereupon he begins that part of his planetary mission designed to illuminate the minds and to inspire the souls of his brethren in the flesh. As teachers, these Sons are exclusively devoted to the spiritual enlightenment of the mortal races on the worlds of their sojourn.

The mortal-bestowal careers of the Michaels and the Avonals, while comparable in most respects, are not identical in all: Never does a Magisterial Son proclaim, "Whosoever has seen the Son has seen the Father," as did your Creator Son when on Urantia and in the flesh. But a bestowed Avonal does declare, "Whosoever has seen me has seen the Eternal Son of God." The Magisterial Sons are not of immediate descent from the Universal Father, nor do they incarnate subject to the Father's will; always do they bestow themselves as Paradise *Sons* subject to the will of the Eternal Son of Paradise.

When the bestowal Sons, Creator or Magisterial, enter the portals of death, they reappear on the third day. But you should not entertain the idea that they always meet with the tragic end encountered by the Creator Son who sojourned on your world nineteen hundred years ago. The extraordinary and unusually cruel experience through which Jesus of Nazareth passed has caused Urantia to become locally known as "the world of the cross." It is not necessary that such inhuman treatment be accorded a Son of God, and the vast majority of planets have afforded them a more considerate reception, allowing them to finish their mortal careers, terminate the age, adjudicate the sleeping survivors, and inaugurate a new dispensation, without imposing a violent death. A bestowal Son must encounter death, must pass through the whole of the actual experience of mortals of the realms, but it is not a requirement of the divine plan that this death be either violent or unusual.

When bestowal Sons are not put to death by violence, they voluntarily relinquish their lives and pass through the portals of death, not to satisfy the demands of "stern justice" or "divine wrath," but rather to complete the bestowal, "to drink the cup" of the career of incarnation and personal experience in all that constitutes a creature's life as it is lived on the planets of mortal existence. Bestowal is a planetary and a universe necessity, and physical death is nothing more than a necessary part of a bestowal mission.

When the mortal incarnation is finished, the Avonal of service proceeds to Paradise, is accepted by the Universal Father, returns to the local universe of assignment, and is acknowledged by the Creator Son. Thereupon the bestowal Avonal and the Creator Son send their conjoint Spirit of Truth to function in the hearts of the mortal races dwelling on the bestowal world. In the presovereignty ages of a local universe, this is the joint spirit of both Sons, implemented by the Creative Spirit. It differs somewhat from the Spirit of Truth which characterizes the local universe ages following a Michael's seventh bestowal.

Upon the completion of a Creator Son's final bestowal the Spirit of Truth previously sent into all Avonal-bestowal worlds of that local universe changes in nature, becoming more literally the spirit of the sovereign Michael. This phenomenon takes place concurrently with the liberation of the Spirit of Truth for service on the Michael-mortal-bestowal planet. Thereafter, each world honored by a Magisterial bestowal will receive the same spirit Comforter from the sevenfold Creator Son, in association with that Magisterial Son, which it would have received had the local universe Sovereign personally incarnated as its bestowal Son.

7. THE TRINITY TEACHER SONS

These highly personal and highly spiritual Paradise Sons are brought into being by the Paradise Trinity. They are known in Havona as the order of Daynals. In Orvonton they are of record as Trinity Teacher Sons, so named because of their parentage. On Salvington they are sometimes denominated the Paradise Spiritual Sons.

In numbers the Teacher Sons are constantly increasing. The last universal census broadcast gave the number of these Trinity Sons functioning in the central and superuniverses as a little more than twenty-one billion, and this is exclusive of the Paradise reserves, which include more than one third of all Trinity Teacher Sons in existence.

The Daynal order of sonship is not an organic part of the local or superuniverse administrations. Its members are neither creators nor retrievers, neither judges nor rulers. They are not so much concerned with universe administration as with moral enlightenment and spiritual development. They are the universal educators, being dedicated to the spiritual awakening and moral guidance of all realms. Their ministry is intimately interrelated with that of the personalities of the Infinite Spirit and is closely associated with the Paradise ascension of creature beings.

These Sons of the Trinity partake of the combined natures of the three Paradise Deities, but in Havona they seem more to reflect the nature of the Universal Father. In the superuniverses they seem to portray the nature of the Eternal Son, while in the local creations they appear to show forth the character of the Infinite Spirit. In all universes they are the embodiment of service and the discretion of wisdom.

Unlike their Paradise brethren, Michaels and Avonals, Trinity Teacher Sons receive no preliminary training in the central universe. They are dispatched directly to the headquarters of the superuniverses and from there are commissioned for service in some local universe. In their ministry to these evolutionary realms they utilize the combined spiritual influence of a Creator Son and the associated Magisterial Sons, for the Daynals do not possess a spiritual drawing power in and of themselves.

8. LOCAL UNIVERSE MINISTRY OF THE DAYNALS

The Paradise Spiritual Sons are unique Trinity-origin beings and the only Trinity creatures to be so completely associated with the conduct of the dual-origin universes. They are affectionately devoted to the educational ministry to mortal creatures and the lower orders of spiritual beings. They begin their labors in the local systems and, in accordance with experience and achievement, are advanced inward through the constellation service to the highest work of the local creation. Upon certification they may become spiritual ambassadors representing the local universes of their service.

The exact number of Teacher Sons in Nebadon I do not know; there are many thousands of them. Many of the heads of departments in the Melchizedek schools belong to this order, while the combined staff of the regularly constituted University of Salvington embraces over one hundred thousand including these Sons. Large numbers are stationed on the various morontia-training worlds, but they are not wholly occupied with the spiritual and intellectual advancement of mortal creatures; they are equally concerned with the instruction of seraphic beings and other natives of the local creations. Many of their assistants are drawn from the ranks of the creature-trinitized beings.

The Teacher Sons compose the faculties who administer all examinations and conduct all tests for the qualification and certification of all subordinate phases of universe service, from the duties of outpost sentinels to those of star students. They conduct an agelong course of training, ranging from the planetary courses up to the high College of Wisdom located on Salvington. Recognition indicative of effort and attainment is granted to all, ascending mortal or ambitious cherubim, who complete these adventures in wisdom and truth.

In all universes all the Sons of God are beholden to these ever-faithful and universally efficient Trinity Teacher Sons. They are the exalted teachers of all spirit personalities, even the tried and true teachers of the Sons of God themselves. But of the endless details of the duties and functions of the Teacher Sons I can hardly instruct you. The vast domain of Daynal-sonship activities will be better understood on Urantia when you are more advanced in intelligence, and after the spiritual isolation of your planet has been terminated.

9. PLANETARY SERVICE OF THE DAYNALS

When the progress of events on an evolutionary world indicates that the time is ripe to initiate a spiritual age, the Trinity Teacher Sons always volunteer for this service. You are not familiar with this order of sonship because Urantia has never experienced a spiritual age, a millennium of cosmic enlightenment. But the Teacher Sons even now visit your world for the purpose of formulating plans concerning their projected sojourn on your sphere. They will be due to appear on Urantia after its inhabitants have gained comparative deliverance from the shackles of animalism and from the fetters of materialism.

Trinity Teacher Sons have nothing to do with terminating planetary dispensations. They neither judge the dead nor translate the living, but on each planetary mission they are accompanied by a Magisterial Son who performs these services. Teacher Sons are wholly concerned with the initiation of a spiritual age, with the dawn of the era of spiritual realities on an evolutionary planet.

They make real the spiritual counterparts of material knowledge and temporal wisdom.

The Teacher Sons usually remain on their visitation planets for one thousand years of planetary time. One Teacher Son presides over the planetary millennial reign and is assisted by seventy associates of his order. The Daynals do not incarnate or otherwise so materialize themselves as to be visible to mortal beings; therefore is contact with the world of visitation maintained through the activities of the Brilliant Evening Stars, local universe personalities who are associated with the Trinity Teacher Sons.

The Daynals may return many times to an inhabited world, and following their final mission the planet will be ushered into the settled status of a sphere of light and life, the evolutionary goal of all the mortal-inhabited worlds of the present universe age. The Mortal Corps of the Finality has much to do with the spheres settled in light and life, and their planetary activities touch upon those of the Teacher Sons. Indeed, the whole order of Daynal sonship is intimately connected with all phases of finaliter activities in the evolutionary creations of time and space.

The Trinity Teacher Sons seem to be so completely identified with the regime of mortal progression through the earlier stages of evolutionary ascension that we are often led to speculate regarding their possible association with the finaliters in the undisclosed career of the future universes. We observe that the administrators of the superuniverses are part Trinity-origin personalities and part Trinity-embraced ascendant evolutionary creatures. We firmly believe that the Teacher Sons and the finaliters are now engaged in acquiring the experience of time-association which may be the preliminary training to prepare them for close association in some unrevealed future destiny. On Uversa it is our belief that, when the superuniverses are finally settled in light and life, these Paradise Teacher Sons, who have become so thoroughly familiar with the problems of evolutionary worlds and have been so long associated with the career of evolutionary mortals, will probably be transferred to eternal association with the Paradise Corps of the Finality.

10. UNITED MINISTRY OF THE PARADISE SONS

All the Paradise Sons of God are divine in origin and in nature. The work of each Paradise Son in behalf of each world is just as if the Son of service were the first and only Son of God.

The Paradise Sons are the divine presentation of the acting natures of the three persons of Deity to the domains of time and space. The Creator, Magisterial, and Teacher Sons are the gifts of the eternal Deities to the children of men and to all other universe creatures of ascension potential. These Sons of God are the divine ministers who are unceasingly devoted to the work of helping the creatures of time attain the high spiritual goal of eternity.

In the Creator Sons the love of the Universal Father is blended with the mercy of the Eternal Son and is disclosed to the local universes in the creative power, loving ministry, and understanding sovereignty of the Michaels. In the Magisterial Sons the mercy of the Eternal Son, united with the ministry of the Infinite Spirit, is revealed to the evolutionary domains in the careers of these Avonals of judgment, service, and bestowal. In the Trinity Teacher Sons the love, mercy, and ministry of the three Paradise Deities are co-ordinated on the highest time-space value-levels and are presented to the universes as living truth, divine goodness, and true spiritual beauty.

In the local universes these orders of sonship collaborate to effect the revelation of the Deities of Paradise to the creatures of space: As the Father of a local universe, a Creator Son portrays the infinite character of the Universal Father. As the bestowal Sons of mercy, the Avonals reveal the matchless nature of the Eternal Son of infinite compassion. As the true teachers of ascending personalities, the Trinity Daynal Sons disclose the teacher personality of the Infinite Spirit. In their divinely perfect co-operation, Michaels, Avonals, and Daynals are contributing to the actualization and revelation of the personality and sovereignty of God the Supreme in and to the time-space universes. In the harmony of their triune activities these Paradise Sons of God ever function in the vanguard of the personalities of Deity as they follow the never-ending expansion of the divinity of the First Great Source and Center from the everlasting Isle of Paradise into the unknown depths of space.

[Presented by a Perfector of Wisdom from Uversa.]

PAPER 21

THE PARADISE CREATOR SONS

THE Creator Sons are the makers and rulers of the local universes of time and space. These universe creators and sovereigns are of dual origin, embodying the characteristics of God the Father and God the Son. But each Creator Son is different from every other; each is unique in nature as well as in personality; each is the "only-begotten Son" of the perfect deity ideal of his origin.

In the vast work of organizing, evolving, and perfecting a local universe, these high Sons always enjoy the sustaining approval of the Universal Father. The relationship of the Creator Sons with their Paradise Father is touching and superlative. No doubt the profound affection of the Deity parents for their divine progeny is the wellspring of that beautiful and well-nigh divine love which even mortal parents bear their children.

These primary Paradise Sons are personalized as Michaels. As they go forth from Paradise to found their universes, they are known as Creator Michaels. When settled in supreme authority, they are called Master Michaels. Sometimes we refer to the sovereign of your universe of Nebadon as Christ Michael. Always and forever do they reign after the "order of Michael," that being the designation of the first Son of their order and nature.

The original or first-born Michael has never experienced incarnation as a material being, but seven times he passed through the experience of spiritual creature ascent on the seven circuits of Havona, advancing from the outer spheres to the innermost circuit of the central creation. The order of Michael knows the grand universe from one end to the other; there is no essential experience of any of the children of time and space in which the Michaels have not personally participated; they are in fact partakers not only of the divine nature but also of your nature, meaning all natures, from the highest to the lowest.

The original Michael is the presiding head of the primary Paradise Sons when they assemble for conference at the center of all things. Not long since on Uversa we recorded a universal broadcast of a conclave extraordinary on the eternal Isle of one hundred fifty thousand Creator Sons assembled in the parental presence and engaged in deliberations having to do with the progress of the unification and stabilization of the universe of universes. This was a selected group of Sovereign Michaels, sevenfold bestowal Sons.

1. ORIGIN AND NATURE OF CREATOR SONS

When the fullness of absolute spiritual ideation in the Eternal Son encounters the fullness of absolute personality concept in the Universal Father, when such a creative union is finally and fully attained, when such absolute identity of spirit and such infinite oneness of personality concept occur, then, right then and there, without the loss of anything of personality or prerogative by either of the infinite Deities, there flashes into full-fledged being a new and original Creator Son, the only-begotten Son of the perfect ideal and the powerful idea whose union produces this new creator personality of power and perfection.

Each Creator Son is the only-begotten and only-begettable offspring of the perfect union of the original concepts of the two infinite and eternal and perfect minds of the ever-existent Creators of the universe of universes. There never can be another such Son because each Creator Son is the unqualified, finished, and final expression and embodiment of all of every phase of every feature of every possibility of every divine reality that could, throughout all eternity, ever be found in, expressed by, or evolved from, those divine creative potentials which united to bring this Michael Son into existence. Each Creator Son is the absolute of the united deity concepts which constitute his divine origin.

The divine natures of these Creator Sons are, in principle, derived equally from the attributes of both Paradise parents. All partake of the fullness of the divine nature of the Universal Father and of the creative prerogatives of the Eternal Son, but as we observe the practical outworking of the Michael functions in the universes, we discern apparent differences. Some Creator Sons appear to be more like God the Father; others more like God the Son. For example: The trend of administration in the universe of Nebadon suggests that its Creator and ruling Son is one whose nature and character more resemble that of the Eternal Mother Son. It should be further stated that some universes are presided over by Paradise Michaels who appear equally to resemble God the Father and God the Son. And these observations are in no sense implied criticisms; they are simply a recording of fact.

I do not know the exact number of Creator Sons in existence, but I have good reasons for believing that there are more than seven hundred thousand. Now, we know that there are exactly seven hundred thousand Unions of Days and no more are being created. We also observe that the ordained plans of the present universe age seem to indicate that one Union of Days is to be stationed in each local universe as the counseling ambassador of the Trinity. We note further that the constantly increasing number of Creator Sons already exceeds the stationary number of the Unions of Days. But concerning the destiny of the Michaels beyond seven hundred thousand, we have never been informed.

2. THE CREATORS OF LOCAL UNIVERSES

The Paradise Sons of the primary order are the designers, creators, builders, and administrators of their respective domains, the local universes of time and space, the basic creative units of the seven evolutionary superuniverses. A Creator Son is permitted to choose the space site of his future cosmic activity, but before he may begin even the physical organization of his universe, he must spend a long period of observation devoted to the study of the efforts of his older brothers in various creations located in the superuniverse of his projected action. And prior to all this, the Michael Son will have completed his long and unique experience of Paradise observation and Havona training.

When a Creator Son departs from Paradise to embark upon the adventure of universe making, to become the head—virtually the God—of the local universe of his own organization, then, for the first time, he finds himself in intimate contact with, and in many respects dependent upon, the Third Source and Center. The Infinite Spirit, though abiding with the Father and the Son at the center of all things, is destined to function as the actual and effective helper of each Creator Son. Therefore is each Creator Son accompanied by a Creative Daughter of the Infinite Spirit, that being who is destined to become the Divine Minister, the Mother Spirit of the new local universe.

The departure of a Michael Son on this occasion forever liberates his creator prerogatives from the Paradise Sources and Centers, subject only to certain limitations inherent in the pre-existence of these Sources and Centers and to certain other antecedent powers and presences. Among these limitations to the otherwise all-powerful creator prerogatives of a local universe Father are the following:

1. *Energy-matter* is dominated by the Infinite Spirit. Before any new forms of things, great or small, may be created, before any new transformations of energy-matter may be attempted, a Creator Son must secure the consent and working co-operation of the Infinite Spirit.

2. *Creature designs and types* are controlled by the Eternal Son. Before a Creator Son may engage in the creation of any new type of being, any new design of creature, he must secure the consent of the Eternal and Original Mother Son.

3. *Personality* is designed and bestowed by the Universal Father.

The types and patterns of *mind* are determined by the precreature factors of being. After these have been associated to constitute a creature (personal or otherwise), mind is the endowment of the Third Source and Center, the universal source of mind ministry to all beings below the level of Paradise Creators.

The control of *spirit* designs and types depends on the level of their manifestation. In the last analysis, spiritual design is controlled by the Trinity or by the pre-Trinity spirit endowments of the Trinity personalities—Father, Son, and Spirit.

When such a perfect and divine Son has taken possession of the space site of his chosen universe; when the initial problems of universe materialization and of gross equilibrium have been resolved; when he has formed an effective and co-operative working union with the complemental Daughter of the Infinite Spirit—then do this Universe Son and this Universe Spirit initiate that liaison which is designed to give origin to the innumerable hosts of their local universe children. In connection with this event the Creative Spirit focalization of the Paradise Infinite Spirit becomes changed in nature, taking on the personal qualities of the Mother Spirit of a local universe.

Notwithstanding that all Creator Sons are divinely like their Paradise parents, none exactly resembles another; each is unique, diverse, exclusive, and original in *nature* as well as in personality. And since they are the architects and makers of the life plans of their respective realms, this very diversity insures that their domains will also be diverse in every form and phase of Michael-derived living existence which may be created or subsequently evolved therein. Hence the orders of creatures native to the local universes are quite varied. No two are administered or inhabited by dual-origin native beings who are in all respects identical. Within any superuniverse, one half of their inherent attributes are quite alike, being derived from the uniform Creative Spirits; the other half vary, being derived from the diversified Creator Sons. But such diversity does not characterize those creatures of sole origin in the Creative Spirit nor those imported beings who are native to the central or superuniverses.

When a Michael Son is absent from his universe, its government is directed by the first-born native being, the Bright and Morning Star, the local universe chief executive. The advice and counsel of the Union of Days is invaluable at such times. During these absences a Creator Son is able to invest the associated Mother Spirit with the overcontrol of his spiritual presence on the inhabited worlds and in the hearts of his mortal children. And the Mother Spirit of a local universe remains always at its headquarters, extending her fostering care and spiritual ministry to the uttermost parts of such an evolutionary domain.

The personal presence of a Creator Son in his local universe is not necessary to the smooth running of an established material creation. Such Sons may journey to Paradise, and still their universes swing on through space. They may lay down their lines of power to incarnate as the children of time; still their realms whirl on about their respective centers. No material organization is independent of the absolute-gravity grasp of Paradise or of the cosmic overcontrol inherent in the space presence of the Unqualified Absolute.

3. LOCAL UNIVERSE SOVEREIGNTY

A Creator Son is given the range of a universe by the consent of the Paradise Trinity and with the confirmation of the supervising Master Spirit of the superuniverse concerned. Such action constitutes title of physical possession, a cosmic leasehold. But the elevation of a Michael Son from this initial and self-limited stage of rulership to the experiential supremacy of self-earned sovereignty comes as a result of his own personal experiences in the work of universe creation and incarnated bestowal. Until the achievement of bestowal-earned sovereignty, he rules as vicegerent of the Universal Father.

A Creator Son could assert full sovereignty over his personal creation at any time, but he wisely chooses not to. If, prior to passing through the creature bestowals, he assumed an unearned supreme sovereignty, the Paradise personalities resident in his local universe would withdraw. But this has never happened throughout all the creations of time and space.

The fact of creatorship implies the fullness of sovereignty, but the Michaels choose to experientially *earn* it, thereby retaining the full co-operation of all Paradise personalities attached to the local universe administration. We know of no Michael who ever did otherwise; but they all could, they are truly freewill Sons.

The sovereignty of a Creator Son in a local universe passes through six, perhaps seven, stages of experiential manifestation. These appear in the following order:

1. Initial vicegerent sovereignty—the solitary provisional authority exercised by a Creator Son before the acquirement of personal qualities by the associated Creative Spirit.

2. Conjoint vicegerent sovereignty—the joint rule of the Paradise pair subsequent to the personality achievement of the Universe Mother Spirit.

3. Augmenting vicegerent sovereignty—the advancing authority of a Creator Son during the period of his seven creature bestowals.

4. Supreme sovereignty—the settled authority following the completion of the seventh bestowal. In Nebadon, supreme sovereignty dates from the completion of Michael's bestowal on Urantia. It has existed just slightly over nineteen hundred years of your planetary time.

5. Augmenting supreme sovereignty—the advanced relationship growing out of the settling of a majority of the creature domains in light and life. This stage pertains to the unachieved future of your local universe.

6. Trinitarian sovereignty—exercised subsequent to the settling of the entire local universe in light and life.

7. Unrevealed sovereignty—the unknown relationships of a future universe age.

In accepting the initial vicegerent sovereignty of a projected local universe, a Creator Michael takes an oath to the Trinity not to assume supreme sovereignty until the seven creature bestowals have been completed and certified by the superuniverse rulers. But if a Michael Son could not, at will, assert such unearned sovereignty, there would be no meaning in taking an oath not to do so.

Even in the prebestowal ages a Creator Son rules his domain well-nigh supremely when there is no dissent in any of its parts. Limited rulership would hardly be manifest if sovereignty were never challenged. The sovereignty exercised by a prebestowal Creator Son in a universe without rebellion is no greater than in a universe with rebellion; but in the first instance sovereignty limitations are not apparent; in the second, they are.

If ever the authority or administration of a Creator Son is challenged, attacked, or jeopardized, he is eternally pledged to uphold, protect, defend, and if necessary retrieve his personal creation. Such Sons can be troubled or harassed only by the creatures of their own making or by higher beings of their own choosing. It might be inferred that "higher beings," those of origin on levels above a local universe, would be unlikely to trouble a Creator Son, and this is true. But they could if they chose to. Virtue is volitional with personality; righteousness is not automatic in freewill creatures.

Before the completion of the bestowal career a Creator Son rules with certain self-imposed limitations of sovereignty, but subsequent to his finished bestowal service he rules by virtue of his actual experience in the form and likeness of his manifold creatures. When a Creator has seven times sojourned among his creatures, when the bestowal career is finished, then is he supremely settled in universe authority; he has become a Master Son, a sovereign and supreme ruler.

The technique of obtaining supreme sovereignty over a local universe involves the following seven experiential steps:

1. Experientially to penetrate seven creature levels of being through the technique of incarnated bestowal in the very likeness of the creatures on the level concerned.

2. To make an experiential consecration to each phase of the sevenfold will of Paradise Deity as it is personified in the Seven Master Spirits.

3. To traverse each of the seven experiences on the creature levels simultaneously with the execution of one of the seven consecrations to the will of Paradise Deity.

4. On each creature level, experientially to portray the acme of creature life to Paradise Deity and to all universe intelligences.

5. On each creature level, experientially to reveal one phase of the sevenfold will of Deity to the bestowal level and to all the universe.

6. Experientially to unify the sevenfold creature experience with the sevenfold experience of consecration to the revelation of the nature and will of Deity.

7. To achieve new and higher relationship with the Supreme Being. The repercussion of the totality of this Creator-creature experience augments the superuniverse reality of God the Supreme and the time-space sovereignty of the Almighty Supreme and factualizes the supreme local universe sovereignty of a Paradise Michael.

In settling the question of sovereignty in a local universe, the Creator Son is not only demonstrating his own fitness to rule but is also revealing the nature and portraying the sevenfold attitude of the Paradise Deities. The finite understanding and creature appreciation of the Father's primacy is concerned in the adventure of a Creator Son when he condescends to take upon himself the form and experiences of his creatures. These primary Paradise Sons are the real revealers of the Father's loving nature and beneficent authority, the same Father who, in association with the Son and the Spirit, is the universal head of all power, personality, and government throughout all the universal realms.

4. THE MICHAEL BESTOWALS

There are seven groups of bestowal Creator Sons, and they are so classified in accordance with the number of times they have bestowed themselves upon the creatures of their realms. They range from the initial experience up through five additional spheres of progressive bestowal until they attain the seventh and final episode of creature-Creator experience.

Avonal bestowals are always in the likeness of mortal flesh, but the seven bestowals of a Creator Son involve his appearing on seven creature levels of being and pertain to the revelation of the seven primary expressions of the will and nature of Deity. Without exception, all Creator Sons pass through this seven times giving of themselves to their created children before they assume settled and supreme jurisdiction over the universes of their own creation.

Though these seven bestowals vary in the different sectors and universes, they always embrace the mortal-bestowal adventure. In the final bestowal a Creator Son appears as a member of one of the higher mortal races on some inhabited world, usually as a member of that racial group which contains the largest hereditary legacy of the Adamic stock which has previously been imported to upstep the physical status of the animal-origin peoples. Only once in his sevenfold career as a bestowal Son is a Paradise Michael born of woman as you have the record of the babe of Bethlehem. Only once does he live and die as a member of the lowest order of evolutionary will creatures.

After each of his bestowals a Creator Son proceeds to the "right hand of the Father," there to gain the Father's acceptance of the bestowal and to receive instruction preparatory to the next episode of universe service. Following the seventh and final bestowal a Creator Son receives from the Universal Father supreme authority and jurisdiction over his universe.

It is of record that the divine Son of last appearance on your planet was a Paradise Creator Son who had completed six phases of his bestowal career; consequently, when he gave up the conscious grasp of the incarnated life on Urantia, he could, and did, truly say, "It is finished"—it was literally finished. His death on Urantia completed his bestowal career; it was the last step in fulfilling the sacred oath of a Paradise Creator Son. And when this experience has been acquired, such Sons are supreme universe sovereigns; no longer do they rule as vicegerents of the Father but in their own right and name as "King of Kings and Lord of Lords." With certain stated exceptions these sevenfold bestowal Sons are unqualifiedly supreme in the universes of their abode. Concerning his local universe, "all power in heaven and on earth" was relegated to this triumphant and enthroned Master Son.

Creator Sons, subsequent to the completion of their bestowal careers, are reckoned as a separate order, sevenfold Master Sons. In person the Master Sons are identical with the Creator Sons, but they have undergone such a unique bestowal experience that they are commonly regarded as a different order. When a Creator deigns to effect a bestowal, a real and permanent change is destined to take place. True, the bestowal Son is still and none the less a Creator, but he has added to his nature the experience of a creature, which forever removes him from the divine level of a Creator Son and elevates him to the experiential plane of a Master Son, one who has fully earned the right to rule a universe and administer its worlds. Such beings embody all that can be secured from divine parentage and embrace everything to be derived from perfected-creature experience. Why should man bemoan his lowly origin and enforced evolutionary career when the very Gods must pass through an equivalent experience before they are accounted experientially worthy and competent finally and fully to rule over their universe domains!

5. RELATION OF MASTER SONS TO THE UNIVERSE

The power of a Master Michael is unlimited because derived from experienced association with the Paradise Trinity, is unquestioned because derived from actual experience as the very creatures subject to such authority. The nature of the sovereignty of a sevenfold Creator Son is supreme because it:

1. Embraces the sevenfold viewpoint of Paradise Deity.
2. Embodies a sevenfold attitude of time-space creatures.
3. Perfectly synthesizes Paradise attitude and creature viewpoint.

This experiential sovereignty is thus all-inclusive of the divinity of God the Sevenfold culminating in the Supreme Being. And the personal sovereignty of a sevenfold Son is like the future sovereignty of the sometime-to-be-completed Supreme Being, embracing as it does the fullest possible content of the power and authority of the Paradise Trinity manifestable within the time-space limits concerned.

With the achievement of supreme local universe sovereignty, there passes from a Michael Son the power and opportunity to create entirely new types of creature beings during the present universe age. But a Master Son's loss of power to originate entirely new orders of beings in no way interferes with the work of life elaboration already established and in process of unfoldment; this vast program of universe evolution goes on without interruption or curtailment. The acquirement of supreme sovereignty by a Master Son implies the responsibility of personal devotion to the fostering and the administering of that which has already been designed and created, and of that which will subsequently be produced by those who have been thus designed and created. In time there may develop an almost endless evolution of diverse beings, but no entirely new pattern or type of intelligent creature will henceforth take direct origin from a Master Son. This is the first step, the beginning, of a settled administration in any local universe.

The elevation of a sevenfold bestowal Son to the unquestioned sovereignty of his universe means the beginning of the end of agelong uncertainty and relative confusion. Subsequent to this event, that which cannot be sometime spiritualized will eventually be disorganized; that which cannot be sometime co-ordinated with cosmic reality will eventually be destroyed. When the provisions of endless mercy and nameless patience have been exhausted in an effort to win the loyalty and devotion of the will creatures of the realms, justice and righteousness will prevail. That which mercy cannot rehabilitate justice will eventually annihilate.

The Master Michaels are supreme in their own local universes when once they have been installed as sovereign rulers. The few limitations upon their rule are those inherent in the cosmic pre-existence of certain forces and personalities. Otherwise these Master Sons are supreme in authority, responsibility, and administrative power in their respective universes; they are as Creators and Gods, supreme in virtually all things. There is no penetration beyond their wisdom regarding the functioning of a given universe.

After his elevation to settled sovereignty in a local universe a Paradise Michael is in full control of all other Sons of God functioning in his domain, and he may freely rule in accordance with his concept of the needs of his realms. A Master Son may at will vary the order of the spiritual adjudication and evolutionary adjustment of the inhabited planets. And such Sons do make and carry out the plans of their own choosing in all matters of special planetary needs, in particular regarding the worlds of their creature sojourn and still more concerning the realm of terminal bestowal, the planet of incarnation in the likeness of mortal flesh.

The Master Sons seem to be in perfect communication with their bestowal worlds, not only the worlds of their personal sojourn but all worlds whereon a Magisterial Son has bestowed himself. This contact is maintained by their own spiritual presence, the Spirit of Truth, which they are able to "pour out upon all flesh." These Master Sons also maintain an unbroken connection with the Eternal Mother Son at the center of all things. They possess a sympathetic reach which extends from the Universal Father on high to the lowly races of planetary life in the realms of time.

6. DESTINY OF THE MASTER MICHAELS

No one may with finality of authority presume to discuss either the natures or the destinies of the sevenfold Master Sovereigns of the local universes; nevertheless, we all speculate much regarding these matters. We are taught, and we believe, that each Paradise Michael is the *absolute* of the dual deity concepts of his origin; thus he embodies actual phases of the infinity of the Universal Father and the Eternal Son. The Michaels must be partial in relation to total infinity, but they are probably absolute in relation to that part of infinity concerned in their origin. But as we observe their work in the present universe age, we detect no action that is more than finite; any conjectured superfinite capacities must be self-contained and as yet unrevealed.

The completion of the creature-bestowal careers and the elevation to supreme universe sovereignty must signify the completed liberation of a Michael's finite-action capacities accompanied by the appearance of capacity for more-than-finite service. For in this connection we note that such Master Sons are then restricted in the production of new types of creature beings, a restriction undoubtedly made necessary by the liberation of their superfinite potentialities.

It is highly probable that these undisclosed creator powers will remain self-contained throughout the present universe age. But sometime in the far-distant future, in the now mobilizing universes of outer space, we believe that the liaison between a sevenfold Master Son and a seventh-stage Creative Spirit may attain to absonite levels of service attended by the appearance of new things, meanings, and values on transcendental levels of ultimate universe significance.

Just as the Deity of the Supreme is actualizing by virtue of experiential service, so are the Creator Sons achieving the personal realization of the Paradise-divinity potentials bound up in their unfathomable natures. When on Urantia, Christ Michael once said, "I am the way, the truth, and the life." And we believe that in eternity the Michaels are literally destined to be "the way, the truth, and the life," ever blazing the path for all universe personalities as it leads from supreme divinity through ultimate absonity to eternal deity finality.

[Presented by a Perfector of Wisdom from Uversa.]

PAPER 22

THE TRINITIZED SONS OF GOD

THERE are three groups of beings who are called Sons of God. In addition to descending and ascending orders of sonship there is a third group known as the Trinitized Sons of God. The trinitized order of sonship is subdivided into three primary divisions in accordance with the origins of its many types of personalities, revealed and unrevealed. These primary divisions are:

1. Deity-trinitized Sons.
2. Trinity-embraced Sons.
3. Creature-trinitized Sons.

Irrespective of origin all Trinitized Sons of God have in common the experience of trinitization, either as a part of their origin or as an experience of Trinity embrace subsequently attained. The Deity-trinitized Sons are unrevealed in these narratives; therefore will this presentation be confined to a portrayal of the remaining two groups, more particularly the Trinity-embraced sons of God.

1. THE TRINITY-EMBRACED SONS

All Trinity-embraced sons are originally of dual or single origin, but subsequent to the Trinity embrace they are forever devoted to Trinity service and assignment. This corps, as revealed and as organized for superuniverse service, embraces seven orders of personalities:

1. Mighty Messengers.
2. Those High in Authority.
3. Those without Name and Number.
4. Trinitized Custodians.
5. Trinitized Ambassadors.
6. Celestial Guardians.
7. High Son Assistants.

These seven groups of personalities are further classified, according to origin, nature, and function, into three major divisions: the Trinitized Sons of Attainment, the Trinitized Sons of Selection, and the Trinitized Sons of Perfection.

The Trinitized Sons of Attainment—the Mighty Messengers, Those High in Authority, and Those without Name and Number—are all Adjuster-fused ascendant mortals who have attained Paradise and the Corps of the Finality. But they are not finaliters; when they have been Trinity embraced, their names are removed from the finaliter roll call. The new sons of this order pass through specific courses of training, for comparatively short periods, on the circuit headquarters planets of the Havona circuits under the direction of the Eternals of Days. Thereafter they are assigned to the services of the Ancients of Days in the seven superuniverses.

The Trinitized Sons of Selection embrace the Trinitized Custodians and the Trinitized Ambassadors. They are recruited from certain of the evolutionary seraphim and translated midway creatures who have traversed Havona and have attained Paradise, as well as from certain of the Spirit-fused and the Son-fused mortals who have likewise ascended to the central Isle of Light and Life. Subsequent to their embrace by the Paradise Trinity and after a brief training in Havona, the Trinitized Sons of Selection are assigned to the courts of the Ancients of Days.

The Trinitized Sons of Perfection. The Celestial Guardians and their coordinates, the High Son Assistants, comprise a unique group of twice-trinitized personalities. They are the creature-trinitized sons of Paradise-Havona personalities or of perfected ascendant mortals who have long distinguished themselves in the Corps of the Finality. Some of these creature-trinitized sons, after service with the Supreme Executives of the Seven Master Spirits and after serving under the Trinity Teacher Sons, are retrinitized (embraced) by the Paradise Trinity and then commissioned to the courts of the Ancients of Days as Celestial Guardians and as High Son Assistants. Trinitized Sons of Perfection are assigned directly to the superuniverse service without further training.

Our Trinity-origin associates—Perfectors of Wisdom, Divine Counselors, and Universal Censors—are of stationary numbers, but the Trinity-embraced sons are constantly increasing. All seven orders of Trinity-embraced sons are commissioned as members of one of the seven superuniverse governments, and the number in the service of each superuniverse is exactly the same; not one has ever been lost. Trinity-embraced beings have never gone astray; they may stumble temporarily, but not one has ever been adjudged in contempt of the superuniverse governments. The Sons of Attainment and the Sons of Selection have never faltered in the service of Orvonton, but the Trinitized Sons of Perfection have sometimes erred in judgment and thereby caused transient confusion.

Under the direction of the Ancients of Days all seven orders function very much as self-governing groups. Their scope of service is far-flung; Trinitized Sons of Perfection do not leave the superuniverse of assignment, but their trinitized associates range the grand universe, journeying from the evolutionary worlds of time and space to the eternal Isle of Paradise. They may function in any of the superuniverses, but they do so always as members of the supergovernment of original designation.

Apparently the Trinity-embraced sons have been permanently assigned to the service of the seven superuniverses; certainly this assignment is for the duration of the present universe age, but we have never been informed that it is to be eternal.

2. THE MIGHTY MESSENGERS

Mighty Messengers belong to the ascendant group of the Trinitized Sons. They are a class of perfected mortals who have been rebellion tested or otherwise equally proved as to their personal loyalty; all have passed through some definite test of universe allegiance. At some time in their Paradise ascent they stood firm and loyal in the face of the disloyalty of their superiors, and some did actively and loyally function in the places of such unfaithful leaders.

With such personal records of fidelity and devotion, these ascending mortals pass on through Havona with the stream of the pilgrims of time, attain Paradise, graduate therefrom, and are mustered into the Corps of the Finality. Thereupon they are trinitized in the secret embrace of the Paradise Trinity and subsequently are commissioned to become associated with the Ancients of Days in the administration of the governments of the seven superuniverses.

Every ascendant mortal of insurrectionary experience who functions loyally in the face of rebellion is eventually destined to become a Mighty Messenger of the superuniverse service. Likewise is any ascendant creature who effectively prevents such upheavals of error, evil, or sin; for action designed to prevent rebellion or to effect higher types of loyalty in a universe crisis is regarded as of even greater value than loyalty in the face of actual rebellion.

The senior Mighty Messengers were chosen from those ascendant mortals of time and space who were among the earlier Paradise arrivals, many having traversed Havona in the times of Grandfanda. But the first trinitizing of Mighty Messengers was not effected until the candidate corps contained representatives from each of the seven superuniverses. And the last group of this order to qualify on Paradise embraced ascendant pilgrims from the local universe of Nebadon.

Mighty Messengers are embraced by the Paradise Trinity in classes of seven hundred thousand, one hundred thousand for assignment to each superuniverse. Almost one trillion Mighty Messengers are commissioned on Uversa, and there is every reason to believe that the number serving in each of the seven superuniverses is exactly the same.

I am a Mighty Messenger, and it may interest Urantians to know that the companion and associate of my mortal experience was also triumphant in the great test, and that, though we were many times and for long periods separated in the agelong inward ascent to Havona, we were embraced in the same seven-hundred-thousand group, and that we spent our time passing through Vicegerington in close and loving association. We were finally commissioned and together assigned to Uversa of Orvonton, and we are often dispatched in company for the execution of assignments requiring the services of two Messengers.

Mighty Messengers, in common with all Trinity-embraced sons, are assigned to all phases of superuniverse activities. They maintain constant connection with their headquarters through the superuniverse reflectivity service. Mighty Messengers serve in all sectors of a superuniverse and frequently execute missions to the local universes and even to the individual worlds, as I do on this occasion.

In the superuniverse courts, Mighty Messengers act as defenders of both individuals and planets when they come up for adjudication; they also assist the Perfections of Days in the direction of the affairs of the major sectors. As a group, their chief assignment is that of superuniverse observers. They are stationed on the various headquarters worlds and on individual planets of importance as the official observers of the Ancients of Days. When so assigned, they also serve as advisers to the authorities directing the affairs of the spheres of their sojourn. The Messengers take active part in all phases of the ascendant scheme of mortal progression. With their associates of mortal origin they keep the supergovernments in close and personal touch with the status and progression of the plans of the descending Sons of God.

Mighty Messengers are fully conscious of their entire ascendant careers, and that is why they are such useful and sympathetic ministers, understanding messengers, for service on any world of space and to any creature of time. As soon as you are delivered from the flesh, you will communicate freely and understandingly with us since we spring from all the races on all the evolutionary worlds of space, that is, from those mortal races that are indwelt by, and subsequently fused with, Thought Adjusters.

3. THOSE HIGH IN AUTHORITY

Those High in Authority, the second group of the Trinitized Sons of Attainment, are all Adjuster-fused beings of mortal origin. These are the perfected mortals who have exhibited superior administrative ability and have shown extraordinary executive genius throughout their long ascending careers. They are the cream of governing ability derived from the surviving mortals of space.

Seventy thousand of Those High in Authority are trinitized at each Trinity liaison. Though the local universe of Nebadon is a comparatively young creation, it has representatives among a recently trinitized class of this order. There are now commissioned in Orvonton more than ten billion of these skillful administrators. Like all separate orders of celestial beings, they maintain their own headquarters on Uversa, and like the other Trinity-embraced sons, their reserves on Uversa act as the central directing body of their order in Orvonton.

Those High in Authority are administrators without limitation. They are the everywhere-present and always-efficient executives of the Ancients of Days. They serve on any sphere, on any inhabited world, and in any phase of activity in any of the seven superuniverses.

Having superb administrative wisdom and unusual executive skill, these brilliant beings assume to present the cause of justice in behalf of the superuniverse tribunals; they foster the execution of justice and the rectification of misadaptations in the evolutionary universes. Therefore, if you should ever be cited for errors of judgment while you are ascending the worlds and spheres of your ordained cosmic progression, it is hardly likely that you would suffer injustice since your prosecutors would be onetime ascendant creatures who are personally familiar with every step of the career you have traversed and are traversing.

4. THOSE WITHOUT NAME AND NUMBER

Those without Name and Number constitute the third and last group of the Trinitized Sons of Attainment; they are the ascendant souls who have developed the ability to worship beyond the skill of all the sons and daughters of the evolutionary races from the worlds of time and space. They have acquired a spiritual concept of the eternal purpose of the Universal Father which comparatively transcends the comprehension of the evolutionary creatures of name or number; therefore are they denominated Those without Name and Number. More strictly translated, their name would be "Those *above* Name and Number."

This order of sons is embraced by the Paradise Trinity in groups of seven thousand. There are of record on Uversa over one hundred million of these sons commissioned in Orvonton.

Since Those without Name and Number are the superior spiritual minds of the survival races, they are especially qualified to sit in judgment and to render opinions when a spiritual viewpoint is desirable, and when experience in the ascendant career is essential to an adequate comprehension of the questions involved in the problem to be adjudicated. They are the supreme jurors of Orvonton. A maladministered jury system may be more or less of a travesty of justice on some worlds, but on Uversa and its extension tribunals we employ the highest type of evolved spiritual mentality as juror-judges. Adjudication is the highest function of any government, and those who are intrusted with verdict rendering should be chosen from the highest and most noble types of the most experienced and understanding individuals.

The selection of candidates for the trinitization classes of Mighty Messengers, Those High in Authority, and Those without Name and Number is inherent and automatic. The selective techniques of Paradise are not in any sense arbitrary. Personal experience and spiritual values determine the personnel of the Trinitized Sons of Attainment. Such beings are equal in authority and uniform in administrative status, but they all possess individuality and diverse characters; they are not standardized beings. All are characteristically different, depending on the differentials of their ascendant careers.

In addition to these experiential qualifications, the Trinitized Sons of Attainment have been trinitized in the divine embrace of the Paradise Deities. Consequently they function as the co-ordinate associates of the Stationary Sons of the Trinity, for the Trinity embrace does seem to precipitate out of the stream of future time many of the unrealized potentials of creature beings. But this is true concerning only that which pertains to the present universe age.

This group of sons is chiefly, but not wholly, concerned with the services of the ascendant career of the time-space mortals. If the viewpoint of a mortal creature is ever in doubt, the question is settled by appeal to an ascendant commission consisting of a Mighty Messenger, One High in Authority, and One without Name and Number.

You mortals who read this message may yourselves ascend to Paradise, attain the Trinity embrace, and in remote future ages be attached to the service of the Ancients of Days in one of the seven superuniverses, and sometime be assigned to enlarge the revelation of truth to some evolving inhabited planet, even as I am now functioning on Urantia.

5. THE TRINITIZED CUSTODIANS

The Trinitized Custodians are Trinitized Sons of Selection. Not only do your races and other mortals of survival value traverse Havona, attain Paradise, and sometimes find themselves destined to superuniverse service with the Stationary Sons of the Trinity, but your faithful seraphic guardians and your equally faithful midway associates may also become candidates for the same Trinity recognition and superb personality destiny.

Trinitized Custodians are ascendant seraphim and translated midway creatures who have passed through Havona and have attained Paradise and the Corps of the Finality. Subsequently they were embraced by the Paradise Trinity and were assigned to the service of the Ancients of Days.

The candidates for the Trinity embrace from among the ascendant seraphim are accorded this recognition because of their valiant co-operation with some ascendant mortal who attained the Corps of the Finality and was subsequently trinitized. My own seraphic guardian of the mortal career went through with me, was later trinitized, and now is attached to the Uversa government as a Trinitized Custodian.

And so with the midway creatures; many are translated and achieve Paradise and, along with the seraphim and for the same reasons, are Trinity embraced and commissioned as Custodians in the superuniverses.

The Trinitized Custodians are embraced by the Paradise Trinity in groups of seventy thousand, and one seventh of each group is assigned to a superuniverse. There are now in the service of Orvonton slightly over ten million of these trusted and high Custodians. They serve on Uversa and on the major and minor headquarters spheres. In their labors they are assisted by a corps of several billion seconaphim and other able superuniverse personalities.

The Trinitized Custodians start out their careers as custodians, and they continue as such in the affairs of the supergovernments. In a way, they are officers of their superuniverse governments, but they do not deal with individuals, as do the Celestial Guardians. The Trinitized Custodians administer group affairs and foster collective projects. They are the custodians of records, plans, and institutions; they act as the trustees of undertakings, personality groups, ascendant projects, morontia plans, universe projections, and innumerable other enterprises.

6. THE TRINITIZED AMBASSADORS

Trinitized Ambassadors are the second order of the Trinitized Sons of Selection and like their associates, the Custodians, are recruited from two types of ascendant creatures. Not all ascending mortals are Adjuster or Father fused; some are Spirit fused, some are Son fused. Certain of these Spirit- and Son-fused mortals reach Havona and attain Paradise. From among these Paradise ascenders, candidates are selected for the Trinity embrace, and from time to time they are trinitized in classes of seven thousand. They are then commissioned in the superuniverses as Trinitized Ambassadors of the Ancients of Days. Almost one-half billion are registered on Uversa.

Trinitized Ambassadors are selected for the Trinity embrace upon the advices of their Havona teachers. They represent the superior minds of their respective groups and are, therefore, best qualified to assist the superuniverse rulers in understanding and in administering the interests of those worlds from which the Spirit-fused mortals hail. The Son-fused Ambassadors are of great assistance in our dealings with problems involving the Son-fused order of personality.

Trinitized Ambassadors are the emissaries of the Ancients of Days for any and all purposes, to any and all worlds or universes within the superuniverse of their assignment. They render particular and important services on the headquarters of the minor sectors, and they perform the numberless miscellaneous assignments of a superuniverse. They are the emergency or reserve corps of the Trinitized Sons of the supergovernments, and they are therefore available for a great range of duties. They engage in thousands upon thousands of undertakings in superuniverse affairs which it is impossible to portray to human minds since there is nothing transpiring on Urantia that is in any way analogous to these activities.

7. TECHNIQUE OF TRINITIZATION

I cannot fully unfold to the material mind the experience of the supreme creative performance of perfect and perfected spiritual beings—the act of trinitization. The techniques of trinitization are among the secrets of Vicegerington and Solitarington and are revealable to, and understandable by, none save those who have passed through these unique experiences. Therefore is it beyond the possibility of any being successfully to portray to the human mind the nature and purport of this extraordinary transaction.

Aside from the Deities, only Paradise-Havona personalities and certain members of each of the finaliter corps engage in trinitization. Under specialized conditions of Paradise perfection, these superb beings may embark upon the unique adventure of concept-identity, and they are many times successful in the production of a new being, a creature-trinitized son.

The glorified creatures who engage in such adventures of trinitization may participate in only one such experience, whereas with the Paradise Deities there seems to be no limit to the continued enactment of trinitization episodes. Deity seems to be limited in just one respect: There can be only one Original and Infinite Spirit, only one infinite executive of the united will of the Father-Son.

The ascendant Adjuster-fused mortal finaliters who have attained certain levels of Paradise culture and spiritual development are among those who can essay to trinitize a creature being. Mortal-finaliter companies, when stationed on Paradise, are granted a recess every millennium of Havona time. There are seven different ways such finaliters may elect to spend this duty-free period, and one of these is, in association with some fellow finaliter or some Paradise-Havona personality, to attempt the enactment of creature trinitization.

If two mortal finaliters, on going before the Architects of the Master Universe, demonstrate that they have independently chosen an identical concept for trinitization, the Architects are empowered, on their own discretion, to promulgate mandates permitting these glorified mortal ascenders to extend their recess and to remove themselves for a time to the trinitizing sector of the Paradise Citizens. At the end of this assigned retreat, if they report that they have singly and jointly elected to make the paradisiacal effort to spiritualize, idealize, and actualize a selected and original concept which has not theretofore been trinitized, then does Master Spirit Number Seven issue orders authorizing such an extraordinary undertaking.

Unbelievably long periods of time are sometimes consumed in these adventures; an age seems to pass before these faithful and determined onetime mortals—and sometimes Paradise-Havona personalities—finally achieve their goal, really succeed in bringing their chosen concept of universal truth into actual being. And not always do these devoted couples meet with success; many times they fail, and that through no discoverable error on their part. Candidates for trinitization who thus fail are admitted to a special group of finaliters who are designated as beings who have made the supreme effort and sustained the supreme disappointment. When the Paradise Deities unite to trinitize, they always succeed, but not so with a homogeneous pair of creatures, the attempted union of two members of the same order of being.

When a new and original being is trinitized by the Gods, the divine parents are in deity potential unchanged; but when exalted creature beings enact such a creative episode, one of the contracting and participating individuals undergoes a unique personality modification. The two ancestors of a creature-trinitized son become in a certain sense spiritually as one. We believe that this status of bi-unification of certain spiritual phases of personality will probably prevail until such time as the Supreme Being shall have attained full and completed manifestation of personality in the grand universe.

Simultaneously with the appearance of a new creature-trinitized son, there occurs this functional spiritual union of the two ancestors; the two trinitizing parents become one on the ultimate functional level. No created being in the universe can fully explain this amazing phenomenon; it is a near-divine experience. When the Father and the Son united to eternalize the Infinite Spirit, upon the accomplishment of their purpose they immediately became as one and ever since have been one. And while the trinitization union of two creatures is on the order of the infinite scope of the perfect Deity union of the Universal Father and the Eternal Son, the repercussions of creature trinitization are not eternal in nature; they will terminate upon the completed factualization of the experiential Deities.

While these parents of creature-trinitized sons become as one in their universe assignments, they continue to be reckoned as two personalities in the make-up and roll calls of the Corps of the Finality and of the Architects of the Master Universe. During the current universe age, all trinitization-united parents are inseparable in assignment and function; where one goes the other goes, what one does the other does. If parental bi-unification involves a mortal (or other) finaliter and a Paradise-Havona personality, the united parental beings function neither with the Paradisers, Havoners, nor finaliters. Such mixed unions forgather in a special corps made up of similar beings. And in all trinitization unions, mixed or otherwise, the parental beings are conscious of, and can communicate with, each other, and they can perform duties that neither could have previously discharged.

The Seven Master Spirits have authority to sanction the trinitizing union of finaliters and Paradise-Havona personalities, and such mixed liaisons are always successful. The resultant magnificent creature-trinitized sons are representative of concepts unsuited to the comprehension of either the eternal creatures of Paradise or the time creatures of space; hence they become the wards of the Architects of the Master Universe. These trinitized sons of destiny embody ideas, ideals, and *experience* which apparently pertain to a future universe age and are therefore of no immediate practical value to either the super- or central universe administrations. These unique sons of the children of time and the citizens of eternity are all held in reserve on Vicegerington, where they are engaged in the study of the concepts of time and the realities of eternity in a special sector of the sphere occupied by the secret colleges of the corps of the Creator Sons.

The Supreme Being is the unification of three phases of Deity reality: God the Supreme, the spiritual unification of certain finite aspects of the Paradise Trinity; the Almighty Supreme, the power unification of the grand universe Creators; and the Supreme Mind, the individual contribution of the Third Source and Center and his co-ordinates to the reality of the Supreme Being. In their trinitization adventures the superb creatures of the central universe and Paradise are engaged in a threefold exploration of the Deity of the Supreme which results in the production of three orders of creature-trinitized sons:

1. *Ascender-trinitized Sons.* In their creative efforts the finaliters are attempting to trinitize certain conceptual realities of the Almighty Supreme which they have experientially acquired in their ascension through time and space to Paradise.

2. *Paradise-Havona-trinitized Sons.* The creative efforts of the Paradise Citizens and the Havoners result in the trinitization of certain high spiritual aspects of the Supreme Being which they have experientially acquired on a super-supreme background bordering on the Ultimate and the Eternal.

3. *Trinitized Sons of Destiny.* But when a finaliter and a Paradise-Havoner together trinitize a new creature, this conjoint effort repercusses in certain phases of the Supreme-Ultimate Mind. The resulting creature-trinitized sons are supercreational; they represent actualities of Supreme-Ultimate Deity which have not been otherwise experientially attained, and which, therefore, automatically fall within the province of the Architects of the Master Universe, custodians of those things which transcend the creational limits of the present universe age. The trinitized sons of destiny embody certain aspects of the unrevealed master universe function of the Supreme-Ultimate. We do not know a great deal about these conjoint children of time and eternity, but we know much more than we are permitted to reveal.

8. THE CREATURE-TRINITIZED SONS

In addition to the creature-trinitized sons considered in this narrative, there are numerous unrevealed orders of creature-trinitized beings—the diverse progeny of the multiple liaisons of seven finaliter corps and Paradise-Havona personalities. But all these creature-trinitized beings, revealed and unrevealed, are endowed with personality by the Universal Father.

When new ascender-trinitized and Paradise-Havona-trinitized sons are young and untrained, they are usually dispatched for long periods of service on the seven Paradise spheres of the Infinite Spirit, where they serve under the tutelage of the Seven Supreme Executives. Subsequently they may be adopted for further training in the local universes by the Trinity Teacher Sons.

These adopted sons of high and glorified creature origin are the apprentices, student helpers, of the Teacher Sons, and as regards classification they are often temporarily numbered with these Sons. They may and do execute many noble assignments in self-denial in behalf of their chosen realms of service.

The Teacher Sons in the local universes may nominate their creature-trinitized wards for embrace by the Paradise Trinity. Emerging from this embrace as Trinitized Sons of Perfection, they enter the service of the Ancients of Days in the seven superuniverses, that being the present known destiny of this unique group of twice-trinitized beings.

Not all creature-trinitized sons are Trinity embraced; many become the associates and ambassadors of the Seven Master Spirits of Paradise, of the Reflective Spirits of the superuniverses, and of the Mother Spirits of the local creations. Others may accept special assignments on the eternal Isle. Still others may enter the special services on the secret worlds of the Father and on the Paradise spheres of the Spirit. Eventually many find their way into the conjoint corps of the Trinitized Sons on the inner circuit of Havona.

Excepting the Trinitized Sons of Perfection and those who are forgathering on Vicegerington, the supreme destiny of all creature-trinitized sons appears to be entrance into the Corps of Trinitized Finaliters, one of the seven Paradise Corps of the Finality.

9. THE CELESTIAL GUARDIANS

Creature-trinitized sons are embraced by the Paradise Trinity in classes of seven thousand. These trinitized offspring of perfected humans and of Paradise-Havona personalities are all equally embraced by the Deities, but they are assigned to the superuniverses in accordance with the advice of their former instructors, the Trinity Teacher Sons. Those of more acceptable service are commissioned High Son Assistants; those of less distinguished performance are designated Celestial Guardians.

When these unique beings have been Trinity embraced, they become valuable adjuncts to the superuniverse governments. They are versed in the affairs of the ascendant career, not by personal ascension, but as a result of their service with the Trinity Teacher Sons on the worlds of space.

Almost one billion Celestial Guardians have been commissioned in Orvonton. They are chiefly assigned to the administrations of the Perfections of Days on the headquarters of the major sectors and are ably assisted by a corps of ascendant Son-fused mortals.

The Celestial Guardians are the officers of the courts of the Ancients of Days, functioning as court messengers and as bearers of the summonses and decisions of the various tribunals of the superuniverse governments. They are the apprehending agents of the Ancients of Days; they go forth from Uversa to bring back beings whose presence is required before the superuniverse judges; they execute the mandates for the detention of any personality in the superuniverse. They also accompany Spirit-fused mortals of the local universes when, for any reason, their presence is required on Uversa.

The Celestial Guardians and their associates, the High Son Assistants, have never been indwelt by Adjusters. Neither are they Spirit nor Son fused. The embrace of the Paradise Trinity does, however, compensate for the nonfused status of the Trinitized Sons of Perfection. The Trinity embrace may act solely upon the idea which is personified in a creature-trinitized son, leaving the embraced son otherwise unchanged, but such a limitation occurs only when so planned.

These twice-trinitized sons are marvelous beings, but they are neither as versatile nor dependable as their ascendant associates; they lack that tremendous and profound personal experience which the rest of the sons belonging to this group have acquired by actually climbing up to glory from the dark domains of space. We of the ascendant career love them and do all in our power to compensate their deficiencies, but they make us ever grateful for our lowly origin and our capacity for experience. Their willingness to recognize and acknowledge their deficiencies in the experiencible realities of universe ascension is transcendently beautiful and sometimes most touchingly pathetic.

Trinitized Sons of Perfection are limited in contrast to other Trinity-embraced sons because their experiential capacity is time-space inhibited. They are experience-deficient, despite long training with the Supreme Executives and the Teacher Sons, and if this were not the case, experiential saturation would preclude their being left in reserve for acquiring experience in a future universe age. There is simply nothing in all universal existence which can take the place of actual personal experience, and these creature-trinitized sons are held in reserve for experiential function in some future universe epoch.

On the mansion worlds I have often seen these dignified officers of the high courts of the superuniverse look so longingly and appealingly at even the recent arrivals from the evolutionary worlds of space that one could not help realizing that these possessors of nonexperiential trinitization really envied their supposedly less fortunate brethren who ascend the universal path by steps of bona fide experience and actual living. Notwithstanding their handicaps and limitations they are a wonderfully useful and ever-willing corps of workers when it comes to the execution of the complex administrative plans of the superuniverse governments.

10. HIGH SON ASSISTANTS

The High Son Assistants are the superior group of the retrinitized trinitized sons of glorified ascendant beings of the Mortal Corps of the Finality and of their eternal associates, the Paradise-Havona personalities. They are assigned to the superuniverse service and function as personal aids to the high sons of the governments of the Ancients of Days. They might fittingly be denominated private secretaries. They act, from time to time, as clerks for special commissions and other group associations of the high sons. They serve Perfectors of Wisdom, Divine Counselors, Universal Censors, Mighty Messengers, Those High in Authority, and Those without Name and Number.

If, in discussing the Celestial Guardians, I have seemed to call attention to the limitations and handicaps of these twice-trinitized sons, let me now, in all fairness, call attention to their one point of great strength, the attribute which makes them almost invaluable to us. These beings owe their very existence to the fact that they are the personification of a single and supreme concept. They are the personality embodiment of some divine idea, some universal ideal, as it has never before been conceived, expressed, or trinitized. And they have subsequently been Trinity embraced; thus they show forth and actually embody the very wisdom of the divine Trinity as concerns the idea-ideal of their personality existence. As far as that particular concept is revealable to the universes, these personalities embody all of everything that any creature or Creator intelligence could possibly conceive, express, or exemplify. *They are that idea personified.*

Can you not see that such living concentrations of a single supreme concept of universe reality would be of untold service to those who are intrusted with the administration of the superuniverses?

Not long since I was directed to head a commission of six—one of each of the high sons—assigned to the study of three problems pertaining to a group of new universes in the south parts of Orvonton. I was made acutely aware of the value of the High Son Assistants when I made requisition on the chief of their order on Uversa for temporary assignment of such secretaries to my commission. The first of our ideas was represented by a High Son Assistant on Uversa, who was forthwith attached to our group. Our second problem was embodied in a High Son Assistant assigned to superuniverse number three. We secured much help from this source through the central universe clearinghouse for the co-ordination and dissemination of essential knowledge, but nothing comparable to the assistance afforded by the actual presence of a personality who *is* a concept creature-trinitized in supremacy and Deity-trinitized in finality. Concerning our third problem, the records of Paradise disclosed that such an idea had never been creature trinitized.

High Son Assistants are unique and original personalizations of tremendous concepts and stupendous ideals. And as such they are able to impart inexpressible illumination to our deliberations from time to time. When I am acting on some remote assignment out in the universes of space, think what it means, by way of assistance, if I am so fortunate as to have attached to my mission a High Son Assistant who is the fullness of divine concept regarding the very problem I have been sent to attack and solve; and I have repeatedly had this very experience. The only difficulty with this plan is that no superuniverse can have a complete edition of these trinitized ideas; we only get one seventh of these beings; so it is only about one time in seven that we enjoy the personal association of these beings even when the records indicate that the idea has been trinitized.

We could use to great advantage much larger numbers of these beings on Uversa. Because of their value to the superuniverse administrations, we, in every way possible, encourage the pilgrims of space and also the residents of Paradise to attempt trinitization after they have contributed to one another those experiential realities which are essential to the enactment of such creative adventures.

We now have in our superuniverse about one and a quarter million High Son Assistants, and they serve on both the major and minor sectors, even as they function on Uversa. They very often accompany us on our assignments to the remote universes. High Son Assistants are not permanently assigned to any Son or to any commission. They are in constant circulation, serving where the idea or ideal which they *are* can best further the eternal purposes of the Paradise Trinity, whose sons they have become.

They are touchingly affectionate, superbly loyal, exquisitely intelligent, supremely wise—regarding a single idea—and transcendently humble. While they can impart to you the lore of the universe concerning their one idea or ideal, it is well-nigh pathetic to observe them seeking knowledge and information on hosts of other subjects, even from the ascending mortals.

And this is the narrative of the origin, nature, and functioning of certain of those who are called the Trinitized Sons of God, more particularly of those who have passed through the divine embrace of the Paradise Trinity, and who have then been assigned to the services of the superuniverses, there to give wise and understanding co-operation with the administrators of the Ancients of Days in their untiring efforts to facilitate the inward progress of the ascending mortals of time toward their immediate Havona destination and their eventual Paradise goal.

[Narrated by a Mighty Messenger of the revelatory corps of Orvonton.]

PAPER 23

THE SOLITARY MESSENGERS

SOLITARY Messengers are the personal and universal corps of the Conjoint Creator; they are the first and senior order of the Higher Personalities of the Infinite Spirit. They represent the initial creative action of the Infinite Spirit in solitary function for the purpose of bringing into existence solitary personality spirits. Neither the Father nor the Son directly participated in this stupendous spiritualization.

These spirit messengers were personalized in a single creative episode, and their number is stationary. Although I have one of these extraordinary beings associated with me on this present mission, I do not know how many such personalities exist in the universe of universes. I only know, from time to time, how many are of registry-record as functioning for the time being within the jurisdiction of our superuniverse. From the last Uversa report I observe that there were almost 7,690 trillion Solitary Messengers then operating within the boundaries of Orvonton; and I conjecture that this is considerably less than one seventh of their total number.

1. NATURE AND ORIGIN OF SOLITARY MESSENGERS

Immediately following the creation of the Seven Spirits of the Havona Circuits the Infinite Spirit brought into being the vast corps of Solitary Messengers. There is no part of the universal creation which is pre-existent to the Solitary Messengers except Paradise and the Havona circuits; they have functioned throughout the grand universe from near eternity. They are fundamental to the divine technique of the Infinite Spirit for self-revelation to, and personal contact with, the far-flung creations of time and space.

Notwithstanding that these messengers are existent from the near times of eternity, they are all aware of a beginning of selfhood. They are conscious of time, being the first of the creation of the Infinite Spirit to possess such a time consciousness. They are the first-born creatures of the Infinite Spirit to be personalized in time and spiritualized in space.

These solitary spirits came forth in the dawn of time as full-fledged and perfectly endowed spirit beings. They are all equal, and there are no classes or subdivisions founded on personal variation. Their classifications are based wholly on the type of work to which they are assigned from time to time.

Mortals start out as well-nigh material beings on the worlds of space and ascend inward towards the Great Centers; these solitary spirits start out at the center of all things and crave assignment to the remote creations, even to the individual worlds of the outermost local universes and even on beyond.

Though denominated Solitary Messengers, they are not lonesome spirits, for they truly like to work alone. They are the only beings in all creation who can and do enjoy a solitary existence, albeit they equally enjoy association with the very few orders of universe intelligence with whom they can fraternize.

Solitar Messengers are not isolated in their service; they are constantly in touch wit the wealth of the intellect of all creation as they are capable of "listening i" on all the broadcasts of the realms of their sojourn. They can also intercommicate with members of their own immediate corps, those beings doing the se kind of work in the same superuniverse. They could communicate with other f their number, but they have been directed by the council of the Seven Mas Spirits not to do so, and they are a loyal group; they do not disobey or de lt. There is no record that a Solitary Messenger ever stumbled into darkne

The Soli Messengers, like the Universe Power Directors, are among the very few ty of beings operating throughout the realms who are exempt from apprehensio detention by the tribunals of time and space. They could be cited to app before no one except the Seven Master Spirits, but not in all the annals of th aster universe has this Paradise council ever been called upon to adjudicat case of a Solitary Messenger.

These me gers of solitary assignment are a dependable, self-reliant, versatile, thoro spiritual, and broadly sympathetic group of created beings derived from Third Source and Center; they operate by the authority of the Infinite Spiri dent on the central Isle of Paradise and as personalized on the headqua spheres of the local universes. They are constant partakers of the direct emanating from the Infinite Spirit, even when they function in the local cr s under the immediate influence of the local universe Mother Spirits.

There is a ical reason why these Solitary Messengers must travel and work alone. F rt periods and when stationary, they can collaborate in a group, but wh s ensembled, they are altogether cut off from the sustenance and direction Paradise circuit; they are wholly isolated. When in transit, or when opera the circuits of space and the currents of time, if two or more of this order a se proximity, both or all are thrown out of liaison with the higher circula ces. They are "short circuited" as you might describe it in illustrative . Therefore they have inherent within them a power of automatic alar rning signal, which unerringly operates to apprise them of approaching ts and unfailingly keeps them sufficiently separated as not to interfere eir proper and effective functioning. They also possess inherent and a powers which detect and indicate the proximity of both the Inspired Tr rits and the divine Thought Adjusters.

These messe sess no power of personality extension or reproduction, but there is pra o work of the universes in which they cannot engage, and to which th contribute something essential and helpful. Especially are they the gre vers for those who are concerned in the administration of universe af hey assist us all, from the highest to the lowest.

ASSIMENTS OF SOLITARY MESSENGERS

Soli ssenger e not permanently attached to any individual or group of cel sonalitie They are on duty, always by assignment, and during such service they work under the immediate supervision of those whodirect the realms of their attachment. Among themselves they have neither or;anization nor government of any kind; they are *Solitary* Messengers.

Solitary Messengers are assigned by the Infinite Spirit to the follo;ing seven divisions of service:

1. Messengers of the Paradise Trinity.
2. Messengers of the Havona Circuits.
3. Messengers of the Superuniverses.
4. Messengers of the Local Universes.
5. Explorers of Undirected Assignment.
6. Ambassadors and Emissaries of Special Assignment.
7. Revelators of Truth.

These spirit messengers are in every sense interchangeable 1 one type of service to another; such transfers are constantly taking place ere are no separate orders of Solitary Messengers; they are spiritually alikd in every sense equal. While they are generally designated by number, thre known to the Infinite Spirit by personal names. They are known to tbt of us by the name or number designative of their current assignment.

1. *Messengers of the Paradise Trinity.* I am not permitted veal much of the work of the group of messengers assigned to the Trinitey are the trusted and secret servants of the Deities, and when intrusted wecial messages which involve the unrevealed policies and future conduct Gods, they have never been known to divulge a secret or betray the confi reposed in their order. And all this is related in this connection, not to aboastful of their perfection, but rather to point out that the Deities can andate *perfect beings.*

The confusion and turmoil of Urantia do not signify that thdise Rulers lack either interest or ability to manage affairs differently. Thers are possessed of full power to make Urantia a veritable paradise, h an Eden would not contribute to the development of those strong, nobl xperienced characters which the Gods are so surely forging out on your etween the anvils of necessity and the hammers of anguish. Your anxietie rows, your trials and disappointments, are just as much a part of the dan on your sphere as are the exquisite perfection and infinite adaptatil things to their supreme purpose on the worlds of the central and perferse.

2. *Messengers of the Havona Circuits.* Throughout thlant career you will be vaguely, but increasingly, able to detect the prethe Solitary Messengers, but not until you reach Havona will you reciem unmistakably. The first of the messengers you will see face to be those of the Havona circuits.

Solitary Messengers enjoy special relations with the nthe Havona worlds. These messengers, who are so functionally handi en associating with one another, can and do have a very close anc communion with the Havona natives. But it is quite impossible to c uman minds the supreme satisfactions consequent upon the contac ds of these divinely perfect beings with the spirits of such near-tracen sonalities.

3. *Messengers of the Superuniverses.* The Ancients of Days, those personalities of Trinity origin who preside over the destinies of the seven superuniverses, those trios of divine power and administrative wisdom, are bountifully supplied with Solitary Messengers. It is only through this order of messengers that the triune rulers of one superuniverse can directly and personally communicate with the rulers of another. Solitary Messengers are the only available type of spirit intelligence—aside, possibly, from the Inspired Trinity Spirits—that can be dispatched from the headquarters of one superuniverse directly to the headquarters of another. All other personalities must make such excursions by way of Havona and the executive worlds of the Master Spirits.

There are some kinds of information which cannot be obtained either by Gravity Messengers, reflectivity, or broadcast. And when the Ancients of Days would certainly know these things, they must dispatch a Solitary Messenger to the source of knowledge. Long before the presence of life on Urantia the messenger now associated with me was assigned on a mission out of Uversa to the central universe—was absent from the roll calls of Orvonton for almost a million years but returned in due time with the desired information.

There is no limitation upon the service of Solitary Messengers in the superuniverses; they may function as executioners of the high tribunals or as intelligence gatherers for the good of the realm. Of all the supercreations they most delight to serve in Orvonton because here the need is greatest and the opportunities for heroic effort are greatly multiplied. In the more needy realms we all enjoy the satisfaction of a more replete function.

4. *Messengers of the Local Universes.* In the services of a local universe there is no limit upon the functioning of the Solitary Messengers. They are the faithful revealers of the motives and intent of the local universe Mother Spirit, although they are under the full jurisdiction of the reigning Master Son. And this is true of all messengers operating in a local universe, whether they are traveling out directly from universe headquarters, or whether they are acting temporarily in liaison with Constellation Fathers, System Sovereigns, or Planetary Princes. Before the concentration of all power in the hands of a Creator Son at the time of his elevation as sovereign ruler of his universe, these messengers of the local universes function under the general direction of the Ancients of Days and are immediately responsible to their resident representative, the Union of Days.

5. *Explorers of Undirected Assignment.* When the reserve corps of the Solitary Messengers is overrecruited, there issues from one of the Seven Supreme Power Directors a call for exploration volunteers; and there is never a lack of volunteers, for they delight to be dispatched as free and untrammeled explorers, to experience the thrill of finding the organizing nucleuses of new worlds and universes.

They go forth to investigate the clues furnished by the space contemplators of the realms. Undoubtedly the Paradise Deities know of the existence of these undiscovered energy systems of space, but they never divulge such information. If the Solitary Messengers did not explore and chart these newly organizing energy centers, such phenomena would long remain unnoticed even by the intelligences of adjacent realms. Solitary Messengers, as a class, are highly sensitive to gravity; accordingly they can sometimes detect the probable presence of very small dark planets, the very worlds which are best adapted to life experiments.

These messenger-explorers of undirected assignment patrol the master universe. They are constantly out on exploring expeditions to the uncharted regions of all outer space. Very much of the information which we possess of transactions in the realms of outer space, we owe to the explorations of the Solitary Messengers as they often work and study with the celestial astronomers.

6. *Ambassadors and Emissaries of Special Assignment.* Local universes situated within the same superuniverse customarily exchange ambassadors selected from their native orders of sonship. But to avoid delay, Solitary Messengers are frequently asked to go as ambassadors from one local creation to another, to represent and interpret one realm to another. For example: When a newly inhabited realm is discovered, it may prove to be so remote in space that a long time will pass before an enseraphimed ambassador can reach this far-distant universe. An enseraphimed being cannot possibly exceed the velocity of 558,840 Urantia miles in one second of your time. Massive stars, crosscurrents, and detours, as well as attraction tangents, will all tend to retard such speed so that on a long journey the velocity will average about 550,000 miles per second.

When it develops that it will require hundreds of years for a native ambassador to reach a far-distant local universe, a Solitary Messenger is often asked to proceed there immediately to act as ambassador ad interim. Solitary Messengers can go in very short order, not independently of time and space as do the Gravity Messengers, but nearly so. They also serve in other circumstances as emissaries of special assignment.

7. *Revelators of Truth.* The Solitary Messengers regard the assignment to reveal truth as the highest trust of their order. And they function ever and anon in this capacity, from the superuniverses to the individual planets of space. They are frequently attached to commissions which are sent to enlarge the revelation of truth to the worlds and systems.

3. TIME AND SPACE SERVICES OF SOLITARY MESSENGERS

The Solitary Messengers are the highest type of perfect and confidential personality available in all realms for the quick transmission of important and urgent messages when it is inexpedient to utilize either the broadcast service or the reflectivity mechanism. They serve in an endless variety of assignments, helping out the spiritual and material beings of the realms, particularly where the element of time is involved. Of all orders assigned to the services of the superuniverse domains, they are the highest and most versatile personalized beings who can come so near to defying time and space.

The universe is well supplied with spirits who utilize gravity for purposes of transit; they can go anywhere any time—instanter—but they are not persons. Certain other gravity traversers are personal beings, such as Gravity Messengers and Transcendental Recorders, but they are not available to the super- and the local universe administrators. The worlds teem with angels and men and other highly personal beings, but they are handicapped by time and space: The limit of velocity for most nonenseraphimed beings is 186,280 miles of your world per second of your time; the midway creatures and certain others can, often do, attain double velocity—372,560 miles per second—while the seraphim and others can traverse space at triple velocity, about 558,840 miles per second.

There are, however, no transit or messenger personalities who function between the instantaneous velocities of the gravity traversers and the comparatively slow speeds of the seraphim, except the Solitary Messengers.

Solitary Messengers are, therefore, generally used for dispatch and service in those situations where personality is essential to the achievement of the assignment, and where it is desired to avoid the loss of time which would be occasioned by the sending of any other readily available type of personal messenger. They are the only definitely personalized beings who can synchronize with the combined universal currents of the grand universe. Their velocity in traversing space is variable, depending on a great variety of interfering influences, but the record shows that on the journey to fulfill this mission my associate messenger proceeded at the rate of 841,621,642,000 of your miles per second of your time.

It is wholly beyond my ability to explain to the material type of mind how a spirit can be a real person and at the same time traverse space at such tremendous velocities. But these very Solitary Messengers actually come to, and go from, Urantia at these incomprehensible speeds; indeed, the whole economy of universal administration would be largely deprived of its personal element were this not a fact.

The Solitary Messengers are able to function as emergency lines of communication throughout remote space regions, realms not embraced within the established circuits of the grand universe. It develops that one messenger, when so functioning, can transmit a message or send an impulse through space to a fellow messenger about one hundred light-years away as Urantia astronomers estimate stellar distances.

Of the myriads of beings who co-operate with us in the conduct of the affairs of the superuniverse, none are more important in practical helpfulness and time-saving assistance. In the universes of space we must reckon with the handicaps of time; hence the great service of the Solitary Messengers, who, by means of their personal prerogatives of communication, are somewhat independent of space and, by virtue of their tremendous transit velocities, are so nearly independent of time.

I am at a loss to explain to Urantia mortals how the Solitary Messengers can be without form and yet possess real and definite personalities. Although they are without that form which would naturally be associated with personality, they do possess a spirit presence which is discernible by all higher types of spirit beings. The Solitary Messengers are the only class of beings who seem to be possessed of well-nigh all the advantages of a formless spirit coupled with all the prerogatives of a full-fledged personality. They are true persons, yet endowed with nearly all of the attributes of impersonal spirit manifestation.

In the seven superuniverses, ordinarily—but not always—everything which tends to increase any creature's liberation from the handicaps of time and space proportionately diminishes personality prerogatives. Solitary Messengers are an exception to this general law. They are in their activities all but unrestricted in the utilization of any and all of the limitless avenues of spiritual expression, divine service, personal ministry, and cosmic communication. If you could view these extraordinary beings in the light of my experience in universe administration, you would comprehend how difficult it would be to co-ordinate superuniverse affairs were it not for their versatile co-operation.

No matter how much the universe may enlarge, no more Solitary Messengers will probably ever be created. As the universes grow, the expanded work of administration must be increasingly borne by other types of spirit ministers and by those beings who take origin in these new creations, such as the creatures of the Sovereign Sons and the local universe Mother Spirits.

4. SPECIAL MINISTRY OF SOLITARY MESSENGERS

The Solitary Messengers seem to be personality co-ordinators for all types of spirit beings. Their ministry helps to make all the personalities of the far-flung spiritual world akin. They contribute much to the development, in all spirit beings, of a consciousness of group identity. Every type of spirit being is served by special groups of Solitary Messengers who foster the ability of such beings to understand and fraternize with all other types and orders, however dissimilar.

The Solitary Messengers demonstrate such an amazing ability to co-ordinate all types and orders of finite personality—even to make contact with the absonite regime of the master universe overcontrollers—that some of us postulate that the creation of these messengers by the Infinite Spirit is in some manner related to the Conjoint Actor's bestowal of Supreme-Ultimate Mind.

When a finaliter and a Paradise Citizen co-operate in the trinitization of a "child of time and eternity"—a transaction involving the unrevealed mind potentials of the Supreme-Ultimate—and when such an unclassified personality is dispatched to Vicegerington, a Solitary Messenger (a conjectured personality repercussion of the bestowal of such deity mind) is always assigned as guardian-companion to such a creature-trinitized son. This messenger accompanies the new son of destiny to the world of his assignment and nevermore leaves Vicegerington. When thus attached to the destinies of a child of time and eternity, a Solitary Messenger is forever transferred to the sole supervision of the Architects of the Master Universe. What the future of such an extraordinary association may be, we do not know. For ages these partnerships of unique personalities have continued to forgather on Vicegerington, but not even a single pair has ever gone forth therefrom.

Solitary Messengers are of stationary numbers, but the trinitization of the sons of destiny is apparently an unlimited technique. Since each trinitized son of destiny has assigned to him a Solitary Messenger, it appears to us that at some time in the remote future the supply of messengers will become exhausted. Who will take up their work in the grand universe? Will their service be assumed by some new development among the Inspired Trinity Spirits? Is the grand universe at some remote period going to be more nearly administered by Trinity-origin beings while the single- and dual-origin creatures move on into the realms of outer space? If the messengers return to their former service, will these sons of destiny accompany them? Will the trinitizations between finaliters and Paradise-Havoners cease when the supply of Solitary Messengers has been absorbed as guardian-companions of these sons of destiny? Are all our efficient Solitary Messengers going to be concentrated on Vicegerington? Are these extraordinary spirit personalities going to be eternally associated with these trinitized sons of unrevealed destiny? What significance should we attach to the fact that these couples forgathering on Vicegerington are under the exclusive direction of those mighty mystery beings, the Architects of the Master Universe? These and many similar questions we ask ourselves, and ask numerous other orders of celestial beings, but we do not know the answers.

This transaction, together with many similar occurrences in universe administration, unmistakably indicates that the personnel of the grand universe, even that of Havona and Paradise, is undergoing a definite and certain reorganization in co-ordination with, and with reference to, the vast energy evolutions now taking place throughout the realms of outer space.

We incline to the belief that the eternal future will witness phenomena of universe evolution which will far transcend all that the eternal past has experienced. And we anticipate such tremendous adventures, even as you should, with keen relish and ever-heightening expectation.

[Presented by a Divine Counselor from Uversa.]

PAPER 24

HIGHER PERSONALITIES OF THE INFINITE SPIRIT

ON UVERSA we divide all personalities and entities of the Conjoint Creator into three grand divisions: the Higher Personalities of the Infinite Spirit, the Messenger Hosts of Space, and the Ministering Spirits of Time, those spirit beings who are concerned with teaching and ministering to the will creatures of the ascendant scheme of mortal progression.

Those Higher Personalities of the Infinite Spirit that find mention in these narratives function throughout the grand universe in seven divisions:

1. Solitary Messengers.
2. Universe Circuit Supervisors.
3. Census Directors.
4. Personal Aids of the Infinite Spirit.
5. Associate Inspectors.
6. Assigned Sentinels.
7. Graduate Guides.

Solitary Messengers, Circuit Supervisors, Census Directors, and the Personal Aids are characterized by the possession of tremendous endowments of antigravity. The Solitary Messengers are without known general headquarters; they roam the universe of universes. The Universe Circuit Supervisors and the Census Directors maintain headquarters on the capitals of the superuniverses. The Personal Aids of the Infinite Spirit are stationed on the central Isle of Light. The Associate Inspectors and the Assigned Sentinels are respectively stationed on the capitals of the local universes and on the capitals of their component systems. The Graduate Guides are resident in the Havona universe and function on all its billion worlds. Most of these higher personalities have stations in the local universes, but they are not organically attached to the administrations of the evolutionary realms.

Of the seven classes composing this group, only the Solitary Messengers and perhaps the Personal Aids range the universe of universes. Solitary Messengers are encountered from Paradise outward: through the Havona circuits to the superuniverse capitals and thence out through the sectors and local universes, with their subdivisions, and even to the inhabited worlds. Although Solitary Messengers belong to the Higher Personalities of the Infinite Spirit, their origin, nature, and service have been discussed in the preceding paper.

1. THE UNIVERSE CIRCUIT SUPERVISORS

The vast power currents of space and the circuits of spirit energy may seem to operate automatically; they may appear to function without let or hindrance, but such is not the case. All these stupendous systems of energy are under control; they are subject to intelligent supervision. Universe Circuit Supervisors are concerned, not with the realms of purely physical or material energy—the domain of the Universe Power Directors—but with the circuits of relative spiritual energy and with those modified circuits which are essential to the maintenance of both the highly developed spiritual beings and the morontia or transition type of intelligent creatures. The supervisors do not give origin to circuits of energy and superessence of divinity, but in general they have to do with all higher spirit circuits of time and eternity and with all relative spirit circuits concerned in the administration of the component parts of the grand universe. They direct and manipulate all such spirit-energy circuits outside the Isle of Paradise.

Universe Circuit Supervisors are the exclusive creation of the Infinite Spirit, and they function solely as the agents of the Conjoint Actor. They are personalized for service in the following four orders:

1. Supreme Circuit Supervisors.
2. Associate Circuit Supervisors.
3. Secondary Circuit Supervisors.
4. Tertiary Circuit Supervisors.

The supreme supervisors of Havona and the associate supervisors of the seven superuniverses are of completed numbers; no more of these orders are being created. The supreme supervisors are seven in number and are stationed on the pilot worlds of the seven Havona circuits. The circuits of the seven superuniverses are in the charge of a marvelous group of seven associate supervisors, who maintain headquarters on the seven Paradise spheres of the Infinite Spirit, the worlds of the Seven Supreme Executives. From here they supervise and direct the circuits of the superuniverses of space.

On these Paradise spheres of the Spirit the seven associate circuit supervisors and the first order of the Supreme Power Centers effect a liaison which, under the direction of the Supreme Executives, results in the sub-Paradise co-ordination of all material and spiritual circuits passing out to the seven superuniverses.

On the headquarters worlds of each superuniverse are stationed the secondary supervisors for the local universes of time and space. The major and minor sectors are administrative divisions of the supergovernments but are not concerned in these matters of spirit-energy supervision. I do not know how many secondary circuit supervisors there are in the grand universe, but on Uversa there are 84,691 of these beings. Secondary supervisors are being created right along; from time to time they appear in groups of seventy on the worlds of the Supreme Executives. We obtain them on requisition as we arrange for the establishment of separate circuits of spirit energy and liaison power to the newly evolving universes of our jurisdiction.

A tertiary circuit supervisor functions on the headquarters world of every local universe. This order, like the secondary supervisors, is of continuous creation, being created in groups of seven hundred. They are assigned to the local universes by the Ancients of Days.

Circuit supervisors are created for their specific tasks, and they eternally serve in the groups of their original assignment. They are not rotated in service and hence make an agelong study of the problems found in the realms of their original assignment. For example: Tertiary circuit supervisor number 572,842 has functioned on Salvington since the early concept of your local universe, and he is a member of the personal staff of Michael of Nebadon.

Whether acting in the local or higher universes, circuit supervisors direct all concerned as to the proper circuits to employ for the transmission of all spirit messages and for the transit of all personalities. In their work of circuit supervision these efficient beings utilize all agencies, forces, and personalities in the universe of universes. They employ the unrevealed "high spirit personalities of circuit control" and are ably assisted by numerous staffs composed of personalities of the Infinite Spirit. It is they who would isolate an evolutionary world if its Planetary Prince should rebel against the Universal Father and his vicegerent Son. They are able to throw any world out of certain universe circuits of the higher spiritual order, but they cannot annul the material currents of the power directors.

The Universe Circuit Supervisors have something of the same relationship to spirit circuits that the Universe Power Directors have to material circuits. The two orders are complemental, together having the oversight of all spirit and all material circuits that are controllable and manipulatable by creatures.

The circuit supervisors exercise certain oversight of those mind circuits which are spirit associated much as the power directors have certain jurisdiction over those phases of mind which are physical-energy associated—mechanical mind. In general the functions of each order are expanded by liaison with the other, but the circuits of pure mind are subject to the supervision of neither. Neither are the two orders co-ordinate; in all their manifold labors the Universe Circuit Supervisors are subject to the Seven Supreme Power Directors and their subordinates.

While the circuit supervisors are entirely alike within their respective orders, they are all distinct individuals. They are truly personal beings, but they possess a type of other-than-Father-endowed personality not encountered in any other type of creature in all universal existence.

Although you will recognize and know them as you journey inward towards Paradise, you will have no personal relations with them. They are circuit supervisors, and they attend strictly and efficiently to their business. They deal solely with those personalities and entities having the oversight of those activities which are concerned with the circuits subject to their supervision.

2. THE CENSUS DIRECTORS

Notwithstanding that the cosmic mind of the Universal Intelligence is cognizant of the presence and whereabouts of all *thinking* creatures, there is operative in the universe of universes an independent method of keeping count of all *will* creatures.

The Census Directors are a special and completed creation of the Infinite Spirit, and they exist in numbers unknown to us. They are so created as to be able to maintain perfect synchrony with the reflectivity technique of the superuniverses, while at the same time they are personally sensitive and responsive to intelligent *will.* These directors, by a not-fully-understood technique, are made immediately aware of the birth of will in any part of the grand universe. They are, therefore, always competent to give us the number, nature, and whereabouts of all will creatures in any part of the central creation and the seven superuniverses. But they do not function on Paradise; there is no need for them there. On Paradise knowledge is inherent; the Deities know all things.

Seven Census Directors operate in Havona, one being stationed on the pilot world of each Havona circuit. Excepting these seven and the reserves of the order on the Paradise worlds of the Spirit, all Census Directors function under the jurisdiction of the Ancients of Days.

One Census Director presides at the headquarters of each superuniverse, while subject to such a chief director are thousands upon thousands, one on the capital of every local universe. All personalities of this order are equal excepting those on the Havona pilot worlds and the seven superuniverse chiefs.

In the seventh superuniverse there are one hundred thousand Census Directors. And this number consists entirely of those assignable to local universes; it does not include the personal staff of Usatia, the superuniverse chief of all Orvonton directors. Usatia, like the other superuniverse chiefs, is not directly attuned to the registration of intelligent will. He is solely attuned to his subordinates stationed in the Orvonton universes; thus he acts as a magnificent totaling personality for their reports coming in from the capitals of the local creations.

From time to time the official recorders of Uversa place on their records the status of the superuniverse as it is indicated by the registrations in and upon the personality of Usatia. Such census data is indigenous to the superuniverses; these reports are transmitted neither to Havona nor to Paradise.

The Census Directors are concerned with human beings—as with other will creatures—only to the extent of recording the fact of will function. They are not concerned with the records of your life and its doings; they are not in any sense recording personalities. The Census Director of Nebadon, number 81,412 of Orvonton, now stationed on Salvington, is at this very moment personally conscious and aware of your living presence here on Urantia; and he will afford the records confirmation of your death the moment you cease to function as a will creature.

Census Directors register the existence of a new will creature when the first act of will is performed; they indicate the death of a will creature when the last act of will takes place. The partial emergence of will observed in the reactions of certain of the higher animals does not belong to the domain of the Census Directors. They keep count of nothing but bona fide will creatures, and they are responsive to nothing but *will function.* Exactly how they register the function of will, we do not know.

These beings always have been, and always will be, Census Directors. They would be comparatively useless in any other division of universe labor. But they are infallible in function; they never default, neither do they falsify. And notwithstanding their marvelous powers and unbelievable prerogatives, they are persons; they have recognizable spirit presence and form.

3. PERSONAL AIDS OF THE INFINITE SPIRIT

We have no authentic knowledge as to the time or manner of the creation of the Personal Aids. Their number must be legion, but it is not of record on Uversa. From conservative deductions based on our knowledge of their work, I venture to estimate that their number extends high into the trillions. We hold the opinion that the Infinite Spirit is not limited as to numbers in the creation of these Personal Aids.

The Personal Aids of the Infinite Spirit exist for the exclusive assistance of the Paradise presence of the Third Person of Deity. Although attached directly to the Infinite Spirit and located on Paradise, they flash to and fro to the uttermost parts of creation. Wherever the circuits of the Conjoint Creator extend, there these Personal Aids may appear for the purpose of executing the bidding of the Infinite Spirit. They traverse space much as do the Solitary Messengers but are not persons in the sense that the messengers are.

The Personal Aids are all equal and identical; they disclose no differentiation of individuality. Though the Conjoint Actor looks upon them as true personalities, it is difficult for others to regard them as real persons; they do not manifest a spirit presence to other spirit beings. Paradise-origin beings are always aware of the proximity of these Aids; but we do not recognize a personality presence. The lack of such a presence-form undoubtedly renders them all the more serviceable to the Third Person of Deity.

Of all the revealed orders of spirit beings taking origin in the Infinite Spirit, the Personal Aids are about the only ones you will not encounter on your inward ascent to Paradise.

4. THE ASSOCIATE INSPECTORS

The Seven Supreme Executives, on the seven Paradise spheres of the Infinite Spirit, collectively function as the administrative board of supermanagers for the seven superuniverses. The Associate Inspectors are the personal embodiment of the authority of the Supreme Executives to the local universes of time and space. These high observers of the affairs of the local creations are the joint offspring of the Infinite Spirit and the Seven Master Spirits of Paradise. In the near times of eternity seven hundred thousand were personalized, and their reserve corps abides on Paradise.

Associate Inspectors work under the direct supervision of the Seven Supreme Executives, being their personal and powerful representatives to the local universes of time and space. An inspector is stationed on the headquarters sphere of each local creation and is a close associate of the resident Union of Days.

The Associate Inspectors receive reports and recommendations only from their subordinates, the Assigned Sentinels, stationed on the capitals of the local systems of inhabited worlds, while they make reports only to their immediate superior, the Supreme Executive of the superuniverse concerned.

5. THE ASSIGNED SENTINELS

The Assigned Sentinels are co-ordinating personalities and liaison representatives of the Seven Supreme Executives. They were personalized on Paradise by the Infinite Spirit and were created for the specific purposes of their assignment. They are of stationary numbers, and there are exactly seven billion in existence.

Much as an Associate Inspector represents the Seven Supreme Executives to a whole local universe, so in each of the ten thousand systems of that local creation there is an Assigned Sentinel, who acts as the direct representative of the far-distant and supreme board of supercontrol for the affairs of all seven superuniverses. The sentinels on duty in the local system governments of Orvonton are acting under the direct authority of Supreme Executive Number Seven, the co-ordinator of the seventh superuniverse. But in their administrative organization all sentinels commissioned in a local universe are subordinate to the Associate Inspector stationed at universe headquarters.

Within a local creation the Assigned Sentinels serve in rotation, being transferred from system to system. They are usually changed every millennium of local universe time. They are among the highest ranking personalities stationed on a system capital, but they never participate in deliberations concerned with system affairs. In the local systems they serve as the ex officio heads of the four and twenty administrators hailing from the evolutionary worlds, but otherwise, ascending mortals have little contact with them. The sentinels are almost exclusively concerned in keeping the Associate Inspector of their universe fully informed on all matters relating to the welfare and state of the systems of their assignment.

Assigned Sentinels and Associate Inspectors do not report to the Supreme Executives through a superuniverse headquarters. They are responsible solely to the Supreme Executive of the superuniverse concerned; their activities are distinct from the administration of the Ancients of Days.

The Supreme Executives, Associate Inspectors, and Assigned Sentinels, together with the omniaphim and a host of unrevealed personalities, constitute an efficient, direct, centralized, but far-flung system of advisory and administrative co-ordination of all the grand universe of things and beings.

6. THE GRADUATE GUIDES

The Graduate Guides, as a group, sponsor and conduct the high university of technical instruction and spiritual training which is so essential to mortal attainment of the goal of the ages: God, rest, and then eternity of perfected service. These highly personal beings take their name from the nature and purpose of their work. They are exclusively devoted to the tasks of guiding the mortal graduates from the superuniverses of time through the Havona course of instruction and training which serves to prepare the ascending pilgrims for admission to Paradise and the Corps of the Finality.

I am not forbidden to undertake to tell you of the work of these Graduate Guides, but it is so ultraspiritual that I despair of being able to adequately portray to the material mind a concept of their manifold activities. On the mansion worlds, after your vision range is extended and you are freed from the fetters of material comparisons, you can begin to comprehend the meaning of those realities which "eye cannot see nor ear hear, and which have never entered the concept of human minds," even those things which "God has prepared for those who love such eternal verities." You are not always to be so limited in the range of your vision and spiritual comprehension.

The Graduate Guides are engaged in piloting the pilgrims of time through the seven circuits of Havona worlds. The guide who greets you upon your arrival on the receiving world of the outer Havona circuit will remain with you throughout your entire career on the heavenly circuits. Though you will associate with countless other personalities during your sojourn on a billion worlds, your Graduate Guide will follow you to the end of your Havona progression and will witness your entrance into the terminal slumber of time, the sleep of eternity transit to the Paradise goal, where, upon awakening, you will be greeted by the Paradise Companion assigned to welcome you and perhaps to remain with you until you are initiated as a member of the Mortal Corps of the Finality.

The number of Graduate Guides is beyond the power of human minds to grasp, and they continue to appear. Their origin is something of a mystery. They have not existed from eternity; they mysteriously appear as they are needed. There is no record of a Graduate Guide in all the realms of the central universe until that far-distant day when the first mortal pilgrim of all time made his way to the outer belt of the central creation. The instant he arrived on the pilot world of the outer circuit, he was met with friendly greetings by Malvorian, the first of the Graduate Guides and now the chief of their supreme council and the director of their vast educational organization.

On the Paradise records of Havona, in the section denominated "Graduate Guides," there appears this initial entry:

"And Malvorian, the first of this order, did greet and instruct the pilgrim discoverer of Havona and did conduct him from the outer circuits of initial experience, step by step and circuit by circuit, until he stood in the very presence of the Source and Destiny of all personality, subsequently crossing the threshold of eternity to Paradise."

At that far-distant time I was attached to the service of the Ancients of Days on Uversa, and we all rejoiced in the assurance that, eventually, pilgrims from our superuniverse would reach Havona. For ages we had been taught that the evolutionary creatures of space would attain Paradise, and the thrill of all time swept through the heavenly courts when the first pilgrim actually arrived.

The name of this pilgrim discoverer of Havona is *Grandfanda,* and he hailed from planet 341 of system 84 in constellation 62 of local universe 1,131 situated in superuniverse number one. His arrival was the signal for the establishment of the broadcast service of the universe of universes. Theretofore only the broadcasts of the superuniverses and the local universes had been in operation, but the announcement of the arrival of Grandfanda at the portals of Havona signalized the inauguration of the "space reports of glory," so named because the initial universe broadcast reported the Havona arrival of the first of the evolutionary beings to attain entrance upon the goal of ascendant existence.

Graduate Guides never leave the Havona worlds; they are dedicated to the service of the graduate pilgrims of time and space. And you will sometime meet these noble beings face to face if you do not reject the certain and all-perfected plan designed to effect your survival and ascension.

7. ORIGIN OF THE GRADUATE GUIDES

Though evolution is not the order of the central universe, we believe that the Graduate Guides are the perfected or more experienced members of another order of central universe creatures, the Havona Servitals. Graduate Guides show such a breadth of sympathy and such a capacity for understanding the ascendant creatures that we are convinced they have gained this culture by actual service in the superuniverse realms as the Havona Servitals of universal ministry. If this view is not correct, how then can we account for the continuous disappearance of the senior or more experienced servitals?

A servital will be long absent from Havona on superuniverse assignment, having been on many such missions previously, will return home, be granted the privilege of "personal contact" with the Paradise Central Shining, will be embraced by the Luminous Persons, and disappear from the recognition of his spirit fellows, never more to reappear among those of his kind.

On returning from superuniverse service, a Havona Servital may enjoy numerous divine embraces and emerge therefrom merely an exalted servital. Experiencing the luminous embrace does not necessarily signify that the servital must translate into a Graduate Guide, but almost one quarter of those who achieve the divine embrace never return to the service of the realms.

There appears on the high records a succession of such entries as this:

"And servital number 842,842,682,846,782 of Havona, named Sudna, came over from the superuniverse service, was received on Paradise, knew the Father, entered the divine embrace, and is not."

When such an entry appears on the records, the career of such a servital is closed. But in just three moments (a little less than three days of your time) a newborn Graduate Guide "spontaneously" appears on the outer circuit of the Havona universe. And the number of Graduate Guides, allowing for a slight difference, due no doubt to those in transition, exactly equals the number of vanished servitals.

There is an additional reason for supposing the Graduate Guides to be evolved Havona Servitals, and that is the unfailing tendency of these guides and their associated servitals to form such extraordinary attachments. The manner in which these supposedly separate orders of beings understand and sympathize with one another is wholly inexplicable. It is refreshing and inspiring to witness their mutual devotion.

The Seven Master Spirits and the associated Seven Supreme Power Directors, respectively, are the personal repositories of the mind potential and of the power potential of the Supreme Being which he does not, as yet, operate personally. And when these Paradise associates collaborate to create the Havona Servitals, the latter are inherently involved in certain phases of Supremacy. Havona Servitals are thus, in actuality, a reflection in the perfect central universe of certain evolutionary potentialities of the time-space domains, all of which is disclosed when a servital undergoes transformation and re-creation. We believe that this transformation takes place in response to the will of the Infinite Spirit, undoubtedly acting in behalf of the Supreme. Graduate Guides are not created by the Supreme Being, but we all conjecture that experiential Deity is in some way concerned in those transactions which bring these beings into existence.

The Havona now traversed by ascending mortals differs in many respects from the central universe as it was before the times of Grandfanda. The arrival of mortal ascenders on the Havona circuits inaugurated sweeping modifications in the organization of the central and divine creation, modifications undoubtedly initiated by the Supreme Being—the God of evolutionary creatures—in response to the arrival of the first of his experiential children from the seven superuniverses. The appearance of the Graduate Guides, together with the creation of the tertiary supernaphim, is indicative of these performances of God the Supreme.

[Presented by a Divine Counselor of Uversa.]

PAPER 25

THE MESSENGER HOSTS OF SPACE

RANKING intermediately in the family of the Infinite Spirit are the Messenger Hosts of Space. These versatile beings function as the connecting links between the higher personalities and the ministering spirits. The messenger hosts include the following orders of celestial beings:

1. Havona Servitals.
2. Universal Conciliators.
3. Technical Advisers.
4. Custodians of Records on Paradise.
5. Celestial Recorders.
6. Morontia Companions.
7. Paradise Companions.

Of the seven groups enumerated, only three—servitals, conciliators, and Morontia Companions—are created as such; the remaining four represent attainment levels of the angelic orders. In accordance with inherent nature and attained status, the messenger hosts variously serve in the universe of universes but always subject to the direction of those who rule the realms of their assignment.

1. THE HAVONA SERVITALS

Though denominated servitals, these "midway creatures" of the central universe are not servants in any menial sense of the word. In the spiritual world there is no such thing as menial work; all service is sacred and exhilarating; neither do the higher orders of beings look down upon the lower orders of existence.

The Havona Servitals are the joint creative work of the Seven Master Spirits and their associates, the Seven Supreme Power Directors. This creative collaboration comes the nearest to being the pattern for the long list of reproductions of the dual order in the evolutionary universes, extending from the creation of a Bright and Morning Star by a Creator Son-Creative Spirit liaison down to sex procreation on worlds like Urantia.

The number of servitals is prodigious, and more are being created all the time. They appear in groups of one thousand on the third moment following the assembly of the Master Spirits and the Supreme Power Directors at their joint area in the far northerly sector of Paradise. Every fourth servital is more physical in type than the others; that is, out of each thousand, seven hundred and fifty are apparently true to spirit type, but two hundred and fifty are semiphysical in nature. These *fourth creatures* are somewhat on the order of material beings (material in the Havona sense), resembling the physical power directors more than the Master Spirits.

In personality relationships the spiritual is dominant over the material, even though it does not now so appear on Urantia; and in the production of Havona Servitals the law of spirit dominance prevails; the established ratio yields three spiritual beings to one semiphysical.

The newly created servitals, together with newly appearing Graduate Guides, all pass through the courses of training which the senior guides continuously conduct on each of the seven Havona circuits. Servitals are then assigned to the activities for which they are best adapted, and since they are of two types—spiritual and semiphysical—there are few limits to the range of work these versatile beings can do. The higher or spirit groups are assigned selectively to the services of the Father, the Son, and the Spirit, and to the work of the Seven Master Spirits. In large numbers they are dispatched, from time to time, to serve on the study worlds encircling the headquarters spheres of the seven superuniverses, the worlds devoted to the final training and spiritual culture of the ascending souls of time who are preparing for advancement to the circuits of Havona. Both spirit servitals and their more physical fellows are also designated assistants and associates of the Graduate Guides in helping and instructing the various orders of ascending creatures who have attained Havona, and who seek to attain Paradise.

The Havona Servitals and the Graduate Guides manifest a transcendent devotion to their work and a touching affection for one another, an affection which, while spiritual, you could only understand by comparison with the phenomenon of human love. There is divine pathos in the separation of the servitals from the guides, as so often occurs when the servitals are dispatched on missions beyond the limits of the central universe; but they go with joy and not with sorrow. The satisfying joy of high duty is the eclipsing emotion of spiritual beings. Sorrow cannot exist in the face of the consciousness of divine duty faithfully performed. And when man's ascending soul stands before the Supreme Judge, the decision of eternal import will not be determined by material successes or quantitative achievements; the verdict reverberating through the high courts declares: "Well done, good and *faithful* servant; you have been faithful over a few essentials; you shall be made ruler over universe realities."

On superuniverse service the Havona Servitals are always assigned to that domain presided over by the Master Spirit whom they most resemble in general and special spirit prerogatives. They serve only on the educational worlds surrounding the capitals of the seven superuniverses, and the last report of Uversa indicates that almost 138 billion servitals were ministering on its 490 satellites. They engage in an endless variety of activities in connection with the work of these educational worlds comprising the superuniversities of the superuniverse of Orvonton. Here they are your companions; they have come down from your next career to study you and to inspire you with the reality and certainty of your eventual graduation from the universes of time to the realms of eternity. And in these contacts the servitals gain that preliminary experience of ministering to the ascending creatures of time which is so helpful in their subsequent work on the Havona circuits as associates of the Graduate Guides or—as translated servitals—as Graduate Guides themselves.

2. THE UNIVERSAL CONCILIATORS

For every Havona Servital created, seven Universal Conciliators are brought into being, one in each superuniverse. This creative enactment involves a definite superuniverse technique of reflective response to transactions taking place on Paradise.

On the headquarters worlds of the seven superuniverses there function the seven reflections of the Seven Master Spirits. It is difficult to undertake to portray the natures of these Reflective Spirits to material minds. They are true personalities; still each member of a superuniverse group is perfectly reflective of just one of the Seven Master Spirits. And every time the Master Spirits associate themselves with the power directors for the purpose of creating a group of Havona Servitals, there is a simultaneous focalization upon one of the Reflective Spirits in each of the superuniverse groups, and forthwith and full-fledgedly an equal number of Universal Conciliators appear on the headquarters worlds of the supercreations. If, in the creation of servitals, Master Spirit Number Seven should take the initiative, none but the Reflective Spirits of the seventh order would become pregnant with conciliators; and concurrently with the creation of one thousand Orvontonlike servitals, one thousand of the seventh-order conciliators would appear on each superuniverse capital. Out of these episodes, reflecting the sevenfold nature of the Master Spirits, arise the seven created orders of conciliators serving in each superuniverse.

Conciliators of pre-Paradise status do not serve interchangeably between superuniverses, being restricted to their native segments of creation. Every superuniverse corps, embracing one seventh of each created order, therefore spends a very long time under the influence of one of the Master Spirits to the exclusion of the others, for, while all seven are *reflected* on the superuniverse capitals, only one is *dominant* in each supercreation.

Each of the seven supercreations is actually pervaded by that one of the Master Spirits who presides over its destinies. Each superuniverse thus becomes like a gigantic mirror reflecting the nature and character of the supervising Master Spirit, and all of this is further continued in every subsidiary local universe by the presence and function of the Creative Mother Spirits. The effect of such an environment upon evolutionary growth is so profound that in their postsuperuniverse careers the conciliators collectively manifest forty-nine experiential viewpoints, or insights, each angular—hence incomplete—but all mutually compensatory and together tending to encompass the circle of Supremacy.

In each superuniverse the Universal Conciliators find themselves strangely and innately segregated into groups of four, associations in which they continue to serve. In each group, three are spirit personalities, and one, like the fourth creatures of the servitals, is a semimaterial being. This quartet constitutes a conciliating commission and is made up as follows:

1. *The Judge-Arbiter.* The one unanimously designated by the other three as the most competent and best qualified to act as judicial head of the group.

2. *The Spirit-Advocate.* The one appointed by the judge-arbiter to present evidence and to safeguard the rights of all personalities involved in any matter assigned to the adjudication of the conciliating commission.

3. *The Divine Executioner.* The conciliator qualified by inherent nature to make contact with the material beings of the realms and to execute the decisions of the commission. Divine executioners, being fourth creatures—quasi-material beings—are almost, but not quite, visible to the short-range vision of the mortal races.

4. *The Recorder.* The remaining member of the commission automatically becomes the recorder, the clerk of the tribunal. He makes certain that all records are properly prepared for the archives of the superuniverse and for the records of the local universe. If the commission is serving on an evolutionary world, a third report, with the assistance of the executioner, is prepared for the physical records of the system government of jurisdiction.

When in session a commission functions as a group of three since the advocate is detached during adjudication and participates in the formulation of the verdict only at the conclusion of the hearing. Hence these commissions are sometimes called referee trios.

The conciliators are of great value in keeping the universe of universes running smoothly. Traversing space at the seraphic rate of triple velocity, they serve as the traveling courts of the worlds, commissions devoted to the quick adjudication of minor difficulties. Were it not for these mobile and eminently fair commissions, the tribunals of the spheres would be hopelessly overspread with the minor misunderstandings of the realms.

These referee trios do not pass upon matters of eternal import; the soul, the eternal prospects of a creature of time, is never placed in jeopardy by their acts. Conciliators do not deal with questions extending beyond the temporal existence and the cosmic welfare of the creatures of time. But when a commission has once accepted jurisdiction of a problem, its rulings are final and always unanimous; there is no appeal from the decision of the judge-arbiter.

3. THE FAR-REACHING SERVICE OF CONCILIATORS

Conciliators maintain group headquarters on the capital of their superuniverse, where their primary reserve corps is held. Their secondary reserves are stationed on the capitals of the local universes. The younger and less experienced commissioners begin their service on the lower worlds, worlds like Urantia, and are advanced to the adjudication of greater problems after they have acquired riper experience.

The order of conciliators is wholly dependable; not one has ever gone astray. Though not infallible in wisdom and judgment, they are of unquestioned reliability and unerring in faithfulness. They take origin on the headquarters of a superuniverse and eventually return thereto, advancing through the following levels of universe service:

1. *Conciliators to the Worlds.* Whenever the supervising personalities of the individual worlds become greatly perplexed or actually deadlocked concerning the proper procedure under existing circumstances, and if the matter is not of sufficient importance to be brought before the regularly constituted tribunals of the realm, then, upon the receipt of a petition of two personalities, one from each contention, a conciliating commission will begin to function forthwith.

When these administrative and jurisdictional difficulties have been placed in the hands of the conciliators for study and adjudication, they are supreme in authority. But they will not formulate a decision until all the evidence has been heard, and there is absolutely no limit to their authority to call witnesses from anywhere and everywhere. And while their decisions may not be appealed, sometimes matters so develop that the commission closes its records at a given point, concludes its opinions, and transfers the whole question to the higher tribunals of the realm.

The commissioners' decisions are placed on the planetary records and, if necessary, are put into effect by the divine executioner. His power is very great, and the range of his activities on an inhabited world is very wide. Divine executioners are masterful manipulators of that which is in the interests of that which ought to be. Their work is sometimes carried out for the apparent welfare of the realm, and sometimes their acts on the worlds of time and space are difficult of explanation. Though executing decrees in defiance of neither natural law nor the ordained usages of the realm, they do ofttimes effect their strange doings and enforce the mandates of the conciliators in accordance with the higher laws of the system administration.

2. *Conciliators to the System Headquarters.* From service on the evolutionary worlds these commissions of four are advanced to duty on a system headquarters. Here they have much work to do, and they prove to be the understanding friends of men, angels, and other spirit beings. The referee trios are not so much concerned with personal differences as with group contentions and with misunderstandings arising between different orders of creatures; and on a system headquarters there live both spiritual and material beings, as well as the combined types, such as the Material Sons.

The moment the Creators bring into existence evolving individuals with the power of choice, that moment a departure is made from the smooth working of divine perfection; misunderstandings are certain to arise, and provision for the fair adjustment of these honest differences of viewpoint must be made. We should all remember that the all-wise and all-powerful Creators could have made the local universes just as perfect as Havona. No conciliating commissions need function in the central universe. But the Creators did not choose in their all-wisdom to do this. And while they have produced universes which abound in differences and teem with difficulties, they have likewise provided the mechanisms and the means for composing all these differences and for harmonizing all this seeming confusion.

3. *The Constellation Conciliators.* From service in the systems the conciliators are promoted to the adjudication of the problems of a constellation, taking up the minor difficulties arising between its one hundred systems of inhabited worlds. Not many problems developing on the constellation headquarters fall under their jurisdiction, but they are kept busy going from system to system gathering evidence and preparing preliminary statements. If the contention is honest, if the difficulties arise out of sincere differences of opinion and honest diversity of viewpoints, no matter how few persons may be involved, no matter how apparently trivial the misunderstanding, a conciliating commission can always be had to pass upon the merits of the controversy.

4. *Conciliators to the Local Universes.* In this larger work of a universe the commissioners are of great assistance to both the Melchizedeks and the Magisterial

Sons and to the constellation rulers and the hosts of personalities concerned with the co-ordination and administration of the one hundred constellations. The different orders of seraphim and other residents of the headquarters spheres of a local universe also avail themselves of the help and decisions of the referee trios.

It is almost impossible to explain the nature of those differences which may arise in the detailed affairs of a system, a constellation, or a universe. Difficulties do develop, but they are very unlike the petty trials and travails of material existence as it is lived on the evolutionary worlds.

5. *Conciliators to the Superuniverse Minor Sectors.* From the problems of local universes the commissioners are advanced to the study of questions arising in the minor sectors of their superuniverse. The farther they ascend inward from the individual planets, the fewer are the material duties of the divine executioner; gradually he assumes a new role of mercy-justice interpreter, at the same time—being quasi-material—keeping the commission as a whole in sympathetic touch with the material aspects of its investigations.

6. *Conciliators to the Superuniverse Major Sectors.* The character of the work of the commissioners continues to change as they advance. There is less and less of misunderstanding to adjudicate and more and more of mysterious phenomena to explain and interpret. From stage to stage they are evolving from arbiters of differences to *explainers of mysteries*—judges evolving into interpretative teachers. Arbiters of those who through ignorance permit difficulties and misunderstandings to arise, they once were; but they are now becoming instructors of those who are sufficiently intelligent and tolerant to avoid clashes of mind and wars of opinions. The higher a creature's education, the more respect he has for the knowledge, experience, and opinions of others.

7. *Conciliators to the Superuniverse.* Here the conciliators become co-ordinate—four mutually understood and perfectly functioning arbiter-teachers. The divine executioner is divested of retributive power and becomes the physical voice of the spirit trio. By this time these counselors and teachers have become expertly familiar with most of the actual problems and difficulties encountered in the conduct of superuniverse affairs. Thus they become wonderful advisers and wise teachers of the ascending pilgrims who are in residence on the educational spheres surrounding the headquarters worlds of the superuniverses.

All conciliators serve under the general supervision of the Ancients of Days and under the immediate direction of the Image Aids until such time as they are advanced to Paradise. During the Paradise sojourn they report to the Master Spirit who presides over the superuniverse of their origin.

The superuniverse registries do not enumerate those conciliators who have passed beyond their jurisdiction, and such commissions are widely scattered through the grand universe. The last report of registry on Uversa gives the number operating in Orvonton as almost eighteen trillion commissions—over seventy trillion individuals. But these are only a very small fraction of the multitude of conciliators that have been created in Orvonton; that number is of an altogether higher magnitude and is the equivalent of the total number of Havona Servitals, with allowances for the transmutation into Graduate Guides.

From time to time, as the numbers of the superuniverse conciliators increase, they are translated to the council of perfection on Paradise, from which they subsequently emerge as the co-ordinating corps evolved by the Infinite Spirit for the universe of universes, a marvelous group of beings which is constantly increasing in numbers and efficiency. By experiential ascent and Paradise training they have acquired a unique grasp of the emerging reality of the Supreme Being, and they roam the universe of universes on special assignment.

The members of a conciliating commission are never separated. A group of four forever serve together just as they were originally associated. Even in their glorified service they continue to function as quartets of accumulated cosmic experience and perfected experiential wisdom. They are eternally associated as the embodiment of the supreme justice of time and space.

4. TECHNICAL ADVISERS

These legal and technical minds of the spirit world were not created as such. From the early supernaphim and omniaphim, one million of the most orderly minds were chosen by the Infinite Spirit as the nucleus of this vast and versatile group. And ever since that far-distant time, actual experience in the application of the laws of perfection to the plans of evolutionary creation has been required of all who aspire to become Technical Advisers.

The Technical Advisers are recruited from the ranks of the following personality orders:

1. The Supernaphim.
2. The Seconaphim.
3. The Tertiaphim.
4. The Omniaphim.
5. The Seraphim.
6. Certain Types of Ascending Mortals.
7. Certain Types of Ascending Midwayers.

At the present time, not counting the mortals and midwayers who are all of transient attachment, the number of Technical Advisers registered on Uversa and operating in Orvonton is slightly in excess of sixty-one trillion.

Technical Advisers frequently function as individuals but are organized for service and maintain common headquarters on the spheres of assignment in groups of seven. In each group at least five must be of permanent status, while two may be of temporary association. Ascending mortals and ascending midway creatures serve on these advisory commissions while pursuing the Paradise ascent, but they do not enter the regular courses of training for Technical Advisers, nor do they ever become permanent members of the order.

Those mortals and midwayers who serve transiently with the advisers are chosen for such work because of their expertness in the concept of universal law and supreme justice. As you journey toward your Paradise goal, constantly acquiring added knowledge and enhanced skill, you are continuously afforded the opportunity to give out to others the wisdom and experience you have already accumulated; all the way in to Havona you enact the role of a pupil-teacher. You will work your way through the ascending levels of this vast experiential university by imparting to those just below you the new-found knowledge of your advancing career. In the universal regime you are not reckoned as having possessed yourself of knowledge and truth until you have demonstrated your ability and your willingness to impart this knowledge and truth to others.

After long training and actual experience, any of the ministering spirits above the status of cherubim are permitted to receive permanent appointment as Technical Advisers. All candidates voluntarily enter this order of service; but having once assumed such responsibilities, they may not relinquish them. Only the Ancients of Days can transfer these advisers to other activities.

The training of Technical Advisers, begun in the Melchizedek colleges of the local universes, continues to the courts of the Ancients of Days. From this superuniverse training they proceed to the "schools of the seven circles" located on the pilot worlds of the Havona circuits. And from the pilot worlds they are received into the "college of the ethics of law and the technique of Supremacy," the Paradise training school for the perfecting of Technical Advisers.

These advisers are more than legal experts; they are students and teachers of *applied* law, the laws of the universe applied to the lives and destinies of all who inhabit the vast domains of the far-flung creation. As time passes, they become the living law libraries of time and space, preventing endless trouble and needless delays by instructing the personalities of time regarding the forms and modes of procedure most acceptable to the rulers of eternity. They are able so to counsel the workers of space as to enable them to function in harmony with the requirements of Paradise; they are the teachers of all creatures concerning the technique of the Creators.

Such a living library of applied law could not be created; such beings must be evolved by actual experience. The infinite Deities are existential, hence are compensated for lack of experience; they know all even before they experience all, but they do not impart this nonexperiential knowledge to their subordinate creatures.

Technical Advisers are dedicated to the work of preventing delay, facilitating progress, and counseling achievement. There is always a *best* and *right* way to do things; there is always the technique of perfection, a divine method, and these advisers know how to direct us all in the finding of this better way.

These exceedingly wise and practical beings are always closely associated with the service and work of the Universal Censors. The Melchizedeks are provided with an able corps. The rulers of the systems, constellations, universes, and superuniverse sectors are all bountifully supplied with these technical or legal reference minds of the spiritual world. A special group act as law counselors to the Life Carriers, advising these Sons concerning the extent of permissible departure from the established order of life propagation and otherwise instructing them respecting their prerogatives and latitudes of function. They are the advisers of all classes of beings regarding the proper usages and techniques of all spirit-world transactions. But they do not directly and personally deal with the material creatures of the realms.

Besides counseling regarding legal usages, Technical Advisers are equally devoted to the efficient interpretation of all laws concerning creature beings—physical, mindal, and spiritual. They are available to the Universal Conciliators and to all others who desire to know the truth of law; in other words, to know how the Supremacy of Deity may be depended upon to react in a given situation having factors of an established physical, mindal, and spiritual order. They even essay to elucidate the technique of the Ultimate.

Technical Advisers are selected and tested beings; I have never known one of them to go astray. We have no records on Uversa of their ever having been adjudged in contempt of the divine laws they so effectively interpret and so eloquently expound. There is no known limit to the domain of their service, neither has any been placed upon their progress. They continue as advisers even to the portals of Paradise; the whole universe of law and experience is open to them.

5. THE CUSTODIANS OF RECORDS ON PARADISE

From among the tertiary supernaphim in Havona, certain of the senior chief recorders are chosen as Custodians of Records, as keepers of the formal archives of the Isle of Light, those archives which stand in contrast to the living records of registry in the minds of the custodians of knowledge, sometimes designated the "living library of Paradise."

The recording angels of the inhabited planets are the source of all individual records. Throughout the universes other recorders function regarding both formal records and living records. From Urantia to Paradise, both recordings are encountered: in a local universe, more of the written records and less of the living; on Paradise, more of the living and less of the formal; on Uversa, both are equally available.

Every occurrence of significance in the organized and inhabited creation is a matter of record. While events of no more than local importance find only a local recording, those of wider significance are dealt with accordingly. From the planets, systems, and constellations of Nebadon, everything of universe import is posted on Salvington; and from such universe capitals those episodes are advanced to higher recording which pertain to the affairs of the sector and supergovernments. Paradise also has a relevant summary of superuniverse and Havona data; and this historic and cumulative story of the universe of universes is in the custody of these exalted tertiary supernaphim.

While certain of these beings have been dispatched to the superuniverses to serve as Chiefs of Records directing the activities of the Celestial Recorders, not one has ever been transferred from the permanent roll call of their order.

6. THE CELESTIAL RECORDERS

These are the recorders who execute all records in duplicate, making an original spirit recording and a semimaterial counterpart—what might be called a carbon copy. This they can do because of their peculiar ability simultaneously to manipulate both spiritual and material energy. Celestial Recorders are not created as such; they are ascendant seraphim from the local universes. They are received, classified, and assigned to their spheres of work by the councils of the Chiefs of Records on the headquarters of the seven superuniverses. There also are located the schools for training Celestial Recorders. The school on Uversa is conducted by the Perfectors of Wisdom and the Divine Counselors.

As the recorders advance in universe service, they continue their system of dual recording, thus making their records always available to all classes of beings, from those of the material order to the high spirits of light. In your transition experience, as you ascend from this material world, you will always be able to consult the records of, and to be otherwise conversant with, the history and traditions of your status sphere.

The recorders are a tested and tried corps. Never have I known of the defection of a Celestial Recorder, and never has there been discovered a falsification in their records. They are subjected to a dual inspection, their records being scrutinized by their exalted fellows from Uversa and by the Mighty Messengers, who certify to the correctness of the quasi-physical duplicates of the original spirit records.

While the advancing recorders stationed on the subordinate spheres of record in the Orvonton universes number trillions upon trillions, those of attained status on Uversa are not quite eight million in number. These senior or graduate recorders are the superuniverse custodians and forwarders of the sponsored records of time and space. Their permanent headquarters are in the circular abodes surrounding the area of records on Uversa. They never leave the custody of these records to others; as individuals they may be absent, but never in large numbers.

Like those supernaphim who have become Custodians of Records, the corps of Celestial Recorders is of permanent assignment. Once seraphim and supernaphim are mustered into these services, they will respectively remain Celestial Recorders and Custodians of Records until the day of the new and modified administration of the full personalization of God the Supreme.

On Uversa these senior Celestial Recorders can show the records of everything of cosmic import in all Orvonton since the far-distant times of the arrival of the Ancients of Days, while on the eternal Isle the Custodians of Records guard the archives of that realm which testify to the transactions of Paradise since the times of the personification of the Infinite Spirit.

7. THE MORONTIA COMPANIONS

These children of the local universe Mother Spirits are the friends and associates of all who live the ascending morontia life. They are not indispensable to an ascender's real work of creature progression, neither do they in any sense displace the work of the seraphic guardians who often accompany their mortal associates on the Paradise journey. The Morontia Companions are simply gracious hosts to those who are just beginning the long inward ascent. They are also skillful play sponsors and are ably assisted in this work by the reversion directors.

Though you will have earnest and progressively difficult tasks to perform on the morontia training worlds of Nebadon, you will always be provided with regular seasons of rest and reversion. Throughout the journey to Paradise there will always be time for rest and spirit play; and in the career of light and life there is always time for worship and new achievement.

These Morontia Companions are such friendly associates that, when you finally leave the last phase of the morontia experience, as you prepare to embark upon the superuniverse spirit adventure, you will truly regret that these companionable creatures cannot accompany you, but they serve exclusively in the local universes. At every stage of the ascending career all contactable personalities will be friendly and companionable, but not until you meet the Paradise Companions will you find another group so devoted to friendship and companionship.

The work of the Morontia Companions is more fully depicted in those narratives dealing with the affairs of your local universe.

8. THE PARADISE COMPANIONS

The Paradise Companions are a composite or assembled group recruited from the ranks of the seraphim, seconaphim, supernaphim, and omniaphim. Though serving for what you would regard as an extraordinary length of time, they are not of permanent status. When this ministry has been completed, as a rule (but not invariably) they return to those duties they performed when summoned to Paradise service.

Members of the angelic hosts are nominated for this service by the local universe Mother Spirits, by the superuniverse Reflective Spirits, and by Majeston of Paradise. They are summoned to the central Isle and are commissioned as Paradise Companions by one of the Seven Master Spirits. Aside from permanent status on Paradise, this temporary service of Paradise companionship is the highest honor ever conferred upon the ministering spirits.

These selected angels are dedicated to the service of companionship and are assigned as associates to all classes of beings who may chance to be alone on Paradise, chiefly to the ascendant mortals but also to all others who are alone on the central Isle. Paradise Companions have nothing especial to accomplish in behalf of those with whom they fraternize; they are simply companions. Almost every other being you mortals will encounter during your Paradise sojourn—aside from your fellow pilgrims—will have something definite to do with you or for you; but these companions are assigned only to be with you and to commune with you as personality associates. They are often assisted in their ministry by the gracious and brilliant Paradise Citizens.

Mortals come from races that are very social. The Creators well know that it is "not good for man to be alone," and provision is accordingly made for companionship, even on Paradise.

If you, as an ascendant mortal, should reach Paradise in the company of the companion or close associate of your earthly career, or if your seraphic guardian of destiny should chance to arrive with you or were waiting for you, then no permanent companion would be assigned you. But if you arrive alone, a companion will certainly welcome you as you awaken on the Isle of Light from the terminal sleep of time. Even if it is known that you will be accompanied by someone of ascendant association, temporary companions will be designated to welcome you to the eternal shores and to escort you to the reservation made ready for the reception of you and your associates. You may be certain of being warmly welcomed when you experience the resurrection into eternity on the everlasting shores of Paradise.

Reception companions are assigned during the terminal days of the ascenders' sojourn on the last circuit of Havona, and they carefully examine the records of mortal origin and eventful ascent through the worlds of space and the circles of Havona. When they greet the mortals of time, they are already well versed in the careers of these arriving pilgrims and immediately prove to be sympathetic and intriguing companions.

During your prefinaliter sojourn on Paradise, if for any reason you should be temporarily separated from your associate of the ascending career—mortal or seraphic—a Paradise Companion would be forthwith assigned for counsel and companionship. When once assigned to an ascendant mortal of solitary residence on Paradise, the companion remains with this person until he either is rejoined by his ascendant associates or is duly mustered into the Corps of the Finality.

Paradise Companions are assigned in order of waiting except that an ascender is never placed in the charge of a companion whose nature is unlike his superuniverse type. If a Urantia mortal were arriving on Paradise today, there would be assigned to him the first waiting companion either of origin in Orvonton or otherwise of the nature of the Seventh Master Spirit. Hence the omniaphim serve not with the ascendant creatures from the seven superuniverses.

Many additional services are performed by the Paradise Companions: If an ascending mortal should reach the central universe alone and, while traversing Havona, should fail in some phase of the Deity adventure, in due course he would be remanded to the universes of time, and forthwith a call would be made to the reserves of the Paradise Companions. One of this order would be assigned to follow the defeated pilgrim, to be with him and to comfort and cheer him, and to remain with him until he returned to the central universe to resume the Paradise ascent.

If an ascending pilgrim met defeat in the Deity adventure while traversing Havona in the company of an ascending seraphim, the guardian angel of the mortal career, she would elect to accompany her mortal associate. These seraphim always volunteer and are permitted to accompany their long-time mortal comrades back to the service of time and space.

But not so with two closely associated mortal ascenders: If one attains God while the other temporarily fails, the successful individual invariably chooses to go back to the evolutionary creations with the disappointed personality, but this is not permitted. Instead, a call is made to the reserves of the Paradise Companions, and one of the volunteers is selected to accompany the disappointed pilgrim. A volunteer Paradise Citizen then becomes associated with the successful mortal, who tarries on the central Isle awaiting the Havona return of the defeated comrade and in the meantime teaches in certain Paradise schools, presenting the adventurous story of the evolutionary ascent.

[Sponsored by One High in Authority from Uversa.]

PAPER 26

MINISTERING SPIRITS OF THE CENTRAL UNIVERSE

SUPERNAPHIM are the ministering spirits of Paradise and the central universe; they are the highest order of the lowest group of the children of the Infinite Spirit—the angelic hosts. Such ministering spirits are to be encountered from the Isle of Paradise to the worlds of time and space. No major part of the organized and inhabited creation is without their services.

1. THE MINISTERING SPIRITS

Angels are the ministering-spirit associates of the evolutionary and ascending will creatures of all space; they are also the colleagues and working associates of the higher hosts of the divine personalities of the spheres. The angels of all orders are distinct personalities and are highly individualized. They all have a large capacity for appreciation of the ministrations of the reversion directors. Together with the Messenger Hosts of Space, the ministering spirits enjoy seasons of rest and change; they possess very social natures and have an associative capacity far transcending that of human beings.

The ministering spirits of the grand universe are classified as follows:

1. Supernaphim.
2. Seconaphim.
3. Tertiaphim.
4. Omniaphim.
5. Seraphim.
6. Cherubim and Sanobim.
7. Midway Creatures.

The individual members of the angelic orders are not altogether stationary as to personal status in the universe. Angels of certain orders may become Paradise Companions for a season; some become Celestial Recorders; others ascend to the ranks of the Technical Advisers. Certain of the cherubim may aspire to seraphic status and destiny, while evolutionary seraphim can achieve the spiritual levels of the ascending Sons of God.

The seven orders of ministering spirits, as revealed, are grouped for presentation in accordance with their functions of greatest importance to ascending creatures:

1. *The Ministering Spirits of the Central Universe.* The three orders of *supernaphim* serve in the Paradise-Havona system. Primary or Paradise supernaphim are created by the Infinite Spirit. The secondary and tertiary orders,

serving in Havona, are respectively the offspring of the Master Spirits and of the Spirits of the Circuits.

2. *The Ministering Spirits of the Superuniverses*—the seconaphim, the tertiaphim, and the omniaphim. *Seconaphim,* the children of the Reflective Spirits, variously serve in the seven superuniverses. *Tertiaphim,* of origin in the Infinite Spirit, are eventually dedicated to the liaison service of the Creator Sons and the Ancients of Days. *Omniaphim* are created concertedly by the Infinite Spirit and the Seven Supreme Executives, and they are the exclusive servants of the latter. The discussion of these three orders forms the subject of a succeeding narrative in this series.

3. *The Ministering Spirits of the Local Universes* embrace the *seraphim* and their assistants, the *cherubim.* With these offspring of a Universe Mother Spirit mortal ascenders have initial contact. The *midway creatures,* of nativity on the inhabited worlds, are not really of the angelic orders proper, though often functionally grouped with the ministering spirits. Their story, with an account of the seraphim and cherubim, is presented in those papers dealing with the affairs of your local universe.

All orders of the angelic hosts are devoted to the various universe services, and they minister in one way or another to the higher orders of celestial beings; but it is the supernaphim, seconaphim, and seraphim who, in large numbers, are employed in the furtherance of the ascending scheme of progressive perfection for the children of time. Functioning in the central, super-, and local universes, they form that unbroken chain of spirit ministers which has been provided by the Infinite Spirit for the help and guidance of all who seek to attain the Universal Father through the Eternal Son.

Supernaphim are limited in "spirit polarity" regarding only one phase of action, that with the Universal Father. They can work singly except when directly employing the exclusive circuits of the Father. When they are in power reception on the Father's direct ministry, supernaphim must voluntarily associate in pairs to be able to function. Seconaphim are likewise limited and in addition must work in pairs in order to synchronize with the circuits of the Eternal Son. Seraphim can work singly as discrete and localized personalities, but they are able to encircuit only when polarized as liaison pairs. When such spirit beings are associated as pairs, the one is spoken of as complemental to the other. Complemental relationships may be transient; they are not necessarily of a permanent nature.

These brilliant creatures of light are sustained directly by the intake of the spiritual energy of the primary circuits of the universe. Urantia mortals must obtain light-energy through the vegetative incarnation, but the angelic hosts are encircuited; they "have food that you know not." They also partake of the circulating teachings of the marvelous Trinity Teacher Sons; they have a reception of knowledge and an intake of wisdom much resembling their technique of assimilating the life energies.

2. THE MIGHTY SUPERNAPHIM

The supernaphim are the skilled ministers to all types of beings who sojourn on Paradise and in the central universe. These high angels are created in three major orders: primary, secondary, and tertiary.

Primary supernaphim are the exclusive offspring of the Conjoint Creator. They divide their ministry about equally between certain groups of the Paradise Citizens and the ever-enlarging corps of ascendant pilgrims. These angels of the eternal Isle are highly efficacious in furthering the essential training of both groups of Paradise dwellers. They contribute much that is helpful to the mutual understanding of these two unique orders of universe creatures—the one being the highest type of divine and perfect will creature, and the other, the perfected evolution of the lowest type of will creature in all the universe of universes.

The work of the primary supernaphim is so unique and distinctive that it will be separately considered in the succeeding narrative.

Secondary supernaphim are the directors of the affairs of ascending beings on the seven circuits of Havona. They are equally concerned in ministering to the educational training of numerous orders of Paradise Citizens who sojourn for long periods on the world circuits of the central creation, but we may not discuss this phase of their service.

There are seven types of these high angels, each of origin in one of the Seven Master Spirits and in nature patterned accordingly. Collectively, the Seven Master Spirits create many different groups of unique beings and entities, and the individual members of each order are comparatively uniform in nature. But when these same Seven Spirits create individually, the resulting orders are always sevenfold in nature; the children of each Master Spirit partake of the nature of their creator and are accordingly diverse from the others. Such is the origin of the secondary supernaphim, and the angels of all seven created types function in all channels of activity open to their entire order, chiefly on the seven circuits of the central and divine universe.

Each of the seven planetary circuits of Havona is under the direct supervision of one of the Seven Spirits of the Circuits, themselves the collective—hence uniform—creation of the Seven Master Spirits. Though partaking of the nature of the Third Source and Center, these seven subsidiary Spirits of Havona were not a part of the original pattern universe. They were in function after the original (eternal) creation but long before the times of Grandfanda. They undoubtedly appeared as a creative response of the Master Spirits to the emerging purpose of the Supreme Being, and they were discovered in function upon the organization of the grand universe. The Infinite Spirit and all his creative associates, as universal co-ordinators, seem abundantly endowed with the ability to make suitable creative responses to the simultaneous developments in the experiential Deities and in the evolving universes.

Tertiary supernaphim take origin in these Seven Spirits of the Circuits. Each one of them, on the separate Havona circles, is empowered by the Infinite Spirit to create a sufficient number of high superaphic ministers of the tertiary order to meet the needs of the central universe. While the Circuit Spirits produced comparatively few of these angelic ministers prior to the arrival in Havona of the pilgrims of time, the Seven Master Spirits did not even begin the creation of secondary supernaphim until the landing of Grandfanda. As the older of the two orders, the tertiary supernaphim will therefore receive first consideration.

3. THE TERTIARY SUPERNAPHIM

These servants of the Seven Master Spirits are the angelic specialists of the various circuits of Havona, and their ministry extends to both the ascending pilgrims of time and the descending pilgrims of eternity. On the billion study worlds of the perfect central creation, your superaphic associates of all orders will be fully visible to you. There you will all be, in the highest sense, fraternal and understanding beings of mutual contact and sympathy. You will also fully recognize and exquisitely fraternize with the descending pilgrims, the Paradise Citizens, who traverse these circuits from within outward, entering Havona through the pilot world of the first circuit and proceeding outward to the seventh.

The ascending pilgrims from the seven superuniverses pass through Havona in the opposite direction, entering by way of the pilot world of the seventh circuit and proceeding inward. There is no time limit set on the progress of the ascending creatures from world to world and from circuit to circuit, just as no fixed span of time is arbitrarily assigned to residence on the morontia worlds. But, whereas adequately developed individuals may be exempted from sojourn on one or more of the local universe training worlds, no pilgrim may avoid passing through all seven of the Havona circuits of progressive spiritualization.

That corps of tertiary supernaphim which is chiefly assigned to the service of the pilgrims of time is classified as follows:

1. *The Harmony Supervisors.* It must be apparent that some sort of co-ordinating influence would be required, even in perfect Havona, to maintain system and to insure harmony in all the work of preparing the pilgrims of time for their subsequent Paradise achievements. Such is the real mission of the harmony supervisors—to keep everything moving along smoothly and expeditiously. Originating on the first circuit, they serve throughout Havona, and their presence on the circuits means that nothing can possibly go amiss. A great ability to co-ordinate a diversity of activities involving personalities of differing orders—even multiple levels—enables these supernaphim to give assistance wherever and whenever required. They contribute enormously to the mutual understanding of the pilgrims of time and the pilgrims of eternity.

2. *The Chief Recorders.* These angels are created on the second circuit but operate everywhere in the central universe. They record in triplicate, executing records for the literal files of Havona, for the spiritual files of their order, and for the formal records of Paradise. In addition they automatically transmit the transactions of true-knowledge import to the living libraries of Paradise, the custodians of knowledge of the primary order of supernaphim.

3. *The Broadcasters.* The children of the third Circuit Spirit function throughout Havona, although their official station is located on planet number seventy in the outermost circle. These master technicians are the broadcast receivers and senders of the central creation and the directors of the space reports of all Deity phenomena on Paradise. They can operate all of the basic circuits of space.

4. *The Messengers* take origin on circuit number four. They range the Paradise-Havona system as bearers of all messages requiring personal transmission.

They serve their fellows, the celestial personalities, the Paradise pilgrims, and even the ascendant souls of time.

5. *The Intelligence Co-ordinators.* These tertiary supernaphim, the children of the fifth Circuit Spirit, are always the wise and sympathetic promoters of fraternal association between the ascending and the descending pilgrims. They minister to all the inhabitants of Havona, and especially to the ascenders, by keeping them currently informed regarding the affairs of the universe of universes. By virtue of personal contacts with the broadcasters and the reflectors, these "living newspapers" of Havona are instantly conversant with all information passing over the vast news circuits of the central universe. They secure intelligence by the Havona graph method, which enables them automatically to assimilate as much information in one hour of Urantia time as would require a thousand years for your most rapid telegraphic technique to record.

6. *The Transport Personalities.* These beings, of origin on circuit number six, usually operate from planet number forty in the outermost circuit. It is they who take away the disappointed candidates who transiently fail in the Deity adventure. They stand ready to serve all who must come and go in the service of Havona, and who are not space traversers.

7. *The Reserve Corps.* The fluctuations in the work with the ascendant beings, the Paradise pilgrims, and other orders of beings sojourning in Havona, make it necessary to maintain these reserves of supernaphim on the pilot world of the seventh circle, where they take origin. They are created without special design and are competent to take up service in the less exacting phases of any of the duties of their superaphic associates of the tertiary order.

4. THE SECONDARY SUPERNAPHIM

The secondary supernaphim are ministers to the seven planetary circuits of the central universe. Part are devoted to the service of the pilgrims of time, and one half of the entire order is assigned to the training of the Paradise pilgrims of eternity. These Paradise Citizens, in their pilgrimage through the Havona circuits, are also attended by volunteers from the Mortal Finality Corps, an arrangement that has prevailed since the completion of the first finaliter group.

According to their periodic assignment to the ministry of the ascending pilgrims, secondary supernaphim work in the following seven groups:

1. Pilgrim Helpers.
2. Supremacy Guides.
3. Trinity Guides.
4. Son Finders.
5. Father Guides.
6. Counselors and Advisers.
7. Complements of Rest.

Each of these working groups contains angels of all seven created types, and a pilgrim of space is always tutored by secondary supernaphim of origin in the Master Spirit who presides over that pilgrim's superuniverse of nativity. When you mortals of Urantia attain Havona, you will certainly be piloted by supernaphim whose created natures—like your own evolved natures—are derived from the Master Spirit of Orvonton. And since your tutors spring from the Master Spirit of your own superuniverse, they are especially qualified to understand, comfort, and assist you in all your efforts to attain Paradise perfection.

The pilgrims of time are transported past the dark gravity bodies of Havona to the outer planetary circuit by the transport personalities of the primary order of seconaphim, operating from the headquarters of the seven superuniverses. A majority, but not all, of the seraphim of planetary and local universe service who have been accredited for the Paradise ascent will part with their mortal associates before the long flight to Havona and will at once begin a long and intense training for supernal assignment, expecting to achieve, as seraphim, perfection of existence and supremacy of service. And this they do, hoping to rejoin the pilgrims of time, to be reckoned among those who forever follow the course of such mortals as have attained the Universal Father and have received assignment to the undisclosed service of the Corps of the Finality.

The pilgrim lands on the receiving planet of Havona, the pilot world of the seventh circuit, with only one endowment of perfection, perfection of purpose. The Universal Father has decreed: "Be you perfect, even as I am perfect." That is the astounding invitation-command broadcast to the finite children of the worlds of space. The promulgation of that injunction has set all creation astir in the co-operative effort of the celestial beings to assist in bringing about the fulfillment and realization of that tremendous command of the First Great Source and Center.

When, through and by the ministry of all the helper hosts of the universal scheme of survival, you are finally deposited on the receiving world of Havona, you arrive with only one sort of perfection—*perfection of purpose*. Your purpose has been thoroughly proved; your faith has been tested. You are known to be disappointment proof. Not even the failure to discern the Universal Father can shake the faith or seriously disturb the trust of an ascendant mortal who has passed through the experience that all must traverse in order to attain the perfect spheres of Havona. By the time you reach Havona, your sincerity has become sublime. Perfection of purpose and divinity of desire, with steadfastness of faith, have secured your entrance to the settled abodes of eternity; your deliverance from the uncertainties of time is full and complete; and now must you come face to face with the problems of Havona and the immensities of Paradise, to meet which you have so long been in training in the experiential epochs of time on the world schools of space.

Faith has won for the ascendant pilgrim a perfection of purpose which admits the children of time to the portals of eternity. Now must the pilgrim helpers begin the work of developing that perfection of understanding and that technique of comprehension which are so indispensable to Paradise perfection of personality.

Ability to comprehend is the mortal passport to Paradise. Willingness to believe is the key to Havona. The acceptance of sonship, co-operation with the indwelling Adjuster, is the price of evolutionary survival.

5. THE PILGRIM HELPERS

The first of the seven groups of secondary supernaphim to be encountered are the pilgrim helpers, those beings of quick understanding and broad sympathy who welcome the much-traveled ascenders of space to the stabilized worlds and settled economy of the central universe. Simultaneously these high ministers begin their work for the Paradise pilgrims of eternity, the first of whom arrived on the pilot world of the inner Havona circuit concomitantly with the landing of Grandfanda on the pilot world of the outer circuit. Back in those far-distant days the pilgrims from Paradise and the pilgrims of time first met on the receiving world of circuit number four.

These pilgrim helpers, functioning on the seventh circle of Havona worlds, conduct their work for the ascending mortals in three major divisions: first, the supreme understanding of the Paradise Trinity; second, the spiritual comprehension of the Father-Son partnership; and third, the intellectual recognition of the Infinite Spirit. Each of these phases of instruction is divided into seven branches of twelve minor divisions of seventy subsidiary groups; and each of these seventy subsidiary groupings of instruction is presented in one thousand classifications. More detailed instruction is provided on subsequent circles, but an outline of every Paradise requirement is taught by the pilgrim helpers.

That, then, is the primary or elementary course which confronts the faith-tested and much-traveled pilgrims of space. But long before reaching Havona, these ascendant children of time have learned to feast upon uncertainty, to fatten upon disappointment, to enthuse over apparent defeat, to invigorate in the presence of difficulties, to exhibit indomitable courage in the face of immensity, and to exercise unconquerable faith when confronted with the challenge of the inexplicable. Long since, the battle cry of these pilgrims became: "In liaison with God, nothing—absolutely nothing—is impossible."

There is a definite requirement of the pilgrims of time on each of the Havona circles; and while every pilgrim continues under the tutelage of supernaphim by nature adapted to helping that particular type of ascendant creature, the course that must be mastered is fairly uniform for all ascenders who reach the central universe. This course of achievement is quantitative, qualitative, and experiential—intellectual, spiritual, and supreme.

Time is of little consequence on the Havona circles. In a limited manner it enters into the possibilities of advancement, but achievement is the final and supreme test. The very moment your superaphic associate deems you to be competent to pass inward to the next circle, you will be taken before the twelve adjutants of the seventh Circuit Spirit. Here you will be required to pass the tests of the circle determined by the superuniverse of your origin and by the system of your nativity. The divinity attainment of this circle takes place on the pilot world and consists in the spiritual recognition and realization of the Master Spirit of the ascending pilgrim's superuniverse.

When the work of the outer Havona circle is finished and the course presented is mastered, the pilgrim helpers take their subjects to the pilot world of the next circle and commit them to the care of the supremacy guides. The pilgrim helpers always tarry for a season to assist in making the transfer both pleasant and profitable.

6. THE SUPREMACY GUIDES

Ascenders of space are designated "spiritual graduates" when translated from the seventh to the sixth circle and are placed under the immediate supervision of the supremacy guides. These guides should not be confused with the Graduate Guides—belonging to the Higher Personalities of the Infinite Spirit—who, with their servital associates, minister on all circuits of Havona to both ascending and descending pilgrims. The supremacy guides function only on the sixth circle of the central universe.

It is in this circle that the ascenders achieve a new realization of Supreme Divinity. Through their long careers in the evolutionary universes the pilgrims of time have been experiencing a growing awareness of the reality of an almighty overcontrol of the time-space creations. Here, on this Havona circuit, they come near to encountering the central universe source of time-space unity—the spiritual reality of God the Supreme.

I am somewhat at a loss to explain what takes place on this circle. No personalized presence of Supremacy is perceptible to the ascenders. In certain respects, new relationships with the Seventh Master Spirit compensate this noncontactability of the Supreme Being. But regardless of our inability to grasp the technique, each ascending creature seems to undergo a transforming growth, a new integration of consciousness, a new spiritualization of purpose, a new sensitivity for divinity, which can hardly be satisfactorily explained without assuming the unrevealed activity of the Supreme Being. To those of us who have observed these mysterious transactions, it appears as if God the Supreme were affectionately bestowing upon his experiential children, up to the very limits of their experiential capacities, those enhancements of intellectual grasp, of spiritual insight, and of personality outreach which they will so need, in all their efforts at penetrating the divinity level of the Trinity of Supremacy, to achieve the eternal and existential Deities of Paradise.

When the supremacy guides deem their pupils ripe for advancement, they bring them before the commission of seventy, a mixed group serving as examiners on the pilot world of circuit number six. After satisfying this commission as to their comprehension of the Supreme Being and of the Trinity of Supremacy, the pilgrims are certified for translation to the fifth circuit.

7. THE TRINITY GUIDES

Trinity guides are the tireless ministers of the fifth circle of the Havona training of the advancing pilgrims of time and space. The spiritual graduates are here designated "candidates for the Deity adventure" since it is on this circle, under the direction of the Trinity guides, that the pilgrims receive advanced instruction concerning the divine Trinity in preparation for the attempt to achieve the personality recognition of the Infinite Spirit. And here the ascending pilgrims discover what true study and real mental effort mean as they begin to discern the nature of the still-more-taxing and far-more-arduous spiritual exertion that will be required to meet the demands of the high goal set for their achievement on the worlds of this circuit.

Most faithful and efficient are the Trinity guides; and each pilgrim receives the undivided attention, and enjoys the whole affection, of a secondary supernaphim belonging to this order. Never would a pilgrim of time find the first approachable person of the Paradise Trinity were it not for the help and assistance of these guides and the host of other spiritual beings engaged in instructing the ascenders respecting the nature and technique of the forthcoming Deity adventure.

After the completion of the course of training on this circuit the Trinity guides take their pupils to its pilot world and present them before one of the many triune commissions functioning as examiners and certifiers of candidates for the Deity adventure. These commissions consist of one fellow of the finaliters, one of the directors of conduct of the order of primary supernaphim, and either a Solitary Messenger of space or a Trinitized Son of Paradise.

When an ascendant soul actually starts for Paradise, he is accompanied only by the transit trio: the superaphic circle associate, the Graduate Guide, and the ever-present servital associate of the latter. These excursions from the Havona circles to Paradise are trial trips; the ascenders are not yet of Paradise status. They do not achieve residential status on Paradise until they have passed through the terminal rest of time subsequent to the attainment of the Universal Father and the final clearance of the Havona circuits. Not until after the divine rest do they partake of the "essence of divinity" and the "spirit of supremacy" and thus really begin to function in the circle of eternity and in the presence of the Trinity.

The ascender's companions of the transit trio are not required to enable him to locate the geographic presence of the spiritual luminosity of the Trinity, rather to afford all possible assistance to a pilgrim in his difficult task of recognizing, discerning, and comprehending the Infinite Spirit sufficiently to constitute personality recognition. Any ascendant pilgrim on Paradise can discern the geographic or locational presence of the Trinity, the great majority are able to contact the intellectual reality of the Deities, especially the Third Person, but not all can recognize or even partially comprehend the reality of the spiritual presence of the Father and the Son. Still more difficult is even the minimum spiritual comprehension of the Universal Father.

Seldom does the quest for the Infinite Spirit fail of consummation, and when their subjects have succeeded in this phase of the Deity adventure, the Trinity guides prepare to transfer them to the ministry of the Son finders on the fourth circle of Havona.

8. THE SON FINDERS

The fourth Havona circuit is sometimes called the "circuit of the Sons." From the worlds of this circuit the ascending pilgrims go to Paradise to achieve an understanding contact with the Eternal Son, while on the worlds of this circuit the descending pilgrims achieve a new comprehension of the nature and mission of the Creator Sons of time and space. There are seven worlds in this circuit on which the reserve corps of the Paradise Michaels maintain special service schools of mutual ministry to both the ascending and descending pilgrims; and it is on these worlds of the Michael Sons that the pilgrims of time and the pilgrims of eternity arrive at their first truly mutual understanding of one another. In many respects the experiences of this circuit are the most intriguing of the entire Havona sojourn.

The Son finders are the superaphic ministers to the ascending mortals of the fourth circuit. In addition to the general work of preparing their candidates for a realization of the Trinity relationships of the Eternal Son, these Son finders must so fully instruct their subjects that they will be wholly successful: first, in the adequate spiritual comprehension of the Son; second, in the satisfactory personality recognition of the Son; and third, in the proper differentiation of the Son from the personality of the Infinite Spirit.

After the attainment of the Infinite Spirit, no more examinations are conducted. The tests of the inner circles are the performances of the pilgrim candidates when in the embrace of the enshroudment of the Deities. Advancement is determined purely by the spirituality of the individual, and no one but the Gods presumes to pass upon this possession. In the event of failure no reasons are ever assigned, neither are the candidates themselves nor their various tutors and guides ever chided or criticized. On Paradise, disappointment is never regarded as defeat; postponement is never looked upon as disgrace; the apparent failures of time are never confused with the significant delays of eternity.

Not many pilgrims experience the delay of seeming failure in the Deity adventure. Nearly all attain the Infinite Spirit, though occasionally a pilgrim from superuniverse number one does not succeed on the first attempt. The pilgrims who attain the Spirit seldom fail in finding the Son; of those who do fail on the first adventure, almost all hail from superuniverses three and five. The great majority of those who fail on the first adventure to attain the Father, after finding both the Spirit and the Son, hail from superuniverse number six, though a few from numbers two and three are likewise unsuccessful. And all this seems clearly to indicate that there is some good and sufficient reason for these apparent failures; in reality, simply unescapable delays.

The defeated candidates for the Deity adventure are placed under the jurisdiction of the chiefs of assignment, a group of primary supernaphim, and are remanded to the work of the realms of space for a period of not less than one millennium. They never return to the superuniverse of their nativity, always to that supercreation most propitious for their retraining in preparation for the second Deity adventure. Following this service, on their own motion, they return to the outer circle of Havona, are immediately escorted to the circle of their interrupted career, and at once resume their preparations for the Deity adventure. Never do the secondary supernaphim fail to pilot their subjects successfully on the second attempt, and the same superaphic ministers and other guides always attend these candidates during this second adventure.

9. THE FATHER GUIDES

When the pilgrim soul attains the third circle of Havona, he comes under the tutelage of the Father guides, the older, highly skilled, and most experienced of the superaphic ministers. On the worlds of this circuit the Father guides maintain schools of wisdom and colleges of technique wherein all the beings inhabiting the central universe serve as teachers. Nothing is neglected which would be of service to a creature of time in this transcendent adventure of eternity attainment.

The attainment of the Universal Father is the passport to eternity, notwithstanding the remaining circuits to be traversed. It is therefore a momentous occasion on the pilot world of circle number three when the transit trio announce that the last venture of time is about to ensue; that another creature of space seeks entry to Paradise through the portals of eternity.

The test of time is almost over; the race for eternity has been all but run. The days of uncertainty are ending; the temptation to doubt is vanishing; the injunction to be *perfect* has been obeyed. From the very bottom of intelligent existence the creature of time and material personality has ascended the evolutionary spheres of space, thus proving the feasibility of the ascension plan while forever demonstrating the justice and righteousness of the command of the Universal Father to his lowly creatures of the worlds: "Be you perfect, even as I am perfect."

Step by step, life by life, world by world, the ascendant career has been mastered, and the goal of Deity has been attained. Survival is complete in perfection, and perfection is replete in the supremacy of divinity. Time is lost in eternity; space is swallowed up in worshipful identity and harmony with the Universal Father. The broadcasts of Havona flash forth the space reports of glory, the good news that in very truth the conscientious creatures of animal nature and material origin have, through evolutionary ascension, become in reality and eternally the perfected sons of God.

10. THE COUNSELORS AND ADVISERS

The superaphic counselors and advisers of the second circle are the instructors of the children of time regarding the career of eternity. The attainment of Paradise entails responsibilities of a new and higher order, and the sojourn on the second circle affords ample opportunity to receive the helpful counsel of these devoted supernaphim.

Those who are unsuccessful in the first effort at Deity attainment are advanced from the circle of failure directly to the second circle before they are returned to superuniverse service. Thus the counselors and advisers also serve as the counselors and comforters of these disappointed pilgrims. They have just encountered their greatest disappointment, in no way differing from the long list of such experiences whereon they climbed, as on a ladder, from chaos to glory—except in its magnitude. These are they who have drained the experiential cup to its dregs; and I have observed that they temporarily return to the services of the superuniverses as the highest type of loving ministrators to the children of time and temporal disappointments.

After a long sojourn on circuit number two the subjects of disappointment are examined by the councils of perfection sitting on the pilot world of this circle and are certified as having passed the Havona test; and this, so far as nonspiritual status is concerned, grants them the same standing in the universes of time as if they had actually succeeded in the Deity adventure. The spirit of such candidates was wholly acceptable; their failure was inherent in some phase of the technique of approach or in some part of their experiential background.

They are then taken by the counselors of the circle before the chiefs of assignment on Paradise and are remanded to the service of time on the worlds of space; and they go with joy and gladness to the tasks of former days and ages. In another day they will return to the circle of their greatest disappointment and attempt anew the Deity adventure.

For the successful pilgrims on the second circuit the stimulus of evolutionary uncertainty is over, but the adventure of the eternal assignment has not yet begun; and while the sojourn on this circle is wholly pleasurable and highly profitable, it lacks some of the anticipative enthusiasm of the former circles. Many are the pilgrims who, at such a time, look back upon the long, long struggle with a joyous envy, really wishing they might somehow go back to the worlds of time and begin it all over again, just as you mortals, in approaching advanced age, sometimes look back over the struggles of youth and early life and truly wish you might live your lives over once again.

But the traversal of the innermost circle lies just ahead, and soon thereafter the last transit sleep will terminate, and the new adventure of the eternal career will begin. The counselors and advisers on the second circle begin the preparation of their subjects for this great and final rest, the inevitable sleep which ever intervenes between the epochal stages of the ascendant career.

When those ascendant pilgrims who have attained the Universal Father complete the second-circle experience, their ever-attendant Graduate Guides issue the order admitting them to the final circle. These guides personally pilot their subjects to the inner circle and there place them in the custody of the complements of rest, the last of those orders of secondary supernaphim assigned to the ministry of the pilgrims of time on the world circuits of Havona.

11. THE COMPLEMENTS OF REST

Much of an ascender's time on the last circuit is devoted to a continuation of the study of the impending problems of Paradise residence. A vast and diverse host of beings, the majority unrevealed, are permanent and transient residents of this inner ring of Havona worlds. And the commingling of these manifold types provides the superaphic complements of rest with a rich situational environment which they effectively utilize in furthering the education of the ascending pilgrims, especially with regard to the problems of adjustment to the many groups of beings soon to be encountered on Paradise.

Among those who dwell on this inner circuit are the creature-trinitized sons. The primary and the secondary supernaphim are the general custodians of the conjoint corps of these sons, including the trinitized offspring of the mortal finaliters and similar progeny of the Paradise Citizens. Certain of these sons are Trinity embraced and commissioned in the supergovernments, others are variously assigned, but the great majority are being gathered together in the conjoint corps on the perfect worlds of the inner Havona circuit. Here, under the supervision of the supernaphim, they are being prepared for some future work by a special and unnamed corps of high Paradise Citizens who were, prior to the times of Grandfanda, first executive assistants to the Eternals of Days. There are many reasons for conjecturing that these two unique groups of trinitized beings are going to work together in the remote future, not the least of which is their common destiny in the reserves of the Paradise Corps of Trinitized Finaliters.

On this innermost circuit, both the ascending and the descending pilgrims fraternize with each other and with the creature-trinitized sons. Like their parents, these sons derive great benefits from interassociation, and it is the special mission of the supernaphim to facilitate and to insure the confraternity of the trinitized sons of the mortal finaliters and the trinitized sons of the Paradise Citizens. The superaphic complements of rest are not so much concerned with their training as with promoting their understanding association with diverse groups.

Mortals have received the Paradise command: "Be you perfect, even as your Paradise Father is perfect." To these trinitized sons of the conjoint corps the supervising supernaphim never cease to proclaim: "Be you understanding of your ascendant brethren, even as the Paradise Creator Sons know and love them."

The mortal creature must find God. The Creator Son never stops until he finds man—the lowest will creature. Beyond doubt, the Creator Sons and their mortal children are preparing for some future and unknown universe service. Both traverse the gamut of the experiential universe and so are educated and trained for their eternal mission. Throughout the universes there is occurring this unique blending of the human and the divine, the commingling of creature and Creator. Unthinking mortals have referred to the manifestation of divine mercy and tenderness, especially towards the weak and in behalf of the needy, as indicative of an anthropomorphic God. What a mistake! Rather should such manifestations of mercy and forbearance by human beings be taken as evidence that mortal man is indwelt by the spirit of the living God; that the creature is, after all, divinity motivated.

Near the end of the first-circle sojourn the ascending pilgrims first meet the instigators of rest of the primary order of supernaphim. These are the angels of Paradise coming out to greet those who stand at the threshold of eternity and to complete their preparation for the transition slumber of the last resurrection. You are not really a child of Paradise until you have traversed the inner circle and have experienced the resurrection of eternity from the terminal sleep of time. The perfected pilgrims begin this rest, go to sleep, on the first circle of Havona, but they awaken on the shores of Paradise. Of all who ascend to the eternal Isle, only those who thus arrive are the children of eternity; the others go as visitors, as guests without residential status.

And now, at the culmination of the Havona career, as you mortals go to sleep on the pilot world of the inner circuit, you go not alone to your rest as you did on the worlds of your origin when you closed your eyes in the natural sleep of mortal death, nor as you did when you entered the long transit trance preparatory for the journey to Havona. Now, as you prepare for the attainment rest, there moves over by your side your long-time associate of the first circle, the majestic complement of rest, who prepares to enter the rest as one with you, as the pledge of Havona that your transition is complete, and that you await only the final touches of perfection.

Your first transition was indeed death, the second an ideal sleep, and now the third metamorphosis is the true rest, the relaxation of the ages.

[Presented by a Perfector of Wisdom from Uversa.]

PAPER 27

MINISTRY OF THE PRIMARY SUPERNAPHIM

PRIMARY supernaphim are the supernal servants of the Deities on the eternal Isle of Paradise. Never have they been known to depart from the paths of light and righteousness. The roll calls are complete; from eternity not one of this magnificent host has been lost. These high supernaphim are perfect beings, supreme in perfection, but they are not absonite, neither are they absolute. Being of the essence of perfection, these children of the Infinite Spirit work interchangeably and at will in all phases of their manifold duties. They do not function extensively outside Paradise, though they do participate in the various millennial gatherings and group reunions of the central universe. They also go forth as special messengers of the Deities, and in large numbers they ascend to become Technical Advisers.

Primary supernaphim are also placed in command of the seraphic hosts ministering on worlds isolated because of rebellion. When a Paradise Son is bestowed upon such a world, completes his mission, ascends to the Universal Father, is accepted, and returns as the accredited deliverer of this isolated world, a primary supernaphim is always designated by the chiefs of assignment to assume command of the ministering spirits on duty in the newly reclaimed sphere. Supernaphim in this special service are periodically rotated. On Urantia the present "chief of seraphim" is the second of this order to be on duty since the times of the bestowal of Christ Michael.

From eternity the primary supernaphim have served on the Isle of Light and have gone forth on missions of leadership to the worlds of space, but they have functioned as now classified only since the arrival on Paradise of the Havona pilgrims of time. These high angels now minister chiefly in the following seven orders of service:

1. Conductors of Worship.
2. Masters of Philosophy.
3. Custodians of Knowledge.
4. Directors of Conduct.
5. Interpreters of Ethics.
6. Chiefs of Assignment.
7. Instigators of Rest.

Not until the ascending pilgrims actually attain Paradise residence do they come under the direct influence of these supernaphim, and then they pass through a training experience under the direction of these angels in the reverse order of their naming. That is, you enter upon your Paradise career under the tutelage of the instigators of rest and, after successive seasons with the intervening orders, finish this training period with the conductors of worship. Thereupon are you ready to begin the endless career of a finaliter.

1. INSTIGATORS OF REST

The instigators of rest are the inspectors of Paradise who go forth from the central Isle to the inner circuit of Havona, there to collaborate with their colleagues, the complements of rest of the secondary order of supernaphim. The one essential to the enjoyment of Paradise is rest, divine rest; and these instigators of rest are the final instructors who make ready the pilgrims of time for their introduction to eternity. They begin their work on the final attainment circle of the central universe and continue it when the pilgrim awakes from the last transition sleep, the slumber which graduates a creature of space into the realm of the eternal.

Rest is of a sevenfold nature: There is the rest of sleep and of play in the lower life orders, discovery in the higher beings, and worship in the highest type of spirit personality. There is also the normal rest of energy intake, the recharging of beings with physical or with spiritual energy. And then there is the transit sleep, the unconscious slumber when enseraphimed, when in passage from one sphere to another. Entirely different from all of these is the deep sleep of metamorphosis, the transition rest from one stage of being to another, from one life to another, from one state of existence to another, the sleep which ever attends transition from actual universe *status* in contrast to evolution through various *stages* of any one status.

But the last metamorphic sleep is something more than those previous transition slumbers which have marked the successive status attainments of the ascendant career; thereby do the creatures of time and space traverse the innermost margins of the temporal and the spatial to attain residential status in the timeless and spaceless abodes of Paradise. The instigators and the complements of rest are just as essential to this transcending metamorphosis as are the seraphim and associated beings to the mortal creature's survival of death.

You enter the rest on the final Havona circuit and are eternally resurrected on Paradise. And as you there spiritually repersonalize, you will immediately recognize the instigator of rest who welcomes you to the eternal shores as the very primary supernaphim who produced the final sleep on the innermost circuit of Havona; and you will recall the last grand stretch of faith as you once again made ready to commend the keeping of your identity into the hands of the Universal Father.

The last rest of time has been enjoyed; the last transition sleep has been experienced; now you awake to life everlasting on the shores of the eternal abode. "And there shall be no more sleep. The presence of God and his Son are before you, and you are eternally his servants; you have seen his face, and his name is your spirit. There shall be no night there; and they need no light of the sun, for the Great Source and Center gives them light; they shall live forever and ever. And God shall wipe away all tears from their eyes; there shall be no more death, neither sorrow nor crying, neither shall there be any more pain, for the former things have passed away."

2. CHIEFS OF ASSIGNMENT

This is the group designated from time to time by the chief supernaphim, "the original pattern angel," to preside over the organization of all three orders of these angels—primary, secondary, and tertiary. The supernaphim, as a body, are wholly self-governing and self-regulatory except for the functions of their mutual chief, the first angel of Paradise, who ever presides over all these spirit personalities.

The angels of assignment have much to do with glorified mortal residents of Paradise before they are admitted to the Corps of the Finality. Study and instruction are not the exclusive occupations of Paradise arrivals; service also plays its essential part in the prefinaliter educational experiences of Paradise. And I have observed that, when the ascendant mortals have periods of leisure, they evince a predilection to fraternize with the reserve corps of the superaphic chiefs of assignment.

When you mortal ascenders attain Paradise, your societal relationships involve a great deal more than contact with a host of exalted and divine beings and with a familiar multitude of glorified fellow mortals. You must also fraternize with upwards of three thousand different orders of Paradise Citizens, with the various groups of the Transcendentalers, and with numerous other types of Paradise inhabitants, permanent and transient, who have not been revealed on Urantia. After sustained contact with these mighty intellects of Paradise, it is very restful to visit with the angelic types of mind; they remind the mortals of time of the seraphim with whom they have had such long contact and such refreshing association.

3. INTERPRETERS OF ETHICS

The higher you ascend in the scale of life, the more attention must be paid to universe ethics. Ethical awareness is simply the recognition by any individual of the rights inherent in the existence of any and all other individuals. But spiritual ethics far transcends the mortal and even the morontia concept of personal and group relations.

Ethics has been duly taught and adequately learned by the pilgrims of time in their long ascent to the glories of Paradise. As this inward-ascending career has unfolded from the nativity worlds of space, the ascenders have continued to add group after group to their ever-widening circle of universe associates. Every new group of colleagues met with adds one more level of ethics to be recognized and complied with until, by the time the mortals of ascent reach Paradise, they really need someone to provide helpful and friendly counsel regarding ethical interpretations. They do not need to be taught ethics, but they do need to have what they have so laboriously learned properly *interpreted* to them as they are brought face to face with the extraordinary task of contacting with so much that is new.

The interpreters of ethics are of inestimable assistance to the Paradise arrivals in helping them to adjust to numerous groups of majestic beings during that eventful period extending from the attainment of residential status to formal induction into the Corps of Mortal Finaliters. Many of the numerous types of Paradise Citizens the ascendant pilgrims have already met on the seven circuits of Havona. The glorified mortals have also enjoyed intimate contact with the creature-trinitized sons of the conjoint corps on the inner Havona circuit, where these beings are receiving much of their education. And on the other circuits the ascending pilgrims have met numerous unrevealed residents of the Paradise-Havona system who are there pursuing group training in preparation for the unrevealed assignments of the future.

All these celestial companionships are invariably mutual. As ascending mortals you not only derive benefit from these successive universe companions and such numerous orders of increasingly divine associates, but you also impart to each of these fraternal beings something from your own personality and experience which forever makes every one of them different and better for having been associated with an ascending mortal from the evolutionary worlds of time and space.

4. DIRECTORS OF CONDUCT

Having already been fully instructed in the ethics of Paradise relationships —neither meaningless formalities nor the dictations of artificial castes but rather the inherent proprieties—the ascendant mortals find it helpful to receive the counsel of the superaphic directors of conduct, who instruct the new members of Paradise society in the usages of the perfect conduct of the high beings who sojourn on the central Isle of Light and Life.

Harmony is the keynote of the central universe, and detectable order prevails on Paradise. Proper conduct is essential to progress by way of knowledge, through philosophy, to the spiritual heights of spontaneous worship. There is a divine technique in the approach to Divinity; and the acquirement of this technique must await the pilgrims' arrival on Paradise. The spirit of it has been imparted on the circles of Havona, but the final touches of the training of the pilgrims of time can be applied only after they actually attain the Isle of Light.

All Paradise conduct is wholly spontaneous, in every sense natural and free. But there still is a proper and perfect way of doing things on the eternal Isle, and the directors of conduct are ever by the side of the "strangers within the gates" to instruct them and so guide their steps as to put them at perfect ease and at the same time to enable the pilgrims to avoid that confusion and uncertainty which would otherwise be inevitable. Only by such an arrangement could endless confusion be avoided; and confusion never appears on Paradise.

These directors of conduct really serve as glorified teachers and guides. They are chiefly concerned with instructing the new mortal residents regarding the almost endless array of new situations and unfamiliar usages. Notwithstanding all the long preparation therefor and the long journey thereto, Paradise is still inexpressibly strange and unexpectedly new to those who finally attain residential status.

5. THE CUSTODIANS OF KNOWLEDGE

The superaphic custodians of knowledge are the higher "living epistles" known and read by all who dwell on Paradise. They are the divine records of truth, the living books of real knowledge. You have heard about records in the "book of life." The custodians of knowledge are just such living books, records of perfection imprinted upon the eternal tablets of divine life and supreme surety. They are in reality living, automatic libraries. The facts of the universes are inherent in these primary supernaphim, actually recorded in these angels; and it is also inherently impossible for an untruth to gain lodgment in the minds of these perfect and replete repositories of the truth of eternity and the intelligence of time.

These custodians conduct informal courses of instruction for the residents of the eternal Isle, but their chief function is that of reference and verification. Any sojourner on Paradise may at will have by his side the living repository of the particular fact or truth he may wish to know. At the northern extremity of the Isle there are available the living finders of knowledge, who will designate the director of the group holding the information sought, and forthwith will appear the brilliant beings who *are* the very thing you wish to know. No longer must you seek enlightenment from engrossed pages; you now commune with living intelligence face to face. Supreme knowledge you thus obtain from the living beings who are its final custodians.

When you locate that supernaphim who is exactly what you desire to verify, you will find available *all* the known facts of all universes, for these custodians of knowledge are the final and living summaries of the vast network of the recording angels, ranging from the seraphim and seconaphim of the local and superuniverses to the chief recorders of the tertiary supernaphim in Havona. And this living accumulation of knowledge is distinct from the formal records of Paradise, the cumulative summary of universal history.

The wisdom of truth takes origin in the divinity of the central universe, but knowledge, experiential knowledge, largely has its beginnings in the domains of time and space—therefore the necessity for the maintenance of the far-flung superuniverse organizations of the recording seraphim and supernaphim sponsored by the Celestial Recorders.

These primary supernaphim who are inherently in possession of universe knowledge are also responsible for its organization and classification. In constituting themselves the living reference library of the universe of universes, they have classified knowledge into seven grand orders, each having about one million subdivisions. The facility with which the residents of Paradise can consult this vast store of knowledge is solely due to the voluntary and wise efforts of the custodians of knowledge. The custodians are also the exalted teachers of the central universe, freely giving out their living treasures to all beings on any of the Havona circuits, and they are extensively, though indirectly, utilized by the courts of the Ancients of Days. But this living library, which is available to the central and superuniverses, is not accessible to the local creations. Only by indirection and reflectively are the benefits of Paradise knowledge secured in the local universes.

6. MASTERS OF PHILOSOPHY

Next to the supreme satisfaction of worship is the exhilaration of philosophy. Never do you climb so high or advance so far that there do not remain a thousand mysteries which demand the employment of philosophy in an attempted solution.

The master philosophers of Paradise delight to lead the minds of its inhabitants, both native and ascendant, in the exhilarating pursuit of attempting to solve universe problems. These superaphic masters of philosophy are the "wise men of heaven," the beings of wisdom who make use of the truth of knowledge and the facts of experience in their efforts to master the unknown. With them knowledge attains to truth and experience ascends to wisdom. On Paradise the ascendant personalities of space experience the heights of being: They have knowledge; they know the truth; they may philosophize—think the truth; they may even seek to encompass the concepts of the Ultimate and attempt to grasp the techniques of the Absolutes.

At the southern extremity of the vast Paradise domain the masters of philosophy conduct elaborate courses in the seventy functional divisions of wisdom. Here they discourse upon the plans and purposes of Infinity and seek to coordinate the experiences, and to compose the knowledge, of all who have access to their wisdom. They have developed a highly specialized attitude toward various universe problems, but their final conclusions are always in uniform agreement.

These Paradise philosophers teach by every possible method of instruction, including the higher graph technique of Havona and certain Paradise methods of communicating information. All of these higher techniques of imparting knowledge and conveying ideas are utterly beyond the comprehension capacity of even the most highly developed human mind. One hour's instruction on Paradise would be the equivalent of ten thousand years of the word-memory methods of Urantia. You cannot grasp such communication techniques, and there is simply nothing in mortal experience with which they may be compared, nothing to which they can be likened.

The masters of philosophy take supreme pleasure in imparting their interpretation of the universe of universes to those beings who have ascended from the worlds of space. And while philosophy can never be as settled in its conclusions as the facts of knowledge and the truths of experience, yet, when you have listened to these primary supernaphim discourse upon the unsolved problems of eternity and the performances of the Absolutes, you will feel a certain and lasting satisfaction concerning these unmastered questions.

These intellectual pursuits of Paradise are not broadcast; the philosophy of perfection is available only to those who are personally present. The encircling creations know of these teachings only from those who have passed through this experience, and who have subsequently carried this wisdom out to the universes of space.

7. CONDUCTORS OF WORSHIP

Worship is the highest privilege and the first duty of all created intelligences. Worship is the conscious and joyous act of recognizing and acknowledging the truth and fact of the intimate and personal relationships of the Creators with their creatures. The quality of worship is determined by the depth of creature perception; and as the knowledge of the infinite character of the Gods progresses, the act of worship becomes increasingly all-encompassing until it eventually attains the glory of the highest experiential delight and the most exquisite pleasure known to created beings.

While the Isle of Paradise contains certain places of worship, it is more nearly one vast sanctuary of divine service. Worship is the first and dominant passion of all who climb to its blissful shores—the spontaneous ebullition of the beings who have learned enough of God to attain his presence. Circle by circle, during the inward journey through Havona, worship is a growing passion until on Paradise it becomes necessary to direct and otherwise control its expression.

The periodic, spontaneous, group, and other special outbursts of supreme adoration and spiritual praise enjoyed on Paradise are conducted under the leadership of a special corps of primary supernaphim. Under the direction of these conductors of worship, such homage achieves the creature goal of supreme pleasure and attains the heights of the perfection of sublime self-expression and personal enjoyment. All primary supernaphim crave to be conductors of worship; and all ascendant beings would enjoy forever remaining in the attitude of worship did not the chiefs of assignment periodically disperse these assemblages. But no ascendant being is ever required to enter upon the assignments of eternal service until he has attained full satisfaction in worship.

It is the task of the conductors of worship so to teach the ascendant creatures how to worship that they may be enabled to gain this satisfaction of self-expression and at the same time be able to give attention to the essential activities of the Paradise regime. Without improvement in the technique of worship it would require hundreds of years for the average mortal who reaches Paradise to give full and satisfactory expression to his emotions of intelligent appreciation and ascendant gratitude. The conductors of worship open up new and hitherto unknown avenues of expression so that these wonderful children of the womb of space and the travail of time are enabled to gain the full satisfactions of worship in much less time.

All the arts of all the beings of the entire universe which are capable of intensifying and exalting the abilities of self-expression and the conveyance of appreciation, are employed to their highest capacity in the worship of the Paradise Deities. *Worship is the highest joy of Paradise existence;* it is the refreshing play of Paradise. What play does for your jaded minds on earth, worship will do for your perfected souls on Paradise. The mode of worship on Paradise is utterly beyond mortal comprehension, but the spirit of it you can begin to appreciate even down here on Urantia, for the spirits of the Gods even now indwell you, hover over you, and inspire you to true worship.

There are appointed times and places for worship on Paradise, but these are not adequate to accommodate the ever-increasing overflow of the spiritual emotions of the growing intelligence and expanding divinity recognition of the brilliant beings of experiential ascension to the eternal Isle. Never since the times of Grandfanda have the supernaphim been able fully to accommodate the spirit of worship on Paradise. Always is there an excess of worshipfulness as gauged by the preparation therefor. And this is because personalities of inherent perfection never can fully appreciate the tremendous reactions of the spiritual emotions of beings who have slowly and laboriously made their way upward to Paradise glory from the depths of the spiritual darkness of the lower worlds of time and space. When such angels and mortals of time attain the presence of the Powers of Paradise, there occurs the expression of the accumulated emotions of the ages, a spectacle astounding to the angels of Paradise and productive of the supreme joy of divine satisfaction in the Paradise Deities.

Sometimes all Paradise becomes engulfed in a dominating tide of spiritual and worshipful expression. Often the conductors of worship cannot control such phenomena until the appearance of the threefold fluctuation of the light of the

Deity abode, signifying that the divine heart of the Gods has been fully and completely satisfied by the sincere worship of the residents of Paradise, the perfect citizens of glory and the ascendant creatures of time. What a triumph of technique! What a fruition of the eternal plan and purpose of the Gods that the intelligent love of the creature child should give full satisfaction to the infinite love of the Creator Father!

After the attainment of the supreme satisfaction of the fullness of worship, you are qualified for admission to the Corps of the Finality. The ascendant career is well-nigh finished, and the seventh jubilee prepares for celebration. The first jubilee marked the mortal agreement with the Thought Adjuster when the purpose to survive was sealed; the second was the awakening in the morontia life; the third was the fusion with the Thought Adjuster; the fourth was the awakening in Havona; the fifth celebrated the finding of the Universal Father; and the sixth jubilee was the occasion of the Paradise awakening from the final transit slumber of time. The seventh jubilee marks entrance into the mortal finaliter corps and the beginning of the eternity service. The attainment of the seventh stage of spirit realization by a finaliter will probably signalize the celebration of the first of the jubilees of eternity.

And thus ends the story of the Paradise supernaphim, the highest order of all the ministering spirits, those beings who, as a universal class, ever attend you from the world of your origin until you are finally bidden farewell by the conductors of worship as you take the Trinity oath of eternity and are mustered into the Mortal Corps of the Finality.

The endless service of the Paradise Trinity is about to begin; and now the finaliter is face to face with the challenge of God the Ultimate.

[Presented by a Perfector of Wisdom from Uversa.]

PAPER 28

MINISTERING SPIRITS OF THE SUPERUNIVERSES

AS THE supernaphim are the angelic hosts of the central universe and the seraphim of the local universes, so are the seconaphim the ministering spirits of the superuniverses. In degree of divinity and in potential of supremacy, however, these children of the Reflective Spirits are much more like supernaphim than seraphim. They serve not alone in the supercreations, and both numerous and intriguing are the transactions sponsored by their unrevealed associates.

As presented in these narratives, the ministering spirits of the superuniverses embrace the following three orders:

1. The Seconaphim.
2. The Tertiaphim.
3. The Omniaphim.

Since the latter two orders are not so directly concerned with the ascendant scheme of mortal progression, they will be briefly discussed prior to the more extended consideration of seconaphim. Technically, neither tertiaphim nor omniaphim are ministering spirits *of* the superuniverses, though both serve as spirit ministers *in* these domains.

1. THE TERTIAPHIM

These high angels are of record on the superuniverse headquarters, and despite service in the local creations, technically they are residents of these superuniverse capitals inasmuch as they are not native to the local universes. Tertiaphim are children of the Infinite Spirit and are personalized on Paradise in groups of one thousand. These supernal beings of divine originality and near-supreme versatility are the gift of the Infinite Spirit to the Creator Sons of God.

When a Michael Son is detached from the parental regime of Paradise and is made ready to go forth on the universe adventure of space, the Infinite Spirit is delivered of a group of one thousand of these companion spirits. And these majestic tertiaphim accompany this Creator Son when he embarks upon the adventure of universe organization.

Throughout the early times of universe building, these one thousand tertiaphim are the only personal staff of a Creator Son. They acquire a mighty experience as Son assistants during these stirring ages of universe assembling and other astronomical manipulations. They serve by the side of the Creator Son until the day of the personalization of the Bright and Morning Star, the first-born of a local universe. Thereupon the formal resignations of the tertiaphim are tendered and accepted. And with the appearance of the initial orders of native angelic life, they retire from active service in the local universe and become the liaison ministers between the Creator Son of former attachment and the Ancients of Days of the superuniverse concerned.

2. THE OMNIAPHIM

Omniaphim are created by the Infinite Spirit in liaison with the Seven Supreme Executives, and they are the exclusive servants and messengers of these same Supreme Executives. Omniaphim are of grand universe assignment, and in Orvonton their corps maintains headquarters in the northerly parts of Uversa, where they reside as a special courtesy colony. They are not of registry on Uversa, nor are they attached to our administration. Neither are they directly concerned with the ascendant scheme of mortal progression.

The omniaphim are wholly occupied with the oversight of the superuniverses in the interests of administrative co-ordination from the viewpoint of the Seven Supreme Executives. Our colony of omniaphim on Uversa receives instructions from, and makes reports to, only the Supreme Executive of Orvonton, situated on conjoint executive sphere number seven in the outer ring of Paradise satellites.

3. THE SECONAPHIM

The secoraphic hosts are produced by the seven Reflective Spirits assigned to the headquarters of each superuniverse. There is a definite Paradise-responsive technique associated with the creation of these angels in groups of seven. In each seven there are always one primary, three secondary, and three tertiary seconaphim; they always personalize in this exact proportion. When seven such seconaphim are created, one, the primary, becomes attached to the service of the Ancients of Days. The three secondary angels are associated with three groups of Paradise-origin administrators in the supergovernments: the Divine Counselors, the Perfectors of Wisdom, and the Universal Censors. The three tertiary angels are attached to the ascendant trinitized associates of the superuniverse rulers: the Mighty Messengers, Those High in Authority, and Those without Name and Number.

These seconaphim of the superuniverses are the offspring of the Reflective Spirits, and therefore reflectivity is inherent in their nature. They are reflectively responsive to all of each phase of every creature of origin in the Third Source and Center and the Paradise Creator Sons, but they are not directly reflective of the beings and entities, personal or otherwise, of sole origin in the First Source and Center. We possess many evidences of the actuality of the universal intelligence circuits of the Infinite Spirit, but even if we had no other proof, the reflective performances of the seconaphim would be quite sufficient to demonstrate the reality of the universal presence of the infinite mind of the Conjoint Actor.

4. THE PRIMARY SECONAPHIM

The primary seconaphim, of assignment to the Ancients of Days, are living mirrors in the service of these triune rulers. Think what it means in the economy of a superuniverse to be able to turn, as it were, to a living mirror and therein to see and therewith to hear the certain responses of another being a thousand or a hundred thousand light-years distant and to do all this instantly and unerringly. Records are essential to the conduct of the universes, broadcasts are serviceable, the work of the Solitary and other messengers is very helpful, but the Ancients of Days from their position midway between the inhabited worlds and Paradise—between man and God—can instantly look both ways, hear both ways, and *know* both ways.

This ability—to hear and see, as it were, all things—can be perfectly realized in the superuniverses only by the Ancients of Days and only on their respective headquarters worlds. Even there limits are encountered: From Uversa, such communication is limited to the worlds and universes of Orvonton, and while inoperative between the superuniverses, this same reflective technique keeps each one of them in close touch with the central universe and with Paradise. The seven supergovernments, though individually segregated, are thus perfectly reflective of the authority above and are wholly sympathetic, as well as perfectly conversant, with the needs below.

The primary seconaphim are found to incline by inherent nature towards seven types of service, and it is befitting that the first serials of this order should be so endowed as inherently to interpret the mind of the Spirit to the Ancients of Days:

1. *The Voice of the Conjoint Actor.* In each superuniverse the first primary seconaphim and every seventh one of that order subsequently created exhibit a high order of adaptability for understanding and interpreting the mind of the Infinite Spirit to the Ancients of Days and their associates in the supergovernments. This is of great value on the headquarters of the superuniverses, for, unlike the local creations with their Divine Ministers, the seat of a supergovernment does not have a specialized personalization of the Infinite Spirit. Hence these secoraphic voices come the nearest to being the personal representatives of the Third Source and Center on such a capital sphere. True, the seven Reflective Spirits are there, but these mothers of the secoraphic hosts are less truly and automatically reflective of the Conjoint Actor than of the Seven Master Spirits.

2. *The Voice of the Seven Master Spirits.* The second primary seconaphim and every seventh one thereafter created incline towards portraying the collective natures and reactions of the Seven Master Spirits. Though each Master Spirit is already represented on a superuniverse capital by some one of the seven Reflective Spirits of assignment, such representation is individual, not collective. Collectively, they are only reflectively present; therefore do the Master Spirits welcome the services of these highly personal angels, the second serials of the primary seconaphim, who are so competent to represent them before the Ancients of Days.

3. *The Voice of the Creator Sons.* The Infinite Spirit must have had something to do with the creation or training of the Paradise Sons of the order of Michael, for the third primary seconaphim and every seventh serial thereafter possess the remarkable gift of being reflective of the minds of these Creator Sons. If the Ancients of Days would like to know—really know—the attitude of Michael of Nebadon regarding some matter under consideration, they do not have to call him on the lines of space; they need only call for the Chief of Nebadon

Voices, who, upon request, will present the Michael seconaphim of record; and right then and there the Ancients of Days will perceive the voice of the Master Son of Nebadon.

No other order of sonship is thus "reflectible," and no other order of angel can thus function. We do not fully understand just how this is accomplished, and I doubt very much that the Creator Sons themselves fully understand it. But of a certainty we know it works, and that it unfailingly works acceptably we also know, for in all the history of Uversa the secoraphic voices have never erred in their presentations.

You are here beginning to see something of the manner in which divinity encompasses the space of time and masters the time of space. You are here obtaining one of your first fleeting glimpses of the technique of the eternity cycle, divergent for the moment to assist the children of time in their tasks of mastering the difficult handicaps of space. And these phenomena are additional to the established universe technique of the Reflective Spirits.

Though apparently deprived of the personal presence of the Master Spirits above and of the Creator Sons below, the Ancients of Days have at their command living beings attuned to cosmic mechanisms of reflective perfection and ultimate precision whereby they may enjoy the reflective presence of all those exalted beings whose personal presence is denied them. By and through these means, and others unknown to you, God is potentially present on the headquarters of the superuniverses.

The Ancients of Days perfectly deduce the Father's will by equating the Spirit voice-flash from above and the Michael voice-flashes from below. Thus may they be unerringly certain in calculating the Father's will concerning the administrative affairs of the local universes. But to deduce the will of one of the Gods from a knowledge of the other two, the three Ancients of Days must act together; two would not be able to achieve the answer. And for this reason, even were there no others, the superuniverses are always presided over by three Ancients of Days, and not by one or even two.

4. *The Voice of the Angelic Hosts.* The fourth primary seconaphim and every seventh serial prove to be angels peculiarly responsive to the sentiments of all orders of angels, including the supernaphim above and the seraphim below. Thus the attitude of any commanding or supervising angel is immediately available for consideration at any council of the Ancients of Days. Never a day passes on your world that the chief of seraphim on Urantia is not made conscious of the phenomenon of reflective transference, of being drawn upon from Uversa for some purpose; but unless forewarned by a Solitary Messenger, she remains wholly ignorant of what is sought and of how it is secured. These ministering spirits of time are constantly furnishing this sort of unconscious and certainly, therefore, unprejudiced testimony concerning the endless array of matters engaging the attention and counsel of the Ancients of Days and their associates.

5. *Broadcast Receivers.* There is a special class of broadcast messages which are received only by these primary seconaphim. While they are not the regular broadcasters of Uversa, they work in liaison with the angels of the reflective voices for the purpose of synchronizing the reflective vision of the Ancients of Days with certain actual messages coming in over the established circuits of universe communication. Broadcast receivers are the fifth serials, the fifth primary seconaphim to be created and every seventh one thereafter.

6. *Transport Personalities.* These are the seconaphim who carry the pilgrims of time from the headquarters worlds of the superuniverses to the outer circle of Havona. They are the transport corps of the superuniverses, operating inward to Paradise and outward to the worlds of their respective sectors. This corps is composed of the sixth primary seconaphim and every seventh one subsequently created.

7. *The Reserve Corps.* A very large group of seconaphim, the seventh primary serials, are held in reserve for the unclassified duties and the emergency assignments of the realms. Not being highly specialized, they can function fairly well in any of the capacities of their diverse associates, but such specialized work is undertaken only in emergencies. Their usual tasks are the performance of those generalized duties of a superuniverse which do not fall within the scope of the angels of specific assignment.

5. THE SECONDARY SECONAPHIM

Seconaphim of the secondary order are no less reflective than their primary fellows. Being classed as primary, secondary, and tertiary does not indicate a differential of status or function in the case of seconaphim; it merely denotes orders of procedure. Identical qualities are exhibited by all three groups in their activities.

The seven reflective types of secondary seconaphim are assigned to the services of the co-ordinate Trinity-origin associates of the Ancients of Days as follows:

To the Perfectors of Wisdom—the Voices of Wisdom, the Souls of Philosophy, and the Unions of Souls.

To the Divine Counselors—the Hearts of Counsel, the Joys of Existence, and the Satisfactions of Service.

To the Universal Censors—the Discerners of Spirits.

Like the primary order, this group is created serially; that is, the first-born was a Voice of Wisdom, and the seventh thereafter was similar, and so with the six other types of these reflective angels.

1. *The Voice of Wisdom.* Certain of these seconaphim are in perpetual liaison with the living libraries of Paradise, the custodians of knowledge belonging to the primary supernaphim. In specialized reflective service the Voices of Wisdom are living, current, replete, and thoroughly reliable concentrations and focalizations of the co-ordinated wisdom of the universe of universes. To the well-nigh infinite volume of information circulating on the master circuits of the superuniverses, these superb beings are so reflective and selective, so sensitive, as to be able to segregate and receive the essence of wisdom and unerringly to transmit these jewels of mentation to their superiors, the Perfectors of Wisdom. And they so function that the Perfectors of Wisdom not only hear the actual and original expressions of this wisdom but also reflectively see the very beings, of high or lowly origin, who gave voice to it.

It is written, "If any man lack wisdom, let him ask." On Uversa, when it becomes necessary to arrive at the decisions of wisdom in the perplexing situations of the complex affairs of the superuniverse government, when both the wisdom of perfection and of practicability must be forthcoming, then do the Perfectors of Wisdom summon a battery of the Voices of Wisdom and, by the consummate skill of their order, so attune and directionize these living receivers of the enminded and circulating wisdom of the universe of universes that presently, from these secoraphic voices, there ensues a stream of the wisdom of divinity from the universe above and a flood of the wisdom of practicality from the higher minds of the universes below.

If confusion arises regarding the harmonization of these two versions of wisdom, immediate appeal is made to the Divine Counselors, who forthwith rule as to the proper combination of procedures. If there is any doubt as to the authenticity of something coming in from realms where rebellion has been rife, appeal is made to the Censors, who, with their Discerners of Spirits, are able to rule immediately as to "what manner of spirit" actuated the adviser. So are the wisdom of the ages and the intellect of the moment ever present with the Ancients of Days, like an open book before their beneficent gaze.

You can just faintly comprehend what all this means to those who are responsible for the conduct of the superuniverse governments. The immensity and the comprehensiveness of these transactions are quite beyond finite conception. When you stand, as I repeatedly have, in the special receiving chambers of the temple of wisdom on Uversa and see all this in actual operation, you will be moved to adoration by the perfection of the complexity, and by the surety of the working, of the interplanetary communications of the universes. You will pay homage to the divine wisdom and goodness of the Gods, who plan and execute with such superb technique. And these things actually happen just as I have portrayed them.

2. *The Soul of Philosophy.* These wonderful teachers are also attached to the Perfectors of Wisdom and, when not otherwise directionized, remain in focal synchrony with the masters of philosophy on Paradise. Think of stepping up to a huge living mirror, as it were, but instead of beholding the likeness of your finite and material self, of perceiving a reflection of the wisdom of divinity and the philosophy of Paradise. And if it becomes desirable to "incarnate" this philosophy of perfection, so to dilute it as to make it practical of application to, and assimilation by, the lowly peoples of the lower worlds, these living mirrors have only to turn their faces downward to reflect the standards and needs of another world or universe.

By these very techniques do the Perfectors of Wisdom adapt decisions and recommendations to the real needs and actual status of the peoples and worlds under consideration, and always do they act in concert with the Divine Counselors and the Universal Censors. But the sublime repleteness of these transactions is beyond even my ability to comprehend.

3. *The Union of Souls.* Completing the triune staff of attachment to the Perfectors of Wisdom, are these reflectors of the ideals and status of ethical relationships. Of all the problems in the universe requiring an exercise of the consummate wisdom of experience and adaptability, none are more important than those arising out of the relationships and associations of intelligent beings. Whether in human associations of commerce and trade, friendship and marriage, or in the liaisons of the angelic hosts, there continue to arise petty frictions, minor misunderstandings too trivial even to engage the attention of conciliators but sufficiently irritating and disturbing to mar the smooth working of the universe if they were allowed to multiply and continue.

Therefore do the Perfectors of Wisdom make available the wise experience of their order as the "oil of reconciliation" for an entire superuniverse. In all this work these wise men of the superuniverses are ably seconded by their reflective associates, the Unions of Souls, who make available current information regarding the status of the universe and concurrently portray the Paradise ideal of the best adjustment of these perplexing problems. When not specifically directionized elsewhere, these seconaphim remain in reflective liaison with the interpreters of ethics on Paradise.

These are the angels who foster and promote the teamwork of all Orvonton. One of the most important lessons to be learned during your mortal career is *teamwork.* The spheres of perfection are manned by those who have mastered this art of working with other beings. Few are the duties in the universe for the lone servant. The higher you ascend, the more lonely you become when temporarily without the association of your fellows.

4. *The Heart of Counsel.* This is the first group of these reflective geniuses to be placed under the supervision of the Divine Counselors. Seconaphim of this type are in possession of the facts of space, being selective for such data in the circuits of time. Especially are they reflective of the superaphic intelligence co-ordinators, but they are also selectively reflective of the counsel of all beings, whether of high or low estate. Whenever the Divine Counselors are called upon for important advice or decisions, they immediately requisition an ensemble of the Hearts of Counsel, and presently there is handed down a ruling which actually incorporates the co-ordinated wisdom and advice of the most competent minds of the entire superuniverse, all of which has been censored and revised in the light of the counsel of the high minds of Havona and even of Paradise.

5. *The Joy of Existence.* By nature these beings are reflectively attuned to the superaphic harmony supervisors above and to certain of the seraphim below, but it is difficult to explain just what the members of this interesting group really do. Their principal activities are directed toward promoting reactions of joy among the various orders of the angelic hosts and the lower will creatures. The Divine Counselors, to whom they are attached, seldom use them for specific joy finding. In a more general manner and in collaboration with the reversion directors, they function as joy clearinghouses, seeking to upstep the pleasure reactions of the realms while trying to improve the humor taste, to develop a superhumor among mortals and angels. They endeavor to demonstrate that there is inherent joy in freewill existence, independent of all extraneous influences; and they are right, although they meet with great difficulty in inculcating this truth in the minds of primitive men. The higher spirit personalities and the angels are more quickly responsive to these educational efforts.

6. *The Satisfaction of Service.* These angels are highly reflective of the attitude of the directors of conduct on Paradise, and functioning much as do the Joys of Existence, they strive to enhance the value of service and to augment the satisfactions to be derived therefrom. They have done much to illuminate the deferred rewards inherent in unselfish service, service for the extension of the kingdom of truth.

The Divine Counselors, to whom this order is attached, utilize them to reflect from one world to another the benefits to be derived from spiritual service.

And by using the performances of the best to inspire and encourage the mediocre, these seconaphim contribute immensely to the quality of devoted service in the superuniverses. Effective use is made of the fraternal competitive spirit by circulating to any one world information about what the others, particularly the best, are doing. A refreshing and wholesome rivalry is promoted even among the seraphic hosts.

7. *The Discerner of Spirits.* A special liaison exists between the counselors and advisers of the second Havona circle and these reflective angels. They are the only seconaphim attached to the Universal Censors but are probably the most uniquely specialized of all their fellows. Regardless of the source or channel of information, no matter how meager the evidence at hand, when it is subjected to their reflective scrutiny, these discerners will forthwith inform us as to the true motive, the actual purpose, and the real nature of its origin. I marvel at the superb functioning of these angels, who so unerringly reflect the actual moral and spiritual character of any individual concerned in a focal exposure.

The Discerners of Spirits carry on these intricate services by virtue of inherent "spiritual insight," if I may use such words in an endeavor to convey to the human mind the thought that these reflective angels thus function intuitively, inherently, and unerringly. When the Universal Censors behold these presentations, they are face to face with the naked soul of the reflected individual; and this very certainty and perfection of portraiture in part explains why the Censors can always function so justly as righteous judges. The discerners always accompany the Censors on any mission away from Uversa, and they are just as effective out in the universes as at their Uversa headquarters.

I assure you that all these transactions of the spirit world are real, that they take place in accordance with established usages and in harmony with the immutable laws of the universal domains. The beings of every newly created order, immediately upon receiving the breath of life, are instantly reflected on high; a living portrayal of the creature nature and potential is flashed to the superuniverse headquarters. Thus, by means of the discerners, are the Censors made fully cognizant of exactly "what manner of spirit" has been born on the worlds of space.

So it is with mortal man: The Mother Spirit of Salvington knows you fully, for the Holy Spirit on your world "searches all things," and whatsoever the divine Spirit knows of you is immediately available whenever the secoraphic discerners reflect with the Spirit concerning the Spirit's knowledge of you. It should, however, be mentioned that the knowledge and plans of the Father fragments are not reflectible. The discerners can and do reflect the presence of the Adjusters (and the Censors pronounce them divine), but they cannot decipher the content of the mindedness of the Mystery Monitors.

6. THE TERTIARY SECONAPHIM

In the same manner as their fellows, these angels are created serially and in seven reflective types, but these types are not assigned individually to the separate services of the superuniverse administrators. All tertiary seconaphim are collectively assigned to the Trinitized Sons of Attainment, and these ascendant sons use them interchangeably; that is, the Mighty Messengers can and do utilize any of the tertiary types, and so do their co-ordinates, Those High in

Authority and Those without Name and Number. These seven types of tertiary seconaphim are:

1. *The Significance of Origins.* The ascendant Trinitized Sons of a superuniverse government are charged with the responsibility of dealing with all issues growing out of the origin of any individual, race, or world; and the significance of origin is the paramount question in all our plans for the cosmic advancement of the living creatures of the realm. All relationships and the application of ethics grow out of the fundamental facts of origin. Origin is the basis of the relational reaction of the Gods. Always does the Conjoint Actor "take note of the man, in what manner he was born."

With the higher descendant beings, origin is simply a fact to be ascertained; but with the ascending beings, including the lower orders of angels, the nature and circumstances of origin are not always so clear, though of equally vital importance at almost every turn of universe affairs—hence the value of having at our disposal a series of reflective seconaphim who can instantly portray anything required respecting the genesis of any being in either the central universe or throughout the entire realm of a superuniverse.

The Significances of Origins are the living ready-reference genealogies of the vast hosts of beings—men, angels, and others—who inhabit the seven superuniverses. They are always ready to supply their superiors with an up-to-date, replete, and trustworthy estimate of the ancestral factors and the current actual status of any individual on any world of their respective superuniverses; and their computation of possessed facts is always up to the minute.

2. *The Memory of Mercy.* These are the actual, full and replete, living records of the mercy which has been extended to individuals and races by the tender ministrations of the instrumentalities of the Infinite Spirit in the mission of adapting the justice of righteousness to the status of the realms, as disclosed by the portrayals of the Significance of Origins. The Memory of Mercy discloses the moral debt of the children of mercy—their spiritual liabilities—to be set down against their assets of the saving provision established by the Sons of God. In revealing the Father's pre-existent mercy, the Sons of God establish the necessary credit to insure the survival of all. And then, in accordance with the findings of the Significance of Origins, a mercy credit is established for the survival of each rational creature, a credit of lavish proportions and one of sufficient grace to insure the survival of every soul who really desires divine citizenship.

The Memory of Mercy is a living trial balance, a current statement of your account with the supernatural forces of the realms. These are the living records of mercy ministration which are read into the testimony of the courts of Uversa when each individual's right to unending life comes up for adjudication, when "thrones are cast up and the Ancients of Days are seated. The broadcasts of Uversa issue and come forth from before them; thousands upon thousands minister to them, and ten thousand times ten thousand stand before them. The judgment is set, and the books are opened." And the books which are opened on such a momentous occasion are the living records of the tertiary seconaphim of the superuniverses. The formal records are on file to corroborate the testimony of the Memories of Mercy if they are required.

The Memory of Mercy must show that the saving credit established by the Sons of God has been fully and faithfully paid out in the loving ministry of the patient personalities of the Third Source and Center. But when mercy is exhausted, when the "memory" thereof testifies to its depletion, then does justice prevail and righteousness decree. For mercy is not to be thrust upon those who despise it; mercy is not a gift to be trampled under foot by the persistent rebels of time. Nevertheless, though mercy is thus precious and dearly bestowed, your individual drawing credits are always far in excess of your ability to exhaust the reserve if you are sincere of purpose and honest of heart.

The mercy reflectors, with their tertiary associates, engage in numerous superuniverse ministries, including the teaching of the ascending creatures. Among many other things the Significances of Origins teach these ascenders how to apply spirit ethics, and following such training, the Memories of Mercy teach them how to be truly merciful. While the spirit techniques of mercy ministry are beyond your concept, you should even now understand that mercy is a quality of growth. You should realize that there is a great reward of personal satisfaction in being first just, next fair, then patient, then kind. And then, on that foundation, if you choose and have it in your heart, you can take the next step and really show mercy; but you cannot exhibit mercy in and of itself. These steps must be traversed; otherwise there can be no genuine mercy. There may be patronage, condescension, or charity—even pity—but not mercy. True mercy comes only as the beautiful climax to these preceding adjuncts to group understanding, mutual appreciation, fraternal fellowship, spiritual communion, and divine harmony.

3. *The Import of Time.* Time is the one universal endowment of all will creatures; it is the "one talent" intrusted to all intelligent beings. You all have time in which to insure your survival; and time is fatally squandered only when it is buried in neglect, when you fail so to utilize it as to make certain the survival of your soul. Failure to improve one's time to the fullest extent possible does not impose fatal penalties; it merely retards the pilgrim of time in his journey of ascent. If survival is gained, all other losses can be retrieved.

In the assignment of trusts the counsel of the Imports of Time is invaluable. Time is a vital factor in everything this side of Havona and Paradise. In the final judgment before the Ancients of Days, time is an element of evidence. The Imports of Time must always afford testimony to show that every defendant has had ample time for making decisions, achieving choice.

These time evaluators are also the secret of prophecy; they portray the element of time which will be required in the completion of any undertaking, and they are just as dependable as indicators as are the frandalanks and chronoldeks of other living orders. The Gods foresee, hence foreknow; but the ascendant authorities of the universes of time must consult the Imports of Time to be able to forecast events of the future.

You will first encounter these beings on the mansion worlds, and they will there instruct you in the advantageous use of that which you call "time," both in its positive employment, work, and in its negative utilization, rest. Both uses of time are important.

4. *The Solemnity of Trust.* Trust is the crucial test of will creatures. Trustworthiness is the true measure of self-mastery, character. These seconaphim accomplish a double purpose in the economy of the superuniverses: They portray to all will creatures the sense of the obligation, sacredness, and solemnity of

trust. At the same time they unerringly reflect to the governing authorities the exact trustworthiness of any candidate for confidence or trust.

On Urantia, you grotesquely essay to read character and to estimate specific abilities, but on Uversa we actually do these things in perfection. These seconaphim weigh trustworthiness in the living scales of unerring character appraisal, and when they have looked at you, we have only to look at them to know the limitations of your ability to discharge responsibility, execute trust, and fulfill missions. Your assets of trustworthiness are clearly set forth alongside your liabilities of possible default or betrayal.

It is the plan of your superiors to advance you by augmented trusts just as fast as your character is sufficiently developed to gracefully bear these added responsibilities, but to overload the individual only courts disaster and insures disappointment. And the mistake of placing responsibility prematurely upon either man or angel may be avoided by utilizing the ministry of these infallible estimators of the trust capacity of the individuals of time and space. These seconaphim ever accompany Those High in Authority, and never do these executives make assignments until their candidates have been weighed in the secoraphic balances and pronounced "not wanting."

5. *The Sanctity of Service.* The privilege of service immediately follows the discovery of trustworthiness. Nothing can stand between you and opportunity for increased service except your own untrustworthiness, your lack of capacity for appreciation of the solemnity of trust.

Service—purposeful service, not slavery—is productive of the highest satisfaction and is expressive of the divinest dignity. Service—more service, increased service, difficult service, adventurous service, and at last divine and perfect service—is the goal of time and the destination of space. But ever will the play cycles of time alternate with the service cycles of progress. And after the service of time there follows the superservice of eternity. During the play of time you should envision the work of eternity, even as you will, during the service of eternity, reminisce the play of time.

The universal economy is based on intake and output; throughout the eternal career you will never encounter monotony of inaction or stagnation of personality. Progress is made possible by inherent motion, advancement grows out of the divine capacity for action, and achievement is the child of imaginative adventure. But inherent in this capacity for achievement is the responsibility of ethics, the necessity for recognizing that the world and the universe are filled with a multitude of differing types of beings. All of this magnificent creation, *including yourself,* was not made just for you. This is not an egocentric universe. The Gods have decreed, "It is more blessed to give than to receive," and said your Master Son, "He who would be greatest among you let him be server of all."

The real nature of any service, be it rendered by man or angel, is fully revealed in the faces of these secoraphic service indicators, the Sanctities of Service. The full analysis of the true and of the hidden motives is clearly shown. These angels are indeed the mind readers, heart searchers, and soul revealers of the universe. Mortals may employ words to conceal their thoughts, but these high seconaphim lay bare the deep motives of the human heart and of the angelic mind.

6 and 7. *The Secret of Greatness and the Soul of Goodness.* The ascending pilgrims having awakened to the import of time, the way is prepared for the realization of the solemnity of trust and for the appreciation of the sanctity of service. While these are the moral elements of greatness, there are also secrets of greatness. When the spiritual tests of greatness are applied, the moral elements are not disregarded, but the quality of unselfishness revealed in disinterested labor for the welfare of one's earthly fellows, particularly worthy beings in need and in distress, that is the real *measure* of planetary greatness. And the *manifestation* of greatness on a world like Urantia is the exhibition of self-control. The great man is not he who "takes a city" or "overthrows a nation," but rather "he who subdues his own tongue."

Greatness is synonymous with divinity. God is supremely great and good. *Greatness and goodness simply cannot be divorced.* They are forever made one in God. This truth is literally and strikingly illustrated by the reflective interdependence of the Secret of Greatness and the Soul of Goodness, for neither can function without the other. In reflecting other qualities of divinity, the superuniverse seconaphim can and do act alone, but the reflective estimates of greatness and of goodness appear to be inseparable. Hence, on any world, in any universe, must these reflectors of greatness and of goodness work together, always showing a dual and mutually dependent report of every being upon whom they focalize. Greatness cannot be estimated without knowing the content of goodness, while goodness cannot be portrayed without exhibiting its inherent and divine greatness.

The estimate of greatness varies from sphere to sphere. To be great is to be Godlike. And since the quality of greatness is wholly determined by the content of goodness, it follows that, even in your present human estate, if you can through grace become good, you are thereby becoming great. The more steadfastly you behold, and the more persistently you pursue, the concepts of divine goodness, the more certainly will you grow in greatness, in true magnitude of genuine survival character.

7. MINISTRY OF THE SECONAPHIM

The seconaphim have their origin and headquarters on the capitals of the superuniverses, but with their liaison fellows they range from the shores of Paradise to the evolutionary worlds of space. They serve as valued assistants to the members of the deliberative assemblies of the supergovernments and are of great help to the courtesy colonies of Uversa: the star students, millennial tourists, celestial observers, and a host of others, including the ascendant beings in waiting for Havona transport. The Ancients of Days take pleasure in assigning certain of the primary seconaphim to assist the ascending creatures domiciled on the four hundred ninety study worlds surrounding Uversa, and here also do many of the secondary and tertiary orders serve as teachers. These Uversa satellites are the finishing schools of the universes of time, presenting the preparatory course for the seven-circuited university of Havona.

Of the three orders of seconaphim, the tertiary group, attached to the ascendant authorities, minister most extensively to the ascending creatures of time. You will on occasion meet them soon after your departure from Urantia, though you will not freely make use of their services until you reach the tarrying worlds of

Orvonton. You will enjoy their companionship when you become fully acquainted with them during your sojourn on the Uversa school worlds.

These tertiary seconaphim are the timesavers, space abridgers, error detectors, faithful teachers, and everlasting guideposts—living signs of divine surety—in mercy placed at the crossroads of time, there to guide the feet of anxious pilgrims in moments of great perplexity and spiritual uncertainty. Long before attaining the portals of perfection, you will begin to gain access to the tools of divinity and to make contact with the techniques of Deity. Increasingly, from the time you arrive on the initial mansion world until you close your eyes in the Havona sleep preparatory to your Paradise transit, you will avail yourself of the emergency help of these marvelous beings, who are so fully and freely reflective of the sure knowledge and certain wisdom of those safe and dependable pilgrims who have preceded you on the long journey to the portals of perfection.

We are denied the full privilege of using these angels of the reflective order on Urantia. They are frequent visitors on your world, accompanying assigned personalities, but here they cannot freely function. This sphere is still under partial spiritual quarantine, and some of the circuits essential to their services are not here at present. When your world is once more restored to the reflective circuits concerned, much of the work of interplanetary and interuniverse communication will be greatly simplified and expedited. Celestial workers on Urantia encounter many difficulties because of this functional curtailment of their reflective associates. But we go on joyfully conducting our affairs with the instrumentalities at hand, notwithstanding our local deprivation of many of the services of these marvelous beings, the living mirrors of space and the presence projectors of time.

[Sponsored by a Mighty Messenger of Uversa.]

PAPER 29

THE UNIVERSE POWER DIRECTORS

OF ALL the universe personalities concerned in the regulation of interplanetary and interuniverse affairs, the power directors and their associates have been the least understood on Urantia. While your races have long known of the existence of angels and similar orders of celestial beings, little information concerning the controllers and regulators of the physical domain has ever been imparted. Even now I am permitted fully to disclose only the last of the following three groups of living beings having to do with force control and energy regulation in the master universe:

1. Primary Eventuated Master Force Organizers.
2. Associate Transcendental Master Force Organizers.
3. Universe Power Directors.

Though I deem it impossible to portray the individuality of the various groups of directors, centers, and controllers of universe power, I hope to be able to explain something about the domain of their activities. They are a unique group of living beings having to do with the intelligent regulation of energy throughout the grand universe. Including the supreme directors, they embrace the following major divisions:

1. The Seven Supreme Power Directors.
2. The Supreme Power Centers.
3. The Master Physical Controllers.
4. The Morontia Power Supervisors.

The Supreme Power Directors and Centers have existed from the near times of eternity, and as far as we know, no more beings of these orders have been created. The Seven Supreme Directors were personalized by the Seven Master Spirits, and then they collaborated with their parents in the production of more than ten billion associates. Before the days of the power directors the energy circuits of space outside of the central universe were under the intelligent supervision of the Master Force Organizers of Paradise.

Having knowledge about material creatures, you have at least a contrastive conception of spiritual beings; but it is very difficult for the mortal mind to envisage the power directors. In the scheme of ascendant progression to higher levels of existence you have nothing directly to do with either the supreme directors or the power centers. On certain rare occasions you will have dealings with the physical controllers, and you will work freely with the supervisors of morontia power upon reaching the mansion worlds. These Morontia Power Supervisors function so exclusively in the morontia regime of the local creations that it is deemed best to narrate their activities in the section dealing with the local universe.

1. THE SEVEN SUPREME POWER DIRECTORS

The Seven Supreme Power Directors are the physical-energy regulators of the grand universe. Their creation by the Seven Master Spirits is the first recorded instance of the derivation of semimaterial progeny from true spirit ancestry. When the Seven Master Spirits create individually, they bring forth highly spiritual personalities on the angelic order; when they create collectively, they sometimes produce these high types of semimaterial beings. But even these quasi-physical beings would be invisible to the short-range vision of Urantia mortals.

The Supreme Power Directors are seven in number, and they are identical in appearance and function. One cannot be distinguished from another except by that Master Spirit with whom each is in immediate association, and to whom each is in complete functional subservience. Each of the Master Spirits is thus in eternal union with one of their collective offspring. The same director is always in association with the same Spirit, and their working partnership results in a unique association of physical and spiritual energies, of a semiphysical being and a spirit personality.

The Seven Supreme Power Directors are stationed on peripheral Paradise, where their slowly circulating presences indicate the whereabouts of the force-focal headquarters of the Master Spirits. These power directors function singly in the power-energy regulation of the superuniverses but collectively in the administration of the central creation. They operate from Paradise but maintain themselves as effective power centers in all divisions of the grand universe.

These mighty beings are the physical ancestors of the vast host of the power centers and, through them, of the physical controllers scattered throughout the seven superuniverses. Such subordinate physical-control organisms are basically uniform, identical except for the differential toning of each superuniverse corps. In order to change in superuniverse service, they would merely have to return to Paradise for retoning. The physical creation is fundamentally uniform in administration.

2. THE SUPREME POWER CENTERS

The Seven Supreme Power Directors are not able, individually, to reproduce themselves, but collectively, and in association with the Seven Master Spirits, they can and do reproduce—create—other beings like themselves. Such is the origin of the Supreme Power Centers of the grand universe, who function in the following seven groups:

1. Supreme Center Supervisors.
2. Havona Centers.
3. Superuniverse Centers.
4. Local Universe Centers.
5. Constellation Centers.
6. System Centers.
7. Unclassified Centers.

of the superuniverse government of the Ancients of Days or of the local universe administration of the Creator Sons.

These power centers and directors are brought into being by the children of the Infinite Spirit. They are not germane to the administration of the Sons of God, though they affiliate with the Creator Sons during the later epochs of universe material organization. But the power centers are in some way closely associated with the cosmic overcontrol of the Supreme Being.

Power centers and physical controllers undergo no training; they are all created in perfection and are inherently perfect in action. Never do they pass from one function to another; always do they serve as originally assigned. There is no evolution in their ranks, and this is true of all seven divisions of both orders.

Having no ascendant past to revert to in memory, power centers and physical controllers never play; they are thoroughly businesslike in all their actions. They are always on duty; there is no provision in the universal scheme for the interruption of the physical lines of energy; never for a fraction of a second can these beings relinquish their direct supervision of the energy circuits of time and space.

The directors, centers, and controllers of power have nothing to do with anything in all creation except power, material or semiphysical energy; they do not originate it, but they do modify, manipulate, and directionize it. Neither do they have anything whatever to do with physical gravity except to resist its drawing power. Their relation to gravity is wholly negative.

The power centers utilize vast mechanisms and co-ordinations of a material order in liaison with the living mechanisms of the various segregated energy concentrations. Each individual power center is constituted in exactly one million units of functional control, and these energy-modifying units are not stationary as are the vital organs of man's physical body; these "vital organs" of power regulation are mobile and truly kaleidoscopic in associative possibilities.

It is utterly beyond my ability to explain the manner in which these living beings encompass the manipulation and regulation of the master circuits of universe energy. To undertake to inform you further concerning the size and function of these gigantic and almost perfectly efficient power centers, would only add to your confusion and consternation. They are both living and "personal," but they are beyond your comprehension.

Outside of Havona the Supreme Power Centers function only on especially constructed (architectural) spheres or on otherwise suitably constituted space bodies. The architectural worlds are so constructed that the living power centers can act as selective switches to directionize, modify, and concentrate the energies of space as they pour over these spheres. They could not so function on an ordinary evolutionary sun or planet. Certain groups are also concerned in the heating and other material necessities of these special headquarters worlds. And though it is beyond the scope of Urantia knowledge, I may state that these orders of living power personalities have much to do with the distribution of the light that shines without heat. They do not produce this phenomenon, but they are concerned with its dissemination and directionization.

The power centers and their subordinate controllers are assigned to the working of all of the physical energies of organized space. They work with the three basic currents of ten energies each. That is the energy charge of organized space; and organized space is their domain. The Universe Power Directors have nothing whatever to do with those tremendous actions of force which are now taking place outside the present boundaries of the seven superuniverses.

The power centers and controllers exert perfect control over only seven of the ten forms of energy contained in each basic universe current; those forms which are partly or wholly exempt from their control must represent the unpredictable realms of energy manifestation dominated by the Unqualified Absolute. If they exert an influence upon the primordial forces of this Absolute, we are not cognizant of such functions, though there is some slight evidence which would warrant the opinion that certain of the physical controllers are sometimes automatically reactive to certain impulses of the Universal Absolute.

These living power mechanisms are not consciously related to the master universe energy overcontrol of the Unqualified Absolute, but we surmise that their entire and almost perfect scheme of power direction is in some unknown manner subordinated to this supergravity presence. In any local energy situation the centers and controllers exert near-supremacy, but they are always conscious of the superenergy presence and the unrecognizable performance of the Unqualified Absolute.

4. THE MASTER PHYSICAL CONTROLLERS

These beings are the mobile subordinates of the Supreme Power Centers. The physical controllers are endowed with capabilities of individuality metamorphosis of such a nature that they can engage in a remarkable variety of autotransport, being able to traverse local space at velocities approaching the flight of Solitary Messengers. But like all other space traversers they require the assistance of both their fellows and certain other types of beings in overcoming the action of gravity and the resistance of inertia in departing from a material sphere.

The Master Physical Controllers serve throughout the grand universe. They are directly governed from Paradise by the Seven Supreme Power Directors as far as the headquarters of the superuniverses; from here they are directed and distributed by the Council of Equilibrium, the high commissioners of power dispatched by the Seven Master Spirits from the personnel of the Associate Master Force Organizers. These high commissioners are empowered to interpret the readings and registrations of the master frandalanks, those living instruments which indicate the power pressure and the energy charge of an entire superuniverse.

While the presence of the Paradise Deities encircles the grand universe and sweeps around the circle of eternity, the influence of any one of the Seven Master Spirits is limited to a single superuniverse. There is a distinct segregation of energy and a separation of the circuits of power between each of the seven supercreations; hence individualized control methods must and do prevail.

The Master Physical Controllers are the direct offspring of the Supreme Power Centers, and their numbers include the following:

1. Associate Power Directors.
2. Mechanical Controllers.
3. Energy Transformers.

4. Energy Transmitters.
5. Primary Associators.
6. Secondary Dissociators.
7. The Frandalanks and Chronoldeks.

Not all of these orders are persons in the sense of possessing individual powers of choice. Especially do the last four seem to be wholly automatic and mechanical in response to the impulses of their superiors and in reaction to existing energy conditions. But though such response appears wholly mechanistic, it is not; they may seem to be automatons, but all of them disclose the differential function of intelligence.

Personality is not necessarily a concomitant of mind. Mind can think even when deprived of all power of choice, as in numerous of the lower types of animals and in certain of these subordinate physical controllers. Many of these more automatic regulators of physical power are not persons in any sense of the term. They are not endowed with will and independence of decision, being wholly subservient to the mechanical perfection of design for the tasks of their allotment. Nonetheless all of them are highly intelligent beings.

The physical controllers are chiefly occupied in the adjustment of basic energies undiscovered on Urantia. These unknown energies are very essential to the interplanetary system of transport and to certain techniques of communication. When we lay lines of energy for the purpose of conveying sound equivalents or of extending vision, these undiscovered forms of energy are utilized by the living physical controllers and their associates. These same energies are also, on occasion, used by the midway creatures in their routine work.

1. *Associate Power Directors.* These marvelously efficient beings are intrusted with the assignment and dispatch of all orders of the Master Physical Controllers in accordance with the ever-shifting needs of the constantly changing energy status of the realms. The vast reserves of the physical controllers are maintained on the headquarters worlds of the minor sectors, and from these concentration points they are periodically dispatched by the associate power directors to the headquarters of the universes, constellations, and systems, and to the individual planets. When thus assigned, the physical controllers are provisionally subject to the orders of the divine executioners of the conciliating commissions but are otherwise solely amenable to their associate directors and to the Supreme Power Centers.

Three million associate power directors are assigned to each of the Orvonton minor sectors, making a total of three billion as the superuniverse quota of these amazingly versatile beings. Their own reserves are maintained on these same minor sector worlds, where they also serve as instructors of all who study the sciences of the techniques of intelligent energy control and transmutation.

These directors alternate periods of executive service in the minor sectors with equal periods of inspection service to the realms of space. At least one acting inspector is always present in each local system, maintaining headquarters on its capital sphere. They keep the whole vast living energy aggregation in harmonious synchrony.

2. *Mechanical Controllers.* These are the exceedingly versatile and mobile assistants of the associate power directors. Trillions upon trillions of them are commissioned in Ensa, your minor sector. These beings are called mechanical

controllers because they are so completely dominated by their superiors, so fully subservient to the will of the associate power directors. Nevertheless they are, themselves, very intelligent, and their work, though mechanical and matter-of-fact in nature, is skillfully performed.

Of all the Master Physical Controllers assigned to the inhabited worlds, the mechanical controllers are by far the most powerful. Possessing the living endowment of antigravity in excess of all other beings, each controller has a gravity resistance equaled only by enormous spheres revolving at tremendous velocity. Ten of these controllers are now stationed on Urantia, and one of their most important planetary activities is to facilitate the departure of seraphic transports. In so functioning, all ten of the mechanical controllers act in unison while a battery of one thousand energy transmitters provides the initial momentum for the seraphic departure.

The mechanical controllers are competent to directionize the flow of energy and to facilitate its concentration into the specialized currents or circuits. These mighty beings have much to do with the segregation, directionization, and intensification of the physical energies and with the equalization of the pressures of the interplanetary circuits. They are expert in the manipulation of twenty-one of the thirty physical energies of space, constituting the power charge of a superuniverse. They are also able to accomplish much towards the management and control of six of the nine more subtle forms of physical energy. By placing these controllers in proper technical relationship to each other and to certain of the power centers, the associate power directors are enabled to effect unbelievable changes in power adjustment and energy control.

The Master Physical Controllers often function in batteries of hundreds, thousands, and even millions and by varying their positions and formations are able to effect energy control in a collective as well as an individual capacity. As requirements vary, they can upstep and accelerate the energy volume and movement or detain, condense, and retard the energy currents. They influence energy and power transformations somewhat as so-called catalytic agents augment chemical reactions. They function by inherent ability and in co-operation with the Supreme Power Centers.

3. *Energy Transformers.* The number of these beings in a superuniverse is unbelievable. There are almost one million in Satania alone, and the usual quota is one hundred for each inhabited world.

The energy transformers are the conjoint creation of the Seven Supreme Power Directors and the Seven Center Supervisors. They are among the more personal orders of physical controllers, and except when an associate power director is present on an inhabited world, the transformers are in command. They are the planetary inspectors of all departing seraphic transports. All classes of celestial life can utilize the less personal orders of the physical controllers only by liaison with the more personal orders of the associate directors and the energy transformers.

These transformers are powerful and effective living switches, being able to dispose themselves for or against a given power disposition or directionization. They are also skillful in their efforts to insulate the planets against the powerful energy streams passing between gigantic planetary and starry neighbors. Their energy-transmutive attributes render them most serviceable in the important task of maintaining universal energy balance, or power equilibrium. At one time they seem to consume or store energy; at other times they appear to exude or liberate energy. The transformers are able to increase or to diminish the "storage-battery" potential of the living and dead energies of their respective realms. But they deal only with physical and semimaterial energies, they do not directly function in the domain of life, neither do they change the forms of living beings.

In some respects the energy transformers are the most remarkable and mysterious of all semimaterial living creatures. They are in some unknown manner physically differentiated, and by varying their liaison relationships, they are able to exert a profound influence upon the energy which passes through their associated presences. The status of the physical realms seems to undergo a transformation under their skillful manipulation. *They can and do change the physical form of the energies of space.* With the aid of their fellow controllers they are actually able to change the form and potential of twenty-seven of the thirty physical energies of the superuniverse power charge. That three of these energies are beyond their control proves that they are not instrumentalities of the Unqualified Absolute.

The remaining four groups of the Master Physical Controllers are hardly persons within any acceptable definition of that word. These transmitters, associators, dissociators, and frandalanks are wholly automatic in their reactions; nevertheless they are in every sense intelligent. We are greatly limited in our knowledge of these wonderful entities because we cannot communicate with them. They appear to understand the language of the realm, but they cannot communicate with us. They seem fully able to receive our communications but quite powerless to make response.

4. *Energy Transmitters.* These beings function chiefly, but not wholly, in an intraplanetary capacity. They are marvelous dispatchers of energy as it is manifested on the individual worlds.

When energy is to be diverted to a new circuit, the transmitters deploy themselves in a line along the desired energy path, and by virtue of their unique attributes of energy-attraction, they can actually induce an increased energy flow in the desired direction. This they do just as literally as certain metallic circuits directionize the flow of certain forms of electric energy; and they are living superconductors for more than half of the thirty forms of physical energy.

Transmitters form skillful liaisons which are effective in rehabilitating the weakening currents of specialized energy passing from planet to planet and from station to station on an individual planet. They can detect currents which are much too feeble to be recognized by any other type of living being, and they can so augment these energies that the accompanying message becomes perfectly intelligible. Their services are invaluable to the broadcast receivers.

Energy transmitters can function with regard to all forms of communicable perception; they can render a distant scene "visible" as well as a distant sound "audible." They provide the emergency lines of communication in the local systems and on the individual planets. These services must be used by practically all creatures for purposes of communication outside of the regularly established circuits.

These beings, together with the energy transformers, are indispensable to the maintenance of mortal existence on those worlds having an impoverished atmosphere, and they are an integral part of the technique of life on the non-breathing planets.

5. *Primary Associators.* These interesting and invaluable entities are masterly energy conservators and custodians. Somewhat as a plant stores solar light, so do these living organisms store energy during times of plus manifestations. They work on a gigantic scale, converting the energies of space into a physical state not known on Urantia. They are also able to carry forward these transformations to the point of producing some of the primitive units of material existence. These beings simply act by their presence. They are in no way exhausted or depleted by this function; they act like living catalytic agents.

During seasons of minus manifestations they are empowered to release these accumulated energies. But your knowledge of energy and matter is not sufficiently advanced to make it possible to explain the technique of this phase of their work. They always labor in compliance with universal law, handling and manipulating atoms, electrons, and ultimatons much as you maneuver adjustable type to make the same alphabetical symbols tell vastly different stories.

The associators are the first group of life to appear on an organizing material sphere, and they can function at physical temperatures which you would regard as utterly incompatible with the existence of living beings. They represent an order of life which is simply beyond the range of human imagination. Together with their co-workers, the dissociators, they are the most slavish of all intelligent creatures.

6. *Secondary Dissociators.* Compared with the primary associators, these beings of enormous antigravity endowment are the reverse workers. There is never any danger that the special or modified forms of physical energy on the local worlds or in the local systems will be exhausted, for these living organizations are endowed with the unique power of evolving limitless supplies of energy. They are chiefly concerned with the evolution of a form of energy which is hardly known on Urantia from a form of matter which is recognized still less. They are truly the alchemists of space and the wonder-workers of time. But in all the wonders they work, they never transgress the mandates of Cosmic Supremacy.

7. *The Frandalanks.* These beings are the joint creation of all three orders of energy-control beings: the primary and secondary force organizers and the power directors. Frandalanks are the most numerous of all the Master Physical Controllers; the number functioning in Satania alone is beyond your numerical concept. They are stationed on all inhabited worlds and are always attached to the higher orders of physical controllers. They function interchangeably in the central and superuniverses and in the domains of outer space.

The frandalanks are created in thirty divisions, one for each form of basic universe force, and they function exclusively as living and automatic presence, pressure, and velocity gauges. These living barometers are solely concerned with the automatic and unerring registration of the status of all forms of force-energy. They are to the physical universe what the vast reflectivity mechanism is to the minded universe. The frandalanks that register time in addition to quantitative and qualitative energy presence are called *chronoldeks.*

I recognize that the frandalanks are intelligent, but I cannot classify them as other than living machines. About the only way I can help you to understand these living mechanisms is to compare them to your own mechanical contrivances which perform with almost intelligentlike precision and accuracy. Then if you would conceive of these beings, draw upon your imagination to the extent of recognizing that in the grand universe we actually have intelligent and *living* mechanisms (entities) that can perform more intricate tasks involving more stupendous computations with even greater delicacy of accuracy, even with ultimacy of precision.

5. THE MASTER FORCE ORGANIZERS

The force organizers are resident on Paradise, but they function throughout the master universe, more particularly in the domains of unorganized space. These extraordinary beings are neither creators nor creatures, and they comprise two grand divisions of service:

1. Primary Eventuated Master Force Organizers.
2. Associate Transcendental Master Force Organizers.

These two mighty orders of primordial-force manipulators work exclusively under the supervision of the Architects of the Master Universe, and at the present time they do not function extensively within the boundaries of the grand universe.

Primary Master Force Organizers are the manipulators of the primordial or basic space-forces of the Unqualified Absolute; they are nebulae creators. They are the living instigators of the energy cyclones of space and the early organizers and directionizers of these gigantic manifestations. These force organizers transmute *primordial force* (pre-energy not responsive to direct Paradise gravity) into primary or *puissant energy,* energy transmuting from the exclusive grasp of the Unqualified Absolute to the gravity grasp of the Isle of Paradise. They are thereupon succeeded by the associate force organizers, who continue the process of energy transmutation from the primary through the secondary or *gravity-energy* stage.

Upon the completion of the plans for the creation of a local universe, signalized by the arrival of a Creator Son, the Associate Master Force Organizers give way to the orders of power directors acting in the superuniverse of astronomic jurisdiction. But in the absence of such plans the associate force organizers continue on indefinitely in charge of these material creations, even as they now operate in outer space.

The Master Force Organizers withstand temperatures and function under physical conditions which would be intolerable even to the versatile power centers and physical controllers of Orvonton. The only other types of revealed beings capable of functioning in these realms of outer space are the Solitary Messengers and the Inspired Trinity Spirits.

[Sponsored by a Universal Censor acting by authority of the Ancients of Days on Uversa.]

PAPER 30

PERSONALITIES OF THE GRAND UNIVERSE

THE personalities and other-than-personal entities now functioning on Paradise and in the grand universe constitute a well-nigh limitless number of living beings. Even the number of major orders and types would stagger the human imagination, let alone the countless subtypes and variations. It is, however, desirable to present something of two basic classifications of living beings—a suggestion of the Paradise classification and an abbreviation of the Uversa Personality Register.

It is not possible to formulate comprehensive and entirely consistent classifications of the personalities of the grand universe because *all* of the groups are not revealed. It would require numerous additional papers to cover the further revelation required to systematically classify all groups. Such conceptual expansion would hardly be desirable as it would deprive the thinking mortals of the next thousand years of that stimulus to creative speculation which these partially revealed concepts supply. It is best that man not have an overrevelation; it stifles imagination.

1. THE PARADISE CLASSIFICATION OF LIVING BEINGS

Living beings are classified on Paradise in accordance with inherent and attained relationship to the Paradise Deities. During the grand gatherings of the central and superuniverses those present are often grouped in accordance with origin: those of triune origin, or of Trinity attainment; those of dual origin; and those of single origin. It is difficult to interpret the Paradise classification of living beings to the mortal mind, but we are authorized to present the following:

I. *TRIUNE-ORIGIN BEINGS.* Beings created by all three Paradise Deities, either as such or as the Trinity, together with the Trinitized Corps, which designation refers to all groups of trinitized beings, revealed and unrevealed.

A. *The Supreme Spirits.*

1. The Seven Master Spirits.
2. The Seven Supreme Executives.
3. The Seven Orders of Reflective Spirits.

B. *The Stationary Sons of the Trinity.*

1. Trinitized Secrets of Supremacy.
2. Eternals of Days.
3. Ancients of Days.
4. Perfections of Days.

5. Recents of Days.
6. Unions of Days.
7. Faithfuls of Days.
8. Perfectors of Wisdom.
9. Divine Counselors.
10. Universal Censors.

C. *Trinity-origin and Trinitized Beings.*

1. Trinity Teacher Sons.
2. Inspired Trinity Spirits.
3. Havona Natives.
4. Paradise Citizens.
5. Unrevealed Trinity-origin Beings.
6. Unrevealed Deity-trinitized Beings.
7. Trinitized Sons of Attainment.
8. Trinitized Sons of Selection.
9. Trinitized Sons of Perfection.
10. Creature-trinitized Sons.

II. *DUAL-ORIGIN BEINGS.* Those of origin in any two of the Paradise Deities or otherwise created by any two beings of direct or indirect descent from the Paradise Deities.

A. *The Descending Orders.*

1. Creator Sons.
2. Magisterial Sons.
3. Bright and Morning Stars.
4. Father Melchizedeks.
5. The Melchizedeks.
6. The Vorondadeks.
7. The Lanonandeks.
8. Brilliant Evening Stars.
9. The Archangels.
10. Life Carriers.
11. Unrevealed Universe Aids.
12. Unrevealed Sons of God.

B. *The Stationary Orders.*

1. Abandonters.
2. Susatia.
3. Univitatia.
4. Spironga.
5. Unrevealed Dual-origin Beings.

C. *The Ascending Orders.*

1. Adjuster-fused Mortals.
2. Son-fused Mortals.
3. Spirit-fused Mortals.
4. Translated Midwayers.
5. Unrevealed Ascenders.

III. *SINGLE-ORIGIN BEINGS.* Those of origin in any one of the Paradise Deities or otherwise created by any one being of direct or indirect descent from the Paradise Deities.

A. *The Supreme Spirits.*

1. Gravity Messengers.
2. The Seven Spirits of the Havona Circuits.
3. The Twelvefold Adjutants of the Havona Circuits.
4. The Reflective Image Aids.
5. Universe Mother Spirits.
6. The Sevenfold Adjutant Mind-Spirits.
7. Unrevealed Deity-origin Beings.

B. *The Ascending Orders.*

1. Personalized Adjusters.
2. Ascending Material Sons.
3. Evolutionary Seraphim.
4. Evolutionary Cherubim.
5. Unrevealed Ascenders.

C. *The Family of the Infinite Spirit.*

1. Solitary Messengers.
2. Universe Circuit Supervisors.
3. Census Directors.
4. Personal Aids of the Infinite Spirit.
5. Associate Inspectors.
6. Assigned Sentinels.
7. Graduate Guides.
8. Havona Servitals.
9. Universal Conciliators.
10. Morontia Companions.
11. Supernaphim.
12. Seconaphim.
13. Tertiaphim.
14. Omniaphim.
15. Seraphim.
16. Cherubim and Sanobim.
17. Unrevealed Spirit-origin Beings.
18. The Seven Supreme Power Directors.
19. The Supreme Power Centers.
20. The Master Physical Controllers.
21. The Morontia Power Supervisors.

IV. *EVENTUATED TRANSCENDENTAL BEINGS.* There is to be found on Paradise a vast host of transcendental beings whose origin is not ordinarily disclosed to the universes of time and space until they are settled in light and life. These Transcendentalers are neither creators nor creatures; they are the *eventuated* children of divinity, ultimacy, and eternity. These "eventuators" are neither finite nor infinite—they are *absonite;* and absonity is neither infinity nor absoluteness.

These uncreated noncreators are ever loyal to the Paradise Trinity and obedient to the Ultimate. They are existent on four ultimate levels of personality activity and are functional on the seven levels of the absonite in twelve grand divisions consisting of one thousand major working groups of seven classes each. These eventuated beings include the following orders:

1. The Architects of the Master Universe.
2. Transcendental Recorders.
3. Other Transcendentalers.
4. Primary Eventuated Master Force Organizers.
5. Associate Transcendental Master Force Organizers.

God, as a superperson, eventuates; God, as a person, creates; God, as a prepreson, fragments; and such an Adjuster fragment of himself evolves the spirit soul upon the material and mortal mind in accordance with the freewill choosing of the personality which has been bestowed upon such a mortal creature by the parental act of God as a Father.

V. *FRAGMENTED ENTITIES OF DEITY.* This order of living existence, originating in the Universal Father, is best typified by the Thought Adjusters, though these entities are by no means the only fragmentations of the prepersonal reality of the First Source and Center. The functions of the other-than-Adjuster fragments are manifold and little known. Fusion with an Adjuster or other such fragment constitutes the creature a *Father-fused being.*

The fragmentations of the premind spirit of the Third Source and Center, though hardly comparable to the Father fragments, should be here recorded. Such entities differ very greatly from Adjusters; they do not as such dwell on Spiritington, nor do they as such traverse the mind-gravity circuits; neither do they indwell mortal creatures during the life in the flesh. They are not prepersonal in the sense that the Adjusters are, but such fragments of premind spirit are bestowed upon certain of the surviving mortals, and fusion therewith constitutes them *Spirit-fused mortals* in contradistinction to Adjuster-fused mortals.

Still more difficult of description is the individualized spirit of a Creator Son, union with which constitutes the creature a *Son-fused mortal.* And there are still other fragmentations of Deity.

VI. *SUPERPERSONAL BEINGS.* There is a vast host of other-than-personal beings of divine origin and of manifold service in the universe of universes. Certain of these beings are resident on the Paradise worlds of the Son; others, like the superpersonal representatives of the Eternal Son, are encountered elsewhere. They are for the most part unmentioned in these narratives, and it would be quite futile to attempt their description to *personal* creatures.

VII. *UNCLASSIFIED AND UNREVEALED ORDERS.* During the present universe age it would not be possible to place all beings, personal or otherwise, within classifications pertaining to the present universe age; nor have all such categories been revealed in these narratives; hence numerous orders have been omitted from these lists. Consider the following:

The Consummator of Universe Destiny.

The Qualified Vicegerents of the Ultimate.

The Unqualified Supervisors of the Supreme.

The Unrevealed Creative Agencies of the Ancients of Days.

Majeston of Paradise.

The Unnamed Reflectivator Liaisons of Majeston.

The Midsonite Orders of the Local Universes.

No especial significance need attach to the listing of these orders together except that none of them appear in the Paradise classification as revealed herein. These are the unclassified few; you have yet to learn of the unrevealed many.

There are spirits: spirit entities, spirit presences, personal spirits, prepersonal spirits, superpersonal spirits, spirit existences, spirit personalities—but neither mortal language nor mortal intellect are adequate. We may however state that there are no personalities of "pure mind"; no entity has personality unless he is endowed with it by God who is spirit. Any mind entity that is not associated with either spiritual or physical energy is not a personality. But in the same sense that there are spirit personalities who have mind there are mind personalities who have spirit. Majeston and his associates are fairly good illustrations of mind-dominated beings, but there are better illustrations of this type of personality unknown to you. There are even whole unrevealed orders of such *mind personalities,* but they are always spirit associated. Certain other unrevealed creatures are what might be termed *mindal- and physical-energy personalities.* This type of being is nonresponsive to spirit gravity but is nonetheless a true personality—is within the Father's circuit.

These papers do not—cannot—even begin to exhaust the story of the living creatures, creators, eventuators, and still-otherwise-existent beings who live and worship and serve in the swarming universes of time and in the central universe of eternity. You mortals are persons; hence we can describe beings who are *personalized,* but how could an *absonitized* being ever be explained to you?

2. THE UVERSA PERSONALITY REGISTER

The divine family of living beings is registered on Uversa in seven grand divisions:

1. The Paradise Deities.
2. The Supreme Spirits.
3. The Trinity-origin Beings.
4. The Sons of God.
5. Personalities of the Infinite Spirit.
6. The Universe Power Directors.
7. The Corps of Permanent Citizenship.

These groups of will creatures are divided into numerous classes and minor subdivisions. The presentation of this classification of the personalities of the grand universe is however chiefly concerned in setting forth those orders of intelligent beings who have been revealed in these narratives, most of whom will be encountered in the ascendant experience of the mortals of time on their progressive climb to Paradise. The following listings make no mention of vast orders of universe beings who carry forward their work apart from the mortal ascension scheme.

I. *THE PARADISE DEITIES.*

1. The Universal Father.
2. The Eternal Son.
3. The Infinite Spirit.

II. *THE SUPREME SPIRITS.*

1. The Seven Master Spirits.
2. The Seven Supreme Executives.
3. The Seven Groups of Reflective Spirits.
4. The Reflective Image Aids.
5. The Seven Spirits of the Circuits.
6. Local Universe Creative Spirits.
7. Adjutant Mind-Spirits.

III. *THE TRINITY-ORIGIN BEINGS.*

1. Trinitized Secrets of Supremacy.
2. Eternals of Days.
3. Ancients of Days.
4. Perfections of Days.
5. Recents of Days.
6. Unions of Days.
7. Faithfuls of Days.
8. Trinity Teacher Sons.
9. Perfectors of Wisdom.
10. Divine Counselors.
11. Universal Censors.
12. Inspired Trinity Spirits.
13. Havona Natives.
14. Paradise Citizens.

IV. *THE SONS OF GOD.*

A. *Descending Sons.*

1. Creator Sons—Michaels.
2. Magisterial Sons—Avonals.
3. Trinity Teacher Sons—Daynals.
4. Melchizedek Sons.
5. Vorondadek Sons.
6. Lanonandek Sons.
7. Life Carrier Sons.

B. *Ascending Sons.*

1. Father-fused Mortals.
2. Son-fused Mortals.
3. Spirit-fused Mortals.
4. Evolutionary Seraphim.
5. Ascending Material Sons.
6. Translated Midwayers.
7. Personalized Adjusters.

C. *Trinitized Sons.*

1. Mighty Messengers.
2. Those High in Authority.
3. Those without Name and Number.
4. Trinitized Custodians.
5. Trinitized Ambassadors.
6. Celestial Guardians.
7. High Son Assistants.
8. Ascender-trinitized Sons.
9. Paradise-Havona-trinitized Sons.
10. Trinitized Sons of Destiny.

V. *PERSONALITIES OF THE INFINITE SPIRIT.*

A. *Higher Personalities of the Infinite Spirit.*

1. Solitary Messengers.
2. Universe Circuit Supervisors.
3. Census Directors.
4. Personal Aids of the Infinite Spirit.
5. Associate Inspectors.
6. Assigned Sentinels.
7. Graduate Guides.

B. *The Messenger Hosts of Space.*

1. Havona Servitals.
2. Universal Conciliators.
3. Technical Advisers.
4. Custodians of Records on Paradise.
5. Celestial Recorders.
6. Morontia Companions.
7. Paradise Companions.

C. *The Ministering Spirits.*

1. Supernaphim.
2. Seconaphim.
3. Tertiaphim.
4. Omniaphim.
5. Seraphim.
6. Cherubim and Sanobim.
7. Midwayers.

VI. *THE UNIVERSE POWER DIRECTORS.*

A. *The Seven Supreme Power Directors.*

B. *Supreme Power Centers.*

1. Supreme Center Supervisors.
2. Havona Centers.
3. Superuniverse Centers.
4. Local Universe Centers.
5. Constellation Centers.
6. System Centers.
7. Unclassified Centers.

C. *Master Physical Controllers.*

1. Associate Power Directors.
2. Mechanical Controllers.
3. Energy Transformers.
4. Energy Transmitters.
5. Primary Associators.
6. Secondary Dissociators.
7. Frandalanks and Chronoldeks.

D. *Morontia Power Supervisors.*

1. Circuit Regulators.
2. System Co-ordinators.
3. Planetary Custodians.
4. Combined Controllers.
5. Liaison Stabilizers.
6. Selective Assorters.
7. Associate Registrars.

VII. *THE CORPS OF PERMANENT CITIZENSHIP.*

1. The Planetary Midwayers.
2. The Adamic Sons of the Systems.
3. The Constellation Univitatia.
4. The Local Universe Susatia.
5. Spirit-fused Mortals of the Local Universes.
6. The Superuniverse Abandonters.
7. Son-fused Mortals of the Superuniverses.
8. The Havona Natives.
9. Natives of the Paradise Spheres of the Spirit.
10. Natives of the Father's Paradise Spheres.
11. The Created Citizens of Paradise.
12. Adjuster-fused Mortal Citizens of Paradise.

This is the working classification of the personalities of the universes as they are of record on the headquarters world of Uversa.

COMPOSITE PERSONALITY GROUPS. There are on Uversa the records of numerous additional groups of intelligent beings, beings that are also closely related to the organization and administration of the grand universe. Among such orders are the following three composite personality groups:

A. *The Paradise Corps of the Finality.*

1. The Corps of Mortal Finaliters.
2. The Corps of Paradise Finaliters.
3. The Corps of Trinitized Finaliters.
4. The Corps of Conjoint Trinitized Finaliters.
5. The Corps of Havona Finaliters.
6. The Corps of Transcendental Finaliters.
7. The Corps of Unrevealed Sons of Destiny.

The Mortal Corps of the Finality is dealt with in the next and final paper of this series.

B. *The Universe Aids.*

1. Bright and Morning Stars.
2. Brilliant Evening Stars.
3. Archangels.
4. Most High Assistants.
5. High Commissioners.
6. Celestial Overseers.
7. Mansion World Teachers.

On all headquarters worlds of both local and superuniverses, provision is made for these beings who are engaged in specific missions for the Creator Sons, the local universe rulers. We welcome these *Universe Aids* on Uversa, but we have no jurisdiction over them. Such emissaries prosecute their work and carry on their observations under authority of the Creator Sons. Their activities are more fully described in the narrative of your local universe.

C. *The Seven Courtesy Colonies.*

1. Star Students.
2. Celestial Artisans.
3. Reversion Directors.
4. Extension-school Instructors.
5. The Various Reserve Corps.
6. Student Visitors.
7. Ascending Pilgrims.

These seven groups of beings will be found thus organized and governed on all headquarters worlds from the local systems up to the capitals of the superuniverses, particularly the latter. The capitals of the seven superuniverses are the meeting places for almost all classes and orders of intelligent beings. With the exception of numerous groups of Paradise-Havoners, here the will creatures of every phase of existence may be observed and studied.

3. THE COURTESY COLONIES

The seven courtesy colonies sojourn on the architectural spheres for a longer or shorter time while engaged in the furtherance of their missions and in the execution of their special assignments. Their work may be described as follows:

1. *The Star Students,* the celestial astronomers, choose to work on spheres like Uversa because such specially constructed worlds are unusually favorable for their observations and calculations. Uversa is favorably situated for the work of this colony, not only because of its central location, but also because there are no gigantic living or dead suns near at hand to disturb the energy currents. These students are not in any manner organically connected with the affairs of the superuniverse; they are merely guests.

The astronomical colony of Uversa contains individuals from many near-by realms, from the central universe, and even from Norlatiadek. Any being on any world in any system of any universe may become a star student, may aspire to join some corps of celestial astronomers. The only requisites are: continuing life and sufficient knowledge of the worlds of space, especially their physical laws of evolution and control. Star students are not required to serve eternally in this corps, but no one admitted to this group may withdraw under one millennium of Uversa time.

The star-observer colony of Uversa now numbers over one million. These astronomers come and go, though some remain for comparatively long periods. They carry on their work with the aid of a multitude of mechanical instruments and physical appliances; they are also greatly assisted by the Solitary Messengers and other spirit explorers. These celestial astronomers make constant use of the living energy transformers and transmitters, as well as of the reflective personalities, in their work of star study and space survey. They study all forms and phases of space material and energy manifestations, and they are just as much interested in force function as in stellar phenomena; nothing in all space escapes their scrutiny.

Similar astronomer colonies are to be found on the sector headquarters worlds of the superuniverse as well as on the architectural capitals of the local universes and their administrative subdivisions. Except on Paradise, knowledge is not inherent; understanding of the physical universe is largely dependent on observation and research.

2. *The Celestial Artisans* serve throughout the seven superuniverses. Ascending mortals have their initial contact with these groups in the morontia career of the local universe in connection with which these artisans will be more fully discussed.

3. *The Reversion Directors* are the promoters of relaxation and humor—reversion to past memories. They are of great service in the practical operation of the ascending scheme of mortal progression, especially during the earlier phases of morontia transition and spirit experience. Their story belongs to the narrative of the mortal career in the local universe.

4. *Extension-School Instructors.* The next higher residential world of the ascendant career always maintains a strong corps of teachers on the world just below, a sort of preparatory school for the progressing residents of that sphere; this is a phase of the ascendant scheme for advancing the pilgrims of time. These schools, their methods of instruction and examinations, are wholly unlike anything which you essay to conduct on Urantia.

The entire ascendant plan of mortal progression is characterized by the practice of giving out to other beings new truth and experience just as soon as acquired. You work your way through the long school of Paradise attainment by serving as teachers to those pupils just behind you in the scale of progression.

5. *The Various Reserve Corps.* Vast reserves of beings not under our immediate supervision are mobilized on Uversa as the reserve-corps colony. There are seventy primary divisions of this colony on Uversa, and it is a liberal education to be permitted to spend a season with these extraordinary personalities. Similar general reserves are maintained on Salvington and other universe capitals; they are dispatched on active service on the requisition of their respective group directors.

6. *The Student Visitors.* From all the universe a constant stream of celestial visitors pours through the various headquarters worlds. As individuals and as classes these various types of beings flock in upon us as observers, exchange pupils, and student helpers. On Uversa, at present, there are over one billion

persons in this courtesy colony. Some of these visitors may tarry a day, others may remain a year, all dependent on the nature of their mission. This colony contains almost every class of universe beings except Creator personalities and morontia mortals.

Morontia mortals are student visitors only within the confines of the local universe of their origin. They may visit in a superuniverse capacity only after they have attained spirit status. Fully one half of our visitor colony consists of "stopovers," beings en route elsewhere who pause to visit the Orvonton capital. These personalities may be executing a universe assignment, or they may be enjoying a period of leisure—freedom from assignment. The privilege of intrauniverse travel and observation is a part of the career of all ascending beings. The human desire to travel and observe new peoples and worlds will be fully gratified during the long and eventful climb to Paradise through the local, super-, and central universes.

7. *The Ascending Pilgrims.* As the ascending pilgrims are assigned to various services in connection with their Paradise progression, they are domiciled as a courtesy colony on the various headquarters spheres. While functioning here and there throughout a superuniverse, such groups are largely self-governing. They are an ever-shifting colony embracing all orders of evolutionary mortals and their ascending associates.

4. THE ASCENDING MORTALS

While the mortal survivors of time and space are denominated *ascending pilgrims* when accredited for the progressive ascent to Paradise, these evolutionary creatures occupy such an important place in these narratives that we here desire to present a synopsis of the following seven stages of the ascending universe career:

1. Planetary Mortals.
2. Sleeping Survivors.
3. Mansion World Students.
4. Morontia Progressors.
5. Superuniverse Wards.
6. Havona Pilgrims.
7. Paradise Arrivals.

The following narrative presents the universe career of an Adjuster-indwelt mortal. The Son- and Spirit-fused mortals share portions of this career, but we have elected to tell this story as it pertains to the Adjuster-fused mortals, for such a destiny may be anticipated by all of the human races of Urantia.

1. *Planetary Mortals.* Mortals are all animal-origin evolutionary beings of ascendant potential. In origin, nature, and destiny these various groups and types of human beings are not wholly unlike the Urantia peoples. The human races of each world receive the same ministry of the Sons of God and enjoy the presence of the ministering spirits of time. After natural death all types of ascenders fraternize as one morontia family on the mansion worlds.

2. *Sleeping Survivors.* All mortals of survival status, in the custody of personal guardians of destiny, pass through the portals of natural death and, on the third period, personalize on the mansion worlds. Those accredited beings who have, for any reason, been unable to attain that level of intelligence mastery and endowment of spirituality which would entitle them to personal guardians, cannot thus immediately and directly go to the mansion worlds. Such surviving souls must rest in unconscious sleep until the judgment day of a new epoch, a new dispensation, the coming of a Son of God to call the rolls of the age and adjudicate the realm, and this is the general practice throughout all Nebadon. It was said of Christ Michael that, when he ascended on high at the conclusion of his work on earth, "He led a great multitude of captives." And these captives were the sleeping survivors from the days of Adam to the day of the Master's resurrection on Urantia.

The passing of time is of no moment to sleeping mortals; they are wholly unconscious and oblivious to the length of their rest. On reassembly of personality at the end of an age, those who have slept five thousand years will react no differently than those who have rested five days. Aside from this time delay these survivors pass on through the ascension regime identically with those who avoid the longer or shorter sleep of death.

These dispensational classes of world pilgrims are utilized for group morontia activities in the work of the local universes. There is a great advantage in the mobilization of such enormous groups; they are thus kept together for long periods of effective service.

3. *Mansion World Students.* All surviving mortals who reawaken on the mansion worlds belong to this class.

The physical body of mortal flesh is not a part of the reassembly of the sleeping survivor; the physical body has returned to dust. The seraphim of assignment sponsors the new body, the morontia form, as the new life vehicle for the immortal soul and for the indwelling of the returned Adjuster. The Adjuster is the custodian of the spirit transcript of the mind of the sleeping survivor. The assigned seraphim is the keeper of the surviving identity—the immortal soul—as far as it has evolved. And when these two, the Adjuster and the seraphim, reunite their personality trusts, the new individual constitutes the resurrection of the old personality, the survival of the evolving morontia identity of the soul. Such a reassociation of soul and Adjuster is quite properly called a resurrection, a reassembly of personality factors; but even this does not entirely explain the reappearance of the surviving *personality.* Though you will probably never understand the fact of such an inexplicable transaction, you will sometime experientially know the truth of it if you do not reject the plan of mortal survival.

The plan of initial mortal detention on seven worlds of progressive training is nearly universal in Orvonton. In each local system of approximately one thousand inhabited planets there are seven mansion worlds, usually satellites or subsatellites of the system capital. They are the receiving worlds for the majority of ascending mortals.

Sometimes all training worlds of mortal residence are called universe "mansions," and it was to such spheres that Jesus alluded when he said: "In my Father's house are many mansions." From here on, within a given group of spheres like the mansion worlds, ascenders will progress individually from one sphere to another and from one phase of life to another, but they will always advance from one stage of universe study to another in class formation.

4. *Morontia Progressors.* From the mansion worlds on up through the spheres of the system, constellation, and the universe, mortals are classed as morontia progressors; they are traversing the transition spheres of mortal ascension. As the ascending mortals progress from the lower to the higher of the morontia worlds, they serve on countless assignments in association with their teachers and in company with their more advanced and senior brethren.

Morontia progression pertains to continuing advancement of intellect, spirit, and personality form. Survivors are still three-natured beings. Throughout the entire morontia experience they are wards of the local universe. The regime of the superuniverse does not function until the spirit career begins.

Mortals acquire real spirit identity just before they leave the local universe headquarters for the receiving worlds of the minor sectors of the superuniverse. Passing from the final morontia stage to the first or lowest spirit status is but a slight transition. The mind, personality, and character are unchanged by such an advance; only does the form undergo modification. But the spirit form is just as real as the morontia body, and it is equally discernible.

Before departing from their native local universes for the superuniverse receiving worlds, the mortals of time are recipients of spirit confirmation from the Creator Son and the local universe Mother Spirit. From this point on, the status of the ascending mortal is forever settled. Superuniverse wards have never been known to go astray. Ascending seraphim are also advanced in angelic standing at the time of their departure from the local universes.

5. *Superuniverse Wards.* All ascenders arriving on the training worlds of the superuniverses become the wards of the Ancients of Days; they have traversed the morontia life of the local universe and are now accredited spirits. As young spirits they begin the ascension of the superuniverse system of training and culture, extending from the receiving spheres of their minor sector in through the study worlds of the ten major sectors and on to the higher cultural spheres of the superuniverse headquarters.

There are three orders of student spirits in accordance with their sojourn upon the minor sector, major sectors, and the superuniverse headquarters worlds of spirit progression. As morontia ascenders studied and worked on the worlds of the local universe, so spirit ascenders continue to master new worlds while they practice at giving out to others that which they have imbibed at the experiential founts of wisdom. But going to school as a spirit being in the superuniverse career is very unlike anything that has ever entered the imaginative realms of the material mind of man.

Before leaving the superuniverse for Havona, these ascending spirits receive the same thorough course in superuniverse management that they received during their morontia experience in local universe supervision. Before spirit mortals reach Havona, their chief study, but not exclusive occupation, is the mastery of local and superuniverse administration. The reason for all of this experience is not now fully apparent, but no doubt such training is wise and necessary in view of their possible future destiny as members of the Corps of the Finality.

The superuniverse regime is not the same for all ascending mortals. They receive the same general education, but special groups and classes are carried through special courses of instruction and are put through specific courses of training.

6. *Havona Pilgrims.* When spirit development is complete, even though not replete, then the surviving mortal prepares for the long flight to Havona, the haven of evolutionary spirits. On earth you were a creature of flesh and blood; through the local universe you were a morontia being; through the superuniverse you were an evolving spirit; with your arrival on the receiving worlds of Havona your spiritual education begins in reality and in earnest; your eventual appearance on Paradise will be as a perfected spirit.

The journey from the superuniverse headquarters to the Havona receiving spheres is always made alone. From now on no more class or group instruction will be administered. You are through with the technical and administrative training of the evolutionary worlds of time and space. Now begins your *personal education,* your individual spiritual training. From first to last, throughout all Havona, the instruction is personal and threefold in nature: intellectual, spiritual, and experiential.

The first act of your Havona career will be to recognize and thank your transport seconaphim for the long and safe journey. Then you are presented to those beings who will sponsor your early Havona activities. Next you go to register your arrival and prepare your message of thanksgiving and adoration for dispatch to the Creator Son of your local universe, the universe Father who made possible your sonship career. This concludes the formalities of the Havona arrival; whereupon you are accorded a long period of leisure for free observation, and this affords opportunity for looking up your friends, fellows, and associates of the long ascension experience. You may also consult the broadcasts to ascertain who of your fellow pilgrims have departed for Havona since the time of your leaving Uversa.

The fact of your arrival on the receiving worlds of Havona will be duly transmitted to the headquarters of your local universe and personally conveyed to your seraphic guardian, wherever that seraphim may chance to be.

The ascendant mortals have been thoroughly trained in the affairs of the evolutionary worlds of space; now they begin their long and profitable contact with the created spheres of perfection. What a preparation for some future work is afforded by this combined, unique, and extraordinary experience! But I cannot tell you about Havona; you must see these worlds to appreciate their glory or to understand their grandeur.

7. *Paradise Arrivals.* On reaching Paradise with residential status, you begin the progressive course in divinity and absonity. Your residence on Paradise signifies that you have found God, and that you are to be mustered into the Mortal Corps of the Finality. Of all the creatures of the grand universe, only those who are Father fused are mustered into the Mortal Corps of the Finality. Only such individuals take the finaliter oath. Other beings of Paradise perfection or attainment may be temporarily attached to this finality corps, but they are not of eternal assignment to the unknown and unrevealed mission of this accumulating host of the evolutionary and perfected veterans of time and space.

Paradise arrivals are accorded a period of freedom, after which they begin their associations with the seven groups of the primary supernaphim. They are designated Paradise graduates when they have finished their course with the conductors of worship and then, as finaliters, are assigned on observational and co-operative service to the ends of the far-flung creation. As yet there seems to be no specific or settled employment for the Mortal Corps of Finaliters, though they serve in many capacities on worlds settled in light and life.

If there should be no future or unrevealed destiny for the Mortal Corps of the Finality, the present assignment of these ascendant beings would be altogether adequate and glorious. Their present destiny wholly justifies the universal plan of evolutionary ascent. But the future ages of the evolution of the spheres of outer space will undoubtedly further elaborate, and with more repleteness divinely illuminate, the wisdom and loving-kindness of the Gods in the execution of their divine plan of human survival and mortal ascension.

This narrative, together with what has been revealed to you and with what you may acquire in connection with instruction respecting your own world, presents an outline of the career of an ascending mortal. The story varies considerably in the different superuniverses, but this recital affords a glimpse of the average plan of mortal progression as it is operative in the local universe of Nebadon and in the seventh segment of the grand universe, the superuniverse of Orvonton.

[Sponsored by a Mighty Messenger from Uversa.]

PAPER 31

THE CORPS OF THE FINALITY

THE Corps of Mortal Finaliters represents the present known destination of the ascending Adjuster-fused mortals of time. But there are other groups who are also assigned to this corps. The primary finaliter corps is composed of the following:

1. Havona Natives.
2. Gravity Messengers.
3. Glorified Mortals.
4. Adopted Seraphim.
5. Glorified Material Sons.
6. Glorified Midway Creatures.

These six groups of glorified beings compose this unique body of eternal destiny. We think we know their future work, but we are not certain. While the Corps of the Mortal Finality is mobilizing on Paradise, and while they now so extensively minister to the universes of space and administer the worlds settled in light and life, their future destination must be the now-organizing universes of outer space. At least that is the conjecture of Uversa.

The corps is organized in accordance with the working associations of the worlds of space and in keeping with the associative experience acquired throughout the long and eventful ascendant career. All the ascendant creatures admitted to this corps are received in equality, but this exalted equality in no way abrogates individuality or destroys personal identity. We can immediately discern, in communicating with a finaliter, whether he is an ascendant mortal, Havona native, adopted seraphim, midway creature, or Material Son.

During the present universe age the finaliters return to serve in the universes of time. They are assigned to labor successively in the different superuniverses and never in their native superuniverses until after they have served in all the other six supercreations. Thus may they acquire the sevenfold concept of the Supreme Being.

One or more companies of the mortal finaliters are constantly in service on Urantia. There is no domain of universe service to which they are not assigned; they function universally and with alternating and equal periods of assigned duty and free service.

We have no idea as to the nature of the future organization of this extraordinary group, but the finaliters are now wholly a self-governing body. They choose their own permanent, periodic, and assignment leaders and directors. No outside influence can ever be brought to bear upon their policies, and their oath of allegiance is only to the Paradise Trinity.

The finaliters maintain their own headquarters on Paradise, in the superuniverses, in the local universes, and on all the divisional capitals. They are a separate order of evolutionary creation. We do not directly manage them or control them, and yet they are absolutely loyal and always co-operative with all our plans. They are indeed the accumulating tried and true souls of time and space—the evolutionary salt of the universe—and they are forever proof against evil and secure against sin.

1. THE HAVONA NATIVES

Many of the Havona natives who serve as teachers in the pilgrim-training schools of the central universe become greatly attached to the ascending mortals and still more intrigued with the future work and destiny of the Corps of Mortal Finaliters. On Paradise there is maintained, at the administrative headquarters of the corps, a registry for Havona volunteers presided over by the associate of Grandfanda. Today, you will find millions upon millions of Havona natives upon this waiting list. These perfect beings of direct and divine creation are of great assistance to the Mortal Corps of Finality, and they will undoubtedly be of even greater service in the far-distant future. They provide the viewpoint of one born in perfection and divine repleteness. The finaliters thus embrace both phases of experiential existence—perfect and perfected.

Havona natives must achieve certain experiential developments in liaison with evolutionary beings which will create reception capacity for the bestowal of a fragment of the spirit of the Universal Father. The Mortal Finaliter Corps has as permanent members only such beings as have been fused with the spirit of the First Source and Center, or who, like the Gravity Messengers, innately embody this spirit of God the Father.

The inhabitants of the central universe are received into the corps in the ratio of one in a thousand—a finaliter company. The corps is organized for temporary service in companies of one thousand, the ascendant creatures numbering 997 to one Havona native and one Gravity Messenger. Finaliters are thus mobilized in companies, but the finality oath is administered individually. It is an oath of sweeping implications and eternal import. The Havona native takes the same oath and becomes forever attached to the corps.

The Havona recruits follow the company of their assignment; wherever the group goes, they go. And you should see their enthusiasm in the new work of the finaliters. The possibility of attaining the Corps of the Finality is one of the superb thrills of Havona; the possibility of becoming a finaliter is one of the supreme adventures of these perfect races.

The Havona natives are also received, in the same ratio, into the Corps of Conjoint Trinitized Finaliters on Vicegerington and into the Corps of Transcendental Finaliters on Paradise. The Havona citizens regard these three destinies as constituting the supreme goals of their supernal careers, together with their possible admission to the Corps of Havona Finaliters.

2. GRAVITY MESSENGERS

Wherever and whenever Gravity Messengers are functioning, the finaliters are in command. All Gravity Messengers are under the exclusive jurisdiction of Grandfanda, and they are assigned only to the primary Corps of the Finality.

They are invaluable to the finaliters even now, and they will be all-serviceable in the eternal future. No other group of intelligent creatures possesses such a personalized messenger corps able to transcend time and space. Similar types of messenger-recorders attached to other finaliter corps are not personalized; they are absonitized.

Gravity Messengers hail from Divinington, and they are modified and personalized Adjusters, but no one of our Uversa group will undertake to explain the nature of one of these messengers. We know they are highly personal beings, divine, intelligent, and touchingly understanding, but we do not comprehend their timeless technique of traversing space. They seem to be competent to utilize any and all energies, circuits, and even gravity. Finaliters of the mortal corps cannot defy time and space, but they have associated with them and subject to their command all but infinite spirit personalities who can. We presume to call Gravity Messengers personalities, but in reality they are superspirit beings, unlimited and boundless personalities. They are of an entirely different order of personality as compared with Solitary Messengers.

Gravity Messengers may be attached to a finaliter company in unlimited numbers, but only one messenger, the chief of his fellows, is mustered into the Mortal Corps of the Finality. This chief however has assigned to him a permanent staff of 999 fellow messengers, and as occasion may require, he may call upon the reserves of the order for assistants in unlimited numbers.

Gravity Messengers and glorified mortal finaliters achieve a touching and profound affection for one another; they have much in common: One is a direct personalization of a fragment of the Universal Father, the other a creature personality existent in the surviving immortal soul fused with a fragment of the same Universal Father, the spirit Thought Adjuster.

3. GLORIFIED MORTALS

Ascendant Adjuster-fused mortals compose the bulk of the primary Corps of the Finality. Together with the adopted and glorified seraphim they usually constitute 990 in each finaliter company. The proportion of mortals and angels in any one group varies, though the mortals far outnumber the seraphim. The Havona natives, glorified Material Sons, glorified midway creatures, the Gravity Messengers, and the unknown and missing member make up only one per cent of the corps; each company of one thousand finaliters has places for just ten of these nonmortal and nonseraphic personalities.

We of Uversa do not know the "finality destiny" of the ascendant mortals of time. At present they reside on Paradise and temporarily serve in the Corps of Light and Life, but such a tremendous course of ascendant training and such lengthy universe discipline must be designed to qualify them for even greater tests of trust and more sublime services of responsibility.

Notwithstanding that these ascendant mortals have attained Paradise, have been mustered into the Corps of the Finality, and have been sent back in large numbers to participate in the conduct of local universes and to assist in the administration of superuniverse affairs—in the face of even this *apparent* destiny, there remains the significant fact that they are of record as only sixth-stage spirits. There undoubtedly remains one more step in the career of the Mortal

Corps of the Finality. We do not know the nature of that step, but we have taken cognizance of, and here call attention to, three facts:

1. We know from the records that mortals are spirits of the first order during their sojourn in the minor sectors, and that they advance to the second order when translated to the major sectors, and to the third when they go forward to the central training worlds of the superuniverse. Mortals become quartan or graduate spirits after reaching the sixth circle of Havona and become spirits of the fifth order when they find the Universal Father. They subsequently attain the sixth stage of spirit existence upon taking the oath that musters them forever into the eternity assignment of the Corps of the Mortal Finality.

We observe that spirit classification, or designation, has been determined by actual advancement from one realm of universe service to another realm of universe service or from one universe to another universe; and we surmise that the bestowal of seventh-spirit classification upon the Mortal Corps of the Finality will be simultaneous with their advancement to eternal assignment for service on hitherto unrecorded and unrevealed spheres and concomitant with their attainment of God the Supreme. But aside from these bold conjectures, we really know no more about all this than you do; our knowledge of the mortal career does not go beyond present Paradise destiny.

2. The mortal finaliters have fully complied with the injunction of the ages, "Be you perfect"; they have ascended the universal path of mortal attainment; they have found God, and they have been duly inducted into the Corps of the Finality. Such beings have attained the present limit of spirit progression but not *finality of ultimate spirit status.* They have achieved the present limit of creature perfection but not *finality of creature service.* They have experienced the fullness of Deity worship but not *finality of experiential Deity attainment.*

3. The glorified mortals of the Paradise Corps of Finality are ascendant beings in possession of experiential knowledge of every step of the actuality and philosophy of the fullest possible life of intelligent existence, while during the ages of this ascent from the lowest material worlds to the spiritual heights of Paradise, these surviving creatures have been trained to the limits of their capacity respecting every detail of every divine principle of the just and efficient, as well as merciful and patient, administration of all the universal creation of time and space.

We deem that human beings are entitled to share our opinions, and that you are free to conjecture with us respecting the mystery of the ultimate destiny of the Paradise Corps of Finality. It seems evident to us that the present assignments of the perfected evolutionary creatures partake of the nature of postgraduate courses in universe understanding and superuniverse administration; and we all ask, "Why should the Gods be so concerned in so thoroughly training surviving mortals in the technique of universe management?"

4. ADOPTED SERAPHIM

Many of the faithful seraphic guardians of mortals are permitted to go through the ascendant career with their human wards, and many of these guardian angels, after becoming Father fused, join their subjects in taking the finaliter oath of eternity and forever accept the destiny of their mortal associates. Angels who pass through the ascending experience of mortal beings may share the destiny of human nature; they may equally and eternally be mustered into this Corps of the Finality. Large numbers of the adopted and glorified seraphim are attached to the various nonmortal finaliter corps.

5. GLORIFIED MATERIAL SONS

There is provision in the universes of time and space whereby the Adamic citizens of the local systems, when long delayed in receiving planetary assignment, may initiate a petition for release from permanent-citizenship status. And if granted, they join the ascending pilgrims on the universe capitals and thence proceed onward to Paradise and the Corps of the Finality.

When an advanced evolutionary world attains the later eras of the age of light and life, the Material Sons, the Planetary Adam and Eve, may elect to humanize, receive Adjusters, and embark upon the evolutionary course of universe ascent leading to the Corps of Mortal Finaliters. Certain of these Material Sons have partially failed or technically defaulted in their mission as biologic accelerators, as Adam did on Urantia; and then are they compelled to take the natural course of the peoples of the realm, receive Adjusters, pass through death, and progress by faith through the ascendant regime, subsequently attaining Paradise and the Corps of the Finality.

These Material Sons are not to be found in many finaliter companies. Their presence lends great potential to the possibilities of high service for such a group, and they are invariably chosen as its leaders. If both of the Edenic pair are attached to the same group, they are usually permitted to function jointly, as one personality. Such ascendant pairs are far more successful in the adventure of trinitizing than are the ascendant mortals.

6. GLORIFIED MIDWAY CREATURES

On many planets the midway creatures are produced in large numbers, but they seldom tarry on their native world subsequent to its being settled in light and life. Then, or soon thereafter, they are released from permanent-citizenship status and start on the ascension to Paradise, passing through the morontia worlds, the superuniverse, and Havona in company with the mortals of time and space.

The midway creatures from various universes differ greatly in origin and nature, but they are all destined to one or another of the Paradise finality corps. The secondary midwayers are all eventually Adjuster fused and are mustered into the mortal corps. Many finaliter companies have one of these glorified beings in their group.

7. THE EVANGELS OF LIGHT

At the present time every finaliter company numbers 999 personalities of oath status, permanent members. The vacant place is occupied by the chief of attached Evangels of Light assigned on any single mission. But these beings are only transient members of the corps.

Any celestial personality assigned to the service of any finaliter corps is denominated an Evangel of Light. These beings do not take the finaliter oath, and though subject to the corps organization they are not of permanent attachment. This group may embrace Solitary Messengers, supernaphim, seconaphim, Paradise Citizens, or their trinitized offspring—any being required in the prosecution of a transient finaliter assignment. Whether or not the corps is to have these beings attached to the eternal mission, we do not know. At the conclusion of attachment these Evangels of Light resume their former status.

As the Mortal Corps of the Finality is at present constituted, there are just six classes of permanent members. The finaliters, as might be expected, engage in much speculation as to the identity of their future comrades, but there is little agreement among them.

We of Uversa often conjecture respecting the identity of the seventh group of finaliters. We entertain many ideas, embracing possible assignment of some of the accumulating corps of the numerous trinitized groups on Paradise, Vicegerington, and the inner Havona circuit. It is even conjectured that the Corps of the Finality may be permitted to trinitize many of their assistants in the work of universe administration in the event they are destined to the service of universes now in the making.

One of us holds the opinion that this vacant place in the corps will be filled by some type of being of origin in the new universe of their future service; the other inclines to the belief that this place will be occupied by some type of Paradise personality not yet created, eventuated, or trinitized. But we will most likely await the entrance of the finaliters upon their seventh stage of spirit attainment before we really know.

8. THE TRANSCENDENTALERS

Part of the perfected mortal's experience on Paradise as a finaliter consists in the effort to achieve comprehension of the nature and function of more than one thousand groups of the transcendental supercitizens of Paradise, eventuated beings of absonite attributes. In their association with these superpersonalities, the ascendant finaliters receive great assistance from the helpful guidance of numerous orders of transcendental ministers who are assigned to the task of introducing the evolved finaliters to their new Paradise brethren. The entire order of the Transcendentalers live in the west of Paradise in a vast area which they exclusively occupy.

In the discussion of Transcendentalers we are restricted, not only by the limitations of human comprehension, but also by the terms of the mandate governing these disclosures concerning the personalities of Paradise. These beings are in no way connected with the mortal ascent to Havona. The vast host of the Paradise Transcendentalers have nothing whatever to do with the affairs of either Havona or the seven superuniverses, being concerned only with the superadministration of the affairs of the master universe.

You, being a creature, can conceive of a Creator, but you can hardly comprehend that there exists an enormous and diversified aggregation of intelligent beings who are neither Creators nor creatures. These Transcendentalers create no beings, neither were they ever created. In speaking of their origin, in order to avoid using a new term—an arbitrary and meaningless designation—we deem it best to say that Transcendentalers simply *eventuate*. The Deity Absolute may well have been concerned in their origin and may be implicated in their destiny, but these unique beings are not now dominated by the Deity Absolute. They are subject to God the Ultimate, and their present Paradise sojourn is in every way Trinity supervised and directed.

Although all mortals who attain Paradise frequently fraternize with the Transcendentalers as they do with the Paradise Citizens, it develops that man's first serious contact with a Transcendentaler occurs on that eventful occasion when, as a member of a new finaliter group, the mortal ascender stands in the finaliter receiving circle as the Trinity oath of eternity is administered by the chief of Transcendentalers, the presiding head of the Architects of the Master Universe.

9. ARCHITECTS OF THE MASTER UNIVERSE

The Architects of the Master Universe are the governing corps of the Paradise Transcendentalers. This governing corps numbers 28,011 personalities possessing master minds, superb spirits, and supernal absonites. The presiding officer of this magnificent group, the senior Master Architect, is the co-ordinating head of all Paradise intelligences below the level of Deity.

The sixteenth proscription of the mandate authorizing these narratives says: "If deemed wise, the existence of the Architects of the Master Universe and their associates may be disclosed, but their origin, nature, and destiny may not be fully revealed." We may, however, inform you that these Master Architects exist in seven levels of the absonite. These seven groups are classified as follows:

1. *The Paradise Level.* Only the senior or first-eventuated Architect functions on this highest level of the absonite. This ultimate personality—neither Creator nor creature—eventuated in the dawn of eternity and now functions as the exquisite co-ordinator of Paradise and its twenty-one worlds of associated activities.

2. *The Havona Level.* The second Architect eventuation yielded three master planners and absonite administrators, and they have always been devoted to the co-ordination of the one billion perfect spheres of the central universe. Paradise tradition asserts that these three Architects, with the counsel of the pre-eventuated senior Architect, contributed to the planning of Havona, but we really do not know.

3. *The Superuniverse Level.* The third absonite level embraces the seven Master Architects of the seven superuniverses, who now, as a group, spend about equal time in the company of the Seven Master Spirits on Paradise and with the Seven Supreme Executives on the seven special worlds of the Infinite Spirit. They are the superco-ordinators of the grand universe.

4. *The Primary Space Level.* This group numbers seventy Architects, and we conjecture that they are concerned with the ultimate plans for the first universe of outer space, now mobilizing beyond the borders of the present seven superuniverses.

5. *The Secondary Space Level.* This fifth corps of Architects numbers 490, and again we conjecture that they must be concerned with the second universe of outer space, where already our physicists have detected definite energy mobilizations.

6. *The Tertiary Space Level.* This sixth group of Master Architects numbers 3,430, and we likewise infer that they may be occupied with the gigantic plans for the third universe of outer space.

7. *The Quartan Space Level.* This, the final and largest corps, consists of 24,010 Master Architects, and if our former conjectures are valid, it must be related to the fourth and last of the ever-increasing-sized universes of outer space.

These seven groups of Master Architects total 28,011 universe planners. On Paradise there is a tradition that far back in eternity there was attempted the eventuation of the 28,012th Master Architect, but that this being failed to absonitize, experiencing personality seizure by the Universal Absolute. It is possible that the ascending series of the Master Architects attained the limit of absonity in the 28,011th Architect, and that the 28,012th attempt encountered the mathematical level of the presence of the Absolute. In other words, at the 28,012th eventuation level the quality of absonity equivalated to the level of the Universal and attained the value of the Absolute.

In their functional organization the three supervising Architects of Havona act as associate assistants to the solitary Paradise Architect. The seven Architects of the superuniverses act as co-ordinates of the three supervisors of Havona. The seventy planners of the universes of the primary outer space level are at present serving as associate assistants to the seven Architects of the seven superuniverses.

The Architects of the Master Universe have at their disposal numerous groups of assistants and helpers, including two vast orders of force organizers, the primary eventuated and the associate transcendental. These Master Force Organizers are not to be confused with the power directors, who are germane to the grand universe.

All beings produced by the union of the children of time and eternity, such as the trinitized offspring of the finaliters and the Paradise Citizens, become wards of the Master Architects. But of all other creatures or entities revealed as functioning in the present organized universes, only Solitary Messengers and Inspired Trinity Spirits maintain any organic association with the Transcendentalers and the Architects of the Master Universe.

The Master Architects contribute technical approval of the assignment of the Creator Sons to their space sites for the organization of the local universes. There is a very close association between the Master Architects and the Paradise Creator Sons, and while this relationship is unrevealed, you have been informed of the association of the Architects and the grand universe Supreme Creators in the relationship of the first experiential Trinity. These two groups, together with the evolving and experiential Supreme Being, constitute the Trinity Ultimate of transcendental values and master universe meanings.

10. THE ULTIMATE ADVENTURE

The senior Master Architect has the oversight of the seven Corps of the Finality, and they are:

1. The Corps of Mortal Finaliters.
2. The Corps of Paradise Finaliters.
3. The Corps of Trinitized Finaliters.

4. The Corps of Conjoint Trinitized Finaliters.
5. The Corps of Havona Finaliters.
6. The Corps of Transcendental Finaliters.
7. The Corps of Unrevealed Sons of Destiny.

Each of these destiny corps has a presiding head, and the seven constitute the Supreme Council of Destiny on Paradise; and during the present universe age Grandfanda is the chief of this supreme body of universe assignment for the children of ultimate destiny.

The gathering together of these seven finaliter corps signifies reality mobilization of potentials, personalities, minds, spirits, absonites, and experiential actualities that probably transcend even the future master universe functions of the Supreme Being. These seven finaliter corps probably signify the present activity of the Ultimate Trinity engaged in mustering the forces of the finite and the absonite in preparation for inconceivable developments in the universes of outer space. Nothing like this mobilization has taken place since the near times of eternity when the Paradise Trinity similarly mobilized the then existing personalities of Paradise and Havona and commissioned them as administrators and rulers of the projected seven superuniverses of time and space. The seven finaliter corps represent the divinity response of the grand universe to the future needs of the undeveloped potentials in the outer universes of future-eternal activities.

We venture the forecast of future and greater outer universes of inhabited worlds, new spheres peopled with new orders of exquisite and unique beings, a material universe sublime in its ultimacy, a vast creation lacking in only one important detail—the presence of actual *finite experience* in the universal life of ascendant existence. Such a universe will come into being under a tremendous experiential handicap: the deprivation of participation in the evolution of the Almighty Supreme. These outer universes will all enjoy the matchless ministry and supernal overcontrol of the Supreme Being, but the very fact of his active presence precludes their participation in the actualization of the Supreme Deity.

During the present universe age the evolving personalities of the grand universe suffer many difficulties due to the incomplete actualization of the sovereignty of God the Supreme, but we are all sharing the unique experience of his evolution. We evolve in him and he evolves in us. Sometime in the eternal future the evolution of Supreme Deity will become a completed fact of universe history, and the opportunity to participate in this wonderful experience will have passed from the stage of cosmic action.

But those of us who have acquired this unique experience during the youth of the universe will treasure it throughout all future eternity. And many of us speculate that it may be the mission of the gradually accumulating reserves of the ascendant and perfected mortals of the Corps of the Finality, in association with the other six similarly recruiting corps, to administer these outer universes in an effort to compensate their experiential deficiencies in not having participated in the time-space evolution of the Supreme Being.

These deficiencies are inevitable on all levels of universe existence. During the present universe age we of the higher levels of spiritual existences now come down to administer the evolutionary universes and minister to the ascending mortals, thus endeavoring to atone for their deficiencies in the realities of the higher spiritual experience.

But though we really know nothing about the plans of the Architects of the Master Universe respecting these outer creations, nevertheless, of three things we are certain:

1. There actually is a vast and new system of universes gradually organizing in the domains of outer space. New orders of physical creations, enormous and gigantic circles of swarming universes upon universes far out beyond the present bounds of the peopled and organized creations, are actually visible through your telescopes. At present, these outer creations are wholly physical; they are apparently uninhabited and seem to be devoid of creature administration.

2. For ages upon ages there continues the unexplained and wholly mysterious Paradise mobilization of the perfected and ascendant beings of time and space, in association with the six other finaliter corps.

3. Concomitantly with these transactions the Supreme Person of Deity is powerizing as the almighty sovereign of the supercreations.

As we view this triune development, embracing creatures, universes, and Deity, can we be criticized for anticipating that something new and unrevealed is approaching culmination in the master universe? Is it not natural that we should associate this agelong mobilization and organization of physical universes on such a hitherto unknown scale and the personality emergence of the Supreme Being with this stupendous scheme of upstepping the mortals of time to divine perfection and with their subsequent mobilization on Paradise in the Corps of the Finality—a designation and destiny enshrouded in universe mystery? It is increasingly the belief of all Uversa that the assembling Corps of the Finality are destined to some future service in the universes of outer space, where we already are able to identify the clustering of at least seventy thousand aggregations of matter, each of which is greater than any one of the present superuniverses.

Evolutionary mortals are born on the planets of space, pass through the morontia worlds, ascend the spirit universes, traverse the Havona spheres, find God, attain Paradise, and are mustered into the primary Corps of the Finality, therein to await the next assignment of universe service. There are six other assembling finality corps, but Grandfanda, the first mortal ascender, presides as Paradise chief of all orders of finaliters. And as we view this sublime spectacle, we all exclaim: What a glorious destiny for the animal-origin children of time, the material sons of space!

[Jointly sponsored by a Divine Counselor and One without Name and Number authorized so to function by the Ancients of Days on Uversa.]

* * * * *

These thirty-one papers depicting the nature of Deity, the reality of Paradise, the organization and working of the central and superuniverses, the personalities of the grand universe, and the high destiny of evolutionary mortals, were sponsored, formulated, and put into English by a high commission consisting of twenty-four Orvonton administrators acting in accordance with a mandate issued by the Ancients of Days of Uversa directing that we should do this on Urantia, 606 of Satania, in Norlatiadek of Nebadon, in the year A.D. 1934.

PART II

THE LOCAL UNIVERSE

Sponsored by a Nebadon Corps of Local Universe
Personalities acting by authority of
Gabriel of Salvington.

PART II

The Local Universe

PAPER 32

THE EVOLUTION OF LOCAL UNIVERSES

A LOCAL universe is the handiwork of a Creator Son of the Paradise order of Michael. It comprises one hundred constellations, each embracing one hundred systems of inhabited worlds. Each system will eventually contain approximately one thousand inhabited spheres.

These universes of time and space are all evolutionary. The creative plan of the Paradise Michaels always proceeds along the path of gradual evolvement and progressive development of the physical, intellectual, and spiritual natures and capacities of the manifold creatures who inhabit the varied orders of spheres comprising such a local universe.

Urantia belongs to a local universe whose sovereign is the God-man of Nebadon, Jesus of Nazareth and Michael of Salvington. And all of Michael's plans for this local universe were fully approved by the Paradise Trinity before he ever embarked upon the supreme adventure of space.

The Sons of God may choose the realms of their creator activities, but these material creations were originally projected and planned by the Paradise Architects of the Master Universe.

1. PHYSICAL EMERGENCE OF UNIVERSES

The preuniverse manipulations of space-force and the primordial energies are the work of the Paradise Master Force Organizers; but in the superuniverse domains, when emergent energy becomes responsive to local or linear gravity, they retire in favor of the power directors of the superuniverse concerned.

These power directors function alone in the prematerial and postforce phases of a local universe creation. There is no opportunity for a Creator Son to begin universe organization until the power directors have effected the mobilization of the space-energies sufficiently to provide a material foundation—literal suns and material spheres—for the emerging universe.

The local universes are all approximately of the same energy potential, though they differ greatly in physical dimensions and may vary in visible-matter content from time to time. The power charge and potential-matter endowment of a local universe are determined by the manipulations of the power directors and their predecessors as well as by the Creator Son's activities and by the endowment of the inherent physical control possessed by his creative associate.

The energy charge of a local universe is approximately one one-hundred-thousandth of the force endowment of its superuniverse. In the case of Nebadon, your local universe, the mass materialization is a trifle less. Physically speaking, Nebadon possesses all of the physical endowment of energy and matter that may be found in any of the Orvonton local creations. The only physical limitation upon the developmental expansion of the Nebadon universe consists in the quantitative charge of space-energy held captive by the gravity control of the associated powers and personalities of the combined universe mechanism.

When energy-matter has attained a certain stage in mass materialization, a Paradise Creator Son appears upon the scene, accompanied by a Creative Daughter of the Infinite Spirit. Simultaneously with the arrival of the Creator Son, work is begun upon the architectural sphere which is to become the headquarters world of the projected local universe. For long ages such a local creation evolves, suns become stabilized, planets form and swing into their orbits, while the work of creating the architectural worlds which are to serve as constellation headquarters and system capitals continues.

2. UNIVERSE ORGANIZATION

The Creator Sons are preceded in universe organization by the power directors and other beings originating in the Third Source and Center. From the energies of space, thus previously organized, Michael, your Creator Son, established the inhabited realms of the universe of Nebadon and ever since has been painstakingly devoted to their administration. From pre-existent energy these divine Sons materialize visible matter, project living creatures, and with the co-operation of the universe presence of the Infinite Spirit, create a diverse retinue of spirit personalities.

These power directors and energy controllers who long preceded the Creator Son in the preliminary physical work of universe organization later serve in magnificent liaison with this Universe Son, forever remaining in associated control of those energies which they originally organized and circuitized. On Salvington there now function the same one hundred power centers who co-operated with your Creator Son in the original formation of this local universe.

The first completed act of physical creation in Nebadon consisted in the organization of the headquarters world, the architectural sphere of Salvington, with its satellites. From the time of the initial moves of the power centers and physical controllers to the arrival of the living staff on the completed spheres of Salvington, there intervened a little over one billion years of your present planetary time. The construction of Salvington was immediately followed by the creation of the one hundred headquarters worlds of the projected constellations and the ten thousand headquarters spheres of the projected local systems of planetary control and administration, together with their architectural satellites. Such architectural worlds are designed to accommodate both physical and spiritual personalities as well as the intervening morontia or transition stages of being.

Salvington, the headquarters of Nebadon, is situated at the exact energy-mass center of the local universe. But your local universe is not a single astronomic system, though a large system does exist at its physical center.

Salvington is the personal headquarters of Michael of Nebadon, but he will not always be found there. While the smooth functioning of your local universe no longer requires the fixed presence of the Creator Son at the capital sphere, this was not true of the earlier epochs of physical organization. A Creator Son is unable to leave his headquarters world until such a time as gravity stabilization of the realm has been effected through the materialization of sufficient energy to enable the various circuits and systems to counterbalance one another by mutual material attraction.

Presently, the physical plan of a universe is completed, and the Creator Son, in association with the Creative Spirit, projects his plan of life creation; whereupon does this representation of the Infinite Spirit begin her universe function as a distinct creative personality. When this first creative act is formulated and executed, there springs into being the Bright and Morning Star, the personification of this initial creative concept of identity and ideal of divinity. This is the chief executive of the universe, the personal associate of the Creator Son, one like him in all aspects of character, though markedly limited in the attributes of divinity.

And now that the right-hand helper and chief executive of the Creator Son has been provided, there ensues the bringing into existence of a vast and wonderful array of diverse creatures. The sons and daughters of the local universe are forthcoming, and soon thereafter the government of such a creation is provided, extending from the supreme councils of the universe to the fathers of the constellations and the sovereigns of the local systems—the aggregations of those worlds which are designed subsequently to become the homes of the varied mortal races of will creatures; and each of these worlds will be presided over by a Planetary Prince.

And then, when such a universe has been so completely organized and so repletely manned, does the Creator Son enter into the Father's proposal to create mortal man in their divine image.

The organization of planetary abodes is still progressing in Nebadon, for this universe is, indeed, a young cluster in the starry and planetary realms of Orvonton. At the last registry there were 3,840,101 inhabited planets in Nebadon, and Satania, the local system of your world, is fairly typical of other systems.

Satania is not a uniform physical system, a single astronomic unit or organization. Its 619 inhabited worlds are located in over five hundred different physical systems. Only five have more than two inhabited worlds, and of these only one has four peopled planets, while there are forty-six having two inhabited worlds.

The Satania system of inhabited worlds is far removed from Uversa and that great sun cluster which functions as the physical or astronomic center of the seventh superuniverse. From Jerusem, the headquarters of Satania, it is over two hundred thousand light-years to the physical center of the superuniverse of Orvonton, far, far away in the dense diameter of the Milky Way. Satania is on the periphery of the local universe, and Nebadon is now well out towards the edge of Orvonton. From the outermost system of inhabited worlds to the center of the superuniverse is a trifle less than two hundred and fifty thousand light-years.

The universe of Nebadon now swings far to the south and east in the superuniverse circuit of Orvonton. The nearest neighboring universes are: Avalon, Henselon, Sanselon, Portalon, Wolvering, Fanoving, and Alvoring.

But the evolution of a local universe is a long narrative. Papers dealing with the superuniverse introduce this subject, those of this section, treating of the local creations, continue it, while those to follow, touching upon the history and destiny of Urantia, complete the story. But you can adequately comprehend the destiny of the mortals of such a local creation only by a perusal of the narratives of the life and teachings of your Creator Son as he once lived the life of man, in the likeness of mortal flesh, on your own evolutionary world.

3. THE EVOLUTIONARY IDEA

The only creation that is perfectly settled is Havona, the central universe, which was made directly by the thought of the Universal Father and the word of the Eternal Son. Havona is an existential, perfect, and replete universe, surrounding the home of the eternal Deities, the center of all things. The creations of the seven superuniverses are finite, evolutionary, and consistently progressive.

The physical systems of time and space are all evolutionary in origin. They are not even physically stabilized until they are swung into the settled circuits of their superuniverses. Neither is a local universe settled in light and life until its physical possibilities of expansion and development have been exhausted, and until the spiritual status of all its inhabited worlds has been forever settled and stabilized.

Except in the central universe, perfection is a progressive attainment. In the central creation we have a pattern of perfection, but all other realms must attain that perfection by the methods established for the advancement of those particular worlds or universes. And an almost infinite variety characterizes the plans of the Creator Sons for organizing, evolving, disciplining, and settling their respective local universes.

With the exception of the deity presence of the Father, every local universe is, in a certain sense, a duplication of the administrative organization of the central or pattern creation. Although the Universal Father is personally present in the residential universe, he does not indwell the minds of the beings originating in that universe as he does literally dwell with the souls of the mortals of time and space. There seems to be an all-wise compensation in the adjustment and regulation of the spiritual affairs of the far-flung creation. In the central universe the Father is personally present as such but absent in the minds of the children of that perfect creation; in the universes of space the Father is absent in person, being represented by his Sovereign Sons, while he is intimately present in the minds of his mortal children, being spiritually represented by the prepersonal presence of the Mystery Monitors that reside in the minds of these will creatures.

On the headquarters of a local universe there reside all those creator and creative personalities who represent self-contained authority and administrative autonomy except the personal presence of the Universal Father. In the local universe there are to be found something of everyone and someone of almost every class of intelligent beings existing in the central universe except the Universal Father. Although the Universal Father is not personally present in a local universe, he is personally represented by its Creator Son, sometime vicegerent of God and subsequently supreme and sovereign ruler in his own right.

The farther down the scale of life we go, the more difficult it becomes to locate, with the eye of faith, the invisible Father. The lower creatures—and sometimes even the higher personalities—find it difficult always to envisage the Universal Father in his Creator Sons. And so, pending the time of their spiritual exaltation, when perfection of development will enable them to see God in person, they grow weary in progression, entertain spiritual doubts, stumble into confusion, and thus isolate themselves from the progressive spiritual aims of their time and universe. In this way they lose the ability to see the Father when beholding the Creator Son. The surest safeguard for the creature throughout the long struggle to attain the Father, during this time when inherent conditions make such attainment impossible, is tenaciously to hold on to the truth-fact of the Father's presence in his Sons. Literally and figuratively, spiritually and personally, the Father and the Sons are one. It is a fact: He who has seen a Creator Son has seen the Father.

The personalities of a given universe are settled and dependable, at the start, only in accordance with their degree of kinship to Deity. When creature origin departs sufficiently far from the original and divine Sources, whether we are dealing with the Sons of God or the creatures of ministry belonging to the Infinite Spirit, there is an increase in the possibility of disharmony, confusion, and sometimes rebellion—sin.

Excepting perfect beings of Deity origin, all will creatures in the superuniverses are of evolutionary nature, beginning in lowly estate and climbing ever upward, in reality inward. Even highly spiritual personalities continue to ascend the scale of life by progressive translations from life to life and from sphere to sphere. And in the case of those who entertain the Mystery Monitors, there is indeed no limit to the possible heights of their spiritual ascent and universe attainment.

The perfection of the creatures of time, when finally achieved, is wholly an acquirement, a bona fide personality possession. While the elements of grace are freely admixed, nevertheless, the creature attainments are the result of individual effort and actual living, personality reaction to the existing environment.

The fact of animal evolutionary origin does not attach stigma to any personality in the sight of the universe as that is the exclusive method of producing one of the two basic types of finite intelligent will creatures. When the heights of perfection and eternity are attained, all the more honor to those who began at the bottom and joyfully climbed the ladder of life, round by round, and who, when they do reach the heights of glory, will have gained a personal experience which embodies an actual knowledge of every phase of life from the bottom to the top.

In all this is shown the wisdom of the Creators. It would be just as easy for the Universal Father to make all mortals perfect beings, to impart perfection by his divine word. But that would deprive them of the wonderful experience of the adventure and training associated with the long and gradual inward climb, an experience to be had only by those who are so fortunate as to begin at the very bottom of living existence.

In the universes encircling Havona there are provided only a sufficient number of perfect creatures to meet the need for pattern teacher guides for those who are ascending the evolutionary scale of life. The experiential nature of the evolutionary type of personality is the natural cosmic complement of the ever-perfect natures of the Paradise-Havona creatures. In reality, both perfect and perfected creatures are incomplete as regards finite totality. But in the complemental association of the existentially perfect creatures of the Paradise-Havona system with the experientially perfected finaliters ascending from the evolutionary universes, both types find release from inherent limitations and thus may conjointly attempt to reach the sublime heights of the ultimate of creature status.

These creature transactions are the universe repercussions of actions and reactions within the Sevenfold Deity, wherein the eternal divinity of the Paradise Trinity is conjoined with the evolving divinity of the Supreme Creators of the time-space universes in, by, and through the power-actualizing Deity of the Supreme Being.

The divinely perfect creature and the evolutionary perfected creature are equal in degree of divinity potential, but they differ in kind. Each must depend on the other to attain supremacy of service. The evolutionary superuniverses depend on perfect Havona to provide the final training for their ascending citizens, but so does the perfect central universe require the existence of the perfecting superuniverses to provide for the full development of its descending inhabitants.

The two prime manifestations of finite reality, innate perfection and evolved perfection, be they personalities or universes, are co-ordinate, dependent, and integrated. Each requires the other to achieve completion of function, service, and destiny.

4. GOD'S RELATION TO A LOCAL UNIVERSE

Do not entertain the idea that, since the Universal Father has delegated so much of himself and his power to others, he is a silent or inactive member of the Deity partnership. Aside from personality domains and Adjuster bestowal, he is apparently the least active of the Paradise Deities in that he allows his Deity co-ordinates, his Sons, and numerous created intelligences to perform so much in the carrying out of his eternal purpose. He is the silent member of the creative trio only in that he never does aught which any of his co-ordinate or subordinate associates can do.

God has full understanding of the need of every intelligent creature for function and experience, and therefore, in every situation, be it concerned with the destiny of a universe or the welfare of the humblest of his creatures, God retires from activity in favor of the galaxy of creature and Creator personalities who inherently intervene between himself and any given universe situation or creative event. But notwithstanding this retirement, this exhibition of infinite co-ordination, there is on God's part an actual, literal, and personal participation in these events by and through these ordained agencies and personalities. The Father is working in and through all these channels for the welfare of all his far-flung creation.

As regards the policies, conduct, and administration of a local universe, the Universal Father acts in the person of his Creator Son. In the interrelationships of the Sons of God, in the group associations of the personalities of origin in the Third Source and Center, or in the relationship between any other creatures, such as human beings—as concerns such associations the Universal Father never intervenes. The law of the Creator Son, the rule of the Constellation Fathers, the System Sovereigns, and the Planetary Princes—the ordained policies and procedures for that universe—always prevail. There is no division of authority; never is there a cross working of divine power and purpose. The Deities are in perfect and eternal unanimity.

The Creator Son rules supreme in all matters of ethical associations, the relations of any division of creatures to any other class of creatures or of two or more individuals within any given group; but such a plan does not mean that the Universal Father may not in his own way intervene and do aught that pleases the divine mind with any *individual creature* throughout all creation, as pertains to that individual's present status or future prospects and as concerns the Father's eternal plan and infinite purpose.

In the mortal will creatures the Father is actually present in the indwelling Adjuster, a fragment of his prepersonal spirit; and the Father is also the source of the personality of such a mortal will creature.

These Thought Adjusters, the bestowals of the Universal Father, are comparatively isolated; they indwell human minds but have no discernible connection with the ethical affairs of a local creation. They are not directly co-ordinated with the seraphic service nor with the administration of systems, constellations, or a local universe, not even with the rule of a Creator Son, whose will is the supreme law of his universe.

The indwelling Adjusters are one of God's separate but unified modes of contact with the creatures of his all but infinite creation. Thus does he who is invisible to mortal man manifest his presence, and could he do so, he would show himself to us in still other ways, but such further revelation is not divinely possible.

We can see and understand the mechanism whereby the Sons enjoy intimate and complete knowledge regarding the universes of their jurisdiction; but we cannot fully comprehend the methods whereby God is so fully and personally conversant with the details of the universe of universes, although we at least can recognize the avenue whereby the Universal Father can receive information regarding, and manifest his presence to, the beings of his immense creation. Through the personality circuit the Father is cognizant—has personal knowledge—of all the thoughts and acts of all the beings in all the systems of all the universes of all creation. Though we cannot fully grasp this technique of God's communion with his children, we can be strengthened in the assurance that the "Lord knows his children," and that of each one of us "he takes note where we were born."

In your universe and in your heart the Universal Father is present, spiritually speaking, by one of the Seven Master Spirits of central abode and, specifically, by the divine Adjuster who lives and works and waits in the depths of the mortal mind.

God is not a self-centered personality; the Father freely distributes himself to his creation and to his creatures. He lives and acts, not only in the Deities, but also in his Sons, whom he intrusts with the doing of everything that it is divinely possible for them to do. The Universal Father has truly divested himself of every function which it is possible for another being to perform. And this is just as true of mortal man as of the Creator Son who rules in God's stead at the headquarters of a local universe. Thus we behold the outworking of the ideal and infinite love of the Universal Father.

In this universal bestowal of himself we have abundant proof of both the magnitude and the magnanimity of the Father's divine nature. If God has withheld aught of himself from the universal creation, then of that residue he is in lavish generosity bestowing the Thought Adjusters upon the mortals of the realms, the Mystery Monitors of time, who so patiently indwell the mortal candidates for life everlasting.

The Universal Father has poured out himself, as it were, to make all creation rich in personality possession and potential spiritual attainment. God has given us himself that we may be like him, and he has reserved for himself of power and glory only that which is necessary for the maintenance of those things for the love of which he has thus divested himself of all things else.

5. THE ETERNAL AND DIVINE PURPOSE

There is a great and glorious purpose in the march of the universes through space. All of your mortal struggling is not in vain. We are all part of an immense plan, a gigantic enterprise, and it is the vastness of the undertaking that renders it impossible to see very much of it at any one time and during any one life. We are all a part of an eternal project which the Gods are supervising and outworking. The whole marvelous and universal mechanism moves on majestically through space to the music of the meter of the infinite thought and the eternal purpose of the First Great Source and Center.

The eternal purpose of the eternal God is a high spiritual ideal. The events of time and the struggles of material existence are but the transient scaffolding which bridges over to the other side, to the promised land of spiritual reality and supernal existence. Of course, you mortals find it difficult to grasp the idea of an eternal purpose; you are virtually unable to comprehend the thought of eternity, something never beginning and never ending. Everything familiar to you has an end.

As regards an individual life, the duration of a realm, or the chronology of any connected series of events, it would seem that we are dealing with an isolated stretch of time; everything seems to have a beginning and an end. And it would appear that a series of such experiences, lives, ages, or epochs, when successively arranged, constitutes a straightaway drive, an isolated event of time flashing momentarily across the infinite face of eternity. But when we look at all this from behind the scenes, a more comprehensive view and a more complete understanding suggest that such an explanation is inadequate, disconnected, and wholly unsuited properly to account for, and otherwise to correlate, the transactions of time with the underlying purposes and basic reactions of eternity.

To me it seems more fitting, for purposes of explanation to the mortal mind, to conceive of eternity as a cycle and the eternal purpose as an endless circle, a cycle of eternity in some way synchronized with the transient material cycles of time. As regards the sectors of time connected with, and forming a part of, the cycle of eternity, we are forced to recognize that such temporary epochs are born, live, and die just as the temporary beings of time are born, live, and die. Most human beings die because, having failed to achieve the spirit level of Adjuster fusion, the metamorphosis of death constitutes the only possible procedure whereby they may escape the fetters of time and the bonds of material creation, thereby being enabled to strike spiritual step with the progressive procession of eternity. Having survived the trial life of time and material existence, it becomes possible for you to continue on in touch with, even as a part of, eternity, swinging on forever with the worlds of space around the circle of the eternal ages.

The sectors of time are like the flashes of personality in temporal form; they appear for a season, and then they are lost to human sight, only to reappear as new actors and continuing factors in the higher life of the endless swing around the eternal circle. Eternity can hardly be conceived as a straightaway drive, in view of our belief in a delimited universe moving over a vast, elongated circle around the central dwelling place of the Universal Father.

Frankly, eternity is incomprehensible to the finite mind of time. You simply cannot grasp it; you cannot comprehend it. I do not completely visualize it, and even if I did, it would be impossible for me to convey my concept to the human mind. Nevertheless, I have done my best to portray something of our viewpoint, to tell you somewhat of our understanding of things eternal. I am endeavoring to aid you in the crystallization of your thoughts about these values which are of infinite nature and eternal import.

There is in the mind of God a plan which embraces every creature of all his vast domains, and this plan is an eternal purpose of boundless opportunity, unlimited progress, and endless life. And the infinite treasures of such a matchless career are yours for the striving!

The goal of eternity is ahead! The adventure of divinity attainment lies before you! The race for perfection is on! whosoever will may enter, and certain victory will crown the efforts of every human being who will run the race of faith and trust, depending every step of the way on the leading of the indwelling Adjuster and on the guidance of that good spirit of the Universe Son, which so freely has been poured out upon all flesh.

[Presented by a Mighty Messenger temporarily attached to the Supreme Council of Nebadon and assigned to this mission by Gabriel of Salvington.]

PAPER 33

ADMINISTRATION OF THE LOCAL UNIVERSE

WHILE the Universal Father most certainly rules over his vast creation, he functions in a local universe administration through the person of the Creator Son. The Father does not otherwise personally function in the administrative affairs of a local universe. These matters are intrusted to the Creator Son and to the local universe Mother Spirit and to their manifold children. The plans, policies, and administrative acts of the local universe are formed and executed by this Son, who, in conjunction with his Spirit associate, delegates executive power to Gabriel and jurisdictional authority to the Constellation Fathers, System Sovereigns, and Planetary Princes.

1. MICHAEL OF NEBADON

Our Creator Son is the personification of the 611,121st original concept of infinite identity of simultaneous origin in the Universal Father and the Eternal Son. The Michael of Nebadon is the "only-begotten Son" personalizing this 611,121st universal concept of divinity and infinity. His headquarters is in the threefold mansion of light on Salvington. And this dwelling is so ordered because Michael has experienced the living of all three phases of intelligent creature existence: spiritual, morontial, and material. Because of the name associated with his seventh and final bestowal on Urantia, he is sometimes spoken of as Christ Michael.

Our Creator Son is not the Eternal Son, the existential Paradise associate of the Universal Father and the Infinite Spirit. Michael of Nebadon is not a member of the Paradise Trinity. Nevertheless our Master Son possesses in his realm all of the divine attributes and powers that the Eternal Son himself would manifest were he actually to be present on Salvington and functioning in Nebadon. Michael possesses even additional power and authority, for he not only personifies the Eternal Son but also fully represents and actually embodies the personality presence of the Universal Father to and in this local universe. He even represents the Father-Son. These relationships constitute a Creator Son the most powerful, versatile, and influential of all divine beings who are capable of direct administration of evolutionary universes and of personality contact with immature creature beings.

Our Creator Son exerts the same spiritual drawing power, spirit gravity, from the headquarters of the local universe that the Eternal Son of Paradise would exert if he were personally present on Salvington, and *more;* this Universe Son is also the personification of the Universal Father to the universe of Nebadon. Creator Sons are personality centers for the spiritual forces of the Paradise

Father-Son. Creator Sons are the final power-personality focalizations of the mighty time-space attributes of God the Sevenfold.

The Creator Son is the vicegerent personalization of the Universal Father, the divinity co-ordinate of the Eternal Son, and the creative associate of the Infinite Spirit. To our universe and all its inhabited worlds the Sovereign Son is, to all practical intents and purposes, God. He personifies all of the Paradise Deities which evolving mortals can discerningly comprehend. This Son and his Spirit associate *are* your creator parents. To you, Michael, the Creator Son, is the supreme personality; to you, the Eternal Son is supersupreme—an infinite Deity personality.

In the person of the Creator Son we have a ruler and divine parent who is just as mighty, efficient, and beneficent as would be the Universal Father and the Eternal Son if both were present on Salvington and engaged in the administration of the affairs of the universe of Nebadon.

2. THE SOVEREIGN OF NEBADON

Observation of Creator Sons discloses that some resemble more the Father, some the Son, while others are a blend of both their infinite parents. Our Creator Son very definitely manifests traits and attributes which more resemble the Eternal Son.

Michael elected to organize this local universe, and herein he now reigns supreme. His personal power is limited by the pre-existent gravity circuits centering at Paradise and by the reservation on the part of the Ancients of Days of the superuniverse government of all final executive judgments regarding the extinction of personality. Personality is the sole bestowal of the Father, but the Creator Sons, with the approval of the Eternal Son, do initiate new creature designs, and with the working co-operation of their Spirit associates they may attempt new transformations of energy-matter.

Michael is the personification of the Paradise Father-Son to and in the local universe of Nebadon; therefore, when the Creative Mother Spirit, the local universe representation of the Infinite Spirit, subordinated herself to Christ Michael upon the return from his final bestowal on Urantia, the Master Son thereby acquired jurisdiction over "all power in heaven and on earth."

This subordination of the Divine Ministers to the Creator Sons of the local universes constitutes these Master Sons the personal repositories of the finitely manifestable divinity of the Father, Son, and Spirit, while the creature-bestowal experiences of the Michaels qualify them to portray the experiential divinity of the Supreme Being. No other beings in the universes have thus personally exhausted the potentials of present finite experience, and no other beings in the universes possess such qualifications for solitary sovereignty.

Although Michael's headquarters is officially located on Salvington, the capital of Nebadon, he spends much of his time visiting the constellation and system headquarters and even the individual planets. Periodically he journeys to Paradise and often to Uversa, where he counsels with the Ancients of Days. When he is away from Salvington, his place is assumed by Gabriel, who then functions as regent of the universe of Nebadon.

3. THE UNIVERSE SON AND SPIRIT

While pervading all the universes of time and space, the Infinite Spirit functions from the headquarters of each local universe as a specialized focalization acquiring full personality qualities by the technique of creative co-operation with the Creator Son. As concerns a local universe, the administrative authority of a Creator Son is supreme; the Infinite Spirit, as the Divine Minister, is wholly co-operative though perfectly co-ordinate.

The Universe Mother Spirit of Salvington, the associate of Michael in the control and administration of Nebadon, is of the sixth group of Supreme Spirits, being the 611,121st of that order. She volunteered to accompany Michael on the occasion of his liberation from Paradise obligations and has ever since functioned with him in creating and governing his universe.

The Master Creator Son is the personal sovereign of his universe, but in all the details of its management the Universe Spirit is codirector with the Son. While the Spirit ever acknowledges the Son as sovereign and ruler, the Son always accords the Spirit a co-ordinate position and equality of authority in all the affairs of the realm. In all his work of love and life bestowal the Creator Son is always and ever perfectly sustained and ably assisted by the all-wise and ever-faithful Universe Spirit and by all of her diversified retinue of angelic personalities. Such a Divine Minister is in reality the mother of spirits and spirit personalities, the ever-present and all-wise adviser of the Creator Son, a faithful and true manifestation of the Paradise Infinite Spirit.

The Son functions as a father in his local universe. The Spirit, as mortal creatures would understand, enacts the role of a mother, always assisting the Son and being everlastingly indispensable to the administration of the universe. In the face of insurrection only the Son and his associated Sons can function as deliverers. Never can the Spirit undertake to contest rebellion or defend authority, but ever does the Spirit sustain the Son in all of everything he may be required to experience in his efforts to stabilize government and uphold authority on worlds tainted with evil or dominated by sin. Only a Son can retrieve the work of their joint creation, but no Son could hope for final success without the incessant co-operation of the Divine Minister and her vast assemblage of spirit helpers, the daughters of God, who so faithfully and valiantly struggle for the welfare of mortal men and the glory of their divine parents.

Upon the completion of the Creator Son's seventh and final creature bestowal, the uncertainties of periodic isolation terminate for the Divine Minister, and the Son's universe helper becomes forever settled in surety and control. It is at the enthronement of the Creator Son as a Master Son, at the jubilee of jubilees, that the Universe Spirit, before the assembled hosts, first makes public and universal acknowledgment of subordination to the Son, pledging fidelity and obedience. This event occurred in Nebadon at the time of Michael's return to Salvington after the Urantian bestowal. Never before this momentous occasion did the Universe Spirit acknowledge subordination to the Universe Son, and not until after this voluntary relinquishment of power and authority by the Spirit could it be truthfully proclaimed of the Son that "all power in heaven and on earth has been committed to his hand."

After this pledge of subordination by the Creative Mother Spirit, Michael of Nebadon nobly acknowledged his eternal dependence on his Spirit companion, constituting the Spirit coruler of his universe domains and requiring all their creatures to pledge themselves in loyalty to the Spirit as they had to the Son; and there issued and went forth the final "Proclamation of Equality." Though he was the sovereign of this local universe, the Son published to the worlds the fact of the Spirit's equality with him in all endowments of personality and attributes of divine character. And this becomes the transcendent pattern for the family organization and government of even the lowly creatures of the worlds of space. This is, in deed and in truth, the high ideal of the family and the human institution of voluntary marriage.

The Son and the Spirit now preside over the universe much as a father and mother watch over, and minister to, their family of sons and daughters. It is not altogether out of place to refer to the Universe Spirit as the creative companion of the Creator Son and to regard the creatures of the realms as their sons and daughters—a grand and glorious family but one of untold responsibilities and endless watchcare.

The Son initiates the creation of certain of the universe children, while the Spirit is solely responsible for bringing into existence the numerous orders of spirit personalities who minister and serve under the direction and guidance of this selfsame Mother Spirit. In the creation of other types of universe personalities, both the Son and the Spirit function together, and in no creative act does the one do aught without the counsel and approval of the other.

4. GABRIEL—THE CHIEF EXECUTIVE

The Bright and Morning Star is the personalization of the first concept of identity and ideal of personality conceived by the Creator Son and the local universe manifestation of the Infinite Spirit. Going back to the early days of the local universe, before the union of the Creator Son and the Mother Spirit in the bonds of creative association, back to the times before the beginning of the creation of their versatile family of sons and daughters, the first conjoint act of this early and free association of these two divine persons results in the creation of the highest spirit personality of the Son and the Spirit, the Bright and Morning Star.

Only one such being of wisdom and majesty is brought forth in each local universe. The Universal Father and the Eternal Son can, in fact do, create an unlimited number of Sons in divinity equal to themselves; but such Sons, in union with the Daughters of the Infinite Spirit, can create only one Bright and Morning Star in each universe, a being like themselves and partaking freely of their combined natures but not of their creative prerogatives. Gabriel of Salvington is like the Universe Son in divinity of nature though considerably limited in the attributes of Deity.

This first-born of the parents of a new universe is a unique personality possessing many wonderful traits not visibly present in either ancestor, a being of unprecedented versatility and unimagined brilliance. This supernal personality embraces the divine will of the Son combined with the creative imagination of the Spirit. The thoughts and acts of the Bright and Morning Star will ever be fully representative of both the Creator Son and the Creative Spirit. Such a being is also capable of a broad understanding of, and sympathetic contact with, both the spiritual seraphic hosts and the material evolutionary will creatures.

The Bright and Morning Star is not a creator, but he is a marvelous administrator, being the personal administrative representative of the Creator Son. Aside from creation and life impartation the Son and the Spirit never confer upon important universe procedures without Gabriel's presence.

Gabriel of Salvington is the chief executive of the universe of Nebadon and the arbiter of all executive appeals respecting its administration. This universe executive was created fully endowed for his work, but he has gained experience with the growth and evolution of our local creation.

Gabriel is the chief officer of execution for superuniverse mandates relating to nonpersonal affairs in the local universe. Most matters pertaining to mass judgment and dispensational resurrections, adjudicated by the Ancients of Days, are also delegated to Gabriel and his staff for execution. Gabriel is thus the combined chief executive of both the super- and the local universe rulers. He has at his command an able corps of administrative assistants, created for their special work, who are unrevealed to evolutionary mortals. In addition to these assistants, Gabriel may employ any and all of the orders of celestial beings functioning in Nebadon, and he is also the commander in chief of "the armies of heaven"—the celestial hosts.

Gabriel and his staff are not teachers; they are administrators. They were never known to depart from their regular work except when Michael was incarnated on a creature bestowal. During such bestowals Gabriel was ever attendant on the will of the incarnated Son, and with the collaboration of the Union of Days, he became the actual director of universe affairs during the later bestowals. Gabriel has been closely identified with the history and development of Urantia ever since the mortal bestowal of Michael.

Aside from meeting Gabriel on the bestowal worlds and at the times of general- and special-resurrection roll calls, mortals will seldom encounter him as they ascend through the local universe until they are inducted into the administrative work of the local creation. As administrators, of whatever order or degree, you will come under the direction of Gabriel.

5. THE TRINITY AMBASSADORS

The administration of Trinity-origin personalities ends with the government of the superuniverses. The local universes are characterized by dual supervision, the beginning of the father-mother concept. The universe father is the Creator Son; the universe mother is the Divine Minister, the local universe Creative Spirit. Every local universe is, however, blessed with the presence of certain personalities from the central universe and Paradise. At the head of this Paradise group in Nebadon is the ambassador of the Paradise Trinity—Immanuel of Salvington—the Union of Days assigned to the local universe of Nebadon. In a certain sense this high Trinity Son is also the personal representative of the Universal Father to the court of the Creator Son; hence his name, Immanuel.

Immanuel of Salvington, number 611,121 of the sixth order of Supreme Trinity Personalities, is a being of sublime dignity and of such superb condescension that he refuses the worship and adoration of all living creatures. He bears the distinction of being the only personality in all Nebadon who has never acknowledged subordination to his brother Michael. He functions as adviser to the Sovereign Son but gives counsel only on request. In the absence of the Creator Son he might preside over any high universe council but would not otherwise participate in the executive affairs of the universe except as requested.

This ambassador of Paradise to Nebadon is not subject to the jurisdiction of the local universe government. Neither does he exercise authoritative jurisdiction in the executive affairs of an evolving local universe except in the supervision of his liaison brethren, the Faithfuls of Days, serving on the headquarters of the constellations.

The Faithfuls of Days, like the Union of Days, never proffer advice or offer assistance to the constellation rulers unless it is asked for. These Paradise ambassadors to the constellations represent the final personal presence of the Stationary Sons of the Trinity functioning in advisory roles in the local universes. Constellations are more closely related to the superuniverse administration than local systems, which are administered exclusively by personalities native to the local universe.

6. GENERAL ADMINISTRATION

Gabriel is the chief executive and actual administrator of Nebadon. Michael's absence from Salvington in no way interferes with the orderly conduct of universe affairs. During the absence of Michael, as recently on the mission of reunion of Orvonton Master Sons on Paradise, Gabriel is the regent of the universe. At such times Gabriel always seeks the counsel of Immanuel of Salvington regarding all major problems.

The Father Melchizedek is Gabriel's first assistant. When the Bright and Morning Star is absent from Salvington, his responsibilities are assumed by this original Melchizedek Son.

The various subadministrations of the universe have assigned to them certain special domains of responsibility. While, in general, a system government looks after the welfare of its planets, it is more particularly concerned with the physical status of living beings, with biologic problems. In turn, the constellation rulers pay especial attention to the social and governmental conditions prevailing on the different planets and systems. A constellation government is chiefly exercised over unification and stabilization. Still higher up, the universe rulers are more occupied with the spiritual status of the realms.

Ambassadors are appointed by judicial decree and represent universes to other universes. Consuls are representatives of constellations to one another and to the universe headquarters; they are appointed by legislative decree and function only within the confines of the local universe. Observers are commissioned by executive decree of a System Sovereign to represent that system to other systems and at the constellation capital, and they, too, function only within the confines of the local universe.

From Salvington, broadcasts are simultaneously directed to the constellation headquarters, the system headquarters, and to individual planets. All higher orders of celestial beings are able to utilize this service for communication with their fellows scattered throughout the universe. The universe broadcast is extended to all inhabited worlds regardless of their spiritual status.

Planetary intercommunication is denied only those worlds under spiritual quarantine.

Constellation broadcasts are periodically sent out from the headquarters of the constellation by the chief of the Constellation Fathers.

Chronology is reckoned, computed, and rectified by a special group of beings on Salvington. The standard day of Nebadon is equal to eighteen days and six hours of Urantia time, plus two and one-half minutes. The Nebadon year consists of a segment of the time of universe swing in relation to the Uversa circuit and is equal to one hundred days of standard universe time, about five years of Urantia time.

Nebadon time, broadcast from Salvington, is the standard for all constellations and systems in this local universe. Each constellation conducts its affairs by Nebadon time, but the systems maintain their own chronology, as do the individual planets.

The day in Satania, as reckoned on Jerusem, is a little less (1 hour, 4 minutes, 15 seconds) than three days of Urantia time. These times are generally known as Salvington or universe time, and Satania or system time. Standard time is universe time.

7. THE COURTS OF NEBADON

The Master Son, Michael, is supremely concerned with but three things: creation, sustenance, and ministry. He does not personally participate in the judicial work of the universe. Creators never sit in judgment on their creatures; that is the exclusive function of creatures of high training and actual creature experience.

The entire judicial mechanism of Nebadon is under the supervision of Gabriel. The high courts, located on Salvington, are occupied with problems of general universe import and with the appellate cases coming up from the system tribunals. There are seventy branches of these universe courts, and they function in seven divisions of ten sections each. In all matters of adjudication there presides a dual magistracy consisting of one judge of perfection antecedents and one magistrate of ascendant experience.

As regards jurisdiction, the local universe courts are limited in the following matters:

1. The administration of the local universe is concerned with creation, evolution, maintenance, and ministry. The universe tribunals are, therefore, denied the right to pass upon those cases involving the question of eternal life and death. This has no reference to natural death as it obtains on Urantia, but if the question of the right of continued existence, life eternal, comes up for adjudication, it must be referred to the tribunals of Orvonton, and if decided adversely to the individual, all sentences of extinction are carried out upon the orders, and through the agencies, of the rulers of the supergovernment.

2. The default or defection of any of the Local Universe Sons of God which jeopardizes their status and authority as Sons is never adjudicated in the tribunals of a Son; such a misunderstanding would be immediately carried to the superuniverse courts.

3. The question of the readmission of any constituent part of a local universe—such as a local system—to the fellowship of full spiritual status in the

local creation subsequent to spiritual isolation must be concurred in by the high assembly of the superuniverse.

In all other matters the courts of Salvington are final and supreme. There is no appeal and no escape from their decisions and decrees.

However unfairly human contentions may sometimes appear to be adjudicated on Urantia, in the universe justice and divine equity do prevail. You are living in a well-ordered universe, and sooner or later you may depend upon being dealt with justly, even mercifully.

8. THE LEGISLATIVE AND EXECUTIVE FUNCTIONS

On Salvington, the headquarters of Nebadon, there are no true legislative bodies. The universe headquarters worlds are concerned largely with adjudication. The legislative assemblies of the local universe are located on the headquarters of the one hundred constellations. The systems are chiefly concerned with the executive and administrative work of the local creations. The System Sovereigns and their associates enforce the legislative mandates of the constellation rulers and execute the judicial decrees of the high courts of the universe.

While true legislation is not enacted at the universe headquarters, there do function on Salvington a variety of advisory and research assemblies, variously constituted and conducted in accordance with their scope and purpose. Some are permanent; others disband upon the accomplishment of their objective.

The supreme council of the local universe is made up of three members from each system and seven representatives from each constellation. Systems in isolation do not have representation in this assembly, but they are permitted to send observers who attend and study all its deliberations.

The one hundred councils of supreme sanction are also situated on Salvington. The presidents of these councils constitute the immediate working cabinet of Gabriel.

All findings of the high universe advisory councils are referred either to the Salvington judicial bodies or to the legislative assemblies of the constellations. These high councils are without authority or power to enforce their recommendations. If their advice is founded on the fundamental laws of the universe, then will the Nebadon courts issue rulings of execution; but if their recommendations have to do with local or emergency conditions, they must pass down to the legislative assemblies of the constellation for deliberative enactment and then to the system authorities for execution. These high councils are, in reality, the universe superlegislatures, but they function without the authority of enactment and without the power of execution.

While we speak of universe administration in terms of "courts" and "assemblies," it should be understood that these spiritual transactions are very different from the more primitive and material activities of Urantia which bear corresponding names.

[Presented by the Chief of the Archangels of Nebadon.]

PAPER 34

THE LOCAL UNIVERSE MOTHER SPIRIT

WHEN a Creator Son is personalized by the Universal Father and the Eternal Son, then does the Infinite Spirit individualize a new and unique representation of himself to accompany this Creator Son to the realms of space, there to be his companion, first, in physical organization and, later, in creation and ministry to the creatures of the newly projected universe.

A Creative Spirit reacts to both physical and spiritual realities; so does a Creator Son; and thus are they co-ordinate and associate in the administration of a local universe of time and space.

These Daughter Spirits are of the essence of the Infinite Spirit, but they cannot function in the work of physical creation and spiritual ministry simultaneously. In physical creation the Universe Son provides the pattern while the Universe Spirit initiates the materialization of physical realities. The Son operates in the power designs, but the Spirit transforms these energy creations into physical substances. Although it is somewhat difficult to portray this early universe presence of the Infinite Spirit as a person, nevertheless, to the Creator Son the Spirit associate is personal and has always functioned as a distinct individual.

1. PERSONALIZATION OF THE CREATIVE SPIRIT

After the completion of the physical organization of a starry and planetary cluster and the establishment of the energy circuits by the superuniverse power centers, subsequent to this preliminary work of creation by the agencies of the Infinite Spirit, operating through, and under the direction of, his local universe creative focalization, there goes forth the proclamation of the Michael Son that life is next to be projected in the newly organized universe. Upon the Paradise recognition of this declaration of intention, there occurs a reaction of approval in the Paradise Trinity, followed by the disappearance in the spiritual shining of the Deities of the Master Spirit in whose superuniverse this new creation is organizing. Meanwhile the other Master Spirits draw near this central lodgment of the Paradise Deities, and subsequently, when the Deity-embraced Master Spirit emerges to the recognition of his fellows, there occurs what is known as a "primary eruption." This is a tremendous spiritual flash, a phenomenon clearly discernible as far away as the headquarters of the superuniverse concerned; and simultaneously with this little-understood Trinity manifestation there occurs a marked change in the nature of the creative spirit presence and power of the Infinite Spirit resident in the local universe concerned. In response to these Paradise phenomena there immediately personalizes, in the very presence of the Creator Son, a new personal representation of the Infinite Spirit. This is the

Divine Minister. The individualized Creative Spirit helper of the Creator Son has become his personal creative associate, the local universe Mother Spirit.

From and through this new personal segregation of the Conjoint Creator there proceed the established currents and the ordained circuits of spirit power and spiritual influence destined to pervade all the worlds and beings of that local universe. In reality, this new and personal presence is but a transformation of the pre-existent and less personal associate of the Son in his earlier work of physical universe organization.

This is the relation of a stupendous drama in few words, but it represents about all that can be told regarding these momentous transactions. They are instantaneous, inscrutable, and incomprehensible; the secret of the technique and procedure resides in the bosom of the Paradise Trinity. Of only one thing are we certain: The Spirit presence in the local universe during the time of purely physical creation or organization was incompletely differentiated from the spirit of the Paradise Infinite Spirit; whereas, after the reappearance of the supervising Master Spirit from the secret embrace of the Gods and following the flash of spiritual energy, the local universe manifestation of the Infinite Spirit suddenly and completely changes to the personal likeness of that Master Spirit who was in transmuting liaison with the Infinite Spirit. The local universe Mother Spirit thus acquires a personal nature tinged by that of the Master Spirit of the superuniverse of astronomic jurisdiction.

This personalized presence of the Infinite Spirit, the Creative Mother Spirit of the local universe, is known in Satania as the Divine Minister. To all practical intents and spiritual purposes this manifestation of Deity is a divine individual, a spirit person. And she is so recognized and regarded by the Creator Son. It is through this localization and personalization of the Third Source and Center in our local universe that the Spirit could subsequently become so fully subject to the Creator Son that of this Son it was truly said, "All power in heaven and on earth has been intrusted to him."

2. NATURE OF THE DIVINE MINISTER

Having undergone marked personality metamorphosis at the time of life creation, the Divine Minister thereafter functions as a person and co-operates in a very personal manner with the Creator Son in the planning and management of the extensive affairs of their local creation. To many universe types of being, even this representation of the Infinite Spirit may not appear to be wholly personal during the ages preceding the final Michael bestowal; but subsequent to the elevation of the Creator Son to the sovereign authority of a Master Son, the Creative Mother Spirit becomes so augmented in personal qualities as to be personally recognized by all contacting individuals.

From the earliest association with the Creator Son the Universe Spirit possesses all the physical-control attributes of the Infinite Spirit, including the full endowment of antigravity. Upon the attainment of personal status the Universe Spirit exerts just as full and complete control of mind gravity, in the local universe, as would the Infinite Spirit if personally present.

In each local universe the Divine Minister functions in accordance with the nature and inherent characteristics of the Infinite Spirit as embodied in one of the Seven Master Spirits of Paradise. While there is a basic uniformity of character in all Universe Spirits, there is also a diversity of function, determined by their origin through one of the Seven Master Spirits. This differential of origin accounts for the diverse techniques in the function of the local universe Mother Spirits in different superuniverses. But in all essential spiritual attributes these Spirits are identical, equally spiritual and wholly divine, irrespective of superuniverse differentiation.

The Creative Spirit is coresponsible with the Creator Son in producing the creatures of the worlds and never fails the Son in all efforts to uphold and conserve these creations. Life is ministered and maintained through the agency of the Creative Spirit. "You send forth your Spirit, and they are created. You renew the face of the earth."

In the creation of a universe of intelligent creatures the Creative Mother Spirit functions first in the sphere of universe perfection, collaborating with the Son in the production of the Bright and Morning Star. Subsequently the offspring of the Spirit increasingly approach the order of created beings on the planets, even as the Sons grade downward from the Melchizedeks to the Material Sons, who actually contact with the mortals of the realms. In the later evolution of mortal creatures the Life Carrier Sons provide the physical body, fabricated out of the existing organized material of the realm, while the Universe Spirit contributes the "breath of life."

While the seventh segment of the grand universe may, in many respects, be tardy in development, thoughtful students of our problems look forward to the evolution of an extraordinarily well-balanced creation in the ages to come. We predict this high degree of symmetry in Orvonton because the presiding Spirit of this superuniverse is the chief of the Master Spirits on high, being a spirit intelligence embodying the balanced union and perfect co-ordination of the traits and character of all three of the eternal Deities. We are tardy and backward in comparison with other sectors, but there undoubtedly awaits us a transcendent development and an unprecedented achievement sometime in the eternal ages of the future.

3. THE SON AND SPIRIT IN TIME AND SPACE

Neither the Eternal Son nor the Infinite Spirit is limited or conditioned by either time or space, but most of their offspring are.

The Infinite Spirit pervades all space and indwells the circle of eternity. Still, in their personal contact with the children of time, the personalities of the Infinite Spirit must often reckon with temporal elements, though not so much with space. Many mind ministries ignore space but suffer a time lag in effecting co-ordination of diverse levels of universe reality. A Solitary Messenger is virtually independent of space except that time is actually required in traveling from one location to another; and there are similar entities unknown to you.

In personal prerogatives a Creative Spirit is wholly and entirely independent of space, but not of time. There is no specialized personal presence of such a Universe Spirit on either the constellation or system headquarters. She is equally and diffusely present throughout her entire local universe and is, therefore, just as literally and personally present on one world as on any other.

Only as regards the element of time is a Creative Spirit ever limited in her universe ministrations. A Creator Son acts instantaneously throughout his universe; but the Creative Spirit must reckon with time in the ministration of the universal mind except as she consciously and designedly avails herself of the personal prerogatives of the Universe Son. In pure-spirit function the Creative Spirit also acts independently of time as well as in her collaboration with the mysterious function of universe reflectivity.

Though the spirit-gravity circuit of the Eternal Son operates independently of both time and space, all functions of the Creator Sons are not exempt from space limitations. If the transactions of the evolutionary worlds are excepted, these Michael Sons seem to be able to operate relatively independent of time. A Creator Son is not handicapped by time, but he is conditioned by space; he cannot personally be in two places at the same time. Michael of Nebadon acts timelessly within his own universe and by reflectivity practically so in the superuniverse. He communicates timelessly with the Eternal Son directly.

The Divine Minister is the understanding helper of the Creator Son, enabling him to overcome and atone for his inherent limitations regarding space, for when these two function in administrative union, they are practically independent of time *and* space within the confines of their local creation. Therefore, as practically observed throughout a local universe, the Creator Son and the Creative Spirit usually function independently of both time and space since there is always available to each the time and the space liberation of the other.

Only absolute beings are independent of time and space in the absolute sense. The majority of the subordinate persons of both the Eternal Son and the Infinite Spirit are subject to both time and space.

When a Creative Spirit becomes "space conscious," she is preparing to recognize a circumscribed "space domain" as hers, a realm in which to be space free in contradistinction to all other space by which she would be conditioned. One is free to choose and act only within the realm of one's consciousness.

4. THE LOCAL UNIVERSE CIRCUITS

There are three distinct spirit circuits in the local universe of Nebadon:

1. The bestowal spirit of the Creator Son, the Comforter, the Spirit of Truth.
2. The spirit circuit of the Divine Minister, the Holy Spirit.
3. The intelligence-ministry circuit, including the more or less unified activities but diverse functioning of the seven adjutant mind-spirits.

The Creator Sons are endowed with a spirit of universe presence in many ways analogous to that of the Seven Master Spirits of Paradise. This is the Spirit of Truth which is poured out upon a world by a bestowal Son after he receives spiritual title to such a sphere. This bestowed Comforter is the spiritual force which ever draws all truth seekers towards Him who is the personification of truth in the local universe. This spirit is an inherent endowment of the Creator Son, emerging from his divine nature just as the master circuits of the grand universe are derived from the personality presences of the Paradise Deities.

The Creator Son may come and go; his personal presence may be in the local universe or elsewhere; yet the Spirit of Truth functions undisturbed, for this divine presence, while derived from the personality of the Creator Son, is functionally centered in the person of the Divine Minister.

The Universe Mother Spirit, however, never leaves the local universe headquarters world. The spirit of the Creator Son may and does function independently of the personal presence of the Son, but not so with her personal spirit. The Holy Spirit of the Divine Minister would become nonfunctional if her personal presence should be removed from Salvington. Her spirit presence seems to be fixed on the universe headquarters world, and it is this very fact that enables the spirit of the Creator Son to function independently of the whereabouts of the Son. The Universe Mother Spirit acts as the universe focus and center of the Spirit of Truth as well as of her own personal influence, the Holy Spirit.

The Creator Father-Son and the Creative Mother Spirit both contribute variously to the mind endowment of their local universe children. But the Creative Spirit does not bestow mind until she is endowed with personal prerogatives.

The superevolutionary orders of personality in a local universe are endowed with the local universe type of the superuniverse pattern of mind. The human and the subhuman orders of evolutionary life are endowed with the adjutant spirit types of mind ministration.

The seven adjutant mind-spirits are the creation of the Divine Minister of a local universe. These mind-spirits are similar in character but diverse in power, and all partake alike of the nature of the Universe Spirit, although they are hardly regarded as personalities apart from their Mother Creator. The seven adjutants have been given the following names: the spirit of *wisdom,* the spirit of *worship,* the spirit of *counsel,* the spirit of *knowledge,* the spirit of *courage,* the spirit of *understanding,* the spirit of *intuition*—of quick perception.

These are the "seven spirits of God," "like lamps burning before the throne," which the prophet saw in the symbols of vision. But he did not see the seats of the four and twenty sentinels about these seven adjutant mind-spirits. This record represents the confusion of two presentations, one pertaining to the universe headquarters and the other to the system capital. The seats of the four and twenty elders are on Jerusem, the headquarters of your local system of inhabited worlds.

But it was of Salvington that John wrote: "And out of the throne proceeded lightnings and thunderings and voices"—the universe broadcasts to the local systems. He also envisaged the directional control creatures of the local universe, the living compasses of the headquarters world. This directional control in Nebadon is maintained by the four control creatures of Salvington, who operate over the universe currents and are ably assisted by the first functioning mind-spirit, the adjutant of intuition, the spirit of "quick understanding." But the description of these four creatures—called beasts—has been sadly marred; they are of unparalleled beauty and exquisite form.

The four points of the compass are universal and inherent in the life of Nebadon. All living creatures possess bodily units which are sensitive and responsive to these directional currents. These creature creations are duplicated on down through the universe to the individual planets and, in conjunction with the magnetic forces of the worlds, so activate the hosts of microscopic bodies in the animal organism that these direction cells ever point north and south. Thus is the sense of orientation forever fixed in the living beings of the universe. This sense is not wholly wanting as a conscious possession by mankind. These bodies were first observed on Urantia about the time of this narration.

5. THE MINISTRY OF THE SPIRIT

The Divine Minister co-operates with the Creator Son in the formulation of life and the creation of new orders of beings up to the time of his seventh bestowal and, subsequently, after his elevation to the full sovereignty of the universe, continues to collaborate with the Son and the Son's bestowed spirit in the further work of world ministry and planetary progression.

On the inhabited worlds the Spirit begins the work of evolutionary progression, starting with the lifeless material of the realm, first endowing vegetable life, then the animal organisms, then the first orders of human existence; and each succeeding impartation contributes to the further unfolding of the evolutionary potential of planetary life from the initial and primitive stages to the appearance of will creatures. This labor of the Spirit is largely effected through the seven adjutants, the spirits of promise, the unifying and co-ordinating spirit-mind of the evolving planets, ever and unitedly leading the races of men towards higher ideas and spiritual ideals.

Mortal man first experiences the ministry of the Spirit in conjunction with mind when the purely animal mind of evolutionary creatures develops reception capacity for the adjutants of worship and of wisdom. This ministry of the sixth and seventh adjutants indicates mind evolution crossing the threshold of spiritual ministry. And immediately are such minds of worship- and wisdom-function included in the spiritual circuits of the Divine Minister.

When mind is thus endowed with the ministry of the Holy Spirit, it possesses the capacity for (consciously or unconsciously) choosing the spiritual presence of the Universal Father—the Thought Adjuster. But it is not until a bestowal Son has liberated the Spirit of Truth for planetary ministry to all mortals that all normal minds are automatically prepared for the reception of the Thought Adjusters. The Spirit of Truth works as one with the presence of the spirit of the Divine Minister. This dual spirit liaison hovers over the worlds, seeking to teach truth and to spiritually enlighten the minds of men, to inspire the souls of the creatures of the ascending races, and to lead the peoples dwelling on the evolutionary planets ever towards their Paradise goal of divine destiny.

Though the Spirit of Truth is poured out upon all flesh, this spirit of the Son is almost wholly limited in function and power by man's personal reception of that which constitutes the sum and substance of the mission of the bestowal Son. The Holy Spirit is partly independent of human attitude and partially conditioned by the decisions and co-operation of the will of man. Nevertheless, the ministry of the Holy Spirit becomes increasingly effective in the sanctification and spiritualization of the inner life of those mortals who the more fully *obey* the divine leadings.

As individuals you do not personally possess a segregated portion or entity of the spirit of the Creator Father-Son or the Creative Mother Spirit; these ministries do not contact with, nor indwell, the thinking centers of the individual's mind as do the Mystery Monitors. Thought Adjusters are definite individualizations of the prepersonal reality of the Universal Father, actually indwelling the mortal mind as a very part of that mind, and they ever work in perfect harmony with the combined spirits of the Creator Son and Creative Spirit.

The presence of the Holy Spirit of the Universe Daughter of the Infinite Spirit, of the Spirit of Truth of the Universe Son of the Eternal Son, and of the Adjuster-spirit of the Paradise Father in or with an evolutionary mortal, denotes symmetry of spiritual endowment and ministry and qualifies such a mortal consciously to realize the faith-fact of sonship with God.

6. THE SPIRIT IN MAN

With the advancing evolution of an inhabited planet and the further spiritualization of its inhabitants, additional spiritual influences may be received by such mature personalities. As mortals progress in mind control and spirit perception, these multiple spirit ministries become more and more co-ordinate in function; they become increasingly blended with the overministry of the Paradise Trinity.

Although Divinity may be plural in manifestation, in human experience Deity is singular, always *one.* Neither is spiritual ministry plural in human experience. Regardless of plurality of origin, all spirit influences are one in function. Indeed they are one, being the spirit ministry of God the Sevenfold in and to the creatures of the grand universe; and as creatures grow in appreciation of, and receptivity for, this unifying ministry of the spirit, it becomes in their experience the ministry of God the Supreme.

From the heights of eternal glory the divine Spirit descends, by a long series of steps, to meet you as you are and where you are and then, in the partnership of faith, lovingly to embrace the soul of mortal origin and to embark on the sure and certain retracement of those steps of condescension, never stopping until the evolutionary soul is safely exalted to the very heights of bliss from which the divine Spirit originally sallied forth on this mission of mercy and ministry.

Spiritual forces unerringly seek and attain their own original levels. Having gone out from the Eternal, they are certain to return thereto, bringing with them all those children of time and space who have espoused the leading and teaching of the indwelling Adjuster, those who have been truly "born of the Spirit," the faith sons of God.

The divine Spirit is the source of continual ministry and encouragement to the children of men. Your power and achievement is "according to his mercy, through the renewing of the Spirit." Spiritual life, like physical energy, is consumed. Spiritual effort results in relative spiritual exhaustion. The whole ascendant experience is real as well as spiritual; therefore, it is truly written, "It is the Spirit that quickens." "The Spirit gives life."

The dead theory of even the highest religious doctrines is powerless to transform human character or to control mortal behavior. What the world of today needs is the truth which your teacher of old declared: "Not in word only but also in power and in the Holy Spirit." The seed of theoretical truth is dead, the highest moral concepts without effect, unless and until the divine Spirit breathes upon the forms of truth and quickens the formulas of righteousness.

Those who have received and recognized the indwelling of God have been born of the Spirit. "You are the temple of God, and the spirit of God dwells in you." It is not enough that this spirit be poured out upon you; the divine Spirit must dominate and control every phase of human experience.

It is the presence of the divine Spirit, the water of life, that prevents the consuming thirst of mortal discontent and that indescribable hunger of the unspiritualized human mind. Spirit-motivated beings "never thirst, for this spiritual water shall be in them a well of satisfaction springing up into life everlasting." Such divinely watered souls are all but independent of material environment as regards the joys of living and the satisfactions of earthly existence. They are spiritually illuminated and refreshed, morally strengthened and endowed.

In every mortal there exists a dual nature: the inheritance of animal tendencies and the high urge of spirit endowment. During the short life you live on Urantia, these two diverse and opposing urges can seldom be fully reconciled; they can hardly be harmonized and unified; but throughout your lifetime the combined Spirit ever ministers to assist you in subjecting the flesh more and more to the leading of the Spirit. Even though you must live your material life through, even though you cannot escape the body and its necessities, nonetheless, in purpose and ideals you are empowered increasingly to subject the animal nature to the mastery of the Spirit. There truly exists within you a conspiracy of spiritual forces, a confederation of divine powers, whose exclusive purpose is to effect your final deliverance from material bondage and finite handicaps.

The purpose of all this ministration is, "That you may be strengthened with power through His spirit in the inner man." And all this represents but the preliminary steps to the final attainment of the perfection of faith and service, that experience wherein you shall be "filled with all the fullness of God," "for all those who are led by the spirit of God are the sons of God."

The Spirit never *drives,* only leads. If you are a willing learner, if you want to attain spirit levels and reach divine heights, if you sincerely desire to reach the eternal goal, then the divine Spirit will gently and lovingly lead you along the pathway of sonship and spiritual progress. Every step you take must be one of willingness, intelligent and cheerful co-operation. The domination of the Spirit is never tainted with coercion nor compromised by compulsion.

And when such a life of spirit guidance is freely and intelligently accepted, there gradually develops within the human mind a positive consciousness of divine contact and assurance of spirit communion; sooner or later "the Spirit bears witness with your spirit (the Adjuster) that you are a child of God." Already has your own Thought Adjuster told you of your kinship to God so that the record testifies that the Spirit bears witness *"with* your spirit," not *to* your spirit.

The consciousness of the spirit domination of a human life is presently attended by an increasing exhibition of the characteristics of the Spirit in the life reactions of such a spirit-led mortal, "for the fruits of the spirit are love, joy, peace, long-suffering, gentleness, goodness, faith, meekness, and temperance." Such spirit-guided and divinely illuminated mortals, while they yet tread the lowly paths of toil and in human faithfulness perform the duties of their earthly assignments, have already begun to discern the lights of eternal life as they glimmer on the faraway shores of another world; already have they begun to comprehend the reality of that inspiring and comforting truth, "The kingdom of God is not meat and drink but righteousness, peace, and joy in the Holy Spirit." And throughout every trial and in the presence of every hardship, spirit-born souls are sustained by that hope which transcends all fear because the love of God is shed abroad in all hearts by the presence of the divine Spirit.

7. THE SPIRIT AND THE FLESH

The flesh, the inherent nature derived from the animal-origin races, does not naturally bear the fruits of the divine Spirit. When the mortal nature has been upstepped by the addition of the nature of the Material Sons of God, as the Urantia races were in a measure advanced by the bestowal of Adam, then is the way better prepared for the Spirit of Truth to co-operate with the indwelling Adjuster to bring forth the beautiful harvest of the character fruits of the spirit. If you do not reject this spirit, even though eternity may be required to fulfill the commission, "he will guide you into all truth."

Evolutionary mortals inhabiting normal worlds of spiritual progress do not experience the acute conflicts between the spirit and the flesh which characterize the present-day Urantia races. But even on the most ideal planets, pre-Adamic man must put forth positive efforts to ascend from the purely animalistic plane of existence up through successive levels of increasingly intellectual meanings and higher spiritual values.

The mortals of a normal world do not experience constant warfare between their physical and spiritual natures. They are confronted with the necessity of climbing up from the animal levels of existence to the higher planes of spiritual living, but this ascent is more like undergoing an educational training when compared with the intense conflicts of Urantia mortals in this realm of the divergent material and spiritual natures.

The Urantia peoples are suffering the consequences of a double deprivation of help in this task of progressive planetary spiritual attainment. The Caligastia upheaval precipitated world-wide confusion and robbed all subsequent generations of the moral assistance which a well-ordered society would have provided. But even more disastrous was the Adamic default in that it deprived the races of that superior type of physical nature which would have been more consonant with spiritual aspirations.

Urantia mortals are compelled to undergo such marked struggling between the spirit and the flesh because their remote ancestors were not more fully Adamized by the Edenic bestowal. It was the divine plan that the mortal races of Urantia should have had physical natures more naturally spirit responsive.

Notwithstanding this double disaster to man's nature and his environment, present-day mortals would experience less of this apparent warfare between the flesh and the spirit if they would enter the spirit kingdom, wherein the faith sons of God enjoy comparative deliverance from the slave-bondage of the flesh in the enlightened and liberating service of wholehearted devotion to doing the will of the Father in heaven. Jesus showed mankind the new way of mortal living whereby human beings may very largely escape the dire consequences of the Caligastic rebellion and most effectively compensate for the deprivations resulting from the Adamic default. "The spirit of the life of Christ Jesus has made us free from the law of animal living and the temptations of evil and sin." "This is the victory that overcomes the flesh, even your faith."

Those God-knowing men and women who have been born of the Spirit experience no more conflict with their mortal natures than do the inhabitants of the most normal of worlds, planets which have never been tainted with sin nor touched by rebellion. Faith sons work on intellectual levels and live on spiritual planes far above the conflicts produced by unrestrained or unnatural physical desires. The normal urges of animal beings and the natural appetites and impulses of the physical nature are not in conflict with even the highest spiritual attainment except in the minds of ignorant, mistaught, or unfortunately overconscientious persons.

Having started out on the way of life everlasting, having accepted the assignment and received your orders to advance, do not fear the dangers of human forgetfulness and mortal inconstancy, do not be troubled with doubts of failure or by perplexing confusion, do not falter and question your status and standing, for in every dark hour, at every crossroad in the forward struggle, the Spirit of Truth will always speak, saying, "This is the way."

[Presented by a Mighty Messenger temporarily assigned to service on Urantia.]

PAPER 35

THE LOCAL UNIVERSE SONS OF GOD

THE Sons of God previously introduced have had a Paradise origin. They are the offspring of the divine Rulers of the universal domains. Of the first Paradise order of sonship, the Creator Sons, there is in Nebadon only one, Michael, the universe father and sovereign. Of the second order of Paradise sonship, the Avonal or Magisterial Sons, Nebadon has its full quota—1,062. And these "lesser Christs" are just as effective and all-powerful in their planetary bestowals as was the Creator and Master Son on Urantia. The third order, being of Trinity origin, do not register in a local universe, but I estimate there are in Nebadon between fifteen and twenty thousand Trinity Teacher Sons exclusive of 9,642 creature-trinitized assistants of record. These Paradise Daynals are neither magistrates nor administrators; they are superteachers.

The types of Sons about to be considered are of local universe origin; they are the offspring of a Paradise Creator Son in varied association with the complemental Universe Mother Spirit. The following orders of local universe sonship find mention in these narratives:

1. Melchizedek Sons.
2. Vorondadek Sons.
3. Lanonandek Sons.
4. Life Carrier Sons.

Triune Paradise Deity functions for the creation of three orders of sonship: the Michaels, the Avonals, and the Daynals. Dual Deity in the local universe, the Son and the Spirit, also functions in the creation of three high orders of Sons: the Melchizedeks, the Vorondadeks, and the Lanonandeks; and having achieved this threefold expression, they collaborate with the next level of God the Sevenfold in the production of the versatile order of Life Carriers. These beings are classified with the descending Sons of God, but they are a unique and original form of universe life. Their consideration will occupy the whole of the next paper.

1. THE FATHER MELCHIZEDEK

After bringing into existence the beings of personal aid, such as the Bright and Morning Star and other administrative personalities, in accordance with the divine purpose and creative plans of a given universe, there occurs a new form of creative union between the Creator Son and the Creative Spirit, the local universe Daughter of the Infinite Spirit. The personality offspring resulting from this creative partnership is the original Melchizedek—the Father

Melchizedek—that unique being who subsequently collaborates with the Creator Son and the Creative Spirit to bring into existence the entire group of that name.

In the universe of Nebadon the Father Melchizedek acts as the first executive associate of the Bright and Morning Star. Gabriel is occupied more with universe policies, Melchizedek with practical procedures. Gabriel presides over the regularly constituted tribunals and councils of Nebadon, Melchizedek over the special, extraordinary, and emergency commissions and advisory bodies. Gabriel and the Father Melchizedek are never away from Salvington at the same time, for in Gabriel's absence the Father Melchizedek functions as the chief executive of Nebadon.

The Melchizedeks of our universe were all created within one millennial period of standard time by the Creator Son and the Creative Spirit in liaison with the Father Melchizedek. Being an order of sonship wherein one of their own number functioned as co-ordinate creator, Melchizedeks are in constitution partly of self-origin and therefore candidates for the realization of a supernal type of self-government. They periodically elect their own administrative chief for a term of seven years of standard time and otherwise function as a self-regulating order, though the original Melchizedek does exercise certain inherent coparental prerogatives. From time to time this Father Melchizedek designates certain individuals of his order to function as special Life Carriers to the midsonite worlds, a type of inhabited planet not heretofore revealed on Urantia.

The Melchizedeks do not function extensively outside the local universe except when they are called as witnesses in matters pending before the tribunals of the superuniverse, and when designated special ambassadors, as they sometimes are, representing one universe to another in the same superuniverse. The original or first-born Melchizedek of each universe is always at liberty to journey to the neighboring universes or to Paradise on missions having to do with the interests and duties of his order.

2. THE MELCHIZEDEK SONS

The Melchizedeks are the first order of divine Sons to approach sufficiently near the lower creature life to be able to function directly in the ministry of mortal uplift, to serve the evolutionary races without the necessity of incarnation. These Sons are naturally at the mid-point of the great personality descent, by origin being just about midway between the highest Divinity and the lowest creature life of will endowment. They thus become the natural intermediaries between the higher and divine levels of living existence and the lower, even the material, forms of life on the evolutionary worlds. The seraphic orders, the angels, delight to work with the Melchizedeks; in fact, all forms of intelligent life find in these Sons understanding friends, sympathetic teachers, and wise counselors.

The Melchizedeks are a self-governing order. With this unique group we encounter the first attempt at self-determination on the part of local universe beings and observe the highest type of true self-government. These Sons organize their own machinery for their group and home-planet administration, as well as that for the six associated spheres and their tributary worlds. And it should be recorded that they have never abused their prerogatives; not once throughout all the superuniverse of Orvonton have these Melchizedek Sons ever betrayed their trust. They are the hope of every universe group which aspires to self-government; they are the pattern and the teachers of self-government to all the spheres of Nebadon. All orders of intelligent beings, superiors from above and subordinates from below, are wholehearted in their praise of the government of the Melchizedeks.

The Melchizedek order of sonship occupies the position, and assumes the responsibility, of the eldest son in a large family. Most of their work is regular and somewhat routine, but much of it is voluntary and altogether self-imposed. A majority of the special assemblies which, from time to time, convene on Salvington are called on motion of the Melchizedeks. On their own initiative these Sons patrol their native universe. They maintain an autonomous organization devoted to universe intelligence, making periodical reports to the Creator Son independent of all information coming up to universe headquarters through the regular agencies concerned with the routine administration of the realm. They are by nature unprejudiced observers; they have the full confidence of all classes of intelligent beings.

The Melchizedeks function as mobile and advisory review courts of the realms; these universe Sons go in small groups to the worlds to serve as advisory commissions, to take depositions, to receive suggestions, and to act as counselors, thus helping to compose the major difficulties and settle the serious differences which arise from time to time in the affairs of the evolutionary domains.

These eldest Sons of a universe are the chief aids of the Bright and Morning Star in carrying out the mandates of the Creator Son. When a Melchizedek goes to a remote world in the name of Gabriel, he may, for the purposes of that particular mission, be deputized in the name of the sender and in that event will appear on the planet of assignment with the full authority of the Bright and Morning Star. Especially is this true on those spheres where a higher Son has not yet appeared in the likeness of the creatures of the realm.

When a Creator Son enters upon the bestowal career on an evolutionary world, he goes alone; but when one of his Paradise brothers, an Avonal Son, enters upon a bestowal, he is accompanied by the Melchizedek supporters, twelve in number, who so efficiently contribute to the success of the bestowal mission. They also support the Paradise Avonals on magisterial missions to the inhabited worlds, and in these assignments the Melchizedeks are visible to mortal eyes if the Avonal Son is also thus manifest.

There is no phase of planetary spiritual need to which they do not minister. They are the teachers who so often win whole worlds of advanced life to the final and full recognition of the Creator Son and his Paradise Father.

The Melchizedeks are well-nigh perfect in wisdom, but they are not infallible in judgment. When detached and alone on planetary missions, they have sometimes erred in minor matters, that is, they have elected to do certain things which their supervisors did not subsequently approve. Such an error of judgment temporarily disqualifies a Melchizedek until he goes to Salvington and, in audience with the Creator Son, receives that instruction which effectually purges him of the disharmony which caused disagreement with his fellows; and then, following the correctional rest, reinstatement to service ensues on the third day. But these minor misadaptations in Melchizedek function have rarely occurred in Nebadon.

These Sons are not an increasing order; their number is stationary, although varying in each local universe. The number of Melchizedeks of record on their headquarters planet in Nebadon is upward of ten million.

3. THE MELCHIZEDEK WORLDS

The Melchizedeks occupy a world of their own near Salvington, the universe headquarters. This sphere, by name Melchizedek, is the pilot world of the Salvington circuit of seventy primary spheres, each of which is encircled by six tributary spheres devoted to specialized activities. These marvelous spheres—seventy primaries and 420 tributaries—are often spoken of as the Melchizedek University. Ascending mortals from all the constellations of Nebadon pass through training on all 490 worlds in the acquirement of residential status on Salvington. But the education of ascenders is only one phase of the manifold activities taking place on the Salvington cluster of architectural spheres.

The 490 spheres of the Salvington circuit are divided into ten groups, each containing seven primary and forty-two tributary spheres. Each of these groups is under the general supervision of some one of the major orders of universe life. The first group, embracing the pilot world and the next six primary spheres in the encircling planetary procession, is under the supervision of the Melchizedeks. These Melchizedek worlds are:

1. The pilot world—the home world of the Melchizedek Sons.
2. The world of the physical-life schools and the laboratories of living energies.
3. The world of morontia life.
4. The sphere of initial spirit life.
5. The world of mid-spirit life.
6. The sphere of advancing spirit life.
7. The domain of co-ordinate and supreme self-realization.

The six tributary worlds of each of these Melchizedek spheres are devoted to activities germane to the work of the associated primary sphere.

The pilot world, the sphere *Melchizedek,* is the common meeting ground for all beings who are engaged in educating and spiritualizing the ascending mortals of time and space. To an ascender this world is probably the most interesting place in all Nebadon. All evolutionary mortals who graduate from their constellation training are destined to land on Melchizedek, where they are initiated into the regime of the disciplines and spirit progression of the Salvington educational system. And never will you forget your reactions to the first day of life on this unique world, not even after you have reached your Paradise destination.

Ascending mortals maintain residence on the Melchizedek world while pursuing their training on the six encircling planets of specialized education. And this same method is adhered to throughout their sojourn on the seventy cultural worlds, the primary spheres of the Salvington circuit.

Many diverse activities occupy the time of the numerous beings who reside on the six tributary worlds of the Melchizedek sphere, but as concerns the ascending mortals, these satellites are devoted to the following special phases of study:

1. Sphere number one is occupied with the review of the initial planetary life of the ascending mortals. This work is carried on in classes composed of those who hail from a given world of mortal origin. Those from Urantia pursue such an experiential review together.

2. The special work of sphere number two consists in a similar review of the experiences passed through on the mansion worlds encircling the premier satellite of the local system headquarters.

3. The reviews of this sphere pertain to the sojourn on the capital of the local system and embrace the activities of the remainder of the architectural worlds of the system headquarters cluster.

4. The fourth sphere is occupied with a review of the experiences of the seventy tributary worlds of the constellation and of their associated spheres.

5. On the fifth sphere there is conducted the review of the ascendant sojourn on the constellation headquarters world.

6. The time on sphere number six is devoted to an attempt to correlate these five epochs and thus achieve co-ordination of experience preparatory to entering the Melchizedek primary schools of universe training.

The schools of universe administration and spiritual wisdom are located on the Melchizedek home world, where also are to be found those schools devoted to a single line of research, such as energy, matter, organization, communication, records, ethics, and comparative creature existence.

In the Melchizedek College of Spiritual Endowment all orders—even the Paradise orders—of the Sons of God co-operate with the Melchizedek and the seraphic teachers in training the hosts who go forth as evangels of destiny, proclaiming spiritual liberty and divine sonship even to the remote worlds of the universe. This particular school of the Melchizedek University is an exclusive universe institution; student visitors are not received from other realms.

The highest course of training in universe administration is given by the Melchizedeks on their home world. This College of High Ethics is presided over by the original Father Melchizedek. It is to these schools that the various universes send exchange students. While the young universe of Nebadon stands low in the scale of universes as regards spiritual achievement and high ethical development, nevertheless, our administrative troubles have so turned the whole universe into a vast clinic for other near-by creations that the Melchizedek colleges are thronged with student visitors and observers from other realms. Besides the immense group of local registrants there are always upward of one hundred thousand foreign students in attendance upon the Melchizedek schools, for the order of Melchizedeks in Nebadon is renowned throughout all Splandon.

4. SPECIAL WORK OF THE MELCHIZEDEKS

A highly specialized branch of Melchizedek activities has to do with the supervision of the progressive morontia career of the ascending mortals. Much of this training is conducted by the patient and wise seraphic ministers, assisted by mortals who have ascended to relatively higher levels of universe attainment, but all of this educational work is under the general supervision of the Melchizedeks in association with the Trinity Teacher Sons.

While the Melchizedek orders are chiefly devoted to the vast educational system and experiential training regime of the local universe, they also function in unique assignments and in unusual circumstances. In an evolving universe eventually embracing approximately ten million inhabited worlds, many things out of the ordinary are destined to happen, and it is in such emergencies that the Melchizedeks act. On Edentia, your constellation headquarters, they are known as emergency Sons. They are always ready to serve in all exigencies—physical, intellectual, or spiritual—whether on a planet, in a system, in a constellation, or in the universe. Whenever and wherever special help is needed, there you will find one or more of the Melchizedek Sons.

When failure of some feature of the Creator Son's plan is threatened, forthwith will go a Melchizedek to render assistance. But not often are they summoned to function in the presence of sinful rebellion, such as occurred in Satania.

The Melchizedeks are the first to act in all emergencies of whatever nature on all worlds where will creatures dwell. They sometimes act as temporary custodians on wayward planets, serving as receivers of a defaulting planetary government. In a planetary crisis these Melchizedek Sons serve in many unique capacities. It is easily possible for such a Son to make himself visible to mortal beings, and sometimes one of this order has even incarnated in the likeness of mortal flesh. Seven times in Nebadon has a Melchizedek served on an evolutionary world in the similitude of mortal flesh, and on numerous occasions these Sons have appeared in the likeness of other orders of universe creatures. They are indeed the versatile and volunteer emergency ministers to all orders of universe intelligences and to all the worlds and systems of worlds.

The Melchizedek who lived on Urantia during the time of Abraham was locally known as Prince of Salem because he presided over a small colony of truth seekers residing at a place called Salem. He volunteered to incarnate in the likeness of mortal flesh and did so with the approval of the Melchizedek receivers of the planet, who feared that the light of life would become extinguished during that period of increasing spiritual darkness. And he did foster the truth of his day and safely pass it on to Abraham and his associates.

5. THE VORONDADEK SONS

After the creation of the personal aids and the first group of the versatile Melchizedeks, the Creator Son and the local universe Creative Spirit planned for, and brought into existence, the second great and diverse order of universe sonship, the Vorondadeks. They are more generally known as Constellation Fathers because a Son of this order is uniformly found at the head of each constellation government in every local universe.

The number of Vorondadeks varies in each local universe, just one million being the recorded number in Nebadon. These Sons, like their co-ordinates, the Melchizedeks, possess no power of reproduction. There exists no known method whereby they can increase their numbers.

In many respects these Sons are a self-governing body; as individuals and as groups, even as a whole, they are largely self-determinative, much as are the

Melchizedeks, but Vorondadeks do not function through such a wide range of activities. They do not equal their Melchizedek brethren in brilliant versatility, but they are even more reliable and efficient as rulers and farseeing administrators. Neither are they quite the administrative peers of their subordinates, the Lanonandek System Sovereigns, but they excel all orders of universe sonship in stability of purpose and in divinity of judgment.

Although the decisions and rulings of this order of Sons are always in accordance with the spirit of divine sonship and in harmony with the policies of the Creator Son, they have been cited for error to the Creator Son, and in details of technique their decisions have sometimes been reversed on appeal to the superior tribunals of the universe. But these Sons rarely fall into error, and they have never gone into rebellion; never in all the history of Nebadon has a Vorondadek been found in contempt of the universe government.

The service of the Vorondadeks in the local universes is extensive and varied. They serve as ambassadors to other universes and as consuls representing constellations within their native universe. Of all orders of local universe sonship they are the most often intrusted with the full delegation of sovereign powers to be exercised in critical universe situations.

On those worlds segregated in spiritual darkness, those spheres which have, through rebellion and default, suffered planetary isolation, an observer Vorondadek is usually present pending the restoration of normal status. In certain emergencies this Most High observer could exercise absolute and arbitrary authority over every celestial being assigned to that planet. It is of record on Salvington that the Vorondadeks have sometimes exercised such authority as Most High regents of such planets. And this has also been true even of inhabited worlds that were untouched by rebellion.

Often a corps of twelve or more Vorondadek Sons sits en banc as a high court of review and appeal concerning special cases involving the status of a planet or a system. But their work more largely pertains to the legislative functions indigenous to the constellation governments. As a result of all these services, the Vorondadek Sons have become the historians of the local universes; they are personally familiar with all the political struggles and the social upheavals of the inhabited worlds.

6. THE CONSTELLATION FATHERS

At least three Vorondadeks are assigned to the rulership of each of the one hundred constellations of a local universe. These Sons are selected by the Creator Son and are commissioned by Gabriel as the *Most Highs* of the constellations for service during one dekamillennium—10,000 standard years, about 50,000 years of Urantia time. The reigning Most High, the Constellation Father, has two associates, a senior and a junior. At each change of administration the senior associate becomes the head of the government, the junior assumes the duties of the senior, while the unassigned Vorondadeks resident on the Salvington worlds nominate one of their number as candidate for selection to assume the responsibilities of junior associate. Thus each of the Most High rulers, in accordance with present policy, has a period of service on the headquarters of a constellation of three dekamillenniums, about 150,000 Urantia years.

The one hundred Constellation Fathers, the actual presiding heads of the constellation governments, constitute the supreme advisory cabinet of the Creator

Son. This council is in frequent session at universe headquarters and is unlimited in the scope and range of its deliberations but is chiefly concerned with the welfare of the constellations and with the unification of the administration of the entire local universe.

When a Constellation Father is in attendance upon duties at the universe headquarters, as he frequently is, the senior associate becomes acting director of constellation affairs. The normal function of the senior associate is the oversight of spiritual affairs, while the junior associate is personally occupied with the physical welfare of the constellation. No major policy, however, is ever carried out in a constellation unless all three of the Most Highs are agreed upon all the details of its execution.

The entire mechanism of spirit intelligence and communication channels is at the disposal of the constellation Most Highs. They are in perfect touch with their superiors on Salvington and with their direct subordinates, the sovereigns of the local systems. They frequently convene in council with these System Sovereigns to deliberate upon the state of the constellation.

The Most Highs surround themselves with a corps of counselors, which varies in number and personnel from time to time in accordance with the presence of the various groups at constellation headquarters and also as the local requirements vary. During times of stress they may ask for, and will quickly receive, additional Sons of the Vorondadek order to assist with the administrative work. Norlatiadek, your own constellation, is at present administered by twelve Vorondadek Sons.

7. THE VORONDADEK WORLDS

The second group of seven worlds in the circuit of seventy primary spheres surrounding Salvington comprise the Vorondadek planets. Each of these spheres, with its six encircling satellites, is devoted to a special phase of Vorondadek activities. On these forty-nine realms the ascending mortals secure the acme of their education respecting universe legislation.

The ascending mortals have observed the legislative assemblies as they functioned on the headquarters worlds of the constellations, but here on these Vorondadek worlds they participate in the enactment of the actual general legislation of the local universe under the tutelage of the senior Vorondadeks. Such enactments are designed to co-ordinate the varied pronouncements of the autonomous legislative assemblies of the one hundred constellations. The instruction to be had in the Vorondadek schools is unexcelled even on Uversa. This training is progressive, extending from the first sphere, with supplemental work on its six satellites, on up through the remaining six primary spheres and their associated satellite groups.

The ascending pilgrims will be introduced to numerous new activities on these worlds of study and practical work. We are not forbidden to undertake the revelation of these new and undreamed-of pursuits, but we despair of being able to portray these undertakings to the material mind of mortal beings. We are without words to convey the meanings of these supernal activities, and there are no analogous human engagements which might be utilized as illustrations of these new occupations of the ascending mortals as they pursue their studies on these forty-nine worlds. And many other activities, not a part of the ascendant regime, are centered on these Vorondadek worlds of the Salvington circuit.

8. THE LANONANDEK SONS

After the creation of the Vorondadeks, the Creator Son and the Universe Mother Spirit unite for the purpose of bringing into existence the third order of universe sonship, the Lanonandeks. Although occupied with varied tasks connected with the system administrations, they are best known as System Sovereigns, the rulers of the local systems, and as Planetary Princes, the administrative heads of the inhabited worlds.

Being a later and lower—as concerns divinity levels—order of sonship creation, these beings were required to pass through certain courses of training on the Melchizedek worlds in preparation for subsequent service. They were the first students in the Melchizedek University and were classified and certified by their Melchizedek teachers and examiners according to ability, personality, and attainment.

The universe of Nebadon began its existence with exactly twelve million Lanonandeks, and when they had passed through the Melchizedek sphere, they were divided in the final tests into three classes:

1. *Primary Lanonandeks.* Of the highest rank there were 709,841. These are the Sons designated as System Sovereigns and assistants to the supreme councils of the constellations and as counselors in the higher administrative work of the universe.

2. *Secondary Lanonandeks.* Of this order emerging from Melchizedek there were 10,234,601. They are assigned as Planetary Princes and to the reserves of that order.

3. *Tertiary Lanonandeks.* This group contained 1,055,558. These Sons function as subordinate assistants, messengers, custodians, commissioners, observers, and prosecute the miscellaneous duties of a system and its component worlds.

It is not possible, as it is with evolutionary beings, for these Sons to progress from one group to another. When subjected to the Melchizedek training, when once tested and classified, they serve continuously in the rank assigned. Neither do these Sons engage in reproduction; their number in the universe is stationary.

In round numbers the Lanonandek order of Sons is classified on Salvington as follows:

Universe Co-ordinators and Constellation Counselors	100,000
System Sovereigns and Assistants	600,000
Planetary Princes and Reserves	10,000,000
Messenger Corps	400,000
Custodians and Recorders	100,000
Reserve Corps	800,000

Since Lanonandeks are a somewhat lower order of sonship than the Melchizedeks and the Vorondadeks, they are of even greater service in the subordinate units of the universe, for they are capable of drawing nearer the lower creatures of the intelligent races. They also stand in greater danger of going astray, of departing from the acceptable technique of universe government. But these Lanonandeks, especially the primary order, are the most able and versatile of all local universe administrators. In executive ability they are excelled only by Gabriel and his unrevealed associates.

9. THE LANONANDEK RULERS

The Lanonandeks are the continuous rulers of the planets and the rotating sovereigns of the systems. Such a Son now rules on Jerusem, the headquarters of your local system of inhabited worlds.

The System Sovereigns rule in commissions of two or three on the headquarters of each system of inhabited worlds. The Constellation Father names one of these Lanonandeks as chief every dekamillennium. Sometimes no change in the head of the trio is made, the matter being entirely optional with the constellation rulers. System governments do not suddenly change in personnel unless a tragedy of some sort occurs.

When System Sovereigns or assistants are recalled, their places are filled by selections made by the supreme council located on the constellation headquarters from the reserves of that order, a group which is larger on Edentia than the average indicated.

The supreme Lanonandek councils are stationed on the various constellation headquarters. Such a body is presided over by the senior Most High associate of the Constellation Father, while the junior associate supervises the reserves of the secondary order.

The System Sovereigns are true to their names; they are well-nigh sovereign in the local affairs of the inhabited worlds. They are almost paternal in their direction of the Planetary Princes, the Material Sons, and the ministering spirits. The personal grasp of the sovereign is all but complete. These rulers are not supervised by Trinity observers from the central universe. They are the executive division of the local universe, and as custodians of the enforcement of legislative mandates and as executives for the application of judicial verdicts, they present the one place in all universe administration where personal disloyalty to the will of the Michael Son could most easily and readily intrench itself and seek to assert itself.

Our local universe has been unfortunate in that over seven hundred Sons of the Lanonandek order have rebelled against the universe government, thus precipitating confusion in several systems and on numerous planets. Of this entire number of failures only three were System Sovereigns; practically all of these Sons belonged to the second and third orders, Planetary Princes and tertiary Lanonandeks.

The large number of these Sons who have lapsed from integrity does not indicate any fault in creatorship. They could have been made divinely perfect, but they were so created that they might better understand, and draw near to, the evolutionary creatures dwelling on the worlds of time and space.

Of all the local universes in Orvonton, our universe has, with the exception of Henselon, lost the largest number of this order of Sons. On Uversa it is the consensus that we have had so much administrative trouble in Nebadon because our Sons of the Lanonandek order have been created with such a large degree of personal liberty in choosing and planning. I do not make this observation by way of criticism. The Creator of our universe has full authority and power to do this. It is the contention of our high rulers that, while such free-choosing

Sons make excessive trouble in the earlier ages of the universe, when things are fully sifted and finally settled, the gains of higher loyalty and fuller volitional service on the part of these thoroughly tested Sons will far more than compensate for the confusion and tribulations of earlier times.

In the event of rebellion on a system headquarters, a new sovereign is usually installed within a comparatively short time, but not so on the individual planets. They are the component units of the material creation, and creature free will is a factor in the final adjudication of all such problems. Successor Planetary Princes are designated for isolated worlds, planets whose princes of authority may have gone astray, but they do not assume active rulership of such worlds until the results of insurrection are partially overcome and removed by the remedial measures adopted by the Melchizedeks and other ministering personalities. Rebellion by a Planetary Prince instantly isolates his planet; the local spiritual circuits are immediately severed. Only a bestowal Son can reestablish interplanetary lines of communication on such a spiritually isolated world.

There exists a plan for saving these wayward and unwise Sons, and many have availed themselves of this merciful provision; but never again may they function in those positions wherein they defaulted. After rehabilitation they are assigned to custodial duties and to departments of physical administration.

10. THE LANONANDEK WORLDS

The third group of seven worlds in the Salvington circuit of seventy planets, with their respective forty-two satellites, constitute the Lanonandek cluster of administrative spheres. On these realms the experienced Lanonandeks belonging to the ex-System Sovereign corps officiate as administrative teachers of the ascending pilgrims and the seraphic hosts. The evolutionary mortals observe the system administrators at work on the system capitals, but here they participate in the actual co-ordination of the administrative pronouncements of the ten thousand local systems.

These administrative schools of the local universe are supervised by a corps of Lanonandek Sons who have had long experience as System Sovereigns and as constellation counselors. These executive colleges are excelled only by the administrative schools of Ensa.

While serving as training spheres for ascending mortals, the Lanonandek worlds are the centers for extensive undertakings having to do with the normal and routine administrative operations of the universe. All the way in to Paradise the ascending pilgrims pursue their studies in the practical schools of applied knowledge—actual training in really doing the things they are being taught. The universe educational system sponsored by the Melchizedeks is practical, progressive, meaningful, and experiential. It embraces training in things material, intellectual, morontial, and spiritual.

It is in connection with these administrative spheres of the Lanonandeks that most of the salvaged Sons of that order serve as custodians and directors of planetary affairs. And these defaulting Planetary Princes and their associates in rebellion who choose to accept the proffered rehabilitation will continue to serve in these routine capacities, at least until the universe of Nebadon is settled in light and life.

Many of the Lanonandek Sons in the older systems, however, have established wonderful records of service, administration, and spiritual achievement. They are a noble, faithful, and loyal group, notwithstanding their tendency to fall into error through fallacies of personal liberty and fictions of self-determination.

[Sponsored by the Chief of Archangels acting by authority of Gabriel of Salvington.]

PAPER 36

THE LIFE CARRIERS

LIFE does not originate spontaneously. Life is constructed according to plans formulated by the (unrevealed) Architects of Being and appears on the inhabited planets either by direct importation or as a result of the operations of the Life Carriers of the local universes. These carriers of life are among the most interesting and versatile of the diverse family of universe Sons. They are intrusted with designing and carrying creature life to the planetary spheres. And after planting this life on such new worlds, they remain there for long periods to foster its development.

1. ORIGIN AND NATURE OF LIFE CARRIERS

Though the Life Carriers belong to the family of divine sonship, they are a peculiar and distinct type of universe Sons, being the only group of intelligent life in a local universe in whose creation the rulers of a superuniverse participate. The Life Carriers are the offspring of three pre-existent personalities: the Creator Son, the Universe Mother Spirit, and, by designation, one of the three Ancients of Days presiding over the destinies of the superuniverse concerned. These Ancients of Days, who alone can decree the extinction of intelligent life, participate in the creation of the Life Carriers, who are intrusted with establishing physical life on the evolving worlds.

In the universe of Nebadon we have on record the creation of one hundred million Life Carriers. This efficient corps of life disseminators is not a truly self-governing group. They are directed by the life-determining trio, consisting of Gabriel, the Father Melchizedek, and Nambia, the original and first-born Life Carrier of Nebadon. But in all phases of their divisional administration they are self-governing.

Life Carriers are graded into three grand divisions: The first division is the senior Life Carriers, the second, assistants, and the third, custodians. The primary division is subdivided into twelve groups of specialists in the various forms of life manifestation. The segregation of these three divisions was effected by the Melchizedeks, who conducted tests for such purposes on the Life Carriers' headquarters sphere. The Melchizedeks have ever since been closely associated with the Life Carriers and always accompany them when they go forth to establish life on a new planet.

When an evolutionary planet is finally settled in light and life, the Life Carriers are organized into the higher deliberative bodies of advisory capacity to assist in the further administration and development of the world and its glorified beings. In the later and settled ages of an evolving universe these Life Carriers are intrusted with many new duties.

2. THE LIFE CARRIER WORLDS

The Melchizedeks have the general oversight of the fourth group of seven primary spheres in the Salvington circuit. These worlds of the Life Carriers are designated as follows:

1. The Life Carrier headquarters.
2. The life-planning sphere.
3. The life-conservation sphere.
4. The sphere of life evolution.
5. The sphere of life associated with mind.
6. The sphere of mind and spirit in living beings.
7. The sphere of unrevealed life.

Each of these primary spheres is surrounded by six satellites, on which the special phases of all the Life Carrier activities in the universe are centered.

World Number One, the headquarters sphere, together with its six tributary satellites, is devoted to the study of universal life, life in all of its known phases of manifestation. Here is located the college of life planning, wherein function teachers and advisers from Uversa and Havona, even from Paradise. And I am permitted to reveal that the seven central emplacements of the adjutant mind-spirits are situated on this world of the Life Carriers.

The number ten—the decimal system—is inherent in the physical universe but not in the spiritual. The domain of life is characterized by three, seven, and twelve or by multiples and combinations of these basic numbers. There are three primal and essentially different life plans, after the order of the three Paradise Sources and Centers, and in the universe of Nebadon these three basic forms of life are segregated on three different types of planets. There were, originally, twelve distinct and divine concepts of transmissible life. This number twelve, with its subdivisions and multiples, runs throughout all basic life patterns of all seven superuniverses. There are also seven architectural types of life design, fundamental arrangements of the reproducing configurations of living matter. The Orvonton life patterns are configured as twelve inheritance carriers. The differing orders of will creatures are configured as 12, 24, 48, 96, 192, 384, and 768. On Urantia there are forty-eight units of pattern control—trait determiners —in the sex cells of human reproduction.

The Second World is the life-designing sphere; here all new modes of life organization are worked out. While the original life designs are provided by the Creator Son, the actual outworking of these plans is intrusted to the Life Carriers and their associates. When the general life plans for a new world have been formulated, they are transmitted to the headquarters sphere, where they are minutely scrutinized by the supreme council of the senior Life Carriers in collaboration with a corps of consulting Melchizedeks. If the plans are a departure from previously accepted formulas, they must be passed upon, and endorsed by, the Creator Son. The chief of Melchizedeks often represents the Creator Son in these deliberations.

Planetary life, therefore, while similar in some respects, differs in many ways on each evolutionary world. Even in a uniform life series in a single family of worlds, life is not exactly the same on any two planets; there is always a planetary type, for the Life Carriers work constantly in an effort to improve the vital formulas committed to their keeping.

There are over one million fundamental or cosmic chemical formulas which constitute the parent patterns and the numerous basic functional variations of life manifestations. Satellite number one of the life-planning sphere is the realm of the universe physicists and electrochemists who serve as technical assistants to the Life Carriers in the work of capturing, organizing, and manipulating the essential units of energy which are employed in building up the material vehicles of life transmission, the so-called germ plasm.

The planetary life-planning laboratories are situated on the second satellite of this world number two. In these laboratories the Life Carriers and all their associates collaborate with the Melchizedeks in the effort to modify and possibly improve the life designed for implantation on the *decimal planets* of Nebadon. The life now evolving on Urantia was planned and partially worked out on this very world, for Urantia is a decimal planet, a life-experiment world. On one world in each ten a greater variance in the standard life designs is permitted than on the other (nonexperimental) worlds.

World Number Three is devoted to the conservation of life. Here various modes of life protection and preservation are studied and developed by the assistants and custodians of the Life Carrier corps. The life plans for every new world always provide for the early establishment of the life-conservation commission, consisting of custodian specialists in the expert manipulation of the basic life patterns. On Urantia there were twenty-four such custodian commissioners, two for each fundamental or parent pattern of the architectural organization of the life material. On planets such as yours the highest form of life is reproduced by a life-carrying bundle which possesses twenty-four pattern units. (And since the intellectual life grows out of, and upon the foundation of, the physical, there come into existence the four and twenty basic orders of psychic organization.)

Sphere Number Four and its tributary satellites are devoted to the study of the evolution of creature life in general and to the evolutionary antecedents of any one life level in particular. The original life plasm of an evolutionary world must contain the full potential for all future developmental variations and for all subsequent evolutionary changes and modifications. The provision for such far-reaching projects of life metamorphosis may require the appearance of many apparently useless forms of animal and vegetable life. Such by-products of planetary evolution, foreseen or unforeseen, appear upon the stage of action only to disappear, but in and through all this long process there runs the thread of the wise and intelligent formulations of the original designers of the planetary life plan and species scheme. The manifold by-products of biologic evolution are all essential to the final and full function of the higher intelligent forms of life, notwithstanding that great outward disharmony may prevail from time to time in the long upward struggle of the higher creatures to effect the mastery of the lower forms of life, many of which are sometimes so antagonistic to the peace and comfort of the evolving will creatures.

Number Five World is concerned wholly with life associated with mind. Each of its satellites is devoted to the study of a single phase of creature mind correlated with creature life. Mind such as man comprehends is an endowment of the seven adjutant mind-spirits superimposed on the nonteachable or mechanical levels of mind by the agencies of the Infinite Spirit. The life patterns are variously responsive to these adjutants and to the different spirit ministries operating throughout the universes of time and space. The capacity of material creatures to effect spirit response is entirely dependent on the associated mind endowment, which, in turn, has directionized the course of the biologic evolution of these same mortal creatures.

World Number Six is dedicated to the correlation of mind with spirit as they are associated with living forms and organisms. This world and its six tributaries embrace the schools of creature co-ordination, wherein teachers from both the central universe and the superuniverse collaborate with the Nebadon instructors in presenting the highest levels of creature attainment in time and space.

The Seventh Sphere of the Life Carriers is dedicated to the unrevealed domains of evolutionary creature life as it is related to the cosmic philosophy of the expanding factualization of the Supreme Being.

3. LIFE TRANSPLANTATION

Life does not spontaneously appear in the universes; the Life Carriers must initiate it on the barren planets. They are the carriers, disseminators, and guardians of life as it appears on the evolutionary worlds of space. All life of the order and forms known on Urantia arises with these Sons, though not all forms of planetary life are existent on Urantia.

The corps of Life Carriers commissioned to plant life upon a new world usually consists of one hundred senior carriers, one hundred assistants, and one thousand custodians. The Life Carriers often carry actual life plasm to a new world, but not always. They sometimes organize the life patterns after arriving on the planet of assignment in accordance with formulas previously approved for a new adventure in life establishment. Such was the origin of the planetary life of Urantia.

When, in accordance with approved formulas, the physical patterns have been provided, then do the Life Carriers catalyze this lifeless material, imparting through their persons the vital spirit spark; and forthwith do the inert patterns become living matter.

The vital spark—the mystery of life—is bestowed through the Life Carriers, not by them. They do indeed supervise such transactions, they formulate the life plasm itself, but it is the Universe Mother Spirit who supplies the essential factor of the living plasm. From the Creative Daughter of the Infinite Spirit comes that *energy spark which* enlivens the body and presages the mind.

In the bestowal of life the Life Carriers transmit nothing of their personal natures, not even on those spheres where new orders of life are projected. At such times they simply initiate and transmit the spark of life, start the required revolutions of matter in accordance with the physical, chemical, and electrical specifications of the ordained plans and patterns. Life Carriers are living catalytic presences which agitate, organize, and vitalize the otherwise inert elements of the material order of existence.

The Life Carriers of a planetary corps are given a certain period in which to establish life on a new world, approximately one-half million years of the time of that planet. At the termination of this period, indicated by certain developmental attainments of the planetary life, they cease implantation efforts, and they may not subsequently add anything new or supplemental to the life of that planet.

During the ages intervening between life establishment and the emergence of human creatures of moral status, the Life Carriers are permitted to manipulate the life environment and otherwise favorably directionize the course of biologic evolution. And this they do for long periods of time.

When the Life Carriers operating on a new world have once succeeded in producing a being with will, with the power of moral decision and spiritual choice, then and there their work terminates—they are through; they may manipulate the evolving life no further. From this point forward the evolution of living things must proceed in accordance with the endowment of the inherent nature and tendencies which have already been imparted to, and established in, the planetary life formulas and patterns. The Life Carriers are not permitted to experiment or to interfere with will; they are not allowed to dominate or arbitrarily influence moral creatures.

Upon the arrival of a Planetary Prince they prepare to leave, though two of the senior carriers and twelve custodians may volunteer, by taking temporary renunciation vows, to remain indefinitely on the planet as advisers in the matter of the further development and conservation of the life plasm. Two such Sons and their twelve associates are now serving on Urantia.

4. MELCHIZEDEK LIFE CARRIERS

In every local system of inhabited worlds throughout Nebadon there is a single sphere whereon the Melchizedeks have functioned as life carriers. These abodes are known as the system *midsonite* worlds, and on each of them a materially modified Melchizedek Son has mated with a selected Daughter of the material order of sonship. The Mother Eves of such midsonite worlds are dispatched from the system headquarters of jurisdiction, having been chosen by the designated Melchizedek life carrier from among the numerous volunteers who respond to the call of the System Sovereign addressed to the Material Daughters of his sphere.

The progeny of a Melchizedek life carrier and a Material Daughter are known as *midsoniters.* The Melchizedek father of such a race of supernal creatures eventually leaves the planet of his unique life function, and the Mother Eve of this special order of universe beings also departs upon the appearance of the seventh generation of planetary offspring. The direction of such a world then devolves upon her eldest son.

The midsonite creatures live and function as reproducing beings on their magnificent worlds until they are one thousand standard years of age; whereupon they are translated by seraphic transport. Midsoniters are nonreproducing beings thereafter because the technique of dematerialization which they pass through in preparation for enseraphiming forever deprives them of reproductive prerogatives.

The present status of these beings can hardly be reckoned as either mortal or immortal, neither can they be definitely classified as human or divine. These creatures are not Adjuster indwelt, hence hardly immortal. But neither do they seem to be mortal; no midsoniter has experienced death. All midsoniters ever born in Nebadon are alive today, functioning on their native worlds, on some intervening sphere, or on the Salvington midsonite sphere in the finaliters' group of worlds.

The Salvington Worlds of the Finaliters. The Melchizedek life carriers, as well as the associated Mother Eves, go from the system midsonite spheres to the finaliters' worlds of the Salvington circuit, where their offspring are also destined to forgather.

It should be explained in this connection that the fifth group of seven primary worlds in the Salvington circuit are the Nebadon worlds of the finaliters. The children of the Melchizedek life carriers and the Material Daughters are domiciled on the seventh world of the finaliters, the Salvington midsonite sphere.

The satellites of the seven primary worlds of the finaliters are the rendezvous of the personalities of the super- and central universes who may be executing assignments in Nebadon. While the ascending mortals go about freely on all of the cultural worlds and training spheres of the 490 worlds comprising the Melchizedek University, there are certain special schools and numerous restricted zones which they are not permitted to enter. This is especially true of the forty-nine spheres under the jurisdiction of the finaliters.

The purpose of the midsonite creatures is not at present known, but it would appear that these personalities are forgathering on the seventh finaliter world in preparation for some future eventuality in universe evolution. Our inquiries concerning the midsonite races are always referred to the finaliters, and always do the finaliters decline to discuss the destiny of their wards. Regardless of our uncertainty as to the future of the midsoniters, we do know that every local universe in Orvonton harbors such an accumulating corps of these mysterious beings. It is the belief of the Melchizedek life carriers that their midsonite children will some day be endowed with the transcendental and eternal spirit of absonity by God the Ultimate.

5. THE SEVEN ADJUTANT MIND-SPIRITS

It is the presence of the seven adjutant mind-spirits on the primitive worlds that conditions the course of organic evolution; that explains why evolution is purposeful and not accidental. These adjutants represent that function of the mind ministry of the Infinite Spirit which is extended to the lower orders of intelligent life through the operations of a local universe Mother Spirit. The adjutants are the children of the Universe Mother Spirit and constitute her personal ministry to the material minds of the realms. Wherever and whenever such mind is manifest, these spirits are variously functioning.

The seven adjutant mind-spirits are called by names which are the equivalents of the following designations: intuition, understanding, courage, knowledge, counsel, worship, and wisdom. These mind-spirits send forth their influence into all the inhabited worlds as a differential urge, each seeking receptivity capacity for manifestation quite apart from the degree to which its fellows may find reception and opportunity for function.

The central lodgments of the adjutant spirits on the Life Carrier headquarters world indicate to the Life Carrier supervisors the extent and quality of the mind function of the adjutants on any world and in any given living organism of intellect status. These life-mind emplacements are perfect indicators of living mind function for the first five adjutants. But with regard to the sixth and seventh adjutant spirits—worship and wisdom—these central lodgments record only a qualitative function. The quantitative activity of the adjutant of worship and the adjutant of wisdom is registered in the immediate presence of the Divine Minister on Salvington, being a personal experience of the Universe Mother Spirit.

The seven adjutant mind-spirits always accompany the Life Carriers to a new planet, but they should not be regarded as entities; they are more like circuits. The spirits of the seven universe adjutants do not function as personalities apart from the universe presence of the Divine Minister; they are in fact a level of consciousness of the Divine Minister and are always subordinate to the action and presence of their creative mother.

We are handicapped for words adequately to designate these seven adjutant mind-spirits. They are ministers of the lower levels of experiential mind, and they may be described, in the order of evolutionary attainment, as follows:

1. *The spirit of intuition*—quick perception, the primitive physical and inherent reflex instincts, the directional and other self-preservative endowments of all mind creations; the only one of the adjutants to function so largely in the lower orders of animal life and the only one to make extensive functional contact with the nonteachable levels of mechanical mind.

2. *The spirit of understanding*—the impulse of co-ordination, the spontaneous and apparently automatic association of ideas. This is the gift of the co-ordination of acquired knowledge, the phenomenon of quick reasoning, rapid judgment, and prompt decision.

3. *The spirit of courage*—the fidelity endowment—in personal beings, the basis of character acquirement and the intellectual root of moral stamina and spiritual bravery. When enlightened by facts and inspired by truth, this becomes the secret of the urge of evolutionary ascension by the channels of intelligent and conscientious self-direction.

4. *The spirit of knowledge*—the curiosity-mother of adventure and discovery, the scientific spirit; the guide and faithful associate of the spirits of courage and counsel; the urge to direct the endowments of courage into useful and progressive paths of growth.

5. *The spirit of counsel*—the social urge, the endowment of species cooperation; the ability of will creatures to harmonize with their fellows; the origin of the gregarious instinct among the more lowly creatures.

6. *The spirit of worship*—the religious impulse, the first differential urge separating mind creatures into the two basic classes of mortal existence. The spirit of worship forever distinguishes the animal of its association from the soulless creatures of mind endowment. Worship is the badge of spiritual-ascension candidacy.

7. *The spirit of wisdom*—the inherent tendency of all moral creatures towards orderly and progressive evolutionary advancement. This is the highest of the adjutants, the spirit co-ordinator and articulator of the work of all the

others. This spirit is the secret of that inborn urge of mind creatures which initiates and maintains the practical and effective program of the ascending scale of existence; that gift of living things which accounts for their inexplicable ability to survive and, in survival, to utilize the co-ordination of all their past experience and present opportunities for the acquisition of all of everything that all of the other six mental ministers can mobilize in the mind of the organism concerned. Wisdom is the acme of intellectual performance. Wisdom is the goal of a purely mental and moral existence.

The adjutant mind-spirits experientially grow, but they never become personal. They evolve in function, and the function of the first five in the animal orders is to a certain extent essential to the function of all seven as human intellect. This animal relationship makes the adjutants more practically effective as human mind; hence animals are to a certain extent indispensable to man's intellectual as well as to his physical evolution.

These mind-adjutants of a local universe Mother Spirit are related to creature life of intelligence status much as the power centers and physical controllers are related to the nonliving forces of the universe. They perform invaluable service in the mind circuits on the inhabited worlds and are effective collaborators with the Master Physical Controllers, who also serve as controllers and directors of the preadjutant mind levels, the levels of nonteachable or mechanical mind.

Living mind, prior to the appearance of capacity to learn from experience, is the ministry domain of the Master Physical Controllers. Creature mind, before acquiring the ability to recognize divinity and worship Deity, is the exclusive domain of the adjutant spirits. With the appearance of the spiritual response of the creature intellect, such created minds at once become superminded, being instantly encircuited in the spirit cycles of the local universe Mother Spirit.

The adjutant mind-spirits are in no manner directly related to the diverse and highly spiritual function of the spirit of the personal presence of the Divine Minister, the Holy Spirit of the inhabited worlds; but they are functionally antecedent to, and preparatory for, the appearance of this very spirit in evolutionary man. The adjutants afford the Universe Mother Spirit a varied contact with, and control over, the material living creatures of a local universe, but they do not repercuss in the Supreme Being when acting on prepersonality levels.

Nonspiritual mind is either a spirit-energy manifestation or a physical-energy phenomenon. Even human mind, personal mind, has no survival qualities apart from spirit identification. Mind is a divinity bestowal, but it is not immortal when it functions without spirit insight, and when it is devoid of the ability to worship and crave survival.

6. LIVING FORCES

Life is both mechanistic and vitalistic—material and spiritual. Ever will Urantia physicists and chemists progress in their understanding of the protoplasmic forms of vegetable and animal life, but never will they be able to produce living organisms. Life is something different from all energy manifestations; even the material life of physical creatures is not inherent in matter.

Things material may enjoy an independent existence, but life springs only from life. Mind can be derived only from pre-existent mind. Spirit takes origin only from spirit ancestors. The creature may produce the forms of life, but only a creator personality or a creative force can supply the activating living spark.

Life Carriers can organize the material forms, or physical patterns, of living beings, but the Spirit provides the initial spark of life and bestows the endowment of mind. Even the living forms of experimental life which the Life Carriers organize on their Salvington worlds are always devoid of reproductive powers. When the life formulas and the vital patterns are correctly assembled and properly organized, the presence of a Life Carrier is sufficient to initiate life, but all such living organisms are lacking in two essential attributes—mind endowment and reproductive powers. Animal mind and human mind are gifts of the local universe Mother Spirit, functioning through the seven adjutant mind-spirits, while creature ability to reproduce is the specific and personal impartation of the Universe Spirit to the ancestral life plasm inaugurated by the Life Carriers.

When the Life Carriers have designed the patterns of life, after they have organized the energy systems, there must occur an additional phenomenon; the "breath of life" must be imparted to these lifeless forms. The Sons of God can construct the forms of life, but it is the Spirit of God who really contributes the vital spark. And when the life thus imparted is spent, then again the remaining material body becomes dead matter. When the bestowed life is exhausted, the body returns to the bosom of the material universe from which it was borrowed by the Life Carriers to serve as a transient vehicle for that life endowment which they conveyed to such a visible association of energy-matter.

The life bestowed upon plants and animals by the Life Carriers does not return to the Life Carriers upon the death of plant or animal. The departing life of such a living thing possesses neither identity nor personality; it does not individually survive death. During its existence and the time of its sojourn in the body of matter, it has undergone a change; it has undergone energy evolution and survives only as a part of the cosmic forces of the universe; it does not survive as individual life. The survival of mortal creatures is wholly predicated on the evolvement of an immortal soul within the mortal mind.

We speak of life as "energy" and as "force," but it is really neither. Force-energy is variously gravity responsive; life is not. Pattern is also nonresponsive to gravity, being a configuration of energies that have already fulfilled all gravity-responsive obligations. Life, as such, constitutes the animation of some pattern-configured or otherwise segregated system of energy—material, mindal, or spiritual.

There are some things connected with the elaboration of life on the evolutionary planets which are not altogether clear to us. We fully comprehend the physical organization of the electrochemical formulas of the Life Carriers, but we do not wholly understand the nature and source of the *life-activation spark.* We know that life flows from the Father through the Son and *by* the Spirit. It is more than possible that the Master Spirits are the sevenfold channel of the river of life which is poured out upon all creation. But we do not comprehend the technique whereby the supervising Master Spirit participates in the initial episode of life bestowal on a new planet. The Ancients of Days, we are confident, also have some part in this inauguration of life on a new world, but we are wholly ignorant of the nature thereof. We do know that the Universe Mother Spirit actually vitalizes the lifeless patterns and imparts to such activated plasm the prerogatives of organismal reproduction. We observe that these three are the levels of God the Sevenfold, sometimes designated as the Supreme Creators of time and space; but otherwise we know little more than Urantia mortals—simply that concept is inherent in the Father, expression in the Son, and life realization in the Spirit.

[Indited by a Vorondadek Son stationed on Urantia as an observer and acting in this capacity by request of the Melchizedek Chief of the Supervising Revelatory Corps.]

PAPER 37

PERSONALITIES OF THE LOCAL UNIVERSE

AT THE head of all personality in Nebadon stands the Creator and Master Son, Michael, the universe father and sovereign. Co-ordinate in divinity and complemental in creative attributes is the local universe Mother Spirit, the Divine Minister of Salvington. And these creators are in a very literal sense the Father-Son and the Spirit-Mother of all the native creatures of Nebadon.

Preceding papers have dealt with the created orders of sonship; succeeding narratives will portray the ministering spirits and the ascending orders of sonship. This paper is chiefly concerned with an intervening group, the Universe Aids, but it will also give brief consideration to certain of the higher spirits stationed in Nebadon and to certain of the orders of permanent citizenship in the local universe.

1. THE UNIVERSE AIDS

Many of the unique orders generally grouped in this category are unrevealed, but as presented in these papers, the Universe Aids include the following seven orders:

1. Bright and Morning Stars.
2. Brilliant Evening Stars.
3. Archangels.
4. Most High Assistants.
5. High Commissioners.
6. Celestial Overseers.
7. Mansion World Teachers.

Of the first order of Universe Aids, the Bright and Morning Stars, there is just one in each local universe, and he is the first-born of all creatures native to a local universe. The Bright and Morning Star of our universe is known as Gabriel of Salvington. He is the chief executive of all Nebadon, functioning as the personal representative of the Sovereign Son and as spokesman for his creative consort.

During the earlier times of Nebadon, Gabriel worked quite alone with Michael and the Creative Spirit. As the universe grew and administrative problems multiplied, he was provided with a personal staff of unrevealed assistants, and eventually this group was augmented by the creation of the Nebadon corps of Evening Stars.

2. THE BRILLIANT EVENING STARS

These brilliant creatures were planned by the Melchizedeks and were then brought into being by the Creator Son and the Creative Spirit. They serve in many capacities but chiefly as liaison officers of Gabriel, the local universe chief executive. One or more of these beings function as his representatives at the capital of every constellation and system in Nebadon.

As chief executive of Nebadon, Gabriel is ex officio chairman of, or observer at, most of the Salvington conclaves, and as many as one thousand of these are often in session simultaneously. The Brilliant Evening Stars represent Gabriel on these occasions; he cannot be in two places at the same time, and these superangels compensate for this limitation. They perform an analogous service for the corps of the Trinity Teacher Sons.

Though personally occupied with administrative duties, Gabriel maintains contact with all other phases of universe life and affairs through the Brilliant Evening Stars. They always accompany him on his planetary tours and frequently go on special missions to the individual planets as his personal representatives. On such assignments they have sometimes been known as "the angel of the Lord." They frequently go to Uversa to represent the Bright and Morning Star before the courts and assemblies of the Ancients of Days, but they seldom journey beyond the confines of Orvonton.

The Brilliant Evening Stars are a unique twofold order, embracing some of created dignity and others of attained service. The Nebadon corps of these superangels now numbers 13,641. There are 4,832 of created dignity, while 8,809 are ascendant spirits who have attained this goal of exalted service. Many of these ascendant Evening Stars started their universe careers as seraphim; others have ascended from unrevealed levels of creature life. As an attainment goal this high corps is never closed to ascension candidates so long as a universe is not settled in light and life.

Both types of Brilliant Evening Stars are easily visible to morontia personalities and certain types of supermortal material beings. The created beings of this interesting and versatile order possess a spirit force which can be manifested independently of their personal presence.

The head of these superangels is Gavalia, the first-born of this order in Nebadon. Since the return of Christ Michael from his triumphant bestowal on Urantia, Gavalia has been assigned to the ascendant mortal ministry, and for the last nineteen hundred Urantia years his associate, Galantia, has maintained headquarters on Jerusem, where he spends about half of his time. Galantia is the first of the ascendant superangels to attain this high estate.

No grouping or company organization of the Brilliant Evening Stars exists other than their customary association in pairs on many assignments. They are not extensively assigned on missions pertaining to the ascendant career of mortals, but when thus commissioned, they never function alone. They always work in pairs—one a created being, the other an ascendant Evening Star.

One of the high duties of the Evening Stars is to accompany the Avonal bestowal Sons on their planetary missions, even as Gabriel accompanied Michael on his Urantia bestowal. The two attending superangels are the ranking personalities of such missions, serving as cocommanders of the archangels and all others assigned to these undertakings. It is the senior of these superangel commanders who, at the significant time and age, bids the Avonal bestowal Son, "Be about your brother's business."

Similar pairs of these superangels are assigned to the planetary corps of Trinity Teacher Sons that functions to establish the postbestowal or dawning spiritual age of an inhabited world. On such assignments the Evening Stars serve as liaisons between the mortals of the realm and the invisible corps of Teacher Sons.

The Worlds of the Evening Stars. The sixth group of seven Salvington worlds and their forty-two tributary satellites are assigned to the administration of the Brilliant Evening Stars. The seven primary worlds are presided over by the created orders of these superangels, while the tributary satellites are administered by ascendant Evening Stars.

The satellites of the first three worlds are devoted to the schools of the Teacher Sons and the Evening Stars dedicated to the spirit personalities of the local universe. The next three groups are occupied by similar joint schools devoted to the training of ascending mortals. The seventh-world satellites are reserved for the triune deliberations of the Teacher Sons, the Evening Stars, and the finaliters. During recent times these superangels have been closely identified with the local universe work of the Corps of the Finality, and they have long been associated with the Teacher Sons. There exists a liaison of tremendous power and import between the Evening Stars and the Gravity Messengers attached to the finaliter working groups. The seventh primary world itself is reserved for those unrevealed matters which pertain to the future relationship that will obtain between the Teacher Sons, the finaliters, and the Evening Stars consequent upon the completed emergence of the superuniverse manifestation of the personality of God the Supreme.

3. THE ARCHANGELS

Archangels are the offspring of the Creator Son and the Universe Mother Spirit. They are the highest type of high spirit being produced in large numbers in a local universe, and at the time of the last registry there were almost eight hundred thousand in Nebadon.

Archangels are one of the few groups of local universe personalities who are not normally under the jurisdiction of Gabriel. They are not in any manner concerned with the routine administration of the universe, being dedicated to the work of creature survival and to the furtherance of the ascending career of the mortals of time and space. While not ordinarily subject to the direction of the Bright and Morning Star, the archangels do sometimes function by his authority. They also collaborate with others of the Universe Aids, such as the Evening Stars, as is illustrated by certain transactions depicted in the narrative of life transplantation on your world.

The archangel corps of Nebadon is directed by the first-born of this order, and in more recent times a divisional headquarters of the archangels has been maintained on Urantia. It is this unusual fact that soon arrests the attention of extra-Nebadon student visitors. Among their early observations of intrauniverse transactions is the discovery that many ascendant activities of the Brilliant Evening Stars are directed from the capital of a local system, Satania. On further examination they discover that certain archangel activities are directed from a small and apparently insignificant inhabited world called Urantia. And then ensues the revelation of Michael's bestowal on Urantia and their immediately quickened interest in you and your lowly sphere.

Do you grasp the significance of the fact that your lowly and confused planet has become a divisional headquarters for the universe administration and direction of certain archangel activities having to do with the Paradise ascension scheme? This undoubtedly presages the future concentration of other ascendant activities on the bestowal world of Michael and lends a tremendous and solemn import to the Master's personal promise, "I will come again."

In general, the archangels are assigned to the service and ministry of the Avonal order of sonship, but not until they have passed through extensive preliminary training in all phases of the work of the various ministering spirits. A corps of one hundred accompanies every Paradise bestowal Son to an inhabited world, being temporarily assigned to him for the duration of such a bestowal. If the Magisterial Son should become temporary ruler of the planet, these archangels would act as the directing heads of all celestial life on that sphere.

Two senior archangels are always assigned as the personal aids of a Paradise Avonal on all planetary missions, whether involving judicial actions, magisterial missions, or bestowal incarnations. When this Paradise Son has finished the judgment of a realm and the dead are called to record (the so-called resurrection), it is literally true that the seraphic guardians of the slumbering personalities respond to "the voice of the archangel." The roll call of a dispensation termination is promulgated by an attendant archangel. This is the archangel of the resurrection, sometimes referred to as the "archangel of Michael."

The Worlds of the Archangels. The seventh group of the encircling Salvington worlds, with their associated satellites, is assigned to the archangels. Sphere number one and all of its six tributary satellites are occupied by the personality record keepers. This enormous corps of recorders busy themselves with keeping straight the record of each mortal of time from the moment of birth up through the universe career until such an individual either leaves Salvington for the superuniverse regime or is "blotted out of recorded existence" by the mandate of the Ancients of Days.

It is on these worlds that personality records and identification sureties are classified, filed, and preserved during that time which intervenes between mortal death and the hour of repersonalization, the resurrection from death.

4. MOST HIGH ASSISTANTS

The Most High Assistants are a group of volunteering beings, of origin outside the local universe, who are temporarily assigned as central and superuniverse representatives to, or observers of, the local creations. Their number varies constantly but is always far up in the millions.

From time to time we thus benefit from the ministry and assistance of such Paradise-origin beings as Perfectors of Wisdom, Divine Counselors, Universal Censors, Inspired Trinity Spirits, Trinitized Sons, Solitary Messengers, supernaphim, seconaphim, tertiaphim, and other gracious ministers, who sojourn with us for the purpose of helping our native personalities in the effort to bring all Nebadon into fuller harmony with the ideas of Orvonton and the ideals of Paradise.

Any of these beings may be voluntarily serving in Nebadon and hence be technically outside our jurisdiction, but when functioning by assignment, such personalities of the super- and central universes are not wholly exempt from the regulations of the local universe of their sojourn, though they continue to function as representatives of the higher universes and to work in accordance with the instructions which constitute their mission in our realm. Their general headquarters is situated in the Salvington sector of the Union of Days, and they operate in Nebadon subject to the oversupervision of this ambassador of the Paradise Trinity. When serving in unattached groups, these personalities from the higher realms are usually self-directing, but when serving on request, they often voluntarily place themselves wholly under the jurisdiction of the supervising directors of the realms of assigned function.

Most High Assistants serve in local universe and in constellation capacities but are not directly attached to the system or planetary governments. They may, however, function anywhere in the local universe and may be assigned to any phase of Nebadon activity—administrative, executive, educational, and others.

Most of this corps is enlisted in assisting the Nebadon Paradise personalities—the Union of Days, the Creator Son, the Faithfuls of Days, the Magisterial Sons, and the Trinity Teacher Sons. Now and then in the transaction of the affairs of a local creation it becomes wise to withhold certain details, temporarily, from the knowledge of practically all of the native personalities of that local universe. Certain advanced plans and complex rulings are also better grasped and more fully understood by the more mature and farseeing corps of Most High Assistants, and it is in such situations, and many others, that they are so highly serviceable to the universe rulers and administrators.

5. HIGH COMMISSIONERS

The High Commissioners are Spirit-fused ascendant mortals; they are not Adjuster fused. You quite well understand about the universe-ascension career of a mortal candidate for Adjuster fusion, that being the high destiny in prospect for all Urantia mortals since the bestowal of Christ Michael. But this is not the exclusive destiny of all mortals in the prebestowal ages of worlds like yours, and there is another type of world whose inhabitants are never permanently indwelt by Thought Adjusters. Such mortals are never permanently joined in union with a Mystery Monitor of Paradise bestowal; nevertheless, the Adjusters do transiently indwell them, serving as guides and patterns for the duration of the life in the flesh. During this temporary sojourn they foster the evolution of an immortal soul just as in those beings with whom they hope to fuse, but when the mortal race is run, they take eternal leave of the creatures of temporary association.

Surviving souls of this order attain immortality by eternal fusion with an individualized fragment of the spirit of the local universe Mother Spirit. They are not a numerous group, at least not in Nebadon. On the mansion worlds you will meet and fraternize with these Spirit-fused mortals as they ascend the Paradise path with you as far as Salvington, where they stop. Some of them may subsequently ascend to higher universe levels, but the majority will forever remain in the service of the local universe; as a class they are not destined to attain Paradise.

Not being Adjuster fused, they never become finaliters, but they do eventually become enrolled in the local universe Corps of Perfection. They have in spirit obeyed the Father's command, "Be you perfect."

After attaining the Nebadon Corps of Perfection, Spirit-fused ascenders may accept assignment as Universe Aids, this being one of the avenues of continuing experiential growth which is open to them. Thus do they become candidates for commissions to the high service of interpreting the viewpoints of the evolving creatures of the material worlds to the celestial authorities of the local universe.

The High Commissioners begin their service on the planets as race commissioners. In this capacity they interpret the viewpoints and portray the needs of the various human races. They are supremely devoted to the welfare of the mortal races whose spokesmen they are, ever seeking to obtain for them mercy, justice, and fair treatment in all relationships with other peoples. Race commissioners function in an endless series of planetary crises and serve as the articulate expression of whole groups of struggling mortals.

After long experience in problem solving on the inhabited worlds, these race commissioners are advanced to the higher levels of function, eventually attaining the status of High Commissioners of and in the local universe. The last registration recorded slightly over one and one-half billion of these High Commissioners in Nebadon. These beings are not finaliters, but they are ascendant beings of long experience and of great service to their native realm.

We invariably find these commissioners in all the tribunals of justice, from the lowest to the highest. Not that they participate in the proceedings of justice, but they do act as friends of the court, advising the presiding magistrates respecting the antecedents, environment, and inherent nature of those concerned in the adjudication.

High Commissioners are attached to the various messenger hosts of space and always to the ministering spirits of time. They are encountered on the programs of various universe assemblies, and these same mortal-wise commissioners are always attached to the missions of the Sons of God to the worlds of space.

Whenever fairness and justice require an understanding of how a contemplated policy or procedure would affect the evolutionary races of time, these commissioners are at hand to present their recommendations; they are always present to speak for those who cannot be present to speak for themselves.

The Worlds of the Spirit-fused Mortals. The eighth group of seven primary worlds and tributary satellites in the Salvington circuit are the exclusive possession of the Spirit-fused mortals of Nebadon. Ascending Adjuster-fused mortals are not concerned with these worlds except to enjoy many pleasant and profitable sojourns as the invited guests of the Spirit-fused residents.

Except for those few who attain Uversa and Paradise, these worlds are the permanent residence of the Spirit-fused survivors. Such designed limitation of mortal ascent reacts to the good of the local universes by insuring the retention of a permanent evolved population whose augmenting experience will continue to enhance the future stabilization and diversification of the local universe administration. These beings may not attain Paradise, but they achieve an experiential wisdom in the mastery of Nebadon problems that utterly surpasses anything attained by the transient ascenders. And these surviving souls continue as unique combinations of the human and the divine, being increasingly able to unite the viewpoints of these two widely separate levels and to present such a dual viewpoint with ever-heightening wisdom.

6. CELESTIAL OVERSEERS

The Nebadon educational system is jointly administered by the Trinity Teacher Sons and the Melchizedek teaching corps, but much of the work designed to effect its maintenance and upbuilding is carried on by the Celestial Overseers. These beings are a recruited corps embracing all types of individuals connected with the scheme of educating and training the ascending mortals. There are upward of three million of them in Nebadon, and they are all volunteers who have qualified by experience to serve as educational advisers to the entire realm. From their headquarters on the Salvington worlds of the Melchizedeks, these overseers range the local universe as inspectors of the Nebadon school technique designed to effect the mind training and the spirit education of the ascending creatures.

This training of mind and education of spirit is carried on from the worlds of human origin up through the system mansion worlds and the other spheres of progress associated with Jerusem, on the seventy socializing realms attached to Edentia, and on the four hundred and ninety spheres of spirit progress encircling Salvington. On the universe headquarters itself are numerous Melchizedek schools, the colleges of the Universe Sons, the seraphic universities, and the schools of the Teacher Sons and the Union of Days. Every possible provision is made to qualify the various personalities of the universe for advancing service and improving function. The entire universe is one vast school.

The methods employed in many of the higher schools are beyond the human concept of the art of teaching truth, but this is the keynote of the whole educational system: character acquired by enlightened experience. The teachers provide the enlightenment; the universe station and the ascender's status afford the opportunity for experience; the wise utilization of these two augments character.

Fundamentally, the Nebadon educational system provides for your assignment to a task and then affords you opportunity to receive instruction as to the ideal and divine method of best performing that task. You are given a definite task to perform, and at the same time you are provided with teachers who are qualified to instruct you in the best method of executing your assignment. The divine plan of education provides for the intimate association of work and instruction. We teach you how best to execute the things we command you to do.

The purpose of all this training and experience is to prepare you for admission to the higher and more spiritual training spheres of the superuniverse. Progress within a given realm is individual, but transition from one phase to another is usually by classes.

The progression of eternity does not consist solely in spiritual development. Intellectual acquisition is also a part of universal education. The experience of the mind is broadened equally with the expansion of the spiritual horizon. Mind and spirit are afforded like opportunities for training and advancement. But in all this superb training of mind and spirit you are forever free from the handicaps of mortal flesh. No longer must you constantly referee the conflicting contentions of your divergent spiritual and material natures. At last you are qualified to enjoy the unified urge of a glorified mind long since divested of primitive animalistic trends towards things material.

Before leaving the universe of Nebadon, most Urantia mortals will be afforded opportunity to serve for a longer or shorter time as members of the Nebadon corps of Celestial Overseers.

7. MANSION WORLD TEACHERS

The Mansion World Teachers are recruited and glorified cherubim. Like most other instructors in Nebadon they are commissioned by the Melchizedeks. They function in most of the educational enterprises of the morontia life, and their number is quite beyond the comprehension of mortal mind.

As an attainment level of cherubim and sanobim, the Mansion World Teachers will receive further consideration in the next paper, while as teachers playing an important part in the morontia life, they will be more extensively discussed in the paper of that name.

8. HIGHER SPIRIT ORDERS OF ASSIGNMENT

Besides the power centers and the physical controllers, certain of the higher-origin spirit beings of the family of the Infinite Spirit are of permanent assignment to the local universe. Of the higher spirit orders of the family of the Infinite Spirit the following are so assigned:

The *Solitary Messengers,* when functionally attached to the local universe administration, render invaluable service to us in our efforts to overcome the handicaps of time and space. When they are not thus assigned, we of the local universes have absolutely no authority over them, but even then these unique beings are always willing to help us with the solution of our problems and with the execution of our mandates.

Andovontia is the name of the tertiary *Universe Circuit Supervisor* stationed in our local universe. He is concerned only with spirit and morontia circuits, not with those under the jurisdiction of the power directors. It was he who isolated Urantia at the time of the Caligastia betrayal of the planet during the testing seasons of the Lucifer rebellion. In sending greetings to the mortals of Urantia, he expresses pleasure in the anticipation of your sometime restoration to the universe circuits of his supervision.

The Nebadon *Census Director,* Salsatia, maintains headquarters within the Gabriel sector of Salvington. He is automatically cognizant of the birth and death of will and currently registers the exact number of will creatures functioning in the local universe. He works in close association with the personality recorders domiciled on the record worlds of the archangels.

An *Associate Inspector* is resident on Salvington. He is the personal representative of the Supreme Executive of Orvonton. His associates, the *Assigned Sentinels* in the local systems, are also representatives of the Supreme Executive of Orvonton.

The *Universal Conciliators* are the traveling courts of the universes of time and space, functioning from the evolutionary worlds up through every section of the local universe and on beyond. These referees are registered on Uversa; the exact number operating in Nebadon is not of record, but I estimate that there are in the neighborhood of one hundred million conciliating commissions in our local universe.

Of the *Technical Advisers,* the legal minds of the realm, we have our quota, about one-half billion. These beings are the living and circulating experiential law libraries of all space.

Of the *Celestial Recorders,* the ascendant seraphim, we have in Nebadon seventy-five. These are the senior or supervising recorders. The advancing students of this order in training number almost four billion.

The ministry of the seventy billion *Morontia Companions* in Nebadon is described in those narratives dealing with the transition planets of the pilgrims of time.

Each universe has its own native angelic corps; nevertheless, there are occasions on which it is very helpful to have the assistance of those higher spirits of origin outside the local creation. Supernaphim perform certain rare and unique services; the present chief of Urantia seraphim is a primary supernaphim of Paradise. The reflective seconaphim are encountered wherever the superuniverse personnel is functioning, and a great many tertiaphim are of temporary service as Most High Assistants.

9. PERMANENT CITIZENS OF THE LOCAL UNIVERSE

As with the super- and central universes, the local universe has its orders of permanent citizenship. These include the following created types:

1. Susatia.
2. Univitatia.
3. Material Sons.
4. Midway Creatures.

These natives of the local creation, together with the Spirit-fused ascenders and the spironga (who are otherwise classified), constitute a relatively permanent citizenship. These orders of beings are by and large neither ascending nor descending. They are all experiential creatures, but their enlarging experience continues to be available to the universe on their level of origin. While this is not wholly true of the Adamic Sons and midway creatures, it is relatively true of these orders.

The Susatia. These marvelous beings reside and function as permanent citizens on Salvington, the headquarters of this local universe. They are the brilliant offspring of the Creator Son and Creative Spirit and are closely associated with the ascendant citizens of the local universe, the Spirit-fused mortals of the Nebadon Corps of Perfection.

The Univitatia. Each of the one hundred constellation headquarters clusters of architectural spheres enjoys the continuous ministry of a residential order of beings known as the univitatia. These children of the Creator Son and the

Creative Spirit constitute the permanent population of the constellation headquarters worlds. They are nonreproducing beings existing on a plane of life about halfway between the semimaterial status of the Material Sons domiciled on the system headquarters and the more definitely spiritual plane of the Spirit-fused mortals and the susatia of Salvington; but the univitatia are not morontia beings. They accomplish for ascending mortals during the traversal of the constellation spheres what the Havona natives contribute to the pilgrim spirits passing through the central creation.

The Material Sons of God. When a creative liaison between the Creator Son and the universe representative of the Infinite Spirit, the Universe Mother Spirit, has completed its cycle, when no more offspring of the combined nature are forthcoming, then does the Creator Son personalize in dual form his last concept of being, thus finally confirming his own and original dual origin. In and of himself he then creates the beautiful and superb Sons and Daughters of the material order of universe sonship. This is the origin of the original Adam and Eve of each local system of Nebadon. They are a reproducing order of sonship, being created male and female. Their progeny function as the relatively permanent citizens of a system capital, though some are commissioned as Planetary Adams.

On a planetary mission the Material Son and Daughter are commissioned to found the Adamic race of that world, a race designed eventually to amalgamate with the mortal inhabitants of that sphere. Planetary Adams are both descending and ascending Sons, but we ordinarily class them as ascending.

The Midway Creatures. In the early days of most inhabited worlds, certain superhuman but materialized beings are of assignment, but they usually retire upon the arrival of the Planetary Adams. The transactions of such beings and the efforts of the Material Sons to improve the evolutionary races often result in the appearance of a limited number of creatures who are difficult to classify. These unique beings are often midway between the Material Sons and the evolutionary creatures; hence their designation, midway creatures. In a comparative sense these midwayers are the permanent citizens of the evolutionary worlds. From the early days of the arrival of a Planetary Prince to the far-distant time of the settling of the planet in light and life, they are the only group of intelligent beings to remain continuously on the sphere. On Urantia the midway ministers are in reality the actual custodians of the planet; they are, practically speaking, the citizens of Urantia. Mortals are indeed the physical and material inhabitants of an evolutionary world, but you are all so short-lived; you tarry on your nativity planet such a short time. You are born, live, die, and pass on to other worlds of evolutionary progression. Even the superhuman beings who serve on the planets as celestial ministers are of transient assignment; few of them are long attached to a given sphere. The midway creatures, however, provide continuity of planetary administration in the face of ever-changing celestial ministries and constantly shifting mortal inhabitants. Throughout all of this never-ceasing changing and shifting, the midway creatures remain on the planet uninterruptedly carrying on their work.

In like manner, all divisions of the administrative organization of the local universes and superuniverses have their more or less permanent populations, inhabitants of citizenship status. As Urantia has its midwayers, Jerusem, your system capital, has the Material Sons and Daughters; Edentia, your constellation headquarters, has the univitatia, while the citizens of Salvington are twofold, the created susatia and the evolved Spirit-fused mortals. The administrative worlds of the minor and major sectors of the superuniverses do not have permanent citizens. But the Uversa headquarters spheres are continuously fostered by an amazing group of beings known as the *abandonters,* the creation of the unrevealed agents of the Ancients of Days and the seven Reflective Spirits resident on the capital of Orvonton. These residential citizens on Uversa are at present administering the routine affairs of their world under the immediate supervision of the Uversa corps of the Son-fused mortals. Even Havona has its native beings, and the central Isle of Light and Life is the home of the various groups of Paradise Citizens.

10. OTHER LOCAL UNIVERSE GROUPS

Besides the seraphic and mortal orders, who will be considered in later papers, there are numerous additional beings concerned in the maintenance and perfecting of such a gigantic organization as the universe of Nebadon, which even now has more than three million inhabited worlds, with ten million in prospect. The various Nebadon types of life are much too numerous to be catalogued in this paper, but there are two unusual orders that function extensively on the 647,591 architectural spheres of the local universe, that may be mentioned.

The *Spironga* are the spirit offspring of the Bright and Morning Star and the Father Melchizedek. They are exempt from personality termination but are not evolutionary or ascending beings. Neither are they functionally concerned with the evolutionary ascension regime. They are the spirit helpers of the local universe, executing the routine spirit tasks of Nebadon.

The *Spornagia.* The architectural headquarters worlds of the local universe are real worlds—physical creations. There is much work connected with their physical upkeep, and herein we have the assistance of a group of physical creatures called spornagia. They are devoted to the care and culture of the material phases of these headquarters worlds, from Jerusem to Salvington. Spornagia are neither spirits nor persons; they are an animal order of existence, but if you could see them, you would agree that they seem to be perfect animals.

The various *courtesy colonies* are domiciled on Salvington and elsewhere. We especially profit from the ministry of the celestial artisans on the constellations and benefit from the activities of the reversion directors, who operate chiefly on the capitals of the local systems.

Always there is attached to the universe service a corps of ascending mortals, including the glorified midway creatures. These ascenders, after attaining Salvington, are used in an almost endless variety of activities in the conduct of universe affairs. From each level of achievement these advancing mortals reach back and down to extend a helping hand to their fellows who follow them in the upward climb. Such mortals of temporary sojourn on Salvington are assigned on requisition to practically all corps of celestial personalities as helpers, students, observers, and teachers.

There are still other types of intelligent life concerned with the administration of a local universe, but the plan of this narrative does not provide for the further revelation of these orders of creation. Enough of the life and administration of this universe is being herewith portrayed to afford the mortal mind a grasp of the reality and grandeur of the survival existence. Further experience in your advancing careers will increasingly reveal these interesting and charming beings. This narrative cannot be more than a brief outline of the nature and work of the manifold personalities who throng the universes of space administering these creations as enormous training schools, schools wherein the pilgrims of time advance from life to life and from world to world until they are lovingly dispatched from the borders of the universe of their origin to the higher educational regime of the superuniverse and thence on to the spirit-training worlds of Havona and eventually to Paradise and the high destiny of the finaliters—the eternal assignment on missions not yet revealed to the universes of time and space.

[Dictated by a Brilliant Evening Star of Nebadon, Number 1,146 of the Created Corps.]

PAPER 38

MINISTERING SPIRITS OF THE LOCAL UNIVERSE

THERE are three distinct orders of the personalities of the Infinite Spirit. The impetuous apostle understood this when he wrote respecting Jesus, "who has gone to heaven and is on the right hand of God, angels and authorities and powers being made subject to him." Angels are the ministering spirits of time; authorities, the messenger hosts of space; powers, the higher personalities of the Infinite Spirit.

As the supernaphim in the central universe and the seconaphim in a superuniverse, so the seraphim, with the associated cherubim and sanobim, constitute the angelic corps of a local universe.

The seraphim are all fairly uniform in design. From universe to universe, throughout all seven of the superuniverses, they show a minimum of variation; they are the most nearly standard of all spirit types of personal beings. Their various orders constitute the corps of the skilled and common ministers of the local creations.

1. ORIGIN OF SERAPHIM

Seraphim are created by the Universe Mother Spirit and have been projected in unit formation—41,472 at a time—ever since the creation of the "pattern angels" and certain angelic archetypes in the early times of Nebadon. The Creator Son and the universe representation of the Infinite Spirit collaborate in the creation of a large number of Sons and other universe personalities. Following the completion of this united effort, the Son engages in the creation of the Material Sons, the first of the sex creatures, while the Universe Mother Spirit concurrently engages in her initial solitary effort at spirit reproduction. Thus begins the creation of the seraphic hosts of a local universe.

These angelic orders are projected at the time of planning for the evolution of mortal will creatures. The creation of seraphim dates from the attainment of relative personality by the Universe Mother Spirit, not as the later co-ordinate of the Master Son, but as the early creative helper of the Creator Son. Previous to this event the seraphim on duty in Nebadon were temporarily loaned by a neighboring universe.

Seraphim are still being periodically created; the universe of Nebadon is still in the making. The Universe Mother Spirit never ceases creative activity in a growing and perfecting universe.

2. ANGELIC NATURES

Angels do not have material bodies, but they are definite and discrete beings; they are of spirit nature and origin. Though invisible to mortals, they perceive you as you are in the flesh without the aid of transformers or translators; they intellectually understand the mode of mortal life, and they share all of man's nonsensuous emotions and sentiments. They appreciate and greatly enjoy your efforts in music, art, and real humor. They are fully cognizant of your moral struggles and spiritual difficulties. They love human beings, and only good can result from your efforts to understand and love them.

Though seraphim are very affectionate and sympathetic beings, they are not sex-emotion creatures. They are much as you will be on the mansion worlds, where you will "neither marry nor be given in marriage but will be as the angels of heaven." For all who "shall be accounted worthy to attain the mansion worlds neither marry nor are given in marriage; neither do they die any more, for they are equal to the angels." Nevertheless, in dealing with sex creatures it is our custom to speak of those beings of more direct descent from the Father and the Son as the sons of God, while referring to the children of the Spirit as the daughters of God. Angels are, therefore, commonly designated by feminine pronouns on the sex planets.

The seraphim are so created as to function on both spiritual and literal levels. There are few phases of morontia or spirit activity which are not open to their ministrations. While in personal status angels are not so far removed from human beings, in certain functional performances seraphim far transcend them. They possess many powers far beyond human comprehension. For example: You have been told that the "very hairs of your head are numbered," and it is true they are, but a seraphim does not spend her time counting them and keeping the number corrected up to date. Angels possess inherent and automatic (that is, automatic as far as you could perceive) powers of knowing such things; you would truly regard a seraphim as a mathematical prodigy. Therefore, numerous duties which would be tremendous tasks for mortals are performed with exceeding ease by seraphim.

Angels are superior to you in spiritual status, but they are not your judges or accusers. No matter what your faults, "the angels, although greater in power and might, bring no accusation against you." Angels do not sit in judgment on mankind, neither should individual mortals prejudge their fellow creatures.

You do well to love them, but you should not adore them; angels are not objects of worship. The great seraphim, Loyalatia, when your seer "fell down to worship before the feet of the angel," said: "See that you do it not; I am a fellow servant with you and with your races, who are all enjoined to worship God."

In nature and personality endowment the seraphim are just a trifle ahead of mortal races in the scale of creature existence. Indeed, when you are delivered from the flesh, you become very much like them. On the mansion worlds you will begin to appreciate the seraphim, on the constellation spheres to enjoy them, while on Salvington they will share their places of rest and worship with you. Throughout the whole morontia and subsequent spirit ascent, your fraternity with the seraphim will be ideal; your companionship will be superb.

3. UNREVEALED ANGELS

Numerous orders of spirit beings function throughout the domains of the local universe that are unrevealed to mortals because they are in no manner connected with the evolutionary plan of Paradise ascension. In this paper the word "angel" is purposely limited to the designation of those seraphic and associated offspring of the Universe Mother Spirit who are so largely concerned with the operation of the plans of mortal survival. There serve in the local universe six other orders of related beings, the unrevealed angels, who are not in any specific manner connected with those universe activities pertaining to the Paradise ascent of evolutionary mortals. These six groups of angelic associates are never called seraphim, neither are they referred to as ministering spirits. These personalities are wholly occupied with the administrative and other affairs of Nebadon, engagements which are in no way related to man's progressive career of spiritual ascent and perfection attainment.

4. THE SERAPHIC WORLDS

The ninth group of seven primary spheres in the Salvington circuit are the worlds of the seraphim. Each of these worlds has six tributary satellites, whereon are the special schools devoted to all phases of seraphic training. While the seraphim have access to all forty-nine worlds comprising this group of Salvington spheres, they exclusively occupy only the first cluster of seven. The remaining six clusters are occupied by the six orders of angelic associates unrevealed on Urantia; each such group maintains headquarters on one of these six primary worlds and carries on specialized activities on the six tributary satellites. Each angelic order has free access to all the worlds of these seven diverse groups.

These headquarters worlds are among the magnificent realms of Nebadon; the seraphic estates are characterized by both beauty and vastness. Here each seraphim has a real home, and "home" means the domicile of two seraphim; they live in pairs.

Though not male and female as are the Material Sons and the mortal races, seraphim are negative and positive. In the majority of assignments it requires two angels to accomplish the task. When they are not encircuited, they can work alone; neither do they require complements of being when stationary. Ordinarily they retain their original complements of being, but not necessarily. Such associations are primarily necessitated by function; they are not characterized by sex emotion, though they are exceedingly personal and truly affectionate.

Besides designated homes, seraphim also have group, company, battalion, and unit headquarters. They forgather for reunions every millennium and are all present in accordance with the time of their creation. If a seraphim bears responsibilities which forbid absence from duty, she alternates attendance with her complement, being relieved by a seraphim of another birth date. Each seraphic partner is thereby present at least every other reunion.

5. SERAPHIC TRAINING

Seraphim spend their first millennium as noncommissioned observers on Salvington and its associated world schools. The second millennium is spent on the seraphic worlds of the Salvington circuit. Their central training school is now presided over by the first one hundred thousand Nebadon seraphim, and at their head is the original or first-born angel of this local universe. The first created group of Nebadon seraphim were trained by a corps of one thousand seraphim from Avalon; subsequently our angels have been taught by their own seniors. The Melchizedeks also have a large part in the education and training of all local universe angels—seraphim, cherubim, and sanobim.

At the termination of this period of training on the seraphic worlds of Salvington, seraphim are mobilized in the conventional groups and units of the angelic organization and are assigned to some one of the constellations. They are not yet commissioned as ministering spirits, although they have well entered upon the precommissioned phases of angelic training.

Seraphim are initiated as ministering spirits by serving as observers on the lowest of the evolutionary worlds. After this experience they return to the associate worlds of the headquarters of the assigned constellation to begin their advanced studies and more definitely to prepare for service in some particular local system. Following this general education they are advanced to the service of some one of the local systems. On the architectural worlds associated with the capital of some Nebadon system our seraphim complete their training and are commissioned as ministering spirits of time.

When once seraphim are commissioned, they may range all Nebadon, even Orvonton, on assignment. Their work in the universe is without bounds and limitations; they are closely associated with the material creatures of the worlds and are ever in the service of the lower orders of spiritual personalities, making contact between these beings of the spirit world and the mortals of the material realms.

6. SERAPHIC ORGANIZATION

After the second millennium of sojourn at seraphic headquarters the seraphim are organized under chiefs into groups of twelve (12 pairs, 24 seraphim), and twelve such groups constitute a company (144 pairs, 288 seraphim), which is commanded by a leader. Twelve companies under a commander constitute a battalion (1,728 pairs or 3,456 seraphim), and twelve battalions under a director equal a seraphic unit (20,736 pairs or 41,472 individuals), while twelve units, subject to the command of a supervisor, constitute a legion numbering 248,832 pairs or 497,664 individuals. Jesus alluded to such a group of angels that night in the garden of Gethsemane when he said: "I can even now ask my Father, and he will presently give me more than twelve legions of angels."

Twelve legions of angels comprise a host numbering 2,985,984 pairs or 5,971,968 individuals, and twelve such hosts (35,831,808 pairs or 71,663,616 individuals) make up the largest operating organization of seraphim, an angelic army. A seraphic host is commanded by an archangel or by some other personality of co-ordinate status, while the angelic armies are directed by the Brilliant Evening Stars or by other immediate lieutenants of Gabriel. And Gabriel is the "supreme commander of the armies of heaven," the chief executive of the Sovereign of Nebadon, "the Lord God of hosts."

Though serving under the direct supervision of the Infinite Spirit as personalized on Salvington, since the bestowal of Michael on Urantia, seraphim and all other local universe orders have become subject to the sovereignty of the

Master Son. Even when Michael was born of the flesh on Urantia, there issued the superuniverse broadcast to all Nebadon which proclaimed, "And let all the angels worship him." All ranks of angels are subject to his sovereignty; they are a part of that group which has been denominated "his mighty angels."

7. CHERUBIM AND SANOBIM

In all essential endowments cherubim and sanobim are similar to seraphim. They have the same origin but not always the same destiny. They are wonderfully intelligent, marvelously efficient, touchingly affectionate, and almost human. They are the lowest order of angels, hence all the nearer of kin to the more progressive types of human beings on the evolutionary worlds.

Cherubim and sanobim are inherently associated, functionally united. One is an energy positive personality; the other, energy negative. The right-hand deflector, or positively charged angel, is the cherubim—the senior or controlling personality. The left-hand deflector, or negatively charged angel, is the sanobim—the complement of being. Each type of angel is very limited in solitary function; hence they usually serve in pairs. When serving independently of their seraphic directors, they are more than ever dependent on mutual contact and always function together.

Cherubim and sanobim are the faithful and efficient aids of the seraphic ministers, and all seven orders of seraphim are provided with these subordinate assistants. Cherubim and sanobim serve for ages in these capacities, but they do not accompany seraphim on assignments beyond the confines of the local universe.

The cherubim and sanobim are the routine spirit workers on the individual worlds of the systems. On a nonpersonal assignment and in an emergency, they may serve in the place of a seraphic pair, but they never function, even temporarily, as attending angels to human beings; that is an exclusive seraphic privilege.

When assigned to a planet, cherubim enter the local courses of training, including a study of planetary usages and languages. The ministering spirits of time are all bilingual, speaking the language of the local universe of their origin and that of their native superuniverse. By study in the schools of the realms they acquire additional tongues. Cherubim and sanobim, like seraphim and all other orders of spirit beings, are continuously engaged in efforts at self-improvement. Only such as the subordinate beings of power control and energy direction are incapable of progression; all creatures having actual or potential personality volition seek new achievements.

Cherubim and sanobim are by nature very near the morontia level of existence, and they prove to be most efficient in the borderland work of the physical, morontial, and spiritual domains. These children of the local universe Mother Spirit are characterized by "fourth creatures" much as are the Havona Servitals and the conciliating commissions. Every fourth cherubim and every fourth sanobim are quasi-material, very definitely resembling the morontia level of existence.

These angelic fourth creatures are of great assistance to the seraphim in the more literal phases of their universe and planetary activities. Such morontia cherubim also perform many indispensable borderline tasks on the morontia training worlds and are assigned to the service of the Morontia Companions in large numbers. They are to the morontia spheres about what the midway creatures are to the evolutionary planets. On the inhabited worlds these morontia cherubim frequently work in liaison with the midway creatures. Cherubim and midway creatures are distinctly separate orders of beings; they have dissimilar origins, but they disclose great similarity in nature and function.

8. EVOLUTION OF CHERUBIM AND SANOBIM

Numerous avenues of advancing service are open to cherubim and sanobim leading to an enhancement of status, which may be still further augmented by the embrace of the Divine Minister. There are three great classes of cherubim and sanobim with regard to evolutionary potential:

1. *Ascension Candidates.* These beings are by nature candidates for seraphic status. Cherubim and sanobim of this order are brilliant, though not by inherent endowment equal to the seraphim; but by application and experience it is possible for them to attain full seraphic standing.

2. *Mid-phase Cherubim.* All cherubim and sanobim are not equal in ascension potential, and these are the inherently limited beings of the angelic creations. Most of them will remain cherubim and sanobim, although the more gifted individuals may achieve limited seraphic service.

3. *Morontia Cherubim.* These "fourth creatures" of the angelic orders always retain their quasi-material characteristics. They will continue on as cherubim and sanobim, together with a majority of their mid-phase brethren, pending the completed factualization of the Supreme Being.

While the second and third groups are somewhat limited in growth potential, the ascension candidates may attain the heights of universal seraphic service. Many of the more experienced of these cherubim are attached to the seraphic guardians of destiny and are thus placed in direct line for advancement to the status of Mansion World Teachers when deserted by their seraphic seniors. Guardians of destiny do not have cherubim and sanobim as helpers when their mortal wards attain the morontia life. And when other types of evolutionary seraphim are granted clearance for Seraphington and Paradise, they must forsake their former subordinates when they pass out of the confines of Nebadon. Such deserted cherubim and sanobim are usually embraced by the Universe Mother Spirit, thus achieving a level equivalent to that of a Mansion World Teacher in the attainment of seraphic status.

When, as Mansion World Teachers, the once-embraced cherubim and sanobim have long served on the morontia spheres, from the lowest to the highest, and when their corps on Salvington is overrecruited, the Bright and Morning Star summons these faithful servants of the creatures of time to appear in his presence. The oath of personality transformation is administered; and thereupon, in groups of seven thousand, these advanced and senior cherubim and sanobim are re-embraced by the Universe Mother Spirit. From this second embrace they emerge as full-fledged seraphim. Henceforth, the full and complete career of a seraphim, with all of its Paradise possibilities, is open to such reborn cherubim and sanobim. Such angels may be assigned as guardians of destiny to some mortal being, and if the mortal ward attains survival, then do they become eligible for advancement to Seraphington and the seven circles of seraphic attainment, even to Paradise and the Corps of the Finality.

9. THE MIDWAY CREATURES

The midway creatures have a threefold classification: They are properly classified with the ascending Sons of God; they are factually grouped with the orders of permanent citizenship, while they are functionally reckoned with the ministering spirits of time because of their intimate and effective association with the angelic hosts in the work of serving mortal man on the individual worlds of space.

These unique creatures appear on the majority of the inhabited worlds and are always found on the decimal or life-experiment planets, such as Urantia. Midwayers are of two types—primary and secondary—and they appear by the following techniques:

1. *Primary Midwayers,* the more spiritual group, are a somewhat standardized order of beings who are uniformly derived from the modified ascendant-mortal staffs of the Planetary Princes. The number of primary midway creatures is always fifty thousand, and no planet enjoying their ministry has a larger group.

2. *Secondary Midwayers,* the more material group of these creatures, vary greatly in numbers on the different worlds, though the average is around fifty thousand. They are variously derived from the planetary biologic uplifters, the Adams and Eves, or from their immediate progeny. There are no less than twenty-four diverse techniques involved in the production of these secondary midway creatures on the evolutionary worlds of space. The mode of origin for this group on Urantia was unusual and extraordinary.

Neither of these groups is an evolutionary accident; both are essential features in the predetermined plans of the universe architects, and their appearance on the evolving worlds at the opportune juncture is in accordance with the original designs and developmental plans of the supervising Life Carriers.

Primary midwayers are energized intellectually and spiritually by the angelic technique and are uniform in intellectual status. The seven adjutant mind-spirits make no contact with them; and only the sixth and the seventh, the spirit of worship and the spirit of wisdom, are able to minister to the secondary group.

Secondary midwayers are physically energized by the Adamic technique, spiritually encircuited by the seraphic, and intellectually endowed with the morontia transition type of mind. They are divided into four physical types, seven orders spiritually, and twelve levels of intellectual response to the joint ministry of the last two adjutant spirits and the morontia mind. These diversities determine their differential of activity and of planetary assignment.

Primary midwayers resemble angels more than mortals; the secondary orders are much more like human beings. Each renders invaluable assistance to the other in the execution of their manifold planetary assignments. The primary ministers can achieve liaison co-operation with both morontia- and spirit-energy controllers and mind circuiters. The secondary group can establish working connections only with the physical controllers and the material-circuit manipulators. But since each order of midwayer can establish perfect synchrony of contact

to the headquarters of the Planetary Prince of some evolutionary world. Here they begin the study of the languages, history, and local habits of the races of mankind. Seraphim must acquire knowledge and gain experience much as do human beings. They are not far removed from you in certain personality attributes. And they all crave to start at the bottom, on the lowest possible level of ministry; thus may they hope to achieve the highest possible level of experiential destiny.

1. SUPREME SERAPHIM

These seraphim are the highest of the seven revealed orders of local universe angels. They function in seven groups, each of which is closely associated with the angelic ministers of the Seraphic Corps of Completion.

1. *Son-Spirit Ministers.* The first group of the supreme seraphim are assigned to the service of the high Sons and Spirit-origin beings resident and functioning in the local universe. This group of angelic ministers also serve the Universe Son and the Universe Spirit and are closely affiliated with the intelligence corps of the Bright and Morning Star, the universe chief executive of the united wills of the Creator Son and the Creative Spirit.

Being of assignment to the high Sons and Spirits, these seraphim are naturally associated with the far-flung services of the Paradise Avonals, the divine offspring of the Eternal Son and the Infinite Spirit. The Paradise Avonals are always attended on all magisterial and bestowal missions by this high and experienced order of seraphim, who are at such times devoted to organizing and administering the special work connected with the termination of one planetary dispensation and the inauguration of a new age. But they are not concerned in the work of adjudication which might be incidental to such a change in dispensations.

Bestowal Attendants. Paradise Avonals, but not Creator Sons, when on a bestowal mission are always accompanied by a corps of 144 bestowal attendants. These 144 angels are the chiefs of all other Son-Spirit ministers who may be associated with a bestowal mission. There might possibly be legions of angels subject to the command of an incarnated Son of God on a planetary bestowal, but all these seraphim would be organized and directed by the 144 bestowal attendants. Higher orders of angels, supernaphim and seconaphim, might also form a part of the attending host, and though their missions are distinct from those of the seraphim, all these activities would be co-ordinated by the bestowal attendants.

These bestowal attendants are completion seraphim; they have all traversed the circles of Seraphington and have attained the Seraphic Corps of Completion. And they have been further especially trained to meet the difficulties and to cope with the emergencies associated with the bestowals of the Sons of God for the advancement of the children of time. Such seraphim have all achieved Paradise and the personal embrace of the Second Source and Center, the Eternal Son.

Seraphim equally crave assignment to the missions of the incarnated Sons and attachment as destiny guardians to the mortals of the realms; the latter is the surest seraphic passport to Paradise, while the bestowal attendants have achieved the highest local universe service of the completion seraphim of Paradise attainment.

2. *Court Advisers.* These are the seraphic advisers and helpers attached to all orders of adjudication, from the conciliators up to the highest tribunals of the realm. It is not the purpose of such tribunals to determine punitive sentences but rather to adjudicate honest differences of opinion and to decree the everlasting survival of ascending mortals. Herein lies the duty of the court advisers: to see that all charges against mortal creatures are stated in justice and adjudicated in mercy. In this work they are closely associated with the High Commissioners, Spirit-fused ascendant mortals serving in the local universe.

The seraphic court advisers serve extensively as defenders of mortals. Not that there ever exists any disposition to be unfair to the lowly creatures of the realms, but while justice demands the adjudication of every default in the climb towards divine perfection, mercy requires that every such misstep be fairly adjudged in accordance with the creature nature and the divine purpose. These angels are the exponents and exemplification of the element of mercy inherent in divine justice—of fairness based on the knowledge of the underlying facts of personal motives and racial tendencies.

This order of angels serves from the councils of the Planetary Princes to the highest tribunals of the local universe, while their associates of the Seraphic Corps of Completion function in the higher realms of Orvonton, even to the courts of the Ancients of Days on Uversa.

3. *Universe Orientators.* These are the true friends and postgraduate counselors of all those ascending creatures who are pausing for the last time on Salvington, in their universe of origin, as they stand on the brink of the spirit adventure stretching out before them in the vast superuniverse of Orvonton. And at such a time many an ascender has a feeling which mortals could understand only by comparison with the human emotion of nostalgia. Behind lie the realms of achievement, realms grown familiar by long service and morontia attainment; ahead lies the challenging mystery of a greater and vaster universe.

It is the task of the universe orientators to facilitate the passage of the ascending pilgrims from the attained to the unattained level of universe service, to help these pilgrims in making those kaleidoscopic adjustments in the comprehension of meanings and values inherent in the realization that a first-stage spirit being stands, not at the end and climax of the local universe morontia ascent, but rather at the very bottom of the long ladder of spiritual ascent to the Universal Father on Paradise.

Many of the Seraphington graduates, members of the Seraphic Corps of Completion who are associated with these seraphim, engage in extensive teaching in certain Salvington schools concerned with the preparation of the creatures of Nebadon for the relationships of the next universe age.

4. *The Teaching Counselors.* These angels are the invaluable assistants of the spiritual teaching corps of the local universe. Teaching counselors are secretaries to all orders of teachers, from the Melchizedeks and the Trinity Teacher Sons down to the morontia mortals who are assigned as helpers to those of their kind who are just behind them in the scale of ascendant life. You will first *see* these associate teaching seraphim on some one of the seven mansion worlds surrounding Jerusem.

These seraphim become associates of the division chiefs of the numerous educational and training institutions of the local universes, and they are attached in large numbers to the faculties of the seven training worlds of the local systems and of the seventy educational spheres of the constellations. These ministrations extend on down to the individual worlds. Even the true and consecrated teachers of time are assisted, and often attended, by these counselors of the supreme seraphim.

The fourth creature bestowal of the Creator Son was in the likeness of a teaching counselor of the supreme seraphim of Nebadon.

5. *Directors of Assignment.* A body of 144 supreme seraphim is elected from time to time by the angels serving on the evolutionary and on the architectural spheres of creature habitation. This is the highest angelic council on any sphere, and it co-ordinates the self-directed phases of seraphic service and assignment. These angels preside over all seraphic assemblies pertaining to the line of duty or the call to worship.

6. *The Recorders.* These are the official recorders for the supreme seraphim. Many of these high angels were born with their gifts fully developed; others have qualified for their positions of trust and responsibility by diligent application to study and faithful performance of similar duties while attached to lower or less responsible orders.

7. *Unattached Ministers.* Large numbers of unattached seraphim of the supreme order are self-directed servers on the architectural spheres and on the inhabited planets. Such ministers voluntarily meet the differential of demand for the service of the supreme seraphim, thus constituting the general reserve of this order.

2. SUPERIOR SERAPHIM

Superior seraphim receive their name, not because they are in any sense qualitatively superior to other orders of angels, but because they are in charge of the higher activities of a local universe. Very many of the first two groups of this seraphic corps are attainment seraphim, angels who have served in all phases of training and have returned to a glorified assignment as directors of their kind in the spheres of their earlier activities. Being a young universe, Nebadon does not have many of this order.

The superior seraphim function in the following seven groups:

1. *The Intelligence Corps.* These seraphim belong to the personal staff of Gabriel, the Bright and Morning Star. They range the local universe gathering the information of the realms for his guidance in the councils of Nebadon. They are the intelligence corps of the mighty hosts over which Gabriel presides as vicegerent of the Master Son. These seraphim are not directly affiliated with either the systems or the constellations, and their information pours in direct to Salvington upon a continuous, direct, and independent circuit.

The intelligence corps of the various local universes can and do intercommunicate but only within a given superuniverse. There is a differential of energy which effectively segregates the business and transactions of the various supergovernments. One superuniverse can ordinarily communicate with another superuniverse only through the provisions and facilities of the Paradise clearinghouse.

2. *The Voice of Mercy.* Mercy is the keynote of seraphic service and angelic ministry. It is therefore fitting that there should be a corps of angels who, in a special manner, portray mercy. These seraphim are the real mercy ministers of the local universes. They are the inspired leaders who foster the higher impulses and holier emotions of men and angels. The directors of these legions are now always completion seraphim who are also graduate guardians of mortal destiny; that is, each angelic pair has guided at least one soul of animal origin during the life in the flesh and has subsequently traversed the circles of Seraphington and has been mustered into the Seraphic Corps of Completion.

3. *Spirit Co-ordinators.* The third group of superior seraphim are based on Salvington but function in the local universe anywhere they can be of fruitful service. While their tasks are essentially spiritual and therefore beyond the real understanding of human minds, you will perhaps grasp something of their ministry to mortals if it is explained that these angels are intrusted with the task of preparing the ascendant sojourners on Salvington for their last transition in the local universe—from the highest morontia level to the status of newborn spirit beings. As the mind planners on the mansion worlds help the surviving creature to adjust to, and make effective use of, the potentials of morontia mind, so do these seraphim instruct the morontia graduates on Salvington regarding the newly attained capacities of the mind of the spirit. And they serve the ascendant mortals in many other ways.

4. *Assistant Teachers.* The assistant teachers are the helpers and associates of their fellow seraphim, the teaching counselors. They are also individually connected with the extensive educational enterprises of the local universe, especially with the sevenfold scheme of training operative on the mansion worlds of the local systems. A marvelous corps of this order of seraphim functions on Urantia for the purpose of fostering and furthering the cause of truth and righteousness.

5. *The Transporters.* All groups of ministering spirits have their transport corps, angelic orders dedicated to the ministry of transporting those personalities who are unable, of themselves, to journey from one sphere to another. The fifth group of the superior seraphim are headquartered on Salvington and serve as space traversers to and from the headquarters of the local universe. Like other subdivisions of the superior seraphim, some were created as such while others have risen from the lower or less endowed groups.

The "energy range" of seraphim is wholly adequate for local universe and even for superuniverse requirements, but they could never withstand the energy demands entailed by such a long journey as that from Uversa to Havona. Such an exhaustive journey requires the special powers of a primary seconaphim of transport endowments. Transporters take on energy for flight while in transit and recuperate personal power at the end of the journey.

Even on Salvington ascending mortals do not possess personal transit forms. Ascenders must depend upon seraphic transport in advancing from world to world until after the last rest of sleep on the inner circle of Havona and the eternal awakening on Paradise. Subsequently you will not be dependent on angels for transport from universe to universe.

The process of being enseraphimed is not unlike the experience of death or sleep except that there is an automatic time element in the transit slumber. You are consciously unconscious during seraphic rest. But the Thought Adjuster is wholly and fully conscious, in fact, exceptionally efficient since you are unable to oppose, resist, or otherwise hinder creative and transforming work.

When enseraphimed, you go to sleep for a specified time, and you will awake at the designated moment. The length of a journey when in transit sleep is immaterial. You are not directly aware of the passing of time. It is as if you went to sleep on a transport vehicle in one city and, after resting in peaceful slumber all night, awakened in another and distant metropolis. You journeyed while you slumbered. And so you take flight through space, enseraphimed, while you rest—sleep. The transit sleep is induced by the liaison between the Adjusters and the seraphic transporters.

The angels cannot transport combustion bodies—flesh and blood—such as you now have, but they can transport all others, from the lowest morontia to the higher spirit forms. They do not function in the event of natural death. When you finish your earthly career, your body remains on this planet. Your Thought Adjuster proceeds to the bosom of the Father, and these angels are not directly concerned in your subsequent personality reassembly on the identification mansion world. There your new body is a morontia form, one that can enseraphim. You "sow a mortal body" in the grave; you "reap a morontia form" on the mansion worlds.

6. *The Recorders.* These personalities are especially concerned with the reception, filing, and redispatch of the records of Salvington and its associated worlds. They also serve as special recorders for resident groups of superuniverse and higher personalities and as clerks of the courts of Salvington and secretaries to the rulers thereof.

Broadcasters—receivers and dispatchers—are a specialized subdivision of the seraphic recorders, being concerned with the dispatch of records and with the dissemination of essential information. Their work is of a high order, being so multicircuited that 144,000 messages can simultaneously traverse the same lines of energy. They adapt the higher ideographic techniques of the superaphic chief recorders and with these common symbols maintain reciprocal contact with both the intelligence co-ordinators of the tertiary supernaphim and the glorified intelligence co-ordinators of the Seraphic Corps of Completion.

Seraphic recorders of the superior order thus effect a close liaison with the intelligence corps of their own order and with all subordinate recorders, while the broadcasts enable them to maintain constant communication with the higher recorders of the superuniverse and, through this channel, with the recorders of Havona and the custodians of knowledge on Paradise. Many of the superior order of recorders are seraphim ascended from similar duties in lower sections of the universe.

7. *The Reserves.* Large reserves of all types of the superior seraphim are held on Salvington, instantly available for dispatch to the farthermost worlds of Nebadon as they are requisitioned by the directors of assignment or upon the request of the universe administrators. The reserves of superior seraphim also furnish messenger aids upon requisition by the chief of the Brilliant Evening Stars, who is intrusted with the custody and dispatch of all personal communications. A local universe is fully provided with adequate means of

intercommunication, but there is always a residue of messages which requires dispatch by personal messengers.

The basic reserves for the entire local universe are held on the seraphic worlds of Salvington. This corps includes all types of all groups of angels.

3. SUPERVISOR SERAPHIM

This versatile order of universe angels is assigned to the exclusive service of the constellations. These able ministers make their headquarters on the constellation capitals but function throughout all Nebadon in the interests of their assigned realms.

1. *Supervising Assistants.* The first order of the supervising seraphim are assigned to the collective work of the Constellation Fathers, and they are the ever-efficient helpers of the Most Highs. These seraphim are primarily concerned with the unification and stabilization of a whole constellation.

2. *Law Forecasters.* The intellectual foundation of justice is law, and in a local universe law originates in the legislative assemblies of the constellations. These deliberative bodies codify and formally promulgate the basic laws of Nebadon, laws designed to afford the greatest possible co-ordination of a whole constellation consistent with the fixed policy of noninfringement of the moral free will of personal creatures. It is the duty of the second order of supervisor seraphim to place before the constellation lawmakers a forecast of how any proposed enactment would affect the lives of freewill creatures. This service they are well qualified to perform by virtue of long experience in the local systems and on the inhabited worlds. These seraphim seek no special favors for one group or another, but they do appear before the celestial lawmakers to speak for those who cannot be present to speak for themselves. Even mortal man may contribute to the evolution of universe law, for these very seraphim do faithfully and fully portray, not necessarily man's transient and conscious desires, but rather the true longings of the inner man, the evolving morontia soul of the material mortal on the worlds of space.

3. *Social Architects.* From the individual planets up through the morontia training worlds, these seraphim labor to enhance all sincere social contacts and to further the social evolution of universe creatures. These are the angels who seek to divest the associations of intelligent beings of all artificiality while endeavoring to facilitate the interassociation of will creatures on a basis of real self-understanding and genuine mutual appreciation.

Social architects do everything within their province and power to bring together suitable individuals that they may constitute efficient and agreeable working groups on earth; and sometimes such groups have found themselves reassociated on the mansion worlds for continued fruitful service. But not always do these seraphim attain their ends; not always are they able to bring together those who would form the most ideal group to achieve a given purpose or to accomplish a certain task; under these conditions they must utilize the best of the material available.

These angels continue their ministry on the mansion and higher morontia worlds. They are concerned with any undertaking having to do with progress on the morontia worlds and which concerns three or more persons. Two beings are regarded as operating on the mating, complemental, or partnership basis, but when three or more are grouped for service, they constitute a social problem and therefore fall within the jurisdiction of the social architects. These efficient seraphim are organized in seventy divisions on Edentia, and these divisions minister on the seventy morontia progress worlds encircling the headquarters sphere.

4. *Ethical Sensitizers.* It is the mission of these seraphim to foster and to promote the growth of creature appreciation of the morality of interpersonal relationships, for such is the seed and secret of the continued and purposeful growth of society and government, human or superhuman. These enhancers of ethical appreciation function anywhere and everywhere they may be of service, as volunteer counselors to the planetary rulers and as exchange teachers on the system training worlds. You will not, however, come under their full guidance until you reach the brotherhood schools on Edentia, where they will quicken your appreciation of those very truths of fraternity which you will even then be so earnestly exploring by the actual experience of living with the univitatia in the social laboratories of Edentia, the seventy satellites of the Norlatiadek capital.

5. *The Transporters.* The fifth group of supervisor seraphim operate as personality transporters, carrying beings to and from the headquarters of the constellations. Such transport seraphim, while in flight from one sphere to another, are fully conscious of their velocity, direction, and astronomic whereabouts. They are not traversing space as would an inanimate projectile. They may pass near one another during space flight without the least danger of collision. They are fully able to vary speed of progression and to alter direction of flight, even to change destinations if their directors should so instruct them at any space junction of the universe intelligence circuits.

These transit personalities are so organized that they can simultaneously utilize all three of the universally distributed lines of energy, each having a clear space velocity of 186,280 miles per second. These transporters are thus able to superimpose velocity of energy upon velocity of power until they attain an average speed on their long journeys varying anywhere from 555,000 to almost 559,000 of your miles per second of your time. The velocity is affected by the mass and proximity of neighboring matter and by the strength and direction of the near-by main circuits of universe power. There are numerous types of beings, similar to the seraphim, who are able to traverse space, and who also are able to transport other beings who have been properly prepared.

6. *The Recorders.* The sixth order of supervising seraphim act as the special recorders of constellation affairs. A large and efficient corps functions on Edentia, the headquarters of the constellation of Norlatiadek, to which your system and planet belong.

7. *The Reserves.* General reserves of the supervisor seraphim are held on the headquarters of the constellations. Such angelic reservists are in no sense inactive; many serve as messenger aids to the constellation rulers; others are attached to the Salvington reserves of unassigned Vorondadeks; still others may be attached to Vorondadek Sons on special assignment, such as the Vorondadek observer, and sometimes Most High regent, of Urantia.

4. ADMINISTRATOR SERAPHIM

The fourth order of seraphim are assigned to the administrative duties of the local systems. They are indigenous to the system capitals but are stationed in large numbers on the mansion and morontia spheres and on the inhabited worlds. Fourth-order seraphim are by nature endowed with unusual administrative ability. They are the able assistants of the directors of the lower divisions of the universe government of a Creator Son and are mainly occupied with the affairs of the local systems and their component worlds. They are organized for service as follows:

1. *Administrative Assistants.* These able seraphim are the immediate assistants of a System Sovereign, a primary Lanonandek Son. They are invaluable aids in the execution of the intricate details of the executive work of the system headquarters. They also serve as the personal agents of the system rulers, journeying back and forth in large numbers to the various transition worlds and to the inhabited planets, executing many commissions for the welfare of the system and in the physical and biologic interests of its inhabited worlds.

These same seraphic administrators are also attached to the governments of the world rulers, the Planetary Princes. The majority of planets in a given universe are under the jurisdiction of a secondary Lanonandek Son, but on certain worlds, such as Urantia, there has been a miscarriage of the divine plan. In the event of the defection of a Planetary Prince, these seraphim become attached to the Melchizedek receivers and their successors in planetary authority. The present acting ruler of Urantia is assisted by a corps of one thousand of this versatile order of seraphim.

2. *Justice Guides.* These are the angels who present the summary of evidence concerning the eternal welfare of men and angels when such matters come up for adjudication in the tribunals of a system or a planet. They prepare the statements for all preliminary hearings involving mortal survival, statements which are subsequently carried with the records of such cases to the higher tribunals of the universe and the superuniverse. The defense of all cases of doubtful survival is prepared by these seraphim, who have a perfect understanding of all the details of every feature of every count in the indictments drawn by the administrators of universe justice.

It is not the mission of these angels to defeat or to delay justice but rather to insure that unerring justice is dealt out with generous mercy in fairness to all creatures. These seraphim often function on the local worlds, commonly appearing before the referee trios of the conciliating commissions—the courts for minor misunderstandings. Many who at one time served as justice guides in the lower realms later appear as Voices of Mercy in the higher spheres and on Salvington.

In the Lucifer rebellion in Satania very few of the justice guides were lost, but more than one quarter of the other administrator seraphim and of the lower orders of seraphic ministers were misled and deluded by the sophistries of unbridled personal liberty.

3. *Interpreters of Cosmic Citizenship.* When ascending mortals have completed the mansion world training, the first student apprenticeship in the universe

career, they are permitted to enjoy the transient satisfactions of relative maturity—citizenship on the system capital. While the attainment of each ascendant goal is a factual achievement, in the larger sense such goals are simply milestones on the long ascending path to Paradise. But however relative such successes may be, no evolutionary creature is ever denied the full though transient satisfaction of goal attainment. Ever and anon there is a pause in the Paradise ascent, a short breathing spell, during which universe horizons stand still, creature status is stationary, and the personality tastes the sweetness of goal fulfillment.

The first of such periods in the career of a mortal ascender occurs on the capital of a local system. During this pause you will, as a citizen of Jerusem, attempt to express in creature life those things which you have acquired during the eight preceding life experiences—embracing Urantia and the seven mansion worlds.

The seraphic interpreters of cosmic citizenship guide the new citizens of the system capitals and quicken their appreciation of the responsibilities of universe government. These seraphim are also closely associated with the Material Sons in the system administration, while they portray the responsibility and morality of cosmic citizenship to the material mortals on the inhabited worlds.

4. *Quickeners of Morality.* On the mansion worlds you begin to learn self-government for the benefit of all concerned. Your mind learns co-operation, learns how to plan with other and wiser beings. On the system headquarters the seraphic teachers will further quicken your appreciation of cosmic morality—of the interactions of liberty and loyalty.

What is loyalty? It is the fruit of an intelligent appreciation of universe brotherhood; one could not take so much and give nothing. As you ascend the personality scale, first you learn to be loyal, then to love, then to be filial, and then may you be free; but not until you are a finaliter, not until you have attained perfection of loyalty, can you self-realize finality of liberty.

These seraphim teach the fruitfulness of patience: That stagnation is certain death, but that overrapid growth is equally suicidal; that as a drop of water from a higher level falls to a lower and, flowing onward, passes ever downward through a succession of short falls, so ever upward is progress in the morontia and spirit worlds—and just as slowly and by just such gradual stages.

To the inhabited worlds the quickeners of morality portray mortal life as an unbroken chain of many links. Your short sojourn on Urantia, on this sphere of mortal infancy, is only a single link, the very first in the long chain that is to stretch across universes and through the eternal ages. It is not so much what you learn in this first life; it is the experience of living this life that is important. Even the *work* of this world, paramount though it is, is not nearly so important as the *way* in which you do this work. There is no material reward for righteous living, but there is profound satisfaction—consciousness of achievement—and this transcends any conceivable material reward.

The keys of the kingdom of heaven are: sincerity, more sincerity, and more sincerity. All men have these keys. Men use them—advance in spirit status—by decisions, by more decisions, and by more decisions. The highest moral choice is the choice of the highest possible value, and always—in any sphere, in all of them—this is to choose to do the will of God. If man thus chooses, he *is* great, though he be the humblest citizen of Jerusem or even the least of mortals on Urantia.

5. *The Transporters.* These are the transport seraphim who function in the local systems. In Satania, your system, they carry passengers back and forth from Jerusem and otherwise serve as interplanetary transporters. Seldom does a day pass in which a transport seraphim of Satania does not deposit some student visitor or some other traveler of spirit or semispirit nature on the shores of Urantia. These very space traversers will sometime carry you to and from the various worlds of the system headquarters group, and when you have finished the Jerusem assignment, they will carry you forward to Edentia. But under no circumstances will they carry you backward to the world of human origin. A mortal never returns to his native planet during the dispensation of his temporal existence, and if he should return during a subsequent dispensation, he would be escorted by a transport seraphim of the universe headquarters group.

6. *The Recorders.* These seraphim are the keepers of the threefold records of the local systems. The temple of records on a system capital is a unique structure, one third material, constructed of luminous metals and crystals; one third morontial, fabricated of the liaison of spiritual and material energy but beyond the range of mortal vision; and one third spiritual. The recorders of this order preside over and maintain this threefold system of records. Ascending mortals will at first consult the material archives, Material Sons and the higher transition beings consult those of the morontia halls, while seraphim and the higher spirit personalities of the realm peruse the records of the spirit section.

7. *The Reserves.* The reserve corps of administrator seraphim on Jerusem spend much of their waiting time in visiting, as spirit companions, with the newly arrived ascending mortals from the various worlds of the system—the accredited graduates of the mansion worlds. One of the delights of your sojourn on Jerusem will be to talk and visit, during recess periods, with these much-traveled and many-experienced seraphim of the waiting reserve corps.

It is just such friendly relationships as these that so endear a system capital to the ascending mortals. On Jerusem you will find the first intermingling of Material Sons, angels, and ascending pilgrims. Here fraternize beings who are wholly spiritual and semispiritual and individuals just emerging from material existence. Mortal forms are there so modified and human ranges of light reaction so extended that all are able to enjoy mutual recognition and sympathetic personality understanding.

5. PLANETARY HELPERS

These seraphim maintain headquarters on the system capitals and, though closely associated with the resident Adamic citizens, are primarily assigned to the service of the Planetary Adams, the biologic or physical uplifters of the material races on the evolutionary worlds. The ministering work of angels becomes of increasing interest as it nears the inhabited worlds, as it nears the actual problems faced by the men and women of time who are preparing themselves for the attempt to attain the goal of eternity.

On Urantia the majority of the planetary helpers were removed upon the collapse of the Adamic regime, and the seraphic supervision of your world devolved to a greater extent upon the administrators, the transition ministers, and the guardians of destiny. But these seraphic aids of your defaulting Material Sons still serve Urantia in the following groups:

1. *The Voices of the Garden.* When the planetary course of human evolution is attaining its highest biologic level, there always appear the Material Sons and Daughters, the Adams and Eves, to augment the further evolution of the races by an actual contribution of their superior life plasm. The planetary headquarters of such an Adam and Eve is usually denominated the Garden of Eden, and their personal seraphim are often known as the "voices of the Garden." These seraphim are of invaluable service to the Planetary Adams in all their projects for the physical and intellectual upstepping of the evolutionary races. After the Adamic default on Urantia, some of these seraphim were left on the planet and were assigned to Adam's successors in authority.

2. *The Spirits of Brotherhood.* It should be apparent that, when an Adam and Eve arrive on an evolutionary world, the task of achieving racial harmony and social co-operation among its diverse races is one of considerable proportions. Seldom do these races of different colors and varied natures take kindly to the plan of human brotherhood. These primitive men only come to realize the wisdom of peaceful interassociation as a result of ripened human experience and through the faithful ministry of the seraphic spirits of brotherhood. Without the work of these seraphim the efforts of the Material Sons to harmonize and advance the races of an evolving world would be greatly delayed. And had your Adam adhered to the original plan for the advancement of Urantia, by this time these spirits of brotherhood would have worked unbelievable transformations in the human race. In view of the Adamic default, it is indeed remarkable that these seraphic orders have been able to foster and bring to realization even as much of brotherhood as you now have on Urantia.

3. *The Souls of Peace.* The early millenniums of the upward strivings of evolutionary men are marked by many a struggle. Peace is not the natural state of the material realms. The worlds first realize "peace on earth and good will among men" through the ministry of the seraphic souls of peace. Although these angels were largely thwarted in their early efforts on Urantia, Vevona, chief of the souls of peace in Adam's day, was left on Urantia and is now attached to the staff of the resident governor general. And it was this same Vevona who, when Michael was born, heralded to the worlds, as the leader of the angelic host, "Glory to God in Havona and on earth peace and good will among men."

In the more advanced epochs of planetary evolution these seraphim are instrumental in supplanting the atonement idea by the concept of divine attunement as a philosophy of mortal survival.

4. *The Spirits of Trust.* Suspicion is the inherent reaction of primitive men; the survival struggles of the early ages do not naturally breed trust. Trust is a new human acquisition brought about by the ministry of these planetary seraphim of the Adamic regime. It is their mission to inculcate trust into the minds of evolving men. The Gods are very trustful; the Universal Father is willing freely to trust himself—the Adjuster—to man's association.

This entire group of seraphim was transferred to the new regime after the Adamic miscarriage, and they have ever since continued their labors on Urantia. And they have not been wholly unsuccessful since a civilization is now evolving which embodies much of their ideals of confidence and trust.

In the more advanced planetary ages these seraphim enhance man's appreciation of the truth that uncertainty is the secret of contented continuity. They help the mortal philosophers to realize that, when ignorance is essential to success, it would be a colossal blunder for the creature to know the future. They heighten man's taste for the sweetness of uncertainty, for the romance and charm of the indefinite and unknown future.

5. *The Transporters.* The planetary transporters serve the individual worlds. The majority of enseraphimed beings brought to this planet are in transit; they merely stop over; they are in custody of their own special seraphic transporters; but there are a large number of such seraphim stationed on Urantia. These are the transport personalities operating from the local planets, as from Urantia to Jerusem.

Your conventional idea of angels has been derived in the following way: During moments just prior to physical death a reflective phenomenon sometimes occurs in the human mind, and this dimming consciousness seems to visualize something of the form of the attending angel, and this is immediately translated into terms of the habitual concept of angels held in that individual's mind.

The erroneous idea that angels possess wings is not wholly due to olden notions that they must have wings to fly through the air. Human beings have sometimes been permitted to observe seraphim that were being prepared for transport service, and the traditions of these experiences have largely determined the Urantian concept of angels. In observing a transport seraphim being made ready to receive a passenger for interplanetary transit, there may be seen what are apparently double sets of wings extending from the head to the foot of the angel. In reality these wings are energy insulators—friction shields.

When celestial beings are to be enseraphimed for transfer from one world to another, they are brought to the headquarters of the sphere and, after due registry, are inducted into the transit sleep. Meantime, the transport seraphim moves into a horizontal position immediately above the universe energy pole of the planet. While the energy shields are wide open, the sleeping personality is skillfully deposited, by the officiating seraphic assistants, directly on top of the transport angel. Then both the upper and lower pairs of shields are carefully closed and adjusted.

And now, under the influence of the transformers and the transmitters, a strange metamorphosis begins as the seraphim is made ready to swing into the energy currents of the universe circuits. To outward appearance the seraphim grows pointed at both extremities and becomes so enshrouded in a queer light of amber hue that very soon it is impossible to distinguish the enseraphimed personality. When all is in readiness for departure, the chief of transport makes the proper inspection of the carriage of life, carries out the routine tests to ascertain whether or not the angel is properly encircuited, and then announces that the traveler is properly enseraphimed, that the energies are adjusted, that the angel is insulated, and that everything is in readiness for the departing flash.

The mechanical controllers, two of them, next take their positions. By this time the transport seraphim has become an almost transparent, vibrating, torpedo-shaped outline of glistening luminosity. Now the transport dispatcher of the realm summons the auxiliary batteries of the living energy transmitters, usually one thousand in number; as he announces the destination of the transport, he reaches out and touches the near point of the seraphic carriage, which shoots forward with lightninglike speed, leaving a trail of celestial luminosity as far as the planetary atmospheric investment extends. In less than ten minutes the marvelous spectacle will be lost even to reinforced seraphic vision.

While planetary space reports are received at noon at the meridian of the designated spiritual headquarters, the transporters are dispatched from this same place at midnight. That is the most favorable time for departure and is the standard hour when not otherwise specified.

6. *The Recorders.* These are the custodians of the major affairs of the planet as it functions as a part of the system, and as it is related to, and concerned in, the universe government. They function in the recording of planetary affairs but are not concerned with matters of individual life and existence.

7. *The Reserves.* The Satania reserve corps of the planetary seraphim is maintained on Jerusem in close association with the reserves of the Material Sons. These abundant reserves repletely provide for every phase of the manifold activities of this seraphic order. These angels are also the personal message bearers of the local systems. They serve transition mortals, angels, and the Material Sons as well as others domiciled on the system headquarters. While Urantia is, at present, outside the spiritual circuits of Satania and Norlatiadek, you are otherwise in intimate touch with interplanetary affairs, for these messengers from Jerusem frequently come to this world as to all the other spheres of the system.

6. TRANSITION MINISTERS

As their name might suggest, seraphim of transitional ministry serve wherever they can contribute to creature transition from the material to the spiritual estate. These angels serve from the inhabited worlds to the system capitals, but those in Satania at present direct their greatest efforts toward the education of the surviving mortals on the seven mansion worlds. This ministry is diversified in accordance with the following seven orders of assignment:

1. Seraphic Evangels.
2. Racial Interpreters.
3. Mind Planners.
4. Morontia Counselors.
5. Technicians.
6. Recorder-Teachers.
7. Ministering Reserves.

More about these seraphic ministers to transitional ascenders you will learn in connection with the narratives dealing with the mansion worlds and the morontia life.

7. SERAPHIM OF THE FUTURE

These angels do not minister extensively except in older realms and on the more advanced planets of Nebadon. Large numbers of them are held in reserve on the seraphic worlds near Salvington, where they are engaged in pursuits relevant to the sometime dawning of the age of light and life in Nebadon. These seraphim do function in connection with the ascendant-mortal career but minister almost exclusively to those mortals who survive by some one of the modified orders of ascension.

Inasmuch as these angels are not now directly concerned with either Urantia or Urantians, it is deemed best to withhold the description of their fascinating activities.

8. SERAPHIC DESTINY

Seraphim are of origin in the local universes, and in these very realms of their nativity some achieve service destiny. With the help and counsel of the senior archangels some seraphim may be elevated to the exalted duties of Brilliant Evening Stars, while others attain the status and service of the unrevealed co-ordinates of the Evening Stars. Still other adventures in local universe destiny may be attempted, but Seraphington ever remains the eternal goal of all angels. Seraphington is the angelic threshold to Paradise and Deity attainment, the transition sphere from the ministry of time to the exalted service of eternity.

Seraphim may attain Paradise in scores—hundreds—of ways, but the most important as elaborated in these narratives are the following:

1. To gain admission to the Paradise seraphic abode in a personal capacity by achieving perfection of specialized service as a celestial artisan, a Technical Adviser, or a Celestial Recorder. To become a Paradise Companion and, having thus attained the center of all things, perhaps then to become an eternal minister and adviser to the seraphic orders and others.

2. To be summoned to Seraphington. Under certain conditions seraphim are commanded on high; in other circumstances angels sometimes achieve Paradise in a much shorter time than mortals. But no matter how fitted any seraphic pair may be, they cannot initiate departure for Seraphington or elsewhere. None but successful destiny guardians can be sure of proceeding to Paradise by a progressive path of evolutionary ascent. All others must patiently await the arrival of the Paradise messengers of the tertiary supernaphim who come with the summons commanding them to appear on high.

3. To attain Paradise by the evolutionary mortal technique. The supreme choice of seraphim in the career of time is the post of guardian angel in order that they may attain the career of finality and be qualified for assignment to the eternal spheres of seraphic service. Such personal guides of the children of time are called guardians of destiny, signifying that they guard mortal creatures in the path of divine destiny, and that in so doing they are determining their own high destiny.

Guardians of destiny are drawn from the ranks of the more experienced angelic personalities of all orders of seraphim who have qualified for this service.

All surviving mortals of Adjuster-fusion destiny have temporary guardians assigned, and these associates may become permanently attached when mortal survivors attain the requisite intellectual and spiritual development. Before mortal ascenders leave the mansion worlds, they all have permanent seraphic associates. This group of ministering spirits is discussed in connection with the Urantia narratives.

It is not possible for angels to attain God from the human level of origin, for they are created a "little higher than you"; but it has been wisely arranged that, while they cannot possibly start up from the very bottom, the spiritual lowlands of mortal existence, they may go down to those who do start from the bottom and pilot such creatures, step by step, world by world, to the portals of Havona. When mortal ascenders leave Uversa to begin the circles of Havona, those guardians of attachment subsequent to the life in the flesh will bid their pilgrim associates a temporary farewell while they journey to Seraphington, the angelic destination of the grand universe. Here will these guardians attempt, and undoubtedly achieve, the seven circles of seraphic light.

Many, but not all, of those seraphim assigned as destiny guardians during the material life accompany their mortal associates through the Havona circles, and certain other seraphim pass through the circuits of the central universe in a way that is wholly different from the mortal ascent. But irrespective of the route of ascent, all evolutionary seraphim traverse Seraphington, and the majority pass through this experience instead of the Havona circuits.

Seraphington is the destiny sphere for angels, and their attainment of this world is quite different from the experiences of the mortal pilgrims on Ascendington. Angels are not absolutely sure of their eternal future until they have attained Seraphington. No angel attaining Seraphington has ever been known to go astray; sin will never find response in the heart of a seraphim of completion.

The graduates of Seraphington are variously assigned: Destiny guardians of Havona-circle experience usually enter the Mortal Finaliter Corps. Other guardians, having passed their Havona separation tests, frequently rejoin their mortal associates on Paradise, and some become the everlasting associates of the mortal finaliters, while others enter the various nonmortal finaliter corps, and many are mustered into the Corps of Seraphic Completion.

9. THE CORPS OF SERAPHIC COMPLETION

After attainment of the Father of spirits and admission to the seraphic service of completion, angels are sometimes assigned to the ministry of worlds settled in light and life. They gain attachment to the high trinitized beings of the universes and to the exalted services of Paradise and Havona. These seraphim of the local universes have experientially compensated the differential in divinity potential formerly setting them apart from the ministering spirits of the central and superuniverses. Angels of the Seraphic Corps of Completion serve as associates of the superuniverse seconaphim and as assistants to the high Paradise-Havona orders of supernaphim. For such angels the career of time is finished; henceforth and forever they are the servants of God, the consorts of divine personalities, and the peers of the Paradise finaliters.

Large numbers of the completion seraphim return to their native universes, there to complement the ministry of divine endowment by the ministry of experiential perfection. Nebadon is, comparatively speaking, one of the younger universes and therefore does not have so many of these returned Seraphington graduates as would be found in an older realm; nonetheless our local universe is adequately supplied with the completion seraphim, for it is significant that the evolutionary realms disclose increasing need for their services as they near the status of light and life. Completion seraphim now serve more extensively with the supreme orders of seraphim, but some serve with each of the other angelic orders. Even your world enjoys the extensive ministry of twelve specialized groups of the Seraphic Corps of Completion; these master seraphim of planetary supervision accompany each newly commissioned Planetary Prince to the inhabited worlds.

Many fascinating avenues of ministry are open to the completion seraphim, but just as they all craved assignment as destiny guardians in the pre-Paradise days, so in the post-Paradise experience they most desire to serve as bestowal attendants of the incarnated Paradise Sons. They are still supremely devoted to that universal plan of starting the mortal creatures of the evolutionary worlds out upon the long and enticing journey towards the Paradise goal of divinity and eternity. Throughout the whole mortal adventure of finding God and of achieving divine perfection, these spirit ministers of seraphic completion, together with the faithful ministering spirits of time, are always and forever your true friends and unfailing helpers.

[Presented by a Melchizedek acting by request of the Chief of the Seraphic Hosts of Nebadon.]

PAPER 40

THE ASCENDING SONS OF GOD

AS IN many of the major groups of universe beings, seven general classes of the Ascending Sons of God have been revealed:

1. Father-fused Mortals.
2. Son-fused Mortals.
3. Spirit-fused Mortals.
4. Evolutionary Seraphim.
5. Ascending Material Sons.
6. Translated Midwayers.
7. Personalized Adjusters.

The story of these beings, from the lowly animal-origin mortals of the evolutionary worlds to the Personalized Adjusters of the Universal Father, presents a glorious recital of the unstinted bestowal of divine love and gracious condescension throughout all time and in all universes of the far-flung creation of the Paradise Deities.

These presentations began with a description of the Deities, and group by group, the narrative has descended the universal scale of living beings until it has reached the lowest order of life endowed with the potential of immortality; and now am I dispatched from Salvington—onetime a mortal of origin on an evolutionary world of space—to elaborate and continue the recital of the eternal purpose of the Gods respecting the ascending orders of sonship, more particularly with regard to the mortal creatures of time and space.

Since the greater part of this narrative will be devoted to a discussion of the three basic orders of ascending mortals, consideration will first be given to the nonmortal ascending orders of sonship—seraphic, Adamic, midwayer, and Adjuster.

1. EVOLUTIONARY SERAPHIM

Mortal creatures of animal origin are not the only beings privileged to enjoy sonship; the angelic hosts also share the supernal opportunity to attain Paradise. Guardian seraphim, through experience and service with the ascending mortals of time, also achieve the status of ascendant sonship. Such angels attain Paradise through Seraphington, and many are even mustered into the Corps of Mortal Finality.

To climb to the supernal heights of finaliter sonship with God is a masterly achievement for an angel, an accomplishment far transcending your attainment of eternal survival through the plan of the Eternal Son and the ever-present help of the indwelling Adjuster; but the guardian seraphim, and occasionally others, do actually effect such ascensions.

2. ASCENDING MATERIAL SONS

The Material Sons of God are created in the local universe along with the Melchizedeks and their associates, who are all classified as descending Sons. And indeed, the Planetary Adams—the Material Sons and Daughters of the evolutionary worlds—are descending Sons, coming down to the inhabited worlds from their spheres of origin, the capitals of the local systems.

When such an Adam and Eve are wholly successful in their joint planetary mission as biologic uplifters, they share the destiny of the inhabitants of their world. When such a world is settled in the advanced stages of light and life, this faithful Material Son and Daughter are permitted to resign all planetary administrative duties, and after being thus liberated from the descending adventure, they are permitted to register themselves as perfected Material Sons on the records of the local universe. Likewise, when planetary assignment is long delayed, may the Material Sons of stationary status—the citizens of the local systems—withdraw from the activities of their status spheres and similarly register as perfected Material Sons. After these formalities such liberated Adams and Eves are accredited as ascending Sons of God and may immediately begin the long journey to Havona and Paradise, starting at the exact point of their then present status and spiritual attainment. And they make this journey in company with the mortal and other ascending Sons, continuing until they have found God and have achieved the Corps of Mortal Finality in the eternal service of the Paradise Deities.

3. TRANSLATED MIDWAYERS

Although deprived of the immediate benefits of the planetary bestowals of the descending Sons of God, though the Paradise ascent is long deferred, nevertheless, soon after an evolutionary planet has attained the intermediate epochs of light and life (if not before), both groups of midway creatures are released from planetary duty. Sometimes the majority of them are translated, along with their human cousins, on the day of the descent of the temple of light and the elevation of the Planetary Prince to the dignity of Planetary Sovereign. Upon being relieved of planetary service, both orders are registered in the local universe as ascending Sons of God and immediately begin the long Paradise ascent by the very routes ordained for the progression of the mortal races of the material worlds. The primary group are destined to various finaliter corps, but the secondary or Adamic midwayers are all routed for enrollment in the Mortal Corps of Finality.

4. PERSONALIZED ADJUSTERS

When the mortals of time fail to achieve the eternal survival of their souls in planetary association with the spirit gifts of the Universal Father, such failure is never in any way due to neglect of duty, ministry, service, or devotion on the part of the Adjuster. At mortal death, such deserted Monitors return to Divinington, and subsequently, following the adjudication of the nonsurvivor, they may be reassigned to the worlds of time and space. Sometimes, after repeated services of this sort or following some unusual experience, such as functioning as the indwelling Adjuster of an incarnated bestowal Son, these efficient Adjusters are personalized by the Universal Father.

Personalized Adjusters are beings of a unique and unfathomable order. Originally of existential prepersonal status, they have experientialized by participation in the lives and careers of the lowly mortals of the material worlds. And since the personality bestowed upon these experienced Thought Adjusters takes origin, and has its wellspring, in the Universal Father's personal and continuing ministry of the bestowals of experiential personality upon his creature creation, these Personalized Adjusters are classified as ascending Sons of God, the highest of all such orders of sonship.

5. MORTALS OF TIME AND SPACE

Mortals represent the last link in the chain of those beings who are called sons of God. The personal touch of the Original and Eternal Son passes on down through a series of decreasingly divine and increasingly human personalizations until there arrives a being much like yourselves, one you can see, hear, and touch. And then you are made spiritually aware of the great truth which your faith may grasp—sonship with the eternal God!

Likewise does the Original and Infinite Spirit, by a long series of decreasingly divine and increasingly human orders, draw nearer and nearer to the struggling creatures of the realms, reaching the limit of expression in the angels—than whom you were created but a little lower—who personally guard and guide you in the life journey of the mortal career of time.

God the Father does not, cannot, thus downstep himself to make such near personal contact with the almost limitless number of ascending creatures throughout the universe of universes. But the Father is not deprived of personal contact with his lowly creatures; you are not without the divine presence. Although God the Father cannot be with you by direct personality manifestation, he is in you and of you in the identity of the indwelling Thought Adjusters, the divine Monitors. Thus does the Father, who is the farthest from you in personality and in spirit, draw the nearest to you in the personality circuit and in the spirit touch of inner communion with the very souls of his mortal sons and daughters.

Spirit identification constitutes the secret of personal survival and determines the destiny of spiritual ascension. And since the Thought Adjusters are the only spirits of fusion potential to be identified with man during the life in the flesh, the mortals of time and space are primarily classified in accordance with their relation to these divine gifts, the indwelling Mystery Monitors. This classification is as follows:

1. Mortals of the transient or experiential Adjuster sojourn.
2. Mortals of the non-Adjuster-fusion types.
3. Mortals of Adjuster-fusion potential.

Series one—mortals of the transient or experiential Adjuster sojourn. This series designation is temporary for any evolving planet, being used during the early stages of all inhabited worlds except those of the second series.

Mortals of series one inhabit the worlds of space during the earlier epochs of the evolution of mankind and embrace the most primitive types of human minds.

On many worlds like pre-Adamic Urantia great numbers of the higher and more advanced types of primitive men acquire survival capacity but fail to attain Adjuster fusion. For ages upon ages, before man's ascent to the level of higher spiritual volition, the Adjusters occupy the minds of these struggling creatures during their short lives in the flesh, and the moment such will creatures are indwelt by Adjusters, the group guardian angels begin to function. While these mortals of the first series do not have personal guardians, they do have group custodians.

An experiential Adjuster remains with a primitive human being throughout his entire lifetime in the flesh. The Adjusters contribute much to the advancement of primitive men but are unable to form eternal unions with such mortals. This transient ministry of the Adjusters accomplishes two things: First, they gain valuable and actual experience in the nature and working of the evolutionary intellect, an experience which will be invaluable in connection with later contacts on other worlds with beings of higher development. Second, the transient sojourn of the Adjusters contributes much towards preparing their mortal subjects for possible subsequent Spirit fusion. All God-seeking souls of this type achieve eternal life through the spiritual embrace of the Mother Spirit of the local universe, thus becoming ascending mortals of the local universe regime. Many persons from pre-Adamic Urantia were thus advanced to the mansion worlds of Satania.

The Gods who ordained that mortal man should climb to higher levels of spiritual intelligence through long ages of evolutionary trials and tribulations, take note of his status and needs at every stage of the ascent; and always are they divinely fair and just, even charmingly merciful, in the final judgments of these struggling mortals of the early days of the evolving races.

Series two—mortals of the non-Adjuster-fusion types. These are specialized types of human beings who are not able to effect eternal union with their indwelling Adjusters. Type classification among the one-, two-, and three-brained races is not a factor in Adjuster fusion; all such mortals are akin, but these non-Adjuster-fusion types are a wholly different and markedly modified order of will creatures. Many of the nonbreathers belong to this series, and there are numerous other groups who do not ordinarily fuse with Adjusters.

Like series number one, each member of this group enjoys the ministry of a single Adjuster during lifetime in the flesh. During temporal life these Adjusters do everything for their subjects of temporary indwelling that is done on other worlds where the mortals are of fusion potential. The mortals of this second series are often indwelt by virgin Adjusters, but the higher human types are often in liaison with masterful and experienced Monitors.

In the ascendant plan for upstepping the animal-origin creatures, these beings enjoy the same devoted service of the Sons of God as is extended to the Urantia type of mortals. Seraphic co-operation with Adjusters on the nonfusion planets is just as fully provided as on the worlds of fusion potential; the guardians of destiny minister on such spheres just as on Urantia and similarly function at the time of mortal survival, at which time the surviving soul becomes Spirit fused.

When you encounter these modified mortal types on the mansion worlds, you will find no difficulty in communicating with them. There they speak the same system language but by a modified technique. These beings are identical with your order of creature life in spirit and personality manifestations, differing only in certain physical features and in the fact that they are nonfusible with Thought Adjusters.

As to just why this type of creature is never able to fuse with the Adjusters of the Universal Father, I am unable to say. Some of us incline to the belief that the Life Carriers, in their efforts to formulate beings capable of maintaining existence in an unusual planetary environment, are confronted with the necessity of making such radical modifications in the universe plan of intelligent will creatures that it becomes inherently impossible to bring about permanent union with the Adjusters. Often have we asked: Is this an intended or an unintended part of the ascension plan? but we have not found the answer.

Series three—mortals of Adjuster-fusion potential. All Father-fused mortals are of animal origin, just like the Urantia races. They embrace mortals of the one-brained, two-brained, and three-brained types of Adjuster-fusion potential. Urantians are of the intermediate or two-brained type, being in many ways humanly superior to the one-brained groups but definitely limited in comparison with the three-brained orders. These three types of physical-brain endowment are not factors in Adjuster bestowal, in seraphic service, or in any other phase of spirit ministry. The intellectual and spiritual differential between the three brain types characterizes individuals who are otherwise quite alike in mind endowment and spiritual potential, being greatest in the temporal life and tending to diminish as the mansion worlds are traversed one by one. From the system headquarters on, the progression of these three types is the same, and their eventual Paradise destiny is identical.

The unnumbered series. These narratives cannot possibly embrace all of the fascinating variations in the evolutionary worlds. You know that every tenth world is a decimal or experimental planet, but you know nothing of the other variables that punctuate the processional of the evolutionary spheres. There are differences too numerous to narrate even between the revealed orders of living creatures as between planets of the same group, but this presentation makes clear the essential differences in relation to the ascension career. And the ascension career is the most important factor in any consideration of the mortals of time and space.

As to the chances of mortal survival, let it be made forever clear: All souls of every possible phase of mortal existence will survive provided they manifest willingness to co-operate with their indwelling Adjusters and exhibit a desire to find God and to attain divine perfection, even though these desires be but the first faint flickers of the primitive comprehension of that "true light which lights every man who comes into the world."

6. THE FAITH SONS OF GOD

The mortal races stand as the representatives of the lowest order of intelligent and personal creation. You mortals are divinely beloved, and every one of you may choose to accept the certain destiny of a glorious experience, but you are not yet by nature of the divine order; you are wholly mortal. You will be reckoned as ascending sons the instant fusion takes place, but the status of the mortals of time and space is that of faith sons prior to the event of the final amalgamation of the surviving mortal soul with some type of eternal and immortal spirit.

It is a solemn and supernal fact that such lowly and material creatures as Urantia human beings are the sons of God, faith children of the Highest. "Behold, what manner of love the Father has bestowed upon us that we should be called the sons of God." "As many as received him, to them gave he the power to recognize that they are the sons of God." While "it does not yet appear what you shall be," even now "you are the faith sons of God"; "for you have not received the spirit of bondage again to fear, but you have received the spirit of sonship, whereby you cry, 'our Father.'" Spoke the prophet of old in the name of the eternal God: "Even to them will I give in my house a place and a name better than sons; I will give them an everlasting name, one that shall not be cut off." "And because you are sons, God has sent forth the spirit of his Son into your hearts."

All evolutionary worlds of mortal habitation harbor these faith sons of God, sons of grace and mercy, mortal beings belonging to the divine family and accordingly called the sons of God. Urantia mortals are entitled to regard themselves as being the sons of God because:

1. You are sons of spiritual promise, faith sons; you have accepted the status of sonship. You believe in the reality of your sonship, and thus does your sonship with God become eternally real.

2. A Creator Son of God became one of you; he is your elder brother in fact; and if in spirit you become truly related brothers of Christ, the victorious Michael, then in spirit must you also be sons of that Father which you have in common—even the Universal Father of all.

3. You are sons because the spirit of a Son has been poured out upon you, has been freely and certainly bestowed upon all Urantia races. This spirit ever draws you toward the divine Son, who is its source, and toward the Paradise Father, who is the source of that divine Son.

4. Of his divine free-willness, the Universal Father has given you your creature personalities. You have been endowed with a measure of that divine spontaneity of freewill action which God shares with all who may become his sons.

5. There dwells within you a fragment of the Universal Father, and you are thus directly related to the divine Father of all the Sons of God.

7. FATHER-FUSED MORTALS

The sending of Adjusters, their indwelling, is indeed one of the unfathomable mysteries of God the Father. These fragments of the divine nature of the Universal Father carry with them the potential of creature immortality. Adjusters are immortal spirits, and union with them confers eternal life upon the soul of the fused mortal.

Your own races of surviving mortals belong to this group of the ascending Sons of God. You are now planetary sons, evolutionary creatures derived from the Life Carrier implantations and modified by the Adamic-life infusion, hardly yet ascending sons; but you are indeed sons of ascension potential—even to the highest heights of glory and divinity attainment—and this spiritual status of ascending sonship you may attain by faith and by freewill co-operation with the spiritualizing activities of the indwelling Adjuster. When you and your Adjusters are finally and forever fused, when you two are made one, even as in Christ Michael the Son of God and the Son of Man are one, then in fact have you become the ascending sons of God.

The details of the Adjuster career of indwelling ministry on a probationary and evolutionary planet are not a part of my assignment; the elaboration of this great truth embraces your whole career. I include the mention of certain Adjuster functions in order to make a replete statement regarding Adjuster-fused mortals. These indwelling fragments of God are with your order of being from the early days of physical existence through all of the ascending career in Nebadon and Orvonton and on through Havona to Paradise itself. Thereafter, in the eternal adventure, this same Adjuster is one with you and of you.

These are the mortals who have been commanded by the Universal Father, "Be you perfect, even as I am perfect." The Father has bestowed himself upon you, placed his own spirit within you; *therefore* does he demand ultimate perfection of you. The narrative of human ascent from the mortal spheres of time to the divine realms of eternity constitutes an intriguing recital not included in my assignment, but this supernal adventure should be the supreme study of mortal man.

Fusion with a fragment of the Universal Father is equivalent to a divine validation of eventual Paradise attainment, and such Adjuster-fused mortals are the only class of human beings who all traverse the Havona circuits and find God on Paradise. To the Adjuster-fused mortal the career of universal service is wide open. What dignity of destiny and glory of attainment await every one of you! Do you fully appreciate what has been done for you? Do you comprehend the grandeur of the heights of eternal achievement which are spread out before you?—even you who now trudge on in the lowly path of life through your so-called "vale of tears"?

8. SON-FUSED MORTALS

While practically all surviving mortals are fused with their Adjusters on one of the mansion worlds or immediately upon their arrival on the higher morontia spheres, there are certain cases of delayed fusion, some not experiencing this final surety of survival until they reach the last educational worlds of the universe headquarters; and a few of these mortal candidates for never-ending life utterly fail to attain identity fusion with their faithful Adjusters.

Such mortals have been deemed worthy of survival by the adjudicational authorities, and even their Adjusters, by returning from Divinington, have concurred in their ascension to the mansion worlds. Such beings have ascended through a system, a constellation, and through the educational worlds of the Salvington circuit; they have enjoyed the "seventy times seven" opportunities for fusion and still have been unable to attain oneness with their Adjusters.

When it becomes apparent that some synchronizing difficulty is inhibiting Father fusion, the survival referees of the Creator Son are convened. And when this court of inquiry, sanctioned by a personal representative of the Ancients of Days, finally determines that the ascending mortal is not guilty of any discoverable cause for failure to attain fusion, they so certify on the records of the local universe and duly transmit this finding to the Ancients of Days. Thereupon does the indwelling Adjuster return forthwith to Divinington for confirmation by the Personalized Monitors, and upon this leave-taking the morontia mortal is immediately fused with an individualized gift of the spirit of the Creator Son.

Much as the morontia spheres of Nebadon are shared with the Spirit-fused mortals, so do these Son-fused creatures share the services of Orvonton with their Adjuster-fused brethren who are journeying inward towards the far-distant Isle of Paradise. They are truly your brethren, and you will greatly enjoy their association as you pass through the training worlds of the superuniverse.

Son-fused mortals are not a numerous group, there being less than one million of them in the superuniverse of Orvonton. Aside from residential destiny on Paradise they are in every way the equals of their Adjuster-fused associates. They frequently journey to Paradise on superuniverse assignment but seldom permanently reside there, being, as a class, confined to the superuniverse of their nativity.

9. SPIRIT-FUSED MORTALS

Ascending Spirit-fused mortals are not Third Source personalities; they are included in the Father's personality circuit, but they have fused with individualizations of the premind spirit of the Third Source and Center. Such Spirit fusion never occurs during the span of natural life; it takes place only at the time of mortal reawakening in the morontia existence on the mansion worlds. In the fusion experience there is no overlapping; the will creature is either Spirit fused, Son fused, or Father fused. Those who are Adjuster or Father fused are never Spirit or Son fused.

The fact that these types of mortal creatures are not Adjuster-fusion candidates does not prevent the Adjusters from indwelling them during the life in the flesh. Adjusters do work in the minds of such beings during the span of material life but never become everlastingly one with their pupil souls. During this temporary sojourn the Adjusters effectively build up the same spirit counterpart of mortal nature—the soul—that they do in the candidates for Adjuster fusion. Up to the time of mortal death the work of the Adjusters is wholly akin to their function in your own races, but upon mortal dissolution the Adjusters take eternal leave of these Spirit-fusion candidates and, proceeding directly to Divinington, the headquarters of all divine Monitors, there await the new assignments of their order.

When such sleeping survivors are repersonalized on the mansion worlds, the place of the departed Adjuster is filled by an individualization of the spirit of the Divine Minister, the representative of the Infinite Spirit in the local universe concerned. This spirit infusion constitutes these surviving creatures Spirit-fused mortals. Such beings are in every way your equals in mind and spirit; and they are indeed your contemporaries, sharing the mansion and morontia spheres in common with your order of fusion candidates and with those who are to be Son fused.

There is, however, one particular in which Spirit-fused mortals differ from their ascendant brethren: Mortal memory of human experience on the material worlds of origin survives death in the flesh because the indwelling Adjuster has acquired a spirit counterpart, or transcript, of those events of human life which were of spiritual significance. But with Spirit-fused mortals there exists no such mechanism whereby human memory may persist. The Adjuster transcripts of memory are full and intact, but these acquisitions are experiential possessions of the departed Adjusters and are not available to the creatures of their former indwelling, who therefore awaken in the resurrection halls of the morontia spheres of Nebadon as if they were newly created beings, creatures without consciousness of former existence.

Such children of the local universe are enabled to repossess themselves of much of their former human memory experience through having it retold by the associated seraphim and cherubim and by consulting the records of the mortal career filed by the recording angels. This they can do with undoubted assurance because the surviving soul, of experiential origin in the material and mortal life, while having no memory of mortal events, does have a residual experiential-recognition-response to these unremembered events of past experience.

When a Spirit-fused mortal is told about the events of the unremembered past experience, there is an immediate response of experiential recognition within the soul (identity) of such a survivor which instantly invests the narrated event with the emotional tinge of reality and with the intellectual quality of fact; and this dual response constitutes the reconstruction, recognition, and validation of an unremembered facet of mortal experience.

Even with Adjuster-fusion candidates, only those human experiences which were of spiritual value are common possessions of the surviving mortal and the returning Adjuster and hence are immediately remembered subsequent to mortal survival. Concerning those happenings which were not of spiritual significance, even these Adjuster-fusers must depend upon the attribute of recognition-response in the surviving soul. And since any one event may have a spiritual connotation to one mortal but not to another, it becomes possible for a group of contemporary ascenders from the same planet to pool their store of Adjuster-remembered events and thus to reconstruct any experience which they had in common, and which was of spiritual value in the life of any one of them.

While we understand such techniques of memory reconstruction fairly well, we do not grasp the technique of personality recognition. Personalities of one-time association mutually respond quite independently of the operation of memory, albeit, memory itself and the techniques of its reconstruction are necessary to invest such mutual personality response with the fullness of recognition.

A Spirit-fused survivor is also able to learn much about the life he lived in the flesh by revisiting his nativity world subsequent to the planetary dispensation in which he lived. Such children of Spirit fusion are enabled to enjoy these opportunities for investigating their human careers since they are in general confined to the service of the local universe. They do not share your high and exalted destiny in the Paradise Corps of the Finality; only Adjuster-fused mortals or other especially embraced ascendant beings are mustered into the ranks of those who await the eternal Deity adventure. Spirit-fused mortals are the permanent citizens of the local universes; they may aspire to Paradise destiny, but they cannot be sure of it. In Nebadon their universe home is the eighth group of worlds encircling Salvington, a destiny-heaven of nature and location much like the one envisioned by the planetary traditions of Urantia.

10. ASCENDANT DESTINIES

Spirit-fused mortals are, generally speaking, confined to a local universe; Son-fused survivors are restricted to a superuniverse; Adjuster-fused mortals are destined to penetrate the universe of universes. The spirits of mortal fusion always ascend to the level of origin; such spirit entities unfailingly return to the sphere of primal source.

Spirit-fused mortals are of the local universe; they do not, ordinarily, ascend beyond the confines of their native realm, beyond the boundaries of the space range of the spirit that pervades them. Son-fused ascenders likewise rise to the source of spirit endowment, for much as the Truth Spirit of a Creator Son focalizes in the associated Divine Minister, so is his "fusion spirit" implemented in the Reflective Spirits of the higher universes. Such spirit relationship between the local and the superuniverse levels of God the Sevenfold may be difficult of explanation but not of discernment, being unmistakably revealed in those children of the Reflective Spirits—the secoraphic Voices of the Creator Sons. The Thought Adjuster, hailing from the Father on Paradise, never stops until the mortal son stands face to face with the eternal God.

The mysterious variable in associative technique whereby a mortal being does not or cannot become eternally fused with the indwelling Thought Adjuster may seem to disclose a flaw in the ascension scheme; Son and Spirit fusion do, superficially, resemble compensations of unexplained failures in some detail of the Paradise-attainment plan; but all such conclusions stand in error; we are taught that all these happenings unfold in obedience to the established laws of the Supreme Universe Rulers.

We have analyzed this problem and have reached the undoubted conclusion that the consignment of all mortals to an ultimate Paradise destiny would be unfair to the time-space universes inasmuch as the courts of the Creator Sons and of the Ancients of Days would then be wholly dependent on the services of those who were in transit to higher realms. And it does seem to be no more than fitting that the local and the superuniverse governments should each be provided with a permanent group of ascendant citizenship; that the functions of these administrations should be enriched by the efforts of certain groups of glorified mortals who are of permanent status, evolutionary complements of the abandonters and of the susatia. Now it is quite obvious that the present ascension scheme effectively provides the time-space administrations with just such groups of ascendant creatures; and we have many times wondered: Does all this represent an intended part of the all-wise plans of the Architects of the Master Universe designed to provide the Creator Sons and the Ancients of Days with a permanent ascendant population? with evolved orders of citizenship that will become increasingly competent to carry forward the affairs of these realms in the universe ages to come?

That mortal destinies do thus vary in no wise proves that one is necessarily greater or lesser than another, merely that they differ. Adjuster-fused ascenders do indeed have a grand and glorious career as finaliters spread out before them in the eternal future, but this does not mean that they are preferred above their ascendant brethren. There is no favoritism, nothing arbitrary, in the selective operation of the divine plan of mortal survival.

While the Adjuster-fused finaliters obviously enjoy the widest service opportunity of all, the attainment of this goal automatically shuts them off from the chance to participate in the agelong struggle of some one universe or superuniverse, from the earlier and less settled epochs to the later and established eras of relative perfection attainment. Finaliters acquire a marvelous and far-flung experience of transient service in all seven segments of the grand universe, but they do not ordinarily acquire that intimate knowledge of any one universe which even now characterizes the Spirit-fused veterans of the Nebadon Corps of Completion. These individuals enjoy an opportunity to witness the ascending processional of the planetary ages as they unfold one by one on ten million inhabited worlds. And in the faithful service of such local universe citizens, experience superimposes upon experience until the fullness of time ripens that high quality of wisdom which is engendered by focalized experience—*authoritative* wisdom—and this in itself is a vital factor in the settling of any local universe.

As it is with the Spirit fusers, so is it with those Son-fused mortals who have achieved residential status on Uversa. Some of these beings hail from the earliest epochs of Orvonton, and they represent a slowly accumulating body of insight-deepening wisdom which is making ever-augmenting service contributions to the welfare and eventual settlement of the seventh superuniverse.

What the ultimate destiny of these stationary orders of local and of superuniverse citizenship will be we do not know, but it is quite possible that, when the Paradise finaliters are pioneering the expanding frontiers of divinity in the planetary systems of the first outer space level, their Son- and Spirit-fused brethren of the ascendant evolutionary struggle will be acceptably contributing to the maintenance of the experiential equilibrium of the perfected superuniverses while they stand ready to welcome the incoming stream of Paradise pilgrims who may, at that distant day, pour in through Orvonton and its sister creations as a vast spirit-questing torrent from these now uncharted and uninhabited galaxies of outer space.

While the majority of Spirit fusers serve permanently as citizens of the local universes, all do not. If some phase of their universe ministry should require their personal presence in the superuniverse, then would such transformations of being be wrought in these citizens as would enable them to ascend to the higher universe; and upon the arrival of the Celestial Guardians with orders to present such Spirit-fused mortals at the courts of the Ancients of Days, they would so ascend, never to return. They become wards of the superuniverse, serving as assistants to the Celestial Guardians and permanently, save for those few who are in turn summoned to the service of Paradise and Havona.

Like their Spirit-fused brethren, the Son fusers neither traverse Havona nor attain Paradise unless they have undergone certain modifying transformations. For good and sufficient reasons, such changes have been wrought in certain Son-fused survivors, and these beings are to be encountered ever and anon on the seven circuits of the central universe. Thus it is that certain numbers of both the Son- and the Spirit-fused mortals do actually ascend to Paradise, do attain a goal in many ways equal to that which awaits the Father-fused mortals.

Father-fused mortals are potential finaliters; their destination is the Universal Father, and him they do attain, but within the purview of the present universe age, finaliters, as such, are not destiny attainers. They remain unfinished creatures—sixth-stage spirits—and hence nonactive in the evolutionary domains of prelight-and-life status.

When a mortal finaliter is Trinity embraced—becomes a Trinitized Son, such as a Mighty Messenger—then has that finaliter attained destiny, at least for the present universe age. Mighty Messengers and their fellows may not in the exact sense be seventh-stage spirits, but in addition to other things the Trinity embrace endows them with everything which a finaliter will sometime achieve as a seventh-stage spirit. After Spirit-fused or Son-fused mortals are trinitized, they pass through the Paradise experience with the Adjuster-fused ascenders, with whom they are then identical in all matters pertaining to superuniverse administration. These Trinitized Sons of Selection or of Attainment at least for now are finished creatures, in contrast to the finaliters, who are at present unfinished creatures.

Thus, in the final analysis, it would be hardly proper to use the words "greater" or "lesser" in contrasting the destinies of the ascending orders of sonship. Every such son of God shares the fatherhood of God, and God loves each of his creature sons alike; he is no more a respecter of ascendant destinies than is he of the creatures who may attain such destinies. The Father loves *each* of his sons, and that affection is not less than true, holy, divine, unlimited, eternal, and unique—a love bestowed upon *this* son and upon *that* son, individually, personally, and exclusively. And such a love utterly eclipses all other facts. Sonship is the supreme relationship of the creature to the Creator.

As mortals you can now recognize your place in the family of divine sonship and begin to sense the obligation to avail yourselves of the advantages so freely provided in and by the Paradise plan for mortal survival, which plan has been so enhanced and illuminated by the life experience of a bestowal Son. Every facility and all power have been provided for insuring your ultimate attainment of the Paradise goal of divine perfection.

[Presented by a Mighty Messenger temporarily attached to the staff of Gabriel of Salvington.]

make up the administrative organization of the constellation of Norlatiadek, having as immediate neighbors the systems of Sandmatia, Assuntia, Porogia, Sortoria, Rantulia, and Glantonia. The Norlatiadek systems differ in many respects, but all are evolutionary and progressive, very much like Satania.

Satania itself is composed of over seven thousand astronomical groups, or physical systems, few of which had an origin similar to that of your solar system. The astronomic center of Satania is an enormous dark island of space which, with its attendant spheres, is situated not far from the headquarters of the system government.

Except for the presence of the assigned power center, the supervision of the entire physical-energy system of Satania is centered on Jerusem. A Master Physical Controller, stationed on this headquarters sphere, works in coordination with the system power center, serving as liaison chief of the power inspectors headquartered on Jerusem and functioning throughout the local system.

The circuitizing and channelizing of energy is supervised by the five hundred thousand living and intelligent energy manipulators scattered throughout Satania. Through the action of such physical controllers the supervising power centers are in complete and perfect control of a majority of the basic energies of space, including the emanations of highly heated orbs and the dark energy-charged spheres. This group of living entities can mobilize, transform, transmute, manipulate, and transmit nearly all of the physical energies of organized space.

Life has inherent capacity for the mobilization and transmutation of universal energy. You are familiar with the action of vegetable life in transforming the material energy of light into the varied manifestations of the vegetable kingdom. You also know something of the method whereby this vegetative energy can be converted into the phenomena of animal activities, but you know practically nothing of the technique of the power directors and the physical controllers, who are endowed with ability to mobilize, transform, directionize, and concentrate the manifold energies of space.

These beings of the energy realms do not directly concern themselves with energy as a component factor of living creatures, not even with the domain of physiological chemistry. They are sometimes concerned with the physical preliminaries of life, with the elaboration of those energy systems which may serve as the physical vehicles for the living energies of elementary material organisms. In a way the physical controllers are related to the preliving manifestations of material energy as the adjutant mind-spirits are concerned with the prespiritual functions of material mind.

These intelligent creatures of power control and energy direction must adjust their technique on each sphere in accordance with the physical constitution and architecture of that planet. They unfailingly utilize the calculations and deductions of their respective staffs of physicists and other technical advisers regarding the local influence of highly heated suns and other types of supercharged stars. Even the enormous cold and dark giants of space and the swarming clouds of star dust must be reckoned with; all of these material things are concerned in the practical problems of energy manipulation.

The power-energy supervision of the evolutionary inhabited worlds is the responsibility of the Master Physical Controllers, but these beings are not responsible for all energy misbehavior on Urantia. There are a number of reasons for such disturbances, some of which are beyond the domain and control of the physical custodians. Urantia is in the lines of tremendous energies, a small planet in the circuit of enormous masses, and the local controllers sometimes employ enormous numbers of their order in an effort to equalize these lines of energy. They do fairly well with regard to the physical circuits of Satania but have trouble insulating against the powerful Norlatiadek currents.

3. OUR STARRY ASSOCIATES

There are upward of two thousand brilliant suns pouring forth light and energy in Satania, and your own sun is an average blazing orb. Of the thirty suns nearest yours, only three are brighter. The Universe Power Directors initiate the specialized currents of energy which play between the individual stars and their respective systems. These solar furnaces, together with the dark giants of space, serve the power centers and physical controllers as way stations for the effective concentrating and directionizing of the energy circuits of the material creations.

The suns of Nebadon are not unlike those of other universes. The material composition of all suns, dark islands, planets, and satellites, even meteors, is quite identical. These suns have an average diameter of about one million miles, that of your own solar orb being slightly less. The largest star in the universe, the stellar cloud Antares, is four hundred and fifty times the diameter of your sun and is sixty million times its volume. But there is abundant space to accommodate all of these enormous suns. They have just as much comparative elbow room in space as one dozen oranges would have if they were circulating about throughout the interior of Urantia, and were the planet a hollow globe.

When suns that are too large are thrown off a nebular mother wheel, they soon break up or form double stars. All suns are originally truly gaseous, though they may later transiently exist in a semiliquid state. When your sun attained this quasi-liquid state of supergas pressure, it was not sufficiently large to split equatorially, this being one type of double star formation.

When less than one tenth the size of your sun, these fiery spheres rapidly contract, condense, and cool. When upwards of thirty times its size—rather thirty times the gross content of actual material—suns readily split into two separate bodies, either becoming the centers of new systems or else remaining in each other's gravity grasp and revolving about a common center as one type of double star.

The most recent of the major cosmic eruptions in Orvonton was the extraordinary double star explosion, the light of which reached Urantia in A. D. 1572. This conflagration was so intense that the explosion was clearly visible in broad daylight.

Not all stars are solid, but many of the older ones are. Some of the reddish, faintly glimmering stars have acquired a density at the center of their enormous masses which would be expressed by saying that one cubic inch of such a star, if on Urantia, would weigh six thousand pounds. The enormous pressure, accompanied by loss of heat and circulating energy, has resulted in bringing the orbits of the basic material units closer and closer together until they now closely approach the status of electronic condensation. This process of cooling and contraction may continue to the limiting and critical explosion point of ultimatonic condensation.

Most of the giant suns are relatively young; most of the dwarf stars are old, but not all. The collisional dwarfs may be very young and may glow with an intense white light, never having known an initial red stage of youthful shining. Both very young and very old suns usually shine with a reddish glow. The yellow tinge indicates moderate youth or approaching old age, but the brilliant white light signifies robust and extended adult life.

While all adolescent suns do not pass through a pulsating stage, at least not visibly, when looking out into space you may observe many of these younger stars whose gigantic respiratory heaves require from two to seven days to complete a cycle. Your own sun still carries a diminishing legacy of the mighty upswellings of its younger days, but the period has lengthened from the former three and one-half day pulsations to the present eleven and one-half year sunspot cycles.

Stellar variables have numerous origins. In some double stars the tides caused by rapidly changing distances as the two bodies swing around their orbits also occasion periodic fluctuations of light. These gravity variations produce regular and recurrent flares, just as the capture of meteors by the accretion of energy-material at the surface would result in a comparatively sudden flash of light which would speedily recede to normal brightness for that sun. Sometimes a sun will capture a stream of meteors in a line of lessened gravity opposition, and occasionally collisions cause stellar flare-ups, but the majority of such phenomena are wholly due to internal fluctuations.

In one group of variable stars the period of light fluctuation is directly dependent on luminosity, and knowledge of this fact enables astronomers to utilize such suns as universe lighthouses or accurate measuring points for the further exploration of distant star clusters. By this technique it is possible to measure stellar distances most precisely up to more than one million light-years. Better methods of space measurement and improved telescopic technique will sometime more fully disclose the ten grand divisions of the superuniverse of Orvonton; you will at least recognize eight of these immense sectors as enormous and fairly symmetrical star clusters.

4. SUN DENSITY

The mass of your sun is slightly greater than the estimate of your physicists, who have reckoned it as about two octillion (2×10^{27}) tons. It now exists about halfway between the most dense and the most diffuse stars, having about one and one-half times the density of water. But your sun is neither a liquid nor a solid—it is gaseous—and this is true notwithstanding the difficulty of explaining how gaseous matter can attain this and even much greater densities.

Gaseous, liquid, and solid states are matters of atomic-molecular relationships, but density is a relationship of space and mass. Density varies directly with the quantity of mass in space and inversely with the amount of space in mass, the space between the central cores of matter and the particles which whirl around these centers as well as the space within such material particles.

Cooling stars can be physically gaseous and tremendously dense at the same time. You are not familiar with the solar *supergases,* but these and other unusual forms of matter explain how even nonsolid suns can attain a density equal to iron—about the same as Urantia—and yet be in a highly heated gaseous state and continue to function as suns. The atoms in these dense supergases are exceptionally small; they contain few electrons. Such suns have also largely lost their free ultimatonic stores of energy.

One of your near-by suns, which started life with about the same mass as yours, has now contracted almost to the size of Urantia, having become forty thousand times as dense as your sun. The weight of this hot-cold gaseous-solid is about one ton per cubic inch. And still this sun shines with a faint reddish glow, the senile glimmer of a dying monarch of light.

Most of the suns, however, are not so dense. One of your nearer neighbors has a density exactly equal to that of your atmosphere at sea level. If you were in the interior of this sun, you would be unable to discern anything. And temperature permitting, you could penetrate the majority of the suns which twinkle in the night sky and notice no more matter than you perceive in the air of your earthly living rooms.

The massive sun of Veluntia, one of the largest in Orvonton, has a density only one one-thousandth that of Urantia's atmosphere. Were it in composition similar to your atmosphere and not superheated, it would be such a vacuum that human beings would speedily suffocate if they were in or on it.

Another of the Orvonton giants now has a surface temperature a trifle under three thousand degrees. Its diameter is over three hundred million miles—ample room to accommodate your sun and the present orbit of the earth. And yet, for all this enormous size, over forty million times that of your sun, its mass is only about thirty times greater. These enormous suns have an extending fringe that reaches almost from one to the other.

5. SOLAR RADIATION

That the suns of space are not very dense is proved by the steady streams of escaping light-energies. Too great a density would retain light by opacity until the light-energy pressure reached the explosion point. There is a tremendous light or gas pressure within a sun to cause it to shoot forth such a stream of energy as to penetrate space for millions upon millions of miles to energize, light, and heat the distant planets. Fifteen feet of surface of the density of Urantia would effectually prevent the escape of all X rays and light-energies from a sun until the rising internal pressure of accumulating energies resulting from atomic dismemberment overcame gravity with a tremendous outward explosion.

Light, in the presence of the propulsive gases, is highly explosive when confined at high temperatures by opaque retaining walls. Light is real. As you value energy and power on your world, sunlight would be economical at a million dollars a pound.

The interior of your sun is a vast X-ray generator. The suns are supported from within by the incessant bombardment of these mighty emanations.

It requires more than one-half million years for an X-ray-stimulated electron to work its way from the very center of an average sun up to the solar surface, whence it starts out on its space adventure, maybe to warm an inhabited planet, to be captured by a meteor, to participate in the birth of an atom, to be attracted by a highly charged dark island of space, or to find its space flight terminated by a final plunge into the surface of a sun similar to the one of its origin.

The X rays of a sun's interior charge the highly heated and agitated electrons with sufficient energy to carry them out through space, past the hosts of detaining influences of intervening matter and, in spite of divergent gravity attractions, on to the distant spheres of the remote systems. The great energy of velocity required to escape the gravity clutch of a sun is sufficient to insure that the sunbeam will travel on with unabated velocity until it encounters considerable masses of matter; whereupon it is quickly transformed into heat with the liberation of other energies.

Energy, whether as light or in other forms, in its flight through space moves straight forward. The actual particles of material existence traverse space like a fusillade. They go in a straight and unbroken line or procession except as they are acted on by superior forces, and except as they ever obey the linear-gravity pull inherent in material mass and the circular-gravity presence of the Isle of Paradise.

Solar energy may seem to be propelled in waves, but that is due to the action of coexistent and diverse influences. A given form of organized energy does not proceed in waves but in direct lines. The presence of a second or a third form of force-energy may cause the stream under observation to *appear* to travel in wavy formation, just as, in a blinding rainstorm accompanied by a heavy wind, the water sometimes appears to fall in sheets or to descend in waves. The raindrops are coming down in a direct line of unbroken procession, but the action of the wind is such as to give the visible appearance of sheets of water and waves of raindrops.

The action of certain secondary and other undiscovered energies present in the space regions of your local universe is such that solar-light emanations appear to execute certain wavy phenomena as well as to be chopped up into infinitesimal portions of definite length and weight. And, practically considered, that is exactly what happens. You can hardly hope to arrive at a better understanding of the behavior of light until such a time as you acquire a clearer concept of the interaction and interrelationship of the various space-forces and solar energies operating in the space regions of Nebadon. Your present confusion is also due to your incomplete grasp of this problem as it involves the interassociated activities of the personal and nonpersonal control of the master universe—the presences, the performances, and the co-ordination of the Conjoint Actor and the Unqualified Absolute.

6. CALCIUM—THE WANDERER OF SPACE

In deciphering spectral phenomena, it should be remembered that space is not empty; that light, in traversing space, is sometimes slightly modified by the various forms of energy and matter which circulate in all organized space. Some of the lines indicating unknown matter which appear in the spectra of your sun are due to modifications of well-known elements which are floating throughout space in shattered form, the atomic casualties of the fierce encounters of the solar elemental battles. Space is pervaded by these wandering derelicts, especially sodium and calcium.

Calcium is, in fact, the chief element of the matter-permeation of space throughout Orvonton. Our whole superuniverse is sprinkled with minutely pulverized stone. Stone is literally the basic building matter for the planets and spheres of space. The cosmic cloud, the great space blanket, consists for the most part of the modified atoms of calcium. The stone atom is one of the most prevalent and persistent of the elements. It not only endures solar ionization—splitting—but persists in an associative identity even after it has been battered by the destructive X rays and shattered by the high solar temperatures. Calcium possesses an individuality and a longevity excelling all of the more common forms of matter.

As your physicists have suspected, these mutilated remnants of solar calcium literally ride the light beams for varied distances, and thus their widespread dissemination throughout space is tremendously facilitated. The sodium atom, under certain modifications, is also capable of light and energy locomotion. The calcium feat is all the more remarkable since this element has almost twice the mass of sodium. Local space-permeation by calcium is due to the fact that it escapes from the solar photosphere, in modified form, by literally riding the outgoing sunbeams. Of all the solar elements, calcium, notwithstanding its comparative bulk—containing as it does twenty revolving electrons—is the most successful in escaping from the solar interior to the realms of space. This explains why there is a calcium layer, a gaseous stone surface, on the sun six thousand miles thick; and this despite the fact that nineteen lighter elements, and numerous heavier ones, are underneath.

Calcium is an active and versatile element at solar temperatures. The stone atom has two agile and loosely attached electrons in the two outer electronic circuits, which are very close together. Early in the atomic struggle it loses its outer electron; whereupon it engages in a masterful act of juggling the nineteenth electron back and forth between the nineteenth and twentieth circuits of electronic revolution. By tossing this nineteenth electron back and forth between its own orbit and that of its lost companion more than twenty-five thousand times a second, a mutilated stone atom is able partially to defy gravity and thus successfully to ride the emerging streams of light and energy, the sunbeams, to liberty and adventure. This calcium atom moves outward by alternate jerks of forward propulsion, grasping and letting go the sunbeam about twenty-five thousand times each second. And this is why stone is the chief component of the worlds of space. Calcium is the most expert solar-prison escaper.

The agility of this acrobatic calcium electron is indicated by the fact that, when tossed by the temperature-X-ray solar forces to the circle of the higher orbit, it only remains in that orbit for about one one-millionth of a second; but before the electric-gravity power of the atomic nucleus pulls it back into its old orbit, it is able to complete one million revolutions about the atomic center.

Your sun has parted with an enormous quantity of its calcium, having lost tremendous amounts during the times of its convulsive eruptions in connection with the formation of the solar system. Much of the solar calcium is now in the outer crust of the sun.

It should be remembered that spectral analyses show only sun-surface compositions. For example: Solar spectra exhibit many iron lines, but iron is not the chief element in the sun. This phenomenon is almost wholly due to the present temperature of the sun's surface, a little less than 6,000 degrees, this temperature being very favorable to the registry of the iron spectrum.

7. SOURCES OF SOLAR ENERGY

The internal temperature of many of the suns, even your own, is much higher than is commonly believed. In the interior of a sun practically no whole atoms exist; they are all more or less shattered by the intensive X-ray bombardment which is indigenous to such high temperatures. Regardless of what material elements may appear in the outer layers of a sun, those in the interior are rendered very similar by the dissociative action of the disruptive X rays. X ray is the great leveler of atomic existence.

The surface temperature of your sun is almost 6,000 degrees, but it rapidly increases as the interior is penetrated until it attains the unbelievable height of about 35,000,000 degrees in the central regions. (All of these temperatures refer to your Fahrenheit scale.)

All of these phenomena are indicative of enormous energy expenditure, and the sources of solar energy, named in the order of their importance, are:

1. Annihilation of atoms and, eventually, of electrons.

2. Transmutation of elements, including the radioactive group of energies thus liberated.

3. The accumulation and transmission of certain universal space-energies.

4. Space matter and meteors which are incessantly diving into the blazing suns.

5. Solar contraction; the cooling and consequent contraction of a sun yields energy and heat sometimes greater than that supplied by space matter.

6. Gravity action at high temperatures transforms certain circuitized power into radiative energies.

7. Recaptive light and other matter which are drawn back into the sun after having left it, together with other energies having extrasolar origin.

There exists a regulating blanket of hot gases (sometimes millions of degrees in temperature) which envelops the suns, and which acts to stabilize heat loss and otherwise prevent hazardous fluctuations of heat dissipation. During the active life of a sun the internal temperature of 35,000,000 degrees remains about the same quite regardless of the progressive fall of the external temperature.

You might try to visualize 35,000,000 degrees of heat, in association with certain gravity pressures, as the electronic boiling point. Under such pressure and at such temperature all atoms are degraded and broken up into their electronic and other ancestral components; even the electrons and other associations of ultimatons may be broken up, but the suns are not able to degrade the ultimatons.

These solar temperatures operate to enormously speed up the ultimatons and the electrons, at least such of the latter as continue to maintain their existence under these conditions. You will realize what high temperature means by way of the acceleration of ultimatonic and electronic activities when you pause to consider that one drop of ordinary water contains over one billion trillions of atoms. This is the energy of more than one hundred horsepower exerted continuously for two years. The total heat now given out by the solar system sun each second is sufficient to boil all the water in all the oceans on Urantia in just one second of time.

Only those suns which function in the direct channels of the main streams of universe energy can shine on forever. Such solar furnaces blaze on indefinitely, being able to replenish their material losses by the intake of space-force and analogous circulating energy. But stars far removed from these chief channels of recharging are destined to undergo energy depletion—gradually cool off and eventually burn out.

Such dead or dying suns can be rejuvenated by collisional impact or can be recharged by certain nonluminous energy islands of space or through gravity-robbery of near-by smaller suns or systems. The majority of dead suns will experience revivification by these or other evolutionary techniques. Those which are not thus eventually recharged are destined to undergo disruption by mass explosion when the gravity condensation attains the critical level of ultimatonic condensation of energy pressure. Such disappearing suns thus become energy of the rarest form, admirably adapted to energize other more favorably situated suns.

8. SOLAR-ENERGY REACTIONS

In those suns which are encircuited in the space-energy channels, solar energy is liberated by various complex nuclear-reaction chains, the most common of which is the hydrogen-carbon-helium reaction. In this metamorphosis, carbon acts as an energy catalyst since it is in no way actually changed by this process of converting hydrogen into helium. Under certain conditions of high temperature the hydrogen penetrates the carbon nuclei. Since the carbon cannot hold more than four such protons, when this saturation state is attained, it begins to emit protons as fast as new ones arrive. In this reaction the ingoing hydrogen particles come forth as a helium atom.

Reduction of hydrogen content increases the luminosity of a sun. In the suns destined to burn out, the height of luminosity is attained at the point of hydrogen exhaustion. Subsequent to this point, brilliance is maintained by the resultant process of gravity contraction. Eventually, such a star will become a so-called white dwarf, a highly condensed sphere.

In large suns—small circular nebulae—when hydrogen is exhausted and gravity contraction ensues, if such a body is not sufficiently opaque to retain the internal pressure of support for the outer gas regions, then a sudden collapse occurs. The gravity-electric changes give origin to vast quantities of tiny particles devoid of electric potential, and such particles readily escape from the solar interior, thus bringing about the collapse of a gigantic sun within a few days. It was such an emigration of these "runaway particles" that occasioned the collapse of the giant nova of the Andromeda nebula about fifty years ago. This vast stellar body collapsed in forty minutes of Urantia time.

As a rule, the vast extrusion of matter continues to exist about the residual cooling sun as extensive clouds of nebular gases. And all this explains the origin of many types of irregular nebulae, such as the Crab nebula, which had its origin about nine hundred years ago, and which still exhibits the mother sphere as a lone star near the center of this irregular nebular mass.

9. SUN STABILITY

The larger suns maintain such a gravity control over their electrons that light escapes only with the aid of the powerful X rays. These helper rays penetrate all space and are concerned in the maintenance of the basic ultimatonic associations of energy. The great energy losses in the early days of a sun, subsequent to its attainment of maximum temperature—upwards of 35,000,000 degrees—are not so much due to light escape as to ultimatonic leakage. These ultimaton energies escape out into space, to engage in the adventure of electronic association and energy materialization, as a veritable energy blast during adolescent solar times.

Atoms and electrons are subject to gravity. The ultimatons are *not* subject to local gravity, the interplay of material attraction, but they are fully obedient to absolute or Paradise gravity, to the trend, the swing, of the universal and eternal circle of the universe of universes. Ultimatonic energy does not obey the linear or direct gravity attraction of near-by or remote material masses, but it does ever swing true to the circuit of the great ellipse of the far-flung creation.

Your own solar center radiates almost one hundred billion tons of actual matter annually, while the giant suns lose matter at a prodigious rate during their earlier growth, the first billion years. A sun's life becomes stable after the maximum of internal temperature is reached, and the subatomic energies begin to be released. And it is just at this critical point that the larger suns are given to convulsive pulsations.

Sun stability is wholly dependent on the equilibrium between gravity-heat contention—tremendous pressures counterbalanced by unimagined temperatures. The interior gas elasticity of the suns upholds the overlying layers of varied materials, and when gravity and heat are in equilibrium, the weight of the outer materials exactly equals the temperature pressure of the underlying and interior gases. In many of the younger stars continued gravity condensation produces ever-heightening internal temperatures, and as internal heat increases, the interior X-ray pressure of supergas winds becomes so great that, in connection with the centrifugal motion, a sun begins to throw its exterior layers off into space, thus redressing the imbalance between gravity and heat.

Your own sun has long since attained relative equilibrium between its expansion and contraction cycles, those disturbances which produce the gigantic pulsations of many of the younger stars. Your sun is now passing out of its six billionth year. At the present time it is functioning through the period of greatest economy. It will shine on as of present efficiency for more than twenty-five billion years. It will probably experience a partially efficient period of decline as long as the combined periods of its youth and stabilized function.

10. ORIGIN OF INHABITED WORLDS

Some of the variable stars, in or near the state of maximum pulsation, are in process of giving origin to subsidiary systems, many of which will eventually be much like your own sun and its revolving planets. Your sun was in just such a state of mighty pulsation when the massive Angona system swung into near approach, and the outer surface of the sun began to erupt veritable streams—

continuous sheets—of matter. This kept up with ever-increasing violence until nearest apposition, when the limits of solar cohesion were reached and a vast pinnacle of matter, the ancestor of the solar system, was disgorged. In similar circumstances the closest approach of the attracting body sometimes draws off whole planets, even a quarter or third of a sun. These major extrusions form certain peculiar cloud-bound types of worlds, spheres much like Jupiter and Saturn.

The majority of solar systems, however, had an origin entirely different from yours, and this is true even of those which were produced by gravity-tidal technique. But no matter what technique of world building obtains, gravity always produces the solar system type of creation; that is, a central sun or dark island with planets, satellites, subsatellites, and meteors.

The physical aspects of the individual worlds are largely determined by mode of origin, astronomical situation, and physical environment. Age, size, rate of revolution, and velocity through space are also determining factors. Both the gas-contraction and the solid-accretion worlds are characterized by mountains and, during their earlier life, when not too small, by water and air. The molten-split and collisional worlds are sometimes without extensive mountain ranges.

During the earlier ages of all these new worlds, earthquakes are frequent, and they are all characterized by great physical disturbances; especially is this true of the gas-contraction spheres, the worlds born of the immense nebular rings which are left behind in the wake of the early condensation and contraction of certain individual suns. Planets having a dual origin like Urantia pass through a less violent and stormy youthful career. Even so, your world experienced an early phase of mighty upheavals, characterized by volcanoes, earthquakes, floods, and terrific storms.

Urantia is comparatively isolated on the outskirts of Satania, your solar system, with one exception, being the farthest removed from Jerusem, while Satania itself is next to the outermost system of Norlatiadek, and this constellation is now traversing the outer fringe of Nebadon. You were truly among the least of all creation until Michael's bestowal elevated your planet to a position of honor and great universe interest. Sometimes the last is first, while truly the least becomes greatest.

[Presented by an Archangel in collaboration with the Chief of Nebadon Power Centers.]

PAPER 42

ENERGY—MIND AND MATTER

THE foundation of the universe is material in the sense that energy is the basis of all existence, and pure energy is controlled by the Universal Father. Force, energy, is the one thing which stands as an everlasting monument demonstrating and proving the existence and presence of the Universal Absolute. This vast stream of energy proceeding from the Paradise Presences has never lapsed, never failed; there has never been a break in the infinite upholding.

The manipulation of universe energy is ever in accordance with the personal will and the all-wise mandates of the Universal Father. This personal control of manifested power and circulating energy is modified by the co-ordinate acts and decisions of the Eternal Son, as well as by the united purposes of the Son and the Father executed by the Conjoint Actor. These divine beings act personally and as individuals; they also function in the persons and powers of an almost unlimited number of subordinates, each variously expressive of the eternal and divine purpose in the universe of universes. But these functional and provisional modifications or transmutations of divine power in no way lessen the truth of the statement that all force-energy is under the ultimate control of a personal God resident at the center of all things.

1. PARADISE FORCES AND ENERGIES

The foundation of the universe is material, but the essence of life is spirit. The Father of spirits is also the ancestor of universes; the eternal Father of the Original Son is also the eternity-source of the original pattern, the Isle of Paradise.

Matter—energy—for they are but diverse manifestations of the same cosmic reality, as a universe phenomenon is inherent in the Universal Father. "In him all things consist." Matter may appear to manifest inherent energy and to exhibit self-contained powers, but the lines of gravity involved in the energies concerned in all these physical phenomena are derived from, and are dependent on, Paradise. The ultimaton, the first measurable form of energy, has Paradise as its nucleus.

There is innate in matter and present in universal space a form of energy not known on Urantia. When this discovery is finally made, then will physicists feel that they have solved, almost at least, the mystery of matter. And so will they have approached one step nearer the Creator; so will they have mastered one more phase of the divine technique; but in no sense will they have found

God, neither will they have established the existence of matter or the operation of natural laws apart from the cosmic technique of Paradise and the motivating purpose of the Universal Father.

Subsequent to even still greater progress and further discoveries, after Urantia has advanced immeasurably in comparison with present knowledge, though you should gain control of the energy revolutions of the electrical units of matter to the extent of modifying their physical manifestations—even after all such possible progress, forever will scientists be powerless to create one atom of matter or to originate one flash of energy or ever to add to matter that which we call life.

The creation of energy and the bestowal of life are the prerogatives of the Universal Father and his associate Creator personalities. The river of energy and life is a continuous outpouring from the Deities, the universal and united stream of Paradise force going forth to all space. This divine energy pervades all creation. The force organizers initiate those changes and institute those modifications of space-force which eventuate in energy; the power directors transmute energy into matter; thus the material worlds are born. The Life Carriers initiate those processes in dead matter which we call life, material life. The Morontia Power Supervisors likewise perform throughout the transition realms between the material and the spiritual worlds. The higher spirit Creators inaugurate similar processes in divine forms of energy, and there ensue the higher spirit forms of intelligent life.

Energy proceeds from Paradise, fashioned after the divine order. Energy—pure energy—partakes of the nature of the divine organization; it is fashioned after the similitude of the three Gods embraced in one, as they function at the headquarters of the universe of universes. And all force is circuited in Paradise, comes from the Paradise Presences and returns thereto, and is in essence a manifestation of the uncaused Cause—the Universal Father; and without the Father would not anything exist that does exist.

Force derived from self-existent Deity is in itself ever existent. Force-energy is imperishable, indestructible; these manifestations of the Infinite may be subject to unlimited transmutation, endless transformation, and eternal metamorphosis; but in no sense or degree, not even to the slightest imaginable extent, could they or ever shall they suffer extinction. But energy, though springing from the Infinite, is not infinitely manifest; there are outer limits to the presently conceived master universe.

Energy is eternal but not infinite; it ever responds to the all-embracing grasp of Infinity. Forever force and energy go on; having gone out from Paradise, they must return thereto, even if age upon age be required for the completion of the ordained circuit. That which is of Paradise Deity origin can have only a Paradise destination or a Deity destiny.

And all this confirms our belief in a circular, somewhat limited, but orderly and far-flung universe of universes. If this were not true, then evidence of energy depletion at some point would sooner or later appear. All laws, organizations, administration, and the testimony of universe explorers—everything points to the existence of an infinite God but, as yet, a finite universe, a circularity of endless existence, well-nigh limitless but, nevertheless, finite in contrast with infinity.

2. UNIVERSAL NONSPIRITUAL ENERGY SYSTEMS (PHYSICAL ENERGIES)

It is indeed difficult to find suitable words in the English language whereby to designate and wherewith to describe the various levels of force and energy—physical, mindal, or spiritual. These narratives cannot altogether follow your accepted definitions of force, energy, and power. There is such paucity of language that we must use these terms in multiple meanings. In this paper, for example, the word *energy* is used to denote all phases and forms of phenomenal motion, action, and potential, while *force* is applied to the pregravity, and *power* to the postgravity, stages of energy.

I will, however, endeavor to lessen conceptual confusion by suggesting the advisability of adopting the following classification for cosmic force, emergent energy, and universe power—physical energy:

1. *Space potency.* This is the unquestioned free space presence of the Unqualified Absolute. The extension of this concept connotes the universe force-space potential inherent in the functional totality of the Unqualified Absolute, while the intension of this concept implies the totality of cosmic reality—universes—which emanated eternitywise from the never-beginning, never-ending, never-moving, never-changing Isle of Paradise.

The phenomena indigenous to the nether side of Paradise probably embrace three zones of absolute force presence and performance: the fulcral zone of the Unqualified Absolute, the zone of the Isle of Paradise itself, and the intervening zone of certain unidentified equalizing and compensating agencies or functions. These triconcentric zones are the centrum of the Paradise cycle of cosmic reality.

Space potency is a prereality; it is the domain of the Unqualified Absolute and is responsive only to the personal grasp of the Universal Father, notwithstanding that it is seemingly modifiable by the presence of the Primary Master Force Organizers.

On Uversa, space potency is spoken of as ABSOLUTA.

2. *Primordial force.* This represents the first basic change in space potency and may be one of the nether Paradise functions of the Unqualified Absolute. We know that the space presence going out from nether Paradise is modified in some manner from that which is incoming. But regardless of any such possible relationships, the openly recognized transmutation of space potency into primordial force is the primary differentiating function of the tension-presence of the living Paradise force organizers.

Passive and potential force becomes active and primordial in response to the resistance afforded by the space presence of the Primary Eventuated Master Force Organizers. Force is now emerging from the exclusive domain of the Unqualified Absolute into the realms of multiple response—response to certain primal motions initiated by the God of Action and thereupon to certain compensating motions emanating from the Universal Absolute. Primordial force is seemingly reactive to transcendental causation in proportion to absoluteness.

Primordial force is sometimes spoken of as *pure energy;* on Uversa we refer to it as SEGREGATA.

3. *Emergent energies.* The passive presence of the primary force organizers is sufficient to transform space potency into primordial force, and it is upon such an activated space field that these same force organizers begin their initial and active operations. Primordial force is destined to pass through two distinct phases of transmutation in the realms of energy manifestation before appearing as universe power. These two levels of emerging energy are:

a. *Puissant energy.* This is the powerful-directional, mass-movemented, mighty-tensioned, and forcible-reacting energy—gigantic energy systems set in motion by the activities of the primary force organizers. This primary or puissant energy is not at first definitely responsive to the Paradise-gravity pull though probably yielding an aggregate-mass or space-directional response to the collective group of absolute influences operative from the nether side of Paradise. When energy emerges to the level of initial response to the circular and absolute-gravity grasp of Paradise, the primary force organizers give way to the functioning of their secondary associates.

b. *Gravity energy.* The now-appearing gravity-responding energy carries the potential of universe power and becomes the active ancestor of all universe matter. This secondary or gravity energy is the product of the energy elaboration resulting from the pressure-presence and the tension-trends set up by the Associate Transcendental Master Force Organizers. In response to the work of these force manipulators, space-energy rapidly passes from the puissant to the gravity stage, thus becoming directly responsive to the circular grasp of Paradise (absolute) gravity while disclosing a certain potential for sensitivity to the linear-gravity pull inherent in the soon appearing material mass of the electronic and the postelectronic stages of energy and matter. Upon the appearance of gravity response, the Associate Master Force Organizers may retire from the energy cyclones of space provided the Universe Power Directors are assignable to that field of action.

We are quite uncertain regarding the exact causes of the early stages of force evolution, but we recognize the intelligent action of the Ultimate in both levels of emergent-energy manifestation. Puissant and gravity energies, when regarded collectively, are spoken of on Uversa as ULTIMATA.

4. *Universe power.* Space-force has been changed into space-energy and thence into the energy of gravity control. Thus has physical energy been ripened to that point where it can be directed into channels of power and made to serve the manifold purposes of the universe Creators. This work is carried on by the versatile directors, centers, and controllers of physical energy in the grand universe—the organized and inhabited creations. These Universe Power Directors assume the more or less complete control of twenty-one of the thirty phases of energy constituting the present energy system of the seven superuniverses. This domain of power-energy-matter is the realm of the intelligent activities of the Sevenfold, functioning under the time-space overcontrol of the Supreme.

On Uversa we refer to the realm of universe power as GRAVITA.

5. *Havona energy.* In concept this narrative has been moving Paradiseward as transmuting space-force has been followed, level by level, to the working level of the energy-power of the universes of time and space. Continuing Paradiseward, there is next encountered a pre-existent phase of energy which is characteristic of the central universe. Here the evolutionary cycle seems to

The power centers and their associates are much concerned in the work of transmuting the ultimaton into the circuits and revolutions of the electron. These unique beings control and compound power by their skillful manipulation of the basic units of materialized energy, the ultimatons. They are masters of energy as it circulates in this primitive state. In liaison with the physical controllers they are able to effectively control and direct energy even after it has transmuted to the electrical level, the so-called electronic stage. But their range of action is enormously curtailed when electronically organized energy swings into the whirls of the atomic systems. Upon such materialization, these energies fall under the complete grasp of the drawing power of linear gravity.

Gravity acts positively on the power lanes and energy channels of the power centers and the physical controllers, but these beings have only a negative relation to gravity—the exercise of their antigravity endowments.

Throughout all space, cold and other influences are at work creatively organizing ultimatons into electrons. Heat is the measurement of electronic activity, while cold merely signifies absence of heat—comparative energy rest—the status of the universal force-charge of space provided neither emergent energy nor organized matter were present and responding to gravity.

Gravity presence and action is what prevents the appearance of the theoretical absolute zero, for interstellar space does not have the temperature of absolute zero. Throughout all organized space there are gravity-responding energy currents, power circuits, and ultimatonic activities, as well as organizing electronic energies. Practically speaking, space is not empty. Even the atmosphere of Urantia thins out increasingly until at about three thousand miles it begins to shade off into the average space matter in this section of the universe. The most nearly empty space known in Nebadon would yield about one hundred ultimatons—the equivalent of one electron—in each cubic inch. Such scarcity of matter is regarded as practically empty space.

Temperature—heat and cold—is secondary only to gravity in the realms of energy and matter evolution. Ultimatons are humbly obedient to temperature extremes. Low temperatures favor certain forms of electronic construction and atomic assembly, while high temperatures facilitate all sorts of atomic breakup and material disintegration.

When subjected to the heat and pressure of certain internal solar states, all but the most primitive associations of matter may be broken up. Heat can thus largely overcome gravity stability. But no known solar heat or pressure can convert ultimatons back into puissant energy.

The blazing suns can transform matter into various forms of energy, but the dark worlds and all outer space can slow down electronic and ultimatonic activity to the point of converting these energies into the matter of the realms. Certain electronic associations of a close nature, as well as many of the basic associations of nuclear matter, are formed in the exceedingly low temperatures of open space, being later augmented by association with larger accretions of materializing energy.

Throughout all of this never-ending metamorphosis of energy and matter we must reckon with the influence of gravity pressure and with the antigravity behavior of the ultimatonic energies under certain conditions of temperature, velocity, and revolution. Temperature, energy currents, distance, and the presence of the living force organizers and the power directors also have a bearing on all transmutation phenomena of energy and matter.

The increase of mass in matter is equal to the increase of energy divided by the square of the velocity of light. In a dynamic sense the work which resting matter can perform is equal to the energy expended in bringing its parts together from Paradise minus the resistance of the forces overcome in transit and the attraction exerted by the parts of matter on one another.

The existence of pre-electronic forms of matter is indicated by the two atomic weights of lead. The lead of original formation weighs slightly more than that produced through uranium disintegration by way of radium emanations; and this difference in atomic weight represents the actual loss of energy in the atomic breakup.

The relative integrity of matter is assured by the fact that energy can be absorbed or released only in those exact amounts which Urantia scientists have designated quanta. This wise provision in the material realms serves to maintain the universes as going concerns.

The quantity of energy taken in or given out when electronic or other positions are shifted is always a "quantum" or some multiple thereof, but the vibratory or wavelike behavior of such units of energy is wholly determined by the dimensions of the material structures concerned. Such wavelike energy ripples are 860 times the diameters of the ultimatons, electrons, atoms, or other units thus performing. The never-ending confusion attending the observation of the wave mechanics of quantum behavior is due to the superimposition of energy waves: Two crests can combine to make a double-height crest, while a crest and a trough may combine, thus producing mutual cancellation.

5. WAVE-ENERGY MANIFESTATIONS

In the superuniverse of Orvonton there are one hundred octaves of wave energy. Of these one hundred groups of energy manifestations, sixty-four are wholly or partially recognized on Urantia. The sun's rays constitute four octaves in the superuniverse scale, the visible rays embracing a single octave, number forty-six in this series. The ultraviolet group comes next, while ten octaves up are the X rays, followed by the gamma rays of radium. Thirty-two octaves above the visible light of the sun are the outer-space energy rays so frequently commingled with their associated highly energized minute particles of matter. Next downward from visible sunlight appear the infrared rays, and thirty octaves below are the radio transmission group.

Wavelike energy manifestations—from the standpoint of twentieth-century Urantia scientific enlightenment—may be classified into the following ten groups:

1. *Infraultimatonic rays*—the borderland revolutions of ultimatons as they begin to assume definite form. This is the first stage of emergent energy in which wavelike phenomena can be detected and measured.

2. *Ultimatonic rays.* The assembly of energy into the minute spheres of the ultimatons occasions vibrations in the content of space which are discernible and measurable. And long before physicists ever discover the ultimaton, they will undoubtedly detect the phenomena of these rays as they shower in upon Urantia. These short and powerful rays represent the initial activity of the

ultimatons as they are slowed down to that point where they veer towards the electronic organization of matter. As the ultimatons aggregate into electrons, condensation occurs with a consequent storage of energy.

3. *The short space rays.* These are the shortest of all purely electronic vibrations and represent the preatomic stage of this form of matter. These rays require extraordinarily high or low temperatures for their production. There are two sorts of these space rays: one attendant upon the birth of atoms and the other indicative of atomic disruption. They emanate in the largest quantities from the densest plane of the superuniverse, the Milky Way, which is also the densest plane of the outer universes.

4. *The electronic stage.* This stage of energy is the basis of all materialization in the seven superuniverses. When electrons pass from higher to lower energy levels of orbital revolution, quanta are always given off. Orbital shifting of electrons results in the ejection or the absorption of very definite and uniform measurable particles of light-energy, while the individual electron always gives up a particle of light-energy when subjected to collision. Wavelike energy manifestations also attend upon the performances of the positive bodies and the other members of the electronic stage.

5. *Gamma rays*—those emanations which characterize the spontaneous dissociation of atomic matter. The best illustration of this form of electronic activity is in the phenomena associated with radium disintegration.

6. *The X-ray group.* The next step in the slowing down of the electron yields the various forms of solar X rays together with artificially generated X rays. The electronic charge creates an electric field; movement gives rise to an electric current; the current produces a magnetic field. When an electron is suddenly stopped, the resultant electromagnetic commotion produces the X ray; the X ray is *that* disturbance. The solar X rays are identical with those which are mechanically generated for exploring the interior of the human body except that they are a trifle longer.

7. *The ultraviolet* or chemical rays of sunlight and the various mechanical productions.

8. *The white light*—the whole visible light of the suns.

9. *Infrared rays*—the slowing down of electronic activity still nearer the stage of appreciable heat.

10. *Hertzian waves*—those energies utilized on Urantia for broadcasting.

Of all these ten phases of wavelike energy activity, the human eye can react to just one octave, the whole light of ordinary sunlight.

The so-called ether is merely a collective name to designate a group of force and energy activities occurring in space. Ultimatons, electrons, and other mass aggregations of energy are uniform particles of matter, and in their transit through space they really proceed in direct lines. Light and all other forms of recognizable energy manifestations consist of a succession of definite energy particles which proceed in direct lines except as modified by gravity and other intervening forces. That these processions of energy particles appear as wave phenomena when subjected to certain observations is due to the resistance of the undifferentiated force blanket of all space, the hypothetical ether, and to the intergravity tension of the associated aggregations of matter. The spacing of the particle-intervals of matter, together with the initial velocity of the energy beams, establishes the undulatory appearance of many forms of energy-matter.

The excitation of the content of space produces a wavelike reaction to the passage of rapidly moving particles of matter, just as the passage of a ship through water initiates waves of varying amplitude and interval.

Primordial-force behavior does give rise to phenomena which are in many ways analogous to your postulated ether. Space is not empty; the spheres of all space whirl and plunge on through a vast ocean of outspread force-energy; neither is the space content of an atom empty. Nevertheless there is no ether, and the very absence of this hypothetical ether enables the inhabited planet to escape falling into the sun and the encircling electron to resist falling into the nucleus.

6. ULTIMATONS, ELECTRONS, AND ATOMS

While the space charge of universal force is homogeneous and undifferentiated, the organization of evolved energy into matter entails the concentration of energy into discrete masses of definite dimensions and established weight—precise gravity reaction.

Local or linear gravity becomes fully operative with the appearance of the atomic organization of matter. Preatomic matter becomes slightly gravity responsive when activated by X ray and other similar energies, but no measurable linear-gravity pull is exerted on free, unattached, and uncharged electronic-energy particles or on unassociated ultimatons.

Ultimatons function by mutual attraction, responding only to the circular Paradise-gravity pull. Without linear-gravity response they are thus held in the universal space drift. Ultimatons are capable of accelerating revolutionary velocity to the point of partial antigravity behavior, but they cannot, independent of force organizers or power directors, attain the critical escape velocity of deindividuation, return to the puissant-energy stage. In nature, ultimatons escape the status of physical existence only when participating in the terminal disruption of a cooled-off and dying sun.

The ultimatons, unknown on Urantia, slow down through many phases of physical activity before they attain the revolutionary-energy prerequisites to electronic organization. Ultimatons have three varieties of motion: mutual resistance to cosmic force, individual revolutions of antigravity potential, and the intraelectronic positions of the one hundred mutually interassociated ultimatons.

Mutual attraction holds one hundred ultimatons together in the constitution of the electron; and there are never more nor less than one hundred ultimatons in a typical electron. The loss of one or more ultimatons destroys typical electronic identity, thus bringing into existence one of the ten modified forms of the electron.

Ultimatons do not describe orbits or whirl about in circuits within the electrons, but they do spread or cluster in accordance with their axial revolutionary velocities, thus determining the differential electronic dimensions. This same ultimatonic velocity of axial revolution also determines the negative or positive reactions of the several types of electronic units. The entire segregation and grouping of electronic matter, together with the electric differentiation of negative and positive bodies of energy-matter, result from these various functions of the component ultimatonic interassociation.

Each atom is a trifle over 1/100,000,000th of an inch in diameter, while an electron weighs a little more than 1/2,000th of the smallest atom, hydrogen. The positive proton, characteristic of the atomic nucleus, while it may be no larger than a negative electron, weighs almost two thousand times more.

If the mass of matter should be magnified until that of an electron equaled one tenth of an ounce, then were size to be proportionately magnified, the volume of such an electron would become as large as that of the earth. If the volume of a proton—eighteen hundred times as heavy as an electron—should be magnified to the size of the head of a pin, then, in comparison, a pin's head would attain a diameter equal to that of the earth's orbit around the sun.

7. ATOMIC MATTER

The formation of all matter is on the order of the solar system. There is at the center of every minute universe of energy a relatively stable, comparatively stationary, nuclear portion of material existence. This central unit is endowed with a threefold possibility of manifestation. Surrounding this energy center there whirl, in endless profusion but in fluctuating circuits, the energy units which are faintly comparable to the planets encircling the sun of some starry group like your own solar system.

Within the atom the electrons revolve about the central proton with about the same comparative room the planets have as they revolve about the sun in the space of the solar system. There is the same relative distance, in comparison with actual size, between the atomic nucleus and the inner electronic circuit as exists between the inner planet, Mercury, and your sun.

The electronic axial revolutions and their orbital velocities about the atomic nucleus are both beyond the human imagination, not to mention the velocities of their component ultimatons. The positive particles of radium fly off into space at the rate of ten thousand miles a second, while the negative particles attain a velocity approximating that of light.

The local universes are of decimal construction. There are just one hundred distinguishable atomic materializations of space-energy in a dual universe; that is the maximum possible organization of matter in Nebadon. These one hundred forms of matter consist of a regular series in which from one to one hundred electrons revolve around a central and relatively compact nucleus. It is this orderly and dependable association of various energies that constitutes matter.

Not every world will show one hundred recognizable elements at the surface, but they are somewhere present, have been present, or are in process of evolution. Conditions surrounding the origin and subsequent evolution of a planet determine how many of the one hundred atomic types will be observable. The heavier atoms are not found on the surface of many worlds. Even on Urantia the known heavier elements manifest a tendency to fly to pieces, as is illustrated by radium behavior.

Stability of the atom depends on the number of electrically inactive neutrons in the central body. Chemical behavior is wholly dependent on the activity of the freely revolving electrons.

In Orvonton it has never been possible naturally to assemble over one hundred orbital electrons in one atomic system. When one hundred and one have been artificially introduced into the orbital field, the result has always been the instantaneous disruption of the central proton with the wild dispersion of the electrons and other liberated energies.

While atoms may contain from one to one hundred orbital electrons, only the outer ten electrons of the larger atoms revolve about the central nucleus as distinct and discrete bodies, intactly and compactly swinging around on precise and definite orbits. The thirty electrons nearest the center are difficult of observation or detection as separate and organized bodies. This same comparative ratio of electronic behavior in relation to nuclear proximity obtains in all atoms regardless of the number of electrons embraced. The nearer the nucleus, the less there is of electronic individuality. The wavelike energy extension of an electron may so spread out as to occupy the whole of the lesser atomic orbits; especially is this true of the electrons nearest the atomic nucleus.

The thirty innermost orbital electrons have individuality, but their energy systems tend to intermingle, extending from electron to electron and well-nigh from orbit to orbit. The next thirty electrons constitute the second family, or energy zone, and are of advancing individuality, bodies of matter exerting a more complete control over their attendant energy systems. The next thirty electrons, the third energy zone, are still more individualized and circulate in more distinct and definite orbits. The last ten electrons, present in only the ten heaviest elements, are possessed of the dignity of independence and are, therefore, able to escape more or less freely from the control of the mother nucleus. With a minimum variation in temperature and pressure, the members of this fourth and outermost group of electrons will escape from the grasp of the central nucleus, as is illustrated by the spontaneous disruption of uranium and kindred elements.

The first twenty-seven atoms, those containing from one to twenty-seven orbital electrons, are more easy of comprehension than the rest. From twenty-eight upward we encounter more and more of the unpredictability of the supposed presence of the Unqualified Absolute. But some of this electronic unpredictability is due to differential ultimatonic axial revolutionary velocities and to the unexplained "huddling" proclivity of ultimatons. Other influences—physical, electrical, magnetic, and gravitational—also operate to produce variable electronic behavior. Atoms therefore are similar to persons as to predictability. Statisticians may announce laws governing a large number of either atoms or persons but not for a single individual atom or person.

8. ATOMIC COHESION

While gravity is one of several factors concerned in holding together a tiny atomic energy system, there is also present in and among these basic physical units a powerful and unknown energy, the secret of their basic constitution and ultimate behavior, a force which remains to be discovered on Urantia. This universal influence permeates all the space embraced within this tiny energy organization.

The interelectronic space of an atom is not empty. Throughout an atom this interelectronic space is activated by wavelike manifestations which are perfectly synchronized with electronic velocity and ultimatonic revolutions. This force is not wholly dominated by your recognized laws of positive and negative attraction; its behavior is therefore sometimes unpredictable. This unnamed influence seems to be a space-force reaction of the Unqualified Absolute.

The charged protons and the uncharged neutrons of the nucleus of the atom are held together by the reciprocating function of the mesotron, a particle of matter 180 times as heavy as the electron. Without this arrangement the electric charge carried by the protons would be disruptive of the atomic nucleus.

As atoms are constituted, neither electric nor gravitational forces could hold the nucleus together. The integrity of the nucleus is maintained by the reciprocal cohering function of the mesotron, which is able to hold charged and uncharged particles together because of superior force-mass power and by the further function of causing protons and neutrons constantly to change places. The mesotron causes the electric charge of the nuclear particles to be incessantly tossed back and forth between protons and neutrons. At one infinitesimal part of a second a given nuclear particle is a charged proton and the next an uncharged neutron. And these alternations of energy status are so unbelievably rapid that the electric charge is deprived of all opportunity to function as a disruptive influence. Thus does the mesotron function as an "energy-carrier" particle which mightily contributes to the nuclear stability of the atom.

The presence and function of the mesotron also explains another atomic riddle. When atoms perform radioactively, they emit far more energy than would be expected. This excess of radiation is derived from the breaking up of the mesotron "energy carrier," which thereby becomes a mere electron. The mesotronic disintegration is also accompanied by the emission of certain small uncharged particles.

The mesotron explains certain cohesive properties of the atomic nucleus, but it does not account for the cohesion of proton to proton nor for the adhesion of neutron to neutron. The paradoxical and powerful force of atomic cohesive integrity is a form of energy as yet undiscovered on Urantia.

These mesotrons are found abundantly in the space rays which so incessantly impinge upon your planet.

9. NATURAL PHILOSOPHY

Religion is not alone dogmatic; natural philosophy equally tends to dogmatize. When a renowned religious teacher reasoned that the number seven was fundamental to nature because there are seven openings in the human head, if he had known more of chemistry, he might have advocated such a belief founded on a true phenomenon of the physical world. There is in all the physical universes of time and space, notwithstanding the universal manifestation of the decimal constitution of energy, the ever-present reminder of the reality of the sevenfold electronic organization of prematter.

The number seven is basic to the central universe and the spiritual system of inherent transmissions of character, but the number ten, the decimal system, is inherent in energy, matter, and the material creation. Nevertheless the atomic world does display a certain periodic characterization which recurs in groups of seven—a birthmark carried by this material world indicative of its far-distant spiritual origin.

This sevenfold persistence of creative constitution is exhibited in the chemical domains as a recurrence of similar physical and chemical properties in segregated periods of seven when the basic elements are arranged in the order of their atomic weights. When the Urantia chemical elements are thus arranged in a row, any given quality or property tends to recur by sevens. This periodic change by sevens recurs diminishingly and with variations throughout the entire chemical table, being most markedly observable in the earlier or lighter atomic groupings. Starting from any one element, after noting some one property, such a quality will change for six consecutive elements, but on reaching the eighth, it tends to reappear, that is, the eighth chemically active element resembles the first, the ninth the second, and so on. Such a fact of the physical world unmistakably points to the sevenfold constitution of ancestral energy and is indicative of the fundamental reality of the sevenfold diversity of the creations of time and space. Man should also note that there are seven colors in the natural spectrum.

But not all the suppositions of natural philosophy are valid; for example, the hypothetical ether, which represents an ingenious attempt of man to unify his ignorance of space phenomena. The philosophy of the universe cannot be predicated on the observations of so-called science. If such a metamorphosis could not be seen, a scientist would be inclined to deny the possibility of developing a butterfly out of a caterpillar.

Physical stability associated with biologic elasticity is present in nature only because of the well-nigh infinite wisdom possessed by the Master Architects of creation. Nothing less than transcendental wisdom could ever design units of matter which are at the same time so stable and so efficiently flexible.

10. UNIVERSAL NONSPIRITUAL ENERGY SYSTEMS (MATERIAL MIND SYSTEMS)

The endless sweep of relative cosmic reality, from the absoluteness of Paradise monota to the absoluteness of space potency, is suggestive of certain evolutions of relationship in the nonspiritual realities of the First Source and Center —those realities which are concealed in space potency, revealed in monota, and provisionally disclosed on intervening cosmic levels. This eternal cycle of energy, being circuited in the Father of universes, is absolute and, being absolute, is expansile in neither fact nor value; nevertheless the Primal Father is even now—as always—self-realizing of an ever-expanding arena of time-space, and of time-space-transcended, meanings, an arena of changing relationships wherein energy-matter is being progressively subjected to the overcontrol of living and divine spirit through the experiential striving of living and personal mind.

The universal nonspiritual energies are reassociated in the living systems of non-Creator minds on various levels, certain of which may be depicted as follows:

1. *Preadjutant-spirit minds.* This level of mind is nonexperiencing and on the inhabited worlds is ministered by the Master Physical Controllers. This is mechanical mind, the nonteachable intellect of the most primitive forms of material life, but the nonteachable mind functions on many levels beside that of primitive planetary life.

2. *Adjutant-spirit minds.* This is the ministry of a local universe Mother Spirit functioning through her seven adjutant mind-spirits on the teachable (nonmechanical) level of material mind. On this level material mind is experiencing: as subhuman (animal) intellect in the first five adjutants; as human (moral) intellect in the seven adjutants; as superhuman (midwayer) intellect in the last two adjutants.

3. *Evolving morontia minds*—the expanding consciousness of evolving personalities in the local universe ascending careers. This is the bestowal of the local universe Mother Spirit in liaison with the Creator Son. This mind level connotes the organization of the morontia type of life vehicle, a synthesis of the material and the spiritual which is effected by the Morontia Power Supervisors of a local universe. Morontia mind functions differentially in response to the 570 levels of morontia life, disclosing increasing associative capacity with the cosmic mind on the higher levels of attainment. This is the evolutionary course of mortal creatures, but mind of a nonmorontia order is also bestowed by a Universe Son and a Universe Spirit upon the nonmorontia children of the local creations.

The cosmic mind. This is the sevenfold diversified mind of time and space, one phase of which is ministered by each of the Seven Master Spirits to one of the seven superuniverses. The cosmic mind encompasses all finite-mind levels and co-ordinates experientially with the evolutionary-deity levels of the Supreme Mind and transcendentally with the existential levels of absolute mind—the direct circuits of the Conjoint Actor.

On Paradise, mind is absolute; in Havona, absonite; in Orvonton, finite. Mind always connotes the presence-activity of living ministry plus varied energy systems, and this is true of all levels and of all kinds of mind. But beyond the cosmic mind it becomes increasingly difficult to portray the relationships of mind to nonspiritual energy. Havona mind is subabsolute but superevolutionary; being existential-experiential, it is nearer the absonite than any other concept revealed to you. Paradise mind is beyond human understanding; it is existential, nonspatial, and nontemporal. Nevertheless, all of these levels of mind are overshadowed by the universal presence of the Conjoint Actor—by the mind-gravity grasp of the God of mind on Paradise.

11. UNIVERSE MECHANISMS

In the evaluation and recognition of mind it should be remembered that the universe is neither mechanical nor magical; it is a creation of mind and a mechanism of law. But while in practical application the laws of nature operate in what seems to be the dual realms of the physical and the spiritual, in reality they are one. The First Source and Center is the primal cause of all materialization and at the same time the first and final Father of all spirits. The Paradise Father appears personally in the extra-Havona universes only as pure energy and pure spirit—as the Thought Adjusters and other similar fragmentations.

Mechanisms do not absolutely dominate the total creation; the universe of universes *in toto* is mind planned, mind made, and mind administered. But the divine mechanism of the universe of universes is altogether too perfect for the scientific methods of the finite mind of man to discern even a trace of the dominance of the infinite mind. For this creating, controlling, and upholding mind is neither material mind nor creature mind; it is spirit-mind functioning on and from creator levels of divine reality.

The ability to discern and discover mind in universe mechanisms depends entirely on the ability, scope, and capacity of the investigating mind engaged in such a task of observation. Time-space minds, organized out of the energies of time and space, are subject to the mechanisms of time and space.

Motion and universe gravitation are twin facets of the impersonal time-space mechanism of the universe of universes. The levels of gravity response for spirit, mind, and matter are quite independent of time, but only true spirit levels of reality are independent of space (nonspatial). The higher mind levels of the universe—the spirit-mind levels—may also be nonspatial, but the levels of material mind, such as human mind, are responsive to the interactions of universe gravitation, losing this response only in proportion to spirit identification. Spirit-reality levels are recognized by their spirit content, and spirituality in time and space is measured inversely to the linear-gravity response.

Linear-gravity response is a quantitative measure of nonspirit energy. All mass—organized energy—is subject to this grasp except as motion and mind act upon it. Linear gravity is the short-range cohesive force of the macrocosmos somewhat as the forces of intra-atomic cohesion are the short-range forces of the microcosmos. Physical materialized energy, organized as so-called matter, cannot traverse space without affecting linear-gravity response. Although such gravity response is directly proportional to mass, it is so modified by intervening space that the final result is no more than roughly approximated when expressed as inversely according to the square of the distance. Space eventually conquers linear gravitation because of the presence therein of the antigravity influences of numerous supermaterial forces which operate to neutralize gravity action and all responses thereto.

Extremely complex and highly automatic-appearing cosmic mechanisms always tend to conceal the presence of the originative or creative indwelling mind from any and all intelligences very far below the universe levels of the nature and capacity of the mechanism itself. Therefore is it inevitable that the higher universe mechanisms must appear to be mindless to the lower orders of creatures. The only possible exception to such a conclusion would be the implication of mindedness in the amazing phenomenon of an *apparently self-maintaining universe*—but that is a matter of philosophy rather than one of actual experience.

Since mind co-ordinates the universe, fixity of mechanisms is nonexistent. The phenomenon of progressive evolution associated with cosmic self-maintenance is universal. The evolutionary capacity of the universe is inexhaustible in the infinity of spontaneity. Progress towards harmonious unity, a growing experiential synthesis superimposed on an ever-increasing complexity of relationships, could be effected only by a purposive and dominant mind.

The higher the universe mind associated with any universe phenomenon, the more difficult it is for the lower types of mind to discover it. And since the mind of the universe mechanism is creative spirit-mind (even the mindedness of the Infinite), it can never be discovered or discerned by the lower-level minds of the universe, much less by the *lowest* mind of all, the human. The evolving animal mind, while naturally God-seeking, is not alone and of itself inherently God-knowing.

12. PATTERN AND FORM—MIND DOMINANCE

The evolution of mechanisms implies and indicates the concealed presence and dominance of creative mind. The ability of the mortal intellect to conceive, design, and create automatic mechanisms demonstrates the superior, creative, and purposive qualities of man's mind as the dominant influence on the planet. Mind always reaches out towards:

1. Creation of material mechanisms.
2. Discovery of hidden mysteries.
3. Exploration of remote situations.
4. Formulation of mental systems.
5. Attainment of wisdom goals.
6. Achievement of spirit levels.
7. The accomplishment of divine destinies—supreme, ultimate, and absolute.

Mind is always creative. The mind endowment of an individual animal, mortal, morontian, spirit ascender, or finality attainer is always competent to produce a suitable and serviceable body for the living creature identity. But the presence phenomenon of a personality or the pattern of an identity, as such, is not a manifestation of energy, either physical, mindal, or spiritual. The personality form is the *pattern* aspect of a living being; it connotes the *arrangement* of energies, and this, plus life and motion, is the *mechanism* of creature existence.

Even spirit beings have form, and these spirit forms (patterns) are real. Even the highest type of spirit personalities have forms—personality presences in every sense analogous to Urantia mortal bodies. Nearly all beings encountered in the seven superuniverses are possessed of forms. But there are a few exceptions to this general rule: Thought Adjusters appear to be without form until after fusion with the surviving souls of their mortal associates. Solitary Messengers, Inspired Trinity Spirits, Personal Aids of the Infinite Spirit, Gravity Messengers, Transcendental Recorders, and certain others are also without discoverable form. But these are typical of the exceptional few; the great majority have bona fide personality forms, forms which are individually characteristic, and which are recognizable and personally distinguishable.

The liaison of the cosmic mind and the ministry of the adjutant mind-spirits evolve a suitable physical tabernacle for the evolving human being. Likewise does the morontia mind individualize the morontia form for all mortal survivors. As the mortal body is personal and characteristic for every human being, so will the morontia form be highly individual and adequately characteristic of the creative mind which dominates it. No two morontia forms are any more alike than any two human bodies. The Morontia Power Supervisors sponsor, and the attending seraphim provide, the undifferentiated morontia material wherewith the morontia life can begin to work. And after the morontia life it will be found that spirit forms are equally diverse, personal, and characteristic of their respective spirit-mind indwellers.

On a material world you think of a body as having a spirit, but we regard the spirit as having a body. The material eyes are truly the windows of the spirit-born soul. The spirit is the architect, the mind is the builder, the body is the material building.

Physical, spiritual, and mindal energies, as such and in their pure states, do not fully interact as actuals of the phenomenal universes. On Paradise the three energies are co-ordinate, in Havona co-ordinated, while in the universe levels of finite activities there must be encountered all ranges of material, mindal, and spiritual dominance. In nonpersonal situations of time and space, physical energy seems to predominate, but it also appears that the more nearly spirit-mind function approaches divinity of purpose and supremacy of action, the more nearly does the spirit phase become dominant; that on the ultimate level spirit-mind may become all but completely dominant. On the absolute level spirit certainly is dominant. And from there on out through the realms of time and space, wherever a divine spirit reality is present, whenever a real spirit-mind is functioning, there always tends to be produced a material or physical counterpart of that spirit reality.

The spirit is the creative reality; the physical counterpart is the time-space reflection of the spirit reality, the physical repercussion of the creative action of spirit-mind.

Mind universally dominates matter, even as it is in turn responsive to the ultimate overcontrol of spirit. And with mortal man, only that mind which freely submits itself to the spirit direction can hope to survive the mortal time-space existence as an immortal child of the eternal spirit world of the Supreme, the Ultimate, and the Absolute: the Infinite.

[Presented by a Mighty Messenger on duty in Nebadon and by the request of Gabriel.]

PAPER 43

THE CONSTELLATIONS

URANTIA is commonly referred to as 606 of Satania in Norlatiadek of Nebadon, meaning the six hundred sixth inhabited world in the local system of Satania, situated in the constellation of Norlatiadek, one of the one hundred constellations of the local universe of Nebadon. Constellations being the primary divisions of a local universe, their rulers link the local systems of inhabited worlds to the central administration of the local universe on Salvington and by reflectivity to the superadministration of the Ancients of Days on Uversa.

The government of your constellation is situated in a cluster of 771 architectural spheres, the centermost and largest of which is Edentia, the seat of the administration of the Constellation Fathers, the Most Highs of Norlatiadek. Edentia itself is approximately one hundred times as large as your world. The seventy major spheres surrounding Edentia are about ten times the size of Urantia, while the ten satellites which revolve around each of these seventy worlds are about the size of Urantia. These 771 architectural spheres are quite comparable in size to those of other constellations.

Edentia time reckoning and distance measurement are those of Salvington, and like the spheres of the universe capital, the constellation headquarters worlds are fully supplied with all orders of celestial intelligences. In general, these personalities are not very different from those described in connection with the universe administration.

The supervisor seraphim, the third order of local universe angels, are assigned to the service of the constellations. They make their headquarters on the capital spheres and minister extensively to the encircling morontia-training worlds. In Norlatiadek the seventy major spheres, together with the seven hundred minor satellites, are inhabited by the univitatia, the permanent citizens of the constellation. All these architectural worlds are fully administered by the various groups of native life, for the greater part unrevealed but including the efficient spironga and the beautiful spornagia. Being the mid-point in the morontia-training regime, as you might suspect, the morontia life of the constellations is both typical and ideal.

1. THE CONSTELLATION HEADQUARTERS

Edentia abounds in fascinating highlands, extensive elevations of physical matter crowned with morontia life and overspread with spiritual glory, but there are no rugged mountain ranges such as appear on Urantia. There are tens of thousands of sparkling lakes and thousands upon thousands of interconnecting streams, but there are no great oceans nor torrential rivers. Only the highlands are devoid of these surface streams.

The water of Edentia and similar architectural spheres is no different from the water of the evolutionary planets. The water systems of such spheres are both surface and subterranean, and the moisture is in constant circulation. Edentia can be circumnavigated via these various water routes, though the chief channel of transportation is the atmosphere. Spirit beings would naturally travel above the surface of the sphere, while the morontia and material beings make use of material and semimaterial means to negotiate atmospheric passage.

Edentia and its associated worlds have a true atmosphere, the usual three-gas mixture which is characteristic of such architectural creations, and which embodies the two elements of Urantian atmosphere plus that morontia gas suitable for the respiration of morontia creatures. But while this atmosphere is both material and morontial, there are no storms or hurricanes; neither is there summer nor winter. This absence of atmospheric disturbances and of seasonal variation makes it possible to embellish all outdoors on these especially created worlds.

The Edentia highlands are magnificent physical features, and their beauty is enhanced by the endless profusion of life which abounds throughout their length and breadth. Excepting a few rather isolated structures, these highlands contain no work of creature hands. Material and morontial ornamentations are limited to the dwelling areas. The lesser elevations are the sites of special residences and are beautifully embellished with both biologic and morontia art.

Situated on the summit of the seventh highland range are the resurrection halls of Edentia, wherein awaken the ascending mortals of the secondary modified order of ascension. These chambers of creature reassembly are under the supervision of the Melchizedeks. The first of the receiving spheres of Edentia (like the planet Melchizedek near Salvington) also has special resurrection halls, wherein the mortals of the modified orders of ascension are reassembled.

The Melchizedeks also maintain two special colleges on Edentia. One, the emergency school, is devoted to the study of problems growing out of the Satania rebellion. The other, the bestowal school, is dedicated to the mastery of the new problems arising out of the fact that Michael made his final bestowal on one of the worlds of Norlatiadek. This latter college was established almost forty thousand years ago, immediately after the announcement by Michael that Urantia had been selected as the world for his final bestowal.

The sea of glass, the receiving area of Edentia, is near the administrative center and is encircled by the headquarters amphitheater. Surrounding this area are the governing centers for the seventy divisions of constellation affairs. One half of Edentia is divided into seventy triangular sections, whose boundaries converge at the headquarters buildings of their respective sectors. The remainder of this sphere is one vast natural park, the gardens of God.

During your periodic visits to Edentia, though the entire planet is open to your inspection, most of your time will be spent in that administrative triangle whose number corresponds to that of your current residential world. You will always be welcome as an observer in the legislative assemblies.

The morontia area assigned to ascending mortals resident on Edentia is located in the mid-zone of the thirty-fifth triangle adjoining the headquarters of the finaliters, situated in the thirty-sixth triangle. The general headquarters of the univitatia occupies an enormous area in the mid-region of the thirty-fourth triangle immediately adjoining the residential reservation of the morontia citizens. From these arrangements it may be seen that provision is made for the accommodation of at least seventy major divisions of celestial life, and also that each of these seventy triangular areas is correlated with some one of the seventy major spheres of morontia training.

The Edentia sea of glass is one enormous circular crystal about one hundred miles in circumference and about thirty miles in depth. This magnificent crystal serves as the receiving field for all transport seraphim and other beings arriving from points outside the sphere; such a sea of glass greatly facilitates the landing of transport seraphim.

A crystal field on this order is found on almost all architectural worlds; and it serves many purposes aside from its decorative value, being utilized for portraying superuniverse reflectivity to assembled groups and as a factor in the energy-transformation technique for modifying the currents of space and for adapting other incoming physical-energy streams.

2. THE CONSTELLATION GOVERNMENT

The constellations are the autonomous units of a local universe, each constellation being administered according to its own legislative enactments. When the courts of Nebadon sit in judgment on universe affairs, all internal matters are adjudicated in accordance with the laws prevailing in the constellation concerned. These judicial decrees of Salvington, together with the legislative enactments of the constellations, are executed by the administrators of the local systems.

Constellations thus function as the legislative or lawmaking units, while the local systems serve as the executive or enforcement units. The Salvington government is the supreme judicial and co-ordinating authority.

While the supreme judicial function rests with the central administration of a local universe, there are two subsidiary but major tribunals at the headquarters of each constellation, the Melchizedek council and the court of the Most High.

All judicial problems are first reviewed by the council of the Melchizedeks. Twelve of this order who have had certain requisite experience on the evolutionary planets and on the system headquarters worlds are empowered to review evidence, digest pleas, and formulate provisional verdicts, which are passed on to the court of the Most High, the reigning Constellation Father. The mortal division of this latter tribunal consists of seven judges, all of whom are ascendant mortals. The higher you ascend in the universe, the more certain you are to be judged by those of your own kind.

The constellation legislative body is divided into three groups. The legislative program of a constellation originates in the lower house of ascenders, a group presided over by a finaliter and consisting of one thousand representative mortals. Each system nominates ten members to sit in this deliberative assembly. On Edentia this body is not fully recruited at the present time.

The mid-chamber of legislators is composed of the seraphic hosts and their associates, other children of the local universe Mother Spirit. This group numbers one hundred and is nominated by the supervising personalities who preside over the various activities of such beings as they function within the constellation.

The advisory or highest body of constellation legislators consists of the house of peers—the house of the divine Sons. This corps is chosen by the Most High Fathers and numbers ten. Only Sons of special experience may serve in this upper house. This is the fact-finding and timesaving group which very effectively serves both of the lower divisions of the legislative assembly.

The combined council of legislators consists of three members from each of these separate branches of the constellation deliberative assembly and is presided over by the reigning junior Most High. This group sanctions the final form of all enactments and authorizes their promulgation by the broadcasters. The approval of this supreme commission renders legislative enactments the law of the realm; their acts are final. The legislative pronouncements of Edentia constitute the fundamental law of all Norlatiadek.

3. THE MOST HIGHS OF NORLATIADEK

The rulers of the constellations are of the Vorondadek order of local universe sonship. When commissioned to active duty in the universe as constellation rulers or otherwise, these Sons are known as the *Most Highs* since they embody the highest administrative wisdom, coupled with the most farseeing and intelligent loyalty, of all the orders of the Local Universe Sons of God. Their personal integrity and their group loyalty have never been questioned; no disaffection of the Vorondadek Sons has ever occurred in Nebadon.

At least three Vorondadek Sons are commissioned by Gabriel as the Most Highs of each of the Nebadon constellations. The presiding member of this trio is known as the *Constellation Father* and his two associates as the *senior Most High* and the *junior Most High*. A Constellation Father reigns for ten thousand standard years (about 50,000 Urantia years), having previously served as junior associate and as senior associate for equal periods.

The Psalmist knew that Edentia was ruled by three Constellation Fathers and accordingly spoke of their abode in the plural: "There is a river, the streams whereof shall make glad the city of God, the most holy place of the tabernacles of the Most Highs."

Down through the ages there has been great confusion on Urantia regarding the various universe rulers. Many later teachers confused their vague and indefinite tribal deities with the Most High Fathers. Still later, the Hebrews merged all of these celestial rulers into a composite Deity. One teacher understood that the Most Highs were not the Supreme Rulers, for he said, "He who dwells in the secret place of the Most High shall abide under the shadow of the Almighty." In the Urantia records it is very difficult at times to know exactly who is referred to by the term "Most High." But Daniel fully understood these matters. He said, "The Most High rules in the kingdom of men and gives it to whomsoever he will."

The Constellation Fathers are little occupied with the individuals of an inhabited planet, but they are closely associated with those legislative and lawmaking functions of the constellations which so greatly concern every mortal *race* and national *group* of the inhabited worlds.

Although the constellation regime stands between you and the universe administration, as individuals you would ordinarily be little concerned with the constellation government. Your great interest would normally center in the local system, Satania; but temporarily, Urantia is closely related to the constellation rulers because of certain system and planetary conditions growing out of the Lucifer rebellion.

The Edentia Most Highs seized certain phases of planetary authority on the rebellious worlds at the time of the Lucifer secession. They have continued to exercise this power, and the Ancients of Days long since confirmed this assumption of control over these wayward worlds. They will no doubt continue to exercise this assumed jurisdiction as long as Lucifer lives. Much of this authority would ordinarily, in a loyal system, be invested in the System Sovereign.

But there is still another way in which Urantia became peculiarly related to the Most Highs. When Michael, the Creator Son, was on his terminal bestowal mission, since the successor of Lucifer was not in full authority in the local system, all Urantia affairs which concerned the Michael bestowal were immediately supervised by the Most Highs of Norlatiadek.

4. MOUNT ASSEMBLY—THE FAITHFUL OF DAYS

The most holy mount of assembly is the dwelling place of the Faithful of Days, the representative of the Paradise Trinity who functions on Edentia.

This Faithful of Days is a Trinity Son of Paradise and has been present on Edentia as the personal representative of Immanuel since the creation of the headquarters world. Ever the Faithful of Days stands at the right hand of the Constellation Fathers to counsel them, but never does he proffer advice unless it is asked for. The high Sons of Paradise never participate in the conduct of the affairs of a local universe except upon the petition of the acting rulers of such domains. But all that a Union of Days is to a Creator Son, a Faithful of Days is to the Most Highs of a constellation.

The residence of the Edentia Faithful of Days is the constellation center of the Paradise system of extrauniverse communication and intelligence. These Trinity Sons, with their staffs of Havona and Paradise personalities, in liaison with the supervising Union of Days, are in direct and constant communication with their order throughout all the universes, even to Havona and Paradise.

The most holy mount is exquisitely beautiful and marvelously appointed, but the actual residence of the Paradise Son is modest in comparison with the central abode of the Most Highs and the surrounding seventy structures comprising the residential unit of the Vorondadek Sons. These appointments are exclusively residential; they are entirely separate from the extensive administrative headquarters buildings wherein the affairs of the constellation are transacted.

The residence of the Faithful of Days on Edentia is located to the north of these residences of the Most Highs and is known as the "mount of Paradise assembly." On this consecrated highland the ascending mortals periodically assemble to hear this Son of Paradise tell of the long and intriguing journey of progressing mortals through the one billion perfection worlds of Havona and on to the indescribable delights of Paradise. And it is at these special gatherings on Mount Assembly that the morontia mortals become more fully acquainted with the various groups of personalities of origin in the central universe.

The traitorous Lucifer, onetime sovereign of Satania, in announcing his claims to increased jurisdiction, sought to displace all superior orders of sonship in the governmental plan of the local universe. He purposed in his heart, saying: "I will exalt my throne above the Sons of God; I will sit upon the mount of assembly in the north; I will be like the Most High."

The one hundred System Sovereigns come periodically to the Edentia conclaves which deliberate on the welfare of the constellation. After the Satania rebellion the archrebels of Jerusem were wont to come up to these Edentia councils just as they had on former occasions. And there was found no way to stop this arrogant effrontery until after the bestowal of Michael on Urantia and his subsequent assumption of unlimited sovereignty throughout all Nebadon. Never, since that day, have these instigators of sin been permitted to sit in the Edentia councils of the loyal System Sovereigns.

That the teachers of olden times knew of these things is shown by the record: "And there was a day when the Sons of God came to present themselves before the Most Highs, and Satan came also and presented himself among them." And this is a statement of fact regardless of the connection in which it chances to appear.

Since the triumph of Christ, all Norlatiadek is being cleansed of sin and rebels. Sometime before Michael's death in the flesh the fallen Lucifer's associate, Satan, sought to attend such an Edentia conclave, but the solidification of sentiment against the archrebels had reached the point where the doors of sympathy were so well-nigh universally closed that there could be found no standing ground for the Satania adversaries. When there exists no open door for the reception of evil, there exists no opportunity for the entertainment of sin. The doors of the hearts of all Edentia closed against Satan; he was unanimously rejected by the assembled System Sovereigns, and it was at this time that the Son of Man "beheld Satan fall as lightning from heaven."

Since the Lucifer rebellion a new structure has been provided near the residence of the Faithful of Days. This temporary edifice is the headquarters of the Most High liaison, who functions in close touch with the Paradise Son as adviser to the constellation government in all matters respecting the policy and attitude of the order of Days toward sin and rebellion.

5. THE EDENTIA FATHERS SINCE THE LUCIFER REBELLION

The rotation of the Most Highs on Edentia was suspended at the time of the Lucifer rebellion. We now have the same rulers who were on duty at that time. We infer that no change in these rulers will be made until Lucifer and his associates are finally disposed of.

The present government of the constellation, however, has been expanded to include twelve Sons of the Vorondadek order. These twelve are as follows:

1. The Constellation Father. The present Most High ruler of Norlatiadek is number 617,318 of the Vorondadek series of Nebadon. He saw service in many constellations throughout our local universe before taking up his Edentia responsibilities.

2. The senior Most High associate.

3. The junior Most High associate.

4. The Most High adviser, the personal representative of Michael since his attainment of the status of a Master Son.

5. The Most High executive, the personal representative of Gabriel stationed on Edentia ever since the Lucifer rebellion.

6. The Most High chief of planetary observers, the director of the Vorondadek observers stationed on the isolated worlds of Satania.

7. The Most High referee, the Vorondadek Son intrusted with the duty of adjusting all difficulties consequential to rebellion within the constellation.

8. The Most High emergency administrator, the Vorondadek Son charged with the task of adapting the emergency enactments of the Norlatiadek legislature to the rebellion-isolated worlds of Satania.

9. The Most High mediator, the Vorondadek Son assigned to harmonize the special bestowal adjustments on Urantia with the routine administration of the constellation. The presence of certain archangel activities and numerous other irregular ministrations on Urantia, together with the special activities of the Brilliant Evening Stars on Jerusem, necessitates the functioning of this Son.

10. The Most High judge-advocate, the head of the emergency tribunal devoted to the adjustment of the special problems of Norlatiadek growing out of the confusion consequent upon the Satania rebellion.

11. The Most High liaison, the Vorondadek Son attached to the Edentia rulers but commissioned as a special counselor with the Faithful of Days regarding the best course to pursue in the management of problems pertaining to rebellion and creature disloyalty.

12. The Most High director, the president of the emergency council of Edentia. All personalities assigned to Norlatiadek because of the Satania upheaval constitute the emergency council, and their presiding officer is a Vorondadek Son of extraordinary experience.

And this takes no account of the numerous Vorondadeks, envoys of Nebadon constellations, and others who are also resident on Edentia.

Ever since the Lucifer rebellion the Edentia Fathers have exercised a special care over Urantia and the other isolated worlds of Satania. Long ago the prophet recognized the controlling hand of the Constellation Fathers in the affairs of nations. "When the Most High divided to the nations their inheritance, when he separated the sons of Adam, he set the bounds of the people."

Every quarantined or isolated world has a Vorondadek Son acting as an observer. He does not participate in planetary administration except when ordered by the Constellation Father to intervene in the affairs of the nations. Actually it is this Most High observer who "rules in the kingdoms of men." Urantia is one of the isolated worlds of Norlatiadek, and a Vorondadek observer has been stationed on the planet ever since the Caligastia betrayal. When Machiventa Melchizedek ministered in semimaterial form on Urantia, he paid respectful homage to the Most High observer then on duty, as it is written, "And Melchizedek, king of Salem, was the priest of the Most High." Melchizedek revealed the relations of this Most High observer to Abraham when he said, "And blessed be the Most High, who has delivered your enemies into your hand."

6. THE GARDENS OF GOD

The system capitals are particularly beautified with material and mineral constructions, while the universe headquarters is more reflective of spiritual glory, but the capitals of the constellations are the acme of morontia activities and living embellishments. On the constellation headquarters worlds living embellishment is more generally utilized, and it is this preponderance of life—botanic artistry—that causes these worlds to be called "the gardens of God."

About one half of Edentia is devoted to the exquisite gardens of the Most Highs, and these gardens are among the most entrancing morontia creations of the local universe. This explains why the extraordinarily beautiful places on the inhabited worlds of Norlatiadek are so often called "the garden of Eden."

Centrally located in this magnificent garden is the worship shrine of the Most Highs. The Psalmist must have known something about these things, for he wrote: "Who shall ascend the hill of the Most Highs? Who shall stand in this holy place? He who has clean hands and a pure heart, who has not lifted up his soul to vanity nor sworn deceitfully." At this shrine the Most Highs, on every tenth day of relaxation, lead all Edentia in the worshipful contemplation of God the Supreme.

The architectural worlds enjoy ten forms of life of the material order. On Urantia there is plant and animal life, but on such a world as Edentia there are ten divisions of the material orders of life. Were you to view these ten divisions of Edentia life, you would quickly classify the first three as vegetable and the last three as animal, but you would be utterly unable to comprehend the nature of the intervening four groups of prolific and fascinating forms of life.

Even the distinctively animal life is very different from that of the evolutionary worlds, so different that it is quite impossible to portray to mortal minds the unique character and affectionate nature of these nonspeaking creatures. There are thousands upon thousands of living creatures which your imagination could not possibly picture. The whole animal creation is of an entirely different order from the gross animal species of the evolutionary planets. But all this animal life is most intelligent and exquisitely serviceable, and all the various species are surprisingly gentle and touchingly companionable. There are no carnivorous creatures on such architectural worlds; there is nothing in all Edentia to make any living being afraid.

The vegetable life is also very different from that of Urantia, consisting of both material and morontia varieties. The material growths have a characteristic green coloration, but the morontia equivalents of vegetative life have a violet or orchid tinge of varying hue and reflection. Such morontia vegetation is purely an energy growth; when eaten there is no residual portion.

Being endowed with ten divisions of physical life, not to mention the morontia variations, these architectural worlds provide tremendous possibilities for the biologic beautification of the landscape and of the material and the morontia structures. The celestial artisans direct the native spornagia in this extensive work of botanic decoration and biologic embellishment. Whereas your artists must resort to inert paint and lifeless marble to portray their concepts, the celestial artisans and the univitatia more frequently utilize living materials to represent their ideas and to capture their ideals.

creatures do not merely double their personal potentials of universe achievement by partnership technique; they more nearly quadruple their attainment and accomplishment possibilities.

We have portrayed Edentia socialization as an association of a morontia mortal with a univitatia family group consisting of ten intellectually dissimilar individuals concomitant with a similar association with ten fellow morontians. But on the first seven major worlds only one ascending mortal lives with ten univitatia. On the second group of seven major worlds two mortals abide with each native group of ten, and so on up until, on the last group of seven major spheres, ten morontia beings are domiciled with ten univitatia. As you learn how better to socialize with the univitatia, you will practice such improved ethics in your relations with your fellow morontia progressors.

As ascending mortals you will enjoy your sojourn on the progress worlds of Edentia, but you will not experience that personal thrill of satisfaction which characterizes your initial contact with universe affairs on the system headquarters or your farewell touch with these realities on the final worlds of the universe capital.

9. CITIZENSHIP ON EDENTIA

After graduation from world number seventy, ascending mortals take up residence on Edentia. Ascenders now, for the first time, attend the "assemblies of Paradise" and hear the story of their far-flung career as it is depicted by the Faithful of Days, the first of the Supreme Trinity-origin Personalities they have met.

This entire sojourn on the constellation training worlds, culminating in Edentia citizenship, is a period of true and heavenly bliss for the morontia progressors. Throughout your sojourn on the system worlds you were evolving from a near-animal to a morontia creature; you were more material than spiritual. On the Salvington spheres you will be evolving from a morontia being to the status of a true spirit; you will be more spiritual than material. But on Edentia, ascenders are midway between their former and their future estates, midway in their passage from evolutionary animal to ascending spirit. During your whole stay on Edentia and its worlds you are "as the angels"; you are constantly progressing but all the while maintaining a general and a typical morontia status.

This constellation sojourn of an ascending mortal is the most uniform and stabilized epoch in the entire career of morontia progression. This experience constitutes the prespirit socialization training of the ascenders. It is analogous to the prefinaliter spiritual experience of Havona and to the preabsonite training on Paradise.

Ascending mortals on Edentia are chiefly occupied with the assignments on the seventy progressive univitatia worlds. They also serve in varied capacities on Edentia itself, mainly in conjunction with the constellation program concerned with group, racial, national, and planetary welfare. The Most Highs are not so much engaged in fostering individual advancement on the inhabited worlds; they rule in the kingdoms of men rather than in the hearts of individuals.

And on that day when you are prepared to leave Edentia for the Salvington career, you will pause and look back on one of the most beautiful and most refreshing of all your epochs of training this side of Paradise. But the glory of it all augments as you ascend inward and achieve increased capacity for enlarged appreciation of divine meanings and spiritual values.

[Sponsored by Malavatia Melchizedek.]

PAPER 44

THE CELESTIAL ARTISANS

AMONG the courtesy colonies of the various divisional and universe headquarters worlds may be found the unique order of composite personalities denominated the celestial artisans. These beings are the master artists and artisans of the morontia and lower spirit realms. They are the spirits and semispirits who are engaged in morontia embellishment and in spiritual beautification. Such artisans are distributed throughout the grand universe—on the headquarters worlds of the superuniverses, the local universes, the constellations, and systems, as well as on all spheres settled in light and life; but their chief realm of activity is in the constellations and especially on the seven hundred seventy worlds surrounding each headquarters sphere.

Though their work may be almost incomprehensible to the material mind, it should be understood that the morontia and spirit worlds are not without their high arts and supernal cultures.

The celestial artisans are not created as such; they are a selected and recruited corps of beings composed of certain teacher personalities native to the central universe and their volunteer pupils drawn from the ascending mortals and numerous other celestial groups. The original teaching corps of these artisans was sometime assigned by the Infinite Spirit in collaboration with the Seven Master Spirits and consisted of seven thousand Havona instructors, one thousand to each of the seven divisions of artisans. With such a nucleus to start with, there has developed through the ages this brilliant body of skillful workers in spirit and morontia affairs.

Any morontia personality or spirit entity is eligible for admission to the corps of the celestial artisans; that is, any being below the rank of inherent divine sonship. Ascending sons of God from the evolutionary spheres may, after their arrival on the morontia worlds, apply for admission to the artisan corps and, if sufficiently gifted, may choose such a career for a longer or shorter period. But no one may enlist with the celestial artisans for less than one millennium, one thousand years of superuniverse time.

All celestial artisans are registered on the superuniverse headquarters but are directed by morontia supervisors on the local universe capitals. They are commissioned in the following seven major divisions of activity by the central corps of morontia supervisors functioning on the headquarters world of each local universe:

1. Celestial Musicians.
2. Heavenly Reproducers.
3. Divine Builders.
4. Thought Recorders.

5. Energy Manipulators.
6. Designers and Embellishers.
7. Harmony Workers.

The original teachers of these seven groups all hailed from the perfect worlds of Havona, and Havona contains the patterns, the pattern studies, for all phases and forms of spirit artistry. While it is a gigantic task to undertake to transfer these arts of Havona to the worlds of space, the celestial artisans have improved in technique and execution from age to age. As in all other phases of the ascending career those who are most advanced in any line of endeavor are required constantly to impart their superior knowledge and skill to their less favored fellows.

You will first begin to glimpse these transplanted arts of Havona on the mansion worlds, and their beauty and your appreciation of their beauty will heighten and brighten until you stand in the spirit halls of Salvington and behold the inspiring masterpieces of the supernal artists of the spirit realms.

All these activities of the morontia and spirit worlds are real. To spirit beings the spirit world is a reality. To us the material world is the more unreal. The higher forms of spirits freely pass through ordinary matter. High spirits are reactive to nothing material excepting certain of the basic energies. To material beings the spirit world is more or less unreal; to spirit beings the material world is almost entirely unreal, being merely a shadow of the substance of spirit realities.

I cannot, with exclusive spirit vision, perceive the building in which this narrative is being translated and recorded. A Divine Counselor from Uversa who chances to stand by my side perceives still less of these purely material creations. We discern how these material structures appear to you by viewing a spirit counterpart presented to our minds by one of our attending energy transformers. This material building is not exactly real to me, a spirit being, but it is, of course, very real and very serviceable to material mortals.

There are certain types of beings who are capable of discerning the reality of the creatures of both the spirit and the material worlds. Belonging to this class are the so-called fourth creatures of the Havona Servitals and the fourth creatures of the conciliators. The angels of time and space are endowed with the ability to discern both spirit and material beings as also are the ascending mortals subsequent to deliverance from the life in the flesh. After attainment of the higher spirit levels the ascenders are able to recognize material, morontia, and spirit realities.

There is also here with me a Mighty Messenger from Uversa, an ascendant Adjuster-fused, onetime mortal being, and he perceives you as you are, and at the same time he visualizes the Solitary Messenger, the supernaphim, and other celestial beings present. Never in your long ascendancy will you lose the power to recognize your associates of former existences. Always, as you ascend inward in the scale of life, will you retain the ability to recognize and fraternize with the fellow beings of your previous and lower levels of experience. Each new translation or resurrection will add one more group of spirit beings to your vision range without in the least depriving you of the ability to recognize your friends and fellows of former estates.

All this is made possible in the experience of ascending mortals by the action of the indwelling Thought Adjusters. Through their retention of the duplicates of your entire life's experiences, you are assured of never losing any true attribute you once had; and these Adjusters are going through with you, as a part of you, in reality, as *you*.

But I almost despair of being able to convey to the material mind the nature of the work of the celestial artisans. I am under the necessity of constantly perverting thought and distorting language in an effort to unfold to the mortal mind the reality of these morontia transactions and near-spirit phenomena. Your comprehension is incapable of grasping, and your language is inadequate for conveying, the meaning, value, and relationship of these semispirit activities. And I proceed with this effort to enlighten the human mind concerning these realities with the full understanding of the utter impossibility of my being very successful in such an undertaking.

I can do no more than attempt to sketch a crude parallelism between mortal material activities and the manifold functions of the celestial artisans. If the Urantia races were more advanced in art and other cultural accomplishments, then could I go that much farther in an effort to project the human mind from the things of matter to those of morontia. About all I can hope to accomplish is to make emphatic the fact of the reality of these transactions of the morontia and the spirit worlds.

1. THE CELESTIAL MUSICIANS

With the limited range of mortal hearing, you can hardly conceive of morontia melodies. There is even a material range of beautiful sound unrecognized by the human sense of hearing, not to mention the inconceivable scope of morontia and spirit harmony. Spirit melodies are not material sound waves but spirit pulsations received by the spirits of celestial personalities. There is a vastness of range and a soul of expression, as well as a grandeur of execution, associated with the melody of the spheres, that are wholly beyond human comprehension. I have seen millions of enraptured beings held in sublime ecstasy while the melody of the realm rolled in upon the spirit energy of the celestial circuits. These marvelous melodies can be broadcast to the uttermost parts of a universe.

The celestial musicians are occupied with the production of celestial harmony by the manipulation of the following spirit forces:

1. *Spiritual sound*—spirit current interruptions.

2. *Spiritual light*—the control and intensification of the light of the morontia and spiritual realms.

3. *Energy impingements*—melody produced by the skillful management of the morontia and spirit energies.

4. *Color symphonies*—melody of morontia color tones; this ranks among the highest accomplishments of the celestial musicians.

5. *Harmony of associated spirits*—the very arrangement and association of different orders of morontia and spirit beings produce majestic melodies.

6. *Melody of thought*—the thinking of spiritual thoughts can be so perfected as to burst forth in the melodies of Havona.

7. *The music of space*—by proper attunement the melodies of other spheres can be picked up on the universe broadcast circuits.

There are over one hundred thousand different modes of sound, color, and energy manipulation, techniques analogous to the human employment of musical instruments. Your ensembles of dancing undoubtedly represent a crude and grotesque attempt of material creatures to approach the celestial harmony of being placement and personality arrangement. The other five forms of morontia melody are unrecognized by the sensory mechanism of material bodies.

Harmony, the music of the seven levels of melodious association, is the one universal code of spirit communication. Music, such as Urantia mortals understand, attains its highest expression in the schools of Jerusem, the system headquarters, where semimaterial beings are taught the harmonies of sound. Mortals do not react to the other forms of morontia melody and celestial harmony.

Appreciation of music on Urantia is both physical and spiritual; and your human musicians have done much to elevate musical taste from the barbarous monotony of your early ancestors to the higher levels of sound appreciation. The majority of Urantia mortals react to music so largely with the material muscles and so slightly with the mind and spirit; but there has been a steady improvement in musical appreciation for more than thirty-five thousand years.

Tuneful syncopation represents a transition from the musical monotony of primitive man to the expressionful harmony and meaningful melodies of your later-day musicians. These earlier types of rhythm stimulate the reaction of the music-loving sense without entailing the exertion of the higher intellectual powers of harmony appreciation and thus more generally appeal to immature or spiritually indolent individuals.

The best music of Urantia is just a fleeting echo of the magnificent strains heard by the celestial associates of your musicians, who left but snatches of these harmonies of morontia forces on record as the musical melodies of sound harmonics. Spirit-morontia music not infrequently employs all seven modes of expression and reproduction, so that the human mind is tremendously handicapped in any attempt to reduce these melodies of the higher spheres to mere notes of musical sound. Such an effort would be something like endeavoring to reproduce the strains of a great orchestra by means of a single musical instrument.

While you have assembled some beautiful melodies on Urantia, you have not progressed musically nearly so far as many of your neighboring planets in Satania. If Adam and Eve had only survived, then would you have had music in reality; but the gift of harmony, so large in their natures, has been so diluted by strains of unmusical tendencies that only once in a thousand mortal lives is there any great appreciation of harmonics. But be not discouraged; some day a real musician may appear on Urantia, and whole peoples will be enthralled by the magnificent strains of his melodies. One such human being could forever change the course of a whole nation, even the entire civilized world. It is literally true, "melody has power a whole world to transform." Forever, music will remain the universal language of men, angels, and spirits. Harmony is the speech of Havona.

2. THE HEAVENLY REPRODUCERS

Mortal man can hardly hope for more than a meager and distorted concept of the functions of the heavenly reproducers, which I must attempt to illustrate through the gross and limited symbolism of your material language. The spirit-morontia world has a thousand and one things of supreme value, things worthy of reproduction but unknown on Urantia, experiences that belong in the category of the activities which have hardly "entered into the mind of man," those realities which God has in waiting for those who survive the life in the flesh.

There are seven groups of the heavenly reproducers, and I will attempt to illustrate their work by the following classification:

1. *The singers*—harmonists who reiterate the specific harmonies of the past and interpret the melodies of the present. But all of this is effected on the morontia level.

2. *The color workers*—those artists of light and shade you might call sketchers and painters, artists who preserve passing scenes and transient episodes for future morontia enjoyment.

3. *The light picturizers*—the makers of the real semispirit-phenomena preservations of which motion pictures would be a very crude illustration.

4. *The historic pageanteers*—those who dramatically reproduce the crucial events of universe records and history.

5. *The prophetic artists*—those who project the meanings of history into the future.

6. *The life-story tellers*—those who perpetuate the meaning and significance of life experience. The projection of present personal experiences into future attainment values.

7. *The administrative enactors*—those who depict the significance of governmental philosophy and administrative technique, the celestial dramatists of sovereignty.

Very often and effectively the heavenly reproducers collaborate with the reversion directors in combining memory recapitulation with certain forms of mind rest and personality diversion. Before the morontia conclaves and spirit assemblies these reproducers sometimes associate themselves in tremendous dramatic spectacles representative of the purpose of such gatherings. I recently witnessed such a stupendous presentation in which more than one million actors produced a succession of one thousand scenes.

The higher intellectual teachers and the transition ministers freely and effectively utilize these various groups of reproducers in their morontia educational activities. But not all of their efforts are devoted to transient illustration; much, very much, of their work is of a permanent nature and will forever remain as a legacy to all future time. So versatile are these artisans that, when they function en masse, they are able to re-enact an age, and in collaboration with the seraphic ministers they can actually portray the eternal values of the spirit world to the mortal seers of time.

3. THE DIVINE BUILDERS

There are cities "whose builder and maker is God." In spirit counterpart we have all that you mortals are familiar with and inexpressibly more. We have homes, spirit comforts, and morontia necessities. For every material satisfaction which humans are capable of enjoying, we have thousands of spiritual realities that serve to enrich and enlarge our existence. The divine builders function in seven groups:

1. *The home designers and builders*—those who construct and remodel the abodes assigned to individuals and working groups. These morontia and spirit domiciles are real. They would be invisible to your short-range vision, but they are very real and beautiful to us. To a certain extent, all spirit beings may share with the builders certain details of the planning and creation of their morontia or spirit abodes. These homes are fitted up and embellished in accordance with the needs of the morontia or of the spirit creatures who are to inhabit them. There is abundant variety and ample opportunity for individual expression in all these constructions.

2. *The vocation builders*—those who function in designing and assembling the abodes of the regular and routine workers of the spirit and morontia realms. These builders are comparable to those who construct the Urantia workshops and other industrial plants. The transition worlds have a necessary economy of mutual ministry and specialized division of labor. We do not all do everything; there is diversity of function among morontia beings and evolving spirits, and these vocation builders not only build better workshops but also contribute to the vocational enhancement of the worker.

3. *The play builders.* Enormous edifices are utilized during the seasons of rest, what mortals would call recreation and, in a certain sense, play. Provision is made for a suitable setting for the reversion directors, the humorists of the morontia worlds, those transition spheres whereon takes place the training of ascendant beings but recently removed from the evolutionary planets. Even the higher spirits engage in a certain form of reminiscent humor during their periods of spiritual recharging.

4. *The worship builders*—the experienced architects of the spirit and the morontia temples. All the worlds of mortal ascent have temples of worship, and they are the most exquisite creations of the morontia realms and the spirit spheres.

5. *The education builders*—those who build the headquarters of morontia training and advanced spirit learning. Always is the way open to acquire more knowledge, to gain additional information respecting one's present and future work as well as universal cultural knowledge, information designed to make ascending mortals more intelligent and effective citizens of the morontia and spirit worlds.

6. *Morontia planners*—those who build for the co-ordinate association of all the personalities of all realms as they are at any one time present on any one sphere. These planners collaborate with the Morontia Power Supervisors to enrich the co-ordination of the progressive morontia life.

7. *The public builders*—the artisans who plan and construct the designated places of assembly other than those of worship. Great and magnificent are the places of common assembly.

While neither these structures nor their embellishment would be exactly real to the sensory comprehension of material mortals, they are very real to us. You would be unable to see these temples could you be there in the flesh; nevertheless, all of these supermaterial creations are actually there, and we clearly discern them and just as fully enjoy them.

4. THE THOUGHT RECORDERS

These artisans are devoted to the preservation and reproduction of the superior thought of the realms, and they function in seven groups:

1. *Thought preservers.* These are the artisans dedicated to the preservation of the higher thought of the realms. On the morontia worlds they truly treasure the gems of mentation. Before first coming to Urantia, I saw records and heard broadcasts of the ideation of some of the great minds of this planet. Thought recorders preserve such noble ideas in the tongue of Uversa.

Each superuniverse has its own language, a tongue spoken by its personalities and prevailing throughout its sectors. This is known as the tongue of Uversa in our superuniverse. Each local universe also has its own language. All of the higher orders of Nebadon are bilingual, speaking both the language of Nebadon and the tongue of Uversa. When two individuals from different local universes meet, they communicate in the tongue of Uversa; if, however, one of them hails from another superuniverse, they must have recourse to a translator. In the central universe there is little need of a language; there exists perfect and well-nigh complete understanding; there, only the Gods are not fully comprehended. We are taught that a chance meeting on Paradise reveals more of mutual understanding than could be communicated by a mortal language in a thousand years. Even on Salvington we "know as we are known."

The ability to translate thought into language in the morontia and spirit spheres is beyond mortal comprehension. Our rate of reducing thought to a permanent record can be so speeded up by the expert recorders that the equivalent of over half a million words, or thought symbols, can be registered in one minute of Urantia time. These universe languages are far more replete than the speech of the evolving worlds. The concept symbols of Uversa embrace more than a billion characters, although the basic alphabet contains only seventy symbols. The language of Nebadon is not quite so elaborate, the basic symbols, or alphabet, being forty-eight in number.

2. *Concept recorders.* This second group of recorders are concerned with the preservation of concept pictures, idea patterns. This is a form of permanent recording unknown on the material realms, and by this method I could gain more knowledge in one hour of your time than you could gain in one hundred years of perusing ordinary written language.

3. *Ideograph recorders.* We have the equivalent of both your written and spoken word, but in preserving thought, we usually employ concept picturization and ideograph techniques. Those who preserve ideographs are able to improve one thousandfold upon the work of the concept recorders.

4. *Promoters of oratory.* This group of recorders are occupied with the task of preserving thought for reproduction by oratory. But in the language of Nebadon we could, in a half hour's address, cover the subject matter of the entire lifetime of a Urantia mortal. Your only hope of comprehending these transactions is to pause and consider the technique of your disordered and garbled dream life—how you can in a few seconds traverse years of experience in these fantasies of the night season.

The oratory of the spirit world is one of the rare treats which await you who have heard only the crude and stumbling orations of Urantia. There is harmony of music and euphony of expression in the orations of Salvington and Edentia which are inspiring beyond description. These burning concepts are like gems of beauty in diadems of glory. But I cannot do it! I cannot convey to the human mind the breadth and depth of these realities of another world!

5. *The broadcast directors.* The broadcasts of Paradise, the superuniverses, and the local universes are under the general supervision of this group of thought conservers. They serve as censors and editors as well as co-ordinators of the broadcast material, making a superuniverse adaptation of all Paradise broadcasts and adapting and translating the broadcasts of the Ancients of Days into the individual tongues of the local universes.

The local universe broadcasts must also be modified for reception by the systems and the individual planets. The transmittal of these space reports is carefully supervised, and there is always a back registry to insure the proper reception of every report on every world in a given circuit. These broadcast directors are technically expert in the utilization of the currents of space for all purposes of intelligence communication.

6. *The rhythm recorders.* Urantians would undoubtedly denominate these artisans poets, although their work is very different from, and almost infinitely transcends, your poetic productions. Rhythm is less exhausting to both morontia and spirit beings, and so an effort is frequently made to increase efficiency, as well as to augment pleasure, by executing numerous functions in rhythmic form. I only wish you might be privileged to hear some of the poetic broadcasts of the Edentia assemblies and to enjoy the richness of the color and tone of the constellation geniuses who are masters of this exquisite form of self-expression and social harmonization.

7. *The morontia recorders.* I am at a loss to know how to depict to the material mind the function of this important group of thought recorders assigned to the work of preserving the ensemble pictures of the various groupings of morontia affairs and spirit transactions; crudely illustrated, they are the group photographers of the transition worlds. They save for the future the vital scenes and associations of these progressive epochs, preserving them in the archives of the morontia halls of records.

5. THE ENERGY MANIPULATORS

These interesting and effective artisans are concerned with every kind of energy: physical, mindal, and spiritual.

1. *Physical-energy manipulators.* The physical-energy manipulators serve for long periods with the power directors and are experts in the manipulation and control of many phases of physical energy. They are conversant with the three basic currents and the thirty subsidiary energy segregations of the superuniverses. These beings are of inestimable assistance to the Morontia Power Supervisors of the transition worlds. They are the persistent students of the cosmic projections of Paradise.

2. *Mind-energy manipulators.* These are the experts of intercommunication between morontia and other types of intelligent beings. This form of communication between mortals is practically nonexistent on Urantia. These are

the specialists who promote the ability of the ascending morontia beings to communicate with one another, and their work embraces numerous unique adventures in intellect liaison which are far beyond my power to portray to the material mind. These artisans are the keen students of the mind circuits of the Infinite Spirit.

3. *Spiritual-energy manipulators.* The manipulators of spiritual energy are an intriguing group. Spiritual energy acts in accordance with established laws, just as does physical energy. That is, spirit force, when studied, yields dependable deductions and can be precisely dealt with, even as can the physical energies. There are just as certain and reliable laws in the spirit world as obtain in the material realms. During the last few millions of years many improved techniques for the intake of spiritual energy have been effected by these students of the fundamental laws of the Eternal Son governing spirit energy as applied to the morontia and other orders of celestial beings throughout the universes.

4. *The compound manipulators.* This is the adventurous group of well-trained beings who are dedicated to the functional association of the three original phases of divine energy manifested throughout the universes as physical, mindal, and spiritual energies. These are the keen personalities who are in reality seeking to discover the universe presence of God the Supreme, for in this Deity personality there must occur the experiential unification of all grand universe divinity. And to a certain extent, these artisans have in recent times met with some success.

5. *The transport advisers.* This corps of technical advisers to the transport seraphim are most proficient in collaborating with the star students in working out routings and in otherwise assisting the chiefs of transport on the worlds of space. They are the traffic supervisors of the spheres and are present on all inhabited planets. Urantia is served by a corps of seventy transport advisers.

6. *The experts of communication.* Urantia, likewise, is served by twelve technicians of interplanetary and interuniverse communication. These long-experienced beings are expert in the knowledge of the laws of transmittal and interference as applied to the communications of the realms. This corps is concerned with all forms of space messages except those of Gravity and Solitary Messengers. On Urantia much of their work must be accomplished over the archangels' circuit.

7. *The teachers of rest.* Divine rest is associated with the technique of spiritual-energy intake. Morontia and spirit energy must be replenished just as certainly as physical energy, but not for the same reasons. I am, perforce, compelled to employ crude illustrations in my attempts to enlighten you; nevertheless, we of the spirit world must stop our regular activities periodically and betake ourselves to suitable places of rendezvous where we enter the divine rest and thus recuperate our depleting energies.

You will receive your first lessons in these matters when you reach the mansion worlds after you have become morontia beings and have begun to experience the technique of spirit affairs. You know of the innermost circle of Havona and that, after the pilgrims of space have traversed the preceding circles, they must be inducted into the long and revivifying rest of Paradise. This is not only a technical requirement of transit from the career of time to the service of eternity, but it is also a necessity, a form of rest required to replenish the energy losses incident to the final steps of the ascendant experience and to store reserves of spirit power for the next stage of the endless career.

These energy manipulators also function in hundreds of other ways too numerous to catalogue, such as counseling with the seraphim, cherubim, and sanobim regarding the most efficient modes of energy intake and as to the maintenance of the most helpful balances of divergent forces between active cherubim and passive sanobim. In many other ways do these experts lend assistance to morontia and spirit creatures in their efforts to understand the divine rest, which is so essential to the effective utilization of the basic energies of space.

6. THE DESIGNERS AND EMBELLISHERS

How I wish I knew how to portray the exquisite work of these unique artisans! Every attempt on my part to explain the work of spirit embellishment would only recall to material minds your own pitiful but worthy efforts to do these things on your world of mind and matter.

This corps, while embracing over one thousand subdivisions of activity, is grouped under the following seven major heads:

1. *The craftworkers of color.* These are they who make the ten thousand color tones of spirit reflection peal forth their exquisite messages of harmonious beauty. Aside from color perception there is nothing in human experience to which these activities may be compared.

2. *The sound designers.* Spirit waves of diverse identity and morontia appreciation are depicted by these designers of what you would call sound. These impulses are in reality the superb reflections of the naked and glorious spirit-souls of the celestial hosts.

3. *The emotion designers.* These enhancers and conservators of feeling are those who preserve the sentiments of morontia and the emotions of divinity for the study and edification of the children of time and for the inspiration and beautification of morontia progressors and advancing spirits.

4. *The artists of odor.* This comparison of supernal spirit activities to the physical recognition of chemical odors is, indeed, unfortunate, but Urantia mortals could hardly recognize this ministry by any other name. These artisans create their varied symphonies for the edification and delight of the advancing children of light. You have nothing on earth to which this type of spiritual grandeur can be even remotely compared.

5. *The presence embellishers.* These artisans are not occupied with the arts of self-adornment or the technique of creature beautification. They are devoted to the production of multitudinous and joyous reactions in individual morontia and spirit creatures by dramatizing the significance of relationship through the positional values assigned to different morontia and spirit orders in the composite ensembles of these diversified beings. These artists arrange supermaterial beings as you would living musical notes, odors, sights, and then blend them into the anthems of glory.

6. *The taste designers.* And how can you be told of these artists! Faintly I might suggest that they are improvers of morontia taste, and they also endeavor to increase the appreciation of beauty through the sharpening of the evolving spirit senses.

7. *The morontia synthesizers.* These are the master craftsmen who, when all others have made their respective contributions, then add the culminating and finishing touches to the morontia ensemble, thus achieving an inspiring portrayal of the divinely beautiful, an enduring inspiration to spirit beings and their morontia associates. But you must await your deliverance from the animal body before you can begin to conceive of the artistic glories and aesthetic beauties of the morontia and spirit worlds.

7. THE HARMONY WORKERS

These artists are not concerned with music, painting, or anything similar, as you might be led to surmise. They are occupied with the manipulation and organization of specialized forces and energies which are present in the spirit world, but which are not recognized by mortals. If I had the least possible basis for comparison, I would attempt to portray this unique field of spirit achievement, but I despair—there is no hope of conveying to mortal minds this sphere of celestial artistry. Nevertheless, that which cannot be described may still be implied:

Beauty, rhythm, and harmony are intellectually associated and spiritually akin. Truth, fact, and relationship are intellectually inseparable and associated with the philosophic concepts of beauty. Goodness, righteousness, and justice are philosophically interrelated and spiritually bound up together with living truth and divine beauty.

Cosmic concepts of true philosophy, the portrayal of celestial artistry, or the mortal attempt to depict the human recognition of divine beauty can never be truly satisfying if such attempted creature progression is ununified. These expressions of the divine urge within the evolving creature may be intellectually true, emotionally beautiful, and spiritually good; but the real soul of expression is absent unless these realities of truth, meanings of beauty, and values of goodness are unified in the life experience of the artisan, the scientist, or the philosopher.

These divine qualities are perfectly and absolutely unified in God. And every God-knowing man or angel possesses the potential of unlimited self-expression on ever-progressive levels of unified self-realization by the technique of the never-ending achievement of Godlikeness—the experiential blending in the evolutionary experience of eternal truth, universal beauty, and divine goodness.

8. MORTAL ASPIRATIONS AND MORONTIA ACHIEVEMENTS

Although celestial artisans do not personally work on material planets, such as Urantia, they do come, from time to time, from the headquarters of the system to proffer help to the naturally gifted individuals of the mortal races. When thus assigned, these artisans temporarily work under the supervision of the planetary angels of progress. The seraphic hosts co-operate with these artisans in attempting to assist those mortal artists who possess inherent endowments, and who also possess Adjusters of special and previous experience.

There are three possible sources of special human ability: At the bottom *always* there exists the natural or inherent aptitude. Special ability is never an arbitrary gift of the Gods; there is always an ancestral foundation for every outstanding talent. In addition to this natural ability, or rather supplemental thereto, there may be contributed the leadings of the Thought Adjuster in those individuals whose indwelling Adjusters may have had actual and bona fide experiences along such lines on other worlds and in other mortal creatures. In those cases where both the human mind and the indwelling Adjuster are unusually skillful, the spirit artisans may be delegated to act as harmonizers of these talents and otherwise to assist and inspire these mortals to seek for ever-perfecting ideals and to attempt their enhanced portrayal for the edification of the realm.

There is no caste in the ranks of spirit artisans. No matter how lowly your origin, if you have ability and the gift of expression, you will gain adequate recognition and receive due appreciation as you ascend upward in the scale of morontia experience and spiritual attainment. There can be no handicap of human heredity or deprivation of mortal environment which the morontia career will not fully compensate and wholly remove. And all such satisfactions of artistic achievement and expressionful self-realization will be effected by your own personal efforts in progressive advancement. At last the aspirations of evolutionary mediocrity may be realized. While the Gods do not arbitrarily bestow talents and ability upon the children of time, they do provide for the attainment of the satisfaction of all their noble longings and for the gratification of all human hunger for supernal self-expression.

But every human being should remember: Many ambitions to excel which tantalize mortals in the flesh will not persist with these same mortals in the morontia and spirit careers. The ascending morontians learn to socialize their former purely selfish longings and egoistic ambitions. Nevertheless, those things which you so earnestly longed to do on earth and which circumstances so persistently denied you, if, after acquiring true mota insight in the morontia career, you still desire to do, then will you most certainly be granted every opportunity fully to satisfy your long-cherished desires.

Before ascending mortals leave the local universe to embark upon their spirit careers, they will be satiated respecting every intellectual, artistic, and social longing or true ambition which ever characterized their mortal or morontia planes of existence. This is the achievement of equality of the satisfaction of self-expression and self-realization but not the attainment of identical experiential status nor the complete obliteration of characteristic individuality in skill, technique, and expression. But the new spirit differential of personal experiential attainment will not become thus leveled off and equalized until after you have finished the last circle of the Havona career. And then will the Paradise residents be confronted with the necessity of adjusting to that absonite differential of personal experience which can be leveled off only by the group attainment of the ultimate of creature status—the seventh-stage-spirit destiny of the mortal finaliters.

And this is the story of the celestial artisans, that cosmopolitan body of exquisite workers who do so much to glorify the architectural spheres with the artistic portrayals of the divine beauty of the Paradise Creators.

[Indited by an Archangel of Nebadon.]

PAPER 45

THE LOCAL SYSTEM ADMINISTRATION

THE administrative center of Satania consists of a cluster of architectural spheres, fifty-seven in number—Jerusem itself, the seven major satellites, and the forty-nine subsatellites. Jerusem, the system capital, is almost one hundred times the size of Urantia, although its gravity is a trifle less. Jerusem's major satellites are the seven transition worlds, each of which is about ten times as large as Urantia, while the seven subsatellites of these transition spheres are just about the size of Urantia.

The seven mansion worlds are the seven subsatellites of transition world number one.

This entire system of fifty-seven architectural worlds is independently lighted, heated, watered, and energized by the co-ordination of the Satania Power Center and the Master Physical Controllers in accordance with the established technique of the physical organization and arrangement of these specially created spheres. They are also physically cared for and otherwise maintained by the native spornagia.

1. TRANSITIONAL CULTURE WORLDS

The seven major worlds swinging around Jerusem are generally known as the transitional culture spheres. Their rulers are designated from time to time by the Jerusem supreme executive council. These spheres are numbered and named as follows:

Number 1. The Finaliter World. This is the headquarters of the finaliter corps of the local system and is surrounded by the receiving worlds, the seven mansion worlds, dedicated so fully to the scheme of mortal ascension. The finaliter world is accessible to the inhabitants of all seven mansion worlds. Transport seraphim carry ascending personalities back and forth on these pilgrimages, which are designed to cultivate their faith in the ultimate destiny of transition mortals. Although the finaliters and their structures are not ordinarily perceptible to morontia vision, you will be more than thrilled, from time to time, when the energy transformers and the Morontia Power Supervisors enable you momentarily to glimpse these high spirit personalities who have actually completed the Paradise ascension, and who have returned to the very worlds where you are beginning this long journey, as the pledge of assurance that you may and can complete the stupendous undertaking. All mansion world sojourners go to the finaliter sphere at least once a year for these assemblies of finaliter visualization.

Number 2. The Morontia World. This planet is the headquarters of the supervisors of morontia life and is surrounded by the seven spheres whereon the morontia chiefs train their associates and helpers, both morontia beings and ascending mortals.

In passing through the seven mansion worlds, you will also progress through these cultural and social spheres of increasing morontia contact. When you advance from the first to the second mansion world, you will become eligible for a visitor's permit to transitional headquarters number two, the morontia world, and so on. And when present on any one of these six cultural spheres, you may, on invitation, become a visitor and observer on any of the seven surrounding worlds of associated group activities.

Number 3. The Angelic World. This is the headquarters of all the seraphic hosts engaged in system activities and is surrounded by the seven worlds of angelic training and instruction. These are the seraphic social spheres.

Number 4. The Superangel World. This sphere is the Satania home of the Brilliant Evening Stars and a vast concourse of co-ordinate and near-co-ordinate beings. The seven satellites of this world are assigned to the seven major groups of these unnamed celestial beings.

Number 5. The World of the Sons. This planet is the headquarters of the divine Sons of all orders, including the creature-trinitized sons. The surrounding seven worlds are devoted to certain individual groupings of these divinely related sons.

Number 6. The World of the Spirit. This sphere serves as the system rendezvous of the high personalities of the Infinite Spirit. Its seven surrounding satellites are assigned to individual groups of these diverse orders. But on transition world number six there is no representation of the Spirit, neither is such a presence to be observed on the system capitals; the Divine Minister of Salvington is *everywhere* in Nebadon.

Number 7. The World of the Father. This is the silent sphere of the system. No group of beings is domiciled on it. The great temple of light occupies a central place, but no one can be discerned therein. All beings of all the system worlds are welcomed as worshipers.

The seven satellites surrounding the Father's world are variously utilized in the different systems. In Satania they are now used as the detention spheres for the interned groups of the Lucifer rebellion. The constellation capital, Edentia, has no analogous prison worlds; the few seraphim and cherubim who went over to the rebels in the Satania rebellion have been long since confined on these isolation worlds of Jerusem.

As a sojourner on the seventh mansion world, you have access to the seventh transition world, the sphere of the Universal Father, and are also permitted to visit the Satania prison worlds surrounding this planet, whereon are now confined Lucifer and the majority of those personalities who followed him in rebellion against Michael. And this sad spectacle has been observable during these recent ages and will continue to serve as a solemn warning to all Nebadon until the Ancients of Days shall adjudicate the sin of Lucifer and his fallen associates who rejected the salvation proffered by Michael, their universe Father.

2. THE SYSTEM SOVEREIGN

The chief executive of a local system of inhabited worlds is a primary Lanonandek Son, the System Sovereign. In our local universe these sovereigns are intrusted with large executive responsibilities, unusual personal prerogatives. Not all universes, even in Orvonton, are so organized as to permit the System Sovereigns to exercise such unusually wide powers of personal discretion in the direction of system affairs. But in all the history of Nebadon these untrammeled executives have exhibited disloyalty only three times. The Lucifer rebellion in the system of Satania was the last and the most widespread of all.

In Satania, even after this disastrous upheaval, absolutely no changes have been made in the technique of system administration. The present System Sovereign possesses all the power and exercises all the authority that were invested in his unworthy predecessor except for certain matters now under the supervision of the Constellation Fathers which the Ancients of Days have not yet fully restored to Lanaforge, the successor of Lucifer.

The present head of Satania is a gracious and brilliant ruler, and he is a rebellion-tested sovereign. When serving as an assistant System Sovereign, Lanaforge was faithful to Michael in an earlier upheaval in the universe of Nebadon. This mighty and brilliant Lord of Satania is a tried and tested administrator. At the time of the second system rebellion in Nebadon, when the System Sovereign stumbled and fell into darkness, Lanaforge, the first assistant to the erring chief, seized the reins of government and so conducted the affairs of the system that comparatively few personalities were lost either on the headquarters worlds or on the inhabited planets of that unfortunate system. Lanaforge bears the distinction of being the only primary Lanonandek Son in all Nebadon who thus functioned loyally in the service of Michael and in the very presence of the default of his brother of superior authority and antecedent rank. Lanaforge will probably not be removed from Jerusem until all the results of the former folly have been overcome and the products of rebellion removed from Satania.

While all the affairs of the isolated worlds of Satania have not been returned to his jurisdiction, Lanaforge discloses great interest in their welfare, and he is a frequent visitor on Urantia. As in other and normal systems, the Sovereign presides over the system council of world rulers, the Planetary Princes and the resident governors general of the isolated worlds. This planetary council assembles from time to time on the headquarters of the system—"When the Sons of God come together."

Once a week, every ten days on Jerusem, the Sovereign holds a conclave with some one group of the various orders of personalities domiciled on the headquarters world. These are the charmingly informal hours of Jerusem, and they are never-to-be-forgotten occasions. On Jerusem there exists the utmost fraternity between all the various orders of beings and between each of these groups and the System Sovereign.

These unique assemblages occur on the sea of glass, the great gathering field of the system capital. They are purely social and spiritual occasions; nothing pertaining to the planetary administration or even to the ascendant plan is ever discussed. Ascending mortals come together at these times merely to enjoy themselves and to meet their fellow Jerusemites. Those groups which are not being entertained by the Sovereign at these weekly relaxations meet at their own headquarters.

3. THE SYSTEM GOVERNMENT

The chief executive of a local system, the System Sovereign, is always supported by two or three Lanonandek Sons, who function as first and second assistants. But at the present time the system of Satania is administered by a staff of seven Lanonandeks:

1. *The System Sovereign*—Lanaforge, number 2,709 of the primary order and successor to the apostate Lucifer.

2. *The first assistant Sovereign*—Mansurotia, number 17,841 of the tertiary Lanonandeks. He was dispatched to Satania along with Lanaforge.

3. *The second assistant Sovereign*—Sadib, number 271,402 of the tertiary order. Sadib also came to Satania with Lanaforge.

4. *The custodian of the system*—Holdant, number 19 of the tertiary corps, the holder and controller of all interned spirits above the order of mortal existence. Holdant likewise came to Satania with Lanaforge.

5. *The system recorder*—Vilton, secretary of the Lanonandek ministry of Satania, number 374 of the third order. Vilton was a member of the original Lanaforge group.

6. *The bestowal director*—Fortant, number 319,847 of the reserves of the secondary Lanonandeks and temporary director of all universe activities transplanted to Jerusem since Michael's bestowal on Urantia. Fortant has been attached to the staff of Lanaforge for nineteen hundred years of Urantia time.

7. *The high counselor*—Hanavard, number 67 of the primary Lanonandek Sons and a member of the high corps of universe counselors and co-ordinators. He functions as acting chairman of the executive council of Satania. Hanavard is the twelfth of this order so to serve on Jerusem since the Lucifer rebellion.

This executive group of seven Lanonandeks constitutes the expanded emergency administration made necessary by the exigencies of the Lucifer rebellion. There are only minor courts on Jerusem since the system is the unit of administration, not adjudication, but the Lanonandek administration is supported by the Jerusem executive council, the supreme advisory body of Satania. This council consists of twelve members:

1. Hanavard, the Lanonandek chairman.
2. Lanaforge, the System Sovereign.
3. Mansurotia, the first assistant Sovereign.
4. The chief of Satania Melchizedeks.
5. The acting director of the Satania Life Carriers.
6. The chief of the Satania finaliters.
7. The original Adam of Satania, the supervising head of the Material Sons.
8. The director of the Satania seraphic hosts.
9. The chief of the Satania physical controllers.
10. The director of the system Morontia Power Supervisors.

11. The acting director of system midway creatures.
12. The acting head of the corps of ascending mortals.

This council periodically chooses three members to represent the local system on the supreme council at universe headquarters, but this representation is suspended by rebellion. Satania now has an observer at the headquarters of the local universe, but since the bestowal of Michael the system has resumed the election of ten members to the Edentia legislature.

4. THE FOUR AND TWENTY COUNSELORS

At the center of the seven angelic residential circles on Jerusem is located the headquarters of the Urantia advisory council, the four and twenty counselors. John the Revelator called them the four and twenty elders: "And round about the throne were four and twenty seats, and upon the seats I saw four and twenty elders sitting, clothed in white raiment." The throne in the center of this group is the judgment seat of the presiding archangel, the throne of the resurrection roll call of mercy and justice for all Satania. This judgment seat has always been on Jerusem, but the twenty-four surrounding seats were placed in position no more than nineteen hundred years ago, soon after Christ Michael was elevated to the full sovereignty of Nebadon. These four and twenty counselors are his personal agents on Jerusem, and they have authority to represent the Master Son in all matters concerning the roll calls of Satania and in many other phases of the scheme of mortal ascension on the isolated worlds of the system. They are the designated agents for executing the special requests of Gabriel and the unusual mandates of Michael.

These twenty-four counselors have been recruited from the eight Urantia races, and the last of this group were assembled at the time of the resurrection roll call of Michael, nineteen hundred years ago. This Urantia advisory council is made up of the following members:

1. *Onagar,* the master mind of the pre-Planetary Prince age, who directed his fellows in the worship of "The Breath Giver."

2. *Mansant,* the great teacher of the post-Planetary Prince age on Urantia, who pointed his fellows to the veneration of "The Great Light."

3. *Onamonalonton,* a far-distant leader of the red man and the one who directed this race from the worship of many gods to the veneration of "The Great Spirit."

4. *Orlandof,* a prince of the blue men and their leader in the recognition of the divinity of "The Supreme Chief."

5. *Porshunta,* the oracle of the extinct orange race and the leader of this people in the worship of "The Great Teacher."

6. *Singlangton,* the first of the yellow men to teach and lead his people in the worship of "One Truth" instead of many. Thousands of years ago the yellow man knew of the one God.

7. *Fantad,* the deliverer of the green men from darkness and their leader in the worship of "The One Source of Life."

8. *Orvonon,* the enlightener of the indigo races and their leader in the onetime service of "The God of Gods."

9. *Adam,* the discredited but rehabilitated planetary father of Urantia, a Material Son of God who was relegated to the likeness of mortal flesh, but who survived and was subsequently elevated to this position by the decree of Michael.

10. *Eve,* the mother of the violet race of Urantia, who suffered the penalty of default with her mate and was also rehabilitated with him and assigned to serve with this group of mortal survivors.

11. *Enoch,* the first of the mortals of Urantia to fuse with the Thought Adjuster during the mortal life in the flesh.

12. *Moses,* the emancipator of a remnant of the submerged violet race and the instigator of the revival of the worship of the Universal Father under the name of "The God of Israel."

13. *Elijah,* a translated soul of brilliant spiritual achievement during the post-Material Son age.

14. *Machiventa Melchizedek,* the only Son of this order to bestow himself upon the Urantia races. While still numbered as a Melchizedek, he has become "forever a minister of the Most Highs," eternally assuming the assignment of service as a mortal ascender, having sojourned on Urantia in the likeness of mortal flesh at Salem in the days of Abraham. This Melchizedek has latterly been proclaimed vicegerent Planetary Prince of Urantia with headquarters on Jerusem and authority to act in behalf of Michael, who is actually the Planetary Prince of the world whereon he experienced his terminal bestowal in human form. Notwithstanding this, Urantia is still supervised by successive resident governors general, members of the four and twenty counselors.

15. *John the Baptist,* the forerunner of Michael's mission on Urantia and, in the flesh, distant cousin of the Son of Man.

16. *1-2-3 the First,* the leader of the loyal midway creatures in the service of Gabriel at the time of the Caligastia betrayal, elevated to this position by Michael soon after his entrance upon unconditioned sovereignty.

These selected personalities are exempt from the ascension regime for the time being, on Gabriel's request, and we have no idea how long they may serve in this capacity.

Seats numbers 17, 18, 19, and 20 are not permanently occupied. They are temporarily filled by the unanimous consent of the sixteen permanent members, being kept open for later assignment to ascending mortals from the present post-bestowal Son age on Urantia.

Numbers 21, 22, 23, and 24 are likewise temporarily filled while being held in reserve for the great teachers of other and subsequent ages which undoubtedly will follow the present age. Eras of the Magisterial Sons and Teacher Sons and the ages of light and life are to be anticipated on Urantia, regardless of unexpected visitations of divine Sons which may or may not occur.

5. THE MATERIAL SONS

The great divisions of celestial life have their headquarters and immense preserves on Jerusem, including the various orders of divine Sons, high spirits, superangels, angels, and midway creatures. The central abode of this wonderful sector is the chief temple of the Material Sons.

Mansion world students who have one or more children in the probationary nursery on the finaliters' world, and who are deficient in essential parental experience, may apply for a Melchizedek permit which will effect their temporary transfer from ascension duties on the mansion worlds to the finaliter world, where they are granted opportunity to function as associate parents to their own and other children. This service of parental ministry may be later accredited on Jerusem as the fulfillment of one half of the training which such ascenders are required to undergo in the families of the Material Sons and Daughters.

The probation nursery itself is supervised by one thousand couples of Material Sons and Daughters, volunteers from the Jerusem colony of their order. They are immediately assisted by about an equal number of volunteer midsonite parental groups who stop off here to render this service on their way from the midsonite world of Satania to the unrevealed destiny on their special worlds of reservation among the finaliter spheres of Salvington.

7. THE MELCHIZEDEK SCHOOLS

The Melchizedeks are the directors of that large corps of instructors—partially spiritualized will creatures and others—who function so acceptably on Jerusem and its associated worlds but especially on the seven mansion worlds. These are the detention planets, where those mortals who fail to achieve fusion with their indwelling Adjusters during the life in the flesh are rehabilitated in transient form to receive further help and to enjoy extended opportunity for continuing their strivings for spiritual attainment, those very efforts which were prematurely interrupted by death. Or if, for any other reason of hereditary handicap, unfavorable environment, or conspiracy of circumstances, this soul attainment was not completed, no matter what the reason, all who are true of purpose and worthy in spirit find themselves, as themselves, present on the continuing planets, where they must learn to master the essentials of the eternal career, to possess themselves of traits which they could not, or did not, acquire during the lifetime in the flesh.

The Brilliant Evening Stars (and their unnamed co-ordinates) frequently serve as teachers in the various educational enterprises of the universe, including those sponsored by the Melchizedeks. Also do the Trinity Teacher Sons collaborate, and they impart the touches of Paradise perfection to these progressive training schools. But all these activities are not exclusively devoted to the advancement of ascending mortals; many are equally occupied with the progressive training of the native spirit personalities of Nebadon.

The Melchizedek Sons conduct upward of thirty different educational centers on Jerusem. These training schools begin with the college of self-evaluation and end with the schools of Jerusem citizenship, wherein the Material Sons and Daughters join with the Melchizedeks and others in their supreme effort to qualify the mortal survivors for the assumption of the high responsibilities of representative government. The entire universe is organized and administered on the *representative* plan. Representative government is the divine ideal of self-government among nonperfect beings.

Every one hundred years of universe time each system selects its ten representatives to sit in the constellation legislature. They are chosen by the Jerusem council of one thousand, an elective body charged with the duty of representing the system groups in all such delegated or appointive matters. All representatives or other delegates are selected by the council of one thousand electors, and they must be graduates of the highest school of the Melchizedek College of Administration, as also are all of those who constitute this group of one thousand electors. This school is fostered by the Melchizedeks, latterly assisted by the finaliters.

There are many elective bodies on Jerusem, and they are voted into authority from time to time by three orders of citizenship—the Material Sons and Daughters, the seraphim and their associates, including midway creatures, and the ascending mortals. To receive nomination for representative honor a candidate must have gained requisite recognition from the Melchizedek schools of administration.

Suffrage is universal on Jerusem among these three groups of citizenship, but the vote is differentially cast in accordance with the recognized and duly registered personal possession of mota—morontia wisdom. The vote cast at a Jerusem election by any one personality has a value ranging from one up to one thousand. Jerusem citizens are thus classified in accordance with their mota achievement.

From time to time Jerusem citizens present themselves to the Melchizedek examiners, who certify to their attainment of morontia wisdom. Then they go before the examining corps of the Brilliant Evening Stars or their designates, who ascertain the degree of spirit insight. Next they appear in the presence of the four and twenty counselors and their associates, who pass upon their status of experiential attainment of socialization. These three factors are then carried to the citizenship registrars of representative government, who quickly compute the mota status and assign suffrage qualifications in accordance therewith.

Under the supervision of the Melchizedeks the ascending mortals, especially those who are tardy in their personality unification on the new morontia levels, are taken in hand by the Material Sons and are given intensive training designed to rectify such deficiencies. No ascending mortal leaves the system headquarters for the more extensive and varied socialization career of the constellation until these Material Sons certify to the achievement of mota personality—an individuality combining the completed mortal existence in experiential association with the budding morontia career, both being duly blended by the spiritual overcontrol of the Thought Adjuster.

[Presented by a Melchizedek of temporary assignment on Urantia.]

PAPER 46

THE LOCAL SYSTEM HEADQUARTERS

JERUSEM, the headquarters of Satania, is an average capital of a local system, and aside from numerous irregularities occasioned by the Lucifer rebellion and the bestowal of Michael on Urantia, it is typical of similar spheres. Your local system has passed through some stormy experiences, but it is at present being administered most efficiently, and as the ages pass, the results of disharmony are being slowly but surely eradicated. Order and good will are being restored, and the conditions on Jerusem are more and more approaching the heavenly status of your traditions, for the system headquarters is truly the heaven visualized by the majority of twentieth-century religious believers.

1. PHYSICAL ASPECTS OF JERUSEM

Jerusem is divided into one thousand latitudinal sectors and ten thousand longitudinal zones. The sphere has seven major capitals and seventy minor administrative centers. The seven sectional capitals are concerned with diverse activities, and the System Sovereign is present in each at least once a year.

The standard mile of Jerusem is equivalent to about seven Urantia miles. The standard weight, the "gradant," is built up through the decimal system from the mature ultimaton and represents almost exactly ten ounces of your weight. The Satania day equals three days of Urantia time, less one hour, four minutes, and fifteen seconds, that being the time of the axial revolution of Jerusem. The system year consists of one hundred Jerusem days. The time of the system is broadcast by the master chronoldeks.

The energy of Jerusem is superbly controlled and circulates about the sphere in the zone channels, which are directly fed from the energy charges of space and expertly administered by the Master Physical Controllers. The natural resistance to the passage of these energies through the physical channels of conduction yields the heat required for the production of the equable temperature of Jerusem. The full-light temperature is maintained at about 70 degrees Fahrenheit, while during the period of light recession it falls to a little lower than 50 degrees.

The lighting system of Jerusem should not be so difficult for you to comprehend. There are no days and nights, no seasons of heat and cold. The power transformers maintain one hundred thousand centers from which rarefied energies are projected upward through the planetary atmosphere, undergoing certain changes, until they reach the electric air-ceiling of the sphere; and then these energies are reflected back and down as a gentle, sifting, and even light of about the intensity of Urantia sunlight when the sun is shining overhead at ten o'clock in the morning.

Under such conditions of lighting, the light rays do not seem to come from one place; they just sift out of the sky, emanating equally from all space directions. This light is very similar to natural sunlight except that it contains very much less heat. Thus it will be recognized that such headquarters worlds are not luminous in space; if Jerusem were very near Urantia, it would not be visible.

The gases which reflect this light-energy from the Jerusem upper ionosphere back to the ground are very similar to those in the Urantia upper air belts which are concerned with the auroral phenomena of your so-called northern lights, although these are produced by different causes. On Urantia it is this same gas shield which prevents the escape of the terrestrial broadcast waves, reflecting them earthward when they strike this gas belt in their direct outward flight. In this way broadcasts are held near the surface as they journey through the air around your world.

This lighting of the sphere is uniformly maintained for seventy-five per cent of the Jerusem day, and then there is a gradual recession until, at the time of minimum illumination, the light is about that of your full moon on a clear night. This is the quiet hour for all Jerusem. Only the broadcast-receiving stations are in operation during this period of rest and rehabilitation.

Jerusem receives faint light from several near-by suns—a sort of brilliant starlight—but it is not dependent on them; worlds like Jerusem are not subject to the vicissitudes of sun disturbances, neither are they confronted with the problem of a cooling or dying sun.

The seven transitional study worlds and their forty-nine satellites are heated, lighted, energized, and watered by the Jerusem technique.

2. PHYSICAL FEATURES OF JERUSEM

On Jerusem you will miss the rugged mountain ranges of Urantia and other evolved worlds since there are neither earthquakes nor rainfalls, but you will enjoy the beauteous highlands and other unique variations of topography and landscape. Enormous areas of Jerusem are preserved in a "natural state," and the grandeur of such districts is quite beyond the powers of human imagination.

There are thousands upon thousands of small lakes but no raging rivers nor expansive oceans. There is no rainfall, neither storms nor blizzards, on any of the architectural worlds, but there is the daily precipitation of the condensation of moisture during the time of lowest temperature attending the light recession. (The dew point is higher on a three-gas world than on a two-gas planet like Urantia.) The physical plant life and the morontia world of living things both require moisture, but this is largely supplied by the subsoil system of circulation which extends all over the sphere, even up to the very tops of the highlands. This water system is not entirely subsurface, for there are many canals interconnecting the sparkling lakes of Jerusem.

The atmosphere of Jerusem is a three-gas mixture. This air is very similar to that of Urantia with the addition of a gas adapted to the respiration of the morontia order of life. This third gas in no way unfits the air for the respiration of animals or plants of the material orders.

The transportation system is allied with the circulatory streams of energy movement, these main energy currents being located at ten-mile intervals. By adjustment of physical mechanisms the material beings of the planet can proceed at a pace varying from two to five hundred miles per hour. The transport birds fly at about one hundred miles an hour. The air mechanisms of the Material Sons travel around five hundred miles per hour. Material and early morontia beings must utilize these mechanical means of transport, but spirit personalities proceed by liaison with the superior forces and spirit sources of energy.

Jerusem and its associated worlds are endowed with the ten standard divisions of physical life characteristic of the architectural spheres of Nebadon. And since there is no organic evolution on Jerusem, there are no conflicting forms of life, no struggle for existence, no survival of the fittest. Rather is there a creative adaptation which foreshadows the beauty, the harmony, and the perfection of the eternal worlds of the central and divine universe. And in all this creative perfection there is the most amazing intermingling of physical and of morontia life, artistically contrasted by the celestial artisans and their fellows.

Jerusem is indeed a foretaste of paradisiacal glory and grandeur. But you can never hope to gain an adequate idea of these glorious architectural worlds by any attempted description. There is so little that can be compared with aught on your world, and even then the things of Jerusem so transcend the things of Urantia that the comparison is almost grotesque. Until you actually arrive on Jerusem, you can hardly entertain anything like a true concept of the heavenly worlds, but that is not so long a time in the future when your coming experience on the system capital is compared with your sometime arrival on the more remote training spheres of the universe, the superuniverse, and Havona.

The manufacturing or laboratory sector of Jerusem is an extensive domain, one which Urantians would hardly recognize since it has no smoking chimneys; nevertheless, there is an intricate material economy associated with these special worlds, and there is a perfection of mechanical technique and physical achievement which would astonish and even awe your most experienced chemists and inventors. Pause to consider that this first world of detention in the Paradise journey is far more material than spiritual. Throughout your stay on Jerusem and its transition worlds you are far nearer your earth life of material things than your later life of advancing spirit existence.

Mount Seraph is the highest elevation on Jerusem, almost fifteen thousand feet, and is the point of departure for all transport seraphim. Numerous mechanical developments are used in providing initial energy for escaping the planetary gravity and overcoming the air resistance. A seraphic transport departs every three seconds of Urantia time throughout the light period and, sometimes, far into the recession. The transporters take off at about twenty-five standard miles per second of Urantia time and do not attain standard velocity until they are over two thousand miles away from Jerusem.

Transports arrive on the crystal field, the so-called sea of glass. Around this area are the receiving stations for the various orders of beings who traverse space by seraphic transport. Near the polar crystal receiving station for student visitors you may ascend the pearly observatory and view the immense relief map of the entire headquarters planet.

3. THE JERUSEM BROADCASTS

The superuniverse and Paradise-Havona broadcasts are received on Jerusem in liaison with Salvington and by a technique involving the polar crystal, the sea of glass. In addition to provisions for the reception of these extra-Nebadon communications, there are three distinct groups of receiving stations. These separate but tricircular groups of stations are adjusted to the reception of broadcasts from the local worlds, from the constellation headquarters, and from the capital of the local universe. All these broadcasts are automatically displayed so as to be discernible by all types of beings present in the central broadcast amphitheater; of all preoccupations for an ascendant mortal on Jerusem, none is more engaging and engrossing than that of listening in on the never-ending stream of universe space reports.

This Jerusem broadcast-receiving station is encircled by an enormous amphitheater, constructed of scintillating materials largely unknown on Urantia and seating over five billion beings—material and morontia—besides accommodating innumerable spirit personalities. It is the favorite diversion for all Jerusem to spend their leisure at the broadcast station, there to learn of the welfare and state of the universe. And this is the only planetary activity which is not slowed down during the recession of light.

At this broadcast-receiving amphitheater the Salvington messages are coming in continuously. Near by, the Edentia word of the Most High Constellation Fathers is received at least once a day. Periodically the regular and special broadcasts of Uversa are relayed through Salvington, and when Paradise messages are in reception, the entire population is assembled around the sea of glass, and the Uversa friends add the reflectivity phenomena to the technique of the Paradise broadcast so that everything heard becomes visible. And it is in this manner that continual foretastes of advancing beauty and grandeur are afforded the mortal survivors as they journey inward on the eternal adventure.

The Jerusem sending station is located at the opposite pole of the sphere. All broadcasts to the individual worlds are relayed from the system capitals except the Michael messages, which sometimes go direct to their destinations over the archangels' circuit.

4. RESIDENTIAL AND ADMINISTRATIVE AREAS

Considerable portions of Jerusem are assigned as residential areas, while other portions of the system capital are given over to the necessary administrative functions involving the supervision of the affairs of 619 inhabited spheres, 56 transitional-culture worlds, and the system capital itself. On Jerusem and in Nebadon these arrangements are designed as follows:

1. *The circles*—the nonnative residential areas.
2. *The squares*—the system executive-administrative areas.
3. *The rectangles*—the rendezvous of the lower native life.
4. *The triangles*—the local or Jerusem administrative areas.

This arrangement of the system activities into circles, squares, rectangles, and triangles is common to all the system capitals of Nebadon. In another universe an entirely different arrangement might prevail. These are matters determined by the diverse plans of the Creator Sons.

Our narrative of these residential and administrative areas takes no account of the vast and beautiful estates of the Material Sons of God, the permanent citizens of Jerusem, neither do we mention numerous other fascinating orders of spirit and near-spirit creatures. For example: Jerusem enjoys the efficient services of the spironga of design for system function. These beings are devoted to spiritual ministry in behalf of the supermaterial residents and visitors. They are a wonderful group of intelligent and beautiful beings who are the transition servants of the higher morontia creatures and of the morontia helpers who labor for the upkeep and embellishment of all morontia creations. They are on Jerusem what the midway creatures are on Urantia, midway helpers functioning between the material and the spiritual.

The system capitals are unique in that they are the only worlds which exhibit well-nigh perfectly all three phases of universe existence: the material, the morontial, and the spiritual. Whether you are a material, morontia, or spirit personality, you will feel at home on Jerusem; so also do the combined beings, such as the midway creatures and the Material Sons.

Jerusem has great buildings of both material and morontia types, while the embellishment of the purely spiritual zones is no less exquisite and replete. If I only had words to tell you of the morontia counterparts of the marvelous physical equipment of Jerusem! If I could only go on to portray the sublime grandeur and exquisite perfection of the spiritual appointments of this headquarters world! Your most imaginative concept of perfection of beauty and repleteness of appointment would hardly approach these grandeurs. And Jerusem is but the first step on the way to the supernal perfection of Paradise beauty.

5. THE JERUSEM CIRCLES

The residential reservations assigned to the major groups of universe life are designated the Jerusem circles. Those circle groups which find mention in these narratives are the following:

1. The circles of the Sons of God.
2. The circles of the angels and higher spirits.
3. The circles of the Universe Aids, including the creature-trinitized sons not assigned to the Trinity Teacher Sons.
4. The circles of the Master Physical Controllers.
5. The circles of the assigned ascending mortals, including the midway creatures.
6. The circles of the courtesy colonies.
7. The circles of the Corps of the Finality.

Each of these residential groupings consists of seven concentric and successively elevated circles. They are all constructed along the same lines but are of different sizes and are fashioned of differing materials. They are all surrounded by far-reaching enclosures, which mount up to form extensive promenades entirely encompassing every group of seven concentric circles.

1. *Circles of the Sons of God.* Though the Sons of God possess a social planet of their own, one of the transitional-culture worlds, they also occupy these extensive domains on Jerusem. On their transitional-culture world the ascending mortals freely mingle with all orders of divine sonship. There you will personally know and love these Sons, but their social life is largely confined to this special world and its satellites. In the Jerusem circles, however, these various groups of sonship may be observed at work. And since morontia vision is of enormous range, you can walk about on the Sons' promenades and overlook the intriguing activities of their numerous orders.

These seven circles of the Sons are concentric and successively elevated so that each of the outer and larger circles overlooks the inner and smaller ones, each being surrounded by a public promenade wall. These walls are constructed of crystal gems of gleaming brightness and are so elevated as to overlook all of their respective residential circles. The many gates—from fifty to one hundred and fifty thousand—which penetrate each of these walls consist of single pearly crystals.

The first circle of the domain of the Sons is occupied by the Magisterial Sons and their personal staffs. Here center all of the plans and immediate activities of the bestowal and adjudicational services of these juridical Sons. It is also through this center that the Avonals of the system maintain contact with the universe.

The second circle is occupied by the Trinity Teacher Sons. In this sacred domain the Daynals and their associates carry forward the training of the newly arrived primary Teacher Sons. And in all of this work they are ably assisted by a division of certain co-ordinates of the Brilliant Evening Stars. The creature-trinitized sons occupy a sector of the Daynal circle. The Trinity Teacher Sons come the nearest to being the personal representatives of the Universal Father in a local system; they are at least Trinity-origin beings. This second circle is a domain of extraordinary interest to all the peoples of Jerusem.

The third circle is devoted to the Melchizedeks. Here the system chiefs reside and supervise the almost endless activities of these versatile Sons. From the first of the mansion worlds on through all the Jerusem career of ascending mortals, the Melchizedeks are foster fathers and ever-present advisers. It would not be amiss to say that they are the dominant influence on Jerusem aside from the ever-present activities of the Material Sons and Daughters.

The fourth circle is the home of the Vorondadeks and all other orders of the visiting and observer Sons who are not otherwise provided for. The Most High Constellation Fathers take up their abode in this circle when on visits of inspection to the local system. Perfectors of Wisdom, Divine Counselors, and Universal Censors all reside in this circle when on duty in the system.

The fifth circle is the abode of the Lanonandeks, the sonship order of the System Sovereigns and the Planetary Princes. The three groups mingle as one when at home in this domain. The system reserves are held in this circle, while the System Sovereign has a temple situated at the center of the governing group of structures on administration hill.

The sixth circle is the tarrying place of the system Life Carriers. All orders of these Sons are here assembled, and from here they go forth on their world assignments.

The seventh circle is the rendezvous of the ascending sons, those assigned mortals who may be temporarily functioning on the system headquarters, together with their seraphic consorts. All ex-mortals above the status of Jerusem citizens and below that of finaliters are reckoned as belonging to the group having its headquarters in this circle.

These circular reservations of the Sons occupy an enormous area, and until nineteen hundred years ago there existed a great open space at its center. This central region is now occupied by the Michael memorial, completed some five hundred years ago. Four hundred and ninety-five years ago, when this temple was dedicated, Michael was present in person, and all Jerusem heard the touching story of the Master Son's bestowal on Urantia, the least of Satania. The Michael memorial is now the center of all activities embraced in the modified management of the system occasioned by Michael's bestowal, including most of the more recently transplanted Salvington activities. The memorial staff consists of over one million personalities.

2. *The circles of the angels.* Like the residential area of the Sons, these circles of the angels consist of seven concentric and successively elevated circles, each overlooking the inner areas.

The first circle of the angels is occupied by the Higher Personalities of the Infinite Spirit who may be stationed on the headquarters world—Solitary Messengers and their associates. The second circle is dedicated to the messenger hosts, Technical Advisers, companions, inspectors, and recorders as they may chance to function on Jerusem from time to time. The third circle is held by the ministering spirits of the higher orders and groupings.

The fourth circle is held by the administrator seraphim, and the seraphim serving in a local system like Satania are an "innumerable host of angels." The fifth circle is occupied by the planetary seraphim, while the sixth is the home of the transition ministers. The seventh circle is the tarrying sphere of certain unrevealed orders of seraphim. The recorders of all these groups of angels do not sojourn with their fellows, being domiciled in the Jerusem temple of records. All records are preserved in triplicate in this threefold hall of archives. On a system headquarters, records are always preserved in material, in morontia, and in spirit form.

These seven circles are surrounded by the exhibit panorama of Jerusem, five thousand standard miles in circumference, which is devoted to the presentation of the advancing status of the peopled worlds of Satania and is constantly revised so as to truly represent up-to-date conditions on the individual planets. I doubt not that this vast promenade overlooking the circles of the angels will be the first sight of Jerusem to claim your attention when you are permitted extended leisure on your earlier visits.

These exhibits are in charge of the native life of Jerusem, but they are assisted by the ascenders from the various Satania worlds who are tarrying on Jerusem en route to Edentia. The portrayal of planetary conditions and world progress is effected by many methods, some known to you, but mostly by techniques unknown on Urantia. These exhibits occupy the outer edge of this vast wall. The remainder of the promenade is almost entirely open, being highly and magnificently embellished.

3. *The circles of the Universe Aids* have the headquarters of the Evening Stars situated in the enormous central space. Here is located the system headquarters of Galantia, the associate head of this powerful group of superangels,

being the first commissioned of all the ascendant Evening Stars. This is one of the most magnificent of all the administrative sectors of Jerusem, even though it is among the more recent constructions. This center is fifty miles in diameter. The Galantia headquarters is a monolithic cast crystal, wholly transparent. These material-morontia crystals are greatly appreciated by both morontia and material beings. The created Evening Stars exert their influence all over Jerusem, being possessed of such extrapersonality attributes. The entire world has been rendered spiritually fragrant since so many of their activities were transferred here from Salvington.

4. *The circles of the Master Physical Controllers.* The various orders of the Master Physical Controllers are concentrically arranged around the vast temple of power, wherein presides the power chief of the system in association with the chief of the Morontia Power Supervisors. This temple of power is one of two sectors on Jerusem where ascending mortals and midway creatures are not permitted. The other one is the dematerializing sector in the area of the Material Sons, a series of laboratories wherein the transport seraphim transform material beings into a state quite like that of the morontia order of existence.

5. *The circles of the ascending mortals.* The central area of the circles of the ascending mortals is occupied by a group of 619 planetary memorials representative of the inhabited worlds of the system, and these structures periodically undergo extensive changes. It is the privilege of the mortals from each world to agree, from time to time, upon certain of the alterations or additions to their planetary memorials. Many changes are even now being made in the Urantia structures. The center of these 619 temples is occupied by a working model of Edentia and its many worlds of ascendant culture. This model is forty miles in diameter and is an actual reproduction of the Edentia system, true to the original in every detail.

Ascenders enjoy their Jerusem services and take pleasure in observing the techniques of other groups. Everything done in these various circles is open to the full observation of all Jerusem.

The activities of such a world are of three distinct varieties: work, progress, and play. Stated otherwise, they are: service, study, and relaxation. The composite activities consist of social intercourse, group entertainment, and divine worship. There is great educational value in mingling with diverse groups of personalities, orders very different from one's own fellows.

6. *The circles of the courtesy colonies.* The seven circles of the courtesy colonies are graced by three enormous structures: the vast astronomic observatory of Jerusem, the gigantic art gallery of Satania, and the immense assembly hall of the reversion directors, the theater of morontia activities devoted to rest and recreation.

The celestial artisans direct the spornagia and provide the host of creative decorations and monumental memorials which abound in every place of public assembly. The studios of these artisans are among the largest and most beautiful of all the matchless structures of this wonderful world. The other courtesy colonies maintain extensive and beautiful headquarters. Many of these buildings are constructed wholly of crystal gems. All the architectural worlds abound in crystals and the so-called precious metals.

7. *The circles of the finaliters* have a unique structure at the center. And this same vacant temple is found on every system headquarters world throughout Nebadon. This edifice on Jerusem is sealed with the insignia of Michael, and it bears this inscription: "Undedicated to the seventh stage of spirit—to the eternal assignment." Gabriel placed the seal on this temple of mystery, and none but Michael can or may break the seal of sovereignty affixed by the Bright and Morning Star. Some day you shall look upon this silent temple, even though you may not penetrate its mystery.

Other Jerusem circles: In addition to these residential circles there are on Jerusem numerous additional designated abodes.

6. THE EXECUTIVE-ADMINISTRATIVE SQUARES

The executive-administrative divisions of the system are located in the immense departmental squares, one thousand in number. Each administrative unit is divided into one hundred subdivisions of ten subgroups each. These one thousand squares are clustered in ten grand divisions, thus constituting the following ten administrative departments:

1. Physical maintenance and material improvement, the domains of physical power and energy.
2. Arbitration, ethics, and administrative adjudication.
3. Planetary and local affairs.
4. Constellation and universe affairs.
5. Education and other Melchizedek activities.
6. Planetary and system physical progress, the scientific domains of Satania activities.
7. Morontia affairs.
8. Pure spirit activities and ethics.
9. Ascendant ministry.
10. Grand universe philosophy.

These structures are transparent; hence all system activities can be viewed even by student visitors.

7. THE RECTANGLES—THE SPORNAGIA

The one thousand *rectangles* of Jerusem are occupied by the lower native life of the headquarters planet, and at their center is situated the vast circular headquarters of the spornagia.

On Jerusem you will be amazed by the agricultural achievements of the wonderful spornagia. There the land is cultivated largely for aesthetic and ornamental effects. The spornagia are the landscape gardeners of the headquarters worlds, and they are both original and artistic in their treatment of the open spaces of Jerusem. They utilize both animals and numerous mechanical contrivances in the culture of the soil. They are intelligently expert in the employment of the power agencies of their realms as well as in the utilization of numerous orders of their lesser brethren of the lower animal creations, many of which are provided them on these special worlds. This order of animal life is now largely directed by the ascending midway creatures from the evolutionary spheres.

Spornagia are not Adjuster indwelt. They do not possess survival souls, but they do enjoy long lives, sometimes to the extent of forty to fifty thousand standard years. Their number is legion, and they afford physical ministry to all orders of universe personalities requiring material service.

Although spornagia neither possess nor evolve survival souls, though they do not have personality, nevertheless, they do evolve an individuality which can experience reincarnation. When, with the passing of time, the physical bodies of these unique creatures deteriorate from usage and age, their creators, in collaboration with the Life Carriers, fabricate new bodies in which the old spornagia re-establish their residences.

Spornagia are the only creatures in all the universe of Nebadon who experience this or any other sort of reincarnation. They are only reactive to the first five of the adjutant mind-spirits; they are not responsive to the spirits of worship and wisdom. But the five-adjutant mind equivalates to a totality or sixth reality level, and it is this factor which persists as an experiential identity.

I am quite without comparisons in undertaking to describe these useful and unusual creatures as there are no animals on the evolutionary worlds comparable to them. They are not evolutionary beings, having been projected by the Life Carriers in their present form and status. They are bisexual and procreate as they are required to meet the needs of a growing population.

Perhaps I can best suggest to Urantia minds something of the nature of these beautiful and serviceable creatures by saying that they embrace the combined traits of a faithful horse and an affectionate dog and manifest an intelligence exceeding that of the highest type of chimpanzee. And they are very beautiful, as judged by the physical standards of Urantia. They are most appreciative of the attentions shown them by the material and semimaterial sojourners on these architectural worlds. They have a vision which permits them to recognize—in addition to material beings—the morontia creations, the lower angelic orders, midway creatures, and some of the lower orders of spirit personalities. They do not comprehend worship of the Infinite, nor do they grasp the import of the Eternal, but they do, through affection for their masters, join in the outward spiritual devotions of their realms.

There are those who believe that, in a future universe age, these faithful spornagia will escape from their animal level of existence and attain a worthy evolutional destiny of progressive intellectual growth and even spiritual achievement.

8. THE JERUSEM TRIANGLES

The purely local and routine affairs of Jerusem are directed from the one hundred *triangles.* These units are clustered around the ten marvelous structures domiciling the local administration of Jerusem. The triangles are surrounded by the panoramic depiction of the system headquarters history. At present there is an erasure of over two standard miles in this circular story. This sector will be restored upon the readmission of Satania into the constellation family. Every provision for this event has been made by the decrees of

Michael, but the tribunal of the Ancients of Days has not yet finished the adjudication of the affairs of the Lucifer rebellion. Satania may not come back into the full fellowship of Norlatiadek so long as it harbors archrebels, high created beings who have fallen from light into darkness.

When Satania can return to the constellation fold, then will come up for consideration the readmission of the isolated worlds into the system family of inhabited planets, accompanied by their restoration to the spiritual communion of the realms. But even if Urantia were restored to the system circuits, you would still be embarrassed by the fact that your whole system rests under a Norlatiadek quarantine partially segregating it from all other systems.

But ere long, the adjudication of Lucifer and his associates will restore the Satania system to the Norlatiadek constellation, and subsequently, Urantia and the other isolated spheres will be restored to the Satania circuits, and again will such worlds enjoy the privileges of interplanetary communication and intersystem communion.

There will come an end for rebels and rebellion. The Supreme Rulers are merciful and patient, but the law of deliberately nourished evil is universally and unerringly executed. "The wages of sin is death"—eternal obliteration.

[Presented by an Archangel of Nebadon.]

PAPER 47

THE SEVEN MANSION WORLDS

THE Creator Son, when on Urantia, spoke of the "many mansions in the Father's universe." In a certain sense, all fifty-six of the encircling worlds of Jerusem are devoted to the transitional culture of ascending mortals, but the seven satellites of world number one are more specifically known as the mansion worlds.

Transition world number one itself is quite exclusively devoted to ascendant activities, being the headquarters of the finaliter corps assigned to Satania. This world now serves as the headquarters for more than one hundred thousand companies of finaliters, and there are one thousand glorified beings in each of these groups.

When a system is settled in light and life, and as the mansion worlds one by one cease to serve as mortal-training stations, they are taken over by the increasing finaliter population which accumulates in these older and more highly perfected systems.

The seven mansion worlds are in charge of the morontia supervisors and the Melchizedeks. There is an acting governor on each world who is directly responsible to the Jerusem rulers. The Uversa conciliators maintain headquarters on each of the mansion worlds, while adjoining is the local rendezvous of the Technical Advisers. The reversion directors and celestial artisans maintain group headquarters on each of these worlds. The spironga function from mansion world number two onward, while all seven, in common with the other transitional-culture planets and the headquarters world, are abundantly provided with spornagia of standard creation.

1. THE FINALITERS' WORLD

Although only finaliters and certain groups of salvaged children and their caretakers are resident on transitional world number one, provision is made for the entertainment of all classes of spirit beings, transition mortals, and student visitors. The spornagia, who function on all of these worlds, are hospitable hosts to all beings whom they can recognize. They have a vague feeling concerning the finaliters but cannot visualize them. They must regard them much as you do the angels in your present physical state.

Though the finaliter world is a sphere of exquisite physical beauty and extraordinary morontia embellishment, the great spirit abode located at the center of activities, the temple of the finaliters, is not visible to the unaided material or early morontia vision. But the energy transformers are able to visualize many of these realities to ascending mortals, and from time to time they do thus function, as on the occasions of the class assemblies of the mansion world students on this cultural sphere.

All through the mansion world experience you are in a way spiritually aware of the presence of your glorified brethren of Paradise attainment, but it is very refreshing, now and then, actually to perceive them as they function in their headquarters abodes. You will not spontaneously visualize finaliters until you acquire true spirit vision.

On the first mansion world all survivors must pass the requirements of the parental commission from their native planets. The present Urantia commission consists of twelve parental couples, recently arrived, who have had mortal experience in rearing three or more children to the pubescent age. Service on this commission is rotational and is for only ten years as a rule. All who fail to satisfy these commissioners as to their parental experience must further qualify by service in the homes of the Material Sons on Jerusem or in part in the probationary nursery on the finaliters' world.

But irrespective of parental experience, mansion world parents who have growing children in the probation nursery are given every opportunity to collaborate with the morontia custodians of such children regarding their instruction and training. These parents are permitted to journey there for visits as often as four times a year. And it is one of the most touchingly beautiful scenes of all the ascending career to observe the mansion world parents embrace their material offspring on the occasions of their periodic pilgrimages to the finaliter world. While one or both parents may leave a mansion world ahead of the child, they are quite often contemporary for a season.

No ascending mortal can escape the experience of rearing children—their own or others—either on the material worlds or subsequently on the finaliter world or on Jerusem. Fathers must pass through this essential experience just as certainly as mothers. It is an unfortunate and mistaken notion of modern peoples on Urantia that child culture is largely the task of mothers. Children need fathers as well as mothers, and fathers need this parental experience as much as do mothers.

2. THE PROBATIONARY NURSERY

The infant-receiving schools of Satania are situated on the finaliter world, the first of the Jerusem transition-culture spheres. These infant-receiving schools are enterprises devoted to the nurture and training of the children of time, including those who have died on the evolutionary worlds of space before the acquirement of individual status on the universe records. In the event of the survival of either or both of such a child's parents, the guardian of destiny deputizes her associated cherubim as the custodian of the child's potential identity, charging the cherubim with the responsibility of delivering this undeveloped soul into the hands of the Mansion World Teachers in the probationary nurseries of the morontia worlds.

It is these same deserted cherubim who, as Mansion World Teachers, under the supervision of the Melchizedeks, maintain such extensive educational facilities for the training of the probationary wards of the finaliters. These wards of the finaliters, these infants of ascending mortals, are always personalized as of their exact physical status at the time of death except for reproductive potential. This awakening occurs at the exact time of the parental arrival on the first mansion world. And then are these children given every opportunity, as they are, to choose the heavenly way just as they would have made such a choice on the worlds where death so untimely terminated their careers.

On the nursery world, probationary creatures are grouped according to whether or not they have Adjusters, for the Adjusters come to indwell these material children just as on the worlds of time. Children of pre-Adjuster ages are cared for in families of five, ranging in ages from one year and under up to approximately five years, or that age when the Adjuster arrives.

All children on the evolving worlds who have Thought Adjusters, but who before death had not made a choice concerning the Paradise career, are also repersonalized on the finaliter world of the system, where they likewise grow up in the families of the Material Sons and their associates as do those little ones who arrived without Adjusters, but who will subsequently receive the Mystery Monitors after attaining the requisite age of moral choice.

The Adjuster-indwelt children and youths on the finaliter world are also reared in families of five, ranging in ages from six to fourteen; approximately, these families consist of children whose ages are six, eight, ten, twelve, and fourteen. Any time after sixteen, if final choice has been made, they translate to the first mansion world and begin their Paradise ascent. Some make a choice before this age and go on to the ascension spheres, but very few children under sixteen years of age, as reckoned by Urantia standards, will be found on the mansion worlds.

The guardian seraphim attend these youths in the probationary nursery on the finaliter world just as they spiritually minister to mortals on the evolutionary planets, while the faithful spornagia minister to their physical necessities. And so do these children grow up on the transition world until such time as they make their final choice.

When material life has run its course, if no choice has been made for the ascendant life, or if these children of time definitely decide against the Havona adventure, death automatically terminates their probationary careers. There is no adjudication of such cases; there is no resurrection from such a second death. They simply become as though they had not been.

But if they choose the Paradise path of perfection, they are immediately made ready for translation to the first mansion world, where many of them arrive in time to join their parents in the Havona ascent. After passing through Havona and attaining the Deities, these salvaged souls of mortal origin constitute the permanent ascendant citizenship of Paradise. These children who have been deprived of the valuable and essential evolutionary experience on the worlds of mortal nativity are not mustered into the Corps of the Finality.

3. THE FIRST MANSION WORLD

On the mansion worlds the resurrected mortal survivors resume their lives just where they left off when overtaken by death. When you go from Urantia to the first mansion world, you will notice considerable change, but if you had come from a more normal and progressive sphere of time, you would hardly notice the difference except for the fact that you were in possession of a different body; the tabernacle of flesh and blood has been left behind on the world of nativity.

The very center of all activities on the first mansion world is the resurrection hall, the enormous temple of personality assembly. This gigantic structure consists of the central rendezvous of the seraphic destiny guardians, the Thought

Adjusters, and the archangels of the resurrection. The Life Carriers also function with these celestial beings in the resurrection of the dead.

The mortal-mind transcripts and the active creature-memory patterns as transformed from the material levels to the spiritual are the individual possession of the detached Thought Adjusters; these spiritized factors of mind, memory, and creature personality are forever a part of such Adjusters. The creature mind-matrix and the passive potentials of identity are present in the morontia soul intrusted to the keeping of the seraphic destiny guardians. And it is the reuniting of the morontia-soul trust of the seraphim and the spirit-mind trust of the Adjuster that reassembles creature personality and constitutes resurrection of a sleeping survivor.

If a transitory personality of mortal origin should never be thus reassembled, the spirit elements of the nonsurviving mortal creature would forever continue as an integral part of the individual experiential endowment of the onetime indwelling Adjuster.

From the Temple of New Life there extend seven radial wings, the resurrection halls of the mortal races. Each of these structures is devoted to the assembly of one of the seven races of time. There are one hundred thousand personal resurrection chambers in each of these seven wings terminating in the circular class assembly halls, which serve as the awakening chambers for as many as one million individuals. These halls are surrounded by the personality assembly chambers of the blended races of the normal post-Adamic worlds. Regardless of the technique which may be employed on the individual worlds of time in connection with special or dispensational resurrections, the real and conscious reassembly of actual and complete personality takes place in the resurrection halls of mansonia number one. Throughout all eternity you will recall the profound memory impressions of your first witnessing of these resurrection mornings.

From the resurrection halls you proceed to the Melchizedek sector, where you are assigned permanent residence. Then you enter upon ten days of personal liberty. You are free to explore the immediate vicinity of your new home and to familiarize yourself with the program which lies immediately ahead. You also have time to gratify your desire to consult the registry and call upon your loved ones and other earth friends who may have preceded you to these worlds. At the end of your ten-day period of leisure you begin the second step in the Paradise journey, for the mansion worlds are actual training spheres, not merely detention planets.

On mansion world number one (or another in case of advanced status) you will resume your intellectual training and spiritual development at the exact level whereon they were interrupted by death. Between the time of planetary death or translation and resurrection on the mansion world, mortal man gains absolutely nothing aside from experiencing the fact of survival. You begin over there right where you leave off down here.

Almost the entire experience of mansion world number one pertains to deficiency ministry. Survivors arriving on this first of the detention spheres present so many and such varied defects of creature character and deficiencies of mortal experience that the major activities of the realm are occupied with the correction and cure of these manifold legacies of the life in the flesh on the material evolutionary worlds of time and space.

The sojourn on mansion world number one is designed to develop mortal survivors at least up to the status of the post-Adamic dispensation on the normal evolutionary worlds. Spiritually, of course, the mansion world students are far in advance of such a state of mere human development.

If you are not to be detained on mansion world number one, at the end of ten days you will enter the translation sleep and proceed to world number two, and every ten days thereafter you will thus advance until you arrive on the world of your assignment.

The center of the seven major circles of the first mansion world administration is occupied by the temple of the Morontia Companions, the personal guides assigned to ascending mortals. These companions are the offspring of the local universe Mother Spirit, and there are several million of them on the morontia worlds of Satania. Aside from those assigned as group companions, you will have much to do with the interpreters and translators, the building custodians, and the excursion supervisors. And all of these companions are most cooperative with those who have to do with developing your personality factors of mind and spirit within the morontia body.

As you start out on the first mansion world, one Morontia Companion is assigned to each company of one thousand ascending mortals, but you will encounter larger numbers as you progress through the seven mansion spheres. These beautiful and versatile beings are companionable associates and charming guides. They are free to accompany individuals or selected groups to any of the transition-culture spheres, including their satellite worlds. They are the excursion guides and leisure associates of all ascending mortals. They often accompany survivor groups on periodic visits to Jerusem, and on any day you are there, you can go to the registry sector of the system capital and meet ascending mortals from all seven of the mansion worlds since they freely journey back and forth between their residential abodes and the system headquarters.

4. THE SECOND MANSION WORLD

It is on this sphere that you are more fully inducted into the mansonia life. The groupings of the morontia life begin to take form; working groups and social organizations start to function, communities take on formal proportions, and the advancing mortals inaugurate new social orders and governmental arrangements.

Spirit-fused survivors occupy the mansion worlds in common with the Adjuster-fused ascending mortals. While the various orders of celestial life differ, they are all friendly and fraternal. In all the worlds of ascension you will find nothing comparable to human intolerance and the discriminations of inconsiderate caste systems.

As you ascend the mansion worlds one by one, they become more crowded with the morontia activities of advancing survivors. As you go forward, you will recognize more and more of the Jerusem features added to the mansion worlds. The sea of glass makes its appearance on the second mansonia.

A newly developed and suitably adjusted morontia body is acquired at the time of each advance from one mansion world to another. You go to sleep with the seraphic transport and awake with the new but undeveloped body in the resurrection halls, much as when you first arrived on mansion world number one except that the Thought Adjuster does not leave you during these transit sleeps between the mansion worlds. Your personality remains intact after you once pass from the evolutionary worlds to the initial mansion world.

Your Adjuster memory remains fully intact as you ascend the morontia life. Those mental associations that were purely animalistic and wholly material naturally perished with the physical brain, but everything in your mental life which was worth while, and which had survival value, was counterparted by the Adjuster and is retained as a part of personal memory all the way through the ascendant career. You will be conscious of all your worth-while experiences as you advance from one mansion world to another and from one section of the universe to another—even to Paradise.

Though you have morontia bodies, you continue, through all seven of these worlds, to eat, drink, and rest. You partake of the morontia order of food, a kingdom of living energy unknown on the material worlds. Both food and water are fully utilized in the morontia body; there is no residual waste. Pause to consider: Mansonia number one is a very material sphere, presenting the early beginnings of the morontia regime. You are still a near human and not far removed from the limited viewpoints of mortal life, but each world discloses definite progress. From sphere to sphere you grow less material, more intellectual, and slightly more spiritual. The spiritual progress is greatest on the last three of these seven progressive worlds.

Biological deficiencies were largely made up on the first mansion world. There defects in planetary experiences pertaining to sex life, family association, and parental function were either corrected or were projected for future rectification among the Material Son families on Jerusem.

Mansonia number two more specifically provides for the removal of all phases of intellectual conflict and for the cure of all varieties of mental disharmony. The effort to master the significance of morontia mota, begun on the first mansion world, is here more earnestly continued. The development on mansonia number two compares with the intellectual status of the post-Magisterial Son culture of the ideal evolutionary worlds.

5. THE THIRD MANSION WORLD

Mansonia the third is the headquarters of the Mansion World Teachers. Though they function on all seven of the mansion spheres, they maintain their group headquarters at the center of the school circles of world number three. There are millions of these instructors on the mansion and higher morontia worlds. These advanced and glorified cherubim serve as morontia teachers all the way up from the mansion worlds to the last sphere of local universe ascendant training. They will be among the last to bid you an affectionate adieu when the farewell time draws near, the time when you bid good-bye—at least for a few ages—to the universe of your origin, when you enseraphim for transit to the receiving worlds of the minor sector of the superuniverse.

When sojourning on the first mansion world, you have permission to visit the first of the transition worlds, the headquarters of the finaliters and the system probationary nursery for the nurture of undeveloped evolutionary children. When you arrive on mansonia number two, you receive permission periodically to visit transition world number two, where are located the morontia supervisor headquarters for all Satania and the training schools for the various morontia orders. When you reach mansion world number three, you are immediately granted a permit to visit the third transition sphere, the headquarters of the angelic orders and the home of their various system training schools. Visits to Jerusem from this world are increasingly profitable and are of ever-heightening interest to the advancing mortals.

Mansonia the third is a world of great personal and social achievement for all who have not made the equivalent of these circles of culture prior to release from the flesh on the mortal nativity worlds. On this sphere more positive educational work is begun. The training of the first two mansion worlds is mostly of a deficiency nature—negative—in that it has to do with supplementing the experience of the life in the flesh. On this third mansion world the survivors really begin their progressive morontia culture. The chief purpose of this training is to enhance the understanding of the correlation of morontia mota and mortal logic, the co-ordination of morontia mota and human philosophy. Surviving mortals now gain practical insight into true metaphysics. This is the real introduction to the intelligent comprehension of cosmic meanings and universe interrelationships. The culture of the third mansion world partakes of the nature of the postbestowal Son age of a normal inhabited planet.

6. THE FOURTH MANSION WORLD

When you arrive on the fourth mansion world, you have well entered upon the morontia career; you have progressed a long way from the initial material existence. Now are you given permission to make visits to transition world number four, there to become familiar with the headquarters and training schools of the superangels, including the Brilliant Evening Stars. Through the good offices of these superangels of the fourth transition world the morontia visitors are enabled to draw very close to the various orders of the Sons of God during the periodic visits to Jerusem, for new sectors of the system capital are gradually opening up to the advancing mortals as they make these repeated visits to the headquarters world. New grandeurs are progressively unfolding to the expanding minds of these ascenders.

On the fourth mansonia the individual ascender more fittingly finds his place in the group working and class functions of the morontia life. Ascenders here develop increased appreciation of the broadcasts and other phases of local universe culture and progress.

It is during the period of training on world number four that the ascending mortals are really first introduced to the demands and delights of the true social life of morontia creatures. And it is indeed a new experience for evolutionary creatures to participate in social activities which are predicated neither on personal aggrandizement nor on self-seeking conquest. A new social order is being introduced, one based on the understanding sympathy of mutual appreciation, the unselfish love of mutual service, and the overmastering motivation of the realization of a common and supreme destiny—the Paradise goal of worshipful and divine perfection. Ascenders are all becoming self-conscious of God-knowing, God-revealing, God-seeking, and God-finding.

The intellectual and social culture of this fourth mansion world is comparable to the mental and social life of the post-Teacher Son age on the planets of normal evolution. The spiritual status is much in advance of such a mortal dispensation.

7. THE FIFTH MANSION WORLD

Transport to the fifth mansion world represents a tremendous forward step in the life of a morontia progressor. The experience on this world is a real foretaste of Jerusem life. Here you begin to realize the high destiny of the loyal evolutionary worlds since they may normally progress to this stage during their natural planetary development. The culture of this mansion world corresponds in general to that of the early era of light and life on the planets of normal evolutionary progress. And from this you can understand why it is so arranged that the highly cultured and progressive types of beings who sometimes inhabit these advanced evolutionary worlds are exempt from passing through one or more, or even all, of the mansion spheres.

Having mastered the local universe language before leaving the fourth mansion world, you now devote more time to the perfection of the tongue of Uversa to the end that you may be proficient in both languages before arriving on Jerusem with residential status. All ascending mortals are bilingual from the system headquarters up to Havona. And then it is only necessary to enlarge the superuniverse vocabulary, still additional enlargement being required for residence on Paradise.

Upon arrival on mansonia number five the pilgrim is given permission to visit the transition world of corresponding number, the Sons' headquarters. Here the ascendant mortal becomes personally familiar with the various groups of divine sonship. He has heard of these superb beings and has already met them on Jerusem, but now he comes really to know them.

On the fifth mansonia you begin to learn of the constellation study worlds. Here you meet the first of the instructors who begin to prepare you for the subsequent constellation sojourn. More of this preparation continues on worlds six and seven, while the finishing touches are supplied in the sector of the ascending mortals on Jerusem.

A real birth of cosmic consciousness takes place on mansonia number five. You are becoming universe minded. This is indeed a time of expanding horizons. It is beginning to dawn upon the enlarging minds of the ascending mortals that some stupendous and magnificent, some supernal and divine, destiny awaits all who complete the progressive Paradise ascension, which has been so laboriously but so joyfully and auspiciously begun. At about this point the average mortal ascender begins to manifest bona fide experiential enthusiasm for the Havona ascent. Study is becoming voluntary, unselfish service natural, and worship spontaneous. A real morontia character is budding; a real morontia creature is evolving.

8. THE SIXTH MANSION WORLD

Sojourners on this sphere are permitted to visit transition world number six, where they learn more about the high spirits of the superuniverse, although they are not able to visualize many of these celestial beings. Here they also receive their first lessons in the prospective spirit career which so immediately follows graduation from the morontia training of the local universe.

The assistant System Sovereign makes frequent visits to this world, and the initial instruction is here begun in the technique of universe administration. The first lessons embracing the affairs of a whole universe are now imparted.

This is a brilliant age for ascending mortals and usually witnesses the perfect fusion of the human mind and the divine Adjuster. In potential, this fusion may have occurred previously, but the actual working identity many times is not achieved until the time of the sojourn on the fifth mansion world or even the sixth.

The union of the evolving immortal soul with the eternal and divine Adjuster is signalized by the seraphic summoning of the supervising superangel for resurrected survivors and of the archangel of record for those going to judgment on the third day; and then, in the presence of such a survivor's morontia associates, these messengers of confirmation speak: "This is a beloved son in whom I am well pleased." This simple ceremony marks the entrance of an ascending mortal upon the eternal career of Paradise service.

Immediately upon the confirmation of Adjuster fusion the new morontia being is introduced to his fellows for the first time by his new name and is granted the forty days of spiritual retirement from all routine activities wherein to commune with himself and to choose some one of the optional routes to Havona and to select from the differential techniques of Paradise attainment.

But still are these brilliant beings more or less material; they are far from being true spirits; they are more like supermortals, spiritually speaking, still a little lower than the angels. But they are truly becoming marvelous creatures.

During the sojourn on world number six the mansion world students achieve a status which is comparable with the exalted development characterizing those evolutionary worlds which have normally progressed beyond the initial stage of light and life. The organization of society on this mansonia is of a high order. The shadow of the mortal nature grows less and less as these worlds are ascended one by one. You are becoming more and more adorable as you leave behind the coarse vestiges of planetary animal origin. "Coming up through great tribulation" serves to make glorified mortals very kind and understanding, very sympathetic and tolerant.

9. THE SEVENTH MANSION WORLD

The experience on this sphere is the crowning achievement of the immediate postmortal career. During your sojourn here you will receive the instruction of many teachers, all of whom will co-operate in the task of preparing you for residence on Jerusem. Any discernible differences between those mortals hailing from the isolated and retarded worlds and those survivors from the more advanced and enlightened spheres are virtually obliterated during the sojourn on the seventh mansion world. Here you will be purged of all the remnants of unfortunate heredity, unwholesome environment, and unspiritual planetary tendencies. The last remnants of the "mark of the beast" are here eradicated.

While sojourning on mansonia number seven, permission is granted to visit transition world number seven, the world of the Universal Father. Here you begin a new and more spiritual worship of the unseen Father, a habit you will increasingly pursue all the way up through your long ascending career. You find the Father's temple on this world of transitional culture, but you do not see the Father.

Now begins the formation of classes for graduation to Jerusem. You have gone from world to world as individuals, but now you prepare to depart for

Jerusem in groups, although, within certain limits, an ascender may elect to tarry on the seventh mansion world for the purpose of enabling a tardy member of his earthly or mansonia working group to catch up with him.

The personnel of the seventh mansonia assemble on the sea of glass to witness your departure for Jerusem with residential status. Hundreds or thousands of times you may have visited Jerusem, but always as a guest; never before have you proceeded toward the system capital in the company of a group of your fellows who were bidding an eternal farewell to the whole mansonia career as ascending mortals. You will soon be welcomed on the receiving field of the headquarters world as Jerusem citizens.

You will greatly enjoy your progress through the seven dematerializing worlds; they are really demortalizing spheres. You are mostly human on the first mansion world, just a mortal being minus a material body, a human mind housed in a morontia form—a material body of the morontia world but not a mortal house of flesh and blood. You really pass from the mortal state to the immortal status at the time of Adjuster fusion, and by the time you have finished the Jerusem career, you will be full-fledged morontians.

10. JERUSEM CITIZENSHIP

The reception of a new class of mansion world graduates is the signal for all Jerusem to assemble as a committee of welcome. Even the spornagia enjoy the arrival of these triumphant ascenders of evolutionary origin, those who have run the planetary race and finished the mansion world progression. Only the physical controllers and Morontia Power Supervisors are absent from these occasions of rejoicing.

John the Revelator saw a vision of the arrival of a class of advancing mortals from the seventh mansion world to their first heaven, the glories of Jerusem. He recorded: "And I saw as it were a sea of glass mingled with fire; and those who had gained the victory over the beast that was originally in them and over the image that persisted through the mansion worlds and finally over the last mark and trace, standing on the sea of glass, having the harps of God, and singing the song of deliverance from mortal fear and death." (Perfected space communication is to be had on all these worlds; and your anywhere reception of such communications is made possible by carrying the "harp of God," a morontia contrivance compensating for the inability to directly adjust the immature morontia sensory mechanism to the reception of space communications.)

Paul also had a view of the ascendant-citizen corps of perfecting mortals on Jerusem, for he wrote: "But you have come to Mount Zion and to the city of the living God, the heavenly Jerusalem, and to an innumerable company of angels, to the grand assembly of Michael, and to the spirits of just men being made perfect."

After mortals have attained residence on the system headquarters, no more literal resurrections will be experienced. The morontia form granted you on departure from the mansion world career is such as will see you through to the end of the local universe experience. Changes will be made from time to time, but you will retain this same form until you bid it farewell when you emerge as first-stage spirits preparatory for transit to the superuniverse worlds of ascending culture and spirit training.

Seven times do those mortals who pass through the entire mansonia career experience the adjustment sleep and the resurrection awakening. But the last resurrection hall, the final awakening chamber, was left behind on the seventh mansion world. No more will a form-change necessitate the lapse of consciousness or a break in the continuity of personal memory.

The mortal personality initiated on the evolutionary worlds and tabernacled in the flesh—indwelt by the Mystery Monitors and invested by the Spirit of Truth—is not fully mobilized, realized, and unified until that day when such a Jerusem citizen is given clearance for Edentia and proclaimed a true member of the morontia corps of Nebadon—an immortal survivor of Adjuster association, a Paradise ascender, a personality of morontia status, and a true child of the Most Highs.

Mortal death is a technique of escape from the material life in the flesh; and the mansonia experience of progressive life through seven worlds of corrective training and cultural education represents the introduction of mortal survivors to the morontia career, the transition life which intervenes between the evolutionary material existence and the higher spirit attainment of the ascenders of time who are destined to achieve the portals of eternity.

[Sponsored by a Brilliant Evening Star.]

PAPER 48

THE MORONTIA LIFE

THE Gods cannot—at least they do not—transform a creature of gross animal nature into a perfected spirit by some mysterious act of creative magic. When the Creators desire to produce perfect beings, they do so by direct and original creation, but they never undertake to convert animal-origin and material creatures into beings of perfection in a single step.

The morontia life, extending as it does over the various stages of the local universe career, is the only possible approach whereby material mortals could attain the threshold of the spirit world. What magic could death, the natural dissolution of the material body, hold that such a simple step should instantly transform the mortal and material mind into an immortal and perfected spirit? Such beliefs are but ignorant superstitions and pleasing fables.

Always this morontia transition intervenes between the mortal estate and the subsequent spirit status of surviving human beings. This intermediate state of universe progress differs markedly in the various local creations, but in intent and purpose they are all quite similar. The arrangement of the mansion and higher morontia worlds in Nebadon is fairly typical of the morontia transition regimes in this part of Orvonton.

1. MORONTIA MATERIALS

The morontia realms are the local universe liaison spheres between the material and spiritual levels of creature existence. This morontia life has been known on Urantia since the early days of the Planetary Prince. From time to time this transition state has been taught to mortals, and the concept, in distorted form, has found a place in present-day religions.

The morontia spheres are the transition phases of mortal ascension through the progression worlds of the local universe. Only the seven worlds surrounding the finaliters' sphere of the local systems are called mansion worlds, but all fifty-six of the system transition abodes, in common with the higher spheres around the constellations and the universe headquarters, are called morontia worlds. These creations partake of the physical beauty and the morontia grandeur of the local universe headquarters spheres.

All of these worlds are architectural spheres, and they have just double the number of elements of the evolved planets. Such made-to-order worlds not only abound in the heavy metals and crystals, having one hundred physical elements, but likewise have exactly one hundred forms of a unique energy organization called *morontia material.* The Master Physical Controllers and the Morontia Power Supervisors are able so to modify the revolutions of the primary units of matter and at the same time so to transform these associations of energy as to create this new substance.

The early morontia life in the local systems is very much like that of your present material world, becoming less physical and more truly morontial on the constellation study worlds. And as you advance to the Salvington spheres, you increasingly attain spiritual levels.

The Morontia Power Supervisors are able to effect a union of material and of spiritual energies, thereby organizing a morontia form of materialization which is receptive to the superimposition of a controlling spirit. When you traverse the morontia life of Nebadon, these same patient and skillful Morontia Power Supervisors will successively provide you with 570 morontia bodies, each one a phase of your progressive transformation. From the time of leaving the material worlds until you are constituted a first-stage spirit on Salvington, you will undergo just 570 separate and ascending morontia changes. Eight of these occur in the system, seventy-one in the constellation, and 491 during the sojourn on the spheres of Salvington.

In the days of the mortal flesh the divine spirit indwells you, almost as a thing apart—in reality an invasion of man by the bestowed spirit of the Universal Father. But in the morontia life the spirit will become a real part of your personality, and as you successively pass through the 570 progressive transformations, you ascend from the material to the spiritual estate of creature life.

Paul learned of the existence of the morontia worlds and of the reality of morontia materials, for he wrote, "They have in heaven a better and more enduring substance." And these morontia materials are real, literal, even as in "the city which has foundations, whose builder and maker is God." And each of these marvelous spheres is "a better country, that is, a heavenly one."

2. MORONTIA POWER SUPERVISORS

These unique beings are exclusively concerned with the supervision of those activities which represent a working combination of spiritual and physical or semimaterial energies. They are exclusively devoted to the ministry of morontia progression. Not that they so much minister to mortals during the transition experience, but they rather make possible the transition environment for the progressing morontia creatures. They are the channels of morontia power which sustain and energize the morontia phases of the transition worlds.

Morontia Power Supervisors are the offspring of a local universe Mother Spirit. They are fairly standard in design though differing slightly in nature in the various local creations. They are created for their specific function and require no training before entering upon their responsibilities.

The creation of the first Morontia Power Supervisors is simultaneous with the arrival of the first mortal survivor on the shores of some one of the first mansion worlds in a local universe. They are created in groups of one thousand, classified as follows:

1.	Circuit Regulators	400
2.	System Co-ordinators	200
3.	Planetary Custodians	100

4. Combined Controllers 100
5. Liaison Stabilizers 100
6. Selective Assorters 50
7. Associate Registrars 50

The power supervisors always serve in their native universe. They are directed exclusively by the joint spirit activity of the Universe Son and the Universe Spirit but are otherwise a wholly self-governing group. They maintain headquarters on each of the first mansion worlds of the local systems, where they work in close association with both the physical controllers and the seraphim but function in a world of their own as regards energy manifestation and spirit application.

They also sometimes work in connection with supermaterial phenomena on the evolutionary worlds as ministers of temporary assignment. But they rarely serve on the inhabited planets; neither do they work on the higher training worlds of the superuniverse, being chiefly devoted to the transition regime of morontia progression in a local universe.

1. *Circuit Regulators.* These are the unique beings who co-ordinate physical and spiritual energy and regulate its flow into the segregated channels of the morontia spheres, and these circuits are exclusively planetary, limited to a single world. The morontia circuits are distinct from, and supplementary to, both physical and spiritual circuits on the transition worlds, and it requires millions of these regulators to energize even a system of mansion worlds like that of Satania.

Circuit regulators initiate those changes in material energies which render them subject to the control and regulation of their associates. These beings are morontia power generators as well as circuit regulators. Much as a dynamo apparently generates electricity out of the atmosphere, so do these living morontia dynamos seem to transform the everywhere energies of space into those materials which the morontia supervisors weave into the bodies and life activities of the ascending mortals.

2. *System Co-ordinators.* Since each morontia world has a separate order of morontia energy, it is exceedingly difficult for humans to visualize these spheres. But on each successive transition sphere, mortals will find the plant life and everything else pertaining to the morontia existence progressively modified to correspond with the advancing spiritization of the ascending survivor. And since the energy system of each world is thus individualized, these co-ordinators operate to harmonize and blend such differing power systems into a working unit for the associated spheres of any particular group.

Ascending mortals gradually progress from the physical to the spiritual as they advance from one morontia world to another; hence the necessity for providing an ascending scale of morontia spheres and an ascending scale of morontia forms.

When mansion world ascenders pass from one sphere to another, they are delivered by the transport seraphim to the receivers of the system co-ordinators on the advanced world. Here in those unique temples at the center of the seventy radiating wings wherein are the chambers of transition similar to the resurrection halls on the initial world of reception for earth-origin mortals, the necessary changes in creature form are skillfully effected by the system co-ordinators.

These early morontia-form changes require about seven days of standard time for their accomplishment.

3. *Planetary Custodians.* Each morontia world, from the mansion spheres up to the universe headquarters, is in the custody—as regards morontia affairs—of seventy guardians. They constitute the local planetary council of supreme morontia authority. This council grants material for morontia forms to all ascending creatures who land on the spheres and authorizes those changes in creature form which make it possible for an ascender to proceed to the succeeding sphere. After the mansion worlds have been traversed, you will translate from one phase of morontia life to another without having to surrender consciousness. Unconsciousness attends only the earlier metamorphoses and the later transitions from one universe to another and from Havona to Paradise.

4. *Combined Controllers.* One of these highly mechanical beings is always stationed at the center of each administrative unit of a morontia world. A combined controller is sensitive to, and functional with, physical, spiritual, and morontial energies; and with this being there are always associated two system co-ordinators, four circuit regulators, one planetary custodian, one liaison stabilizer, and either an associate registrar or a selective assorter.

5. *Liaison Stabilizers.* These are the regulators of the morontia energy in association with the physical and spirit forces of the realm. They make possible the conversion of morontia energy into morontia material. The whole morontia organization of existence is dependent on the stabilizers. They slow down the energy revolutions to that point where physicalization can occur. But I have no terms with which I can compare or illustrate the ministry of such beings. It is quite beyond human imagination.

6. *Selective Assorters.* As you progress from one class or phase of a morontia world to another, you must be re-keyed or advance-tuned, and it is the task of the selective assorters to keep you in progressive synchrony with the morontia life.

While the basic morontia forms of life and matter are identical from the first mansion world to the last universe transition sphere, there is a functional progression which gradually extends from the material to the spiritual. Your adaptation to this basically uniform but successively advancing and spiritizing creation is effected by this selective re-keying. Such an adjustment in the mechanism of personality is tantamount to a new creation, notwithstanding that you retain the same morontia form.

You may repeatedly subject yourself to the test of these examiners, and as soon as you register adequate spiritual achievement, they will gladly certify you for advanced standing. These progressive changes result in altered reactions to the morontia environment, such as modifications in food requirements and numerous other personal practices.

The selective assorters are also of great service in the grouping of morontia personalities for purposes of study, teaching, and other projects. They naturally indicate those who will best function in temporary association.

7. *Associate Registrars.* The morontia world has its own recorders, who serve in association with the spirit recorders in the supervision and custody of

the records and other data indigenous to the morontia creations. The morontia records are available to all orders of personalities.

All morontia transition realms are accessible alike to material and spirit beings. As morontia progressors you will remain in full contact with the material world and with material personalities, while you will increasingly discern and fraternize with spirit beings; and by the time of departure from the morontia regime, you will have seen all orders of spirits with the exception of a few of the higher types, such as Solitary Messengers.

3. MORONTIA COMPANIONS

These hosts of the mansion and morontia worlds are the offspring of a local universe Mother Spirit. They are created from age to age in groups of one hundred thousand, and in Nebadon there are at present over seventy billion of these unique beings.

Morontia Companions are trained for service by the Melchizedeks on a special planet near Salvington; they do not pass through the central Melchizedek schools. In service they range from the lowest mansion worlds of the systems to the highest study spheres of Salvington, but they are seldom encountered on the inhabited worlds. They serve under the general supervision of the Sons of God and under the immediate direction of the Melchizedeks.

The Morontia Companions maintain ten thousand headquarters in a local universe—on each of the first mansion worlds of the local systems. They are almost wholly a self-governing order and are, in general, an intelligent and loyal group of beings; but every now and then, in connection with certain unfortunate celestial upheavals, they have been known to go astray. Thousands of these useful creatures were lost during the times of the Lucifer rebellion in Satania. Your local system now has its full quota of these beings, the loss of the Lucifer rebellion having only recently been made up.

There are two distinct types of Morontia Companions; one type is aggressive, the other retiring, but otherwise they are equal in status. They are not sex creatures, but they manifest a touchingly beautiful affection for one another. And while they are hardly companionate in the material (human) sense, they are very close of kin to the human races in the order of creature existence. The midway creatures of the worlds are your nearest of kin; then come the morontia cherubim, and after them the Morontia Companions.

These companions are touchingly affectionate and charmingly social beings. They possess distinct personalities, and when you meet them on the mansion worlds, after learning to recognize them as a class, you will soon discern their individuality. Mortals all resemble one another; at the same time each of you possesses a distinct and recognizable personality.

Something of an idea of the nature of the work of these Morontia Companions may be derived from the following classification of their activities in a local system:

1. *Pilgrim Guardians* are not assigned to specific duties in their association with the morontia progressors. These companions are responsible for the whole of the morontia career and are therefore the co-ordinators of the work of all other morontia and transition ministers.

2. *Pilgrim Receivers and Free Associators.* These are the social companions of the new arrivals on the mansion worlds. One of them will certainly be on hand to welcome you when you awaken on the initial mansion world from the first transit sleep of time, when you experience the resurrection from the death of the flesh into the morontia life. And from the time you are thus formally welcomed on awakening to that day when you leave the local universe as a first-stage spirit, these Morontia Companions are ever with you.

Companions are not assigned permanently to individuals. An ascending mortal on one of the mansion or higher worlds might have a different companion on each of several successive occasions and again might go for long periods without one. It would all depend on the requirements and also on the supply of companions available.

3. *Hosts to Celestial Visitors.* These gracious creatures are dedicated to the entertainment of the superhuman groups of student visitors and other celestials who may chance to sojourn on the transition worlds. You will have ample opportunity to visit within any realm you have experientially attained. Student visitors are allowed on all inhabited planets, even those in isolation.

4. *Co-ordinators and Liaison Directors.* These companions are dedicated to the facilitation of morontia intercourse and to the prevention of confusion. They are the instructors of social conduct and morontia progress, sponsoring classes and other group activities among the ascending mortals. They maintain extensive areas wherein they assemble their pupils and from time to time make requisition on the celestial artisans and the reversion directors for the embellishment of their programs. As you progress, you will come in intimate contact with these companions, and you will grow exceedingly fond of both groups. It is a matter of chance as to whether you will be associated with an aggressive or a retiring type of companion.

5. *Interpreters and Translators.* During the early mansonia career you will have frequent recourse to the interpreters and the translators. They know and speak all the tongues of a local universe; they are the linguists of the realms.

You will not acquire new languages automatically; you will learn a language over there much as you do down here, and these brilliant beings will be your language teachers. The first study on the mansion worlds will be the tongue of Satania and then the language of Nebadon. And while you are mastering these new tongues, the Morontia Companions will be your efficient interpreters and patient translators. You will never encounter a visitor on any of these worlds but that some one of the Morontia Companions will be able to officiate as interpreter.

6. *Excursion and Reversion Supervisors.* These companions will accompany you on the longer trips to the headquarters sphere and to the surrounding worlds of transition culture. They plan, conduct, and supervise all such individual and group tours about the system worlds of training and culture.

7. *Area and Building Custodians.* Even the material and morontia structures increase in perfection and grandeur as you advance in the mansonia career. As individuals and as groups you are permitted to make certain changes in the abodes assigned as headquarters for your sojourn on the different mansion

worlds. Many of the activities of these spheres take place in the open enclosures of the variously designated circles, squares, and triangles. The majority of the mansion world structures are roofless, being enclosures of magnificent construction and exquisite embellishment. The climatic and other physical conditions prevailing on the architectural worlds make roofs wholly unnecessary.

These custodians of the transition phases of ascendant life are supreme in the management of morontia affairs. They were created for this work, and pending the factualization of the Supreme Being, always will they remain Morontia Companions; never do they perform other duties.

As systems and universes are settled in light and life, the mansion worlds increasingly cease to function as transition spheres of morontia training. More and more the finaliters institute their new training regime, which appears to be designed to translate the cosmic consciousness from the present level of the grand universe to that of the future outer universes. The Morontia Companions are destined to function increasingly in association with the finaliters and in numerous other realms not at present revealed on Urantia.

You can forecast that these beings are probably going to contribute much to your enjoyment of the mansion worlds, whether your sojourn is to be long or short. And you will continue to enjoy them all the way up to Salvington. They are not, technically, essential to any part of your survival experience. You could reach Salvington without them, but you would greatly miss them. They are the personality luxury of your ascending career in the local universe.

4. THE REVERSION DIRECTORS

Joyful mirth and the smile-equivalent are as universal as music. There is a morontial and a spiritual equivalent of mirth and laughter. The ascendant life is about equally divided between work and play—freedom from assignment.

Celestial relaxation and superhuman humor are quite different from their human analogues, but we all actually indulge in a form of both; and they really accomplish for us, in our state, just about what ideal humor is able to do for you on Urantia. The Morontia Companions are skillful play sponsors, and they are most ably supported by the reversion directors.

You would probably best understand the work of the reversion directors if they were likened to the higher types of humorists on Urantia, though that would be an exceedingly crude and somewhat unfortunate way in which to try to convey an idea of the function of these directors of change and relaxation, these ministers of the exalted humor of the morontia and spirit realms.

In discussing spirit humor, first let me tell you what it is *not.* Spirit jest is never tinged with the accentuation of the misfortunes of the weak and erring. Neither is it ever blasphemous of the righteousness and glory of divinity. Our humor embraces three general levels of appreciation:

1. *Reminiscent jests.* Quips growing out of the memories of past episodes in one's experience of combat, struggle, and sometimes fearfulness, and ofttimes foolish and childish anxiety. To us, this phase of humor derives from the deep-seated and abiding ability to draw upon the past for memory material with which pleasantly to flavor and otherwise lighten the heavy loads of the present.

2. *Current humor.* The senselessness of much that so often causes us serious concern, the joy at discovering the unimportance of much of our serious personal anxiety. We are most appreciative of this phase of humor when we are best able to discount the anxieties of the present in favor of the certainties of the future.

3. *Prophetic joy.* It will perhaps be difficult for mortals to envisage this phase of humor, but we do get a peculiar satisfaction out of the assurance "that all things work together for good"—for spirits and morontians as well as for mortals. This aspect of celestial humor grows out of our faith in the loving overcare of our superiors and in the divine stability of our Supreme Directors.

But the reversion directors of the realms are not concerned exclusively with depicting the high humor of the various orders of intelligent beings; they are also occupied with the leadership of diversion, spiritual recreation and morontia entertainment. And in this connection they have the hearty co-operation of the celestial artisans.

The reversion directors themselves are not a created group; they are a recruited corps embracing beings ranging from the Havona natives down through the messenger hosts of space and the ministering spirits of time to the morontia progressors from the evolutionary worlds. All are volunteers, giving themselves to the work of assisting their fellows in the achievement of thought change and mind rest, for such attitudes are most helpful in recuperating depleted energies.

When partially exhausted by the efforts of attainment, and while awaiting the reception of new energy charges, there is agreeable pleasure in living over again the enactments of other days and ages. *The early experiences of the race or the order are restful to reminisce.* And that is exactly why these artists are called reversion directors—they assist in reverting the memory to a former state of development or to a less experienced status of being.

All beings enjoy this sort of reversion except those who are inherent Creators, hence automatic self-rejuvenators, and certain highly specialized types of creatures, such as the power centers and the physical controllers, who are always and eternally thoroughly businesslike in all their reactions. These periodic releases from the tension of functional duty are a regular part of life on all worlds throughout the universe of universes but not on the Isle of Paradise. Beings indigenous to the central abode are incapable of depletion and are not, therefore, subject to re-energizing. And with such beings of eternal Paradise perfection there can be no such reversion to evolutionary experiences.

Most of us have come up through lower stages of existence or through progressive levels of our orders, and it is refreshing and in a measure amusing to look back upon certain episodes of our early experience. There is a restfulness in the contemplation of that which is old to one's order, and which lingers as a memory possession of the mind. The future signifies struggle and advancement; it bespeaks work, effort, and achievement; but the past savors of things already mastered and achieved; contemplation of the past permits of relaxation and such a carefree review as to provoke spirit mirth and a morontia state of mind verging on merriment.

Even mortal humor becomes most hearty when it depicts episodes affecting those just a little beneath one's present developmental state, or when it portrays one's supposed superiors falling victim to the experiences which are commonly associated with supposed inferiors. You of Urantia have allowed much that is at once vulgar and unkind to become confused with your humor, but on the whole, you are to be congratulated on a comparatively keen sense of humor. Some of your races have a rich vein of it and are greatly helped in their earthly careers thereby. Apparently you received much in the way of humor from your Adamic inheritance, much more than was secured of either music or art.

All Satania, during times of play, those times when its inhabitants refreshingly resurrect the memories of a lower stage of existence, is edified by the pleasant humor of a corps of reversion directors from Urantia. The sense of celestial humor we have with us always, even when engaged in the most difficult of assignments. It helps to avoid an overdevelopment of the notion of one's self-importance. But we do not give rein to it freely, as you might say, "have fun," except when we are in recess from the serious assignments of our respective orders.

When we are tempted to magnify our self-importance, if we stop to contemplate the infinity of the greatness and grandeur of our Makers, our own self-glorification becomes sublimely ridiculous, even verging on the humorous. One of the functions of humor is to help all of us take ourselves less seriously. *Humor is the divine antidote for exaltation of ego.*

The need for the relaxation and diversion of humor is greatest in those orders of ascendant beings who are subjected to sustained stress in their upward struggles. The two extremes of life have little need for humorous diversions. Primitive men have no capacity therefor, and beings of Paradise perfection have no need thereof. The hosts of Havona are naturally a joyous and exhilarating assemblage of supremely happy personalities. On Paradise the quality of worship obviates the necessity for reversion activities. But among those who start their careers far below the goal of Paradise perfection, there is a large place for the ministry of the reversion directors.

The higher the mortal species, the greater the stress and the greater the capacity for humor as well as the necessity for it. In the spirit world the opposite is true: The higher we ascend, the less the need for the diversions of reversion experiences. But proceeding down the scale of spirit life from Paradise to the seraphic hosts, there is an increasing need for the mission of mirth and the ministry of merriment. Those beings who most need the refreshment of periodic reversion to the intellectual status of previous experiences are the higher types of the human species, the morontians, angels, and the Material Sons, together with all similar types of personality.

Humor should function as an automatic safety valve to prevent the building up of excessive pressures due to the monotony of sustained and serious self-contemplation in association with the intense struggle for developmental progress and noble achievement. Humor also functions to lessen the shock of the unexpected impact of fact or of truth, rigid unyielding fact and flexible ever-living truth. The mortal personality, never sure as to which will next be encountered, through humor swiftly grasps—sees the point and achieves insight—the unexpected nature of the situation be it fact or be it truth.

While the humor of Urantia is exceedingly crude and most inartistic, it does serve a valuable purpose both as a health insurance and as a liberator of emotional pressure, thus preventing injurious nervous tension and overserious self-contemplation. Humor and play—relaxation—are never reactions of progressive exertion; always are they the echoes of a backward glance, a reminiscence of the past. Even on Urantia and as you now are, you always find it rejuvenating when for a short time you can suspend the exertions of the newer and higher intellectual efforts and revert to the more simple engagements of your ancestors.

The principles of Urantian play life are philosophically sound and continue to apply on up through your ascending life, through the circuits of Havona to the eternal shores of Paradise. As ascendant beings you are in possession of personal memories of all former and lower existences, and without such identity memories of the past there would be no basis for the humor of the present, either mortal laughter or morontia mirth. It is this recalling of past experiences that provides the basis for present diversion and amusement. And so you will enjoy the celestial equivalents of your earthly humor all the way up through your long morontia, and then increasingly spiritual, careers. And that part of God (the Adjuster) which becomes an eternal part of the personality of an ascendant mortal contributes the overtones of divinity to the joyous expressions, even spiritual laughter, of the ascending creatures of time and space.

5. THE MANSION WORLD TEACHERS

The Mansion World Teachers are a corps of deserted but glorified cherubim and sanobim. When a pilgrim of time advances from a trial world of space to the mansion and associated worlds of morontia training, he is accompanied by his personal or group seraphim, the guardian of destiny. In the worlds of mortal existence the seraphim is ably assisted by cherubim and sanobim; but when her mortal ward is delivered from the bonds of the flesh and starts out on the ascendant career, when the postmaterial or morontia life begins, the attending seraphim has no further need of the ministrations of her former lieutenants, the cherubim and sanobim.

These deserted assistants of the ministering seraphim are often summoned to universe headquarters, where they pass into the intimate embrace of the Universe Mother Spirit and then go forth to the system training spheres as Mansion World Teachers. These teachers often visit the material worlds and function from the lowest mansion worlds on up to the highest of the educational spheres connected with the universe headquarters. Upon their own motion they may return to their former associative work with the ministering seraphim.

There are billions upon billions of these teachers in Satania, and their numbers constantly increase because, in the majority of instances, when a seraphim proceeds inward with an Adjuster-fused mortal, both a cherubim and a sanobim are left behind.

Mansion World Teachers, like most of the other instructors, are commissioned by the Melchizedeks. They are generally supervised by the Morontia Companions, but as individuals and as teachers they are supervised by the acting heads of the schools or spheres wherein they may be functioning as instructors.

These advanced cherubim usually work in pairs as they did when attached to the seraphim. They are by nature very near the morontia type of existence, and they are inherently sympathetic teachers of the ascending mortals and most efficiently conduct the program of the mansion world and morontia educational system.

In the schools of the morontia life these teachers engage in individual, group, class, and mass teaching. On the mansion worlds such schools are organized in three general groups of one hundred divisions each: the schools of thinking, the schools of feeling, and the schools of doing. When you reach the constellation, there are added the schools of ethics, the schools of administration, and the schools of social adjustment. On the universe headquarters worlds you will enter the schools of philosophy, divinity, and pure spirituality.

Those things which you might have learned on earth, but which you failed to learn, must be acquired under the tutelage of these faithful and patient teachers. There are no royal roads, short cuts, or easy paths to Paradise. Irrespective of the individual variations of the route, you master the lessons of one sphere before you proceed to another; at least this is true after you once leave the world of your nativity.

One of the purposes of the morontia career is to effect the permanent eradication from the mortal survivors of such animal vestigial traits as procrastination, equivocation, insincerity, problem avoidance, unfairness, and ease seeking. The mansonia life early teaches the young morontia pupils that postponement is in no sense avoidance. After the life in the flesh, time is no longer available as a technique of dodging situations or of circumventing disagreeable obligations.

Beginning service on the lowest of the tarrying spheres, the Mansion World Teachers advance, with experience, through the educational spheres of the system and the constellation to the training worlds of Salvington. They are subjected to no special discipline either before or after their embrace by the Universe Mother Spirit. They have already been trained for their work while serving as seraphic associates on the worlds native to their pupils of mansion world sojourn. They have had actual experience with these advancing mortals on the inhabited worlds. They are practical and sympathetic teachers, wise and understanding instructors, able and efficient guides. They are entirely familiar with the ascendant plans and thoroughly experienced in the initial phases of the progression career.

Many of the older of these teachers, those who have long served on the worlds of the Salvington circuit, are re-embraced by the Universe Mother Spirit, and from this second embrace these cherubim and sanobim emerge with the status of seraphim.

6. MORONTIA WORLD SERAPHIM—TRANSITION MINISTERS

While all orders of angels, from the planetary helpers to the supreme seraphim, minister on the morontia worlds, the transition ministers are more exclusively assigned to these activities. These angels are of the sixth order of seraphic servers, and their ministry is devoted to facilitating the transit of material and mortal creatures from the temporal life in the flesh on into the early stages of morontia existence on the seven mansion worlds.

You should understand that the morontia life of an ascending mortal is really initiated on the inhabited worlds at the conception of the soul, at that moment when the creature mind of moral status is indwelt by the spirit Adjuster. And from that moment on, the mortal soul has potential capacity for supermortal function, even for recognition on the higher levels of the morontia spheres of the local universe.

You will not, however, be conscious of the ministry of the transition seraphim until you attain the mansion worlds, where they labor untiringly for the advancement of their mortal pupils, being assigned for service in the following seven divisions:

1. *Seraphic Evangels.* The moment you consciousize on the mansion worlds, you are classified as evolving spirits in the records of the system. True, you are not yet spirits in reality, but you are no longer mortal or material beings; you have embarked upon the prespirit career and have been duly admitted to the morontia life.

On the mansion worlds the seraphic evangels will help you to choose wisely among the optional routes to Edentia, Salvington, Uversa, and Havona. If there are a number of equally advisable routes, these will be put before you, and you will be permitted to select the one that most appeals to you. These seraphim then make recommendations to the four and twenty advisers on Jerusem concerning that course which would be most advantageous for each ascending soul.

You are not given unrestricted choice as to your future course; but you may choose within the limits of that which the transition ministers and their superiors wisely determine to be most suitable for your future spirit attainment. The spirit world is governed on the principle of respecting your freewill choice provided the course you may choose is not detrimental to you or injurious to your fellows.

These seraphic evangels are dedicated to the proclamation of the gospel of eternal progression, the triumph of perfection attainment. On the mansion worlds they proclaim the great law of the conservation and dominance of goodness: No act of good is ever wholly lost; it may be long thwarted but never wholly annulled, and it is eternally potent in proportion to the divinity of its motivation.

Even on Urantia they counsel the human teachers of truth and righteousness to adhere to the preaching of "the goodness of God, which leads to repentance," to proclaim "the love of God, which casts out all fear." Even so have these truths been declared on your world:

The Gods are my caretakers; I shall not stray;
Side by side they lead me in the beautiful paths and glorious refreshing of life everlasting.
I shall not, in this Divine Presence, want for food nor thirst for water.
Though I go down into the valley of uncertainty or ascend up into the worlds of doubt,
Though I move in loneliness or with the fellows of my kind,
Though I triumph in the choirs of light or falter in the solitary places of the spheres,
Your good spirit shall minister to me, and your glorious angel will comfort me.
Though I descend into the depths of darkness and death itself,
I shall not doubt you nor fear you,
For I know that in the fullness of time and the glory of your name
You will raise me up to sit with you on the battlements on high.

That is the story whispered in the night season to the shepherd boy. He could not retain it word for word, but to the best of his memory he gave it much as it is recorded today.

These seraphim are also the evangels of the gospel of perfection attainment for the whole system as well as for the individual ascender. Even now in the young system of Satania their teachings and plans encompass provisions for the future ages when the mansion worlds will no longer serve the mortal ascenders as steppingstones to the spheres on high.

2. *Racial Interpreters.* All races of mortal beings are not alike. True, there is a planetary pattern running through the physical, mental, and spiritual natures and tendencies of the various races of a given world; but there are also distinct racial types, and very definite social tendencies characterize the offspring of these different basic types of human beings. On the worlds of time the seraphic racial interpreters further the efforts of the race commissioners to harmonize the varied viewpoints of the races, and they continue to function on the mansion worlds, where these same differences tend to persist in a measure. On a confused planet, such as Urantia, these brilliant beings have hardly had a fair opportunity to function, but they are the skillful sociologists and the wise ethnic advisers of the first heaven.

You should consider the statement about "heaven" and the "heaven of heavens." The heaven conceived by most of your prophets was the first of the mansion worlds of the local system. When the apostle spoke of being "caught up to the third heaven," he referred to that experience in which his Adjuster was detached during sleep and in this unusual state made a projection to the third of the seven mansion worlds. Some of your wise men saw the vision of the greater heaven, "the heaven of heavens," of which the sevenfold mansion world experience was but the first; the second being Jerusem; the third, Edentia and its satellites; the fourth, Salvington and the surrounding educational spheres; the fifth, Uversa; the sixth, Havona; and the seventh, Paradise.

3. *Mind Planners.* These seraphim are devoted to the effective grouping of morontia beings and to organizing their teamwork on the mansion worlds. They are the psychologists of the first heaven. The majority of this particular division of seraphic ministers have had previous experience as guardian angels to the children of time, but their wards, for some reason, failed to personalize on the mansion worlds or else survived by the technique of Spirit fusion.

It is the task of the mind planners to study the nature, experience, and status of the Adjuster souls in transit through the mansion worlds and to facilitate their grouping for assignment and advancement. But these mind planners do not scheme, manipulate, or otherwise take advantage of the ignorance or other limitations of mansion world students. They are wholly fair and eminently just. They respect your newborn morontia will; they regard you as independent volitional beings, and they seek to encourage your speedy development and advancement. Here you are face to face with true friends and understanding counselors, angels who are really able to help you "to see yourself as others see you" and "to know yourself as angels know you."

Even on Urantia, these seraphim teach the everlasting truth: If your own mind does not serve you well, you can exchange it for the mind of Jesus of Nazareth, who always serves you well.

4. *Morontia Counselors.* These ministers receive their name because they are assigned to teach, direct, and counsel the surviving mortals from the worlds of human origin, souls in transit to the higher schools of the system headquarters. They are the teachers of those who seek insight into the experiential unity of divergent life levels, those who are attempting the integration of meanings and the unification of values. This is the function of philosophy in mortal life, of mota on the morontia spheres.

Mota is more than a superior philosophy; it is to philosophy as two eyes are to one; it has a stereoscopic effect on meanings and values. Material man sees the universe, as it were, with but one eye—flat. Mansion world students achieve cosmic perspective—depth—by superimposing the perceptions of the morontia life upon the perceptions of the physical life. And they are enabled to bring these material and morontial viewpoints into true focus largely through the untiring ministry of their seraphic counselors, who so patiently teach the mansion world students and the morontia progressors. Many of the teaching counselors of the supreme order of seraphim began their careers as advisers of the newly liberated souls of the mortals of time.

5. *Technicians.* These are the seraphim who help new ascenders adjust themselves to the new and comparatively strange environment of the morontia spheres. Life on the transition worlds entails real contact with the energies and materials of both the physical and morontia levels and to a certain extent with spiritual realities. Ascenders must acclimatize to every new morontia level, and in all of this they are greatly helped by the seraphic technicians. These seraphim act as liaisons with the Morontia Power Supervisors and with the Master Physical Controllers and function extensively as instructors of the ascending pilgrims concerning the nature of those energies which are utilized on the transition spheres. They serve as emergency space traversers and perform numerous other regular and special duties.

6. *Recorder-Teachers.* These seraphim are the recorders of the borderland transactions of the spiritual and the physical, of the relationships of men and angels, of the morontia transactions of the lower universe realms. They also serve as instructors regarding the efficient and effective techniques of fact recording. There is an artistry in the intelligent assembly and co-ordination of related data, and this art is heightened in collaboration with the celestial artisans, and even the ascending mortals become thus affiliated with the recording seraphim.

The recorders of all the seraphic orders devote a certain amount of time to the education and training of the morontia progressors. These angelic custodians of the facts of time are the ideal instructors of all fact seekers. Before leaving Jerusem, you will become quite familiar with the history of Satania and its 619 inhabited worlds, and much of this story will be imparted by the seraphic recorders.

These angels are all in the chain of recorders extending from the lowest to the highest custodians of the facts of time and the truths of eternity. Some day they will teach you to seek truth as well as fact, to expand your soul as well as your mind. Even now you should learn to water the garden of your heart as well as to seek for the dry sands of knowledge. Forms are valueless when lessons are learned. No chick may be had without the shell, and no shell is of any worth after the chick is hatched. But sometimes error is so great that its rectification by revelation would be fatal to those slowly emerging truths which are essential to its experiential overthrow. When children have their ideals, do not dislodge them; let them grow. And while you are learning to think as men, you should also be learning to pray as children.

Law is life itself and not the rules of its conduct. Evil is a transgression of law, not a violation of the rules of conduct pertaining to life, which *is* the law. Falsehood is not a matter of narration technique but something premeditated as a perversion of truth. The creation of new pictures out of old facts, the restatement of parental life in the lives of offspring—these are the artistic triumphs of truth. The shadow of a hair's turning, premeditated for an untrue purpose, the slightest twisting or perversion of that which is principle—these constitute falseness. But the fetish of factualized truth, fossilized truth, the iron band of so-called unchanging truth, holds one blindly in a closed circle of cold fact. One can be technically right as to fact and everlastingly wrong in the truth.

7. *Ministering Reserves.* A large corps of all orders of the transition seraphim is held on the first mansion world. Next to the destiny guardians, these transition ministers draw the nearest to humans of all orders of seraphim, and many of your leisure moments will be spent with them. Angels take delight in service and, when unassigned, often minister as volunteers. The soul of many an ascending mortal has for the first time been kindled by the divine fire of the will-to-service through personal friendship with the volunteer servers of the seraphic reserves.

From them you will learn to let pressure develop stability and certainty; to be faithful and earnest and, withal, cheerful; to accept challenges without complaint and to face difficulties and uncertainties without fear. They will ask: If you fail, will you rise indomitably to try anew? If you succeed, will you maintain a well-balanced poise—a stabilized and spiritualized attitude—throughout every effort in the long struggle to break the fetters of material inertia, to attain the freedom of spirit existence?

Even as mortals, so have these angels been father to many disappointments, and they will point out that sometimes your most disappointing disappointments have become your greatest blessings. Sometimes the planting of a seed necessitates its death, the death of your fondest hopes, before it can be reborn to bear the fruits of new life and new opportunity. And from them you will learn to suffer less through sorrow and disappointment, first, by making fewer personal plans concerning other personalities, and then, by accepting your lot when you have faithfully performed your duty.

You will learn that you increase your burdens and decrease the likelihood of success by taking yourself too seriously. Nothing can take precedence over the work of your status sphere—this world or the next. Very important is the work of preparation for the next higher sphere, but nothing equals the importance of the work of the world in which you are actually living. But though the *work* is important, the *self* is not. When you feel important, you lose energy to the wear and tear of ego dignity so that there is little energy left to do the work. Self-importance, not work-importance, exhausts immature creatures; it is the self element that exhausts, not the effort to achieve. You can do important work if you do not become self-important; you can do several things as easily as one if you leave yourself out. Variety is restful; monotony is what wears and exhausts. Day after day is alike—just life or the alternative of death.

7. MORONTIA MOTA

The lower planes of morontia mota join directly with the higher levels of human philosophy. On the first mansion world it is the practice to teach the less advanced students by the parallel technique; that is, in one column are presented the more simple concepts of mota meanings, and in the opposite column citation is made of analogous statements of mortal philosophy.

Not long since, while executing an assignment on the first mansion world of Satania, I had occasion to observe this method of teaching; and though I may not undertake to present the mota content of the lesson, I am permitted to record the twenty-eight statements of human philosophy which this morontia instructor was utilizing as illustrative material designed to assist these new mansion world sojourners in their early efforts to grasp the significance and meaning of mota. These illustrations of human philosophy were:

1. A display of specialized skill does not signify possession of spiritual capacity. Cleverness is not a substitute for true character.

2. Few persons live up to the faith which they really have. Unreasoned fear is a master intellectual fraud practiced upon the evolving mortal soul.

3. Inherent capacities cannot be exceeded; a pint can never hold a quart. The spirit concept cannot be mechanically forced into the material memory mold.

4. Few mortals ever dare to draw anything like the sum of personality credits established by the combined ministries of nature and grace. The majority of impoverished souls are truly rich, but they refuse to believe it.

5. Difficulties may challenge mediocrity and defeat the fearful, but they only stimulate the true children of the Most Highs.

6. To enjoy privilege without abuse, to have liberty without license, to possess power and steadfastly refuse to use it for self-aggrandizement—these are the marks of high civilization.

7. Blind and unforeseen accidents do not occur in the cosmos. Neither do the celestial beings assist the lower being who refuses to act upon his light of truth.

8. Effort does not always produce joy, but there is no happiness without intelligent effort.

9. Action achieves strength; moderation eventuates in charm.

10. Righteousness strikes the harmony chords of truth, and the melody vibrates throughout the cosmos, even to the recognition of the Infinite.

11. The weak indulge in resolutions, but the strong act. Life is but a day's work—do it well. The act is ours; the consequences God's.

12. The greatest affliction of the cosmos is never to have been afflicted. Mortals only learn wisdom by experiencing tribulation.

13. Stars are best discerned from the lonely isolation of experiential depths, not from the illuminated and ecstatic mountain tops.

14. Whet the appetites of your associates for truth; give advice only when it is asked for.

15. Affectation is the ridiculous effort of the ignorant to appear wise, the attempt of the barren soul to appear rich.

16. You cannot perceive spiritual truth until you feelingly experience it, and many truths are not really felt except in adversity.

17. Ambition is dangerous until it is fully socialized. You have not truly acquired any virtue until your acts make you worthy of it.

18. Impatience is a spirit poison; anger is like a stone hurled into a hornet's nest.

19. Anxiety must be abandoned. The disappointments hardest to bear are those which never come.

20. Only a poet can discern poetry in the commonplace prose of routine existence.

21. The high mission of any art is, by its illusions, to foreshadow a higher universe reality, to crystallize the emotions of time into the thought of eternity.

22. The evolving soul is not made divine by what it does, but by what it strives to do.

23. Death added nothing to the intellectual possession or to the spiritual endowment, but it did add to the experiential status the consciousness of *survival.*

24. The destiny of eternity is determined moment by moment by the achievements of the day by day living. The acts of today are the destiny of tomorrow.

25. Greatness lies not so much in possessing strength as in making a wise and divine use of such strength.

26. Knowledge is possessed only by sharing; it is safeguarded by wisdom and socialized by love.

27. Progress demands development of individuality; mediocrity seeks perpetuation in standardization.

28. The argumentative defense of any proposition is inversely proportional to the truth contained.

Such is the work of the beginners on the first mansion world while the more advanced pupils on the later worlds are mastering the higher levels of cosmic insight and morontia mota.

8. THE MORONTIA PROGRESSORS

From the time of graduation from the mansion worlds to the attainment of spirit status in the superuniverse career, ascending mortals are denominated morontia progressors. Your passage through this wonderful borderland life will be an unforgettable experience, a charming memory. It is the evolutionary portal to spirit life and the eventual attainment of creature perfection by which ascenders achieve the goal of time—the finding of God on Paradise.

There is a definite and divine purpose in all this morontia and subsequent spirit scheme of mortal progression, this elaborate universe training school for ascending creatures. It is the design of the Creators to afford the creatures of time a graduated opportunity to master the details of the operation and administration of the grand universe, and this long course of training is best carried forward by having the surviving mortal climb up gradually and by actual participation in every step of the ascent.

The mortal-survival plan has a practical and serviceable objective; you are not the recipients of all this divine labor and painstaking training only that you may survive just to enjoy endless bliss and eternal ease. There is a goal of transcendent service concealed beyond the horizon of the present universe age. If the Gods designed merely to take you on one long and eternal joy excursion, they certainly would not so largely turn the whole universe into one vast and intricate practical training school, requisition a substantial part of the celestial creation as teachers and instructors, and then spend ages upon ages piloting you, one by one, through this gigantic universe school of experiential training. The furtherance of the scheme of mortal progression seems to be one of the chief businesses of the present organized universe, and the majority of innumerable orders of created intelligences are either directly or indirectly engaged in advancing some phase of this progressive perfection plan.

In traversing the ascending scale of living existence from mortal man to the Deity embrace, you actually live the very life of every possible phase and stage of perfected creature existence within the limits of the present universe age. From mortal man to Paradise finaliter embraces all that now can be—encompasses everything presently possible to the living orders of intelligent, perfected finite creature beings. If the future destiny of the Paradise finaliters is service in new universes now in the making, it is assured that in this new and future creation there will be no created orders of experiential beings whose lives will be wholly different from those which mortal finaliters have lived on some world as a part of their ascending training, as one of the stages of their agelong progress from animal to angel and from angel to spirit and from spirit to God.

[Presented by an Archangel of Nebadon.]

PAPER 49

THE INHABITED WORLDS

ALL mortal-inhabited worlds are evolutionary in origin and nature. These spheres are the spawning ground, the evolutionary cradle, of the mortal races of time and space. Each unit of the ascendant life is a veritable training school for the stage of existence just ahead, and this is true of every stage of man's progressive Paradise ascent; just as true of the initial mortal experience on an evolutionary planet as of the final universe headquarters school of the Melchizedeks, a school which is not attended by ascending mortals until just before their translation to the regime of the superuniverse and the attainment of first-stage spirit existence.

All inhabited worlds are basically grouped for celestial administration into the local systems, and each of these local systems is limited to about one thousand evolutionary worlds. This limitation is by the decree of the Ancients of Days, and it pertains to actual evolutionary planets whereon mortals of survival status are living. Neither worlds finally settled in light and life nor planets in the prehuman stage of life development are reckoned in this group.

Satania itself is an unfinished system containing only 619 inhabited worlds. Such planets are numbered serially in accordance with their registration as inhabited worlds, as worlds inhabited by will creatures. Thus was Urantia given the number *606 of Satania,* meaning the 606th world in this local system on which the long evolutionary life process culminated in the appearance of human beings. There are thirty-six uninhabited planets nearing the life-endowment stage, and several are now being made ready for the Life Carriers. There are nearly two hundred spheres which are evolving so as to be ready for life implantation within the next few million years.

Not all planets are suited to harbor mortal life. Small ones having a high rate of axial revolution are wholly unsuited for life habitats. In several of the physical systems of Satania the planets revolving around the central sun are too large for habitation, their great mass occasioning oppressive gravity. Many of these enormous spheres have satellites, sometimes a half dozen or more, and these moons are often in size very near that of Urantia, so that they are almost ideal for habitation.

The oldest inhabited world of Satania, world number one, is Anova, one of the forty-four satellites revolving around an enormous dark planet but exposed to the differential light of three neighboring suns. Anova is in an advanced stage of progressive civilization.

1. THE PLANETARY LIFE

The universes of time and space are gradual in development; the progression of life—terrestrial or celestial—is neither arbitrary nor magical. Cosmic evolution may not always be understandable (predictable), but it is strictly nonaccidental.

The biologic unit of material life is the protoplasmic cell, the communal association of chemical, electrical, and other basic energies. The chemical formulas differ in each system, and the technique of living cell reproduction is slightly different in each local universe, but the Life Carriers are always the living catalyzers who initiate the primordial reactions of material life; they are the instigators of the energy circuits of living matter.

All the worlds of a local system disclose unmistakable physical kinship; nevertheless, each planet has its own scale of life, no two worlds being exactly alike in plant and animal endowment. These planetary variations in the system life types result from the decisions of the Life Carriers. But these beings are neither capricious nor whimsical; the universes are conducted in accordance with law and order. The laws of Nebadon are the divine mandates of Salvington, and the evolutionary order of life in Satania is in consonance with the evolutionary pattern of Nebadon.

Evolution is the rule of human development, but the process itself varies greatly on different worlds. Life is sometimes initiated in one center, sometimes in three, as it was on Urantia. On the atmospheric worlds it usually has a marine origin, but not always; much depends on the physical status of a planet. The Life Carriers have great latitude in their function of life initiation.

In the development of planetary life the vegetable form always precedes the animal and is quite fully developed before the animal patterns differentiate. All animal types are developed from the basic patterns of the preceding vegetable kingdom of living things; they are not separately organized.

The early stages of life evolution are not altogether in conformity with your present-day views. *Mortal man is not an evolutionary accident.* There is a precise system, a universal law, which determines the unfolding of the planetary life plan on the spheres of space. Time and the production of large numbers of a species are not the controlling influences. Mice reproduce much more rapidly than elephants, yet elephants evolve more rapidly than mice.

The process of planetary evolution is orderly and controlled. The development of higher organisms from lower groupings of life is not accidental. Sometimes evolutionary progress is temporarily delayed by the destruction of certain favorable lines of life plasm carried in a selected species. It often requires ages upon ages to recoup the damage occasioned by the loss of a single superior strain of human heredity. These selected and superior strains of living protoplasm should be jealously and intelligently guarded when once they make their appearance. And on most of the inhabited worlds these superior potentials of life are valued much more highly than on Urantia.

2. PLANETARY PHYSICAL TYPES

There is a standard and basic pattern of vegetable and animal life in each system. But the Life Carriers are oftentimes confronted with the necessity of modifying these basic patterns to conform to the varying physical conditions which confront them on numerous worlds of space. They foster a generalized system type of mortal creature, but there are seven distinct physical types as well as thousands upon thousands of minor variants of these seven outstanding differentiations:

1. Atmospheric types.
2. Elemental types.
3. Gravity types.
4. Temperature types.
5. Electric types.
6. Energizing types.
7. Unnamed types.

The Satania system contains all of these types and numerous intermediate groups, although some are very sparingly represented.

1. *The atmospheric types.* The physical differences of the worlds of mortal habitation are chiefly determined by the nature of the atmosphere; other influences which contribute to the planetary differentiation of life are relatively minor.

The present atmospheric status of Urantia is almost ideal for the support of the breathing type of man, but the human type can be so modified that it can live on both the superatmospheric and the subatmospheric planets. Such modifications also extend to the animal life, which differs greatly on the various inhabited spheres. There is a very great modification of animal orders on both the sub- and the superatmospheric worlds.

Of the atmospheric types in Satania, about two and one-half per cent are subbreathers, about five per cent superbreathers, and over ninety-one per cent are mid-breathers, altogether accounting for ninety-eight and one-half per cent of the Satania worlds.

Beings such as the Urantia races are classified as mid-breathers; you represent the average or typical breathing order of mortal existence. If intelligent creatures should exist on a planet with an atmosphere similar to that of your near neighbor, Venus, they would belong to the superbreather group, while those inhabiting a planet with an atmosphere as thin as that of your outer neighbor, Mars, would be denominated subbreathers.

If mortals should inhabit a planet devoid of air, like your moon, they would belong to the separate order of nonbreathers. This type represents a radical or extreme adjustment to the planetary environment and is separately considered. Nonbreathers account for the remaining one and one-half per cent of Satania worlds.

2. *The elemental types.* These differentiations have to do with the relation of mortals to water, air, and land, and there are four distinct species of intelligent life as they are related to these habitats. The Urantia races are of the land order.

It is quite impossible for you to envisage the environment which prevails during the early ages of some worlds. These unusual conditions make it necessary for the evolving animal life to remain in its marine nursery habitat for longer periods than on those planets which very early provide a hospitable land-and-atmosphere environment. Conversely, on some worlds of the superbreathers, when the planet is not too large, it is sometimes expedient to provide for a mortal type which can readily negotiate atmospheric passage. These air navigators sometimes intervene between the water and land groups, and they always live in a measure upon the ground, eventually evolving into land dwellers.

But on some worlds, for ages they continue to fly even after they have become land-type beings.

It is both amazing and amusing to observe the early civilization of a primitive race of human beings taking shape, in one case, in the air and treetops and, in another, midst the shallow waters of sheltered tropic basins, as well as on the bottom, sides, and shores of these marine gardens of the dawn races of such extraordinary spheres. Even on Urantia there was a long age during which primitive man preserved himself and advanced his primitive civilization by living for the most part in the treetops as did his earlier arboreal ancestors. And on Urantia you still have a group of diminutive mammals (the bat family) that are air navigators, and your seals and whales, of marine habitat, are also of the mammalian order.

In Satania, of the elemental types, seven per cent are water, ten per cent air, seventy per cent land, and thirteen per cent combined land-and-air types. But these modifications of early intelligent creatures are neither human fishes nor human birds. They are of the human and prehuman types, neither superfishes nor glorified birds but distinctly mortal.

3. *The gravity types.* By modification of creative design, intelligent beings are so constructed that they can freely function on spheres both smaller and larger than Urantia, thus being, in measure, accommodated to the gravity of those planets which are not of ideal size and density.

The various planetary types of mortals vary in height, the average in Nebadon being a trifle under seven feet. Some of the larger worlds are peopled with beings who are only about two and one-half feet in height. Mortal stature ranges from here on up through the average heights on the average-sized planets to around ten feet on the smaller inhabited spheres. In Satania there is only one race under four feet in height. Twenty per cent of the Satania inhabited worlds are peopled with mortals of the modified gravity types occupying the larger and the smaller planets.

4. *The temperature types.* It is possible to create living beings who can withstand temperatures both much higher and much lower than the life range of the Urantia races. There are five distinct orders of beings as they are classified with reference to heat-regulating mechanisms. In this scale the Urantia races are number three. Thirty per cent of Satania worlds are peopled with races of modified temperature types. Twelve per cent belong to the higher temperature ranges, eighteen per cent to the lower, as compared with Urantians, who function in the mid-temperature group.

5. *The electric types.* The electric, magnetic, and electronic behavior of the worlds varies greatly. There are ten designs of mortal life variously fashioned to withstand the differential energy of the spheres. These ten varieties also react in slightly different ways to the chemical rays of ordinary sunlight. But these slight physical variations in no way affect the intellectual or the spiritual life.

Of the electric groupings of mortal life, almost twenty-three per cent belong to class number four, the Urantia type of existence. These types are distributed as follows: number 1, one per cent; number 2, two per cent; number 3, five per cent; number 4, twenty-three per cent; number 5, twenty-seven per cent;

number 6, twenty-four per cent; number 7, eight per cent; number 8, five per cent; number 9, three per cent; number 10, two per cent—in whole percentages.

6. *The energizing types.* Not all worlds are alike in the manner of taking in energy. Not all inhabited worlds have an atmospheric ocean suited to respiratory exchange of gases, such as is present on Urantia. During the earlier and the later stages of many planets, beings of your present order could not exist; and when the respiratory factors of a planet are very high or very low, but when all other prerequisites to intelligent life are adequate, the Life Carriers often establish on such worlds a modified form of mortal existence, beings who are competent to effect their life-process exchanges directly by means of light-energy and the firsthand power transmutations of the Master Physical Controllers.

There are six differing types of animal and mortal nutrition: The subbreathers employ the first type of nutrition, the marine dwellers the second, the mid-breathers the third, as on Urantia. The superbreathers employ the fourth type of energy intake, while the nonbreathers utilize the fifth order of nutrition and energy. The sixth technique of energizing is limited to the midway creatures.

7. *The unnamed types.* There are numerous additional physical variations in planetary life, but all of these differences are wholly matters of anatomical modification, physiologic differentiation, and electrochemical adjustment. Such distinctions do not concern the intellectual or the spiritual life.

3. WORLDS OF THE NONBREATHERS

The majority of inhabited planets are peopled with the breathing type of intelligent beings. But there are also orders of mortals who are able to live on worlds with little or no air. Of the Orvonton inhabited worlds this type amounts to less than seven per cent. In Nebadon this percentage is less than three. In all Satania there are only nine such worlds.

There are so very few of the nonbreather type of inhabited worlds in Satania because this more recently organized section of Norlatiadek still abounds in meteoric space bodies; and worlds without a protective friction atmosphere are subject to incessant bombardment by these wanderers. Even some of the comets consist of meteor swarms, but as a rule they are disrupted smaller bodies of matter.

Millions upon millions of meteorites enter the atmosphere of Urantia daily, coming in at the rate of almost two hundred miles a second. On the nonbreathing worlds the advanced races must do much to protect themselves from meteor damage by making electrical installations which operate to consume or shunt the meteors. Great danger confronts them when they venture beyond these protected zones. These worlds are also subject to disastrous electrical storms of a nature unknown on Urantia. During such times of tremendous energy fluctuation the inhabitants must take refuge in their special structures of protective insulation.

Life on the worlds of the nonbreathers is radically different from what it is on Urantia. The nonbreathers do not eat food or drink water as do the Urantia races. The reactions of the nervous system, the heat-regulating mechanism, and the metabolism of these specialized peoples are radically different from such functions of Urantia mortals. Almost every act of living, aside from reproduction, differs, and even the methods of procreation are somewhat different.

On the nonbreathing worlds the animal species are radically unlike those found on the atmospheric planets. The nonbreathing plan of life varies from the technique of existence on an atmospheric world; even in survival their peoples differ, being candidates for Spirit fusion. Nevertheless, these beings enjoy life and carry forward the activities of the realm with the same relative trials and joys that are experienced by the mortals living on atmospheric worlds. In mind and character the nonbreathers do not differ from other mortal types.

You would be more than interested in the planetary conduct of this type of mortal because such a race of beings inhabits a sphere in close proximity to Urantia.

4. EVOLUTIONARY WILL CREATURES

There are great differences between the mortals of the different worlds, even among those belonging to the same intellectual and physical types, but all mortals of will dignity are erect animals, bipeds.

There are six basic evolutionary races: three primary—red, yellow, and blue; and three secondary—orange, green, and indigo. Most inhabited worlds have all of these races, but many of the three-brained planets harbor only the three primary types. Some local systems also have only these three races.

The average special physical-sense endowment of human beings is twelve, though the special senses of the three-brained mortals are extended slightly beyond those of the one- and two-brained types; they can see and hear considerably more than the Urantia races.

Young are usually born singly, multiple births being the exception, and the family life is fairly uniform on all types of planets. Sex equality prevails on all advanced worlds; male and female are equal in mind endowment and spiritual status. We do not regard a planet as having emerged from barbarism so long as one sex seeks to tyrannize over the other. This feature of creature experience is always greatly improved after the arrival of a Material Son and Daughter.

Seasons and temperature variations occur on all sunlighted and sun-heated planets. Agriculture is universal on all atmospheric worlds; tilling the soil is the one pursuit that is common to the advancing races of all such planets.

Mortals all have the same general struggles with microscopic foes in their early days, such as you now experience on Urantia, though perhaps not so extensive. The length of life varies on the different planets from twenty-five years on the primitive worlds to near five hundred on the more advanced and older spheres.

Human beings are all gregarious, both tribal and racial. These group segregations are inherent in their origin and constitution. Such tendencies can be modified only by advancing civilization and by gradual spiritualization. The social, economic, and governmental problems of the inhabited worlds vary in accordance with the age of the planets and the degree to which they have been influenced by the successive sojourns of the divine Sons.

Mind is the bestowal of the Infinite Spirit and functions quite the same in diverse environments. The mind of mortals is akin, regardless of certain structural and chemical differences which characterize the physical natures of the will creatures of the local systems. Regardless of personal or physical planetary differences, the mental life of all these various orders of mortals is very similar, and their immediate careers after death are very much alike.

But mortal mind without immortal spirit cannot survive. The mind of man is mortal; only the bestowed spirit is immortal. Survival is dependent on spiritualization by the ministry of the Adjuster—on the birth and evolution of the immortal soul; at least, there must not have developed an antagonism towards the Adjuster's mission of effecting the spiritual transformation of the material mind.

5. THE PLANETARY SERIES OF MORTALS

It will be somewhat difficult to make an adequate portrayal of the planetary series of mortals because you know so little about them, and because there are so many variations. Mortal creatures may, however, be studied from numerous viewpoints, among which are the following:

1. Adjustment to planetary environment.
2. Brain-type series.
3. Spirit-reception series.
4. Planetary-mortal epochs.
5. Creature-kinship serials.
6. Adjuster-fusion series.
7. Techniques of terrestrial escape.

The inhabited spheres of the seven superuniverses are peopled with mortals who simultaneously classify in some one or more categories of each of these seven generalized classes of evolutionary creature life. But even these general classifications make no provision for such beings as midsoniters nor for certain other forms of intelligent life. The inhabited worlds, as they have been presented in these narratives, are peopled with evolutionary mortal creatures, but there are other life forms.

1. *Adjustment to planetary environment.* There are three general groups of inhabited worlds from the standpoint of the adjustment of creature life to the planetary environment: the normal adjustment group, the radical adjustment group, and the experimental group.

Normal adjustments to planetary conditions follow the general physical patterns previously considered. The worlds of the nonbreathers typify the radical or extreme adjustment, but other types are also included in this group. Experimental worlds are usually ideally adapted to the typical life forms, and on these decimal planets the Life Carriers attempt to produce beneficial variations in the standard life designs. Since your world is an experimental planet, it differs markedly from its sister spheres in Satania; many forms of life have appeared on Urantia that are not found elsewhere; likewise are many common species absent from your planet.

In the universe of Nebadon, all the life-modification worlds are serially linked together and constitute a special domain of universe affairs which is given attention by designated administrators; and all of these experimental worlds are periodically inspected by a corps of universe directors whose chief is the veteran finaliter known in Satania as Tabamantia.

2. *Brain-type series.* The one physical uniformity of mortals is the brain and nervous system; nevertheless, there are three basic organizations of the brain mechanism: the one-, the two-, and the three-brained types. Urantians are of the two-brained type, somewhat more imaginative, adventurous, and philosophical than the one-brained mortals but somewhat less spiritual, ethical, and worshipful than the three-brained orders. These brain differences characterize even the prehuman animal existences.

From the two-hemisphere type of the Urantian cerebral cortex you can, by analogy, grasp something of the one-brained type. The third brain of the three-brained orders is best conceived as an evolvement of your lower or rudimentary form of brain, which is developed to the point where it functions chiefly in control of physical activities, leaving the two superior brains free for higher engagements: one for intellectual functions and the other for the spiritual-counterparting activities of the Thought Adjuster.

While the terrestrial attainments of the one-brained races are slightly limited in comparison with the two-brained orders, the older planets of the three-brained group exhibit civilizations that would astound Urantians, and which would somewhat shame yours by comparison. In mechanical development and material civilization, even in intellectual progress, the two-brained mortal worlds are able to equal the three-brained spheres. But in the higher control of mind and development of intellectual and spiritual reciprocation, you are somewhat inferior.

All such comparative estimates concerning the intellectual progress or the spiritual attainments of any world or group of worlds should in fairness recognize planetary age; much, very much, depends on age, the help of the biologic uplifters, and the subsequent missions of the various orders of the divine Sons.

While the three-brained peoples are capable of a slightly higher planetary evolution than either the one- or two-brained orders, all have the same type of life plasm and carry on planetary activities in very similar ways, much as do human beings on Urantia. These three types of mortals are distributed throughout the worlds of the local systems. In the majority of cases planetary conditions had very little to do with the decisions of the Life Carriers to project these varied orders of mortals on the different worlds; it is a prerogative of the Life Carriers thus to plan and execute.

These three orders stand on an equal footing in the ascension career. Each must traverse the same intellectual scale of development, and each must master the same spiritual tests of progression. The system administration and the constellation overcontrol of these different worlds are uniformly free from discrimination; even the regimes of the Planetary Princes are identical.

3. *Spirit-reception series.* There are three groups of mind design as related to contact with spirit affairs. This classification does not refer to the one-, two-, and three-brained orders of mortals; it refers primarily to gland chemistry, more particularly to the organization of certain glands comparable to the pituitary bodies. The races on some worlds have one gland, on others two, as do Urantians, while on still other spheres the races have three of these unique bodies. The inherent imagination and spiritual receptivity is definitely influenced by this differential chemical endowment.

Of the spirit-reception types, sixty-five per cent are of the second group, like the Urantia races. Twelve per cent are of the first type, naturally less receptive, while twenty-three per cent are more spiritually inclined during terrestrial life. But such distinctions do not survive natural death; all of these racial differences pertain only to the life in the flesh.

4. *Planetary-mortal epochs.* This classification recognizes the succession of temporal dispensations as they affect man's terrestrial status and his reception of celestial ministry.

Life is initiated on the planets by the Life Carriers, who watch over its development until sometime after the evolutionary appearance of mortal man. Before the Life Carriers leave a planet, they duly install a Planetary Prince as ruler of the realm. With this ruler there arrives a full quota of subordinate auxiliaries and ministering helpers, and the first adjudication of the living and the dead is simultaneous with his arrival.

With the emergence of human groupings, this Planetary Prince arrives to inaugurate human civilization and to focalize human society. Your world of confusion is no criterion of the early days of the reign of the Planetary Princes, for it was near the beginning of such an administration on Urantia that your Planetary Prince, Caligastia, cast his lot with the rebellion of the System Sovereign, Lucifer. Your planet has pursued a stormy course ever since.

On a normal evolutionary world, racial progress attains its natural biologic peak during the regime of the Planetary Prince, and shortly thereafter the System Sovereign dispatches a Material Son and Daughter to that planet. These imported beings are of service as biologic uplifters; their default on Urantia further complicated your planetary history.

When the intellectual and ethical progress of a human race has reached the limits of evolutionary development, there comes an Avonal Son of Paradise on a magisterial mission; and later on, when the spiritual status of such a world is nearing its limit of natural attainment, the planet is visited by a Paradise bestowal Son. The chief mission of a bestowal Son is to establish the planetary status, release the Spirit of Truth for planetary function, and thus effect the universal coming of the Thought Adjusters.

Here, again, Urantia deviates: There has never been a magisterial mission on your world, neither was your bestowal Son of the Avonal order; your planet enjoyed the signal honor of becoming the mortal home planet of the Sovereign Son, Michael of Nebadon.

As a result of the ministry of all the successive orders of divine sonship, the inhabited worlds and their advancing races begin to approach the apex of planetary evolution. Such worlds now become ripe for the culminating mission, the arrival of the Trinity Teacher Sons. This epoch of the Teacher Sons is the vestibule to the final planetary age—evolutionary utopia—the age of light and life.

This classification of human beings will receive particular attention in a succeeding paper.

5. *Creature-kinship serials.* Planets are not only organized vertically into systems, constellations, and so on, but the universe administration also provides for horizontal groupings according to type, series, and other relationships. This lateral administration of the universe pertains more particularly to the coordination of activities of a kindred nature which have been independently fostered on different spheres. These related classes of universe creatures are

periodically inspected by certain composite corps of high personalities presided over by long-experienced finaliters.

These kinship factors are manifest on all levels, for kinship serials exist among nonhuman personalities as well as among mortal creatures—even between human and superhuman orders. Intelligent beings are vertically related in twelve great groups of seven major divisions each. The co-ordination of these uniquely related groups of living beings is probably effected by some not fully comprehended technique of the Supreme Being.

6. *Adjuster-fusion series.* The spiritual classification or grouping of all mortals during their prefusion experience is wholly determined by the relation of the personality status to the indwelling Mystery Monitor. Almost ninety per cent of the inhabited worlds of Nebadon are peopled with Adjuster-fusion mortals in contrast with a near-by universe where scarcely more than one half of the worlds harbor beings who are Adjuster-indwelt candidates for eternal fusion.

7. *Techniques of terrestrial escape.* There is fundamentally only one way in which individual human life can be initiated on the inhabited worlds, and that is through creature procreation and natural birth; but there are numerous techniques whereby man escapes his terrestrial status and gains access to the inward moving stream of Paradise ascenders.

6. TERRESTRIAL ESCAPE

All of the differing physical types and planetary series of mortals alike enjoy the ministry of Thought Adjusters, guardian angels, and the various orders of the messenger hosts of the Infinite Spirit. All alike are liberated from the bonds of flesh by the emancipation of natural death, and all alike go thence to the morontia worlds of spiritual evolution and mind progress.

From time to time, on motion of the planetary authorities or the system rulers, special resurrections of the sleeping survivors are conducted. Such resurrections occur at least every millennium of planetary time, when not all but "many of those who sleep in the dust awake." These special resurrections are the occasion for mobilizing special groups of ascenders for specific service in the local universe plan of mortal ascension. There are both practical reasons and sentimental associations connected with these special resurrections.

Throughout the earlier ages of an inhabited world, many are called to the mansion spheres at the special and the millennial resurrections, but most survivors are repersonalized at the inauguration of a new dispensation associated with the advent of a divine Son of planetary service.

1. *Mortals of the dispensational or group order of survival.* With the arrival of the first Adjuster on an inhabited world the guardian seraphim also make their appearance; they are indispensable to terrestrial escape. Throughout the life-lapse period of the sleeping survivors the spiritual values and eternal realities of their newly evolved and immortal souls are held as a sacred trust by the personal or by the group guardian seraphim.

The group guardians of assignment to the sleeping survivors always function with the judgment Sons on their world advents. "He shall send his angels, and they shall gather together his elect from the four winds." With each seraphim of assignment to the repersonalization of a sleeping mortal there functions the returned Adjuster, the same immortal Father fragment that lived in him during the days in the flesh, and thus is identity restored and personality resurrected. During the sleep of their subjects these waiting Adjusters serve on Divinington; they never indwell another mortal mind in this interim.

While the older worlds of mortal existence harbor those highly developed and exquisitely spiritual types of human beings who are virtually exempt from the morontia life, the earlier ages of the animal-origin races are characterized by primitive mortals who are so immature that fusion with their Adjusters is impossible. The reawakening of these mortals is accomplished by the guardian seraphim in conjunction with an individualized portion of the immortal spirit of the Third Source and Center.

Thus are the sleeping survivors of a planetary age repersonalized in the dispensational roll calls. But with regard to the nonsalvable personalities of a realm, no immortal spirit is present to function with the group guardians of destiny, and this constitutes cessation of creature existence. While some of your records have pictured these events as taking place on the planets of mortal death, they all really occur on the mansion worlds.

2. *Mortals of the individual orders of ascension.* The individual progress of human beings is measured by their successive attainment and traversal (mastery) of the seven cosmic circles. These circles of mortal progression are levels of associated intellectual, social, spiritual, and cosmic-insight values. Starting out in the seventh circle, mortals strive for the first, and all who have attained the third immediately have personal guardians of destiny assigned to them. These mortals may be repersonalized in the morontia life independent of dispensational or other adjudications.

Throughout the earlier ages of an evolutionary world, few mortals go to judgment on the third day. But as the ages pass, more and more the personal guardians of destiny are assigned to the advancing mortals, and thus increasing numbers of these evolving creatures are repersonalized on the first mansion world on the third day after natural death. On such occasions the return of the Adjuster signalizes the awakening of the human soul, and this is the repersonalization of the dead just as literally as when the en masse roll is called at the end of a dispensation on the evolutionary worlds.

There are three groups of individual ascenders: The less advanced land on the initial or first mansion world. The more advanced group may take up the morontia career on any of the intermediate mansion worlds in accordance with previous planetary progression. The most advanced of these orders really begin their morontia experience on the seventh mansion world.

3. *Mortals of the probationary-dependent orders of ascension.* The arrival of an Adjuster constitutes identity in the eyes of the universe, and all indwelt beings are on the roll calls of justice. But temporal life on the evolutionary worlds is uncertain, and many die in youth before choosing the Paradise career. Such Adjuster-indwelt children and youths follow the parent of most advanced spiritual status, thus going to the system finaliter world (the probationary nursery) on the third day, at a special resurrection, or at the regular millennial and dispensational roll calls.

Children who die when too young to have Thought Adjusters are repersonalized on the finaliter world of the local systems concomitant with the arrival of either parent on the mansion worlds. A child acquires physical entity at mortal birth, but in the matter of survival all Adjusterless children are reckoned as still attached to their parents.

In due course Thought Adjusters come to indwell these little ones, while the seraphic ministry to both groups of the probationary-dependent orders of survival is in general similar to that of the more advanced parent or is equivalent to that of the parent in case only one survives. Those attaining the third circle, regardless of the status of their parents, are accorded personal guardians.

Similar probation nurseries are maintained on the finaliter spheres of the constellation and the universe headquarters for the Adjusterless children of the primary and secondary modified orders of ascenders.

4. *Mortals of the secondary modified orders of ascension.* These are the progressive human beings of the intermediate evolutionary worlds. As a rule they are not immune to natural death, but they are exempt from passing through the seven mansion worlds.

The less perfected group reawaken on the headquarters of their local system, passing by only the mansion worlds. The intermediate group go to the constellation training worlds; they pass by the entire morontia regime of the local system. Still farther on in the planetary ages of spiritual striving, many survivors awaken on the constellation headquarters and there begin the Paradise ascent.

But before any of these groups may go forward, they must journey back as instructors to the worlds they missed, gaining many experiences as teachers in those realms which they passed by as students. They all subsequently proceed to Paradise by the ordained routes of mortal progression.

5. *Mortals of the primary modified order of ascension.* These mortals belong to the Adjuster-fused type of evolutionary life, but they are most often representative of the final phases of human development on an evolving world. These glorified beings are exempt from passing through the portals of death; they are submitted to Son seizure; they are translated from among the living and appear immediately in the presence of the Sovereign Son on the headquarters of the local universe.

These are the mortals who fuse with their Adjusters during mortal life, and such Adjuster-fused personalities traverse space freely before being clothed with morontia forms. These fused souls go by direct Adjuster transit to the resurrection halls of the higher morontia spheres, where they receive their initial morontia investiture just as do all other mortals arriving from the evolutionary worlds.

This primary modified order of mortal ascension may apply to individuals in any of the planetary series from the lowest to the highest stages of the Adjuster-fusion worlds, but it more frequently functions on the older of these spheres after they have received the benefits of numerous sojourns of the divine Sons.

With the establishment of the planetary era of light and life, many go to the universe morontia worlds by the primary modified order of translation. Further along in the advanced stages of settled existence, when the majority of the mortals leaving a realm are embraced in this class, the planet is regarded as belonging to this series. Natural death becomes decreasingly frequent on these spheres long settled in light and life.

[Presented by a Melchizedek of the Jerusem School of Planetary Administration.]

PAPER 50

THE PLANETARY PRINCES

WHILE belonging to the order of Lanonandek Sons, the Planetary Princes are so specialized in service that they are commonly regarded as a distinct group. After their Melchizedek certification as secondary Lanonandeks, these local universe Sons are assigned to the reserves of their order on the constellation headquarters. From here they are assigned to various duties by the System Sovereign and eventually commissioned as Planetary Princes and sent forth to rule the evolving inhabited worlds.

The signal for a System Sovereign to act in the matter of assigning a ruler to a given planet is the reception of a request from the Life Carriers for the dispatch of an administrative head to function on this planet whereon they have established life and developed intelligent evolutionary beings. All planets which are inhabited by evolutionary mortal creatures have assigned to them a planetary ruler of this order of sonship.

1. MISSION OF THE PRINCES

The Planetary Prince and his assistant brethren represent the nearest personalized approach (aside from incarnation) that the Eternal Son of Paradise can make to the lowly creatures of time and space. True, the Creator Son touches the creatures of the realms through his spirit, but the Planetary Prince is the last of the orders of personal Sons extending out from Paradise to the children of men. The Infinite Spirit comes very near in the persons of the guardians of destiny and other angelic beings; the Universal Father lives in man by the prepersonal presence of the Mystery Monitors; but the Planetary Prince represents the last effort of the Eternal Son and his Sons to draw near you. On a newly inhabited world the Planetary Prince is the sole representative of complete divinity, springing from the Creator Son (the offspring of the Universal Father and the Eternal Son) and the Divine Minister (the universe Daughter of the Infinite Spirit).

The prince of a newly inhabited world is surrounded by a loyal corps of helpers and assistants and by large numbers of the ministering spirits. But the directing corps of such new worlds must be of the lower orders of the administrators of a system in order to be innately sympathetic with, and understanding of, the planetary problems and difficulties. And all of this effort to provide sympathetic rulership for the evolutionary worlds entails the increased liability that these near-human personalities may be led astray by the exaltation of their own minds over and above the will of the Supreme Rulers.

Being quite alone as representatives of divinity on the individual planets, these Sons are tested severely, and Nebadon has suffered the misfortune of several rebellions. In the creation of the System Sovereigns and the Planetary Princes there occurs the personalization of a concept that has been getting farther and farther away from the Universal Father and the Eternal Son, and there is an increasing danger of losing the sense of proportion as to one's self-importance and a greater likelihood of failure to keep a proper grasp of the values and relationships of the numerous orders of divine beings and their gradations of authority. That the Father is not personally present in the local universe also imposes a certain test of faith and loyalty on all these Sons.

But not often do these world princes fail in their missions of organizing and administering the inhabited spheres, and their success greatly facilitates the subsequent missions of the Material Sons, who come to engraft the higher forms of creature life on the primitive men of the worlds. Their rule also does much to prepare the planets for the Paradise Sons of God, who subsequently come to judge the worlds and to inaugurate successive dispensations.

2. PLANETARY ADMINISTRATION

All Planetary Princes are under the universe administrative jurisdiction of Gabriel, the chief executive of Michael, while in immediate authority they are subject to the executive mandates of the System Sovereigns.

The Planetary Princes may at any time seek the counsel of the Melchizedeks, their former instructors and sponsors, but they are not arbitrarily required to ask for such assistance, and if such aid is not voluntarily requested, the Melchizedeks do not interfere with the planetary administration. These world rulers may also avail themselves of the advice of the four and twenty counselors, assembled from the bestowal worlds of the system. In Satania these counselors are at present all natives of Urantia. And there is an analogous council of seventy at the constellation headquarters also selected from the evolutionary beings of the realms.

The rule of the evolutionary planets in their early and unsettled careers is largely autocratic. The Planetary Princes organize their specialized groups of assistants from among their corps of planetary aids. They usually surround themselves with a supreme council of twelve, but this is variously chosen and diversely constituted on the different worlds. A Planetary Prince may also have as assistants one or more of the third order of his own group of sonship and sometimes, on certain worlds, one of his own order, a secondary Lanonandek associate.

The entire staff of a world ruler consists of personalities of the Infinite Spirit and certain types of higher evolved beings and ascending mortals from other worlds. Such a staff averages about one thousand, and as the planet progresses, this corps of helpers may be increased up to one hundred thousand or more. At any time need is felt for more helpers, the Planetary Princes have only to make request of their brothers, the System Sovereigns, and the petition is granted forthwith.

Planets vary greatly in nature and organization and in administration, but all provide for tribunals of justice. The judicial system of the local universe has its beginnings in the tribunals of a Planetary Prince, which are presided over by a member of his personal staff; the decrees of such courts reflect a highly fatherly and discretionary attitude. All problems involving more than the regulation of the planetary inhabitants are subject to appeal to the higher tribunals, but the affairs of his world domain are largely adjusted in accordance with the personal discretion of the prince.

The roving commissions of conciliators serve and supplement the planetary tribunals, and both spirit and physical controllers are subject to the findings of these conciliators. But no arbitrary execution is ever carried out without the consent of the Constellation Father, for the "Most Highs rule in the kingdoms of men."

The controllers and transformers of planetary assignment are also able to collaborate with angels and other orders of celestial beings in rendering these latter personalities visible to mortal creatures. On special occasions the seraphic helpers and even the Melchizedeks can and do make themselves visible to the inhabitants of the evolutionary worlds. The principal reason for bringing mortal ascenders from the system capital as a part of the staff of the Planetary Prince is to facilitate communication with the inhabitants of the realm.

3. THE PRINCE'S CORPOREAL STAFF

On going to a young world, a Planetary Prince usually takes with him a group of volunteer ascending beings from the local system headquarters. These ascenders accompany the prince as advisers and helpers in the work of early race improvement. This corps of material helpers constitutes the connecting link between the prince and the world races. The Urantia Prince, Caligastia, had a corps of one hundred such helpers.

Such volunteer assistants are citizens of a system capital, and none of them have fused with their indwelling Adjusters. The status of the Adjusters of such volunteer servers remains as of the residential standing on the system headquarters while these morontia progressors temporarily revert to a former material state.

The Life Carriers, the architects of form, provide such volunteers with new physical bodies, which they occupy for the periods of their planetary sojourn. These personality forms, while exempt from the ordinary diseases of the realms, are, like the early morontia bodies, subject to certain accidents of a mechanical nature.

The prince's corporeal staff are usually removed from the planet in connection with the next adjudication at the time of the second Son's arrival on the sphere. Before leaving, they customarily assign their various duties to their mutual offspring and to certain superior native volunteers. On those worlds where these helpers of the prince have been permitted to mate with the superior groups of the native races, such offspring usually succeed them.

These assistants to the Planetary Prince seldom mate with the world races, but they do always mate among themselves. Two classes of beings result from these unions: the primary type of midway creatures and certain high types of material beings who remain attached to the prince's staff after their parents have been removed from the planet at the time of the arrival of Adam and Eve. These children do not mate with the mortal races except in certain emergencies and then only by direction of the Planetary Prince. In such an event, their children—the grandchildren of the corporeal staff—are in status as of the superior races of their day and generation. All the offspring of these semimaterial assistants of the Planetary Prince are Adjuster indwelt.

At the end of the prince's dispensation, when the time comes for this "reversion staff" to be returned to the system headquarters for the resumption of the Paradise career, these ascenders present themselves to the Life Carriers for the purpose of yielding up their material bodies. They enter the transition slumber and awaken delivered from their mortal investment and clothed with morontia forms, ready for seraphic transportation back to the system capital, where their detached Adjusters await them. They are a whole dispensation behind their Jerusem class, but they have gained a unique and extraordinary experience, a rare chapter in the career of an ascending mortal.

4. THE PLANETARY HEADQUARTERS AND SCHOOLS

The prince's corporeal staff early organize the planetary schools of training and culture, wherein the cream of the evolutionary races are instructed and then sent forth to teach these better ways to their people. These schools of the prince are located at the material headquarters of the planet.

Much of the physical work connected with the establishment of this headquarters city is performed by the corporeal staff. Such headquarters cities, or settlements, of the early times of the Planetary Prince are very different from what a Urantia mortal might imagine. They are, in comparison with later ages, simple, being characterized by mineral embellishment and by relatively advanced material construction. And all of this stands in contrast with the Adamic regime centering around a garden headquarters, from which their work in behalf of the races is prosecuted during the second dispensation of the universe Sons.

In the headquarters settlement on your world every human habitation was provided with abundance of land. Although the remote tribes continued in hunting and food foraging, the students and teachers in the Prince's schools were all agriculturists and horticulturists. The time was about equally divided between the following pursuits:

1. *Physical labor.* Cultivation of the soil, associated with home building and embellishment.

2. *Social activities.* Play performances and cultural social groupings.

3. *Educational application.* Individual instruction in connection with family-group teaching, supplemented by specialized class training.

4. *Vocational training.* Schools of marriage and homemaking, the schools of art and craft training, and the classes for the training of teachers—secular, cultural, and religious.

5. *Spiritual culture.* The teacher brotherhood, the enlightenment of childhood and youth groups, and the training of adopted native children as missionaries to their people.

A Planetary Prince is not visible to mortal beings; it is a test of faith to believe the representations of the semimaterial beings of his staff. But these schools of culture and training are well adapted to the needs of each planet, and there soon develops a keen and laudatory rivalry among the races of men in their efforts to gain entrance to these various institutions of learning.

From such a world center of culture and achievement there gradually radiates to all peoples an uplifting and civilizing influence which slowly and certainly transforms the evolutionary races. Meantime the educated and spiritualized children of the surrounding peoples who have been adopted and trained in the prince's schools are returning to their native groups and, to the best of their ability, are there establishing new and potent centers of learning and culture which they carry on according to the plan of the prince's schools.

On Urantia these plans for planetary progress and cultural advancement were well under way, proceeding most satisfactorily, when the whole enterprise was brought to a rather sudden and most inglorious end by Caligastia's adherence to the Lucifer rebellion.

It was one of the most profoundly shocking episodes of this rebellion for me to learn of the callous perfidy of one of my own order of sonship, Caligastia, who, in deliberation and with malice aforethought, systematically perverted the instruction and poisoned the teaching provided in all the Urantia planetary schools in operation at that time. The wreck of these schools was speedy and complete.

Many of the offspring of the ascenders of the Prince's materialized staff remained loyal, deserting the ranks of Caligastia. These loyalists were encouraged by the Melchizedek receivers of Urantia, and in later times their descendants did much to uphold the planetary concepts of truth and righteousness. The work of these loyal evangels helped to prevent the total obliteration of spiritual truth on Urantia. These courageous souls and their descendants kept alive some knowledge of the Father's rule and preserved for the world races the concept of the successive planetary dispensations of the various orders of divine Sons.

5. PROGRESSIVE CIVILIZATION

The loyal princes of the inhabited worlds are permanently attached to the planets of their original assignment. Paradise Sons and their dispensations may come and go, but a successful Planetary Prince continues on as the ruler of his realm. His work is quite independent of the missions of the higher Sons, being designed to foster the development of planetary civilization.

The progress of civilization is hardly alike on any two planets. The details of the unfoldment of mortal evolution are very different on numerous dissimilar worlds. Notwithstanding these many diversifications of planetary development along physical, intellectual, and social lines, all evolutionary spheres progress in certain well-defined directions.

Under the benign rule of a Planetary Prince, augmented by the Material Sons and punctuated by the periodic missions of the Paradise Sons, the mortal races on an average world of time and space will successively pass through the following seven developmental epochs:

1. *The nutrition epoch.* The prehuman creatures and the dawn races of primitive man are chiefly concerned with food problems. These evolving beings spend their waking hours either in seeking food or in fighting, offensively or defensively. The food quest is paramount in the minds of these early ancestors of subsequent civilization.

2. *The security age.* Just as soon as the primitive hunter can spare any time from the search for food, he turns this leisure to augmenting his security.

More and more attention is devoted to the technique of war. Homes are fortified, and the clans are solidified by mutual fear and by the inculcation of hate for foreign groups. Self-preservation is a pursuit which always follows self-maintenance.

3. *The material-comfort era.* After food problems have been partially solved and some degree of security has been attained, the additional leisure is utilized to promote personal comfort. Luxury vies with necessity in occupying the center of the stage of human activities. Such an age is all too often characterized by tyranny, intolerance, gluttony, and drunkenness. The weaker elements of the races incline towards excesses and brutality. Gradually these pleasure-seeking weaklings are subjugated by the more strong and truth-loving elements of the advancing civilization.

4. *The quest for knowledge and wisdom.* Food, security, pleasure, and leisure provide the foundation for the development of culture and the spread of knowledge. The effort to execute knowledge results in wisdom, and when a culture has learned how to profit and improve by experience, civilization has really arrived. Food, security, and material comfort still dominate society, but many forward-looking individuals are hungering for knowledge and thirsting for wisdom. Every child is provided an opportunity to learn by doing; education is the watchword of these ages.

5. *The epoch of philosophy and brotherhood.* When mortals learn to think and begin to profit by experience, they become philosophical—they start out to reason within themselves and to exercise discriminative judgment. The society of this age becomes ethical, and the mortals of such an era are truly becoming moral beings. Wise moral beings are capable of establishing human brotherhood on such a progressing world. Ethical and moral beings can learn how to live in accordance with the golden rule.

6. *The age of spiritual striving.* When evolving mortals have passed through the physical, intellectual, and social stages of development, sooner or later they attain those levels of personal insight which impel them to seek for spiritual satisfactions and cosmic understandings. Religion is completing the ascent from the emotional domains of fear and superstition to the high levels of cosmic wisdom and personal spiritual experience. Education aspires to the attainment of meanings, and culture grasps at cosmic relationships and true values. Such evolving mortals are genuinely cultured, truly educated, and exquisitely God-knowing.

7. *The era of light and life.* This is the flowering of the successive ages of physical security, intellectual expansion, social culture, and spiritual achievement. These human accomplishments are now blended, associated, and co-ordinated in cosmic unity and unselfish service. Within the limitations of finite nature and material endowments there are no bounds set upon the possibilities of evolutionary attainment by the advancing generations who successively live upon these supernal and settled worlds of time and space.

After serving their spheres through successive dispensations of world history and the progressing epochs of planetary progress, the Planetary Princes are elevated to the position of Planetary Sovereigns upon the inauguration of the era of light and life.

6. PLANETARY CULTURE

The isolation of Urantia renders it impossible to undertake the presentation of many details of the life and environment of your Satania neighbors. In these presentations we are limited by the planetary quarantine and by the system isolation. We must be guided by these restrictions in all our efforts to enlighten Urantia mortals, but in so far as is permissible, you have been instructed in the progress of an average evolutionary world, and you are able to compare such a world's career with the present state of Urantia.

The development of civilization on Urantia has not differed so greatly from that of other worlds which have sustained the misfortune of spiritual isolation. But when compared with the loyal worlds of the universe, your planet seems most confused and greatly retarded in all phases of intellectual progress and spiritual attainment.

Because of your planetary misfortunes, Urantians are prevented from understanding very much about the culture of normal worlds. But you should not envisage the evolutionary worlds, even the most ideal, as spheres whereon life is a flowery bed of ease. The initial life of the mortal races is always attended by struggle. Effort and decision are an essential part of the acquirement of survival values.

Culture presupposes quality of mind; culture cannot be enhanced unless mind is elevated. Superior intellect will seek a noble culture and find some way to attain such a goal. Inferior minds will spurn the highest culture even when presented to them ready-made. Much depends, also, upon the successive missions of the divine Sons and upon the extent to which enlightenment is received by the ages of their respective dispensations.

You should not forget that for two hundred thousand years all the worlds of Satania have rested under the spiritual ban of Norlatiadek in consequence of the Lucifer rebellion. And it will require age upon age to retrieve the resultant handicaps of sin and secession. Your world still continues to pursue an irregular and checkered career as a result of the double tragedy of a rebellious Planetary Prince and a defaulting Material Son. Even the bestowal of Christ Michael on Urantia did not immediately set aside the temporal consequences of these serious blunders in the earlier administration of the world.

7. THE REWARDS OF ISOLATION

On first thought it might appear that Urantia and its associated isolated worlds are most unfortunate in being deprived of the beneficent presence and influence of such superhuman personalities as a Planetary Prince and a Material Son and Daughter. But isolation of these spheres affords their races a unique opportunity for the exercise of faith and for the development of a peculiar quality of confidence in cosmic reliability which is not dependent on sight or any other material consideration. It may turn out, eventually, that mortal creatures hailing from the worlds quarantined in consequence of rebellion are extremely fortunate. We have discovered that such ascenders are very early intrusted with numerous special assignments to cosmic undertakings where unquestioned faith and sublime confidence are essential to achievement.

On Jerusem the ascenders from these isolated worlds occupy a residential sector by themselves and are known as the *agondonters,* meaning evolutionary will creatures who can believe without seeing, persevere when isolated, and triumph over insuperable difficulties even when alone. This functional grouping of the agondonters persists throughout the ascension of the local universe and the traversal of the superuniverse; it disappears during the sojourn in Havona but promptly reappears upon the attainment of Paradise and definitely persists in the Corps of the Mortal Finality. Tabamantia is an *agondonter* of finaliter status, having survived from one of the quarantined spheres involved in the first rebellion ever to take place in the universes of time and space.

All through the Paradise career, reward follows effort as the result of causes. Such rewards set off the individual from the average, provide a differential of creature experience, and contribute to the versatility of ultimate performances in the collective body of the finaliters.

[Presented by a Secondary Lanonandek Son of the Reserve Corps.]

PAPER 51

THE PLANETARY ADAMS

DURING the dispensation of a Planetary Prince, primitive man reaches the limit of natural evolutionary development, and this biologic attainment signals the System Sovereign to dispatch to such a world the second order of sonship, the biologic uplifters. These Sons, for there are two of them —the Material Son and Daughter—are usually known on a planet as Adam and Eve. The original Material Son of Satania is Adam, and those who go to the system worlds as biologic uplifters always carry the name of this first and original Son of their unique order.

These Sons are the material gift of the Creator Son to the inhabited worlds. Together with the Planetary Prince, they remain on their planet of assignment throughout the evolutionary course of such a sphere. Such an adventure on a world having a Planetary Prince is not much of a hazard, but on an apostate planet, a realm without a spiritual ruler and deprived of interplanetary communication, such a mission is fraught with grave danger.

Although you cannot hope to know all about the work of these Sons on all the worlds of Satania and other systems, other papers depict more fully the life and experiences of the interesting pair, Adam and Eve, who came from the corps of the biologic uplifters of Jerusem to upstep the Urantia races. While there was a miscarriage of the ideal plans for improving your native races, still, Adam's mission was not in vain; Urantia has profited immeasurably from the gift of Adam and Eve, and among their fellows and in the councils on high their work is not reckoned as a total loss.

1. ORIGIN AND NATURE OF THE MATERIAL SONS OF GOD

The material or sex Sons and Daughters are the offspring of the Creator Son; the Universe Mother Spirit does not participate in the production of these beings who are destined to function as physical uplifters on the evolutionary worlds.

The material order of sonship is not uniform throughout the local universe. The Creator Son produces only one pair of these beings in each local system; these original pairs are diverse in nature, being attuned to the life pattern of their respective systems. This is a necessary provision since otherwise the reproductive potential of the Adams would be nonfunctional with that of the evolving mortal beings of the worlds of any one particular system. The Adam and Eve who came to Urantia were descended from the original Satania pair of Material Sons.

Material Sons vary in height from eight to ten feet, and their bodies glow with the brilliance of radiant light of a violet hue. While material blood circulates through their material bodies, they are also surcharged with divine energy and saturated with celestial light. These Material Sons (the Adams) and Material Daughters (the Eves) are equal to each other, differing only in reproductive nature and in certain chemical endowments. They are equal but differential, male and female—hence complemental—and are designed to serve on almost all assignments in pairs.

The Material Sons enjoy a dual nutrition; they are really dual in nature and constitution, partaking of materialized energy much as do the physical beings of the realm, while their immortal existence is fully maintained by the direct and automatic intake of certain sustaining cosmic energies. Should they fail on some mission of assignment or even consciously and deliberately rebel, this order of Sons becomes isolated, cut off from connection with the universe source of light and life. Thereupon they become practically material beings, destined to take the course of material life on the world of their assignment and compelled to look to the universe magistrates for adjudication. Material death will eventually terminate the planetary career of such an unfortunate and unwise Material Son or Daughter.

An original or directly created Adam and Eve are immortal by inherent endowment just as are all other orders of local universe sonship, but a diminution of immortality potential characterizes their sons and daughters. This original couple cannot transmit unconditioned immortality to their procreated sons and daughters. Their progeny are dependent for continuing life on unbroken intellectual synchrony with the mind-gravity circuit of the Spirit. Since the inception of the system of Satania, thirteen Planetary Adams have been lost in rebellion and default and 681,204 in the subordinate positions of trust. Most of these defections occurred at the time of the Lucifer rebellion.

While living as permanent citizens on the system capitals, even when functioning on descending missions to the evolutionary planets, the Material Sons do not possess Thought Adjusters, but it is through these very services that they acquire experiential capacity for Adjuster indwellment and the Paradise ascension career. These unique and wonderfully useful beings are the connecting links between the spiritual and physical worlds. They are concentrated on the system headquarters, where they reproduce and carry on as material citizens of the realm, and whence they are dispatched to the evolutionary worlds.

Unlike the other created Sons of planetary service, the material order of sonship is not, by nature, invisible to material creatures like the inhabitants of Urantia. These Sons of God can be seen, understood, and can, in turn, actually mingle with the creatures of time, could even procreate with them, though this role of biologic upliftment usually falls to the progeny of the Planetary Adams.

On Jerusem the loyal children of any Adam and Eve are immortal, but the offspring of a Material Son and Daughter procreated subsequent to their arrival on an evolutionary planet are not thus immune to natural death. There occurs a change in the life-transmitting mechanism when these Sons are rematerialized for reproductive function on an evolutionary world. The Life Carriers designedly deprive the Planetary Adams and Eves of the power of begetting undying sons and daughters. If they do not default, an Adam and Eve on a planetary mission can live on indefinitely, but within certain limits their children experience decreasing longevity with each succeeding generation.

2. TRANSIT OF THE PLANETARY ADAMS

Upon receipt of the news that another inhabited world has attained the height of physical evolution, the System Sovereign convenes the corps of Material Sons and Daughters on the system capital; and following the discussion of the needs of such an evolutionary world, two of the volunteering group—an Adam and an Eve of the senior corps of Material Sons—are selected to undertake the adventure, to submit to the deep sleep preparatory to being enseraphimed and transported from their home of associated service to the new realm of new opportunities and new dangers.

Adams and Eves are semimaterial creatures and, as such, are not transportable by seraphim. They must undergo dematerialization on the system capital before they can be enseraphimed for transport to the world of assignment. The transport seraphim are able to effect such changes in the Material Sons and in other semimaterial beings as enable them to be enseraphimed and thus to be transported through space from one world or system to another. About three days of standard time are consumed in this transport preparation, and it requires the co-operation of a Life Carrier to restore such a dematerialized creature to normal existence upon arrival at the end of the seraphic-transport journey.

While there is this dematerializing technique for preparing the Adams for transit from Jerusem to the evolutionary worlds, there is no equivalent method for taking them away from such worlds unless the entire planet is to be emptied, in which event emergency installation of the dematerialization technique is made for the entire salvable population. If some physical catastrophe should doom the planetary residence of an evolving race, the Melchizedeks and the Life Carriers would install the technique of dematerialization for all survivors, and by seraphic transport these beings would be carried away to the new world prepared for their continuing existence. The evolution of a human race, once initiated on a world of space, must proceed quite independently of the physical survival of that planet, but during the evolutionary ages it is not otherwise intended that a Planetary Adam or Eve shall leave their chosen world.

Upon arrival at their planetary destination the Material Son and Daughter are rematerialized under the direction of the Life Carriers. This entire process takes ten to twenty-eight days of Urantia time. The unconsciousness of the seraphic slumber continues throughout this entire period of reconstruction. When the reassembly of the physical organism is completed, these Material Sons and Daughters stand in their new homes and on their new worlds to all intents and purposes just as they were before submitting to the dematerializing process on Jerusem.

3. THE ADAMIC MISSIONS

On the inhabited worlds the Material Sons and Daughters construct their own garden homes, soon being assisted by their own children. Usually the site of the garden has been selected by the Planetary Prince, and his corporeal staff do much of the preliminary work of preparation with the help of many of the higher types of native races.

These Gardens of Eden are so named in honor of Edentia, the constellation capital, and because they are patterned after the botanic grandeur of the headquarters world of the Most High Fathers. Such garden homes are usually located in a secluded section and in a near-tropic zone. They are wonderful creations on an average world. You can judge nothing of these beautiful centers of culture by the fragmentary account of the aborted development of such an undertaking on Urantia.

A Planetary Adam and Eve are, in potential, the full gift of physical grace to the mortal races. The chief business of such an imported pair is to multiply and to uplift the children of time. But there is no immediate interbreeding between the people of the garden and those of the world; for many generations Adam and Eve remain biologically segregated from the evolutionary mortals while they build up a strong race of their order. This is the origin of the violet race on the inhabited worlds.

The plans for race upstepping are prepared by the Planetary Prince and his staff and are executed by Adam and Eve. And this was where your Material Son and his companion were placed at great disadvantage when they arrived on Urantia. Caligastia offered crafty and effective opposition to the Adamic mission; and notwithstanding that the Melchizedek receivers of Urantia had duly warned both Adam and Eve concerning the planetary dangers inherent in the presence of the rebellious Planetary Prince, this archrebel, by a wily stratagem, outmaneuvered the Edenic pair and entrapped them into a violation of the covenant of their trusteeship as the visible rulers of your world. The traitorous Planetary Prince did succeed in compromising your Adam and Eve, but he failed in his effort to involve them in the Lucifer rebellion.

The fifth order of angels, the planetary helpers, are attached to the Adamic mission, always accompanying the Planetary Adams on their world adventures. The corps of initial assignment is usually about one hundred thousand. When the work of the Urantia Adam and Eve was prematurely launched, when they departed from the ordained plan, it was one of the seraphic Voices of the Garden who remonstrated with them concerning their reprehensible conduct. And your narrative of this occurrence well illustrates the manner in which your planetary traditions have tended to ascribe everything supernatural to the Lord God. Because of this, Urantians have often become confused concerning the nature of the Universal Father since the words and acts of all his associates and subordinates have been so generally attributed to him. In the case of Adam and Eve, the angel of the Garden was none other than the chief of the planetary helpers then on duty. This seraphim, Solonia, proclaimed the miscarriage of the divine plan and requisitioned the return of the Melchizedek receivers to Urantia.

The secondary midway creatures are indigenous to the Adamic missions. As with the corporeal staff of the Planetary Prince, the descendants of the Material Sons and Daughters are of two orders: their physical children and the secondary order of midway creatures. These material but ordinarily invisible planetary ministers contribute much to the advancement of civilization and even to the subjection of insubordinate minorities who may seek to subvert social development and spiritual progress.

The secondary midwayers should not be confused with the primary order, who date from the near times of the arrival of the Planetary Prince. On Urantia a majority of these earlier midway creatures went into rebellion with Caligastia and have, since Pentecost, been interned. Many of the Adamic group who did not remain loyal to the planetary administration are likewise interned.

On the day of Pentecost the loyal primary and the secondary midwayers effected a voluntary union and have functioned as one unit in world affairs ever since. They serve under the leadership of loyal midwayers alternately chosen from the two groups.

Your world has been visited by four orders of sonship: Caligastia, the Planetary Prince; Adam and Eve of the Material Sons of God; Machiventa Melchizedek, the "sage of Salem" in the days of Abraham; and Christ Michael, who came as the Paradise bestowal Son. How much more effective and beautiful it would have been had Michael, the supreme ruler of the universe of Nebadon, been welcomed to your world by a loyal and efficient Planetary Prince and a devoted and successful Material Son, both of whom could have done so much to enhance the lifework and mission of the bestowal Son! But not all worlds have been so unfortunate as Urantia, neither has the mission of the Planetary Adams always been so difficult or so hazardous. When they are successful, they contribute to the development of a great people, continuing as the visible heads of planetary affairs even far into the age when such a world is settled in light and life.

4. THE SIX EVOLUTIONARY RACES

The race of dominance during the early ages of the inhabited worlds is the red man, who ordinarily is the first to attain human levels of development. But while the red man is the senior race of the planets, the succeeding colored peoples begin to make their appearances very early in the age of mortal emergence.

The earlier races are somewhat superior to the later; the red man stands far above the indigo—black—race. The Life Carriers impart the full bestowal of the living energies to the initial or red race, and each succeeding evolutionary manifestation of a distinct group of mortals represents variation at the expense of the original endowment. Even mortal stature tends to decrease from the red man down to the indigo race, although on Urantia unexpected strains of giantism appeared among the green and orange peoples.

On those worlds having all six evolutionary races the superior peoples are the first, third, and fifth races—the red, the yellow, and the blue. The evolutionary races thus alternate in capacity for intellectual growth and spiritual development, the second, fourth, and sixth being somewhat less endowed. These secondary races are the peoples that are missing on certain worlds; they are the ones that have been exterminated on many others. It is a misfortune on Urantia that you so largely lost your superior blue men, except as they persist in your amalgamated "white race." The loss of your orange and green stocks is not of such serious concern.

The evolution of six—or of three—colored races, while seeming to deteriorate the original endowment of the red man, provides certain very desirable variations in mortal types and affords an otherwise unattainable expression of diverse human potentials. These modifications are beneficial to the progress of mankind as a whole provided they are subsequently upstepped by the imported Adamic or violet race. On Urantia this usual plan of amalgamation was not extensively carried out, and this failure to execute the plan of race evolution makes it impossible for you to understand very much about the status of these peoples on an average inhabited planet by observing the remnants of these early races on your world.

In the early days of racial development there is a slight tendency for the red, the yellow, and the blue men to interbreed; there is a similar tendency for the orange, green, and indigo races to intermingle.

The more backward humans are usually employed as laborers by the more progressive races. This accounts for the origin of slavery on the planets during the early ages. The orange men are usually subdued by the red and reduced to the status of servants—sometimes exterminated. The yellow and red men often fraternize, but not always. The yellow race usually enslaves the green, while the blue man subdues the indigo. These races of primitive men think no more of utilizing the services of their backward fellows in compulsory labor than Urantians would of buying and selling horses and cattle.

On most normal worlds involuntary servitude does not survive the dispensation of the Planetary Prince, although mental defectives and social delinquents are often still compelled to perform involuntary labor. But on all normal spheres this sort of primitive slavery is abolished soon after the arrival of the imported violet or Adamic race.

These six evolutionary races are destined to be blended and exalted by amalgamation with the progeny of the Adamic uplifters. But before these peoples are blended, the inferior and unfit are largely eliminated. The Planetary Prince and the Material Son, with other suitable planetary authorities, pass upon the fitness of the reproducing strains. The difficulty of executing such a radical program on Urantia consists in the absence of competent judges to pass upon the biologic fitness or unfitness of the individuals of your world races. Notwithstanding this obstacle, it seems that you ought to be able to agree upon the biologic disfellowshiping of your more markedly unfit, defective, degenerate, and antisocial stocks.

5. RACIAL AMALGAMATION— BESTOWAL OF THE ADAMIC BLOOD

When a Planetary Adam and Eve arrive on an inhabited world, they have been fully instructed by their superiors as to the best way to effect the improvement of the existing races of intelligent beings. The plan of procedure is not uniform; much is left to the judgment of the ministering pair, and mistakes are not infrequent, especially on disordered, insurrectionary worlds, such as Urantia.

Usually the violet peoples do not begin to amalgamate with the planetary natives until their own group numbers over one million. But in the meantime the staff of the Planetary Prince proclaims that the children of the Gods have come down, as it were, to be one with the races of men; and the people eagerly look forward to the day when announcement will be made that those who have qualified as belonging to the superior racial strains may proceed to the Garden of Eden and be there chosen by the sons and daughters of Adam as the evolutionary fathers and mothers of the new and blended order of mankind.

On normal worlds the Planetary Adam and Eve never mate with the evolutionary races. This work of biologic betterment is a function of the Adamic progeny. But these Adamites do not go out among the races; the prince's staff bring to the Garden of Eden the superior men and women for voluntary mating with the Adamic offspring. And on most worlds it is considered the highest honor to be selected as a candidate for mating with the sons and daughters of the garden.

For the first time the racial wars and other tribal struggles are diminished, while the world races increasingly strive to qualify for recognition and admission to the garden. You can at best have but a very meager idea of how this competitive struggle comes to occupy the center of all activities on a normal planet. This whole scheme of race improvement was early wrecked on Urantia.

The violet race is a monogamous people, and every evolutionary man or woman uniting with the Adamic sons and daughters pledges not to take other mates and to instruct his or her children in single-matedness. The children of each of these unions are educated and trained in the schools of the Planetary Prince and then are permitted to go forth to the race of their evolutionary parent, there to marry among the selected groups of superior mortals.

When this strain of the Material Sons is added to the evolving races of the worlds, a new and greater era of evolutionary progress is initiated. Following this procreative outpouring of imported ability and superevolutionary traits there ensues a succession of rapid strides in civilization and racial development; in one hundred thousand years more progress is made than in a million years of former struggle. On your world, even in the face of the miscarriage of the ordained plans, great progress has been made since the gift to your peoples of Adam's life plasm.

But while the pure-line children of a planetary Garden of Eden can bestow themselves upon the superior members of the evolutionary races and thereby upstep the biologic level of mankind, it would not prove beneficial for the higher strains of Urantia mortals to mate with the lower races; such an unwise procedure would jeopardize all civilization on your world. Having failed to achieve race harmonization by the Adamic technique, you must now work out your planetary problem of race improvement by other and largely human methods of adaptation and control.

6. THE EDENIC REGIME

On most of the inhabited worlds the Gardens of Eden remain as superb cultural centers and continue to function as the social patterns of planetary conduct and usage age after age. Even in early times when the violet peoples are relatively segregated, their schools receive suitable candidates from among the world races, while the industrial developments of the garden open up new channels of commercial intercourse. Thus do the Adams and Eves and their progeny contribute to the sudden expansion of culture and to the rapid improvement of the evolutionary races of their worlds. And all of these relationships are augmented and sealed by the amalgamation of the evolutionary races and the sons of Adam, resulting in the immediate upstepping of biologic status, the quickening of intellectual potential, and the enhancement of spiritual receptivity.

On normal worlds the garden headquarters of the violet race becomes the second center of world culture and, jointly with the headquarters city of the Planetary Prince, sets the pace for the development of civilization. For centuries the city headquarters schools of the Planetary Prince and the garden schools of Adam and Eve are contemporary. They are usually not very far apart, and they work together in harmonious co-operation.

Think what it would mean on your world if somewhere in the Levant there were a world center of civilization, a great planetary university of culture, which had functioned uninterruptedly for 37,000 years. And again, pause to consider how the moral authority of even such an ancient center would be reinforced were there situated not far-distant still another and older headquarters of celestial ministry whose traditions would exert a cumulative force of 500,000 years of integrated evolutionary influence. It is custom which eventually spreads the ideals of Eden to a whole world.

The schools of the Planetary Prince are primarily concerned with philosophy, religion, morals, and the higher intellectual and artistic achievements. The garden schools of Adam and Eve are usually devoted to practical arts, fundamental intellectual training, social culture, economic development, trade relations, physical efficiency, and civil government. Eventually these world centers amalgamate, but this actual affiliation sometimes does not occur until the times of the first Magisterial Son.

The continuing existence of the Planetary Adam and Eve, together with the pure-line nucleus of the violet race, imparts that stability of growth to Edenic culture by virtue of which it comes to act upon the civilization of a world with the compelling force of tradition. In these immortal Material Sons and Daughters we encounter the last and the indispensable link connecting God with man, bridging the almost infinite gulf between the eternal Creator and the lowest finite personalities of time. Here is a being of high origin who is physical, material, even a sex creature like Urantia mortals, one who can see and comprehend the invisible Planetary Prince and interpret him to the mortal creatures of the realm, for the Material Sons and Daughters are able to see all of the lower orders of spirit beings; they visualize the Planetary Prince and his entire staff, visible and invisible.

With the passing of centuries, through the amalgamation of their progeny with the races of men, this same Material Son and Daughter become accepted as the common ancestors of mankind, the common parents of the now blended descendants of the evolutionary races. It is intended that mortals who start out from an inhabited world have the experience of recognizing seven fathers:

1. The biologic father—the father in the flesh.

2. The father of the realm—the Planetary Adam.

3. The father of the spheres—the System Sovereign.

4. The Most High Father—the Constellation Father.

5. The universe Father—the Creator Son and supreme ruler of the local creations.

6. The super-Fathers—the Ancients of Days who govern the superuniverse.

7. The spirit or Havona Father—the Universal Father, who dwells on Paradise and bestows his spirit to live and work in the minds of the lowly creatures who inhabit the universe of universes.

7. UNITED ADMINISTRATION

From time to time the Avonal Sons of Paradise come to the inhabited worlds for judicial actions, but the first Avonal to arrive on a magisterial mission inaugurates the fourth dispensation of an evolutionary world of time and space. On some planets where this Magisterial Son is universally accepted, he remains for one age; and thus the planet prospers under the joint rulership of three Sons: the Planetary Prince, the Material Son, and the Magisterial Son, the latter two being visible to all the inhabitants of the realm.

Before the first Magisterial Son concludes his mission on a normal evolutionary world, there has been effected the union of the educational and administrative work of the Planetary Prince and the Material Son. This amalgamation of the dual supervision of a planet brings into existence a new and effective order of world administration. Upon the retirement of the Magisterial Son the Planetary Adam assumes the outward direction of the sphere. The Material Son and Daughter thus act jointly as planetary administrators until the settling of the world in the era of light and life; whereupon the Planetary Prince is elevated to the position of Planetary Sovereign. During this age of advanced evolution, Adam and Eve become what might be called joint prime ministers of the glorified realm.

As soon as the new and consolidated capital of the evolving world has become well established, and just as fast as competent subordinate administrators can be properly trained, subcapitals are founded on remote land bodies and among the different peoples. Before the arrival of another dispensational Son, from fifty to one hundred of these subcenters will have been organized.

The Planetary Prince and his staff still foster the spiritual and philosophic domains of activity. Adam and Eve pay particular attention to the physical, scientific, and economic status of the realm. Both groups equally devote their energies to the promotion of the arts, social relations, and intellectual achievements.

By the time of the inauguration of the fifth dispensation of world affairs, a magnificent administration of planetary activities has been achieved. Mortal existence on such a well-managed sphere is indeed stimulating and profitable. And if Urantians could only observe life on such a planet, they would immediately appreciate the value of those things which their world has lost through embracing evil and participating in rebellion.

[Presented by a Secondary Lanonandek Son of the Reserve Corps.]

PAPER 52
PLANETARY MORTAL EPOCHS

FROM the inception of life on an evolutionary planet to the time of its final flowering in the era of light and life, there appear upon the stage of world action at least seven epochs of human life. These successive ages are determined by the planetary missions of the divine Sons, and on an average inhabited world these epochs appear in the following order:

1. Pre-Planetary Prince Man.
2. Post-Planetary Prince Man.
3. Post-Adamic Man.
4. Post-Magisterial Son Man.
5. Post-Bestowal Son Man.
6. Post-Teacher Son Man.
7. The Era of Light and Life.

The worlds of space, as soon as they are physically suitable for life, are placed on the registry of the Life Carriers, and in due time these Sons are dispatched to such planets for the purpose of initiating life. The entire period from life initiation to the appearance of man is designated the prehuman era and precedes the successive mortal epochs considered in this narrative.

1. PRIMITIVE MAN

From the time of man's emergence from the animal level—when he can choose to worship the Creator—to the arrival of the Planetary Prince, mortal will creatures are called *primitive men.* There are six basic types or races of primitive men, and these early peoples successively appear in the order of the spectrum colors, beginning with the red. The length of time consumed in this early life evolution varies greatly on the different worlds, ranging from one hundred and fifty thousand years to over one million years of Urantia time.

The evolutionary races of color—red, orange, yellow, green, blue, and indigo —begin to appear about the time that primitive man is developing a simple language and is beginning to exercise the creative imagination. By this time man is well accustomed to standing erect.

Primitive men are mighty hunters and fierce fighters. The law of this age is the physical survival of the fittest; the government of these times is wholly tribal. During the early racial struggles on many worlds some of the evolutionary races are obliterated, as occurred on Urantia. Those who survive are usually subsequently blended with the later imported violet race, the Adamic peoples.

In the light of subsequent civilization, this era of primitive man is a long, dark, and bloody chapter. The ethics of the jungle and the morals of the primeval forests are not in keeping with the standards of later dispensations of revealed religion and higher spiritual development. On normal and nonexperimental worlds this epoch is very different from the prolonged and extraordinarily brutal struggles which characterized this age on Urantia. When you have emerged from your first world experience, you will begin to see why this long and painful struggle on the evolutionary worlds occurs, and as you go forward in the Paradise path, you will increasingly understand the wisdom of these apparently strange doings. But notwithstanding all the vicissitudes of the early ages of human emergence, the performances of primitive man represent a splendid, even a heroic, chapter in the annals of an evolutionary world of time and space.

Early evolutionary man is not a colorful creature. In general, these primitive mortals are cave dwellers or cliff residents. They also build crude huts in the large trees. Before they acquire a high order of intelligence, the planets are sometimes overrun with the larger types of animals. But early in this era mortals learn to kindle and maintain fire, and with the increase of inventive imagination and the improvement in tools, evolving man soon vanquishes the larger and more unwieldy animals. The early races also make extensive use of the larger flying animals. These enormous birds are able to carry one or two average-sized men for a nonstop flight of over five hundred miles. On some planets these birds are of great service since they possess a high order of intelligence, often being able to speak many words of the languages of the realm. These birds are most intelligent, very obedient, and unbelievably affectionate. Such passenger birds have been long extinct on Urantia, but your early ancestors enjoyed their services.

Man's acquirement of ethical judgment, moral will, is usually coincident with the appearance of early language. Upon attaining the human level, after this emergence of mortal will, these beings become receptive to the temporary indwelling of the divine Adjusters, and upon death many are duly elected as survivors and sealed by the archangels for subsequent resurrection and Spirit fusion. The archangels always accompany the Planetary Princes, and a dispensational adjudication of the realm is simultaneous with the prince's arrival.

All mortals who are indwelt by Thought Adjusters are potential worshipers; they have been "lighted by the true light," and they possess capacity for seeking reciprocal contact with divinity. Nevertheless, the early or biologic religion of primitive man is largely a persistence of animal fear coupled with ignorant awe and tribal superstition. The survival of superstition in the Urantia races is hardly complimentary to your evolutionary development nor compatible with your otherwise splendid achievements in material progress. But this early fear religion serves a very valuable purpose in subduing the fiery tempers of these primitive creatures. It is the forerunner of civilization and the soil for the subsequent planting of the seeds of revealed religion by the Planetary Prince and his ministers.

Within one hundred thousand years from the time man acquires erect posture, the Planetary Prince usually arrives, having been dispatched by the System Sovereign upon the report of the Life Carriers that will is functioning, even though comparatively few individuals have thus developed. Primitive mortals usually welcome the Planetary Prince and his visible staff; in fact, they often look upon them with awe and reverence, almost with worshipfulness, if they are not restrained.

2. POST-PLANETARY PRINCE MAN

With the arrival of the Planetary Prince a new dispensation begins. Government appears on earth, and the advanced tribal epoch is attained. Great social strides are made during a few thousand years of this regime. Under normal conditions mortals attain a high state of civilization during this age. They do not struggle so long in barbarism as did the Urantia races. But life on an inhabited world is so changed by rebellion that you can have little or no idea of such a regime on a normal planet.

The average length of this dispensation is around five hundred thousand years, some longer, some shorter. During this era the planet is established in the circuits of the system, and a full quota of seraphic and other celestial helpers is assigned to its administration. The Thought Adjusters come in increasing numbers, and the seraphic guardians amplify their regime of mortal supervision.

When the Planetary Prince arrives on a primitive world, the evolved religion of fear and ignorance prevails. The prince and his staff make the first revelations of higher truth and universe organization. These initial presentations of revealed religion are very simple, and they usually pertain to the affairs of the local system. Religion is wholly an evolutionary process prior to the arrival of the Planetary Prince. Subsequently, religion progresses by graduated revelation as well as by evolutionary growth. Each dispensation, each mortal epoch, receives an enlarged presentation of spiritual truth and religious ethics. The evolution of the religious capacity of receptivity in the inhabitants of a world largely determines their rate of spiritual advancement and the extent of religious revelation.

This dispensation witnesses a spiritual dawn, and the different races and their various tribes tend to develop specialized systems of religious and philosophic thought. There uniformly run through all of these racial religions two strains: the early fears of primitive men and the later revelations of the Planetary Prince. In some respects Urantians do not seem to have wholly emerged from this stage of planetary evolution. As you pursue this study, you will the more clearly discern how far your world departs from the average course of evolutionary progress and development.

But the Planetary Prince is not "the Prince of Peace." Racial struggles and tribal wars continue over into this dispensation but with diminishing frequency and severity. This is the great age of racial dispersion, and it culminates in a period of intense nationalism. Color is the basis of tribal and national groupings, and the different races often develop separate languages. Each expanding group of mortals tends to seek isolation. This segregation is favored by the existence of many languages. Before the unification of the several races their relentless warfare sometimes results in the obliteration of whole peoples; the orange and green men are particularly subject to such extinction.

On average worlds, during the latter part of the prince's rule, national life begins to replace tribal organization or rather to be superimposed upon the existing tribal groupings. But the great social achievement of the prince's epoch is the emergence of family life. Heretofore, human relationships have been chiefly tribal; now, the home begins to materialize.

This is the dispensation of the realization of sex equality. On some planets the male may rule the female; on others the reverse prevails. During this age normal worlds establish full equality of the sexes, this being preliminary to the fuller realization of the ideals of home life. This is the dawn of the golden age of the home. The idea of tribal rule gradually gives way to the dual concept of national life and family life.

During this age agriculture makes its appearance. The growth of the family idea is incompatible with the roving and unsettled life of the hunter. Gradually the practices of settled habitations and the cultivation of the soil become established. The domestication of animals and the development of home arts proceed apace. Upon reaching the apex of biologic evolution, a high level of civilization has been attained, but there is little development of a mechanical order; invention is the characteristic of the succeeding age.

The races are purified and brought up to a high state of physical perfection and intellectual strength before the end of this era. The early development of a normal world is greatly helped by the plan of promoting the increase of the higher types of mortals with proportionate curtailment of the lower. And it is the failure of your early peoples to thus discriminate between these types that accounts for the presence of so many defective and degenerate individuals among the present-day Urantia races.

One of the great achievements of the age of the prince is this restriction of the multiplication of mentally defective and socially unfit individuals. Long before the times of the arrival of the second Sons, the Adams, most worlds seriously address themselves to the tasks of race purification, something which the Urantia peoples have not even yet seriously undertaken.

This problem of race improvement is not such an extensive undertaking when it is attacked at this early date in human evolution. The preceding period of tribal struggles and rugged competition in race survival has weeded out most of the abnormal and defective strains. An idiot does not have much chance of survival in a primitive and warring tribal social organization. It is the false sentiment of your partially perfected civilizations that fosters, protects, and perpetuates the hopelessly defective strains of evolutionary human stocks.

It is neither tenderness nor altruism to bestow futile sympathy upon degenerated human beings, unsalvable abnormal and inferior mortals. There exist on even the most normal of the evolutionary worlds sufficient differences between individuals and between numerous social groups to provide for the full exercise of all those noble traits of altruistic sentiment and unselfish mortal ministry without perpetuating the socially unfit and the morally degenerate strains of evolving humanity. There is abundant opportunity for the exercise of tolerance and the function of altruism in behalf of those unfortunate and needy individuals who have not irretrievably lost their moral heritage and forever destroyed their spiritual birthright.

3. POST-ADAMIC MAN

When the original impetus of evolutionary life has run its biologic course, when man has reached the apex of animal development, there arrives the second order of sonship, and the second dispensation of grace and ministry is inaugurated. This is true on all evolutionary worlds. When the highest possible level of evolutionary life has been attained, when primitive man has ascended as far as possible in the biologic scale, a Material Son and Daughter always appear on the planet, having been dispatched by the System Sovereign.

Thought Adjusters are increasingly bestowed upon the post-Adamic men, and in constantly augmented numbers these mortals attain capacity for subsequent Adjuster fusion. While functioning as descending Sons, the Adams do not possess Adjusters, but their planetary offspring—direct and mixed—become legitimate candidates for the reception, in due time, of the Mystery Monitors. By the termination of the post-Adamic age the planet is in possession of its full quota of celestial ministers; only the fusion Adjusters are not yet universally bestowed.

It is the prime purpose of the Adamic regime to influence evolving man to complete the transit from the hunter and herder stage of civilization to that of the agriculturist and horticulturist, to be later supplemented by the appearance of the urban and industrial adjuncts to civilization. Ten thousand years of this dispensation of the biologic uplifters is sufficient to effect a marvelous transformation. Twenty-five thousand years of such an administration of the conjoint wisdom of the Planetary Prince and the Material Sons usually ripens the sphere for the advent of a Magisterial Son.

This age usually witnesses the completion of the elimination of the unfit and the still further purification of the racial strains; on normal worlds the defective bestial tendencies are very nearly eliminated from the reproducing stocks of the realm.

The Adamic progeny never amalgamate with the inferior strains of the evolutionary races. Neither is it the divine plan for the Planetary Adam or Eve to mate, personally, with the evolutionary peoples. This race-improvement project is the task of their progeny. But the offspring of the Material Son and Daughter are mobilized for generations before the racial-amalgamation ministry is inaugurated.

The result of the gift of the Adamic life plasm to the mortal races is an immediate upstepping of intellectual capacity and an acceleration of spiritual progress. There is usually some physical improvement also. On an average world the post-Adamic dispensation is an age of great invention, energy control, and mechanical development. This is the era of the appearance of multiform manufacture and the control of natural forces; it is the golden age of exploration and the final subduing of the planet. Much of the material progress of a world occurs during this time of the inauguration of the development of the physical sciences, just such an epoch as Urantia is now experiencing. Your world is a full dispensation and more behind the average planetary schedule.

By the end of the Adamic dispensation on a normal planet the races are practically blended, so that it can be truly proclaimed that "God has made of one blood all the nations," and that his Son "has made of one color all peoples." The color of such an amalgamated race is somewhat of an olive shade of the violet hue, the racial "white" of the spheres.

Primitive man is for the most part carnivorous; the Material Sons and Daughters do not eat meat, but their offspring within a few generations usually gravitate to the omnivorous level, although whole groups of their descendants sometimes remain nonflesh eaters. This double origin of the post-Adamic races explains how such blended human stocks exhibit anatomic vestiges belonging to both the herbivorous and carnivorous animal groups.

Within ten thousand years of racial amalgamation the resultant stocks show varying degrees of anatomic blend, some strains carrying more of the marks of the nonflesh-eating ancestry, others exhibiting more of the distinguishing traits and physical characteristics of their carnivorous evolutionary progenitors. The majority of these world races soon become omnivorous, subsisting upon a wide range of viands from both the animal and vegetable kingdoms.

The post-Adamic epoch is the dispensation of internationalism. With the near completion of the task of race blending, nationalism wanes, and the brotherhood of man really begins to materialize. Representative government begins to take the place of the monarchial or paternal form of rulership. The educational system becomes world-wide, and gradually the languages of the races give way to the tongue of the violet people. Universal peace and cooperation are seldom attained until the races are fairly well blended, and until they speak a common language.

During the closing centuries of the post-Adamic age there develops new interest in art, music, and literature, and this world-wide awakening is the signal for the appearance of a Magisterial Son. The crowning development of this era is the universal interest in intellectual realities, true philosophy. Religion becomes less nationalistic, becomes more and more a planetary affair. New revelations of truth characterize these ages, and the Most Highs of the constellations begin to rule in the affairs of men. Truth is revealed up to the administration of the constellations.

Great ethical advancement characterizes this era; the brotherhood of man is the goal of its society. World-wide peace—the cessation of race conflict and national animosity—is the indicator of planetary ripeness for the advent of the third order of sonship, the Magisterial Son.

4. POST-MAGISTERIAL SON MAN

On normal and loyal planets this age opens with the mortal races blended and biologically fit. There are no race or color problems; literally all nations and races are of one blood. The brotherhood of man flourishes, and the nations are learning to live on earth in peace and tranquillity. Such a world stands on the eve of a great and culminating intellectual development.

When an evolutionary world becomes thus ripe for the magisterial age, one of the high order of Avonal Sons makes his appearance on a magisterial mission. The Planetary Prince and the Material Sons are of local universe origin; the Magisterial Son hails from Paradise.

When the Paradise Avonals come to the mortal spheres on judicial actions, solely as dispensation adjudicators, they are never incarnated. But when they come on magisterial missions, at least the initial one, they are always incarnated, though they do not experience birth, neither do they die the death of the realm. They may live on for generations in those cases where they remain as rulers on certain planets. When their missions are concluded, they yield up their planetary lives and return to their former status of divine sonship.

Each new dispensation extends the horizon of revealed religion, and the Magisterial Sons extend the revelation of truth to portray the affairs of the local universe and all its tributaries.

After the initial visitation of a Magisterial Son the races soon effect their economic liberation. The daily work required to sustain one's independence would be represented by two and one-half hours of your time. It is perfectly safe to liberate such ethical and intelligent mortals. Such refined peoples well know how to utilize leisure for self-improvement and planetary advancement. This age witnesses the further purification of the racial stocks by the restriction of reproduction among the less fit and poorly endowed individuals.

The political government and social administration of the races continue to improve, self-government being fairly well established by the end of this age. By self-government we refer to the highest type of representative government. Such worlds advance and honor only those leaders and rulers who are most fit to bear social and political responsibilities.

During this epoch the majority of the world mortals are Adjuster indwelt. But even yet the bestowal of divine Monitors is not always universal. The Adjusters of fusion destiny are not yet bestowed upon all planetary mortals; it is still necessary for the will creatures to choose the Mystery Monitors.

During the closing ages of this dispensation, society begins to return to more simplified forms of living. The complex nature of an advancing civilization is running its course, and mortals are learning to live more naturally and effectively. And this trend increases with each succeeding epoch. This is the age of the flowering of art, music, and higher learning. The physical sciences have already reached their height of development. The termination of this age, on an ideal world, witnesses the fullness of a great religious awakening, a world-wide spiritual enlightenment. And this extensive arousal of the spiritual natures of the races is the signal for the arrival of the bestowal Son and for the inauguration of the fifth mortal epoch.

On many worlds it develops that the planet is not made ready for a bestowal Son by one magisterial mission; in that event there will be a second, even a succession of Magisterial Sons, each of whom will advance the races from one dispensation to another until the planet is made ready for the gift of the bestowal Son. On the second and subsequent missions the Magisterial Sons may or may not be incarnated. But no matter how many Magisterial Sons may appear—and they may also come as such after the bestowal Son—the advent of each one marks the end of one dispensation and the beginning of another.

These dispensations of the Magisterial Sons cover anywhere from twenty-five thousand to fifty thousand years of Urantia time. Sometimes such an epoch is much shorter and in rare instances even longer. But in the fullness of time one of these same Magisterial Sons will be born as the Paradise bestowal Son.

5. POST-BESTOWAL SON MAN

When a certain standard of intellectual and spiritual development is attained on an inhabited world, a Paradise bestowal Son always arrives. On normal worlds he does not appear in the flesh until the races have ascended to the highest levels of intellectual development and ethical attainment. But on Urantia the bestowal Son, even your own Creator Son, appeared at the close of the Adamic dispensation, but that is not the usual order of events on the worlds of space.

When the worlds have become ripe for spiritualization, the bestowal Son arrives. These Sons always belong to the Magisterial or Avonal order except in that case, once in each local universe, when the Creator Son prepares for his terminal bestowal on some evolutionary world, as occurred when Michael of

Nebadon appeared on Urantia to bestow himself upon your mortal races. Only one world in near ten million can enjoy such a gift; all other worlds are spiritually advanced by the bestowal of a Paradise Son of the Avonal order.

The bestowal Son arrives on a world of high educational culture and encounters a race spiritually trained and prepared to assimilate advanced teachings and to appreciate the bestowal mission. This is an age characterized by the world-wide pursuit of moral culture and spiritual truth. The mortal passion of this dispensation is the penetration of cosmic reality and communion with spiritual reality. The revelations of truth are extended to include the superuniverse. Entirely new systems of education and government grow up to supplant the crude regimes of former times. The joy of living takes on new color, and the reactions of life are exalted to heavenly heights of tone and timbre.

The bestowal Son lives and dies for the spiritual uplift of the mortal races of a world. He establishes the "new and living way"; his life is an incarnation of Paradise truth in mortal flesh, that very truth—even the Spirit of Truth—in the knowledge of which men shall be free.

On Urantia the establishment of this "new and living way" was a matter of fact as well as of truth. The isolation of Urantia in the Lucifer rebellion had suspended the procedure whereby mortals can pass, upon death, directly to the shores of the mansion worlds. Before the days of Christ Michael on Urantia all souls slept on until the dispensational or special millennial resurrections. Even Moses was not permitted to go over to the other side until the occasion of a special resurrection, the fallen Planetary Prince, Caligastia, contesting such a deliverance. But ever since the day of Pentecost, Urantia mortals again may proceed directly to the morontia spheres.

Upon the resurrection of a bestowal Son, on the third day after yielding up his incarnated life, he ascends to the right hand of the Universal Father, receives the assurance of the acceptance of the bestowal mission, and returns to the Creator Son at the headquarters of the local universe. Thereupon the bestowal Avonal and the Creator Michael send their joint spirit, the Spirit of Truth, into the bestowal world. This is the occasion when the "spirit of the triumphant Son is poured out upon all flesh." The Universe Mother Spirit also participates in this bestowal of the Spirit of Truth, and concomitant therewith there issues the bestowal edict of the Thought Adjusters. Thereafter all normal-minded will creatures of that world will receive Adjusters as soon as they attain the age of moral responsibility, of spiritual choice.

If such a bestowal Avonal should return to a world after the bestowal mission, he would not incarnate but would come "in glory with the seraphic hosts."

The postbestowal Son age may extend from ten thousand to a hundred thousand years. There is no arbitrary time allotted to any of these dispensational eras. This is a time of great ethical and spiritual progress. Under the spiritual influence of these ages, human character undergoes tremendous transformations and experiences phenomenal development. It becomes possible to put the golden rule into practical operation. The teachings of Jesus are really applicable to a mortal world which has had the preliminary training of the prebestowal Sons with their dispensations of character ennoblement and culture augmentation.

During this era the problems of disease and delinquency are virtually solved. Degeneracy has already been largely eliminated by selective reproduction. Disease has been practically mastered through the high resistant qualities of the

Adamic strains and by the intelligent and world-wide application of the discoveries of the physical sciences of preceding ages. The average length of life, during this period, climbs well above the equivalent of three hundred years of Urantia time.

Throughout this epoch there is a gradual lessening of governmental supervision. True self-government is beginning to function; fewer and fewer restrictive laws are necessary. The military branches of national resistance are passing away; the era of international harmony is really arriving. There are many nations, mostly determined by land distribution, but only one race, one language, and one religion. Mortal affairs are almost, but not quite, utopian. This truly is a great and glorious age!

6. URANTIA'S POST-BESTOWAL AGE

The bestowal Son is the Prince of Peace. He arrives with the message, "Peace on earth and good will among men." On normal worlds this is a dispensation of world-wide peace; the nations no more learn war. But such salutary influences did not attend the coming of your bestowal Son, Christ Michael. Urantia is not proceeding in the normal order. Your world is out of step in the planetary procession. Your Master, when on earth, warned his disciples that his advent would not bring the usual reign of peace on Urantia. He distinctly told them that there would be "wars and rumors of wars," and that nation would rise against nation. At another time he said, "Think not that I have come to bring peace upon earth."

Even on normal evolutionary worlds the realization of the world-wide brotherhood of man is not an easy accomplishment. On a confused and disordered planet like Urantia such an achievement requires a much longer time and necessitates far greater effort. Unaided social evolution can hardly achieve such happy results on a spiritually isolated sphere. Religious revelation is essential to the realization of brotherhood on Urantia. While Jesus has shown the way to the immediate attainment of spiritual brotherhood, the realization of social brotherhood on your world depends much on the achievement of the following personal transformations and planetary adjustments:

1. *Social fraternity.* Multiplication of international and interracial social contacts and fraternal associations through travel, commerce, and competitive play. Development of a common language and the multiplication of multilinguists. The racial and national interchange of students, teachers, industrialists, and religious philosophers.

2. *Intellectual cross-fertilization.* Brotherhood is impossible on a world whose inhabitants are so primitive that they fail to recognize the folly of unmitigated selfishness. There must occur an exchange of national and racial literature. Each race must become familiar with the thought of all races; each nation must know the feelings of all nations. Ignorance breeds suspicion, and suspicion is incompatible with the essential attitude of sympathy and love.

3. *Ethical awakening.* Only ethical consciousness can unmask the immorality of human intolerance and the sinfulness of fratricidal strife. Only a moral conscience can condemn the evils of national envy and racial jealousy. Only moral beings will ever seek for that spiritual insight which is essential to living the golden rule.

4. *Political wisdom.* Emotional maturity is essential to self-control. Only emotional maturity will insure the substitution of international techniques of civilized adjudication for the barbarous arbitrament of war. Wise statesmen will sometime work for the welfare of humanity even while they strive to promote the interest of their national or racial groups. Selfish political sagacity is ultimately suicidal—destructive of all those enduring qualities which insure planetary group survival.

5. *Spiritual insight.* The brotherhood of man is, after all, predicated on the recognition of the fatherhood of God. The quickest way to realize the brotherhood of man on Urantia is to effect the spiritual transformation of present-day humanity. The only technique for accelerating the natural trend of social evolution is that of applying spiritual pressure from above, thus augmenting moral insight while enhancing the soul capacity of every mortal to understand and love every other mortal. Mutual understanding and fraternal love are transcendent civilizers and mighty factors in the world-wide realization of the brotherhood of man.

If you could be transplanted from your backward and confused world to some normal planet now in the postbestowal Son age, you would think you had been translated to the heaven of your traditions. You would hardly believe that you were observing the normal evolutionary workings of a mortal sphere of human habitation. These worlds are in the spiritual circuits of their realm, and they enjoy all the advantages of the universe broadcasts and the reflectivity services of the superuniverse.

7. POST-TEACHER SON MAN

The Sons of the next order to arrive on the average evolutionary world are the Trinity Teacher Sons, the divine Sons of the Paradise Trinity. Again we find Urantia out of step with its sister spheres in that your Jesus has promised to return. That promise he will certainly fulfill, but no one knows whether his second coming will precede or follow the appearances of Magisterial or Teacher Sons on Urantia.

The Teacher Sons come in groups to the spiritualizing worlds. A planetary Teacher Son is assisted and supported by seventy primary Sons, twelve secondary Sons, and three of the highest and most experienced of the supreme order of Daynals. This corps will remain for some time on the world, long enough to effect the transition from the evolutionary ages to the era of light and life—not less than one thousand years of planetary time and often considerably longer. This mission is a Trinity contribution to the antecedent efforts of all the divine personalities who have ministered to an inhabited world.

The revelation of truth is now extended to the central universe and to Paradise. The races are becoming highly spiritual. A great people has evolved and a great age is approaching. The educational, economic, and administrative systems of the planet are undergoing radical transformations. New values and relationships are being established. The kingdom of heaven is appearing on earth, and the glory of God is being shed abroad in the world.

This is the dispensation when many mortals are translated from among the living. As the era of Trinity Teacher Sons progresses, the spiritual allegiance of the mortals of time becomes more and more universal. Natural death becomes less frequent as the Adjusters increasingly fuse with their subjects during the lifetime in the flesh. The planet eventually is classed as of the primary modified order of mortal ascension.

Life during this era is pleasant and profitable. Degeneracy and the antisocial end products of the long evolutionary struggle have been virtually obliterated. The length of life approaches five hundred Urantia years, and the reproductive rate of racial increase is intelligently controlled. An entirely new order of society has arrived. There are still great differences among mortals, but the state of society more nearly approaches the ideals of social brotherhood and spiritual equality. Representative government is vanishing, and the world is passing under the rule of individual self-control. The function of government is chiefly directed to collective tasks of social administration and economic co-ordination. The golden age is coming on apace; the temporal goal of the long and intense planetary evolutionary struggle is in sight. The reward of the ages is soon to be realized; the wisdom of the Gods is about to be manifested.

The physical administration of a world during this age requires about one hour each day on the part of every adult individual; that is, the equivalent of one Urantia hour. The planet is in close touch with universe affairs, and its people scan the latest broadcasts with the same keen interest you now manifest in the latest editions of your daily newspapers. These races are occupied with a thousand things of interest unknown on your world.

Increasingly, true planetary allegiance to the Supreme Being grows. Generation after generation, more and more of the race step into line with those who practice justice and live mercy. Slowly but surely the world is being won to the joyous service of the Sons of God. The physical difficulties and material problems have been largely solved; the planet is ripening for advanced life and a more settled existence.

From time to time throughout their dispensation, Teacher Sons continue to come to these peaceful worlds. They do not leave a world until they observe that the evolutionary plan, as it concerns that planet, is working smoothly. A Magisterial Son of judgment usually accompanies the Teacher Sons on their successive missions, while another such Son functions at the time of their departure, and these judicial actions continue from age to age throughout the duration of the mortal regime of time and space.

Each recurring mission of the Trinity Teacher Sons successively exalts such a supernal world to ever-ascending heights of wisdom, spirituality, and cosmic illumination. But the noble natives of such a sphere are still finite and mortal. Nothing is perfect; nevertheless, there is evolving a quality of near perfection in the operation of an imperfect world and in the lives of its human inhabitants.

The Trinity Teacher Sons may return many times to the same world. But sooner or later, in connection with the termination of one of their missions, the Planetary Prince is elevated to the position of Planetary Sovereign, and the System Sovereign appears to proclaim the entrance of such a world upon the era of light and life.

It was of the conclusion of the terminal mission of the Teacher Sons (at least that would be the chronology on a normal world) that John wrote: "I saw a new heaven and a new earth and the new Jerusalem coming down from God out of heaven, prepared as a princess adorned for the prince."

This is the same renovated earth, the advanced planetary stage, that the olden seer envisioned when he wrote: "'For, as the new heavens and the new earth, which I will make, shall remain before me, so shall you and your children survive; and it shall come to pass that from one new moon to another and from one Sabbath to another all flesh shall come to worship before me,' says the Lord."

It is the mortals of such an age who are described as "a chosen generation, a royal priesthood, a holy nation, an exalted people; and you shall show forth the praises of Him who has called you out of darkness into this marvelous light."

No matter what the special natural history of an individual planet may be, no difference whether a realm has been wholly loyal, tainted with evil, or cursed by sin—no matter what the antecedents may be—sooner or later the grace of God and the ministry of angels will usher in the day of the advent of the Trinity Teacher Sons; and their departure, following their final mission, will inaugurate this superb era of light and life.

All the worlds of Satania can join in the hope of the one who wrote: "Nevertheless we, according to His promise, look for a new heaven and a new earth, wherein dwells righteousness. Wherefore, beloved, seeing that you look for such things, be diligent that you may be found by Him in peace, without spot and blameless."

The departure of the Teacher Son corps, at the end of their first or some subsequent reign, ushers in the dawn of the era of light and life—the threshold of the transition from time to the vestibule of eternity. The planetary realization of this era of light and life far more than equals the fondest expectations of Urantia mortals who have entertained no more farseeing concepts of the future life than those embraced within religious beliefs which depict heaven as the immediate destiny and final dwelling place of surviving mortals.

[Sponsored by a Mighty Messenger temporarily attached to the staff of Gabriel.]

PAPER 53

THE LUCIFER REBELLION

LUCIFER was a brilliant primary Lanonandek Son of Nebadon. He had experienced service in many systems, had been a high counselor of his group, and was distinguished for wisdom, sagacity, and efficiency. Lucifer was number 37 of his order, and when commissioned by the Melchizedeks, he was designated as one of the one hundred most able and brilliant personalities in more than seven hundred thousand of his kind. From such a magnificent beginning, through evil and error, he embraced sin and now is numbered as one of three System Sovereigns in Nebadon who have succumbed to the urge of self and surrendered to the sophistry of spurious personal liberty—rejection of universe allegiance and disregard of fraternal obligations, blindness to cosmic relationships.

In the universe of Nebadon, the domain of Christ Michael, there are ten thousand systems of inhabited worlds. In all the history of Lanonandek Sons, in all their work throughout these thousands of systems and at the universe headquarters, only three System Sovereigns have ever been found in contempt of the government of the Creator Son.

1. THE LEADERS OF REBELLION

Lucifer was not an ascendant being; he was a created Son of the local universe, and of him it was said: "You were perfect in all your ways from the day you were created till unrighteousness was found in you." Many times had he been in counsel with the Most Highs of Edentia. And Lucifer reigned "upon the holy mountain of God," the administrative mount of Jerusem, for he was the chief executive of a great system of 607 inhabited worlds.

Lucifer was a magnificent being, a brilliant personality; he stood next to the Most High Fathers of the constellations in the direct line of universe authority. Notwithstanding Lucifer's transgression, subordinate intelligences refrained from showing him disrespect and disdain prior to Michael's bestowal on Urantia. Even the archangel of Michael, at the time of Moses' resurrection, "did not bring against him an accusing judgment but simply said, 'the Judge rebuke you.'" Judgment in such matters belongs to the Ancients of Days, the rulers of the superuniverse.

Lucifer is now the fallen and deposed Sovereign of Satania. Self-contemplation is most disastrous, even to the exalted personalities of the celestial world. Of Lucifer it was said: "Your heart was lifted up because of your beauty; you corrupted your wisdom because of your brightness." Your olden prophet saw his sad estate when he wrote: "How are you fallen from heaven, O Lucifer, son of the morning! How are you cast down, you who dared to confuse the worlds!"

Very little was heard of Lucifer on Urantia owing to the fact that he assigned his first lieutenant, Satan, to advocate his cause on your planet. Satan was a member of the same primary group of Lanonandeks but had never functioned as a System Sovereign; he entered fully into the Lucifer insurrection. The "devil" is none other than Caligastia, the deposed Planetary Prince of Urantia and a Son of the secondary order of Lanonandeks. At the time Michael was on Urantia in the flesh, Lucifer, Satan, and Caligastia were leagued together to effect the miscarriage of his bestowal mission. But they signally failed.

Abaddon was the chief of the staff of Caligastia. He followed his master into rebellion and has ever since acted as chief executive of the Urantia rebels. Beelzebub was the leader of the disloyal midway creatures who allied themselves with the forces of the traitorous Caligastia.

The dragon eventually became the symbolic representation of all these evil personages. Upon the triumph of Michael, "Gabriel came down from Salvington and bound the dragon (all the rebel leaders) for an age." Of the Jerusem seraphic rebels it is written: "And the angels who kept not their first estate but left their own habitation, he has reserved in sure chains of darkness to the judgment of the great day."

2. THE CAUSES OF REBELLION

Lucifer and his first assistant, Satan, had reigned on Jerusem for more than five hundred thousand years when in their hearts they began to array themselves against the Universal Father and his then vicegerent Son, Michael.

There were no peculiar or special conditions in the system of Satania which suggested or favored rebellion. It is our belief that the idea took origin and form in Lucifer's mind, and that he might have instigated such a rebellion no matter where he might have been stationed. Lucifer first announced his plans to Satan, but it required several months to corrupt the mind of his able and brilliant associate. However, when once converted to the rebel theories, he became a bold and earnest advocate of "self-assertion and liberty."

No one ever suggested rebellion to Lucifer. The idea of self-assertion in opposition to the will of Michael and to the plans of the Universal Father, as they are represented in Michael, had its origin in his own mind. His relations with the Creator Son had been intimate and always cordial. At no time prior to the exaltation of his own mind did Lucifer openly express dissatisfaction about the universe administration. Notwithstanding his silence, for more than one hundred years of standard time the Union of Days on Salvington had been reflectivating to Uversa that all was not at peace in Lucifer's mind. This information was also communicated to the Creator Son and the Constellation Fathers of Norlatiadek.

Throughout this period Lucifer became increasingly critical of the entire plan of universe administration but always professed wholehearted loyalty to the Supreme Rulers. His first outspoken disloyalty was manifested on the occasion of a visit of Gabriel to Jerusem just a few days before the open proclamation of the Lucifer Declaration of Liberty. Gabriel was so profoundly impressed with the certainty of the impending outbreak that he went direct to Edentia to confer with the Constellation Fathers regarding the measures to be employed in case of open rebellion.

It is very difficult to point out the exact cause or causes which finally culminated in the Lucifer rebellion. We are certain of only one thing, and that is: Whatever these first beginnings were, they had their origin in Lucifer's mind. There must have been a pride of self that nourished itself to the point of self-deception, so that Lucifer for a time really persuaded himself that his contemplation of rebellion was actually for the good of the system, if not of the universe. By the time his plans had developed to the point of disillusionment, no doubt he had gone too far for his original and mischief-making pride to permit him to stop. At some point in this experience he became insincere, and evil evolved into deliberate and willful sin. That this happened is proved by the subsequent conduct of this brilliant executive. He was long offered opportunity for repentance, but only some of his subordinates ever accepted the proffered mercy. The Faithful of Days of Edentia, on the request of the Constellation Fathers, in person presented the plan of Michael for the saving of these flagrant rebels, but always was the mercy of the Creator Son rejected and rejected with increasing contempt and disdain.

3. THE LUCIFER MANIFESTO

Whatever the early origins of trouble in the hearts of Lucifer and Satan, the final outbreak took form as the Lucifer Declaration of Liberty. The cause of the rebels was stated under three heads:

1. *The reality of the Universal Father.* Lucifer charged that the Universal Father did not really exist, that physical gravity and space-energy were inherent in the universe, and that the Father was a myth invented by the Paradise Sons to enable them to maintain the rule of the universes in the Father's name. He denied that personality was a gift of the Universal Father. He even intimated that the finaliters were in collusion with the Paradise Sons to foist fraud upon all creation since they never brought back a very clear-cut idea of the Father's actual personality as it is discernible on Paradise. He traded on reverence as ignorance. The charge was sweeping, terrible, and blasphemous. It was this veiled attack upon the finaliters that no doubt influenced the ascendant citizens then on Jerusem to stand firm and remain steadfast in resistance to all the rebel's proposals.

2. *The universe government of the Creator Son—Michael.* Lucifer contended that the local systems should be autonomous. He protested against the right of Michael, the Creator Son, to assume sovereignty of Nebadon in the name of a hypothetical Paradise Father and require all personalities to acknowledge allegiance to this unseen Father. He asserted that the whole plan of worship was a clever scheme to aggrandize the Paradise Sons. He was willing to acknowledge Michael as his Creator-father but not as his God and rightful ruler.

Most bitterly did he attack the right of the Ancients of Days—"foreign potentates"—to interfere in the affairs of the local systems and universes. These rulers he denounced as tyrants and usurpers. He exhorted his followers to believe that none of these rulers could do aught to interfere with the operation of complete home rule if men and angels only had the courage to assert themselves and boldly claim their rights.

He contended that the executioners of the Ancients of Days could be debarred from functioning in the local systems if the native beings would only assert their independence. He maintained that immortality was inherent in the system personalities, that resurrection was natural and automatic, and that all beings would live eternally except for the arbitrary and unjust acts of the executioners of the Ancients of Days.

3. *The attack upon the universal plan of ascendant mortal training.* Lucifer maintained that far too much time and energy were expended upon the scheme of so thoroughly training ascending mortals in the principles of universe administration, principles which he alleged were unethical and unsound. He protested against the agelong program for preparing the mortals of space for some unknown destiny and pointed to the presence of the finaliter corps on Jerusem as proof that these mortals had spent ages of preparation for some destiny of pure fiction. With derision he pointed out that the finaliters had encountered a destiny no more glorious than to be returned to humble spheres similar to those of their origin. He intimated that they had been debauched by overmuch discipline and prolonged training, and that they were in reality traitors to their mortal fellows since they were now co-operating with the scheme of enslaving all creation to the fictions of a mythical eternal destiny for ascending mortals. He advocated that ascenders should enjoy the liberty of individual self-determination. He challenged and condemned the entire plan of mortal ascension as sponsored by the Paradise Sons of God and supported by the Infinite Spirit.

And it was with such a Declaration of Liberty that Lucifer launched his orgy of darkness and death.

4. OUTBREAK OF THE REBELLION

The Lucifer manifesto was issued at the annual conclave of Satania on the sea of glass, in the presence of the assembled hosts of Jerusem, on the last day of the year, about two hundred thousand years ago, Urantia time. Satan proclaimed that worship could be accorded the universal forces—physical, intellectual, and spiritual—but that allegiance could be acknowledged only to the actual and present ruler, Lucifer, the "friend of men and angels" and the "God of liberty."

Self-assertion was the battle cry of the Lucifer rebellion. One of his chief arguments was that, if self-government was good and right for the Melchizedeks and other groups, it was equally good for all orders of intelligence. He was bold and persistent in the advocacy of the "equality of mind" and "the brotherhood of intelligence." He maintained that all government should be limited to the local planets and their voluntary confederation into the local systems. All other supervision he disallowed. He promised the Planetary Princes that they should rule the worlds as supreme executives. He denounced the location of legislative activities on the constellation headquarters and the conduct of judicial affairs on the universe capital. He contended that all these functions of government should be concentrated on the system capitals and proceeded to set up his own legislative assembly and organized his own tribunals under the jurisdiction of Satan. And he directed that the princes on the apostate worlds do the same.

The entire administrative cabinet of Lucifer went over in a body and were sworn in publicly as the officers of the administration of the new head of "the liberated worlds and systems."

While there had been two previous rebellions in Nebadon, they were in distant constellations. Lucifer held that these insurrections were unsuccessful because the majority of the intelligences failed to follow their leaders. He contended that "majorities rule," that "mind is infallible." The freedom allowed him by the universe rulers apparently sustained many of his nefarious contentions. He defied all his superiors; yet they apparently took no note of his doings. He was given a free hand to prosecute his seductive plan without let or hindrance.

All the merciful delays of justice Lucifer pointed to as evidence of the inability of the government of the Paradise Sons to stop the rebellion. He would openly defy and arrogantly challenge Michael, Immanuel, and the Ancients of Days and then point to the fact that no action ensued as positive evidence of the impotency of the universe and the superuniverse governments.

Gabriel was personally present throughout all these disloyal proceedings and only announced that he would, in due time, speak for Michael, and that all beings would be left free and unmolested in their choice; that the "government of the Sons for the Father desired only that loyalty and devotion which was voluntary, wholehearted, and sophistry-proof."

Lucifer was permitted fully to establish and thoroughly to organize his rebel government before Gabriel made any effort to contest the right of secession or to counterwork the rebel propaganda. But the Constellation Fathers immediately confined the action of these disloyal personalities to the system of Satania. Nevertheless, this period of delay was a time of great trial and testing to the loyal beings of all Satania. All was chaotic for a few years, and there was great confusion on the mansion worlds.

5. NATURE OF THE CONFLICT

Upon the outbreak of the Satania rebellion, Michael took counsel of his Paradise brother, Immanuel. Following this momentous conference, Michael announced that he would pursue the same policy which had characterized his dealings with similar upheavals in the past, an attitude of noninterference.

At the time of this rebellion and the two which preceded it there was no absolute and personal sovereign authority in the universe of Nebadon. Michael ruled by divine right, as vicegerent of the Universal Father, but not yet in his own personal right. He had not completed his bestowal career; he had not yet been vested with "all power in heaven and on earth."

From the outbreak of rebellion to the day of his enthronement as sovereign ruler of Nebadon, Michael never interfered with the rebel forces of Lucifer; they were allowed to run a free course for almost two hundred thousand years of Urantia time. Christ Michael now has ample power and authority to deal promptly, even summarily, with such outbreaks of disloyalty, but we doubt that this sovereign authority would lead him to act differently if another such upheaval should occur.

Since Michael elected to remain aloof from the actual warfare of the Lucifer rebellion, Gabriel called his personal staff together on Edentia and, in counsel with the Most Highs, elected to assume command of the loyal hosts of Satania. Michael remained on Salvington while Gabriel proceeded to Jerusem, and establishing himself on the sphere dedicated to the Father—the same Universal

Father whose personality Lucifer and Satan had questioned—in the presence of the forgathered hosts of loyal personalities, he displayed the banner of Michael, the material emblem of the Trinity government of all creation, the three azure blue concentric circles on a white background.

The Lucifer emblem was a banner of white with one red circle, in the center of which a black solid circle appeared.

"There was war in heaven; Michael's commander and his angels fought against the dragon (Lucifer, Satan, and the apostate princes); and the dragon and his rebellious angels fought but prevailed not." This "war in heaven" was not a physical battle as such a conflict might be conceived on Urantia. In the early days of the struggle Lucifer held forth continuously in the planetary amphitheater. Gabriel conducted an unceasing exposure of the rebel sophistries from his headquarters taken up near at hand. The various personalities present on the sphere who were in doubt as to their attitude would journey back and forth between these discussions until they arrived at a final decision.

But this war in heaven was very terrible and very real. While displaying none of the barbarities so characteristic of physical warfare on the immature worlds, this conflict was far more deadly; material life is in jeopardy in material combat, but the war in heaven was fought in terms of life eternal.

6. A LOYAL SERAPHIC COMMANDER

There were many noble and inspiring acts of devotion and loyalty which were performed by numerous personalities during the interim between the outbreak of hostilities and the arrival of the new system ruler and his staff. But the most thrilling of all these daring feats of devotion was the courageous conduct of Manotia, the second in command of the Satania headquarters' seraphim.

At the outbreak of rebellion on Jerusem the head of the seraphic hosts joined the Lucifer cause. This no doubt explains why such a large number of the fourth order, the system administrator seraphim, went astray. The seraphic leader was spiritually blinded by the brilliant personality of Lucifer; his charming ways fascinated the lower orders of celestial beings. They simply could not comprehend that it was possible for such a dazzling personality to go wrong.

Not long since, in describing the experiences associated with the onset of the Lucifer rebellion, Manotia said: "But my most exhilarating moment was the thrilling adventure connected with the Lucifer rebellion when, as second seraphic commander, I refused to participate in the projected insult to Michael; and the powerful rebels sought my destruction by means of the liaison forces they had arranged. There was a tremendous upheaval on Jerusem, but not a single loyal seraphim was harmed.

"Upon the default of my immediate superior it devolved upon me to assume command of the angelic hosts of Jerusem as the titular director of the confused seraphic affairs of the system. I was morally upheld by the Melchizedeks, ably assisted by a majority of the Material Sons, deserted by a tremendous group of my own order, but magnificently supported by the ascendant mortals on Jerusem.

"Having been automatically thrown out of the constellation circuits by the secession of Lucifer, we were dependent on the loyalty of our intelligence corps, who forwarded calls for help to Edentia from the near-by system of Rantulia; and we found that the kingdom of order, the intellect of loyalty, and the spirit of truth were inherently triumphant over rebellion, self-assertion, and so-called personal liberty; we were able to carry on until the arrival of the new System Sovereign, the worthy successor of Lucifer. And immediately thereafter I was assigned to the corps of the Melchizedek receivership of Urantia, assuming jurisdiction over the loyal seraphic orders on the world of the traitorous Caligastia, who had proclaimed his sphere a member of the newly projected system of 'liberated worlds and emancipated personalities' proposed in the infamous Declaration of Liberty issued by Lucifer in his call to the 'liberty-loving, free-thinking, and forward-looking intelligences of the misruled and maladministered worlds of Satania.'"

This angel is still in service on Urantia, functioning as associate chief of seraphim.

7. HISTORY OF THE REBELLION

The Lucifer rebellion was system wide. Thirty-seven seceding Planetary Princes swung their world administrations largely to the side of the archrebel. Only on Panoptia did the Planetary Prince fail to carry his people with him. On this world, under the guidance of the Melchizedeks, the people rallied to the support of Michael. Ellanora, a young woman of that mortal realm, grasped the leadership of the human races, and not a single soul on that strife-torn world enlisted under the Lucifer banner. And ever since have these loyal Panoptians served on the seventh Jerusem transition world as the caretakers and builders on the Father's sphere and its surrounding seven detention worlds. The Panoptians not only act as the literal custodians of these worlds, but they also execute the personal orders of Michael for the embellishment of these spheres for some future and unknown use. They do this work as they tarry en route to Edentia.

Throughout this period Caligastia was advocating the cause of Lucifer on Urantia. The Melchizedeks ably opposed the apostate Planetary Prince, but the sophistries of unbridled liberty and the delusions of self-assertion had every opportunity for deceiving the primitive peoples of a young and undeveloped world.

All secession propaganda had to be carried on by personal effort because the broadcast service and all other avenues of interplanetary communication were suspended by the action of the system circuit supervisors. Upon the actual outbreak of the insurrection the entire system of Satania was isolated in both the constellation and the universe circuits. During this time all incoming and outgoing messages were dispatched by seraphic agents and Solitary Messengers. The circuits to the fallen worlds were also cut off, so that Lucifer could not utilize this avenue for the furtherance of his nefarious scheme. And these circuits will not be restored so long as the archrebel lives within the confines of Satania.

This was a Lanonandek rebellion. The higher orders of local universe sonship did not join the Lucifer secession, although a few of the Life Carriers stationed on the rebel planets were somewhat influenced by the rebellion of the disloyal princes. None of the Trinitized Sons went astray. The Melchizedeks, archangels, and the Brilliant Evening Stars were all loyal to Michael and, with Gabriel, valiantly contended for the Father's will and the Son's rule.

No beings of Paradise origin were involved in disloyalty. Together with the Solitary Messengers they took up headquarters on the world of the Spirit and remained under the leadership of the Faithful of Days of Edentia. None of the conciliators apostatized, nor did a single one of the Celestial Recorders go astray. But a heavy toll was taken of the Morontia Companions and the Mansion World Teachers.

Of the supreme order of seraphim, not an angel was lost, but a considerable group of the next order, the superior, were deceived and ensnared. Likewise a few of the third or supervisor order of angels were misled. But the terrible breakdown came in the fourth group, the administrator angels, those seraphim who are normally assigned to the duties of the system capitals. Manotia saved almost two thirds of them, but slightly over one third followed their chief into the rebel ranks. One third of all the Jerusem cherubim attached to the administrator angels were lost with their disloyal seraphim.

Of the planetary angelic helpers, those assigned to the Material Sons, about one third were deceived, and almost ten per cent of the transition ministers were ensnared. In symbol John saw this when he wrote of the great red dragon, saying: "And his tail drew a third part of the stars of heaven and cast them down in darkness."

The greatest loss occurred in the angelic ranks, but most of the lower orders of intelligence were involved in disloyalty. Of the 681,217 Material Sons lost in Satania, ninety-five per cent were casualties of the Lucifer rebellion. Large numbers of midway creatures were lost on those individual planets whose Planetary Princes joined the Lucifer cause.

In many respects this rebellion was the most widespread and disastrous of all such occurrences in Nebadon. More personalities were involved in this insurrection than in both of the others. And it is to their everlasting dishonor that the emissaries of Lucifer and Satan spared not the infant-training schools on the finaliter cultural planet but rather sought to corrupt these developing minds in mercy salvaged from the evolutionary worlds.

The ascending mortals were vulnerable, but they withstood the sophistries of rebellion better than the lower spirits. While many on the lower mansion worlds, those who had not attained final fusion with their Adjusters, fell, it is recorded to the glory of the wisdom of the ascension scheme that not a single member of the Satania ascendant citizenship resident on Jerusem participated in the Lucifer rebellion.

Hour by hour and day by day the broadcast stations of all Nebadon were thronged by the anxious watchers of every imaginable class of celestial intelligence, who intently perused the bulletins of the Satania rebellion and rejoiced as the reports continuously narrated the unswerving loyalty of the ascending mortals who, under their Melchizedek leadership, successfully withstood the combined and protracted efforts of all the subtle evil forces which so swiftly gathered around the banners of secession and sin.

It was over two years of system time from the beginning of the "war in heaven" until the installation of Lucifer's successor. But at last the new Sovereign came, landing on the sea of glass with his staff. I was among the reserves mobilized on Edentia by Gabriel, and I well remember the first message of Lanaforge to the Constellation Father of Norlatiadek. It read: "Not a single Jerusem citizen was lost. Every ascendant mortal survived the fiery trial and emerged from the crucial test triumphant and altogether victorious." And on to Salvington, Uversa, and Paradise went this message of assurance that the survival experience of mortal ascension is the greatest security against rebellion and the surest safeguard against sin. This noble Jerusem band of faithful mortals numbered just 187,432,811.

With the arrival of Lanaforge the archrebels were dethroned and shorn of all governing powers, though they were permitted freely to go about Jerusem, the morontia spheres, and even to the individual inhabited worlds. They continued their deceptive and seductive efforts to confuse and mislead the minds of men and angels. But as concerned their work on the administrative mount of Jerusem, "their place was found no more."

While Lucifer was deprived of all administrative authority in Satania, there then existed no local universe power nor tribunal which could detain or destroy this wicked rebel; at that time Michael was not a sovereign ruler. The Ancients of Days sustained the Constellation Fathers in their seizure of the system government, but they have never handed down any subsequent decisions in the many appeals still pending with regard to the present status and future disposition of Lucifer, Satan, and their associates.

Thus were these archrebels allowed to roam the entire system to seek further penetration for their doctrines of discontent and self-assertion. But in almost two hundred thousand Urantia years they have been unable to deceive another world. No Satania worlds have been lost since the fall of the thirty-seven, not even those younger worlds peopled since that day of rebellion.

8. THE SON OF MAN ON URANTIA

Lucifer and Satan freely roamed the Satania system until the completion of the bestowal mission of Michael on Urantia. They were last on your world together during the time of their combined assault upon the Son of Man.

Formerly, when the Planetary Princes, the "Sons of God," were periodically assembled, "Satan came also," claiming that he represented all of the isolated worlds of the fallen Planetary Princes. But he has not been accorded such liberty on Jerusem since Michael's terminal bestowal. Subsequent to their effort to corrupt Michael when in the bestowal flesh, all sympathy for Lucifer and Satan has perished throughout all Satania, that is, outside the isolated worlds of sin.

The bestowal of Michael terminated the Lucifer rebellion in all Satania aside from the planets of the apostate Planetary Princes. And this was the significance of Jesus' personal experience, just before his death in the flesh, when he one day exclaimed to his disciples, "And I beheld Satan fall as lightning from heaven." He had come with Lucifer to Urantia for the last crucial struggle.

The Son of Man was confident of success, and he knew that his triumph on your world would forever settle the status of his agelong enemies, not only in Satania but also in the other two systems where sin had entered. There was survival for mortals and security for angels when your Master, in reply to the Lucifer proposals, calmly and with divine assurance replied, "Get you behind me, Satan." That was, in principle, the real end of the Lucifer rebellion. True, the Uversa tribunals have not yet rendered the executive decision regarding the appeal of Gabriel praying for the destruction of the rebels, but such a decree will, no doubt, be forthcoming in the fullness of time since the first step in the hearing of this case has already been taken.

Caligastia was recognized by the Son of Man as the technical Prince of Urantia up to near the time of his death. Said Jesus: "Now is the judgment of this world; now shall the prince of this world be cast down." And then still nearer the completion of his lifework he announced, "The prince of this world is judged." And it is this same dethroned and discredited Prince who was once termed "God of Urantia."

The last act of Michael before leaving Urantia was to offer mercy to Caligastia and Daligastia, but they spurned his tender proffer. Caligastia, your apostate Planetary Prince, is still free on Urantia to prosecute his nefarious designs, but he has absolutely no power to enter the minds of men, neither can he draw near to their souls to tempt or corrupt them unless they really desire to be cursed with his wicked presence.

Before the bestowal of Michael these rulers of darkness sought to maintain their authority on Urantia, and they persistently withstood the minor and subordinate celestial personalities. But since the day of Pentecost this traitorous Caligastia and his equally contemptible associate, Daligastia, are servile before the divine majesty of the Paradise Thought Adjusters and the protective Spirit of Truth, the spirit of Michael, which has been poured out upon all flesh.

But even so, no fallen spirit ever did have the power to invade the minds or to harass the souls of the children of God. Neither Satan nor Caligastia could ever touch or approach the faith sons of God; faith is an effective armor against sin and iniquity. It is true: "He who is born of God keeps himself, and the wicked one touches him not."

In general, when weak and dissolute mortals are supposed to be under the influence of devils and demons, they are merely being dominated by their own inherent and debased tendencies, being led away by their own natural propensities. The devil has been given a great deal of credit for evil which does not belong to him. Caligastia has been comparatively impotent since the cross of Christ.

9. PRESENT STATUS OF THE REBELLION

Early in the days of the Lucifer rebellion, salvation was offered all rebels by Michael. To all who would show proof of sincere repentance, he offered, upon his attainment of complete universe sovereignty, forgiveness and reinstatement in some form of universe service. None of the leaders accepted this merciful proffer. But thousands of the angels and the lower orders of celestial beings, including hundreds of the Material Sons and Daughters, accepted the mercy proclaimed by the Panoptians and were given rehabilitation at the time of Jesus' resurrection nineteen hundred years ago. These beings have since been transferred to the Father's world of Jerusem, where they must be held, technically, until the Uversa courts hand down a decision in the matter of Gabriel *vs.* Lucifer. But no one doubts that, when the annihilation verdict is issued, these repentant and salvaged personalities will be exempted from the decree of extinction. These probationary souls now labor with the Panoptians in the work of caring for the Father's world.

The archdeceiver has never been on Urantia since the days when he sought to turn back Michael from the purpose to complete the bestowal and to establish himself finally and securely as the unqualified ruler of Nebadon. Upon Michael's becoming the settled head of the universe of Nebadon, Lucifer was taken into custody by the agents of the Uversa Ancients of Days and has since been a prisoner on satellite number one of the Father's group of the transition spheres of Jerusem. And here the rulers of other worlds and systems behold the end of the unfaithful Sovereign of Satania. Paul knew of the status of these rebellious leaders following Michael's bestowal, for he wrote of Caligastia's chiefs as "spiritual hosts of wickedness in the heavenly places."

Michael, upon assuming the supreme sovereignty of Nebadon, petitioned the Ancients of Days for authority to intern all personalities concerned in the Lucifer rebellion pending the rulings of the superuniverse tribunals in the case of Gabriel *vs.* Lucifer, placed on the records of the Uversa supreme court almost two hundred thousand years ago, as you reckon time. Concerning the system capital group, the Ancients of Days granted the Michael petition with but a single exception: Satan was allowed to make periodic visits to the apostate princes on the fallen worlds until another Son of God should be accepted by such apostate worlds, or until such time as the courts of Uversa should begin the adjudication of the case of Gabriel *vs.* Lucifer.

Satan could come to Urantia because you had no Son of standing in residence —neither Planetary Prince nor Material Son. Machiventa Melchizedek has since been proclaimed vicegerent Planetary Prince of Urantia, and the opening of the case of Gabriel *vs.* Lucifer has signalized the inauguration of temporary planetary regimes on all the isolated worlds. It is true that Satan did periodically visit Caligastia and others of the fallen princes right up to the time of the presentation of these revelations, when there occurred the first hearing of Gabriel's plea for the annihilation of the archrebels. Satan is now unqualifiedly detained on the Jerusem prison worlds.

Since Michael's final bestowal no one in all Satania has desired to go to the prison worlds to minister to the interned rebels. And no more beings have been won to the deceiver's cause. For nineteen hundred years the status has been unchanged.

We do not look for a removal of the present Satania restrictions until the Ancients of Days make final disposition of the archrebels. The system circuits will not be reinstated so long as Lucifer lives. Meantime, he is wholly inactive.

The rebellion has ended on Jerusem. It ends on the fallen worlds as fast as divine Sons arrive. We believe that all rebels who will ever accept mercy have done so. We await the flashing broadcast that will deprive these traitors of personality existence. We anticipate the verdict of Uversa will be announced by the executionary broadcast which will effect the annihilation of these interned rebels. Then will you look for their places, but they shall not be found. "And they who know you among the worlds will be astonished at you; you have been a terror, but never shall you be any more." And thus shall all of these unworthy traitors "become as though they had not been." All await the Uversa decree.

But for ages the seven prison worlds of spiritual darkness in Satania have constituted a solemn warning to all Nebadon, eloquently and effectively proclaiming the great truth "that the way of the transgressor is hard"; "that within every sin is concealed the seed of its own destruction"; that "the wages of sin is death."

[Presented by Manovandet Melchizedek, onetime attached to the receivership of Urantia.]

PAPER 54

PROBLEMS OF THE LUCIFER REBELLION

EVOLUTIONARY man finds it difficult fully to comprehend the significance and to grasp the meanings of evil, error, sin, and iniquity. Man is slow to perceive that contrastive perfection and imperfection produce potential evil; that conflicting truth and falsehood create confusing error; that the divine endowment of freewill choice eventuates in the divergent realms of sin and righteousness; that the persistent pursuit of divinity leads to the kingdom of God as contrasted with its continuous rejection, which leads to the domains of iniquity.

The Gods neither create evil nor permit sin and rebellion. Potential evil is time-existent in a universe embracing differential levels of perfection meanings and values. Sin is potential in all realms where imperfect beings are endowed with the ability to choose between good and evil. The very conflicting presence of truth and untruth, fact and falsehood, constitutes the potentiality of error. The deliberate choice of evil constitutes sin; the willful rejection of truth is error; the persistent pursuit of sin and error is iniquity.

1. TRUE AND FALSE LIBERTY

Of all the perplexing problems growing out of the Lucifer rebellion, none has occasioned more difficulty than the failure of immature evolutionary mortals to distinguish between true and false liberty.

True liberty is the quest of the ages and the reward of evolutionary progress. False liberty is the subtle deception of the error of time and the evil of space. Enduring liberty is predicated on the reality of justice—intelligence, maturity, fraternity, and equity.

Liberty is a self-destroying technique of cosmic existence when its motivation is unintelligent, unconditioned, and uncontrolled. True liberty is progressively related to reality and is ever regardful of social equity, cosmic fairness, universe fraternity, and divine obligations.

Liberty is suicidal when divorced from material justice, intellectual fairness, social forbearance, moral duty, and spiritual values. Liberty is nonexistent apart from cosmic reality, and all personality reality is proportional to its divinity relationships.

Unbridled self-will and unregulated self-expression equal unmitigated selfishness, the acme of ungodliness. Liberty without the associated and ever-increasing conquest of self is a figment of egoistic mortal imagination. Self-motivated liberty is a conceptual illusion, a cruel deception. License masquerading in the garments of liberty is the forerunner of abject bondage.

True liberty is the associate of genuine self-respect; false liberty is the consort of self-admiration. True liberty is the fruit of self-control; false liberty, the assumption of self-assertion. Self-control leads to altruistic service; self-admiration tends towards the exploitation of others for the selfish aggrandizement of such a mistaken individual as is willing to sacrifice righteous attainment for the sake of possessing unjust power over his fellow beings.

Even wisdom is divine and safe only when it is cosmic in scope and spiritual in motivation.

There is no error greater than that species of self-deception which leads intelligent beings to crave the exercise of power over other beings for the purpose of depriving these persons of their natural liberties. The golden rule of human fairness cries out against all such fraud, unfairness, selfishness, and unrighteousness. Only true and genuine liberty is compatible with the reign of love and the ministry of mercy.

How dare the self-willed creature encroach upon the rights of his fellows in the name of personal liberty when the Supreme Rulers of the universe stand back in merciful respect for these prerogatives of will and potentials of personality! No being, in the exercise of his supposed personal liberty, has a right to deprive any other being of those privileges of existence conferred by the Creators and duly respected by all their loyal associates, subordinates, and subjects.

Evolutionary man may have to contend for his material liberties with tyrants and oppressors on a world of sin and iniquity or during the early times of a primitive evolving sphere, but not so on the morontia worlds or on the spirit spheres. War is the heritage of early evolutionary man, but on worlds of normal advancing civilization physical combat as a technique of adjusting racial misunderstandings has long since fallen into disrepute.

2. THE THEFT OF LIBERTY

With the Son and in the Spirit did God project eternal Havona, and ever since has there obtained the eternal pattern of co-ordinate participation in creation—sharing. This pattern of sharing is the master design for every one of the Sons and Daughters of God who go out into space to engage in the attempt to duplicate in time the central universe of eternal perfection.

Every creature of every evolving universe who aspires to do the Father's will is destined to become the partner of the time-space Creators in this magnificent adventure of experiential perfection attainment. Were this not true, the Father would have hardly endowed such creatures with creative free will, neither would he indwell them, actually go into partnership with them by means of his own spirit.

Lucifer's folly was the attempt to do the nondoable, to short-circuit time in an experiential universe. Lucifer's crime was the attempted creative disenfranchisement of every personality in Satania, the unrecognized abridgment of the creature's personal participation—freewill participation—in the long evolutionary struggle to attain the status of light and life both individually and collectively. In so doing this onetime Sovereign of your system set the temporal purpose of his own will directly athwart the eternal purpose of God's will as it is revealed in the bestowal of free will upon all personal creatures. The Lucifer rebellion thus threatened the maximum possible infringement of the freewill choice of the ascenders and servers of the system of Satania—a threat forevermore to deprive every one of these beings of the thrilling experience of contributing something personal and unique to the slowly erecting monument to experiential wisdom which will sometime exist as the perfected system of Satania. Thus does the Lucifer manifesto, masquerading in the habiliments of liberty, stand forth in the clear light of reason as a monumental threat to consummate the theft of personal liberty and to do it on a scale that has been approached only twice in all the history of Nebadon.

In short, what God had given men and angels Lucifer would have taken away from them, that is, the divine privilege of participating in the creation of their own destinies and of the destiny of this local system of inhabited worlds.

No being in all the universe has the rightful liberty to deprive any other being of true liberty, the right to love and be loved, the privilege of worshiping God and of serving his fellows.

3. THE TIME LAG OF JUSTICE

The moral will creatures of the evolutionary worlds are always bothered with the unthinking question as to why the all-wise Creators permit evil and sin. They fail to comprehend that both are inevitable if the creature is to be truly free. The free will of evolving man or exquisite angel is not a mere philosophic concept, a symbolic ideal. Man's ability to choose good or evil is a universe reality. This liberty to choose for oneself is an endowment of the Supreme Rulers, and they will not permit any being or group of beings to deprive a single personality in the wide universe of this divinely bestowed liberty—not even to satisfy such misguided and ignorant beings in the enjoyment of this misnamed personal liberty.

Although conscious and wholehearted identification with evil (sin) is the equivalent of nonexistence (annihilation), there must always intervene between the time of such personal identification with sin and the execution of the penalty—the automatic result of such a willful embrace of evil—a period of time of sufficient length to allow for such an adjudication of such an individual's universe status as will prove entirely satisfactory to all related universe personalities, and which will be so fair and just as to win the approval of the sinner himself.

But if this universe rebel against the reality of truth and goodness refuses to approve the verdict, and if the guilty one knows in his heart the justice of his condemnation but refuses to make such confession, then must the execution of sentence be delayed in accordance with the discretion of the Ancients of Days. And the Ancients of Days refuse to annihilate any being until all moral values and all spiritual realities are extinct, both in the evildoer and in all related supporters and possible sympathizers.

4. THE MERCY TIME LAG

Another problem somewhat difficult of explanation in the constellation of Norlatiadek pertains to the reasons for permitting Lucifer, Satan, and the fallen princes to work mischief so long before being apprehended, interned, and adjudicated.

Parents, those who have borne and reared children, are better able to understand why Michael, a Creator-father, might be slow to condemn and destroy his own Sons. Jesus' story of the prodigal son well illustrates how a loving father can long wait for the repentance of an erring child.

The very fact that an evil-doing creature can actually choose to do wrong—commit sin—establishes the fact of free-willness and fully justifies any length delay in the execution of justice provided the extended mercy might conduce to repentance and rehabilitation.

Most of the liberties which Lucifer sought he already had; others he was to receive in the future. All these precious endowments were lost by giving way to impatience and yielding to a desire to possess what one craves now and to possess it in defiance of all obligation to respect the rights and liberties of all other beings composing the universe of universes. Ethical obligations are innate, divine, and universal.

There are many reasons known to us why the Supreme Rulers did not immediately destroy or intern the leaders of the Lucifer rebellion. There are no doubt still other and possibly better reasons unknown to us. The mercy features of this delay in the execution of justice were extended personally by Michael of Nebadon. Except for the affection of this Creator-father for his erring Sons, the supreme justice of the superuniverse would have acted. If such an episode as the Lucifer rebellion had occurred in Nebadon while Michael was incarnated on Urantia, the instigators of such evil might have been instantly and absolutely annihilated.

Supreme justice can act instantly when not restrained by divine mercy. But the ministry of mercy to the children of time and space always provides for this time lag, this saving interval between seedtime and harvest. If the seed sowing is good, this interval provides for the testing and upbuilding of character; if the seed sowing is evil, this merciful delay provides time for repentance and rectification. This time delay in the adjudication and execution of evildoers is inherent in the mercy ministry of the seven superuniverses. This restraint of justice by mercy proves that God is love, and that such a God of love dominates the universes and in mercy controls the fate and judgment of all his creatures.

The mercy delays of time are by the mandate of the free will of the Creators. There is good to be derived in the universe from this technique of patience in dealing with sinful rebels. While it is all too true that good cannot come of evil to the one who contemplates and performs evil, it is equally true that all things (including evil, potential and manifest) work together for good to all beings who know God, love to do his will, and are ascending Paradiseward according to his eternal plan and divine purpose.

But these mercy delays are not interminable. Notwithstanding the long delay (as time is reckoned on Urantia) in adjudicating the Lucifer rebellion, we may record that, during the time of effecting this revelation, the first hearing in the pending case of Gabriel *vs.* Lucifer was held on Uversa, and soon thereafter there issued the mandate of the Ancients of Days directing that Satan be henceforth confined to the prison world with Lucifer. This ends the ability of Satan to pay further visits to any of the fallen worlds of Satania. Justice in a mercy-dominated universe may be slow, but it is certain.

5. THE WISDOM OF DELAY

Of the many reasons known to me as to why Lucifer and his confederates were not sooner interned or adjudicated, I am permitted to recite the following:

1. Mercy requires that every wrongdoer have sufficient time in which to formulate a deliberate and fully chosen attitude regarding his evil thoughts and sinful acts.

2. Supreme justice is dominated by a Father's love; therefore will justice never destroy that which mercy can save. Time to accept salvation is vouchsafed every evildoer.

3. No affectionate father is ever precipitate in visiting punishment upon an erring member of his family. Patience cannot function independently of time.

4. While wrongdoing is always deleterious to a family, wisdom and love admonish the upright children to bear with an erring brother during the time granted by the affectionate father in which the sinner may see the error of his way and embrace salvation.

5. Regardless of Michael's attitude toward Lucifer, notwithstanding his being Lucifer's Creator-father, it was not in the province of the Creator Son to exercise summary jurisdiction over the apostate System Sovereign because he had not then completed his bestowal career, thereby attaining unqualified sovereignty of Nebadon.

6. The Ancients of Days could have immediately annihilated these rebels, but they seldom execute wrongdoers without a full hearing. In this instance they refused to overrule the Michael decisions.

7. It is evident that Immanuel counseled Michael to remain aloof from the rebels and allow rebellion to pursue a natural course of self-obliteration. And the wisdom of the Union of Days is the time reflection of the united wisdom of the Paradise Trinity.

8. The Faithful of Days on Edentia advised the Constellation Fathers to allow the rebels free course to the end that all sympathy for these evildoers should be the sooner uprooted in the hearts of every present and future citizen of Norlatiadek—every mortal, morontia, or spirit creature.

9. On Jerusem the personal representative of the Supreme Executive of Orvonton counseled Gabriel to foster full opportunity for every living creature to mature a deliberate choice in those matters involved in the Lucifer Declaration of Liberty. The issues of rebellion having been raised, the Paradise emergency adviser of Gabriel portrayed that, if such full and free opportunity were not given all Norlatiadek creatures, then would the Paradise quarantine against all such possible halfhearted or doubt-stricken creatures be extended in self-protection against the entire constellation. To keep open the Paradise doors of ascension to the beings of Norlatiadek, it was necessary to provide for the full development of rebellion and to insure the complete determination of attitude on the part of all beings in any way concerned therewith.

10. The Divine Minister of Salvington issued as her third independent proclamation a mandate directing that nothing be done to half cure, cowardly suppress, or otherwise hide the hideous visage of rebels and rebellion. The

angelic hosts were directed to work for full disclosure and unlimited opportunity for sin-expression as the quickest technique of achieving the perfect and final cure of the plague of evil and sin.

11. An emergency council of ex-mortals consisting of Mighty Messengers, glorified mortals who had had personal experience with like situations, together with their colleagues, was organized on Jerusem. They advised Gabriel that at least three times the number of beings would be led astray if arbitrary or summary methods of suppression were attempted. The entire Uversa corps of counselors concurred in advising Gabriel to permit the rebellion to take its full and natural course, even if it should require a million years to wind up the consequences.

12. Time, even in a universe of time, is relative: If a Urantia mortal of average length of life should commit a crime which precipitated world-wide pandemonium, and if he were apprehended, tried, and executed within two or three days of the commission of the crime, would it seem a long time to you? And yet that would be nearer a comparison with the length of Lucifer's life even if his adjudication, now begun, should not be completed for a hundred thousand Urantia years. The relative lapse of time from the viewpoint of Uversa, where the litigation is pending, could be indicated by saying that the crime of Lucifer was being brought to trial within two and a half seconds of its commission. From the Paradise viewpoint the adjudication is simultaneous with the enactment.

There are an equal number of reasons for not arbitrarily stopping the Lucifer rebellion which would be partially comprehensible to you, but which I am not permitted to narrate. I may inform you that on Uversa we teach forty-eight reasons for permitting evil to run the full course of its own moral bankruptcy and spiritual extinction. I doubt not that there are just as many additional reasons not known to me.

6. THE TRIUMPH OF LOVE

Whatever the difficulties evolutionary mortals may encounter in their efforts to understand the Lucifer rebellion, it should be clear to all reflective thinkers that the technique of dealing with the rebels is a vindication of divine love. The loving mercy extended to the rebels does seem to have involved many innocent beings in trials and tribulations, but all these distraught personalities may securely depend upon the all-wise Judges to adjudicate their destinies in mercy as well as justice.

In all their dealings with intelligent beings, both the Creator Son and his Paradise Father are love dominated. It is impossible to comprehend many phases of the attitude of the universe rulers toward rebels and rebellion—sin and sinners—unless it be remembered that God as a Father takes precedence over all other phases of Deity manifestation in all the dealings of divinity with humanity. It should also be recalled that the Paradise Creator Sons are all mercy motivated.

If an affectionate father of a large family chooses to show mercy to one of his children guilty of grievous wrongdoing, it may well be that the extension of mercy to this misbehaving child will work a temporary hardship upon all the other and well-behaved children. Such eventualities are inevitable; such a risk is inseparable from the reality situation of having a loving parent and of being a member of a family group. Each member of a family profits by the righteous conduct of every other member; likewise must each member suffer the immediate time-consequences of the misconduct of every other member. Families, groups, nations, races, worlds, systems, constellations, and universes are relationships of association which possess individuality; and therefore does every member of any such group, large or small, reap the benefits and suffer the consequences of the rightdoing and the wrongdoing of all other members of the group concerned.

But one thing should be made clear: If you are made to suffer the evil consequences of the sin of some member of your family, some fellow citizen or fellow mortal, even rebellion in the system or elsewhere—no matter what you may have to endure because of the wrongdoing of your associates, fellows, or superiors—you may rest secure in the eternal assurance that such tribulations are transient afflictions. None of these fraternal consequences of misbehavior in the group can ever jeopardize your eternal prospects or in the least degree deprive you of your divine right of Paradise ascension and God attainment.

And there is compensation for these trials, delays, and disappointments which invariably accompany the sin of rebellion. Of the many valuable repercussions of the Lucifer rebellion which might be named, I will only call attention to the enhanced careers of those mortal ascenders, the Jerusem citizens, who, by withstanding the sophistries of sin, placed themselves in line for becoming future Mighty Messengers, fellows of my own order. Every being who stood the test of that evil episode thereby immediately advanced his administrative status and enhanced his spiritual worth.

At first the Lucifer upheaval appeared to be an unmitigated calamity to the system and to the universe. Gradually benefits began to accrue. With the passing of twenty-five thousand years of system time (twenty thousand years of Urantia time), the Melchizedeks began to teach that the good resulting from Lucifer's folly had come to equal the evil incurred. The sum of evil had by that time become almost stationary, continuing to increase only on certain isolated worlds, while the beneficial repercussions continued to multiply and extend out through the universe and superuniverse, even to Havona. The Melchizedeks now teach that the good resulting from the Satania rebellion is more than a thousand times the sum of all the evil.

But such an extraordinary and beneficent harvest of wrongdoing could only be brought about by the wise, divine, and merciful attitude of all of Lucifer's superiors, extending from the Constellation Fathers on Edentia to the Universal Father on Paradise. The passing of time has enhanced the consequential good to be derived from the Lucifer folly; and since the evil to be penalized was quite fully developed within a comparatively short time, it is apparent that the all-wise and farseeing universe rulers would be certain to extend the time in which to reap increasingly beneficial results. Regardless of the many additional reasons for delaying the apprehension and adjudication of the Satania rebels, this one gain would have been enough to explain why these sinners were not sooner interned, and why they have not been adjudicated and destroyed.

Shortsighted and time-bound mortal minds should be slow to criticize the time delays of the farseeing and all-wise administrators of universe affairs.

One error of human thinking respecting these problems consists in the idea that all evolutionary mortals on an evolving planet would choose to enter upon the Paradise career if sin had not cursed their world. The ability to decline survival does not date from the times of the Lucifer rebellion. Mortal man has always possessed the endowment of freewill choice regarding the Paradise career.

As you ascend in the survival experience, you will broaden your universe concepts and extend your horizon of meanings and values; and thus will you be able the better to understand why such beings as Lucifer and Satan are permitted to continue in rebellion. You will also better comprehend how ultimate (if not immediate) good can be derived from time-limited evil. After you attain Paradise, you will really be enlightened and comforted when you listen to the superaphic philosophers discuss and explain these profound problems of universe adjustment. But even then, I doubt that you will be fully satisfied in your own minds. At least I was not even when I had thus attained the acme of universe philosophy. I did not achieve a full comprehension of these complexities until after I had been assigned to administrative duties in the superuniverse, where by actual experience I have acquired conceptual capacity adequate for the comprehension of such many-sided problems in cosmic equity and spiritual philosophy. As you ascend Paradiseward, you will increasingly learn that many problematic features of universe administration can only be comprehended subsequent to the acquirement of increased experiential capacity and to the achievement of enhanced spiritual insight. Cosmic wisdom is essential to the understanding of cosmic situations.

[Presented by a Mighty Messenger of experiential survival in the first system rebellion in the universes of time now attached to the superuniverse government of Orvonton and acting in this matter by request of Gabriel of Salvington.]

PAPER 55

THE SPHERES OF LIGHT AND LIFE

THE age of light and life is the final evolutionary attainment of a world of time and space. From the early times of primitive man, such an inhabited world has passed through the successive planetary ages—the pre- and the post-Planetary Prince ages, the post-Adamic age, the post-Magisterial Son age, and the postbestowal Son age. And then is such a world made ready for the culminating evolutionary attainment, the settled status of light and life, by the ministry of the successive planetary missions of the Trinity Teacher Sons with their ever-advancing revelations of divine truth and cosmic wisdom. In these endeavors the Teacher Sons enjoy the assistance of the Brilliant Evening Stars always, and the Melchizedeks sometimes, in establishing the final planetary age.

This era of light and life, inaugurated by the Teacher Sons at the conclusion of their final planetary mission, continues indefinitely on the inhabited worlds. Each advancing stage of settled status may be segregated by the judicial actions of the Magisterial Sons into a succession of dispensations; but all such judicial actions are purely technical, in no way modifying the course of planetary events.

Only those planets which attain existence in the main circuits of the superuniverse are assured of continuous survival, but as far as we know, these worlds settled in light and life are destined to go on throughout the eternal ages of all future time.

There are seven stages in the unfoldment of the era of light and life on an evolutionary world, and in this connection it should be noted that the worlds of the Spirit-fused mortals evolve along lines identical with those of the Adjuster-fusion series. These seven stages of light and life are:

1. The first or planetary stage.
2. The second or system stage.
3. The third or constellation stage.
4. The fourth or local universe stage.
5. The fifth or minor sector stage.
6. The sixth or major sector stage.
7. The seventh or superuniverse stage.

At the conclusion of this narrative these stages of advancing development are described as they relate to the universe organization, but the planetary values of any stage may be attained by any world quite independent of the development of other worlds or of the superplanetary levels of universe administration.

1. THE MORONTIA TEMPLE

The presence of a morontia temple at the capital of an inhabited world is the certificate of the admission of such a sphere to the settled ages of light and life. Before the Teacher Sons leave a world at the conclusion of their terminal mission, they inaugurate this final epoch of evolutionary attainment; they preside on that day when the "holy temple comes down upon earth." This event, signalizing the dawn of the era of light and life, is always honored by the personal presence of the Paradise bestowal Son of that planet, who comes to witness this great day. There in this temple of unparalleled beauty, this bestowal Son of Paradise proclaims the long-time Planetary Prince as the new Planetary Sovereign and invests such a faithful Lanonandek Son with new powers and extended authority over planetary affairs. The System Sovereign is also present and speaks in confirmation of these pronouncements.

A morontia temple has three parts: Centermost is the sanctuary of the Paradise bestowal Son. On the right is the seat of the former Planetary Prince, now Planetary Sovereign; and when present in the temple, this Lanonandek Son is visible to the more spiritual individuals of the realm. On the left is the seat of the acting chief of finaliters attached to the planet.

Although the planetary temples have been spoken of as "coming down from heaven," in reality no actual material is transported from the system headquarters. The architecture of each is worked out in miniature on the system capital, and the Morontia Power Supervisors subsequently bring these approved plans to the planet. Here, in association with the Master Physical Controllers, they proceed to build the morontia temple according to specifications.

The average morontia temple seats about three hundred thousand spectators. These edifices are not used for worship, play, or for receiving broadcasts; they are devoted to the special ceremonies of the planet, such as: communications with the System Sovereign or with the Most Highs, special visualization ceremonies designed to reveal the personality presence of spirit beings, and silent cosmic contemplation. The schools of cosmic philosophy here conduct their graduation exercises, and here also do the mortals of the realm receive planetary recognition for achievements of high social service and for other outstanding attainments.

Such a morontia temple also serves as the place of assembly for witnessing the translation of living mortals to the morontia existence. It is because the translation temple is composed of morontia material that it is not destroyed by the blazing glory of the consuming fire which so completely obliterates the physical bodies of those mortals who therein experience final fusion with their divine Adjusters. On a large world these departure flares are almost continuous, and as the number of translations increases, subsidiary morontia life shrines are provided in different areas of the planet. Not long since I sojourned on a world in the far north whereon twenty-five morontia shrines were functioning.

On presettled worlds, planets without morontia temples, these fusion flashes many times occur in the planetary atmosphere, where the material body of a translation candidate is elevated by the midway creatures and the physical controllers.

2. DEATH AND TRANSLATION

Natural, physical death is not a mortal inevitability. The majority of advanced evolutionary beings, citizens on worlds existing in the final era of light and life, do not die; they are translated directly from the life in the flesh to the morontia existence.

This experience of translation from the material life to the morontia state —fusion of the immortal soul with the indwelling Adjuster—increases in frequency commensurate with the evolutionary progress of the planet. At first only a few mortals in each age attain translation levels of spiritual progress, but with the onset of the successive ages of the Teacher Sons, more and more Adjuster fusions occur before the termination of the lengthening lives of these progressing mortals; and by the time of the terminal mission of the Teacher Sons, approximately one quarter of these superb mortals are exempt from natural death.

Farther along in the era of light and life the midway creatures or their associates sense the approaching status of probable soul-Adjuster union and signify this to the destiny guardians, who in turn communicate these matters to the finaliter group under whose jurisdiction this mortal may be functioning; then there is issued the summons of the Planetary Sovereign for such a mortal to resign all planetary duties, bid farewell to the world of his origin, and repair to the inner temple of the Planetary Sovereign, there to await morontia transit, the translation flash, from the material domain of evolution to the morontia level of prespirit progression.

When the family, friends, and working group of such a fusion candidate have forgathered in the morontia temple, they are distributed around the central stage whereon the fusion candidates are resting, meantime freely conversing with their assembled friends. A circle of intervening celestial personalities is arranged to protect the material mortals from the action of the energies manifest at the instant of the "life flash" which delivers the ascension candidate from the bonds of material flesh, thereby doing for such an evolutionary mortal everything that natural death does for those who are thereby delivered from the flesh.

Many fusion candidates may be assembled in the spacious temple at the same time. And what a beautiful occasion when mortals thus forgather to witness the ascension of their loved ones in spiritual flames, and what a contrast to those earlier ages when mortals must commit their dead to the embrace of the terrestrial elements! The scenes of weeping and wailing characteristic of earlier epochs of human evolution are now replaced by ecstatic joy and the sublimest enthusiasm as these God-knowing mortals bid their loved ones a transient farewell as they are removed from their material associations by the spiritual fires of consuming grandeur and ascending glory. On worlds settled in light and life, "funerals" are occasions of supreme joy, profound satisfaction, and inexpressible hope.

The souls of these progressing mortals are increasingly filled with faith, hope, and assurance. The spirit permeating those gathered around the translation shrine resembles that of the joyful friends and relatives who might assemble at a graduating exercise for one of their group, or who might come together to witness the conferring of some great honor upon one of their number. And it would be decidedly helpful if less advanced mortals could only learn to view natural death with something of this same cheerfulness and lightheartedness.

Mortal observers can see nothing of their translated associates subsequent to the fusion flash. Such translated souls proceed by Adjuster transit direct to the resurrection hall of the appropriate morontia-training world. These transactions concerned with the translation of living human beings to the morontia world are supervised by an archangel who was assigned to such a world on the day when it was first settled in light and life.

By the time a world attains the fourth stage of light and life, more than half the mortals leave the planet by translation from among the living. Such diminishment of death continues on and on, but I know of no system whose inhabited worlds, even though long settled in life, are entirely free from natural death as the technique of escape from the bonds of flesh. And until such a high state of planetary evolution is uniformly attained, the morontia-training worlds of the local universe must continue in service as educational and cultural spheres for the evolving morontia progressors. The elimination of death is theoretically possible, but it has not yet occurred according to my observation. Perhaps such a status may be attained during the faraway stretches of the succeeding epochs of the seventh stage of settled planetary life.

The translated souls of the flowering ages of the settled spheres do not pass through the mansion worlds. Neither do they sojourn, as students, on the morontia worlds of the system or constellation. They do not pass through any of the earlier phases of morontia life. They are the only ascending mortals who so nearly escape the morontia transition from material existence to semispirit status. The initial experience of such *Son-seized* mortals in the ascension career is in the services of the progression worlds of the universe headquarters. And from these study worlds of Salvington they go back as teachers to the very worlds they passed by, subsequently going on inward to Paradise by the established route of mortal ascension.

Could you but visit a planet in an advanced stage of development, you would quickly grasp the reasons for providing for the differential reception of ascending mortals on the mansion and higher morontia worlds. You would readily understand that beings passing on from such highly evolved spheres are prepared to resume their Paradise ascent far in advance of the average mortal arriving from a disordered and backward world like Urantia.

No matter from what level of planetary attainment human beings may ascend to the morontia worlds, the seven mansion spheres afford them ample opportunity to gain in experience as teacher-students all of everything which they failed to pass through because of the advanced status of their native planets.

The universe is unfailing in the application of these equalizing techniques designed to insure that no ascender shall be deprived of aught which is essential to his ascension experience.

3. THE GOLDEN AGES

During this age of light and life the world increasingly prospers under the fatherly rule of the Planetary Sovereign. By this time the worlds are progressing under the momentum of one language, one religion, and, on normal spheres, one race. But this age is not perfect. These worlds still have well-appointed hospitals, homes for the care of the sick. There still remain the problems of caring for accidental injuries and the inescapable infirmities attendant upon the decrepitude of old age and the disorders of senility. Disease has not been entirely vanquished, neither have the earth animals been subdued in perfection; but such worlds are like Paradise in comparison with the early times of primitive man during the pre-Planetary Prince age. You would instinctively describe such a realm—could you be suddenly transported to a planet in this stage of development—as heaven on earth.

Human government in the conduct of material affairs continues to function throughout this age of relative progress and perfection. The public activities of a world in the first stage of light and life which I recently visited were financed by the tithing technique. Every adult worker—and all able-bodied citizens worked at something—paid ten per cent of his income or increase to the public treasury, and it was disbursed as follows:

1. Three per cent was expended in the promotion of truth—science, education, and philosophy.

2. Three per cent was devoted to beauty—play, social leisure, and art.

3. Three per cent was dedicated to goodness—social service, altruism, and religion.

4. One per cent was assigned to the insurance reserves against the risk of incapacity for labor resultant from accident, disease, old age, or unpreventable disasters.

The natural resources of this planet were administered as social possessions, community property.

On this world the highest honor conferred upon a citizen was the order of "supreme service," being the only degree of recognition ever to be granted in the morontia temple. This recognition was bestowed upon those who had long distinguished themselves in some phase of supermaterial discovery or planetary social service.

The majority of social and administrative posts were held jointly by men and women. Most of the teaching was also done jointly; likewise all judicial trusts were discharged by similar associated couples.

On these superb worlds the childbearing period is not greatly prolonged. It is not best for too many years to intervene between the ages of a family of children. When close together in age, children are able to contribute much more to their mutual training. And on these worlds they are magnificently trained by the competitive systems of keen striving in the advanced domains and divisions of diverse achievement in the mastery of truth, beauty, and goodness. Never fear but that even such glorified spheres present plenty of evil, real and potential, which is stimulative of the choosing between truth and error, good and evil, sin and righteousness.

Nevertheless, there is a certain, inevitable penalty attaching to mortal existence on such advanced evolutionary planets. When a settled world progresses beyond the third stage of light and life, all ascenders are destined, before attaining the minor sector, to receive some sort of transient assignment on a planet passing through the earlier stages of evolution.

Each of these successive ages represents advancing achievements in all phases of planetary attainment. In the initial age of light the revelation of truth was enlarged to embrace the workings of the universe of universes, while the Deity study of the second age is the attempt to master the protean concept of the nature, mission, ministry, associations, origin, and destiny of the Creator Sons, the first level of God the Sevenfold.

A planet the size of Urantia, when fairly well settled, would have about one hundred subadministrative centers. These subordinate centers would be presided over by one of the following groups of qualified administrators:

1. Young Material Sons and Daughters brought from the system headquarters to act as assistants to the ruling Adam and Eve.

2. The progeny of the semimortal staff of the Planetary Prince who were procreated on certain worlds for this and other similar responsibilities.

3. The direct planetary progeny of Adam and Eve.

4. Materialized and humanized midway creatures.

5. Mortals of Adjuster-fusion status who, upon their own petition, are temporarily exempted from translation by the order of the Personalized Adjuster of universe chieftainship in order that they may continue on the planet in certain important administrative posts.

6. Specially trained mortals of the planetary schools of administration who have also received the order of supreme service of the morontia temple.

7. Certain elective commissions of three properly qualified citizens who are sometimes chosen by the citizenry by direction of the Planetary Sovereign in accordance with their special ability to accomplish some definite task which is needful in that particular planetary sector.

The great handicap confronting Urantia in the matter of attaining the high planetary destiny of light and life is embraced in the problems of disease, degeneracy, war, multicolored races, and multilingualism.

No evolutionary world can hope to progress beyond the first stage of settledness in light until it has achieved one language, one religion, and one philosophy. Being of one race greatly facilitates such achievement, but the many peoples of Urantia do not preclude the attainment of higher stages.

4. ADMINISTRATIVE READJUSTMENTS

In the successive stages of settled existence the inhabited worlds make marvelous progress under the wise and sympathetic administration of the volunteer Corps of the Finality, ascenders of Paradise attainment who have come back to minister to their brethren in the flesh. These finaliters are active in co-operation with the Trinity Teacher Sons, but they do not begin their real participation in world affairs until the morontia temple appears on earth.

Upon the formal inauguration of the planetary ministry of the Corps of the Finality, the majority of the celestial hosts withdraw. But the seraphic guardians of destiny continue their personal ministry to the progressing mortals in light; indeed such angels come in ever-increasing numbers throughout the settled ages since larger and larger groups of human beings reach the third cosmic circle of co-ordinate mortal attainment during the planetary life span.

This is merely the first of the successive administrative adjustments which attend the unfolding of the successive ages of increasingly brilliant attainment on the inhabited worlds as they pass from the first to the seventh stage of settled existence.

1. *The first stage of light and life.* A world in this initial settled stage is being administered by three rulers:

a. The Planetary Sovereign, presently to be advised by a counseling Trinity Teacher Son, in all probability the chief of the terminal corps of such Sons to function on the planet.

b. The chief of the planetary corps of finaliters.

c. Adam and Eve, who function jointly as the unifiers of the dual leadership of the Prince-Sovereign and the chief of finaliters.

Acting as interpreters for the seraphic guardians and the finaliters are the exalted and liberated midway creatures. One of the last acts of the Trinity Teacher Sons on their terminal mission is to liberate the midwayers of the realm and to promote (or restore) them to advanced planetary status, assigning them to responsible places in the new administration of the settled sphere. Such changes have already been made in the range of human vision as enable mortals to recognize these heretofore invisible cousins of the early Adamic regime. This is made possible by the final discoveries of physical science in liaison with the enlarged planetary functions of the Master Physical Controllers.

The System Sovereign has authority to release midway creatures any time after the first settled stage so that they may humanize in the morontia by the aid of the Life Carriers and the physical controllers and, after receiving Thought Adjusters, start out on their Paradise ascension.

In the third and subsequent stages, some of the midwayers are still functioning, chiefly as contact personalities for the finaliters, but as each stage of light and life is entered, new orders of liaison ministers largely replace the midwayers; very few of them ever remain beyond the fourth stage of light. The seventh stage will witness the coming of the first absonite ministers from Paradise to serve in the places of certain universe creatures.

2. *The second stage of light and life.* This epoch is signalized on the worlds by the arrival of a Life Carrier who becomes the volunteer adviser of the planetary rulers regarding the further efforts to purify and stabilize the mortal race. Thus do the Life Carriers actively participate in the further evolution of the human race—physically, socially, and economically. And then they extend their supervision to the further purification of the mortal stock by the drastic elimination of the retarded and persisting remnants of inferior potential of an intellectual, philosophic, cosmic, and spiritual nature. Those who design and plant life on an inhabited world are fully competent to advise the Material Sons and Daughters, who have full and unquestioned authority to purge the evolving race of all detrimental influences.

From the second stage on throughout the career of a settled planet the Teacher Sons serve as counselors to the finaliters. During such missions they serve as volunteers and not by assignment; and they serve exclusively with the finaliter corps except that, upon the consent of the System Sovereign, they may be had as advisers to the Planetary Adam and Eve.

3. *The third stage of light and life.* During this epoch the inhabited worlds arrive at a new appreciation of the Ancients of Days, the second phase of God the Sevenfold, and the representatives of these superuniverse rulers enter into new relationships with the planetary administration.

In each succeeding age of settled existence the finaliters function in ever-increasing capacities. There exists a close working connection between the finaliters, the Evening Stars (the superangels), and the Trinity Teacher Sons.

During this or the following age a Teacher Son, assisted by the ministering-spirit quartette, becomes attached to the elective mortal chief executive, who now becomes associated with the Planetary Sovereign as joint administrator of world affairs. These mortal chief executives serve for twenty-five years of planetary time, and it is this new development that makes it easy for the Planetary Adam and Eve to secure release from their world of long-time assignment during the following ages.

The ministering-spirit quartettes consist of: the seraphic chief of the sphere, the superuniverse secoraphic counselor, the archangel of translations, and the omniaphim who functions as the personal representative of the Assigned Sentinel stationed on the system headquarters. But these advisers never proffer counsel unless it is asked for.

4. *The fourth stage of light and life.* On these worlds the Trinity Teacher Sons appear in new roles. Assisted by the creature-trinitized sons so long associated with their order, they now come to the worlds as volunteer counselors and advisers to the Planetary Sovereign and his associates. Such couples—Paradise-Havona-trinitized sons and ascender-trinitized sons—represent differing universe viewpoints and diverse personal experiences which are highly serviceable to the planetary rulers.

At any time after this age the Planetary Adam and Eve can petition the Sovereign Creator Son for release from planetary duties in order to begin their Paradise ascent; or they can remain on the planet as directors of the newly appearing order of increasingly spiritual society composed of advanced mortals striving to comprehend the philosophic teachings of the finaliters portrayed by the Brilliant Evening Stars, who are now assigned to these worlds to collaborate in pairs with the seconaphim from the headquarters of the superuniverse.

The finaliters are chiefly engaged in initiating the new and supermaterial activities of society—social, cultural, philosophic, cosmic, and spiritual. As far as we can discern, they will continue this ministry far into the seventh epoch of evolutionary stability, when, possibly, they may go forth to minister in outer space; whereupon we conjecture their places may be taken by absonite beings from Paradise.

5. *The fifth stage of light and life.* The readjustments of this stage of settled existence pertain almost entirely to the physical domains and are of primary concern to the Master Physical Controllers.

6. *The sixth stage of light and life* witnesses the development of new functions of the mind circuits of the realm. Cosmic wisdom seems to become constitutive in the universe ministry of mind.

7. *The seventh stage of light and life.* Early in the seventh epoch the Trinity Teacher counselor of the Planetary Sovereign is joined by a volunteer

adviser sent by the Ancients of Days, and later on they will be augmented by a third counselor coming from the superuniverse Supreme Executive.

During this epoch, if not before, Adam and Eve are always relieved of planetary duties. If there is a Material Son in the finaliter corps, he may become associated with the mortal chief executive, and sometimes it is a Melchizedek who volunteers to function in this capacity. If a midwayer is among the finaliters, all of that order remaining on the planet are immediately released.

Upon obtaining release from their agelong assignment, a Planetary Adam and Eve may select careers as follows:

1. They can secure planetary release and from the universe headquarters start out immediately on the Paradise career, receiving Thought Adjusters at the conclusion of the morontia experience.
2. Very often a Planetary Adam and Eve will receive Adjusters while yet serving on a world settled in light concomitant with the receiving of Adjusters by some of their imported pure-line children who have volunteered for a term of planetary service. Subsequently they may all go to universe headquarters and there begin the Paradise career.
3. A Planetary Adam and Eve may elect—as do Material Sons and Daughters from the system capital—to go direct to the midsonite world for a brief sojourn, there to receive their Adjusters.
4. They may decide to return to the system headquarters, there for a time to occupy seats on the supreme court, after which service they will receive Adjusters and begin the Paradise ascent.
5. They may choose to go from their administrative duties back to their native world to serve as teachers for a season and to become Adjuster indwelt at the time of transfer to the universe headquarters.

Throughout all of these epochs the imported assisting Material Sons and Daughters exert a tremendous influence on the progressing social and economic orders. They are potentially immortal, at least until such time as they elect to humanize, receive Adjusters, and start for Paradise.

On the evolutionary worlds a being must humanize to receive a Thought Adjuster. All ascendant members of the Mortal Corps of Finaliters have been Adjuster indwelt and fused except seraphim, and they are Father indwelt by another type of spirit at the time of being mustered into this corps.

5. THE ACME OF MATERIAL DEVELOPMENT

Mortal creatures living on a sin-stricken, evil-dominated, self-seeking, isolated world, such as Urantia, can hardly conceive of the physical perfection, the intellectual attainment, and the spiritual development which characterize these advanced epochs of evolution on a sinless sphere.

The advanced stages of a world settled in light and life represent the acme of evolutionary material development. On these cultured worlds, gone are the idleness and friction of the earlier primitive ages. Poverty and social inequality have all but vanished, degeneracy has disappeared, and delinquency is rarely observed. Insanity has practically ceased to exist, and feeble-mindedness is a rarity.

The economic, social, and administrative status of these worlds is of a high and perfected order. Science, art, and industry flourish, and society is a smoothly working mechanism of high material, intellectual, and cultural achievement. Industry has been largely diverted to serving the higher aims of such a superb civilization. The economic life of such a world has become ethical.

War has become a matter of history, and there are no more armies or police forces. Government is gradually disappearing. Self-control is slowly rendering laws of human enactment obsolete. The extent of civil government and statutory regulation, in an intermediate state of advancing civilization, is in inverse proportion to the morality and spirituality of the citizenship.

Schools are vastly improved and are devoted to the training of mind and the expansion of soul. The art centers are exquisite and the musical organizations superb. The temples of worship with their associated schools of philosophy and experiential religion are creations of beauty and grandeur. The open-air arenas of worship assembly are equally sublime in the simplicity of their artistic appointment.

The provisions for competitive play, humor, and other phases of personal and group achievement are ample and appropriate. A special feature of the competitive activities on such a highly cultured world concerns the efforts of individuals and groups to excel in the sciences and philosophies of cosmology. Literature and oratory flourish, and language is so improved as to be symbolic of concepts as well as to be expressive of ideas. Life is refreshingly simple; man has at last co-ordinated a high state of mechanical development with an inspiring intellectual attainment and has overshadowed both with an exquisite spiritual achievement. The pursuit of happiness is an experience of joy and satisfaction.

6. THE INDIVIDUAL MORTAL

As worlds advance in the settled status of light and life, society becomes increasingly peaceful. The individual, while no less independent and devoted to his family, has become more altruistic and fraternal.

On Urantia, and as you are, you can have little appreciation of the advanced status and progressive nature of the enlightened races of these perfected worlds. These people are the flowering of the evolutionary races. But such beings are still mortal; they continue to breathe, eat, sleep, and drink. This great evolution is not heaven, but it is a sublime foreshadowing of the divine worlds of the Paradise ascent.

On a normal world the biologic fitness of the mortal race was long since brought up to a high level during the post-Adamic epochs; and now, from age to age throughout the settled eras the physical evolution of man continues. Both vision and hearing are extended. By now the population has become stationary in numbers. Reproduction is regulated in accordance with planetary requirements and innate hereditary endowments: The mortals on a planet during this age are divided into from five to ten groups, and the lower groups are permitted to produce only one half as many children as the higher. The continued improvement of such a magnificent race throughout the era of light and life is largely a matter of the selective reproduction of those racial strains which exhibit superior qualities of a social, philosophic, cosmic, and spiritual nature.

The Adjusters continue to come as in former evolutionary eras, and as the epochs pass, these mortals are increasingly able to commune with the indwelling

Father fragment. During the embryonic and prespiritual stages of development the adjutant mind-spirits are still functioning. The Holy Spirit and the ministry of angels are even more effective as the successive epochs of settled life are experienced. In the fourth stage of light and life the advanced mortals seem to experience considerable conscious contact with the spirit presence of the Master Spirit of superuniverse jurisdiction, while the philosophy of such a world is focused upon the attempt to comprehend the new revelations of God the Supreme. More than one half of the human inhabitants on planets of this advanced status experience translation to the morontia state from among the living. Even so, "old things are passing away; behold, all things are becoming new."

We conceive that physical evolution will have attained its full development by the end of the fifth epoch of the light-and-life era. We observe that the upper limits of spiritual development associated with evolving human mind are determined by the Adjuster-fusion level of conjoint morontia values and cosmic meanings. But concerning wisdom: While we do not really know, we conjecture that there can never be a limit to intellectual evolution and the attainment of wisdom. On a seventh-stage world, wisdom can exhaust the material potentials, enter upon mota insight, and eventually even taste of absonite grandeur.

We observe that on these highly evolved and long seventh-stage worlds human beings fully learn the local universe language before they are translated; and I have visited a few very old planets where abandonters were teaching the older mortals the tongue of the superuniverse. And on these worlds I have observed the technique whereby the absonite personalities reveal the presence of the finaliters in the morontia temple.

This is the story of the magnificent goal of mortal striving on the evolutionary worlds; and it all takes place even before human beings enter upon their morontia careers; all of this splendid development is attainable by material mortals on the inhabited worlds, the very first stage of that endless and incomprehensible career of Paradise ascension and divinity attainment.

But can you possibly imagine what sort of evolutionary mortals are now coming up from worlds long existing in the seventh epoch of settled light and life? It is such as these who go on to the morontia worlds of the local universe capital to begin their ascension careers.

If the mortals of distraught Urantia could only view one of these more advanced worlds long settled in light and life, they would nevermore question the wisdom of the evolutionary scheme of creation. Were there no future of eternal creature progression, still the superb evolutionary attainments of the mortal races on such settled worlds of perfected achievement would amply justify man's creation on the worlds of time and space.

We often ponder: If the grand universe should be settled in light and life, would the ascending exquisite mortals still be destined to the Corps of the Finality? But we do not know.

7. THE FIRST OR PLANETARY STAGE

This epoch extends from the appearance of the morontia temple at the new planetary headquarters to the time of the settling of the entire system in light and life. This age is inaugurated by the Trinity Teacher Sons at the close of their successive world missions when the Planetary Prince is elevated to the status of Planetary Sovereign by the mandate and personal presence of the Paradise bestowal Son of that sphere. Concomitant therewith the finaliters inaugurate their active participation in planetary affairs.

To outward and visible appearances the actual rulers, or directors, of such a world settled in light and life are the Material Son and Daughter, the Planetary Adam and Eve. The finaliters are invisible, as also is the Prince-Sovereign except when in the morontia temple. The actual and literal heads of the planetary regime are therefore the Material Son and Daughter. It is the knowledge of these arrangements that has given prestige to the idea of kings and queens throughout the universe realms. And kings and queens are a great success under these ideal circumstances, when a world can command such high personalities to act in behalf of still higher but invisible rulers.

When such an era is attained on your world, no doubt Machiventa Melchizedek, now the vicegerent Planetary Prince of Urantia, will occupy the seat of the Planetary Sovereign; and it has long been conjectured on Jerusem that he will be accompanied by a son and daughter of the Urantia Adam and Eve who are now held on Edentia as wards of the Most Highs of Norlatiadek. These children of Adam might so serve on Urantia in association with the Melchizedek-Sovereign since they were deprived of procreative powers almost 37,000 years ago at the time they gave up their material bodies on Urantia in preparation for transit to Edentia.

This settled age continues on and on until every inhabited planet in the system attains the era of stabilization; and then, when the youngest world—the last to achieve light and life—has experienced such settledness for one millennium of system time, the entire system enters the stabilized status, and the individual worlds are ushered into the system epoch of the era of light and life.

8. THE SECOND OR SYSTEM STAGE

When an entire system becomes settled in life, a new order of government is inaugurated. The Planetary Sovereigns become members of the system conclave, and this new administrative body, subject to the veto of the Constellation Fathers, is supreme in authority. Such a system of inhabited worlds becomes virtually self-governing. The system legislative assembly is constituted on the headquarters world, and each planet sends its ten representatives thereto. Courts are now established on the system capitals, and only appeals are taken to the universe headquarters.

With the settling of the system the Assigned Sentinel, representative of the superuniverse Supreme Executive, becomes the volunteer adviser to the system supreme court and actual presiding officer of the new legislative assembly.

After the settling of an entire system in light and life the System Sovereigns will no more come and go. Such a sovereign remains perpetually at the head of his system. The assistant sovereigns continue to change as in former ages.

During this epoch of stabilization, for the first time midsoniters come from the universe headquarters worlds of their sojourn to act as counselors to the legislative assemblies and advisers to the adjudicational tribunals. These midsoniters also carry on certain efforts to inculcate new mota meanings of supreme value into the teaching enterprises which they sponsor jointly with the finaliters.

What the Material Sons did for the mortal races biologically, the midsonite creatures now do for these unified and glorified humans in the ever-advancing realms of philosophy and spiritualized thinking.

On the inhabited worlds the Teacher Sons become voluntary collaborators with the finaliters, and these same Teacher Sons also accompany the finaliters to the mansion worlds when those spheres are no longer to be utilized as differential receiving worlds after an entire system is settled in light and life; at least this is true by the time the entire constellation has thus evolved. But there are no groups that far advanced in Nebadon.

We are not permitted to reveal the nature of the work of the finaliters who will supervise such rededicated mansion worlds. You have, however, been informed that there are throughout the universes various types of intelligent creatures who have not been portrayed in these narratives.

And now, as the systems one by one become settled in light by virtue of the progress of their component worlds, the time comes when the last system in a given constellation attains stabilization, and the universe administrators—the Master Son, the Union of Days, and the Bright and Morning Star—arrive on the capital of the constellation to proclaim the Most Highs the unqualified rulers of the newly perfected family of one hundred settled systems of inhabited worlds.

9. THE THIRD OR CONSTELLATION STAGE

The unification of a whole constellation of settled systems is attended by new distributions of executive authority and additional readjustments of universe administration. This epoch witnesses advanced attainment on every inhabited world but is particularly characterized by readjustments on the constellation headquarters, with marked modification of relationships with both the system supervision and the local universe government. During this age many constellation and universe activities are transferred to the system capitals, and the representatives of the superuniverse assume new and more intimate relations with the planetary, system, and universe rulers. Concomitant with these new associations, certain superuniverse administrators establish themselves on the constellation capitals as volunteer advisers to the Most High Fathers.

When a constellation is thus settled in light, the legislative function ceases, and the house of System Sovereigns, presided over by the Most Highs, functions instead. Now, for the first time, such administrative groups deal directly with the superuniverse government in matters pertaining to Havona and Paradise relationships. Otherwise the constellation remains related to the local universe as before. From stage to stage in the settled life the univitatia continue to administer the constellation morontia worlds.

As the ages pass, the Constellation Fathers take over more and more of the detailed administrative or supervising functions which were formerly centered on the universe headquarters. By the attainment of the sixth stage of stabilization these unified constellations will have reached the position of well-nigh complete autonomy. Entrance upon the seventh stage of settledness will no doubt witness the exaltation of these rulers to the true dignity signified by their names, the Most Highs. To all intents and purposes the constellations will then deal directly with the superuniverse rulers, while the local universe government will expand to grasp the responsibilities of new grand universe obligations.

10. THE FOURTH OR LOCAL UNIVERSE STAGE

When a universe becomes settled in light and life, it soon swings into the established superuniverse circuits, and the Ancients of Days proclaim the establishment of the *supreme council of unlimited authority.* This new governing body consists of the one hundred Faithfuls of Days, presided over by the Union of Days, and the first act of this supreme council is to acknowledge the continued sovereignty of the Master Creator Son.

The universe administration, as far as concerns Gabriel and the Father Melchizedek, is quite unchanged. This council of unlimited authority is chiefly concerned with the new problems and the new conditions arising out of the advanced status of light and life.

The Associate Inspector now mobilizes all Assigned Sentinels to constitute the *stabilization corps of the local universe* and asks the Father Melchizedek to share its supervision with him. And now, for the first time, a corps of the Inspired Trinity Spirits are assigned to the service of the Union of Days.

The settling of an entire local universe in light and life inaugurates profound readjustments in the entire scheme of administration, from the individual inhabited worlds to the universe headquarters. New relationships extend down to the constellations and systems. The local universe Mother Spirit experiences new liaison relations with the Master Spirit of the superuniverse, and Gabriel establishes direct contact with the Ancients of Days to be effective when and as the Master Son may be absent from the headquarters world.

During this and subsequent ages the Magisterial Sons continue to function as dispensational adjudicators, while one hundred of these Avonal Sons of Paradise constitute the new high council of the Bright and Morning Star on the universe capital. Later on, and as requested by the System Sovereigns, one of these Magisterial Sons will become the supreme counselor stationed on the headquarters world of each local system until the seventh stage of unity is attained.

During this epoch the Trinity Teacher Sons are volunteer advisers, not only to the Planetary Sovereigns, but in groups of three they similarly serve the Constellation Fathers. And at last these Sons find their place in the local universe, for at this time they are removed from the jurisdiction of the local creation and are assigned to the service of the supreme council of unlimited authority.

The finaliter corps now, for the first time, acknowledges the jurisdiction of an extra-Paradise authority, the supreme council. Heretofore the finaliters have recognized no supervision this side of Paradise.

The Creator Sons of such settled universes spend much of their time on Paradise and its associated worlds and in counseling the numerous finaliter groups serving throughout the local creation. In this way the man of Michael will find a fuller fraternity of association with the glorified finaliter mortals.

Speculation concerning the function of these Creator Sons in connection with the outer universes now in process of preliminary assembly is wholly futile. But we all engage in such postulations from time to time. On attaining this fourth stage of development the Creator Son becomes administratively free; the Divine Minister is progressively blending her ministry with that of the superuniverse Master Spirit and the Infinite Spirit. There seems to be evolving a new and sublime relationship between the Creator Son, the Creative Spirit, the Evening Stars, the Teacher Sons, and the ever-increasing finaliter corps.

If Michael should ever leave Nebadon, Gabriel would undoubtedly become chief administrator with the Father Melchizedek as his associate. At the same time new status would be imparted to all orders of permanent citizenship, such as Material Sons, univitatia, midsoniters, susatia, and Spirit-fused mortals. But as long as evolution continues, the seraphim and the archangels will be required in universe administration.

We are, however, satisfied regarding two features of our speculations: If the Creator Sons are destined to the outer universes, the Divine Ministers will undoubtedly accompany them. We are equally sure that the Melchizedeks are to remain with the universes of their origin. We hold that the Melchizedeks are destined to play ever-increasingly responsible parts in local universe government and administration.

11. THE MINOR AND MAJOR SECTOR STAGES

Minor and major sectors of the superuniverse do not figure directly in the plan of being settled in light and life. Such an evolutionary progression pertains primarily to the local universe as a unit and concerns only the components of a local universe. A superuniverse is settled in light and life when all of its component local universes are thus perfected. But not one of the seven superuniverses has attained a level of progression even approaching this.

The minor sector age. As far as observations can penetrate, the fifth or minor sector stage of stabilization has exclusively to do with physical status and with the co-ordinate settling of the one hundred associated local universes in the established circuits of the superuniverse. Apparently none but the power centers and their associates are concerned in these realignments of the material creation.

The major sector age. Concerning the sixth stage, or major sector stabilization, we can only conjecture since none of us have witnessed such an event. Nevertheless, we can postulate much concerning the administrative and other readjustments which would probably accompany such an advanced status of inhabited worlds and their universe groupings.

Since the minor sector status has to do with co-ordinate physical equilibrium, we infer that major sector unification will be concerned with certain new intellectual levels of attainment, possibly some advanced achievements in the supreme realization of cosmic wisdom.

We arrive at conclusions regarding the readjustments which would probably attend the realization of hitherto unattained levels of evolutionary progress by observing the results of such achievements on the individual worlds and in the experiences of individual mortals living on these older and highly developed spheres.

Let it be made clear that the administrative mechanisms and governmental techniques of a universe or a superuniverse cannot in any manner limit or retard the evolutionary development or spiritual progress of an individual inhabited planet or of any individual mortal on such a sphere.

In some of the older universes we find worlds settled in the fifth and the sixth stages of light and life—even far extended into the seventh epoch—whose local systems are not yet settled in light. Younger planets may delay system unification, but this does not in the least handicap the progress of an older and advanced world. Neither can environmental limitations, even on an isolated world, thwart the personal attainment of the individual mortal; Jesus of Nazareth, as a man among men, personally achieved the status of light and life over nineteen hundred years ago on Urantia.

It is by observing what takes place on long-settled worlds that we arrive at fairly reliable conclusions as to what will happen when a whole superuniverse is settled in light, even if we cannot safely postulate the event of the stabilization of the seven superuniverses.

12. THE SEVENTH OR SUPERUNIVERSE STAGE

We cannot positively forecast what would occur when a superuniverse became settled in light because such an event has never factualized. From the teachings of the Melchizedeks, which have never been contradicted, we infer that sweeping changes would be made in the entire organization and administration of every unit of the creations of time and space extending from the inhabited worlds to the superuniverse headquarters.

It is generally believed that large numbers of the otherwise unattached creature-trinitized sons are to be assembled on the headquarters and divisional capitals of the settled superuniverses. This may be in anticipation of the sometime arrival of outer-spacers on their way in to Havona and Paradise; but we really do not know.

If and when a superuniverse should be settled in light and life, we believe that the now advisory Unqualified Supervisors of the Supreme would become the high administrative body on the headquarters world of the superuniverse. These are the personalities who are able to contact directly with the absonite administrators, who will forthwith become active in the settled superuniverse. Although these Unqualified Supervisors have long functioned as advisers and counselors in advanced evolutionary units of creation, they do not assume administrative responsibilities until the authority of the Supreme Being becomes sovereign.

The Unqualified Supervisors of the Supreme, who function more extensively during this epoch, are not finite, absonite, ultimate, or infinite; they *are* supremacy and only represent God the Supreme. They are the personalization of time-space supremacy and therefore do not function in Havona. They function only as supreme unifiers. They may possibly be involved in the technique of universe reflectivity, but we are not certain.

None of us entertain a satisfactory concept of what will happen when the grand universe (the seven superuniverses as dependent on Havona) becomes entirely settled in light and life. That event will undoubtedly be the most profound occurrence in the annals of eternity since the appearance of the central universe. There are those who hold that the Supreme Being himself will emerge from the Havona mystery enshrouding his spirit person and will become residential on the headquarters of the seventh superuniverse as the almighty and experiential sovereign of the perfected creations of time and space. But we really do not know.

[Presented by a Mighty Messenger temporarily assigned to the Archangel Council on Urantia.]

PAPER 56

UNIVERSAL UNITY

GOD is unity. Deity is universally co-ordinated. The universe of universes is one vast integrated mechanism which is absolutely controlled by one infinite mind. The physical, intellectual, and spiritual domains of universal creation are divinely correlated. The perfect and imperfect are truly interrelated, and therefore may the finite evolutionary creature ascend to Paradise in obedience to the Universal Father's mandate: "Be you perfect, even as I am perfect."

The diverse levels of creation are all unified in the plans and administration of the Architects of the Master Universe. To the circumscribed minds of time-space mortals the universe may present many problems and situations which apparently portray disharmony and indicate absence of effective co-ordination; but those of us who are able to observe wider stretches of universal phenomena, and who are more experienced in this art of detecting the basic unity which underlies creative diversity and of discovering the divine oneness which overspreads all this functioning of plurality, better perceive the divine and single purpose exhibited in all these manifold manifestations of universal creative energy.

1. PHYSICAL CO-ORDINATION

The physical or material creation is not infinite, but it is perfectly co-ordinated. There are force, energy, and power, but they are all one in origin. The seven superuniverses are seemingly dual; the central universe, triune; but Paradise is of single constitution. And Paradise is the actual source of all material universes—past, present, and future. But this cosmic derivation is an *eternity* event; at no *time*—past, present, or future—does either space or the material cosmos come forth from the nuclear Isle of Light. As the cosmic source, Paradise functions prior to space and before time; hence would its derivations seem to be orphaned in time and space did they not emerge through the Unqualified Absolute, their ultimate repository in space and their revealer and regulator in time.

The Unqualified Absolute upholds the physical universe, while the Deity Absolute motivates the exquisite overcontrol of all material reality; and both Absolutes are functionally unified by the Universal Absolute. This cohesive correlation of the material universe is best understood by all personalities—material, morontia, absonite, or spiritual—by the observation of the gravity response of all bona fide material reality to the gravity centering on nether Paradise.

Gravity unification is universal and unvarying; pure-energy response is likewise universal and inescapable. Pure energy (primordial force) and pure spirit are wholly preresponsive to gravity. These primal forces, inhering in the Absolutes, are personally controlled by the Universal Father; hence does all gravity center in the personal presence of the Paradise Father of pure energy and pure spirit and in his supermaterial abode.

Pure energy is the ancestor of all relative, nonspirit functional realities, while pure spirit is the potential of the divine and directive overcontrol of all basic energy systems. And these realities, so diverse as manifested throughout space and as observed in the motions of time, are both centered in the person of the Paradise Father. In him they are one—must be unified—because God is one. The Father's personality is absolutely unified.

In the infinite nature of God the Father there could not possibly exist duality of reality, such as physical and spiritual; but the instant we look aside from the infinite levels and absolute reality of the personal values of the Paradise Father, we observe the existence of these two realities and recognize that they are fully responsive to his personal presence; in him all things consist.

The moment you depart from the unqualified concept of the infinite personality of the Paradise Father, you must postulate MIND as the inevitable technique of unifying the ever-widening divergence of these dual universe manifestations of the original monothetic Creator personality, the First Source and Center—the I AM.

2. INTELLECTUAL UNITY

The Thought-Father realizes spirit expression in the Word-Son and attains reality expansion through Paradise in the far-flung material universes. The spiritual expressions of the Eternal Son are correlated with the material levels of creation by the functions of the Infinite Spirit, by whose spirit-responsive ministry of mind, and in whose physical-directive acts of mind, the spiritual realities of Deity and the material repercussions of Deity are correlated the one with the other.

Mind is the functional endowment of the Infinite Spirit, therefore infinite in potential and universal in bestowal. The primal thought of the Universal Father eternalizes in dual expression: the Isle of Paradise and his Deity equal, the spiritual and Eternal Son. Such duality of eternal reality renders the mind God, the Infinite Spirit, inevitable. Mind is the indispensable channel of communication between spiritual and material realities. The material evolutionary creature can conceive and comprehend the indwelling spirit only by the ministry of mind.

This infinite and universal mind is ministered in the universes of time and space as the cosmic mind; and though extending from the primitive ministry of the adjutant spirits up to the magnificent mind of the chief executive of a universe, even this cosmic mind is adequately unified in the supervision of the Seven Master Spirits, who are in turn co-ordinated with the Supreme Mind of time and space and perfectly correlated with the all-embracing mind of the Infinite Spirit.

3. SPIRITUAL UNIFICATION

As the universal mind gravity is centered in the Paradise personal presence of the Infinite Spirit, so does the universal spirit gravity center in the Paradise personal presence of the Eternal Son. The Universal Father is one, but to time-space he is revealed in the dual phenomena of pure energy and pure spirit.

Paradise spirit realities are likewise one, but in all time-space situations and relations this single spirit is revealed in the dual phenomena of the spirit personalities and emanations of the Eternal Son and the spirit personalities and influences of the Infinite Spirit and associated creations; and there is yet a third—pure-spirit fragmentations—the Father's bestowal of the Thought Adjusters and other spirit entities which are prepersonal.

No matter on what level of universe activities you may encounter spiritual phenomena or contact with spirit beings, you may know that they are all derived from the God who is spirit by the ministry of the Spirit Son and the Infinite Mind Spirit. And this far-flung spirit functions as a phenomenon on the evolutionary worlds of time as it is directed from the headquarters of the local universes. From these capitals of the Creator Sons come the Holy Spirit and the Spirit of Truth, together with the ministry of the adjutant mind-spirits, to the lower and evolving levels of material minds.

While mind is more unified on the level of the Master Spirits in association with the Supreme Being and as the cosmic mind in subordination to the Absolute Mind, the spirit ministry to the evolving worlds is more directly unified in the personalities resident on the headquarters of the local universes and in the persons of the presiding Divine Ministers, who are in turn well-nigh perfectly correlated with the Paradise gravity circuit of the Eternal Son, wherein occurs final unification of all time-space spirit manifestations.

Perfected creature existence can be attained, sustained, and eternalized by the fusion of self-conscious mind with a fragment of the pre-Trinity spirit endowment of some one of the persons of the Paradise Trinity. The mortal mind is the creation of the Sons and Daughters of the Eternal Son and the Infinite Spirit and, when fused with the Thought Adjuster from the Father, partakes of the threefold spirit endowment of the evolutionary realms. But these three spirit expressions become perfectly unified in the finaliters, even as they were in eternity so unified in the Universal I AM ere he ever became the Universal Father of the Eternal Son and the Infinite Spirit.

Spirit must always and ultimately become threefold in expression and Trinity-unified in final realization. Spirit originates from one source through a threefold expression; and in finality it must and does attain its full realization in that divine unification which is experienced in finding God—oneness with divinity—in eternity, and by means of the ministry of the cosmic mind of the infinite expression of the eternal word of the Father's universal thought.

4. PERSONALITY UNIFICATION

The Universal Father is a divinely unified personality; hence will all his ascendant children who are carried to Paradise by the rebound momentum of the Thought Adjusters, who went forth from Paradise to indwell material mortals in obedience to the Father's mandate, likewise be fully unified personalities ere they reach Havona.

Personality inherently reaches out to unify all constituent realities. The infinite personality of the First Source and Center, the Universal Father, unifies all seven constituent Absolutes of Infinity; and the personality of mortal man, being an exclusive and direct bestowal of the Universal Father, likewise possesses the potential of unifying the constituent factors of the mortal creature. Such unifying creativity of all creature personality is a birthmark of its high and exclusive source and is further evidential of its unbroken contact with this same source through the personality circuit, by means of which the personality of the creature maintains direct and sustaining contact with the Father of all personality on Paradise.

Notwithstanding that God is manifest from the domains of the Sevenfold up through supremacy and ultimacy to God the Absolute, the personality circuit, centering on Paradise and in the person of God the Father, provides for the complete and perfect unification of all these diverse expressions of divine personality so far as concerns all creature personalities on all levels of intelligent existence and in all the realms of the perfect, perfected, and perfecting universes.

While God is to and in the universes all that we have portrayed, nevertheless, to you and to all other God-knowing creatures he is one, your Father and their Father. To personality God cannot be plural. God is Father to each of his creatures, and it is literally impossible for any child to have more than one father.

Philosophically, cosmically, and with reference to differential levels and locations of manifestation, you may and perforce must conceive of the functioning of plural Deities and postulate the existence of plural Trinities; but in the worshipful experience of the personal contact of every worshiping personality throughout the master universe, God is one; and that unified and personal Deity is our Paradise parent, God the Father, the bestower, conservator, and Father of all personalities from mortal man on the inhabited worlds to the Eternal Son on the central Isle of Light.

5. DEITY UNITY

The oneness, the indivisibility, of Paradise Deity is existential and absolute. There are three eternal personalizations of Deity—the Universal Father, the Eternal Son, and the Infinite Spirit—but in the Paradise Trinity they are *actually* one Deity, undivided and indivisible.

From the original Paradise-Havona level of existential reality, two subabsolute levels have differentiated, and thereon have the Father, Son, and Spirit engaged in the creation of numerous personal associates and subordinates. And while it is inappropriate in this connection to undertake the consideration of absonite deity unification on transcendental levels of ultimacy, it is feasible to look at some features of the unifying function of the various Deity personalizations in whom divinity is functionally manifest to the diverse sectors of creation and to the different orders of intelligent beings.

The present functioning of divinity in the superuniverses is actively manifest in the operations of the Supreme Creators—the local universe Creator Sons and Spirits, the superuniverse Ancients of Days, and the Seven Master Spirits of Paradise. These beings constitute the first three levels of God the Sevenfold leading inward to the Universal Father, and this entire domain of God the Sevenfold is co-ordinating on the first level of experiential deity in the evolving Supreme Being.

On Paradise and in the central universe, Deity unity is a fact of existence. Throughout the evolving universes of time and space, Deity unity is an achievement.

6. UNIFICATION OF EVOLUTIONARY DEITY

When the three eternal persons of Deity function as undivided Deity in the Paradise Trinity, they achieve perfect unity; likewise, when they create, either associatively or severally, their Paradise progeny exhibit the characteristic unity of divinity. And this divinity of purpose manifested by the Supreme Creators and Rulers of the time-space domains eventuates in the unifying power potential of the sovereignty of experiential supremacy which, in the presence of the impersonal energy unity of the universe, constitutes a reality tension that can be resolved only through adequate unification with the experiential personality realities of experiential Deity.

The personality realities of the Supreme Being come forth from the Paradise Deities and on the pilot world of the outer Havona circuit unify with the power prerogatives of the Almighty Supreme coming up from the Creator divinities of the grand universe. God the Supreme as a person existed in Havona before the creation of the seven superuniverses, but he functioned only on spiritual levels. The evolution of the Almighty power of Supremacy by diverse divinity synthesis in the evolving universes eventuated in a new power presence of Deity which co-ordinated with the spiritual person of the Supreme in Havona by means of the Supreme Mind, which concomitantly translated from the potential resident in the infinite mind of the Infinite Spirit to the active functional mind of the Supreme Being.

The material-minded creatures of the evolutionary worlds of the seven superuniverses can comprehend Deity unity only as it is evolving in this power-personality synthesis of the Supreme Being. On any level of existence God cannot exceed the conceptual capacity of the beings who live on such a level. Mortal man must, through the recognition of truth, the appreciation of beauty, and the worship of goodness, evolve the recognition of a God of love and then progress through ascending deity levels to the comprehension of the Supreme. Deity, having been thus grasped as unified in power, can then be personalized in spirit to creature understanding and attainment.

While ascending mortals achieve power comprehension of the Almighty on the capitals of the superuniverses and personality comprehension of the Supreme on the outer circuits of Havona, they do not actually find the Supreme Being as they are destined to find the Paradise Deities. Even the finaliters, sixth-stage spirits, have not found the Supreme Being, nor are they likely to until they have achieved seventh-stage-spirit status, and until the Supreme has become actually functional in the activities of the future outer universes.

But when ascenders find the Universal Father as the seventh level of God the Sevenfold, they have attained the personality of the First Person of *all* deity levels of personal relationships with universe creatures.

7. UNIVERSAL EVOLUTIONARY REPERCUSSIONS

The steady progress of evolution in the time-space universes is accompanied by ever-enlarging revelations of Deity to all intelligent creatures. The attainment of the height of evolutionary progress on a world, in a system, constellation, universe, superuniverse, or in the grand universe signalizes corresponding enlargements of deity function to and in these progressive units of creation. And every such local enhancement of divinity realization is accompanied by certain well-defined repercussions of enlarged deity manifestation to all other sectors of creation. Extending outward from Paradise, each new domain of realized and attained evolution constitutes a new and enlarged revelation of experiential Deity to the universe of universes.

As the components of a local universe are progressively settled in light and life, God the Sevenfold is increasingly made manifest. Time-space evolution begins on a planet with the first expression of God the Sevenfold—the Creator Son-Creative Spirit association—in control. With the settling of a system in light, this Son-Spirit liaison attains the fullness of function; and when an entire constellation is thus settled, the second phase of God the Sevenfold becomes more active throughout such a realm. The completed administrative evolution of a local universe is attended by new and more direct ministrations of the superuniverse Master Spirits; and at this point there also begins that ever-expanding revelation and realization of God the Supreme which culminates in the ascender's comprehension of the Supreme Being while passing through the worlds of the sixth Havona circuit.

The Universal Father, the Eternal Son, and the Infinite Spirit are existential deity manifestations to intelligent creatures and are not, therefore, similarly expanded in personality relations with the mind and spirit creatures of all creation.

It should be noted that ascending mortals may experience the impersonal presence of successive levels of Deity long before they become sufficiently spiritual and adequately educated to attain experiential personal recognition of, and contact with, these Deities as personal beings.

Each new evolutionary attainment within a sector of creation, as well as every new invasion of space by divinity manifestations, is attended by simultaneous expansions of Deity functional-revelation within the then existing and previously organized units of all creation. This new invasion of the administrative work of the universes and their component units may not always appear to be executed exactly in accordance with the technique herewith outlined because it is the practice to send forth advance groups of administrators to prepare the way for the subsequent and successive eras of new administrative overcontrol. Even God the Ultimate foreshadows his transcendental overcontrol of the universes during the later stages of a local universe settled in light and life.

It is a fact that, as the creations of time and space are progressively settled in evolutionary status, there is observed a new and fuller functioning of God the Supreme concomitant with a corresponding withdrawing of the first three manifestations of God the Sevenfold. If and when the grand universe becomes settled in light and life, what then will be the future function of the Creator-Creative manifestations of God the Sevenfold if God the Supreme assumes direct control of these creations of time and space? Are these organizers and pioneers of the time-space universes to be liberated for similar activities in outer space? We do not know, but we speculate much concerning these and related matters.

As the frontiers of experiential Deity are extended out into the domains of the Unqualified Absolute, we envision the activity of God the Sevenfold during the earlier evolutionary epochs of these creations of the future. We are not all in agreement respecting the future status of the Ancients of Days and the superuniverse Master Spirits. Neither do we know whether or not the Supreme Being will therein function as in the seven superuniverses. But we all conjecture that the Michaels, the Creator Sons, are destined to function in these outer universes. Some hold that the future ages will witness some closer form of union between the associated Creator Sons and Divine Ministers; it is even possible that such a creator union might eventuate in some new expression of associate-creator identity of an ultimate nature. But we really know nothing about these possibilities of the unrevealed future.

We do know, however, that in the universes of time and space, God the Sevenfold provides a progressive approach to the Universal Father, and that this evolutionary approach is experientially unified in God the Supreme. We might conjecture that such a plan must prevail in the outer universes; on the other hand, the new orders of beings that may sometime inhabit these universes may be able to approach Deity on ultimate levels and by absonite techniques. In short, we have not the slightest concept of what technique of deity approach may become operative in the future universes of outer space.

Nevertheless, we deem that the perfected superuniverses will in some way become a part of the Paradise-ascension careers of those beings who may inhabit these outer creations. It is quite possible that in that future age we may witness outer-spacers approaching Havona through the seven superuniverses, administered by God the Supreme with or without the collaboration of the Seven Master Spirits.

8. THE SUPREME UNIFIER

The Supreme Being has a threefold function in the experience of mortal man: First, he is the unifier of time-space divinity, God the Sevenfold; second, he is the maximum of Deity which finite creatures can actually comprehend; third, he is mortal man's only avenue of approach to the transcendental experience of consorting with absonite mind, eternal spirit, and Paradise personality.

Ascendant finaliters, having been born in the local universes, nurtured in the superuniverses, and trained in the central universe, embrace in their personal experiences the full potential of the comprehension of the time-space divinity of God the Sevenfold unifying in the Supreme. Finaliters serve successively in superuniverses other than those of nativity, thereby superimposing experience upon experience until the fullness of the sevenfold diversity of possible creature experience has been encompassed. Through the ministry of the indwelling Adjusters the finaliters are enabled to *find* the Universal Father, but it is by these techniques of experience that such finaliters come really to *know* the Supreme Being, and they are destined to the service and the *revelation* of this Supreme Deity in and to the future universes of outer space.

Bear in mind, all that God the Father and his Paradise Sons do for us, we in turn and in spirit have the opportunity to do for and in the emerging Supreme Being. The experience of love, joy, and service in the universe is mutual. God the Father does not need that his sons should return to him all that he bestows upon them, but they do (or may) in turn bestow all of this upon their fellows and upon the evolving Supreme Being.

All creational phenomena are reflective of antecedent creator-spirit activities. Said Jesus, and it is literally true, "The Son does only those things which he sees the Father do." In time you mortals may begin the revelation of the Supreme to your fellows, and increasingly may you augment this revelation as you ascend Paradiseward. In eternity you may be permitted to make increasing revelations of this God of evolutionary creatures on supreme levels—even ultimate—as seventh-stage finaliters.

9. UNIVERSAL ABSOLUTE UNITY

The Unqualified Absolute and the Deity Absolute are unified in the Universal Absolute. The Absolutes are co-ordinated in the Ultimate, conditioned in the Supreme, and time-space modified in God the Sevenfold. On subinfinite levels there are *three* Absolutes, but in infinity they appear to be *one.* On Paradise there are three personalizations of Deity, but in the Trinity they *are* one.

The major philosophic proposition of the master universe is this: Did the Absolute (the three Absolutes as one in infinity) exist before the Trinity? and is the Absolute ancestral to the Trinity? or is the Trinity antecedent to the Absolute?

Is the Unqualified Absolute a force presence independent of the Trinity? Does the presence of the Deity Absolute connote the unlimited function of the Trinity? and is the Universal Absolute the final function of the Trinity, even a Trinity of Trinities?

On first thought, a concept of the Absolute as ancestor to all things—even the Trinity—seems to afford transitory satisfaction of consistency gratification and philosophic unification, but any such conclusion is invalidated by the actuality of the eternity of the Paradise Trinity. We are taught, and we believe, that the Universal Father and his Trinity associates are eternal in nature and existence. There is, then, but one consistent philosophic conclusion, and that is: The Absolute is, to all universe intelligences, the impersonal and co-ordinate reaction of the Trinity (of Trinities) to all basic and primary space situations, intrauniversal and extrauniversal. To all personality intelligences of the grand universe the Paradise Trinity forever stands in finality, eternity, supremacy, and ultimacy and, for all practical purposes of personal comprehension and creature realization, as absolute.

As creature minds may view this problem, they are led to the final postulate of the Universal I AM as the primal cause and the unqualified source of both the Trinity and the Absolute. When, therefore, we crave to entertain a personal concept of the Absolute, we revert to our ideas and ideals of the Paradise Father. When we desire to facilitate comprehension or to augment consciousness of this otherwise impersonal Absolute, we revert to the fact that the Universal Father is the existential Father of absolute personality; the Eternal Son is the Absolute Person, though not, in the experiential sense, the personalization of the Absolute.

And then we go on to envisage the experiential Trinities as culminating in the experiential personalization of the Deity Absolute, while conceiving the Universal Absolute as constituting the universe and the extrauniverse phenomena of the manifest presence of the impersonal activities of the unified and co-ordinated Deity associations of supremacy, ultimacy, and infinity—the Trinity of Trinities.

God the Father is discernible on all levels from the finite to the infinite, and though his creatures from Paradise to the evolutionary worlds have variously perceived him, only the Eternal Son and the Infinite Spirit know him as an infinity.

Spiritual personality is absolute only on Paradise, and the concept of the Absolute is unqualified only in infinity. Deity presence is absolute only on Paradise, and the revelation of God must always be partial, relative, and progressive until his power becomes experientially infinite in the space potency of the Unqualified Absolute, while his personality manifestation becomes experientially infinite in the manifest presence of the Deity Absolute, and while these two potentials of infinity become reality-unified in the Universal Absolute.

But beyond subinfinite levels the three Absolutes *are* one, and thereby is infinity Deity-realized regardless of whether any other order of existence ever self-realizes consciousness of infinity.

Existential status in eternity implies existential self-consciousness of infinity, even though another eternity may be required to experience self-realization of the experiential potentialities inherent in an infinity eternity—an eternal infinity.

And God the Father is the personal source of all manifestations of Deity and reality to all intelligent creatures and spirit beings throughout all the universe of universes. As personalities, now or in the successive universe experiences of the eternal future, no matter if you achieve the attainment of God the Sevenfold, comprehend God the Supreme, find God the Ultimate, or attempt to grasp the concept of God the Absolute, you will discover to your eternal satisfaction that in the consummation of each adventure you have, on new experiential levels, rediscovered the eternal God—the Paradise Father of all universe personalities.

The Universal Father is the explanation of universal unity as it must be supremely, even ultimately, realized in the postultimate unity of absolute values and meanings—unqualified Reality.

The Master Force Organizers go out into space and mobilize its energies to become gravity responsive to the Paradise pull of the Universal Father; and subsequently there come the Creator Sons, who organize these gravity-responding forces into inhabited universes and therein evolve intelligent creatures who receive unto themselves the spirit of the Paradise Father and subsequently ascend to the Father to become like him in all possible divinity attributes.

The ceaseless and expanding march of the Paradise creative forces through space seems to presage the ever-extending domain of the gravity grasp of the Universal Father and the never-ending multiplication of varied types of intelligent creatures who are able to love God and be loved by him, and who, by thus becoming God-knowing, may choose to be like him, may elect to attain Paradise and find God.

The universe of universes is altogether unified. God is one in power and personality. There is co-ordination of all levels of energy and all phases of personality. Philosophically and experientially, in concept and in reality, all things and beings center in the Paradise Father. God is all and in all, and no things or beings exist without him.

10. TRUTH, BEAUTY, AND GOODNESS

As the worlds settled in life and light progress from the initial stage to the seventh epoch, they successively grasp for the realization of the reality of God the Sevenfold, ranging from the adoration of the Creator Son to the worship of his Paradise Father. Throughout the continuing seventh stage of such a world's history the ever-progressing mortals grow in the knowledge of God the Supreme, while they vaguely discern the reality of the overshadowing ministry of God the Ultimate.

Throughout this glorious age the chief pursuit of the ever-advancing mortals is the quest for a better understanding and a fuller realization of the comprehensible elements of Deity—truth, beauty, and goodness. This represents man's effort to discern God in mind, matter, and spirit. And as the mortal pursues this quest, he finds himself increasingly absorbed in the experiential study of philosophy, cosmology, and divinity.

Philosophy you somewhat grasp, and divinity you comprehend in worship, social service, and personal spiritual experience, but the pursuit of beauty—cosmology—you all too often limit to the study of man's crude artistic endeavors. Beauty, art, is largely a matter of the unification of contrasts. Variety is essential to the concept of beauty. The supreme beauty, the height of finite art, is the drama of the unification of the vastness of the cosmic extremes of Creator and creature. Man finding God and God finding man—the creature becoming perfect as is the Creator—that is the supernal achievement of the supremely beautiful, the attainment of the apex of cosmic art.

Hence materialism, atheism, is the maximation of ugliness, the climax of the finite antithesis of the beautiful. Highest beauty consists in the panorama of the unification of the variations which have been born of pre-existent harmonious reality.

The attainment of cosmologic levels of thought includes:

1. *Curiosity.* Hunger for harmony and thirst for beauty. Persistent attempts to discover new levels of harmonious cosmic relationships.

2. *Aesthetic appreciation.* Love of the beautiful and ever-advancing appreciation of the artistic touch of all creative manifestations on all levels of reality.

3. *Ethic sensitivity.* Through the realization of truth the appreciation of beauty leads to the sense of the eternal fitness of those things which impinge upon the recognition of divine goodness in Deity relations with all beings; and thus even cosmology leads to the pursuit of divine reality values—to God-consciousness.

The worlds settled in light and life are so fully concerned with the comprehension of truth, beauty, and goodness because these quality values embrace the revelation of Deity to the realms of time and space. The meanings of eternal truth make a combined appeal to the intellectual and spiritual natures of mortal man. Universal beauty embraces the harmonious relations and rhythms of the cosmic creation; this is more distinctly the intellectual appeal and leads towards unified and synchronous comprehension of the material universe. Divine goodness represents the revelation of infinite values to the finite mind, therein to be perceived and elevated to the very threshold of the spiritual level of human comprehension.

Truth is the basis of science and philosophy, presenting the intellectual foundation of religion. Beauty sponsors art, music, and the meaningful rhythms of all human experience. Goodness embraces the sense of ethics, morality, and religion—experiential perfection-hunger.

The existence of beauty implies the presence of appreciative creature mind just as certainly as the fact of progressive evolution indicates the dominance of the Supreme Mind. Beauty is the intellectual recognition of the harmonious time-space synthesis of the far-flung diversification of phenomenal reality, all of which stems from pre-existent and eternal oneness.

Goodness is the mental recognition of the relative values of the diverse levels of divine perfection. The recognition of goodness implies a mind of moral status, a personal mind with ability to discriminate between good and evil. But the possession of goodness, greatness, is the measure of real divinity attainment.

The recognition of *true relations* implies a mind competent to discriminate between truth and error. The bestowal Spirit of Truth which invests the human minds of Urantia is unerringly responsive to truth—the living spirit relationship of all things and all beings as they are co-ordinated in the eternal ascent Godward.

Every impulse of every electron, thought, or spirit is an acting unit in the whole universe. Only sin is isolated and evil gravity resisting on the mental and spiritual levels. The universe is a whole; no thing or being exists or lives in isolation. Self-realization is potentially evil if it is antisocial. It is literally true: "No man lives by himself." Cosmic socialization constitutes the highest form of personality unification. Said Jesus: "He who would be greatest among you, let him become server of all."

Even truth, beauty, and goodness—man's intellectual approach to the universe of mind, matter, and spirit—must be combined into one unified concept of a divine and supreme *ideal.* As mortal personality unifies the human experience with matter, mind, and spirit, so does this divine and supreme ideal become power-unified in Supremacy and then personalized as a God of fatherly love.

All insight into the relations of the parts to any given whole requires an understanding grasp of the relation of all parts to that whole; and in the universe this means the relation of created parts to the Creative Whole. Deity thus becomes the transcendental, even the infinite, goal of universal and eternal attainment.

Universal beauty is the recognition of the reflection of the Isle of Paradise in the material creation, while eternal truth is the special ministry of the Paradise Sons who not only bestow themselves upon the mortal races but even pour out their Spirit of Truth upon all peoples. Divine goodness is more fully shown forth in the loving ministry of the manifold personalities of the Infinite Spirit.

But love, the sum total of these three qualities, is man's perception of God as his spirit Father.

Physical matter is the time-space shadow of the Paradise energy-shining of the absolute Deities. Truth meanings are the mortal-intellect repercussions of the eternal word of Deity—the time-space comprehension of supreme concepts. The goodness values of divinity are the merciful ministries of the spirit personalities of the Universal, the Eternal, and the Infinite to the time-space finite creatures of the evolutionary spheres.

These meaningful reality values of divinity are blended in the Father's relation with each personal creature as divine love. They are co-ordinated in the Son and his Sons as divine mercy. They manifest their qualities through the Spirit and his spirit children as divine ministry, the portrayal of loving mercy to the children of time. These three divinities are primarily manifested by the Supreme Being as power-personality synthesis. They are variously shown forth by God the Sevenfold in seven differing associations of divine meanings and values on seven ascending levels.

To finite man truth, beauty, and goodness embrace the full revelation of divinity reality. As this love-comprehension of Deity finds spiritual expression in the lives of God-knowing mortals, there are yielded the fruits of divinity: intellectual peace, social progress, moral satisfaction, spiritual joy, and cosmic wisdom. The advanced mortals on a world in the seventh stage of light and life have learned that love is the greatest thing in the universe—and they know that God is love.

Love is the desire to do good to others.

[Presented by a Mighty Messenger visiting on Urantia, by request of the Nebadon Revelatory Corps and in collaboration with a certain Melchizedek, the vicegerent Planetary Prince of Urantia.]

* * * * *

This paper on Universal Unity is the twenty-fifth of a series of presentations by various authors, having been sponsored as a group by a commission of Nebadon personalities numbering twelve and acting under the direction of Mantutia Melchizedek. We indited these narratives and put them in the English language, by a technique authorized by our superiors, in the year 1934 of Urantia time.

PART III

THE HISTORY OF URANTIA

These papers were sponsored by a Corps of Local Universe Personalities acting by authority of Gabriel of Salvington.

PART III
The History of Urantia

PAPER 57
THE ORIGIN OF URANTIA

IN PRESENTING excerpts from the archives of Jerusem for the records of Urantia respecting its antecedents and early history, we are directed to reckon time in terms of current usage—the present leap-year calendar of 365¼ days to the year. As a rule, no attempt will be made to give exact years, though they are of record. We will use the nearest whole numbers as the better method of presenting these historic facts.

When referring to an event as of one or two millions of years ago, we intend to date such an occurrence back that number of years from the early decades of the twentieth century of the Christian era. We will thus depict these far-distant events as occurring in even periods of thousands, millions, and billions of years.

1. THE ANDRONOVER NEBULA

Urantia is of origin in your sun, and your sun is one of the multifarious offspring of the Andronover nebula, which was onetime organized as a component part of the physical power and material matter of the local universe of Nebadon. And this great nebula itself took origin in the universal force-charge of space in the superuniverse of Orvonton, long, long ago.

At the time of the beginning of this recital, the Primary Master Force Organizers of Paradise had long been in full control of the space-energies which were later organized as the Andronover nebula.

987,000,000,000 years ago associate force organizer and then acting inspector number 811,307 of the Orvonton series, traveling out from Uversa, reported to the Ancients of Days that space conditions were favorable for the initiation of materialization phenomena in a certain sector of the, then, easterly segment of Orvonton.

900,000,000,000 years ago, the Uversa archives testify, there was recorded a permit issued by the Uversa Council of Equilibrium to the superuniverse government authorizing the dispatch of a force organizer and staff to the region previously designated by inspector number 811,307. The Orvonton authorities commissioned the original discoverer of this potential universe to execute the mandate of the Ancients of Days calling for the organization of a new material creation.

The recording of this permit signifies that the force organizer and staff had already departed from Uversa on the long journey to that easterly space sector where they were subsequently to engage in those protracted activities which would terminate in the emergence of a new physical creation in Orvonton.

875,000,000,000 years ago the enormous Andronover nebula number 876,926 was duly initiated. Only the presence of the force organizer and the liaison staff was required to inaugurate the energy whirl which eventually grew into this vast cyclone of space. Subsequent to the initiation of such nebular revolutions, the living force organizers simply withdraw at right angles to the plane of the revolutionary disk, and from that time forward, the inherent qualities of energy insure the progressive and orderly evolution of such a new physical system.

At about this time the narrative shifts to the functioning of the personalities of the superuniverse. In reality the story has its proper beginning at this point—at just about the time the Paradise force organizers are preparing to withdraw, having made the space-energy conditions ready for the action of the power directors and physical controllers of the superuniverse of Orvonton.

2. THE PRIMARY NEBULAR STAGE

All evolutionary material creations are born of circular and gaseous nebulae, and all such primary nebulae are circular throughout the early part of their gaseous existence. As they grow older, they usually become spiral, and when their function of sun formation has run its course, they often terminate as clusters of stars or as enormous suns surrounded by a varying number of planets, satellites, and smaller groups of matter in many ways resembling your own diminutive solar system.

800,000,000,000 years ago the Andronover creation was well established as one of the magnificent primary nebulae of Orvonton. As the astronomers of near-by universes looked out upon this phenomenon of space, they saw very little to attract their attention. Gravity estimates made in adjacent creations indicated that space materializations were taking place in the Andronover regions, but that was all.

700,000,000,000 years ago the Andronover system was assuming gigantic proportions, and additional physical controllers were dispatched to nine surrounding material creations to afford support and supply co-operation to the power centers of this new material system which was so rapidly evolving. At this distant date all of the material bequeathed to the subsequent creations was held within the confines of this gigantic space wheel, which continued ever to whirl and, after reaching its maximum of diameter, to whirl faster and faster as it continued to condense and contract.

600,000,000,000 years ago the height of the Andronover energy-mobilization period was attained; the nebula had acquired its maximum of mass. At this time it was a gigantic circular gas cloud in shape somewhat like a flattened spheroid. This was the early period of differential mass formation and varying revolutionary velocity. Gravity and other influences were about to begin their work of converting space gases into organized matter.

3. THE SECONDARY NEBULAR STAGE

The enormous nebula now began gradually to assume the spiral form and to become clearly visible to the astronomers of even distant universes. This is the natural history of most nebulae; before they begin to throw off suns and start upon the work of universe building, these secondary space nebulae are usually observed as *spiral phenomena.*

The near-by star students of that faraway era, as they observed this metamorphosis of the Andronover nebula, saw exactly what twentieth-century astronomers see when they turn their telescopes spaceward and view the present-age spiral nebulae of adjacent outer space.

About the time of the attainment of the maximum of mass, the gravity control of the gaseous content commenced to weaken, and there ensued the stage of gas escapement, the gas streaming forth as two gigantic and distinct arms, which took origin on opposite sides of the mother mass. The rapid revolutions of this enormous central core soon imparted a spiral appearance to these two projecting gas streams. The cooling and subsequent condensation of portions of these protruding arms eventually produced their knotted appearance. These denser portions were vast systems and subsystems of physical matter whirling through space in the midst of the gaseous cloud of the nebula while being held securely within the gravity grasp of the mother wheel.

But the nebula had begun to contract, and the increase in the rate of revolution further lessened gravity control; and erelong, the outer gaseous regions began actually to escape from the immediate embrace of the nebular nucleus, passing out into space on circuits of irregular outline, returning to the nuclear regions to complete their circuits, and so on. But this was only a temporary stage of nebular progression. The ever-increasing rate of whirling was soon to throw enormous suns off into space on independent circuits.

And this is what happened in Andronover ages upon ages ago. The energy wheel grew and grew until it attained its maximum of expansion, and then, when contraction set in, it whirled on faster and faster until, eventually, the critical centrifugal stage was reached and the great breakup began.

500,000,000,000 years ago the first Andronover sun was born. This blazing streak broke away from the mother gravity grasp and tore out into space on an independent adventure in the cosmos of creation. Its orbit was determined by its path of escape. Such young suns quickly become spherical and start out on their long and eventful careers as the stars of space. Excepting terminal nebular nucleuses, the vast majority of Orvonton suns have had an analogous birth. These escaping suns pass through varied periods of evolution and subsequent universe service.

400,000,000,000 years ago began the recaptive period of the Andronover nebula. Many of the near-by and smaller suns were recaptured as a result of the gradual enlargement and further condensation of the mother nucleus. Very soon there was inaugurated the terminal phase of nebular condensation, the period which always precedes the final segregation of these immense space aggregations of energy and matter.

It was scarcely a million years subsequent to this epoch that Michael of Nebadon, a Creator Son of Paradise, selected this disintegrating nebula as the site of his adventure in universe building. Almost immediately the architectural worlds of Salvington and the one hundred constellation headquarters groups of planets were begun. It required almost one million years to complete these clusters of specially created worlds. The local system headquarters planets were constructed over a period extending from that time to about five billion years ago.

300,000,000,000 years ago the Andronover solar circuits were well established, and the nebular system was passing through a transient period of relative physical stability. About this time the staff of Michael arrived on Salvington, and the Uversa government of Orvonton extended physical recognition to the local universe of Nebadon.

200,000,000,000 years ago witnessed the progression of contraction and condensation with enormous heat generation in the Andronover central cluster, or nuclear mass. Relative space appeared even in the regions near the central mother-sun wheel. The outer regions were becoming more stabilized and better organized; some planets revolving around the newborn suns had cooled sufficiently to be suitable for life implantation. The oldest inhabited planets of Nebadon date from these times.

Now the completed universe mechanism of Nebadon first begins to function, and Michael's creation is registered on Uversa as a universe of inhabitation and progressive mortal ascension.

100,000,000,000 years ago the nebular apex of condensation tension was reached; the point of maximum heat tension was attained. This critical stage of gravity-heat contention sometimes lasts for ages, but sooner or later, heat wins the struggle with gravity, and the spectacular period of sun dispersion begins. And this marks the end of the secondary career of a space nebula.

4. TERTIARY AND QUARTAN STAGES

The primary stage of a nebula is circular; the secondary, spiral; the tertiary stage is that of the first sun dispersion, while the quartan embraces the second and last cycle of sun dispersion, with the mother nucleus ending either as a globular cluster or as a solitary sun functioning as the center of a terminal solar system.

75,000,000,000 years ago this nebula had attained the height of its sun-family stage. This was the apex of the first period of sun losses. The majority of these suns have since possessed themselves of extensive systems of planets, satellites, dark islands, comets, meteors, and cosmic dust clouds.

50,000,000,000 years ago this first period of sun dispersion was completed; the nebula was fast finishing its tertiary cycle of existence, during which it gave origin to 876,926 sun systems.

25,000,000,000 years ago witnessed the completion of the tertiary cycle of nebular life and brought about the organization and relative stabilization of the far-flung starry systems derived from this parent nebula. But the process of physical contraction and increased heat production continued in the central mass of the nebular remnant.

augmented by the capture of enormous quantities of meteors. Indeed they still continue to capture meteors, but in greatly lessened numbers.

The planets do not swing around the sun in the equatorial plane of their solar mother, which they would do if they had been thrown off by solar revolution. Rather, they travel in the plane of the Angona solar extrusion, which existed at a considerable angle to the plane of the sun's equator.

While Angona was unable to capture any of the solar mass, your sun did add to its metamorphosing planetary family some of the circulating space material of the visiting system. Due to the intense gravity field of Angona, its tributary planetary family pursued orbits of considerable distance from the dark giant; and shortly after the extrusion of the solar system ancestral mass and while Angona was yet in the vicinity of the sun, three of the major planets of the Angona system swung so near to the massive solar system ancestor that its gravitational pull, augmented by that of the sun, was sufficient to overbalance the gravity grasp of Angona and to permanently detach these three tributaries of the celestial wanderer.

All of the solar system material derived from the sun was originally endowed with a homogeneous direction of orbital swing, and had it not been for the intrusion of these three foreign space bodies, all solar system material would still maintain the same direction of orbital movement. As it was, the impact of the three Angona tributaries injected new and foreign directional forces into the emerging solar system with the resultant appearance of *retrograde motion.* Retrograde motion in any astronomic system is always accidental and always appears as a result of the collisional impact of foreign space bodies. Such collisions may not always produce retrograde motion, but no retrograde ever appears except in a system containing masses which have diverse origins.

6. THE SOLAR SYSTEM STAGE—THE PLANET-FORMING ERA

Subsequent to the birth of the solar system a period of diminishing solar disgorgement ensued. Decreasingly, for another five hundred thousand years, the sun continued to pour forth diminishing volumes of matter into surrounding space. But during these early times of erratic orbits, when the surrounding bodies made their nearest approach to the sun, the solar parent was able to recapture a large portion of this meteoric material.

The planets nearest the sun were the first to have their revolutions slowed down by tidal friction. Such gravitational influences also contribute to the stabilization of planetary orbits while acting as a brake on the rate of planetary-axial revolution, causing a planet to revolve ever slower until axial revolution ceases, leaving one hemisphere of the planet always turned toward the sun or larger body, as is illustrated by the planet Mercury and by the moon, which always turns the same face toward Urantia.

When the tidal frictions of the moon and the earth become equalized, the earth will always turn the same hemisphere toward the moon, and the day and month will be analogous—in length about forty-seven days. When such stability of orbits is attained, tidal frictions will go into reverse action, no longer driving the moon farther away from the earth but gradually drawing the satellite toward the planet. And then, in that far-distant future when the moon approaches to within about eleven thousand miles of the earth, the gravity action of the latter will cause the moon to disrupt, and this tidal-gravity explosion will shatter the moon into small particles, which may assemble about the world as rings of matter resembling those of Saturn or may be gradually drawn into the earth as meteors.

If space bodies are similar in size and density, collisions may occur. But if two space bodies of similar density are relatively unequal in size, then, if the smaller progressively approaches the larger, the disruption of the smaller body will occur when the radius of its orbit becomes less than two and one-half times the radius of the larger body. Collisions among the giants of space are rare indeed, but these gravity-tidal explosions of lesser bodies are quite common.

Shooting stars occur in swarms because they are the fragments of larger bodies of matter which have been disrupted by tidal gravity exerted by near-by and still larger space bodies. Saturn's rings are the fragments of a disrupted satellite. One of the moons of Jupiter is now approaching dangerously near the critical zone of tidal disruption and, within a few million years, will either be claimed by the planet or will undergo gravity-tidal disruption. The fifth planet of the solar system of long, long ago traversed an irregular orbit, periodically making closer and closer approach to Jupiter until it entered the critical zone of gravity-tidal disruption, was swiftly fragmentized, and became the present-day cluster of asteroids.

4,000,000,000 years ago witnessed the organization of the Jupiter and Saturn systems much as observed today except for their moons, which continued to increase in size for several billions of years. In fact, all of the planets and satellites of the solar system are still growing as the result of continued meteoric captures.

3,500,000,000 years ago the condensation nucleuses of the other ten planets were well formed, and the cores of most of the moons were intact, though some of the smaller satellites later united to make the present-day larger moons. This age may be regarded as the era of planetary assembly.

3,000,000,000 years ago the solar system was functioning much as it does today. Its members continued to grow in size as space meteors continued to pour in upon the planets and their satellites at a prodigious rate.

About this time your solar system was placed on the physical registry of Nebadon and given its name, Monmatia.

2,500,000,000 years ago the planets had grown immensely in size. Urantia was a well-developed sphere about one tenth its present mass and was still growing rapidly by meteoric accretion.

All of this tremendous activity is a normal part of the making of an evolutionary world on the order of Urantia and constitutes the astronomic preliminaries to the setting of the stage for the beginning of the physical evolution of such worlds of space in preparation for the life adventures of time.

7. THE METEORIC ERA—THE VOLCANIC AGE THE PRIMITIVE PLANETARY ATMOSPHERE

Throughout these early times the space regions of the solar system were swarming with small disruptive and condensation bodies, and in the absence of a protective combustion atmosphere such space bodies crashed directly on the surface of Urantia. These incessant impacts kept the surface of the planet more or less heated, and this, together with the increased action of gravity as the sphere grew larger, began to set in operation those influences which gradually caused the heavier elements, such as iron, to settle more and more toward the center of the planet.

2,000,000,000 years ago the earth began decidedly to gain on the moon. Always had the planet been larger than its satellite, but there was not so much difference in size until about this time, when enormous space bodies were captured by the earth. Urantia was then about one fifth its present size and had become large enough to hold the primitive atmosphere which had begun to appear as a result of the internal elemental contest between the heated interior and the cooling crust.

Definite volcanic action dates from these times. The internal heat of the earth continued to be augmented by the deeper and deeper burial of the radioactive or heavier elements brought in from space by the meteors. The study of these radioactive elements will reveal that Urantia is more than one billion years old on its surface. The radium clock is your most reliable timepiece for making scientific estimates of the age of the planet, but all such estimates are too short because the radioactive materials open to your scrutiny are all derived from the earth's surface and hence represent Urantia's comparatively recent acquirements of these elements.

1,500,000,000 years ago the earth was two thirds its present size, while the moon was nearing its present mass. Earth's rapid gain over the moon in size enabled it to begin the slow robbery of the little atmosphere which its satellite originally had.

Volcanic action is now at its height. The whole earth is a veritable fiery inferno, the surface resembling its earlier molten state before the heavier metals gravitated toward the center. *This is the volcanic age.* Nevertheless, a crust, consisting chiefly of the comparatively lighter granite, is gradually forming. The stage is being set for a planet which can someday support life.

The primitive planetary atmosphere is slowly evolving, now containing some water vapor, carbon monoxide, carbon dioxide, and hydrogen chloride, but there is little or no free nitrogen or free oxygen. The atmosphere of a world in the volcanic age presents a queer spectacle. In addition to the gases enumerated it is heavily charged with numerous volcanic gases and, as the air belt matures, with the combustion products of the heavy meteoric showers which are constantly hurtling in upon the planetary surface. Such meteoric combustion keeps the atmospheric oxygen very nearly exhausted, and the rate of meteoric bombardment is still tremendous.

Presently, the atmosphere became more settled and cooled sufficiently to start precipitation of rain on the hot rocky surface of the planet. For thousands of years Urantia was enveloped in one vast and continuous blanket of steam. And during these ages the sun never shone upon the earth's surface.

Much of the carbon of the atmosphere was abstracted to form the carbonates of the various metals which abounded in the superficial layers of the planet. Later on, much greater quantities of these carbon gases were consumed by the early and prolific plant life.

Even in the later periods the continuing lava flows and the incoming meteors kept the oxygen of the air almost completely used up. Even the early deposits of the soon appearing primitive ocean contain no colored stones or shales. And for a long time after this ocean appeared, there was virtually no free oxygen in the atmosphere; and it did not appear in significant quantities until it was later generated by the seaweeds and other forms of vegetable life.

The primitive planetary atmosphere of the volcanic age affords little protection against the collisional impacts of the meteoric swarms. Millions upon millions of meteors are able to penetrate such an air belt to smash against the planetary crust as solid bodies. But as time passes, fewer and fewer prove large enough to resist the ever-stronger friction shield of the oxygen-enriching atmosphere of the later eras.

8. CRUSTAL STABILIZATION THE AGE OF EARTHQUAKES THE WORLD OCEAN AND THE FIRST CONTINENT

1,000,000,000 years ago is the date of the actual beginning of Urantia history. The planet had attained approximately its present size. And about this time it was placed upon the physical registries of Nebadon and given its name, *Urantia.*

The atmosphere, together with incessant moisture precipitation, facilitated the cooling of the earth's crust. Volcanic action early equalized internal-heat pressure and crustal contraction; and as volcanoes rapidly decreased, earthquakes made their appearance as this epoch of crustal cooling and adjustment progressed.

The real geologic history of Urantia begins with the cooling of the earth's crust sufficiently to cause the formation of the first ocean. Water-vapor condensation on the cooling surface of the earth, once begun, continued until it was virtually complete. By the end of this period the ocean was world-wide, covering the entire planet to an average depth of over one mile. The tides were then in play much as they are now observed, but this primitive ocean was not salty; it was practically a fresh-water covering for the world. In those days, most of the chlorine was combined with various metals, but there was enough, in union with hydrogen, to render this water faintly acid.

At the opening of this faraway era, Urantia should be envisaged as a water-bound planet. Later on, deeper and hence denser lava flows came out upon the bottom of the present Pacific Ocean, and this part of the water-covered surface became considerably depressed. The first continental land mass emerged from the world ocean in compensatory adjustment of the equilibrium of the gradually thickening earth's crust.

950,000,000 years ago Urantia presents the picture of one great continent of land and one large body of water, the Pacific Ocean. Volcanoes are still widespread and earthquakes are both frequent and severe. Meteors continue to bombard the earth, but they are diminishing in both frequency and size. The atmosphere is clearing up, but the amount of carbon dioxide continues large. The earth's crust is gradually stabilizing.

It was at about this time that Urantia was assigned to the system of Satania for planetary administration and was placed on the life registry of Norlatiadek.

Then began the administrative recognition of the small and insignificant sphere which was destined to be the planet whereon Michael would subsequently engage in the stupendous undertaking of mortal bestowal, would participate in those experiences which have since caused Urantia to become locally known as the "world of the cross."

900,000,000 years ago witnessed the arrival on Urantia of the first Satania scouting party sent out from Jerusem to examine the planet and make a report on its adaptation for a life-experiment station. This commission consisted of twenty-four members, embracing Life Carriers, Lanonandek Sons, Melchizedeks, seraphim, and other orders of celestial life having to do with the early days of planetary organization and administration.

After making a painstaking survey of the planet, this commission returned to Jerusem and reported favorably to the System Sovereign, recommending that Urantia be placed on the life-experiment registry. Your world was accordingly registered on Jerusem as a decimal planet, and the Life Carriers were notified that they would be granted permission to institute new patterns of mechanical, chemical, and electrical mobilization at the time of their subsequent arrival with life transplantation and implantation mandates.

In due course arrangements for the planetary occupation were completed by the mixed commission of twelve on Jerusem and approved by the planetary commission of seventy on Edentia. These plans, proposed by the advisory counselors of the Life Carriers, were finally accepted on Salvington. Soon thereafter the Nebadon broadcasts carried the announcement that Urantia would become the stage whereon the Life Carriers would execute their sixtieth Satania experiment designed to amplify and improve the Satania type of the Nebadon life patterns.

Shortly after Urantia was first recognized on the universe broadcasts to all Nebadon, it was accorded full universe status. Soon thereafter it was registered in the records of the minor and the major sector headquarters planets of the superuniverse; and before this age was over, Urantia had found entry on the planetary-life registry of Uversa.

This entire age was characterized by frequent and violent storms. The early crust of the earth was in a state of continual flux. Surface cooling alternated with immense lava flows. Nowhere can there be found on the surface of the world anything of this original planetary crust. It has all been mixed up too many times with extruding lavas of deep origins and admixed with subsequent deposits of the early world-wide ocean.

Nowhere on the surface of the world will there be found more of the modified remnants of these ancient preocean rocks than in northeastern Canada around Hudson Bay. This extensive granite elevation is composed of stone belonging to the preoceanic ages. These rock layers have been heated, bent, twisted, upcrumpled, and again and again have they passed through these distorting metamorphic experiences.

Throughout the oceanic ages, enormous layers of fossil-free stratified stone were deposited on this ancient ocean bottom. (Limestone can form as a result of chemical precipitation; not all of the older limestone was produced by marine-life deposition.) In none of these ancient rock formations will there be found evidences of life; they contain no fossils unless, by some chance, later deposits of the water ages have become mixed with these older prelife layers.

The earth's early crust was highly unstable, but mountains were not in process of formation. The planet contracted under gravity pressure as it formed. Mountains are not the result of the collapse of the cooling crust of a contracting sphere; they appear later on as a result of the action of rain, gravity, and erosion.

The continental land mass of this era increased until it covered almost ten per cent of the earth's surface. Severe earthquakes did not begin until the continental mass of land emerged well above the water. When they once began, they increased in frequency and severity for ages. For millions upon millions of years earthquakes have diminished, but Urantia still has an average of fifteen daily.

850,000,000 years ago the first real epoch of the stabilization of the earth's crust began. Most of the heavier metals had settled down toward the center of the globe; the cooling crust had ceased to cave in on such an extensive scale as in former ages. There was established a better balance between the land extrusion and the heavier ocean bed. The flow of the subcrustal lava bed became well-nigh world-wide, and this compensated and stabilized the fluctuations due to cooling, contracting, and superficial shifting.

Volcanic eruptions and earthquakes continued to diminish in frequency and severity. The atmosphere was clearing of volcanic gases and water vapor, but the percentage of carbon dioxide was still high.

Electric disturbances in the air and in the earth were also decreasing. The lava flows had brought to the surface a mixture of elements which diversified the crust and better insulated the planet from certain space-energies. And all of this did much to facilitate the control of terrestrial energy and to regulate its flow, as is disclosed by the functioning of the magnetic poles.

800,000,000 years ago witnessed the inauguration of the first great land epoch, the age of increased continental emergence.

Since the condensation of the earth's hydrosphere, first into the world ocean and subsequently into the Pacific Ocean, this latter body of water should be visualized as then covering nine tenths of the earth's surface. Meteors falling into the sea accumulated on the ocean bottom, and meteors are, generally speaking, composed of heavy materials. Those falling on the land were largely oxidized, subsequently worn down by erosion, and washed into the ocean basins. Thus the ocean bottom grew increasingly heavy, and added to this was the weight of a body of water at some places ten miles deep.

The increasing downthrust of the Pacific Ocean operated further to upthrust the continental land mass. Europe and Africa began to rise out of the Pacific depths along with those masses now called Australia, North and South America, and the continent of Antarctica, while the bed of the Pacific Ocean engaged in a further compensatory sinking adjustment. By the end of this period almost one third of the earth's surface consisted of land, all in one continental body.

With this increase in land elevation the first climatic differences of the planet appeared. Land elevation, cosmic clouds, and oceanic influences are the chief factors in climatic fluctuation. The backbone of the Asiatic land mass reached a height of almost nine miles at the time of the maximum land emergence. Had there been much moisture in the air hovering over these highly elevated regions, enormous ice blankets would have formed; the ice age would have arrived long before it did. It was several hundred millions of years before so much land again appeared above water.

750,000,000 years ago the first breaks in the continental land mass began as the great north-and-south cracking, which later admitted the ocean waters and prepared the way for the westward drift of the continents of North and South America, including Greenland. The long east-and-west cleavage separated Africa from Europe and severed the land masses of Australia, the Pacific Islands, and Antarctica from the Asiatic continent.

700,000,000 years ago Urantia was approaching the ripening of conditions suitable for the support of life. The continental land drift continued; increasingly the ocean penetrated the land as long fingerlike seas providing those shallow waters and sheltered bays which are so suitable as a habitat for marine life.

650,000,000 years ago witnessed the further separation of the land masses and, in consequence, a further extension of the continental seas. And these waters were rapidly attaining that degree of saltiness which was essential to Urantia life.

It was these seas and their successors that laid down the life records of Urantia, as subsequently discovered in well-preserved stone pages, volume upon volume, as era succeeded era and age grew upon age. These inland seas of olden times were truly the cradle of evolution.

[Presented by a Life Carrier, a member of the original Urantia Corps and now a resident observer.]

PAPER 58

LIFE ESTABLISHMENT ON URANTIA

IN ALL Satania there are only sixty-one worlds similar to Urantia, life-modification planets. The majority of inhabited worlds are peopled in accordance with established techniques; on such spheres the Life Carriers are afforded little leeway in their plans for life implantation. But about one world in ten is designated as a *decimal planet* and assigned to the special registry of the Life Carriers; and on such planets we are permitted to undertake certain life experiments in an effort to modify or possibly improve the standard universe types of living beings.

1. PHYSICAL-LIFE PREREQUISITES

600,000,000 years ago the commission of Life Carriers sent out from Jerusem arrived on Urantia and began the study of physical conditions preparatory to launching life on world number 606 of the Satania system. This was to be our six hundred and sixth experience with the initiation of the Nebadon life patterns in Satania and our sixtieth opportunity to make changes and institute modifications in the basic and standard life designs of the local universe.

It should be made clear that Life Carriers cannot initiate life until a sphere is ripe for the inauguration of the evolutionary cycle. Neither can we provide for a more rapid life development than can be supported and accommodated by the physical progress of the planet.

The Satania Life Carriers had projected a sodium chloride pattern of life; therefore no steps could be taken toward planting it until the ocean waters had become sufficiently briny. The Urantia type of protoplasm can function only in a suitable salt solution. All ancestral life—vegetable and animal—evolved in a salt-solution habitat. And even the more highly organized land animals could not continue to live did not this same essential salt solution circulate throughout their bodies in the blood stream which freely bathes, literally submerses, every tiny living cell in this "briny deep."

Your primitive ancestors freely circulated about in the salty ocean; today, this same oceanlike salty solution freely circulates about in your bodies, bathing each individual cell with a chemical liquid in all essentials comparable to the salt water which stimulated the first protoplasmic reactions of the first living cells to function on the planet.

But as this era opens, Urantia is in every way evolving toward a state favorable for the support of the initial forms of marine life. Slowly but surely physical developments on earth and in adjacent space regions are preparing the stage for the later attempts to establish such life forms as we had decided would be best adapted to the unfolding physical environment—both terrestrial and spatial.

Subsequently the Satania commission of Life Carriers returned to Jerusem, preferring to await the further breakup of the continental land mass, which would afford still more inland seas and sheltered bays, before actually beginning life implantation.

On a planet where life has a marine origin, the ideal conditions for life implantation are provided by a large number of inland seas, by an extensive shore line of shallow waters and sheltered bays; and just such a distribution of the earth's waters was rapidly developing. These ancient inland seas were seldom over five or six hundred feet deep, and sunlight can penetrate ocean water for more than six hundred feet.

And it was from such seashores of the mild and equable climes of a later age that primitive plant life found its way onto the land. There the high degree of carbon in the atmosphere afforded the new land varieties of life opportunity for speedy and luxuriant growth. Though this atmosphere was then ideal for plant growth, it contained such a high degree of carbon dioxide that no animal, much less man, could have lived on the face of the earth.

2. THE URANTIA ATMOSPHERE

The planetary atmosphere filters through to the earth about one two-billionth of the sun's total light emanation. If the light falling upon North America were paid for at the rate of two cents per kilowatt-hour, the annual light bill would be upward of 800 quadrillion dollars. Chicago's bill for sunshine would amount to considerably over 100 million dollars a day. And it should be remembered that you receive from the sun other forms of energy—light is not the only solar contribution reaching your atmosphere. Vast solar energies pour in upon Urantia embracing wave lengths ranging both above and below the recognition range of human vision.

The earth's atmosphere is all but opaque to much of the solar radiation at the extreme ultraviolet end of the spectrum. Most of these short wave lengths are absorbed by a layer of ozone which exists throughout a level about ten miles above the surface of the earth, and which extends spaceward for another ten miles. The ozone permeating this region, at conditions prevailing on the earth's surface, would make a layer only one tenth of an inch thick; nevertheless, this relatively small and apparently insignificant amount of ozone protects Urantia inhabitants from the excess of these dangerous and destructive ultraviolet radiations present in sunlight. But were this ozone layer just a trifle thicker, you would be deprived of the highly important and health-giving ultraviolet rays which now reach the earth's surface, and which are ancestral to one of the most essential of your vitamins.

And yet some of the less imaginative of your mortal mechanists insist on viewing material creation and human evolution as an accident. The Urantia midwayers have assembled over fifty thousand facts of physics and chemistry which they deem to be incompatible with the laws of accidental chance, and which they contend unmistakably demonstrate the presence of intelligent purpose in the material creation. And all of this takes no account of their catalogue of more than one hundred thousand findings outside the domain of physics and chemistry which they maintain prove the presence of mind in the planning, creation, and maintenance of the material cosmos.

Your sun pours forth a veritable flood of death-dealing rays, and your pleasant life on Urantia is due to the "fortuitous" influence of more than two-score apparently accidental protective operations similar to the action of this unique ozone layer.

Were it not for the "blanketing" effect of the atmosphere at night, heat would be lost by radiation so rapidly that life would be impossible of maintenance except by artificial provision.

The lower five or six miles of the earth's atmosphere is the troposphere; this is the region of winds and air currents which provide weather phenomena. Above this region is the inner ionosphere and next above is the stratosphere. Ascending from the surface of the earth, the temperature steadily falls for six or eight miles, at which height it registers around 70 degrees below zero F. This temperature range of from 65 to 70 degrees below zero F. is unchanged in the further ascent for forty miles; this realm of constant temperature is the stratosphere. At a height of forty-five or fifty miles, the temperature begins to rise, and this increase continues until, at the level of the auroral displays, a temperature of 1200° F. is attained, and it is this intense heat that ionizes the oxygen. But temperature in such a rarefied atmosphere is hardly comparable with heat reckoning at the surface of the earth. Bear in mind that one half of all your atmosphere is to be found in the first three miles. The height of the earth's atmosphere is indicated by the highest auroral streamers—about four hundred miles.

Auroral phenomena are directly related to sunspots, those solar cyclones which whirl in opposite directions above and below the solar equator, even as do the terrestrial tropical hurricanes. Such atmospheric disturbances whirl in opposite directions when occurring above or below the equator.

The power of sunspots to alter light frequencies shows that these solar storm centers function as enormous magnets. Such magnetic fields are able to hurl charged particles from the sunspot craters out through space to the earth's outer atmosphere, where their ionizing influence produces such spectacular auroral displays. Therefore do you have the greatest auroral phenomena when sunspots are at their height—or soon thereafter—at which time the spots are more generally equatorially situated.

Even the compass needle is responsive to this solar influence since it turns slightly to the east as the sun rises and slightly to the west as the sun nears setting. This happens every day, but during the height of sunspot cycles this variation of the compass is twice as great. These diurnal wanderings of the compass are in response to the increased ionization of the upper atmosphere, which is produced by the sunlight.

It is the presence of two different levels of electrified conducting regions in the superstratosphere that accounts for the long-distance transmission of your long- and short-wave radiobroadcasts. Your broadcasting is sometimes disturbed by the terrific storms which occasionally rage in the realms of these outer ionospheres.

3. SPATIAL ENVIRONMENT

During the earlier times of universe materialization the space regions are interspersed with vast hydrogen clouds, just such astronomic dust clusters as now characterize many regions throughout remote space. Much of the organized matter which the blazing suns break down and disperse as radiant energy was originally built up in these early appearing hydrogen clouds of space. Under certain unusual conditions atom disruption also occurs at the nucleus of the larger hydrogen masses. And all of these phenomena of atom building and atom dissolution, as in the highly heated nebulae, are attended by the emergence of flood tides of short space rays of radiant energy. Accompanying these diverse radiations is a form of space-energy unknown on Urantia.

This short-ray energy charge of universe space is four hundred times greater than all other forms of radiant energy existing in the organized space domains. The output of short space rays, whether coming from the blazing nebulae, tense electric fields, outer space, or the vast hydrogen dust clouds, is modified qualitatively and quantitatively by fluctuations of, and sudden tension changes in, temperature, gravity, and electronic pressures.

These eventualities in the origin of the space rays are determined by many cosmic occurrences as well as by the orbits of circulating matter, which vary from modified circles to extreme ellipses. Physical conditions may also be greatly altered because the electron spin is sometimes in the opposite direction from that of the grosser matter behavior, even in the same physical zone.

The vast hydrogen clouds are veritable cosmic chemical laboratories, harboring all phases of evolving energy and metamorphosing matter. Great energy actions also occur in the marginal gases of the great binary stars which so frequently overlap and hence extensively commingle. But none of these tremendous and far-flung energy activities of space exerts the least influence upon the phenomena of organized life—the germ plasm of living things and beings. These energy conditions of space are germane to the essential environment of life establishment, but they are not effective in the subsequent modification of the inheritance factors of the germ plasm as are some of the longer rays of radiant energy. The implanted life of the Life Carriers is fully resistant to all of this amazing flood of the short space rays of universe energy.

All of these essential cosmic conditions had to evolve to a favorable status before the Life Carriers could actually begin the establishment of life on Urantia.

4. THE LIFE-DAWN ERA

That we are called Life Carriers should not confuse you. We can and do carry life to the planets, but we brought no life to Urantia. Urantia life is unique, original with the planet. This sphere is a life-modification world; all life appearing hereon was formulated by us right here on the planet; and there is no other world in all Satania, even in all Nebadon, that has a life existence just like that of Urantia.

550,000,000 years ago the Life Carrier corps returned to Urantia. In cooperation with spiritual powers and superphysical forces we organized and initiated the original life patterns of this world and planted them in the hospitable waters of the realm. All planetary life (aside from extraplanetary personalities) down to the days of Caligastia, the Planetary Prince, had its origin in our three original, identical, and simultaneous marine-life implantations. These three life implantations have been designated as: the *central* or Eurasian-African, the *eastern* or Australasian, and the *western,* embracing Greenland and the Americas.

500,000,000 years ago primitive marine vegetable life was well established on Urantia. Greenland and the arctic land mass, together with North and South America, were beginning their long and slow westward drift. Africa moved slightly south, creating an east and west trough, the Mediterranean basin, between itself and the mother body. Antarctica, Australia, and the land indicated by the islands of the Pacific broke away on the south and east and have drifted far away since that day.

We had planted the primitive form of marine life in the sheltered tropic bays of the central seas of the east-west cleavage of the breaking-up continental land mass. Our purpose in making three marine-life implantations was to insure that each great land mass would carry this life with it, in its warm-water seas, as the land subsequently separated. We foresaw that in the later era of the emergence of land life large oceans of water would separate these drifting continental land masses.

5. THE CONTINENTAL DRIFT

The continental land drift continued. The earth's core had become as dense and rigid as steel, being subjected to a pressure of almost 25,000 tons to the square inch, and owing to the enormous gravity pressure, it was and still is very hot in the deep interior. The temperature increases from the surface downward until at the center it is slightly above the surface temperature of the sun.

The outer one thousand miles of the earth's mass consists principally of different kinds of rock. Underneath are the denser and heavier metallic elements. Throughout the early and preatmospheric ages the world was so nearly fluid in its molten and highly heated state that the heavier metals sank deep into the interior. Those found near the surface today represent the exudate of ancient volcanoes, later and extensive lava flows, and the more recent meteoric deposits.

The outer crust was about forty miles thick. This outer shell was supported by, and rested directly upon, a molten sea of basalt of varying thickness, a mobile layer of molten lava held under high pressure but always tending to flow hither and yon in equalization of shifting planetary pressures, thereby tending to stabilize the earth's crust.

Even today the continents continue to float upon this noncrystallized cushiony sea of molten basalt. Were it not for this protective condition, the more severe earthquakes would literally shake the world to pieces. Earthquakes are caused by sliding and shifting of the solid outer crust and not by volcanoes.

The lava layers of the earth's crust, when cooled, form granite. The average density of Urantia is a little more than five and one-half times that of water; the density of granite is less than three times that of water. The earth's core is twelve times as dense as water.

The sea bottoms are more dense than the land masses, and this is what keeps the continents above water. When the sea bottoms are extruded above the sea level, they are found to consist largely of basalt, a form of lava considerably heavier than the granite of the land masses. Again, if the continents were not lighter than the ocean beds, gravity would draw the edges of the oceans up onto the land, but such phenomena are not observable.

The weight of the oceans is also a factor in the increase of pressure on the sea beds. The lower but comparatively heavier ocean beds, plus the weight of the overlying water, approximate the weight of the higher but much lighter continents. But all continents tend to creep into the oceans. The continental pressure at ocean-bottom levels is about 20,000 pounds to the square inch. That is, this would be the pressure of a continental mass standing 15,000 feet above the ocean floor. The ocean-floor water pressure is only about 5,000 pounds to the square inch. These differential pressures tend to cause the continents to slide toward the ocean beds.

Depression of the ocean bottom during the prelife ages had upthrust a solitary continental land mass to such a height that its lateral pressure tended to cause the eastern, western, and southern fringes to slide downhill, over the underlying semiviscous lava beds, into the waters of the surrounding Pacific Ocean. This so fully compensated the continental pressure that a wide break did not occur on the eastern shore of this ancient Asiatic continent, but ever since has that eastern coast line hovered over the precipice of its adjoining oceanic depths, threatening to slide into a watery grave.

6. THE TRANSITION PERIOD

450,000,000 years ago the *transition from vegetable to animal life* occurred. This metamorphosis took place in the shallow waters of the sheltered tropic bays and lagoons of the extensive shore lines of the separating continents. And this development, all of which was inherent in the original life patterns, came about gradually. There were many transitional stages between the early primitive vegetable forms of life and the later well-defined animal organisms. Even today the transition slime molds persist, and they can hardly be classified either as plants or as animals.

Although the evolution of vegetable life can be traced into animal life, and though there have been found graduated series of plants and animals which progressively lead up from the most simple to the most complex and advanced organisms, you will not be able to find such connecting links between the great divisions of the animal kingdom nor between the highest of the prehuman animal types and the dawn men of the human races. These so-called "missing links" will forever remain missing, for the simple reason that they never existed.

From era to era radically new species of animal life arise. They do not evolve as the result of the gradual accumulation of small variations; they appear as full-fledged and new orders of life, and they appear *suddenly*.

The *sudden* appearance of new species and diversified orders of living organisms is wholly biologic, strictly natural. There is nothing supernatural connected with these genetic mutations.

At the proper degree of saltiness in the oceans animal life evolved, and it was comparatively simple to allow the briny waters to circulate through the animal bodies of marine life. But when the oceans were contracted and the percentage of salt was greatly increased, these same animals evolved the ability to reduce the saltiness of their body fluids just as those organisms which learned to live in fresh water acquired the ability to maintain the proper degree of sodium chloride in their body fluids by ingenious techniques of salt conservation.

Study of the rock-embraced fossils of marine life reveals the early adjustment struggles of these primitive organisms. Plants and animals never cease to make these adjustment experiments. Ever the environment is changing, and always are living organisms striving to accommodate themselves to these never-ending fluctuations.

The physiologic equipment and the anatomic structure of all new orders of life are in response to the action of physical law, but the subsequent endowment of mind is a bestowal of the adjutant mind-spirits in accordance with innate brain capacity. Mind, while not a physical evolution, is wholly dependent on the brain capacity afforded by purely physical and evolutionary developments.

Through almost endless cycles of gains and losses, adjustments and readjustments, all living organisms swing back and forth from age to age. Those that attain cosmic unity persist, while those that fall short of this goal cease to exist.

7. THE GEOLOGIC HISTORY BOOK

The vast group of rock systems which constituted the outer crust of the world during the life-dawn or Proterozoic era does not now appear at many points on the earth's surface. And when it does emerge from below all the accumulations of subsequent ages, there will be found only the fossil remains of vegetable and early primitive animal life. Some of these older water-deposited rocks are commingled with subsequent layers, and sometimes they yield fossil remains of some of the earlier forms of vegetable life, while on the topmost layers occasionally may be found some of the more primitive forms of the early marine-animal organisms. In many places these oldest stratified rock layers, bearing the fossils of the early marine life, both animal and vegetable, may be found directly on top of the older undifferentiated stone.

Fossils of this era yield algae, corallike plants, primitive Protozoa, and spongelike transition organisms. But the absence of such fossils in the early rock layers does not necessarily prove that living things were not elsewhere in existence at the time of their deposition. Life was sparse throughout these early times and only slowly made its way over the face of the earth.

The rocks of this olden age are now at the earth's surface, or very near the surface, over about one eighth of the present land area. The average thickness of this transition stone, the oldest stratified rock layers, is about one and one-half miles. At some points these ancient rock systems are as much as four miles thick, but many of the layers which have been ascribed to this era belong to later periods.

In North America this ancient and primitive fossil-bearing stone layer comes to the surface over the eastern, central, and northern regions of Canada. There is also an intermittent east-west ridge of this rock which extends from Pennsylvania and the ancient Adirondack Mountains on west through Michigan, Wisconsin, and Minnesota. Other ridges run from Newfoundland to Alabama and from Alaska to Mexico.

The rocks of this era are exposed here and there all over the world, but none are so easy of interpretation as those about Lake Superior and in the Grand Canyon of the Colorado River, where these primitive fossil-bearing rocks, existing in several layers, testify to the upheavals and surface fluctuations of those faraway times.

This stone layer, the oldest fossil-bearing stratum in the crust of the earth, has been crumpled, folded, and grotesquely twisted as a result of the upheavals of earthquakes and the early volcanoes. The lava flows of this age brought much iron, copper, and lead up near the planetary surface.

There are few places on the earth where such activities are more graphically shown than in the St. Croix valley of Wisconsin. In this region there occurred one hundred and twenty-seven successive lava flows on land with succeeding water submergence and consequent rock deposition. Although much of the upper rock sedimentation and intermittent lava flow is absent today, and though the bottom of this system is buried deep in the earth, nevertheless, about sixty-five or seventy of these stratified records of past ages are now exposed to view.

In these early ages when much land was near sea level, there occurred many successive submergences and emergences. The earth's crust was just entering upon its later period of comparative stabilization. The undulations, rises and dips, of the earlier continental drift contributed to the frequency of the periodic submergence of the great land masses.

During these times of primitive marine life, extensive areas of the continental shores sank beneath the seas from a few feet to half a mile. Much of the older sandstone and conglomerates represents the sedimentary accumulations of these ancient shores. The sedimentary rocks belonging to this early stratification rest directly upon those layers which date back far beyond the origin of life, back to the early appearance of the world-wide ocean.

Some of the upper layers of these transition rock deposits contain small amounts of shale or slate of dark colors, indicating the presence of organic carbon and testifying to the existence of the ancestors of those forms of plant life which overran the earth during the succeeding Carboniferous or coal age. Much of the copper in these rock layers results from water deposition. Some is found in the cracks of the older rocks and is the concentrate of the sluggish swamp water of some ancient sheltered shore line. The iron mines of North America and Europe are located in deposits and extrusions lying partly in the older unstratified rocks and partly in these later stratified rocks of the transition periods of life formation.

This era witnesses the spread of life throughout the waters of the world; marine life has become well established on Urantia. The bottoms of the shallow and extensive inland seas are being gradually overrun by a profuse and luxuriant growth of vegetation, while the shore-line waters are swarming with the simple forms of animal life.

All of this story is graphically told within the fossil pages of the vast "stone book" of world record. And the pages of this gigantic biogeologic record unfailingly tell the truth if you but acquire skill in their interpretation. Many of these ancient sea beds are now elevated high upon land, and their deposits of age upon age tell the story of the life struggles of those early days. It is literally true, as your poet has said, "The dust we tread upon was once alive."

[Presented by a member of the Urantia Life Carrier Corps now resident on the planet.]

PAPER 59

THE MARINE-LIFE ERA ON URANTIA

WE RECKON the history of Urantia as beginning about one billion years ago and extending through five major eras:

1. *The prelife era* extends over the initial four hundred and fifty million years, from about the time the planet attained its present size to the time of life establishment. Your students have designated this period as the *Archeozoic.*

2. *The life-dawn era* extends over the next one hundred and fifty million years. This epoch intervenes between the preceding prelife or cataclysmic age and the following period of more highly developed marine life. This era is known to your researchers as the *Proterozoic.*

3. *The marine-life era* covers the next two hundred and fifty million years and is best known to you as the *Paleozoic.*

4. *The early land-life era* extends over the next one hundred million years and is known as the *Mesozoic.*

5. *The mammalian era* occupies the last fifty million years. This recent-times era is known as the *Cenozoic.*

The marine-life era thus covers about one quarter of your planetary history. It may be subdivided into six long periods, each characterized by certain well-defined developments in both the geologic realms and the biologic domains.

As this era begins, the sea bottoms, the extensive continental shelves, and the numerous shallow near-shore basins are covered with prolific vegetation. The more simple and primitive forms of animal life have already developed from preceding vegetable organisms, and the early animal organisms have gradually made their way along the extensive coast lines of the various land masses until the many inland seas are teeming with primitive marine life. Since so few of these early organisms had shells, not many have been preserved as fossils. Nevertheless the stage is set for the opening chapters of that great "stone book" of the life-record preservation which was so methodically laid down during the succeeding ages.

The continent of North America is wonderfully rich in the fossil-bearing deposits of the entire marine-life era. The very first and oldest layers are separated from the later strata of the preceding period by extensive erosion deposits which clearly segregate these two stages of planetary development.

1. EARLY MARINE LIFE IN THE SHALLOW SEAS THE TRILOBITE AGE

By the dawn of this period of relative quiet on the earth's surface, life is confined to the various inland seas and the oceanic shore line; as yet no form of land organism has evolved. Primitive marine animals are well established and are prepared for the next evolutionary development. Amebas are typical survivors of this initial stage of animal life, having made their appearance toward the close of the preceding transition period.

400,000,000 years ago marine life, both vegetable and animal, is fairly well distributed over the whole world. The world climate grows slightly warmer and becomes more equable. There is a general inundation of the seashores of the various continents, particularly of North and South America. New oceans appear, and the older bodies of water are greatly enlarged.

Vegetation now for the first time crawls out upon the land and soon makes considerable progress in adaptation to a nonmarine habitat.

Suddenly and without gradation ancestry the first multicellular animals make their appearance. The trilobites have evolved, and for ages they dominate the seas. From the standpoint of marine life this is the trilobite age.

In the later portion of this time segment much of North America and Europe emerged from the sea. The crust of the earth was temporarily stabilized; mountains, or rather high elevations of land, rose along the Atlantic and Pacific coasts, over the West Indies, and in southern Europe. The entire Caribbean region was highly elevated.

390,000,000 years ago the land was still elevated. Over parts of eastern and western America and western Europe may be found the stone strata laid down during these times, and these are the oldest rocks which contain trilobite fossils. There were many long fingerlike gulfs projecting into the land masses in which were deposited these fossil-bearing rocks.

Within a few million years the Pacific Ocean began to invade the American continents. The sinking of the land was principally due to crustal adjustment, although the lateral land spread, or continental creep, was also a factor.

380,000,000 years ago Asia was subsiding, and all other continents were experiencing a short-lived emergence. But as this epoch progressed, the newly appearing Atlantic Ocean made extensive inroads on all adjacent coast lines. The northern Atlantic or Arctic seas were then connected with the southern Gulf waters. When this southern sea entered the Appalachian trough, its waves broke upon the east against mountains as high as the Alps, but in general the continents were uninteresting lowlands, utterly devoid of scenic beauty.

The sedimentary deposits of these ages are of four sorts:

1. Conglomerates—matter deposited near the shore lines.
2. Sandstones—deposits made in shallow water but where the waves were sufficient to prevent mud settling.
3. Shales—deposits made in the deeper and more quiet water.
4. Limestone—including the deposits of trilobite shells in deep water.

The trilobite fossils of these times present certain basic uniformities coupled with certain well-marked variations. The early animals developing from the three original life implantations were characteristic; those appearing in the Western Hemisphere were slightly different from those of the Eurasian group and from the Australasian or Australian-Antarctic type.

370,000,000 years ago the great and almost total submergence of North and South America occurred, followed by the sinking of Africa and Australia. Only certain parts of North America remained above these shallow Cambrian seas. Five million years later the seas were retreating before the rising land. And all of these phenomena of land sinking and land rising were undramatic, taking place slowly over millions of years.

The trilobite fossil-bearing strata of this epoch outcrop here and there throughout all the continents except in central Asia. In many regions these rocks are horizontal, but in the mountains they are tilted and distorted because of pressure and folding. And such pressure has, in many places, changed the original character of these deposits. Sandstone has been turned into quartz, shale has been changed to slate, while limestone has been converted into marble.

360,000,000 years ago the land was still rising. North and South America were well up. Western Europe and the British Isles were emerging, except parts of Wales, which were deeply submerged. There were no great ice sheets during these ages. The supposed glacial deposits appearing in connection with these strata in Europe, Africa, China, and Australia are due to isolated mountain glaciers or to the displacement of glacial debris of later origin. The world climate was oceanic, not continental. The southern seas were warmer then than now, and they extended northward over North America up to the polar regions. The Gulf Stream coursed over the central portion of North America, being deflected eastward to bathe and warm the shores of Greenland, making that now ice-mantled continent a veritable tropic paradise.

The marine life was much alike the world over and consisted of the seaweeds, one-celled organisms, simple sponges, trilobites, and other crustaceans—shrimps, crabs, and lobsters. Three thousand varieties of brachiopods appeared at the close of this period, only two hundred of which have survived. These animals represent a variety of early life which has come down to the present time practically unchanged.

But the trilobites were the dominant living creatures. They were sexed animals and existed in many forms; being poor swimmers, they sluggishly floated in the water or crawled along the sea bottoms, curling up in self-protection when attacked by their later appearing enemies. They grew in length from two inches to one foot and developed into four distinct groups: carnivorous, herbivorous, omnivorous, and "mud eaters." The ability of the latter group largely to subsist on inorganic matter—being the last multicelled animal that could—explains their great increase and long survival.

This was the biogeologic picture of Urantia at the end of that long period of the world's history, embracing fifty million years, designated by your geologists as the *Cambrian.*

2. THE FIRST CONTINENTAL FLOOD STAGE THE INVERTEBRATE-ANIMAL AGE

The periodic phenomena of land elevation and land sinking characteristic of these times were all gradual and nonspectacular, being accompanied by little or no volcanic action. Throughout all of these successive land elevations and depressions the Asiatic mother continent did not fully share the history of the other land bodies. It experienced many inundations, dipping first in one direction and then another, more particularly in its earlier history, but it does not present the uniform rock deposits which may be discovered on the other continents. In recent ages Asia has been the most stable of all the land masses.

350,000,000 years ago saw the beginning of the great flood period of all the continents except central Asia. The land masses were repeatedly covered with water; only the coastal highlands remained above these shallow but widespread oscillatory inland seas. Three major inundations characterized this period, but before it ended, the continents again arose, the total land emergence being fifteen per cent greater than now exists. The Caribbean region was highly elevated. This period is not well marked off in Europe because the land fluctuations were less, while the volcanic action was more persistent.

340,000,000 years ago there occurred another extensive land sinking except in Asia and Australia. The waters of the world's oceans were generally commingled. This was a great limestone age, much of its stone being laid down by lime-secreting algae.

A few million years later large portions of the American continents and Europe began to emerge from the water. In the Western Hemisphere only an arm of the Pacific Ocean remained over Mexico and the present Rocky Mountain regions, but near the close of this epoch the Atlantic and Pacific coasts again began to sink.

330,000,000 years ago marks the beginning of a time sector of comparative quiet all over the world, with much land again above water. The only exception to this reign of terrestrial quiet was the eruption of the great North American volcano of eastern Kentucky, one of the greatest single volcanic activities the world has ever known. The ashes of this volcano covered five hundred square miles to a depth of from fifteen to twenty feet.

320,000,000 years ago the third major flood of this period occurred. The waters of this inundation covered all the land submerged by the preceding deluge, while extending farther in many directions all over the Americas and Europe. Eastern North America and western Europe were from 10,000 to 15,000 feet under water.

310,000,000 years ago the land masses of the world were again well up excepting the southern parts of North America. Mexico emerged, thus creating the Gulf Sea, which has ever since maintained its identity.

The life of this period continues to evolve. The world is once again quiet and relatively peaceful; the climate remains mild and equable; the land plants are migrating farther and farther from the seashores. The life patterns are well developed, although few plant fossils of these times are to be found.

This was the great age of individual animal organismal evolution, though many of the basic changes, such as the transition from plant to animal, had previously occurred. The marine fauna developed to the point where every type of life below the vertebrate scale was represented in the fossils of those rocks which were laid down during these times. But all of these animals were marine organisms. No land animals had yet appeared except a few types of worms which burrowed along the seashores, nor had the land plants yet overspread the continents; there was still too much carbon dioxide in the air to permit of the existence of air breathers. Primarily, all animals except certain of the more primitive ones are directly or indirectly dependent on plant life for their existence.

The trilobites were still prominent. These little animals existed in tens of thousands of patterns and were the predecessors of modern crustaceans. Some of the trilobites had from twenty-five to four thousand tiny eyelets; others had aborted eyes. As this period closed, the trilobites shared domination of the seas with several other forms of invertebrate life. But they utterly perished during the beginning of the next period.

Lime-secreting algae were widespread. There existed thousands of species of the early ancestors of the corals. Sea worms were abundant, and there were many varieties of jellyfish which have since become extinct. Corals and the later types of sponges evolved. The cephalopods were well developed, and they have survived as the modern pearly nautilus, octopus, cuttlefish, and squid.

There were many varieties of shell animals, but their shells were not then so much needed for defensive purposes as in subsequent ages. The gastropods were present in the waters of the ancient seas, and they included single-shelled drills, periwinkles, and snails. The bivalve gastropods have come on down through the intervening millions of years much as they then existed and embrace the mussels, clams, oysters, and scallops. The valve-shelled organisms also evolved, and these brachiopods lived in those ancient waters much as they exist today; they even had hinged, notched, and other sorts of protective arrangements of their valves.

So ends the evolutionary story of the second great period of marine life, which is known to your geologists as the *Ordovician.*

3. THE SECOND GREAT FLOOD STAGE
THE CORAL PERIOD—THE BRACHIOPOD AGE

300,000,000 years ago another great period of land submergence began. The southward and northward encroachment of the ancient Silurian seas made ready to engulf most of Europe and North America. The land was not elevated far above the sea so that not much deposition occurred about the shore lines. The seas teemed with lime-shelled life, and the falling of these shells to the sea bottom gradually built up very thick layers of limestone. This is the first widespread limestone deposit, and it covers practically all of Europe and North America but only appears at the earth's surface in a few places. The thickness of this ancient rock layer averages about one thousand feet, but many of these deposits have since been greatly deformed by tilting, upheavals, and faulting, and many have been changed to quartz, shale, and marble.

No fire rocks or lava are found in the stone layers of this period except those of the great volcanoes of southern Europe and eastern Maine and the lava flows of Quebec. Volcanic action was largely past. This was the height of great water deposition; there was little or no mountain building.

290,000,000 years ago the sea had largely withdrawn from the continents, and the bottoms of the surrounding oceans were sinking. The land masses were little changed until they were again submerged. The early mountain movements of all the continents were beginning, and the greatest of these crustal upheavals were the Himalayas of Asia and the great Caledonian Mountains, extending from Ireland through Scotland and on to Spitzbergen.

It is in the deposits of this age that much of the gas, oil, zinc, and lead are found, the gas and oil being derived from the enormous collections of vegetable and animal matter carried down at the time of the previous land submergence, while the mineral deposits represent the sedimentation of sluggish bodies of water. Many of the rock salt deposits belong to this period.

The trilobites rapidly declined, and the center of the stage was occupied by the larger mollusks, or cephalopods. These animals grew to be fifteen feet long and one foot in diameter and became masters of the seas. This species of animal appeared *suddenly* and assumed dominance of sea life.

The great volcanic activity of this age was in the European sector. Not in millions upon millions of years had such violent and extensive volcanic eruptions occurred as now took place around the Mediterranean trough and especially in the neighborhood of the British Isles. This lava flow over the British Isles region today appears as alternate layers of lava and rock 25,000 feet thick. These rocks were laid down by the intermittent lava flows which spread out over a shallow sea bed, thus interspersing the rock deposits, and all of this was subsequently elevated high above the sea. Violent earthquakes took place in northern Europe, notably in Scotland.

The oceanic climate remained mild and uniform, and the warm seas bathed the shores of the polar lands. Brachiopod and other marine-life fossils may be found in these deposits right up to the North Pole. Gastropods, brachiopods, sponges, and reef-making corals continued to increase.

The close of this epoch witnesses the second advance of the Silurian seas with another commingling of the waters of the southern and northern oceans. The cephalopods dominate marine life, while associated forms of life progressively develop and differentiate.

280,000,000 years ago the continents had largely emerged from the second Silurian inundation. The rock deposits of this submergence are known in North America as Niagara limestone because this is the stratum of rock over which Niagara Falls now flows. This layer of rock extends from the eastern mountains to the Mississippi valley region but not farther west except to the south. Several layers extend over Canada, portions of South America, Australia, and most of Europe, the average thickness of this Niagara series being about six hundred feet. Immediately overlying the Niagara deposit, in many regions may be found a collection of conglomerate, shale, and rock salt. This is the accumulation of secondary subsidences. This salt settled in great lagoons which were alternately opened up to the sea and then cut off so that evaporation occurred with deposition of salt along with other matter held in solution. In some regions these rock salt beds are seventy feet thick.

The climate is even and mild, and marine fossils are laid down in the arctic regions. But by the end of this epoch the seas are so excessively salty that little life survives.

Toward the close of the final Silurian submergence there is a great increase in the echinoderms—the stone lilies—as is evidenced by the crinoid limestone deposits. The trilobites have nearly disappeared, and the mollusks continue monarchs of the seas; coral-reef formation increases greatly. During this age, in the more favorable locations the primitive water scorpions first evolve. Soon thereafter, and *suddenly,* the true scorpions—actual air breathers—make their appearance.

These developments terminate the third marine-life period, covering twenty-five million years and known to your researchers as the *Silurian.*

4. THE GREAT LAND-EMERGENCE STAGE
THE VEGETATIVE LAND-LIFE PERIOD
THE AGE OF FISHES

In the agelong struggle between land and water, for long periods the sea has been comparatively victorious, but times of land victory are just ahead. And the continental drifts have not proceeded so far but that, at times, practically all of the land of the world is connected by slender isthmuses and narrow land bridges.

As the land emerges from the last Silurian inundation, an important period in world development and life evolution comes to an end. It is the dawn of a new age on earth. The naked and unattractive landscape of former times is becoming clothed with luxuriant verdure, and the first magnificent forests will soon appear.

The marine life of this age was very diverse due to the early species segregation, but later on there was free commingling and association of all these different types. The brachiopods early reached their climax, being succeeded by the arthropods, and barnacles made their first appearance. But the greatest event of all was the sudden appearance of the fish family. This became the age of fishes, that period of the world's history characterized by the *vertebrate* type of animal.

270,000,000 years ago the continents were all above water. In millions upon millions of years not so much land had been above water at one time; it was one of the greatest land-emergence epochs in all world history.

Five million years later the land areas of North and South America, Europe, Africa, northern Asia, and Australia were briefly inundated, in North America the submergence at one time or another being almost complete; and the resulting limestone layers run from 500 to 5,000 feet in thickness. These various Devonian seas extended first in one direction and then in another so that the immense arctic North American inland sea found an outlet to the Pacific Ocean through northern California.

260,000,000 years ago, toward the end of this land-depression epoch, North America was partially overspread by seas having simultaneous connection with the Pacific, Atlantic, Arctic, and Gulf waters. The deposits of these later stages of the first Devonian flood average about one thousand feet in thickness. The coral reefs characterizing these times indicate that the inland seas were clear and shallow. Such coral deposits are exposed in the banks of the Ohio River near Louisville, Kentucky, and are about one hundred feet thick, embracing more than two hundred varieties. These coral formations extend through Canada and northern Europe to the arctic regions.

Following these submergences, many of the shore lines were considerably elevated so that the earlier deposits were covered by mud or shale. There is also a red sandstone stratum which characterizes one of the Devonian sedimentations, and this red layer extends over much of the earth's surface, being found in North and South America, Europe, Russia, China, Africa, and Australia. Such red deposits are suggestive of arid or semiarid conditions, but the climate of this epoch was still mild and even.

Throughout all of this period the land southeast of the Cincinnati Island remained well above water. But very much of western Europe, including the British Isles, was submerged. In Wales, Germany, and other places in Europe the Devonian rocks are 20,000 feet thick.

250,000,000 years ago witnessed the appearance of the fish family, the vertebrates, one of the most important steps in all prehuman evolution.

The arthropods, or crustaceans, were the ancestors of the first vertebrates. The forerunners of the fish family were two modified arthropod ancestors; one had a long body connecting a head and tail, while the other was a backboneless, jawless prefish. But these preliminary types were quickly destroyed when the fishes, the first vertebrates of the animal world, made their *sudden* appearance from the north.

Many of the largest true fish belong to this age, some of the teeth-bearing varieties being twenty-five to thirty feet long; the present-day sharks are the survivors of these ancient fishes. The lung and armored fishes reached their evolutionary apex, and before this epoch had ended, fishes had adapted to both fresh and salt waters.

Veritable bone beds of fish teeth and skeletons may be found in the deposits laid down toward the close of this period, and rich fossil beds are situated along the coast of California since many sheltered bays of the Pacific Ocean extended into the land of that region.

The earth was being rapidly overrun by the new orders of land vegetation. Heretofore few plants grew on land except about the water's edge. Now, and *suddenly,* the prolific *fern family* appeared and quickly spread over the face of the rapidly rising land in all parts of the world. Tree types, two feet thick and forty feet high, soon developed; later on, leaves evolved, but these early varieties had only rudimentary foliage. There were many smaller plants, but their fossils are not found since they were usually destroyed by the still earlier appearing bacteria.

As the land rose, North America became connected with Europe by land bridges extending to Greenland. And today Greenland holds the remains of these early land plants beneath its mantle of ice.

240,000,000 years ago the land over parts of both Europe and North and South America began to sink. This subsidence marked the appearance of the last and least extensive of the Devonian floods. The arctic seas again moved southward over much of North America, the Atlantic inundated a large part of Europe and western Asia, while the southern Pacific covered most of India. This inundation was slow in appearing and equally slow in retreating. The Catskill Mountains along the west bank of the Hudson River are one of the largest geologic monuments of this epoch to be found on the surface of North America.

230,000,000 years ago the seas were continuing their retreat. Much of North America was above water, and great volcanic activity occurred in the St.

Lawrence region. Mount Royal, at Montreal, is the eroded neck of one of these volcanoes. The deposits of this entire epoch are well shown in the Appalachian Mountains of North America where the Susquehanna River has cut a valley exposing these successive layers, which attained a thickness of over 13,000 feet.

The elevation of the continents proceeded, and the atmosphere was becoming enriched with oxygen. The earth was overspread by vast forests of ferns one hundred feet high and by the peculiar trees of those days, silent forests; not a sound was heard, not even the rustle of a leaf, for such trees had no leaves.

And thus drew to a close one of the longest periods of marine-life evolution, the *age of fishes.* This period of the world's history lasted almost fifty million years; it has become known to your researchers as the *Devonian.*

5. THE CRUSTAL-SHIFTING STAGE THE FERN-FOREST CARBONIFEROUS PERIOD THE AGE OF FROGS

The appearance of fish during the preceding period marks the apex of marine-life evolution. From this point onward the evolution of land life becomes increasingly important. And this period opens with the stage almost ideally set for the appearance of the first land animals.

220,000,000 years ago many of the continental land areas, including most of North America, were above water. The land was overrun by luxurious vegetation; this was indeed the *age of ferns.* Carbon dioxide was still present in the atmosphere but in lessening degree.

Shortly thereafter the central portion of North America was inundated, creating two great inland seas. Both the Atlantic and Pacific coastal highlands were situated just beyond the present shore lines. These two seas presently united, commingling their different forms of life, and the union of these marine fauna marked the beginning of the rapid and world-wide decline in marine life and the opening of the subsequent land-life period.

210,000,000 years ago the warm-water arctic seas covered most of North America and Europe. The south polar waters inundated South America and Australia, while both Africa and Asia were highly elevated.

When the seas were at their height, a new evolutionary development *suddenly* occurred. Abruptly, the first of the land animals appeared. There were numerous species of these animals that were able to live on land or in water. These air-breathing amphibians developed from the arthropods, whose swim bladders had evolved into lungs.

From the briny waters of the seas there crawled out upon the land snails, scorpions, and frogs. Today frogs still lay their eggs in water, and their young first exist as little fishes, tadpoles. This period could well be known as the *age of frogs.*

Very soon thereafter the insects first appeared and, together with spiders, scorpions, cockroaches, crickets, and locusts, soon overspread the continents of the world. Dragon flies measured thirty inches across. One thousand species of cockroaches developed, and some grew to be four inches long.

Two groups of echinoderms became especially well developed, and they are in reality the guide fossils of this epoch. The large shell-feeding sharks were also highly evolved, and for more than five million years they dominated the oceans. The climate was still mild and equable; the marine life was little changed. Fresh-water fish were developing and the trilobites were nearing extinction. Corals were scarce, and much of the limestone was being made by the crinoids. The finer building limestones were laid down during this epoch.

The waters of many of the inland seas were so heavily charged with lime and other minerals as greatly to interfere with the progress and development of many marine species. Eventually the seas cleared up as the result of an extensive stone deposit, in some places containing zinc and lead.

The deposits of this early Carboniferous age are from 500 to 2,000 feet thick, consisting of sandstone, shale, and limestone. The oldest strata yield the fossils of both land and marine animals and plants, along with much gravel and basin sediments. Little workable coal is found in these older strata. These depositions throughout Europe are very similar to those laid down over North America.

Toward the close of this epoch the land of North America began to rise. There was a short interruption, and the sea returned to cover about half of its previous beds. This was a short inundation, and most of the land was soon well above water. South America was still connected with Europe by way of Africa.

This epoch witnessed the beginning of the Vosges, Black Forest, and Ural mountains. Stumps of other and older mountains are to be found all over Great Britain and Europe.

200,000,000 years ago the really active stages of the Carboniferous period began. For twenty million years prior to this time the earlier coal deposits were being laid down, but now the more extensive coal-formation activities were in process. The length of the actual coal-deposition epoch was a little over twenty-five million years.

The land was periodically going up and down due to the shifting sea level occasioned by activities on the ocean bottoms. This crustal uneasiness—the settling and rising of the land—in connection with the prolific vegetation of the coastal swamps, contributed to the production of extensive coal deposits, which have caused this period to be known as the *Carboniferous.* And the climate was still mild the world over.

The coal layers alternate with shale, stone, and conglomerate. These coal beds over central and eastern United States vary in thickness from forty to fifty feet. But many of these deposits were washed away during subsequent land elevations. In some parts of North America and Europe the coal-bearing strata are 18,000 feet in thickness.

The presence of roots of trees as they grew in the clay underlying the present coal beds demonstrates that coal was formed exactly where it is now found. Coal is the water-preserved and pressure-modified remains of the rank vegetation growing in the bogs and on the swamp shores of this faraway age. Coal layers often hold both gas and oil. Peat beds, the remains of past vegetable growth, would be converted into a type of coal if subjected to proper pressure and heat. Anthracite has been subjected to more pressure and heat than other coal.

In North America the layers of coal in the various beds, which indicate the number of times the land fell and rose, vary from ten in Illinois, twenty in Pennsylvania, thirty-five in Alabama, to seventy-five in Canada. Both fresh- and salt-water fossils are found in the coal beds.

Throughout this epoch the mountains of North and South America were active, both the Andes and the southern ancestral Rocky Mountains rising. The great Atlantic and Pacific high coastal regions began to sink, eventually becoming so eroded and submerged that the coast lines of both oceans withdrew to approximately their present positions. The deposits of this inundation average about one thousand feet in thickness.

190,000,000 years ago witnessed a westward extension of the North American Carboniferous sea over the present Rocky Mountain region, with an outlet to the Pacific Ocean through northern California. Coal continued to be laid down throughout the Americas and Europe, layer upon layer, as the coastlands rose and fell during these ages of seashore oscillations.

180,000,000 years ago brought the close of the Carboniferous period, during which coal had been formed all over the world—in Europe, India, China, North Africa, and the Americas. At the close of the coal-formation period North America east of the Mississippi valley rose, and most of this section has ever since remained above the sea. This land-elevation period marks the beginning of the modern mountains of North America, both in the Appalachian regions and in the west. Volcanoes were active in Alaska and California and in the mountain-forming regions of Europe and Asia. Eastern America and western Europe were connected by the continent of Greenland.

Land elevation began to modify the marine climate of the preceding ages and to substitute therefor the beginnings of the less mild and more variable continental climate.

The plants of these times were spore bearing, and the wind was able to spread them far and wide. The trunks of the Carboniferous trees were commonly seven feet in diameter and often one hundred and twenty-five feet high. The modern ferns are truly relics of these bygone ages.

In general, these were the epochs of development for fresh-water organisms; little change occurred in the previous marine life. But the important characteristic of this period was the *sudden* appearance of the frogs and their many cousins. The life features of the coal age were *ferns* and *frogs*.

6. THE CLIMATIC TRANSITION STAGE
THE SEED-PLANT PERIOD
THE AGE OF BIOLOGIC TRIBULATION

This period marks the end of pivotal evolutionary development in marine life and the opening of the transition period leading to the subsequent ages of land animals.

This age was one of great life impoverishment. Thousands of marine species perished, and life was hardly yet established on land. This was a time of biologic tribulation, the age when life nearly vanished from the face of the earth and from the depths of the oceans. Toward the close of the long marine-life era there were more than one hundred thousand species of living things on earth. At the close of this period of transition less than five hundred had survived.

The peculiarities of this new period were not due so much to the cooling of the earth's crust or to the long absence of volcanic action as to an unusual combination of commonplace and pre-existing influences—restrictions of the seas and increasing elevation of enormous land masses. The mild marine climate of former times was disappearing, and the harsher continental type of weather was fast developing.

170,000,000 years ago great evolutionary changes and adjustments were taking place over the entire face of the earth. Land was rising all over the world as the ocean beds were sinking. Isolated mountain ridges appeared. The eastern part of North America was high above the sea; the west was slowly rising. The continents were covered by great and small salt lakes and numerous inland seas which were connected with the oceans by narrow straits. The strata of this transition period vary in thickness from 1,000 to 7,000 feet.

The earth's crust folded extensively during these land elevations. This was a time of continental emergence except for the disappearance of certain land bridges, including the continents which had so long connected South America with Africa and North America with Europe.

Gradually the inland lakes and seas were drying up all over the world. Isolated mountain and regional glaciers began to appear, especially over the Southern Hemisphere, and in many regions the glacial deposit of these local ice formations may be found even among some of the upper and later coal deposits. Two new climatic factors appeared—glaciation and aridity. Many of the earth's higher regions had become arid and barren.

Throughout these times of climatic change, great variations also occurred in the land plants. The *seed plants* first appeared, and they afforded a better food supply for the subsequently increased land-animal life. The insects underwent a radical change. The *resting stages* evolved to meet the demands of suspended animation during winter and drought.

Among the land animals the frogs reached their climax in the preceding age and rapidly declined, but they survived because they could long live even in the drying-up pools and ponds of these far-distant and extremely trying times. During this declining frog age, in Africa, the first step in the evolution of the frog into the reptile occurred. And since the land masses were still connected, this prereptilian creature, an air breather, spread over all the world. By this time the atmosphere had been so changed that it served admirably to support animal respiration. It was soon after the arrival of these prereptilian frogs that North America was temporarily isolated, cut off from Europe, Asia, and South America.

The gradual cooling of the ocean waters contributed much to the destruction of oceanic life. The marine animals of those ages took temporary refuge in three favorable retreats: the present Gulf of Mexico region, the Ganges Bay of India, and the Sicilian Bay of the Mediterranean basin. And it was from these three regions that the new marine species, born to adversity, later went forth to replenish the seas.

160,000,000 years ago the land was largely covered with vegetation adapted to support land-animal life, and the atmosphere had become ideal for animal respiration. Thus ends the period of marine-life curtailment and those testing times of biologic adversity which eliminated all forms of life except such as had survival value, and which were therefore entitled to function as the ancestors of the more rapidly developing and highly differentiated life of the ensuing ages of planetary evolution.

The ending of this period of biologic tribulation, known to your students as the *Permian,* also marks the end of the long *Paleozoic* era, which covers one quarter of the planetary history, two hundred and fifty million years.

The vast oceanic nursery of life on Urantia has served its purpose. During the long ages when the land was unsuited to support life, before the atmosphere contained sufficient oxygen to sustain the higher land animals, the sea mothered and nurtured the early life of the realm. Now the biologic importance of the sea progressively diminishes as the second stage of evolution begins to unfold on the land.

[Presented by a Life Carrier of Nebadon, one of the original corps assigned to Urantia.]

PAPER 60

URANTIA DURING THE EARLY LAND-LIFE ERA

THE era of exclusive marine life has ended. Land elevation, cooling crust and cooling oceans, sea restriction and consequent deepening, together with a great increase of land in northern latitudes, all conspired greatly to change the world's climate in all regions far removed from the equatorial zone.

The closing epochs of the preceding era were indeed the age of frogs, but these ancestors of the land vertebrates were no longer dominant, having survived in greatly reduced numbers. Very few types outlived the rigorous trials of the preceding period of biologic tribulation. Even the spore-bearing plants were nearly extinct.

1. THE EARLY REPTILIAN AGE

The erosion deposits of this period were mostly conglomerates, shale, and sandstone. The gypsum and red layers throughout these sedimentations over both America and Europe indicate that the climate of these continents was arid. These arid districts were subjected to great erosion from the violent and periodic cloudbursts on the surrounding highlands.

Few fossils are to be found in these layers, but numerous sandstone footprints of the land reptiles may be observed. In many regions the one thousand feet of red sandstone deposit of this period contains no fossils. The life of land animals was continuous only in certain parts of Africa.

These deposits vary in thickness from 3,000 to 10,000 feet, even being 18,000 on the Pacific coast. Lava was later forced in between many of these layers. The Palisades of the Hudson River were formed by the extrusion of basalt lava between these Triassic strata. Volcanic action was extensive in different parts of the world.

Over Europe, especially Germany and Russia, may be found deposits of this period. In England the New Red Sandstone belongs to this epoch. Limestone was laid down in the southern Alps as the result of a sea invasion and may now be seen as the peculiar dolomite limestone walls, peaks, and pillars of those regions. This layer is to be found all over Africa and Australia. The Carrara marble comes from such modified limestone. Nothing of this period will be found in the southern regions of South America as that part of the continent remained down and hence presents only a water or marine deposit continuous with the preceding and succeeding epochs.

150,000,000 years ago the early land-life periods of the world's history began. Life, in general, did not fare well but did better than at the strenuous and hostile close of the marine-life era.

As this era opens, the eastern and central parts of North America, the northern half of South America, most of Europe, and all of Asia are well above water. North America for the first time is geographically isolated, but not for long as the Bering Strait land bridge soon again emerges, connecting the continent with Asia.

Great troughs developed in North America, paralleling the Atlantic and Pacific coasts. The great eastern-Connecticut fault appeared, one side eventually sinking two miles. Many of these North American troughs were later filled with erosion deposits, as also were many of the basins of the fresh- and salt-water lakes of the mountain regions. Later on, these filled land depressions were greatly elevated by lava flows which occurred underground. The petrified forests of many regions belong to this epoch.

The Pacific coast, usually above water during the continental submergences, went down excepting the southern part of California and a large island which then existed in what is now the Pacific Ocean. This ancient California sea was rich in marine life and extended eastward to connect with the old sea basin of the midwestern region.

140,000,000 years ago, *suddenly* and with only the hint of the two prereptilian ancestors that developed in Africa during the preceding epoch, the reptiles appeared in full-fledged form. They developed rapidly, soon yielding crocodiles, scaled reptiles, and eventually both sea serpents and flying reptiles. Their transition ancestors speedily disappeared.

These rapidly evolving reptilian dinosaurs soon became the monarchs of this age. They were egg layers and are distinguished from all animals by their small brains, having brains weighing less than one pound to control bodies later weighing as much as forty tons. But earlier reptiles were smaller, carnivorous, and walked kangaroolike on their hind legs. They had hollow avian bones and subsequently developed only three toes on their hind feet, and many of their fossil footprints have been mistaken for those of giant birds. Later on, the herbivorous dinosaurs evolved. They walked on all fours, and one branch of this group developed a protective armor.

Several million years later the first mammals appeared. They were nonplacental and proved a speedy failure; none survived. This was an experimental effort to improve mammalian types, but it did not succeed on Urantia.

The marine life of this period was meager but improved rapidly with the new invasion of the sea, which again produced extensive coast lines of shallow waters. Since there was more shallow water around Europe and Asia, the richest fossil beds are to be found about these continents. Today, if you would study the life of this age, examine the Himalayan, Siberian, and Mediterranean regions, as well as India and the islands of the southern Pacific basin. A prominent feature of the marine life was the presence of hosts of the beautiful ammonites, whose fossil remains are found all over the world.

130,000,000 years ago the seas had changed very little. Siberia and North America were connected by the Bering Strait land bridge. A rich and unique marine life appeared on the Californian Pacific coast, where over one thousand species of ammonites developed from the higher types of cephalopods. The life changes of this period were indeed revolutionary notwithstanding that they were transitional and gradual.

This period extended over twenty-five million years and is known as the *Triassic.*

2. THE LATER REPTILIAN AGE

120,000,000 years ago a new phase of the reptilian age began. The great event of this period was the evolution and decline of the dinosaurs. Land-animal life reached its greatest development, in point of size, and had virtually perished from the face of the earth by the end of this age. The dinosaurs evolved in all sizes from a species less than two feet long up to the huge noncarnivorous dinosaurs, seventy-five feet long, that have never since been equaled in bulk by any living creature.

The largest of the dinosaurs originated in western North America. These monstrous reptiles are buried throughout the Rocky Mountain regions, along the whole of the Atlantic coast of North America, over western Europe, South Africa, and India, but not in Australia.

These massive creatures became less active and strong as they grew larger and larger; but they required such an enormous amount of food and the land was so overrun by them that they literally starved to death and became extinct—they lacked the intelligence to cope with the situation.

By this time most of the eastern part of North America, which had long been elevated, had been leveled down and washed into the Atlantic Ocean so that the coast extended several hundred miles farther out than now. The western part of the continent was still up, but even these regions were later invaded by both the northern sea and the Pacific, which extended eastward to the Dakota Black Hills region.

This was a fresh-water age characterized by many inland lakes, as is shown by the abundant fresh-water fossils of the so-called Morrison beds of Colorado, Montana, and Wyoming. The thickness of these combined salt- and fresh-water deposits varies from 2,000 to 5,000 feet; but very little limestone is present in these layers.

The same polar sea that extended so far down over North America likewise covered all of South America except the soon appearing Andes Mountains. Most of China and Russia was inundated, but the water invasion was greatest in Europe. It was during this submergence that the beautiful lithographic stone of southern Germany was laid down, those strata in which fossils, such as the most delicate wings of olden insects, are preserved as of but yesterday.

The flora of this age was much like that of the preceding. Ferns persisted, while conifers and pines became more and more like the present-day varieties. Some coal was still being formed along the northern Mediterranean shores.

The return of the seas improved the weather. Corals spread to European waters, testifying that the climate was still mild and even, but they never again appeared in the slowly cooling polar seas. The marine life of these times improved and developed greatly, especially in European waters. Both corals and crinoids temporarily appeared in larger numbers than heretofore, but the ammonites dominated the invertebrate life of the oceans, their average size ranging from three to four inches, though one species attained a diameter of eight feet. Sponges were everywhere, and both cuttlefish and oysters continued to evolve.

110,000,000 years ago the potentials of marine life were continuing to unfold. The sea urchin was one of the outstanding mutations of this epoch. Crabs, lobsters, and the modern types of crustaceans matured. Marked changes occurred in the fish family, a sturgeon type first appearing, but the ferocious sea serpents, descended from the land reptiles, still infested all the seas, and they threatened the destruction of the entire fish family.

This continued to be, pre-eminently, the age of the dinosaurs. They so overran the land that two species had taken to the water for sustenance during the preceding period of sea encroachment. These sea serpents represent a backward step in evolution. While some new species are progressing, certain strains remain stationary and others gravitate backward, reverting to a former state. And this is what happened when these two types of reptiles forsook the land.

As time passed, the sea serpents grew to such size that they became very sluggish and eventually perished because they did not have brains large enough to afford protection for their immense bodies. Their brains weighed less than two ounces notwithstanding the fact that these huge ichthyosaurs sometimes grew to be fifty feet long, the majority being over thirty-five feet in length. The marine crocodilians were also a reversion from the land type of reptile, but unlike the sea serpents, these animals always returned to the land to lay their eggs.

Soon after two species of dinosaurs migrated to the water in a futile attempt at self-preservation, two other types were driven to the air by the bitter competition of life on land. But these flying pterosaurs were not the ancestors of the true birds of subsequent ages. They evolved from the hollow-boned leaping dinosaurs, and their wings were of batlike formation with a spread of twenty to twenty-five feet. These ancient flying reptiles grew to be ten feet long, and they had separable jaws much like those of modern snakes. For a time these flying reptiles appeared to be a success, but they failed to evolve along lines which would enable them to survive as air navigators. They represent the nonsurviving strains of bird ancestry.

Turtles increased during this period, first appearing in North America. Their ancestors came over from Asia by way of the northern land bridge.

One hundred million years ago the reptilian age was drawing to a close. The dinosaurs, for all their enormous mass, were all but brainless animals, lacking the intelligence to provide sufficient food to nourish such enormous bodies. And so did these sluggish land reptiles perish in ever-increasing numbers. Henceforth, evolution will follow the growth of brains, not physical bulk, and the development of brains will characterize each succeeding epoch of animal evolution and planetary progress.

This period, embracing the height and the beginning decline of the reptiles, extended nearly twenty-five million years and is known as the *Jurassic*.

3. THE CRETACEOUS STAGE
THE FLOWERING-PLANT PERIOD
THE AGE OF BIRDS

The great Cretaceous period derives its name from the predominance of the prolific chalk-making foraminifers in the seas. This period brings Urantia to near the end of the long reptilian dominance and witnesses the appearance of flowering plants and bird life on land. These are also the times of the termination of the westward and southward drift of the continents, accompanied by tremendous crustal deformations and concomitant widespread lava flows and great volcanic activities.

Near the close of the preceding geologic period much of the continental land was up above water, although as yet there were no mountain peaks. But as the continental land drift continued, it met with the first great obstruction on the deep floor of the Pacific. This contention of geologic forces gave impetus to the formation of the whole vast north and south mountain range extending from Alaska down through Mexico to Cape Horn.

This period thus becomes the *modern mountain-building stage* of geologic history. Prior to this time there were few mountain peaks, merely elevated land ridges of great width. Now the Pacific coast range was beginning to elevate, but it was located seven hundred miles west of the present shore line. The Sierras were beginning to form, their gold-bearing quartz strata being the product of lava flows of this epoch. In the eastern part of North America, Atlantic sea pressure was also working to cause land elevation.

100,000,000 years ago the North American continent and a part of Europe were well above water. The warping of the American continents continued, resulting in the metamorphosing of the South American Andes and in the gradual elevation of the western plains of North America. Most of Mexico sank beneath the sea, and the southern Atlantic encroached on the eastern coast of South America, eventually reaching the present shore line. The Atlantic and Indian Oceans were then about as they are today.

95,000,000 years ago the American and European land masses again began to sink. The southern seas commenced the invasion of North America and gradually extended northward to connect with the Arctic Ocean, constituting the second greatest submergence of the continent. When this sea finally withdrew, it left the continent about as it now is. Before this great submergence began, the eastern Appalachian highlands had been almost completely worn down to the water's level. The many colored layers of pure clay now used for the manufacture of earthenware were laid down over the Atlantic coast regions during this age, their average thickness being about 2,000 feet.

Great volcanic actions occurred south of the Alps and along the line of the present California coast-range mountains. The greatest crustal deformations in millions upon millions of years took place in Mexico. Great changes also occurred in Europe, Russia, Japan, and southern South America. The climate became increasingly diversified.

90,000,000 years ago the angiosperms emerged from these early Cretaceous seas and soon overran the continents. These land plants *suddenly* appeared along with fig trees, magnolias, and tulip trees. Soon after this time fig trees, breadfruit trees, and palms overspread Europe and the western plains of North America. No new land animals appeared.

85,000,000 years ago the Bering Strait closed, shutting off the cooling waters of the northern seas. Theretofore the marine life of the Atlantic-Gulf waters and that of the Pacific Ocean had differed greatly, owing to the temperature variations of these two bodies of water, which now became uniform.

The deposits of chalk and greensand marl give name to this period. The sedimentations of these times are variegated, consisting of chalk, shale, sandstone, and small amounts of limestone, together with inferior coal or lignite, and in many regions they contain oil. These layers vary in thickness from 200 feet in some places to 10,000 feet in western North America and numerous European localities. Along the eastern borders of the Rocky Mountains these deposits may be observed in the uptilted foothills.

All over the world these strata are permeated with chalk, and these layers of porous semirock pick up water at upturned outcrops and convey it downward to furnish the water supply of much of the earth's present arid regions.

80,000,000 years ago great disturbances occurred in the earth's crust. The western advance of the continental drift was coming to a standstill, and the enormous energy of the sluggish momentum of the hinter continental mass upcrumpled the Pacific shore line of both North and South America and initiated profound repercussional changes along the Pacific shores of Asia. This circumpacific land elevation, which culminated in present-day mountain ranges, is more than twenty-five thousand miles long. And the upheavals attendant upon its birth were the greatest surface distortions to take place since life appeared on Urantia. The lava flows, both above and below ground, were extensive and widespread.

75,000,000 years ago marks the end of the continental drift. From Alaska to Cape Horn the long Pacific coast mountain ranges were completed, but there were as yet few peaks.

The backthrust of the halted continental drift continued the elevation of the western plains of North America, while in the east the worn-down Appalachian Mountains of the Atlantic coast region were projected straight up, with little or no tilting.

70,000,000 years ago the crustal distortions connected with the maximum elevation of the Rocky Mountain region took place. A large segment of rock was overthrust fifteen miles at the surface in British Columbia; here the Cambrian rocks are obliquely thrust out over the Cretaceous layers. On the eastern slope of the Rocky Mountains, near the Canadian border, there was another spectacular overthrust; here may be found the prelife stone layers shoved out over the then recent Cretaceous deposits.

This was an age of volcanic activity all over the world, giving rise to numerous small isolated volcanic cones. Submarine volcanoes broke out in the submerged Himalayan region. Much of the rest of Asia, including Siberia, was also still under water.

65,000,000 years ago there occurred one of the greatest lava flows of all time. The deposition layers of these and preceding lava flows are to be found all over the Americas, North and South Africa, Australia, and parts of Europe.

The land animals were little changed, but because of greater continental emergence, especially in North America, they rapidly multiplied. North America was the great field of the land-animal evolution of these times, most of Europe being under water.

The climate was still warm and uniform. The arctic regions were enjoying weather much like that of the present climate in central and southern North America.

Great plant-life evolution was taking place. Among the land plants the angiosperms predominated, and many present-day trees first appeared, including beech, birch, oak, walnut, sycamore, maple, and modern palms. Fruits, grasses, and cereals were abundant, and these seed-bearing grasses and trees were to the plant world what the ancestors of man were to the animal world—they were second in evolutionary importance only to the appearance of man himself. *Suddenly* and without previous gradation, the great family of flowering plants mutated. And this new flora soon overspread the entire world.

60,000,000 years ago, though the land reptiles were on the decline, the dinosaurs continued as monarchs of the land, the lead now being taken by the more agile and active types of the smaller leaping kangaroo varieties of the carnivorous dinosaurs. But sometime previously there had appeared new types of the herbivorous dinosaurs, whose rapid increase was due to the appearance of the grass family of land plants. One of these new grass-eating dinosaurs was a true quadruped having two horns and a capelike shoulder flange. The land type of turtle, twenty feet across, appeared as did also the modern crocodile and true snakes of the modern type. Great changes were also occurring among the fishes and other forms of marine life.

The wading and swimming prebirds of earlier ages had not been a success in the air, nor had the flying dinosaurs. They were a short-lived species, soon becoming extinct. They, too, were subject to the dinosaur doom, destruction, because of having too little brain substance in comparison with body size. This second attempt to produce animals that could navigate the atmosphere failed, as did the abortive attempt to produce mammals during this and a preceding age.

55,000,000 years ago the evolutionary march was marked by the *sudden* appearance of the first of the *true birds,* a small pigeonlike creature which was the ancestor of all bird life. This was the third type of flying creature to appear on earth, and it sprang directly from the reptilian group, not from the contemporary flying dinosaurs nor from the earlier types of toothed land birds. And so this becomes known as the *age of birds* as well as the declining age of reptiles.

4. THE END OF THE CHALK PERIOD

The great Cretaceous period was drawing to a close, and its termination marks the end of the great sea invasions of the continents. Particularly is this true of North America, where there had been just twenty-four great inundations. And though there were subsequent minor submergences, none of these can be compared with the extensive and lengthy marine invasions of this and previous ages. These alternate periods of land and sea dominance have occurred in million-year cycles. There has been an agelong rhythm associated with this rise and fall of ocean floor and continental land levels. And these same rhythmical crustal movements will continue from this time on throughout the earth's history but with diminishing frequency and extent.

This period also witnesses the end of the continental drift and the building of the modern mountains of Urantia. But the pressure of the continental masses and the thwarted momentum of their agelong drift are not the exclusive influences in mountain building. The chief and underlying factor in determining the location of a mountain range is the pre-existent lowland, or trough, which has become filled up with the comparatively lighter deposits of the land erosion and marine drifts of the preceding ages. These lighter areas of land are sometimes 15,000 to 20,000 feet thick; therefore, when the crust is subjected to pressure from any cause, these lighter areas are the first to crumple up, fold, and rise upward to afford compensatory adjustment for the contending and conflicting forces and pressures at work in the earth's crust or underneath the crust. Sometimes these upthrusts of land occur without folding. But in connection with the rise of the Rocky Mountains, great folding and tilting occurred, coupled with enormous overthrusts of the various layers, both underground and at the surface.

The oldest mountains of the world are located in Asia, Greenland, and northern Europe among those of the older east-west systems. The mid-age mountains are in the circumpacific group and in the second European east-west system, which was born at about the same time. This gigantic uprising is almost ten thousand miles long, extending from Europe over into the West Indies land elevations. The youngest mountains are in the Rocky Mountain system, where, for ages, land elevations had occurred only to be successively covered by the sea, though some of the higher lands remained as islands. Subsequent to the formation of the mid-age mountains, a real mountain highland was elevated which was destined, subsequently, to be carved into the present Rocky Mountains by the combined artistry of nature's elements.

The present North American Rocky Mountain region is not the original elevation of land; that elevation had been long since leveled by erosion and then re-elevated. The present front range of mountains is what is left of the remains of the original range which was re-elevated. Pikes Peak and Longs Peak are outstanding examples of this mountain activity, extending over two or more generations of mountain lives. These two peaks held their heads above water during several of the preceding inundations.

Biologically as well as geologically this was an eventful and active age on land and under water. Sea urchins increased while corals and crinoids decreased. The ammonites, of preponderant influence during a previous age, also rapidly declined. On land the fern forests were largely replaced by pine and other modern trees, including the gigantic redwoods. By the end of this period, while the placental mammal has not yet evolved, the biologic stage is fully set for the appearance, in a subsequent age, of the early ancestors of the future mammalian types.

And thus ends a long era of world evolution, extending from the early appearance of land life down to the more recent times of the immediate ancestors of the human species and its collateral branches. This, the *Cretaceous age,* covers fifty million years and brings to a close the premammalian era of land life, which extends over a period of one hundred million years and is known as the *Mesozoic*.

[Presented by a Life Carrier of Nebadon assigned to Satania and now functioning on Urantia.]

families also sprang up. The angiosperms were the principal food of the rapidly increasing mammals, the modern land flora, including the majority of present-day plants and trees, having appeared during earlier periods.

35,000,000 years ago marks the beginning of the age of placental-mammalian world domination. The southern land bridge was extensive, reconnecting the then enormous Antarctic continent with South America, South Africa, and Australia. In spite of the massing of land in high latitudes, the world climate remained relatively mild because of the enormous increase in the size of the tropic seas, nor was the land elevated sufficiently to produce glaciers. Extensive lava flows occurred in Greenland and Iceland, some coal being deposited between these layers.

Marked changes were taking place in the fauna of the planet. The sea life was undergoing great modification; most of the present-day orders of marine life were in existence, and foraminifers continued to play an important role. The insect life was much like that of the previous era. The Florissant fossil beds of Colorado belong to the later years of these far-distant times. Most of the living insect families go back to this period, but many then in existence are now extinct, though their fossils remain.

On land this was pre-eminently the age of mammalian renovation and expansion. Of the earlier and more primitive mammals, over one hundred species were extinct before this period ended. Even the mammals of large size and small brain soon perished. Brains and agility had replaced armor and size in the progress of animal survival. And with the dinosaur family on the decline, the mammals slowly assumed domination of the earth, speedily and completely destroying the remainder of their reptilian ancestors.

Along with the disappearance of the dinosaurs, other and great changes occurred in the various branches of the saurian family. The surviving members of the early reptilian families are turtles, snakes, and crocodiles, together with the venerable frog, the only remaining group representative of man's earlier ancestors.

Various groups of mammals had their origin in a unique animal now extinct. This carnivorous creature was something of a cross between a cat and a seal; it could live on land or in water and was highly intelligent and very active. In Europe the ancestor of the canine family evolved, soon giving rise to many species of small dogs. About the same time the gnawing rodents, including beavers, squirrels, gophers, mice, and rabbits, appeared and soon became a notable form of life, very little change having since occurred in this family. The later deposits of this period contain the fossil remains of dogs, cats, coons, and weasels in ancestral form.

30,000,000 years ago the modern types of mammals began to make their appearance. Formerly the mammals had lived for the greater part in the hills, being of the mountainous types; *suddenly* there began the evolution of the plains or hoofed type, the grazing species, as differentiated from the clawed flesh eaters. These grazers sprang from an undifferentiated ancestor having five toes and forty-four teeth, which perished before the end of the age. Toe evolution did not progress beyond the three-toed stage throughout this period.

The horse, an outstanding example of evolution, lived during these times in both North America and Europe, though his development was not fully completed until the later ice age. While the rhinoceros family appeared at the close of this period, it underwent its greatest expansion subsequently. A small hoglike creature also developed which became the ancestor of the many species of swine, peccaries, and hippopotamuses. Camels and llamas had their origin in North America about the middle of this period and overran the western plains. Later, the llamas migrated to South America, the camels to Europe, and soon both were extinct in North America, though a few camels survived up to the ice age.

About this time a notable thing occurred in western North America: The early ancestors of the ancient lemurs first made their appearance. While this family cannot be regarded as true lemurs, their coming marked the establishment of the line from which the true lemurs subsequently sprang.

Like the land serpents of a previous age which betook themselves to the seas, now a whole tribe of placental mammals deserted the land and took up their residence in the oceans. And they have ever since remained in the sea, yielding the modern whales, dolphins, porpoises, seals, and sea lions.

The bird life of the planet continued to develop, but with few important evolutionary changes. The majority of modern birds were existent, including gulls, herons, flamingoes, buzzards, falcons, eagles, owls, quails, and ostriches.

By the close of this *Oligocene* period, covering ten million years, the plant life, together with the marine life and the land animals, had very largely evolved and was present on earth much as today. Considerable specialization has subsequently appeared, but the ancestral forms of most living things were then alive.

3. THE MODERN MOUNTAIN STAGE AGE OF THE ELEPHANT AND THE HORSE

Land elevation and sea segregation were slowly changing the world's weather, gradually cooling it, but the climate was still mild. Sequoias and magnolias grew in Greenland, but the subtropical plants were beginning to migrate southward. By the end of this period these warm-climate plants and trees had largely disappeared from the northern latitudes, their places being taken by more hardy plants and the deciduous trees.

There was a great increase in the varieties of grasses, and the teeth of many mammalian species gradually altered to conform to the present-day grazing type.

25,000,000 years ago there was a slight land submergence following the long epoch of land elevation. The Rocky Mountain region remained highly elevated so that the deposition of erosion material continued throughout the lowlands to the east. The Sierras were well re-elevated; in fact, they have been rising ever since. The great four-mile vertical fault in the California region dates from this time.

20,000,000 years ago was indeed the golden age of mammals. The Bering Strait land bridge was up, and many groups of animals migrated to North America from Asia, including the four-tusked mastodons, short-legged rhinoceroses, and many varieties of the cat family.

The first deer appeared, and North America was soon overrun by ruminants—deer, oxen, camels, bison, and several species of rhinoceroses—but the giant pigs, more than six feet tall, became extinct.

The huge elephants of this and subsequent periods possessed large brains as well as large bodies, and they soon overran the entire world except Australia. For once the world was dominated by a huge animal with a brain sufficiently large to enable it to carry on. Confronted by the highly intelligent life of these ages, no animal the size of an elephant could have survived unless it had possessed a brain of large size and superior quality. In intelligence and adaptation the elephant is approached only by the horse and is surpassed only by man himself. Even so, of the fifty species of elephants in existence at the opening of this period, only two have survived.

15,000,000 years ago the mountain regions of Eurasia were rising, and there was some volcanic activity throughout these regions, but nothing comparable to the lava flows of the Western Hemisphere. These unsettled conditions prevailed all over the world.

The Strait of Gibraltar closed, and Spain was connected with Africa by the old land bridge, but the Mediterranean flowed into the Atlantic through a narrow channel which extended across France, the mountain peaks and highlands appearing as islands above this ancient sea. Later on, these European seas began to withdraw. Still later, the Mediterranean was connected with the Indian Ocean, while at the close of this period the Suez region was elevated so that the Mediterranean became, for a time, an inland salt sea.

The Iceland land bridge submerged, and the arctic waters commingled with those of the Atlantic Ocean. The Atlantic coast of North America rapidly cooled, but the Pacific coast remained warmer than at present. The great ocean currents were in function and affected climate much as they do today.

Mammalian life continued to evolve. Enormous herds of horses joined the camels on the western plains of North America; this was truly the age of horses as well as of elephants. The horse's brain is next in animal quality to that of the elephant, but in one respect it is decidedly inferior, for the horse never fully overcame the deep-seated propensity to flee when frightened. The horse lacks the emotional control of the elephant, while the elephant is greatly handicapped by size and lack of agility. During this period an animal evolved which was somewhat like both the elephant and the horse, but it was soon destroyed by the rapidly increasing cat family.

As Urantia is entering the so-called "horseless age," you should pause and ponder what this animal meant to your ancestors. Men first used horses for food, then for travel, and later in agriculture and war. The horse has long served mankind and has played an important part in the development of human civilization.

The biologic developments of this period contributed much toward the setting of the stage for the subsequent appearance of man. In central Asia the true types of both the primitive monkey and the gorilla evolved, having a common ancestor, now extinct. But neither of these species is concerned in the line of living beings which were, later on, to become the ancestors of the human race.

The dog family was represented by several groups, notably wolves and foxes; the cat tribe, by panthers and large saber-toothed tigers, the latter first evolving in North America. The modern cat and dog families increased in numbers all over the world. Weasels, martens, otters, and raccoons thrived and developed throughout the northern latitudes.

Birds continued to evolve, though few marked changes occurred. Reptiles were similar to modern types—snakes, crocodiles, and turtles.

Thus drew to a close a very eventful and interesting period of the world's history. This age of the elephant and the horse is known as the *Miocene.*

4. THE RECENT CONTINENTAL-ELEVATION STAGE THE LAST GREAT MAMMALIAN MIGRATION

This is the period of preglacial land elevation in North America, Europe, and Asia. The land was greatly altered in topography. Mountain ranges were born, streams changed their courses, and isolated volcanoes broke out all over the world.

10,000,000 years ago began an age of widespread local land deposits on the lowlands of the continents, but most of these sedimentations were later removed. Much of Europe, at this time, was still under water, including parts of England, Belgium, and France, and the Mediterranean Sea covered much of northern Africa. In North America extensive depositions were made at the mountain bases, in lakes, and in the great land basins. These deposits average only about two hundred feet, are more or less colored, and fossils are rare. Two great fresh-water lakes existed in western North America. The Sierras were elevating; Shasta, Hood, and Rainier were beginning their mountain careers. But it was not until the subsequent ice age that North America began its creep toward the Atlantic depression.

For a short time all the land of the world was again joined excepting Australia, and the last great world-wide animal migration took place. North America was connected with both South America and Asia, and there was a free exchange of animal life. Asiatic sloths, armadillos, antelopes, and bears entered North America, while North American camels went to China. Rhinoceroses migrated over the whole world except Australia and South America, but they were extinct in the Western Hemisphere by the close of this period.

In general, the life of the preceding period continued to evolve and spread. The cat family dominated the animal life, and marine life was almost at a standstill. Many of the horses were still three-toed, but the modern types were arriving; llamas and giraffelike camels mingled with the horses on the grazing plains. The giraffe appeared in Africa, having just as long a neck then as now. In South America sloths, armadillos, anteaters, and the South American type of primitive monkeys evolved. Before the continents were finally isolated, those massive animals, the mastodons, migrated everywhere except to Australia.

5,000,000 years ago the horse evolved as it now is and from North America migrated to all the world. But the horse had become extinct on the continent of its origin long before the red man arrived.

The climate was gradually getting cooler; the land plants were slowly moving southward. At first it was the increasing cold in the north that stopped animal migrations over the northern isthmuses; subsequently these North American land bridges went down. Soon afterwards the land connection between Africa and South America finally submerged, and the Western Hemisphere was isolated much as it is today. From this time forward distinct types of life began to develop in the Eastern and Western Hemispheres.

And thus does this period of almost ten million years' duration draw to a close, and not yet has the ancestor of man appeared. This is the time usually designated as the *Pliocene*.

5. THE EARLY ICE AGE

By the close of the preceding period the lands of the northeastern part of North America and of northern Europe were highly elevated on an extensive scale, in North America vast areas rising up to 30,000 feet and more. Mild climates had formerly prevailed over these northern regions, and the arctic waters were all open to evaporation, and they continued to be ice-free until almost the close of the glacial period.

Simultaneously with these land elevations the ocean currents shifted, and the seasonal winds changed their direction. These conditions eventually produced an almost constant precipitation of moisture from the movement of the heavily saturated atmosphere over the northern highlands. Snow began to fall on these elevated and therefore cool regions, and it continued to fall until it had attained a depth of 20,000 feet. The areas of the greatest depth of snow, together with altitude, determined the central points of subsequent glacial pressure flows. And the ice age persisted just as long as this excessive precipitation continued to cover these northern highlands with this enormous mantle of snow, which soon metamorphosed into solid but creeping ice.

The great ice sheets of this period were all located on elevated highlands, not in mountainous regions where they are found today. One half of the glacial ice was in North America, one fourth in Eurasia, and one fourth elsewhere, chiefly in Antarctica. Africa was little affected by the ice, but Australia was almost covered with the antarctic ice blanket.

The northern regions of this world have experienced six separate and distinct ice invasions, although there were scores of advances and recessions associated with the activity of each individual ice sheet. The ice in North America collected in two and, later, three centers. Greenland was covered, and Iceland was completely buried beneath the ice flow. In Europe the ice at various times covered the British Isles excepting the coast of southern England, and it overspread western Europe down to France.

2,000,000 years ago the first North American glacier started its southern advance. The ice age was now in the making, and this glacier consumed nearly one million years in its advance from, and retreat back toward, the northern pressure centers. The central ice sheet extended south as far as Kansas; the eastern and western ice centers were not then so extensive.

1,500,000 years ago the first great glacier was retreating northward. In the meantime, enormous quantities of snow had been falling on Greenland and on the northeastern part of North America, and erelong this eastern ice mass began to flow southward. This was the second invasion of the ice.

These first two ice invasions were not extensive in Eurasia. During these early epochs of the ice age North America was overrun with mastodons, woolly mammoths, horses, camels, deer, musk oxen, bison, ground sloths, giant beavers, saber-toothed tigers, sloths as large as elephants, and many groups of the cat and dog families. But from this time forward they were rapidly reduced in numbers by the increasing cold of the glacial period. Toward the close of the ice age the majority of these animal species were extinct in North America.

Away from the ice the land and water life of the world was little changed. Between the ice invasions the climate was about as mild as at present, perhaps a little warmer. The glaciers were, after all, local phenomena, though they spread out to cover enormous areas. The coastwise climate varied greatly between the times of glacial inaction and those times when enormous icebergs were sliding off the coast of Maine into the Atlantic, slipping out through Puget Sound into the Pacific, and thundering down Norwegian fiords into the North Sea.

6. PRIMITIVE MAN IN THE ICE AGE

The great event of this glacial period was the evolution of primitive man. Slightly to the west of India, on land now under water and among the offspring of Asiatic migrants of the older North American lemur types, the dawn mammals *suddenly* appeared. These small animals walked mostly on their hind legs, and they possessed large brains in proportion to their size and in comparison with the brains of other animals. In the seventieth generation of this order of life a new and higher group of animals *suddenly* differentiated. These new mid-mammals—almost twice the size and height of their ancestors and possessing proportionately increased brain power—had only well established themselves when the Primates, the third vital mutation, *suddenly* appeared. (At this same time, a retrograde development within the mid-mammal stock gave origin to the simian ancestry; and from that day to this the human branch has gone forward by progressive evolution, while the simian tribes have remained stationary or have actually retrogressed.)

1,000,000 years ago Urantia was registered as an *inhabited world*. A mutation within the stock of the progressing Primates *suddenly* produced two primitive human beings, the actual ancestors of mankind.

This event occurred at about the time of the beginning of the third glacial advance; thus it may be seen that your early ancestors were born and bred in a stimulating, invigorating, and difficult environment. And the sole survivors of these Urantia aborigines, the Eskimos, even now prefer to dwell in frigid northern climes.

Human beings were not present in the Western Hemisphere until near the close of the ice age. But during the interglacial epochs they passed westward around the Mediterranean and soon overran the continent of Europe. In the caves of western Europe may be found human bones mingled with the remains of both tropic and arctic animals, testifying that man lived in these regions throughout the later epochs of the advancing and retreating glaciers.

7. THE CONTINUING ICE AGE

Throughout the glacial period other activities were in progress, but the action of the ice overshadows all other phenomena in the northern latitudes. No other terrestrial activity leaves such characteristic evidence on the topography. The distinctive boulders and surface cleavages, such as potholes, lakes, displaced stone, and rock flour, are to be found in connection with no other phenomenon in nature. The ice is also responsible for those gentle swells, or surface undulations, known as drumlins. And a glacier, as it advances, displaces rivers and changes the whole face of the earth. Glaciers alone leave behind them those telltale drifts—the ground, lateral, and terminal moraines. These drifts, particularly the ground moraines, extend from the eastern seaboard north and westward in North America and are found in Europe and Siberia.

750,000 years ago the fourth ice sheet, a union of the North American central and eastern ice fields, was well on its way south; at its height it reached to southern Illinois, displacing the Mississippi River fifty miles to the west, and in the east it extended as far south as the Ohio River and central Pennsylvania.

In Asia the Siberian ice sheet made its southernmost invasion, while in Europe the advancing ice stopped just short of the mountain barrier of the Alps.

500,000 years ago, during the fifth advance of the ice, a new development accelerated the course of human evolution. *Suddenly* and in one generation the six colored races mutated from the aboriginal human stock. This is a doubly important date since it also marks the arrival of the Planetary Prince.

In North America the advancing fifth glacier consisted of a combined invasion by all three ice centers. The eastern lobe, however, extended only a short distance below the St. Lawrence valley, and the western ice sheet made little southern advance. But the central lobe reached south to cover most of the state of Iowa. In Europe this invasion of the ice was not so extensive as the preceding one.

250,000 years ago the sixth and last glaciation began. And despite the fact that the northern highlands had begun to sink slightly, this was the period of greatest snow deposition on the northern ice fields.

In this invasion the three great ice sheets coalesced into one vast ice mass, and all of the western mountains participated in this glacial activity. This was the largest of all ice invasions in North America; the ice moved south over fifteen hundred miles from its pressure centers, and North America experienced its lowest temperatures.

200,000 years ago, during the advance of the last glacier, there occurred an episode which had much to do with the march of events on Urantia—the Lucifer rebellion.

150,000 years ago the sixth and last glacier reached its farthest points of southern extension, the western ice sheet crossing just over the Canadian border; the central coming down into Kansas, Missouri, and Illinois; the eastern sheet advancing south and covering the greater portion of Pennsylvania and Ohio.

This is the glacier that sent forth the many tongues, or ice lobes, which carved out the present-day lakes, great and small. During its retreat the North American system of Great Lakes was produced. And Urantian geologists have very accurately deduced the various stages of this development and have correctly surmised that these bodies of water did, at different times, empty first into the Mississippi valley, then eastward into the Hudson valley, and finally by a northern route into the St. Lawrence. It is thirty-seven thousand years since the connected Great Lakes system began to empty out over the present Niagara route.

100,000 years ago, during the retreat of the last glacier, the vast polar ice sheets began to form, and the center of ice accumulation moved considerably northward. And as long as the polar regions continue to be covered with ice, it is hardly possible for another glacial age to occur, regardless of future land elevations or modification of ocean currents.

This last glacier was one hundred thousand years advancing, and it required a like span of time to complete its northern retreat. The temperate regions have been free from the ice for a little over fifty thousand years.

The rigorous glacial period destroyed many species and radically changed numerous others. Many were sorely sifted by the to-and-fro migration which was made necessary by the advancing and retreating ice. Those animals which followed the glaciers back and forth over the land were the bear, bison, reindeer, musk ox, mammoth, and mastodon.

The mammoth sought the open prairies, but the mastodon preferred the sheltered fringes of the forest regions. The mammoth, until a late date, ranged from Mexico to Canada; the Siberian variety became wool covered. The mastodon persisted in North America until exterminated by the red man much as the white man later killed off the bison.

In North America, during the last glaciation, the horse, tapir, llama, and saber-toothed tiger became extinct. In their places sloths, armadillos, and water hogs came up from South America.

The enforced migration of life before the advancing ice led to an extraordinary commingling of plants and of animals, and with the retreat of the final ice invasion, many arctic species of both plants and animals were left stranded high upon certain mountain peaks, whither they had journeyed to escape destruction by the glacier. And so, today, these dislocated plants and animals may be found high up on the Alps of Europe and even on the Appalachian Mountains of North America.

The ice age is the last completed geologic period, the so-called *Pleistocene,* over two million years in length.

35,000 years ago marks the termination of the great ice age excepting in the polar regions of the planet. This date is also significant in that it approximates the arrival of a Material Son and Daughter and the beginning of the Adamic dispensation, roughly corresponding to the beginning of the *Holocene* or post-glacial period.

This narrative, extending from the rise of mammalian life to the retreat of the ice and on down to historic times, covers a span of almost fifty million years. This is the last—the current—geologic period and is known to your researchers as the *Cenozoic* or recent-times era.

[Sponsored by a Resident Life Carrier.]

PAPER 62

THE DAWN RACES OF EARLY MAN

ABOUT one million years ago the immediate ancestors of mankind made their appearance by three successive and sudden mutations stemming from early stock of the lemur type of placental mammal. The dominant factors of these early lemurs were derived from the western or later American group of the evolving life plasm. But before establishing the direct line of human ancestry, this strain was reinforced by contributions from the central life implantation evolved in Africa. The eastern life group contributed little or nothing to the actual production of the human species.

1. THE EARLY LEMUR TYPES

The early lemurs concerned in the ancestry of the human species were not directly related to the pre-existent tribes of gibbons and apes then living in Eurasia and northern Africa, whose progeny have survived to the present time. Neither were they the offspring of the modern type of lemur, though springing from an ancestor common to both but long since extinct.

While these early lemurs evolved in the Western Hemisphere, the establishment of the direct mammalian ancestry of mankind took place in southwestern Asia, in the original area of the central life implantation but on the borders of the eastern regions. Several million years ago the North American type lemurs had migrated westward over the Bering land bridge and had slowly made their way southwestward along the Asiatic coast. These migrating tribes finally reached the salubrious region lying between the then expanded Mediterranean Sea and the elevating mountainous regions of the Indian peninsula. In these lands to the west of India they united with other and favorable strains, thus establishing the ancestry of the human race.

With the passing of time the seacoast of India southwest of the mountains gradually submerged, completely isolating the life of this region. There was no avenue of approach to, or escape from, this Mesopotamian or Persian peninsula except to the north, and that was repeatedly cut off by the southern invasions of the glaciers. And it was in this then almost paradisiacal area, and from the superior descendants of this lemur type of mammal, that there sprang two great groups, the simian tribes of modern times and the present-day human species.

2. THE DAWN MAMMALS

A little more than one million years ago the Mesopotamian dawn mammals, the direct descendants of the North American lemur type of placental mammal, *suddenly* appeared. They were active little creatures, almost three feet tall; and while they did not habitually walk on their hind legs, they could easily stand erect. They were hairy and agile and chattered in monkeylike fashion, but unlike the simian tribes, they were flesh eaters. They had a primitive opposable thumb as well as a highly useful grasping big toe. From this point onward the prehuman species successively developed the opposable thumb while they progressively lost the grasping power of the great toe. The later ape tribes retained the grasping big toe but never developed the human type of thumb.

These dawn mammals attained full growth when three or four years of age, having a potential life span, on the average, of about twenty years. As a rule offspring were born singly, although twins were occasional.

The members of this new species had the largest brains for their size of any animal that had theretofore existed on earth. They experienced many of the emotions and shared numerous instincts which later characterized primitive man, being highly curious and exhibiting considerable elation when successful at any undertaking. Food hunger and sex craving were well developed, and a definite sex selection was manifested in a crude form of courtship and choice of mates. They would fight fiercely in defense of their kindred and were quite tender in family associations, possessing a sense of self-abasement bordering on shame and remorse. They were very affectionate and touchingly loyal to their mates, but if circumstances separated them, they would choose new partners.

Being small of stature and having keen minds to realize the dangers of their forest habitat, they developed an extraordinary fear which led to those wise precautionary measures that so enormously contributed to survival, such as their construction of crude shelters in the high treetops which eliminated many of the perils of ground life. The beginning of the fear tendencies of mankind more specifically dates from these days.

These dawn mammals developed more of a tribal spirit than had ever been previously exhibited. They were, indeed, highly gregarious but nevertheless exceedingly pugnacious when in any way disturbed in the ordinary pursuit of their routine life, and they displayed fiery tempers when their anger was fully aroused. Their bellicose natures, however, served a good purpose; superior groups did not hesitate to make war on their inferior neighbors, and thus, by selective survival, the species was progressively improved. They very soon dominated the life of the smaller creatures of this region, and very few of the older noncarnivorous monkeylike tribes survived.

These aggressive little animals multiplied and spread over the Mesopotamian peninsula for more than one thousand years, constantly improving in physical type and general intelligence. And it was just seventy generations after this new tribe had taken origin from the highest type of lemur ancestor that the next epoch-making development occurred—the *sudden* differentiation of the ancestors of the next vital step in the evolution of human beings on Urantia.

3. THE MID-MAMMALS

Early in the career of the dawn mammals, in the treetop abode of a superior pair of these agile creatures, twins were born, one male and one female. Compared with their ancestors, they were really handsome little creatures. They had little hair on their bodies, but this was no disability as they lived in a warm and equable climate.

These children grew to be a little over four feet in height. They were in every way larger than their parents, having longer legs and shorter arms. They had almost perfectly opposable thumbs, just about as well adapted for diversified work as the present human thumb. They walked upright, having feet almost as well suited for walking as those of the later human races.

Their brains were inferior to, and smaller than, those of human beings but very superior to, and comparatively much larger than, those of their ancestors. The twins early displayed superior intelligence and were soon recognized as the heads of the whole tribe of dawn mammals, really instituting a primitive form of social organization and a crude economic division of labor. This brother and sister mated and soon enjoyed the society of twenty-one children much like themselves, all more than four feet tall and in every way superior to the ancestral species. This new group formed the nucleus of the mid-mammals.

When the numbers of this new and superior group grew great, war, relentless war, broke out; and when the terrible struggle was over, not a single individual of the pre-existent and ancestral race of dawn mammals remained alive. The less numerous but more powerful and intelligent offshoot of the species had survived at the expense of their ancestors.

And now, for almost fifteen thousand years (six hundred generations), this creature became the terror of this part of the world. All of the great and vicious animals of former times had perished. The large beasts native to these regions were not carnivorous, and the larger species of the cat family, lions and tigers, had not yet invaded this peculiarly sheltered nook of the earth's surface. Therefore did these mid-mammals wax valiant and subdue the whole of their corner of creation.

Compared with the ancestral species, the mid-mammals were an improvement in every way. Even their potential life span was longer, being about twenty-five years. A number of rudimentary human traits appeared in this new species. In addition to the innate propensities exhibited by their ancestors, these mid-mammals were capable of showing disgust in certain repulsive situations. They further possessed a well-defined hoarding instinct; they would hide food for subsequent use and were greatly given to the collection of smooth round pebbles and certain types of round stones suitable for defensive and offensive ammunition.

These mid-mammals were the first to exhibit a definite construction propensity, as shown in their rivalry in the building of both treetop homes and their many-tunneled subterranean retreats; they were the first species of mammals ever to provide for safety in both arboreal and underground shelters. They largely forsook the trees as places of abode, living on the ground during the day and sleeping in the treetops at night.

As time passed, the natural increase in numbers eventually resulted in serious food competition and sex rivalry, all of which culminated in a series of internecine battles that nearly destroyed the entire species. These struggles continued until only one group of less than one hundred individuals was left alive. But peace once more prevailed, and this lone surviving tribe built anew its treetop bedrooms and once again resumed a normal and semipeaceful existence.

You can hardly realize by what narrow margins your prehuman ancestors missed extinction from time to time. Had the ancestral frog of all humanity jumped two inches less on a certain occasion, the whole course of evolution would have been markedly changed. The immediate lemurlike mother of the dawn-mammal species escaped death no less than five times by mere hairbreadth margins before she gave birth to the father of the new and higher mammalian order. But the closest call of all was when lightning struck the tree in which the prospective mother of the Primates twins was sleeping. Both of these mid-mammal parents were severely shocked and badly burned; three of their seven children were killed by this bolt from the skies. These evolving animals were almost superstitious. This couple whose treetop home had been struck were really the leaders of the more progressive group of the mid-mammal species; and following their example, more than half the tribe, embracing the more intelligent families, moved about two miles away from this locality and began the construction of new treetop abodes and new ground shelters—their transient retreats in time of sudden danger.

Soon after the completion of their home, this couple, veterans of so many struggles, found themselves the proud parents of twins, the most interesting and important animals ever to have been born into the world up to that time, for they were the first of the new species of *Primates* constituting the next vital step in prehuman evolution.

Contemporaneously with the birth of these Primates twins, another couple—a peculiarly retarded male and female of the mid-mammal tribe, a couple that were both mentally and physically inferior—also gave birth to twins. These twins, one male and one female, were indifferent to conquest; they were concerned only with obtaining food and, since they would not eat flesh, soon lost all interest in seeking prey. These retarded twins became the founders of the modern simian tribes. Their descendants sought the warmer southern regions with their mild climates and an abundance of tropical fruits, where they have continued much as of that day except for those branches which mated with the earlier types of gibbons and apes and have greatly deteriorated in consequence.

And so it may be readily seen that man and the ape are related only in that they sprang from the mid-mammals, a tribe in which there occurred the contemporaneous birth and subsequent segregation of two pairs of twins: the inferior pair destined to produce the modern types of monkey, baboon, chimpanzee, and gorilla; the superior pair destined to continue the line of ascent which evolved into man himself.

Modern man and the simians did spring from the same tribe and species but not from the same parents. Man's ancestors are descended from the superior strains of the selected remnant of this mid-mammal tribe, whereas the modern simians (excepting certain pre-existent types of lemurs, gibbons, apes, and other monkeylike creatures) are the descendants of the most inferior couple of this mid-mammal group, a couple who only survived by hiding themselves in a subterranean food-storage retreat for more than two weeks during the last fierce battle of their tribe, emerging only after the hostilities were well over.

4. THE PRIMATES

Going back to the birth of the superior twins, one male and one female, to the two leading members of the mid-mammal tribe: These animal babies were of an unusual order; they had still less hair on their bodies than their parents and, when very young, insisted on walking upright. Their ancestors had always learned to walk on their hind legs, but these Primates twins stood erect from the beginning. They attained a height of over five feet, and their heads grew larger in comparison with others among the tribe. While early learning to communicate with each other by means of signs and sounds, they were never able to make their people understand these new symbols.

When about fourteen years of age, they fled from the tribe, going west to raise their family and establish the new species of Primates. And these new creatures are very properly denominated *Primates* since they were the direct and immediate animal ancestors of the human family itself.

Thus it was that the Primates came to occupy a region on the west coast of the Mesopotamian peninsula as it then projected into the southern sea, while the less intelligent and closely related tribes lived around the peninsula point and up the eastern shore line.

The Primates were more human and less animal than their mid-mammal predecessors. The skeletal proportions of this new species were very similar to those of the primitive human races. The human type of hand and foot had fully developed, and these creatures could walk and even run as well as any of their later-day human descendants. They largely abandoned tree life, though continuing to resort to the treetops as a safety measure at night, for like their earlier ancestors, they were greatly subject to fear. The increased use of their hands did much to develop inherent brain power, but they did not yet possess minds that could really be called human.

Although in emotional nature the Primates differed little from their forebears, they exhibited more of a human trend in all of their propensities. They were, indeed, splendid and superior animals, reaching maturity at about ten years of age and having a natural life span of about forty years. That is, they might have lived that long had they died natural deaths, but in those early days very few animals ever died a natural death; the struggle for existence was altogether too intense.

And now, after almost nine hundred generations of development, covering about twenty-one thousand years from the origin of the dawn mammals, the Primates *suddenly* gave birth to two remarkable creatures, the first true human beings.

Thus it was that the dawn mammals, springing from the North American lemur type, gave origin to the mid-mammals, and these mid-mammals in turn produced the superior Primates, who became the immediate ancestors of the primitive human race. The Primates tribes were the last vital link in the evolution of man, but in less than five thousand years not a single individual of these extraordinary tribes was left.

5. THE FIRST HUMAN BEINGS

From the year A.D. 1934 back to the birth of the first two human beings is just 993,419 years.

These two remarkable creatures were true human beings. They possessed perfect human thumbs, as had many of their ancestors, while they had just as perfect feet as the present-day human races. They were walkers and runners, not climbers; the grasping function of the big toe was absent, completely absent.

When danger drove them to the treetops, they climbed just like the humans of today would. They would climb up the trunk of a tree like a bear and not as would a chimpanzee or a gorilla, swinging up by the branches.

These first human beings (and their descendants) reached full maturity at twelve years of age and possessed a potential life span of about seventy-five years.

Many new emotions early appeared in these human twins. They experienced admiration for both objects and other beings and exhibited considerable vanity. But the most remarkable advance in emotional development was the sudden appearance of a new group of really human feelings, the worshipful group, embracing awe, reverence, humility, and even a primitive form of gratitude. Fear, joined with ignorance of natural phenomena, is about to give birth to primitive religion.

Not only were such human feelings manifested in these primitive humans, but many more highly evolved sentiments were also present in rudimentary form. They were mildly cognizant of pity, shame, and reproach and were acutely conscious of love, hate, and revenge, being also susceptible to marked feelings of jealousy.

These first two humans—the twins—were a great trial to their Primates parents. They were so curious and adventurous that they nearly lost their lives on numerous occasions before they were eight years old. As it was, they were rather well scarred up by the time they were twelve.

Very early they learned to engage in verbal communication; by the age of ten they had worked out an improved sign and word language of almost half a hundred ideas and had greatly improved and expanded the crude communicative technique of their ancestors. But try as hard as they might, they were able to teach only a few of their new signs and symbols to their parents.

When about nine years of age, they journeyed off down the river one bright day and held a momentous conference. Every celestial intelligence stationed on Urantia, including myself, was present as an observer of the transactions of this noontide tryst. On this eventful day they arrived at an understanding to live with and for each other, and this was the first of a series of such agreements which finally culminated in the decision to flee from their inferior animal associates and to journey northward, little knowing that they were thus to found the human race.

While we were all greatly concerned with what these two little savages were planning, we were powerless to control the working of their minds; we did not—could not—arbitrarily influence their decisions. But within the permissible limits of planetary function, we, the Life Carriers, together with our associates, all conspired to lead the human twins northward and far from their hairy and partially tree-dwelling people. And so, by reason of their own intelligent choice, the twins did *migrate,* and because of our supervision they migrated *northward* to a secluded region where they escaped the possibility of biologic degradation through admixture with their inferior relatives of the Primates tribes.

Shortly before their departure from the home forests they lost their mother in a gibbon raid. While she did not possess their intelligence, she did have a worthy mammalian affection of a high order for her offspring, and she fearlessly gave her life in the attempt to save the wonderful pair. Nor was her sacrifice in vain, for she held off the enemy until the father arrived with reinforcements and put the invaders to rout.

Soon after this young couple forsook their associates to found the human race, their Primates father became disconsolate—he was heartbroken. He refused to eat, even when food was brought to him by his other children. His brilliant offspring having been lost, life did not seem worth living among his ordinary fellows; so he wandered off into the forest, was set upon by hostile gibbons and beaten to death.

6. EVOLUTION OF THE HUMAN MIND

We, the Life Carriers on Urantia, had passed through the long vigil of watchful waiting since the day we first planted the life plasm in the planetary waters, and naturally the appearance of the first really intelligent and volitional beings brought to us great joy and supreme satisfaction.

We had been watching the twins develop mentally through our observation of the functioning of the seven adjutant mind-spirits assigned to Urantia at the time of our arrival on the planet. Throughout the long evolutionary development of planetary life, these tireless mind ministers had ever registered their increasing ability to contact with the successively expanding brain capacities of the progressively superior animal creatures.

At first only the *spirit of intuition* could function in the instinctive and reflex behavior of the primordial animal life. With the differentiation of higher types, the *spirit of understanding* was able to endow such creatures with the gift of spontaneous association of ideas. Later on we observed the *spirit of courage* in operation; evolving animals really developed a crude form of protective self-consciousness. Subsequent to the appearance of the mammalian groups, we beheld the *spirit of knowledge* manifesting itself in increased measure. And the evolution of the higher mammals brought the function of the *spirit of counsel,* with the resulting growth of the herd instinct and the beginnings of primitive social development.

Increasingly, on down through the dawn mammals, the mid-mammals, and the Primates, we had observed the augmented service of the first five adjutants. But never had the remaining two, the highest mind ministers, been able to function in the Urantia type of evolutionary mind.

Imagine our joy one day—the twins were about ten years old—when the *spirit of worship* made its first contact with the mind of the female twin and shortly thereafter with the male. We knew that something closely akin to human mind was approaching culmination; and when, about a year later, they finally resolved, as a result of meditative thought and purposeful decision, to flee from home and journey north, then did the *spirit of wisdom* begin to function on Urantia and in these two now recognized human minds.

There was an immediate and new order of mobilization of the seven adjutant mind-spirits. We were alive with expectation; we realized that the long-waited-for hour was approaching; we knew we were upon the threshold of the realization of our protracted effort to evolve will creatures on Urantia.

7. RECOGNITION AS AN INHABITED WORLD

We did not have to wait long. At noon, the day after the runaway of the twins, there occurred the initial test flash of the universe circuit signals at the planetary reception-focus of Urantia. We were, of course, all astir with the realization that a great event was impending; but since this world was a life-experiment station, we had not the slightest idea of just how we would be apprised of the recognition of intelligent life on the planet. But we were not long in suspense. On the third day after the elopement of the twins, and before the Life Carrier corps departed, there arrived the Nebadon archangel of initial planetary circuit establishment.

It was an eventful day on Urantia when our small group gathered about the planetary pole of space communication and received the first message from Salvington over the newly established mind circuit of the planet. And this first message, dictated by the chief of the archangel corps, said:

"To the Life Carriers on Urantia—Greetings! We transmit assurance of great pleasure on Salvington, Edentia, and Jerusem in honor of the registration on the headquarters of Nebadon of the signal of the existence on Urantia of mind of will dignity. The purposeful decision of the twins to flee northward and segregate their offspring from their inferior ancestors has been noted. This is the first decision of mind—the human type of mind—on Urantia and automatically establishes the circuit of communication over which this initial message of acknowledgment is transmitting."

Next over this new circuit came the greetings of the Most Highs of Edentia, containing instructions for the resident Life Carriers forbidding us to interfere with the pattern of life we had established. We were directed not to intervene in the affairs of human progress. It should not be inferred that Life Carriers ever arbitrarily and mechanically interfere with the natural outworking of the planetary evolutionary plans, for we do not. But up to this time we had been permitted to manipulate the environment and shield the life plasm in a special manner, and it was this extraordinary, but wholly natural, supervision that was to be discontinued.

And no sooner had the Most Highs left off speaking than the beautiful message of Lucifer, then sovereign of the Satania system, began to planetize. Now the Life Carriers heard the welcome words of their own chief and received his permission to return to Jerusem. This message from Lucifer contained the official acceptance of the Life Carriers' work on Urantia and absolved us from all future criticism of any of our efforts to improve the life patterns of Nebadon as established in the Satania system.

These messages from Salvington, Edentia, and Jerusem formally marked the termination of the Life Carriers' agelong supervision of the planet. For ages we had been on duty, assisted only by the seven adjutant mind-spirits and the Master Physical Controllers. And now, will, the power of choosing to worship and to ascend, having appeared in the evolutionary creatures of the planet, we realized that our work was finished, and our group prepared to depart. Urantia being a life-modification world, permission was granted to leave behind two senior Life Carriers with twelve assistants, and I was chosen as one of this group and have ever since been on Urantia.

It is just 993,408 years ago (from the year A.D. 1934) that Urantia was formally recognized as a planet of human habitation in the universe of Nebadon. Biologic evolution had once again achieved the human levels of will dignity; man had arrived on planet 606 of Satania.

[Sponsored by a Life Carrier of Nebadon resident on Urantia.]

PAPER 63

THE FIRST HUMAN FAMILY

URANTIA was registered as an inhabited world when the first two human beings—the twins—were eleven years old, and before they had become the parents of the first-born of the second generation of actual human beings. And the archangel message from Salvington, on this occasion of formal planetary recognition, closed with these words:

"Man-mind has appeared on 606 of Satania, and these parents of the new race shall be called *Andon* and *Fonta.* And all archangels pray that these creatures may speedily be endowed with the personal indwelling of the gift of the spirit of the Universal Father."

Andon is the Nebadon name which signifies "the first Fatherlike creature to exhibit human perfection hunger." Fonta signifies "the first Sonlike creature to exhibit human perfection hunger." Andon and Fonta never knew these names until they were bestowed upon them at the time of fusion with their Thought Adjusters. Throughout their mortal sojourn on Urantia they called each other Sonta-an and Sonta-en, Sonta-an meaning "loved by mother," Sonta-en signifying "loved by father." They gave themselves these names, and the meanings are significant of their mutual regard and affection.

1. ANDON AND FONTA

In many respects, Andon and Fonta were the most remarkable pair of human beings that have ever lived on the face of the earth. This wonderful pair, the actual parents of all mankind, were in every way superior to many of their immediate descendants, and they were radically different from all of their ancestors, both immediate and remote.

The parents of this first human couple were apparently little different from the average of their tribe, though they were among its more intelligent members, that group which first learned to throw stones and to use clubs in fighting. They also made use of sharp spicules of stone, flint, and bone.

While still living with his parents, Andon had fastened a sharp piece of flint on the end of a club, using animal tendons for this purpose, and on no less than a dozen occasions he made good use of such a weapon in saving both his own life and that of his equally adventurous and inquisitive sister, who unfailingly accompanied him on all of his tours of exploration.

The decision of Andon and Fonta to flee from the Primates tribes implies a quality of mind far above the baser intelligence which characterized so many of their later descendants who stooped to mate with their retarded cousins of the simian tribes. But their vague feeling of being something more than mere animals was due to the possession of personality and was augmented by the indwelling presence of the Thought Adjusters.

2. THE FLIGHT OF THE TWINS

After Andon and Fonta had decided to flee northward, they succumbed to their fears for a time, especially the fear of displeasing their father and immediate family. They envisaged being set upon by hostile relatives and thus recognized the possibility of meeting death at the hands of their already jealous tribesmen. As youngsters, the twins had spent most of their time in each other's company and for this reason had never been overly popular with their animal cousins of the Primates tribe. Nor had they improved their standing in the tribe by building a separate, and a very superior, tree home.

And it was in this new home among the treetops, one night after they had been awakened by a violent storm, and as they held each other in fearful and fond embrace, that they finally and fully made up their minds to flee from the tribal habitat and the home treetops.

They had already prepared a crude treetop retreat some half-day's journey to the north. This was their secret and safe hiding place for the first day away from the home forests. Notwithstanding that the twins shared the Primates' deathly fear of being on the ground at nighttime, they sallied forth shortly before nightfall on their northern trek. While it required unusual courage for them to undertake this night journey, even with a full moon, they correctly concluded that they were less likely to be missed and pursued by their tribesmen and relatives. And they safely made their previously prepared rendezvous shortly after midnight.

On their northward journey they discovered an exposed flint deposit and, finding many stones suitably shaped for various uses, gathered up a supply for the future. In attempting to chip these flints so that they would be better adapted for certain purposes, Andon discovered their sparking quality and conceived the idea of building fire. But the notion did not take firm hold of him at the time as the climate was still salubrious and there was little need of fire.

But the autumn sun was getting lower in the sky, and as they journeyed northward, the nights grew cooler and cooler. Already they had been forced to make use of animal skins for warmth. Before they had been away from home one moon, Andon signified to his mate that he thought he could make fire with the flint. They tried for two months to utilize the flint spark for kindling a fire but only met with failure. Each day this couple would strike the flints and endeavor to ignite the wood. Finally, one evening about the time of the setting of the sun, the secret of the technique was unraveled when it occurred to Fonta to climb a near-by tree to secure an abandoned bird's nest. The nest was dry and highly inflammable and consequently flared right up into a full blaze the moment the spark fell upon it. They were so surprised and startled at their success that they almost lost the fire, but they saved it by the addition of suitable fuel, and then began the first search for firewood by the parents of all mankind.

This was one of the most joyous moments in their short but eventful lives. All night long they sat up watching their fire burn, vaguely realizing that they had made a discovery which would make it possible for them to defy climate and thus forever to be independent of their animal relatives of the southern lands. After three days' rest and enjoyment of the fire, they journeyed on.

The Primates ancestors of Andon had often replenished fire which had been kindled by lightning, but never before had the creatures of earth possessed a method of starting fire at will. But it was a long time before the twins learned that dry moss and other materials would kindle fire just as well as birds' nests.

3. ANDON'S FAMILY

It was almost two years from the night of the twins' departure from home before their first child was born. They named him Sontad; and Sontad was the first creature to be born on Urantia who was wrapped in protective coverings at the time of birth. The human race had begun, and with this new evolution there appeared the instinct properly to care for the increasingly enfeebled infants which would characterize the progressive development of mind of the intellectual order as contrasted with the more purely animal type.

Andon and Fonta had nineteen children in all, and they lived to enjoy the association of almost half a hundred grandchildren and half a dozen great-grandchildren. The family was domiciled in four adjoining rock shelters, or semicaves, three of which were interconnected by hallways which had been excavated in the soft limestone with flint tools devised by Andon's children.

These early Andonites evinced a very marked clannish spirit; they hunted in groups and never strayed very far from the homesite. They seemed to realize that they were an isolated and unique group of living beings and should therefore avoid becoming separated. This feeling of intimate kinship was undoubtedly due to the enhanced mind ministry of the adjutant spirits.

Andon and Fonta labored incessantly for the nurture and uplift of the clan. They lived to the age of forty-two, when both were killed at the time of an earthquake by the falling of an overhanging rock. Five of their children and eleven grandchildren perished with them, and almost a score of their descendants suffered serious injuries.

Upon the death of his parents, Sontad, despite a seriously injured foot, immediately assumed the leadership of the clan and was ably assisted by his wife, his eldest sister. Their first task was to roll up stones to effectively entomb their dead parents, brothers, sisters, and children. Undue significance should not attach to this act of burial. Their ideas of survival after death were very vague and indefinite, being largely derived from their fantastic and variegated dream life.

This family of Andon and Fonta held together until the twentieth generation, when combined food competition and social friction brought about the beginning of dispersion.

4. THE ANDONIC CLANS

Primitive man—the Andonites—had black eyes and a swarthy complexion, something of a cross between yellow and red. Melanin is a coloring substance which is found in the skins of all human beings. It is the original Andonic skin pigment. In general appearance and skin color these early Andonites more nearly resembled the present-day Eskimo than any other type of living human beings. They were the first creatures to use the skins of animals as a protection against cold; they had little more hair on their bodies than present-day humans.

The tribal life of the animal ancestors of these early men had foreshadowed the beginnings of numerous social conventions, and with the expanding emotions and augmented brain powers of these beings, there was an immediate development in social organization and a new division of clan labor. They were exceedingly imitative, but the play instinct was only slightly developed, and the sense of humor was almost entirely absent. Primitive man smiled occasionally, but he never indulged in hearty laughter. Humor was the legacy of the later Adamic race. These early human beings were not so sensitive to pain nor so reactive to unpleasant situations as were many of the later evolving mortals. Childbirth was not a painful or distressing ordeal to Fonta and her immediate progeny.

They were a wonderful tribe. The males would fight heroically for the safety of their mates and their offspring; the females were affectionately devoted to their children. But their patriotism was wholly limited to the immediate clan. They were very loyal to their families; they would die without question in defense of their children, but they were not able to grasp the idea of trying to make the world a better place for their grandchildren. Altruism was as yet unborn in the human heart, notwithstanding that all of the emotions essential to the birth of religion were already present in these Urantia aborigines.

These early men possessed a touching affection for their comrades and certainly had a real, although crude, idea of friendship. It was a common sight in later times, during their constantly recurring battles with the inferior tribes, to see one of these primitive men valiantly fighting with one hand while he struggled on, trying to protect and save an injured fellow warrior. Many of the most noble and highly human traits of subsequent evolutionary development were touchingly foreshadowed in these primitive peoples.

The original Andonic clan maintained an unbroken line of leadership until the twenty-seventh generation, when, no male offspring appearing among Sontad's direct descendants, two rival would-be rulers of the clan fell to fighting for supremacy.

Before the extensive dispersion of the Andonic clans a well-developed language had evolved from their early efforts to intercommunicate. This language continued to grow, and almost daily additions were made to it because of the new inventions and adaptations to environment which were developed by these active, restless, and curious people. And this language became the word of Urantia, the tongue of the early human family, until the later appearance of the colored races.

As time passed, the Andonic clans grew in number, and the contact of the expanding families developed friction and misunderstandings. Only two things came to occupy the minds of these peoples: hunting to obtain food and fighting to avenge themselves against some real or supposed injustice or insult at the hands of the neighboring tribes.

Family feuds increased, tribal wars broke out, and serious losses were sustained among the very best elements of the more able and advanced groups. Some of these losses were irreparable; some of the most valuable strains of ability and intelligence were forever lost to the world. This early race and its primitive civilization were threatened with extinction by this incessant warfare of the clans.

It is impossible to induce such primitive beings long to live together in peace. Man is the descendant of fighting animals, and when closely associated, uncultured people irritate and offend each other. The Life Carriers know this tendency among evolutionary creatures and accordingly make provision for the eventual separation of developing human beings into at least three, and more often six, distinct and separate races.

5. DISPERSION OF THE ANDONITES

The early Andon races did not penetrate very far into Asia, and they did not at first enter Africa. The geography of those times pointed them north, and farther and farther north these people journeyed until they were hindered by the slowly advancing ice of the third glacier.

Before this extensive ice sheet reached France and the British Isles, the descendants of Andon and Fonta had pushed on westward over Europe and had established more than one thousand separate settlements along the great rivers leading to the then warm waters of the North Sea.

These Andonic tribes were the early river dwellers of France; they lived along the river Somme for tens of thousands of years. The Somme is the one river unchanged by the glaciers, running down to the sea in those days much as it does today. And that explains why so much evidence of the Andonic descendants is found along the course of this river valley.

These aborigines of Urantia were not tree dwellers, though in emergencies they still betook themselves to the treetops. They regularly dwelt under the shelter of overhanging cliffs along the rivers and in hillside grottoes which afforded a good view of the approaches and sheltered them from the elements. They could thus enjoy the comfort of their fires without being too much inconvenienced by the smoke. They were not really cave dwellers either, though in subsequent times the later ice sheets came farther south and drove their descendants to the caves. They preferred to camp near the edge of a forest and beside a stream.

They very early became remarkably clever in disguising their partially sheltered abodes and showed great skill in constructing stone sleeping chambers, dome-shaped stone huts, into which they crawled at night. The entrance to such a hut was closed by rolling a stone in front of it, a large stone which had been placed inside for this purpose before the roof stones were finally put in place.

The Andonites were fearless and successful hunters and, with the exception of wild berries and certain fruits of the trees, lived exclusively on flesh. As Andon had invented the stone ax, so his descendants early discovered and made effective use of the throwing stick and the harpoon. At last a tool-creating mind was functioning in conjunction with an implement-using hand, and these early humans became highly skillful in the fashioning of flint tools. They traveled far and wide in search of flint, much as present-day humans journey to the ends of the earth in quest of gold, platinum, and diamonds.

And in many other ways these Andon tribes manifested a degree of intelligence which their retrogressing descendants did not attain in half a million years, though they did again and again rediscover various methods of kindling fire.

6. ONAGAR—THE FIRST TRUTH TEACHER

As the Andonic dispersion extended, the cultural and spiritual status of the clans retrogressed for nearly ten thousand years until the days of Onagar, who assumed the leadership of these tribes, brought peace among them, and for the first time, led all of them in the worship of the "Breath Giver to men and animals."

Andon's philosophy had been most confused; he had barely escaped becoming a fire worshiper because of the great comfort derived from his accidental discovery of fire. Reason, however, directed him from his own discovery to the sun as a superior and more awe-inspiring source of heat and light, but it was too remote, and so he failed to become a sun worshiper.

The Andonites early developed a fear of the elements—thunder, lightning, rain, snow, hail, and ice. But hunger was the constantly recurring urge of these early days, and since they largely subsisted on animals, they eventually evolved a form of animal worship. To Andon, the larger food animals were symbols of creative might and sustaining power. From time to time it became the custom to designate various of these larger animals as objects of worship. During the vogue of a particular animal, crude outlines of it would be drawn on the walls of the caves, and later on, as continued progress was made in the arts, such an animal god was engraved on various ornaments.

Very early the Andonic peoples formed the habit of refraining from eating the flesh of the animal of tribal veneration. Presently, in order more suitably to impress the minds of their youths, they evolved a ceremony of reverence which was carried out about the body of one of these venerated animals; and still later on, this primitive performance developed into the more elaborate sacrificial ceremonies of their descendants. And this is the origin of sacrifices as a part of worship. This idea was elaborated by Moses in the Hebrew ritual and was preserved, in principle, by the Apostle Paul as the doctrine of atonement for sin by "the shedding of blood."

That food was the all-important thing in the lives of these primitive human beings is shown by the prayer taught these simple folks by Onagar, their great teacher. And this prayer was:

"O Breath of Life, give us this day our daily food, deliver us from the curse of the ice, save us from our forest enemies, and with mercy receive us into the Great Beyond."

Onagar maintained headquarters on the northern shores of the ancient Mediterranean in the region of the present Caspian Sea at a settlement called Oban, the tarrying place on the westward turning of the travel trail leading up northward from the Mesopotamian southland. From Oban he sent out teachers to the remote settlements to spread his new doctrines of one Deity and his concept of the hereafter, which he called the Great Beyond. These emissaries of Onagar were the world's first missionaries; they were also the first human beings to cook meat, the first regularly to use fire in the preparation of food. They cooked flesh on the ends of sticks and also on hot stones; later on they roasted large pieces in the fire, but their descendants almost entirely reverted to the use of raw flesh.

Onagar was born 983,323 years ago (from A.D. 1934), and he lived to be sixty-nine years of age. The record of the achievements of this master mind and spiritual leader of the pre-Planetary Prince days is a thrilling recital of the organization of these primitive peoples into a real society. He instituted an efficient tribal government, the like of which was not attained by succeeding generations in many millenniums. Never again, until the arrival of the Planetary Prince, was there such a high spiritual civilization on earth. These simple people had a real though primitive religion, but it was subsequently lost to their deteriorating descendants.

Although both Andon and Fonta had received Thought Adjusters, as had many of their descendants, it was not until the days of Onagar that the Adjusters and guardian seraphim came in great numbers to Urantia. This was, indeed, the golden age of primitive man.

7. THE SURVIVAL OF ANDON AND FONTA

Andon and Fonta, the splendid founders of the human race, received recognition at the time of the adjudication of Urantia upon the arrival of the Planetary Prince, and in due time they emerged from the regime of the mansion worlds with citizenship status on Jerusem. Although they have never been permitted to return to Urantia, they are cognizant of the history of the race they founded. They grieved over the Caligastia betrayal, sorrowed because of the Adamic failure, but rejoiced exceedingly when announcement was received that Michael had selected their world as the theater for his final bestowal.

On Jerusem both Andon and Fonta were fused with their Thought Adjusters, as also were several of their children, including Sontad, but the majority of even their immediate descendants only achieved Spirit fusion.

Andon and Fonta, shortly after their arrival on Jerusem, received permission from the System Sovereign to return to the first mansion world to serve with the morontia personalities who welcome the pilgrims of time from Urantia to the heavenly spheres. And they have been assigned indefinitely to this service. They sought to send greetings to Urantia in connection with these revelations, but this request was wisely denied them.

And this is the recital of the most heroic and fascinating chapter in all the history of Urantia, the story of the evolution, life struggles, death, and eternal survival of the unique parents of all mankind.

[Presented by a Life Carrier resident on Urantia.]

PAPER 64

THE EVOLUTIONARY RACES OF COLOR

THIS is the story of the evolutionary races of Urantia from the days of Andon and Fonta, almost one million years ago, down through the times of the Planetary Prince to the end of the ice age.

The human race is almost one million years old, and the first half of its story roughly corresponds to the pre-Planetary Prince days of Urantia. The latter half of the history of mankind begins at the time of the arrival of the Planetary Prince and the appearance of the six colored races and roughly corresponds to the period commonly regarded as the Old Stone Age.

1. THE ANDONIC ABORIGINES

Primitive man made his evolutionary appearance on earth a little less than one million years ago, and he had a vigorous experience. He instinctively sought to escape the danger of mingling with the inferior simian tribes. But he could not migrate eastward because of the arid Tibetan land elevations, 30,000 feet above sea level; neither could he go south nor west because of the expanded Mediterranean Sea, which then extended eastward to the Indian Ocean; and as he went north, he encountered the advancing ice. But even when further migration was blocked by the ice, and though the dispersing tribes became increasingly hostile, the more intelligent groups never entertained the idea of going southward to live among their hairy tree-dwelling cousins of inferior intellect.

Many of man's earliest religious emotions grew out of his feeling of helplessness in the shut-in environment of this geographic situation—mountains to the right, water to the left, and ice in front. But these progressive Andonites would not turn back to their inferior tree-dwelling relatives in the south.

These Andonites avoided the forests in contrast with the habits of their nonhuman relatives. In the forests man has always deteriorated; human evolution has made progress only in the open and in the higher latitudes. The cold and hunger of the open lands stimulate action, invention, and resourcefulness. While these Andonic tribes were developing the pioneers of the present human race amidst the hardships and privations of these rugged northern climes, their backward cousins were luxuriating in the southern tropical forests of the land of their early common origin.

These events occurred during the times of the third glacier, the first according to the reckoning of geologists. The first two glaciers were not extensive in northern Europe.

During most of the ice age England was connected by land with France, while later on Africa was joined to Europe by the Sicilian land bridge. At the time of the Andonic migrations there was a continuous land path from England in the west on through Europe and Asia to Java in the east; but Australia was again isolated, which further accentuated the development of its own peculiar fauna.

950,000 years ago the descendants of Andon and Fonta had migrated far to the east and to the west. To the west they passed over Europe to France and England. In later times they penetrated eastward as far as Java, where their bones were so recently found—the so-called Java man—and then journeyed on to Tasmania.

The groups going west became less contaminated with the backward stocks of mutual ancestral origin than those going east, who mingled so freely with their retarded animal cousins. These unprogressive individuals drifted southward and presently mated with the inferior tribes. Later on, increasing numbers of their mongrel descendants returned to the north to mate with the rapidly expanding Andonic peoples, and such unfortunate unions unfailingly deteriorated the superior stock. Fewer and fewer of the primitive settlements maintained the worship of the Breath Giver. This early dawn civilization was threatened with extinction.

And thus it has ever been on Urantia. Civilizations of great promise have successively deteriorated and have finally been extinguished by the folly of allowing the superior freely to procreate with the inferior.

2. THE FOXHALL PEOPLES

900,000 years ago the arts of Andon and Fonta and the culture of Onagar were vanishing from the face of the earth; culture, religion, and even flintworking were at their lowest ebb.

These were the times when large numbers of inferior mongrel groups were arriving in England from southern France. These tribes were so largely mixed with the forest apelike creatures that they were scarcely human. They had no religion but were crude flintworkers and possessed sufficient intelligence to kindle fire.

They were followed in Europe by a somewhat superior and prolific people, whose descendants soon spread over the entire continent from the ice in the north to the Alps and Mediterranean in the south. These tribes are the so-called *Heidelberg race.*

During this long period of cultural decadence the Foxhall peoples of England and the Badonan tribes northwest of India continued to hold on to some of the traditions of Andon and certain remnants of the culture of Onagar.

The Foxhall peoples were farthest west and succeeded in retaining much of the Andonic culture; they also preserved their knowledge of flintworking, which they transmitted to their descendants, the ancient ancestors of the Eskimos.

Though the remains of the Foxhall peoples were the last to be discovered in England, these Andonites were really the first human beings to live in those regions. At that time the land bridge still connected France with England; and since most of the early settlements of the Andon descendants were located along the rivers and seashores of that early day, they are now under the waters of the English Channel and the North Sea, but some three or four are still above water on the English coast.

Many of the more intelligent and spiritual of the Foxhall peoples maintained their racial superiority and perpetuated their primitive religious customs. And these people, as they were later admixed with subsequent stocks, journeyed on west from England after a later ice visitation and have survived as the present-day Eskimos.

3. THE BADONAN TRIBES

Besides the Foxhall peoples in the west, another struggling center of culture persisted in the east. This group was located in the foothills of the northwestern Indian highlands among the tribes of Badonan, a great-great-grandson of Andon. These people were the only descendants of Andon who never practiced human sacrifice.

These highland Badonites occupied an extensive plateau surrounded by forests, traversed by streams, and abounding in game. Like some of their cousins in Tibet, they lived in crude stone huts, hillside grottoes, and semiunderground passages.

While the tribes of the north grew more and more to fear the ice, those living near the homeland of their origin became exceedingly fearful of the water. They observed the Mesopotamian peninsula gradually sinking into the ocean, and though it emerged several times, the traditions of these primitive races grew up around the dangers of the sea and the fear of periodic engulfment. And this fear, together with their experience with river floods, explains why they sought out the highlands as a safe place in which to live.

To the east of the Badonan peoples, in the Siwalik Hills of northern India, may be found fossils that approach nearer to transition types between man and the various prehuman groups than any others on earth.

850,000 years ago the superior Badonan tribes began a warfare of extermination directed against their inferior and animalistic neighbors. In less than one thousand years most of the borderland animal groups of these regions had been either destroyed or driven back to the southern forests. This campaign for the extermination of inferiors brought about a slight improvement in the hill tribes of that age. And the mixed descendants of this improved Badonite stock appeared on the stage of action as an apparently new people—the *Neanderthal race.*

4. THE NEANDERTHAL RACES

The Neanderthalers were excellent fighters, and they traveled extensively. They gradually spread from the highland centers in northwest India to France on the west, China on the east, and even down into northern Africa. They dominated the world for almost half a million years until the times of the migration of the evolutionary races of color.

800,000 years ago game was abundant; many species of deer, as well as elephants and hippopotamuses, roamed over Europe. Cattle were plentiful; horses and wolves were everywhere. The Neanderthalers were great hunters, and the tribes in France were the first to adopt the practice of giving the most successful hunters the choice of women for wives.

The reindeer was highly useful to these Neanderthal peoples, serving as food, clothing, and for tools, since they made various uses of the horns and bones. They had little culture, but they greatly improved the work in flint until it almost reached the levels of the days of Andon. Large flints attached to wooden handles came back into use and served as axes and picks.

750,000 years ago the fourth ice sheet was well on its way south. With their improved implements the Neanderthalers made holes in the ice covering the northern rivers and thus were able to spear the fish which came up to these vents. Ever these tribes retreated before the advancing ice, which at this time made its most extensive invasion of Europe.

In these times the Siberian glacier was making its southernmost march, compelling early man to move southward, back toward the lands of his origin. But the human species had so differentiated that the danger of further mingling with its nonprogressive simian relatives was greatly lessened.

700,000 years ago the fourth glacier, the greatest of all in Europe, was in recession; men and animals were returning north. The climate was cool and moist, and primitive man again thrived in Europe and western Asia. Gradually the forests spread north over land which had been so recently covered by the glacier.

Mammalian life had been little changed by the great glacier. These animals persisted in that narrow belt of land lying between the ice and the Alps and, upon the retreat of the glacier, again rapidly spread out over all Europe. There arrived from Africa, over the Sicilian land bridge, straight-tusked elephants, broad-nosed rhinoceroses, hyenas, and African lions, and these new animals virtually exterminated the saber-toothed tigers and the hippopotamuses.

650,000 years ago witnessed the continuation of the mild climate. By the middle of the interglacial period it had become so warm that the Alps were almost denuded of ice and snow.

600,000 years ago the ice had reached its then northernmost point of retreat and, after a pause of a few thousand years, started south again on its fifth excursion. But there was little modification of climate for fifty thousand years. Man and the animals of Europe were little changed. The slight aridity of the former period lessened, and the alpine glaciers descended far down the river valleys.

550,000 years ago the advancing glacier again pushed man and the animals south. But this time man had plenty of room in the wide belt of land stretching northeast into Asia and lying between the ice sheet and the then greatly expanded Black Sea extension of the Mediterranean.

These times of the fourth and fifth glaciers witnessed the further spread of the crude culture of the Neanderthal races. But there was so little progress that it truly appeared as though the attempt to produce a new and modified type of intelligent life on Urantia was about to fail. For almost a quarter of a million years these primitive peoples drifted on, hunting and fighting, by spells improving in certain directions, but, on the whole, steadily retrogressing as compared with their superior Andonic ancestors.

During these spiritually dark ages the culture of superstitious mankind reached its lowest levels. The Neanderthalers really had no religion beyond a shameful superstition. They were deathly afraid of clouds, more especially of mists and fogs. A primitive religion of the fear of natural forces gradually developed, while animal worship declined as improvement in tools, with abundance of game, enabled these people to live with lessened anxiety about food; the sex rewards of the chase tended greatly to improve hunting skill. This new religion of fear led to attempts to placate the invisible forces behind these natural elements and culminated, later on, in the sacrificing of humans to appease these invisible and unknown physical forces. And this terrible practice of human sacrifice has been perpetuated by the more backward peoples of Urantia right on down to the twentieth century.

These early Neanderthalers could hardly be called sun worshipers. They rather lived in fear of the dark; they had a mortal dread of nightfall. As long as the moon shone a little, they managed to get along, but in the dark of the moon they grew panicky and began the sacrifice of their best specimens of manhood and womanhood in an effort to induce the moon again to shine. The sun, they early learned, would regularly return, but the moon they conjectured only returned because they sacrificed their fellow tribesmen. As the race advanced, the object and purpose of sacrifice progressively changed, but the offering of human sacrifice as a part of religious ceremonial long persisted.

5. ORIGIN OF THE COLORED RACES

500,000 years ago the Badonan tribes of the northwestern highlands of India became involved in another great racial struggle. For more than one hundred years this relentless warfare raged, and when the long fight was finished, only about one hundred families were left. But these survivors were the most intelligent and desirable of all the then living descendants of Andon and Fonta.

And now, among these highland Badonites there was a new and strange occurrence. A man and woman living in the northeastern part of the then inhabited highland region began *suddenly* to produce a family of unusually intelligent children. This was the *Sangik family,* the ancestors of all of the six colored races of Urantia.

These Sangik children, nineteen in number, were not only intelligent above their fellows, but their skins manifested a unique tendency to turn various colors upon exposure to sunlight. Among these nineteen children were five red, two orange, four yellow, two green, four blue, and two indigo. These colors became more pronounced as the children grew older, and when these youths later mated with their fellow tribesmen, all of their offspring tended toward the skin color of the Sangik parent.

And now I interrupt the chronological narrative, after calling attention to the arrival of the Planetary Prince at about this time, while we separately consider the six Sangik races of Urantia.

6. THE SIX SANGIK RACES OF URANTIA

On an average evolutionary planet the six evolutionary races of color appear one by one; the red man is the first to evolve, and for ages he roams the world before the succeeding colored races make their appearance. The simultaneous emergence of all six races on Urantia, *and in one family,* was most unusual.

The appearance of the earlier Andonites on Urantia was also something new in Satania. On no other world in the local system has such a race of will creatures evolved in advance of the evolutionary races of color.

1. *The red man.* These peoples were remarkable specimens of the human race, in many ways superior to Andon and Fonta. They were a most intelligent group and were the first of the Sangik children to develop a tribal civilization and government. They were always monogamous; even their mixed descendants seldom practiced plural mating.

In later times they had serious and prolonged trouble with their yellow brethren in Asia. They were aided by their early invention of the bow and arrow, but they had unfortunately inherited much of the tendency of their ancestors to fight among themselves, and this so weakened them that the yellow tribes were able to drive them off the Asiatic continent.

About eighty-five thousand years ago the comparatively pure remnants of the red race went en masse across to North America, and shortly thereafter the Bering land isthmus sank, thus isolating them. No red man ever returned to Asia. But throughout Siberia, China, central Asia, India, and Europe they left behind much of their stock blended with the other colored races.

When the red man crossed over into America, he brought along much of the teachings and traditions of his early origin. His immediate ancestors had been in touch with the later activities of the world headquarters of the Planetary Prince. But in a short time after reaching the Americas, the red men began to lose sight of these teachings, and there occurred a great decline in intellectual and spiritual culture. Very soon these people again fell to fighting so fiercely among themselves that it appeared that these tribal wars would result in the speedy extinction of this remnant of the comparatively pure red race.

Because of this great retrogression the red men seemed doomed when, about sixty-five thousand years ago, Onamonalonton appeared as their leader and spiritual deliverer. He brought temporary peace among the American red men and revived their worship of the "Great Spirit." Onamonalonton lived to be ninety-six years of age and maintained his headquarters among the great redwood trees of California. Many of his later descendants have come down to modern times among the Blackfoot Indians.

As time passed, the teachings of Onamonalonton became hazy traditions. Internecine wars were resumed, and never after the days of this great teacher did another leader succeed in bringing universal peace among them. Increasingly the more intelligent strains perished in these tribal struggles; otherwise a great civilization would have been built upon the North American continent by these able and intelligent red men.

After crossing over to America from China, the northern red man never again came in contact with other world influences (except the Eskimo) until he was later discovered by the white man. It was most unfortunate that the red man almost completely missed his opportunity of being upstepped by the admixture of the later Adamic stock. As it was, the red man could not rule the white man, and he would not willingly serve him. In such a circumstance, if the two races do not blend, one or the other is doomed.

2. *The orange man.* The outstanding characteristic of this race was their peculiar urge to build, to build anything and everything, even to the piling up

of vast mounds of stone just to see which tribe could build the largest mound. Though they were not a progressive people, they profited much from the schools of the Prince and sent delegates there for instruction.

The orange race was the first to follow the coast line southward toward Africa as the Mediterranean Sea withdrew to the west. But they never secured a favorable footing in Africa and were wiped out of existence by the later arriving green race.

Before the end came, this people lost much cultural and spiritual ground. But there was a great revival of higher living as a result of the wise leadership of Porshunta, the master mind of this unfortunate race, who ministered to them when their headquarters was at Armageddon some three hundred thousand years ago.

The last great struggle between the orange and the green men occurred in the region of the lower Nile valley in Egypt. This long-drawn-out battle was waged for almost one hundred years, and at its close very few of the orange race were left alive. The shattered remnants of these people were absorbed by the green and by the later arriving indigo men. But as a race the orange man ceased to exist about one hundred thousand years ago.

3. *The yellow man.* The primitive yellow tribes were the first to abandon the chase, establish settled communities, and develop a home life based on agriculture. Intellectually they were somewhat inferior to the red man, but socially and collectively they proved themselves superior to all of the Sangik peoples in the matter of fostering racial civilization. Because they developed a fraternal spirit, the various tribes learning to live together in relative peace, they were able to drive the red race before them as they gradually expanded into Asia.

They traveled far from the influences of the spiritual headquarters of the world and drifted into great darkness following the Caligastia apostasy; but there occurred one brilliant age among this people when Singlangton, about one hundred thousand years ago, assumed the leadership of these tribes and proclaimed the worship of the "One Truth."

The survival of comparatively large numbers of the yellow race is due to their intertribal peacefulness. From the days of Singlangton to the times of modern China, the yellow race has been numbered among the more peaceful of the nations of Urantia. This race received a small but potent legacy of the later imported Adamic stock.

4. *The green man.* The green race was one of the less able groups of primitive men, and they were greatly weakened by extensive migrations in different directions. Before their dispersion these tribes experienced a great revival of culture under the leadership of Fantad, some three hundred and fifty thousand years ago.

The green race split into three major divisions: The northern tribes were subdued, enslaved, and absorbed by the yellow and blue races. The eastern group were amalgamated with the Indian peoples of those days, and remnants still persist among them. The southern nation entered Africa, where they destroyed their almost equally inferior orange cousins.

In many ways both groups were evenly matched in this struggle since each carried strains of the giant order, many of their leaders being eight and nine feet in height. These giant strains of the green man were mostly confined to this southern or Egyptian nation.

The remnants of the victorious green men were subsequently absorbed by the indigo race, the last of the colored peoples to develop and emigrate from the original Sangik center of race dispersion.

5. *The blue man.* The blue men were a great people. They early invented the spear and subsequently worked out the rudiments of many of the arts of modern civilization. The blue man had the brain power of the red man associated with the soul and sentiment of the yellow man. The Adamic descendants preferred them to all of the later persisting colored races.

The early blue men were responsive to the persuasions of the teachers of Prince Caligastia's staff and were thrown into great confusion by the subsequent perverted teachings of those traitorous leaders. Like other primitive races they never fully recovered from the turmoil produced by the Caligastia betrayal, nor did they ever completely overcome their tendency to fight among themselves.

About five hundred years after Caligastia's downfall a widespread revival of learning and religion of a primitive sort—but none the less real and beneficial—occurred. Orlandof became a great teacher among the blue race and led many of the tribes back to the worship of the true God under the name of the "Supreme Chief." This was the greatest advance of the blue man until those later times when this race was so greatly upstepped by the admixture of the Adamic stock.

The European researches and explorations of the Old Stone Age have largely to do with unearthing the tools, bones, and artcraft of these ancient blue men, for they persisted in Europe until recent times. The so-called *white races* of Urantia are the descendants of these blue men as they were first modified by slight mixture with yellow and red, and as they were later greatly upstepped by assimilating the greater portion of the violet race.

6. *The indigo race.* As the red men were the most advanced of all the Sangik peoples, so the black men were the least progressive. They were the last to migrate from their highland homes. They journeyed to Africa, taking possession of the continent, and have ever since remained there except when they have been forcibly taken away, from age to age, as slaves.

Isolated in Africa, the indigo peoples, like the red man, received little or none of the race elevation which would have been derived from the infusion of the Adamic stock. Alone in Africa, the indigo race made little advancement until the days of Orvonon, when they experienced a great spiritual awakening. While they later almost entirely forgot the "God of Gods" proclaimed by Orvonon, they did not entirely lose the desire to worship the Unknown; at least they maintained a form of worship up to a few thousand years ago.

Notwithstanding their backwardness, these indigo peoples have exactly the same standing before the celestial powers as any other earthly race.

These were ages of intense struggles between the various races, but near the headquarters of the Planetary Prince the more enlightened and more recently taught groups lived together in comparative harmony, though no great cultural conquest of the world races had been achieved up to the time of the serious disruption of this regime by the outbreak of the Lucifer rebellion.

From time to time all of these different peoples experienced cultural and spiritual revivals. Mansant was a great teacher of the post-Planetary Prince days. But mention is made only of those outstanding leaders and teachers who markedly influenced and inspired a whole race. With the passing of time, many lesser teachers arose in different regions; and in the aggregate they contributed much to the sum total of those saving influences which prevented the total collapse of cultural civilization, especially during the long and dark ages between the Caligastia rebellion and the arrival of Adam.

There are many good and sufficient reasons for the plan of evolving either three or six colored races on the worlds of space. Though Urantia mortals may not be in a position fully to appreciate all of these reasons, we would call attention to the following:

1. Variety is indispensable to opportunity for the wide functioning of natural selection, differential survival of superior strains.

2. Stronger and better races are to be had from the interbreeding of diverse peoples when these different races are carriers of superior inheritance factors. And the Urantia races would have benefited by such an early amalgamation provided such a conjoint people could have been subsequently effectively upstepped by a thoroughgoing admixture with the superior Adamic stock. The attempt to execute such an experiment on Urantia under present racial conditions would be highly disastrous.

3. Competition is healthfully stimulated by diversification of races.

4. Differences in status of the races and of groups within each race are essential to the development of human tolerance and altruism.

5. Homogeneity of the human race is not desirable until the peoples of an evolving world attain comparatively high levels of spiritual development.

7. DISPERSION OF THE COLORED RACES

When the colored descendants of the Sangik family began to multiply, and as they sought opportunity for expansion into adjacent territory, the fifth glacier, the third of geologic count, was well advanced on its southern drift over Europe and Asia. These early colored races were extraordinarily tested by the rigors and hardships of the glacial age of their origin. This glacier was so extensive in Asia that for thousands of years migration to eastern Asia was cut off. And not until the later retreat of the Mediterranean Sea, consequent upon the elevation of Arabia, was it possible for them to reach Africa.

Thus it was that for almost one hundred thousand years these Sangik peoples spread out around the foothills and mingled together more or less, notwithstanding the peculiar but natural antipathy which early manifested itself between the different races.

Between the times of the Planetary Prince and Adam, India became the home of the most cosmopolitan population ever to be found on the face of the earth. But it was unfortunate that this mixture came to contain so much of the green, orange, and indigo races. These secondary Sangik peoples found existence more easy and agreeable in the southlands, and many of them subsequently migrated to Africa. The primary Sangik peoples, the superior races, avoided the tropics, the red man going northeast to Asia, closely followed by the yellow man, while the blue race moved northwest into Europe.

The red men early began to migrate to the northeast, on the heels of the retreating ice, passing around the highlands of India and occupying all of northeastern Asia. They were closely followed by the yellow tribes, who subsequently drove them out of Asia into North America.

When the relatively pure-line remnants of the red race forsook Asia, there were eleven tribes, and they numbered a little over seven thousand men, women, and children. These tribes were accompanied by three small groups of mixed ancestry, the largest of these being a combination of the orange and blue races. These three groups never fully fraternized with the red man and early journeyed southward to Mexico and Central America, where they were later joined by a small group of mixed yellows and reds. These peoples all intermarried and founded a new and amalgamated race, one which was much less warlike than the pure-line red men. Within five thousand years this amalgamated race broke up into three groups, establishing the civilizations respectively of Mexico, Central America, and South America. The South American offshoot did receive a faint touch of the blood of Adam.

To a certain extent the early red and yellow men mingled in Asia, and the offspring of this union journeyed on to the east and along the southern seacoast and, eventually, were driven by the rapidly increasing yellow race onto the peninsulas and near-by islands of the sea. They are the present-day brown men.

The yellow race has continued to occupy the central regions of eastern Asia. Of all the six colored races they have survived in greatest numbers. While the yellow men now and then engaged in racial war, they did not carry on such incessant and relentless wars of extermination as were waged by the red, green, and orange men. These three races virtually destroyed themselves before they were finally all but annihilated by their enemies of other races.

Since the fifth glacier did not extend so far south in Europe, the way was partially open for these Sangik peoples to migrate to the northwest; and upon the retreat of the ice the blue men, together with a few other small racial groups, migrated westward along the old trails of the Andon tribes. They invaded Europe in successive waves, occupying most of the continent.

In Europe they soon encountered the Neanderthal descendants of their early and common ancestor, Andon. These older European Neanderthalers had been driven south and east by the glacier and thus were in position quickly to encounter and absorb their invading cousins of the Sangik tribes.

In general and to start with, the Sangik tribes were more intelligent than, and in most ways far superior to, the deteriorated descendants of the early Andonic plainsmen; and the mingling of these Sangik tribes with the Neanderthal peoples led to the immediate improvement of the older race. It was this infusion of Sangik blood, more especially that of the blue man, which produced that marked improvement in the Neanderthal peoples exhibited by the successive waves of increasingly intelligent tribes that swept over Europe from the east.

During the following interglacial period this new Neanderthal race extended from England to India. The remnant of the blue race left in the old Persian peninsula later amalgamated with certain others, primarily the yellow; and the resultant blend, subsequently somewhat upstepped by the violet race of Adam, has persisted as the swarthy nomadic tribes of modern Arabs.

All efforts to identify the Sangik ancestry of modern peoples must take into account the later improvement of the racial strains by the subsequent admixture of Adamic blood.

The superior races sought the northern or temperate climes, while the orange, green, and indigo races successively gravitated to Africa over the newly elevated land bridge which separated the westward retreating Mediterranean from the Indian Ocean.

The last of the Sangik peoples to migrate from their center of race origin was the indigo man. About the time the green man was killing off the orange race in Egypt and greatly weakening himself in so doing, the great black exodus started south through Palestine along the coast; and later, when these physically strong indigo peoples overran Egypt, they wiped the green man out of existence by sheer force of numbers. These indigo races absorbed the remnants of the orange man and much of the stock of the green man, and certain of the indigo tribes were considerably improved by this racial amalgamation.

And so it appears that Egypt was first dominated by the orange man, then by the green, followed by the indigo (black) man, and still later by a mongrel race of indigo, blue, and modified green men. But long before Adam arrived, the blue men of Europe and the mixed races of Arabia had driven the indigo race out of Egypt and far south on the African continent.

As the Sangik migrations draw to a close, the green and orange races are gone, the red man holds North America, the yellow man eastern Asia, the blue man Europe, and the indigo race has gravitated to Africa. India harbors a blend of the secondary Sangik races, and the brown man, a blend of the red and yellow, holds the islands off the Asiatic coast. An amalgamated race of rather superior potential occupies the highlands of South America. The purer Andonites live in the extreme northern regions of Europe and in Iceland, Greenland, and northeastern North America.

During the periods of farthest glacial advance the westernmost of the Andon tribes came very near being driven into the sea. They lived for years on a narrow southern strip of the present island of England. And it was the tradition of these repeated glacial advances that drove them to take to the sea when the sixth and last glacier finally appeared. They were the first marine adventurers. They built boats and started in search of new lands which they hoped might be free from the terrifying ice invasions. And some of them reached Iceland, others Greenland, but the vast majority perished from hunger and thirst on the open sea.

A little more than eighty thousand years ago, shortly after the red man entered northwestern North America, the freezing over of the north seas and the advance of local ice fields on Greenland drove these Eskimo descendants of the Urantia aborigines to seek a better land, a new home; and they were successful, safely crossing the narrow straits which then separated Greenland from the northeastern land masses of North America. They reached the continent about twenty-one hundred years after the red man arrived in Alaska. Subsequently some of the mixed stock of the blue man journeyed westward and amalgamated with the later-day Eskimos, and this union was slightly beneficial to the Eskimo tribes.

About five thousand years ago a chance meeting occurred between an Indian tribe and a lone Eskimo group on the southeastern shores of Hudson Bay.

These two tribes found it difficult to communicate with each other, but very soon they intermarried with the result that these Eskimos were eventually absorbed by the more numerous red men. And this represents the only contact of the North American red man with any other human stock down to about one thousand years ago, when the white man first chanced to land on the Atlantic coast.

The struggles of these early ages were characterized by courage, bravery, and even heroism. And we all regret that so many of those sterling and rugged traits of your early ancestors have been lost to the later-day races. While we appreciate the value of many of the refinements of advancing civilization, we miss the magnificent persistency and superb devotion of your early ancestors, which oftentimes bordered on grandeur and sublimity.

[Presented by a Life Carrier resident on Urantia.]

PAPER 65

THE OVERCONTROL OF EVOLUTION

BASIC evolutionary material life—premind life—is the formulation of the Master Physical Controllers and the life-impartation ministry of the Seven Master Spirits in conjunction with the active ministration of the ordained Life Carriers. As a result of the co-ordinate function of this threefold creativity there develops organismal physical capacity for mind—material mechanisms for intelligent reaction to external environmental stimuli and, later on, to internal stimuli, influences taking origin in the organismal mind itself.

There are, then, three distinct levels of life production and evolution:

1. The physical-energy domain—mind-capacity production.

2. The mind ministry of the adjutant spirits—impinging upon spirit capacity.

3. The spirit endowment of mortal mind—culminating in Thought Adjuster bestowal.

The mechanical-nonteachable levels of organismal environmental response are the domains of the physical controllers. The adjutant mind-spirits activate and regulate the adaptative or nonmechanical-teachable types of mind—those response mechanisms of organisms capable of learning from experience. And as the spirit adjutants thus manipulate mind potentials, so do the Life Carriers exercise considerable discretionary control over the environmental aspects of evolutionary processes right up to the time of the appearance of human will—the ability to know God and the power of choosing to worship him.

It is the integrated functioning of the Life Carriers, the physical controllers, and the spirit adjutants that conditions the course of organic evolution on the inhabited worlds. And this is why evolution—on Urantia or elsewhere—is always purposeful and never accidental.

1. LIFE CARRIER FUNCTIONS

The Life Carriers are endowed with potentials of personality metamorphosis which but few orders of creatures possess. These Sons of the local universe are capable of functioning in three diverse phases of being. They ordinarily perform their duties as mid-phase Sons, that being the state of their origin. But a Life Carrier in such a stage of existence could not possibly function in the electrochemical domains as a fabricator of physical energies and material particles into units of living existence.

Life Carriers are able to function and do function on the following three levels:

1. The physical level of electrochemistry.

2. The usual mid-phase of quasi-morontial existence.

3. The advanced semispiritual level.

When the Life Carriers make ready to engage in life implantation, and after they have selected the sites for such an undertaking, they summon the archangel commission of Life Carrier transmutation. This group consists of ten orders of diverse personalities, including the physical controllers and their associates, and is presided over by the chief of archangels, who acts in this capacity by the mandate of Gabriel and with the permission of the Ancients of Days. When these beings are properly encircuited, they can effect such modifications in the Life Carriers as will enable them immediately to function on the physical levels of electrochemistry.

After the life patterns have been formulated and the material organizations have been duly completed, the supermaterial forces concerned in life propagation become forthwith active, and life is existent. Whereupon the Life Carriers are immediately returned to their normal mid-phase of personality existence, in which estate they can manipulate the living units and maneuver the evolving organisms, even though they are shorn of all ability to organize—create—new patterns of living matter.

After organic evolution has run a certain course and free will of the human type has appeared in the highest evolving organisms, the Life Carriers must either leave the planet or take renunciation vows; that is, they must pledge themselves to refrain from all attempts further to influence the course of organic evolution. And when such vows are voluntarily taken by those Life Carriers who choose to remain on the planet as future advisers to those who shall be intrusted with the fostering of the newly evolved will creatures, there is summoned a commission of twelve, presided over by the chief of the Evening Stars, acting by authority of the System Sovereign and with permission of Gabriel; and forthwith these Life Carriers are transmuted to the third phase of personality existence—the semispiritual level of being. And I have functioned on Urantia in this third phase of existence ever since the times of Andon and Fonta.

We look forward to a time when the universe may be settled in light and life, to a possible fourth stage of being wherein we shall be wholly spiritual, but it has never been revealed to us by what technique we may attain this desirable and advanced estate.

2. THE EVOLUTIONARY PANORAMA

The story of man's ascent from seaweed to the lordship of earthly creation is indeed a romance of biologic struggle and mind survival. Man's primordial ancestors were literally the slime and ooze of the ocean bed in the sluggish and warm-water bays and lagoons of the vast shore lines of the ancient inland seas, those very waters in which the Life Carriers established the three independent life implantations on Urantia.

Very few species of the early types of marine vegetation that participated in those epochal changes which resulted in the animallike borderland organisms are in existence today. The sponges are the survivors of one of these early midway types, those organisms through which the *gradual* transition from the vegetable to the animal took place. These early transition forms, while not identical with modern sponges, were much like them; they were true borderline organisms—neither vegetable nor animal—but they eventually led to the development of the true animal forms of life.

The bacteria, simple vegetable organisms of a very primitive nature, are very little changed from the early dawn of life; they even exhibit a degree of retrogression in their parasitic behavior. Many of the fungi also represent a retrograde movement in evolution, being plants which have lost their chlorophyll-making ability and have become more or less parasitic. The majority of disease-causing bacteria and their auxiliary virus bodies really belong to this group of renegade parasitic fungi. During the intervening ages all of the vast kingdom of plant life has evolved from ancestors from which the bacteria have also descended.

The higher protozoan type of animal life soon appeared, and appeared *suddenly.* And from these far-distant times the ameba, the typical single-celled animal organism, has come on down but little modified. He disports himself today much as he did when he was the last and greatest achievement in life evolution. This minute creature and his protozoan cousins are to the animal creation what bacteria are to the plant kingdom; they represent the survival of the first early evolutionary steps in life differentiation together with *failure of subsequent development.*

Before long the early single-celled animal types associated themselves in communities, first on the plan of the Volvox and presently along the lines of the Hydra and jellyfish. Still later there evolved the starfish, stone lilies, sea urchins, sea cucumbers, centipedes, insects, spiders, crustaceans, and the closely related groups of earthworms and leeches, soon followed by the mollusks—the oyster, octopus, and snail. Hundreds upon hundreds of species intervened and perished; mention is made only of those which survived the long, long struggle. Such nonprogressive specimens, together with the later appearing fish family, today represent the stationary types of early and lower animals, branches of the tree of life which failed to progress.

The stage was thus set for the appearance of the first backboned animals, the fishes. From this fish family there sprang two unique modifications, the frog and the salamander. And it was the frog which began that series of progressive differentiations in animal life that finally culminated in man himself.

The frog is one of the earliest of surviving human-race ancestors, but it also failed to progress, persisting today much as in those remote times. The frog is the only species ancestor of the early dawn races now living on the face of the earth. The human race has no surviving ancestry between the frog and the Eskimo.

The frogs gave rise to the Reptilia, a great animal family which is virtually extinct, but which, before passing out of existence, gave origin to the whole bird family and the numerous orders of mammals.

Probably the greatest single leap of all prehuman evolution was executed when the reptile became a bird. The bird types of today—eagles, ducks, pigeons, and ostriches—all descended from the enormous reptiles of long, long ago.

The kingdom of reptiles, descended from the frog family, is today represented by four surviving divisions: two nonprogressive, snakes and lizards, together with their cousins, alligators and turtles; one partially progressive, the bird family, and the fourth, the ancestors of mammals and the direct line of descent of the human species. But though long departed, the massiveness of the passing Reptilia found echo in the elephant and mastodon, while their peculiar forms were perpetuated in the leaping kangaroos.

Only fourteen phyla have appeared on Urantia, the fishes being the last, and no new classes have developed since birds and mammals.

It was from an agile little reptilian dinosaur of carnivorous habits but having a comparatively large brain that the placental mammals *suddenly* sprang. These mammals developed rapidly and in many different ways, not only giving rise to the common modern varieties but also evolving into marine types, such as whales and seals, and into air navigators like the bat family.

Man thus evolved from the higher mammals derived principally from the *western implantation* of life in the ancient east-west sheltered seas. The *eastern* and *central groups* of living organisms were early progressing favorably toward the attainment of prehuman levels of animal existence. But as the ages passed, the eastern focus of life emplacement failed to attain a satisfactory level of intelligent prehuman status, having suffered such repeated and irretrievable losses of its highest types of germ plasm that it was forever shorn of the power to rehabilitate human potentialities.

Since the quality of the mind capacity for development in this eastern group was so definitely inferior to that of the other two groups, the Life Carriers, with the consent of their superiors, so manipulated the environment as further to circumscribe these inferior prehuman strains of evolving life. To all outward appearances the elimination of these inferior groups of creatures was accidental, but in reality it was altogether purposeful.

Later in the evolutionary unfolding of intelligence, the lemur ancestors of the human species were far more advanced in North America than in other regions; and they were therefore led to migrate from the arena of western life implantation over the Bering land bridge and down the coast to southwestern Asia, where they continued to evolve and to benefit by the addition of certain strains of the central life group. Man thus evolved out of certain western and central life strains but in the central to near-eastern regions.

In this way the life that was planted on Urantia evolved until the ice age, when man himself first appeared and began his eventful planetary career. And this appearance of primitive man on earth during the ice age was not just an accident; it was by design. The rigors and climatic severity of the glacial era were in every way adapted to the purpose of fostering the production of a hardy type of human being with tremendous survival endowment.

3. THE FOSTERING OF EVOLUTION

It will hardly be possible to explain to the present-day human mind many of the queer and apparently grotesque occurrences of early evolutionary progress. A purposeful plan was functioning throughout all of these seemingly strange evolutions of living things, but we are not allowed arbitrarily to interfere with the development of the life patterns after they have once been set in operation.

Life Carriers may employ every possible natural resource and may utilize any and all fortuitous circumstances which will enhance the developmental progress of the life experiment, but we are not permitted mechanically to intervene in, or arbitrarily to manipulate the conduct and course of, either plant or animal evolution.

You have been informed that Urantia mortals evolved by way of primitive frog development, and that this ascending strain, carried in potential in a single frog, narrowly escaped extinction on a certain occasion. But it should not be inferred that the evolution of mankind would have been terminated by an accident at this juncture. At that very moment we were observing and fostering no less than one thousand different and remotely situated mutating strains of life which could have been directed into various different patterns of prehuman development. This particular ancestral frog represented our third selection, the two prior life strains having perished in spite of all our efforts toward their conservation.

Even the loss of Andon and Fonta before they had offspring, though delaying human evolution, would not have prevented it. Subsequent to the appearance of Andon and Fonta and before the mutating human potentials of animal life were exhausted, there evolved no less than seven thousand favorable strains which could have achieved some sort of human type of development. And many of these better stocks were subsequently assimilated by the various branches of the expanding human species.

Long before the Material Son and Daughter, the biologic uplifters, arrive on a planet, the human potentials of the evolving animal species have been exhausted. This biologic status of animal life is disclosed to the Life Carriers by the phenomenon of the third phase of adjutant spirit mobilization, which automatically occurs concomitantly with the exhaustion of the capacity of all animal life to give origin to the mutant potentials of prehuman individuals.

Mankind on Urantia must solve its problems of mortal development with the human stocks it has—no more races will evolve from prehuman sources throughout all future time. But this fact does not preclude the possibility of the attainment of vastly higher levels of human development through the intelligent fostering of the evolutionary potentials still resident in the mortal races. That which we, the Life Carriers, do toward fostering and conserving the life strains before the appearance of human will, man must do for himself after such an event and subsequent to our retirement from active participation in evolution. In a general way, man's evolutionary destiny is in his own hands, and scientific intelligence must sooner or later supersede the random functioning of uncontrolled natural selection and chance survival.

And in discussing the fostering of evolution, it would not be amiss to point out that, in the long future ahead, when you may sometime be attached to a corps of Life Carriers, you will have abundant and ample opportunity to offer suggestions and make any possible improvements in the plans and technique of life management and transplantation. Be patient! If you have good ideas, if your minds are fertile with better methods of administration for any part of the universal domains, you are certainly going to have an opportunity to present them to your associates and fellow administrators in the ages to come.

4. THE URANTIA ADVENTURE

Do not overlook the fact that Urantia was assigned to us as a life-experiment world. On this planet we made our sixtieth attempt to modify and, if possible, improve the Satania adaptation of the Nebadon life designs, and it is of record that we achieved numerous beneficial modifications of the standard life patterns. To be specific, on Urantia we worked out and have satisfactorily demonstrated not less than twenty-eight features of life modification which will be of service to all Nebadon throughout all future time.

But the establishment of life on no world is ever experimental in the sense that something untried and unknown is attempted. The evolution of life is a technique ever progressive, differential, and variable, but never haphazard, uncontrolled, nor wholly experimental, in the accidental sense.

Many features of human life afford abundant evidence that the phenomenon of mortal existence was intelligently planned, that organic evolution is not a mere cosmic accident. When a living cell is injured, it possesses the ability to elaborate certain chemical substances which are empowered so to stimulate and activate the neighboring normal cells that they immediately begin the secretion of certain substances which facilitate healing processes in the wound; and at the same time these normal and uninjured cells begin to proliferate—they actually start to work creating new cells to replace any fellow cells which may have been destroyed by the accident.

This chemical action and reaction concerned in wound healing and cell reproduction represents the choice of the Life Carriers of a formula embracing over one hundred thousand phases and features of possible chemical reactions and biologic repercussions. More than half a million specific experiments were made by the Life Carriers in their laboratories before they finally settled upon this formula for the Urantia life experiment.

When Urantia scientists know more of these healing chemicals, they will become more efficient in the treatment of injuries, and indirectly they will know more about controlling certain serious diseases.

Since life was established on Urantia, the Life Carriers have improved this healing technique as it has been introduced on another Satania world, in that it affords more pain relief and exercises better control over the proliferation capacity of the associated normal cells.

There were many unique features of the Urantia life experiment, but the two outstanding episodes were the appearance of the Andonic race prior to the evolution of the six colored peoples and the later simultaneous appearance of the Sangik mutants in a single family. Urantia is the first world in Satania where the six colored races sprang from the same human family. They ordinarily arise in diversified strains from independent mutations within the prehuman animal stock and usually appear on earth one at a time and successively over long periods of time, beginning with the red man and passing on down through the colors to indigo.

Another outstanding variation of procedure was the late arrival of the Planetary Prince. As a rule, the prince appears on a planet about the time of will development; and if such a plan had been followed, Caligastia might have come to Urantia even during the lifetimes of Andon and Fonta instead of almost five hundred thousand years later, simultaneously with the appearance of the six Sangik races.

On an ordinary inhabited world a Planetary Prince would have been granted on the request of the Life Carriers at, or sometime after, the appearance of Andon and Fonta. But Urantia having been designated a life-modification planet, it was by preagreement that the Melchizedek observers, twelve in number, were sent as advisers to the Life Carriers and as overseers of the planet until the subsequent arrival of the Planetary Prince. These Melchizedeks came at the time Andon and Fonta made the decisions which enabled Thought Adjusters to indwell their mortal minds.

On Urantia the endeavors of the Life Carriers to improve the Satania life patterns necessarily resulted in the production of many apparently useless forms of transition life. But the gains already accrued are sufficient to justify the Urantia modifications of the standard life designs.

It was our intention to produce an early manifestation of will in the evolutionary life of Urantia, and we succeeded. Ordinarily, will does not emerge until the colored races have long been in existence, usually first appearing among the superior types of the red man. Your world is the only planet in Satania where the human type of will has appeared in a precolored race.

But in our effort to provide for that combination and association of inheritance factors which finally gave rise to the mammalian ancestors of the human race, we were confronted with the necessity of permitting hundreds and thousands of other and comparatively useless combinations and associations of inheritance factors to take place. Many of these seemingly strange by-products of our efforts are certain to meet your gaze as you dig back into the planetary past, and I can well understand how puzzling some of these things must be to the limited human viewpoint.

5. LIFE-EVOLUTION VICISSITUDES

It was a source of regret to the Life Carriers that our special efforts to modify intelligent life on Urantia should have been so handicapped by tragic perversions beyond our control: the Caligastia betrayal and the Adamic default.

But throughout all of this biologic adventure our greatest disappointment grew out of the reversion of certain primitive plant life to the prechlorophyll levels of parasitic bacteria on such an extensive and unexpected scale. This eventuality in plant-life evolution caused many distressful diseases in the higher mammals, particularly in the more vulnerable human species. When we were confronted with this perplexing situation, we somewhat discounted the difficulties involved because we knew that the subsequent admixture of the Adamic life plasm would so reinforce the resisting powers of the resulting blended race as to make it practically immune to all diseases produced by the vegetable type of organism. But our hopes were doomed to disappointment owing to the misfortune of the Adamic default.

The universe of universes, including this small world called Urantia, is not being managed merely to meet our approval nor just to suit our convenience, much less to gratify our whims and satisfy our curiosity. The wise and all-powerful beings who are responsible for universe management undoubtedly know exactly what they are about; and so it becomes Life Carriers and behooves mortal minds to enlist in patient waiting and hearty co-operation with the rule of wisdom, the reign of power, and the march of progress.

There are, of course, certain compensations for tribulation, such as Michael's bestowal on Urantia. But irrespective of all such considerations, the later celestial supervisors of this planet express complete confidence in the ultimate evolutionary triumph of the human race and in the eventual vindication of our original plans and life patterns.

6. EVOLUTIONARY TECHNIQUES OF LIFE

It is impossible accurately to determine, simultaneously, the exact location and the velocity of a moving object; any attempt at measurement of either inevitably involves change in the other. The same sort of a paradox confronts mortal man when he undertakes the chemical analysis of protoplasm. The chemist can elucidate the chemistry of *dead* protoplasm, but he cannot discern either the physical organization or the dynamic performance of *living* protoplasm. Ever will the scientist come nearer and nearer the secrets of life, but never will he find them and for no other reason than that he must kill protoplasm in order to analyze it. Dead protoplasm weighs the same as living protoplasm, but it is not the same.

There is original endowment of adaptation in living things and beings. In every *living* plant or animal cell, in every *living* organism—material or spiritual—there is an insatiable craving for the attainment of ever-increasing perfection of environmental adjustment, organismal adaptation, and augmented life realization. These interminable efforts of all living things evidence the existence within them of an innate striving for perfection.

The most important step in plant evolution was the development of chlorophyll-making ability, and the second greatest advance was the evolution of the spore into the complex seed. The spore is most efficient as a reproductive agent, but it lacks the potentials of variety and versatility inherent in the seed.

One of the most serviceable and complex episodes in the evolution of the higher types of animals consisted in the development of the ability of the iron in the circulating blood cells to perform in the double role of oxygen carrier and carbon dioxide remover. And this performance of the red blood cells illustrates how evolving organisms are able to adapt their functions to varying or changing environment. The higher animals, including man, oxygenate their tissues by the action of the iron of the red blood cells, which carries oxygen to the living cells and just as efficiently removes the carbon dioxide. But other metals can be made to serve the same purpose. The cuttlefish employs copper for this function, and the sea squirt utilizes vanadium.

The continuation of such biologic adjustments is illustrated by the evolution of teeth in the higher Urantia mammals; these attained to thirty-six in man's remote ancestors, and then began an adaptative readjustment toward thirty-two in the dawn man and his near relatives. Now the human species is slowly gravitating toward twenty-eight. The process of evolution is still actively and adaptatively in progress on this planet.

But many seemingly mysterious adjustments of living organisms are purely chemical, wholly physical. At any moment of time, in the blood stream of any human being there exists the possibility of upward of 15,000,000 chemical reactions between the hormone output of a dozen ductless glands.

The lower forms of plant life are wholly responsive to physical, chemical, and electrical environment. But as the scale of life ascends, one by one the mind ministries of the seven adjutant spirits become operative, and the mind becomes increasingly adjustive, creative, co-ordinative, and dominative. The ability of animals to adapt themselves to air, water, and land is not a supernatural endowment, but it is a superphysical adjustment.

Physics and chemistry alone cannot explain how a human being evolved out of the primeval protoplasm of the early seas. The ability to learn, memory and differential response to environment, is the endowment of mind. The laws of physics are not responsive to training; they are immutable and unchanging. The reactions of chemistry are not modified by education; they are uniform and dependable. Aside from the presence of the Unqualified Absolute, electrical and chemical reactions are predictable. But mind can profit from experience, can learn from reactive habits of behavior in response to repetition of stimuli.

Preintelligent organisms react to environmental stimuli, but those organisms which are reactive to mind ministry can adjust and manipulate the environment itself.

The physical brain with its associated nervous system possesses innate capacity for response to mind ministry just as the developing mind of a personality possesses a certain innate capacity for spirit receptivity and therefore contains the potentials of spiritual progress and attainment. Intellectual, social, moral, and spiritual evolution are dependent on the mind ministry of the seven adjutant spirits and their superphysical associates.

7. EVOLUTIONARY MIND LEVELS

The seven adjutant mind-spirits are the versatile mind ministers to the lower intelligent existences of a local universe. This order of mind is ministered from the local universe headquarters or from some world connected therewith, but there is influential direction of lower-mind function from the system capitals.

On an evolutionary world much, very much, depends on the work of these seven adjutants. But they are mind ministers; they are not concerned in physical evolution, the domain of the Life Carriers. Nevertheless, the perfect integration of these spirit endowments with the ordained and natural procedure of the unfolding and inherent regime of the Life Carriers is responsible for the mortal inability to discern, in the phenomenon of mind, aught but the hand of nature and the outworking of natural processes, albeit you are occasionally somewhat perplexed in explaining all of everything connected with the natural reactions of mind as it is associated with matter. And if Urantia were operating more in accordance with the original plans, you would observe even less to arrest your attention in the phenomenon of mind.

The seven adjutant spirits are more circuitlike than entitylike, and on ordinary worlds they are encircuited with other adjutant functionings throughout the local universe. On life-experiment planets, however, they are relatively isolated. And on Urantia, owing to the unique nature of the life patterns, the lower adjutants experienced far more difficulty in contacting with the evolutionary organisms than would have been the case in a more standardized type of life endowment.

Again, on an average evolutionary world the seven adjutant spirits are far better synchronized with the advancing stages of animal development than they were on Urantia. With but a single exception, the adjutants experienced the greatest difficulty in contacting with the evolving minds of Urantia organisms that they had ever had in all their functioning throughout the universe of Nebadon. On this world there developed many forms of border phenomena—confusional combinations of the mechanical-nonteachable and the nonmechanical-teachable types of organismal response.

The seven adjutant spirits do not make contact with the purely mechanical orders of organismal environmental response. Such preintelligent responses of living organisms pertain purely to the energy domains of the power centers, the physical controllers, and their associates.

The acquisition of the potential of the ability to *learn* from experience marks the beginning of the functioning of the adjutant spirits, and they function from the lowliest minds of primitive and invisible existences up to the highest types in the evolutionary scale of human beings. They are the source and pattern for the otherwise more or less mysterious behavior and incompletely understood quick reactions of mind to the material environment. Long must these faithful and always dependable influences carry forward their preliminary ministry before the animal mind attains the human levels of spirit receptivity.

The adjutants function exclusively in the evolution of experiencing mind up to the level of the sixth phase, the spirit of worship. At this level there occurs that inevitable overlapping of ministry—the phenomenon of the higher reaching down to co-ordinate with the lower in anticipation of subsequent attainment of advanced levels of development. And still additional spirit ministry accompanies the action of the seventh and last adjutant, the spirit of wisdom. Throughout the ministry of the spirit world the individual never experiences abrupt transitions of spirit co-operation; always are these changes gradual and reciprocal.

Always should the domains of the physical (electrochemical) and the mental response to environmental stimuli be differentiated, and in turn must they all be recognized as phenomena apart from spiritual activities. The domains of physical, mental, and spiritual gravity are distinct realms of cosmic reality, notwithstanding their intimate interrelations.

8. EVOLUTION IN TIME AND SPACE

Time and space are indissolubly linked; there is an innate association. The delays of time are inevitable in the presence of certain space conditions.

If spending so much time in effecting the evolutionary changes of life development occasions perplexity, I would say that we cannot time the life processes to unfold any faster than the physical metamorphoses of a planet will permit. We must wait upon the natural, physical development of a planet; we have absolutely no control over geologic evolution. If the physical conditions would allow, we could arrange for the completed evolution of life in considerably less than one million years. But we are all under the jurisdiction of the Supreme Rulers of Paradise, and time is nonexistent on Paradise.

The individual's yardstick for time measurement is the length of his life. All creatures are thus time conditioned, and therefore do they regard evolution as being a long-drawn-out process. To those of us whose life span is not limited by a temporal existence, evolution does not seem to be such a protracted transaction. On Paradise, where time is nonexistent, these things are all *present* in the mind of Infinity and the acts of Eternity.

As mind evolution is dependent on, and delayed by, the slow development of physical conditions, so is spiritual progress dependent on mental expansion and unfailingly delayed by intellectual retardation. But this does not mean that spiritual evolution is dependent on education, culture, or wisdom. The soul may evolve regardless of mental culture but not in the absence of mental capacity and desire—the choice of survival and the decision to achieve ever-increasing perfection—to do the will of the Father in heaven. Although survival may not depend on the possession of knowledge and wisdom, progression most certainly does.

In the cosmic evolutionary laboratories mind is always dominant over matter, and spirit is ever correlated with mind. Failure of these diverse endowments to synchronize and co-ordinate may cause time delays, but if the individual really knows God and desires to find him and become like him, then survival is assured regardless of the handicaps of time. Physical status may handicap mind, and mental perversity may delay spiritual attainment, but none of these obstacles can defeat the whole-souled choice of will.

When physical conditions are ripe, *sudden* mental evolutions may take place; when mind status is propitious, *sudden* spiritual transformations may occur; when spiritual values receive proper recognition, then cosmic meanings become discernible, and increasingly the personality is released from the handicaps of time and delivered from the limitations of space.

[Sponsored by a Life Carrier of Nebadon resident on Urantia.]

PAPER 66

THE PLANETARY PRINCE OF URANTIA

THE advent of a Lanonandek Son on an average world signifies that will, the ability to choose the path of eternal survival, has developed in the mind of primitive man. But on Urantia the Planetary Prince arrived almost half a million years after the appearance of human will.

About five hundred thousand years ago and concurrent with the appearance of the six colored or Sangik races, Caligastia, the Planetary Prince, arrived on Urantia. There were almost one-half billion primitive human beings on earth at the time of the Prince's arrival, and they were well scattered over Europe, Asia, and Africa. The Prince's headquarters, established in Mesopotamia, was at about the center of world population.

1. PRINCE CALIGASTIA

Caligastia was a Lanonandek Son, number 9,344 of the secondary order. He was experienced in the administration of the affairs of the local universe in general and, during later ages, with the management of the local system of Satania in particular.

Prior to the reign of Lucifer in Satania, Caligastia had been attached to the council of the Life Carrier advisers on Jerusem. Lucifer elevated Caligastia to a position on his personal staff, and he acceptably filled five successive assignments of honor and trust.

Caligastia very early sought a commission as Planetary Prince, but repeatedly, when his request came up for approval in the constellation councils, it would fail to receive the assent of the Constellation Fathers. Caligastia seemed especially desirous of being sent as planetary ruler to a decimal or life-modification world. His petition had several times been disapproved before he was finally assigned to Urantia.

Caligastia went forth from Jerusem to his trust of world dominion with an enviable record of loyalty and devotion to the welfare of the universe of his origin and sojourn, notwithstanding a certain characteristic restlessness coupled with a tendency to disagree with the established order in certain minor matters.

I was present on Jerusem when the brilliant Caligastia departed from the system capital. No prince of the planets ever embarked upon a career of world rulership with a richer preparatory experience or with better prospects than did Caligastia on that eventful day one-half million years ago. One thing is certain: As I executed my assignment of putting the narrative of that event on the broadcasts of the local universe, I never for one moment entertained even in the slightest degree any idea that this noble Lanonandek would so shortly betray his sacred trust of planetary custody and so horribly stain the fair name of his exalted order of universe sonship. I really regarded Urantia as being among the five or six most fortunate planets in all Satania in that it was to have such an experienced, brilliant, and original mind at the helm of world affairs. I did not then comprehend that Caligastia was insidiously falling in love with himself; I did not then so fully understand the subtleties of personality pride.

2. THE PRINCE'S STAFF

The Planetary Prince of Urantia was not sent out on his mission alone but was accompanied by the usual corps of assistants and administrative helpers.

At the head of this group was Daligastia, the associate-assistant of the Planetary Prince. Daligastia was also a secondary Lanonandek Son, being number 319,407 of that order. He ranked as an assistant at the time of his assignment as Caligastia's associate.

The planetary staff included a large number of angelic co-operators and a host of other celestial beings assigned to advance the interests and promote the welfare of the human races. But from your standpoint the most interesting group of all were the corporeal members of the Prince's staff—sometimes referred to as *the Caligastia one hundred.*

These one hundred rematerialized members of the Prince's staff were chosen by Caligastia from over 785,000 ascendant citizens of Jerusem who volunteered for embarkation on the Urantia adventure. Each one of the chosen one hundred was from a different planet, and none of them were from Urantia.

These Jerusemite volunteers were brought by seraphic transport direct from the system capital to Urantia, and upon arrival they were held enseraphimed until they could be provided with personality forms of the dual nature of special planetary service, literal bodies consisting of flesh and blood but also attuned to the life circuits of the system.

Sometime before the arrival of these one hundred Jerusem citizens, the two supervising Life Carriers resident on Urantia, having previously perfected their plans, petitioned Jerusem and Edentia for permission to transplant the life plasm of one hundred selected survivors of the Andon and Fonta stock into the material bodies to be projected for the corporeal members of the Prince's staff. The request was granted on Jerusem and approved on Edentia.

Accordingly, fifty males and fifty females of the Andon and Fonta posterity, representing the survival of the best strains of that unique race, were chosen by the Life Carriers. With one or two exceptions these Andonite contributors to the advancement of the race were strangers to one another. They were assembled from widely separated places by co-ordinated Thought Adjuster direction and seraphic guidance at the threshold of the planetary headquarters of the Prince. Here the one hundred human subjects were given into the hands of the highly skilled volunteer commission from Avalon, who directed the material extraction of a portion of the life plasm of these Andon descendants. This living material was then transferred to the material bodies constructed for the use of the one hundred Jerusemite members of the Prince's staff. Meantime, these newly arrived citizens of the system capital were held in the sleep of seraphic transport.

These transactions, together with the literal creation of special bodies for the Caligastia one hundred, gave origin to numerous legends, many of which subsequently became confused with the later traditions concerning the planetary installation of Adam and Eve.

The entire transaction of repersonalization, from the time of the arrival of the seraphic transports bearing the one hundred Jerusem volunteers until they became conscious, threefold beings of the realm, consumed exactly ten days.

3. DALAMATIA—THE CITY OF THE PRINCE

The headquarters of the Planetary Prince was situated in the Persian Gulf region of those days, in the district corresponding to later Mesopotamia.

The climate and landscape in the Mesopotamia of those times were in every way favorable to the undertakings of the Prince's staff and their assistants, very different from conditions which have sometimes since prevailed. It was necessary to have such a favoring climate as a part of the natural environment designed to induce primitive Urantians to make certain initial advances in culture and civilization. The one great task of those ages was to transform man from a hunter to a herder, with the hope that later on he would evolve into a peace-loving, home-abiding farmer.

The headquarters of the Planetary Prince on Urantia was typical of such stations on a young and developing sphere. The nucleus of the Prince's settlement was a very simple but beautiful city, enclosed within a wall forty feet high. This world center of culture was named Dalamatia in honor of Daligastia.

The city was laid out in ten subdivisions with the headquarters mansions of the ten councils of the corporeal staff situated at the centers of these subdivisions. Centermost in the city was the temple of the unseen Father. The administrative headquarters of the Prince and his associates was arranged in twelve chambers immediately grouped about the temple itself.

The buildings of Dalamatia were all one story except the council headquarters, which were two stories, and the central temple of the Father of all, which was small but three stories in height.

The city represented the best practices of those early days in building material—brick. Very little stone or wood was used. Home building and village architecture among the surrounding peoples were greatly improved by the Dalamatian example.

Near the Prince's headquarters there dwelt all colors and strata of human beings. And it was from these near-by tribes that the first students of the Prince's schools were recruited. Although these early schools of Dalamatia were crude, they provided all that could be done for the men and women of that primitive age.

The Prince's corporeal staff continuously gathered about them the superior individuals of the surrounding tribes and, after training and inspiring these students, sent them back as teachers and leaders of their respective peoples.

4. EARLY DAYS OF THE ONE HUNDRED

The arrival of the Prince's staff created a profound impression. While it required almost a thousand years for the news to spread abroad, those tribes near the Mesopotamian headquarters were tremendously influenced by the teachings and conduct of the one hundred new sojourners on Urantia. And much of your subsequent mythology grew out of the garbled legends of these early days when these members of the Prince's staff were repersonalized on Urantia as supermen.

The serious obstacle to the good influence of such extraplanetary teachers is the tendency of mortals to regard them as gods, but aside from the technique of their appearance on earth the Caligastia one hundred—fifty men and fifty women—did not resort to supernatural methods nor superhuman manipulations.

But the corporeal staff were nonetheless superhuman. They began their mission on Urantia as extraordinary threefold beings:

1. They were corporeal and relatively human, for they embodied the actual life plasm of one of the human races, the Andonic life plasm of Urantia.

These one hundred members of the Prince's staff were divided equally as to sex and in accordance with their previous mortal status. Each person of this group was capable of becoming coparental to some new order of physical being, but they had been carefully instructed to resort to parenthood only under certain conditions. It is customary for the corporeal staff of a Planetary Prince to procreate their successors sometime prior to retiring from special planetary service. Usually this is at, or shortly after, the time of the arrival of the Planetary Adam and Eve.

These special beings therefore had little or no idea as to what type of material creature would be produced by their sexual union. And they never did know; before the time for such a step in the prosecution of their world work the entire regime was upset by rebellion, and those who later functioned in the parental role had been isolated from the life currents of the system.

In skin color and language these materialized members of Caligastia's staff followed the Andonic race. They partook of food as did the mortals of the realm with this difference: The re-created bodies of this group were fully satisfied by a nonflesh diet. This was one of the considerations which determined their residence in a warm region abounding in fruits and nuts. The practice of subsisting on a nonflesh diet dates from the times of the Caligastia one hundred, for this custom spread near and far to affect the eating habits of many surrounding tribes, groups of origin in the once exclusively meat-eating evolutionary races.

2. The one hundred were material but superhuman beings, having been reconstituted on Urantia as unique men and women of a high and special order.

This group, while enjoying provisional citizenship on Jerusem, were as yet unfused with their Thought Adjusters; and when they volunteered and were accepted for planetary service in liaison with the descending orders of sonship, their Adjusters were detached. But these Jerusemites were superhuman beings—they possessed souls of ascendant growth. During the mortal life in the flesh the soul is of embryonic estate; it is born (resurrected) in the morontia life and experiences growth through the successive morontia worlds. And the souls of the Caligastia one hundred had thus expanded through the progressive experiences of the seven mansion worlds to citizenship status on Jerusem.

In conformity to their instructions the staff did not engage in sexual reproduction, but they did painstakingly study their personal constitutions, and they carefully explored every imaginable phase of intellectual (mind) and morontia (soul) liaison. And it was during the thirty-third year of their sojourn in Dalamatia, long before the wall was completed, that number two and number seven of the Danite group accidentally discovered a phenomenon attendant upon the liaison of their morontia selves (supposedly nonsexual and nonmaterial);

and the result of this adventure proved to be the first of the primary midway creatures. This new being was wholly visible to the planetary staff and to their celestial associates but was not visible to the men and women of the various human tribes. Upon authority of the Planetary Prince the entire corporeal staff undertook the production of similar beings, and all were successful, following the instructions of the pioneer Danite pair. Thus did the Prince's staff eventually bring into being the original corps of 50,000 primary midwayers.

These mid-type creatures were of great service in carrying on the affairs of the world's headquarters. They were invisible to human beings, but the primitive sojourners at Dalamatia were taught about these unseen semispirits, and for ages they constituted the sum total of the spirit world to these evolving mortals.

3. The Caligastia one hundred were personally immortal, or undying. There circulated through their material forms the antidotal complements of the life currents of the system; and had they not lost contact with the life circuits through rebellion, they would have lived on indefinitely until the arrival of a subsequent Son of God, or until their sometime later release to resume the interrupted journey to Havona and Paradise.

These antidotal complements of the Satania life currents were derived from the fruit of the tree of life, a shrub of Edentia which was sent to Urantia by the Most Highs of Norlatiadek at the time of Caligastia's arrival. In the days of Dalamatia this tree grew in the central courtyard of the temple of the unseen Father, and it was the fruit of the tree of life that enabled the material and otherwise mortal beings of the Prince's staff to live on indefinitely as long as they had access to it.

While of no value to the evolutionary races, this supersustenance was quite sufficient to confer continuous life upon the Caligastia one hundred and also upon the one hundred modified Andonites who were associated with them.

It should be explained in this connection that, at the time the one hundred Andonites contributed their human germ plasm to the members of the Prince's staff, the Life Carriers introduced into their mortal bodies the complement of the system circuits; and thus were they enabled to live on concurrently with the staff, century after century, in defiance of physical death.

Eventually the one hundred Andonites were made aware of their contribution to the new forms of their superiors, and these same one hundred children of the Andon tribes were kept at headquarters as the personal attendants of the Prince's corporeal staff.

5. ORGANIZATION OF THE ONE HUNDRED

The one hundred were organized for service in ten autonomous councils of ten members each. When two or more of these ten councils met in joint session, such liaison gatherings were presided over by Daligastia. These ten groups were constituted as follows:

1. *The council on food and material welfare.* This group was presided over by Ang. Food, water, clothes, and the material advancement of the human species were fostered by this able corps. They taught well digging, spring control, and irrigation. They taught those from the higher altitudes and from the north

improved methods of treating skins for use as clothing, and weaving was later introduced by the teachers of art and science.

Great advances were made in methods of food storage. Food was preserved by cooking, drying, and smoking; it thus became the earliest property. Man was taught to provide for the hazards of famine, which periodically decimated the world.

2. *The board of animal domestication and utilization.* This council was dedicated to the task of selecting and breeding those animals best adapted to help human beings in bearing burdens and transporting themselves, to supply food, and later on to be of service in the cultivation of the soil. This able corps was directed by Bon.

Several types of useful animals, now extinct, were tamed, together with some that have continued as domesticated animals to the present day. Man had long lived with the dog, and the blue man had already been successful in taming the elephant. The cow was so improved by careful breeding as to become a valuable source of food; butter and cheese became common articles of human diet. Men were taught to use oxen for burden bearing, but the horse was not domesticated until a later date. The members of this corps first taught men to use the wheel for the facilitation of traction.

It was in these days that carrier pigeons were first used, being taken on long journeys for the purpose of sending messages or calls for help. Bon's group were successful in training the great fandors as passenger birds, but they became extinct more than thirty thousand years ago.

3. *The advisers regarding the conquest of predatory animals.* It was not enough that early man should try to domesticate certain animals, but he must also learn how to protect himself from destruction by the remainder of the hostile animal world. This group was captained by Dan.

The purpose of an ancient city wall was to protect against ferocious beasts as well as to prevent surprise attacks by hostile humans. Those living without the walls and in the forest were dependent on tree dwellings, stone huts, and the maintenance of night fires. It was therefore very natural that these teachers should devote much time to instructing their pupils in the improvement of human dwellings. By employing improved techniques and by the use of traps, great progress was made in animal subjugation.

4. *The faculty on dissemination and conservation of knowledge.* This group organized and directed the purely educational endeavors of those early ages. It was presided over by Fad. The educational methods of Fad consisted in supervision of employment accompanied by instruction in improved methods of labor. Fad formulated the first alphabet and introduced a writing system. This alphabet contained twenty-five characters. For writing material these early peoples utilized tree barks, clay tablets, stone slabs, a form of parchment made of hammered hides, and a crude form of paperlike material made from wasps' nests. The Dalamatia library, destroyed soon after the Caligastia disaffection, comprised more than two million separate records and was known as the "house of Fad."

The blue man was partial to alphabet writing and made the greatest progress along such lines. The red man preferred pictorial writing, while the yellow races drifted into the use of symbols for words and ideas, much like those they now employ. But the alphabet and much more was subsequently lost to the world during the confusion attendant upon rebellion. The Caligastia defection destroyed the hope of the world for a universal language, at least for untold ages.

5. *The commission on industry and trade.* This council was employed in fostering industry within the tribes and in promoting trade between the various peace groups. Its leader was Nod. Every form of primitive manufacture was encouraged by this corps. They contributed directly to the elevation of standards of living by providing many new commodities to attract the fancy of primitive men. They greatly expanded the trade in the improved salt produced by the council on science and art.

It was among these enlightened groups educated in the Dalamatia schools that the first commercial credit was practiced. From a central exchange of credits they secured tokens which were accepted in lieu of the actual objects of barter. The world did not improve upon these business methods for hundreds of thousands of years.

6. *The college of revealed religion.* This body was slow in functioning. Urantia civilization was literally forged out between the anvil of necessity and the hammers of fear. But this group had made considerable progress in their attempt to substitute Creator fear for creature fear (ghost worship) before their labors were interrupted by the later confusion attendant upon the secession upheaval. The head of this council was Hap.

None of the Prince's staff would present revelation to complicate evolution; they presented revelation only as the climax of their exhaustion of the forces of evolution. But Hap did yield to the desire of the inhabitants of the city for the establishment of a form of religious service. His group provided the Dalamatians with the seven chants of worship and also gave them the daily praise-phrase and eventually taught them "the Father's prayer," which was:

"Father of all, whose Son we honor, look down upon us with favor. Deliver us from the fear of all save you. Make us a pleasure to our divine teachers and forever put truth on our lips. Deliver us from violence and anger; give us respect for our elders and that which belongs to our neighbors. Give us this season green pastures and fruitful flocks to gladden our hearts. We pray for the hastening of the coming of the promised uplifter, and we would do your will on this world as others do on worlds beyond."

Although the Prince's staff were limited to natural means and ordinary methods of race improvement, they held out the promise of the Adamic gift of a new race as the goal of subsequent evolutionary growth upon the attainment of the height of biologic development.

7. *The guardians of health and life.* This council was concerned with the introduction of sanitation and the promotion of primitive hygiene and was led by Lut.

Its members taught much that was lost during the confusion of subsequent ages, never to be rediscovered until the twentieth century. They taught mankind that cooking, boiling and roasting, was a means of avoiding sickness; also that such cooking greatly reduced infant mortality and facilitated early weaning.

Many of the early teachings of Lut's guardians of health persisted among the tribes of earth on down to the days of Moses, even though they became much garbled and were greatly changed.

The great obstacle in the way of promoting hygiene among these ignorant peoples consisted in the fact that the real causes of many diseases were too small to be seen by the naked eye, and also because they all held fire in superstitious regard. It required thousands of years to persuade them to burn refuse. In the meantime they were urged to bury their decaying rubbish. The great sanitary advance of this epoch came from the dissemination of knowledge regarding the health-giving and disease-destroying properties of sunlight.

Before the Prince's arrival, bathing had been an exclusively religious ceremonial. It was indeed difficult to persuade primitive men to wash their bodies as a health practice. Lut finally induced the religious teachers to include cleansing with water as a part of the purification ceremonies to be practiced in connection with the noontime devotions, once a week, in the worship of the Father of all.

These guardians of health also sought to introduce handshaking in substitution for saliva exchange or blood drinking as a seal of personal friendship and as a token of group loyalty. But when out from under the compelling pressure of the teachings of their superior leaders, these primitive peoples were not slow in reverting to their former health-destroying and disease-breeding practices of ignorance and superstition.

8. *The planetary council on art and science.* This corps did much to improve the industrial technique of early man and to elevate his concepts of beauty. Their leader was Mek.

Art and science were at a low ebb throughout the world, but the rudiments of physics and chemistry were taught the Dalamatians. Pottery was advanced, decorative arts were all improved, and the ideals of human beauty were greatly enhanced. But music made little progress until after the arrival of the violet race.

These primitive men would not consent to experiment with steam power, notwithstanding the repeated urgings of their teachers; never could they overcome their great fear of the explosive power of confined steam. They were, however, finally persuaded to work with metals and fire, although a piece of red-hot metal was a terrorizing object to early man.

Mek did a great deal to advance the culture of the Andonites and to improve the art of the blue man. A blend of the blue man with the Andon stock produced an artistically gifted type, and many of them became master sculptors. They did not work in stone or marble, but their works of clay, hardened by baking, adorned the gardens of Dalamatia.

Great progress was made in the home arts, most of which were lost in the long and dark ages of rebellion, never to be rediscovered until modern times.

9. *The governors of advanced tribal relations.* This was the group intrusted with the work of bringing human society up to the level of statehood. Their chief was Tut.

These leaders contributed much to bringing about intertribal marriages. They fostered courtship and marriage after due deliberation and full opportunity to become acquainted. The purely military war dances were refined and made to serve valuable social ends. Many competitive games were introduced, but these ancient folk were a serious people; little humor graced these early tribes. Few of these practices survived the subsequent disintegration of planetary insurrection.

Tut and his associates labored to promote group associations of a peaceful nature, to regulate and humanize warfare, to co-ordinate intertribal relations, and to improve tribal governments. In the vicinity of Dalamatia there developed a more advanced culture, and these improved social relations were very helpful in influencing more remote tribes. But the pattern of civilization prevailing at the Prince's headquarters was quite different from the barbaric society evolving elsewhere, just as the twentieth-century society of Capetown, South Africa, is totally unlike the crude culture of the diminutive Bushmen to the north.

10. *The supreme court of tribal co-ordination and racial co-operation.* This supreme council was directed by Van and was the court of appeals for all of the other nine special commissions charged with the supervision of human affairs. This council was one of wide function, being intrusted with all matters of earthly concern which were not specifically assigned to the other groups. This selected corps had been approved by the Constellation Fathers of Edentia before they were authorized to assume the functions of the supreme court of Urantia.

6. THE PRINCE'S REIGN

The degree of a world's culture is measured by the social heritage of its native beings, and the rate of cultural expansion is wholly determined by the ability of its inhabitants to comprehend new and advanced ideas.

Slavery to tradition produces stability and co-operation by sentimentally linking the past with the present, but it likewise stifles initiative and enslaves the creative powers of the personality. The whole world was caught in the stalemate of tradition-bound mores when the Caligastia one hundred arrived and began the proclamation of the new gospel of individual initiative within the social groups of that day. But this beneficent rule was so soon interrupted that the races never have been wholly liberated from the slavery of custom; fashion still unduly dominates Urantia.

The Caligastia one hundred—graduates of the Satania mansion worlds—well knew the arts and culture of Jerusem, but such knowledge is nearly valueless on a barbaric planet populated by primitive humans. These wise beings knew better than to undertake the *sudden* transformation, or the en masse uplifting, of the primitive races of that day. They well understood the slow evolution of the human species, and they wisely refrained from any radical attempts at modifying man's mode of life on earth.

Each of the ten planetary commissions set about *slowly* and naturally to advance the interests intrusted to them. Their plan consisted in attracting the best minds of the surrounding tribes and, after training them, sending them back to their people as emissaries of social uplift.

Foreign emissaries were never sent to a race except upon the specific request of that people. Those who labored for the uplift and advancement of a given tribe or race were always natives of that tribe or race. The one hundred would not attempt to impose the habits and mores of even a superior race upon another tribe. Always they patiently worked to uplift and advance the time-tried mores of each race. The simple folk of Urantia brought their social customs to Dalamatia, not to exchange them for new and better practices, but to have them uplifted by contact with a higher culture and by association with superior minds. The process was slow but very effectual.

The Dalamatia teachers sought to add conscious social selection to the purely natural selection of biologic evolution. They did not derange human society, but they did markedly accelerate its normal and natural evolution. Their motive was progression by evolution and not revolution by revelation. The human race had spent ages in acquiring the little religion and morals it had, and these supermen knew better than to rob mankind of these few advances by the confusion and dismay which always result when enlightened and superior beings undertake to uplift the backward races by overteaching and overenlightenment.

When Christian missionaries go into the heart of Africa, where sons and daughters are supposed to remain under the control and direction of their parents throughout the lifetime of the parents, they only bring about confusion and the breakdown of all authority when they seek, in a single generation, to supplant this practice by teaching that these children should be free from all parental restraint after they have attained the age of twenty-one.

7. LIFE IN DALAMATIA

The Prince's headquarters, though exquisitely beautiful and designed to awe the primitive men of that age, was altogether modest. The buildings were not especially large as it was the motive of these imported teachers to encourage the eventual development of agriculture through the introduction of animal husbandry. The land provision within the city walls was sufficient to provide for pasturage and gardening for the support of a population of about twenty thousand.

The interiors of the central temple of worship and the ten council mansions of the supervising groups of supermen were indeed beautiful works of art. And while the residential buildings were models of neatness and cleanliness, everything was very simple and altogether primitive in comparison with later-day developments. At this headquarters of culture no methods were employed which did not naturally belong on Urantia.

The Prince's corporeal staff presided over simple and exemplary abodes which they maintained as homes designed to inspire and favorably impress the student observers sojourning at the world's social center and educational headquarters.

The definite order of family life and the living of one family together in one residence of comparatively settled location date from these times of Dalamatia and were chiefly due to the example and teachings of the one hundred and their pupils. The home as a social unit never became a success until the supermen and superwomen of Dalamatia led mankind to love and plan for their grandchildren and their grandchildren's children. Savage man loves his child, but civilized man loves also his grandchild.

The Prince's staff lived together as fathers and mothers. True, they had no children of their own, but the fifty pattern homes of Dalamatia never sheltered less than five hundred adopted little ones assembled from the superior families of the Andonic and Sangik races; many of these children were orphans. They were favored with the discipline and training of these superparents; and then, after three years in the schools of the Prince (they entered from thirteen to fifteen), they were eligible for marriage and ready to receive their commissions as emissaries of the Prince to the needy tribes of their respective races.

Fad sponsored the Dalamatia plan of teaching that was carried out as an industrial school in which the pupils learned by doing, and through which they worked their way by the daily performance of useful tasks. This plan of education did not ignore thinking and feeling in the development of character; but it gave first place to manual training. The instruction was individual and collective. The pupils were taught by both men and women and by the two acting conjointly. One half of this group instruction was by sexes; the other half was coeducational. Students were taught manual dexterity as individuals and were socialized in groups or classes. They were trained to fraternize with younger groups, older groups, and adults, as well as to do teamwork with those of their own ages. They were also familiarized with such associations as family groups, play squads, and school classes.

Among the later students trained in Mesopotamia for work with their respective races were Andonites from the highlands of western India together with representatives of the red men and the blue men; still later a small number of the yellow race were also received.

Hap presented the early races with a moral law. This code was known as "The Father's Way" and consisted of the following seven commands:

1. You shall not fear nor serve any God but the Father of all.
2. You shall not disobey the Father's Son, the world's ruler, nor show disrespect to his superhuman associates.
3. You shall not speak a lie when called before the judges of the people.
4. You shall not kill men, women, or children.
5. You shall not steal your neighbor's goods or cattle.
6. You shall not touch your friend's wife.
7. You shall not show disrespect to your parents or to the elders of the tribe.

This was the law of Dalamatia for almost three hundred thousand years. And many of the stones on which this law was inscribed now lie beneath the waters off the shores of Mesopotamia and Persia. It became the custom to hold one of these commands in mind for each day of the week, using it for salutations and mealtime thanksgiving.

The time measurement of these days was the lunar month, this period being reckoned as twenty-eight days. That, with the exception of day and night, was the only time reckoning known to the early peoples. The seven-day week was introduced by the Dalamatia teachers and grew out of the fact that seven was one fourth of twenty-eight. The significance of the number seven in the superuniverse undoubtedly afforded them opportunity to introduce a spiritual reminder into the common reckoning of time. But there is no natural origin for the weekly period.

The country around the city was quite well settled within a radius of one hundred miles. Immediately surrounding the city, hundreds of graduates of the Prince's schools engaged in animal husbandry and otherwise carried out the instruction they had received from his staff and their numerous human helpers. A few engaged in agriculture and horticulture.

Mankind was not consigned to agricultural toil as the penalty of supposed sin. "In the sweat of your face shall you eat the fruit of the fields" was not a sentence of punishment pronounced because of man's participation in the follies of the Lucifer rebellion under the leadership of the traitorous Caligastia. The cultivation of the soil is inherent in the establishment of an advancing civilization on the evolutionary worlds, and this injunction was the center of all teaching of the Planetary Prince and his staff throughout the three hundred thousand years which intervened between their arrival on Urantia and those tragic days when Caligastia threw in his lot with the rebel Lucifer. Work with the soil is not a curse; rather is it the highest blessing to all who are thus permitted to enjoy the most human of all human activities.

At the outbreak of the rebellion, Dalamatia had a resident population of almost six thousand. This number includes the regular students but does not embrace the visitors and observers, who always numbered more than one thousand. But you can have little or no concept of the marvelous progress of those faraway times; practically all of the wonderful human gains of those days were wiped out by the horrible confusion and abject spiritual darkness which followed the Caligastia catastrophe of deception and sedition.

8. MISFORTUNES OF CALIGASTIA

In looking back over the long career of Caligastia, we find only one outstanding feature of his conduct that might have challenged attention; he was ultraindividualistic. He was inclined to take sides with almost every party of protest, and he was usually sympathetic with those who gave mild expression to implied criticism. We detect the early appearance of this tendency to be restless under authority, to mildly resent all forms of supervision. While slightly resentful of senior counsel and somewhat restive under superior authority, nonetheless, whenever a test had come, he had always proved loyal to the universe rulers and obedient to the mandates of the Constellation Fathers. No real fault was ever found in him up to the time of his shameful betrayal of Urantia.

It should be noted that both Lucifer and Caligastia had been patiently instructed and lovingly warned respecting their critical tendencies and the subtle development of their pride of self and its associated exaggeration of the feeling of self-importance. But all of these attempts to help had been misconstrued as unwarranted criticism and as unjustified interference with personal liberties. Both Caligastia and Lucifer judged their friendly advisers as being actuated by the very reprehensible motives which were beginning to dominate their own distorted thinking and misguided planning. They judged their unselfish advisers by their own evolving selfishness.

From the arrival of Prince Caligastia, planetary civilization progressed in a fairly normal manner for almost three hundred thousand years. Aside from being a life-modification sphere and therefore subject to numerous irregularities and unusual episodes of evolutionary fluctuation, Urantia progressed very satisfactorily in its planetary career up to the times of the Lucifer rebellion and the concurrent Caligastia betrayal. All subsequent history has been definitely modified by this catastrophic blunder as well as by the later failure of Adam and Eve to fulfill their planetary mission.

The Prince of Urantia went into darkness at the time of the Lucifer rebellion, thus precipitating the long confusion of the planet. He was subsequently deprived of sovereign authority by the co-ordinate action of the constellation rulers and other universe authorities. He shared the inevitable vicissitudes of isolated Urantia down to the time of Adam's sojourn on the planet and contributed something to the miscarriage of the plan to uplift the mortal races through the infusion of the lifeblood of the new violet race—the descendants of Adam and Eve.

The power of the fallen Prince to disturb human affairs was enormously curtailed by the mortal incarnation of Machiventa Melchizedek in the days of Abraham; and subsequently, during the life of Michael in the flesh, this traitorous Prince was finally shorn of all authority on Urantia.

The doctrine of a personal devil on Urantia, though it had some foundation in the planetary presence of the traitorous and iniquitous Caligastia, was nevertheless wholly fictitious in its teachings that such a "devil" could influence the normal human mind against its free and natural choosing. Even before Michael's bestowal on Urantia, neither Caligastia nor Daligastia was ever able to oppress mortals or to coerce any normal individual into doing anything against the human will. The free will of man is supreme in moral affairs; even the indwelling Thought Adjuster refuses to compel man to think a single thought or to perform a single act against the choosing of man's own will.

And now this rebel of the realm, shorn of all power to harm his former subjects, awaits the final adjudication, by the Uversa Ancients of Days, of all who participated in the Lucifer rebellion.

[Presented by a Melchizedek of Nebadon.]

PAPER 67

THE PLANETARY REBELLION

THE problems associated with human existence on Urantia are impossible of understanding without a knowledge of certain great epochs of the past, notably the occurrence and consequences of the planetary rebellion. Although this upheaval did not seriously interfere with the progress of organic evolution, it did markedly modify the course of social evolution and of spiritual development. The entire superphysical history of the planet was profoundly influenced by this devastating calamity.

1. THE CALIGASTIA BETRAYAL

For three hundred thousand years Caligastia had been in charge of Urantia when Satan, Lucifer's assistant, made one of his periodic inspection calls. And when Satan arrived on the planet, his appearance in no way resembled your caricatures of his nefarious majesty. He was, and still is, a Lanonandek Son of great brilliance. "And no marvel, for Satan himself is a brilliant creature of light."

In the course of this inspection Satan informed Caligastia of Lucifer's then proposed "Declaration of Liberty," and as we now know, the Prince agreed to betray the planet upon the announcement of the rebellion. The loyal universe personalities look with peculiar disdain upon Prince Caligastia because of this premeditated betrayal of trust. The Creator Son voiced this contempt when he said: "You are like your leader, Lucifer, and you have sinfully perpetuated his iniquity. He was a falsifier from the beginning of his self-exaltation because he abode not in the truth."

In all the administrative work of a local universe no high trust is deemed more sacred than that reposed in a Planetary Prince who assumes responsibility for the welfare and guidance of the evolving mortals on a newly inhabited world. And of all forms of evil, none are more destructive of personality status than betrayal of trust and disloyalty to one's confiding friends. In committing this deliberate sin, Caligastia so completely distorted his personality that his mind has never since been able fully to regain its equilibrium.

There are many ways of looking at sin, but from the universe philosophic viewpoint sin is the attitude of a personality who is knowingly resisting cosmic reality. Error might be regarded as a misconception or distortion of reality. Evil is a partial realization of, or maladjustment to, universe realities. But sin is a purposeful resistance to divine reality—a conscious choosing to oppose spiritual progress—while iniquity consists in an open and persistent defiance of recognized reality and signifies such a degree of personality disintegration as to border on cosmic insanity.

Error suggests lack of intellectual keenness; evil, deficiency of wisdom; sin, abject spiritual poverty; but iniquity is indicative of vanishing personality control.

And when sin has so many times been chosen and so often been repeated, it may become habitual. Habitual sinners can easily become iniquitous, become wholehearted rebels against the universe and all of its divine realities. While all manner of sins may be forgiven, we doubt whether the established iniquiter would ever sincerely experience sorrow for his misdeeds or accept forgiveness for his sins.

2. THE OUTBREAK OF REBELLION

Shortly after Satan's inspection and when the planetary administration was on the eve of the realization of great things on Urantia, one day, midwinter of the northern continents, Caligastia held a prolonged conference with his associate, Daligastia, after which the latter called the ten councils of Urantia in session extraordinary. This assembly was opened with the statement that Prince Caligastia was about to proclaim himself absolute sovereign of Urantia and demanded that all administrative groups abdicate by resigning all of their functions and powers into the hands of Daligastia as trustee, pending the reorganization of the planetary government and the subsequent redistribution of these offices of administrative authority.

The presentation of this astounding demand was followed by the masterly appeal of Van, chairman of the supreme council of co-ordination. This distinguished administrator and able jurist branded the proposed course of Caligastia as an act bordering on planetary rebellion and appealed to his conferees to abstain from all participation until an appeal could be taken to Lucifer, the System Sovereign of Satania; and he won the support of the entire staff. Accordingly, appeal was taken to Jerusem, and forthwith came back the orders designating Caligastia as supreme sovereign on Urantia and commanding absolute and unquestioning allegiance to his mandates. And it was in reply to this amazing message that the noble Van made his memorable address of seven hours' length in which he formally drew his indictment of Daligastia, Caligastia, and Lucifer as standing in contempt of the sovereignty of the universe of Nebadon; and he appealed to the Most Highs of Edentia for support and confirmation.

Meantime the system circuits had been severed; Urantia was isolated. Every group of celestial life on the planet found itself suddenly and without warning isolated, utterly cut off from all outside counsel and advice.

Daligastia formally proclaimed Caligastia "God of Urantia and supreme over all." With this proclamation before them, the issues were clearly drawn; and each group drew off by itself and began deliberations, discussions destined eventually to determine the fate of every superhuman personality on the planet.

Seraphim and cherubim and other celestial beings were involved in the decisions of this bitter struggle, this long and sinful conflict. Many superhuman groups that chanced to be on Urantia at the time of its isolation were detained here and, like the seraphim and their associates, were compelled to choose between sin and righteousness—between the ways of Lucifer and the will of the unseen Father.

For more than seven years this struggle continued. Not until every personality concerned had made a final decision, would or did the authorities of Edentia interfere or intervene. Not until then did Van and his loyal associates receive vindication and release from their prolonged anxiety and intolerable suspense.

3. THE SEVEN CRUCIAL YEARS

The outbreak of rebellion on Jerusem, the capital of Satania, was broadcast by the Melchizedek council. The emergency Melchizedeks were immediately dispatched to Jerusem, and Gabriel volunteered to act as the representative of the Creator Son, whose authority had been challenged. With this broadcast of the fact of rebellion in Satania the system was isolated, quarantined, from her sister systems. There was "war in heaven," the headquarters of Satania, and it spread to every planet in the local system.

On Urantia forty members of the corporeal staff of one hundred (including Van) refused to join the insurrection. Many of the staff's human assistants (modified and otherwise) were also brave and noble defenders of Michael and his universe government. There was a terrible loss of personalities among seraphim and cherubim. Almost one half of the administrator and transition seraphim assigned to the planet joined their leader and Daligastia in support of the cause of Lucifer. Forty thousand one hundred and nineteen of the primary midway creatures joined hands with Caligastia, but the remainder of these beings remained true to their trust.

The traitorous Prince marshaled the disloyal midway creatures and other groups of rebel personalities and organized them to execute his bidding, while Van assembled the loyal midwayers and other faithful groups and began the great battle for the salvation of the planetary staff and other marooned celestial personalities.

During the times of this struggle the loyalists dwelt in an unwalled and poorly protected settlement a few miles to the east of Dalamatia, but their dwellings were guarded day and night by the alert and ever-watchful loyal midway creatures, and they had possession of the priceless tree of life.

Upon the outbreak of rebellion, loyal cherubim and seraphim, with the aid of three faithful midwayers, assumed the custody of the tree of life and permitted only the forty loyalists of the staff and their associated modified mortals to partake of the fruit and leaves of this energy plant. There were fifty-six of these modified Andonite associates of the staff, sixteen of the Andonite attendants of the disloyal staff refusing to go into rebellion with their masters.

Throughout the seven crucial years of the Caligastia rebellion, Van was wholly devoted to the work of ministry to his loyal army of men, midwayers, and angels. The spiritual insight and moral steadfastness which enabled Van to maintain such an unshakable attitude of loyalty to the universe government was the product of clear thinking, wise reasoning, logical judgment, sincere motivation, unselfish purpose, intelligent loyalty, experiential memory, disciplined character, and the unquestioning dedication of his personality to the doing of the will of the Father in Paradise.

This seven years of waiting was a time of heart searching and soul discipline. Such crises in the affairs of a universe demonstrate the tremendous influence of mind as a factor in spiritual choosing. Education, training, and experience are factors in most of the vital decisions of all evolutionary moral creatures. But it is entirely possible for the indwelling spirit to make direct contact with the decision-determining powers of the human personality so as to empower the fully consecrated will of the creature to perform amazing acts of loyal devotion to the will and the way of the Father in Paradise. And this is just what occurred in the experience of Amadon, the modified human associate of Van.

Amadon is the outstanding human hero of the Lucifer rebellion. This male descendant of Andon and Fonta was one of the one hundred who contributed life plasm to the Prince's staff, and ever since that event he had been attached to Van as his associate and human assistant. Amadon elected to stand with his chief throughout the long and trying struggle. And it was an inspiring sight to behold this child of the evolutionary races standing unmoved by the sophistries of Daligastia while throughout the seven-year struggle he and his loyal associates resisted with unyielding fortitude all of the deceptive teachings of the brilliant Caligastia.

Caligastia, with a maximum of intelligence and a vast experience in universe affairs, went astray—embraced sin. Amadon, with a minimum of intelligence and utterly devoid of universe experience, remained steadfast in the service of the universe and in loyalty to his associate. Van utilized both mind and spirit in a magnificent and effective combination of intellectual determination and spiritual insight, thereby achieving an experiential level of personality realization of the highest attainable order. Mind and spirit, when fully united, are potential for the creation of superhuman values, even morontia realities.

There is no end to the recital of the stirring events of these tragic days. But at last the final decision of the last personality was made, and then, but only then, did a Most High of Edentia arrive with the emergency Melchizedeks to seize authority on Urantia. The Caligastia panoramic reign-records on Jerusem were obliterated, and the probationary era of planetary rehabilitation was inaugurated.

4. THE CALIGASTIA ONE HUNDRED AFTER REBELLION

When the final roll was called, the corporeal members of the Prince's staff were found to have aligned themselves as follows: Van and his entire court of co-ordination had remained loyal. Ang and three members of the food council had survived. The board of animal husbandry were all swept into rebellion as were all of the animal-conquest advisers. Fad and five members of the educational faculty were saved. Nod and all of the commission on industry and trade joined Caligastia. Hap and the entire college of revealed religion remained loyal with Van and his noble band. Lut and the whole board of health were lost. The council of art and science remained loyal in its entirety, but Tut and the commission on tribal government all went astray. Thus were forty out of the one hundred saved, later to be transferred to Jerusem, where they resumed their Paradise journey.

The sixty members of the planetary staff who went into rebellion chose Nod as their leader. They worked wholeheartedly for the rebel Prince but soon discovered that they were deprived of the sustenance of the system life circuits. They awakened to the fact that they had been degraded to the status of mortal beings. They were indeed superhuman but, at the same time, material and mortal. In an effort to increase their numbers, Daligastia ordered immediate resort to sexual reproduction, knowing full well that the original sixty and their forty-four modified Andonite associates were doomed to suffer extinction by death, sooner or later. After the fall of Dalamatia the disloyal staff migrated to the north and the east. Their descendants were long known as the Nodites, and their dwelling place as "the land of Nod."

The presence of these extraordinary supermen and superwomen, stranded by rebellion and presently mating with the sons and daughters of earth, easily gave origin to those traditional stories of the gods coming down to mate with mortals. And thus originated the thousand and one legends of a mythical nature, but founded on the facts of the postrebellion days, which later found a place in the folk tales and traditions of the various peoples whose ancestors had participated in these contacts with the Nodites and their descendants.

The staff rebels, deprived of spiritual sustenance, eventually died a natural death. And much of the subsequent idolatry of the human races grew out of the desire to perpetuate the memory of these highly honored beings of the days of Caligastia.

When the staff of one hundred came to Urantia, they were temporarily detached from their Thought Adjusters. Immediately upon the arrival of the Melchizedek receivers the loyal personalities (except Van) were returned to Jerusem and were reunited with their waiting Adjusters. We know not the fate of the sixty staff rebels; their Adjusters still tarry on Jerusem. Matters will undoubtedly rest as they now are until the entire Lucifer rebellion is finally adjudicated and the fate of all participants decreed.

It was very difficult for such beings as angels and midwayers to conceive of brilliant and trusted rulers like Caligastia and Daligastia going astray—committing traitorous sin. Those beings who fell into sin—they did not deliberately or premeditatedly enter upon rebellion—were misled by their superiors, deceived by their trusted leaders. It was likewise easy to win the support of the primitive-minded evolutionary mortals.

The vast majority of all human and superhuman beings who were victims of the Lucifer rebellion on Jerusem and the various misled planets have long since heartily repented of their folly; and we truly believe that all such sincere penitents will in some manner be rehabilitated and restored to some phase of universe service when the Ancients of Days finally complete the adjudication of the affairs of the Satania rebellion, which they have so recently begun.

5. IMMEDIATE RESULTS OF REBELLION

Great confusion reigned in Dalamatia and thereabout for almost fifty years after the instigation of rebellion. The complete and radical reorganization of the whole world was attempted; revolution displaced evolution as the policy of cultural advancement and racial improvement. Among the superior and partially trained sojourners in and near Dalamatia there appeared a sudden advancement in cultural status, but when these new and radical methods were attempted on the outlying peoples, indescribable confusion and racial pandemonium was the immediate result. Liberty was quickly translated into license by the half-evolved primitive men of those days.

Very soon after the rebellion the entire staff of sedition were engaged in energetic defense of the city against the hordes of semisavages who besieged its walls as a result of the doctrines of liberty which had been prematurely taught them. And years before the beautiful headquarters went down beneath the southern waves, the misled and mistaught tribes of the Dalamatia hinterland had already swept down in semisavage assault on the splendid city, driving the secession staff and their associates northward.

The Caligastia scheme for the immediate reconstruction of human society in accordance with his ideas of individual freedom and group liberties, proved a swift and more or less complete failure. Society quickly sank back to its old biologic level, and the forward struggle began all over, starting not very far in advance of where it was at the beginning of the Caligastia regime, this upheaval having left the world in confusion worse confounded.

One hundred and sixty-two years after the rebellion a tidal wave swept up over Dalamatia, and the planetary headquarters sank beneath the waters of the sea, and this land did not again emerge until almost every vestige of the noble culture of those splendid ages had been obliterated.

When the first capital of the world was engulfed, it harbored only the lowest types of the Sangik races of Urantia, renegades who had already converted the Father's temple into a shrine dedicated to Nog, the false god of light and fire.

6. VAN—THE STEADFAST

The followers of Van early withdrew to the highlands west of India, where they were exempt from attacks by the confused races of the lowlands, and from which place of retirement they planned for the rehabilitation of the world as their early Badonite predecessors had once all unwittingly worked for the welfare of mankind just before the days of the birth of the Sangik tribes.

Before the arrival of the Melchizedek receivers, Van placed the administration of human affairs in the hands of ten commissions of four each, groups identical with those of the Prince's regime. The senior resident Life Carriers assumed temporary leadership of this council of forty, which functioned throughout the seven years of waiting. Similar groups of Amadonites assumed these responsibilities when the thirty-nine loyal staff members returned to Jerusem.

These *Amadonites* were derived from the group of 144 loyal Andonites to which Amadon belonged, and who have become known by his name. This group comprised thirty-nine men and one hundred and five women. Fifty-six of this number were of immortality status, and all (except Amadon) were translated along with the loyal members of the staff. The remainder of this noble band continued on earth to the end of their mortal days under the leadership of Van and Amadon. They were the biologic leaven which multiplied and continued to furnish leadership for the world down through the long dark ages of the postrebellion era.

Van was left on Urantia until the time of Adam, remaining as titular head of all superhuman personalities functioning on the planet. He and Amadon were sustained by the technique of the tree of life in conjunction with the specialized life ministry of the Melchizedeks for over one hundred and fifty thousand years.

The affairs of Urantia were for a long time administered by a council of planetary receivers, twelve Melchizedeks, confirmed by the mandate of the senior constellation ruler, the Most High Father of Norlatiadek. Associated with the Melchizedek receivers was an advisory council consisting of: one of the loyal aids of the fallen Prince, the two resident Life Carriers, a Trinitized Son in apprenticeship training, a volunteer Teacher Son, a Brilliant Evening Star of Avalon (periodically), the chiefs of seraphim and cherubim, advisers from two neighboring planets, the director general of subordinate angelic life, and Van, the commander in chief of the midway creatures. And thus was Urantia governed and administered until the arrival of Adam. It is not strange that the courageous and loyal Van was assigned a place on the council of planetary receivers which for so long administered the affairs of Urantia.

The twelve Melchizedek receivers of Urantia did heroic work. They preserved the remnants of civilization, and their planetary policies were faithfully executed by Van. Within one thousand years after the rebellion he had more than three hundred and fifty advanced groups scattered abroad in the world. These outposts of civilization consisted largely of the descendants of the loyal Andonites slightly admixed with the Sangik races, particularly the blue men, and with the Nodites.

Notwithstanding the terrible setback of rebellion there were many good strains of biologic promise on earth. Under the supervision of the Melchizedek receivers, Van and Amadon continued the work of fostering the natural evolution of the human race, carrying forward the physical evolution of man until it reached that culminating attainment which warranted the dispatch of a Material Son and Daughter to Urantia.

Van and Amadon remained on earth until shortly after the arrival of Adam and Eve. Some years thereafter they were translated to Jerusem, where Van was reunited with his waiting Adjuster. Van now serves in behalf of Urantia while awaiting the order to go forward on the long, long trail to Paradise perfection and the unrevealed destiny of the assembling Corps of Mortal Finality.

It should be recorded that, when Van appealed to the Most Highs of Edentia after Lucifer had sustained Caligastia on Urantia, the Constellation Fathers dispatched an immediate decision sustaining Van on every point of his contention. This verdict failed to reach him because the planetary circuits of communication were severed while it was in transit. Only recently was this actual ruling discovered lodged in the possession of a relay energy transmitter where it had been marooned ever since the isolation of Urantia. Without this discovery, made as the result of the investigations of the Urantia midwayers, the release of this decision would have awaited the restoration of Urantia to the constellation circuits. And this apparent accident of interplanetary communication was possible because energy transmitters can receive and transmit intelligence, but they cannot initiate communication.

The technical status of Van on the legal records of Satania was not actually and finally settled until this ruling of the Edentia Fathers was recorded on Jerusem.

7. REMOTE REPERCUSSIONS OF SIN

The personal (centripetal) consequences of the creature's willful and persistent rejection of light are both inevitable and individual and are of concern only to Deity and to that personal creature. Such a soul-destroying harvest of iniquity is the inner reaping of the iniquitous will creature.

But not so with the external repercussions of sin: The impersonal (centrifugal) consequences of embraced sin are both inevitable and collective, being of concern to every creature functioning within the affect-range of such events.

By fifty thousand years after the collapse of the planetary administration, earthly affairs were so disorganized and retarded that the human race had gained very little over the general evolutionary status existing at the time of Caligastia's arrival three hundred and fifty thousand years previously. In certain respects progress had been made; in other directions much ground had been lost.

Sin is never purely local in its effects. The administrative sectors of the universes are organismal; the plight of one personality must to a certain extent be shared by all. Sin, being an attitude of the person toward reality, is destined to exhibit its inherent negativistic harvest upon any and all related levels of universe values. But the full consequences of erroneous thinking, evil-doing, or sinful planning are experienced only on the level of actual performance. The transgression of universe law may be fatal in the physical realm without seriously involving the mind or impairing the spiritual experience. Sin is fraught with fatal consequences to personality survival only when it is the attitude of the whole being, when it stands for the choosing of the mind and the willing of the soul.

Evil and sin visit their consequences in material and social realms and may sometimes even retard spiritual progress on certain levels of universe reality, but never does the sin of any being rob another of the realization of the divine right of personality survival. Eternal survival can be jeopardized only by the decisions of the mind and the choice of the soul of the individual himself.

Sin on Urantia did very little to delay biologic evolution, but it did operate to deprive the mortal races of the full benefit of the Adamic inheritance. Sin enormously retards intellectual development, moral growth, social progress, and mass spiritual attainment. But it does not prevent the highest spiritual achievement by any individual who chooses to know God and sincerely do his divine will.

Caligastia rebelled, Adam and Eve did default, but no mortal subsequently born on Urantia has suffered in his personal spiritual experience because of these blunders. Every mortal born on Urantia since Caligastia's rebellion has been in some manner time-penalized, but the future welfare of such souls has never been in the least eternity-jeopardized. No person is ever made to suffer vital spiritual deprivation because of the sin of another. Sin is wholly personal as to moral guilt or spiritual consequences, notwithstanding its far-flung repercussions in administrative, intellectual, and social domains.

While we cannot fathom the wisdom that permits such catastrophes, we can always discern the beneficial outworking of these local disturbances as they are reflected out upon the universe at large.

8. THE HUMAN HERO OF THE REBELLION

The Lucifer rebellion was withstood by many courageous beings on the various worlds of Satania; but the records of Salvington portray Amadon as the outstanding character of the entire system in his glorious rejection of the flood tides of sedition and in his unswerving devotion to Van—they stood together unmoved in their loyalty to the supremacy of the invisible Father and his Son Michael.

At the time of these momentous transactions I was stationed on Edentia, and I am still conscious of the exhilaration I experienced as I perused the Salvington broadcasts which told from day to day of the unbelievable steadfastness, the transcendent devotion, and the exquisite loyalty of this onetime semisavage springing from the experimental and original stock of the Andonic race.

From Edentia up through Salvington and even on to Uversa, for seven long years the first inquiry of all subordinate celestial life regarding the Satania rebellion, ever and always, was: "What of Amadon of Urantia, does he still stand unmoved?"

If the Lucifer rebellion has handicapped the local system and its fallen worlds, if the loss of this Son and his misled associates has temporarily hampered the progress of the constellation of Norlatiadek, then weigh the effect of the far-flung presentation of the inspiring performance of this one child of nature and his determined band of 143 comrades in standing steadfast for the higher concepts of universe management and administration in the face of such tremendous and adverse pressure exerted by his disloyal superiors. And let me assure you, this has already done more good in the universe of Nebadon and the superuniverse of Orvonton than can ever be outweighed by the sum total of all the evil and sorrow of the Lucifer rebellion.

And all this is a beautifully touching and superbly magnificent illumination of the wisdom of the Father's universal plan for mobilizing the Corps of Mortal Finality on Paradise and for recruiting this vast group of mysterious servants of the future largely from the common clay of the mortals of ascending progression—just such mortals as the impregnable Amadon.

[Presented by a Melchizedek of Nebadon.]

PAPER 68

THE DAWN OF CIVILIZATION

THIS is the beginning of the narrative of the long, long forward struggle of the human species from a status that was little better than an animal existence, through the intervening ages, and down to the later times when a real, though imperfect, civilization had evolved among the higher races of mankind.

Civilization is a racial acquirement; it is not biologically inherent; hence must all children be reared in an environment of culture, while each succeeding generation of youth must receive anew its education. The superior qualities of civilization—scientific, philosophic, and religious—are not transmitted from one generation to another by direct inheritance. These cultural achievements are preserved only by the enlightened conservation of social inheritance.

Social evolution of the co-operative order was initiated by the Dalamatia teachers, and for three hundred thousand years mankind was nurtured in the idea of group activities. The blue man most of all profited by these early social teachings, the red man to some extent, and the black man least of all. In more recent times the yellow race and the white race have presented the most advanced social development on Urantia.

1. PROTECTIVE SOCIALIZATION

When brought closely together, men often learn to like one another, but primitive man was not naturally overflowing with the spirit of brotherly feeling and the desire for social contact with his fellows. Rather did the early races learn by sad experience that "in union there is strength"; and it is this lack of natural brotherly attraction that now stands in the way of immediate realization of the brotherhood of man on Urantia.

Association early became the price of survival. The lone man was helpless unless he bore a tribal mark which testified that he belonged to a group which would certainly avenge any assault made upon him. Even in the days of Cain it was fatal to go abroad alone without some mark of group association. Civilization has become man's insurance against violent death, while the premiums are paid by submission to society's numerous law demands.

Primitive society was thus founded on the reciprocity of necessity and on the enhanced safety of association. And human society has evolved in agelong cycles as a result of this isolation fear and by means of reluctant co-operation.

Primitive human beings early learned that groups are vastly greater and stronger than the mere sum of their individual units. One hundred men united and working in unison can move a great stone; a score of well-trained guardians of the peace can restrain an angry mob. And so society was born, not of mere association of numbers, but rather as a result of the *organization* of intelligent co-operators. But co-operation is not a natural trait of man; he learns to co-operate first through fear and then later because he discovers it is most beneficial in meeting the difficulties of time and guarding against the supposed perils of eternity.

The peoples who thus early organized themselves into a primitive society became more successful in their attacks on nature as well as in defense against their fellows; they possessed greater survival possibilities; hence has civilization steadily progressed on Urantia, notwithstanding its many setbacks. And it is only because of the enhancement of survival value in association that man's many blunders have thus far failed to stop or destroy human civilization.

That contemporary cultural society is a rather recent phenomenon is well shown by the present-day survival of such primitive social conditions as characterize the Australian natives and the Bushmen and Pygmies of Africa. Among these backward peoples may be observed something of the early group hostility, personal suspicion, and other highly antisocial traits which were so characteristic of all primitive races. These miserable remnants of the nonsocial peoples of ancient times bear eloquent testimony to the fact that the natural individualistic tendency of man cannot successfully compete with the more potent and powerful organizations and associations of social progression. These backward and suspicious antisocial races that speak a different dialect every forty or fifty miles illustrate what a world you might now be living in but for the combined teaching of the corporeal staff of the Planetary Prince and the later labors of the Adamic group of racial uplifters.

The modern phrase, "back to nature," is a delusion of ignorance, a belief in the reality of the onetime fictitious "golden age." The only basis for the legend of the golden age is the historic fact of Dalamatia and Eden. But these improved societies were far from the realization of utopian dreams.

2. FACTORS IN SOCIAL PROGRESSION

Civilized society is the result of man's early efforts to overcome his dislike of *isolation.* But this does not necessarily signify mutual affection, and the present turbulent state of certain primitive groups well illustrates what the early tribes came up through. But though the individuals of a civilization may collide with each other and struggle against one another, and though civilization itself may appear to be an inconsistent mass of striving and struggling, it does evidence earnest striving, not the deadly monotony of stagnation.

While the level of intelligence has contributed considerably to the rate of cultural progress, society is essentially designed to lessen the risk element in the individual's mode of living, and it has progressed just as fast as it has succeeded in lessening pain and increasing the pleasure element in life. Thus does the whole social body push on slowly toward the goal of destiny—extinction or survival—depending on whether that goal is self-maintenance or self-gratification. Self-maintenance originates society, while excessive self-gratification destroys civilization.

Society is concerned with self-perpetuation, self-maintenance, and self-gratification, but human self-realization is worthy of becoming the immediate goal of many cultural groups.

The herd instinct in natural man is hardly sufficient to account for the development of such a social organization as now exists on Urantia. Though this innate gregarious propensity lies at the bottom of human society, much of man's sociability is an acquirement. Two great influences which contributed to the early association of human beings were food hunger and sex love; these instinctive urges man shares with the animal world. Two other emotions which drove human beings together and *held* them together were vanity and fear, more particularly ghost fear.

History is but the record of man's agelong food struggle. *Primitive man only thought when he was hungry;* food saving was his first self-denial, self-discipline. With the growth of society, food hunger ceased to be the only incentive for mutual association. Numerous other sorts of hunger, the realization of various needs, all led to the closer association of mankind. But today society is top-heavy with the overgrowth of supposed human needs. Occidental civilization of the twentieth century groans wearily under the tremendous overload of luxury and the inordinate multiplication of human desires and longings. Modern society is enduring the strain of one of its most dangerous phases of far-flung inter-association and highly complicated interdependence.

Hunger, vanity, and ghost fear were continuous in their social pressure, but sex gratification was transient and spasmodic. The sex urge alone did not impel primitive men and women to assume the heavy burdens of home maintenance. The early home was founded upon the sex restlessness of the male when deprived of frequent gratification and upon that devoted mother love of the human female, which in measure she shares with the females of all the higher animals. The presence of a helpless baby determined the early differentiation of male and female activities; the woman had to maintain a settled residence where she could cultivate the soil. And from earliest times, where woman was has always been regarded as the home.

Woman thus early became indispensable to the evolving social scheme, not so much because of the fleeting sex passion as in consequence of *food requirement;* she was an essential partner in self-maintenance. She was a food provider, a beast of burden, and a companion who would stand great abuse without violent resentment, and in addition to all of these desirable traits, she was an ever-present means of sex gratification.

Almost everything of lasting value in civilization has its roots in the family. The family was the first successful peace group, the man and woman learning how to adjust their antagonisms while at the same time teaching the pursuits of peace to their children.

The function of marriage in evolution is the insurance of race survival, not merely the realization of personal happiness; self-maintenance and self-perpetuation are the real objects of the home. Self-gratification is incidental and not essential except as an incentive insuring sex association. Nature demands survival, but the arts of civilization continue to increase the pleasures of marriage and the satisfactions of family life.

If vanity be enlarged to cover pride, ambition, and honor, then we may discern not only how these propensities contribute to the formation of human associations, but how they also hold men together, since such emotions are futile without an audience to parade before. Soon vanity associated with itself other emotions and impulses which required a social arena wherein they might exhibit and gratify themselves. This group of emotions gave origin to the early beginnings of all art, ceremonial, and all forms of sportive games and contests.

Vanity contributed mightily to the birth of society; but at the time of these revelations the devious strivings of a vainglorious generation threaten to swamp and submerge the whole complicated structure of a highly specialized civilization. Pleasure-want has long since superseded hunger-want; the legitimate social aims of self-maintenance are rapidly translating themselves into base and threatening forms of self-gratification. Self-maintenance builds society; unbridled self-gratification unfailingly destroys civilization.

3. SOCIALIZING INFLUENCE OF GHOST FEAR

Primitive desires produced the original society, but ghost fear held it together and imparted an extrahuman aspect to its existence. Common fear was physiological in origin: fear of physical pain, unsatisfied hunger, or some earthly calamity; but ghost fear was a new and sublime sort of terror.

Probably the greatest single factor in the evolution of human society was the ghost dream. Although most dreams greatly perturbed the primitive mind, the ghost dream actually terrorized early men, driving these superstitious dreamers into each other's arms in willing and earnest association for mutual protection against the vague and unseen imaginary dangers of the spirit world. The ghost dream was one of the earliest appearing differences between the animal and human types of mind. Animals do not visualize survival after death.

Except for this ghost factor, all society was founded on fundamental needs and basic biologic urges. But ghost fear introduced a new factor in civilization, a fear which reaches out and away from the elemental needs of the individual, and which rises far above even the struggles to maintain the group. The dread of the departed spirits of the dead brought to light a new and amazing form of fear, an appalling and powerful terror, which contributed to whipping the loose social orders of early ages into the more thoroughly disciplined and better controlled primitive groups of ancient times. This senseless superstition, some of which still persists, prepared the minds of men, through superstitious fear of the unreal and the supernatural, for the later discovery of "the fear of the Lord which is the beginning of wisdom." The baseless fears of evolution are designed to be supplanted by the awe for Deity inspired by revelation. The early cult of ghost fear became a powerful social bond, and ever since that far-distant day mankind has been striving more or less for the attainment of spirituality.

Hunger and love drove men together; vanity and ghost fear held them together. But these emotions alone, without the influence of peace-promoting revelations, are unable to endure the strain of the suspicions and irritations of human interassociations. Without help from superhuman sources the strain of society breaks down upon reaching certain limits, and these very influences of social mobilization—hunger, love, vanity, and fear—conspire to plunge mankind into war and bloodshed.

The peace tendency of the human race is not a natural endowment; it is derived from the teachings of revealed religion, from the accumulated experience of the progressive races, but more especially from the teachings of Jesus, the Prince of Peace.

4. EVOLUTION OF THE MORES

All modern social institutions arise from the evolution of the primitive customs of your savage ancestors; the conventions of today are the modified and expanded customs of yesterday. What habit is to the individual, custom is to the group; and group customs develop into folkways or tribal traditions—mass conventions. From these early beginnings all of the institutions of present-day human society take their humble origin.

It must be borne in mind that the mores originated in an effort to adjust group living to the conditions of mass existence; the mores were man's first social institution. And all of these tribal reactions grew out of the effort to avoid pain and humiliation while at the same time seeking to enjoy pleasure and power. The origin of folkways, like the origin of languages, is always unconscious and unintentional and therefore always shrouded in mystery.

Ghost fear drove primitive man to envision the supernatural and thus securely laid the foundations for those powerful social influences of ethics and religion which in turn preserved inviolate the mores and customs of society from generation to generation. The one thing which early established and crystallized the mores was the belief that the dead were jealous of the ways by which they had lived and died; therefore would they visit dire punishment upon those living mortals who dared to treat with careless disdain the rules of living which they had honored when in the flesh. All this is best illustrated by the present reverence of the yellow race for their ancestors. Later developing primitive religion greatly reinforced ghost fear in stabilizing the mores, but advancing civilization has increasingly liberated mankind from the bondage of fear and the slavery of superstition.

Prior to the liberating and liberalizing instruction of the Dalamatia teachers, ancient man was held a helpless victim of the ritual of the mores; the primitive savage was hedged about by an endless ceremonial. Everything he did from the time of awakening in the morning to the moment he fell asleep in his cave at night had to be done just so—in accordance with the folkways of the tribe. He was a slave to the tyranny of usage; his life contained nothing free, spontaneous, or original. There was no natural progress toward a higher mental, moral, or social existence.

Early man was mightily gripped by custom; the savage was a veritable slave to usage; but there have arisen ever and anon those variations from type who have dared to inaugurate new ways of thinking and improved methods of living. Nevertheless, the inertia of primitive man constitutes the biologic safety brake against precipitation too suddenly into the ruinous maladjustment of a too rapidly advancing civilization.

But these customs are not an unmitigated evil; their evolution should continue. It is nearly fatal to the continuance of civilization to undertake their wholesale modification by radical revolution. Custom has been the thread of continuity which has held civilization together. The path of human history is strewn with the remnants of discarded customs and obsolete social practices; but no civilization has endured which abandoned its mores except for the adoption of better and more fit customs.

The survival of a society depends chiefly on the progressive evolution of its mores. The process of custom evolution grows out of the desire for experimentation;

new ideas are put forward—competition ensues. A progressing civilization embraces the progressive idea and endures; time and circumstance finally select the fitter group for survival. But this does not mean that each separate and isolated change in the composition of human society has been for the better. No! indeed no! for there have been many, many retrogressions in the long forward struggle of Urantia civilization.

5. LAND TECHNIQUES—MAINTENANCE ARTS

Land is the stage of society; men are the actors. And man must ever adjust his performances to conform to the land situation. The evolution of the mores is always dependent on the land-man ratio. This is true notwithstanding the difficulty of its discernment. Man's land technique, or maintenance arts, plus his standards of living, equal the sum total of the folkways, the mores. And the sum of man's adjustment to the life demands equals his cultural civilization.

The earliest human cultures arose along the rivers of the Eastern Hemisphere, and there were four great steps in the forward march of civilization. They were:

1. *The collection stage.* Food coercion, hunger, led to the first form of industrial organization, the primitive food-gathering lines. Sometimes such a line of hunger march would be ten miles long as it passed over the land gleaning food. This was the primitive nomadic stage of culture and is the mode of life now followed by the African Bushmen.

2. *The hunting stage.* The invention of weapon tools enabled man to become a hunter and thus to gain considerable freedom from food slavery. A thoughtful Andonite who had severely bruised his fist in a serious combat rediscovered the idea of using a long stick for his arm and a piece of hard flint, bound on the end with sinews, for his fist. Many tribes made independent discoveries of this sort, and these various forms of hammers represented one of the great forward steps in human civilization. Today some Australian natives have progressed little beyond this stage.

The blue men became expert hunters and trappers; by fencing the rivers they caught fish in great numbers, drying the surplus for winter use. Many forms of ingenious snares and traps were employed in catching game, but the more primitive races did not hunt the larger animals.

3. *The pastoral stage.* This phase of civilization was made possible by the domestication of animals. The Arabs and the natives of Africa are among the more recent pastoral peoples.

Pastoral living afforded further relief from food slavery; man learned to live on the interest of his capital, the increase in his flocks; and this provided more leisure for culture and progress.

Prepastoral society was one of sex co-operation, but the spread of animal husbandry reduced women to the depths of social slavery. In earlier times it was man's duty to secure the animal food, woman's business to provide the vegetable edibles. Therefore, when man entered the pastoral era of his existence, woman's dignity fell greatly. She must still toil to produce the vegetable necessities of life, whereas the man need only go to his herds to provide an abundance of animal food. Man thus became relatively independent of woman; throughout the entire pastoral age woman's status steadily declined. By the close of this era she had become scarcely more than a human animal, consigned to work and to bear human offspring, much as the animals of the herd were expected to labor and bring forth young. The men of the pastoral ages had great love for their cattle; all the more pity they could not have developed a deeper affection for their wives.

4. *The agricultural stage.* This era was brought about by the domestication of plants, and it represents the highest type of material civilization. Both Caligastia and Adam endeavored to teach horticulture and agriculture. Adam and Eve were gardeners, not shepherds, and gardening was an advanced culture in those days. The growing of plants exerts an ennobling influence on all races of mankind.

Agriculture more than quadrupled the land-man ratio of the world. It may be combined with the pastoral pursuits of the former cultural stage. When the three stages overlap, men hunt and women till the soil.

There has always been friction between the herders and the tillers of the soil. The hunter and herder were militant, warlike; the agriculturist is a more peace-loving type. Association with animals suggests struggle and force; association with plants instills patience, quiet, and peace. Agriculture and industrialism are the activities of peace. But the weakness of both, as world social activities, is that they lack excitement and adventure.

Human society has evolved from the hunting stage through that of the herders to the territorial stage of agriculture. And each stage of this progressive civilization was accompanied by less and less of nomadism; more and more man began to live at home.

And now is industry supplementing agriculture, with consequently increased urbanization and multiplication of nonagricultural groups of citizenship classes. But an industrial era cannot hope to survive if its leaders fail to recognize that even the highest social developments must ever rest upon a sound agricultural basis.

6. EVOLUTION OF CULTURE

Man is a creature of the soil, a child of nature; no matter how earnestly he may try to escape from the land, in the last reckoning he is certain to fail. "Dust you are and to dust shall you return" is literally true of all mankind. The basic struggle of man was, and is, and ever shall be, for land. The first social associations of primitive human beings were for the purpose of winning these land struggles. The land-man ratio underlies all social civilization.

Man's intelligence, by means of the arts and sciences, increased the land yield; at the same time the natural increase in offspring was somewhat brought under control, and thus was provided the sustenance and leisure to build a cultural civilization.

Human society is controlled by a law which decrees that the population must vary directly in accordance with the land arts and inversely with a given standard of living. Throughout these early ages, even more than at present, the law of supply and demand as concerned men and land determined the estimated value of both. During the times of plentiful land—unoccupied territory—the need for men was great, and therefore the value of human life was much enhanced; hence the loss of life was more horrifying. During periods of land scarcity and associated overpopulation, human life became comparatively cheapened so that war, famine, and pestilence were regarded with less concern.

When the land yield is reduced or the population is increased, the inevitable struggle is renewed; the very worst traits of human nature are brought to the surface. The improvement of the land yield, the extension of the mechanical arts, and the reduction of population all tend to foster the development of the better side of human nature.

Frontier society develops the unskilled side of humanity; the fine arts and true scientific progress, together with spiritual culture, have all thrived best in the larger centers of life when supported by an agricultural and industrial population slightly under the land-man ratio. Cities always multiply the power of their inhabitants for either good or evil.

The size of the family has always been influenced by the standards of living. The higher the standard the smaller the family, up to the point of established status or gradual extinction.

All down through the ages the standards of living have determined the quality of a surviving population in contrast with mere quantity. Local class standards of living give origin to new social castes, new mores. When standards of living become too complicated or too highly luxurious, they speedily become suicidal. Caste is the direct result of the high social pressure of keen competition produced by dense populations.

The early races often resorted to practices designed to restrict population; all primitive tribes killed deformed and sickly children. Girl babies were frequently killed before the times of wife purchase. Children were sometimes strangled at birth, but the favorite method was exposure. The father of twins usually insisted that one be killed since multiple births were believed to be caused either by magic or by infidelity. As a rule, however, twins of the same sex were spared. While these taboos on twins were once well-nigh universal, they were never a part of the Andonite mores; these peoples always regarded twins as omens of good luck.

Many races learned the technique of abortion, and this practice became very common after the establishment of the taboo on childbirth among the unmarried. It was long the custom for a maiden to kill her offspring, but among more civilized groups these illegitimate children became the wards of the girl's mother. Many primitive clans were virtually exterminated by the practice of both abortion and infanticide. But regardless of the dictates of the mores, very few children were ever destroyed after having once been suckled—maternal affection is too strong.

Even in the twentieth century there persist remnants of these primitive population controls. There is a tribe in Australia whose mothers refuse to rear more than two or three children. Not long since, one cannibalistic tribe ate every fifth child born. In Madagascar some tribes still destroy all children born on certain unlucky days, resulting in the death of about twenty-five per cent of all babies.

From a world standpoint, overpopulation has never been a serious problem in the past, but if war is lessened and science increasingly controls human diseases, it may become a serious problem in the near future. At such a time the great test of the wisdom of world leadership will present itself. Will Urantia rulers have the insight and courage to foster the multiplication of the average or stabilized human being instead of the extremes of the supernormal and the enormously increasing groups of the subnormal? The normal man should be fostered; he is the backbone of civilization and the source of the mutant geniuses of the race. The subnormal man should be kept under society's control; no more should be produced than are required to administer the lower levels of industry, those tasks requiring intelligence above the animal level but making such low-grade demands as to prove veritable slavery and bondage for the higher types of mankind.

[Presented by a Melchizedek sometime stationed on Urantia.]

PAPER 69
PRIMITIVE HUMAN INSTITUTIONS

EMOTIONALLY, man transcends his animal ancestors in his ability to appreciate humor, art, and religion. Socially, man exhibits his superiority in that he is a toolmaker, a communicator, and an institution builder.

When human beings long maintain social groups, such aggregations always result in the creation of certain activity trends which culminate in institutionalization. Most of man's institutions have proved to be laborsaving while at the same time contributing something to the enhancement of group security.

Civilized man takes great pride in the character, stability, and continuity of his established institutions, but all human institutions are merely the accumulated mores of the past as they have been conserved by taboos and dignified by religion. Such legacies become traditions, and traditions ultimately metamorphose into conventions.

1. BASIC HUMAN INSTITUTIONS

All human institutions minister to some social need, past or present, notwithstanding that their overdevelopment unfailingly detracts from the worthwhileness of the individual in that personality is overshadowed and initiative is diminished. Man should control his institutions rather than permit himself to be dominated by these creations of advancing civilization.

Human institutions are of three general classes:

1. *The institutions of self-maintenance.* These institutions embrace those practices growing out of food hunger and its associated instincts of self-preservation. They include industry, property, war for gain, and all the regulative machinery of society. Sooner or later the fear instinct fosters the establishment of these institutions of survival by means of taboo, convention, and religious sanction. But fear, ignorance, and superstition have played a prominent part in the early origin and subsequent development of all human institutions.

2. *The institutions of self-perpetuation.* These are the establishments of society growing out of sex hunger, maternal instinct, and the higher tender emotions of the races. They embrace the social safeguards of the home and the school, of family life, education, ethics, and religion. They include marriage customs, war for defense, and home building.

3. *The institutions of self-gratification.* These are the practices growing out of vanity proclivities and pride emotions; and they embrace customs in dress and personal adornment, social usages, war for glory, dancing, amusement, games, and other phases of sensual gratification. But civilization has never evolved distinctive institutions of self-gratification.

These three groups of social practices are intimately interrelated and minutely interdependent the one upon the other. On Urantia they represent a complex organization which functions as a single social mechanism.

2. THE DAWN OF INDUSTRY

Primitive industry slowly grew up as an insurance against the terrors of famine. Early in his existence man began to draw lessons from some of the animals that, during a harvest of plenty, store up food against the days of scarcity.

Before the dawn of early frugality and primitive industry the lot of the average tribe was one of destitution and real suffering. Early man had to compete with the whole animal world for his food. Competition-gravity ever pulls man down toward the beast level; poverty is his natural and tyrannical estate. Wealth is not a natural gift; it results from labor, knowledge, and organization.

Primitive man was not slow to recognize the advantages of association. Association led to organization, and the first result of organization was division of labor, with its immediate saving of time and materials. These specializations of labor arose by adaptation to pressure—pursuing the paths of lessened resistance. Primitive savages never did any real work cheerfully or willingly. With them conformity was due to the coercion of necessity.

Primitive man disliked hard work, and he would not hurry unless confronted by grave danger. The time element in labor, the idea of doing a given task within a certain time limit, is entirely a modern notion. The ancients were never rushed. It was the double demands of the intense struggle for existence and of the ever-advancing standards of living that drove the naturally inactive races of early man into avenues of industry.

Labor, the efforts of design, distinguishes man from the beast, whose exertions are largely instinctive. The necessity for labor is man's paramount blessing. The Prince's staff all worked; they did much to ennoble physical labor on Urantia. Adam was a gardener; the God of the Hebrews labored—he was the creator and upholder of all things. The Hebrews were the first tribe to put a supreme premium on industry; they were the first people to decree that "he who does not work shall not eat." But many of the religions of the world reverted to the early ideal of idleness. Jupiter was a reveler, and Buddha became a reflective devotee of leisure.

The Sangik tribes were fairly industrious when residing away from the tropics. But there was a long, long struggle between the lazy devotees of magic and the apostles of work—those who exercised foresight.

The first human foresight was directed toward the preservation of fire, water, and food. But primitive man was a natural-born gambler; he always wanted to get something for nothing, and all too often during these early times the success which accrued from patient practice was attributed to charms. Magic was slow to give way before foresight, self-denial, and industry.

3. THE SPECIALIZATION OF LABOR

The divisions of labor in primitive society were determined first by natural, and then by social, circumstances. The early order of specialization in labor was:

1. *Specialization based on sex.* Woman's work was derived from the selective presence of the child; women naturally love babies more than men do. Thus woman became the routine worker, while man became the hunter and fighter, engaging in accentuated periods of work and rest.

All down through the ages the taboos have operated to keep woman strictly in her own field. Man has most selfishly chosen the more agreeable work, leaving the routine drudgery to woman. Man has always been ashamed to do woman's work, but woman has never shown any reluctance to doing man's work. But strange to record, both men and women have always worked together in building and furnishing the home.

2. *Modification consequent upon age and disease.* These differences determined the next division of labor. The old men and cripples were early set to work making tools and weapons. They were later assigned to building irrigation works.

3. *Differentiation based on religion.* The medicine men were the first human beings to be exempted from physical toil; they were the pioneer professional class. The smiths were a small group who competed with the medicine men as magicians. Their skill in working with metals made the people afraid of them. The "white smiths" and the "black smiths" gave origin to the early beliefs in white and black magic. And this belief later became involved in the superstition of good and bad ghosts, good and bad spirits.

Smiths were the first nonreligious group to enjoy special privileges. They were regarded as neutrals during war, and this extra leisure led to their becoming, as a class, the politicians of primitive society. But through gross abuse of these privileges the smiths became universally hated, and the medicine men lost no time in fostering hatred for their competitors. In this first contest between science and religion, religion (superstition) won. After being driven out of the villages, the smiths maintained the first inns, public lodginghouses, on the outskirts of the settlements.

4. *Master and slave.* The next differentiation of labor grew out of the relations of the conqueror to the conquered, and that meant the beginning of human slavery.

5. *Differentiation based on diverse physical and mental endowments.* Further divisions of labor were favored by the inherent differences in men; all human beings are not born equal.

The early specialists in industry were the flint flakers and stone masons; next came the smiths. Subsequently group specialization developed; whole families and clans dedicated themselves to certain sorts of labor. The origin of one of the earliest castes of priests, apart from the tribal medicine men, was due to the superstitious exaltation of a family of expert swordmakers.

The first group specialists in industry were rock salt exporters and potters. Women made the plain pottery and men the fancy. Among some tribes sewing and weaving were done by women, in others by the men.

The early traders were women; they were employed as spies, carrying on commerce as a side line. Presently trade expanded, the women acting as intermediaries—jobbers. Then came the merchant class, charging a commission, profit, for their services. Growth of group barter developed into commerce; and following the exchange of commodities came the exchange of skilled labor.

4. THE BEGINNINGS OF TRADE

Just as marriage by contract followed marriage by capture, so trade by barter followed seizure by raids. But a long period of piracy intervened between the early practices of silent barter and the later trade by modern exchange methods.

The first barter was conducted by armed traders who would leave their goods on a neutral spot. Women held the first markets; they were the earliest traders, and this was because they were the burden bearers; the men were warriors. Very early the trading counter was developed, a wall wide enough to prevent the traders reaching each other with weapons.

A fetish was used to stand guard over the deposits of goods for silent barter. Such market places were secure against theft; nothing would be removed except by barter or purchase; with a fetish on guard the goods were always safe. The early traders were scrupulously honest within their own tribes but regarded it as all right to cheat distant strangers. Even the early Hebrews recognized a separate code of ethics in their dealings with the gentiles.

For ages silent barter continued before men would meet, unarmed, on the sacred market place. These same market squares became the first places of sanctuary and in some countries were later known as "cities of refuge." Any fugitive reaching the market place was safe and secure against attack.

The first weights were grains of wheat and other cereals. The first medium of exchange was a fish or a goat. Later the cow became a unit of barter.

Modern writing originated in the early trade records; the first literature of man was a trade-promotion document, a salt advertisement. Many of the earlier wars were fought over natural deposits, such as flint, salt, and metals. The first formal tribal treaty concerned the intertribalizing of a salt deposit. These treaty spots afforded opportunity for friendly and peaceful interchange of ideas and the intermingling of various tribes.

Writing progressed up through the stages of the "message stick," knotted cords, picture writing, hieroglyphics, and wampum belts, to the early symbolic alphabets. Message sending evolved from the primitive smoke signal up through runners, animal riders, railroads, and airplanes, as well as telegraph, telephone, and wireless communication.

New ideas and better methods were carried around the inhabited world by the ancient traders. Commerce, linked with adventure, led to exploration and discovery. And all of these gave birth to transportation. Commerce has been the great civilizer through promoting the cross-fertilization of culture.

5. THE BEGINNINGS OF CAPITAL

Capital is labor applied as a renunciation of the present in favor of the future. Savings represent a form of maintenance and survival insurance. Food hoarding developed self-control and created the first problems of capital and labor. The man who had food, provided he could protect it from robbers, had a distinct advantage over the man who had no food.

The early banker was the valorous man of the tribe. He held the group treasures on deposit, while the entire clan would defend his hut in event of attack. Thus the accumulation of individual capital and group wealth immediately led to military organization. At first such precautions were designed to defend property against foreign raiders, but later on it became the custom to keep the military organization in practice by inaugurating raids on the property and wealth of neighboring tribes.

The basic urges which led to the accumulation of capital were:

1. *Hunger—associated with foresight.* Food saving and preservation meant power and comfort for those who possessed sufficient *foresight* thus to provide for future needs. Food storage was adequate insurance against famine and disaster. And the entire body of primitive mores was really designed to help man subordinate the present to the future.

2. *Love of family*—desire to provide for their wants. Capital represents the saving of property in spite of the pressure of the wants of today in order to insure against the demands of the future. A part of this future need may have to do with one's posterity.

3. *Vanity*—longing to display one's property accumulations. Extra clothing was one of the first badges of distinction. Collection vanity early appealed to the pride of man.

4. *Position*—eagerness to buy social and political prestige. There early sprang up a commercialized nobility, admission to which depended on the performance of some special service to royalty or was granted frankly for the payment of money.

5. *Power*—the craving to be master. Treasure lending was carried on as a means of enslavement, one hundred per cent a year being the loan rate of these ancient times. The moneylenders made themselves kings by creating a standing army of debtors. Bond servants were among the earliest form of property to be accumulated, and in olden days debt slavery extended even to the control of the body after death.

6. *Fear of the ghosts of the dead*—priest fees for protection. Men early began to give death presents to the priests with a view to having their property used to facilitate their progress through the next life. The priesthoods thus became very rich; they were chief among ancient capitalists.

7. *Sex urge*—the desire to buy one or more wives. Man's first form of trading was woman exchange; it long preceded horse trading. But never did the barter in sex slaves advance society; such traffic was and is a racial disgrace, for at one and the same time it hindered the development of family life and polluted the biologic fitness of superior peoples.

8. *Numerous forms of self-gratification.* Some sought wealth because it conferred power; others toiled for property because it meant ease. Early man (and some later-day ones) tended to squander his resources on luxury. Intoxicants and drugs intrigued the primitive races.

As civilization developed, men acquired new incentives for saving; new wants were rapidly added to the original food hunger. Poverty became so abhorred that only the rich were supposed to go direct to heaven when they died. Property became so highly valued that to give a pretentious feast would wipe a dishonor from one's name.

Accumulations of wealth early became the badge of social distinction. Individuals in certain tribes would accumulate property for years just to create an impression by burning it up on some holiday or by freely distributing it to fellow tribesmen. This made them great men. Even modern peoples revel in the lavish distribution of Christmas gifts, while rich men endow great institutions of philanthropy and learning. Man's technique varies, but his disposition remains quite unchanged.

But it is only fair to record that many an ancient rich man distributed much of his fortune because of the fear of being killed by those who coveted his treasures. Wealthy men commonly sacrificed scores of slaves to show disdain for wealth.

Though capital has tended to liberate man, it has greatly complicated his social and industrial organization. The abuse of capital by unfair capitalists does not destroy the fact that it is the basis of modern industrial society. Through capital and invention the present generation enjoys a higher degree of freedom than any that ever preceded it on earth. This is placed on record as a fact and not in justification of the many misuses of capital by thoughtless and selfish custodians.

6. FIRE IN RELATION TO CIVILIZATION

Primitive society with its four divisions—industrial, regulative, religious, and military—rose through the instrumentality of fire, animals, slaves, and property.

Fire building, by a single bound, forever separated man from animal; it is the basic human invention, or discovery. Fire enabled man to stay on the ground at night as all animals are afraid of it. Fire encouraged eventide social intercourse; it not only protected against cold and wild beasts but was also employed as security against ghosts. It was at first used more for light than heat; many backward tribes refuse to sleep unless a flame burns all night.

Fire was a great civilizer, providing man with his first means of being altruistic without loss by enabling him to give live coals to a neighbor without depriving himself. The household fire, which was attended by the mother or eldest daughter, was the first educator, requiring watchfulness and dependability. The early home was not a building but the family gathered about the fire, the family hearth. When a son founded a new home, he carried a firebrand from the family hearth.

Though Andon, the discoverer of fire, avoided treating it as an object of worship, many of his descendants regarded the flame as a fetish or as a spirit. They failed to reap the sanitary benefits of fire because they would not burn refuse. Primitive man feared fire and always sought to keep it in good humor, hence the sprinkling of incense. Under no circumstances would the ancients spit in a fire, nor would they ever pass between anyone and a burning fire. Even the iron pyrites and flints used in striking fire were held sacred by early mankind.

It was a sin to extinguish a flame; if a hut caught fire, it was allowed to burn. The fires of the temples and shrines were sacred and were never permitted to go out except that it was the custom to kindle new flames annually or after some calamity. Women were selected as priests because they were custodians of the home fires.

The early myths about how fire came down from the gods grew out of the observations of fire caused by lightning. These ideas of supernatural origin led directly to fire worship, and fire worship led to the custom of "passing through fire," a practice carried on up to the times of Moses. And there still persists the idea of passing through fire after death. The fire myth was a great bond in early times and still persists in the symbolism of the Parsees.

Fire led to cooking, and "raw eaters" became a term of derision. And cooking lessened the expenditure of vital energy necessary for the digestion of food and so left early man some strength for social culture, while animal husbandry, by reducing the effort necessary to secure food, provided time for social activities.

It should be remembered that fire opened the doors to metalwork and led to the subsequent discovery of steam power and the present-day uses of electricity.

7. THE UTILIZATION OF ANIMALS

To start with, the entire animal world was man's enemy; human beings had to learn to protect themselves from the beasts. First, man ate the animals but later learned to domesticate and make them serve him.

The domestication of animals came about accidentally. The savage would hunt herds much as the American Indians hunted the bison. By surrounding the herd they could keep control of the animals, thus being able to kill them as they were required for food. Later, corrals were constructed, and entire herds would be captured.

It was easy to tame some animals, but like the elephant, many of them would not reproduce in captivity. Still further on it was discovered that certain species of animals would submit to man's presence, and that they would reproduce in captivity. The domestication of animals was thus promoted by selective breeding, an art which has made great progress since the days of Dalamatia.

The dog was the first animal to be domesticated, and the difficult experience of taming it began when a certain dog, after following a hunter around all day, actually went home with him. For ages dogs were used for food, hunting, transportation, and companionship. At first dogs only howled, but later on they learned to bark. The dog's keen sense of smell led to the notion it could see spirits, and thus arose the dog-fetish cults. The employment of watchdogs made it first possible for the whole clan to sleep at night. It then became the custom to employ watchdogs to protect the home against spirits as well as material enemies. When the dog barked, man or beast approached, but when the dog howled, spirits were near. Even now many still believe that a dog's howling at night betokens death.

When man was a hunter, he was fairly kind to woman, but after the domestication of animals, coupled with the Caligastia confusion, many tribes shamefully treated their women. They treated them altogether too much as they treated their animals. Man's brutal treatment of woman constitutes one of the darkest chapters of human history.

8. SLAVERY AS A FACTOR IN CIVILIZATION

Primitive man never hesitated to enslave his fellows. Woman was the first slave, a family slave. Pastoral man enslaved woman as his inferior sex partner.

This sort of sex slavery grew directly out of man's decreased dependence upon woman.

Not long ago enslavement was the lot of those military captives who refused to accept the conqueror's religion. In earlier times captives were either eaten, tortured to death, set to fighting each other, sacrificed to spirits, or enslaved. Slavery was a great advancement over massacre and cannibalism.

Enslavement was a forward step in the merciful treatment of war captives. The ambush of Ai, with the wholesale slaughter of men, women, and children, only the king being saved to gratify the conqueror's vanity, is a faithful picture of the barbaric slaughter practiced by even supposedly civilized peoples. The raid upon Og, the king of Bashan, was equally brutal and effective. The Hebrews "utterly destroyed" their enemies, taking all their property as spoils. They put all cities under tribute on pain of the "destruction of all males." But many of the contemporary tribes, those having less tribal egotism, had long since begun to practice the adoption of superior captives.

The hunter, like the American red man, did not enslave. He either adopted or killed his captives. Slavery was not prevalent among the pastoral peoples, for they needed few laborers. In war the herders made a practice of killing all men captives and taking as slaves only the women and children. The Mosaic code contained specific directions for making wives of these women captives. If not satisfactory, they could be sent away, but the Hebrews were not allowed to sell such rejected consorts as slaves—that was at least one advance in civilization. Though the social standards of the Hebrews were crude, they were far above those of the surrounding tribes.

The herders were the first capitalists; their herds represented capital, and they lived on the interest—the natural increase. And they were disinclined to trust this wealth to the keeping of either slaves or women. But later on they took male prisoners and forced them to cultivate the soil. This is the early origin of serfdom—man attached to the land. The Africans could easily be taught to till the soil; hence they became the great slave race.

Slavery was an indispensable link in the chain of human civilization. It was the bridge over which society passed from chaos and indolence to order and civilized activities; it compelled backward and lazy peoples to work and thus provide wealth and leisure for the social advancement of their superiors.

The institution of slavery compelled man to invent the regulative mechanism of primitive society; it gave origin to the beginnings of government. Slavery demands strong regulation and during the European Middle Ages virtually disappeared because the feudal lords could not control the slaves. The backward tribes of ancient times, like the native Australians of today, never had slaves.

True, slavery was oppressive, but it was in the schools of oppression that man learned industry. Eventually the slaves shared the blessings of a higher society which they had so unwillingly helped create. Slavery creates an organization of culture and social achievement but soon insidiously attacks society internally as the gravest of all destructive social maladies.

Modern mechanical invention rendered the slave obsolete. Slavery, like polygamy, is passing because it does not pay. But it has always proved disastrous suddenly to liberate great numbers of slaves; less trouble ensues when they are gradually emancipated.

Today, men are not social slaves, but thousands allow ambition to enslave them to debt. Involuntary slavery has given way to a new and improved form of modified industrial servitude.

While the ideal of society is universal freedom, idleness should never be tolerated. All able-bodied persons should be compelled to do at least a self-sustaining amount of work.

Modern society is in reverse. Slavery has nearly disappeared; domesticated animals are passing. Civilization is reaching back to fire—the inorganic world—for power. Man came up from savagery by way of fire, animals, and slavery; today he reaches back, discarding the help of slaves and the assistance of animals, while he seeks to wrest new secrets and sources of wealth and power from the elemental storehouse of nature.

9. PRIVATE PROPERTY

While primitive society was virtually communal, primitive man did not adhere to the modern doctrines of communism. The communism of these early times was not a mere theory or social doctrine; it was a simple and practical automatic adjustment. Communism prevented pauperism and want; begging and prostitution were almost unknown among these ancient tribes.

Primitive communism did not especially level men down, nor did it exalt mediocrity, but it did put a premium on inactivity and idleness, and it did stifle industry and destroy ambition. Communism was indispensable scaffolding in the growth of primitive society, but it gave way to the evolution of a higher social order because it ran counter to four strong human proclivities:

1. *The family.* Man not only craves to accumulate property; he desires to bequeath his capital goods to his progeny. But in early communal society a man's capital was either immediately consumed or distributed among the group at his death. There was no inheritance of property—the inheritance tax was one hundred per cent. The later capital-accumulation and property-inheritance mores were a distinct social advance. And this is true notwithstanding the subsequent gross abuses attendant upon the misuse of capital.

2. *Religious tendencies.* Primitive man also wanted to save up property as a nucleus for starting life in the next existence. This motive explains why it was so long the custom to bury a man's personal belongings with him. The ancients believed that only the rich survived death with any immediate pleasure and dignity. The teachers of revealed religion, more especially the Christian teachers, were the first to proclaim that the poor could have salvation on equal terms with the rich.

3. *The desire for liberty and leisure.* In the earlier days of social evolution the apportionment of individual earnings among the group was virtually a form of slavery; the worker was made slave to the idler. This was the suicidal weakness of communism: The improvident habitually lived off the thrifty. Even in modern times the improvident depend on the state (thrifty taxpayers) to take care of them. Those who have no capital still expect those who have to feed them.

4. *The urge for security and power.* Communism was finally destroyed by the deceptive practices of progressive and successful individuals who resorted to

diverse subterfuges in an effort to escape enslavement to the shiftless idlers of their tribes. But at first all hoarding was secret; primitive insecurity prevented the outward accumulation of capital. And even at a later time it was most dangerous to amass too much wealth; the king would be sure to trump up some charge for confiscating a rich man's property, and when a wealthy man died, the funeral was held up until the family donated a large sum to public welfare or to the king, an inheritance tax.

In earliest times women were the property of the community, and the mother dominated the family. The early chiefs owned all the land and were proprietors of all the women; marriage required the consent of the tribal ruler. With the passing of communism, women were held individually, and the father gradually assumed domestic control. Thus the home had its beginning, and the prevailing polygamous customs were gradually displaced by monogamy. (Polygamy is the survival of the female-slavery element in marriage. Monogamy is the slave-free ideal of the matchless association of one man and one woman in the exquisite enterprise of home building, offspring rearing, mutual culture, and self-improvement.)

At first, all property, including tools and weapons, was the common possession of the tribe. Private property first consisted of all things personally touched. If a stranger drank from a cup, the cup was henceforth his. Next, any place where blood was shed became the property of the injured person or group.

Private property was thus originally respected because it was supposed to be charged with some part of the owner's personality. Property honesty rested safely on this type of superstition; no police were needed to guard personal belongings. There was no stealing within the group, though men did not hesitate to appropriate the goods of other tribes. Property relations did not end with death; early, personal effects were burned, then buried with the dead, and later, inherited by the surviving family or by the tribe.

The ornamental type of personal effects originated in the wearing of charms. Vanity plus ghost fear led early man to resist all attempts to relieve him of his favorite charms, such property being valued above necessities.

Sleeping space was one of man's earliest properties. Later, homesites were assigned by the tribal chiefs, who held all real estate in trust for the group. Presently a fire site conferred ownership; and still later, a well constituted title to the adjacent land.

Water holes and wells were among the first private possessions. The whole fetish practice was utilized to guard water holes, wells, trees, crops, and honey. Following the loss of faith in the fetish, laws were evolved to protect private belongings. But game laws, the right to hunt, long preceded land laws. The American red man never understood private ownership of land; he could not comprehend the white man's view.

Private property was early marked by family insignia, and this is the early origin of family crests. Real estate could also be put under the watchcare of spirits. The priests would "consecrate" a piece of land, and it would then rest under the protection of the magic taboos erected thereon. Owners thereof were said to have a "priest's title." The Hebrews had great respect for these family landmarks: "Cursed be he who removes his neighbor's landmark." These stone markers bore the priest's initials. Even trees, when initialed, became private property.

In early days only the crops were private, but successive crops conferred title; agriculture was thus the genesis of the private ownership of land. Individuals were first given only a life tenureship; at death land reverted to the tribe. The very first land titles granted by tribes to individuals were graves—family burying grounds. In later times land belonged to those who fenced it. But the cities always reserved certain lands for public pasturage and for use in case of siege; these "commons" represent the survival of the earlier form of collective ownership.

Eventually the state assigned property to the individual, reserving the right of taxation. Having made secure their titles, landlords could collect rents, and land became a source of income—capital. Finally land became truly negotiable, with sales, transfers, mortgages, and foreclosures.

Private ownership brought increased liberty and enhanced stability; but private ownership of land was given social sanction only after communal control and direction had failed, and it was soon followed by a succession of slaves, serfs, and landless classes. But improved machinery is gradually setting men free from slavish toil.

The right to property is not absolute; it is purely social. But all government, law, order, civil rights, social liberties, conventions, peace, and happiness, as they are enjoyed by modern peoples, have grown up around the private ownership of property.

The present social order is not necessarily right—not divine or sacred—but mankind will do well to move slowly in making changes. That which you have is vastly better than any system known to your ancestors. Make certain that when you change the social order you change for the better. Do not be persuaded to experiment with the discarded formulas of your forefathers. Go forward, not backward! Let evolution proceed! Do not take a backward step.

[Presented by a Melchizedek of Nebadon.]

PAPER 70

THE EVOLUTION OF HUMAN GOVERNMENT

NO SOONER had man partially solved the problem of making a living than he was confronted with the task of regulating human contacts. The development of industry demanded law, order, and social adjustment; private property necessitated government.

On an evolutionary world, antagonisms are natural; peace is secured only by some sort of social regulative system. Social regulation is inseparable from social organization; association implies some controlling authority. Government compels the co-ordination of the antagonisms of the tribes, clans, families, and individuals.

Government is an unconscious development; it evolves by trial and error. It does have survival value; therefore it becomes traditional. Anarchy augmented misery; therefore government, comparative law and order, slowly emerged or is emerging. The coercive demands of the struggle for existence literally drove the human race along the progressive road to civilization.

1. THE GENESIS OF WAR

War is the natural state and heritage of evolving man; peace is the social yardstick measuring civilization's advancement. Before the partial socialization of the advancing races man was exceedingly individualistic, extremely suspicious, and unbelievably quarrelsome. Violence is the law of nature, hostility the automatic reaction of the children of nature, while war is but these same activities carried on collectively. And wherever and whenever the fabric of civilization becomes stressed by the complications of society's advancement, there is always an immediate and ruinous reversion to these early methods of violent adjustment of the irritations of human interassociations.

War is an animalistic reaction to misunderstandings and irritations; peace attends upon the civilized solution of all such problems and difficulties. The Sangik races, together with the later deteriorated Adamites and Nodites, were all belligerent. The Andonites were early taught the golden rule, and, even today, their Eskimo descendants live very much by that code; custom is strong among them, and they are fairly free from violent antagonisms.

Andon taught his children to settle disputes by each beating a tree with a stick, meanwhile cursing the tree; the one whose stick broke first was the victor. The later Andonites used to settle disputes by holding a public show at which the disputants made fun of and ridiculed each other, while the audience decided the winner by its applause.

But there could be no such phenomenon as war until society had evolved sufficiently far to actually experience periods of peace and to sanction warlike practices. The very concept of war implies some degree of organization.

With the emergence of social groupings, individual irritations began to be submerged in the group feelings, and this promoted intratribal tranquillity but at the expense of intertribal peace. Peace was thus first enjoyed by the in-group, or tribe, who always disliked and hated the out-group, foreigners. Early man regarded it a virtue to shed alien blood.

But even this did not work at first. When the early chiefs would try to iron out misunderstandings, they often found it necessary, at least once a year, to permit the tribal stone fights. The clan would divide up into two groups and engage in an all-day battle. And this for no other reason than just the fun of it; they really enjoyed fighting.

Warfare persists because man is human, evolved from an animal, and all animals are bellicose. Among the early causes of war were:

1. *Hunger,* which led to food raids. Scarcity of land has always brought on war, and during these struggles the early peace tribes were practically exterminated.

2. *Woman scarcity*—an attempt to relieve a shortage of domestic help. Woman stealing has always caused war.

3. *Vanity*—the desire to exhibit tribal prowess. Superior groups would fight to impose their mode of life upon inferior peoples.

4. *Slaves*—need of recruits for the labor ranks.

5. *Revenge* was the motive for war when one tribe believed that a neighboring tribe had caused the death of a fellow tribesman. Mourning was continued until a head was brought home. The war for vengeance was in good standing right on down to comparatively modern times.

6. *Recreation*—war was looked upon as recreation by the young men of these early times. If no good and sufficient pretext for war arose, when peace became oppressive, neighboring tribes were accustomed to go out in semifriendly combat to engage in a foray as a holiday, to enjoy a sham battle.

7. *Religion*—the desire to make converts to the cult. The primitive religions all sanctioned war. Only in recent times has religion begun to frown upon war. The early priesthoods were, unfortunately, usually allied with the military power. One of the great peace moves of the ages has been the attempt to separate church and state.

Always these olden tribes made war at the bidding of their gods, at the behest of their chiefs or medicine men. The Hebrews believed in such a "God of battles"; and the narrative of their raid on the Midianites is a typical recital of the atrocious cruelty of the ancient tribal wars; this assault, with its slaughter of all the males and the later killing of all male children and all women who were not virgins, would have done honor to the mores of a tribal chieftain of two hundred thousand years ago. And all this was executed in the "name of the Lord God of Israel."

This is a narrative of the evolution of society—the natural outworking of the problems of the races—man working out his own destiny on earth. Such atrocities are not instigated by Deity, notwithstanding the tendency of man to place the responsibility on his gods.

Military mercy has been slow in coming to mankind. Even when a woman, Deborah, ruled the Hebrews, the same wholesale cruelty persisted. Her general in his victory over the gentiles caused "all the host to fall upon the sword; there was not one left."

Very early in the history of the race, poisoned weapons were used. All sorts of mutilations were practiced. Saul did not hesitate to require one hundred Philistine foreskins as the dowry David should pay for his daughter Michal.

Early wars were fought between tribes as a whole, but in later times, when two individuals in different tribes had a dispute, instead of both tribes fighting, the two disputants engaged in a duel. It also became a custom for two armies to stake all on the outcome of a contest between a representative chosen from each side, as in the instance of David and Goliath.

The first refinement of war was the taking of prisoners. Next, women were exempted from hostilities, and then came the recognition of noncombatants. Military castes and standing armies soon developed to keep pace with the increasing complexity of combat. Such warriors were early prohibited from associating with women, and women long ago ceased to fight, though they have always fed and nursed the soldiers and urged them on to battle.

The practice of declaring war represented great progress. Such declarations of intention to fight betokened the arrival of a sense of fairness, and this was followed by the gradual development of the rules of "civilized" warfare. Very early it became the custom not to fight near religious sites and, still later, not to fight on certain holy days. Next came the general recognition of the right of asylum; political fugitives received protection.

Thus did warfare gradually evolve from the primitive man hunt to the somewhat more orderly system of the later-day "civilized" nations. But only slowly does the social attitude of amity displace that of enmity.

2. THE SOCIAL VALUE OF WAR

In past ages a fierce war would institute social changes and facilitate the adoption of new ideas such as would not have occurred naturally in ten thousand years. The terrible price paid for these certain war advantages was that society was temporarily thrown back into savagery; civilized reason had to abdicate. War is strong medicine, very costly and most dangerous; while often curative of certain social disorders, it sometimes kills the patient, destroys the society.

The constant necessity for national defense creates many new and advanced social adjustments. Society, today, enjoys the benefit of a long list of useful innovations which were at first wholly military and is even indebted to war for the dance, one of the early forms of which was a military drill.

War has had a social value to past civilizations because it:

1. Imposed discipline, enforced co-operation.

2. Put a premium on fortitude and courage.

3. Fostered and solidified nationalism.

4. Destroyed weak and unfit peoples.

5. Dissolved the illusion of primitive equality and selectively stratified society.

War has had a certain evolutionary and selective value, but like slavery, it must sometime be abandoned as civilization slowly advances. Olden wars promoted travel and cultural intercourse; these ends are now better served by modern methods of transport and communication. Olden wars strengthened nations, but modern struggles disrupt civilized culture. Ancient warfare resulted in the decimation of inferior peoples; the net result of modern conflict is the selective destruction of the best human stocks. Early wars promoted organization and efficiency, but these have now become the aims of modern industry. During past ages war was a social ferment which pushed civilization forward; this result is now better attained by ambition and invention. Ancient warfare supported the concept of a God of battles, but modern man has been told that God is love. War has served many valuable purposes in the past, it has been an indispensable scaffolding in the building of civilization, but it is rapidly becoming culturally bankrupt—incapable of producing dividends of social gain in any way commensurate with the terrible losses attendant upon its invocation.

At one time physicians believed in bloodletting as a cure for many diseases, but they have since discovered better remedies for most of these disorders. And so must the international bloodletting of war certainly give place to the discovery of better methods for curing the ills of nations.

The nations of Urantia have already entered upon the gigantic struggle between nationalistic militarism and industrialism, and in many ways this conflict is analogous to the agelong struggle between the herder-hunter and the farmer. But if industrialism is to triumph over militarism, it must avoid the dangers which beset it. The perils of budding industry on Urantia are:

1. The strong drift toward materialism, spiritual blindness.
2. The worship of wealth-power, value distortion.
3. The vices of luxury, cultural immaturity.
4. The increasing dangers of indolence, service insensitivity.
5. The growth of undesirable racial softness, biologic deterioration.
6. The threat of standardized industrial slavery, personality stagnation. Labor is ennobling but drudgery is benumbing.

Militarism is autocratic and cruel—savage. It promotes social organization among the conquerors but disintegrates the vanquished. Industrialism is more civilized and should be so carried on as to promote initiative and to encourage individualism. Society should in every way possible foster originality.

Do not make the mistake of glorifying war; rather discern what it has done for society so that you may the more accurately visualize what its substitutes must provide in order to continue the advancement of civilization. And if such adequate substitutes are not provided, then you may be sure that war will long continue.

Man will never accept peace as a normal mode of living until he has been thoroughly and repeatedly convinced that peace is best for his material welfare, and until society has wisely provided peaceful substitutes for the gratification of that inherent tendency periodically to let loose a collective drive designed to liberate those ever-accumulating emotions and energies belonging to the self-preservation reactions of the human species.

But even in passing, war should be honored as the school of experience which compelled a race of arrogant individualists to submit themselves to highly concentrated authority—a chief executive. Old-fashioned war did select the innately great men for leadership, but modern war no longer does this. To discover leaders society must now turn to the conquests of peace: industry, science, and social achievement.

3. EARLY HUMAN ASSOCIATIONS

In the most primitive society the *horde* is everything; even children are its common property. The evolving family displaced the horde in child rearing, while the emerging clans and tribes took its place as the social unit.

Sex hunger and mother love establish the family. But real government does not appear until superfamily groups have begun to form. In the prefamily days of the horde, leadership was provided by informally chosen individuals. The African Bushmen have never progressed beyond this primitive stage; they do not have chiefs in the horde.

Families became united by blood ties in clans, aggregations of kinsmen; and these subsequently evolved into tribes, territorial communities. Warfare and external pressure forced the tribal organization upon the kinship clans, but it was commerce and trade that held these early and primitive groups together with some degree of internal peace.

The peace of Urantia will be promoted far more by international trade organizations than by all the sentimental sophistry of visionary peace planning. Trade relations have been facilitated by development of language and by improved methods of communication as well as by better transportation.

The absence of a common language has always impeded the growth of peace groups, but money has become the universal language of modern trade. Modern society is largely held together by the industrial market. The gain motive is a mighty civilizer when augmented by the desire to serve.

In the early ages each tribe was surrounded by concentric circles of increasing fear and suspicion; hence it was once the custom to kill all strangers, later on, to enslave them. The old idea of friendship meant adoption into the clan; and clan membership was believed to survive death—one of the earliest concepts of eternal life.

The ceremony of adoption consisted in drinking each other's blood. In some groups saliva was exchanged in the place of blood drinking, this being the ancient origin of the practice of social kissing. And all ceremonies of association, whether marriage or adoption, were always terminated by feasting.

In later times, blood diluted with red wine was used, and eventually wine alone was drunk to seal the adoption ceremony, which was signified in the touching of the wine cups and consummated by the swallowing of the beverage. The Hebrews employed a modified form of this adoption ceremony. Their Arab ancestors made use of the oath taken while the hand of the candidate rested upon the generative organ of the tribal native. The Hebrews treated adopted aliens kindly and fraternally. "The stranger that dwells with you shall be as one born among you, and you shall love him as yourself."

"Guest friendship" was a relation of temporary hospitality. When visiting guests departed, a dish would be broken in half, one piece being given the departing friend so that it would serve as a suitable introduction for a third party who might arrive on a later visit. It was customary for guests to pay their way by telling tales of their travels and adventures. The storytellers of olden times became so popular that the mores eventually forbade their functioning during either the hunting or harvest seasons.

The first treaties of peace were the "blood bonds." The peace ambassadors of two warring tribes would meet, pay their respects, and then proceed to prick the skin until it bled; whereupon they would suck each other's blood and declare peace.

The earliest peace missions consisted of delegations of men bringing their choice maidens for the sex gratification of their onetime enemies, the sex appetite being utilized in combating the war urge. The tribe so honored would pay a return visit, with its offering of maidens; whereupon peace would be firmly established. And soon intermarriages between the families of the chiefs were sanctioned.

4. CLANS AND TRIBES

The first peace group was the family, then the clan, the tribe, and later on the nation, which eventually became the modern territorial state. The fact that the present-day peace groups have long since expanded beyond blood ties to embrace nations is most encouraging, despite the fact that Urantia nations are still spending vast sums on war preparations.

The clans were blood-tie groups within the tribe, and they owed their existence to certain common interests, such as:

1. Tracing origin back to a common ancestor.
2. Allegiance to a common religious totem.
3. Speaking the same dialect.
4. Sharing a common dwelling place.
5. Fearing the same enemies.
6. Having had a common military experience.

The clan headmen were always subordinate to the tribal chief, the early tribal governments being a loose confederation of clans. The native Australians never developed a tribal form of government.

The clan peace chiefs usually ruled through the mother line; the tribal war chiefs established the father line. The courts of the tribal chiefs and early kings consisted of the headmen of the clans, whom it was customary to invite into the king's presence several times a year. This enabled him to watch them and the better secure their co-operation. The clans served a valuable purpose in local self-government, but they greatly delayed the growth of large and strong nations.

5. THE BEGINNINGS OF GOVERNMENT

Every human institution had a beginning, and civil government is a product of progressive evolution just as much as are marriage, industry, and religion. From the early clans and primitive tribes there gradually developed the successive orders of human government which have come and gone right on down to those forms of social and civil regulation that characterize the second third of the twentieth century.

With the gradual emergence of the family units the foundations of government were established in the clan organization, the grouping of consanguineous families. The first real governmental body was the *council of the elders.* This regulative group was composed of old men who had distinguished themselves in some efficient manner. Wisdom and experience were early appreciated even by barbaric man, and there ensued a long age of the domination of the elders. This reign of the oligarchy of age gradually grew into the patriarchal idea.

In the early council of the elders there resided the potential of all governmental functions: executive, legislative, and judicial. When the council interpreted the current mores, it was a court; when establishing new modes of social usage, it was a legislature; to the extent that such decrees and enactments were enforced, it was the executive. The chairman of the council was one of the forerunners of the later tribal chief.

Some tribes had female councils, and from time to time many tribes had women rulers. Certain tribes of the red man preserved the teaching of Onamonalonton in following the unanimous rule of the "council of seven."

It has been hard for mankind to learn that neither peace nor war can be run by a debating society. The primitive "palavers" were seldom useful. The race early learned that an army commanded by a group of clan heads had no chance against a strong one-man army. War has always been a kingmaker.

At first the war chiefs were chosen only for military service, and they would relinquish some of their authority during peacetimes, when their duties were of a more social nature. But gradually they began to encroach upon the peace intervals, tending to continue to rule from one war on through to the next. They often saw to it that one war was not too long in following another. These early war lords were not fond of peace.

In later times some chiefs were chosen for other than military service, being selected because of unusual physique or outstanding personal abilities. The red men often had two sets of chiefs—the sachems, or peace chiefs, and the hereditary war chiefs. The peace rulers were also judges and teachers.

Some early communities were ruled by medicine men, who often acted as chiefs. One man would act as priest, physician, and chief executive. Quite often the early royal insignias had originally been the symbols or emblems of priestly dress.

And it was by these steps that the executive branch of government gradually came into existence. The clan and tribal councils continued in an advisory capacity and as forerunners of the later appearing legislative and judicial branches. In Africa, today, all these forms of primitive government are in actual existence among the various tribes.

6. MONARCHIAL GOVERNMENT

Effective state rule only came with the arrival of a chief with full executive authority. Man found that effective government could be had only by conferring power on a personality, not by endowing an idea.

Rulership grew out of the idea of family authority or wealth. When a patriarchal kinglet became a real king, he was sometimes called "father of his people." Later on, kings were thought to have sprung from heroes. And still further on, rulership became hereditary, due to belief in the divine origin of kings.

Hereditary kingship avoided the anarchy which had previously wrought such havoc between the death of a king and the election of a successor. The family had a biologic head; the clan, a selected natural leader; the tribe and later state had no natural leader, and this was an additional reason for making the chief-kings hereditary. The idea of royal families and aristocracy was also based on the mores of "name ownership" in the clans.

The succession of kings was eventually regarded as supernatural, the royal blood being thought to extend back to the times of the materialized staff of Prince Caligastia. Thus kings became fetish personalities and were inordinately feared, a special form of speech being adopted for court usage. Even in recent times it was believed that the touch of kings would cure disease, and some Urantia peoples still regard their rulers as having had a divine origin.

The early fetish king was often kept in seclusion; he was regarded as too sacred to be viewed except on feast days and holy days. Ordinarily a representative was chosen to impersonate him, and this is the origin of prime ministers. The first cabinet officer was a food administrator; others shortly followed. Rulers soon appointed representatives to be in charge of commerce and religion; and the development of a cabinet was a direct step toward depersonalization of executive authority. These assistants of the early kings became the accepted nobility, and the king's wife gradually rose to the dignity of queen as women came to be held in higher esteem.

Unscrupulous rulers gained great power by the discovery of poison. Early court magic was diabolical; the king's enemies soon died. But even the most despotic tyrant was subject to some restrictions; he was at least restrained by the ever-present fear of assassination. The medicine men, witch doctors, and priests have always been a powerful check on the kings. Subsequently, the landowners, the aristocracy, exerted a restraining influence. And ever and anon the clans and tribes would simply rise up and overthrow their despots and tyrants. Deposed rulers, when sentenced to death, were often given the option of committing suicide, which gave origin to the ancient social vogue of suicide in certain circumstances.

7. PRIMITIVE CLUBS AND SECRET SOCIETIES

Blood kinship determined the first social groups; association enlarged the kinship clan. Intermarriage was the next step in group enlargement, and the resultant complex tribe was the first true political body. The next advance in social development was the evolution of religious cults and the political clubs. These first appeared as secret societies and originally were wholly religious; subsequently they became regulative. At first they were men's clubs; later women's groups appeared. Presently they became divided into two classes: sociopolitical and religio-mystical.

There were many reasons for the secrecy of these societies, such as:

1. Fear of incurring the displeasure of the rulers because of the violation of some taboo.
2. In order to practice minority religious rites.
3. For the purpose of preserving valuable "spirit" or trade secrets.
4. For the enjoyment of some special charm or magic.

The very secrecy of these societies conferred on all members the power of mystery over the rest of the tribe. Secrecy also appeals to vanity; the initiates were the social aristocracy of their day. After initiation the boys hunted with the men; whereas before they had gathered vegetables with the women. And it was the supreme humiliation, a tribal disgrace, to fail to pass the puberty tests and thus be compelled to remain outside the men's abode with the women and children, to be considered effeminate. Besides, noninitiates were not allowed to marry.

Primitive people very early taught their adolescent youths sex control. It became the custom to take boys away from parents from puberty to marriage, their education and training being intrusted to the men's secret societies. And one of the chief functions of these clubs was to keep control of adolescent young men, thus preventing illegitimate children.

Commercialized prostitution began when these men's clubs paid money for the use of women from other tribes. But the earlier groups were remarkably free from sex laxity.

The puberty initiation ceremony usually extended over a period of five years. Much self-torture and painful cutting entered into these ceremonies. Circumcision was first practiced as a rite of initiation into one of these secret fraternities. The tribal marks were cut on the body as a part of the puberty initiation; the tattoo originated as such a badge of membership. Such torture, together with much privation, was designed to harden these youths, to impress them with the reality of life and its inevitable hardships. This purpose is better accomplished by the later appearing athletic games and physical contests.

But the secret societies did aim at the improvement of adolescent morals; one of the chief purposes of the puberty ceremonies was to impress upon the boy that he must leave other men's wives alone.

Following these years of rigorous discipline and training and just before marriage, the young men were usually released for a short period of leisure and freedom, after which they returned to marry and to submit to lifelong subjection to the tribal taboos. And this ancient custom has continued down to modern times as the foolish notion of "sowing wild oats."

Many later tribes sanctioned the formation of women's secret clubs, the purpose of which was to prepare adolescent girls for wifehood and motherhood. After initiation girls were eligible for marriage and were permitted to attend the "bride show," the coming-out party of those days. Women's orders pledged against marriage early came into existence.

Presently nonsecret clubs made their appearance when groups of unmarried men and groups of unattached women formed their separate organizations. These associations were really the first schools. And while men's and women's clubs were often given to persecuting each other, some advanced tribes, after contact with the Dalamatia teachers, experimented with coeducation, having boarding schools for both sexes.

Secret societies contributed to the building up of social castes chiefly by the mysterious character of their initiations. The members of these societies first wore masks to frighten the curious away from their mourning rites—ancestor worship. Later this ritual developed into a pseudo seance at which ghosts were reputed to have appeared. The ancient societies of the "new birth" used signs and employed a special secret language; they also forswore certain foods and drinks. They acted as night police and otherwise functioned in a wide range of social activities.

All secret associations imposed an oath, enjoined confidence, and taught the keeping of secrets. These orders awed and controlled the mobs; they also acted as vigilance societies, thus practicing lynch law. They were the first spies when the tribes were at war and the first secret police during times of peace. Best of all they kept unscrupulous kings on the anxious seat. To offset them, the kings fostered their own secret police.

These societies gave rise to the first political parties. The first party government was "the strong" *vs.* "the weak." In ancient times a change of administration only followed civil war, abundant proof that the weak had become strong.

These clubs were employed by merchants to collect debts and by rulers to collect taxes. Taxation has been a long struggle, one of the earliest forms being the tithe, one tenth of the hunt or spoils. Taxes were originally levied to keep up the king's house, but it was found that they were easier to collect when disguised as an offering for the support of the temple service.

By and by these secret associations grew into the first charitable organizations and later evolved into the earlier religious societies—the forerunners of churches. Finally some of these societies became intertribal, the first international fraternities.

8. SOCIAL CLASSES

The mental and physical inequality of human beings insures that social classes will appear. The only worlds without social strata are the most primitive and the most advanced. A dawning civilization has not yet begun the differentiation of social levels, while a world settled in light and life has largely effaced these divisions of mankind, which are so characteristic of all intermediate evolutionary stages.

As society emerged from savagery to barbarism, its human components tended to become grouped in classes for the following general reasons:

1. *Natural*—contact, kinship, and marriage; the first social distinctions were based on sex, age, and blood—kinship to the chief.

2. *Personal*—the recognition of ability, endurance, skill, and fortitude; soon followed by the recognition of language mastery, knowledge, and general intelligence.

3. *Chance*—war and emigration resulted in the separating of human groups. Class evolution was powerfully influenced by conquest, the relation of the victor to the vanquished, while slavery brought about the first general division of society into free and bond.

4. *Economic*—rich and poor. Wealth and the possession of slaves was a genetic basis for one class of society.

5. *Geographic*—classes arose consequent upon urban or rural settlement. City and country have respectively contributed to the differentiation of the herder-agriculturist and the trader-industrialist, with their divergent viewpoints and reactions.

6. *Social*—classes have gradually formed according to popular estimate of the social worth of different groups. Among the earliest divisions of this sort were the demarcations between priest-teachers, ruler-warriors, capitalist-traders,

common laborers, and slaves. The slave could never become a capitalist, though sometimes the wage earner could elect to join the capitalistic ranks.

7. *Vocational*—as vocations multiplied, they tended to establish castes and guilds. Workers divided into three groups: the professional classes, including the medicine men, then the skilled workers, followed by the unskilled laborers.

8. *Religious*—the early cult clubs produced their own classes within the clans and tribes, and the piety and mysticism of the priests have long perpetuated them as a separate social group.

9. *Racial*—the presence of two or more races within a given nation or territorial unit usually produces color castes. The original caste system of India was based on color, as was that of early Egypt.

10. *Age*—youth and maturity. Among the tribes the boy remained under the watchcare of his father as long as the father lived, while the girl was left in the care of her mother until married.

Flexible and shifting social classes are indispensable to an evolving civilization, but when *class* becomes *caste,* when social levels petrify, the enhancement of social stability is purchased by diminishment of personal initiative. Social caste solves the problem of finding one's place in industry, but it also sharply curtails individual development and virtually prevents social co-operation.

Classes in society, having naturally formed, will persist until man gradually achieves their evolutionary obliteration through intelligent manipulation of the biologic, intellectual, and spiritual resources of a progressing civilization, such as:

1. Biologic renovation of the racial stocks—the selective elimination of inferior human strains. This will tend to eradicate many mortal inequalities.

2. Educational training of the increased brain power which will arise out of such biologic improvement.

3. Religious quickening of the feelings of mortal kinship and brotherhood.

But these measures can bear their true fruits only in the distant millenniums of the future, although much social improvement will immediately result from the intelligent, wise, and *patient* manipulation of these acceleration factors of cultural progress. Religion is the mighty lever that lifts civilization from chaos, but it is powerless apart from the fulcrum of sound and normal mind resting securely on sound and normal heredity.

9. HUMAN RIGHTS

Nature confers no rights on man, only life and a world in which to live it. Nature does not even confer the right to live, as might be deduced by considering what would likely happen if an unarmed man met a hungry tiger face to face in the primitive forest. Society's prime gift to man is security.

Gradually society asserted its rights and, at the present time, they are:

1. Assurance of food supply.

2. Military defense—security through preparedness.

3. Internal peace preservation—prevention of personal violence and social disorder.

4. Sex control—marriage, the family institution.
5. Property—the right to own.
6. Fostering of individual and group competition.
7. Provision for educating and training youth.
8. Promotion of trade and commerce—industrial development.
9. Improvement of labor conditions and rewards.
10. The guarantee of the freedom of religious practices to the end that all of these other social activities may be exalted by becoming spiritually motivated.

When rights are old beyond knowledge of origin, they are often called *natural rights.* But human rights are not really natural; they are entirely social. They are relative and ever changing, being no more than the rules of the game—recognized adjustments of relations governing the ever-changing phenomena of human competition.

What may be regarded as right in one age may not be so regarded in another. The survival of large numbers of defectives and degenerates is not because they have any natural right thus to encumber twentieth-century civilization, but simply because the society of the age, the mores, thus decrees.

Few human rights were recognized in the European Middle Ages; then every man belonged to someone else, and rights were only privileges or favors granted by state or church. And the revolt from this error was equally erroneous in that it led to the belief that all men are born equal.

The weak and the inferior have always contended for equal rights; they have always insisted that the state compel the strong and superior to supply their wants and otherwise make good those deficiencies which all too often are the natural result of their own indifference and indolence.

But this equality ideal is the child of civilization; it is not found in nature. Even culture itself demonstrates conclusively the inherent inequality of men by their very unequal capacity therefor. The sudden and nonevolutionary realization of supposed natural equality would quickly throw civilized man back to the crude usages of primitive ages. Society cannot offer equal rights to all, but it can promise to administer the varying rights of each with fairness and equity. It is the business and duty of society to provide the child of nature with a fair and peaceful opportunity to pursue self-maintenance, participate in self-perpetuation, while at the same time enjoying some measure of self-gratification, the sum of all three constituting human happiness.

10. EVOLUTION OF JUSTICE

Natural justice is a man-made theory; it is not a reality. In nature, justice is purely theoretic, wholly a fiction. Nature provides but one kind of justice—inevitable conformity of results to causes.

Justice, as conceived by man, means getting one's rights and has, therefore, been a matter of progressive evolution. The concept of justice may well be constitutive in a spirit-endowed mind, but it does not spring full-fledgedly into existence on the worlds of space.

Primitive man assigned all phenomena to a person. In case of death the savage asked, not *what* killed him, but *who?* Accidental murder was not therefore recognized, and in the punishment of crime the motive of the criminal was wholly disregarded; judgment was rendered in accordance with the injury done.

In the earliest primitive society public opinion operated directly; officers of law were not needed. There was no privacy in primitive life. A man's neighbors were responsible for his conduct; therefore their right to pry into his personal affairs. Society was regulated on the theory that the group membership should have an interest in, and some degree of control over, the behavior of each individual.

It was very early believed that ghosts administered justice through the medicine men and priests; this constituted these orders the first crime detectors and officers of the law. Their early methods of detecting crime consisted in conducting ordeals of poison, fire, and pain. These savage ordeals were nothing more than crude techniques of arbitration; they did not necessarily settle a dispute justly. For example: When poison was administered, if the accused vomited, he was innocent.

The Old Testament records one of these ordeals, a marital guilt test: If a man suspected his wife of being untrue to him, he took her to the priest and stated his suspicions, after which the priest would prepare a concoction consisting of holy water and sweepings from the temple floor. After due ceremony, including threatening curses, the accused wife was made to drink the nasty potion. If she was guilty, "the water that causes the curse shall enter into her and become bitter, and her belly shall swell, and her thighs shall rot, and the woman shall be accursed among her people." If, by any chance, any woman could quaff this filthy draught and not show symptoms of physical illness, she was acquitted of the charges made by her jealous husband.

These atrocious methods of crime detection were practiced by almost all the evolving tribes at one time or another. Dueling is a modern survival of the trial by ordeal.

It is not to be wondered that the Hebrews and other semicivilized tribes practiced such primitive techniques of justice administration three thousand years ago, but it is most amazing that thinking men would subsequently retain such a relic of barbarism within the pages of a collection of sacred writings. Reflective thinking should make it clear that no divine being ever gave mortal man such unfair instructions regarding the detection and adjudication of suspected marital unfaithfulness.

Society early adopted the paying-back attitude of retaliation: an eye for an eye, a life for a life. The evolving tribes all recognized this right of blood vengeance. Vengeance became the aim of primitive life, but religion has since greatly modified these early tribal practices. The teachers of revealed religion have always proclaimed, "'Vengeance is mine,' says the Lord." Vengeance killing in early times was not altogether unlike present-day murders under the pretense of the unwritten law.

Suicide was a common mode of retaliation. If one were unable to avenge himself in life, he died entertaining the belief that, as a ghost, he could return and visit wrath upon his enemy. And since this belief was very general, the threat of suicide on an enemy's doorstep was usually sufficient to bring him to terms. Primitive man did not hold life very dear; suicide over trifles was common, but the teachings of the Dalamatians greatly lessened this custom, while in more recent times leisure, comforts, religion, and philosophy have united to make life sweeter and more desirable. Hunger strikes are, however, a modern analogue of this old-time method of retaliation.

One of the earliest formulations of advanced tribal law had to do with the taking over of the blood feud as a tribal affair. But strange to relate, even then a man could kill his wife without punishment provided he had fully paid for her. The Eskimos of today, however, still leave the penalty for a crime, even for murder, to be decreed and administered by the family wronged.

Another advance was the imposition of fines for taboo violations, the provision of penalties. These fines constituted the first public revenue. The practice of paying "blood money" also came into vogue as a substitute for blood vengeance. Such damages were usually paid in women or cattle; it was a long time before actual fines, monetary compensation, were assessed as punishment for crime. And since the idea of punishment was essentially compensation, everything, including human life, eventually came to have a price which could be paid as damages. The Hebrews were the first to abolish the practice of paying blood money. Moses taught that they should "take no satisfaction for the life of a murderer, who is guilty of death; he shall surely be put to death."

Justice was thus first meted out by the family, then by the clan, and later on by the tribe. The administration of true justice dates from the taking of revenge from private and kin groups and lodging it in the hands of the social group, the state.

Punishment by burning alive was once a common practice. It was recognized by many ancient rulers, including Hammurabi and Moses, the latter directing that many crimes, particularly those of a grave sex nature, should be punished by burning at the stake. If "the daughter of a priest" or other leading citizen turned to public prostitution, it was the Hebrew custom to "burn her with fire."

Treason—the "selling out" or betrayal of one's tribal associates—was the first capital crime. Cattle stealing was universally punished by summary death, and even recently horse stealing has been similarly punished. But as time passed, it was learned that the severity of the punishment was not so valuable a deterrent to crime as was its certainty and swiftness.

When society fails to punish crimes, group resentment usually asserts itself as lynch law; the provision of sanctuary was a means of escaping this sudden group anger. Lynching and dueling represent the unwillingness of the individual to surrender private redress to the state.

11. LAWS AND COURTS

It is just as difficult to draw sharp distinctions between mores and laws as to indicate exactly when, at the dawning, night is succeeded by day. Mores are laws and police regulations in the making. When long established, the undefined mores tend to crystallize into precise laws, concrete regulations, and well-defined social conventions.

Law is always at first negative and prohibitive; in advancing civilizations it becomes increasingly positive and directive. Early society operated negatively, granting the individual the right to live by imposing upon all others the command, "you shall not kill." Every grant of rights or liberty to the individual involves curtailment of the liberties of all others, and this is effected by the taboo, primitive law. The whole idea of the taboo is inherently negative, for primitive society was wholly negative in its organization, and the early administration of justice consisted in the enforcement of the taboos. But originally these laws applied only to fellow tribesmen, as is illustrated by the later-day Hebrews, who had a different code of ethics for dealing with the gentiles.

The oath originated in the days of Dalamatia in an effort to render testimony more truthful. Such oaths consisted in pronouncing a curse upon oneself. Formerly no individual would testify against his native group.

Crime was an assault upon the tribal mores, sin was the transgression of those taboos which enjoyed ghost sanction, and there was long confusion due to the failure to segregate crime and sin.

Self-interest established the taboo on killing, society sanctified it as traditional mores, while religion consecrated the custom as moral law, and thus did all three conspire in rendering human life more safe and sacred. Society could not have held together during early times had not rights had the sanction of religion; superstition was the moral and social police force of the long evolutionary ages. The ancients all claimed that their olden laws, the taboos, had been given to their ancestors by the gods.

Law is a codified record of long human experience, public opinion crystallized and legalized. The mores were the raw material of accumulated experience out of which later ruling minds formulated the written laws. The ancient judge had no laws. When he handed down a decision, he simply said, "It is the custom."

Reference to precedent in court decisions represents the effort of judges to adapt written laws to the changing conditions of society. This provides for progressive adaptation to altering social conditions combined with the impressiveness of traditional continuity.

Property disputes were handled in many ways, such as:

1. By destroying the disputed property.
2. By force—the contestants fought it out.
3. By arbitration—a third party decided.
4. By appeal to the elders—later to the courts.

The first courts were regulated fistic encounters; the judges were merely umpires or referees. They saw to it that the fight was carried on according to approved rules. On entering a court combat, each party made a deposit with the judge to pay the costs and fine after one had been defeated by the other. "Might was still right." Later on, verbal arguments were substituted for physical blows.

The whole idea of primitive justice was not so much to be fair as to dispose of the contest and thus prevent public disorder and private violence. But primitive man did not so much resent what would now be regarded as an injustice; it was taken for granted that those who had power would use it selfishly. Nevertheless, the status of any civilization may be very accurately determined by the thoroughness and equity of its courts and by the integrity of its judges.

12. ALLOCATION OF CIVIL AUTHORITY

The great struggle in the evolution of government has concerned the concentration of power. The universe administrators have learned from experience that the evolutionary peoples on the inhabited worlds are best regulated by the representative type of civil government when there is maintained proper balance of power between the well-co-ordinated executive, legislative, and judicial branches.

While primitive authority was based on strength, physical power, the ideal government is the representative system wherein leadership is based on ability, but in the days of barbarism there was entirely too much war to permit representative government to function effectively. In the long struggle between division of authority and unity of command, the dictator won. The early and diffuse powers of the primitive council of elders were gradually concentrated in the person of the absolute monarch. After the arrival of real kings the groups of elders persisted as quasi-legislative-judicial advisory bodies; later on, legislatures of co-ordinate status made their appearance, and eventually supreme courts of adjudication were established separate from the legislatures.

The king was the executor of the mores, the original or unwritten law. Later he enforced the legislative enactments, the crystallization of public opinion. A popular assembly as an expression of public opinion, though slow in appearing, marked a great social advance.

The early kings were greatly restricted by the mores—by tradition or public opinion. In recent times some Urantia nations have codified these mores into documentary bases for government.

Urantia mortals are entitled to liberty; they should create their systems of government; they should adopt their constitutions or other charters of civil authority and administrative procedure. And having done this, they should select their most competent and worthy fellows as chief executives. For representatives in the legislative branch they should elect only those who are qualified intellectually and morally to fulfill such sacred responsibilities. As judges of their high and supreme tribunals only those who are endowed with natural ability and who have been made wise by replete experience should be chosen.

If men would maintain their freedom, they must, after having chosen their charter of liberty, provide for its wise, intelligent, and fearless interpretation to the end that there may be prevented:

1. Usurpation of unwarranted power by either the executive or legislative branches.
2. Machinations of ignorant and superstitious agitators.
3. Retardation of scientific progress.
4. Stalemate of the dominance of mediocrity.
5. Domination by vicious minorities.
6. Control by ambitious and clever would-be dictators.
7. Disastrous disruption of panics.
8. Exploitation by the unscrupulous.
9. Taxation enslavement of the citizenry by the state.
10. Failure of social and economic fairness.
11. Union of church and state.
12. Loss of personal liberty.

These are the purposes and aims of constitutional tribunals acting as governors upon the engines of representative government on an evolutionary world.

Mankind's struggle to perfect government on Urantia has to do with perfecting channels of administration, with adapting them to ever-changing current needs, with improving power distribution within government, and then with selecting such administrative leaders as are truly wise. While there is a divine and ideal form of government, such cannot be revealed but must be slowly and laboriously discovered by the men and women of each planet throughout the universes of time and space.

[Presented by a Melchizedek of Nebadon.]

PAPER 71

DEVELOPMENT OF THE STATE

THE state is a useful evolution of civilization; it represents society's net gain from the ravages and sufferings of war. Even statecraft is merely the accumulated technique for adjusting the competitive contest of force between the struggling tribes and nations.

The modern state is the institution which survived in the long struggle for group power. Superior power eventually prevailed, and it produced a creature of fact—the state—together with the moral myth of the absolute obligation of the citizen to live and die for the state. But the state is not of divine genesis; it was not even produced by volitionally intelligent human action; it is purely an evolutionary institution and was wholly automatic in origin.

1. THE EMBRYONIC STATE

The state is a territorial social regulative organization, and the strongest, most efficient, and enduring state is composed of a single nation whose people have a common language, mores, and institutions.

The early states were small and were all the result of conquest. They did not originate in voluntary associations. Many were founded by conquering nomads, who would swoop down on peaceful herders or settled agriculturists to overpower and enslave them. Such states, resulting from conquest, were, perforce, stratified; classes were inevitable, and class struggles have ever been selective.

The northern tribes of the American red men never attained real statehood. They never progressed beyond a loose confederation of tribes, a very primitive form of state. Their nearest approach was the Iroquois federation, but this group of six nations never quite functioned as a state and failed to survive because of the absence of certain essentials to modern national life, such as:

1. Acquirement and inheritance of private property.
2. Cities plus agriculture and industry.
3. Helpful domestic animals.
4. Practical family organization. These red men clung to the mother-family and nephew inheritance.
5. Definite territory.
6. A strong executive head.
7. Enslavement of captives—they either adopted or massacred them.
8. Decisive conquests.

The red men were too democratic; they had a good government, but it failed. Eventually they would have evolved a state had they not prematurely encountered the more advanced civilization of the white man, who was pursuing the governmental methods of the Greeks and the Romans.

The successful Roman state was based on:

1. The father-family.
2. Agriculture and the domestication of animals.
3. Condensation of population—cities.
4. Private property and land.
5. Slavery—classes of citizenship.
6. Conquest and reorganization of weak and backward peoples.
7. Definite territory with roads.
8. Personal and strong rulers.

The great weakness in Roman civilization, and a factor in the ultimate collapse of the empire, was the supposed liberal and advanced provision for the emancipation of the boy at twenty-one and the unconditional release of the girl so that she was at liberty to marry a man of her own choosing or to go abroad in the land to become immoral. The harm to society consisted not in these reforms themselves but rather in the sudden and extensive manner of their adoption. The collapse of Rome indicates what may be expected when a state undergoes too rapid extension associated with internal degeneration.

The embryonic state was made possible by the decline of the blood bond in favor of the territorial, and such tribal federations were usually firmly cemented by conquest. While a sovereignty that transcends all minor struggles and group differences is the characteristic of the true state, still, many classes and castes persist in the later state organizations as remnants of the clans and tribes of former days. The later and larger territorial states had a long and bitter struggle with these smaller consanguineous clan groups, the tribal government proving a valuable transition from family to state authority. During later times many clans grew out of trades and other industrial associations.

Failure of state integration results in retrogression to prestate conditions of governmental techniques, such as the feudalism of the European Middle Ages. During these dark ages the territorial state collapsed, and there was a reversion to the small castle groups, the reappearance of the clan and tribal stages of development. Similar semistates even now exist in Asia and Africa, but not all of them are evolutionary reversions; many are the embryonic nucleuses of states of the future.

2. THE EVOLUTION OF REPRESENTATIVE GOVERNMENT

Democracy, while an ideal, is a product of civilization, not of evolution. Go slowly! select carefully! for the dangers of democracy are:

1. Glorification of mediocrity.
2. Choice of base and ignorant rulers.
3. Failure to recognize the basic facts of social evolution.
4. Danger of universal suffrage in the hands of uneducated and indolent majorities.
5. Slavery to public opinion; the majority is not always right.

Public opinion, common opinion, has always delayed society; nevertheless, it is valuable, for, while retarding social evolution, it does preserve civilization. Education of public opinion is the only safe and true method of accelerating civilization; force is only a temporary expedient, and cultural growth will increasingly accelerate as bullets give way to ballots. Public opinion, the mores, is the basic and elemental energy in social evolution and state development, but to be of state value it must be nonviolent in expression.

The measure of the advance of society is directly determined by the degree to which public opinion can control personal behavior and state regulation through nonviolent expression. The really civilized government had arrived when public opinion was clothed with the powers of personal franchise. Popular elections may not always decide things rightly, but they represent the right way even to do a wrong thing. Evolution does not at once produce superlative perfection but rather comparative and advancing practical adjustment.

There are ten steps, or stages, to the evolution of a practical and efficient form of representative government, and these are:

1. *Freedom of the person.* Slavery, serfdom, and all forms of human bondage must disappear.

2. *Freedom of the mind.* Unless a free people are educated—taught to think intelligently and plan wisely—freedom usually does more harm than good.

3. *The reign of law.* Liberty can be enjoyed only when the will and whims of human rulers are replaced by legislative enactments in accordance with accepted fundamental law.

4. *Freedom of speech.* Representative government is unthinkable without freedom of all forms of expression for human aspirations and opinions.

5. *Security of property.* No government can long endure if it fails to provide for the right to enjoy personal property in some form. Man craves the right to use, control, bestow, sell, lease, and bequeath his personal property.

6. *The right of petition.* Representative government assumes the right of citizens to be heard. The privilege of petition is inherent in free citizenship.

7. *The right to rule.* It is not enough to be heard; the power of petition must progress to the actual management of the government.

8. *Universal suffrage.* Representative government presupposes an intelligent, efficient, and universal electorate. The character of such a government will ever be determined by the character and caliber of those who compose it. As civilization progresses, suffrage, while remaining universal for both sexes, will be effectively modified, regrouped, and otherwise differentiated.

9. *Control of public servants.* No civil government will be serviceable and effective unless the citizenry possess and use wise techniques of guiding and controlling officeholders and public servants.

10. *Intelligent and trained representation.* The survival of democracy is dependent on successful representative government; and that is conditioned upon the practice of electing to public offices only those individuals who are technically trained, intellectually competent, socially loyal, and morally fit. Only by such provisions can government of the people, by the people, and for the people be preserved.

3. THE IDEALS OF STATEHOOD

The political or administrative form of a government is of little consequence provided it affords the essentials of civil progress—liberty, security, education, and social co-ordination. It is not what a state is but what it does that determines the course of social evolution. And after all, no state can transcend the moral values of its citizenry as exemplified in their chosen leaders. Ignorance and selfishness will insure the downfall of even the highest type of government.

Much as it is to be regretted, national egotism has been essential to social survival. The chosen people doctrine has been a prime factor in tribal welding and nation building right on down to modern times. But no state can attain ideal levels of functioning until every form of intolerance is mastered; it is everlastingly inimical to human progress. And intolerance is best combated by the co-ordination of science, commerce, play, and religion.

The ideal state functions under the impulse of three mighty and co-ordinated drives:

1. Love loyalty derived from the realization of human brotherhood.
2. Intelligent patriotism based on wise ideals.
3. Cosmic insight interpreted in terms of planetary facts, needs, and goals.

The laws of the ideal state are few in number, and they have passed out of the negativistic taboo age into the era of the positive progress of individual liberty consequent upon enhanced self-control. The exalted state not only compels its citizens to work but also entices them into profitable and uplifting utilization of the increasing leisure which results from toil liberation by the advancing machine age. Leisure must produce as well as consume.

No society has progressed very far when it permits idleness or tolerates poverty. But poverty and dependence can never be eliminated if the defective and degenerate stocks are freely supported and permitted to reproduce without restraint.

A moral society should aim to preserve the self-respect of its citizenry and afford every normal individual adequate opportunity for self-realization. Such a plan of social achievement would yield a cultural society of the highest order. Social evolution should be encouraged by governmental supervision which exercises a minimum of regulative control. That state is best which co-ordinates most while governing least.

The ideals of statehood must be attained by evolution, by the slow growth of civic consciousness, the recognition of the obligation and privilege of social service. At first men assume the burdens of government as a duty, following the end of the administration of political spoilsmen, but later on they seek such ministry as a privilege, as the greatest honor. The status of any level of civilization is faithfully portrayed by the caliber of its citizens who volunteer to accept the responsibilities of statehood.

In a real commonwealth the business of governing cities and provinces is conducted by experts and is managed just as are all other forms of economic and commercial associations of people.

In advanced states, political service is esteemed as the highest devotion of the citizenry. The greatest ambition of the wisest and noblest of citizens is to gain civil recognition, to be elected or appointed to some position of governmental trust, and such governments confer their highest honors of recognition for service upon their civil and social servants. Honors are next bestowed in the order named upon philosophers, educators, scientists, industrialists, and militarists. Parents are duly rewarded by the excellency of their children, and purely religious leaders, being ambassadors of a spiritual kingdom, receive their real rewards in another world.

4. PROGRESSIVE CIVILIZATION

Economics, society, and government must evolve if they are to remain. Static conditions on an evolutionary world are indicative of decay; only those institutions which move forward with the evolutionary stream persist.

The progressive program of an expanding civilization embraces:

1. Preservation of individual liberties.
2. Protection of the home.
3. Promotion of economic security.
4. Prevention of disease.
5. Compulsory education.
6. Compulsory employment.
7. Profitable utilization of leisure.
8. Care of the unfortunate.
9. Race improvement.
10. Promotion of science and art.
11. Promotion of philosophy—wisdom.
12. Augmentation of cosmic insight—spirituality.

And this progress in the arts of civilization leads directly to the realization of the highest human and divine goals of mortal endeavor—the social achievement of the brotherhood of man and the personal status of God-consciousness, which becomes revealed in the supreme desire of every individual to do the will of the Father in heaven.

The appearance of genuine brotherhood signifies that a social order has arrived in which all men delight in bearing one another's burdens; they actually desire to practice the golden rule. But such an ideal society cannot be realized when either the weak or the wicked lie in wait to take unfair and unholy advantage of those who are chiefly actuated by devotion to the service of truth, beauty, and goodness. In such a situation only one course is practical: The "golden rulers" may establish a progressive society in which they live according to their ideals while maintaining an adequate defense against their benighted fellows who might seek either to exploit their pacific predilections or to destroy their advancing civilization.

Idealism can never survive on an evolving planet if the idealists in each generation permit themselves to be exterminated by the baser orders of humanity. And here is the great test of idealism: Can an advanced society maintain that military preparedness which renders it secure from all attack by its war-loving neighbors without yielding to the temptation to employ this military strength in offensive operations against other peoples for purposes of selfish gain or national aggrandizement? National survival demands preparedness, and religious idealism alone can prevent the prostitution of preparedness into aggression. Only love, brotherhood, can prevent the strong from oppressing the weak.

5. THE EVOLUTION OF COMPETITION

Competition is essential to social progress, but competition, unregulated, breeds violence. In current society, competition is slowly displacing war in that it determines the individual's place in industry, as well as decreeing the survival of the industries themselves. (Murder and war differ in their status before the mores, murder having been outlawed since the early days of society, while war has never yet been outlawed by mankind as a whole.)

The ideal state undertakes to regulate social conduct only enough to take violence out of individual competition and to prevent unfairness in personal initiative. Here is a great problem in statehood: How can you guarantee peace and quiet in industry, pay the taxes to support state power, and at the same time prevent taxation from handicapping industry and keep the state from becoming parasitical or tyrannical?

Throughout the earlier ages of any world, competition is essential to progressive civilization. As the evolution of man progresses, co-operation becomes increasingly effective. In advanced civilizations co-operation is more efficient than competition. Early man is stimulated by competition. Early evolution is characterized by the survival of the biologically fit, but later civilizations are the better promoted by intelligent co-operation, understanding fraternity, and spiritual brotherhood.

True, competition in industry is exceedingly wasteful and highly ineffective, but no attempt to eliminate this economic lost motion should be countenanced if such adjustments entail even the slightest abrogation of any of the basic liberties of the individual.

6. THE PROFIT MOTIVE

Present-day profit-motivated economics is doomed unless profit motives can be augmented by service motives. Ruthless competition based on narrow-minded self-interest is ultimately destructive of even those things which it seeks to maintain. Exclusive and self-serving profit motivation is incompatible with Christian ideals—much more incompatible with the teachings of Jesus.

In economics, profit motivation is to service motivation what fear is to love in religion. But the profit motive must not be suddenly destroyed or removed; it keeps many otherwise slothful mortals hard at work. It is not necessary, however, that this social energy arouser be forever selfish in its objectives.

The profit motive of economic activities is altogether base and wholly unworthy of an advanced order of society; nevertheless, it is an indispensable factor throughout the earlier phases of civilization. Profit motivation must not be taken away from men until they have firmly possessed themselves of superior types of nonprofit motives for economic striving and social serving—the transcendent urges of superlative wisdom, intriguing brotherhood, and excellency of spiritual attainment.

7. EDUCATION

The enduring state is founded on culture, dominated by ideals, and motivated by service. The purpose of education should be acquirement of skill, pursuit of wisdom, realization of selfhood, and attainment of spiritual values.

In the ideal state, education continues throughout life, and philosophy sometime becomes the chief pursuit of its citizens. The citizens of such a commonwealth pursue wisdom as an enhancement of insight into the significance of human relations, the meanings of reality, the nobility of values, the goals of living, and the glories of cosmic destiny.

Urantians should get a vision of a new and higher cultural society. Education will jump to new levels of value with the passing of the purely profit-motivated system of economics. Education has too long been localistic, militaristic, ego exalting, and success seeking; it must eventually become world-wide, idealistic, self-realizing, and cosmic grasping.

Education recently passed from the control of the clergy to that of lawyers and businessmen. Eventually it must be given over to the philosophers and the scientists. Teachers must be free beings, real leaders, to the end that philosophy, the search for wisdom, may become the chief educational pursuit.

Education is the business of living; it must continue throughout a lifetime so that mankind may gradually experience the ascending levels of mortal wisdom, which are:

1. The knowledge of things.
2. The realization of meanings.
3. The appreciation of values.
4. The nobility of work—duty.
5. The motivation of goals—morality.
6. The love of service—character.
7. Cosmic insight—spiritual discernment.

And then, by means of these achievements, many will ascend to the mortal ultimate of mind attainment, God-consciousness.

8. THE CHARACTER OF STATEHOOD

The only sacred feature of any human government is the division of statehood into the three domains of executive, legislative, and judicial functions. The universe is administered in accordance with such a plan of segregation of functions and authority. Aside from this divine concept of effective social regulation or civil government, it matters little what form of state a people may elect to have provided the citizenry is ever progressing toward the goal of augmented self-control and increased social service. The intellectual keenness, economic wisdom, social cleverness, and moral stamina of a people are all faithfully reflected in statehood.

The evolution of statehood entails progress from level to level, as follows:

1. The creation of a threefold government of executive, legislative, and judicial branches.
2. The freedom of social, political, and religious activities.

3. The abolition of all forms of slavery and human bondage.

4. The ability of the citizenry to control the levying of taxes.

5. The establishment of universal education—learning extended from the cradle to the grave.

6. The proper adjustment between local and national governments.

7. The fostering of science and the conquest of disease.

8. The due recognition of sex equality and the co-ordinated functioning of men and women in the home, school, and church, with specialized service of women in industry and government.

9. The elimination of toiling slavery by machine invention and the subsequent mastery of the machine age.

10. The conquest of dialects—the triumph of a universal language.

11. The ending of war—international adjudication of national and racial differences by continental courts of nations presided over by a supreme planetary tribunal automatically recruited from the periodically retiring heads of the continental courts. The continental courts are authoritative; the world court is advisory—moral.

12. The world-wide vogue of the pursuit of wisdom—the exaltation of philosophy. The evolution of a world religion, which will presage the entrance of the planet upon the earlier phases of settlement in light and life.

These are the prerequisites of progressive government and the earmarks of ideal statehood. Urantia is far from the realization of these exalted ideals, but the civilized races have made a beginning—mankind is on the march toward higher evolutionary destinies.

[Sponsored by a Melchizedek of Nebadon.]

PAPER 72

GOVERNMENT ON A NEIGHBORING PLANET

BY PERMISSION of Lanaforge and with the approval of the Most Highs of Edentia, I am authorized to narrate something of the social, moral, and political life of the most advanced human race living on a not far-distant planet belonging to the Satania system.

Of all the Satania worlds which became isolated because of participation in the Lucifer rebellion, this planet has experienced a history most like that of Urantia. The similarity of the two spheres undoubtedly explains why permission to make this extraordinary presentation was granted, for it is most unusual for the system rulers to consent to the narration on one planet of the affairs of another.

This planet, like Urantia, was led astray by the disloyalty of its Planetary Prince in connection with the Lucifer rebellion. It received a Material Son shortly after Adam came to Urantia, and this Son also defaulted, leaving the sphere isolated, since a Magisterial Son has never been bestowed upon its mortal races.

1. THE CONTINENTAL NATION

Notwithstanding all these planetary handicaps a very superior civilization is evolving on an isolated continent about the size of Australia. This nation numbers about 140 million. Its people are a mixed race, predominantly blue and yellow, having a slightly greater proportion of violet than the so-called white race of Urantia. These different races are not yet fully blended, but they fraternize and socialize very acceptably. The average length of life on this continent is now ninety years, fifteen per cent higher than that of any other people on the planet.

The industrial mechanism of this nation enjoys a certain great advantage derived from the unique topography of the continent. The high mountains, on which heavy rains fall eight months in the year, are situated at the very center of the country. This natural arrangement favors the utilization of water power and greatly facilitates the irrigation of the more arid western quarter of the continent.

These people are self-sustaining, that is, they can live indefinitely without importing anything from the surrounding nations. Their natural resources are replete, and by scientific techniques they have learned how to compensate for their deficiencies in the essentials of life. They enjoy a brisk domestic commerce but have little foreign trade owing to the universal hostility of their less progressive neighbors.

This continental nation, in general, followed the evolutionary trend of the planet: The development from the tribal stage to the appearance of strong rulers and kings occupied thousands of years. The unconditional monarchs were succeeded by many different orders of government—abortive republics, communal states, and dictators came and went in endless profusion. This growth continued until about five hundred years ago when, during a politically fermenting period, one of the nation's powerful dictator-triumvirs had a change of heart. He volunteered to abdicate upon condition that one of the other rulers, the baser of the remaining two, also vacate his dictatorship. Thus was the sovereignty of the continent placed in the hands of one ruler. The unified state progressed under strong monarchial rule for over one hundred years, during which there evolved a masterful charter of liberty.

The subsequent transition from monarchy to a representative form of government was gradual, the kings remaining as mere social or sentimental figureheads, finally disappearing when the male line of descent ran out. The present republic has now been in existence just two hundred years, during which time there has been a continuous progression toward the governmental techniques about to be narrated, the last developments in industrial and political realms having been made within the past decade.

2. POLITICAL ORGANIZATION

This continental nation now has a representative government with a centrally located national capital. The central government consists of a strong federation of one hundred comparatively free states. These states elect their governors and legislators for ten years, and none are eligible for re-election. State judges are appointed for life by the governors and confirmed by their legislatures, which consist of one representative for each one hundred thousand citizens.

There are five different types of metropolitan government, depending on the size of the city, but no city is permitted to have more than one million inhabitants. On the whole, these municipal governing schemes are very simple, direct, and economical. The few offices of city administration are keenly sought by the highest types of citizens.

The federal government embraces three co-ordinate divisions: executive, legislative, and judicial. The federal chief executive is elected every six years by universal territorial suffrage. He is not eligible for re-election except upon the petition of at least seventy-five state legislatures concurred in by the respective state governors, and then but for one term. He is advised by a supercabinet composed of all living ex-chief executives.

The legislative division embraces three houses:

1. The *upper house* is elected by industrial, professional, agricultural, and other groups of workers, balloting in accordance with economic function.

2. The *lower house* is elected by certain organizations of society embracing the social, political, and philosophic groups not included in industry or the professions. All citizens in good standing participate in the election of both classes of representatives, but they are differently grouped, depending on whether the election pertains to the upper or lower house.

3. The *third house*—the elder statesmen—embraces the veterans of civic service and includes many distinguished persons nominated by the chief

executive, by the regional (subfederal) executives, by the chief of the supreme tribunal, and by the presiding officers of either of the other legislative houses. This group is limited to one hundred, and its members are elected by the majority action of the elder statesmen themselves. Membership is for life, and when vacancies occur, the person receiving the largest ballot among the list of nominees is thereby duly elected. The scope of this body is purely advisory, but it is a mighty regulator of public opinion and exerts a powerful influence upon all branches of the government.

Very much of the federal administrative work is carried on by the ten regional (subfederal) authorities, each consisting of the association of ten states. These regional divisions are wholly executive and administrative, having neither legislative nor judicial functions. The ten regional executives are the personal appointees of the federal chief executive, and their term of office is concurrent with his—six years. The federal supreme tribunal approves the appointment of these ten regional executives, and while they may not be reappointed, the retiring executive automatically becomes the associate and adviser of his successor. Otherwise, these regional chiefs choose their own cabinets of administrative officials.

This nation is adjudicated by two major court systems—the law courts and the socioeconomic courts. The law courts function on the following three levels:

1. *Minor courts* of municipal and local jurisdiction, whose decisions may be appealed to the high state tribunals.

2. *State supreme courts,* whose decisions are final in all matters not involving the federal government or jeopardy of citizenship rights and liberties. The regional executives are empowered to bring any case at once to the bar of the federal supreme court.

3. *Federal supreme court*—the high tribunal for the adjudication of national contentions and the appellate cases coming up from the state courts. This supreme tribunal consists of twelve men over forty and under seventy-five years of age who have served two or more years on some state tribunal, and who have been appointed to this high position by the chief executive with the majority approval of the supercabinet and the third house of the legislative assembly. All decisions of this supreme judicial body are by at least a two-thirds vote.

The socioeconomic courts function in the following three divisions:

1. *Parental courts,* associated with the legislative and executive divisions of the home and social system.

2. *Educational courts*—the juridical bodies connected with the state and regional school systems and associated with the executive and legislative branches of the educational administrative mechanism.

3. *Industrial courts*—the jurisdictional tribunals vested with full authority for the settlement of all economic misunderstandings.

The federal supreme court does not pass upon socioeconomic cases except upon the three-quarters vote of the third legislative branch of the national government, the house of elder statesmen. Otherwise, all decisions of the parental, educational, and industrial high courts are final.

3. THE HOME LIFE

On this continent it is against the law for two families to live under the same roof. And since group dwellings have been outlawed, most of the tenement type of buildings have been demolished. But the unmarried still live in clubs, hotels, and other group dwellings. The smallest homesite permitted must provide fifty thousand square feet of land. All land and other property used for home purposes are free from taxation up to ten times the minimum homesite allotment.

The home life of this people has greatly improved during the last century. Attendance of parents, both fathers and mothers, at the parental schools of child culture is compulsory. Even the agriculturists who reside in small country settlements carry on this work by correspondence, going to the near-by centers for oral instruction once in ten days—every two weeks, for they maintain a five-day week.

The average number of children in each family is five, and they are under the full control of their parents or, in case of the demise of one or both, under that of the guardians designated by the parental courts. It is considered a great honor for any family to be awarded the guardianship of a full orphan. Competitive examinations are held among parents, and the orphan is awarded to the home of those displaying the best parental qualifications.

These people regard the home as the basic institution of their civilization. It is expected that the most valuable part of a child's education and character training will be secured from his parents and at home, and fathers devote almost as much attention to child culture as do mothers.

All sex instruction is administered in the home by parents or by legal guardians. Moral instruction is offered by teachers during the rest periods in the school shops, but not so with religious training, which is deemed to be the exclusive privilege of parents, religion being looked upon as an integral part of home life. Purely religious instruction is given publicly only in the temples of philosophy, no such exclusively religious institutions as the Urantia churches having developed among this people. In their philosophy, religion is the striving to know God and to manifest love for one's fellows through service for them, but this is not typical of the religious status of the other nations on this planet. Religion is so entirely a family matter among these people that there are no public places devoted exclusively to religious assembly. Politically, church and state, as Urantians are wont to say, are entirely separate, but there is a strange overlapping of religion and philosophy.

Until twenty years ago the spiritual teachers (comparable to Urantia pastors), who visit each family periodically to examine the children to ascertain if they have been properly instructed by their parents, were under governmental supervision. These spiritual advisers and examiners are now under the direction of the newly created Foundation of Spiritual Progress, an institution supported by voluntary contributions. Possibly this institution may not further evolve until after the arrival of a Paradise Magisterial Son.

Children remain legally subject to their parents until they are fifteen, when the first initiation into civic responsibility is held. Thereafter, every five years for five successive periods similar public exercises are held for such age groups at which their obligations to parents are lessened, while new civic and social responsibilities to the state are assumed. Suffrage is conferred at twenty, the right to marry without parental consent is not bestowed until twenty-five, and children must leave home on reaching the age of thirty.

Marriage and divorce laws are uniform throughout the nation. Marriage before twenty—the age of civil enfranchisement—is not permitted. Permission to marry is only granted after one year's notice of intention, and after both bride and groom present certificates showing that they have been duly instructed in the parental schools regarding the responsibilities of married life.

Divorce regulations are somewhat lax, but decrees of separation, issued by the parental courts, may not be had until one year after application therefor has been recorded, and the year on this planet is considerably longer than on Urantia. Notwithstanding their easy divorce laws, the present rate of divorces is only one tenth that of the civilized races of Urantia.

4. THE EDUCATIONAL SYSTEM

The educational system of this nation is compulsory and coeducational in the precollege schools that the student attends from the ages of five to eighteen. These schools are vastly different from those of Urantia. There are no classrooms, only one study is pursued at a time, and after the first three years all pupils become assistant teachers, instructing those below them. Books are used only to secure information that will assist in solving the problems arising in the school shops and on the school farms. Much of the furniture used on the continent and the many mechanical contrivances—this is a great age of invention and mechanization—are produced in these shops. Adjacent to each shop is a working library where the student may consult the necessary reference books. Agriculture and horticulture are also taught throughout the entire educational period on the extensive farms adjoining every local school.

The feeble-minded are trained only in agriculture and animal husbandry, and are committed for life to special custodial colonies where they are segregated by sex to prevent parenthood, which is denied all subnormals. These restrictive measures have been in operation for seventy-five years; the commitment decrees are handed down by the parental courts.

Everyone takes one month's vacation each year. The precollege schools are conducted for nine months out of the year of ten, the vacation being spent with parents or friends in travel. This travel is a part of the adult-education program and is continued throughout a lifetime, the funds for meeting such expenses being accumulated by the same methods as those employed in old-age insurance.

One quarter of the school time is devoted to play—competitive athletics—the pupils progressing in these contests from the local, through the state and regional, and on to the national trials of skill and prowess. Likewise, the oratorical and musical contests, as well as those in science and philosophy, occupy the attention of students from the lower social divisions on up to the contests for national honors.

The school government is a replica of the national government with its three correlated branches, the teaching staff functioning as the third or advisory legislative division. The chief object of education on this continent is to make every pupil a self-supporting citizen.

Every child graduating from the precollege school system at eighteen is a skilled artisan. Then begins the study of books and the pursuit of special knowledge, either in the adult schools or in the colleges. When a brilliant student completes his work ahead of schedule, he is granted an award of time and means wherewith he may execute some pet project of his own devising. The entire educational system is designed to adequately train the individual.

5. INDUSTRIAL ORGANIZATION

The industrial situation among this people is far from their ideals; capital and labor still have their troubles, but both are becoming adjusted to the plan of sincere co-operation. On this unique continent the workers are increasingly becoming shareholders in all industrial concerns; every intelligent laborer is slowly becoming a small capitalist.

Social antagonisms are lessening, and good will is growing apace. No grave economic problems have arisen out of the abolition of slavery (over one hundred years ago) since this adjustment was effected gradually by the liberation of two per cent each year. Those slaves who satisfactorily passed mental, moral, and physical tests were granted citizenship; many of these superior slaves were war captives or children of such captives. Some fifty years ago they deported the last of their inferior slaves, and still more recently they are addressing themselves to the task of reducing the numbers of their degenerate and vicious classes.

These people have recently developed new techniques for the adjustment of industrial misunderstandings and for the correction of economic abuses which are marked improvements over their older methods of settling such problems. Violence has been outlawed as a procedure in adjusting either personal or industrial differences. Wages, profits, and other economic problems are not rigidly regulated, but they are in general controlled by the industrial legislatures, while all disputes arising out of industry are passed upon by the industrial courts.

The industrial courts are only thirty years old but are functioning very satisfactorily. The most recent development provides that hereafter the industrial courts shall recognize legal compensation as falling in three divisions:

1. Legal rates of interest on invested capital.
2. Reasonable salary for skill employed in industrial operations.
3. Fair and equitable wages for labor.

These shall first be met in accordance with contract, or in the face of decreased earnings they shall share proportionally in transient reduction. And thereafter all earnings in excess of these fixed charges shall be regarded as dividends and shall be prorated to all three divisions: capital, skill, and labor.

Every ten years the regional executives adjust and decree the lawful hours of daily gainful toil. Industry now operates on a five-day week, working four and playing one. These people labor six hours each working day and, like students, nine months in the year of ten. Vacation is usually spent in travel, and new methods of transportation having been so recently developed, the whole nation is travel bent. The climate favors travel about eight months in the year, and they are making the most of their opportunities.

Two hundred years ago the profit motive was wholly dominant in industry, but today it is being rapidly displaced by other and higher driving forces.

Competition is keen on this continent, but much of it has been transferred from industry to play, skill, scientific achievement, and intellectual attainment. It is most active in social service and governmental loyalty. Among this people public service is rapidly becoming the chief goal of ambition. The richest man on the continent works six hours a day in the office of his machine shop and then hastens over to the local branch of the school of statesmanship, where he seeks to qualify for public service.

Labor is becoming more honorable on this continent, and all able-bodied citizens over eighteen work either at home and on farms, at some recognized industry, on the public works where the temporarily unemployed are absorbed, or else in the corps of compulsory laborers in the mines.

These people are also beginning to foster a new form of social disgust—disgust for both idleness and unearned wealth. Slowly but certainly they are conquering their machines. Once they, too, struggled for political liberty and subsequently for economic freedom. Now are they entering upon the enjoyment of both while in addition they are beginning to appreciate their well-earned leisure, which can be devoted to increased self-realization.

6. OLD-AGE INSURANCE

This nation is making a determined effort to replace the self-respect-destroying type of charity by dignified government-insurance guarantees of security in old age. This nation provides every child an education and every man a job; therefore can it successfully carry out such an insurance scheme for the protection of the infirm and aged.

Among this people all persons must retire from gainful pursuit at sixty-five unless they secure a permit from the state labor commissioner which will entitle them to remain at work until the age of seventy. This age limit does not apply to government servants or philosophers. The physically disabled or permanently crippled can be placed on the retired list at any age by court order countersigned by the pension commissioner of the regional government.

The funds for old-age pensions are derived from four sources:

1. One day's earnings each month are requisitioned by the federal government for this purpose, and in this country everybody works.

2. Bequests—many wealthy citizens leave funds for this purpose.

3. The earnings of compulsory labor in the state mines. After the conscript workers support themselves and set aside their own retirement contributions, all excess profits on their labor are turned over to this pension fund.

4. The income from natural resources. All natural wealth on the continent is held as a social trust by the federal government, and the income therefrom is utilized for social purposes, such as disease prevention, education of geniuses, and expenses of especially promising individuals in the statesmanship schools. One half of the income from natural resources goes to the old-age pension fund.

Although state and regional actuarial foundations supply many forms of protective insurance, old-age pensions are solely administered by the federal government through the ten regional departments.

These government funds have long been honestly administered. Next to treason and murder, the heaviest penalties meted out by the courts are attached to betrayal of public trust. Social and political disloyalty are now looked upon as being the most heinous of all crimes.

7. TAXATION

The federal government is paternalistic only in the administration of old-age pensions and in the fostering of genius and creative originality; the state governments are slightly more concerned with the individual citizen, while the local governments are much more paternalistic or socialistic. The city (or some subdivision thereof) concerns itself with such matters as health, sanitation, building regulations, beautification, water supply, lighting, heating, recreation, music, and communication.

In all industry first attention is paid to health; certain phases of physical well-being are regarded as industrial and community prerogatives, but individual and family health problems are matters of personal concern only. In medicine, as in all other purely personal matters, it is increasingly the plan of government to refrain from interfering.

Cities have no taxing power, neither can they go in debt. They receive per capita allowances from the state treasury and must supplement such revenue from the earnings of their socialistic enterprises and by licensing various commercial activities.

The rapid-transit facilities, which make it practical greatly to extend the city boundaries, are under municipal control. The city fire departments are supported by the fire-prevention and insurance foundations, and all buildings, in city or country, are fireproof—have been for over seventy-five years.

There are no municipally appointed peace officers; the police forces are maintained by the state governments. This department is recruited almost entirely from the unmarried men between twenty-five and fifty. Most of the states assess a rather heavy bachelor tax, which is remitted to all men joining the state police. In the average state the police force is now only one tenth as large as it was fifty years ago.

There is little or no uniformity among the taxation schemes of the one hundred comparatively free and sovereign states as economic and other conditions vary greatly in different sections of the continent. Every state has ten basic constitutional provisions which cannot be modified except by consent of the federal supreme court, and one of these articles prevents levying a tax of more than one per cent on the value of any property in any one year, homesites, whether in city or country, being exempted.

The federal government cannot go in debt, and a three-fourths referendum is required before any state can borrow except for purposes of war. Since the federal government cannot incur debt, in the event of war the National Council of Defense is empowered to assess the states for money, as well as for men and materials, as it may be required. But no debt may run for more than twenty-five years.

Income to support the federal government is derived from the following five sources:

1. *Import duties.* All imports are subject to a tariff designed to protect the standard of living on this continent, which is far above that of any other

nation on the planet. These tariffs are set by the highest industrial court after both houses of the industrial congress have ratified the recommendations of the chief executive of economic affairs, who is the joint appointee of these two legislative bodies. The upper industrial house is elected by labor, the lower by capital.

2. *Royalties.* The federal government encourages invention and original creations in the ten regional laboratories, assisting all types of geniuses—artists, authors, and scientists—and protecting their patents. In return the government takes one half the profits realized from all such inventions and creations, whether pertaining to machines, books, artistry, plants, or animals.

3. *Inheritance tax.* The federal government levies a graduated inheritance tax ranging from one to fifty per cent, depending on the size of an estate as well as on other conditions.

4. *Military equipment.* The government earns a considerable sum from the leasing of military and naval equipment for commercial and recreational usages.

5. *Natural resources.* The income from natural resources, when not fully required for the specific purposes designated in the charter of federal statehood, is turned into the national treasury.

Federal appropriations, except war funds assessed by the National Council of Defense, are originated in the upper legislative house, concurred in by the lower house, approved by the chief executive, and finally validated by the federal budget commission of one hundred. The members of this commission are nominated by the state governors and elected by the state legislatures to serve for twenty-four years, one quarter being elected every six years. Every six years this body, by a three-fourths ballot, chooses one of its number as chief, and he thereby becomes director-controller of the federal treasury.

8. THE SPECIAL COLLEGES

In addition to the basic compulsory education program extending from the ages of five to eighteen, special schools are maintained as follows:

1. *Statesmanship schools.* These schools are of three classes: national, regional, and state. The public offices of the nation are grouped in four divisions. The first division of public trust pertains principally to the national administration, and all officeholders of this group must be graduates of both regional and national schools of statesmanship. Individuals may accept political, elective, or appointive office in the second division upon graduating from any one of the ten regional schools of statesmanship; their trusts concern responsibilities in the regional administration and the state governments. Division three includes state responsibilities, and such officials are only required to have state degrees of statesmanship. The fourth and last division of officeholders are not required to hold statesmanship degrees, such offices being wholly appointive. They represent minor positions of assistantship, secretaryships, and technical trusts which are discharged by the various learned professions functioning in governmental administrative capacities.

Judges of the minor and state courts hold degrees from the state schools of statesmanship. Judges of the jurisdictional tribunals of social, educational, and industrial matters hold degrees from the regional schools. Judges of the federal supreme court must hold degrees from all these schools of statesmanship.

2. *Schools of philosophy.* These schools are affiliated with the temples of philosophy and are more or less associated with religion as a public function.

3. *Institutions of science.* These technical schools are co-ordinated with industry rather than with the educational system and are administered under fifteen divisions.

4. *Professional training schools.* These special institutions provide the technical training for the various learned professions, twelve in number.

5. *Military and naval schools.* Near the national headquarters and at the twenty-five coastal military centers are maintained those institutions devoted to the military training of volunteer citizens from eighteen to thirty years of age. Parental consent is required before twenty-five in order to gain entrance to these schools.

9. THE PLAN OF UNIVERSAL SUFFRAGE

Although candidates for all public offices are restricted to graduates of the state, regional, or federal schools of statesmanship, the progressive leaders of this nation discovered a serious weakness in their plan of universal suffrage and about fifty years ago made constitutional provision for a modified scheme of voting which embraces the following features:

1. Every man and woman of twenty years and over has one vote. Upon attaining this age, all citizens must accept membership in two voting groups: They will join the first in accordance with their economic function—industrial, professional, agricultural, or trade; they will enter the second group according to their political, philosophic, and social inclinations. All workers thus belong to some economic franchise group, and these guilds, like the noneconomic associations, are regulated much as is the national government with its threefold division of powers. Registration in these groups cannot be changed for twelve years.

2. Upon nomination by the state governors or by the regional executives and by the mandate of the regional supreme councils, individuals who have rendered great service to society, or who have demonstrated extraordinary wisdom in government service, may have additional votes conferred upon them not oftener than every five years and not to exceed nine such superfranchises. The maximum suffrage of any multiple voter is ten. Scientists, inventors, teachers, philosophers, and spiritual leaders are also thus recognized and honored with augmented political power. These advanced civic privileges are conferred by the state and regional supreme councils much as degrees are bestowed by the special colleges, and the recipients are proud to attach the symbols of such civic recognition, along with their other degrees, to their lists of personal achievements.

3. All individuals sentenced to compulsory labor in the mines and all governmental servants supported by tax funds are, for the periods of such services, disenfranchised. This does not apply to aged persons who may be retired on pensions at sixty-five.

4. There are five brackets of suffrage reflecting the average yearly taxes paid for each half-decade period. Heavy taxpayers are permitted extra votes

up to five. This grant is independent of all other recognition, but in no case can any person cast over ten ballots.

5. At the time this franchise plan was adopted, the territorial method of voting was abandoned in favor of the economic or functional system. All citizens now vote as members of industrial, social, or professional groups, regardless of their residence. Thus the electorate consists of solidified, unified, and intelligent groups who elect only their best members to positions of governmental trust and responsibility. There is one exception to this scheme of functional or group suffrage: The election of a federal chief executive every six years is by nation-wide ballot, and no citizen casts over one vote.

Thus, except in the election of the chief executive, suffrage is exercised by economic, professional, intellectual, and social groupings of the citizenry. The ideal state is organic, and every free and intelligent group of citizens represents a vital and functioning organ within the larger governmental organism.

The schools of statesmanship have power to start proceedings in the state courts looking toward the disenfranchisement of any defective, idle, indifferent, or criminal individual. These people recognize that, when fifty per cent of a nation is inferior or defective and possesses the ballot, such a nation is doomed. They believe the dominance of mediocrity spells the downfall of any nation. Voting is compulsory, heavy fines being assessed against all who fail to cast their ballots.

10. DEALING WITH CRIME

The methods of this people in dealing with crime, insanity, and degeneracy, while in some ways pleasing, will, no doubt, in others prove shocking to most Urantians. Ordinary criminals and the defectives are placed, by sexes, in different agricultural colonies and are more than self-supporting. The more serious habitual criminals and the incurably insane are sentenced to death in the lethal gas chambers by the courts. Numerous crimes aside from murder, including betrayal of governmental trust, also carry the death penalty, and the visitation of justice is sure and swift.

These people are passing out of the negative into the positive era of law. Recently they have gone so far as to attempt the prevention of crime by sentencing those who are believed to be potential murderers and major criminals to life service in the detention colonies. If such convicts subsequently demonstrate that they have become more normal, they may be either paroled or pardoned. The homicide rate on this continent is only one per cent of that among the other nations.

Efforts to prevent the breeding of criminals and defectives were begun over one hundred years ago and have already yielded gratifying results. There are no prisons or hospitals for the insane. For one reason, there are only about ten per cent as many of these groups as are found on Urantia.

11. MILITARY PREPAREDNESS

Graduates of the federal military schools may be commissioned as "guardians of civilization" in seven ranks, in accordance with ability and experience, by the president of the National Council of Defense. This council consists of twenty-five members, nominated by the highest parental, educational, and industrial tribunals, confirmed by the federal supreme court, and presided over ex officio by the chief of staff of co-ordinated military affairs. Such members serve until they are seventy years of age.

The courses pursued by such commissioned officers are four years in length and are invariably correlated with the mastery of some trade or profession. Military training is never given without this associated industrial, scientific, or professional schooling. When military training is finished, the individual has, during his four years' course, received one half of the education imparted in any of the special schools where the courses are likewise four years in length. In this way the creation of a professional military class is avoided by providing this opportunity for a large number of men to support themselves while securing the first half of a technical or professional training.

Military service during peacetime is purely voluntary, and the enlistments in all branches of the service are for four years, during which every man pursues some special line of study in addition to the mastery of military tactics. Training in music is one of the chief pursuits of the central military schools and of the twenty-five training camps distributed about the periphery of the continent. During periods of industrial slackness many thousands of unemployed are automatically utilized in upbuilding the military defenses of the continent on land and sea and in the air.

Although these people maintain a powerful war establishment as a defense against invasion by the surrounding hostile peoples, it may be recorded to their credit that they have not in over one hundred years employed these military resources in an offensive war. They have become civilized to that point where they can vigorously defend civilization without yielding to the temptation to utilize their war powers in aggression. There have been no civil wars since the establishment of the united continental state, but during the last two centuries these people have been called upon to wage nine fierce defensive conflicts, three of which were against mighty confederations of world powers. Although this nation maintains adequate defense against attack by hostile neighbors, it pays far more attention to the training of statesmen, scientists, and philosophers.

When at peace with the world, all mobile defense mechanisms are quite fully employed in trade, commerce, and recreation. When war is declared, the entire nation is mobilized. Throughout the period of hostilities military pay obtains in all industries, and the chiefs of all military departments become members of the chief executive's cabinet.

12. THE OTHER NATIONS

Although the society and government of this unique people are in many respects superior to those of the Urantia nations, it should be stated that on the other continents (there are eleven on this planet) the governments are decidedly inferior to the more advanced nations of Urantia.

Just now this superior government is planning to establish ambassadorial relations with the inferior peoples, and for the first time a great religious leader has arisen who advocates the sending of missionaries to these surrounding nations. We fear they are about to make the mistake that so many others have made when they have endeavored to force a superior culture and religion upon other races. What a wonderful thing could be done on this world if this continental nation of advanced culture would only go out and bring to itself the best of the neighboring peoples and then, after educating them, send them back as emissaries of culture to their benighted brethren! Of course, if a Magisterial Son should soon come to this advanced nation, great things could quickly happen on this world.

This recital of the affairs of a neighboring planet is made by special permission with the intent of advancing civilization and augmenting governmental evolution on Urantia. Much more could be narrated that would no doubt interest and intrigue Urantians, but this disclosure covers the limits of our permissive mandate.

Urantians should, however, take note that their sister sphere in the Satania family has benefited by neither magisterial nor bestowal missions of the Paradise Sons. Neither are the various peoples of Urantia set off from each other by such disparity of culture as separates the continental nation from its planetary fellows.

The pouring out of the Spirit of Truth provides the spiritual foundation for the realization of great achievements in the interests of the human race of the bestowal world. Urantia is therefore far better prepared for the more immediate realization of a planetary government with its laws, mechanisms, symbols, conventions, and language—all of which could contribute so mightily to the establishment of world-wide peace under law and could lead to the sometime dawning of a real age of spiritual striving; and such an age is the planetary threshold to the utopian ages of light and life.

[Presented by a Melchizedek of Nebadon.]

PAPER 73

THE GARDEN OF EDEN

THE cultural decadence and spiritual poverty resulting from the Caligastia downfall and consequent social confusion had little effect on the physical or biologic status of the Urantia peoples. Organic evolution proceeded apace, quite regardless of the cultural and moral setback which so swiftly followed the disaffection of Caligastia and Daligastia. And there came a time in the planetary history, almost forty thousand years ago, when the Life Carriers on duty took note that, from a purely biologic standpoint, the developmental progress of the Urantia races was nearing its apex. The Melchizedek receivers, concurring in this opinion, readily agreed to join the Life Carriers in a petition to the Most Highs of Edentia asking that Urantia be inspected with a view to authorizing the dispatch of biologic uplifters, a Material Son and Daughter.

This request was addressed to the Most Highs of Edentia because they had exercised direct jurisdiction over many of Urantia's affairs ever since Caligastia's downfall and the temporary vacation of authority on Jerusem.

Tabamantia, sovereign supervisor of the series of decimal or experimental worlds, came to inspect the planet and, after his survey of racial progress, duly recommended that Urantia be granted Material Sons. In a little less than one hundred years from the time of this inspection, Adam and Eve, a Material Son and Daughter of the local system, arrived and began the difficult task of attempting to untangle the confused affairs of a planet retarded by rebellion and resting under the ban of spiritual isolation.

1. THE NODITES AND THE AMADONITES

On a normal planet the arrival of the Material Son would ordinarily herald the approach of a great age of invention, material progress, and intellectual enlightenment. The post-Adamic era is the great scientific age of most worlds, but not so on Urantia. Though the planet was peopled by races physically fit, the tribes languished in the depths of savagery and moral stagnation.

Ten thousand years after the rebellion practically all the gains of the Prince's administration had been effaced; the races of the world were little better off than if this misguided Son had never come to Urantia. Only among the Nodites and the Amadonites was there persistence of the traditions of Dalamatia and the culture of the Planetary Prince.

The *Nodites* were the descendants of the rebel members of the Prince's staff, their name deriving from their first leader, Nod, onetime chairman of the Dalamatia commission on industry and trade. The *Amadonites* were the descendants of those Andonites who chose to remain loyal with Van and Amadon.

"Amadonite" is more of a cultural and religious designation than a racial term; racially considered the Amadonites were essentially *Andonites*. "Nodite" is both a cultural and racial term, for the Nodites themselves constituted the eighth race of Urantia.

There existed a traditional enmity between the Nodites and the Amadonites. This feud was constantly coming to the surface whenever the offspring of these two groups would try to engage in some common enterprise. Even later, in the affairs of Eden, it was exceedingly difficult for them to work together in peace.

Shortly after the destruction of Dalamatia the followers of Nod became divided into three major groups. The central group remained in the immediate vicinity of their original home near the headwaters of the Persian Gulf. The eastern group migrated to the highland regions of Elam just east of the Euphrates valley. The western group was situated on the northeastern Syrian shores of the Mediterranean and in adjacent territory.

These Nodites had freely mated with the Sangik races and had left behind an able progeny. And some of the descendants of the rebellious Dalamatians subsequently joined Van and his loyal followers in the lands north of Mesopotamia. Here, in the vicinity of Lake Van and the southern Caspian Sea region, the Nodites mingled and mixed with the Amadonites, and they were numbered among the "mighty men of old."

Prior to the arrival of Adam and Eve these groups—Nodites and Amadonites—were the most advanced and cultured races on earth.

2. PLANNING FOR THE GARDEN

For almost one hundred years prior to Tabamantia's inspection, Van and his associates, from their highland headquarters of world ethics and culture, had been preaching the advent of a promised Son of God, a racial uplifter, a teacher of truth, and the worthy successor of the traitorous Caligastia. Though the majority of the world's inhabitants of those days exhibited little or no interest in such a prediction, those who were in immediate contact with Van and Amadon took such teaching seriously and began to plan for the actual reception of the promised Son.

Van told his nearest associates the story of the Material Sons on Jerusem; what he had known of them before ever he came to Urantia. He well knew that these Adamic Sons always lived in simple but charming garden homes and proposed, eighty-three years before the arrival of Adam and Eve, that they devote themselves to the proclamation of their advent and to the preparation of a garden home for their reception.

From their highland headquarters and from sixty-one far-scattered settlements, Van and Amadon recruited a corps of over three thousand willing and enthusiastic workers who, in solemn assembly, dedicated themselves to this mission of preparing for the promised—at least expected—Son.

Van divided his volunteers into one hundred companies with a captain over each and an associate who served on his personal staff as a liaison officer, keeping Amadon as his own associate. These commissions all began in earnest their preliminary work, and the committee on location for the Garden sallied forth in search of the ideal spot.

Although Caligastia and Daligastia had been deprived of much of their power for evil, they did everything possible to frustrate and hamper the work of preparing the Garden. But their evil machinations were largely offset by the faithful activities of the almost ten thousand loyal midway creatures who so tirelessly labored to advance the enterprise.

3. THE GARDEN SITE

The committee on location was absent for almost three years. It reported favorably concerning three possible locations: The first was an island in the Persian Gulf; the second, the river location subsequently occupied as the second garden; the third, a long narrow peninsula—almost an island—projecting westward from the eastern shores of the Mediterranean Sea.

The committee almost unanimously favored the third selection. This site was chosen, and two years were occupied in transferring the world's cultural headquarters, including the tree of life, to this Mediterranean peninsula. All but a single group of the peninsula dwellers peaceably vacated when Van and his company arrived.

This Mediterranean peninsula had a salubrious climate and an equable temperature; this stabilized weather was due to the encircling mountains and to the fact that this area was virtually an island in an inland sea. While it rained copiously on the surrounding highlands, it seldom rained in Eden proper. But each night, from the extensive network of artificial irrigation channels, a "mist would go up" to refresh the vegetation of the Garden.

The coast line of this land mass was considerably elevated, and the neck connecting with the mainland was only twenty-seven miles wide at the narrowest point. The great river that watered the Garden came down from the higher lands of the peninsula and flowed east through the peninsular neck to the mainland and thence across the lowlands of Mesopotamia to the sea beyond. It was fed by four tributaries which took origin in the coastal hills of the Edenic peninsula, and these are the "four heads" of the river which "went out of Eden," and which later became confused with the branches of the rivers surrounding the second garden.

The mountains surrounding the Garden abounded in precious stones and metals, though these received very little attention. The dominant idea was to be the glorification of horticulture and the exaltation of agriculture.

The site chosen for the Garden was probably the most beautiful spot of its kind in all the world, and the climate was then ideal. Nowhere else was there a location which could have lent itself so perfectly to becoming such a paradise of botanic expression. In this rendezvous the cream of the civilization of Urantia was forgathering. Without and beyond, the world lay in darkness, ignorance, and savagery. Eden was the one bright spot on Urantia; it was naturally a dream of loveliness, and it soon became a poem of exquisite and perfected landscape glory.

4. ESTABLISHING THE GARDEN

When Material Sons, the biologic uplifters, begin their sojourn on an evolutionary world, their place of abode is often called the Garden of Eden because it is characterized by the floral beauty and the botanic grandeur of Edentia, the constellation capital. Van well knew of these customs and accordingly provided that the entire peninsula be given over to the Garden. Pasturage and animal husbandry were projected for the adjoining mainland. Of animal life, only the birds and the various domesticated species were to be found in the park. Van's instructions were that Eden was to be a garden, and only a garden. No animals were ever slaughtered within its precincts. All flesh eaten by the Garden workers throughout all the years of construction was brought in from the herds maintained under guard on the mainland.

The first task was the building of the brick wall across the neck of the peninsula. This once completed, the real work of landscape beautification and home building could proceed unhindered.

A zoological garden was created by building a smaller wall just outside the main wall; the intervening space, occupied by all manner of wild beasts, served as an additional defense against hostile attacks. This menagerie was organized in twelve grand divisions, and walled paths led between these groups to the twelve gates of the Garden, the river and its adjacent pastures occupying the central area.

In the preparation of the Garden only volunteer laborers were employed; no hirelings were ever used. They cultivated the Garden and tended their herds for support; contributions of food were also received from near-by believers. And this great enterprise was carried through to completion in spite of the difficulties attendant upon the confused status of the world during these troublous times.

But it was a cause for great disappointment when Van, not knowing how soon the expected Son and Daughter might come, suggested that the younger generation also be trained in the work of carrying on the enterprise in case their arrival should be delayed. This seemed like an admission of lack of faith on Van's part and made considerable trouble, caused many desertions; but Van went forward with his plan of preparedness, meantime filling the places of the deserters with younger volunteers.

5. THE GARDEN HOME

At the center of the Edenic peninsula was the exquisite stone temple of the Universal Father, the sacred shrine of the Garden. To the north the administrative headquarters was established; to the south were built the homes for the workers and their families; to the west was provided the allotment of ground for the proposed schools of the educational system of the expected Son, while in the "east of Eden" were built the domiciles intended for the promised Son and his immediate offspring. The architectural plans for Eden provided homes and abundant land for one million human beings.

At the time of Adam's arrival, though the Garden was only one-fourth finished, it had thousands of miles of irrigation ditches and more than twelve thousand miles of paved paths and roads. There were a trifle over five thousand brick buildings in the various sectors, and the trees and plants were almost beyond number. Seven was the largest number of houses composing any one cluster in the park. And though the structures of the Garden were simple, they were most artistic. The roads and paths were well built, and the landscaping was exquisite.

The sanitary arrangements of the Garden were far in advance of anything that had been attempted theretofore on Urantia. The drinking water of Eden was kept wholesome by the strict observance of the sanitary regulations designed to conserve its purity. During these early times much trouble came about from neglect of these rules, but Van gradually impressed upon his associates the importance of allowing nothing to fall into the water supply of the Garden.

Before the later establishment of a sewage-disposal system the Edenites practiced the scrupulous burial of all waste or decomposing material. Amadon's inspectors made their rounds each day in search for possible causes of sickness. Urantians did not again awaken to the importance of the prevention of human diseases until the later times of the nineteenth and twentieth centuries. Before the disruption of the Adamic regime a covered brick-conduit disposal system had been constructed which ran beneath the walls and emptied into the river of Eden almost a mile beyond the outer or lesser wall of the Garden.

By the time of Adam's arrival most of the plants of that section of the world were growing in Eden. Already had many of the fruits, cereals, and nuts been greatly improved. Many modern vegetables and cereals were first cultivated here, but scores of varieties of food plants were subsequently lost to the world.

About five per cent of the Garden was under high artificial cultivation, fifteen per cent partially cultivated, the remainder being left in a more or less natural state pending the arrival of Adam, it being thought best to finish the park in accordance with his ideas.

And so was the Garden of Eden made ready for the reception of the promised Adam and his consort. And this Garden would have done honor to a world under perfected administration and normal control. Adam and Eve were well pleased with the general plan of Eden, though they made many changes in the furnishings of their own personal dwelling.

Although the work of embellishment was hardly finished at the time of Adam's arrival, the place was already a gem of botanic beauty; and during the early days of his sojourn in Eden the whole Garden took on new form and assumed new proportions of beauty and grandeur. Never before this time nor after has Urantia harbored such a beautiful and replete exhibition of horticulture and agriculture.

6. THE TREE OF LIFE

In the center of the Garden temple Van planted the long-guarded tree of life, whose leaves were for the "healing of the nations," and whose fruit had so long sustained him on earth. Van well knew that Adam and Eve would also be dependent on this gift of Edentia for their life maintenance after they once appeared on Urantia in material form.

The Material Sons on the system capitals do not require the tree of life for sustenance. Only in the planetary repersonalization are they dependent on this adjunct to physical immortality.

The "tree of the knowledge of good and evil" may be a figure of speech, a symbolic designation covering a multitude of human experiences, but the "tree of life" was not a myth; it was real and for a long time was present on Urantia. When the Most Highs of Edentia approved the commission of Caligastia as Planetary Prince of Urantia and those of the one hundred Jerusem citizens as his administrative staff, they sent to the planet, by the Melchizedeks, a shrub of Edentia, and this plant grew to be the tree of life on Urantia. This form of nonintelligent life is native to the constellation headquarters spheres, being also found on the headquarters worlds of the local and superuniverses as well as on the Havona spheres, but not on the system capitals.

This superplant stored up certain space-energies which were antidotal to the age-producing elements of animal existence. The fruit of the tree of life was like a superchemical storage battery, mysteriously releasing the life-extension force of the universe when eaten. This form of sustenance was wholly useless to the ordinary evolutionary beings on Urantia, but specifically it was serviceable to the one hundred materialized members of Caligastia's staff and to the one hundred modified Andonites who had contributed of their life plasm to the Prince's staff, and who, in return, were made possessors of that complement of life which made it possible for them to utilize the fruit of the tree of life for an indefinite extension of their otherwise mortal existence.

During the days of the Prince's rule the tree was growing from the earth in the central and circular courtyard of the Father's temple. Upon the outbreak of the rebellion it was regrown from the central core by Van and his associates in their temporary camp. This Edentia shrub was subsequently taken to their highland retreat, where it served both Van and Amadon for more than one hundred and fifty thousand years.

When Van and his associates made ready the Garden for Adam and Eve, they transplanted the Edentia tree to the Garden of Eden, where, once again, it grew in a central, circular courtyard of another temple to the Father. And Adam and Eve periodically partook of its fruit for the maintenance of their dual form of physical life.

When the plans of the Material Son went astray, Adam and his family were not permitted to carry the core of the tree away from the Garden. When the Nodites invaded Eden, they were told that they would become as "gods if they partook of the fruit of the tree." Much to their surprise they found it unguarded. They ate freely of the fruit for years, but it did nothing for them; they were all material mortals of the realm; they lacked that endowment which acted as a complement to the fruit of the tree. They became enraged at their inability to benefit from the tree of life, and in connection with one of their internal wars, the temple and the tree were both destroyed by fire; only the stone wall stood until the Garden was subsequently submerged. This was the second temple of the Father to perish.

And now must all flesh on Urantia take the natural course of life and death. Adam, Eve, their children, and their children's children, together with their associates, all perished in the course of time, thus becoming subject to the ascension scheme of the local universe wherein mansion world resurrection follows material death.

7. THE FATE OF EDEN

After the first garden was vacated by Adam, it was occupied variously by the Nodites, Cutites, and the Suntites. It later became the dwelling place of the northern Nodites who opposed co-operation with the Adamites. The peninsula had been overrun by these lower-grade Nodites for almost four thousand years after Adam left the Garden when, in connection with the violent activity of the surrounding volcanoes and the submergence of the Sicilian land bridge to Africa, the eastern floor of the Mediterranean Sea sank, carrying down beneath the waters the whole of the Edenic peninsula. Concomitant with this vast submergence the coast line of the eastern Mediterranean was greatly elevated. And this was the end of the most beautiful natural creation that Urantia has ever harbored. The sinking was not sudden, several hundred years being required completely to submerge the entire peninsula.

We cannot regard this disappearance of the Garden as being in any way a result of the miscarriage of the divine plans or as a result of the mistakes of Adam and Eve. We do not regard the submergence of Eden as anything but a natural occurrence, but it does seem to us that the sinking of the Garden was timed to occur at just about the date of the accumulation of the reserves of the violet race for undertaking the work of rehabilitating the world peoples.

The Melchizedeks counseled Adam not to initiate the program of racial uplift and blending until his own family had numbered one-half million. It was never intended that the Garden should be the permanent home of the Adamites. They were to become emissaries of a new life to all the world; they were to mobilize for unselfish bestowal upon the needy races of earth.

The instructions given Adam by the Melchizedeks implied that he was to establish racial, continental, and divisional headquarters to be in charge of his immediate sons and daughters, while he and Eve were to divide their time between these various world capitals as advisers and co-ordinators of the world-wide ministry of biologic uplift, intellectual advancement, and moral rehabilitation.

[Presented by Solonia, the seraphic "voice in the Garden."]

PAPER 74

ADAM AND EVE

ADAM AND EVE arrived on Urantia, from the year A.D. 1934, 37,848 years ago. It was in midseason when the Garden was in the height of bloom that they arrived. At high noon and unannounced, the two seraphic transports, accompanied by the Jerusem personnel intrusted with the transportation of the biologic uplifters to Urantia, settled slowly to the surface of the revolving planet in the vicinity of the temple of the Universal Father. All the work of rematerializing the bodies of Adam and Eve was carried on within the precincts of this newly created shrine. And from the time of their arrival ten days passed before they were re-created in dual human form for presentation as the world's new rulers. They regained consciousness simultaneously. The Material Sons and Daughters always serve together. It is the essence of their service at all times and in all places never to be separated. They are designed to work in pairs; seldom do they function alone.

1. ADAM AND EVE ON JERUSEM

The Planetary Adam and Eve of Urantia were members of the senior corps of Material Sons on Jerusem, being jointly number 14,311. They belonged to the third physical series and were a little more than eight feet in height.

At the time Adam was chosen to come to Urantia, he was employed, with his mate, in the trial-and-testing physical laboratories of Jerusem. For more than fifteen thousand years they had been directors of the division of experimental energy as applied to the modification of living forms. Long before this they had been teachers in the citizenship schools for new arrivals on Jerusem. And all this should be borne in mind in connection with the narration of their subsequent conduct on Urantia.

When the proclamation was issued calling for volunteers for the mission of Adamic adventure on Urantia, the entire senior corps of Material Sons and Daughters volunteered. The Melchizedek examiners, with the approval of Lanaforge and the Most Highs of Edentia, finally selected the Adam and Eve who subsequently came to function as the biologic uplifters of Urantia.

Adam and Eve had remained loyal to Michael during the Lucifer rebellion; nevertheless, the pair were called before the System Sovereign and his entire cabinet for examination and instruction. The details of Urantia affairs were fully presented; they were exhaustively instructed as to the plans to be pursued in accepting the responsibilities of rulership on such a strife-torn world. They were put under joint oaths of allegiance to the Most Highs of Edentia and to Michael of Salvington. And they were duly advised to regard themselves as subject to the Urantia corps of Melchizedek receivers until that governing body should see fit to relinquish rule on the world of their assignment.

This Jerusem pair left behind them on the capital of Satania and elsewhere, one hundred offspring—fifty sons and fifty daughters—magnificent creatures who had escaped the pitfalls of progression, and who were all in commission as faithful stewards of universe trust at the time of their parents' departure for Urantia. And they were all present in the beautiful temple of the Material Sons attendant upon the farewell exercises associated with the last ceremonies of the bestowal acceptance. These children accompanied their parents to the dematerialization headquarters of their order and were the last to bid them farewell and divine speed as they fell asleep in the personality lapse of consciousness which precedes the preparation for seraphic transport. The children spent some time together at the family rendezvous rejoicing that their parents were soon to become the visible heads, in reality the sole rulers, of planet 606 in the system of Satania.

And thus did Adam and Eve leave Jerusem amidst the acclaim and well-wishing of its citizens. They went forth to their new responsibilities adequately equipped and fully instructed concerning every duty and danger to be encountered on Urantia.

2. ARRIVAL OF ADAM AND EVE

Adam and Eve fell asleep on Jerusem, and when they awakened in the Father's temple on Urantia in the presence of the mighty throng assembled to welcome them, they were face to face with two beings of whom they had heard much, Van and his faithful associate Amadon. These two heroes of the Caligastia secession were the first to welcome them in their new garden home.

The tongue of Eden was an Andonic dialect as spoken by Amadon. Van and Amadon had markedly improved this language by creating a new alphabet of twenty-four letters, and they had hoped to see it become the tongue of Urantia as the Edenic culture would spread throughout the world. Adam and Eve had fully mastered this human dialect before they departed from Jerusem so that this son of Andon heard the exalted ruler of his world address him in his own tongue.

And on that day there was great excitement and joy throughout Eden as the runners went in great haste to the rendezvous of the carrier pigeons assembled from near and far, shouting: "Let loose the birds; let them carry the word that the promised Son has come." Hundreds of believer settlements had faithfully, year after year, kept up the supply of these home-reared pigeons for just such an occasion.

As the news of Adam's arrival spread abroad, thousands of the near-by tribesmen accepted the teachings of Van and Amadon, while for months and months pilgrims continued to pour into Eden to welcome Adam and Eve and to do homage to their unseen Father.

Soon after their awakening, Adam and Eve were escorted to the formal reception on the great mound to the north of the temple. This natural hill had been enlarged and made ready for the installation of the world's new rulers. Here, at noon, the Urantia reception committee welcomed this Son and Daughter of the system of Satania. Amadon was chairman of this committee, which consisted of twelve members embracing a representative of each of the six Sangik races; the acting chief of the midwayers; Annan, a loyal daughter and spokesman for the Nodites; Noah, the son of the architect and builder of the Garden and executive of his deceased father's plans; and the two resident Life Carriers.

The next act was the delivery of the charge of planetary custody to Adam and Eve by the senior Melchizedek, chief of the council of receivership on Urantia. The Material Son and Daughter took the oath of allegiance to the Most Highs of Norlatiadek and to Michael of Nebadon and were proclaimed rulers of Urantia by Van, who thereby relinquished the titular authority which for over one hundred and fifty thousand years he had held by virtue of the action of the Melchizedek receivers.

And Adam and Eve were invested with kingly robes on this occasion, the time of their formal induction into world rulership. Not all of the arts of Dalamatia had been lost to the world; weaving was still practiced in the days of Eden.

Then was heard the archangels' proclamation, and the broadcast voice of Gabriel decreed the second judgment roll call of Urantia and the resurrection of the sleeping survivors of the second dispensation of grace and mercy on 606 of Satania. The dispensation of the Prince has passed; the age of Adam, the third planetary epoch, opens amidst scenes of simple grandeur; and the new rulers of Urantia start their reign under seemingly favorable conditions, notwithstanding the world-wide confusion occasioned by lack of the co-operation of their predecessor in authority on the planet.

3. ADAM AND EVE LEARN ABOUT THE PLANET

And now, after their formal installation, Adam and Eve became painfully aware of their planetary isolation. Silent were the familiar broadcasts, and absent were all the circuits of extraplanetary communication. Their Jerusem fellows had gone to worlds running along smoothly with a well-established Planetary Prince and an experienced staff ready to receive them and competent to co-operate with them during their early experience on such worlds. But on Urantia rebellion had changed everything. Here the Planetary Prince was very much present, and though shorn of most of his power to work evil, he was still able to make the task of Adam and Eve difficult and to some extent hazardous. It was a serious and disillusioned Son and Daughter of Jerusem who walked that night through the Garden under the shining of the full moon, discussing plans for the next day.

Thus ended the first day of Adam and Eve on isolated Urantia, the confused planet of the Caligastia betrayal; and they walked and talked far into the night, their first night on earth—and it was so lonely.

Adam's second day on earth was spent in session with the planetary receivers and the advisory council. From the Melchizedeks, and their associates, Adam and Eve learned more about the details of the Caligastia rebellion and the result of that upheaval upon the world's progress. And it was, on the whole, a disheartening story, this long recital of the mismanagement of world affairs. They learned all the facts regarding the utter collapse of the Caligastia scheme for accelerating the process of social evolution. They also arrived at a full realization of the folly of attempting to achieve planetary advancement independently of the divine plan of progression. And thus ended a sad but enlightening day—their second on Urantia.

The third day was devoted to an inspection of the Garden. From the large passenger birds—the fandors—Adam and Eve looked down upon the vast stretches of the Garden while being carried through the air over this, the most beautiful spot on earth. This day of inspection ended with an enormous banquet in honor of all who had labored to create this garden of Edenic beauty and grandeur. And again, late into the night of their third day, the Son and his mate walked in the Garden and talked about the immensity of their problems.

On the fourth day Adam and Eve addressed the Garden assembly. From the inaugural mount they spoke to the people concerning their plans for the rehabilitation of the world and outlined the methods whereby they would seek to redeem the social culture of Urantia from the low levels to which it had fallen as a result of sin and rebellion. This was a great day, and it closed with a feast for the council of men and women who had been selected to assume responsibilities in the new administration of world affairs. Take note! women as well as men were in this group, and that was the first time such a thing had occurred on earth since the days of Dalamatia. It was an astounding innovation to behold Eve, a woman, sharing the honors and responsibilities of world affairs with a man. And thus ended the fourth day on earth.

The fifth day was occupied with the organization of the temporary government, the administration which was to function until the Melchizedek receivers should leave Urantia.

The sixth day was devoted to an inspection of the numerous types of men and animals. Along the walls eastward in Eden, Adam and Eve were escorted all day, viewing the animal life of the planet and arriving at a better understanding as to what must be done to bring order out of the confusion of a world inhabited by such a variety of living creatures.

It greatly surprised those who accompanied Adam on this trip to observe how fully he understood the nature and function of the thousands upon thousands of animals shown him. The instant he glanced at an animal, he would indicate its nature and behavior. Adam could give names descriptive of the origin, nature, and function of all material creatures on sight. Those who conducted him on this tour of inspection did not know that the world's new ruler was one of the most expert anatomists of all Satania; and Eve was equally proficient. Adam amazed his associates by describing hosts of living things too small to be seen by human eyes.

When the sixth day of their sojourn on earth was over, Adam and Eve rested for the first time in their new home in "the east of Eden." The first six days of the Urantia adventure had been very busy, and they looked forward with great pleasure to an entire day of freedom from all activities.

But circumstances dictated otherwise. The experience of the day just past in which Adam had so intelligently and so exhaustively discussed the animal life of Urantia, together with his masterly inaugural address and his charming manner, had so won the hearts and overcome the intellects of the Garden dwellers that they were not only wholeheartedly disposed to accept the newly arrived Son and Daughter of Jerusem as rulers, but the majority were about ready to fall down and worship them as gods.

4. THE FIRST UPHEAVAL

That night, the night following the sixth day, while Adam and Eve slumbered, strange things were transpiring in the vicinity of the Father's temple in the central sector of Eden. There, under the rays of the mellow moon, hundreds of enthusiastic and excited men and women listened for hours to the impassioned pleas of their leaders. They meant well, but they simply could not understand the simplicity of the fraternal and democratic manner of their new rulers. And long before daybreak the new and temporary administrators of world affairs reached a virtually unanimous conclusion that Adam and his mate were altogether too modest and unassuming. They decided that Divinity had descended to earth in bodily form, that Adam and Eve were in reality gods or else so near such an estate as to be worthy of reverent worship.

The amazing events of the first six days of Adam and Eve on earth were entirely too much for the unprepared minds of even the world's best men; their heads were in a whirl; they were swept along with the proposal to bring the noble pair up to the Father's temple at high noon in order that everyone might bow down in respectful worship and prostrate themselves in humble submission. And the Garden dwellers were really sincere in all of this.

Van protested. Amadon was absent, being in charge of the guard of honor which had remained behind with Adam and Eve overnight. But Van's protest was swept aside. He was told that he was likewise too modest, too unassuming; that he was not far from a god himself, else how had he lived so long on earth, and how had he brought about such a great event as the advent of Adam? And as the excited Edenites were about to seize him and carry him up to the mount for adoration, Van made his way out through the throng and, being able to communicate with the midwayers, sent their leader in great haste to Adam.

It was near the dawn of their seventh day on earth that Adam and Eve heard the startling news of the proposal of these well-meaning but misguided mortals; and then, even while the passenger birds were swiftly winging to bring them to the temple, the midwayers, being able to do such things, transported Adam and Eve to the Father's temple. It was early on the morning of this seventh day and from the mount of their so recent reception that Adam held forth in explanation of the orders of divine sonship and made clear to these earth minds that only the Father and those whom he designates may be worshiped. Adam made it plain that he would accept any honor and receive all respect, but worship never!

It was a momentous day, and just before noon, about the time of the arrival of the seraphic messenger bearing the Jerusem acknowledgment of the installation of the world's rulers, Adam and Eve, moving apart from the throng, pointed to the Father's temple and said: "Go you now to the material emblem of the Father's invisible presence and bow down in worship of him who made us all and who keeps us living. And let this act be the sincere pledge that you never will again be tempted to worship anyone but God." They all did as Adam directed. The Material Son and Daughter stood alone on the mount with bowed heads while the people prostrated themselves about the temple.

And this was the origin of the Sabbath-day tradition. Always in Eden the seventh day was devoted to the noontide assembly at the temple; long it was the custom to devote this day to self-culture. The forenoon was devoted to physical improvement, the noontime to spiritual worship, the afternoon to mind culture, while the evening was spent in social rejoicing. This was never the law in Eden, but it was the custom as long as the Adamic administration held sway on earth.

5. ADAM'S ADMINISTRATION

For almost seven years after Adam's arrival the Melchizedek receivers remained on duty, but the time finally came when they turned the administration of world affairs over to Adam and returned to Jerusem.

The farewell of the receivers occupied the whole of a day, and during the evening the individual Melchizedeks gave Adam and Eve their parting advice and best wishes. Adam had several times requested his advisers to remain on earth with him, but always were these petitions denied. The time had come when the Material Sons must assume full responsibility for the conduct of world affairs. And so, at midnight, the seraphic transports of Satania left the planet with fourteen beings for Jerusem, the translation of Van and Amadon occurring simultaneously with the departure of the twelve Melchizedeks.

All went fairly well for a time on Urantia, and it appeared that Adam would, eventually, be able to develop some plan for promoting the gradual extension of the Edenic civilization. Pursuant to the advice of the Melchizedeks, he began to foster the arts of manufacture with the idea of developing trade relations with the outside world. When Eden was disrupted, there were over one hundred primitive manufacturing plants in operation, and extensive trade relations with the near-by tribes had been established.

For ages Adam and Eve had been instructed in the technique of improving a world in readiness for their specialized contributions to the advancement of evolutionary civilization; but now they were face to face with pressing problems, such as the establishment of law and order in a world of savages, barbarians, and semicivilized human beings. Aside from the cream of the earth's population, assembled in the Garden, only a few groups, here and there, were at all ready for the reception of the Adamic culture.

Adam made a heroic and determined effort to establish a world government, but he met with stubborn resistance at every turn. Adam had already put in operation a system of group control throughout Eden and had federated all of these companies into the Edenic league. But trouble, serious trouble, ensued when he went outside the Garden and sought to apply these ideas to the outlying tribes. The moment Adam's associates began to work outside the Garden, they met the direct and well-planned resistance of Caligastia and Daligastia. The fallen Prince had been deposed as world ruler, but he had not been removed from the planet. He was still present on earth and able, at least to some extent, to resist all of Adam's plans for the rehabilitation of human society. Adam tried to warn the races against Caligastia, but the task was made very difficult because his archenemy was invisible to the eyes of mortals.

Even among the Edenites there were those confused minds that leaned toward the Caligastia teaching of unbridled personal liberty; and they caused Adam no end of trouble; always were they upsetting the best-laid plans for orderly progression and substantial development. He was finally compelled to withdraw his program for immediate socialization; he fell back on Van's method of organization, dividing the Edenites into companies of one hundred with captains over each and with lieutenants in charge of groups of ten.

Adam and Eve had come to institute representative government in the place of monarchial, but they found no government worthy of the name on the face of the whole earth. For the time being Adam abandoned all effort to establish representative government, and before the collapse of the Edenic regime he succeeded in establishing almost one hundred outlying trade and social centers where strong individuals ruled in his name. Most of these centers had been organized aforetime by Van and Amadon.

The sending of ambassadors from one tribe to another dates from the times of Adam. This was a great forward step in the evolution of government.

6. HOME LIFE OF ADAM AND EVE

The Adamic family grounds embraced a little over five square miles. Immediately surrounding this homesite, provision had been made for the care of more than three hundred thousand of the pure-line offspring. But only the first unit of the projected buildings was ever constructed. Before the size of the Adamic family outgrew these early provisions, the whole Edenic plan had been disrupted and the Garden vacated.

Adamson was the first-born of the violet race of Urantia, being followed by his sister and Eveson, the second son of Adam and Eve. Eve was the mother of five children before the Melchizedeks left—three sons and two daughters. The next two were twins. She bore sixty-three children, thirty-two daughters and thirty-one sons, before the default. When Adam and Eve left the Garden, their family consisted of four generations numbering 1,647 pure-line descendants. They had forty-two children after leaving the Garden besides the two offspring of joint parentage with the mortal stock of earth. And this does not include the Adamic parentage to the Nodite and evolutionary races.

The Adamic children did not take milk from animals when they ceased to nurse the mother's breast at one year of age. Eve had access to the milk of a great variety of nuts and to the juices of many fruits, and knowing full well the chemistry and energy of these foods, she suitably combined them for the nourishment of her children until the appearance of teeth.

While cooking was universally employed outside of the immediate Adamic sector of Eden, there was no cooking in Adam's household. They found their foods—fruits, nuts, and cereals—ready prepared as they ripened. They ate once a day, shortly after noontime. Adam and Eve also imbibed "light and energy" direct from certain space emanations in conjunction with the ministry of the tree of life.

The bodies of Adam and Eve gave forth a shimmer of light, but they always wore clothing in conformity with the custom of their associates. Though wearing very little during the day, at eventide they donned night wraps. The origin of the traditional halo encircling the heads of supposed pious and holy men dates back to the days of Adam and Eve. Since the light emanations of their bodies were so largely obscured by clothing, only the radiating glow from their heads was discernible. The descendants of Adamson always thus portrayed their concept of individuals believed to be extraordinary in spiritual development.

Adam and Eve could communicate with each other and with their immediate children over a distance of about fifty miles. This thought exchange was effected by means of the delicate gas chambers located in close proximity to their brain structures. By this mechanism they could send and receive thought oscillations. But this power was instantly suspended upon the mind's surrender to the discord and disruption of evil.

The Adamic children attended their own schools until they were sixteen, the younger being taught by the elder. The little folks changed activities every thirty minutes, the older every hour. And it was certainly a new sight on Urantia to observe these children of Adam and Eve at play, joyous and exhilarating activity just for the sheer fun of it. The play and humor of the present-day races are largely derived from the Adamic stock. The Adamites all had a great appreciation of music as well as a keen sense of humor.

The average age of betrothal was eighteen, and these youths then entered upon a two years' course of instruction in preparation for the assumption of marital responsibilities. At twenty they were eligible for marriage; and after marriage they began their lifework or entered upon special preparation therefor.

The practice of some subsequent nations of permitting the royal families, supposedly descended from the gods, to marry brother to sister, dates from the traditions of the Adamic offspring—mating, as they must needs, with one another. The marriage ceremonies of the first and second generations of the Garden were always performed by Adam and Eve.

7. LIFE IN THE GARDEN

The children of Adam, except for four years' attendance at the western schools, lived and worked in the "east of Eden." They were trained intellectually until they were sixteen in accordance with the methods of the Jerusem schools. From sixteen to twenty they were taught in the Urantia schools at the other end of the Garden, serving there also as teachers in the lower grades.

The entire purpose of the western school system of the Garden was *socialization.* The forenoon periods of recess were devoted to practical horticulture and agriculture, the afternoon periods to competitive play. The evenings were employed in social intercourse and the cultivation of personal friendships. Religious and sexual training were regarded as the province of the home, the duty of parents.

The teaching in these schools included instruction regarding:

1. Health and the care of the body.
2. The golden rule, the standard of social intercourse.
3. The relation of individual rights to group rights and community obligations.
4. History and culture of the various earth races.
5. Methods of advancing and improving world trade.
6. Co-ordination of conflicting duties and emotions.
7. The cultivation of play, humor, and competitive substitutes for physical fighting.

The schools, in fact every activity of the Garden, were always open to visitors. Unarmed observers were freely admitted to Eden for short visits. To sojourn in the Garden a Urantian had to be "adopted." He received instructions in the plan and purpose of the Adamic bestowal, signified his intention to adhere to this mission, and then made declaration of loyalty to the social rule of Adam and the spiritual sovereignty of the Universal Father.

The laws of the Garden were based on the older codes of Dalamatia and were promulgated under seven heads:

1. The laws of health and sanitation.
2. The social regulations of the Garden.
3. The code of trade and commerce.
4. The laws of fair play and competition.
5. The laws of home life.
6. The civil codes of the golden rule.
7. The seven commands of supreme moral rule.

The moral law of Eden was little different from the seven commandments of Dalamatia. But the Adamites taught many additional reasons for these commands; for instance, regarding the injunction against murder, the indwelling of the Thought Adjuster was presented as an additional reason for not destroying human life. They taught that "whoso sheds man's blood by man shall his blood be shed, for in the image of God made he man."

The public worship hour of Eden was noon; sunset was the hour of family worship. Adam did his best to discourage the use of set prayers, teaching that effective prayer must be wholly individual, that it must be the "desire of the soul"; but the Edenites continued to use the prayers and forms handed down from the times of Dalamatia. Adam also endeavored to substitute the offerings of the fruit of the land for the blood sacrifices in the religious ceremonies but had made little progress before the disruption of the Garden.

Adam endeavored to teach the races sex equality. The way Eve worked by the side of her husband made a profound impression upon all dwellers in the Garden. Adam definitely taught them that the woman, equally with the man, contributes those life factors which unite to form a new being. Theretofore, mankind had presumed that all procreation resided in the "loins of the father." They had looked upon the mother as being merely a provision for nurturing the unborn and nursing the newborn.

Adam taught his contemporaries all they could comprehend, but that was not very much, comparatively speaking. Nevertheless, the more intelligent of the races of earth looked forward eagerly to the time when they would be permitted to intermarry with the superior children of the violet race. And what a different world Urantia would have become if this great plan of uplifting the races had been carried out! Even as it was, tremendous gains resulted from the small amount of the blood of this imported race which the evolutionary peoples incidentally secured.

And thus did Adam work for the welfare and uplift of the world of his sojourn. But it was a difficult task to lead these mixed and mongrel peoples in the better way.

8. THE LEGEND OF CREATION

The story of the creation of Urantia in six days was based on the tradition that Adam and Eve had spent just six days in their initial survey of the Garden. This circumstance lent almost sacred sanction to the time period of the week, which had been originally introduced by the Dalamatians. Adam's spending six days inspecting the Garden and formulating preliminary plans for organization was not prearranged; it was worked out from day to day. The choosing of the seventh day for worship was wholly incidental to the facts herewith narrated.

The legend of the making of the world in six days was an afterthought, in fact, more than thirty thousand years afterwards. One feature of the narrative, the sudden appearance of the sun and moon, may have taken origin in the traditions of the onetime sudden emergence of the world from a dense space cloud of minute matter which had long obscured both sun and moon.

The story of creating Eve out of Adam's rib is a confused condensation of the Adamic arrival and the celestial surgery connected with the interchange of living substances associated with the coming of the corporeal staff of the Planetary Prince more than four hundred and fifty thousand years previously.

The majority of the world's peoples have been influenced by the tradition that Adam and Eve had physical forms created for them upon their arrival on Urantia. The belief in man's having been created from clay was well-nigh universal in the Eastern Hemisphere; this tradition can be traced from the Philippine Islands around the world to Africa. And many groups accepted this story of man's clay origin by some form of special creation in the place of the earlier beliefs in progressive creation—evolution.

Away from the influences of Dalamatia and Eden, mankind tended toward the belief in the gradual ascent of the human race. The fact of evolution is not a modern discovery; the ancients understood the slow and evolutionary character of human progress. The early Greeks had clear ideas of this despite their proximity to Mesopotamia. Although the various races of earth became sadly mixed up in their notions of evolution, nevertheless, many of the primitive tribes believed and taught that they were the descendants of various animals. Primitive peoples made a practice of selecting for their "totems" the animals of their supposed ancestry. Certain North American Indian tribes believed they originated from beavers and coyotes. Certain African tribes teach that they are descended from the hyena, a Malay tribe from the lemur, a New Guinea group from the parrot.

The Babylonians, because of immediate contact with the remnants of the civilization of the Adamites, enlarged and embellished the story of man's creation; they taught that he had descended directly from the gods. They held to an aristocratic origin for the race which was incompatible with even the doctrine of creation out of clay.

The Old Testament account of creation dates from long after the time of Moses; he never taught the Hebrews such a distorted story. But he did present a simple and condensed narrative of creation to the Israelites, hoping thereby to augment his appeal to worship the Creator, the Universal Father, whom he called the Lord God of Israel.

In his early teachings, Moses very wisely did not attempt to go back of Adam's time, and since Moses was the supreme teacher of the Hebrews, the stories of Adam became intimately associated with those of creation. That the earlier traditions recognized pre-Adamic civilization is clearly shown by the fact that later editors, intending to eradicate all reference to human affairs before Adam's time, neglected to remove the telltale reference to Cain's emigration to the "land of Nod," where he took himself a wife.

The Hebrews had no written language in general usage for a long time after they reached Palestine. They learned the use of an alphabet from the neighboring Philistines, who were political refugees from the higher civilization of Crete. The Hebrews did little writing until about 900 B.C., and having no written language until such a late date, they had several different stories of creation in circulation, but after the Babylonian captivity they inclined more toward accepting a modified Mesopotamian version.

Jewish tradition became crystallized about Moses, and because he endeavored to trace the lineage of Abraham back to Adam, the Jews assumed that Adam was the first of all mankind. Yahweh was the creator, and since Adam was supposed to be the first man, he must have made the world just prior to making Adam. And then the tradition of Adam's six days got woven into the story, with the result that almost a thousand years after Moses' sojourn on earth the tradition of creation in six days was written out and subsequently credited to him.

When the Jewish priests returned to Jerusalem, they had already completed the writing of their narrative of the beginning of things. Soon they made claims that this recital was a recently discovered story of creation written by Moses. But the contemporary Hebrews of around 500 B.C. did not consider these writings to be divine revelations; they looked upon them much as later peoples regard mythological narratives.

This spurious document, reputed to be the teachings of Moses, was brought to the attention of Ptolemy, the Greek king of Egypt, who had it translated into Greek by a commission of seventy scholars for his new library at Alexandria. And so this account found its place among those writings which subsequently became a part of the later collections of the "sacred scriptures" of the Hebrew and Christian religions. And through identification with these theological systems, such concepts for a long time profoundly influenced the philosophy of many Occidental peoples.

The Christian teachers perpetuated the belief in the fiat creation of the human race, and all this led directly to the formation of the hypothesis of a onetime golden age of utopian bliss and the theory of the fall of man or superman which accounted for the nonutopian condition of society. These outlooks on life and man's place in the universe were at best discouraging since they were predicated upon a belief in retrogression rather than progression, as well as implying a vengeful Deity, who had vented wrath upon the human race in retribution for the errors of certain onetime planetary administrators.

The "golden age" is a myth, but Eden was a fact, and the Garden civilization was actually overthrown. Adam and Eve carried on in the Garden for one hundred and seventeen years when, through the impatience of Eve and the errors of judgment of Adam, they presumed to turn aside from the ordained way, speedily bringing disaster upon themselves and ruinous retardation upon the developmental progression of all Urantia.

[Narrated by Solonia, the seraphic "voice in the Garden."]

PAPER 75

THE DEFAULT OF ADAM AND EVE

AFTER more than one hundred years of effort on Urantia, Adam was able to see very little progress outside the Garden; the world at large did not seem to be improving much. The realization of race betterment appeared to be a long way off, and the situation seemed so desperate as to demand something for relief not embraced in the original plans. At least that is what often passed through Adam's mind, and he so expressed himself many times to Eve. Adam and his mate were loyal, but they were isolated from their kind, and they were sorely distressed by the sorry plight of their world.

1. THE URANTIA PROBLEM

The Adamic mission on experimental, rebellion-seared, and isolated Urantia was a formidable undertaking. And the Material Son and Daughter early became aware of the difficulty and complexity of their planetary assignment. Nevertheless, they courageously set about the task of solving their manifold problems. But when they addressed themselves to the all-important work of eliminating the defectives and degenerates from among the human strains, they were quite dismayed. They could see no way out of the dilemma, and they could not take counsel with their superiors on either Jerusem or Edentia. Here they were, isolated and day by day confronted with some new and complicated tangle, some problem that seemed to be unsolvable.

Under normal conditions the first work of a Planetary Adam and Eve would be the co-ordination and blending of the races. But on Urantia such a project seemed just about hopeless, for the races, while biologically fit, had never been purged of their retarded and defective strains.

Adam and Eve found themselves on a sphere wholly unprepared for the proclamation of the brotherhood of man, a world groping about in abject spiritual darkness and cursed with confusion worse confounded by the miscarriage of the mission of the preceding administration. Mind and morals were at a low level, and instead of beginning the task of effecting religious unity, they must begin all anew the work of converting the inhabitants to the most simple forms of religious belief. Instead of finding one language ready for adoption, they were confronted by the world-wide confusion of hundreds upon hundreds of local dialects. No Adam of the planetary service was ever set down on a more difficult world; the obstacles seemed insuperable and the problems beyond creature solution.

They were isolated, and the tremendous sense of loneliness which bore down upon them was all the more heightened by the early departure of the Melchizedek receivers. Only indirectly, by means of the angelic orders, could they communicate with any being off the planet. Slowly their courage weakened, their spirits drooped, and sometimes their faith almost faltered.

And this is the true picture of the consternation of these two noble souls as they pondered the tasks which confronted them. They were both keenly aware of the enormous undertaking involved in the execution of their planetary assignment.

Probably no Material Sons of Nebadon were ever faced with such a difficult and seemingly hopeless task as confronted Adam and Eve in the sorry plight of Urantia. But they would have sometime met with success had they been more farseeing and *patient.* Both of them, especially Eve, were altogether too impatient; they were not willing to settle down to the long, long endurance test. They wanted to see some immediate results, and they did, but the results thus secured proved most disastrous both to themselves and to their world.

2. CALIGASTIA'S PLOT

Caligastia paid frequent visits to the Garden and held many conferences with Adam and Eve, but they were adamant to all his suggestions of compromise and short-cut adventures. They had before them enough of the results of rebellion to produce effective immunity against all such insinuating proposals. Even the young offspring of Adam were uninfluenced by the overtures of Daligastia. And of course neither Caligastia nor his associate had power to influence any individual against his will, much less to persuade the children of Adam to do wrong.

It must be remembered that Caligastia was still the titular Planetary Prince of Urantia, a misguided but nevertheless high Son of the local universe. He was not finally deposed until the times of Christ Michael on Urantia.

But the fallen Prince was persistent and determined. He soon gave up working on Adam and decided to try a wily flank attack on Eve. The evil one concluded that the only hope for success lay in the adroit employment of suitable persons belonging to the upper strata of the Nodite group, the descendants of his onetime corporeal-staff associates. And the plans were accordingly laid for entrapping the mother of the violet race.

It was farthest from Eve's intention ever to do anything which would militate against Adam's plans or jeopardize their planetary trust. Knowing the tendency of woman to look upon immediate results rather than to plan farsightedly for more remote effects, the Melchizedeks, before departing, had especially enjoined Eve as to the peculiar dangers besetting their isolated position on the planet and had in particular warned her never to stray from the side of her mate, that is, to attempt no personal or secret methods of furthering their mutual undertakings. Eve had most scrupulously carried out these instructions for more than one hundred years, and it did not occur to her that any danger would attach to the increasingly private and confidential visits she was enjoying with a certain Nodite leader named Serapatatia. The whole affair developed so gradually and naturally that she was taken unawares.

The Garden dwellers had been in contact with the Nodites since the early days of Eden. From these mixed descendants of the defaulting members of Caligastia's staff they had received much valuable help and co-operation, and through them the Edenic regime was now to meet its complete undoing and final overthrow.

3. THE TEMPTATION OF EVE

Adam had just finished his first one hundred years on earth when Serapatatia, upon the death of his father, came to the leadership of the western or Syrian confederation of the Nodite tribes. Serapatatia was a brown-tinted man, a brilliant descendant of the onetime chief of the Dalamatia commission on health mated with one of the master female minds of the blue race of those distant days. All down through the ages this line had held authority and wielded a great influence among the western Nodite tribes.

Serapatatia had made several visits to the Garden and had become deeply impressed with the righteousness of Adam's cause. And shortly after assuming the leadership of the Syrian Nodites, he announced his intention of establishing an affiliation with the work of Adam and Eve in the Garden. The majority of his people joined him in this program, and Adam was cheered by the news that the most powerful and the most intelligent of all the neighboring tribes had swung over almost bodily to the support of the program for world improvement; it was decidedly heartening. And shortly after this great event, Serapatatia and his new staff were entertained by Adam and Eve in their own home.

Serapatatia became one of the most able and efficient of all of Adam's lieutenants. He was entirely honest and thoroughly sincere in all of his activities; he was never conscious, even later on, that he was being used as a circumstantial tool of the wily Caligastia.

Presently, Serapatatia became the associate chairman of the Edenic commission on tribal relations, and many plans were laid for the more vigorous prosecution of the work of winning the remote tribes to the cause of the Garden.

He held many conferences with Adam and Eve—especially with Eve—and they talked over many plans for improving their methods. One day, during a talk with Eve, it occurred to Serapatatia that it would be very helpful if, while awaiting the recruiting of large numbers of the violet race, something could be done in the meantime immediately to advance the needy waiting tribes. Serapatatia contended that, if the Nodites, as the most progressive and cooperative race, could have a leader born to them of part origin in the violet stock, it would constitute a powerful tie binding these peoples more closely to the Garden. And all of this was soberly and honestly considered to be for the good of the world since this child, to be reared and educated in the Garden, would exert a great influence for good over his father's people.

It should again be emphasized that Serapatatia was altogether honest and wholly sincere in all that he proposed. He never once suspected that he was playing into the hands of Caligastia and Daligastia. Serapatatia was entirely loyal to the plan of building up a strong reserve of the violet race before attempting the world-wide upstepping of the confused peoples of Urantia. But this would require hundreds of years to consummate, and he was impatient; he wanted to see some immediate results—something in his own lifetime. He made it clear to Eve that Adam was oftentimes discouraged by the little that had been accomplished toward uplifting the world.

For more than five years these plans were secretly matured. At last they had developed to the point where Eve consented to have a secret conference with

Cano, the most brilliant mind and active leader of the near-by colony of friendly Nodites. Cano was very sympathetic with the Adamic regime; in fact, he was the sincere spiritual leader of those neighboring Nodites who favored friendly relations with the Garden.

The fateful meeting occurred during the twilight hours of the autumn evening, not far from the home of Adam. Eve had never before met the beautiful and enthusiastic Cano—and he was a magnificent specimen of the survival of the superior physique and outstanding intellect of his remote progenitors of the Prince's staff. And Cano also thoroughly believed in the righteousness of the Serapatatia project. (Outside of the Garden, multiple mating was a common practice.)

Influenced by flattery, enthusiasm, and great personal persuasion, Eve then and there consented to embark upon the much-discussed enterprise, to add her own little scheme of world saving to the larger and more far-reaching divine plan. Before she quite realized what was transpiring, the fatal step had been taken. It was done.

4. THE REALIZATION OF DEFAULT

The celestial life of the planet was astir. Adam recognized that something was wrong, and he asked Eve to come aside with him in the Garden. And now, for the first time, Adam heard the entire story of the long-nourished plan for accelerating world improvement by operating simultaneously in two directions: the prosecution of the divine plan concomitantly with the execution of the Serapatatia enterprise.

And as the Material Son and Daughter thus communed in the moonlit Garden, "the voice in the Garden" reproved them for disobedience. And that voice was none other than my own announcement to the Edenic pair that they had transgressed the Garden covenant; that they had disobeyed the instructions of the Melchizedeks; that they had defaulted in the execution of their oaths of trust to the sovereign of the universe.

Eve had consented to participate in the practice of good and evil. Good is the carrying out of the divine plans; sin is a deliberate transgression of the divine will; evil is the misadaptation of plans and the maladjustment of techniques resulting in universe disharmony and planetary confusion.

Every time the Garden pair had partaken of the fruit of the tree of life, they had been warned by the archangel custodian to refrain from yielding to the suggestions of Caligastia to combine good and evil. They had been thus admonished: "In the day that you commingle good and evil, you shall surely become as the mortals of the realm; you shall surely die."

Eve had told Cano of this oft-repeated warning on the fateful occasion of their secret meeting, but Cano, not knowing the import or significance of such admonitions, had assured her that men and women with good motives and true intentions could do no evil; that she should surely not die but rather live anew in the person of their offspring, who would grow up to bless and stabilize the world.

Even though this project of modifying the divine plan had been conceived and executed with entire sincerity and with only the highest motives concerning the welfare of the world, it constituted evil because it represented the wrong way to achieve righteous ends, because it departed from the right way, the divine plan.

True, Eve had found Cano pleasant to the eyes, and she realized all that her seducer promised by way of "new and increased knowledge of human affairs and quickened understanding of human nature as supplemental to the comprehension of the Adamic nature."

I talked to the father and mother of the violet race that night in the Garden as became my duty under the sorrowful circumstances. I listened fully to the recital of all that led up to the default of Mother Eve and gave both of them advice and counsel concerning the immediate situation. Some of this advice they followed; some they disregarded. This conference appears in your records as "the Lord God calling to Adam and Eve in the Garden and asking, 'Where are you?'" It was the practice of later generations to attribute everything unusual and extraordinary, whether natural or spiritual, directly to the personal intervention of the Gods.

5. REPERCUSSIONS OF DEFAULT

Eve's disillusionment was truly pathetic. Adam discerned the whole predicament and, while heartbroken and dejected, entertained only pity and sympathy for his erring mate.

It was in the despair of the realization of failure that Adam, the day after Eve's misstep, sought out Laotta, the brilliant Nodite woman who was head of the western schools of the Garden, and with premeditation committed the folly of Eve. But do not misunderstand; Adam was not beguiled; he knew exactly what he was about; he deliberately chose to share the fate of Eve. He loved his mate with a supermortal affection, and the thought of the possibility of a lonely vigil on Urantia without her was more than he could endure.

When they learned what had happened to Eve, the infuriated inhabitants of the Garden became unmanageable; they declared war on the near-by Nodite settlement. They swept out through the gates of Eden and down upon these unprepared people, utterly destroying them—not a man, woman, or child was spared. And Cano, the father of Cain yet unborn, also perished.

Upon the realization of what had happened, Serapatatia was overcome with consternation and beside himself with fear and remorse. The next day he drowned himself in the great river.

The children of Adam sought to comfort their distracted mother while their father wandered in solitude for thirty days. At the end of that time judgment asserted itself, and Adam returned to his home and began to plan for their future course of action.

The consequences of the follies of misguided parents are so often shared by their innocent children. The upright and noble sons and daughters of Adam and Eve were overwhelmed by the inexplicable sorrow of the unbelievable tragedy which had been so suddenly and so ruthlessly thrust upon them. Not in fifty years did the older of these children recover from the sorrow and sadness of those tragic days, especially the terror of that period of thirty days during which their father was absent from home while their distracted mother was in complete ignorance of his whereabouts or fate.

And those same thirty days were as long years of sorrow and suffering to Eve. Never did this noble soul fully recover from the effects of that excruciating period of mental suffering and spiritual sorrow. No feature of their subsequent deprivations and material hardships ever began to compare in Eve's memory with those terrible days and awful nights of loneliness and unbearable uncertainty. She learned of the rash act of Serapatatia and did not know whether her mate had in sorrow destroyed himself or had been removed from the world in retribution for her misstep. And when Adam returned, Eve experienced a satisfaction of joy and gratitude that never was effaced by their long and difficult life partnership of toiling service.

Time passed, but Adam was not certain of the nature of their offense until seventy days after the default of Eve, when the Melchizedek receivers returned to Urantia and assumed jurisdiction over world affairs. And then he knew they had failed.

But still more trouble was brewing: The news of the annihilation of the Nodite settlement near Eden was not slow in reaching the home tribes of Serapatatia to the north, and presently a great host was assembling to march on the Garden. And this was the beginning of a long and bitter warfare between the Adamites and the Nodites, for these hostilities kept up long after Adam and his followers emigrated to the second garden in the Euphrates valley. There was intense and lasting "enmity between that man and the woman, between his seed and her seed."

6. ADAM AND EVE LEAVE THE GARDEN

When Adam learned that the Nodites were on the march, he sought the counsel of the Melchizedeks, but they refused to advise him, only telling him to do as he thought best and promising their friendly co-operation, as far as possible, in any course he might decide upon. The Melchizedeks had been forbidden to interfere with the personal plans of Adam and Eve.

Adam knew that he and Eve had failed; the presence of the Melchizedek receivers told him that, though he still knew nothing of their personal status or future fate. He held an all-night conference with some twelve hundred loyal followers who pledged themselves to follow their leader, and the next day at noon these pilgrims went forth from Eden in quest of new homes. Adam had no liking for war and accordingly elected to leave the first garden to the Nodites unopposed.

The Edenic caravan was halted on the third day out from the Garden by the arrival of the seraphic transports from Jerusem. And for the first time Adam and Eve were informed of what was to become of their children. While the transports stood by, those children who had arrived at the age of choice (twenty years) were given the option of remaining on Urantia with their parents or of becoming wards of the Most Highs of Norlatiadek. Two thirds chose to go to Edentia; about one third elected to remain with their parents. All children of prechoice age were taken to Edentia. No one could have beheld the sorrowful parting of this Material Son and Daughter and their children without realizing that the way of the transgressor is hard. These offspring of Adam and Eve are now on Edentia; we do not know what disposition is to be made of them.

It was a sad, sad caravan that prepared to journey on. Could anything have been more tragic! To have come to a world in such high hopes, to have been so auspiciously received, and then to go forth in disgrace from Eden, only to lose more than three fourths of their children even before finding a new abiding place!

7. DEGRADATION OF ADAM AND EVE

It was while the Edenic caravan was halted that Adam and Eve were informed of the nature of their transgressions and advised concerning their fate. Gabriel appeared to pronounce judgment. And this was the verdict: The Planetary Adam and Eve of Urantia are adjudged in default; they have violated the covenant of their trusteeship as the rulers of this inhabited world.

While downcast by the sense of guilt, Adam and Eve were greatly cheered by the announcement that their judges on Salvington had absolved them from all charges of standing in "contempt of the universe government." They had not been held guilty of rebellion.

The Edenic pair were informed that they had degraded themselves to the status of the mortals of the realm; that they must henceforth conduct themselves as man and woman of Urantia, looking to the future of the world races for their future.

Long before Adam and Eve left Jerusem, their instructors had fully explained to them the consequences of any vital departure from the divine plans. I had personally and repeatedly warned them, both before and after they arrived on Urantia, that reduction to the status of mortal flesh would be the certain result, the sure penalty, which would unfailingly attend default in the execution of their planetary mission. But a comprehension of the immortality status of the material order of sonship is essential to a clear understanding of the consequences attendant upon the default of Adam and Eve.

1. Adam and Eve, like their fellows on Jerusem, maintained immortal status through intellectual association with the mind-gravity circuit of the Spirit. When this vital sustenance is broken by mental disjunction, then, regardless of the spiritual level of creature existence, immortality status is lost. Mortal status followed by physical dissolution was the inevitable consequence of the intellectual default of Adam and Eve.

2. The Material Son and Daughter of Urantia, being also personalized in the similitude of the mortal flesh of this world, were further dependent on the maintenance of a dual circulatory system, the one derived from their physical natures, the other from the superenergy stored in the fruit of the tree of life. Always had the archangel custodian admonished Adam and Eve that default of trust would culminate in degradation of status, and access to this source of energy was denied them subsequent to their default.

Caligastia did succeed in trapping Adam and Eve, but he did not accomplish his purpose of leading them into open rebellion against the universe government. What they had done was indeed evil, but they were never guilty of contempt for truth, neither did they knowingly enlist in rebellion against the righteous rule of the Universal Father and his Creator Son.

8. THE SO-CALLED FALL OF MAN

Adam and Eve did fall from their high estate of material sonship down to the lowly status of mortal man. But that was not the fall of man. The human race has been uplifted despite the immediate consequences of the Adamic default. Although the divine plan of giving the violet race to the Urantia peoples miscarried, the mortal races have profited enormously from the limited contribution which Adam and his descendants made to the Urantia races.

There has been no "fall of man." The history of the human race is one of progressive evolution, and the Adamic bestowal left the world peoples greatly improved over their previous biologic condition. The more superior stocks of Urantia now contain inheritance factors derived from as many as four separate sources: Andonite, Sangik, Nodite, and Adamic.

Adam should not be regarded as the cause of a curse on the human race. While he did fail in carrying forward the divine plan, while he did transgress his covenant with Deity, while he and his mate were most certainly degraded in creature status, notwithstanding all this, their contribution to the human race did much to advance civilization on Urantia.

In estimating the results of the Adamic mission on your world, justice demands the recognition of the condition of the planet. Adam was confronted with a well-nigh hopeless task when, with his beautiful mate, he was transported from Jerusem to this dark and confused planet. But had they been guided by the counsel of the Melchizedeks and their associates, and *had they been more patient,* they would have eventually met with success. But Eve listened to the insidious propaganda of personal liberty and planetary freedom of action. She was led to experiment with the life plasm of the material order of sonship in that she allowed this life trust to become prematurely commingled with that of the then mixed order of the original design of the Life Carriers which had been previously combined with that of the reproducing beings once attached to the staff of the Planetary Prince.

Never, in all your ascent to Paradise, will you gain anything by impatiently attempting to circumvent the established and divine plan by short cuts, personal inventions, or other devices for improving on the way of perfection, to perfection, and for eternal perfection.

All in all, there probably never was a more disheartening miscarriage of wisdom on any planet in all Nebadon. But it is not surprising that these missteps occur in the affairs of the evolutionary universes. We are a part of a gigantic creation, and it is not strange that everything does not work in perfection; our universe was not created in perfection. Perfection is our eternal goal, not our origin.

If this were a mechanistic universe, if the First Great Source and Center were only a force and not also a personality, if all creation were a vast aggregation of physical matter dominated by precise laws characterized by unvarying energy actions, then might perfection obtain, even despite the incompleteness of universe status. There would be no disagreement; there would be no friction. But in our evolving universe of relative perfection and imperfection we rejoice that disagreement and misunderstanding are possible, for thereby is evidenced the fact and the act of personality in the universe. And if our creation is an existence dominated by personality, then can you be assured of the possibilities of personality survival, advancement, and achievement; we can be confident of personality growth, experience, and adventure. What a glorious universe, in that it is personal and progressive, not merely mechanical or even passively perfect!

[Presented by Solonia, the seraphic "voice in the Garden."]

PAPER 76
THE SECOND GARDEN

WHEN Adam elected to leave the first garden to the Nodites unopposed, he and his followers could not go west, for the Edenites had no boats suitable for such a marine adventure. They could not go north; the northern Nodites were already on the march toward Eden. They feared to go south; the hills of that region were infested with hostile tribes. The only way open was to the east, and so they journeyed eastward toward the then pleasant regions between the Tigris and Euphrates rivers. And many of those who were left behind later journeyed eastward to join the Adamites in their new valley home.

Cain and Sansa were both born before the Adamic caravan had reached its destination between the rivers in Mesopotamia. Laotta, the mother of Sansa, perished at the birth of her daughter; Eve suffered much but survived, owing to superior strength. Eve took Sansa, the child of Laotta, to her bosom, and she was reared along with Cain. Sansa grew up to be a woman of great ability. She became the wife of Sargan, the chief of the northern blue races, and contributed to the advancement of the blue men of those times.

1. THE EDENITES ENTER MESOPOTAMIA

It required almost a full year for the caravan of Adam to reach the Euphrates River. Finding it in flood tide, they remained camped on the plains west of the stream almost six weeks before they made their way across to the land between the rivers which was to become the second garden.

When word had reached the dwellers in the land of the second garden that the king and high priest of the Garden of Eden was marching on them, they had fled in haste to the eastern mountains. Adam found all of the desired territory vacated when he arrived. And here in this new location Adam and his helpers set themselves to work to build new homes and establish a new center of culture and religion.

This site was known to Adam as one of the three original selections of the committee assigned to choose possible locations for the Garden proposed by Van and Amadon. The two rivers themselves were a good natural defense in those days, and a short way north of the second garden the Euphrates and Tigris came close together so that a defense wall extending fifty-six miles could be built for the protection of the territory to the south and between the rivers.

After getting settled in the new Eden, it became necessary to adopt crude methods of living; it seemed entirely true that the ground had been cursed. Nature was once again taking its course. Now were the Adamites compelled to wrest a living from unprepared soil and to cope with the realities of life in the face of the natural hostilities and incompatibilities of mortal existence. They found the first garden partially prepared for them, but the second had to be created by the labor of their own hands and in the "sweat of their faces."

2. CAIN AND ABEL

Less than two years after Cain's birth, Abel was born, the first child of Adam and Eve to be born in the second garden. When Abel grew up to the age of twelve years, he elected to be a herder; Cain had chosen to follow agriculture.

Now, in those days it was customary to make offerings to the priesthood of the things at hand. Herders would bring of their flocks, farmers of the fruits of the fields; and in accordance with this custom, Cain and Abel likewise made periodic offerings to the priests. The two boys had many times argued about the relative merits of their vocations, and Abel was not slow to note that preference was shown for his animal sacrifices. In vain did Cain appeal to the traditions of the first Eden, to the former preference for the fruits of the fields. But this Abel would not allow, and he taunted his older brother in his discomfiture.

In the days of the first Eden, Adam had indeed sought to discourage the offering of animal sacrifice so that Cain had a justifiable precedent for his contentions. It was, however, difficult to organize the religious life of the second Eden. Adam was burdened with a thousand and one details associated with the work of building, defense, and agriculture. Being much depressed spiritually, he intrusted the organization of worship and education to those of Nodite extraction who had served in these capacities in the first garden; and in even so short a time the officiating Nodite priests were reverting to the standards and rulings of pre-Adamic times.

The two boys never got along well, and this matter of sacrifices further contributed to the growing hatred between them. Abel knew he was the son of both Adam and Eve and never failed to impress upon Cain that Adam was not his father. Cain was not pure violet as his father was of the Nodite race later admixed with the blue and the red man and with the aboriginal Andonic stock. And all of this, with Cain's natural bellicose inheritance, caused him to nourish an ever-increasing hatred for his younger brother.

The boys were respectively eighteen and twenty years of age when the tension between them was finally resolved, one day, when Abel's taunts so infuriated his bellicose brother that Cain turned upon him in wrath and slew him.

The observation of Abel's conduct establishes the value of environment and education as factors in character development. Abel had an ideal inheritance, and heredity lies at the bottom of all character; but the influence of an inferior environment virtually neutralized this magnificent inheritance. Abel, especially during his younger years, was greatly influenced by his unfavorable surroundings. He would have become an entirely different person had he lived to be twenty-five or thirty; his superb inheritance would then have shown itself. While a good environment cannot contribute much toward really overcoming the character handicaps of a base heredity, a bad environment can very effectively spoil an excellent inheritance, at least during the younger years of life. Good social environment and proper education are indispensable soil and atmosphere for getting the most out of a good inheritance.

The death of Abel became known to his parents when his dogs brought the flocks home without their master. To Adam and Eve, Cain was fast becoming the grim reminder of their folly, and they encouraged him in his decision to leave the garden.

Cain's life in Mesopotamia had not been exactly happy since he was in such a peculiar way symbolic of the default. It was not that his associates were unkind to him, but he had not been unaware of their subconscious resentment of his presence. But Cain knew that, since he bore no tribal mark, he would be killed by the first neighboring tribesmen who might chance to meet him. Fear, and some remorse, led him to repent. Cain had never been indwelt by an Adjuster, had always been defiant of the family discipline and disdainful of his father's religion. But he now went to Eve, his mother, and asked for spiritual help and guidance, and when he honestly sought divine assistance, an Adjuster indwelt him. And this Adjuster, dwelling within and looking out, gave Cain a distinct advantage of superiority which classed him with the greatly feared tribe of Adam.

And so Cain departed for the land of Nod, east of the second Eden. He became a great leader among one group of his father's people and did, to a certain degree, fulfill the predictions of Serapatatia, for he did promote peace between this division of the Nodites and the Adamites throughout his lifetime. Cain married Remona, his distant cousin, and their first son, Enoch, became the head of the Elamite Nodites. And for hundreds of years the Elamites and the Adamites continued to be at peace.

3. LIFE IN MESOPOTAMIA

As time passed in the second garden, the consequences of default became increasingly apparent. Adam and Eve greatly missed their former home of beauty and tranquillity as well as their children who had been deported to Edentia. It was indeed pathetic to observe this magnificent couple reduced to the status of the common flesh of the realm; but they bore their diminished estate with grace and fortitude.

Adam wisely spent most of the time training his children and their associates in civil administration, educational methods, and religious devotions. Had it not been for this foresight, pandemonium would have broken loose upon his death. As it was, the death of Adam made little difference in the conduct of the affairs of his people. But long before Adam and Eve passed away, they recognized that their children and followers had gradually learned to forget the days of their glory in Eden. And it was better for the majority of their followers that they did forget the grandeur of Eden; they were not so likely to experience undue dissatisfaction with their less fortunate environment.

The civil rulers of the Adamites were derived hereditarily from the sons of the first garden. Adam's first son, Adamson (Adam ben Adam), founded a secondary center of the violet race to the north of the second Eden. Adam's second son, Eveson, became a masterly leader and administrator; he was the great helper of his father. Eveson lived not quite so long as Adam, and his eldest son, Jansad, became the successor of Adam as the head of the Adamite tribes.

The religious rulers, or priesthood, originated with Seth, the eldest surviving son of Adam and Eve born in the second garden. He was born one hundred and twenty-nine years after Adam's arrival on Urantia. Seth became absorbed in the work of improving the spiritual status of his father's people, becoming the head of the new priesthood of the second garden. His son, Enos, founded the new order of worship, and his grandson, Kenan, instituted the foreign missionary service to the surrounding tribes, near and far.

The Sethite priesthood was a threefold undertaking, embracing religion, health, and education. The priests of this order were trained to officiate at religious ceremonies, to serve as physicians and sanitary inspectors, and to act as teachers in the schools of the garden.

Adam's caravan had carried the seeds and bulbs of hundreds of plants and cereals of the first garden with them to the land between the rivers; they also had brought along extensive herds and some of all the domesticated animals. Because of this they possessed great advantages over the surrounding tribes. They enjoyed many of the benefits of the previous culture of the original Garden.

Up to the time of leaving the first garden, Adam and his family had always subsisted on fruits, cereals, and nuts. On the way to Mesopotamia they had, for the first time, partaken of herbs and vegetables. The eating of meat was early introduced into the second garden, but Adam and Eve never partook of flesh as a part of their regular diet. Neither did Adamson nor Eveson nor the other children of the first generation of the first garden become flesh eaters.

The Adamites greatly excelled the surrounding peoples in cultural achievement and intellectual development. They produced the third alphabet and otherwise laid the foundations for much that was the forerunner of modern art, science, and literature. Here in the lands between the Tigris and Euphrates they maintained the arts of writing, metalworking, pottery making, and weaving and produced a type of architecture that was not excelled in thousands of years.

The home life of the violet peoples was, for their day and age, ideal. Children were subjected to courses of training in agriculture, craftsmanship, and animal husbandry or else were educated to perform the threefold duty of a Sethite: to be priest, physician, and teacher.

And when thinking of the Sethite priesthood, do not confuse those high-minded and noble teachers of health and religion, those true educators, with the debased and commercial priesthoods of the later tribes and surrounding nations. Their religious concepts of Deity and the universe were advanced and more or less accurate, their health provisions were, for their time, excellent, and their methods of education have never since been surpassed.

4. THE VIOLET RACE

Adam and Eve were the founders of the violet race of men, the ninth human race to appear on Urantia. Adam and his offspring had blue eyes, and the violet peoples were characterized by fair complexions and light hair color—yellow, red, and brown.

Eve did not suffer pain in childbirth; neither did the early evolutionary races. Only the mixed races produced by the union of evolutionary man with the Nodites and later with the Adamites suffered the severe pangs of childbirth.

Adam and Eve, like their brethren on Jerusem, were energized by dual nutrition, subsisting on both food and light, supplemented by certain superphysical energies unrevealed on Urantia. Their Urantia offspring did not inherit the parental endowment of energy intake and light circulation. They had a single circulation, the human type of blood sustenance. They were designedly mortal though long-lived, albeit longevity gravitated toward the human norm with each succeeding generation.

Adam and Eve and their first generation of children did not use the flesh of animals for food. They subsisted wholly upon "the fruits of the trees." After the first generation all of the descendants of Adam began to partake of dairy products, but many of them continued to follow a nonflesh diet. Many of the southern tribes with whom they later united were also nonflesh eaters. Later on, most of these vegetarian tribes migrated to the east and survived as now admixed in the peoples of India.

Both the physical and spiritual visions of Adam and Eve were far superior to those of the present-day peoples. Their special senses were much more acute, and they were able to see the midwayers and the angelic hosts, the Melchizedeks, and the fallen Prince Caligastia, who several times came to confer with his noble successor. They retained the ability to see these celestial beings for over one hundred years after the default. These special senses were not so acutely present in their children and tended to diminish with each succeeding generation.

The Adamic children were usually Adjuster indwelt since they all possessed undoubted survival capacity. These superior offspring were not so subject to fear as the children of evolution. So much of fear persists in the present-day races of Urantia because your ancestors received so little of Adam's life plasm, owing to the early miscarriage of the plans for racial physical uplift.

The body cells of the Material Sons and their progeny are far more resistant to disease than are those of the evolutionary beings indigenous to the planet. The body cells of the native races are akin to the living disease-producing microscopic and ultramicroscopic organisms of the realm. These facts explain why the Urantia peoples must do so much by way of scientific effort to withstand so many physical disorders. You would be far more disease resistant if your races carried more of the Adamic life.

After becoming established in the second garden on the Euphrates, Adam elected to leave behind as much of his life plasm as possible to benefit the world after his death. Accordingly, Eve was made the head of a commission of twelve on race improvement, and before Adam died this commission had selected 1,682 of the highest type of women on Urantia, and these women were impregnated with the Adamic life plasm. Their children all grew up to maturity except 112, so that the world, in this way, was benefited by the addition of 1,570 superior men and women. Though these candidate mothers were selected from all the surrounding tribes and represented most of the races on earth, the majority were chosen from the highest strains of the Nodites, and they constituted the early beginnings of the mighty Andite race. These children were born and reared in the tribal surroundings of their respective mothers.

5. DEATH OF ADAM AND EVE

Not long after the establishment of the second Eden, Adam and Eve were duly informed that their repentance was acceptable, and that, while they were doomed to suffer the fate of the mortals of their world, they should certainly become eligible for admission to the ranks of the sleeping survivors of Urantia. They fully believed this gospel of resurrection and rehabilitation which the Melchizedeks so touchingly proclaimed to them. Their transgression had been an error of judgment and not the sin of conscious and deliberate rebellion.

Adam and Eve did not, as citizens of Jerusem, have Thought Adjusters, nor were they Adjuster indwelt when they functioned on Urantia in the first garden. But shortly after their reduction to mortal status they became conscious of a new presence within them and awakened to the realization that human status coupled with sincere repentance had made it possible for Adjusters to indwell them. It was this knowledge of being Adjuster indwelt that greatly heartened Adam and Eve throughout the remainder of their lives; they knew that they had failed as Material Sons of Satania, but they also knew that the Paradise career was still open to them as ascending sons of the universe.

Adam knew about the dispensational resurrection which occurred simultaneously with his arrival on the planet, and he believed that he and his companion would probably be repersonalized in connection with the advent of the next order of sonship. He did not know that Michael, the sovereign of this universe, was so soon to appear on Urantia; he expected that the next Son to arrive would be of the Avonal order. Even so, it was always a comfort to Adam and Eve, as well as something difficult for them to understand, to ponder the only personal message they ever received from Michael. This message, among other expressions of friendship and comfort, said: "I have given consideration to the circumstances of your default, I have remembered the desire of your hearts ever to be loyal to my Father's will, and you will be called from the embrace of mortal slumber when I come to Urantia if the subordinate Sons of my realm do not send for you before that time."

And this was a great mystery to Adam and Eve. They could comprehend the veiled promise of a possible special resurrection in this message, and such a possibility greatly cheered them, but they could not grasp the meaning of the intimation that they might rest until the time of a resurrection associated with Michael's personal appearance on Urantia. And so the Edenic pair always proclaimed that a Son of God would sometime come, and they communicated to their loved ones the belief, at least the longing hope, that the world of their blunders and sorrows might possibly be the realm whereon the ruler of this universe would elect to function as the Paradise bestowal Son. It seemed too good to be true, but Adam did entertain the thought that strife-torn Urantia might, after all, turn out to be the most fortunate world in the system of Satania, the envied planet of all Nebadon.

Adam lived for 530 years; he died of what might be termed old age. His physical mechanism simply wore out; the process of disintegration gradually gained on the process of repair, and the inevitable end came. Eve had died nineteen years previously of a weakened heart. They were both buried in the center of the temple of divine service which had been built in accordance with their plans soon after the wall of the colony had been completed. And this was the origin of the practice of burying noted and pious men and women under the floors of the places of worship.

The supermaterial government of Urantia, under the direction of the Melchizedeks, continued, but direct physical contact with the evolutionary races had been severed. From the distant days of the arrival of the corporeal staff of the Planetary Prince, down through the times of Van and Amadon to the arrival of Adam and Eve, physical representatives of the universe government had been stationed on the planet. But with the Adamic default this regime, extending over a period of more than four hundred and fifty thousand years, came to an end. In the spiritual spheres, angelic helpers continued to struggle in conjunction with the Thought Adjusters, both working heroically for the salvage of the individual; but no comprehensive plan for far-reaching world welfare was promulgated to the mortals of earth until the arrival of Machiventa Melchizedek, in the times of Abraham, who, with the power, patience, and authority of a Son of God, did lay the foundations for the further uplift and spiritual rehabilitation of unfortunate Urantia.

Misfortune has not, however, been the sole lot of Urantia; this planet has also been the most fortunate in the local universe of Nebadon. Urantians should count it all gain if the blunders of their ancestors and the mistakes of their early world rulers so plunged the planet into such a hopeless state of confusion, all the more confounded by evil and sin, that this very background of darkness should so appeal to Michael of Nebadon that he selected this world as the arena wherein to reveal the loving personality of the Father in heaven. It is not that Urantia needed a Creator Son to set its tangled affairs in order; it is rather that the evil and sin on Urantia afforded the Creator Son a more striking background against which to reveal the matchless love, mercy, and patience of the Paradise Father.

6. SURVIVAL OF ADAM AND EVE

Adam and Eve went to their mortal rest with strong faith in the promises made to them by the Melchizedeks that they would sometime awake from the sleep of death to resume life on the mansion worlds, worlds all so familiar to them in the days preceding their mission in the material flesh of the violet race on Urantia.

They did not long rest in the oblivion of the unconscious sleep of the mortals of the realm. On the third day after Adam's death, the second following his reverent burial, the orders of Lanaforge, sustained by the acting Most High of Edentia and concurred in by the Union of Days on Salvington, acting for Michael, were placed in Gabriel's hands, directing the special roll call of the distinguished survivors of the Adamic default on Urantia. And in accordance with this mandate of special resurrection, number twenty-six of the Urantia series, Adam and Eve were repersonalized and reassembled in the resurrection halls of the mansion worlds of Satania together with 1,316 of their associates in the experience of the first garden. Many other loyal souls had already been translated at the time of Adam's arrival, which was attended by a dispensational adjudication of both the sleeping survivors and of the living qualified ascenders.

Adam and Eve quickly passed through the worlds of progressive ascension until they attained citizenship on Jerusem, once again to be residents of the planet of their origin but this time as members of a different order of universe personalities. They left Jerusem as permanent citizens—Sons of God; they returned as ascendant citizens—sons of man. They were immediately attached to the Urantia service on the system capital, later being assigned membership among the four and twenty counselors who constitute the present advisory-control body of Urantia.

And thus ends the story of the Planetary Adam and Eve of Urantia, a story of trial, tragedy, and triumph, at least personal triumph for your well-meaning but deluded Material Son and Daughter and undoubtedly, in the end, a story of ultimate triumph for their world and its rebellion-tossed and evil-harassed inhabitants. When all is summed up, Adam and Eve made a mighty contribution to the speedy civilization and accelerated biologic progress of the human race. They left a great culture on earth, but it was not possible for such an advanced civilization to survive in the face of the early dilution and the eventual submergence of the Adamic inheritance. It is the people who make a civilization; civilization does not make the people.

[Presented by Solonia, the seraphic "voice in the Garden."]

PAPER 77

THE MIDWAY CREATURES

MOST of the inhabited worlds of Nebadon harbor one or more groups of unique beings existing on a life-functioning level about midway between those of the mortals of the realms and of the angelic orders; hence are they called *midway* creatures. They appear to be an accident of time, but they occur so widespreadly and are so valuable as helpers that we have all long since accepted them as one of the essential orders of our combined planetary ministry.

On Urantia there function two distinct orders of midwayers: the primary or senior corps, who came into being back in the days of Dalamatia, and the secondary or younger group, whose origin dates from the times of Adam.

1. THE PRIMARY MIDWAYERS

The primary midwayers have their genesis in a unique interassociation of the material and the spiritual on Urantia. We know of the existence of similar creatures on other worlds and in other systems, but they originated by dissimilar techniques.

It is well always to bear in mind that the successive bestowals of the Sons of God on an evolving planet produce marked changes in the spiritual economy of the realm and sometimes so modify the workings of the interassociation of spiritual and material agencies on a planet as to create situations indeed difficult of understanding. The status of the one hundred corporeal members of Prince Caligastia's staff illustrates just such a unique interassociation: As ascendant morontia citizens of Jerusem they were supermaterial creatures without reproductive prerogatives. As descendant planetary ministers on Urantia they were material sex creatures capable of procreating material offspring (as some of them later did). What we cannot satisfactorily explain is how these one hundred could function in the parental role on a supermaterial level, but that is exactly what happened. A supermaterial (nonsexual) liaison of a male and a female member of the corporeal staff resulted in the appearance of the first-born of the primary midwayers.

It was immediately discovered that a creature of this order, midway between the mortal and angelic levels, would be of great service in carrying on the affairs of the Prince's headquarters, and each couple of the corporeal staff was accordingly granted permission to produce a similar being. This effort resulted in the first group of fifty midway creatures.

After a year of observing the work of this unique group, the Planetary Prince authorized the reproduction of midwayers without restriction. This plan was carried out as long as the power to create continued, and the original corps of 50,000 was accordingly brought into being.

A period of one-half year intervened between the production of each midwayer, and when one thousand such beings had been born to each couple, no more were ever forthcoming. And there is no explanation available as to why this power was exhausted upon the appearance of the one thousandth offspring. No amount of further experimentation ever resulted in anything but failure.

These creatures constituted the intelligence corps of the Prince's administration. They ranged far and wide, studying and observing the world races and rendering other invaluable services to the Prince and his staff in the work of influencing human society remote from the planetary headquarters.

This regime continued until the tragic days of the planetary rebellion, which ensnared a little over four fifths of the primary midwayers. The loyal corps entered the service of the Melchizedek receivers, functioning under the titular leadership of Van until the days of Adam.

2. THE NODITE RACE

While this is the narrative of the origin, nature, and function of the midway creatures of Urantia, the kinship between the two orders—primary and secondary—makes it necessary to interrupt the story of the primary midwayers at this point in order to follow out the line of descent from the rebel members of the corporeal staff of Prince Caligastia from the days of the planetary rebellion to the times of Adam. It was this line of inheritance which, in the early days of the second garden, furnished one half of the ancestry for the secondary order of midway creatures.

The physical members of the Prince's staff had been constituted sex creatures for the purpose of participating in the plan of procreating offspring embodying the combined qualities of their special order united with those of the selected stock of the Andon tribes, and all of this was in anticipation of the subsequent appearance of Adam. The Life Carriers had planned a new type of mortal embracing the union of the conjoint offspring of the Prince's staff with the first-generation offspring of Adam and Eve. They had thus projected a plan envisioning a new order of planetary creatures whom they hoped would become the teacher-rulers of human society. Such beings were designed for social sovereignty, not civil sovereignty. But since this project almost completely miscarried, we shall never know what an aristocracy of benign leadership and matchless culture Urantia was thus deprived of. For when the corporeal staff later reproduced, it was subsequent to the rebellion and after they had been deprived of their connection with the life currents of the system.

The postrebellion era on Urantia witnessed many unusual happenings. A great civilization—the culture of Dalamatia—was going to pieces. "The Nephilim (Nodites) were on earth in those days, and when these sons of the gods went in to the daughters of men and they bore to them, their children were the 'mighty men of old,' the 'men of renown.'" While hardly "sons of the gods," the staff and their early descendants were so regarded by the evolutionary mortals of those distant days; even their stature came to be magnified by tradition. This, then, is the origin of the well-nigh universal folk tale of the gods who came down to earth and there with the daughters of men begot an ancient race of heroes. And all this legend became further confused with the race mixtures of the later appearing Adamites in the second garden.

Since the one hundred corporeal members of the Prince's staff carried germ plasm of the Andonic human strains, it would naturally be expected that, if they engaged in sexual reproduction, their progeny would altogether resemble the offspring of other Andonite parents. But when the sixty rebels of the staff, the followers of Nod, actually engaged in sexual reproduction, their children proved to be far superior in almost every way to both the Andonite and the Sangik peoples. This unexpected excellence characterized not only physical and intellectual qualities but also spiritual capacities.

These mutant traits appearing in the first Nodite generation resulted from certain changes which had been wrought in the configuration and in the chemical constituents of the inheritance factors of the Andonic germ plasm. These changes were caused by the presence in the bodies of the staff members of the powerful life-maintenance circuits of the Satania system. These life circuits caused the chromosomes of the specialized Urantia pattern to reorganize more after the patterns of the standardized Satania specialization of the ordained Nebadon life manifestation. The technique of this germ plasm metamorphosis by the action of the system life currents is not unlike those procedures whereby Urantia scientists modify the germ plasm of plants and animals by the use of X rays.

Thus did the Nodite peoples arise out of certain peculiar and unexpected modifications occurring in the life plasm which had been transferred from the bodies of the Andonite contributors to those of the corporeal staff members by the Avalon surgeons.

It will be recalled that the one hundred Andonite germ plasm contributors were in turn made possessors of the organic complement of the tree of life so that the Satania life currents likewise invested their bodies. The forty-four modified Andonites who followed the staff into rebellion also mated among themselves and made a great contribution to the better strains of the Nodite people.

These two groups, embracing 104 individuals who carried the modified Andonite germ plasm, constitute the ancestry of the Nodites, the eighth race to appear on Urantia. And this new feature of human life on Urantia represents another phase of the outworking of the original plan of utilizing this planet as a life-modification world, except that this was one of the unforeseen developments.

The pure-line Nodites were a magnificent race, but they gradually mingled with the evolutionary peoples of earth, and before long great deterioration had occurred. Ten thousand years after the rebellion they had lost ground to the point where their average length of life was little more than that of the evolutionary races.

When archaeologists dig up the clay-tablet records of the later-day Sumerian descendants of the Nodites, they discover lists of Sumerian kings running back for several thousand years; and as these records go further back, the reigns of the individual kings lengthen from around twenty-five or thirty years up to one hundred and fifty years and more. This lengthening of the reigns of these older kings signifies that some of the early Nodite rulers (immediate descendants of the Prince's staff) did live longer than their later-day successors and also indicates an effort to stretch the dynasties back to Dalamatia.

The records of such long-lived individuals are also due to the confusion of months and years as time periods. This may also be observed in the Biblical genealogy of Abraham and in the early records of the Chinese. The confusion of the twenty-eight-day month, or season, with the later introduced year of more than three hundred and fifty days is responsible for the traditions of such long human lives. There are records of a man who lived over nine hundred "years." This period represents not quite seventy years, and such lives were regarded for ages as very long, "threescore years and ten" as such a life span was later designated.

The reckoning of time by the twenty-eight-day month persisted long after the days of Adam. But when the Egyptians undertook to reform the calendar, about seven thousand years ago, they did it with great accuracy, introducing the year of 365 days.

3. THE TOWER OF BABEL

After the submergence of Dalamatia the Nodites moved north and east, presently founding the new city of Dilmun as their racial and cultural headquarters. And about fifty thousand years after the death of Nod, when the offspring of the Prince's staff had become too numerous to find subsistence in the lands immediately surrounding their new city of Dilmun, and after they had reached out to intermarry with the Andonite and Sangik tribes adjoining their borders, it occurred to their leaders that something should be done to preserve their racial unity. Accordingly a council of the tribes was called, and after much deliberation the plan of Bablot, a descendant of Nod, was endorsed.

Bablot proposed to erect a pretentious temple of racial glorification at the center of their then occupied territory. This temple was to have a tower the like of which the world had never seen. It was to be a monumental memorial to their passing greatness. There were many who wished to have this monument erected in Dilmun, but others contended that such a great structure should be placed a safe distance from the dangers of the sea, remembering the traditions of the engulfment of their first capital, Dalamatia.

Bablot planned that the new buildings should become the nucleus of the future center of the Nodite culture and civilization. His counsel finally prevailed, and construction was started in accordance with his plans. The new city was to be named *Bablot* after the architect and builder of the tower. This location later became known as Bablod and eventually as Babel.

But the Nodites were still somewhat divided in sentiment as to the plans and purposes of this undertaking. Neither were their leaders altogether agreed concerning either construction plans or usage of the buildings after they should be completed. After four and one-half years of work a great dispute arose about the object and motive for the erection of the tower. The contentions became so bitter that all work stopped. The food carriers spread the news of the dissension, and large numbers of the tribes began to forgather at the building site. Three differing views were propounded as to the purpose of building the tower:

1. The largest group, almost one half, desired to see the tower built as a memorial of Nodite history and racial superiority. They thought it ought to be a great and imposing structure which would challenge the admiration of all future generations.

2. The next largest faction wanted the tower designed to commemorate the Dilmun culture. They foresaw that Bablot would become a great center of commerce, art, and manufacture.

3. The smallest and minority contingent held that the erection of the tower presented an opportunity for making atonement for the folly of their progenitors in participating in the Caligastia rebellion. They maintained that the tower should be devoted to the worship of the Father of all, that the whole purpose of the new city should be to take the place of Dalamatia—to function as the cultural and religious center for the surrounding barbarians.

The religious group were promptly voted down. The majority rejected the teaching that their ancestors had been guilty of rebellion; they resented such a racial stigma. Having disposed of one of the three angles to the dispute and failing to settle the other two by debate, they fell to fighting. The religionists, the noncombatants, fled to their homes in the south, while their fellows fought until well-nigh obliterated.

About twelve thousand years ago a second attempt to erect the tower of Babel was made. The mixed races of the Andites (Nodites and Adamites) undertook to raise a new temple on the ruins of the first structure, but there was not sufficient support for the enterprise; it fell of its own pretentious weight. This region was long known as the land of Babel.

4. NODITE CENTERS OF CIVILIZATION

The dispersion of the Nodites was an immediate result of the internecine conflict over the tower of Babel. This internal war greatly reduced the numbers of the purer Nodites and was in many ways responsible for their failure to establish a great pre-Adamic civilization. From this time on Nodite culture declined for over one hundred and twenty thousand years until it was upstepped by Adamic infusion. But even in the times of Adam the Nodites were still an able people. Many of their mixed descendants were numbered among the Garden builders, and several of Van's group captains were Nodites. Some of the most capable minds serving on Adam's staff were of this race.

Three out of the four great Nodite centers were established immediately following the Bablot conflict:

1. *The western or Syrian Nodites.* The remnants of the nationalistic or racial memorialists journeyed northward, uniting with the Andonites to found the later Nodite centers to the northwest of Mesopotamia. This was the largest group of the dispersing Nodites, and they contributed much to the later appearing Assyrian stock.

2. *The eastern or Elamite Nodites.* The culture and commerce advocates migrated in large numbers eastward into Elam and there united with the mixed Sangik tribes. The Elamites of thirty to forty thousand years ago had become largely Sangik in nature, although they continued to maintain a civilization superior to that of the surrounding barbarians.

After the establishment of the second garden it was customary to allude to this near-by Nodite settlement as "the land of Nod"; and during the long period of relative peace between this Nodite group and the Adamites, the two races were greatly blended, for it became more and more the custom for the Sons of God (the Adamites) to intermarry with the daughters of men (the Nodites).

3. *The central or pre-Sumerian Nodites.* A small group at the mouth of the Tigris and Euphrates rivers maintained more of their racial integrity. They persisted for thousands of years and eventually furnished the Nodite ancestry which blended with the Adamites to found the Sumerian peoples of historic times.

And all this explains how the Sumerians appeared so suddenly and mysteriously on the stage of action in Mesopotamia. Investigators will never be able to trace out and follow these tribes back to the beginning of the Sumerians, who had their origin two hundred thousand years ago after the submergence of Dalamatia. Without a trace of origin elsewhere in the world, these ancient tribes suddenly loom upon the horizon of civilization with a full-grown and superior culture, embracing temples, metalwork, agriculture, animals, pottery, weaving, commercial law, civil codes, religious ceremonial, and an old system of writing. At the beginning of the historical era they had long since lost the alphabet of Dalamatia, having adopted the peculiar writing system originating in Dilmun. The Sumerian language, though virtually lost to the world, was not Semitic; it had much in common with the so-called Aryan tongues.

The elaborate records left by the Sumerians describe the site of a remarkable settlement which was located on the Persian Gulf near the earlier city of Dilmun. The Egyptians called this city of ancient glory Dilmat, while the later Adamized Sumerians confused both the first and second Nodite cities with Dalamatia and called all three Dilmun. And already have archaeologists found these ancient Sumerian clay tablets which tell of this earthly paradise "where the Gods first blessed mankind with the example of civilized and cultured life." And these tablets, descriptive of Dilmun, the paradise of men and God, are now silently resting on the dusty shelves of many museums.

The Sumerians well knew of the first and second Edens but, despite extensive intermarriage with the Adamites, continued to regard the garden dwellers to the north as an alien race. Sumerian pride in the more ancient Nodite culture led them to ignore these later vistas of glory in favor of the grandeur and paradisiacal traditions of the city of Dilmun.

4. *The northern Nodites and Amadonites—the Vanites.* This group arose prior to the Bablot conflict. These northernmost Nodites were descendants of those who had forsaken the leadership of Nod and his successors for that of Van and Amadon.

Some of the early associates of Van subsequently settled about the shores of the lake which still bears his name, and their traditions grew up about this locality. Ararat became their sacred mountain, having much the same meaning to later-day Vanites that Sinai had to the Hebrews. Ten thousand years ago the Vanite ancestors of the Assyrians taught that their moral law of seven commandments had been given to Van by the Gods upon Mount Ararat. They firmly believed that Van and his associate Amadon were taken alive from the planet while they were up on the mountain engaged in worship.

Mount Ararat was the sacred mountain of northern Mesopotamia, and since much of your tradition of these ancient times was acquired in connection with the Babylonian story of the flood, it is not surprising that Mount Ararat and its region were woven into the later Jewish story of Noah and the universal flood.

About 35,000 B.C. Adamson visited one of the easternmost of the old Vanite settlements to found his center of civilization.

5. ADAMSON AND RATTA

Having delineated the Nodite antecedents of the ancestry of the secondary midwayers, this narrative should now give consideration to the Adamic half of their ancestry, for the secondary midwayers are also the grandchildren of Adamson, the first-born of the violet race of Urantia.

Adamson was among that group of the children of Adam and Eve who elected to remain on earth with their father and mother. Now this eldest son of Adam had often heard from Van and Amadon the story of their highland home in the north, and sometime after the establishment of the second garden he determined to go in search of this land of his youthful dreams.

Adamson was 120 years old at this time and had been the father of thirty-two pure-line children of the first garden. He wanted to remain with his parents and assist them in upbuilding the second garden, but he was greatly disturbed by the loss of his mate and their children, who had all elected to go to Edentia along with those other Adamic children who chose to become wards of the Most Highs.

Adamson would not desert his parents on Urantia, he was disinclined to flee from hardship or danger, but he found the associations of the second garden far from satisfying. He did much to forward the early activities of defense and construction but decided to leave for the north at the earliest opportunity. And though his departure was wholly pleasant, Adam and Eve were much grieved to lose their eldest son, to have him go out into a strange and hostile world, as they feared, never to return.

A company of twenty-seven followed Adamson northward in quest of these people of his childhood fantasies. In a little over three years Adamson's party actually found the object of their adventure, and among these people he discovered a wonderful and beautiful woman, twenty years old, who claimed to be the last pure-line descendant of the Prince's staff. This woman, Ratta, said that her ancestors were all descendants of two of the fallen staff of the Prince. She was the last of her race, having no living brothers or sisters. She had about decided not to mate, had about made up her mind to die without issue, but she lost her heart to the majestic Adamson. And when she heard the story of Eden, how the predictions of Van and Amadon had really come to pass, and as she listened to the recital of the Garden default, she was encompassed with but a single thought—to marry this son and heir of Adam. And quickly the idea grew upon Adamson. In a little more than three months they were married.

Adamson and Ratta had a family of sixty-seven children. They gave origin to a great line of the world's leadership, but they did something more. It should be remembered that both of these beings were really superhuman. Every fourth child born to them was of a unique order. It was often invisible. Never in the world's history had such a thing occurred. Ratta was greatly perturbed—even superstitious—but Adamson well knew of the existence of the primary midwayers, and he concluded that something similar was transpiring before his eyes. When the second strangely behaving offspring arrived, he decided to mate them, since one was male and the other female, and this is the origin of the secondary order of midwayers. Within one hundred years, before this phenomenon ceased, almost two thousand were brought into being.

Adamson lived for 396 years. Many times he returned to visit his father and mother. Every seven years he and Ratta journeyed south to the second garden, and meanwhile the midwayers kept him informed regarding the welfare of his people. During Adamson's life they did great service in upbuilding a new and independent world center for truth and righteousness.

Adamson and Ratta thus had at their command this corps of marvelous helpers, who labored with them throughout their long lives to assist in the propagation of advanced truth and in the spread of higher standards of spiritual, intellectual, and physical living. And the results of this effort at world betterment never did become fully eclipsed by subsequent retrogressions.

The Adamsonites maintained a high culture for almost seven thousand years from the times of Adamson and Ratta. Later on they became admixed with the neighboring Nodites and Andonites and were also included among the "mighty men of old." And some of the advances of that age persisted to become a latent part of the cultural potential which later blossomed into European civilization.

This center of civilization was situated in the region east of the southern end of the Caspian Sea, near the Kopet Dagh. A short way up in the foothills of Turkestan are the vestiges of what was onetime the Adamsonite headquarters of the violet race. In these highland sites, situated in a narrow and ancient fertile belt lying in the lower foothills of the Kopet range, there successively arose at various periods four diverse cultures respectively fostered by four different groups of Adamson's descendants. It was the second of these groups which migrated westward to Greece and the islands of the Mediterranean. The residue of Adamson's descendants migrated north and west to enter Europe with the blended stock of the last Andite wave coming out of Mesopotamia, and they were also numbered among the Andite-Aryan invaders of India.

6. THE SECONDARY MIDWAYERS

While the primary midwayers had a well-nigh superhuman origin, the secondary order are the offspring of the pure Adamic stock united with a humanized descendant of ancestors common to the parentage of the senior corps.

Among the children of Adamson there were just sixteen of the peculiar progenitors of the secondary midwayers. These unique children were equally divided as regards sex, and each couple was capable of producing a secondary midwayer every seventy days by a combined technique of sex and nonsex liaison. And such a phenomenon was never possible on earth before that time, nor has it ever occurred since.

These sixteen children lived and died (except for their peculiarities) as mortals of the realm, but their electrically energized offspring live on and on, not being subject to the limitations of mortal flesh.

Each of the eight couples eventually produced 248 midwayers, and thus did the original secondary corps—1,984 in number—come into existence. There are eight subgroups of secondary midwayers. They are designated as A-B-C the first, second, third, and so on. And then there are D-E-F the first, second, and so on.

After the default of Adam the primary midwayers returned to the service of the Melchizedek receivers, while the secondary group were attached to the Adamson center until his death. Thirty-three of these secondary midwayers, the chiefs of their organization at the death of Adamson, endeavored to swing the whole order over to the service of the Melchizedeks, thus effecting a liaison with the primary corps. But failing to accomplish this, they deserted their companions and went over in a body to the service of the planetary receivers.

After the death of Adamson the remainder of the secondary midwayers became a strange, unorganized, and unattached influence on Urantia. From that time to the days of Machiventa Melchizedek they led an irregular and unorganized existence. They were partially brought under control by this Melchizedek but were still productive of much mischief up to the days of Christ Michael. And during his sojourn on earth they all made final decisions as to their future destiny, the loyal majority then enlisting under the leadership of the primary midwayers.

7. THE REBEL MIDWAYERS

The majority of the primary midwayers went into sin at the time of the Lucifer rebellion. When the devastation of the planetary rebellion was reckoned up, among other losses it was discovered that of the original 50,000, 40,119 had joined the Caligastia secession.

The original number of secondary midwayers was 1,984, and of these 873 failed to align themselves with the rule of Michael and were duly interned in connection with the planetary adjudication of Urantia on the day of Pentecost. No one can forecast the future of these fallen creatures.

Both groups of rebel midwayers are now held in custody awaiting the final adjudication of the affairs of the system rebellion. But they did many strange things on earth prior to the inauguration of the present planetary dispensation.

These disloyal midwayers were able to reveal themselves to mortal eyes under certain circumstances, and especially was this true of the associates of Beelzebub, the leader of the apostate secondary midwayers. But these unique creatures must not be confused with certain of the rebel cherubim and seraphim who also were on earth up to the time of Christ's death and resurrection. Some of the older writers designated these rebellious midway creatures as evil spirits and demons, and the apostate seraphim as evil angels.

On no world can evil spirits possess any mortal mind subsequent to the life of a Paradise bestowal Son. But before the days of Christ Michael on Urantia—before the universal coming of the Thought Adjusters and the pouring out of the Master's spirit upon all flesh—these rebel midwayers were actually able to influence the minds of certain inferior mortals and somewhat to control their actions. This was accomplished in much the same way as the loyal midway creatures function when they serve as efficient contact guardians of the human minds of the Urantia reserve corps of destiny at those times when the Adjuster is, in effect, detached from the personality during a season of contact with superhuman intelligences.

It is no mere figure of speech when the record states: "And they brought to Him all sorts of sick people, those who were possessed by devils and those who were lunatics." Jesus knew and recognized the difference between insanity and demoniacal possession, although these states were greatly confused in the minds of those who lived in his day and generation.

Even prior to Pentecost no rebel spirit could dominate a normal human mind, and since that day even the weak minds of inferior mortals are free from such possibilities. The supposed casting out of devils since the arrival of the Spirit of Truth has been a matter of confounding a belief in demoniacal possession with hysteria, insanity, and feeble-mindedness. But just because Michael's bestowal has forever liberated all human minds on Urantia from the possibility of demoniacal possession, do not imagine that such was not a reality in former ages.

The entire group of rebel midwayers is at present held prisoner by order of the Most Highs of Edentia. No more do they roam this world on mischief bent. Regardless of the presence of the Thought Adjusters, the pouring out of the Spirit of Truth upon all flesh forever made it impossible for disloyal spirits of any sort or description ever again to invade even the most feeble of human minds. Since the day of Pentecost there never again can be such a thing as demoniacal possession.

8. THE UNITED MIDWAYERS

At the last adjudication of this world, when Michael removed the slumbering survivors of time, the midway creatures were left behind, left to assist in the spiritual and semispiritual work on the planet. They now function as a single corps, embracing both orders and numbering 10,992. *The United Midwayers of Urantia* are at present governed alternately by the senior member of each order. This regime has obtained since their amalgamation into one group shortly after Pentecost.

The members of the older or primary order are generally known by numerals; they are often given names such as 1-2-3 the first, 4-5-6 the first, and so on. On Urantia the Adamic midwayers are designated alphabetically in order to distinguish them from the numerical designation of the primary midwayers.

Both orders are nonmaterial beings as regards nutrition and energy intake, but they partake of many human traits and are able to enjoy and follow your humor as well as your worship. When attached to mortals, they enter into the spirit of human work, rest, and play. But midwayers do not sleep, neither do they possess powers of procreation. In a certain sense the secondary group are differentiated along the lines of maleness and femaleness, often being spoken of as "he" or "she." They often work together in such pairs.

Midwayers are not men, neither are they angels, but secondary midwayers are, in nature, nearer man than angel; they are, in a way, of your races and are, therefore, very understanding and sympathetic in their contact with human beings; they are invaluable to the seraphim in their work for and with the various races of mankind, and both orders are indispensable to the seraphim who serve as personal guardians to mortals.

The United Midwayers of Urantia are organized for service with the planetary seraphim in accordance with innate endowments and acquired skills, in the following groups:

1. *Midway messengers.* This group bear names; they are a small corps and are of great assistance on an evolutionary world in the service of quick and reliable personal communication.

2. *Planetary sentinels.* Midwayers are the guardians, the sentinels, of the worlds of space. They perform the important duties of observers for all the numerous phenomena and types of communication which are of import to the

supernatural beings of the realm. They patrol the invisible spirit realm of the planet.

3. *Contact personalities.* In the contacts made with the mortal beings of the material worlds, such as with the subject through whom these communications were transmitted, the midway creatures are always employed. They are an essential factor in such liaisons of the spiritual and the material levels.

4. *Progress helpers.* These are the more spiritual of the midway creatures, and they are distributed as assistants to the various orders of seraphim who function in special groups on the planet.

Midwayers vary greatly in their abilities to make contact with the seraphim above and with their human cousins below. It is exceedingly difficult, for instance, for the primary midwayers to make direct contact with material agencies. They are considerably nearer the angelic type of being and are therefore usually assigned to working with, and ministering to, the spiritual forces resident on the planet. They act as companions and guides for celestial visitors and student sojourners, whereas the secondary creatures are almost exclusively attached to the ministry of the material beings of the realm.

The 1,111 loyal secondary midwayers are engaged in important missions on earth. As compared with their primary associates, they are decidedly material. They exist just outside the range of mortal vision and possess sufficient latitude of adaptation to make, at will, physical contact with what humans call "material things." These unique creatures have certain definite powers over the things of time and space, not excepting the beasts of the realm.

Many of the more literal phenomena ascribed to angels have been performed by the secondary midway creatures. When the early teachers of the gospel of Jesus were thrown into prison by the ignorant religious leaders of that day, an actual "angel of the Lord" "by night opened the prison doors and brought them forth." But in the case of Peter's deliverance after the killing of James by Herod's order, it was a secondary midwayer who performed the work ascribed to an angel.

Their chief work today is that of unperceived personal-liaison associates of those men and women who constitute the planetary reserve corps of destiny. It was the work of this secondary group, ably seconded by certain of the primary corps, that brought about the co-ordination of personalities and circumstances on Urantia which finally induced the planetary celestial supervisors to initiate those petitions that resulted in the granting of the mandates making possible the series of revelations of which this presentation is a part. But it should be made clear that the midway creatures are not involved in the sordid performances taking place under the general designation of "spiritualism." The midwayers at present on Urantia, all of whom are of honorable standing, are not connected with the phenomena of so-called "mediumship"; and they do not, ordinarily, permit humans to witness their sometimes necessary physical activities or other contacts with the material world, as they are perceived by human senses.

9. THE PERMANENT CITIZENS OF URANTIA

Midwayers may be regarded as the first group of the permanent inhabitants to be found on the various orders of worlds throughout the universes in contrast with evolutionary ascenders like the mortal creatures and the angelic hosts. Such permanent citizens are encountered at various points in the Paradise ascent.

Unlike the various orders of celestial beings who are assigned to *minister* on a planet, the midwayers *live* on an inhabited world. The seraphim come and go, but the midway creatures remain and will remain, albeit they are nonetheless ministers for being natives of the planet, and they provide the one continuing regime which harmonizes and connects the changing administrations of the seraphic hosts.

As actual citizens of Urantia, the midwayers have a kinship interest in the destiny of this sphere. They are a determined association, persistently working for the progress of their native planet. Their determination is suggested by the motto of their order: "What the United Midwayers undertake, the United Midwayers do."

Although their ability to traverse the energy circuits makes planetary departure feasible to any midwayer, they have individually pledged themselves not to leave the planet prior to their sometime release by the universe authorities. Midwayers are anchored on a planet until the ages of settled light and life. With the exception of 1-2-3 the first, no loyal midway creatures have ever departed from Urantia.

1-2-3 the first, the eldest of the primary order, was released from immediate planetary duties shortly after Pentecost. This noble midwayer stood steadfast with Van and Amadon during the tragic days of the planetary rebellion, and his fearless leadership was instrumental in reducing the casualties in his order. He serves at present on Jerusem as a member of the twenty-four counselors, having already functioned as governor general of Urantia once since Pentecost.

Midwayers are planet bound, but much as mortals talk with travelers from afar and thus learn about remote places on the planet, so do midwayers converse with celestial travelers to learn about the far places of the universe. So do they become conversant with this system and universe, even with Orvonton and its sister creations, and so do they prepare themselves for citizenship on the higher levels of creature existence.

While the midwayers were brought into existence fully developed—experiencing no period of growth or development from immaturity—they never cease to grow in wisdom and experience. Like mortals they are evolutionary creatures, and they have a culture which is a bona fide evolutionary attainment. There are many great minds and mighty spirits among the Urantia midway corps.

In the larger aspect the civilization of Urantia is the joint product of the Urantia mortals and the Urantia midwayers, and this is true despite the present differential between the two levels of culture, a differential which will not be compensated prior to the ages of light and life.

The midway culture, being the product of an immortal planetary citizenry, is relatively immune to those temporal vicissitudes which beset human civilization. The generations of men forget; the corps of midwayers remembers, and that memory is the treasure house of the traditions of your inhabited world. Thus does the culture of a planet remain ever present on that planet, and in proper circumstances such treasured memories of past events are made available, even as the story of the life and teachings of Jesus has been given by the midwayers of Urantia to their cousins in the flesh.

Midwayers are the skillful ministers who compensate that gap between the material and spiritual affairs of Urantia which appeared upon the death of Adam and Eve. They are likewise your elder brethren, comrades in the long struggle to attain a settled status of light and life on Urantia. The United Midwayers are a rebellion-tested corps, and they will faithfully enact their part in planetary evolution until this world attains the goal of the ages, until that distant day when in fact peace does reign on earth and in truth is there good will in the hearts of men.

Because of the valuable work performed by these midwayers, we have concluded that they are a truly essential part of the spirit economy of the realms. And where rebellion has not marred a planet's affairs, they are of still greater assistance to the seraphim.

The entire organization of high spirits, angelic hosts, and midway fellows is enthusiastically devoted to the furtherance of the Paradise plan for the progressive ascension and perfection attainment of evolutionary mortals, one of the supernal businesses of the universe—the superb survival plan of bringing God down to man and then, by a sublime sort of partnership, carrying man up to God and on to eternity of service and divinity of attainment—alike for mortal and midwayer.

[Presented by an Archangel of Nebadon.]

PAPER 78

THE VIOLET RACE AFTER THE DAYS OF ADAM

THE second Eden was the cradle of civilization for almost thirty thousand years. Here in Mesopotamia the Adamic peoples held forth, sending out their progeny to the ends of the earth, and latterly, as amalgamated with the Nodite and Sangik tribes, were known as the Andites. From this region went those men and women who initiated the doings of historic times, and who have so enormously accelerated cultural progress on Urantia.

This paper depicts the planetary history of the violet race, beginning soon after the default of Adam, about 35,000 B.C., and extending down through its amalgamation with the Nodite and Sangik races, about 15,000 B.C., to form the Andite peoples and on to its final disappearance from the Mesopotamian homelands, about 2000 B.C.

1. RACIAL AND CULTURAL DISTRIBUTION

Although the minds and morals of the races were at a low level at the time of Adam's arrival, physical evolution had gone on quite unaffected by the exigencies of the Caligastia rebellion. Adam's contribution to the biologic status of the races, notwithstanding the partial failure of the undertaking, enormously upstepped the people of Urantia.

Adam and Eve also contributed much that was of value to the social, moral, and intellectual progress of mankind; civilization was immensely quickened by the presence of their offspring. But thirty-five thousand years ago the world at large possessed little culture. Certain centers of civilization existed here and there, but most of Urantia languished in savagery. Racial and cultural distribution was as follows:

1. *The violet race—Adamites and Adamsonites.* The chief center of Adamite culture was in the second garden, located in the triangle of the Tigris and Euphrates rivers; this was indeed the cradle of Occidental and Indian civilizations. The secondary or northern center of the violet race was the Adamsonite headquarters, situated east of the southern shore of the Caspian Sea near the Kopet mountains. From these two centers there went forth to the surrounding lands the culture and life plasm which so immediately quickened all the races.

2. *Pre-Sumerians and other Nodites.* There were also present in Mesopotamia, near the mouth of the rivers, remnants of the ancient culture of the days of Dalamatia. With the passing millenniums, this group became thoroughly admixed with the Adamites to the north, but they never entirely lost their Nodite traditions. Various other Nodite groups that had settled in the Levant were, in general, absorbed by the later expanding violet race.

3. *The Andonites* maintained five or six fairly representative settlements to the north and east of the Adamson headquarters. They were also scattered throughout Turkestan, while isolated islands of them persisted throughout Eurasia, especially in mountainous regions. These aborigines still held the northlands of the Eurasian continent, together with Iceland and Greenland, but they had long since been driven from the plains of Europe by the blue man and from the river valleys of farther Asia by the expanding yellow race.

4. *The red man* occupied the Americas, having been driven out of Asia over fifty thousand years before the arrival of Adam.

5. *The yellow race.* The Chinese peoples were well established in control of eastern Asia. Their most advanced settlements were situated to the northwest of modern China in regions bordering on Tibet.

6. *The blue race.* The blue men were scattered all over Europe, but their better centers of culture were situated in the then fertile valleys of the Mediterranean basin and in northwestern Europe. Neanderthal absorption had greatly retarded the culture of the blue man, but he was otherwise the most aggressive, adventurous, and exploratory of all the evolutionary peoples of Eurasia.

7. *Pre-Dravidian India.* The complex mixture of races in India—embracing every race on earth, but especially the green, orange, and black—maintained a culture slightly above that of the outlying regions.

8. *The Sahara civilization.* The superior elements of the indigo race had their most progressive settlements in what is now the great Sahara desert. This indigo-black group carried extensive strains of the submerged orange and green races.

9. *The Mediterranean basin.* The most highly blended race outside of India occupied what is now the Mediterranean basin. Here blue men from the north and Saharans from the south met and mingled with Nodites and Adamites from the east.

This was the picture of the world prior to the beginnings of the great expansions of the violet race, about twenty-five thousand years ago. The hope of future civilization lay in the second garden between the rivers of Mesopotamia. Here in southwestern Asia there existed the potential of a great civilization, the possibility of the spread to the world of the ideas and ideals which had been salvaged from the days of Dalamatia and the times of Eden.

Adam and Eve had left behind a limited but potent progeny, and the celestial observers on Urantia waited anxiously to find out how these descendants of the erring Material Son and Daughter would acquit themselves.

2. THE ADAMITES IN THE SECOND GARDEN

For thousands of years the sons of Adam labored along the rivers of Mesopotamia, working out their irrigation and flood-control problems to the south, perfecting their defenses to the north, and attempting to preserve their traditions of the glory of the first Eden.

The heroism displayed in the leadership of the second garden constitutes one of the amazing and inspiring epics of Urantia's history. These splendid souls never wholly lost sight of the purpose of the Adamic mission, and therefore did they valiantly fight off the influences of the surrounding and inferior tribes while they willingly sent forth their choicest sons and daughters in a steady stream as emissaries to the races of earth. Sometimes this expansion was depleting to the home culture, but always these superior peoples would rehabilitate themselves.

The civilization, society, and cultural status of the Adamites were far above the general level of the evolutionary races of Urantia. Only among the old settlements of Van and Amadon and the Adamsonites was there a civilization in any way comparable. But the civilization of the second Eden was an artificial structure—*it had not been evolved*—and was therefore doomed to deteriorate until it reached a natural evolutionary level.

Adam left a great intellectual and spiritual culture behind him, but it was not advanced in mechanical appliances since every civilization is limited by available natural resources, inherent genius, and sufficient leisure to insure inventive fruition. The civilization of the violet race was predicated on the presence of Adam and on the traditions of the first Eden. After Adam's death and as these traditions grew dim through the passing millenniums, the cultural level of the Adamites steadily deteriorated until it reached a state of reciprocal balance with the status of the surrounding peoples and the naturally evolving cultural capacities of the violet race.

But the Adamites were a real nation around 19,000 B.C., numbering four and a half million, and already they had poured forth millions of their progeny into the surrounding peoples.

3. EARLY EXPANSIONS OF THE ADAMITES

The violet race retained the Edenic traditions of peacefulness for many millenniums, which explains their long delay in making territorial conquests. When they suffered from population pressure, instead of making war to secure more territory, they sent forth their excess inhabitants as teachers to the other races. The cultural effect of these earlier migrations was not enduring, but the absorption of the Adamite teachers, traders, and explorers was biologically invigorating to the surrounding peoples.

Some of the Adamites early journeyed westward to the valley of the Nile; others penetrated eastward into Asia, but these were a minority. The mass movement of the later days was extensively northward and thence westward. It was, in the main, a gradual but unremitting northward push, the greater number making their way north and then circling westward around the Caspian Sea into Europe.

About twenty-five thousand years ago many of the purer elements of the Adamites were well on their northern trek. And as they penetrated northward, they became less and less Adamic until, by the times of their occupation of Turkestan, they had become thoroughly admixed with the other races, particularly the Nodites. Very few of the pure-line violet peoples ever penetrated far into Europe or Asia.

From about 30,000 to 10,000 B.C. epoch-making racial mixtures were taking place throughout southwestern Asia. The highland inhabitants of Turkestan were a virile and vigorous people. To the northwest of India much of the culture of the days of Van persisted. Still to the north of these settlements the best of the early Andonites had been preserved. And both of these superior races of culture and character were absorbed by the northward-moving Adamites. This amalgamation led to the adoption of many new ideas; it facilitated the progress of civilization and greatly advanced all phases of art, science, and social culture.

As the period of the early Adamic migrations ended, about 15,000 B.C., there were already more descendants of Adam in Europe and central Asia than anywhere else in the world, even than in Mesopotamia. The European blue races had been largely infiltrated. The lands now called Russia and Turkestan were occupied throughout their southern stretches by a great reservoir of the Adamites mixed with Nodites, Andonites, and red and yellow Sangiks. Southern Europe and the Mediterranean fringe were occupied by a mixed race of Andonite and Sangik peoples—orange, green, and indigo—with a sprinkling of the Adamite stock. Asia Minor and the central-eastern European lands were held by tribes that were predominantly Andonite.

A blended colored race, about this time greatly reinforced by arrivals from Mesopotamia, held forth in Egypt and prepared to take over the disappearing culture of the Euphrates valley. The black peoples were moving farther south in Africa and, like the red race, were virtually isolated.

The Saharan civilization had been disrupted by drought and that of the Mediterranean basin by flood. The blue races had, as yet, failed to develop an advanced culture. The Andonites were still scattered over the Arctic and central Asian regions. The green and orange races had been exterminated as such. The indigo race was moving south in Africa, there to begin its slow but long-continued racial deterioration.

The peoples of India lay stagnant, with a civilization that was unprogressing; the yellow man was consolidating his holdings in central Asia; the brown man had not yet begun his civilization on the near-by islands of the Pacific.

These racial distributions, associated with extensive climatic changes, set the world stage for the inauguration of the Andite era of Urantia civilization. These early migrations extended over a period of ten thousand years, from 25,000 to 15,000 B.C. The later or Andite migrations extended from about 15,000 to 6000 B.C.

It took so long for the earlier waves of Adamites to pass over Eurasia that their culture was largely lost in transit. Only the later Andites moved with sufficient speed to retain the Edenic culture at any great distance from Mesopotamia.

4. THE ANDITES

The Andite races were the primary blends of the pure-line violet race and the Nodites plus the evolutionary peoples. In general, Andites should be thought of as having a far greater percentage of Adamic blood than the modern races. In the main, the term Andite is used to designate those peoples whose racial inheritance was from one-eighth to one-sixth violet. Modern Urantians, even the northern white races, contain much less than this percentage of the blood of Adam.

The earliest Andite peoples took origin in the regions adjacent to Mesopotamia more than twenty-five thousand years ago and consisted of a blend of the Adamites and Nodites. The second garden was surrounded by concentric circles of diminishing violet blood, and it was on the periphery of this racial melting pot that the Andite race was born. Later on, when the migrating Adamites and Nodites entered the then fertile regions of Turkestan, they soon blended with the superior inhabitants, and the resultant race mixture extended the Andite type northward.

The Andites were the best all-round human stock to appear on Urantia since the days of the pure-line violet peoples. They embraced most of the highest types of the surviving remnants of the Adamite and Nodite races and, later, some of the best strains of the yellow, blue, and green men.

These early Andites were not Aryan; they were pre-Aryan. They were not white; they were pre-white. They were neither an Occidental nor an Oriental people. But it is Andite inheritance that gives to the polyglot mixture of the so-called white races that generalized homogeneity which has been called Caucasoid.

The purer strains of the violet race had retained the Adamic tradition of peace-seeking, which explains why the earlier race movements had been more in the nature of peaceful migrations. But as the Adamites united with the Nodite stocks, who were by this time a belligerent race, their Andite descendants became, for their day and age, the most skillful and sagacious militarists ever to live on Urantia. Thenceforth the movements of the Mesopotamians grew increasingly military in character and became more akin to actual conquests.

These Andites were adventurous; they had roving dispositions. An increase of either Sangik or Andonite stock tended to stabilize them. But even so, their later descendants never stopped until they had circumnavigated the globe and discovered the last remote continent.

5. THE ANDITE MIGRATIONS

For twenty thousand years the culture of the second garden persisted, but it experienced a steady decline until about 15,000 B.C., when the regeneration of the Sethite priesthood and the leadership of Amosad inaugurated a brilliant era. The massive waves of civilization which later spread over Eurasia immediately followed the great renaissance of the Garden consequent upon the extensive union of the Adamites with the surrounding mixed Nodites to form the Andites.

These Andites inaugurated new advances throughout Eurasia and North Africa. From Mesopotamia through Sinkiang the Andite culture was dominant, and the steady migration toward Europe was continuously offset by new arrivals from Mesopotamia. But it is hardly correct to speak of the Andites as a race in Mesopotamia proper until near the beginning of the terminal migrations of the mixed descendants of Adam. By this time even the races in the second garden had become so blended that they could no longer be considered Adamites.

The civilization of Turkestan was constantly being revived and refreshed by the newcomers from Mesopotamia, especially by the later Andite cavalrymen. The so-called Aryan mother tongue was in process of formation in the highlands of Turkestan; it was a blend of the Andonic dialect of that region with the language of the Adamsonites and later Andites. Many modern languages are derived from this early speech of these central Asian tribes who conquered Europe, India, and the upper stretches of the Mesopotamian plains. This ancient language gave the Occidental tongues all of that similarity which is called Aryan.

By 12,000 B.C. three quarters of the Andite stock of the world was resident in northern and eastern Europe, and when the later and final exodus from

Mesopotamia took place, sixty-five per cent of these last waves of emigration entered Europe.

The Andites not only migrated to Europe but to northern China and India, while many groups penetrated to the ends of the earth as missionaries, teachers, and traders. They contributed considerably to the northern groups of the Saharan Sangik peoples. But only a few teachers and traders ever penetrated farther south in Africa than the headwaters of the Nile. Later on, mixed Andites and Egyptians followed down both the east and west coasts of Africa well below the equator, but they did not reach Madagascar.

These Andites were the so-called Dravidian and later Aryan conquerors of India; and their presence in central Asia greatly upstepped the ancestors of the Turanians. Many of this race journeyed to China by way of both Sinkiang and Tibet and added desirable qualities to the later Chinese stocks. From time to time small groups made their way into Japan, Formosa, the East Indies, and southern China, though very few entered southern China by the coastal route.

One hundred and thirty-two of this race, embarking in a fleet of small boats from Japan, eventually reached South America and by intermarriage with the natives of the Andes established the ancestry of the later rulers of the Incas. They crossed the Pacific by easy stages, tarrying on the many islands they found along the way. The islands of the Polynesian group were both more numerous and larger then than now, and these Andite sailors, together with some who followed them, biologically modified the native groups in transit. Many flourishing centers of civilization grew up on these now submerged lands as a result of Andite penetration. Easter Island was long a religious and administrative center of one of these lost groups. But of the Andites who navigated the Pacific of long ago none but the one hundred and thirty-two ever reached the mainland of the Americas.

The migratory conquests of the Andites continued on down to their final dispersions, from 8000 to 6000 B.C. As they poured out of Mesopotamia, they continuously depleted the biologic reserves of their homelands while markedly strengthening the surrounding peoples. And to every nation to which they journeyed, they contributed humor, art, adventure, music, and manufacture. They were skillful domesticators of animals and expert agriculturists. For the time being, at least, their presence usually improved the religious beliefs and moral practices of the older races. And so the culture of Mesopotamia quietly spread out over Europe, India, China, northern Africa, and the Pacific Islands.

6. THE LAST ANDITE DISPERSIONS

The last three waves of Andites poured out of Mesopotamia between 8000 and 6000 B.C. These three great waves of culture were forced out of Mesopotamia by the pressure of the hill tribes to the east and the harassment of the plainsmen of the west. The inhabitants of the Euphrates valley and adjacent territory went forth in their final exodus in several directions:

Sixty-five per cent entered Europe by the Caspian Sea route to conquer and amalgamate with the newly appearing white races—the blend of the blue men and the earlier Andites.

Ten per cent, including a large group of the Sethite priests, moved eastward through the Elamite highlands to the Iranian plateau and Turkestan. Many of their descendants were later driven into India with their Aryan brethren from the regions to the north.

Ten per cent of the Mesopotamians turned eastward in their northern trek, entering Sinkiang, where they blended with the Andite-yellow inhabitants. The majority of the able offspring of this racial union later entered China and contributed much to the immediate improvement of the northern division of the yellow race.

Ten per cent of these fleeing Andites made their way across Arabia and entered Egypt.

Five per cent of the Andites, the very superior culture of the coastal district about the mouths of the Tigris and Euphrates who had kept themselves free from intermarriage with the inferior neighboring tribesmen, refused to leave their homes. This group represented the survival of many superior Nodite and Adamite strains.

The Andites had almost entirely evacuated this region by 6000 B.C., though their descendants, largely mixed with the surrounding Sangik races and the Andonites of Asia Minor, were there to give battle to the northern and eastern invaders at a much later date.

The cultural age of the second garden was terminated by the increasing infiltration of the surrounding inferior stocks. Civilization moved westward to the Nile and the Mediterranean islands, where it continued to thrive and advance long after its fountainhead in Mesopotamia had deteriorated. And this unchecked influx of inferior peoples prepared the way for the later conquest of all Mesopotamia by the northern barbarians who drove out the residual strains of ability. Even in later years the cultured residue still resented the presence of these ignorant and uncouth invaders.

7. THE FLOODS IN MESOPOTAMIA

The river dwellers were accustomed to rivers overflowing their banks at certain seasons; these periodic floods were annual events in their lives. But new perils threatened the valley of Mesopotamia as a result of progressive geologic changes to the north.

For thousands of years after the submergence of the first Eden the mountains about the eastern coast of the Mediterranean and those to the northwest and northeast of Mesopotamia continued to rise. This elevation of the highlands was greatly accelerated about 5000 B.C., and this, together with greatly increased snowfall on the northern mountains, caused unprecedented floods each spring throughout the Euphrates valley. These spring floods grew increasingly worse so that eventually the inhabitants of the river regions were driven to the eastern highlands. For almost a thousand years scores of cities were practically deserted because of these extensive deluges.

Almost five thousand years later, as the Hebrew priests in Babylonian captivity sought to trace the Jewish people back to Adam, they found great difficulty in piecing the story together; and it occurred to one of them to abandon the effort, to let the whole world drown in its wickedness at the time of Noah's flood, and thus to be in a better position to trace Abraham right back to one of the three surviving sons of Noah.

The traditions of a time when water covered the whole of the earth's surface are universal. Many races harbor the story of a world-wide flood some time during past ages. The Biblical story of Noah, the ark, and the flood is an invention of the Hebrew priesthood during the Babylonian captivity. There has never been a universal flood since life was established on Urantia. The only time the surface of the earth was completely covered by water was during those Archeozoic ages before the land had begun to appear.

But Noah really lived; he was a wine maker of Aram, a river settlement near Erech. He kept a written record of the days of the river's rise from year to year. He brought much ridicule upon himself by going up and down the river valley advocating that all houses be built of wood, boat fashion, and that the family animals be put on board each night as the flood season approached. He would go to the neighboring river settlements every year and warn them that in so many days the floods would come. Finally a year came in which the annual floods were greatly augmented by unusually heavy rainfall so that the sudden rise of the waters wiped out the entire village; only Noah and his immediate family were saved in their houseboat.

These floods completed the disruption of Andite civilization. With the ending of this period of deluge, the second garden was no more. Only in the south and among the Sumerians did any trace of the former glory remain.

The remnants of this, one of the oldest civilizations, are to be found in these regions of Mesopotamia and to the northeast and northwest. But still older vestiges of the days of Dalamatia exist under the waters of the Persian Gulf, and the first Eden lies submerged under the eastern end of the Mediterranean Sea.

8. THE SUMERIANS—LAST OF THE ANDITES

When the last Andite dispersion broke the biologic backbone of Mesopotamian civilization, a small minority of this superior race remained in their homeland near the mouths of the rivers. These were the Sumerians, and by 6000 B.C. they had become largely Andite in extraction, though their culture was more exclusively Nodite in character, and they clung to the ancient traditions of Dalamatia. Nonetheless, these Sumerians of the coastal regions were the last of the Andites in Mesopotamia. But the races of Mesopotamia were already thoroughly blended by this late date, as is evidenced by the skull types found in the graves of this era.

It was during the floodtimes that Susa so greatly prospered. The first and lower city was inundated so that the second or higher town succeeded the lower as the headquarters for the peculiar artcrafts of that day. With the later diminution of these floods, Ur became the center of the pottery industry. About seven thousand years ago Ur was on the Persian Gulf, the river deposits having since built up the land to its present limits. These settlements suffered less from the floods because of better controlling works and the widening mouths of the rivers.

The peaceful grain growers of the Euphrates and Tigris valleys had long been harassed by the raids of the barbarians of Turkestan and the Iranian plateau. But now a concerted invasion of the Euphrates valley was brought about by the increasing drought of the highland pastures. And this invasion was all the more serious because these surrounding herdsmen and hunters possessed large numbers of tamed horses. It was the possession of horses which gave them a tremendous military advantage over their rich neighbors to the south. In a short time they overran all Mesopotamia, driving forth the last waves of culture which spread out over all of Europe, western Asia, and northern Africa.

These conquerors of Mesopotamia carried in their ranks many of the better Andite strains of the mixed northern races of Turkestan, including some of the Adamson stock. These less advanced but more vigorous tribes from the north quickly and willingly assimilated the residue of the civilization of Mesopotamia and presently developed into those mixed peoples found in the Euphrates valley at the beginning of historic annals. They quickly revived many phases of the passing civilization of Mesopotamia, adopting the arts of the valley tribes and much of the culture of the Sumerians. They even sought to build a third tower of Babel and later adopted the term as their national name.

When these barbarian cavalrymen from the northeast overran the whole Euphrates valley, they did not conquer the remnants of the Andites who dwelt about the mouth of the river on the Persian Gulf. These Sumerians were able to defend themselves because of superior intelligence, better weapons, and their extensive system of military canals, which were an adjunct to their irrigation scheme of interconnecting pools. They were a united people because they had a uniform group religion. They were thus able to maintain their racial and national integrity long after their neighbors to the northwest were broken up into isolated city-states. No one of these city groups was able to overcome the united Sumerians.

And the invaders from the north soon learned to trust and prize these peace-loving Sumerians as able teachers and administrators. They were greatly respected and sought after as teachers of art and industry, as directors of commerce, and as civil rulers by all peoples to the north and from Egypt in the west to India in the east.

After the breakup of the early Sumerian confederation the later city-states were ruled by the apostate descendants of the Sethite priests. Only when these priests made conquests of the neighboring cities did they call themselves kings. The later city kings failed to form powerful confederations before the days of Sargon because of deity jealousy. Each city believed its municipal god to be superior to all other gods, and therefore they refused to subordinate themselves to a common leader.

The end of this long period of the weak rule of the city priests was terminated by Sargon, the priest of Kish, who proclaimed himself king and started out on the conquest of the whole of Mesopotamia and adjoining lands. And for the time, this ended the city-states, priest-ruled and priest-ridden, each city having its own municipal god and its own ceremonial practices.

After the breakup of this Kish confederation there ensued a long period of constant warfare between these valley cities for supremacy. And the rulership variously shifted between Sumer, Akkad, Kish, Erech, Ur, and Susa.

About 2500 B.C. the Sumerians suffered severe reverses at the hands of the northern Suites and Guites. Lagash, the Sumerian capital built on flood mounds, fell. Erech held out for thirty years after the fall of Akkad. By the time of the establishment of the rule of Hammurabi the Sumerians had become absorbed into the ranks of the northern Semites, and the Mesopotamian Andites passed from the pages of history.

From 2500 to 2000 B.C. the nomads were on a rampage from the Atlantic to the Pacific. The Nerites constituted the final eruption of the Caspian group of the Mesopotamian descendants of the blended Andonite and Andite races. What the barbarians failed to do to effect the ruination of Mesopotamia, subsequent climatic changes succeeded in accomplishing.

And this is the story of the violet race after the days of Adam and of the fate of their homeland between the Tigris and Euphrates. Their ancient civilization finally fell due to the emigration of superior peoples and the immigration of their inferior neighbors. But long before the barbarian cavalrymen conquered the valley, much of the Garden culture had spread to Asia, Africa, and Europe, there to produce the ferments which have resulted in the twentieth-century civilization of Urantia.

[Presented by an Archangel of Nebadon.]

PAPER 79
ANDITE EXPANSION IN THE ORIENT

ASIA is the homeland of the human race. It was on a southern peninsula of this continent that Andon and Fonta were born; in the highlands of what is now Afghanistan, their descendant Badonan founded a primitive center of culture that persisted for over one-half million years. Here at this eastern focus of the human race the Sangik peoples differentiated from the Andonic stock, and Asia was their first home, their first hunting ground, their first battlefield. Southwestern Asia witnessed the successive civilizations of Dalamatians, Nodites, Adamites, and Andites, and from these regions the potentials of modern civilization spread to the world.

1. THE ANDITES OF TURKESTAN

For over twenty-five thousand years, on down to nearly 2000 B.C., the heart of Eurasia was predominantly, though diminishingly, Andite. In the lowlands of Turkestan the Andites made the westward turning around the inland lakes into Europe, while from the highlands of this region they infiltrated eastward. Eastern Turkestan (Sinkiang) and, to a lesser extent, Tibet were the ancient gateways through which these peoples of Mesopotamia penetrated the mountains to the northern lands of the yellow men. The Andite infiltration of India proceeded from the Turkestan highlands into the Punjab and from the Iranian grazing lands through Baluchistan. These earlier migrations were in no sense conquests; they were, rather, the continual drifting of the Andite tribes into western India and China.

For almost fifteen thousand years centers of mixed Andite culture persisted in the basin of the Tarim River in Sinkiang and to the south in the highland regions of Tibet, where the Andites and Andonites had extensively mingled. The Tarim valley was the easternmost outpost of the true Andite culture. Here they built their settlements and entered into trade relations with the progressive Chinese to the east and with the Andonites to the north. In those days the Tarim region was a fertile land; the rainfall was plentiful. To the east the Gobi was an open grassland where the herders were gradually turning to agriculture. This civilization perished when the rain winds shifted to the southeast, but in its day it rivaled Mesopotamia itself.

By 8000 B.C. the slowly increasing aridity of the highland regions of central Asia began to drive the Andites to the river bottoms and the seashores. This increasing drought not only drove them to the valleys of the Nile, Euphrates, Indus, and Yellow rivers, but it produced a new development in Andite civilization. A new class of men, the traders, began to appear in large numbers.

When climatic conditions made hunting unprofitable for the migrating Andites, they did not follow the evolutionary course of the older races by becoming herders. Commerce and urban life made their appearance. From Egypt through Mesopotamia and Turkestan to the rivers of China and India, the more highly civilized tribes began to assemble in cities devoted to manufacture and trade. Adonia became the central Asian commercial metropolis, being located near the present city of Ashkhabad. Commerce in stone, metal, wood, and pottery was accelerated on both land and water.

But ever-increasing drought gradually brought about the great Andite exodus from the lands south and east of the Caspian Sea. The tide of migration began to veer from northward to southward, and the Babylonian cavalrymen began to push into Mesopotamia.

Increasing aridity in central Asia further operated to reduce population and to render these people less warlike; and when the diminishing rainfall to the north forced the nomadic Andonites southward, there was a tremendous exodus of Andites from Turkestan. This is the terminal movement of the so-called Aryans into the Levant and India. It culminated that long dispersal of the mixed descendants of Adam during which every Asiatic and most of the island peoples of the Pacific were to some extent improved by these superior races.

Thus, while they dispersed over the Eastern Hemisphere, the Andites were dispossessed of their homelands in Mesopotamia and Turkestan, for it was this extensive southward movement of Andonites that diluted the Andites in central Asia nearly to the vanishing point.

But even in the twentieth century after Christ there are traces of Andite blood among the Turanian and Tibetan peoples, as is witnessed by the blond types occasionally found in these regions. The early Chinese annals record the presence of the red-haired nomads to the north of the peaceful settlements of the Yellow River, and there still remain paintings which faithfully record the presence of both the blond-Andite and the brunet-Mongolian types in the Tarim basin of long ago.

The last great manifestation of the submerged military genius of the central Asiatic Andites was in A.D. 1200, when the Mongols under Genghis Khan began the conquest of the greater portion of the Asiatic continent. And like the Andites of old, these warriors proclaimed the existence of "one God in heaven." The early breakup of their empire long delayed cultural intercourse between Occident and Orient and greatly handicapped the growth of the monotheistic concept in Asia.

2. THE ANDITE CONQUEST OF INDIA

India is the only locality where all the Urantia races were blended, the Andite invasion adding the last stock. In the highlands northwest of India the Sangik races came into existence, and without exception members of each penetrated the subcontinent of India in their early days, leaving behind them the most heterogeneous race mixture ever to exist on Urantia. Ancient India acted as a catch basin for the migrating races. The base of the peninsula was formerly somewhat narrower than now, much of the deltas of the Ganges and Indus being the work of the last fifty thousand years.

The earliest race mixtures in India were a blending of the migrating red and yellow races with the aboriginal Andonites. This group was later weakened by absorbing the greater portion of the extinct eastern green peoples as well as large numbers of the orange race, was slightly improved through limited admixture with the blue man, but suffered exceedingly through assimilation of large numbers of the indigo race. But the so-called aborigines of India are hardly representative of these early people; they are rather the most inferior southern and eastern fringe, which was never fully absorbed by either the early Andites or their later appearing Aryan cousins.

By 20,000 B.C. the population of western India had already become tinged with the Adamic blood, and never in the history of Urantia did any one people combine so many different races. But it was unfortunate that the secondary Sangik strains predominated, and it was a real calamity that both the blue and the red man were so largely missing from this racial melting pot of long ago; more of the primary Sangik strains would have contributed very much toward the enhancement of what might have been an even greater civilization. As it developed, the red man was destroying himself in the Americas, the blue man was disporting himself in Europe, and the early descendants of Adam (and most of the later ones) exhibited little desire to admix with the darker colored peoples, whether in India, Africa, or elsewhere.

About 15,000 B.C. increasing population pressure throughout Turkestan and Iran occasioned the first really extensive Andite movement toward India. For over fifteen centuries these superior peoples poured in through the highlands of Baluchistan, spreading out over the valleys of the Indus and Ganges and slowly moving southward into the Deccan. This Andite pressure from the northwest drove many of the southern and eastern inferiors into Burma and southern China but not sufficiently to save the invaders from racial obliteration.

The failure of India to achieve the hegemony of Eurasia was largely a matter of topography; population pressure from the north only crowded the majority of the people southward into the decreasing territory of the Deccan, surrounded on all sides by the sea. Had there been adjacent lands for emigration, then would the inferiors have been crowded out in all directions, and the superior stocks would have achieved a higher civilization.

As it was, these earlier Andite conquerors made a desperate attempt to preserve their identity and stem the tide of racial engulfment by the establishment of rigid restrictions regarding intermarriage. Nonetheless, the Andites had become submerged by 10,000 B.C., but the whole mass of the people had been markedly improved by this absorption.

Race mixture is always advantageous in that it favors versatility of culture and makes for a progressive civilization, but if the inferior elements of racial stocks predominate, such achievements will be short-lived. A polyglot culture can be preserved only if the superior stocks reproduce themselves in a safe margin over the inferior. Unrestrained multiplication of inferiors, with decreasing reproduction of superiors, is unfailingly suicidal of cultural civilization.

Had the Andite conquerors been in numbers three times what they were, or had they driven out or destroyed the least desirable third of the mixed orange-green-indigo inhabitants, then would India have become one of the world's leading centers of cultural civilization and undoubtedly would have attracted more of the later waves of Mesopotamians that flowed into Turkestan and thence northward to Europe.

3. DRAVIDIAN INDIA

The blending of the Andite conquerors of India with the native stock eventually resulted in that mixed people which has been called Dravidian. The earlier and purer Dravidians possessed a great capacity for cultural achievement, which was continuously weakened as their Andite inheritance became progressively attenuated. And this is what doomed the budding civilization of India almost twelve thousand years ago. But the infusion of even this small amount of the blood of Adam produced a marked acceleration in social development. This composite stock immediately produced the most versatile civilization then on earth.

Not long after conquering India, the Dravidian Andites lost their racial and cultural contact with Mesopotamia, but the later opening up of the sea lanes and the caravan routes re-established these connections; and at no time within the last ten thousand years has India ever been entirely out of touch with Mesopotamia on the west and China to the east, although the mountain barriers greatly favored western intercourse.

The superior culture and religious leanings of the peoples of India date from the early times of Dravidian domination and are due, in part, to the fact that so many of the Sethite priesthood entered India, both in the earlier Andite and in the later Aryan invasions. The thread of monotheism running through the religious history of India thus stems from the teachings of the Adamites in the second garden.

As early as 16,000 B.C. a company of one hundred Sethite priests entered India and very nearly achieved the religious conquest of the western half of that polyglot people. But their religion did not persist. Within five thousand years their doctrines of the Paradise Trinity had degenerated into the triune symbol of the fire god.

But for more than seven thousand years, down to the end of the Andite migrations, the religious status of the inhabitants of India was far above that of the world at large. During these times India bid fair to produce the leading cultural, religious, philosophic, and commercial civilization of the world. And but for the complete submergence of the Andites by the peoples of the south, this destiny would probably have been realized.

The Dravidian centers of culture were located in the river valleys, principally of the Indus and Ganges, and in the Deccan along the three great rivers flowing through the Eastern Ghats to the sea. The settlements along the seacoast of the Western Ghats owed their prominence to maritime relationships with Sumeria.

The Dravidians were among the earliest peoples to build cities and to engage in an extensive export and import business, both by land and sea. By 7000 B.C. camel trains were making regular trips to distant Mesopotamia; Dravidian shipping was pushing coastwise across the Arabian Sea to the Sumerian cities of the Persian Gulf and was venturing on the waters of the Bay of Bengal as far as the East Indies. An alphabet, together with the art of writing, was imported from Sumeria by these seafarers and merchants.

These commercial relationships greatly contributed to the further diversification of a cosmopolitan culture, resulting in the early appearance of many of the refinements and even luxuries of urban life. When the later appearing Aryans entered India, they did not recognize in the Dravidians their Andite cousins submerged in the Sangik races, but they did find a well-advanced civilization. Despite biologic limitations, the Dravidians founded a superior civilization. It was well diffused throughout all India and has survived on down to modern times in the Deccan.

4. THE ARYAN INVASION OF INDIA

The second Andite penetration of India was the Aryan invasion during a period of almost five hundred years in the middle of the third millennium before Christ. This migration marked the terminal exodus of the Andites from their homelands in Turkestan.

The early Aryan centers were scattered over the northern half of India, notably in the northwest. These invaders never completed the conquest of the country and subsequently met their undoing in this neglect since their lesser numbers made them vulnerable to absorption by the Dravidians of the south, who subsequently overran the entire peninsula except the Himalayan provinces.

The Aryans made very little racial impression on India except in the northern provinces. In the Deccan their influence was cultural and religious more than racial. The greater persistence of the so-called Aryan blood in northern India is not only due to their presence in these regions in greater numbers but also because they were reinforced by later conquerors, traders, and missionaries. Right on down to the first century before Christ there was a continuous infiltration of Aryan blood into the Punjab, the last influx being attendant upon the campaigns of the Hellenistic peoples.

On the Gangetic plain Aryan and Dravidian eventually mingled to produce a high culture, and this center was later reinforced by contributions from the northeast, coming from China.

In India many types of social organizations flourished from time to time, from the semidemocratic systems of the Aryans to despotic and monarchial forms of government. But the most characteristic feature of society was the persistence of the great social castes that were instituted by the Aryans in an effort to perpetuate racial identity. This elaborate caste system has been preserved on down to the present time.

Of the four great castes, all but the first were established in the futile effort to prevent racial amalgamation of the Aryan conquerors with their inferior subjects. But the premier caste, the teacher-priests, stems from the Sethites; the Brahmans of the twentieth century after Christ are the lineal cultural descendants of the priests of the second garden, albeit their teachings differ greatly from those of their illustrious predecessors.

When the Aryans entered India, they brought with them their concepts of Deity as they had been preserved in the lingering traditions of the religion of the second garden. But the Brahman priests were never able to withstand the pagan momentum built up by the sudden contact with the inferior religions of the Deccan after the racial obliteration of the Aryans. Thus the vast majority of the population fell into the bondage of the enslaving superstitions of inferior religions; and so it was that India failed to produce the high civilization which had been foreshadowed in earlier times.

The spiritual awakening of the sixth century before Christ did not persist in India, having died out even before the Mohammedan invasion. But someday a greater Gautama may arise to lead all India in the search for the living God, and then the world will observe the fruition of the cultural potentialities of a versatile people so long comatose under the benumbing influence of an unprogressing spiritual vision.

Culture does rest on a biologic foundation, but caste alone could not perpetuate the Aryan culture, for religion, true religion, is the indispensable source of that higher energy which drives men to establish a superior civilization based on human brotherhood.

5. RED MAN AND YELLOW MAN

While the story of India is that of Andite conquest and eventual submergence in the older evolutionary peoples, the narrative of eastern Asia is more properly that of the primary Sangiks, particularly the red man and the yellow man. These two races largely escaped that admixture with the debased Neanderthal strain which so greatly retarded the blue man in Europe, thus preserving the superior potential of the primary Sangik type.

While the early Neanderthalers were spread out over the entire breadth of Eurasia, the eastern wing was the more contaminated with debased animal strains. These subhuman types were pushed south by the fifth glacier, the same ice sheet which so long blocked Sangik migration into eastern Asia. And when the red man moved northeast around the highlands of India, he found northeastern Asia free from these subhuman types. The tribal organization of the red races was formed earlier than that of any other peoples, and they were the first to migrate from the central Asian focus of the Sangiks. The inferior Neanderthal strains were destroyed or driven off the mainland by the later migrating yellow tribes. But the red man had reigned supreme in eastern Asia for almost one hundred thousand years before the yellow tribes arrived.

More than three hundred thousand years ago the main body of the yellow race entered China from the south as coastwise migrants. Each millennium they penetrated farther and farther inland, but they did not make contact with their migrating Tibetan brethren until comparatively recent times.

Growing population pressure caused the northward-moving yellow race to begin to push into the hunting grounds of the red man. This encroachment, coupled with natural racial antagonism, culminated in increasing hostilities, and thus began the crucial struggle for the fertile lands of farther Asia.

The story of this agelong contest between the red and yellow races is an epic of Urantia history. For over two hundred thousand years these two superior races waged bitter and unremitting warfare. In the earlier struggles the red men were generally successful, their raiding parties spreading havoc among the yellow settlements. But the yellow man was an apt pupil in the art of warfare, and he early manifested a marked ability to live peaceably with his compatriots; the Chinese were the first to learn that in union there is strength. The red tribes continued their internecine conflicts, and presently they began to suffer repeated defeats at the aggressive hands of the relentless Chinese, who continued their inexorable march northward.

One hundred thousand years ago the decimated tribes of the red race were fighting with their backs to the retreating ice of the last glacier, and when the land passage to the West, over the Bering isthmus, became passable, these tribes were not slow in forsaking the inhospitable shores of the Asiatic continent. It is eighty-five thousand years since the last of the pure red men departed from Asia, but the long struggle left its genetic imprint upon the victorious yellow race. The northern Chinese peoples, together with the Andonite Siberians, assimilated much of the red stock and were in considerable measure benefited thereby.

The North American Indians never came in contact with even the Andite offspring of Adam and Eve, having been dispossessed of their Asiatic homelands some fifty thousand years before the coming of Adam. During the age of Andite migrations the pure red strains were spreading out over North America as nomadic tribes, hunters who practiced agriculture to a small extent. These races and cultural groups remained almost completely isolated from the remainder of the world from their arrival in the Americas down to the end of the first millennium of the Christian era, when they were discovered by the white races of Europe. Up to that time the Eskimos were the nearest to white men the northern tribes of red men had ever seen.

The red and the yellow races are the only human stocks that ever achieved a high degree of civilization apart from the influences of the Andites. The oldest Amerindian culture was the Onamonalonton center in California, but this had long since vanished by 35,000 B.C. In Mexico, Central America, and in the mountains of South America the later and more enduring civilizations were founded by a race predominantly red but containing a considerable admixture of the yellow, orange, and blue.

These civilizations were evolutionary products of the Sangiks, notwithstanding that traces of Andite blood reached Peru. Excepting the Eskimos in North America and a few Polynesian Andites in South America, the peoples of the Western Hemisphere had no contact with the rest of the world until the end of the first millennium after Christ. In the original Melchizedek plan for the improvement of the Urantia races it had been stipulated that one million of the pure-line descendants of Adam should go to upstep the red men of the Americas.

6. DAWN OF CHINESE CIVILIZATION

Sometime after driving the red man across to North America, the expanding Chinese cleared the Andonites from the river valleys of eastern Asia, pushing them north into Siberia and west into Turkestan, where they were soon to come in contact with the superior culture of the Andites.

In Burma and the peninsula of Indo-China the cultures of India and China mixed and blended to produce the successive civilizations of those regions. Here the vanished green race has persisted in larger proportion than anywhere else in the world.

Many different races occupied the islands of the Pacific. In general, the southern and then more extensive islands were occupied by peoples carrying a heavy percentage of green and indigo blood. The northern islands were held by Andonites and, later on, by races embracing large proportions of the yellow and red stocks. The ancestors of the Japanese people were not driven off the mainland until 12,000 B.C., when they were dislodged by a powerful southern-coastwise thrust of the northern Chinese tribes. Their final exodus was not so much due to population pressure as to the initiative of a chieftain whom they came to regard as a divine personage.

Like the peoples of India and the Levant, victorious tribes of the yellow man established their earliest centers along the coast and up the rivers. The coastal settlements fared poorly in later years as the increasing floods and the shifting courses of the rivers made the lowland cities untenable.

Twenty thousand years ago the ancestors of the Chinese had built up a dozen strong centers of primitive culture and learning, especially along the Yellow River and the Yangtze. And now these centers began to be reinforced by the arrival of a steady stream of superior blended peoples from Sinkiang and Tibet. The migration from Tibet to the Yangtze valley was not so extensive as in the north, neither were the Tibetan centers so advanced as those of the Tarim basin. But both movements carried a certain amount of Andite blood eastward to the river settlements.

The superiority of the ancient yellow race was due to four great factors:

1. *Genetic.* Unlike their blue cousins in Europe, both the red and yellow races had largely escaped mixture with debased human stocks. The northern Chinese, already strengthened by small amounts of the superior red and Andonic strains, were soon to benefit by a considerable influx of Andite blood. The southern Chinese did not fare so well in this regard, and they had long suffered from absorption of the green race, while later on they were to be further weakened by the infiltration of the swarms of inferior peoples crowded out of India by the Dravidian-Andite invasion. And today in China there is a definite difference between the northern and southern races.

2. *Social.* The yellow race early learned the value of peace among themselves. Their internal peaceableness so contributed to population increase as to insure the spread of their civilization among many millions. From 25,000 to 5000 B.C. the highest mass civilization on Urantia was in central and northern China. The yellow man was first to achieve a racial solidarity—the first to attain a large-scale cultural, social, and political civilization.

The Chinese of 15,000 B.C. were aggressive militarists; they had not been weakened by an overreverence for the past, and numbering less than twelve million, they formed a compact body speaking a common language. During this age they built up a real nation, much more united and homogeneous than their political unions of historic times.

3. *Spiritual.* During the age of Andite migrations the Chinese were among the more spiritual peoples of earth. Long adherence to the worship of the One Truth proclaimed by Singlangton kept them ahead of most of the other races. The stimulus of a progressive and advanced religion is often a decisive factor in cultural development; as India languished, so China forged ahead under the invigorating stimulus of a religion in which truth was enshrined as the supreme Deity.

This worship of truth was provocative of research and fearless exploration of the laws of nature and the potentials of mankind. The Chinese of even six thousand years ago were still keen students and aggressive in their pursuit of truth.

4. *Geographic.* China is protected by the mountains to the west and the Pacific to the east. Only in the north is the way open to attack, and from the days of the red man to the coming of the later descendants of the Andites, the north was not occupied by any aggressive race.

And but for the mountain barriers and the later decline in spiritual culture, the yellow race undoubtedly would have attracted to itself the larger part of the Andite migrations from Turkestan and unquestionably would have quickly dominated world civilization.

7. THE ANDITES ENTER CHINA

About fifteen thousand years ago the Andites, in considerable numbers, were traversing the pass of Ti Tao and spreading out over the upper valley of the Yellow River among the Chinese settlements of Kansu. Presently they penetrated eastward to Honan, where the most progressive settlements were situated. This infiltration from the west was about half Andonite and half Andite.

The northern centers of culture along the Yellow River had always been more progressive than the southern settlements on the Yangtze. Within a few thousand years after the arrival of even the small numbers of these superior mortals, the settlements along the Yellow River had forged ahead of the Yangtze villages and had achieved an advanced position over their brethren in the south which has ever since been maintained.

It was not that there were so many of the Andites, nor that their culture was so superior, but amalgamation with them produced a more versatile stock. The northern Chinese received just enough of the Andite strain to mildly stimulate their innately able minds but not enough to fire them with the restless, exploratory curiosity so characteristic of the northern white races. This more limited infusion of Andite inheritance was less disturbing to the innate stability of the Sangik type.

The later waves of Andites brought with them certain of the cultural advances of Mesopotamia; this is especially true of the last waves of migration from the west. They greatly improved the economic and educational practices of the northern Chinese; and while their influence upon the religious culture of the yellow race was short-lived, their later descendants contributed much to a subsequent spiritual awakening. But the Andite traditions of the beauty of Eden and Dalamatia did influence Chinese traditions; early Chinese legends place "the land of the gods" in the west.

The Chinese people did not begin to build cities and engage in manufacture until after 10,000 B.C., subsequent to the climatic changes in Turkestan and the arrival of the later Andite immigrants. The infusion of this new blood did not add so much to the civilization of the yellow man as it stimulated the further and rapid development of the latent tendencies of the superior Chinese stocks. From Honan to Shensi the potentials of an advanced civilization were coming to fruit. Metalworking and all the arts of manufacture date from these days.

The similarities between certain of the early Chinese and Mesopotamian methods of time reckoning, astronomy, and governmental administration were due to the commercial relationships between these two remotely situated centers. Chinese merchants traveled the overland routes through Turkestan to Mesopotamia even in the days of the Sumerians. Nor was this exchange one-sided—the valley of the Euphrates benefited considerably thereby, as did the peoples of the Gangetic plain. But the climatic changes and the nomadic invasions of the third millennium before Christ greatly reduced the volume of trade passing over the caravan trails of central Asia.

8. LATER CHINESE CIVILIZATION

While the red man suffered from too much warfare, it is not altogether amiss to say that the development of statehood among the Chinese was delayed by the thoroughness of their conquest of Asia. They had a great potential of racial solidarity, but it failed properly to develop because the continuous driving stimulus of the ever-present danger of external aggression was lacking.

With the completion of the conquest of eastern Asia the ancient military state gradually disintegrated—past wars were forgotten. Of the epic struggle with the red race there persisted only the hazy tradition of an ancient contest with the archer peoples. The Chinese early turned to agricultural pursuits, which contributed further to their pacific tendencies, while a population well below the land-man ratio for agriculture still further contributed to the growing peacefulness of the country.

Consciousness of past achievements (somewhat diminished in the present), the conservatism of an overwhelmingly agricultural people, and a well-developed family life equaled the birth of ancestor veneration, culminating in the custom of so honoring the men of the past as to border on worship. A very similar attitude prevailed among the white races in Europe for some five hundred years following the disruption of Greco-Roman civilization.

The belief in, and worship of, the "One Truth" as taught by Singlangton never entirely died out; but as time passed, the search for new and higher truth became overshadowed by a growing tendency to venerate that which was already established. Slowly the genius of the yellow race became diverted from the pursuit of the unknown to the preservation of the known. And this is the reason for the stagnation of what had been the world's most rapidly progressing civilization.

Between 4000 and 500 B.C. the political reunification of the yellow race was consummated, but the cultural union of the Yangtze and Yellow river centers had already been effected. This political reunification of the later tribal groups was not without conflict, but the societal opinion of war remained low; ancestor worship, increasing dialects, and no call for military action for thousands upon thousands of years had rendered this people ultrapeaceful.

Despite failure to fulfill the promise of an early development of advanced statehood, the yellow race did progressively move forward in the realization of the arts of civilization, especially in the realms of agriculture and horticulture. The hydraulic problems faced by the agriculturists in Shensi and Honan demanded group co-operation for solution. Such irrigation and soil-conservation difficulties contributed in no small measure to the development of interdependence with the consequent promotion of peace among farming groups.

Soon developments in writing, together with the establishment of schools, contributed to the dissemination of knowledge on a previously unequaled scale. But the cumbersome nature of the ideographic writing system placed a numerical limit upon the learned classes despite the early appearance of printing. And above all else, the process of social standardization and religio-philosophic dogmatization continued apace. The religious development of ancestor veneration became further complicated by a flood of superstitions involving nature worship, but lingering vestiges of a real concept of God remained preserved in the imperial worship of Shang-ti.

The great weakness of ancestor veneration is that it promotes a backward-looking philosophy. However wise it may be to glean wisdom from the past, it is folly to regard the past as the exclusive source of truth. Truth is relative and expanding; it *lives* always in the present, achieving new expression in each generation of men—even in each human life.

The great strength in a veneration of ancestry is the value that such an attitude places upon the family. The amazing stability and persistence of Chinese culture is a consequence of the paramount position accorded the family, for civilization is directly dependent on the effective functioning of the family; and in China the family attained a social importance, even a religious significance, approached by few other peoples.

The filial devotion and family loyalty exacted by the growing cult of ancestor worship insured the building up of superior family relationships and of enduring family groups, all of which facilitated the following factors in the preservation of civilization:

1. Conservation of property and wealth.
2. Pooling of the experience of more than one generation.
3. Efficient education of children in the arts and sciences of the past.
4. Development of a strong sense of duty, the enhancement of morality, and the augmentation of ethical sensitivity.

The formative period of Chinese civilization, opening with the coming of the Andites, continues on down to the great ethical, moral, and semireligious awakening of the sixth century before Christ. And Chinese tradition preserves the hazy record of the evolutionary past; the transition from mother- to father-family, the establishment of agriculture, the development of architecture, the initiation of industry — all these are successively narrated. And this story presents, with greater accuracy than any other similar account, the picture of the magnificent ascent of a superior people from the levels of barbarism. During this time they passed from a primitive agricultural society to a higher social organization embracing cities, manufacture, metalworking, commercial exchange, government, writing, mathematics, art, science, and printing.

And so the ancient civilization of the yellow race has persisted down through the centuries. It is almost forty thousand years since the first important advances were made in Chinese culture, and though there have been many retrogressions, the civilization of the sons of Han comes the nearest of all to presenting an unbroken picture of continual progression right on down to the times of the twentieth century. The mechanical and religious developments of the white races have been of a high order, but they have never excelled the Chinese in family loyalty, group ethics, or personal morality.

This ancient culture has contributed much to human happiness; millions of human beings have lived and died, blessed by its achievements. For centuries this great civilization has rested upon the laurels of the past, but it is even now reawakening to envision anew the transcendent goals of mortal existence, once again to take up the unremitting struggle for never-ending progress.

[Presented by an Archangel of Nebadon.]

PAPER 80

ANDITE EXPANSION IN THE OCCIDENT

ALTHOUGH the European blue man did not of himself achieve a great cultural civilization, he did supply the biologic foundation which, when its Adamized strains were blended with the later Andite invaders, produced one of the most potent stocks for the attainment of aggressive civilization ever to appear on Urantia since the times of the violet race and their Andite successors.

The modern white peoples incorporate the surviving strains of the Adamic stock which became admixed with the Sangik races, some red and yellow but more especially the blue. There is a considerable percentage of the original Andonite stock in all the white races and still more of the early Nodite strains.

1. THE ADAMITES ENTER EUROPE

Before the last Andites were driven out of the Euphrates valley, many of their brethren had entered Europe as adventurers, teachers, traders, and warriors. During the earlier days of the violet race the Mediterranean trough was protected by the Gibraltar isthmus and the Sicilian land bridge. Some of man's very early maritime commerce was established on these inland lakes, where blue men from the north and the Saharans from the south met Nodites and Adamites from the east.

In the eastern trough of the Mediterranean the Nodites had established one of their most extensive cultures and from these centers had penetrated somewhat into southern Europe but more especially into northern Africa. The broad-headed Nodite-Andonite Syrians very early introduced pottery and agriculture in connection with their settlements on the slowly rising Nile delta. They also imported sheep, goats, cattle, and other domesticated animals and brought in greatly improved methods of metalworking, Syria then being the center of that industry.

For more than thirty thousand years Egypt received a steady stream of Mesopotamians, who brought along their art and culture to enrich that of the Nile valley. But the ingress of large numbers of the Sahara peoples greatly deteriorated the early civilization along the Nile so that Egypt reached its lowest cultural level some fifteen thousand years ago.

But during earlier times there was little to hinder the westward migration of the Adamites. The Sahara was an open grazing land overspread by herders and agriculturists. These Saharans never engaged in manufacture, nor were they city builders. They were an indigo-black group which carried extensive strains of the extinct green and orange races. But they received a very limited amount of the violet inheritance before the upthrust of land and the shifting water-laden winds dispersed the remnants of this prosperous and peaceful civilization.

Adam's blood has been shared with most of the human races, but some secured more than others. The mixed races of India and the darker peoples of Africa were not attractive to the Adamites. They would have mixed freely with the red man had he not been far removed in the Americas, and they were kindly disposed toward the yellow man, but he was likewise difficult of access in far-away Asia. Therefore, when actuated by either adventure or altruism, or when driven out of the Euphrates valley, they very naturally chose union with the blue races of Europe.

The blue men, then dominant in Europe, had no religious practices which were repulsive to the earlier migrating Adamites, and there was great sex attraction between the violet and the blue races. The best of the blue men deemed it a high honor to be permitted to mate with the Adamites. Every blue man entertained the ambition of becoming so skillful and artistic as to win the affection of some Adamite woman, and it was the highest aspiration of a superior blue woman to receive the attentions of an Adamite.

Slowly these migrating sons of Eden united with the higher types of the blue race, invigorating their cultural practices while ruthlessly exterminating the lingering strains of Neanderthal stock. This technique of race blending, combined with the elimination of inferior strains, produced a dozen or more virile and progressive groups of superior blue men, one of which you have denominated the Cro-Magnons.

For these and other reasons, not the least of which was more favorable paths of migration, the early waves of Mesopotamian culture made their way almost exclusively to Europe. And it was these circumstances that determined the antecedents of modern European civilization.

2. CLIMATIC AND GEOLOGIC CHANGES

The early expansion of the violet race into Europe was cut short by certain rather sudden climatic and geologic changes. With the retreat of the northern ice fields the water-laden winds from the west shifted to the north, gradually turning the great open pasture regions of Sahara into a barren desert. This drought dispersed the smaller-statured brunets, dark-eyed but long-headed dwellers of the great Sahara plateau.

The purer indigo elements moved southward to the forests of central Africa, where they have ever since remained. The more mixed groups spread out in three directions: The superior tribes to the west migrated to Spain and thence to adjacent parts of Europe, forming the nucleus of the later Mediterranean long-headed brunet races. The least progressive division to the east of the Sahara plateau migrated to Arabia and thence through northern Mesopotamia and India to faraway Ceylon. The central group moved north and east to the Nile valley and into Palestine.

It is this secondary Sangik substratum that suggests a certain degree of kinship among the modern peoples scattered from the Deccan through Iran, Mesopotamia, and along both shores of the Mediterranean Sea.

About the time of these climatic changes in Africa, England separated from the continent, and Denmark arose from the sea, while the isthmus of Gibraltar, protecting the western basin of the Mediterranean, gave way as the result of an earthquake, quickly raising this inland lake to the level of the Atlantic Ocean.

Presently the Sicilian land bridge submerged, creating one sea of the Mediterranean and connecting it with the Atlantic Ocean. This cataclysm of nature flooded scores of human settlements and occasioned the greatest loss of life by flood in all the world's history.

This engulfment of the Mediterranean basin immediately curtailed the westward movements of the Adamites, while the great influx of Saharans led them to seek outlets for their increasing numbers to the north and east of Eden. As the descendants of Adam journeyed northward from the valleys of the Tigris and Euphrates, they encountered mountainous barriers and the then expanded Caspian Sea. And for many generations the Adamites hunted, herded, and tilled the soil around their settlements scattered throughout Turkestan. Slowly this magnificent people extended their territory into Europe. But now the Adamites enter Europe from the east and find the culture of the blue man thousands of years behind that of Asia since this region has been almost entirely out of touch with Mesopotamia.

3. THE CRO-MAGNOID BLUE MAN

The ancient centers of the culture of the blue man were located along all the rivers of Europe, but only the Somme now flows in the same channel which it followed during preglacial times.

While we speak of the blue man as pervading the European continent, there were scores of racial types. Even thirty-five thousand years ago the European blue races were already a highly blended people carrying strains of both red and yellow, while on the Atlantic coastlands and in the regions of present-day Russia they had absorbed a considerable amount of Andonite blood and to the south were in contact with the Saharan peoples. But it would be fruitless to attempt to enumerate the many racial groups.

The European civilization of this early post-Adamic period was a unique blend of the vigor and art of the blue men with the creative imagination of the Adamites. The blue men were a race of great vigor, but they greatly deteriorated the cultural and spiritual status of the Adamites. It was very difficult for the latter to impress their religion upon the Cro-Magnoids because of the tendency of so many to cheat and to debauch the maidens. For ten thousand years religion in Europe was at a low ebb as compared with the developments in India and Egypt.

The blue men were perfectly honest in all their dealings and were wholly free from the sexual vices of the mixed Adamites. They respected maidenhood, only practicing polygamy when war produced a shortage of males.

These Cro-Magnon peoples were a brave and farseeing race. They maintained an efficient system of child culture. Both parents participated in these labors, and the services of the older children were fully utilized. Each child was carefully trained in the care of the caves, in art, and in flint making. At an early age the women were well versed in the domestic arts and in crude agriculture, while the men were skilled hunters and courageous warriors.

The blue men were hunters, fishers, and food gatherers; they were expert boatbuilders. They made stone axes, cut down trees, erected log huts, partly below ground and roofed with hides. And there are peoples who still build similar huts in Siberia. The southern Cro-Magnons generally lived in caves and grottoes.

It was not uncommon during the rigors of winter for their sentinels standing on night guard at cave entrances to freeze to death. They had courage, but above all they were artists; the Adamic mixture suddenly accelerated creative imagination. The height of the blue man's art was about fifteen thousand years ago, before the days when the darker-skinned races came north from Africa through Spain.

About fifteen thousand years ago the Alpine forests were spreading extensively. The European hunters were being driven to the river valleys and to the seashores by the same climatic coercion that had turned the world's happy hunting grounds into dry and barren deserts. As the rain winds shifted to the north, the great open grazing lands of Europe became covered by forests. These great and relatively sudden climatic modifications drove the races of Europe to change from open-space hunters to herders, and in some measure to fishers and tillers of the soil.

These changes, while resulting in cultural advances, produced certain biologic retrogressions. During the previous hunting era the superior tribes had intermarried with the higher types of war captives and had unvaryingly destroyed those whom they deemed inferior. But as they commenced to establish settlements and engage in agriculture and commerce, they began to save many of the mediocre captives as slaves. And it was the progeny of these slaves that subsequently so greatly deteriorated the whole Cro-Magnon type. This retrogression of culture continued until it received a fresh impetus from the east when the final and en masse invasion of the Mesopotamians swept over Europe, quickly absorbing the Cro-Magnon type and culture and initiating the civilization of the white races.

4. THE ANDITE INVASIONS OF EUROPE

While the Andites poured into Europe in a steady stream, there were seven major invasions, the last arrivals coming on horseback in three great waves. Some entered Europe by way of the islands of the Aegean and up the Danube valley, but the majority of the earlier and purer strains migrated to northwestern Europe by the northern route across the grazing lands of the Volga and the Don.

Between the third and fourth invasions a horde of Andonites entered Europe from the north, having come from Siberia by way of the Russian rivers and the Baltic. They were immediately assimilated by the northern Andite tribes.

The earlier expansions of the purer violet race were far more pacific than were those of their later semimilitary and conquest-loving Andite descendants. The Adamites were pacific; the Nodites were belligerent. The union of these stocks, as later mingled with the Sangik races, produced the able, aggressive Andites who made actual military conquests.

But the horse was the evolutionary factor which determined the dominance of the Andites in the Occident. The horse gave the dispersing Andites the hitherto nonexistent advantage of mobility, enabling the last groups of Andite cavalrymen to progress quickly around the Caspian Sea to overrun all of Europe. All previous waves of Andites had moved so slowly that they tended to disintegrate at any great distance from Mesopotamia. But these later waves moved so rapidly that they reached Europe as coherent groups, still retaining some measure of higher culture.

The whole inhabited world, outside of China and the Euphrates region, had made very limited cultural progress for ten thousand years when the hard-riding Andite horsemen made their appearance in the sixth and seventh millenniums before Christ. As they moved westward across the Russian plains, absorbing the best of the blue man and exterminating the worst, they became blended into one people. These were the ancestors of the so-called Nordic races, the forefathers of the Scandinavian, German, and Anglo-Saxon peoples.

It was not long before the superior blue strains had been fully absorbed by the Andites throughout all northern Europe. Only in Lapland (and to a certain extent in Brittany) did the older Andonites retain even a semblance of identity.

5. THE ANDITE CONQUEST OF NORTHERN EUROPE

The tribes of northern Europe were being continuously reinforced and upstepped by the steady stream of migrants from Mesopotamia through the Turkestan-south Russian regions, and when the last waves of Andite cavalry swept over Europe, there were already more men with Andite inheritance in that region than were to be found in all the rest of the world.

For three thousand years the military headquarters of the northern Andites was in Denmark. From this central point there went forth the successive waves of conquest, which grew decreasingly Andite and increasingly white as the passing centuries witnessed the final blending of the Mesopotamian conquerors with the conquered peoples.

While the blue man had been absorbed in the north and eventually succumbed to the white cavalry raiders who penetrated the south, the advancing tribes of the mixed white race met with stubborn and protracted resistance from the Cro-Magnons, but superior intelligence and ever-augmenting biologic reserves enabled them to wipe the older race out of existence.

The decisive struggles between the white man and the blue man were fought out in the valley of the Somme. Here, the flower of the blue race bitterly contested the southward-moving Andites, and for over five hundred years these Cro-Magnoids successfully defended their territories before succumbing to the superior military strategy of the white invaders. Thor, the victorious commander of the armies of the north in the final battle of the Somme, became the hero of the northern white tribes and later on was revered as a god by some of them.

The strongholds of the blue man which persisted longest were in southern France, but the last great military resistance was overcome along the Somme. The later conquest progressed by commercial penetration, population pressure along the rivers, and by continued intermarriage with the superiors, coupled with the ruthless extermination of the inferiors.

When the tribal council of the Andite elders had adjudged an inferior captive to be unfit, he was, by elaborate ceremony, committed to the shaman priests, who escorted him to the river and administered the rites of initiation to the "happy hunting grounds"—lethal submergence. In this way the white invaders of Europe exterminated all peoples encountered who were not quickly absorbed into their own ranks, and thus did the blue man come to an end—and quickly.

The Cro-Magnoid blue man constituted the biologic foundation for the modern European races, but they have survived only as absorbed by the later and virile conquerors of their homelands. The blue strain contributed many sturdy traits and much physical vigor to the white races of Europe, but the humor and imagination of the blended European peoples were derived from the Andites. This Andite-blue union, resulting in the northern white races, produced an immediate lapse of Andite civilization, a retardation of a transient nature. Eventually, the latent superiority of these northern barbarians manifested itself and culminated in present-day European civilization.

By 5000 B.C. the evolving white races were dominant throughout all of northern Europe, including northern Germany, northern France, and the British Isles. Central Europe was for some time controlled by the blue man and the round-headed Andonites. The latter were mainly situated in the Danube valley and were never entirely displaced by the Andites.

6. THE ANDITES ALONG THE NILE

From the times of the terminal Andite migrations, culture declined in the Euphrates valley, and the immediate center of civilization shifted to the valley of the Nile. Egypt became the successor of Mesopotamia as the headquarters of the most advanced group on earth.

The Nile valley began to suffer from floods shortly before the Mesopotamian valleys but fared much better. This early setback was more than compensated by the continuing stream of Andite immigrants, so that the culture of Egypt, though really derived from the Euphrates region, seemed to forge ahead. But in 5000 B.C., during the flood period in Mesopotamia, there were seven distinct groups of human beings in Egypt; all of them, save one, came from Mesopotamia.

When the last exodus from the Euphrates valley occurred, Egypt was fortunate in gaining so many of the most skillful artists and artisans. These Andite artisans found themselves quite at home in that they were thoroughly familiar with river life, its floods, irrigations, and dry seasons. They enjoyed the sheltered position of the Nile valley; they were there much less subject to hostile raids and attacks than along the Euphrates. And they added greatly to the metalworking skill of the Egyptians. Here they worked iron ores coming from Mount Sinai instead of from the Black Sea regions.

The Egyptians very early assembled their municipal deities into an elaborate national system of gods. They developed an extensive theology and had an equally extensive but burdensome priesthood. Several different leaders sought to revive the remnants of the early religious teachings of the Sethites, but these endeavors were short-lived. The Andites built the first stone structures in Egypt. The first and most exquisite of the stone pyramids was erected by Imhotep, an Andite architectural genius, while serving as prime minister. Previous buildings had been constructed of brick, and while many stone structures had been erected in different parts of the world, this was the first in Egypt. But the art of building steadily declined from the days of this great architect.

This brilliant epoch of culture was cut short by internal warfare along the Nile, and the country was soon overrun, as Mesopotamia had been, by the inferior tribes from inhospitable Arabia and by the blacks from the south. As a result, social progress steadily declined for more than five hundred years.

7. ANDITES OF THE MEDITERRANEAN ISLES

During the decline of culture in Mesopotamia there persisted for some time a superior civilization on the islands of the eastern Mediterranean.

About 12,000 B.C. a brilliant tribe of Andites migrated to Crete. This was the only island settled so early by such a superior group, and it was almost two thousand years before the descendants of these mariners spread to the neighboring isles. This group were the narrow-headed, smaller-statured Andites who had intermarried with the Vanite division of the northern Nodites. They were all under six feet in height and had been literally driven off the mainland by their larger and inferior fellows. These emigrants to Crete were highly skilled in textiles, metals, pottery, plumbing, and the use of stone for building material. They engaged in writing and carried on as herders and agriculturists.

Almost two thousand years after the settlement of Crete a group of the tall descendants of Adamson made their way over the northern islands to Greece, coming almost directly from their highland home north of Mesopotamia. These progenitors of the Greeks were led westward by Sato, a direct descendant of Adamson and Ratta.

The group which finally settled in Greece consisted of three hundred and seventy-five of the selected and superior people comprising the end of the second civilization of the Adamsonites. These later sons of Adamson carried the then most valuable strains of the emerging white races. They were of a high intellectual order and, physically regarded, the most beautiful of men since the days of the first Eden.

Presently Greece and the Aegean Islands region succeeded Mesopotamia and Egypt as the Occidental center of trade, art, and culture. But as it was in Egypt, so again practically all of the art and science of the Aegean world was derived from Mesopotamia except for the culture of the Adamsonite forerunners of the Greeks. All the art and genius of these latter people is a direct legacy of the posterity of Adamson, the first son of Adam and Eve, and his extraordinary second wife, a daughter descended in an unbroken line from the pure Nodite staff of Prince Caligastia. No wonder the Greeks had mythological traditions that they were directly descended from gods and superhuman beings.

The Aegean region passed through five distinct cultural stages, each less spiritual than the preceding, and erelong the last glorious era of art perished beneath the weight of the rapidly multiplying mediocre descendants of the Danubian slaves who had been imported by the later generations of Greeks.

It was during this age in Crete that the *mother cult* of the descendants of Cain attained its greatest vogue. This cult glorified Eve in the worship of the "great mother." Images of Eve were everywhere. Thousands of public shrines were erected throughout Crete and Asia Minor. And this mother cult persisted on down to the times of Christ, becoming later incorporated in the early Christian religion under the guise of the glorification and worship of Mary the earth mother of Jesus.

By about 6500 B.C. there had occurred a great decline in the spiritual heritage of the Andites. The descendants of Adam were widespreadly dispersed and had been virtually swallowed up in the older and more numerous human races. And this decadence of Andite civilization, together with the disappearance of their religious standards, left the spiritually impoverished races of the world in a deplorable condition.

By 5000 B.C. the three purest strains of Adam's descendants were in Sumeria, northern Europe, and Greece. The whole of Mesopotamia was being slowly deteriorated by the stream of mixed and darker races which filtered in from Arabia. And the coming of these inferior peoples contributed further to the scattering abroad of the biologic and cultural residue of the Andites. From all over the fertile crescent the more adventurous peoples poured westward to the islands. These migrants cultivated both grain and vegetables, and they brought domesticated animals with them.

About 5000 B.C. a mighty host of progressive Mesopotamians moved out of the Euphrates valley and settled upon the island of Cyprus; this civilization was wiped out about two thousand years subsequently by the barbarian hordes from the north.

Another great colony settled on the Mediterranean near the later site of Carthage. And from north Africa large numbers of Andites entered Spain and later mingled in Switzerland with their brethren who had earlier come to Italy from the Aegean Islands.

When Egypt followed Mesopotamia in cultural decline, many of the more able and advanced families fled to Crete, thus greatly augmenting this already advanced civilization. And when the arrival of inferior groups from Egypt later threatened the civilization of Crete, the more cultured families moved on west to Greece.

The Greeks were not only great teachers and artists, they were also the world's greatest traders and colonizers. Before succumbing to the flood of inferiority which eventually engulfed their art and commerce, they succeeded in planting so many outposts of culture to the west that a great many of the advances in early Greek civilization persisted in the later peoples of southern Europe, and many of the mixed descendants of these Adamsonites became incorporated in the tribes of the adjacent mainlands.

8. THE DANUBIAN ANDONITES

The Andite peoples of the Euphrates valley migrated north to Europe to mingle with the blue men and west into the Mediterranean regions to mix with the remnants of the commingled Saharans and the southern blue men. And these two branches of the white race were, and now are, widely separated by the broad-headed mountain survivors of the earlier Andonite tribes which had long inhabited these central regions.

These descendants of Andon were dispersed through most of the mountainous regions of central and southeastern Europe. They were often reinforced by arrivals from Asia Minor, which region they occupied in considerable strength. The ancient Hittites stemmed directly from the Andonite stock; their pale skins and broad heads were typical of that race. This strain was carried in Abraham's ancestry and contributed much to the characteristic facial appearance of his later Jewish descendants who, while having a culture and religion derived from the Andites, spoke a very different language. Their tongue was distinctly Andonite.

The tribes that dwelt in houses erected on piles or log piers over the lakes of Italy, Switzerland, and southern Europe were the expanding fringes of the African, Aegean, and, more especially, the Danubian migrations.

The Danubians were Andonites, farmers and herders who had entered Europe through the Balkan peninsula and were moving slowly northward by way of the Danube valley. They made pottery and tilled the land, preferring to live in the valleys. The most northerly settlement of the Danubians was at Liege in Belgium. These tribes deteriorated rapidly as they moved away from the center and source of their culture. The best pottery is the product of the earlier settlements.

The Danubians became mother worshipers as the result of the work of the missionaries from Crete. These tribes later amalgamated with groups of Andonite sailors who came by boats from the coast of Asia Minor, and who were also mother worshipers. Much of central Europe was thus early settled by these mixed types of the broad-headed white races which practiced mother worship and the religious rite of cremating the dead, for it was the custom of the mother cultists to burn their dead in stone huts.

9. THE THREE WHITE RACES

The racial blends in Europe toward the close of the Andite migrations became generalized into the three white races as follows:

1. *The northern white race.* This so-called Nordic race consisted primarily of the blue man plus the Andite but also contained a considerable amount of Andonite blood, together with smaller amounts of the red and yellow Sangik. The northern white race thus encompassed these four most desirable human stocks. But the largest inheritance was from the blue man. The typical early Nordic was long-headed, tall, and blond. But long ago this race became thoroughly mixed with all of the branches of the white peoples.

The primitive culture of Europe, which was encountered by the invading Nordics, was that of the retrograding Danubians blended with the blue man. The Nordic-Danish and the Danubian-Andonite cultures met and mingled on the Rhine as is witnessed by the existence of two racial groups in Germany today.

The Nordics continued the trade in amber from the Baltic coast, building up a great commerce with the broadheads of the Danube valley via the Brenner Pass. This extended contact with the Danubians led these northerners into mother worship, and for several thousands of years cremation of the dead was almost universal throughout Scandinavia. This explains why remains of the earlier white races, although buried all over Europe, are not to be found—only their ashes in stone and clay urns. These white men also built dwellings; they never lived in caves. And again this explains why there are so few evidences of the white man's early culture, although the preceding Cro-Magnon type is well preserved where it has been securely sealed up in caves and grottoes. As it were, one day in northern Europe there is a primitive culture of the retrogressing Danubians and the blue man and the next that of a suddenly appearing and vastly superior white man.

2. *The central white race.* While this group includes strains of blue, yellow, and Andite, it is predominantly Andonite. These people are broad-headed, swarthy, and stocky. They are driven like a wedge between the Nordic and

Mediterranean races, with the broad base resting in Asia and the apex penetrating eastern France.

For almost twenty thousand years the Andonites had been pushed farther and farther to the north of central Asia by the Andites. By 3000 B.C. increasing aridity was driving these Andonites back into Turkestan. This Andonite push southward continued for over a thousand years and, splitting around the Caspian and Black seas, penetrated Europe by way of both the Balkans and the Ukraine. This invasion included the remaining groups of Adamson's descendants and, during the latter half of the invasion period, carried with it considerable numbers of the Iranian Andites as well as many of the descendants of the Sethite priests.

By 2500 B.C. the westward thrust of the Andonites reached Europe. And this overrunning of all Mesopotamia, Asia Minor, and the Danube basin by the barbarians of the hills of Turkestan constituted the most serious and lasting of all cultural setbacks up to that time. These invaders definitely Andonized the character of the central European races, which have ever since remained characteristically Alpine.

3. *The southern white race.* This brunet Mediterranean race consisted of a blend of the Andite and the blue man, with a smaller Andonite strain than in the north. This group also absorbed a considerable amount of secondary Sangik blood through the Saharans. In later times this southern division of the white race was infused by strong Andite elements from the eastern Mediterranean.

The Mediterranean coastlands did not, however, become permeated by the Andites until the times of the great nomadic invasions of 2500 B.C. Land traffic and trade were nearly suspended during these centuries when the nomads invaded the eastern Mediterranean districts. This interference with land travel brought about the great expansion of sea traffic and trade; Mediterranean sea-borne commerce was in full swing about forty-five hundred years ago. And this development of marine traffic resulted in the sudden expansion of the descendants of the Andites throughout the entire coastal territory of the Mediterranean basin.

These racial mixtures laid the foundations for the southern European race, the most highly mixed of all. And since these days this race has undergone still further admixture, notably with the blue-yellow-Andite peoples of Arabia. This Mediterranean race is, in fact, so freely admixed with the surrounding peoples as to be virtually indiscernible as a separate type, but in general its members are short, long-headed, and brunet.

In the north the Andites, through warfare and marriage, obliterated the blue men, but in the south they survived in greater numbers. The Basques and the Berbers represent the survival of two branches of this race, but even these peoples have been thoroughly admixed with the Saharans.

This was the picture of race mixture presented in central Europe about 3000 B.C. In spite of the partial Adamic default, the higher types did blend.

These were the times of the New Stone Age overlapping the oncoming Bronze Age. In Scandinavia it was the Bronze Age associated with mother worship. In southern France and Spain it was the New Stone Age associated with sun worship. This was the time of the building of the circular and roofless sun temples. The European white races were energetic builders, delighting to set up great stones as tokens to the sun, much as did their later-day descendants at Stonehenge. The vogue of sun worship indicates that this was a great period of agriculture in southern Europe.

The superstitions of this comparatively recent sun-worshiping era even now persist in the folkways of Brittany. Although Christianized for over fifteen hundred years, these Bretons still retain charms of the New Stone Age for warding off the evil eye. They still keep thunderstones in the chimney as protection against lightning. The Bretons never mingled with the Scandinavian Nordics. They are survivors of the original Andonite inhabitants of western Europe, mixed with the Mediterranean stock.

But it is a fallacy to presume to classify the white peoples as Nordic, Alpine, and Mediterranean. There has been altogether too much blending to permit such a grouping. At one time there was a fairly well-defined division of the white race into such classes, but widespread intermingling has since occurred, and it is no longer possible to identify these distinctions with any clarity. Even in 3000 B.C. the ancient social groups were no more of one race than are the present inhabitants of North America.

This European culture for five thousand years continued to grow and to some extent intermingle. But the barrier of language prevented the full reciprocation of the various Occidental nations. During the past century this culture has been experiencing its best opportunity for blending in the cosmopolitan population of North America; and the future of that continent will be determined by the quality of the racial factors which are permitted to enter into its present and future populations, as well as by the level of the social culture which is maintained.

[Presented by an Archangel of Nebadon.]

PAPER 81

DEVELOPMENT OF MODERN CIVILIZATION

REGARDLESS of the ups and downs of the miscarriage of the plans for world betterment projected in the missions of Caligastia and Adam, the basic organic evolution of the human species continued to carry the races forward in the scale of human progress and racial development. Evolution can be delayed but it cannot be stopped.

The influence of the violet race, though in numbers smaller than had been planned, produced an advance in civilization which, since the days of Adam, has far exceeded the progress of mankind throughout its entire previous existence of almost a million years.

1. THE CRADLE OF CIVILIZATION

For about thirty-five thousand years after the days of Adam, the cradle of civilization was in southwestern Asia, extending from the Nile valley eastward and slightly to the north across northern Arabia, through Mesopotamia, and on into Turkestan. And *climate* was the decisive factor in the establishment of civilization in that area.

It was the great climatic and geologic changes in northern Africa and western Asia that terminated the early migrations of the Adamites, barring them from Europe by the expanded Mediterranean and diverting the stream of migration north and east into Turkestan. By the time of the completion of these land elevations and associated climatic changes, about 15,000 B.C., civilization had settled down to a world-wide stalemate except for the cultural ferments and biologic reserves of the Andites still confined by mountains to the east in Asia and by the expanding forests in Europe to the west.

Climatic evolution is now about to accomplish what all other efforts had failed to do, that is, to compel Eurasian man to abandon hunting for the more advanced callings of herding and farming. Evolution may be slow, but it is terribly effective.

Since slaves were so generally employed by the earlier agriculturists, the farmer was formerly looked down on by both the hunter and the herder. For ages it was considered menial to till the soil; wherefore the idea that soil toil is a curse, whereas it is the greatest of all blessings. Even in the days of Cain and Abel the sacrifices of the pastoral life were held in greater esteem than the offerings of agriculture.

Man ordinarily evolved into a farmer from a hunter by transition through the era of the herder, and this was also true among the Andites, but more often the evolutionary coercion of climatic necessity would cause whole tribes to pass directly from hunters to successful farmers. But this phenomenon of passing immediately from hunting to agriculture only occurred in those regions where there was a high degree of race mixture with the violet stock.

The evolutionary peoples (notably the Chinese) early learned to plant seeds and to cultivate crops through observation of the sprouting of seeds accidentally moistened or which had been put in graves as food for the departed. But throughout southwest Asia, along the fertile river bottoms and adjacent plains, the Andites were carrying out the improved agricultural techniques inherited from their ancestors, who had made farming and gardening the chief pursuits within the boundaries of the second garden.

For thousands of years the descendants of Adam had grown wheat and barley, as improved in the Garden, throughout the highlands of the upper border of Mesopotamia. The descendants of Adam and Adamson here met, traded, and socially mingled.

It was these enforced changes in living conditions which caused such a large proportion of the human race to become omnivorous in dietetic practice. And the combination of the wheat, rice, and vegetable diet with the flesh of the herds marked a great forward step in the health and vigor of these ancient peoples.

2. THE TOOLS OF CIVILIZATION

The growth of culture is predicated upon the development of the tools of civilization. And the tools which man utilized in his ascent from savagery were effective just to the extent that they released man power for the accomplishment of higher tasks.

You who now live amid latter-day scenes of budding culture and beginning progress in social affairs, who actually have some little spare time in which to *think* about society and civilization, must not overlook the fact that your early ancestors had little or no leisure which could be devoted to thoughtful reflection and social thinking.

The first four great advances in human civilization were:

1. The taming of fire.
2. The domestication of animals.
3. The enslavement of captives.
4. Private property.

While fire, the first great discovery, eventually unlocked the doors of the scientific world, it was of little value in this regard to primitive man. He refused to recognize natural causes as explanations for commonplace phenomena.

When asked where fire came from, the simple story of Andon and the flint was soon replaced by the legend of how some Prometheus stole it from heaven. The ancients sought a supernatural explanation for all natural phenomena not within the range of their personal comprehension; and many moderns continue to do this. The depersonalization of so-called natural phenomena has required ages, and it is not yet completed. But the frank, honest, and fearless search for true causes gave birth to modern science: It turned astrology into astronomy, alchemy into chemistry, and magic into medicine.

In the premachine age the only way in which man could accomplish work without doing it himself was to use an animal. Domestication of animals placed in his hands living tools, the intelligent use of which prepared the way for both agriculture and transportation. And without these animals man could not have risen from his primitive estate to the levels of subsequent civilization.

Most of the animals best suited to domestication were found in Asia, especially in the central to southwest regions. This was one reason why civilization progressed faster in that locality than in other parts of the world. Many of these animals had been twice before domesticated, and in the Andite age they were retamed once again. But the dog had remained with the hunters ever since being adopted by the blue man long, long before.

The Andites of Turkestan were the first peoples to extensively domesticate the horse, and this is another reason why their culture was for so long predominant. By 5000 B.C. the Mesopotamian, Turkestan, and Chinese farmers had begun the raising of sheep, goats, cows, camels, horses, fowls, and elephants. They employed as beasts of burden the ox, camel, horse, and yak. Man was himself at one time the beast of burden. One ruler of the blue race once had one hundred thousand men in his colony of burden bearers.

The institutions of slavery and private ownership of land came with agriculture. Slavery raised the master's standard of living and provided more leisure for social culture.

The savage is a slave to nature, but scientific civilization is slowly conferring increasing liberty on mankind. Through animals, fire, wind, water, electricity, and other undiscovered sources of energy, man has liberated, and will continue to liberate, himself from the necessity for unremitting toil. Regardless of the transient trouble produced by the prolific invention of machinery, the ultimate benefits to be derived from such mechanical inventions are inestimable. Civilization can never flourish, much less be established, until man has *leisure* to think, to plan, to imagine new and better ways of doing things.

Man first simply appropriated his shelter, lived under ledges or dwelt in caves. Next he adapted such natural materials as wood and stone to the creation of family huts. Lastly he entered the creative stage of home building, learned to manufacture brick and other building materials.

The peoples of the Turkestan highlands were the first of the more modern races to build their homes of wood, houses not at all unlike the early log cabins of the American pioneer settlers. Throughout the plains human dwellings were made of brick; later on, of burned bricks.

The older river races made their huts by setting tall poles in the ground in a circle; the tops were then brought together, making the skeleton frame for the hut, which was interlaced with transverse reeds, the whole creation resembling a huge inverted basket. This structure could then be daubed over with clay and, after drying in the sun, would make a very serviceable weatherproof habitation.

It was from these early huts that the subsequent idea of all sorts of basket weaving independently originated. Among one group the idea of making pottery arose from observing the effects of smearing these pole frameworks with moist clay. The practice of hardening pottery by baking was discovered when one of these clay-covered primitive huts accidentally burned. The arts of olden days were many times derived from the accidental occurrences attendant upon the daily life of early peoples. At least, this was almost wholly true of the evolutionary progress of mankind up to the coming of Adam.

While pottery had been first introduced by the staff of the Prince about one-half million years ago, the making of clay vessels had practically ceased for over one hundred and fifty thousand years. Only the gulf coast pre-Sumerian Nodites continued to make clay vessels. The art of pottery making was revived during Adam's time. The dissemination of this art was simultaneous with the extension of the desert areas of Africa, Arabia, and central Asia, and it spread in successive waves of improving technique from Mesopotamia out over the Eastern Hemisphere.

These civilizations of the Andite age cannot always be traced by the stages of their pottery or other arts. The smooth course of human evolution was tremendously complicated by the regimes of both Dalamatia and Eden. It often occurs that the later vases and implements are inferior to the earlier products of the purer Andite peoples.

3. CITIES, MANUFACTURE, AND COMMERCE

The climatic destruction of the rich, open grassland hunting and grazing grounds of Turkestan, beginning about 12,000 B.C., compelled the men of those regions to resort to new forms of industry and crude manufacturing. Some turned to the cultivation of domesticated flocks, others became agriculturists or collectors of water-borne food, but the higher type of Andite intellects chose to engage in trade and manufacture. It even became the custom for entire tribes to dedicate themselves to the development of a single industry. From the valley of the Nile to the Hindu Kush and from the Ganges to the Yellow River, the chief business of the superior tribes became the cultivation of the soil, with commerce as a side line.

The increase in trade and in the manufacture of raw materials into various articles of commerce was directly instrumental in producing those early and semipeaceful communities which were so influential in spreading the culture and the arts of civilization. Before the era of extensive world trade, social communities were tribal—expanded family groups. Trade brought into fellowship different sorts of human beings, thus contributing to a more speedy cross-fertilization of culture.

About twelve thousand years ago the era of the independent cities was dawning. And these primitive trading and manufacturing cities were always surrounded by zones of agriculture and cattle raising. While it is true that industry was promoted by the elevation of the standards of living, you should have no misconception regarding the refinements of early urban life. The early races were not overly neat and clean, and the average primitive community rose from one to two feet every twenty-five years as the result of the mere accumulation of dirt and trash. Certain of these olden cities also rose above the surrounding ground very quickly because their unbaked mud huts were short-lived, and it was the custom to build new dwellings directly on top of the ruins of the old.

The widespread use of metals was a feature of this era of the early industrial and trading cities. You have already found a bronze culture in Turkestan dating before 9000 B.C., and the Andites early learned to work in iron, gold, and copper, as well. But conditions were very different away from the more advanced centers of civilization. There were no distinct periods, such as the Stone, Bronze, and Iron Ages; all three existed at the same time in different localities.

Gold was the first metal to be sought by man; it was easy to work and, at first, was used only as an ornament. Copper was next employed but not extensively until it was admixed with tin to make the harder bronze. The discovery of mixing copper and tin to make bronze was made by one of the Adamsonites of Turkestan whose highland copper mine happened to be located alongside a tin deposit.

With the appearance of crude manufacture and beginning industry, commerce quickly became the most potent influence in the spread of cultural civilization. The opening up of the trade channels by land and by sea greatly facilitated travel and the mixing of cultures as well as the blending of civilizations. By 5000 B.C. the horse was in general use throughout civilized and semicivilized lands. These later races not only had the domesticated horse but also various sorts of wagons and chariots. Ages before, the wheel had been used, but now vehicles so equipped became universally employed both in commerce and war.

The traveling trader and the roving explorer did more to advance historic civilization than all other influences combined. Military conquests, colonization, and missionary enterprises fostered by the later religions were also factors in the spread of culture; but these were all secondary to the trading relations, which were ever accelerated by the rapidly developing arts and sciences of industry.

Infusion of the Adamic stock into the human races not only quickened the pace of civilization, but it also greatly stimulated their proclivities toward adventure and exploration to the end that most of Eurasia and northern Africa was presently occupied by the rapidly multiplying mixed descendants of the Andites.

4. THE MIXED RACES

As contact is made with the dawn of historic times, all of Eurasia, northern Africa, and the Pacific Islands is overspread with the composite races of mankind. And these races of today have resulted from a blending and reblending of the five basic human stocks of Urantia.

Each of the Urantia races was identified by certain distinguishing physical characteristics. The Adamites and Nodites were long-headed; the Andonites were broad-headed. The Sangik races were medium-headed, with the yellow and blue men tending to broad-headedness. The blue races, when mixed with the Andonite stock, were decidedly broad-headed. The secondary Sangiks were medium- to long-headed.

Although these skull dimensions are serviceable in deciphering racial origins, the skeleton as a whole is far more dependable. In the early development of the Urantia races there were originally five distinct types of skeletal structure:

1. Andonic, Urantia aborigines.
2. Primary Sangik, red, yellow, and blue.
3. Secondary Sangik, orange, green, and indigo.
4. Nodites, descendants of the Dalamatians.
5. Adamites, the violet race.

As these five great racial groups extensively intermingled, continual mixture tended to obscure the Andonite type by Sangik hereditary dominance. The

Lapps and the Eskimos are blends of Andonite and Sangik-blue races. Their skeletal structures come the nearest to preserving the aboriginal Andonic type. But the Adamites and the Nodites have become so admixed with the other races that they can be detected only as a generalized Caucasoid order.

In general, therefore, as the human remains of the last twenty thousand years are unearthed, it will be impossible clearly to distinguish the five original types. Study of such skeletal structures will disclose that mankind is now divided into approximately three classes:

1. *The Caucasoid*—the Andite blend of the Nodite and Adamic stocks, further modified by primary and (some) secondary Sangik admixture and by considerable Andonic crossing. The Occidental white races, together with some Indian and Turanian peoples, are included in this group. The unifying factor in this division is the greater or lesser proportion of Andite inheritance.

2. *The Mongoloid*—the primary Sangik type, including the original red, yellow, and blue races. The Chinese and Amerinds belong to this group. In Europe the Mongoloid type has been modified by secondary Sangik and Andonic mixture; still more by Andite infusion. The Malayan and other Indonesian peoples are included in this classification, though they contain a high percentage of secondary Sangik blood.

3. *The Negroid*—the secondary Sangik type, which originally included the orange, green, and indigo races. This is the type best illustrated by the Negro, and it will be found through Africa, India, and Indonesia wherever the secondary Sangik races located.

In North China there is a certain blending of Caucasoid and Mongoloid types; in the Levant the Caucasoid and Negroid have intermingled; in India, as in South America, all three types are represented. And the skeletal characteristics of the three surviving types still persist and help to identify the later ancestry of present-day human races.

5. CULTURAL SOCIETY

Biologic evolution and cultural civilization are not necessarily correlated; organic evolution in any age may proceed unhindered in the very midst of cultural decadence. But when lengthy periods of human history are surveyed, it will be observed that eventually evolution and culture become related as cause and effect. Evolution may advance in the absence of culture, but cultural civilization does not flourish without an adequate background of antecedent racial progression. Adam and Eve introduced no art of civilization foreign to the progress of human society, but the Adamic blood did augment the inherent ability of the races and did accelerate the pace of economic development and industrial progression. Adam's bestowal improved the brain power of the races, thereby greatly hastening the processes of natural evolution.

Through agriculture, animal domestication, and improved architecture, mankind gradually escaped the worst of the incessant struggle to live and began to cast about to find wherewith to sweeten the process of living; and this was the beginning of the striving for higher and ever higher standards of material comfort. Through manufacture and industry man is gradually augmenting the pleasure content of mortal life.

But cultural society is no great and beneficent club of inherited privilege into which all men are born with free membership and entire equality. Rather is it an exalted and ever-advancing guild of earth workers, admitting to its ranks only the nobility of those toilers who strive to make the world a better place in which their children and their children's children may live and advance in subsequent ages. And this guild of civilization exacts costly admission fees, imposes strict and rigorous disciplines, visits heavy penalties on all dissenters and nonconformists, while it confers few personal licenses or privileges except those of enhanced security against common dangers and racial perils.

Social association is a form of survival insurance which human beings have learned is profitable; therefore are most individuals willing to pay those premiums of self-sacrifice and personal-liberty curtailment which society exacts from its members in return for this enhanced group protection. In short, the present-day social mechanism is a trial-and-error insurance plan designed to afford some degree of assurance and protection against a return to the terrible and antisocial conditions which characterized the early experiences of the human race.

Society thus becomes a co-operative scheme for securing civil freedom through institutions, economic freedom through capital and invention, social liberty through culture, and freedom from violence through police regulation.

Might does not make right, but it does enforce the commonly recognized rights of each succeeding generation. The prime mission of government is the definition of the right, the just and fair regulation of class differences, and the enforcement of equality of opportunity under the rules of law. Every human right is associated with a social duty; group privilege is an insurance mechanism which unfailingly demands the full payment of the exacting premiums of group service. And group rights, as well as those of the individual, must be protected, including the regulation of the sex propensity.

Liberty subject to group regulation is the legitimate goal of social evolution. Liberty without restrictions is the vain and fanciful dream of unstable and flighty human minds.

6. THE MAINTENANCE OF CIVILIZATION

While biologic evolution has proceeded ever upward, much of cultural evolution went out from the Euphrates valley in waves, which successively weakened as time passed until finally the whole of the pure-line Adamic posterity had gone forth to enrich the civilizations of Asia and Europe. The races did not fully blend, but their civilizations did to a considerable extent mix. Culture did slowly spread throughout the world. And this civilization must be maintained and fostered, for there exist today no new sources of culture, no Andites to invigorate and stimulate the slow progress of the evolution of civilization.

The civilization which is now evolving on Urantia grew out of, and is predicated on, the following factors:

1. *Natural circumstances.* The nature and extent of a material civilization is in large measure determined by the natural resources available. Climate, weather, and numerous physical conditions are factors in the evolution of culture.

At the opening of the Andite era there were only two extensive and fertile open hunting areas in all the world. One was in North America and was overspread by the Amerinds; the other was to the north of Turkestan and was partly occupied by an Andonic-yellow race. The decisive factors in the evolution of a superior culture in southwestern Asia were race and climate. The Andites were a great people, but the crucial factor in determining the course of their civilization was the increasing aridity of Iran, Turkestan, and Sinkiang, which *forced* them to invent and adopt new and advanced methods of wresting a livelihood from their decreasingly fertile lands.

The configuration of continents and other land-arrangement situations are very influential in determining peace or war. Very few Urantians have ever had such a favorable opportunity for continuous and unmolested development as has been enjoyed by the peoples of North America—protected on practically all sides by vast oceans.

2. *Capital goods.* Culture is never developed under conditions of poverty; leisure is essential to the progress of civilization. Individual character of moral and spiritual value may be acquired in the absence of material wealth, but a cultural civilization is only derived from those conditions of material prosperity which foster leisure combined with ambition.

During primitive times life on Urantia was a serious and sober business. And it was to escape this incessant struggle and interminable toil that mankind constantly tended to drift toward the salubrious climate of the tropics. While these warmer zones of habitation afforded some remission from the intense struggle for existence, the races and tribes who thus sought ease seldom utilized their unearned leisure for the advancement of civilization. Social progress has invariably come from the thoughts and plans of those races that have, by their intelligent toil, learned how to wrest a living from the land with lessened effort and shortened days of labor and thus have been able to enjoy a well-earned and profitable margin of leisure.

3. *Scientific knowledge.* The material aspects of civilization must always await the accumulation of scientific data. It was a long time after the discovery of the bow and arrow and the utilization of animals for power purposes before man learned how to harness wind and water, to be followed by the employment of steam and electricity. But slowly the tools of civilization improved. Weaving, pottery, the domestication of animals, and metalworking were followed by an age of writing and printing.

Knowledge is power. Invention always precedes the acceleration of cultural development on a world-wide scale. Science and invention benefited most of all from the printing press, and the interaction of all these cultural and inventive activities has enormously accelerated the rate of cultural advancement.

Science teaches man to speak the new language of mathematics and trains his thoughts along lines of exacting precision. And science also stabilizes philosophy through the elimination of error, while it purifies religion by the destruction of superstition.

4. *Human resources.* Man power is indispensable to the spread of civilization. All things equal, a numerous people will dominate the civilization of a smaller race. Hence failure to increase in numbers up to a certain point prevents the full realization of national destiny, but there comes a point in population

increase where further growth is suicidal. Multiplication of numbers beyond the optimum of the normal man-land ratio means either a lowering of the standards of living or an immediate expansion of territorial boundaries by peaceful penetration or by military conquest, forcible occupation.

You are sometimes shocked at the ravages of war, but you should recognize the necessity for producing large numbers of mortals so as to afford ample opportunity for social and moral development; with such planetary fertility there soon occurs the serious problem of overpopulation. Most of the inhabited worlds are small. Urantia is average, perhaps a trifle undersized. The optimum stabilization of national population enhances culture and prevents war. And it is a wise nation which knows when to cease growing.

But the continent richest in natural deposits and the most advanced mechanical equipment will make little progress if the intelligence of its people is on the decline. Knowledge can be had by education, but wisdom, which is indispensable to true culture, can be secured only through experience and by men and women who are innately intelligent. Such a people are able to learn from experience; they may become truly wise.

5. *Effectiveness of material resources.* Much depends on the wisdom displayed in the utilization of natural resources, scientific knowledge, capital goods, and human potentials. The chief factor in early civilization was the *force* exerted by wise social masters; primitive man had civilization literally thrust upon him by his superior contemporaries. Well-organized and superior minorities have largely ruled this world.

Might does not make right, but might does make what is and what has been in history. Only recently has Urantia reached that point where society is willing to debate the ethics of might and right.

6. *Effectiveness of language.* The spread of civilization must wait upon language. Live and growing languages insure the expansion of civilized thinking and planning. During the early ages important advances were made in language. Today, there is great need for further linguistic development to facilitate the expression of evolving thought.

Language evolved out of group associations, each local group developing its own system of word exchange. Language grew up through gestures, signs, cries, imitative sounds, intonation, and accent to the vocalization of subsequent alphabets. Language is man's greatest and most serviceable thinking tool, but it never flourished until social groups acquired some leisure. The tendency to play with language develops new words—slang. If the majority adopt the slang, then usage constitutes it language. The origin of dialects is illustrated by the indulgence in "baby talk" in a family group.

Language differences have ever been the great barrier to the extension of peace. The conquest of dialects must precede the spread of a culture throughout a race, over a continent, or to a whole world. A universal language promotes peace, insures culture, and augments happiness. Even when the tongues of a world are reduced to a few, the mastery of these by the leading cultural peoples mightily influences the achievement of world-wide peace and prosperity.

While very little progress has been made on Urantia toward developing an international language, much has been accomplished by the establishment of international commercial exchange. And all these international relations should be fostered, whether they involve language, trade, art, science, competitive play, or religion.

7. *Effectiveness of mechanical devices.* The progress of civilization is directly related to the development and possession of tools, machines, and channels of distribution. Improved tools, ingenious and efficient machines, determine the survival of contending groups in the arena of advancing civilization.

In the early days the only energy applied to land cultivation was man power. It was a long struggle to substitute oxen for men since this threw men out of employment. Latterly, machines have begun to displace men, and every such advance is directly contributory to the progress of society because it liberates man power for the accomplishment of more valuable tasks.

Science, guided by wisdom, may become man's great social liberator. A mechanical age can prove disastrous only to a nation whose intellectual level is too low to discover those wise methods and sound techniques for successfully adjusting to the transition difficulties arising from the sudden loss of employment by large numbers consequent upon the too rapid invention of new types of laborsaving machinery.

8. *Character of torchbearers.* Social inheritance enables man to stand on the shoulders of all who have preceded him, and who have contributed aught to the sum of culture and knowledge. In this work of passing on the cultural torch to the next generation, the home will ever be the basic institution. The play and social life comes next, with the school last but equally indispensable in a complex and highly organized society.

Insects are born fully educated and equipped for life—indeed, a very narrow and purely instinctive existence. The human baby is born without an education; therefore man possesses the power, by controlling the educational training of the younger generation, greatly to modify the evolutionary course of civilization.

The greatest twentieth-century influences contributing to the furtherance of civilization and the advancement of culture are the marked increase in world travel and the unparalleled improvements in methods of communication. But the improvement in education has not kept pace with the expanding social structure; neither has the modern appreciation of ethics developed in correspondence with growth along more purely intellectual and scientific lines. And modern civilization is at a standstill in spiritual development and the safeguarding of the home institution.

9. *The racial ideals.* The ideals of one generation carve out the channels of destiny for immediate posterity. The *quality* of the social torchbearers will determine whether civilization goes forward or backward. The homes, churches, and schools of one generation predetermine the character trend of the succeeding generation. The moral and spiritual momentum of a race or a nation largely determines the cultural velocity of that civilization.

Ideals elevate the source of the social stream. And no stream will rise any higher than its source no matter what technique of pressure or directional control may be employed. The driving power of even the most material aspects of a cultural civilization is resident in the least material of society's achievements. Intelligence may control the mechanism of civilization, wisdom may direct it, but spiritual idealism is the energy which really uplifts and advances human culture from one level of attainment to another.

At first life was a struggle for existence; now, for a standard of living; next it will be for quality of thinking, the coming earthly goal of human existence.

10. *Co-ordination of specialists.* Civilization has been enormously advanced by the early division of labor and by its later corollary of specialization. Civilization is now dependent on the effective co-ordination of specialists. As society expands, some method of drawing together the various specialists must be found.

Social, artistic, technical, and industrial specialists will continue to multiply and increase in skill and dexterity. And this diversification of ability and dissimilarity of employment will eventually weaken and disintegrate human society if effective means of co-ordination and co-operation are not developed. But the intelligence which is capable of such inventiveness and such specialization should be wholly competent to devise adequate methods of control and adjustment for all problems resulting from the rapid growth of invention and the accelerated pace of cultural expansion.

11. *Place-finding devices.* The next age of social development will be embodied in a better and more effective co-operation and co-ordination of ever-increasing and expanding specialization. And as labor more and more diversifies, some technique for directing individuals to suitable employment must be devised. Machinery is not the only cause for unemployment among the civilized peoples of Urantia. Economic complexity and the steady increase of industrial and professional specialism add to the problems of labor placement.

It is not enough to train men for work; in a complex society there must also be provided efficient methods of place finding. Before training citizens in the highly specialized techniques of earning a living, they should be trained in one or more methods of commonplace labor, trades or callings which could be utilized when they were transiently unemployed in their specialized work. No civilization can survive the long-time harboring of large classes of unemployed. In time, even the best of citizens will become distorted and demoralized by accepting support from the public treasury. Even private charity becomes pernicious when long extended to able-bodied citizens.

Such a highly specialized society will not take kindly to the ancient communal and feudal practices of olden peoples. True, many common services can be acceptably and profitably socialized, but highly trained and ultraspecialized human beings can best be managed by some technique of intelligent co-operation. Modernized co-ordination and fraternal regulation will be productive of longer-lived co-operation than will the older and more primitive methods of communism or dictatorial regulative institutions based on force.

12. *The willingness to co-operate.* One of the great hindrances to the progress of human society is the conflict between the interests and welfare of the larger, more socialized human groups and of the smaller, contrary-minded asocial associations of mankind, not to mention antisocially-minded single individuals.

No national civilization long endures unless its educational methods and religious ideals inspire a high type of intelligent patriotism and national devotion.

Without this sort of intelligent patriotism and cultural solidarity, all nations tend to disintegrate as a result of provincial jealousies and local self-interests.

The maintenance of world-wide civilization is dependent on human beings learning how to live together in peace and fraternity. Without effective co-ordination, industrial civilization is jeopardized by the dangers of ultraspecialization: monotony, narrowness, and the tendency to breed distrust and jealousy.

13. *Effective and wise leadership.* In civilization much, very much, depends on an enthusiastic and effective load-pulling spirit. Ten men are of little more value than one in lifting a great load unless they lift together—all at the same moment. And such teamwork—social co-operation—is dependent on leadership. The cultural civilizations of the past and the present have been based upon the intelligent co-operation of the citizenry with wise and progressive leaders; and until man evolves to higher levels, civilization will continue to be dependent on wise and vigorous leadership.

High civilizations are born of the sagacious correlation of material wealth, intellectual greatness, moral worth, social cleverness, and cosmic insight.

14. *Social changes.* Society is not a divine institution; it is a phenomenon of progressive evolution; and advancing civilization is always delayed when its leaders are slow in making those changes in the social organization which are essential to keeping pace with the scientific developments of the age. For all that, things must not be despised just because they are old, neither should an idea be unconditionally embraced just because it is novel and new.

Man should be unafraid to experiment with the mechanisms of society. But always should these adventures in cultural adjustment be controlled by those who are fully conversant with the history of social evolution; and always should these innovators be counseled by the wisdom of those who have had practical experience in the domains of contemplated social or economic experiment. *No great social or economic change should be attempted suddenly.* Time is essential to all types of human adjustment—physical, social, or economic. Only moral and spiritual adjustments can be made on the spur of the moment, and even these require the passing of time for the full outworking of their material and social repercussions. The ideals of the race are the chief support and assurance during the critical times when civilization is in transit from one level to another.

15. *The prevention of transitional breakdown.* Society is the offspring of age upon age of trial and error; it is what survived the selective adjustments and readjustments in the successive stages of mankind's agelong rise from animal to human levels of planetary status. The great danger to any civilization —at any one moment—is the threat of breakdown during the time of transition from the established methods of the past to those new and better, but untried, procedures of the future.

Leadership is vital to progress. Wisdom, insight, and foresight are indispensable to the endurance of nations. Civilization is never really jeopardized until able leadership begins to vanish. And the quantity of such wise leadership has never exceeded one per cent of the population.

And it was by these rungs on the evolutionary ladder that civilization climbed to that place where those mighty influences could be initiated which have culminated in the rapidly expanding culture of the twentieth century. And only by adherence to these essentials can man hope to maintain his present-day civilizations while providing for their continued development and certain survival.

This is the gist of the long, long struggle of the peoples of earth to establish civilization since the age of Adam. Present-day culture is the net result of this strenuous evolution. Before the discovery of printing, progress was relatively slow since one generation could not so rapidly benefit from the achievements of its predecessors. But now human society is plunging forward under the force of the accumulated momentum of all the ages through which civilization has struggled.

[Sponsored by an Archangel of Nebadon.]

PAPER 82

THE EVOLUTION OF MARRIAGE

MARRIAGE—mating—grows out of bisexuality. Marriage is man's reactional adjustment to such bisexuality, while the family life is the sum total resulting from all such evolutionary and adaptative adjustments. Marriage is enduring; it is not inherent in biologic evolution, but it is the basis of all social evolution and is therefore certain of continued existence in some form. Marriage has given mankind the home, and the home is the crowning glory of the whole long and arduous evolutionary struggle.

While religious, social, and educational institutions are all essential to the survival of cultural civilization, *the family is the master civilizer.* A child learns most of the essentials of life from his family and the neighbors.

The humans of olden times did not possess a very rich social civilization, but such as they had they faithfully and effectively passed on to the next generation. And you should recognize that most of these civilizations of the past continued to evolve with a bare minimum of other institutional influences because the home was effectively functioning. Today the human races possess a rich social and cultural heritage, and it should be wisely and effectively passed on to succeeding generations. The family as an educational institution must be maintained.

1. THE MATING INSTINCT

Notwithstanding the personality gulf between men and women, the sex urge is sufficient to insure their coming together for the reproduction of the species. This instinct operated effectively long before humans experienced much of what was later called love, devotion, and marital loyalty. Mating is an innate propensity, and marriage is its evolutionary social repercussion.

Sex interest and desire were not dominating passions in primitive peoples; they simply took them for granted. The entire reproductive experience was free from imaginative embellishment. The all-absorbing sex passion of the more highly civilized peoples is chiefly due to race mixtures, especially where the evolutionary nature has been stimulated by the associative imagination and beauty appreciation of the Nodites and Adamites. But this Andite inheritance was absorbed by the evolutionary races in such limited amounts as to fail to provide sufficient self-control for the animal passions thus quickened and aroused by the endowment of keener sex consciousness and stronger mating urges. Of the evolutionary races, the red man had the highest sex code.

The regulation of sex in relation to marriage indicates:

1. The relative progress of civilization. Civilization has increasingly demanded that sex be gratified in useful channels and in accordance with the mores.

2. The amount of Andite stock in any people. Among such groups sex has become expressive of both the highest and the lowest in both the physical and emotional natures.

The Sangik races had normal animal passion, but they displayed little imagination or appreciation of the beauty and physical attractiveness of the opposite sex. What is called sex appeal is virtually absent even in present-day primitive races; these unmixed peoples have a definite mating instinct but insufficient sex attraction to create serious problems requiring social control.

The mating instinct is one of the dominant physical driving forces of human beings; it is the one emotion which, in the guise of individual gratification, effectively tricks selfish man into putting race welfare and perpetuation high above individual ease and personal freedom from responsibility.

As an institution, marriage, from its early beginnings down to modern times, pictures the social evolution of the biologic propensity for self-perpetuation. The perpetuation of the evolving human species is made certain by the presence of this racial mating impulse, an urge which is loosely called sex attraction. This great biologic urge becomes the impulse hub for all sorts of associated instincts, emotions, and usages—physical, intellectual, moral, and social.

With the savage, the food supply was the impelling motivation, but when civilization insures plentiful food, the sex urge many times becomes a dominant impulse and therefore ever stands in need of social regulation. In animals, instinctive periodicity checks the mating propensity, but since man is so largely a self-controlled being, sex desire is not altogether periodic; therefore does it become necessary for society to impose self-control upon the individual.

No human emotion or impulse, when unbridled and overindulged, can produce so much harm and sorrow as this powerful sex urge. Intelligent submission of this impulse to the regulations of society is the supreme test of the actuality of any civilization. Self-control, more and more self-control, is the ever-increasing demand of advancing mankind. Secrecy, insincerity, and hypocrisy may obscure sex problems, but they do not provide solutions, nor do they advance ethics.

2. THE RESTRICTIVE TABOOS

The story of the evolution of marriage is simply the history of sex control through the pressure of social, religious, and civil restrictions. Nature hardly recognizes individuals; it takes no cognizance of so-called morals; it is only and exclusively interested in the reproduction of the species. Nature compellingly insists on reproduction but indifferently leaves the consequential problems to be solved by society, thus creating an ever-present and major problem for evolutionary mankind. This social conflict consists in the unending war between basic instincts and evolving ethics.

Among the early races there was little or no regulation of the relations of the sexes. Because of this sex license, no prostitution existed. Today, the Pygmies and other backward groups have no marriage institution; a study of these peoples reveals the simple mating customs followed by primitive races. But all ancient peoples should always be studied and judged in the light of the moral standards of the mores of their own times.

Free love, however, has never been in good standing above the scale of rank savagery. The moment societal groups began to form, marriage codes and marital restrictions began to develop. Mating has thus progressed through a multitude of transitions from a state of almost complete sex license to the twentieth-century standards of relatively complete sex restriction.

In the earliest stages of tribal development the mores and restrictive taboos were very crude, but they did keep the sexes apart—this favored quiet, order, and industry—and the long evolution of marriage and the home had begun. The sex customs of dress, adornment, and religious practices had their origin in these early taboos which defined the range of sex liberties and thus eventually created concepts of vice, crime, and sin. But it was long the practice to suspend all sex regulations on high festival days, especially May Day.

Women have always been subject to more restrictive taboos than men. The early mores granted the same degree of sex liberty to unmarried women as to men, but it has always been required of wives that they be faithful to their husbands. Primitive marriage did not much curtail man's sex liberties, but it did render further sex license taboo to the wife. Married women have always borne some mark which set them apart as a class by themselves, such as hairdress, clothing, veil, seclusion, ornamentation, and rings.

3. EARLY MARRIAGE MORES

Marriage is the institutional response of the social organism to the ever-present biologic tension of man's unremitting urge to reproduction—self-propagation. Mating is universally natural, and as society evolved from the simple to the complex, there was a corresponding evolution of the mating mores, the genesis of the marital institution. Wherever social evolution has progressed to the stage at which mores are generated, marriage will be found as an evolving institution.

There always have been and always will be two distinct realms of marriage: the mores, the laws regulating the external aspects of mating, and the otherwise secret and personal relations of men and women. Always has the individual been rebellious against the sex regulations imposed by society; and this is the reason for this agelong sex problem: Self-maintenance is individual but is carried on by the group; self-perpetuation is social but is secured by individual impulse.

The mores, when respected, have ample power to restrain and control the sex urge, as has been shown among all races. Marriage standards have always been a true indicator of the current power of the mores and the functional integrity of the civil government. But the early sex and mating mores were a mass of inconsistent and crude regulations. Parents, children, relatives, and society all had conflicting interests in the marriage regulations. But in spite of all this, those races which exalted and practiced marriage naturally evolved to higher levels and survived in increased numbers.

In primitive times marriage was the price of social standing; the possession of a wife was a badge of distinction. The savage looked upon his wedding day as marking his entrance upon responsibility and manhood. In one age, marriage has been looked upon as a social duty; in another, as a religious obligation; and in still another, as a political requirement to provide citizens for the state.

Many early tribes required feats of stealing as a qualification for marriage; later peoples substituted for such raiding forays, athletic contests and competitive games. The winners in these contests were awarded the first prize—choice of the season's brides. Among the head-hunters a youth might not marry until he possessed at least one head, although such skulls were sometimes purchasable. As the buying of wives declined, they were won by riddle contests, a practice that still survives among many groups of the black man.

With advancing civilization, certain tribes put the severe marriage tests of male endurance in the hands of the women; they thus were able to favor the men of their choice. These marriage tests embraced skill in hunting, fighting, and ability to provide for a family. The groom was long required to enter the bride's family for at least one year, there to live and labor and prove that he was worthy of the wife he sought.

The qualifications of a wife were the ability to perform hard work and to bear children. She was required to execute a certain piece of agricultural work within a given time. And if she had borne a child before marriage, she was all the more valuable; her fertility was thus assured.

The fact that ancient peoples regarded it as a disgrace, or even a sin, not to be married, explains the origin of child marriages; since one must be married, the earlier the better. It was also a general belief that unmarried persons could not enter spiritland, and this was a further incentive to child marriages even at birth and sometimes before birth, contingent upon sex. The ancients believed that even the dead must be married. The original matchmakers were employed to negotiate marriages for deceased individuals. One parent would arrange for these intermediaries to effect the marriage of a dead son with a dead daughter of another family.

Among later peoples, puberty was the common age of marriage, but this has advanced in direct proportion to the progress of civilization. Early in social evolution peculiar and celibate orders of both men and women arose; they were started and maintained by individuals more or less lacking normal sex urge.

Many tribes allowed members of the ruling group to have sex relations with the bride just before she was to be given to her husband. Each of these men would give the girl a present, and this was the origin of the custom of giving wedding presents. Among some groups it was expected that a young woman would earn her dowry, which consisted of the presents received in reward for her sex service in the bride's exhibition hall.

Some tribes married the young men to the widows and older women and then, when they were subsequently left widowers, would allow them to marry the young girls, thus insuring, as they expressed it, that both parents would not be fools, as they conceived would be the case if two youths were allowed to mate. Other tribes limited mating to similar age groups. It was the limitation of marriage to certain age groups that first gave origin to ideas of incest. (In India there are even now no age restrictions on marriage.)

Under certain mores widowhood was greatly to be feared, widows being either killed or allowed to commit suicide on their husbands' graves, for they were supposed to go over into spiritland with their spouses. The surviving widow was almost invariably blamed for her husband's death. Some tribes burned them alive. If a widow continued to live, her life was one of continuous mourning and unbearable social restriction since remarriage was generally disapproved.

In olden days many practices now regarded as immoral were encouraged. Primitive wives not infrequently took great pride in their husbands' affairs with other women. Chastity in girls was a great hindrance to marriage; the bearing of a child before marriage greatly increased a girl's desirability as a wife since the man was sure of having a fertile companion.

Many primitive tribes sanctioned trial marriage until the woman became pregnant, when the regular marriage ceremony would be performed; among other groups the wedding was not celebrated until the first child was born. If a wife was barren, she had to be redeemed by her parents, and the marriage was annulled. The mores demanded that every pair have children.

These primitive trial marriages were entirely free from all semblance of license; they were simply sincere tests of fecundity. The contracting individuals married permanently just as soon as fertility was established. When modern couples marry with the thought of convenient divorce in the background of their minds if they are not wholly pleased with their married life, they are in reality entering upon a form of trial marriage and one that is far beneath the status of the honest adventures of their less civilized ancestors.

4. MARRIAGE UNDER THE PROPERTY MORES

Marriage has always been closely linked with both property and religion. Property has been the stabilizer of marriage; religion, the moralizer.

Primitive marriage was an investment, an economic speculation; it was more a matter of business than an affair of flirtation. The ancients married for the advantage and welfare of the group; wherefore their marriages were planned and arranged by the group, their parents and elders. And that the property mores were effective in stabilizing the marriage institution is borne out by the fact that marriage was more permanent among the early tribes than it is among many modern peoples.

As civilization advanced and private property gained further recognition in the mores, stealing became the great crime. Adultery was recognized as a form of stealing, an infringement of the husband's property rights; it is not therefore specifically mentioned in the earlier codes and mores. Woman started out as the property of her father, who transferred his title to her husband, and all legalized sex relations grew out of these pre-existent property rights. The Old Testament deals with women as a form of property; the Koran teaches their inferiority. Man had the right to lend his wife to a friend or guest, and this custom still obtains among certain peoples.

Modern sex jealousy is not innate; it is a product of the evolving mores. Primitive man was not jealous of his wife; he was just guarding his property. The reason for holding the wife to stricter sex account than the husband was because her marital infidelity involved descent and inheritance. Very early in the march of civilization the illegitimate child fell into disrepute. At first only the woman was punished for adultery; later on, the mores also decreed the chastisement of her partner, and for long ages the offended husband or the protector father had the full right to kill the male trespasser. Modern peoples retain these mores, which allow so-called crimes of honor under the unwritten law.

Since the chastity taboo had its origin as a phase of the property mores, it applied at first to married women but not to unmarried girls. In later years, chastity was more demanded by the father than by the suitor; a virgin was a commercial asset to the father—she brought a higher price. As chastity came more into demand, it was the practice to pay the father a bride fee in recognition of the service of properly rearing a chaste bride for the husband-to-be. When once started, this idea of female chastity took such hold on the races that it became the practice literally to cage up girls, actually to imprison them for years, in order to assure their virginity. And so the more recent standards and virginity tests automatically gave origin to the professional prostitute classes; they were the rejected brides, those women who were found by the grooms' mothers not to be virgins.

5. ENDOGAMY AND EXOGAMY

Very early the savage observed that race mixture improved the quality of the offspring. It was not that inbreeding was always bad, but that outbreeding was always comparatively better; therefore the mores tended to crystallize in restriction of sex relations among near relatives. It was recognized that outbreeding greatly increased the selective opportunity for evolutionary variation and advancement. The outbred individuals were more versatile and had greater ability to survive in a hostile world; the inbreeders, together with their mores, gradually disappeared. This was all a slow development; the savage did not consciously reason about such problems. But the later and advancing peoples did, and they also made the observation that general weakness sometimes resulted from excessive inbreeding.

While the inbreeding of good stock sometimes resulted in the upbuilding of strong tribes, the spectacular cases of the bad results of the inbreeding of hereditary defectives more forcibly impressed the mind of man, with the result that the advancing mores increasingly formulated taboos against all marriages among near relatives.

Religion has long been an effective barrier against outmarriage; many religious teachings have proscribed marriage outside the faith. Woman has usually favored the practice of in-marriage; man, outmarriage. Property has always influenced marriage, and sometimes, in an effort to conserve property within a clan, mores have arisen compelling women to choose husbands within their fathers' tribes. Rulings of this sort led to a great multiplication of cousin marriages. In-mating was also practiced in an effort to preserve craft secrets; skilled workmen sought to keep the knowledge of their craft within the family.

Superior groups, when isolated, always reverted to consanguineous mating. The Nodites for over one hundred and fifty thousand years were one of the great in-marriage groups. The later-day in-marriage mores were tremendously influenced by the traditions of the violet race, in which, at first, matings were, perforce, between brother and sister. And brother and sister marriages were common in early Egypt, Syria, Mesopotamia, and throughout the lands once occupied by the Andites. The Egyptians long practiced brother and sister marriages in an effort to keep the royal blood pure, a custom which persisted even longer in Persia. Among the Mesopotamians, before the days of Abraham, cousin marriages were obligatory; cousins had prior marriage rights to cousins. Abraham himself married his half sister, but such unions were not allowed under the later mores of the Jews.

The first move away from brother and sister marriages came about under the plural-wife mores because the sister-wife would arrogantly dominate the other wife or wives. Some tribal mores forbade marriage to a dead brother's widow but required the living brother to beget children for his departed brother. There is no biologic instinct against any degree of in-marriage; such restrictions are wholly a matter of taboo.

Outmarriage finally dominated because it was favored by the man; to get a wife from the outside insured greater freedom from in-laws. Familiarity breeds contempt; so, as the element of individual choice began to dominate mating, it became the custom to choose partners from outside the tribe.

Many tribes finally forbade marriages within the clan; others limited mating to certain castes. The taboo against marriage with a woman of one's own totem gave impetus to the custom of stealing women from neighboring tribes. Later on, marriages were regulated more in accordance with territorial residence than with kinship. There were many steps in the evolution of in-marriage into the modern practice of outmarriage. Even after the taboo rested upon in-marriages for the common people, chiefs and kings were permitted to marry those of close kin in order to keep the royal blood concentrated and pure. The mores have usually permitted sovereign rulers certain licenses in sex matters.

The presence of the later Andite peoples had much to do with increasing the desire of the Sangik races to mate outside their own tribes. But it was not possible for out-mating to become prevalent until neighboring groups had learned to live together in relative peace.

Outmarriage itself was a peace promoter; marriages between the tribes lessened hostilities. Outmarriage led to tribal co-ordination and to military alliances; it became dominant because it provided increased strength; it was a nation builder. Outmarriage was also greatly favored by increasing trade contacts; adventure and exploration contributed to the extension of the mating bounds and greatly facilitated the cross-fertilization of racial cultures.

The otherwise inexplicable inconsistencies of the racial marriage mores are largely due to this outmarriage custom with its accompanying wife stealing and buying from foreign tribes, all of which resulted in a compounding of the separate tribal mores. That these taboos respecting in-marriage were sociologic, not biologic, is well illustrated by the taboos on kinship marriages, which embraced many degrees of in-law relationships, cases representing no blood relation whatsoever.

6. RACIAL MIXTURES

There are no pure races in the world today. The early and original evolutionary peoples of color have only two representative races persisting in the world, the yellow man and the black man; and even these two races are much admixed with the extinct colored peoples. While the so-called white race is predominantly descended from the ancient blue man, it is admixed more or less with all other races much as is the red man of the Americas.

Of the six colored Sangik races, three were primary and three were secondary. Though the primary races—blue, red, and yellow—were in many respects superior to the three secondary peoples, it should be remembered that these secondary races had many desirable traits which would have considerably enhanced the primary peoples if their better strains could have been absorbed.

Present-day prejudice against "half-castes," "hybrids," and "mongrels" arises because modern racial crossbreeding is, for the greater part, between the grossly inferior strains of the races concerned. You also get unsatisfactory offspring when the degenerate strains of the same race intermarry.

If the present-day races of Urantia could be freed from the curse of their lowest strata of deteriorated, antisocial, feeble-minded, and outcast specimens, there would be little objection to a limited race amalgamation. And if such racial mixtures could take place between the highest types of the several races, still less objection could be offered.

Hybridization of superior and dissimilar stocks is the secret of the creation of new and more vigorous strains. And this is true of plants, animals, and the human species. Hybridization augments vigor and increases fertility. Race mixtures of the average or superior strata of various peoples greatly increase *creative* potential, as is shown in the present population of the United States of North America. When such matings take place between the lower or inferior strata, creativity is diminished, as is shown by the present-day peoples of southern India.

Race blending greatly contributes to the sudden appearance of *new* characteristics, and if such hybridization is the union of superior strains, then these new characteristics will also be *superior* traits.

As long as present-day races are so overloaded with inferior and degenerate strains, race intermingling on a large scale would be most detrimental, but most of the objections to such experiments rest on social and cultural prejudices rather than on biological considerations. Even among inferior stocks, hybrids often are an improvement on their ancestors. Hybridization makes for species improvement because of the role of the *dominant genes*. Racial intermixture increases the likelihood of a larger number of the desirable *dominants* being present in the hybrid.

For the past hundred years more racial hybridization has been taking place on Urantia than has occurred in thousands of years. The danger of gross disharmonies as a result of crossbreeding of human stocks has been greatly exaggerated. The chief troubles of "half-breeds" are due to social prejudices.

The Pitcairn experiment of blending the white and Polynesian races turned out fairly well because the white men and the Polynesian women were of fairly good racial strains. Interbreeding between the highest types of the white, red, and yellow races would immediately bring into existence many new and biologically effective characteristics. These three peoples belong to the primary Sangik races. Mixtures of the white and black races are not so desirable in their immediate results, neither are such mulatto offspring so objectionable as social and racial prejudice would seek to make them appear. Physically, such white-black hybrids are excellent specimens of humanity, notwithstanding their slight inferiority in some other respects.

When a primary Sangik race amalgamates with a secondary Sangik race, the latter is considerably improved at the expense of the former. And on a small scale—extending over long periods of time—there can be little serious objection to such a sacrificial contribution by the primary races to the betterment of the secondary groups. Biologically considered, the secondary Sangiks were in some respects superior to the primary races.

After all, the real jeopardy of the human species is to be found in the unrestrained multiplication of the inferior and degenerate strains of the various civilized peoples rather than in any supposed danger of their racial interbreeding.

[Presented by the Chief of Seraphim stationed on Urantia.]

PAPER 83

THE MARRIAGE INSTITUTION

THIS is the recital of the early beginnings of the institution of marriage. It has progressed steadily from the loose and promiscuous matings of the herd through many variations and adaptations, even to the appearance of those marriage standards which eventually culminated in the realization of pair matings, the union of one man and one woman to establish a home of the highest social order.

Marriage has been many times in jeopardy, and the marriage mores have drawn heavily on both property and religion for support; but the real influence which forever safeguards marriage and the resultant family is the simple and innate biologic fact that men and women positively will not live without each other, be they the most primitive savages or the most cultured mortals.

It is because of the sex urge that selfish man is lured into making something better than an animal out of himself. The self-regarding and self-gratifying sex relationship entails the certain consequences of self-denial and insures the assumption of altruistic duties and numerous race-benefiting home responsibilities. Herein has sex been the unrecognized and unsuspected civilizer of the savage; for this same sex impulse automatically and unerringly *compels man to think* and eventually *leads him to love.*

1. MARRIAGE AS A SOCIETAL INSTITUTION

Marriage is society's mechanism designed to regulate and control those many human relations which arise out of the physical fact of bisexuality. As such an institution, marriage functions in two directions:

1. In the regulation of personal sex relations.

2. In the regulation of descent, inheritance, succession, and social order, this being its older and original function.

The family, which grows out of marriage, is itself a stabilizer of the marriage institution together with the property mores. Other potent factors in marriage stability are pride, vanity, chivalry, duty, and religious convictions. But while marriages may be approved or disapproved on high, they are hardly made in heaven. The human family is a distinctly human institution, an evolutionary development. Marriage is an institution of society, not a department of the church. True, religion should mightily influence it but should not undertake exclusively to control and regulate it.

Primitive marriage was primarily industrial; and even in modern times it is often a social or business affair. Through the influence of the mixture of the Andite stock and as a result of the mores of advancing civilization, marriage is slowly becoming mutual, romantic, parental, poetical, affectionate, ethical, and even idealistic. Selection and so-called romantic love, however, were at a minimum in primitive mating. During early times husband and wife were not much together; they did not even eat together very often. But among the ancients, personal affection was not strongly linked to sex attraction; they became fond of one another largely because of living and working together.

2. COURTSHIP AND BETROTHAL

Primitive marriages were always planned by the parents of the boy and girl. The transition stage between this custom and the times of free choosing was occupied by the marriage broker or professional matchmaker. These matchmakers were at first the barbers; later, the priests. Marriage was originally a group affair; then a family matter; only recently has it become an individual adventure.

Coercion, not attraction, was the approach to primitive marriage. In early times woman had no sex aloofness, only sex inferiority as inculcated by the mores. As raiding preceded trading, so marriage by capture preceded marriage by contract. Some women would connive at capture in order to escape the domination of the older men of their tribe; they preferred to fall into the hands of men of their own age from another tribe. This pseudo elopement was the transition stage between capture by force and subsequent courtship by charming.

An early type of wedding ceremony was the mimic flight, a sort of elopement rehearsal which was once a common practice. Later, mock capture became a part of the regular wedding ceremony. A modern girl's pretensions to resist "capture," to be reticent toward marriage, are all relics of olden customs. The carrying of the bride over the threshold is reminiscent of a number of ancient practices, among others, of the days of wife stealing.

Woman was long denied full freedom of self-disposal in marriage, but the more intelligent women have always been able to circumvent this restriction by the clever exercise of their wits. Man has usually taken the lead in courtship, but not always. Woman sometimes formally, as well as covertly, initiates marriage. And as civilization has progressed, women have had an increasing part in all phases of courtship and marriage.

Increasing love, romance, and personal selection in premarital courtship are an Andite contribution to the world races. The relations between the sexes are evolving favorably; many advancing peoples are gradually substituting somewhat idealized concepts of sex attraction for those older motives of utility and ownership. Sex impulse and feelings of affection are beginning to displace cold calculation in the choosing of life partners.

The betrothal was originally equivalent to marriage; and among early peoples sex relations were conventional during the engagement. In recent times, religion has established a sex taboo on the period between betrothal and marriage.

3. PURCHASE AND DOWRY

The ancients mistrusted love and promises; they thought that abiding unions must be guaranteed by some tangible security, property. For this reason, the purchase price of a wife was regarded as a forfeit or deposit which the husband was doomed to lose in case of divorce or desertion. Once the purchase price of a bride had been paid, many tribes permitted the husband's brand to be burned upon her. Africans still buy their wives. A love wife, or a white man's wife, they compare to a cat because she costs nothing.

The bride shows were occasions for dressing up and decorating daughters for public exhibition with the idea of their bringing higher prices as wives. But they were not sold as animals—among the later tribes such a wife was not transferable. Neither was her purchase always just a cold-blooded money transaction; service was equivalent to cash in the purchase of a wife. If an otherwise desirable man could not pay for his wife, he could be adopted as a son by the girl's father and then could marry. And if a poor man sought a wife and could not meet the price demanded by a grasping father, the elders would often bring pressure to bear upon the father which would result in a modification of his demands, or else there might be an elopement.

As civilization progressed, fathers did not like to appear to sell their daughters, and so, while continuing to accept the bride purchase price, they initiated the custom of giving the pair valuable presents which about equaled the purchase money. And upon the later discontinuance of payment for the bride, these presents became the bride's dowry.

The idea of a dowry was to convey the impression of the bride's independence, to suggest far removal from the times of slave wives and property companions. A man could not divorce a dowered wife without paying back the dowry in full. Among some tribes a mutual deposit was made with the parents of both bride and groom to be forfeited in case either deserted the other, in reality a marriage bond. During the period of transition from purchase to dowry, if the wife were purchased, the children belonged to the father; if not, they belonged to the wife's family.

4. THE WEDDING CEREMONY

The wedding ceremony grew out of the fact that marriage was originally a community affair, not just the culmination of a decision of two individuals. Mating was of group concern as well as a personal function.

Magic, ritual, and ceremony surrounded the entire life of the ancients, and marriage was no exception. As civilization advanced, as marriage became more seriously regarded, the wedding ceremony became increasingly pretentious. Early marriage was a factor in property interests, even as it is today, and therefore required a legal ceremony, while the social status of subsequent children demanded the widest possible publicity. Primitive man had no records; therefore must the marriage ceremony be witnessed by many persons.

At first the wedding ceremony was more on the order of a betrothal and consisted only in public notification of intention of living together; later it consisted in formal eating together. Among some tribes the parents simply took their daughter to the husband; in other cases the only ceremony was the formal exchange of presents, after which the bride's father would present her to the groom. Among many Levantine peoples it was the custom to dispense with all formality, marriage being consummated by sex relations. The red man was the first to develop the more elaborate celebration of weddings.

Childlessness was greatly dreaded, and since barrenness was attributed to spirit machinations, efforts to insure fecundity also led to the association of marriage with certain magical or religious ceremonials. And in this effort to insure a happy and fertile marriage, many charms were employed; even the astrologers were consulted to ascertain the birth stars of the contracting parties.

At one time the human sacrifice was a regular feature of all weddings among well-to-do people.

Lucky days were sought out, Thursday being most favorably regarded, and weddings celebrated at the full of the moon were thought to be exceptionally fortunate. It was the custom of many Near Eastern peoples to throw grain upon the newlyweds; this was a magical rite which was supposed to insure fecundity. Certain Oriental peoples used rice for this purpose.

Fire and water were always considered the best means of resisting ghosts and evil spirits; hence altar fires and lighted candles, as well as the baptismal sprinkling of holy water, were usually in evidence at weddings. For a long time it was customary to set a false wedding day and then suddenly postpone the event so as to put the ghosts and spirits off the track.

The teasing of newlyweds and the pranks played upon honeymooners are all relics of those far-distant days when it was thought best to appear miserable and ill at ease in the sight of the spirits so as to avoid arousing their envy. The wearing of the bridal veil is a relic of the times when it was considered necessary to disguise the bride so that ghosts might not recognize her and also to hide her beauty from the gaze of the otherwise jealous and envious spirits. The bride's feet must never touch the ground just prior to the ceremony. Even in the twentieth century it is still the custom under the Christian mores to stretch carpets from the carriage landing to the church altar.

One of the most ancient forms of the wedding ceremony was to have a priest bless the wedding bed to insure the fertility of the union; this was done long before any formal wedding ritual was established. During this period in the evolution of the marriage mores the wedding guests were expected to file through the bedchamber at night, thus constituting legal witness to the consummation of marriage.

The luck element, that in spite of all premarital tests certain marriages turned out bad, led primitive man to seek insurance protection against marriage failure; led him to go in quest of priests and magic. And this movement culminated directly in modern church weddings. But for a long time marriage was generally recognized as consisting in the decisions of the contracting parents—later of the pair—while for the last five hundred years church and state have assumed jurisdiction and now presume to make pronouncements of marriage.

5. PLURAL MARRIAGES

In the early history of marriage the unmarried women belonged to the men of the tribe. Later on, a woman had only one husband at a time. This practice of *one-man-at-a-time* was the first step away from the promiscuity of the herd. While a woman was allowed but one man, her husband could sever such temporary relationships at will. But these loosely regulated associations were the first step toward living pairwise in distinction to living herdwise. In this stage of marriage development children usually belonged to the mother.

The next step in mating evolution was the *group marriage*. This communal phase of marriage had to intervene in the unfolding of family life because the marriage mores were not yet strong enough to make pair associations permanent. The brother and sister marriages belonged to this group; five brothers of one family would marry five sisters of another. All over the world the looser forms of communal marriage gradually evolved into various types of group marriage.

And these group associations were largely regulated by the totem mores. Family life slowly and surely developed because sex and marriage regulation favored the survival of the tribe itself by insuring the survival of larger numbers of children.

Group marriages gradually gave way before the emerging practices of polygamy—polygyny and polyandry—among the more advanced tribes. But polyandry was never general, being usually limited to queens and rich women; furthermore, it was customarily a family affair, one wife for several brothers. Caste and economic restrictions sometimes made it necessary for several men to content themselves with one wife. Even then, the woman would marry only one, the others being loosely tolerated as "uncles" of the joint progeny.

The Jewish custom requiring that a man consort with his deceased brother's widow for the purpose of "raising up seed for his brother," was the custom of more than half the ancient world. This was a relic of the time when marriage was a family affair rather than an individual association.

The institution of polygyny recognized, at various times, four sorts of wives:

1. The ceremonial or legal wives.
2. Wives of affection and permission.
3. Concubines, contractual wives.
4. Slave wives.

True polygyny, where all the wives are of equal status and all the children equal, has been very rare. Usually, even with plural marriages, the home was dominated by the head wife, the status companion. She alone had the ritual wedding ceremony, and only the children of such a purchased or dowered spouse could inherit unless by special arrangement with the status wife.

The status wife was not necessarily the love wife; in early times she usually was not. The love wife, or sweetheart, did not appear until the races were considerably advanced, more particularly after the blending of the evolutionary tribes with the Nodites and Adamites.

The taboo wife—one wife of legal status—created the concubine mores. Under these mores a man might have only one wife, but he could maintain sex relations with any number of concubines. Concubinage was the steppingstone to monogamy, the first move away from frank polygyny. The concubines of the Jews, Romans, and Chinese were very frequently the handmaidens of the wife. Later on, as among the Jews, the legal wife was looked upon as the mother of all children born to the husband.

The olden taboos on sex relations with a pregnant or nursing wife tended greatly to foster polygyny. Primitive women aged very early because of frequent childbearing coupled with hard work. (Such overburdened wives only managed to exist by virtue of the fact that they were put in isolation one week out of each month when they were not heavy with child.) Such a wife often grew tired of bearing children and would request her husband to take a second and younger wife, one able to help with both childbearing and the domestic work. The new wives were therefore usually hailed with delight by the older spouses; there existed nothing on the order of sex jealousy.

The number of wives was only limited by the ability of the man to provide for them. Wealthy and able men wanted large numbers of children, and since the infant mortality was very high, it required an assembly of wives to recruit a large family. Many of these plural wives were mere laborers, slave wives.

Human customs evolve, but very slowly. The purpose of a harem was to build up a strong and numerous body of blood kin for the support of the throne. A certain chief was once convinced that he should not have a harem, that he should be contented with one wife; so he promptly dismissed his harem. The dissatisfied wives went to their homes, and their offended relatives swept down on the chief in wrath and did away with him then and there.

6. TRUE MONOGAMY—PAIR MARRIAGE

Monogamy is monopoly; it is good for those who attain this desirable state, but it tends to work a biologic hardship on those who are not so fortunate. But quite regardless of the effect on the individual, monogamy is decidedly best for the children.

The earliest monogamy was due to force of circumstances, poverty. Monogamy is cultural and societal, artificial and unnatural, that is, unnatural to evolutionary man. It was wholly natural to the purer Nodites and Adamites and has been of great cultural value to all advanced races.

The Chaldean tribes recognized the right of a wife to impose a premarital pledge upon her spouse not to take a second wife or concubine; both the Greeks and the Romans favored monogamous marriage. Ancestor worship has always fostered monogamy, as has the Christian error of regarding marriage as a sacrament. Even the elevation of the standard of living has consistently militated against plural wives. By the time of Michael's advent on Urantia practically all of the civilized world had attained the level of theoretical monogamy. But this passive monogamy did not mean that mankind had become habituated to the practice of real pair marriage.

While pursuing the monogamic goal of the ideal pair marriage, which is, after all, something of a monopolistic sex association, society must not overlook the unenviable situation of those unfortunate men and women who fail to find a place in this new and improved social order, even when having done their best to co-operate with, and enter into, its requirements. Failure to gain mates in the social arena of competition may be due to insurmountable difficulties or multitudinous restrictions which the current mores have imposed. Truly, monogamy is ideal for those who are in, but it must inevitably work great hardship on those who are left out in the cold of solitary existence.

Always have the unfortunate few had to suffer that the majority might advance under the developing mores of evolving civilization; but always should the favored majority look with kindness and consideration on their less fortunate fellows who must pay the price of failure to attain membership in the ranks of those ideal sex partnerships which afford the satisfaction of all biologic urges under the sanction of the highest mores of advancing social evolution.

Monogamy always has been, now is, and forever will be the idealistic goal of human sex evolution. This ideal of true pair marriage entails self-denial, and therefore does it so often fail just because one or both of the contracting parties are deficient in that acme of all human virtues, rugged self-control.

Monogamy is the yardstick which measures the advance of social civilization as distinguished from purely biologic evolution. Monogamy is not necessarily biologic or natural, but it is indispensable to the immediate maintenance and further development of social civilization. It contributes to a delicacy of sentiment, a refinement of moral character, and a spiritual growth which are utterly impossible in polygamy. A woman never can become an ideal mother when she is all the while compelled to engage in rivalry for her husband's affections.

Pair marriage favors and fosters that intimate understanding and effective co-operation which is best for parental happiness, child welfare, and social efficiency. Marriage, which began in crude coercion, is gradually evolving into a magnificent institution of self-culture, self-control, self-expression, and self-perpetuation.

7. THE DISSOLUTION OF WEDLOCK

In the early evolution of the marital mores, marriage was a loose union which could be terminated at will, and the children always followed the mother; the mother-child bond is instinctive and has functioned regardless of the developmental stage of the mores.

Among primitive peoples only about one half the marriages proved satisfactory. The most frequent cause for separation was barrenness, which was always blamed on the wife; and childless wives were believed to become snakes in the spirit world. Under the more primitive mores, divorce was had at the option of the man alone, and these standards have persisted to the twentieth century among some peoples.

As the mores evolved, certain tribes developed two forms of marriage: the ordinary, which permitted divorce, and the priest marriage, which did not allow for separation. The inauguration of wife purchase and wife dowry, by introducing a property penalty for marriage failure, did much to lessen separation. And, indeed, many modern unions are stabilized by this ancient property factor.

The social pressure of community standing and property privileges has always been potent in the maintenance of the marriage taboos and mores. Down through the ages marriage has made steady progress and stands on advanced ground in the modern world, notwithstanding that it is threateningly assailed by widespread dissatisfaction among those peoples where individual choice—a new liberty—figures most largely. While these upheavals of adjustment appear among the more progressive races as a result of suddenly accelerated social evolution, among the less advanced peoples marriage continues to thrive and slowly improve under the guidance of the older mores.

The new and sudden substitution of the more ideal but extremely individualistic love motive in marriage for the older and long-established property motive, has unavoidably caused the marriage institution to become temporarily unstable. Man's marriage motives have always far transcended actual marriage morals, and in the nineteenth and twentieth centuries the Occidental ideal of marriage has suddenly far outrun the self-centered and but partially controlled sex impulses of the races. The presence of large numbers of unmarried persons in any society indicates the temporary breakdown or the transition of the mores.

The real test of marriage, all down through the ages, has been that continuous intimacy which is inescapable in all family life. Two pampered and spoiled youths, educated to expect every indulgence and full gratification of vanity and ego, can hardly hope to make a great success of marriage and home building—a lifelong partnership of self-effacement, compromise, devotion, and unselfish dedication to child culture.

The high degree of imagination and fantastic romance entering into courtship is largely responsible for the increasing divorce tendencies among modern Occidental peoples, all of which is further complicated by woman's greater personal freedom and increased economic liberty. Easy divorce, when the result of lack of self-control or failure of normal personality adjustment, only leads directly back to those crude societal stages from which man has emerged so recently and as the result of so much personal anguish and racial suffering.

But just so long as society fails to properly educate children and youths, so long as the social order fails to provide adequate premarital training, and so long as unwise and immature youthful idealism is to be the arbiter of the entrance upon marriage, just so long will divorce remain prevalent. And in so far as the social group falls short of providing marriage preparation for youths, to that extent must divorce function as the social safety valve which prevents still worse situations during the ages of the rapid growth of the evolving mores.

The ancients seem to have regarded marriage just about as seriously as some present-day people do. And it does not appear that many of the hasty and unsuccessful marriages of modern times are much of an improvement over the ancient practices of qualifying young men and women for mating. The great inconsistency of modern society is to exalt love and to idealize marriage while disapproving of the fullest examination of both.

8. THE IDEALIZATION OF MARRIAGE

Marriage which culminates in the home is indeed man's most exalted institution, but it is essentially human; it should never have been called a sacrament. The Sethite priests made marriage a religious ritual; but for thousands of years after Eden, mating continued as a purely social and civil institution.

The likening of human associations to divine associations is most unfortunate. The union of husband and wife in the marriage-home relationship is a material function of the mortals of the evolutionary worlds. True, indeed, much spiritual progress may accrue consequent upon the sincere human efforts of husband and wife to progress, but this does not mean that marriage is necessarily sacred. Spiritual progress is attendant upon sincere application to other avenues of human endeavor.

Neither can marriage be truly compared to the relation of the Adjuster to man nor to the fraternity of Christ Michael and his human brethren. At scarcely any point are such relationships comparable to the association of husband and wife. And it is most unfortunate that the human misconception of these relationships has produced so much confusion as to the status of marriage.

It is also unfortunate that certain groups of mortals have conceived of marriage as being consummated by divine action. Such beliefs lead directly to the concept of the indissolubility of the marital state regardless of the circumstances or wishes of the contracting parties. But the very fact of marriage dissolution itself indicates that Deity is not a conjoining party to such unions. If God has once joined any two things or persons together, they will remain thus joined until such a time as the divine will decrees their separation. But, regarding marriage, which is a human institution, who shall presume to sit in judgment, to say which marriages are unions that might be approved by the universe supervisors in contrast with those which are purely human in nature and origin?

Nevertheless, there is an ideal of marriage on the spheres on high. On the capital of each local system the Material Sons and Daughters of God do portray the height of the ideals of the union of man and woman in the bonds of marriage and for the purpose of procreating and rearing offspring. After all, the ideal mortal marriage is *humanly* sacred.

Marriage always has been and still is man's supreme dream of temporal ideality. Though this beautiful dream is seldom realized in its entirety, it endures as a glorious ideal, ever luring progressing mankind on to greater strivings for human happiness. But young men and women should be taught something of the realities of marriage before they are plunged into the exacting demands of the interassociations of family life; youthful idealization should be tempered with some degree of premarital disillusionment.

The youthful idealization of marriage should not, however, be discouraged; such dreams are the visualization of the future goal of family life. This attitude is both stimulating and helpful providing it does not produce an insensitivity to the realization of the practical and commonplace requirements of marriage and subsequent family life.

The ideals of marriage have made great progress in recent times; among some peoples woman enjoys practically equal rights with her consort. In concept, at least, the family is becoming a loyal partnership for rearing offspring, accompanied by sexual fidelity. But even this newer version of marriage need not presume to swing so far to the extreme as to confer mutual monopoly of all personality and individuality. Marriage is not just an individualistic ideal; it is the evolving social partnership of a man and a woman, existing and functioning under the current mores, restricted by the taboos, and enforced by the laws and regulations of society.

Twentieth-century marriages stand high in comparison with those of past ages, notwithstanding that the home institution is now undergoing a serious testing because of the problems so suddenly thrust upon the social organization by the precipitate augmentation of woman's liberties, rights so long denied her in the tardy evolution of the mores of past generations.

[Presented by the Chief of Seraphim stationed on Urantia.]

PAPER 84

MARRIAGE AND FAMILY LIFE

MATERIAL necessity founded marriage, sex hunger embellished it, religion sanctioned and exalted it, the state demanded and regulated it, while in later times evolving love is beginning to justify and glorify marriage as the ancestor and creator of civilization's most useful and sublime institution, the home. And home building should be the center and essence of all educational effort.

Mating is purely an act of self-perpetuation associated with varying degrees of self-gratification; marriage, home building, is largely a matter of self-maintenance, and it implies the evolution of society. Society itself is the aggregated structure of family units. Individuals are very temporary as planetary factors—only families are continuing agencies in social evolution. The family is the channel through which the river of culture and knowledge flows from one generation to another.

The home is basically a sociologic institution. Marriage grew out of co-operation in self-maintenance and partnership in self-perpetuation, the element of self-gratification being largely incidental. Nevertheless, the home does embrace all three of the essential functions of human existence, while life propagation makes it the fundamental human institution, and sex sets it off from all other social activities.

1. PRIMITIVE PAIR ASSOCIATIONS

Marriage was not founded on sex relations; they were incidental thereto. Marriage was not needed by primitive man, who indulged his sex appetite freely without encumbering himself with the responsibilities of wife, children, and home.

Woman, because of physical and emotional attachment to her offspring, is dependent on co-operation with the male, and this urges her into the sheltering protection of marriage. But no direct biologic urge led man into marriage—much less held him in. It was not love that made marriage attractive to man, but food hunger which first attracted savage man to woman and the primitive shelter shared by her children.

Marriage was not even brought about by the conscious realization of the obligations of sex relations. Primitive man comprehended no connection between sex indulgence and the subsequent birth of a child. It was once universally believed that a virgin could become pregnant. The savage early conceived the idea that babies were made in spiritland; pregnancy was believed to be the result of a woman's being entered by a spirit, an evolving ghost. Both diet and the evil eye were also believed to be capable of causing pregnancy in a virgin or unmarried woman, while later beliefs connected the beginnings of life with the breath and with sunlight.

Many early peoples associated ghosts with the sea; hence virgins were greatly restricted in their bathing practices; young women were far more afraid of bathing in the sea at high tide than of having sex relations. Deformed or premature babies were regarded as the young of animals which had found their way into a woman's body as a result of careless bathing or through malevolent spirit activity. Savages, of course, thought nothing of strangling such offspring at birth.

The first step in enlightenment came with the belief that sex relations opened up the way for the impregnating ghost to enter the female. Man has since discovered that father and mother are equal contributors of the living inheritance factors which initiate offspring. But even in the twentieth century many parents still endeavor to keep their children in more or less ignorance as to the origin of human life.

A family of some simple sort was insured by the fact that the reproductive function entails the mother-child relationship. Mother love is instinctive; it did not originate in the mores as did marriage. All mammalian mother love is the inherent endowment of the adjutant mind-spirits of the local universe and is in strength and devotion always directly proportional to the length of the helpless infancy of the species.

The mother and child relation is natural, strong, and instinctive, and one which, therefore, constrained primitive women to submit to many strange conditions and to endure untold hardships. This compelling mother love is the handicapping emotion which has always placed woman at such a tremendous disadvantage in all her struggles with man. Even at that, maternal instinct in the human species is not overpowering; it may be thwarted by ambition, selfishness, and religious conviction.

While the mother-child association is neither marriage nor home, it was the nucleus from which both sprang. The great advance in the evolution of mating came when these temporary partnerships lasted long enough to rear the resultant offspring, for that was homemaking.

Regardless of the antagonisms of these early pairs, notwithstanding the looseness of the association, the chances for survival were greatly improved by these male-female partnerships. A man and a woman, co-operating, even aside from family and offspring, are vastly superior in most ways to either two men or two women. This pairing of the sexes enhanced survival and was the very beginning of human society. The sex division of labor also made for comfort and increased happiness.

2. THE EARLY MOTHER-FAMILY

The woman's periodic hemorrhage and her further loss of blood at childbirth early suggested blood as the creator of the child (even as the seat of the soul) and gave origin to the blood-bond concept of human relationships. In early times all descent was reckoned in the female line, that being the only part of inheritance which was at all certain.

The primitive family, growing out of the instinctive biologic blood bond of mother and child, was inevitably a mother-family; and many tribes long held to this arrangement. The mother-family was the only possible transition from the stage of group marriage in the horde to the later and improved home life of the polygamous and monogamous father-families. The mother-family was natural and biologic; the father-family is social, economic, and political. The persistence of the mother-family among the North American red men is one of the chief reasons why the otherwise progressive Iroquois never became a real state.

Under the mother-family mores the wife's mother enjoyed virtually supreme authority in the home; even the wife's brothers and their sons were more active in family supervision than was the husband. Fathers were often renamed after their own children.

The earliest races gave little credit to the father, looking upon the child as coming altogether from the mother. They believed that children resembled the father as a result of association, or that they were "marked" in this manner because the mother desired them to look like the father. Later on, when the switch came from the mother-family to the father-family, the father took all credit for the child, and many of the taboos on a pregnant woman were subsequently extended to include her husband. The prospective father ceased work as the time of delivery approached, and at childbirth he went to bed, along with the wife, remaining at rest from three to eight days. The wife might arise the next day and engage in hard labor, but the husband remained in bed to receive congratulations; this was all a part of the early mores designed to establish the father's right to the child.

At first, it was the custom for the man to go to his wife's people, but in later times, after a man had paid or worked out the bride price, he could take his wife and children back to his own people. The transition from the mother-family to the father-family explains the otherwise meaningless prohibitions of some types of cousin marriages while others of equal kinship are approved.

With the passing of the hunter mores, when herding gave man control of the chief food supply, the mother-family came to a speedy end. It failed simply because it could not successfully compete with the newer father-family. Power lodged with the male relatives of the mother could not compete with power concentrated in the husband-father. Woman was not equal to the combined tasks of childbearing and of exercising continuous authority and increasing domestic power. The oncoming of wife stealing and later wife purchase hastened the passing of the mother-family.

The stupendous change from the mother-family to the father-family is one of the most radical and complete right-about-face adjustments ever executed by the human race. This change led at once to greater social expression and increased family adventure.

3. THE FAMILY UNDER FATHER DOMINANCE

It may be that the instinct of motherhood led woman into marriage, but it was man's superior strength, together with the influence of the mores, that virtually compelled her to remain in wedlock. Pastoral living tended to create a new system of mores, the patriarchal type of family life; and the basis of family unity under the herder and early agricultural mores was the unquestioned and arbitrary authority of the father. All society, whether national or familial, passed through the stage of the autocratic authority of a patriarchal order.

The scant courtesy paid womankind during the Old Testament era is a true reflection of the mores of the herdsmen. The Hebrew patriarchs were all herdsmen, as is witnessed by the saying, "The Lord is my Shepherd."

But man was no more to blame for his low opinion of woman during past ages than was woman herself. She failed to get social recognition during primitive times because she did not function in an emergency; she was not a spectacular or crisis hero. Maternity was a distinct disability in the existence struggle; mother love handicapped women in the tribal defense.

Primitive women also unintentionally created their dependence on the male by their admiration and applause for his pugnacity and virility. This exaltation of the warrior elevated the male ego while it equally depressed that of the female and made her more dependent; a military uniform still mightily stirs the feminine emotions.

Among the more advanced races, women are not so large or so strong as men. Woman, being the weaker, therefore became the more tactful; she early learned to trade upon her sex charms. She became more alert and conservative than man, though slightly less profound. Man was woman's superior on the battlefield and in the hunt; but at home woman has usually outgeneraled even the most primitive of men.

The herdsman looked to his flocks for sustenance, but throughout these pastoral ages woman must still provide the vegetable food. Primitive man shunned the soil; it was altogether too peaceful, too unadventuresome. There was also an old superstition that women could raise better plants; they were mothers. In many backward tribes today, the men cook the meat, the women the vegetables, and when the primitive tribes of Australia are on the march, the women never attack game, while a man would not stoop to dig a root.

Woman has always had to work; at least right up to modern times the female has been a real producer. Man has usually chosen the easier path, and this inequality has existed throughout the entire history of the human race. Woman has always been the burden bearer, carrying the family property and tending the children, thus leaving the man's hands free for fighting or hunting.

Woman's first liberation came when man consented to till the soil, consented to do what had theretofore been regarded as woman's work. It was a great step forward when male captives were no longer killed but were enslaved as agriculturists. This brought about the liberation of woman so that she could devote more time to homemaking and child culture.

The provision of milk for the young led to earlier weaning of babies, hence to the bearing of more children by the mothers thus relieved of their sometimes temporary barrenness, while the use of cow's milk and goat's milk greatly reduced infant mortality. Before the herding stage of society, mothers used to nurse their babies until they were four and five years old.

Decreasing primitive warfare greatly lessened the disparity between the division of labor based on sex. But women still had to do the real work while men did picket duty. No camp or village could be left unguarded day or night, but even this task was alleviated by the domestication of the dog. In general, the coming of agriculture has enhanced woman's prestige and social standing; at least this was true up to the time man himself turned agriculturist. And as soon as man addressed himself to the tilling of the soil, there immediately ensued great improvement in methods of agriculture, extending on down through successive generations. In hunting and war man had learned the value of organization, and he introduced these techniques into industry and later, when taking over much of woman's work, greatly improved on her loose methods of labor.

4. WOMAN'S STATUS IN EARLY SOCIETY

Generally speaking, during any age woman's status is a fair criterion of the evolutionary progress of marriage as a social institution, while the progress of marriage itself is a reasonably accurate gauge registering the advances of human civilization.

Woman's status has always been a social paradox; she has always been a shrewd manager of men; she has always capitalized man's stronger sex urge for her own interests and to her own advancement. By trading subtly upon her sex charms, she has often been able to exercise dominant power over man, even when held by him in abject slavery.

Early woman was not to man a friend, sweetheart, lover, and partner but rather a piece of property, a servant or slave and, later on, an economic partner, plaything, and childbearer. Nonetheless, proper and satisfactory sex relations have always involved the element of choice and co-operation by woman, and this has always given intelligent women considerable influence over their immediate and personal standing, regardless of their social position as a sex. But man's distrust and suspicion were not helped by the fact that women were all along compelled to resort to shrewdness in the effort to alleviate their bondage.

The sexes have had great difficulty in understanding each other. Man found it hard to understand woman, regarding her with a strange mixture of ignorant mistrust and fearful fascination, if not with suspicion and contempt. Many tribal and racial traditions relegate trouble to Eve, Pandora, or some other representative of womankind. These narratives were always distorted so as to make it appear that the woman brought evil upon man; and all this indicates the onetime universal distrust of woman. Among the reasons cited in support of a celibate priesthood, the chief was the baseness of woman. The fact that most supposed witches were women did not improve the olden reputation of the sex.

Men have long regarded women as peculiar, even abnormal. They have even believed that women did not have souls; therefore were they denied names. During early times there existed great fear of the first sex relation with a woman; hence it became the custom for a priest to have initial intercourse with a virgin. Even a woman's shadow was thought to be dangerous.

Childbearing was once generally looked upon as rendering a woman dangerous and unclean. And many tribal mores decreed that a mother must undergo extensive purification ceremonies subsequent to the birth of a child. Except among those groups where the husband participated in the lying-in, the expectant mother was shunned, left alone. The ancients even avoided having a child born in the house. Finally, the old women were permitted to attend the mother during labor, and this practice gave origin to the profession of midwifery. During labor, scores of foolish things were said and done in an effort to facilitate delivery. It was the custom to sprinkle the newborn with holy water to prevent ghost interference.

Among the unmixed tribes, childbirth was comparatively easy, occupying only two or three hours; it is seldom so easy among the mixed races. If a woman died in childbirth, especially during the delivery of twins, she was believed to have been guilty of spirit adultery. Later on, the higher tribes looked upon death in childbirth as the will of heaven; such mothers were regarded as having perished in a noble cause.

The so-called modesty of women respecting their clothing and the exposure of the person grew out of the deadly fear of being observed at the time of a menstrual period. To be thus detected was a grievous sin, the violation of a taboo. Under the mores of olden times, every woman, from adolescence to the end of the childbearing period, was subjected to complete family and social quarantine one full week each month. Everything she might touch, sit upon, or lie upon was "defiled." It was for long the custom to brutally beat a girl after each monthly period in an effort to drive the evil spirit out of her body. But when a woman passed beyond the childbearing age, she was usually treated more considerately, being accorded more rights and privileges. In view of all this it was not strange that women were looked down upon. Even the Greeks held the menstruating woman as one of the three great causes of defilement, the other two being pork and garlic.

However foolish these olden notions were, they did some good since they gave overworked females, at least when young, one week each month for welcome rest and profitable meditation. Thus could they sharpen their wits for dealing with their male associates the rest of the time. This quarantine of women also protected men from over-sex indulgence, thereby indirectly contributing to the restriction of population and to the enhancement of self-control.

A great advance was made when a man was denied the right to kill his wife at will. Likewise, it was a forward step when a woman could own the wedding gifts. Later, she gained the legal right to own, control, and even dispose of property, but she was long deprived of the right to hold office in either church or state. Woman has always been treated more or less as property, right up to and in the twentieth century after Christ. She has not yet gained world-wide freedom from seclusion under man's control. Even among advanced peoples, man's attempt to protect woman has always been a tacit assertion of superiority.

But primitive women did not pity themselves as their more recently liberated sisters are wont to do. They were, after all, fairly happy and contented; they did not dare to envision a better or different mode of existence.

5. WOMAN UNDER THE DEVELOPING MORES

In self-perpetuation woman is man's equal, but in the partnership of self-maintenance she labors at a decided disadvantage, and this handicap of enforced maternity can only be compensated by the enlightened mores of advancing civilization and by man's increasing sense of acquired fairness.

As society evolved, the sex standards rose higher among women because they suffered more from the consequences of the transgression of the sex mores. Man's sex standards are only tardily improving as a result of the sheer sense of that fairness which civilization demands. Nature knows nothing of fairness—makes woman alone suffer the pangs of childbirth.

The modern idea of sex equality is beautiful and worthy of an expanding civilization, but it is not found in nature. When might is right, man lords it over woman; when more justice, peace, and fairness prevail, she gradually emerges from slavery and obscurity. Woman's social position has generally varied inversely with the degree of militarism in any nation or age.

But man did not consciously nor intentionally seize woman's rights and then gradually and grudgingly give them back to her; all this was an unconscious and unplanned episode of social evolution. When the time really came for woman to enjoy added rights, she got them, and all quite regardless of man's conscious attitude. Slowly but surely the mores change so as to provide for those social adjustments which are a part of the persistent evolution of civilization. The advancing mores slowly provided increasingly better treatment for females; those tribes which persisted in cruelty to them did not survive.

The Adamites and Nodites accorded women increased recognition, and those groups which were influenced by the migrating Andites have tended to be influenced by the Edenic teachings regarding women's place in society.

The early Chinese and the Greeks treated women better than did most surrounding peoples. But the Hebrews were exceedingly distrustful of them. In the Occident woman has had a difficult climb under the Pauline doctrines which became attached to Christianity, although Christianity did advance the mores by imposing more stringent sex obligations upon man. Woman's estate is little short of hopeless under the peculiar degradation which attaches to her in Mohammedanism, and she fares even worse under the teachings of several other Oriental religions.

Science, not religion, really emancipated woman; it was the modern factory which largely set her free from the confines of the home. Man's physical abilities became no longer a vital essential in the new maintenance mechanism; science so changed the conditions of living that man power was no longer so superior to woman power.

These changes have tended toward woman's liberation from domestic slavery and have brought about such a modification of her status that she now enjoys a degree of personal liberty and sex determination that practically equals man's. Once a woman's value consisted in her food-producing ability, but invention and wealth have enabled her to create a new world in which to function—spheres of grace and charm. Thus has industry won its unconscious and unintended fight for woman's social and economic emancipation. And again has evolution succeeded in doing what even revelation failed to accomplish.

The reaction of enlightened peoples from the inequitable mores governing woman's place in society has indeed been pendulumlike in its extremeness. Among industrialized races she has received almost all rights and enjoys exemption from many obligations, such as military service. Every easement of the struggle for existence has redounded to the liberation of woman, and she has directly benefited from every advance toward monogamy. The weaker always makes disproportionate gains in every adjustment of the mores in the progressive evolution of society.

In the ideals of pair marriage, woman has finally won recognition, dignity, independence, equality, and education; but will she prove worthy of all this new and unprecedented accomplishment? Will modern woman respond to this great achievement of social liberation with idleness, indifference, barrenness, and infidelity? Today, in the twentieth century, woman is undergoing the crucial test of her long world existence!

Woman is man's equal partner in race reproduction, hence just as important in the unfolding of racial evolution; therefore has evolution increasingly worked toward the realization of women's rights. But women's rights are by no means men's rights. Woman cannot thrive on man's rights any more than man can prosper on woman's rights.

Each sex has its own distinctive sphere of existence, together with its own rights within that sphere. If woman aspires literally to enjoy all of man's rights, then, sooner or later, pitiless and emotionless competition will certainly replace that chivalry and special consideration which many women now enjoy, and which they have so recently won from men.

Civilization never can obliterate the behavior gulf between the sexes. From age to age the mores change, but instinct never. Innate maternal affection will never permit emancipated woman to become man's serious rival in industry. Forever each sex will remain supreme in its own domain, domains determined by biologic differentiation and by mental dissimilarity.

Each sex will always have its own special sphere, albeit they will ever and anon overlap. Only socially will men and women compete on equal terms.

6. THE PARTNERSHIP OF MAN AND WOMAN

The reproductive urge unfailingly brings men and women together for self-perpetuation but, alone, does not insure their remaining together in mutual co-operation—the founding of a home.

Every successful human institution embraces antagonisms of personal interest which have been adjusted to practical working harmony, and homemaking is no exception. Marriage, the basis of home building, is the highest manifestation of that antagonistic co-operation which so often characterizes the contacts of nature and society. The conflict is inevitable. Mating is inherent; it is natural. But marriage is not biologic; it is sociologic. Passion insures that man and woman will come together, but the weaker parental instinct and the social mores hold them together.

Male and female are, practically regarded, two distinct varieties of the same species living in close and intimate association. Their viewpoints and entire life reactions are essentially different; they are wholly incapable of full and real comprehension of each other. Complete understanding between the sexes is not attainable.

Women seem to have more intuition than men, but they also appear to be somewhat less logical. Woman, however, has always been the moral standard-bearer and the spiritual leader of mankind. The hand that rocks the cradle still fraternizes with destiny.

The differences of nature, reaction, viewpoint, and thinking between men and women, far from occasioning concern, should be regarded as highly beneficial to mankind, both individually and collectively. Many orders of universe creatures are created in dual phases of personality manifestation. Among mortals, Material Sons, and midsoniters, this difference is described as male and female; among seraphim, cherubim, and Morontia Companions, it has been denominated positive or aggressive and negative or retiring. Such dual associations greatly multiply versatility and overcome inherent limitations, even as do certain triune associations in the Paradise-Havona system.

Men and women need each other in their morontial and spiritual as well as in their mortal careers. The differences in viewpoint between male and female persist even beyond the first life and throughout the local and superuniverse ascensions. And even in Havona, the pilgrims who were once men and women will still be aiding each other in the Paradise ascent. Never, even in the Corps of the Finality, will the creature metamorphose so far as to obliterate the personality trends that humans call male and female; always will these two basic variations of humankind continue to intrigue, stimulate, encourage, and assist each other; always will they be mutually dependent on co-operation in the solution of perplexing universe problems and in the overcoming of manifold cosmic difficulties.

While the sexes never can hope fully to understand each other, they are effectively complementary, and though co-operation is often more or less personally antagonistic, it is capable of maintaining and reproducing society. Marriage is an institution designed to compose sex differences, meanwhile effecting the continuation of civilization and insuring the reproduction of the race.

Marriage is the mother of all human institutions, for it leads directly to home founding and home maintenance, which is the structural basis of society. The family is vitally linked to the mechanism of self-maintenance; it is the sole hope of race perpetuation under the mores of civilization, while at the same time it most effectively provides certain highly satisfactory forms of self-gratification. The family is man's greatest purely human achievement, combining as it does the evolution of the biologic relations of male and female with the social relations of husband and wife.

7. THE IDEALS OF FAMILY LIFE

Sex mating is instinctive, children are the natural result, and the family thus automatically comes into existence. As are the families of the race or nation, so is its society. If the families are good, the society is likewise good. The great cultural stability of the Jewish and of the Chinese peoples lies in the strength of their family groups.

Woman's instinct to love and care for children conspired to make her the interested party in promoting marriage and primitive family life. Man was only forced into home building by the pressure of the later mores and social conventions; he was slow to take an interest in the establishment of marriage and home because the sex act imposes no biologic consequences upon him.

Sex association is natural, but marriage is social and has always been regulated by the mores. The mores (religious, moral, and ethical), together with property, pride, and chivalry, stabilize the institutions of marriage and family. Whenever the mores fluctuate, there is fluctuation in the stability of the home-marriage institution. Marriage is now passing out of the property stage into the personal era. Formerly man protected woman because she was his chattel, and she obeyed for the same reason. Regardless of its merits this system did provide stability. Now, woman is no longer regarded as property, and new mores are emerging designed to stabilize the marriage-home institution:

1. The new role of religion—the teaching that parental experience is essential, the idea of procreating cosmic citizens, the enlarged understanding of the privilege of procreation—giving sons to the Father.

2. The new role of science—procreation is becoming more and more voluntary, subject to man's control. In ancient times lack of understanding insured the appearance of children in the absence of all desire therefor.

3. The new function of pleasure lures—this introduces a new factor into racial survival; ancient man exposed undesired children to die; moderns refuse to bear them.

4. The enhancement of parental instinct—each generation now tends to eliminate from the reproductive stream of the race those individuals in whom parental instinct is insufficiently strong to insure the procreation of children, the prospective parents of the next generation.

But the home as an institution, a partnership between one man and one woman, dates more specifically from the days of Dalamatia, about one-half million years ago, the monogamous practices of Andon and his immediate descendants having been abandoned long before. Family life, however, was not much to boast of before the days of the Nodites and the later Adamites. Adam and Eve exerted a lasting influence on all mankind; for the first time in the history of the world men and women were observed working side by side in the Garden. The Edenic ideal, the whole family as gardeners, was a new idea on Urantia.

The early family embraced a related working group, including the slaves, all living in one dwelling. Marriage and family life have not always been identical but have of necessity been closely associated. Woman always wanted the individual family, and eventually she had her way.

Love of offspring is almost universal and is of distinct survival value. The ancients always sacrificed the mother's interests for the welfare of the child; an Eskimo mother even yet licks her baby in lieu of washing. But primitive mothers only nourished and cared for their children when very young; like the animals, they discarded them as soon as they grew up. Enduring and continuous human associations have never been founded on biologic affection alone. The animals love their children; man—civilized man—loves his children's children. The higher the civilization, the greater the joy of parents in the children's advancement and success; thus the new and higher realization of *name* pride comes into existence.

The large families among ancient peoples were not necessarily affectional. Many children were desired because:

1. They were valuable as laborers.
2. They were old-age insurance.
3. Daughters were salable.
4. Family pride required extension of name.
5. Sons afforded protection and defense.
6. Ghost fear produced a dread of being alone.
7. Certain religions required offspring.

Ancestor worshipers view the failure to have sons as the supreme calamity for all time and eternity. They desire above all else to have sons to officiate in the post-mortem feasts, to offer the required sacrifices for the ghost's progress through spiritland.

Among ancient savages, discipline of children was begun very early; and the child early realized that disobedience meant failure or even death just as it did to the animals. It is civilization's protection of the child from the natural consequences of foolish conduct that contributes so much to modern insubordination.

Eskimo children thrive on so little discipline and correction simply because they are naturally docile little animals; the children of both the red and the yellow men are almost equally tractable. But in races containing Andite inheritance, children are not so placid; these more imaginative and adventurous youths require more training and discipline. Modern problems of child culture are rendered increasingly difficult by:

1. The large degree of race mixture.
2. Artificial and superficial education.
3. Inability of the child to gain culture by imitating parents—the parents are absent from the family picture so much of the time.

The olden ideas of family discipline were biologic, growing out of the realization that parents were creators of the child's being. The advancing ideals of family life are leading to the concept that bringing a child into the world, instead of conferring certain parental rights, entails the supreme responsibility of human existence.

Civilization regards the parents as assuming all duties, the child as having all the rights. Respect of the child for his parents arises, not in knowledge of the obligation implied in parental procreation, but naturally grows as a result of the care, training, and affection which are lovingly displayed in assisting the child to win the battle of life. The true parent is engaged in a continuous service-ministry which the wise child comes to recognize and appreciate.

In the present industrial and urban era the marriage institution is evolving along new economic lines. Family life has become more and more costly, while children, who used to be an asset, have become economic liabilities. But the security of civilization itself still rests on the growing willingness of one generation to invest in the welfare of the next and future generations. And any attempt to shift parental responsibility to state or church will prove suicidal to the welfare and advancement of civilization.

Marriage, with children and consequent family life, is stimulative of the highest potentials in human nature and simultaneously provides the ideal avenue for the expression of these quickened attributes of mortal personality. The family provides for the biologic perpetuation of the human species. The home is the natural social arena wherein the ethics of blood brotherhood may be grasped by the growing children. The family is the fundamental unit of fraternity in which parents and children learn those lessons of patience, altruism, tolerance, and forbearance which are so essential to the realization of brotherhood among all men.

Human society would be greatly improved if the civilized races would more generally return to the family-council practices of the Andites. They did not maintain the patriarchal or autocratic form of family government. They were very brotherly and associative, freely and frankly discussing every proposal and regulation of a family nature. They were ideally fraternal in all their family government. In an ideal family filial and parental affection are both augmented by fraternal devotion.

Family life is the progenitor of true morality, the ancestor of the consciousness of loyalty to duty. The enforced associations of family life stabilize personality and stimulate its growth through the compulsion of necessitous adjustment to other and diverse personalities. But even more, a true family—a good family—reveals to the parental procreators the attitude of the Creator to his children, while at the same time such true parents portray to their children the first of a long series of ascending disclosures of the love of the Paradise parent of all universe children.

8. DANGERS OF SELF-GRATIFICATION

The great threat against family life is the menacing rising tide of self-gratification, the modern pleasure mania. The prime incentive to marriage used to be economic; sex attraction was secondary. Marriage, founded on self-maintenance, led to self-perpetuation and concomitantly provided one of the most desirable forms of self-gratification. It is the only institution of human society which embraces all three of the great incentives for living.

Originally, property was the basic institution of self-maintenance, while marriage functioned as the unique institution of self-perpetuation. Although food satisfaction, play, and humor, along with periodic sex indulgence, were means of self-gratification, it remains a fact that the evolving mores have failed to build any distinct institution of self-gratification. And it is due to this failure to evolve specialized techniques of pleasurable enjoyment that all human institutions are so completely shot through with this pleasure pursuit. Property accumulation is becoming an instrument for augmenting all forms of self-gratification, while marriage is often viewed only as a means of pleasure. And this overindulgence, this widely spread pleasure mania, now constitutes the greatest threat that has ever been leveled at the social evolutionary institution of family life, the home.

The violet race introduced a new and only imperfectly realized characteristic into the experience of humankind—the play instinct coupled with the sense of humor. It was there in measure in the Sangiks and Andonites, but the Adamic strain elevated this primitive propensity into the *potential of pleasure*, a new and glorified form of self-gratification. The basic type of self-gratification, aside from appeasing hunger, is sex gratification, and this form of sensual pleasure was enormously heightened by the blending of the Sangiks and the Andites.

There is real danger in the combination of restlessness, curiosity, adventure, and pleasure-abandon characteristic of the post-Andite races. The hunger of the soul cannot be satisfied with physical pleasures; the love of home and children is not augmented by the unwise pursuit of pleasure. Though you exhaust the resources of art, color, sound, rhythm, music, and adornment of person, you cannot hope thereby to elevate the soul or to nourish the spirit. Vanity and fashion cannot minister to home building and child culture; pride and rivalry are powerless to enhance the survival qualities of succeeding generations.

Advancing celestial beings all enjoy rest and the ministry of the reversion directors. All efforts to obtain wholesome diversion and to engage in uplifting play are sound; refreshing sleep, rest, recreation, and all pastimes which prevent the boredom of monotony are worth while. Competitive games, storytelling, and even the taste of good food may serve as forms of self-gratification. (When you use salt to savor food, pause to consider that, for almost a million years, man could obtain salt only by dipping his food in ashes.)

Let man enjoy himself; let the human race find pleasure in a thousand and one ways; let evolutionary mankind explore all forms of legitimate self-gratification, the fruits of the long upward biologic struggle. Man has well earned some of his present-day joys and pleasures. But look you well to the goal of destiny! Pleasures are indeed suicidal if they succeed in destroying property, which has become the institution of self-maintenance; and self-gratifications have indeed cost a fatal price if they bring about the collapse of marriage, the decadence of family life, and the destruction of the home—man's supreme evolutionary acquirement and civilization's only hope of survival.

[Presented by the Chief of Seraphim stationed on Urantia.]

PAPER 85
THE ORIGINS OF WORSHIP

PRIMITIVE religion had a biologic origin, a natural evolutionary development, aside from moral associations and apart from all spiritual influences. The higher animals have fears but no illusions, hence no religion. Man creates his primitive religions out of his fears and by means of his illusions.

In the evolution of the human species, worship in its primitive manifestations appears long before the mind of man is capable of formulating the more complex concepts of life now and in the hereafter which deserve to be called religion. Early religion was wholly intellectual in nature and was entirely predicated on associational circumstances. The objects of worship were altogether suggestive; they consisted of the things of nature which were close at hand, or which loomed large in the commonplace experience of the simple-minded primitive Urantians.

When religion once evolved beyond nature worship, it acquired roots of spirit origin but was nevertheless always conditioned by the social environment. As nature worship developed, man's concepts envisioned a division of labor in the supermortal world; there were nature spirits for lakes, trees, waterfalls, rain, and hundreds of other ordinary terrestrial phenomena.

At one time or another mortal man has worshiped everything on the face of the earth, including himself. He has also worshiped about everything imaginable in the sky and beneath the surface of the earth. Primitive man feared all manifestations of power; he worshiped every natural phenomenon he could not comprehend. The observation of powerful natural forces, such as storms, floods, earthquakes, landslides, volcanoes, fire, heat, and cold, greatly impressed the expanding mind of man. The inexplicable things of life are still termed "acts of God" and "mysterious dispensations of Providence."

1. WORSHIP OF STONES AND HILLS

The first object to be worshiped by evolving man was a stone. Today the Kateri people of southern India still worship a stone, as do numerous tribes in northern India. Jacob slept on a stone because he venerated it; he even anointed it. Rachel concealed a number of sacred stones in her tent.

Stones first impressed early man as being out of the ordinary because of the manner in which they would so suddenly appear on the surface of a cultivated field or pasture. Men failed to take into account either erosion or the results of the overturning of soil. Stones also greatly impressed early peoples because of their frequent resemblance to animals. The attention of civilized man is arrested by numerous stone formations in the mountains which so much resemble the faces of animals and even men. But the most profound influence was exerted by meteoric stones which primitive humans beheld hurtling through the atmosphere in flaming grandeur. The shooting star was awesome to early man, and he easily believed that such blazing streaks marked the passage of a spirit on its way to earth. No wonder men were led to worship such phenomena, especially when they subsequently discovered the meteors. And this led to greater reverence for all other stones. In Bengal many worship a meteor which fell to earth in A.D. 1880.

All ancient clans and tribes had their sacred stones, and most modern peoples manifest a degree of veneration for certain types of stones—their jewels. A group of five stones was reverenced in India; in Greece it was a cluster of thirty; among the red men it was usually a circle of stones. The Romans always threw a stone into the air when invoking Jupiter. In India even to this day a stone can be used as a witness. In some regions a stone may be employed as a talisman of the law, and by its prestige an offender can be haled into court. But simple mortals do not always identify Deity with an object of reverent ceremony. Such fetishes are many times mere symbols of the real object of worship.

The ancients had a peculiar regard for holes in stones. Such porous rocks were supposed to be unusually efficacious in curing diseases. Ears were not perforated to carry stones, but the stones were put in to keep the ear holes open. Even in modern times superstitious persons make holes in coins. In Africa the natives make much ado over their fetish stones. In fact, among all backward tribes and peoples stones are still held in superstitious veneration. Stone worship is even now widespread over the world. The tombstone is a surviving symbol of images and idols which were carved in stone in connection with beliefs in ghosts and the spirits of departed fellow beings.

Hill worship followed stone worship, and the first hills to be venerated were large stone formations. It presently became the custom to believe that the gods inhabited the mountains, so that high elevations of land were worshiped for this additional reason. As time passed, certain mountains were associated with certain gods and therefore became holy. The ignorant and superstitious aborigines believed that caves led to the underworld, with its evil spirits and demons, in contrast with the mountains, which were identified with the later evolving concepts of good spirits and deities.

2. WORSHIP OF PLANTS AND TREES

Plants were first feared and then worshiped because of the intoxicating liquors which were derived therefrom. Primitive man believed that intoxication rendered one divine. There was supposed to be something unusual and sacred about such an experience. Even in modern times alcohol is known as "spirits."

Early man looked upon sprouting grain with dread and superstitious awe. The Apostle Paul was not the first to draw profound spiritual lessons from, and predicate religious beliefs on, the sprouting grain.

The cults of tree worship are among the oldest religious groups. All early marriages were held under the trees, and when women desired children, they would sometimes be found out in the forest affectionately embracing a sturdy oak. Many plants and trees were venerated because of their real or fancied medicinal powers. The savage believed that all chemical effects were due to the direct activity of supernatural forces.

Ideas about tree spirits varied greatly among different tribes and races. Some trees were indwelt by kindly spirits; others harbored the deceptive and cruel. The Finns believed that most trees were occupied by kind spirits. The Swiss long mistrusted the trees, believing they contained tricky spirits. The inhabitants of

India and eastern Russia regard the tree spirits as being cruel. The Patagonians still worship trees, as did the early Semites. Long after the Hebrews ceased tree worship, they continued to venerate their various deities in the groves. Except in China, there once existed a universal cult of the *tree of life.*

The belief that water or precious metals beneath the earth's surface can be detected by a wooden divining rod is a relic of the ancient tree cults. The Maypole, the Christmas tree, and the superstitious practice of rapping on wood perpetuate certain of the ancient customs of tree worship and the later-day tree cults.

Many of these earliest forms of nature veneration became blended with the later evolving techniques of worship, but the earliest mind-adjutant-activated types of worship were functioning long before the newly awakening religious nature of mankind became fully responsive to the stimulus of spiritual influences.

3. THE WORSHIP OF ANIMALS

Primitive man had a peculiar and fellow feeling for the higher animals. His ancestors had lived with them and even mated with them. In southern Asia it was early believed that the souls of men came back to earth in animal form. This belief was a survival of the still earlier practice of worshiping animals.

Early men revered the animals for their power and their cunning. They thought the keen scent and the farseeing eyes of certain creatures betokened spirit guidance. The animals have all been worshiped by one race or another at one time or another. Among such objects of worship were creatures that were regarded as half human and half animal, such as centaurs and mermaids.

The Hebrews worshiped serpents down to the days of King Hezekiah, and the Hindus still maintain friendly relations with their house snakes. The Chinese worship of the dragon is a survival of the snake cults. The wisdom of the serpent was a symbol of Greek medicine and is still employed as an emblem by modern physicians. The art of snake charming has been handed down from the days of the female shamans of the *snake love cult,* who, as the result of daily snake bites, became immune, in fact, became genuine venom addicts and could not get along without this poison.

The worship of insects and other animals was promoted by a later misinterpretation of the golden rule—doing to others (every form of life) as you would be done by. The ancients once believed that all winds were produced by the wings of birds and therefore both feared and worshiped all winged creatures. The early Nordics thought that eclipses were caused by a wolf that devoured a portion of the sun or moon. The Hindus often show Vishnu with a horse's head. Many times an animal symbol stands for a forgotten god or a vanished cult. Early in evolutionary religion the lamb became the typical sacrificial animal and the dove the symbol of peace and love.

In religion, symbolism may be either good or bad just to the extent that the symbol does or does not displace the original worshipful idea. And symbolism must not be confused with direct idolatry wherein the material object is directly and actually worshiped.

4. WORSHIP OF THE ELEMENTS

Mankind has worshiped earth, air, water, and fire. The primitive races venerated springs and worshiped rivers. Even now in Mongolia there flourishes an influential river cult. Baptism became a religious ceremonial in Babylon, and the Greeks practiced the annual ritual bath. It was easy for the ancients to imagine that the spirits dwelt in the bubbling springs, gushing fountains, flowing rivers, and raging torrents. Moving waters vividly impressed these simple minds with beliefs of spirit animation and supernatural power. Sometimes a drowning man would be refused succor for fear of offending some river god.

Many things and numerous events have functioned as religious stimuli to different peoples in different ages. A rainbow is yet worshiped by many of the hill tribes of India. In both India and Africa the rainbow is thought to be a gigantic celestial snake; Hebrews and Christians regard it as "the bow of promise." Likewise, influences regarded as beneficent in one part of the world may be looked upon as malignant in other regions. The east wind is a god in South America, for it brings rain; in India it is a devil because it brings dust and causes drought. The ancient Bedouins believed that a nature spirit produced the sand whirls, and even in the times of Moses belief in nature spirits was strong enough to insure their perpetuation in Hebrew theology as angels of fire, water, and air.

Clouds, rain, and hail have all been feared and worshiped by numerous primitive tribes and by many of the early nature cults. Windstorms with thunder and lightning overawed early man. He was so impressed with these elemental disturbances that thunder was regarded as the voice of an angry god. The worship of fire and the fear of lightning were linked together and were widespread among many early groups.

Fire was mixed up with magic in the minds of primitive fear-ridden mortals. A devotee of magic will vividly remember one positive chance result in the practice of his magic formulas, while he nonchalantly forgets a score of negative results, out-and-out failures. Fire reverence reached its height in Persia, where it long persisted. Some tribes worshiped fire as a deity itself; others revered it as the flaming symbol of the purifying and purging spirit of their venerated deities. Vestal virgins were charged with the duty of watching sacred fires, and in the twentieth century candles still burn as a part of the ritual of many religious services.

5. WORSHIP OF THE HEAVENLY BODIES

The worship of rocks, hills, trees, and animals naturally developed up through fearful veneration of the elements to the deification of the sun, moon, and stars. In India and elsewhere the stars were regarded as the glorified souls of great men who had departed from the life in the flesh. The Chaldean star cultists considered themselves to be the children of the sky father and the earth mother.

Moon worship preceded sun worship. Veneration of the moon was at its height during the hunting era, while sun worship became the chief religious ceremony of the subsequent agricultural ages. Solar worship first took extensive root in India, and there it persisted the longest. In Persia sun veneration gave rise to the later Mithraic cult. Among many peoples the sun was regarded as the ancestor of their kings. The Chaldeans put the sun in the center of "the seven circles of the universe." Later civilizations honored the sun by giving its name to the first day of the week.

The sun god was supposed to be the mystic father of the virgin-born sons of destiny who ever and anon were thought to be bestowed as saviors upon favored races. These supernatural infants were always put adrift upon some sacred river to be rescued in an extraordinary manner, after which they would grow up to become miraculous personalities and the deliverers of their peoples.

6. WORSHIP OF MAN

Having worshiped everything else on the face of the earth and in the heavens above, man has not hesitated to honor himself with such adoration. The simple-minded savage makes no clear distinction between beasts, men, and gods.

Early man regarded all unusual persons as superhuman, and he so feared such beings as to hold them in reverential awe; to some degree he literally worshiped them. Even having twins was regarded as being either very lucky or very unlucky. Lunatics, epileptics, and the feeble-minded were often worshiped by their normal-minded fellows, who believed that such abnormal beings were indwelt by the gods. Priests, kings, and prophets were worshiped; the holy men of old were looked upon as inspired by the deities.

Tribal chiefs died and were *deified.* Later, distinguished souls passed on and were *sainted.* Unaided evolution never originated gods higher than the glorified, exalted, and evolved spirits of deceased humans. In early evolution religion creates its own gods. In the course of revelation the Gods formulate religion. Evolutionary religion creates its gods in the image and likeness of mortal man; revelatory religion seeks to evolve and transform mortal man into the image and likeness of God.

The ghost gods, who are of supposed human origin, should be distinguished from the nature gods, for nature worship did evolve a pantheon—nature spirits elevated to the position of gods. The nature cults continued to develop along with the later appearing ghost cults, and each exerted an influence upon the other. Many religious systems embraced a dual concept of deity, nature gods and ghost gods; in some theologies these concepts are confusingly intertwined, as is illustrated by Thor, a ghost hero who was also master of the lightning.

But the worship of man by man reached its height when temporal rulers commanded such veneration from their subjects and, in substantiation of such demands, claimed to have descended from deity.

7. THE ADJUTANTS OF WORSHIP AND WISDOM

Nature worship may seem to have arisen naturally and spontaneously in the minds of primitive men and women, and so it did; but there was operating all this time in these same primitive minds the sixth adjutant spirit, which had been bestowed upon these peoples as a directing influence of this phase of human evolution. And this spirit was constantly stimulating the worship urge of the human species, no matter how primitive its first manifestations might be. The spirit of worship gave definite origin to the human impulse to worship, notwithstanding that animal fear motivated the expression of worshipfulness, and that its early practice became centered upon objects of nature.

You must remember that feeling, not thinking, was the guiding and controlling influence in all evolutionary development. To the primitive mind there is little difference between fearing, shunning, honoring, and worshiping.

When the worship urge is admonished and directed by wisdom—meditative and experiential thinking—it then begins to develop into the phenomenon of real religion. When the seventh adjutant spirit, the spirit of wisdom, achieves effective ministration, then in worship man begins to turn away from nature and natural objects to the God of nature and to the eternal Creator of all things natural.

[Presented by a Brilliant Evening Star of Nebadon.]

PAPER 86

EARLY EVOLUTION OF RELIGION

THE evolution of religion from the preceding and primitive worship urge is not dependent on revelation. The normal functioning of the human mind under the directive influence of the sixth and seventh mind-adjutants of universal spirit bestowal is wholly sufficient to insure such development.

Man's earliest prereligious fear of the forces of nature gradually became religious as nature became personalized, spiritized, and eventually deified in human consciousness. Religion of a primitive type was therefore a natural biologic consequence of the psychologic inertia of evolving animal minds after such minds had once entertained concepts of the supernatural.

1. CHANCE: GOOD LUCK AND BAD LUCK

Aside from the natural worship urge, early evolutionary religion had its roots of origin in the human experiences of chance—so-called luck, commonplace happenings. Primitive man was a food hunter. The results of hunting must ever vary, and this gives certain origin to those experiences which man interprets as *good luck* and *bad luck.* Mischance was a great factor in the lives of men and women who lived constantly on the ragged edge of a precarious and harassed existence.

The limited intellectual horizon of the savage so concentrates the attention upon chance that luck becomes a constant factor in his life. Primitive Urantians struggled for existence, not for a standard of living; they lived lives of peril in which chance played an important role. The constant dread of unknown and unseen calamity hung over these savages as a cloud of despair which effectively eclipsed every pleasure; they lived in constant dread of doing something that would bring bad luck. Superstitious savages always feared a run of good luck; they viewed such good fortune as a certain harbinger of calamity.

This ever-present dread of bad luck was paralyzing. Why work hard and reap bad luck—nothing for something—when one might drift along and encounter good luck—something for nothing? Unthinking men forget good luck—take it for granted—but they painfully remember bad luck.

Early man lived in uncertainty and in constant fear of chance—bad luck. Life was an exciting game of chance; existence was a gamble. It is no wonder that partially civilized people still believe in chance and evince lingering predispositions to gambling. Primitive man alternated between two potent interests: the passion of getting something for nothing and the fear of getting nothing for something. And this gamble of existence was the main interest and the supreme fascination of the early savage mind.

The later herders held the same views of chance and luck, while the still later agriculturists were increasingly conscious that crops were immediately influenced by many things over which man had little or no control. The farmer found himself the victim of drought, floods, hail, storms, pests, and plant diseases, as well as heat and cold. And as all of these natural influences affected individual prosperity, they were regarded as good luck or bad luck.

This notion of chance and luck strongly pervaded the philosophy of all ancient peoples. Even in recent times in the Wisdom of Solomon it is said: "I returned and saw that the race is not to the swift, nor the battle to the strong, neither bread to the wise, nor riches to men of understanding, nor favor to men of skill; but fate and chance befall them all. For man knows not his fate; as fishes are taken in an evil net, and as birds are caught in a snare, so are the sons of men snared in an evil time when it falls suddenly upon them."

2. THE PERSONIFICATION OF CHANCE

Anxiety was a natural state of the savage mind. When men and women fall victims to excessive anxiety, they are simply reverting to the natural estate of their far-distant ancestors; and when anxiety becomes actually painful, it inhibits activity and unfailingly institutes evolutionary changes and biologic adaptations. Pain and suffering are essential to progressive evolution.

The struggle for life is so painful that certain backward tribes even yet howl and lament over each new sunrise. Primitive man constantly asked, "Who is tormenting me?" Not finding a material source for his miseries, he settled upon a spirit explanation. And so was religion born of the fear of the mysterious, the awe of the unseen, and the dread of the unknown. Nature fear thus became a factor in the struggle for existence first because of chance and then because of mystery.

The primitive mind was logical but contained few ideas for intelligent association; the savage mind was uneducated, wholly unsophisticated. If one event followed another, the savage considered them to be cause and effect. What civilized man regards as superstition was just plain ignorance in the savage. Mankind has been slow to learn that there is not necessarily any relationship between purposes and results. Human beings are only just beginning to realize that the reactions of existence appear between acts and their consequences. The savage strives to personalize everything intangible and abstract, and thus both nature and chance become personalized as ghosts—spirits—and later on as gods.

Man naturally tends to believe that which he deems best for him, that which is in his immediate or remote interest; self-interest largely obscures logic. The difference between the minds of savage and civilized men is more one of content than of nature, of degree rather than of quality.

But to continue to ascribe things difficult of comprehension to supernatural causes is nothing less than a lazy and convenient way of avoiding all forms of intellectual hard work. Luck is merely a term coined to cover the inexplicable in any age of human existence; it designates those phenomena which men are unable or unwilling to penetrate. Chance is a word which signifies that man is too ignorant or too indolent to determine causes. Men regard a natural occurrence as an accident or as bad luck only when they are destitute of curiosity and imagination, when the races lack initiative and adventure. Exploration of the phenomena of life sooner or later destroys man's belief in chance, luck, and so-called accidents, substituting therefor a universe of law and order wherein all effects are preceded by definite causes. Thus is the fear of existence replaced by the joy of living.

The savage looked upon all nature as alive, as possessed by something. Civilized man still kicks and curses those inanimate objects which get in his way and bump him. Primitive man never regarded anything as accidental; always was everything intentional. To primitive man the domain of fate, the function of luck, the spirit world, was just as unorganized and haphazard as was primitive society. Luck was looked upon as the whimsical and temperamental reaction of the spirit world; later on, as the humor of the gods.

But all religions did not develop from animism. Other concepts of the supernatural were contemporaneous with animism, and these beliefs also led to worship. Naturalism is not a religion—it is the offspring of religion.

3. DEATH—THE INEXPLICABLE

Death was the supreme shock to evolving man, the most perplexing combination of chance and mystery. Not the sanctity of life but the shock of death inspired fear and thus effectively fostered religion. Among savage peoples death was ordinarily due to violence, so that nonviolent death became increasingly mysterious. Death as a natural and expected end of life was not clear to the consciousness of primitive people, and it has required age upon age for man to realize its inevitability.

Early man accepted life as a fact, while he regarded death as a visitation of some sort. All races have their legends of men who did not die, vestigial traditions of the early attitude toward death. Already in the human mind there existed the nebulous concept of a hazy and unorganized spirit world, a domain whence came all that is inexplicable in human life, and death was added to this long list of unexplained phenomena.

All human disease and natural death was at first believed to be due to spirit influence. Even at the present time some civilized races regard disease as having been produced by "the enemy" and depend upon religious ceremonies to effect healing. Later and more complex systems of theology still ascribe death to the action of the spirit world, all of which has led to such doctrines as original sin and the fall of man.

It was the realization of impotency before the mighty forces of nature, together with the recognition of human weakness before the visitations of sickness and death, that impelled the savage to seek for help from the supermaterial world, which he vaguely visualized as the source of these mysterious vicissitudes of life.

4. THE DEATH-SURVIVAL CONCEPT

The concept of a supermaterial phase of mortal personality was born of the unconscious and purely accidental association of the occurrences of everyday life plus the ghost dream. The simultaneous dreaming about a departed chief by several members of his tribe seemed to constitute convincing evidence that the old chief had really returned in some form. It was all very real to the savage who would awaken from such dreams reeking with sweat, trembling, and screaming.

The dream origin of the belief in a future existence explains the tendency always to imagine unseen things in the terms of things seen. And presently this new dream-ghost-future-life concept began effectively to antidote the death fear associated with the biologic instinct of self-preservation.

Early man was also much concerned about his breath, especially in cold climates, where it appeared as a cloud when exhaled. The *breath of life* was regarded as the one phenomenon which differentiated the living and the dead. He knew the breath could leave the body, and his dreams of doing all sorts of queer things while asleep convinced him that there was something immaterial about a human being. The most primitive idea of the human soul, the ghost, was derived from the breath-dream idea-system.

Eventually the savage conceived of himself as a double—body and breath. The breath minus the body equaled a spirit, a ghost. While having a very definite human origin, ghosts, or spirits, were regarded as superhuman. And this belief in the existence of disembodied spirits seemed to explain the occurrence of the unusual, the extraordinary, the infrequent, and the inexplicable.

The primitive doctrine of survival after death was not necessarily a belief in immortality. Beings who could not count over twenty could hardly conceive of infinity and eternity; they rather thought of recurring incarnations.

The orange race was especially given to belief in transmigration and reincarnation. This idea of reincarnation originated in the observance of hereditary and trait resemblance of offspring to ancestors. The custom of naming children after grandparents and other ancestors was due to belief in reincarnation. Some later-day races believed that man died from three to seven times. This belief (residual from the teachings of Adam about the mansion worlds), and many other remnants of revealed religion, can be found among the otherwise absurd doctrines of twentieth-century barbarians.

Early man entertained no ideas of hell or future punishment. The savage looked upon the future life as just like this one, minus all ill luck. Later on, a separate destiny for good ghosts and bad ghosts—heaven and hell—was conceived. But since many primitive races believed that man entered the next life just as he left this one, they did not relish the idea of becoming old and decrepit. The aged much preferred to be killed before becoming too infirm.

Almost every group had a different idea regarding the destiny of the ghost soul. The Greeks believed that weak men must have weak souls; so they invented Hades as a fit place for the reception of such anemic souls; these unrobust specimens were also supposed to have shorter shadows. The early Andites thought their ghosts returned to the ancestral homelands. The Chinese and Egyptians once believed that soul and body remained together. Among the Egyptians this led to careful tomb construction and efforts at body preservation. Even modern peoples seek to arrest the decay of the dead. The Hebrews conceived that a phantom replica of the individual went down to Sheol; it could not return to the land of the living. They did make that important advance in the doctrine of the evolution of the soul.

5. THE GHOST-SOUL CONCEPT

The nonmaterial part of man has been variously termed ghost, spirit, shade, phantom, specter, and latterly *soul.* The soul was early man's dream double; it was in every way exactly like the mortal himself except that it was not responsive to touch. The belief in dream doubles led directly to the notion that all things animate and inanimate had souls as well as men. This concept tended long to perpetuate the nature-spirit beliefs; the Eskimos still conceive that everything in nature has a spirit.

The ghost soul could be heard and seen, but not touched. Gradually the dream life of the race so developed and expanded the activities of this evolving spirit world that death was finally regarded as "giving up the ghost." All primitive tribes, except those little above animals, have developed some concept of the soul. As civilization advances, this superstitious concept of the soul is destroyed, and man is wholly dependent on revelation and personal religious experience for his new idea of the soul as the joint creation of the God-knowing mortal mind and its indwelling divine spirit, the Thought Adjuster.

Early mortals usually failed to differentiate the concepts of an indwelling spirit and a soul of evolutionary nature. The savage was much confused as to whether the ghost soul was native to the body or was an external agency in possession of the body. The absence of reasoned thought in the presence of perplexity explains the gross inconsistencies of the savage view of souls, ghosts, and spirits.

The soul was thought of as being related to the body as the perfume to the flower. The ancients believed that the soul could leave the body in various ways, as in:

1. Ordinary and transient fainting.
2. Sleeping, natural dreaming.
3. Coma and unconsciousness associated with disease and accidents.
4. Death, permanent departure.

The savage looked upon sneezing as an abortive attempt of the soul to escape from the body. Being awake and on guard, the body was able to thwart the soul's attempted escape. Later on, sneezing was always accompanied by some religious expression, such as "God bless you!"

Early in evolution sleep was regarded as proving that the ghost soul could be absent from the body, and it was believed that it could be called back by speaking or shouting the sleeper's name. In other forms of unconsciousness the soul was thought to be farther away, perhaps trying to escape for good—impending death. Dreams were looked upon as the experiences of the soul during sleep while temporarily absent from the body. The savage believes his dreams to be just as real as any part of his waking experience. The ancients made a practice of awaking sleepers gradually so that the soul might have time to get back into the body.

All down through the ages men have stood in awe of the apparitions of the night season, and the Hebrews were no exception. They truly believed that God spoke to them in dreams, despite the injunctions of Moses against this idea. And Moses was right, for ordinary dreams are not the methods employed by the personalities of the spiritual world when they seek to communicate with material beings.

The ancients believed that souls could enter animals or even inanimate objects. This culminated in the werewolf ideas of animal identification. A person could be a law-abiding citizen by day, but when he fell asleep, his soul could enter a wolf or some other animal to prowl about on nocturnal depredations.

Primitive men thought that the soul was associated with the breath, and that its qualities could be imparted or transferred by the breath. The brave chief would breathe upon the newborn child, thereby imparting courage. Among early Christians the ceremony of bestowing the Holy Spirit was accompanied by breathing on the candidates. Said the Psalmist: "By the word of the Lord were the heavens made and all the host of them by the breath of his mouth." It was long the custom of the eldest son to try to catch the last breath of his dying father.

The shadow came, later on, to be feared and revered equally with the breath. The reflection of oneself in the water was also sometimes looked upon as proof of the double self, and mirrors were regarded with superstitious awe. Even now many civilized persons turn the mirror to the wall in the event of death. Some backward tribes still believe that the making of pictures, drawings, models, or images removes all or a part of the soul from the body; hence such are forbidden.

The soul was generally thought of as being identified with the breath, but it was also located by various peoples in the head, hair, heart, liver, blood, and fat. The "crying out of Abel's blood from the ground" is expressive of the onetime belief in the presence of the ghost in the blood. The Semites taught that the soul resided in the bodily fat, and among many the eating of animal fat was taboo. Head hunting was a method of capturing an enemy's soul, as was scalping. In recent times the eyes have been regarded as the windows of the soul.

Those who held the doctrine of three or four souls believed that the loss of one soul meant discomfort, two illness, three death. One soul lived in the breath, one in the head, one in the hair, one in the heart. The sick were advised to stroll about in the open air with the hope of recapturing their strayed souls. The greatest of the medicine men were supposed to exchange the sick soul of a diseased person for a new one, the "new birth."

The children of Badonan developed a belief in two souls, the breath and the shadow. The early Nodite races regarded man as consisting of two persons, soul and body. This philosophy of human existence was later reflected in the Greek viewpoint. The Greeks themselves believed in three souls; the vegetative resided in the stomach, the animal in the heart, the intellectual in the head. The Eskimos believe that man has three parts: body, soul, and name.

6. THE GHOST-SPIRIT ENVIRONMENT

Man inherited a natural environment, acquired a social environment, and imagined a ghost environment. The state is man's reaction to his natural environment, the home to his social environment, the church to his illusory ghost environment.

Very early in the history of mankind the realities of the imaginary world of ghosts and spirits became universally believed, and this newly imagined spirit world became a power in primitive society. The mental and moral life of all mankind was modified for all time by the appearance of this new factor in human thinking and acting.

Into this major premise of illusion and ignorance, mortal fear has packed all of the subsequent superstition and religion of primitive peoples. This was man's only religion up to the times of revelation, and today many of the world's races have only this crude religion of evolution.

As evolution progressed, good luck became associated with good spirits and bad luck with bad spirits. The discomfort of enforced adaptation to a changing environment was regarded as ill luck, the displeasure of the spirit ghosts. Primitive man slowly evolved religion out of his innate worship urge and his misconception of chance. Civilized man provides schemes of insurance to overcome these chance occurrences; modern science puts an actuary with mathematical reckoning in the place of fictitious spirits and whimsical gods.

Each passing generation smiles at the foolish superstitions of its ancestors while it goes on entertaining those fallacies of thought and worship which will give cause for further smiling on the part of enlightened posterity.

But at last the mind of primitive man was occupied with thoughts which transcended all of his inherent biologic urges; at last man was about to evolve an art of living based on something more than response to material stimuli. The beginnings of a primitive philosophic life policy were emerging. A supernatural standard of living was about to appear, for, if the spirit ghost in anger visits ill luck and in pleasure good fortune, then must human conduct be regulated accordingly. The concept of right and wrong had at last evolved; and all of this long before the times of any revelation on earth.

With the emergence of these concepts, there was initiated the long and wasteful struggle to appease the ever-displeased spirits, the slavish bondage to evolutionary religious fear, that long waste of human effort upon tombs, temples, sacrifices, and priesthoods. It was a terrible and frightful price to pay, but it was worth all it cost, for man therein achieved a natural consciousness of relative right and wrong; human ethics was born!

7. THE FUNCTION OF PRIMITIVE RELIGION

The savage felt the need of insurance, and he therefore willingly paid his burdensome premiums of fear, superstition, dread, and priest gifts toward his policy of magic insurance against ill luck. Primitive religion was simply the payment of premiums on insurance against the perils of the forests; civilized man pays material premiums against the accidents of industry and the exigencies of modern modes of living.

Modern society is removing the business of insurance from the realm of priests and religion, placing it in the domain of economics. Religion is concerning itself increasingly with the insurance of life beyond the grave. Modern men, at least those who think, no longer pay wasteful premiums to control luck. Religion is slowly ascending to higher philosophic levels in contrast with its former function as a scheme of insurance against bad luck.

But these ancient ideas of religion prevented men from becoming fatalistic and hopelessly pessimistic; they believed they could at least do something to influence fate. The religion of ghost fear impressed upon men that they must *regulate their conduct,* that there was a supermaterial world which was in control of human destiny.

Modern civilized races are just emerging from ghost fear as an explanation of luck and the commonplace inequalities of existence. Mankind is achieving emancipation from the bondage of the ghost-spirit explanation of ill luck. But while men are giving up the erroneous doctrine of a spirit cause of the vicissitudes of life, they exhibit a surprising willingness to accept an almost equally fallacious teaching which bids them attribute all human inequalities to political misadaptation, social injustice, and industrial competition. But new legislation, increasing philanthropy, and more industrial reorganization, however good in and of themselves, will not remedy the facts of birth and the accidents of living. Only comprehension of facts and wise manipulation within the laws of nature will enable man to get what he wants and to avoid what he does not want. Scientific knowledge, leading to scientific action, is the only antidote for so-called accidental ills.

Industry, war, slavery, and civil government arose in response to the social evolution of man in his natural environment; religion similarly arose as his response to the illusory environment of the imaginary ghost world. Religion was an evolutionary development of self-maintenance, and it has worked, notwithstanding that it was originally erroneous in concept and utterly illogical.

Primitive religion prepared the soil of the human mind, by the powerful and awesome force of false fear, for the bestowal of a bona fide spiritual force of supernatural origin, the Thought Adjuster. And the divine Adjusters have ever since labored to transmute God-fear into God-love. Evolution may be slow, but it is unerringly effective.

[Presented by an Evening Star of Nebadon.]

PAPER 87
THE GHOST CULTS

THE ghost cult evolved as an offset to the hazards of bad luck; its primitive religious observances were the outgrowth of anxiety about bad luck and of the inordinate fear of the dead. None of these early religions had much to do with the recognition of Deity or with reverence for the superhuman; their rites were mostly negative, designed to avoid, expel, or coerce ghosts. The ghost cult was nothing more nor less than insurance against disaster; it had nothing to do with investment for higher and future returns.

Man has had a long and bitter struggle with the ghost cult. Nothing in human history is designed to excite more pity than this picture of man's abject slavery to ghost-spirit fear. With the birth of this very fear mankind started on the upgrade of religious evolution. Human imagination cast off from the shores of self and will not again find anchor until it arrives at the concept of a true Deity, a real God.

1. GHOST FEAR

Death was feared because death meant the liberation of another ghost from its physical body. The ancients did their best to prevent death, to avoid the trouble of having to contend with a new ghost. They were always anxious to induce the ghost to leave the scene of death, to embark on the journey to deadland. The ghost was feared most of all during the supposed transition period between its emergence at the time of death and its later departure for the ghost homeland, a vague and primitive concept of pseudo heaven.

Though the savage credited ghosts with supernatural powers, he hardly conceived of them as having supernatural intelligence. Many tricks and stratagems were practiced in an effort to hoodwink and deceive the ghosts; civilized man still pins much faith on the hope that an outward manifestation of piety will in some manner deceive even an omniscient Deity.

The primitives feared sickness because they observed it was often a harbinger of death. If the tribal medicine man failed to cure an afflicted individual, the sick man was usually removed from the family hut, being taken to a smaller one or left in the open air to die alone. A house in which death had occurred was usually destroyed; if not, it was always avoided, and this fear prevented early man from building substantial dwellings. It also militated against the establishment of permanent villages and cities.

The savages sat up all night and talked when a member of the clan died; they feared they too would die if they fell asleep in the vicinity of a corpse. Contagion from the corpse substantiated the fear of the dead, and all peoples, at one time or another, have employed elaborate purification ceremonies designed to cleanse an individual after contact with the dead. The ancients believed that light must be provided for a corpse; a dead body was never permitted to remain in the dark. In the twentieth century, candles are still burned in death chambers, and men still sit up with the dead. So-called civilized man has hardly yet completely eliminated the fear of dead bodies from his philosophy of life.

But despite all this fear, men still sought to trick the ghost. If the death hut was not destroyed, the corpse was removed through a hole in the wall, never by way of the door. These measures were taken to confuse the ghost, to prevent its tarrying, and to insure against its return. Mourners also returned from a funeral by a different road, lest the ghost follow. Backtracking and scores of other tactics were practiced to insure that the ghost would not return from the grave. The sexes often exchanged clothes in order to deceive the ghost. Mourning costumes were designed to disguise survivors; later on, to show respect for the dead and thus appease the ghosts.

2. GHOST PLACATION

In religion the negative program of ghost placation long preceded the positive program of spirit coercion and supplication. The first acts of human worship were phenomena of defense, not reverence. Modern man deems it wise to insure against fire; so the savage thought it the better part of wisdom to provide insurance against ghost bad luck. The effort to secure this protection constituted the techniques and rituals of the ghost cult.

It was once thought that the great desire of a ghost was to be quickly "laid" so that it might proceed undisturbed to deadland. Any error of commission or omission in the acts of the living in the ritual of laying the ghost was sure to delay its progress to ghostland. This was believed to be displeasing to the ghost, and an angered ghost was supposed to be a source of calamity, misfortune, and unhappiness.

The funeral service originated in man's effort to induce the ghost soul to depart for its future home, and the funeral sermon was originally designed to instruct the new ghost how to get there. It was the custom to provide food and clothes for the ghost's journey, these articles being placed in or near the grave. The savage believed that it required from three days to a year to "lay the ghost" —to get it away from the vicinity of the grave. The Eskimos still believe that the soul stays with the body three days.

Silence or mourning was observed after a death so that the ghost would not be attracted back home. Self-torture—wounds—was a common form of mourning. Many advanced teachers tried to stop this, but they failed. Fasting and other forms of self-denial were thought to be pleasing to the ghosts, who took pleasure in the discomfort of the living during the transition period of lurking about before their actual departure for deadland.

Long and frequent periods of mourning inactivity were one of the great obstacles to civilization's advancement. Weeks and even months of each year were literally wasted in this nonproductive and useless mourning. The fact that professional mourners were hired for funeral occasions indicates that mourning was a ritual, not an evidence of sorrow. Moderns may mourn the dead out of respect and because of bereavement, but the ancients did this because of *fear.*

The names of the dead were never spoken. In fact, they were often banished from the language. These names became taboo, and in this way the languages were constantly impoverished. This eventually produced a multiplication of symbolic speech and figurative expression, such as "the name or day one never mentions."

The ancients were so anxious to get rid of a ghost that they offered it everything which might have been desired during life. Ghosts wanted wives and servants; a well-to-do savage expected that at least one slave wife would be buried alive at his death. It later became the custom for a widow to commit suicide on her husband's grave. When a child died, the mother, aunt, or grandmother was often strangled in order that an adult ghost might accompany and care for the child ghost. And those who thus gave up their lives usually did so willingly; indeed, had they lived in violation of custom, their fear of ghost wrath would have denuded life of such few pleasures as the primitives enjoyed.

It was customary to dispatch a large number of subjects to accompany a dead chief; slaves were killed when their master died that they might serve him in ghostland. The Borneans still provide a courier companion; a slave is speared to death to make the ghost journey with his deceased master. Ghosts of murdered persons were believed to be delighted to have the ghosts of their murderers as slaves; this notion motivated men to head hunting.

Ghosts supposedly enjoyed the smell of food; food offerings at funeral feasts were once universal. The primitive method of saying grace was, before eating, to throw a bit of food into the fire for the purpose of appeasing the spirits, while mumbling a magic formula.

The dead were supposed to use the ghosts of the tools and weapons that were theirs in life. To break an article was to "kill it," thus releasing its ghost to pass on for service in ghostland. Property sacrifices were also made by burning or burying. Ancient funeral wastes were enormous. Later races made paper models and substituted drawings for real objects and persons in these death sacrifices. It was a great advance in civilization when the inheritance of kin replaced the burning and burying of property. The Iroquois Indians made many reforms in funeral waste. And this conservation of property enabled them to become the most powerful of the northern red men. Modern man is not supposed to fear ghosts, but custom is strong, and much terrestrial wealth is still consumed on funeral rituals and death ceremonies.

3. ANCESTOR WORSHIP

The advancing ghost cult made ancestor worship inevitable since it became the connecting link between common ghosts and the higher spirits, the evolving gods. The early gods were simply glorified departed humans.

Ancestor worship was originally more of a fear than a worship, but such beliefs did definitely contribute to the further spread of ghost fear and worship. Devotees of the early ancestor-ghost cults even feared to yawn lest a malignant ghost enter their bodies at such a time.

The custom of adopting children was to make sure that someone would provide offerings after death for the peace and progress of the soul. The savage lived in fear of the ghosts of his fellows and spent his spare time planning for the safe conduct of his own ghost after death.

Most tribes instituted an all-souls' feast at least once a year. The Romans had twelve ghost feasts and accompanying ceremonies each year. Half the days of the year were dedicated to some sort of ceremony associated with these ancient cults. One Roman emperor tried to reform these practices by reducing the number of feast days to 135 a year.

The ghost cult was in continuous evolution. As ghosts were envisioned as passing from the incomplete to the higher phase of existence, so did the cult eventually progress to the worship of spirits, and even gods. But regardless of varying beliefs in more advanced spirits, all tribes and races once believed in ghosts.

4. GOOD AND BAD SPIRIT GHOSTS

Ghost fear was the fountainhead of all world religion; and for ages many tribes clung to the old belief in one class of ghosts. They taught that man had good luck when the ghost was pleased, bad luck when he was angered.

As the cult of ghost fear expanded, there came about the recognition of higher types of spirits, spirits not definitely identifiable with any individual human. They were graduate or glorified ghosts who had progressed beyond the domain of ghostland to the higher realms of spiritland.

The notion of two kinds of spirit ghosts made slow but sure progress throughout the world. This new dual spiritism did not have to spread from tribe to tribe; it sprang up independently all over the world. In influencing the expanding evolutionary mind, the power of an idea lies not in its reality or reasonableness but rather in its *vividness* and the universality of its ready and simple application.

Still later the imagination of man envisioned the concept of both good and bad supernatural agencies; some ghosts never evolved to the level of good spirits. The early monospiritism of ghost fear was gradually evolving into a dual spiritism, a new concept of the invisible control of earthly affairs. At last good luck and bad luck were pictured as having their respective controllers. And of the two classes, the group that brought bad luck were believed to be the more active and numerous.

When the doctrine of good and bad spirits finally matured, it became the most widespread and persistent of all religious beliefs. This dualism represented a great religio-philosophic advance because it enabled man to account for both good luck and bad luck while at the same time believing in supermortal beings who were to some extent consistent in their behavior. The spirits could be counted on to be either good or bad; they were not thought of as being completely temperamental as the early ghosts of the monospiritism of most primitive religions had been conceived to be. Man was at last able to conceive of supermortal forces that were consistent in behavior, and this was one of the most momentous discoveries of truth in the entire history of the evolution of religion and in the expansion of human philosophy.

Evolutionary religion has, however, paid a terrible price for the concept of dual spiritism. Man's early philosophy was able to reconcile spirit constancy with the vicissitudes of temporal fortune only by postulating two kinds of spirits, one good and the other bad. And while this belief did enable man to reconcile the variables of chance with a concept of unchanging supermortal forces, this doctrine has ever since made it difficult for religionists to conceive of cosmic unity. The gods of evolutionary religion have generally been opposed by the forces of darkness.

The tragedy of all this lies in the fact that, when these ideas were taking root in the primitive mind of man, there really were no bad or disharmonious spirits in all the world. Such an unfortunate situation did not develop until after the Caligastic rebellion and only persisted until Pentecost. The concept of good and evil as cosmic co-ordinates is, even in the twentieth century, very much alive in human philosophy; most of the world's religions still carry this cultural birthmark of the long-gone days of the emerging ghost cults.

5. THE ADVANCING GHOST CULT

Primitive man viewed the spirits and ghosts as having almost unlimited rights but no duties; the spirits were thought to regard man as having manifold duties but no rights. The spirits were believed to look down upon man as constantly failing in the discharge of his spiritual duties. It was the general belief of mankind that ghosts levied a continuous tribute of service as the price of noninterference in human affairs, and the least mischance was laid to ghost activities. Early humans were so afraid they might overlook some honor due the gods that, after they had sacrificed to all known spirits, they did another turn to the "unknown gods," just to be thoroughly safe.

And now the simple ghost cult is followed by the practices of the more advanced and relatively complex spirit-ghost cult, the service and worship of the higher spirits as they evolved in man's primitive imagination. Religious ceremonial must keep pace with spirit evolution and progress. The expanded cult was but the art of self-maintenance practiced in relation to belief in supernatural beings, self-adjustment to spirit environment. Industrial and military organizations were adjustments to natural and social environments. And as marriage arose to meet the demands of bisexuality, so did religious organization evolve in response to the belief in higher spirit forces and spiritual beings. Religion represents man's adjustment to his illusions of the mystery of chance. Spirit fear and subsequent worship were adopted as insurance against misfortune, as prosperity policies.

The savage visualizes the good spirits as going about their business, requiring little from human beings. It is the bad ghosts and spirits who must be kept in good humor. Accordingly, primitive peoples paid more attention to their malevolent ghosts than to their benign spirits.

Human prosperity was supposed to be especially provocative of the envy of evil spirits, and their method of retaliation was to strike back through a human agency and by the technique of the *evil eye.* That phase of the cult which had to do with spirit avoidance was much concerned with the machinations of the evil eye. The fear of it became almost world-wide. Pretty women were veiled to protect them from the evil eye; subsequently many women who desired to be considered beautiful adopted this practice. Because of this fear of bad spirits, children were seldom allowed out after dark, and the early prayers always included the petition, "deliver us from the evil eye."

The Koran contains a whole chapter devoted to the evil eye and magic spells, and the Jews fully believed in them. The whole phallic cult grew up as a defense against the evil eye. The organs of reproduction were thought to be the only fetish which could render it powerless. The evil eye gave origin to the first superstitions respecting prenatal marking of children, maternal impressions, and the cult was at one time well-nigh universal.

Envy is a deep-seated human trait; therefore did primitive man ascribe it to his early gods. And since man had once practiced deception upon the ghosts, he soon began to deceive the spirits. Said he, "If the spirits are jealous of our beauty and prosperity, we will disfigure ourselves and speak lightly of our success." Early humility was not, therefore, debasement of ego but rather an attempt to foil and deceive the envious spirits.

The method adopted to prevent the spirits from becoming jealous of human prosperity was to heap vituperation upon some lucky or much loved thing or person. The custom of depreciating complimentary remarks regarding oneself or family had its origin in this way, and it eventually evolved into civilized modesty, restraint, and courtesy. In keeping with the same motive, it became the fashion to look ugly. Beauty aroused the envy of spirits; it betokened sinful human pride. The savage sought for an ugly name. This feature of the cult was a great handicap to the advancement of art, and it long kept the world somber and ugly.

Under the spirit cult, life was at best a gamble, the result of spirit control. One's future was not the result of effort, industry, or talent except as they might be utilized to influence the spirits. The ceremonies of spirit propitiation constituted a heavy burden, rendering life tedious and virtually unendurable. From age to age and from generation to generation, race after race has sought to improve this superghost doctrine, but no generation has ever yet dared to wholly reject it.

The intention and will of the spirits were studied by means of omens, oracles, and signs. And these spirit messages were interpreted by divination, soothsaying, magic, ordeals, and astrology. The whole cult was a scheme designed to placate, satisfy, and buy off the spirits through this disguised bribery.

And thus there grew up a new and expanded world philosophy consisting in:

1. *Duty*—those things which must be done to keep the spirits favorably disposed, at least neutral.

2. *Right*—the correct conduct and ceremonies designed to win the spirits actively to one's interests.

3. *Truth*—the correct understanding of, and attitude toward, spirits, and hence toward life and death.

It was not merely out of curiosity that the ancients sought to know the future; they wanted to dodge ill luck. Divination was simply an attempt to avoid trouble. During these times, dreams were regarded as prophetic, while everything out of the ordinary was considered an omen. And even today the civilized races are cursed with the belief in signs, tokens, and other superstitious remnants of the advancing ghost cult of old. Slow, very slow, is man to abandon those methods whereby he so gradually and painfully ascended the evolutionary scale of life.

6. COERCION AND EXORCISM

When men believed in ghosts only, religious ritual was more personal, less organized, but the recognition of higher spirits necessitated the employment of "higher spiritual methods" in dealing with them. This attempt to improve upon, and to elaborate, the technique of spirit propitiation led directly to the creation of defenses against the spirits. Man felt helpless indeed before the uncontrollable forces operating in terrestrial life, and his feeling of inferiority drove him to attempt to find some compensating adjustment, some technique for evening the odds in the one-sided struggle of man versus the cosmos.

In the early days of the cult, man's efforts to influence ghost action were confined to propitiation, attempts by bribery to buy off ill luck. As the evolution of the ghost cult progressed to the concept of good as well as bad spirits, these ceremonies turned toward attempts of a more positive nature, efforts to win good luck. Man's religion no longer was completely negativistic, nor did he stop with the effort to win good luck; he shortly began to devise schemes whereby he could compel spirit co-operation. No longer does the religionist stand defenseless before the unceasing demands of the spirit phantasms of his own devising; the savage is beginning to invent weapons wherewith he may coerce spirit action and compel spirit assistance.

Man's first efforts at defense were directed against the ghosts. As the ages passed, the living began to devise methods of resisting the dead. Many techniques were developed for frightening ghosts and driving them away, among which may be cited the following:

1. Cutting off the head and tying up the body in the grave.
2. Stoning the death house.
3. Castration or breaking the legs of the corpse.
4. Burying under stones, one origin of the modern tombstone.
5. Cremation, a later-day invention to prevent ghost trouble.
6. Casting the body into the sea.
7. Exposure of the body to be eaten by wild animals.

Ghosts were supposed to be disturbed and frightened by noise; shouting, bells, and drums drove them away from the living; and these ancient methods are still in vogue at "wakes" for the dead. Foul-smelling concoctions were utilized to banish unwelcome spirits. Hideous images of the spirits were constructed so that they would flee in haste when they beheld themselves. It was believed that dogs could detect the approach of ghosts, and that they gave warning by howling; that cocks would crow when they were near. The use of a cock as a weather vane is in perpetuation of this superstition.

Water was regarded as the best protection against ghosts. Holy water was superior to all other forms, water in which the priests had washed their feet. Both fire and water were believed to constitute impassable barriers to ghosts. The Romans carried water three times around the corpse; in the twentieth century the body is sprinkled with holy water, and hand washing at the cemetery is still a Jewish ritual. Baptism was a feature of the later water ritual; primitive bathing was a religious ceremony. Only in recent times has bathing become a sanitary practice.

But man did not stop with ghost coercion; through religious ritual and other practices he was soon attempting to compel spirit action. Exorcism was the employment of one spirit to control or banish another, and these tactics were also utilized for frightening ghosts and spirits. The dual-spiritism concept of good and bad forces offered man ample opportunity to attempt to pit one agency against another, for, if a powerful man could vanquish a weaker one, then certainly a strong spirit could dominate an inferior ghost. Primitive cursing was a coercive practice designed to overawe minor spirits. Later this custom expanded into the pronouncing of curses upon enemies.

It was long believed that by reverting to the usages of the more ancient mores the spirits and demigods could be forced into desirable action. Modern man is guilty of the same procedure. You address one another in common, everyday language, but when you engage in prayer, you resort to the older style of another generation, the so-called solemn style.

This doctrine also explains many religious-ritual reversions of a sex nature, such as temple prostitution. These reversions to primitive customs were considered sure guards against many calamities. And with these simple-minded peoples all such performances were entirely free from what modern man would term promiscuity.

Next came the practice of ritual vows, soon to be followed by religious pledges and sacred oaths. Most of these oaths were accompanied by self-torture and self-mutilation; later on, by fasting and prayer. Self-denial was subsequently looked upon as being a sure coercive; this was especially true in the matter of sex suppression. And so primitive man early developed a decided austerity in his religious practices, a belief in the efficacy of self-torture and self-denial as rituals capable of coercing the unwilling spirits to react favorably toward all such suffering and deprivation.

Modern man no longer attempts openly to coerce the spirits, though he still evinces a disposition to bargain with Deity. And he still swears, knocks on wood, crosses his fingers, and follows expectoration with some trite phrase; once it was a magical formula.

7. NATURE OF CULTISM

The cult type of social organization persisted because it provided a symbolism for the preservation and stimulation of moral sentiments and religious loyalties. The cult grew out of the traditions of "old families" and was perpetuated as an established institution; all families have a cult of some sort. Every inspiring ideal grasps for some perpetuating symbolism—seeks some technique for cultural manifestation which will insure survival and augment realization—and the cult achieves this end by fostering and gratifying emotion.

From the dawn of civilization every appealing movement in social culture or religious advancement has developed a ritual, a symbolic ceremonial. The more this ritual has been an unconscious growth, the stronger it has gripped its devotees. The cult preserved sentiment and satisfied emotion, but it has always been the greatest obstacle to social reconstruction and spiritual progress.

Notwithstanding that the cult has always retarded social progress, it is regrettable that so many modern believers in moral standards and spiritual ideals have no adequate symbolism—no cult of mutual support—nothing to *belong* to. But a religious cult cannot be manufactured; it must grow. And those of no two groups will be identical unless their rituals are arbitrarily standardized by authority.

The early Christian cult was the most effective, appealing, and enduring of any ritual ever conceived or devised, but much of its value has been destroyed in a scientific age by the destruction of so many of its original underlying tenets. The Christian cult has been devitalized by the loss of many fundamental ideas.

In the past, truth has grown rapidly and expanded freely when the cult has been elastic, the symbolism expansile. Abundant truth and an adjustable cult have favored rapidity of social progression. A meaningless cult vitiates religion when it attempts to supplant philosophy and to enslave reason; a genuine cult grows.

Regardless of the drawbacks and handicaps, every new revelation of truth has given rise to a new cult, and even the restatement of the religion of Jesus must develop a new and appropriate symbolism. Modern man must find some adequate symbolism for his new and expanding ideas, ideals, and loyalties. This enhanced symbol must arise out of religious living, spiritual experience. And this higher symbolism of a higher civilization must be predicated on the concept of the Fatherhood of God and be pregnant with the mighty ideal of the brotherhood of man.

The old cults were too egocentric; the new must be the outgrowth of applied love. The new cult must, like the old, foster sentiment, satisfy emotion, and promote loyalty; but it must do more: It must facilitate spiritual progress, enhance cosmic meanings, augment moral values, encourage social development, and stimulate a high type of personal religious living. The new cult must provide supreme goals of living which are both temporal and eternal—social and spiritual.

No cult can endure and contribute to the progress of social civilization and individual spiritual attainment unless it is based on the biologic, sociologic, and religious significance of the *home.* A surviving cult must symbolize that which is permanent in the presence of unceasing change; it must glorify that which unifies the stream of ever-changing social metamorphosis. It must recognize true meanings, exalt beautiful relations, and glorify the good values of real nobility.

But the great difficulty of finding a new and satisfying symbolism is because modern men, as a group, adhere to the scientific attitude, eschew superstition, and abhor ignorance, while as individuals they all crave mystery and venerate the unknown. No cult can survive unless it embodies some masterful mystery and conceals some worthful unattainable. Again, the new symbolism must not only be significant for the group but also meaningful to the individual. The forms of any serviceable symbolism must be those which the individual can carry out on his own initiative, and which he can also enjoy with his fellows. If the new cult could only be dynamic instead of static, it might really contribute something worth while to the progress of mankind, both temporal and spiritual.

But a cult—a symbolism of rituals, slogans, or goals—will not function if it is too complex. And there must be the demand for devotion, the response of loyalty. Every effective religion unerringly develops a worthy symbolism, and its devotees would do well to prevent the crystallization of such a ritual into cramping, deforming, and stifling stereotyped ceremonials which can only handicap and retard all social, moral, and spiritual progress. No cult can survive if it retards moral growth and fails to foster spiritual progress. The cult is the skeletal structure around which grows the living and dynamic body of personal spiritual experience—true religion.

[Presented by a Brilliant Evening Star of Nebadon.]

PAPER 88

FETISHES, CHARMS, AND MAGIC

THE concept of a spirit's entering into an inanimate object, an animal, or a human being, is a very ancient and honorable belief, having prevailed since the beginning of the evolution of religion. This doctrine of spirit possession is nothing more nor less than *fetishism.* The savage does not necessarily worship the fetish; he very logically worships and reverences the spirit resident therein.

At first, the spirit of a fetish was believed to be the ghost of a dead man; later on, the higher spirits were supposed to reside in fetishes. And so the fetish cult eventually incorporated all of the primitive ideas of ghosts, souls, spirits, and demon possession.

1. BELIEF IN FETISHES

Primitive man always wanted to make anything extraordinary into a fetish; chance therefore gave origin to many. A man is sick, something happens, and he gets well. The same thing is true of the reputation of many medicines and the chance methods of treating disease. Objects connected with dreams were likely to be converted into fetishes. Volcanoes, but not mountains, became fetishes; comets, but not stars. Early man regarded shooting stars and meteors as indicating the arrival on earth of special visiting spirits.

The first fetishes were peculiarly marked pebbles, and "sacred stones" have ever since been sought by man; a string of beads was once a collection of sacred stones, a battery of charms. Many tribes had fetish stones, but few have survived as have the Kaaba and the Stone of Scone. Fire and water were also among the early fetishes, and fire worship, together with belief in holy water, still survives.

Tree fetishes were a later development, but among some tribes the persistence of nature worship led to belief in charms indwelt by some sort of nature spirit. When plants and fruits became fetishes, they were taboo as food. The apple was among the first to fall into this category; it was never eaten by the Levantine peoples.

If an animal ate human flesh, it became a fetish. In this way the dog came to be the sacred animal of the Parsees. If the fetish is an animal and the ghost is permanently resident therein, then fetishism may impinge on reincarnation. In many ways the savages envied the animals; they did not feel superior to them and were often named after their favorite beasts.

When animals became fetishes, there ensued the taboos on eating the flesh of the fetish animal. Apes and monkeys, because of resemblance to man, early became fetish animals; later, snakes, birds, and swine were also similarly regarded.

At one time the cow was a fetish, the milk being taboo while the excreta were highly esteemed. The serpent was revered in Palestine, especially by the Phoenicians, who, along with the Jews, considered it to be the mouthpiece of evil spirits. Even many moderns believe in the charm powers of reptiles. From Arabia on through India to the snake dance of the Moqui tribe of red men the serpent has been revered.

Certain days of the week were fetishes. For ages Friday has been regarded as an unlucky day and the number thirteen as an evil numeral. The lucky numbers three and seven came from later revelations; four was the lucky number of primitive man and was derived from the early recognition of the four points of the compass. It was held unlucky to count cattle or other possessions; the ancients always opposed the taking of a census, "numbering the people."

Primitive man did not make an undue fetish out of sex; the reproductive function received only a limited amount of attention. The savage was natural minded, not obscene or prurient.

Saliva was a potent fetish; devils could be driven out by spitting on a person. For an elder or superior to spit on one was the highest compliment. Parts of the human body were looked upon as potential fetishes, particularly the hair and nails. The long-growing fingernails of the chiefs were highly prized, and the trimmings thereof were a powerful fetish. Belief in skull fetishes accounts for much of later-day head-hunting. The umbilical cord was a highly prized fetish; even today it is so regarded in Africa. Mankind's first toy was a preserved umbilical cord. Set with pearls, as was often done, it was man's first necklace.

Hunchbacked and crippled children were regarded as fetishes; lunatics were believed to be moon-struck. Primitive man could not distinguish between genius and insanity; idiots were either beaten to death or revered as fetish personalities. Hysteria increasingly confirmed the popular belief in witchcraft; epileptics often were priests and medicine men. Drunkenness was looked upon as a form of spirit possession; when a savage went on a spree, he put a leaf in his hair for the purpose of disavowing responsibility for his acts. Poisons and intoxicants became fetishes; they were deemed to be possessed.

Many people looked upon geniuses as fetish personalities possessed by a wise spirit. And these talented humans soon learned to resort to fraud and trickery for the advancement of their selfish interests. A fetish man was thought to be more than human; he was divine, even infallible. Thus did chiefs, kings, priests, prophets, and church rulers eventually wield great power and exercise unbounded authority.

2. EVOLUTION OF THE FETISH

It was a supposed preference of ghosts to indwell some object which had belonged to them when alive in the flesh. This belief explains the efficacy of many modern relics. The ancients always revered the bones of their leaders, and the skeletal remains of saints and heroes are still regarded with superstitious awe by many. Even today, pilgrimages are made to the tombs of great men.

Belief in relics is an outgrowth of the ancient fetish cult. The relics of modern religions represent an attempt to rationalize the fetish of the savage and thus elevate it to a place of dignity and respectability in the modern religious systems. It is heathenish to believe in fetishes and magic but supposedly all right to accept relics and miracles.

The hearth—fireplace—became more or less of a fetish, a sacred spot. The shrines and temples were at first fetish places because the dead were buried there. The fetish hut of the Hebrews was elevated by Moses to that place where it harbored a superfetish, the then existent concept of the law of God. But the Israelites never gave up the peculiar Canaanite belief in the stone altar: "And this stone which I have set up as a pillar shall be God's house." They truly believed that the spirit of their God dwelt in such stone altars, which were in reality fetishes.

The earliest images were made to preserve the appearance and memory of the illustrious dead; they were really monuments. Idols were a refinement of fetishism. The primitives believed that a ceremony of consecration caused the spirit to enter the image; likewise, when certain objects were blessed, they became charms.

Moses, in the addition of the second commandment to the ancient Dalamatian moral code, made an effort to control fetish worship among the Hebrews. He carefully directed that they should make no sort of image that might become consecrated as a fetish. He made it plain, "You shall not make a graven image or any likeness of anything that is in heaven above, or on the earth beneath, or in the waters of the earth." While this commandment did much to retard art among the Jews, it did lessen fetish worship. But Moses was too wise to attempt suddenly to displace the olden fetishes, and he therefore consented to the putting of certain relics alongside the law in the combined war altar and religious shrine which was the ark.

Words eventually became fetishes, more especially those which were regarded as God's words; in this way the sacred books of many religions have become fetishistic prisons incarcerating the spiritual imagination of man. Moses' very effort against fetishes became a supreme fetish; his commandment was later used to stultify art and to retard the enjoyment and adoration of the beautiful.

In olden times the fetish word of authority was a fear-inspiring *doctrine,* the most terrible of all tyrants which enslave men. A doctrinal fetish will lead mortal man to betray himself into the clutches of bigotry, fanaticism, superstition, intolerance, and the most atrocious of barbarous cruelties. Modern respect for wisdom and truth is but the recent escape from the fetish-making tendency up to the higher levels of thinking and reasoning. Concerning the accumulated fetish writings which various religionists hold as *sacred books,* it is not only believed that what is in the book is true, but also that every truth is contained in the book. If one of these sacred books happens to speak of the earth as being flat, then, for long generations, otherwise sane men and women will refuse to accept positive evidence that the planet is round.

The practice of opening one of these sacred books to let the eye chance upon a passage, the following of which may determine important life decisions or projects, is nothing more nor less than arrant fetishism. To take an oath on a "holy book" or to swear by some object of supreme veneration is a form of refined fetishism.

But it does represent real evolutionary progress to advance from the fetish fear of a savage chief's fingernail trimmings to the adoration of a superb collection of letters, laws, legends, allegories, myths, poems, and chronicles which, after all, reflect the winnowed moral wisdom of many centuries, at least up to the time and event of their being assembled as a "sacred book."

To become fetishes, words had to be considered inspired, and the invocation of supposed divinely inspired writings led directly to the establishment of the *authority* of the church, while the evolution of civil forms led to the fruition of the *authority* of the state.

3. TOTEMISM

Fetishism ran through all the primitive cults from the earliest belief in sacred stones, through idolatry, cannibalism, and nature worship, to totemism.

Totemism is a combination of social and religious observances. Originally it was thought that respect for the totem animal of supposed biologic origin insured the food supply. Totems were at one and the same time symbols of the group and their god. Such a god was the clan personified. Totemism was one phase of the attempted socialization of otherwise personal religion. The totem eventually evolved into the flag, or national symbol, of the various modern peoples.

A fetish bag, a medicine bag, was a pouch containing a reputable assortment of ghost-impregnated articles, and the medicine man of old never allowed his bag, the symbol of his power, to touch the ground. Civilized peoples in the twentieth century see to it that their flags, emblems of national consciousness, likewise never touch the ground.

The insignia of priestly and kingly office were eventually regarded as fetishes, and the fetish of the state supreme has passed through many stages of development, from clans to tribes, from suzerainty to sovereignty, from totems to flags. Fetish kings have ruled by "divine right," and many other forms of government have obtained. Men have also made a fetish of democracy, the exaltation and adoration of the common man's ideas when collectively called "public opinion." One man's opinion, when taken by itself, is not regarded as worth much, but when many men are collectively functioning as a democracy, this same mediocre judgment is held to be the arbiter of justice and the standard of righteousness.

4. MAGIC

Civilized man attacks the problems of a real environment through his science; savage man attempted to solve the real problems of an illusory ghost environment by magic. Magic was the technique of manipulating the conjectured spirit environment whose machinations endlessly explained the inexplicable; it was the art of obtaining voluntary spirit co-operation and of coercing involuntary spirit aid through the use of fetishes or other and more powerful spirits.

The object of magic, sorcery, and necromancy was twofold:

1. To secure insight into the future.
2. Favorably to influence environment.

The objects of science are identical with those of magic. Mankind is progressing from magic to science, not by meditation and reason, but rather through long experience, gradually and painfully. Man is gradually backing into the truth, beginning in error, progressing in error, and finally attaining the threshold of truth. Only with the arrival of the scientific method has he faced forward. But primitive man had to experiment or perish.

The fascination of early superstition was the mother of the later scientific curiosity. There was progressive dynamic emotion—fear plus curiosity—in these primitive superstitions; there was progressive driving power in the olden magic. These superstitions represented the emergence of the human desire to know and to control planetary environment.

Magic gained such a strong hold upon the savage because he could not grasp the concept of natural death. The later idea of original sin helped much to weaken the grip of magic on the race in that it accounted for natural death. It was at one time not at all uncommon for ten innocent persons to be put to death because of supposed responsibility for one natural death. This is one reason why ancient peoples did not increase faster, and it is still true of some African tribes. The accused individual usually confessed guilt, even when facing death.

Magic is natural to a savage. He believes that an enemy can actually be killed by practicing sorcery on his shingled hair or fingernail trimmings. The fatality of snake bites was attributed to the magic of the sorcerer. The difficulty in combating magic arises from the fact that fear can kill. Primitive peoples so feared magic that it did actually kill, and such results were sufficient to substantiate this erroneous belief. In case of failure there was always some plausible explanation; the cure for defective magic was more magic.

5. MAGICAL CHARMS

Since anything connected with the body could become a fetish, the earliest magic had to do with hair and nails. Secrecy attendant upon body elimination grew up out of fear that an enemy might get possession of something derived from the body and employ it in detrimental magic; all excreta of the body were therefore carefully buried. Public spitting was refrained from because of the fear that saliva would be used in deleterious magic; spittle was always covered. Even food remnants, clothing, and ornaments could become instruments of magic. The savage never left any remnants of his meal on the table. And all this was done through fear that one's enemies might use these things in magical rites, not from any appreciation of the hygienic value of such practices.

Magical charms were concocted from a great variety of things: human flesh, tiger claws, crocodile teeth, poison plant seeds, snake venom, and human hair. The bones of the dead were very magical. Even the dust from footprints could be used in magic. The ancients were great believers in love charms. Blood and other forms of bodily secretions were able to insure the magic influence of love.

Images were supposed to be effective in magic. Effigies were made, and when treated ill or well, the same effects were believed to rest upon the real person. When making purchases, superstitious persons would chew a bit of hard wood in order to soften the heart of the seller.

The milk of a black cow was highly magical; so also were black cats. The staff or wand was magical, along with drums, bells, and knots. All ancient objects were magical charms. The practices of a new or higher civilization were looked upon with disfavor because of their supposedly evil magical nature. Writing, printing, and pictures were long so regarded.

Primitive man believed that names must be treated with respect, especially names of the gods. The name was regarded as an entity, an influence distinct from the physical personality; it was esteemed equally with the soul and the shadow. Names were pawned for loans; a man could not use his name until it had been redeemed by payment of the loan. Nowadays one signs his name to a note. An individual's name soon became important in magic. The savage had two names; the important one was regarded as too sacred to use on ordinary occasions, hence the second or everyday name—a nickname. He never told his real name to strangers. Any experience of an unusual nature caused him to change his name; sometimes it was in an effort to cure disease or to stop bad luck. The savage could get a new name by buying it from the tribal chief; men still invest in titles and degrees. But among the most primitive tribes, such as the African Bushmen, individual names do not exist.

6. THE PRACTICE OF MAGIC

Magic was practiced through the use of wands, "medicine" ritual, and incantations, and it was customary for the practitioner to work unclothed. Women outnumbered the men among primitive magicians. In magic, "medicine" means mystery, not treatment. The savage never doctored himself; he never used medicines except on the advice of the specialists in magic. And the voodoo doctors of the twentieth century are typical of the magicians of old.

There was both a public and a private phase to magic. That performed by the medicine man, shaman, or priest was supposed to be for the good of the whole tribe. Witches, sorcerers, and wizards dispensed private magic, personal and selfish magic which was employed as a coercive method of bringing evil on one's enemies. The concept of dual spiritism, good and bad spirits, gave rise to the later beliefs in white and black magic. And as religion evolved, magic was the term applied to spirit operations outside one's own cult, and it also referred to older ghost beliefs.

Word combinations, the ritual of chants and incantations, were highly magical. Some early incantations finally evolved into prayers. Presently, imitative magic was practiced; prayers were acted out; magical dances were nothing but dramatic prayers. Prayer gradually displaced magic as the associate of sacrifice.

Gesture, being older than speech, was the more holy and magical, and mimicry was believed to have strong magical power. The red men often staged a buffalo dance in which one of their number would play the part of a buffalo and, in being caught, would insure the success of the impending hunt. The sex festivities of May Day were simply imitative magic, a suggestive appeal to the sex passions of the plant world. The doll was first employed as a magic talisman by the barren wife.

Magic was the branch off the evolutionary religious tree which eventually bore the fruit of a scientific age. Belief in astrology led to the development of astronomy; belief in a philosopher's stone led to the mastery of metals, while belief in magic numbers founded the science of mathematics.

But a world so filled with charms did much to destroy all personal ambition and initiative. The fruits of extra labor or of diligence were looked upon as magical. If a man had more grain in his field than his neighbor, he might be haled before the chief and charged with enticing this extra grain from the indolent neighbor's field. Indeed, in the days of barbarism it was dangerous to know very much; there was always the chance of being executed as a black artist.

Gradually science is removing the gambling element from life. But if modern methods of education should fail, there would be an almost immediate reversion to the primitive beliefs in magic. These superstitions still linger in the minds of many so-called civilized people. Language contains many fossils which testify that the race has long been steeped in magical superstition, such words as spellbound, ill-starred, possessions, inspiration, spirit away, ingenuity, entrancing, thunderstruck, and astonished. And intelligent human beings still believe in good luck, the evil eye, and astrology.

Ancient magic was the cocoon of modern science, indispensable in its time but now no longer useful. And so the phantasms of ignorant superstition agitated the primitive minds of men until the concepts of science could be born. Today, Urantia is in the twilight zone of this intellectual evolution. One half the world is grasping eagerly for the light of truth and the facts of scientific discovery, while the other half languishes in the arms of ancient superstition and but thinly disguised magic.

[Presented by a Brilliant Evening Star of Nebadon.]

PAPER 89

SIN, SACRIFICE, AND ATONEMENT

PRIMITIVE man regarded himself as being in debt to the spirits, as standing in need of redemption. As the savages looked at it, in justice the spirits might have visited much more bad luck upon them. As time passed, this concept developed into the doctrine of sin and salvation. The soul was looked upon as coming into the world under forfeit—original sin. The soul must be ransomed; a scapegoat must be provided. The head-hunter, in addition to practicing the cult of skull worship, was able to provide a substitute for his own life, a scapeman.

The savage was early possessed with the notion that spirits derive supreme satisfaction from the sight of human misery, suffering, and humiliation. At first, man was only concerned with sins of commission, but later he became exercised over sins of omission. And the whole subsequent sacrificial system grew up around these two ideas. This new ritual had to do with the observance of the propitiation ceremonies of sacrifice. Primitive man believed that something special must be done to win the favor of the gods; only advanced civilization recognizes a consistently even-tempered and benevolent God. Propitiation was insurance against immediate ill luck rather than investment in future bliss. And the rituals of avoidance, exorcism, coercion, and propitiation all merge into one another.

1. THE TABOO

Observance of a taboo was man's effort to dodge ill luck, to keep from offending the spirit ghosts by the avoidance of something. The taboos were at first nonreligious, but they early acquired ghost or spirit sanction, and when thus reinforced, they became lawmakers and institution builders. The taboo is the source of ceremonial standards and the ancestor of primitive self-control. It was the earliest form of societal regulation and for a long time the only one; it is still a basic unit of the social regulative structure.

The respect which these prohibitions commanded in the mind of the savage exactly equaled his fear of the powers who were supposed to enforce them. Taboos first arose because of chance experience with ill luck; later they were proposed by chiefs and shamans—fetish men who were thought to be directed by a spirit ghost, even by a god. The fear of spirit retribution is so great in the mind of a primitive that he sometimes dies of fright when he has violated a taboo, and this dramatic episode enormously strengthens the hold of the taboo on the minds of the survivors.

Among the earliest prohibitions were restrictions on the appropriation of women and other property. As religion began to play a larger part in the evolution of the taboo, the article resting under ban was regarded as unclean, subsequently as unholy. The records of the Hebrews are full of the mention of things clean and unclean, holy and unholy, but their beliefs along these lines were far less cumbersome and extensive than were those of many other peoples.

The seven commandments of Dalamatia and Eden, as well as the ten injunctions of the Hebrews, were definite taboos, all expressed in the same negative form as were the most ancient prohibitions. But these newer codes were truly emancipating in that they took the place of thousands of pre-existent taboos. And more than this, these later commandments definitely promised something in return for obedience.

The early food taboos originated in fetishism and totemism. The swine was sacred to the Phoenicians, the cow to the Hindus. The Egyptian taboo on pork has been perpetuated by the Hebraic and Islamic faiths. A variant of the food taboo was the belief that a pregnant woman could think so much about a certain food that the child, when born, would be the echo of that food. Such viands would be taboo to the child.

Methods of eating soon became taboo, and so originated ancient and modern table etiquette. Caste systems and social levels are vestigial remnants of olden prohibitions. The taboos were highly effective in organizing society, but they were terribly burdensome; the negative-ban system not only maintained useful and constructive regulations but also obsolete, outworn, and useless taboos.

There would, however, be no civilized society to sit in criticism upon primitive man except for these far-flung and multifarious taboos, and the taboo would never have endured but for the upholding sanctions of primitive religion. Many of the essential factors in man's evolution have been highly expensive, have cost vast treasure in effort, sacrifice, and self-denial, but these achievements of self-control were the real rungs on which man climbed civilization's ascending ladder.

2. THE CONCEPT OF SIN

The fear of chance and the dread of bad luck literally drove man into the invention of primitive religion as supposed insurance against these calamities. From magic and ghosts, religion evolved through spirits and fetishes to taboos. Every primitive tribe had its tree of forbidden fruit, literally the apple but figuratively consisting of a thousand branches hanging heavy with all sorts of taboos. And the forbidden tree always said, "Thou shalt not."

As the savage mind evolved to that point where it envisaged both good and bad spirits, and when the taboo received the solemn sanction of evolving religion, the stage was all set for the appearance of the new conception of *sin*. The idea of sin was universally established in the world before revealed religion ever made its entry. It was only by the concept of sin that natural death became logical to the primitive mind. Sin was the transgression of taboo, and death was the penalty of sin.

Sin was ritual, not rational; an act, not a thought. And this entire concept of sin was fostered by the lingering traditions of Dilmun and the days of a little paradise on earth. The tradition of Adam and the Garden of Eden also lent substance to the dream of a onetime "golden age" of the dawn of the races. And all this confirmed the ideas later expressed in the belief that man had his origin in a special creation, that he started his career in perfection, and that transgression of the taboos—sin—brought him down to his later sorry plight.

The habitual violation of a taboo became a vice; primitive law made vice a crime; religion made it a sin. Among the early tribes the violation of a taboo was a combined crime and sin. Community calamity was always regarded as punishment for tribal sin. To those who believed that prosperity and righteousness went together, the apparent prosperity of the wicked occasioned so much worry that it was necessary to invent hells for the punishment of taboo violators; the numbers of these places of future punishment have varied from one to five.

The idea of confession and forgiveness early appeared in primitive religion. Men would ask forgiveness at a public meeting for sins they intended to commit the following week. Confession was merely a rite of remission, also a public notification of defilement, a ritual of crying "unclean, unclean!" Then followed all the ritualistic schemes of purification. All ancient peoples practiced these meaningless ceremonies. Many apparently hygienic customs of the early tribes were largely ceremonial.

3. RENUNCIATION AND HUMILIATION

Renunciation came as the next step in religious evolution; fasting was a common practice. Soon it became the custom to forgo many forms of physical pleasure, especially of a sexual nature. The ritual of the fast was deeply rooted in many ancient religions and has been handed down to practically all modern theologic systems of thought.

Just about the time barbarian man was recovering from the wasteful practice of burning and burying property with the dead, just as the economic structure of the races was beginning to take shape, this new religious doctrine of renunciation appeared, and tens of thousands of earnest souls began to court poverty. Property was regarded as a spiritual handicap. These notions of the spiritual dangers of material possession were widespreadly entertained in the times of Philo and Paul, and they have markedly influenced European philosophy ever since.

Poverty was just a part of the ritual of the mortification of the flesh which, unfortunately, became incorporated into the writings and teachings of many religions, notably Christianity. Penance is the negative form of this ofttimes foolish ritual of renunciation. But all this taught the savage *self-control,* and that was a worth-while advancement in social evolution. Self-denial and self-control were two of the greatest social gains from early evolutionary religion. Self-control gave man a new philosophy of life; it taught him the art of augmenting life's fraction by lowering the denominator of personal demands instead of always attempting to increase the numerator of selfish gratification.

These olden ideas of self-discipline embraced flogging and all sorts of physical torture. The priests of the mother cult were especially active in teaching the virtue of physical suffering, setting the example by submitting themselves to castration. The Hebrews, Hindus, and Buddhists were earnest devotees of this doctrine of physical humiliation.

All through the olden times men sought in these ways for extra credits on the self-denial ledgers of their gods. It was once customary, when under some emotional stress, to make vows of self-denial and self-torture. In time these vows assumed the form of contracts with the gods and, in that sense, represented true evolutionary progress in that the gods were supposed to do something definite in return for this self-torture and mortification of the flesh. Vows were both negative and positive. Pledges of this harmful and extreme nature are best observed today among certain groups in India.

It was only natural that the cult of renunciation and humiliation should have paid attention to sexual gratification. The continence cult originated as a ritual among soldiers prior to engaging in battle; in later days it became the practice of "saints." This cult tolerated marriage only as an evil lesser than fornication. Many of the world's great religions have been adversely influenced by this ancient cult, but none more markedly than Christianity. The Apostle Paul was a devotee of this cult, and his personal views are reflected in the teachings which he fastened onto Christian theology: "It is good for a man not to touch a woman." "I would that all men were even as I myself." "I say, therefore, to the unmarried and widows, it is good for them to abide even as I." Paul well knew that such teachings were not a part of Jesus' gospel, and his acknowledgment of this is illustrated by his statement, "I speak this by permission and not by commandment." But this cult led Paul to look down upon women. And the pity of it all is that his personal opinions have long influenced the teachings of a great world religion. If the advice of the tentmaker-teacher were to be literally and universally obeyed, then would the human race come to a sudden and inglorious end. Furthermore, the involvement of a religion with the ancient continence cult leads directly to a war against marriage and the home, society's veritable foundation and the basic institution of human progress. And it is not to be wondered at that all such beliefs fostered the formation of celibate priesthoods in the many religions of various peoples.

Someday man should learn how to enjoy liberty without license, nourishment without gluttony, and pleasure without debauchery. Self-control is a better human policy of behavior regulation than is extreme self-denial. Nor did Jesus ever teach these unreasonable views to his followers.

4. ORIGINS OF SACRIFICE

Sacrifice as a part of religious devotions, like many other worshipful rituals, did not have a simple and single origin. The tendency to bow down before power and to prostrate oneself in worshipful adoration in the presence of mystery is foreshadowed in the fawning of the dog before its master. It is but one step from the impulse of worship to the act of sacrifice. Primitive man gauged the value of his sacrifice by the pain which he suffered. When the idea of sacrifice first attached itself to religious ceremonial, no offering was contemplated which was not productive of pain. The first sacrifices were such acts as plucking hair, cutting the flesh, mutilations, knocking out teeth, and cutting off fingers. As civilization advanced, these crude concepts of sacrifice were elevated to the level of the rituals of self-abnegation, asceticism, fasting, deprivation, and the later Christian doctrine of sanctification through sorrow, suffering, and the mortification of the flesh.

Early in the evolution of religion there existed two conceptions of the sacrifice: the idea of the gift sacrifice, which connoted the attitude of thanksgiving, and the debt sacrifice, which embraced the idea of redemption. Later there developed the notion of substitution.

Man still later conceived that his sacrifice of whatever nature might function as a message bearer to the gods; it might be as a sweet savor in the nostrils of deity. This brought incense and other aesthetic features of sacrificial rituals which developed into sacrificial feasting, in time becoming increasingly elaborate and ornate.

As religion evolved, the sacrificial rites of conciliation and propitiation replaced the older methods of avoidance, placation, and exorcism.

The earliest idea of the sacrifice was that of a neutrality assessment levied by ancestral spirits; only later did the idea of atonement develop. As man got away from the notion of the evolutionary origin of the race, as the traditions of the days of the Planetary Prince and the sojourn of Adam filtered down through time, the concept of sin and of original sin became widespread, so that sacrifice for accidental and personal sin evolved into the doctrine of sacrifice for the atonement of racial sin. The atonement of the sacrifice was a blanket insurance device which covered even the resentment and jealousy of an unknown god.

Surrounded by so many sensitive spirits and grasping gods, primitive man was face to face with such a host of creditor deities that it required all the priests, ritual, and sacrifices throughout an entire lifetime to get him out of spiritual debt. The doctrine of original sin, or racial guilt, started every person out in serious debt to the spirit powers.

Gifts and bribes are given to men; but when tendered to the gods, they are described as being dedicated, made sacred, or are called sacrifices. Renunciation was the negative form of propitiation; sacrifice became the positive form. The act of propitiation included praise, glorification, flattery, and even entertainment. And it is the remnants of these positive practices of the olden propitiation cult that constitute the modern forms of divine worship. Present-day forms of worship are simply the ritualization of these ancient sacrificial techniques of positive propitiation.

Animal sacrifice meant much more to primitive man than it could ever mean to modern races. These barbarians regarded the animals as their actual and near kin. As time passed, man became shrewd in his sacrificing, ceasing to offer up his work animals. At first he sacrificed the *best* of everything, including his domesticated animals.

It was no empty boast that a certain Egyptian ruler made when he stated that he had sacrificed: 113,433 slaves, 493,386 head of cattle, 88 boats, 2,756 golden images, 331,702 jars of honey and oil, 228,380 jars of wine, 680,714 geese, 6,744,428 loaves of bread, and 5,740,352 sacks of corn. And in order to do this he must needs have sorely taxed his toiling subjects.

Sheer necessity eventually drove these semisavages to eat the material part of their sacrifices, the gods having enjoyed the soul thereof. And this custom found justification under the pretense of the ancient sacred meal, a communion service according to modern usage.

5. SACRIFICES AND CANNIBALISM

Modern ideas of early cannibalism are entirely wrong; it was a part of the mores of early society. While cannibalism is traditionally horrible to modern civilization, it was a part of the social and religious structure of primitive society. Group interests dictated the practice of cannibalism. It grew up through the urge of necessity and persisted because of the slavery of superstition and ignorance. It was a social, economic, religious, and military custom.

Early man was a cannibal; he enjoyed human flesh, and therefore he offered it as a food gift to the spirits and his primitive gods. Since ghost spirits were merely modified men, and since food was man's greatest need, then food must likewise be a spirit's greatest need.

Cannibalism was once well-nigh universal among the evolving races. The Sangiks were all cannibalistic, but originally the Andonites were not, nor were the Nodites and Adamites; neither were the Andites until after they had become grossly admixed with the evolutionary races.

The taste for human flesh grows. Having been started through hunger, friendship, revenge, or religious ritual, the eating of human flesh goes on to habitual cannibalism. Man-eating has arisen through food scarcity, though this has seldom been the underlying reason. The Eskimos and early Andonites, however, seldom were cannibalistic except in times of famine. The red men, especially in Central America, were cannibals. It was once a general practice for primitive mothers to kill and eat their own children in order to renew the strength lost in childbearing, and in Queensland the first child is still frequently thus killed and devoured. In recent times cannibalism has been deliberately resorted to by many African tribes as a war measure, a sort of frightfulness with which to terrorize their neighbors.

Some cannibalism resulted from the degeneration of once superior stocks, but it was mostly prevalent among the evolutionary races. Man-eating came on at a time when men experienced intense and bitter emotions regarding their enemies. Eating human flesh became part of a solemn ceremony of revenge; it was believed that an enemy's ghost could, in this way, be destroyed or fused with that of the eater. It was once a widespread belief that wizards attained their powers by eating human flesh.

Certain groups of man-eaters would consume only members of their own tribes, a pseudospiritual inbreeding which was supposed to accentuate tribal solidarity. But they also ate enemies for revenge with the idea of appropriating their strength. It was considered an honor to the soul of a friend or fellow tribesman if his body were eaten, while it was no more than just punishment to an enemy thus to devour him. The savage mind made no pretensions to being consistent.

Among some tribes aged parents would seek to be eaten by their children; among others it was customary to refrain from eating near relations; their bodies were sold or exchanged for those of strangers. There was considerable commerce in women and children who had been fattened for slaughter. When disease or war failed to control population, the surplus was unceremoniously eaten.

Cannibalism has been gradually disappearing because of the following influences:

1. It sometimes became a communal ceremony, the assumption of collective responsibility for inflicting the death penalty upon a fellow tribesman. The blood guilt ceases to be a crime when participated in by all, by society. The last of cannibalism in Asia was this eating of executed criminals.

2. It very early became a religious ritual, but the growth of ghost fear did not always operate to reduce man-eating.

3. Eventually it progressed to the point where only certain parts or organs of the body were eaten, those parts supposed to contain the soul or portions of

the spirit. Blood drinking became common, and it was customary to mix the "edible" parts of the body with medicines.

4. It became limited to men; women were forbidden to eat human flesh.

5. It was next limited to the chiefs, priests, and shamans.

6. Then it became taboo among the higher tribes. The taboo on man-eating originated in Dalamatia and slowly spread over the world. The Nodites encouraged cremation as a means of combating cannibalism since it was once a common practice to dig up buried bodies and eat them.

7. Human sacrifice sounded the death knell of cannibalism. Human flesh having become the food of superior men, the chiefs, it was eventually reserved for the still more superior spirits; and thus the offering of human sacrifices effectively put a stop to cannibalism, except among the lowest tribes. When human sacrifice was fully established, man-eating became taboo; human flesh was food only for the gods; man could eat only a small ceremonial bit, a sacrament.

Finally animal substitutes came into general use for sacrificial purposes, and even among the more backward tribes dog-eating greatly reduced man-eating. The dog was the first domesticated animal and was held in high esteem both as such and as food.

6. EVOLUTION OF HUMAN SACRIFICE

Human sacrifice was an indirect result of cannibalism as well as its cure. Providing spirit escorts to the spirit world also led to the lessening of man-eating as it was never the custom to eat these death sacrifices. No race has been entirely free from the practice of human sacrifice in some form and at some time, even though the Andonites, Nodites, and Adamites were the least addicted to cannibalism.

Human sacrifice has been virtually universal; it persisted in the religious customs of the Chinese, Hindus, Egyptians, Hebrews, Mesopotamians, Greeks, Romans, and many other peoples, even on to recent times among the backward African and Australian tribes. The later American Indians had a civilization emerging from cannibalism and, therefore, steeped in human sacrifice, especially in Central and South America. The Chaldeans were among the first to abandon the sacrificing of humans for ordinary occasions, substituting therefor animals. About two thousand years ago a tenderhearted Japanese emperor introduced clay images to take the place of human sacrifices, but it was less than a thousand years ago that these sacrifices died out in northern Europe. Among certain backward tribes, human sacrifice is still carried on by volunteers, a sort of religious or ritual suicide. A shaman once ordered the sacrifice of a much respected old man of a certain tribe. The people revolted; they refused to obey. Whereupon the old man had his own son dispatch him; the ancients really believed in this custom.

There is no more tragic and pathetic experience on record, illustrative of the heart-tearing contentions between ancient and time-honored religious customs and the contrary demands of advancing civilization, than the Hebrew narrative of Jephthah and his only daughter. As was common custom, this well-meaning man had made a foolish vow, had bargained with the "god of battles," agreeing to pay a certain price for victory over his enemies. And this price was to make a sacrifice of that which first came out of his house to meet him when he returned to his home. Jephthah thought that one of his trusty slaves would thus be on hand to greet him, but it turned out that his daughter and only child came out to welcome him home. And so, even at that late date and among a supposedly civilized people, this beautiful maiden, after two months to mourn her fate, was actually offered as a human sacrifice by her father, and with the approval of his fellow tribesmen. And all this was done in the face of Moses' stringent rulings against the offering of human sacrifice. But men and women are addicted to making foolish and needless vows, and the men of old held all such pledges to be highly sacred.

In olden times, when a new building of any importance was started, it was customary to slay a human being as a "foundation sacrifice." This provided a ghost spirit to watch over and protect the structure. When the Chinese made ready to cast a bell, custom decreed the sacrifice of at least one maiden for the purpose of improving the tone of the bell; the girl chosen was thrown alive into the molten metal.

It was long the practice of many groups to build slaves alive into important walls. In later times the northern European tribes substituted the walling in of the shadow of a passerby for this custom of entombing living persons in the walls of new buildings. The Chinese buried in a wall those workmen who died while constructing it.

A petty king in Palestine, in building the walls of Jericho, "laid the foundation thereof in Abiram, his first-born, and set up the gates thereof in his youngest son, Segub." At that late date, not only did this father put two of his sons alive in the foundation holes of the city's gates, but his action is also recorded as being "according to the word of the Lord." Moses had forbidden these foundation sacrifices, but the Israelites reverted to them soon after his death. The twentieth-century ceremony of depositing trinkets and keepsakes in the cornerstone of a new building is reminiscent of the primitive foundation sacrifices.

It was long the custom of many peoples to dedicate the first fruits to the spirits. And these observances, now more or less symbolic, are all survivals of the early ceremonies involving human sacrifice. The idea of offering the first-born as a sacrifice was widespread among the ancients, especially among the Phoenicians, who were the last to give it up. It used to be said upon sacrificing, "life for life." Now you say at death, "dust to dust."

The spectacle of Abraham constrained to sacrifice his son Isaac, while shocking to civilized susceptibilities, was not a new or strange idea to the men of those days. It was long a prevalent practice for fathers, at times of great emotional stress, to sacrifice their first-born sons. Many peoples have a tradition analogous to this story, for there once existed a world-wide and profound belief that it was necessary to offer a human sacrifice when anything extraordinary or unusual happened.

7. MODIFICATIONS OF HUMAN SACRIFICE

Moses attempted to end human sacrifices by inaugurating the ransom as a substitute. He established a systematic schedule which enabled his people to escape the worst results of their rash and foolish vows. Lands, properties, and children could be redeemed according to the established fees, which were payable to the priests. Those groups which ceased to sacrifice their first-born soon possessed great advantages over less advanced neighbors who continued these atrocious acts. Many such backward tribes were not only greatly weakened by this loss of sons, but even the succession of leadership was often broken.

An outgrowth of the passing child sacrifice was the custom of smearing blood on the house doorposts for the protection of the first-born. This was often done in connection with one of the sacred feasts of the year, and this ceremony once obtained over most of the world from Mexico to Egypt.

Even after most groups had ceased the ritual killing of children, it was the custom to put an infant away by itself, off in the wilderness or in a little boat on the water. If the child survived, it was thought that the gods had intervened to preserve him, as in the traditions of Sargon, Moses, Cyrus, and Romulus. Then came the practice of dedicating the first-born sons as sacred or sacrificial, allowing them to grow up and then exiling them in lieu of death; this was the origin of colonization. The Romans adhered to this custom in their scheme of colonization.

Many of the peculiar associations of sex laxity with primitive worship had their origin in connection with human sacrifice. In olden times, if a woman met head-hunters, she could redeem her life by sexual surrender. Later, a maiden consecrated to the gods as a sacrifice might elect to redeem her life by dedicating her body for life to the sacred sex service of the temple; in this way she could earn her redemption money. The ancients regarded it as highly elevating to have sex relations with a woman thus engaged in ransoming her life. It was a religious ceremony to consort with these sacred maidens, and in addition, this whole ritual afforded an acceptable excuse for commonplace sexual gratification. This was a subtle species of self-deception which both the maidens and their consorts delighted to practice upon themselves. The mores always drag behind in the evolutionary advance of civilization, thus providing sanction for the earlier and more savagelike sex practices of the evolving races.

Temple harlotry eventually spread throughout southern Europe and Asia. The money earned by the temple prostitutes was held sacred among all peoples—a high gift to present to the gods. The highest types of women thronged the temple sex marts and devoted their earnings to all kinds of sacred services and works of public good. Many of the better classes of women collected their dowries by temporary sex service in the temples, and most men preferred to have such women for wives.

8. REDEMPTION AND COVENANTS

Sacrificial redemption and temple prostitution were in reality modifications of human sacrifice. Next came the mock sacrifice of daughters. This ceremony consisted in bloodletting, with dedication to lifelong virginity, and was a moral reaction to the older temple harlotry. In more recent times virgins dedicated themselves to the service of tending the sacred temple fires.

Men eventually conceived the idea that the offering of some part of the body could take the place of the older and complete human sacrifice. Physical mutilation was also considered to be an acceptable substitute. Hair, nails, blood, and even fingers and toes were sacrificed. The later and well-nigh universal ancient rite of circumcision was an outgrowth of the cult of partial sacrifice; it was purely sacrificial, no thought of hygiene being attached thereto. Men were circumcised; women had their ears pierced.

Subsequently it became the custom to bind fingers together instead of cutting them off. Shaving the head and cutting the hair were likewise forms of religious devotion. The making of eunuchs was at first a modification of the idea of human sacrifice. Nose and lip piercing is still practiced in Africa, and tattooing is an artistic evolution of the earlier crude scarring of the body.

The custom of sacrifice eventually became associated, as a result of advancing teachings, with the idea of the covenant. At last, the gods were conceived of as entering into real agreements with man; and this was a major step in the stabilization of religion. Law, a covenant, takes the place of luck, fear, and superstition.

Man could never even dream of entering into a contract with Deity until his concept of God had advanced to the level whereon the universe controllers were envisioned as dependable. And man's early idea of God was so anthropomorphic that he was unable to conceive of a dependable Deity until he himself became relatively dependable, moral, and ethical.

But the idea of making a covenant with the gods did finally arrive. *Evolutionary man eventually acquired such moral dignity that he dared to bargain with his gods.* And so the business of offering sacrifices gradually developed into the game of man's philosophic bargaining with God. And all this represented a new device for insuring against bad luck or, rather, an enhanced technique for the more definite purchase of prosperity. Do not entertain the mistaken idea that these early sacrifices were a free gift to the gods, a spontaneous offering of gratitude or thanksgiving; they were not expressions of true worship.

Primitive forms of prayer were nothing more nor less than bargaining with the spirits, an argument with the gods. It was a kind of bartering in which pleading and persuasion were substituted for something more tangible and costly. The developing commerce of the races had inculcated the spirit of trade and had developed the shrewdness of barter; and now these traits began to appear in man's worship methods. And as some men were better traders than others, so some were regarded as better prayers than others. The prayer of a just man was held in high esteem. A just man was one who had paid all accounts to the spirits, had fully discharged every ritual obligation to the gods.

Early prayer was hardly worship; it was a bargaining petition for health, wealth, and life. And in many respects prayers have not much changed with the passing of the ages. They are still read out of books, recited formally, and written out for emplacement on wheels and for hanging on trees, where the blowing of the winds will save man the trouble of expending his own breath.

9. SACRIFICES AND SACRAMENTS

The human sacrifice, throughout the course of the evolution of Urantian rituals, has advanced from the bloody business of man-eating to higher and more symbolic levels. The early rituals of sacrifice bred the later ceremonies of sacrament. In more recent times the priest alone would partake of a bit of the cannibalistic sacrifice or a drop of human blood, and then all would partake of the animal substitute. These early ideas of ransom, redemption, and covenants have evolved into the later-day sacramental services. And all this ceremonial evolution has exerted a mighty socializing influence.

In connection with the Mother of God cult, in Mexico and elsewhere, a sacrament of cakes and wine was eventually utilized in lieu of the flesh and blood of the older human sacrifices. The Hebrews long practiced this ritual as a part of their Passover ceremonies, and it was from this ceremonial that the later Christian version of the sacrament took its origin.

The ancient social brotherhoods were based on the rite of blood drinking; the early Jewish fraternity was a sacrificial blood affair. Paul started out to build a new Christian cult on "the blood of the everlasting covenant." And while he may have unnecessarily encumbered Christianity with teachings about blood and sacrifice, he did once and for all make an end of the doctrines of redemption through human or animal sacrifices. His theologic compromises indicate that even revelation must submit to the graduated control of evolution. According to Paul, Christ became the last and all-sufficient human sacrifice; the divine Judge is now fully and forever satisfied.

And so, after long ages the cult of the sacrifice has evolved into the cult of the sacrament. Thus are the sacraments of modern religions the legitimate successors of those shocking early ceremonies of human sacrifice and the still earlier cannibalistic rituals. Many still depend upon blood for salvation, but it has at least become figurative, symbolic, and mystic.

10. FORGIVENESS OF SIN

Ancient man only attained consciousness of favor with God through sacrifice. Modern man must develop new techniques of achieving the self-consciousness of salvation. The consciousness of sin persists in the mortal mind, but the thought patterns of salvation therefrom have become outworn and antiquated. The reality of the spiritual need persists, but intellectual progress has destroyed the olden ways of securing peace and consolation for mind and soul.

Sin must be redefined as deliberate disloyalty to Deity. There are degrees of disloyalty: the partial loyalty of indecision; the divided loyalty of confliction; the dying loyalty of indifference; and the death of loyalty exhibited in devotion to godless ideals.

The sense or feeling of guilt is the consciousness of the violation of the mores; it is not necessarily sin. There is no real sin in the absence of conscious disloyalty to Deity.

The possibility of the recognition of the sense of guilt is a badge of transcendent distinction for mankind. It does not mark man as mean but rather sets him apart as a creature of potential greatness and ever-ascending glory. Such a sense of unworthiness is the initial stimulus that should lead quickly and surely to those faith conquests which translate the mortal mind to the superb levels of moral nobility, cosmic insight, and spiritual living; thus are all the meanings of human existence changed from the temporal to the eternal, and all values are elevated from the human to the divine.

The confession of sin is a manful repudiation of disloyalty, but it in no wise mitigates the time-space consequences of such disloyalty. But confession—sincere recognition of the nature of sin—is essential to religious growth and spiritual progress.

The forgiveness of sin by Deity is the renewal of loyalty relations following a period of the human consciousness of the lapse of such relations as the consequence of conscious rebellion. The forgiveness does not have to be sought, only received as the consciousness of re-establishment of loyalty relations between the creature and the Creator. And all the loyal sons of God are happy, service-loving, and ever-progressive in the Paradise ascent.

[Presented by a Brilliant Evening Star of Nebadon.]

PAPER 90

SHAMANISM—MEDICINE MEN AND PRIESTS

THE evolution of religious observances progressed from placation, avoidance, exorcism, coercion, conciliation, and propitiation to sacrifice, atonement, and redemption. The technique of religious ritual passed from the forms of the primitive cult through fetishes to magic and miracles; and as ritual became more complex in response to man's increasingly complex concept of the supermaterial realms, it was inevitably dominated by medicine men, shamans, and priests.

In the advancing concepts of primitive man the spirit world was eventually regarded as being unresponsive to the ordinary mortal. Only the exceptional among humans could catch the ear of the gods; only the extraordinary man or woman would be heard by the spirits. Religion thus enters upon a new phase, a stage wherein it gradually becomes secondhanded; always does a medicine man, a shaman, or a priest intervene between the religionist and the object of worship. And today most Urantia systems of organized religious belief are passing through this level of evolutionary development.

Evolutionary religion is born of a simple and all-powerful fear, the fear which surges through the human mind when confronted with the unknown, the inexplicable, and the incomprehensible. Religion eventually achieves the profoundly simple realization of an all-powerful love, the love which sweeps irresistibly through the human soul when awakened to the conception of the limitless affection of the Universal Father for the sons of the universe. But in between the beginning and the consummation of religious evolution, there intervene the long ages of the shamans, who presume to stand between man and God as intermediaries, interpreters, and intercessors.

1. THE FIRST SHAMANS—THE MEDICINE MEN

The shaman was the ranking medicine man, the ceremonial fetishman, and the focus personality for all the practices of evolutionary religion. In many groups the shaman outranked the war chief, marking the beginning of the church domination of the state. The shaman sometimes functioned as a priest and even as a priest-king. Some of the later tribes had both the earlier shaman-medicine men (seers) and the later appearing shaman-priests. And in many cases the office of shaman became hereditary.

Since in olden times anything abnormal was ascribed to spirit possession, any striking mental or physical abnormality constituted qualification for being a medicine man. Many of these men were epileptic, many of the women hysteric, and these two types accounted for a good deal of ancient inspiration as well as spirit and devil possession. Quite a few of these earliest of priests were of a class which has since been denominated paranoiac.

While they may have practiced deception in minor matters, the great majority of the shamans believed in the fact of their spirit possession. Women who were able to throw themselves into a trance or a cataleptic fit became powerful shamanesses; later, such women became prophets and spirit mediums. Their cataleptic trances usually involved alleged communications with the ghosts of the dead. Many female shamans were also professional dancers.

But not all shamans were self-deceived; many were shrewd and able tricksters. As the profession developed, a novice was required to serve an apprenticeship of ten years of hardship and self-denial to qualify as a medicine man. The shamans developed a professional mode of dress and affected a mysterious conduct. They frequently employed drugs to induce certain physical states which would impress and mystify the tribesmen. Sleight-of-hand feats were regarded as supernatural by the common folk, and ventriloquism was first used by shrewd priests. Many of the olden shamans unwittingly stumbled onto hypnotism; others induced autohypnosis by prolonged staring at their navels.

While many resorted to these tricks and deceptions, their reputation as a class, after all, stood on apparent achievement. When a shaman failed in his undertakings, if he could not advance a plausible alibi, he was either demoted or killed. Thus the honest shamans early perished; only the shrewd actors survived.

It was shamanism that took the exclusive direction of tribal affairs out of the hands of the old and the strong and lodged it in the hands of the shrewd, the clever, and the farsighted.

2. SHAMANISTIC PRACTICES

Spirit conjuring was a very precise and highly complicated procedure, comparable to present-day church rituals conducted in an ancient tongue. The human race very early sought for superhuman help, for *revelation;* and men believed that the shaman actually received such revelations. While the shamans utilized the great power of suggestion in their work, it was almost invariably negative suggestion; only in very recent times has the technique of positive suggestion been employed. In the early development of their profession the shamans began to specialize in such vocations as rain making, disease healing, and crime detecting. To heal diseases was not, however, the chief function of a shamanic medicine man; it was, rather, to know and to control the hazards of living.

Ancient black art, both religious and secular, was called white art when practiced by either priests, seers, shamans, or medicine men. The practitioners of the black art were called sorcerers, magicians, wizards, witches, enchanters, necromancers, conjurers, and soothsayers. As time passed, all such purported contact with the supernatural was classified either as witchcraft or shamancraft.

Witchcraft embraced the *magic* performed by earlier, irregular, and unrecognized spirits; shamancraft had to do with *miracles* performed by regular spirits and recognized gods of the tribe. In later times the witch became associated with the devil, and thus was the stage set for the many comparatively recent exhibitions of religious intolerance. Witchcraft was a religion with many primitive tribes.

The shamans were great believers in the mission of chance as revelatory of the will of the spirits; they frequently cast lots to arrive at decisions. Modern survivals of this proclivity for casting lots are illustrated, not only in the many games of chance, but also in the well-known "counting-out" rhymes. Once, the person counted out must die; now, he is only *it* in some childish game. That which was serious business to primitive man has survived as a diversion of the modern child.

The medicine men put great trust in signs and omens, such as, "When you hear the sound of a rustling in the tops of the mulberry trees, then shall you bestir yourself." Very early in the history of the race the shamans turned their attention to the stars. Primitive astrology was a world-wide belief and practice; dream interpreting also became widespread. All this was soon followed by the appearance of those temperamental shamanesses who professed to be able to communicate with the spirits of the dead.

Though of ancient origin, the rain makers, or weather shamans, have persisted right on down through the ages. A severe drought meant death to the early agriculturists; weather control was the object of much ancient magic. Civilized man still makes the weather the common topic of conversation. The olden peoples all believed in the power of the shaman as a rain maker, but it was customary to kill him when he failed, unless he could offer a plausible excuse to account for the failure.

Again and again did the Caesars banish the astrologers, but they invariably returned because of the popular belief in their powers. They could not be driven out, and even in the sixteenth century after Christ the directors of Occidental church and state were the patrons of astrology. Thousands of supposedly intelligent people still believe that one may be born under the domination of a lucky or an unlucky star; that the juxtaposition of the heavenly bodies determines the outcome of various terrestrial adventures. Fortunetellers are still patronized by the credulous.

The Greeks believed in the efficacy of oracular advice, the Chinese used magic as protection against demons, shamanism flourished in India, and it still openly persists in central Asia. It is an only recently abandoned practice throughout much of the world.

Ever and anon, true prophets and teachers arose to denounce and expose shamanism. Even the vanishing red man had such a prophet within the past hundred years, the Shawnee Tenskwatawa, who predicted the eclipse of the sun in 1806 and denounced the vices of the white man. Many true teachers have appeared among the various tribes and races all through the long ages of evolutionary history. And they will ever continue to appear to challenge the shamans or priests of any age who oppose general education and attempt to thwart scientific progress.

In many ways and by devious methods the olden shamans established their reputations as voices of God and custodians of providence. They sprinkled the newborn with water and conferred names upon them; they circumcised the males. They presided over all burial ceremonies and made due announcement of the safe arrival of the dead in spiritland.

The shamanic priests and medicine men often became very wealthy through the accretion of their various fees which were ostensibly offerings to the spirits. Not infrequently a shaman would accumulate practically all the material wealth of his tribe. Upon the death of a wealthy man it was customary to divide his property equally with the shaman and some public enterprise or charity. This practice still obtains in some parts of Tibet, where one half the male population belongs to this class of nonproducers.

The shamans dressed well and usually had a number of wives; they were the original aristocracy, being exempt from all tribal restrictions. They were very often of low-grade mind and morals. They suppressed their rivals by denominating them witches or sorcerers and very frequently rose to such positions of influence and power that they were able to dominate the chiefs or kings.

Primitive man regarded the shaman as a necessary evil; he feared him but did not love him. Early man respected knowledge; he honored and rewarded wisdom. The shaman was mostly fraud, but the veneration for shamanism well illustrates the premium put upon wisdom in the evolution of the race.

3. THE SHAMANIC THEORY OF DISEASE AND DEATH

Since ancient man regarded himself and his material environment as being directly responsive to the whims of the ghosts and the fancies of the spirits, it is not strange that his religion should have been so exclusively concerned with material affairs. Modern man attacks his material problems directly; he recognizes that matter is responsive to the intelligent manipulation of mind. Primitive man likewise desired to modify and even to control the life and energies of the physical domains; and since his limited comprehension of the cosmos led him to the belief that ghosts, spirits, and gods were personally and immediately concerned with the detailed control of life and matter, he logically directed his efforts to winning the favor and support of these superhuman agencies.

Viewed in this light, much of the inexplicable and irrational in the ancient cults is understandable. The ceremonies of the cult were primitive man's attempt to control the material world in which he found himself. And many of his efforts were directed to the end of prolonging life and insuring health. Since all diseases and death itself were originally regarded as spirit phenomena, it was inevitable that the shamans, while functioning as medicine men and priests, should also have labored as doctors and surgeons.

The primitive mind may be handicapped by lack of facts, but it is for all that logical. When thoughtful men observe disease and death, they set about to determine the causes of these visitations, and in accordance with their understanding, the shamans and the scientists have propounded the following theories of affliction:

1. *Ghosts—direct spirit influences.* The earliest hypothesis advanced in explanation of disease and death was that spirits caused disease by enticing the soul out of the body; if it failed to return, death ensued. The ancients so feared the malevolent action of disease-producing ghosts that ailing individuals would often be deserted without even food or water. Regardless of the erroneous basis for these beliefs, they did effectively isolate afflicted individuals and prevent the spread of contagious disease.

2. *Violence—obvious causes.* The causes for some accidents and deaths were so easy to identify that they were early removed from the category of ghost action. Fatalities and wounds attendant upon war, animal combat, and other readily identifiable agencies were considered as natural occurrences. But it was long believed that the spirits were still responsible for delayed healing or for the infection of wounds of even "natural" causation. If no observable natural agent could be discovered, the spirit ghosts were still held responsible for disease and death.

Today, in Africa and elsewhere may be found primitive peoples who kill someone every time a nonviolent death occurs. Their medicine men indicate the guilty parties. If a mother dies in childbirth, the child is immediately strangled—a life for a life.

3. *Magic—the influence of enemies.* Much sickness was thought to be caused by bewitchment, the action of the evil eye and the magic pointing bow. At one time it was really dangerous to point a finger at anyone; it is still regarded as ill-mannered to point. In cases of obscure disease and death the ancients would hold a formal inquest, dissect the body, and settle upon some finding as the cause of death; otherwise the death would be laid to witchcraft, thus necessitating the execution of the witch responsible therefor. These ancient coroner's inquests saved many a supposed witch's life. Among some it was believed that a tribesman could die as a result of his own witchcraft, in which event no one was accused.

4. *Sin—punishment for taboo violation.* In comparatively recent times it has been believed that sickness is a punishment for sin, personal or racial. Among peoples traversing this level of evolution the prevailing theory is that one cannot be afflicted unless one has violated a taboo. To regard sickness and suffering as "arrows of the Almighty within them" is typical of such beliefs. The Chinese and Mesopotamians long regarded disease as the result of the action of evil demons, although the Chaldeans also looked upon the stars as the cause of suffering. This theory of disease as a consequence of divine wrath is still prevalent among many reputedly civilized groups of Urantians.

5. *Natural causation.* Mankind has been very slow to learn the material secrets of the interrelationship of cause and effect in the physical domains of energy, matter, and life. The ancient Greeks, having preserved the traditions of Adamson's teachings, were among the first to recognize that all disease is the result of natural causes. Slowly and certainly the unfolding of a scientific era is destroying man's age-old theories of sickness and death. Fever was one of the first human ailments to be removed from the category of supernatural disorders, and progressively the era of science has broken the fetters of ignorance which so long imprisoned the human mind. An understanding of old age and contagion is gradually obliterating man's fear of ghosts, spirits, and gods as the personal perpetrators of human misery and mortal suffering.

Evolution unerringly achieves its end: It imbues man with that superstitious fear of the unknown and dread of the unseen which is the scaffolding for the God concept. And having witnessed the birth of an advanced comprehension of Deity, through the co-ordinate action of revelation, this same technique of evolution then unerringly sets in motion those forces of thought which will inexorably obliterate the scaffolding, which has served its purpose.

4. MEDICINE UNDER THE SHAMANS

The entire life of ancient men was prophylactic; their religion was in no small measure a technique for disease prevention. And regardless of the error in their theories, they were wholehearted in putting them into effect; they had unbounded faith in their methods of treatment, and that, in itself, is a powerful remedy.

The faith required to get well under the foolish ministrations of one of these ancient shamans was, after all, not materially different from that which is required to experience healing at the hands of some of his later-day successors who engage in the nonscientific treatment of disease.

The more primitive tribes greatly feared the sick, and for long ages they were carefully avoided, shamefully neglected. It was a great advance in humanitarianism when the evolution of shamancraft produced priests and medicine men who consented to treat disease. Then it became customary for the entire clan to crowd into the sickroom to assist the shaman in howling the disease ghosts away. It was not uncommon for a woman to be the diagnosing shaman, while a man would administer treatment. The usual method of diagnosing disease was to examine the entrails of an animal.

Disease was treated by chanting, howling, laying on of hands, breathing on the patient, and many other techniques. In later times the resort to temple sleep, during which healing supposedly took place, became widespread. The medicine men eventually essayed actual surgery in connection with temple slumber; among the first operations was that of trephining the skull to allow a headache spirit to escape. The shamans learned to treat fractures and dislocations, to open boils and abscesses; the shamanesses became adept at midwifery.

It was a common method of treatment to rub something magical on an infected or blemished spot on the body, throw the charm away, and supposedly experience a cure. If anyone should chance to pick up the discarded charm, it was believed he would immediately acquire the infection or blemish. It was a long time before herbs and other real medicines were introduced. Massage was developed in connection with incantation, rubbing the spirit out of the body, and was preceded by efforts to rub medicine in, even as moderns attempt to rub liniments in. Cupping and sucking the affected parts, together with bloodletting, were thought to be of value in getting rid of a disease-producing spirit.

Since water was a potent fetish, it was utilized in the treatment of many ailments. For long it was believed that the spirit causing the sickness could be eliminated by sweating. Vapor baths were highly regarded; natural hot springs soon blossomed as primitive health resorts. Early man discovered that heat would relieve pain; he used sunlight, fresh animal organs, hot clay, and hot stones, and many of these methods are still employed. Rhythm was practiced in an effort to influence the spirits; the tom-toms were universal.

Among some people disease was thought to be caused by a wicked conspiracy between spirits and animals. This gave rise to the belief that there existed a beneficent plant remedy for every animal-caused disease. The red men were especially devoted to the plant theory of universal remedies; they always put a drop of blood in the root hole left when the plant was pulled up.

Fasting, dieting, and counterirritants were often used as remedial measures. Human secretions, being definitely magical, were highly regarded; blood and urine were thus among the earliest medicines and were soon augmented by roots and various salts. The shamans believed that disease spirits could be driven out of the body by foul-smelling and bad-tasting medicines. Purging very early became a routine treatment, and the values of raw cocoa and quinine were among the earliest pharmaceutical discoveries.

The Greeks were the first to evolve truly rational methods of treating the sick. Both the Greeks and the Egyptians received their medical knowledge from the Euphrates valley. Oil and wine was a very early medicine for treating wounds; castor oil and opium were used by the Sumerians. Many of these ancient and effective secret remedies lost their power when they became known; secrecy has always been essential to the successful practice of fraud and superstition. Only facts and truth court the full light of comprehension and rejoice in the illumination and enlightenment of scientific research.

5. PRIESTS AND RITUALS

The essence of the ritual is the perfection of its performance; among savages it must be practiced with exact precision. It is only when the ritual has been correctly carried out that the ceremony possesses compelling power over the spirits. If the ritual is faulty, it only arouses the anger and resentment of the gods. Therefore, since man's slowly evolving mind conceived that the *technique of ritual* was the decisive factor in its efficacy, it was inevitable that the early shamans should sooner or later evolve into a priesthood trained to direct the meticulous practice of the ritual. And so for tens of thousands of years endless rituals have hampered society and cursed civilization, have been an intolerable burden to every act of life, every racial undertaking.

Ritual is the technique of sanctifying custom; ritual creates and perpetuates myths as well as contributing to the preservation of social and religious customs. Again, ritual itself has been fathered by myths. Rituals are often at first social, later becoming economic and finally acquiring the sanctity and dignity of religious ceremonial. Ritual may be personal or group in practice—or both—as illustrated by prayer, dancing, and drama.

Words become a part of ritual, such as the use of terms like amen and selah. The habit of swearing, profanity, represents a prostitution of former ritualistic repetition of holy names. The making of pilgrimages to sacred shrines is a very ancient ritual. The ritual next grew into elaborate ceremonies of purification, cleansing, and sanctification. The initiation ceremonies of the primitive tribal secret societies were in reality a crude religious rite. The worship technique of the olden mystery cults was just one long performance of accumulated religious ritual. Ritual finally developed into the modern types of social ceremonials and religious worship, services embracing prayer, song, responsive reading, and other individual and group spiritual devotions.

The priests evolved from shamans up through oracles, diviners, singers, dancers, weathermakers, guardians of religious relics, temple custodians, and foretellers of events, to the status of actual directors of religious worship. Eventually the office became hereditary, a continuous priestly caste arose.

As religion evolved, priests began to specialize according to their innate talents or special predilections. Some became singers, others prayers, and still others sacrificers; later came the orators—preachers. And when religion became institutionalized, these priests claimed to "hold the keys of heaven."

The priests have always sought to impress and awe the common people by conducting the religious ritual in an ancient tongue and by sundry magical passes so to mystify the worshipers as to enhance their own piety and authority. The great danger in all this is that the ritual tends to become a substitute for religion.

The priesthoods have done much to delay scientific development and to hinder spiritual progress, but they have contributed to the stabilization of civilization and to the enhancement of certain kinds of culture. But many modern priests have ceased to function as directors of the ritual of the worship of God, having turned their attention to theology—the attempt to define God.

It is not denied that the priests have been a millstone about the neck of the races, but the true religious leaders have been invaluable in pointing the way to higher and better realities.

[Presented by a Melchizedek of Nebadon.]

PAPER 91

THE EVOLUTION OF PRAYER

PRAYER, as an agency of religion, evolved from previous nonreligious monologue and dialogue expressions. With the attainment of self-consciousness by primitive man there occurred the inevitable corollary of other-consciousness, the dual potential of social response and God recognition.

The earliest prayer forms were not addressed to Deity. These expressions were much like what you would say to a friend as you entered upon some important undertaking, "Wish me luck." Primitive man was enslaved to magic; luck, good and bad, entered into all the affairs of life. At first, these luck petitions were monologues—just a kind of thinking out loud by the magic server. Next, these believers in luck would enlist the support of their friends and families, and presently some form of ceremony would be performed which included the whole clan or tribe.

When the concepts of ghosts and spirits evolved, these petitions became superhuman in address, and with the consciousness of gods, such expressions attained to the levels of genuine prayer. As an illustration of this, among certain Australian tribes primitive religious prayers antedated their belief in spirits and superhuman personalities.

The Toda tribe of India now observes this practice of praying to no one in particular, just as did the early peoples before the times of religious consciousness. Only, among the Todas, this represents a regression of their degenerating religion to this primitive level. The present-day rituals of the dairymen priests of the Todas do not represent a religious ceremony since these impersonal prayers do not contribute anything to the conservation or enhancement of any social, moral, or spiritual values.

Prereligious praying was part of the mana practices of the Melanesians, the oudah beliefs of the African Pygmies, and the manitou superstitions of the North American Indians. The Baganda tribes of Africa have only recently emerged from the mana level of prayer. In this early evolutionary confusion men pray to gods—local and national—to fetishes, amulets, ghosts, rulers, and to ordinary people.

1. PRIMITIVE PRAYER

The function of early evolutionary religion is to conserve and augment the essential social, moral, and spiritual values which are slowly taking form. This mission of religion is not consciously observed by mankind, but it is chiefly effected by the function of prayer. The practice of prayer represents the unintended, but nonetheless personal and collective, effort of any group to secure (to actualize) this conservation of higher values. But for the safeguarding of prayer, all holy days would speedily revert to the status of mere holidays.

Religion and its agencies, the chief of which is prayer, are allied only with those values which have general social recognition, group approval. Therefore, when primitive man attempted to gratify his baser emotions or to achieve unmitigated selfish ambitions, he was deprived of the consolation of religion and the assistance of prayer. If the individual sought to accomplish anything antisocial, he was obliged to seek the aid of nonreligious magic, resort to sorcerers, and thus be deprived of the assistance of prayer. Prayer, therefore, very early became a mighty promoter of social evolution, moral progress, and spiritual attainment.

But the primitive mind was neither logical nor consistent. Early men did not perceive that material things were not the province of prayer. These simple-minded souls reasoned that food, shelter, rain, game, and other material goods enhanced the social welfare, and therefore they began to pray for these physical blessings. While this constituted a perversion of prayer, it encouraged the effort to realize these material objectives by social and ethical actions. Such a prostitution of prayer, while debasing the spiritual values of a people, nevertheless directly elevated their economic, social, and ethical mores.

Prayer is only monologuous in the most primitive type of mind. It early becomes a dialogue and rapidly expands to the level of group worship. Prayer signifies that the premagical incantations of primitive religion have evolved to that level where the human mind recognizes the reality of beneficent powers or beings who are able to enhance social values and to augment moral ideals, and further, that these influences are superhuman and distinct from the ego of the self-conscious human and his fellow mortals. True prayer does not, therefore, appear until the agency of religious ministry is visualized as *personal.*

Prayer is little associated with animism, but such beliefs may exist alongside emerging religious sentiments. Many times, religion and animism have had entirely separate origins.

With those mortals who have not been delivered from the primitive bondage of fear, there is a real danger that all prayer may lead to a morbid sense of sin, unjustified convictions of guilt, real or fancied. But in modern times it is not likely that many will spend sufficient time at prayer to lead to this harmful brooding over their unworthiness or sinfulness. The dangers attendant upon the distortion and perversion of prayer consist in ignorance, superstition, crystallization, devitalization, materialism, and fanaticism.

2. EVOLVING PRAYER

The first prayers were merely verbalized wishes, the expression of sincere desires. Prayer next became a technique of achieving spirit co-operation. And then it attained to the higher function of assisting religion in the conservation of all worth-while values.

Both prayer and magic arose as a result of man's adjustive reactions to Urantian environment. But aside from this generalized relationship, they have little in common. Prayer has always indicated positive action by the praying ego; it has been always psychic and sometimes spiritual. Magic has usually signified an attempt to manipulate reality without affecting the ego of the manipulator, the practitioner of magic. Despite their independent origins, magic and prayer often have been interrelated in their later stages of development. Magic has sometimes ascended by goal elevation from formulas through rituals and incantations to the threshold of true prayer. Prayer has sometimes become so materialistic that it has degenerated into a pseudomagical technique of avoiding the expenditure of that effort which is requisite for the solution of Urantian problems.

When man learned that prayer could not coerce the gods, then it became more of a petition, favor seeking. But the truest prayer is in reality a communion between man and his Maker.

The appearance of the sacrifice idea in any religion unfailingly detracts from the higher efficacy of true prayer in that men seek to substitute the offerings of material possessions for the offering of their own consecrated wills to the doing of the will of God.

When religion is divested of a personal God, its prayers translate to the levels of theology and philosophy. When the highest God concept of a religion is that of an impersonal Deity, such as in pantheistic idealism, although affording the basis for certain forms of mystic communion, it proves fatal to the potency of true prayer, which always stands for man's communion with a personal and superior being.

During the earlier times of racial evolution and even at the present time, in the day-by-day experience of the average mortal, prayer is very much a phenomenon of man's intercourse with his own subconscious. But there is also a domain of prayer wherein the intellectually alert and spiritually progressing individual attains more or less contact with the superconscious levels of the human mind, the domain of the indwelling Thought Adjuster. In addition, there is a definite spiritual phase of true prayer which concerns its reception and recognition by the spiritual forces of the universe, and which is entirely distinct from all human and intellectual association.

Prayer contributes greatly to the development of the religious sentiment of an evolving human mind. It is a mighty influence working to prevent isolation of personality.

Prayer represents one technique associated with the natural religions of racial evolution which also forms a part of the experiential values of the higher religions of ethical excellence, the religions of revelation.

3. PRAYER AND THE ALTER EGO

Children, when first learning to make use of language, are prone to think out loud, to express their thoughts in words, even if no one is present to hear them. With the dawn of creative imagination they evince a tendency to converse with imaginary companions. In this way a budding ego seeks to hold communion with a fictitious *alter ego*. By this technique the child early learns to convert his monologue conversations into pseudo dialogues in which this alter ego makes replies to his verbal thinking and wish expression. Very much of an adult's thinking is mentally carried on in conversational form.

The early and primitive form of prayer was much like the semimagical recitations of the present-day Toda tribe, prayers that were not addressed to anyone in particular. But such techniques of praying tend to evolve into the dialogue type of communication by the emergence of the idea of an alter ego. In time the alter-ego concept is exalted to a superior status of divine dignity, and prayer as an agency of religion has appeared. Through many phases and during long ages this primitive type of praying is destined to evolve before attaining the level of intelligent and truly ethical prayer.

As it is conceived by successive generations of praying mortals, the alter ego evolves up through ghosts, fetishes, and spirits to polytheistic gods, and eventually to the One God, a divine being embodying the highest ideals and the loftiest aspirations of the praying ego. And thus does prayer function as the most potent agency of religion in the conservation of the highest values and ideals of those who pray. From the moment of the conceiving of an alter ego to the appearance of the concept of a divine and heavenly Father, prayer is always a socializing, moralizing, and spiritualizing practice.

The simple prayer of faith evidences a mighty evolution in human experience whereby the ancient conversations with the fictitious symbol of the alter ego of primitive religion have become exalted to the level of communion with the spirit of the Infinite and to that of a bona fide consciousness of the reality of the eternal God and Paradise Father of all intelligent creation.

Aside from all that is superself in the experience of praying, it should be remembered that ethical prayer is a splendid way to elevate one's ego and reinforce the self for better living and higher attainment. Prayer induces the human ego to look both ways for help: for material aid to the subconscious reservoir of mortal experience, for inspiration and guidance to the superconscious borders of the contact of the material with the spiritual, with the Mystery Monitor.

Prayer ever has been and ever will be a twofold human experience: a psychologic procedure interassociated with a spiritual technique. And these two functions of prayer can never be fully separated.

Enlightened prayer must recognize not only an external and personal God but also an internal and impersonal Divinity, the indwelling Adjuster. It is altogether fitting that man, when he prays, should strive to grasp the concept of the Universal Father on Paradise; but the more effective technique for most practical purposes will be to revert to the concept of a near-by alter ego, just as the primitive mind was wont to do, and then to recognize that the idea of this alter ego has evolved from a mere fiction to the truth of God's indwelling mortal man in the factual presence of the Adjuster so that man can talk face to face, as it were, with a real and genuine and divine alter ego that indwells him and is the very presence and essence of the living God, the Universal Father.

4. ETHICAL PRAYING

No prayer can be ethical when the petitioner seeks for selfish advantage over his fellows. Selfish and materialistic praying is incompatible with the ethical religions which are predicated on unselfish and divine love. All such unethical praying reverts to the primitive levels of pseudo magic and is unworthy of advancing civilizations and enlightened religions. Selfish praying transgresses the spirit of all ethics founded on loving justice.

Prayer must never be so prostituted as to become a substitute for action. All ethical prayer is a stimulus to action and a guide to the progressive striving for idealistic goals of superself-attainment.

In all your praying be *fair;* do not expect God to show partiality, to love you more than his other children, your friends, neighbors, even enemies. But the prayer of the natural or evolved religions is not at first ethical, as it is in the later revealed religions. All praying, whether individual or communal, may be either egoistic or altruistic. That is, the prayer may be centered upon the self or upon others. When the prayer seeks nothing for the one who prays nor anything for his fellows, then such attitudes of the soul tend to the levels of true worship. Egoistic prayers involve confessions and petitions and often consist in requests for material favors. Prayer is somewhat more ethical when it deals with forgiveness and seeks wisdom for enhanced self-control.

While the nonselfish type of prayer is strengthening and comforting, materialistic praying is destined to bring disappointment and disillusionment as advancing scientific discoveries demonstrate that man lives in a physical universe of law and order. The childhood of an individual or a race is characterized by primitive, selfish, and materialistic praying. And, to a certain extent, all such petitions are efficacious in that they unvaryingly lead to those efforts and exertions which are contributory to achieving the answers to such prayers. The real prayer of faith always contributes to the augmentation of the technique of living, even if such petitions are not worthy of spiritual recognition. But the spiritually advanced person should exercise great caution in attempting to discourage the primitive or immature mind regarding such prayers.

Remember, even if prayer does not change God, it very often effects great and lasting changes in the one who prays in faith and confident expectation. Prayer has been the ancestor of much peace of mind, cheerfulness, calmness, courage, self-mastery, and fair-mindedness in the men and women of the evolving races.

5. SOCIAL REPERCUSSIONS OF PRAYER

In ancestor worship, prayer leads to the cultivation of ancestral ideals. But prayer, as a feature of Deity worship, transcends all other such practices since it leads to the cultivation of divine ideals. As the concept of the alter ego of prayer becomes supreme and divine, so are man's ideals accordingly elevated from mere human toward supernal and divine levels, and the result of all such praying is the enhancement of human character and the profound unification of human personality.

But prayer need not always be individual. Group or congregational praying is very effective in that it is highly socializing in its repercussions. When a group engages in community prayer for moral enhancement and spiritual uplift, such devotions are reactive upon the individuals composing the group; they are all made better because of participation. Even a whole city or an entire nation can be helped by such prayer devotions. Confession, repentance, and prayer have led individuals, cities, nations, and whole races to mighty efforts of reform and courageous deeds of valorous achievement.

If you truly desire to overcome the habit of criticizing some friend, the quickest and surest way of achieving such a change of attitude is to establish the habit of praying for that person every day of your life. But the social repercussions of such prayers are dependent largely on two conditions:

1. The person who is prayed for should know that he is being prayed for.

2. The person who prays should come into intimate social contact with the person for whom he is praying.

Prayer is the technique whereby, sooner or later, every religion becomes institutionalized. And in time prayer becomes associated with numerous secondary agencies, some helpful, others decidedly deleterious, such as priests, holy books, worship rituals, and ceremonials.

But the minds of greater spiritual illumination should be patient with, and tolerant of, those less endowed intellects that crave symbolism for the mobilization of their feeble spiritual insight. The strong must not look with disdain upon the weak. Those who are God-conscious without symbolism must not deny the grace-ministry of the symbol to those who find it difficult to worship Deity and to revere truth, beauty, and goodness without form and ritual. In prayerful worship, most mortals envision some symbol of the object-goal of their devotions.

6. THE PROVINCE OF PRAYER

Prayer, unless in liaison with the will and actions of the personal spiritual forces and material supervisors of a realm, can have no direct effect upon one's physical environment. While there is a very definite limit to the province of the petitions of prayer, such limits do not equally apply to the *faith* of those who pray.

Prayer is not a technique for curing real and organic diseases, but it has contributed enormously to the enjoyment of abundant health and to the cure of numerous mental, emotional, and nervous ailments. And even in actual bacterial disease, prayer has many times added to the efficacy of other remedial procedures. Prayer has turned many an irritable and complaining invalid into a paragon of patience and made him an inspiration to all other human sufferers.

No matter how difficult it may be to reconcile the scientific doubtings regarding the efficacy of prayer with the ever-present urge to seek help and guidance from divine sources, never forget that the sincere prayer of faith is a mighty force for the promotion of personal happiness, individual self-control, social harmony, moral progress, and spiritual attainment.

Prayer, even as a purely human practice, a dialogue with one's alter ego, constitutes a technique of the most efficient approach to the realization of those reserve powers of human nature which are stored and conserved in the unconscious realms of the human mind. Prayer is a sound psychologic practice, aside from its religious implications and its spiritual significance. It is a fact of human experience that most persons, if sufficiently hard pressed, will pray in some way to some source of help.

Do not be so slothful as to ask God to solve your difficulties, but never hesitate to ask him for wisdom and spiritual strength to guide and sustain you while you yourself resolutely and courageously attack the problems at hand.

Prayer has been an indispensable factor in the progress and preservation of religious civilization, and it still has mighty contributions to make to the further enhancement and spiritualization of society if those who pray will only do so in the light of scientific facts, philosophic wisdom, intellectual sincerity, and spiritual faith. Pray as Jesus taught his disciples—honestly, unselfishly, with fairness, and without doubting.

But the efficacy of prayer in the personal spiritual experience of the one who prays is in no way dependent on such a worshiper's intellectual understanding, philosophic acumen, social level, cultural status, or other mortal acquirements. The psychic and spiritual concomitants of the prayer of faith are immediate, personal, and experiential. There is no other technique whereby every man, regardless of all other mortal accomplishments, can so effectively and immediately approach the threshold of that realm wherein he can communicate with his Maker, where the creature contacts with the reality of the Creator, with the indwelling Thought Adjuster.

7. MYSTICISM, ECSTASY, AND INSPIRATION

Mysticism, as the technique of the cultivation of the consciousness of the presence of God, is altogether praiseworthy, but when such practices lead to social isolation and culminate in religious fanaticism, they are all but reprehensible. Altogether too frequently that which the overwrought mystic evaluates as divine inspiration is the uprisings of his own deep mind. The contact of the mortal mind with its indwelling Adjuster, while often favored by devoted meditation, is more frequently facilitated by wholehearted and loving service in unselfish ministry to one's fellow creatures.

The great religious teachers and the prophets of past ages were not extreme mystics. They were God-knowing men and women who best served their God by unselfish ministry to their fellow mortals. Jesus often took his apostles away by themselves for short periods to engage in meditation and prayer, but for the most part he kept them in service-contact with the multitudes. The soul of man requires spiritual exercise as well as spiritual nourishment.

Religious ecstasy is permissible when resulting from sane antecedents, but such experiences are more often the outgrowth of purely emotional influences than a manifestation of deep spiritual character. Religious persons must not regard every vivid psychologic presentiment and every intense emotional experience as a divine revelation or a spiritual communication. Genuine spiritual ecstasy is usually associated with great outward calmness and almost perfect emotional control. But true prophetic vision is a superpsychologic presentiment. Such visitations are not pseudo hallucinations, neither are they trancelike ecstasies.

The human mind may perform in response to so-called inspiration when it is sensitive either to the uprisings of the subconscious or to the stimulus of the superconscious. In either case it appears to the individual that such augmentations of the content of consciousness are more or less foreign. Unrestrained mystical enthusiasm and rampant religious ecstasy are not the credentials of inspiration, supposedly divine credentials.

The practical test of all these strange religious experiences of mysticism, ecstasy, and inspiration is to observe whether these phenomena cause an individual:

1. To enjoy better and more complete physical health.
2. To function more efficiently and practically in his mental life.
3. More fully and joyfully to socialize his religious experience.
4. More completely to spiritualize his day-by-day living while faithfully discharging the commonplace duties of routine mortal existence.

5. To enhance his love for, and appreciation of, truth, beauty, and goodness.

6. To conserve currently recognized social, moral, ethical, and spiritual values.

7. To increase his spiritual insight—God-consciousness.

But prayer has no real association with these exceptional religious experiences. When prayer becomes overmuch aesthetic, when it consists almost exclusively in beautiful and blissful contemplation of paradisiacal divinity, it loses much of its socializing influence and tends toward mysticism and the isolation of its devotees. There is a certain danger associated with overmuch private praying which is corrected and prevented by group praying, community devotions.

8. PRAYING AS A PERSONAL EXPERIENCE

There is a truly spontaneous aspect to prayer, for primitive man found himself praying long before he had any clear concept of a God. Early man was wont to pray in two diverse situations: When in dire need, he experienced the impulse to reach out for help; and when jubilant, he indulged the impulsive expression of joy.

Prayer is not an evolution of magic; they each arose independently. Magic was an attempt to adjust Deity to conditions; prayer is the effort to adjust the personality to the will of Deity. True prayer is both moral and religious; magic is neither.

Prayer may become an established custom; many pray because others do. Still others pray because they fear something direful may happen if they do not offer their regular supplications.

To some individuals prayer is the calm expression of gratitude; to others, a group expression of praise, social devotions; sometimes it is the imitation of another's religion, while in true praying it is the sincere and trusting communication of the spiritual nature of the creature with the anywhere presence of the spirit of the Creator.

Prayer may be a spontaneous expression of God-consciousness or a meaningless recitation of theologic formulas. It may be the ecstatic praise of a God-knowing soul or the slavish obeisance of a fear-ridden mortal. It is sometimes the pathetic expression of spiritual craving and sometimes the blatant shouting of pious phrases. Prayer may be joyous praise or a humble plea for forgiveness.

Prayer may be the childlike plea for the impossible or the mature entreaty for moral growth and spiritual power. A petition may be for daily bread or may embody a wholehearted yearning to find God and to do his will. It may be a wholly selfish request or a true and magnificent gesture toward the realization of unselfish brotherhood.

Prayer may be an angry cry for vengeance or a merciful intercession for one's enemies. It may be the expression of a hope of changing God or the powerful technique of changing one's self. It may be the cringing plea of a lost sinner before a supposedly stern Judge or the joyful expression of a liberated son of the living and merciful heavenly Father.

Modern man is perplexed by the thought of talking things over with God in a purely personal way. Many have abandoned regular praying; they only pray when under unusual pressure—in emergencies. Man should be unafraid to talk to God, but only a spiritual child would undertake to persuade, or presume to change, God.

But real praying does attain reality. Even when the air currents are ascending, no bird can soar except by outstretched wings. Prayer elevates man because it is a technique of progressing by the utilization of the ascending spiritual currents of the universe.

Genuine prayer adds to spiritual growth, modifies attitudes, and yields that satisfaction which comes from communion with divinity. It is a spontaneous outburst of God-consciousness.

God answers man's prayer by giving him an increased revelation of truth, an enhanced appreciation of beauty, and an augmented concept of goodness. Prayer is a subjective gesture, but it contacts with mighty objective realities on the spiritual levels of human experience; it is a meaningful reach by the human for superhuman values. It is the most potent spiritual-growth stimulus.

Words are irrelevant to prayer; they are merely the intellectual channel in which the river of spiritual supplication may chance to flow. The word value of a prayer is purely autosuggestive in private devotions and sociosuggestive in group devotions. God answers the soul's attitude, not the words.

Prayer is not a technique of escape from conflict but rather a stimulus to growth in the very face of conflict. Pray only for values, not things; for growth, not for gratification.

9. CONDITIONS OF EFFECTIVE PRAYER

If you would engage in effective praying, you should bear in mind the laws of prevailing petitions:

1. You must qualify as a potent prayer by sincerely and courageously facing the problems of universe reality. You must possess cosmic stamina.

2. You must have honestly exhausted the human capacity for human adjustment. You must have been industrious.

3. You must surrender every wish of mind and every craving of soul to the transforming embrace of spiritual growth. You must have experienced an enhancement of meanings and an elevation of values.

4. You must make a wholehearted choice of the divine will. You must obliterate the dead center of indecision.

5. You not only recognize the Father's will and choose to do it, but you have effected an unqualified consecration, and a dynamic dedication, to the actual doing of the Father's will.

6. Your prayer will be directed exclusively for divine wisdom to solve the specific human problems encountered in the Paradise ascension—the attainment of divine perfection.

7. And you must have faith—living faith.

[Presented by the Chief of the Urantia Midwayers.]

PAPER 92

THE LATER EVOLUTION OF RELIGION

MAN possessed a religion of natural origin as a part of his evolutionary experience long before any systematic revelations were made on Urantia. But this religion of *natural* origin was, in itself, the product of man's superanimal endowments. Evolutionary religion arose slowly throughout the millenniums of mankind's experiential career through the ministry of the following influences operating within, and impinging upon, savage, barbarian, and civilized man:

1. *The adjutant of worship*—the appearance in animal consciousness of superanimal potentials for reality perception. This might be termed the primordial human instinct for Deity.

2. *The adjutant of wisdom*—the manifestation in a worshipful mind of the tendency to direct its adoration in higher channels of expression and toward ever-expanding concepts of Deity reality.

3. *The Holy Spirit*—this is the initial supermind bestowal, and it unfailingly appears in all bona fide human personalities. This ministry to a worship-craving and wisdom-desiring mind creates the capacity to self-realize the postulate of human survival, both in theologic concept and as an actual and factual personality experience.

The co-ordinate functioning of these three divine ministrations is quite sufficient to initiate and prosecute the growth of evolutionary religion. These influences are later augmented by Thought Adjusters, seraphim, and the Spirit of Truth, all of which accelerate the rate of religious development. These agencies have long functioned on Urantia, and they will continue here as long as this planet remains an inhabited sphere. Much of the potential of these divine agencies has never yet had opportunity for expression; much will be revealed in the ages to come as mortal religion ascends, level by level, toward the supernal heights of morontia value and spirit truth.

1. THE EVOLUTIONARY NATURE OF RELIGION

The evolution of religion has been traced from early fear and ghosts down through many successive stages of development, including those efforts first to coerce and then to cajole the spirits. Tribal fetishes grew into totems and tribal gods; magic formulas became modern prayers. Circumcision, at first a sacrifice, became a hygienic procedure.

Religion progressed from nature worship up through ghost worship to fetishism throughout the savage childhood of the races. With the dawn of civilization the human race espoused the more mystic and symbolic beliefs, while now, with approaching maturity, mankind is ripening for the appreciation of real religion, even a beginning of the revelation of truth itself.

Religion arises as a biologic reaction of mind to spiritual beliefs and the environment; it is the last thing to perish or change in a race. Religion is society's adjustment, in any age, to that which is mysterious. As a social institution it embraces rites, symbols, cults, scriptures, altars, shrines, and temples. Holy water, relics, fetishes, charms, vestments, bells, drums, and priesthoods are common to all religions. And it is impossible entirely to divorce purely evolved religion from either magic or sorcery.

Mystery and power have always stimulated religious feelings and fears, while emotion has ever functioned as a powerful conditioning factor in their development. Fear has always been the basic religious stimulus. Fear fashions the gods of evolutionary religion and motivates the religious ritual of the primitive believers. As civilization advances, fear becomes modified by reverence, admiration, respect, and sympathy and is then further conditioned by remorse and repentance.

One Asiatic people taught that "God is a great fear"; that is the outgrowth of purely evolutionary religion. Jesus, the revelation of the highest type of religious living, proclaimed that "God is love."

2. RELIGION AND THE MORES

Religion is the most rigid and unyielding of all human institutions, but it does tardily adjust to changing society. Eventually, evolutionary religion does reflect the changing mores, which, in turn, may have been affected by revealed religion. Slowly, surely, but grudgingly, does religion (worship) follow in the wake of wisdom—knowledge directed by experiential reason and illuminated by divine revelation.

Religion clings to the mores; that which *was* is ancient and supposedly sacred. For this reason and no other, stone implements persisted long into the age of bronze and iron. This statement is of record: "And if you will make me an altar of stone, you shall not build it of hewn stone, for, if you use your tools in making it, you have polluted it." Even today, the Hindus kindle their altar fires by using a primitive fire drill. In the course of evolutionary religion, novelty has always been regarded as sacrilege. The sacrament must consist, not of new and manufactured food, but of the most primitive of viands: "The flesh roasted with fire and unleavened bread served with bitter herbs." All types of social usage and even legal procedures cling to the old forms.

When modern man wonders at the presentation of so much in the scriptures of different religions that may be regarded as obscene, he should pause to consider that passing generations have feared to eliminate what their ancestors deemed to be holy and sacred. A great deal that one generation might look upon as obscene, preceding generations have considered a part of their accepted mores, even as approved religious rituals. A considerable amount of religious controversy has been occasioned by the never-ending attempts to reconcile olden but reprehensible practices with newly advanced reason, to find plausible theories in justification of creedal perpetuation of ancient and outworn customs.

But it is only foolish to attempt the too sudden acceleration of religious growth. A race or nation can only assimilate from any advanced religion that which is reasonably consistent and compatible with its current evolutionary status, plus its genius for adaptation. Social, climatic, political, and economic conditions are all influential in determining the course and progress of religious evolution. Social morality is not determined by religion, that is, by evolutionary religion; rather are the forms of religion dictated by the racial morality.

Races of men only superficially accept a strange and new religion; they actually adjust it to their mores and old ways of believing. This is well illustrated by the example of a certain New Zealand tribe whose priests, after nominally accepting Christianity, professed to have received direct revelations from Gabriel to the effect that this selfsame tribe had become the chosen people of God and directing that they be permitted freely to indulge in loose sex relations and numerous other of their olden and reprehensible customs. And immediately all of the new-made Christians went over to this new and less exacting version of Christianity.

Religion has at one time or another sanctioned all sorts of contrary and inconsistent behavior, has at some time approved of practically all that is now regarded as immoral or sinful. Conscience, untaught by experience and unaided by reason, never has been, and never can be, a safe and unerring guide to human conduct. Conscience is not a divine voice speaking to the human soul. It is merely the sum total of the moral and ethical content of the mores of any current stage of existence; it simply represents the humanly conceived ideal of reaction in any given set of circumstances.

3. THE NATURE OF EVOLUTIONARY RELIGION

The study of human religion is the examination of the fossil-bearing social strata of past ages. The mores of the anthropomorphic gods are a truthful reflection of the morals of the men who first conceived such deities. Ancient religions and mythology faithfully portray the beliefs and traditions of peoples long since lost in obscurity. These olden cult practices persist alongside newer economic customs and social evolutions and, of course, appear grossly inconsistent. The remnants of the cult present a true picture of the racial religions of the past. Always remember, the cults are formed, not to discover truth, but rather to promulgate their creeds.

Religion has always been largely a matter of rites, rituals, observances, ceremonies, and dogmas. It has usually become tainted with that persistently mischief-making error, the chosen-people delusion. The cardinal religious ideas of incantation, inspiration, revelation, propitiation, repentance, atonement, intercession, sacrifice, prayer, confession, worship, survival after death, sacrament, ritual, ransom, salvation, redemption, covenant, uncleanness, purification, prophecy, original sin—they all go back to the early times of primordial ghost fear.

Primitive religion is nothing more nor less than the struggle for material existence extended to embrace existence beyond the grave. The observances of such a creed represented the extension of the self-maintenance struggle into the domain of an imagined ghost-spirit world. But when tempted to criticize evolutionary religion, be careful. Remember, that is *what happened;* it is a historical fact. And further recall that the power of any idea lies, not in its certainty or truth, but rather in the vividness of its human appeal.

Evolutionary religion makes no provision for change or revision; unlike science, it does not provide for its own progressive correction. Evolved religion commands respect because its followers believe it is *The Truth;* "the faith once delivered to the saints" must, in theory, be both final and infallible. The cult resists development because real progress is certain to modify or destroy the cult itself; therefore must revision always be forced upon it.

Only two influences can modify and uplift the dogmas of natural religion: the pressure of the slowly advancing mores and the periodic illumination of epochal revelation. And it is not strange that progress was slow; in ancient days, to be progressive or inventive meant to be killed as a sorcerer. The cult advances slowly in generation epochs and agelong cycles. But it does move forward. Evolutionary belief in ghosts laid the foundation for a philosophy of revealed religion which will eventually destroy the superstition of its origin.

Religion has handicapped social development in many ways, but without religion there would have been no enduring morality nor ethics, no worth-while civilization. Religion enmothered much nonreligious culture: Sculpture originated in idol making, architecture in temple building, poetry in incantations, music in worship chants, drama in the acting for spirit guidance, and dancing in the seasonal worship festivals.

But while calling attention to the fact that religion was essential to the development and preservation of civilization, it should be recorded that natural religion has also done much to cripple and handicap the very civilization which it otherwise fostered and maintained. Religion has hampered industrial activities and economic development; it has been wasteful of labor and has squandered capital; it has not always been helpful to the family; it has not adequately fostered peace and good will; it has sometimes neglected education and retarded science; it has unduly impoverished life for the pretended enrichment of death. Evolutionary religion, human religion, has indeed been guilty of all these and many more mistakes, errors, and blunders; nevertheless, it did maintain cultural ethics, civilized morality, and social coherence, and made it possible for later revealed religion to compensate for these many evolutionary shortcomings.

Evolutionary religion has been man's most expensive but incomparably effective institution. Human religion can be justified only in the light of evolutionary civilization. If man were not the ascendant product of animal evolution, then would such a course of religious development stand without justification.

Religion facilitated the accumulation of capital; it fostered work of certain kinds; the leisure of the priests promoted art and knowledge; the race, in the end, gained much as a result of all these early errors in ethical technique. The shamans, honest and dishonest, were terribly expensive, but they were worth all they cost. The learned professions and science itself emerged from the parasitical priesthoods. Religion fostered civilization and provided societal continuity; it has been the moral police force of all time. Religion provided that human discipline and self-control which made *wisdom* possible. Religion is the efficient scourge of evolution which ruthlessly drives indolent and suffering humanity from its natural state of intellectual inertia forward and upward to the higher levels of reason and wisdom.

And this sacred heritage of animal ascent, evolutionary religion, must ever continue to be refined and ennobled by the continuous censorship of revealed religion and by the fiery furnace of genuine science.

4. THE GIFT OF REVELATION

Revelation is evolutionary but always progressive. Down through the ages of a world's history, the revelations of religion are ever-expanding and successively more enlightening. It is the mission of revelation to sort and censor the successive religions of evolution. But if revelation is to exalt and upstep the religions of evolution, then must such divine visitations portray teachings which are not too far removed from the thought and reactions of the age in which they are presented. Thus must and does revelation always keep in touch with evolution. Always must the religion of revelation be limited by man's capacity of receptivity.

But regardless of apparent connection or derivation, the religions of revelation are always characterized by a belief in some Deity of final value and in some concept of the survival of personality identity after death.

Evolutionary religion is sentimental, not logical. It is man's reaction to belief in a hypothetical ghost-spirit world—the human belief-reflex, excited by the realization and fear of the unknown. Revelatory religion is propounded by the real spiritual world; it is the response of the superintellectual cosmos to the mortal hunger to believe in, and depend upon, the universal Deities. Evolutionary religion pictures the circuitous gropings of humanity in quest of truth; revelatory religion *is* that very truth.

There have been many events of religious revelation but only five of epochal significance. These were as follows:

1. *The Dalamatian teachings.* The true concept of the First Source and Center was first promulgated on Urantia by the one hundred corporeal members of Prince Caligastia's staff. This expanding revelation of Deity went on for more than three hundred thousand years until it was suddenly terminated by the planetary secession and the disruption of the teaching regime. Except for the work of Van, the influence of the Dalamatian revelation was practically lost to the whole world. Even the Nodites had forgotten this truth by the time of Adam's arrival. Of all who received the teachings of the one hundred, the red men held them longest, but the idea of the Great Spirit was but a hazy concept in Amerindian religion when contact with Christianity greatly clarified and strengthened it.

2. *The Edenic teachings.* Adam and Eve again portrayed the concept of the Father of all to the evolutionary peoples. The disruption of the first Eden halted the course of the Adamic revelation before it had ever fully started. But the aborted teachings of Adam were carried on by the Sethite priests, and some of these truths have never been entirely lost to the world. The entire trend of Levantine religious evolution was modified by the teachings of the Sethites. But by 2500 B.C. mankind had largely lost sight of the revelation sponsored in the days of Eden.

3. *Melchizedek of Salem.* This emergency Son of Nebadon inaugurated the third revelation of truth on Urantia. The cardinal precepts of his teachings were *trust* and *faith.* He taught trust in the omnipotent beneficence of God and proclaimed that faith was the act by which men earned God's favor. His teachings gradually commingled with the beliefs and practices of various evolutionary

religions and finally developed into those theologic systems present on Urantia at the opening of the first millennium after Christ.

4. *Jesus of Nazareth.* Christ Michael presented for the fourth time to Urantia the concept of God as the Universal Father, and this teaching has generally persisted ever since. The essence of his teaching was *love* and *service,* the loving worship which a creature son voluntarily gives in recognition of, and response to, the loving ministry of God his Father; the freewill service which such creature sons bestow upon their brethren in the joyous realization that in this service they are likewise serving God the Father.

5. *The Urantia Papers.* The papers, of which this is one, constitute the most recent presentation of truth to the mortals of Urantia. These papers differ from all previous revelations, for they are not the work of a single universe personality but a composite presentation by many beings. But no revelation short of the attainment of the Universal Father can ever be complete. All other celestial ministrations are no more than partial, transient, and practically adapted to local conditions in time and space. While such admissions as this may possibly detract from the immediate force and authority of all revelations, the time has arrived on Urantia when it is advisable to make such frank statements, even at the risk of weakening the future influence and authority of this, the most recent of the revelations of truth to the mortal races of Urantia.

5. THE GREAT RELIGIOUS LEADERS

In evolutionary religion, the gods are conceived to exist in the likeness of man's image; in revelatory religion, men are taught that they are God's sons—even fashioned in the finite image of divinity; in the synthesized beliefs compounded from the teachings of revelation and the products of evolution, the God concept is a blend of:

1. The pre-existent ideas of the evolutionary cults.
2. The sublime ideals of revealed religion.
3. The personal viewpoints of the great religious leaders, the prophets and teachers of mankind.

Most great religious epochs have been inaugurated by the life and teachings of some outstanding personality; leadership has originated a majority of the worth-while moral movements of history. And men have always tended to venerate the leader, even at the expense of his teachings; to revere his personality, even though losing sight of the truths which he proclaimed. And this is not without reason; there is an instinctive longing in the heart of evolutionary man for help from above and beyond. This craving is designed to anticipate the appearance on earth of the Planetary Prince and the later Material Sons. On Urantia man has been deprived of these superhuman leaders and rulers, and therefore does he constantly seek to make good this loss by enshrouding his human leaders with legends pertaining to supernatural origins and miraculous careers.

Many races have conceived of their leaders as being born of virgins; their careers are liberally sprinkled with miraculous episodes, and their return is always expected by their respective groups. In central Asia the tribesmen still look for the return of Genghis Khan; in Tibet, China, and India it is Buddha; in Islam it is Mohammed; among the Amerinds it was Hesunanin Onamonalonton;

with the Hebrews it was, in general, Adam's return as a material ruler. In Babylon the god Marduk was a perpetuation of the Adam legend, the son-of-God idea, the connecting link between man and God. Following the appearance of Adam on earth, so-called sons of God were common among the world races.

But regardless of the superstitious awe in which they were often held, it remains a fact that these teachers were the temporal personality fulcrums on which the levers of revealed truth depended for the advancement of the morality, philosophy, and religion of mankind.

There have been hundreds upon hundreds of religious leaders in the million-year human history of Urantia from Onagar to Guru Nanak. During this time there have been many ebbs and flows of the tide of religious truth and spiritual faith, and each renaissance of Urantian religion has, in the past, been identified with the life and teachings of some religious leader. In considering the teachers of recent times, it may prove helpful to group them into the seven major religious epochs of post-Adamic Urantia:

1. *The Sethite period.* The Sethite priests, as regenerated under the leadership of Amosad, became the great post-Adamic teachers. They functioned throughout the lands of the Andites, and their influence persisted longest among the Greeks, Sumerians, and Hindus. Among the latter they have continued to the present time as the Brahmans of the Hindu faith. The Sethites and their followers never entirely lost the Trinity concept revealed by Adam.

2. *Era of the Melchizedek missionaries.* Urantia religion was in no small measure regenerated by the efforts of those teachers who were commissioned by Machiventa Melchizedek when he lived and taught at Salem almost two thousand years before Christ. These missionaries proclaimed faith as the price of favor with God, and their teachings, though unproductive of any immediately appearing religions, nevertheless formed the foundations on which later teachers of truth were to build the religions of Urantia.

3. *The post-Melchizedek era.* Though Amenemope and Ikhnaton both taught in this period, the outstanding religious genius of the post-Melchizedek era was the leader of a group of Levantine Bedouins and the founder of the Hebrew religion—Moses. Moses taught monotheism. Said he: "Hear, O Israel, the Lord our God is one God." "The Lord he is God. There is none beside him." He persistently sought to uproot the remnants of the ghost cult among his people, even prescribing the death penalty for its practitioners. The monotheism of Moses was adulterated by his successors, but in later times they did return to many of his teachings. The greatness of Moses lies in his wisdom and sagacity. Other men have had greater concepts of God, but no one man was ever so successful in inducing large numbers of people to adopt such advanced beliefs.

4. *The sixth century before Christ.* Many men arose to proclaim truth in this, one of the greatest centuries of religious awakening ever witnessed on Urantia. Among these should be recorded Gautama, Confucius, Lao-tse, Zoroaster, and the Jainist teachers. The teachings of Gautama have become widespread in Asia, and he is revered as the Buddha by millions. Confucius was to Chinese morality what Plato was to Greek philosophy, and while there were religious repercussions to the teachings of both, strictly speaking, neither was a religious teacher; Lao-tse envisioned more of God in Tao than did Confucius in humanity or Plato in idealism. Zoroaster, while much affected by the prevalent

concept of dual spiritism, the good and the bad, at the same time definitely exalted the idea of one eternal Deity and of the ultimate victory of light over darkness.

5. *The first century after Christ.* As a religious teacher, Jesus of Nazareth started out with the cult which had been established by John the Baptist and progressed as far as he could away from fasts and forms. Aside from Jesus, Paul of Tarsus and Philo of Alexandria were the greatest teachers of this era. Their concepts of religion have played a dominant part in the evolution of that faith which bears the name of Christ.

6. *The sixth century after Christ.* Mohammed founded a religion which was superior to many of the creeds of his time. His was a protest against the social demands of the faiths of foreigners and against the incoherence of the religious life of his own people.

7. *The fifteenth century after Christ.* This period witnessed two religious movements: the disruption of the unity of Christianity in the Occident and the synthesis of a new religion in the Orient. In Europe institutionalized Christianity had attained that degree of inelasticity which rendered further growth incompatible with unity. In the Orient the combined teachings of Islam, Hinduism, and Buddhism were synthesized by Nanak and his followers into Sikhism, one of the most advanced religions of Asia.

The future of Urantia will doubtless be characterized by the appearance of teachers of religious truth—the Fatherhood of God and the fraternity of all creatures. But it is to be hoped that the ardent and sincere efforts of these future prophets will be directed less toward the strengthening of interreligious barriers and more toward the augmentation of the religious brotherhood of spiritual worship among the many followers of the differing intellectual theologies which so characterize Urantia of Satania.

6. THE COMPOSITE RELIGIONS

Twentieth-century Urantia religions present an interesting study of the social evolution of man's worship impulse. Many faiths have progressed very little since the days of the ghost cult. The Pygmies of Africa have no religious reactions as a class, although some of them believe slightly in a spirit environment. They are today just where primitive man was when the evolution of religion began. The basic belief of primitive religion was survival after death. The idea of worshiping a personal God indicates advanced evolutionary development, even the first stage of revelation. The Dyaks have evolved only the most primitive religious practices. The comparatively recent Eskimos and Amerinds had very meager concepts of God; they believed in ghosts and had an indefinite idea of survival of some sort after death. Present-day native Australians have only a ghost fear, dread of the dark, and a crude ancestor veneration. The Zulus are just evolving a religion of ghost fear and sacrifice. Many African tribes, except through missionary work of Christians and Mohammedans, are not yet beyond the fetish stage of religious evolution. But some groups have long held to the idea of monotheism, like the onetime Thracians, who also believed in immortality.

On Urantia, evolutionary and revelatory religion are progressing side by side while they blend and coalesce into the diversified theologic systems found in the world in the times of the inditement of these papers. These religions, the religions of twentieth-century Urantia, may be enumerated as follows:

1. Hinduism—the most ancient.
2. The Hebrew religion.
3. Buddhism.
4. The Confucian teachings.
5. The Taoist beliefs.
6. Zoroastrianism.
7. Shinto.
8. Jainism.
9. Christianity.
10. Islam.
11. Sikhism—the most recent.

The most advanced religions of ancient times were Judaism and Hinduism, and each respectively has greatly influenced the course of religious development in Orient and Occident. Both Hindus and Hebrews believed that their religions were inspired and revealed, and they believed all others to be decadent forms of the one true faith.

India is divided among Hindu, Sikh, Mohammedan, and Jain, each picturing God, man, and the universe as these are variously conceived. China follows the Taoist and the Confucian teachings; Shinto is revered in Japan.

The great international, interracial faiths are the Hebraic, Buddhist, Christian, and Islamic. Buddhism stretches from Ceylon and Burma through Tibet and China to Japan. It has shown an adaptability to the mores of many peoples that has been equaled only by Christianity.

The Hebrew religion encompasses the philosophic transition from polytheism to monotheism; it is an evolutionary link between the religions of evolution and the religions of revelation. The Hebrews were the only western people to follow their early evolutionary gods straight through to the God of revelation. But this truth never became widely accepted until the days of Isaiah, who once again taught the blended idea of a racial deity combined with a Universal Creator: "O Lord of Hosts, God of Israel, you are God, even you alone; you have made heaven and earth." At one time the hope of the survival of Occidental civilization lay in the sublime Hebraic concepts of goodness and the advanced Hellenic concepts of beauty.

The Christian religion is the religion about the life and teachings of Christ based upon the theology of Judaism, modified further through the assimilation of certain Zoroastrian teachings and Greek philosophy, and formulated primarily by three individuals: Philo, Peter, and Paul. It has passed through many phases of evolution since the time of Paul and has become so thoroughly Occidentalized that many non-European peoples very naturally look upon Christianity as a strange revelation of a strange God and for strangers.

Islam is the religio-cultural connective of North Africa, the Levant, and southeastern Asia. It was Jewish theology in connection with the later Christian teachings that made Islam monotheistic. The followers of Mohammed stumbled at the advanced teachings of the Trinity; they could not comprehend the doctrine of three divine personalities and one Deity. It is always difficult to induce evolutionary minds *suddenly* to accept avanced revealed truth. Man is an evolutionary creature and in the main must get his religion by evolutionary techniques.

Ancestor worship onetime constituted a decided advance in religious evolution, but it is both amazing and regrettable that this primitive concept persists in China, Japan, and India amidst so much that is relatively more advanced, such as Buddhism and Hinduism. In the Occident, ancestor worship developed into the veneration of national gods and respect for racial heroes. In the twentieth century this hero-venerating nationalistic religion makes its appearance in the various radical and nationalistic secularisms which characterize many races and nations of the Occident. Much of this same attitude is also found in the great universities and the larger industrial communities of the English-speaking peoples. Not very different from these concepts is the idea that religion is but "a shared quest of the good life." The "national religions" are nothing more than a reversion to the early Roman emperor worship and to Shinto—worship of the state in the imperial family.

7. THE FURTHER EVOLUTION OF RELIGION

Religion can never become a scientific fact. Philosophy may, indeed, rest on a scientific basis, but religion will ever remain either evolutionary or revelatory, or a possible combination of both, as it is in the world today.

New religions cannot be invented; they are either evolved, or else they are *suddenly revealed.* All new evolutionary religions are merely advancing expressions of the old beliefs, new adaptations and adjustments. The old does not cease to exist; it is merged with the new, even as Sikhism budded and blossomed out of the soil and forms of Hinduism, Buddhism, Islam, and other contemporary cults. Primitive religion was very democratic; the savage was quick to borrow or lend. Only with revealed religion did autocratic and intolerant theologic egotism appear.

The many religions of Urantia are all good to the extent that they bring man to God and bring the realization of the Father to man. It is a fallacy for any group of religionists to conceive of their creed as *The Truth;* such attitudes bespeak more of theological arrogance than of certainty of faith. There is not a Urantia religion that could not profitably study and assimilate the best of the truths contained in every other faith, for all contain truth. Religionists would do better to borrow the best in their neighbors' living spiritual faith rather than to denounce the worst in their lingering superstitions and outworn rituals.

All these religions have arisen as a result of man's variable intellectual response to his identical spiritual leading. They can never hope to attain a uniformity of creeds, dogmas, and rituals—these are intellectual; but they can, and some day will, realize a unity in true worship of the Father of all, for this is spiritual, and it is forever true, in the spirit all men are equal.

Primitive religion was largely a material-value consciousness, but civilization elevates religious values, for true religion is the devotion of the self to the service of meaningful and supreme values. As religion evolves, ethics becomes the philosophy of morals, and morality becomes the discipline of self by the standards of highest meanings and supreme values—divine and spiritual ideals. And thus religion becomes a spontaneous and exquisite devotion, the living experience of the loyalty of love.

The quality of a religion is indicated by:

1. Level of values—loyalties.

2. Depth of meanings—the sensitization of the individual to the idealistic appreciation of these highest values.

3. Consecration intensity—the degree of devotion to these divine values.

4. The unfettered progress of the personality in this cosmic path of idealistic spiritual living, realization of sonship with God and never-ending progressive citizenship in the universe.

Religious meanings progress in self-consciousness when the child transfers his ideas of omnipotence from his parents to God. And the entire religious experience of such a child is largely dependent on whether fear or love has dominated the parent-child relationship. Slaves have always experienced great difficulty in transferring their master-fear into concepts of God-love. Civilization, science, and advanced religions must deliver mankind from those fears born of the dread of natural phenomena. And so should greater enlightenment deliver educated mortals from all dependence on intermediaries in communion with Deity.

These intermediate stages of idolatrous hesitation in the transfer of veneration from the human and the visible to the divine and invisible are inevitable, but they should be shortened by the consciousness of the facilitating ministry of the indwelling divine spirit. Nevertheless, man has been profoundly influenced, not only by his concepts of Deity, but also by the character of the heroes whom he has chosen to honor. It is most unfortunate that those who have come to venerate the divine and risen Christ should have overlooked the man—the valiant and courageous hero—Joshua ben Joseph.

Modern man is adequately self-conscious of religion, but his worshipful customs are confused and discredited by his accelerated social metamorphosis and unprecedented scientific developments. Thinking men and women want religion redefined, and this demand will compel religion to re-evaluate itself.

Modern man is confronted with the task of making more readjustments of human values in one generation than have been made in two thousand years. And this all influences the social attitude toward religion, for religion is a way of living as well as a technique of thinking.

True religion must ever be, at one and the same time, the eternal foundation and the guiding star of all enduring civilizations.

[Presented by a Melchizedek of Nebadon.]

PAPER 93

MACHIVENTA MELCHIZEDEK

THE Melchizedeks are widely known as emergency Sons, for they engage in an amazing range of activities on the worlds of a local universe. When any extraordinary problem arises, or when something unusual is to be attempted, it is quite often a Melchizedek who accepts the assignment. The ability of the Melchizedek Sons to function in emergencies and on widely divergent levels of the universe, even on the physical level of personality manifestation, is peculiar to their order. Only the Life Carriers share to any degree this metamorphic range of personality function.

The Melchizedek order of universe sonship has been exceedingly active on Urantia. A corps of twelve served in conjunction with the Life Carriers. A later corps of twelve became receivers for your world shortly after the Caligastia secession and continued in authority until the time of Adam and Eve. These twelve Melchizedeks returned to Urantia upon the default of Adam and Eve, and they continued thereafter as planetary receivers on down to the day when Jesus of Nazareth, as the Son of Man, became the titular Planetary Prince of Urantia.

1. THE MACHIVENTA INCARNATION

Revealed truth was threatened with extinction during the millenniums which followed the miscarriage of the Adamic mission on Urantia. Though making progress intellectually, the human races were slowly losing ground spiritually. About 3000 B.C. the concept of God had grown very hazy in the minds of men.

The twelve Melchizedek receivers knew of Michael's impending bestowal on their planet, but they did not know how soon it would occur; therefore they convened in solemn council and petitioned the Most Highs of Edentia that some provision be made for maintaining the light of truth on Urantia. This plea was dismissed with the mandate that "the conduct of affairs on 606 of Satania is fully in the hands of the Melchizedek custodians." The receivers then appealed to the Father Melchizedek for help but only received word that they should continue to uphold truth in the manner of their own election "until the arrival of a bestowal Son," who "would rescue the planetary titles from forfeiture and uncertainty."

And it was in consequence of having been thrown so completely on their own resources that Machiventa Melchizedek, one of the twelve planetary receivers, volunteered to do that which had been done only six times in all the history of Nebadon: to personalize on earth as a temporary man of the realm, to bestow himself as an emergency Son of world ministry. Permission was granted for this adventure by the Salvington authorities, and the actual incarnation of

Machiventa Melchizedek was consummated near what was to become the city of Salem, in Palestine. The entire transaction of the materialization of this Melchizedek Son was completed by the planetary receivers with the co-operation of the Life Carriers, certain of the Master Physical Controllers, and other celestial personalities resident on Urantia.

2. THE SAGE OF SALEM

It was 1,973 years before the birth of Jesus that Machiventa was bestowed upon the human races of Urantia. His coming was unspectacular; his materialization was not witnessed by human eyes. He was first observed by mortal man on that eventful day when he entered the tent of Amdon, a Chaldean herder of Sumerian extraction. And the proclamation of his mission was embodied in the simple statement which he made to this shepherd, "I am Melchizedek, priest of El Elyon, the Most High, the one and only God."

When the herder had recovered from his astonishment, and after he had plied this stranger with many questions, he asked Melchizedek to sup with him, and this was the first time in his long universe career that Machiventa had partaken of material food, the nourishment which was to sustain him throughout his ninety-four years of life as a material being.

And that night, as they talked out under the stars, Melchizedek began his mission of the revelation of the truth of the reality of God when, with a sweep of his arm, he turned to Amdon, saying, "El Elyon, the Most High, is the divine creator of the stars of the firmament and even of this very earth on which we live, and he is also the supreme God of heaven."

Within a few years Melchizedek had gathered around himself a group of pupils, disciples, and believers who formed the nucleus of the later community of Salem. He was soon known throughout Palestine as the priest of El Elyon, the Most High, and as the sage of Salem. Among some of the surrounding tribes he was often referred to as the sheik, or king, of Salem. Salem was the site which after the disappearance of Melchizedek became the city of Jebus, subsequently being called Jerusalem.

In personal appearance, Melchizedek resembled the then blended Nodite and Sumerian peoples, being almost six feet in height and possessing a commanding presence. He spoke Chaldean and a half dozen other languages. He dressed much as did the Canaanite priests except that on his breast he wore an emblem of three concentric circles, the Satania symbol of the Paradise Trinity. In the course of his ministry this insignia of three concentric circles became regarded as so sacred by his followers that they never dared to use it, and it was soon forgotten with the passing of a few generations.

Though Machiventa lived after the manner of the men of the realm, he never married, nor could he have left offspring on earth. His physical body, while resembling that of the human male, was in reality on the order of those especially constructed bodies used by the one hundred materialized members of Prince Caligastia's staff except that it did not carry the life plasm of any human race. Nor was there available on Urantia the tree of life. Had Machiventa remained for any long period on earth, his physical mechanism would have gradually deteriorated; as it was, he terminated his bestowal mission in ninety-four years long before his material body had begun to disintegrate.

This incarnated Melchizedek received a Thought Adjuster, who indwelt his superhuman personality as the monitor of time and the mentor of the flesh, thus gaining that experience and practical introduction to Urantian problems and to the technique of indwelling an incarnated Son which enabled this spirit of the Father to function so valiantly in the human mind of the later Son of God, Michael, when he appeared on earth in the likeness of mortal flesh. And this is the only Thought Adjuster who ever functioned in two minds on Urantia, but both minds were divine as well as human.

During the incarnation in the flesh, Machiventa was in full contact with his eleven fellows of the corps of planetary custodians, but he could not communicate with other orders of celestial personalities. Aside from the Melchizedek receivers, he had no more contact with superhuman intelligences than a human being.

3. MELCHIZEDEK'S TEACHINGS

With the passing of a decade, Melchizedek organized his schools at Salem, patterning them on the olden system which had been developed by the early Sethite priests of the second Eden. Even the idea of a tithing system, which was introduced by his later convert Abraham, was also derived from the lingering traditions of the methods of the ancient Sethites.

Melchizedek taught the concept of one God, a universal Deity, but he allowed the people to associate this teaching with the Constellation Father of Norlatiadek, whom he termed El Elyon—the Most High. Melchizedek remained all but silent as to the status of Lucifer and the state of affairs on Jerusem. Lanaforge, the System Sovereign, had little to do with Urantia until after the completion of Michael's bestowal. To a majority of the Salem students Edentia was heaven and the Most High was God.

The symbol of the three concentric circles, which Melchizedek adopted as the insignia of his bestowal, a majority of the people interpreted as standing for the three kingdoms of men, angels, and God. And they were allowed to continue in that belief; very few of his followers ever knew that these three circles were emblematic of the infinity, eternity, and universality of the Paradise Trinity of divine maintenance and direction; even Abraham rather regarded this symbol as standing for the three Most Highs of Edentia, as he had been instructed that the three Most Highs functioned as one. To the extent that Melchizedek taught the Trinity concept symbolized in his insignia, he usually associated it with the three Vorondadek rulers of the constellation of Norlatiadek.

To the rank and file of his followers he made no effort to present teaching beyond the fact of the rulership of the Most Highs of Edentia—Gods of Urantia. But to some, Melchizedek taught advanced truth, embracing the conduct and organization of the local universe, while to his brilliant disciple Nordan the Kenite and his band of earnest students he taught the truths of the superuniverse and even of Havona.

The members of the family of Katro, with whom Melchizedek lived for more than thirty years, knew many of these higher truths and long perpetuated them in their family, even to the days of their illustrious descendant Moses, who thus had a compelling tradition of the days of Melchizedek handed down to him on this, his father's side, as well as through other sources on his mother's side.

Melchizedek taught his followers all they had capacity to receive and assimilate. Even many modern religious ideas about heaven and earth, of man, God, and angels, are not far removed from these teachings of Melchizedek. But this great teacher subordinated everything to the doctrine of one God, a universe Deity, a heavenly Creator, a divine Father. Emphasis was placed upon this teaching for the purpose of appealing to man's adoration and of preparing the way for the subsequent appearance of Michael as the Son of this same Universal Father.

Melchizedek taught that at some future time another Son of God would come in the flesh as he had come, but that he would be born of a woman; and that is why numerous later teachers held that Jesus was a priest, or minister, "forever after the order of Melchizedek."

And thus did Melchizedek prepare the way and set the monotheistic stage of world tendency for the bestowal of an actual Paradise Son of the one God, whom he so vividly portrayed as the Father of all, and whom he represented to Abraham as a God who would accept man on the simple terms of personal faith. And Michael, when he appeared on earth, confirmed all that Melchizedek had taught concerning the Paradise Father.

4. THE SALEM RELIGION

The ceremonies of the Salem worship were very simple. Every person who signed or marked the clay-tablet rolls of the Melchizedek church committed to memory, and subscribed to, the following belief:

1. I believe in El Elyon, the Most High God, the only Universal Father and Creator of all things.

2. I accept the Melchizedek covenant with the Most High, which bestows the favor of God on my faith, not on sacrifices and burnt offerings.

3. I promise to obey the seven commandments of Melchizedek and to tell the good news of this covenant with the Most High to all men.

And that was the whole of the creed of the Salem colony. But even such a short and simple declaration of faith was altogether too much and too advanced for the men of those days. They simply could not grasp the idea of getting divine favor for nothing—by faith. They were too deeply confirmed in the belief that man was born under forfeit to the gods. Too long and too earnestly had they sacrificed and made gifts to the priests to be able to comprehend the good news that salvation, divine favor, was a free gift to all who would believe in the Melchizedek covenant. But Abraham did believe halfheartedly, and even that was "counted for righteousness."

The seven commandments promulgated by Melchizedek were patterned along the lines of the ancient Dalamatian supreme law and very much resembled the seven commands taught in the first and second Edens. These commands of the Salem religion were:

1. You shall not serve any God but the Most High Creator of heaven and earth.

2. You shall not doubt that faith is the only requirement for eternal salvation.

3. You shall not bear false witness.

4. You shall not kill.

5. You shall not steal.

6. You shall not commit adultery.

7. You shall not show disrespect for your parents and elders.

While no sacrifices were permitted within the colony, Melchizedek well knew how difficult it is to suddenly uproot long-established customs and accordingly had wisely offered these people the substitute of a sacrament of bread and wine for the older sacrifice of flesh and blood. It is of record, "Melchizedek, king of Salem, brought forth bread and wine." But even this cautious innovation was not altogether successful; the various tribes all maintained auxiliary centers on the outskirts of Salem where they offered sacrifices and burnt offerings. Even Abraham resorted to this barbarous practice after his victory over Chedorlaomer; he simply did not feel quite at ease until he had offered a conventional sacrifice. And Melchizedek never did succeed in fully eradicating this proclivity to sacrifice from the religious practices of his followers, even of Abraham.

Like Jesus, Melchizedek attended strictly to the fulfillment of the mission of his bestowal. He did not attempt to reform the mores, to change the habits of the world, nor to promulgate even advanced sanitary practices or scientific truths. He came to achieve two tasks: to keep alive on earth the truth of the one God and to prepare the way for the subsequent mortal bestowal of a Paradise Son of that Universal Father.

Melchizedek taught elementary revealed truth at Salem for ninety-four years, and during this time Abraham attended the Salem school three different times. He finally became a convert to the Salem teachings, becoming one of Melchizedek's most brilliant pupils and chief supporters.

5. THE SELECTION OF ABRAHAM

Although it may be an error to speak of "chosen people," it is not a mistake to refer to Abraham as a chosen individual. Melchizedek did lay upon Abraham the responsibility of keeping alive the truth of one God as distinguished from the prevailing belief in plural deities.

The choice of Palestine as the site for Machiventa's activities was in part predicated upon the desire to establish contact with some human family embodying the potentials of leadership. At the time of the incarnation of Melchizedek there were many families on earth just as well prepared to receive the doctrine of Salem as was that of Abraham. There were equally endowed families among the red men, the yellow men, and the descendants of the Andites to the west and north. But, again, none of these localities were so favorably situated for Michael's subsequent appearance on earth as was the eastern shore of the Mediterranean Sea. The Melchizedek mission in Palestine and the subsequent appearance of Michael among the Hebrew people were in no small measure determined by geography, by the fact that Palestine was centrally located with reference to the then existent trade, travel, and civilization of the world.

For some time the Melchizedek receivers had been observing the ancestors of Abraham, and they confidently expected offspring in a certain generation who would be characterized by intelligence, initiative, sagacity, and sincerity. The children of Terah, the father of Abraham, in every way met these expectations. It was this possibility of contact with these versatile children of Terah that had considerable to do with the appearance of Machiventa at Salem, rather than in Egypt, China, India, or among the northern tribes.

Terah and his whole family were halfhearted converts to the Salem religion, which had been preached in Chaldea; they learned of Melchizedek through the preaching of Ovid, a Phoenician teacher who proclaimed the Salem doctrines in Ur. They left Ur intending to go directly through to Salem, but Nahor, Abraham's brother, not having seen Melchizedek, was lukewarm and persuaded them to tarry at Haran. And it was a long time after they arrived in Palestine before they were willing to destroy *all* of the household gods they had brought with them; they were slow to give up the many gods of Mesopotamia for the one God of Salem.

A few weeks after the death of Abraham's father, Terah, Melchizedek sent one of his students, Jaram the Hittite, to extend this invitation to both Abraham and Nahor: "Come to Salem, where you shall hear our teachings of the truth of the eternal Creator, and in the enlightened offspring of you two brothers shall all the world be blessed." Now Nahor had not wholly accepted the Melchizedek gospel; he remained behind and built up a strong city-state which bore his name; but Lot, Abraham's nephew, decided to go with his uncle to Salem.

Upon arriving at Salem, Abraham and Lot chose a hilly fastness near the city where they could defend themselves against the many surprise attacks of northern raiders. At this time the Hittites, Assyrians, Philistines, and other groups were constantly raiding the tribes of central and southern Palestine. From their stronghold in the hills Abraham and Lot made frequent pilgrimages to Salem.

Not long after they had established themselves near Salem, Abraham and Lot journeyed to the valley of the Nile to obtain food supplies as there was then a drought in Palestine. During his brief sojourn in Egypt Abraham found a distant relative on the Egyptian throne, and he served as the commander of two very successful military expeditions for this king. During the latter part of his sojourn on the Nile he and his wife, Sarah, lived at court, and when leaving Egypt, he was given a share of the spoils of his military campaigns.

It required great determination for Abraham to forgo the honors of the Egyptian court and return to the more spiritual work sponsored by Machiventa. But Melchizedek was revered even in Egypt, and when the full story was laid before Pharaoh, he strongly urged Abraham to return to the execution of his vows to the cause of Salem.

Abraham had kingly ambitions, and on the way back from Egypt he laid before Lot his plan to subdue all Canaan and bring its people under the rule of Salem. Lot was more bent on business; so, after a later disagreement, he went to Sodom to engage in trade and animal husbandry. Lot liked neither a military nor a herder's life.

Upon returning with his family to Salem, Abraham began to mature his military projects. He was soon recognized as the civil ruler of the Salem territory and had confederated under his leadership seven near-by tribes. Indeed, it was with great difficulty that Melchizedek restrained Abraham, who was fired with a zeal to go forth and round up the neighboring tribes with the sword that they might thus more quickly be brought to a knowledge of the Salem truths.

Melchizedek maintained peaceful relations with all the surrounding tribes; he was not militaristic and was never attacked by any of the armies as they moved back and forth. He was entirely willing that Abraham should formulate a defensive policy for Salem such as was subsequently put into effect, but he would not approve of his pupil's ambitious schemes for conquest; so there occurred a friendly severance of relationship, Abraham going over to Hebron to establish his military capital.

Abraham, because of his close connection with the illustrious Melchizedek, possessed great advantage over the surrounding petty kings; they all revered Melchizedek and unduly feared Abraham. Abraham knew of this fear and only awaited an opportune occasion to attack his neighbors, and this excuse came when some of these rulers presumed to raid the property of his nephew Lot, who dwelt in Sodom. Upon hearing of this, Abraham, at the head of his seven confederated tribes, moved on the enemy. His own bodyguard of 318 officered the army, numbering more than 4,000, which struck at this time.

When Melchizedek heard of Abraham's declaration of war, he went forth to dissuade him but only caught up with his former disciple as he returned victorious from the battle. Abraham insisted that the God of Salem had given him victory over his enemies and persisted in giving a tenth of his spoils to the Salem treasury. The other ninety per cent he removed to his capital at Hebron.

After this battle of Siddim, Abraham became leader of a second confederation of eleven tribes and not only paid tithes to Melchizedek but saw to it that all others in that vicinity did the same. His diplomatic dealings with the king of Sodom, together with the fear in which he was so generally held, resulted in the king of Sodom and others joining the Hebron military confederation; Abraham was really well on the way to establishing a powerful state in Palestine.

6. Melchizedek's Covenant with Abraham

Abraham envisaged the conquest of all Canaan. His determination was only weakened by the fact that Melchizedek would not sanction the undertaking. But Abraham had about decided to embark upon the enterprise when the thought that he had no son to succeed him as ruler of this proposed kingdom began to worry him. He arranged another conference with Melchizedek; and it was in the course of this interview that the priest of Salem, the visible Son of God, persuaded Abraham to abandon his scheme of material conquest and temporal rule in favor of the spiritual concept of the kingdom of heaven.

Melchizedek explained to Abraham the futility of contending with the Amorite confederation but made it equally clear that these backward clans were certainly committing suicide by their foolish practices so that in a few generations they would be so weakened that the descendants of Abraham, meanwhile greatly increased, could easily overcome them.

And Melchizedek made a formal covenant with Abraham at Salem. Said he to Abraham: "Look now up to the heavens and number the stars if you are able; so numerous shall your seed be." And Abraham believed Melchizedek, "and it was counted to him for righteousness." And then Melchizedek told Abraham the story of the future occupation of Canaan by his offspring after their sojourn in Egypt.

This covenant of Melchizedek with Abraham represents the great Urantian agreement between divinity and humanity whereby God agrees to do *everything;* man only agrees to *believe* God's promises and follow his instructions. Heretofore it had been believed that salvation could be secured only by works—sacrifices and offerings; now, Melchizedek again brought to Urantia the good news that salvation, favor with God, is to be had by *faith.* But this gospel of simple faith in God was too advanced; the Semitic tribesmen subsequently preferred to go back to the older sacrifices and atonement for sin by the shedding of blood.

It was not long after the establishment of this covenant that Isaac, the son of Abraham, was born in accordance with the promise of Melchizedek. After the birth of Isaac, Abraham took a very solemn attitude toward his covenant with Melchizedek, going over to Salem to have it stated in writing. It was at this public and formal acceptance of the covenant that he changed his name from Abram to Abraham.

Most of the Salem believers had practiced circumcision, though it had never been made obligatory by Melchizedek. Now Abraham had always so opposed circumcision that on this occasion he decided to solemnize the event by formally accepting this rite in token of the ratification of the Salem covenant.

It was following this real and public surrender of his personal ambitions in behalf of the larger plans of Melchizedek that the three celestial beings appeared to him on the plains of Mamre. This was an appearance of fact, notwithstanding its association with the subsequently fabricated narratives relating to the natural destruction of Sodom and Gomorrah. And these legends of the happenings of those days indicate how retarded were the morals and ethics of even so recent a time.

Upon the consummation of the solemn covenant, the reconciliation between Abraham and Melchizedek was complete. Abraham again assumed the civil and military leadership of the Salem colony, which at its height carried over one hundred thousand regular tithe payers on the rolls of the Melchizedek brotherhood. Abraham greatly improved the Salem temple and provided new tents for the entire school. He not only extended the tithing system but also instituted many improved methods of conducting the business of the school, besides contributing greatly to the better handling of the department of missionary propaganda. He also did much to effect improvement of the herds and the reorganization of the Salem dairying projects. Abraham was a shrewd and efficient business man, a wealthy man for his day; he was not overly pious, but he was thoroughly sincere, and he did believe in Machiventa Melchizedek.

7. THE MELCHIZEDEK MISSIONARIES

Melchizedek continued for some years to instruct his students and to train the Salem missionaries, who penetrated to all the surrounding tribes, especially to Egypt, Mesopotamia, and Asia Minor. And as the decades passed, these teachers journeyed farther and farther from Salem, carrying with them Machiventa's gospel of belief and faith in God.

The descendants of Adamson, clustered about the shores of the lake of Van, were willing listeners to the Hittite teachers of the Salem cult. From this onetime Andite center, teachers were dispatched to the remote regions of both Europe and Asia. Salem missionaries penetrated all Europe, even to the British Isles. One group went by way of the Faroes to the Andonites of Iceland, while another traversed China and reached the Japanese of the eastern islands. The lives and experiences of the men and women who ventured forth from Salem, Mesopotamia, and Lake Van to enlighten the tribes of the Eastern Hemisphere present a heroic chapter in the annals of the human race.

But the task was so great and the tribes were so backward that the results were vague and indefinite. From one generation to another the Salem gospel found lodgment here and there, but except in Palestine, never was the idea of one God able to claim the continued allegiance of a whole tribe or race. Long before the coming of Jesus the teachings of the early Salem missionaries had become generally submerged in the older and more universal superstitions and beliefs. The original Melchizedek gospel had been almost wholly absorbed in the beliefs in the Great Mother, the Sun, and other ancient cults.

You who today enjoy the advantages of the art of printing little understand how difficult it was to perpetuate truth during these earlier times; how easy it was to lose sight of a new doctrine from one generation to another. There was always a tendency for the new doctrine to become absorbed into the older body of religious teaching and magical practice. A new revelation is always contaminated by the older evolutionary beliefs.

8. DEPARTURE OF MELCHIZEDEK

It was shortly after the destruction of Sodom and Gomorrah that Machiventa decided to end his emergency bestowal on Urantia. Melchizedek's decision to terminate his sojourn in the flesh was influenced by numerous conditions, chief of which was the growing tendency of the surrounding tribes, and even of his immediate associates, to regard him as a demigod, to look upon him as a supernatural being, which indeed he was; but they were beginning to reverence him unduly and with a highly superstitious fear. In addition to these reasons, Melchizedek wanted to leave the scene of his earthly activities a sufficient length of time before Abraham's death to insure that the truth of the one and only God would become strongly established in the minds of his followers. Accordingly Machiventa retired one night to his tent at Salem, having said good night to his human companions, and when they went to call him in the morning, he was not there, for his fellows had taken him.

9. AFTER MELCHIZEDEK'S DEPARTURE

It was a great trial for Abraham when Melchizedek so suddenly disappeared. Although he had fully warned his followers that he must sometime go as he had come, they were not reconciled to the loss of their wonderful leader. The great organization built up at Salem nearly disappeared, though the traditions of these days were what Moses built upon when he led the Hebrew slaves out of Egypt.

The loss of Melchizedek produced a sadness in the heart of Abraham that he never fully overcame. Hebron he had abandoned when he gave up the ambition of building a material kingdom; and now, upon the loss of his associate in the building of the spiritual kingdom, he departed from Salem, going south to live near his interests at Gerar.

Abraham became fearful and timid immediately after the disappearance of Melchizedek. He withheld his identity upon arrival at Gerar, so that Abimelech appropriated his wife. (Shortly after his marriage to Sarah, Abraham one night had overheard a plot to murder him in order to get his brilliant wife. This dread became a terror to the otherwise brave and daring leader; all his life he feared that someone would kill him secretly in order to get Sarah. And this explains why, on three separate occasions, this brave man exhibited real cowardice.)

But Abraham was not long to be deterred in his mission as the successor of Melchizedek. Soon he made converts among the Philistines and of Abimelech's people, made a treaty with them, and, in turn, became contaminated with many of their superstitions, particularly with their practice of sacrificing first-born sons. Thus did Abraham again become a great leader in Palestine. He was held in reverence by all groups and honored by all kings. He was the spiritual leader of all the surrounding tribes, and his influence continued for some time after his death. During the closing years of his life he once more returned to Hebron, the scene of his earlier activities and the place where he had worked in association with Melchizedek. Abraham's last act was to send trusty servants to the city of his brother, Nahor, on the border of Mesopotamia, to secure a woman of his own people as a wife for his son Isaac. It had long been the custom of Abraham's people to marry their cousins. And Abraham died confident in that faith in God which he had learned from Melchizedek in the vanished schools of Salem.

It was hard for the next generation to comprehend the story of Melchizedek; within five hundred years many regarded the whole narrative as a myth. Isaac held fairly well to the teachings of his father and nourished the gospel of the Salem colony, but it was harder for Jacob to grasp the significance of these traditions. Joseph was a firm believer in Melchizedek and was, largely because of this, regarded by his brothers as a dreamer. Joseph's honor in Egypt was chiefly due to the memory of his great-grandfather Abraham. Joseph was offered military command of the Egyptian armies, but being such a firm believer in the traditions of Melchizedek and the later teachings of Abraham and Isaac, he elected to serve as a civil administrator, believing that he could thus better labor for the advancement of the kingdom of heaven.

The teaching of Melchizedek was full and replete, but the records of these days seemed impossible and fantastic to the later Hebrew priests, although many had some understanding of these transactions, at least up to the times of the en masse editing of the Old Testament records in Babylon.

What the Old Testament records describe as conversations between Abraham and God were in reality conferences between Abraham and Melchizedek. Later scribes regarded the term Melchizedek as synonymous with God. The record of so many contacts of Abraham and Sarah with "the angel of the Lord" refers to their numerous visits with Melchizedek.

The Hebrew narratives of Isaac, Jacob, and Joseph are far more reliable than those about Abraham, although they also contain many diversions from the facts, alterations made intentionally and unintentionally at the time of the compilation of these records by the Hebrew priests during the Babylonian captivity. Keturah was not a wife of Abraham; like Hagar, she was merely a concubine. All of Abraham's property went to Isaac, the son of Sarah, the status wife. Abraham was not so old as the records indicate, and his wife was much younger. These ages were deliberately altered in order to provide for the subsequent alleged miraculous birth of Isaac.

The national ego of the Jews was tremendously depressed by the Babylonian captivity. In their reaction against national inferiority they swung to the other extreme of national and racial egotism, in which they distorted and perverted their traditions with the view of exalting themselves above all races as the chosen people of God; and hence they carefully edited all their records for the purpose of raising Abraham and their other national leaders high up above all other persons, not excepting Melchizedek himself. The Hebrew scribes therefore destroyed every record of these momentous times which they could find, preserving only the narrative of the meeting of Abraham and Melchizedek after the battle of Siddim, which they deemed reflected great honor upon Abraham.

And thus, in losing sight of Melchizedek, they also lost sight of the teaching of this emergency Son regarding the spiritual mission of the promised bestowal Son; lost sight of the nature of this mission so fully and completely that very few of their progeny were able or willing to recognize and receive Michael when he appeared on earth and in the flesh as Machiventa had foretold.

But one of the writers of the Book of Hebrews understood the mission of Melchizedek, for it is written: "This Melchizedek, priest of the Most High, was also king of peace; without father, without mother, without pedigree, having neither beginning of days nor end of life but made like a Son of God, he abides a priest continually." This writer designated Melchizedek as a type of the later bestowal of Michael, affirming that Jesus was "a minister forever on the order of Melchizedek." While this comparison was not altogether fortunate, it was literally true that Christ did receive provisional title to Urantia "upon the orders of the twelve Melchizedek receivers" on duty at the time of his world bestowal.

10. PRESENT STATUS OF MACHIVENTA MELCHIZEDEK

During the years of Machiventa's incarnation the Urantia Melchizedek receivers functioned as eleven. When Machiventa considered that his mission as an emergency Son was finished, he signalized this fact to his eleven associates, and they immediately made ready the technique whereby he was to be released from the flesh and safely restored to his original Melchizedek status. And on the third day after his disappearance from Salem he appeared among his eleven fellows of the Urantia assignment and resumed his interrupted career as one of the planetary receivers of 606 of Satania.

Machiventa terminated his bestowal as a creature of flesh and blood just as suddenly and unceremoniously as he had begun it. Neither his appearance nor departure were accompanied by any unusual announcement or demonstration; neither resurrection roll call nor ending of planetary dispensation marked his appearance on Urantia; his was an emergency bestowal. But Machiventa did not end his sojourn in the flesh of human beings until he had been duly released by the Father Melchizedek and had been informed that his emergency bestowal had received the approval of the chief executive of Nebadon, Gabriel of Salvington.

Machiventa Melchizedek continued to take a great interest in the affairs of the descendants of those men who had believed in his teachings when he was in the flesh. But the progeny of Abraham through Isaac as intermarried with the Kenites were the only line which long continued to nourish any clear concept of the Salem teachings.

This same Melchizedek continued to collaborate throughout the nineteen succeeding centuries with the many prophets and seers, thus endeavoring to keep alive the truths of Salem until the fullness of the time for Michael's appearance on earth.

Machiventa continued as a planetary receiver up to the times of the triumph of Michael on Urantia. Subsequently, he was attached to the Urantia service on Jerusem as one of the four and twenty directors, only just recently having been elevated to the position of personal ambassador on Jerusem of the Creator Son, bearing the title Vicegerent Planetary Prince of Urantia. It is our belief that, as long as Urantia remains an inhabited planet, Machiventa Melchizedek will not be fully returned to the duties of his order of sonship but will remain, speaking in the terms of time, forever a planetary minister representing Christ Michael.

As his was an emergency bestowal on Urantia, it does not appear from the records what Machiventa's future may be. It may develop that the Melchizedek corps of Nebadon have sustained the permanent loss of one of their number. Recent rulings handed down from the Most Highs of Edentia, and later confirmed by the Ancients of Days of Uversa, strongly suggest that this bestowal Melchizedek is destined to take the place of the fallen Planetary Prince, Caligastia. If our conjectures in this respect are correct, it is altogether possible that Machiventa Melchizedek may again appear in person on Urantia and in some modified manner resume the role of the dethroned Planetary Prince, or else appear on earth to function as vicegerent Planetary Prince representing Christ Michael, who now actually holds the title of Planetary Prince of Urantia. While it is far from clear to us as to what Machiventa's destiny may be, nevertheless, events which have so recently taken place strongly suggest that the foregoing conjectures are probably not far from the truth.

We well understand how, by his triumph on Urantia, Michael became the successor of both Caligastia and Adam; how he became the planetary Prince of Peace and the second Adam. And now we behold the conferring upon this Melchizedek of the title Vicegerent Planetary Prince of Urantia. Will he also be constituted Vicegerent Material Son of Urantia? Or is there a possibility that an unexpected and unprecedented event is to take place, the sometime return to the planet of Adam and Eve or certain of their progeny as representatives of Michael with the titles vicegerents of the second Adam of Urantia?

And all these speculations associated with the certainty of future appearances of both Magisterial and Trinity Teacher Sons, in conjunction with the explicit promise of the Creator Son to return sometime, make Urantia a planet of future uncertainty and render it one of the most interesting and intriguing spheres in all the universe of Nebadon. It is altogether possible that, in some future age when Urantia is approaching the era of light and life, after the affairs of the Lucifer rebellion and the Caligastia secession have been finally adjudicated, we may witness the presence on Urantia, simultaneously, of Machiventa, Adam, Eve, and Christ Michael, as well as either a Magisterial Son or even Trinity Teacher Sons.

It has long been the opinion of our order that Machiventa's presence on the Jerusem corps of Urantia directors, the four and twenty counselors, is sufficient evidence to warrant the belief that he is destined to follow the mortals of Urantia on through the universe scheme of progression and ascension even to the Paradise Corps of the Finality. We know that Adam and Eve are thus destined to accompany their earth fellows on the Paradise adventure when Urantia has become settled in light and life.

Less than a thousand years ago this same Machiventa Melchizedek, the onetime sage of Salem, was invisibly present on Urantia for a period of one hundred years, acting as resident governor general of the planet; and if the present system of directing planetary affairs should continue, he will be due to return in the same capacity in a little over one thousand years.

This is the story of Machiventa Melchizedek, one of the most unique of all characters ever to become connected with the history of Urantia and a personality who may be destined to play an important role in the future experience of your irregular and unusual world.

[Presented by a Melchizedek of Nebadon.]

PAPER 94

THE MELCHIZEDEK TEACHINGS IN THE ORIENT

THE early teachers of the Salem religion penetrated to the remotest tribes of Africa and Eurasia, ever preaching Machiventa's gospel of man's faith and trust in the one universal God as the only price of obtaining divine favor. Melchizedek's covenant with Abraham was the pattern for all the early propaganda that went out from Salem and other centers. Urantia has never had more enthusiastic and aggressive missionaries of any religion than these noble men and women who carried the teachings of Melchizedek over the entire Eastern Hemisphere. These missionaries were recruited from many peoples and races, and they largely spread their teachings through the medium of native converts. They established training centers in different parts of the world where they taught the natives the Salem religion and then commissioned these pupils to function as teachers among their own people.

1. THE SALEM TEACHINGS IN VEDIC INDIA

In the days of Melchizedek, India was a cosmopolitan country which had recently come under the political and religious dominance of the Aryan-Andite invaders from the north and west. At this time only the northern and western portions of the peninsula had been extensively permeated by the Aryans. These Vedic newcomers had brought along with them their many tribal deities. Their religious forms of worship followed closely the ceremonial practices of their earlier Andite forebears in that the father still functioned as a priest and the mother as a priestess, and the family hearth was still utilized as an altar.

The Vedic cult was then in process of growth and metamorphosis under the direction of the Brahman caste of teacher-priests, who were gradually assuming control over the expanding ritual of worship. The amalgamation of the onetime thirty-three Aryan deities was well under way when the Salem missionaries penetrated the north of India.

The polytheism of these Aryans represented a degeneration of their earlier monotheism occasioned by their separation into tribal units, each tribe having its venerated god. This devolution of the original monotheism and trinitarianism of Andite Mesopotamia was in process of resynthesis in the early centuries of the second millennium before Christ. The many gods were organized into a pantheon under the triune leadership of Dyaus pitar, the lord of heaven; Indra, the tempestuous lord of the atmosphere; and Agni, the three-headed fire god, lord of the earth and the vestigial symbol of an earlier Trinity concept.

Definite henotheistic developments were paving the way for an evolved monotheism. Agni, the most ancient deity, was often exalted as the father-head of the entire pantheon. The deity-father principle, sometimes called Prajapati, sometimes termed Brahma, was submerged in the theologic battle which the Brahman priests later fought with the Salem teachers. *The Brahman* was conceived as the energy-divinity principle activating the entire Vedic pantheon.

The Salem missionaries preached the one God of Melchizedek, the Most High of heaven. This portrayal was not altogether disharmonious with the emerging concept of the Father-Brahma as the source of all gods, but the Salem doctrine was nonritualistic and hence ran directly counter to the dogmas, traditions, and teachings of the Brahman priesthood. Never would the Brahman priests accept the Salem teaching of salvation through faith, favor with God apart from ritualistic observances and sacrificial ceremonials.

The rejection of the Melchizedek gospel of trust in God and salvation through faith marked a vital turning point for India. The Salem missionaries had contributed much to the loss of faith in all the ancient Vedic gods, but the leaders, the priests of Vedism, refused to accept the Melchizedek teaching of one God and one simple faith.

The Brahmans culled the sacred writings of their day in an effort to combat the Salem teachers, and this compilation, as later revised, has come on down to modern times as the Rig-Veda, one of the most ancient of sacred books. The second, third, and fourth Vedas followed as the Brahmans sought to crystallize, formalize, and fix their rituals of worship and sacrifice upon the peoples of those days. Taken at their best, these writings are the equal of any other body of similar character in beauty of concept and truth of discernment. But as this superior religion became contaminated with the thousands upon thousands of superstitions, cults, and rituals of southern India, it progressively metamorphosed into the most variegated system of theology ever developed by mortal man. An examination of the Vedas will disclose some of the highest and some of the most debased concepts of Deity ever to be conceived.

2. BRAHMANISM

As the Salem missionaries penetrated southward into the Dravidian Deccan, they encountered an increasing caste system, the scheme of the Aryans to prevent loss of racial identity in the face of a rising tide of the secondary Sangik peoples. Since the Brahman priest caste was the very essence of this system, this social order greatly retarded the progress of the Salem teachers. This caste system failed to save the Aryan race, but it did succeed in perpetuating the Brahmans, who, in turn, have maintained their religious hegemony in India to the present time.

And now, with the weakening of Vedism through the rejection of higher truth, the cult of the Aryans became subject to increasing inroads from the Deccan. In a desperate effort to stem the tide of racial extinction and religious obliteration, the Brahman caste sought to exalt themselves above all else. They taught that the sacrifice to deity in itself was all-efficacious, that it was all-compelling in its potency. They proclaimed that, of the two essential divine principles of the universe, one was Brahman the deity, and the other was the Brahman priesthood. Among no other Urantia peoples did the priests presume to exalt themselves above even their gods, to relegate to themselves the honors due their gods. But they went so absurdly far with these presumptuous claims that the whole precarious system collapsed before the debasing cults which poured in from the surrounding and less advanced civilizations. The vast Vedic priesthood itself floundered and sank beneath the black flood of inertia and pessimism which their own selfish and unwise presumption had brought upon all India.

The undue concentration on self led certainly to a fear of the nonevolutionary perpetuation of self in an endless round of successive incarnations as man, beast, or weeds. And of all the contaminating beliefs which could have become fastened upon what may have been an emerging monotheism, none was so stultifying as this belief in transmigration—the doctrine of the reincarnation of souls—which came from the Dravidian Deccan. This belief in the weary and monotonous round of repeated transmigrations robbed struggling mortals of their long-cherished hope of finding that deliverance and spiritual advancement in death which had been a part of the earlier Vedic faith.

This philosophically debilitating teaching was soon followed by the invention of the doctrine of the eternal escape from self by submergence in the universal rest and peace of absolute union with Brahman, the oversoul of all creation. Mortal desire and human ambition were effectually ravished and virtually destroyed. For more than two thousand years the better minds of India have sought to escape from all desire, and thus was opened wide the door for the entrance of those later cults and teachings which have virtually shackled the souls of many Hindu peoples in the chains of spiritual hopelessness. Of all civilizations, the Vedic-Aryan paid the most terrible price for its rejection of the Salem gospel.

Caste alone could not perpetuate the Aryan religio-cultural system, and as the inferior religions of the Deccan permeated the north, there developed an age of despair and hopelessness. It was during these dark days that the cult of taking no life arose, and it has ever since persisted. Many of the new cults were frankly atheistic, claiming that such salvation as was attainable could come only by man's own unaided efforts. But throughout a great deal of all this unfortunate philosophy, distorted remnants of the Melchizedek and even the Adamic teachings can be traced.

These were the times of the compilation of the later scriptures of the Hindu faith, the Brahmanas and the Upanishads. Having rejected the teachings of personal religion through the personal faith experience with the one God, and having become contaminated with the flood of debasing and debilitating cults and creeds from the Deccan, with their anthropomorphisms and reincarnations, the Brahmanic priesthood experienced a violent reaction against these vitiating beliefs; there was a definite effort to seek and to find *true reality.* The Brahmans set out to deanthropomorphize the Indian concept of deity, but in so doing they stumbled into the grievous error of depersonalizing the concept of God, and they emerged, not with a lofty and spiritual ideal of the Paradise Father, but with a distant and metaphysical idea of an all-encompassing Absolute.

In their efforts at self-preservation the Brahmans had rejected the one God of Melchizedek, and now they found themselves with the hypothesis of Brahman, that indefinite and illusive philosophic self, that impersonal and impotent *it* which has left the spiritual life of India helpless and prostrate from that unfortunate day to the twentieth century.

It was during the times of the writing of the Upanishads that Buddhism arose in India. But despite its successes of a thousand years, it could not compete with later Hinduism; despite a higher morality, its early portrayal of God was even less well-defined than was that of Hinduism, which provided for lesser and personal deities. Buddhism finally gave way in northern India before the onslaught of a militant Islam with its clear-cut concept of Allah as the supreme God of the universe.

3. BRAHMANIC PHILOSOPHY

While the highest phase of Brahmanism was hardly a religion, it was truly one of the most noble reaches of the mortal mind into the domains of philosophy and metaphysics. Having started out to discover final reality, the Indian mind did not stop until it had speculated about almost every phase of theology excepting the essential dual concept of religion: the existence of the Universal Father of all universe creatures and the fact of the ascending experience in the universe of these very creatures as they seek to attain the eternal Father, who has commanded them to be perfect, even as he is perfect.

In the concept of Brahman the minds of those days truly grasped at the idea of some all-pervading Absolute, for this postulate was at one and the same time identified as creative energy and cosmic reaction. Brahman was conceived to be beyond all definition, capable of being comprehended only by the successive negation of all finite qualities. It was definitely a belief in an absolute, even an infinite, being, but this concept was largely devoid of personality attributes and was therefore not experiencible by individual religionists.

Brahman-Narayana was conceived as the Absolute, the infinite IT IS, the primordial creative potency of the potential cosmos, the Universal Self existing static and potential throughout all eternity. Had the philosophers of those days been able to make the next advance in deity conception, had they been able to conceive of the Brahman as associative and creative, as a personality approachable by created and evolving beings, then might such a teaching have become the most advanced portraiture of Deity on Urantia since it would have encompassed the first five levels of total deity function and might possibly have envisioned the remaining two.

In certain phases the concept of the One Universal Oversoul as the totality of the summation of all creature existence led the Indian philosophers very close to the truth of the Supreme Being, but this truth availed them naught because they failed to evolve any reasonable or rational personal approach to the attainment of their theoretic monotheistic goal of Brahman-Narayana.

The karma principle of causality continuity is, again, very close to the truth of the repercussional synthesis of all time-space actions in the Deity presence of the Supreme; but this postulate never provided for the co-ordinate personal attainment of Deity by the individual religionist, only for the ultimate engulfment of all personality by the Universal Oversoul.

The philosophy of Brahmanism also came very near to the realization of the indwelling of the Thought Adjusters, only to become perverted through the misconception of truth. The teaching that the soul is the indwelling of the Brahman would have paved the way for an advanced religion had not this concept been completely vitiated by the belief that there is no human individuality apart from this indwelling of the Universal One.

In the doctrine of the merging of the self-soul with the Oversoul, the theologians of India failed to provide for the survival of something human, something new and unique, something born of the union of the will of man and the will of God. The teaching of the soul's return to the Brahman is closely parallel to the truth of the Adjuster's return to the bosom of the Universal Father, but there is something distinct from the Adjuster which also survives, the morontial counterpart of mortal personality. And this vital concept was fatally absent from Brahmanic philosophy.

Brahmanic philosophy has approximated many of the facts of the universe and has approached numerous cosmic truths, but it has all too often fallen victim to the error of failing to differentiate between the several levels of reality, such as absolute, transcendental, and finite. It has failed to take into account that what may be finite-illusory on the absolute level may be absolutely real on the finite level. And it has also taken no cognizance of the essential personality of the Universal Father, who is personally contactable on all levels from the evolutionary creature's limited experience with God on up to the limitless experience of the Eternal Son with the Paradise Father.

4. THE HINDU RELIGION

With the passing of the centuries in India, the populace returned in measure to the ancient rituals of the Vedas as they had been modified by the teachings of the Melchizedek missionaries and crystallized by the later Brahman priesthood. This, the oldest and most cosmopolitan of the world's religions, has undergone further changes in response to Buddhism and Jainism and to the later appearing influences of Mohammedanism and Christianity. But by the time the teachings of Jesus arrived, they had already become so Occidentalized as to be a "white man's religion," hence strange and foreign to the Hindu mind.

Hindu theology, at present, depicts four descending levels of deity and divinity:

1. *The Brahman,* the Absolute, the Infinite One, the IT IS.

2. *The Trimurti,* the supreme trinity of Hinduism. In this association *Brahma,* the first member, is conceived as being self-created out of the Brahman—infinity. Were it not for close identification with the pantheistic Infinite One, Brahma could constitute the foundation for a concept of the Universal Father. Brahma is also identified with fate.

The worship of the second and third members, Siva and Vishnu, arose in the first millennium after Christ. *Siva* is lord of life and death, god of fertility, and master of destruction. *Vishnu* is extremely popular due to the belief that he periodically incarnates in human form. In this way, Vishnu becomes real and living in the imaginations of the Indians. Siva and Vishnu are each regarded by some as supreme over all.

3. *Vedic and post-Vedic deities.* Many of the ancient gods of the Aryans, such as Agni, Indra, and Soma, have persisted as secondary to the three members of the Trimurti. Numerous additional gods have arisen since the early days of Vedic India, and these have also been incorporated into the Hindu pantheon.

4. *The demigods:* supermen, semigods, heroes, demons, ghosts, evil spirits, sprites, monsters, goblins, and saints of the later-day cults.

While Hinduism has long failed to vivify the Indian people, at the same time it has usually been a tolerant religion. Its great strength lies in the fact that it has proved to be the most adaptive, amorphic religion to appear on Urantia. It is capable of almost unlimited change and possesses an unusual range of flexible adjustment from the high and semimonotheistic speculations of the intellectual Brahman to the arrant fetishism and primitive cult practices of the debased and depressed classes of ignorant believers.

Hinduism has survived because it is essentially an integral part of the basic social fabric of India. It has no great hierarchy which can be disturbed or destroyed; it is interwoven into the life pattern of the people. It has an adaptability to changing conditions that excels all other cults, and it displays a tolerant attitude of adoption toward many other religions, Gautama Buddha and even Christ himself being claimed as incarnations of Vishnu.

Today, in India, the great need is for the portrayal of the Jesusonian gospel —the Fatherhood of God and the sonship and consequent brotherhood of all men, which is personally realized in loving ministry and social service. In India the philosophical framework is existent, the cult structure is present; all that is needed is the vitalizing spark of the dynamic love portrayed in the original gospel of the Son of Man, divested of the Occidental dogmas and doctrines which have tended to make Michael's life bestowal a white man's religion.

5. THE STRUGGLE FOR TRUTH IN CHINA

As the Salem missionaries passed through Asia, spreading the doctrine of the Most High God and salvation through faith, they absorbed much of the philosophy and religious thought of the various countries traversed. But the teachers commissioned by Melchizedek and his successors did not default in their trust; they did penetrate to all peoples of the Eurasian continent, and it was in the middle of the second millennium before Christ that they arrived in China. At See Fuch, for more than one hundred years, the Salemites maintained their headquarters, there training Chinese teachers who taught throughout all the domains of the yellow race.

It was in direct consequence of this teaching that the earliest form of Taoism arose in China, a vastly different religion than the one which bears that name today. Early or proto-Taoism was a compound of the following factors:

1. The lingering teachings of Singlangton, which persisted in the concept of Shang-ti, the God of Heaven. In the times of Singlangton the Chinese people became virtually monotheistic; they concentrated their worship on the One Truth, later known as the Spirit of Heaven, the universe ruler. And the yellow race never fully lost this early concept of Deity, although in subsequent centuries many subordinate gods and spirits insidiously crept into their religion.

2. The Salem religion of a Most High Creator Deity who would bestow his favor upon mankind in response to man's faith. But it is all too true that, by the time the Melchizedek missionaries had penetrated to the lands of the yellow race, their original message had become considerably changed from the simple doctrines of Salem in the days of Machiventa.

3. The Brahman-Absolute concept of the Indian philosophers, coupled with the desire to escape all evil. Perhaps the greatest extraneous influence in the eastward spread of the Salem religion was exerted by the Indian teachers of the Vedic faith, who injected their conception of the Brahman—the Absolute—into the salvationistic thought of the Salemites.

This composite belief spread through the lands of the yellow and brown races as an underlying influence in religio-philosophic thought. In Japan this proto-Taoism was known as Shinto, and in this country, far-distant from Salem of Palestine, the peoples learned of the incarnation of Machiventa Melchizedek, who dwelt upon earth that the name of God might not be forgotten by mankind.

In China all of these beliefs were later confused and compounded with the ever-growing cult of ancestor worship. But never since the time of Singlangton have the Chinese fallen into helpless slavery to priestcraft. The yellow race was the first to emerge from barbaric bondage into orderly civilization because it was the first to achieve some measure of freedom from the abject fear of the gods, not even fearing the ghosts of the dead as other races feared them. China met her defeat because she failed to progress beyond her early emancipation from priests; she fell into an almost equally calamitous error, the worship of ancestors.

But the Salemites did not labor in vain. It was upon the foundations of their gospel that the great philosophers of sixth-century China built their teachings. The moral atmosphere and the spiritual sentiments of the times of Lao-tse and Confucius grew up out of the teachings of the Salem missionaries of an earlier age.

6. LAO-TSE AND CONFUCIUS

About six hundred years before the arrival of Michael, it seemed to Melchizedek, long since departed from the flesh, that the purity of his teaching on earth was being unduly jeopardized by general absorption into the older Urantia beliefs. It appeared for a time that his mission as a forerunner of Michael might be in danger of failing. And in the sixth century before Christ, through an unusual co-ordination of spiritual agencies, not all of which are understood even by the planetary supervisors, Urantia witnessed a most unusual presentation of manifold religious truth. Through the agency of several human teachers the Salem gospel was restated and revitalized, and as it was then presented, much has persisted to the times of this writing.

This unique century of spiritual progress was characterized by great religious, moral, and philosophic teachers all over the civilized world. In China, the two outstanding teachers were Lao-tse and Confucius.

Lao-tse built directly upon the concepts of the Salem traditions when he declared Tao to be the One First Cause of all creation. Lao was a man of great spiritual vision. He taught that man's eternal destiny was "everlasting union with Tao, Supreme God and Universal King." His comprehension of ultimate causation was most discerning, for he wrote: "Unity arises out of the Absolute Tao, and from Unity there appears cosmic Duality, and from such Duality, Trinity springs forth into existence, and Trinity is the primal source of all reality." "All reality is ever in balance between the potentials and the actuals of the cosmos, and these are eternally harmonized by the spirit of divinity."

Lao-tse also made one of the earliest presentations of the doctrine of returning good for evil: "Goodness begets goodness, but to the one who is truly good, evil also begets goodness."

He taught the return of the creature to the Creator and pictured life as the emergence of a personality from the cosmic potentials, while death was like the returning home of this creature personality. His concept of true faith was unusual, and he too likened it to the "attitude of a little child."

His understanding of the eternal purpose of God was clear, for he said: "The Absolute Deity does not strive but is always victorious; he does not coerce mankind but always stands ready to respond to their true desires; the will of God is eternal in patience and eternal in the inevitability of its expression." And of the true religionist he said, in expressing the truth that it is more blessed to give than to receive: "The good man seeks not to retain truth for himself but rather attempts to bestow these riches upon his fellows, for that is the realization of truth. The will of the Absolute God always benefits, never destroys; the purpose of the true believer is always to act but never to coerce."

Lao's teaching of nonresistance and the distinction which he made between *action* and *coercion* became later perverted into the beliefs of "seeing, doing, and thinking nothing." But Lao never taught such error, albeit his presentation of nonresistance has been a factor in the further development of the pacific predilections of the Chinese peoples.

But the popular Taoism of twentieth-century Urantia has very little in common with the lofty sentiments and the cosmic concepts of the old philosopher who taught the truth as he perceived it, which was: That faith in the Absolute God is the source of that divine energy which will remake the world, and by which man ascends to spiritual union with Tao, the Eternal Deity and Creator Absolute of the universes.

Confucius (Kung Fu-tze) was a younger contemporary of Lao in sixth-century China. Confucius based his doctrines upon the better moral traditions of the long history of the yellow race, and he was also somewhat influenced by the lingering traditions of the Salem missionaries. His chief work consisted in the compilation of the wise sayings of ancient philosophers. He was a rejected teacher during his lifetime, but his writings and teachings have ever since exerted a great influence in China and Japan. Confucius set a new pace for the shamans in that he put morality in the place of magic. But he built too well; he made a new fetish out of *order* and established a respect for ancestral conduct that is still venerated by the Chinese at the time of this writing.

The Confucian preachment of morality was predicated on the theory that the earthly way is the distorted shadow of the heavenly way; that the true pattern of temporal civilization is the mirror reflection of the eternal order of heaven. The potential God concept in Confucianism was almost completely subordinated to the emphasis placed upon the Way of Heaven, the pattern of the cosmos.

The teachings of Lao have been lost to all but a few in the Orient, but the writings of Confucius have ever since constituted the basis of the moral fabric of the culture of almost a third of Urantians. These Confucian precepts, while perpetuating the best of the past, were somewhat inimical to the very Chinese spirit of investigation that had produced those achievements which were so venerated. The influence of these doctrines was unsuccessfully combated both by the imperial efforts of Ch'in Shih Huang Ti and by the teachings of Mo Ti, who proclaimed a brotherhood founded not on ethical duty but on the love of God. He sought to rekindle the ancient quest for new truth, but his teachings failed before the vigorous opposition of the disciples of Confucius.

Like many other spiritual and moral teachers, both Confucius and Lao-tse were eventually deified by their followers in those spiritually dark ages of China which intervened between the decline and perversion of the Taoist faith and the coming of the Buddhist missionaries from India. During these spiritually decadent centuries the religion of the yellow race degenerated into a pitiful theology wherein swarmed devils, dragons, and evil spirits, all betokening the returning fears of the unenlightened mortal mind. And China, once at the head of human society because of an advanced religion, then fell behind because of temporary failure to progress in the true path of the development of that God-consciousness which is indispensable to the true progress, not only of the individual mortal, but also of the intricate and complex civilizations which characterize the advance of culture and society on an evolutionary planet of time and space.

7. GAUTAMA SIDDHARTHA

Contemporary with Lao-tse and Confucius in China, another great teacher of truth arose in India. Gautama Siddhartha was born in the sixth century before Christ in the north Indian province of Nepal. His followers later made it appear that he was the son of a fabulously wealthy ruler, but, in truth, he was the heir apparent to the throne of a petty chieftain who ruled by sufferance over a small and secluded mountain valley in the southern Himalayas.

Gautama formulated those theories which grew into the philosophy of Buddhism after six years of the futile practice of Yoga. Siddhartha made a determined but unavailing fight against the growing caste system. There was a lofty sincerity and a unique unselfishness about this young prophet prince that greatly appealed to the men of those days. He detracted from the practice of seeking individual salvation through physical affliction and personal pain. And he exhorted his followers to carry his gospel to all the world.

Amid the confusion and extreme cult practices of India, the saner and more moderate teachings of Gautama came as a refreshing relief. He denounced gods, priests, and their sacrifices, but he too failed to perceive the *personality* of the One Universal. Not believing in the existence of individual human souls, Gautama, of course, made a valiant fight against the time-honored belief in transmigration of the soul. He made a noble effort to deliver men from fear, to make them feel at ease and at home in the great universe, but he failed to show them the pathway to that real and supernal home of ascending mortals—Paradise—and to the expanding service of eternal existence.

Gautama was a real prophet, and had he heeded the instruction of the hermit Godad, he might have aroused all India by the inspiration of the revival of the Salem gospel of salvation by faith. Godad was descended through a family that had never lost the traditions of the Melchizedek missionaries.

At Benares Gautama founded his school, and it was during its second year that a pupil, Bautan, imparted to his teacher the traditions of the Salem missionaries about the Melchizedek covenant with Abraham; and while Siddhartha did not have a very clear concept of the Universal Father, he took an advanced stand on salvation through faith—simple belief. He so declared himself before his followers and began sending his students out in groups of sixty to proclaim to the people of India "the glad tidings of free salvation; that all men, high and low, can attain bliss by faith in righteousness and justice."

Gautama's wife believed her husband's gospel and was the founder of an order of nuns. His son became his successor and greatly extended the cult; he grasped the new idea of salvation through faith but in his later years wavered regarding the Salem gospel of divine favor through faith alone, and in his old age his dying words were, "Work out your own salvation."

When proclaimed at its best, Gautama's gospel of universal salvation, free from sacrifice, torture, ritual, and priests, was a revolutionary and amazing doctrine for its time. And it came surprisingly near to being a revival of the Salem gospel. It brought succor to millions of despairing souls, and notwithstanding its grotesque perversion during later centuries, it still persists as the hope of millions of human beings.

Siddhartha taught far more truth than has survived in the modern cults bearing his name. Modern Buddhism is no more the teachings of Gautama Siddhartha than is Christianity the teachings of Jesus of Nazareth.

8. THE BUDDHIST FAITH

To become a Buddhist, one merely made public profession of the faith by reciting the Refuge: "I take my refuge in the Buddha; I take my refuge in the Doctrine; I take my refuge in the Brotherhood."

Buddhism took origin in a historic person, not in a myth. Gautama's followers called him Sasta, meaning master or teacher. While he made no superhuman claims for either himself or his teachings, his disciples early began to call him *the enlightened one,* the Buddha; later on, Sakyamuni Buddha.

The original gospel of Gautama was based on the four noble truths:

1. The noble truths of suffering.
2. The origins of suffering.
3. The destruction of suffering.
4. The way to the destruction of suffering.

Closely linked to the doctrine of suffering and the escape therefrom was the philosophy of the Eightfold Path: right views, aspirations, speech, conduct, livelihood, effort, mindfulness, and contemplation. It was not Gautama's intention to attempt to destroy all effort, desire, and affection in the escape from suffering; rather was his teaching designed to picture to mortal man the futility of pinning all hope and aspirations entirely on temporal goals and material objectives. It was not so much that love of one's fellows should be shunned as that the true believer should also look beyond the associations of this material world to the realities of the eternal future.

The moral commandments of Gautama's preachment were five in number:

1. You shall not kill.
2. You shall not steal.
3. You shall not be unchaste.
4. You shall not lie.
5. You shall not drink intoxicating liquors.

There were several additional or secondary commandments, whose observance was optional with believers.

Siddhartha hardly believed in the immortality of the human personality; his philosophy only provided for a sort of functional continuity. He never clearly defined what he meant to include in the doctrine of Nirvana. The fact that it could theoretically be experienced during mortal existence would indicate that it was not viewed as a state of complete annihilation. It implied a condition of supreme enlightenment and supernal bliss wherein all fetters binding man to the material world had been broken; there was freedom from the desires of mortal life and deliverance from all danger of ever again experiencing incarnation.

According to the original teachings of Gautama, salvation is achieved by human effort, apart from divine help; there is no place for saving faith or prayers to superhuman powers. Gautama, in his attempt to minimize the superstitions of India, endeavored to turn men away from the blatant claims of magical salvation. And in making this effort, he left the door wide open for his successors to misinterpret his teaching and to proclaim that all human striving for attainment is distasteful and painful. His followers overlooked the fact that the highest happiness is linked with the intelligent and enthusiastic pursuit of worthy goals, and that such achievements constitute true progress in cosmic self-realization.

The great truth of Siddhartha's teaching was his proclamation of a universe of absolute justice. He taught the best godless philosophy ever invented by mortal man; it was the ideal humanism and most effectively removed all grounds for superstition, magical rituals, and fear of ghosts or demons.

The great weakness in the original gospel of Buddhism was that it did not produce a religion of unselfish social service. The Buddhistic brotherhood was, for a long time, not a fraternity of believers but rather a community of student teachers. Gautama forbade their receiving money and thereby sought to prevent the growth of hierarchal tendencies. Gautama himself was highly social; indeed, his life was much greater than his preachment.

9. THE SPREAD OF BUDDHISM

Buddhism prospered because it offered salvation through belief in the Buddha, the enlightened one. It was more representative of the Melchizedek truths than any other religious system to be found throughout eastern Asia. But Buddhism did not become widespread as a religion until it was espoused in self-protection by the low-caste monarch Asoka, who, next to Ikhnaton in Egypt, was one of the most remarkable civil rulers between Melchizedek and Michael. Asoka built a great Indian empire through the propaganda of his Buddhist missionaries. During a period of twenty-five years he trained and sent forth more than seventeen thousand missionaries to the farthest frontiers of all the known world. In one generation he made Buddhism the dominant religion of one half the world. It soon became established in Tibet, Kashmir, Ceylon, Burma, Java, Siam, Korea, China, and Japan. And generally speaking, it was a religion vastly superior to those which it supplanted or upstepped.

The spread of Buddhism from its homeland in India to all of Asia is one of the thrilling stories of the spiritual devotion and missionary persistence of sincere religionists. The teachers of Gautama's gospel not only braved the perils of the overland caravan routes but faced the dangers of the China Seas as they pursued their mission over the Asiatic continent, bringing to all peoples the message of their faith. But this Buddhism was no longer the simple doctrine of Gautama; it was the miraculized gospel which made him a god. And the farther Buddhism spread from its highland home in India, the more unlike the teachings of Gautama it became, and the more like the religions it supplanted, it grew to be.

Buddhism, later on, was much affected by Taoism in China, Shinto in Japan, and Christianity in Tibet. After a thousand years, in India Buddhism simply withered and expired. It became Brahmanized and later abjectly surrendered to Islam, while throughout much of the rest of the Orient it degenerated into a ritual which Gautama Siddhartha would never have recognized.

In the south the fundamentalist stereotype of the teachings of Siddhartha persisted in Ceylon, Burma, and the Indo-China peninsula. This is the Hinayana division of Buddhism which clings to the early or asocial doctrine.

But even before the collapse in India, the Chinese and north Indian groups of Gautama's followers had begun the development of the Mahayana teaching of the "Great Road" to salvation in contrast with the purists of the south who held to the Hinayana, or "Lesser Road." And these Mahayanists cast loose from the social limitations inherent in the Buddhist doctrine, and ever since has this northern division of Buddhism continued to evolve in China and Japan.

Buddhism is a living, growing religion today because it succeeds in conserving many of the highest moral values of its adherents. It promotes calmness and self-control, augments serenity and happiness, and does much to prevent sorrow and mourning. Those who believe this philosophy live better lives than many who do not.

10. RELIGION IN TIBET

In Tibet may be found the strangest association of the Melchizedek teachings combined with Buddhism, Hinduism, Taoism, and Christianity. When the Buddhist missionaries entered Tibet, they encountered a state of primitive savagery very similar to that which the early Christian missionaries found among the northern tribes of Europe.

These simple-minded Tibetans would not wholly give up their ancient magic and charms. Examination of the religious ceremonials of present-day Tibetan rituals reveals an overgrown brotherhood of priests with shaven heads who practice an elaborate ritual embracing bells, chants, incense, processionals, rosaries, images, charms, pictures, holy water, gorgeous vestments, and elaborate choirs. They have rigid dogmas and crystallized creeds, mystic rites and special fasts. Their hierarchy embraces monks, nuns, abbots, and the Grand Lama. They pray to angels, saints, a Holy Mother, and the gods. They practice confessions and believe in purgatory. Their monasteries are extensive and their cathedrals magnificent. They keep up an endless repetition of sacred rituals and believe that such ceremonials bestow salvation. Prayers are fastened to a wheel, and with its turning they believe the petitions become efficacious. Among no other people of modern times can be found the observance of so much from so many religions; and it is inevitable that such a cumulative liturgy would become inordinately cumbersome and intolerably burdensome.

The Tibetans have something of all the leading world religions except the simple teachings of the Jesusonian gospel: sonship with God, brotherhood with man, and ever-ascending citizenship in the eternal universe.

11. BUDDHIST PHILOSOPHY

Buddhism entered China in the first millennium after Christ, and it fitted well into the religious customs of the yellow race. In ancestor worship they had long prayed to the dead; now they could also pray for them. Buddhism soon amalgamated with the lingering ritualistic practices of disintegrating Taoism. This new synthetic religion with its temples of worship and definite religious ceremonial soon became the generally accepted cult of the peoples of China, Korea, and Japan.

While in some respects it is unfortunate that Buddhism was not carried to the world until after Gautama's followers had so perverted the traditions and teachings of the cult as to make of him a divine being, nonetheless this myth of his human life, embellished as it was with a multitude of miracles, proved very appealing to the auditors of the northern or Mahayana gospel of Buddhism.

Some of his later followers taught that Sakyamuni Buddha's spirit returned periodically to earth as a living Buddha, thus opening the way for an indefinite perpetuation of Buddha images, temples, rituals, and impostor "living Buddhas." Thus did the religion of the great Indian protestant eventually find itself shackled with those very ceremonial practices and ritualistic incantations against which he had so fearlessly fought, and which he had so valiantly denounced.

The great advance made in Buddhist philosophy consisted in its comprehension of the relativity of all truth. Through the mechanism of this hypothesis Buddhists have been able to reconcile and correlate the divergencies within their own religious scriptures as well as the differences between their own and many others. It was taught that the small truth was for little minds, the large truth for great minds.

This philosophy also held that the Buddha (divine) nature resided in all men; that man, through his own endeavors, could attain to the realization of this inner divinity. And this teaching is one of the clearest presentations of the truth of the indwelling Adjusters ever to be made by a Urantian religion.

But a great limitation in the original gospel of Siddhartha, as it was interpreted by his followers, was that it attempted the complete liberation of the human self from all the limitations of the mortal nature by the technique of isolating the self from objective reality. True cosmic self-realization results from identification with cosmic reality and with the finite cosmos of energy, mind, and spirit, bounded by space and conditioned by time.

But though the ceremonies and outward observances of Buddhism became grossly contaminated with those of the lands to which it traveled, this degeneration was not altogether the case in the philosophical life of the great thinkers who, from time to time, embraced this system of thought and belief. Through more than two thousand years, many of the best minds of Asia have concentrated upon the problem of ascertaining absolute truth and the truth of the Absolute.

The evolution of a high concept of the Absolute was achieved through many channels of thought and by devious paths of reasoning. The upward ascent of this doctrine of infinity was not so clearly defined as was the evolution of the God concept in Hebrew theology. Nevertheless, there were certain broad levels which the minds of the Buddhists reached, tarried upon, and passed through on their way to the envisioning of the Primal Source of universes:

1. *The Gautama legend.* At the base of the concept was the historic fact of the life and teachings of Siddhartha, the prophet prince of India. This legend grew in myth as it traveled through the centuries and across the broad lands of Asia until it surpassed the status of the idea of Gautama as the enlightened one and began to take on additional attributes.

2. *The many Buddhas.* It was reasoned that, if Gautama had come to the peoples of India, then, in the remote past and in the remote future, the races of mankind must have been, and undoubtedly would be, blessed with other teachers of truth. This gave rise to the teaching that there were many Buddhas, an unlimited and infinite number, even that anyone could aspire to become one—to attain the divinity of a Buddha.

3. *The Absolute Buddha.* By the time the number of Buddhas was approaching infinity, it became necessary for the minds of those days to reunify this unwieldy concept. Accordingly it began to be taught that all Buddhas were but the manifestation of some higher essence, some Eternal One of infinite and unqualified existence, some Absolute Source of all reality. From here on, the Deity concept of Buddhism, in its highest form, becomes divorced from the human person of Gautama Siddhartha and casts off from the anthropomorphic limitations which have held it in leash. This final conception of the Buddha Eternal can well be identified as the Absolute, sometimes even as the infinite I AM.

While this idea of Absolute Deity never found great popular favor with the peoples of Asia, it did enable the intellectuals of these lands to unify their philosophy and to harmonize their cosmology. The concept of the Buddha Absolute is at times quasi-personal, at times wholly impersonal—even an infinite creative force. Such concepts, though helpful to philosophy, are not vital to religious development. Even an anthropomorphic Yahweh is of greater religious value than an infinitely remote Absolute of Buddhism or Brahmanism.

At times the Absolute was even thought of as contained within the infinite I AM. But these speculations were chill comfort to the hungry multitudes who craved to hear words of promise, to hear the simple gospel of Salem, that faith in God would assure divine favor and eternal survival.

12. THE GOD CONCEPT OF BUDDHISM

The great weakness in the cosmology of Buddhism was twofold: its contamination with many of the superstitions of India and China and its sublimation of Gautama, first as the enlightened one, and then as the Eternal Buddha. Just as Christianity has suffered from the absorption of much erroneous human philosophy, so does Buddhism bear its human birthmark. But the teachings of Gautama have continued to evolve during the past two and one-half millenniums. The concept of Buddha, to an enlightened Buddhist, is no more the human personality of Gautama than the concept of Jehovah is identical with the spirit demon of Horeb to an enlightened Christian. Paucity of terminology, together with the sentimental retention of olden nomenclature, is often provocative of the failure to understand the true significance of the evolution of religious concepts.

Gradually the concept of God, as contrasted with the Absolute, began to appear in Buddhism. Its sources are back in the early days of this differentiation of the followers of the Lesser Road and the Greater Road. It was among the latter division of Buddhism that the dual conception of God and the Absolute finally matured. Step by step, century by century, the God concept has evolved until, with the teachings of Ryonin, Honen Shonin, and Shinran in Japan, this concept finally came to fruit in the belief in Amida Buddha.

Among these believers it is taught that the soul, upon experiencing death, may elect to enjoy a sojourn in Paradise prior to entering Nirvana, the ultimate of existence. It is proclaimed that this new salvation is attained by faith in the divine mercies and loving care of Amida, God of the Paradise in the west. In their philosophy, the Amidists hold to an Infinite Reality which is beyond all finite mortal comprehension; in their religion, they cling to faith in the all-merciful Amida, who so loves the world that he will not suffer one mortal who calls on his name in true faith and with a pure heart to fail in the attainment of the supernal happiness of Paradise.

The great strength of Buddhism is that its adherents are free to choose truth from all religions; such freedom of choice has seldom characterized a Urantian faith. In this respect the Shin sect of Japan has become one of the most progressive religious groups in the world; it has revived the ancient missionary spirit of Gautama's followers and has begun to send teachers to other peoples. This willingness to appropriate truth from any and all sources is indeed a commendable tendency to appear among religious believers during the first half of the twentieth century after Christ.

Buddhism itself is undergoing a twentieth-century renaissance. Through contact with Christianity the social aspects of Buddhism have been greatly enhanced. The desire to learn has been rekindled in the hearts of the monk priests of the brotherhood, and the spread of education throughout this faith will be certainly provocative of new advances in religious evolution.

At the time of this writing, much of Asia rests its hope in Buddhism. Will this noble faith, that has so valiantly carried on through the dark ages of the past, once again receive the truth of expanded cosmic realities even as the disciples of the great teacher in India once listened to his proclamation of new truth? Will this ancient faith respond once more to the invigorating stimulus of the presentation of new concepts of God and the Absolute for which it has so long searched?

All Urantia is waiting for the proclamation of the ennobling message of Michael, unencumbered by the accumulated doctrines and dogmas of nineteen centuries of contact with the religions of evolutionary origin. The hour is striking for presenting to Buddhism, to Christianity, to Hinduism, even to the peoples of all faiths, not the gospel about Jesus, but the living, spiritual reality of the gospel of Jesus.

[Presented by a Melchizedek of Nebadon.]

PAPER 95

THE MELCHIZEDEK TEACHINGS IN THE LEVANT

AS INDIA gave rise to many of the religions and philosophies of eastern Asia, so the Levant was the homeland of the faiths of the Occidental world. The Salem missionaries spread out all over southwestern Asia, through Palestine, Mesopotamia, Egypt, Iran, and Arabia, everywhere proclaiming the good news of the gospel of Machiventa Melchizedek. In some of these lands their teachings bore fruit; in others they met with varying success. Sometimes their failures were due to lack of wisdom, sometimes to circumstances beyond their control.

1. THE SALEM RELIGION IN MESOPOTAMIA

By 2000 B.C. the religions of Mesopotamia had just about lost the teachings of the Sethites and were largely under the influence of the primitive beliefs of two groups of invaders, the Bedouin Semites who had filtered in from the western desert and the barbarian horsemen who had come down from the north.

But the custom of the early Adamite peoples in honoring the seventh day of the week never completely disappeared in Mesopotamia. Only, during the Melchizedek era, the seventh day was regarded as the worst of bad luck. It was taboo-ridden; it was unlawful to go on a journey, cook food, or make a fire on the evil seventh day. The Jews carried back to Palestine many of the Mesopotamian taboos which they had found resting on the Babylonian observance of the seventh day, the Shabattum.

Although the Salem teachers did much to refine and uplift the religions of Mesopotamia, they did not succeed in bringing the various peoples to the permanent recognition of one God. Such teaching gained the ascendancy for more than one hundred and fifty years and then gradually gave way to the older belief in a multiplicity of deities.

The Salem teachers greatly reduced the number of the gods of Mesopotamia, at one time bringing the chief deities down to seven: Bel, Shamash, Nabu, Anu, Ea, Marduk, and Sin. At the height of the new teaching they exalted three of these gods to supremacy over all others, the Babylonian triad: Bel, Ea, and Anu, the gods of earth, sea, and sky. Still other triads grew up in different localities, all reminiscent of the trinity teachings of the Andites and the Sumerians and based on the belief of the Salemites in Melchizedek's insignia of the three circles.

Never did the Salem teachers fully overcome the popularity of Ishtar, the mother of gods and the spirit of sex fertility. They did much to refine the worship of this goddess, but the Babylonians and their neighbors had never completely outgrown their disguised forms of sex worship. It had become a universal practice throughout Mesopotamia for all women to submit, at least once in early life, to the embrace of strangers; this was thought to be a devotion required by Ishtar, and it was believed that fertility was largely dependent on this sex sacrifice.

The early progress of the Melchizedek teaching was highly gratifying until Nabodad, the leader of the school at Kish, decided to make a concerted attack upon the prevalent practices of temple harlotry. But the Salem missionaries failed in their effort to bring about this social reform, and in the wreck of this failure all their more important spiritual and philosophic teachings went down in defeat.

This defeat of the Salem gospel was immediately followed by a great increase in the cult of Ishtar, a ritual which had already invaded Palestine as Ashtoreth, Egypt as Isis, Greece as Aphrodite, and the northern tribes as Astarte. And it was in connection with this revival of the worship of Ishtar that the Babylonian priests turned anew to stargazing; astrology experienced its last great Mesopotamian revival, fortunetelling became the vogue, and for centuries the priesthood increasingly deteriorated.

Melchizedek had warned his followers to teach about the one God, the Father and Maker of all, and to preach only the gospel of divine favor through faith alone. But it has often been the error of the teachers of new truth to attempt too much, to attempt to supplant slow evolution by sudden revolution. The Melchizedek missionaries in Mesopotamia raised a moral standard too high for the people; they attempted too much, and their noble cause went down in defeat. They had been commissioned to preach a definite gospel, to proclaim the truth of the reality of the Universal Father, but they became entangled in the apparently worthy cause of reforming the mores, and thus was their great mission sidetracked and virtually lost in frustration and oblivion.

In one generation the Salem headquarters at Kish came to an end, and the propaganda of the belief in one God virtually ceased throughout Mesopotamia. But remnants of the Salem schools persisted. Small bands scattered here and there continued their belief in the one Creator and fought against the idolatry and immorality of the Mesopotamian priests.

It was the Salem missionaries of the period following the rejection of their teaching who wrote many of the Old Testament Psalms, inscribing them on stone, where later-day Hebrew priests found them during the captivity and subsequently incorporated them among the collection of hymns ascribed to Jewish authorship. These beautiful psalms from Babylon were not written in the temples of Bel-Marduk; they were the work of the descendants of the earlier Salem missionaries, and they are a striking contrast to the magical conglomerations of the Babylonian priests. The Book of Job is a fairly good reflection of the teachings of the Salem school at Kish and throughout Mesopotamia.

Much of the Mesopotamian religious culture found its way into Hebrew literature and liturgy by way of Egypt through the work of Amenemope and Ikhnaton. The Egyptians remarkably preserved the teachings of social obligation derived from the earlier Andite Mesopotamians and so largely lost by the later Babylonians who occupied the Euphrates valley.

2. EARLY EGYPTIAN RELIGION

The original Melchizedek teachings really took their deepest root in Egypt, from where they subsequently spread to Europe. The evolutionary religion of the Nile valley was periodically augmented by the arrival of superior strains of Nodite, Adamite, and later Andite peoples of the Euphrates valley. From time to time, many of the Egyptian civil administrators were Sumerians. As India in these days harbored the highest mixture of the world races, so Egypt fostered the most thoroughly blended type of religious philosophy to be found on Urantia, and from the Nile valley it spread to many parts of the world. The Jews received much of their idea of the creation of the world from the Babylonians, but they derived the concept of divine Providence from the Egyptians.

It was political and moral, rather than philosophic or religious, tendencies that rendered Egypt more favorable to the Salem teaching than Mesopotamia. Each tribal leader in Egypt, after fighting his way to the throne, sought to perpetuate his dynasty by proclaiming his tribal god the original deity and creator of all other gods. In this way the Egyptians gradually got used to the idea of a supergod, a steppingstone to the later doctrine of a universal creator Deity. The idea of monotheism wavered back and forth in Egypt for many centuries, the belief in one God always gaining ground but never quite dominating the evolving concepts of polytheism.

For ages the Egyptian peoples had been given to the worship of nature gods; more particularly did each of the two-score separate tribes have a special group god, one worshiping the bull, another the lion, a third the ram, and so on. Still earlier they had been totem tribes, very much like the Amerinds.

In time the Egyptians observed that dead bodies placed in brickless graves were preserved—embalmed—by the action of the soda-impregnated sand, while those buried in brick vaults decayed. These observations led to those experiments which resulted in the later practice of embalming the dead. The Egyptians believed that preservation of the body facilitated one's passage through the future life. That the individual might properly be identified in the distant future after the decay of the body, they placed a burial statue in the tomb along with the corpse, carving a likeness on the coffin. The making of these burial statues led to great improvement in Egyptian art.

For centuries the Egyptians placed their faith in tombs as the safeguard of the body and of consequent pleasurable survival after death. The later evolution of magical practices, while burdensome to life from the cradle to the grave, most effectually delivered them from the religion of the tombs. The priests would inscribe the coffins with charm texts which were believed to be protection against a "man's having his heart taken away from him in the nether world." Presently a diverse assortment of these magical texts was collected and preserved as The Book of the Dead. But in the Nile valley magical ritual early became involved with the realms of conscience and character to a degree not often attained by the rituals of those days. And subsequently these ethical and moral ideals, rather than elaborate tombs, were depended upon for salvation.

The superstitions of these times are well illustrated by the general belief in the efficacy of spittle as a healing agent, an idea which had its origin in Egypt and spread therefrom to Arabia and Mesopotamia. In the legendary battle of Horus with Set the young god lost his eye, but after Set was vanquished, this eye was restored by the wise god Thoth, who spat upon the wound and healed it.

The Egyptians long believed that the stars twinkling in the night sky represented the survival of the souls of the worthy dead; other survivors they thought were absorbed into the sun. During a certain period, solar veneration became a species of ancestor worship. The sloping entrance passage of the great pyramid pointed directly toward the Pole Star so that the soul of the king, when emerging from the tomb, could go straight to the stationary and established constellations of the fixed stars, the supposed abode of the kings.

When the oblique rays of the sun were observed penetrating earthward through an aperture in the clouds, it was believed that they betokened the letting down of a celestial stairway whereon the king and other righteous souls might ascend. "King Pepi has put down his radiance as a stairway under his feet whereon to ascend to his mother."

When Melchizedek appeared in the flesh, the Egyptians had a religion far above that of the surrounding peoples. They believed that a disembodied soul, if properly armed with magic formulas, could evade the intervening evil spirits and make its way to the judgment hall of Osiris, where, if innocent of "murder, robbery, falsehood, adultery, theft, and selfishness," it would be admitted to the realms of bliss. If this soul were weighed in the balances and found wanting, it would be consigned to hell, to the Devouress. And this was, relatively, an advanced concept of a future life in comparison with the beliefs of many surrounding peoples.

The concept of judgment in the hereafter for the sins of one's life in the flesh on earth was carried over into Hebrew theology from Egypt. The word judgment appears only once in the entire Book of Hebrew Psalms, and that particular psalm was written by an Egyptian.

3. EVOLUTION OF MORAL CONCEPTS

Although the culture and religion of Egypt were chiefly derived from Andite Mesopotamia and largely transmitted to subsequent civilizations through the Hebrews and Greeks, much, very much, of the social and ethical idealism of the Egyptians arose in the valley of the Nile as a purely evolutionary development. Notwithstanding the importation of much truth and culture of Andite origin, there evolved in Egypt more of moral culture as a purely human development than appeared by similar natural techniques in any other circumscribed area prior to the bestowal of Michael.

Moral evolution is not wholly dependent on revelation. High moral concepts can be derived from man's own experience. Man can even evolve spiritual values and derive cosmic insight from his personal experiential living because a divine spirit indwells him. Such natural evolutions of conscience and character were also augmented by the periodic arrival of teachers of truth, in ancient times from the second Eden, later on from Melchizedek's headquarters at Salem.

Thousands of years before the Salem gospel penetrated to Egypt, its moral leaders taught justice, fairness, and the avoidance of avarice. Three thousand years before the Hebrew scriptures were written, the motto of the Egyptians was: "Established is the man whose standard is righteousness; who walks according to its way." They taught gentleness, moderation, and discretion. The message of one of the great teachers of this epoch was: "Do right and deal justly with all." The Egyptian triad of this age was Truth-Justice-Righteousness. Of all the purely human religions of Urantia none ever surpassed the social ideals and the moral grandeur of this onetime humanism of the Nile valley.

In the soil of these evolving ethical ideas and moral ideals the surviving doctrines of the Salem religion flourished. The concepts of good and evil found ready response in the hearts of a people who believed that "Life is given to the peaceful and death to the guilty." "The peaceful is he who does what is loved; the guilty is he who does what is hated." For centuries the inhabitants of the Nile valley had lived by these emerging ethical and social standards before they ever entertained the later concepts of right and wrong—good and bad.

Egypt was intellectual and moral but not overly spiritual. In six thousand years only four great prophets arose among the Egyptians. Amenemope they followed for a season; Okhban they murdered; Ikhnaton they accepted but half-heartedly for one short generation; Moses they rejected. Again was it political rather than religious circumstances that made it easy for Abraham and, later on, for Joseph to exert great influence throughout Egypt in behalf of the Salem teachings of one God. But when the Salem missionaries first entered Egypt, they encountered this highly ethical culture of evolution blended with the modified moral standards of Mesopotamian immigrants. These early Nile valley teachers were the first to proclaim conscience as the mandate of God, the voice of Deity.

4. THE TEACHINGS OF AMENEMOPE

In due time there grew up in Egypt a teacher called by many the "son of man" and by others Amenemope. This seer exalted conscience to its highest pinnacle of arbitrament between right and wrong, taught punishment for sin, and proclaimed salvation through calling upon the solar deity.

Amenemope taught that riches and fortune were the gift of God, and this concept thoroughly colored the later appearing Hebrew philosophy. This noble teacher believed that God-consciousness was the determining factor in all conduct; that every moment should be lived in the realization of the presence of, and responsibility to, God. The teachings of this sage were subsequently translated into Hebrew and became the sacred book of that people long before the Old Testament was reduced to writing. The chief preachment of this good man had to do with instructing his son in uprightness and honesty in governmental positions of trust, and these noble sentiments of long ago would do honor to any modern statesman.

This wise man of the Nile taught that "riches take themselves wings and fly away"—that all things earthly are evanescent. His great prayer was to be "saved from fear." He exhorted all to turn away from "the words of men" to "the acts of God." In substance he taught: Man proposes but God disposes. His teachings, translated into Hebrew, determined the philosophy of the Old Testament Book of Proverbs. Translated into Greek, they gave color to all subsequent Hellenic religious philosophy. The later Alexandrian philosopher, Philo, possessed a copy of the Book of Wisdom.

Amenemope functioned to conserve the ethics of evolution and the morals of revelation and in his writings passed them on both to the Hebrews and to the Greeks. He was not the greatest of the religious teachers of this age, but he was the most influential in that he colored the subsequent thought of two vital links in the growth of Occidental civilization—the Hebrews, among whom evolved the acme of Occidental religious faith, and the Greeks, who developed pure philosophic thought to its greatest European heights.

In the Book of Hebrew Proverbs, chapters fifteen, seventeen, twenty, and chapter twenty-two, verse seventeen, to chapter twenty-four, verse twenty-two, are taken almost verbatim from Amenemope's Book of Wisdom. The first psalm of the Hebrew Book of Psalms was written by Amenemope and is the heart of the teachings of Ikhnaton.

5. THE REMARKABLE IKHNATON

The teachings of Amenemope were slowly losing their hold on the Egyptian mind when, through the influence of an Egyptian Salemite physician, a woman of the royal family espoused the Melchizedek teachings. This woman prevailed upon her son, Ikhnaton, Pharaoh of Egypt, to accept these doctrines of One God.

Since the disappearance of Melchizedek in the flesh, no human being up to that time had possessed such an amazingly clear concept of the revealed religion of Salem as Ikhnaton. In some respects this young Egyptian king is one of the most remarkable persons in human history. During this time of increasing spiritual depression in Mesopotamia, he kept alive the doctrine of El Elyon, the One God, in Egypt, thus maintaining the philosophic monotheistic channel which was vital to the religious background of the then future bestowal of Michael. And it was in recognition of this exploit, among other reasons, that the child Jesus was taken to Egypt, where some of the spiritual successors of Ikhnaton saw him and to some extent understood certain phases of his divine mission to Urantia.

Moses, the greatest character between Melchizedek and Jesus, was the joint gift to the world of the Hebrew race and the Egyptian royal family; and had Ikhnaton possessed the versatility and ability of Moses, had he manifested a political genius to match his surprising religious leadership, then would Egypt have become the great monotheistic nation of that age; and if this had happened, it is barely possible that Jesus might have lived the greater portion of his mortal life in Egypt.

Never in all history did any king so methodically proceed to swing a whole nation from polytheism to monotheism as did this extraordinary Ikhnaton. With the most amazing determination this young ruler broke with the past, changed his name, abandoned his capital, built an entirely new city, and created a new art and literature for a whole people. But he went too fast; he built too much, more than could stand when he had gone. Again, he failed to provide for the material stability and prosperity of his people, all of which reacted unfavorably against his religious teachings when the subsequent floods of adversity and oppression swept over the Egyptians.

Had this man of amazingly clear vision and extraordinary singleness of purpose had the political sagacity of Moses, he would have changed the whole history of the evolution of religion and the revelation of truth in the Occidental world. During his lifetime he was able to curb the activities of the priests, whom he generally discredited, but they maintained their cults in secret and sprang into action as soon as the young king passed from power; and they were not slow to connect all of Egypt's subsequent troubles with the establishment of monotheism during his reign.

Very wisely Ikhnaton sought to establish monotheism under the guise of the sun-god. This decision to approach the worship of the Universal Father by absorbing all gods into the worship of the sun was due to the counsel of the Salemite physician. Ikhnaton took the generalized doctrines of the then existent Aton faith regarding the fatherhood and motherhood of Deity and created a religion which recognized an intimate worshipful relation between man and God.

Ikhnaton was wise enough to maintain the outward worship of Aton, the sun-god, while he led his associates in the disguised worship of the One God, creator of Aton and supreme Father of all. This young teacher-king was a prolific writer, being author of the exposition entitled "The One God," a book of thirty-one chapters, which the priests, when returned to power, utterly destroyed. Ikhnaton also wrote one hundred and thirty-seven hymns, twelve of which are now preserved in the Old Testament Book of Psalms, credited to Hebrew authorship.

The supreme word of Ikhnaton's religion in daily life was "righteousness," and he rapidly expanded the concept of right doing to embrace international as well as national ethics. This was a generation of amazing personal piety and was characterized by a genuine aspiration among the more intelligent men and women to find God and to know him. In those days social position or wealth gave no Egyptian any advantage in the eyes of the law. The family life of Egypt did much to preserve and augment moral culture and was the inspiration of the later superb family life of the Jews in Palestine.

The fatal weakness of Ikhnaton's gospel was its greatest truth, the teaching that Aton was not only the creator of Egypt but also of the "whole world, man and beasts, and all the foreign lands, even Syria and Kush, besides this land of Egypt. He sets all in their place and provides all with their needs." These concepts of Deity were high and exalted, but they were not nationalistic. Such sentiments of internationality in religion failed to augment the morale of the Egyptian army on the battlefield, while they provided effective weapons for the priests to use against the young king and his new religion. He had a Deity concept far above that of the later Hebrews, but it was too advanced to serve the purposes of a nation builder.

Though the monotheistic ideal suffered with the passing of Ikhnaton, the idea of one God persisted in the minds of many groups. The son-in-law of Ikhnaton went along with the priests, back to the worship of the old gods, changing his name to Tutankhamen. The capital returned to Thebes, and the priests waxed fat upon the land, eventually gaining possession of one seventh of all Egypt; and presently one of this same order of priests made bold to seize the crown.

But the priests could not fully overcome the monotheistic wave. Increasingly they were compelled to combine and hyphenate their gods; more and more the family of gods contracted. Ikhnaton had associated the flaming disc of the heavens with the creator God, and this idea continued to flame up in the hearts of men, even of the priests, long after the young reformer had passed on. Never did the concept of monotheism die out of the hearts of men in Egypt and in the world. It persisted even to the arrival of the Creator Son of that same divine Father, the one God whom Ikhnaton had so zealously proclaimed for the worship of all Egypt.

The weakness of Ikhnaton's doctrine lay in the fact that he proposed such an advanced religion that only the educated Egyptians could fully comprehend his teachings. The rank and file of the agricultural laborers never really grasped his gospel and were, therefore, ready to return with the priests to the old-time worship of Isis and her consort Osiris, who was supposed to have been miraculously resurrected from a cruel death at the hands of Set, the god of darkness and evil.

The teaching of immortality for all men was too advanced for the Egyptians. Only kings and the rich were promised a resurrection; therefore did they so carefully embalm and preserve their bodies in tombs against the day of judgment. But the democracy of salvation and resurrection as taught by Ikhnaton eventually prevailed, even to the extent that the Egyptians later believed in the survival of dumb animals.

Although the effort of this Egyptian ruler to impose the worship of one God upon his people appeared to fail, it should be recorded that the repercussions of his work persisted for centuries both in Palestine and Greece, and that Egypt thus became the agent for transmitting the combined evolutionary culture of the Nile and the revelatory religion of the Euphrates to all of the subsequent peoples of the Occident.

The glory of this great era of moral development and spiritual growth in the Nile valley was rapidly passing at about the time the national life of the Hebrews was beginning, and consequent upon their sojourn in Egypt these Bedouins carried away much of these teachings and perpetuated many of Ikhnaton's doctrines in their racial religion.

6. The Salem Doctrines in Iran

From Palestine some of the Melchizedek missionaries passed on through Mesopotamia and to the great Iranian plateau. For more than five hundred years the Salem teachers made headway in Iran, and the whole nation was swinging to the Melchizedek religion when a change of rulers precipitated a bitter persecution which practically ended the monotheistic teachings of the Salem cult. The doctrine of the Abrahamic covenant was virtually extinct in Persia when, in that great century of moral renaissance, the sixth before Christ, Zoroaster appeared to revive the smouldering embers of the Salem gospel.

This founder of a new religion was a virile and adventurous youth, who, on his first pilgrimage to Ur in Mesopotamia, had learned of the traditions of the Caligastia and the Lucifer rebellion—along with many other traditions—all of which had made a strong appeal to his religious nature. Accordingly, as the result of a dream while in Ur, he settled upon a program of returning to his northern home to undertake the remodeling of the religion of his people. He had imbibed the Hebraic idea of a God of justice, the Mosaic concept of divinity. The idea of a supreme God was clear in his mind, and he set down all other gods as devils, consigned them to the ranks of the demons of which he had heard in Mesopotamia. He had learned of the story of the Seven Master Spirits as the tradition lingered in Ur, and, accordingly, he created a galaxy of seven supreme gods with Ahura-Mazda at its head. These subordinate gods he associated with the idealization of Right Law, Good Thought, Noble Government, Holy Character, Health, and Immortality.

And this new religion was one of action—work—not prayers and rituals. Its God was a being of supreme wisdom and the patron of civilization; it was a militant religious philosophy which dared to battle with evil, inaction, and backwardness.

Zoroaster did not teach the worship of fire but sought to utilize the flame as a symbol of the pure and wise Spirit of universal and supreme dominance. (All too true, his later followers did both reverence and worship this symbolic fire.)

Finally, upon the conversion of an Iranian prince, this new religion was spread by the sword. And Zoroaster heroically died in battle for that which he believed was the "truth of the Lord of light."

Zoroastrianism is the only Urantian creed that perpetuates the Dalamatian and Edenic teachings about the Seven Master Spirits. While failing to evolve the Trinity concept, it did in a certain way approach that of God the Sevenfold. Original Zoroastrianism was not a pure dualism; though the early teachings did picture evil as a time co-ordinate of goodness, it was definitely eternity-submerged in the ultimate reality of the good. Only in later times did the belief gain credence that good and evil contended on equal terms.

The Jewish traditions of heaven and hell and the doctrine of devils as recorded in the Hebrew scriptures, while founded on the lingering traditions of Lucifer and Caligastia, were principally derived from the Zoroastrians during the times when the Jews were under the political and cultural dominance of the Persians. Zoroaster, like the Egyptians, taught the "day of judgment," but he connected this event with the end of the world.

Even the religion which succeeded Zoroastrianism in Persia was markedly influenced by it. When the Iranian priests sought to overthrow the teachings of Zoroaster, they resurrected the ancient worship of Mithra. And Mithraism spread throughout the Levant and Mediterranean regions, being for some time a contemporary of both Judaism and Christianity. The teachings of Zoroaster thus came successively to impress three great religions: Judaism and Christianity and, through them, Mohammedanism.

But it is a far cry from the exalted teachings and noble psalms of Zoroaster to the modern perversions of his gospel by the Parsees with their great fear of the dead, coupled with the entertainment of beliefs in sophistries which Zoroaster never stooped to countenance.

This great man was one of that unique group that sprang up in the sixth century before Christ to keep the light of Salem from being fully and finally extinguished as it so dimly burned to show man in his darkened world the path of light leading to everlasting life.

7. THE SALEM TEACHINGS IN ARABIA

The Melchizedek teachings of the one God became established in the Arabian Desert at a comparatively recent date. As in Greece, so in Arabia the Salem missionaries failed because of their misunderstanding of Machiventa's instructions regarding overorganization. But they were not thus hindered by their interpretation of his admonition against all efforts to extend the gospel through military force or civil compulsion.

Not even in China or Rome did the Melchizedek teachings fail more completely than in this desert region so very near Salem itself. Long after the majority of the peoples of the Orient and Occident had become respectively Buddhist and Christian, the desert of Arabia continued as it had for thousands of years. Each tribe worshiped its olden fetish, and many individual families had their own household gods. Long the struggle continued between Babylonian Ishtar, Hebrew Yahweh, Iranian Ahura, and Christian Father of the Lord Jesus Christ. Never was one concept able fully to displace the others.

Here and there throughout Arabia were families and clans that held on to the hazy idea of the one God. Such groups treasured the traditions of Melchizedek, Abraham, Moses, and Zoroaster. There were numerous centers that might have responded to the Jesusonian gospel, but the Christian missionaries of the desert lands were an austere and unyielding group in contrast with the compromisers and innovators who functioned as missionaries in the Mediterranean countries. Had the followers of Jesus taken more seriously his injunction to "go into all the world and preach the gospel," and had they been more gracious in that preaching, less stringent in collateral social requirements of their own devising, then many lands would gladly have received the simple gospel of the carpenter's son, Arabia among them.

Despite the fact that the great Levantine monotheisms failed to take root in Arabia, this desert land was capable of producing a faith which, though less demanding in its social requirements, was nonetheless monotheistic.

There was only one factor of a tribal, racial, or national nature about the primitive and unorganized beliefs of the desert, and that was the peculiar and general respect which almost all Arabian tribes were willing to pay to a certain black stone fetish in a certain temple at Mecca. This point of common contact and reverence subsequently led to the establishment of the Islamic religion. What Yahweh, the volcano spirit, was to the Jewish Semites, the Kaaba stone became to their Arabic cousins.

The strength of Islam has been its clear-cut and well-defined presentation of Allah as the one and only Deity; its weakness, the association of military force with its promulgation, together with its degradation of woman. But it has steadfastly held to its presentation of the One Universal Deity of all, "who knows the invisible and the visible. He is the merciful and the compassionate." "Truly God is plenteous in goodness to all men." "And when I am sick, it is he who heals me." "For whenever as many as three speak together, God is present as a fourth," for is he not "the first and the last, also the seen and the hidden"?

[Presented by a Melchizedek of Nebadon.]

PAPER 96

YAHWEH—GOD OF THE HEBREWS

IN CONCEIVING of Deity, man first includes all gods, then subordinates all foreign gods to his tribal deity, and finally excludes all but the one God of final and supreme value. The Jews synthesized all gods into their more sublime concept of the Lord God of Israel. The Hindus likewise combined their multifarious deities into the "one spirituality of the gods" portrayed in the Rig-Veda, while the Mesopotamians reduced their gods to the more centralized concept of Bel-Marduk. These ideas of monotheism matured all over the world not long after the appearance of Machiventa Melchizedek at Salem in Palestine. But the Melchizedek concept of Deity was unlike that of the evolutionary philosophy of inclusion, subordination, and exclusion; it was based exclusively on *creative power* and very soon influenced the highest deity concepts of Mesopotamia, India, and Egypt.

The Salem religion was revered as a tradition by the Kenites and several other Canaanite tribes. And this was one of the purposes of Melchizedek's incarnation: That a religion of one God should be so fostered as to prepare the way for the earth bestowal of a Son of that one God. Michael could hardly come to Urantia until there existed a people believing in the Universal Father among whom he could appear.

The Salem religion persisted among the Kenites in Palestine as their creed, and this religion as it was later adopted by the Hebrews was influenced, first, by Egyptian moral teachings; later, by Babylonian theologic thought; and lastly, by Iranian conceptions of good and evil. Factually the Hebrew religion is predicated upon the covenant between Abraham and Machiventa Melchizedek, evolutionally it is the outgrowth of many unique situational circumstances, but culturally it has borrowed freely from the religion, morality, and philosophy of the entire Levant. It is through the Hebrew religion that much of the morality and religious thought of Egypt, Mesopotamia, and Iran was transmitted to the Occidental peoples.

1. DEITY CONCEPTS AMONG THE SEMITES

The early Semites regarded everything as being indwelt by a spirit. There were spirits of the animal and vegetable worlds; annual spirits, the lord of progeny; spirits of fire, water, and air; a veritable pantheon of spirits to be feared and worshiped. And the teaching of Melchizedek regarding a Universal Creator never fully destroyed the belief in these subordinate spirits or nature gods.

The progress of the Hebrews from polytheism through henotheism to monotheism was not an unbroken and continuous conceptual development. They experienced many retrogressions in the evolution of their Deity concepts, while during any one epoch there existed varying ideas of God among different groups of Semite believers. From time to time numerous terms were applied to their concepts of God, and in order to prevent confusion these various Deity titles will be defined as they pertain to the evolution of Jewish theology:

1. *Yahweh* was the god of the southern Palestinian tribes, who associated this concept of deity with Mount Horeb, the Sinai volcano. Yahweh was merely one of the hundreds and thousands of nature gods which held the attention and claimed the worship of the Semitic tribes and peoples.

2. *El Elyon.* For centuries after Melchizedek's sojourn at Salem his doctrine of Deity persisted in various versions but was generally connoted by the term El Elyon, the Most High God of heaven. Many Semites, including the immediate descendants of Abraham, at various times worshiped both Yahweh and El Elyon.

3. *El Shaddai.* It is difficult to explain what El Shaddai stood for. This idea of God was a composite derived from the teachings of Amenemope's Book of Wisdom modified by Ikhnaton's doctrine of Aton and further influenced by Melchizedek's teachings embodied in the concept of El Elyon. But as the concept of El Shaddai permeated the Hebrew mind, it became thoroughly colored with the Yahweh beliefs of the desert.

One of the dominant ideas of the religion of this era was the Egyptian concept of divine Providence, the teaching that material prosperity was a reward for serving El Shaddai.

4. *El.* Amid all this confusion of terminology and haziness of concept, many devout believers sincerely endeavored to worship all of these evolving ideas of divinity, and there grew up the practice of referring to this composite Deity as El. And this term included still other of the Bedouin nature gods.

5. *Elohim.* In Kish and Ur there long persisted Sumerian-Chaldean groups who taught a three-in-one God concept founded on the traditions of the days of Adam and Melchizedek. This doctrine was carried to Egypt, where this Trinity was worshiped under the name of Elohim, or in the singular as Eloah. The philosophic circles of Egypt and later Alexandrian teachers of Hebraic extraction taught this unity of pluralistic Gods, and many of Moses' advisers at the time of the exodus believed in this Trinity. But the concept of the trinitarian Elohim never became a real part of Hebrew theology until after they had come under the political influence of the Babylonians.

6. *Sundry names.* The Semites disliked to speak the name of their Deity, and they therefore resorted to numerous appellations from time to time, such as: The Spirit of God, The Lord, The Angel of the Lord, The Almighty, The Holy One, The Most High, Adonai, The Ancient of Days, The Lord God of Israel, The Creator of Heaven and Earth, Kyrios, Jah, The Lord of Hosts, and The Father in Heaven.

Jehovah is a term which in recent times has been employed to designate the completed concept of Yahweh which finally evolved in the long Hebrew experience. But the name Jehovah did not come into use until fifteen hundred years after the times of Jesus.

Up to about 2000 B.C., Mount Sinai was intermittently active as a volcano, occasional eruptions occurring as late as the time of the sojourn of the Israelites in this region. The fire and smoke, together with the thunderous detonations associated with the eruptions of this volcanic mountain, all impressed and awed the Bedouins of the surrounding regions and caused them greatly to fear Yahweh. This spirit of Mount Horeb later became the god of the Hebrew Semites, and they eventually believed him to be supreme over all other gods.

The Canaanites had long revered Yahweh, and although many of the Kenites believed more or less in El Elyon, the supergod of the Salem religion, a majority of the Canaanites held loosely to the worship of the old tribal deities. They were hardly willing to abandon their national deities in favor of an international, not to say an interplanetary, God. They were not universal-deity minded, and therefore these tribes continued to worship their tribal deities, including Yahweh and the silver and golden calves which symbolized the Bedouin herders' concept of the spirit of the Sinai volcano.

The Syrians, while worshiping their gods, also believed in Yahweh of the Hebrews, for their prophets said to the Syrian king: "Their gods are gods of the hills; therefore they were stronger than we; but let us fight against them on the plain, and surely we shall be stronger than they."

As man advances in culture, the lesser gods are subordinated to a supreme deity; the great Jove persists only as an exclamation. The monotheists keep their subordinate gods as spirits, demons, fates, Nereids, fairies, brownies, dwarfs, banshees, and the evil eye. The Hebrews passed through henotheism and long believed in the existence of gods other than Yahweh, but they increasingly held that these foreign deities were subordinate to Yahweh. They conceded the actuality of Chemosh, god of the Amorites, but maintained that he was subordinate to Yahweh.

The idea of Yahweh has undergone the most extensive development of all the mortal theories of God. Its progressive evolution can only be compared with the metamorphosis of the Buddha concept in Asia, which in the end led to the concept of the Universal Absolute even as the Yahweh concept finally led to the idea of the Universal Father. But as a matter of historic fact, it should be understood that, while the Jews thus changed their views of Deity from the tribal god of Mount Horeb to the loving and merciful Creator Father of later times, they did not change his name; they continued all the way along to call this evolving concept of Deity, Yahweh.

2. THE SEMITIC PEOPLES

The Semites of the East were well-organized and well-led horsemen who invaded the eastern regions of the fertile crescent and there united with the Babylonians. The Chaldeans near Ur were among the most advanced of the eastern Semites. The Phoenicians were a superior and well-organized group of mixed Semites who held the western section of Palestine, along the Mediterranean coast. Racially the Semites were among the most blended of Urantia peoples, containing hereditary factors from almost all of the nine world races.

Again and again the Arabian Semites fought their way into the northern Promised Land, the land that "flowed with milk and honey," but just as often were they ejected by the better-organized and more highly civilized northern Semites and Hittites. Later, during an unusually severe famine, these roving

Bedouins entered Egypt in large numbers as contract laborers on the Egyptian public works, only to find themselves undergoing the bitter experience of enslavement at the hard daily toil of the common and downtrodden laborers of the Nile valley.

It was only after the days of Machiventa Melchizedek and Abraham that certain tribes of Semites, because of their peculiar religious beliefs, were called the children of Israel and later on Hebrews, Jews, and the "chosen people." Abraham was not the racial father of all the Hebrews; he was not even the progenitor of all the Bedouin Semites who were held captive in Egypt. True, his offspring, coming up out of Egypt, did form the nucleus of the later Jewish people, but the vast majority of the men and women who became incorporated into the clans of Israel had never sojourned in Egypt. They were merely fellow nomads who chose to follow the leadership of Moses as the children of Abraham and their Semite associates from Egypt journeyed through northern Arabia.

The Melchizedek teaching concerning El Elyon, the Most High, and the covenant of divine favor through faith, had been largely forgotten by the time of the Egyptian enslavement of the Semite peoples who were shortly to form the Hebrew nation. But throughout this period of captivity these Arabian nomads maintained a lingering traditional belief in Yahweh as their racial deity.

Yahweh was worshiped by more than one hundred separate Arabian tribes, and except for the tinge of the El Elyon concept of Melchizedek which persisted among the more educated classes of Egypt, including the mixed Hebrew and Egyptian stocks, the religion of the rank and file of the Hebrew captive slaves was a modified version of the old Yahweh ritual of magic and sacrifice.

3. THE MATCHLESS MOSES

The beginning of the evolution of the Hebraic concepts and ideals of a Supreme Creator dates from the departure of the Semites from Egypt under that great leader, teacher, and organizer, Moses. His mother was of the royal family of Egypt; his father was a Semitic liaison officer between the government and the Bedouin captives. Moses thus possessed qualities derived from superior racial sources; his ancestry was so highly blended that it is impossible to classify him in any one racial group. Had he not been of this mixed type, he would never have displayed that unusual versatility and adaptability which enabled him to manage the diversified horde which eventually became associated with those Bedouin Semites who fled from Egypt to the Arabian Desert under his leadership.

Despite the enticements of the culture of the Nile kingdom, Moses elected to cast his lot with the people of his father. At the time this great organizer was formulating his plans for the eventual freeing of his father's people, the Bedouin captives hardly had a religion worthy of the name; they were virtually without a true concept of God and without hope in the world.

No leader ever undertook to reform and uplift a more forlorn, downcast, dejected, and ignorant group of human beings. But these slaves carried latent possibilities of development in their hereditary strains, and there were a sufficient number of educated leaders who had been coached by Moses in preparation for the day of revolt and the strike for liberty to constitute a corps of efficient organizers. These superior men had been employed as native overseers of their people; they had received some education because of Moses' influence with the Egyptian rulers.

Moses endeavored to negotiate diplomatically for the freedom of his fellow Semites. He and his brother entered into a compact with the king of Egypt whereby they were granted permission peaceably to leave the valley of the Nile for the Arabian Desert. They were to receive a modest payment of money and goods in token of their long service in Egypt. The Hebrews for their part entered into an agreement to maintain friendly relations with the Pharaohs and not to join in any alliance against Egypt. But the king later saw fit to repudiate this treaty, giving as his reason the excuse that his spies had discovered disloyalty among the Bedouin slaves. He claimed they sought freedom for the purpose of going into the desert to organize the nomads against Egypt.

But Moses was not discouraged; he bided his time, and in less than a year, when the Egyptian military forces were fully occupied in resisting the simultaneous onslaughts of a strong Libyan thrust from the south and a Greek naval invasion from the north, this intrepid organizer led his compatriots out of Egypt in a spectacular night flight. This dash for liberty was carefully planned and skillfully executed. And they were successful, notwithstanding that they were hotly pursued by Pharaoh and a small body of Egyptians, who all fell before the fugitives' defense, yielding much booty, all of which was augmented by the loot of the advancing host of escaping slaves as they marched on toward their ancestral desert home.

4. THE PROCLAMATION OF YAHWEH

The evolution and elevation of the Mosaic teaching has influenced almost one half of all the world, and still does even in the twentieth century. While Moses comprehended the more advanced Egyptian religious philosophy, the Bedouin slaves knew little about such teachings, but they had never entirely forgotten the god of Mount Horeb, whom their ancestors had called Yahweh.

Moses had heard of the teachings of Machiventa Melchizedek from both his father and his mother, their commonness of religious belief being the explanation for the unusual union between a woman of royal blood and a man from a captive race. Moses' father-in-law was a Kenite worshiper of El Elyon, but the emancipator's parents were believers in El Shaddai. Moses thus was educated an El Shaddaist; through the influence of his father-in-law he became an El Elyonist; and by the time of the Hebrew encampment about Mount Sinai after the flight from Egypt, he had formulated a new and enlarged concept of Deity (derived from all his former beliefs), which he wisely decided to proclaim to his people as an expanded concept of their olden tribal god, Yahweh.

Moses had endeavored to teach these Bedouins the idea of El Elyon, but before leaving Egypt, he had become convinced they would never fully comprehend this doctrine. Therefore he deliberately determined upon the compromise adoption of their tribal god of the desert as the one and only god of his followers. Moses did not specifically teach that other peoples and nations might not have other gods, but he did resolutely maintain that Yahweh was over and above all, especially to the Hebrews. But always was he plagued by the awkward predicament of trying to present his new and higher idea of Deity to these ignorant slaves under the guise of the ancient term Yahweh, which had always been symbolized by the golden calf of the Bedouin tribes.

The fact that Yahweh was the god of the fleeing Hebrews explains why they tarried so long before the holy mountain of Sinai, and why they there received the ten commandments which Moses promulgated in the name of Yahweh, the god of Horeb. During this lengthy sojourn before Sinai the religious ceremonials of the newly evolving Hebrew worship were further perfected.

It does not appear that Moses would ever have succeeded in the establishment of his somewhat advanced ceremonial worship and in keeping his followers intact for a quarter of a century had it not been for the violent eruption of Horeb during the third week of their worshipful sojourn at its base. "The mountain of Yahweh was consumed in fire, and the smoke ascended like the smoke of a furnace, and the whole mountain quaked greatly." In view of this cataclysm it is not surprising that Moses could impress upon his brethren the teaching that their God was "mighty, terrible, a devouring fire, fearful, and all-powerful."

Moses proclaimed that Yahweh was the Lord God of Israel, who had singled out the Hebrews as his chosen people; he was building a new nation, and he wisely nationalized his religious teachings, telling his followers that Yahweh was a hard taskmaster, a "jealous God." But nonetheless he sought to enlarge their concept of divinity when he taught them that Yahweh was the "God of the spirits of all flesh," and when he said, "The eternal God is your refuge, and underneath are the everlasting arms." Moses taught that Yahweh was a covenant-keeping God; that he "will not forsake you, neither destroy you, nor forget the covenant of your fathers because the Lord loves you and will not forget the oath by which he swore to your fathers."

Moses made a heroic effort to uplift Yahweh to the dignity of a supreme Deity when he presented him as the "God of truth and without iniquity, just and right in all his ways." And yet, despite this exalted teaching, the limited understanding of his followers made it necessary to speak of God as being in man's image, as being subject to fits of anger, wrath, and severity, even that he was vengeful and easily influenced by man's conduct.

Under the teachings of Moses this tribal nature god, Yahweh, became the Lord God of Israel, who followed them through the wilderness and even into exile, where he presently was conceived of as the God of all peoples. The later captivity that enslaved the Jews in Babylon finally liberated the evolving concept of Yahweh to assume the monotheistic role of the God of all nations.

The most unique and amazing feature of the religious history of the Hebrews concerns this continuous evolution of the concept of Deity from the primitive god of Mount Horeb up through the teachings of their successive spiritual leaders to the high level of development depicted in the Deity doctrines of the Isaiahs, who proclaimed that magnificent concept of the loving and merciful Creator Father.

5. THE TEACHINGS OF MOSES

Moses was an extraordinary combination of military leader, social organizer, and religious teacher. He was the most important individual world teacher and leader between the times of Machiventa and Jesus. Moses attempted to introduce many reforms in Israel of which there is no record. In the space of one man's life he led the polyglot horde of so-called Hebrews out of slavery and uncivilized roaming while he laid the foundation for the subsequent birth of a nation and the perpetuation of a race.

There is so little on record of the great work of Moses because the Hebrews had no written language at the time of the exodus. The record of the times and doings of Moses was derived from the traditions extant more than one thousand years after the death of the great leader.

Many of the advances which Moses made over and above the religion of the Egyptians and the surrounding Levantine tribes were due to the Kenite traditions of the time of Melchizedek. Without the teaching of Machiventa to Abraham and his contemporaries, the Hebrews would have come out of Egypt in hopeless darkness. Moses and his father-in-law, Jethro, gathered up the residue of the traditions of the days of Melchizedek, and these teachings, joined to the learning of the Egyptians, guided Moses in the creation of the improved religion and ritual of the Israelites. Moses was an organizer; he selected the best in the religion and mores of Egypt and Palestine and, associating these practices with the traditions of the Melchizedek teachings, organized the Hebrew ceremonial system of worship.

Moses was a believer in Providence; he had become thoroughly tainted with the doctrines of Egypt concerning the supernatural control of the Nile and the other elements of nature. He had a great vision of God, but he was thoroughly sincere when he taught the Hebrews that, if they would obey God, "He will love you, bless you, and multiply you. He will multiply the fruit of your womb and the fruit of your land—the corn, wine, oil, and your flocks. You shall be prospered above all people, and the Lord your God will take away from you all sickness and will put none of the evil diseases of Egypt upon you." He even said: "Remember the Lord your God, for it is he who gives you the power to get wealth." "You shall lend to many nations, but you shall not borrow. You shall reign over many nations, but they shall not reign over you."

But it was truly pitiful to watch this great mind of Moses trying to adapt his sublime concept of El Elyon, the Most High, to the comprehension of the ignorant and illiterate Hebrews. To his assembled leaders he thundered, "The Lord your God is one God; there is none beside him"; while to the mixed multitude he declared, "Who is like your God among all the gods?" Moses made a brave and partly successful stand against fetishes and idolatry, declaring, "You saw no similitude on the day that your God spoke to you at Horeb out of the midst of the fire." He also forbade the making of images of any sort.

Moses feared to proclaim the mercy of Yahweh, preferring to awe his people with the fear of the justice of God, saying: "The Lord your God is God of Gods, and Lord of Lords, a great God, a mighty and terrible God, who regards not man." Again he sought to control the turbulent clans when he declared that "your God kills when you disobey him; he heals and gives life when you obey him." But Moses taught these tribes that they would become the chosen people of God only on condition that they "kept all his commandments and obeyed all his statutes."

Little of the mercy of God was taught the Hebrews during these early times. They learned of God as "the Almighty; the Lord is a man of war, God of battles, glorious in power, who dashes in pieces his enemies." "The Lord your God walks in the midst of the camp to deliver you." The Israelites thought of their God as one who loved them, but who also "hardened Pharaoh's heart" and "cursed their enemies."

While Moses presented fleeting glimpses of a universal and beneficent Deity to the children of Israel, on the whole, their day-by-day concept of Yahweh was that of a God but little better than the tribal gods of the surrounding peoples. Their concept of God was primitive, crude, and anthropomorphic; when Moses passed on, these Bedouin tribes quickly reverted to the semibarbaric ideas of their olden gods of Horeb and the desert. The enlarged and more sublime vision of God which Moses every now and then presented to his leaders was soon lost to view, while most of the people turned to the worship of their fetish golden calves, the Palestinian herdsman's symbol of Yahweh.

When Moses turned over the command of the Hebrews to Joshua, he had already gathered up thousands of the collateral descendants of Abraham, Nahor, Lot, and other of the related tribes and had whipped them into a self-sustaining and partially self-regulating nation of pastoral warriors.

6. THE GOD CONCEPT AFTER MOSES' DEATH

Upon the death of Moses his lofty concept of Yahweh rapidly deteriorated. Joshua and the leaders of Israel continued to harbor the Mosaic traditions of the all-wise, beneficent, and almighty God, but the common people rapidly reverted to the older desert idea of Yahweh. And this backward drift of the concept of Deity continued increasingly under the successive rule of the various tribal sheiks, the so-called Judges.

The spell of the extraordinary personality of Moses had kept alive in the hearts of his followers the inspiration of an increasingly enlarged concept of God; but when they once reached the fertile lands of Palestine, they quickly evolved from nomadic herders into settled and somewhat sedate farmers. And this evolution of life practices and change of religious viewpoint demanded a more or less complete change in the character of their conception of the nature of their God, Yahweh. During the times of the beginning of the transmutation of the austere, crude, exacting, and thunderous desert god of Sinai into the later appearing concept of a God of love, justice, and mercy, the Hebrews almost lost sight of Moses' lofty teachings. They came near losing all concept of monotheism; they nearly lost their opportunity of becoming the people who would serve as a vital link in the spiritual evolution of Urantia, the group who would conserve the Melchizedek teaching of one God until the times of the incarnation of a bestowal Son of that Father of all.

Desperately Joshua sought to hold the concept of a supreme Yahweh in the minds of the tribesmen, causing it to be proclaimed: "As I was with Moses, so will I be with you; I will not fail you nor forsake you." Joshua found it necessary to preach a stern gospel to his disbelieving people, people all too willing to believe their old and native religion but unwilling to go forward in the religion of faith and righteousness. The burden of Joshua's teaching became: "Yahweh is a holy God; he is a jealous God; he will not forgive your transgressions nor your sins." The highest concept of this age pictured Yahweh as a "God of power, judgment, and justice."

But even in this dark age, every now and then a solitary teacher would arise proclaiming the Mosaic concept of divinity: "You children of wickedness cannot serve the Lord, for he is a holy God." "Shall mortal man be more just than God? shall a man be more pure than his Maker?" "Can you by searching find out God? Can you find out the Almighty to perfection? Behold, God is great and we know him not. Touching the Almighty, we cannot find him out."

7. PSALMS AND THE BOOK OF JOB

Under the leadership of their sheiks and priests the Hebrews became loosely established in Palestine. But they soon drifted back into the benighted beliefs of the desert and became contaminated with the less advanced Canaanite religious practices. They became idolatrous and licentious, and their idea of Deity fell far below the Egyptian and Mesopotamian concepts of God that were maintained by certain surviving Salem groups, and which are recorded in some of the Psalms and in the so-called Book of Job.

The Psalms are the work of a score or more of authors; many were written by Egyptian and Mesopotamian teachers. During these times when the Levant worshiped nature gods, there were still a goodly number who believed in the supremacy of El Elyon, the Most High.

No collection of religious writings gives expression to such a wealth of devotion and inspirational ideas of God as the Book of Psalms. And it would be very helpful if, in the perusal of this wonderful collection of worshipful literature, consideration could be given to the source and chronology of each separate hymn of praise and adoration, bearing in mind that no other single collection covers such a great range of time. This Book of Psalms is the record of the varying concepts of God entertained by the believers of the Salem religion throughout the Levant and embraces the entire period from Amenemope to Isaiah. In the Psalms God is depicted in all phases of conception, from the crude idea of a tribal deity to the vastly expanded ideal of the later Hebrews, wherein Yahweh is pictured as a loving ruler and merciful Father.

And when thus regarded, this group of Psalms constitutes the most valuable and helpful assortment of devotional sentiments ever assembled by man up to the times of the twentieth century. The worshipful spirit of this collection of hymns transcends that of all other sacred books of the world.

The variegated picture of Deity presented in the Book of Job was the product of more than a score of Mesopotamian religious teachers extending over a period of almost three hundred years. And when you read the lofty concept of divinity found in this compilation of Mesopotamian beliefs, you will recognize that it was in the neighborhood of Ur of Chaldea that the idea of a real God was best preserved during the dark days in Palestine.

In Palestine the wisdom and all-pervasiveness of God was often grasped but seldom his love and mercy. The Yahweh of these times "sends evil spirits to dominate the souls of his enemies"; he prospers his own and obedient children, while he curses and visits dire judgments upon all others. "He disappoints the devices of the crafty; he takes the wise in their own deceit."

Only at Ur did a voice arise to cry out the mercy of God, saying: "He shall pray to God and shall find favor with him and shall see his face with joy, for God will give to man divine righteousness." Thus from Ur there is preached salvation, divine favor, by faith: "He is gracious to the repentant and says, 'Deliver him from going down in the pit, for I have found a ransom.' If any say, 'I have sinned and perverted that which was right, and it profited me not,' God will deliver his soul from going into the pit, and he shall see the light." Not since the times of Melchizedek had the Levantine world heard such a ringing and cheering message of human salvation as this extraordinary teaching of Elihu, the prophet of Ur and priest of the Salem believers, that is, the remnant of the onetime Melchizedek colony in Mesopotamia.

And thus did the remnants of the Salem missionaries in Mesopotamia maintain the light of truth during the period of the disorganization of the Hebrew peoples until the appearance of the first of that long line of the teachers of Israel who never stopped as they built, concept upon concept, until they had achieved the realization of the ideal of the Universal and Creator Father of all, the acme of the evolution of the Yahweh concept.

[Presented by a Melchizedek of Nebadon.]

PAPER 97

EVOLUTION OF THE GOD CONCEPT AMONG THE HEBREWS

THE spiritual leaders of the Hebrews did what no others before them had ever succeeded in doing—they deanthropomorphized their God concept without converting it into an abstraction of Deity comprehensible only to philosophers. Even common people were able to regard the matured concept of Yahweh as a Father, if not of the individual, at least of the race.

The concept of the personality of God, while clearly taught at Salem in the days of Melchizedek, was vague and hazy at the time of the flight from Egypt and only gradually evolved in the Hebraic mind from generation to generation in response to the teaching of the spiritual leaders. The perception of Yahweh's personality was much more continuous in its progressive evolution than was that of many other of the Deity attributes. From Moses to Malachi there occurred an almost unbroken ideational growth of the personality of God in the Hebrew mind, and this concept was eventually heightened and glorified by the teachings of Jesus about the Father in heaven.

1. SAMUEL—FIRST OF THE HEBREW PROPHETS

Hostile pressure of the surrounding peoples in Palestine soon taught the Hebrew sheiks they could not hope to survive unless they confederated their tribal organizations into a centralized government. And this centralization of administrative authority afforded a better opportunity for Samuel to function as a teacher and reformer.

Samuel sprang from a long line of the Salem teachers who had persisted in maintaining the truths of Melchizedek as a part of their worship forms. This teacher was a virile and resolute man. Only his great devotion, coupled with his extraordinary determination, enabled him to withstand the almost universal opposition which he encountered when he started out to turn all Israel back to the worship of the supreme Yahweh of Mosaic times. And even then he was only partially successful; he won back to the service of the higher concept of Yahweh only the more intelligent half of the Hebrews; the other half continued in the worship of the tribal gods of the country and in the baser conception of Yahweh.

Samuel was a rough-and-ready type of man, a practical reformer who could go out in one day with his associates and overthrow a score of Baal sites. The progress he made was by sheer force of compulsion; he did little preaching, less teaching, but he did act. One day he was mocking the priest of Baal; the next, chopping in pieces a captive king. He devotedly believed in the one God, and he had a clear concept of that one God as creator of heaven and earth: "The pillars of the earth are the Lord's, and he has set the world upon them."

But the great contribution which Samuel made to the development of the concept of Deity was his ringing pronouncement that Yahweh was *changeless,* forever the same embodiment of unerring perfection and divinity. In these times Yahweh was conceived to be a fitful God of jealous whims, always regretting that he had done thus and so; but now, for the first time since the Hebrews sallied forth from Egypt, they heard these startling words, "The Strength of Israel will not lie nor repent, for he is not a man, that he should repent." Stability in dealing with Divinity was proclaimed. Samuel reiterated the Melchizedek covenant with Abraham and declared that the Lord God of Israel was the source of all truth, stability, and constancy. Always had the Hebrews looked upon their God as a man, a superman, an exalted spirit of unknown origin; but now they heard the onetime spirit of Horeb exalted as an unchanging God of creator perfection. Samuel was aiding the evolving God concept to ascend to heights above the changing state of men's minds and the vicissitudes of mortal existence. Under his teaching, the God of the Hebrews was beginning the ascent from an idea on the order of the tribal gods to the ideal of an all-powerful and changeless Creator and *Supervisor* of all creation.

And he preached anew the story of God's sincerity, his covenant-keeping reliability. Said Samuel: "The Lord will not forsake his people." "He has made with us an everlasting covenant, ordered in all things and sure." And so, throughout all Palestine there sounded the call back to the worship of the supreme Yahweh. Ever this energetic teacher proclaimed, "You are great, O Lord God, for there is none like you, neither is there any God beside you."

Theretofore the Hebrews had regarded the favor of Yahweh mainly in terms of material prosperity. It was a great shock to Israel, and almost cost Samuel his life, when he dared to proclaim: "The Lord enriches and impoverishes; he debases and exalts. He raises the poor out of the dust and lifts up the beggars to set them among princes to make them inherit the throne of glory." Not since Moses had such comforting promises for the humble and the less fortunate been proclaimed, and thousands of despairing among the poor began to take hope that they could improve their spiritual status.

But Samuel did not progress very far beyond the concept of a tribal god. He proclaimed a Yahweh who made all men but was occupied chiefly with the Hebrews, his chosen people. Even so, as in the days of Moses, once more the God concept portrayed a Deity who is holy and upright. "There is none as holy as the Lord. Who can be compared to this holy Lord God?"

As the years passed, the grizzled old leader progressed in the understanding of God, for he declared: "The Lord is a God of knowledge, and actions are weighed by him. The Lord will judge the ends of the earth, showing mercy to the merciful, and with the upright man he will also be upright." Even here is the dawn of mercy, albeit it is limited to those who are merciful. Later he went one step further when, in their adversity, he exhorted his people: "Let us fall now into the hands of the Lord, for his mercies are great." "There is no restraint upon the Lord to save many or few."

And this gradual development of the concept of the character of Yahweh continued under the ministry of Samuel's successors. They attempted to present Yahweh as a covenant-keeping God but hardly maintained the pace set by Samuel; they failed to develop the idea of the mercy of God as Samuel had later conceived it. There was a steady drift back toward the recognition of other gods, despite the maintenance that Yahweh was above all. "Yours is the kingdom, O Lord, and you are exalted as head above all."

The keynote of this era was divine power; the prophets of this age preached a religion designed to foster the king upon the Hebrew throne. "Yours, O Lord, is the greatness and the power and the glory and the victory and the majesty. In your hand is power and might, and you are able to make great and to give strength to all." And this was the status of the God concept during the time of Samuel and his immediate successors.

2. ELIJAH AND ELISHA

In the tenth century before Christ the Hebrew nation became divided into two kingdoms. In both of these political divisions many truth teachers endeavored to stem the reactionary tide of spiritual decadence that had set in, and which continued disastrously after the war of separation. But these efforts to advance the Hebraic religion did not prosper until that determined and fearless warrior for righteousness, Elijah, began his teaching. Elijah restored to the northern kingdom a concept of God comparable with that held in the days of Samuel. Elijah had little opportunity to present an advanced concept of God; he was kept busy, as Samuel had been before him, overthrowing the altars of Baal and demolishing the idols of false gods. And he carried forward his reforms in the face of the opposition of an idolatrous monarch; his task was even more gigantic and difficult than that which Samuel had faced.

When Elijah was called away, Elisha, his faithful associate, took up his work and, with the invaluable assistance of the little-known Micaiah, kept the light of truth alive in Palestine.

But these were not times of progress in the concept of Deity. Not yet had the Hebrews ascended even to the Mosaic ideal. The era of Elijah and Elisha closed with the better classes returning to the worship of the supreme Yahweh and witnessed the restoration of the idea of the Universal Creator to about that place where Samuel had left it.

3. YAHWEH AND BAAL

The long-drawn-out controversy between the believers in Yahweh and the followers of Baal was a socioeconomic clash of ideologies rather than a difference in religious beliefs.

The inhabitants of Palestine differed in their attitude toward private ownership of land. The southern or wandering Arabian tribes (the Yahwehites) looked upon land as an inalienable—as a gift of Deity to the clan. They held that land could not be sold or mortgaged. "Yahweh spoke, saying, 'The land shall not be sold, for the land is mine.'"

The northern and more settled Canaanites (the Baalites) freely bought, sold, and mortgaged their lands. The word Baal means owner. The Baal cult was founded on two major doctrines: First, the validation of property exchange, contracts, and covenants—the right to buy and sell land. Second, Baal was supposed to send rain—he was a god of fertility of the soil. Good crops depended on the favor of Baal. The cult was largely concerned with *land,* its ownership and fertility.

In general, the Baalites owned houses, lands, and slaves. They were the aristocratic landlords and lived in the cities. Each Baal had a sacred place, a priesthood, and the "holy women," the ritual prostitutes.

Out of this basic difference in the regard for land, there evolved the bitter antagonisms of social, economic, moral, and religious attitudes exhibited by the Canaanites and the Hebrews. This socioeconomic controversy did not become a definite religious issue until the times of Elijah. From the days of this aggressive prophet the issue was fought out on more strictly religious lines—Yahweh *vs.* Baal—and it ended in the triumph of Yahweh and the subsequent drive toward monotheism.

Elijah shifted the Yahweh-Baal controversy from the land issue to the religious aspect of Hebrew and Canaanite ideologies. When Ahab murdered the Naboths in the intrigue to get possession of their land, Elijah made a moral issue out of the olden land mores and launched his vigorous campaign against the Baalites. This was also a fight of the country folk against domination by the cities. It was chiefly under Elijah that Yahweh became Elohim. The prophet began as an agrarian reformer and ended up by exalting Deity. Baals were many, Yahweh was *one*—monotheism won over polytheism.

4. AMOS AND HOSEA

A great step in the transition of the tribal god—the god who had so long been served with sacrifices and ceremonies, the Yahweh of the earlier Hebrews—to a God who would punish crime and immorality among even his own people, was taken by Amos, who appeared from among the southern hills to denounce the criminality, drunkenness, oppression, and immorality of the northern tribes. Not since the times of Moses had such ringing truths been proclaimed in Palestine.

Amos was not merely a restorer or reformer; he was a discoverer of new concepts of Deity. He proclaimed much about God that had been announced by his predecessors and courageously attacked the belief in a Divine Being who would countenance sin among his so-called chosen people. For the first time since the days of Melchizedek the ears of man heard the denunciation of the double standard of national justice and morality. For the first time in their history Hebrew ears heard that their own God, Yahweh, would no more tolerate crime and sin in their lives than he would among any other people. Amos envisioned the stern and just God of Samuel and Elijah, but he also saw a God who thought no differently of the Hebrews than of any other nation when it came to the punishment of wrongdoing. This was a direct attack on the egoistic doctrine of the "chosen people," and many Hebrews of those days bitterly resented it.

Said Amos: "He who formed the mountains and created the wind, seek him who formed the seven stars and Orion, who turns the shadow of death into the morning and makes the day dark as night." And in denouncing his half-religious, timeserving, and sometimes immoral fellows, he sought to portray the inexorable justice of an unchanging Yahweh when he said of the evildoers: "Though they dig into hell, thence shall I take them; though they climb up to heaven, thence will I bring them down." "And though they go into captivity before their enemies, thence will I direct the sword of justice, and it shall slay them." Amos further startled his hearers when, pointing a reproving and accusing finger at them, he declared in the name of Yahweh: "Surely I will never forget any of your works." "And I will sift the house of Israel among all nations as wheat is sifted in a sieve."

Amos proclaimed Yahweh the "God of all nations" and warned the Israelites that ritual must not take the place of righteousness. And before this courageous teacher was stoned to death, he had spread enough leaven of truth to save the doctrine of the supreme Yahweh; he had insured the further evolution of the Melchizedek revelation.

Hosea followed Amos and his doctrine of a universal God of justice by the resurrection of the Mosaic concept of a God of love. Hosea preached forgiveness through repentance, not by sacrifice. He proclaimed a gospel of loving-kindness and divine mercy, saying: "I will betroth you to me forever; yes, I will betroth you to me in righteousness and judgment and in loving-kindness and in mercies. I will even betroth you to me in faithfulness." "I will love them freely, for my anger is turned away."

Hosea faithfully continued the moral warnings of Amos, saying of God, "It is my desire that I chastise them." But the Israelites regarded it as cruelty bordering on treason when he said: "I will say to those who were not my people, 'you are my people'; and they will say, 'you are our God.'" He continued to preach repentance and forgiveness, saying, "I will heal their backsliding; I will love them freely, for my anger is turned away." Always Hosea proclaimed hope and forgiveness. The burden of his message ever was: "I will have mercy upon my people. They shall know no God but me, for there is no savior beside me."

Amos quickened the national conscience of the Hebrews to the recognition that Yahweh would not condone crime and sin among them because they were supposedly the chosen people, while Hosea struck the opening notes in the later merciful chords of divine compassion and loving-kindness which were so exquisitely sung by Isaiah and his associates.

5. THE FIRST ISAIAH

These were the times when some were proclaiming threatenings of punishment against personal sins and national crime among the northern clans while others predicted calamity in retribution for the transgressions of the southern kingdom. It was in the wake of this arousal of conscience and consciousness in the Hebrew nations that the first Isaiah made his appearance.

Isaiah went on to preach the eternal nature of God, his infinite wisdom, his unchanging perfection of reliability. He represented the God of Israel as saying: "Judgment also will I lay to the line and righteousness to the plummet." "The Lord will give you rest from your sorrow and from your fear and from the hard bondage wherein man has been made to serve." "And your ears shall hear a word behind you, saying, 'this is the way, walk in it.'" "Behold God is my salvation; I will trust and not be afraid, for the Lord is my strength and my song." "'Come now and let us reason together,' says the Lord, 'though your sins be as scarlet, they shall be as white as snow; though they be red like the crimson, they shall be as wool.'"

Speaking to the fear-ridden and soul-hungry Hebrews, this prophet said: "Arise and shine, for your light has come, and the glory of the Lord has risen upon you." "The spirit of the Lord is upon me because he has anointed me to preach good tidings to the meek; he has sent me to bind up the brokenhearted, to proclaim liberty to the captives and the opening of the prison to those who are bound." "I will greatly rejoice in the Lord, my soul shall be joyful in my God, for he has clothed me with the garments of salvation and has covered me with his robe of righteousness." "In all their afflictions he was afflicted, and the angel of his presence saved them. In his love and in his pity he redeemed them."

This Isaiah was followed by Micah and Obadiah, who confirmed and embellished his soul-satisfying gospel. And these two brave messengers boldly denounced the priest-ridden ritual of the Hebrews and fearlessly attacked the whole sacrificial system.

Micah denounced "the rulers who judge for reward and the priests who teach for hire and the prophets who divine for money." He taught of a day of freedom from superstition and priestcraft, saying: "But every man shall sit under his own vine, and no one shall make him afraid, for all people will live, each one according to his understanding of God."

Ever the burden of Micah's message was: "Shall I come before God with burnt offerings? Will the Lord be pleased with a thousand rams or with ten thousand rivers of oil? Shall I give my first-born for my transgression, the fruit of my body for the sin of my soul? He has shown me, O man, what is good; and what does the Lord require of you but to do justly and to love mercy and to walk humbly with your God?" And it was a great age; these were indeed stirring times when mortal man heard, and some even believed, such emancipating messages more than two and a half millenniums ago. And but for the stubborn resistance of the priests, these teachers would have overthrown the whole bloody ceremonial of the Hebrew ritual of worship.

6. JEREMIAH THE FEARLESS

While several teachers continued to expound the gospel of Isaiah, it remained for Jeremiah to take the next bold step in the internationalization of Yahweh, God of the Hebrews.

Jeremiah fearlessly declared that Yahweh was not on the side of the Hebrews in their military struggles with other nations. He asserted that Yahweh was God of all the earth, of all nations and of all peoples. Jeremiah's teaching was the crescendo of the rising wave of the internationalization of the God of Israel; finally and forever did this intrepid preacher proclaim that Yahweh was God of all nations, and that there was no Osiris for the Egyptians, Bel for the Babylonians, Ashur for the Assyrians, or Dagon for the Philistines. And thus did the religion of the Hebrews share in that renaissance of monotheism throughout the world at about and following this time; at last the concept of Yahweh had ascended to a Deity level of planetary and even cosmic dignity. But many of Jeremiah's associates found it difficult to conceive of Yahweh apart from the Hebrew nation.

Jeremiah also preached of the just and loving God described by Isaiah, declaring: "Yes, I have loved you with an everlasting love; therefore with loving-kindness have I drawn you." "For he does not afflict willingly the children of men."

Said this fearless prophet: "Righteous is our Lord, great in counsel and mighty in work. His eyes are open upon all the ways of all the sons of men, to give every one according to his ways and according to the fruit of his doings." But it was considered blasphemous treason when, during the siege of Jerusalem, he said: "And now have I given these lands into the hand of Nebuchadnezzar, the king of Babylon, my servant." And when Jeremiah counseled the surrender of the city, the priests and civil rulers cast him into the miry pit of a dismal dungeon.

7. THE SECOND ISAIAH

The destruction of the Hebrew nation and their captivity in Mesopotamia would have proved of great benefit to their expanding theology had it not been for the determined action of their priesthood. Their nation had fallen before the armies of Babylon, and their nationalistic Yahweh had suffered from the international preachments of the spiritual leaders. It was resentment of the loss of their national god that led the Jewish priests to go to such lengths in the invention of fables and the multiplication of miraculous appearing events in Hebrew history in an effort to restore the Jews as the chosen people of even the new and expanded idea of an internationalized God of all nations.

During the captivity the Jews were much influenced by Babylonian traditions and legends, although it should be noted that they unfailingly improved the moral tone and spiritual significance of the Chaldean stories which they adopted, notwithstanding that they invariably distorted these legends to reflect honor and glory upon the ancestry and history of Israel.

These Hebrew priests and scribes had a single idea in their minds, and that was the rehabilitation of the Jewish nation, the glorification of Hebrew traditions, and the exaltation of their racial history. If there is resentment of the fact that these priests have fastened their erroneous ideas upon such a large part of the Occidental world, it should be remembered that they did not intentionally do this; they did not claim to be writing by inspiration; they made no profession to be writing a sacred book. They were merely preparing a textbook designed to bolster up the dwindling courage of their fellows in captivity. They were definitely aiming at improving the national spirit and morale of their compatriots. It remained for later-day men to assemble these and other writings into a guide book of supposedly infallible teachings.

The Jewish priesthood made liberal use of these writings subsequent to the captivity, but they were greatly hindered in their influence over their fellow captives by the presence of a young and indomitable prophet, Isaiah the second, who was a full convert to the elder Isaiah's God of justice, love, righteousness, and mercy. He also believed with Jeremiah that Yahweh had become the God of all nations. He preached these theories of the nature of God with such telling effect that he made converts equally among the Jews and their captors. And this young preacher left on record his teachings, which the hostile and unforgiving priests sought to divorce from all association with him, although sheer respect for their beauty and grandeur led to their incorporation among the writings of the earlier Isaiah. And thus may be found the writings of this second Isaiah in the book of that name, embracing chapters forty to fifty-five inclusive.

No prophet or religious teacher from Machiventa to the time of Jesus attained the high concept of God that Isaiah the second proclaimed during these days of the captivity. It was no small, anthropomorphic, man-made God that this spiritual leader proclaimed. "Behold he takes up the isles as a very little thing." "And as the heavens are higher than the earth, so are my ways higher than your ways and my thoughts higher than your thoughts."

At last Machiventa Melchizedek beheld human teachers proclaiming a real God to mortal man. Like Isaiah the first, this leader preached a God of universal creation and upholding. "I have made the earth and put man upon it. I have created it not in vain; I formed it to be inhabited." "I am the first and the last; there is no God beside me." Speaking for the Lord God of Israel, this new prophet said: "The heavens may vanish and the earth wax old, but my righteousness shall endure forever and my salvation from generation to generation." "Fear you not, for I am with you; be not dismayed, for I am your God." "There is no God beside me—a just God and a Savior."

And it comforted the Jewish captives, as it has thousands upon thousands ever since, to hear such words as: "Thus says the Lord, 'I have created you, I have redeemed you, I have called you by your name; you are mine.'" "When you pass through the waters, I will be with you since you are precious in my sight." "Can a woman forget her suckling child that she should not have compassion on her son? Yes, she may forget, yet will I not forget my children, for behold I have graven them upon the palms of my hands; I have even covered them with the shadow of my hands." "Let the wicked forsake his ways and the unrighteous man his thoughts, and let him return to the Lord, and he will have mercy upon him, and to our God, for he will abundantly pardon."

Listen again to the gospel of this new revelation of the God of Salem: "He shall feed his flock like a shepherd; he shall gather the lambs in his arms and carry them in his bosom. He gives power to the faint, and to those who have no might he increases strength. Those who wait upon the Lord shall renew their strength; they shall mount up with wings as eagles; they shall run and not be weary; they shall walk and not faint."

This Isaiah conducted a far-flung propaganda of the gospel of the enlarging concept of a supreme Yahweh. He vied with Moses in the eloquence with which he portrayed the Lord God of Israel as the Universal Creator. He was poetic in his portrayal of the infinite attributes of the Universal Father. No more beautiful pronouncements about the heavenly Father have ever been made. Like the Psalms, the writings of Isaiah are among the most sublime and true presentations of the spiritual concept of God ever to greet the ears of mortal man prior to the arrival of Michael on Urantia. Listen to his portrayal of Deity: "I am the high and lofty one who inhabits eternity." "I am the first and the last, and beside me there is no other God." "And the Lord's hand is not shortened that it cannot save, neither his ear heavy that it cannot hear." And it was a new doctrine in Jewry when this benign but commanding prophet persisted in the preachment of divine constancy, God's faithfulness. He declared that "God would not forget, would not forsake."

This daring teacher proclaimed that man was very closely related to God, saying: "Every one who is called by my name I have created for my glory, and they shall show forth my praise. I, even I, am he who blots out their transgressions for my own sake, and I will not remember their sins."

Hear this great Hebrew demolish the concept of a national God while in glory he proclaims the divinity of the Universal Father, of whom he says, "The heavens are my throne, and the earth is my footstool." And Isaiah's God was none the less holy, majestic, just, and unsearchable. The concept of the angry, vengeful, and jealous Yahweh of the desert Bedouins has almost vanished. A new concept of the supreme and universal Yahweh has appeared in the mind of mortal man, never to be lost to human view. The realization of divine justice has begun the destruction of primitive magic and biologic fear. At last, man is introduced to a universe of law and order and to a universal God of dependable and final attributes.

And this preacher of a supernal God never ceased to proclaim this *God of love*. "I dwell in the high and holy place, also with him who is of a contrite and humble spirit." And still further words of comfort did this great teacher speak to his contemporaries: "And the Lord will guide you continually and satisfy your soul. You shall be like a watered garden and like a spring whose waters fail not. And if the enemy shall come in like a flood, the spirit of the Lord will lift up a defense against him." And once again did the fear-destroying gospel of Melchizedek and the trust-breeding religion of Salem shine forth for the blessing of mankind.

The farseeing and courageous Isaiah effectively eclipsed the nationalistic Yahweh by his sublime portraiture of the majesty and universal omnipotence of the supreme Yahweh, God of love, ruler of the universe, and affectionate Father of all mankind. Ever since those eventful days the highest God concept in the Occident has embraced universal justice, divine mercy, and eternal righteousness. In superb language and with matchless grace this great teacher portrayed the all-powerful Creator as the all-loving Father.

This prophet of the captivity preached to his people and to those of many nations as they listened by the river in Babylon. And this second Isaiah did much to counteract the many wrong and racially egoistic concepts of the mission of the promised Messiah. But in this effort he was not wholly successful. Had the priests not dedicated themselves to the work of building up a misconceived nationalism, the teachings of the two Isaiahs would have prepared the way for the recognition and reception of the promised Messiah.

8. SACRED AND PROFANE HISTORY

The custom of looking upon the record of the experiences of the Hebrews as sacred history and upon the transactions of the rest of the world as profane history is responsible for much of the confusion existing in the human mind as to the interpretation of history. And this difficulty arises because there is no secular history of the Jews. After the priests of the Babylonian exile had prepared their new record of God's supposedly miraculous dealings with the Hebrews, the sacred history of Israel as portrayed in the Old Testament, they carefully and completely destroyed the existing records of Hebrew affairs—such books as "The Doings of the Kings of Israel" and "The Doings of the Kings of Judah," together with several other more or less accurate records of Hebrew history.

In order to understand how the devastating pressure and the inescapable coercion of secular history so terrorized the captive and alien-ruled Jews that they attempted the complete rewriting and recasting of their history, we should briefly survey the record of their perplexing national experience. It must be remembered that the Jews failed to evolve an adequate nontheologic philosophy of life. They struggled with their original and Egyptian concept of divine rewards for righteousness coupled with dire punishments for sin. The drama of Job was something of a protest against this erroneous philosophy. The frank pessimism of Ecclesiastes was a worldly wise reaction to these overoptimistic beliefs in Providence.

But five hundred years of the overlordship of alien rulers was too much for even the patient and long-suffering Jews. The prophets and priests began to cry: "How long, O Lord, how long?" As the honest Jew searched the Scriptures, his confusion became worse confounded. An olden seer promised that God would protect and deliver his "chosen people." Amos had threatened that God would abandon Israel unless they re-established their standards of national righteousness. The scribe of Deuteronomy had portrayed the Great Choice—as between the good and the evil, the blessing and the curse. Isaiah the first had preached a beneficent king-deliverer. Jeremiah had proclaimed an era of inner righteousness—the covenant written on the tablets of the heart. The second Isaiah talked about salvation by sacrifice and redemption. Ezekiel proclaimed deliverance through the service of devotion, and Ezra promised prosperity by adherence to the law. But in spite of all this they lingered on in bondage, and deliverance was deferred. Then Daniel presented the drama of the impending "crisis"—the smiting of the great image and the immediate establishment of the everlasting reign of righteousness, the Messianic kingdom.

And all of this false hope led to such a degree of racial disappointment and frustration that the leaders of the Jews were so confused they failed to recognize and accept the mission and ministry of a divine Son of Paradise when he presently came to them in the likeness of mortal flesh—incarnated as the Son of Man.

All modern religions have seriously blundered in the attempt to put a miraculous interpretation on certain epochs of human history. While it is true that God has many times thrust a Father's hand of providential intervention into the stream of human affairs, it is a mistake to regard theologic dogmas and religious superstition as a supernatural sedimentation appearing by miraculous action in this stream of human history. The fact that the "Most Highs rule in the kingdoms of men" does not convert secular history into so-called sacred history.

New Testament authors and later Christian writers further complicated the distortion of Hebrew history by their well-meant attempts to transcendentalize the Jewish prophets. Thus has Hebrew history been disastrously exploited by both Jewish and Christian writers. Secular Hebrew history has been thoroughly dogmatized. It has been converted into a fiction of sacred history and has become inextricably bound up with the moral concepts and religious teachings of the so-called Christian nations.

A brief recital of the high points in Hebrew history will illustrate how the facts of the record were so altered in Babylon by the Jewish priests as to turn the everyday secular history of their people into a fictitious and sacred history.

9. HEBREW HISTORY

There never were twelve tribes of the Israelites—only three or four tribes settled in Palestine. The Hebrew nation came into being as the result of the union of the so-called Israelites and the Canaanites. "And the children of Israel dwelt among the Canaanites. And they took their daughters to be their wives and gave their daughters to the sons of the Canaanites." The Hebrews never drove the Canaanites out of Palestine, notwithstanding that the priests' record of these things unhesitatingly declared that they did.

The Israelitish consciousness took origin in the hill country of Ephraim; the later Jewish consciousness originated in the southern clan of Judah. The Jews

(Judahites) always sought to defame and blacken the record of the northern Israelites (Ephraimites).

Pretentious Hebrew history begins with Saul's rallying the northern clans to withstand an attack by the Ammonites upon their fellow tribesmen—the Gileadites—east of the Jordan. With an army of a little more than three thousand he defeated the enemy, and it was this exploit that led the hill tribes to make him king. When the exiled priests rewrote this story, they raised Saul's army to 330,000 and added "Judah" to the list of tribes participating in the battle.

Immediately following the defeat of the Ammonites, Saul was made king by popular election by his troops. No priest or prophet participated in this affair. But the priests later on put it in the record that Saul was crowned king by the prophet Samuel in accordance with divine directions. This they did in order to establish a "divine line of descent" for David's Judahite kingship.

The greatest of all distortions of Jewish history had to do with David. After Saul's victory over the Ammonites (which he ascribed to Yahweh) the Philistines became alarmed and began attacks on the northern clans. David and Saul never could agree. David with six hundred men entered into a Philistine alliance and marched up the coast to Esdraelon. At Gath the Philistines ordered David off the field; they feared he might go over to Saul. David retired; the Philistines attacked and defeated Saul. They could not have done this had David been loyal to Israel. David's army was a polyglot assortment of malcontents, being for the most part made up of social misfits and fugitives from justice.

Saul's tragic defeat at Gilboa by the Philistines brought Yahweh to a low point among the gods in the eyes of the surrounding Canaanites. Ordinarily, Saul's defeat would have been ascribed to apostasy from Yahweh, but this time the Judahite editors attributed it to ritual errors. They required the tradition of Saul and Samuel as a background for the kingship of David.

David with his small army made his headquarters at the non-Hebrew city of Hebron. Presently his compatriots proclaimed him king of the new kingdom of Judah. Judah was made up mostly of non-Hebrew elements—Kenites, Calebites, Jebusites, and other Canaanites. They were nomads—herders—and so were devoted to the Hebrew idea of land ownership. They held the ideologies of the desert clans.

The difference between sacred and profane history is well illustrated by the two differing stories concerning making David king as they are found in the Old Testament. A part of the secular story of how his immediate followers (his army) made him king was inadvertently left in the record by the priests who subsequently prepared the lengthy and prosaic account of the sacred history wherein is depicted how the prophet Samuel, by divine direction, selected David from among his brethren and proceeded formally and by elaborate and solemn ceremonies to anoint him king over the Hebrews and then to proclaim him Saul's successor.

So many times did the priests, after preparing their fictitious narratives of God's miraculous dealings with Israel, fail fully to delete the plain and matter-of-fact statements which already rested in the records.

David sought to build himself up politically by first marrying Saul's daughter, then the widow of Nabal the rich Edomite, and then the daughter of Talmai, the king of Geshur. He took six wives from the women of Jebus, not to mention Bathsheba, the wife of the Hittite.

And it was by such methods and out of such people that David built up the fiction of a divine kingdom of Judah as the successor of the heritage and traditions of the vanishing northern kingdom of Ephraimite Israel. David's cosmopolitan tribe of Judah was more gentile than Jewish; nevertheless the oppressed elders of Ephraim came down and "anointed him king of Israel." After a military threat, David then made a compact with the Jebusites and established his capital of the united kingdom at Jebus (Jerusalem), which was a strong-walled city midway between Judah and Israel. The Philistines were aroused and soon attacked David. After a fierce battle they were defeated, and once more Yahweh was established as "The Lord God of Hosts."

But Yahweh must, perforce, share some of this glory with the Canaanite gods, for the bulk of David's army was non-Hebrew. And so there appears in your record (overlooked by the Judahite editors) this telltale statement: "Yahweh has broken my enemies before me. Therefore he called the name of the place Baal-Perazim." And they did this because eighty per cent of David's soldiers were Baalites.

David explained Saul's defeat at Gilboa by pointing out that Saul had attacked a Canaanite city, Gibeon, whose people had a peace treaty with the Ephraimites. Because of this, Yahweh forsook him. Even in Saul's time David had defended the Canaanite city of Keilah against the Philistines, and then he located his capital in a Canaanite city. In keeping with the policy of compromise with the Canaanites, David turned seven of Saul's descendants over to the Gibeonites to be hanged.

After the defeat of the Philistines, David gained possession of the "ark of Yahweh," brought it to Jerusalem, and made the worship of Yahweh official for his kingdom. He next laid heavy tribute on the neighboring tribes—the Edomites, Moabites, Ammonites, and Syrians.

David's corrupt political machine began to get personal possession of land in the north in violation of the Hebrew mores and presently gained control of the caravan tariffs formerly collected by the Philistines. And then came a series of atrocities climaxed by the murder of Uriah. All judicial appeals were adjudicated at Jerusalem; no longer could "the elders" mete out justice. No wonder rebellion broke out. Today, Absalom might be called a demagogue; his mother was a Canaanite. There were a half dozen contenders for the throne besides the son of Bathsheba—Solomon.

After David's death Solomon purged the political machine of all northern influences but continued all of the tyranny and taxation of his father's regime. Solomon bankrupted the nation by his lavish court and by his elaborate building program: There was the house of Lebanon, the palace of Pharaoh's daughter, the temple of Yahweh, the king's palace, and the restoration of the walls of many cities. Solomon created a vast Hebrew navy, operated by Syrian sailors and trading with all the world. His harem numbered almost one thousand.

By this time Yahweh's temple at Shiloh was discredited, and all the worship of the nation was centered at Jebus in the gorgeous royal chapel. The northern kingdom returned more to the worship of Elohim. They enjoyed the favor of the Pharaohs, who later enslaved Judah, putting the southern kingdom under tribute.

There were ups and downs—wars between Israel and Judah. After four years of civil war and three dynasties, Israel fell under the rule of city despots who began to trade in land. Even King Omri attempted to buy Shemer's estate.

But the end drew on apace when Shalmaneser III decided to control the Mediterranean coast. King Ahab of Ephraim gathered ten other groups and resisted at Karkar; the battle was a draw. The Assyrian was stopped but the allies were decimated. This great fight is not even mentioned in the Old Testament.

New trouble started when King Ahab tried to buy land from Naboth. His Phoenician wife forged Ahab's name to papers directing that Naboth's land be confiscated on the charge that he had blasphemed the names of "Elohim and the king." He and his sons were promptly executed. The vigorous Elijah appeared on the scene denouncing Ahab for the murder of the Naboths. Thus Elijah, one of the greatest of the prophets, began his teaching as a defender of the old land mores as against the land-selling attitude of the Baalim, against the attempt of the cities to dominate the country. But the reform did not succeed until the country landlord Jehu joined forces with the gypsy chieftain Jehonadab to destroy the prophets (real estate agents) of Baal at Samaria.

New life appeared as Jehoash and his son Jeroboam delivered Israel from its enemies. But by this time there ruled in Samaria a gangster-nobility whose depredations rivaled those of the Davidic dynasty of olden days. State and church went along hand in hand. The attempt to suppress freedom of speech led Elijah, Amos, and Hosea to begin their secret writing, and this was the real beginning of the Jewish and Christian Bibles.

But the northern kingdom did not vanish from history until the king of Israel conspired with the king of Egypt and refused to pay further tribute to Assyria. Then began the three years' siege followed by the total dispersion of the northern kingdom. Ephraim (Israel) thus vanished. Judah—the Jews, the "remnant of Israel"—had begun the concentration of land in the hands of the few, as Isaiah said, "Adding house to house and field to field." Presently there was in Jerusalem a temple of Baal alongside the temple of Yahweh. This reign of terror was ended by a monotheistic revolt led by the boy king Joash, who crusaded for Yahweh for thirty-five years.

The next king, Amaziah, had trouble with the revolting tax-paying Edomites and their neighbors. After a signal victory he turned to attack his northern neighbors and was just as signally defeated. Then the rural folk revolted; they assassinated the king and put his sixteen-year-old son on the throne. This was Azariah, called Uzziah by Isaiah. After Uzziah, things went from bad to worse, and Judah existed for a hundred years by paying tribute to the kings of Assyria. Isaiah the first told them that Jerusalem, being the city of Yahweh, would never fall. But Jeremiah did not hesitate to proclaim its downfall.

The real undoing of Judah was effected by a corrupt and rich ring of politicians operating under the rule of a boy king, Manasseh. The changing economy favored the return of the worship of Baal, whose private land dealings were against the ideology of Yahweh. The fall of Assyria and the ascendancy of Egypt brought deliverance to Judah for a time, and the country folk took over. Under Josiah they destroyed the Jerusalem ring of corrupt politicians.

But this era came to a tragic end when Josiah presumed to go out to intercept Necho's mighty army as it moved up the coast from Egypt for the aid of Assyria against Babylon. He was wiped out, and Judah went under tribute to Egypt. The Baal political party returned to power in Jerusalem, and thus began the *real* Egyptian bondage. Then ensued a period in which the Baalim politicians controlled both the courts and the priesthood. Baal worship was an economic and social system dealing with property rights as well as having to do with soil fertility.

With the overthrow of Necho by Nebuchadnezzar, Judah fell under the rule of Babylon and was given ten years of grace, but soon rebelled. When Nebuchadnezzar came against them, the Judahites started social reforms, such as releasing slaves, to influence Yahweh. When the Babylonian army temporarily withdrew, the Hebrews rejoiced that their magic of reform had delivered them. It was during this period that Jeremiah told them of the impending doom, and presently Nebuchadnezzar returned.

And so the end of Judah came suddenly. The city was destroyed, and the people were carried away into Babylon. The Yahweh-Baal struggle ended with the captivity. And the captivity shocked the remnant of Israel into monotheism.

In Babylon the Jews arrived at the conclusion that they could not exist as a small group in Palestine, having their own peculiar social and economic customs, and that, if their ideologies were to prevail, they must convert the gentiles. Thus originated their new concept of destiny—the idea that the Jews must become the chosen servants of Yahweh. The Jewish religion of the Old Testament really evolved in Babylon during the captivity.

The doctrine of immortality also took form at Babylon. The Jews had thought that the idea of the future life detracted from the emphasis of their gospel of social justice. Now for the first time theology displaced sociology and economics. Religion was taking shape as a system of human thought and conduct more and more to be separated from politics, sociology, and economics.

And so does the truth about the Jewish people disclose that much which has been regarded as sacred history turns out to be little more than the chronicle of ordinary profane history. Judaism was the soil out of which Christianity grew, but the Jews were not a miraculous people.

10. THE HEBREW RELIGION

Their leaders had taught the Israelites that they were a chosen people, not for special indulgence and monopoly of divine favor, but for the special service of carrying the truth of the one God over all to every nation. And they had promised the Jews that, if they would fulfill this destiny, they would become the spiritual leaders of all peoples, and that the coming Messiah would reign over them and all the world as the Prince of Peace.

When the Jews had been freed by the Persians, they returned to Palestine only to fall into bondage to their own priest-ridden code of laws, sacrifices, and rituals. And as the Hebrew clans rejected the wonderful story of God presented in the farewell oration of Moses for the rituals of sacrifice and penance, so did these remnants of the Hebrew nation reject the magnificent concept of the second Isaiah for the rules, regulations, and rituals of their growing priesthood.

National egotism, false faith in a misconceived promised Messiah, and the increasing bondage and tyranny of the priesthood forever silenced the voices of the spiritual leaders (excepting Daniel, Ezekiel, Haggai, and Malachi); and from that day to the time of John the Baptist all Israel experienced an increasing spiritual retrogression. But the Jews never lost the concept of the Universal Father; even to the twentieth century after Christ they have continued to follow this Deity conception.

From Moses to John the Baptist there extended an unbroken line of faithful teachers who passed the monotheistic torch of light from one generation to another while they unceasingly rebuked unscrupulous rulers, denounced commercializing priests, and ever exhorted the people to adhere to the worship of the supreme Yahweh, the Lord God of Israel.

As a nation the Jews eventually lost their political identity, but the Hebrew religion of sincere belief in the one and universal God continues to live in the hearts of the scattered exiles. And this religion survives because it has effectively functioned to conserve the highest values of its followers. The Jewish religion did preserve the ideals of a people, but it failed to foster progress and encourage philosophic creative discovery in the realms of truth. The Jewish religion had many faults—it was deficient in philosophy and almost devoid of aesthetic qualities—but it did conserve moral values; therefore it persisted. The supreme Yahweh, as compared with other concepts of Deity, was clear-cut, vivid, personal, and moral.

The Jews loved justice, wisdom, truth, and righteousness as have few peoples, but they contributed least of all peoples to the intellectual comprehension and to the spiritual understanding of these divine qualities. Though Hebrew theology refused to expand, it played an important part in the development of two other world religions, Christianity and Mohammedanism.

The Jewish religion persisted also because of its institutions. It is difficult for religion to survive as the private practice of isolated individuals. This has ever been the error of the religious leaders: Seeing the evils of institutionalized religion, they seek to destroy the technique of group functioning. In place of destroying all ritual, they would do better to reform it. In this respect Ezekiel was wiser than his contemporaries; though he joined with them in insisting on personal moral responsibility, he also set about to establish the faithful observance of a superior and purified ritual.

And thus the successive teachers of Israel accomplished the greatest feat in the evolution of religion ever to be effected on Urantia: the gradual but continuous transformation of the barbaric concept of the savage demon Yahweh, the jealous and cruel spirit god of the fulminating Sinai volcano, to the later exalted and supernal concept of the supreme Yahweh, creator of all things and the loving and merciful Father of all mankind. And this Hebraic concept of God was the highest human visualization of the Universal Father up to that time when it was further enlarged and so exquisitely amplified by the personal teachings and life example of his Son, Michael of Nebadon.

[Presented by a Melchizedek of Nebadon.]

PAPER 98

THE MELCHIZEDEK TEACHINGS IN THE OCCIDENT

THE Melchizedek teachings entered Europe along many routes, but chiefly they came by way of Egypt and were embodied in Occidental philosophy after being thoroughly Hellenized and later Christianized. The ideals of the Western world were basically Socratic, and its later religious philosophy became that of Jesus as it was modified and compromised through contact with evolving Occidental philosophy and religion, all of which culminated in the Christian church.

For a long time in Europe the Salem missionaries carried on their activities, becoming gradually absorbed into many of the cults and ritual groups which periodically arose. Among those who maintained the Salem teachings in the purest form must be mentioned the Cynics. These preachers of faith and trust in God were still functioning in Roman Europe in the first century after Christ, being later incorporated into the newly forming Christian religion.

Much of the Salem doctrine was spread in Europe by the Jewish mercenary soldiers who fought in so many of the Occidental military struggles. In ancient times the Jews were famed as much for military valor as for theologic peculiarities.

The basic doctrines of Greek philosophy, Jewish theology, and Christian ethics were fundamentally repercussions of the earlier Melchizedek teachings.

1. THE SALEM RELIGION AMONG THE GREEKS

The Salem missionaries might have built up a great religious structure among the Greeks had it not been for their strict interpretation of their oath of ordination, a pledge imposed by Machiventa which forbade the organization of exclusive congregations for worship, and which exacted the promise of each teacher never to function as a priest, never to receive fees for religious service, only food, clothing, and shelter. When the Melchizedek teachers penetrated to pre-Hellenic Greece, they found a people who still fostered the traditions of Adamson and the days of the Andites, but these teachings had become greatly adulterated with the notions and beliefs of the hordes of inferior slaves that had been brought to the Greek shores in increasing numbers. This adulteration produced a reversion to a crude animism with bloody rites, the lower classes even making ceremonial out of the execution of condemned criminals.

The early influence of the Salem teachers was nearly destroyed by the so-called Aryan invasion from southern Europe and the East. These Hellenic invaders brought along with them anthropomorphic God concepts similar to those which their Aryan fellows had carried to India. This importation inaugurated the evolution of the Greek family of gods and goddesses. This new religion was partly based on the cults of the incoming Hellenic barbarians, but it also shared in the myths of the older inhabitants of Greece.

The Hellenic Greeks found the Mediterranean world largely dominated by the mother cult, and they imposed upon these peoples their man-god, Dyaus-Zeus, who had already become, like Yahweh among the henotheistic Semites, head of the whole Greek pantheon of subordinate gods. And the Greeks would have eventually achieved a true monotheism in the concept of Zeus except for their retention of the overcontrol of Fate. A God of final value must, himself, be the arbiter of fate and the creator of destiny.

As a consequence of these factors in religious evolution, there presently developed the popular belief in the happy-go-lucky gods of Mount Olympus, gods more human than divine, and gods which the intelligent Greeks never did regard very seriously. They neither greatly loved nor greatly feared these divinities of their own creation. They had a patriotic and racial feeling for Zeus and his family of half men and half gods, but they hardly reverenced or worshiped them.

The Hellenes became so impregnated with the antipriestcraft doctrines of the earlier Salem teachers that no priesthood of any importance ever arose in Greece. Even the making of images to the gods became more of a work in art than a matter of worship.

The Olympian gods illustrate man's typical anthropomorphism. But the Greek mythology was more aesthetic than ethic. The Greek religion was helpful in that it portrayed a universe governed by a deity group. But Greek morals, ethics, and philosophy presently advanced far beyond the god concept, and this imbalance between intellectual and spiritual growth was as hazardous to Greece as it had proved to be in India.

2. GREEK PHILOSOPHIC THOUGHT

A lightly regarded and superficial religion cannot endure, especially when it has no priesthood to foster its forms and to fill the hearts of the devotees with fear and awe. The Olympian religion did not promise salvation, nor did it quench the spiritual thirst of its believers; therefore was it doomed to perish. Within a millennium of its inception it had nearly vanished, and the Greeks were without a national religion, the gods of Olympus having lost their hold upon the better minds.

This was the situation when, during the sixth century before Christ, the Orient and the Levant experienced a revival of spiritual consciousness and a new awakening to the recognition of monotheism. But the West did not share in this new development; neither Europe nor northern Africa extensively participated in this religious renaissance. The Greeks, however, did engage in a magnificent intellectual advancement. They had begun to master fear and no longer sought religion as an antidote therefor, but they did not perceive that true religion is the cure for soul hunger, spiritual disquiet, and moral despair. They sought for the solace of the soul in deep thinking—philosophy and metaphysics. They turned from the contemplation of self-preservation—salvation—to self-realization and self-understanding.

By rigorous thought the Greeks attempted to attain that consciousness of security which would serve as a substitute for the belief in survival, but they utterly failed. Only the more intelligent among the higher classes of the Hellenic peoples could grasp this new teaching; the rank and file of the progeny of the slaves of former generations had no capacity for the reception of this new substitute for religion.

The philosophers disdained all forms of worship, notwithstanding that they practically all held loosely to the background of a belief in the Salem doctrine of "the Intelligence of the universe," "the idea of God," and "the Great Source." In so far as the Greek philosophers gave recognition to the divine and the superfinite, they were frankly monotheistic; they gave scant recognition to the whole galaxy of Olympian gods and goddesses.

The Greek poets of the fifth and sixth centuries, notably Pindar, attempted the reformation of Greek religion. They elevated its ideals, but they were more artists than religionists. They failed to develop a technique for fostering and conserving supreme values.

Xenophanes taught one God, but his deity concept was too pantheistic to be a personal Father to mortal man. Anaxagoras was a mechanist except that he did recognize a First Cause, an Initial Mind. Socrates and his successors, Plato and Aristotle, taught that virtue is knowledge; goodness, health of the soul; that it is better to suffer injustice than to be guilty of it, that it is wrong to return evil for evil, and that the gods are wise and good. Their cardinal virtues were: wisdom, courage, temperance, and justice.

The evolution of religious philosophy among the Hellenic and Hebrew peoples affords a contrastive illustration of the function of the church as an institution in the shaping of cultural progress. In Palestine, human thought was so priest-controlled and scripture-directed that philosophy and aesthetics were entirely submerged in religion and morality. In Greece, the almost complete absence of priests and "sacred scriptures" left the human mind free and unfettered, resulting in a startling development in depth of thought. But religion as a personal experience failed to keep pace with the intellectual probings into the nature and reality of the cosmos.

In Greece, believing was subordinated to thinking; in Palestine, thinking was held subject to believing. Much of the strength of Christianity is due to its having borrowed heavily from both Hebrew morality and Greek thought.

In Palestine, religious dogma became so crystallized as to jeopardize further growth; in Greece, human thought became so abstract that the concept of God resolved itself into a misty vapor of pantheistic speculation not at all unlike the impersonal Infinity of the Brahman philosophers.

But the average men of these times could not grasp, nor were they much interested in, the Greek philosophy of self-realization and an abstract Deity; they rather craved promises of salvation, coupled with a personal God who could hear their prayers. They exiled the philosophers, persecuted the remnants of the Salem cult, both doctrines having become much blended, and made ready for that terrible orgiastic plunge into the follies of the mystery cults which were then overspreading the Mediterranean lands. The Eleusinian mysteries grew up within the Olympian pantheon, a Greek version of the worship of fertility; Dionysus nature worship flourished; the best of the cults was the Orphic brotherhood, whose moral preachments and promises of salvation made a great appeal to many.

All Greece became involved in these new methods of attaining salvation, these emotional and fiery ceremonials. No nation ever attained such heights of artistic philosophy in so short a time; none ever created such an advanced system of ethics practically without Deity and entirely devoid of the promise of human salvation; no nation ever plunged so quickly, deeply, and violently into such depths of intellectual stagnation, moral depravity, and spiritual poverty as these same Greek peoples when they flung themselves into the mad whirl of the mystery cults.

Religions have long endured without philosophical support, but few philosophies, as such, have long persisted without some identification with religion. Philosophy is to religion as conception is to action. But the ideal human estate is that in which philosophy, religion, and science are welded into a meaningful unity by the conjoined action of wisdom, faith, and experience.

3. THE MELCHIZEDEK TEACHINGS IN ROME

Having grown out of the earlier religious forms of worship of the family gods into the tribal reverence for Mars, the god of war, it was natural that the later religion of the Latins was more of a political observance than were the intellectual systems of the Greeks and Brahmans or the more spiritual religions of several other peoples.

In the great monotheistic renaissance of Melchizedek's gospel during the sixth century before Christ, too few of the Salem missionaries penetrated Italy, and those who did were unable to overcome the influence of the rapidly spreading Etruscan priesthood with its new galaxy of gods and temples, all of which became organized into the Roman state religion. This religion of the Latin tribes was not trivial and venal like that of the Greeks, neither was it austere and tyrannical like that of the Hebrews; it consisted for the most part in the observance of mere forms, vows, and taboos.

Roman religion was greatly influenced by extensive cultural importations from Greece. Eventually most of the Olympian gods were transplanted and incorporated into the Latin pantheon. The Greeks long worshiped the fire of the family hearth—Hestia was the virgin goddess of the hearth; Vesta was the Roman goddess of the home. Zeus became Jupiter; Aphrodite, Venus; and so on down through the many Olympian deities.

The religious initiation of Roman youths was the occasion of their solemn consecration to the service of the state. Oaths and admissions to citizenship were in reality religious ceremonies. The Latin peoples maintained temples, altars, and shrines and, in a crisis, would consult the oracles. They preserved the bones of heroes and later on those of the Christian saints.

This formal and unemotional form of pseudoreligious patriotism was doomed to collapse, even as the highly intellectual and artistic worship of the Greeks had gone down before the fervid and deeply emotional worship of the mystery cults. The greatest of these devastating cults was the mystery religion of the Mother of God sect, which had its headquarters, in those days, on the exact site of the present church of St. Peter's in Rome.

The emerging Roman state conquered politically but was in turn conquered by the cults, rituals, mysteries, and god concepts of Egypt, Greece, and the Levant. These imported cults continued to flourish throughout the Roman state up to the time of Augustus, who, purely for political and civic reasons, made a heroic and somewhat successful effort to destroy the mysteries and revive the older political religion.

One of the priests of the state religion told Augustus of the earlier attempts of the Salem teachers to spread the doctrine of one God, a final Deity presiding over all supernatural beings; and this idea took such a firm hold on the emperor that he built many temples, stocked them well with beautiful images, reorganized the state priesthood, re-established the state religion, appointed himself acting high priest of all, and as emperor did not hesitate to proclaim himself the supreme god.

This new religion of Augustus worship flourished and was observed throughout the empire during his lifetime except in Palestine, the home of the Jews. And this era of the human gods continued until the official Roman cult had a roster of more than twoscore self-elevated human deities, all claiming miraculous births and other superhuman attributes.

The last stand of the dwindling band of Salem believers was made by an earnest group of preachers, the Cynics, who exhorted the Romans to abandon their wild and senseless religious rituals and return to a form of worship embodying Melchizedek's gospel as it had been modified and contaminated through contact with the philosophy of the Greeks. But the people at large rejected the Cynics; they preferred to plunge into the rituals of the mysteries, which not only offered hopes of personal salvation but also gratified the desire for diversion, excitement, and entertainment.

4. THE MYSTERY CULTS

The majority of people in the Greco-Roman world, having lost their primitive family and state religions and being unable or unwilling to grasp the meaning of Greek philosophy, turned their attention to the spectacular and emotional mystery cults from Egypt and the Levant. The common people craved promises of salvation—religious consolation for today and assurances of hope for immortality after death.

The three mystery cults which became most popular were:

1. The Phrygian cult of Cybele and her son Attis.
2. The Egyptian cult of Osiris and his mother Isis.
3. The Iranian cult of the worship of Mithras as the savior and redeemer of sinful mankind.

The Phrygian and Egyptian mysteries taught that the divine son (respectively Attis and Osiris) had experienced death and had been resurrected by divine power, and further that all who were properly initiated into the mystery, and who reverently celebrated the anniversary of the god's death and resurrection, would thereby become partakers of his divine nature and his immortality.

The Phrygian ceremonies were imposing but degrading; their bloody festivals indicate how degraded and primitive these Levantine mysteries became. The most holy day was Black Friday, the "day of blood," commemorating the self-inflicted death of Attis. After three days of the celebration of the sacrifice and death of Attis the festival was turned to joy in honor of his resurrection.

The rituals of the worship of Isis and Osiris were more refined and impressive than were those of the Phrygian cult. This Egyptian ritual was built around the legend of the Nile god of old, a god who died and was resurrected, which concept was derived from the observation of the annually recurring stoppage of vegetation growth followed by the springtime restoration of all living plants. The frenzy of the observance of these mystery cults and the orgies of their ceremonials, which were supposed to lead up to the "enthusiasm" of the realization of divinity, were sometimes most revolting.

5. THE CULT OF MITHRAS

The Phrygian and Egyptian mysteries eventually gave way before the greatest of all the mystery cults, the worship of Mithras. The Mithraic cult made its appeal to a wide range of human nature and gradually supplanted both of its predecessors. Mithraism spread over the Roman Empire through the propagandizing of Roman legions recruited in the Levant, where this religion was the vogue, for they carried this belief wherever they went. And this new religious ritual was a great improvement over the earlier mystery cults.

The cult of Mithras arose in Iran and long persisted in its homeland despite the militant opposition of the followers of Zoroaster. But by the time Mithraism reached Rome, it had become greatly improved by the absorption of many of Zoroaster's teachings. It was chiefly through the Mithraic cult that Zoroaster's religion exerted an influence upon later appearing Christianity.

The Mithraic cult portrayed a militant god taking origin in a great rock, engaging in valiant exploits, and causing water to gush forth from a rock struck with his arrows. There was a flood from which one man escaped in a specially built boat and a last supper which Mithras celebrated with the sun-god before he ascended into the heavens. This sun-god, or Sol Invictus, was a degeneration of the Ahura-Mazda deity concept of Zoroastrianism. Mithras was conceived as the surviving champion of the sun-god in his struggle with the god of darkness. And in recognition of his slaying the mythical sacred bull, Mithras was made immortal, being exalted to the station of intercessor for the human race among the gods on high.

The adherents of this cult worshiped in caves and other secret places, chanting hymns, mumbling magic, eating the flesh of the sacrificial animals, and drinking the blood. Three times a day they worshiped, with special weekly ceremonials on the day of the sun-god and with the most elaborate observance of all on the annual festival of Mithras, December twenty-fifth. It was believed that the partaking of the sacrament ensured eternal life, the immediate passing, after death, to the bosom of Mithras, there to tarry in bliss until the judgment day. On the judgment day the Mithraic keys of heaven would unlock the gates of Paradise for the reception of the faithful; whereupon all the unbaptized of the living and the dead would be annihilated upon the return of Mithras to earth. It was taught that, when a man died, he went before Mithras for judgment, and that at the end of the world Mithras would summon all the dead from their graves to face the last judgment. The wicked would be destroyed by fire, and the righteous would reign with Mithras forever.

At first it was a religion only for men, and there were seven different orders into which believers could be successively initiated. Later on, the wives and daughters of believers were admitted to the temples of the Great Mother, which adjoined the Mithraic temples. The women's cult was a mixture of Mithraic ritual and the ceremonies of the Phrygian cult of Cybele, the mother of Attis.

6. MITHRAISM AND CHRISTIANITY

Prior to the coming of the mystery cults and Christianity, personal religion hardly developed as an independent institution in the civilized lands of North Africa and Europe; it was more of a family, city-state, political, and imperial affair. The Hellenic Greeks never evolved a centralized worship system; the ritual was local; they had no priesthood and no "sacred book." Much as the Romans, their religious institutions lacked a powerful driving agency for the preservation of higher moral and spiritual values. While it is true that the institutionalization of religion has usually detracted from its spiritual quality, it is also a fact that no religion has thus far succeeded in surviving without the aid of institutional organization of some degree, greater or lesser.

Occidental religion thus languished until the days of the Skeptics, Cynics, Epicureans, and Stoics, but most important of all, until the times of the great contest between Mithraism and Paul's new religion of Christianity.

During the third century after Christ, Mithraic and Christian churches were very similar both in appearance and in the character of their ritual. A majority of such places of worship were underground, and both contained altars whose backgrounds variously depicted the sufferings of the savior who had brought salvation to a sin-cursed human race.

Always had it been the practice of Mithraic worshipers, on entering the temple, to dip their fingers in holy water. And since in some districts there were those who at one time belonged to both religions, they introduced this custom into the majority of the Christian churches in the vicinity of Rome. Both religions employed baptism and partook of the sacrament of bread and wine. The one great difference between Mithraism and Christianity, aside from the characters of Mithras and Jesus, was that the one encouraged militarism while the other was ultrapacific. Mithraism's tolerance for other religions (except later Christianity) led to its final undoing. But the deciding factor in the struggle between the two was the admission of women into the full fellowship of the Christian faith.

In the end the nominal Christian faith dominated the Occident. Greek philosophy supplied the concepts of ethical value; Mithraism, the ritual of worship observance; and Christianity, as such, the technique for the conservation of moral and social values.

7. THE CHRISTIAN RELIGION

A Creator Son did not incarnate in the likeness of mortal flesh and bestow himself upon the humanity of Urantia to reconcile an angry God but rather to win all mankind to the recognition of the Father's love and to the realization of their sonship with God. After all, even the great advocate of the atonement doctrine realized something of this truth, for he declared that "God was in Christ reconciling the world to himself."

It is not the province of this paper to deal with the origin and dissemination of the Christian religion. Suffice it to say that it is built around the person of Jesus of Nazareth, the humanly incarnate Michael Son of Nebadon, known to Urantia as the Christ, the anointed one. Christianity was spread throughout the Levant and Occident by the followers of this Galilean, and their missionary zeal equaled that of their illustrious predecessors, the Sethites and Salemites, as well as that of their earnest Asiatic contemporaries, the Buddhist teachers.

The Christian religion, as a Urantian system of belief, arose through the compounding of the following teachings, influences, beliefs, cults, and personal individual attitudes:

1. The Melchizedek teachings, which are a basic factor in all the religions of Occident and Orient that have arisen in the last four thousand years.

2. The Hebraic system of morality, ethics, theology, and belief in both Providence and the supreme Yahweh.

3. The Zoroastrian conception of the struggle between cosmic good and evil, which had already left its imprint on both Judaism and Mithraism. Through prolonged contact attendant upon the struggles between Mithraism and Christianity, the doctrines of the Iranian prophet became a potent factor in determining the theologic and philosophic cast and structure of the dogmas, tenets, and cosmology of the Hellenized and Latinized versions of the teachings of Jesus.

4. The mystery cults, especially Mithraism but also the worship of the Great Mother in the Phrygian cult. Even the legends of the birth of Jesus on Urantia became tainted with the Roman version of the miraculous birth of the Iranian savior-hero, Mithras, whose advent on earth was supposed to have been witnessed by only a handful of gift-bearing shepherds who had been informed of this impending event by angels.

5. The historic fact of the human life of Joshua ben Joseph, the reality of Jesus of Nazareth as the glorified Christ, the Son of God.

6. The personal viewpoint of Paul of Tarsus. And it should be recorded that Mithraism was the dominant religion of Tarsus during his adolescence. Paul little dreamed that his well-intentioned letters to his converts would someday be regarded by still later Christians as the "word of God." Such well-meaning teachers must not be held accountable for the use made of their writings by later-day successors.

7. The philosophic thought of the Hellenistic peoples, from Alexandria and Antioch through Greece to Syracuse and Rome. The philosophy of the Greeks was more in harmony with Paul's version of Christianity than with any other current religious system and became an important factor in the success of Christianity in the Occident. Greek philosophy, coupled with Paul's theology, still forms the basis of European ethics.

As the original teachings of Jesus penetrated the Occident, they became Occidentalized, and as they became Occidentalized, they began to lose their potentially universal appeal to all races and kinds of men. Christianity, today, has become a religion well adapted to the social, economic, and political mores of the white races. It has long since ceased to be the religion of Jesus, although it still valiantly portrays a beautiful religion about Jesus to such individuals as sincerely seek to follow in the way of its teaching. It has glorified Jesus as the Christ, the Messianic anointed one from God, but has largely forgotten the Master's personal gospel: the Fatherhood of God and the universal brotherhood of all men.

And this is the long story of the teachings of Machiventa Melchizedek on Urantia. It is nearly four thousand years since this emergency Son of Nebadon bestowed himself on Urantia, and in that time the teachings of the "priest of El Elyon, the Most High God," have penetrated to all races and peoples. And Machiventa was successful in achieving the purpose of his unusual bestowal; when Michael made ready to appear on Urantia, the God concept was existent in the hearts of men and women, the same God concept that still flames anew in the living spiritual experience of the manifold children of the Universal Father as they live their intriguing temporal lives on the whirling planets of space.

[Presented by a Melchizedek of Nebadon.]

PAPER 99
THE SOCIAL PROBLEMS OF RELIGION

RELIGION achieves its highest social ministry when it has least connection with the secular institutions of society. In past ages, since social reforms were largely confined to the moral realms, religion did not have to adjust its attitude to extensive changes in economic and political systems. The chief problem of religion was the endeavor to replace evil with good within the existing social order of political and economic culture. Religion has thus indirectly tended to perpetuate the established order of society, to foster the maintenance of the existent type of civilization.

But religion should not be directly concerned either with the creation of new social orders or with the preservation of old ones. True religion does oppose violence as a technique of social evolution, but it does not oppose the intelligent efforts of society to adapt its usages and adjust its institutions to new economic conditions and cultural requirements.

Religion did approve the occasional social reforms of past centuries, but in the twentieth century it is of necessity called upon to face adjustment to extensive and continuing social reconstruction. Conditions of living alter so rapidly that institutional modifications must be greatly accelerated, and religion must accordingly quicken its adaptation to this new and ever-changing social order.

1. RELIGION AND SOCIAL RECONSTRUCTION

Mechanical inventions and the dissemination of knowledge are modifying civilization; certain economic adjustments and social changes are imperative if cultural disaster is to be avoided. This new and oncoming social order will not settle down complacently for a millennium. The human race must become reconciled to a procession of changes, adjustments, and readjustments. Mankind is on the march toward a new and unrevealed planetary destiny.

Religion must become a forceful influence for moral stability and spiritual progression functioning dynamically in the midst of these ever-changing conditions and never-ending economic adjustments.

Urantia society can never hope to settle down as in past ages. The social ship has steamed out of the sheltered bays of established tradition and has begun its cruise upon the high seas of evolutionary destiny; and the soul of man, as never before in the world's history, needs carefully to scrutinize its charts of morality and painstakingly to observe the compass of religious guidance. The paramount mission of religion as a social influence is to stabilize the ideals of mankind during these dangerous times of transition from one phase of civilization to another, from one level of culture to another.

Religion has no new duties to perform, but it is urgently called upon to function as a wise guide and experienced counselor in all of these new and rapidly changing human situations. Society is becoming more mechanical, more compact, more complex, and more critically interdependent. Religion must function to prevent these new and intimate interassociations from becoming mutually retrogressive or even destructive. Religion must act as the cosmic salt which prevents the ferments of progression from destroying the cultural savor of civilization. These new social relations and economic upheavals can result in lasting brotherhood only by the ministry of religion.

A godless humanitarianism is, humanly speaking, a noble gesture, but true religion is the only power which can lastingly increase the responsiveness of one social group to the needs and sufferings of other groups. In the past, institutional religion could remain passive while the upper strata of society turned a deaf ear to the sufferings and oppression of the helpless lower strata, but in modern times these lower social orders are no longer so abjectly ignorant nor so politically helpless.

Religion must not become organically involved in the secular work of social reconstruction and economic reorganization. But it must actively keep pace with all these advances in civilization by making clear-cut and vigorous restatements of its moral mandates and spiritual precepts, its progressive philosophy of human living and transcendent survival. The spirit of religion is eternal, but the form of its expression must be restated every time the dictionary of human language is revised.

2. WEAKNESS OF INSTITUTIONAL RELIGION

Institutional religion cannot afford inspiration and provide leadership in this impending world-wide social reconstruction and economic reorganization because it has unfortunately become more or less of an organic part of the social order and the economic system which is destined to undergo reconstruction. Only the real religion of personal spiritual experience can function helpfully and creatively in the present crisis of civilization.

Institutional religion is now caught in the stalemate of a vicious circle. It cannot reconstruct society without first reconstructing itself; and being so much an integral part of the established order, it cannot reconstruct itself until society has been radically reconstructed.

Religionists must function in society, in industry, and in politics as individuals, not as groups, parties, or institutions. A religious group which presumes to function as such, apart from religious activities, immediately becomes a political party, an economic organization, or a social institution. Religious collectivism must confine its efforts to the furtherance of religious causes.

Religionists are of no more value in the tasks of social reconstruction than nonreligionists except in so far as their religion has conferred upon them enhanced cosmic foresight and endowed them with that superior social wisdom which is born of the sincere desire to love God supremely and to love every man as a brother in the heavenly kingdom. An ideal social order is that in which every man loves his neighbor as he loves himself.

The institutionalized church may have appeared to serve society in the past by glorifying the established political and economic orders, but it must speedily cease such action if it is to survive. Its only proper attitude consists in the teaching of nonviolence, the doctrine of peaceful evolution in the place of violent revolution—peace on earth and good will among all men.

Modern religion finds it difficult to adjust its attitude toward the rapidly shifting social changes only because it has permitted itself to become so thoroughly traditionalized, dogmatized, and institutionalized. The religion of living experience finds no difficulty in keeping ahead of all these social developments and economic upheavals, amid which it ever functions as a moral stabilizer, social guide, and spiritual pilot. True religion carries over from one age to another the worth-while culture and that wisdom which is born of the experience of knowing God and striving to be like him.

3. RELIGION AND THE RELIGIONIST

Early Christianity was entirely free from all civil entanglements, social commitments, and economic alliances. Only did later institutionalized Christianity become an organic part of the political and social structure of Occidental civilization.

The kingdom of heaven is neither a social nor economic order; it is an exclusively spiritual brotherhood of God-knowing individuals. True, such a brotherhood is in itself a new and amazing social phenomenon attended by astounding political and economic repercussions.

The religionist is not unsympathetic with social suffering, not unmindful of civil injustice, not insulated from economic thinking, neither insensible to political tyranny. Religion influences social reconstruction directly because it spiritualizes and idealizes the individual citizen. Indirectly, cultural civilization is influenced by the attitude of these individual religionists as they become active and influential members of various social, moral, economic, and political groups.

The attainment of a high cultural civilization demands, first, the ideal type of citizen and, then, ideal and adequate social mechanisms wherewith such a citizenry may control the economic and political institutions of such an advanced human society.

The church, because of overmuch false sentiment, has long ministered to the underprivileged and the unfortunate, and this has all been well, but this same sentiment has led to the unwise perpetuation of racially degenerate stocks which have tremendously retarded the progress of civilization.

Many individual social reconstructionists, while vehemently repudiating institutionalized religion, are, after all, zealously religious in the propagation of their social reforms. And so it is that religious motivation, personal and more or less unrecognized, is playing a great part in the present-day program of social reconstruction.

The great weakness of all this unrecognized and unconscious type of religious activity is that it is unable to profit from open religious criticism and thereby attain to profitable levels of self-correction. It is a fact that religion does not grow unless it is disciplined by constructive criticism, amplified by philosophy, purified by science, and nourished by loyal fellowship.

There is always the great danger that religion will become distorted and perverted into the pursuit of false goals, as when in times of war each contending nation prostitutes its religion into military propaganda. Loveless zeal is always harmful to religion, while persecution diverts the activities of religion into the achievement of some sociologic or theologic drive.

Religion can be kept free from unholy secular alliances only by:

1. A critically corrective philosophy.

2. Freedom from all social, economic, and political alliances.

3. Creative, comforting, and love-expanding fellowships.

4. Progressive enhancement of spiritual insight and the appreciation of cosmic values.

5. Prevention of fanaticism by the compensations of the scientific mental attitude.

Religionists, as a group, must never concern themselves with anything but *religion,* albeit any one such religionist, as an individual citizen, may become the outstanding leader of some social, economic, or political reconstruction movement.

It is the business of religion to create, sustain, and inspire such a cosmic loyalty in the individual citizen as will direct him to the achievement of success in the advancement of all these difficult but desirable social services.

4. TRANSITION DIFFICULTIES

Genuine religion renders the religionist socially fragrant and creates insights into human fellowship. But the formalization of religious groups many times destroys the very values for the promotion of which the group was organized. Human friendship and divine religion are mutually helpful and significantly illuminating if the growth in each is equalized and harmonized. Religion puts new meaning into all group associations—families, schools, and clubs. It imparts new values to play and exalts all true humor.

Social leadership is transformed by spiritual insight; religion prevents all collective movements from losing sight of their true objectives. Together with children, religion is the great unifier of family life, provided it is a living and growing faith. Family life cannot be had without children; it can be lived without religion, but such a handicap enormously multiplies the difficulties of this intimate human association. During the early decades of the twentieth century, family life, next to personal religious experience, suffers most from the decadence consequent upon the transition from old religious loyalties to the emerging new meanings and values.

True religion is a meaningful way of living dynamically face to face with the commonplace realities of everyday life. But if religion is to stimulate individual development of character and augment integration of personality, it must not be standardized. If it is to stimulate evaluation of experience and serve as a value-lure, it must not be stereotyped. If religion is to promote supreme loyalties, it must not be formalized.

No matter what upheavals may attend the social and economic growth of civilization, religion is genuine and worth while if it fosters in the individual an experience in which the sovereignty of truth, beauty, and goodness prevails, for such is the true spiritual concept of supreme reality. And through love and worship this becomes meaningful as fellowship with man and sonship with God.

After all, it is what one believes rather than what one knows that determines conduct and dominates personal performances. Purely factual knowledge exerts very little influence upon the average man unless it becomes emotionally activated. But the activation of religion is superemotional, unifying the entire human experience on transcendent levels through contact with, and release of, spiritual energies in the mortal life.

During the psychologically unsettled times of the twentieth century, amid the economic upheavals, the moral crosscurrents, and the sociologic rip tides of the cyclonic transitions of a scientific era, thousands upon thousands of men and women have become humanly dislocated; they are anxious, restless, fearful, uncertain, and unsettled; as never before in the world's history they need the consolation and stabilization of sound religion. In the face of unprecedented scientific achievement and mechanical development there is spiritual stagnation and philosophic chaos.

There is no danger in religion's becoming more and more of a private matter—a personal experience—provided it does not lose its motivation for unselfish and loving social service. Religion has suffered from many secondary influences: sudden mixing of cultures, intermingling of creeds, diminution of ecclesiastical authority, changing of family life, together with urbanization and mechanization.

Man's greatest spiritual jeopardy consists in partial progress, the predicament of unfinished growth: forsaking the evolutionary religions of fear without immediately grasping the revelatory religion of love. Modern science, particularly psychology, has weakened only those religions which are so largely dependent upon fear, superstition, and emotion.

Transition is always accompanied by confusion, and there will be little tranquillity in the religious world until the great struggle between the three contending philosophies of religion is ended:

1. The spiritistic belief (in a providential Deity) of many religions.
2. The humanistic and idealistic belief of many philosophies.
3. The mechanistic and naturalistic conceptions of many sciences.

And these three partial approaches to the reality of the cosmos must eventually become harmonized by the revelatory presentation of religion, philosophy, and cosmology which portrays the triune existence of spirit, mind, and energy proceeding from the Trinity of Paradise and attaining time-space unification within the Deity of the Supreme.

5. SOCIAL ASPECTS OF RELIGION

While religion is exclusively a personal spiritual experience—knowing God as a Father—the corollary of this experience—knowing man as a brother—entails the adjustment of the self to other selves, and that involves the social or group aspect of religious life. Religion is first an inner or personal adjustment, and then it becomes a matter of social service or group adjustment. The fact of man's gregariousness perforce determines that religious groups will come into existence. What happens to these religious groups depends very much on intelligent leadership. In primitive society the religious group is not always very different from economic or political groups. Religion has always been a conservator of morals and a stabilizer of society. And this is still true, notwithstanding the contrary teaching of many modern socialists and humanists.

Always keep in mind: True religion is to know God as your Father and man as your brother. Religion is not a slavish belief in threats of punishment or magical promises of future mystical rewards.

The religion of Jesus is the most dynamic influence ever to activate the human race. Jesus shattered tradition, destroyed dogma, and called mankind to the achievement of its highest ideals in time and eternity—to be perfect, even as the Father in heaven is perfect.

Religion has little chance to function until the religious group becomes separated from all other groups—the social association of the spiritual membership of the kingdom of heaven.

The doctrine of the total depravity of man destroyed much of the potential of religion for effecting social repercussions of an uplifting nature and of inspirational value. Jesus sought to restore man's dignity when he declared that all men are the children of God.

Any religious belief which is effective in spiritualizing the believer is certain to have powerful repercussions in the social life of such a religionist. Religious experience unfailingly yields the "fruits of the spirit" in the daily life of the spirit-led mortal.

Just as certainly as men share their religious beliefs, they create a religious group of some sort which eventually creates common goals. Someday religionists will get together and actually effect co-operation on the basis of unity of ideals and purposes rather than attempting to do so on the basis of psychological opinions and theological beliefs. Goals rather than creeds should unify religionists. Since true religion is a matter of personal spiritual experience, it is inevitable that each individual religionist must have his own and personal interpretation of the realization of that spiritual experience. Let the term "faith" stand for the individual's relation to God rather than for the creedal formulation of what some group of mortals have been able to agree upon as a common religious attitude. "Have you faith? Then have it to yourself."

That faith is concerned only with the grasp of ideal values is shown by the New Testament definition which declares that faith is the substance of things hoped for and the evidence of things not seen.

Primitive man made little effort to put his religious convictions into words. His religion was danced out rather than thought out. Modern men have thought out many creeds and created many tests of religious faith. Future religionists must live out their religion, dedicate themselves to the wholehearted service of the brotherhood of man. It is high time that man had a religious experience so personal and so sublime that it could be realized and expressed only by "feelings that lie too deep for words."

Jesus did not require of his followers that they should periodically assemble and recite a form of words indicative of their common beliefs. He only ordained that they should gather together to actually *do something*—partake of the communal supper of the remembrance of his bestowal life on Urantia.

What a mistake for Christians to make when, in presenting Christ as the supreme ideal of spiritual leadership, they dare to require God-conscious men and women to reject the historic leadership of the God-knowing men who have contributed to their particular national or racial illumination during past ages.

6. INSTITUTIONAL RELIGION

Sectarianism is a disease of institutional religion, and dogmatism is an enslavement of the spiritual nature. It is far better to have a religion without a church than a church without religion. The religious turmoil of the twentieth century does not, in and of itself, betoken spiritual decadence. Confusion goes before growth as well as before destruction.

There is a real purpose in the socialization of religion. It is the purpose of group religious activities to dramatize the loyalties of religion; to magnify the lures of truth, beauty, and goodness; to foster the attractions of supreme values; to enhance the service of unselfish fellowship; to glorify the potentials of family life; to promote religious education; to provide wise counsel and spiritual guidance; and to encourage group worship. And all live religions encourage human friendship, conserve morality, promote neighborhood welfare, and facilitate the spread of the essential gospel of their respective messages of eternal salvation.

But as religion becomes institutionalized, its power for good is curtailed, while the possibilities for evil are greatly multiplied. The dangers of formalized religion are: fixation of beliefs and crystallization of sentiments; accumulation of vested interests with increase of secularization; tendency to standardize and fossilize truth; diversion of religion from the service of God to the service of the church; inclination of leaders to become administrators instead of ministers; tendency to form sects and competitive divisions; establishment of oppressive ecclesiastical authority; creation of the aristocratic "chosen-people" attitude; fostering of false and exaggerated ideas of sacredness; the routinizing of religion and the petrification of worship; tendency to venerate the past while ignoring present demands; failure to make up-to-date interpretations of religion; entanglement with functions of secular institutions; it creates the evil discrimination of religious castes; it becomes an intolerant judge of orthodoxy; it fails to hold the interest of adventurous youth and gradually loses the saving message of the gospel of eternal salvation.

Formal religion restrains men in their personal spiritual activities instead of releasing them for heightened service as kingdom builders.

7. RELIGION'S CONTRIBUTION

Though churches and all other religious groups should stand aloof from all secular activities, at the same time religion must do nothing to hinder or retard the social co-ordination of human institutions. Life must continue to grow in meaningfulness; man must go on with his reformation of philosophy and his clarification of religion.

Political science must effect the reconstruction of economics and industry by the techniques it learns from the social sciences and by the insights and motives supplied by religious living. In all social reconstruction religion provides a stabilizing loyalty to a transcendent object, a steadying goal beyond and above the immediate and temporal objective. In the midst of the confusions of a rapidly changing environment mortal man needs the sustenance of a far-flung cosmic perspective.

Religion inspires man to live courageously and joyfully on the face of the earth; it joins patience with passion, insight to zeal, sympathy with power, and ideals with energy.

Man can never wisely decide temporal issues or transcend the selfishness of personal interests unless he meditates in the presence of the sovereignty of God and reckons with the realities of divine meanings and spiritual values.

Economic interdependence and social fraternity will ultimately conduce to brotherhood. Man is naturally a dreamer, but science is sobering him so that religion can presently activate him with far less danger of precipitating fanatical reactions. Economic necessities tie man up with reality, and personal religious experience brings this same man face to face with the eternal realities of an ever-expanding and progressing cosmic citizenship.

[Presented by a Melchizedek of Nebadon.]

PAPER 100

RELIGION IN HUMAN EXPERIENCE

THE experience of dynamic religious living transforms the mediocre individual into a personality of idealistic power. Religion ministers to the progress of all through fostering the progress of each individual, and the progress of each is augmented through the achievement of all.

Spiritual growth is mutually stimulated by intimate association with other religionists. Love supplies the soil for religious growth—an objective lure in the place of subjective gratification—yet it yields the supreme subjective satisfaction. And religion ennobles the commonplace drudgery of daily living.

1. RELIGIOUS GROWTH

While religion produces growth of meanings and enhancement of values, evil always results when purely personal evaluations are elevated to the levels of absolutes. A child evaluates experience in accordance with the content of pleasure; maturity is proportional to the substitution of higher meanings for personal pleasure, even loyalties to the highest concepts of diversified life situations and cosmic relations.

Some persons are too busy to grow and are therefore in grave danger of spiritual fixation. Provision must be made for growth of meanings at differing ages, in successive cultures, and in the passing stages of advancing civilization. The chief inhibitors of growth are prejudice and ignorance.

Give every developing child a chance to grow his own religious experience; do not force a ready-made adult experience upon him. Remember, year-by-year progress through an established educational regime does not necessarily mean intellectual progress, much less spiritual growth. Enlargement of vocabulary does not signify development of character. Growth is not truly indicated by mere products but rather by progress. Real educational growth is indicated by enhancement of ideals, increased appreciation of values, new meanings of values, and augmented loyalty to supreme values.

Children are permanently impressed only by the loyalties of their adult associates; precept or even example is not lastingly influential. Loyal persons are growing persons, and growth is an impressive and inspiring reality. Live loyally today—grow—and tomorrow will attend to itself. The quickest way for a tadpole to become a frog is to live loyally each moment as a tadpole.

The soil essential for religious growth presupposes a progressive life of self-realization, the co-ordination of natural propensities, the exercise of curiosity and the enjoyment of reasonable adventure, the experiencing of feelings of satisfaction, the functioning of the fear stimulus of attention and awareness, the wonder-lure, and a normal consciousness of smallness, humility. Growth is also predicated on the discovery of selfhood accompanied by self-criticism—conscience, for conscience is really the criticism of oneself by one's own value-habits, personal ideals.

Religious experience is markedly influenced by physical health, inherited temperament, and social environment. But these temporal conditions do not inhibit inner spiritual progress by a soul dedicated to the doing of the will of the Father in heaven. There are present in all normal mortals certain innate drives toward growth and self-realization which function if they are not specifically inhibited. The certain technique of fostering this constitutive endowment of the potential of spiritual growth is to maintain an attitude of wholehearted devotion to supreme values.

Religion cannot be bestowed, received, loaned, learned, or lost. It is a personal experience which grows proportionally to the growing quest for final values. Cosmic growth thus attends on the accumulation of meanings and the ever-expanding elevation of values. But nobility itself is always an unconscious growth.

Religious habits of thinking and acting are contributory to the economy of spiritual growth. One can develop religious predispositions toward favorable reaction to spiritual stimuli, a sort of conditioned spiritual reflex. Habits which favor religious growth embrace cultivated sensitivity to divine values, recognition of religious living in others, reflective meditation on cosmic meanings, worshipful problem solving, sharing one's spiritual life with one's fellows, avoidance of selfishness, refusal to presume on divine mercy, living as in the presence of God. The factors of religious growth may be intentional, but the growth itself is unvaryingly unconscious.

The unconscious nature of religious growth does not, however, signify that it is an activity functioning in the supposed subconscious realms of human intellect; rather does it signify creative activities in the superconscious levels of mortal mind. The experience of the realization of the reality of unconscious religious growth is the one positive proof of the functional existence of the superconsciousness.

2. SPIRITUAL GROWTH

Spiritual development depends, first, on the maintenance of a living spiritual connection with true spiritual forces and, second, on the continuous bearing of spiritual fruit: yielding the ministry to one's fellows of that which has been received from one's spiritual benefactors. Spiritual progress is predicated on intellectual recognition of spiritual poverty coupled with the self-consciousness of perfection-hunger, the desire to know God and be like him, the wholehearted purpose to do the will of the Father in heaven.

Spiritual growth is first an awakening to needs, next a discernment of meanings, and then a discovery of values. The evidence of true spiritual development consists in the exhibition of a human personality motivated by love, activated by unselfish ministry, and dominated by the wholehearted worship of the perfection ideals of divinity. And this entire experience constitutes the reality of religion as contrasted with mere theological beliefs.

Religion can progress to that level of experience whereon it becomes an enlightened and wise technique of spiritual reaction to the universe. Such a glorified religion can function on three levels of human personality: the intellectual, the morontial, and the spiritual; upon the mind, in the evolving soul, and with the indwelling spirit.

Spirituality becomes at once the indicator of one's nearness to God and the measure of one's usefulness to fellow beings. Spirituality enhances the ability to discover beauty in things, recognize truth in meanings, and discover goodness in values. Spiritual development is determined by capacity therefor and is directly proportional to the elimination of the selfish qualities of love.

Actual spiritual status is the measure of Deity attainment, Adjuster attunement. The achievement of finality of spirituality is equivalent to the attainment of the maximum of reality, the maximum of Godlikeness. Eternal life is the endless quest for infinite values.

The goal of human self-realization should be spiritual, not material. The only realities worth striving for are divine, spiritual, and eternal. Mortal man is entitled to the enjoyment of physical pleasures and to the satisfaction of human affections; he is benefited by loyalty to human associations and temporal institutions; but these are not the eternal foundations upon which to build the immortal personality which must transcend space, vanquish time, and achieve the eternal destiny of divine perfection and finaliter service.

Jesus portrayed the profound surety of the God-knowing mortal when he said: "To a God-knowing kingdom believer, what does it matter if all things earthly crash?" Temporal securities are vulnerable, but spiritual sureties are impregnable. When the flood tides of human adversity, selfishness, cruelty, hate, malice, and jealousy beat about the mortal soul, you may rest in the assurance that there is one inner bastion, the citadel of the spirit, which is absolutely unassailable; at least this is true of every human being who has dedicated the keeping of his soul to the indwelling spirit of the eternal God.

After such spiritual attainment, whether secured by gradual growth or specific crisis, there occurs a new orientation of personality as well as the development of a new standard of values. Such spirit-born individuals are so remotivated in life that they can calmly stand by while their fondest ambitions perish and their keenest hopes crash; they positively know that such catastrophes are but the redirecting cataclysms which wreck one's temporal creations preliminary to the rearing of the more noble and enduring realities of a new and more sublime level of universe attainment.

3. CONCEPTS OF SUPREME VALUE

Religion is not a technique for attaining a static and blissful peace of mind; it is an impulse for organizing the soul for dynamic service. It is the enlistment of the totality of selfhood in the loyal service of loving God and serving man. Religion pays any price essential to the attainment of the supreme goal, the eternal prize. There is a consecrated completeness in religious loyalty which is superbly sublime. And these loyalties are socially effective and spiritually progressive.

To the religionist the word God becomes a symbol signifying the approach to supreme reality and the recognition of divine value. Human likes and dislikes do not determine good and evil; moral values do not grow out of wish fulfillment or emotional frustration.

In the contemplation of values you must distinguish between that which *is* value and that which *has* value. You must recognize the relation between pleasurable activities and their meaningful integration and enhanced realization on ever progressively higher and higher levels of human experience.

Meaning is something which experience adds to value; it is the appreciative consciousness of values. An isolated and purely selfish pleasure may connote a virtual devaluation of meanings, a meaningless enjoyment bordering on relative evil. Values are experiential when realities are meaningful and mentally associated, when such relationships are recognized and appreciated by mind.

Values can never be static; reality signifies change, growth. Change without growth, expansion of meaning and exaltation of value, is valueless—is potential evil. The greater the quality of cosmic adaptation, the more of meaning any experience possesses. Values are not conceptual illusions; they are real, but always they depend on the fact of relationships. Values are always both actual and potential—not what was, but what is and is to be.

The association of actuals and potentials equals growth, the experiential realization of values. But growth is not mere progress. Progress is always meaningful, but it is relatively valueless without growth. The supreme value of human life consists in growth of values, progress in meanings, and realization of the cosmic interrelatedness of both of these experiences. And such an experience is the equivalent of God-consciousness. Such a mortal, while not supernatural, is truly becoming superhuman; an immortal soul is evolving.

Man cannot cause growth, but he can supply favorable conditions. Growth is always unconscious, be it physical, intellectual, or spiritual. Love thus grows; it cannot be created, manufactured, or purchased; it must grow. Evolution is a cosmic technique of growth. Social growth cannot be secured by legislation, and moral growth is not had by improved administration. Man may manufacture a machine, but its real value must be derived from human culture and personal appreciation. Man's sole contribution to growth is the mobilization of the total powers of his personality—living faith.

4. PROBLEMS OF GROWTH

Religious living is devoted living, and devoted living is creative living, original and spontaneous. New religious insights arise out of conflicts which initiate the choosing of new and better reaction habits in the place of older and inferior reaction patterns. New meanings only emerge amid conflict; and conflict persists only in the face of refusal to espouse the higher values connoted in superior meanings.

Religious perplexities are inevitable; there can be no growth without psychic conflict and spiritual agitation. The organization of a philosophic standard of living entails considerable commotion in the philosophic realms of the mind. Loyalties are not exercised in behalf of the great, the good, the true, and the noble without a struggle. Effort is attendant upon clarification of spiritual vision and enhancement of cosmic insight. And the human intellect protests against being weaned from subsisting upon the nonspiritual energies of temporal existence. The slothful animal mind rebels at the effort required to wrestle with cosmic problem solving.

But the great problem of religious living consists in the task of unifying the soul powers of the personality by the dominance of LOVE. Health, mental efficiency, and happiness arise from the unification of physical systems, mind systems, and spirit systems. Of health and sanity man understands much, but of happiness he has truly realized very little. The highest happiness is indissolubly linked with spiritual progress. Spiritual growth yields lasting joy, peace which passes all understanding.

In physical life the senses tell of the existence of things; mind discovers the reality of meanings; but the spiritual experience reveals to the individual the true values of life. These high levels of human living are attained in the supreme love of God and in the unselfish love of man. If you love your fellow men, you must have discovered their values. Jesus loved men so much because he placed such a high value upon them. You can best discover values in your associates by discovering their motivation. If someone irritates you, causes feelings of resentment, you should sympathetically seek to discern his viewpoint, his reasons for such objectionable conduct. If once you understand your neighbor, you will become tolerant, and this tolerance will grow into friendship and ripen into love.

In the mind's eye conjure up a picture of one of your primitive ancestors of cave-dwelling times—a short, misshapen, filthy, snarling hulk of a man standing, legs spread, club upraised, breathing hate and animosity as he looks fiercely just ahead. Such a picture hardly depicts the divine dignity of man. But allow us to enlarge the picture. In front of this animated human crouches a saber-toothed tiger. Behind him, a woman and two children. Immediately you recognize that such a picture stands for the beginnings of much that is fine and noble in the human race, but the man is the same in both pictures. Only, in the second sketch you are favored with a widened horizon. You therein discern the motivation of this evolving mortal. His attitude becomes praiseworthy because you understand him. If you could only fathom the motives of your associates, how much better you would understand them. If you could only know your fellows, you would eventually fall in love with them.

You cannot truly love your fellows by a mere act of the will. Love is only born of thoroughgoing understanding of your neighbor's motives and sentiments. It is not so important to love all men today as it is that each day you learn to love one more human being. If each day or each week you achieve an understanding of one more of your fellows, and if this is the limit of your ability, then you are certainly socializing and truly spiritualizing your personality. Love is infectious, and when human devotion is intelligent and wise, love is more catching than hate. But only genuine and unselfish love is truly contagious. If each mortal could only become a focus of dynamic affection, this benign virus of love would soon pervade the sentimental emotion-stream of humanity to such an extent that all civilization would be encompassed by love, and that would be the realization of the brotherhood of man.

5. CONVERSION AND MYSTICISM

The world is filled with lost souls, not lost in the theologic sense but lost in the directional meaning, wandering about in confusion among the isms and cults of a frustrated philosophic era. Too few have learned how to install a philosophy of living in the place of religious authority. (The symbols of socialized religion are not to be despised as channels of growth, albeit the river bed is not the river.)

The progression of religious growth leads from stagnation through conflict to co-ordination, from insecurity to undoubting faith, from confusion of cosmic consciousness to unification of personality, from the temporal objective to the eternal, from the bondage of fear to the liberty of divine sonship.

It should be made clear that professions of loyalty to the supreme ideals—the psychic, emotional, and spiritual awareness of God-consciousness—may be a natural and gradual growth or may sometimes be experienced at certain junctures, as in a crisis. The Apostle Paul experienced just such a sudden and spectacular conversion that eventful day on the Damascus road. Gautama Siddhartha had a similar experience the night he sat alone and sought to penetrate the mystery of final truth. Many others have had like experiences, and many true believers have progressed in the spirit without sudden conversion.

Most of the spectacular phenomena associated with so-called religious conversions are entirely psychologic in nature, but now and then there do occur experiences which are also spiritual in origin. When the mental mobilization is absolutely total on any level of the psychic upreach toward spirit attainment, when there exists perfection of the human motivation of loyalties to the divine idea, then there very often occurs a sudden down-grasp of the indwelling spirit to synchronize with the concentrated and consecrated purpose of the superconscious mind of the believing mortal. And it is such experiences of unified intellectual and spiritual phenomena that constitute the conversion which consists in factors over and above purely psychologic involvement.

But emotion alone is a false conversion; one must have faith as well as feeling. To the extent that such psychic mobilization is partial, and in so far as such human-loyalty motivation is incomplete, to that extent will the experience of conversion be a blended intellectual, emotional, and spiritual reality.

If one is disposed to recognize a theoretical subconscious mind as a practical working hypothesis in the otherwise unified intellectual life, then, to be consistent, one should postulate a similar and corresponding realm of ascending intellectual activity as the superconscious level, the zone of immediate contact with the indwelling spirit entity, the Thought Adjuster. The great danger in all these psychic speculations is that visions and other so-called mystic experiences, along with extraordinary dreams, may be regarded as divine communications to the human mind. In times past, divine beings have revealed themselves to certain God-knowing persons, not because of their mystic trances or morbid visions, but in spite of all these phenomena.

In contrast with conversion-seeking, the better approach to the morontia zones of possible contact with the Thought Adjuster would be through living faith and sincere worship, wholehearted and unselfish prayer. Altogether too much of the uprush of the memories of the unconscious levels of the human mind has been mistaken for divine revelations and spirit leadings.

There is great danger associated with the habitual practice of religious daydreaming; mysticism may become a technique of reality avoidance, albeit it has sometimes been a means of genuine spiritual communion. Short seasons of retreat from the busy scenes of life may not be seriously dangerous, but prolonged isolation of personality is most undesirable. Under no circumstances should the trancelike state of visionary consciousness be cultivated as a religious experience.

The characteristics of the mystical state are diffusion of consciousness with vivid islands of focal attention operating on a comparatively passive intellect.

All of this gravitates consciousness toward the subconscious rather than in the direction of the zone of spiritual contact, the superconscious. Many mystics have carried their mental dissociation to the level of abnormal mental manifestations.

The more healthful attitude of spiritual meditation is to be found in reflective worship and in the prayer of thanksgiving. The direct communion with one's Thought Adjuster, such as occurred in the later years of Jesus' life in the flesh, should not be confused with these so-called mystical experiences. The factors which contribute to the initiation of mystic communion are indicative of the danger of such psychic states. The mystic status is favored by such things as: physical fatigue, fasting, psychic dissociation, profound aesthetic experiences, vivid sex impulses, fear, anxiety, rage, and wild dancing. Much of the material arising as a result of such preliminary preparation has its origin in the subconscious mind.

However favorable may have been the conditions for mystic phenomena, it should be clearly understood that Jesus of Nazareth never resorted to such methods for communion with the Paradise Father. Jesus had no subconscious delusions or superconscious illusions.

6. MARKS OF RELIGIOUS LIVING

Evolutionary religions and revelatory religions may differ markedly in method, but in motive there is great similarity. Religion is not a specific function of life; rather is it a mode of living. True religion is a wholehearted devotion to some reality which the religionist deems to be of supreme value to himself and for all mankind. And the outstanding characteristics of all religions are: unquestioning loyalty and wholehearted devotion to supreme values. This religious devotion to supreme values is shown in the relation of the supposedly irreligious mother to her child and in the fervent loyalty of nonreligionists to an espoused cause.

The accepted supreme value of the religionist may be base or even false, but it is nevertheless religious. A religion is genuine to just the extent that the value which is held to be supreme is truly a cosmic reality of genuine spiritual worth.

The marks of human response to the religious impulse embrace the qualities of nobility and grandeur. The sincere religionist is conscious of universe citizenship and is aware of making contact with sources of superhuman power. He is thrilled and energized with the assurance of belonging to a superior and ennobled fellowship of the sons of God. The consciousness of self-worth has become augmented by the stimulus of the quest for the highest universe objectives—supreme goals.

The self has surrendered to the intriguing drive of an all-encompassing motivation which imposes heightened self-discipline, lessens emotional conflict, and makes mortal life truly worth living. The morbid recognition of human limitations is changed to the natural consciousness of mortal shortcomings, associated with moral determination and spiritual aspiration to attain the highest universe and superuniverse goals. And this intense striving for the attainment of supermortal ideals is always characterized by increasing patience, forbearance, fortitude, and tolerance.

But true religion is a living love, a life of service. The religionist's detachment from much that is purely temporal and trivial never leads to social isolation, and it should not destroy the sense of humor. Genuine religion takes nothing away from human existence, but it does add new meanings to all of life; it generates new types of enthusiasm, zeal, and courage. It may even engender the spirit of the crusader, which is more than dangerous if not controlled by spiritual insight and loyal devotion to the commonplace social obligations of human loyalties.

One of the most amazing earmarks of religious living is that dynamic and sublime peace, that peace which passes all human understanding, that cosmic poise which betokens the absence of all doubt and turmoil. Such levels of spiritual stability are immune to disappointment. Such religionists are like the Apostle Paul, who said: "I am persuaded that neither death, nor life, nor angels, nor principalities, nor powers, nor things present, nor things to come, nor height, nor depth, nor anything else shall be able to separate us from the love of God."

There is a sense of security, associated with the realization of triumphing glory, resident in the consciousness of the religionist who has grasped the reality of the Supreme, and who pursues the goal of the Ultimate.

Even evolutionary religion is all of this in loyalty and grandeur because it is a genuine experience. But revelatory religion is *excellent* as well as genuine. The new loyalties of enlarged spiritual vision create new levels of love and devotion, of service and fellowship; and all this enhanced social outlook produces an enlarged consciousness of the Fatherhood of God and the brotherhood of man.

The characteristic difference between evolved and revealed religion is a new quality of divine wisdom which is added to purely experiential human wisdom. But it is experience in and with the human religions that develops the capacity for subsequent reception of increased bestowals of divine wisdom and cosmic insight.

7. THE ACME OF RELIGIOUS LIVING

Although the average mortal of Urantia cannot hope to attain the high perfection of character which Jesus of Nazareth acquired while sojourning in the flesh, it is altogether possible for every mortal believer to develop a strong and unified personality along the perfected lines of the Jesus personality. The unique feature of the Master's personality was not so much its perfection as its symmetry, its exquisite and balanced unification. The most effective presentation of Jesus consists in following the example of the one who said, as he gestured toward the Master standing before his accusers, "Behold the man!"

The unfailing kindness of Jesus touched the hearts of men, but his stalwart strength of character amazed his followers. He was truly sincere; there was nothing of the hypocrite in him. He was free from affectation; he was always so refreshingly genuine. He never stooped to pretense, and he never resorted to shamming. He lived the truth, even as he taught it. He was the truth. He was constrained to proclaim saving truth to his generation, even though such sincerity sometimes caused pain. He was unquestioningly loyal to all truth.

But the Master was so reasonable, so approachable. He was so practical in all his ministry, while all his plans were characterized by such sanctified common sense. He was so free from all freakish, erratic, and eccentric tendencies. He was never capricious, whimsical, or hysterical. In all his teaching and in everything he did there was always an exquisite discrimination associated with an extraordinary sense of propriety.

The Son of Man was always a well-poised personality. Even his enemies maintained a wholesome respect for him; they even feared his presence. Jesus was unafraid. He was surcharged with divine enthusiasm, but he never became fanatical. He was emotionally active but never flighty. He was imaginative but always practical. He frankly faced the realities of life, but he was never dull or prosaic. He was courageous but never reckless; prudent but never cowardly. He was sympathetic but not sentimental; unique but not eccentric. He was pious but not sanctimonious. And he was so well-poised because he was so perfectly unified.

Jesus' originality was unstifled. He was not bound by tradition or handicapped by enslavement to narrow conventionality. He spoke with undoubted confidence and taught with absolute authority. But his superb originality did not cause him to overlook the gems of truth in the teachings of his predecessors and contemporaries. And the most original of his teachings was the emphasis of love and mercy in the place of fear and sacrifice.

Jesus was very broad in his outlook. He exhorted his followers to preach the gospel to all peoples. He was free from all narrow-mindedness. His sympathetic heart embraced all mankind, even a universe. Always his invitation was, "Whosoever will, let him come."

Of Jesus it was truly said, "He trusted God." As a man among men he most sublimely trusted the Father in heaven. He trusted his Father as a little child trusts his earthly parent. His faith was perfect but never presumptuous. No matter how cruel nature might appear to be or how indifferent to man's welfare on earth, Jesus never faltered in his faith. He was immune to disappointment and impervious to persecution. He was untouched by apparent failure.

He loved men as brothers, at the same time recognizing how they differed in innate endowments and acquired qualities. "He went about doing good."

Jesus was an unusually cheerful person, but he was not a blind and unreasoning optimist. His constant word of exhortation was, "Be of good cheer." He could maintain this confident attitude because of his unswerving trust in God and his unshakable confidence in man. He was always touchingly considerate of all men because he loved them and believed in them. Still he was always true to his convictions and magnificently firm in his devotion to the doing of his Father's will.

The Master was always generous. He never grew weary of saying, "It is more blessed to give than to receive." Said he, "Freely you have received, freely give." And yet, with all of his unbounded generosity, he was never wasteful or extravagant. He taught that you must believe to receive salvation. "For every one who seeks shall receive."

He was candid, but always kind. Said he, "If it were not so, I would have told you." He was frank, but always friendly. He was outspoken in his love for the sinner and in his hatred for sin. But throughout all this amazing frankness he was unerringly *fair*.

Jesus was consistently cheerful, notwithstanding he sometimes drank deeply of the cup of human sorrow. He fearlessly faced the realities of existence, yet was he filled with enthusiasm for the gospel of the kingdom. But he controlled his enthusiasm; it never controlled him. He was unreservedly dedicated to "the Father's business." This divine enthusiasm led his unspiritual brethren to think he was beside himself, but the onlooking universe appraised him as the model of sanity and the pattern of supreme mortal devotion to the high standards of spiritual living. And his controlled enthusiasm was contagious; his associates were constrained to share his divine optimism.

This man of Galilee was not a man of sorrows; he was a soul of gladness. Always was he saying, "Rejoice and be exceedingly glad." But when duty required, he was willing to walk courageously through the "valley of the shadow of death." He was gladsome but at the same time humble.

His courage was equaled only by his patience. When pressed to act prematurely, he would only reply, "My hour has not yet come." He was never in a hurry; his composure was sublime. But he was often indignant at evil, intolerant of sin. He was often mightily moved to resist that which was inimical to the welfare of his children on earth. But his indignation against sin never led to anger at the sinner.

His courage was magnificent, but he was never foolhardy. His watchword was, "Fear not." His bravery was lofty and his courage often heroic. But his courage was linked with discretion and controlled by reason. It was courage born of faith, not the recklessness of blind presumption. He was truly brave but never audacious.

The Master was a pattern of reverence. The prayer of even his youth began, "Our Father who is in heaven, hallowed be your name." He was even respectful of the faulty worship of his fellows. But this did not deter him from making attacks on religious traditions or assaulting errors of human belief. He was reverential of true holiness, and yet he could justly appeal to his fellows, saying, "Who among you convicts me of sin?"

Jesus was great because he was good, and yet he fraternized with the little children. He was gentle and unassuming in his personal life, and yet he was the perfected man of a universe. His associates called him Master unbidden.

Jesus was the perfectly unified human personality. And today, as in Galilee, he continues to unify mortal experience and to co-ordinate human endeavors. He unifies life, ennobles character, and simplifies experience. He enters the human mind to elevate, transform, and transfigure it. It is literally true: "If any man has Christ Jesus within him, he is a new creature; old things are passing away; behold, all things are becoming new."

[Presented by a Melchizedek of Nebadon.]

PAPER 101

THE REAL NATURE OF RELIGION

RELIGION, as a human experience, ranges from the primitive fear slavery of the evolving savage up to the sublime and magnificent faith liberty of those civilized mortals who are superbly conscious of sonship with the eternal God.

Religion is the ancestor of the advanced ethics and morals of progressive social evolution. But religion, as such, is not merely a moral movement, albeit the outward and social manifestations of religion are mightily influenced by the ethical and moral momentum of human society. Always is religion the inspiration of man's evolving nature, but it is not the secret of that evolution.

Religion, the conviction-faith of the personality, can always triumph over the superficially contradictory logic of despair born in the unbelieving material mind. There really is a true and genuine inner voice, that "true light which lights every man who comes into the world." And this spirit leading is distinct from the ethical prompting of human conscience. The feeling of religious assurance is more than an emotional feeling. The assurance of religion transcends the reason of the mind, even the logic of philosophy. Religion *is* faith, trust, and assurance.

1. TRUE RELIGION

True religion is not a system of philosophic belief which can be reasoned out and substantiated by natural proofs, neither is it a fantastic and mystic experience of indescribable feelings of ecstasy which can be enjoyed only by the romantic devotees of mysticism. Religion is not the product of reason, but viewed from within, it is altogether reasonable. Religion is not derived from the logic of human philosophy, but as a mortal experience it is altogether logical. Religion is the experiencing of divinity in the consciousness of a moral being of evolutionary origin; it represents true experience with eternal realities in time, the realization of spiritual satisfactions while yet in the flesh.

The Thought Adjuster has no special mechanism through which to gain self-expression; there is no mystic religious faculty for the reception or expression of religious emotions. These experiences are made available through the naturally ordained mechanism of mortal mind. And therein lies one explanation of the Adjuster's difficulty in engaging in direct communication with the material mind of its constant indwelling.

The divine spirit makes contact with mortal man, not by feelings or emotions, but in the realm of the highest and most spiritualized thinking. It is your *thoughts,* not your feelings, that lead you Godward. The divine nature may be perceived only with the eyes of the mind. But the mind that really discerns God, hears the indwelling Adjuster, is the pure mind. "Without holiness no man may see the Lord." All such inner and spiritual communion is termed spiritual insight. Such religious experiences result from the impress made upon the mind of man by the combined operations of the Adjuster and the Spirit of Truth as they function amid and upon the ideas, ideals, insights, and spirit strivings of the evolving sons of God.

Religion lives and prospers, then, not by sight and feeling, but rather by faith and insight. It consists not in the discovery of new facts or in the finding of a unique experience, but rather in the discovery of new and spiritual *meanings* in facts already well known to mankind. The highest religious experience is not dependent on prior acts of belief, tradition, and authority; neither is religion the offspring of sublime feelings and purely mystical emotions. It is, rather, a profoundly deep and actual experience of spiritual communion with the spirit influences resident within the human mind, and as far as such an experience is definable in terms of psychology, it is simply the experience of experiencing the reality of believing in God as the reality of such a purely personal experience.

While religion is not the product of the rationalistic speculations of a material cosmology, it is, nonetheless, the creation of a wholly rational insight which originates in man's mind-experience. Religion is born neither of mystic meditations nor of isolated contemplations, albeit it is ever more or less mysterious and always indefinable and inexplicable in terms of purely intellectual reason and philosophic logic. The germs of true religion originate in the domain of man's moral consciousness, and they are revealed in the growth of man's spiritual insight, that faculty of human personality which accrues as a consequence of the presence of the God-revealing Thought Adjuster in the God-hungry mortal mind.

Faith unites moral insight with conscientious discriminations of values, and the pre-existent evolutionary sense of duty completes the ancestry of true religion. The experience of religion eventually results in the certain consciousness of God and in the undoubted assurance of the survival of the believing personality.

Thus it may be seen that religious longings and spiritual urges are not of such a nature as would merely lead men to *want* to believe in God, but rather are they of such nature and power that men are profoundly impressed with the conviction that they *ought* to believe in God. The sense of evolutionary duty and the obligations consequent upon the illumination of revelation make such a profound impression upon man's moral nature that he finally reaches that position of mind and that attitude of soul where he concludes that he *has no right not to believe in God.* The higher and superphilosophic wisdom of such enlightened and disciplined individuals ultimately instructs them that to doubt God or distrust his goodness would be to prove untrue to the *realest* and *deepest* thing within the human mind and soul—the divine Adjuster.

2. THE FACT OF RELIGION

The fact of religion consists wholly in the religious experience of rational and average human beings. And this is the only sense in which religion can ever be regarded as scientific or even psychological. The proof that revelation is revelation is this same fact of human experience: the fact that revelation does synthesize the apparently divergent sciences of nature and the theology of religion into a consistent and logical universe philosophy, a co-ordinated and unbroken explanation of both science and religion, thus creating a harmony of mind and satisfaction of spirit which answers in human experience those questionings of the mortal mind which craves to know *how* the Infinite works out his will and plans in matter, with minds, and on spirit.

Reason is the method of science; faith is the method of religion; logic is the attempted technique of philosophy. Revelation compensates for the absence of the morontia viewpoint by providing a technique for achieving unity in the comprehension of the reality and relationships of matter and spirit by the mediation of mind. And true revelation never renders science unnatural, religion unreasonable, or philosophy illogical.

Reason, through the study of science, may lead back through nature to a First Cause, but it requires religious faith to transform the First Cause of science into a God of salvation; and revelation is further required for the validation of such a faith, such spiritual insight.

There are two basic reasons for believing in a God who fosters human survival:

1. Human experience, personal assurance, the somehow registered hope and trust initiated by the indwelling Thought Adjuster.
2. The revelation of truth, whether by direct personal ministry of the Spirit of Truth, by the world bestowal of divine Sons, or through the revelations of the written word.

Science ends its reason-search in the hypothesis of a First Cause. Religion does not stop in its flight of faith until it is sure of a God of salvation. The discriminating study of science logically suggests the reality and existence of an Absolute. Religion believes unreservedly in the existence and reality of a God who fosters personality survival. What metaphysics fails utterly in doing, and what even philosophy fails partially in doing, revelation does; that is, affirms that this First Cause of science and religion's God of salvation are *one and the same Deity.*

Reason is the proof of science, faith the proof of religion, logic the proof of philosophy, but revelation is validated only by human *experience.* Science yields knowledge; religion yields happiness; philosophy yields unity; revelation confirms the experiential harmony of this triune approach to universal reality.

The contemplation of nature can only reveal a God of nature, a God of motion. Nature exhibits only matter, motion, and animation—life. Matter plus energy, under certain conditions, is manifested in living forms, but while natural life is thus relatively continuous as a phenomenon, it is wholly transient as to individualities. Nature does not afford ground for logical belief in human-personality survival. The religious man who finds God in nature has already and first found this same personal God in his own soul.

Faith reveals God in the soul. Revelation, the substitute for morontia insight on an evolutionary world, enables man to see the same God in nature that faith exhibits in his soul. Thus does revelation successfully bridge the gulf between the material and the spiritual, even between the creature and the Creator, between man and God.

The contemplation of nature does logically point in the direction of intelligent guidance, even living supervision, but it does not in any satisfactory manner reveal a personal God. On the other hand, nature discloses nothing which would preclude the universe from being looked upon as the handiwork of the God of religion. God cannot be found through nature alone, but man having otherwise found him, the study of nature becomes wholly consistent with a higher and more spiritual interpretation of the universe.

Revelation as an epochal phenomenon is periodic; as a personal human experience it is continuous. Divinity functions in mortal personality as the Adjuster gift of the Father, as the Spirit of Truth of the Son, and as the Holy Spirit of the Universe Spirit, while these three supermortal endowments are unified in human experiential evolution as the ministry of the Supreme.

True religion is an insight into reality, the faith-child of the moral consciousness, and not a mere intellectual assent to any body of dogmatic doctrines. True religion consists in the experience that "the Spirit itself bears witness with our spirit that we are the children of God." Religion consists not in theologic propositions but in spiritual insight and the sublimity of the soul's trust.

Your deepest nature—the divine Adjuster—creates within you a hunger and thirst for righteousness, a certain craving for divine perfection. Religion is the faith act of the recognition of this inner urge to divine attainment; and thus is brought about that soul trust and assurance of which you become conscious as the way of salvation, the technique of the survival of personality and all those values which you have come to look upon as being true and good.

The realization of religion never has been, and never will be, dependent on great learning or clever logic. It is spiritual insight, and that is just the reason why some of the world's greatest religious teachers, even the prophets, have sometimes possessed so little of the wisdom of the world. Religious faith is available alike to the learned and the unlearned.

Religion must ever be its own critic and judge; it can never be observed, much less understood, from the outside. Your only assurance of a personal God consists in your own insight as to your belief in, and experience with, things spiritual. To all of your fellows who have had a similar experience, no argument about the personality or reality of God is necessary, while to all other men who are not thus sure of God no possible argument could ever be truly convincing.

Psychology may indeed attempt to study the phenomena of religious reactions to the social environment, but never can it hope to penetrate to the real and inner motives and workings of religion. Only theology, the province of faith and the technique of revelation, can afford any sort of intelligent account of the nature and content of religious experience.

3. THE CHARACTERISTICS OF RELIGION

Religion is so vital that it persists in the absence of learning. It lives in spite of its contamination with erroneous cosmologies and false philosophies; it survives even the confusion of metaphysics. In and through all the historic vicissitudes of religion there ever persists that which is indispensable to human progress and survival: the ethical conscience and the moral consciousness.

Faith-insight, or spiritual intuition, is the endowment of the cosmic mind in association with the Thought Adjuster, which is the Father's gift to man. Spiritual reason, soul intelligence, is the endowment of the Holy Spirit, the Creative Spirit's gift to man. Spiritual philosophy, the wisdom of spirit realities, is the endowment of the Spirit of Truth, the combined gift of the bestowal Sons to the children of men. And the co-ordination and interassociation of these spirit endowments constitute man a spirit personality in potential destiny.

It is this same spirit personality, in primitive and embryonic form, the Adjuster possession of which survives the natural death in the flesh. This composite entity of spirit origin in association with human experience is enabled, by means of the living way provided by the divine Sons, to survive (in Adjuster custody) the dissolution of the material self of mind and matter when such a transient partnership of the material and the spiritual is divorced by the cessation of vital motion.

Through religious faith the soul of man reveals itself and demonstrates the potential divinity of its emerging nature by the characteristic manner in which it induces the mortal personality to react to certain trying intellectual and testing social situations. Genuine spiritual faith (true moral consciousness) is revealed in that it:

1. Causes ethics and morals to progress despite inherent and adverse animalistic tendencies.

2. Produces a sublime trust in the goodness of God even in the face of bitter disappointment and crushing defeat.

3. Generates profound courage and confidence despite natural adversity and physical calamity.

4. Exhibits inexplicable poise and sustaining tranquillity notwithstanding baffling diseases and even acute physical suffering.

5. Maintains a mysterious poise and composure of personality in the face of maltreatment and the rankest injustice.

6. Maintains a divine trust in ultimate victory in spite of the cruelties of seemingly blind fate and the apparent utter indifference of natural forces to human welfare.

7. Persists in the unswerving belief in God despite all contrary demonstrations of logic and successfully withstands all other intellectual sophistries.

8. Continues to exhibit undaunted faith in the soul's survival regardless of the deceptive teachings of false science and the persuasive delusions of unsound philosophy.

9. Lives and triumphs irrespective of the crushing overload of the complex and partial civilizations of modern times.

10. Contributes to the continued survival of altruism in spite of human selfishness, social antagonisms, industrial greeds, and political maladjustments.

11. Steadfastly adheres to a sublime belief in universe unity and divine guidance regardless of the perplexing presence of evil and sin.

12. Goes right on worshiping God in spite of anything and everything. Dares to declare, "Even though he slay me, yet will I serve him."

We know, then, by three phenomena, that man has a divine spirit or spirits dwelling within him: first, by personal experience—religious faith; second, by revelation—personal and racial; and third, by the amazing exhibition of such extraordinary and unnatural reactions to his material environment as are illustrated by the foregoing recital of twelve spiritlike performances in the presence of the actual and trying situations of real human existence. And there are still others.

And it is just such a vital and vigorous performance of faith in the domain of religion that entitles mortal man to affirm the personal possession and spiritual reality of that crowning endowment of human nature, religious experience.

4. THE LIMITATIONS OF REVELATION

Because your world is generally ignorant of origins, even of physical origins, it has appeared to be wise from time to time to provide instruction in cosmology. And always has this made trouble for the future. The laws of revelation hamper us greatly by their proscription of the impartation of unearned or premature knowledge. Any cosmology presented as a part of revealed religion is destined to be outgrown in a very short time. Accordingly, future students of such a revelation are tempted to discard any element of genuine religious truth it may contain because they discover errors on the face of the associated cosmologies therein presented.

Mankind should understand that we who participate in the revelation of truth are very rigorously limited by the instructions of our superiors. We are not at liberty to anticipate the scientific discoveries of a thousand years. Revelators must act in accordance with the instructions which form a part of the revelation mandate. We see no way of overcoming this difficulty, either now or at any future time. We full well know that, while the historic facts and religious truths of this series of revelatory presentations will stand on the records of the ages to come, within a few short years many of our statements regarding the physical sciences will stand in need of revision in consequence of additional scientific developments and new discoveries. These new developments we even now foresee, but we are forbidden to include such humanly undiscovered facts in the revelatory records. Let it be made clear that revelations are not necessarily inspired. The cosmology of these revelations is *not inspired.* It is limited by our permission for the co-ordination and sorting of present-day knowledge. While divine or spiritual insight is a gift, *human wisdom must evolve.*

Truth is always a revelation: autorevelation when it emerges as a result of the work of the indwelling Adjuster; epochal revelation when it is presented by the function of some other celestial agency, group, or personality.

In the last analysis, religion is to be judged by its fruits, according to the manner and the extent to which it exhibits its own inherent and divine excellence.

Truth may be but relatively inspired, even though revelation is invariably a spiritual phenomenon. While statements with reference to cosmology are never inspired, such revelations are of immense value in that they at least transiently clarify knowledge by:

1. The reduction of confusion by the authoritative elimination of error.

2. The co-ordination of known or about-to-be-known facts and observations.

3. The restoration of important bits of lost knowledge concerning epochal transactions in the distant past.

4. The supplying of information which will fill in vital missing gaps in otherwise earned knowledge.

5. Presenting cosmic data in such a manner as to illuminate the spiritual teachings contained in the accompanying revelation.

5. RELIGION EXPANDED BY REVELATION

Revelation is a technique whereby ages upon ages of time are saved in the necessary work of sorting and sifting the errors of evolution from the truths of spirit acquirement.

Science deals with *facts;* religion is concerned only with *values.* Through enlightened philosophy the mind endeavors to unite the meanings of both facts and values, thereby arriving at a concept of complete *reality.* Remember that science is the domain of knowledge, philosophy the realm of wisdom, and religion the sphere of the faith experience. But religion, nonetheless, presents two phases of manifestation:

1. Evolutionary religion. The experience of primitive worship, the religion which is a mind derivative.

2. Revealed religion. The universe attitude which is a spirit derivative; the assurance of, and belief in, the conservation of eternal realities, the survival of personality, and the eventual attainment of the cosmic Deity, whose purpose has made all this possible. It is a part of the plan of the universe that, sooner or later, evolutionary religion is destined to receive the spiritual expansion of revelation.

Both science and religion start out with the assumption of certain generally accepted bases for logical deductions. So, also, must philosophy start its career upon the assumption of the reality of three things:

1. The material body.

2. The supermaterial phase of the human being, the soul or even the indwelling spirit.

3. The human mind, the mechanism for intercommunication and interassociation between spirit and matter, between the material and the spiritual.

Scientists assemble facts, philosophers co-ordinate ideas, while prophets exalt ideals. Feeling and emotion are invariable concomitants of religion, but they are not religion. Religion may be the feeling of experience, but it is hardly the experience of feeling. Neither logic (rationalization) nor emotion (feeling) is essentially a part of religious experience, although both may variously be associated with the exercise of faith in the furtherance of spiritual insight into reality, all according to the status and temperamental tendency of the individual mind.

Evolutionary religion is the outworking of the endowment of the local universe mind adjutant charged with the creation and fostering of the worship trait in evolving man. Such primitive religions are directly concerned with ethics and morals, the sense of human *duty.* Such religions are predicated on the assurance of conscience and result in the stabilization of relatively ethical civilizations.

Personally revealed religions are sponsored by the bestowal spirits representing the three persons of the Paradise Trinity and are especially concerned with the expansion of *truth.* Evolutionary religion drives home to the individual the idea of personal duty; revealed religion lays increasing emphasis on loving, the golden rule.

Evolved religion rests wholly on faith. Revelation has the additional assurance of its expanded presentation of the truths of divinity and reality and the still more valuable testimony of the actual experience which accumulates in consequence of the practical working union of the faith of evolution and the truth of revelation. Such a working union of human faith and divine truth constitutes the possession of a character well on the road to the actual acquirement of a morontial personality.

Evolutionary religion provides only the assurance of faith and the confirmation of conscience; revelatory religion provides the assurance of faith plus the truth of a living experience in the realities of revelation. The third step in religion, or the third phase of the experience of religion, has to do with the morontia state, the firmer grasp of mota. Increasingly in the morontia progression the truths of revealed religion are expanded; more and more you will know the truth of supreme values, divine goodnesses, universal relationships, eternal realities, and ultimate destinies.

Increasingly throughout the morontia progression the assurance of truth replaces the assurance of faith. When you are finally mustered into the actual spirit world, then will the assurances of pure spirit insight operate in the place of faith and truth or, rather, in conjunction with, and superimposed upon, these former techniques of personality assurance.

6. PROGRESSIVE RELIGIOUS EXPERIENCE

The morontia phase of revealed religion has to do with the *experience of survival,* and its great urge is the attainment of spirit perfection. There also is present the higher urge of worship, associated with an impelling call to increased ethical service. Morontia insight entails an ever-expanding consciousness of the Sevenfold, the Supreme, and even the Ultimate.

Throughout all religious experience, from its earliest inception on the material level up to the time of the attainment of full spirit status, the Adjuster is the secret of the personal realization of the reality of the existence of the Supreme; and this same Adjuster also holds the secrets of your faith in the transcendental attainment of the Ultimate. The experiential personality of evolving man, united to the Adjuster essence of the existential God, constitutes the potential completion of supreme existence and is inherently the basis for the superfinite eventuation of transcendental personality.

Moral will embraces decisions based on reasoned knowledge, augmented by wisdom, and sanctioned by religious faith. Such choices are acts of moral nature and evidence the existence of moral personality, the forerunner of morontia personality and eventually of true spirit status.

The evolutionary type of knowledge is but the accumulation of protoplasmic memory material; this is the most primitive form of creature consciousness. Wisdom embraces the ideas formulated from protoplasmic memory in process of association and recombination, and such phenomena differentiate human mind from mere animal mind. Animals have knowledge, but only man possesses wisdom capacity. Truth is made accessible to the wisdom-endowed individual by the bestowal on such a mind of the spirits of the Father and the Sons, the Thought Adjuster and the Spirit of Truth.

Christ Michael, when bestowed on Urantia, lived under the reign of evolutionary religion up to the time of his baptism. From that moment up to and including the event of his crucifixion he carried forward his work by the combined guidance of evolutionary and revealed religion. From the morning of his resurrection until his ascension he traversed the manifold phases of the morontia life of mortal transition from the world of matter to that of spirit. After his ascension Michael became master of the experience of Supremacy, the realization of the Supreme; and being the one person in Nebadon possessed of unlimited capacity to experience the reality of the Supreme, he forthwith attained to the status of the sovereignty of supremacy in and to his local universe.

With man, the eventual fusion and resultant oneness with the indwelling Adjuster—the personality synthesis of man and the essence of God—constitute him, in potential, a living part of the Supreme and insure for such a onetime mortal being the eternal birthright of the endless pursuit of finality of universe service for and with the Supreme.

Revelation teaches mortal man that, to start such a magnificent and intriguing adventure through space by means of the progression of time, he should begin by the organization of knowledge into idea-decisions; next, mandate wisdom to labor unremittingly at its noble task of transforming self-possessed ideas into increasingly practical but nonetheless supernal ideals, even those concepts which are so reasonable as ideas and so logical as ideals that the Adjuster dares so to combine and spiritize them as to render them available for such association in the finite mind as will constitute them the actual human complement thus made ready for the action of the Truth Spirit of the Sons, the time-space manifestations of Paradise truth—universal truth. The co-ordination of idea-decisions, logical ideals, and divine truth constitutes the possession of a righteous character, the prerequisite for mortal admission to the ever-expanding and increasingly spiritual realities of the morontia worlds.

The teachings of Jesus constituted the first Urantian religion which so fully embraced a harmonious co-ordination of knowledge, wisdom, faith, truth, and love as completely and simultaneously to provide temporal tranquillity, intellectual certainty, moral enlightenment, philosophic stability, ethical sensitivity, God-consciousness, and the positive assurance of personal survival. The faith of Jesus pointed the way to finality of human salvation, to the ultimate of mortal universe attainment, since it provided for:

1. Salvation from material fetters in the personal realization of sonship with God, who is spirit.

2. Salvation from intellectual bondage: man shall know the truth, and the truth shall set him free.

3. Salvation from spiritual blindness, the human realization of the fraternity of mortal beings and the morontian awareness of the brotherhood of all universe creatures; the service-discovery of spiritual reality and the ministry-revelation of the goodness of spirit values.

4. Salvation from incompleteness of self through the attainment of the spirit levels of the universe and through the eventual realization of the harmony of Havona and the perfection of Paradise.

5. Salvation from self, deliverance from the limitations of self-consciousness through the attainment of the cosmic levels of the Supreme Mind and by co-ordination with the attainments of all other self-conscious beings.

6. Salvation from time, the achievement of an eternal life of unending progression in God-recognition and God-service.

7. Salvation from the finite, the perfected oneness with Deity in and through the Supreme by which the creature attempts the transcendental discovery of the Ultimate on the postfinaliter levels of the absonite.

Such a sevenfold salvation is the equivalent of the completeness and perfection of the realization of the ultimate experience of the Universal Father. And all this, in potential, is contained within the reality of the faith of the human experience of religion. And it can be so contained since the faith of Jesus was nourished by, and was revelatory of, even realities beyond the ultimate; the faith of Jesus approached the status of a universe absolute in so far as such is possible of manifestation in the evolving cosmos of time and space.

Through the appropriation of the faith of Jesus, mortal man can foretaste in time the realities of eternity. Jesus made the discovery, in human experience, of the Final Father, and his brothers in the flesh of mortal life can follow him along this same experience of Father discovery. They can even attain, as they are, the same satisfaction in this experience with the Father as did Jesus as he was. New potentials were actualized in the universe of Nebadon consequent upon the terminal bestowal of Michael, and one of these was the new illumination of the path of eternity that leads to the Father of all, and which can be traversed even by the mortals of material flesh and blood in the initial life on the planets of space. Jesus was and is the new and living way whereby man can come into the divine inheritance which the Father has decreed shall be his for but the asking. In Jesus there is abundantly demonstrated both the beginnings and endings of the faith experience of humanity, even of divine humanity.

7. A PERSONAL PHILOSOPHY OF RELIGION

An idea is only a theoretical plan for action, while a positive decision is a validated plan of action. A stereotype is a plan of action accepted without validation. The materials out of which to build a personal philosophy of religion are derived from both the inner and the environmental experience of the individual. The social status, economic conditions, educational opportunities, moral trends, institutional influences, political developments, racial tendencies, and the religious teachings of one's time and place all become factors in the formulation of a personal philosophy of religion. Even the inherent temperament and intellectual bent markedly determine the pattern of religious philosophy. Vocation, marriage, and kindred all influence the evolution of one's personal standards of life.

A philosophy of religion evolves out of a basic growth of ideas plus experimental living as both are modified by the tendency to imitate associates. The soundness of philosophic conclusions depends on keen, honest, and discriminating thinking in connection with sensitivity to meanings and accuracy of evaluation.

Moral cowards never achieve high planes of philosophic thinking; it requires courage to invade new levels of experience and to attempt the exploration of unknown realms of intellectual living.

Presently new systems of values come into existence; new formulations of principles and standards are achieved; habits and ideals are reshaped; some idea of a personal God is attained, followed by enlarging concepts of relationship thereto.

The great difference between a religious and a nonreligious philosophy of living consists in the nature and level of recognized values and in the object of loyalties. There are four phases in the evolution of religious philosophy: Such an experience may become merely conformative, resigned to submission to tradition and authority. Or it may be satisfied with slight attainments, just enough to stabilize the daily living, and therefore becomes early arrested on such an adventitious level. Such mortals believe in letting well enough alone. A third group progress to the level of logical intellectuality but there stagnate in consequence of cultural slavery. It is indeed pitiful to behold giant intellects held so securely within the cruel grasp of cultural bondage. It is equally pathetic to observe those who trade their cultural bondage for the materialistic fetters of a science, falsely so called. The fourth level of philosophy attains freedom from all conventional and traditional handicaps and dares to think, act, and live honestly, loyally, fearlessly, and truthfully.

The acid test for any religious philosophy consists in whether or not it distinguishes between the realities of the material and the spiritual worlds while at the same moment recognizing their unification in intellectual striving and in social serving. A sound religious philosophy does not confound the things of God with the things of Caesar. Neither does it recognize the aesthetic cult of pure wonder as a substitute for religion.

Philosophy transforms that primitive religion which was largely a fairy tale of conscience into a living experience in the ascending values of cosmic reality.

8. FAITH AND BELIEF

Belief has attained the level of faith when it motivates life and shapes the mode of living. The acceptance of a teaching as true is not faith; that is mere belief. Neither is certainty nor conviction faith. A state of mind attains to faith levels only when it actually dominates the mode of living. Faith is a living attribute of genuine personal religious experience. One believes truth, admires beauty, and reverences goodness, but does not worship them; such an attitude of saving faith is centered on God alone, who is all of these personified and infinitely more.

Belief is always limiting and binding; faith is expanding and releasing. Belief fixates, faith liberates. But living religious faith is more than the association of noble beliefs; it is more than an exalted system of philosophy; it is a living experience concerned with spiritual meanings, divine ideals, and supreme values; it is God-knowing and man-serving. Beliefs may become group possessions, but faith must be personal. Theologic beliefs can be suggested to a group, but faith can rise up only in the heart of the individual religionist.

Faith has falsified its trust when it presumes to deny realities and to confer upon its devotees assumed knowledge. Faith is a traitor when it fosters betrayal of intellectual integrity and belittles loyalty to supreme values and divine ideals. Faith never shuns the problem-solving duty of mortal living. Living faith does not foster bigotry, persecution, or intolerance.

Faith does not shackle the creative imagination, neither does it maintain an unreasoning prejudice toward the discoveries of scientific investigation. Faith vitalizes religion and constrains the religionist heroically to live the golden rule. The zeal of faith is according to knowledge, and its strivings are the preludes to sublime peace.

9. RELIGION AND MORALITY

No professed revelation of religion could be regarded as authentic if it failed to recognize the duty demands of ethical obligation which had been created and fostered by preceding evolutionary religion. Revelation unfailingly enlarges the ethical horizon of evolved religion while it simultaneously and unfailingly expands the moral obligations of all prior revelations.

When you presume to sit in critical judgment on the primitive religion of man (or on the religion of primitive man), you should remember to judge such savages and to evaluate their religious experience in accordance with their enlightenment and status of conscience. Do not make the mistake of judging another's religion by your own standards of knowledge and truth.

True religion is that sublime and profound conviction within the soul which compellingly admonishes man that it would be wrong for him not to believe in those morontial realities which constitute his highest ethical and moral concepts, his highest interpretation of life's greatest values and the universe's deepest realities. And such a religion is simply the experience of yielding intellectual loyalty to the highest dictates of spiritual consciousness.

The search for beauty is a part of religion only in so far as it is ethical and to the extent that it enriches the concept of the moral. Art is only religious when it becomes diffused with purpose which has been derived from high spiritual motivation.

The enlightened spiritual consciousness of civilized man is not concerned so much with some specific intellectual belief or with any one particular mode of living as with discovering the truth of living, the good and right technique of reacting to the ever-recurring situations of mortal existence. Moral consciousness is just a name applied to the human recognition and awareness of those ethical and emerging morontial values which duty demands that man shall abide by in the day-by-day control and guidance of conduct.

Though recognizing that religion is imperfect, there are at least two practical manifestations of its nature and function:

1. The spiritual urge and philosophic pressure of religion tend to cause man to project his estimation of moral values directly outward into the affairs of his fellows—the ethical reaction of religion.

2. Religion creates for the human mind a spiritualized consciousness of divine reality based on, and by faith derived from, antecedent concepts of moral values and co-ordinated with superimposed concepts of spiritual values. Religion thereby becomes a censor of mortal affairs, a form of glorified moral trust and confidence in reality, the enhanced realities of time and the more enduring realities of eternity.

Faith becomes the connection between moral consciousness and the spiritual concept of enduring reality. Religion becomes the avenue of man's escape from the material limitations of the temporal and natural world to the supernal realities of the eternal and spiritual world by and through the technique of salvation, the progressive morontia transformation.

10. Religion as Man's Liberator

Intelligent man knows that he is a child of nature, a part of the material universe; he likewise discerns no survival of individual personality in the motions and tensions of the mathematical level of the energy universe. Nor can man ever discern spiritual reality through the examination of physical causes and effects.

A human being is also aware that he is a part of the ideational cosmos, but though concept may endure beyond a mortal life span, there is nothing inherent in concept which indicates the personal survival of the conceiving personality. Nor will the exhaustion of the possibilities of logic and reason ever reveal to the logician or to the reasoner the eternal truth of the survival of personality.

The material level of law provides for causality continuity, the unending response of effect to antecedent action; the mind level suggests the perpetuation of ideational continuity, the unceasing flow of conceptual potentiality from pre-existent conceptions. But neither of these levels of the universe discloses to the inquiring mortal an avenue of escape from partiality of status and from the intolerable suspense of being a transient reality in the universe, a temporal personality doomed to be extinguished upon the exhaustion of the limited life energies.

It is only through the morontial avenue leading to spiritual insight that man can ever break the fetters inherent in his mortal status in the universe. Energy and mind do lead back to Paradise and Deity, but neither the energy endowment nor the mind endowment of man proceeds directly from such Paradise Deity. Only in the spiritual sense is man a child of God. And this is true because it is only in the spiritual sense that man is at present endowed and indwelt by the Paradise Father. Mankind can never discover divinity except through the avenue of religious experience and by the exercise of true faith. The faith acceptance of the truth of God enables man to escape from the circumscribed confines of material limitations and affords him a rational hope of achieving safe conduct from the material realm, whereon is death, to the spiritual realm, wherein is life eternal.

The purpose of religion is not to satisfy curiosity about God but rather to afford intellectual constancy and philosophic security, to stabilize and enrich human living by blending the mortal with the divine, the partial with the perfect, man and God. It is through religious experience that man's concepts of ideality are endowed with reality.

Never can there be either scientific or logical proofs of divinity. Reason alone can never validate the values and goodnesses of religious experience. But it will always remain true: Whosoever wills to do the will of God shall comprehend the validity of spiritual values. This is the nearest approach that can be made on the mortal level to offering proofs of the reality of religious experience. Such faith affords the only escape from the mechanical clutch of the material world and from the error distortion of the incompleteness of the intellectual world; it is the only discovered solution to the impasse in mortal thinking regarding the continuing survival of the individual personality. It is the only passport to completion of reality and to eternity of life in a universal creation of love, law, unity, and progressive Deity attainment.

Religion effectually cures man's sense of idealistic isolation or spiritual loneliness; it enfranchises the believer as a son of God, a citizen of a new and meaningful universe. Religion assures man that, in following the gleam of righteousness discernible in his soul, he is thereby identifying himself with the plan of the Infinite and the purpose of the Eternal. Such a liberated soul immediately begins to feel at home in this new universe, his universe.

When you experience such a transformation of faith, you are no longer a slavish part of the mathematical cosmos but rather a liberated volitional son of the Universal Father. No longer is such a liberated son fighting alone against the inexorable doom of the termination of temporal existence; no longer does he combat all nature, with the odds hopelessly against him; no longer is he staggered by the paralyzing fear that, perchance, he has put his trust in a hopeless phantasm or pinned his faith to a fanciful error.

Now, rather, are the sons of God enlisted together in fighting the battle of reality's triumph over the partial shadows of existence. At last all creatures become conscious of the fact that God and all the divine hosts of a well-nigh limitless universe are on their side in the supernal struggle to attain eternity of life and divinity of status. Such faith-liberated sons have certainly enlisted in the struggles of time on the side of the supreme forces and divine personalities of eternity; even the stars in their courses are now doing battle for them; at last they gaze upon the universe from within, from God's viewpoint, and all is transformed from the uncertainties of material isolation to the sureties of eternal spiritual progression. Even time itself becomes but the shadow of eternity cast by Paradise realities upon the moving panoply of space.

[Presented by a Melchizedek of Nebadon.]

PAPER 102

THE FOUNDATIONS OF RELIGIOUS FAITH

TO THE unbelieving materialist, man is simply an evolutionary accident. His hopes of survival are strung on a figment of mortal imagination; his fears, loves, longings, and beliefs are but the reaction of the incidental juxtaposition of certain lifeless atoms of matter. No display of energy nor expression of trust can carry him beyond the grave. The devotional labors and inspirational genius of the best of men are doomed to be extinguished by death, the long and lonely night of eternal oblivion and soul extinction. Nameless despair is man's only reward for living and toiling under the temporal sun of mortal existence. Each day of life slowly and surely tightens the grasp of a pitiless doom which a hostile and relentless universe of matter has decreed shall be the crowning insult to everything in human desire which is beautiful, noble, lofty, and good.

But such is not man's end and eternal destiny; such a vision is but the cry of despair uttered by some wandering soul who has become lost in spiritual darkness, and who bravely struggles on in the face of the mechanistic sophistries of a material philosophy, blinded by the confusion and distortion of a complex learning. And all this doom of darkness and all this destiny of despair are forever dispelled by one brave stretch of faith on the part of the most humble and unlearned of God's children on earth.

This saving faith has its birth in the human heart when the moral consciousness of man realizes that human values may be translated in mortal experience from the material to the spiritual, from the human to the divine, from time to eternity.

1. ASSURANCES OF FAITH

The work of the Thought Adjuster constitutes the explanation of the translation of man's primitive and evolutionary sense of duty into that higher and more certain faith in the eternal realities of revelation. There must be perfection hunger in man's heart to insure capacity for comprehending the faith paths to supreme attainment. If any man chooses to do the divine will, he shall know the way of truth. It is literally true, "Human things must be known in order to be loved, but divine things must be loved in order to be known." But honest doubts and sincere questionings are not sin; such attitudes merely spell delay in the progressive journey toward perfection attainment. Childlike trust secures man's entrance into the kingdom of heavenly ascent, but progress is wholly dependent on the vigorous exercise of the robust and confident faith of the full-grown man.

The reason of science is based on the observable facts of time; the faith of religion argues from the spirit program of eternity. What knowledge and reason cannot do for us, true wisdom admonishes us to allow faith to accomplish through religious insight and spiritual transformation.

Owing to the isolation of rebellion, the revelation of truth on Urantia has all too often been mixed up with the statements of partial and transient cosmologies. Truth remains unchanged from generation to generation, but the associated teachings about the physical world vary from day to day and from year to year. Eternal truth should not be slighted because it chances to be found in company with obsolete ideas regarding the material world. The more of science you know, the less sure you can be; the more of religion you *have,* the more certain you are.

The certainties of science proceed entirely from the intellect; the certitudes of religion spring from the very foundations of the *entire personality.* Science appeals to the understanding of the mind; religion appeals to the loyalty and devotion of the body, mind, and spirit, even to the whole personality.

God is so all real and absolute that no material sign of proof or no demonstration of so-called miracle may be offered in testimony of his reality. Always will we know him because we trust him, and our belief in him is wholly based on our personal participation in the divine manifestations of his infinite reality.

The indwelling Thought Adjuster unfailingly arouses in man's soul a true and searching hunger for perfection together with a far-reaching curiosity which can be adequately satisfied only by communion with God, the divine source of that Adjuster. The hungry soul of man refuses to be satisfied with anything less than the personal realization of the living God. Whatever more God may be than a high and perfect moral personality, he cannot, in our hungry and finite concept, be anything less.

2. RELIGION AND REALITY

Observing minds and discriminating souls know religion when they find it in the lives of their fellows. Religion requires no definition; we all know its social, intellectual, moral, and spiritual fruits. And this all grows out of the fact that religion is the property of the human race; it is not a child of culture. True, one's perception of religion is still human and therefore subject to the bondage of ignorance, the slavery of superstition, the deceptions of sophistication, and the delusions of false philosophy.

One of the characteristic peculiarities of genuine religious assurance is that, notwithstanding the absoluteness of its affirmations and the stanchness of its attitude, the spirit of its expression is so poised and tempered that it never conveys the slightest impression of self-assertion or egoistic exaltation. The wisdom of religious experience is something of a paradox in that it is both humanly original and Adjuster derivative. Religious force is not the product of the individual's personal prerogatives but rather the outworking of that sublime partnership of man and the everlasting source of all wisdom. Thus do the words and acts of true and undefiled religion become compellingly authoritative for all enlightened mortals.

It is difficult to identify and analyze the factors of a religious experience, but it is not difficult to observe that such religious practitioners live and carry on as if already in the presence of the Eternal. Believers react to this temporal life as if immortality already were within their grasp. In the lives of such mortals there is a valid originality and a spontaneity of expression that forever segregate them from those of their fellows who have imbibed only the wisdom of the world. Religionists seem to live in effective emancipation from harrying haste and the painful stress of the vicissitudes inherent in the temporal currents of time; they exhibit a stabilization of personality and a tranquillity of character not explained by the laws of physiology, psychology, and sociology.

Time is an invariable element in the attainment of knowledge; religion makes its endowments immediately available, albeit there is the important factor of growth in grace, definite advancement in all phases of religious experience. Knowledge is an eternal quest; always are you learning, but never are you able to arrive at the full knowledge of absolute truth. In knowledge alone there can never be absolute certainty, only increasing probability of approximation; but the religious soul of spiritual illumination *knows,* and knows *now.* And yet this profound and positive certitude does not lead such a sound-minded religionist to take any less interest in the ups and downs of the progress of human wisdom, which is bound up on its material end with the developments of slow-moving science.

Even the discoveries of science are not truly *real* in the consciousness of human experience until they are unraveled and correlated, until their relevant facts actually become *meaning* through encircuitment in the thought streams of mind. Mortal man views even his physical environment from the mind level, from the perspective of its psychological registry. It is not, therefore, strange that man should place a highly unified interpretation upon the universe and then seek to identify this energy unity of his science with the spirit unity of his religious experience. Mind is unity; mortal consciousness lives on the mind level and perceives the universal realities through the eyes of the mind endowment. The mind perspective will not yield the existential unity of the source of reality, the First Source and Center, but it can and sometime will portray to man the experiential synthesis of energy, mind, and spirit in and as the Supreme Being. But mind can never succeed in this unification of the diversity of reality unless such mind is firmly aware of material things, intellectual meanings, and spiritual values; only in the harmony of the triunity of functional reality is there unity, and only in unity is there the personality satisfaction of the realization of cosmic constancy and consistency.

Unity is best found in human experience through philosophy. And while the body of philosophic thought must ever be founded on material facts, the soul and energy of true philosophic dynamics is mortal spiritual insight.

Evolutionary man does not naturally relish hard work. To keep pace in his life experience with the impelling demands and the compelling urges of a growing religious experience means incessant activity in spiritual growth, intellectual expansion, factual enlargement, and social service. There is no real religion apart from a highly active personality. Therefore do the more indolent of men often seek to escape the rigors of truly religious activities by a species of ingenious self-deception through resorting to a retreat to the false shelter of stereotyped religious doctrines and dogmas. But true religion is alive. Intellectual crystallization of religious concepts is the equivalent of spiritual death. You cannot conceive of religion without ideas, but when religion once becomes reduced only to an *idea,* it is no longer religion; it has become merely a species of human philosophy.

Again, there are other types of unstable and poorly disciplined souls who would use the sentimental ideas of religion as an avenue of escape from the irritating demands of living. When certain vacillating and timid mortals attempt to escape from the incessant pressure of evolutionary life, religion, as they conceive it, seems to present the nearest refuge, the best avenue of escape. But it is the mission of religion to prepare man for bravely, even heroically, facing the vicissitudes of life. Religion is evolutionary man's supreme endowment, the one thing which enables him to carry on and "endure as seeing Him who is invisible." Mysticism, however, is often something of a retreat from life which is embraced by those humans who do not relish the more robust activities of living a religious life in the open arenas of human society and commerce. True religion must *act.* Conduct will be the result of religion when man actually has it, or rather when religion is permitted truly to possess the man. Never will religion be content with mere thinking or unacting feeling.

We are not blind to the fact that religion often acts unwisely, even irreligiously, but it *acts.* Aberrations of religious conviction have led to bloody persecutions, but always and ever religion does something; it is dynamic!

3. KNOWLEDGE, WISDOM, AND INSIGHT

Intellectual deficiency or educational poverty unavoidably handicaps higher religious attainment because such an impoverished environment of the spiritual nature robs religion of its chief channel of philosophic contact with the world of scientific knowledge. The intellectual factors of religion are important, but their overdevelopment is likewise sometimes very handicapping and embarrassing. Religion must continually labor under a paradoxical necessity: the necessity of making effective use of thought while at the same time discounting the spiritual serviceableness of all thinking.

Religious speculation is inevitable but always detrimental; speculation invariably falsifies its object. Speculation tends to translate religion into something material or humanistic, and thus, while directly interfering with the clarity of logical thought, it indirectly causes religion to appear as a function of the temporal world, the very world with which it should everlastingly stand in contrast. Therefore will religion always be characterized by paradoxes, the paradoxes resulting from the absence of the experiential connection between the material and the spiritual levels of the universe—morontia mota, the superphilosophic sensitivity for truth discernment and unity perception.

Material feelings, human emotions, lead directly to material actions, selfish acts. Religious insights, spiritual motivations, lead directly to religious actions, unselfish acts of social service and altruistic benevolence.

Religious desire is the hunger quest for divine reality. Religious experience is the realization of the consciousness of having found God. And when a human being does find God, there is experienced within the soul of that being such an indescribable restlessness of triumph in discovery that he is impelled to seek loving service-contact with his less illuminated fellows, not to disclose that he has found God, but rather to allow the overflow of the welling-up of eternal goodness within his own soul to refresh and ennoble his fellows. Real religion leads to increased social service.

Science, knowledge, leads to *fact* consciousness; religion, experience, leads to *value* consciousness; philosophy, wisdom, leads to *co-ordinate* consciousness; revelation (the substitute for morontia mota) leads to the consciousness of *true reality;* while the co-ordination of the consciousness of fact, value, and true reality constitutes awareness of personality reality, maximum of being, together with the belief in the possibility of the survival of that very personality.

Knowledge leads to placing men, to originating social strata and castes. Religion leads to serving men, thus creating ethics and altruism. Wisdom leads to the higher and better fellowship of both ideas and one's fellows. Revelation liberates men and starts them out on the eternal adventure.

Science sorts men; religion loves men, even as yourself; wisdom does justice to differing men; but revelation glorifies man and discloses his capacity for partnership with God.

Science vainly strives to create the brotherhood of culture; religion brings into being the brotherhood of the spirit. Philosophy strives for the brotherhood of wisdom; revelation portrays the eternal brotherhood, the Paradise Corps of the Finality.

Knowledge yields pride in the fact of personality; wisdom is the consciousness of the meaning of personality; religion is the experience of cognizance of the value of personality; revelation is the assurance of personality survival.

Science seeks to identify, analyze, and classify the segmented parts of the limitless cosmos. Religion grasps the idea-of-the-whole, the entire cosmos. Philosophy attempts the identification of the material segments of science with the spiritual-insight concept of the whole. Wherein philosophy fails in this attempt, revelation succeeds, affirming that the cosmic circle is universal, eternal, absolute, and infinite. This cosmos of the Infinite I AM is therefore endless, limitless, and all-inclusive—timeless, spaceless, and unqualified. And we bear testimony that the Infinite I AM is also the Father of Michael of Nebadon and the God of human salvation.

Science indicates Deity as a *fact;* philosophy presents the *idea* of an Absolute; religion envisions God as a loving *spiritual personality.* Revelation affirms the *unity* of the fact of Deity, the idea of the Absolute, and the spiritual personality of God and, further, presents this concept as our Father—the universal fact of existence, the eternal idea of mind, and the infinite spirit of life.

The pursuit of knowledge constitutes science; the search for wisdom is philosophy; the love for God is religion; the hunger for truth *is* a revelation. But it is the indwelling Thought Adjuster that attaches the feeling of reality to man's spiritual insight into the cosmos.

In science, the idea precedes the expression of its realization; in religion, the experience of realization precedes the expression of the idea. There is a vast difference between the evolutionary will-to-believe and the product of enlightened reason, religious insight, and revelation—the *will that believes.*

In evolution, religion often leads to man's creating his concepts of God; revelation exhibits the phenomenon of God's evolving man himself, while in the earth life of Christ Michael we behold the phenomenon of God's revealing himself to man. Evolution tends to make God manlike; revelation tends to make man Godlike.

Science is only satisfied with first causes, religion with supreme personality, and philosophy with unity. Revelation affirms that these three are one, and that all are good. The *eternal real* is the good of the universe and not the time illusions of space evil. In the spiritual experience of all personalities, always is it true that the real is the good and the good is the real.

4. THE FACT OF EXPERIENCE

Because of the presence in your minds of the Thought Adjuster, it is no more of a mystery for you to know the mind of God than for you to be sure of the consciousness of knowing any other mind, human or superhuman. Religion and social consciousness have this in common: They are predicated on the consciousness of other-mindness. The technique whereby you can accept another's idea as yours is the same whereby you may "let the mind which was in Christ be also in you."

What is human experience? It is simply any interplay between an active and questioning self and any other active and external reality. The mass of experience is determined by depth of concept plus totality of recognition of the reality of the external. The motion of experience equals the force of expectant imagination plus the keenness of the sensory discovery of the external qualities of contacted reality. The fact of experience is found in self-consciousness plus other-existences —other-thingness, other-mindness, and other-spiritness.

Man very early becomes conscious that he is not alone in the world or the universe. There develops a natural spontaneous self-consciousness of other-mindness in the environment of selfhood. Faith translates this natural experience into religion, the recognition of God as the reality—source, nature, and destiny —of *other-mindness.* But such a knowledge of God is ever and always a reality of personal experience. If God were not a personality, he could not become a living part of the real religious experience of a human personality.

The element of error present in human religious experience is directly proportional to the content of materialism which contaminates the spiritual concept of the Universal Father. Man's prespirit progression in the universe consists in the experience of divesting himself of these erroneous ideas of the nature of God and of the reality of pure and true spirit. Deity is more than spirit, but the spiritual approach is the only one possible to ascending man.

Prayer is indeed a part of religious experience, but it has been wrongly emphasized by modern religions, much to the neglect of the more essential communion of worship. The reflective powers of the mind are deepened and broadened by worship. Prayer may enrich the life, but worship illuminates destiny.

Revealed religion is the unifying element of human existence. Revelation unifies history, co-ordinates geology, astronomy, physics, chemistry, biology, sociology, and psychology. Spiritual experience is the real soul of man's cosmos.

5. THE SUPREMACY OF PURPOSIVE POTENTIAL

Although the establishment of the fact of belief is not equivalent to establishing the fact of that which is believed, nevertheless, the evolutionary progression of simple life to the status of personality does demonstrate the fact of the existence of the potential of personality to start with. And in the time universes, potential is always supreme over the actual. In the evolving cosmos the potential is what is to be, and what is to be is the unfolding of the purposive mandates of Deity.

This same purposive supremacy is shown in the evolution of mind ideation when primitive animal fear is transmuted into the constantly deepening reverence for God and into increasing awe of the universe. Primitive man had more religious fear than faith, and the supremacy of spirit potentials over mind actuals is demonstrated when this craven fear is translated into living faith in spiritual realities.

You can psychologize evolutionary religion but not the personal-experience religion of spiritual origin. Human morality may recognize values, but only religion can conserve, exalt, and spiritualize such values. But notwithstanding such actions, religion is something more than emotionalized morality. Religion is to morality as love is to duty, as sonship is to servitude, as essence is to substance. Morality discloses an almighty Controller, a Deity to be served; religion discloses an all-loving Father, a God to be worshiped and loved. And again this is because the spiritual potentiality of religion is dominant over the duty actuality of the morality of evolution.

6. THE CERTAINTY OF RELIGIOUS FAITH

The philosophic elimination of religious fear and the steady progress of science add greatly to the mortality of false gods; and even though these casualties of man-made deities may momentarily befog the spiritual vision, they eventually destroy that ignorance and superstition which so long obscured the living God of eternal love. The relation between the creature and the Creator is a living experience, a dynamic religious faith, which is not subject to precise definition. To isolate part of life and call it religion is to disintegrate life and to distort religion. And this is just why the God of worship claims all allegiance or none.

The gods of primitive men may have been no more than shadows of themselves; the living God is the divine light whose interruptions constitute the creation shadows of all space.

The religionist of philosophic attainment has faith in a personal God of personal salvation, something more than a reality, a value, a level of achievement, an exalted process, a transmutation, the ultimate of time-space, an idealization, the personalization of energy, the entity of gravity, a human projection, the idealization of self, nature's upthrust, the inclination to goodness, the forward impulse of evolution, or a sublime hypothesis. The religionist has faith in a God of love. Love is the essence of religion and the wellspring of superior civilization.

Faith transforms the philosophic God of probability into the saving God of certainty in the personal religious experience. Skepticism may challenge the theories of theology, but confidence in the dependability of personal experience affirms the truth of that belief which has grown into faith.

Convictions about God may be arrived at through wise reasoning, but the individual becomes God-knowing only by faith, through personal experience. In much that pertains to life, probability must be reckoned with, but when contacting with cosmic reality, certainty may be experienced when such meanings and values are approached by living faith. The God-knowing soul dares to say,

"I know," even when this knowledge of God is questioned by the unbeliever who denies such certitude because it is not wholly supported by intellectual logic. To every such doubter the believer only replies, "How do you know that I do not know?"

Though reason can always question faith, faith can always supplement both reason and logic. Reason creates the probability which faith can transform into a moral certainty, even a spiritual experience. God is the first truth and the last fact; therefore does all truth take origin in him, while all facts exist relative to him. God is absolute truth. As truth one may know God, but to understand—to explain—God, one must explore the fact of the universe of universes. The vast gulf between the experience of the truth of God and ignorance as to the fact of God can be bridged only by living faith. Reason alone cannot achieve harmony between infinite truth and universal fact.

Belief may not be able to resist doubt and withstand fear, but faith is always triumphant over doubting, for faith is both positive and living. The positive always has the advantage over the negative, truth over error, experience over theory, spiritual realities over the isolated facts of time and space. The convincing evidence of this spiritual certainty consists in the social fruits of the spirit which such believers, faithers, yield as a result of this genuine spiritual experience. Said Jesus: "If you love your fellows as I have loved you, then shall all men know that you are my disciples."

To science God is a possibility, to psychology a desirability, to philosophy a probability, to religion a certainty, an actuality of religious experience. Reason demands that a philosophy which cannot find the God of probability should be very respectful of that religious faith which can and does find the God of certitude. Neither should science discount religious experience on grounds of credulity, not so long as it persists in the assumption that man's intellectual and philosophic endowments emerged from increasingly lesser intelligences the further back they go, finally taking origin in primitive life which was utterly devoid of all thinking and feeling.

The facts of evolution must not be arrayed against the truth of the reality of the certainty of the spiritual experience of the religious living of the God-knowing mortal. Intelligent men should cease to reason like children and should attempt to use the consistent logic of adulthood, logic which tolerates the concept of truth alongside the observation of fact. Scientific materialism has gone bankrupt when it persists, in the face of each recurring universe phenomenon, in refunding its current objections by referring what is admittedly higher back into that which is admittedly lower. Consistency demands the recognition of the activities of a purposive Creator.

Organic evolution is a fact; purposive or progressive evolution is a truth which makes consistent the otherwise contradictory phenomena of the ever-ascending achievements of evolution. The higher any scientist progresses in his chosen science, the more will he abandon the theories of materialistic fact in favor of the cosmic truth of the dominance of the Supreme Mind. Materialism cheapens human life; the gospel of Jesus tremendously enhances and supernally exalts every mortal. Mortal existence must be visualized as consisting in the intriguing and fascinating experience of the realization of the reality of the meeting of the human upreach and the divine and saving downreach.

7. THE CERTITUDE OF THE DIVINE

The Universal Father, being self-existent, is also self-explanatory; he actually lives in every rational mortal. But you cannot be sure about God unless you know him; sonship is the only experience which makes fatherhood certain. The universe is everywhere undergoing change. A changing universe is a dependent universe; such a creation cannot be either final or absolute. A finite universe is wholly dependent on the Ultimate and the Absolute. The universe and God are not identical; one is cause, the other effect. The cause is absolute, infinite, eternal, and changeless; the effect, time-space and transcendental but ever changing, always growing.

God is the one and only self-caused fact in the universe. He is the secret of the order, plan, and purpose of the whole creation of things and beings. The everywhere-changing universe is regulated and stabilized by absolutely unchanging laws, the habits of an unchanging God. The fact of God, the divine law, is changeless; the truth of God, his relation to the universe, is a relative revelation which is ever adaptable to the constantly evolving universe.

Those who would invent a religion without God are like those who would gather fruit without trees, have children without parents. You cannot have effects without causes; only the I AM is causeless. The fact of religious experience implies God, and such a God of personal experience must be a personal Deity. You cannot pray to a chemical formula, supplicate a mathematical equation, worship a hypothesis, confide in a postulate, commune with a process, serve an abstraction, or hold loving fellowship with a law.

True, many apparently religious traits can grow out of nonreligious roots. Man can, intellectually, deny God and yet be morally good, loyal, filial, honest, and even idealistic. Man may graft many purely humanistic branches onto his basic spiritual nature and thus apparently prove his contentions in behalf of a godless religion, but such an experience is devoid of survival values, God-knowingness and God-ascension. In such a mortal experience only social fruits are forthcoming, not spiritual. The graft determines the nature of the fruit, notwithstanding that the living sustenance is drawn from the roots of original divine endowment of both mind and spirit.

The intellectual earmark of religion is certainty; the philosophical characteristic is consistency; the social fruits are love and service.

The God-knowing individual is not one who is blind to the difficulties or unmindful of the obstacles which stand in the way of finding God in the maze of superstition, tradition, and materialistic tendencies of modern times. He has encountered all these deterrents and triumphed over them, surmounted them by living faith, and attained the highlands of spiritual experience in spite of them. But it is true that many who are inwardly sure about God fear to assert such feelings of certainty because of the multiplicity and cleverness of those who assemble objections and magnify difficulties about believing in God. It requires no great depth of intellect to pick flaws, ask questions, or raise objections. But it does require brilliance of mind to answer these questions and solve these difficulties; faith certainty is the greatest technique for dealing with all such superficial contentions.

If science, philosophy, or sociology dares to become dogmatic in contending with the prophets of true religion, then should God-knowing men reply to such unwarranted dogmatism with that more farseeing dogmatism of the certainty of personal spiritual experience, "I know what I have experienced because I am a son of I AM." If the personal experience of a faither is to be challenged by dogma, then this faith-born son of the experiencible Father may reply with that unchallengeable dogma, the statement of his actual sonship with the Universal Father.

Only an unqualified reality, an absolute, could dare consistently to be dogmatic. Those who assume to be dogmatic must, if consistent, sooner or later be driven into the arms of the Absolute of energy, the Universal of truth, and the Infinite of love.

If the nonreligious approaches to cosmic reality presume to challenge the certainty of faith on the grounds of its unproved status, then the spirit experiencer can likewise resort to the dogmatic challenge of the facts of science and the beliefs of philosophy on the grounds that they are likewise unproved; they are likewise experiences in the consciousness of the scientist or the philosopher.

Of God, the most inescapable of all presences, the most real of all facts, the most living of all truths, the most loving of all friends, and the most divine of all values, we have the right to be the most certain of all universe experiences.

8. THE EVIDENCES OF RELIGION

The highest evidence of the reality and efficacy of religion consists in the *fact of human experience;* namely, that man, naturally fearful and suspicious, innately endowed with a strong instinct of self-preservation and craving survival after death, is willing fully to trust the deepest interests of his present and future to the keeping and direction of that power and person designated by his faith as God. That is the one central truth of all religion. As to what that power or person requires of man in return for this watchcare and final salvation, no two religions agree; in fact, they all more or less disagree.

Regarding the status of any religion in the evolutionary scale, it may best be judged by its moral judgments and its ethical standards. The higher the type of any religion, the more it encourages and is encouraged by a constantly improving social morality and ethical culture. We cannot judge religion by the status of its accompanying civilization; we had better estimate the real nature of a civilization by the purity and nobility of its religion. Many of the world's most notable religious teachers have been virtually unlettered. The wisdom of the world is not necessary to an exercise of saving faith in eternal realities.

The difference in the religions of various ages is wholly dependent on the difference in man's comprehension of reality and on his differing recognition of moral values, ethical relationships, and spirit realities.

Ethics is the external social or racial mirror which faithfully reflects the otherwise unobservable progress of internal spiritual and religious developments. Man has always thought of God in the terms of the best he knew, his deepest ideas and highest ideals. Even historic religion has always created its God conceptions out of its highest recognized values. Every intelligent creature gives the name of God to the best and highest thing he knows.

Religion, when reduced to terms of reason and intellectual expression, has always dared to criticize civilization and evolutionary progress as judged by its own standards of ethical culture and moral progress.

While personal religion precedes the evolution of human morals, it is regretfully recorded that institutional religion has invariably lagged behind the slowly changing mores of the human races. Organized religion has proved to be conservatively tardy. The prophets have usually led the people in religious development; the theologians have usually held them back. Religion, being a matter of inner or personal experience, can never develop very far in advance of the intellectual evolution of the races.

But religion is never enhanced by an appeal to the so-called miraculous. The quest for miracles is a harking back to the primitive religions of magic. True religion has nothing to do with alleged miracles, and never does revealed religion point to miracles as proof of authority. Religion is ever and always rooted and grounded in personal experience. And your highest religion, the life of Jesus, was just such a personal experience: man, mortal man, seeking God and finding him to the fullness during one short life in the flesh, while in the same human experience there appeared God seeking man and finding him to the full satisfaction of the perfect soul of infinite supremacy. And that is religion, even the highest yet revealed in the universe of Nebadon—the earth life of Jesus of Nazareth.

[Presented by a Melchizedek of Nebadon.]

PAPER 103

THE REALITY OF RELIGIOUS EXPERIENCE

ALL of man's truly religious reactions are sponsored by the early ministry of the adjutant of worship and are censored by the adjutant of wisdom. Man's first supermind endowment is that of personality encircuitment in the Holy Spirit of the Universe Creative Spirit; and long before either the bestowals of the divine Sons or the universal bestowal of the Adjusters, this influence functions to enlarge man's viewpoint of ethics, religion, and spirituality. Subsequent to the bestowals of the Paradise Sons the liberated Spirit of Truth makes mighty contributions to the enlargement of the human capacity to perceive religious truths. As evolution advances on an inhabited world, the Thought Adjusters increasingly participate in the development of the higher types of human religious insight. The Thought Adjuster is the cosmic window through which the finite creature may faith-glimpse the certainties and divinities of limitless Deity, the Universal Father.

The religious tendencies of the human races are innate; they are universally manifested and have an apparently natural origin; primitive religions are always evolutionary in their genesis. As natural religious experience continues to progress, periodic revelations of truth punctuate the otherwise slow-moving course of planetary evolution.

On Urantia, today, there are four kinds of religion:

1. Natural or evolutionary religion.

2. Supernatural or revelatory religion.

3. Practical or current religion, varying degrees of the admixture of natural and supernatural religions.

4. Philosophic religions, man-made or philosophically thought-out theologic doctrines and reason-created religions.

1. PHILOSOPHY OF RELIGION

The unity of religious experience among a social or racial group derives from the identical nature of the God fragment indwelling the individual. It is this divine in man that gives origin to his unselfish interest in the welfare of other men. But since personality is unique—no two mortals being alike—it inevitably follows that no two human beings can similarly interpret the leadings and urges of the spirit of divinity which lives within their minds. A group of mortals can experience spiritual unity, but they can never attain philosophic uniformity. And this diversity of the interpretation of religious thought and experience is shown by the fact that twentieth-century theologians and philosophers have formulated upward of five hundred different definitions of religion. In reality, every human being defines religion in the terms of his own experiential interpretation of the divine impulses emanating from the God spirit that indwells him, and therefore must such an interpretation be unique and wholly different from the religious philosophy of all other human beings.

When one mortal is in full agreement with the religious philosophy of a fellow mortal, that phenomenon indicates that these two beings have had a similar *religious experience* touching the matters concerned in their similarity of philosophic religious interpretation.

While your religion is a matter of personal experience, it is most important that you should be exposed to the knowledge of a vast number of other religious experiences (the diverse interpretations of other and diverse mortals) to the end that you may prevent your religious life from becoming egocentric—circumscribed, selfish, and unsocial.

Rationalism is wrong when it assumes that religion is at first a primitive belief in something which is then followed by the pursuit of values. Religion is primarily a pursuit of values, and then there formulates a system of interpretative beliefs. It is much easier for men to agree on religious values—goals—than on beliefs—interpretations. And this explains how religion can agree on values and goals while exhibiting the confusing phenomenon of maintaining a belief in hundreds of conflicting beliefs—creeds. This also explains why a given person can maintain his religious experience in the face of giving up or changing many of his religious beliefs. Religion persists in spite of revolutionary changes in religious beliefs. Theology does not produce religion; it is religion that produces theologic philosophy.

That religionists have believed so much that was false does not invalidate religion because religion is founded on the recognition of values and is validated by the faith of personal religious experience. Religion, then, is based on experience and religious thought; theology, the philosophy of religion, is an honest attempt to interpret that experience. Such interpretative beliefs may be right or wrong, or a mixture of truth and error.

The realization of the recognition of spiritual values is an experience which is superideational. There is no word in any human language which can be employed to designate this "sense," "feeling," "intuition," or "experience" which we have elected to call God-consciousness. The spirit of God that dwells in man is not personal—the Adjuster is prepersonal—but this Monitor presents a value, exudes a flavor of divinity, which is personal in the highest and infinite sense. If God were not at least personal, he could not be conscious, and if not conscious, then would he be infrahuman.

2. RELIGION AND THE INDIVIDUAL

Religion is functional in the human mind and has been realized in experience prior to its appearance in human consciousness. A child has been in existence about nine months before it experiences *birth*. But the "birth" of religion is not sudden; it is rather a gradual emergence. Nevertheless, sooner or later there is a "birth day." You do not enter the kingdom of heaven unless you have been "born again"—born of the Spirit. Many spiritual births are accompanied by much anguish of spirit and marked psychological perturbations, as many physical births are characterized by a "stormy labor" and other abnormalities of "delivery." Other spiritual births are a natural and normal growth of the recognition of supreme values with an enhancement of spiritual experience, albeit no religious development occurs without conscious effort and positive and individual determinations. Religion is never a passive experience, a negative attitude. What is termed the "birth of religion" is not directly associated with so-called conversion experiences which usually characterize religious episodes occurring later in life as a result of mental conflict, emotional repression, and temperamental upheavals.

But those persons who were so reared by their parents that they grew up in the consciousness of being children of a loving heavenly Father, should not look askance at their fellow mortals who could only attain such consciousness of fellowship with God through a psychological crisis, an emotional upheaval.

The evolutionary soil in the mind of man in which the seed of revealed religion germinates is the moral nature that so early gives origin to a social consciousness. The first promptings of a child's moral nature have not to do with sex, guilt, or personal pride, but rather with impulses of justice, fairness, and urges to kindness—helpful ministry to one's fellows. And when such early moral awakenings are nurtured, there occurs a gradual development of the religious life which is comparatively free from conflicts, upheavals, and crises.

Every human being very early experiences something of a conflict between his self-seeking and his altruistic impulses, and many times the first experience of God-consciousness may be attained as the result of seeking for superhuman help in the task of resolving such moral conflicts.

The psychology of a child is naturally positive, not negative. So many mortals are negative because they were so trained. When it is said that the child is positive, reference is made to his moral impulses, those powers of mind whose emergence signals the arrival of the Thought Adjuster.

In the absence of wrong teaching, the mind of the normal child moves positively, in the emergence of religious consciousness, toward moral righteousness and social ministry, rather than negatively, away from sin and guilt. There may or may not be conflict in the development of religious experience, but there are always present the inevitable decisions, effort, and function of the human will.

Moral choosing is usually accompanied by more or less moral conflict. And this very first conflict in the child mind is between the urges of egoism and the impulses of altruism. The Thought Adjuster does not disregard the personality values of the egoistic motive but does operate to place a slight preference upon the altruistic impulse as leading to the goal of human happiness and to the joys of the kingdom of heaven.

When a moral being chooses to be unselfish when confronted by the urge to be selfish, that is primitive religious experience. No animal can make such a choice; such a decision is both human and religious. It embraces the fact of God-consciousness and exhibits the impulse of social service, the basis of the brotherhood of man. When mind chooses a right moral judgment by an act of the free will, such a decision constitutes a religious experience.

But before a child has developed sufficiently to acquire moral capacity and therefore to be able to choose altruistic service, he has already developed a strong and well-unified egoistic nature. And it is this factual situation that gives rise to the theory of the struggle between the "higher" and the "lower" natures, between the "old man of sin" and the "new nature" of grace. Very early in life the normal child begins to learn that it is "more blessed to give than to receive."

Man tends to identify the urge to be self-serving with his ego—himself. In contrast he is inclined to identify the will to be altruistic with some influence outside himself—God. And indeed is such a judgment right, for all such nonself desires do actually have their origin in the leadings of the indwelling Thought Adjuster, and this Adjuster is a fragment of God. The impulse of the spirit Monitor is realized in human consciousness as the urge to be altruistic, fellow-creature minded. At least this is the early and fundamental experience of the child mind. When the growing child fails of personality unification, the altruistic drive may become so overdeveloped as to work serious injury to the welfare of the self. A misguided conscience can become responsible for much conflict, worry, sorrow, and no end of human unhappiness.

3. RELIGION AND THE HUMAN RACE

While the belief in spirits, dreams, and diverse other superstitions all played a part in the evolutionary origin of primitive religions, you should not overlook the influence of the clan or tribal spirit of solidarity. In the group relationship there was presented the exact social situation which provided the challenge to the egoistic-altruistic conflict in the moral nature of the early human mind. In spite of their belief in spirits, primitive Australians still focus their religion upon the clan. In time, such religious concepts tend to personalize, first, as animals, and later, as a superman or as a God. Even such inferior races as the African Bushmen, who are not even totemic in their beliefs, do have a recognition of the difference between the self-interest and the group-interest, a primitive distinction between the values of the secular and the sacred. But the social group is not the source of religious experience. Regardless of the influence of all these primitive contributions to man's early religion, the fact remains that the true religious impulse has its origin in genuine spirit presences activating the will to be unselfish.

Later religion is foreshadowed in the primitive belief in natural wonders and mysteries, the impersonal mana. But sooner or later the evolving religion requires that the individual should make some personal sacrifice for the good of his social group, should do something to make other people happier and better. Ultimately, religion is destined to become the service of God and of man.

Religion is designed to change man's environment, but much of the religion found among mortals today has become helpless to do this. Environment has all too often mastered religion.

Remember that in the religion of all ages the experience which is paramount is the feeling regarding moral values and social meanings, not the thinking regarding theologic dogmas or philosophic theories. Religion evolves favorably as the element of magic is replaced by the concept of morals.

Man evolved through the superstitions of mana, magic, nature worship, spirit fear, and animal worship to the various ceremonials whereby the religious attitude of the individual became the group reactions of the clan. And then these ceremonies became focalized and crystallized into tribal beliefs, and eventually these fears and faiths became personalized into gods. But in all of this religious evolution the moral element was never wholly absent. The impulse of the God within man was always potent. And these powerful influences—one human and the other divine—insured the survival of religion throughout the vicissitudes of the ages and that notwithstanding it was so often threatened with extinction by a thousand subversive tendencies and hostile antagonisms.

4. SPIRITUAL COMMUNION

The characteristic difference between a social occasion and a religious gathering is that in contrast with the secular the religious is pervaded by the atmosphere of *communion.* In this way human association generates a feeling of fellowship with the divine, and this is the beginning of group worship. Partaking of a common meal was the earliest type of social communion, and so did early religions provide that some portion of the ceremonial sacrifice should be eaten by the worshipers. Even in Christianity the Lord's Supper retains this mode of communion. The atmosphere of the communion provides a refreshing and comforting period of truce in the conflict of the self-seeking ego with the altruistic urge of the indwelling spirit Monitor. And this is the prelude to true worship—the practice of the presence of God which eventuates in the emergence of the brotherhood of man.

When primitive man felt that his communion with God had been interrupted, he resorted to sacrifice of some kind in an effort to make atonement, to restore friendly relationship. The hunger and thirst for righteousness leads to the discovery of truth, and truth augments ideals, and this creates new problems for the individual religionists, for our ideals tend to grow by geometrical progression, while our ability to live up to them is enhanced only by arithmetical progression.

The sense of guilt (not the consciousness of sin) comes either from interrupted spiritual communion or from the lowering of one's moral ideals. Deliverance from such a predicament can only come through the realization that one's highest moral ideals are not necessarily synonymous with the will of God. Man cannot hope to live up to his highest ideals, but he can be true to his purpose of finding God and becoming more and more like him.

Jesus swept away all of the ceremonials of sacrifice and atonement. He destroyed the basis of all this fictitious guilt and sense of isolation in the universe by declaring that man is a child of God; the creature-Creator relationship was placed on a child-parent basis. God becomes a loving Father to his mortal sons and daughters. All ceremonials not a legitimate part of such an intimate family relationship are forever abrogated.

God the Father deals with man his child on the basis, not of actual virtue or worthiness, but in recognition of the child's motivation—the creature purpose and intent. The relationship is one of parent-child association and is actuated by divine love.

5. THE ORIGIN OF IDEALS

The early evolutionary mind gives origin to a feeling of social duty and moral obligation derived chiefly from emotional fear. The more positive urge of social service and the idealism of altruism are derived from the direct impulse of the divine spirit indwelling the human mind.

This idea-ideal of doing good to others—the impulse to deny the ego something for the benefit of one's neighbor—is very circumscribed at first. Primitive man regards as neighbor only those very close to him, those who treat him neighborly; as religious civilization advances, one's neighbor expands in concept to embrace the clan, the tribe, the nation. And then Jesus enlarged the neighbor scope to embrace the whole of humanity, even that we should love our enemies. And there is something inside of every normal human being that tells him this teaching is moral—right. Even those who practice this ideal least, admit that it is right in theory.

All men recognize the morality of this universal human urge to be unselfish and altruistic. The humanist ascribes the origin of this urge to the natural working of the material mind; the religionist more correctly recognizes that the truly unselfish drive of mortal mind is in response to the inner spirit leadings of the Thought Adjuster.

But man's interpretation of these early conflicts between the ego-will and the other-than-self-will is not always dependable. Only a fairly well unified personality can arbitrate the multiform contentions of the ego cravings and the budding social consciousness. The self has rights as well as one's neighbors. Neither has exclusive claims upon the attention and service of the individual. Failure to resolve this problem gives origin to the earliest type of human guilt feelings.

Human happiness is achieved only when the ego desire of the self and the altruistic urge of the higher self (divine spirit) are co-ordinated and reconciled by the unified will of the integrating and supervising personality. The mind of evolutionary man is ever confronted with the intricate problem of refereeing the contest between the natural expansion of emotional impulses and the moral growth of unselfish urges predicated on spiritual insight—genuine religious reflection.

The attempt to secure equal good for the self and for the greatest number of other selves presents a problem which cannot always be satisfactorily resolved in a time-space frame. Given an eternal life, such antagonisms can be worked out, but in one short human life they are incapable of solution. Jesus referred to such a paradox when he said: "Whosoever shall save his life shall lose it, but whosoever shall lose his life for the sake of the kingdom, shall find it."

The pursuit of the ideal—the striving to be Godlike—is a continuous effort before death and after. The life after death is no different in the essentials than the mortal existence. Everything we do in this life which is good contributes directly to the enhancement of the future life. Real religion does not foster moral indolence and spiritual laziness by encouraging the vain hope of having all the virtues of a noble character bestowed upon one as a result of passing through the portals of natural death. True religion does not belittle man's efforts to progress during the mortal lease on life. Every mortal gain is a direct contribution to the enrichment of the first stages of the immortal survival experience.

It is fatal to man's idealism when he is taught that all of his altruistic impulses are merely the development of his natural herd instincts. But he is ennobled and mightily energized when he learns that these higher urges of his soul emanate from the spiritual forces that indwell his mortal mind.

It lifts man out of himself and beyond himself when he once fully realizes that there lives and strives within him something which is eternal and divine. And so it is that a living faith in the superhuman origin of our ideals validates our belief that we are the sons of God and makes real our altruistic convictions, the feelings of the brotherhood of man.

Man, in his spiritual domain, does have a free will. Mortal man is neither a helpless slave of the inflexible sovereignty of an all-powerful God nor the victim of the hopeless fatality of a mechanistic cosmic determinism. Man is most truly the architect of his own eternal destiny.

But man is not saved or ennobled by pressure. Spirit growth springs from within the evolving soul. Pressure may deform the personality, but it never stimulates growth. Even educational pressure is only negatively helpful in that it may aid in the prevention of disastrous experiences. Spiritual growth is greatest where all external pressures are at a minimum. "Where the spirit of the Lord is, there is freedom." Man develops best when the pressures of home, community, church, and state are least. But this must not be construed as meaning that there is no place in a progressive society for home, social institutions, church, and state.

When a member of a social religious group has complied with the requirements of such a group, he should be encouraged to enjoy religious liberty in the full expression of his own personal interpretation of the truths of religious belief and the facts of religious experience. The security of a religious group depends on spiritual unity, not on theological uniformity. A religious group should be able to enjoy the liberty of freethinking without having to become "freethinkers." There is great hope for any church that worships the living God, validates the brotherhood of man, and dares to remove all creedal pressure from its members.

6. PHILOSOPHIC CO-ORDINATION

Theology is the study of the actions and reactions of the human spirit; it can never become a science since it must always be combined more or less with psychology in its personal expression and with philosophy in its systematic portrayal. Theology is always the study of *your* religion; the study of another's religion is psychology.

When man approaches the study and examination of his universe from the *outside,* he brings into being the various physical sciences; when he approaches the research of himself and the universe from the *inside,* he gives origin to theology and metaphysics. The later art of philosophy develops in an effort to harmonize the many discrepancies which are destined at first to appear between the findings and teachings of these two diametrically opposite avenues of approaching the universe of things and beings.

Religion has to do with the spiritual viewpoint, the awareness of the *insideness* of human experience. Man's spiritual nature affords him the opportunity of turning the universe outside in. It is therefore true that, viewed exclusively from the insideness of personality experience, all creation appears to be spiritual in nature.

When man analytically inspects the universe through the material endowments of his physical senses and associated mind perception, the cosmos appears to be mechanical and energy-material. Such a technique of studying reality consists in turning the universe inside out.

A logical and consistent philosophic concept of the universe cannot be built up on the postulations of either materialism or spiritism, for both of these systems of thinking, when universally applied, are compelled to view the cosmos in distortion, the former contacting with a universe turned inside out, the latter realizing the nature of a universe turned outside in. Never, then, can either science or religion, in and of themselves, standing alone, hope to gain an adequate understanding of universal truths and relationships without the guidance of human philosophy and the illumination of divine revelation.

Always must man's inner spirit depend for its expression and self-realization upon the mechanism and technique of the mind. Likewise must man's outer experience of material reality be predicated on the mind consciousness of the experiencing personality. Therefore are the spiritual and the material, the inner and the outer, human experiences always correlated with the mind function and conditioned, as to their conscious realization, by the mind activity. Man experiences matter in his mind; he experiences spiritual reality in the soul but becomes conscious of this experience in his mind. The intellect is the harmonizer and the ever-present conditioner and qualifier of the sum total of mortal experience. Both energy-things and spirit values are colored by their interpretation through the mind media of consciousness.

Your difficulty in arriving at a more harmonious co-ordination between science and religion is due to your utter ignorance of the intervening domain of the morontia world of things and beings. The local universe consists of three degrees, or stages, of reality manifestation: matter, morontia, and spirit. The morontia angle of approach erases all divergence between the findings of the physical sciences and the functioning of the spirit of religion. Reason is the understanding technique of the sciences; faith is the insight technique of religion; mota is the technique of the morontia level. Mota is a supermaterial reality sensitivity which is beginning to compensate incomplete growth, having for its substance knowledge-reason and for its essence faith-insight. Mota is a superphilosophical reconciliation of divergent reality perception which is nonattainable by material personalities; it is predicated, in part, on the experience of having survived the material life of the flesh. But many mortals have recognized the desirability of having some method of reconciling the interplay between the widely separated domains of science and religion; and metaphysics is the result of man's unavailing attempt to span this well-recognized chasm. But human metaphysics has proved more confusing than illuminating. Metaphysics stands for man's well-meant but futile effort to compensate for the absence of the mota of morontia.

Metaphysics has proved a failure; mota, man cannot perceive. Revelation is the only technique which can compensate for the absence of the truth sensitivity of mota in a material world. Revelation authoritatively clarifies the muddle of reason-developed metaphysics on an evolutionary sphere.

Science is man's attempted study of his physical environment, the world of energy-matter; religion is man's experience with the cosmos of spirit values; philosophy has been developed by man's mind effort to organize and correlate the findings of these widely separated concepts into something like a reasonable and unified attitude toward the cosmos. Philosophy, clarified by revelation, functions acceptably in the absence of mota and in the presence of the breakdown and failure of man's reason substitute for mota—metaphysics.

Early man did not differentiate between the energy level and the spirit level. It was the violet race and their Andite successors who first attempted to divorce the mathematical from the volitional. Increasingly has civilized man followed in the footsteps of the earliest Greeks and the Sumerians who distinguished between the inanimate and the animate. And as civilization progresses, philosophy will have to bridge ever-widening gulfs between the spirit concept and the energy concept. But in the time of space these divergencies are at one in the Supreme.

Science must always be grounded in reason, although imagination and conjecture are helpful in the extension of its borders. Religion is forever dependent on faith, albeit reason is a stabilizing influence and a helpful handmaid. And always there have been, and ever will be, misleading interpretations of the phenomena of both the natural and the spiritual worlds, sciences and religions falsely so called.

Out of his incomplete grasp of science, his faint hold upon religion, and his abortive attempts at metaphysics, man has attempted to construct his formulations of philosophy. And modern man would indeed build a worthy and engaging philosophy of himself and his universe were it not for the breakdown of his all-important and indispensable metaphysical connection between the worlds of matter and spirit, the failure of metaphysics to bridge the morontia gulf between the physical and the spiritual. Mortal man lacks the concept of morontia mind and material; and *revelation* is the only technique for atoning for this deficiency in the conceptual data which man so urgently needs in order to construct a logical philosophy of the universe and to arrive at a satisfying understanding of his sure and settled place in that universe.

Revelation is evolutionary man's only hope of bridging the morontia gulf. Faith and reason, unaided by mota, cannot conceive and construct a logical universe. Without the insight of mota, mortal man cannot discern goodness, love, and truth in the phenomena of the material world.

When the philosophy of man leans heavily toward the world of matter, it becomes rationalistic or *naturalistic.* When philosophy inclines particularly toward the spiritual level, it becomes *idealistic* or even mystical. When philosophy is so unfortunate as to lean upon metaphysics, it unfailingly becomes *skeptical,* confused. In past ages, most of man's knowledge and intellectual evaluations have fallen into one of these three distortions of perception. Philosophy dare not project its interpretations of reality in the linear fashion of logic; it must never fail to reckon with the elliptic symmetry of reality and with the essential curvature of all relation concepts.

The highest attainable philosophy of mortal man must be logically based on the reason of science, the faith of religion, and the truth insight afforded by revelation. By this union man can compensate somewhat for his failure to develop an adequate metaphysics and for his inability to comprehend the mota of the morontia.

7. SCIENCE AND RELIGION

Science is sustained by reason, religion by faith. Faith, though not predicated on reason, is reasonable; though independent of logic, it is nonetheless encouraged by sound logic. Faith cannot be nourished even by an ideal philosophy; indeed, it is, with science, the very source of such a philosophy. Faith, human religious insight, can be surely instructed only by revelation, can be surely elevated only by personal mortal experience with the spiritual Adjuster presence of the God who is spirit.

True salvation is the technique of the divine evolution of the mortal mind from matter identification through the realms of morontia liaison to the high universe status of spiritual correlation. And as material intuitive instinct precedes the appearance of reasoned knowledge in terrestrial evolution, so does the manifestation of spiritual intuitive insight presage the later appearance of morontia and spirit reason and experience in the supernal program of celestial evolution, the business of transmuting the potentials of man the temporal into the actuality and divinity of man the eternal, a Paradise finaliter.

But as ascending man reaches inward and Paradiseward for the God experience, he will likewise be reaching outward and spaceward for an energy understanding of the material cosmos. The progression of science is not limited to the terrestrial life of man; his universe and superuniverse ascension experience will to no small degree be the study of energy transmutation and material metamorphosis. God is spirit, but Deity is unity, and the unity of Deity not only embraces the spiritual values of the Universal Father and the Eternal Son but is also cognizant of the energy facts of the Universal Controller and the Isle of Paradise, while these two phases of universal reality are perfectly correlated in the mind relationships of the Conjoint Actor and unified on the finite level in the emerging Deity of the Supreme Being.

The union of the scientific attitude and the religious insight by the mediation of experiential philosophy is part of man's long Paradise-ascension experience. The approximations of mathematics and the certainties of insight will always require the harmonizing function of mind logic on all levels of experience short of the maximum attainment of the Supreme.

But logic can never succeed in harmonizing the findings of science and the insights of religion unless both the scientific and the religious aspects of a personality are truth dominated, sincerely desirous of following the truth wherever it may lead regardless of the conclusions which it may reach.

Logic is the technique of philosophy, its method of expression. Within the domain of true science, reason is always amenable to genuine logic; within the domain of true religion, faith is always logical from the basis of an inner viewpoint, even though such faith may appear to be quite unfounded from the inlooking viewpoint of the scientific approach. From outward, looking within, the universe may appear to be material; from within, looking out, the same universe appears to be wholly spiritual. Reason grows out of material awareness, faith out of spiritual awareness, but through the mediation of a philosophy strengthened by revelation, logic may confirm both the inward and the outward view, thereby effecting the stabilization of both science and religion. Thus, through common contact with the logic of philosophy, may both science and religion become increasingly tolerant of each other, less and less skeptical.

What both developing science and religion need is more searching and fearless self-criticism, a greater awareness of incompleteness in evolutionary status. The teachers of both science and religion are often altogether too self-confident and dogmatic. Science and religion can only be self-critical of their *facts*. The moment departure is made from the stage of facts, reason abdicates or else rapidly degenerates into a consort of false logic.

The truth—an understanding of cosmic relationships, universe facts, and spiritual values—can best be had through the ministry of the Spirit of Truth and can best be criticized by *revelation*. But revelation originates neither a science nor a religion; its function is to co-ordinate both science and religion with the truth of reality. Always, in the absence of revelation or in the failure to accept or grasp it, has mortal man resorted to his futile gesture of metaphysics, that being the only human substitute for the revelation of truth or for the mota of morontia personality.

The science of the material world enables man to control, and to some extent dominate, his physical environment. The religion of the spiritual experience is the source of the fraternity impulse which enables men to live together in the complexities of the civilization of a scientific age. Metaphysics, but more certainly revelation, affords a common meeting ground for the discoveries of both science and religion and makes possible the human attempt logically to correlate these separate but interdependent domains of thought into a well-balanced philosophy of scientific stability and religious certainty.

In the mortal state, nothing can be absolutely proved; both science and religion are predicated on assumptions. On the morontia level, the postulates of both science and religion are capable of partial proof by mota logic. On the spiritual level of maximum status, the need for finite proof gradually vanishes before the actual experience of and with reality; but even then there is much beyond the finite that remains unproved.

All divisions of human thought are predicated on certain assumptions which are accepted, though unproved, by the constitutive reality sensitivity of the mind endowment of man. Science starts out on its vaunted career of reasoning by *assuming* the reality of three things: matter, motion, and life. Religion starts out with the assumption of the validity of three things: mind, spirit, and the universe—the Supreme Being.

Science becomes the thought domain of mathematics, of the energy and material of time in space. Religion assumes to deal not only with finite and temporal spirit but also with the spirit of eternity and supremacy. Only through a long experience in mota can these two extremes of universe perception be made to yield analogous interpretations of origins, functions, relations, realities, and destinies. The maximum harmonization of the energy-spirit divergence is in the encircuitment of the Seven Master Spirits; the first unification thereof, in the Deity of the Supreme; the finality unity thereof, in the infinity of the First Source and Center, the I AM.

Reason is the act of recognizing the conclusions of consciousness with regard to the experience in and with the physical world of energy and matter. *Faith* is the act of recognizing the validity of spiritual consciousness—something which is incapable of other mortal proof. *Logic* is the synthetic truth-seeking progression of the unity of faith and reason and is founded on the constitutive mind endowments of mortal beings, the innate recognition of things, meanings, and values.

There is a real proof of spiritual reality in the presence of the Thought Adjuster, but the validity of this presence is not demonstrable to the external world, only to the one who thus experiences the indwelling of God. The consciousness of the Adjuster is based on the intellectual reception of truth, the supermind perception of goodness, and the personality motivation to love.

Science discovers the material world, religion evaluates it, and philosophy endeavors to interpret its meanings while co-ordinating the scientific material viewpoint with the religious spiritual concept. But history is a realm in which science and religion may never fully agree.

8. PHILOSOPHY AND RELIGION

Although both science and philosophy may assume the probability of God by their reason and logic, only the personal religious experience of a spirit-led man can affirm the certainty of such a supreme and personal Deity. By the technique of such an incarnation of living truth the philosophic hypothesis of the probability of God becomes a religious reality.

The confusion about the experience of the certainty of God arises out of the dissimilar interpretations and relations of that experience by separate individuals and by different races of men. The experiencing of God may be wholly valid, but the discourse *about* God, being intellectual and philosophical, is divergent and oftentimes confusingly fallacious.

A good and noble man may be consummately in love with his wife but utterly unable to pass a satisfactory written examination on the psychology of marital love. Another man, having little or no love for his spouse, might pass such an examination most acceptably. The imperfection of the lover's insight into the true nature of the beloved does not in the least invalidate either the reality or sincerity of his love.

If you truly believe in God—by faith know him and love him—do not permit the reality of such an experience to be in any way lessened or detracted from by the doubting insinuations of science, the caviling of logic, the postulates of philosophy, or the clever suggestions of well-meaning souls who would create a religion without God.

The certainty of the God-knowing religionist should not be disturbed by the uncertainty of the doubting materialist; rather should the uncertainty of the unbeliever be mightily challenged by the profound faith and unshakable certainty of the experiential believer.

Philosophy, to be of the greatest service to both science and religion, should avoid the extremes of both materialism and pantheism. Only a philosophy which recognizes the reality of personality—permanence in the presence of change—can be of moral value to man, can serve as a liaison between the theories of material science and spiritual religion. Revelation is a compensation for the frailties of evolving philosophy.

9. THE ESSENCE OF RELIGION

Theology deals with the intellectual content of religion, metaphysics (revelation) with the philosophic aspects. Religious experience *is* the spiritual content of religion. Notwithstanding the mythologic vagaries and the psychologic illusions of the intellectual content of religion, the metaphysical assumptions of error and the techniques of self-deception, the political distortions and the socioeconomic perversions of the philosophic content of religion, the spiritual experience of personal religion remains genuine and valid.

Religion has to do with feeling, acting, and living, not merely with thinking. Thinking is more closely related to the material life and should be in the main, but not altogether, dominated by reason and the facts of science and, in its nonmaterial reaches toward the spirit realms, by truth. No matter how illusory and erroneous one's theology, one's religion may be wholly genuine and everlastingly true.

Buddhism in its original form is one of the best religions without a God which has arisen throughout all the evolutionary history of Urantia, although, as this faith developed, it did not remain godless. Religion without faith is a contradiction; without God, a philosophic inconsistency and an intellectual absurdity.

The magical and mythological parentage of natural religion does not invalidate the reality and truth of the later revelational religions and the consummate saving gospel of the religion of Jesus. Jesus' life and teachings finally divested religion of the superstitions of magic, the illusions of mythology, and the bondage of traditional dogmatism. But this early magic and mythology very effectively prepared the way for later and superior religion by assuming the existence and reality of supermaterial values and beings.

Although religious experience is a purely spiritual subjective phenomenon, such an experience embraces a positive and living faith attitude toward the highest realms of universe objective reality. The ideal of religious philosophy is such a faith-trust as would lead man unqualifiedly to depend upon the absolute love of the infinite Father of the universe of universes. Such a genuine religious experience far transcends the philosophic objectification of idealistic desire; it actually takes salvation for granted and concerns itself only with learning and doing the will of the Father in Paradise. The earmarks of such a religion are: faith in a supreme Deity, hope of eternal survival, and love, especially of one's fellows.

When theology masters religion, religion dies; it becomes a doctrine instead of a life. The mission of theology is merely to facilitate the self-consciousness of personal spiritual experience. Theology constitutes the religious effort to define, clarify, expound, and justify the experiential claims of religion, which, in the last analysis, can be validated only by living faith. In the higher philosophy of the universe, wisdom, like reason, becomes allied to faith. Reason, wisdom, and faith are man's highest human attainments. Reason introduces man to the world of facts, to things; wisdom introduces him to a world of truth, to relationships; faith initiates him into a world of divinity, spiritual experience.

Faith most willingly carries reason along as far as reason can go and then goes on with wisdom to the full philosophic limit; and then it dares to launch out upon the limitless and never-ending universe journey in the sole company of TRUTH.

Science (knowledge) is founded on the inherent (adjutant spirit) assumption that reason is valid, that the universe can be comprehended. Philosophy (co-ordinate comprehension) is founded on the inherent (spirit of wisdom) assumption that wisdom is valid, that the material universe can be co-ordinated with the spiritual. Religion (the truth of personal spiritual experience) is founded on the inherent (Thought Adjuster) assumption that faith is valid, that God can be known and attained.

The full realization of the reality of mortal life consists in a progressive willingness to believe these assumptions of reason, wisdom, and faith. Such a life is one motivated by truth and dominated by love; and these are the ideals of objective cosmic reality whose existence cannot be materially demonstrated.

When reason once recognizes right and wrong, it exhibits wisdom; when wisdom chooses between right and wrong, truth and error, it demonstrates spirit leading. And thus are the functions of mind, soul, and spirit ever closely united and functionally interassociated. Reason deals with factual knowledge; wisdom, with philosophy and revelation; faith, with living spiritual experience. Through truth man attains beauty and by spiritual love ascends to goodness.

Faith leads to knowing God, not merely to a mystical feeling of the divine presence. Faith must not be overmuch influenced by its emotional consequences. True religion is an experience of believing and knowing as well as a satisfaction of feeling.

There is a reality in religious experience that is proportional to the spiritual content, and such a reality is transcendent to reason, science, philosophy, wisdom, and all other human achievements. The convictions of such an experience are unassailable; the logic of religious living is incontrovertible; the certainty of such knowledge is superhuman; the satisfactions are superbly divine, the courage indomitable, the devotions unquestioning, the loyalties supreme, and the destinies final—eternal, ultimate, and universal.

[Presented by a Melchizedek of Nebadon.]

PAPER 104

GROWTH OF THE TRINITY CONCEPT

THE Trinity concept of revealed religion must not be confused with the triad beliefs of evolutionary religions. The ideas of triads arose from many suggestive relationships but chiefly because of the three joints of the fingers, because three legs were the fewest which could stabilize a stool, because three support points could keep up a tent; furthermore, primitive man, for a long time, could not count beyond three.

Aside from certain natural couplets, such as past and present, day and night, hot and cold, and male and female, man generally tends to think in triads: yesterday, today, and tomorrow; sunrise, noon, and sunset; father, mother, and child. Three cheers are given the victor. The dead are buried on the third day, and the ghost is placated by three ablutions of water.

As a consequence of these natural associations in human experience, the triad made its appearance in religion, and this long before the Paradise Trinity of Deities, or even any of their representatives, had been revealed to mankind. Later on, the Persians, Hindus, Greeks, Egyptians, Babylonians, Romans, and Scandinavians all had triad gods, but these were still not true trinities. Triad deities all had a natural origin and have appeared at one time or another among most of the intelligent peoples of Urantia. Sometimes the concept of an evolutionary triad has become mixed with that of a revealed Trinity; in these instances it is often impossible to distinguish one from the other.

1. URANTIAN TRINITY CONCEPTS

The first Urantian revelation leading to the comprehension of the Paradise Trinity was made by the staff of Prince Caligastia about one-half million years ago. This earliest Trinity concept was lost to the world in the unsettled times following the planetary rebellion.

The second presentation of the Trinity was made by Adam and Eve in the first and second gardens. These teachings had not been wholly obliterated even in the times of Machiventa Melchizedek about thirty-five thousand years later, for the Trinity concept of the Sethites persisted in both Mesopotamia and Egypt but more especially in India, where it was long perpetuated in Agni, the Vedic three-headed fire god.

The third presentation of the Trinity was made by Machiventa Melchizedek, and this doctrine was symbolized by the three concentric circles which the sage of Salem wore on his breast plate. But Machiventa found it very difficult to teach the Palestinian Bedouins about the Universal Father, the Eternal Son, and the Infinite Spirit. Most of his disciples thought that the Trinity consisted of the three Most Highs of Norlatiadek; a few conceived of the Trinity as the

System Sovereign, the Constellation Father, and the local universe Creator Deity; still fewer even remotely grasped the idea of the Paradise association of the Father, Son, and Spirit.

Through the activities of the Salem missionaries the Melchizedek teachings of the Trinity gradually spread throughout much of Eurasia and northern Africa. It is often difficult to distinguish between the triads and the trinities in the later Andite and the post-Melchizedek ages, when both concepts to a certain extent intermingled and coalesced.

Among the Hindus the trinitarian concept took root as Being, Intelligence, and Joy. (A later Indian conception was Brahma, Siva, and Vishnu.) While the earlier Trinity portrayals were brought to India by the Sethite priests, the later ideas of the Trinity were imported by the Salem missionaries and were developed by the native intellects of India through a compounding of these doctrines with the evolutionary triad conceptions.

The Buddhist faith developed two doctrines of a trinitarian nature: The earlier was Teacher, Law, and Brotherhood; that was the presentation made by Gautama Siddhartha. The later idea, developing among the northern branch of the followers of Buddha, embraced Supreme Lord, Holy Spirit, and Incarnate Savior.

And these ideas of the Hindus and Buddhists were real trinitarian postulates, that is, the idea of a threefold manifestation of a monotheistic God. A true trinity conception is not just a grouping together of three separate gods.

The Hebrews knew about the Trinity from the Kenite traditions of the days of Melchizedek, but their monotheistic zeal for the one God, Yahweh, so eclipsed all such teachings that by the time of Jesus' appearance the Elohim doctrine had been practically eradicated from Jewish theology. The Hebrew mind could not reconcile the trinitarian concept with the monotheistic belief in the One Lord, the God of Israel.

The followers of the Islamic faith likewise failed to grasp the idea of the Trinity. It is always difficult for an emerging monotheism to tolerate trinitarianism when confronted by polytheism. The trinity idea takes best hold of those religions which have a firm monotheistic tradition coupled with doctrinal elasticity. The great monotheists, the Hebrews and Mohammedans, found it difficult to distinguish between worshiping three gods, polytheism, and trinitarianism, the worship of one Deity existing in a triune manifestation of divinity and personality.

Jesus taught his apostles the truth regarding the persons of the Paradise Trinity, but they thought he spoke figuratively and symbolically. Having been nurtured in Hebraic monotheism, they found it difficult to entertain any belief that seemed to conflict with their dominating concept of Yahweh. And the early Christians inherited the Hebraic prejudice against the Trinity concept.

The first Trinity of Christianity was proclaimed at Antioch and consisted of God, his Word, and his Wisdom. Paul knew of the Paradise Trinity of Father, Son, and Spirit, but he seldom preached about it and made mention thereof in only a few of his letters to the newly forming churches. Even then, as did his fellow apostles, Paul confused Jesus, the Creator Son of the local universe, with the Second Person of Deity, the Eternal Son of Paradise.

The Christian concept of the Trinity, which began to gain recognition near the close of the first century after Christ, was comprised of the Universal Father, the Creator Son of Nebadon, and the Divine Minister of Salvington—Mother Spirit of the local universe and creative consort of the Creator Son.

Not since the times of Jesus has the factual identity of the Paradise Trinity been known on Urantia (except by a few individuals to whom it was especially revealed) until its presentation in these revelatory disclosures. But though the Christian concept of the Trinity erred in fact, it was practically true with respect to spiritual relationships. Only in its philosophic implications and cosmological consequences did this concept suffer embarrassment: It has been difficult for many who are cosmic minded to believe that the Second Person of Deity, the second member of an infinite Trinity, once dwelt on Urantia; and while in spirit this is true, in actuality it is not a fact. The Michael Creators fully embody the divinity of the Eternal Son, but they are not the absolute personality.

2. TRINITY UNITY AND DEITY PLURALITY

Monotheism arose as a philosophic protest against the inconsistency of polytheism. It developed first through pantheon organizations with the departmentalization of supernatural activities, then through the henotheistic exaltation of one god above the many, and finally through the exclusion of all but the One God of final value.

Trinitarianism grows out of the experiential protest against the impossibility of conceiving the oneness of a deanthropomorphized solitary Deity of unrelated universe significance. Given a sufficient time, philosophy tends to abstract the personal qualities from the Deity concept of pure monotheism, thus reducing this idea of an unrelated God to the status of a pantheistic Absolute. It has always been difficult to understand the personal nature of a God who has no personal relationships in equality with other and co-ordinate personal beings. Personality in Deity demands that such Deity exist in relation to other and equal personal Deity.

Through the recognition of the Trinity concept the mind of man can hope to grasp something of the interrelationship of love and law in the time-space creations. Through spiritual faith man gains insight into the love of God but soon discovers that this spiritual faith has no influence on the ordained laws of the material universe. Irrespective of the firmness of man's belief in God as his Paradise Father, expanding cosmic horizons demand that he also give recognition to the reality of Paradise Deity as universal law, that he recognize the Trinity sovereignty extending outward from Paradise and overshadowing even the evolving local universes of the Creator Sons and Creative Daughters of the three eternal persons whose deity union *is* the fact and reality and eternal indivisibility of the Paradise Trinity.

And this selfsame Paradise Trinity is a real entity—not a personality but nonetheless a true and absolute reality; not a personality but nonetheless compatible with coexistent personalities—the personalities of the Father, the Son, and the Spirit. The Trinity is a supersummative Deity reality eventuating out of the conjoining of the three Paradise Deities. The qualities, characteristics, and functions of the Trinity are not the simple sum of the attributes of the three Paradise Deities; Trinity functions are something unique, original, and not wholly predictable from an analysis of the attributes of Father, Son, and Spirit.

For example: The Master, when on earth, admonished his followers that justice is never a *personal* act; it is always a *group* function. Neither do the Gods, as persons, administer justice. But they perform this very function as a collective whole, as the Paradise Trinity.

The conceptual grasp of the Trinity association of Father, Son, and Spirit prepares the human mind for the further presentation of certain other threefold relationships. Theological reason may be fully satisfied by the concept of the Paradise Trinity, but philosophical and cosmological reason demand the recognition of the other triune associations of the First Source and Center, those triunities in which the Infinite functions in various non-Father capacities of universal manifestation—the relationships of the God of force, energy, power, causation, reaction, potentiality, actuality, gravity, tension, pattern, principle, and unity.

3. TRINITIES AND TRIUNITIES

While mankind has sometimes grasped at an understanding of the Trinity of the three persons of Deity, consistency demands that the human intellect perceive that there are certain relationships between all seven Absolutes. But all that which is true of the Paradise Trinity is not necessarily true of a *triunity,* for a triunity is something other than a trinity. In certain functional aspects a triunity may be analogous to a trinity, but it is never homologous in nature with a trinity.

Mortal man is passing through a great age of expanding horizons and enlarging concepts on Urantia, and his cosmic philosophy must accelerate in evolution to keep pace with the expansion of the intellectual arena of human thought. As the cosmic consciousness of mortal man expands, he perceives the interrelatedness of all that he finds in his material science, intellectual philosophy, and spiritual insight. Still, with all this belief in the unity of the cosmos, man perceives the diversity of all existence. In spite of all concepts concerning the immutability of Deity, man perceives that he lives in a universe of constant change and experiential growth. Regardless of the realization of the survival of spiritual values, man has ever to reckon with the mathematics and premathematics of force, energy, and power.

In some manner the eternal repleteness of infinity must be reconciled with the time-growth of the evolving universes and with the incompleteness of the experiential inhabitants thereof. In some way the conception of total infinitude must be so segmented and qualified that the mortal intellect and the morontia soul can grasp this concept of final value and spiritualizing significance.

While reason demands a monotheistic unity of cosmic reality, finite experience requires the postulate of plural Absolutes and of their co-ordination in cosmic relationships. Without co-ordinate existences there is no possibility for the appearance of diversity of absolute relationships, no chance for the operation of differentials, variables, modifiers, attenuators, qualifiers, or diminishers.

In these papers total reality (infinity) has been presented as it exists in the seven Absolutes:

1. The Universal Father.
2. The Eternal Son.
3. The Infinite Spirit.

4. The Isle of Paradise.
5. The Deity Absolute.
6. The Universal Absolute.
7. The Unqualified Absolute.

The First Source and Center, who is Father to the Eternal Son, is also Pattern to the Paradise Isle. He is personality unqualified in the Son but personality potentialized in the Deity Absolute. The Father is energy revealed in Paradise-Havona and at the same time energy concealed in the Unqualified Absolute. The Infinite is ever disclosed in the ceaseless acts of the Conjoint Actor while he is eternally functioning in the compensating but enshrouded activities of the Universal Absolute. Thus is the Father related to the six coordinate Absolutes, and thus do all seven encompass the circle of infinity throughout the endless cycles of eternity.

It would seem that triunity of absolute relationships is inevitable. Personality seeks other personality association on absolute as well as on all other levels. And the association of the three Paradise personalities eternalizes the first triunity, the personality union of the Father, the Son, and the Spirit. For when these three persons, *as persons,* conjoin for united function, they thereby constitute a triunity of functional unity, not a trinity—an organic entity—but nonetheless a triunity, a threefold functional aggregate unanimity.

The Paradise Trinity is not a triunity; it is not a functional unanimity; rather is it undivided and indivisible Deity. The Father, Son, and Spirit (as persons) can sustain a relationship to the Paradise Trinity, for the Trinity *is* their undivided Deity. The Father, Son, and Spirit sustain no such personal relationship to the first triunity, for that *is* their functional union as three persons. Only as the Trinity—as undivided Deity—do they collectively sustain an external relationship to the triunity of their personal aggregation.

Thus does the Paradise Trinity stand unique among absolute relationships; there are several existential triunities but only one existential Trinity. A triunity is *not* an entity. It is functional rather than organic. Its members are partners rather than corporative. The components of the triunities may be entities, but a triunity itself is an association.

There is, however, one point of comparison between trinity and triunity: Both eventuate in functions that are something other than the discernible sum of the attributes of the component members. But while they are thus comparable from a functional standpoint, they otherwise exhibit no categorical relationship. They are roughly related as the relation of function to structure. But the function of the triunity association is not the function of the trinity structure or entity.

The triunities are nonetheless real; they are very real. In them is total reality functionalized, and through them does the Universal Father exercise immediate and personal control over the master functions of infinity.

4. THE SEVEN TRIUNITIES

In attempting the description of seven triunities, attention is directed to the fact that the Universal Father is the primal member of each. He is, was, and ever will be: the First Universal Father-Source, Absolute Center, Primal

Cause, Universal Controller, Limitless Energizer, Original Unity, Unqualified Upholder, First Person of Deity, Primal Cosmic Pattern, and Essence of Infinity. The Universal Father is the personal cause of the Absolutes; he is the absolute of Absolutes.

The nature and meaning of the seven triunities may be suggested as:

The First Triunity—the personal-purposive triunity. This is the grouping of the three Deity personalities:

1. The Universal Father.
2. The Eternal Son.
3. The Infinite Spirit.

This is the threefold union of love, mercy, and ministry—the purposive and personal association of the three eternal Paradise personalities. This is the divinely fraternal, creature-loving, fatherly-acting, and ascension-promoting association. The divine personalities of this first triunity are personality-bequeathing, spirit-bestowing, and mind-endowing Gods.

This is the triunity of infinite volition; it acts throughout the eternal present and in all of the past-present-future flow of time. This association yields volitional infinity and provides the mechanisms whereby personal Deity becomes self-revelatory to the creatures of the evolving cosmos.

The Second Triunity—the power-pattern triunity. Whether it be a tiny ultimaton, a blazing star, or a whirling nebula, even the central or superuniverses, from the smallest to the largest material organizations, always is the physical pattern—the cosmic configuration—derived from the function of this triunity. This association consists of:

1. The Father-Son.
2. The Paradise Isle.
3. The Conjoint Actor.

Energy is organized by the cosmic agents of the Third Source and Center; energy is fashioned after the pattern of Paradise, the absolute materialization; but behind all of this ceaseless manipulation is the presence of the Father-Son, whose union first activated the Paradise pattern in the appearance of Havona concomitant with the birth of the Infinite Spirit, the Conjoint Actor.

In religious experience, creatures make contact with the God who is love, but such spiritual insight must never eclipse the intelligent recognition of the universe fact of the pattern which is Paradise. The Paradise personalities enlist the freewill adoration of all creatures by the compelling power of divine love and lead all such spirit-born personalities into the supernal delights of the unending service of the finaliter sons of God. The second triunity is the architect of the space stage whereon these transactions unfold; it determines the patterns of cosmic configuration.

Love may characterize the divinity of the first triunity, but pattern is the galactic manifestation of the second triunity. What the first triunity is to evolving personalities, the second triunity is to the evolving universes. Pattern and personality are two of the great manifestations of the acts of the First Source and Center; and no matter how difficult it may be to comprehend, it is nonetheless true that the power-pattern and the loving person are one and the same universal reality; the Paradise Isle and the Eternal Son are co-ordinate but antipodal revelations of the unfathomable nature of the Universal Father-Force.

The Third Triunity—the spirit-evolutional triunity. The entirety of spiritual manifestation has its beginning and end in this association, consisting of:

1. The Universal Father.
2. The Son-Spirit.
3. The Deity Absolute.

From spirit potency to Paradise spirit, all spirit finds reality expression in this triune association of the pure spirit essence of the Father, the active spirit values of the Son-Spirit, and the unlimited spirit potentials of the Deity Absolute. The existential values of spirit have their primordial genesis, complete manifestation, and final destiny in this triunity.

The Father exists before spirit; the Son-Spirit functions as active creative spirit; the Deity Absolute exists as all-encompassing spirit, even beyond spirit.

The Fourth Triunity—the triunity of energy infinity. Within this triunity there eternalizes the beginnings and the endings of all energy reality, from space potency to monota. This grouping embraces the following:

1. The Father-Spirit.
2. The Paradise Isle.
3. The Unqualified Absolute.

Paradise is the center of the force-energy activation of the cosmos—the universe position of the First Source and Center, the cosmic focal point of the Unqualified Absolute, and the source of all energy. Existentially present within this triunity is the energy potential of the cosmos-infinite, of which the grand universe and the master universe are only partial manifestations.

The fourth triunity absolutely controls the fundamental units of cosmic energy and releases them from the grasp of the Unqualified Absolute in direct proportion to the appearance in the experiential Deities of subabsolute capacity to control and stabilize the metamorphosing cosmos.

This triunity *is* force and energy. The endless possibilities of the Unqualified Absolute are centered around the absolutum of the Isle of Paradise, whence emanate the unimaginable agitations of the otherwise static quiescence of the Unqualified. And the endless throbbing of the material Paradise heart of the infinite cosmos beats in harmony with the unfathomable pattern and the unsearchable plan of the Infinite Energizer, the First Source and Center.

The Fifth Triunity—the triunity of reactive infinity. This association consists of:

1. The Universal Father.
2. The Universal Absolute.
3. The Unqualified Absolute.

This grouping yields the eternalization of the functional infinity realization of all that is actualizable within the domains of nondeity reality. This triunity manifests unlimited reactive capacity to the volitional, causative, tensional, and patternal actions and presences of the other triunities.

The Sixth Triunity—the triunity of cosmic-associated Deity. This grouping consists of:

1. The Universal Father.
2. The Deity Absolute.
3. The Universal Absolute.

This is the association of Deity-in-the-cosmos, the immanence of Deity in conjunction with the transcendence of Deity. This is the last outreach of divinity on the levels of infinity toward those realities which lie outside the domain of deified reality.

The Seventh Triunity—the triunity of infinite unity. This is the unity of infinity functionally manifest in time and eternity, the co-ordinate unification of actuals and potentials. This group consists of:

1. The Universal Father.
2. The Conjoint Actor.
3. The Universal Absolute.

The Conjoint Actor universally integrates the varying functional aspects of all actualized reality on all levels of manifestation, from finites through transcendentals and on to absolutes. The Universal Absolute perfectly compensates the differentials inherent in the varying aspects of all incomplete reality, from the limitless potentialities of active-volitional and causative Deity reality to the boundless possibilities of static, reactive, nondeity reality in the incomprehensible domains of the Unqualified Absolute.

As they function in this triunity, the Conjoint Actor and the Universal Absolute are alike responsive to Deity and to nondeity presences, as also is the First Source and Center, who in this relationship is to all intents and purposes conceptually indistinguishable from the I AM.

These approximations are sufficient to elucidate the concept of the triunities. Not knowing the ultimate level of the triunities, you cannot fully comprehend the first seven. While we do not deem it wise to attempt any further elaboration, we may state that there are fifteen triune associations of the First Source and Center, eight of which are unrevealed in these papers. These unrevealed associations are concerned with realities, actualities, and potentialities which are beyond the experiential level of supremacy.

The triunities are the functional balance wheel of infinity, the unification of the uniqueness of the Seven Infinity Absolutes. It is the existential presence of the triunities that enables the Father-I AM to experience functional infinity unity despite the diversification of infinity into seven Absolutes. The First Source and Center is the unifying member of all triunities; in him all things have their unqualified beginnings, eternal existences, and infinite destinies—"in him all things consist."

Although these associations cannot augment the infinity of the Father-I AM, they do appear to make possible the subinfinite and subabsolute manifestations of his reality. The seven triunities multiply versatility, eternalize new depths, deitize new values, disclose new potentialities, reveal new meanings; and all these diversified manifestations in time and space and in the eternal cosmos are existent in the hypothetical stasis of the original infinity of the I AM.

5. TRIODITIES

There are certain other triune relationships which are non-Father in constitution, but they are not real triunities, and they are always distinguished from the Father triunities. They are called variously, associate triunities, co-ordinate triunities, and *triodities.* They are consequential to the existence of the triunities. Two of these associations are constituted as follows:

The Triodity of Actuality. This triodity consists in the interrelationship of the three absolute actuals:

1. The Eternal Son.
2. The Paradise Isle.
3. The Conjoint Actor.

The Eternal Son is the absolute of spirit reality, the absolute personality. The Paradise Isle is the absolute of cosmic reality, the absolute pattern. The Conjoint Actor is the absolute of mind reality, the co-ordinate of absolute spirit reality, and the existential Deity synthesis of personality and power. This triune association eventuates the co-ordination of the sum total of actualized reality—spirit, cosmic, or mindal. It is unqualified in actuality.

The Triodity of Potentiality. This triodity consists in the association of the three Absolutes of potentiality:

1. The Deity Absolute.
2. The Universal Absolute.
3. The Unqualified Absolute.

Thus are interassociated the infinity reservoirs of all latent energy reality—spirit, mindal, or cosmic. This association yields the integration of all latent energy reality. It is infinite in potential.

As the triunities are primarily concerned with the functional unification of infinity, so are triodities involved in the cosmic appearance of experiential Deities. The triunities are indirectly concerned, but the triodities are directly concerned, in the experiential Deities—Supreme, Ultimate, and Absolute. They appear in the emerging power-personality synthesis of the Supreme Being. And to the time creatures of space the Supreme Being is a revelation of the unity of the I AM.

[Presented by a Melchizedek of Nebadon.]

PAPER 105

DEITY AND REALITY

TO EVEN high orders of universe intelligences infinity is only partially comprehensible, and the finality of reality is only relatively understandable. The human mind, as it seeks to penetrate the eternity-mystery of the origin and destiny of all that is called *real,* may helpfully approach the problem by conceiving eternity-infinity as an almost limitless ellipse which is produced by one absolute cause, and which functions throughout this universal circle of endless diversification, ever seeking some absolute and infinite potential of destiny.

When the mortal intellect attempts to grasp the concept of reality totality, such a finite mind is face to face with infinity-reality; reality totality *is* infinity and therefore can never be fully comprehended by any mind that is subinfinite in concept capacity.

The human mind can hardly form an adequate concept of eternity existences, and without such comprehension it is impossible to portray even our concepts of reality totality. Nevertheless, we may attempt such a presentation, although we are fully aware that our concepts must be subjected to profound distortion in the process of translation-modification to the comprehension level of mortal mind.

1. THE PHILOSOPHIC CONCEPT OF THE I AM

Absolute primal causation in infinity the philosophers of the universes attribute to the Universal Father functioning as the infinite, the eternal, and the absolute I AM.

There are many elements of danger attendant upon the presentation to the mortal intellect of this idea of an infinite I AM since this concept is so remote from human experiential understanding as to involve serious distortion of meanings and misconception of values. Nevertheless, the philosophic concept of the I AM does afford finite beings some basis for an attempted approach to the partial comprehension of absolute origins and infinite destinies. But in all our attempts to elucidate the genesis and fruition of reality, let it be made clear that this concept of the I AM is, in all personality meanings and values, synonymous with the First Person of Deity, the Universal Father of all personalities. But this postulate of the I AM is not so clearly identifiable in undeified realms of universal reality.

The I AM is the Infinite; the I AM is also infinity. From the sequential, time viewpoint, all reality has its origin in the infinite I AM, whose solitary existence in past infinite eternity must be a finite creature's premier philosophic postulate. The concept of the I AM connotes *unqualified infinity,* the undifferentiated reality of all that could ever be in all of an infinite eternity.

As an existential concept the I AM is neither deified nor undeified, neither actual nor potential, neither personal nor impersonal, neither static nor dynamic. No qualification can be applied to the Infinite except to state that the I AM *is.* The philosophic postulate of the I AM is one universe concept which is somewhat more difficult of comprehension than that of the Unqualified Absolute.

To the finite mind there simply must be a beginning, and though there never was a real beginning to reality, still there are certain source relationships which reality manifests to infinity. The prereality, primordial, eternity situation may be thought of something like this: At some infinitely distant, hypothetical, past-eternity moment, the I AM may be conceived as both thing and no thing, as both cause and effect, as both volition and response. At this hypothetical eternity moment there is no differentiation throughout all infinity. Infinity is filled by the Infinite; the Infinite encompasses infinity. This is the hypothetical static moment of eternity; actuals are still contained within their potentials, and potentials have not yet appeared within the infinity of the I AM. But even in this conjectured situation we must assume the existence of the possibility of self-will.

Ever remember that man's comprehension of the Universal Father is a personal experience. God, as your spiritual Father, is comprehensible to you and to all other mortals; but *your experiential worshipful concept of the Universal Father must always be less than your philosophic postulate of the infinity of the First Source and Center, the I AM*. When we speak of the Father, we mean God as he is understandable by his creatures both high and low, but there is much more of Deity which is not comprehensible to universe creatures. God, your Father and my Father, is that phase of the Infinite which we perceive in our personalities as an actual experiential reality, but the I AM ever remains as our hypothesis of all that we feel is unknowable of the First Source and Center. And even that hypothesis probably falls far short of the unfathomed infinity of original reality.

The universe of universes, with its innumerable host of inhabiting personalities, is a vast and complex organism, but the First Source and Center is infinitely more complex than the universes and personalities which have become real in response to his willful mandates. When you stand in awe of the magnitude of the master universe, pause to consider that even this inconceivable creation can be no more than a partial revelation of the Infinite.

Infinity is indeed remote from the experience level of mortal comprehension, but even in this age on Urantia your concepts of infinity are growing, and they will continue to grow throughout your endless careers stretching onward into future eternity. Unqualified infinity is meaningless to the finite creature, but infinity is capable of self-limitation and is susceptible of reality expression to all levels of universe existences. And the face which the Infinite turns toward all universe personalities is the face of a Father, the Universal Father of love.

2. THE I AM AS TRIUNE AND AS SEVENFOLD

In considering the genesis of reality, ever bear in mind that all absolute reality is from eternity and is without beginning of existence. By absolute reality we refer to the three existential persons of Deity, the Isle of Paradise, and the three Absolutes. These seven realities are co-ordinately eternal, notwithstanding that we resort to time-space language in presenting their sequential origins to human beings.

In following the chronological portrayal of the origins of reality, there must be a postulated theoretical moment of "first" volitional expression and "first" repercussional reaction within the I AM. In our attempts to portray the genesis and generation of reality, this stage may be conceived as the self-differentiation of *The Infinite One* from *The Infinitude,* but the postulation of this dual relationship must always be expanded to a triune conception by the recognition of the eternal continuum of *The Infinity,* the I AM.

This self-metamorphosis of the I AM culminates in the multiple differentiation of deified reality and of undeified reality, of potential and actual reality, and of certain other realities that can hardly be so classified. These differentiations of the theoretical monistic I AM are eternally integrated by simultaneous relationships arising within the same I AM—the prepotential, preactual, prepersonal, monothetic prereality which, though infinite, is revealed as absolute in the presence of the First Source and Center and as personality in the limitless love of the Universal Father.

By these internal metamorphoses the I AM is establishing the basis for a sevenfold self-relationship. The philosophic (time) concept of the solitary I AM and the transitional (time) concept of the I AM as triune can now be enlarged to encompass the I AM as sevenfold. This sevenfold—or seven phase—nature may be best suggested in relation to the Seven Absolutes of Infinity:

1. *The Universal Father.* I AM father of the Eternal Son. This is the primal personality relationship of actualities. The absolute personality of the Son makes absolute the fact of God's fatherhood and establishes the potential sonship of all personalities. This relationship establishes the personality of the Infinite and consummates its spiritual revelation in the personality of the Original Son. This phase of the I AM is partially experiencible on spiritual levels even by mortals who, while yet in the flesh, may worship our Father.

2. *The Universal Controller.* I AM cause of eternal Paradise. This is the primal impersonal relationship of actualities, the original nonspiritual association. The Universal Father is God-as-love; the Universal Controller is God-as-pattern. This relationship establishes the potential of form—configuration—and determines the master pattern of impersonal and nonspiritual relationship—the master pattern from which all copies are made.

3. *The Universal Creator.* I AM one with the Eternal Son. This union of the Father and the Son (in the presence of Paradise) initiates the creative cycle, which is consummated in the appearance of conjoint personality and the eternal universe. From the finite mortal's viewpoint, reality has its true beginnings with the eternity appearance of the Havona creation. This creative act of Deity is by and through the God of Action, who is in essence the unity of the Father-Son manifested on and to all levels of the actual. Therefore is divine creativity unfailingly characterized by unity, and this unity is the outward reflection of the absolute oneness of the duality of the Father-Son and of the Trinity of the Father-Son-Spirit.

4. *The Infinite Upholder.* I AM self-associative. This is the primordial association of the statics and potentials of reality. In this relationship, all qualifieds and unqualifieds are compensated. This phase of the I AM is best understood as the Universal Absolute—the unifier of the Deity and the Unqualified Absolutes.

5. *The Infinite Potential.* I AM self-qualified. This is the infinity bench mark bearing eternal witness to the volitional self-limitation of the I AM by virtue of which there was achieved threefold self-expression and self-revelation. This phase of the I AM is usually understood as the Deity Absolute.

6. *The Infinite Capacity.* I AM static-reactive. This is the endless matrix, the possibility for all future cosmic expansion. This phase of the I AM is perhaps best conceived as the supergravity presence of the Unqualified Absolute.

7. *The Universal One of Infinity.* I AM as I AM. This is the stasis or self-relationship of Infinity, the eternal fact of infinity-reality and the universal truth of reality-infinity. In so far as this relationship is discernible as personality, it is revealed to the universes in the divine Father of all personality—even of absolute personality. In so far as this relationship is impersonally expressible, it is contacted by the universe as the absolute coherence of pure energy and of pure spirit in the presence of the Universal Father. In so far as this relationship is conceivable as an absolute, it is revealed in the primacy of the First Source and Center; in him we all live and move and have our being, from the creatures of space to the citizens of Paradise; and this is just as true of the master universe as of the infinitesimal ultimaton, just as true of what is to be as of that which is and of what has been.

3. THE SEVEN ABSOLUTES OF INFINITY

The seven prime relationships within the I AM eternalize as the Seven Absolutes of Infinity. But though we may portray reality origins and infinity differentiation by a sequential narrative, in fact all seven Absolutes are unqualifiedly and co-ordinately eternal. It may be necessary for mortal minds to conceive of their beginnings, but always should this conception be overshadowed by the realization that the seven Absolutes had no beginning; they are eternal and as such have always been. The seven Absolutes are the premise of reality. They have been described in these papers as follows:

1. *The First Source and Center.* First Person of Deity and primal nondeity pattern, God, the Universal Father, creator, controller, and upholder; universal love, eternal spirit, and infinite energy; potential of all potentials and source of all actuals; stability of all statics and dynamism of all change; source of pattern and Father of persons. Collectively, all seven Absolutes equivalate to infinity, but the Universal Father himself actually is infinite.

2. *The Second Source and Center.* Second Person of Deity, the Eternal and Original Son; the absolute personality realities of the I AM and the basis for the realization-revelation of "I AM personality." No personality can hope to attain the Universal Father except through his Eternal Son; neither can

personality attain to spirit levels of existence apart from the action and aid of this absolute pattern for all personalities. In the Second Source and Center spirit is unqualified while personality is absolute.

3. *The Paradise Source and Center.* Second nondeity pattern, the eternal Isle of Paradise; the basis for the realization-revelation of "I AM force" and the foundation for the establishment of gravity control throughout the universes. Regarding all actualized, nonspiritual, impersonal, and nonvolitional reality, Paradise is the absolute of patterns. Just as spirit energy is related to the Universal Father through the absolute personality of the Mother-Son, so is all cosmic energy grasped in the gravity control of the First Source and Center through the absolute pattern of the Paradise Isle. Paradise is not in space; space exists relative to Paradise, and the chronicity of motion is determined through Paradise relationship. The eternal Isle is absolutely at rest; all other organized and organizing energy is in eternal motion; in all space, only the presence of the Unqualified Absolute is quiescent, and the Unqualified is co-ordinate with Paradise. Paradise exists at the focus of space, the Unqualified pervades it, and all relative existence has its being within this domain.

4. *The Third Source and Center.* Third Person of Deity, the Conjoint Actor; infinite integrator of Paradise cosmic energies with the spirit energies of the Eternal Son; perfect co-ordinator of the motives of will and the mechanics of force; unifier of all actual and actualizing reality. Through the ministrations of his manifold children the Infinite Spirit reveals the mercy of the Eternal Son while at the same time functioning as the infinite manipulator, forever weaving the pattern of Paradise into the energies of space. This selfsame Conjoint Actor, this God of Action, is the perfect expression of the limitless plans and purposes of the Father-Son while functioning himself as the source of mind and the bestower of intellect upon the creatures of a far-flung cosmos.

5. *The Deity Absolute.* The causational, potentially personal possibilities of universal reality, the totality of all Deity potential. The Deity Absolute is the purposive qualifier of the unqualified, absolute, and nondeity realities. The Deity Absolute is the qualifier of the absolute and the absolutizer of the qualified—the destiny inceptor.

6. *The Unqualified Absolute.* Static, reactive, and abeyant; the unrevealed cosmic infinity of the I AM; totality of nondeified reality and finality of all nonpersonal potential. Space limits the function of the Unqualified, but the presence of the Unqualified is without limit, infinite. There is a concept periphery to the master universe, but the presence of the Unqualified is limitless; even eternity cannot exhaust the boundless quiescence of this nondeity Absolute.

7. *The Universal Absolute.* Unifier of the deified and the undeified; correlator of the absolute and the relative. The Universal Absolute (being static, potential, and associative) compensates the tension between the ever-existent and the uncompleted.

The Seven Absolutes of Infinity constitute the beginnings of reality. As mortal minds would regard it, the First Source and Center would appear to be antecedent to all absolutes. But such a postulate, however helpful, is invalidated by the eternity coexistence of the Son, the Spirit, the three Absolutes, and the Paradise Isle.

It is a *truth* that the Absolutes are manifestations of the I AM-First Source and Center; it is a *fact* that these Absolutes never had a beginning but are coordinate eternals with the First Source and Center. The relationships of absolutes in eternity cannot always be presented without involving paradoxes in the language of time and in the concept patterns of space. But regardless of any confusion concerning the origin of the Seven Absolutes of Infinity, it is both fact and truth that all reality is predicated upon their eternity existence and infinity relationships.

4. UNITY, DUALITY, AND TRIUNITY

The universe philosophers postulate the eternity existence of the I AM as the primal source of all reality. And concomitant therewith they postulate the self-segmentation of the I AM into the primary self-relationships—the seven phases of infinity. And simultaneous with this assumption is the third postulate—the eternity appearance of the Seven Absolutes of Infinity and the eternalization of the duality association of the seven phases of the I AM and these seven Absolutes.

The self-revelation of the I AM thus proceeds from static self through self-segmentation and self-relationship to absolute relationships, relationships with self-derived Absolutes. Duality becomes thus existent in the eternal association of the Seven Absolutes of Infinity with the sevenfold infinity of the self-segmented phases of the self-revealing I AM. These dual relationships, eternalizing to the universes as the seven Absolutes, eternalize the basic foundations for all universe reality.

It has been sometime stated that unity begets duality, that duality begets triunity, and that triunity is the eternal ancestor of all things. There are, indeed, three great classes of primordial relationships, and they are:

1. *Unity relationships.* Relations existent within the I AM as the unity thereof is conceived as a threefold and then as a sevenfold self-differentiation.

2. *Duality relationships.* Relations existent between the I AM as sevenfold and the Seven Absolutes of Infinity.

3. *Triunity relationships.* These are the functional associations of the Seven Absolutes of Infinity.

Triunity relationships arise upon duality foundations because of the inevitability of Absolute interassociation. Such triunity associations eternalize the potential of all reality; they encompass both deified and undeified reality.

The I AM is unqualified infinity as *unity.* The dualities eternalize reality *foundations.* The triunities eventuate the realization of infinity as universal *function.*

Pre-existentials become existential in the seven Absolutes, and existentials become functional in the triunities, the basic association of Absolutes. And concomitant with the eternalization of the triunities the universe stage is set—the potentials are existent and the actuals are present—and the fullness of eternity witnesses the diversification of cosmic energy, the outspreading of Paradise spirit, and the endowment of mind together with the bestowal of personality, by virtue of which all of these Deity and Paradise derivatives are unified in experience on the creature level and by other techniques on the supercreature level.

5. PROMULGATION OF FINITE REALITY

Just as the original diversification of the I AM must be attributed to inherent and self-contained volition, so must the promulgation of finite reality be ascribed to the volitional acts of Paradise Deity and to the repercussional adjustments of the functional triunities.

Prior to the deitization of the finite, it would appear that all reality diversification took place on absolute levels; but the volitional act promulgating finite reality connotes a qualification of absoluteness and implies the appearance of relativities.

While we present this narrative as a sequence and portray the historic appearance of the finite as a direct derivative of the absolute, it should be borne in mind that transcendentals both preceded and succeeded all that is finite. Transcendental ultimates are, in relation to the finite, both causal and consummational.

Finite possibility is inherent in the Infinite, but the transmutation of possibility to probability and inevitability must be attributed to the self-existent free will of the First Source and Center, activating all triunity associations. Only the infinity of the Father's will could ever have so qualified the absolute level of existence as to eventuate an ultimate or to create a finite.

With the appearance of relative and qualified reality there comes into being a new cycle of reality—the growth cycle—a majestic downsweep from the heights of infinity to the domain of the finite, forever swinging inward to Paradise and Deity, always seeking those high destinies commensurate with an infinity source.

These inconceivable transactions mark the beginning of universe history, mark the coming into existence of time itself. To a creature, the beginning of the finite *is* the genesis of reality; as viewed by creature mind, there is no actuality conceivable prior to the finite. This newly appearing finite reality exists in two original phases:

1. *Primary maximums,* the supremely perfect reality, the Havona type of universe and creature.

2. *Secondary maximums,* the supremely perfected reality, the superuniverse type of creature and creation.

These, then, are the two original manifestations: the constitutively perfect and the evolutionally perfected. The two are co-ordinate in eternity relationships, but within the limits of time they are seemingly different. A time factor means growth to that which grows; secondary finites grow; hence those that are growing must appear as incomplete in time. But these differences, which are so important this side of Paradise, are nonexistent in eternity.

We speak of the perfect and the perfected as primary and secondary maximums, but there is still another type: Trinitizing and other relationships between the primaries and the secondaries result in the appearance of *tertiary maximums* —things, meanings, and values that are neither perfect nor perfected yet are co-ordinate with both ancestral factors.

6. REPERCUSSIONS OF FINITE REALITY

The entire promulgation of finite existences represents a transference from potentials to actuals within the absolute associations of functional infinity. Of the many repercussions to creative actualization of the finite, there may be cited:

1. *The deity response,* the appearance of the three levels of experiential supremacy: the actuality of personal-spirit supremacy in Havona, the potential for personal-power supremacy in the grand universe to be, and the capacity for some unknown function of experiential mind acting on some level of supremacy in the future master universe.

2. *The universe response* involved an activation of the architectural plans for the superuniverse space level, and this evolution is still progressing throughout the physical organization of the seven superuniverses.

3. *The creature repercussion* to finite-reality promulgation resulted in the appearance of perfect beings on the order of the eternal inhabitants of Havona and of perfected evolutionary ascenders from the seven superuniverses. But to attain perfection as an evolutionary (time-creative) experience implies something other-than-perfection as a point of departure. Thus arises imperfection in the evolutionary creations. And this is the origin of potential evil. Misadaptation, disharmony, and conflict, all these things are inherent in evolutionary growth, from physical universes to personal creatures.

4. *The divinity response* to the imperfection inherent in the time lag of evolution is disclosed in the compensating presence of God the Sevenfold, by whose activities that which is perfecting is integrated with both the perfect and the perfected. This time lag is inseparable from evolution, which is creativity in time. Because of it, as well as for other reasons, the almighty power of the Supreme is predicated on the divinity successes of God the Sevenfold. This time lag makes possible creature participation in divine creation by permitting creature personalities to become partners with Deity in the attainment of maximum development. Even the material mind of the mortal creature thus becomes partner with the divine Adjuster in the dualization of the immortal soul. God the Sevenfold also provides techniques of compensation for the experiential limitations of inherent perfection as well as compensating the preascension limitations of imperfection.

7. EVENTUATION OF TRANSCENDENTALS

Transcendentals are subinfinite and subabsolute but superfinite and supercreatural. Transcendentals eventuate as an integrating level correlating the supervalues of absolutes with the maximum values of finites. From the creature standpoint, that which is transcendental would appear to have eventuated as a consequence of the finite; from the eternity viewpoint, in anticipation of the finite; and there are those who have considered it as a "pre-echo" of the finite.

That which is transcendental is not necessarily nondevelopmental, but it is superevolutional in the finite sense; neither is it nonexperiential, but it is superexperience as such is meaningful to creatures. Perhaps the best illustration of such a paradox is the central universe of perfection: It is hardly absolute—only the Paradise Isle is truly absolute in the "materialized" sense. Neither is it a finite evolutionary creation as are the seven superuniverses. Havona is eternal but not changeless in the sense of being a universe of nongrowth. It is inhabited by creatures (Havona natives) who never were actually created, for they are eternally existent. Havona thus illustrates something which is not exactly finite nor yet absolute. Havona further acts as a buffer between absolute Paradise and finite creations, still further illustrating the function of transcendentals. But Havona itself is not a transcendental—it is Havona.

As the Supreme is associated with finites, so the Ultimate is identified with transcendentals. But though we thus compare Supreme and Ultimate, they differ by something more than degree; the difference is also a matter of quality. The Ultimate is something more than a super-Supreme projected on the transcendental level. The Ultimate is all of that, but more: The Ultimate is an eventuation of new Deity realities, the qualification of new phases of the theretofore unqualified.

Among those realities which are associated with the transcendental level are the following:

1. The Deity presence of the Ultimate.
2. The concept of the master universe.
3. The Architects of the Master Universe.
4. The two orders of Paradise force organizers.
5. Certain modifications in space potency.
6. Certain values of spirit.
7. Certain meanings of mind.
8. Absonite qualities and realities.
9. Omnipotence, omniscience, and omnipresence.
10. Space.

The universe in which we now live may be thought of as existing on finite, transcendental, and absolute levels. This is the cosmic stage on which is enacted the endless drama of personality performance and energy metamorphosis.

And all of these manifold realities are unified *absolutely* by the several triunities, *functionally* by the Architects of the Master Universe, and *relatively* by the Seven Master Spirits, the subsupreme co-ordinators of the divinity of God the Sevenfold.

God the Sevenfold represents the personality and divinity revelation of the Universal Father to creatures of both maximum and submaximum status, but there are other sevenfold relationships of the First Source and Center which do not pertain to the manifestation of the divine spiritual ministry of the God who is spirit.

In the eternity of the past the forces of the Absolutes, the spirits of the Deities, and the personalities of the Gods stirred in response to the primordial self-will of self-existent self-will. In this universe age we are all witnessing the stupendous repercussions of the far-flung cosmic panorama of the subabsolute manifestations of the limitless potentials of all these realities. And it is altogether possible that the continued diversification of the original reality of the First Source and

Center may proceed onward and outward throughout age upon age, on and on, into the faraway and inconceivable stretches of absolute infinity.

[Presented by a Melchizedek of Nebadon.]

PAPER 106

UNIVERSE LEVELS OF REALITY

IT IS not enough that the ascending mortal should know something of the relations of Deity to the genesis and manifestations of cosmic reality; he should also comprehend something of the relationships existing between himself and the numerous levels of existential and experiential realities, of potential and actual realities. Man's terrestrial orientation, his cosmic insight, and his spiritual directionization are all enhanced by a better comprehension of universe realities and their techniques of interassociation, integration, and unification.

The present grand universe and the emerging master universe are made up of many forms and phases of reality which, in turn, are existent on several levels of functional activity. These manifold existents and latents have been previously suggested in these papers, and they are now grouped for conceptual convenience in the following categories:

1. *Incomplete finites.* This is the present status of the ascending creatures of the grand universe, the present status of Urantia mortals. This level embraces creature existence from the planetary human up to, but not including, destiny attainers. It pertains to universes from early physical beginnings up to, but not including, settlement in light and life. This level constitutes the present periphery of creative activity in time and space. It appears to be moving outward from Paradise, for the closing of the present universe age, which will witness the grand universe attainment of light and life, will also and surely witness the appearance of some new order of developmental growth in the first outer space level.

2. *Maximum finites.* This is the present status of all experiential creatures who have attained destiny—destiny as revealed within the scope of the present universe age. Even universes can attain to the maximum of status, both spiritually and physically. But the term "maximum" is itself a relative term—maximum in relation to what? And that which is maximum, seemingly final, in the present universe age may be no more than a real beginning in terms of the ages to come. Some phases of Havona appear to be on the maximum order.

3. *Transcendentals.* This superfinite level (antecedently) follows finite progression. It implies the prefinite genesis of finite beginnings and the postfinite significance of all apparent finite endings or destinies. Much of Paradise-Havona appears to be on the transcendental order.

4. *Ultimates.* This level encompasses that which is of master universe significance and impinges on the destiny level of the completed master universe. Paradise-Havona (especially the circuit of the Father's worlds) is in many respects of ultimate significance.

5. *Coabsolutes.* This level implies the projection of experientials upon a supermaster universe field of creative expression.

6. *Absolutes.* This level connotes the eternity presence of the seven existential Absolutes. It may also involve some degree of associative experiential attainment, but if so, we do not understand how, perhaps through the contact potential of personality.

7. *Infinity.* This level is pre-existential and postexperiential. Unqualified unity of infinity is a hypothetical reality before all beginnings and after all destinies.

These levels of reality are convenient compromise symbolizations of the present universe age and for the mortal perspective. There are a number of other ways of looking at reality from other-than-mortal perspective and from the standpoint of other universe ages. Thus it should be recognized that the concepts herewith presented are entirely relative, relative in the sense of being conditioned and limited by:

1. The limitations of mortal language.
2. The limitations of the mortal mind.
3. The limited development of the seven superuniverses.
4. Your ignorance of the six prime purposes of superuniverse development which do not pertain to the mortal ascent to Paradise.
5. Your inability to grasp even a partial eternity viewpoint.
6. The impossibility of depicting cosmic evolution and destiny in relation to all universe ages, not just in regard to the present age of the evolutionary unfolding of the seven superuniverses.
7. The inability of any creature to grasp what is really meant by pre-existentials or by postexperientials—that which lies before beginnings and after destinies.

Reality growth is conditioned by the circumstances of the successive universe ages. The central universe underwent no evolutionary change in the Havona age, but in the present epochs of the superuniverse age it is undergoing certain progressive changes induced by co-ordination with the evolutionary superuniverses. The seven superuniverses, now evolving, will sometime attain the settled status of light and life, will attain the growth limit for the present universe age. But beyond doubt, the next age, the age of the first outer space level, will release the superuniverses from the destiny limitations of the present age. Repletion is continually being superimposed upon completion.

These are some of the limitations which we encounter in attempting to present a unified concept of the cosmic growth of things, meanings, and values and of their synthesis on ever-ascending levels of reality.

1. PRIMARY ASSOCIATION OF FINITE FUNCTIONALS

The primary or spirit-origin phases of finite reality find immediate expression on creature levels as perfect personalities and on universe levels as the perfect Havona creation. Even experiential Deity is thus expressed in the spirit person of God the Supreme in Havona. But the secondary, evolutionary, time-and-matter-conditioned phases of the finite become cosmically integrated only as a result of growth and attainment. Eventually all secondary or perfecting finites are to attain a level equal to that of primary perfection, but such destiny is subject to a time delay, a constitutive superuniverse qualification which is not genetically found in the central creation. (We know of the existence of tertiary finites, but the technique of their integration is as yet unrevealed.)

This superuniverse time lag, this obstacle to perfection attainment, provides for creature participation in evolutionary growth. It thus makes it possible for the creature to enter into partnership with the Creator in the evolution of that selfsame creature. And during these times of expanding growth the incomplete is correlated with the perfect through the ministry of God the Sevenfold.

God the Sevenfold signifies the recognition by Paradise Deity of the barriers of time in the evolutionary universes of space. No matter how remote from Paradise, how deep in space, a material survival personality may take origin, God the Sevenfold will be found there present and engaged in the loving and merciful ministry of truth, beauty, and goodness to such an incomplete, struggling, and evolutionary creature. The divinity ministry of the Sevenfold reaches inward through the Eternal Son to the Paradise Father and outward through the Ancients of Days to the universe Fathers—the Creator Sons.

Man, being personal and ascending by spiritual progression, finds the personal and spiritual divinity of the Sevenfold Deity; but there are other phases of the Sevenfold which are not concerned with the progression of personality. The divinity aspects of this Deity grouping are at present integrated in the liaison between the Seven Master Spirits and the Conjoint Actor, but they are destined to be eternally unified in the emerging personality of the Supreme Being. The other phases of the Sevenfold Deity are variously integrated in the present universe age, but all are likewise destined to be unified in the Supreme. The Sevenfold, in all phases, is the source of the relative unity of the functional reality of the present grand universe.

2. SECONDARY SUPREME FINITE INTEGRATION

As God the Sevenfold functionally co-ordinates finite evolution, so does the Supreme Being eventually synthesize destiny attainment. The Supreme Being is the deity culmination of grand universe evolution—physical evolution around a spirit nucleus and eventual dominance of the spirit nucleus over the encircling and whirling domains of physical evolution. And all of this takes place in accordance with the mandates of personality: Paradise personality in the highest sense, Creator personality in the universe sense, mortal personality in the human sense, Supreme personality in the culminating or experiential totaling sense.

The concept of the Supreme must provide for the differential recognition of spirit person, evolutionary power, and power-personality synthesis—the unification of evolutionary power with, and its dominance by, spirit personality.

Spirit, in the last analysis, comes from Paradise through Havona. Energy-matter seemingly evolves in the depths of space and is organized as power by the children of the Infinite Spirit in conjunction with the Creator Sons of God. And all of this is experiential; it is a transaction in time and space involving a wide range of living beings including even Creator divinities and evolutionary creatures.

The power mastery of the Creator divinities in the grand universe slowly expands to encompass the evolutionary settling and stabilizing of the time-space creations, and this is the flowering of the experiential power of God the Sevenfold. It encompasses the whole gamut of divinity attainment in time and space from the Adjuster bestowals of the Universal Father to the life bestowals of the Paradise Sons. This is earned power, demonstrated power, experiential power; it stands in contrast to the eternity power, the unfathomable power, the existential power of the Paradise Deities.

This experiential power arising out of the divinity achievements of God the Sevenfold itself manifests the cohesive qualities of divinity by synthesizing—totalizing—as the almighty power of the attained experiential mastery of the evolving creations. And this almighty power in turn finds spirit-personality cohesion on the pilot sphere of the outer belt of Havona worlds in union with the spirit personality of the Havona presence of God the Supreme. Thus does experiential Deity culminate the long evolutionary struggle by investing the power product of time and space with the spirit presence and divine personality resident in the central creation.

Thus does the Supreme Being eventually attain to the embrace of all of everything evolving in time and space while investing these qualities with spirit personality. Since creatures, even mortals, are personality participants in this majestic transaction, so do they certainly attain the capacity to know the Supreme and to perceive the Supreme as true children of such an evolutionary Deity.

Michael of Nebadon is like the Paradise Father because he shares his Paradise perfection; so will evolutionary mortals sometime attain to kinship with the experiential Supreme, for they will truly share his evolutionary perfection.

God the Supreme is experiential; therefore is he completely experiencible. The existential realities of the seven Absolutes are not perceivable by the technique of experience; only the *personality realities* of the Father, Son, and Spirit can be grasped by the personality of the finite creature in the prayer-worship attitude.

Within the completed power-personality synthesis of the Supreme Being there will be associated all of the absoluteness of the several triodities which could be so associated, and this majestic personality of evolution will be experientially attainable and understandable by all finite personalities. When ascenders attain the postulated seventh stage of spirit existence, they will therein experience the realization of a new meaning-value of the absoluteness and infinity of the triodities as such is revealed on subabsolute levels in the Supreme Being, who is experiencible. But the attainment of these stages of maximum development will probably await the co-ordinate settling of the entire grand universe in light and life.

3. TRANSCENDENTAL TERTIARY REALITY ASSOCIATION

The absonite architects eventuate the plan; the Supreme Creators bring it into existence; the Supreme Being will consummate its fullness as it was time created by the Supreme Creators, and as it was space forecast by the Master Architects.

During the present universe age the administrative co-ordination of the master universe is the function of the Architects of the Master Universe. But the appearance of the Almighty Supreme at the termination of the present universe age will signify that the evolutionary finite has attained the first stage of experiential destiny. This happening will certainly lead to the completed function of the first experiential Trinity—the union of the Supreme Creators, the Supreme Being, and the Architects of the Master Universe. This Trinity is destined to effect the further evolutionary integration of the master creation.

The Paradise Trinity is truly one of infinity, and no Trinity can possibly be infinite that does not include this original Trinity. But the original Trinity is an eventuality of the exclusive association of absolute Deities; subabsolute beings had nothing to do with this primal association. The subsequently appearing and experiential Trinities embrace the contributions of even creature personalities. Certainly this is true of the Trinity Ultimate, wherein the very presence of the Master Creator Sons among the Supreme Creator members thereof betokens the concomitant presence of actual and bona fide creature experience *within* this Trinity association.

The first experiential Trinity provides for group attainment of ultimate eventualities. Group associations are enabled to anticipate, even to transcend, individual capacities; and this is true even beyond the finite level. In the ages to come, after the seven superuniverses have been settled in light and life, the Corps of the Finality will doubtless be promulgating the purposes of the Paradise Deities as they are dictated by the Trinity Ultimate, and as they are power-personality unified in the Supreme Being.

Throughout all the gigantic universe developments of past and future eternity, we detect the expansion of the comprehensible elements of the Universal Father. As the I AM, we philosophically postulate his permeation of total infinity, but no creature is able experientially to encompass such a postulate. As the universes expand, and as gravity and love reach out into time-organizing space, we are able to understand more and more of the First Source and Center. We observe gravity action penetrating the space presence of the Unqualified Absolute, and we detect spirit creatures evolving and expanding within the divinity presence of the Deity Absolute while both cosmic and spirit evolution are by mind and experience unifying on finite deity levels as the Supreme Being and are co-ordinating on transcendental levels as the Trinity Ultimate.

4. ULTIMATE QUARTAN INTEGRATION

The Paradise Trinity certainly co-ordinates in the ultimate sense but functions in this respect as a self-qualified absolute; the experiential Trinity Ultimate co-ordinates the transcendental as a transcendental. In the eternal future this experiential Trinity will, through augmenting unity, further activate the eventuating presence of Ultimate Deity.

While the Trinity Ultimate is destined to co-ordinate the master creation, God the Ultimate is the transcendental power-personalization of the directionization of the entire master universe. The completed eventuation of the Ultimate implies the completion of the master creation and connotes the full emergence of this transcendental Deity.

What changes will be inaugurated by the full emergence of the Ultimate we do not know. But as the Supreme is now spiritually and personally present in Havona, so also is the Ultimate there present but in the absonite and superpersonal sense. And you have been informed of the existence of the Qualified Vicegerents of the Ultimate, though you have not been informed of their present whereabouts or function.

But irrespective of the administrative repercussions attendant upon the emergence of Ultimate Deity, the personal values of his transcendental divinity will be experiencible by all personalities who have been participants in the actualization of this Deity level. Transcendence of the finite can lead only to ultimate attainment. God the Ultimate exists in transcendence of time and space but is nonetheless subabsolute notwithstanding inherent capacity for functional association with absolutes.

5. COABSOLUTE OR FIFTH-PHASE ASSOCIATION

The Ultimate is the apex of transcendental reality even as the Supreme is the capstone of evolutionary-experiential reality. And the actual emergence of these two experiential Deities lays the foundation for the second experiential Trinity. This is the Trinity Absolute, the union of God the Supreme, God the Ultimate, and the unrevealed Consummator of Universe Destiny. And this Trinity has theoretical capacity to activate the Absolutes of potentiality—Deity, Universal, and Unqualified. But the completed formation of this Trinity Absolute could take place only after the completed evolution of the entire master universe, from Havona to the fourth and outermost space level.

It should be made clear that these experiential Trinities are correlative, not only of the personality qualities of experiential Divinity, but also of all the other-than-personal qualities which characterize their attained Deity unity. While this presentation deals primarily with the personal phases of the unification of the cosmos, it is nonetheless true that the impersonal aspects of the universe of universes are likewise destined to undergo unification as is illustrated by the power-personality synthesis now going on in connection with the evolution of the Supreme Being. The spirit-personal qualities of the Supreme are inseparable from the power prerogatives of the Almighty, and both are complemented by the unknown potential of Supreme Mind. Neither can God the Ultimate as a person be considered apart from the other-than-personal aspects of Ultimate Deity. And on the absolute level the Deity and the Unqualified Absolutes are inseparable and indistinguishable in the presence of the Universal Absolute.

Trinities are, in and of themselves, not personal, but neither do they contravene personality. Rather do they encompass it and correlate it, in a collective sense, with impersonal functions. Trinities are, then, always *deity* reality but never *personality* reality. The personality aspects of a trinity are inherent in its individual members, and as individual persons they are *not* that trinity. Only as a collective are they trinity; that *is* trinity. But always is trinity inclusive of all encompassed deity; trinity is deity unity.

The three Absolutes—Deity, Universal, and Unqualified—are not trinity, for all are not deity. Only the deified can become trinity; all other associations are triunities or triodities.

6. ABSOLUTE OR SIXTH-PHASE INTEGRATION

The present potential of the master universe is hardly absolute, though it may well be near-ultimate, and we deem it impossible to achieve the full revelation of absolute meaning-values within the scope of a subabsolute cosmos. We therefore encounter considerable difficulty in attempting to conceive of a total expression of the limitless possibilities of the three Absolutes or even in attempting to visualize the experiential personalization of God the Absolute on the now impersonal level of the Deity Absolute.

The space-stage of the master universe seems to be adequate for the actualization of the Supreme Being, for the formation and full function of the Trinity Ultimate, for the eventuation of God the Ultimate, and even for the inception of the Trinity Absolute. But our concepts regarding the full function of this second experiential Trinity seem to imply something beyond even the wide-spreading master universe.

If we assume a cosmos-infinite—some illimitable cosmos on beyond the master universe—and if we conceive that the final developments of the Absolute Trinity will take place out on such a superultimate stage of action, then it becomes possible to conjecture that the completed function of the Trinity Absolute will achieve final expression in the creations of infinity and will consummate the absolute actualization of *all* potentials. The integration and association of ever-enlarging segments of reality will approach absoluteness of status proportional to the inclusion of all reality within the segments thus associated.

Stated otherwise: The Trinity Absolute, as its name implies, is really absolute in total function. We do not know how an absolute function can achieve total expression on a qualified, limited, or otherwise restricted basis. Hence we must assume that any such totality function will be unconditioned (in potential). And it would also appear that the unconditioned would also be unlimited, at least from a qualitative standpoint, though we are not so sure regarding quantitative relationships.

Of this, however, we are certain: While the existential Paradise Trinity is infinite, and while the experiential Trinity Ultimate is subinfinite, the Trinity Absolute is not so easy to classify. Though experiential in genesis and constitution, it definitely impinges upon the existential Absolutes of potentiality.

While it is hardly profitable for the human mind to seek to grasp such faraway and superhuman concepts, we would suggest that the eternity action of the Trinity Absolute may be thought of as culminating in some kind of experientialization of the Absolutes of potentiality. This would appear to be a reasonable conclusion with respect to the Universal Absolute, if not the Unqualified Absolute; at least we know that the Universal Absolute is not only static and potential but also associative in the total Deity sense of those words. But in regard to the conceivable values of divinity and personality, these conjectured happenings imply the personalization of the Deity Absolute and the appearance of those superpersonal values and those ultrapersonal meanings inherent in the personality completion of God the Absolute—the third and last of the experiential Deities.

7. FINALITY OF DESTINY

Some of the difficulties in forming concepts of infinite reality integration are inherent in the fact that all such ideas embrace something of the finality of universal development, some kind of an experiential realization of all that could ever be. And it is inconceivable that quantitative infinity could ever be completely realized in finality. Always there must remain unexplored possibilities in the three potential Absolutes which no quantity of experiential development could ever exhaust. Eternity itself, though absolute, is not more than absolute.

Even a tentative concept of final integration is inseparable from the fruitions of unqualified eternity and is, therefore, practically nonrealizable at any conceivable future time.

Destiny is established by the volitional act of the Deities who constitute the Paradise Trinity; destiny is established in the vastness of the three great potentials whose absoluteness encompasses the possibilities of all future development; destiny is probably consummated by the act of the Consummator of Universe Destiny, and this act is probably involved with the Supreme and the Ultimate in the Trinity Absolute. Any experiential destiny can be at least partially comprehended by experiencing creatures; but a destiny which impinges on infinite existentials is hardly comprehensible. Finality destiny is an existential-experiential attainment which appears to involve the Deity Absolute. But the Deity Absolute stands in eternity relationship with the Unqualified Absolute by virtue of the Universal Absolute. And these three Absolutes, experiential in possibility, are actually existential and more, being limitless, timeless, spaceless, boundless, and measureless—truly infinite.

The improbability of goal attainment does not, however, prevent philosophical theorizing about such hypothetical destinies. The actualization of the Deity Absolute as an attainable absolute God may be practically impossible of realization; nevertheless, such a finality fruition remains a theoretical possibility. The involvement of the Unqualified Absolute in some inconceivable cosmos-infinite may be measurelessly remote in the futurity of endless eternity, but such a hypothesis is nonetheless valid. Mortals, morontians, spirits, finaliters, Transcendentalers, and others, together with the universes themselves and all other phases of reality, certainly do have a *potentially final destiny that is absolute in value;* but we doubt that any being or universe will ever completely attain all of the aspects of such a destiny.

No matter how much you may grow in Father comprehension, your mind will always be staggered by the unrevealed infinity of the Father-I AM, the unexplored vastness of which will always remain unfathomable and incomprehensible throughout all the cycles of eternity. No matter how much of God you may attain, there will always remain much more of him, the existence of which you will not even suspect. And we believe that this is just as true on transcendental levels as it is in the domains of finite existence. The quest for God is endless!

Such inability to attain God in a final sense should in no manner discourage universe creatures; indeed, you can and do attain Deity levels of the Sevenfold, the Supreme, and the Ultimate, which mean to you what the infinite realization of God the Father means to the Eternal Son and to the Conjoint Actor in their absolute status of eternity existence. Far from harassing the creature, the infinity of God should be the supreme assurance that throughout all endless futurity an ascending personality will have before him the possibilities of personality development and Deity association which even eternity will neither exhaust nor terminate.

To finite creatures of the grand universe the concept of the master universe seems to be well-nigh infinite, but doubtless the absonite architects thereof perceive its relatedness to future and unimagined developments within the unending I AM. Even space itself is but an ultimate condition, a condition of qualification *within* the relative absoluteness of the quiet zones of midspace.

At the inconceivably distant future eternity moment of the final completion of the entire master universe, no doubt we will all look back upon its entire history as only the beginning, simply the creation of certain finite and transcendental foundations for even greater and more enthralling metamorphoses in uncharted infinity. At such a future eternity moment the master universe will still seem youthful; indeed, it will be always young in the face of the limitless possibilities of never-ending eternity.

The improbability of infinite destiny attainment does not in the least prevent the entertainment of ideas about such destiny, and we do not hesitate to say that, if the three absolute potentials could ever become completely actualized, it would be possible to conceive of the final integration of total reality. This developmental realization is predicated on the completed actualization of the Unqualified, Universal, and Deity Absolutes, the three potentialities whose union constitutes the latency of the I AM, the suspended realities of eternity, the abeyant possibilities of all futurity, and more.

Such eventualities are rather remote to say the least; nevertheless, in the mechanisms, personalities, and associations of the three Trinities we believe we detect the theoretical possibility of the reuniting of the seven absolute phases of the Father-I AM. And this brings us face to face with the concept of the threefold Trinity encompassing the Paradise Trinity of existential status and the two subsequently appearing Trinities of experiential nature and origin.

8. THE TRINITY OF TRINITIES

The nature of the Trinity of Trinities is difficult to portray to the human mind; it is the actual summation of the entirety of experiential infinity as such is manifested in a theoretical infinity of eternity realization. In the Trinity of Trinities the experiential infinite attains to identity with the existential infinite, and both are as one in the pre-experiential, pre-existential I AM. The Trinity of Trinities is the final expression of all that is implied in the fifteen triunities and associated triodities. Finalities are difficult for relative beings to comprehend, be they existential or experiential; therefore must they always be presented as relativities.

The Trinity of Trinities exists in several phases. It contains possibilities, probabilities, and inevitabilities that stagger the imaginations of beings far above the human level. It has implications that are probably unsuspected by the celestial philosophers, for its implications are in the triunities, and the triunities are, in the last analysis, unfathomable.

There are a number of ways in which the Trinity of Trinities can be portrayed. We elect to present the three-level concept, which is as follows:

1. The level of the three Trinities.
2. The level of experiential Deity.
3. The level of the I AM.

These are levels of increasing unification. Actually the Trinity of Trinities is the first level, while the second and third levels are unification-derivatives of the first.

THE FIRST LEVEL: On this initial level of association it is believed that the three Trinities function as perfectly synchronized, though distinct, groupings of Deity personalities.

1. *The Paradise Trinity,* the association of the three Paradise Deities—Father, Son, and Spirit. It should be remembered that the Paradise Trinity implies a threefold function—an absolute function, a transcendental function (Trinity of Ultimacy), and a finite function (Trinity of Supremacy). The Paradise Trinity is any and all of these at any and all times.

2. *The Ultimate Trinity.* This is the deity association of the Supreme Creators, God the Supreme, and the Architects of the Master Universe. While this is an adequate presentation of the divinity aspects of this Trinity, it should be recorded that there are other phases of this Trinity, which, however, appear to be perfectly co-ordinating with the divinity aspects.

3. *The Absolute Trinity.* This is the grouping of God the Supreme, God the Ultimate, and the Consummator of Universe Destiny in regard to all divinity values. Certain other phases of this triune grouping have to do with other-than-divinity values in the expanding cosmos. But these are unifying with the divinity phases just as the power and the personality aspects of the experiential Deities are now in process of experiential synthesis.

The association of these three Trinities in the Trinity of Trinities provides for a possible unlimited integration of reality. This grouping contains causes, intermediates, and finals; inceptors, realizers, and consummators; beginnings, existences, and destinies. The Father-Son partnership has become Son-Spirit and then Spirit-Supreme and on to Supreme-Ultimate and Ultimate-Absolute, even to Absolute and Father-Infinite—the completion of the cycle of reality. Likewise, in other phases not so immediately concerned with divinity and personality, does the First Great Source and Center self-realize the limitlessness of reality around the circle of eternity, from the absoluteness of self-existence, through the endlessness of self-revelation, to the finality of self-realization—from the absolute of existentials to the finality of experientials.

THE SECOND LEVEL: The co-ordination of the three Trinities inevitably involves the associative union of the experiential Deities, who are genetically associated with these Trinities. The nature of this second level has been sometimes presented as:

1. *The Supreme.* This is the deity consequence of the unity of the Paradise Trinity in experiential liaison with the Creator-Creative children of the Paradise Deities. The Supreme is the deity embodiment of the completion of the first stage of finite evolution.

2. *The Ultimate.* This is the deity consequence of the eventuated unity of the second Trinity, the transcendental and absonite personification of divinity. The Ultimate consists in a variably regarded unity of many qualities, and the human conception thereof would do well to include at least those phases of ultimacy which are control directing, personally experiencible, and tensionally unifying, but there are many other unrevealed aspects of the eventuated Deity. While the Ultimate and the Supreme are comparable, they are not identical, neither is the Ultimate merely an amplification of the Supreme.

3. *The Absolute.* There are many theories held as to the character of the third member of the second level of the Trinity of Trinities. God the Absolute is undoubtedly involved in this association as the personality consequence of the final function of the Trinity Absolute, yet the Deity Absolute is an existential reality of eternity status.

The concept difficulty regarding this third member is inherent in the fact that the presupposition of such a membership really implies just one Absolute. Theoretically, if such an event could take place, we should witness the *experiential* unification of the three Absolutes as one. And we are taught that, in infinity and *existentially,* there is one Absolute. While it is least clear as to who this third member can be, it is often postulated that such may consist of the Deity, Universal, and Unqualified Absolutes in some form of unimagined liaison and cosmic manifestation. Certainly, the Trinity of Trinities could hardly attain to complete function short of the full unification of the three Absolutes, and the three Absolutes can hardly be unified short of the complete realization of all infinite potentials.

It will probably represent a minimum distortion of truth if the third member of the Trinity of Trinities is conceived as the Universal Absolute, provided this conception envisions the Universal not only as static and potential but also as associative. But we still do not perceive the relationship to the creative and evolutional aspects of the function of total Deity.

Though a completed concept of the Trinity of Trinities is difficult to form, a qualified concept is not so difficult. If the second level of the Trinity of Trinities is conceived as essentially personal, it becomes quite possible to postulate the union of God the Supreme, God the Ultimate, and God the Absolute as the personal repercussion of the union of the personal Trinities who are ancestral to these experiential Deities. We venture the opinion that these three experiential Deities will certainly unify on the second level as the direct consequence of the growing unity of their ancestral and causative Trinities who constitute the first level.

The first level consists of three Trinities; the second level exists as the personality association of experiential-evolved, experiential-eventuated, and experiential-existential Deity personalities. And regardless of any conceptual difficulty in understanding the complete Trinity of Trinities, the personal association of these three Deities on the second level has become manifest to our own universe age in the phenomenon of the deitization of Majeston, who was actualized on this second level by the Deity Absolute, acting through the Ultimate and in response to the initial creative mandate of the Supreme Being.

THE THIRD LEVEL: In an unqualified hypothesis of the second level of the Trinity of Trinities, there is embraced the correlation of every phase of every kind of reality that is, or was, or could be in the entirety of infinity. The Supreme Being is not only spirit but also mind and power and experience. The Ultimate is all this and much more, while, in the conjoined concept of the oneness of the Deity, Universal, and Unqualified Absolutes, there is included the absolute finality of all reality realization.

In the union of the Supreme, Ultimate, and the complete Absolute, there could occur the functional reassembly of those aspects of infinity which were originally segmentalized by the I AM, and which resulted in the appearance of the Seven

Absolutes of Infinity. Though the universe philosophers deem this to be a most remote probability, still, we often ask this question: If the second level of the Trinity of Trinities could ever achieve trinity unity, what then would transpire as a consequence of such deity unity? We do not know, but we are confident that it would lead directly to the realization of the I AM as an experiential attainable. From the standpoint of personal beings it could mean that the unknowable I AM had become experiencible as the Father-Infinite. What these absolute destinies might mean from a nonpersonal standpoint is another matter and one which only eternity could possibly clarify. But as we view these remote eventualities as personal creatures, we deduce that the final destiny of all personalities is the final knowing of the Universal Father of these selfsame personalities.

As we philosophically conceive of the I AM in past eternity, he is alone, there is none beside him. Looking forward into future eternity, we do not see that the I AM could possibly change as an existential, but we are inclined to forecast a vast experiential difference. Such a concept of the I AM implies full self-realization—it embraces that limitless galaxy of personalities who have become volitional participants in the self-revelation of the I AM, and who will remain eternally as absolute volitional parts of the totality of infinity, final sons of the absolute Father.

9. EXISTENTIAL INFINITE UNIFICATION

In the concept of the Trinity of Trinities we postulate the possible experiential unification of limitless reality, and we sometimes theorize that all this may happen in the utter remoteness of far-distant eternity. But there is nonetheless an actual and present unification of infinity in this very age as in all past and future universe ages; such unification is existential in the Paradise Trinity. Infinity unification as an experiential reality is unthinkably remote, but an unqualified unity of infinity now dominates the present moment of universe existence and unites the divergencies of all reality with an existential majesty that is *absolute*.

When finite creatures attempt to conceive of infinite unification on the finality levels of consummated eternity, they are face to face with intellect limitations inherent in their finite existences. Time, space, and experience constitute barriers to creature concept; and yet, without time, apart from space, and except for experience, no creature could achieve even a limited comprehension of universe reality. Without time sensitivity, no evolutionary creature could possibly perceive the relations of sequence. Without space perception, no creature could fathom the relations of simultaneity. Without experience, no evolutionary creature could even exist; only the Seven Absolutes of Infinity really transcend experience, and even these may be experiential in certain phases.

Time, space, and experience are man's greatest aids to relative reality perception and yet his most formidable obstacles to complete reality perception. Mortals and many other universe creatures find it necessary to think of potentials as being actualized in space and evolving to fruition in time, but this entire process is a time-space phenomenon which does not actually take place on Paradise and in eternity. On the absolute level there is neither time nor space; all potentials may be there perceived as actuals.

The concept of the unification of all reality, be it in this or any other universe age, is basically twofold: existential and experiential. Such a unity is in process of experiential realization in the Trinity of Trinities, but the degree of the apparent actualization of this threefold Trinity is directly proportional to the disappearance of the qualifications and imperfections of reality in the cosmos. But total integration of reality is unqualifiedly and eternally and existentially present in the Paradise Trinity, within which, at this very universe moment, infinite reality is absolutely unified.

The paradox created by the experiential and the existential viewpoints is inevitable and is predicated in part on the fact that the Paradise Trinity and the Trinity of Trinities are each an eternity relationship which mortals can only perceive as a time-space relativity. The human concept of the gradual experiential actualization of the Trinity of Trinities—the time viewpoint—must be supplemented by the additional postulate that this *is* already a factualization—the eternity viewpoint. But how can these two viewpoints be reconciled? To finite mortals we suggest the acceptance of the truth that the Paradise Trinity is the existential unification of infinity, and that the inability to detect the actual presence and completed manifestation of the experiential Trinity of Trinities is in part due to reciprocal distortion because of:

1. The limited human viewpoint, the inability to grasp the concept of unqualified eternity.

2. The imperfect human status, the remoteness from the absolute level of experientials.

3. The purpose of human existence, the fact that mankind is designed to evolve by the technique of experience and, therefore, must be inherently and constitutively dependent on experience. Only an Absolute can be both existential and experiential.

The Universal Father in the Paradise Trinity is the I AM of the Trinity of Trinities, and the failure to experience the Father as infinite is due to finite limitations. The concept of the *existential,* solitary, pre-Trinity nonattainable I AM and the postulate of the *experiential* post-Trinity of Trinities and attainable I AM are one and the same hypothesis; no actual change has taken place in the Infinite; all apparent developments are due to increased capacities for reality reception and cosmic appreciation.

The I AM, in the final analysis, must exist *before* all existentials and *after* all experientials. While these ideas may not clarify the paradoxes of eternity and infinity in the human mind, they should at least stimulate such finite intellects to grapple anew with these never-ending problems, problems which will continue to intrigue you on Salvington and later as finaliters and on throughout the unending future of your eternal careers in the wide-spreading universes.

Sooner or later all universe personalities begin to realize that the final quest of eternity is the endless exploration of infinity, the never-ending voyage of discovery into the absoluteness of the First Source and Center. Sooner or later we all become aware that all creature growth is proportional to Father identification. We arrive at the understanding that living the will of God is the eternal passport to the endless possibility of infinity itself. Mortals will sometime realize that success in the quest of the Infinite is directly proportional to the achievement of Fatherlikeness, and that in this universe age the realities of the Father are revealed within the qualities of divinity. And these qualities of divinity are personally appropriated by universe creatures in the experience of living divinely, and to live divinely means actually to live the will of God.

To material, evolutionary, finite creatures, a life predicated on the living of the Father's will leads directly to the attainment of spirit supremacy in the personality arena and brings such creatures one step nearer the comprehension of the Father-Infinite. Such a Father life is one predicated on truth, sensitive to beauty, and dominated by goodness. Such a God-knowing person is inwardly illuminated by worship and outwardly devoted to the wholehearted service of the universal brotherhood of all personalities, a service ministry which is filled with mercy and motivated by love, while all these life qualities are unified in the evolving personality on ever-ascending levels of cosmic wisdom, self-realization, God-finding, and Father worship.

[Presented by a Melchizedek of Nebadon.]

PAPER 107

ORIGIN AND NATURE OF THOUGHT ADJUSTERS

ALTHOUGH the Universal Father is personally resident on Paradise, at the very center of the universes, he is also actually present on the worlds of space in the minds of his countless children of time, for he indwells them as the Mystery Monitors. The eternal Father is at one and the same time farthest removed from, and most intimately associated with, his planetary mortal sons.

The Adjusters are the actuality of the Father's love incarnate in the souls of men; they are the veritable promise of man's eternal career imprisoned within the mortal mind; they are the essence of man's perfected finaliter personality, which he can foretaste in time as he progressively masters the divine technique of achieving the living of the Father's will, step by step, through the ascension of universe upon universe until he actually attains the divine presence of his Paradise Father.

God, having commanded man to be perfect, even as he is perfect, has descended as the Adjuster to become man's experiential partner in the achievement of the supernal destiny which has been thus ordained. The fragment of God which indwells the mind of man is the absolute and unqualified assurance that man can find the Universal Father in association with this divine Adjuster, which came forth from God to find man and sonship him even in the days of the flesh.

Any mortal who has seen a Creator Son has seen the Universal Father, and he who is indwelt by a divine Adjuster is indwelt by the Paradise Father. Every mortal who is consciously or unconsciously following the leading of his indwelling Adjuster is living in accordance with the will of God. Consciousness of Adjuster presence is consciousness of God's presence. Eternal fusion of the Adjuster with the evolutionary soul of man is the factual experience of eternal union with God as a universe associate of Deity.

It is the Adjuster who creates within man that unquenchable yearning and incessant longing to be like God, to attain Paradise, and there before the actual person of Deity to worship the infinite source of the divine gift. The Adjuster is the living presence which actually links the mortal son with his Paradise Father and draws him nearer and nearer to the Father. The Adjuster is our compensatory equalization of the enormous universe tension which is created by the distance of man's removal from God and by the degree of his partiality in contrast with the universality of the eternal Father.

The Adjuster is an absolute essence of an infinite being imprisoned within the mind of a finite creature which, depending on the choosing of such a mortal, can eventually consummate this temporary union of God and man and veritably actualize a new order of being for unending universe service. The Adjuster is the divine universe reality which factualizes the truth that God is man's Father. The Adjuster is man's infallible cosmic compass, always and unerringly pointing the soul Godward.

On the evolutionary worlds, will creatures traverse three general developmental stages of being: From the arrival of the Adjuster to comparative full growth, about twenty years of age on Urantia, the Monitors are sometimes designated Thought Changers. From this time to the attainment of the age of discretion, about forty years, the Mystery Monitors are called Thought Adjusters. From the attainment of discretion to deliverance from the flesh, they are often referred to as Thought Controllers. These three phases of mortal life have no connection with the three stages of Adjuster progress in mind duplication and soul evolution.

1. ORIGIN OF THOUGHT ADJUSTERS

Since Thought Adjusters are of the essence of original Deity, no one may presume to discourse authoritatively upon their nature and origin; I can only impart the traditions of Salvington and the beliefs of Uversa; I can only explain how we regard these Mystery Monitors and their associated entities throughout the grand universe.

Though there are diverse opinions regarding the mode of the bestowal of Thought Adjusters, there exist no such differences concerning their origin; all are agreed that they proceed direct from the Universal Father, the First Source and Center. They are not created beings; they are fragmentized entities constituting the factual presence of the infinite God. Together with their many unrevealed associates, the Adjusters are undiluted and unmixed divinity, unqualified and unattenuated parts of Deity; they are of God, and as far as we are able to discern, *they are God.*

As to the time of their beginning separate existences apart from the absoluteness of the First Source and Center, we do not know; neither do we know their number. We know very little concerning their careers until they arrive on the planets of time to indwell human minds, but from that time on we are more or less familiar with their cosmic progressions up to and including the consummation of their triune destinies: attainment of personality by fusion with some mortal ascender, attainment of personality by fiat of the Universal Father, or liberation from the known assignments of Thought Adjusters.

Although we do not know, we presume that Adjusters are being constantly individualized as the universe enlarges, and as the candidates for Adjuster fusion increase in numbers. But it may be equally possible that we are in error in attempting to assign a numerical magnitude to the Adjusters; like God himself, these fragments of his unfathomable nature may be existentially infinite.

The technique of the origin of the Thought Adjusters is one of the unrevealed functions of the Universal Father. We have every reason to believe that none of the other absolute associates of the First Source and Center have aught to do with the production of Father fragments. Adjusters are simply and eternally the divine gifts; they are of God and from God, and they are like God.

In their relationship to fusion creatures they reveal a supernal love and spiritual ministry that is profoundly confirmative of the declaration that God is spirit. But there is much that takes place in addition to this transcendent ministry that has never been revealed to Urantia mortals. Neither do we fully understand just what really transpires when the Universal Father gives of himself to be a part of the personality of a creature of time. Nor has the ascending progression of the Paradise finaliters as yet disclosed the full possibilities inherent in this supernal partnership of man and God. In the last analysis, the Father fragments must be the gift of the absolute God to those creatures whose destiny encompasses the possibility of the attainment of God as absolute.

As the Universal Father fragmentizes his prepersonal Deity, so does the Infinite Spirit individuate portions of his premind spirit to indwell and actually to fuse with the evolutionary souls of the surviving mortals of the spirit-fusion series. But the nature of the Eternal Son is not thus fragmentable; the spirit of the Original Son is either diffuse or discretely personal. Son-fused creatures are united with individualized bestowals of the spirit of the Creator Sons of the Eternal Son.

2. CLASSIFICATION OF ADJUSTERS

Adjusters are individuated as virgin entities, and all are destined to become either liberated, fused, or Personalized Monitors. We understand that there are seven orders of Thought Adjusters, although we do not altogether comprehend these divisions. We often refer to the different orders as follows:

1. *Virgin Adjusters,* those serving on their initial assignment in the minds of evolutionary candidates for eternal survival. Mystery Monitors are eternally uniform in divine nature. They are also uniform in experiential nature as they first go out from Divinington; subsequent experiential differentiation is the result of actual experience in universe ministry.

2. *Advanced Adjusters,* those who have served one or more seasons with will creatures on worlds where the final fusion takes place between the identity of the creature of time and an individualized portion of the spirit of the local universe manifestation of the Third Source and Center.

3. *Supreme Adjusters,* those Monitors that have served in the adventure of time on the evolutionary worlds, but whose human partners for some reason declined eternal survival, and those that have been subsequently assigned to other adventures in other mortals on other evolving worlds. A supreme Adjuster, though no more divine than a virgin Monitor, has had more experience, can do things in the human mind which a less experienced Adjuster could not do.

4. *Vanished Adjusters.* Here occurs a break in our efforts to follow the careers of the Mystery Monitors. There is a fourth stage of service about which we are not sure. The Melchizedeks teach that the fourth-stage Adjusters are on detached assignments, roaming the universe of universes. The Solitary Messengers are inclined to believe that they are at one with the First Source and Center, enjoying a period of refreshing association with the Father himself. And it is entirely possible that an Adjuster could be roaming the master universe simultaneously with being at one with the omnipresent Father.

5. *Liberated Adjusters,* those Mystery Monitors that have been eternally liberated from the service of time for the mortals of the evolving spheres. What functions may be theirs, we do not know.

6. *Fused Adjusters*—finaliters—those who have become one with the ascending creatures of the superuniverses, the eternity partners of the time ascenders of the Paradise Corps of the Finality. Thought Adjusters ordinarily become fused with the ascending mortals of time, and with such surviving mortals they are registered in and out of Ascendington; they follow the course of ascendant beings. Upon fusion with the ascending evolutionary soul, it appears that the Adjuster translates from the absolute existential level of the universe to the finite experiential level of functional association with an ascending personality. While retaining all of the character of the existential divine nature, a fused Adjuster becomes indissolubly linked with the ascending career of a surviving mortal.

7. *Personalized Adjusters,* those who have served with the incarnated Paradise Sons, together with many who have achieved unusual distinction during the mortal indwelling, but whose subjects rejected survival. We have reasons for believing that such Adjusters are personalized on the recommendations of the Ancients of Days of the superuniverse of their assignment.

There are many ways in which these mysterious God fragments can be classified: according to universe assignment, by the measure of success in the indwelling of an individual mortal, or even by the racial ancestry of the mortal candidate for fusion.

3. THE DIVININGTON HOME OF ADJUSTERS

All universe activities related to the dispatch, management, direction, and return of the Mystery Monitors from service in all of the seven superuniverses seem to be centered on the sacred sphere of Divinington. As far as I know, none but Adjusters and other entities of the Father have been on that sphere. It seems likely that numerous unrevealed prepersonal entities share Divinington as a home sphere with the Adjusters. We conjecture that these fellow entities may in some manner be associated with the present and future ministry of the Mystery Monitors. But we really do not know.

When Thought Adjusters return to the Father, they go back to the realm of supposed origin, Divinington; and probably as a part of this experience, there is actual contact with the Father's Paradise personality as well as with the specialized manifestation of the Father's divinity which is reported to be situated on this secret sphere.

Although we know something of all the seven secret spheres of Paradise, we know less of Divinington than of the others. Beings of high spiritual orders receive only three divine injunctions, and they are:

1. Always to show adequate respect for the experience and endowments of their seniors and superiors.

2. Always to be considerate of the limitations and inexperience of their juniors and subordinates.

3. Never to attempt a landing on the shores of Divinington.

I have often reflected that it would be quite useless for me to go to Divinington; I probably should be unable to see any resident beings except such as the Personalized Adjusters, and I have seen them elsewhere. I am very sure there is nothing on Divinington of real value or profit to me, nothing essential to my growth and development, or I should not have been forbidden to go there.

Since we can learn little or nothing of the nature and origin of Adjusters from Divinington, we are compelled to gather information from a thousand and one different sources, and it is necessary to assemble, associate, and correlate this accumulated data in order that such knowledge may be informative.

The valor and wisdom exhibited by Thought Adjusters suggest that they have undergone a training of tremendous scope and range. Since they are not personalities, this training must be imparted in the educational institutions of Divinington. The unique Personalized Adjusters no doubt constitute the personnel of the Adjuster training schools of Divinington. And we do know that this central and supervising corps is presided over by the now Personalized Adjuster of the first Paradise Son of the Michael order to complete his sevenfold bestowal upon the races and peoples of his universe realms.

We really know very little about the nonpersonalized Adjusters; we only contact and communicate with the personalized orders. These are christened on Divinington and are always known by name and not by number. The Personalized Adjusters are permanently domiciled on Divinington; that sacred sphere is their home. They go out from that abode only by the will of the Universal Father. Very few are found in the domains of the local universes, but larger numbers are present in the central universe.

4. NATURE AND PRESENCE OF ADJUSTERS

To say that a Thought Adjuster is divine is merely to recognize the nature of origin. It is highly probable that such purity of divinity embraces the essence of the potential of all attributes of Deity which can be contained within such a fragment of the absolute essence of the universal presence of the eternal and infinite Paradise Father.

The actual source of the Adjuster must be infinite, and before fusion with the immortal soul of an evolving mortal, the reality of the Adjuster must border on absoluteness. Adjusters are not absolutes in the universal sense, in the Deity sense, but they are probably true absolutes within the potentialities of their fragmented nature. They are qualified as to universality but not as to nature; in extensiveness they are limited, but in intensiveness of meaning, value, and fact *they are absolute.* For this reason we sometimes denominate the divine gifts as the qualified absolute fragments of the Father.

No Adjuster has ever been disloyal to the Paradise Father; the lower orders of personal creatures may sometimes have to contend with disloyal fellows, but never the Adjusters; they are supreme and infallible in their supernal sphere of creature ministry and universe function.

Nonpersonalized Adjusters are visible only to Personalized Adjusters. My order, the Solitary Messengers, together with Inspired Trinity Spirits, can detect the presence of Adjusters by means of spiritual reactive phenomena; and even seraphim can sometimes discern the spirit luminosity of supposed association with the presence of Monitors in the material minds of men; but none of us are able actually to discern the real presence of Adjusters, not unless they have been personalized, albeit their natures are perceivable in union with the fused personalities of the ascending mortals from the evolutionary worlds.

The universal invisibility of the Adjusters is strongly suggestive of their high and exclusive divine origin and nature.

There is a characteristic light, a spirit luminosity, which accompanies this divine presence, and which has become generally associated with Thought Adjusters. In the universe of Nebadon this Paradise luminosity is widespreadly known as the "pilot light"; on Uversa it is called the "light of life." On Urantia this phenomenon has sometimes been referred to as that "true light which lights every man who comes into the world."

To all beings who have attained the Universal Father, the Personalized Thought Adjusters are visible. Adjusters of all stages, together with all other beings, entities, spirits, personalities, and spirit manifestations, are always discernible by those Supreme Creator Personalities who originate in the Paradise Deities, and who preside over the major governments of the grand universe.

Can you really realize the true significance of the Adjuster's indwelling? Do you really fathom what it means to have an absolute fragment of the absolute and infinite Deity, the Universal Father, indwelling and fusing with your finite mortal natures? When mortal man fuses with an actual fragment of the existential Cause of the total cosmos, no limit can ever be placed upon the destiny of such an unprecedented and unimaginable partnership. In eternity, man will be discovering not only the infinity of the objective Deity but also the unending potentiality of the subjective fragment of this same God. Always will the Adjuster be revealing to the mortal personality the wonder of God, and never can this supernal revelation come to an end, for the Adjuster is of God and as God to mortal man.

5. ADJUSTER MINDEDNESS

Evolutionary mortals are prone to look upon mind as a cosmic mediation between spirit and matter, for that is indeed the principal ministry of mind as discernible by you. Hence it is quite difficult for humans to perceive that Thought Adjusters have minds, for Adjusters are fragmentations of God on an absolute level of reality which is not only prepersonal but also prior to all energy and spirit divergence. On a monistic level antecedent to energy and spirit differentiation there could be no mediating function of mind, for there are no divergencies to be mediated.

Since Adjusters can plan, work, and love, they must have powers of selfhood which are commensurate with mind. They are possessed of unlimited ability to communicate with each other, that is, all forms of Monitors above the first or virgin groups. As to the nature and purport of their intercommunications, we can reveal very little, for we do not know. And we further know that they must be minded in some manner else they could never be personalized.

The mindedness of the Thought Adjuster is like the *mindedness* of the Universal Father and the Eternal Son—that which is ancestral to the *minds* of the Conjoint Actor.

The type of mind postulated in an Adjuster must be similar to the mind endowment of numerous other orders of prepersonal entities which presumably likewise originate in the First Source and Center. Though many of these orders have not been revealed on Urantia, they all disclose minded qualities. It is also possible for these individuations of original Deity to become unified with numerous evolving types of nonmortal beings and even with a limited number of nonevolutionary beings who have developed capacity for fusion with such Deity fragments.

When a Thought Adjuster is fused with the evolving immortal morontia soul of the surviving human, the mind of the Adjuster can only be identified as persisting apart from the creature's mind until the ascending mortal attains spirit levels of universe progression.

Upon the attainment of the finaliter levels of ascendant experience, these spirits of the sixth stage appear to transmute some mind factor representing a union of certain phases of the mortal and Adjuster minds which had previously functioned as liaison between the divine and human phases of such ascending personalities. This experiential mind quality probably "supremacizes" and subsequently augments the experiential endowment of evolutionary Deity—the Supreme Being.

6. ADJUSTERS AS PURE SPIRITS

As Thought Adjusters are encountered in creature experience, they disclose the presence and leading of a spirit influence. The Adjuster is indeed a spirit, pure spirit, but spirit plus. We have never been able satisfactorily to classify Mystery Monitors; all that can certainly be said of them is that they are truly Godlike.

The Adjuster is man's eternity possibility; man is the Adjuster's personality possibility. Your individual Adjusters work to spiritize you in the hope of eternalizing your temporal identity. The Adjusters are saturated with the beautiful and self-bestowing love of the Father of spirits. They truly and divinely love you; they are the prisoners of spirit hope confined within the minds of men. They long for the divinity attainment of your mortal minds that their loneliness may end, that they may be delivered with you from the limitations of material investiture and the habiliments of time.

Your path to Paradise is the path of spirit attainment, and the Adjuster nature will faithfully unfold the revelation of the spiritual nature of the Universal Father. Beyond the Paradise ascent and in the postfinaliter stages of the eternal career, the Adjuster may possibly contact with the onetime human partner in other than spirit ministry; but the Paradise ascent and the finaliter career are the partnership between the God-knowing spiritualizing mortal and the spiritual ministry of the God-revealing Adjuster.

We know that Thought Adjusters are spirits, pure spirits, presumably absolute spirits. But the Adjuster must also be something more than exclusive spirit reality. In addition to conjectured mindedness, factors of pure energy are also present. If you will remember that God is the source of pure energy and of pure spirit, it will not be so difficult to perceive that his fragments would be both. It is a fact that the Adjusters traverse space over the instantaneous and universal gravity circuits of the Paradise Isle.

That the Mystery Monitors are thus associated with the material circuits of the universe of universes is indeed puzzling. But it remains a fact that they flash throughout the entire grand universe over the material-gravity circuits. It is entirely possible that they may even penetrate the outer space levels; they certainly could follow the gravity presence of Paradise into these regions, and though my order of personality can traverse the mind circuits of the Conjoint Actor also beyond the confines of the grand universe, we have never been sure of detecting the presence of Adjusters in the uncharted regions of outer space.

And yet, while the Adjusters utilize the material-gravity circuits, they are not subject thereto as is material creation. The Adjusters are fragments of the ancestor of gravity, not the consequentials of gravity; they have segmentized on a universe level of existence which is hypothetically antecedent to gravity appearance.

Thought Adjusters have no relaxation from the time of their bestowal until the day of their release to start for Divinington upon the natural death of their mortal subjects. And those whose subjects do not pass through the portals of natural death do not even experience this temporary respite. Thought Adjusters do not require energy intake; they are energy, energy of the highest and most divine order.

7. ADJUSTERS AND PERSONALITY

Thought Adjusters are not personalities, but they are real entities; they are truly and perfectly individualized, although they are never, while indwelling mortals, actually personalized. Thought Adjusters are not true personalities; they are *true realities,* realities of the purest order known in the universe of universes—they are the divine presence. Though not personal, these marvelous fragments of the Father are commonly referred to as beings and sometimes, in view of the spiritual phases of their present ministry to mortals, as spirit entities.

If Thought Adjusters are not personalities having prerogatives of will and powers of choice, how then can they select mortal subjects and volunteer to indwell these creatures of the evolutionary worlds? This is a question easy to ask, but probably no being in the universe of universes has ever found the exact answer. Even my order of personality, the Solitary Messengers, does not fully understand the endowment of will, choice, and love in entities that are not personal.

We have often speculated that Thought Adjusters must have volition on all *prepersonal* levels of choice. They volunteer to indwell human beings, they lay plans for man's eternal career, they adapt, modify, and substitute in accordance with circumstances, and these activities connote genuine volition. They have affection for mortals, they function in universe crises, they are always waiting to act decisively in accordance with human choice, and all these are highly volitional reactions. In all situations not concerned with the domain of the human will, they unquestionably exhibit conduct which betokens the exercise of powers in every sense the equivalent of will, maximated decision.

Why then, if Thought Adjusters possess volition, are they subservient to the mortal will? We believe it is because Adjuster volition, though absolute in nature, is prepersonal in manifestation. Human will functions on the personality level of universe reality, and throughout the cosmos the impersonal—the nonpersonal, the subpersonal, and the prepersonal—is ever responsive to the will and acts of existent personality.

Throughout a universe of created beings and nonpersonal energies we do not observe will, volition, choice, and love manifested apart from personality. Except in the Adjusters and other similar entities we do not witness these attributes of personality functioning in association with impersonal realities. It would not be correct to designate an Adjuster as subpersonal, neither would it be proper to allude to such an entity as superpersonal, but it would be entirely permissible to term such a being prepersonal.

To our orders of being these fragments of Deity are known as the divine gifts. We recognize that the Adjusters are divine in origin, and that they constitute the probable proof and demonstration of a reservation by the Universal Father of the possibility of direct and unlimited communication with any and all material creatures throughout his virtually infinite realms, and all of this quite apart from his presence in the personalities of his Paradise Sons or through his indirect ministrations in the personalities of the Infinite Spirit.

There are no created beings that would not delight to be hosts to the Mystery Monitors, but no orders of beings are thus indwelt excepting evolutionary will creatures of finaliter destiny.

[Presented by a Solitary Messenger of Orvonton.]

PAPER 108

MISSION AND MINISTRY OF THOUGHT ADJUSTERS

THE mission of the Thought Adjusters to the human races is to represent, to be, the Universal Father to the mortal creatures of time and space; that is the fundamental work of the divine gifts. Their mission is also that of elevating the mortal minds and of translating the immortal souls of men up to the divine heights and spiritual levels of Paradise perfection. And in the experience of thus transforming the human nature of the temporal creature into the divine nature of the eternal finaliter, the Adjusters bring into existence a unique type of being, a being consisting in the eternal union of the perfect Adjuster and the perfected creature which it would be impossible to duplicate by any other universe technique.

Nothing in the entire universe can substitute for the fact of experience on nonexistential levels. The infinite God is, as always, replete and complete, infinitely inclusive of all things except evil and creature experience. God cannot do wrong; he is infallible. God cannot experientially know what he has never personally experienced; God's preknowledge is existential. Therefore does the spirit of the Father descend from Paradise to participate with finite mortals in every bona fide experience of the ascending career; it is only by such a method that the existential God could become in truth and in fact man's experiential Father. The infinity of the eternal God encompasses the potential for finite experience, which indeed becomes actual in the ministry of the Adjuster fragments that actually share the life vicissitude experiences of human beings.

1. SELECTION AND ASSIGNMENT

When Adjusters are dispatched for mortal service from Divinington, they are identical in the endowment of existential divinity, but they vary in experiential qualities proportional to previous contact in and with evolutionary creatures. We cannot explain the basis of Adjuster assignment, but we conjecture that these divine gifts are bestowed in accordance with some wise and efficient policy of eternal fitness of adaptation to the indwelt personality. We do observe that the more experienced Adjuster is often the indweller of the higher type of human mind; human inheritance must therefore be a considerable factor in determining selection and assignment.

Although we do not definitely know, we firmly believe that all Thought Adjusters are volunteers. But before ever they volunteer, they are in possession of full data respecting the candidate for indwelling. The seraphic drafts of ancestry and projected patterns of life conduct are transmitted via Paradise to the reserve corps of Adjusters on Divinington by the reflectivity technique extending inward from the capitals of the local universes to the headquarters of the superuniverses. This forecast covers not only the hereditary antecedents of the mortal candidate but also the estimate of probable intellectual endowment and spiritual capacity. The Adjusters thus volunteer to indwell minds of whose intimate natures they have been fully apprised.

The volunteering Adjuster is particularly interested in three qualifications of the human candidate:

1. *Intellectual capacity.* Is the mind normal? What is the intellectual potential, the intelligence capacity? Can the individual develop into a bona fide will creature? Will wisdom have an opportunity to function?

2. *Spiritual perception.* The prospects of reverential development, the birth and growth of the religious nature. What is the potential of soul, the probable spiritual capacity of receptivity?

3. *Combined intellectual and spiritual powers.* The degree to which these two endowments may possibly be associated, combined, so as to produce strength of human character and contribute to the certain evolution of an immortal soul of survival value.

With these facts before them, it is our belief that the Monitors freely volunteer for assignment. Probably more than one Adjuster volunteers; perhaps the supervising personalized orders select from this group of volunteering Adjusters the one best suited to the task of spiritualizing and eternalizing the personality of the mortal candidate. (In the assignment and service of the Adjusters the sex of the creature is of no consideration.)

The short time intervening between the volunteering and the actual dispatch of the Adjuster is presumably spent in the Divinington schools of the Personalized Monitors where a working pattern of the waiting mortal mind is utilized in instructing the assigned Adjuster as to the most effective plans for personality approach and mind spiritization. This mind model is formulated through a combination of data supplied by the superuniverse reflectivity service. At least this is our understanding, a belief which we hold as the result of putting together information secured by contact with many Personalized Adjusters throughout the long universe careers of the Solitary Messengers.

When once the Adjusters are actually dispatched from Divinington, practically no time intervenes between that moment and the hour of their appearance in the minds of their chosen subjects. The average transit time of an Adjuster from Divinington to Urantia is 117 hours, 42 minutes, and 7 seconds. Virtually all of this time is occupied with registration on Uversa.

2. PREREQUISITES OF ADJUSTER INDWELLING

Though the Adjusters volunteer for service as soon as the personality forecasts have been relayed to Divinington, they are not actually assigned until the human subjects make their first moral personality decision. The first moral choice of the human child is automatically indicated in the seventh mind-adjutant and registers instantly, by way of the local universe Creative Spirit, over the universal mind-gravity circuit of the Conjoint Actor in the presence of the Master Spirit of superuniverse jurisdiction, who forthwith dispatches this intelligence to Divinington. Adjusters reach their human subjects on

Urantia, on the average, just prior to the sixth birthday. In the present generation it is running five years, ten months, and four days; that is, on the 2,134th day of terrestrial life.

The Adjusters cannot invade the mortal mind until it has been duly prepared by the indwelling ministry of the adjutant mind-spirits and encircuited in the Holy Spirit. And it requires the co-ordinate function of all seven adjutants to thus qualify the human mind for the reception of an Adjuster. Creature mind must exhibit the worship outreach and indicate wisdom function by exhibiting the ability to choose between the emerging values of good and evil—moral choice.

Thus is the stage of the human mind set for the reception of Adjusters, but as a general rule they do not immediately appear to indwell such minds except on those worlds where the Spirit of Truth is functioning as a spiritual co-ordinator of these different spirit ministries. If this spirit of the bestowal Sons is present, the Adjusters unfailingly come the instant the seventh adjutant mind-spirit begins to function and signalizes to the Universe Mother Spirit that it has achieved in potential the co-ordination of the associated six adjutants of prior ministry to such a mortal intellect. Therefore have the divine Adjusters been universally bestowed upon all normal minds of moral status on Urantia ever since the day of Pentecost.

Even with a Spirit of Truth endowed mind, the Adjusters cannot arbitrarily invade the mortal intellect prior to the appearance of moral decision. But when such a moral decision has been made, this spirit helper assumes jurisdiction direct from Divinington. There are no intermediaries or other intervening authorities or powers functioning between the divine Adjusters and their human subjects; God and man are directly related.

Before the times of the pouring out of the Spirit of Truth upon the inhabitants of an evolutionary world, the Adjusters' bestowal appears to be determined by many spirit influences and personality attitudes. We do not fully comprehend the laws governing such bestowals; we do not understand just what determines the release of the Adjusters who have volunteered to indwell such evolving minds. But we do observe numerous influences and conditions which appear to be associated with the arrival of the Adjusters in such minds prior to the bestowal of the Spirit of Truth, and they are:

1. The assignment of personal seraphic guardians. If a mortal has not been previously indwelt by an Adjuster, the assignment of a personal guardian brings the Adjuster forthwith. There exists some very definite but unknown relation between the ministry of Adjusters and the ministry of personal seraphic guardians.

2. The attainment of the third circle of intellectual achievement and spiritual attainment. I have observed Adjusters arrive in mortal minds upon the conquest of the third circle even before such an accomplishment could be signalized to the local universe personalities concerned with such matters.

3. Upon the making of a supreme decision of unusual spiritual import. Such human behavior in a personal planetary crisis usually is attended by the immediate arrival of the waiting Adjuster.

4. The spirit of brotherhood. Regardless of the attainment of the psychic circles and the assignment of personal guardians—in the absence of anything

resembling a crisis decision—when an evolving mortal becomes dominated by the love of his fellows and consecrated to unselfish ministry to his brethren in the flesh, the waiting Adjuster unvaryingly descends to indwell the mind of such a mortal minister.

5. Declaration of intention to do the will of God. We observe that many mortals on the worlds of space may be apparently in readiness to receive Adjusters, and yet the Monitors do not appear. We go on watching such creatures as they live from day to day, and presently they quietly, almost unconsciously, arrive at the decision to begin the pursuit of the doing of the will of the Father in heaven. And then we observe the immediate dispatch of the Thought Adjusters.

6. Influence of the Supreme Being. On worlds where the Adjusters do not fuse with the evolving souls of the mortal inhabitants, we observe Adjusters sometimes bestowed in response to influences which are wholly beyond our comprehension. We conjecture that such bestowals are determined by some cosmic reflex action originating in the Supreme Being. As to why these Adjusters can not or do not fuse with these certain types of evolving mortal minds we do not know. Such transactions have never been revealed to us.

3. ORGANIZATION AND ADMINISTRATION

As far as we know, Adjusters are organized as an independent working unit in the universe of universes and are apparently administered directly from Divinington. They are uniform throughout the seven superuniverses, all local universes being served by identical types of Mystery Monitors. We do know from observation that there are numerous series of Adjusters involving a serial organization that extends through races, over dispensations, and to worlds, systems, and universes. It is, however, exceedingly difficult to keep track of these divine gifts since they function interchangeably throughout the grand universe.

Adjusters are of complete record (outside of Divinington) only on the headquarters of the seven superuniverses. The number and order of each Adjuster indwelling each ascending creature are reported out by the Paradise authorities to the headquarters of the superuniverse, and from there are communicated to the headquarters of the local universe concerned and relayed to the particular planet involved. But the local universe records do not disclose the full number of the Thought Adjusters; the Nebadon records contain only the local universe assignment number as designated by the representatives of the Ancients of Days. The real significance of the Adjuster's complete number is known only on Divinington.

Human subjects are often known by the numbers of their Adjusters; mortals do not receive real universe names until after Adjuster fusion, which union is signalized by the bestowal of the new name upon the new creature by the destiny guardian.

Though we have the records of Thought Adjusters in Orvonton, and though we have absolutely no authority over them or administrative connection with them, we firmly believe that there is a very close administrative connection between the individual worlds of the local universes and the central lodgment of the divine gifts on Divinington. We do know that, following the appearance of a Paradise bestowal Son, an evolutionary world has a Personalized Adjuster assigned to it as the planetary supervisor of Adjusters.

It is interesting to note that local universe inspectors always address themselves, when carrying out a planetary examination, to the planetary chief of Thought Adjusters, just as they deliver charges to the chiefs of seraphim and to the leaders of other orders of beings attached to the administration of an evolving world. Not long since, Urantia underwent such a periodic inspection by Tabamantia, the sovereign supervisor of all life-experiment planets in the universe of Nebadon. And the records reveal that, in addition to his admonitions and indictments delivered to the various chiefs of superhuman personalities, he also delivered the following acknowledgment to the chief of Adjusters, whether located on the planet, on Salvington, Uversa, or Divinington, we do not definitely know, but he said:

"Now to you, superiors far above me, I come as one placed in temporary authority over the experimental planetary series; and I come to express admiration and profound respect for this magnificent group of celestial ministers, the Mystery Monitors, who have volunteered to serve on this irregular sphere. No matter how trying the crises, you never falter. Not on the records of Nebadon nor before the commissions of Orvonton has there ever been offered an indictment of a divine Adjuster. You have been true to your trusts; you have been divinely faithful. You have helped to adjust the mistakes and to compensate for the shortcomings of all who labor on this confused planet. You are marvelous beings, guardians of the good in the souls of this backward realm. I pay you respect even while you are apparently under my jurisdiction as volunteer ministers. I bow before you in humble recognition of your exquisite unselfishness, your understanding ministry, and your impartial devotion. You deserve the name of the Godlike servers of the mortal inhabitants of this strife-torn, grief-stricken, and disease-afflicted world. I honor you! I all but worship you!"

As a result of many suggestive lines of evidence, we believe that the Adjusters are thoroughly organized, that there exists a profoundly intelligent and efficient directive administration of these divine gifts from some far-distant and central source, probably Divinington. We know that they come from Divinington to the worlds, and undoubtedly they return thereto upon the deaths of their subjects.

Among the higher spirit orders it is exceedingly difficult to discover the mechanisms of administration. My order of personalities, while engaged in the prosecution of our specific duties, is undoubtedly unconsciously participating with numerous other personal and impersonal sub-Deity groups who unitedly are functioning as far-flung universe correlators. We suspect that we are thus serving because we are the only group of personalized creatures (aside from Personalized Adjusters) who are uniformly conscious of the presence of numerous orders of the prepersonal entities.

We are aware of the presence of the Adjusters, who are fragments of the prepersonal Deity of the First Source and Center. We sense the presence of the Inspired Trinity Spirits, who are superpersonal expressions of the Paradise Trinity. We likewise unfailingly detect the spirit presence of certain unrevealed orders springing from the Eternal Son and the Infinite Spirit. And we are not wholly unresponsive to still other entities unrevealed to you.

The Melchizedeks of Nebadon teach that the Solitary Messengers are the personality co-ordinators of these various influences as they register in the expanding Deity of the evolutionary Supreme Being. It is very possible that we may be participants in the experiential unification of many of the unexplained phenomena of time, but we are not consciously certain of thus functioning.

4. RELATION TO OTHER SPIRITUAL INFLUENCES

Apart from possible co-ordination with other Deity fragments, the Adjusters are quite alone in their sphere of activity in the mortal mind. The Mystery Monitors eloquently bespeak the fact that, though the Father may have apparently resigned the exercise of all direct personal power and authority throughout the grand universe, notwithstanding this act of abnegation in behalf of the Supreme Creator children of the Paradise Deities, the Father has certainly reserved to himself the unchallengeable right to be present in the minds and souls of his evolving creatures to the end that he may so act as to draw all creature creation to himself, co-ordinately with the spiritual gravity of the Paradise Sons. Said your Paradise bestowal Son when yet on Urantia, "I, if I am lifted up, will draw all men." This spiritual drawing power of the Paradise Sons and their creative associates we recognize and understand, but we do not so fully comprehend the methods of the all-wise Father's functioning in and through these Mystery Monitors that live and work so valiantly within the human mind.

While not subordinate to, co-ordinate with, or apparently related to, the work of the universe of universes, though acting independently in the minds of the children of men, unceasingly do these mysterious presences urge the creatures of their indwelling toward divine ideals, always luring them upward toward the purposes and aims of a future and better life. These Mystery Monitors are continually assisting in the establishment of the spiritual dominion of Michael throughout the universe of Nebadon while mysteriously contributing to the stabilization of the sovereignty of the Ancients of Days in Orvonton. The Adjusters *are* the will of God, and since the Supreme Creator children of God also personally embody that same will, it is inevitable that the actions of Adjusters and the sovereignty of the universe rulers should be mutually interdependent. Though apparently unconnected, the Father presence of the Adjusters and the Father sovereignty of Michael of Nebadon must be diverse manifestations of the same divinity.

Thought Adjusters appear to come and go quite independent of any and all other spiritual presences; they seem to function in accordance with universe laws quite apart from those which govern and control the performances of all other spirit influences. But regardless of such apparent independence, long-range observation unquestionably discloses that they function in the human mind in perfect synchrony and co-ordination with all other spirit ministries, including adjutant mind-spirits, Holy Spirit, Spirit of Truth, and other influences.

When a world is isolated by rebellion, when a planet is cut off from all outside encircuited communication, as was Urantia after the Caligastia upheaval, aside from personal messengers there remains but one possibility of direct interplanetary or universe communication, and that is through the liaison of the Adjusters of the spheres. No matter what happens on a world or in a universe, the Adjusters are never directly concerned. The isolation of a planet in no way affects the Adjusters and their ability to communicate with any part of the local universe, superuniverse, or the central universe. And this is the reason why contacts with the supreme and the self-acting Adjusters of the reserve corps of destiny are so frequently made on quarantined worlds. Recourse is had to such a technique as a means of circumventing the handicaps of planetary isolation. In recent years the archangels' circuit has functioned on Urantia, but that means of communication is largely limited to the transactions of the archangel corps itself.

We are cognizant of many spirit phenomena in the far-flung universe which we are at a loss fully to understand. We are not yet masters of all that is transpiring about us; and I believe that much of this inscrutable work is wrought by the Gravity Messengers and certain types of Mystery Monitors. I do not believe that Adjusters are devoted solely to the remaking of mortal minds. I am persuaded that the Personalized Monitors and other orders of unrevealed prepersonal spirits are representative of the Universal Father's direct and unexplained contact with the creatures of the realms.

5. THE ADJUSTER'S MISSION

The Adjusters accept a difficult assignment when they volunteer to indwell such composite beings as live on Urantia. But they have assumed the task of existing in your minds, there to receive the admonitions of the spiritual intelligences of the realms and then to undertake to redictate or translate these spiritual messages to the material mind; they are indispensable to the Paradise ascension.

What the Thought Adjuster cannot utilize in your present life, those truths which he cannot successfully transmit to the man of his betrothal, he will faithfully preserve for use in the next stage of existence, just as he now carries over from circle to circle those items which he fails to register in the experience of the human subject, owing to the creature's inability, or failure, to give a sufficient degree of co-operation.

One thing you can depend upon: The Adjusters will never lose anything committed to their care; never have we known these spirit helpers to default. Angels and other high types of spirit beings, not excepting the local universe type of Sons, may occasionally embrace evil, may sometimes depart from the divine way, but Adjusters never falter. They are absolutely dependable, and this is equally true of all seven groups.

Your Adjuster is the potential of your new and next order of existence, the advance bestowal of your eternal sonship with God. By and with the consent of your will, the Adjuster has the power to subject the creature trends of the material mind to the transforming actions of the motivations and purposes of the emerging morontial soul.

The Mystery Monitors are not thought helpers; they are thought adjusters. They labor with the material mind for the purpose of constructing, by adjustment and spiritualization, a new mind for the new worlds and the new name of your future career. Their mission chiefly concerns the future life, not this life. They are called heavenly helpers, not earthly helpers. They are not interested in making the mortal career easy; rather are they concerned in making your life reasonably difficult and rugged, so that decisions will be stimulated and multiplied. The presence of a great Thought Adjuster does not bestow ease of living and freedom from strenuous thinking, but such a divine gift should confer a sublime peace of mind and a superb tranquillity of spirit.

Your transient and ever-changing emotions of joy and sorrow are in the main purely human and material reactions to your internal psychic climate and to your external material environment. Do not, therefore, look to the Adjuster for selfish consolation and mortal comfort. It is the business of the Adjuster to prepare you for the eternal adventure, to assure your survival. It is not the mission of the Mystery Monitor to smooth your ruffled feelings or to minister to your injured pride; it is the preparation of your soul for the long ascending career that engages the attention and occupies the time of the Adjuster.

I doubt that I am able to explain to you just what the Adjusters do in your minds and for your souls. I do not know that I am fully cognizant of what is really going on in the cosmic association of a divine Monitor and a human mind. It is all somewhat of a mystery to us, not as to the plan and purpose but as to the actual mode of accomplishment. And this is just why we are confronted with such difficulty in finding an appropriate name for these supernal gifts to mortal men.

The Thought Adjusters would like to change your feelings of fear to convictions of love and confidence; but they cannot mechanically and arbitrarily do such things; that is your task. In executing those decisions which deliver you from the fetters of fear, you literally supply the psychic fulcrum on which the Adjuster may subsequently apply a spiritual lever of uplifting and advancing illumination.

When it comes to the sharp and well-defined conflicts between the higher and lower tendencies of the races, between what *really is* right or wrong (not merely what you may call right and wrong), you can depend upon it that the Adjuster will always participate in some definite and active manner in such experiences. The fact that such Adjuster activity may be unconscious to the human partner does not in the least detract from its value and reality.

If you have a personal guardian of destiny and should fail of survival, that guardian angel must be adjudicated in order to receive vindication as to the faithful execution of her trust. But Thought Adjusters are not thus subjected to examination when their subjects fail to survive. We all know that, while an angel might possibly fall short of the perfection of ministry, Thought Adjusters work in the manner of Paradise perfection; their ministry is characterized by a flawless technique which is beyond the possibility of criticism by any being outside of Divinington. You have perfect guides; therefore is the goal of perfection certainly attainable.

6. GOD IN MAN

It is indeed a marvel of divine condescension for the exalted and perfect Adjusters to offer themselves for actual existence in the minds of material creatures, such as the mortals of Urantia, really to consummate a probationary union with the animal-origin beings of earth.

No matter what the previous status of the inhabitants of a world, subsequent to the bestowal of a divine Son and after the bestowal of the Spirit of Truth upon all humans, the Adjusters flock to such a world to indwell the minds of all normal will creatures. Following the completion of the mission of a Paradise bestowal Son, these Monitors truly become the "kingdom of heaven within you." Through the bestowal of the divine gifts the Father makes the closest possible approach to sin and evil, for it is literally true that the Adjuster must coexist in the mortal mind even in the very midst of human unrighteousness. The indwelling Adjusters are particularly tormented by those thoughts which are purely sordid and selfish; they are distressed by irreverence for that which is beautiful and divine, and they are virtually thwarted in their work by many of man's foolish animal fears and childish anxieties.

The Mystery Monitors are undoubtedly the bestowal of the Universal Father, the reflection of the image of God abroad in the universe. A great teacher once admonished men that they should be renewed in the spirit of their minds; that they become new men who, like God, are created in righteousness and in the completion of truth. The Adjuster is the mark of divinity, the presence of God. The "image of God" does not refer to physical likeness nor to the circumscribed limitations of material creature endowment but rather to the gift of the spirit presence of the Universal Father in the supernal bestowal of the Thought Adjusters upon the humble creatures of the universes.

The Adjuster is the wellspring of spiritual attainment and the hope of divine character within you. He is the power, privilege, and the possibility of survival, which so fully and forever distinguishes you from mere animal creatures. He is the higher and truly internal spiritual stimulus of thought in contrast with the external and physical stimulus, which reaches the mind over the nerve-energy mechanism of the material body.

These faithful custodians of the future career unfailingly duplicate every mental creation with a spiritual counterpart; they are thus slowly and surely re-creating you as you really are (only spiritually) for resurrection on the survival worlds. And all of these exquisite spirit re-creations are being preserved in the emerging reality of your evolving and immortal soul, your morontia self. These realities are actually there, notwithstanding that the Adjuster is seldom able to exalt these duplicate creations sufficiently to exhibit them to the light of consciousness.

And as you are the human parent, so is the Adjuster the divine parent of the real you, your higher and advancing self, your better morontial and future spiritual self. And it is this evolving morontial soul that the judges and censors discern when they decree your survival and pass you upward to new worlds and never-ending existence in eternal liaison with your faithful partner—God, the Adjuster.

The Adjusters are the eternal ancestors, the divine originals, of your evolving immortal souls; they are the unceasing urge that leads man to attempt the mastery of the material and present existence in the light of the spiritual and future career. The Monitors are the prisoners of undying hope, the founts of everlasting progression. And how they do enjoy communicating with their subjects in more or less direct channels! How they rejoice when they can dispense with symbols and other methods of indirection and flash their messages straight to the intellects of their human partners!

You humans have begun an endless unfolding of an almost infinite panorama, a limitless expanding of never-ending, ever-widening spheres of opportunity for exhilarating service, matchless adventure, sublime uncertainty, and boundless attainment. When the clouds gather overhead, your faith should accept the fact of the presence of the indwelling Adjuster, and thus you should be able to look beyond the mists of mortal uncertainty into the clear shining of the sun of eternal righteousness on the beckoning heights of the mansion worlds of Satania.

[Presented by a Solitary Messenger of Orvonton.]

PAPER 109

RELATION OF ADJUSTERS TO UNIVERSE CREATURES

THE Thought Adjusters are the children of the universe career, and indeed the virgin Adjusters must gain experience while mortal creatures grow and develop. As the personality of the human child expands for the struggles of evolutionary existence, so does the Adjuster wax great in the rehearsals of the next stage of ascending life. As the child acquires adaptative versatility for his adult activities through the social and play life of early childhood, so does the indwelling Adjuster achieve skill for the next stage of cosmic life by virtue of the preliminary mortal planning and rehearsing of those activities which have to do with the morontia career. Human existence constitutes a period of practice which is effectively utilized by the Adjuster in preparing for the increased responsibilities and the greater opportunities of a future life. But the Adjuster's efforts, while living within you, are not so much concerned with the affairs of temporal life and planetary existence. Today, the Thought Adjusters are, as it were, rehearsing the realities of the universe career in the evolving minds of human beings.

1. DEVELOPMENT OF ADJUSTERS

There must be a comprehensive and elaborate plan for the training and development of virgin Adjusters before they are sent forth from Divinington, but we really do not know very much about it. There undoubtedly also exists an extensive system for retraining Adjusters of indwelling experience before they embark upon new missions of mortal association, but, again, we do not actually know.

I have been told by Personalized Adjusters that every time a Monitor-indwelt mortal fails of survival, when the Adjuster returns to Divinington, an extended course of training is engaged in. This additional training is made possible by the experience of having indwelt a human being, and it is always imparted before the Adjuster is remanded to the evolutionary worlds of time.

Actual living experience has no cosmic substitute. The perfection of the divinity of a newly formed Thought Adjuster does not in any manner endow this Mystery Monitor with experienced ministrative ability. Experience is inseparable from a living existence; it is the one thing which no amount of divine endowment can absolve you from the necessity of securing by *actual living.* Therefore, in common with all beings living and functioning within the present sphere of the Supreme, Thought Adjusters must acquire experience; they must evolve from the lower, inexperienced, to the higher, more experienced, groups.

Adjusters pass through a definite developmental career in the mortal mind; they achieve a reality of attainment which is eternally theirs. They progressively acquire Adjuster skill and ability as a result of any and all contacts with the material races, regardless of the survival or nonsurvival of their particular mortal subjects. They are also equal partners of the human mind in fostering the evolution of the immortal soul of survival capacity.

The first stage of Adjuster evolution is attained in fusion with the surviving soul of a mortal being. Thus, while you are in nature evolving inward and upward from man to God, the Adjusters are in nature evolving outward and downward from God to man; and so will the final product of this union of divinity and humanity eternally be the son of man and the son of God.

2. SELF-ACTING ADJUSTERS

You have been informed of the classification of Adjusters in relation to experience—virgin, advanced, and supreme. You should also recognize a certain functional classification—the self-acting Adjusters. A self-acting Adjuster is one who:

1. Has had certain requisite experience in the evolving life of a will creature, either as a temporary indweller on a type of world where Adjusters are only loaned to mortal subjects or on an actual fusion planet where the human failed of survival. Such a Monitor is either an advanced or a supreme Adjuster.

2. Has acquired the balance of spiritual power in a human who has made the third psychic circle and has had assigned to him a personal seraphic guardian.

3. Has a subject who has made the supreme decision, has entered into a solemn and sincere betrothal with the Adjuster. The Adjuster looks beforehand to the time of actual fusion and reckons the union as an event of fact.

4. Has a subject who has been mustered into one of the reserve corps of destiny on an evolutionary world of mortal ascension.

5. At some time, during human sleep, has been temporarily detached from the mind of mortal incarceration to perform some exploit of liaison, contact, reregistration, or other extrahuman service associated with the spiritual administration of the world of assignment.

6. Has served in a time of crisis in the experience of some human being who was the material complement of a spirit personality intrusted with the enactment of some cosmic achievement essential to the spiritual economy of the planet.

Self-acting Adjusters seem to possess a marked degree of will in all matters not involving the human personalities of their immediate indwelling, as is indicated by their numerous exploits both within and without the mortal subjects of attachment. Such Adjusters participate in numerous activities of the realm, but more frequently they function as undetected indwellers of the earthly tabernacles of their own choosing.

Undoubtedly these higher and more experienced types of Adjusters can communicate with those in other realms. But while self-acting Adjusters do thus intercommunicate, they do so only on the levels of their mutual work and for the purpose of preserving custodial data essential to the Adjuster ministry of the realms of their sojourn, though on occasions they have been known to function in interplanetary matters during times of crisis.

Supreme and self-acting Adjusters can leave the human body at will. The indwellers are not an organic or biologic part of mortal life; they are divine superimpositions thereon. In the original life plans they were provided for, but they are not indispensable to material existence. Nevertheless it should be recorded that they very rarely, even temporarily, leave their mortal tabernacles after they once take up their indwelling.

The superacting Adjusters are those who have achieved the conquest of their intrusted tasks and only await the dissolution of the material-life vehicle or the translation of the immortal soul.

3. RELATION OF ADJUSTERS TO MORTAL TYPES

The character of the detailed work of Mystery Monitors varies in accordance with the nature of their assignments, as to whether or not they are *liaison* or *fusion* Adjusters. Some Adjusters are merely loaned for the temporal lifetimes of their subjects; others are bestowed as personality candidates with permission for everlasting fusion if their subjects survive. There is also a slight variation in their work among the different planetary types as well as in different systems and universes. But, on the whole, their labors are remarkably uniform, more so than are the duties of any of the created orders of celestial beings.

On certain primitive worlds (the series one group) the Adjuster indwells the mind of the creature as an experiential training, chiefly for self-culture and progressive development. Virgin Adjusters are usually sent to such worlds during the earlier times when primitive men are arriving in the valley of decision, but when comparatively few will elect to ascend the moral heights beyond the hills of self-mastery and character acquirement to attain the higher levels of emerging spirituality. (Many, however, who fail of Adjuster fusion do survive as Spirit-fused ascenders.) The Adjusters receive valuable training and acquire wonderful experience in transient association with primitive minds, and they are able subsequently to utilize this experience for the benefit of superior beings on other worlds. *Nothing of survival value is ever lost in all the wide universe.*

On another type of world (the series two group) the Adjusters are merely loaned to mortal beings. Here the Monitors can never attain fusion personality through such indwelling, but they do afford great help to their human subjects during the mortal lifetime, far more than they are able to give to Urantia mortals. The Adjusters are here loaned to the mortal creatures for a single life span as patterns for their higher spiritual attainment, temporary helpers in the intriguing task of perfecting a survival character. The Adjusters do not return after natural death; these surviving mortals attain eternal life through Spirit fusion.

On worlds such as Urantia (the series three group) there is a real betrothal with the divine gifts, a life and death engagement. If you survive, there is to be an eternal union, an everlasting fusion, the making of man and Adjuster one being.

In the three-brained mortals of this series of worlds, the Adjusters are able to gain far more actual contact with their subjects during the temporal life than in the one- and two-brained types. But in the career after death, the three-brained type proceed just as do the one-brained type and the two-brained peoples—the Urantia races.

On the two-brain worlds, subsequent to the sojourn of a Paradise bestowal Son, virgin Adjusters are seldom assigned to persons who have unquestioned capacity for survival. It is our belief that on such worlds practically all Adjusters indwelling intelligent men and women of survival capacity belong to the advanced or to the supreme type.

In many of the early evolutionary races of Urantia, three groups of beings existed. There were those who were so animalistic that they were utterly lacking in Adjuster capacity. There were those who exhibited undoubted capacity for Adjusters and promptly received them when the age of moral responsibility was attained. There was a third class who occupied a borderline position; they had capacity for Adjuster reception, but the Monitors could only indwell the mind on the personal petition of the individual.

But with those beings who are virtually disqualified for survival by disinheritance through the agency of unfit and inferior ancestors, many a virgin Adjuster has served a valuable preliminary experience in contacting evolutionary mind and thus has become better qualified for a subsequent assignment to a higher type of mind on some other world.

4. ADJUSTERS AND HUMAN PERSONALITY

The higher forms of intelligent intercommunication between human beings are greatly helped by the indwelling Adjusters. Animals do have fellow feelings, but they do not communicate concepts to each other; they can express emotions but not ideas and ideals. Neither do men of animal origin experience a high type of intellectual intercourse or spiritual communion with their fellows until the Thought Adjusters have been bestowed, albeit, when such evolutionary creatures develop speech, they are on the highroad to receiving Adjusters.

Animals do, in a crude way, communicate with each other, but there is little or no *personality* in such primitive contact. Adjusters are not personality; they are prepersonal beings. But they do hail from the source of personality, and their presence does augment the qualitative manifestations of human personality; especially is this true if the Adjuster has had previous experience.

The type of Adjuster has much to do with the potential for expression of the human personality. On down through the ages, many of the great intellectual and spiritual leaders of Urantia have exerted their influence chiefly because of the superiority and previous experience of their indwelling Adjusters.

The indwelling Adjusters have in no small measure co-operated with other spiritual influences in transforming and humanizing the descendants of the primitive men of olden ages. If the Adjusters indwelling the minds of the inhabitants of Urantia were to be withdrawn, the world would slowly return to many of the scenes and practices of the men of primitive times; the divine Monitors are one of the real potentials of advancing civilization.

I have observed a Thought Adjuster indwelling a mind on Urantia who has, according to the records on Uversa, indwelt fifteen minds previously in Orvonton. We do not know whether this Monitor has had similar experiences in other superuniverses, but I suspect so. This is a marvelous Adjuster and one of the most useful and potent forces on Urantia during this present age. What others have lost, in that they refused to survive, this human being (and your whole world) now gains. From him who has not survival qualities, shall be taken away even that experienced Adjuster which he now has, while to him who has survival prospects, shall be given even the pre-experienced Adjuster of a slothful deserter.

In a sense the Adjusters may be fostering a certain degree of planetary cross-fertilization in the domains of truth, beauty, and goodness. But they are seldom given two indwelling experiences on the same planet; there is no Adjuster now serving on Urantia who has been on this world previously. I know whereof I speak since we have their numbers and records in the archives of Uversa.

5. MATERIAL HANDICAPS TO ADJUSTER INDWELLING

Supreme and self-acting Adjusters are often able to contribute factors of spiritual import to the human mind when it flows freely in the liberated but controlled channels of creative imagination. At such times, and sometimes during sleep, the Adjuster is able to arrest the mental currents, to stay the flow, and then to divert the idea procession; and all this is done in order to effect deep spiritual transformations in the higher recesses of the superconsciousness. Thus are the forces and energies of mind more fully adjusted to the key of the contactual tones of the spiritual level of the present and the future.

It is sometimes possible to have the mind illuminated, to hear the divine voice that continually speaks within you, so that you may become partially conscious of the wisdom, truth, goodness, and beauty of the potential personality constantly indwelling you.

But your unsteady and rapidly shifting mental attitudes often result in thwarting the plans and interrupting the work of the Adjusters. Their work is not only interfered with by the innate natures of the mortal races, but this ministry is also greatly retarded by your own preconceived opinions, settled ideas, and long-standing prejudices. Because of these handicaps, many times only their unfinished creations emerge into consciousness, and confusion of concept is inevitable. Therefore, in scrutinizing mental situations, safety lies only in the prompt recognition of each and every thought and experience for just what it actually and fundamentally is, disregarding entirely what it might have been.

The great problem of life is the adjustment of the ancestral tendencies of living to the demands of the spiritual urges initiated by the divine presence of the Mystery Monitor. While in the universe and superuniverse careers no man can serve two masters, in the life you now live on Urantia every man must perforce serve two masters. He must become adept in the art of a continuous human temporal compromise while he yields spiritual allegiance to but one master; and this is why so many falter and fail, grow weary and succumb to the stress of the evolutionary struggle.

While the hereditary legacy of cerebral endowment and that of electrochemical overcontrol both operate to delimit the sphere of efficient Adjuster activity, no hereditary handicap (in normal minds) ever prevents eventual spiritual achievement. Heredity may interfere with the rate of personality conquest, but it does not prevent eventual consummation of the ascendant adventure. If you will co-operate with your Adjuster, the divine gift will, sooner or later, evolve the immortal morontia soul and, subsequent to fusion therewith, will present the new creature to the sovereign Master Son of the local universe and eventually to the Father of Adjusters on Paradise.

6. THE PERSISTENCE OF TRUE VALUES

Adjusters never fail; nothing worth surviving is ever lost; every meaningful value in every will creature is certain of survival, irrespective of the survival or nonsurvival of the meaning-discovering or evaluating personality. And so it is, a mortal creature may reject survival; still the life experience is not wasted; the eternal Adjuster carries the worth-while features of such an apparent life of failure over into some other world and there bestows these surviving meanings and values upon some higher type of mortal mind, one of survival capacity. No worth-while experience ever happens in vain; no true meaning or real value ever perishes.

As related to fusion candidates, if a Mystery Monitor is deserted by the mortal associate, if the human partner declines to pursue the ascending career, when released by natural death (or prior thereto), the Adjuster carries away everything of survival value which has evolved in the mind of that nonsurviving creature. If an Adjuster should repeatedly fail to attain fusion personality because of the nonsurvival of successive human subjects, and if this Monitor should subsequently be personalized, all the acquired experience of having indwelt and mastered all these mortal minds would become the actual possession of such a newly Personalized Adjuster, an endowment to be enjoyed and utilized throughout all future ages. A Personalized Adjuster of this order is a composite assembly of all the survival traits of all his former creature hosts.

When Adjusters of long universe experience volunteer to indwell divine Sons on bestowal missions, they full well know that personality attainment can never be achieved through this service. But often does the Father of spirits grant personality to these volunteers and establish them as directors of their kind. These are the personalities honored with authority on Divinington. And their unique natures embody the mosaic humanity of their multiple experiences of mortal indwelling and also the spirit transcript of the human divinity of the Paradise bestowal Son of the terminal indwelling experience.

The activities of Adjusters in your local universe are directed by the Personalized Adjuster of Michael of Nebadon, that very Monitor who guided him step by step when he lived his human life in the flesh of Joshua ben Joseph. Faithful to his trust was this extraordinary Adjuster, and wisely did this valiant Monitor direct the human nature, ever guiding the mortal mind of the Paradise Son in the choosing of the path of the Father's perfect will. This Adjuster had previously served with Machiventa Melchizedek in the days of Abraham and had engaged in tremendous exploits both previous to this indwelling and between these bestowal experiences.

This Adjuster did indeed triumph in Jesus' human mind—that mind which in each of life's recurring situations maintained a consecrated dedication to the Father's will, saying, "Not my will, but yours, be done." Such decisive consecration constitutes the true passport from the limitations of human nature to the finality of divine attainment.

This same Adjuster now reflects in the inscrutable nature of his mighty personality the prebaptismal humanity of Joshua ben Joseph, the eternal and living transcript of the eternal and living values which the greatest of all Urantians created out of the humble circumstances of a commonplace life as it was lived to the complete exhaustion of the spiritual values attainable in mortal experience.

Everything of permanent value which is intrusted to an Adjuster is assured eternal survival. In certain instances the Monitor holds these possessions for bestowal on a mortal mind of future indwelling; in others, and upon personalization, these surviving and conserved realities are held in trust for future utilization in the service of the Architects of the Master Universe.

7. DESTINY OF PERSONALIZED ADJUSTERS

We cannot state whether or not non-Adjuster Father fragments are personalizable, but you have been informed that personality is the sovereign freewill bestowal of the Universal Father. As far as we know, the Adjuster type of Father fragment attains personality only by the acquirement of personal attributes through service-ministry to a personal being. These Personalized Adjusters are at home on Divinington, where they instruct and direct their prepersonal associates.

Personalized Thought Adjusters are the untrammeled, unassigned, and sovereign stabilizers and compensators of the far-flung universe of universes. They combine the Creator and creature experience—existential and experiential. They are conjoint time and eternity beings. They associate the prepersonal and the personal in universe administration.

Personalized Adjusters are the all-wise and powerful executives of the Architects of the Master Universe. They are the personal agents of the full ministry of the Universal Father—personal, prepersonal, and superpersonal. They are the personal ministers of the extraordinary, the unusual, and the unexpected throughout all the realms of the transcendental absonite spheres of the domain of God the Ultimate, even to the levels of God the Absolute.

They are the exclusive beings of the universes who embrace within their being all the known relationships of personality; they are omnipersonal—they are before personality, they are personality, and they are after personality. They minister the personality of the Universal Father as in the eternal past, the eternal present, and the eternal future.

Existential personality on the order of the infinite and absolute, the Father bestowed upon the Eternal Son, but he chose to reserve for his own ministry the experiential personality of the type of the Personalized Adjuster bestowed upon the existential prepersonal Adjuster; and they are thus both destined to the future eternal superpersonality of the transcendental ministry of the absonite realms of the Ultimate, the Supreme-Ultimate, even to the levels of the Ultimate-Absolute.

Seldom are the Personalized Adjusters seen at large in the universes. Occasionally they consult with the Ancients of Days, and sometimes the Personalized Adjusters of the sevenfold Creator Sons come to the headquarters worlds of the constellations to confer with the Vorondadek rulers.

When the planetary Vorondadek observer of Urantia—the Most High custodian who not long since assumed an emergency regency of your world—asserted his authority in the presence of the resident governor general, he began his emergency administration of Urantia with a full staff of his own choosing. He immediately assigned to all his associates and assistants their planetary duties. But he did not choose the three Personalized Adjusters who appeared in his presence the instant he assumed the regency. He did not even know they would thus appear, for they did not so manifest their divine presence at the time of a previous regency. And the Most High regent did not assign service or designate duties for these volunteer Personalized Adjusters. Nevertheless, these three omnipersonal beings were among the most active of the numerous orders of celestial beings then serving on Urantia.

Personalized Adjusters perform a wide range of services for numerous orders of universe personalities, but we are not permitted to discuss these ministries with Adjuster-indwelt evolutionary creatures. These extraordinary human divinities are among the most remarkable personalities of the entire grand universe, and no one dares to predict what their future missions may be.

[Presented by a Solitary Messenger of Orvonton.]

PAPER 110

RELATION OF ADJUSTERS TO INDIVIDUAL MORTALS

THE endowment of imperfect beings with freedom entails inevitable tragedy, and it is the nature of the perfect ancestral Deity to universally and affectionately share these sufferings in loving companionship.

As far as I am conversant with the affairs of a universe, I regard the love and devotion of a Thought Adjuster as the most truly divine affection in all creation. The love of the Sons in their ministry to the races is superb, but the devotion of an Adjuster to the individual is touchingly sublime, divinely Fatherlike. The Paradise Father has apparently reserved this form of personal contact with his individual creatures as an exclusive Creator prerogative. And there is nothing in all the universe of universes exactly comparable to the marvelous ministry of these impersonal entities that so fascinatingly indwell the children of the evolutionary planets.

1. INDWELLING THE MORTAL MIND

Adjusters should not be thought of as living in the material brains of human beings. They are not organic parts of the physical creatures of the realms. The Thought Adjuster may more properly be envisaged as indwelling the mortal mind of man rather than as existing within the confines of a single physical organ. And indirectly and unrecognized the Adjuster is constantly communicating with the human subject, especially during those sublime experiences of the worshipful contact of mind with spirit in the superconsciousness.

I wish it were possible for me to help evolving mortals to achieve a better understanding and attain a fuller appreciation of the unselfish and superb work of the Adjusters living within them, who are so devoutly faithful to the task of fostering man's spiritual welfare. These Monitors are efficient ministers to the higher phases of men's minds; they are wise and experienced manipulators of the spiritual potential of the human intellect. These heavenly helpers are dedicated to the stupendous task of guiding you safely inward and upward to the celestial haven of happiness. These tireless toilers are consecrated to the future personification of the triumph of divine truth in your life everlasting. They are the watchful workers who pilot the God-conscious human mind away from the shoals of evil while expertly guiding the evolving soul of man toward the divine harbors of perfection on far-distant and eternal shores. The Adjusters are loving leaders, your safe and sure guides through the dark and uncertain mazes of your short earthly career; they are the patient teachers who so constantly urge their subjects forward in the paths of progressive perfection. They are the careful custodians of the sublime values of creature character. I wish you could love them more, co-operate with them more fully, and cherish them more affectionately.

Although the divine indwellers are chiefly concerned with your spiritual preparation for the next stage of the never-ending existence, they are also deeply interested in your temporal welfare and in your real achievements on earth. They are delighted to contribute to your health, happiness, and true prosperity. They are not indifferent to your success in all matters of planetary advancement which are not inimical to your future life of eternal progress.

Adjusters are interested in, and concerned with, your daily doings and the manifold details of your life just to the extent that these are influential in the determination of your significant temporal choices and vital spiritual decisions and, hence, are factors in the solution of your problem of soul survival and eternal progress. The Adjuster, while passive regarding purely temporal welfare, is divinely active concerning all the affairs of your eternal future.

The Adjuster remains with you in all disaster and through every sickness which does not wholly destroy the mentality. But how unkind knowingly to defile or otherwise deliberately to pollute the physical body, which must serve as the earthly tabernacle of this marvelous gift from God. All physical poisons greatly retard the efforts of the Adjuster to exalt the material mind, while the mental poisons of fear, anger, envy, jealousy, suspicion, and intolerance likewise tremendously interfere with the spiritual progress of the evolving soul.

Today you are passing through the period of the courtship of your Adjuster; and if you only prove faithful to the trust reposed in you by the divine spirit who seeks your mind and soul in eternal union, there will eventually ensue that morontia oneness, that supernal harmony, that cosmic co-ordination, that divine attunement, that celestial fusion, that never-ending blending of identity, that oneness of being which is so perfect and final that even the most experienced personalities can never segregate or recognize as separate identities the fusion partners—mortal man and divine Adjuster.

2. ADJUSTERS AND HUMAN WILL

When Thought Adjusters indwell human minds, they bring with them the model careers, the ideal lives, as determined and foreordained by themselves and the Personalized Adjusters of Divinington, which have been certified by the Personalized Adjuster of Urantia. Thus they begin work with a definite and predetermined plan for the intellectual and spiritual development of their human subjects, but it is not incumbent upon any human being to accept this plan. You are all subjects of predestination, but it is not foreordained that you must accept this divine predestination; you are at full liberty to reject any part or all of the Thought Adjusters' program. It is their mission to effect such mind changes and to make such spiritual adjustments as you may willingly and intelligently authorize, to the end that they may gain more influence over the personality directionization; but under no circumstances do these divine Monitors ever take advantage of you or in any way arbitrarily influence you in your choices and decisions. The Adjusters respect your sovereignty of personality; *they are always subservient to your will.*

They are persistent, ingenious, and perfect in their methods of work, but they never do violence to the volitional selfhood of their hosts. No human being will ever be spiritualized by a divine Monitor against his will; survival is a gift of the Gods which must be desired by the creatures of time. In the final analysis, whatever the Adjuster has succeeded in doing for you, the records will show that the transformation has been accomplished with your co-operative consent; you will have been a willing partner with the Adjuster in the attainment of every step of the tremendous transformation of the ascension career.

The Adjuster is not trying to control your thinking, as such, but rather to spiritualize it, to eternalize it. Neither angels nor Adjusters are devoted directly to influencing human thought; that is your exclusive personality prerogative. The Adjusters are dedicated to improving, modifying, adjusting, and co-ordinating your thinking processes; but more especially and specifically they are devoted to the work of building up spiritual counterparts of your careers, morontia transcripts of your true advancing selves, for survival purposes.

Adjusters work in the spheres of the higher levels of the human mind, unceasingly seeking to produce morontia duplicates of every concept of the mortal intellect. There are, therefore, two realities which impinge upon, and are centered in, the human mind circuits: one, a mortal self evolved from the original plans of the Life Carriers, the other, an immortal entity from the high spheres of Divinington, an indwelling gift from God. But the mortal self is also a personal self; it has personality.

You as a personal creature have mind and will. The Adjuster as a prepersonal creature has premind and prewill. If you so fully conform to the Adjuster's mind that you see eye to eye, then your minds become one, and you receive the reinforcement of the Adjuster's mind. Subsequently, if your will orders and enforces the execution of the decisions of this new or combined mind, the Adjuster's prepersonal will attains to personality expression through your decision, and as far as that particular project is concerned, you and the Adjuster are one. Your mind has attained to divinity attunement, and the Adjuster's will has achieved personality expression.

To the extent that this identity is realized, you are mentally approaching the morontia order of existence. Morontia mind is a term signifying the substance and sum total of the co-operating minds of diversely material and spiritual natures. Morontia intellect, therefore, connotes a dual mind in the local universe dominated by one will. And with mortals this is a will, human in origin, which is becoming divine through man's identification of the human mind with the mindedness of God.

3. CO-OPERATION WITH THE ADJUSTER

Adjusters are playing the sacred and superb game of the ages; they are engaged in one of the supreme adventures of time in space. And how happy they are when your co-operation permits them to lend assistance in your short struggles of time as they continue to prosecute their larger tasks of eternity. But usually, when your Adjuster attempts to communicate with you, the message is lost in the material currents of the energy streams of human mind; only occasionally do you catch an echo, a faint and distant echo, of the divine voice.

The success of your Adjuster in the enterprise of piloting you through the mortal life and bringing about your survival depends not so much on the theories of your beliefs as upon your decisions, determinations, and steadfast *faith.* All these movements of personality growth become powerful influences aiding in your advancement because they help you to co-operate with the Adjuster; they assist you in ceasing to resist. Thought Adjusters succeed or apparently fail in their terrestrial undertakings just in so far as mortals succeed or fail to co-operate with the scheme whereby they are to be advanced along the ascending path of perfection attainment. The secret of survival is wrapped up in the supreme human desire to be Godlike and in the associated willingness to do and be any and all things which are essential to the final attainment of that overmastering desire.

When we speak of an Adjuster's success or failure, we are speaking in terms of human survival. *Adjusters never fail;* they are of the divine essence, and they always emerge triumphant in each of their undertakings.

I cannot but observe that so many of you spend so much time and thought on mere trifles of living, while you almost wholly overlook the more essential realities of everlasting import, those very accomplishments which are concerned with the development of a more harmonious working agreement between you and your Adjusters. The great goal of human existence is to attune to the divinity of the indwelling Adjuster; the great achievement of mortal life is the attainment of a true and understanding consecration to the eternal aims of the divine spirit who waits and works within your mind. But a devoted and determined effort to realize eternal destiny is wholly compatible with a lighthearted and joyous life and with a successful and honorable career on earth. Co-operation with the Thought Adjuster does not entail self-torture, mock piety, or hypocritical and ostentatious self-abasement; the ideal life is one of loving service rather than an existence of fearful apprehension.

Confusion, being puzzled, even sometimes discouraged and distracted, does not necessarily signify resistance to the leadings of the indwelling Adjuster. Such attitudes may sometimes connote lack of active co-operation with the divine Monitor and may, therefore, somewhat delay spiritual progress, but such intellectual emotional difficulties do not in the least interfere with the certain survival of the God-knowing soul. Ignorance alone can never prevent survival; neither can confusional doubts nor fearful uncertainty. Only conscious resistance to the Adjuster's leading can prevent the survival of the evolving immortal soul.

You must not regard co-operation with your Adjuster as a particularly conscious process, for it is not; but your motives and your decisions, your faithful determinations and your supreme desires, do constitute real and effective co-operation. You can consciously augment Adjuster harmony by:

1. Choosing to respond to divine leading; sincerely basing the human life on the highest consciousness of truth, beauty, and goodness, and then co-ordinating these qualities of divinity through wisdom, worship, faith, and love.

2. Loving God and desiring to be like him—genuine recognition of the divine fatherhood and loving worship of the heavenly Parent.

3. Loving man and sincerely desiring to serve him—wholehearted recognition of the brotherhood of man coupled with an intelligent and wise affection for each of your fellow mortals.

4. Joyful acceptance of cosmic citizenship—honest recognition of your progressive obligations to the Supreme Being, awareness of the interdependence of evolutionary man and evolving Deity. This is the birth of cosmic morality and the dawning realization of universal duty.

4. THE ADJUSTER'S WORK IN THE MIND

Adjusters are able to receive the continuous stream of cosmic intelligence coming in over the master circuits of time and space; they are in full touch with the spirit intelligence and energy of the universes. But these mighty indwellers are unable to transmit very much of this wealth of wisdom and truth to the minds of their mortal subjects because of the lack of commonness of nature and the absence of responsive recognition.

The Thought Adjuster is engaged in a constant effort so to spiritualize your mind as to evolve your morontia soul; but you yourself are mostly unconscious of this inner ministry. You are quite incapable of distinguishing the product of your own material intellect from that of the conjoint activities of your soul and the Adjuster.

Certain abrupt presentations of thoughts, conclusions, and other pictures of mind are sometimes the direct or indirect work of the Adjuster; but far more often they are the sudden emergence into consciousness of ideas which have been grouping themselves together in the submerged mental levels, natural and everyday occurrences of normal and ordinary psychic function inherent in the circuits of the evolving animal mind. (In contrast with these subconscious emanations, the revelations of the Adjuster appear through the realms of the superconscious.)

Trust all matters of mind beyond the dead level of consciousness to the custody of the Adjusters. In due time, if not in this world then on the mansion worlds, they will give good account of their stewardship, and eventually will they bring forth those meanings and values intrusted to their care and keeping. They will resurrect every worthy treasure of the mortal mind if you survive.

There exists a vast gulf between the human and the divine, between man and God. The Urantia races are so largely electrically and chemically controlled, so highly animallike in their common behavior, so emotional in their ordinary reactions, that it becomes exceedingly difficult for the Monitors to guide and direct them. You are so devoid of courageous decisions and consecrated co-operation that your indwelling Adjusters find it next to impossible to communicate directly with the human mind. Even when they do find it possible to flash a gleam of new truth to the evolving mortal soul, this spiritual revelation often so blinds the creature as to precipitate a convulsion of fanaticism or to initiate some other intellectual upheaval which results disastrously. Many a new religion and strange "ism" has arisen from the aborted, imperfect, misunderstood, and garbled communications of the Thought Adjusters.

For many thousands of years, so the records of Jerusem show, in each generation there have lived fewer and fewer beings who could function safely with self-acting Adjusters. This is an alarming picture, and the supervising personalities of Satania look with favor upon the proposals of some of your more immediate planetary supervisors who advocate the inauguration of measures designed to foster and conserve the higher spiritual types of the Urantia races.

5. ERRONEOUS CONCEPTS OF ADJUSTER GUIDANCE

Do not confuse and confound the mission and influence of the Adjuster with what is commonly called conscience; they are not directly related. Conscience is a human and purely psychic reaction. It is not to be despised, but it is hardly the voice of God to the soul, which indeed the Adjuster's would be if such a voice could be heard. Conscience, rightly, admonishes you to do right; but the Adjuster, in addition, endeavors to tell you what truly is right; that is, when and as you are able to perceive the Monitor's leading.

Man's dream experiences, that disordered and disconnected parade of the un-co-ordinated sleeping mind, present adequate proof of the failure of the Adjusters to harmonize and associate the divergent factors of the mind of man. The Adjusters simply cannot, in a single lifetime, arbitrarily co-ordinate and synchronize two such unlike and diverse types of thinking as the human and the divine. When they do, as they sometimes have, such souls are translated directly to the mansion worlds without the necessity of passing through the experience of death.

During the slumber season the Adjuster attempts to achieve only that which the will of the indwelt personality has previously fully approved by the decisions and choosings which were made during times of fully wakeful consciousness, and which have thereby become lodged in the realms of the supermind, the liaison domain of human and divine interrelationship.

While their mortal hosts are asleep, the Adjusters try to register their creations in the higher levels of the material mind, and some of your grotesque dreams indicate their failure to make efficient contact. The absurdities of dream life not only testify to pressure of unexpressed emotions but also bear witness to the horrible distortion of the representations of the spiritual concepts presented by the Adjusters. Your own passions, urges, and other innate tendencies translate themselves into the picture and substitute their unexpressed desires for the divine messages which the indwellers are endeavoring to put into the psychic records during unconscious sleep.

It is extremely dangerous to postulate as to the Adjuster content of the dream life. The Adjusters do work during sleep, but your ordinary dream experiences are purely physiologic and psychologic phenomena. Likewise, it is hazardous to attempt the differentiation of the Adjusters' concept registry from the more or less continuous and conscious reception of the dictations of mortal conscience. These are problems which will have to be solved through individual discrimination and personal decision. But a human being would do better to err in rejecting an Adjuster's expression through believing it to be a purely human experience than to blunder into exalting a reaction of the mortal mind to the sphere of divine dignity. Remember, the influence of a Thought Adjuster is for the most part, though not wholly, a superconscious experience.

In varying degrees and increasingly as you ascend the psychic circles, sometimes directly, but more often indirectly, you do communicate with your Adjusters. But it is dangerous to entertain the idea that every new concept originating in the human mind is the dictation of the Adjuster. More often, in beings of your order, that which you accept as the Adjuster's voice is in reality the emanation of your own intellect. This is dangerous ground, and every human being must settle these problems for himself in accordance with his natural human wisdom and superhuman insight.

The Adjuster of the human being through whom this communication is being made enjoys such a wide scope of activity chiefly because of this human's almost complete indifference to any outward manifestations of the Adjuster's inner presence; it is indeed fortunate that he remains consciously quite unconcerned about the entire procedure. He holds one of the highly experienced Adjusters of his day and generation, and yet his passive reaction to, and inactive concern toward, the phenomena associated with the presence in his mind of this versatile Adjuster is pronounced by the guardian of destiny to be a rare and fortuitous reaction. And all this constitutes a favorable co-ordination of influences, favorable both to the Adjuster in the higher sphere of action and to the human partner from the standpoints of health, efficiency, and tranquillity.

6. THE SEVEN PSYCHIC CIRCLES

The sum total of personality realization on a material world is contained within the successive conquest of the seven psychic circles of mortal potentiality. Entrance upon the seventh circle marks the beginning of true human personality function. Completion of the first circle denotes the relative maturity of the mortal being. Though the traversal of the seven circles of cosmic growth does not equal fusion with the Adjuster, the mastery of these circles marks the attainment of those steps which are preliminary to Adjuster fusion.

The Adjuster is your equal partner in the attainment of the seven circles—the achievement of comparative mortal maturity. The Adjuster ascends the circles with you from the seventh to the first but progresses to the status of supremacy and self-activity quite independent of the active co-operation of the mortal mind.

The psychic circles are not exclusively intellectual, neither are they wholly morontial; they have to do with personality status, mind attainment, soul growth, and Adjuster attunement. The successful traversal of these levels demands the harmonious functioning of the *entire personality,* not merely of some one phase thereof. The growth of the parts does not equal the true maturation of the whole; the parts really grow in proportion to the expansion of the entire self—the whole self—material, intellectual, and spiritual.

When the development of the intellectual nature proceeds faster than that of the spiritual, such a situation renders communication with the Thought Adjuster both difficult and dangerous. Likewise, overspiritual development tends to produce a fanatical and perverted interpretation of the spirit leadings of the divine indweller. Lack of spiritual capacity makes it very difficult to transmit to such a material intellect the spiritual truths resident in the higher superconsciousness. It is to the mind of perfect poise, housed in a body of clean habits, stabilized neural energies, and balanced chemical function—when the physical, mental, and spiritual powers are in triune harmony of development—that a maximum of light and truth can be imparted with a minimum of temporal danger or risk to the real welfare of such a being. By such a balanced growth does man ascend the circles of planetary progression one by one, from the seventh to the first.

The Adjusters are always near you and of you, but rarely can they speak directly, as another being, to you. Circle by circle your intellectual decisions, moral choosings, and spiritual development add to the ability of the Adjuster to function in your mind; circle by circle you thereby ascend from the lower stages of Adjuster association and mind attunement, so that the Adjuster is increasingly enabled to register his picturizations of destiny with augmenting vividness and conviction upon the evolving consciousness of this God-seeking mind-soul.

Every decision you make either impedes or facilitates the function of the Adjuster; likewise do these very decisions determine your advancement in the circles of human achievement. It is true that the supremacy of a decision, its crisis relationship, has a great deal to do with its circle-making influence; nevertheless, numbers of decisions, frequent repetitions, persistent repetitions, are also essential to the habit-forming certainty of such reactions.

It is difficult precisely to define the seven levels of human progression, for the reason that these levels are personal; they are variable for each individual and are apparently determined by the growth capacity of each human being. The conquest of these levels of cosmic evolution is reflected in three ways:

1. *Adjuster attunement.* The spiritizing mind nears the Adjuster presence proportional to circle attainment.

2. *Soul evolution.* The emergence of the morontia soul indicates the extent and depth of circle mastery.

3. *Personality reality.* The degree of selfhood reality is directly determined by circle conquest. Persons become more real as they ascend from the seventh to the first level of mortal existence.

As the circles are traversed, the child of material evolution is growing into the mature human of immortal potentiality. The shadowy reality of the embryonic nature of a seventh circler is giving way to the clearer manifestation of the emerging morontia nature of a local universe citizen.

While it is impossible precisely to define the seven levels, or psychic circles, of human growth, it is permissible to suggest the minimum and maximum limits of these stages of maturity realization:

The seventh circle. This level is entered when human beings develop the powers of personal choice, individual decision, moral responsibility, and the capacity for the attainment of spiritual individuality. This signifies the united function of the seven adjutant mind-spirits under the direction of the spirit of wisdom, the encircuitment of the mortal creature in the influence of the Holy Spirit, and, on Urantia, the first functioning of the Spirit of Truth, together with the reception of a Thought Adjuster in the mortal mind. Entrance upon the seventh circle constitutes a mortal creature a truly potential citizen of the local universe.

The third circle. The Adjuster's work is much more effective after the human ascender attains the third circle and receives a personal seraphic guardian of destiny. While there is no apparent concert of effort between the Adjuster and the seraphic guardian, nonetheless there is to be observed an unmistakable improvement in all phases of cosmic achievement and spiritual development subsequent to the assignment of the personal seraphic attendant. When the third circle is attained, the Adjuster endeavors to morontiaize the mind of man during the remainder of the mortal life span, to make the remaining circles, and achieve the final stage of the divine-human association before natural death dissolves the unique partnership.

The first circle. The Adjuster cannot, ordinarily, speak directly and immediately with you until you attain the first and final circle of progressive mortal achievement. This level represents the highest possible realization of mind-Adjuster relationship in the human experience prior to the liberation of the evolving morontia soul from the habiliments of the material body. Concerning mind, emotions, and cosmic insight, this achievement of the first psychic circle is the nearest possible approach of material mind and spirit Adjuster in human experience.

Perhaps these psychic circles of mortal progression would be better denominated *cosmic levels*—actual meaning grasps and value realizations of progressive approach to the morontia consciousness of initial relationship of the evolutionary soul with the emerging Supreme Being. And it is this very relationship that makes it forever impossible fully to explain the significance of the cosmic circles to the material mind. These circle attainments are only relatively related to God-consciousness. A seventh or sixth circler can be almost as truly God-knowing—sonship conscious—as a second or first circler, but such lower circle beings are far less conscious of experiential relation to the Supreme Being, universe citizenship. The attainment of these cosmic circles will become a part of the ascenders' experience on the mansion worlds if they fail of such achievement before natural death.

The motivation of faith makes experiential the full realization of man's sonship with God, but *action,* completion of decisions, is essential to the evolutionary attainment of consciousness of progressive kinship with the *cosmic actuality* of the Supreme Being. Faith transmutes potentials to actuals in the spiritual world, but potentials become actuals in the finite realms of the Supreme only by and through the realization of choice-experience. But choosing to do the will of God joins spiritual faith to material decisions in personality action and thus supplies a divine and spiritual fulcrum for the more effective functioning of the human and material leverage of God-hunger. Such a wise co-ordination of material and spiritual forces greatly augments both cosmic realization of the Supreme and morontia comprehension of the Paradise Deities.

The mastery of the cosmic circles is related to the quantitative growth of the morontia soul, the comprehension of supreme meanings. But the qualitative status of this immortal soul is *wholly* dependent on the grasp of living faith upon the Paradise-potential fact-value that mortal man is a son of the eternal God. Therefore does a seventh circler go on to the mansion worlds to attain further quantitative realization of cosmic growth just as does a second or even a first circler.

There is only an indirect relation between cosmic-circle attainment and actual spiritual religious experience; such attainments are reciprocal and therefore mutually beneficial. Purely spiritual development may have little to do with planetary material prosperity, but circle attainment always augments the potential of human success and mortal achievement.

From the seventh to the third circle there occurs increased and unified action of the seven adjutant mind-spirits in the task of weaning the mortal mind from its dependence on the realities of the material life mechanisms preparatory to increased introduction to morontia levels of experience. From the third circle onward the adjutant influence progressively diminishes.

The seven circles embrace mortal experience extending from the highest purely animal level to the lowest actual contactual morontia level of self-consciousness as a personality experience. The mastery of the first cosmic circle signalizes the attainment of premorontia mortal maturity and marks the termination of the conjoint ministry of the adjutant mind-spirits as an exclusive influence of mind action in the human personality. Beyond the first circle, mind becomes increasingly akin to the intelligence of the morontia stage of evolution, the conjoined ministry of the cosmic mind and the superadjutant endowment of the Creative Spirit of a local universe.

The great days in the individual careers of Adjusters are: first, when the human subject breaks through into the third psychic circle, thus insuring the Monitor's self-activity and increased range of function (provided the indweller was not already self-acting); then, when the human partner attains the first psychic circle, and they are thereby enabled to intercommunicate, at least to some degree; and last, when they are finally and eternally fused.

7. THE ATTAINMENT OF IMMORTALITY

The achievement of the seven cosmic circles does not equal Adjuster fusion. There are many mortals living on Urantia who have attained their circles; but fusion depends on yet other greater and more sublime spiritual achievements, upon the attainment of a final and complete attunement of the mortal will with the will of God as it is resident in the Thought Adjuster.

When a human being has completed the circles of cosmic achievement, and further, when the final choosing of the mortal will permits the Adjuster to complete the association of human identity with the morontial soul during evolutionary and physical life, then do such consummated liaisons of soul and Adjuster go on independently to the mansion worlds, and there is issued the mandate from Uversa which provides for the immediate fusion of the Adjuster and the morontial soul. This fusion during physical life instantly consumes the material body; the human beings who might witness such a spectacle would only observe the translating mortal disappear "in chariots of fire."

Most Adjusters who have translated their subjects from Urantia were highly experienced and of record as previous indwellers of numerous mortals on other spheres. Remember, Adjusters gain valuable indwelling experience on planets of the loan order; it does not follow that Adjusters only gain experience for advanced work in those mortal subjects who fail to survive.

Subsequent to mortal fusion the Adjusters share your destiny and experience; *they are you.* After the fusion of the immortal morontia soul and the associated Adjuster, all of the experience and all of the values of the one eventually become the possession of the other, so that the two are actually one entity. In a certain sense, this new being is of the eternal past as well as for the eternal future. All that was once human in the surviving soul and all that is experientially divine in the Adjuster now become the actual possession of the new and ever-ascending universe personality. But on each universe level the Adjuster can endow the new creature only with those attributes which are meaningful and of value on that level. An absolute *oneness* with the divine Monitor, a complete exhaustion of the endowment of an Adjuster, can only be achieved in eternity subsequent to the final attainment of the Universal Father, the Father of spirits, ever the source of these divine gifts.

When the evolving soul and the divine Adjuster are finally and eternally fused, each gains all of the experiencible qualities of the other. This co-ordinate personality possesses all of the experiential memory of survival once held by the ancestral mortal mind and then resident in the morontia soul, and in addition thereto this potential finaliter embraces all the experiential memory of the

Adjuster throughout the mortal indwellings of all time. But it will require an eternity of the future for an Adjuster ever completely to endow the personality partnership with the meanings and values which the divine Monitor carries forward from the eternity of the past.

But with the vast majority of Urantians the Adjuster must patiently await the arrival of death deliverance; must await the liberation of the emerging soul from the well-nigh complete domination of the energy patterns and chemical forces inherent in your material order of existence. The chief difficulty you experience in contacting with your Adjusters consists in this very inherent material nature. So few mortals are real thinkers; you do not spiritually develop and discipline your minds to the point of favorable liaison with the divine Adjusters. The ear of the human mind is almost deaf to the spiritual pleas which the Adjuster translates from the manifold messages of the universal broadcasts of love proceeding from the Father of mercies. The Adjuster finds it almost impossible to register these inspiring spirit leadings in an animal mind so completely dominated by the chemical and electrical forces inherent in your physical natures.

Adjusters rejoice to make contact with the mortal mind; but they must be patient through the long years of silent sojourn during which they are unable to break through animal resistance and directly communicate with you. The higher the Thought Adjusters ascend in the scale of service, the more efficient they become. But never can they greet you, in the flesh, with the same full, sympathetic, and expressionful affection as they will when you discern them mind to mind on the mansion worlds.

During mortal life the material body and mind separate you from your Adjuster and prevent free communication; subsequent to death, after the eternal fusion, you and the Adjuster are one—you are not distinguishable as separate beings—and thus there exists no need for communication as you would understand it.

While the voice of the Adjuster is ever within you, most of you will hear it seldom during a lifetime. Human beings below the third and second circles of attainment rarely hear the Adjuster's direct voice except in moments of supreme desire, in a supreme situation, and consequent upon a supreme decision.

During the making and breaking of a contact between the mortal mind of a destiny reservist and the planetary supervisors, sometimes the indwelling Adjuster is so situated that it becomes possible to transmit a message to the mortal partner. Not long since, on Urantia, such a message was transmitted by a self-acting Adjuster to the human associate, a member of the reserve corps of destiny. This message was introduced by these words: "And now, without injury or jeopardy to the subject of my solicitous devotion and without intent to overchastise or discourage, for me, make record of this my plea to him." Then followed a beautifully touching and appealing admonition. Among other things, the Adjuster pleaded "that he more faithfully give me his sincere co-operation, more cheerfully endure the tasks of my emplacement, more faithfully carry out the program of my arrangement, more patiently go through the trials of my selection, more persistently and cheerfully tread the path of my choosing, more humbly receive credit that may accrue as a result of my ceaseless endeavors—thus transmit my admonition to the man of my indwelling.

Upon him I bestow the supreme devotion and affection of a divine spirit. And say further to my beloved subject that I will function with wisdom and power until the very end, until the last earth struggle is over; I will be true to my personality trust. And I exhort him to survival, not to disappoint me, not to deprive me of the reward of my patient and intense struggle. On the human will our achievement of personality depends. Circle by circle I have patiently ascended this human mind, and I have testimony that I am meeting the approval of the chief of my kind. Circle by circle I am passing on to judgment. I await with pleasure and without apprehension the roll call of destiny; I am prepared to submit all to the tribunals of the Ancients of Days."

[Presented by a Solitary Messenger of Orvonton.]

PAPER 111

THE ADJUSTER AND THE SOUL

THE presence of the divine Adjuster in the human mind makes it forever impossible for either science or philosophy to attain a satisfactory comprehension of the evolving soul of the human personality. The morontia soul is the child of the universe and may be really known only through cosmic insight and spiritual discovery.

The concept of a soul and of an indwelling spirit is not new to Urantia; it has frequently appeared in the various systems of planetary beliefs. Many of the Oriental as well as some of the Occidental faiths have perceived that man is divine in heritage as well as human in inheritance. The feeling of the inner presence in addition to the external omnipresence of Deity has long formed a part of many Urantian religions. Men have long believed that there is something growing within the human nature, something vital that is destined to endure beyond the short span of temporal life.

Before man realized that his evolving soul was fathered by a divine spirit, it was thought to reside in different physical organs—the eye, liver, kidney, heart, and later, the brain. The savage associated the soul with blood, breath, shadows and with reflections of the self in water.

In the conception of the *atman* the Hindu teachers really approximated an appreciation of the nature and presence of the Adjuster, but they failed to distinguish the copresence of the evolving and potentially immortal soul. The Chinese, however, recognized two aspects of a human being, the *yang* and the *yin,* the soul and the spirit. The Egyptians and many African tribes also believed in two factors, the *ka* and the *ba;* the soul was not usually believed to be pre-existent, only the spirit.

The inhabitants of the Nile valley believed that each favored individual had bestowed upon him at birth, or soon thereafter, a protecting spirit which they called the ka. They taught that this guardian spirit remained with the mortal subject throughout life and passed before him into the future estate. On the walls of a temple at Luxor, where is depicted the birth of Amenhotep III, the little prince is pictured on the arm of the Nile god, and near him is another child, in appearance identical with the prince, which is a symbol of that entity which the Egyptians called the ka. This sculpture was completed in the fifteenth century before Christ.

The ka was thought to be a superior spirit genius which desired to guide the associated mortal soul into the better paths of temporal living but more especially to influence the fortunes of the human subject in the hereafter. When an Egyptian of this period died, it was expected that his ka would be waiting for him on the other side of the Great River. At first, only kings were supposed to have kas, but presently all righteous men were believed to possess them.

One Egyptian ruler, speaking of the ka within his heart, said: "I did not disregard its speech; I feared to transgress its guidance. I prospered thereby greatly; I was thus successful by reason of that which it caused me to do; I was distinguished by its guidance." Many believed that the ka was "an oracle from God in everybody." Many believed that they were to "spend eternity in gladness of heart in the favor of the God that is in you."

Every race of evolving Urantia mortals has a word equivalent to the concept of soul. Many primitive peoples believed the soul looked out upon the world through human eyes; therefore did they so cravenly fear the malevolence of the evil eye. They have long believed that "the spirit of man is the lamp of the Lord." The Rig-Veda says: "My mind speaks to my heart."

1. THE MIND ARENA OF CHOICE

Though the work of Adjusters is spiritual in nature, they must, perforce, do all their work upon an intellectual foundation. Mind is the human soil from which the spirit Monitor must evolve the morontia soul with the co-operation of the indwelt personality.

There is a cosmic unity in the several mind levels of the universe of universes. Intellectual selves have their origin in the cosmic mind much as nebulae take origin in the cosmic energies of universe space. On the human (hence personal) level of intellectual selves the potential of spirit evolution becomes dominant, with the assent of the mortal mind, because of the spiritual endowments of the human personality together with the creative presence of an entity-point of absolute value in such human selves. But such a spirit dominance of the material mind is conditioned upon two experiences: This mind must have evolved up through the ministry of the seven adjutant mind-spirits, and the material (personal) self must choose to co-operate with the indwelling Adjuster in creating and fostering the morontia self, the evolutionary and potentially immortal soul.

Material mind is the arena in which human personalities live, are self-conscious, make decisions, choose God or forsake him, eternalize or destroy themselves.

Material evolution has provided you a life machine, your body; the Father himself has endowed you with the purest spirit reality known in the universe, your Thought Adjuster. But into your hands, subject to your own decisions, has been given mind, and it is by mind that you live or die. It is within this mind and with this mind that you make those moral decisions which enable you to achieve Adjusterlikeness, and that is Godlikeness.

Mortal mind is a temporary intellect system loaned to human beings for use during a material lifetime, and as they use this mind, they are either accepting or rejecting the potential of eternal existence. Mind is about all you have of universe reality that is subject to your will, and the soul—the morontia self—will faithfully portray the harvest of the temporal decisions which the mortal self is making. Human consciousness rests gently upon the electrochemical mechanism below and delicately touches the spirit-morontia energy system above. Of neither of these two systems is the human being ever completely conscious in his mortal life; therefore must he work in mind, of which he is conscious. And it is not so much what mind comprehends as what mind desires to comprehend that insures survival; it is not so much what mind is like as what mind is striving to be like that constitutes spirit identification. It is not so much that man is conscious of God as that man yearns for God that results in universe ascension. What you are today is not so important as what you are becoming day by day and in eternity.

Mind is the cosmic instrument on which the human will can play the discords of destruction, or upon which this same human will can bring forth the exquisite melodies of God identification and consequent eternal survival. The Adjuster bestowed upon man is, in the last analysis, impervious to evil and incapable of sin, but mortal mind can actually be twisted, distorted, and rendered evil and ugly by the sinful machinations of a perverse and self-seeking human will. Likewise can this mind be made noble, beautiful, true, and good—actually great—in accordance with the spirit-illuminated will of a God-knowing human being.

Evolutionary mind is only fully stable and dependable when manifesting itself upon the two extremes of cosmic intellectuality—the wholly mechanized and the entirely spiritualized. Between the intellectual extremes of pure mechanical control and true spirit nature there intervenes that enormous group of evolving and ascending minds whose stability and tranquillity are dependent upon personality choice and spirit identification.

But man does not passively, slavishly, surrender his will to the Adjuster. Rather does he actively, positively, and co-operatively choose to follow the Adjuster's leading when and as such leading consciously differs from the desires and impulses of the natural mortal mind. The Adjusters manipulate but never dominate man's mind against his will; to the Adjusters the human will is supreme. And they so regard and respect it while they strive to achieve the spiritual goals of thought adjustment and character transformation in the almost limitless arena of the evolving human intellect.

Mind is your ship, the Adjuster is your pilot, the human will is captain. The master of the mortal vessel should have the wisdom to trust the divine pilot to guide the ascending soul into the morontia harbors of eternal survival. Only by selfishness, slothfulness, and sinfulness can the will of man reject the guidance of such a loving pilot and eventually wreck the mortal career upon the evil shoals of rejected mercy and upon the rocks of embraced sin. With your consent, this faithful pilot will safely carry you across the barriers of time and the handicaps of space to the very source of the divine mind and on beyond, even to the Paradise Father of Adjusters.

2. NATURE OF THE SOUL

Throughout the mind functions of cosmic intelligence, the totality of mind is dominant over the parts of intellectual function. Mind, in its essence, is functional unity; therefore does mind never fail to manifest this constitutive unity, even when hampered and hindered by the unwise actions and choices of a misguided self. And this unity of mind invariably seeks for spirit co-ordination on all levels of its association with selves of will dignity and ascension prerogatives.

The material mind of mortal man is the cosmic loom that carries the morontia fabrics on which the indwelling Thought Adjuster threads the spirit patterns of a universe character of enduring values and divine meanings—a surviving soul of ultimate destiny and unending career, a potential finaliter.

The human personality is identified with mind and spirit held together in functional relationship by life in a material body. This functioning relationship of such mind and spirit does not result in some combination of the qualities or attributes of mind and spirit but rather in an entirely new, original, and unique universe value of potentially eternal endurance, the *soul.*

There are three and not two factors in the evolutionary creation of such an immortal soul. These three antecedents of the morontia human soul are:

1. *The human mind* and all cosmic influences antecedent thereto and impinging thereon.
2. *The divine spirit* indwelling this human mind and all potentials inherent in such a fragment of absolute spirituality together with all associated spiritual influences and factors in human life.
3. *The relationship between material mind and divine spirit,* which connotes a value and carries a meaning not found in either of the contributing factors to such an association. The reality of this unique relationship is neither material nor spiritual but morontial. It is the soul.

The midway creatures have long denominated this evolving soul of man the mid-mind in contradistinction to the lower or material mind and the higher or cosmic mind. This mid-mind is really a morontia phenomenon since it exists in the realm between the material and the spiritual. The potential of such a morontia evolution is inherent in the two universal urges of mind: the impulse of the finite mind of the creature to know God and attain the divinity of the Creator, and the impulse of the infinite mind of the Creator to know man and attain the *experience* of the creature.

This supernal transaction of evolving the immortal soul is made possible because the mortal mind is first personal and second is in contact with superanimal realities; it possesses a supermaterial endowment of cosmic ministry which insures the evolution of a moral nature capable of making moral decisions, thereby effecting a bona fide creative contact with the associated spiritual ministries and with the indwelling Thought Adjuster.

The inevitable result of such a contactual spiritualization of the human mind is the gradual birth of a soul, the joint offspring of an adjutant mind dominated by a human will that craves to know God, working in liaison with the spiritual forces of the universe which are under the overcontrol of an actual fragment of the very God of all creation—the Mystery Monitor. And thus does the material and mortal reality of the self transcend the temporal limitations of the physical-life machine and attain a new expression and a new identification in the evolving vehicle for selfhood continuity, the morontia and immortal soul.

3. THE EVOLVING SOUL

The mistakes of mortal mind and the errors of human conduct may markedly delay the evolution of the soul, although they cannot inhibit such a morontia phenomenon when once it has been initiated by the indwelling Adjuster with the consent of the creature will. But at any time prior to mortal death this same material and human will is empowered to rescind such a choice and to reject survival. Even after survival the ascending mortal still retains this prerogative of choosing to reject eternal life; at any time before fusion with the Adjuster the evolving and ascending creature can choose to forsake the will of the Paradise Father. Fusion with the Adjuster signalizes the fact that the ascending mortal has eternally and unreservedly chosen to do the Father's will.

During the life in the flesh the evolving soul is enabled to reinforce the supermaterial decisions of the mortal mind. The soul, being supermaterial, does not of itself function on the material level of human experience. Neither can this subspiritual soul, without the collaboration of some spirit of Deity, such as the Adjuster, function above the morontia level. Neither does the soul make final decisions until death or translation divorces it from material association with the mortal mind except when and as this material mind delegates such authority freely and willingly to such a morontia soul of associated function. During life the mortal will, the personality power of decision-choice, is resident in the material mind circuits; as terrestrial mortal growth proceeds, this self, with its priceless powers of choice, becomes increasingly identified with the emerging morontia-soul entity; after death and following the mansion world resurrection, the human personality is completely identified with the morontia self. The soul is thus the embryo of the future morontia vehicle of personality identity.

This immortal soul is at first wholly morontia in nature, but it possesses such a capacity for development that it invariably ascends to the true spirit levels of fusion value with the spirits of Deity, usually with the same spirit of the Universal Father that initiated such a creative phenomenon in the creature mind.

Both the human mind and the divine Adjuster are conscious of the presence and differential nature of the evolving soul—the Adjuster fully, the mind partially. The soul becomes increasingly conscious of both the mind and the Adjuster as associated identities, proportional to its own evolutionary growth. The soul partakes of the qualities of both the human mind and the divine spirit but persistently evolves toward augmentation of spirit control and divine dominance through the fostering of a mind function whose meanings seek to coordinate with true spirit value.

The mortal career, the soul's evolution, is not so much a probation as an education. Faith in the survival of supreme values is the core of religion; genuine religious experience consists in the union of supreme values and cosmic meanings as a realization of universal reality.

Mind knows quantity, reality, meanings. But quality—values—is *felt.* That which feels is the mutual creation of mind, which knows, and the associated spirit, which reality-izes.

In so far as man's evolving morontia soul becomes permeated by truth, beauty, and goodness as the value-realization of God-consciousness, such a resultant being becomes indestructible. If there is no survival of eternal values in the evolving soul of man, then mortal existence is without meaning, and life itself is a tragic illusion. But it is forever true: What you begin in time you will assuredly finish in eternity—if it is worth finishing.

4. THE INNER LIFE

Recognition is the intellectual process of fitting the sensory impressions received from the external world into the memory patterns of the individual.

Understanding connotes that these recognized sensory impressions and their associated memory patterns have become integrated or organized into a dynamic network of principles.

Meanings are derived from a combination of recognition and understanding. Meanings are nonexistent in a wholly sensory or material world. Meanings and values are only perceived in the inner or supermaterial spheres of human experience.

The advances of true civilization are all born in this inner world of mankind. It is only the inner life that is truly creative. Civilization can hardly progress when the majority of the youth of any generation devote their interests and energies to the materialistic pursuits of the sensory or outer world.

The inner and the outer worlds have a different set of values. Any civilization is in jeopardy when three quarters of its youth enter materialistic professions and devote themselves to the pursuit of the sensory activities of the outer world. Civilization is in danger when youth neglect to interest themselves in ethics, sociology, eugenics, philosophy, the fine arts, religion, and cosmology.

Only in the higher levels of the superconscious mind as it impinges upon the spirit realm of human experience can you find those higher concepts in association with effective master patterns which will contribute to the building of a better and more enduring civilization. Personality is inherently creative, but it thus functions only in the inner life of the individual.

Snow crystals are always hexagonal in form, but no two are ever alike. Children conform to types, but no two are exactly alike, even in the case of twins. Personality follows types but is always unique.

Happiness and joy take origin in the inner life. You cannot experience real joy all by yourself. A solitary life is fatal to happiness. Even families and nations will enjoy life more if they share it with others.

You cannot completely control the external world—environment. It is the creativity of the inner world that is most subject to your direction because there your personality is so largely liberated from the fetters of the laws of antecedent causation. There is associated with personality a limited sovereignty of will.

Since this inner life of man is truly creative, there rests upon each person the responsibility of choosing as to whether this creativity shall be spontaneous and wholly haphazard or controlled, directed, and constructive. How can a creative imagination produce worthy children when the stage whereon it functions is already preoccupied by prejudice, hate, fears, resentments, revenge, and bigotries?

Ideas may take origin in the stimuli of the outer world, but ideals are born only in the creative realms of the inner world. Today the nations of the world are directed by men who have a superabundance of ideas, but they are poverty-stricken in ideals. That is the explanation of poverty, divorce, war, and racial hatreds.

This is the problem: If freewill man is endowed with the powers of creativity in the inner man, then must we recognize that freewill creativity embraces the potential of freewill destructivity. And when creativity is turned to destructivity, you are face to face with the devastation of evil and sin—oppression, war, and destruction. Evil is a partiality of creativity which tends toward disintegration and eventual destruction. All conflict is evil in that it inhibits the creative function of the inner life—it is a species of civil war in the personality.

Inner creativity contributes to ennoblement of character through personality integration and selfhood unification. It is forever true: The past is unchangeable; only the future can be changed by the ministry of the present creativity of the inner self.

5. THE CONSECRATION OF CHOICE

The doing of the will of God is nothing more or less than an exhibition of creature willingness to share the inner life with God—with the very God who has made such a creature life of inner meaning-value possible. Sharing is Godlike—divine. God shares all with the Eternal Son and the Infinite Spirit, while they, in turn, share all things with the divine Sons and spirit Daughters of the universes.

The imitation of God is the key to perfection; the doing of his will is the secret of survival and of perfection in survival.

Mortals live in God, and so God has willed to live in mortals. As men trust themselves to him, so has he—and first—trusted a part of himself to be with men; has consented to live in men and to indwell men subject to the human will.

Peace in this life, survival in death, perfection in the next life, service in eternity—all these are achieved (in spirit) *now* when the creature personality consents—chooses—to subject the creature will to the Father's will. And already has the Father chosen to make a fragment of himself subject to the will of the creature personality.

Such a creature choice is not a surrender of will. It is a consecration of will, an expansion of will, a glorification of will, a perfecting of will; and such choosing raises the creature will from the level of temporal significance to that higher estate wherein the personality of the creature son communes with the personality of the spirit Father.

This choosing of the Father's will is the spiritual finding of the spirit Father by mortal man, even though an age must pass before the creature son may actually stand in the factual presence of God on Paradise. This choosing does not so much consist in the negation of creature will—"Not my will but yours be done"—as it consists in the creature's positive affirmation: "It is *my* will that *your* will be done." And if this choice is made, sooner or later will the God-choosing son find inner union (fusion) with the indwelling God fragment, while this same perfecting son will find supreme personality satisfaction in the worship communion of the personality of man and the personality of his Maker, two personalities whose creative attributes have eternally joined in self-willed mutuality of expression—the birth of another eternal partnership of the will of man and the will of God.

6. THE HUMAN PARADOX

Many of the temporal troubles of mortal man grow out of his twofold relation to the cosmos. Man is a part of nature—he exists in nature—and yet he is able to transcend nature. Man is finite, but he is indwelt by a spark of infinity. Such a dual situation not only provides the potential for evil but also engenders many social and moral situations fraught with much uncertainty and not a little anxiety.

The courage required to effect the conquest of nature and to transcend one's self is a courage that might succumb to the temptations of self-pride. The mortal who can transcend self might yield to the temptation to deify his own self-consciousness. The mortal dilemma consists in the double fact that man is in bondage to nature while at the same time he possesses a unique liberty—freedom of spiritual choice and action. On material levels man finds himself subservient to nature, while on spiritual levels he is triumphant over nature and over all things temporal and finite. Such a paradox is inseparable from temptation, potential evil, decisional errors, and when self becomes proud and arrogant, sin may evolve.

The problem of sin is not self-existent in the finite world. The fact of finiteness is not evil or sinful. The finite world was made by an infinite Creator—it is the handiwork of his divine Sons—and therefore it must be *good.* It is the misuse, distortion, and perversion of the finite that gives origin to evil and sin.

The spirit can dominate mind; so mind can control energy. But mind can control energy only through its own intelligent manipulation of the metamorphic potentials inherent in the mathematical level of the causes and effects of the physical domains. Creature mind does not inherently control energy; that is a Deity prerogative. But creature mind can and does manipulate energy just in so far as it has become master of the energy secrets of the physical universe.

When man wishes to modify physical reality, be it himself or his environment, he succeeds to the extent that he has discovered the ways and means of controlling matter and directing energy. Unaided mind is impotent to influence anything material save its own physical mechanism, with which it is inescapably linked. But through the intelligent use of the body mechanism, mind can create other mechanisms, even energy relationships and living relationships, by the utilization of which this mind can increasingly control and even dominate its physical level in the universe.

Science is the source of facts, and mind cannot operate without facts. They are the building blocks in the construction of wisdom which are cemented together by life experience. Man can find the love of God without facts, and man can discover the laws of God without love, but man can never begin to appreciate the infinite symmetry, the supernal harmony, the exquisite repleteness of the all-inclusive nature of the First Source and Center until he has found divine law and divine love and has experientially unified these in his own evolving cosmic philosophy.

The expansion of material knowledge permits a greater intellectual appreciation of the meanings of ideas and the values of ideals. A human being can find truth in his inner experience, but he needs a clear knowledge of facts to apply his personal discovery of truth to the ruthlessly practical demands of everyday life.

It is only natural that mortal man should be harassed by feelings of insecurity as he views himself inextricably bound to nature while he possesses spiritual powers wholly transcendent to all things temporal and finite. Only religious confidence—living faith—can sustain man amid such difficult and perplexing problems.

Of all the dangers which beset man's mortal nature and jeopardize his spiritual integrity, pride is the greatest. Courage is valorous, but egotism is vainglorious and suicidal. Reasonable self-confidence is not to be deplored. Man's ability to transcend himself is the one thing which distinguishes him from the animal kingdom.

Pride is deceitful, intoxicating, and sin-breeding whether found in an individual, a group, a race, or a nation. It is literally true, "Pride goes before a fall."

7. THE ADJUSTER'S PROBLEM

Uncertainty with security is the essence of the Paradise adventure—uncertainty in time and in mind, uncertainty as to the events of the unfolding Paradise ascent; security in spirit and in eternity, security in the unqualified trust of the creature son in the divine compassion and infinite love of the Universal Father; uncertainty as an inexperienced citizen of the universe; security as an ascending son in the universe mansions of an all-powerful, all-wise, and all-loving Father.

May I admonish you to heed the distant echo of the Adjuster's faithful call to your soul? The indwelling Adjuster cannot stop or even materially alter your career struggle of time; the Adjuster cannot lessen the hardships of life as you journey on through this world of toil. The divine indweller can only patiently forbear while you fight the battle of life as it is lived on your planet; but you could, if you only would—as you work and worry, as you fight and toil—permit the valiant Adjuster to fight with you and for you. You could be so comforted and inspired, so enthralled and intrigued, if you would only allow the Adjuster constantly to bring forth the pictures of the real motive, the final aim, and the eternal purpose of all this difficult, uphill struggle with the commonplace problems of your present material world.

Why do you not aid the Adjuster in the task of showing you the spiritual counterpart of all these strenuous material efforts? Why do you not allow the Adjuster to strengthen you with the spiritual truths of cosmic power while you wrestle with the temporal difficulties of creature existence? Why do you not encourage the heavenly helper to cheer you with the clear vision of the eternal outlook of universal life as you gaze in perplexity at the problems of the passing hour? Why do you refuse to be enlightened and inspired by the universe viewpoint while you toil amidst the handicaps of time and flounder in the maze of uncertainties which beset your mortal life journey? Why not allow the Adjuster to spiritualize your thinking, even though your feet must tread the material paths of earthly endeavor?

The higher human races of Urantia are complexly admixed; they are a blend of many races and stocks of different origin. This composite nature renders it exceedingly difficult for the Monitors to work efficiently during life and adds definitely to the problems of both the Adjuster and the guardian seraphim after death. Not long since I was present on Salvington and heard a guardian of destiny present a formal statement in extenuation of the difficulties of ministering to her mortal subject. This seraphim said:

"Much of my difficulty was due to the unending conflict between the two natures of my subject: the urge of ambition opposed by animal indolence;

the ideals of a superior people crossed by the instincts of an inferior race; the high purposes of a great mind antagonized by the urge of a primitive inheritance; the long-distance view of a far-seeing Monitor counteracted by the nearsightedness of a creature of time; the progressive plans of an ascending being modified by the desires and longings of a material nature; the flashes of universe intelligence cancelled by the chemical-energy mandates of the evolving race; the urge of angels opposed by the emotions of an animal; the training of an intellect annulled by the tendencies of instinct; the experience of the individual opposed by the accumulated propensities of the race; the aims of the best overshadowed by the drift of the worst; the flight of genius neutralized by the gravity of mediocrity; the progress of the good retarded by the inertia of the bad; the art of the beautiful besmirched by the presence of evil; the buoyancy of health neutralized by the debility of disease; the fountain of faith polluted by the poisons of fear; the spring of joy embittered by the waters of sorrow; the gladness of anticipation disillusioned by the bitterness of realization; the joys of living ever threatened by the sorrows of death. Such a life on such a planet! And yet, because of the ever-present help and urge of the Thought Adjuster, this soul did achieve a fair degree of happiness and success and has even now ascended to the judgment halls of mansonia."

[Presented by a Solitary Messenger of Orvonton.]

PAPER 112

PERSONALITY SURVIVAL

THE evolutionary planets are the spheres of human origin, the initial worlds of the ascending mortal career. Urantia is your starting point; here you and your divine Thought Adjuster are joined in temporary union. You have been endowed with a perfect guide; therefore, if you will sincerely run the race of time and gain the final goal of faith, the reward of the ages shall be yours; you will be eternally united with your indwelling Adjuster. Then will begin your real life, the ascending life, to which your present mortal state is but the vestibule. Then will begin your exalted and progressive mission as finaliters in the eternity which stretches out before you. And throughout all of these successive ages and stages of evolutionary growth, there is one part of you that remains absolutely unaltered, and that is personality—permanence in the presence of change.

While it would be presumptuous to attempt the definition of personality, it may prove helpful to recount some of the things which are known about personality:

1. Personality is that quality in reality which is bestowed by the Universal Father himself or by the Conjoint Actor, acting for the Father.

2. It may be bestowed upon any living energy system which includes mind or spirit.

3. It is not wholly subject to the fetters of antecedent causation. It is relatively creative or cocreative.

4. When bestowed upon evolutionary material creatures, it causes spirit to strive for the mastery of energy-matter through the mediation of mind.

5. Personality, while devoid of identity, can unify the identity of any living energy system.

6. It discloses only qualitative response to the personality circuit in contradistinction to the three energies which show both qualitative and quantitative response to gravity.

7. Personality is changeless in the presence of change.

8. It can make a gift to God—dedication of the free will to the doing of the will of God.

9. It is characterized by morality—awareness of relativity of relationship with other persons. It discerns conduct levels and choosingly discriminates between them.

10. Personality is unique, absolutely unique: It is unique in time and space; it is unique in eternity and on Paradise; it is unique when bestowed—there are

no duplicates; it is unique during every moment of existence; it is unique in relation to God—he is no respecter of persons, but neither does he add them together, for they are nonaddable—they are associable but nontotalable.

11. Personality responds directly to other-personality presence.

12. It is one thing which can be added to spirit, thus illustrating the primacy of the Father in relation to the Son. (Mind does not have to be added to spirit.)

13. Personality may survive mortal death with identity in the surviving soul. The Adjuster and the personality are changeless; the relationship between them (in the soul) is nothing but change, continuing evolution; and if this change (growth) ceased, the soul would cease.

14. Personality is uniquely conscious of time, and this is something other than the time perception of mind or spirit.

1. PERSONALITY AND REALITY

Personality is bestowed by the Universal Father upon his creatures as a potentially eternal endowment. Such a divine gift is designed to function on numerous levels and in successive universe situations ranging from the lowly finite to the highest absonite, even to the borders of the absolute. Personality thus performs on three cosmic planes or in three universe phases:

1. *Position status.* Personality functions equally efficiently in the local universe, in the superuniverse, and in the central universe.

2. *Meaning status.* Personality performs effectively on the levels of the finite, the absonite, and even as impinging upon the absolute.

3. *Value status.* Personality can be experientially realized in the progressive realms of the material, the morontial, and the spiritual.

Personality has a perfected range of cosmic dimensional performance. The dimensions of finite personality are three, and they are roughly functional as follows:

1. *Length* represents direction and nature of progression—movement through space and according to time—evolution.

2. *Vertical depth* embraces the organismal drives and attitudes, the varying levels of self-realization and the general phenomenon of reaction to environment.

3. *Breadth* embraces the domain of co-ordination, association, and selfhood organization.

The type of personality bestowed upon Urantia mortals has a potentiality of seven dimensions of self-expression or person-realization. These dimensional phenomena are realizable as three on the finite level, three on the absonite level, and one on the absolute level. On subabsolute levels this seventh or totality dimension is experiencible as the *fact* of personality. This supreme dimension is an associable absolute and, while not infinite, is dimensionally potential for subinfinite penetration of the absolute.

The finite dimensions of personality have to do with cosmic length, depth, and breadth. Length denotes meaning; depth signifies value; breadth embraces insight—the capacity to experience unchallengeable consciousness of cosmic reality.

On the morontia level all of these finite dimensions of the material level are greatly enhanced, and certain new dimensional values are realizable. All these enlarged dimensional experiences of the morontia level are marvelously articulated with the supreme or personality dimension through the influence of mota and also because of the contribution of morontia mathematics.

Much trouble experienced by mortals in their study of human personality could be avoided if the finite creature would remember that dimensional levels and spiritual levels are not co-ordinated in experiential personality realization.

Life is really a process which takes place between the organism (selfhood) and its environment. The personality imparts value of identity and meanings of continuity to this organismal-environmental association. Thus it will be recognized that the phenomenon of stimulus-response is not a mere mechanical process since the personality functions as a factor in the total situation. It is ever true that mechanisms are innately passive; organisms, inherently active.

Physical life is a process taking place not so much within the organism as *between* the organism and the environment. And every such process tends to create and establish organismal patterns of reaction to such an environment. And all such *directive patterns* are highly influential in goal choosing.

It is through the mediation of mind that the self and the environment establish meaningful contact. The ability and willingness of the organism to make such significant contacts with environment (response to a drive) represents the *attitude* of the whole personality.

Personality cannot very well perform in isolation. Man is innately a social creature; he is dominated by the craving of belongingness. It is literally true, "No man lives unto himself."

But the concept of the personality as the meaning of the whole of the living and functioning creature means much more than the integration of relationships; it signifies the *unification* of all factors of reality as well as co-ordination of relationships. Relationships exist between two objects, but three or more objects eventuate a *system,* and such a system is much more than just an enlarged or complex relationship. This distinction is vital, for in a cosmic system the individual members are not connected with each other except in relation to the whole and through the individuality of the whole.

In the human organism the summation of its parts constitutes selfhood—individuality—but such a process has nothing whatever to do with personality, which is the unifier of all these factors as related to cosmic realities.

In aggregations parts are added; in systems parts are *arranged.* Systems are significant because of organization—positional values. In a good system all factors are in cosmic position. In a bad system something is either missing or displaced—deranged. In the human system it is the personality which unifies all activities and in turn imparts the qualities of identity and creativity.

2. THE SELF

It would be helpful in the study of selfhood to remember:

1. That physical systems are subordinate.
2. That intellectual systems are co-ordinate.
3. That personality is superordinate.
4. That the indwelling spiritual force is potentially directive.

In all concepts of selfhood it should be recognized that the fact of life comes first, its evaluation or interpretation later. The human child first *lives* and subsequently *thinks* about his living. In the cosmic economy insight precedes foresight.

The universe fact of God's becoming man has forever changed all meanings and altered all values of human personality. In the true meaning of the word, love connotes mutual regard of whole personalities, whether human or divine or human *and* divine. Parts of the self may function in numerous ways—thinking, feeling, wishing—but only the co-ordinated attributes of the whole personality are focused in intelligent action; and all of these powers are associated with the spiritual endowment of the mortal mind when a human being sincerely and unselfishly loves another being, human or divine.

All mortal concepts of reality are based on the assumption of the actuality of human personality; all concepts of superhuman realities are based on the experience of the human personality with and in the cosmic realities of certain associated spiritual entities and divine personalities. Everything nonspiritual in human experience, excepting personality, is a means to an end. Every true relationship of mortal man with other persons—human or divine—is an end in itself. And such fellowship with the personality of Deity is the eternal goal of universe ascension.

The possession of personality identifies man as a spiritual being since the unity of selfhood and the self-consciousness of personality are endowments of the supermaterial world. The very fact that a mortal materialist can deny the existence of supermaterial realities in and of itself demonstrates the presence, and indicates the working, of spirit synthesis and cosmic consciousness in his human mind.

There exists a great cosmic gulf between matter and thought, and this gulf is immeasurably greater between material mind and spiritual love. Consciousness, much less self-consciousness, cannot be explained by any theory of mechanistic electronic association or materialistic energy phenomena.

As mind pursues reality to its ultimate analysis, matter vanishes to the material senses but may still remain real to mind. When spiritual insight pursues that reality which remains after the disappearance of matter and pursues it to an ultimate analysis, it vanishes to mind, but the insight of spirit can still perceive cosmic realities and supreme values of a spiritual nature. Accordingly does science give way to philosophy, while philosophy must surrender to the conclusions inherent in genuine spiritual experience. Thinking surrenders to wisdom, and wisdom is lost in enlightened and reflective worship.

In science the human self observes the material world; philosophy is the observation of this observation of the material world; religion, true spiritual experience, is the experiential realization of the cosmic reality of the observation of the observation of all this relative synthesis of the energy materials of time and space. To build a philosophy of the universe on an exclusive materialism is to ignore the fact that all things material are initially conceived as real in the experience of human consciousness. The observer cannot be the thing observed; evaluation demands some degree of transcendence of the thing which is evaluated.

In time, thinking leads to wisdom and wisdom leads to worship; in eternity, worship leads to wisdom, and wisdom eventuates in the finality of thought.

The possibility of the unification of the evolving self is inherent in the qualities of its constitutive factors: the basic energies, the master tissues, the fundamental chemical overcontrol, the supreme ideas, the supreme motives, the supreme goals, and the divine spirit of Paradise bestowal—the secret of the self-consciousness of man's spiritual nature.

The purpose of cosmic evolution is to achieve unity of personality through increasing spirit dominance, volitional response to the teaching and leading of the Thought Adjuster. Personality, both human and superhuman, is characterized by an inherent cosmic quality which may be called "the evolution of dominance," the expansion of the control of both itself and its environment.

An ascending onetime human personality passes through two great phases of increasing volitional dominance over the self and in the universe:

1. The prefinaliter or God-seeking experience of augmenting the self-realization through a technique of identity expansion and actualization together with cosmic problem solving and consequent universe mastery.

2. The postfinaliter or God-revealing experience of the creative expansion of self-realization through revealing the Supreme Being of experience to the God-seeking intelligences who have not yet attained the divine levels of God-likeness.

Descending personalities attain analogous experiences through their various universe adventures as they seek for enlarged capacity for ascertaining and executing the divine wills of the Supreme, Ultimate, and Absolute Deities.

The material self, the ego-entity of human identity, is dependent during the physical life on the continuing function of the material life vehicle, on the continued existence of the unbalanced equilibrium of energies and intellect which, on Urantia, has been given the name *life.* But selfhood of survival value, selfhood that can transcend the experience of death, is only evolved by establishing a potential transfer of the seat of the identity of the evolving personality from the transient life vehicle—the material body—to the more enduring and immortal nature of the morontia soul and on beyond to those levels whereon the soul becomes infused with, and eventually attains the status of, spirit reality. This actual transfer from material association to morontia identification is effected by the sincerity, persistence, and steadfastness of the God-seeking decisions of the human creature.

3. THE PHENOMENON OF DEATH

Urantians generally recognize only one kind of death, the physical cessation of life energies; but concerning personality survival there are really three kinds:

1. *Spiritual (soul) death.* If and when mortal man has finally rejected survival, when he has been pronounced spiritually insolvent, morontially bankrupt, in the conjoint opinion of the Adjuster and the surviving seraphim, when such co-ordinate advice has been recorded on Uversa, and after the Censors and their reflective associates have verified these findings, thereupon do the rulers of Orvonton order the immediate release of the indwelling Monitor. But this release of the Adjuster in no way affects the duties of the personal or group

seraphim concerned with that Adjuster-abandoned individual. This kind of death is final in its significance irrespective of the temporary continuation of the living energies of the physical and mind mechanisms. From the cosmic standpoint the mortal is already dead; the continuing life merely indicates the persistence of the material momentum of cosmic energies.

2. *Intellectual (mind) death.* When the vital circuits of higher adjutant ministry are disrupted through the aberrations of intellect or because of the partial destruction of the mechanism of the brain, and if these conditions pass a certain critical point of irreparability, the indwelling Adjuster is immediately released to depart for Divinington. On the universe records a mortal personality is considered to have met with death whenever the essential mind circuits of human will-action have been destroyed. And again, this is death, irrespective of the continuing function of the living mechanism of the physical body. The body minus the volitional mind is no longer human, but according to the prior choosing of the human will, the soul of such an individual may survive.

3. *Physical (body and mind) death.* When death overtakes a human being, the Adjuster remains in the citadel of the mind until it ceases to function as an intelligent mechanism, about the time that the measurable brain energies cease their rhythmic vital pulsations. Following this dissolution the Adjuster takes leave of the vanishing mind, just as unceremoniously as entry was made years before, and proceeds to Divinington by way of Uversa.

After death the material body returns to the elemental world from which it was derived, but two nonmaterial factors of surviving personality persist: The pre-existent Thought Adjuster, with the memory transcription of the mortal career, proceeds to Divinington; and there also remains, in the custody of the destiny guardian, the immortal morontia soul of the deceased human. These phases and forms of soul, these once kinetic but now static formulas of identity, are essential to repersonalization on the morontia worlds; and it is the reunion of the Adjuster and the soul that reassembles the surviving personality, that reconsciousizes you at the time of the morontia awakening.

For those who do not have personal seraphic guardians, the group custodians faithfully and efficiently perform the same service of identity safekeeping and personality resurrection. The seraphim are indispensable to the reassembly of personality.

Upon death the Thought Adjuster temporarily loses personality, but not identity; the human subject temporarily loses identity, but not personality; on the mansion worlds both reunite in eternal manifestation. Never does a departed Thought Adjuster return to earth as the being of former indwelling; never is personality manifested without the human will; and never does a dis-Adjustered human being after death manifest active identity or in any manner establish communication with the living beings of earth. Such dis-Adjustered souls are wholly and absolutely unconscious during the long or short sleep of death. There can be no exhibition of any sort of personality or ability to engage in communications with other personalities until after completion of survival. Those who go to the mansion worlds are not permitted to send messages back to their loved ones. It is the policy throughout the universes to forbid such communication during the period of a current dispensation.

4. ADJUSTERS AFTER DEATH

When death of a material, intellectual, or spiritual nature occurs, the Adjuster bids farewell to the mortal host and departs for Divinington. From the headquarters of the local universe and the superuniverse a reflective contact is made with the supervisors of both governments, and the Monitor is registered out by the same number that recorded entry into the domains of time.

In some way not fully understood, the Universal Censors are able to gain possession of an epitome of the human life as it is embodied in the Adjuster's duplicate transcription of the spiritual values and morontia meanings of the indwelt mind. The Censors are able to appropriate the Adjuster's version of the deceased human's survival character and spiritual qualities, and all this data, together with the seraphic records, is available for presentation at the time of the adjudication of the individual concerned. This information is also used to confirm those superuniverse mandates which make it possible for certain ascenders immediately to begin their morontia careers, upon mortal dissolution to proceed to the mansion worlds ahead of the formal termination of a planetary dispensation.

Subsequent to physical death, except in individuals translated from among the living, the released Adjuster goes immediately to the home sphere of Divinington. The details of what transpires on that world during the time of awaiting the factual reappearance of the surviving mortal depend chiefly on whether the human being ascends to the mansion worlds in his own individual right or awaits a dispensational summoning of the sleeping survivors of a planetary age.

If the mortal associate belongs to a group that will be repersonalized at the end of a dispensation, the Adjuster will not immediately return to the mansion world of the former system of service but will, according to choice, enter upon one of the following temporary assignments:

1. Be mustered into the ranks of vanished Monitors for undisclosed service.
2. Be assigned for a period to the observation of the Paradise regime.
3. Be enrolled in one of the many training schools of Divinington.
4. Be stationed for a time as a student observer on one of the other six sacred spheres which constitute the Father's circuit of Paradise worlds.
5. Be assigned to the messenger service of the Personalized Adjusters.
6. Become an associate instructor in the Divinington schools devoted to the training of Monitors belonging to the virgin group.
7. Be assigned to select a group of possible worlds on which to serve in the event that there is reasonable cause for believing that the human partner may have rejected survival.

If, when death overtakes you, you have attained the third circle or a higher realm and therefore have had assigned to you a personal guardian of destiny, and if the final transcript of the summary of survival character submitted by the Adjuster is unconditionally certified by the destiny guardian—if both seraphim and Adjuster essentially agree in every item of their life records and recommendations—if the Universal Censors and their reflective associates on Uversa confirm this data and do so without equivocation or reservation, in that event the Ancients of Days flash forth the mandate of advanced standing over the communication circuits to Salvington, and, thus released, the tribunals of the Sovereign of Nebadon will decree the immediate passage of the surviving soul to the resurrection halls of the mansion worlds.

If the human individual survives without delay, the Adjuster, so I am instructed, registers at Divinington, proceeds to the Paradise presence of the Universal Father, returns immediately and is embraced by the Personalized Adjusters of the superuniverse and local universe of assignment, receives the recognition of the chief Personalized Monitor of Divinington, and then, at once, passes into the "realization of identity transition," being summoned therefrom on the third period and on the mansion world in the actual personality form made ready for the reception of the surviving soul of the earth mortal as that form has been projected by the guardian of destiny.

5. SURVIVAL OF THE HUMAN SELF

Selfhood is a cosmic reality whether material, morontial, or spiritual. The actuality of the *personal* is the bestowal of the Universal Father acting in and of himself or through his manifold universe agencies. To say that a being is personal is to recognize the relative individuation of such a being within the cosmic organism. The living cosmos is an all but infinitely integrated aggregation of real units, all of which are relatively subject to the destiny of the whole. But those that are personal have been endowed with the actual choice of destiny acceptance or of destiny rejection.

That which comes from the Father is like the Father eternal, and this is just as true of personality, which God gives by his own freewill choice, as it is of the divine Thought Adjuster, an actual fragment of God. Man's personality is eternal but with regard to identity a conditioned eternal reality. Having appeared in response to the Father's will, personality will attain Deity destiny, but man must choose whether or not he will be present at the attainment of such destiny. In default of such choice, personality attains experiential Deity directly, becoming a part of the Supreme Being. The cycle is foreordained, but man's participation therein is optional, personal, and experiential.

Mortal identity is a transient time-life condition in the universe; it is real only in so far as the personality elects to become a continuing universe phenomenon. This is the essential difference between man and an energy system: The energy system must continue, it has no choice; but man has everything to do with determining his own destiny. The Adjuster is truly the path to Paradise, but man himself must pursue that path by his own deciding, his freewill choosing.

Human beings possess identity only in the material sense. Such qualities of the self are expressed by the material mind as it functions in the energy system of the intellect. When it is said that man has identity, it is recognized that he is in possession of a mind circuit which has been placed in subordination to the acts and choosing of the will of the human personality. But this is a material and purely temporary manifestation, just as the human embryo is a transient parasitic stage of human life. Human beings, from a cosmic perspective, are born, live, and die in a relative instant of time; they are not enduring. But mortal personality, through its own choosing, possesses the power of transferring its seat of identity from the passing material-intellect system to the higher morontia-soul system which, in association with the Thought Adjuster, is created as a new vehicle for personality manifestation.

And it is this very power of choice, the universe insignia of freewill creaturehood, that constitutes man's greatest opportunity and his supreme cosmic responsibility. Upon the integrity of the human volition depends the eternal destiny of the future finaliter; upon the sincerity of the mortal free will the divine Adjuster depends for eternal personality; upon the faithfulness of mortal choice the Universal Father depends for the realization of a new ascending son; upon the steadfastness and wisdom of decision-actions the Supreme Being depends for the actuality of experiential evolution.

Though the cosmic circles of personality growth must eventually be attained, if, through no fault of your own, the accidents of time and the handicaps of material existence prevent your mastering these levels on your native planet, if your intentions and desires are of survival value, there are issued the decrees of probation extension. You will be afforded additional time in which to prove yourself.

If ever there is doubt as to the advisability of advancing a human identity to the mansion worlds, the universe governments invariably rule in the personal interests of that individual; they unhesitatingly advance such a soul to the status of a transitional being, while they continue their observations of the emerging morontia intent and spiritual purpose. Thus divine justice is certain of achievement, and divine mercy is accorded further opportunity for extending its ministry.

The governments of Orvonton and Nebadon do not claim absolute perfection for the detail working of the universal plan of mortal repersonalization, but they do claim to, and actually do, manifest patience, tolerance, understanding, and merciful sympathy. We had rather assume the risk of a system rebellion than to court the hazard of depriving one struggling mortal from any evolutionary world of the eternal joy of pursuing the ascending career.

This does not mean that human beings are to enjoy a second opportunity in the face of the rejection of a first, not at all. But it does signify that all will creatures are to experience one true opportunity to make one undoubted, self-conscious, and final choice. The sovereign Judges of the universes will not deprive any being of personality status who has not finally and fully made the eternal choice; the soul of man must and will be given full and ample opportunity to reveal its true intent and real purpose.

When the more spiritually and cosmically advanced mortals die, they proceed immediately to the mansion worlds; in general, this provision operates with those who have had assigned to them personal seraphic guardians. Other mortals may be detained until such time as the adjudication of their affairs has been completed, after which they may proceed to the mansion worlds, or they may be assigned to the ranks of the sleeping survivors who will be repersonalized en masse at the end of the current planetary dispensation.

There are two difficulties that hamper my efforts to explain just what happens to *you* in death, the surviving *you* which is distinct from the departing Adjuster. One of these consists in the impossibility of conveying to your level of comprehension an adequate description of a transaction on the borderland of the physical and morontia realms. The other is brought about by the restrictions placed upon my commission as a revelator of truth by the celestial governing authorities of Urantia. There are many interesting details which might be presented, but I withhold them upon the advice of your immediate planetary supervisors. But within the limits of my permission I can say this much:

There is something real, something of human evolution, something additional to the Mystery Monitor, which survives death. This newly appearing entity is the soul, and it survives the death of both your physical body and your material mind. This entity is the conjoint child of the combined life and efforts of the human you in liaison with the divine you, the Adjuster. This child of human and divine parentage constitutes the surviving element of terrestrial origin; it is the morontia self, the immortal soul.

This child of persisting meaning and surviving value is wholly unconscious during the period from death to repersonalization and is in the keeping of the seraphic destiny guardian throughout this season of waiting. You will not function as a conscious being, following death, until you attain the new consciousness of morontia on the mansion worlds of Satania.

At death the functional identity associated with the human personality is disrupted through the cessation of vital motion. Human personality, while transcending its constituent parts, is dependent on them for functional identity. The stoppage of life destroys the physical brain patterns for mind endowment, and the disruption of mind terminates mortal consciousness. The consciousness of that creature cannot subsequently reappear until a cosmic situation has been arranged which will permit the same human personality again to function in relationship with living energy.

During the transit of surviving mortals from the world of origin to the mansion worlds, whether they experience personality reassembly on the third period or ascend at the time of a group resurrection, the record of personality constitution is faithfully preserved by the archangels on their worlds of special activities. These beings are not the custodians of personality (as the guardian seraphim are of the soul), but it is nonetheless true that every identifiable factor of personality is effectually safeguarded in the custody of these dependable trustees of mortal survival. As to the exact whereabouts of mortal personality during the time intervening between death and survival, we do not know.

The situation which makes repersonalization possible is brought about in the resurrection halls of the morontia receiving planets of a local universe. Here in these life-assembly chambers the supervising authorities provide that relationship of universe energy—morontial, mindal, and spiritual—which makes possible the reconsciousizing of the sleeping survivor. The reassembly of the constituent parts of a onetime material personality involves:

1. The fabrication of a suitable form, a morontia energy pattern, in which the new survivor can make contact with nonspiritual reality, and within which the morontia variant of the cosmic mind can be encircuited.

2. The return of the Adjuster to the waiting morontia creature. The Adjuster is the eternal custodian of your ascending identity; your Monitor is the absolute assurance that you yourself and not another will occupy the morontia form created for your personality awakening. And the Adjuster will be present at your personality reassembly to take up once more the role of Paradise guide to your surviving self.

3. When these prerequisites of repersonalization have been assembled, the seraphic custodian of the potentialities of the slumbering immortal soul, with the assistance of numerous cosmic personalities, bestows this morontia entity upon and in the awaiting morontia mind-body form while committing this evolutionary child of the Supreme to eternal association with the waiting Adjuster. And this completes the repersonalization, reassembly of memory, insight, and consciousness—identity.

The fact of repersonalization consists in the seizure of the encircuited morontia phase of the newly segregated cosmic mind by the awakening human self. The phenomenon of personality is dependent on the persistence of the identity of selfhood reaction to universe environment; and this can only be effected through the medium of mind. Selfhood persists in spite of a continuous change in all the factor components of self; in the physical life the change is gradual; at death and upon repersonalization the change is sudden. The true reality of all selfhood (personality) is able to function responsively to universe conditions by virtue of the unceasing changing of its constituent parts; stagnation terminates in inevitable death. Human life is an endless change of the factors of life unified by the stability of the unchanging personality.

And when you thus awaken on the mansion worlds of Jerusem, you will be so changed, the spiritual transformation will be so great that, were it not for your Thought Adjuster and the destiny guardian, who so fully connect up your new life in the new worlds with your old life in the first world, you would at first have difficulty in connecting the new morontia consciousness with the reviving memory of your previous identity. Notwithstanding the continuity of personal selfhood, much of the mortal life would at first seem to be a vague and hazy dream. But time will clarify many mortal associations.

The Thought Adjuster will recall and rehearse for you only those memories and experiences which are a part of, and essential to, your universe career. If the Adjuster has been a partner in the evolution of aught in the human mind, then will these worth-while experiences survive in the eternal consciousness of the Adjuster. But much of your past life and its memories, having neither spiritual meaning nor morontia value, will perish with the material brain; much of material experience will pass away as onetime scaffolding which, having bridged you over to the morontia level, no longer serves a purpose in the universe. But personality and the relationships between personalities are never scaffolding; mortal memory of personality relationships has cosmic value and will persist. On the mansion worlds you will know and be known, and more, you will remember, and be remembered by, your onetime associates in the short but intriguing life on Urantia.

6. THE MORONTIA SELF

Just as a butterfly emerges from the caterpillar stage, so will the true personalities of human beings emerge on the mansion worlds, for the first time revealed apart from their onetime enshroudment in the material flesh. The morontia career in the local universe has to do with the continued elevation of the personality mechanism from the beginning morontia level of soul existence up to the final morontia level of progressive spirituality.

It is difficult to instruct you regarding your morontia personality forms for the local universe career. You will be endowed with morontia patterns of personality manifestability, and these are investments which, in the last analysis, are beyond your comprehension. Such forms, while entirely real, are not energy patterns of the material order which you now understand. They do, however, serve the same purpose on the local universe worlds as do your material bodies on the planets of human nativity.

To a certain extent, the appearance of the material body-form is responsive to the character of the personality identity; the physical body does, to a limited degree, reflect something of the inherent nature of the personality. Still more so does the morontia form. In the physical life, mortals may be outwardly beautiful though inwardly unlovely; in the morontia life, and increasingly on its higher levels, the personality form will vary directly in accordance with the nature of the inner person. On the spiritual level, outward form and inner nature begin to approximate complete identification, which grows more and more perfect on higher and higher spirit levels.

In the morontia estate the ascending mortal is endowed with the Nebadon modification of the cosmic-mind endowment of the Master Spirit of Orvonton. The mortal intellect, as such, has perished, has ceased to exist as a focalized universe entity apart from the undifferentiated mind circuits of the Creative Spirit. But the meanings and values of the mortal mind have not perished. Certain phases of mind are continued in the surviving soul; certain experiential values of the former human mind are held by the Adjuster; and there persist in the local universe the records of the human life as it was lived in the flesh, together with certain living registrations in the numerous beings who are concerned with the final evaluation of the ascending mortal, beings extending in range from seraphim to Universal Censors and probably on beyond to the Supreme.

Creature volition cannot exist without mind, but it does persist in spite of the loss of the material intellect. During the times immediately following survival, the ascending personality is in great measure guided by the character patterns inherited from the human life and by the newly appearing action of morontia mota. And these guides to mansonia conduct function acceptably in the early stages of the morontia life and prior to the emergence of morontia will as a full-fledged volitional expression of the ascending personality.

There are no influences in the local universe career comparable to the seven adjutant mind-spirits of human existence. The morontia mind must evolve by direct contact with cosmic mind, as this cosmic mind has been modified and translated by the creative source of local universe intellect—the Divine Minister.

Mortal mind, prior to death, is self-consciously independent of the Adjuster presence; adjutant mind needs only the associated material-energy pattern to enable it to operate. But the morontia soul, being superadjutant, does not retain self-consciousness without the Adjuster when deprived of the material-mind mechanism. This evolving soul does, however, possess a continuing character derived from the decisions of its former associated adjutant mind, and this character becomes active memory when the patterns thereof are energized by the returning Adjuster.

The persistence of memory is proof of the retention of the identity of original selfhood; it is essential to complete self-consciousness of personality continuity and expansion. Those mortals who ascend without Adjusters are dependent on the instruction of seraphic associates for the reconstruction of human memory; otherwise the morontia souls of the Spirit-fused mortals are not limited. The pattern of memory persists in the soul, but this pattern requires the presence of the former Adjuster to become *immediately* self-realizable as continuing memory. Without the Adjuster, it requires considerable time for the mortal survivor to re-explore and relearn, to recapture, the memory consciousness of the meanings and values of a former existence.

The soul of survival value faithfully reflects both the qualitative and the quantitative actions and motivations of the material intellect, the former seat of the identity of selfhood. In the choosing of truth, beauty, and goodness, the mortal mind enters upon its premorontia universe career under the tutelage of the seven adjutant mind-spirits unified under the direction of the spirit of wisdom. Subsequently, upon the completion of the seven circles of premorontia attainment, the superimposition of the endowment of morontia mind upon adjutant mind initiates the prespiritual or morontia career of local universe progression.

When a creature leaves his native planet, he leaves the adjutant ministry behind and becomes solely dependent on morontia intellect. When an ascender leaves the local universe, he has attained the spiritual level of existence, having passed beyond the morontia level. This newly appearing spirit entity then becomes attuned to the direct ministry of the cosmic mind of Orvonton.

7. ADJUSTER FUSION

Thought Adjuster fusion imparts eternal actualities to personality which were previously only potential. Among these new endowments may be mentioned: fixation of divinity quality, past-eternity experience and memory, immortality, and a phase of qualified potential absoluteness.

When your earthly course in temporary form has been run, you are to awaken on the shores of a better world, and eventually you will be united with your faithful Adjuster in an eternal embrace. And this fusion constitutes the mystery of making God and man one, the mystery of finite creature evolution, but it is eternally true. Fusion is the secret of the sacred sphere of Ascendington, and no creature, save those who have experienced fusion with the spirit of Deity, can comprehend the true meaning of the actual values which are conjoined when the identity of a creature of time becomes eternally one with the spirit of Paradise Deity.

Fusion with the Adjuster is usually effected while the ascender is resident within his local system. It may occur on the planet of nativity as a transcendence of natural death; it may take place on any one of the mansion worlds or on the headquarters of the system; it may even be delayed until the time of the constellation sojourn; or, in special instances, it may not be consummated until the ascender is on the local universe capital.

When fusion with the Adjuster has been effected, there can be no future danger to the eternal career of such a personality. Celestial beings are tested throughout a long experience, but mortals pass through a relatively short and intensive testing on the evolutionary and morontia worlds.

Fusion with the Adjuster never occurs until the mandates of the superuniverse have pronounced that the human nature has made a final and irrevocable choice for the eternal career. This is the at-onement authorization, which, when issued, constitutes the clearance authority for the fused personality eventually to leave the confines of the local universe to proceed sometime to the headquarters of the superuniverse, from which point the pilgrim of time will, in the distant future, enseconaphim for the long flight to the central universe of Havona and the Deity adventure.

On the evolutionary worlds, selfhood is material; it is a thing in the universe and as such is subject to the laws of material existence. It is a fact in time and is responsive to the vicissitudes thereof. *Survival decisions must here be formulated.* In the morontia state the self has become a new and more enduring universe reality, and its continuing growth is predicated on its increasing attunement to the mind and spirit circuits of the universes. *Survival decisions are now being confirmed.* When the self attains the spiritual level, it has become a secure value in the universe, and this new value is predicated upon the fact that *survival decisions have been made,* which fact has been witnessed by eternal fusion with the Thought Adjuster. And having achieved the status of a true universe value, the creature becomes liberated in potential for the seeking of the highest universe value—God.

Such fused beings are twofold in their universe reactions: They are discrete morontia individuals not altogether unlike seraphim, and they are also beings in potential on the order of the Paradise finaliters.

But the fused individual is really one personality, one being, whose unity defies all attempts at analysis by any intelligence of the universes. And so, having passed the tribunals of the local universe from the lowest to the highest, none of which have been able to identify man or Adjuster, the one apart from the other, you shall finally be taken before the Sovereign of Nebadon, your local universe Father. And there, at the hand of the very being whose creative fatherhood in this universe of time has made possible the fact of your life, you will be granted those credentials which entitle you eventually to proceed upon your superuniverse career in quest of the Universal Father.

Has the triumphant Adjuster won personality by the magnificent service to humanity, or has the valiant human acquired immortality through sincere efforts to achieve Adjusterlikeness? It is neither; but they together have achieved the evolution of a member of one of the unique orders of the ascending personalities of the Supreme, one who will ever be found serviceable, faithful, and efficient, a candidate for further growth and development, ever ranging upward and never ceasing the supernal ascent until the seven circuits of Havona have been traversed and the onetime soul of earthly origin stands in worshipful recognition of the actual personality of the Father on Paradise.

Throughout all this magnificent ascent the Thought Adjuster is the divine pledge of the future and full spiritual stabilization of the ascending mortal. Meanwhile the presence of the mortal free will affords the Adjuster an eternal channel for the liberation of the divine and infinite nature. Now have these two identities become one; no event of time or of eternity can ever separate man and Adjuster; they are inseparable, eternally fused.

On the Adjuster-fusion worlds the destiny of the Mystery Monitor is identical with that of the ascending mortal—the Paradise Corps of the Finality. And neither Adjuster nor mortal can attain that unique goal without the full cooperation and faithful help of the other. This extraordinary partnership is one of the most engrossing and amazing of all the cosmic phenomena of this universe age.

From the time of Adjuster fusion the status of the ascender is that of the evolutionary creature. The human member was the first to enjoy personality and, therefore, outranks the Adjuster in all matters concerned with the recognition of personality. The Paradise headquarters of this fused being is Ascendington, not Divinington, and this unique combination of God and man ranks as an ascending mortal all the way up to the Corps of the Finality.

When once an Adjuster fuses with an ascending mortal, the number of that Adjuster is stricken from the records of the superuniverse. What happens on the records of Divinington, I do not know, but I surmise that the registry of that Adjuster is removed to the secret circles of the inner courts of Grandfanda, the acting head of the Corps of the Finality.

With Adjuster fusion the Universal Father has completed his promise of the gift of himself to his material creatures; he has fulfilled the promise, and consummated the plan, of the eternal bestowal of divinity upon humanity. Now begins the human attempt to realize and to actualize the limitless possibilities that are inherent in the supernal partnership with God which has thus factualized.

The present known destiny of surviving mortals is the Paradise Corps of the Finality; this is also the goal of destiny for all Thought Adjusters who become joined in eternal union with their mortal companions. At present the Paradise finaliters are working throughout the grand universe in many undertakings, but we all conjecture that they will have other and even more supernal tasks to perform in the distant future after the seven superuniverses have become settled in light and life, and when the finite God has finally emerged from the mystery which now surrounds this Supreme Deity.

You have been instructed to a certain extent about the organization and personnel of the central universe, the superuniverses, and the local universes; you have been told something about the character and origin of some of the various personalities who now rule these far-flung creations. You have also been informed that there are in process of organization vast galaxies of universes far out beyond the periphery of the grand universe, in the first outer space level. It has also been intimated in the course of these narratives that the Supreme Being is to disclose his unrevealed tertiary function in these now uncharted regions of outer space; and you have also been told that the finaliters of the Paradise corps are the experiential children of the Supreme.

We believe that the mortals of Adjuster fusion, together with their finaliter associates, are destined to function in some manner in the administration of the universes of the first outer space level. We have not the slightest doubt that in due time these enormous galaxies will become inhabited universes. And we are equally convinced that among the administrators thereof will be found the Paradise finaliters whose natures are the cosmic consequence of the blending of creature and Creator.

What an adventure! What a romance! A gigantic creation to be administered by the children of the Supreme, these personalized and humanized Adjusters, these Adjusterized and eternalized mortals, these mysterious combinations and eternal associations of the highest known manifestation of the essence of the First Source and Center and the lowest form of intelligent life capable of comprehending and attaining the Universal Father. We conceive that such amalgamated beings, such partnerships of Creator and creature, will become superb rulers, matchless administrators, and understanding and sympathetic directors of any and all forms of intelligent life which may come into existence throughout these future universes of the first outer space level.

True it is, you mortals are of earthly, animal origin; your frame is indeed dust. But if you actually will, if you really desire, surely the heritage of the ages is yours, and you shall someday serve throughout the universes in your true characters—children of the Supreme God of experience and divine sons of the Paradise Father of all personalities.

[Presented by a Solitary Messenger of Orvonton.]

PAPER 113

SERAPHIC GUARDIANS OF DESTINY

HAVING presented the narratives of the Ministering Spirits of Time and the Messenger Hosts of Space, we come to the consideration of the guardian angels, seraphim devoted to the ministry to individual mortals, for whose elevation and perfection all of the vast survival scheme of spiritual progression has been provided. In past ages on Urantia, these destiny guardians were about the only group of angels that had recognition. The planetary seraphim are indeed ministering spirits sent forth to do service for those who shall survive. These attending seraphim have functioned as the spiritual helpers of mortal man in all the great events of the past and the present. In many a revelation "the word was spoken by angels"; many of the mandates of heaven have been "received by the ministry of angels."

Seraphim are the traditional angels of heaven; they are the ministering spirits who live so near you and do so much for you. They have ministered on Urantia since the earliest times of human intelligence.

1. THE GUARDIAN ANGELS

The teaching about guardian angels is not a myth; certain groups of human beings do actually have personal angels. It was in recognition of this that Jesus, in speaking of the children of the heavenly kingdom, said: "Take heed that you despise not one of these little ones, for I say to you, their angels do always behold the presence of the spirit of my Father."

Originally, the seraphim were definitely assigned to the separate Urantia races. But since the bestowal of Michael, they are assigned in accordance with human intelligence, spirituality, and destiny. Intellectually, mankind is divided into three classes:

1. The subnormal minded—those who do not exercise normal will power; those who do not make average decisions. This class embraces those who cannot comprehend God; they lack capacity for the intelligent worship of Deity. The subnormal beings of Urantia have a corps of seraphim, one company, with one battalion of cherubim, assigned to minister to them and to witness that justice and mercy are extended to them in the life struggles of the sphere.

2. The average, normal type of human mind. From the standpoint of seraphic ministry, most men and women are grouped in seven classes in accordance with their status in making the circles of human progress and spiritual development.

3. The supernormal minded—those of great decision and undoubted potential of spiritual achievement; men and women who enjoy more or less contact

with their indwelling Adjusters; members of the various reserve corps of destiny. No matter in what circle a human happens to be, if such an individual becomes enrolled in any of the several reserve corps of destiny, right then and there, personal seraphim are assigned, and from that time until the earthly career is finished, that mortal will enjoy the continuous ministry and unceasing watchcare of a guardian angel. Also, when any human being makes *the* supreme decision, when there is a real betrothal with the Adjuster, a personal guardian is immediately assigned to that soul.

In the ministry to so-called normal beings, seraphic assignments are made in accordance with the human attainment of the circles of intellectuality and spirituality. You start out in your mind of mortal investment in the seventh circle and journey inward in the task of self-understanding, self-conquest, and self-mastery; and circle by circle you advance until (if natural death does not terminate your career and transfer your struggles to the mansion worlds) you reach the first or inner circle of relative contact and communion with the indwelling Adjuster.

Human beings in the initial or seventh circle have one guardian angel with one company of assisting cherubim assigned to the watchcare and custody of one thousand mortals. In the sixth circle, a seraphic pair with one company of cherubim is assigned to guide these ascending mortals in groups of five hundred. When the fifth circle is attained, human beings are grouped in companies of approximately one hundred, and a pair of guardian seraphim with a group of cherubim is placed in charge. Upon attainment of the fourth circle, mortal beings are assembled in groups of ten, and again charge is given to a pair of seraphim, assisted by one company of cherubim.

When a mortal mind breaks through the inertia of animal legacy and attains the third circle of human intellectuality and acquired spirituality, a personal angel (in reality two) will henceforth be wholly and exclusively devoted to this ascending mortal. And thus these human souls, in addition to the ever-present and increasingly efficient indwelling Thought Adjusters, receive the undivided assistance of these personal guardians of destiny in all their efforts to finish the third circle, traverse the second, and attain the first.

2. THE DESTINY GUARDIANS

Seraphim are not known as guardians of destiny until such time as they are assigned to the association of a human soul who has realized one or more of three achievements: has made a supreme decision to become Godlike, has entered the third circle, or has been mustered into one of the reserve corps of destiny.

In the evolution of races a guardian of destiny is assigned to the very first being who attains the requisite circle of conquest. On Urantia the first mortal to secure a personal guardian was Rantowoc, a wise man of the red race of long ago.

All angelic assignments are made from a group of volunteering seraphim, and these appointments are always in accordance with human needs and with regard to the status of the angelic pair—in the light of seraphic experience, skill, and wisdom. Only seraphim of long service, the more experienced and tested types, are assigned as destiny guards. Many guardians have gained much valuable experience on those worlds which are of the non-Adjuster fusion series. Like the Adjusters, the seraphim attend these beings for a single lifetime and then are liberated for new assignment. Many guardians on Urantia have had this previous practical experience on other worlds.

When human beings fail to survive, their personal or group guardians may repeatedly serve in similar capacities on the same planet. The seraphim develop a sentimental regard for individual worlds and entertain a special affection for certain races and types of mortal creatures with whom they have been so closely and intimately associated.

The angels develop an abiding affection for their human associates; and you would, if you could only visualize the seraphim, develop a warm affection for them. Divested of material bodies, given spirit forms, you would be very near the angels in many attributes of personality. They share most of your emotions and experience some additional ones. The only emotion actuating you which is somewhat difficult for them to comprehend is the legacy of animal fear that bulks so large in the mental life of the average inhabitant of Urantia. The angels really find it hard to understand why you will so persistently allow your higher intellectual powers, even your religious faith, to be so dominated by fear, so thoroughly demoralized by the thoughtless panic of dread and anxiety.

All seraphim have individual names, but in the records of assignment to world service they are frequently designated by their planetary numbers. At the universe headquarters they are registered by name and number. The destiny guardian of the human subject used in this contactual communication is number 3 of group 17, of company 126, of battalion 4, of unit 384, of legion 6, of host 37, of the 182,314th seraphic army of Nebadon. The current planetary assignment number of this seraphim on Urantia and to this human subject is 3,641,852.

In the ministry of personal guardianship, the assignment of angels as destiny guardians, seraphim always volunteer their services. In the city of this visitation a certain mortal was recently admitted to the reserve corps of destiny, and since all such humans are personally attended by guardian angels, more than one hundred qualified seraphim sought the assignment. The planetary director selected twelve of the more experienced individuals and subsequently appointed the seraphim whom they selected as best adapted to guide this human being through his life journey. That is, they selected a certain pair of equally qualified seraphim; one of this seraphic pair will always be on duty.

Seraphic tasks may be unremitting, but either of the angelic pair can discharge all ministering responsibilities. Like cherubim, seraphim usually serve in pairs, but unlike their less advanced associates, the seraphim sometimes work singly. In practically all their contacts with human beings they can function as individuals. Both angels are required only for communication and service on the higher circuits of the universes.

When a seraphic pair accept guardian assignment, they serve for the remainder of the life of that human being. The complement of being (one of the two angels) becomes the recorder of the undertaking. These complemental seraphim are the recording angels of the mortals of the evolutionary worlds. The records are kept by the pair of cherubim (a cherubim and a sanobim) who are always associated with the seraphic guardians, but these records are always sponsored by one of the seraphim.

For purposes of rest and recharging with the life energy of the universe circuits, the guardian is periodically relieved by her complement, and during her absence the associated cherubim functions as the recorder, as is also the case when the complemental seraphim is similarly absent.

3. RELATION TO OTHER SPIRIT INFLUENCES

One of the most important things a destiny guardian does for her mortal subject is to effect a personal co-ordination of the numerous impersonal spirit influences which indwell, surround, and impinge upon the mind and soul of the evolving material creature. Human beings are personalities, and it is exceedingly difficult for nonpersonal spirits and prepersonal entities to make direct contact with such highly material and discretely personal minds. In the ministry of the guarding angel all of these influences are more or less unified and made more nearly appreciable by the expanding moral nature of the evolving human personality.

More especially can and does this seraphic guardian correlate the manifold agencies and influences of the Infinite Spirit, ranging from the domains of the physical controllers and the adjutant mind-spirits up to the Holy Spirit of the Divine Minister and to the Omnipresent Spirit presence of the Paradise Third Source and Center. Having thus unified and made more personal these vast ministries of the Infinite Spirit, the seraphim then undertakes to correlate this integrated influence of the Conjoint Actor with the spirit presences of the Father and the Son.

The Adjuster is the presence of the Father; the Spirit of Truth, the presence of the Sons. These divine endowments are unified and co-ordinated on the lower levels of human spiritual experience by the ministry of the guardian seraphim. The angelic servers are gifted in combining the love of the Father and the mercy of the Son in their ministry to mortal creatures.

And herein is revealed the reason why the seraphic guardian eventually becomes the personal custodian of the mind patterns, memory formulas, and soul realities of the mortal survivor during that interval between physical death and morontia resurrection. None but the ministering children of the Infinite Spirit could thus function in behalf of the human creature during this phase of transition from one level of the universe to another and higher level. Even when you engage in your terminal transition slumber, when you pass from time to eternity, a high supernaphim likewise shares the transit with you as the custodian of creature identity and the surety of personal integrity.

On the spiritual level, seraphim make personal many otherwise impersonal and prepersonal ministries of the universe; they are co-ordinators. On the intellectual level they are the correlators of mind and morontia; they are interpreters. And on the physical level they manipulate terrestrial environment through their liaison with the Master Physical Controllers and through the cooperative ministry of the midway creatures.

This is a recital of the manifold and intricate function of an attending seraphim; but how does such a subordinate angelic personality, created but a little above the universe level of humanity, do such difficult and complex things? We do not really know, but we conjecture that this phenomenal ministry is in some undisclosed manner facilitated by the unrecognized and unrevealed working of the Supreme Being, the actualizing Deity of the evolving universes of time and space. Throughout the entire realm of progressive survival in and through the Supreme Being, seraphim are an essential part of continuing mortal progression.

4. SERAPHIC DOMAINS OF ACTION

The guardian seraphim are not mind, though they do spring from the same source that also gives origin to mortal mind, the Creative Spirit. Seraphim are mind stimulators; they continually seek to promote circle-making decisions in human mind. They do this, not as does the Adjuster, operating from within and through the soul, but rather from the outside inward, working through the social, ethical, and moral environment of human beings. Seraphim are not the divine Adjuster lure of the Universal Father, but they do function as the personal agency of the ministry of the Infinite Spirit.

Mortal man, subject to Adjuster leading, is also amenable to seraphic guidance. The Adjuster is the essence of man's eternal nature; the seraphim is the teacher of man's evolving nature—in this life the mortal mind, in the next the morontia soul. On the mansion worlds you will be conscious and aware of seraphic instructors, but in the first life men are usually unaware of them.

Seraphim function as teachers of men by guiding the footsteps of the human personality into paths of new and progressive experiences. To accept the guidance of a seraphim rarely means attaining a life of ease. In following this leading you are sure to encounter, and if you have the courage, to traverse, the rugged hills of moral choosing and spiritual progress.

The impulse of worship largely originates in the spirit promptings of the higher mind adjutants, reinforced by the leadings of the Adjuster. But the urge to pray so often experienced by God-conscious mortals very often arises as the result of seraphic influence. The guarding seraphim is constantly manipulating the mortal environment for the purpose of augmenting the cosmic insight of the human ascender to the end that such a survival candidate may acquire enhanced realization of the presence of the indwelling Adjuster and thus be enabled to yield increased co-operation with the spiritual mission of the divine presence.

While there is apparently no communication between the indwelling Adjusters and the encompassing seraphim, they always seem to work in perfect harmony and exquisite accord. The guardians are most active at those times when the Adjusters are least active, but their ministry is in some manner strangely correlated. Such superb co-operation could hardly be either accidental or incidental.

The ministering personality of the guardian seraphim, the God presence of the indwelling Adjuster, the encircuited action of the Holy Spirit, and the Son-consciousness of the Spirit of Truth are all divinely correlated into a meaningful unity of spiritual ministry in and to a mortal personality. Though hailing from different sources and different levels, these celestial influences are all integrated in the enveloping and evolving presence of the Supreme Being.

5. SERAPHIC MINISTRY TO MORTALS

Angels do not invade the sanctity of the human mind; they do not manipulate the will of mortals; neither do they directly contact with the indwelling Adjusters. The guardian of destiny influences you in every possible manner consistent with the dignity of your personality; under no circumstances do these angels interfere with the free action of the human will. Neither angels nor any other order of universe personality have power or authority to curtail or abridge the prerogatives of human choosing.

Angels are so near you and care so feelingly for you that they figuratively "weep because of your willful intolerance and stubbornness." Seraphim do not shed physical tears; they do not have physical bodies; neither do they possess wings. But they do have spiritual emotions, and they do experience feelings and sentiments of a spiritual nature which are in certain ways comparable to human emotions.

The seraphim act in your behalf quite independent of your direct appeals; they are executing the mandates of their superiors, and thus they function regardless of your passing whims or changing moods. This does not imply that you may not make their tasks either easier or more difficult, but rather that angels are not directly concerned with your appeals or with your prayers.

In the life of the flesh the intelligence of angels is not directly available to mortal men. They are not overlords or directors; they are simply guardians. The seraphim *guard* you; they do not seek directly to influence you; you must chart your own course, but these angels then act to make the best possible use of the course you have chosen. They do not (ordinarily) arbitrarily intervene in the routine affairs of human life. But when they receive instructions from their superiors to perform some unusual exploit, you may rest assured that these guardians will find some means of carrying out these mandates. They do not, therefore, intrude into the picture of human drama except in emergencies and then usually on the direct orders of their superiors. They are the beings who are going to follow you for many an age, and they are thus receiving an introduction to their future work and personality association.

Seraphim are able to function as material ministers to human beings under certain circumstances, but their action in this capacity is very rare. They are able, with the assistance of the midway creatures and the physical controllers, to function in a wide range of activities in behalf of human beings, even to make actual contact with mankind, but such occurrences are very unusual. In most instances the circumstances of the material realm proceed unaltered by seraphic action, although occasions have arisen, involving jeopardy to vital links in the chain of human evolution, in which seraphic guardians have acted, and properly, on their own initiative.

6. GUARDIAN ANGELS AFTER DEATH

Having told you something of the ministry of seraphim during natural life, I will endeavor to inform you about the conduct of the guardians of destiny at the time of the mortal dissolution of their human associates. Upon your death, your records, identity specifications, and the morontia entity of the human soul —conjointly evolved by the ministry of mortal mind and the divine Adjuster— are faithfully conserved by the destiny guardian together with all other values related to your future existence, everything that constitutes you, the real you, except the identity of continuing existence represented by the departing Adjuster and the actuality of personality.

The instant the pilot light in the human mind disappears, the spirit luminosity which seraphim associate with the presence of the Adjuster, the attending angel reports in person to the commanding angels, successively, of the group, company, battalion, unit, legion, and host; and after being duly registered for the final adventure of time and space, such an angel receives certification by the planetary chief of seraphim for reporting to the Evening Star (or other lieutenant of Gabriel) in command of the seraphic army of this candidate for universe ascension. And upon being granted permission from the commander of this highest organizational unit, such a guardian of destiny proceeds to the first mansion world and there awaits the consciousizing of her former ward in the flesh.

In case the human soul fails of survival after having received the assignment of a personal angel, the attending seraphim must proceed to the headquarters of the local universe, there to witness to the complete records of her complement as previously reported. Next she goes before the tribunals of the archangels, to be absolved from blame in the matter of the survival failure of her subject; and then she goes back to the worlds, again to be assigned to another mortal of ascending potentiality or to some other division of seraphic ministry.

But angels minister to evolutionary creatures in many ways aside from the services of personal and group guardianship. Personal guardians whose subjects do not go immediately to the mansion worlds do not tarry there in idleness awaiting the dispensational roll calls of judgment; they are reassigned to numerous ministering missions throughout the universe.

The guardian seraphim is the custodial trustee of the survival values of mortal man's slumbering soul as the absent Adjuster *is* the identity of such an immortal universe being. When these two collaborate in the resurrection halls of mansonia in conjunction with the newly fabricated morontia form, there occurs the reassembly of the constituent factors of the personality of the mortal ascender.

The Adjuster will identify you; the guardian seraphim will repersonalize you and then re-present you to the faithful Monitor of your earth days.

And even so, when a planetary age ends, when those in the lower circles of mortal achievement are forgathered, it is their group guardians who reassemble them in the resurrection halls of the mansion spheres, even as your record tells: "And he shall send his angels with a great voice and shall gather together his elect from one end of the realm to another."

The technique of justice demands that personal or group guardians shall respond to the dispensational roll call in behalf of all nonsurviving personalities. The Adjusters of such nonsurvivors do not return, and when the rolls are called, the seraphim respond, but the Adjusters make no answer. This constitutes the "resurrection of the unjust," in reality the formal recognition of the cessation of creature existence. This roll call of justice always immediately follows the roll call of mercy, the resurrection of the sleeping survivors. But these are matters which are of concern to none but the supreme and all-knowing Judges of survival values. Such problems of adjudication do not really concern us.

Group guardians may serve on a planet age after age and eventually become custodians of the slumbering souls of thousands upon thousands of sleeping survivors. They can so serve on many different worlds in a given system since the resurrection response occurs on the mansion worlds.

All personal and group guardians in the system of Satania who went astray in the Lucifer rebellion, notwithstanding that many sincerely repented of their folly, are to be detained on Jerusem until the final adjudication of the rebellion. Already have the Universal Censors arbitrarily taken from these disobedient and unfaithful guardians all aspects of their soul trusts and lodged these morontia realities for safekeeping in the custody of volunteer seconaphim.

7. SERAPHIM AND THE ASCENDANT CAREER

It is indeed an epoch in the career of an ascending mortal, this first awakening on the shores of the mansion world; there, for the first time, actually to see your long-loved and ever-present angelic companions of earth days; there also to become truly conscious of the identity and presence of the divine Monitor who so long indwelt your mind on earth. Such an experience constitutes a glorious awakening, a real resurrection.

On the morontia spheres the attending seraphim (there are two of them) are your open companions. These angels not only consort with you as you progress through the career of the transition worlds, in every way possible assisting you in the acquirement of morontia and spirit status, but they also avail themselves of the opportunity to advance by study in the extension schools for evolutionary seraphim maintained on the mansion worlds.

The human race was created just a little lower than the more simple types of the angelic orders. Therefore will your first assignment of the morontia life be as assistants to the seraphim in the immediate work awaiting at the time you attain personality consciousness subsequent to your liberation from the bonds of the flesh.

Before leaving the mansion worlds, all mortals will have permanent seraphic associates or guardians. And as you ascend the morontia spheres, eventually it is the seraphic guardians who witness and certify the decrees of your eternal union with the Thought Adjusters. Together they have established your personality identities as children of the flesh from the worlds of time. Then, with your attainment of the mature morontia estate, they accompany you through Jerusem and the associated worlds of system progress and culture. After that they go with you to Edentia and its seventy spheres of advanced socialization, and subsequently will they pilot you to the Melchizedeks and follow you through the superb career of the universe headquarters worlds. And when you have learned the wisdom and culture of the Melchizedeks, they will take you on to Salvington, where you will stand face to face with the Sovereign of all Nebadon. And still will these seraphic guides follow you through the minor and major sectors of the superuniverse and on to the receiving worlds of Uversa, remaining with you until you finally enseconaphim for the long Havona flight.

Some of the destiny guardians of attachment during the mortal career follow the course of the ascending pilgrims through Havona. The others bid their long-time mortal associates a temporary farewell, and then, while these mortals traverse the circles of the central universe, these guardians of destiny achieve the circles of Seraphington. And they will be in waiting on the shores of Paradise when their mortal associates awaken from the last transit sleep of time into the new experiences of eternity. Such ascending seraphim subsequently enter upon divergent services in the finaliter corps and in the Seraphic Corps of Completion.

Man and angel may or may not be reunited in eternal service, but wherever seraphic assignment may take them, the seraphim are always in communication with their former wards of the evolutionary worlds, the ascendant mortals of time. The intimate associations and the affectionate attachments of the realms of human origin are never forgotten nor ever completely severed. In the eternal ages men and angels will co-operate in the divine service as they did in the career of time.

For seraphim, the surest way of achieving the Paradise Deities is by successfully guiding a soul of evolutionary origin to the portals of Paradise. Therefore is the assignment of guardian of destiny the most highly prized seraphic duty.

Only destiny guardians are mustered into the primary or mortal Corps of the Finality, and such pairs have engaged in the supreme adventure of identity atoneness; the two beings have achieved spiritual bi-unification on Seraphington prior to their reception into the finaliter corps. In this experience the two angelic natures, so complemental in all universe functions, achieve ultimate spirit two-in-oneness, repercussing in a new capacity for the reception of, and fusion with, a non-Adjuster fragment of the Paradise Father. And so do some of your loving seraphic associates in time also become your finaliter associates in eternity, children of the Supreme and perfected sons of the Paradise Father.

[Presented by the Chief of Seraphim stationed on Urantia.]

PAPER 114

SERAPHIC PLANETARY GOVERNMENT

THE Most Highs rule in the kingdoms of men through many celestial forces and agencies but chiefly through the ministry of seraphim.

At noon today the roll call of planetary angels, guardians, and others on Urantia was 501,234,619 pairs of seraphim. There were assigned to my command two hundred seraphic hosts—597,196,800 pairs of seraphim, or 1,194,393,600 individual angels. The registry, however, shows 1,002,469,238 individuals; it follows therefore that 191,924,362 angels were absent from this world on transport, messenger, and death duty. (On Urantia there are about the same number of cherubim as seraphim, and they are similarly organized.)

Seraphim and their associated cherubim have much to do with the details of the superhuman government of a planet, especially of worlds which have been isolated by rebellion. The angels, ably assisted by the midwayers, function on Urantia as the actual supermaterial ministers who execute the mandates of the resident governor general and all his associates and subordinates. Seraphim as a class are occupied with many assignments other than those of personal and group guardianship.

Urantia is not without proper and effective supervision from the system, constellation, and universe rulers. But the planetary government is unlike that of any other world in the Satania system, even in all Nebadon. This uniqueness in your plan of supervision is due to a number of unusual circumstances:

1. The life modification status of Urantia.

2. The exigencies of the Lucifer rebellion.

3. The disruptions of the Adamic default.

4. The irregularities growing out of the fact that Urantia was one of the bestowal worlds of the Universe Sovereign. Michael of Nebadon is the Planetary Prince of Urantia.

5. The special function of the twenty-four planetary directors.

6. The location on the planet of an archangels' circuit.

7. The more recent designation of the onetime incarnated Machiventa Melchizedek as vicegerent Planetary Prince.

1. THE SOVEREIGNTY OF URANTIA

The original sovereignty of Urantia was held in trust by the sovereign of the Satania system. It was first delegated by him to a joint commission of Melchizedeks and Life Carriers, and this group functioned on Urantia until the arrival of a regularly constituted Planetary Prince. Subsequent to the downfall of Prince Caligastia, at the time of the Lucifer rebellion, Urantia had no sure and settled relationship with the local universe and its administrative divisions until the completion of Michael's bestowal in the flesh, when he was proclaimed, by the Union of Days, Planetary Prince of Urantia. Such a proclamation in surety and in principle forever settled the status of your world, but in practice the Sovereign Creator Son made no gesture of personal administration of the planet aside from the establishment of the Jerusem commission of twenty-four former Urantians with authority to represent him in the government of Urantia and all other quarantined planets in the system. One of this council is now always resident on Urantia as resident governor general.

Vicegerent authority to act for Michael as Planetary Prince has been recently vested in Machiventa Melchizedek, but this Son of the local universe has made not the slightest move toward modifying the present planetary regime of the successive administrations of the resident governors general.

There is little likelihood that any marked change will be made in the government of Urantia during the present dispensation unless the vicegerent Planetary Prince should arrive to assume his titular responsibilities. It appears to certain of our associates that at some time in the near future the plan of sending one of the twenty-four counselors to Urantia to act as governor general will be superseded by the formal arrival of Machiventa Melchizedek with the vicegerent mandate of the sovereignty of Urantia. As acting Planetary Prince he would undoubtedly continue in charge of the planet until the final adjudication of the Lucifer rebellion and probably on into the distant future of planetary settlement in light and life.

Some believe that Machiventa will not come to take personal direction of Urantian affairs until the end of the current dispensation. Others hold that the vicegerent Prince may not come, as such, until Michael sometime returns to Urantia as he promised when still in the flesh. Still others, including this narrator, look for Melchizedek's appearance any day or hour.

2. THE BOARD OF PLANETARY SUPERVISORS

Since the times of Michael's bestowal on your world the general management of Urantia has been intrusted to a special group on Jerusem of twenty-four onetime Urantians. Qualification for membership on this commission is unknown to us, but we have observed that those who have been thus commissioned have all been contributors to the enlarging sovereignty of the Supreme in the system of Satania. By nature they were all real leaders when they functioned on Urantia, and (excepting Machiventa Melchizedek) these qualities of leadership have been further augmented by mansion world experience and supplemented by the training of Jerusem citizenship. Members are nominated to the twenty-four by the cabinet of Lanaforge, seconded by the Most Highs of Edentia, approved by the Assigned Sentinel of Jerusem, and appointed by Gabriel of Salvington in accordance with the mandate of Michael. The temporary appointees function just as fully as do the permanent members of this commission of special supervisors.

This board of planetary directors is especially concerned with the supervision of those activities on this world which result from the fact that Michael here experienced his terminal bestowal. They are kept in close and immediate touch with Michael by the liaison activities of a certain Brilliant Evening Star, the identical being who attended upon Jesus throughout the mortal bestowal.

At the present time one John, known to you as "the Baptist," is chairman of this council when it is in session on Jerusem. But the ex officio head of this council is the Assigned Sentinel of Satania, the direct and personal representative of the Associate Inspector on Salvington and of the Supreme Executive of Orvonton.

The members of this same commission of former Urantians also act as advisory supervisors of the thirty-six other rebellion-isolated worlds of the system; they perform a very valuable service in keeping Lanaforge, the System Sovereign, in close and sympathetic touch with the affairs of these planets, which still remain more or less under the overcontrol of the Constellation Fathers of Norlatiadek. These twenty-four counselors make frequent trips as individuals to each of the quarantined planets, especially to Urantia.

Each of the other isolated worlds is advised by similar and varying sized commissions of its onetime inhabitants, but these other commissions are subordinate to the Urantian group of twenty-four. While the members of the latter commission are thus actively interested in every phase of human progress on each quarantined world in Satania, they are especially and particularly concerned with the welfare and advancement of the mortal races of Urantia, for they immediately and directly supervise the affairs of none of the planets except Urantia, and even here their authority is not complete excepting in certain domains concerned with mortal survival.

No one knows how long these twenty-four Urantia counselors will continue in their present status, detached from the regular program of universe activities. They will no doubt continue to serve in their present capacities until some change in planetary status ensues, such as the end of a dispensation, the assumption of full authority by Machiventa Melchizedek, the final adjudication of the Lucifer rebellion, or the reappearance of Michael on the world of his final bestowal. The present resident governor general of Urantia seems inclined to the opinion that all but Machiventa may be released for Paradise ascension the moment the system of Satania is restored to the constellation circuits. But other opinions are also current.

3. THE RESIDENT GOVERNOR GENERAL

Every one hundred years of Urantia time, the Jerusem corps of twenty-four planetary supervisors designate one of their number to sojourn on your world to act as their executive representative, as resident governor general. During the times of the preparation of these narratives this executive officer was changed, the nineteenth so to serve being succeeded by the twentieth. The name of the current planetary supervisor is withheld from you only because mortal man is so prone to venerate, even to deify, his extraordinary compatriots and superhuman superiors.

The resident governor general has no actual personal authority in the management of world affairs except as the representative of the twenty-four Jerusem counselors. He acts as the co-ordinator of superhuman administration and is the respected head and universally recognized leader of the celestial beings functioning on Urantia. All orders of angelic hosts regard him as their co-ordinating director, while the United Midwayers, since the departure of 1-2-3 the first to become one of the twenty-four counselors, really look upon the successive governors general as their planetary fathers.

Although the governor general does not possess actual and personal authority on the planet, he hands down scores of rulings and decisions each day which are accepted as final by all personalities concerned. He is much more of a fatherly adviser than a technical ruler. In certain ways he functions as would a Planetary Prince, but his administration much more closely resembles that of the Material Sons.

The Urantia government is represented in the councils of Jerusem in accordance with an arrangement whereby the returning governor general sits as a temporary member of the System Sovereign's cabinet of Planetary Princes. It was expected, when Machiventa was designated vicegerent Prince, that he would immediately assume his place in the council of the Planetary Princes of Satania, but thus far he has made no gesture in this direction.

The supermaterial government of Urantia does not maintain a very close organic relationship with the higher units of the local universe. In a way, the resident governor general represents Salvington as well as Jerusem since he acts on behalf of the twenty-four counselors, who are directly representative of Michael and Gabriel. And being a Jerusem citizen, the planetary governor can function as a spokesman for the System Sovereign. The constellation authorities are represented directly by a Vorondadek Son, the Edentia observer.

4. THE MOST HIGH OBSERVER

The sovereignty of Urantia is further complicated by the onetime arbitrary seizure of planetary authority by the government of Norlatiadek shortly after the planetary rebellion. There is still resident on Urantia a Vorondadek Son, an observer for the Most Highs of Edentia and, in the absence of direct action by Michael, trustee of planetary sovereignty. The present Most High observer (and sometime regent) is the twenty-third thus to serve on Urantia.

There are certain groups of planetary problems which are still under the control of the Most Highs of Edentia, jurisdiction over them having been seized at the time of the Lucifer rebellion. Authority in these matters is exercised by a Vorondadek Son, the Norlatiadek observer, who maintains very close advisory relations with the planetary supervisors. The race commissioners are very active on Urantia, and their various group chiefs are informally attached to the resident Vorondadek observer, who acts as their advisory director.

In a crisis the actual and sovereign head of the government, excepting in certain purely spiritual matters, would be this Vorondadek Son of Edentia now on observation duty. (In these exclusively spiritual problems and in certain purely personal matters, the supreme authority seems to be vested in the commanding archangel attached to the divisional headquarters of that order which was recently established on Urantia.)

A Most High observer is empowered, at his discretion, to seize the planetary government in times of grave planetary crises, and it is of record that this has happened thirty-three times in the history of Urantia. At such times the Most High observer functions as the Most High regent, exercising unquestioned authority over all ministers and administrators resident on the planet excepting only the divisional organization of the archangels.

Vorondadek regencies are not peculiar to rebellion-isolated planets, for the Most Highs may intervene at any time in the affairs of the inhabited worlds, interposing the superior wisdom of the constellation rulers in the affairs of the kingdoms of men.

5. THE PLANETARY GOVERNMENT

The actual administration of Urantia is indeed difficult to describe. There exists no formal government along the lines of universe organization, such as separate legislative, executive, and judicial departments. The twenty-four counselors come the nearest to being the legislative branch of the planetary government. The governor general is a provisional and advisory chief executive with the veto power resident in the Most High observer. And there are no absolutely authoritative judicial powers operative on the planet—only the conciliating commissions.

A majority of the problems involving seraphim and midwayers are, by mutual consent, decided by the governor general. But except when voicing the mandates of the twenty-four counselors, his rulings are all subject to appeal to conciliating commissions, to local authorities constituted for planetary function, or even to the System Sovereign of Satania.

The absence of the corporeal staff of a Planetary Prince and the material regime of an Adamic Son and Daughter is partially compensated by the special ministry of seraphim and by the unusual services of the midway creatures. The absence of the Planetary Prince is effectively compensated by the triune presence of the archangels, the Most High observer, and the governor general.

This rather loosely organized and somewhat personally administered planetary government is more than expectedly effective because of the time-saving assistance of the archangels and their ever-ready circuit, which is so frequently utilized in planetary emergencies and administrative difficulties. Technically, the planet is still spiritually isolated in the Norlatiadek circuits, but in an emergency this handicap can now be circumvented through utilization of the archangels' circuit. Planetary isolation is, of course, of little concern to individual mortals since the pouring out of the Spirit of Truth upon all flesh nineteen hundred years ago.

Each administrative day on Urantia begins with a consultative conference, which is attended by the governor general, the planetary chief of archangels, the Most High observer, the supervising supernaphim, the chief of resident Life Carriers, and invited guests from among the high Sons of the universe or from among certain of the student visitors who may chance to be sojourning on the planet.

The direct administrative cabinet of the governor general consists of twelve seraphim, the acting chiefs of the twelve groups of special angels functioning as the immediate superhuman directors of planetary progress and stability.

6. THE MASTER SERAPHIM OF PLANETARY SUPERVISION

When the first governor general arrived on Urantia, concurrent with the outpouring of the Spirit of Truth, he was accompanied by twelve corps of special seraphim, Seraphington graduates, who were immediately assigned to certain special planetary services. These exalted angels are known as the master seraphim of planetary supervision and are, aside from the overcontrol of the planetary

Most High observer, under the immediate direction of the resident governor general.

These twelve groups of angels, while functioning under the general supervision of the resident governor general, are immediately directed by the seraphic council of twelve, the acting chiefs of each group. This council also serves as the volunteer cabinet of the resident governor general.

As planetary chief of seraphim, I preside over this council of seraphic chiefs, and I am a volunteer supernaphim of the primary order serving on Urantia as the successor of the onetime chief of the angelic hosts of the planet who defaulted at the time of the Caligastia secession.

The twelve corps of the master seraphim of planetary supervision are functional on Urantia as follows:

1. *The epochal angels.* These are the angels of the current age, the dispensational group. These celestial ministers are intrusted with the oversight and direction of the affairs of each generation as they are designed to fit into the mosaic of the age in which they occur. The present corps of epochal angels serving on Urantia is the third group assigned to the planet during the current dispensation.

2. *The progress angels.* These seraphim are intrusted with the task of initiating the evolutionary progress of the successive social ages. They foster the development of the inherent progressive trend of evolutionary creatures; they labor incessantly to make things what they ought to be. The group now on duty is the second to be assigned to the planet.

3. *The religious guardians.* These are the "angels of the churches," the earnest contenders for that which is and has been. They endeavor to maintain the ideals of that which has survived for the sake of the safe transit of moral values from one epoch to another. They are the checkmates of the angels of progress, all the while seeking to translate from one generation to another the imperishable values of the old and passing forms into the new and therefore less stabilized patterns of thought and conduct. These angels do contend for spiritual forms, but they are not the source of ultrasectarianism and meaningless controversial divisions of professed religionists. The corps now functioning on Urantia is the fifth thus to serve.

4. *The angels of nation life.* These are the "angels of the trumpets," directors of the political performances of Urantia national life. The group now functioning in the overcontrol of international relations is the fourth corps to serve on the planet. It is particularly through the ministry of this seraphic division that "the Most Highs rule in the kingdoms of men."

5. *The angels of the races.* Those who work for the conservation of the evolutionary races of time, regardless of their political entanglements and religious groupings. On Urantia there are remnants of nine human races which have commingled and combined into the people of modern times. These seraphim are closely associated with the ministry of the race commissioners, and the group now on Urantia is the original corps assigned to the planet soon after the day of Pentecost.

6. *The angels of the future.* These are the projection angels, who forecast a future age and plan for the realization of the better things of a new and

advancing dispensation; they are the architects of the successive eras. The group now on the planet has thus functioned since the beginning of the current dispensation.

7. *The angels of enlightenment.* Urantia is now receiving the help of the third corps of seraphim dedicated to the fostering of planetary education. These angels are occupied with mental and moral training as it concerns individuals, families, groups, schools, communities, nations, and whole races.

8. *The angels of health.* These are the seraphic ministers assigned to the assistance of those mortal agencies dedicated to the promotion of health and the prevention of disease. The present corps is the sixth group to serve during this dispensation.

9. *The home seraphim.* Urantia now enjoys the services of the fifth group of angelic ministers dedicated to the preservation and advancement of the home, the basic institution of human civilization.

10. *The angels of industry.* This seraphic group is concerned with fostering industrial development and improving economic conditions among the Urantia peoples. This corps has been seven times changed since the bestowal of Michael.

11. *The angels of diversion.* These are the seraphim who foster the values of play, humor, and rest. They ever seek to uplift man's recreational diversions and thus to promote the more profitable utilization of human leisure. The present corps is the third of that order to minister on Urantia.

12. *The angels of superhuman ministry.* These are the angels of the angels, those seraphim who are assigned to the ministry of all other superhuman life on the planet, temporary or permanent. This corps has served since the beginning of the current dispensation.

When these groups of master seraphim disagree in matters of planetary policy or procedure, their differences are usually composed by the governor general, but all his rulings are subject to appeal in accordance with the nature and gravity of the issues involved in the disagreement.

None of these angelic groups exercise direct or arbitrary control over the domains of their assignment. They cannot fully control the affairs of their respective realms of action, but they can and do so manipulate planetary conditions and so associate circumstances as favorably to influence the spheres of human activity to which they are attached.

The master seraphim of planetary supervision utilize many agencies for the prosecution of their missions. They function as ideational clearinghouses, mind focalizers, and project promoters. While unable to inject new and higher conceptions into human minds, they often act to intensify some higher ideal which has already appeared within a human intellect.

But aside from these many means of positive action, the master seraphim insure planetary progress against vital jeopardy through the mobilization, training, and maintenance of the reserve corps of destiny. The chief function of these reservists is to insure against breakdown of evolutionary progress; they are the provisions which the celestial forces have made against surprise; they are the guarantees against disaster.

7. THE RESERVE CORPS OF DESTINY

The reserve corps of destiny consists of living men and women who have been admitted to the special service of the superhuman administration of world affairs. This corps is made up of the men and women of each generation who are chosen by the spirit directors of the realm to assist in the conduct of the ministry of mercy and wisdom to the children of time on the evolutionary worlds. It is the general practice in the conduct of the affairs of the ascension plans to begin this liaison utilization of mortal will creatures immediately they are competent and trustworthy to assume such responsibilities. Accordingly, as soon as men and women appear on the stage of temporal action with sufficient mental capacity, adequate moral status, and requisite spirituality, they are quickly assigned to the appropriate celestial group of planetary personalities as human liaisons, mortal assistants.

When human beings are chosen as protectors of planetary destiny, when they become pivotal individuals in the plans which the world administrators are prosecuting, at that time the planetary chief of seraphim confirms their temporal attachment to the seraphic corps and appoints personal destiny guardians to serve with these mortal reservists. All reservists have self-conscious Adjusters, and most of them function in the higher cosmic circles of intellectual achievement and spiritual attainment.

Mortals of the realm are chosen for service in the reserve corps of destiny on the inhabited worlds because of:

1. Special capacity for being secretly rehearsed for numerous possible emergency missions in the conduct of various activities of world affairs.

2. Wholehearted dedication to some special social, economic, political, spiritual, or other cause, coupled with willingness to serve without human recognition and rewards.

3. The possession of a Thought Adjuster of extraordinary versatility and probable pre-Urantia experience in coping with planetary difficulties and contending with impending world emergency situations.

Each division of planetary celestial service is entitled to a liaison corps of these mortals of destiny standing. The average inhabited world employs seventy separate corps of destiny, which are intimately connected with the superhuman current conduct of world affairs. On Urantia there are twelve reserve corps of destiny, one for each of the planetary groups of seraphic supervision.

The twelve groups of Urantia destiny reservists are composed of mortal inhabitants of the sphere who have been rehearsed for numerous crucial positions on earth and are held in readiness to act in possible planetary emergencies. This combined corps now consists of 962 persons. The smallest corps numbers 41 and the largest 172. With the exception of less than a score of contact personalities, the members of this unique group are wholly unconscious of their preparation for possible function in certain planetary crises. These mortal reservists are chosen by the corps to which they are respectively attached and are likewise trained and rehearsed in the deep mind by the combined technique of Thought Adjuster and seraphic guardian ministry. Many times numerous other celestial personalities participate in this unconscious training, and in all this special preparation the midwayers perform valuable and indispensable services.

On many worlds the better adapted secondary midway creatures are able to attain varying degrees of contact with the Thought Adjusters of certain favorably constituted mortals through the skillful penetration of the minds of the latters' indwelling. (And it was by just such a fortuitous combination of cosmic adjustments that these revelations were materialized in the English language on Urantia.) Such potential contact mortals of the evolutionary worlds are mobilized in the numerous reserve corps, and it is, to a certain extent, through these small groups of forward-looking personalities that spiritual civilization is advanced and the Most Highs are able to rule in the kingdoms of men. The men and women of these reserve corps of destiny thus have various degrees of contact with their Adjusters through the intervening ministry of the midway creatures; but these same mortals are little known to their fellows except in those rare social emergencies and spiritual exigencies wherein these reserve personalities function for the prevention of the breakdown of evolutionary culture or the extinction of the light of living truth. On Urantia these reservists of destiny have seldom been emblazoned on the pages of human history.

The reservists unconsciously act as conservators of essential planetary information. Many times, upon the death of a reservist, a transfer of certain vital data from the mind of the dying reservist to a younger successor is made by a liaison of the two Thought Adjusters. The Adjusters undoubtedly function in many other ways unknown to us, in connection with these reserve corps.

On Urantia the reserve corps of destiny, though having no permanent head, does have its own permanent councils which constitute its governing organization. These embrace the judiciary council, the historicity council, the council on political sovereignty, and many others. From time to time, in accordance with the corps organization, titular (mortal) heads of the whole reserve corps have been commissioned by these permanent councils for specific function. The tenure of such reservist chiefs is usually a matter of a few hours' duration, being limited to the accomplishment of some specific task at hand.

The Urantia reserve corps had its largest membership in the days of the Adamites and Andites, steadily declining with the dilution of the violet blood and reaching its low point around the time of Pentecost, since which time reserve corps membership has steadily increased.

(The cosmic reserve corps of universe-conscious citizens on Urantia now numbers over one thousand mortals whose insight of cosmic citizenship far transcends the sphere of their terrestrial abode, but I am forbidden to reveal the real nature of the function of this unique group of living human beings.)

Urantia mortals should not allow the comparative spiritual isolation of their world from certain of the local universe circuits to produce a feeling of cosmic desertion or planetary orphanage. There is operative on the planet a very definite and effective superhuman supervision of world affairs and human destinies.

But it is true that you can have, at best, only a meager idea of an ideal planetary government. Since the early times of the Planetary Prince, Urantia has suffered from the miscarriage of the divine plan of world growth and racial development. The loyal inhabited worlds of Satania are not governed as is Urantia. Nevertheless, compared with the other isolated worlds, your planetary governments have not been so inferior; only one or two worlds may be said to be worse, and a few may be slightly better, but the majority are on a plane of equality with you.

No one in the local universe seems to know when the unsettled status of the planetary administration will terminate. The Nebadon Melchizedeks are inclined to the opinion that little change will occur in the planetary government and administration until Michael's second personal arrival on Urantia. Undoubtedly at this time, if not before, sweeping changes will be effected in planetary management. But as to the nature of such modifications of world administration, no one seems to be able even to conjecture. There is no precedent for such an episode in all the history of the inhabited worlds of the universe of Nebadon. Among the many things difficult to understand concerning the future government of Urantia, a prominent one is the location on the planet of a circuit and divisional headquarters of the archangels.

Your isolated world is not forgotten in the counsels of the universe. Urantia is not a cosmic orphan stigmatized by sin and shut away from divine watchcare by rebellion. From Uversa to Salvington and on down to Jerusem, even in Havona and on Paradise, they all know we are here; and you mortals now dwelling on Urantia are just as lovingly cherished and just as faithfully watched over as if the sphere had never been betrayed by a faithless Planetary Prince, even more so. It is eternally true, "the Father himself loves you."

[Presented by the Chief of Seraphim stationed on Urantia.]

PAPER 115

THE SUPREME BEING

WITH God the Father, sonship is the great relationship. With God the Supreme, achievement is the prerequisite to status—one must do something as well as be something.

1. RELATIVITY OF CONCEPT FRAMES

Partial, incomplete, and evolving intellects would be helpless in the master universe, would be unable to form the first rational thought pattern, were it not for the innate ability of all mind, high or low, to form a *universe frame* in which to think. If mind cannot fathom conclusions, if it cannot penetrate to true origins, then will such mind unfailingly postulate conclusions and invent origins that it may have a means of logical thought within the frame of these mind-created postulates. And while such universe frames for creature thought are indispensable to rational intellectual operations, they are, without exception, erroneous to a greater or lesser degree.

Conceptual frames of the universe are only relatively true; they are serviceable scaffolding which must eventually give way before the expansions of enlarging cosmic comprehension. The understandings of truth, beauty, and goodness, morality, ethics, duty, love, divinity, origin, existence, purpose, destiny, time, space, even Deity, are only relatively true. God is much, much more than a Father, but the Father is man's highest concept of God; nonetheless, the Father-Son portrayal of Creator-creature relationship will be augmented by those supermortal conceptions of Deity which will be attained in Orvonton, in Havona, and on Paradise. Man must think in a mortal universe frame, but that does not mean that he cannot envision other and higher frames within which thought can take place.

In order to facilitate mortal comprehension of the universe of universes, the diverse levels of cosmic reality have been designated as finite, absonite, and absolute. Of these only the absolute is unqualifiedly eternal, truly existential. Absonites and finites are derivatives, modifications, qualifications, and attenuations of the original and primordial absolute reality of infinity.

The realms of the finite exist by virtue of the eternal purpose of God. Finite creatures, high and low, may propound theories, and have done so, as to the necessity of the finite in the cosmic economy, but in the last analysis it exists because God so willed. The universe cannot be explained, neither can a finite creature offer a rational reason for his own individual existence without appealing to the prior acts and pre-existent volition of ancestral beings, Creators or procreators.

2. THE ABSOLUTE BASIS FOR SUPREMACY

From the existential standpoint, nothing new can happen throughout the galaxies, for the completion of infinity inherent in the I AM is eternally present in the seven Absolutes, is functionally associated in the triunities, and is transmitively associated in the triodities. But the fact that infinity is thus existentially present in these absolute associations in no way makes it impossible to realize new cosmic experientials. From a finite creature's viewpoint, infinity contains much that is potential, much that is on the order of a future possibility rather than a present actuality.

Value is a unique element in universe reality. We do not comprehend how the value of anything infinite and divine could possibly be increased. But we discover that *meanings* can be modified if not augmented even in the relations of infinite Deity. To the experiential universes even divine values are increased as actualities by enlarged comprehension of reality meanings.

The entire scheme of universal creation and evolution on all experiencing levels is apparently a matter of the conversion of potentialities into actualities; and this transmutation has to do equally with the realms of space potency, mind potency, and spirit potency.

The apparent method whereby the possibilities of the cosmos are brought into actual existence varies from level to level, being experiential evolution in the finite and experiential eventuation in the absonite. Existential infinity is indeed unqualified in all-inclusiveness, and this very all-inclusiveness must, perforce, encompass even the possibility for evolutionary finite experiencing. And the possibility for such experiential growth becomes a universe actuality through triodity relationships impinging upon and in the Supreme.

3. ORIGINAL, ACTUAL, AND POTENTIAL

The absolute cosmos is conceptually without limit; to define the extent and nature of this primal reality is to place qualifications upon infinity and to attenuate the pure concept of eternity. The idea of the infinite-eternal, the eternal-infinite, is unqualified in extent and absolute in fact. There is no language in the past, present, or future of Urantia adequate to express the reality of infinity or the infinity of reality. Man, a finite creature in an infinite cosmos, must content himself with distorted reflections and attenuated conceptions of that limitless, boundless, never-beginning, never-ending existence the comprehension of which is really beyond his ability.

Mind can never hope to grasp the concept of an Absolute without attempting first to break the unity of such a reality. Mind is unifying of all divergencies, but in the very absence of such divergencies, mind finds no basis upon which to attempt to formulate understanding concepts.

The primordial stasis of infinity requires segmentation prior to human attempts at comprehension. There is a unity in infinity which has been expressed in these papers as the I AM—the premier postulate of the creature mind. But never can a creature understand how it is that this unity becomes duality, triunity, and diversity while yet remaining an unqualified unity. Man encounters a similar problem when he pauses to contemplate the undivided Deity of Trinity alongside the plural personalization of God.

It is only man's distance from infinity that causes this concept to be expressed as one word. While infinity is on the one hand UNITY, on the other it is DIVERSITY without end or limit. Infinity, as it is observed by finite intelligences, is the maximum paradox of creature philosophy and finite metaphysics. Though man's spiritual nature reaches up in the worship experience to the Father who is infinite, man's intellectual comprehension capacity is exhausted by the maximum conception of the Supreme Being. Beyond the Supreme, concepts are increasingly names; less and less are they true designations of reality; more and more do they become the creature's projection of finite understanding toward the superfinite.

One basic conception of the absolute level involves a postulate of three phases:

1. *The Original.* The unqualified concept of the First Source and Center, that source manifestation of the I AM from which all reality takes origin.

2. *The Actual.* The union of the three Absolutes of actuality, the Second, Third, and Paradise Sources and Centers. This triodity of the Eternal Son, the Infinite Spirit, and the Paradise Isle constitutes the actual revelation of the originality of the First Source and Center.

3. *The Potential.* The union of the three Absolutes of potentiality, the Deity, Unqualified, and Universal Absolutes. This triodity of existential potentiality constitutes the potential revelation of the originality of the First Source and Center.

The interassociation of the Original, the Actual, and the Potential yields the tensions within infinity which result in the possibility for all universe growth; and growth is the nature of the Sevenfold, the Supreme, and the Ultimate.

In the association of the Deity, Universal, and Unqualified Absolutes, potentiality is absolute while actuality is emergent; in the association of the Second, Third, and Paradise Sources and Centers, actuality is absolute while potentiality is emergent; in the originality of the First Source and Center, we cannot say that either actuality or potentiality is either existent or emergent—*the Father is.*

From the time viewpoint, the Actual is that which was and is; the Potential is that which is becoming and will be; the Original is that which is. From the eternity viewpoint, the differences between the Original, the Actual, and the Potential are not thus apparent. These triune qualities are not so distinguished on Paradise-eternity levels. In eternity all is—only has all not yet been revealed in time and space.

From a creature's viewpoint, actuality is substance, potentiality is capacity. Actuality exists centermost and expands therefrom into peripheral infinity; potentiality comes inward from the infinity periphery and converges at the center of all things. Originality is that which first causes and then balances the dual motions of the cycle of reality metamorphosis from potentials to actuals and the potentializing of existing actuals.

The three Absolutes of potentiality are operative on the purely eternal level of the cosmos, hence never function as such on subabsolute levels. On the descending levels of reality the triodity of potentiality is manifest with the Ultimate and upon the Supreme. The potential may fail to time-actualize with respect to a part on some subabsolute level, but never in the aggregate. The will of God does ultimately prevail, not always concerning the individual but invariably concerning the total.

It is in the triodity of actuality that the existents of the cosmos have their center; be it spirit, mind, or energy, all center in this association of the Son, the Spirit, and Paradise. The personality of the spirit Son is the master pattern for all personality throughout all universes. The substance of the Paradise Isle is the master pattern of which Havona is a perfect, and the superuniverses are a perfecting, revelation. The Conjoint Actor is at one and the same time the mind activation of cosmic energy, the conceptualization of spirit purpose, and the integration of the mathematical causes and effects of the material levels with the volitional purposes and motives of the spiritual level. In and to a finite universe the Son, Spirit, and Paradise function in and upon the Ultimate as he is conditioned and qualified in the Supreme.

Actuality (of Deity) is what man seeks in the Paradise ascent. Potentiality (of human divinity) is what man evolves in that search. The Original is what makes possible the coexistence and integration of man the actual, man the potential, and man the eternal.

The final dynamics of the cosmos have to do with the continual transfer of reality from potentiality to actuality. In theory, there may be an end to this metamorphosis, but in fact, such is impossible since the Potential and the Actual are both encircuited in the Original (the I AM), and this identification makes it forever impossible to place a limit on the developmental progression of the universe. Whatsoever is identified with the I AM can never find an end to progression since the actuality of the potentials of the I AM is absolute, and the potentiality of the actuals of the I AM is also absolute. Always will actuals be opening up new avenues of the realization of hitherto impossible potentials—every human decision not only actualizes a new reality in human experience but also opens up a new capacity for human growth. The man lives in every child, and the morontia progressor is resident in the mature God-knowing man.

Statics in growth can never appear in the total cosmos since the basis for growth—the absolute actuals—is unqualified, and since the possibilities for growth—the absolute potentials—are unlimited. From a practical viewpoint the philosophers of the universe have come to the conclusion that there is no such thing as an *end.*

From a circumscribed view there are, indeed, many ends, many terminations of activities, but from a larger viewpoint on a higher universe level, there are no endings, merely transitions from one phase of development to another. The major chronicity of the master universe is concerned with the several universe ages, the Havona, the superuniverse, and the outer universe ages. But even these basic divisions of sequence relationships cannot be more than relative landmarks on the unending highway of eternity.

The final penetration of the truth, beauty, and goodness of the Supreme Being could only open up to the progressing creature those absonite qualities of ultimate divinity which lie beyond the concept levels of truth, beauty, and goodness.

4. SOURCES OF SUPREME REALITY

Any consideration of the *origins* of God the Supreme must begin with the Paradise Trinity, for the Trinity is original Deity while the Supreme is derived

Deity. Any consideration of the *growth* of the Supreme must give consideration to the existential triodities, for they encompass all absolute actuality and all infinite potentiality (in conjunction with the First Source and Center). And the evolutionary Supreme is the culminating and personally volitional focus of the transmutation—the transformation—of potentials to actuals in and on the finite level of existence. The two triodities, actual and potential, encompass the totality of the interrelationships of growth in the universes.

The source of the Supreme is in the Paradise Trinity—eternal, actual, and undivided Deity. The Supreme is first of all a spirit person, and this spirit person stems from the Trinity. But the Supreme is secondly a Deity of growth—evolutionary growth—and this growth derives from the two triodities, actual and potential.

If it is difficult to comprehend that the infinite triodities can function on the finite level, pause to consider that their very infinity must in itself contain the potentiality of the finite; infinity encompasses all things ranging from the lowest and most qualified finite existence to the highest and unqualifiedly absolute realities.

It is not so difficult to comprehend that the infinite does contain the finite as it is to understand just how this infinite actually is manifest to the finite. But the Thought Adjusters indwelling mortal man are one of the eternal proofs that even the absolute God (as absolute) can and does actually make direct contact with even the lowest and least of all universe will creatures.

The triodities which collectively encompass the actual and the potential are manifest on the finite level in conjunction with the Supreme Being. The technique of such manifestation is both direct and indirect: direct in so far as triodity relations repercuss directly in the Supreme and indirect in so far as they are derived through the eventuated level of the absonite.

Supreme reality, which is total finite reality, is in process of dynamic growth between the unqualified potentials of outer space and the unqualified actuals at the center of all things. The finite domain thus factualizes through the cooperation of the absonite agencies of Paradise and the Supreme Creator Personalities of time. The act of maturing the qualified possibilities of the three great potential Absolutes is the absonite function of the Architects of the Master Universe and their transcendental associates. And when these eventualities have attained to a certain point of maturation, the Supreme Creator Personalities emerge from Paradise to engage in the agelong task of bringing the evolving universes into factual being.

The growth of Supremacy derives from the triodities; the spirit person of the Supreme, from the Trinity; but the power prerogatives of the Almighty are predicated on the divinity successes of God the Sevenfold, while the conjoining of the power prerogatives of the Almighty Supreme with the spirit person of God the Supreme takes place by virtue of the ministry of the Conjoint Actor, who bestowed the mind of the Supreme as the conjoining factor in this evolutionary Deity.

5. RELATION OF THE SUPREME TO THE PARADISE TRINITY

The Supreme Being is absolutely dependent on the existence and action of the Paradise Trinity for the reality of his personal and spirit nature. While the growth of the Supreme is a matter of triodity relationship, the spirit personality of God the Supreme is dependent upon, and is derived from, the Paradise Trinity, which ever remains as the absolute center-source of perfect and infinite stability around which the evolutionary growth of the Supreme progressively unfolds.

The function of the Trinity is related to the function of the Supreme, for the Trinity is functional on all (total) levels, including the level of the function of Supremacy. But as the age of Havona gives way to the age of the superuniverses, so does the discernible action of the Trinity as immediate creator give way to the creative acts of the children of the Paradise Deities.

6. RELATION OF THE SUPREME TO THE TRIODITIES

The triodity of actuality continues to function directly in the post-Havona epochs; Paradise gravity grasps the basic units of material existence, the spirit gravity of the Eternal Son operates directly upon the fundamental values of spirit existence, and the mind gravity of the Conjoint Actor unerringly clutches all vital meanings of intellectual existence.

But as each stage of creative activity proceeds out through uncharted space, it functions and exists farther and farther removed from direct action by the creative forces and divine personalities of central emplacement—the absolute Isle of Paradise and the infinite Deities resident thereon. These successive levels of cosmic existence become, therefore, increasingly dependent upon developments within the three Absolute potentialities of infinity.

The Supreme Being embraces possibilities for cosmic ministry that are not apparently manifested in the Eternal Son, the Infinite Spirit, or the nonpersonal realities of the Isle of Paradise. This statement is made with due regard for the absoluteness of these three basic actualities, but the growth of the Supreme is not only predicated on these actualities of Deity and Paradise but is also involved in developments within the Deity, Universal, and Unqualified Absolutes.

The Supreme not only grows as the Creators and creatures of the evolving universes attain to Godlikeness, but this finite Deity also experiences growth as a result of the creature and Creator mastery of the finite possibilities of the grand universe. The motion of the Supreme is twofold: intensively toward Paradise and Deity and extensively toward the limitlessness of the Absolutes of potential.

In the present universe age this dual motion is revealed in the descending and ascending personalities of the grand universe. The Supreme Creator Personalities and all their divine associates are reflective of the outward, diverging motion of the Supreme, while the ascending pilgrims from the seven superuniverses are indicative of the inward, converging trend of Supremacy.

Always is the finite Deity seeking for dual correlation, inward toward Paradise and the Deities thereof and outward toward infinity and the Absolutes therein. The mighty eruption of the Paradise-creative divinity personalizing in the Creator Sons and powerizing in the power controllers, signifies the vast outsurge of Supremacy into the domains of potentiality, while the endless procession of the ascending creatures of the grand universe witnesses the mighty insurge of Supremacy toward unity with Paradise Deity.

Human beings have learned that the motion of the invisible may sometimes be discerned by observing its effects on the visible; and we in the universes have long since learned to detect the movements and trends of Supremacy by observing the repercussions of such evolutions in the personalities and patterns of the grand universe.

Though we are not sure, we believe that, as a finite reflection of Paradise Deity, the Supreme is engaged in an eternal progression into outer space; but as a qualification of the three Absolute potentials of outer space, this Supreme Being is forever seeking for Paradise coherence. And these dual motions seem to account for most of the basic activities in the presently organized universes.

7. THE NATURE OF THE SUPREME

In the Deity of the Supreme the Father-I AM has achieved relatively complete liberation from the limitations inherent in infinity of status, eternity of being, and absoluteness of nature. But God the Supreme has been freed from all existential limitations only by having become subject to experiential qualifications of universal function. In attaining capacity for experience, the finite God also becomes subject to the necessity therefor; in achieving liberation from eternity, the Almighty encounters the barriers of time; and the Supreme could only know growth and development as a consequence of partiality of existence and incompleteness of nature, nonabsoluteness of being.

All this must be according to the Father's plan, which has predicated finite progress upon effort, creature achievement upon perseverance, and personality development upon faith. By thus ordaining the experience-evolution of the Supreme, the Father has made it possible for finite creatures to exist in the universes and, by experiential progression, sometime to attain the divinity of Supremacy.

Including the Supreme and even the Ultimate, all reality, excepting the unqualified values of the seven Absolutes, is relative. The fact of Supremacy is predicated on Paradise power, Son personality, and Conjoint action, but the growth of the Supreme is involved in the Deity Absolute, the Unqualified Absolute, and the Universal Absolute. And this synthesizing and unifying Deity—God the Supreme—is the personification of the finite shadow cast athwart the grand universe by the infinite unity of the unsearchable nature of the Paradise Father, the First Source and Center.

To the extent that the triodities are directly operative on the finite level, they impinge upon the Supreme, who is the Deity focalization and cosmic summation of the finite qualifications of the natures of the Absolute Actual and the Absolute Potential.

The Paradise Trinity is considered to be the absolute inevitability; the Seven Master Spirits are apparently Trinity inevitabilities; the power-mind-spirit-personality actualization of the Supreme must be the evolutionary inevitability.

God the Supreme does not appear to have been inevitable in unqualified infinity, but he seems to be on all relativity levels. He is the indispensable focalizer, summarizer, and encompasser of evolutionary experience, effectively unifying the results of this mode of reality perception in his Deity nature. And all this he appears to do for the purpose of contributing to the appearance of the *inevitable eventuation,* the superexperience and superfinite manifestation of God the Ultimate.

The Supreme Being cannot be fully appreciated without taking into consideration source, function, and destiny: relationship to the originating Trinity, the universe of activity, and the Trinity Ultimate of immediate destiny.

By the process of summating evolutionary experience the Supreme connects the finite with the absonite, even as the mind of the Conjoint Actor integrates the divine spirituality of the personal Son with the immutable energies of the Paradise pattern, and as the presence of the Universal Absolute unifies Deity activation with the Unqualified reactivity. And this unity must be a revelation of the undetected working of the original unity of the First Father-Cause and Source-Pattern of all things and all beings.

[Sponsored by a Mighty Messenger temporarily sojourning on Urantia.]

PAPER 116

THE ALMIGHTY SUPREME

IF MAN recognized that his Creators—his immediate supervisors—while being divine were also finite, and that the God of time and space was an evolving and nonabsolute Deity, then would the inconsistencies of temporal inequalities cease to be profound religious paradoxes. No longer would religious faith be prostituted to the promotion of social smugness in the fortunate while serving only to encourage stoical resignation in the unfortunate victims of social deprivation.

When viewing the exquisitely perfect spheres of Havona, it is both reasonable and logical to believe they were made by a perfect, infinite, and absolute Creator. But that same reason and logic would compel any honest being, when viewing the turmoil, imperfections, and inequities of Urantia, to conclude that your world had been made by, and was being managed by, Creators who were subabsolute, preinfinite, and other than perfect.

Experiential growth implies creature-Creator partnership—God and man in association. Growth is the earmark of experiential Deity: Havona did not grow; Havona is and always has been; it is existential like the everlasting Gods who are its source. But growth characterizes the grand universe.

The Almighty Supreme is a living and evolving Deity of power and personality. His present domain, the grand universe, is also a growing realm of power and personality. His destiny is perfection, but his present experience encompasses the elements of growth and incomplete status.

The Supreme Being functions primarily in the central universe as a spirit personality; secondarily in the grand universe as God the Almighty, a personality of power. The tertiary function of the Supreme in the master universe is now latent, existing only as an unknown mind potential. No one knows just what this third development of the Supreme Being will disclose. Some believe that, when the superuniverses are settled in light and life, the Supreme will become functional from Uversa as the almighty and experiential sovereign of the grand universe while expanding in power as the superalmighty of the outer universes. Others speculate that the third stage of Supremacy will involve the third level of Deity manifestation. But none of us really know.

1. THE SUPREME MIND

The experience of every evolving creature personality is a phase of the experience of the Almighty Supreme. The intelligent subjugation of every physical segment of the superuniverses is a part of the growing control of the

Almighty Supreme. The creative synthesis of power and personality is a part of the creative urge of the Supreme Mind and is the very essence of the evolutionary growth of unity in the Supreme Being.

The union of the power and personality attributes of Supremacy is the function of Supreme Mind; and the completed evolution of the Almighty Supreme will result in one unified and personal Deity—not in any loosely co-ordinated association of divine attributes. From the broader perspective, there will be no Almighty apart from the Supreme, no Supreme apart from the Almighty.

Throughout the evolutionary ages the physical power potential of the Supreme is vested in the Seven Supreme Power Directors, and the mind potential reposes in the Seven Master Spirits. The Infinite Mind is the function of the Infinite Spirit; the cosmic mind, the ministry of the Seven Master Spirits; the Supreme Mind is in process of actualizing in the co-ordination of the grand universe and in functional association with the revelation and attainment of God the Sevenfold.

The time-space mind, the cosmic mind, is differently functioning in the seven superuniverses, but it is co-ordinated by some unknown associative technique in the Supreme Being. The Almighty overcontrol of the grand universe is not exclusively physical and spiritual. In the seven superuniverses it is primarily material and spiritual, but there are also present phenomena of the Supreme which are both intellectual and spiritual.

We really know less about the mind of Supremacy than about any other aspect of this evolving Deity. It is unquestionably active throughout the grand universe and is believed to have a potential destiny of master universe function which is of vast extent. But this we do know: Whereas physique may attain completed growth, and whereas spirit may achieve perfection of development, mind never ceases to progress—it is the experiential technique of endless progress. The Supreme is an experiential Deity and therefore never achieves completion of mind attainment.

2. THE ALMIGHTY AND GOD THE SEVENFOLD

The appearance of the universe power presence of the Almighty is concomitant with the appearance on the stage of cosmic action of the high creators and controllers of the evolutionary superuniverses.

God the Supreme derives his spirit and personality attributes from the Paradise Trinity, but he is power-actualizing in the doings of the Creator Sons, the Ancients of Days, and the Master Spirits, whose collective acts are the source of his growing power as almighty sovereign to and in the seven superuniverses.

Unqualified Paradise Deity is incomprehensible to the evolving creatures of time and space. Eternity and infinity connote a level of deity reality which time-space creatures cannot comprehend. Infinity of deity and absoluteness of sovereignty are inherent in the Paradise Trinity, and the Trinity is a reality which lies somewhat beyond the understanding of mortal man. Time-space creatures must have origins, relativities, and destinies in order to grasp universe relationships and to understand the meaning values of divinity. Therefore does Paradise Deity attenuate and otherwise qualify the extra-Paradise personalizations of divinity, thus bringing into existence the Supreme Creators and their associates, who ever carry the light of life farther and farther from its Paradise source until it finds its most distant and beautiful expression in the earth lives of the bestowal Sons on the evolutionary worlds.

And this is the origin of God the Sevenfold, whose successive levels are encountered by mortal man in the following order:

1. The Creator Sons (and Creative Spirits).
2. The Ancients of Days.
3. The Seven Master Spirits.
4. The Supreme Being.
5. The Conjoint Actor.
6. The Eternal Son.
7. The Universal Father.

The first three levels are the Supreme Creators; the last three levels are the Paradise Deities. The Supreme ever intervenes as the experiential spirit personalization of the Paradise Trinity and as the experiential focus of the evolutionary almighty power of the creator children of the Paradise Deities. The Supreme Being is the maximum revelation of Deity to the seven superuniverses and for the present universe age.

By the technique of mortal logic it might be inferred that the experiential reunification of the collective acts of the first three levels of God the Sevenfold would equivalate to the level of Paradise Deity, but such is not the case. Paradise Deity is *existential* Deity. The Supreme Creators, in their divine unity of power and personality, are constitutive and expressive of a new power potential of *experiential* Deity. And this power potential of experiential origin finds inevitable and inescapable union with the experiential Deity of Trinity origin—the Supreme Being.

God the Supreme is not the Paradise Trinity, neither is he any one or all of those superuniverse Creators whose functional activities actually synthesize his evolving almighty power. God the Supreme, while of origin in the Trinity, becomes manifest to evolutionary creatures as a personality of power only through the co-ordinated functions of the first three levels of God the Sevenfold. The Almighty Supreme is now factualizing in time and space through the activities of the Supreme Creator Personalities, even as in eternity the Conjoint Actor flashed into being by the will of the Universal Father and the Eternal Son. These beings of the first three levels of God the Sevenfold are the very nature and source of the power of the Almighty Supreme; therefore must they ever accompany and sustain his administrative acts.

3. THE ALMIGHTY AND PARADISE DEITY

The Paradise Deities not only act directly in their gravity circuits throughout the grand universe, but they also function through their various agencies and other manifestations, such as:

1. *The mind focalizations of the Third Source and Center.* The finite domains of energy and spirit are literally held together by the mind presences of the Conjoint Actor. This is true from the Creative Spirit in a local universe through the Reflective Spirits of a superuniverse to the Master Spirits in the

grand universe. The mind circuits emanating from these varied intelligence focuses represent the cosmic arena of creature choice. Mind is the flexible reality which creatures and Creators can so readily manipulate; it is the vital link connecting matter and spirit. The mind bestowal of the Third Source and Center unifies the spirit person of God the Supreme with the experiential power of the evolutionary Almighty.

2. *The personality revelations of the Second Source and Center.* The mind presences of the Conjoint Actor unify the spirit of divinity with the pattern of energy. The bestowal incarnations of the Eternal Son and his Paradise Sons unify, actually fuse, the divine nature of a Creator with the evolving nature of a creature. The Supreme is both creature and creator; the possibility of his being such is revealed in the bestowal actions of the Eternal Son and his coordinate and subordinate Sons. The bestowal orders of sonship, the Michaels and the Avonals, actually augment their divine natures with bona fide creature natures which have become theirs by the living of the actual creature life on the evolutionary worlds. When divinity becomes like humanity, inherent in this relationship is the possibility that humanity can become divine.

3. *The indwelling presences of the First Source and Center.* Mind unifies spirit causations with energy reactions; bestowal ministry unifies divinity descensions with creature ascensions; and the indwelling fragments of the Universal Father actually unify the evolving creatures with God on Paradise. There are many such presences of the Father which indwell numerous orders of personalities, and in mortal man these divine fragments of God are the Thought Adjusters. The Mystery Monitors are to human beings what the Paradise Trinity is to the Supreme Being. The Adjusters are absolute foundations, and upon absolute foundations freewill choice can cause to be evolved the divine reality of an eternaliter nature, finaliter nature in the case of man, Deity nature in God the Supreme.

The creature bestowals of the Paradise orders of sonship enable these divine Sons to enrich their personalities by the acquisition of the actual nature of universe creatures, while such bestowals unfailingly reveal to the creatures themselves the Paradise path of divinity attainment. The Adjuster bestowals of the Universal Father enable him to draw the personalities of the volitional will creatures to himself. And throughout all these relationships in the finite universes the Conjoint Actor is the ever-present source of the mind ministry by virtue of which these activities take place.

In these and many other ways do the Paradise Deities participate in the evolutions of time as they unfold on the circling planets of space, and as they culminate in the emergence of the Supreme personality consequence of all evolution.

4. THE ALMIGHTY AND THE SUPREME CREATORS

The unity of the Supreme Whole is dependent on the progressive unification of the finite parts; the actualization of the Supreme is resultant from, and productive of, these very unifications of the factors of supremacy—the creators, creatures, intelligences, and energies of the universes.

During those ages in which the sovereignty of Supremacy is undergoing its time development, the almighty power of the Supreme is dependent on the divinity acts of God the Sevenfold, while there seems to be a particularly close relationship between the Supreme Being and the Conjoint Actor together with his primary personalities, the Seven Master Spirits. The Infinite Spirit as the Conjoint Actor functions in many ways which compensate the incompletion of evolutionary Deity and sustains very close relations to the Supreme. This closeness of relationship is shared in measure by all of the Master Spirits but especially by Master Spirit Number Seven, who speaks for the Supreme. This Master Spirit knows—is in personal contact with—the Supreme.

Early in the projection of the superuniverse scheme of creation, the Master Spirits joined with the ancestral Trinity in the cocreation of the forty-nine Reflective Spirits, and concomitantly the Supreme Being functioned creatively as the culminator of the conjoined acts of the Paradise Trinity and the creative children of Paradise Deity. Majeston appeared and ever since has focalized the cosmic presence of the Supreme Mind, while the Master Spirits continue as source-centers for the far-flung ministry of the cosmic mind.

But the Master Spirits continue in supervision of the Reflective Spirits. The Seventh Master Spirit is (in his overall supervision of Orvonton from the central universe) in personal contact with (and has overcontrol of) the seven Reflective Spirits located on Uversa. In his inter- and intrasuperuniverse controls and administrations he is in reflective contact with the Reflective Spirits of his own type located on each superuniverse capital.

These Master Spirits are not only the supporters and augmenters of the sovereignty of Supremacy, but they are in turn affected by the creative purposes of the Supreme. Ordinarily, the collective creations of the Master Spirits are of the quasi-material order (power directors, etc.), while their individual creations are of the spiritual order (supernaphim, etc.). But when the Master Spirits *collectively* produced the Seven Circuit Spirits in response to the will and purpose of the Supreme Being, it is to be noted that the offspring of this creative act are spiritual, not material or quasi-material.

And as it is with the Master Spirits of the superuniverses, so is it with the triune rulers of these supercreations—the Ancients of Days. These personifications of Trinity justice-judgment in time and space are the field fulcrums for the mobilizing almighty power of the Supreme, serving as the sevenfold focal points for the evolution of trinitarian sovereignty in the domains of time and space. From their vantage point midway between Paradise and the evolving worlds, these Trinity-origin sovereigns see both ways, know both ways, and co-ordinate both ways.

But the local universes are the real laboratories in which are worked out the mind experiments, galactic adventures, divinity unfoldings, and personality progressions which, when cosmically totaled, constitute the actual foundation upon which the Supreme is achieving deity evolution in and by experience.

In the local universes even the Creators evolve: The presence of the Conjoint Actor evolves from a living power focus to the status of the divine personality of a Universe Mother Spirit; the Creator Son evolves from the nature of existential Paradise divinity to the experiential nature of supreme sovereignty. The local universes are the starting points of true evolution, the spawning grounds of bona fide imperfect personalities endowed with the freewill choice of becoming cocreators of themselves as they are to be.

The Magisterial Sons in their bestowals upon the evolutionary worlds eventually acquire natures expressive of Paradise divinity in experiential unification with the highest spiritual values of material human nature. And through these and other bestowals the Michael Creators likewise acquire the natures and cosmic viewpoints of their actual local universe children. Such Master Creator Sons approximate the completion of subsupreme experience; and when their local universe sovereignty is enlarged to embrace the associated Creative Spirits, it may be said to approximate the limits of supremacy within the present potentials of the evolutionary grand universe.

When the bestowal Sons reveal new ways for man to find God, they are not creating these paths of divinity attainment; rather are they illuminating the everlasting highways of progression which lead through the presence of the Supreme to the person of the Paradise Father.

The local universe is the starting place for those personalities who are farthest from God, and who can therefore experience the greatest degree of spiritual ascent in the universe, can achieve the maximum of experiential participation in the cocreation of themselves. These same local universes likewise provide the greatest possible depth of experience for the descending personalities, who thereby achieve something which is to them just as meaningful as the Paradise ascent is to an evolving creature.

Mortal man appears to be necessary to the full function of God the Sevenfold as this divinity grouping culminates in the actualizing Supreme. There are many other orders of universe personalities who are equally necessary to the evolution of the almighty power of the Supreme, but this portrayal is presented for the edification of human beings, hence is largely limited to those factors operating in the evolution of God the Sevenfold which are related to mortal man.

5. THE ALMIGHTY AND THE SEVENFOLD CONTROLLERS

You have been instructed in the relationship of God the Sevenfold to the Supreme Being, and you should now recognize that the Sevenfold encompasses the controllers as well as the creators of the grand universe. These sevenfold controllers of the grand universe embrace the following:

1. The Master Physical Controllers.
2. The Supreme Power Centers.
3. The Supreme Power Directors.
4. The Almighty Supreme.
5. The God of Action—the Infinite Spirit.
6. The Isle of Paradise.
7. The Source of Paradise—the Universal Father.

These seven groups are functionally inseparable from God the Sevenfold and constitute the physical-control level of this Deity association.

The bifurcation of energy and spirit (stemming from the conjoint presence of the Eternal Son and the Paradise Isle) was symbolized in the superuniverse sense when the Seven Master Spirits unitedly engaged in their first act of collective creation. This episode witnessed the appearance of the Seven Supreme Power Directors. Concomitant therewith the spiritual circuits of the Master Spirits contrastively differentiated from the physical activities of power director supervision, and immediately did the cosmic mind appear as a new factor co-ordinating matter and spirit.

The Almighty Supreme is evolving as the overcontroller of the physical power of the grand universe. In the present universe age this potential of physical power appears to be centered in the Seven Supreme Power Directors, who operate through the fixed locations of the power centers and through the mobile presences of the physical controllers.

The time universes are not perfect; that is their destiny. The struggle for perfection pertains not only to the intellectual and the spiritual levels but also to the physical level of energy and mass. The settlement of the seven superuniverses in light and life presupposes their attainment of physical stability. And it is conjectured that the final attainment of material equilibrium will signify the completed evolution of the physical control of the Almighty.

In the early days of universe building even the Paradise Creators are primarily concerned with material equilibrium. The pattern of a local universe takes shape not only as a result of the activities of the power centers but also because of the space presence of the Creative Spirit. And throughout these early epochs of local universe building the Creator Son exhibits a little-understood attribute of material control, and he does not leave his capital planet until the gross equilibrium of the local universe has been established.

In the final analysis, all energy responds to mind, and the physical controllers are the children of the mind God, who is the activator of Paradise pattern. The intelligence of the power directors is unremittingly devoted to the task of bringing about material control. Their struggle for physical dominance over the relationships of energy and the motions of mass never ceases until they achieve finite victory over the energies and masses which constitute their perpetual domains of activity.

The spirit struggles of time and space have to do with the evolution of spirit dominance over matter by the mediation of (personal) mind; the physical (nonpersonal) evolution of the universes has to do with bringing cosmic energy into harmony with the equilibrium concepts of mind subject to the overcontrol of spirit. The total evolution of the entire grand universe is a matter of the personality unification of the energy-controlling mind with the spirit-co-ordinated intellect and will be revealed in the full appearance of the almighty power of the Supreme.

The difficulty in arriving at a state of dynamic equilibrium is inherent in the fact of the growing cosmos. The established circuits of physical creation are being continually jeopardized by the appearance of new energy and new mass. A growing universe is an unsettled universe; hence no part of the cosmic whole can find real stability until the fullness of time witnesses the material completion of the seven superuniverses.

In the settled universes of light and life there are no unexpected physical events of major importance. Relatively complete control over the material creation has been achieved; still the problems of the relationship of the settled universes to the evolving universes continue to challenge the skill of the Universe Power Directors. But these problems will gradually vanish with the diminution of new creative activity as the grand universe approaches culmination of evolutionary expression.

6. SPIRIT DOMINANCE

In the evolutionary superuniverses energy-matter is dominant except in personality, where spirit through the mediation of mind is struggling for the mastery. The goal of the evolutionary universes is the subjugation of energy-matter by mind, the co-ordination of mind with spirit, and all of this by virtue of the creative and unifying presence of personality. Thus, in relation to personality, do physical systems become subordinate; mind systems, co-ordinate; and spirit systems, directive.

This union of power and personality is expressive on deity levels in and as the Supreme. But the actual evolution of spirit dominance is a growth which is predicated on the freewill acts of the Creators and creatures of the grand universe.

On absolute levels, energy and spirit are one. But the moment departure is made from such absolute levels, difference appears, and as energy and spirit move spaceward from Paradise, the gulf between them widens until in the local universes they have become quite divergent. They are no longer identical, neither are they alike, and mind must intervene to interrelate them.

That energy can be directionized by the action of controller personalities discloses the responsiveness of energy to mind action. That mass can be stabilized through the action of these same controlling entities indicates the responsiveness of mass to the order-producing presence of mind. And that spirit itself in volitional personality can strive through mind for the mastery of energy-matter discloses the potential unity of all finite creation.

There is an interdependence of all forces and personalities throughout the universe of universes. Creator Sons and Creative Spirits depend on the co-operative function of the power centers and physical controllers in the organization of universes; the Supreme Power Directors are incomplete without the overcontrol of the Master Spirits. In a human being the mechanism of physical life is responsive, in part, to the dictates of (personal) mind. This very mind may, in turn, become dominated by the leadings of purposive spirit, and the result of such evolutionary development is the production of a new child of the Supreme, a new personal unification of the several kinds of cosmic reality.

And as it is with the parts, so it is with the whole; the spirit person of Supremacy requires the evolutionary power of the Almighty to achieve completion of Deity and to attain destiny of Trinity association. The effort is made by the personalities of time and space, but the culmination and consummation of this effort is the act of the Almighty Supreme. And while the growth of the whole is thus a totalizing of the collective growth of the parts, it equally follows that the evolution of the parts is a segmented reflection of the purposive growth of the whole.

On Paradise, monota and spirit are as one—indistinguishable except by name. In Havona, matter and spirit, while distinguishably different, are at the same time innately harmonious. In the seven superuniverses, however, there is great divergence; there is a wide gulf between cosmic energy and divine spirit; therefore is there a greater experiential potential for mind action in harmonizing and eventually unifying physical pattern with spiritual purposes. In the time-evolving universes of space there is greater divinity attenuation, more difficult problems to be solved, and larger opportunity to acquire experience in their solution. And this entire superuniverse situation brings into being a larger arena of evolutionary existence in which the possibility of cosmic experience is made available alike to creature and Creator—even to Supreme Deity.

The dominance of spirit, which is existential on absolute levels, becomes an evolutionary experience on finite levels and in the seven superuniverses. And this experience is shared alike by all, from mortal man to the Supreme Being. All strive, personally strive, in the achievement; all participate, personally participate, in the destiny.

7. THE LIVING ORGANISM OF THE GRAND UNIVERSE

The grand universe is not only a material creation of physical grandeur, spirit sublimity, and intellectual magnitude, it is also a magnificent and responsive living organism. There is actual life pulsating throughout the mechanism of the vast creation of the vibrant cosmos. The physical reality of the universes is symbolic of the perceivable reality of the Almighty Supreme; and this material and living organism is penetrated by intelligence circuits, even as the human body is traversed by a network of neural sensation paths. This physical universe is permeated by energy lanes which effectively activate material creation, even as the human body is nourished and energized by the circulatory distribution of the assimilable energy products of nourishment. The vast universe is not without those co-ordinating centers of magnificent overcontrol which might be compared to the delicate chemical-control system of the human mechanism. But if you only knew something about the physique of a power center, we could, by analogy, tell you so much more about the physical universe.

Much as mortals look to solar energy for life maintenance, so does the grand universe depend upon the unfailing energies emanating from nether Paradise to sustain the material activities and cosmic motions of space.

Mind has been given to mortals wherewith they may become self-conscious of identity and personality; and mind—even a Supreme Mind—has been bestowed upon the totality of the finite whereby the spirit of this emerging personality of the cosmos ever strives for the mastery of energy-matter.

Mortal man is responsive to spirit guidance, even as the grand universe responds to the far-flung spirit-gravity grasp of the Eternal Son, the universal supermaterial cohesion of the eternal spiritual values of all the creations of the finite cosmos of time and space.

Human beings are capable of making an everlasting self-identification with total and indestructible universe reality—fusion with the indwelling Thought Adjuster. Likewise does the Supreme everlastingly depend on the absolute stability of Original Deity, the Paradise Trinity.

Man's urge for Paradise perfection, his striving for God-attainment, creates a genuine divinity tension in the living cosmos which can only be resolved by the evolution of an immortal soul; this is what happens in the experience of a single mortal creature. But when all creatures and all Creators in the grand universe likewise strive for God-attainment and divine perfection, there is built up a profound cosmic tension which can only find resolution in the sublime synthesis of almighty power with the spirit person of the evolving God of all creatures, the Supreme Being.

[Sponsored by a Mighty Messenger temporarily sojourning on Urantia.]

PAPER 117

GOD THE SUPREME

TO THE extent that we do the will of God in whatever universe station we may have our existence, in that measure the almighty potential of the Supreme becomes one step more actual. The will of God is the purpose of the First Source and Center as it is potentialized in the three Absolutes, personalized in the Eternal Son, conjoined for universe action in the Infinite Spirit, and eternalized in the everlasting patterns of Paradise. And God the Supreme is becoming the highest finite manifestation of the total will of God.

If all grand universers should ever relatively achieve the full living of the will of God, then would the time-space creations be settled in light and life, and then would the Almighty, the deity potential of Supremacy, become factual in the emergence of the divine personality of God the Supreme.

When an evolving mind becomes attuned to the circuits of cosmic mind, when an evolving universe becomes stabilized after the pattern of the central universe, when an advancing spirit contacts the united ministry of the Master Spirits, when an ascending mortal personality finally attunes to the divine leading of the indwelling Adjuster, then has the actuality of the Supreme become real by one more degree in the universes; then has the divinity of Supremacy advanced one more step toward cosmic realization.

The parts and individuals of the grand universe evolve as a reflection of the total evolution of the Supreme, while in turn the Supreme is the synthetic cumulative total of all grand universe evolution. From the mortal viewpoint both are evolutionary and experiential reciprocals.

1. NATURE OF THE SUPREME BEING

The Supreme is the beauty of physical harmony, the truth of intellectual meaning, and the goodness of spiritual value. He is the sweetness of true success and the joy of everlasting achievement. He is the oversoul of the grand universe, the consciousness of the finite cosmos, the completion of finite reality, and the personification of Creator-creature experience. Throughout all future eternity God the Supreme will voice the reality of volitional experience in the trinity relationships of Deity.

In the persons of the Supreme Creators the Gods have descended from Paradise to the domains of time and space, there to create and to evolve creatures with Paradise-attainment capacity who can ascend thereto in quest of the Father. This universe procession of descending God-revealing Creators and ascending God-seeking creatures is revelatory of the Deity evolution of the Supreme, in whom both descenders and ascenders achieve mutuality of understanding, the discovery of eternal and universal brotherhood. The Supreme Being thus becomes the finite synthesis of the experience of the perfect-Creator cause and the perfecting-creature response.

The grand universe contains the possibility of, and ever seeks for, complete unification, and this grows out of the fact that this cosmic existence is a consequence of the creative acts and the power mandates of the Paradise Trinity, which is unqualified unity. This very trinitarian unity is expressed in the finite cosmos in the Supreme, whose reality becomes increasingly apparent as the universes attain to the maximum level of Trinity identification.

The will of the Creator and the will of the creature are qualitatively different, but they are also experientially akin, for creature and Creator can collaborate in the achievement of universe perfection. Man can work in liaison with God and thereby cocreate an eternal finaliter. God can work even as humanity in the incarnations of his Sons, who thereby achieve the supremacy of creature experience.

In the Supreme Being, Creator and creature are united in one Deity whose will is expressive of one divine personality. And this will of the Supreme is something more than the will of either creature or Creator, even as the sovereign will of the Master Son of Nebadon is now something more than a combination of the will of divinity and humanity. The union of Paradise perfection and time-space experience yields a new meaning value on deity levels of reality.

The evolving divine nature of the Supreme is becoming a faithful portrayal of the matchless experience of all creatures and of all Creators in the grand universe. In the Supreme, creatorship and creaturehood are at one; they are forever united by that experience which was born of the vicissitudes attendant upon the solution of the manifold problems which beset all finite creation as it pursues the eternal path in quest of perfection and liberation from the fetters of incompleteness.

Truth, beauty, and goodness are correlated in the ministry of the Spirit, the grandeur of Paradise, the mercy of the Son, and the experience of the Supreme. God the Supreme *is* truth, beauty, and goodness, for these concepts of divinity represent finite maximums of ideational experience. The eternal sources of these triune qualities of divinity are on superfinite levels, but a creature could only conceive of such sources as supertruth, superbeauty, and supergoodness.

Michael, a creator, revealed the divine love of the Creator Father for his terrestrial children. And having discovered and received this divine affection, men can aspire to reveal this love to their brethren in the flesh. Such creature affection is a true reflection of the love of the Supreme.

The Supreme is symmetrically inclusive. The First Source and Center is potential in the three great Absolutes, is actual in Paradise, in the Son, and in the Spirit; but the Supreme is both actual and potential, a being of personal supremacy and of almighty power, responsive alike to creature effort and Creator purpose; self-acting upon the universe and self-reactive to the sum total of the universe; and at one and the same time the supreme creator and the supreme creature. The Deity of Supremacy is thus expressive of the sum total of the entire finite.

2. THE SOURCE OF EVOLUTIONARY GROWTH

The Supreme is God-in-time; his is the secret of creature growth in time; his also is the conquest of the incomplete present and the consummation of the perfecting future. And the final fruits of all finite growth are: power controlled through mind by spirit by virtue of the unifying and creative presence of personality. The culminating consequence of all this growth is the Supreme Being.

To mortal man, existence is equivalent to growth. And so indeed it would seem to be, even in the larger universe sense, for spirit-led existence does seem to result in experiential growth—augmentation of status. We have long held, however, that the present growth which characterizes creature existence in the present universe age is a function of the Supreme. We equally hold that this kind of growth is peculiar to the age of the growth of the Supreme, and that it will terminate with the completion of the growth of the Supreme.

Consider the status of the creature-trinitized sons: They are born and live in the present universe age; they have personalities, together with mind and spirit endowments. They have experiences and the memory thereof, but they do not *grow* as do ascenders. It is our belief and understanding that these creature-trinitized sons, while they are *in* the present universe age, are really *of* the next universe age—the age which will follow the completion of the growth of the Supreme. Hence they are not *in* the Supreme as of his present status of incompleteness and consequent growth. Thus they are nonparticipating in the experiential growth of the present universe age, being held in reserve for the next universe age.

My own order, the Mighty Messengers, being Trinity embraced, are nonparticipating in the growth of the present universe age. In a sense we are in status as of the preceding universe age as in fact are the Stationary Sons of the Trinity. One thing is certain: Our status is fixed by the Trinity embrace, and experience no longer eventuates in growth.

This is not true of the finaliters nor of any other of the evolutionary and experiential orders which are participants in the growth process of the Supreme. You mortals now living on Urantia who may aspire to Paradise attainment and finaliter status should understand that such a destiny is only realizable because you are in and of the Supreme, hence are participants in the cycle of the growth of the Supreme.

There will come an end sometime to the growth of the Supreme; his status will achieve completion (in the energy-spirit sense). This termination of the evolution of the Supreme will also witness the ending of creature evolution as a part of Supremacy. What kind of growth may characterize the universes of outer space, we do not know. But we are very sure that it will be something very different from anything that has been seen in the present age of the evolution of the seven superuniverses. It will undoubtedly be the function of the evolutionary citizens of the grand universe to compensate the outer-spacers for this deprivation of the growth of Supremacy.

As existent upon the consummation of the present universe age, the Supreme Being will function as an experiential sovereign in the grand universe. Outer-spacers—citizens of the next universe age—will have a postsuperuniverse growth potential, a capacity for evolutionary attainment presupposing the sovereignty of the Almighty Supreme, hence excluding creature participation in the power-personality synthesis of the present universe age.

Thus may the incompleteness of the Supreme be regarded as a virtue since it makes possible the evolutionary growth of the creature-creation of the present universes. Emptiness does have its virtue, for it may become experientially filled.

One of the most intriguing questions in finite philosophy is this: Does the Supreme Being actualize in response to the evolution of the grand universe, or does this finite cosmos progressively evolve in response to the gradual actualization of the Supreme? Or is it possible that they are mutually interdependent for their development? that they are evolutionary reciprocals, each initiating the growth of the other? Of this we are certain: Creatures and universes, high and low, are evolving within the Supreme, and as they evolve, there is appearing the unified summation of the entire finite activity of this universe age. And this is the appearance of the Supreme Being, to all personalities the evolution of the almighty power of God the Supreme.

3. SIGNIFICANCE OF THE SUPREME TO UNIVERSE CREATURES

The cosmic reality variously designated as the Supreme Being, God the Supreme, and the Almighty Supreme, is the complex and universal synthesis of the emerging phases of all finite realities. The far-flung diversification of eternal energy, divine spirit, and universal mind attains finite culmination in the evolution of the Supreme, who is the sum total of all finite growth, self-realized on deity levels of finite maximum completion.

The Supreme is the divine channel through which flows the creative infinity of the triodities that crystallizes into the galactic panorama of space, against which takes place the magnificent personality drama of time: the spirit conquest of energy-matter through the mediation of mind.

Said Jesus: "I am the living way," and so he is the living way from the material level of self-consciousness to the spiritual level of God-consciousness. And even as he is this living way of ascension from the self to God, so is the Supreme the living way from finite consciousness to transcendence of consciousness, even to the insight of absonity.

Your Creator Son can actually be such a living channel from humanity to divinity since he has personally experienced the fullness of the traversal of this universe path of progression, from the true humanity of Joshua ben Joseph, the Son of Man, to the Paradise divinity of Michael of Nebadon, the Son of the infinite God. Similarly can the Supreme Being function as the universe approach to the transcendence of finite limitations, for he is the actual embodiment and personal epitome of all creature evolution, progression, and spiritualization. Even the grand universe experiences of the descending personalities from Paradise are that part of his experience which is complemental to his summation of the ascending experiences of the pilgrims of time.

Mortal man is more than figuratively made in the image of God. From a physical standpoint this statement is hardly true, but with reference to certain universe potentialities it is an actual fact. In the human race, something of the same drama of evolutionary attainment is being unfolded as takes place, on a vastly larger scale, in the universe of universes. Man, a volitional personality, becomes creative in liaison with an Adjuster, an impersonal entity, in the presence of the finite potentialities of the Supreme, and the result is the flowering of an immortal soul. In the universes the Creator personalities of time and space function in liaison with the impersonal spirit of the Paradise Trinity and become thereby creative of a new power potential of Deity reality.

Mortal man, being a creature, is not exactly like the Supreme Being, who is deity, but man's evolution does in some ways resemble the growth of the Supreme. Man consciously grows from the material toward the spiritual by the strength, power, and persistency of his own decisions; he also grows as his Thought Adjuster develops new techniques for reaching down from the spiritual to the morontial soul levels; and once the soul comes into being, it begins to grow in and of itself.

This is somewhat like the way in which the Supreme Being expands. His sovereignty grows in and out of the acts and achievements of the Supreme Creator Personalities; that is the evolution of the majesty of his power as the ruler of the grand universe. His deity nature is likewise dependent on the pre-existent unity of the Paradise Trinity. But there is still another aspect to the evolution of God the Supreme: He is not only Creator-evolved and Trinity-derived; he is also self-evolved and self-derived. God the Supreme is himself a volitional, creative participant in his own deity actualization. The human morontial soul is likewise a volitional, cocreative partner in its own immortalization.

The Father collaborates with the Conjoint Actor in manipulating the energies of Paradise and in rendering these responsive to the Supreme. The Father collaborates with the Eternal Son in the production of Creator personalities whose acts will sometime culminate in the sovereignty of the Supreme. The Father collaborates with both Son and Spirit in the creation of Trinity personalities to function as rulers of the grand universe until such time as the completed evolution of the Supreme qualifies him to assume that sovereignty. The Father co-operates with his Deity and non-Deity co-ordinates in these and many other ways in the furtherance of the evolution of Supremacy, but he also functions alone in these matters. And his solitary function is probably best revealed in the ministry of the Thought Adjusters and their associated entities.

Deity is unity, existential in the Trinity, experiential in the Supreme, and, in mortals, creature-realized in Adjuster fusion. The presence of the Thought Adjusters in mortal man reveals the essential unity of the universe, for man, the lowest possible type of universe personality, contains within himself an actual fragment of the highest and eternal reality, even the original Father of all personalities.

The Supreme Being evolves by virtue of his liaison with the Paradise Trinity and in consequence of the divinity successes of the creator and administrator children of that Trinity. Man's immortal soul evolves its own eternal destiny by association with the divine presence of the Paradise Father and in accordance with the personality decisions of the human mind. What the Trinity is to God the Supreme, the Adjuster is to evolving man.

During the present universe age the Supreme Being is apparently unable to function directly as a creator except in those instances where the finite possibilities of action have been exhausted by the creative agencies of time and space. Thus far in universe history this has transpired but once; when the possibilities of finite action in the matter of universe reflectivity had been exhausted, then did the Supreme function as the creative culminator of all antecedent creator actions. And we believe he will again function as a culminator in future ages whenever antecedent creatorship has completed an appropriate cycle of creative activity.

The Supreme Being did not create man, but man was literally created out of, his very life was derived from, the potentiality of the Supreme. Nor does he evolve man; yet is the Supreme himself the very essence of evolution. From the finite standpoint, we actually live, move, and have our being within the immanence of the Supreme.

The Supreme apparently cannot initiate original causation but appears to be the catalyzer of all universe growth and is seemingly destined to provide totality culmination as regards the destiny of all experiential-evolutionary beings. The Father originates the concept of a finite cosmos; the Creator Sons factualize this idea in time and space with the consent and co-operation of the Creative Spirits; the Supreme culminates the total finite and establishes its relationship with the destiny of the absonite.

4. THE FINITE GOD

As we view the ceaseless struggles of the creature creation for perfection of status and divinity of being, we cannot but believe that these unending efforts bespeak the unceasing struggle of the Supreme for divine self-realization. God the Supreme is the finite Deity, and he must cope with the problems of the finite in the total sense of that word. Our struggles with the vicissitudes of time in the evolutions of space are reflections of his efforts to achieve reality of self and completion of sovereignty within the sphere of action which his evolving nature is expanding to the outermost limits of possibility.

Throughout the grand universe the Supreme struggles for expression. His divine evolution is in measure predicated on the wisdom-action of every personality in existence. When a human being chooses eternal survival, he is co-creating destiny; and in the life of this ascending mortal the finite God finds an increased measure of personality self-realization and an enlargement of experiential sovereignty. But if a creature rejects the eternal career, that part of the Supreme which was dependent on this creature's choice experiences inescapable delay, a deprivation which must be compensated by substitutional or collateral experience; as for the personality of the nonsurvivor, it is absorbed into the oversoul of creation, becoming a part of the Deity of the Supreme.

God is so trusting, so loving, that he gives a portion of his divine nature into the hands of even human beings for safekeeping and self-realization. The Father nature, the Adjuster presence, is indestructible regardless of the choice of the mortal being. The child of the Supreme, the evolving self, can be destroyed notwithstanding that the potentially unifying personality of such a misguided self will persist as a factor of the Deity of Supremacy.

The human personality can truly destroy individuality of creaturehood, and though all that was worth while in the life of such a cosmic suicide will persist, *these qualities will not persist as an individual creature.* The Supreme will again find expression in the creatures of the universes but never again as that particular person; the unique personality of a nonascender returns to the Supreme as a drop of water returns to the sea.

Any isolated action of the personal parts of the finite is comparatively irrelevant to the eventual appearance of the Supreme Whole, but the whole is nonetheless dependent on the total acts of the manifold parts. The personality of the individual mortal is insignificant in the face of the total of Supremacy, but the personality of each human being represents an irreplaceable meaning-value in the finite; personality, having once been expressed, never again finds identical expression except in the continuing existence of that living personality.

And so, as we strive for self-expression, the Supreme is striving in us, and with us, for deity expression. As we find the Father, so has the Supreme again found the Paradise Creator of all things. As we master the problems of self-realization, so is the God of experience achieving almighty supremacy in the universes of time and space.

Mankind does not ascend effortlessly in the universe, neither does the Supreme evolve without purposeful and intelligent action. Creatures do not attain perfection by mere passivity, nor can the spirit of Supremacy factualize the power of the Almighty without unceasing service ministry to the finite creation.

The temporal relation of man to the Supreme is the foundation for cosmic morality, the universal sensitivity to, and acceptance of, *duty*. This is a morality which transcends the temporal sense of relative right and wrong; it is a morality directly predicated on the self-conscious creature's appreciation of experiential obligation to experiential Deity. Mortal man and all other finite creatures are created out of the living potential of energy, mind, and spirit existent in the Supreme. It is upon the Supreme that the Adjuster-mortal ascender draws for the creation of the immortal and divine character of a finaliter. It is out of the very reality of the Supreme that the Adjuster, with the consent of the human will, weaves the patterns of the eternal nature of an ascending son of God.

The evolution of Adjuster progress in the spiritualizing and eternalizing of a human personality is directly productive of an enlargement of the sovereignty of the Supreme. Such achievements in human evolution are at the same time achievements in the evolutionary actualization of the Supreme. While it is true that creatures could not evolve without the Supreme, it is probably also true that the evolution of the Supreme can never be fully attained independent of the completed evolution of all creatures. Herein lies the great cosmic responsibility of self-conscious personalities: That Supreme Deity is in a certain sense dependent on the choosing of the mortal will. And the mutual progression of creature evolution and of Supreme evolution is faithfully and fully indicated to the Ancients of Days over the inscrutable mechanisms of universe reflectivity.

The great challenge that has been given to mortal man is this: Will you decide to personalize the experiencible value meanings of the cosmos into your own evolving selfhood? or by rejecting survival, will you allow these secrets of Supremacy to lie dormant, awaiting the action of another creature at some other time who will in *his* way attempt a creature contribution to the evolution of the finite God? But that will be his contribution to the Supreme, not yours.

The great struggle of this universe age is between the potential and the actual—the seeking for actualization by all that is as yet unexpressed. If mortal man proceeds upon the Paradise adventure, he is following the motions of time, which flow as currents within the stream of eternity; if mortal man rejects the eternal career, he is moving counter to the stream of events in the finite universes. The mechanical creation moves on inexorably in accordance with the unfolding purpose of the Paradise Father, but the volitional creation has the choice of accepting or of rejecting the role of personality participation in the adventure of eternity. Mortal man cannot destroy the supreme values of human existence, but he can very definitely prevent the evolution of these values in his own personal experience. To the extent that the human self thus refuses to take part in the Paradise ascent, to just that extent is the Supreme delayed in achieving divinity expression in the grand universe.

Into the keeping of mortal man has been given not only the Adjuster presence of the Paradise Father but also control over the destiny of an infinitesimal fraction of the future of the Supreme. For as man attains human destiny, so does the Supreme achieve destiny on deity levels.

And so the decision awaits each of you as it once awaited each of us: Will you fail the God of time, who is so dependent upon the decisions of the finite mind? will you fail the Supreme personality of the universes by the slothfulness of animalistic retrogression? will you fail the great brother of all creatures, who is so dependent on each creature? can you allow yourself to pass into the realm of the unrealized when before you lies the enchanting vista of the universe career—the divine discovery of the Paradise Father and the divine participation in the search for, and the evolution of, the God of Supremacy?

God's gifts—his bestowal of reality—are not divorcements from himself; he does not alienate creation from himself, but he has set up tensions in the creations circling Paradise. God first loves man and confers upon him the potential of immortality—eternal reality. And as man loves God, so does man become eternal in actuality. And here is mystery: The more closely man approaches God through love, the greater the reality—actuality—of that man. The more man withdraws from God, the more nearly he approaches nonreality—cessation of existence. When man consecrates his will to the doing of the Father's will, when man gives God all that he *has,* then does God make that man more than he is.

5. THE OVERSOUL OF CREATION

The great Supreme is the cosmic oversoul of the grand universe. In him the qualities and quantities of the cosmos do find their deity reflection; his deity nature is the mosaic composite of the total vastness of all creature-Creator nature throughout the evolving universes. And the Supreme is also an actualizing Deity embodying a creative will which embraces an evolving universe purpose.

The intellectual, potentially personal selves of the finite emerge from the Third Source and Center and achieve finite time-space Deity synthesis in the Supreme. When the creature submits to the will of the Creator, he does not submerge or surrender his personality; the individual personality participants in the actualization of the finite God do not lose their volitional selfhood by so functioning. Rather are such personalities progressively augmented by participation in this great Deity adventure; by such union with divinity man exalts, enriches, spiritualizes, and unifies his evolving self to the very threshold of supremacy.

The evolving immortal soul of man, the joint creation of the material mind and the Adjuster, ascends as such to Paradise and subsequently, when mustered into the Corps of the Finality, becomes allied in some new way with the spirit-gravity circuit of the Eternal Son by a technique of experience known as *finaliter transcendation.* Such finaliters thus become acceptable candidates for experiential recognition as personalities of God the Supreme. And when these mortal intellects in the unrevealed future assignments of the Corps of the Finality attain the seventh stage of spirit existence, such dual minds will become triune. These two attuned minds, the human and the divine, will become glorified in union with the experiential mind of the then actualized Supreme Being.

In the eternal future, God the Supreme will be actualized—creatively expressed and spiritually portrayed—in the spiritualized mind, the immortal soul, of ascendant man, even as the Universal Father was so revealed in the earth life of Jesus.

Man does not unite with the Supreme and submerge his personal identity, but the universe repercussions of the experience of all men do thus form a part of the divine experiencing of the Supreme. "The act is ours, the consequences God's."

The progressing personality leaves a trail of actualized reality as it passes through the ascending levels of the universes. Be they mind, spirit, or energy, the growing creations of time and space are modified by the progression of personality through their domains. When man acts, the Supreme reacts, and this transaction constitutes the fact of progression.

The great circuits of energy, mind, and spirit are never the permanent possessions of ascending personality; these ministries remain forever a part of Supremacy. In the mortal experience the human intellect resides in the rhythmic pulsations of the adjutant mind-spirits and effects its decisions within the arena produced by encircuitment within this ministry. Upon mortal death the human self is everlastingly divorced from the adjutant circuit. While these adjutants never seem to transmit experience from one personality to another, they can and do transmit the impersonal repercussions of decision-action through God the Sevenfold to God the Supreme. (At least this is true of the adjutants of worship and wisdom.)

And so it is with the spiritual circuits: Man utilizes these in his ascent through the universes, but he never possesses them as a part of his eternal personality. But these circuits of spiritual ministry, whether Spirit of Truth, Holy Spirit, or superuniverse spirit presences, are receptive and reactive to the emerging values in ascending personality, and these values are faithfully transmitted through the Sevenfold to the Supreme.

While such spiritual influences as the Holy Spirit and the Spirit of Truth are local universe ministrations, their guidance is not wholly confined to the geographic limitations of a given local creation. As the ascending mortal passes beyond the boundaries of his local universe of origin, he is not entirely deprived of the ministry of the Spirit of Truth which has so constantly taught and guided him through the philosophic mazes of the material and morontial worlds, in every crisis of ascension unfailingly directing the Paradise pilgrim, ever saying:

"This is the way." When you leave the domains of the local universe, through the ministry of the spirit of the emerging Supreme Being and through the provisions of superuniverse reflectivity, you will still be guided in your Paradise ascent by the comforting directive spirit of the Paradise bestowal Sons of God.

How do these manifold circuits of cosmic ministry register the meanings, values, and facts of evolutionary experience in the Supreme? We are not exactly certain, but we believe that this registry takes place through the persons of the Supreme Creators of Paradise origin who are the immediate bestowers of these circuits of time and space. The mind-experience accumulations of the seven adjutant mind-spirits, in their ministry to the physical level of intellect, are a part of the local universe experience of the Divine Minister, and through this Creative Spirit they probably find registry in the mind of Supremacy. Likewise are mortal experiences with the Spirit of Truth and the Holy Spirit probably registered by similar techniques in the person of Supremacy.

Even the experience of man and Adjuster must find echo in the divinity of God the Supreme, for, as the Adjusters experience, they are like the Supreme, and the evolving soul of mortal man is created out of the pre-existent possibility for such experience within the Supreme.

In this manner do the manifold experiences of all creation become a part of the evolution of Supremacy. Creatures merely utilize the qualities and quantities of the finite as they ascend to the Father; the impersonal consequences of such utilization remain forever a part of the living cosmos, the Supreme person.

What man himself takes with him as a personality possession are the character consequences of the experience of having used the mind and spirit circuits of the grand universe in his Paradise ascent. When man decides, and when he consummates this decision in action, man experiences, and the meanings and the values of this experience are forever a part of his eternal character on all levels, from the finite to the final. Cosmically moral and divinely spiritual character represents the creature's capital accumulation of personal decisions which have been illuminated by sincere worship, glorified by intelligent love, and consummated in brotherly service.

The evolving Supreme will eventually compensate finite creatures for their inability ever to achieve more than limited experience contact with the universe of universes. Creatures can attain the Paradise Father, but their evolutionary minds, being finite, are incapable of really understanding the infinite and absolute Father. But since all creature experiencing registers in, and is a part of, the Supreme, when all creatures attain the final level of finite existence, and after total universe development makes possible their attainment of God the Supreme as an actual divinity presence, then, inherent in the fact of such contact, is contact with total experience. The finite of time contains within itself the seeds of eternity; and we are taught that, when the fullness of evolution witnesses the exhaustion of the capacity for cosmic growth, the total finite will embark upon the absonite phases of the eternal career in quest of the Father as Ultimate.

6. THE QUEST FOR THE SUPREME

We seek the Supreme in the universes, but we find him not. "He is the within and the without of all things and beings, moving and quiescent.

Unrecognizable in his mystery, though distant, yet is he near." The Almighty Supreme is "the form of the yet unformed, the pattern of the yet uncreated." The Supreme is your universe home, and when you find him, it will be like returning home. He is your experiential parent, and even as in the experience of human beings, so has he grown in the experience of divine parenthood. He knows you because he is creaturelike as well as creatorlike.

If you truly desire to find God, you cannot help having born in your minds the consciousness of the Supreme. As God is your divine Father, so is the Supreme your divine Mother, in whom you are nurtured throughout your lives as universe creatures. "How universal is the Supreme—he is on all sides! The limitless things of creation depend on his presence for life, and none are refused."

What Michael is to Nebadon, the Supreme is to the finite cosmos; his Deity is the great avenue through which the love of the Father flows outward to all creation, and he is the great avenue through which finite creatures pass inward in their quest of the Father, who is love. Even Thought Adjusters are related to him; in original nature and divinity they are like the Father, but when they experience the transactions of time in the universes of space, they become like the Supreme.

The act of the creature's choosing to do the will of the Creator is a cosmic value and has a universe meaning which is immediately reacted to by some unrevealed but ubiquitous force of co-ordination, probably the functioning of the ever-enlarging action of the Supreme Being.

The morontia soul of an evolving mortal is really the son of the Adjuster action of the Universal Father and the child of the cosmic reaction of the Supreme Being, the Universal Mother. The mother influence dominates the human personality throughout the local universe childhood of the growing soul. The influence of the Deity parents becomes more equal after the Adjuster fusion and during the superuniverse career, but when the creatures of time begin the traversal of the central universe of eternity, the Father nature becomes increasingly manifest, attaining its height of finite manifestation upon the recognition of the Universal Father and the admission into the Corps of the Finality.

In and through the experience of finaliter attainment the experiential mother qualities of the ascending self become tremendously affected by contact and infusion with the spirit presence of the Eternal Son and the mind presence of the Infinite Spirit. Then, throughout the realms of finaliter activity in the grand universe, there appears a new awakening of the latent mother potential of the Supreme, a new realization of experiential meanings, and a new synthesis of experiential values of the entire ascension career. It appears that this realization of self will continue in the universe careers of the sixth-stage finaliters until the mother inheritance of the Supreme attains to finite synchrony with the Adjuster inheritance of the Father. This intriguing period of grand universe function represents the continuing adult career of the ascendant and perfected mortal.

Upon the completion of the sixth stage of existence and the entrance upon the seventh and final stage of spirit status, there will probably ensue the advancing ages of enriching experience, ripening wisdom, and divinity realization. In the nature of the finaliter this will probably equal the completed attainment of the mind struggle for spirit self-realization, the completion of the co-ordination of the ascendant man-nature with the divine Adjuster-nature within the limits of finite possibilities. Such a magnificent universe self thus becomes the eternal finaliter son of the Paradise Father as well as the eternal universe child of the Mother Supreme, a universe self qualified to represent both the Father and Mother of universes and personalities in any activity or undertaking pertaining to the finite administration of created, creating, or evolving things and beings.

All soul-evolving humans are literally the evolutionary sons of God the Father and God the Mother, the Supreme Being. But until such time as mortal man becomes soul-conscious of his divine heritage, this assurance of Deity kinship must be faith realized. Human life experience is the cosmic cocoon in which the universe endowments of the Supreme Being and the universe presence of the Universal Father (none of which are personalities) are evolving the morontia soul of time and the human-divine finaliter character of universe destiny and eternal service.

Men all too often forget that God is the greatest experience in human existence. Other experiences are limited in their nature and content, but the experience of God has no limits save those of the creature's comprehension capacity, and this very experience is in itself capacity enlarging. When men search for God, they are searching for everything. When they find God, they have found everything. The search for God is the unstinted bestowal of love attended by amazing discoveries of new and greater love to be bestowed.

All true love is from God, and man receives the divine affection as he himself bestows this love upon his fellows. Love is dynamic. It can never be captured; it is alive, free, thrilling, and always moving. Man can never take the love of the Father and imprison it within his heart. The Father's love can become real to mortal man only by passing through that man's personality as he in turn bestows this love upon his fellows. The great circuit of love is from the Father, through sons to brothers, and hence to the Supreme. The love of the Father appears in the mortal personality by the ministry of the indwelling Adjuster. Such a God-knowing son reveals this love to his universe brethren, and this fraternal affection is the essence of the love of the Supreme.

There is no approach to the Supreme except through experience, and in the current epochs of creation there are only three avenues of creature approach to Supremacy:

1. The Paradise Citizens descend from the eternal Isle through Havona, where they acquire capacity for Supremacy comprehension through observation of the Paradise-Havona reality differential and by exploratory discovery of the manifold activities of the Supreme Creator Personalities, ranging from the Master Spirits to the Creator Sons.

2. The time-space ascenders coming up from the evolutionary universes of the Supreme Creators make close approach to the Supreme in the traversal of Havona as a preliminary to the augmenting appreciation of the unity of the Paradise Trinity.

3. The Havona natives acquire a comprehension of the Supreme through contacts with descending pilgrims from Paradise and ascending pilgrims from the seven superuniverses. Havona natives are inherently in position to harmonize the essentially different viewpoints of the citizens of the eternal Isle and the citizens of the evolutionary universes.

To evolutionary creatures there are seven great approaches to the Universal Father, and each of these Paradise ascensions passes through the divinity of one of the Seven Master Spirits; and each such approach is made possible by an enlargement of experience receptivity consequent upon the creature's having served in the superuniverse reflective of the nature of that Master Spirit. The sum total of these seven experiences constitutes the present-known limits of a creature's consciousness of the reality and actuality of God the Supreme.

It is not only man's own limitations which prevent him from finding the finite God; it is also the incompletion of the universe; even the incompletion of all creatures—past, present, and future—makes the Supreme inaccessible. God the Father can be found by any individual who has attained the divine level of Godlikeness, but God the Supreme will never be personally discovered by any *one* creature until that far-distant time when, through the universal attainment of perfection, *all* creatures will simultaneously find him.

Despite the fact that you cannot, in this universe age, personally find him as you can and will find the Father, the Son, and the Spirit, nevertheless, the Paradise ascent and subsequent universe career will gradually create in your consciousness the recognition of the universe presence and the cosmic action of the God of all experience. The fruits of the spirit are the substance of the Supreme as he is realizable in human experience.

Man's sometime attainment of the Supreme is consequent upon his fusion with the spirit of Paradise Deity. With Urantians this spirit is the Adjuster presence of the Universal Father; and though the Mystery Monitor is from the Father and like the Father, we doubt that even such a divine gift can achieve the impossible task of revealing the nature of the infinite God to a finite creature. We suspect that what the Adjusters will reveal to future seventh-stage finaliters will be the divinity and nature of God the Supreme. And this revelation will be to a finite creature what the revelation of the Infinite would be to an absolute being.

The Supreme is not infinite, but he probably embraces all of infinity that a finite creature can ever really comprehend. To understand more than the Supreme is to be more than finite!

All experiential creations are interdependent in their realization of destiny. Only existential reality is self-contained and self-existent. Havona and the seven superuniverses require each other to achieve the maximum of finite attainment; likewise will they be sometime dependent on the future universes of outer space for finite transcendence.

A human ascender can find the Father; God is existential and therefore real, irrespective of the status of experience in the total universe. But no single ascender will ever find the Supreme until all ascenders have reached that maximum universe maturity which qualifies them simultaneously to participate in this discovery.

The Father is no respecter of persons; he treats each of his ascending sons as cosmic individuals. The Supreme likewise is no respecter of persons; he treats his experiential children as a single cosmic total.

Man can discover the Father in his heart, but he will have to search for the Supreme in the hearts of all other men; and when all creatures perfectly reveal the love of the Supreme, then will he become a universe actuality to all creatures. And that is just another way of saying that the universes will be settled in light and life.

The attainment of perfected self-realization by all personalities plus the attainment of perfected equilibrium throughout the universes equals the attainment of the Supreme and witnesses the liberation of all finite reality from the limitations of incomplete existence. Such an exhaustion of all finite potentials yields the completed attainment of the Supreme and may be otherwise defined as the completed evolutionary actualization of the Supreme Being himself.

Men do not find the Supreme suddenly and spectacularly as an earthquake tears chasms into the rocks, but they find him slowly and patiently as a river quietly wears away the soil beneath.

When you find the Father, you will find the great cause of your spiritual ascent in the universes; when you find the Supreme, you will discover the great result of your career of Paradise progression.

But no God-knowing mortal can ever be lonely in his journey through the cosmos, for he knows that the Father walks beside him each step of the way, while the very way that he is traversing is the presence of the Supreme.

7. THE FUTURE OF THE SUPREME

The completed realization of all finite potentials equals the completion of the realization of all evolutionary experience. This suggests the final emergence of the Supreme as an almighty Deity presence in the universes. We believe that the Supreme, in this stage of development, will be as discretely personalized as is the Eternal Son, as concretely powerized as is the Isle of Paradise, as completely unified as is the Conjoint Actor, and all of this within the limitations of the finite possibilities of Supremacy at the culmination of the present universe age.

While this is an entirely proper concept of the future of the Supreme, we would call attention to certain problems inherent in this concept:

1. The Unqualified Supervisors of the Supreme could hardly be deitized at any stage prior to his completed evolution, and yet these same supervisors even now qualifiedly exercise the sovereignty of supremacy concerning the universes settled in light and life.

2. The Supreme could hardly function in the Trinity Ultimate until he had attained complete actuality of universe status, and yet the Trinity Ultimate is even now a qualified reality, and you have been informed of the existence of the Qualified Vicegerents of the Ultimate.

3. The Supreme is not completely real to universe creatures, but there are many reasons for deducing that he is quite real to the Sevenfold Deity, extending from the Universal Father on Paradise to the Creator Sons and the Creative Spirits of the local universes.

It may be that on the upper limits of the finite, where time conjoins transcended time, there is some sort of blurring and blending of sequence. It may be that the Supreme is able to forecast his universe presence onto these supertime levels and then to a limited degree anticipate future evolution by reflecting this future forecast back to the created levels as the Immanence of the Projected Incomplete. Such phenomena may be observed wherever finite makes contact with superfinite, as in the experiences of human beings who are indwelt by Thought Adjusters that are veritable predictions of man's future universe attainments throughout all eternity.

When mortal ascenders are admitted to the finaliter corps of Paradise, they take an oath to the Paradise Trinity, and in taking this oath of allegiance, they are thereby pledging eternal fidelity to God the Supreme, who *is* the Trinity as comprehended by all finite creature personalities. Subsequently, as the finaliter companies function throughout the evolving universes, they are solely amenable to the mandates of Paradise origin until the eventful times of the settling of local universes in light and life. As the new governmental organizations of these perfected creations begin to be reflective of the emerging sovereignty of the Supreme, we observe that the outlying finaliter companies then acknowledge the jurisdictional authority of such new governments. It appears that God the Supreme is evolving as the unifier of the evolutionary Corps of the Finality, but it is highly probable that the eternal destiny of these seven corps will be directed by the Supreme as a member of the Ultimate Trinity.

The Supreme Being contains three superfinite possibilities for universe manifestation:

1. Absonite collaboration in the first experiential Trinity.

2. Coabsolute relationship in the second experiential Trinity.

3. Coinfinite participation in the Trinity of Trinities, but we have no satisfactory concept as to what this really means.

This is one of the generally accepted hypotheses of the future of the Supreme, but there are also many speculations concerning his relations to the present grand universe subsequent to its attainment of the status of light and life.

The present goal of the superuniverses is to become, as they are and within their potentials, perfect, even as is Havona. This perfection pertains to physical and spiritual attainment, even to administrative, governmental, and fraternal development. It is believed that, in the ages to come, the possibilities for disharmony, maladjustment, and misadaptation will be eventually exhausted in the superuniverses. The energy circuits will be in perfect balance and in complete subjugation to mind, while spirit, in the presence of personality, will have achieved the dominance of mind.

It is conjectured that at this far-distant time the spirit person of the Supreme and attained power of the Almighty will have achieved co-ordinate development, and that both, as unified in and by the Supreme Mind, will factualize as the Supreme Being, a completed actuality in the universes—an actuality which will be observable by all creature intelligences, reacted to by all created energies, co-ordinated in all spiritual entities, and experienced by all universe personalities.

This concept implies the actual sovereignty of the Supreme in the grand universe. It is altogether likely that the present Trinity administrators will continue as his vicegerents, but we believe that the present demarcations between the seven superuniverses will gradually disappear, and that the entire grand universe will function as a perfected whole.

It is possible that the Supreme may then be personally resident on Uversa, the headquarters of Orvonton, from which he will direct the administration of the time creations, but this is really only a conjecture. Certainly, though, the personality of the Supreme Being will be definitely contactable at some specific locality, although the ubiquity of his Deity presence will probably continue to permeate the universe of universes. What the relation of the superuniverse citizens of that age will be to the Supreme we do not know, but it may be something like the present relationship between the Havona natives and the Paradise Trinity.

The perfected grand universe of those future days will be vastly different from what it is at present. Gone will be the thrilling adventures of the organization of the galaxies of space, the planting of life on the uncertain worlds of time, and the evolving of harmony out of chaos, beauty out of potentials, truth out of meanings, and goodness out of values. The time universes will have achieved the fulfillment of finite destiny! And perhaps for a space there will be rest, relaxation from the agelong struggle for evolutionary perfection. But not for long! Certainly, surely, and inexorably the enigma of the emerging Deity of God the Ultimate will challenge these perfected citizens of the settled universes just as their struggling evolutionary forebears were once challenged by the quest for God the Supreme. The curtain of cosmic destiny will draw back to reveal the transcendent grandeur of the alluring absonite quest for the attainment of the Universal Father on those new and higher levels revealed in the ultimate of creature experience.

[Sponsored by a Mighty Messenger temporarily sojourning on Urantia.]

PAPER 118

SUPREME AND ULTIMATE—TIME AND SPACE

CONCERNING the several natures of Deity, it may be said:

1. The Father is self-existent self.
2. The Son is coexistent self.
3. The Spirit is conjoint-existent self.
4. The Supreme is evolutionary-experiential self.
5. The Sevenfold is self-distributive divinity.
6. The Ultimate is transcendental-experiential self.
7. The Absolute is existential-experiential self.

While God the Sevenfold is indispensable to the evolutionary attainment of the Supreme, the Supreme is also indispensable to the eventual emergence of the Ultimate. And the dual presence of the Supreme and the Ultimate constitutes the basic association of subabsolute and derived Deity, for they are interdependently complemental in the attainment of destiny. Together they constitute the experiential bridge linking the beginnings and the completions of all creative growth in the master universe.

Creative growth is unending but ever satisfying, endless in extent but always punctuated by those personality-satisfying moments of transient goal attainment which serve so effectively as the mobilization preludes to new adventures in cosmic growth, universe exploration, and Deity attainment.

While the domain of mathematics is beset with qualitative limitations, it does provide the finite mind with a conceptual basis of contemplating infinity. There is no quantitative limitation to numbers, even in the comprehension of the finite mind. No matter how large the number conceived, you can always envisage one more being added. And also, you can comprehend that that is short of infinity, for no matter how many times you repeat this addition to number, still always one more can be added.

At the same time, the infinite series can be totaled at any given point, and this total (more properly, a subtotal) provides the fullness of the sweetness of goal attainment for a given person at a given time and status. But sooner or later, this same person begins to hunger and yearn for new and greater goals, and such adventures in growth will be forever forthcoming in the fullness of time and the cycles of eternity.

Each successive universe age is the antechamber of the following era of cosmic growth, and each universe epoch provides immediate destiny for all preceding stages. Havona, in and of itself, is a perfect, but perfection-limited, creation; Havona perfection, expanding out into the evolutionary superuniverses, finds not only cosmic destiny but also liberation from the limitations of pre-evolutionary existence.

1. TIME AND ETERNITY

It is helpful to man's cosmic orientation to attain all possible comprehension of Deity's relation to the cosmos. While absolute Deity is eternal in nature, the Gods are related to time as an experience in eternity. In the evolutionary universes eternity is temporal everlastingness—the everlasting *now*.

The personality of the mortal creature may eternalize by self-identification with the indwelling spirit through the technique of choosing to do the will of the Father. Such a consecration of will is tantamount to the realization of eternity-reality of purpose. This means that the purpose of the creature has become fixed with regard to the succession of moments; stated otherwise, that the succession of moments will witness no change in creature purpose. A million or a billion moments makes no difference. Number has ceased to have meaning with regard to the creature's purpose. Thus does creature choice plus God's choice eventuate in the eternal realities of the never-ending union of the spirit of God and the nature of man in the everlasting service of the children of God and of their Paradise Father.

There is a direct relationship between maturity and the unit of time consciousness in any given intellect. The time unit may be a day, a year, or a longer period, but inevitably it is the criterion by which the conscious self evaluates the circumstances of life, and by which the conceiving intellect measures and evaluates the facts of temporal existence.

Experience, wisdom, and judgment are the concomitants of the lengthening of the time unit in mortal experience. As the human mind reckons backward into the past, it is evaluating past experience for the purpose of bringing it to bear on a present situation. As mind reaches out into the future, it is attempting to evaluate the future significance of possible action. And having thus reckoned with both experience and wisdom, the human will exercises judgment-decision in the present, and the plan of action thus born of the past and the future becomes existent.

In the maturity of the developing self, the past and future are brought together to illuminate the true meaning of the present. As the self matures, it reaches further and further back into the past for experience, while its wisdom forecasts seek to penetrate deeper and deeper into the unknown future. And as the conceiving self extends this reach ever further into both past and future, so does judgment become less and less dependent on the momentary present. In this way does decision-action begin to escape from the fetters of the moving present, while it begins to take on the aspects of past-future significance.

Patience is exercised by those mortals whose time units are short; true maturity transcends patience by a forbearance born of real understanding.

To become mature is to live more intensely in the present, at the same time escaping from the limitations of the present. The plans of maturity, founded on past experience, are coming into being in the present in such manner as to enhance the values of the future.

The time unit of immaturity concentrates meaning-value into the present moment in such a way as to divorce the present of its true relationship to the not-present—the past-future. The time unit of maturity is proportioned so to reveal the co-ordinate relationship of past-present-future that the self begins to gain insight into the wholeness of events, begins to view the landscape of time from the panoramic perspective of broadened horizons, begins perhaps to suspect the nonbeginning, nonending eternal continuum, the fragments of which are called time.

On the levels of the infinite and the absolute the moment of the present contains all of the past as well as all of the future. I AM signifies also I WAS and I WILL BE. And this represents our best concept of eternity and the eternal.

On the absolute and eternal level, potential reality is just as meaningful as actual reality. Only on the finite level and to time-bound creatures does there appear to be such a vast difference. To God, as absolute, an ascending mortal who has made the eternal decision is already a Paradise finaliter. But the Universal Father, through the indwelling Thought Adjuster, is not thus limited in awareness but can also know of, and participate in, every temporal struggle with the problems of the creature ascent from animallike to Godlike levels of existence.

2. OMNIPRESENCE AND UBIQUITY

The ubiquity of Deity must not be confused with the ultimacy of the divine omnipresence. It is volitional with the Universal Father that the Supreme, the Ultimate, and the Absolute should compensate, co-ordinate, and unify his time-space ubiquity and his time-space-transcended omnipresence with his timeless and spaceless universal and absolute presence. And you should remember that, while Deity ubiquity may be so often space associated, it is not necessarily time conditioned.

As mortal and morontia ascenders you progressively discern God through the ministry of God the Sevenfold. Through Havona you discover God the Supreme. On Paradise you find him as a person, and then as finaliters you will presently attempt to know him as Ultimate. Being finaliters, there would seem to be but one course to pursue after having attained the Ultimate, and that would be to begin the quest of the Absolute. No finaliter will be disturbed by the uncertainties of the attainment of the Deity Absolute since at the end of the supreme and ultimate ascensions he encountered God the Father. Such finaliters will no doubt believe that, even if they should be successful in finding God the Absolute, they would only be discovering the same God, the Paradise Father manifesting himself on more nearly infinite and universal levels. Undoubtedly the attainment of God in absolute would reveal the Primal Ancestor of universes as well as the Final Father of personalities.

God the Supreme may not be a demonstration of the time-space omnipresence of Deity, but he is literally a manifestation of divine ubiquity. Between the spiritual presence of the Creator and the material manifestations of creation there exists a vast domain of the ubiquitous *becoming*—the universe emergence of evolutionary Deity.

If God the Supreme ever assumes direct control of the universes of time and space, we are confident such a Deity administration will function under the overcontrol of the Ultimate. In such an event God the Ultimate would begin to become manifest to the universes of time as the transcendental

Almighty (the Omnipotent) exercising the overcontrol of supertime and transcended space concerning the administrative functions of the Almighty Supreme.

The mortal mind may ask, even as we do: If the evolution of God the Supreme to administrative authority in the grand universe is attended by augmented manifestations of God the Ultimate, will a corresponding emergence of God the Ultimate in the postulated universes of outer space be attended by similar and enhanced revelations of God the Absolute? But we really do not know.

3. TIME-SPACE RELATIONSHIPS

Only by ubiquity could Deity unify time-space manifestations to the finite conception, for time is a succession of instants while space is a system of associated points. You do, after all, perceive time by analysis and space by synthesis. You co-ordinate and associate these two dissimilar conceptions by the integrating insight of personality. Of all the animal world only man possesses this time-space perceptibility. To an animal, motion has a meaning, but motion exhibits value only to a creature of personality status.

Things are time conditioned, but truth is timeless. The more truth you know, the more truth you *are,* the more of the past you can understand and of the future you can comprehend.

Truth is inconcussible—forever exempt from all transient vicissitudes, albeit never dead and formal, always vibrant and adaptable—radiantly alive. But when truth becomes linked with fact, then both time and space condition its meanings and correlate its values. Such realities of truth wedded to fact become concepts and are accordingly relegated to the domain of relative cosmic realities.

The linking of the absolute and eternal truth of the Creator with the factual experience of the finite and temporal creature eventuates a new and emerging value of the Supreme. The concept of the Supreme is essential to the coordination of the divine and unchanging overworld with the finite and everchanging underworld.

Space comes the nearest of all nonabsolute things to being absolute. Space is apparently absolutely ultimate. The real difficulty we have in understanding space on the material level is due to the fact that, while material bodies exist in space, space also exists in these same material bodies. While there is much about space that is absolute, that does not mean that space is absolute.

It may help to an understanding of space relationships if you would conjecture that, relatively speaking, space is after all a property of all material bodies. Hence, when a body moves through space, it also takes all its properties with it, even the space which is in and of such a moving body.

All patterns of reality occupy space on the material levels, but spirit patterns only exist in relation to space; they do not occupy or displace space, neither do they contain it. But to us the master riddle of space pertains to the pattern of an idea. When we enter the mind domain, we encounter many a puzzle. Does the pattern—the reality—of an idea occupy space? We really do not know, albeit we are sure that an idea pattern does not contain space. But it would hardly be safe to postulate that the immaterial is always nonspatial.

4. PRIMARY AND SECONDARY CAUSATION

Many of the theologic difficulties and the metaphysical dilemmas of mortal man are due to man's mislocation of Deity personality and consequent assignment of infinite and absolute attributes to subordinate Divinity and to evolutionary Deity. You must not forget that, while there is indeed a true First Cause, there are also a host of co-ordinate and subordinate causes, both associate and secondary causes.

The vital distinction between first causes and second causes is that first causes produce original effects which are free from inheritance of any factor derived from any antecedent causation. Secondary causes yield effects which invariably exhibit inheritance from other and preceding causation.

The purely static potentials inherent in the Unqualified Absolute are reactive to those causations of the Deity Absolute which are produced by the actions of the Paradise Trinity. In the presence of the Universal Absolute these causative-impregnated static potentials forthwith become active and responsive to the influence of certain transcendental agencies whose actions result in the transmutation of these activated potentials to the status of true universe possibilities for development, actualized capacities for growth. It is upon such matured potentials that the creators and controllers of the grand universe enact the never-ending drama of cosmic evolution.

Causation, disregarding existentials, is threefold in its basic constitution. As it operates in this universe age and concerning the finite level of the seven superuniverses, it may be conceived as follows:

1. *Activation of static potentials.* The establishment of destiny in the Universal Absolute by the actions of the Deity Absolute, operating in and upon the Unqualified Absolute and in consequence of the volitional mandates of the Paradise Trinity.

2. *Eventuation of universe capacities.* This involves the transformation of undifferentiated potentials into segregated and defined plans. This is the act of the Ultimacy of Deity and of the manifold agencies of the transcendental level. Such acts are in perfect anticipation of the future needs of the entire master universe. It is in connection with the segregation of potentials that the Architects of the Master Universe exist as the veritable embodiments of the Deity concept of the universes. Their plans appear to be ultimately space limited in extent by the concept periphery of the master universe, but *as plans* they are not otherwise conditioned by time or space.

3. *Creation and evolution of universe actuals.* It is upon a cosmos impregnated by the capacity-producing presence of the Ultimacy of Deity that the Supreme Creators operate to effect the time transmutations of matured potentials into experiential actuals. Within the master universe all actualization of potential reality is limited by ultimate capacity for development and is time-space conditioned in the final stages of emergence. The Creator Sons going out from Paradise are, in actuality, *transformative* creators in the cosmic sense. But this in no manner invalidates man's concept of them as creators; from the finite viewpoint they certainly can and do create.

5. OMNIPOTENCE AND COMPOSSIBILITY

The omnipotence of Deity does not imply the power to do the nondoable. Within the time-space frame and from the intellectual reference point of mortal comprehension, even the infinite God cannot create square circles or produce evil that is inherently good. God cannot do the ungodlike thing. Such a contradiction of philosophic terms is the equivalent of nonentity and implies that nothing is thus created. A personality trait cannot at the same time be Godlike and ungodlike. Compossibility is innate in divine power. And all of this is derived from the fact that omnipotence not only creates things with a nature but also gives origin to the nature of all things and beings.

In the beginning the Father does all, but as the panorama of eternity unfolds in response to the will and mandates of the Infinite, it becomes increasingly apparent that creatures, even men, are to become God's partners in the realization of finality of destiny. And this is true even in the life in the flesh; when man and God enter into partnership, no limitation can be placed upon the future possibilities of such a partnership. When man realizes that the Universal Father is his partner in eternal progression, when he fuses with the indwelling Father presence, he has, in spirit, broken the fetters of time and has already entered upon the progressions of eternity in the quest for the Universal Father.

Mortal consciousness proceeds from the fact, to the meaning, and then to the value. Creator consciousness proceeds from the thought-value, through the word-meaning, to the fact of action. Always must God act to break the deadlock of the unqualified unity inherent in existential infinity. Always must Deity provide the pattern universe, the perfect personalities, the original truth, beauty, and goodness for which all subdeity creations strive. Always must God first find man that man may later find God. Always must there be a Universal Father before there can ever be universal sonship and consequent universal brotherhood.

6. OMNIPOTENCE AND OMNIFICENCE

God is truly omnipotent, but he is not omnificent—he does not personally do all that is done. Omnipotence embraces the power-potential of the Almighty Supreme and the Supreme Being, but the volitional acts of God the Supreme are not the personal doings of God the Infinite.

To advocate the omnificence of primal Deity would be equal to disenfranchising well-nigh a million Creator Sons of Paradise, not to mention the innumerable hosts of various other orders of concurring creative assistants. There is but one uncaused Cause in the whole universe. All other causes are derivatives of this one First Great Source and Center. And none of this philosophy does any violence to the free-willness of the myriads of the children of Deity scattered through a vast universe.

Within a local frame, volition may appear to function as an uncaused cause, but it unfailingly exhibits inheritance factors which establish relationship with the unique, original, and absolute First Causes.

All volition is relative. In the originating sense, only the Father-I AM possesses finality of volition; in the absolute sense, only the Father, the Son, and the Spirit exhibit the prerogatives of volition unconditioned by time and unlimited by space. Mortal man is endowed with free will, the power of choice, and though such choosing is not absolute, nevertheless, it is relatively final on the finite level and concerning the destiny of the choosing personality.

Volition on any level short of the absolute encounters limitations which are constitutive in the very personality exercising the power of choice. Man cannot choose beyond the range of that which is choosable. He cannot, for instance, choose to be other than a human being except that he can elect to become more than a man; he can choose to embark upon the voyage of universe ascension, but this is because the human choice and the divine will happen to be coincident upon this point. And what a son desires and the Father wills will certainly come to pass.

In the mortal life, paths of differential conduct are continually opening and closing, and during the times when choice is possible the human personality is constantly deciding between these many courses of action. Temporal volition is linked to time, and it must await the passing of time to find opportunity for expression. Spiritual volition has begun to taste liberation from the fetters of time, having achieved partial escape from time sequence, and that is because spiritual volition is self-identifying with the will of God.

Volition, the act of choosing, must function within the universe frame which has actualized in response to higher and prior choosing. The entire range of human will is strictly finite-limited except in one particular: When man chooses to find God and to be like him, such a choice is superfinite; only eternity can disclose whether this choice is also superabsonite.

To recognize Deity omnipotence is to enjoy security in your experience of cosmic citizenship, to possess assurance of safety in the long journey to Paradise. But to accept the fallacy of omnificence is to embrace the colossal error of pantheism.

7. OMNISCIENCE AND PREDESTINATION

The function of Creator will and creature will, in the grand universe, operates within the limits, and in accordance with the possibilities, established by the Master Architects. This foreordination of these maximum limits does not, however, in the least abridge the sovereignty of creature will within these boundaries. Neither does ultimate foreknowledge—full allowance for all finite choice—constitute an abrogation of finite volition. A mature and farseeing human being might be able to forecast the decision of some younger associate most accurately, but this foreknowledge takes nothing away from the freedom and genuineness of the decision itself. The Gods have wisely limited the range of the action of immature will, but it is true will, nonetheless, within these defined limits.

Even the supreme correlation of all past, present, and future choice does not invalidate the authenticity of such choosings. It rather indicates the foreordained trend of the cosmos and suggests foreknowledge of those volitional beings who may, or may not, elect to become contributory parts of the experiential actualization of all reality.

Error in finite choosing is time bound and time limited. It can exist only in time and *within* the evolving presence of the Supreme Being. Such mistaken choosing is time possible and indicates (besides the incompleteness of the Supreme) that certain range of choice with which immature creatures must be endowed in order to enjoy universe progression by making freewill contact with reality.

Sin in time-conditioned space clearly proves the temporal liberty—even license—of the finite will. Sin depicts immaturity dazzled by the freedom of the relatively sovereign will of personality while failing to perceive the supreme obligations and duties of cosmic citizenship.

Iniquity in the finite domains reveals the transient reality of all God-unidentified selfhood. Only as a creature becomes God identified, does he become truly real in the universes. Finite personality is not self-created, but in the superuniverse arena of choice it does self-determine destiny.

The bestowal of life renders material-energy systems capable of self-perpetuation, self-propagation, and self-adaptation. The bestowal of personality imparts to living organisms the further prerogatives of self-determination, self-evolution, and self-identification with a fusion spirit of Deity.

Subpersonal living things indicate mind activating energy-matter, first as physical controllers, and then as adjutant mind-spirits. Personality endowment comes from the Father and imparts unique prerogatives of choice to the living system. But if personality has the prerogative of exercising volitional choice of reality identification, and if this is a true and free choice, then must evolving personality also have the possible choice of becoming self-confusing, self-disrupting, and self-destroying. The possibility of cosmic self-destruction cannot be avoided if the evolving personality is to be truly free in the exercise of finite will.

Therefore is there increased safety in narrowing the limits of personality choice throughout the lower levels of existence. Choice becomes increasingly liberated as the universes are ascended; choice eventually approximates divine freedom when the ascending personality achieves divinity of status, supremacy of consecration to the purposes of the universe, completion of cosmic-wisdom attainment, and finality of creature identification with the will and the way of God.

8. CONTROL AND OVERCONTROL

In the time-space creations, free will is hedged about with restraints, with limitations. Material-life evolution is first mechanical, then mind activated, and (after the bestowal of personality) it may become spirit directed. Organic evolution on the inhabited worlds is physically limited by the potentials of the original physical-life implantations of the Life Carriers.

Mortal man is a machine, a living mechanism; his roots are truly in the physical world of energy. Many human reactions are mechanical in nature; much of life is machinelike. But man, a mechanism, is much more than a machine; he is mind endowed and spirit indwelt; and though he can never throughout his material life escape the chemical and electrical mechanics of his existence, he can increasingly learn how to subordinate this physical-life machine to the directive wisdom of experience by the process of consecrating the human mind to the execution of the spiritual urges of the indwelling Thought Adjuster.

The spirit liberates, and the mechanism limits, the function of will. Imperfect choice, uncontrolled by mechanism, unidentified with spirit, is dangerous and unstable. Mechanical dominance insures stability at the expense of progress; spirit alliance liberates choice from the physical level and at the same time assures the divine stability produced by augmented universe insight and increased cosmic comprehension.

The great danger that besets the creature is that, in achieving liberation from the fetters of the life mechanism, he will fail to compensate this loss of stability by effecting a harmonious working liaison with spirit. Creature choice, when relatively liberated from mechanical stability, may attempt further self-liberation independent of greater spirit identification.

The whole principle of biologic evolution makes it impossible for primitive man to appear on the inhabited worlds with any large endowment of self-restraint. Therefore does the same creative design which purposed evolution likewise provide those external restraints of time and space, hunger and fear, which effectively circumscribe the subspiritual choice range of such uncultured creatures. As man's mind successfully overstrides increasingly difficult barriers, this same creative design has also provided for the slow accumulation of the racial heritage of painfully garnered experiential wisdom—in other words, for the maintenance of a balance between the diminishing external restraints and the augmenting internal restraints.

The slowness of evolution, of human cultural progress, testifies to the effectiveness of that brake—material inertia—which so efficiently operates to retard dangerous velocities of progress. Thus does time itself cushion and distribute the otherwise lethal results of premature escape from the next-encompassing barriers to human action. For when culture advances overfast, when material achievement outruns the evolution of worship-wisdom, then does civilization contain within itself the seeds of retrogression; and unless buttressed by the swift augmentation of experiential wisdom, such human societies will recede from high but premature levels of attainment, and the "dark ages" of the interregnum of wisdom will bear witness to the inexorable restoration of the imbalance between self-liberty and self-control.

The iniquity of Caligastia was the by-passing of the time governor of progressive human liberation—the gratuitous destruction of restraining barriers, barriers which the mortal minds of those times had not experientially overridden.

That mind which can effect a partial abridgment of time and space, by this very act proves itself possessed of the seeds of wisdom which can effectively serve in lieu of the transcended barrier of restraint.

Lucifer similarly sought to disrupt the time governor operating in restraint of the premature attainment of certain liberties in the local system. A local system settled in light and life has experientially achieved those viewpoints and insights which make feasible the operation of many techniques that would be disruptive and destructive in the presettled eras of that very realm.

As man shakes off the shackles of fear, as he bridges continents and oceans with his machines, generations and centuries with his records, he must substitute for each transcended restraint a new and voluntarily assumed restraint in accordance with the moral dictates of expanding human wisdom. These self-imposed restraints are at once the most powerful and the most tenuous of all the factors of human civilization—concepts of justice and ideals of brotherhood. Man even qualifies himself for the restraining garments of mercy when he dares to love his fellow men, while he achieves the beginnings of spiritual brotherhood when he elects to mete out to them that treatment which he himself would be accorded, even that treatment which he conceives that God would accord them.

An automatic universe reaction is stable and, in some form, continuing in the cosmos. A personality who knows God and desires to do his will, who has spirit insight, is divinely stable and eternally existent. Man's great universe adventure consists in the transit of his mortal mind from the stability of mechanical statics to the divinity of spiritual dynamics, and he achieves this transformation by the force and constancy of his own personality decisions, in each of life's situations declaring, "It is my will that your will be done."

9. UNIVERSE MECHANISMS

Time and space are a conjoined mechanism of the master universe. They are the devices whereby finite creatures are enabled to coexist in the cosmos with the Infinite. Finite creatures are effectively insulated from the absolute levels by time and space. But these insulating media, without which no mortal could exist, operate directly to limit the range of finite action. Without them no creature could act, but by them the acts of every creature are definitely limited.

Mechanisms produced by higher minds function to liberate their creative sources but to some degree unvaryingly limit the action of all subordinate intelligences. To the creatures of the universes this limitation becomes apparent as the mechanism of the universes. Man does not have unfettered free will; there are limits to his range of choice, but within the radius of this choice his will is relatively sovereign.

The life mechanism of the mortal personality, the human body, is the product of supermortal creative design; therefore it can never be perfectly controlled by man himself. Only when ascending man, in liaison with the fused Adjuster, self-creates the mechanism for personality expression, will he achieve perfected control thereof.

The grand universe is mechanism as well as organism, mechanical and living—a living mechanism activated by a Supreme Mind, co-ordinating with a Supreme Spirit, and finding expression on maximum levels of power and personality unification as the Supreme Being. But to deny the mechanism of the finite creation is to deny fact and to disregard reality.

Mechanisms are the products of mind, creative mind acting on and in cosmic potentials. Mechanisms are the fixed crystallizations of Creator thought, and they ever function true to the volitional concept that gave them origin. But the purposiveness of any mechanism is in its origin, not in its function.

These mechanisms should not be thought of as limiting the action of Deity; rather is it true that in these very mechanics Deity has achieved one phase of eternal expression. The basic universe mechanisms have come into existence in response to the absolute will of the First Source and Center, and they will therefore eternally function in perfect harmony with the plan of the Infinite; they are, indeed, the nonvolitional patterns of that very plan.

We understand something of how the mechanism of Paradise is correlated with the personality of the Eternal Son; this is the function of the Conjoint Actor. And we have theories regarding the operations of the Universal Absolute with respect to the theoretical mechanisms of the Unqualified and the potential person of the Deity Absolute. But in the evolving Deities of Supreme and Ultimate we observe that certain impersonal phases are being actually united with their volitional counterparts, and thus there is evolving a new relationship between pattern and person.

In the eternity of the past the Father and the Son found union in the unity of the expression of the Infinite Spirit. If, in the eternity of the future, the Creator Sons and the Creative Spirits of the local universes of time and space should attain creative union in the realms of outer space, what would their unity create as the combined expression of their divine natures? It may well be that we are to witness a hitherto unrevealed manifestation of Ultimate Deity, a new type of superadministrator. Such beings would embrace unique prerogatives of personality, being the union of personal Creator, impersonal Creative Spirit, mortal-creature experience, and progressive personalization of the Divine Minister. Such beings could be ultimate in that they would embrace personal and impersonal reality, while they would combine the experiences of Creator and creature. Whatever the attributes of such third persons of these postulated functioning trinities of the creations of outer space, they will sustain something of the same relation to their Creator Fathers and their Creative Mothers that the Infinite Spirit does to the Universal Father and the Eternal Son.

God the Supreme is the personalization of all universe experience, the focalization of all finite evolution, the maximation of all creature reality, the consummation of cosmic wisdom, the embodiment of the harmonious beauties of the galaxies of time, the truth of cosmic mind meanings, and the goodness of supreme spirit values. And God the Supreme will, in the eternal future, synthesize these manifold finite diversities into one experientially meaningful whole, even as they are now existentially united on absolute levels in the Paradise Trinity.

10. FUNCTIONS OF PROVIDENCE

Providence does not mean that God has decided all things for us and in advance. God loves us too much to do that, for that would be nothing short of cosmic tyranny. Man does have relative powers of choice. Neither is the divine love that shortsighted affection which would pamper and spoil the children of men.

The Father, Son, and Spirit—as the Trinity—are not the Almighty Supreme, but the supremacy of the Almighty can never be manifest without them. The *growth* of the Almighty is centered on the Absolutes of actuality and predicated on the Absolutes of potentiality. But the *functions* of the Almighty Supreme are related to the functions of the Paradise Trinity.

It would appear that, in the Supreme Being, all phases of universe activity are being partially reunited by the personality of this experiential Deity. When, therefore, we desire to view the Trinity as one God, and if we limit this concept to the present known and organized grand universe, we discover that the evolving Supreme Being is the partial portraiture of the Paradise Trinity. And we further find that this Supreme Deity is evolving as the personality synthesis of finite matter, mind, and spirit in the grand universe.

The Gods have attributes but the Trinity has functions, and like the Trinity, providence *is* a function, the composite of the other-than-personal overcontrol of the universe of universes, extending from the evolutionary levels of the Sevenfold synthesizing in the power of the Almighty on up through the transcendental realms of the Ultimacy of Deity.

God loves each creature as a child, and that love overshadows each creature throughout all time and eternity. Providence functions with regard to the total and deals with the function of any creature as such function is related to the total. Providential intervention with regard to any being is indicative of the importance of the *function* of that being as concerns the evolutionary growth of some total; such total may be the total race, the total nation, the total planet, or even a higher total. It is the importance of the function of the creature that occasions providential intervention, not the importance of the creature as a person.

Nevertheless, the Father as a person may at any time interpose a fatherly hand in the stream of cosmic events all in accordance with the will of God and in consonance with the wisdom of God and as motivated by the love of God.

But what man calls providence is all too often the product of his own imagination, the fortuitous juxtaposition of the circumstances of chance. There is, however, a real and emerging providence in the finite realm of universe existence, a true and actualizing correlation of the energies of space, the motions of time, the thoughts of intellect, the ideals of character, the desires of spiritual natures, and the purposive volitional acts of evolving personalities. The circumstances of the material realms find final finite integration in the interlocking presences of the Supreme and the Ultimate.

As the mechanisms of the grand universe are perfected to a point of final precision through the overcontrol of mind, and as creature mind ascends to the perfection of divinity attainment through perfected integration with spirit, and as the Supreme consequently emerges as an *actual* unifier of all these universe phenomena, so does providence become increasingly discernible.

Some of the amazingly fortuitous conditions occasionally prevailing on the evolutionary worlds may be due to the gradually emerging presence of the Supreme, the foretasting of his future universe activities. Most of what a mortal would call providential is not; his judgment of such matters is very handicapped by lack of farsighted vision into the true meanings of the circumstances of life. Much of what a mortal would call good luck might really be bad luck; the smile of fortune that bestows unearned leisure and undeserved wealth may be the greatest of human afflictions; the apparent cruelty of a perverse fate that heaps tribulation upon some suffering mortal may in reality be the tempering fire that is transmuting the soft iron of immature personality into the tempered steel of real character.

There is a providence in the evolving universes, and it can be discovered by creatures to just the extent that they have attained capacity to perceive the purpose of the evolving universes. Complete capacity to discern universe purposes equals the evolutionary completion of the creature and may otherwise be expressed as the attainment of the Supreme within the limits of the present state of the incomplete universes.

The love of the Father operates directly in the heart of the individual, independent of the actions or reactions of all other individuals; the relationship is personal—man and God. The impersonal presence of Deity (Almighty Supreme and Paradise Trinity) manifests regard for the whole, not for the part. The providence of the overcontrol of Supremacy becomes increasingly apparent as the successive parts of the universe progress in the attainment of finite destinies. As the systems, constellations, universes, and superuniverses become settled in light and life, the Supreme increasingly emerges as the meaningful correlator of all that is transpiring, while the Ultimate gradually emerges as the transcendental unifier of all things.

In the beginnings on an evolutionary world the natural occurrences of the material order and the personal desires of human beings often appear to be antagonistic. Much that takes place on an evolving world is rather hard for mortal man to understand—natural law is so often apparently cruel, heartless, and indifferent to all that is true, beautiful, and good in human comprehension. But as humanity progresses in planetary development, we observe that this viewpoint is modified by the following factors:

1. *Man's augmenting vision*—his increased understanding of the world in which he lives; his enlarging capacity for the comprehension of the material facts of time, the meaningful ideas of thought, and the valuable ideals of spiritual insight. As long as men measure only by the yardstick of the things of a physical nature, they can never hope to find unity in time and space.

2. *Man's increasing control*—the gradual accumulation of the knowledge of the laws of the material world, the purposes of spiritual existence, and the possibilities of the philosophic co-ordination of these two realities. Man, the savage, was helpless before the onslaughts of natural forces, was slavish before the cruel mastery of his own inner fears. Semicivilized man is beginning to unlock the storehouse of the secrets of the natural realms, and his science is slowly but effectively destroying his superstitions while at the same time providing a new and enlarged factual basis for the comprehension of the meanings of philosophy and the values of true spiritual experience. Man, the civilized, will someday achieve relative mastery of the physical forces of his planet; the love of God in his heart will be effectively outpoured as love for his fellow men, while the values of human existence will be nearing the limits of mortal capacity.

3. *Man's universe integration*—the increase of human insight plus the increase of human experiential achievement brings him into closer harmony with the unifying presences of Supremacy—Paradise Trinity and Supreme Being. And this is what establishes the sovereignty of the Supreme on the worlds long settled in light and life. Such advanced planets are indeed poems of harmony, pictures of the beauty of achieved goodness attained through the pursuit of cosmic truth. And if such things can happen to a planet, then even greater things can happen to a system and the larger units of the grand universe as they too achieve a settledness indicating the exhaustion of the potentials for finite growth.

On a planet of this advanced order, providence has become an actuality, the circumstances of life are correlated, but this is not only because man has come to dominate the material problems of his world; it is also because he has begun to live according to the trend of the universes; he is following the pathway of Supremacy to the attainment of the Universal Father.

The kingdom of God is in the hearts of men, and when this kingdom becomes actual in the heart of every individual on a world, then God's rule has become actual on that planet; and this is the attained sovereignty of the Supreme Being.

To realize providence in time, man must accomplish the task of achieving perfection. But man can even now foretaste this providence in its eternity meanings as he ponders the universe fact that all things, be they good or evil, work together for the advancement of God-knowing mortals in their quest for the Father of all.

Providence becomes increasingly discernible as men reach upward from the material to the spiritual. The attainment of completed spiritual insight enables the ascending personality to detect harmony in what was theretofore chaos. Even morontia mota represents a real advance in this direction.

Providence is in part the overcontrol of the incomplete Supreme manifested in the incomplete universes, and it must therefore ever be:

1. *Partial*—due to the incompleteness of the actualization of the Supreme Being, and

2. *Unpredictable*—due to the fluctuations in creature attitude, which ever varies from level to level, thus causing apparently variable reciprocal response in the Supreme.

When men pray for providential intervention in the circumstances of life, many times the answer to their prayer is their own changed attitudes toward life. But providence is not whimsical, neither is it fantastic nor magical. It is the slow and sure emergence of the mighty sovereign of the finite universes, whose majestic presence the evolving creatures occasionally detect in their universe progressions. Providence is the sure and certain march of the galaxies of space and the personalities of time toward the goals of eternity, first in the Supreme, then in the Ultimate, and perhaps in the Absolute. And in infinity we believe there is the same providence, and this is the will, the actions, the purpose of the Paradise Trinity thus motivating the cosmic panorama of universes upon universes.

[Sponsored by a Mighty Messenger temporarily sojourning on Urantia.]

PAPER 119

THE BESTOWALS OF CHRIST MICHAEL

CHIEF of the Evening Stars of Nebadon, I am assigned to Urantia by Gabriel on the mission of revealing the story of the seven bestowals of the Universe Sovereign, Michael of Nebadon, and my name is Gavalia. In making this presentation, I will adhere strictly to the limitations imposed by my commission.

The attribute of bestowal is inherent in the Paradise Sons of the Universal Father. In their desire to come close to the life experiences of their subordinate living creatures, the various orders of the Paradise Sons are reflecting the divine nature of their Paradise parents. The Eternal Son of the Paradise Trinity led the way in this practice, having seven times bestowed himself upon the seven circuits of Havona during the times of the ascension of Grandfanda and the first of the pilgrims from time and space. And the Eternal Son continues to bestow himself upon the local universes of space in the persons of his representatives, the Michael and Avonal Sons.

When the Eternal Son bestows a Creator Son upon a projected local universe, that Creator Son assumes full responsibility for the completion, control, and composure of that new universe, including the solemn oath to the eternal Trinity not to assume full sovereignty of the new creation until his seven creature bestowals shall have been successfully completed and certified by the Ancients of Days of the superuniverse of jurisdiction. This obligation is assumed by every Michael Son who volunteers to go out from Paradise to engage in universe organization and creation.

The purpose of these creature incarnations is to enable such Creators to become wise, sympathetic, just, and understanding sovereigns. These divine Sons are innately just, but they become understandingly merciful as a result of these successive bestowal experiences; they are naturally merciful, but these experiences make them merciful in new and additional ways. These bestowals are the last steps in their education and training for the sublime tasks of ruling the local universes in divine righteousness and by just judgment.

Though numerous incidental benefits accrue to the various worlds, systems, and constellations, as well as to the different orders of universe intelligences affected and benefited by these bestowals, still they are primarily designed to complete the personal training and universe education of a Creator Son himself. These bestowals are not essential to the wise, just, and efficient management of a local universe, but they are absolutely necessary to a fair, merciful, and understanding administration of such a creation, teeming with its varied forms of life and its myriads of intelligent but imperfect creatures.

The Michael Sons begin their work of universe organization with a full and just sympathy for the various orders of beings whom they have created. They have vast stores of mercy for all these differing creatures, even pity for those who err and flounder in the selfish mire of their own production. But such endowments of justice and righteousness will not suffice in the estimate of the Ancients of Days. These triune rulers of the superuniverses will never certify a Creator Son as Universe Sovereign until he has really acquired the viewpoint of his own creatures by actual experience in the environment of their existence and as these very creatures themselves. In this way such Sons become intelligent and understanding rulers; they come to *know* the various groups over which they rule and exercise universe authority. By living experience they possess themselves of practical mercy, fair judgment, and the patience born of experiential creature existence.

The local universe of Nebadon is now ruled by a Creator Son who has completed his service of bestowal; he reigns in just and merciful supremacy over all the vast realms of his evolving and perfecting universe. Michael of Nebadon is the 611,121st bestowal of the Eternal Son upon the universes of time and space, and he began the organization of your local universe about four hundred billion years ago. Michael made ready for his first bestowal adventure about the time Urantia was taking on its present form, one billion years ago. His bestowals have occurred about one hundred and fifty million years apart, the last taking place on Urantia nineteen hundred years ago. I will now proceed to unfold the nature and character of these bestowals as fully as my commission permits.

1. THE FIRST BESTOWAL

It was a solemn occasion on Salvington almost one billion years ago when the assembled directors and chiefs of the universe of Nebadon heard Michael announce that his elder brother, Immanuel, would presently assume authority in Nebadon while he (Michael) would be absent on an unexplained mission. No other announcement was made about this transaction except that the farewell broadcast to the Constellation Fathers, among other instructions, said: "And for this period I place you under the care and keeping of Immanuel while I go to do the bidding of my Paradise Father."

After sending this farewell broadcast, Michael appeared on the dispatching field of Salvington, just as on many previous occasions when preparing for departure to Uversa or Paradise except that he came alone. He concluded his statement of departure with these words: "I leave you but for a short season. Many of you, I know, would go with me, but whither I go you cannot come. That which I am about to do, you cannot do. I go to do the will of the Paradise Deities, and when I have finished my mission and have acquired this experience, I will return to my place among you." And having thus spoken, Michael of Nebadon vanished from the sight of all those assembled and did not reappear for twenty years of standard time. In all Salvington, only the Divine Minister and Immanuel knew what was taking place, and the Union of Days shared his secret only with the chief executive of the universe, Gabriel, the Bright and Morning Star.

All the inhabitants of Salvington and those dwelling on the constellation and system headquarters worlds assembled about their respective receiving stations for universe intelligence, hoping to get some word of the mission and whereabouts of the Creator Son. Not until the third day after Michael's departure was any message of possible significance received. On this day a communication was registered on Salvington from the Melchizedek sphere, the headquarters of that order in Nebadon, which simply recorded this extraordinary and never-before-heard-of transaction: "At noon today there appeared on the receiving field of this world a strange Melchizedek Son, not of our number but wholly like our order. He was accompanied by a solitary omniaphim who bore credentials from Uversa and presented orders addressed to our chief, derived from the Ancients of Days and concurred in by Immanuel of Salvington, directing that this new Melchizedek Son be received into our order and assigned to the emergency service of the Melchizedeks of Nebadon. And it has been so ordered; it has been done."

And this is about all that appears on the records of Salvington regarding the first Michael bestowal. Nothing more appears until after one hundred years of Urantia time, when there was recorded the fact of Michael's return and unannounced resumption of the direction of universe affairs. But a strange record is to be found on the Melchizedek world, a recital of the service of this unique Melchizedek Son of the emergency corps of that age. This record is preserved in a simple temple which now occupies the foreground of the home of the Father Melchizedek, and it comprises the narration of the service of this transitory Melchizedek Son in connection with his assignment to twenty-four missions of universe emergency. And this record, which I have so recently reviewed, ends thus:

"And at noon on this day, without previous announcement and witnessed by only three of our brotherhood, this visiting Son of our order disappeared from our world as he came, accompanied only by a solitary omniaphim; and this record is now closed with the certification that this visitor lived as a Melchizedek, in the likeness of a Melchizedek he worked as a Melchizedek, and he faithfully performed all of his assignments as an emergency Son of our order. By universal consent he has become chief of Melchizedeks, having earned our love and adoration by his matchless wisdom, supreme love, and superb devotion to duty. He loved us, understood us, and served with us, and forever we are his loyal and devoted fellow Melchizedeks, for this stranger on our world has now eternally become a universe minister of Melchizedek nature."

And that is all I am permitted to tell you of the first bestowal of Michael. We, of course, fully understand that this strange Melchizedek who so mysteriously served with the Melchizedeks a billion years ago was none other than the incarnated Michael on the mission of his first bestowal. The records do not specifically state that this unique and efficient Melchizedek was Michael, but it is universally believed that he was. Probably the actual statement of that fact cannot be found outside of the records of Sonarington, and the records of that secret world are not open to us. Only on this sacred world of the divine Sons are the mysteries of incarnation and bestowal fully known. We all know of the facts of the Michael bestowals, but we do not understand how they are effected. We do not know how the ruler of a universe, the creator of the Melchizedeks, can so suddenly and mysteriously become one of their number and, as one of them, live among them and work as a Melchizedek Son for one hundred years. But it so happened.

2. THE SECOND BESTOWAL

For almost one hundred and fifty million years after the Melchizedek bestowal of Michael, all went well in the universe of Nebadon, when trouble began to brew in system 11 of constellation 37. This trouble involved a misunderstanding by a Lanonandek Son, a System Sovereign, which had been adjudicated by the Constellation Fathers and approved by the Faithful of Days, the Paradise counselor to that constellation, but the protesting System Sovereign was not fully reconciled to the verdict. After more than one hundred years of dissatisfaction he led his associates in one of the most widespread and disastrous rebellions against the sovereignty of the Creator Son ever instigated in the universe of Nebadon, a rebellion long since adjudicated and ended by the action of the Ancients of Days on Uversa.

This rebel System Sovereign, Lutentia, reigned supreme on his headquarters planet for more than twenty years of standard Nebadon time; whereupon, the Most Highs, with approval from Uversa, ordered his segregation and requisitioned the Salvington rulers for the designation of a new System Sovereign to assume direction of that strife-torn and confused system of inhabited worlds.

Simultaneously with the reception of this request on Salvington, Michael initiated the second of those extraordinary proclamations of intention to be absent from the universe headquarters for the purpose of "doing the bidding of my Paradise Father," promising to "return in due season" and concentrating all authority in the hands of his Paradise brother, Immanuel, the Union of Days.

And then, by the same technique observed at the time of his departure in connection with the Melchizedek bestowal, Michael again took leave of his headquarters sphere. Three days after this unexplained leave-taking there appeared among the reserve corps of the primary Lanonandek Sons of Nebadon, a new and unknown member. This new Son appeared at noon, unannounced and accompanied by a lone tertiaphim who bore credentials from the Uversa Ancients of Days, certified by Immanuel of Salvington, directing that this new Son be assigned to system 11 of constellation 37 as the successor of the deposed Lutentia and with full authority as acting System Sovereign pending the appointment of a new sovereign.

For more than seventeen years of universe time this strange and unknown temporary ruler administered the affairs and wisely adjudicated the difficulties of this confused and demoralized local system. No System Sovereign was ever more ardently loved or more widespreadly honored and respected. In justice and mercy this new ruler set the turbulent system in order while he painstakingly ministered to all his subjects, even offering his rebellious predecessor the privilege of sharing the system throne of authority if he would only apologize to Immanuel for his indiscretions. But Lutentia spurned these overtures of mercy, well knowing that this new and strange System Sovereign was none other than Michael, the very universe ruler whom he had so recently defied. But millions of his misguided and deluded followers accepted the forgiveness of this new ruler, known in that age as the Savior Sovereign of the system of Palonia.

And then came that eventful day on which there arrived the newly appointed System Sovereign, designated by the universe authorities as the permanent successor of the deposed Lutentia, and all Palonia mourned the departure of the most noble and the most benign system ruler that Nebadon had ever known. He was beloved by all the system and adored by his fellows of all groups of the Lanonandek Sons. His departure was not unceremonious; a great celebration was arranged when he left the system headquarters. Even his erring predecessor sent this message: "Just and righteous are you in all your ways. While I continue in rejection of the Paradise rule, I am compelled to confess that you are a just and merciful administrator."

And then did this transient ruler of a rebellious system take leave of the planet of his short administrative sojourn, while on the third day thereafter Michael appeared on Salvington and resumed the direction of the universe of Nebadon. There soon followed the third Uversa proclamation of the advancing jurisdiction of the sovereignty and authority of Michael. The first proclamation was made at the time of his arrival in Nebadon, the second was issued soon after the completion of the Melchizedek bestowal, and now the third follows upon the termination of the second or Lanonandek mission.

3. THE THIRD BESTOWAL

The supreme council on Salvington had just finished the consideration of the call of the Life Carriers on planet 217 in system 87 in constellation 61 for the dispatch to their assistance of a Material Son. Now this planet was situated in a system of inhabited worlds where another System Sovereign had gone astray, the second such rebellion in all Nebadon up to that time.

Upon the request of Michael, action on the petition of the Life Carriers of this planet was deferred pending its consideration by Immanuel and his report thereon. This was an irregular procedure, and I well remember how we all anticipated something unusual, and we were not long held in suspense. Michael proceeded to place universe direction in the hands of Immanuel, while he intrusted command of the celestial forces to Gabriel, and having thus disposed of his administrative responsibilities, he took leave of the Universe Mother Spirit and vanished from the dispatching field of Salvington precisely as he had done on two previous occasions.

And, as might have been expected, on the third day thereafter there appeared, unannounced, on the headquarters world of system 87 in constellation 61, a strange Material Son, accompanied by a lone seconaphim, accredited by the Uversa Ancients of Days, and certified by Immanuel of Salvington. Immediately the acting System Sovereign appointed this new and mysterious Material Son acting Planetary Prince of world 217, and this designation was at once confirmed by the Most Highs of constellation 61.

Thus did this unique Material Son begin his difficult career on a quarantined world of secession and rebellion, located in a beleaguered system without any direct communication with the outside universe, working alone for one whole generation of planetary time. This emergency Material Son effected the repentance and reclamation of the defaulting Planetary Prince and his entire staff and witnessed the restoration of the planet to the loyal service of the Paradise rule as established in the local universes. In due time a Material Son and Daughter arrived on this rejuvenated and redeemed world, and when they had been duly installed as visible planetary rulers, the transitory or emergency Planetary Prince took formal leave, disappearing at noon one day. On the third day thereafter, Michael appeared in his accustomed place on Salvington, and very soon the superuniverse broadcasts carried the fourth proclamation of the Ancients of Days announcing the further advancement of the sovereignty of Michael in Nebadon.

I regret that I do not have permission to narrate the patience, fortitude, and skill with which this Material Son met the trying situations on this confused planet. The reclamation of this isolated world is one of the most beautifully touching chapters in the annals of salvation throughout Nebadon. By the end of this mission it had become evident to all Nebadon as to why their beloved ruler chose to engage in these repeated bestowals in the likeness of some subordinate order of intelligent being.

The bestowals of Michael as a Melchizedek Son, then as a Lanonandek Son, and next as a Material Son are all equally mysterious and beyond explanation. In each instance he appeared *suddenly* and as a fully developed individual of the bestowal group. The mystery of such incarnations will never be known except to those who have access to the inner circle of the records on the sacred sphere of Sonarington.

Never, since this marvelous bestowal as the Planetary Prince of a world in isolation and rebellion, have any of the Material Sons or Daughters in Nebadon been tempted to complain of their assignments or to find fault with the difficulties of their planetary missions. For all time the Material Sons know that in the Creator Son of the universe they have an understanding sovereign and a sympathetic friend, one who has in "all points been tried and tested," even as they must also be tried and tested.

Each of these missions was followed by an age of increasing service and loyalty among all celestial intelligences of universe origin, while each succeeding bestowal age was characterized by advancement and improvement in all methods of universe administration and in all techniques of government. Since this bestowal no Material Son or Daughter has ever knowingly joined in rebellion against Michael; they love and honor him too devotedly ever consciously to reject him. Only through deception and sophistry have the Adams of recent times been led astray by higher types of rebel personalities.

4. THE FOURTH BESTOWAL

It was at the end of one of the periodic millennial roll calls of Uversa that Michael proceeded to place the government of Nebadon in the hands of Immanuel and Gabriel; and, of course, recalling what had happened in times past following such action, we all prepared to witness Michael's disappearance on his fourth mission of bestowal, and we were not long kept waiting, for he shortly went out upon the Salvington dispatching field and was lost to our view.

On the third day after this bestowal disappearance we observed, in the universe broadcasts to Uversa, this significant news item from the seraphic headquarters of Nebadon: "Reporting the unannounced arrival of an unknown seraphim, accompanied by a solitary supernaphim and Gabriel of Salvington. This unregistered seraphim qualifies as of the Nebadon order and bears credentials from the Uversa Ancients of Days, certified by Immanuel of Salvington. This seraphim tests out as belonging to the supreme order of the angels of a local universe and has already been assigned to the corps of the teaching counselors."

Michael was absent from Salvington during this, the seraphic bestowal, for a period of over forty standard universe years. During this time he was attached as a seraphic teaching counselor, what you might denominate a private secretary, to twenty-six different master teachers, functioning on twenty-two different worlds. His last or terminal assignment was as counselor and helper attached to a bestowal mission of a Trinity Teacher Son on world 462 in system 84 of constellation 3 in the universe of Nebadon.

Never, throughout the seven years of this assignment, was this Trinity Teacher Son wholly persuaded as to the identity of his seraphic associate. True, all seraphim during that age were regarded with peculiar interest and scrutiny. Full well we all knew that our beloved Sovereign was abroad in the universe, disguised as a seraphim, but never could we be certain of his identity. Never was he positively identified until the time of his attachment to the bestowal mission of this Trinity Teacher Son. But always throughout this era were the supreme seraphim regarded with special solicitude, lest any of us should find that we had unawares been host to the Sovereign of the universe on a mission of creature bestowal. And so it has become forever true, concerning angels, that their Creator and Ruler has been "in all points tried and tested in the likeness of seraphic personality."

As these successive bestowals partook increasingly of the nature of the lower forms of universe life, Gabriel became more and more an associate of these incarnation adventures, functioning as the universe liaison between the bestowed Michael and the acting universe ruler, Immanuel.

Now has Michael passed through the bestowal experience of three orders of his created universe Sons: the Melchizedeks, the Lanonandeks, and the Material Sons. Next he condescends to personalize in the likeness of angelic life as a supreme seraphim before turning his attention to the various phases of the ascending careers of his lowest form of will creatures, the evolutionary mortals of time and space.

5. THE FIFTH BESTOWAL

A little over three hundred million years ago, as time is reckoned on Urantia, we witnessed another of those transfers of universe authority to Immanuel and observed the preparations of Michael for departure. This occasion was different from the previous ones in that he announced that his destination was Uversa, headquarters of the superuniverse of Orvonton. In due time our Sovereign departed, but the broadcasts of the superuniverse never made mention of Michael's arrival at the courts of the Ancients of Days. Shortly after his departure from Salvington there did appear in the Uversa broadcasts this significant statement: "There arrived today an unannounced and unnumbered ascendant pilgrim of mortal origin from the universe of Nebadon, certified by Immanuel of Salvington and accompanied by Gabriel of Nebadon. This unidentified being presents the status of a true spirit and has been received into our fellowship."

If you should visit Uversa today, you would hear the recounting of the days when Eventod sojourned there, this particular and unknown pilgrim of time and space being known on Uversa by that name. And this ascending mortal, at least a superb personality in the exact likeness of the spirit stage of the ascending mortals, lived and functioned on Uversa for a period of eleven years of Orvonton standard time. This being received the assignments and performed the duties of a spirit mortal in common with his fellows from the various local universes of Orvonton. In "all points he was tested and tried, even as his fellows," and on all occasions he proved worthy of the confidence and trust of his superiors, while he unfailingly commanded the respect and loyal admiration of his fellow spirits.

On Salvington we followed the career of this spirit pilgrim with consummate interest, knowing full well, by the presence of Gabriel, that this unassuming and unnumbered pilgrim spirit was none other than the bestowed ruler of our local universe. This first appearance of Michael incarnated in the role of one stage of mortal evolution was an event which thrilled and enthralled all Nebadon. We had heard of such things but now we beheld them. He appeared on Uversa as a fully developed and perfectly trained spirit mortal and, as such, continued his career up to the occasion of the advancement of a group of ascending mortals to Havona; whereupon he held converse with the Ancients of Days and immediately, in the company of Gabriel, took sudden and unceremonious leave of Uversa, appearing shortly thereafter in his accustomed place on Salvington.

Not until the completion of this bestowal did it finally dawn upon us that Michael was probably going to incarnate in the likeness of his various orders of universe personalities, from the highest Melchizedeks right on down to the mortals of flesh and blood on the evolutionary worlds of time and space. About this time the Melchizedek colleges began to teach the probability of Michael's sometime incarnating as a mortal of the flesh, and there occurred much speculation as to the possible technique of such an inexplicable bestowal. That Michael had in person performed in the role of an ascending mortal lent new and added interest to the whole scheme of creature progression all the way up through both the local universe and the superuniverse.

Still, the technique of these successive bestowals remained a mystery. Even Gabriel confesses that he does not comprehend the method whereby this Paradise Son and universe Creator could, at will, assume the personality and live the life of one of his own subordinate creatures.

6. THE SIXTH BESTOWAL

Now that all Salvington was familiar with the preliminaries of an impending bestowal, Michael called the sojourners on the headquarters planet together and, for the first time, unfolded the remainder of the incarnation plan, announcing that he was soon to leave Salvington for the purpose of assuming the career of a morontia mortal at the courts of the Most High Fathers on the headquarters planet of the fifth constellation. And then we heard for the first time the announcement that his seventh and final bestowal would be made on some evolutionary world in the likeness of mortal flesh.

Before leaving Salvington for the sixth bestowal, Michael addressed the assembled inhabitants of the sphere and departed in full view of everyone, accompanied by a lone seraphim and the Bright and Morning Star of Nebadon. While the direction of the universe had again been intrusted to Immanuel, there was a wider distribution of administrative responsibilities.

Michael appeared on the headquarters of constellation five as a full-fledged morontia mortal of ascending status. I regret that I am forbidden to reveal the details of this unnumbered morontia mortal's career, for it was one of the most extraordinary and amazing epochs in Michael's bestowal experience, not even excepting his dramatic and tragic sojourn on Urantia. But among the many restrictions imposed upon me in accepting this commission is one which forbids my undertaking to unfold the details of this wonderful career of Michael as the morontia mortal of Endantum.

When Michael returned from this morontia bestowal, it was apparent to all of us that our Creator had become a fellow creature, that the Universe Sovereign was also the friend and sympathetic helper of even the lowest form of created intelligence in his realms. We had noted this progressive acquirement of the creature's viewpoint in universe administration before this, for it had been gradually appearing, but it became more apparent after the completion of the morontia mortal bestowal, even still more so after his return from the career of the carpenter's son on Urantia.

We were informed in advance by Gabriel of the time of Michael's release from the morontia bestowal, and accordingly we arranged a suitable reception on Salvington. Millions upon millions of beings were assembled from the constellation headquarters worlds of Nebadon, and a majority of the sojourners on the worlds adjacent to Salvington were gathered together to welcome him back to the rulership of his universe. In response to our many addresses of welcome and expressions of appreciation of a Sovereign so vitally interested in his creatures, he only replied: "I have simply been about my Father's business. I am only doing the pleasure of the Paradise Sons who love and crave to understand their creatures."

But from that day down to the hour when Michael embarked upon his Urantia adventure as the Son of Man, all Nebadon continued to discuss the many exploits of their Sovereign Ruler as he functioned on Endantum as the bestowal incarnation of a morontia mortal of evolutionary ascension, being in all points tested like his fellows assembled from the material worlds of the entire constellation of his sojourn.

7. THE SEVENTH AND FINAL BESTOWAL

For tens of thousands of years we all looked forward to the seventh and final bestowal of Michael. Gabriel had taught us that this terminal bestowal would be made in the likeness of mortal flesh, but we were wholly ignorant of the time, place, and manner of this culminating adventure.

The public announcement that Michael had selected Urantia as the theater for his final bestowal was made shortly after we learned about the default of Adam and Eve. And thus, for more than thirty-five thousand years, your world occupied a very conspicuous place in the councils of the entire universe. There was no secrecy (aside from the incarnation mystery) connected with any step in the Urantia bestowal. From first to last, up to the final and triumphant return of Michael to Salvington as supreme Universe Sovereign, there was the fullest universe publicity of all that transpired on your small but highly honored world.

While we believed that this would be the method, we never knew, until the time of the event itself, that Michael would appear on earth as a helpless infant of the realm. Theretofore had he always appeared as a fully developed individual of the personality group of the bestowal selection, and it was a thrilling announcement which was broadcast from Salvington telling that the babe of Bethlehem had been born on Urantia.

We then not only realized that our Creator and friend was taking the most precarious step in all his career, apparently risking his position and authority on this bestowal as a helpless infant, but we also understood that his experience in this final and mortal bestowal would eternally enthrone him as the undisputed and supreme sovereign of the universe of Nebadon. For a third of a century of earth time all eyes in all parts of this local universe were focused on Urantia. All intelligences realized that the last bestowal was in progress, and as we had long known of the Lucifer rebellion in Satania and of the Caligastia disaffection on Urantia, we well understood the intensity of the struggle which would ensue when our ruler condescended to incarnate on Urantia in the humble form and likeness of mortal flesh.

Joshua ben Joseph, the Jewish baby, was conceived and was born into the world just as all other babies before and since *except* that this particular baby was the incarnation of Michael of Nebadon, a divine Son of Paradise and the creator of all this local universe of things and beings. And this mystery of the incarnation of Deity within the human form of Jesus, otherwise of natural origin on the world, will forever remain unsolved. Even in eternity you will never know the technique and method of the incarnation of the Creator in the form and likeness of his creatures. That is the secret of Sonarington, and such mysteries are the exclusive possession of those divine Sons who have passed through the bestowal experience.

Certain wise men of earth knew of Michael's impending arrival. Through the contacts of one world with another, these wise men of spiritual insight learned of the forthcoming bestowal of Michael on Urantia. And the seraphim did, through the midway creatures, make announcement to a group of Chaldean priests whose leader was Ardnon. These men of God visited the newborn child in the manger. The only supernatural event associated with the birth of Jesus was this announcement to Ardnon and his associates by the seraphim of former attachment to Adam and Eve in the first garden.

Jesus' human parents were average people of their day and generation, and this incarnated Son of God was thus born of woman and was reared in the ordinary manner of the children of that race and age.

The story of Michael's sojourn on Urantia, the narrative of the mortal bestowal of the Creator Son on your world, is a matter beyond the scope and purpose of this narrative.

8. MICHAEL'S POSTBESTOWAL STATUS

After Michael's final and successful bestowal on Urantia he was not only accepted by the Ancients of Days as sovereign ruler of Nebadon, but he was also recognized by the Universal Father as the established director of the local universe of his own creation. Upon his return to Salvington this Michael, the Son of Man and the Son of God, was proclaimed the settled ruler of Nebadon. From Uversa came the eighth proclamation of Michael's sovereignty, while from Paradise came the joint pronouncement of the Universal Father and the Eternal Son constituting this union of God and man sole head of the universe and directing the Union of Days stationed on Salvington to signify his intention of withdrawing to Paradise. The Faithfuls of Days on the constellation headquarters were also instructed to retire from the councils of the Most Highs. But Michael would not consent to the withdrawal of the Trinity Sons of counsel and co-operation. He assembled them on Salvington and personally requested them forever to remain on duty in Nebadon. They signified their desire to comply with this request to their directors on Paradise, and shortly thereafter there were issued those mandates of Paradise divorcement which forever attached these Sons of the central universe to the court of Michael of Nebadon.

It required almost one billion years of Urantia time to complete the bestowal career of Michael and to effect the final establishment of his supreme authority in the universe of his own creation. Michael was born a creator, educated an administrator, trained an executive, but he was required to earn his sovereignty by experience. And thus has your little world become known throughout all Nebadon as the arena wherein Michael completed the experience which is required of every Paradise Creator Son before he is given unlimited control and direction of the universe of his own making. As you ascend the local universe, you will learn more about the ideals of the personalities concerned in Michael's previous bestowals.

In completing his creature bestowals, Michael was not only establishing his own sovereignty but also was augmenting the evolving sovereignty of God the Supreme. In the course of these bestowals the Creator Son not only engaged in a descending exploration of the various natures of creature personality, but he also achieved the revelation of the variously diversified wills of the Paradise Deities, whose synthetic unity, as revealed by the Supreme Creators, is revelatory of the will of the Supreme Being.

These various will aspects of the Deities are eternally personalized in the differing natures of the Seven Master Spirits, and each of Michael's bestowals was peculiarly revelatory of one of these divinity manifestations. On his Melchizedek bestowal he manifested the united will of the Father, Son, and Spirit, on his Lanonandek bestowal the will of the Father and the Son; on the Adamic bestowal he revealed the will of the Father and the Spirit, on the seraphic bestowal the will of the Son and the Spirit; on the Uversa mortal bestowal he portrayed the will of the Conjoint Actor, on the morontia mortal bestowal the will of the Eternal Son; and on the Urantia material bestowal he lived the will of the Universal Father, even as a mortal of flesh and blood.

The completion of these seven bestowals resulted in the liberation of Michael's supreme sovereignty and also in the creation of the possibility for the sovereignty of the Supreme in Nebadon. On none of Michael's bestowals did he reveal God the Supreme, but the sum total of all seven bestowals is a new Nebadon revelation of the Supreme Being.

In the experience of descending from God to man, Michael was concomitantly experiencing the ascent from partiality of manifestability to supremacy of finite action and finality of the liberation of his potential for absonite function. Michael, a Creator Son, is a time-space creator, but Michael, a sevenfold Master Son, is a member of one of the divine corps constituting the Trinity Ultimate.

In passing through the experience of revealing the Seven Master Spirit wills of the Trinity, the Creator Son has passed through the experience of revealing the will of the Supreme. In functioning as a revelator of the will of Supremacy, Michael, together with all other Master Sons, has identified himself eternally with the Supreme. In this universe age he reveals the Supreme and participates in the actualization of the sovereignty of Supremacy. But in the next universe age we believe he will be collaborating with the Supreme Being in the first experiential Trinity for and in the universes of outer space.

Urantia is the sentimental shrine of all Nebadon, the chief of ten million inhabited worlds, the mortal home of Christ Michael, sovereign of all Nebadon, a Melchizedek minister to the realms, a system savior, an Adamic redeemer, a seraphic fellow, an associate of ascending spirits, a morontia progressor, a Son of Man in the likeness of mortal flesh, and the Planetary Prince of Urantia. And your record tells the truth when it says that this same Jesus has promised sometime to return to the world of his terminal bestowal, the World of the Cross.

[This paper, depicting the seven bestowals of Christ Michael, is the sixty-third of a series of presentations, sponsored by numerous personalities, narrating the history of Urantia down to the time of Michael's appearance on earth in the likeness of mortal flesh. These papers were authorized by a Nebadon commission of twelve acting under the direction of Mantutia Melchizedek. We indited these narratives and put them in the English language, by a technique authorized by our superiors, in the year A.D. 1935 of Urantia time.]

PART IV

THE LIFE AND TEACHINGS OF JESUS

This group of papers was sponsored by a commission of twelve Urantia midwayers acting under the supervision of a Melchizedek revelatory director. The basis of this narrative was supplied by a secondary midwayer who was onetime assigned to the superhuman watchcare of the Apostle Andrew.

PART IV

The Life and Teachings of Jesus

PAPER 120

THE BESTOWAL OF MICHAEL ON URANTIA

ASSIGNED by Gabriel to supervise the restatement of the life of Michael when on Urantia and in the likeness of mortal flesh, I, the Melchizedek director of the revelatory commission intrusted with this task, am authorized to present this narrative of certain events which immediately preceded the Creator Son's arrival on Urantia to embark upon the terminal phase of his universe bestowal experience. To live such identical lives as he imposes upon the intelligent beings of his own creation, thus to bestow himself in the likeness of his various orders of created beings, is a part of the price which every Creator Son must pay for the full and supreme sovereignty of his self-made universe of things and beings.

Before the events I am about to delineate, Michael of Nebadon had bestowed himself six times after the similitude of six differing orders of his diverse creation of intelligent beings. Then he prepared to descend upon Urantia in the likeness of mortal flesh, the lowest order of his intelligent will creatures, and, as such a human of the material realm, to execute the final act in the drama of the acquirement of universe sovereignty in accordance with the mandates of the divine Paradise Rulers of the universe of universes.

In the course of each of these preceding bestowals Michael not only acquired the finite experience of one group of his created beings, but he also acquired an essential experience in Paradise co-operation which would, in and of itself, further contribute to constituting him the sovereign of his self-made universe. At any moment throughout all past local universe time, Michael could have asserted personal sovereignty as a Creator Son and as a Creator Son could have ruled his universe after the manner of his own choosing. In such an event, Immanuel and the associated Paradise Sons would have taken leave of the universe. But Michael did not wish to rule Nebadon merely in his own isolated right, as a Creator Son. He desired to ascend through actual experience in co-operative subordination to the Paradise Trinity to that high place in universe status where he would become qualified to rule his universe and administer its affairs with that perfection of insight and wisdom of execution which will sometime be characteristic of the exalted rule of the Supreme Being. He aspired not to perfection of rule as a Creator Son but to supremacy of administration as the embodiment of the universe wisdom and the divine experience of the Supreme Being.

Michael, therefore, had a double purpose in the making of these seven bestowals upon the various orders of his universe creatures: First, he was completing the required experience in creature understanding which is demanded of all Creator Sons before they assume complete sovereignty. At any time a Creator Son may rule his universe in his own right, but he can rule as the supreme representative of the Paradise Trinity only after passing through the seven universe-creature bestowals. Second, he was aspiring to the privilege of representing the maximum authority of the Paradise Trinity which can be exercised in the direct and personal administration of a local universe. Accordingly, did Michael, during the experience of each of his universe bestowals, successfully and acceptably voluntarily subordinate himself to the variously constituted wills of the diverse associations of the persons of the Paradise Trinity. That is, on the first bestowal he was subject to the combined will of the Father, Son, and Spirit; on the second bestowal to the will of the Father and the Son; on the third bestowal to the will of the Father and the Spirit; on the fourth bestowal to the will of the Son and the Spirit; on the fifth bestowal to the will of the Infinite Spirit; on the sixth bestowal to the will of the Eternal Son; and during the seventh and final bestowal, on Urantia, to the will of the Universal Father.

Michael, therefore, combines in his personal sovereignty the divine will of the sevenfold phases of the universal Creators with the understanding experience of his local universe creatures. Thus has his administration become representative of the greatest possible power and authority although divested of all arbitrary assumptions. His power is unlimited since it is derived from experienced association with the Paradise Deities; his authority is unquestioned inasmuch as it was acquired through actual experience in the likeness of universe creatures; his sovereignty is supreme since it embodies at one and the same time the sevenfold viewpoint of Paradise Deity with the creature viewpoint of time and space.

Having determined the time of his final bestowal and having selected the planet whereon this extraordinary event would take place, Michael held the usual prebestowal conference with Gabriel and then presented himself before his elder brother and Paradise counselor, Immanuel. All powers of universe administration which had not previously been conferred upon Gabriel, Michael now assigned to the custody of Immanuel. And just before Michael's departure for the Urantia incarnation, Immanuel, in accepting the custody of the universe during the time of the Urantia bestowal, proceeded to impart the bestowal counsel which would serve as the incarnation guide for Michael when he would presently grow up on Urantia as a mortal of the realm.

In this connection it should be borne in mind that Michael had elected to execute this bestowal in the likeness of mortal flesh, subject to the will of the Paradise Father. The Creator Son required instructions from no one in order to effect this incarnation for the sole purpose of achieving universe sovereignty, but he had embarked upon a program of the revelation of the Supreme which involved co-operative functioning with the diverse wills of the Paradise Deities. Thus his sovereignty, when finally and personally acquired, would actually be all-inclusive of the sevenfold will of Deity as it culminates in the Supreme. He had, therefore, six times previously been instructed by the personal representatives of the various Paradise Deities and associations thereof; and now he was instructed by the Union of Days, ambassador of the Paradise Trinity to the local universe of Nebadon, acting on behalf of the Universal Father.

There were immediate advantages and tremendous compensations resultant from the willingness of this mighty Creator Son once more voluntarily to subordinate himself to the will of the Paradise Deities, this time to that of the Universal Father. By this decision to effect such associative subordination, Michael would experience in this incarnation, not only the nature of mortal man, but also the will of the Paradise Father of all. And further, he could enter upon this unique bestowal with the complete assurance, not only that Immanuel would exercise the full authority of the Paradise Father in the administration of his universe during his absence on the Urantia bestowal, but also with the comforting knowledge that the Ancients of Days of the superuniverse had decreed the safety of his realm throughout the entire bestowal period.

And this was the setting of the momentous occasion when Immanuel presented the seventh bestowal commission. And from this prebestowal charge of Immanuel to the universe ruler who subsequently became Jesus of Nazareth (Christ Michael) on Urantia, I am permitted to present the following excerpts:

1. THE SEVENTH BESTOWAL COMMISSION

"My Creator brother, I am about to witness your seventh and final universe bestowal. Most faithfully and perfectly have you executed the six previous commissions, and I entertain no thought but that you will be equally triumphant on this, your terminal sovereignty bestowal. Heretofore you have appeared on your bestowal spheres as a fully developed being of the order of your choosing. Now you are about to appear upon Urantia, the disordered and disturbed planet of your choice, not as a fully developed mortal, but as a helpless babe. This, my comrade, will be a new and untried experience for you. You are about to pay the full price of bestowal and to experience the complete enlightenment of the incarnation of a Creator in the likeness of a creature.

"Throughout each of your former bestowals you have voluntarily chosen to subject yourself to the will of the three Paradise Deities and their divine interassociations. Of the seven phases of the will of the Supreme you have in your previous bestowals been subject to all but the personal will of your Paradise Father. Now that you have elected to be wholly subject to your Father's will throughout your seventh bestowal, I, as the personal representative of our Father, assume the unqualified jurisdiction of your universe for the time of your incarnation.

"In entering upon the Urantia bestowal, you have voluntarily divested yourself of all extraplanetary support and special assistance such as might be rendered by any creature of your own creation. As your created sons of Nebadon are wholly dependent upon you for safe conduct throughout their universe careers, so now must you become wholly and unreservedly dependent upon your Paradise Father for safe conduct throughout the unrevealed vicissitudes of your ensuing mortal career. And when you shall have finished this bestowal experience, you will know in very truth the full meaning and the rich significance of that faith-trust which you so unvaryingly require all your creatures to master as a part of their intimate relationship with you as their local universe Creator and Father.

"Throughout your Urantia bestowal you need be concerned with but one thing, the unbroken communion between you and your Paradise Father; and it will be by the perfection of such a relationship that the world of your bestowal, even all the universe of your creation, will behold a new and more understandable revelation of your Father and my Father, the Universal Father of all. Your concern, therefore, has only to do with your personal life on Urantia. I will be fully and efficiently responsible for the security and unbroken administration of your universe from the moment of your voluntary relinquishment of authority until you return to us as Universe Sovereign, confirmed by Paradise, and receive back from my hands, not the vicegerent authority which you now surrender to me, but, instead, the supreme power over, and jurisdiction of, your universe.

"And that you may know with assurance that I am empowered to do all that I am now promising (knowing full well that I am the assurance of all Paradise for the faithful performance of my word), I announce to you that there has just been communicated to me a mandate of the Ancients of Days on Uversa which will prevent all spiritual jeopardy in Nebadon throughout the period of your voluntary bestowal. From the moment you surrender consciousness, upon the beginning of the mortal incarnation, until you return to us as supreme and unconditional sovereign of this universe of your own creation and organization, nothing of serious import can happen in all Nebadon. In this interim of your incarnation, I hold the orders of the Ancients of Days which unqualifiedly mandate the instantaneous and automatic extinction of any being guilty of rebellion or presuming to instigate insurrection in the universe of Nebadon while you are absent on this bestowal. My brother, in view of the authority of Paradise inherent in my presence and augmented by the judicial mandate of Uversa, your universe and all its loyal creatures will be secure during your bestowal. You may proceed upon your mission with but a single thought—the enhanced revelation of our Father to the intelligent beings of your universe.

"As in each of your previous bestowals, I would remind you that I am recipient of your universe jurisdiction as brother-trustee. I exercise all authority and wield all power in your name. I function as would our Paradise Father and in accordance with your explicit request that I thus act in your stead. And such being the fact, all this delegated authority is yours again to exercise at any moment you may see fit to requisition its return. Your bestowal is, throughout, wholly voluntary. As a mortal incarnate in the realm you are without celestial endowments, but all your relinquished power may be had at any time you may choose to reinvest yourself with universe authority. If you should choose to reinstate yourself in power and authority, remember, it will be wholly for *personal* reasons since I am the living and supreme pledge whose presence and promise guarantee the safe administration of your universe in accordance with your Father's will. Rebellion, such as has three times occurred in Nebadon, cannot occur during your absence from Salvington on this bestowal. For the period of the Urantia bestowal the Ancients of Days have decreed that rebellion in Nebadon shall be invested with the automatic seed of its own annihilation.

"As long as you are absent on this final and extraordinary bestowal, I pledge (with Gabriel's co-operation) the faithful administration of your universe; and as I commission you to undertake this ministry of divine revelation and to undergo this experience of perfected human understanding, I act in behalf of my Father and your Father and offer you the following counsel, which should guide you in the living of your earth life as you become progressively self-conscious regarding the divine mission of your continued sojourn in the flesh:

2. THE BESTOWAL LIMITATIONS

"1. In accordance with the usages and in conformity with the technique of Sonarington—in compliance with the mandates of the Eternal Son of Paradise—I have provided in every way for your immediate entrance upon this mortal bestowal in harmony with the plans formulated by you and placed in my keeping by Gabriel. You will grow up on Urantia as a child of the realm, complete your human education—all the while subject to the will of your Paradise Father—live your life on Urantia as you have determined, terminate your planetary sojourn, and prepare for ascension to your Father to receive from him the supreme sovereignty of your universe.

"2. Apart from your earth mission and your universe revelation, but incidental to both, I counsel that you assume, after you are sufficiently self-conscious of your divine identity, the additional task of technically terminating the Lucifer rebellion in the system of Satania, and that you do all this as the *Son of Man;* thus, as a mortal creature of the realm, in weakness made powerful by faith-submission to the will of your Father, I suggest that you graciously achieve all you have repeatedly declined arbitrarily to accomplish by power and might when you were so endowed at the time of the inception of this sinful and unjustified rebellion. I would regard it as a fitting climax of your mortal bestowal if you should return to us as the Son of Man, Planetary Prince of Urantia, as well as the Son of God, supreme sovereign of your universe. As a mortal man, the lowest type of intelligent creature in Nebadon, meet and adjudicate the blasphemous pretensions of Caligastia and Lucifer and, in your assumed humble estate, forever end the shameful misrepresentations of these fallen children of light. Having steadfastly declined to discredit these rebels through the exercise of your creator prerogatives, now it would be fitting that you should, in the likeness of the lowest creatures of your creation, wrest dominion from the hands of these fallen Sons; and so would your whole local universe in all fairness clearly and forever recognize the justice of your doing in the role of mortal flesh those things which mercy admonished you not to do by the power of arbitrary authority. And having thus by your bestowal established the possibility of the sovereignty of the Supreme in Nebadon, you will in effect have brought to a close the unadjudicated affairs of all preceding insurrections, notwithstanding the greater or lesser time lag involved in the realization of this achievement. By this act the pending dissensions of your universe will be in substance liquidated. And with the subsequent endowment of supreme sovereignty over your universe, similar challenges to your authority can never recur in any part of your great personal creation.

"3. When you have succeeded in terminating the Urantia secession, as you undoubtedly will, I counsel you to accept from Gabriel the conference of the title of 'Planetary Prince of Urantia' as the eternal recognition by your universe of your final bestowal experience; and that you further do any and all things, consistent with the purport of your bestowal, to atone for the sorrow and confusion brought upon Urantia by the Caligastia betrayal and the subsequent Adamic default.

"4. In accordance with your request, Gabriel and all concerned will co-operate with you in the expressed desire to end your Urantia bestowal with the pronouncement of a dispensational judgment of the realm, accompanied by the termination of an age, the resurrection of the sleeping mortal survivors, and the establishment of the dispensation of the bestowed Spirit of Truth.

"5. As concerns the planet of your bestowal and the immediate generation of men living thereon at the time of your mortal sojourn, I counsel you to function largely in the role of a teacher. Give attention, first, to the liberation and inspiration of man's spiritual nature. Next, illuminate the darkened human intellect, heal the souls of men, and emancipate their minds from age-old fears. And then, in accordance with your mortal wisdom, minister to the physical well-being and material comfort of your brothers in the flesh. Live the ideal religious life for the inspiration and edification of all your universe.

"6. On the planet of your bestowal, set rebellion-segregated man spiritually free. On Urantia, make a further contribution to the sovereignty of the Supreme, thus extending the establishment of this sovereignty throughout the broad domains of your personal creation. In this, your material bestowal in the likeness of the flesh, you are about to experience the final enlightenment of a time-space Creator, the dual experience of working within the nature of man with the will of your Paradise Father. In your temporal life the will of the finite creature and the will of the infinite Creator are to become as one, even as they are also uniting in the evolving Deity of the Supreme Being. Pour out upon the planet of your bestowal the Spirit of Truth and thus make all normal mortals on that isolated sphere immediately and fully accessible to the ministry of the segregated presence of our Paradise Father, the Thought Adjusters of the realms.

"7. In all that you may perform on the world of your bestowal, bear constantly in mind that you are living a life for the instruction and edification of all your universe. You are *bestowing* this life of mortal incarnation upon Urantia, but you are to *live* such a life for the spiritual inspiration of every human and superhuman intelligence that has lived, now exists, or may yet live on every inhabited world which has formed, now forms, or may yet form a part of the vast galaxy of your administrative domain. Your earth life in the likeness of mortal flesh shall not be so lived as to constitute an *example* for the mortals of Urantia in the days of your earthly sojourn nor for any subsequent generation of human beings on Urantia or on any other world. Rather shall your life in the flesh on Urantia be the *inspiration* for all lives upon all Nebadon worlds throughout all generations in the ages to come.

"8. Your great mission to be realized and experienced in the mortal incarnation is embraced in your decision to live a life wholeheartedly motivated to do the will of your Paradise Father, thus to *reveal God,* your Father, in the flesh and especially to the creatures of the flesh. At the same time you will also *interpret,* with a new enhancement, our Father, to the supermortal beings of all Nebadon. Equally with this ministry of new revelation and augmented interpretation of the Paradise Father to the human and the superhuman type of mind, you will also so function as to make a new revelation of man to God. Exhibit in your one short life in the flesh, as it has never before been seen in all Nebadon, the transcendent possibilities attainable by a God-knowing human during the short career of mortal existence, and make a new and illuminating *interpretation* of man and the vicissitudes of his planetary life to all the superhuman intelligences of all Nebadon, and for all time. You are to go down to Urantia in the likeness of mortal flesh, and living as a man in your day and generation, you will so function as to show your entire universe the ideal of perfected technique in the supreme engagement of the affairs of your vast creation: The achievement of God seeking man and finding him and the phenomenon of man seeking God and finding him; and doing all of this to mutual satisfaction and doing it during one short lifetime in the flesh.

"9. I caution you ever to bear in mind that, while in fact you are to become an ordinary human of the realm, in potential you will remain a Creator Son of the Paradise Father. Throughout this incarnation, although you will live and act as a Son of Man, the creative attributes of your personal divinity will follow you from Salvington to Urantia. It will ever be within your power-of-will to terminate the incarnation at any moment subsequent to the arrival of your Thought Adjuster. Prior to the arrival and reception of the Adjuster I will vouch for your personality integrity. But subsequent to the arrival of your Adjuster and concomitant with your progressive recognition of the nature and import of your bestowal mission, you should refrain from the formulation of any superhuman will-to-attainment, achievement, or power in view of the fact that your creator prerogatives will remain associated with your mortal personality because of the inseparability of these attributes from your personal presence. But no superhuman repercussions will attend your earthly career apart from the will of the Paradise Father unless you should, by an act of conscious and deliberate will, make an undivided decision which would terminate in whole-personality choice.

3. FURTHER COUNSEL AND ADVICE

"And now, my brother, in taking leave of you as you prepare to depart for Urantia and after counseling you regarding the general conduct of your bestowal, allow me to present certain advices that have been arrived at in consultation with Gabriel, and which concern minor phases of your mortal life. We further suggest:

"1. That, in the pursuit of the ideal of your mortal earth life, you also give some attention to the realization and exemplification of some things practical and immediately helpful to your fellow men.

"2. As concerns family relationships, give precedence to the accepted customs of family life as you find them established in the day and generation of your bestowal. Live your family and community life in accordance with the practices of the people among whom you have elected to appear.

"3. In your relations to the social order we advise that you confine your efforts largely to spiritual regeneration and intellectual emancipation. Avoid all entanglements with the economic structure and the political commitments of your day. More especially devote yourself to living the ideal religious life on Urantia.

"4. Under no circumstances and not even in the least detail, should you interfere with the normal and orderly progressive evolution of the Urantia races. But this prohibition must not be interpreted as limiting your efforts to leave behind you on Urantia an enduring and improved system of *positive religious ethics.*

As a dispensational Son you are granted certain privileges pertaining to the advancement of the *spiritual* and *religious* status of the world peoples.

"5. As you may see fit, you are to identify yourself with existing religious and spiritual movements as they may be found on Urantia but in every possible manner seek to avoid the formal establishment of an organized cult, a crystallized religion, or a segregated ethical grouping of mortal beings. Your life and teachings are to become the common heritage of all religions and all peoples.

"6. To the end that you may not unnecessarily contribute to the creation of subsequent stereotyped systems of Urantia religious beliefs or other types of nonprogressive religious loyalties, we advise you still further: Leave no writings behind you on the planet. Refrain from all writing upon permanent materials; enjoin your associates to make no images or other likenesses of yourself in the flesh. See that nothing potentially idolatrous is left on the planet at the time of your departure.

"7. While you will live the normal and average social life of the planet, being a normal individual of the male sex, you will probably not enter the marriage relation, which relation would be wholly honorable and consistent with your bestowal; but I must remind you that one of the incarnation mandates of Sonarington forbids the leaving of human offspring behind on any planet by a bestowal Son of Paradise origin.

"8. In all other details of your oncoming bestowal we would commit you to the leading of the indwelling Adjuster, the teaching of the ever-present divine spirit of human guidance, and the reason-judgment of your expanding human mind of hereditary endowment. Such an association of creature and Creator attributes will enable you to live for us the perfect life of man on the planetary spheres, not necessarily perfect as regarded by any one man in any one generation on any one world (much less on Urantia) but wholly and supremely replete as evaluated on the more highly perfected and perfecting worlds of your far-flung universe.

"And now, may your Father and my Father, who has ever sustained us in all past performances, guide and sustain you and be with you from the moment you leave us and achieve the surrender of your consciousness of personality, throughout your gradual return to recognition of your divine identity incarnate in human form, and then on through the whole of your bestowal experience on Urantia until your deliverance from the flesh and your ascension to our Father's right hand of sovereignty. When I shall again see you on Salvington, we shall welcome your return to us as the supreme and unconditional sovereign of this universe of your own making, serving, and completed understanding.

"In your stead I now reign. I assume jurisdiction of all Nebadon as acting sovereign during the interim of your seventh and mortal bestowal on Urantia. And to you, Gabriel, I commit the safekeeping of the Son of Man about-to-be until he shall presently and in power and glory be returned to me as the Son of Man and the Son of God. And, Gabriel, I am your sovereign until Michael thus returns."

***

Then, immediately, in the presence of all Salvington assembled, Michael removed himself from our midst, and we saw him no more in his accustomed place until his return as the supreme and personal ruler of the universe, subsequent to the completion of his bestowal career on Urantia.

4. THE INCARNATION—MAKING TWO ONE

And so certain unworthy children of Michael, who had accused their Creator-father of selfishly seeking rulership and indulged the insinuation that the Creator Son was arbitrarily and autocratically upheld in power by virtue of the unreasoning loyalty of a deluded universe of subservient creatures, were to be silenced forever and left confounded and disillusioned by the life of self-forgetful service which the Son of God now entered upon as the Son of Man—all the while subject to "the will of the Paradise Father."

But make no mistake; Christ Michael, while truly a dual-origin being, was not a double personality. He was not God in association *with* man but, rather, God *incarnate* in man. And he was always just that combined being. The only progressive factor in such a nonunderstandable relationship was the progressive self-conscious realization and recognition (by the human mind) of this fact of being God and man.

Christ Michael did not progressively become God. God did not, at some vital moment in the earth life of Jesus, become man. Jesus was God *and* man—always and even forevermore. And this God and this man were, and now are, *one,* even as the Paradise Trinity of three beings is in reality *one* Deity.

Never lose sight of the fact that the supreme spiritual purpose of the Michael bestowal was to enhance the *revelation of God.*

Urantia mortals have varying concepts of the miraculous, but to us who live as citizens of the local universe there are few miracles, and of these by far the most intriguing are the incarnational bestowals of the Paradise Sons. The appearance in and on your world, by apparently natural processes, of a divine Son, we regard as a miracle—the operation of universal laws beyond our understanding. Jesus of Nazareth was a miraculous person.

In and through all this extraordinary experience, God the Father chose to manifest himself as he always does—*in the usual way*—in the normal, natural, and dependable way of divine acting.

PAPER 121

THE TIMES OF MICHAEL'S BESTOWAL

ACTING under the supervision of a commission of twelve members of the United Brotherhood of Urantia Midwayers, conjointly sponsored by the presiding head of our order and the Melchizedek of record, I am the secondary midwayer of onetime attachment to the Apostle Andrew, and I am authorized to place on record the narrative of the life transactions of Jesus of Nazareth as they were observed by my order of earth creatures, and as they were subsequently partially recorded by the human subject of my temporal guardianship. Knowing how his Master so scrupulously avoided leaving written records behind him, Andrew steadfastly refused to multiply copies of his written narrative. A similar attitude on the part of the other apostles of Jesus greatly delayed the writing of the Gospels.

1. THE OCCIDENT OF THE FIRST CENTURY AFTER CHRIST

Jesus did not come to this world during an age of spiritual decadence; at the time of his birth Urantia was experiencing such a revival of spiritual thinking and religious living as it had not known in all its previous post-Adamic history nor has experienced in any era since. When Michael incarnated on Urantia, the world presented the most favorable condition for the Creator Son's bestowal that had ever previously prevailed or has since obtained. In the centuries just prior to these times Greek culture and the Greek language had spread over Occident and near Orient, and the Jews, being a Levantine race, in nature part Occidental and part Oriental, were eminently fitted to utilize such cultural and linguistic settings for the effective spread of a new religion to both East and West. These most favorable circumstances were further enhanced by the tolerant political rule of the Mediterranean world by the Romans.

This entire combination of world influences is well illustrated by the activities of Paul, who, being in religious culture a Hebrew of the Hebrews, proclaimed the gospel of a Jewish Messiah in the Greek tongue, while he himself was a Roman citizen.

Nothing like the civilization of the times of Jesus has been seen in the Occident before or since those days. European civilization was unified and co-ordinated under an extraordinary threefold influence:

1. The Roman political and social systems.
2. The Grecian language and culture—and philosophy to a certain extent.
3. The rapidly spreading influence of Jewish religious and moral teachings.

When Jesus was born, the entire Mediterranean world was a unified empire. Good roads, for the first time in the world's history, interconnected many major centers. The seas were cleared of pirates, and a great era of trade and travel was rapidly advancing. Europe did not again enjoy another such period of travel and trade until the nineteenth century after Christ.

Notwithstanding the internal peace and superficial prosperity of the Greco-Roman world, a majority of the inhabitants of the empire languished in squalor and poverty. The small upper class was rich; a miserable and impoverished lower class embraced the rank and file of humanity. There was no happy and prosperous middle class in those days; it had just begun to make its appearance in Roman society.

The first struggles between the expanding Roman and Parthian states had been concluded in the then recent past, leaving Syria in the hands of the Romans. In the times of Jesus, Palestine and Syria were enjoying a period of prosperity, relative peace, and extensive commercial intercourse with the lands to both the East and the West.

2. THE JEWISH PEOPLE

The Jews were a part of the older Semitic race, which also included the Babylonians, the Phoenicians, and the more recent enemies of Rome, the Carthaginians. During the fore part of the first century after Christ, the Jews were the most influential group of the Semitic peoples, and they happened to occupy a peculiarly strategic geographic position in the world as it was at that time ruled and organized for trade.

Many of the great highways joining the nations of antiquity passed through Palestine, which thus became the meeting place, or crossroads, of three continents. The travel, trade, and armies of Babylonia, Assyria, Egypt, Syria, Greece, Parthia, and Rome successively swept over Palestine. From time immemorial, many caravan routes from the Orient passed through some part of this region to the few good seaports of the eastern end of the Mediterranean, whence ships carried their cargoes to all the maritime Occident. And more than half of this caravan traffic passed through or near the little town of Nazareth in Galilee.

Although Palestine was the home of Jewish religious culture and the birthplace of Christianity, the Jews were abroad in the world, dwelling in many nations and trading in every province of the Roman and Parthian states.

Greece provided a language and a culture, Rome built the roads and unified an empire, but the dispersion of the Jews, with their more than two hundred synagogues and well-organized religious communities scattered hither and yon throughout the Roman world, provided the cultural centers in which the new gospel of the kingdom of heaven found initial reception, and from which it subsequently spread to the uttermost parts of the world.

Each Jewish synagogue tolerated a fringe of gentile believers, "devout" or "God-fearing" men, and it was among this fringe of proselytes that Paul made the bulk of his early converts to Christianity. Even the temple at Jerusalem possessed its ornate court of the gentiles. There was very close connection between the culture, commerce, and worship of Jerusalem and Antioch. In Antioch Paul's disciples were first called "Christians."

The centralization of the Jewish temple worship at Jerusalem constituted alike the secret of the survival of their monotheism and the promise of the nurture and sending forth to the world of a new and enlarged concept of that one

God of all nations and Father of all mortals. The temple service at Jerusalem represented the survival of a religious cultural concept in the face of the downfall of a succession of gentile national overlords and racial persecutors.

The Jewish people of this time, although under Roman suzerainty, enjoyed a considerable degree of self-government and, remembering the then only recent heroic exploits of deliverance executed by Judas Maccabee and his immediate successors, were vibrant with the expectation of the immediate appearance of a still greater deliverer, the long-expected Messiah.

The secret of the survival of Palestine, the kingdom of the Jews, as a semi-independent state was wrapped up in the foreign policy of the Roman government, which desired to maintain control of the Palestinian highway of travel between Syria and Egypt as well as the western terminals of the caravan routes between the Orient and the Occident. Rome did not wish any power to arise in the Levant which might curb her future expansion in these regions. The policy of intrigue which had for its object the pitting of Seleucid Syria and Ptolemaic Egypt against each other necessitated fostering Palestine as a separate and independent state. Roman policy, the degeneration of Egypt, and the progressive weakening of the Seleucids before the rising power of Parthia, explain why it was that for several generations a small and unpowerful group of Jews was able to maintain its independence against both Seleucidae to the north and Ptolemies to the south. This fortuitous liberty and independence of the political rule of surrounding and more powerful peoples the Jews attributed to the fact that they were the "chosen people," to the direct interposition of Yahweh. Such an attitude of racial superiority made it all the harder for them to endure Roman suzerainty when it finally fell upon their land. But even in that sad hour the Jews refused to learn that their world mission was spiritual, not political.

The Jews were unusually apprehensive and suspicious during the times of Jesus because they were then ruled by an outsider, Herod the Idumean, who had seized the overlordship of Judea by cleverly ingratiating himself with the Roman rulers. And though Herod professed loyalty to the Hebrew ceremonial observances, he proceeded to build temples for many strange gods.

The friendly relations of Herod with the Roman rulers made the world safe for Jewish travel and thus opened the way for increased Jewish penetration even of distant portions of the Roman Empire and of foreign treaty nations with the new gospel of the kingdom of heaven. Herod's reign also contributed much toward the further blending of Hebrew and Hellenistic philosophies.

Herod built the harbor of Caesarea, which further aided in making Palestine the crossroads of the civilized world. He died in 4 B.C., and his son Herod Antipas governed Galilee and Perea during Jesus' youth and ministry to A.D. 39. Antipas, like his father, was a great builder. He rebuilt many of the cities of Galilee, including the important trade center of Sepphoris.

The Galileans were not regarded with full favor by the Jerusalem religious leaders and rabbinical teachers. Galilee was more gentile than Jewish when Jesus was born.

3. AMONG THE GENTILES

Although the social and economic condition of the Roman state was not of the highest order, the widespread domestic peace and prosperity was propitious for the bestowal of Michael. In the first century after Christ the society of the Mediterranean world consisted of five well-defined strata:

1. *The aristocracy.* The upper classes with money and official power, the privileged and ruling groups.

2. *The business groups.* The merchant princes and the bankers, the traders—the big importers and exporters—the international merchants.

3. *The small middle class.* Although this group was indeed small, it was very influential and provided the moral backbone of the early Christian church, which encouraged these groups to continue in their various crafts and trades. Among the Jews many of the Pharisees belonged to this class of tradesmen.

4. *The free proletariat.* This group had little or no social standing. Though proud of their freedom, they were placed at great disadvantage because they were forced to compete with slave labor. The upper classes regarded them disdainfully, allowing that they were useless except for "breeding purposes."

5. *The slaves.* Half the population of the Roman state were slaves; many were superior individuals and quickly made their way up among the free proletariat and even among the tradesmen. The majority were either mediocre or very inferior.

Slavery, even of superior peoples, was a feature of Roman military conquest. The power of the master over his slave was unqualified. The early Christian church was largely composed of the lower classes and these slaves.

Superior slaves often received wages and by saving their earnings were able to purchase their freedom. Many such emancipated slaves rose to high positions in state, church, and the business world. And it was just such possibilities that made the early Christian church so tolerant of this modified form of slavery.

There was no widespread social problem in the Roman Empire in the first century after Christ. The major portion of the populace regarded themselves as belonging in that group into which they chanced to be born. There was always the open door through which talented and able individuals could ascend from the lower to the higher strata of Roman society, but the people were generally content with their social rank. They were not class conscious, neither did they look upon these class distinctions as being unjust or wrong. Christianity was in no sense an economic movement having for its purpose the amelioration of the miseries of the depressed classes.

Although woman enjoyed more freedom throughout the Roman Empire than in her restricted position in Palestine, the family devotion and natural affection of the Jews far transcended that of the gentile world.

4. GENTILE PHILOSOPHY

The gentiles were, from a moral standpoint, somewhat inferior to the Jews, but there was present in the hearts of the nobler gentiles abundant soil of natural goodness and potential human affection in which it was possible for the seed of Christianity to sprout and bring forth an abundant harvest of moral character and spiritual achievement. The gentile world was then dominated by four great philosophies, all more or less derived from the earlier Platonism of the Greeks. These schools of philosophy were:

1. *The Epicurean.* This school of thought was dedicated to the pursuit of happiness. The better Epicureans were not given to sensual excesses. At least

this doctrine helped to deliver the Romans from a more deadly form of fatalism; it taught that men could do something to improve their terrestrial status. It did effectually combat ignorant superstition.

2. *The Stoic.* Stoicism was the superior philosophy of the better classes. The Stoics believed that a controlling Reason-Fate dominated all nature. They taught that the soul of man was divine; that it was imprisoned in the evil body of physical nature. Man's soul achieved liberty by living in harmony with nature, with God; thus virtue came to be its own reward. Stoicism ascended to a sublime morality, ideals never since transcended by any purely human system of philosophy. While the Stoics professed to be the "offspring of God," they failed to know him and therefore failed to find him. Stoicism remained a philosophy; it never became a religion. Its followers sought to attune their minds to the harmony of the Universal Mind, but they failed to envisage themselves as the children of a loving Father. Paul leaned heavily toward Stoicism when he wrote, "I have learned in whatsoever state I am, therewith to be content."

3. *The Cynic.* Although the Cynics traced their philosophy to Diogenes of Athens, they derived much of their doctrine from the remnants of the teachings of Machiventa Melchizedek. Cynicism had formerly been more of a religion than a philosophy. At least the Cynics made their religio-philosophy democratic. In the fields and in the market places they continually preached their doctrine that "man could save himself if he would." They preached simplicity and virtue and urged men to meet death fearlessly. These wandering Cynic preachers did much to prepare the spiritually hungry populace for the later Christian missionaries. Their plan of popular preaching was much after the pattern, and in accordance with the style, of Paul's Epistles.

4. *The Skeptic.* Skepticism asserted that knowledge was fallacious, and that conviction and assurance were impossible. It was a purely negative attitude and never became widespread.

These philosophies were semireligious; they were often invigorating, ethical, and ennobling but were usually above the common people. With the possible exception of Cynicism, they were philosophies for the strong and the wise, not religions of salvation for even the poor and the weak.

5. THE GENTILE RELIGIONS

Throughout preceding ages religion had chiefly been an affair of the tribe or nation; it had not often been a matter of concern to the individual. Gods were tribal or national, not personal. Such religious systems afforded little satisfaction for the individual spiritual longings of the average person.

In the times of Jesus the religions of the Occident included:

1. *The pagan cults.* These were a combination of Hellenic and Latin mythology, patriotism, and tradition.

2. *Emperor worship.* This deification of man as the symbol of the state was very seriously resented by the Jews and the early Christians and led directly to the bitter persecutions of both churches by the Roman government.

3. *Astrology.* This pseudo science of Babylon developed into a religion throughout the Greco-Roman Empire. Even in the twentieth century man has not been fully delivered from this superstitious belief.

4. *The mystery religions.* Upon such a spiritually hungry world a flood of mystery cults had broken, new and strange religions from the Levant, which had enamored the common people and had promised them *individual* salvation. These religions rapidly became the accepted belief of the lower classes of the Greco-Roman world. And they did much to prepare the way for the rapid spread of the vastly superior Christian teachings, which presented a majestic concept of Deity, associated with an intriguing theology for the intelligent and a profound proffer of salvation for all, including the ignorant but spiritually hungry average man of those days.

The mystery religions spelled the end of national beliefs and resulted in the birth of the numerous personal cults. The mysteries were many but were all characterized by:

1. Some mythical legend, a mystery—whence their name. As a rule this mystery pertained to the story of some god's life and death and return to life, as illustrated by the teachings of Mithraism, which, for a time, were contemporary with, and a competitor of, Paul's rising cult of Christianity.

2. The mysteries were nonnational and interracial. They were personal and fraternal, giving rise to religious brotherhoods and numerous sectarian societies.

3. They were, in their services, characterized by elaborate ceremonies of initiation and impressive sacraments of worship. Their secret rites and rituals were sometimes gruesome and revolting.

4. But no matter what the nature of their ceremonies or the degree of their excesses, these mysteries invariably promised their devotees *salvation,* "deliverance from evil, survival after death, and enduring life in blissful realms beyond this world of sorrow and slavery."

But do not make the mistake of confusing the teachings of Jesus with the mysteries. The popularity of the mysteries reveals man's quest for survival, thus portraying a real hunger and thirst for personal religion and individual righteousness. Although the mysteries failed adequately to satisfy this longing, they did prepare the way for the subsequent appearance of Jesus, who truly brought to this world the bread of life and the water thereof.

Paul, in an effort to utilize the widespread adherence to the better types of the mystery religions, made certain adaptations of the teachings of Jesus so as to render them more acceptable to a larger number of prospective converts. But even Paul's compromise of Jesus' teachings (Christianity) was superior to the best in the mysteries in that:

1. Paul taught a moral redemption, an ethical salvation. Christianity pointed to a new life and proclaimed a new ideal. Paul forsook magic rites and ceremonial enchantments.

2. Christianity presented a religion which grappled with final solutions of the human problem, for it not only offered salvation from sorrow and even from death, but it also promised deliverance from sin followed by the endowment of a righteous character of eternal survival qualities.

3. The mysteries were built upon myths. Christianity, as Paul preached it, was founded upon a historic fact: the bestowal of Michael, the Son of God, upon mankind.

Morality among the gentiles was not necessarily related to either philosophy or religion. Outside of Palestine it not always occurred to people that a priest of religion was supposed to lead a moral life. Jewish religion and subsequently the teachings of Jesus and later the evolving Christianity of Paul were the first European religions to lay one hand upon morals and the other upon ethics, insisting that religionists pay some attention to both.

Into such a generation of men, dominated by such incomplete systems of philosophy and perplexed by such complex cults of religion, Jesus was born in Palestine. And to this same generation he subsequently gave his gospel of personal religion—sonship with God.

6. THE HEBREW RELIGION

By the close of the first century before Christ the religious thought of Jerusalem had been tremendously influenced and somewhat modified by Greek cultural teachings and even by Greek philosophy. In the long contest between the views of the Eastern and Western schools of Hebrew thought, Jerusalem and the rest of the Occident and the Levant in general adopted the Western Jewish or modified Hellenistic viewpoint.

In the days of Jesus three languages prevailed in Palestine: The common people spoke some dialect of Aramaic; the priests and rabbis spoke Hebrew; the educated classes and the better strata of Jews in general spoke Greek. The early translation of the Hebrew scriptures into Greek at Alexandria was responsible in no small measure for the subsequent predominance of the Greek wing of Jewish culture and theology. And the writings of the Christian teachers were soon to appear in the same language. The renaissance of Judaism dates from the Greek translation of the Hebrew scriptures. This was a vital influence which later determined the drift of Paul's Christian cult toward the West instead of toward the East.

Though the Hellenized Jewish beliefs were very little influenced by the teachings of the Epicureans, they were very materially affected by the philosophy of Plato and the self-abnegation doctrines of the Stoics. The great inroad of Stoicism is exemplified by the Fourth Book of the Maccabees; the penetration of both Platonic philosophy and Stoic doctrines is exhibited in the Wisdom of Solomon. The Hellenized Jews brought to the Hebrew scriptures such an allegorical interpretation that they found no difficulty in conforming Hebrew theology with their revered Aristotelian philosophy. But this all led to disastrous confusion until these problems were taken in hand by Philo of Alexandria, who proceeded to harmonize and systemize Greek philosophy and Hebrew theology into a compact and fairly consistent system of religious belief and practice. And it was this later teaching of combined Greek philosophy and Hebrew theology that prevailed in Palestine when Jesus lived and taught, and which Paul utilized as the foundation on which to build his more advanced and enlightening cult of Christianity.

Philo was a great teacher; not since Moses had there lived a man who exerted such a profound influence on the ethical and religious thought of the Occidental world. In the matter of the combination of the better elements in contemporaneous systems of ethical and religious teachings, there have been seven outstanding human teachers: Sethard, Moses, Zoroaster, Lao-tse, Buddha, Philo, and Paul.

Many, but not all, of Philo's inconsistencies resulting from an effort to combine Greek mystical philosophy and Roman Stoic doctrines with the legalistic theology of the Hebrews, Paul recognized and wisely eliminated from his pre-Christian basic theology. Philo led the way for Paul more fully to restore the concept of the Paradise Trinity, which had long been dormant in Jewish theology. In only one matter did Paul fail to keep pace with Philo or to transcend the teachings of this wealthy and educated Jew of Alexandria, and that was the doctrine of the atonement; Philo taught deliverance from the doctrine of forgiveness only by the shedding of blood. He also possibly glimpsed the reality and presence of the Thought Adjusters more clearly than did Paul. But Paul's theory of original sin, the doctrines of hereditary guilt and innate evil and redemption therefrom, was partially Mithraic in origin, having little in common with Hebrew theology, Philo's philosophy, or Jesus' teachings. Some phases of Paul's teachings regarding original sin and the atonement were original with himself.

The Gospel of John, the last of the narratives of Jesus' earth life, was addressed to the Western peoples and presents its story much in the light of the viewpoint of the later Alexandrian Christians, who were also disciples of the teachings of Philo.

At about the time of Christ a strange reversion of feeling toward the Jews occurred in Alexandria, and from this former Jewish stronghold there went forth a virulent wave of persecution, extending even to Rome, from which many thousands were banished. But such a campaign of misrepresentation was short-lived; very soon the imperial government fully restored the curtailed liberties of the Jews throughout the empire.

Throughout the whole wide world, no matter where the Jews found themselves dispersed by commerce or oppression, all with one accord kept their hearts centered on the holy temple at Jerusalem. Jewish theology did survive as it was interpreted and practiced at Jerusalem, notwithstanding that it was several times saved from oblivion by the timely intervention of certain Babylonian teachers.

As many as two and one-half million of these dispersed Jews used to come to Jerusalem for the celebration of their national religious festivals. And no matter what the theologic or philosophic differences of the Eastern (Babylonian) and the Western (Hellenic) Jews, they were all agreed on Jerusalem as the center of their worship and in ever looking forward to the coming of the Messiah.

7. JEWS AND GENTILES

By the times of Jesus the Jews had arrived at a settled concept of their origin, history, and destiny. They had built up a rigid wall of separation between themselves and the gentile world; they looked upon all gentile ways with utter contempt. They worshiped the letter of the law and indulged a form of self-righteousness based upon the false pride of descent. They had formed preconceived notions regarding the promised Messiah, and most of these expectations envisaged a Messiah who would come as a part of their national and racial history. To the Hebrews of those days Jewish theology was irrevocably settled, forever fixed.

The teachings and practices of Jesus regarding tolerance and kindness ran counter to the long-standing attitude of the Jews toward other peoples whom they considered heathen. For generations the Jews had nourished an attitude toward the outside world which made it impossible for them to accept the Master's teachings about the spiritual brotherhood of man. They were unwilling to share Yahweh on equal terms with the gentiles and were likewise unwilling to accept as the Son of God one who taught such new and strange doctrines.

The scribes, the Pharisees, and the priesthood held the Jews in a terrible bondage of ritualism and legalism, a bondage far more real than that of the Roman political rule. The Jews of Jesus' time were not only held in subjugation to the *law* but were equally bound by the slavish demands of the *traditions,* which involved and invaded every domain of personal and social life. These minute regulations of conduct pursued and dominated every loyal Jew, and it is not strange that they promptly rejected one of their number who presumed to ignore their sacred traditions, and who dared to flout their long-honored regulations of social conduct. They could hardly regard with favor the teachings of one who did not hesitate to clash with dogmas which they regarded as having been ordained by Father Abraham himself. Moses had given them their law and they would not compromise.

By the time of the first century after Christ the spoken interpretation of the law by the recognized teachers, the scribes, had become a higher authority than the written law itself. And all this made it easier for certain religious leaders of the Jews to array the people against the acceptance of a new gospel.

These circumstances rendered it impossible for the Jews to fulfill their divine destiny as messengers of the new gospel of religious freedom and spiritual liberty. They could not break the fetters of tradition. Jeremiah had told of the "law to be written in men's hearts," Ezekiel had spoken of a "new spirit to live in man's soul," and the Psalmist had prayed that God would "create a clean heart within and renew a right spirit." But when the Jewish religion of good works and slavery to law fell victim to the stagnation of traditionalistic inertia, the motion of religious evolution passed westward to the European peoples.

And so a different people were called upon to carry an advancing theology to the world, a system of teaching embodying the philosophy of the Greeks, the law of the Romans, the morality of the Hebrews, and the gospel of personality sanctity and spiritual liberty formulated by Paul and based on the teachings of Jesus.

Paul's cult of Christianity exhibited its morality as a Jewish birthmark. The Jews viewed history as the providence of God—Yahweh at work. The Greeks brought to the new teaching clearer concepts of the eternal life. Paul's doctrines were influenced in theology and philosophy not only by Jesus' teachings but also by Plato and Philo. In ethics he was inspired not only by Christ but also by the Stoics.

The gospel of Jesus, as it was embodied in Paul's cult of Antioch Christianity, became blended with the following teachings:

1. The philosophic reasoning of the Greek proselytes to Judaism, including some of their concepts of the eternal life.

2. The appealing teachings of the prevailing mystery cults, especially the Mithraic doctrines of redemption, atonement, and salvation by the sacrifice made by some god.

3. The sturdy morality of the established Jewish religion.

The Mediterranean Roman Empire, the Parthian kingdom, and the adjacent peoples of Jesus' time all held crude and primitive ideas regarding the geography of the world, astronomy, health, and disease; and naturally they were amazed by the new and startling pronouncements of the carpenter of Nazareth. The ideas of spirit possession, good and bad, applied not merely to human beings, but every rock and tree was viewed by many as being spirit possessed. This was an enchanted age, and everybody believed in miracles as commonplace occurrences.

8. PREVIOUS WRITTEN RECORDS

As far as possible, consistent with our mandate, we have endeavored to utilize and to some extent co-ordinate the existing records having to do with the life of Jesus on Urantia. Although we have enjoyed access to the lost record of the Apostle Andrew and have benefited from the collaboration of a vast host of celestial beings who were on earth during the times of Michael's bestowal (notably his now Personalized Adjuster), it has been our purpose also to make use of the so-called Gospels of Matthew, Mark, Luke, and John.

These New Testament records had their origin in the following circumstances:

1. *The Gospel by Mark.* John Mark wrote the earliest (excepting the notes of Andrew), briefest, and most simple record of Jesus' life. He presented the Master as a minister, as man among men. Although Mark was a lad lingering about many of the scenes which he depicts, his record is in reality the Gospel according to Simon Peter. He was early associated with Peter; later with Paul. Mark wrote this record at the instigation of Peter and on the earnest petition of the church at Rome. Knowing how consistently the Master refused to write out his teachings when on earth and in the flesh, Mark, like the apostles and other leading disciples, was hesitant to put them in writing. But Peter felt the church at Rome required the assistance of such a written narrative, and Mark consented to undertake its preparation. He made many notes before Peter died in A.D. 67, and in accordance with the outline approved by Peter and for the church at Rome, he began his writing soon after Peter's death. The Gospel was completed near the end of A.D. 68. Mark wrote entirely from his own memory and Peter's memory. The record has since been considerably changed, numerous passages having been taken out and some later matter added at the end to replace the latter one fifth of the original Gospel, which was lost from the first manuscript before it was ever copied. This record by Mark, in conjunction with Andrew's and Matthew's notes, was the written basis of all subsequent Gospel narratives which sought to portray the life and teachings of Jesus.

2. *The Gospel of Matthew.* The so-called Gospel according to Matthew is the record of the Master's life which was written for the edification of Jewish Christians. The author of this record constantly seeks to show in Jesus' life that much which he did was that "it might be fulfilled which was spoken by the prophet." Matthew's Gospel portrays Jesus as a son of David, picturing him as showing great respect for the law and the prophets.

The Apostle Matthew did not write this Gospel. It was written by Isador, one of his disciples, who had as a help in his work not only Matthew's personal remembrance of these events but also a certain record which the latter had made of the sayings of Jesus directly after the crucifixion. This record by Matthew was written in Aramaic; Isador wrote in Greek. There was no intent to deceive in accrediting the production to Matthew. It was the custom in those days for pupils thus to honor their teachers.

Matthew's original record was edited and added to in A.D. 40 just before he left Jerusalem to engage in evangelistic preaching. It was a private record, the last copy having been destroyed in the burning of a Syrian monastery in A.D. 416.

Isador escaped from Jerusalem in A.D. 70 after the investment of the city by the armies of Titus, taking with him to Pella a copy of Matthew's notes. In the year 71, while living at Pella, Isador wrote the Gospel according to Matthew. He also had with him the first four fifths of Mark's narrative.

3. *The Gospel by Luke.* Luke, the physician of Antioch in Pisidia, was a gentile convert of Paul, and he wrote quite a different story of the Master's life. He began to follow Paul and learn of the life and teachings of Jesus in A.D. 47. Luke preserves much of the "grace of the Lord Jesus Christ" in his record as he gathered up these facts from Paul and others. Luke presents the Master as "the friend of publicans and sinners." He did not formulate his many notes into the Gospel until after Paul's death. Luke wrote in the year 82 in Achaia. He planned three books dealing with the history of Christ and Christianity but died in A.D. 90 just before he finished the second of these works, the "Acts of the Apostles."

As material for the compilation of his Gospel, Luke first depended upon the story of Jesus' life as Paul had related it to him. Luke's Gospel is, therefore, in some ways the Gospel according to Paul. But Luke had other sources of information. He not only interviewed scores of eyewitnesses to the numerous episodes of Jesus' life which he records, but he also had with him a copy of Mark's Gospel, that is, the first four fifths, Isador's narrative, and a brief record made in the year A.D. 78 at Antioch by a believer named Cedes. Luke also had a mutilated and much-edited copy of some notes purported to have been made by the Apostle Andrew.

4. *The Gospel of John.* The Gospel according to John relates much of Jesus' work in Judea and around Jerusalem which is not contained in the other records. This is the so-called Gospel according to John the son of Zebedee, and though John did not write it, he did inspire it. Since its first writing it has several times been edited to make it appear to have been written by John himself. When this record was made, John had the other Gospels, and he saw that much had been omitted; accordingly, in the year A.D. 101 he encouraged his associate, Nathan, a Greek Jew from Caesarea, to begin the writing. John supplied his material from memory and by reference to the three records already in existence. He had no written records of his own. The Epistle known as "First John" was written by John himself as a covering letter for the work which Nathan executed under his direction.

All these writers presented honest pictures of Jesus as they saw, remembered, or had learned of him, and as their concepts of these distant events were affected by their subsequent espousal of Paul's theology of Christianity. And these records, imperfect as they are, have been sufficient to change the course of the history of Urantia for almost two thousand years.

[*Acknowledgment:* In carrying out my commission to restate the teachings and retell the doings of Jesus of Nazareth, I have drawn freely upon all sources of record and planetary information. My ruling motive has been to prepare a record which will not only be enlightening to the generation of men now living, but which may also be helpful to all future generations. From the vast store of information made available to me, I have chosen that which is best suited to the accomplishment of this purpose. As far as possible I have derived my information from purely human sources. Only when such sources failed, have I resorted to those records which are superhuman. When ideas and concepts of Jesus' life and teachings have been acceptably expressed by a human mind, I invariably gave preference to such apparently human thought patterns. Although I have sought to adjust the verbal expression the better to conform to our concept of the real meaning and the true import of the Master's life and teachings, as far as possible, I have adhered to the actual human concept and thought pattern in all my narratives. I well know that those concepts which have had origin in the human mind will prove more acceptable and helpful to all other human minds. When unable to find the necessary concepts in the human records or in human expressions, I have next resorted to the memory resources of my own order of earth creatures, the midwayers. And when that secondary source of information proved inadequate, I have unhesitatingly resorted to the superplanetary sources of information.

The memoranda which I have collected, and from which I have prepared this narrative of the life and teachings of Jesus—aside from the memory of the record of the Apostle Andrew—embrace thought gems and superior concepts of Jesus' teachings assembled from more than two thousand human beings who have lived on earth from the days of Jesus down to the time of the inditing of these revelations, more correctly restatements. The revelatory permission has been utilized only when the human record and human concepts failed to supply an adequate thought pattern. My revelatory commission forbade me to resort to extrahuman sources of either information or expression until such a time as I could testify that I had failed in my efforts to find the required conceptual expression in purely human sources.

While I, with the collaboration of my eleven associate fellow midwayers and under the supervision of the Melchizedek of record, have portrayed this narrative in accordance with my concept of its effective arrangement and in response to my choice of immediate expression, nevertheless, the majority of the ideas and even some of the effective expressions which I have thus utilized had their origin in the minds of the men of many races who have lived on earth during the intervening generations, right on down to those who are still alive at the time of this undertaking. In many ways I have served more as a collector and editor than as an original narrator. I have unhesitatingly appropriated those ideas and concepts, preferably human, which would enable me to create the most effective portraiture of Jesus' life, and which would qualify me to restate his matchless teachings in the most strikingly helpful and universally uplifting phraseology. In behalf of the Brotherhood of the United Midwayers of Urantia, I most gratefully acknowledge our indebtedness to all sources of record and concept which have been hereinafter utilized in the further elaboration of our restatement of Jesus' life on earth.]

PAPER 122
BIRTH AND INFANCY OF JESUS

IT WILL hardly be possible fully to explain the many reasons which led to the selection of Palestine as the land for Michael's bestowal, and especially as to just why the family of Joseph and Mary should have been chosen as the immediate setting for the appearance of this Son of God on Urantia.

After a study of the special report on the status of segregated worlds prepared by the Melchizedeks, in counsel with Gabriel, Michael finally chose Urantia as the planet whereon to enact his final bestowal. Subsequent to this decision Gabriel made a personal visit to Urantia, and, as a result of his study of human groups and his survey of the spiritual, intellectual, racial, and geographic features of the world and its peoples, he decided that the Hebrews possessed those relative advantages which warranted their selection as the bestowal race. Upon Michael's approval of this decision, Gabriel appointed and dispatched to Urantia the Family Commission of Twelve—selected from among the higher orders of universe personalities—which was intrusted with the task of making an investigation of Jewish family life. When this commission ended its labors, Gabriel was present on Urantia and received the report nominating three prospective unions as being, in the opinion of the commission, equally favorable as bestowal families for Michael's projected incarnation.

From the three couples nominated, Gabriel made the personal choice of Joseph and Mary, subsequently making his personal appearance to Mary, at which time he imparted to her the glad tidings that she had been selected to become the earth mother of the bestowal child.

1. JOSEPH AND MARY

Joseph, the human father of Jesus (Joshua ben Joseph), was a Hebrew of the Hebrews, albeit he carried many non-Jewish racial strains which had been added to his ancestral tree from time to time by the female lines of his progenitors. The ancestry of the father of Jesus went back to the days of Abraham and through this venerable patriarch to the earlier lines of inheritance leading to the Sumerians and Nodites and, through the southern tribes of the ancient blue man, to Andon and Fonta. David and Solomon were not in the direct line of Joseph's ancestry, neither did Joseph's lineage go directly back to Adam. Joseph's immediate ancestors were mechanics—builders, carpenters, masons, and smiths. Joseph himself was a carpenter and later a contractor. His family belonged to a long and illustrious line of the nobility of the common people, accentuated ever and anon by the appearance of unusual individuals who had distinguished themselves in connection with the evolution of religion on Urantia.

Mary, the earth mother of Jesus, was a descendant of a long line of unique ancestors embracing many of the most remarkable women in the racial history of Urantia. Although Mary was an average woman of her day and generation, possessing a fairly normal temperament, she reckoned among her ancestors such well-known women as Annon, Tamar, Ruth, Bathsheba, Ansie, Cloa, Eve, Enta, and Ratta. No Jewish woman of that day had a more illustrious lineage of common progenitors or one extending back to more auspicious beginnings. Mary's ancestry, like Joseph's, was characterized by the predominance of strong but average individuals, relieved now and then by numerous outstanding personalities in the march of civilization and the progressive evolution of religion. Racially considered, it is hardly proper to regard Mary as a Jewess. In culture and belief she was a Jew, but in hereditary endowment she was more a composite of Syrian, Hittite, Phoenician, Greek, and Egyptian stocks, her racial inheritance being more general than that of Joseph.

Of all couples living in Palestine at about the time of Michael's projected bestowal, Joseph and Mary possessed the most ideal combination of widespread racial connections and superior average of personality endowments. It was the plan of Michael to appear on earth as an *average* man, that the common people might understand him and receive him; wherefore Gabriel selected just such persons as Joseph and Mary to become the bestowal parents.

2. GABRIEL APPEARS TO ELIZABETH

Jesus' lifework on Urantia was really begun by John the Baptist. Zacharias, John's father, belonged to the Jewish priesthood, while his mother, Elizabeth, was a member of the more prosperous branch of the same large family group to which Mary the mother of Jesus also belonged. Zacharias and Elizabeth, though they had been married many years, were childless.

It was late in the month of June, 8 B.C., about three months after the marriage of Joseph and Mary, that Gabriel appeared to Elizabeth at noontide one day, just as he later made his presence known to Mary. Said Gabriel:

"While your husband, Zacharias, stands before the altar in Jerusalem, and while the assembled people pray for the coming of a deliverer, I, Gabriel, have come to announce that you will shortly bear a son who shall be the forerunner of this divine teacher, and you shall call your son John. He will grow up dedicated to the Lord your God, and when he has come to full years, he will gladden your heart because he will turn many souls to God, and he will also proclaim the coming of the soul-healer of your people and the spirit-liberator of all mankind. Your kinswoman Mary shall be the mother of this child of promise, and I will also appear to her."

This vision greatly frightened Elizabeth. After Gabriel's departure she turned this experience over in her mind, long pondering the sayings of the majestic visitor, but did not speak of the revelation to anyone save her husband until her subsequent visit with Mary in early February of the following year.

For five months, however, Elizabeth withheld her secret even from her husband. Upon her disclosure of the story of Gabriel's visit, Zacharias was very skeptical and for weeks doubted the entire experience, only consenting halfheartedly to believe in Gabriel's visit to his wife when he could no longer question that she was expectant with child. Zacharias was very much perplexed regarding the prospective motherhood of Elizabeth, but he did not doubt the integrity of his wife, notwithstanding his own advanced age. It was not until about six weeks before John's birth that Zacharias, as the result of an impressive dream, became fully convinced that Elizabeth was to become the mother of a son of destiny, one who was to prepare the way for the coming of the Messiah.

Gabriel appeared to Mary about the middle of November, 8 B.C., while she was at work in her Nazareth home. Later on, after Mary knew without doubt that she was to become a mother, she persuaded Joseph to let her journey to the City of Judah, four miles west of Jerusalem, in the hills, to visit Elizabeth. Gabriel had informed each of these mothers-to-be of his appearance to the other. Naturally they were anxious to get together, compare experiences, and talk over the probable futures of their sons. Mary remained with her distant cousin for three weeks. Elizabeth did much to strengthen Mary's faith in the vision of Gabriel, so that she returned home more fully dedicated to the call to mother the child of destiny whom she was so soon to present to the world as a helpless babe, an average and normal infant of the realm.

John was born in the City of Judah, March 25, 7 B.C. Zacharias and Elizabeth rejoiced greatly in the realization that a son had come to them as Gabriel had promised, and when on the eighth day they presented the child for circumcision, they formally christened him John, as they had been directed aforetime. Already had a nephew of Zacharias departed for Nazareth, carrying the message of Elizabeth to Mary proclaiming that a son had been born to her and that his name was to be John.

From his earliest infancy John was judiciously impressed by his parents with the idea that he was to grow up to become a spiritual leader and religious teacher. And the soil of John's heart was ever responsive to the sowing of such suggestive seeds. Even as a child he was found frequently at the temple during the seasons of his father's service, and he was tremendously impressed with the significance of all that he saw.

3. GABRIEL'S ANNOUNCEMENT TO MARY

One evening about sundown, before Joseph had returned home, Gabriel appeared to Mary by the side of a low stone table and, after she had recovered her composure, said: "I come at the bidding of one who is my Master and whom you shall love and nurture. To you, Mary, I bring glad tidings when I announce that the conception within you is ordained by heaven, and that in due time you will become the mother of a son; you shall call him Joshua, and he shall inaugurate the kingdom of heaven on earth and among men. Speak not of this matter save to Joseph and to Elizabeth, your kinswoman, to whom I have also appeared, and who shall presently also bear a son, whose name shall be John, and who will prepare the way for the message of deliverance which your son shall proclaim to men with great power and deep conviction. And doubt not my word, Mary, for this home has been chosen as the mortal habitat of the child of destiny. My benediction rests upon you, the power of the Most Highs will strengthen you, and the Lord of all the earth shall overshadow you."

Mary pondered this visitation secretly in her heart for many weeks until of a certainty she knew she was with child, before she dared to disclose these unusual events to her husband. When Joseph heard all about this, although he had great confidence in Mary, he was much troubled and could not sleep for many nights. At first Joseph had doubts about the Gabriel visitation. Then when he became well-nigh persuaded that Mary had really heard the voice and beheld the form of the divine messenger, he was torn in mind as he pondered how such things could be. How could the offspring of human beings be a child of divine destiny? Never could Joseph reconcile these conflicting ideas until, after several weeks of thought, both he and Mary reached the conclusion that they had been chosen to become the parents of the Messiah, though it had hardly been the Jewish concept that the expected deliverer was to be of divine nature. Upon arriving at this momentous conclusion, Mary hastened to depart for a visit with Elizabeth.

Upon her return, Mary went to visit her parents, Joachim and Hannah. Her two brothers and two sisters, as well as her parents, were always very skeptical about the divine mission of Jesus, though, of course, at this time they knew nothing of the Gabriel visitation. But Mary did confide to her sister Salome that she thought her son was destined to become a great teacher.

Gabriel's announcement to Mary was made the day following the conception of Jesus and was the only event of supernatural occurrence connected with her entire experience of carrying and bearing the child of promise.

4. JOSEPH'S DREAM

Joseph did not become reconciled to the idea that Mary was to become the mother of an extraordinary child until after he had experienced a very impressive dream. In this dream a brilliant celestial messenger appeared to him and, among other things, said: "Joseph, I appear by command of Him who now reigns on high, and I am directed to instruct you concerning the son whom Mary shall bear, and who shall become a great light in the world. In him will be life, and his life shall become the light of mankind. He shall first come to his own people, but they will hardly receive him; but to as many as shall receive him to them will he reveal that they are the children of God." After this experience Joseph never again wholly doubted Mary's story of Gabriel's visit and of the promise that the unborn child was to become a divine messenger to the world.

In all these visitations nothing was said about the house of David. Nothing was ever intimated about Jesus' becoming a "deliverer of the Jews," not even that he was to be the long-expected Messiah. Jesus was not such a Messiah as the Jews had anticipated, but he was the *world's deliverer.* His mission was to all races and peoples, not to any one group.

Joseph was not of the line of King David. Mary had more of the Davidic ancestry than Joseph. True, Joseph did go to the City of David, Bethlehem, to be registered for the Roman census, but that was because, six generations previously, Joseph's paternal ancestor of that generation, being an orphan, was adopted by one Zadoc, who was a direct descendant of David; hence was Joseph also accounted as of the "house of David."

Most of the so-called Messianic prophecies of the Old Testament were made to apply to Jesus long after his life had been lived on earth. For centuries the Hebrew prophets had proclaimed the coming of a deliverer, and these promises had been construed by successive generations as referring to a new Jewish ruler who would sit upon the throne of David and, by the reputed miraculous methods of Moses, proceed to establish the Jews in Palestine as a powerful nation, free from all foreign domination. Again, many figurative passages found throughout the Hebrew scriptures were subsequently misapplied to the life mission of Jesus. Many Old Testament sayings were so distorted as to appear to fit some episode of the Master's earth life. Jesus himself onetime publicly denied any connection with the royal house of David. Even the passage, "a maiden shall bear a son," was made to read, "a virgin shall bear a son." This was also true of the many genealogies of both Joseph and Mary which were constructed subsequent to Michael's career on earth. Many of these lineages contain much of the Master's ancestry, but on the whole they are not genuine and may not be depended upon as factual. The early followers of Jesus all too often succumbed to the temptation to make all the olden prophetic utterances appear to find fulfillment in the life of their Lord and Master.

5. JESUS' EARTH PARENTS

Joseph was a mild-mannered man, extremely conscientious, and in every way faithful to the religious conventions and practices of his people. He talked little but thought much. The sorry plight of the Jewish people caused Joseph much sadness. As a youth, among his eight brothers and sisters, he had been more cheerful, but in the earlier years of married life (during Jesus' childhood) he was subject to periods of mild spiritual discouragement. These temperamental manifestations were greatly improved just before his untimely death and after the economic condition of his family had been enhanced by his advancement from the rank of carpenter to the role of a prosperous contractor.

Mary's temperament was quite opposite to that of her husband. She was usually cheerful, was very rarely downcast, and possessed an ever-sunny disposition. Mary indulged in free and frequent expression of her emotional feelings and was never observed to be sorrowful until after the sudden death of Joseph. And she had hardly recovered from this shock when she had thrust upon her the anxieties and questionings aroused by the extraordinary career of her eldest son, which was so rapidly unfolding before her astonished gaze. But throughout all this unusual experience Mary was composed, courageous, and fairly wise in her relationship with her strange and little-understood first-born son and his surviving brothers and sisters.

Jesus derived much of his unusual gentleness and marvelous sympathetic understanding of human nature from his father; he inherited his gift as a great teacher and his tremendous capacity for righteous indignation from his mother. In emotional reactions to his adult-life environment, Jesus was at one time like his father, meditative and worshipful, sometimes characterized by apparent sadness; but more often he drove forward in the manner of his mother's optimistic and determined disposition. All in all, Mary's temperament tended to dominate the career of the divine Son as he grew up and swung into the momentous strides of his adult life. In some particulars Jesus was a blending of his parents' traits; in other respects he exhibited the traits of one in contrast with those of the other.

From Joseph Jesus secured his strict training in the usages of the Jewish ceremonials and his unusual acquaintance with the Hebrew scriptures; from Mary he derived a broader viewpoint of religious life and a more liberal concept of personal spiritual freedom.

The families of both Joseph and Mary were well educated for their time. Joseph and Mary were educated far above the average for their day and station in life. He was a thinker; she was a planner, expert in adaptation and practical in immediate execution. Joseph was a black-eyed brunet; Mary, a brown-eyed well-nigh blond type.

Had Joseph lived, he undoubtedly would have become a firm believer in the divine mission of his eldest son. Mary alternated between believing and doubting, being greatly influenced by the position taken by her other children and by her friends and relatives, but always was she steadied in her final attitude by the memory of Gabriel's appearance to her immediately after the child was conceived.

Mary was an expert weaver and more than averagely skilled in most of the household arts of that day; she was a good housekeeper and a superior home-maker. Both Joseph and Mary were good teachers, and they saw to it that their children were well versed in the learning of that day.

When Joseph was a young man, he was employed by Mary's father in the work of building an addition to his house, and it was when Mary brought Joseph a cup of water, during a noontime meal, that the courtship of the pair who were destined to become the parents of Jesus really began.

Joseph and Mary were married, in accordance with Jewish custom, at Mary's home in the environs of Nazareth when Joseph was twenty-one years old. This marriage concluded a normal courtship of almost two years' duration. Shortly thereafter they moved into their new home in Nazareth, which had been built by Joseph with the assistance of two of his brothers. The house was located near the foot of the near-by elevated land which so charmingly overlooked the surrounding countryside. In this home, especially prepared, these young and expectant parents had thought to welcome the child of promise, little realizing that this momentous event of a universe was to transpire while they would be absent from home in Bethlehem of Judea.

The larger part of Joseph's family became believers in the teachings of Jesus, but very few of Mary's people ever believed in him until after he departed from this world. Joseph leaned more toward the spiritual concept of the expected Messiah, but Mary and her family, especially her father, held to the idea of the Messiah as a temporal deliverer and political ruler. Mary's ancestors had been prominently identified with the Maccabean activities of the then but recent times.

Joseph held vigorously to the Eastern, or Babylonian, views of the Jewish religion; Mary leaned strongly toward the more liberal and broader Western, or Hellenistic, interpretation of the law and the prophets.

6. THE HOME AT NAZARETH

The home of Jesus was not far from the high hill in the northerly part of Nazareth, some distance from the village spring, which was in the eastern section of the town. Jesus' family dwelt in the outskirts of the city, and this made it all the easier for him subsequently to enjoy frequent strolls in the country and to make trips up to the top of this near-by highland, the highest of all the hills of southern Galilee save the Mount Tabor range to the east and the hill of Nain, which was about the same height. Their home was located a little to the south and east of the southern promontory of this hill and about midway between the base of this elevation and the road leading out of Nazareth toward Cana. Aside from climbing the hill, Jesus' favorite stroll was to follow a narrow trail winding about the base of the hill in a northeasterly direction to a point where it joined the road to Sepphoris.

The home of Joseph and Mary was a one-room stone structure with a flat roof and an adjoining building for housing the animals. The furniture consisted of a low stone table, earthenware and stone dishes and pots, a loom, a lampstand, several small stools, and mats for sleeping on the stone floor. In the back yard, near the animal annex, was the shelter which covered the oven and the mill for grinding grain. It required two persons to operate this type of mill, one to grind and another to feed the grain. As a small boy Jesus often fed grain to this mill while his mother turned the grinder.

In later years, as the family grew in size, they would all squat about the enlarged stone table to enjoy their meals, helping themselves from a common dish, or pot, of food. During the winter, at the evening meal the table would be lighted by a small, flat clay lamp, which was filled with olive oil. After the birth of Martha, Joseph built an addition to this house, a large room, which was used as a carpenter shop during the day and as a sleeping room at night.

7. THE TRIP TO BETHLEHEM

In the month of March, 8 B.C. (the month Joseph and Mary were married), Caesar Augustus decreed that all inhabitants of the Roman Empire should be numbered, that a census should be made which could be used for effecting better taxation. The Jews had always been greatly prejudiced against any attempt to "number the people," and this, in connection with the serious domestic difficulties of Herod, King of Judea, had conspired to cause the postponement of the taking of this census in the Jewish kingdom for one year. Throughout all the Roman Empire this census was registered in the year 8 B.C., except in the Palestinian kingdom of Herod, where it was taken in 7 B.C., one year later.

It was not necessary that Mary should go to Bethlehem for enrollment—Joseph was authorized to register for his family—but Mary, being an adventurous and aggressive person, insisted on accompanying him. She feared being left alone lest the child be born while Joseph was away, and again, Bethlehem being not far from the City of Judah, Mary foresaw a possible pleasurable visit with her kinswoman Elizabeth.

Joseph virtually forbade Mary to accompany him, but it was of no avail; when the food was packed for the trip of three or four days, she prepared double rations and made ready for the journey. But before they actually set forth, Joseph was reconciled to Mary's going along, and they cheerfully departed from Nazareth at the break of day.

Joseph and Mary were poor, and since they had only one beast of burden, Mary, being large with child, rode on the animal with the provisions while Joseph walked, leading the beast. The building and furnishing of a home had been a great drain on Joseph since he had also to contribute to the support of his parents, as his father had been recently disabled. And so this Jewish couple went forth from their humble home early on the morning of August 18, 7 B.C., on their journey to Bethlehem.

Their first day of travel carried them around the foothills of Mount Gilboa, where they camped for the night by the river Jordan and engaged in many speculations as to what sort of a son would be born to them, Joseph adhering to the concept of a spiritual teacher and Mary holding to the idea of a Jewish Messiah, a deliverer of the Hebrew nation.

Bright and early the morning of August 19, Joseph and Mary were again on their way. They partook of their noontide meal at the foot of Mount Sartaba, overlooking the Jordan valley, and journeyed on, making Jericho for the night, where they stopped at an inn on the highway in the outskirts of the city. Following the evening meal and after much discussion concerning the oppressiveness of Roman rule, Herod, the census enrollment, and the comparative influence of Jerusalem and Alexandria as centers of Jewish learning and culture, the Nazareth travelers retired for the night's rest. Early in the morning of August 20 they resumed their journey, reaching Jerusalem before noon, visiting the temple, and going on to their destination, arriving at Bethlehem in midafternoon.

The inn was overcrowded, and Joseph accordingly sought lodgings with distant relatives, but every room in Bethlehem was filled to overflowing. On returning to the courtyard of the inn, he was informed that the caravan stables, hewn out of the side of the rock and situated just below the inn, had been cleared of animals and cleaned up for the reception of lodgers. Leaving the donkey in the courtyard, Joseph shouldered their bags of clothing and provisions and with Mary descended the stone steps to their lodgings below. They found themselves located in what had been a grain storage room to the front of the stalls and mangers. Tent curtains had been hung, and they counted themselves fortunate to have such comfortable quarters.

Joseph had thought to go out at once and enroll, but Mary was weary; she was considerably distressed and besought him to remain by her side, which he did.

8. THE BIRTH OF JESUS

All that night Mary was restless so that neither of them slept much. By the break of day the pangs of childbirth were well in evidence, and at noon, August 21, 7 B.C., with the help and kind ministrations of women fellow travelers, Mary was delivered of a male child. Jesus of Nazareth was born into the world, was wrapped in the clothes which Mary had brought along for such a possible contingency, and laid in a near-by manger.

In just the same manner as all babies before that day and since have come into the world, the promised child was born; and on the eighth day, according to the Jewish practice, he was circumcised and formally named Joshua (Jesus).

The next day after the birth of Jesus, Joseph made his enrollment. Meeting a man they had talked with two nights previously at Jericho, Joseph was taken by him to a well-to-do friend who had a room at the inn, and who said he would gladly exchange quarters with the Nazareth couple. That afternoon they moved up to the inn, where they lived for almost three weeks until they found lodgings in the home of a distant relative of Joseph.

The second day after the birth of Jesus, Mary sent word to Elizabeth that her child had come and received word in return inviting Joseph up to Jerusalem to talk over all their affairs with Zacharias. The following week Joseph went to Jerusalem to confer with Zacharias. Both Zacharias and Elizabeth had become possessed with the sincere conviction that Jesus was indeed to become the Jewish deliverer, the Messiah, and that their son John was to be his chief of aides, his right-hand man of destiny. And since Mary held these same ideas, it was not difficult to prevail upon Joseph to remain in Bethlehem, the City of David, so that Jesus might grow up to become the successor of David on the throne of all Israel. Accordingly, they remained in Bethlehem more than a year, Joseph meantime working some at his carpenter's trade.

At the noontide birth of Jesus the seraphim of Urantia, assembled under their directors, did sing anthems of glory over the Bethlehem manger, but these utterances of praise were not heard by human ears. No shepherds nor any other mortal creatures came to pay homage to the babe of Bethlehem until the day of the arrival of certain priests from Ur, who were sent down from Jerusalem by Zacharias.

These priests from Mesopotamia had been told sometime before by a strange religious teacher of their country that he had had a dream in which he was informed that "the light of life" was about to appear on earth as a babe and among the Jews. And thither went these three teachers looking for this "light of life." After many weeks of futile search in Jerusalem, they were about to return to Ur when Zacharias met them and disclosed his belief that Jesus was the object of their quest and sent them on to Bethlehem, where they found the babe and left their gifts with Mary, his earth mother. The babe was almost three weeks old at the time of their visit.

These wise men saw no star to guide them to Bethlehem. The beautiful legend of the star of Bethlehem originated in this way: Jesus was born August 21 at noon, 7 B.C. On May 29, 7 B.C., there occurred an extraordinary conjunction of Jupiter and Saturn in the constellation of Pisces. And it is a remarkable astronomic fact that similar conjunctions occurred on September 29 and December 5 of the same year. Upon the basis of these extraordinary but wholly natural events the well-meaning zealots of the succeeding generation constructed the appealing legend of the star of Bethlehem and the adoring Magi led thereby to the manger, where they beheld and worshiped the newborn babe. Oriental and near-Oriental minds delight in fairy stories, and they are continually spinning such beautiful myths about the lives of their religious leaders and political heroes. In the absence of printing, when most human knowledge was passed by word of mouth from one generation to another, it was very easy for myths to become traditions and for traditions eventually to become accepted as facts.

9. THE PRESENTATION IN THE TEMPLE

Moses had taught the Jews that every first-born son belonged to the Lord, and that, in lieu of his sacrifice as was the custom among the heathen nations, such a son might live provided his parents would redeem him by the payment of five shekels to any authorized priest. There was also a Mosaic ordinance which directed that a mother, after the passing of a certain period of time, should present herself (or have someone make the proper sacrifice for her) at the temple for purification. It was customary to perform both of these ceremonies at the same time. Accordingly, Joseph and Mary went up to the temple at Jerusalem in person to present Jesus to the priests and effect his redemption and also to make the proper sacrifice to insure Mary's ceremonial purification from the alleged uncleanness of childbirth.

There lingered constantly about the courts of the temple two remarkable characters, Simeon a singer and Anna a poetess. Simeon was a Judean, but Anna was a Galilean. This couple were frequently in each other's company, and both were intimates of the priest Zacharias, who had confided the secret of John and Jesus to them. Both Simeon and Anna longed for the coming of the Messiah, and their confidence in Zacharias led them to believe that Jesus was the expected deliverer of the Jewish people.

Zacharias knew the day Joseph and Mary were expected to appear at the temple with Jesus, and he had prearranged with Simeon and Anna to indicate, by the salute of his upraised hand, which one in the procession of first-born children was Jesus.

For this occasion Anna had written a poem which Simeon proceeded to sing, much to the astonishment of Joseph, Mary, and all who were assembled in the temple courts. And this was their hymn of the redemption of the first-born son:

Blessed be the Lord, the God of Israel,
For he has visited us and wrought redemption for his people;
He has raised up a horn of salvation for all of us
In the house of his servant David.
Even as he spoke by the mouth of his holy prophets—
Salvation from our enemies and from the hand of all who hate us;
To show mercy to our fathers, and remember his holy covenant—
The oath which he swore to Abraham our father,
To grant us that we, being delivered out of the hand of our enemies,
Should serve him without fear,
In holiness and righteousness before him all our days.
Yes, and you, child of promise, shall be called the prophet of the Most
High;
For you shall go before the face of the Lord to establish his kingdom;
To give knowledge of salvation to his people
In the remission of their sins.
Rejoice in the tender mercy of our God because the dayspring from on
high has now visited us
To shine upon those who sit in darkness and the shadow of death;
To guide our feet into ways of peace.
And now let your servant depart in peace, O Lord, according to your word,
For my eyes have seen your salvation,
Which you have prepared before the face of all peoples;
A light for even the unveiling of the gentiles
And the glory of your people Israel.

On the way back to Bethlehem, Joseph and Mary were silent—confused and overawed. Mary was much disturbed by the farewell salutation of Anna, the aged poetess, and Joseph was not in harmony with this premature effort to make Jesus out to be the expected Messiah of the Jewish people.

10. HEROD ACTS

But the watchers for Herod were not inactive. When they reported to him the visit of the priests of Ur to Bethlehem, Herod summoned these Chaldeans to appear before him. He inquired diligently of these wise men about the new "king of the Jews," but they gave him little satisfaction, explaining that the babe had been born of a woman who had come down to Bethlehem with her husband for the census enrollment. Herod, not being satisfied with this answer, sent them forth with a purse and directed that they should find the child so that he too might come and worship him, since they had declared that his kingdom was to be spiritual, not temporal. But when the wise men did not return, Herod grew suspicious. As he turned these things over in his mind, his informers returned and made full report of the recent occurrences in the temple, bringing him a copy of parts of the Simeon song which had been sung at the redemption ceremonies of Jesus. But they had failed to follow Joseph and Mary, and Herod was very angry with them when they could not tell him whither the pair had taken the babe. He then dispatched searchers to locate Joseph and Mary. Knowing Herod pursued the Nazareth family, Zacharias and Elizabeth remained away from Bethlehem. The boy baby was secreted with Joseph's relatives.

Joseph was afraid to seek work, and their small savings were rapidly disappearing. Even at the time of the purification ceremonies at the temple, Joseph deemed himself sufficiently poor to warrant his offering for Mary two young pigeons as Moses had directed for the purification of mothers among the poor.

When, after more than a year of searching, Herod's spies had not located Jesus, and because of the suspicion that the babe was still concealed in Bethlehem, he prepared an order directing that a systematic search be made of every house in Bethlehem, and that all boy babies under two years of age should be killed. In this manner Herod hoped to make sure that this child who was to become "king of the Jews" would be destroyed. And thus perished in one day sixteen boy babies in Bethlehem of Judea. But intrigue and murder, even in his own immediate family, were common occurrences at the court of Herod.

The massacre of these infants took place about the middle of October, 6 B.C., when Jesus was a little over one year of age. But there were believers in the coming Messiah even among Herod's court attachés, and one of these, learning of the order to slaughter the Bethlehem boy babies, communicated with Zacharias, who in turn dispatched a messenger to Joseph; and the night before the massacre Joseph and Mary departed from Bethlehem with the babe for Alexandria in Egypt. In order to avoid attracting attention, they journeyed alone to Egypt with Jesus. They went to Alexandria on funds provided by Zacharias, and there Joseph worked at his trade while Mary and Jesus lodged with well-to-do relatives of Joseph's family. They sojourned in Alexandria two full years, not returning to Bethlehem until after the death of Herod.

PAPER 123

THE EARLY CHILDHOOD OF JESUS

OWING to the uncertainties and anxieties of their sojourn in Bethlehem, Mary did not wean the babe until they had arrived safely in Alexandria, where the family was able to settle down to a normal life. They lived with kinsfolk, and Joseph was well able to support his family as he secured work shortly after their arrival. He was employed as a carpenter for several months and then elevated to the position of foreman of a large group of workmen employed on one of the public buildings then in process of construction. This new experience gave him the idea of becoming a contractor and builder after their return to Nazareth.

All through these early years of Jesus' helpless infancy, Mary maintained one long and constant vigil lest anything befall her child which might jeopardize his welfare or in any way interfere with his future mission on earth; no mother was ever more devoted to her child. In the home where Jesus chanced to be there were two other children about his age, and among the near neighbors there were six others whose ages were sufficiently near his own to make them acceptable playfellows. At first Mary was disposed to keep Jesus close by her side. She feared something might happen to him if he were allowed to play in the garden with the other children, but Joseph, with the assistance of his kinsfolk, was able to convince her that such a course would deprive Jesus of the helpful experience of learning how to adjust himself to children of his own age. And Mary, realizing that such a program of undue sheltering and unusual protection might tend to make him self-conscious and somewhat self-centered, finally gave assent to the plan of permitting the child of promise to grow up just like any other child; and though she was obedient to this decision, she made it her business always to be on watch while the little folks were at play about the house or in the garden. Only an affectionate mother can know the burden that Mary carried in her heart for the safety of her son during these years of his infancy and early childhood.

Throughout the two years of their sojourn at Alexandria, Jesus enjoyed good health and continued to grow normally. Aside from a few friends and relatives no one was told about Jesus' being a "child of promise." One of Joseph's relatives revealed this to a few friends in Memphis, descendants of the distant Ikhnaton, and they, with a small group of Alexandrian believers, assembled at the palatial home of Joseph's relative-benefactor a short time before the return to Palestine to wish the Nazareth family well and to pay their respects to the child. On this occasion the assembled friends presented Jesus with a complete copy of the Greek translation of the Hebrew scriptures. But this copy of the Jewish sacred writings was not placed in Joseph's hands until both he and Mary had finally declined the invitation of their Memphis and Alexandrian friends to remain in Egypt. These believers insisted that the child of destiny would be able to exert a far greater world influence as a resident of Alexandria than of any designated place in Palestine.

These persuasions delayed their departure for Palestine for some time after they received the news of Herod's death.

Joseph and Mary finally took leave of Alexandria on a boat belonging to their friend Ezraeon, bound for Joppa, arriving at that port late in August of the year 4 B.C. They went directly to Bethlehem, where they spent the entire month of September in counsel with their friends and relatives concerning whether they should remain there or return to Nazareth.

Mary had never fully given up the idea that Jesus ought to grow up in Bethlehem, the City of David. Joseph did not really believe that their son was to become a kingly deliverer of Israel. Besides, he knew that he himself was not really a descendant of David; that his being reckoned among the offspring of David was due to the adoption of one of his ancestors into the Davidic line of descent. Mary, of course, thought the City of David the most appropriate place in which the new candidate for David's throne could be reared, but Joseph preferred to take chances with Herod Antipas rather than with his brother Archelaus. He entertained great fears for the child's safety in Bethlehem or in any other city in Judea, and surmised that Archelaus would be more likely to pursue the menacing policies of his father, Herod, than would Antipas in Galilee. And besides all these reasons, Joseph was outspoken in his preference for Galilee as a better place in which to rear and educate the child, but it required three weeks to overcome Mary's objections.

By the first of October Joseph had convinced Mary and all their friends that it was best for them to return to Nazareth. Accordingly, early in October, 4 B.C., they departed from Bethlehem for Nazareth, going by way of Lydda and Scythopolis. They started out early one Sunday morning, Mary and the child riding on their newly acquired beast of burden, while Joseph and five accompanying kinsmen proceeded on foot; Joseph's relatives refused to permit them to make the trip to Nazareth alone. They feared to go to Galilee by Jerusalem and the Jordan valley, and the western routes were not altogether safe for two lone travelers with a child of tender years.

1. BACK IN NAZARETH

On the fourth day of the journey the party reached its destination in safety. They arrived unannounced at the Nazareth home, which had been occupied for more than three years by one of Joseph's married brothers, who was indeed surprised to see them; so quietly had they gone about their business that neither the family of Joseph nor that of Mary knew they had even left Alexandria. The next day Joseph's brother moved his family, and Mary, for the first time since Jesus' birth, settled down with her little family to enjoy life in their own home. In less than a week Joseph secured work as a carpenter, and they were supremely happy.

Jesus was about three years and two months old at the time of their return to Nazareth. He had stood all these travels very well and was in excellent health and full of childish glee and excitement at having premises of his own to run about in and to enjoy. But he greatly missed the association of his Alexandrian playmates.

On the way to Nazareth Joseph had persuaded Mary that it would be unwise to spread the word among their Galilean friends and relatives that Jesus was a child of promise. They agreed to refrain from all mention of these matters to anyone. And they were both very faithful in keeping this promise.

Jesus' entire fourth year was a period of normal physical development and of unusual mental activity. Meantime he had formed a very close attachment for a neighbor boy about his own age named Jacob. Jesus and Jacob were always happy in their play, and they grew up to be great friends and loyal companions.

The next important event in the life of this Nazareth family was the birth of the second child, James, in the early morning hours of April 2, 3 B.C. Jesus was thrilled by the thought of having a baby brother, and he would stand around by the hour just to observe the baby's early activities.

It was midsummer of this same year that Joseph built a small workshop close to the village spring and near the caravan tarrying lot. After this he did very little carpenter work by the day. He had as associates two of his brothers and several other mechanics, whom he sent out to work while he remained at the shop making yokes and plows and doing other woodwork. He also did some work in leather and with rope and canvas. And Jesus, as he grew up, when not at school, spent his time about equally between helping his mother with home duties and watching his father work at the shop, meanwhile listening to the conversation and gossip of the caravan conductors and passengers from the four corners of the earth.

In July of this year, one month before Jesus was four years old, an outbreak of malignant intestinal trouble spread over all Nazareth from contact with the caravan travelers. Mary became so alarmed by the danger of Jesus being exposed to this epidemic of disease that she bundled up both her children and fled to the country home of her brother, several miles south of Nazareth on the Megiddo road near Sarid. They did not return to Nazareth for more than two months; Jesus greatly enjoyed this, his first experience on a farm.

2. THE FIFTH YEAR (2 B.C.)

In something more than a year after the return to Nazareth the boy Jesus arrived at the age of his first personal and wholehearted moral decision; and there came to abide with him a Thought Adjuster, a divine gift of the Paradise Father, which had aforetime served with Machiventa Melchizedek, thus gaining the experience of functioning in connection with the incarnation of a supermortal being living in the likeness of mortal flesh. This event occurred on February 11, 2 B.C. Jesus was no more aware of the coming of the divine Monitor than are the millions upon millions of other children who, before and since that day, have likewise received these Thought Adjusters to indwell their minds and work for the ultimate spiritualization of these minds and the eternal survival of their evolving immortal souls.

On this day in February the direct and personal supervision of the Universe Rulers, as it was related to the integrity of the childlike incarnation of Michael, terminated. From that time on throughout the human unfolding of the incarnation, the guardianship of Jesus was destined to rest in the keeping of this indwelling Adjuster and the associated seraphic guardians, supplemented from time to time by the ministry of midway creatures assigned for the performance of certain definite duties in accordance with the instruction of their planetary superiors.

Jesus was five years old in August of this year, and we will, therefore, refer to this as his fifth (calendar) year of life. In this year, 2 B.C., a little more than one month before his fifth birthday anniversary, Jesus was made very happy by the coming of his sister Miriam, who was born on the night of July 11. During the evening of the following day Jesus had a long talk with his father concerning the manner in which various groups of living things are born into the world as separate individuals. The most valuable part of Jesus' early education was secured from his parents in answer to his thoughtful and searching inquiries. Joseph never failed to do his full duty in taking pains and spending time answering the boy's numerous questions. From the time Jesus was five years old until he was ten, he was one continuous question mark. While Joseph and Mary could not always answer his questions, they never failed fully to discuss his inquiries and in every other possible way to assist him in his efforts to reach a satisfactory solution of the problem which his alert mind had suggested.

Since returning to Nazareth, theirs had been a busy household, and Joseph had been unusually occupied building his new shop and getting his business started again. So fully was he occupied that he had found no time to build a cradle for James, but this was corrected long before Miriam came, so that she had a very comfortable crib in which to nestle while the family admired her. And the child Jesus heartily entered into all these natural and normal home experiences. He greatly enjoyed his little brother and his baby sister and was of great help to Mary in their care.

There were few homes in the gentile world of those days that could give a child a better intellectual, moral, and religious training than the Jewish homes of Galilee. These Jews had a systematic program for rearing and educating their children. They divided a child's life into seven stages:

1. The newborn child, the first to the eighth day.
2. The suckling child.
3. The weaned child.
4. The period of dependence on the mother, lasting up to the end of the fifth year.
5. The beginning independence of the child and, with sons, the father assuming responsibility for their education.
6. The adolescent youths and maidens.
7. The young men and the young women.

It was the custom of the Galilean Jews for the mother to bear the responsibility for a child's training until the fifth birthday, and then, if the child were a boy, to hold the father responsible for the lad's education from that time on. This year, therefore, Jesus entered upon the fifth stage of a Galilean Jewish child's career, and accordingly on August 21, 2 B.C., Mary formally turned him over to Joseph for further instruction.

Though Joseph was now assuming the direct responsibility for Jesus' intellectual and religious education, his mother still interested herself in his home training. She taught him to know and care for the vines and flowers growing about the garden walls which completely surrounded the home plot. She also provided on the roof of the house (the summer bedroom) shallow boxes of sand in which Jesus worked out maps and did much of his early practice at writing Aramaic, Greek, and later on, Hebrew, for in time he learned to read, write, and speak, fluently, all three languages.

Jesus appeared to be a well-nigh perfect child physically and continued to make normal progress mentally and emotionally. He experienced a mild digestive upset, his first minor illness, in the latter part of this, his fifth (calendar) year.

Though Joseph and Mary often talked about the future of their eldest child, had you been there, you would only have observed the growing up of a normal, healthy, carefree, but exceedingly inquisitive child of that time and place.

3. EVENTS OF THE SIXTH YEAR (1 B.C.)

Already, with his mother's help, Jesus had mastered the Galilean dialect of the Aramaic tongue; and now his father began teaching him Greek. Mary spoke little Greek, but Joseph was a fluent speaker of both Aramaic and Greek. The textbook for the study of the Greek language was the copy of the Hebrew scriptures—a complete version of the law and the prophets, including the Psalms—which had been presented to them on leaving Egypt. There were only two complete copies of the Scriptures in Greek in all Nazareth, and the possession of one of them by the carpenter's family made Joseph's home a much-sought place and enabled Jesus, as he grew up, to meet an almost endless procession of earnest students and sincere truth seekers. Before this year ended, Jesus had assumed custody of this priceless manuscript, having been told on his sixth birthday that the sacred book had been presented to him by Alexandrian friends and relatives. And in a very short time he could read it readily.

The first great shock of Jesus' young life occurred when he was not quite six years old. It had seemed to the lad that his father—at least his father and mother together—knew everything. Imagine, therefore, the surprise of this inquiring child, when he asked his father the cause of a mild earthquake which had just occurred, to hear Joseph say, "My son, I really do not know." Thus began that long and disconcerting disillusionment in the course of which Jesus found out that his earthly parents were not all-wise and all-knowing.

Joseph's first thought was to tell Jesus that the earthquake had been caused by God, but a moment's reflection admonished him that such an answer would immediately be provocative of further and still more embarrassing inquiries. Even at an early age it was very difficult to answer Jesus' questions about physical or social phenomena by thoughtlessly telling him that either God or the devil was responsible. In harmony with the prevailing belief of the Jewish people, Jesus was long willing to accept the doctrine of good spirits and evil spirits as the possible explanation of mental and spiritual phenomena, but he very early became doubtful that such unseen influences were responsible for the physical happenings of the natural world.

Before Jesus was six years of age, in the early summer of 1 B.C., Zacharias and Elizabeth and their son John came to visit the Nazareth family. Jesus and John had a happy time during this, their first visit within their memories. Although the visitors could remain only a few days, the parents talked over many things, including the future plans for their sons. While they were thus engaged, the lads played with blocks in the sand on top of the house and in many other ways enjoyed themselves in true boyish fashion.

Having met John, who came from near Jerusalem, Jesus began to evince an unusual interest in the history of Israel and to inquire in great detail as to the meaning of the Sabbath rites, the synagogue sermons, and the recurring feasts of commemoration. His father explained to him the meaning of all these seasons. The first was the midwinter festive illumination, lasting eight days, starting out with one candle the first night and adding one each successive night; this commemorated the dedication of the temple after the restoration of the Mosaic services by Judas Maccabee. Next came the early springtime celebration of Purim, the feast of Esther and Israel's deliverance through her. Then followed the solemn Passover, which the adults celebrated in Jerusalem whenever possible, while at home the children would remember that no leavened bread was to be eaten for the whole week. Later came the feast of the first-fruits, the harvest ingathering; and last, the most solemn of all, the feast of the new year, the day of atonement. While some of these celebrations and observances were difficult for Jesus' young mind to understand, he pondered them seriously and then entered fully into the joy of the feast of tabernacles, the annual vacation season of the whole Jewish people, the time when they camped out in leafy booths and gave themselves up to mirth and pleasure.

During this year Joseph and Mary had trouble with Jesus about his prayers. He insisted on talking to his heavenly Father much as he would talk to Joseph, his earthly father. This departure from the more solemn and reverent modes of communication with Deity was a bit disconcerting to his parents, especially to his mother, but there was no persuading him to change; he would say his prayers just as he had been taught, after which he insisted on having "just a little talk with my Father in heaven."

In June of this year Joseph turned the shop in Nazareth over to his brothers and formally entered upon his work as a builder. Before the year was over, the family income had more than trebled. Never again, until after Joseph's death, did the Nazareth family feel the pinch of poverty. The family grew larger and larger, and they spent much money on extra education and travel, but always Joseph's increasing income kept pace with the growing expenses.

The next few years Joseph did considerable work at Cana, Bethlehem (of Galilee), Magdala, Nain, Sepphoris, Capernaum, and Endor, as well as much building in and near Nazareth. As James grew up to be old enough to help his mother with the housework and care of the younger children, Jesus made frequent trips away from home with his father to these surrounding towns and villages. Jesus was a keen observer and gained much practical knowledge from these trips away from home; he was assiduously storing up knowledge regarding man and the way he lived on earth.

This year Jesus made great progress in adjusting his strong feelings and vigorous impulses to the demands of family co-operation and home discipline. Mary was a loving mother but a fairly strict disciplinarian. In many ways, however, Joseph exerted the greater control over Jesus as it was his practice to sit down with the boy and fully explain the real and underlying reasons for the necessity of disciplinary curtailment of personal desires in deference to the welfare and tranquillity of the entire family. When the situation had been explained to Jesus, he was always intelligently and willingly co-operative with parental wishes and family regulations.

Much of his spare time—when his mother did not require his help about the house—was spent studying the flowers and plants by day and the stars by night. He evinced a troublesome penchant for lying on his back and gazing wonderingly up into the starry heavens long after his usual bedtime in this well-ordered Nazareth household.

4. THE SEVENTH YEAR (A.D. 1)

This was, indeed, an eventful year in Jesus' life. Early in January a great snowstorm occurred in Galilee. Snow fell two feet deep, the heaviest snowfall Jesus saw during his lifetime and one of the deepest at Nazareth in a hundred years.

The play life of Jewish children in the times of Jesus was rather circumscribed; all too often the children played at the more serious things they observed their elders doing. They played much at weddings and funerals, ceremonies which they so frequently saw and which were so spectacular. They danced and sang but had few organized games, such as children of later days so much enjoy.

Jesus, in company with a neighbor boy and later his brother James, delighted to play in the far corner of the family carpenter shop, where they had great fun with the shavings and the blocks of wood. It was always difficult for Jesus to comprehend the harm of certain sorts of play which were forbidden on the Sabbath, but he never failed to conform to his parents' wishes. He had a capacity for humor and play which was afforded little opportunity for expression in the environment of his day and generation, but up to the age of fourteen he was cheerful and lighthearted most of the time.

Mary maintained a dovecote on top of the animal house adjoining the home, and they used the profits from the sale of doves as a special charity fund, which Jesus administered after he deducted the tithe and turned it over to the officer of the synagogue.

The only real accident Jesus had up to this time was a fall down the back-yard stone stairs which led up to the canvas-roofed bedroom. It happened during an unexpected July sandstorm from the east. The hot winds, carrying blasts of fine sand, usually blew during the rainy season, especially in March and April. It was extraordinary to have such a storm in July. When the storm came up, Jesus was on the housetop playing, as was his habit, for during much of the dry season this was his accustomed playroom. He was blinded by the sand when descending the stairs and fell. After this accident Joseph built a balustrade up both sides of the stairway.

There was no way in which this accident could have been prevented. It was not chargeable to neglect by the midway temporal guardians, one primary and one secondary midwayer having been assigned to the watchcare of the lad; neither was it chargeable to the guardian seraphim. It simply could not have been avoided. But this slight accident, occurring while Joseph was absent in Endor, caused such great anxiety to develop in Mary's mind that she unwisely tried to keep Jesus very close to her side for some months.

Material accidents, commonplace occurrences of a physical nature, are not arbitrarily interfered with by celestial personalities. Under ordinary circumstances only midway creatures can intervene in material conditions to safeguard the persons of men and women of destiny, and even in special situations these beings can so act only in obedience to the specific mandates of their superiors.

And this was but one of a number of such minor accidents which subsequently befell this inquisitive and adventurous youth. If you envisage the average childhood and youth of an aggressive boy, you will have a fairly good idea of the youthful career of Jesus, and you will be able to imagine just about how much anxiety he caused his parents, particularly his mother.

The fourth member of the Nazareth family, Joseph, was born Wednesday morning, March 16, A.D. 1.

5. SCHOOL DAYS IN NAZARETH

Jesus was now seven years old, the age when Jewish children were supposed to begin their formal education in the synagogue schools. Accordingly, in August of this year he entered upon his eventful school life at Nazareth. Already this lad was a fluent reader, writer, and speaker of two languages, Aramaic and Greek. He was now to acquaint himself with the task of learning to read, write, and speak the Hebrew language. And he was truly eager for the new school life which was ahead of him.

For three years—until he was ten—he attended the elementary school of the Nazareth synagogue. For these three years he studied the rudiments of the Book of the Law as it was recorded in the Hebrew tongue. For the following three years he studied in the advanced school and committed to memory, by the method of repeating aloud, the deeper teachings of the sacred law. He graduated from this school of the synagogue during his thirteenth year and was turned over to his parents by the synagogue rulers as an educated "son of the commandment"—henceforth a responsible citizen of the commonwealth of Israel, all of which entailed his attendance at the Passovers in Jerusalem; accordingly, he attended his first Passover that year in company with his father and mother.

At Nazareth the pupils sat on the floor in a semicircle, while their teacher, the chazan, an officer of the synagogue, sat facing them. Beginning with the Book of Leviticus, they passed on to the study of the other books of the law, followed by the study of the Prophets and the Psalms. The Nazareth synagogue possessed a complete copy of the Scriptures in Hebrew. Nothing but the Scriptures was studied prior to the twelfth year. In the summer months the hours for school were greatly shortened.

Jesus early became a master of Hebrew, and as a young man, when no visitor of prominence happened to be sojourning in Nazareth, he would often be asked to read the Hebrew scriptures to the faithful assembled in the synagogue at the regular Sabbath services.

These synagogue schools, of course, had no textbooks. In teaching, the chazan would utter a statement while the pupils would in unison repeat it after him. When having access to the written books of the law, the student learned his lesson by reading aloud and by constant repetition.

Next, in addition to his more formal schooling, Jesus began to make contact with human nature from the four quarters of the earth as men from many lands passed in and out of his father's repair shop. When he grew older, he mingled freely with the caravans as they tarried near the spring for rest and nourishment. Being a fluent speaker of Greek, he had little trouble in conversing with the majority of the caravan travelers and conductors.

Nazareth was a caravan way station and crossroads of travel and largely gentile in population; at the same time it was widely known as a center of liberal interpretation of Jewish traditional law. In Galilee the Jews mingled more freely with the gentiles than was their practice in Judea. And of all the cities of Galilee, the Jews of Nazareth were most liberal in their interpretation of the social restrictions based on the fears of contamination as a result of contact with the gentiles. And these conditions gave rise to the common saying in Jerusalem, "Can any good thing come out of Nazareth?"

Jesus received his moral training and spiritual culture chiefly in his own home. He secured much of his intellectual and theological education from the chazan. But his real education—that equipment of mind and heart for the actual test of grappling with the difficult problems of life—he obtained by mingling with his fellow men. It was this close association with his fellow men, young and old, Jew and gentile, that afforded him the opportunity to know the human race. Jesus was highly educated in that he thoroughly understood men and devotedly loved them.

Throughout his years at the synagogue he was a brilliant student, possessing a great advantage since he was conversant with three languages. The Nazareth chazan, on the occasion of Jesus' finishing the course in his school, remarked to Joseph that he feared he "had learned more from Jesus' searching questions" than he had "been able to teach the lad."

Throughout his course of study Jesus learned much and derived great inspiration from the regular Sabbath sermons in the synagogue. It was customary to ask distinguished visitors, stopping over the Sabbath in Nazareth, to address the synagogue. As Jesus grew up, he heard many great thinkers of the entire Jewish world expound their views, and many also who were hardly orthodox Jews since the synagogue of Nazareth was an advanced and liberal center of Hebrew thought and culture.

When entering school at seven years (at this time the Jews had just inaugurated a compulsory education law), it was customary for the pupils to choose their "birthday text," a sort of golden rule to guide them throughout their studies, one upon which they often expatiated at their graduation when thirteen years old. The text which Jesus chose was from the Prophet Isaiah: "The spirit of the Lord God is upon me, for the Lord has anointed me; he has sent me to bring good news to the meek, to bind up the brokenhearted, to proclaim liberty to the captives, and to set the spiritual prisoners free."

Nazareth was one of the twenty-four priest centers of the Hebrew nation. But the Galilean priesthood was more liberal in the interpretation of the traditional laws than were the Judean scribes and rabbis. And at Nazareth they were also more liberal regarding the observance of the Sabbath. It was therefore the custom for Joseph to take Jesus out for walks on Sabbath afternoons, one of their favorite jaunts being to climb the high hill near their home, from which they could obtain a panoramic view of all Galilee. To the northwest, on clear days, they could see the long ridge of Mount Carmel running down to the sea; and many times Jesus heard his father relate the story of Elijah, one of the first of that long line of Hebrew prophets, who reproved Ahab and exposed the priests of Baal. To the north Mount Hermon raised its snowy peak in majestic splendor and monopolized the skyline, almost 3,000 feet of the upper slopes glistening white with perpetual snow. Far to the east they could discern the Jordan valley and, far beyond, the rocky hills of Moab. Also to the south and the east, when the sun shone upon their marble walls, they could see the Greco-Roman cities of the Decapolis, with their amphitheaters and pretentious temples. And when they lingered toward the going down of the sun, to the west they could make out the sailing vessels on the distant Mediterranean.

From four directions Jesus could observe the caravan trains as they wended their way in and out of Nazareth, and to the south he could overlook the broad and fertile plain country of Esdraelon, stretching off toward Mount Gilboa and Samaria.

When they did not climb the heights to view the distant landscape, they strolled through the countryside and studied nature in her various moods in accordance with the seasons. Jesus' earliest training, aside from that of the home hearth, had to do with a reverent and sympathetic contact with nature.

Before he was eight years of age, he was known to all the mothers and young women of Nazareth, who had met him and talked with him at the spring, which was not far from his home, and which was one of the social centers of contact and gossip for the entire town. This year Jesus learned to milk the family cow and care for the other animals. During this and the following year he also learned to make cheese and to weave. When he was ten years of age, he was an expert loom operator. It was about this time that Jesus and the neighbor boy Jacob became great friends of the potter who worked near the flowing spring; and as they watched Nathan's deft fingers mold the clay on the potter's wheel, many times both of them determined to be potters when they grew up. Nathan was very fond of the lads and often gave them clay to play with, seeking to stimulate their creative imaginations by suggesting competitive efforts in modeling various objects and animals.

6. HIS EIGHTH YEAR (A.D. 2)

This was an interesting year at school. Although Jesus was not an unusual student, he was a diligent pupil and belonged to the more progressive third of the class, doing his work so well that he was excused from attendance one week out of each month. This week he usually spent either with his fisherman uncle on the shores of the Sea of Galilee near Magdala or on the farm of another uncle (his mother's brother) five miles south of Nazareth.

Although his mother had become unduly anxious about his health and safety, she gradually became reconciled to these trips away from home. Jesus' uncles and aunts were all very fond of him, and there ensued a lively competition among them to secure his company for these monthly visits throughout this and immediately subsequent years. His first week's sojourn on his uncle's farm (since infancy) was in January of this year; the first week's fishing experience on the Sea of Galilee occurred in the month of May.

About this time Jesus met a teacher of mathematics from Damascus, and learning some new techniques of numbers, he spent much time on mathematics for several years. He developed a keen sense of numbers, distances, and proportions.

Jesus began to enjoy his brother James very much and by the end of this year had begun to teach him the alphabet.

This year Jesus made arrangements to exchange dairy products for lessons on the harp. He had an unusual liking for everything musical. Later on he did much to promote an interest in vocal music among his youthful associates. By the time he was eleven years of age, he was a skillful harpist and greatly enjoyed entertaining both family and friends with his extraordinary interpretations and able improvisations.

While Jesus continued to make enviable progress at school, all did not run smoothly for either parents or teachers. He persisted in asking many embarrassing questions concerning both science and religion, particularly regarding geography and astronomy. He was especially insistent on finding out why there was a dry season and a rainy season in Palestine. Repeatedly he sought the explanation for the great difference between the temperatures of Nazareth and the Jordan valley. He simply never ceased to ask such intelligent but perplexing questions.

His third brother, Simon, was born on Friday evening, April 14, of this year, A.D. 2.

In February, Nahor, one of the teachers in a Jerusalem academy of the rabbis, came to Nazareth to observe Jesus, having been on a similar mission to Zacharias's home near Jerusalem. He came to Nazareth at the instigation of John's father. While at first he was somewhat shocked by Jesus' frankness and unconventional manner of relating himself to things religious, he attributed it to the remoteness of Galilee from the centers of Hebrew learning and culture and advised Joseph and Mary to allow him to take Jesus back with him to Jerusalem, where he could have the advantages of education and training at the center of Jewish culture. Mary was half persuaded to consent; she was convinced her eldest son was to become the Messiah, the Jewish deliverer; Joseph hesitated; he was equally persuaded that Jesus was to grow up to become a man of destiny, but what that destiny would prove to be he was profoundly uncertain. But he never really doubted that his son was to fulfill some great mission on earth. The more he thought about Nahor's advice, the more he questioned the wisdom of the proposed sojourn in Jerusalem.

Because of this difference of opinion between Joseph and Mary, Nahor requested permission to lay the whole matter before Jesus. Jesus listened attentively, talked with Joseph, Mary, and a neighbor, Jacob the stone mason, whose son was his favorite playmate, and then, two days later, reported that since there was such a difference of opinion among his parents and advisers, and since he did not feel competent to assume the responsibility for such a decision, not feeling strongly one way or the other, in view of the whole situation, he had finally decided to "talk with my Father who is in heaven"; and while he was not perfectly sure about the answer, he rather felt he should remain at home "with my father and mother," adding, "they who love me so much should be able to do more for me and guide me more safely than strangers who can only view my body and observe my mind but can hardly truly know me." They all marveled, and Nahor went his way, back to Jerusalem. And it was many years before the subject of Jesus' going away from home again came up for consideration.

PAPER 124

THE LATER CHILDHOOD OF JESUS

ALTHOUGH Jesus might have enjoyed a better opportunity for schooling at Alexandria than in Galilee, he could not have had such a splendid environment for working out his own life problems with a minimum of educational guidance, at the same time enjoying the great advantage of constantly contacting with such a large number of all classes of men and women hailing from every part of the civilized world. Had he remained at Alexandria, his education would have been directed by Jews and along exclusively Jewish lines. At Nazareth he secured an education and received a training which more acceptably prepared him to understand the gentiles, and which gave him a better and more balanced idea of the relative merits of the Eastern, or Babylonian, and the Western, or Hellenic, views of Hebrew theology.

1. JESUS' NINTH YEAR (A.D. 3)

Though it could hardly be said that Jesus was ever seriously ill, he did have some of the minor ailments of childhood this year, along with his brothers and baby sister.

School went on and he was still a favored pupil, having one week each month at liberty, and he continued to divide his time about equally between trips to neighboring cities with his father, sojourns on his uncle's farm south of Nazareth, and fishing excursions out from Magdala.

The most serious trouble as yet to come up at school occurred in late winter when Jesus dared to challenge the chazan regarding the teaching that all images, pictures, and drawings were idolatrous in nature. Jesus delighted in drawing landscapes as well as in modeling a great variety of objects in potter's clay. Everything of that sort was strictly forbidden by Jewish law, but up to this time he had managed to disarm his parents' objection to such an extent that they had permitted him to continue in these activities.

But trouble was again stirred up at school when one of the more backward pupils discovered Jesus drawing a charcoal picture of the teacher on the floor of the schoolroom. There it was, plain as day, and many of the elders had viewed it before the committee went to call on Joseph to demand that something be done to suppress the lawlessness of his eldest son. And though this was not the first time complaints had come to Joseph and Mary about the doings of their versatile and aggressive child, this was the most serious of all the accusations which had thus far been lodged against him. Jesus listened to the indictment of his artistic efforts for some time, being seated on a large stone just outside the back door. He resented their blaming his father for his alleged misdeeds; so in he marched, fearlessly confronting his accusers. The elders were thrown into confusion. Some were inclined to view the episode humorously, while one or two seemed to think the boy was sacrilegious if not blasphemous. Joseph was nonplused, Mary indignant, but Jesus insisted on being heard. He had his say, courageously defended his viewpoint, and with consummate self-control announced that he would abide by the decision of his father in this as in all other matters controversial. And the committee of elders departed in silence.

Mary endeavored to influence Joseph to permit Jesus to model in clay at home, provided he promised not to carry on any of these questionable activities at school, but Joseph felt impelled to rule that the rabbinical interpretation of the second commandment should prevail. And so Jesus no more drew or modeled the likeness of anything from that day as long as he lived in his father's house. But he was unconvinced of the wrong of what he had done, and to give up such a favorite pastime constituted one of the great trials of his young life.

In the latter part of June, Jesus, in company with his father, first climbed to the summit of Mount Tabor. It was a clear day and the view was superb. It seemed to this nine-year-old lad that he had really gazed upon the entire world excepting India, Africa, and Rome.

Jesus' second sister, Martha, was born Thursday night, September 13. Three weeks after the coming of Martha, Joseph, who was home for awhile, started the building of an addition to their house, a combined workshop and bedroom. A small workbench was built for Jesus, and for the first time he possessed tools of his own. At odd times for many years he worked at this bench and became highly expert in the making of yokes.

This winter and the next were the coldest in Nazareth for many decades. Jesus had seen snow on the mountains, and several times it had fallen in Nazareth, remaining on the ground only a short time; but not until this winter had he seen ice. The fact that water could be had as a solid, a liquid, and a vapor—he had long pondered over the escaping steam from the boiling pots—caused the lad to think a great deal about the physical world and its constitution; and yet the personality embodied in this growing youth was all this while the actual creator and organizer of all these things throughout a far-flung universe.

The climate of Nazareth was not severe. January was the coldest month, the temperature averaging around 50° F. During July and August, the hottest months, the temperature would vary from 75° to 90° F. From the mountains to the Jordan and the Dead Sea valley the climate of Palestine ranged from the frigid to the torrid. And so, in a way, the Jews were prepared to live in about any and all of the world's varying climates.

Even during the warmest summer months a cool sea breeze usually blew from the west from 10:00 A.M. until about 10:00 P.M. But every now and then terrific hot winds from the eastern desert would blow across all Palestine. These hot blasts usually came in February and March, near the end of the rainy season. In those days the rain fell in refreshing showers from November to April, but it did not rain steadily. There were only two seasons in Palestine, summer and winter, the dry and rainy seasons. In January the flowers began to bloom, and by the end of April the whole land was one vast flower garden.

In May of this year, on his uncle's farm, Jesus for the first time helped with the harvest of the grain. Before he was thirteen, he had managed to find out something about practically everything that men and women worked at around

Nazareth except metal working, and he spent several months in a smith's shop when older, after the death of his father.

When work and caravan travel were slack, Jesus made many trips with his father on pleasure or business to near-by Cana, Endor, and Nain. Even as a lad he frequently visited Sepphoris, only a little over three miles from Nazareth to the northwest, and from 4 B.C. to about A.D. 25 the capital of Galilee and one of the residences of Herod Antipas.

Jesus continued to grow physically, intellectually, socially, and spiritually. His trips away from home did much to give him a better and more generous understanding of his own family, and by this time even his parents were beginning to learn from him as well as to teach him. Jesus was an original thinker and a skillful teacher, even in his youth. He was in constant collision with the so-called "oral law," but he always sought to adapt himself to the practices of his family. He got along fairly well with the children of his age, but he often grew discouraged with their slow-acting minds. Before he was ten years old, he had become the leader of a group of seven lads who formed themselves into a society for promoting the acquirements of manhood—physical, intellectual, and religious. Among these boys Jesus succeeded in introducing many new games and various improved methods of physical recreation.

2. THE TENTH YEAR (A.D. 4)

It was the fifth of July, the first Sabbath of the month, when Jesus, while strolling through the countryside with his father, first gave expression to feelings and ideas which indicated that he was becoming self-conscious of the unusual nature of his life mission. Joseph listened attentively to the momentous words of his son but made few comments; he volunteered no information. The next day Jesus had a similar but longer talk with his mother. Mary likewise listened to the pronouncements of the lad, but neither did she volunteer any information. It was almost two years before Jesus again spoke to his parents concerning this increasing revelation within his own consciousness regarding the nature of his personality and the character of his mission on earth.

He entered the advanced school of the synagogue in August. At school he was constantly creating trouble by the questions he persisted in asking. Increasingly he kept all Nazareth in more or less of a hubbub. His parents were loath to forbid his asking these disquieting questions, and his chief teacher was greatly intrigued by the lad's curiosity, insight, and hunger for knowledge.

Jesus' playmates saw nothing supernatural in his conduct; in most ways he was altogether like themselves. His interest in study was somewhat above the average but not wholly unusual. He did ask more questions at school than others in his class.

Perhaps his most unusual and outstanding trait was his unwillingness to fight for his rights. Since he was such a well-developed lad for his age, it seemed strange to his playfellows that he was disinclined to defend himself even from injustice or when subjected to personal abuse. As it happened, he did not suffer much on account of this trait because of the friendship of Jacob, a neighbor boy, who was one year older. He was the son of the stone mason, a business associate of Joseph. Jacob was a great admirer of Jesus and made it his business to see that no one was permitted to impose upon Jesus because of his aversion to physical combat. Several times older and uncouth youths attacked Jesus, relying upon his reputed docility, but they always suffered swift and certain retribution at the hands of his self-appointed champion and ever-ready defender, Jacob the stone mason's son.

Jesus was the generally accepted leader of the Nazareth lads who stood for the higher ideals of their day and generation. He was really loved by his youthful associates, not only because he was fair, but also because he possessed a rare and understanding sympathy that betokened love and bordered on discreet compassion.

This year he began to show a marked preference for the company of older persons. He delighted in talking over things cultural, educational, social, economic, political, and religious with older minds, and his depth of reasoning and keenness of observation so charmed his adult associates that they were always more than willing to visit with him. Until he became responsible for the support of the home, his parents were constantly seeking to influence him to associate with those of his own age, or more nearly his age, rather than with older and better-informed individuals for whom he evinced such a preference.

Late this year he had a fishing experience of two months with his uncle on the Sea of Galilee, and he was very successful. Before attaining manhood, he had become an expert fisherman.

His physical development continued; he was an advanced and privileged pupil at school; he got along fairly well at home with his younger brothers and sisters, having the advantage of being three and one-half years older than the oldest of the other children. He was well thought of in Nazareth except by the parents of some of the duller children, who often spoke of Jesus as being too pert, as lacking in proper humility and youthful reserve. He manifested a growing tendency to direct the play activities of his youthful associates into more serious and thoughtful channels. He was a born teacher and simply could not refrain from so functioning, even when supposedly engaged in play.

Joseph early began to instruct Jesus in the diverse means of gaining a livelihood, explaining the advantages of agriculture over industry and trade. Galilee was a more beautiful and prosperous district than Judea, and it cost only about one fourth as much to live there as in Jerusalem and Judea. It was a province of agricultural villages and thriving industrial cities, containing more than two hundred towns of over five thousand population and thirty of over fifteen thousand.

When on his first trip with his father to observe the fishing industry on the lake of Galilee, Jesus had just about made up his mind to become a fisherman; but close association with his father's vocation later on influenced him to become a carpenter, while still later a combination of influences led him to the final choice of becoming a religious teacher of a new order.

3. THE ELEVENTH YEAR (A.D. 5)

Throughout this year the lad continued to make trips away from home with his father, but he also frequently visited his uncle's farm and occasionally went over to Magdala to engage in fishing with the uncle who made his headquarters near that city.

Joseph and Mary were often tempted to show some special favoritism for Jesus or otherwise to betray their knowledge that he was a child of promise, a son of destiny. But both of his parents were extraordinarily wise and sagacious in all these matters. The few times they did in any manner exhibit any preference for him, even in the slightest degree, the lad was quick to refuse all such special consideration.

Jesus spent considerable time at the caravan supply shop, and by conversing with the travelers from all parts of the world, he acquired a store of information about international affairs that was amazing, considering his age. This was the last year in which he enjoyed much free play and youthful joyousness. From this time on difficulties and responsibilities rapidly multiplied in the life of this youth.

On Wednesday evening, June 24, A.D. 5, Jude was born. Complications attended the birth of this, the seventh child. Mary was so very ill for several weeks that Joseph remained at home. Jesus was very much occupied with errands for his father and with many duties occasioned by his mother's serious illness. Never again did this youth find it possible to return to the childlike attitude of his earlier years. From the time of his mother's illness—just before he was eleven years old—he was compelled to assume the responsibilities of the first-born son and to do all this one or two full years before these burdens should normally have fallen on his shoulders.

The chazan spent one evening each week with Jesus, helping him to master the Hebrew scriptures. He was greatly interested in the progress of his promising pupil; therefore was he willing to assist him in many ways. This Jewish pedagogue exerted a great influence upon this growing mind, but he was never able to comprehend why Jesus was so indifferent to all his suggestions regarding the prospects of going to Jerusalem to continue his education under the learned rabbis.

About the middle of May the lad accompanied his father on a business trip to Scythopolis, the chief Greek city of the Decapolis, the ancient Hebrew city of Beth-shean. On the way Joseph recounted much of the olden history of King Saul, the Philistines, and the subsequent events of Israel's turbulent history. Jesus was tremendously impressed with the clean appearance and well-ordered arrangement of this so-called heathen city. He marveled at the open-air theater and admired the beautiful marble temple dedicated to the worship of the "heathen" gods. Joseph was much perturbed by the lad's enthusiasm and sought to counteract these favorable impressions by extolling the beauty and grandeur of the Jewish temple at Jerusalem. Jesus had often gazed curiously upon this magnificent Greek city from the hill of Nazareth and had many times inquired about its extensive public works and ornate buildings, but his father had always sought to avoid answering these questions. Now they were face to face with the beauties of this gentile city, and Joseph could not gracefully ignore Jesus' inquiries.

It so happened that just at this time the annual competitive games and public demonstrations of physical prowess between the Greek cities of the Decapolis were in progress at the Scythopolis amphitheater, and Jesus was insistent that his father take him to see the games, and he was so insistent that Joseph hesitated to deny him. The boy was thrilled with the games and entered most heartily into the spirit of the demonstrations of physical development and athletic skill. Joseph was inexpressibly shocked to observe his son's enthusiasm as he beheld these exhibitions of "heathen" vaingloriousness. After the games were finished,

Joseph received the surprise of his life when he heard Jesus express his approval of them and suggest that it would be good for the young men of Nazareth if they could be thus benefited by wholesome outdoor physical activities. Joseph talked earnestly and long with Jesus concerning the evil nature of such practices, but he well knew that the lad was unconvinced.

The only time Jesus ever saw his father angry with him was that night in their room at the inn when, in the course of their discussions, the boy so far forgot the trends of Jewish thought as to suggest that they go back home and work for the building of an amphitheater at Nazareth. When Joseph heard his first-born son express such un-Jewish sentiments, he forgot his usual calm demeanor and, seizing Jesus by the shoulder, angrily exclaimed, "My son, never again let me hear you give utterance to such an evil thought as long as you live." Jesus was startled by his father's display of emotion; he had never before been made to feel the personal sting of his father's indignation and was astonished and shocked beyond expression. He only replied, "Very well, my father, it shall be so." And never again did the boy even in the slightest manner allude to the games and other athletic activities of the Greeks as long as his father lived.

Later on, Jesus saw the Greek amphitheater at Jerusalem and learned how hateful such things were from the Jewish point of view. Nevertheless, throughout his life he endeavored to introduce the idea of wholesome recreation into his personal plans and, as far as Jewish practice would permit, into the later program of regular activities for his twelve apostles.

At the end of this eleventh year Jesus was a vigorous, well-developed, moderately humorous, and fairly lighthearted youth, but from this year on he was more and more given to peculiar seasons of profound meditation and serious contemplation. He was much given to thinking about how he was to carry out his obligations to his family and at the same time be obedient to the call of his mission to the world; already he had conceived that his ministry was not to be limited to the betterment of the Jewish people.

4. THE TWELFTH YEAR (A.D. 6)

This was an eventful year in Jesus' life. He continued to make progress at school and was indefatigable in his study of nature, while increasingly he prosecuted his study of the methods whereby men make a living. He began doing regular work in the home carpenter shop and was permitted to manage his own earnings, a very unusual arrangement to obtain in a Jewish family. This year he also learned the wisdom of keeping such matters a secret in the family. He was becoming conscious of the way in which he had caused trouble in the village, and henceforth he became increasingly discreet in concealing everything which might cause him to be regarded as different from his fellows.

Throughout this year he experienced many seasons of uncertainty, if not actual doubt, regarding the nature of his mission. His naturally developing human mind did not yet fully grasp the reality of his dual nature. The fact that he had a single personality rendered it difficult for his consciousness to recognize the double origin of those factors which composed the nature associated with that selfsame personality.

From this time on he became more successful in getting along with his brothers and sisters. He was increasingly tactful, always compassionate and considerate of their welfare and happiness, and enjoyed good relations with them up to the beginning of his public ministry. To be more explicit: He got along with James, Miriam, and the two younger (as yet unborn) children, Amos and Ruth, most excellently. He always got along with Martha fairly well. What trouble he had at home largely arose out of friction with Joseph and Jude, particularly the latter.

It was a trying experience for Joseph and Mary to undertake the rearing of this unprecedented combination of divinity and humanity, and they deserve great credit for so faithfully and successfully discharging their parental responsibilities. Increasingly Jesus' parents realized that there was something superhuman resident within this eldest son, but they never even faintly dreamed that this son of promise was indeed and in truth the actual creator of this local universe of things and beings. Joseph and Mary lived and died without ever learning that their son Jesus really was the Universe Creator incarnate in mortal flesh.

This year Jesus paid more attention than ever to music, and he continued to teach the home school for his brothers and sisters. It was at about this time that the lad became keenly conscious of the difference between the viewpoints of Joseph and Mary regarding the nature of his mission. He pondered much over his parents' differing opinions, often hearing their discussions when they thought he was sound asleep. More and more he inclined to the view of his father, so that his mother was destined to be hurt by the realization that her son was gradually rejecting her guidance in matters having to do with his life career. And, as the years passed, this breach of understanding widened. Less and less did Mary comprehend the significance of Jesus' mission, and increasingly was this good mother hurt by the failure of her favorite son to fulfill her fond expectations.

Joseph entertained a growing belief in the spiritual nature of Jesus' mission. And but for other and more important reasons it does seem unfortunate that he could not have lived to see the fulfillment of his concept of Jesus' bestowal on earth.

During his last year at school, when he was twelve years old, Jesus remonstrated with his father about the Jewish custom of touching the bit of parchment nailed upon the doorpost each time on going into, or coming out of, the house and then kissing the finger that touched the parchment. As a part of this ritual it was customary to say, "The Lord shall preserve our going out and our coming in, from this time forth and even forevermore." Joseph and Mary had repeatedly instructed Jesus as to the reasons for not making images or drawing pictures, explaining that such creations might be used for idolatrous purposes. Though Jesus failed fully to grasp their proscriptions against images and pictures, he possessed a high concept of consistency and therefore pointed out to his father the essentially idolatrous nature of this habitual obeisance to the doorpost parchment. And Joseph removed the parchment after Jesus had thus remonstrated with him.

As time passed, Jesus did much to modify their practice of religious forms, such as the family prayers and other customs. And it was possible to do many such things at Nazareth, for its synagogue was under the influence of a liberal school of rabbis, exemplified by the renowned Nazareth teacher, Jose.

Throughout this and the two following years Jesus suffered great mental distress as the result of his constant effort to adjust his personal views of religious practices and social amenities to the established beliefs of his parents. He was distraught by the conflict between the urge to be loyal to his own convictions and the conscientious admonition of dutiful submission to his parents; his supreme conflict was between two great commands which were uppermost in his youthful mind. The one was: "Be loyal to the dictates of your highest convictions of truth and righteousness." The other was: "Honor your father and mother, for they have given you life and the nurture thereof." However, he never shirked the responsibility of making the necessary daily adjustments between these realms of loyalty to one's personal convictions and duty toward one's family, and he achieved the satisfaction of effecting an increasingly harmonious blending of personal convictions and family obligations into a masterful concept of group solidarity based upon loyalty, fairness, tolerance, and love.

5. HIS THIRTEENTH YEAR (A.D. 7)

In this year the lad of Nazareth passed from boyhood to the beginning of young manhood; his voice began to change, and other features of mind and body gave evidence of the oncoming status of manhood.

On Sunday night, January 9, A.D. 7, his baby brother, Amos, was born. Jude was not yet two years of age, and the baby sister, Ruth, was yet to come; so it may be seen that Jesus had a sizable family of small children left to his watchcare when his father met his accidental death the following year.

It was about the middle of February that Jesus became humanly assured that he was destined to perform a mission on earth for the enlightenment of man and the revelation of God. Momentous decisions, coupled with far-reaching plans, were formulating in the mind of this youth, who was, to outward appearances, an average Jewish lad of Nazareth. The intelligent life of all Nebadon looked on with fascination and amazement as all this began to unfold in the thinking and acting of the now adolescent carpenter's son.

On the first day of the week, March 20, A.D. 7, Jesus graduated from the course of training in the local school connected with the Nazareth synagogue. This was a great day in the life of any ambitious Jewish family, the day when the first-born son was pronounced a "son of the commandment" and the ransomed first-born of the Lord God of Israel, a "child of the Most High" and servant of the Lord of all the earth.

Friday of the week before, Joseph had come over from Sepphoris, where he was in charge of the work on a new public building, to be present on this glad occasion. Jesus' teacher confidently believed that his alert and diligent pupil was destined to some outstanding career, some distinguished mission. The elders, notwithstanding all their trouble with Jesus' nonconformist tendencies, were very proud of the lad and had already begun laying plans which would enable him to go to Jerusalem to continue his education in the renowned Hebrew academies.

As Jesus heard these plans discussed from time to time, he became increasingly sure that he would never go to Jerusalem to study with the rabbis. But he little dreamed of the tragedy, so soon to occur, which would insure the abandonment of all such plans by causing him to assume the responsibility for the support and direction of a large family, presently to consist of five brothers and three sisters as well as his mother and himself. Jesus had a larger and longer experience rearing this family than was accorded to Joseph, his father; and he did measure up to the standard which he subsequently set for himself: to become a wise, patient, understanding, and effective teacher and eldest brother to this family—his family—so suddenly sorrow-stricken and so unexpectedly bereaved.

6. THE JOURNEY TO JERUSALEM

Jesus, having now reached the threshold of young manhood and having been formally graduated from the synagogue schools, was qualified to proceed to Jerusalem with his parents to participate with them in the celebration of his first Passover. The Passover feast of this year fell on Saturday, April 9, A.D. 7. A considerable company (103) made ready to depart from Nazareth early Monday morning, April 4, for Jerusalem. They journeyed south toward Samaria, but on reaching Jezreel, they turned east, going around Mount Gilboa into the Jordan valley in order to avoid passing through Samaria. Joseph and his family would have enjoyed going down through Samaria by way of Jacob's well and Bethel, but since the Jews disliked to deal with the Samaritans, they decided to go with their neighbors by way of the Jordan valley.

The much-dreaded Archelaus had been deposed, and they had little to fear in taking Jesus to Jerusalem. Twelve years had passed since the first Herod had sought to destroy the babe of Bethlehem, and no one would now think of associating that affair with this obscure lad of Nazareth.

Before reaching the Jezreel junction, and as they journeyed on, very soon, on the left, they passed the ancient village of Shunem, and Jesus heard again about the most beautiful maiden of all Israel who once lived there and also about the wonderful works Elisha performed there. In passing by Jezreel, Jesus' parents recounted the doings of Ahab and Jezebel and the exploits of Jehu. In passing around Mount Gilboa, they talked much about Saul, who took his life on the slopes of this mountain, King David, and the associations of this historic spot.

As they rounded the base of Gilboa, the pilgrims could see the Greek city of Scythopolis on the right. They gazed upon the marble structures from a distance but went not near the gentile city lest they so defile themselves that they could not participate in the forthcoming solemn and sacred ceremonies of the Passover at Jerusalem. Mary could not understand why neither Joseph nor Jesus would speak of Scythopolis. She did not know about their controversy of the previous year as they had never revealed this episode to her.

The road now led immediately down into the tropical Jordan valley, and soon Jesus was to have exposed to his wondering gaze the crooked and ever-winding Jordan with its glistening and rippling waters as it flowed down toward the Dead Sea. They laid aside their outer garments as they journeyed south in this tropical valley, enjoying the luxurious fields of grain and the beautiful oleanders laden with their pink blossoms, while massive snow-capped Mount Hermon stood far to the north, in majesty looking down on the historic valley. A little over three hours' travel from opposite Scythopolis they came upon a bubbling spring, and here they camped for the night, out under the starlit heavens.

On their second day's journey they passed by where the Jabbok, from the east, flows into the Jordan, and looking east up this river valley, they recounted the days of Gideon, when the Midianites poured into this region to overrun the land. Toward the end of the second day's journey they camped near the base of the highest mountain overlooking the Jordan valley, Mount Sartaba, whose summit was occupied by the Alexandrian fortress where Herod had imprisoned one of his wives and buried his two strangled sons.

The third day they passed by two villages which had been recently built by Herod and noted their superior architecture and their beautiful palm gardens. By nightfall they reached Jericho, where they remained until the morrow. That evening Joseph, Mary, and Jesus walked a mile and a half to the site of the ancient Jericho, where Joshua, for whom Jesus was named, had performed his renowned exploits, according to Jewish tradition.

By the fourth and last day's journey the road was a continuous procession of pilgrims. They now began to climb the hills leading up to Jerusalem. As they neared the top, they could look across the Jordan to the mountains beyond and south over the sluggish waters of the Dead Sea. About halfway up to Jerusalem, Jesus gained his first view of the Mount of Olives (the region to be so much a part of his subsequent life), and Joseph pointed out to him that the Holy City lay just beyond this ridge, and the lad's heart beat fast with joyous anticipation of soon beholding the city and house of his heavenly Father.

On the eastern slopes of Olivet they paused for rest in the borders of a little village called Bethany. The hospitable villagers poured forth to minister to the pilgrims, and it happened that Joseph and his family had stopped near the house of one Simon, who had three children about the same age as Jesus—Mary, Martha, and Lazarus. They invited the Nazareth family in for refreshment, and a lifelong friendship sprang up between the two families. Many times afterward, in his eventful life, Jesus stopped in this home.

They pressed on, soon standing on the brink of Olivet, and Jesus saw for the first time (in his memory) the Holy City, the pretentious palaces, and the inspiring temple of his Father. At no time in his life did Jesus ever experience such a purely human thrill as that which at this time so completely enthralled him as he stood there on this April afternoon on the Mount of Olives, drinking in his first view of Jerusalem. And in after years, on this same spot he stood and wept over the city which was about to reject another prophet, the last and the greatest of her heavenly teachers.

But they hurried on to Jerusalem. It was now Thursday afternoon. On reaching the city, they journeyed past the temple, and never had Jesus beheld such throngs of human beings. He meditated deeply on how these Jews had assembled here from the uttermost parts of the known world.

Soon they reached the place prearranged for their accommodation during the Passover week, the large home of a well-to-do relative of Mary's, one who knew something of the early history of both John and Jesus, through Zacharias. The following day, the day of preparation, they made ready for the appropriate celebration of the Passover Sabbath.

While all Jerusalem was astir in preparation for the Passover, Joseph found time to take his son around to visit the academy where it had been arranged for him to resume his education two years later, as soon as he reached the required age of fifteen. Joseph was truly puzzled when he observed how little interest Jesus evinced in all these carefully laid plans.

Jesus was profoundly impressed by the temple and all the associated services and other activities. For the first time since he was four years old, he was too much preoccupied with his own meditations to ask many questions. He did, however, ask his father several embarrassing questions (as he had on previous occasions) as to why the heavenly Father required the slaughter of so many innocent and helpless animals. And his father well knew from the expression on the lad's face that his answers and attempts at explanation were unsatisfactory to his deep-thinking and keen-reasoning son.

On the day before the Passover Sabbath, flood tides of spiritual illumination swept through the mortal mind of Jesus and filled his human heart to overflowing with affectionate pity for the spiritually blind and morally ignorant multitudes assembled for the celebration of the ancient Passover commemoration. This was one of the most extraordinary days that the Son of God spent in the flesh; and during the night, for the first time in his earth career, there appeared to him an assigned messenger from Salvington, commissioned by Immanuel, who said: "The hour has come. It is time that you began to be about your Father's business."

And so, even ere the heavy responsibilities of the Nazareth family descended upon his youthful shoulders, there now arrived the celestial messenger to remind this lad, not quite thirteen years of age, that the hour had come to begin the resumption of the responsibilities of a universe. This was the first act of a long succession of events which finally culminated in the completion of the Son's bestowal on Urantia and the replacing of "the government of a universe on his human-divine shoulders."

As time passed, the mystery of the incarnation became, to all of us, more and more unfathomable. We could hardly comprehend that this lad of Nazareth was the creator of all Nebadon. Neither do we nowadays understand how the spirit of this same Creator Son and the spirit of his Paradise Father are associated with the souls of mankind. With the passing of time, we could see that his human mind was increasingly discerning that, while he lived his life in the flesh, in spirit on his shoulders rested the responsibility of a universe.

Thus ends the career of the Nazareth lad, and begins the narrative of that adolescent youth—the increasingly self-conscious divine human—who now begins the contemplation of his world career as he strives to integrate his expanding life purpose with the desires of his parents and his obligations to his family and the society of his day and age.

PAPER 125
JESUS AT JERUSALEM

NO INCIDENT in all Jesus' eventful earth career was more engaging, more humanly thrilling, than this, his first remembered visit to Jerusalem. He was especially stimulated by the experience of attending the temple discussions by himself, and it long stood out in his memory as the great event of his later childhood and early youth. This was his first opportunity to enjoy a few days of independent living, the exhilaration of going and coming without restraint and restrictions. This brief period of undirected living, during the week following the Passover, was the first complete freedom from responsibility he had ever enjoyed. And it was many years subsequent to this before he again had a like period of freedom from all sense of responsibility, even for a short time.

Women seldom went to the Passover feast at Jerusalem; they were not required to be present. Jesus, however, virtually refused to go unless his mother would accompany them. And when his mother decided to go, many other Nazareth women were led to make the journey, so that the Passover company contained the largest number of women, in proportion to men, ever to go up to the Passover from Nazareth. Ever and anon, on the way to Jerusalem, they chanted the one hundred and thirtieth Psalm.

From the time they left Nazareth until they reached the summit of the Mount of Olives, Jesus experienced one long stress of expectant anticipation. All through a joyful childhood he had reverently heard of Jerusalem and its temple; now he was soon to behold them in reality. From the Mount of Olives and from the outside, on closer inspection, the temple had been all and more than Jesus had expected; but when he once entered its sacred portals, the great disillusionment began.

In company with his parents Jesus passed through the temple precincts on his way to join that group of new sons of the law who were about to be consecrated as citizens of Israel. He was a little disappointed by the general demeanor of the temple throngs, but the first great shock of the day came when his mother took leave of them on her way to the women's gallery. It had never occurred to Jesus that his mother was not to accompany him to the consecration ceremonies, and he was thoroughly indignant that she was made to suffer from such unjust discrimination. While he strongly resented this, aside from a few remarks of protest to his father, he said nothing. But he thought, and thought deeply, as his questions to the scribes and teachers a week later disclosed.

He passed through the consecration rituals but was disappointed by their perfunctory and routine natures. He missed that personal interest which characterized the ceremonies of the synagogue at Nazareth. He then returned to greet his mother and prepared to accompany his father on his first trip about the temple and its various courts, galleries, and corridors. The temple precincts could accommodate over two hundred thousand worshipers at one time, and while the vastness of these buildings—in comparison with any he had ever seen—greatly impressed his mind, he was more intrigued by the contemplation of the spiritual significance of the temple ceremonies and their associated worship.

Though many of the temple rituals very touchingly impressed his sense of the beautiful and the symbolic, he was always disappointed by the explanation of the real meanings of these ceremonies which his parents would offer in answer to his many searching inquiries. Jesus simply would not accept explanations of worship and religious devotion which involved belief in the wrath of God or the anger of the Almighty. In further discussion of these questions, after the conclusion of the temple visit, when his father became mildly insistent that he acknowledge acceptance of the orthodox Jewish beliefs, Jesus turned suddenly upon his parents and, looking appealingly into the eyes of his father, said: "My father, it cannot be true—the Father in heaven cannot so regard his erring children on earth. The heavenly Father cannot love his children less than you love me. And I well know, no matter what unwise thing I might do, you would never pour out wrath upon me nor vent anger against me. If you, my earthly father, possess such human reflections of the Divine, how much more must the heavenly Father be filled with goodness and overflowing with mercy. I refuse to believe that my Father in heaven loves me less than my father on earth."

When Joseph and Mary heard these words of their first-born son, they held their peace. And never again did they seek to change his mind about the love of God and the mercifulness of the Father in heaven.

1. JESUS VIEWS THE TEMPLE

Everywhere Jesus went throughout the temple courts, he was shocked and sickened by the spirit of irreverence which he observed. He deemed the conduct of the temple throngs to be inconsistent with their presence in "his Father's house." But he received the shock of his young life when his father escorted him into the court of the gentiles with its noisy jargon, loud talking and cursing, mingled indiscriminately with the bleating of sheep and the babble of noises which betrayed the presence of the money-changers and the vendors of sacrificial animals and sundry other commercial commodities.

But most of all was his sense of propriety outraged by the sight of the frivolous courtesans parading about within this precinct of the temple, just such painted women as he had so recently seen when on a visit to Sepphoris. This profanation of the temple fully aroused all his youthful indignation, and he did not hesitate to express himself freely to Joseph.

Jesus admired the sentiment and service of the temple, but he was shocked by the spiritual ugliness which he beheld on the faces of so many of the unthinking worshipers.

They now passed down to the priests' court beneath the rock ledge in front of the temple, where the altar stood, to observe the killing of the droves of animals and the washing away of the blood from the hands of the officiating slaughter priests at the bronze fountain. The bloodstained pavement, the gory hands of the priests, and the sounds of the dying animals were more than this nature-loving lad could stand. The terrible sight sickened this boy of Nazareth; he clutched his father's arm and begged to be taken away. They walked back through the court of the gentiles, and even the coarse laughter and profane jesting which he there heard were a relief from the sights he had just beheld.

Joseph saw how his son had sickened at the sight of the temple rites and wisely led him around to view the "Gate Beautiful," the artistic gate made of Corinthian bronze. But Jesus had had enough for his first visit at the temple. They returned to the upper court for Mary and walked about in the open air and away from the crowds for an hour, viewing the Asmonean palace, the stately home of Herod, and the tower of the Roman guards. During this stroll Joseph explained to Jesus that only the inhabitants of Jerusalem were permitted to witness the daily sacrifices in the temple, and that the dwellers in Galilee came up only three times a year to participate in the temple worship: at the Passover, at the feast of Pentecost (seven weeks after Passover), and at the feast of tabernacles in October. These feasts were established by Moses. They then discussed the two later established feasts of the dedication and of Purim. Afterward they went to their lodgings and made ready for the celebration of the Passover.

2. JESUS AND THE PASSOVER

Five Nazareth families were guests of, or associates with, the family of Simon of Bethany in the celebration of the Passover, Simon having purchased the paschal lamb for the company. It was the slaughter of these lambs in such enormous numbers that had so affected Jesus on his temple visit. It had been the plan to eat the Passover with Mary's relatives, but Jesus persuaded his parents to accept the invitation to go to Bethany.

That night they assembled for the Passover rites, eating the roasted flesh with unleavened bread and bitter herbs. Jesus, being a new son of the covenant, was asked to recount the origin of the Passover, and this he well did, but he somewhat disconcerted his parents by the inclusion of numerous remarks mildly reflecting the impressions made on his youthful but thoughtful mind by the things which he had so recently seen and heard. This was the beginning of the seven-day ceremonies of the feast of the Passover.

Even at this early date, though he said nothing about such matters to his parents, Jesus had begun to turn over in his mind the propriety of celebrating the Passover without the slaughtered lamb. He felt assured in his own mind that the Father in heaven was not pleased with this spectacle of sacrificial offerings, and as the years passed, he became increasingly determined someday to establish the celebration of a bloodless Passover.

Jesus slept very little that night. His rest was greatly disturbed by revolting dreams of slaughter and suffering. His mind was distraught and his heart torn by the inconsistencies and absurdities of the theology of the whole Jewish ceremonial system. His parents likewise slept little. They were greatly disconcerted by the events of the day just ended. They were completely upset in their own hearts by the lad's, to them, strange and determined attitude. Mary became nervously agitated during the fore part of the night, but Joseph remained calm, though he was equally puzzled. Both of them feared to talk frankly with the lad about these problems, though Jesus would gladly have talked with his parents if they had dared to encourage him.

The next day's services at the temple were more acceptable to Jesus and did much to relieve the unpleasant memories of the previous day. The following morning young Lazarus took Jesus in hand, and they began a systematic exploration of Jerusalem and its environs. Before the day was over, Jesus discovered the various places about the temple where teaching and question conferences were in progress; and aside from a few visits to the holy of holies to gaze in wonder as to what really was behind the veil of separation, he spent most of his time about the temple at these teaching conferences.

Throughout the Passover week, Jesus kept his place among the new sons of the commandment, and this meant that he must seat himself outside the rail which segregated all persons who were not full citizens of Israel. Being thus made conscious of his youth, he refrained from asking the many questions which surged back and forth in his mind; at least he refrained until the Passover celebration had ended and these restrictions on the newly consecrated youths were lifted.

On Wednesday of the Passover week, Jesus was permitted to go home with Lazarus to spend the night at Bethany. This evening, Lazarus, Martha, and Mary heard Jesus discuss things temporal and eternal, human and divine, and from that night on they all three loved him as if he had been their own brother.

By the end of the week, Jesus saw less of Lazarus since he was not eligible for admission to even the outer circle of the temple discussions, though he attended some of the public talks delivered in the outer courts. Lazarus was the same age as Jesus, but in Jerusalem youths were seldom admitted to the consecration of sons of the law until they were a full thirteen years of age.

Again and again, during the Passover week, his parents would find Jesus sitting off by himself with his youthful head in his hands, profoundly thinking. They had never seen him behave like this, and not knowing how much he was confused in mind and troubled in spirit by the experience through which he was passing, they were sorely perplexed; they did not know what to do. They welcomed the passing of the days of the Passover week and longed to have their strangely acting son safely back in Nazareth.

Day by day Jesus was thinking through his problems. By the end of the week he had made many adjustments; but when the time came to return to Nazareth, his youthful mind was still swarming with perplexities and beset by a host of unanswered questions and unsolved problems.

Before Joseph and Mary left Jerusalem, in company with Jesus' Nazareth teacher they made definite arrangements for Jesus to return when he reached the age of fifteen to begin his long course of study in one of the best-known academies of the rabbis. Jesus accompanied his parents and teacher on their visits to the school, but they were all distressed to observe how indifferent he seemed to all they said and did. Mary was deeply pained at his reactions to the Jerusalem visit, and Joseph was profoundly perplexed at the lad's strange remarks and unusual conduct.

After all, Passover week had been a great event in Jesus' life. He had enjoyed the opportunity of meeting scores of boys about his own age, fellow candidates for the consecration, and he utilized such contacts as a means of learning how people lived in Mesopotamia, Turkestan, and Parthia, as well as in the Far-Western provinces of Rome. He was already fairly conversant with the way in which the youth of Egypt and other regions near Palestine grew up. There were thousands of young people in Jerusalem at this time, and the Nazareth lad personally met, and more or less extensively interviewed, more than one hundred and fifty. He was particularly interested in those who hailed from the Far-

Eastern and the remote Western countries. As a result of these contacts the lad began to entertain a desire to travel about the world for the purpose of learning how the various groups of his fellow men toiled for their livelihood.

3. DEPARTURE OF JOSEPH AND MARY

It had been arranged that the Nazareth party should gather in the region of the temple at midforenoon on the first day of the week after the Passover festival had ended. This they did and started out on the return journey to Nazareth. Jesus had gone into the temple to listen to the discussions while his parents awaited the assembly of their fellow travelers. Presently the company prepared to depart, the men going in one group and the women in another as was their custom in journeying to and from the Jerusalem festivals. Jesus had gone up to Jerusalem in company with his mother and the women. Being now a young man of the consecration, he was supposed to journey back to Nazareth in company with his father and the men. But as the Nazareth party moved on toward Bethany, Jesus was completely absorbed in the discussion of angels, in the temple, being wholly unmindful of the passing of the time for the departure of his parents. And he did not realize that he had been left behind until the noontime adjournment of the temple conferences.

The Nazareth travelers did not miss Jesus because Mary surmised he journeyed with the men, while Joseph thought he traveled with the women since he had gone up to Jerusalem with the women, leading Mary's donkey. They did not discover his absence until they reached Jericho and prepared to tarry for the night. After making inquiry of the last of the party to reach Jericho and learning that none of them had seen their son, they spent a sleepless night, turning over in their minds what might have happened to him, recounting many of his unusual reactions to the events of Passover week, and mildly chiding each other for not seeing to it that he was in the group before they left Jerusalem.

4. FIRST AND SECOND DAYS IN THE TEMPLE

In the meantime, Jesus had remained in the temple throughout the afternoon, listening to the discussions and enjoying the more quiet and decorous atmosphere, the great crowds of Passover week having about disappeared. At the conclusion of the afternoon discussions, in none of which Jesus participated, he betook himself to Bethany, arriving just as Simon's family made ready to partake of their evening meal. The three youngsters were overjoyed to greet Jesus, and he remained in Simon's house for the night. He visited very little during the evening, spending much of the time alone in the garden meditating.

Early next day Jesus was up and on his way to the temple. On the brow of Olivet he paused and wept over the sight his eyes beheld—a spiritually impoverished people, tradition bound and living under the surveillance of the Roman legions. Early forenoon found him in the temple with his mind made up to take part in the discussions. Meanwhile, Joseph and Mary also had arisen with the early dawn with the intention of retracing their steps to Jerusalem. First, they hastened to the house of their relatives, where they had lodged as a family during the Passover week, but inquiry elicited the fact that no one had seen Jesus. After searching all day and finding no trace of him, they returned to their relatives for the night.

At the second conference Jesus had made bold to ask questions, and in a very amazing way he participated in the temple discussions but always in a manner consistent with his youth. Sometimes his pointed questions were somewhat embarrassing to the learned teachers of the Jewish law, but he evinced such a spirit of candid fairness, coupled with an evident hunger for knowledge, that the majority of the temple teachers were disposed to treat him with every consideration. But when he presumed to question the justice of putting to death a drunken gentile who had wandered outside the court of the gentiles and unwittingly entered the forbidden and reputedly sacred precincts of the temple, one of the more intolerant teachers grew impatient with the lad's implied criticisms and, glowering down upon him, asked how old he was. Jesus replied, "thirteen years lacking a trifle more than four months." "Then," rejoined the now irate teacher, "why are you here, since you are not of age as a son of the law?" And when Jesus explained that he had received consecration during the Passover, and that he was a finished student of the Nazareth schools, the teachers with one accord derisively replied, "We might have known; he is from Nazareth." But the leader insisted that Jesus was not to be blamed if the rulers of the synagogue at Nazareth had graduated him, technically, when he was twelve instead of thirteen; and notwithstanding that several of his detractors got up and left, it was ruled that the lad might continue undisturbed as a pupil of the temple discussions.

When this, his second day in the temple, was finished, again he went to Bethany for the night. And again he went out in the garden to meditate and pray. It was apparent that his mind was concerned with the contemplation of weighty problems.

5. THE THIRD DAY IN THE TEMPLE

Jesus' third day with the scribes and teachers in the temple witnessed the gathering of many spectators who, having heard of this youth from Galilee, came to enjoy the experience of seeing a lad confuse the wise men of the law. Simon also came down from Bethany to see what the boy was up to. Throughout this day Joseph and Mary continued their anxious search for Jesus, even going several times into the temple but never thinking to scrutinize the several discussion groups, although they once came almost within hearing distance of his fascinating voice.

Before the day had ended, the entire attention of the chief discussion group of the temple had become focused upon the questions being asked by Jesus. Among his many questions were:

1. What really exists in the holy of holies, behind the veil?

2. Why should mothers in Israel be segregated from the male temple worshipers?

3. If God is a father who loves his children, why all this slaughter of animals to gain divine favor—has the teaching of Moses been misunderstood?

4. Since the temple is dedicated to the worship of the Father in heaven, is it consistent to permit the presence of those who engage in secular barter and trade?

5. Is the expected Messiah to become a temporal prince to sit on the throne of David, or is he to function as the light of life in the establishment of a spiritual kingdom?

And all the day through, those who listened marveled at these questions, and none was more astonished than Simon. For more than four hours this Nazareth youth plied these Jewish teachers with thought-provoking and heart-searching questions. He made few comments on the remarks of his elders. He conveyed his teaching by the questions he would ask. By the deft and subtle phrasing of a question he would at one and the same time challenge their teaching and suggest his own. In the manner of his asking a question there was an appealing combination of sagacity and humor which endeared him even to those who more or less resented his youthfulness. He was always eminently fair and considerate in the asking of these penetrating questions. On this eventful afternoon in the temple he exhibited that same reluctance to take unfair advantage of an opponent which characterized his entire subsequent public ministry. As a youth, and later on as a man, he seemed to be utterly free from all egoistic desire to win an argument merely to experience logical triumph over his fellows, being interested supremely in just one thing: to proclaim everlasting truth and thus effect a fuller revelation of the eternal God.

When the day was over, Simon and Jesus wended their way back to Bethany. For most of the distance both the man and the boy were silent. Again Jesus paused on the brow of Olivet, but as he viewed the city and its temple, he did not weep; he only bowed his head in silent devotion.

After the evening meal at Bethany he again declined to join the merry circle but instead went to the garden, where he lingered long into the night, vainly endeavoring to think out some definite plan of approach to the problem of his lifework and to decide how best he might labor to reveal to his spiritually blinded countrymen a more beautiful concept of the heavenly Father and so set them free from their terrible bondage to law, ritual, ceremonial, and musty tradition. But the clear light did not come to the truth-seeking lad.

6. THE FOURTH DAY IN THE TEMPLE

Jesus was strangely unmindful of his earthly parents; even at breakfast, when Lazarus's mother remarked that his parents must be about home by that time, Jesus did not seem to comprehend that they would be somewhat worried about his having lingered behind.

Again he journeyed to the temple, but he did not pause to meditate at the brow of Olivet. In the course of the morning's discussions much time was devoted to the law and the prophets, and the teachers were astonished that Jesus was so familiar with the Scriptures, in Hebrew as well as Greek. But they were amazed not so much by his knowledge of truth as by his youth.

At the afternoon conference they had hardly begun to answer his question relating to the purpose of prayer when the leader invited the lad to come forward and, sitting beside him, bade him state his own views regarding prayer and worship.

The evening before, Jesus' parents had heard about this strange youth who so deftly sparred with the expounders of the law, but it had not occurred to them that this lad was their son. They had about decided to journey out to the home of Zacharias as they thought Jesus might have gone thither to see Elizabeth and John. Thinking Zacharias might perhaps be at the temple, they stopped there on their way to the City of Judah. As they strolled through the courts of the temple, imagine their surprise and amazement when they recognized the voice of the missing lad and beheld him seated among the temple teachers.

Joseph was speechless, but Mary gave vent to her long-pent-up fear and anxiety when, rushing up to the lad, now standing to greet his astonished parents, she said: "My child, why have you treated us like this? It is now more than three days that your father and I have searched for you sorrowing. Whatever possessed you to desert us?" It was a tense moment. All eyes were turned on Jesus to hear what he would say. His father looked reprovingly at him but said nothing.

It should be remembered that Jesus was supposed to be a young man. He had finished the regular schooling of a child, had been recognized as a son of the law, and had received consecration as a citizen of Israel. And yet his mother more than mildly upbraided him before all the people assembled, right in the midst of the most serious and sublime effort of his young life, thus bringing to an inglorious termination one of the greatest opportunities ever to be granted him to function as a teacher of truth, a preacher of righteousness, a revealer of the loving character of his Father in heaven.

But the lad was equal to the occasion. When you take into fair consideration all the factors which combined to make up this situation, you will be better prepared to fathom the wisdom of the boy's reply to his mother's unintended rebuke. After a moment's thought, Jesus answered his mother, saying: "Why is it that you have so long sought me? Would you not expect to find me in my Father's house since the time has come when I should be about my Father's business?"

Everyone was astonished at the lad's manner of speaking. Silently they all withdrew and left him standing alone with his parents. Presently the young man relieved the embarrassment of all three when he quietly said: "Come, my parents, none has done aught but that which he thought best. Our Father in heaven has ordained these things; let us depart for home."

In silence they started out, arriving at Jericho for the night. Only once did they pause, and that on the brow of Olivet, when the lad raised his staff aloft and, quivering from head to foot under the surging of intense emotion, said: "O Jerusalem, Jerusalem, and the people thereof, what slaves you are—subservient to the Roman yoke and victims of your own traditions—but I will return to cleanse yonder temple and deliver my people from this bondage!"

On the three days' journey to Nazareth Jesus said little; neither did his parents say much in his presence. They were truly at a loss to understand the conduct of their first-born son, but they did treasure in their hearts his sayings, even though they could not fully comprehend their meanings.

Upon reaching home, Jesus made a brief statement to his parents, assuring them of his affection and implying that they need not fear he would again give any occasion for their suffering anxiety because of his conduct. He concluded this momentous statement by saying: "While I must do the will of my Father in heaven, I will also be obedient to my father on earth. I will await my hour."

Though Jesus, in his mind, would many times refuse to *consent* to the well-intentioned but misguided efforts of his parents to dictate the course of his thinking or to establish the plan of his work on earth, still, in every manner consistent with his dedication to the doing of his Paradise Father's will, he did most gracefully *conform* to the desires of his earthly father and to the usages of his family in the flesh. Even when he could not consent, he would do everything possible to conform. He was an artist in the matter of adjusting his dedication to duty to his obligations of family loyalty and social service.

Joseph was puzzled, but Mary, as she reflected on these experiences, gained comfort, eventually viewing his utterance on Olivet as prophetic of the Messianic mission of her son as Israel's deliverer. She set to work with renewed energy to mold his thoughts into patriotic and nationalistic channels and enlisted the efforts of her brother, Jesus' favorite uncle; and in every other way did the mother of Jesus address herself to the task of preparing her first-born son to assume the leadership of those who would restore the throne of David and forever cast off the gentile yoke of political bondage.

PAPER 126

THE TWO CRUCIAL YEARS

OF ALL Jesus' earth-life experiences, the fourteenth and fifteenth years were the most crucial. These two years, after he began to be self-conscious of divinity and destiny, and before he achieved a large measure of communication with his indwelling Adjuster, were the most trying of his eventful life on Urantia. It is this period of two years which should be called the great test, the real temptation. No human youth, in passing through the early confusions and adjustment problems of adolescence, ever experienced a more crucial testing than that which Jesus passed through during his transition from childhood to young manhood.

This important period in Jesus' youthful development began with the conclusion of the Jerusalem visit and with his return to Nazareth. At first Mary was happy in the thought that she had her boy back once more, that Jesus had returned home to be a dutiful son—not that he was ever anything else—and that he would henceforth be more responsive to her plans for his future life. But she was not for long to bask in this sunshine of maternal delusion and unrecognized family pride; very soon she was to be more completely disillusioned. More and more the boy was in the company of his father; less and less did he come to her with his problems, while increasingly both his parents failed to comprehend his frequent alternation between the affairs of this world and the contemplation of his relation to his Father's business. Frankly, they did not understand him, but they did truly love him.

As he grew older, Jesus' pity and love for the Jewish people deepened, but with the passing years, there developed in his mind a growing righteous resentment of the presence in the Father's temple of the politically appointed priests. Jesus had great respect for the sincere Pharisees and the honest scribes, but he held the hypocritical Pharisees and the dishonest theologians in great contempt; he looked with disdain upon all those religious leaders who were not sincere. When he scrutinized the leadership of Israel, he was sometimes tempted to look with favor on the possibility of his becoming the Messiah of Jewish expectation, but he never yielded to such a temptation.

The story of his exploits among the wise men of the temple in Jerusalem was gratifying to all Nazareth, especially to his former teachers in the synagogue school. For a time his praise was on everybody's lips. All the village recounted his childhood wisdom and praiseworthy conduct and predicted that he was destined to become a great leader in Israel; at last a really great teacher was to come out of Nazareth in Galilee. And they all looked forward to the time when he would be fifteen years of age so that he might be permitted regularly to read the Scriptures in the synagogue on the Sabbath day.

1. HIS FOURTEENTH YEAR (A.D. 8)

This is the calendar year of his fourteenth birthday. He had become a good yoke maker and worked well with both canvas and leather. He was also rapidly developing into an expert carpenter and cabinetmaker. This summer he made frequent trips to the top of the hill to the northwest of Nazareth for prayer and meditation. He was gradually becoming more self-conscious of the nature of his bestowal on earth.

This hill, a little more than one hundred years previously, had been the "high place of Baal," and now it was the site of the tomb of Simeon, a reputed holy man of Israel. From the summit of this hill of Simeon, Jesus looked out over Nazareth and the surrounding country. He would gaze upon Megiddo and recall the story of the Egyptian army winning its first great victory in Asia; and how, later on, another such army defeated the Judean king Josiah. Not far away he could look upon Taanach, where Deborah and Barak defeated Sisera. In the distance he could view the hills of Dothan, where he had been taught Joseph's brethren sold him into Egyptian slavery. He then would shift his gaze over to Ebal and Gerizim and recount to himself the traditions of Abraham, Jacob, and Abimelech. And thus he recalled and turned over in his mind the historic and traditional events of his father Joseph's people.

He continued to carry on his advanced courses of reading under the synagogue teachers, and he also continued with the home education of his brothers and sisters as they grew up to suitable ages.

Early this year Joseph arranged to set aside the income from his Nazareth and Capernaum property to pay for Jesus' long course of study at Jerusalem, it having been planned that he should go to Jerusalem in August of the following year when he would be fifteen years of age.

By the beginning of this year both Joseph and Mary entertained frequent doubts about the destiny of their first-born son. He was indeed a brilliant and lovable child, but he was so difficult to understand, so hard to fathom, and again, nothing extraordinary or miraculous ever happened. Scores of times had his proud mother stood in breathless anticipation, expecting to see her son engage in some superhuman or miraculous performance, but always were her hopes dashed down in cruel disappointment. And all this was discouraging, even disheartening. The devout people of those days truly believed that prophets and men of promise always demonstrated their calling and established their divine authority by performing miracles and working wonders. But Jesus did none of these things; wherefore was the confusion of his parents steadily increased as they contemplated his future.

The improved economic condition of the Nazareth family was reflected in many ways about the home and especially in the increased number of smooth white boards which were used as writing slates, the writing being done with charcoal. Jesus was also permitted to resume his music lessons; he was very fond of playing the harp.

Throughout this year it can truly be said that Jesus "grew in favor with man and with God." The prospects of the family seemed good; the future was bright.

2. THE DEATH OF JOSEPH

All did go well until that fateful day of Tuesday, September 25, when a runner from Sepphoris brought to this Nazareth home the tragic news that Joseph had been severely injured by the falling of a derrick while at work on the governor's residence. The messenger from Sepphoris had stopped at the shop on the way to Joseph's home, informing Jesus of his father's accident, and they went together to the house to break the sad news to Mary. Jesus desired to go immediately to his father, but Mary would hear to nothing but that she must hasten to her husband's side. She directed that James, then ten years of age, should accompany her to Sepphoris while Jesus remained home with the younger children until she should return, as she did not know how seriously Joseph had been injured. But Joseph died of his injuries before Mary arrived. They brought him to Nazareth, and on the following day he was laid to rest with his fathers.

Just at the time when prospects were good and the future looked bright, an apparently cruel hand struck down the head of this Nazareth household, the affairs of this home were disrupted, and every plan for Jesus and his future education was demolished. This carpenter lad, now just past fourteen years of age, awakened to the realization that he had not only to fulfill the commission of his heavenly Father to reveal the divine nature on earth and in the flesh, but that his young human nature must also shoulder the responsibility of caring for his widowed mother and seven brothers and sisters—and another yet to be born. This lad of Nazareth now became the sole support and comfort of this so suddenly bereaved family. Thus were permitted those occurrences of the natural order of events on Urantia which would force this young man of destiny so early to assume these heavy but highly educational and disciplinary responsibilities attendant upon becoming the head of a human family, of becoming father to his own brothers and sisters, of supporting and protecting his mother, of functioning as guardian of his father's home, the only home he was to know while on this world.

Jesus cheerfully accepted the responsibilities so suddenly thrust upon him, and he carried them faithfully to the end. At least one great problem and anticipated difficulty in his life had been tragically solved—he would not now be expected to go to Jerusalem to study under the rabbis. It remained always true that Jesus "sat at no man's feet." He was ever willing to learn from even the humblest of little children, but he never derived authority to teach truth from human sources.

Still he knew nothing of the Gabriel visit to his mother before his birth; he only learned of this from John on the day of his baptism, at the beginning of his public ministry.

As the years passed, this young carpenter of Nazareth increasingly measured every institution of society and every usage of religion by the unvarying test: What does it do for the human soul? does it bring God to man? does it bring man to God? While this youth did not wholly neglect the recreational and social aspects of life, more and more he devoted his time and energies to just two purposes: the care of his family and the preparation to do his Father's heavenly will on earth.

This year it became the custom for the neighbors to drop in during the winter evenings to hear Jesus play upon the harp, to listen to his stories (for the lad was a master storyteller), and to hear him read from the Greek scriptures.

The economic affairs of the family continued to run fairly smoothly as there was quite a sum of money on hand at the time of Joseph's death. Jesus early demonstrated the possession of keen business judgment and financial sagacity. He was liberal but frugal; he was saving but generous. He proved to be a wise and efficient administrator of his father's estate.

But in spite of all that Jesus and the Nazareth neighbors could do to bring cheer into the home, Mary, and even the children, were overcast with sadness. Joseph was gone. Joseph was an unusual husband and father, and they all missed him. And it seemed all the more tragic to think that he died ere they could speak to him or hear his farewell blessing.

3. THE FIFTEENTH YEAR (A.D. 9)

By the middle of this fifteenth year—and we are reckoning time in accordance with the twentieth-century calendar, not by the Jewish year—Jesus had taken a firm grasp upon the management of his family. Before this year had passed, their savings had about disappeared, and they were face to face with the necessity of disposing of one of the Nazareth houses which Joseph and his neighbor Jacob owned in partnership.

On Wednesday evening, April 17, A.D. 9, Ruth, the baby of the family, was born, and to the best of his ability Jesus endeavored to take the place of his father in comforting and ministering to his mother during this trying and peculiarly sad ordeal. For almost a score of years (until he began his public ministry) no father could have loved and nurtured his daughter any more affectionately and faithfully than Jesus cared for little Ruth. And he was an equally good father to all the other members of his family.

During this year Jesus first formulated the prayer which he subsequently taught to his apostles, and which to many has become known as "The Lord's Prayer." In a way it was an evolution of the family altar; they had many forms of praise and several formal prayers. After his father's death Jesus tried to teach the older children to express themselves individually in prayer—much as he so enjoyed doing—but they could not grasp his thought and would invariably fall back upon their memorized prayer forms. It was in this effort to stimulate his older brothers and sisters to say individual prayers that Jesus would endeavor to lead them along by suggestive phrases, and presently, without intention on his part, it developed that they were all using a form of prayer which was largely built up from these suggestive lines which Jesus had taught them.

At last Jesus gave up the idea of having each member of the family formulate spontaneous prayers, and one evening in October he sat down by the little squat lamp on the low stone table, and, on a piece of smooth cedar board about eighteen inches square, with a piece of charcoal he wrote out the prayer which became from that time on the standard family petition.

This year Jesus was much troubled with confused thinking. Family responsibility had quite effectively removed all thought of immediately carrying out any plan for responding to the Jerusalem visitation directing him to "be about his Father's business." Jesus rightly reasoned that the watchcare of his earthly father's family must take precedence of all duties; that the support of his family must become his first obligation.

In the course of this year Jesus found a passage in the so-called Book of Enoch which influenced him in the later adoption of the term "Son of Man" as a designation for his bestowal mission on Urantia. He had thoroughly considered the idea of the Jewish Messiah and was firmly convinced that he was not to be that Messiah. He longed to help his father's people, but he never expected to lead Jewish armies in overthrowing the foreign domination of Palestine. He knew he would never sit on the throne of David at Jerusalem. Neither did he believe that his mission was that of a spiritual deliverer or moral teacher solely to the Jewish people. In no sense, therefore, could his life mission be the fulfillment of the intense longings and supposed Messianic prophecies of the Hebrew scriptures; at least, not as the Jews understood these predictions of the prophets. Likewise he was certain he was never to appear as the Son of Man depicted by the Prophet Daniel.

But when the time came for him to go forth as a world teacher, what would he call himself? What claim should he make concerning his mission? By what name would he be called by the people who would become believers in his teachings?

While turning all these problems over in his mind, he found in the synagogue library at Nazareth, among the apocalyptic books which he had been studying, this manuscript called "The Book of Enoch"; and though he was certain that it had not been written by Enoch of old, it proved very intriguing to him, and he read and reread it many times. There was one passage which particularly impressed him, a passage in which this term "Son of Man" appeared. The writer of this so-called Book of Enoch went on to tell about this Son of Man, describing the work he would do on earth and explaining that this Son of Man, before coming down on this earth to bring salvation to mankind, had walked through the courts of heavenly glory with his Father, the Father of all; and that he had turned his back upon all this grandeur and glory to come down on earth to proclaim salvation to needy mortals. As Jesus would read these passages (well understanding that much of the Eastern mysticism which had become admixed with these teachings was erroneous), he responded in his heart and recognized in his mind that of all the Messianic predictions of the Hebrew scriptures and of all the theories about the Jewish deliverer, none was so near the truth as this story tucked away in this only partially accredited Book of Enoch; and he then and there decided to adopt as his inaugural title "the Son of Man." And this he did when he subsequently began his public work. Jesus had an unerring ability for the recognition of truth, and truth he never hesitated to embrace, no matter from what source it appeared to emanate.

By this time he had quite thoroughly settled many things about his forthcoming work for the world, but he said nothing of these matters to his mother, who still held stoutly to the idea of his being the Jewish Messiah.

The great confusion of Jesus' younger days now arose. Having settled something about the nature of his mission on earth, "to be about his Father's business"—to show forth his Father's loving nature to all mankind—he began to ponder anew the many statements in the Scriptures referring to the coming of a national deliverer, a Jewish teacher or king. To what event did these prophecies refer? Was not he a Jew? or was he? Was he or was he not of the house of David? His mother averred he was; his father had ruled that he was not. He decided he was not. But had the prophets confused the nature and mission of the Messiah?

After all, could it be possible that his mother was right? In most matters, when differences of opinion had arisen in the past, she had been right. If he were a new teacher and *not* the Messiah, then how should he recognize the Jewish Messiah if such a one should appear in Jerusalem during the time of his earth mission; and, further, what should be his relation to this Jewish Messiah? And what should be his relation, after embarking on his life mission, to his family? to the Jewish commonwealth and religion? to the Roman Empire? to the gentiles and their religions? Each of these momentous problems this young Galilean turned over in his mind and seriously pondered while he continued to work at the carpenter's bench, laboriously making a living for himself, his mother, and eight other hungry mouths.

Before the end of this year Mary saw the family funds diminishing. She turned the sale of doves over to James. Presently they bought a second cow, and with the aid of Miriam they began the sale of milk to their Nazareth neighbors.

His profound periods of meditation, his frequent journeys to the hilltop for prayer, and the many strange ideas which Jesus advanced from time to time, thoroughly alarmed his mother. Sometimes she thought the lad was beside himself, and then she would steady her fears, remembering that he was, after all, a child of promise and in some manner different from other youths.

But Jesus was learning not to speak of all his thoughts, not to present all his ideas to the world, not even to his own mother. From this year on, Jesus' disclosures about what was going on in his mind steadily diminished; that is, he talked less about those things which an average person could not grasp, and which would lead to his being regarded as peculiar or different from ordinary folks. To all appearances he became commonplace and conventional, though he did long for someone who could understand his problems. He craved a trustworthy and confidential friend, but his problems were too complex for his human associates to comprehend. The uniqueness of the unusual situation compelled him to bear his burdens alone.

4. FIRST SERMON IN THE SYNAGOGUE

With the coming of his fifteenth birthday, Jesus could officially occupy the synagogue pulpit on the Sabbath day. Many times before, in the absence of speakers, Jesus had been asked to read the Scriptures, but now the day had come when, according to law, he could conduct the service. Therefore on the first Sabbath after his fifteenth birthday the chazan arranged for Jesus to conduct the morning service of the synagogue. And when all the faithful in Nazareth had assembled, the young man, having made his selection of Scriptures, stood up and began to read:

"The spirit of the Lord God is upon me, for the Lord has anointed me; he has sent me to bring good news to the meek, to bind up the brokenhearted, to proclaim liberty to the captives, and to set the spiritual prisoners free; to proclaim the year of God's favor and the day of our God's reckoning; to comfort all mourners, to give them beauty for ashes, the oil of joy in the place of mourning, a song of praise instead of the spirit of sorrow, that they may be called trees of righteousness, the planting of the Lord, wherewith he may be glorified.

"Seek good and not evil that you may live, and so the Lord, the God of hosts, shall be with you. Hate the evil and love the good; establish judgment in the gate. Perhaps the Lord God will be gracious to the remnant of Joseph.

"Wash yourselves, make yourselves clean; put away the evil of your doings from before my eyes; cease to do evil and learn to do good; seek justice, relieve the oppressed. Defend the fatherless and plead for the widow.

"Wherewith shall I come before the Lord, to bow myself before the Lord of all the earth? Shall I come before him with burnt offerings, with calves a year old? Will the Lord be pleased with thousands of rams, ten thousands of sheep, or with rivers of oil? Shall I give my first-born for my transgression, the fruit of my body for the sin of my soul? No! for the Lord has showed us, O men, what is good. And what does the Lord require of you but to deal justly, love mercy, and walk humbly with your God?

"To whom, then, will you liken God who sits upon the circle of the earth? Lift up your eyes and behold who has created all these worlds, who brings forth their host by number and calls them all by their names. He does all these things by the greatness of his might, and because he is strong in power, not one fails. He gives power to the weak, and to those who are weary he increases strength. Fear not, for I am with you; be not dismayed, for I am your God. I will strengthen you and I will help you; yes, I will uphold you with the right hand of my righteousness, for I am the Lord your God. And I will hold your right hand, saying to you, fear not, for I will help you.

"And you are my witness, says the Lord, and my servant whom I have chosen that all may know and believe me and understand that I am the Eternal. I, even I, am the Lord, and beside me there is no savior."

And when he had thus read, he sat down, and the people went to their homes, pondering over the words which he had so graciously read to them. Never had his townspeople seen him so magnificently solemn; never had they heard his voice so earnest and so sincere; never had they observed him so manly and decisive, so authoritative.

This Sabbath afternoon Jesus climbed the Nazareth hill with James and, when they returned home, wrote out the Ten Commandments in Greek on two smooth boards in charcoal. Subsequently Martha colored and decorated these boards, and for long they hung on the wall over James's small workbench.

5. THE FINANCIAL STRUGGLE

Gradually Jesus and his family returned to the simple life of their earlier years. Their clothes and even their food became simpler. They had plenty of milk, butter, and cheese. In season they enjoyed the produce of their garden, but each passing month necessitated the practice of greater frugality. Their breakfasts were very plain; they saved their best food for the evening meal. However, among these Jews lack of wealth did not imply social inferiority.

Already had this youth well-nigh encompassed the comprehension of how men lived in his day. And how well he understood life in the home, field, and workshop is shown by his subsequent teachings, which so repletely reveal his intimate contact with all phases of human experience.

The Nazareth chazan continued to cling to the belief that Jesus was to become a great teacher, probably the successor of the renowned Gamaliel at Jerusalem.

Apparently all Jesus' plans for a career were thwarted. The future did not look bright as matters now developed. But he did not falter; he was not discouraged. He lived on, day by day, doing well the present duty and faithfully discharging the *immediate* responsibilities of his station in life. Jesus' life is the everlasting comfort of all disappointed idealists.

The pay of a common day-laboring carpenter was slowly diminishing. By the end of this year Jesus could earn, by working early and late, only the equivalent of about twenty-five cents a day. By the next year they found it difficult to pay the civil taxes, not to mention the synagogue assessments and the temple tax of one-half shekel. During this year the tax collector tried to squeeze extra revenue out of Jesus, even threatening to take his harp.

Fearing that the copy of the Greek scriptures might be discovered and confiscated by the tax collectors, Jesus, on his fifteenth birthday, presented it to the Nazareth synagogue library as his maturity offering to the Lord.

The great shock of his fifteenth year came when Jesus went over to Sepphoris to receive the decision of Herod regarding the appeal taken to him in the dispute about the amount of money due Joseph at the time of his accidental death. Jesus and Mary had hoped for the receipt of a considerable sum of money when the treasurer at Sepphoris had offered them a paltry amount. Joseph's brothers had taken an appeal to Herod himself, and now Jesus stood in the palace and heard Herod decree that his father had nothing due him at the time of his death. And for such an unjust decision Jesus never again trusted Herod Antipas. It is not surprising that he once alluded to Herod as "that fox."

The close work at the carpenter's bench during this and subsequent years deprived Jesus of the opportunity of mingling with the caravan passengers. The family supply shop had already been taken over by his uncle, and Jesus worked altogether in the home shop, where he was near to help Mary with the family. About this time he began sending James up to the camel lot to gather information about world events, and thus he sought to keep in touch with the news of the day.

As he grew up to manhood, he passed through all those conflicts and confusions which the average young persons of previous and subsequent ages have undergone. And the rigorous experience of supporting his family was a sure safeguard against his having overmuch time for idle meditation or the indulgence of mystic tendencies.

This was the year that Jesus rented a considerable piece of land just to the north of their home, which was divided up as a family garden plot. Each of the older children had an individual garden, and they entered into keen competition in their agricultural efforts. Their eldest brother spent some time with them in the garden each day during the season of vegetable cultivation. As Jesus worked with his younger brothers and sisters in the garden, he many times entertained the wish that they were all located on a farm out in the country where they could enjoy the liberty and freedom of an unhampered life. But they did not find themselves growing up in the country; and Jesus, being a thoroughly practical youth as well as an idealist, intelligently and vigorously attacked his problem just as he found it, and did everything within his power to adjust himself and his family to the realities of their situation and to adapt their condition to the highest possible satisfaction of their individual and collective longings.

At one time Jesus faintly hoped that he might be able to gather up sufficient means, provided they could collect the considerable sum of money due his father for work on Herod's palace, to warrant undertaking the purchase of a small farm. He had really given serious thought to this plan of moving his family out into the country. But when Herod refused to pay them any of the funds due Joseph, they gave up the ambition of owning a home in the country. As it was, they contrived to enjoy much of the experience of farm life as they now had three cows, four sheep, a flock of chickens, a donkey, and a dog, in addition to the doves. Even the little tots had their regular duties to perform in the well-regulated scheme of management which characterized the home life of this Nazareth family.

With the close of this fifteenth year Jesus completed the traversal of that dangerous and difficult period in human existence, that time of transition between the more complacent years of childhood and the consciousness of approaching manhood with its increased responsibilities and opportunities for the acquirement of advanced experience in the development of a noble character. The growth period for mind and body had ended, and now began the real career of this young man of Nazareth.

PAPER 127

THE ADOLESCENT YEARS

AS JESUS entered upon his adolescent years, he found himself the head and sole support of a large family. Within a few years after his father's death all their property was gone. As time passed, he became increasingly conscious of his pre-existence; at the same time he began more fully to realize that he was present on earth and in the flesh for the express purpose of revealing his Paradise Father to the children of men.

No adolescent youth who has lived or ever will live on this world or any other world has had or ever will have more weighty problems to resolve or more intricate difficulties to untangle. No youth of Urantia will ever be called upon to pass through more testing conflicts or more trying situations than Jesus himself endured during those strenuous years from fifteen to twenty.

Having thus tasted the actual experience of living these adolescent years on a world beset by evil and distraught by sin, the Son of Man became possessed of full knowledge about the life experience of the youth of all the realms of Nebadon, and thus forever he became the understanding refuge for the distressed and perplexed adolescents of all ages and on all worlds throughout the local universe.

Slowly, but certainly and by actual experience, this divine Son is *earning* the right to become sovereign of his universe, the unquestioned and supreme ruler of all created intelligences on all local universe worlds, the understanding refuge of the beings of all ages and of all degrees of personal endowment and experience.

1. THE SIXTEENTH YEAR (A.D. 10)

The incarnated Son passed through infancy and experienced an uneventful childhood. Then he emerged from that testing and trying transition stage between childhood and young manhood—he became the adolescent Jesus.

This year he attained his full physical growth. He was a virile and comely youth. He became increasingly sober and serious, but he was kind and sympathetic. His eye was kind but searching; his smile was always engaging and reassuring. His voice was musical but authoritative; his greeting cordial but unaffected. Always, even in the most commonplace of contacts, there seemed to be in evidence the touch of a twofold nature, the human and the divine. Ever he displayed this combination of the sympathizing friend and the authoritative teacher. And these personality traits began early to become manifest, even in these adolescent years.

This physically strong and robust youth also acquired the full growth of his human intellect, not the full experience of human thinking but the fullness of capacity for such intellectual development. He possessed a healthy and well-proportioned body, a keen and analytical mind, a kind and sympathetic disposition, a somewhat fluctuating but aggressive temperament, all of which were becoming organized into a strong, striking, and attractive personality.

As time went on, it became more difficult for his mother and his brothers and sisters to understand him; they stumbled over his sayings and misinterpreted his doings. They were all unfitted to comprehend their eldest brother's life because their mother had given them to understand that he was destined to become the deliverer of the Jewish people. After they had received from Mary such intimations as family secrets, imagine their confusion when Jesus would make frank denials of all such ideas and intentions.

This year Simon started to school, and they were compelled to sell another house. James now took charge of the teaching of his three sisters, two of whom were old enough to begin serious study. As soon as Ruth grew up, she was taken in hand by Miriam and Martha. Ordinarily the girls of Jewish families received little education, but Jesus maintained (and his mother agreed) that girls should go to school the same as boys, and since the synagogue school would not receive them, there was nothing to do but conduct a home school especially for them.

Throughout this year Jesus was closely confined to the workbench. Fortunately he had plenty of work; his was of such a superior grade that he was never idle no matter how slack work might be in that region. At times he had so much to do that James would help him.

By the end of this year he had just about made up his mind that he would, after rearing his family and seeing them married, enter publicly upon his work as a teacher of truth and as a revealer of the heavenly Father to the world. He knew he was not to become the expected Jewish Messiah, and he concluded that it was next to useless to discuss these matters with his mother; he decided to allow her to entertain whatever ideas she might choose since all he had said in the past had made little or no impression upon her and he recalled that his father had never been able to say anything that would change her mind. From this year on he talked less and less with his mother, or anyone else, about these problems. His was such a peculiar mission that no one living on earth could give him advice concerning its prosecution.

He was a real though youthful father to the family; he spent every possible hour with the youngsters, and they truly loved him. His mother grieved to see him work so hard; she sorrowed that he was day by day toiling at the carpenter's bench earning a living for the family instead of being, as they had so fondly planned, at Jerusalem studying with the rabbis. While there was much about her son that Mary could not understand, she did love him, and she most thoroughly appreciated the willing manner in which he shouldered the responsibility of the home.

2. THE SEVENTEENTH YEAR (A.D. 11)

At about this time there was considerable agitation, especially at Jerusalem and in Judea, in favor of rebellion against the payment of taxes to Rome. There was coming into existence a strong nationalist party, presently to be called the Zealots. The Zealots, unlike the Pharisees, were not willing to await the coming of the Messiah. They proposed to bring things to a head through political revolt.

A group of organizers from Jerusalem arrived in Galilee and were making good headway until they reached Nazareth. When they came to see Jesus, he listened carefully to them and asked many questions but refused to join the party. He declined fully to disclose his reasons for not enlisting, and his refusal had the effect of keeping out many of his youthful fellows in Nazareth.

Mary did her best to induce him to enlist, but she could not budge him. She went so far as to intimate that his refusal to espouse the nationalist cause at her behest was insubordination, a violation of his pledge made upon their return from Jerusalem that he would be subject to his parents; but in answer to this insinuation he only laid a kindly hand on her shoulder and, looking into her face, said: "My mother, how could you?" And Mary withdrew her statement.

One of Jesus' uncles (Mary's brother Simon) had already joined this group, subsequently becoming an officer in the Galilean division. And for several years there was something of an estrangement between Jesus and his uncle.

But trouble began to brew in Nazareth. Jesus' attitude in these matters had resulted in creating a division among the Jewish youths of the city. About half had joined the nationalist organization, and the other half began the formation of an opposing group of more moderate patriots, expecting Jesus to assume the leadership. They were amazed when he refused the honor offered him, pleading as an excuse his heavy family responsibilities, which they all allowed. But the situation was still further complicated when, presently, a wealthy Jew, Isaac, a moneylender to the gentiles, came forward agreeing to support Jesus' family if he would lay down his tools and assume leadership of these Nazareth patriots.

Jesus, then scarcely seventeen years of age, was confronted with one of the most delicate and difficult situations of his early life. Patriotic issues, especially when complicated by tax-gathering foreign oppressors, are always difficult for spiritual leaders to relate themselves to, and it was doubly so in this case since the Jewish religion was involved in all this agitation against Rome.

Jesus' position was made more difficult because his mother and uncle, and even his younger brother James, all urged him to join the nationalist cause. All the better Jews of Nazareth had enlisted, and those young men who had not joined the movement would all enlist the moment Jesus changed his mind. He had but one wise counselor in all Nazareth, his old teacher, the chazan, who counseled him about his reply to the citizens' committee of Nazareth when they came to ask for his answer to the public appeal which had been made. In all Jesus' young life this was the very first time he had consciously resorted to public strategy. Theretofore, always had he depended upon a frank statement of truth to clarify the situation, but now he could not declare the full truth. He could not intimate that he was more than a man; he could not disclose his idea of the mission which awaited his attainment of a riper manhood. Despite these limitations his religious fealty and national loyalty were directly challenged. His family was in a turmoil, his youthful friends in division, and the entire Jewish contingent of the town in a hubbub. And to think that he was to blame for it all! And how innocent he had been of all intention to make trouble of any kind, much less a disturbance of this sort.

Something had to be done. He must state his position, and this he did bravely and diplomatically to the satisfaction of many, but not all. He adhered to the terms of his original plea, maintaining that his first duty was to his family, that a widowed mother and eight brothers and sisters needed something more than mere money could buy—the physical necessities of life—that they were entitled to a father's watchcare and guidance, and that he could not in clear conscience release himself from the obligation which a cruel accident had thrust upon him.

He paid compliment to his mother and eldest brother for being willing to release him but reiterated that loyalty to a dead father forbade his leaving the family no matter how much money was forthcoming for their material support, making his never-to-be-forgotten statement that "money cannot love." In the course of this address Jesus made several veiled references to his "life mission" but explained that, regardless of whether or not it might be inconsistent with the military idea, it, along with everything else in his life, had been given up in order that he might be able to discharge faithfully his obligation to his family. Everyone in Nazareth well knew he was a good father to his family, and this was a matter so near the heart of every noble Jew that Jesus' plea found an appreciative response in the hearts of many of his hearers; and some of those who were not thus minded were disarmed by a speech made by James, which, while not on the program, was delivered at this time. That very day the chazan had rehearsed James in his speech, but that was their secret.

James stated that he was sure Jesus would help to liberate his people if he (James) were only old enough to assume responsibility for the family, and that, if they would only consent to allow Jesus to remain "with us, to be our father and teacher, then you will have not just one leader from Joseph's family, but presently you will have five loyal nationalists, for are there not five of us boys to grow up and come forth from our brother-father's guidance to serve our nation?" And thus did the lad bring to a fairly happy ending a very tense and threatening situation.

The crisis for the time being was over, but never was this incident forgotten in Nazareth. The agitation persisted; not again was Jesus in universal favor; the division of sentiment was never fully overcome. And this, augmented by other and subsequent occurrences, was one of the chief reasons why he moved to Capernaum in later years. Henceforth Nazareth maintained a division of sentiment regarding the Son of Man.

James graduated at school this year and began full-time work at home in the carpenter shop. He had become a clever worker with tools and now took over the making of yokes and plows while Jesus began to do more house finishing and expert cabinet work.

This year Jesus made great progress in the organization of his mind. Gradually he had brought his divine and human natures together, and he accomplished all this organization of intellect by the force of his own *decisions* and with only the aid of his indwelling Monitor, just such a Monitor as all normal mortals on all postbestowal-Son worlds have within their minds. So far, nothing supernatural had happened in this young man's career except the visit of a messenger, dispatched by his elder brother Immanuel, who once appeared to him during the night at Jerusalem.

3. THE EIGHTEENTH YEAR (A.D. 12)

In the course of this year all the family property, except the home and garden, was disposed of. The last piece of Capernaum property (except an equity in one other), already mortgaged, was sold. The proceeds were used for taxes, to buy some new tools for James, and to make a payment on the old family supply and repair shop near the caravan lot, which Jesus now proposed to buy back since James was old enough to work at the house shop and help Mary about the home.

With the financial pressure thus eased for the time being, Jesus decided to take James to the Passover. They went up to Jerusalem a day early, to be alone, going by way of Samaria. They walked, and Jesus told James about the historic places en route as his father had taught him on a similar journey five years before.

In passing through Samaria, they saw many strange sights. On this journey they talked over many of their problems, personal, family, and national. James was a very religious type of lad, and while he did not fully agree with his mother regarding the little he knew of the plans concerning Jesus' lifework, he did look forward to the time when he would be able to assume responsibility for the family so that Jesus could begin his mission. He was very appreciative of Jesus' taking him up to the Passover, and they talked over the future more fully than ever before.

Jesus did much thinking as they journeyed through Samaria, particularly at Bethel and when drinking from Jacob's well. He and his brother discussed the traditions of Abraham, Isaac, and Jacob. He did much to prepare James for what he was about to witness at Jerusalem, thus seeking to lessen the shock such as he himself had experienced on his first visit to the temple. But James was not so sensitive to some of these sights. He commented on the perfunctory and heartless manner in which some of the priests performed their duties but on the whole greatly enjoyed his sojourn at Jerusalem.

Jesus took James to Bethany for the Passover supper. Simon had been laid to rest with his fathers, and Jesus presided over this household as the head of the Passover family, having brought the paschal lamb from the temple.

After the Passover supper Mary sat down to talk with James while Martha, Lazarus, and Jesus talked together far into the night. The next day they attended the temple services, and James was received into the commonwealth of Israel. That morning, as they paused on the brow of Olivet to view the temple, while James exclaimed in wonder, Jesus gazed on Jerusalem in silence. James could not comprehend his brother's demeanor. That night they again returned to Bethany and would have departed for home the next day, but James was insistent on their going back to visit the temple, explaining that he wanted to hear the teachers. And while this was true, secretly in his heart he wanted to hear Jesus participate in the discussions, as he had heard his mother tell about. Accordingly, they went to the temple and heard the discussions, but Jesus asked no questions. It all seemed so puerile and insignificant to this awakening mind of man and God—he could only pity them. James was disappointed that Jesus said nothing. To his inquiries Jesus only made reply, "My hour has not yet come."

The next day they journeyed home by Jericho and the Jordan valley, and Jesus recounted many things by the way, including his former trip over this road when he was thirteen years old.

Upon returning to Nazareth, Jesus began work in the old family repair shop and was greatly cheered by being able to meet so many people each day from all parts of the country and surrounding districts. Jesus truly loved people—just common folks. Each month he made his payments on the shop and, with James's help, continued to provide for the family.

Several times a year, when visitors were not present thus to function, Jesus continued to read the Sabbath scriptures at the synagogue and many times offered comments on the lesson, but usually he so selected the passages that comment was unnecessary. He was skillful, so arranging the order of the reading of the various passages that the one would illuminate the other. He never failed, weather permitting, to take his brothers and sisters out on Sabbath afternoons for their nature strolls.

About this time the chazan inaugurated a young men's club for philosophic discussion which met at the homes of different members and often at his own home, and Jesus became a prominent member of this group. By this means he was enabled to regain some of the local prestige which he had lost at the time of the recent nationalistic controversies.

His social life, while restricted, was not wholly neglected. He had many warm friends and stanch admirers among both the young men and the young women of Nazareth.

In September, Elizabeth and John came to visit the Nazareth family. John, having lost his father, intended to return to the Judean hills to engage in agriculture and sheep raising unless Jesus advised him to remain in Nazareth to take up carpentry or some other line of work. They did not know that the Nazareth family was practically penniless. The more Mary and Elizabeth talked about their sons, the more they became convinced that it would be good for the two young men to work together and see more of each other.

Jesus and John had many talks together; and they talked over some very intimate and personal matters. When they had finished this visit, they decided not again to see each other until they should meet in their public service after "the heavenly Father should call" them to their work. John was tremendously impressed by what he saw at Nazareth that he should return home and labor for the support of his mother. He became convinced that he was to be a part of Jesus' life mission, but he saw that Jesus was to occupy many years with the rearing of his family; so he was much more content to return to his home and settle down to the care of their little farm and to minister to the needs of his mother. And never again did John and Jesus see each other until that day by the Jordan when the Son of Man presented himself for baptism.

On Saturday afternoon, December 3, of this year, death for the second time struck at this Nazareth family. Little Amos, their baby brother, died after a week's illness with a high fever. After passing through this time of sorrow with her first-born son as her only support, Mary at last and in the fullest sense recognized Jesus as the real head of the family; and he was truly a worthy head.

For four years their standard of living had steadily declined; year by year they felt the pinch of increasing poverty. By the close of this year they faced one of the most difficult experiences of all their uphill struggles. James had not yet begun to earn much, and the expenses of a funeral on top of everything else staggered them. But Jesus would only say to his anxious and grieving mother: "Mother-Mary, sorrow will not help us; we are all doing our best, and mother's smile, perchance, might even inspire us to do better. Day by day we are strengthened for these tasks by our hope of better days ahead." His sturdy and practical optimism was truly contagious; all the children lived in an atmosphere of anticipation of better times and better things. And this hopeful courage contributed mightily to the development of strong and noble characters, in spite of the depressiveness of their poverty.

Jesus possessed the ability effectively to mobilize all his powers of mind, soul, and body on the task immediately in hand. He could concentrate his deep-thinking mind on the one problem which he wished to solve, and this, in connection with his untiring *patience,* enabled him serenely to endure the trials of a difficult mortal existence—to live as if he were "seeing Him who is invisible."

4. THE NINETEENTH YEAR (A.D. 13)

By this time Jesus and Mary were getting along much better. She regarded him less as a son; he had become to her more a father to her children. Each day's life swarmed with practical and immediate difficulties. Less frequently they spoke of his lifework, for, as time passed, all their thought was mutually devoted to the support and upbringing of their family of four boys and three girls.

By the beginning of this year Jesus had fully won his mother to the acceptance of his methods of child training—the positive injunction to do good in the place of the older Jewish method of forbidding to do evil. In his home and throughout his public-teaching career Jesus invariably employed the *positive* form of exhortation. Always and everywhere did he say, "You shall do this—you ought to do that." Never did he employ the negative mode of teaching derived from the ancient taboos. He refrained from placing emphasis on evil by forbidding it, while he exalted the good by commanding its performance. Prayer time in this household was the occasion for discussing anything and everything relating to the welfare of the family.

Jesus began wise discipline upon his brothers and sisters at such an early age that little or no punishment was ever required to secure their prompt and wholehearted obedience. The only exception was Jude, upon whom on sundry occasions Jesus found it necessary to impose penalties for his infractions of the rules of the home. On three occasions when it was deemed wise to punish Jude for self-confessed and deliberate violations of the family rules of conduct, his punishment was fixed by the unanimous decree of the older children and was assented to by Jude himself before it was inflicted.

While Jesus was most methodical and systematic in everything he did, there was also in all his administrative rulings a refreshing elasticity of interpretation and an individuality of adaptation that greatly impressed all the children with the spirit of justice which actuated their father-brother. He never arbitrarily disciplined his brothers and sisters, and such uniform fairness and personal consideration greatly endeared Jesus to all his family.

James and Simon grew up trying to follow Jesus' plan of placating their bellicose and sometimes irate playmates by persuasion and nonresistance, and they were fairly successful; but Joseph and Jude, while assenting to such teachings at home, made haste to defend themselves when assailed by their comrades; in particular was Jude guilty of violating the spirit of these teachings. But nonresistance was not a *rule* of the family. No penalty was attached to the violation of personal teachings.

In general, all of the children, particularly the girls, would consult Jesus about their childhood troubles and confide in him just as they would have in an affectionate father.

James was growing up to be a well-balanced and even-tempered youth, but he was not so spiritually inclined as Jesus. He was a much better student than Joseph, who, while a faithful worker, was even less spiritually minded. Joseph was a plodder and not up to the intellectual level of the other children. Simon was a well-meaning boy but too much of a dreamer. He was slow in getting settled down in life and was the cause of considerable anxiety to Jesus and Mary. But he was always a good and well-intentioned lad. Jude was a firebrand. He had the highest of ideals, but he was unstable in temperament. He had all and more of his mother's determination and aggressiveness, but he lacked much of her sense of proportion and discretion.

Miriam was a well-balanced and level-headed daughter with a keen appreciation of things noble and spiritual. Martha was slow in thought and action but a very dependable and efficient child. Baby Ruth was the sunshine of the home; though thoughtless of speech, she was most sincere of heart. She just about worshiped her big brother and father. But they did not spoil her. She was a beautiful child but not quite so comely as Miriam, who was the belle of the family, if not of the city.

As time passed, Jesus did much to liberalize and modify the family teachings and practices related to Sabbath observance and many other phases of religion, and to all these changes Mary gave hearty assent. By this time Jesus had become the unquestioned head of the house.

This year Jude started to school, and it was necessary for Jesus to sell his harp in order to defray these expenses. Thus disappeared the last of his recreational pleasures. He much loved to play the harp when tired in mind and weary in body, but he comforted himself with the thought that at least the harp was safe from seizure by the tax collector.

5. REBECCA, THE DAUGHTER OF EZRA

Although Jesus was poor, his social standing in Nazareth was in no way impaired. He was one of the foremost young men of the city and very highly regarded by most of the young women. Since Jesus was such a splendid specimen of robust and intellectual manhood, and considering his reputation as a spiritual leader, it was not strange that Rebecca, the eldest daughter of Ezra, a wealthy merchant and trader of Nazareth, should discover that she was slowly falling in love with this son of Joseph. She first confided her affection to Miriam, Jesus' sister, and Miriam in turn talked all this over with her mother. Mary was intensely aroused. Was she about to lose her son, now become the indispensable head of the family? Would troubles never cease? What next could happen? And then she paused to contemplate what effect marriage would have upon Jesus' future career; not often, but at least sometimes, did she recall the fact that Jesus was a "child of promise." After she and Miriam had talked this matter over, they decided to make an effort to stop it before Jesus learned about it, by going direct to Rebecca, laying the whole story before her, and honestly telling her about their belief that Jesus was a son of destiny; that he was to become a great religious leader, perhaps the Messiah.

Rebecca listened intently; she was thrilled with the recital and more than ever determined to cast her lot with this man of her choice and to share his career of leadership. She argued (to herself) that such a man would all the more need a faithful and efficient wife. She interpreted Mary's efforts to dissuade her as a natural reaction to the dread of losing the head and sole support of her family; but knowing that her father approved of her attraction for the carpenter's son, she rightly reckoned that he would gladly supply the family with sufficient income fully to compensate for the loss of Jesus' earnings. When her father agreed to such a plan, Rebecca had further conferences with Mary and Miriam, and when she failed to win their support, she made bold to go directly to Jesus. This she did with the co-operation of her father, who invited Jesus to their home for the celebration of Rebecca's seventeenth birthday.

Jesus listened attentively and sympathetically to the recital of these things, first by the father, then by Rebecca herself. He made kindly reply to the effect that no amount of money could take the place of his obligation personally to rear his father's family, to "fulfill the most sacred of all human trusts—loyalty to one's own flesh and blood." Rebecca's father was deeply touched by Jesus' words of family devotion and retired from the conference. His only remark to Mary, his wife, was: "We can't have him for a son; he is too noble for us."

Then began that eventful talk with Rebecca. Thus far in his life, Jesus had made little distinction in his association with boys and girls, with young men and young women. His mind had been altogether too much occupied with the pressing problems of practical earthly affairs and the intriguing contemplation of his eventual career "about his Father's business" ever to have given serious consideration to the consummation of personal love in human marriage. But now he was face to face with another of those problems which every average human being must confront and decide. Indeed was he "tested in all points like as you are."

After listening attentively, he sincerely thanked Rebecca for her expressed admiration, adding, "it shall cheer and comfort me all the days of my life." He explained that he was not free to enter into relations with any woman other than those of simple brotherly regard and pure friendship. He made it clear that his first and paramount duty was the rearing of his father's family, that he could not consider marriage until that was accomplished; and then he added: "If I am a son of destiny, I must not assume obligations of lifelong duration until such a time as my destiny shall be made manifest."

Rebecca was heartbroken. She refused to be comforted and importuned her father to leave Nazareth until he finally consented to move to Sepphoris. In after years, to the many men who sought her hand in marriage, Rebecca had but one answer. She lived for only one purpose—to await the hour when this, to her, the greatest man who ever lived would begin his career as a teacher of living truth. And she followed him devotedly through his eventful years of public labor, being present (unobserved by Jesus) that day when he rode triumphantly into Jerusalem; and she stood "among the other women" by the side of Mary on that fateful and tragic afternoon when the Son of Man hung upon the cross, to her, as well as to countless worlds on high, "the one altogether lovely and the greatest among ten thousand."

6. HIS TWENTIETH YEAR (A.D. 14)

The story of Rebecca's love for Jesus was whispered about Nazareth and later on at Capernaum, so that, while in the years to follow many women loved Jesus even as men loved him, not again did he have to reject the personal proffer of another good woman's devotion. From this time on human affection for Jesus partook more of the nature of worshipful and adoring regard. Both men and women loved him devotedly and for what he was, not with any tinge of self-satisfaction or desire for affectionate possession. But for many years, whenever the story of Jesus' human personality was recited, the devotion of Rebecca was recounted.

Miriam, knowing fully about the affair of Rebecca and knowing how her brother had forsaken even the love of a beautiful maiden (not realizing the factor of his future career of destiny), came to idealize Jesus and to love him with a touching and profound affection as for a father as well as for a brother.

Although they could hardly afford it, Jesus had a strange longing to go up to Jerusalem for the Passover. His mother, knowing of his recent experience with Rebecca, wisely urged him to make the journey. He was not markedly conscious of it, but what he most wanted was an opportunity to talk with Lazarus and to visit with Martha and Mary. Next to his own family he loved these three most of all.

In making this trip to Jerusalem, he went by way of Megiddo, Antipatris, and Lydda, in part covering the same route traversed when he was brought back to Nazareth on the return from Egypt. He spent four days going up to the Passover and thought much about the past events which had transpired in and around Megiddo, the international battlefield of Palestine.

Jesus passed on through Jerusalem, only pausing to look upon the temple and the gathering throngs of visitors. He had a strange and increasing aversion to this Herod-built temple with its politically appointed priesthood. He wanted most of all to see Lazarus, Martha, and Mary. Lazarus was the same age as Jesus and now head of the house; by the time of this visit Lazarus's mother had also been laid to rest. Martha was a little over one year older than Jesus, while Mary was two years younger. And Jesus was the idolized ideal of all three of them.

On this visit occurred one of those periodic outbreaks of rebellion against tradition—the expression of resentment for those ceremonial practices which Jesus deemed misrepresentative of his Father in heaven. Not knowing Jesus was coming, Lazarus had arranged to celebrate the Passover with friends in an adjoining village down the Jericho road. Jesus now proposed that they celebrate the feast where they were, at Lazarus's house. "But," said Lazarus, "we have no paschal lamb." And then Jesus entered upon a prolonged and convincing dissertation to the effect that the Father in heaven was not truly concerned with such childlike and meaningless rituals. After solemn and fervent prayer they rose, and Jesus said: "Let the childlike and darkened minds of my people serve their God as Moses directed; it is better that they do, but let us who have seen the light of life no longer approach our Father by the darkness of death. Let us be free in the knowledge of the truth of our Father's eternal love."

That evening about twilight these four sat down and partook of the first Passover feast ever to be celebrated by devout Jews without the paschal lamb. The unleavened bread and the wine had been made ready for this Passover, and these emblems, which Jesus termed "the bread of life" and "the water of life," he served to his companions, and they ate in solemn conformity with the teachings just imparted. It was his custom to engage in this sacramental ritual whenever he paid subsequent visits to Bethany. When he returned home, he told all this to his mother. She was shocked at first but came gradually to see his viewpoint; nevertheless, she was greatly relieved when Jesus assured her that he did not intend to introduce this new idea of the Passover in their family. At home with the children he continued, year by year, to eat the Passover "according to the law of Moses."

It was during this year that Mary had a long talk with Jesus about marriage. She frankly asked him if he would get married if he were free from his family responsibilities. Jesus explained to her that, since immediate duty forbade his marriage, he had given the subject little thought. He expressed himself as doubting that he would ever enter the marriage state; he said that all such things must await "my hour," the time when "my Father's work must begin." Having settled already in his mind that he was not to become the father of children in the flesh, he gave very little thought to the subject of human marriage.

This year he began anew the task of further weaving his mortal and divine natures into a simple and effective *human individuality.* And he continued to grow in moral status and spiritual understanding.

Although all their Nazareth property (except their home) was gone, this year they received a little financial help from the sale of an equity in a piece of property in Capernaum. This was the last of Joseph's entire estate. This real estate deal in Capernaum was with a boatbuilder named Zebedee.

Joseph graduated at the synagogue school this year and prepared to begin work at the small bench in the home carpenter shop. Although the estate of their father was exhausted, there were prospects that they would successfully fight off poverty since three of them were now regularly at work.

Jesus is rapidly becoming a man, not just a young man but an adult. He has learned well to bear responsibility. He knows how to carry on in the face of disappointment. He bears up bravely when his plans are thwarted and his purposes temporarily defeated. He has learned how to be fair and just even in the face of injustice. He is learning how to adjust his ideals of spiritual living to the practical demands of earthly existence. He is learning how to plan for the achievement of a higher and distant goal of idealism while he toils earnestly for the attainment of a nearer and immediate goal of necessity. He is steadily acquiring the art of adjusting his aspirations to the commonplace demands of the human occasion. He has very nearly mastered the technique of utilizing the energy of the spiritual drive to turn the mechanism of material achievement. He is slowly learning how to live the heavenly life while he continues on with the earthly existence. More and more he depends upon the ultimate guidance of his heavenly Father while he assumes the fatherly role of guiding and directing the children of his earth family. He is becoming experienced in the skillful wresting of victory from the very jaws of defeat; he is learning how to transform the difficulties of time into the triumphs of eternity.

And so, as the years pass, this young man of Nazareth continues to experience life as it is lived in mortal flesh on the worlds of time and space. He lives a full, representative, and replete life on Urantia. He left this world ripe in the experience which his creatures pass through during the short and strenuous years of their first life, the life in the flesh. And all this human experience is an eternal possession of the Universe Sovereign. He is our understanding brother, sympathetic friend, experienced sovereign, and merciful father.

As a child he accumulated a vast body of knowledge; as a youth he sorted, classified, and correlated this information; and now as a man of the realm he begins to organize these mental possessions preparatory to utilization in his subsequent teaching, ministry, and service in behalf of his fellow mortals on this world and on all other spheres of habitation throughout the entire universe of Nebadon.

Born into the world a babe of the realm, he has lived his childhood life and passed through the successive stages of youth and young manhood; he now stands on the threshold of full manhood, rich in the experience of human living, replete in the understanding of human nature, and full of sympathy for the frailties of human nature. He is becoming expert in the divine art of revealing his Paradise Father to all ages and stages of mortal creatures.

And now as a full-grown man—an adult of the realm—he prepares to continue his supreme mission of revealing God to men and leading men to God.

PAPER 128

JESUS' EARLY MANHOOD

AS JESUS of Nazareth entered upon the early years of his adult life, he had lived, and continued to live, a normal and average human life on earth. Jesus came into this world just as other children come; he had nothing to do with selecting his parents. He did choose this particular world as the planet whereon to carry out his seventh and final bestowal, his incarnation in the likeness of mortal flesh, but otherwise he entered the world in a natural manner, growing up as a child of the realm and wrestling with the vicissitudes of his environment just as do other mortals on this and on similar worlds.

Always be mindful of the twofold purpose of Michael's bestowal on Urantia:

1. The mastering of the experience of living the full life of a human creature in mortal flesh, the completion of his sovereignty in Nebadon.

2. The revelation of the Universal Father to the mortal dwellers on the worlds of time and space and the more effective leading of these same mortals to a better understanding of the Universal Father.

All other creature benefits and universe advantages were incidental and secondary to these major purposes of the mortal bestowal.

1. THE TWENTY-FIRST YEAR (A.D. 15)

With the attainment of adult years Jesus began in earnest and with full self-consciousness the task of completing the experience of mastering the knowledge of the life of his lowest form of intelligent creatures, thereby finally and fully earning the right of unqualified rulership of his self-created universe. He entered upon this stupendous task fully realizing his dual nature. But he had already effectively combined these two natures into one—Jesus of Nazareth.

Joshua ben Joseph knew full well that he was a man, a mortal man, born of woman. This is shown in the selection of his first title, the *Son of Man.* He was truly a partaker of flesh and blood, and even now, as he presides in sovereign authority over the destinies of a universe, he still bears among his numerous well-earned titles that of Son of Man. It is literally true that the creative Word—the Creator Son—of the Universal Father was "made flesh and dwelt as a man of the realm on Urantia." He labored, grew weary, rested, and slept. He hungered and satisfied such cravings with food; he thirsted and quenched his thirst with water. He experienced the full gamut of human feelings and emotions; he was "in all things tested, even as you are," and he suffered and died.

He obtained knowledge, gained experience, and combined these into wisdom, just as do other mortals of the realm. Until after his baptism he availed himself of no supernatural power. He employed no agency not a part of his human endowment as a son of Joseph and Mary.

As to the attributes of his prehuman existence, he emptied himself. Prior to the beginning of his public work his knowledge of men and events was wholly self-limited. He was a true man among men.

It is forever and gloriously true: "We have a high ruler who can be touched with the feeling of our infirmities. We have a Sovereign who was in all points tested and tempted like as we are, yet without sin." And since he himself has suffered, being tested and tried, he is abundantly able to understand and minister to those who are confused and distressed.

The Nazareth carpenter now fully understood the work before him, but he chose to live his human life in the channel of its natural flowing. And in some of these matters he is indeed an example to his mortal creatures, even as it is recorded: "Let this mind be in you which was also in Christ Jesus, who, being of the nature of God, thought it not strange to be equal with God. But he made himself to be of little import and, taking upon himself the form of a creature, was born in the likeness of mankind. And being thus fashioned as a man, he humbled himself and became obedient to death, even the death of the cross."

He lived his mortal life just as all others of the human family may live theirs, "who in the days of the flesh so frequently offered up prayers and supplications, even with strong feelings and tears, to Him who is able to save from all evil, and his prayers were effective because he believed." Wherefore it behooved him *in every respect* to be made like his brethren that he might become a merciful and understanding sovereign ruler over them.

Of his human nature he was never in doubt; it was self-evident and always present in his consciousness. But of his divine nature there was always room for doubt and conjecture, at least this was true right up to the event of his baptism. The self-realization of divinity was a slow and, from the human standpoint, a natural evolutionary revelation. This revelation and self-realization of divinity began in Jerusalem when he was not quite thirteen years old with the first supernatural occurrence of his human existence; and this experience of effecting the self-realization of his divine nature was completed at the time of his second supernatural experience while in the flesh, the episode attendant upon his baptism by John in the Jordan, which event marked the beginning of his public career of ministry and teaching.

Between these two celestial visitations, one in his thirteenth year and the other at his baptism, there occurred nothing supernatural or superhuman in the life of this incarnated Creator Son. Notwithstanding this, the babe of Bethlehem, the lad, youth, and man of Nazareth, was in reality the incarnated Creator of a universe; but he never once used aught of this power, nor did he utilize the guidance of celestial personalities, aside from that of his guardian seraphim, in the living of his human life up to the day of his baptism by John. And we who thus testify know whereof we speak.

And yet, throughout all these years of his life in the flesh he was truly divine. He was actually a Creator Son of the Paradise Father. When once he had espoused his public career, subsequent to the technical completion of his purely mortal experience of sovereignty acquirement, he did not hesitate publicly to admit that he was the Son of God. He did not hesitate to declare, "I am Alpha and Omega, the beginning and the end, the first and the last." He made no protest in later years when he was called Lord of Glory, Ruler of a Universe, the Lord God of all creation, the Holy One of Israel, the Lord of all, our Lord and our God, God with us, having a name above every name and on all worlds, the Omnipotence of a universe, the Universe Mind of this creation, the One in whom are hid all treasures of wisdom and knowledge, the fullness of Him who fills all things, the eternal Word of the eternal God, the One who was before all things and in whom all things consist, the Creator of the heavens and the earth, the Upholder of a universe, the Judge of all the earth, the Giver of life eternal, the True Shepherd, the Deliverer of the worlds, and the Captain of our salvation.

He never objected to any of these titles as they were applied to him subsequent to the emergence from his purely human life into the later years of his self-consciousness of the ministry of divinity in humanity, and for humanity, and to humanity on this world and for all other worlds. Jesus objected to but one title as applied to him: When he was once called Immanuel, he merely replied, "Not I, that is my elder brother."

Always, even after his emergence into the larger life on earth, Jesus was submissively subject to the will of the Father in heaven.

After his baptism he thought nothing of permitting his sincere believers and grateful followers to worship him. Even while he wrestled with poverty and toiled with his hands to provide the necessities of life for his family, his awareness that he was a Son of God was growing; he knew that he was the maker of the heavens and this very earth whereon he was now living out his human existence. And the hosts of celestial beings throughout the great and onlooking universe likewise knew that this man of Nazareth was their beloved Sovereign and Creator-father. A profound suspense pervaded the universe of Nebadon throughout these years; all celestial eyes were continuously focused on Urantia—on Palestine.

This year Jesus went up to Jerusalem with Joseph to celebrate the Passover. Having taken James to the temple for consecration, he deemed it his duty to take Joseph. Jesus never exhibited any degree of partiality in dealing with his family. He went with Joseph to Jerusalem by the usual Jordan valley route, but he returned to Nazareth by the east Jordan way, which led through Amathus. Going down the Jordan, Jesus narrated Jewish history to Joseph and on the return trip told him about the experiences of the reputed tribes of Ruben, Gad, and Gilead that traditionally had dwelt in these regions east of the river.

Joseph asked Jesus many leading questions concerning his life mission, but to most of these inquiries Jesus would only reply, "My hour has not yet come." However, in these intimate discussions many words were dropped which Joseph remembered during the stirring events of subsequent years. Jesus, with Joseph, spent this Passover with his three friends at Bethany, as was his custom when in Jerusalem attending these festival commemorations.

2. The Twenty-Second Year (A.D. 16)

This was one of several years during which Jesus' brothers and sisters were facing the trials and tribulations peculiar to the problems and readjustments of adolescence. Jesus now had brothers and sisters ranging in ages from seven to eighteen, and he was kept busy helping them to adjust themselves to the new awakenings of their intellectual and emotional lives. He had thus to grapple with the problems of adolescence as they became manifest in the lives of his younger brothers and sisters.

This year Simon graduated from school and began work with Jesus' old boyhood playmate and ever-ready defender, Jacob the stone mason. As a result of several family conferences it was decided that it was unwise for all the boys to take up carpentry. It was thought that by diversifying their trades they would be prepared to take contracts for putting up entire buildings. Again, they had not all kept busy since three of them had been working as full-time carpenters.

Jesus continued this year at house finishing and cabinetwork but spent most of his time at the caravan repair shop. James was beginning to alternate with him in attendance at the shop. The latter part of this year, when carpenter work was slack about Nazareth, Jesus left James in charge of the repair shop and Joseph at the home bench while he went over to Sepphoris to work with a smith. He worked six months with metals and acquired considerable skill at the anvil.

Before taking up his new employment at Sepphoris, Jesus held one of his periodic family conferences and solemnly installed James, then just past eighteen years old, as acting head of the family. He promised his brother hearty support and full co-operation and exacted formal promises of obedience to James from each member of the family. From this day James assumed full financial responsibility for the family, Jesus making his weekly payments to his brother. Never again did Jesus take the reins out of James's hands. While working at Sepphoris he could have walked home every night if necessary, but he purposely remained away, assigning weather and other reasons, but his true motive was to train James and Joseph in the bearing of the family responsibility. He had begun the slow process of weaning his family. Each Sabbath Jesus returned to Nazareth, and sometimes during the week when occasion required, to observe the working of the new plan, to give advice and offer helpful suggestions.

Living much of the time in Sepphoris for six months afforded Jesus a new opportunity to become better acquainted with the gentile viewpoint of life. He worked with gentiles, lived with gentiles, and in every possible manner did he make a close and painstaking study of their habits of living and of the gentile mind.

The moral standards of this home city of Herod Antipas were so far below those of even the caravan city of Nazareth that after six months' sojourn at Sepphoris Jesus was not averse to finding an excuse for returning to Nazareth. The group he worked for were to become engaged on public work in both Sepphoris and the new city of Tiberias, and Jesus was disinclined to have anything to do with any sort of employment under the supervision of Herod Antipas. And there were still other reasons which made it wise, in the opinion of Jesus, for him to go back to Nazareth. When he returned to the repair shop, he did not again assume the personal direction of family affairs. He worked in association with James at the shop and as far as possible permitted him to continue oversight of the home. James's management of family expenditures and his administration of the home budget were undisturbed.

It was by just such wise and thoughtful planning that Jesus prepared the way for his eventual withdrawal from active participation in the affairs of his family. When James had had two years' experience as acting head of the family—and two full years before he (James) was to be married—Joseph was placed in charge of the household funds and intrusted with the general management of the home.

3. THE TWENTY-THIRD YEAR (A.D. 17)

This year the financial pressure was slightly relaxed as four were at work. Miriam earned considerable by the sale of milk and butter; Martha had become an expert weaver. The purchase price of the repair shop was over one third paid. The situation was such that Jesus stopped work for three weeks to take Simon to Jerusalem for the Passover, and this was the longest period away from daily toil he had enjoyed since the death of his father.

They journeyed to Jerusalem by way of the Decapolis and through Pella, Gerasa, Philadelphia, Heshbon, and Jericho. They returned to Nazareth by the coast route, touching Lydda, Joppa, Caesarea, thence around Mount Carmel to Ptolemais and Nazareth. This trip fairly well acquainted Jesus with the whole of Palestine north of the Jerusalem district.

At Philadelphia Jesus and Simon became acquainted with a merchant from Damascus who developed such a great liking for the Nazareth couple that he insisted they stop with him at his Jerusalem headquarters. While Simon gave attendance at the temple, Jesus spent much of his time talking with this well-educated and much-traveled man of world affairs. This merchant owned over four thousand caravan camels; he had interests all over the Roman world and was now on his way to Rome. He proposed that Jesus come to Damascus to enter his Oriental import business, but Jesus explained that he did not feel justified in going so far away from his family just then. But on the way back home he thought much about these distant cities and the even more remote countries of the Far West and the Far East, countries he had so frequently heard spoken of by the caravan passengers and conductors.

Simon greatly enjoyed his visit to Jerusalem. He was duly received into the commonwealth of Israel at the Passover consecration of the new sons of the commandment. While Simon attended the Passover ceremonies, Jesus mingled with the throngs of visitors and engaged in many interesting personal conferences with numerous gentile proselytes.

Perhaps the most notable of all these contacts was the one with a young Hellenist named Stephen. This young man was on his first visit to Jerusalem and chanced to meet Jesus on Thursday afternoon of Passover week. While they both strolled about viewing the Asmonean palace, Jesus began the casual conversation that resulted in their becoming interested in each other, and which led to a four-hour discussion of the way of life and the true God and his worship. Stephen was tremendously impressed with what Jesus said; he never forgot his words.

And this was the same Stephen who subsequently became a believer in the teachings of Jesus, and whose boldness in preaching this early gospel resulted in his being stoned to death by irate Jews. Some of Stephen's extraordinary boldness in proclaiming his view of the new gospel was the direct result of this earlier interview with Jesus. But Stephen never even faintly surmised that the Galilean he had talked with some fifteen years previously was the very same person whom he later proclaimed the world's Savior, and for whom he was so soon to die, thus becoming the first martyr of the newly evolving Christian faith. When Stephen yielded up his life as the price of his attack upon the Jewish temple and its traditional practices, there stood by one named Saul, a citizen of Tarsus. And when Saul saw how this Greek could die for his faith, there were aroused in his heart those emotions which eventually led him to espouse the cause for which Stephen died; later on he became the aggressive and indomitable Paul, the philosopher, if not the sole founder, of the Christian religion.

On the Sunday after Passover week Simon and Jesus started on their way back to Nazareth. Simon never forgot what Jesus taught him on this trip. He had always loved Jesus, but now he felt that he had begun to know his father-brother. They had many heart-to-heart talks as they journeyed through the country and prepared their meals by the wayside. They arrived home Thursday noon, and Simon kept the family up late that night relating his experiences.

Mary was much upset by Simon's report that Jesus spent most of the time when in Jerusalem "visiting with the strangers, especially those from the far countries." Jesus' family never could comprehend his great interest in people, his urge to visit with them, to learn about their way of living, and to find out what they were thinking about.

More and more the Nazareth family became engrossed with their immediate and human problems; not often was mention made of the future mission of Jesus, and very seldom did he himself speak of his future career. His mother rarely thought about his being a child of promise. She was slowly giving up the idea that Jesus was to fulfill any divine mission on earth, yet at times her faith was revived when she paused to recall the Gabriel visitation before the child was born.

4. THE DAMASCUS EPISODE

The last four months of this year Jesus spent in Damascus as the guest of the merchant whom he first met at Philadelphia when on his way to Jerusalem. A representative of this merchant had sought out Jesus when passing through Nazareth and escorted him to Damascus. This part-Jewish merchant proposed to devote an extraordinary sum of money to the establishment of a school of religious philosophy at Damascus. He planned to create a center of learning which would outrival Alexandria. And he proposed that Jesus should immediately begin a long tour of the world's educational centers preparatory to becoming the head of this new project. This was one of the greatest temptations that Jesus ever faced in the course of his purely human career.

Presently this merchant brought before Jesus a group of twelve merchants and bankers who agreed to support this newly projected school. Jesus manifested deep interest in the proposed school, helped them plan for its organization, but always expressed the fear that his other and unstated but prior obligations would prevent his accepting the direction of such a pretentious enterprise. His would-be benefactor was persistent, and he profitably employed Jesus at his home doing some translating while he, his wife, and their sons and daughters sought to prevail upon Jesus to accept the proffered honor. But he would not consent. He well knew that his mission on earth was not to be supported by institutions of learning; he knew that he must not obligate himself in the least to be directed by the "councils of men," no matter how well-intentioned.

He who was rejected by the Jerusalem religious leaders, even after he had demonstrated his leadership, was recognized and hailed as a master teacher by the businessmen and bankers of Damascus, and all this when he was an obscure and unknown carpenter of Nazareth.

He never spoke about this offer to his family, and the end of this year found him back in Nazareth going about his daily duties just as if he had never been tempted by the flattering propositions of his Damascus friends. Neither did these men of Damascus ever associate the later citizen of Capernaum who turned all Jewry upside down with the former carpenter of Nazareth who had dared to refuse the honor which their combined wealth might have procured.

Jesus most cleverly and intentionally contrived to detach various episodes of his life so that they never became, in the eyes of the world, associated together as the doings of a single individual. Many times in subsequent years he listened to the recital of this very story of the strange Galilean who declined the opportunity of founding a school in Damascus to compete with Alexandria.

One purpose which Jesus had in mind, when he sought to segregate certain features of his earthly experience, was to prevent the building up of such a versatile and spectacular career as would cause subsequent generations to venerate the teacher in place of obeying the truth which he had lived and taught. Jesus did not want to build up such a human record of achievement as would attract attention from his teaching. Very early he recognized that his followers would be tempted to formulate a religion *about* him which might become a competitor of the gospel of the kingdom that he intended to proclaim to the world. Accordingly, he consistently sought to suppress everything during his eventful career which he thought might be made to serve this natural human tendency to exalt the teacher in place of proclaiming his teachings.

This same motive also explains why he permitted himself to be known by different titles during various epochs of his diversified life on earth. Again, he did not want to bring any undue influence to bear upon his family or others which would lead them to believe in him against their honest convictions. He always refused to take undue or unfair advantage of the human mind. He did not want men to believe in him unless their hearts were responsive to the spiritual realities revealed in his teachings.

By the end of this year the Nazareth home was running fairly smoothly. The children were growing up, and Mary was becoming accustomed to Jesus' being away from home. He continued to turn over his earnings to James for the support of the family, retaining only a small portion for his immediate personal expenses.

As the years passed, it became more difficult to realize that this man was a Son of God on earth. He seemed to become quite like an individual of the realm, just another man among men. And it was ordained by the Father in heaven that the bestowal should unfold in this very way.

5. THE TWENTY-FOURTH YEAR (A.D. 18)

This was Jesus' first year of comparative freedom from family responsibility. James was very successful in managing the home with Jesus' help in counsel and finances.

The week following the Passover of this year a young man from Alexandria came down to Nazareth to arrange for a meeting, later in the year, between Jesus and a group of Alexandrian Jews at some point on the Palestinian coast. This conference was set for the middle of June, and Jesus went over to Caesarea to meet with five prominent Jews of Alexandria, who besought him to establish himself in their city as a religious teacher, offering as an inducement to begin with, the position of assistant to the chazan in their chief synagogue.

The spokesmen for this committee explained to Jesus that Alexandria was destined to become the headquarters of Jewish culture for the entire world; that the Hellenistic trend of Jewish affairs had virtually outdistanced the Babylonian school of thought. They reminded Jesus of the ominous rumblings of rebellion in Jerusalem and throughout Palestine and assured him that any uprising of the Palestinian Jews would be equivalent to national suicide, that the iron hand of Rome would crush the rebellion in three months, and that Jerusalem would be destroyed and the temple demolished, that not one stone would be left upon another.

Jesus listened to all they had to say, thanked them for their confidence, and, in declining to go to Alexandria, in substance said, "My hour has not yet come." They were nonplused by his apparent indifference to the honor they had sought to confer upon him. Before taking leave of Jesus, they presented him with a purse in token of the esteem of his Alexandrian friends and in compensation for the time and expense of coming over to Caesarea to confer with them. But he likewise refused the money, saying: "The house of Joseph has never received alms, and we cannot eat another's bread as long as I have strong arms and my brothers can labor."

His friends from Egypt set sail for home, and in subsequent years, when they heard rumors of the Capernaum boatbuilder who was creating such a commotion in Palestine, few of them surmised that he was the babe of Bethlehem grown up and the same strange-acting Galilean who had so unceremoniously declined the invitation to become a great teacher in Alexandria.

Jesus returned to Nazareth. The remainder of this year was the most uneventful six months of his whole career. He enjoyed this temporary respite from the usual program of problems to solve and difficulties to surmount. He communed much with his Father in heaven and made tremendous progress in the mastery of his human mind.

But human affairs on the worlds of time and space do not run smoothly for long. In December James had a private talk with Jesus, explaining that he was much in love with Esta, a young woman of Nazareth, and that they would sometime like to be married if it could be arranged. He called attention to the fact that Joseph would soon be eighteen years old, and that it would be a good experience for him to have a chance to serve as the acting head of the family. Jesus gave consent for James's marriage two years later, provided he had, during the intervening time, properly trained Joseph to assume direction of the home.

And now things began to happen—marriage was in the air. James's success in gaining Jesus' assent to his marriage emboldened Miriam to approach her brother-father with her plans. Jacob, the younger stone mason, onetime self-appointed champion of Jesus, now business associate of James and Joseph, had long sought to gain Miriam's hand in marriage. After Miriam had laid her plans before Jesus, he directed that Jacob should come to him making formal request for her and promised his blessing for the marriage just as soon as she felt that Martha was competent to assume her duties as eldest daughter.

When at home, he continued to teach the evening school three times a week, read the Scriptures often in the synagogue on the Sabbath, visited with his mother, taught the children, and in general conducted himself as a worthy and respected citizen of Nazareth in the commonwealth of Israel.

6. THE TWENTY-FIFTH YEAR (A.D. 19)

This year began with the Nazareth family all in good health and witnessed the finishing of the regular schooling of all the children with the exception of certain work which Martha must do for Ruth.

Jesus was one of the most robust and refined specimens of manhood to appear on earth since the days of Adam. His physical development was superb. His mind was active, keen, and penetrating—compared with the average mentality of his contemporaries, it had developed gigantic proportions—and his spirit was indeed humanly divine.

The family finances were in the best condition since the disappearance of Joseph's estate. The final payments had been made on the caravan repair shop; they owed no man and for the first time in years had some funds ahead. This being true, and since he had taken his other brothers to Jerusalem for their first Passover ceremonies, Jesus decided to accompany Jude (who had just graduated from the synagogue school) on his first visit to the temple.

They went up to Jerusalem and returned by the same route, the Jordan valley, as Jesus feared trouble if he took his young brother through Samaria. Already at Nazareth Jude had got into slight trouble several times because of his hasty disposition, coupled with his strong patriotic sentiments.

They arrived at Jerusalem in due time and were on their way for a first visit to the temple, the very sight of which had stirred and thrilled Jude to the very depths of his soul, when they chanced to meet Lazarus of Bethany. While Jesus talked with Lazarus and sought to arrange for their joint celebration of the Passover, Jude started up real trouble for them all. Close at hand stood a Roman guard who made some improper remarks regarding a Jewish girl who was passing. Jude flushed with fiery indignation and was not slow in expressing his resentment of such an impropriety directly to and within hearing of the soldier. Now the Roman legionnaires were very sensitive to anything bordering on Jewish disrespect; so the guard promptly placed Jude under arrest. This was too much for the young patriot, and before Jesus could caution him by a warning glance, he had delivered himself of a voluble denunciation of pent-up anti-Roman feelings, all of which only made a bad matter worse. Jude, with Jesus by his side, was taken at once to the military prison.

Jesus endeavored to obtain either an immediate hearing for Jude or else his release in time for the Passover celebration that evening, but he failed in these attempts. Since the next day was a "holy convocation" in Jerusalem, even the Romans would not presume to hear charges against a Jew. Accordingly, Jude remained in confinement until the morning of the second day after his arrest, and Jesus stayed at the prison with him. They were not present in the temple at the ceremony of receiving the sons of the law into the full citizenship of Israel. Jude did not pass through this formal ceremony for several years, until he was next in Jerusalem at a Passover and in connection with his propaganda work in behalf of the Zealots, the patriotic organization to which he belonged and in which he was very active.

The morning following their second day in prison Jesus appeared before the military magistrate in behalf of Jude. By making apologies for his brother's youth and by a further explanatory but judicious statement with reference to the provocative nature of the episode which had led up to the arrest of his brother, Jesus so handled the case that the magistrate expressed the opinion that the young Jew might have had some possible excuse for his violent outburst. After warning Jude not to allow himself again to be guilty of such rashness, he said to Jesus in dismissing them: "You had better keep your eye on the lad; he's liable to make a lot of trouble for all of you." And the Roman judge spoke the truth. Jude did make considerable trouble for Jesus, and always was the trouble of this same nature—clashes with the civil authorities because of his thoughtless and unwise patriotic outbursts.

Jesus and Jude walked over to Bethany for the night, explaining why they had failed to keep their appointment for the Passover supper, and set out for Nazareth the following day. Jesus did not tell the family about his young brother's arrest at Jerusalem, but he had a long talk with Jude about this episode some three weeks after their return. After this talk with Jesus Jude himself told the family. He never forgot the patience and forbearance his brother-father manifested throughout the whole of this trying experience.

This was the last Passover Jesus attended with any member of his own family. Increasingly the Son of Man was to become separated from close association with his own flesh and blood.

This year his seasons of deep meditation were often broken into by Ruth and her playmates. And always was Jesus ready to postpone the contemplation of his future work for the world and the universe that he might share in the childish joy and youthful gladness of these youngsters, who never tired of listening to Jesus relate the experiences of his various trips to Jerusalem. They also greatly enjoyed his stories about animals and nature.

The children were always welcome at the repair shop. Jesus provided sand, blocks, and stones by the side of the shop, and bevies of youngsters flocked there to amuse themselves. When they tired of their play, the more intrepid ones would peek into the shop, and if its keeper were not busy, they would make bold to go in and say, "Uncle Joshua, come out and tell us a big story." Then they would lead him out by tugging at his hands until he was seated on the favorite rock by the corner of the shop, with the children on the ground in a semicircle before him. And how the little folks did enjoy their Uncle Joshua. They were learning to laugh, and to laugh heartily. It was customary for one or two of the smallest of the children to climb upon his knees and sit there, looking up in wonderment at his expressive features as he told his stories. The children loved Jesus, and Jesus loved the children.

It was difficult for his friends to comprehend the range of his intellectual activities, how he could so suddenly and so completely swing from the profound discussion of politics, philosophy, or religion to the lighthearted and joyous playfulness of these tots of from five to ten years of age. As his own brothers and sisters grew up, as he gained more leisure, and before the grandchildren arrived, he paid a great deal of attention to these little ones. But he did not live on earth long enough to enjoy the grandchildren very much.

7. THE TWENTY-SIXTH YEAR (A.D. 20)

As this year began, Jesus of Nazareth became strongly conscious that he possessed a wide range of potential power. But he was likewise fully persuaded that this power was not to be employed by his personality as the Son of Man, at least not until his hour should come.

At this time he thought much but said little about the relation of himself to his Father in heaven. And the conclusion of all this thinking was expressed once in his prayer on the hilltop, when he said: "Regardless of who I am and what power I may or may not wield, I always have been, and always will be, subject to the will of my Paradise Father." And yet, as this man walked about Nazareth to and from his work, it was literally true—as concerned a vast universe—that "in him were hidden all the treasures of wisdom and knowledge."

All this year the family affairs ran smoothly except for Jude. For years James had trouble with his youngest brother, who was not inclined to settle down to work nor was he to be depended upon for his share of the home expenses. While he would live at home, he was not conscientious about earning his share of the family upkeep.

Jesus was a man of peace, and ever and anon was he embarrassed by Jude's belligerent exploits and numerous patriotic outbursts. James and Joseph were in favor of casting him out, but Jesus would not consent. When their patience would be severely tried, Jesus would only counsel: "Be patient. Be wise in your counsel and eloquent in your lives, that your young brother may first know the better way and then be constrained to follow you in it." The wise and loving counsel of Jesus prevented a break in the family; they remained together. But Jude never was brought to his sober senses until after his marriage.

Mary seldom spoke of Jesus' future mission. Whenever this subject was referred to, Jesus only replied, "My hour has not yet come." Jesus had about completed the difficult task of weaning his family from dependence on the immediate presence of his personality. He was rapidly preparing for the day when he could consistently leave this Nazareth home to begin the more active prelude to his real ministry for men.

Never lose sight of the fact that the prime mission of Jesus in his seventh bestowal was the acquirement of creature experience, the achievement of the sovereignty of Nebadon. And in the gathering of this very experience he made the supreme revelation of the Paradise Father to Urantia and to his entire local universe. Incidental to these purposes he also undertook to untangle the complicated affairs of this planet as they were related to the Lucifer rebellion.

This year Jesus enjoyed more than usual leisure, and he devoted much time to training James in the management of the repair shop and Joseph in the direction of home affairs. Mary sensed that he was making ready to leave them. Leave them to go where? To do what? She had about given up the thought that Jesus was the Messiah. She could not understand him; she simply could not fathom her first-born son.

Jesus spent a great deal of time this year with the individual members of his family. He would take them for long and frequent strolls up the hill and through the countryside. Before harvest he took Jude to the farmer uncle south of Nazareth, but Jude did not remain long after the harvest. He ran away, and Simon later found him with the fishermen at the lake. When Simon brought him back home, Jesus talked things over with the runaway lad and, since he wanted to be a fisherman, went over to Magdala with him and put him in the care of a relative, a fisherman; and Jude worked fairly well and regularly from that time on until his marriage, and he continued as a fisherman after his marriage.

At last the day had come when all Jesus' brothers had chosen, and were established in, their lifework. The stage was being set for Jesus' departure from home.

In November a double wedding occurred. James and Esta, and Miriam and Jacob were married. It was truly a joyous occasion. Even Mary was once more happy except every now and then when she realized that Jesus was preparing to go away. She suffered under the burden of a great uncertainty: If Jesus would only sit down and talk it all over freely with her as he had done when he was a boy, but he was consistently uncommunicative; he was profoundly silent about the future.

James and his bride, Esta, moved into a neat little home on the west side of town, the gift of her father. While James continued his support of his mother's home, his quota was cut in half because of his marriage, and Joseph was formally installed by Jesus as head of the family. Jude was now very faithfully sending his share of funds home each month. The weddings of James and Miriam had a very beneficial influence on Jude, and when he left for the fishing grounds, the day after the double wedding, he assured Joseph that he could depend on him "to do my full duty, and more if it is needed." And he kept his promise.

Miriam lived next door to Mary in the home of Jacob, Jacob the elder having been laid to rest with his fathers. Martha took Miriam's place in the home, and the new organization was working smoothly before the year ended.

The day after this double wedding Jesus held an important conference with James. He told James, confidentially, that he was preparing to leave home. He presented full title to the repair shop to James, formally and solemnly abdicated as head of Joseph's house, and most touchingly established his brother James as "head and protector of my father's house." He drew up, and they both signed, a secret compact in which it was stipulated that, in return for the gift of the repair shop, James would henceforth assume full financial responsibility for the family, thus releasing Jesus from all further obligations in these matters. After the contract was signed, after the budget was so arranged that the actual expenses of the family would be met without any contribution from Jesus, Jesus said to James: "But, my son, I will continue to send you something each month until my hour shall have come, but what I send shall be used by you as the occasion demands. Apply my funds to the family necessities or pleasures as you see fit. Use them in case of sickness or apply them to meet the unexpected emergencies which may befall any individual member of the family."

And thus did Jesus make ready to enter upon the second and home-detached phase of his adult life before the public entrance upon his Father's business.

PAPER 129

THE LATER ADULT LIFE OF JESUS

JESUS had fully and finally separated himself from the management of the domestic affairs of the Nazareth family and from the immediate direction of its individuals. He continued, right up to the event of his baptism, to contribute to the family finances and to take a keen personal interest in the spiritual welfare of every one of his brothers and sisters. And always was he ready to do everything humanly possible for the comfort and happiness of his widowed mother.

The Son of Man had now made every preparation for detaching himself permanently from the Nazareth home; and this was not easy for him to do. Jesus naturally loved his people; he loved his family, and this natural affection had been tremendously augmented by his extraordinary devotion to them. The more fully we bestow ourselves upon our fellows, the more we come to love them; and since Jesus had given himself so fully to his family, he loved them with a great and fervent affection.

All the family had slowly awakened to the realization that Jesus was making ready to leave them. The sadness of the anticipated separation was only tempered by this graduated method of preparing them for the announcement of his intended departure. For more than four years they discerned that he was planning for this eventual separation.

1. THE TWENTY-SEVENTH YEAR (A.D. 21)

In January of this year, A.D. 21, on a rainy Sunday morning, Jesus took unceremonious leave of his family, only explaining that he was going over to Tiberias and then on a visit to other cities about the Sea of Galilee. And thus he left them, never again to be a regular member of that household.

He spent one week at Tiberias, the new city which was soon to succeed Sepphoris as the capital of Galilee; and finding little to interest him, he passed on successively through Magdala and Bethsaida to Capernaum, where he stopped to pay a visit to his father's friend Zebedee. Zebedee's sons were fishermen; he himself was a boatbuilder. Jesus of Nazareth was an expert in both designing and building; he was a master at working with wood; and Zebedee had long known of the skill of the Nazareth craftsman. For a long time Zebedee had contemplated making improved boats; he now laid his plans before Jesus and invited the visiting carpenter to join him in the enterprise, and Jesus readily consented.

Jesus worked with Zebedee only a little more than one year, but during that time he created a new style of boat and established entirely new methods of boatmaking. By superior technique and greatly improved methods of steaming the boards, Jesus and Zebedee began to build boats of a very superior type, craft which were far more safe for sailing the lake than were the older types. For several years Zebedee had more work, turning out these new-style boats, than his small establishment could handle; in less than five years practically all the craft on the lake had been built in the shop of Zebedee at Capernaum. Jesus became well known to the Galilean fisherfolk as the designer of the new boats.

Zebedee was a moderately well-to-do man; his boatbuilding shops were on the lake to the south of Capernaum, and his home was situated down the lake shore near the fishing headquarters of Bethsaida. Jesus lived in the home of Zebedee during the year and more he remained at Capernaum. He had long worked alone in the world, that is, without a father, and greatly enjoyed this period of working with a father-partner.

Zebedee's wife, Salome, was a relative of Annas, onetime high priest at Jerusalem and still the most influential of the Sadducean group, having been deposed only eight years previously. Salome became a great admirer of Jesus. She loved him as she loved her own sons, James, John, and David, while her four daughters looked upon Jesus as their elder brother. Jesus often went out fishing with James, John, and David, and they learned that he was an experienced fisherman as well as an expert boatbuilder.

All this year Jesus sent money each month to James. He returned to Nazareth in October to attend Martha's wedding, and he was not again in Nazareth for over two years, when he returned shortly before the double wedding of Simon and Jude.

Throughout this year Jesus built boats and continued to observe how men lived on earth. Frequently he would go down to visit at the caravan station, Capernaum being on the direct travel route from Damascus to the south. Capernaum was a strong Roman military post, and the garrison's commanding officer was a gentile believer in Yahweh, "a devout man," as the Jews were wont to designate such proselytes. This officer belonged to a wealthy Roman family, and he took it upon himself to build a beautiful synagogue in Capernaum, which had been presented to the Jews a short time before Jesus came to live with Zebedee. Jesus conducted the services in this new synagogue more than half the time this year, and some of the caravan people who chanced to attend remembered him as the carpenter from Nazareth.

When it came to the payment of taxes, Jesus registered himself as a "skilled craftsman of Capernaum." From this day on to the end of his earth life he was known as a resident of Capernaum. He never claimed any other legal residence, although he did, for various reasons, permit others to assign his residence to Damascus, Bethany, Nazareth, and even Alexandria.

At the Capernaum synagogue he found many new books in the library chests, and he spent at least five evenings a week at intense study. One evening he devoted to social life with the older folks, and one evening he spent with the young people. There was something gracious and inspiring about the personality of Jesus which invariably attracted young people. He always made them feel at ease in his presence. Perhaps his great secret in getting along with them consisted in the twofold fact that he was always interested in what they were doing, while he seldom offered them advice unless they asked for it.

The Zebedee family almost worshiped Jesus, and they never failed to attend the conferences of questions and answers which he conducted each evening after supper before he departed for the synagogue to study. The youthful neighbors also came in frequently to attend these after-supper meetings. To these little gatherings Jesus gave varied and advanced instruction, just as advanced as they could comprehend. He talked quite freely with them, expressing his ideas and ideals about politics, sociology, science, and philosophy, but never presumed to speak with authoritative finality except when discussing religion—the relation of man to God.

Once a week Jesus held a meeting with the entire household, shop, and shore helpers, for Zebedee had many employees. And it was among these workers that Jesus was first called "the Master." They all loved him. He enjoyed his labors with Zebedee in Capernaum, but he missed the children playing out by the side of the Nazareth carpenter shop.

Of the sons of Zebedee, James was the most interested in Jesus as a teacher, as a philosopher. John cared most for his religious teaching and opinions. David respected him as a mechanic but took little stock in his religious views and philosophic teachings.

Frequently Jude came over on the Sabbath to hear Jesus talk in the synagogue and would tarry to visit with him. And the more Jude saw of his eldest brother, the more he became convinced that Jesus was a truly great man.

This year Jesus made great advances in the ascendant mastery of his human mind and attained new and high levels of conscious contact with his indwelling Thought Adjuster.

This was the last year of his settled life. Never again did Jesus spend a whole year in one place or at one undertaking. The days of his earth pilgrimages were rapidly approaching. Periods of intense activity were not far in the future, but there were now about to intervene between his simple but intensely active life of the past and his still more intense and strenuous public ministry, a few years of extensive travel and highly diversified personal activity. His training as a man of the realm had to be completed before he could enter upon his career of teaching and preaching as the perfected God-man of the divine and posthuman phases of his Urantia bestowal.

2. THE TWENTY-EIGHTH YEAR (A.D. 22)

In March, A.D. 22, Jesus took leave of Zebedee and of Capernaum. He asked for a small sum of money to defray his expenses to Jerusalem. While working with Zebedee he had drawn only small sums of money, which each month he would send to the family at Nazareth. One month Joseph would come down to Capernaum for the money; the next month Jude would come over to Capernaum, get the money from Jesus, and take it up to Nazareth. Jude's fishing headquarters was only a few miles south of Capernaum.

When Jesus took leave of Zebedee's family, he agreed to remain in Jerusalem until Passover time, and they all promised to be present for that event. They even arranged to celebrate the Passover supper together. They all sorrowed when Jesus left them, especially the daughters of Zebedee.

Before leaving Capernaum, Jesus had a long talk with his new-found friend and close companion, John Zebedee. He told John that he contemplated traveling extensively until "my hour shall come" and asked John to act in his stead in the matter of sending some money to the family at Nazareth each month until the funds due him should be exhausted. And John made him this promise: "My Teacher, go about your business, do your work in the world; I will act for you in this or any other matter, and I will watch over your family even as I would foster my own mother and care for my own brothers and sisters. I will disburse your funds which my father holds as you have directed and as they may be needed, and when your money has been expended, if I do not receive more from you, and if your mother is in need, then will I share my own earnings with her. Go your way in peace. I will act in your stead in all these matters."

Therefore, after Jesus had departed for Jerusalem, John consulted with his father, Zebedee, regarding the money due Jesus, and he was surprised that it was such a large sum. As Jesus had left the matter so entirely in their hands, they agreed that it would be the better plan to invest these funds in property and use the income for assisting the family at Nazareth; and since Zebedee knew of a little house in Capernaum which carried a mortgage and was for sale, he directed John to buy this house with Jesus' money and hold the title in trust for his friend. And John did as his father advised him. For two years the rent of this house was applied on the mortgage, and this, augmented by a certain large fund which Jesus presently sent up to John to be used as needed by the family, almost equaled the amount of this obligation; and Zebedee supplied the difference, so that John paid up the remainder of the mortgage when it fell due, thereby securing clear title to this two-room house. In this way Jesus became the owner of a house in Capernaum, but he had not been told about it.

When the family at Nazareth heard that Jesus had departed from Capernaum, they, not knowing of this financial arrangement with John, believed the time had come for them to get along without any further help from Jesus. James remembered his contract with Jesus and, with the help of his brothers, forthwith assumed full responsibility for the care of the family.

But let us go back to observe Jesus in Jerusalem. For almost two months he spent the greater part of his time listening to the temple discussions with occasional visits to the various schools of the rabbis. Most of the Sabbath days he spent at Bethany.

Jesus had carried with him to Jerusalem a letter from Salome, Zebedee's wife, introducing him to the former high priest, Annas, as "one, the same as my own son." Annas spent much time with him, personally taking him to visit the many academies of the Jerusalem religious teachers. While Jesus thoroughly inspected these schools and carefully observed their methods of teaching, he never so much as asked a single question in public. Although Annas looked upon Jesus as a great man, he was puzzled as to how to advise him. He recognized the foolishness of suggesting that he enter any of the schools of Jerusalem as a student, and yet he well knew Jesus would never be accorded the status of a regular teacher inasmuch as he had never been trained in these schools.

Presently the time of the Passover drew near, and along with the throngs from every quarter there arrived at Jerusalem from Capernaum, Zebedee and his entire family. They all stopped at the spacious home of Annas, where they celebrated the Passover as one happy family.

Before the end of this Passover week, by apparent chance, Jesus met a wealthy traveler and his son, a young man about seventeen years of age. These travelers hailed from India, and being on their way to visit Rome and various other points on the Mediterranean, they had arranged to arrive in Jerusalem during the Passover, hoping to find someone whom they could engage as interpreter for both and tutor for the son. The father was insistent that Jesus consent to travel with them. Jesus told him about his family and that it was hardly fair to go away for almost two years, during which time they might find themselves in need. Whereupon, this traveler from the Orient proposed to advance to Jesus the wages of one year so that he could intrust such funds to his friends for the safeguarding of his family against want. And Jesus agreed to make the trip.

Jesus turned this large sum over to John the son of Zebedee. And you have been told how John applied this money toward the liquidation of the mortgage on the Capernaum property. Jesus took Zebedee fully into his confidence regarding this Mediterranean journey, but he enjoined him to tell no man, not even his own flesh and blood, and Zebedee never did disclose his knowledge of Jesus' whereabouts during this long period of almost two years. Before Jesus' return from this trip the family at Nazareth had just about given him up as dead. Only the assurances of Zebedee, who went up to Nazareth with his son John on several occasions, kept hope alive in Mary's heart.

During this time the Nazareth family got along very well; Jude had considerably increased his quota and kept up this extra contribution until he was married. Notwithstanding that they required little assistance, it was the practice of John Zebedee to take presents each month to Mary and Ruth, as Jesus had instructed him.

3. THE TWENTY-NINTH YEAR (A.D. 23)

The whole of Jesus' twenty-ninth year was spent finishing up the tour of the Mediterranean world. The main events, as far as we have permission to reveal these experiences, constitute the subjects of the narratives which immediately follow this paper.

Throughout this tour of the Roman world, for many reasons, Jesus was known as the *Damascus scribe.* At Corinth and other stops on the return trip he was, however, known as the *Jewish tutor.*

This was an eventful period in Jesus' life. While on this journey he made many contacts with his fellow men, but this experience is a phase of his life which he never revealed to any member of his family nor to any of the apostles. Jesus lived out his life in the flesh and departed from this world without anyone (save Zebedee of Bethsaida) knowing that he had made this extensive trip. Some of his friends thought he had returned to Damascus; others thought he had gone to India. His own family inclined to the belief that he was in Alexandria, as they knew that he had once been invited to go there for the purpose of becoming an assistant chazan.

When Jesus returned to Palestine, he did nothing to change the opinion of his family that he had gone from Jerusalem to Alexandria; he permitted them to continue in the belief that all the time he had been absent from Palestine had been spent in that city of learning and culture. Only Zebedee the boatbuilder of Bethsaida knew the facts about these matters, and Zebedee told no one.

In all your efforts to decipher the meaning of Jesus' life on Urantia, you must be mindful of the motivation of the Michael bestowal. If you would comprehend the meaning of many of his apparently strange doings, you must discern the purpose of his sojourn on your world. He was consistently careful not to build up an overattractive and attention-consuming personal career. He wanted to make no unusual or overpowering appeals to his fellow men. He was dedicated to the work of revealing the heavenly Father to his fellow mortals and at the same time was consecrated to the sublime task of living his mortal earth life all the while subject to the will of the same Paradise Father.

It will also always be helpful in understanding Jesus' life on earth if all mortal students of this divine bestowal will remember that, while he lived this life of incarnation *on* Urantia, he lived it *for* his entire universe. There was something special and inspiring associated with the life he lived in the flesh of mortal nature for every single inhabited sphere throughout all the universe of Nebadon. The same is also true of all those worlds which have become habitable since the eventful times of his sojourn on Urantia. And it will likewise be equally true of all worlds which may become inhabited by will creatures in all the future history of this local universe.

The Son of Man, during the time and through the experiences of this tour of the Roman world, practically completed his educational contact-training with the diversified peoples of the world of his day and generation. By the time of his return to Nazareth, through the medium of this travel-training he had just about learned how man lived and wrought out his existence on Urantia.

The real purpose of his trip around the Mediterranean basin was to *know men.* He came very close to hundreds of humankind on this journey. He met and loved all manner of men, rich and poor, high and low, black and white, educated and uneducated, cultured and uncultured, animalistic and spiritual, religious and irreligious, moral and immoral.

On this Mediterranean journey Jesus made great advances in his human task of mastering the material and mortal mind, and his indwelling Adjuster made great progress in the ascension and spiritual conquest of this same human intellect. By the end of this tour Jesus virtually knew—with all human certainty—that he was a Son of God, a Creator Son of the Universal Father. The Adjuster more and more was able to bring up in the mind of the Son of Man shadowy memories of his Paradise experience in association with his divine Father ere he ever came to organize and administer this local universe of Nebadon. Thus did the Adjuster, little by little, bring to Jesus' human consciousness those necessary memories of his former and divine existence in the various epochs of the well-nigh eternal past. The last episode of his prehuman experience to be brought forth by the Adjuster was his farewell conference with Immanuel of Salvington just before his surrender of conscious personality to embark upon the Urantia incarnation. And this final memory picture of prehuman existence was made clear in Jesus' consciousness on the very day of his baptism by John in the Jordan.

4. THE HUMAN JESUS

To the onlooking celestial intelligences of the local universe, this Mediterranean trip was the most enthralling of all Jesus' earth experiences, at least of all his career right up to the event of his crucifixion and mortal death. This was the fascinating period of his *personal ministry* in contrast with the soon-following epoch of public ministry. This unique episode was all the more engrossing because he was at this time still the carpenter of Nazareth, the boatbuilder of Capernaum, the scribe of Damascus; he was still the Son of Man. He had not yet achieved the complete mastery of his human mind; the Adjuster had not fully mastered and counterparted the mortal identity. He was still a man among men.

The purely human religious experience—the personal spiritual growth—of the Son of Man well-nigh reached the apex of attainment during this, the twenty-ninth year. This experience of spiritual development was a consistently gradual growth from the moment of the arrival of his Thought Adjuster until the day of the completion and confirmation of that natural and normal human relationship between the material mind of man and the mind-endowment of the spirit—the phenomenon of the making of these two minds one, the experience which the Son of Man attained in completion and finality, as an incarnated mortal of the realm, on the day of his baptism in the Jordan.

Throughout these years, while he did not appear to engage in so many seasons of formal communion with his Father in heaven, he perfected increasingly effective methods of personal communication with the indwelling spirit presence of the Paradise Father. He lived a real life, a full life, and a truly normal, natural, and average life in the flesh. He knows from personal experience the equivalent of the actuality of the entire sum and substance of the living of the life of human beings on the material worlds of time and space.

The Son of Man experienced those wide ranges of human emotion which reach from superb joy to profound sorrow. He was a child of joy and a being of rare good humor; likewise was he a "man of sorrows and acquainted with grief." In a spiritual sense, he did live through the mortal life from the bottom to the top, from the beginning to the end. From a material point of view, he might appear to have escaped living through both social extremes of human existence, but intellectually he became wholly familiar with the entire and complete experience of humankind.

Jesus knows about the thoughts and feelings, the urges and impulses, of the evolutionary and ascendant mortals of the realms, from birth to death. He has lived the human life from the beginnings of physical, intellectual, and spiritual selfhood up through infancy, childhood, youth, and adulthood—even to the human experience of death. He not only passed through these usual and familiar human periods of intellectual and spiritual advancement, but he *also* fully experienced those higher and more advanced phases of human and Adjuster reconciliation which so few Urantia mortals ever attain. And thus he experienced the full life of mortal man, not only as it is lived on your world, but also as it is lived on all other evolutionary worlds of time and space, even on the highest and most advanced of all the worlds settled in light and life.

Although this perfect life which he lived in the likeness of mortal flesh may not have received the unqualified and universal approval of his fellow mortals, those who chanced to be his contemporaries on earth, still, the life which Jesus of Nazareth lived in the flesh and on Urantia did receive full and unqualified acceptance by the Universal Father as constituting at one and the same time, and in one and the same personality-life, the fullness of the revelation of the eternal God to mortal man and the presentation of perfected human personality to the satisfaction of the Infinite Creator.

And this was his true and supreme purpose. He did not come down to live on Urantia as the perfect and detailed example for any child or adult, any man or woman, in that age or any other. True it is, indeed, that in his full, rich, beautiful, and noble life we may all find much that is exquisitely exemplary, divinely inspiring, but this is because he lived a true and genuinely human life. Jesus did not live his life on earth in order to set an example for all other human beings to copy. He lived this life in the flesh by the same mercy ministry that you all may live your lives on earth; and as he lived his mortal life in his day and *as he was,* so did he thereby set the example for all of us thus to live our lives in our day and *as we are.* You may not aspire to live his life, but you can resolve to *live your lives* even as, and by the same means that, he lived his. Jesus may not be the technical and detailed example for all the mortals of all ages on all the realms of this local universe, but he is everlastingly the inspiration and guide of all Paradise pilgrims from the worlds of initial ascension up through a universe of universes and on through Havona to Paradise. Jesus is the *new and living way* from man to God, from the partial to the perfect, from the earthly to the heavenly, from time to eternity.

By the end of the twenty-ninth year Jesus of Nazareth had virtually finished the living of the life required of mortals as sojourners in the flesh. He came on earth the fullness of God to be manifest to man; he had now become well-nigh the perfection of man awaiting the occasion to become manifest to God. And he did all of this before he was thirty years of age.

PAPER 130

ON THE WAY TO ROME

THE tour of the Roman world consumed most of the twenty-eighth and the entire twenty-ninth year of Jesus' life on earth. Jesus and the two natives from India—Gonod and his son Ganid—left Jerusalem on a Sunday morning, April 26, A.D. 22. They made their journey according to schedule, and Jesus said good-bye to the father and son in the city of Charax on the Persian Gulf on the tenth day of December the following year, A.D. 23.

From Jerusalem they went to Caesarea by way of Joppa. At Caesarea they took a boat for Alexandria. From Alexandria they sailed for Lasea in Crete. From Crete they sailed for Carthage, touching at Cyrene. At Carthage they took a boat for Naples, stopping at Malta, Syracuse, and Messina. From Naples they went to Capua, whence they traveled by the Appian Way to Rome.

After their stay in Rome they went overland to Tarentum, where they set sail for Athens in Greece, stopping at Nicopolis and Corinth. From Athens they went to Ephesus by way of Troas. From Ephesus they sailed for Cyprus, putting in at Rhodes on the way. They spent considerable time visiting and resting on Cyprus and then sailed for Antioch in Syria. From Antioch they journeyed south to Sidon and then went over to Damascus. From there they traveled by caravan to Mesopotamia, passing through Thapsacus and Larissa. They spent some time in Babylon, visited Ur and other places, and then went to Susa. From Susa they journeyed to Charax, from which place Gonod and Ganid embarked for India.

It was while working four months at Damascus that Jesus had picked up the rudiments of the language spoken by Gonod and Ganid. While there he had labored much of the time on translations from Greek into one of the languages of India, being assisted by a native of Gonod's home district.

On this Mediterranean tour Jesus spent about half of each day teaching Ganid and acting as interpreter during Gonod's business conferences and social contacts. The remainder of each day, which was at his disposal, he devoted to making those close personal contacts with his fellow men, those intimate associations with the mortals of the realm, which so characterized his activities during these years that just preceded his public ministry.

From firsthand observation and actual contact Jesus acquainted himself with the higher material and intellectual civilization of the Occident and the Levant; from Gonod and his brilliant son he learned a great deal about the civilization and culture of India and China, for Gonod, himself a citizen of India, had made three extensive trips to the empire of the yellow race.

Ganid, the young man, learned much from Jesus during this long and intimate association. They developed a great affection for each other, and the lad's father many times tried to persuade Jesus to return with them to India, but Jesus always declined, pleading the necessity for returning to his family in Palestine.

1. AT JOPPA—DISCOURSE ON JONAH

During their stay in Joppa, Jesus met Gadiah, a Philistine interpreter who worked for one Simon a tanner. Gonod's agents in Mesopotamia had transacted much business with this Simon; so Gonod and his son desired to pay him a visit on their way to Caesarea. While they tarried at Joppa, Jesus and Gadiah became warm friends. This young Philistine was a truth seeker. Jesus was a truth giver; he *was* the truth for that generation on Urantia. When a great truth seeker and a great truth giver meet, the result is a great and liberating enlightenment born of the experience of new truth.

One day after the evening meal Jesus and the young Philistine strolled down by the sea, and Gadiah, not knowing that this "scribe of Damascus" was so well versed in the Hebrew traditions, pointed out to Jesus the ship landing from which it was reputed that Jonah had embarked on his ill-fated voyage to Tarshish. And when he had concluded his remarks, he asked Jesus this question: "But do you suppose the big fish really did swallow Jonah?" Jesus perceived that this young man's life had been tremendously influenced by this tradition, and that its contemplation had impressed upon him the folly of trying to run away from duty; Jesus therefore said nothing that would suddenly destroy the foundations of Gadiah's present motivation for practical living. In answering this question, Jesus said: "My friend, we are all Jonahs with lives to live in accordance with the will of God, and at all times when we seek to escape the present duty of living by running away to far-off enticements, we thereby put ourselves in the immediate control of those influences which are not directed by the powers of truth and the forces of righteousness. The flight from duty is the sacrifice of truth. The escape from the service of light and life can only result in those distressing conflicts with the difficult whales of selfishness which lead eventually to darkness and death unless such God-forsaking Jonahs shall turn their hearts, even when in the very depths of despair, to seek after God and his goodness. And when such disheartened souls sincerely seek for God—hunger for truth and thirst for righteousness—there is nothing that can hold them in further captivity. No matter into what great depths they may have fallen, when they seek the light with a whole heart, the spirit of the Lord God of heaven will deliver them from their captivity; the evil circumstances of life will spew them out upon the dry land of fresh opportunities for renewed service and wiser living."

Gadiah was mightily moved by Jesus' teaching, and they talked long into the night by the seaside, and before they went to their lodgings, they prayed together and for each other. This was the same Gadiah who listened to the later preaching of Peter, became a profound believer in Jesus of Nazareth, and held a memorable argument with Peter one evening at the home of Dorcas. And Gadiah had very much to do with the final decision of Simon, the wealthy leather merchant, to embrace Christianity.

(In this narrative of the personal work of Jesus with his fellow mortals on this tour of the Mediterranean, we shall, in accordance with our permission, freely translate his words into modern phraseology current on Urantia at the time of this presentation.)

Jesus' last visit with Gadiah had to do with a discussion of good and evil. This young Philistine was much troubled by a feeling of injustice because of the presence of evil in the world alongside the good. He said: "How can God, if he is infinitely good, permit us to suffer the sorrows of evil; after all, who creates evil?" It was still believed by many in those days that God creates both good and evil, but Jesus never taught such error. In answering this question, Jesus said: "My brother, God is love; therefore he must be good, and his goodness is so great and real that it cannot contain the small and unreal things of evil. God is so positively good that there is absolutely no place in him for negative evil. Evil is the immature choosing and the unthinking misstep of those who are resistant to goodness, rejectful of beauty, and disloyal to truth. Evil is only the misadaptation of immaturity or the disruptive and distorting influence of ignorance. Evil is the inevitable darkness which follows upon the heels of the unwise rejection of light. Evil is that which is dark and untrue, and which, when consciously embraced and willfully endorsed, becomes sin.

"Your Father in heaven, by endowing you with the power to choose between truth and error, created the potential negative of the positive way of light and life; but such errors of evil are really nonexistent until such a time as an intelligent creature wills their existence by mischoosing the way of life. And then are such evils later exalted into sin by the knowing and deliberate choice of such a willful and rebellious creature. This is why our Father in heaven permits the good and the evil to go along together until the end of life, just as nature allows the wheat and the tares to grow side by side until the harvest." Gadiah was fully satisfied with Jesus' answer to his question after their subsequent discussion had made clear to his mind the real meaning of these momentous statements.

2. AT CAESAREA

Jesus and his friends tarried in Caesarea beyond the time expected because one of the huge steering paddles of the vessel on which they intended to embark was discovered to be in danger of cleaving. The captain decided to remain in port while a new one was being made. There was a shortage of skilled woodworkers for this task, so Jesus volunteered to assist. During the evenings Jesus and his friends strolled about on the beautiful wall which served as a promenade around the port. Ganid greatly enjoyed Jesus' explanation of the water system of the city and the technique whereby the tides were utilized to flush the city's streets and sewers. This youth of India was much impressed with the temple of Augustus, situated upon an elevation and surmounted by a colossal statue of the Roman emperor. The second afternoon of their stay the three of them attended a performance in the enormous amphitheater which could seat twenty thousand persons, and that night they went to a Greek play at the theater. These were the first exhibitions of this sort Ganid had ever witnessed, and he asked Jesus many questions about them. On the morning of the third day they paid a formal visit to the governor's palace, for Caesarea was the capital of Palestine and the residence of the Roman procurator.

At their inn there also lodged a merchant from Mongolia, and since this Far-Easterner talked Greek fairly well, Jesus had several long visits with him. This man was much impressed with Jesus' philosophy of life and never forgot his words of wisdom regarding "the living of the heavenly life while on earth by means of daily submission to the will of the heavenly Father." This merchant was a Taoist, and he had thereby become a strong believer in the doctrine of a universal Deity. When he returned to Mongolia, he began to teach these advanced truths to his neighbors and to his business associates, and as a direct result of such activities, his eldest son decided to become a Taoist priest. This young man exerted a great influence in behalf of advanced truth throughout his lifetime and was followed by a son and a grandson who likewise were devotedly loyal to the doctrine of the One God—the Supreme Ruler of Heaven.

While the eastern branch of the early Christian church, having its headquarters at Philadelphia, held more faithfully to the teachings of Jesus than did the Jerusalem brethren, it was regrettable that there was no one like Peter to go into China, or like Paul to enter India, where the spiritual soil was then so favorable for planting the seed of the new gospel of the kingdom. These very teachings of Jesus, as they were held by the Philadelphians, would have made just such an immediate and effective appeal to the minds of the spiritually hungry Asiatic peoples as did the preaching of Peter and Paul in the West.

One of the young men who worked with Jesus one day on the steering paddle became much interested in the words which he dropped from hour to hour as they toiled in the shipyard. When Jesus intimated that the Father in heaven was interested in the welfare of his children on earth, this young Greek, Anaxand, said: "If the Gods are interested in me, then why do they not remove the cruel and unjust foreman of this workshop?" He was startled when Jesus replied, "Since you know the ways of kindness and value justice, perhaps the Gods have brought this erring man near that you may lead him into this better way. Maybe you are the salt which is to make this brother more agreeable to all other men; that is, if you have not lost your savor. As it is, this man is your master in that his evil ways unfavorably influence you. Why not assert your mastery of evil by virtue of the power of goodness and thus become the master of all relations between the two of you? I predict that the good in you could overcome the evil in him if you gave it a fair and living chance. There is no adventure in the course of mortal existence more enthralling than to enjoy the exhilaration of becoming the material life partner with spiritual energy and divine truth in one of their triumphant struggles with error and evil. It is a marvelous and transforming experience to become the living channel of spiritual light to the mortal who sits in spiritual darkness. If you are more blessed with truth than is this man, his need should challenge you. Surely you are not the coward who could stand by on the seashore and watch a fellow man who could not swim perish! How much more of value is this man's soul floundering in darkness compared to his body drowning in water!"

Anaxand was mightily moved by Jesus' words. Presently he told his superior what Jesus had said, and that night they both sought Jesus' advice as to the welfare of their souls. And later on, after the Christian message had been proclaimed in Caesarea, both of these men, one a Greek and the other a Roman, believed Philip's preaching and became prominent members of the church which he founded. Later this young Greek was appointed the steward of a Roman centurion, Cornelius, who became a believer through Peter's ministry. Anaxand continued to minister light to those who sat in darkness until the days of Paul's imprisonment at Caesarea, when he perished, by accident, in the great slaughter of twenty thousand Jews while he ministered to the suffering and dying.

Ganid was, by this time, beginning to learn how his tutor spent his leisure in this unusual personal ministry to his fellow men, and the young Indian set about to find out the motive for these incessant activities. He asked, "Why do you occupy yourself so continuously with these visits with strangers?" And Jesus answered: "Ganid, no man is a stranger to one who knows God. In the experience of finding the Father in heaven you discover that all men are your brothers, and does it seem strange that one should enjoy the exhilaration of meeting a newly discovered brother? To become acquainted with one's brothers and sisters, to know their problems and to learn to love them, is the supreme experience of living."

This was a conference which lasted well into the night, in the course of which the young man requested Jesus to tell him the difference between the will of God and that human mind act of choosing which is also called will. In substance Jesus said: The will of God is the way of God, partnership with the choice of God in the face of any potential alternative. To do the will of God, therefore, is the progressive experience of becoming more and more like God, and God is the source and destiny of all that is good and beautiful and true. The will of man is the way of man, the sum and substance of that which the mortal chooses to be and do. Will is the deliberate choice of a self-conscious being which leads to decision-conduct based on intelligent reflection.

That afternoon Jesus and Ganid had both enjoyed playing with a very intelligent shepherd dog, and Ganid wanted to know whether the dog had a soul, whether it had a will, and in response to his questions Jesus said: "The dog has a mind which can know material man, his master, but cannot know God, who is spirit; therefore the dog does not possess a spiritual nature and cannot enjoy a spiritual experience. The dog may have a will derived from nature and augmented by training, but such a power of mind is not a spiritual force, neither is it comparable to the human will, inasmuch as it is not *reflective*—it is not the result of discriminating higher and moral meanings or choosing spiritual and eternal values. It is the possession of such powers of spiritual discrimination and truth choosing that makes mortal man a moral being, a creature endowed with the attributes of spiritual responsibility and the potential of eternal survival." Jesus went on to explain that it is the absence of such mental powers in the animal which makes it forever impossible for the animal world to develop language in time or to experience anything equivalent to personality survival in eternity. As a result of this day's instruction Ganid never again entertained belief in the transmigration of the souls of men into the bodies of animals.

The next day Ganid talked all this over with his father, and it was in answer to Gonod's question that Jesus explained that "human wills which are fully occupied with passing only upon temporal decisions having to do with the material problems of animal existence are doomed to perish in time. Those who make wholehearted moral decisions and unqualified spiritual choices are thus progressively identified with the indwelling and divine spirit, and thereby are they increasingly transformed into the values of eternal survival—unending progression of divine service."

It was on this same day that we first heard that momentous truth which, stated in modern terms, would signify: "Will is that manifestation of the human mind which enables the subjective consciousness to express itself objectively and to experience the phenomenon of aspiring to be Godlike." And it is in this same sense that every reflective and spiritually minded human being can become *creative.*

3. AT ALEXANDRIA

It had been an eventful visit at Caesarea, and when the boat was ready, Jesus and his two friends departed at noon one day for Alexandria in Egypt.

The three enjoyed a most pleasant passage to Alexandria. Ganid was delighted with the voyage and kept Jesus busy answering questions. As they approached the city's harbor, the young man was thrilled by the great lighthouse of Pharos, located on the island which Alexander had joined by a mole to the mainland, thus creating two magnificent harbors and thereby making Alexandria the maritime commercial crossroads of Africa, Asia, and Europe. This great lighthouse was one of the seven wonders of the world and was the forerunner of all subsequent lighthouses. They arose early in the morning to view this splendid lifesaving device of man, and amidst the exclamations of Ganid Jesus said: "And you, my son, will be like this lighthouse when you return to India, even after your father is laid to rest; you will become like the light of life to those who sit about you in darkness, showing all who so desire the way to reach the harbor of salvation in safety." And as Ganid squeezed Jesus' hand, he said, "I will."

And again we remark that the early teachers of the Christian religion made a great mistake when they so exclusively turned their attention to the western civilization of the Roman world. The teachings of Jesus, as they were held by the Mesopotamian believers of the first century, would have been readily received by the various groups of Asiatic religionists.

By the fourth hour after landing they were settled near the eastern end of the long and broad avenue, one hundred feet wide and five miles long, which stretched on out to the western limits of this city of one million people. After the first survey of the city's chief attractions—university (museum), library, the royal mausoleum of Alexander, the palace, temple of Neptune, theater, and gymnasium—Gonod addressed himself to business while Jesus and Ganid went to the library, the greatest in the world. Here were assembled nearly a million manuscripts from all the civilized world: Greece, Rome, Palestine, Parthia, India, China, and even Japan. In this library Ganid saw the largest collection of Indian literature in all the world; and they spent some time here each day throughout their stay in Alexandria. Jesus told Ganid about the translation of the Hebrew scriptures into Greek at this place. And they discussed again and again all the religions of the world, Jesus endeavoring to point out to this young mind the truth in each, always adding: "But Yahweh is the God developed from the revelations of Melchizedek and the covenant of Abraham. The Jews were the offspring of Abraham and subsequently occupied the very land wherein Melchizedek had lived and taught, and from which he sent teachers to all the world; and their religion eventually portrayed a clearer recognition of the Lord God of Israel as the Universal Father in heaven than any other world religion."

Under Jesus' direction Ganid made a collection of the teachings of all those religions of the world which recognized a Universal Deity, even though they might also give more or less recognition to subordinate deities. After much discussion Jesus and Ganid decided that the Romans had no real God in their religion, that their religion was hardly more than emperor worship. The Greeks, they concluded, had a philosophy but hardly a religion with a personal God. The mystery cults they discarded because of the confusion of their multiplicity, and because their varied concepts of Deity seemed to be derived from other and older religions.

Although these translations were made at Alexandria, Ganid did not finally arrange these selections and add his own personal conclusions until near the end of their sojourn in Rome. He was much surprised to discover that the best of the authors of the world's sacred literature all more or less clearly recognized the existence of an eternal God and were much in agreement with regard to his character and his relationship with mortal man.

Jesus and Ganid spent much time in the museum during their stay in Alexandria. This museum was not a collection of rare objects but rather a university of fine art, science, and literature. Learned professors here gave daily lectures, and in those times this was the intellectual center of the Occidental world. Day by day Jesus interpreted the lectures to Ganid; one day during the second week the young man exclaimed: "Teacher Joshua, you know more than these professors; you should stand up and tell them the great things you have told me; they are befogged by much thinking. I shall speak to my father and have him arrange it." Jesus smiled, saying: "You are an admiring pupil, but these teachers are not minded that you and I should instruct them. The pride of unspiritualized learning is a treacherous thing in human experience. The true teacher maintains his intellectual integrity by ever remaining a learner."

Alexandria was the city of the blended culture of the Occident and next to Rome the largest and most magnificent in the world. Here was located the largest Jewish synagogue in the world, the seat of government of the Alexandria Sanhedrin, the seventy ruling elders.

Among the many men with whom Gonod transacted business was a certain Jewish banker, Alexander, whose brother, Philo, was a famous religious philosopher of that time. Philo was engaged in the laudable but exceedingly difficult task of harmonizing Greek philosophy and Hebrew theology. Ganid and Jesus talked much about Philo's teachings and expected to attend some of his lectures, but throughout their stay at Alexandria this famous Hellenistic Jew lay sick abed.

Jesus commended to Ganid much in the Greek philosophy and the Stoic doctrines, but he impressed upon the lad the truth that these systems of belief, like the indefinite teachings of some of his own people, were religions only in the sense that they led men to find God and enjoy a living experience in knowing the Eternal.

4. DISCOURSE ON REALITY

The night before they left Alexandria Ganid and Jesus had a long visit with one of the government professors at the university who lectured on the teachings of Plato. Jesus interpreted for the learned Greek teacher but injected no teaching of his own in refutation of the Greek philosophy. Gonod was away on business that evening; so, after the professor had departed, the teacher and his pupil had a long and heart-to-heart talk about Plato's doctrines. While Jesus gave qualified approval of some of the Greek teachings which had to do with the theory that the material things of the world are shadowy reflections of invisible but more substantial spiritual realities, he sought to lay a more trustworthy foundation for the lad's thinking; so he began a long dissertation concerning the nature of reality in the universe. In substance and in modern phraseology Jesus said to Ganid:

The source of universe reality is the Infinite. The material things of finite creation are the time-space repercussions of the Paradise Pattern and the Universal Mind of the eternal God. Causation in the physical world, self-consciousness in the intellectual world, and progressing selfhood in the spirit world—these realities, projected on a universal scale, combined in eternal relatedness, and experienced with perfection of quality and divinity of value—constitute the *reality of the Supreme.* But in an ever-changing universe the Original Personality of causation, intelligence, and spirit experience is changeless, absolute. All things, even in an eternal universe of limitless values and divine qualities, may, and oftentimes do, change except the Absolutes and that which has attained the physical status, intellectual embrace, or spiritual identity which is absolute.

The highest level to which a finite creature can progress is the recognition of the Universal Father and the knowing of the Supreme. And even then such beings of finality destiny go on experiencing change in the motions of the physical world and in its material phenomena. Likewise do they remain aware of selfhood progression in their continuing ascension of the spiritual universe and of growing consciousness in their deepening appreciation of, and response to, the intellectual cosmos. Only in the perfection, harmony, and unanimity of will can the creature become as one with the Creator; and such a state of divinity is attained and maintained only by the creature's continuing to live in time and eternity by consistently conforming his finite personal will to the divine will of the Creator. Always must the desire to do the Father's will be supreme in the soul and dominant over the mind of an ascending son of God.

A one-eyed person can never hope to visualize depth of perspective. Neither can single-eyed material scientists nor single-eyed spiritual mystics and allegorists correctly visualize and adequately comprehend the true depths of universe reality. All true values of creature experience are concealed in depth of recognition.

Mindless causation cannot evolve the refined and complex from the crude and the simple, neither can spiritless experience evolve the divine characters of eternal survival from the material minds of the mortals of time. The one attribute of the universe which so exclusively characterizes the infinite Deity is this unending creative bestowal of personality which can survive in progressive Deity attainment.

Personality is that cosmic endowment, that phase of universal reality, which can coexist with unlimited change and at the same time retain its identity in the very presence of all such changes, and forever afterward.

Life is an adaptation of the original cosmic causation to the demands and possibilities of universe situations, and it comes into being by the action of the Universal Mind and the activation of the spirit spark of the God who is spirit. The meaning of life is its adaptability; the value of life is its progressability—even to the heights of God-consciousness.

Misadaptation of self-conscious life to the universe results in cosmic disharmony. Final divergence of personality will from the trend of the universes terminates in intellectual isolation, personality segregation. Loss of the indwelling spirit pilot supervenes in spiritual cessation of existence. Intelligent and progressing life becomes then, in and of itself, an incontrovertible proof of the existence of a purposeful universe expressing the will of a divine Creator. And this life, in the aggregate, struggles toward higher values, having for its final goal the Universal Father.

Only in degree does man possess mind above the animal level aside from the higher and quasi-spiritual ministrations of intellect. Therefore animals (not having worship and wisdom) cannot experience superconsciousness, consciousness of consciousness. The animal mind is only conscious of the objective universe.

Knowledge is the sphere of the material or fact-discerning mind. Truth is the domain of the spiritually endowed intellect that is conscious of knowing God. Knowledge is demonstrable; truth is experienced. Knowledge is a possession of the mind; truth an experience of the soul, the progressing self. Knowledge is a function of the nonspiritual level; truth is a phase of the mind-spirit level of the universes. The eye of the material mind perceives a world of factual knowledge; the eye of the spiritualized intellect discerns a world of true values. These two views, synchronized and harmonized, reveal the world of reality, wherein wisdom interprets the phenomena of the universe in terms of progressive personal experience.

Error (evil) is the penalty of imperfection. The qualities of imperfection or facts of misadaptation are disclosed on the material level by critical observation and by scientific analysis; on the moral level, by human experience. The presence of evil constitutes proof of the inaccuracies of mind and the immaturity of the evolving self. Evil is, therefore, also a measure of imperfection in universe interpretation. The possibility of making mistakes is inherent in the acquisition of wisdom, the scheme of progressing from the partial and temporal to the complete and eternal, from the relative and imperfect to the final and perfected. Error is the shadow of relative incompleteness which must of necessity fall across man's ascending universe path to Paradise perfection. Error (evil) is not an actual universe quality; it is simply the observation of a relativity in the relatedness of the imperfection of the incomplete finite to the ascending levels of the Supreme and Ultimate.

Although Jesus told all this to the lad in language best suited to his comprehension, at the end of the discussion Ganid was heavy of eye and was soon lost in slumber. They rose early the next morning to go aboard the boat bound for Lasea on the island of Crete. But before they embarked, the lad had still further questions to ask about evil, to which Jesus replied:

Evil is a relativity concept. It arises out of the observation of the imperfections which appear in the shadow cast by a finite universe of things and beings as such a cosmos obscures the living light of the universal expression of the eternal realities of the Infinite One.

Potential evil is inherent in the necessary incompleteness of the revelation of God as a time-space-limited expression of infinity and eternity. The fact of the partial in the presence of the complete constitutes relativity of reality, creates necessity for intellectual choosing, and establishes value levels of spirit recognition and response. The incomplete and finite concept of the Infinite which is held by the temporal and limited creature mind is, in and of itself, *potential evil.* But the augmenting error of unjustified deficiency in reasonable spiritual rectification of these originally inherent intellectual disharmonies and spiritual insufficiencies, is equivalent to the realization of *actual evil.*

All static, dead, concepts are potentially evil. The finite shadow of relative and living truth is continually moving. Static concepts invariably retard science, politics, society, and religion. Static concepts may represent a certain knowledge, but they are deficient in wisdom and devoid of truth. But do not permit the concept of relativity so to mislead you that you fail to recognize the co-ordination of the universe under the guidance of the cosmic mind, and its stabilized control by the energy and spirit of the Supreme.

5. ON THE ISLAND OF CRETE

The travelers had but one purpose in going to Crete, and that was to play, to walk about over the island, and to climb the mountains. The Cretans of that time did not enjoy an enviable reputation among the surrounding peoples. Nevertheless, Jesus and Ganid won many souls to higher levels of thinking and living and thus laid the foundation for the quick reception of the later gospel teachings when the first preachers from Jerusalem arrived. Jesus loved these Cretans, notwithstanding the harsh words which Paul later spoke concerning them when he subsequently sent Titus to the island to reorganize their churches.

On the mountainside in Crete Jesus had his first long talk with Gonod regarding religion. And the father was much impressed, saying: "No wonder the boy believes everything you tell him, but I never knew they had such a religion even in Jerusalem, much less in Damascus." It was during the island sojourn that Gonod first proposed to Jesus that he go back to India with them, and Ganid was delighted with the thought that Jesus might consent to such an arrangement.

One day when Ganid asked Jesus why he had not devoted himself to the work of a public teacher, he said: "My son, everything must await the coming of its time. You are born into the world, but no amount of anxiety and no manifestation of impatience will help you to grow up. You must, in all such matters, wait upon time. Time alone will ripen the green fruit upon the tree. Season follows season and sundown follows sunrise only with the passing of time. I am now on the way to Rome with you and your father, and that is sufficient for today. My tomorrow is wholly in the hands of my Father in heaven." And then he told Ganid the story of Moses and the forty years of watchful waiting and continued preparation.

One thing happened on a visit to Fair Havens which Ganid never forgot; the memory of this episode always caused him to wish he might do something to change the caste system of his native India. A drunken degenerate was attacking a slave girl on the public highway. When Jesus saw the plight of the girl, he rushed forward and drew the maiden away from the assault of the madman. While the frightened child clung to him, he held the infuriated man at a safe distance by his powerful extended right arm until the poor fellow had exhausted himself beating the air with his angry blows. Ganid felt a strong impulse to help Jesus handle the affair, but his father forbade him. Though they could not speak the girl's language, she could understand their act of mercy and gave token of her heartfelt appreciation as they all three escorted her home. This was probably as near a personal encounter with his fellows as Jesus ever had throughout his entire life in the flesh. But he had a difficult task that evening trying to explain to

Ganid why he did not smite the drunken man. Ganid thought this man should have been struck at least as many times as he had struck the girl.

6. THE YOUNG MAN WHO WAS AFRAID

While they were up in the mountains, Jesus had a long talk with a young man who was fearful and downcast. Failing to derive comfort and courage from association with his fellows, this youth had sought the solitude of the hills; he had grown up with a feeling of helplessness and inferiority. These natural tendencies had been augmented by numerous difficult circumstances which the lad had encountered as he grew up, notably, the loss of his father when he was twelve years of age. As they met, Jesus said: "Greetings, my friend! why so downcast on such a beautiful day? If something has happened to distress you, perhaps I can in some manner assist you. At any rate it affords me real pleasure to proffer my services."

The young man was disinclined to talk, and so Jesus made a second approach to his soul, saying: "I understand you come up in these hills to get away from folks; so, of course, you do not want to talk with me, but I would like to know whether you are familiar with these hills; do you know the direction of the trails? and, perchance, could you inform me as to the best route to Phenix?" Now this youth was very familiar with these mountains, and he really became much interested in telling Jesus the way to Phenix, so much so that he marked out all the trails on the ground and fully explained every detail. But he was startled and made curious when Jesus, after saying good-bye and making as if he were taking leave, suddenly turned to him, saying: "I well know you wish to be left alone with your disconsolation; but it would be neither kind nor fair for me to receive such generous help from you as to how best to find my way to Phenix and then unthinkingly to go away from you without making the least effort to answer your appealing request for help and guidance regarding the best route to the goal of destiny which you seek in your heart while you tarry here on the mountainside. As you so well know the trails to Phenix, having traversed them many times, so do I well know the way to the city of your disappointed hopes and thwarted ambitions. And since you have asked me for help, I will not disappoint you." The youth was almost overcome, but he managed to stammer out, "But—I did not ask you for anything—" And Jesus, laying a gentle hand on his shoulder, said: "No, son, not with words but with longing looks did you appeal to my heart. My boy, to one who loves his fellows there is an eloquent appeal for help in your countenance of discouragement and despair. Sit down with me while I tell you of the service trails and happiness highways which lead from the sorrows of self to the joys of loving activities in the brotherhood of men and in the service of the God of heaven."

By this time the young man very much desired to talk with Jesus, and he knelt at his feet imploring Jesus to help him, to show him the way of escape from his world of personal sorrow and defeat. Said Jesus: "My friend, arise! Stand up like a man! You may be surrounded with small enemies and be retarded by many obstacles, but the big things and the real things of this world and the universe are on your side. The sun rises every morning to salute you just as it does the most powerful and prosperous man on earth. Look—you have a strong body and powerful muscles—your physical equipment is better than the average. Of course, it is just about useless while you sit out here on the mountainside and grieve over your misfortunes, real and fancied. But you could do great things with your body if you would hasten off to where great things are waiting to be done. You are trying to run away from your unhappy self, but it cannot be done. You and your problems of living are real; you cannot escape them as long as you live. But look again, your mind is clear and capable. Your strong body has an intelligent mind to direct it. Set your mind at work to solve its problems; teach your intellect to work for you; refuse longer to be dominated by fear like an unthinking animal. Your mind should be your courageous ally in the solution of your life problems rather than your being, as you have been, its abject fear-slave and the bond servant of depression and defeat. But most valuable of all, your potential of real achievement is the spirit which lives within you, and which will stimulate and inspire your mind to control itself and activate the body if you will release it from the fetters of fear and thus enable your spiritual nature to begin your deliverance from the evils of inaction by the power-presence of living faith. And then, forthwith, will this faith vanquish fear of men by the compelling presence of that new and all-dominating *love of your fellows* which will so soon fill your soul to overflowing because of the consciousness which has been born in your heart that you are a child of God.

"This day, my son, you are to be reborn, re-established as a man of faith, courage, and devoted service to man, for God's sake. And when you become so readjusted to life within yourself, you become likewise readjusted to the universe; you have been born again—born of the spirit—and henceforth will your whole life become one of victorious accomplishment. Trouble will invigorate you; disappointment will spur you on; difficulties will challenge you; and obstacles will stimulate you. Arise, young man! Say farewell to the life of cringing fear and fleeing cowardice. Hasten back to duty and live your life in the flesh as a son of God, a mortal dedicated to the ennobling service of man on earth and destined to the superb and eternal service of God in eternity."

And this youth, Fortune, subsequently became the leader of the Christians in Crete and the close associate of Titus in his labors for the uplift of the Cretan believers.

The travelers were truly rested and refreshed when they made ready about noon one day to sail for Carthage in northern Africa, stopping for two days at Cyrene. It was here that Jesus and Ganid gave first aid to a lad named Rufus, who had been injured by the breakdown of a loaded oxcart. They carried him home to his mother, and his father, Simon, little dreamed that the man whose cross he subsequently bore by orders of a Roman soldier was the stranger who once befriended his son.

7. AT CARTHAGE—DISCOURSE ON TIME AND SPACE

Most of the time en route to Carthage Jesus talked with his fellow travelers about things social, political, and commercial; hardly a word was said about religion. For the first time Gonod and Ganid discovered that Jesus was a good storyteller, and they kept him busy telling tales about his early life in Galilee. They also learned that he was reared in Galilee and not in either Jerusalem or Damascus.

When Ganid inquired what one could do to make friends, having noticed that the majority of persons whom they chanced to meet were attracted to Jesus, his teacher said: "Become interested in your fellows; learn how to love them and watch for the opportunity to do something for them which you are sure they want done," and then he quoted the olden Jewish proverb—"A man who would have friends must show himself friendly."

At Carthage Jesus had a long and memorable talk with a Mithraic priest about immortality, about time and eternity. This Persian had been educated at Alexandria, and he really desired to learn from Jesus. Put into the words of today, in substance Jesus said in answer to his many questions:

Time is the stream of flowing temporal events perceived by creature consciousness. Time is a name given to the succession-arrangement whereby events are recognized and segregated. The universe of space is a time-related phenomenon as it is viewed from any interior position outside of the fixed abode of Paradise. The motion of time is only revealed in relation to something which does not move in space as a time phenomenon. In the universe of universes Paradise and its Deities transcend both time and space. On the inhabited worlds, human personality (indwelt and oriented by the Paradise Father's spirit) is the only physically related reality which can transcend the material sequence of temporal events.

Animals do not sense time as does man, and even to man, because of his sectional and circumscribed view, time appears as a succession of events; but as man ascends, as he progresses inward, the enlarging view of this event procession is such that it is discerned more and more in its wholeness. That which formerly appeared as a succession of events then will be viewed as a whole and perfectly related cycle; in this way will circular simultaneity increasingly displace the onetime consciousness of the linear sequence of events.

There are seven different conceptions of space as it is conditioned by time. Space is measured by time, not time by space. The confusion of the scientist grows out of failure to recognize the reality of space. Space is not merely an intellectual concept of the variation in relatedness of universe objects. Space is not empty, and the only thing man knows which can even partially transcend space is mind. Mind can function independently of the concept of the space-relatedness of material objects. Space is relatively and comparatively finite to all beings of creature status. The nearer consciousness approaches the awareness of seven cosmic dimensions, the more does the concept of potential space approach ultimacy. But the space potential is truly ultimate only on the absolute level.

It must be apparent that universal reality has an expanding and always relative meaning on the ascending and perfecting levels of the cosmos. Ultimately, surviving mortals achieve identity in a seven-dimensional universe.

The time-space concept of a mind of material origin is destined to undergo successive enlargements as the conscious and conceiving personality ascends the levels of the universes. When man attains the mind intervening between the material and the spiritual planes of existence, his ideas of time-space will be enormously expanded both as to quality of perception and quantity of experience. The enlarging cosmic conceptions of an advancing spirit personality are due to augmentations of both depth of insight and scope of consciousness. And as personality passes on, upward and inward, to the transcendental levels of Deity-likeness, the time-space concept will increasingly approximate the timeless and spaceless concepts of the Absolutes. Relatively, and in accordance with transcendental attainment, these concepts of the absolute level are to be envisioned by the children of ultimate destiny.

8. ON THE WAY TO NAPLES AND ROME

The first stop on the way to Italy was at the island of Malta. Here Jesus had a long talk with a downhearted and discouraged young man named Claudus. This fellow had contemplated taking his life, but when he had finished talking with the scribe of Damascus, he said: "I will face life like a man; I am through playing the coward. I will go back to my people and begin all over again." Shortly he became an enthusiastic preacher of the Cynics, and still later on he joined hands with Peter in proclaiming Christianity in Rome and Naples, and after the death of Peter he went on to Spain preaching the gospel. But he never knew that the man who inspired him in Malta was the Jesus whom he subsequently proclaimed the world's Deliverer.

At Syracuse they spent a full week. The notable event of their stop here was the rehabilitation of Ezra, the backslidden Jew, who kept the tavern where Jesus and his companions stopped. Ezra was charmed by Jesus' approach and asked him to help him come back to the faith of Israel. He expressed his hopelessness by saying, "I want to be a true son of Abraham, but I cannot find God." Said Jesus: "If you truly want to find God, that desire is in itself evidence that you have already found him. Your trouble is not that you cannot find God, for the Father has already found you; your trouble is simply that you do not know God. Have you not read in the Prophet Jeremiah, 'You shall seek me and find me when you shall search for me with all your heart'? And again, does not this same prophet say: 'And I will give you a heart to know me, that I am the Lord, and you shall belong to my people, and I will be your God'? And have you not also read in the Scriptures where it says: 'He looks down upon men, and if any will say: I have sinned and perverted that which was right, and it profited me not, then will God deliver that man's soul from darkness, and he shall see the light'?" And Ezra found God and to the satisfaction of his soul. Later, this Jew, in association with a well-to-do Greek proselyte, built the first Christian church in Syracuse.

At Messina they stopped for only one day, but that was long enough to change the life of a small boy, a fruit vendor, of whom Jesus bought fruit and in turn fed with the bread of life. The lad never forgot the words of Jesus and the kindly look which went with them when, placing his hand on the boy's shoulder, he said: "Farewell, my lad, be of good courage as you grow up to manhood and after you have fed the body learn how also to feed the soul. And my Father in heaven will be with you and go before you." The lad became a devotee of the Mithraic religion and later on turned to the Christian faith.

At last they reached Naples and felt they were not far from their destination, Rome. Gonod had much business to transact in Naples, and aside from the time Jesus was required as interpreter, he and Ganid spent their leisure visiting and exploring the city. Ganid was becoming adept at sighting those who appeared to be in need. They found much poverty in this city and distributed many alms. But Ganid never understood the meaning of Jesus' words when, after he had given a coin to a street beggar, he refused to pause and speak comfortingly to the man. Said Jesus: "Why waste words upon one who cannot perceive the meaning of what you say? The spirit of the Father cannot teach and save one who has no capacity for sonship." What Jesus meant was that the man was not of normal mind; that he lacked the ability to respond to spirit leading.

There was no outstanding experience in Naples; Jesus and the young man thoroughly canvassed the city and spread good cheer with many smiles upon hundreds of men, women, and children.

From here they went by way of Capua to Rome, making a stop of three days at Capua. By the Appian Way they journeyed on beside their pack animals toward Rome, all three being anxious to see this mistress of empire and the greatest city in all the world.

PAPER 131

THE WORLD'S RELIGIONS

DURING the Alexandrian sojourn of Jesus, Gonod, and Ganid, the young man spent much of his time and no small sum of his father's money making a collection of the teachings of the world's religions about God and his relations with mortal man. Ganid employed more than threescore learned translators in the making of this abstract of the religious doctrines of the world concerning the Deities. And it should be made plain in this record that all these teachings portraying monotheism were largely derived, directly or indirectly, from the preachments of the missionaries of Machiventa Melchizedek, who went forth from their Salem headquarters to spread the doctrine of one God—the Most High—to the ends of the earth.

There is presented herewith an abstract of Ganid's manuscript, which he prepared at Alexandria and Rome, and which was preserved in India for hundreds of years after his death. He collected this material under ten heads, as follows:

1. CYNICISM

The residual teachings of the disciples of Melchizedek, excepting those which persisted in the Jewish religion, were best preserved in the doctrines of the Cynics. Ganid's selection embraced the following:

"God is supreme; he is the Most High of heaven and earth. God is the perfected circle of eternity, and he rules the universe of universes. He is the sole maker of the heavens and the earth. When he decrees a thing, that thing is. Our God is one God, and he is compassionate and merciful. Everything that is high, holy, true, and beautiful is like our God. The Most High is the light of heaven and earth; he is the God of the east, the west, the north, and the south.

"Even if the earth should pass away, the resplendent face of the Supreme would abide in majesty and glory. The Most High is the first and the last, the beginning and the end of everything. There is but this one God, and his name is Truth. God is self-existent, and he is devoid of all anger and enmity; he is immortal and infinite. Our God is omnipotent and bounteous. While he has many manifestations, we worship only God himself. God knows all—our secrets and our proclamations; he also knows what each of us deserves. His might is equal to all things.

"God is a peace giver and a faithful protector of all who fear and trust him. He gives salvation to all who serve him. All creation exists in the power of the Most High. His divine love springs forth from the holiness of his power, and affection is born of the might of his greatness. The Most High has decreed the union of body and soul and has endowed man with his own spirit. What man does must come to an end, but what the Creator does goes on forever. We gain knowledge from the experience of man, but we derive wisdom from the contemplation of the Most High.

"God pours rain upon the earth, he causes the sun to shine upon the sprouting grain, and he gives us the abundant harvest of the good things of this life and eternal salvation in the world to come. Our God enjoys great authority; his name is Excellent and his nature is unfathomable. When you are sick, it is the Most High who heals you. God is full of goodness toward all men; we have no friend like the Most High. His mercy fills all places and his goodness encompasses all souls. The Most High is changeless; and he is our helper in every time of need. Wherever you turn to pray, there is the face of the Most High and the open ear of our God. You may hide yourself from men, but not from God. God is not a great distance from us; he is omnipresent. God fills all places and lives in the heart of the man who fears his holy name. Creation is in the Creator and the Creator in his creation. We search for the Most High and then find him in our hearts. You go in quest of a dear friend, and then you discover him within your soul.

"The man who knows God looks upon all men as equal; they are his brethren. Those who are selfish, those who ignore their brothers in the flesh, have only weariness as their reward. Those who love their fellows and who have pure hearts shall see God. God never forgets sincerity. He will guide the honest of heart into the truth, for God is truth.

"In your lives overthrow error and overcome evil by the love of the living truth. In all your relations with men do good for evil. The Lord God is merciful and loving; he is forgiving. Let us love God, for he first loved us. By God's love and through his mercy we shall be saved. Poor men and rich men are brothers. God is their Father. The evil you would not have done you, do not to others.

"At all times call upon his name, and as you believe in his name, so shall your prayer be heard. What a great honor it is to worship the Most High! All the worlds and the universes worship the Most High. And with all your prayers give thanks—ascend to worship. Prayerful worship shuns evil and forbids sin. At all times let us praise the name of the Most High. The man who takes shelter in the Most High conceals his defects from the universe. When you stand before God with a clean heart, you become fearless of all creation. The Most High is like a loving father and mother; he really loves us, his children on earth. Our God will forgive us and guide our footsteps into the ways of salvation. He will take us by the hand and lead us to himself. God saves those who trust him; he does not compel man to serve his name.

"If the faith of the Most High has entered your heart, then shall you abide free from fear throughout all the days of your life. Fret not yourself because of the prosperity of the ungodly; fear not those who plot evil; let the soul turn away from sin and put your whole trust in the God of salvation. The weary soul of the wandering mortal finds eternal rest in the arms of the Most High; the wise man hungers for the divine embrace; the earth child longs for the security of the arms of the Universal Father. The noble man seeks for that high estate wherein the soul of the mortal blends with the spirit of the Supreme. God is just: What fruit we receive not from our plantings in this world we shall receive in the next."

2. JUDAISM

The Kenites of Palestine salvaged much of the teaching of Melchizedek, and from these records, as preserved and modified by the Jews, Jesus and Ganid made the following selection:

"In the beginning God created the heavens and the earth and all things therein. And, behold, all he created was very good. The Lord, he is God; there is none beside him in heaven above or upon the earth beneath. Therefore shall you love the Lord your God with all your heart and with all your soul and with all your might. The earth shall be full of the knowledge of the Lord as the waters cover the sea. The heavens declare the glory of God, and the firmament shows his handiwork. Day after day utters speech; night after night shows knowledge. There is no speech or language where their voice is not heard. The Lord's work is great, and in wisdom has he made all things; the greatness of the Lord is unsearchable. He knows the number of the stars; he calls them all by their names.

"The power of the Lord is great and his understanding infinite. Says the Lord: 'As the heavens are higher than the earth, so are my ways higher than your ways, and my thoughts higher than your thoughts.' God reveals the deep and secret things because the light dwells with him. The Lord is merciful and gracious; he is long-suffering and abundant in goodness and truth. The Lord is good and upright; the meek will he guide in judgment. Taste and see that the Lord is good! Blessed is the man who trusts God. God is our refuge and strength, a very present help in trouble.

"The mercy of the Lord is from everlasting to everlasting upon those who fear him and his righteousness even to our children's children. The Lord is gracious and full of compassion. The Lord is good to all, and his tender mercies are over all his creation; he heals the brokenhearted and binds up their wounds. Whither shall I go from God's spirit? whither shall I flee from the divine presence? Thus says the High and Lofty One who inhabits eternity, whose name is Holy: 'I dwell in the high and holy place; also with him who is of a contrite heart and a humble spirit!' None can hide himself from our God, for he fills heaven and earth. Let the heavens be glad and let the earth rejoice. Let all nations say: The Lord reigns! Give thanks to God, for his mercy endures forever.

"The heavens declare God's righteousness, and all the people have seen his glory. It is God who has made us, and not we ourselves; we are his people, the sheep of his pasture. His mercy is everlasting, and his truth endures to all generations. Our God is governor among the nations. Let the earth be filled with his glory! O that men would praise the Lord for his goodness and for his wonderful gifts to the children of men!

"God has made man a little less than divine and has crowned him with love and mercy. The Lord knows the way of the righteous, but the way of the ungodly shall perish. The fear of the Lord is the beginning of wisdom; the knowledge of the Supreme is understanding. Says the Almighty God: 'Walk before me and be perfect.' Forget not that pride goes before destruction and a haughty spirit before a fall. He who rules his own spirit is mightier than he who takes a city. Says the Lord God, the Holy One: 'In returning to your spiritual rest shall you be saved; in quietness and confidence shall be your strength.' They who wait upon the Lord shall renew their strength; they shall mount up with wings like eagles. They shall run and not be weary; they shall walk and not be faint. The Lord shall give you rest from your fear. Says the Lord: 'Fear not, for I am with you. Be not dismayed, for I am your God. I will strengthen you; I will help you; yes, I will uphold you with the right hand of my righteousness.'

"God is our Father; the Lord is our redeemer. God has created the universal hosts, and he preserves them all. His righteousness is like the mountains and his judgment like the great deep. He causes us to drink of the river of his pleasures, and in his light we shall see light. It is good to give thanks to the Lord and to sing praises to the Most High; to show forth loving-kindness in the morning and the divine faithfulness every night. God's kingdom is an everlasting kingdom, and his dominion endures throughout all generations. The Lord is my shepherd; I shall not want. He makes me to lie down in green pastures; he leads me beside still waters. He restores my soul. He leads me in the paths of righteousness. Yes, even though I walk through the valley of the shadow of death, I will fear no evil, for God is with me. Surely goodness and mercy shall follow me all the days of my life, and I shall dwell in the house of the Lord forever.

"Yahweh is the God of my salvation; therefore in the divine name will I put my trust. I will trust in the Lord with all my heart; I will lean not upon my own understanding. In all my ways I will acknowledge him, and he shall direct my paths. The Lord is faithful; he keeps his word with those who serve him; the just shall live by his faith. If you do not well, it is because sin lies at the door; men reap the evil they plough and the sin they sow. Fret not yourself because of evildoers. If you regard iniquity in your heart, the Lord will not hear you; if you sin against God, you also wrong your own soul. God will bring every man's work to judgment with every secret thing, whether it be good or evil. As a man thinks in his heart, so is he.

"The Lord is near all who call upon him in sincerity and in truth. Weeping may endure for a night, but joy comes in the morning. A merry heart does good like a medicine. No good thing will God withhold from those who walk uprightly. Fear God and keep his commandments, for this is the whole duty of man. Thus says the Lord who created the heavens and who formed the earth: 'There is no God beside me, a just God and a savior. Look to me and be saved, all the ends of the earth. If you seek me, you shall find me if you search for me with all your heart.' The meek shall inherit the earth and shall delight themselves in the abundance of peace. Whoever sows iniquity shall reap calamity; they who sow the wind shall reap the whirlwind.

" 'Come now, let us reason together,' says the Lord, 'Though your sins be as scarlet, they shall be as white as snow. Though they be red like crimson, they shall be as wool.' But there is no peace for the wicked; it is your own sins which have withheld the good things from you. God is the health of my countenance and the joy of my soul. The eternal God is my strength; he is our dwelling place, and underneath are the everlasting arms. The Lord is near to those who are brokenhearted; he saves all who have a childlike spirit. Many are the afflictions of the righteous man, but the Lord delivers him out of them all. Commit your way to the Lord—trust him—and he will bring it to pass. He who dwells in the secret place of the Most High shall abide under the shadow of the Almighty.

"Love your neighbor as yourself; bear a grudge against no man. Whatsoever you hate do to no man. Love your brother, for the Lord has said: 'I will love my children freely.' The path of the just is as a shining light which shines more and more until the perfect day. They who are wise shall shine as the brightness of the firmament and they who turn many to righteousness as the stars forever and ever. Let the wicked forsake his evil way and the unrighteous man his rebellious thoughts. Says the Lord: 'Let them return to me, and I will have mercy on them; I will abundantly pardon.'

"Says God, the creator of heaven and earth: 'Great peace have they who love my law. My commandments are: You shall love me with all your heart; you shall have no gods before me; you shall not take my name in vain; remember the Sabbath day to keep it holy; honor your father and mother; you shall not kill; you shall not commit adultery; you shall not steal; you shall not bear false witness; you shall not covet.'

"And to all who love the Lord supremely and their neighbors like themselves, the God of heaven says: 'I will ransom you from the grave; I will redeem you from death. I will be merciful to your children, as well as just. Have I not said of my creatures on earth, you are the sons of the living God? And have I not loved you with an everlasting love? Have I not called you to become like me and to dwell forever with me in Paradise?'"

3. BUDDHISM

Ganid was shocked to discover how near Buddhism came to being a great and beautiful religion without God, without a personal and universal Deity. However, he did find some record of certain earlier beliefs which reflected something of the influence of the teachings of the Melchizedek missionaries who continued their work in India even to the times of Buddha. Jesus and Ganid collected the following statements from the Buddhist literature:

"Out of a pure heart shall gladness spring forth to the Infinite; all my being shall be at peace with this supermortal rejoicing. My soul is filled with content, and my heart overflows with the bliss of peaceful trust. I have no fear; I am free from anxiety. I dwell in security, and my enemies cannot alarm me. I am satisfied with the fruits of my confidence. I have found the approach to the Immortal easy of access. I pray for faith to sustain me on the long journey; I know that faith from beyond will not fail me. I know my brethren will prosper if they become imbued with the faith of the Immortal, even the faith that creates modesty, uprightness, wisdom, courage, knowledge, and perseverance. Let us forsake sorrow and disown fear. By faith let us lay hold upon true righteousness and genuine manliness. Let us learn to meditate on justice and mercy. Faith is man's true wealth; it is the endowment of virtue and glory.

"Unrighteousness is contemptible; sin is despicable. Evil is degrading, whether held in thought or wrought out in deeds. Pain and sorrow follow in the path of evil as the dust follows the wind. Happiness and peace of mind follow pure thinking and virtuous living as the shadow follows the substance of material things. Evil is the fruit of wrongly directed thinking. It is evil to see sin where there is no sin; to see no sin where there is sin. Evil is the path of false doctrines. Those who avoid evil by seeing things as they are gain joy by thus embracing the truth. Make an end of your misery by loathing sin. When you look up to the Noble One, turn away from sin with a whole heart. Make no apology for evil; make no excuse for sin. By your efforts to make amends for past sins you acquire strength to resist future tendencies thereto. Restraint is born of repentance. Leave no fault unconfessed to the Noble One.

"Cheerfulness and gladness are the rewards of deeds well done and to the glory of the Immortal. No man can rob you of the liberty of your own mind. When the faith of your religion has emancipated your heart, when the mind, like a mountain, is settled and immovable, then shall the peace of the soul flow tranquilly like a river of waters. Those who are sure of salvation are forever free from lust, envy, hatred, and the delusions of wealth. While faith is the energy of the better life, nevertheless, must you work out your own salvation with perseverance. If you would be certain of your final salvation, then make sure that you sincerely seek to fulfill all righteousness. Cultivate the assurance of the heart which springs from within and thus come to enjoy the ecstasy of eternal salvation.

"No religionist may hope to attain the enlightenment of immortal wisdom who persists in being slothful, indolent, feeble, idle, shameless, and selfish. But whoso is thoughtful, prudent, reflective, fervent, and earnest—even while he yet lives on earth—may attain the supreme enlightenment of the peace and liberty of divine wisdom. Remember, every act shall receive its reward. Evil results in sorrow and sin ends in pain. Joy and happiness are the outcome of a good life. Even the evildoer enjoys a season of grace before the time of the full ripening of his evil deeds, but inevitably there must come the full harvest of evil-doing. Let no man think lightly of sin, saying in his heart: 'The penalty of wrongdoing shall not come near me.' What you do shall be done to you, in the judgment of wisdom. Injustice done to your fellows shall come back upon you. The creature cannot escape the destiny of his deeds.

"The fool has said in his heart, 'Evil shall not overtake me'; but safety is found only when the soul craves reproof and the mind seeks wisdom. The wise man is a noble soul who is friendly in the midst of his enemies, tranquil among the turbulent, and generous among the grasping. Love of self is like weeds in a goodly field. Selfishness leads to grief; perpetual care kills. The tamed mind yields happiness. He is the greatest of warriors who overcomes and subdues himself. Restraint in all things is good. He alone is a superior person who esteems virtue and is observant of his duty. Let not anger and hate master you. Speak harshly of no one. Contentment is the greatest wealth. What is given wisely is well saved. Do not to others those things you would not wish done to you. Pay good for evil; overcome evil with the good.

"A righteous soul is more to be desired than the sovereignty of all the earth. Immortality is the goal of sincerity; death, the end of thoughtless living. Those who are earnest die not; the thoughtless are dead already. Blessed are they who have insight into the deathless state. Those who torture the living will hardly find happiness after death. The unselfish go to heaven, where they rejoice in the bliss of infinite liberality and continue to increase in noble generosity. Every mortal who thinks righteously, speaks nobly, and acts unselfishly shall not only enjoy virtue here during this brief life but shall also, after the dissolution of the body, continue to enjoy the delights of heaven."

4. HINDUISM

The missionaries of Melchizedek carried the teachings of the one God with them wherever they journeyed. Much of this monotheistic doctrine, together with other and previous concepts, became embodied in the subsequent teachings of Hinduism. Jesus and Ganid made the following excerpts:

"He is the great God, in every way supreme. He is the Lord who encompasses all things. He is the creator and controller of the universe of universes. God is one God; he is alone and by himself; he is the only one. And this one God is our Maker and the last destiny of the soul. The Supreme One is brilliant beyond description; he is the Light of Lights. Every heart and every world is illuminated by this divine light. God is our protector—he stands by the side of his creatures—and those who learn to know him become immortal. God is the great source of energy; he is the Great Soul. He exercises universal lordship over all. This one God is loving, glorious, and adorable. Our God is supreme in power and abides in the supreme abode. This true Person is eternal and divine; he is the primal Lord of heaven. All the prophets have hailed him, and he has revealed himself to us. We worship him. O Supreme Person, source of beings, Lord of creation, and ruler of the universe, reveal to us, your creatures, the power whereby you abide immanent! God has made the sun and the stars; he is bright, pure, and self-existent. His eternal knowledge is divinely wise. The Eternal is unpenetrated by evil. Inasmuch as the universe sprang from God, he does rule it appropriately. He is the cause of creation, and hence are all things established in him.

"God is the sure refuge of every good man when in need; the Immortal One cares for all mankind. God's salvation is strong and his kindness is gracious. He is a loving protector, a blessed defender. Says the Lord: 'I dwell within their own souls as a lamp of wisdom. I am the splendor of the splendid and the goodness of the good. Where two or three gather together, there am I also.' The creature cannot escape the presence of the Creator. The Lord even counts the ceaseless winking of every mortal's eyes; and we worship this divine Being as our inseparable companion. He is all-prevailing, bountiful, omnipresent, and infinitely kind. The Lord is our ruler, shelter, and supreme controller, and his primeval spirit dwells within the mortal soul. The Eternal Witness to vice and virtue dwells within man's heart. Let us long meditate on the adorable and divine Vivifier; let his spirit fully direct our thoughts. From this unreal world lead us to the real! From darkness lead us to the light! From death guide us to immortality!

"With our hearts purged of all hate, let us worship the Eternal. Our God is the Lord of prayer; he hears the cry of his children. Let all men submit their wills to him, the Resolute. Let us delight in the liberality of the Lord of prayer. Make prayer your inmost friend and worship your soul's support. 'If you will but worship me in love,' says the Eternal, 'I will give you the wisdom to attain me, for my worship is the virtue common to all creatures.' God is the illuminator of the gloomy and the power of those who are faint. Since God is our strong friend, we have no more fear. We praise the name of the never-conquered Conqueror. We worship him because he is man's faithful and eternal helper. God is our sure leader and unfailing guide. He is the great parent of heaven and earth, possessed of unlimited energy and infinite wisdom. His splendor is sublime and his beauty divine. He is the supreme refuge of the universe and the changeless guardian of everlasting law. Our God is the Lord of life and the Comforter of all men; he is the lover of mankind and the helper of those who are distressed. He is our life giver and the Good Shepherd of the human flocks. God is our father, brother, and friend. And we long to know this God in our inner being.

"We have learned to win faith by the yearning of our hearts. We have attained wisdom by the restraint of our senses, and by wisdom we have experienced peace in the Supreme. He who is full of faith worships truly when his inner self is intent upon God. Our God wears the heavens as a mantle; he also inhabits the other six wide-spreading universes. He is supreme over all and in all. We crave forgiveness from the Lord for all of our trespasses against our fellows; and we would release our friend from the wrong he has done us. Our spirit loathes all evil; therefore, O Lord, free us from all taint of sin. We pray to God as a comforter, protector, and savior—one who loves us.

"The spirit of the Universe Keeper enters the soul of the simple creature. That man is wise who worships the One God. Those who strive for perfection must indeed know the Lord Supreme. He never fears who knows the blissful security of the Supreme, for the Supreme says to those who serve him, 'Fear not, for I am with you.' The God of providence is our Father. God is truth. And it is the desire of God that his creatures should understand him—come fully to know the truth. Truth is eternal; it sustains the universe. Our supreme desire shall be union with the Supreme. The Great Controller is the generator of all things—all evolves from him. And this is the sum of duty: Let no man do to another what would be repugnant to himself; cherish no malice, smite not him who smites you, conquer anger with mercy, and vanquish hate by benevolence. And all this we should do because God is a kind friend and a gracious father who remits all our earthly offenses.

"God is our Father, the earth our mother, and the universe our birthplace. Without God the soul is a prisoner; to know God releases the soul. By meditation on God, by union with him, there comes deliverance from the illusions of evil and ultimate salvation from all material fetters. When man shall roll up space as a piece of leather, then will come the end of evil because man has found God. O God, save us from the threefold ruin of hell—lust, wrath, and avarice! O soul, gird yourself for the spirit struggle of immortality! When the end of mortal life comes, hesitate not to forsake this body for a more fit and beautiful form and to awake in the realms of the Supreme and Immortal, where there is no fear, sorrow, hunger, thirst, or death. To know God is to cut the cords of death. The God-knowing soul rises in the universe like the cream appears on top of the milk. We worship God, the all-worker, the Great Soul, who is ever seated in the heart of his creatures. And they who know that God is enthroned in the human heart are destined to become like him—immortal. Evil must be left behind in this world, but virtue follows the soul to heaven.

"It is only the wicked who say: The universe has neither truth nor a ruler; it was only designed for our lusts. Such souls are deluded by the smallness of their intellects. They thus abandon themselves to the enjoyment of their lusts and deprive their souls of the joys of virtue and the pleasures of righteousness. What can be greater than to experience salvation from sin? The man who has seen the Supreme is immortal. Man's friends of the flesh cannot survive death; virtue alone walks by man's side as he journeys ever onward toward the gladsome and sunlit fields of Paradise."

5. ZOROASTRIANISM

Zoroaster was himself directly in contact with the descendants of the earlier Melchizedek missionaries, and their doctrine of the one God became a central teaching in the religion which he founded in Persia. Aside from Judaism, no religion of that day contained more of these Salem teachings. From the records of this religion Ganid made the following excerpts:

"All things come from, and belong to, the One God—all-wise, good, righteous, holy, resplendent, and glorious. This, our God, is the source of all luminosity. He is the Creator, the God of all good purposes, and the protector of the justice of the universe. The wise course in life is to act in consonance with the spirit of truth. God is all-seeing, and he beholds both the evil deeds of the wicked and the good works of the righteous; our God observes all things with a flashing eye. His touch is the touch of healing. The Lord is an all-powerful benefactor. God stretches out his beneficent hand to both the righteous and the wicked. God established the world and ordained the rewards for good and for evil. The all-wise God has promised immortality to the pious souls who think purely and act righteously. As you supremely desire, so shall you be. The light of the sun is as wisdom to those who discern God in the universe.

"Praise God by seeking the pleasure of the Wise One. Worship the God of light by joyfully walking in the paths ordained by his revealed religion. There is but one Supreme God, the Lord of Lights. We worship him who made the waters, plants, animals, the earth, and the heavens. Our God is Lord, most beneficent. We worship the most beauteous, the bountiful Immortal, endowed with eternal light. God is farthest from us and at the same time nearest to us in that he dwells within our souls. Our God is the divine and holiest Spirit of Paradise, and yet he is more friendly to man than the most friendly of all creatures. God is most helpful to us in this greatest of all businesses, the knowing of himself. God is our most adorable and righteous friend; he is our wisdom, life, and vigor of soul and body. Through our good thinking the wise Creator will enable us to do his will, thereby attaining the realization of all that is divinely perfect.

"Lord, teach us how to live this life in the flesh while preparing for the next life of the spirit. Speak to us, Lord, and we will do your bidding. Teach us the good paths, and we will go right. Grant us that we may attain union with you. We know that the religion is right which leads to union with righteousness. God is our wise nature, best thought, and righteous act. May God grant us unity with the divine spirit and immortality in himself!

"This religion of the Wise One cleanses the believer from every evil thought and sinful deed. I bow before the God of heaven in repentance if I have offended in thought, word, or act—intentionally or unintentionally—and I offer prayers for mercy and praise for forgiveness. I know when I make confession, if I purpose not to do again the evil thing, that sin will be removed from my soul. I know that forgiveness takes away the bonds of sin. Those who do evil shall receive punishment, but those who follow truth shall enjoy the bliss of an eternal salvation. Through grace lay hold upon us and minister saving power to our souls. We claim mercy because we aspire to attain perfection; we would be like God."

6. SUDUANISM (JAINISM)

The third group of religious believers who preserved the doctrine of one God in India—the survival of the Melchizedek teaching—were known in those days as the Suduanists. Latterly these believers have become known as followers of Jainism. They taught:

"The Lord of Heaven is supreme. Those who commit sin will not ascend on high, but those who walk in the paths of righteousness shall find a place in heaven. We are assured of the life hereafter if we know truth. The soul of man may ascend to the highest heaven, there to develop its true spiritual nature, to attain perfection. The estate of heaven delivers man from the bondage of sin and introduces him to the final beatitudes; the righteous man has already experienced an end of sin and all its associated miseries. Self is man's invincible foe, and self is manifested as man's four greatest passions: anger, pride, deceit, and greed. Man's greatest victory is the conquest of himself. When man looks to God for forgiveness, and when he makes bold to enjoy such liberty, he is thereby delivered from fear. Man should journey through life treating his fellow creatures as he would like to be treated."

7. SHINTO

Only recently had the manuscripts of this Far-Eastern religion been lodged in the Alexandrian library. It was the one world religion of which Ganid had never heard. This belief also contained remnants of the earlier Melchizedek teachings as is shown by the following abstracts:

"Says the Lord: 'You are all recipients of my divine power; all men enjoy my ministry of mercy. I derive great pleasure in the multiplication of righteous men throughout the land. In both the beauties of nature and the virtues of men does the Prince of Heaven seek to reveal himself and to show forth his righteous nature. Since the olden people did not know my name, I manifested myself by being born into the world as a visible existence and endured such abasement even that man should not forget my name. I am the maker of heaven and earth; the sun and the moon and all the stars obey my will. I am the ruler of all creatures on land and in the four seas. Although I am great and supreme, still I have regard for the prayer of the poorest man. If any creature will worship me, I will hear his prayer and grant the desire of his heart.'

"'Every time man yields to anxiety, he takes one step away from the leading of the spirit of his heart.' Pride obscures God. If you would obtain heavenly help, put away your pride; every hair of pride shuts off saving light, as it were, by a great cloud. If you are not right on the inside, it is useless to pray for that which is on the outside. 'If I hear your prayers, it is because you come before me with a clean heart, free from falsehood and hypocrisy, with a soul which reflects truth like a mirror. If you would gain immortality, forsake the world and come to me.'"

8. TAOISM

The messengers of Melchizedek penetrated far into China, and the doctrine of one God became a part of the earlier teachings of several Chinese religions; the one persisting the longest and containing most of the monotheistic truth was Taoism, and Ganid collected the following from the teachings of its founder:

"How pure and tranquil is the Supreme One and yet how powerful and mighty, how deep and unfathomable! This God of heaven is the honored ancestor of all things. If you know the Eternal, you are enlightened and wise. If you know not the Eternal, then does ignorance manifest itself as evil, and thus do the passions of sin arise. This wondrous Being existed before the heavens and the earth were. He is truly spiritual; he stands alone and changes not. He is indeed the world's mother, and all creation moves around him. This Great One imparts himself to men and thereby enables them to excel and to survive. Even if one has but a little knowledge, he can still walk in the ways of the Supreme; he can conform to the will of heaven.

"All good works of true service come from the Supreme. All things depend on the Great Source for life. The Great Supreme seeks no credit for his bestowals. He is supreme in power, yet he remains hidden from our gaze. He unceasingly transmutes his attributes while perfecting his creatures. The heavenly Reason is slow and patient in his designs but sure of his accomplishments. The Supreme overspreads the universe and sustains it all. How great and mighty are his overflowing influence and drawing power! True goodness is like water in that it blesses everything and harms nothing. And like water, true goodness seeks the lowest places, even those levels which others avoid, and that is because it is akin to the Supreme. The Supreme creates all things, in nature nourishing them and in spirit perfecting them. And it is a mystery how the Supreme fosters, protects, and perfects the creature without compelling him. He guides and directs, but without self-assertion. He ministers progression, but without domination.

"The wise man universalizes his heart. A little knowledge is a dangerous thing. Those who aspire to greatness must learn to humble themselves. In creation the Supreme became the world's mother. To know one's mother is to recognize one's sonship. He is a wise man who regards all parts from the point of view of the whole. Relate yourself to every man as if you were in his place. Recompense injury with kindness. If you love people, they will draw near you—you will have no difficulty in winning them.

"The Great Supreme is all-pervading; he is on the left hand and on the right; he supports all creation and indwells all true beings. You cannot find the Supreme, neither can you go to a place where he is not. If a man recognizes the evil of his ways and repents of sin from the heart, then may he seek forgiveness; he may escape the penalty; he may change calamity into blessing. The Supreme is the secure refuge for all creation; he is the guardian and savior of mankind. If you seek for him daily, you shall find him. Since he can forgive sins, he is indeed most precious to all men. Always remember that God does not reward man for what he does but for what he is; therefore should you extend help to your fellows without the thought of rewards. Do good without thought of benefit to the self.

"They who know the laws of the Eternal are wise. Ignorance of the divine law is misery and disaster. They who know the laws of God are liberal minded. If you know the Eternal, even though your body perish, your soul shall survive in spirit service. You are truly wise when you recognize your insignificance. If you abide in the light of the Eternal, you shall enjoy the enlightenment of the Supreme. Those who dedicate their persons to the service of the Supreme are joyous in this pursuit of the Eternal. When man dies, the spirit begins to wing its long flight on the great home journey."

9. CONFUCIANISM

Even the least God-recognizing of the world's great religions acknowledged the monotheism of the Melchizedek missionaries and their persistent successors. Ganid's summary of Confucianism was:

"What Heaven appoints is without error. Truth is real and divine. Everything originates in Heaven, and the Great Heaven makes no mistakes. Heaven has appointed many subordinates to assist in the instruction and uplifting of the inferior creatures. Great, very great, is the One God who rules man from on high. God is majestic in power and awful in judgment. But this Great God has conferred a moral sense even on many inferior people. Heaven's bounty never stops. Benevolence is Heaven's choicest gift to men. Heaven has bestowed its nobility upon the soul of man; the virtues of man are the fruit of this endowment of Heaven's nobility. The Great Heaven is all-discerning and goes with man in all his doings. And we do well when we call the Great Heaven our Father and our Mother. If we are thus servants of our divine ancestors, then may we in confidence pray to Heaven. At all times and in everything let us stand in awe of the majesty of Heaven. We acknowledge, O God, the Most High and sovereign Potentate, that judgment rests with you, and that all mercy proceeds from the divine heart.

"God is with us; therefore we have no fear in our hearts. If there be found any virtue in me, it is the manifestation of Heaven who abides with me. But this Heaven within me often makes hard demands on my faith. If God is with me, I have determined to have no doubt in my heart. Faith must be very near the truth of things, and I do not see how a man can live without this good faith. Good and evil do not befall men without cause. Heaven deals with man's soul in accordance with its purpose. When you find yourself in the wrong, do not hesitate to confess your error and be quick to make amends.

"A wise man is occupied with the search for truth, not in seeking for a mere living. To attain the perfection of Heaven is the goal of man. The superior man is given to self-adjustment, and he is free from anxiety and fear. God is with you; have no doubt in your heart. Every good deed has its recompense. The superior man murmurs not against Heaven nor holds a grudge against men. What you do not like when done to yourself, do not to others. Let compassion be a part of all punishment; in every way endeavor to make punishment a blessing. Such is the way of Great Heaven. While all creatures must die and return to the earth, the spirit of the noble man goes forth to be displayed on high and to ascend to the glorious light of final brightness."

10. "OUR RELIGION"

After the arduous labor of effecting this compilation of the teachings of the world religions concerning the Paradise Father, Ganid set himself to the task of formulating what he deemed to be a summary of the belief he had arrived at regarding God as a result of Jesus' teaching. This young man was in the habit of referring to such beliefs as "our religion." This was his record:

"The Lord our God is one Lord, and you should love him with all your mind and heart while you do your very best to love all his children as you love yourself. This one God is our heavenly Father, in whom all things consist, and who dwells, by his spirit, in every sincere human soul. And we who are the children of God should learn how to commit the keeping of our souls to him as to a faithful Creator. With our heavenly Father all things are possible. Since he is the Creator, having made all things and all beings, it could not be otherwise. Though we cannot see God, we can know him. And by daily living the will of the Father in heaven, we can reveal him to our fellow men.

"The divine riches of God's character must be infinitely deep and eternally wise. We cannot search out God by knowledge, but we can know him in our hearts by personal experience. While his justice may be past finding out, his mercy may be received by the humblest being on earth. While the Father fills the universe, he also lives in our hearts. The mind of man is human, mortal, but the spirit of man is divine, immortal. God is not only all-powerful but also all-wise. If our earth parents, being of evil tendency, know how to love their children and bestow good gifts on them, how much more must the good Father in heaven know how wisely to love his children on earth and to bestow suitable blessings upon them.

"The Father in heaven will not suffer a single child on earth to perish if that child has a desire to find the Father and truly longs to be like him. Our Father even loves the wicked and is always kind to the ungrateful. If more human beings could only know about the goodness of God, they would certainly be led to repent of their evil ways and forsake all known sin. All good things come down from the Father of light, in whom there is no variableness neither shadow of changing. The spirit of the true God is in man's heart. He intends that all men should be brothers. When men begin to feel after God, that is evidence that God has found them, and that they are in quest of knowledge about him. We live in God and God dwells in us.

"I will no longer be satisfied to believe that God is the Father of all my people; I will henceforth believe that he is also *my* Father. Always will I try to worship God with the help of the Spirit of Truth, which is my helper when I have become really God-knowing. But first of all I am going to practice worshiping God by learning how to do the will of God on earth; that is, I am going to do my best to treat each of my fellow mortals just as I think God would like to have him treated. And when we live this sort of a life in the flesh, we may ask many things of God, and he will give us the desire of our hearts that we may be the better prepared to serve our fellows. And all of this loving service of the children of God enlarges our capacity to receive and experience the joys of heaven, the high pleasures of the ministry of the spirit of heaven.

"I will every day thank God for his unspeakable gifts; I will praise him for his wonderful works to the children of men. To me he is the Almighty, the Creator, the Power, and the Mercy, but best of all, he is my spirit Father, and as his earth child I am sometime going forth to see him. And my tutor has said that by searching for him I shall become like him. By faith in God I have attained peace with him. This new religion of ours is very full of joy, and it generates an enduring happiness. I am confident that I shall be faithful even to death, and that I will surely receive the crown of eternal life.

"I am learning to prove all things and adhere to that which is good. Whatsoever I would that men should do to me, that I will do to my fellows. By this new faith I know that man may become the son of God, but it sometimes terrifies me when I stop to think that all men are my brothers, but it must be true. I do not see how I can rejoice in the fatherhood of God while I refuse to accept the brotherhood of man. Whosoever calls upon the name of the Lord shall be saved. If that is true, then all men must be my brothers.

"Henceforth will I do my good deeds in secret; I will also pray most when by myself. I will judge not that I may not be unfair to my fellows. I am going to learn to love my enemies; I have not truly mastered this practice of being Godlike. Though I see God in these other religions, I find him in 'our religion' as being more beautiful, loving, merciful, personal, and positive. But most of all, this great and glorious Being is my spiritual Father; I am his child. And by no other means than my honest desire to be like him, I am eventually to find him and eternally to serve him. At last I have a religion with a God, a marvelous God, and he is a God of eternal salvation."

PAPER 132

THE SOJOURN AT ROME

SINCE Gonod carried greetings from the princes of India to Tiberius, the Roman ruler, on the third day after their arrival in Rome the two Indians and Jesus appeared before him. The morose emperor was unusually cheerful on this day and chatted long with the trio. And when they had gone from his presence, the emperor, referring to Jesus, remarked to the aide standing on his right, "If I had that fellow's kingly bearing and gracious manner, I would be a real emperor, eh?"

While at Rome, Ganid had regular hours for study and for visiting places of interest about the city. His father had much business to transact, and desiring that his son grow up to become a worthy successor in the management of his vast commercial interests, he thought the time had come to introduce the boy to the business world. There were many citizens of India in Rome, and often one of Gonod's own employees would accompany him as interpreter so that Jesus would have whole days to himself; this gave him time in which to become thoroughly acquainted with this city of two million inhabitants. He was frequently to be found in the forum, the center of political, legal, and business life. He often went up to the Capitolium and pondered the bondage of ignorance in which these Romans were held as he beheld this magnificent temple dedicated to Jupiter, Juno, and Minerva. He also spent much time on Palatine hill, where were located the emperor's residence, the temple of Apollo, and the Greek and Latin libraries.

At this time the Roman Empire included all of southern Europe, Asia Minor, Syria, Egypt, and northwest Africa; and its inhabitants embraced the citizens of every country of the Eastern Hemisphere. His desire to study and mingle with this cosmopolitan aggregation of Urantia mortals was the chief reason why Jesus consented to make this journey.

Jesus learned much about men while in Rome, but the most valuable of all the manifold experiences of his six months' sojourn in that city was his contact with, and influence upon, the religious leaders of the empire's capital. Before the end of the first week in Rome Jesus had sought out, and had made the acquaintance of, the worth-while leaders of the Cynics, the Stoics, and the mystery cults, in particular the Mithraic group. Whether or not it was apparent to Jesus that the Jews were going to reject his mission, he most certainly foresaw that his messengers were presently coming to Rome to proclaim the kingdom of heaven; and he therefore set about, in the most amazing manner, to prepare the way for the better and more certain reception of their message. He selected five of the leading Stoics, eleven of the Cynics, and sixteen of the mystery-cult leaders and spent much of his spare time for almost six months in intimate association with these religious teachers. And this was his method of instruction: Never once did he attack their errors or even mention the flaws in their teachings. In each case he would select the truth in what they taught and then proceed so to embellish and illuminate this truth in their minds that in a very short time this enhancement of the truth effectively crowded out the associated error; and thus were these Jesus-taught men and women prepared for the subsequent recognition of additional and similar truths in the teachings of the early Christian missionaries. It was this early acceptance of the teachings of the gospel preachers which gave that powerful impetus to the rapid spread of Christianity in Rome and from there throughout the empire.

The significance of this remarkable doing can the better be understood when we record the fact that, out of this group of thirty-two Jesus-taught religious leaders in Rome, only two were unfruitful; the thirty became pivotal individuals in the establishment of Christianity in Rome, and certain of them also aided in turning the chief Mithraic temple into the first Christian church of that city. We who view human activities from behind the scenes and in the light of nineteen centuries of time recognize just three factors of paramount value in the early setting of the stage for the rapid spread of Christianity throughout Europe, and they are:

1. The choosing and holding of Simon Peter as an apostle.

2. The talk in Jerusalem with Stephen, whose death led to the winning of Saul of Tarsus.

3. The preliminary preparation of these thirty Romans for the subsequent leadership of the new religion in Rome and throughout the empire.

Through all their experiences, neither Stephen nor the thirty chosen ones ever realized that they had once talked with the man whose name became the subject of their religious teaching. Jesus' work in behalf of the original thirty-two was entirely personal. In his labors for these individuals the scribe of Damascus never met more than three of them at one time, seldom more than two, while most often he taught them singly. And he could do this great work of religious training because these men and women were not tradition bound; they were not victims of a settled preconception as to all future religious developments.

Many were the times in the years so soon to follow that Peter, Paul, and the other Christian teachers in Rome heard about this scribe of Damascus who had preceded them, and who had so obviously (and as they supposed unwittingly) prepared the way for their coming with the new gospel. Though Paul never really surmised the identity of this scribe of Damascus, he did, a short time before his death, because of the similarity of personal descriptions, reach the conclusion that the "tentmaker of Antioch" was also the "scribe of Damascus." On one occasion, while preaching in Rome, Simon Peter, on listening to a description of the Damascus scribe, surmised that this individual might have been Jesus but quickly dismissed the idea, knowing full well (so he thought) that the Master had never been in Rome.

1. TRUE VALUES

It was with Angamon, the leader of the Stoics, that Jesus had an all-night talk early during his sojourn in Rome. This man subsequently became a great friend of Paul and proved to be one of the strong supporters of the Christian church at Rome. In substance, and restated in modern phraseology, Jesus taught Angamon:

The standard of true values must be looked for in the spiritual world and on divine levels of eternal reality. To an ascending mortal all lower and material standards must be recognized as transient, partial, and inferior. The scientist, as such, is limited to the discovery of the relatedness of material facts. Technically, he has no right to assert that he is either materialist or idealist, for in so doing he has assumed to forsake the attitude of a true scientist since any and all such assertions of attitude are the very essence of philosophy.

Unless the moral insight and the spiritual attainment of mankind are proportionately augmented, the unlimited advancement of a purely materialistic culture may eventually become a menace to civilization. A purely materialistic science harbors within itself the potential seed of the destruction of all scientific striving, for this very attitude presages the ultimate collapse of a civilization which has abandoned its sense of moral values and has repudiated its spiritual goal of attainment.

The materialistic scientist and the extreme idealist are destined always to be at loggerheads. This is not true of those scientists and idealists who are in possession of a common standard of high moral values and spiritual test levels. In every age scientists and religionists must recognize that they are on trial before the bar of human need. They must eschew all warfare between themselves while they strive valiantly to justify their continued survival by enhanced devotion to the service of human progress. If the so-called science or religion of any age is false, then must it either purify its activities or pass away before the emergence of a material science or spiritual religion of a truer and more worthy order.

2. GOOD AND EVIL

Mardus was the acknowledged leader of the Cynics of Rome, and he became a great friend of the scribe of Damascus. Day after day he conversed with Jesus, and night upon night he listened to his supernal teaching. Among the more important discussions with Mardus was the one designed to answer this sincere Cynic's question about good and evil. In substance, and in twentieth-century phraseology, Jesus said:

My brother, good and evil are merely words symbolizing relative levels of human comprehension of the observable universe. If you are ethically lazy and socially indifferent, you can take as your standard of good the current social usages. If you are spiritually indolent and morally unprogressive, you may take as your standards of good the religious practices and traditions of your contemporaries. But the soul that survives time and emerges into eternity must make a living and personal choice between good and evil as they are determined by the true values of the spiritual standards established by the divine spirit which the Father in heaven has sent to dwell within the heart of man. This indwelling spirit is the standard of personality survival.

Goodness, like truth, is always relative and unfailingly evil-contrasted. It is the perception of these qualities of goodness and truth that enables the evolving souls of men to make those personal decisions of choice which are essential to eternal survival.

The spiritually blind individual who logically follows scientific dictation, social usage, and religious dogma stands in grave danger of sacrificing his moral freedom and losing his spiritual liberty. Such a soul is destined to become an intellectual parrot, a social automaton, and a slave to religious authority.

Goodness is always growing toward new levels of the increasing liberty of moral self-realization and spiritual personality attainment—the discovery of, and identification with, the indwelling Adjuster. An experience is good when it heightens the appreciation of beauty, augments the moral will, enhances the discernment of truth, enlarges the capacity to love and serve one's fellows, exalts the spiritual ideals, and unifies the supreme human motives of time with the eternal plans of the indwelling Adjuster, all of which lead directly to an increased desire to do the Father's will, thereby fostering the divine passion to find God and to be more like him.

As you ascend the universe scale of creature development, you will find increasing goodness and diminishing evil in perfect accordance with your capacity for goodness-experience and truth-discernment. The ability to entertain error or experience evil will not be fully lost until the ascending human soul achieves final spirit levels.

Goodness is living, relative, always progressing, invariably a personal experience, and everlastingly correlated with the discernment of truth and beauty. Goodness is found in the recognition of the positive truth-values of the spiritual level, which must, in human experience, be contrasted with the negative counterpart—the shadows of potential evil.

Until you attain Paradise levels, goodness will always be more of a quest than a possession, more of a goal than an experience of attainment. But even as you hunger and thirst for righteousness, you experience increasing satisfaction in the partial attainment of goodness. The presence of goodness and evil in the world is in itself positive proof of the existence and reality of man's moral will, the personality, which thus identifies these values and is also able to choose between them.

By the time of the attainment of Paradise the ascending mortal's capacity for identifying the self with true spirit values has become so enlarged as to result in the attainment of the perfection of the possession of the light of life. Such a perfected spirit personality becomes so wholly, divinely, and spiritually unified with the positive and supreme qualities of goodness, beauty, and truth that there remains no possibility that such a righteous spirit would cast any negative shadow of potential evil when exposed to the searching luminosity of the divine light of the infinite Rulers of Paradise. In all such spirit personalities, goodness is no longer partial, contrastive, and comparative; it has become divinely complete and spiritually replete; it approaches the purity and perfection of the Supreme.

The *possibility* of evil is necessary to moral choosing, but not the actuality thereof. A shadow is only relatively real. Actual evil is not necessary as a personal experience. Potential evil acts equally well as a decision stimulus in the realms of moral progress on the lower levels of spiritual development. Evil becomes a reality of personal experience only when a moral mind makes evil its choice.

3. TRUTH AND FAITH

Nabon was a Greek Jew and foremost among the leaders of the chief mystery cult in Rome, the Mithraic. While this high priest of Mithraism held many conferences with the Damascus scribe, he was most permanently influenced by their discussion of truth and faith one evening. Nabon had thought to make a convert of Jesus and had even suggested that he return to Palestine as a Mithraic teacher. He little realized that Jesus was preparing him to become one of the early converts to the gospel of the kingdom. Restated in modern phraseology, the substance of Jesus' teaching was:

Truth cannot be defined with words, only by living. Truth is always more than knowledge. Knowledge pertains to things observed, but truth transcends such purely material levels in that it consorts with wisdom and embraces such imponderables as human experience, even spiritual and living realities. Knowledge originates in science; wisdom, in true philosophy; truth, in the religious experience of spiritual living. Knowledge deals with facts; wisdom, with relationships; truth, with reality values.

Man tends to crystallize science, formulate philosophy, and dogmatize truth because he is mentally lazy in adjusting to the progressive struggles of living, while he is also terribly afraid of the unknown. Natural man is slow to initiate changes in his habits of thinking and in his techniques of living.

Revealed truth, personally discovered truth, is the supreme delight of the human soul; it is the joint creation of the material mind and the indwelling spirit. The eternal salvation of this truth-discerning and beauty-loving soul is assured by that hunger and thirst for goodness which leads this mortal to develop a singleness of purpose to do the Father's will, to find God and to become like him. There is never conflict between true knowledge and truth. There may be conflict between knowledge and human beliefs, beliefs colored with prejudice, distorted by fear, and dominated by the dread of facing new facts of material discovery or spiritual progress.

But truth can never become man's possession without the exercise of faith. This is true because man's thoughts, wisdom, ethics, and ideals will never rise higher than his faith, his sublime hope. And all such true faith is predicated on profound reflection, sincere self-criticism, and uncompromising moral consciousness. Faith is the inspiration of the spiritized creative imagination.

Faith acts to release the superhuman activities of the divine spark, the immortal germ, that lives within the mind of man, and which is the potential of eternal survival. Plants and animals survive in time by the technique of passing on from one generation to another identical particles of themselves. The human soul (personality) of man survives mortal death by identity association with this indwelling spark of divinity, which is immortal, and which functions to perpetuate the human personality upon a continuing and higher level of progressive universe existence. The concealed seed of the human soul is an immortal spirit. The second generation of the soul is the first of a succession of personality manifestations of spiritual and progressing existences, terminating only when this divine entity attains the source of its existence, the personal source of all existence, God, the Universal Father.

Human life continues—survives—because it has a universe function, the task of finding God. The faith-activated soul of man cannot stop short of the attainment of this goal of destiny; and when it does once achieve this divine goal, it can never end because it has become like God—eternal.

Spiritual evolution is an experience of the increasing and voluntary choice of goodness attended by an equal and progressive diminution of the possibility of evil. With the attainment of finality of choice for goodness and of completed capacity for truth appreciation, there comes into existence a perfection of beauty and holiness whose righteousness eternally inhibits the possibility of the emergence of even the concept of potential evil. Such a God-knowing soul casts no shadow of doubting evil when functioning on such a high spirit level of divine goodness.

The presence of the Paradise spirit in the mind of man constitutes the revelation promise and the faith pledge of an eternal existence of divine progression for every soul seeking to achieve identity with this immortal and indwelling spirit fragment of the Universal Father.

Universe progress is characterized by increasing personality freedom because it is associated with the progressive attainment of higher and higher levels of self-understanding and consequent voluntary self-restraint. The attainment of perfection of spiritual self-restraint equals completeness of universe freedom and personal liberty. Faith fosters and maintains man's soul in the midst of the confusion of his early orientation in such a vast universe, whereas prayer becomes the great unifier of the various inspirations of the creative imagination and the faith urges of a soul trying to identify itself with the spirit ideals of the indwelling and associated divine presence.

Nabon was greatly impressed by these words, as he was by each of his talks with Jesus. These truths continued to burn within his heart, and he was of great assistance to the later arriving preachers of Jesus' gospel.

4. PERSONAL MINISTRY

Jesus did not devote all his leisure while in Rome to this work of preparing men and women to become future disciples in the oncoming kingdom. He spent much time gaining an intimate knowledge of all races and classes of men who lived in this, the largest and most cosmopolitan city of the world. In each of these numerous human contacts Jesus had a double purpose: He desired to learn their reactions to the life they were living in the flesh, and he was also minded to say or do something to make that life richer and more worth while. His religious teachings during these weeks were no different than those which characterized his later life as teacher of the twelve and preacher to the multitudes.

Always the burden of his message was: the fact of the heavenly Father's love and the truth of his mercy, coupled with the good news that man is a faith-son of this same God of love. Jesus' usual technique of social contact was to draw people out and into talking with him by asking them questions. The interview would usually begin by his asking them questions and end by their asking him questions. He was equally adept in teaching by either asking or answering questions. As a rule, to those he taught the most, he said the least. Those who derived most benefit from his personal ministry were overburdened, anxious, and dejected mortals who gained much relief because of the opportunity to unburden their souls to a sympathetic and understanding listener, and he was all that and more. And when these maladjusted human beings had told Jesus about their troubles, always was he able to offer practical and immediately helpful suggestions looking toward the correction of their real difficulties, albeit he did not neglect to speak words of present comfort and immediate consolation. And invariably would he tell these distressed mortals about the love of God and impart the information, by various and sundry methods, that they were the children of this loving Father in heaven.

In this manner, during the sojourn in Rome, Jesus personally came into affectionate and uplifting contact with upward of five hundred mortals of the realm. He thus gained a knowledge of the different races of mankind which he could never have acquired in Jerusalem and hardly even in Alexandria. He always regarded this six months as one of the richest and most informative of any like period of his earth life.

As might have been expected, such a versatile and aggressive man could not thus function for six months in the world's metropolis without being approached by numerous persons who desired to secure his services in connection with some business or, more often, for some project of teaching, social reform, or religious movement. More than a dozen such proffers were made, and he utilized each one as an opportunity for imparting some thought of spiritual ennoblement by well-chosen words or by some obliging service. Jesus was very fond of doing things—even little things—for all sorts of people.

He talked with a Roman senator on politics and statesmanship, and this one contact with Jesus made such an impression on this legislator that he spent the rest of his life vainly trying to induce his colleagues to change the course of the ruling policy from the idea of the government supporting and feeding the people to that of the people supporting the government. Jesus spent one evening with a wealthy slaveholder, talked about man as a son of God, and the next day this man, Claudius, gave freedom to one hundred and seventeen slaves. He visited at dinner with a Greek physician, telling him that his patients had minds and souls as well as bodies, and thus led this able doctor to attempt a more far-reaching ministry to his fellow men. He talked with all sorts of people in every walk of life. The only place in Rome he did not visit was the public baths. He refused to accompany his friends to the baths because of the sex promiscuity which there prevailed.

To a Roman soldier, as they walked along the Tiber, he said: "Be brave of heart as well as of hand. Dare to do justice and be big enough to show mercy. Compel your lower nature to obey your higher nature as you obey your superiors. Revere goodness and exalt truth. Choose the beautiful in place of the ugly. Love your fellows and reach out for God with a whole heart, for God is your Father in heaven."

To the speaker at the forum he said: "Your eloquence is pleasing, your logic is admirable, your voice is pleasant, but your teaching is hardly true. If you could only enjoy the inspiring satisfaction of knowing God as your spiritual Father, then you might employ your powers of speech to liberate your fellows from the bondage of darkness and from the slavery of ignorance." This was the Marcus who heard Peter preach in Rome and became his successor. When they crucified Simon Peter, it was this man who defied the Roman persecutors and boldly continued to preach the new gospel.

Meeting a poor man who had been falsely accused, Jesus went with him before the magistrate and, having been granted special permission to appear in his behalf, made that superb address in the course of which he said: "Justice makes a nation great, and the greater a nation the more solicitous will it be to see that injustice shall not befall even its most humble citizen. Woe upon any nation when only those who possess money and influence can secure ready justice before its courts! It is the sacred duty of a magistrate to acquit the innocent as well as to punish the guilty. Upon the impartiality, fairness, and integrity of its courts the endurance of a nation depends. Civil government is founded on justice, even as true religion is founded on mercy." The judge reopened the case, and when the evidence had been sifted, he discharged the prisoner. Of all Jesus' activities during these days of personal ministry, this came the nearest to being a public appearance.

5. COUNSELING THE RICH MAN

A certain rich man, a Roman citizen and a Stoic, became greatly interested in Jesus' teaching, having been introduced by Angamon. After many intimate conferences this wealthy citizen asked Jesus what he would do with wealth if he had it, and Jesus answered him: "I would bestow material wealth for the enhancement of material life, even as I would minister knowledge, wisdom, and spiritual service for the enrichment of the intellectual life, the ennoblement of the social life, and the advancement of the spiritual life. I would administer material wealth as a wise and effective trustee of the resources of one generation for the benefit and ennoblement of the next and succeeding generations."

But the rich man was not fully satisfied with Jesus' answer. He made bold to ask again: "But what do you think a man in my position should do with his wealth? Should I keep it, or should I give it away?" And when Jesus perceived that he really desired to know more of the truth about his loyalty to God and his duty to men, he further answered: "My good friend, I discern that you are a sincere seeker after wisdom and an honest lover of truth; therefore am I minded to lay before you my view of the solution of your problems having to do with the responsibilities of wealth. I do this because you have *asked* for my counsel, and in giving you this advice, I am not concerned with the wealth of any other rich man; I am offering advice only to you and for your personal guidance. If you honestly desire to regard your wealth as a trust, if you really wish to become a wise and efficient steward of your accumulated wealth, then would I counsel you to make the following analysis of the sources of your riches: Ask yourself, and do your best to find the honest answer, whence came this wealth? And as a help in the study of the sources of your great fortune, I would suggest that you bear in mind the following ten different methods of amassing material wealth:

"1. Inherited wealth—riches derived from parents and other ancestors.

"2. Discovered wealth—riches derived from the uncultivated resources of mother earth.

"3. Trade wealth—riches obtained as a fair profit in the exchange and barter of material goods.

"4. Unfair wealth—riches derived from the unfair exploitation or the enslavement of one's fellows.

"5. Interest wealth—income derived from the fair and just earning possibilities of invested capital.

"6. Genius wealth—riches accruing from the rewards of the creative and inventive endowments of the human mind.

"7. Accidental wealth—riches derived from the generosity of one's fellows or taking origin in the circumstances of life.

"8. Stolen wealth—riches secured by unfairness, dishonesty, theft, or fraud.

"9. Trust funds—wealth lodged in your hands by your fellows for some specific use, now or in the future.

"10. Earned wealth—riches derived directly from your own personal labor, the fair and just reward of your own daily efforts of mind and body.

"And so, my friend, if you would be a faithful and just steward of your large fortune, before God and in service to men, you must approximately divide your wealth into these ten grand divisions, and then proceed to administer each portion in accordance with the wise and honest interpretation of the laws of justice, equity, fairness, and true efficiency; albeit, the God of heaven would not condemn you if sometimes you erred, in doubtful situations, on the side of merciful and unselfish regard for the distress of the suffering victims of the unfortunate circumstances of mortal life. When in honest doubt about the equity and justice of material situations, let your decisions favor those who are in need, favor those who suffer the misfortune of undeserved hardships."

After discussing these matters for several hours and in response to the rich man's request for further and more detailed instruction, Jesus went on to amplify his advice, in substance saying: "While I offer further suggestions concerning your attitude toward wealth, I would admonish you to receive my counsel as given only to you and for your personal guidance. I speak only for myself and to you as an inquiring friend. I adjure you not to become a dictator as to how other rich men shall regard their wealth. I would advise you:

"1. As steward of inherited wealth you should consider its sources. You are under moral obligation to represent the past generation in the honest transmittal of legitimate wealth to succeeding generations after subtracting a fair toll for the benefit of the present generation. But you are not obligated to perpetuate any dishonesty or injustice involved in the unfair accumulation of wealth by your ancestors. Any portion of your inherited wealth which turns out to have been derived through fraud or unfairness, you may disburse in accordance with your convictions of justice, generosity, and restitution. The remainder of your legitimate inherited wealth you may use in equity and transmit in security as the trustee of one generation for another. Wise discrimination and sound judgment should dictate your decisions regarding the bequest of riches to your successors.

"2. Everyone who enjoys wealth as a result of discovery should remember that one individual can live on earth but a short season and should, therefore, make adequate provision for the sharing of these discoveries in helpful ways by the largest possible number of his fellow men. While the discoverer should not be denied all reward for efforts of discovery, neither should he selfishly presume to lay claim to all of the advantages and blessings to be derived from the uncovering of nature's hoarded resources.

"3. As long as men choose to conduct the world's business by trade and barter, they are entitled to a fair and legitimate profit. Every tradesman deserves wages for his services; the merchant is entitled to his hire. The fairness of trade and the honest treatment accorded one's fellows in the organized business of the world create many different sorts of profit wealth, and all these sources of wealth must be judged by the highest principles of justice, honesty, and fairness. The honest trader should not hesitate to take the same profit which he would gladly accord his fellow trader in a similar transaction. While this sort of wealth is not identical with individually earned income when business dealings are conducted on a large scale, at the same time, such honestly accumulated wealth endows its possessor with a considerable equity as regards a voice in its subsequent distribution.

"4. No mortal who knows God and seeks to do the divine will can stoop to engage in the oppressions of wealth. No noble man will strive to accumulate riches and amass wealth-power by the enslavement or unfair exploitation of his brothers in the flesh. Riches are a moral curse and a spiritual stigma when they are derived from the sweat of oppressed mortal man. All such wealth should be restored to those who have thus been robbed or to their children and their children's children. An enduring civilization cannot be built upon the practice of defrauding the laborer of his hire.

"5. Honest wealth is entitled to interest. As long as men borrow and lend, that which is fair interest may be collected provided the capital lent was legitimate wealth. First cleanse your capital before you lay claim to the interest. Do not become so small and grasping that you would stoop to the practice of usury. Never permit yourself to be so selfish as to employ money-power to gain unfair advantage over your struggling fellows. Yield not to the temptation to take usury from your brother in financial distress.

"6. If you chance to secure wealth by flights of genius, if your riches are derived from the rewards of inventive endowment, do not lay claim to an unfair portion of such rewards. The genius owes something to both his ancestors and his progeny; likewise is he under obligation to the race, nation, and circumstances of his inventive discoveries; he should also remember that it was as man among men that he labored and wrought out his inventions. It would be equally unjust to deprive the genius of all his increment of wealth. And it will ever be impossible for men to establish rules and regulations applicable equally to all these problems of the equitable distribution of wealth. You must first recognize man as your brother, and if you honestly desire to do by him as you would have him do by you, the commonplace dictates of justice, honesty, and fairness will guide you in the just and impartial settlement of every recurring problem of economic rewards and social justice.

"7. Except for the just and legitimate fees earned in administration, no man should lay personal claim to that wealth which time and chance may cause to fall into his hands. Accidental riches should be regarded somewhat in the light of a trust to be expended for the benefit of one's social or economic group. The possessors of such wealth should be accorded the major voice in the determination of the wise and effective distribution of such unearned resources. Civilized man will not always look upon all that he controls as his personal and private possession.

"8. If any portion of your fortune has been knowingly derived from fraud; if aught of your wealth has been accumulated by dishonest practices or unfair methods; if your riches are the product of unjust dealings with your fellows, make haste to restore all these ill-gotten gains to the rightful owners. Make full amends and thus cleanse your fortune of all dishonest riches.

"9. The trusteeship of the wealth of one person for the benefit of others is a solemn and sacred responsibility. Do not hazard or jeopardize such a trust. Take for yourself of any trust only that which all honest men would allow.

"10. That part of your fortune which represents the earnings of your own mental and physical efforts—if your work has been done in fairness and equity—is truly your own. No man can gainsay your right to hold and use such wealth as you may see fit provided your exercise of this right does not work harm upon your fellows."

When Jesus had finished counseling him, this wealthy Roman arose from his couch and, in saying farewell for the night, delivered himself of this promise: "My good friend, I perceive you are a man of great wisdom and goodness, and tomorrow I will begin the administration of all my wealth in accordance with your counsel."

6. SOCIAL MINISTRY

Here in Rome also occurred that touching incident in which the Creator of a universe spent several hours restoring a lost child to his anxious mother. This little boy had wandered away from his home, and Jesus found him crying in distress. He and Ganid were on their way to the libraries, but they devoted themselves to getting the child back home. Ganid never forgot Jesus' comment: "You know, Ganid, most human beings are like the lost child. They spend much of their time crying in fear and suffering in sorrow when, in very truth, they are but a short distance from safety and security, even as this child was only a little way from home. And all those who know the way of truth and enjoy the assurance of knowing God should esteem it a privilege, not a duty, to offer guidance to their fellows in their efforts to find the satisfactions of living. Did we not supremely enjoy this ministry of restoring the child to his mother? So do those who lead men to God experience the supreme satisfaction of human service." And from that day forward, for the remainder of his natural life, Ganid was continually on the lookout for lost children whom he might restore to their homes.

There was the widow with five children whose husband had been accidentally killed. Jesus told Ganid about the loss of his own father by an accident, and they went repeatedly to comfort this mother and her children, while Ganid sought money from his father to provide food and clothing. They did not cease their efforts until they had found a position for the eldest boy so that he could help in the care of the family.

That night, as Gonod listened to the recital of these experiences, he said to Jesus, good-naturedly: "I propose to make a scholar or a businessman of my son, and now you start out to make a philosopher or philanthropist of him." And Jesus smilingly replied: "Perhaps we will make him all four; then can he enjoy a fourfold satisfaction in life as his ear for the recognition of human melody will be able to recognize four tones instead of one." Then said Gonod: "I perceive that you really are a philosopher. You must write a book for future generations." And Jesus replied: "Not a book—my mission is to live a life in this generation and for all generations. I—" but he stopped, saying to Ganid, "My son, it is time to retire."

7. TRIPS ABOUT ROME

Jesus, Gonod, and Ganid made five trips away from Rome to points of interest in the surrounding territory. On their visit to the northern Italian lakes Jesus had the long talk with Ganid concerning the impossibility of teaching a man about God if the man does not desire to know God. They had casually met a thoughtless pagan while on their journey up to the lakes, and Ganid was surprised that Jesus did not follow out his usual practice of enlisting the man in conversation which would naturally lead up to the discussion of spiritual questions. When Ganid asked his teacher why he evinced so little interest in this pagan, Jesus answered:

"Ganid, the man was not hungry for truth. He was not dissatisfied with himself. He was not ready to ask for help, and the eyes of his mind were not open to receive light for the soul. That man was not ripe for the harvest of salvation; he must be allowed more time for the trials and difficulties of life to prepare him for the reception of wisdom and higher learning. Or, if we could have him live with us, we might by our lives show him the Father in heaven, and thus would he become so attracted by our lives as sons of God that he would be constrained to inquire about our Father. You cannot reveal God to those who do not seek for him; you cannot lead unwilling souls into the joys of salvation. Man must become hungry for truth as a result of the experiences of living, or he must desire to know God as the result of contact with the lives of those who are acquainted with the divine Father before another human being can act as the means of leading such a fellow mortal to the Father in heaven. If we know God, our real business on earth is so to live as to permit the Father to reveal himself in our lives, and thus will all God-seeking persons see the Father and ask for our help in finding out more about the God who in this manner finds expression in our lives."

It was on the visit to Switzerland, up in the mountains, that Jesus had an all-day talk with both father and son about Buddhism. Many times Ganid had asked Jesus direct questions about Buddha, but he had always received more or less evasive replies. Now, in the presence of the son, the father asked Jesus a direct question about Buddha, and he received a direct reply. Said Gonod: "I would really like to know what you think of Buddha." And Jesus answered:

"Your Buddha was much better than your Buddhism. Buddha was a great man, even a prophet to his people, but he was an orphan prophet; by that I mean that he early lost sight of his spiritual Father, the Father in heaven. His experience was tragic. He tried to live and teach as a messenger of God, but without God. Buddha guided his ship of salvation right up to the safe harbor, right up to the entrance to the haven of mortal salvation, and there, because of faulty charts of navigation, the good ship ran aground. There it has rested these many generations, motionless and almost hopelessly stranded. And thereon have many of your people remained all these years. They live within hailing distance of the safe waters of rest, but they refuse to enter because the noble craft of the good Buddha met the misfortune of grounding just outside the harbor. And the

Buddhist peoples never will enter this harbor unless they abandon the philosophic craft of their prophet and seize upon his noble spirit. Had your people remained true to the spirit of Buddha, you would have long since entered your haven of spirit tranquillity, soul rest, and assurance of salvation.

"You see, Gonod, Buddha knew God in spirit but failed clearly to discover him in mind; the Jews discovered God in mind but largely failed to know him in spirit. Today, the Buddhists flounder about in a philosophy without God, while my people are piteously enslaved to the fear of a God without a saving philosophy of life and liberty. You have a philosophy without a God; the Jews have a God but are largely without a philosophy of living as related thereto. Buddha, failing to envision God as a spirit and as a Father, failed to provide in his teaching the moral energy and the spiritual driving power which a religion must possess if it is to change a race and exalt a nation."

Then exclaimed Ganid: "Teacher, let's you and I make a new religion, one good enough for India and big enough for Rome, and maybe we can trade it to the Jews for Yahweh." And Jesus replied: "Ganid, religions are not made. The religions of men grow up over long periods of time, while the revelations of God flash upon earth in the lives of the men who reveal God to their fellows." But they did not comprehend the meaning of these prophetic words.

That night after they had retired, Ganid could not sleep. He talked a long time with his father and finally said, "You know, father, I sometimes think Joshua is a prophet." And his father only sleepily replied, "My son, there are others —"

From this day, for the remainder of his natural life, Ganid continued to evolve a religion of his own. He was mightily moved in his own mind by Jesus' broadmindedness, fairness, and tolerance. In all their discussions of philosophy and religion this youth never experienced feelings of resentment or reactions of antagonism.

What a scene for the celestial intelligences to behold, this spectacle of the Indian lad proposing to the Creator of a universe that they make a new religion! And though the young man did not know it, they were making a new and everlasting religion right then and there—this new way of salvation, the revelation of God to man through, and in, Jesus. That which the lad wanted most to do he was unconsciously actually doing. And it was, and is, ever thus. That which the enlightened and reflective human imagination of spiritual teaching and leading wholeheartedly and unselfishly wants to do and be, becomes measurably creative in accordance with the degree of mortal dedication to the divine doing of the Father's will. When man goes in partnership with God, great things may, and do, happen.

PAPER 133

THE RETURN FROM ROME

WHEN preparing to leave Rome, Jesus said good-bye to none of his friends. The scribe of Damascus appeared in Rome without announcement and disappeared in like manner. It was a full year before those who knew and loved him gave up hope of seeing him again. Before the end of the second year small groups of those who had known him found themselves drawn together by their common interest in his teachings and through mutual memory of their good times with him. And these small groups of Stoics, Cynics, and mystery cultists continued to hold these irregular and informal meetings right up to the time of the appearance in Rome of the first preachers of the Christian religion.

Gonod and Ganid had purchased so many things in Alexandria and Rome that they sent all their belongings on ahead by pack train to Tarentum, while the three travelers walked leisurely across Italy over the great Appian Way. On this journey they encountered all sorts of human beings. Many noble Roman citizens and Greek colonists lived along this road, but already the progeny of great numbers of inferior slaves were beginning to make their appearance.

One day while resting at lunch, about halfway to Tarentum, Ganid asked Jesus a direct question as to what he thought of India's caste system. Said Jesus: "Though human beings differ in many ways, the one from another, before God and in the spiritual world all mortals stand on an equal footing. There are only two groups of mortals in the eyes of God: those who desire to do his will and those who do not. As the universe looks upon an inhabited world, it likewise discerns two great classes: those who know God and those who do not. Those who cannot know God are reckoned among the animals of any given realm. Mankind can appropriately be divided into many classes in accordance with differing qualifications, as they may be viewed physically, mentally, socially, vocationally, or morally, but as these different classes of mortals appear before the judgment bar of God, they stand on an equal footing; God is truly no respecter of persons. Although you cannot escape the recognition of differential human abilities and endowments in matters intellectual, social, and moral, you should make no such distinctions in the spiritual brotherhood of men when assembled for worship in the presence of God."

1. MERCY AND JUSTICE

A very interesting incident occurred one afternoon by the roadside as they neared Tarentum. They observed a rough and bullying youth brutally attacking a smaller lad. Jesus hastened to the assistance of the assaulted youth, and when he had rescued him, he tightly held on to the offender until the smaller lad had made his escape. The moment Jesus released the little bully, Ganid pounced upon the boy and began soundly to thrash him, and to Ganid's astonishment Jesus promptly interfered. After he had restrained Ganid and permitted the frightened boy to escape, the young man, as soon as he got his breath, excitedly exclaimed: "I cannot understand you, Teacher. If mercy requires that you rescue the smaller lad, does not justice demand the punishment of the larger and offending youth?" In answering, Jesus said:

"Ganid, it is true, you do not understand. Mercy ministry is always the work of the individual, but justice punishment is the function of the social, governmental, or universe administrative groups. As an individual I am beholden to show mercy; I must go to the rescue of the assaulted lad, and in all consistency I may employ sufficient force to restrain the aggressor. And that is just what I did. I achieved the deliverance of the assaulted lad; that was the end of mercy ministry. Then I forcibly detained the aggressor a sufficient length of time to enable the weaker party to the dispute to make his escape, after which I withdrew from the affair. I did not proceed to sit in judgment on the aggressor, thus to pass upon his motive—to adjudicate all that entered into his attack upon his fellow—and then undertake to execute the punishment which my mind might dictate as just recompense for his wrongdoing. Ganid, mercy may be lavish, but justice is precise. Cannot you discern that no two persons are likely to agree as to the punishment which would satisfy the demands of justice? One would impose forty lashes, another twenty, while still another would advise solitary confinement as a just punishment. Can you not see that on this world such responsibilities had better rest upon the group or be administered by chosen representatives of the group? In the universe, judgment is vested in those who fully know the antecedents of all wrongdoing as well as its motivation. In civilized society and in an organized universe the administration of justice presupposes the passing of just sentence consequent upon fair judgment, and such prerogatives are vested in the juridical groups of the worlds and in the all-knowing administrators of the higher universes of all creation."

For days they talked about this problem of manifesting mercy and administering justice. And Ganid, at least to some extent, understood why Jesus would not engage in personal combat. But Ganid asked one last question, to which he never received a fully satisfactory answer; and that question was: "But, Teacher, if a stronger and ill-tempered creature should attack you and threaten to destroy you, what would you do? Would you make no effort to defend yourself?" Although Jesus could not fully and satisfactorily answer the lad's question, inasmuch as he was not willing to disclose to him that he (Jesus) was living on earth as the exemplification of the Paradise Father's love to an onlooking universe, he did say this much:

"Ganid, I can well understand how some of these problems perplex you, and I will endeavor to answer your question. First, in all attacks which might be made upon my person, I would determine whether or not the aggressor was a son of God—my brother in the flesh—and if I thought such a creature did not possess moral judgment and spiritual reason, I would unhesitatingly defend myself to the full capacity of my powers of resistance, regardless of consequences to the attacker. But I would not thus assault a fellow man of sonship status, even in self-defense. That is, I would not punish him in advance and without judgment for his assault upon me. I would by every possible artifice seek to prevent and dissuade him from making such an attack and to mitigate it in case of my failure to abort it. Ganid, I have absolute confidence in my heavenly Father's overcare; I am consecrated to doing the will of my Father in heaven. I do not believe that *real* harm can befall me; I do not believe that my lifework can really be jeopardized by anything my enemies might wish to visit upon me, and surely we have no violence to fear from our friends. I am absolutely assured that the entire universe is friendly to me—this all-powerful truth I insist on believing with a wholehearted trust in spite of all appearances to the contrary."

But Ganid was not fully satisfied. Many times they talked over these matters, and Jesus told him some of his boyhood experiences and also about Jacob the stone mason's son. On learning how Jacob appointed himself to defend Jesus, Ganid said: "Oh, I begin to see! In the first place very seldom would any normal human being want to attack such a kindly person as you, and even if anyone should be so unthinking as to do such a thing, there is pretty sure to be near at hand some other mortal who will fly to your assistance, even as you always go to the rescue of any person you observe to be in distress. In my heart, Teacher, I agree with you, but in my head I still think that if I had been Jacob, I would have enjoyed punishing those rude fellows who presumed to attack you just because they thought you would not defend yourself. I presume you are fairly safe in your journey through life since you spend much of your time helping others and ministering to your fellows in distress—well, most likely there'll always be someone on hand to defend you." And Jesus replied: "That test has not yet come, Ganid, and when it does, we will have to abide by the Father's will." And that was about all the lad could get his teacher to say on this difficult subject of self-defense and nonresistance. On another occasion he did draw from Jesus the opinion that organized society had every right to employ force in the execution of its just mandates.

2. EMBARKING AT TARENTUM

While tarrying at the ship landing, waiting for the boat to unload cargo, the travelers observed a man mistreating his wife. As was his custom, Jesus intervened in behalf of the person subjected to attack. He stepped up behind the irate husband and, tapping him gently on the shoulder, said: "My friend, may I speak with you in private for a moment?" The angry man was nonplused by such an approach and, after a moment of embarrassing hesitation, stammered out—"er—why—yes, what do you want with me?" When Jesus had led him to one side, he said: "My friend, I perceive that something terrible must have happened to you; I very much desire that you tell me what could happen to such a strong man to lead him to attack his wife, the mother of his children, and that right out here before all eyes. I am sure you must feel that you have some good reason for this assault. What did the woman do to deserve such treatment from her husband? As I look upon you, I think I discern in your face the love of justice if not the desire to show mercy. I venture to say that, if you found me out by the wayside, attacked by robbers, you would unhesitatingly rush to my rescue. I dare say you have done many such brave things in the course of your life. Now, my friend, tell me what is the matter? Did the woman do something wrong, or did you foolishly lose your head and thoughtlessly assault her?" It was not so much what he said that touched this man's heart as the kindly look and the sympathetic smile which Jesus bestowed upon him at the conclusion of his remarks. Said the man: "I perceive you are a priest of the Cynics, and I am thankful you restrained me. My wife has done no great wrong; she is a good woman, but she irritates me by the manner in which she picks on me in public, and I lose my temper. I am sorry for my lack of self-control, and I promise to try to live up to my former pledge to one of your brothers who taught me the better way many years ago. I promise you."

And then, in bidding him farewell, Jesus said: "My brother, always remember that man has no rightful authority over woman unless the woman has willingly and voluntarily given him such authority. Your wife has engaged to go through life with you, to help you fight its battles, and to assume the far greater share of the burden of bearing and rearing your children; and in return for this special service it is only fair that she receive from you that special protection which man can give to woman as the partner who must carry, bear, and nurture the children. The loving care and consideration which a man is willing to bestow upon his wife and their children are the measure of that man's attainment of the higher levels of creative and spiritual self-consciousness. Do you not know that men and women are partners with God in that they co-operate to create beings who grow up to possess themselves of the potential of immortal souls? The Father in heaven treats the Spirit Mother of the children of the universe as one equal to himself. It is Godlike to share your life and all that relates thereto on equal terms with the mother partner who so fully shares with you that divine experience of reproducing yourselves in the lives of your children. If you can only love your children as God loves you, you will love and cherish your wife as the Father in heaven honors and exalts the Infinite Spirit, the mother of all the spirit children of a vast universe."

As they went on board the boat, they looked back upon the scene of the teary-eyed couple standing in silent embrace. Having heard the latter half of Jesus' message to the man, Gonod was all day occupied with meditations thereon, and he resolved to reorganize his home when he returned to India.

The journey to Nicopolis was pleasant but slow as the wind was not favorable. The three spent many hours recounting their experiences in Rome and reminiscing about all that had happened to them since they first met in Jerusalem. Ganid was becoming imbued with the spirit of personal ministry. He began work on the steward of the ship, but on the second day, when he got into deep religious water, he called on Joshua to help him out.

They spent several days at Nicopolis, the city which Augustus had founded some fifty years before as the "city of victory" in commemoration of the battle of Actium, this site being the land whereon he camped with his army before the battle. They lodged in the home of one Jeramy, a Greek proselyte of the Jewish faith, whom they had met on shipboard. The Apostle Paul spent all winter with the son of Jeramy in the same house in the course of his third missionary journey. From Nicopolis they sailed on the same boat for Corinth, the capital of the Roman province of Achaia.

3. AT CORINTH

By the time they reached Corinth, Ganid was becoming very much interested in the Jewish religion, and so it was not strange that, one day as they passed the synagogue and saw the people going in, he requested Jesus to take him to the service. That day they heard a learned rabbi discourse on the "Destiny of Israel," and after the service they met one Crispus, the chief ruler of this synagogue.

Many times they went back to the synagogue services, but chiefly to meet Crispus. Ganid grew to be very fond of Crispus, his wife, and their family of five children. He much enjoyed observing how a Jew conducted his family life.

While Ganid studied family life, Jesus was teaching Crispus the better ways of religious living. Jesus held more than twenty sessions with this forward-looking Jew; and it is not surprising, years afterward, when Paul was preaching in this very synagogue, and when the Jews had rejected his message and had voted to forbid his further preaching in the synagogue, and when he then went to the gentiles, that Crispus with his entire family embraced the new religion, and that he became one of the chief supports of the Christian church which Paul subsequently organized at Corinth.

During the eighteen months Paul preached in Corinth, being later joined by Silas and Timothy, he met many others who had been taught by the "Jewish tutor of the son of an Indian merchant."

At Corinth they met people of every race hailing from three continents. Next to Alexandria and Rome, it was the most cosmopolitan city of the Mediterranean empire. There was much to attract one's attention in this city, and Ganid never grew weary of visiting the citadel which stood almost two thousand feet above the sea. He also spent a great deal of his spare time about the synagogue and in the home of Crispus. He was at first shocked, and later on charmed, by the status of woman in the Jewish home; it was a revelation to this young Indian.

Jesus and Ganid were often guests in another Jewish home, that of Justus, a devout merchant, who lived alongside the synagogue. And many times, subsequently, when the Apostle Paul sojourned in this home, did he listen to the recounting of these visits with the Indian lad and his Jewish tutor, while both Paul and Justus wondered whatever became of such a wise and brilliant Hebrew teacher.

When in Rome, Ganid observed that Jesus refused to accompany them to the public baths. Several times afterward the young man sought to induce Jesus further to express himself in regard to the relations of the sexes. Though he would answer the lad's questions, he never seemed disposed to discuss these subjects at great length. One evening as they strolled about Corinth out near where the wall of the citadel ran down to the sea, they were accosted by two public women. Ganid had imbibed the idea, and rightly, that Jesus was a man of high ideals, and that he abhorred everything which partook of uncleanness or savored of evil; accordingly he spoke sharply to these women and rudely motioned them away. When Jesus saw this, he said to Ganid: "You mean well, but you should not presume thus to speak to the children of God, even though they chance to be his erring children. Who are we that we should sit in judgment on these women? Do you happen to know all of the circumstances which led them to resort to such methods of obtaining a livelihood? Stop here with me while we talk about these matters." The courtesans were astonished at what he said even more than was Ganid.

As they stood there in the moonlight, Jesus went on to say: "There lives within every human mind a divine spirit, the gift of the Father in heaven. This good spirit ever strives to lead us to God, to help us to find God and to know God; but also within mortals there are many natural physical tendencies which the Creator put there to serve the well-being of the individual and the race. Now, oftentimes, men and women become confused in their efforts to understand themselves and to grapple with the manifold difficulties of making a living in a world so largely dominated by selfishness and sin. I perceive, Ganid, that neither of these women is willfully wicked. I can tell by their faces that they have experienced much sorrow; they have suffered much at the hands of an apparently cruel fate; they have not intentionally chosen this sort of life; they have, in discouragement bordering on despair, surrendered to the pressure of the hour and accepted this distasteful means of obtaining a livelihood as the best way out of a situation that to them appeared hopeless. Ganid, some people are really wicked at heart; they deliberately choose to do mean things, but, tell me, as you look into these now tear-stained faces, do you see anything bad or wicked?" And as Jesus paused for his reply, Ganid's voice choked up as he stammered out his answer: "No, Teacher, I do not. And I apologize for my rudeness to them—I crave their forgiveness." Then said Jesus: "And I bespeak for them that they have forgiven you as I speak for my Father in heaven that he has forgiven them. Now all of you come with me to a friend's house where we will seek refreshment and plan for the new and better life ahead." Up to this time the amazed women had not uttered a word; they looked at each other and silently followed as the men led the way.

Imagine the surprise of Justus' wife when, at this late hour, Jesus appeared with Ganid and these two strangers, saying: "You will forgive us for coming at this hour, but Ganid and I desire a bite to eat, and we would share it with these our new-found friends, who are also in need of nourishment; and besides all this, we come to you with the thought that you will be interested in counseling with us as to the best way to help these women get a new start in life. They can tell you their story, but I surmise they have had much trouble, and their very presence here in your house testifies how earnestly they crave to know good people, and how willingly they will embrace the opportunity to show all the world—and even the angels of heaven—what brave and noble women they can become."

When Martha, Justus' wife, had spread the food on the table, Jesus, taking unexpected leave of them, said: "As it is getting late, and since the young man's father will be awaiting us, we pray to be excused while we leave you here together—three women—the beloved children of the Most High. And I will pray for your spiritual guidance while you make plans for a new and better life on earth and eternal life in the great beyond."

Thus did Jesus and Ganid take leave of the women. So far the two courtesans had said nothing; likewise was Ganid speechless. And for a few moments so was Martha, but presently she rose to the occasion and did everything for these strangers that Jesus had hoped for. The elder of these two women died a short time thereafter, with bright hopes of eternal survival, and the younger woman worked at Justus' place of business and later became a lifelong member of the first Christian church in Corinth.

Several times in the home of Crispus, Jesus and Ganid met one Gaius, who subsequently became a loyal supporter of Paul. During these two months in Corinth they held intimate conversations with scores of worth-while individuals, and as a result of all these apparently casual contacts more than half of the individuals so affected became members of the subsequent Christian community.

When Paul first went to Corinth, he had not intended to make a prolonged visit. But he did not know how well the Jewish tutor had prepared the way for his labors. And further, he discovered that great interest had already been aroused by Aquila and Priscilla, Aquila being one of the Cynics with whom Jesus had come in contact when in Rome. This couple were Jewish refugees from Rome, and they quickly embraced Paul's teachings. He lived with them and worked with them, for they were also tentmakers. It was because of these circumstances that Paul prolonged his stay in Corinth.

4. PERSONAL WORK IN CORINTH

Jesus and Ganid had many more interesting experiences in Corinth. They had close converse with a great number of persons who greatly profited by the instruction received from Jesus.

The miller he taught about grinding up the grains of truth in the mill of living experience so as to render the difficult things of divine life readily receivable by even the weak and feeble among one's fellow mortals. Said Jesus: "Give the milk of truth to those who are babes in spiritual perception. In your living and loving ministry serve spiritual food in attractive form and suited to the capacity of receptivity of each of your inquirers."

To the Roman centurion he said: "Render unto Caesar the things which are Caesar's and unto God the things which are God's. The sincere service of God and the loyal service of Caesar do not conflict unless Caesar should presume to arrogate to himself that homage which alone can be claimed by Deity. Loyalty to God, if you should come to know him, would render you all the more loyal and faithful in your devotion to a worthy emperor."

To the earnest leader of the Mithraic cult he said: "You do well to seek for a religion of eternal salvation, but you err to go in quest of such a glorious truth among man-made mysteries and human philosophies. Know you not that the mystery of eternal salvation dwells within your own soul? Do you not know that the God of heaven has sent his spirit to live within you, and that this spirit will lead all truth-loving and God-serving mortals out of this life and through the portals of death up to the eternal heights of light where God waits to receive his children? And never forget: You who know God are the sons of God if you truly yearn to be like him."

To the Epicurean teacher he said: "You do well to choose the best and esteem the good, but are you wise when you fail to discern the greater things of mortal life which are embodied in the spirit realms derived from the realization of the presence of God in the human heart? The great thing in all human experience is the realization of knowing the God whose spirit lives within you and seeks to lead you forth on that long and almost endless journey of attaining the personal presence of our common Father, the God of all creation, the Lord of universes."

To the Greek contractor and builder he said: "My friend, as you build the material structures of men, grow a spiritual character in the similitude of the divine spirit within your soul. Do not let your achievement as a temporal builder outrun your attainment as a spiritual son of the kingdom of heaven. While you build the mansions of time for another, neglect not to secure your title to the mansions of eternity for yourself. Ever remember, there is a city whose foundations are righteousness and truth, and whose builder and maker is God."

To the Roman judge he said: "As you judge men, remember that you yourself will also some day come to judgment before the bar of the Rulers of a universe. Judge justly, even mercifully, even as you shall some day thus crave merciful consideration at the hands of the Supreme Arbiter. Judge as you would be judged under similar circumstances, thus being guided by the spirit of the law as well as by its letter. And even as you accord justice dominated by fairness in the light of the need of those who are brought before you, so shall you have the right to expect justice tempered by mercy when you sometime stand before the Judge of all the earth."

To the mistress of the Greek inn he said: "Minister your hospitality as one who entertains the children of the Most High. Elevate the drudgery of your daily toil to the high levels of a fine art through the increasing realization that you minister to God in the persons whom he indwells by his spirit which has descended to live within the hearts of men, thereby seeking to transform their minds and lead their souls to the knowledge of the Paradise Father of all these bestowed gifts of the divine spirit."

Jesus had many visits with a Chinese merchant. In saying good-bye, he admonished him: "Worship only God, who is your true spirit ancestor. Remember that the Father's spirit ever lives within you and always points your soul-direction heavenward. If you follow the unconscious leadings of this immortal spirit, you are certain to continue on in the uplifted way of finding God. And when you do attain the Father in heaven, it will be because by seeking him you have become more and more like him. And so farewell, Chang, but only for a season, for we shall meet again in the worlds of light where the Father of spirit souls has provided many delightful stopping-places for those who are Paradise-bound."

To the traveler from Britain he said: "My brother, I perceive you are seeking for truth, and I suggest that the spirit of the Father of all truth may chance to dwell within you. Did you ever sincerely endeavor to talk with the spirit of your own soul? Such a thing is indeed difficult and seldom yields consciousness of success; but every honest attempt of the material mind to communicate with its indwelling spirit meets with certain success, notwithstanding that the majority of all such magnificent human experiences must long remain as superconscious registrations in the souls of such God-knowing mortals."

To the runaway lad Jesus said: "Remember, there are two things you cannot run away from—God and yourself. Wherever you may go, you take with you yourself and the spirit of the heavenly Father which lives within your heart. My son, stop trying to deceive yourself; settle down to the courageous practice of facing the facts of life; lay firm hold on the assurances of sonship with God and the certainty of eternal life, as I have instructed you. From this day on purpose to be a real man, a man determined to face life bravely and intelligently."

To the condemned criminal he said at the last hour: "My brother, you have fallen on evil times. You lost your way; you became entangled in the meshes of crime. From talking to you, I well know you did not plan to do the thing which is about to cost you your temporal life. But you did do this evil, and your fellows have adjudged you guilty; they have determined that you shall die. You or I may not deny the state this right of self-defense in the manner of its own choosing. There seems to be no way of humanly escaping the penalty of your wrongdoing. Your fellows must judge you by what you did, but there is a Judge to whom you may appeal for forgiveness, and who will judge you by your real motives and better intentions. You need not fear to meet the judgment of God if your repentance is genuine and your faith sincere. The fact that your error carries with it the death penalty imposed by man does not prejudice the chance of your soul to obtain justice and enjoy mercy before the heavenly courts."

Jesus enjoyed many intimate talks with a large number of hungry souls, too many to find a place in this record. The three travelers enjoyed their sojourn in Corinth. Excepting Athens, which was more renowned as an educational center, Corinth was the most important city in Greece during these Roman times, and their two months' stay in this thriving commercial center afforded opportunity for all three of them to gain much valuable experience. Their sojourn in this city was one of the most interesting of all their stops on the way back from Rome.

Gonod had many interests in Corinth, but finally his business was finished, and they prepared to sail for Athens. They traveled on a small boat which could be carried overland on a land track from one of Corinth's harbors to the other, a distance of ten miles.

5. AT ATHENS—DISCOURSE ON SCIENCE

They shortly arrived at the olden center of Greek science and learning, and Ganid was thrilled with the thought of being in Athens, of being in Greece, the cultural center of the onetime Alexandrian empire, which had extended its borders even to his own land of India. There was little business to transact; so Gonod spent most of his time with Jesus and Ganid, visiting the many points of interest and listening to the interesting discussions of the lad and his versatile teacher.

A great university still thrived in Athens, and the trio made frequent visits to its halls of learning. Jesus and Ganid had thoroughly discussed the teachings of Plato when they attended the lectures in the museum at Alexandria. They all enjoyed the art of Greece, examples of which were still to be found here and there about the city.

Both the father and the son greatly enjoyed the discussion on science which Jesus had at their inn one evening with a Greek philosopher. After this pedant had talked for almost three hours, and when he had finished his discourse, Jesus, in terms of modern thought, said:

Scientists may some day measure the energy, or force manifestations, of gravitation, light, and electricity, but these same scientists can never (scientifically) tell you what these universe phenomena *are.* Science deals with physical-energy activities; religion deals with eternal values. True philosophy grows out of the wisdom which does its best to correlate these quantitative and qualitative observations. There always exists the danger that the purely physical scientist may become afflicted with mathematical pride and statistical egotism, not to mention spiritual blindness.

Logic is valid in the material world, and mathematics is reliable when limited in its application to physical things; but neither is to be regarded as wholly dependable or infallible when applied to life problems. Life embraces phenomena which are not wholly material. Arithmetic says that, if one man could shear a sheep in ten minutes, ten men could shear it in one minute. That is sound mathematics, but it is not true, for the ten men could not so do it; they would get in one another's way so badly that the work would be greatly delayed.

Mathematics asserts that, if one person stands for a certain unit of intellectual and moral value, ten persons would stand for ten times this value. But in dealing with human personality it would be nearer the truth to say that such a personality association is a sum equal to the square of the number of personalities concerned in the equation rather than the simple arithmetical sum. A social group of human beings in co-ordinated working harmony stands for a force far greater than the simple sum of its parts.

Quantity may be identified as a *fact,* thus becoming a scientific uniformity. Quality, being a matter of mind interpretation, represents an estimate of *values,* and must, therefore, remain an experience of the individual. When both science and religion become less dogmatic and more tolerant of criticism, philosophy will then begin to achieve *unity* in the intelligent comprehension of the universe.

There is unity in the cosmic universe if you could only discern its workings in actuality. The real universe is friendly to every child of the eternal God. The real problem is: How can the finite mind of man achieve a logical, true, and corresponding unity of thought? This universe-knowing state of mind can be had only by conceiving that the quantitative fact and the qualitative value have a common causation in the Paradise Father. Such a conception of reality yields a broader insight into the purposeful unity of universe phenomena; it even reveals a spiritual goal of progressive personality achievement. And this is a concept of unity which can sense the unchanging background of a living universe of continually changing impersonal relations and evolving personal relationships.

Matter and spirit and the state intervening between them are three interrelated and interassociated levels of the true unity of the real universe. Regardless of how divergent the universe phenomena of fact and value may appear to be, they are, after all, unified in the Supreme.

Reality of material existence attaches to unrecognized energy as well as to visible matter. When the energies of the universe are so slowed down that they acquire the requisite degree of motion, then, under favorable conditions, these same energies become mass. And forget not, the mind which can alone perceive the presence of apparent realities is itself also real. And the fundamental cause of this universe of energy-mass, mind, and spirit, is eternal—it exists and consists in the nature and reactions of the Universal Father and his absolute co-ordinates.

They were all more than astounded at the words of Jesus, and when the Greek took leave of them, he said: "At last my eyes have beheld a Jew who thinks something besides racial superiority and talks something besides religion." And they retired for the night.

The sojourn in Athens was pleasant and profitable, but it was not particularly fruitful in its human contacts. Too many of the Athenians of that day were either intellectually proud of their reputation of another day or mentally stupid and ignorant, being the offspring of the inferior slaves of those earlier periods when there was glory in Greece and wisdom in the minds of its people. Even then, there were still many keen minds to be found among the citizens of Athens.

6. AT EPHESUS—DISCOURSE ON THE SOUL

On leaving Athens, the travelers went by way of Troas to Ephesus, the capital of the Roman province of Asia. They made many trips out to the famous temple of Artemis of the Ephesians, about two miles from the city. Artemis was the most famous goddess of all Asia Minor and a perpetuation of the still earlier mother goddess of ancient Anatolian times. The crude idol exhibited in the enormous temple dedicated to her worship was reputed to have fallen from heaven. Not all of Ganid's early training to respect images as symbols of divinity had been eradicated, and he thought it best to purchase a little silver shrine in honor of this fertility goddess of Asia Minor. That night they talked at great length about the worship of things made with human hands.

On the third day of their stay they walked down by the river to observe the dredging of the harbor's mouth. At noon they talked with a young Phoenician who was homesick and much discouraged; but most of all he was envious of a certain young man who had received promotion over his head. Jesus spoke comforting words to him and quoted the olden Hebrew proverb: "A man's gift makes room for him and brings him before great men."

Of all the large cities they visited on this tour of the Mediterranean, they here accomplished the least of value to the subsequent work of the Christian missionaries. Christianity secured its start in Ephesus largely through the efforts of Paul, who resided here more than two years, making tents for a living and conducting lectures on religion and philosophy each night in the main audience chamber of the school of Tyrannus.

There was a progressive thinker connected with this local school of philosophy, and Jesus had several profitable sessions with him. In the course of these talks Jesus had repeatedly used the word "soul." This learned Greek finally asked him what he meant by "soul," and he replied:

"The soul is the self-reflective, truth-discerning, and spirit-perceiving part of man which forever elevates the human being above the level of the animal world. Self-consciousness, in and of itself, is not the soul. Moral self-consciousness is true human self-realization and constitutes the foundation of the human soul, and the soul is that part of man which represents the potential survival value of human experience. Moral choice and spiritual attainment, the ability to know God and the urge to be like him, are the characteristics of the soul. The soul of man cannot exist apart from moral thinking and spiritual activity. A stagnant soul is a dying soul. But the soul of man is distinct from the divine spirit which dwells within the mind. The divine spirit arrives simultaneously with the first moral activity of the human mind, and that is the occasion of the birth of the soul.

"The saving or losing of a soul has to do with whether or not the moral consciousness attains survival status through eternal alliance with its associated immortal spirit endowment. Salvation is the spiritualization of the self-realization of the moral consciousness, which thereby becomes possessed of survival value. All forms of soul conflict consist in the lack of harmony between the moral, or spiritual, self-consciousness and the purely intellectual self-consciousness.

"The human soul, when matured, ennobled, and spiritualized, approaches the heavenly status in that it comes near to being an entity intervening between the material and the spiritual, the material self and the divine spirit. The evolving soul of a human being is difficult of description and more difficult of demonstration because it is not discoverable by the methods of either material investigation or spiritual proving. Material science cannot demonstrate the existence of a soul, neither can pure spirit-testing. Notwithstanding the failure of both material science and spiritual standards to discover the existence of the human soul, every morally conscious mortal *knows* of the existence of *his* soul as a *real* and actual personal experience."

7. THE SOJOURN AT CYPRUS—DISCOURSE ON MIND

Shortly the travelers set sail for Cyprus, stopping at Rhodes. They enjoyed the long water voyage and arrived at their island destination much rested in body and refreshed in spirit.

It was their plan to enjoy a period of real rest and play on this visit to Cyprus as their tour of the Mediterranean was drawing to a close. They landed at Paphos and at once began the assembly of supplies for their sojourn of several weeks in the near-by mountains. On the third day after their arrival they started for the hills with their well-loaded pack animals.

For two weeks the trio greatly enjoyed themselves, and then, without warning, young Ganid was suddenly taken grievously ill. For two weeks he suffered from a raging fever, oftentimes becoming delirious; both Jesus and Gonod were kept busy attending the sick boy. Jesus skillfully and tenderly cared for the lad, and the father was amazed by both the gentleness and adeptness manifested in all his ministry to the afflicted youth. They were far from human habitations, and the boy was too ill to be moved; so they prepared as best they could to nurse him back to health right there in the mountains.

During Ganid's convalescence of three weeks Jesus told him many interesting things about nature and her various moods. And what fun they had as they wandered over the mountains, the boy asking questions, Jesus answering them, and the father marveling at the whole performance.

The last week of their sojourn in the mountains Jesus and Ganid had a long talk on the functions of the human mind. After several hours of discussion the lad asked this question: "But, Teacher, what do you mean when you say that man experiences a higher form of self-consciousness than do the higher animals?" And as restated in modern phraseology, Jesus answered:

My son, I have already told you much about the mind of man and the divine spirit that lives therein, but now let me emphasize that self-consciousness is a *reality.* When any animal becomes self-conscious, it becomes a primitive man. Such an attainment results from a co-ordination of function between impersonal energy and spirit-conceiving mind, and it is this phenomenon which warrants the bestowal of an absolute focal point for the human personality, the spirit of the Father in heaven.

Ideas are not simply a record of sensations; ideas are sensations plus the reflective interpretations of the personal self; and the self is more than the sum of one's sensations. There begins to be something of an approach to unity in an evolving selfhood, and that unity is derived from the indwelling presence of a part of absolute unity which spiritually activates such a self-conscious animal-origin mind.

No mere animal could possess a time self-consciousness. Animals possess a physiological co-ordination of associated sensation-recognition and memory thereof, but none experience a meaningful recognition of sensation or exhibit a purposeful association of these combined physical experiences such as is manifested in the conclusions of intelligent and reflective human interpretations. And this fact of self-conscious existence, associated with the reality of his subsequent spiritual experience, constitutes man a potential son of the universe and foreshadows his eventual attainment of the Supreme Unity of the universe.

Neither is the human self merely the sum of the successive states of consciousness. Without the effective functioning of a consciousness sorter and associater there would not exist sufficient unity to warrant the designation of a selfhood. Such an ununified mind could hardly attain conscious levels of human status. If the associations of consciousness were just an accident, the minds of all men would then exhibit the uncontrolled and random associations of certain phases of mental madness.

A human mind, built up solely out of the consciousness of physical sensations, could never attain spiritual levels; this kind of material mind would be utterly lacking in a sense of moral values and would be without a guiding sense of spiritual dominance which is so essential to achieving harmonious personality unity in time, and which is inseparable from personality survival in eternity.

The human mind early begins to manifest qualities which are supermaterial; the truly reflective human intellect is not altogether bound by the limits of time. That individuals so differ in their life performances indicates, not only the varying endowments of heredity and the different influences of the environment, but also the degree of unification with the indwelling spirit of the Father which has been achieved by the self, the measure of the identification of the one with the other.

The human mind does not well stand the conflict of double allegiance. It is a severe strain on the soul to undergo the experience of an effort to serve both good and evil. The supremely happy and efficiently unified mind is the one wholly dedicated to the doing of the will of the Father in heaven. Unresolved conflicts destroy unity and may terminate in mind disruption. But the survival character of a soul is not fostered by attempting to secure peace of mind at any price, by the surrender of noble aspirations, and by the compromise of spiritual ideals; rather is such peace attained by the stalwart assertion of the triumph of that which is true, and this victory is achieved in the overcoming of evil with the potent force of good.

The next day they departed for Salamis, where they embarked for Antioch on the Syrian coast.

8. AT ANTIOCH

Antioch was the capital of the Roman province of Syria, and here the imperial governor had his residence. Antioch had half a million inhabitants; it was the third city of the empire in size and the first in wickedness and flagrant immorality. Gonod had considerable business to transact; so Jesus and Ganid were much by themselves. They visited everything about this polyglot city except the grove of Daphne. Gonod and Ganid visited this notorious shrine of shame, but Jesus declined to accompany them. Such scenes were not so shocking to Indians, but they were repellent to an idealistic Hebrew.

Jesus became sober and reflective as he drew nearer Palestine and the end of their journey. He visited with few people in Antioch; he seldom went about in the city. After much questioning as to why his teacher manifested so little interest in Antioch, Ganid finally induced Jesus to say: "This city is not far from Palestine; maybe I shall come back here sometime."

Ganid had a very interesting experience in Antioch. This young man had proved himself an apt pupil and already had begun to make practical use of some of Jesus' teachings. There was a certain Indian connected with his father's business in Antioch who had become so unpleasant and disgruntled that his dismissal had been considered. When Ganid heard this, he betook himself to his father's place of business and held a long conference with his fellow countryman. This man felt he had been put at the wrong job. Ganid told him about the Father in heaven and in many ways expanded his views of religion. But of all that Ganid said, the quotation of a Hebrew proverb did the most good, and that word of wisdom was: "Whatsoever your hand finds to do, do that with all your might."

After preparing their luggage for the camel caravan, they passed on down to Sidon and thence over to Damascus, and after three days they made ready for the long trek across the desert sands.

9. IN MESOPOTAMIA

The caravan trip across the desert was not a new experience for these much-traveled men. After Ganid had watched his teacher help with the loading of their twenty camels and observed him volunteer to drive their own animal, he exclaimed, "Teacher, is there anything that you cannot do?" Jesus only smiled, saying, "The teacher surely is not without honor in the eyes of a diligent pupil." And so they set forth for the ancient city of Ur.

Jesus was much interested in the early history of Ur, the birthplace of Abraham, and he was equally fascinated with the ruins and traditions of Susa, so much so that Gonod and Ganid extended their stay in these parts three weeks in order to afford Jesus more time to conduct his investigations and also to provide the better opportunity to persuade him to go back to India with them.

It was at Ur that Ganid had a long talk with Jesus regarding the difference between knowledge, wisdom, and truth. And he was greatly charmed with the saying of the Hebrew wise man: "Wisdom is the principal thing; therefore get wisdom. With all your quest for knowledge, get understanding. Exalt wisdom and she will promote you. She will bring you to honor if you will but embrace her."

At last the day came for the separation. They were all brave, especially the lad, but it was a trying ordeal. They were tearful of eye but courageous of heart. In bidding his teacher farewell, Ganid said: "Farewell, Teacher, but not forever. When I come again to Damascus, I will look for you. I love you, for I think the Father in heaven must be something like you; at least I know you are much like what you have told me about him. I will remember your teaching, but most of all, I will never forget you." Said the father, "Farewell to a great teacher, one who has made us better and helped us to know God." And Jesus replied, "Peace be upon you, and may the blessing of the Father in heaven ever abide with you." And Jesus stood on the shore and watched as the small boat carried them out to their anchored ship. Thus the Master left his friends from India at Charax, never to see them again in this world; nor were they, in this world, ever to know that the man who later appeared as Jesus of Nazareth was this same friend they had just taken leave of—Joshua their teacher.

In India, Ganid grew up to become an influential man, a worthy successor of his eminent father, and he spread abroad many of the noble truths which he had learned from Jesus, his beloved teacher. Later on in life, when Ganid heard of the strange teacher in Palestine who terminated his career on a cross, though he recognized the similarity between the gospel of this Son of Man and the teachings of his Jewish tutor, it never occurred to him that these two were actually the same person.

Thus ended that chapter in the life of the Son of Man which might be termed: *The mission of Joshua the teacher.*

PAPER 134

THE TRANSITION YEARS

DURING the Mediterranean journey Jesus had carefully studied the people he met and the countries through which he passed, and at about this time he reached his final decision as to the remainder of his life on earth. He had fully considered and now finally approved the plan which provided that he be born of Jewish parents in Palestine, and he therefore deliberately returned to Galilee to await the beginning of his lifework as a public teacher of truth; he began to lay plans for a public career in the land of his father Joseph's people, and he did this of his own free will.

Jesus had found out through personal and human experience that Palestine was the best place in all the Roman world wherein to set forth the closing chapters, and to enact the final scenes, of his life on earth. For the first time he became fully satisfied with the program of openly manifesting his true nature and of revealing his divine identity among the Jews and gentiles of his native Palestine. He definitely decided to finish his life on earth and to complete his career of mortal existence in the same land in which he entered the human experience as a helpless babe. His Urantia career began among the Jews in Palestine, and he chose to terminate his life in Palestine and among the Jews.

1. THE THIRTIETH YEAR (A.D. 24)

After taking leave of Gonod and Ganid at Charax (in December of A.D. 23), Jesus returned by way of Ur to Babylon, where he joined a desert caravan that was on its way to Damascus. From Damascus he went to Nazareth, stopping only a few hours at Capernaum, where he paused to call on Zebedee's family. There he met his brother James, who had sometime previously come over to work in his place in Zebedee's boatshop. After talking with James and Jude (who also chanced to be in Capernaum) and after turning over to his brother James the little house which John Zebedee had managed to buy, Jesus went on to Nazareth.

At the end of his Mediterranean journey Jesus had received sufficient money to meet his living expenses almost up to the time of the beginning of his public ministry. But aside from Zebedee of Capernaum and the people whom he met on this extraordinary trip, the world never knew that he made this journey. His family always believed that he spent this time in study at Alexandria. Jesus never confirmed these beliefs, neither did he make open denial of such misunderstandings.

During his stay of a few weeks at Nazareth, Jesus visited with his family and friends, spent some time at the repair shop with his brother Joseph, but devoted most of his attention to Mary and Ruth. Ruth was then nearly fifteen years old, and this was Jesus' first opportunity to have long talks with her since she had become a young woman.

Both Simon and Jude had for some time wanted to get married, but they had disliked to do this without Jesus' consent; accordingly they had postponed these events, hoping for their eldest brother's return. Though they all regarded James as the head of the family in most matters, when it came to getting married, they wanted the blessing of Jesus. So Simon and Jude were married at a double wedding in early March of this year, A.D. 24. All the older children were now married; only Ruth, the youngest, remained at home with Mary.

Jesus visited with the individual members of his family quite normally and naturally, but when they were all together, he had so little to say that they remarked about it among themselves. Mary especially was disconcerted by this unusually peculiar behavior of her first-born son.

About the time Jesus was preparing to leave Nazareth, the conductor of a large caravan which was passing through the city was taken violently ill, and Jesus, being a linguist, volunteered to take his place. Since this trip would necessitate his absence for a year, and inasmuch as all his brothers were married and his mother was living at home with Ruth, Jesus called a family conference at which he proposed that his mother and Ruth go to Capernaum to live in the home which he had so recently given to James. Accordingly, a few days after Jesus left with the caravan, Mary and Ruth moved to Capernaum, where they lived for the rest of Mary's life in the home that Jesus had provided. Joseph and his family moved into the old Nazareth home.

This was one of the more unusual years in the inner experience of the Son of Man; great progress was made in effecting working harmony between his human mind and the indwelling Adjuster. The Adjuster had been actively engaged in reorganizing the thinking and in rehearsing the mind for the great events which were in the not then distant future. The personality of Jesus was preparing for his great change in attitude toward the world. These were the in-between times, the transition stage of that being who began life as God appearing as man, and who was now making ready to complete his earth career as man appearing as God.

2. THE CARAVAN TRIP TO THE CASPIAN

It was the first of April, A.D. 24, when Jesus left Nazareth on the caravan trip to the Caspian Sea region. The caravan which Jesus joined as its conductor was going from Jerusalem by way of Damascus and Lake Urmia through Assyria, Media, and Parthia to the southeastern Caspian Sea region. It was a full year before he returned from this journey.

For Jesus this caravan trip was another adventure of exploration and personal ministry. He had an interesting experience with his caravan family—passengers, guards, and camel drivers. Scores of men, women, and children residing along the route followed by the caravan lived richer lives as a result of their contact with Jesus, to them, the extraordinary conductor of a commonplace caravan. Not all who enjoyed these occasions of his personal ministry profited thereby, but the vast majority of those who met and talked with him were made better for the remainder of their natural lives.

Of all his world travels this Caspian Sea trip carried Jesus nearest to the Orient and enabled him to gain a better understanding of the Far-Eastern peoples. He made intimate and personal contact with every one of the surviving races of Urantia excepting the red. He equally enjoyed his personal ministry to each of these varied races and blended peoples, and all of them were receptive to the living truth which he brought them. The Europeans from the Far West and the Asiatics from the Far East alike gave attention to his words of hope and eternal life and were equally influenced by the life of loving service and spiritual ministry which he so graciously lived among them.

The caravan trip was successful in every way. This was a most interesting episode in the human life of Jesus, for he functioned during this year in an executive capacity, being responsible for the material intrusted to his charge and for the safe conduct of the travelers making up the caravan party. And he most faithfully, efficiently, and wisely discharged his multiple duties.

On the return from the Caspian region, Jesus gave up the direction of the caravan at Lake Urmia, where he tarried for slightly over two weeks. He returned as a passenger with a later caravan to Damascus, where the owners of the camels besought him to remain in their service. Declining this offer, he journeyed on with the caravan train to Capernaum, arriving the first of April, A.D. 25. No longer did he regard Nazareth as his home. Capernaum had become the home of Jesus, James, Mary, and Ruth. But Jesus never again lived with his family; when in Capernaum he made his home with the Zebedees.

3. THE URMIA LECTURES

On the way to the Caspian Sea, Jesus had stopped several days for rest and recuperation at the old Persian city of Urmia on the western shores of Lake Urmia. On the largest of a group of islands situated a short distance offshore near Urmia was located a large building—a lecture amphitheater—dedicated to the "spirit of religion." This structure was really a temple of the philosophy of religions.

This temple of religion had been built by a wealthy merchant citizen of Urmia and his three sons. This man was Cymboyton, and he numbered among his ancestors many diverse peoples.

The lectures and discussions in this school of religion began at ten o'clock every morning in the week. The afternoon sessions started at three o'clock, and the evening debates opened at eight o'clock. Cymboyton or one of his three sons always presided at these sessions of teaching, discussion, and debate. The founder of this unique school of religions lived and died without ever revealing his personal religious beliefs.

On several occasions Jesus participated in these discussions, and before he left Urmia, Cymboyton arranged with Jesus to sojourn with them for two weeks on his return trip and give twenty-four lectures on "The Brotherhood of Men," and to conduct twelve evening sessions of questions, discussions, and debates on his lectures in particular and on the brotherhood of men in general.

In accordance with this arrangement, Jesus stopped off on the return trip and delivered these lectures. This was the most systematic and formal of all the Master's teaching on Urantia. Never before or after did he say so much on one subject as was contained in these lectures and discussions on the brotherhood of men. In reality these lectures were on the "Kingdom of God" and the "Kingdoms of Men."

More than thirty religions and religious cults were represented on the faculty of this temple of religious philosophy. These teachers were chosen, supported, and fully accredited by their respective religious groups. At this time there were about seventy-five teachers on the faculty, and they lived in cottages each accommodating about a dozen persons. Every new moon these groups were changed by the casting of lots. Intolerance, a contentious spirit, or any other disposition to interfere with the smooth running of the community would bring about the prompt and summary dismissal of the offending teacher. He would be unceremoniously dismissed, and his alternate in waiting would be immediately installed in his place.

These teachers of the various religions made a great effort to show how similar their religions were in regard to the fundamental things of this life and the next. There was but one doctrine which had to be accepted in order to gain a seat on this faculty—every teacher must represent a religion which recognized God—some sort of supreme Deity. There were five independent teachers on the faculty who did not represent any organized religion, and it was as such an independent teacher that Jesus appeared before them.

[When we, the midwayers, first prepared the summary of Jesus' teachings at Urmia, there arose a disagreement between the seraphim of the churches and the seraphim of progress as to the wisdom of including these teachings in the Urantia Revelation. Conditions of the twentieth century, prevailing in both religion and human governments, are so different from those prevailing in Jesus' day that it was indeed difficult to adapt the Master's teachings at Urmia to the problems of the kingdom of God and the kingdoms of men as these world functions are existent in the twentieth century. We were never able to formulate a statement of the Master's teachings which was acceptable to both groups of these seraphim of planetary government. Finally, the Melchizedek chairman of the revelatory commission appointed a commission of three of our number to prepare our view of the Master's Urmia teachings as adapted to twentieth-century religious and political conditions on Urantia. Accordingly, we three secondary midwayers completed such an adaptation of Jesus' teachings, restating his pronouncements as we would apply them to present-day world conditions, and we now present these statements as they stand after having been edited by the Melchizedek chairman of the revelatory commission.]

4. SOVEREIGNTY—DIVINE AND HUMAN

The brotherhood of men is founded on the fatherhood of God. The family of God is derived from the love of God—God is love. God the Father divinely loves his children, all of them.

The kingdom of heaven, the divine government, is founded on the fact of divine sovereignty—God is spirit. Since God is spirit, this kingdom is spiritual. The kingdom of heaven is neither material nor merely intellectual; it is a spiritual relationship between God and man.

If different religions recognize the spirit sovereignty of God the Father, then will all such religions remain at peace. Only when one religion assumes that it is in some way superior to all others, and that it possesses exclusive authority over other religions, will such a religion presume to be intolerant of other religions or dare to persecute other religious believers.

Religious peace—brotherhood—can never exist unless all religions are willing to completely divest themselves of all ecclesiastical authority and fully surrender all concept of spiritual sovereignty. God alone is spirit sovereign.

You cannot have equality among religions (religious liberty) without having religious wars unless all religions consent to the transfer of all religious sovereignty to some superhuman level, to God himself.

The kingdom of heaven in the hearts of men will create religious unity (not necessarily uniformity) because any and all religious groups composed of such religious believers will be free from all notions of ecclesiastical authority—religious sovereignty.

God is spirit, and God gives a fragment of his spirit self to dwell in the heart of man. Spiritually, all men are equal. The kingdom of heaven is free from castes, classes, social levels, and economic groups. You are all brethren.

But the moment you lose sight of the spirit sovereignty of God the Father, some one religion will begin to assert its superiority over other religions; and then, instead of peace on earth and good will among men, there will start dissensions, recriminations, even religious wars, at least wars among religionists.

Freewill beings who regard themselves as equals, unless they mutually acknowledge themselves as subject to some supersovereignty, some authority over and above themselves, sooner or later are tempted to try out their ability to gain power and authority over other persons and groups. The concept of equality never brings peace except in the mutual recognition of some overcontrolling influence of supersovereignty.

The Urmia religionists lived together in comparative peace and tranquillity because they had fully surrendered all their notions of religious sovereignty. Spiritually, they all believed in a sovereign God; socially, full and unchallengeable authority rested in their presiding head—Cymboyton. They well knew what would happen to any teacher who assumed to lord it over his fellow teachers. There can be no lasting religious peace on Urantia until all religious groups freely surrender all their notions of divine favor, chosen people, and religious sovereignty. Only when God the Father becomes supreme will men become religious brothers and live together in religious peace on earth.

5. POLITICAL SOVEREIGNTY

[While the Master's teaching concerning the sovereignty of God is a truth—only complicated by the subsequent appearance of the religion about him among the world's religions—his presentations concerning political sovereignty are vastly complicated by the political evolution of nation life during the last nineteen hundred years and more. In the times of Jesus there were only two great world powers—the Roman Empire in the West and the Han Empire in the East—and these were widely separated by the Parthian kingdom and other intervening lands of the Caspian and Turkestan regions. We have, therefore, in the following presentation departed more widely from the substance of the Master's teachings at Urmia concerning political sovereignty, at the same time attempting to depict the import of such teachings as they are applicable to the peculiarly critical stage of the evolution of political sovereignty in the twentieth century after Christ.]

War on Urantia will never end so long as nations cling to the illusive notions of unlimited national sovereignty. There are only two levels of relative sovereignty on an inhabited world: the spiritual free will of the individual mortal and the collective sovereignty of mankind as a whole. Between the level of the individual human being and the level of the total of mankind, all groupings and associations are relative, transitory, and of value only in so far as they enhance the welfare, well-being, and progress of the individual and the planetary grand total—man and mankind.

Religious teachers must always remember that the spiritual sovereignty of God overrides all intervening and intermediate spiritual loyalties. Someday civil rulers will learn that the Most Highs rule in the kingdoms of men.

This rule of the Most Highs in the kingdoms of men is not for the especial benefit of any especially favored group of mortals. There is no such thing as a "chosen people." The rule of the Most Highs, the overcontrollers of political evolution, is a rule designed to foster the greatest good to the greatest number of *all* men and for the greatest length of time.

Sovereignty is power and it grows by organization. This growth of the organization of political power is good and proper, for it tends to encompass ever-widening segments of the total of mankind. But this same growth of political organizations creates a problem at every intervening stage between the initial and natural organization of political power—the family—and the final consummation of political growth—the government of all mankind, by all mankind, and for all mankind.

Starting out with parental power in the family group, political sovereignty evolves by organization as families overlap into consanguineous clans which become united, for various reasons, into tribal units—superconsanguineous political groupings. And then, by trade, commerce, and conquest, tribes become unified as a nation, while nations themselves sometimes become unified by empire.

As sovereignty passes from smaller groups to larger groups, wars are lessened. That is, minor wars between smaller nations are lessened, but the potential for greater wars is increased as the nations wielding sovereignty become larger and larger. Presently, when all the world has been explored and occupied, when nations are few, strong, and powerful, when these great and supposedly sovereign nations come to touch borders, when only oceans separate them, then will the stage be set for major wars, world-wide conflicts. So-called sovereign nations cannot rub elbows without generating conflicts and eventuating wars.

The difficulty in the evolution of political sovereignty from the family to all mankind, lies in the inertia-resistance exhibited on all intervening levels. Families have, on occasion, defied their clan, while clans and tribes have often been subversive of the sovereignty of the territorial state. Each new and forward evolution of political sovereignty is (and has always been) embarrassed and hampered by the "scaffolding stages" of the previous developments in political organization. And this is true because human loyalties, once mobilized, are hard to change. The same loyalty which makes possible the evolution of the tribe, makes difficult the evolution of the supertribe—the territorial state. And the same loyalty (patriotism) which makes possible the evolution of the territorial state, vastly complicates the evolutionary development of the government of all mankind.

Political sovereignty is created out of the surrender of self-determinism, first by the individual within the family and then by the families and clans in relation to the tribe and larger groupings. This progressive transfer of self-determination from the smaller to ever larger political organizations has generally proceeded unabated in the East since the establishment of the Ming and the

Mogul dynasties. In the West it obtained for more than a thousand years right on down to the end of the World War, when an unfortunate retrograde movement temporarily reversed this normal trend by re-establishing the submerged political sovereignty of numerous small groups in Europe.

Urantia will not enjoy lasting peace until the so-called sovereign nations intelligently and fully surrender their sovereign powers into the hands of the brotherhood of men—mankind government. Internationalism—Leagues of Nations—can never bring permanent peace to mankind. World-wide confederations of nations will effectively prevent minor wars and acceptably control the smaller nations, but they will not prevent world wars nor control the three, four, or five most powerful governments. In the face of real conflicts, one of these world powers will withdraw from the League and declare war. You cannot prevent nations going to war as long as they remain infected with the delusional virus of national sovereignty. Internationalism is a step in the right direction. An international police force will prevent many minor wars, but it will not be effective in preventing major wars, conflicts between the great military governments of earth.

As the number of truly sovereign nations (great powers) decreases, so do both opportunity and need for mankind government increase. When there are only a few really sovereign (great) powers, either they must embark on the life and death struggle for national (imperial) supremacy, or else, by voluntary surrender of certain prerogatives of sovereignty, they must create the essential nucleus of supernational power which will serve as the beginning of the real sovereignty of all mankind.

Peace will not come to Urantia until every so-called sovereign nation surrenders its power to make war into the hands of a representative government of all mankind. Political sovereignty is innate with the peoples of the world. When all the peoples of Urantia create a world government, they have the right and the power to make such a government SOVEREIGN; and when such a representative or democratic world power controls the world's land, air, and naval forces, peace on earth and good will among men can prevail—but not until then.

To use an important nineteenth- and twentieth-century illustration: The forty-eight states of the American Federal Union have long enjoyed peace. They have no more wars among themselves. They have surrendered their sovereignty to the federal government, and through the arbitrament of war, they have abandoned all claims to the delusions of self-determination. While each state regulates its internal affairs, it is not concerned with foreign relations, tariffs, immigration, military affairs, or interstate commerce. Neither do the individual states concern themselves with matters of citizenship. The forty-eight states suffer the ravages of war only when the federal government's sovereignty is in some way jeopardized.

These forty-eight states, having abandoned the twin sophistries of sovereignty and self-determination, enjoy interstate peace and tranquillity. So will the nations of Urantia begin to enjoy peace when they freely surrender their respective sovereignties into the hands of a global government—the sovereignty of the brotherhood of men. In this world state the small nations will be as powerful as the great, even as the small state of Rhode Island has its two senators in the American Congress just the same as the populous state of New York or the large state of Texas.

The limited (state) sovereignty of these forty-eight states was created by men and for men. The superstate (national) sovereignty of the American Federal Union was created by the original thirteen of these states for their own benefit and for the benefit of men. Sometime the supernational sovereignty of the planetary government of mankind will be similarly created by nations for their own benefit and for the benefit of all men.

Citizens are not born for the benefit of governments; governments are organizations created and devised for the benefit of men. There can be no end to the evolution of political sovereignty short of the appearance of the government of the sovereignty of all men. All other sovereignties are relative in value, intermediate in meaning, and subordinate in status.

With scientific progress, wars are going to become more and more devastating until they become almost racially suicidal. How many world wars must be fought and how many leagues of nations must fail before men will be willing to establish the government of mankind and begin to enjoy the blessings of permanent peace and thrive on the tranquillity of good will—world-wide good will—among men?

6. LAW, LIBERTY, AND SOVEREIGNTY

If one man craves freedom—liberty—he must remember that *all* other men long for the same freedom. Groups of such liberty-loving mortals cannot live together in peace without becoming subservient to such laws, rules, and regulations as will grant each person the same degree of freedom while at the same time safeguarding an equal degree of freedom for all of his fellow mortals. If one man is to be absolutely free, then another must become an absolute slave. And the relative nature of freedom is true socially, economically, and politically. Freedom is the gift of civilization made possible by the enforcement of LAW.

Religion makes it spiritually possible to realize the brotherhood of men, but it will require mankind government to regulate the social, economic, and political problems associated with such a goal of human happiness and efficiency.

There shall be wars and rumors of wars—nation will rise against nation—just as long as the world's political sovereignty is divided up and unjustly held by a group of nation-states. England, Scotland, and Wales were always fighting each other until they gave up their respective sovereignties, reposing them in the United Kingdom.

Another world war will teach the so-called sovereign nations to form some sort of federation, thus creating the machinery for preventing small wars, wars between the lesser nations. But global wars will go on until the government of mankind is created. Global sovereignty will prevent global wars—nothing else can.

The forty-eight American free states live together in peace. There are among the citizens of these forty-eight states all of the various nationalities and races that live in the ever-warring nations of Europe. These Americans represent almost all the religions and religious sects and cults of the whole wide world, and yet here in North America they live together in peace. And all this is made possible because these forty-eight states have surrendered their sovereignty and have abandoned all notions of the supposed rights of self-determination.

It is not a question of armaments or disarmament. Neither does the question of conscription or voluntary military service enter into these problems of maintaining world-wide peace. If you take every form of modern mechanical armaments and all types of explosives away from strong nations, they will fight with fists, stones, and clubs as long as they cling to their delusions of the divine right of national sovereignty.

War is not man's great and terrible disease; war is a symptom, a result. The real disease is the virus of national sovereignty.

Urantia nations have not possessed real sovereignty; they never have had a sovereignty which could protect them from the ravages and devastations of world wars. In the creation of the global government of mankind, the nations are not giving up sovereignty so much as they are actually creating a real, bona fide, and lasting world sovereignty which will henceforth be fully able to protect them from all war. Local affairs will be handled by local governments; national affairs, by national governments; international affairs will be administered by global government.

World peace cannot be maintained by treaties, diplomacy, foreign policies, alliances, balances of power, or any other type of makeshift juggling with the sovereignties of nationalism. World law must come into being and must be enforced by world government—the sovereignty of all mankind.

The individual will enjoy far more liberty under world government. Today, the citizens of the great powers are taxed, regulated, and controlled almost oppressively, and much of this present interference with individual liberties will vanish when the national governments are willing to trustee their sovereignty as regards international affairs into the hands of global government.

Under global government the national groups will be afforded a real opportunity to realize and enjoy the personal liberties of genuine democracy. The fallacy of self-determination will be ended. With global regulation of money and trade will come the new era of world-wide peace. Soon may a global language evolve, and there will be at least some hope of sometime having a global religion—or religions with a global viewpoint.

Collective security will never afford peace until the collectivity includes all mankind.

The political sovereignty of representative mankind government will bring lasting peace on earth, and the spiritual brotherhood of man will forever insure good will among all men. And there is no other way whereby peace on earth and good will among men can be realized.

***

After the death of Cymboyton, his sons encountered great difficulties in maintaining a peaceful faculty. The repercussions of Jesus' teachings would have been much greater if the later Christian teachers who joined the Urmia faculty had exhibited more wisdom and exercised more tolerance.

Cymboyton's eldest son had appealed to Abner at Philadelphia for help, but Abner's choice of teachers was most unfortunate in that they turned out to be unyielding and uncompromising. These teachers sought to make their religion dominant over the other beliefs. They never suspected that the oft-referred-to lectures of the caravan conductor had been delivered by Jesus himself.

As confusion increased in the faculty, the three brothers withdrew their financial support, and after five years the school closed. Later it was reopened as a Mithraic temple and eventually burned down in connection with one of their orgiastic celebrations.

7. THE THIRTY-FIRST YEAR (A.D. 25)

When Jesus returned from the journey to the Caspian Sea, he knew that his world travels were about finished. He made only one more trip outside of Palestine, and that was into Syria. After a brief visit to Capernaum, he went to Nazareth, stopping over a few days to visit. In the middle of April he left Nazareth for Tyre. From there he journeyed on north, tarrying for a few days at Sidon, but his destination was Antioch.

This is the year of Jesus' solitary wanderings through Palestine and Syria. Throughout this year of travel he was known by various names in different parts of the country: the carpenter of Nazareth, the boatbuilder of Capernaum, the scribe of Damascus, and the teacher of Alexandria.

At Antioch the Son of Man lived for over two months, working, observing, studying, visiting, ministering, and all the while learning how man lives, how he thinks, feels, and reacts to the environment of human existence. For three weeks of this period he worked as a tentmaker. He remained longer in Antioch than at any other place he visited on this trip. Ten years later, when the Apostle Paul was preaching in Antioch and heard his followers speak of the doctrines of the *Damascus scribe,* he little knew that his pupils had heard the voice, and listened to the teachings, of the Master himself.

From Antioch Jesus journeyed south along the coast to Caesarea, where he tarried for a few weeks, continuing down the coast to Joppa. From Joppa he traveled inland to Jamnia, Ashdod, and Gaza. From Gaza he took the inland trail to Beersheba, where he remained for a week.

Jesus then started on his final tour, as a private individual, through the heart of Palestine, going from Beersheba in the south to Dan in the north. On this journey northward he stopped at Hebron, Bethlehem (where he saw his birthplace), Jerusalem (he did not visit Bethany), Beeroth, Lebonah, Sychar, Shechem, Samaria, Geba, En-Gannim, Endor, Madon; passing through Magdala and Capernaum, he journeyed on north; and passing east of the Waters of Merom, he went by Karahta to Dan, or Caesarea-Philippi.

The indwelling Thought Adjuster now led Jesus to forsake the dwelling places of men and betake himself up to Mount Hermon that he might finish his work of mastering his human mind and complete the task of effecting his full consecration to the remainder of his lifework on earth.

This was one of those unusual and extraordinary epochs in the Master's earth life on Urantia. Another and very similar one was the experience he passed through when alone in the hills near Pella just subsequent to his baptism. This period of isolation on Mount Hermon marked the termination of his purely human career, that is, the technical termination of the mortal bestowal, while the later isolation marked the beginning of the more divine phase of the bestowal. And Jesus lived alone with God for six weeks on the slopes of Mount Hermon.

8. THE SOJOURN ON MOUNT HERMON

After spending some time in the vicinity of Caesarea-Philippi, Jesus made ready his supplies, and securing a beast of burden and a lad named Tiglath, he proceeded along the Damascus road to a village sometime known as Beit Jenn in the foothills of Mount Hermon. Here, near the middle of August, A.D. 25, he established his headquarters, and leaving his supplies in the custody of Tiglath, he ascended the lonely slopes of the mountain. Tiglath accompanied Jesus this first day up the mountain to a designated point about 6,000 feet above sea level, where they built a stone container in which Tiglath was to deposit food twice a week.

The first day, after he had left Tiglath, Jesus had ascended the mountain only a short way when he paused to pray. Among other things he asked his Father to send back the guardian seraphim to "be with Tiglath." He requested that he be permitted to go up to his last struggle with the realities of mortal existence alone. And his request was granted. He went into the great test with only his indwelling Adjuster to guide and sustain him.

Jesus ate frugally while on the mountain; he abstained from all food only a day or two at a time. The superhuman beings who confronted him on this mountain, and with whom he wrestled in spirit, and whom he defeated in power, were *real;* they were his archenemies in the system of Satania; they were not phantasms of the imagination evolved out of the intellectual vagaries of a weakened and starving mortal who could not distinguish reality from the visions of a disordered mind.

Jesus spent the last three weeks of August and the first three weeks of September on Mount Hermon. During these weeks he finished the mortal task of achieving the circles of mind-understanding and personality-control. Throughout this period of communion with his heavenly Father the indwelling Adjuster also completed the assigned services. The mortal goal of this earth creature was there attained. Only the final phase of mind and Adjuster attunement remained to be consummated.

After more than five weeks of unbroken communion with his Paradise Father, Jesus became absolutely assured of his nature and of the certainty of his triumph over the material levels of time-space personality manifestation. He fully believed in, and did not hesitate to assert, the ascendancy of his divine nature over his human nature.

Near the end of the mountain sojourn Jesus asked his Father if he might be permitted to hold conference with his Satania enemies as the Son of Man, as Joshua ben Joseph. This request was granted. During the last week on Mount Hermon the great temptation, the universe trial, occurred. Satan (representing Lucifer) and the rebellious Planetary Prince, Caligastia, were present with Jesus and were made fully visible to him. And this "temptation," this final trial of human loyalty in the face of the misrepresentations of rebel personalities, had *not to do* with food, temple pinnacles, or presumptuous acts. It had not to do with the kingdoms of this world but with the sovereignty of a mighty and glorious universe. The symbolism of your records was intended for the backward ages of the world's childlike thought. And subsequent generations should understand what a great struggle the Son of Man passed through that eventful day on Mount Hermon.

To the many proposals and counterproposals of the emissaries of Lucifer, Jesus only made reply: "May the will of my Paradise Father prevail, and you, my rebellious son, may the Ancients of Days judge you divinely. I am your

Creator-father; I can hardly judge you justly, and my mercy you have already spurned. I commit you to the adjudication of the Judges of a greater universe."

To all the Lucifer-suggested compromises and makeshifts, to all such specious proposals about the incarnation bestowal, Jesus only made reply, "The will of my Father in Paradise be done." And when the trying ordeal was finished, the detached guardian seraphim returned to Jesus' side and ministered to him.

On an afternoon in late summer, amid the trees and in the silence of nature, Michael of Nebadon won the unquestioned sovereignty of his universe. On that day he completed the task set for Creator Sons to live to the full the incarnated life in the likeness of mortal flesh on the evolutionary worlds of time and space. The universe announcement of this momentous achievement was not made until the day of his baptism, months afterward, but it all really took place that day on the mountain. And when Jesus came down from his sojourn on Mount Hermon, the Lucifer rebellion in Satania and the Caligastia secession on Urantia were virtually settled. Jesus had paid the last price required of him to attain the sovereignty of his universe, which in itself regulates the status of all rebels and determines that all such future upheavals (if they ever occur) may be dealt with summarily and effectively. Accordingly, it may be seen that the so-called "great temptation" of Jesus took place sometime before his baptism and not just after that event.

At the end of this sojourn on the mountain, as Jesus was making his descent, he met Tiglath coming up to the rendezvous with food. Turning him back, he said only: "The period of rest is over; I must return to my Father's business." He was a silent and much changed man as they journeyed back to Dan, where he took leave of the lad, giving him the donkey. He then proceeded south by the same way he had come, to Capernaum.

9. THE TIME OF WAITING

It was now near the end of the summer, about the time of the day of atonement and the feast of tabernacles. Jesus had a family meeting in Capernaum over the Sabbath and the next day started for Jerusalem with John the son of Zebedee, going to the east of the lake and by Gerasa and on down the Jordan valley. While he visited some with his companion on the way, John noted a great change in Jesus.

Jesus and John stopped overnight at Bethany with Lazarus and his sisters, going early the next morning to Jerusalem. They spent almost three weeks in and around the city, at least John did. Many days John went into Jerusalem alone while Jesus walked about over the near-by hills and engaged in many seasons of spiritual communion with his Father in heaven.

Both of them were present at the solemn services of the day of atonement. John was much impressed by the ceremonies of this day of all days in the Jewish religious ritual, but Jesus remained a thoughtful and silent spectator. To the Son of Man this performance was pitiful and pathetic. He viewed it all as misrepresentative of the character and attributes of his Father in heaven. He looked upon the doings of this day as a travesty upon the facts of divine justice and the truths of infinite mercy. He burned to give vent to the declaration of the real truth about his Father's loving character and merciful conduct in the universe, but his faithful Monitor admonished him that his hour had not yet come. But that night, at

Bethany, Jesus did drop numerous remarks which greatly disturbed John; and John never fully understood the real significance of what Jesus said in their hearing that evening.

Jesus planned to remain throughout the week of the feast of tabernacles with John. This feast was the annual holiday of all Palestine; it was the Jewish vacation time. Although Jesus did not participate in the merriment of the occasion, it was evident that he derived pleasure and experienced satisfaction as he beheld the lighthearted and joyous abandon of the young and the old.

In the midst of the week of celebration and ere the festivities were finished, Jesus took leave of John, saying that he desired to retire to the hills where he might the better commune with his Paradise Father. John would have gone with him, but Jesus insisted that he stay through the festivities, saying: "It is not required of you to bear the burden of the Son of Man; only the watchman must keep vigil while the city sleeps in peace." Jesus did not return to Jerusalem. After almost a week alone in the hills near Bethany, he departed for Capernaum. On the way home he spent a day and a night alone on the slopes of Gilboa, near where King Saul had taken his life; and when he arrived at Capernaum, he seemed more cheerful than when he had left John in Jerusalem.

The next morning Jesus went to the chest containing his personal effects, which had remained in Zebedee's workshop, put on his apron, and presented himself for work, saying, "It behooves me to keep busy while I wait for my hour to come." And he worked several months, until January of the following year, in the boatshop, by the side of his brother James. After this period of working with Jesus, no matter what doubts came up to becloud James's understanding of the lifework of the Son of Man, he never again really and wholly gave up his faith in the mission of Jesus.

During this final period of Jesus' work at the boatshop, he spent most of his time on the interior finishing of some of the larger craft. He took great pains with all his handiwork and seemed to experience the satisfaction of human achievement when he had completed a commendable piece of work. Though he wasted little time upon trifles, he was a painstaking workman when it came to the essentials of any given undertaking.

As time passed, rumors came to Capernaum of one John who was preaching while baptizing penitents in the Jordan, and John preached: "The kingdom of heaven is at hand; repent and be baptized." Jesus listened to these reports as John slowly worked his way up the Jordan valley from the ford of the river nearest to Jerusalem. But Jesus worked on, making boats, until John had journeyed up the river to a point near Pella in the month of January of the next year, A.D. 26, when he laid down his tools, declaring, "My hour has come," and presently presented himself to John for baptism.

But a great change had been coming over Jesus. Few of the people who had enjoyed his visits and ministrations as he had gone up and down in the land ever subsequently recognized in the public teacher the same person they had known and loved as a private individual in former years. And there was a reason for this failure of his early beneficiaries to recognize him in his later role of public and authoritative teacher. For long years this transformation of mind and spirit had been in progress, and it was finished during the eventful sojourn on Mount Hermon.

PAPER 135

JOHN THE BAPTIST

JOHN the Baptist was born March 25, 7 B.C., in accordance with the promise that Gabriel made to Elizabeth in June of the previous year. For five months Elizabeth kept secret Gabriel's visitation; and when she told her husband, Zacharias, he was greatly troubled and fully believed her narrative only after he had an unusual dream about six weeks before the birth of John. Excepting the visit of Gabriel to Elizabeth and the dream of Zacharias, there was nothing unusual or supernatural connected with the birth of John the Baptist.

On the eighth day John was circumcised according to the Jewish custom. He grew up as an ordinary child, day by day and year by year, in the small village known in those days as the City of Judah, about four miles west of Jerusalem.

The most eventful occurrence in John's early childhood was the visit, in company with his parents, to Jesus and the Nazareth family. This visit occurred in the month of June, 1 B.C., when he was a little over six years of age.

After their return from Nazareth John's parents began the systematic education of the lad. There was no synagogue school in this little village; however, as he was a priest, Zacharias was fairly well educated, and Elizabeth was far better educated than the average Judean woman; she was also of the priesthood, being a descendant of the "daughters of Aaron." Since John was an only child, they spent a great deal of time on his mental and spiritual training. Zacharias had only short periods of service at the temple in Jerusalem so that he devoted much of his time to teaching his son.

Zacharias and Elizabeth had a small farm on which they raised sheep. They hardly made a living on this land, but Zacharias received a regular allowance from the temple funds dedicated to the priesthood.

1. JOHN BECOMES A NAZARITE

John had no school from which to graduate at the age of fourteen, but his parents had selected this as the appropriate year for him to take the formal Nazarite vow. Accordingly, Zacharias and Elizabeth took their son to Engedi, down by the Dead Sea. This was the southern headquarters of the Nazarite brotherhood, and there the lad was duly and solemnly inducted into this order for life. After these ceremonies and the making of the vows to abstain from all intoxicating drinks, to let the hair grow, and to refrain from touching the dead, the family proceeded to Jerusalem, where, before the temple, John completed the making of the offerings which were required of those taking Nazarite vows.

John took the same life vows that had been administered to his illustrious predecessors, Samson and the prophet Samuel. A life Nazarite was looked upon as a sanctified and holy personality. The Jews regarded a Nazarite with almost the respect and veneration accorded the high priest, and this was not strange since

Nazarites of lifelong consecration were the only persons, except high priests, who were ever permitted to enter the holy of holies in the temple.

John returned home from Jerusalem to tend his father's sheep and grew up to be a strong man with a noble character.

When sixteen years old, John, as a result of reading about Elijah, became greatly impressed with the prophet of Mount Carmel and decided to adopt his style of dress. From that day on John always wore a hairy garment with a leather girdle. At sixteen he was more than six feet tall and almost full grown. With his flowing hair and peculiar mode of dress he was indeed a picturesque youth. And his parents expected great things of this their only son, a child of promise and a Nazarite for life.

2. THE DEATH OF ZACHARIAS

After an illness of several months Zacharias died in July, A.D. 12, when John was just past eighteen years of age. This was a time of great embarrassment to John since the Nazarite vow forbade contact with the dead, even in one's own family. Although John had endeavored to comply with the restrictions of his vow regarding contamination by the dead, he doubted that he had been wholly obedient to the requirements of the Nazarite order; therefore, after his father's burial he went to Jerusalem, where, in the Nazarite corner of the women's court, he offered the sacrifices required for his cleansing.

In September of this year Elizabeth and John made a journey to Nazareth to visit Mary and Jesus. John had just about made up his mind to launch out in his lifework, but he was admonished, not only by Jesus' words but also by his example, to return home, take care of his mother, and await the "coming of the Father's hour." After bidding Jesus and Mary good-bye at the end of this enjoyable visit, John did not again see Jesus until the event of his baptism in the Jordan.

John and Elizabeth returned to their home and began to lay plans for the future. Since John refused to accept the priest's allowance due him from the temple funds, by the end of two years they had all but lost their home; so they decided to go south with the sheep herd. Accordingly, the summer that John was twenty years of age witnessed their removal to Hebron. In the so-called "wilderness of Judea" John tended his sheep along a brook that was tributary to a larger stream which entered the Dead Sea at Engedi. The Engedi colony included not only Nazarites of lifelong and time-period consecration but numerous other ascetic herdsmen who congregated in this region with their herds and fraternized with the Nazarite brotherhood. They supported themselves by sheep raising and from gifts which wealthy Jews made to the order.

As time passed, John returned less often to Hebron, while he made more frequent visits to Engedi. He was so entirely different from the majority of the Nazarites that he found it very difficult fully to fraternize with the brotherhood. But he was very fond of Abner, the acknowledged leader and head of the Engedi colony.

3. THE LIFE OF A SHEPHERD

Along the valley of this little brook John built no less than a dozen stone shelters and night corrals, consisting of piled-up stones, wherein he could watch over and safeguard his herds of sheep and goats. John's life as a shepherd afforded him a great deal of time for thought. He talked much with Ezda, an orphan lad of Beth-zur, whom he had in a way adopted, and who cared for the herds when he made trips to Hebron to see his mother and to sell sheep, as well as when he went down to Engedi for Sabbath services. John and the lad lived very simply, subsisting on mutton, goat's milk, wild honey, and the edible locusts of that region. This, their regular diet, was supplemented by provisions brought from Hebron and Engedi from time to time.

Elizabeth kept John posted about Palestinian and world affairs, and his conviction grew deeper and deeper that the time was fast approaching when the old order was to end; that he was to become the herald of the approach of a new age, "the kingdom of heaven." This rugged shepherd was very partial to the writings of the Prophet Daniel. He read a thousand times Daniel's description of the great image, which Zacharias had told him represented the history of the great kingdoms of the world, beginning with Babylon, then Persia, Greece, and finally Rome. John perceived that already was Rome composed of such polyglot peoples and races that it could never become a strongly cemented and firmly consolidated empire. He believed that Rome was even then divided, as Syria, Egypt, Palestine, and other provinces; and then he further read "in the days of these kings shall the God of heaven set up a kingdom which shall never be destroyed. And this kingdom shall not be left to other people but shall break in pieces and consume all these kingdoms, and it shall stand forever." "And there was given him dominion and glory and a kingdom that all peoples, nations, and languages should serve him. His dominion is an everlasting dominion, which shall not pass away, and his kingdom never shall be destroyed." "And the kingdom and dominion and the greatness of the kingdom under the whole heaven shall be given to the people of the saints of the Most High, whose kingdom is an everlasting kingdom, and all dominions shall serve and obey him."

John was never able completely to rise above the confusion produced by what he had heard from his parents concerning Jesus and by these passages which he read in the Scriptures. In Daniel he read: "I saw in the night visions, and, behold, one like the Son of Man came with the clouds of heaven, and there was given him dominion and glory and a kingdom." But these words of the prophet did not harmonize with what his parents had taught him. Neither did his talk with Jesus, at the time of his visit when he was eighteen years old, correspond with these statements of the Scriptures. Notwithstanding this confusion, throughout all of his perplexity his mother assured him that his distant cousin, Jesus of Nazareth, was the true Messiah, that he had come to sit on the throne of David, and that he (John) was to become his advance herald and chief support.

From all John heard of the vice and wickedness of Rome and the dissoluteness and moral barrenness of the empire, from what he knew of the evil doings of Herod Antipas and the governors of Judea, he was minded to believe that the end of the age was impending. It seemed to this rugged and noble child of nature that the world was ripe for the end of the age of man and the dawn of the new and divine age—the kingdom of heaven. The feeling grew in John's heart that he was to be the last of the old prophets and the first of the new. And he fairly vibrated with the mounting impulse to go forth and proclaim to all men: "Repent! Get right with God! Get ready for the end; prepare yourselves for the appearance of the new and eternal order of earth affairs, the kingdom of heaven."

4. THE DEATH OF ELIZABETH

On August 17, A.D. 22, when John was twenty-eight years of age, his mother suddenly passed away. Elizabeth's friends, knowing of the Nazarite restrictions regarding contact with the dead, even in one's own family, made all arrangements for the burial of Elizabeth before sending for John. When he received word of the death of his mother, he directed Ezda to drive his herds to Engedi and started for Hebron.

On returning to Engedi from his mother's funeral, he presented his flocks to the brotherhood and for a season detached himself from the outside world while he fasted and prayed. John knew only of the old methods of approach to divinity; he knew only of the records of such as Elijah, Samuel, and Daniel. Elijah was his ideal of a prophet. Elijah was the first of the teachers of Israel to be regarded as a prophet, and John truly believed that he was to be the last of this long and illustrious line of the messengers of heaven.

For two and a half years John lived at Engedi, and he persuaded most of the brotherhood that "the end of the age was at hand"; that "the kingdom of heaven was about to appear." And all his early teaching was based upon the current Jewish idea and concept of the Messiah as the promised deliverer of the Jewish nation from the domination of their gentile rulers.

Throughout this period John read much in the sacred writings which he found at the Engedi home of the Nazarites. He was especially impressed by Isaiah and by Malachi, the last of the prophets up to that time. He read and reread the last five chapters of Isaiah, and he believed these prophecies. Then he would read in Malachi: "Behold, I will send you Elijah the prophet before the coming of the great and dreadful day of the Lord; and he shall turn the hearts of the fathers toward the children and the hearts of the children toward their fathers, lest I come and smite the earth with a curse." And it was only this promise of Malachi that Elijah would return that deterred John from going forth to preach about the coming kingdom and to exhort his fellow Jews to flee from the wrath to come. John was ripe for the proclamation of the message of the coming kingdom, but this expectation of the coming of Elijah held him back for more than two years. He knew he was not Elijah. What did Malachi mean? Was the prophecy literal or figurative? How could he know the truth? He finally dared to think that, since the first of the prophets was called Elijah, so the last should be known, eventually, by the same name. Nevertheless, he had doubts, doubts sufficient to prevent his ever calling himself Elijah.

It was the influence of Elijah that caused John to adopt his methods of direct and blunt assault upon the sins and vices of his contemporaries. He sought to dress like Elijah, and he endeavored to talk like Elijah; in every outward aspect he was like the olden prophet. He was just such a stalwart and picturesque child of nature, just such a fearless and daring preacher of righteousness. John was not illiterate, he did well know the Jewish sacred writings, but he was hardly cultured. He was a clear thinker, a powerful speaker, and a fiery denunciator. He was hardly an example to his age, but he was an eloquent rebuke.

At last he thought out the method of proclaiming the new age, the kingdom of God; he settled that he was to become the herald of the Messiah; he swept aside all doubts and departed from Engedi one day in March of A.D. 25 to begin his short but brilliant career as a public preacher.

5. THE KINGDOM OF GOD

In order to understand John's message, account should be taken of the status of the Jewish people at the time he appeared upon the stage of action. For almost one hundred years all Israel had been in a quandary; they were at a loss to explain their continuous subjugation to gentile overlords. Had not Moses taught that righteousness was always rewarded with prosperity and power? Were they not God's chosen people? Why was the throne of David desolate and vacant? In the light of the Mosaic doctrines and the precepts of the prophets the Jews found it difficult to explain their long-continued national desolation.

About one hundred years before the days of Jesus and John a new school of religious teachers arose in Palestine, the apocalyptists. These new teachers evolved a system of belief that accounted for the sufferings and humiliation of the Jews on the ground that they were paying the penalty for the nation's sins. They fell back onto the well-known reasons assigned to explain the Babylonian and other captivities of former times. But, so taught the apocalyptists, Israel should take heart; the days of their affliction were almost over; the discipline of God's chosen people was about finished; God's patience with the gentile foreigners was about exhausted. The end of Roman rule was synonymous with the end of the age and, in a certain sense, with the end of the world. These new teachers leaned heavily on the predictions of Daniel, and they consistently taught that creation was about to pass into its final stage; the kingdoms of this world were about to become the kingdom of God. To the Jewish mind of that day this was the meaning of that phrase—the kingdom of heaven—which runs throughout the teachings of both John and Jesus. To the Jews of Palestine the phrase "kingdom of heaven" had but one meaning: an absolutely righteous state in which God (the Messiah) would rule the nations of earth in perfection of power just as he ruled in heaven—"Your will be done on earth as in heaven."

In the days of John all Jews were expectantly asking, "How soon will the kingdom come?" There was a general feeling that the end of the rule of the gentile nations was drawing near. There was present throughout all Jewry a lively hope and a keen expectation that the consummation of the desire of the ages would occur during the lifetime of that generation.

While the Jews differed greatly in their estimates of the nature of the coming kingdom, they were alike in their belief that the event was impending, near at hand, even at the door. Many who read the Old Testament literally looked expectantly for a new king in Palestine, for a regenerated Jewish nation delivered from its enemies and presided over by the successor of King David, the Messiah who would quickly be acknowledged as the rightful and righteous ruler of all the world. Another, though smaller, group of devout Jews held a vastly different view of this kingdom of God. They taught that the coming kingdom was not of this world, that the world was approaching its certain end, and that "a new heaven and a new earth" were to usher in the establishment of the kingdom of God; that this kingdom was to be an everlasting dominion, that sin was to be ended, and that the citizens of the new kingdom were to become immortal in their enjoyment of this endless bliss.

All were agreed that some drastic purging or purifying discipline would of necessity precede the establishment of the new kingdom on earth. The literalists taught that a world-wide war would ensue which would destroy all unbelievers, while the faithful would sweep on to universal and eternal victory. The spiritists taught that the kingdom would be ushered in by the great judgment of God which would relegate the unrighteous to their well-deserved judgment of punishment and final destruction, at the same time elevating the believing saints of the chosen people to high seats of honor and authority with the Son of Man, who would rule over the redeemed nations in God's name. And this latter group even believed that many devout gentiles might be admitted to the fellowship of the new kingdom.

Some of the Jews held to the opinion that God might possibly establish this new kingdom by direct and divine intervention, but the vast majority believed that he would interpose some representative intermediary, the Messiah. And that was the only possible meaning the term Messiah could have had in the minds of the Jews of the generation of John and Jesus. *Messiah* could not possibly refer to one who merely taught God's will or proclaimed the necessity for righteous living. To all such holy persons the Jews gave the title of *prophet.* The Messiah was to be more than a prophet; the Messiah was to bring in the establishment of the new kingdom, the kingdom of God. No one who failed to do this could be the Messiah in the traditional Jewish sense.

Who would this Messiah be? Again the Jewish teachers differed. The older ones clung to the doctrine of the son of David. The newer taught that, since the new kingdom was a heavenly kingdom, the new ruler might also be a divine personality, one who had long sat at God's right hand in heaven. And strange as it may appear, those who thus conceived of the ruler of the new kingdom looked upon him not as a human Messiah, not as a mere *man,* but as "the Son of Man" —a Son of God—a heavenly Prince, long held in waiting thus to assume the rulership of the earth made new. Such was the religious background of the Jewish world when John went forth proclaiming: "Repent, for the kingdom of heaven is at hand!"

It becomes apparent, therefore, that John's announcement of the coming kingdom had not less than half a dozen different meanings in the minds of those who listened to his impassioned preaching. But no matter what significance they attached to the phrases which John employed, each of these various groups of Jewish-kingdom expectants was intrigued by the proclamations of this sincere, enthusiastic, rough-and-ready preacher of righteousness and repentance, who so solemnly exhorted his hearers to "flee from the wrath to come."

6. JOHN BEGINS TO PREACH

Early in the month of March, A.D. 25, John journeyed around the western coast of the Dead Sea and up the river Jordan to opposite Jericho, the ancient ford over which Joshua and the children of Israel passed when they first entered the promised land; and crossing over to the other side of the river, he established himself near the entrance to the ford and began to preach to the people who passed by on their way back and forth across the river. This was the most frequented of all the Jordan crossings.

It was apparent to all who heard John that he was more than a preacher. The great majority of those who listened to this strange man who had come up from the Judean wilderness went away believing that they had heard the voice of a prophet. No wonder the souls of these weary and expectant Jews were deeply stirred by such a phenomenon. Never in all Jewish history had the devout children of Abraham so longed for the "consolation of Israel" or more ardently anticipated "the restoration of the kingdom." Never in all Jewish history could John's message, "the kingdom of heaven is at hand," have made such a deep and universal appeal as at the very time he so mysteriously appeared on the bank of this southern crossing of the Jordan.

He came from the herdsmen, like Amos. He was dressed like Elijah of old, and he thundered his admonitions and poured forth his warnings in the "spirit and power of Elijah." It is not surprising that this strange preacher created a mighty stir throughout all Palestine as the travelers carried abroad the news of his preaching along the Jordan.

There was still another and a *new* feature about the work of this Nazarite preacher: He baptized every one of his believers in the Jordan "for the remission of sins." Although baptism was not a new ceremony among the Jews, they had never seen it employed as John now made use of it. It had long been the practice thus to baptize the gentile proselytes into the fellowship of the outer court of the temple, but never had the Jews themselves been asked to submit to the baptism of repentance. Only fifteen months intervened between the time John began to preach and baptize and his arrest and imprisonment at the instigation of Herod Antipas, but in this short time he baptized considerably over one hundred thousand penitents.

John preached four months at Bethany ford before starting north up the Jordan. Tens of thousands of listeners, some curious but many earnest and serious, came to hear him from all parts of Judea, Perea, and Samaria. Even a few came from Galilee.

In May of this year, while he still lingered at Bethany ford, the priests and Levites sent a delegation out to inquire of John whether he claimed to be the Messiah, and by whose authority he preached. John answered these questioners by saying: "Go tell your masters that you have heard 'the voice of one crying in the wilderness,' as spoken by the prophet, saying, 'make ready the way of the Lord, make straight a highway for our God. Every valley shall be filled, and every mountain and hill shall be brought low; the uneven ground shall become a plain, while the rough places shall become a smooth valley; and all flesh shall see the salvation of God.'"

John was a heroic but tactless preacher. One day when he was preaching and baptizing on the west bank of the Jordan, a group of Pharisees and a number of Sadducees came forward and presented themselves for baptism. Before leading them down into the water, John, addressing them as a group said: "Who warned you to flee, as vipers before the fire, from the wrath to come? I will baptize you, but I warn you to bring forth fruit worthy of sincere repentance if you would receive the remission of your sins. Tell me not that Abraham is your father. I declare that God is able of these twelve stones here before you to raise up worthy children for Abraham. And even now is the ax laid to the very roots of the trees. Every tree that brings not forth good fruit is destined to be cut down and cast into the fire." (The twelve stones to which he referred were the reputed memorial stones set up by Joshua to commemorate the crossing of the "twelve tribes" at this very point when they first entered the promised land.)

John conducted classes for his disciples, in the course of which he instructed them in the details of their new life and endeavored to answer their many questions. He counseled the teachers to instruct in the spirit as well as the letter of the law. He instructed the rich to feed the poor; to the tax gatherers he said:

"Extort no more than that which is assigned you." To the soldiers he said: "Do no violence and exact nothing wrongfully—be content with your wages." While he counseled all: "Make ready for the end of the age—the kingdom of heaven is at hand."

7. JOHN JOURNEYS NORTH

John still had confused ideas about the coming kingdom and its king. The longer he preached the more confused he became, but never did this intellectual uncertainty concerning the nature of the coming kingdom in the least lessen his conviction of the certainty of the kingdom's immediate appearance. In mind John might be confused, but in spirit never. He was in no doubt about the coming kingdom, but he was far from certain as to whether or not Jesus was to be the ruler of that kingdom. As long as John held to the idea of the restoration of the throne of David, the teachings of his parents that Jesus, born in the City of David, was to be the long-expected deliverer, seemed consistent; but at those times when he leaned more toward the doctrine of a spiritual kingdom and the end of the temporal age on earth, he was sorely in doubt as to the part Jesus would play in such events. Sometimes he questioned everything, but not for long. He really wished he might talk it all over with his cousin, but that was contrary to their expressed agreement.

As John journeyed north, he thought much about Jesus. He paused at more than a dozen places as he traveled up the Jordan. It was at Adam that he first made reference to "another one who is to come after me" in answer to the direct question which his disciples asked him, "Are you the Messiah?" And he went on to say: "There will come after me one who is greater than I, whose sandal straps I am not worthy to stoop down and unloose. I baptize you with water, but he will baptize you with the Holy Spirit. And his shovel is in his hand thoroughly to cleanse his threshing floor; he will gather the wheat into his garner, but the chaff will he burn up with the judgment fire."

In response to the questions of his disciples John continued to expand his teachings, from day to day adding more that was helpful and comforting compared with his early and cryptic message: "Repent and be baptized." By this time throngs were arriving from Galilee and the Decapolis. Scores of earnest believers lingered with their adored teacher day after day.

8. MEETING OF JESUS AND JOHN

By December of A.D. 25, when John reached the neighborhood of Pella in his journey up the Jordan, his fame had extended throughout all Palestine, and his work had become the chief topic of conversation in all the towns about the lake of Galilee. Jesus had spoken favorably of John's message, and this had caused many from Capernaum to join John's cult of repentance and baptism. James and John the fishermen sons of Zebedee had gone down in December, soon after John took up his preaching position near Pella, and had offered themselves for baptism. They went to see John once a week and brought back to Jesus fresh, firsthand reports of the evangelist's work.

Jesus' brothers James and Jude had talked about going down to John for baptism; and now that Jude had come over to Capernaum for the Sabbath services, both he and James, after listening to Jesus' discourse in the synagogue, decided to take counsel with him concerning their plans. This was on Saturday night, January 12, A.D. 26. Jesus requested that they postpone the discussion until the following day, when he would give them his answer. He slept very little that night, being in close communion with the Father in heaven. He had arranged to have noontime lunch with his brothers and to advise them concerning baptism by John. That Sunday morning Jesus was working as usual in the boatshop. James and Jude had arrived with the lunch and were waiting in the lumber room for him, as it was not yet time for the midday recess, and they knew that Jesus was very regular about such matters.

Just before the noon rest, Jesus laid down his tools, removed his work apron, and merely announced to the three workmen in the room with him, "My hour has come." He went out to his brothers James and Jude, repeating, "My hour has come—let us go to John." And they started immediately for Pella, eating their lunch as they journeyed. This was on Sunday, January 13. They tarried for the night in the Jordan valley and arrived on the scene of John's baptizing about noon of the next day.

John had just begun baptizing the candidates for the day. Scores of repentants were standing in line awaiting their turn when Jesus and his two brothers took up their positions in this line of earnest men and women who had become believers in John's preaching of the coming kingdom. John had been inquiring about Jesus of Zebedee's sons. He had heard of Jesus' remarks concerning his preaching, and he was day by day expecting to see him arrive on the scene, but he had not expected to greet him in the line of baptismal candidates.

Being engrossed with the details of rapidly baptizing such a large number of converts, John did not look up to see Jesus until the Son of Man stood in his immediate presence. When John recognized Jesus, the ceremonies were halted for a moment while he greeted his cousin in the flesh and asked, "But why do you come down into the water to greet me?" And Jesus answered, "To be subject to your baptism." John replied: "But I have need to be baptized by you. Why do you come to me?" And Jesus whispered to John: "Bear with me now, for it becomes us to set this example for my brothers standing here with me, and that the people may know that my hour has come."

There was a tone of finality and authority in Jesus' voice. John was atremble with emotion as he made ready to baptize Jesus of Nazareth in the Jordan at noon on Monday, January 14, A.D. 26. Thus did John baptize Jesus and his two brothers James and Jude. And when John had baptized these three, he dismissed the others for the day, announcing that he would resume baptisms at noon the next day. As the people were departing, the four men still standing in the water heard a strange sound, and presently there appeared for a moment an apparition immediately over the head of Jesus, and they heard a voice saying, "This is my beloved Son in whom I am well pleased." A great change came over the countenance of Jesus, and coming up out of the water in silence he took leave of them, going toward the hills to the east. And no man saw Jesus again for forty days.

John followed Jesus a sufficient distance to tell him the story of Gabriel's visit to his mother ere either had been born, as he had heard it so many times from his mother's lips. He allowed Jesus to continue on his way after he had said, "Now I know of a certainty that you are the Deliverer." But Jesus made no reply.

9. FORTY DAYS OF PREACHING

When John returned to his disciples (he now had some twenty-five or thirty who abode with him constantly), he found them in earnest conference, discussing what had just happened in connection with Jesus' baptism. They were all the more astonished when John now made known to them the story of the Gabriel visitation to Mary before Jesus was born, and also that Jesus spoke no word to him even after he had told him about this. There was no rain that evening, and this group of thirty or more talked long into the starlit night. They wondered where Jesus had gone, and when they would see him again.

After the experience of this day the preaching of John took on new and certain notes of proclamation concerning the coming kingdom and the expected Messiah. It was a tense time, these forty days of tarrying, waiting for the return of Jesus. But John continued to preach with great power, and his disciples began at about this time to preach to the overflowing throngs which gathered around John at the Jordan.

In the course of these forty days of waiting, many rumors spread about the countryside and even to Tiberias and Jerusalem. Thousands came over to see the new attraction in John's camp, the reputed Messiah, but Jesus was not to be seen. When the disciples of John asserted that the strange man of God had gone to the hills, many doubted the entire story.

About three weeks after Jesus had left them, there arrived on the scene at Pella a new deputation from the priests and Pharisees at Jerusalem. They asked John directly if he was Elijah or the prophet that Moses promised; and when John said, "I am not," they made bold to ask, "Are you the Messiah?" and John answered, "I am not." Then said these men from Jerusalem: "If you are not Elijah, nor the prophet, nor the Messiah, then why do you baptize the people and create all this stir?" And John replied: "It should be for those who have heard me and received my baptism to say who I am, but I declare to you that, while I baptize with water, there has been among us one who will return to baptize you with the Holy Spirit."

These forty days were a difficult period for John and his disciples. What was to be the relation of John to Jesus? A hundred questions came up for discussion. Politics and selfish preferment began to make their appearance. Intense discussions grew up around the various ideas and concepts of the Messiah. Would he become a military leader and a Davidic king? Would he smite the Roman armies as Joshua had the Canaanites? Or would he come to establish a spiritual kingdom? John rather decided, with the minority, that Jesus had come to establish the kingdom of heaven, although he was not altogether clear in his own mind as to just what was to be embraced within this mission of the establishment of the kingdom of heaven.

These were strenuous days in John's experience, and he prayed for the return of Jesus. Some of John's disciples organized scouting parties to go in search of Jesus, but John forbade, saying: "Our times are in the hands of the God of heaven; he will direct his chosen Son."

It was early on the morning of Sabbath, February 23, that the company of John, engaged in eating their morning meal, looked up toward the north and beheld Jesus coming to them. As he approached them, John stood upon a large rock and, lifting up his sonorous voice, said: "Behold the Son of God, the deliverer of the world! This is he of whom I have said, 'After me there will come one who is preferred before me because he was before me.' For this cause came I out of the wilderness to preach repentance and to baptize with water, proclaiming that the kingdom of heaven is at hand. And now comes one who shall baptize you with the Holy Spirit. And I beheld the divine spirit descending upon this man, and I heard the voice of God declare, 'This is my beloved Son in whom I am well pleased.'"

Jesus bade them return to their food while he sat down to eat with John, his brothers James and Jude having returned to Capernaum.

Early in the morning of the next day he took leave of John and his disciples, going back to Galilee. He gave them no word as to when they would again see him. To John's inquiries about his own preaching and mission Jesus only said, "My Father will guide you now and in the future as he has in the past." And these two great men separated that morning on the banks of the Jordan, never again to greet each other in the flesh.

10. JOHN JOURNEYS SOUTH

Since Jesus had gone north into Galilee, John felt led to retrace his steps southward. Accordingly, on Sunday morning, March 3, John and the remainder of his disciples began their journey south. About one quarter of John's immediate followers had meantime departed for Galilee in quest of Jesus. There was a sadness of confusion about John. He never again preached as he had before baptizing Jesus. He somehow felt that the responsibility of the coming kingdom was no longer on his shoulders. He felt that his work was almost finished; he was disconsolate and lonely. But he preached, baptized, and journeyed on southward.

Near the village of Adam, John tarried for several weeks, and it was here that he made the memorable attack upon Herod Antipas for unlawfully taking the wife of another man. By June of this year (A.D. 26) John was back at the Bethany ford of the Jordan, where he had begun his preaching of the coming kingdom more than a year previously. In the weeks following the baptism of Jesus the character of John's preaching gradually changed into a proclamation of mercy for the common people, while he denounced with renewed vehemence the corrupt political and religious rulers.

Herod Antipas, in whose territory John had been preaching, became alarmed lest he and his disciples should start a rebellion. Herod also resented John's public criticisms of his domestic affairs. In view of all this, Herod decided to put John in prison. Accordingly, very early in the morning of June 12, before the multitude arrived to hear the preaching and witness the baptizing, the agents of Herod placed John under arrest. As weeks passed and he was not released, his disciples scattered over all Palestine, many of them going into Galilee to join the followers of Jesus.

11. JOHN IN PRISON

John had a lonely and somewhat bitter experience in prison. Few of his followers were permitted to see him. He longed to see Jesus but had to be content with hearing of his work through those of his followers who had become believers in the Son of Man. He was often tempted to doubt Jesus and his divine mission. If Jesus were the Messiah, why did he do nothing to deliver him from this unbearable imprisonment? For more than a year and a half this rugged man of God's outdoors languished in that despicable prison. And this experience was a great test of his faith in, and loyalty to, Jesus. Indeed, this whole experience was a great test of John's faith even in God. Many times was he tempted to doubt even the genuineness of his own mission and experience.

After he had been in prison several months, a group of his disciples came to him and, after reporting concerning the public activities of Jesus, said: "So you see, Teacher, that he who was with you at the upper Jordan prospers and receives all who come to him. He even feasts with publicans and sinners. You bore courageous witness to him, and yet he does nothing to effect your deliverance." But John answered his friends: "This man can do nothing unless it has been given him by his Father in heaven. You well remember that I said, 'I am not the Messiah, but I am one sent on before to prepare the way for him.' And that I did. He who has the bride is the bridegroom, but the friend of the bridegroom who stands near by and hears him rejoices greatly because of the bridegroom's voice. This, my joy, therefore is fulfilled. He must increase but I must decrease. I am of this earth and have declared my message. Jesus of Nazareth comes down to the earth from heaven and is above us all. The Son of Man has descended from God, and the words of God he will declare to you. For the Father in heaven gives not the spirit by measure to his own Son. The Father loves his Son and will presently put all things in the hands of this Son. He who believes in the Son has eternal life. And these words which I speak are true and abiding."

These disciples were amazed at John's pronouncement, so much so that they departed in silence. John was also much agitated, for he perceived that he had uttered a prophecy. Never again did he wholly doubt the mission and divinity of Jesus. But it was a sore disappointment to John that Jesus sent him no word, that he came not to see him, and that he exercised none of his great power to deliver him from prison. But Jesus knew all about this. He had great love for John, but being now cognizant of his divine nature and knowing fully the great things in preparation for John when he departed from this world and also knowing that John's work on earth was finished, he constrained himself not to interfere in the natural outworking of the great preacher-prophet's career.

This long suspense in prison was humanly unbearable. Just a few days before his death John again sent trusted messengers to Jesus, inquiring: "Is my work done? Why do I languish in prison? Are you truly the Messiah, or shall we look for another?" And when these two disciples gave this message to Jesus, the Son of Man replied: "Go back to John and tell him that I have not forgotten but to suffer me also this, for it becomes us to fulfill all righteousness. Tell John what you have seen and heard—that the poor have good tidings preached to them—and, finally, tell the beloved herald of my earth mission that he shall be abundantly blessed in the age to come if he finds no occasion to doubt and stumble over me." And this was the last word John received from Jesus. This message greatly comforted him and did much to stabilize his faith and prepare him for the tragic end of his life in the flesh which followed so soon upon the heels of this memorable occasion.

12. DEATH OF JOHN THE BAPTIST

As John was working in southern Perea when arrested, he was taken immediately to the prison of the fortress of Machaerus, where he was incarcerated until his execution. Herod ruled over Perea as well as Galilee, and he maintained residence at this time at both Julias and Machaerus in Perea. In Galilee the official residence had been moved from Sepphoris to the new capital at Tiberias.

Herod feared to release John lest he instigate rebellion. He feared to put him to death lest the multitude riot in the capital, for thousands of Pereans believed that John was a holy man, a prophet. Therefore Herod kept the Nazarite preacher in prison, not knowing what else to do with him. Several times John had been before Herod, but never would he agree either to leave the domains of Herod or to refrain from all public activities if he were released. And this new agitation concerning Jesus of Nazareth, which was steadily increasing, admonished Herod that it was no time to turn John loose. Besides, John was also a victim of the intense and bitter hatred of Herodias, Herod's unlawful wife.

On numerous occasions Herod talked with John about the kingdom of heaven, and while sometimes seriously impressed with his message, he was afraid to release him from prison.

Since much building was still going on at Tiberias, Herod spent considerable time at his Perean residences, and he was partial to the fortress of Machaerus. It was a matter of several years before all the public buildings and the official residence at Tiberias were fully completed.

In celebration of his birthday Herod made a great feast in the Machaerian palace for his chief officers and other men high in the councils of the government of Galilee and Perea. Since Herodias had failed to bring about John's death by direct appeal to Herod, she now set herself to the task of having John put to death by cunning planning.

In the course of the evening's festivities and entertainment, Herodias presented her daughter to dance before the banqueters. Herod was very much pleased with the damsel's performance and, calling her before him, said: "You are charming. I am much pleased with you. Ask me on this my birthday for whatever you desire, and I will give it to you, even to the half of my kingdom." And Herod did all this while well under the influence of his many wines. The young lady drew aside and inquired of her mother what she should ask of Herod. Herodias said, "Go to Herod and ask for the head of John the Baptist." And the young woman, returning to the banquet table, said to Herod, "I request that you forthwith give me the head of John the Baptist on a platter."

Herod was filled with fear and sorrow, but because of his oath and because of all those who sat at meat with him, he would not deny the request. And Herod Antipas sent a soldier, commanding him to bring the head of John. So was John that night beheaded in the prison, the soldier bringing the head of the prophet on a platter and presenting it to the young woman at the rear of the banquet hall. And the damsel gave the platter to her mother. When John's disciples heard of this, they came to the prison for the body of John, and after laying it in a tomb, they went and told Jesus.

PAPER 136

BAPTISM AND THE FORTY DAYS

JESUS began his public work at the height of the popular interest in John's preaching and at a time when the Jewish people of Palestine were eagerly looking for the appearance of the Messiah. There was a great contrast between John and Jesus. John was an eager and earnest worker, but Jesus was a calm and happy laborer; only a few times in his entire life was he ever in a hurry. Jesus was a comforting consolation to the world and somewhat of an example; John was hardly a comfort or an example. He preached the kingdom of heaven but hardly entered into the happiness thereof. Though Jesus spoke of John as the greatest of the prophets of the old order, he also said that the least of those who saw the great light of the new way and entered thereby into the kingdom of heaven was indeed greater than John.

When John preached the coming kingdom, the burden of his message was: Repent! flee from the wrath to come. When Jesus began to preach, there remained the exhortation to repentance, but such a message was always followed by the gospel, the good tidings of the joy and liberty of the new kingdom.

1. CONCEPTS OF THE EXPECTED MESSIAH

The Jews entertained many ideas about the expected deliverer, and each of these different schools of Messianic teaching was able to point to statements in the Hebrew scriptures as proof of their contentions. In a general way, the Jews regarded their national history as beginning with Abraham and culminating in the Messiah and the new age of the kingdom of God. In earlier times they had envisaged this deliverer as "the servant of the Lord," then as "the Son of Man," while latterly some even went so far as to refer to the Messiah as the "Son of God." But no matter whether he was called the "seed of Abraham" or "the son of David," all were agreed that he was to be the Messiah, the "anointed one." Thus did the concept evolve from the "servant of the Lord" to the "son of David," "Son of Man," and "Son of God."

In the days of John and Jesus the more learned Jews had developed an idea of the coming Messiah as the perfected and representative Israelite, combining in himself as the "servant of the Lord" the threefold office of prophet, priest, and king.

The Jews devoutly believed that, as Moses had delivered their fathers from Egyptian bondage by miraculous wonders, so would the coming Messiah deliver the Jewish people from Roman domination by even greater miracles of power and marvels of racial triumph. The rabbis had gathered together almost five hundred passages from the Scriptures which, notwithstanding their apparent contradictions, they averred were prophetic of the coming Messiah. And amidst all these details of time, technique, and function, they almost completely lost sight of the *personality* of the promised Messiah. They were looking for a restoration of Jewish national glory—Israel's temporal exaltation—rather than for the salvation of the world. It therefore becomes evident that Jesus of Nazareth could never satisfy this materialistic Messianic concept of the Jewish mind. Many of their reputed Messianic predictions, had they but viewed these prophetic utterances in a different light, would have very naturally prepared their minds for a recognition of Jesus as the terminator of one age and the inaugurator of a new and better dispensation of mercy and salvation for all nations.

The Jews had been brought up to believe in the doctrine of the *Shekinah*. But this reputed symbol of the Divine Presence was not to be seen in the temple. They believed that the coming of the Messiah would effect its restoration. They held confusing ideas about racial sin and the supposed evil nature of man. Some taught that Adam's sin had cursed the human race, and that the Messiah would remove this curse and restore man to divine favor. Others taught that God, in creating man, had put into his being both good and evil natures; that when he observed the outworking of this arrangement, he was greatly disappointed, and that "He repented that he had thus made man." And those who taught this believed that the Messiah was to come in order to redeem man from this inherent evil nature.

The majority of the Jews believed that they continued to languish under Roman rule because of their national sins and because of the halfheartedness of the gentile proselytes. The Jewish nation had not wholeheartedly *repented;* therefore did the Messiah delay his coming. There was much talk about repentance; wherefore the mighty and immediate appeal of John's preaching, "Repent and be baptized, for the kingdom of heaven is at hand." And the kingdom of heaven could mean only one thing to any devout Jew: The coming of the Messiah.

There was one feature of the bestowal of Michael which was utterly foreign to the Jewish conception of the Messiah, and that was the *union* of the two natures, the human and the divine. The Jews had variously conceived of the Messiah as perfected human, superhuman, and even as divine, but they never entertained the concept of the *union* of the human and the divine. And this was the great stumbling block of Jesus' early disciples. They grasped the human concept of the Messiah as the son of David, as presented by the earlier prophets; as the Son of Man, the superhuman idea of Daniel and some of the later prophets; and even as the Son of God, as depicted by the author of the Book of Enoch and by certain of his contemporaries; but never had they for a single moment entertained the true concept of the union in one earth personality of the two natures, the human and the divine. The incarnation of the Creator in the form of the creature had not been revealed beforehand. It was revealed only in Jesus; the world knew nothing of such things until the Creator Son was made flesh and dwelt among the mortals of the realm.

2. THE BAPTISM OF JESUS

Jesus was baptized at the very height of John's preaching when Palestine was aflame with the expectancy of his message—"the kingdom of God is at hand" —when all Jewry was engaged in serious and solemn self-examination. The Jewish sense of racial solidarity was very profound. The Jews not only believed that the sins of the father might afflict his children, but they firmly believed that the sin of one individual might curse the nation. Accordingly, not all who submitted to John's baptism regarded themselves as being guilty of the specific sins which John denounced. Many devout souls were baptized by John for the good of Israel. They feared lest some sin of ignorance on their part might delay the coming of the Messiah. They felt themselves to belong to a guilty and sin-cursed nation, and they presented themselves for baptism that they might by so doing manifest fruits of race penitence. It is therefore evident that Jesus in no sense received John's baptism as a rite of repentance or for the remission of sins. In accepting baptism at the hands of John, Jesus was only following the example of many pious Israelites.

When Jesus of Nazareth went down into the Jordan to be baptized, he was a mortal of the realm who had attained the pinnacle of human evolutionary ascension in all matters related to the conquest of mind and to self-identification with the spirit. He stood in the Jordan that day a perfected mortal of the evolutionary worlds of time and space. Perfect synchrony and full communication had become established between the mortal mind of Jesus and the indwelling spirit Adjuster, the divine gift of his Father in Paradise. And just such an Adjuster indwells all normal beings living on Urantia since the ascension of Michael to the headship of his universe, except that Jesus' Adjuster had been previously prepared for this special mission by similarly indwelling another superhuman incarnated in the likeness of mortal flesh, Machiventa Melchizedek.

Ordinarily, when a mortal of the realm attains such high levels of personality perfection, there occur those preliminary phenomena of spiritual elevation which terminate in eventual fusion of the matured soul of the mortal with its associated divine Adjuster. And such a change was apparently due to take place in the personality experience of Jesus of Nazareth on that very day when he went down into the Jordan with his two brothers to be baptized by John. This ceremony was the final act of his purely human life on Urantia, and many superhuman observers expected to witness the fusion of the Adjuster with its indwelt mind, but they were all destined to suffer disappointment. Something new and even greater occurred. As John laid his hands upon Jesus to baptize him, the indwelling Adjuster took final leave of the perfected human soul of Joshua ben Joseph. And in a few moments this divine entity returned from Divinington as a Personalized Adjuster and chief of his kind throughout the entire local universe of Nebadon. Thus did Jesus observe his own former divine spirit descending on its return to him in personalized form. And he heard this same spirit of Paradise origin now speak, saying, "This is my beloved Son in whom I am well pleased." And John, with Jesus' two brothers, also heard these words. John's disciples, standing by the water's edge, did not hear these words, neither did they see the apparition of the Personalized Adjuster. Only the eyes of Jesus beheld the Personalized Adjuster.

When the returned and now exalted Personalized Adjuster had thus spoken, all was silence. And while the four of them tarried in the water, Jesus, looking up to the near-by Adjuster, prayed: "My Father who reigns in heaven, hallowed be your name. Your kingdom come! Your will be done on earth, even as it is in heaven." When he had prayed, the "heavens were opened," and the Son of Man saw the vision, presented by the now Personalized Adjuster, of himself as a Son of God as he was before he came to earth in the likeness of mortal flesh, and as he would be when the incarnated life should be finished. This heavenly vision was seen only by Jesus.

It was the voice of the Personalized Adjuster that John and Jesus heard, speaking in behalf of the Universal Father, for the Adjuster is of, and as, the Paradise Father. Throughout the remainder of Jesus' earth life this Personalized Adjuster was associated with him in all his labors; Jesus was in constant communion with this exalted Adjuster.

When Jesus was baptized, he repented of no misdeeds; he made no confession of sin. His was the baptism of consecration to the performance of the will of the heavenly Father. At his baptism he heard the unmistakable call of his Father, the final summons to be about his Father's business, and he went away into private seclusion for forty days to think over these manifold problems. In thus retiring for a season from active personality contact with his earthly associates, Jesus, as he was and on Urantia, was following the very procedure that obtains on the morontia worlds whenever an ascending mortal fuses with the inner presence of the Universal Father.

This day of baptism ended the purely human life of Jesus. The divine Son has found his Father, the Universal Father has found his incarnated Son, and they speak the one to the other.

(Jesus was almost thirty-one and one-half years old when he was baptized. While Luke says that Jesus was baptized in the fifteenth year of the reign of Tiberius Caesar, which would be A.D. 29 since Augustus died in A.D. 14, it should be recalled that Tiberius was coemperor with Augustus for two and one-half years before the death of Augustus, having had coins struck in his honor in October, A.D. 11. The fifteenth year of his actual rule was, therefore, this very year of A.D. 26, that of Jesus' baptism. And this was also the year that Pontius Pilate began his rule as governor of Judea.)

3. THE FORTY DAYS

Jesus had endured the great temptation of his mortal bestowal before his baptism when he had been wet with the dews of Mount Hermon for six weeks. There on Mount Hermon, as an unaided mortal of the realm, he had met and defeated the Urantia pretender, Caligastia, the prince of this world. That eventful day, on the universe records, Jesus of Nazareth had become the Planetary Prince of Urantia. And this Prince of Urantia, so soon to be proclaimed supreme Sovereign of Nebadon, now went into forty days of retirement to formulate the plans and determine upon the technique of proclaiming the new kingdom of God in the hearts of men.

After his baptism he entered upon the forty days of adjusting himself to the changed relationships of the world and the universe occasioned by the personalization of his Adjuster. During this isolation in the Perean hills he determined upon the policy to be pursued and the methods to be employed in the new and changed phase of earth life which he was about to inaugurate.

Jesus did not go into retirement for the purpose of fasting and for the affliction of his soul. He was not an ascetic, and he came forever to destroy all such notions regarding the approach to God. His reasons for seeking this retirement were entirely different from those which had actuated Moses and Elijah, and even John the Baptist. Jesus was then wholly self-conscious concerning his relation to the universe of his making and also to the universe of universes, supervised by the Paradise Father, his Father in heaven. He now fully recalled the bestowal charge and its instructions administered by his elder brother, Immanuel, ere he entered upon his Urantia incarnation. He now clearly and fully comprehended all these far-flung relationships, and he desired to be away for a season of quiet meditation so that he could think out the plans and decide upon the procedures for the prosecution of his public labors in behalf of this world and for all other worlds in his local universe.

While wandering about in the hills, seeking a suitable shelter, Jesus encountered his universe chief executive, Gabriel, the Bright and Morning Star of Nebadon. Gabriel now re-established personal communication with the Creator Son of the universe; they met directly for the first time since Michael took leave of his associates on Salvington when he went to Edentia preparatory to entering upon the Urantia bestowal. Gabriel, by direction of Immanuel and on authority of the Uversa Ancients of Days, now laid before Jesus information indicating that his bestowal experience on Urantia was practically finished so far as concerned the earning of the perfected sovereignty of his universe and the termination of the Lucifer rebellion. The former was achieved on the day of his baptism when the personalization of his Adjuster demonstrated the perfection and completion of his bestowal in the likeness of mortal flesh, and the latter was a fact of history on that day when he came down from Mount Hermon to join the waiting lad, Tiglath. Jesus was now informed, upon the highest authority of the local universe and the superuniverse, that his bestowal work was finished in so far as it affected his personal status in relation to sovereignty and rebellion. He had already had this assurance direct from Paradise in the baptismal vision and in the phenomenon of the personalization of his indwelling Thought Adjuster.

While he tarried on the mountain, talking with Gabriel, the Constellation Father of Edentia appeared to Jesus and Gabriel in person, saying: "The records are completed. The sovereignty of Michael number 611,121 over his universe of Nebadon rests in completion at the right hand of the Universal Father. I bring to you the bestowal release of Immanuel, your sponsor-brother for the Urantia incarnation. You are at liberty now or at any subsequent time, in the manner of your own choosing, to terminate your incarnation bestowal, ascend to the right hand of your Father, receive your sovereignty, and assume your well-earned unconditional rulership of all Nebadon. I also testify to the completion of the records of the superuniverse, by authorization of the Ancients of Days, having to do with the termination of all sin-rebellion in your universe and endowing you with full and unlimited authority to deal with any and all such possible upheavals in the future. Technically, your work on Urantia and in the flesh of the mortal creature is finished. Your course from now on is a matter of your own choosing."

When the Most High Father of Edentia had taken leave, Jesus held long converse with Gabriel regarding the welfare of the universe and, sending greetings to Immanuel, proffered his assurance that, in the work which he was about to undertake on Urantia, he would be ever mindful of the counsel he had received in connection with the prebestowal charge administered on Salvington.

Throughout all of these forty days of isolation James and John the sons of Zebedee were engaged in searching for Jesus. Many times they were not far from his abiding place, but never did they find him.

4. PLANS FOR PUBLIC WORK

Day by day, up in the hills, Jesus formulated the plans for the remainder of his Urantia bestowal. He first decided not to teach contemporaneously with John. He planned to remain in comparative retirement until the work of John achieved its purpose, or until John was suddenly stopped by imprisonment. Jesus well knew that John's fearless and tactless preaching would presently arouse the fears and enmity of the civil rulers. In view of John's precarious situation, Jesus began definitely to plan his program of public labors in behalf of his people and the world, in behalf of every inhabited world throughout his vast universe. Michael's mortal bestowal was *on* Urantia but *for* all worlds of Nebadon.

The first thing Jesus did, after thinking through the general plan of coordinating his program with John's movement, was to review in his mind the instructions of Immanuel. Carefully he thought over the advice given him concerning his methods of labor, and that he was to leave no permanent writing on the planet. Never again did Jesus write on anything except sand. On his next visit to Nazareth, much to the sorrow of his brother Joseph, Jesus destroyed all of his writing that was preserved on the boards about the carpenter shop, and which hung upon the walls of the old home. And Jesus pondered well over Immanuel's advice pertaining to his economic, social, and political attitude toward the world as he should find it.

Jesus did not fast during this forty days' isolation. The longest period he went without food was his first two days in the hills when he was so engrossed with his thinking that he forgot all about eating. But on the third day he went in search of food. Neither was he *tempted* during this time by any evil spirits or rebel personalities of station on this world or from any other world.

These forty days were the occasion of the final conference between the human and the divine minds, or rather the first real functioning of these two minds as now made one. The results of this momentous season of meditation demonstrated conclusively that the divine mind has triumphantly and spiritually dominated the human intellect. The mind of man has become the mind of God from this time on, and though the selfhood of the mind of man is ever present, always does this spiritualized human mind say, "Not my will but yours be done."

The transactions of this eventful time were not the fantastic visions of a starved and weakened mind, neither were they the confused and puerile symbolisms which afterward gained record as the "temptations of Jesus in the wilderness." Rather was this a season for thinking over the whole eventful and varied career of the Urantia bestowal and for the careful laying of those plans for further ministry which would best serve this world while also contributing something to the betterment of all other rebellion-isolated spheres. Jesus thought over the whole span of human life on Urantia, from the days of Andon and Fonta, down through Adam's default, and on to the ministry of the Melchizedek of Salem.

Gabriel had reminded Jesus that there were two ways in which he might manifest himself to the world in case he should choose to tarry on Urantia for a time. And it was made clear to Jesus that his choice in this matter would have nothing to do with either his universe sovereignty or the termination of the Lucifer rebellion. These two ways of world ministry were:

1. His own way—the way that might seem most pleasant and profitable from the standpoint of the immediate needs of this world and the present edification of his own universe.

2. The Father's way—the exemplification of a farseeing ideal of creature life visualized by the high personalities of the Paradise administration of the universe of universes.

It was thus made clear to Jesus that there were two ways in which he could order the remainder of his earth life. Each of these ways had something to be said in its favor as it might be regarded in the light of the immediate situation. The Son of Man clearly saw that his choice between these two modes of conduct would have nothing to do with his reception of universe sovereignty; that was a matter already settled and sealed on the records of the universe of universes and only awaited his demand in person. But it was indicated to Jesus that it would afford his Paradise brother, Immanuel, great satisfaction if he, Jesus, should see fit to finish up his earth career of incarnation as he had so nobly begun it, always subject to the Father's will. On the third day of this isolation Jesus promised himself he would go back to the world to finish his earth career, and that in a situation involving any two ways he would always choose the Father's will. And he lived out the remainder of his earth life always true to that resolve. Even to the bitter end he invariably subordinated his sovereign will to that of his heavenly Father.

The forty days in the mountain wilderness were not a period of great temptation but rather the period of the Master's *great decisions.* During these days of lone communion with himself and his Father's immediate presence—the Personalized Adjuster (he no longer had a personal seraphic guardian)—he arrived, one by one, at the great decisions which were to control his policies and conduct for the remainder of his earth career. Subsequently the tradition of a great temptation became attached to this period of isolation through confusion with the fragmentary narratives of the Mount Hermon struggles, and further because it was the custom to have all great prophets and human leaders begin their public careers by undergoing these supposed seasons of fasting and prayer. It had always been Jesus' practice, when facing any new or serious decisions, to withdraw for communion with his own spirit that he might seek to know the will of God.

In all this planning for the remainder of his earth life, Jesus was always torn in his human heart by two opposing courses of conduct:

1. He entertained a strong desire to win his people—and the whole world—to believe in him and to accept his new spiritual kingdom. And he well knew their ideas concerning the coming Messiah.

2. To live and work as he knew his Father would approve, to conduct his work in behalf of other worlds in need, and to continue, in the establishment of the kingdom, to reveal the Father and show forth his divine character of love.

Throughout these eventful days Jesus lived in an ancient rock cavern, a shelter in the side of the hills near a village sometime called Beit Adis. He drank from the small spring which came from the side of the hill near this rock shelter.

5. THE FIRST GREAT DECISION

On the third day after beginning this conference with himself and his Personalized Adjuster, Jesus was presented with the vision of the assembled celestial hosts of Nebadon sent by their commanders to wait upon the will of their beloved Sovereign. This mighty host embraced twelve legions of seraphim and proportionate numbers of every order of universe intelligence. And the first great decision of Jesus' isolation had to do with whether or not he would make use of these mighty personalities in connection with the ensuing program of his public work on Urantia.

Jesus decided that he would *not* utilize a single personality of this vast assemblage unless it should become evident that this was his *Father's will.* Notwithstanding this general decision, this vast host remained with him throughout the balance of his earth life, always in readiness to obey the least expression of their Sovereign's will. Although Jesus did not constantly behold these attendant personalities with his human eyes, his associated Personalized Adjuster did constantly behold, and could communicate with, all of them.

Before coming down from the forty days' retreat in the hills, Jesus assigned the immediate command of this attendant host of universe personalities to his recently Personalized Adjuster, and for more than four years of Urantia time did these selected personalities from every division of universe intelligences obediently and respectfully function under the wise guidance of this exalted and experienced Personalized Mystery Monitor. In assuming command of this mighty assembly, the Adjuster, being a onetime part and essence of the Paradise Father, assured Jesus that in no case would these superhuman agencies be permitted to serve, or manifest themselves in connection with, or in behalf of, his earth career unless it should develop that the Father willed such intervention. Thus by one great decision Jesus voluntarily deprived himself of all superhuman co-operation in all matters having to do with the remainder of his mortal career unless the Father might independently choose to participate in some certain act or episode of the Son's earth labors.

In accepting this command of the universe hosts in attendance upon Christ Michael, the Personalized Adjuster took great pains to point out to Jesus that, while such an assembly of universe creatures could be limited in their *space* activities by the delegated authority of their Creator, such limitations were not operative in connection with their function in *time.* And this limitation was dependent on the fact that Adjusters are nontime beings when once they are personalized. Accordingly was Jesus admonished that, while the Adjuster's control of the living intelligences placed under his command would be complete and perfect as to all matters involving *space,* there could be no such perfect limitations imposed regarding *time.* Said the Adjuster: "I will, as you have directed, enjoin the employment of this attendant host of universe intelligences in any manner in connection with your earth career except in those cases where the Paradise Father directs me to release such agencies in order that his divine will of your choosing may be accomplished, and in those instances where you may engage in any choice or act of your divine-human will which shall only involve departures from the natural earth order as to *time.* In all such events I am powerless, and your creatures here assembled in perfection and unity of power are likewise helpless. If your united natures once entertain such desires, these mandates of your choice will be forthwith executed. Your wish in all such matters will constitute the abridgment of time, and the thing projected *is* existent. Under my command this constitutes the fullest possible limitation which can be imposed upon your potential sovereignty. In my self-consciousness time is nonexistent, and therefore I cannot limit your creatures in anything related thereto."

Thus did Jesus become apprised of the working out of his decision to go on living as a man among men. He had by a single decision excluded all of his attendant universe hosts of varied intelligences from participating in his ensuing public ministry except in such matters as concerned *time* only. It therefore becomes evident that any possible supernatural or supposedly superhuman accompaniments of Jesus' ministry pertained wholly to the elimination of time unless the Father in heaven specifically ruled otherwise. No miracle, ministry of mercy, or any other possible event occurring in connection with Jesus' remaining earth labors could possibly be of the nature or character of an act transcending the natural laws established and regularly working in the affairs of man as he lives on Urantia *except* in this expressly stated matter of *time.* No limits, of course, could be placed upon the manifestations of "the Father's will." The elimination of time in connection with the expressed desire of this potential Sovereign of a universe could only be avoided by the direct and explicit act of the *will* of this God-man to the effect that time, as related to the act or event in question, *should not be shortened or eliminated.* In order to prevent the appearance of apparent *time miracles,* it was necessary for Jesus to remain constantly time conscious. Any lapse of time consciousness on his part, in connection with the entertainment of definite desire, was equivalent to the enactment of the thing conceived in the mind of this Creator Son, and without the intervention of time.

Through the supervising control of his associated and Personalized Adjuster it was possible for Michael perfectly to limit his personal earth activities with reference to space, but it was not possible for the Son of Man thus to limit his new earth status as potential Sovereign of Nebadon as regards *time.* And this was the actual status of Jesus of Nazareth as he went forth to begin his public ministry on Urantia.

6. THE SECOND DECISION

Having settled his policy concerning all personalities of all classes of his created intelligences, so far as this could be determined in view of the inherent potential of his new status of divinity, Jesus now turned his thoughts toward himself. What would he, now the fully self-conscious creator of all things and beings existent in this universe, do with these creator prerogatives in the recurring life situations which would immediately confront him when he returned to Galilee to resume his work among men? In fact, already, and right where he was in these lonely hills, had this problem forcibly presented itself in the matter of obtaining food. By the third day of his solitary meditations the human body grew hungry. Should he go in quest of food as any ordinary man would, or should he merely exercise his normal creative powers and produce suitable bodily nourishment ready at hand? And this great decision of the Master has been portrayed to you as a temptation—as a challenge by supposed enemies that he "command that these stones become loaves of bread."

Jesus thus settled upon another and consistent policy for the remainder of his earth labors. As far as his personal necessities were concerned, and in general even in his relations with other personalities, he now deliberately chose to pursue the path of normal earthly existence; he definitely decided against a policy which would transcend, violate, or outrage his own established natural laws. But he could not promise himself, as he had already been warned by his Personalized Adjuster, that these natural laws might not, in certain conceivable circumstances, be greatly *accelerated.* In principle, Jesus decided that his lifework should be organized and prosecuted in accordance with natural law and in harmony with the existing social organization. The Master thereby chose a program of living which was the equivalent of deciding against miracles and wonders. Again he decided in favor of "the Father's will"; again he surrendered everything into the hands of his Paradise Father.

Jesus' human nature dictated that the first duty was self-preservation; that is the normal attitude of the natural man on the worlds of time and space, and it is, therefore, a legitimate reaction of a Urantia mortal. But Jesus was not concerned merely with this world and its creatures; he was living a life designed to instruct and inspire the manifold creatures of a far-flung universe.

Before his baptismal illumination he had lived in perfect submission to the will and guidance of his heavenly Father. He emphatically decided to continue on in just such implicit mortal dependence on the Father's will. He purposed to follow the unnatural course—he decided not to seek self-preservation. He chose to go on pursuing the policy of refusing to defend himself. He formulated his conclusions in the words of Scripture familiar to his human mind: "Man shall not live by bread alone but by every word that proceeds from the mouth of God." In reaching this conclusion in regard to the appetite of the physical nature as expressed in hunger for food, the Son of Man made his final declaration concerning all other urges of the flesh and the natural impulses of human nature.

His superhuman power he might possibly use for others, but for himself, never. And he pursued this policy consistently to the very end, when it was jeeringly said of him: "He saved others; himself he cannot save"—because he would not.

The Jews were expecting a Messiah who would do even greater wonders than Moses, who was reputed to have brought forth water from the rock in a desert place and to have fed their forefathers with manna in the wilderness. Jesus knew the sort of Messiah his compatriots expected, and he had all the powers and prerogatives to measure up to their most sanguine expectations, but he decided against such a magnificent program of power and glory. Jesus looked upon such a course of expected miracle working as a harking back to the olden days of ignorant magic and the degraded practices of the savage medicine men. Possibly, for the salvation of his creatures, he might accelerate natural law, but to transcend his own laws, either for the benefit of himself or the overawing of his fellow men, that he would not do. And the Master's decision was final.

Jesus sorrowed for his people; he fully understood how they had been led up to the expectation of the coming Messiah, the time when "the earth will yield its fruits ten thousandfold, and on one vine there will be a thousand branches, and each branch will produce a thousand clusters, and each cluster will produce a thousand grapes, and each grape will produce a gallon of wine." The Jews believed the Messiah would usher in an era of miraculous plenty. The Hebrews had long been nurtured on traditions of miracles and legends of wonders.

He was not a Messiah coming to multiply bread and wine. He came not to minister to temporal needs only; he came to reveal his Father in heaven to his children on earth, while he sought to lead his earth children to join him in a sincere effort so to live as to do the will of the Father in heaven.

In this decision Jesus of Nazareth portrayed to an onlooking universe the folly and sin of prostituting divine talents and God-given abilities for personal aggrandizement or for purely selfish gain and glorification. That was the sin of Lucifer and Caligastia.

This great decision of Jesus portrays dramatically the truth that selfish satisfaction and sensuous gratification, alone and of themselves, are not able to confer happiness upon evolving human beings. There are higher values in mortal existence—intellectual mastery and spiritual achievement—which far transcend the necessary gratification of man's purely physical appetites and urges. Man's natural endowment of talent and ability should be chiefly devoted to the development and ennoblement of his higher powers of mind and spirit.

Jesus thus revealed to the creatures of his universe the technique of the new and better way, the higher moral values of living and the deeper spiritual satisfactions of evolutionary human existence on the worlds of space.

7. THE THIRD DECISION

Having made his decisions regarding such matters as food and physical ministration to the needs of his material body, the care of the health of himself and his associates, there remained yet other problems to solve. What would be his attitude when confronted by personal danger? He decided to exercise normal watchcare over his human safety and to take reasonable precaution to prevent the untimely termination of his career in the flesh but to refrain from all superhuman intervention when the crisis of his life in the flesh should come. As he was formulating this decision, Jesus was seated under the shade of a tree on an overhanging ledge of rock with a precipice right there before him. He fully realized that he could cast himself off the ledge and out into space, and that nothing could happen to harm him provided he would rescind his first great decision not to invoke the interposition of his celestial intelligences in the prosecution of his lifework on Urantia, and provided he would abrogate his second decision concerning his attitude toward self-preservation.

Jesus knew his fellow countrymen were expecting a Messiah who would be above natural law. Well had he been taught that Scripture: "There shall no evil befall you, neither shall any plague come near your dwelling. For he shall give his angels charge over you, to keep you in all your ways. They shall bear you up in their hands lest you dash your foot against a stone." Would this sort of presumption, this defiance of his Father's laws of gravity, be justified in order to protect himself from possible harm or, perchance, to win the confidence of his mistaught and distracted people? But such a course, however gratifying to the sign-seeking Jews, would be, not a revelation of his Father, but a questionable trifling with the established laws of the universe of universes.

Understanding all of this and knowing that the Master refused to work in defiance of his established laws of nature in so far as his personal conduct was concerned, you know of a certainty that he never walked on the water nor did anything else which was an outrage to his material order of administering the world; always, of course, bearing in mind that there had, as yet, been found no way whereby he could be wholly delivered from the lack of control over the element of time in connection with those matters put under the jurisdiction of the Personalized Adjuster.

Throughout his entire earth life Jesus was consistently loyal to this decision. No matter whether the Pharisees taunted him for a sign, or the watchers at Calvary dared him to come down from the cross, he steadfastly adhered to the decision of this hour on the hillside.

8. THE FOURTH DECISION

The next great problem with which this God-man wrestled and which he presently decided in accordance with the will of the Father in heaven, concerned the question as to whether or not any of his superhuman powers should be employed for the purpose of attracting the attention and winning the adherence of his fellow men. Should he in any manner lend his universe powers to the gratification of the Jewish hankering for the spectacular and the marvelous? He decided that he should not. He settled upon a policy of procedure which eliminated all such practices as the method of bringing his mission to the notice of men. And he consistently lived up to this great decision. Even when he permitted the manifestation of numerous time-shortening ministrations of mercy, he almost invariably admonished the recipients of his healing ministry to tell no man about the benefits they had received. And always did he refuse the taunting challenge of his enemies to "show us a sign" in proof and demonstration of his divinity.

Jesus very wisely foresaw that the working of miracles and the execution of wonders would call forth only outward allegiance by overawing the material mind; such performances would not reveal God nor save men. He refused to become a mere wonder-worker. He resolved to become occupied with but a single task—the establishment of the kingdom of heaven.

Throughout all this momentous dialogue of Jesus' communing with himself, there was present the human element of questioning and near-doubting, for Jesus was man as well as God. It was evident he would never be received by the Jews as the Messiah if he did not work wonders. Besides, if he would consent to do just one unnatural thing, the human mind would know of a certainty that it was in subservience to a truly divine mind. Would it be consistent with "the Father's will" for the divine mind to make this concession to the doubting nature of the human mind? Jesus decided that it would not and cited the presence of the Personalized Adjuster as sufficient proof of divinity in partnership with humanity.

Jesus had traveled much; he recalled Rome, Alexandria, and Damascus. He knew the methods of the world—how people gained their ends in politics and commerce by compromise and diplomacy. Would he utilize this knowledge in the furtherance of his mission on earth? No! He likewise decided against all compromise with the wisdom of the world and the influence of riches in the establishment of the kingdom. He again chose to depend exclusively on the Father's will.

Jesus was fully aware of the short cuts open to one of his powers. He knew many ways in which the attention of the nation, and the whole world, could be immediately focused upon himself. Soon the Passover would be celebrated at Jerusalem; the city would be thronged with visitors. He could ascend the pinnacle of the temple and before the bewildered multitude walk out on the air; that would be the kind of a Messiah they were looking for. But he would subsequently disappoint them since he had not come to re-establish David's throne. And he knew the futility of the Caligastia method of trying to get ahead of the natural, slow, and sure way of accomplishing the divine purpose. Again the Son of Man bowed obediently to the Father's way, the Father's will.

Jesus chose to establish the kingdom of heaven in the hearts of mankind by natural, ordinary, difficult, and trying methods, just such procedures as his earth children must subsequently follow in their work of enlarging and extending that heavenly kingdom. For well did the Son of Man know that it would be "through much tribulation that many of the children of all ages would enter into the kingdom." Jesus was now passing through the great test of civilized man, to have power and steadfastly refuse to use it for purely selfish or personal purposes.

In your consideration of the life and experience of the Son of Man, it should be ever borne in mind that the Son of God was incarnate in the mind of a first-century human being, not in the mind of a twentieth-century or other-century mortal. By this we mean to convey the idea that the human endowments of Jesus were of natural acquirement. He was the product of the hereditary and environmental factors of his time, plus the influence of his training and education. His humanity was genuine, natural, wholly derived from the antecedents of, and fostered by, the actual intellectual status and social and economic conditions of that day and generation. While in the experience of this God-man there was always the possibility that the divine mind would transcend the human intellect, nonetheless, when, and as, his human mind functioned, it did perform as would a true mortal mind under the conditions of the human environment of that day.

Jesus portrayed to all the worlds of his vast universe the folly of creating artificial situations for the purpose of exhibiting arbitrary authority or of indulging exceptional power for the purpose of enhancing moral values or accelerating spiritual progress. Jesus decided that he would not lend his mission on earth to a repetition of the disappointment of the reign of the Maccabees. He refused to prostitute his divine attributes for the purpose of acquiring unearned popularity or for gaining political prestige. He would not countenance the transmutation of divine and creative energy into national power or international prestige. Jesus of Nazareth refused to compromise with *evil,* much less to consort with sin. The Master triumphantly put loyalty to his Father's will above every other earthly and temporal consideration.

9. THE FIFTH DECISION

Having settled such questions of policy as pertained to his individual relations to natural law and spiritual power, he turned his attention to the choice of methods to be employed in the proclamation and establishment of the kingdom of God. John had already begun this work; how might he continue the message? How should he take over John's mission? How should he organize his followers for effective effort and intelligent co-operation? Jesus was now reaching the final decision which would forbid that he further regard himself as the Jewish Messiah, at least as the Messiah was popularly conceived in that day.

The Jews envisaged a deliverer who would come in miraculous power to cast down Israel's enemies and establish the Jews as world rulers, free from want and oppression. Jesus knew that this hope would never be realized. He knew that the kingdom of heaven had to do with the overthrow of evil in the hearts of men, and that it was purely a matter of spiritual concern. He thought out the advisability of inaugurating the spiritual kingdom with a brilliant and dazzling display of power—and such a course would have been permissible and wholly within the jurisdiction of Michael—but he fully decided against such a plan. He would not compromise with the revolutionary techniques of Caligastia. He had won the world in potential by submission to the Father's will, and he proposed to finish his work as he had begun it, and as the Son of Man.

You can hardly imagine what would have happened on Urantia had this God-man, now in potential possession of all power in heaven and on earth, once decided to unfurl the banner of sovereignty, to marshal his wonder-working battalions in militant array! But he would not compromise. He would not serve evil that the worship of God might presumably be derived therefrom. He would abide by the Father's will. He would proclaim to an onlooking universe, "You shall worship the Lord your God and him only shall you serve."

As the days passed, with ever-increasing clearness Jesus perceived what kind of a truth-revealer he was to become. He discerned that God's way was not going to be the easy way. He began to realize that the cup of the remainder of his human experience might possibly be bitter, but he decided to drink it.

Even his human mind is saying good-bye to the throne of David. Step by step this human mind follows in the path of the divine. The human mind still asks questions but unfailingly accepts the divine answers as final rulings in this combined life of living as a man in the world while all the time submitting unqualifiedly to the doing of the Father's eternal and divine will.

Rome was mistress of the Western world. The Son of Man, now in isolation and achieving these momentous decisions, with the hosts of heaven at his command, represented the last chance of the Jews to attain world dominion; but this earthborn Jew, who possessed such tremendous wisdom and power, declined to use his universe endowments either for the aggrandizement of himself or for the enthronement of his people. He saw, as it were, "the kingdoms of this world," and he possessed the power to take them. The Most Highs of Edentia had resigned all these powers into his hands, but he did not want them. The kingdoms of earth were paltry things to interest the Creator and Ruler of a universe. He had only one objective, the further revelation of God to man, the establishment of the kingdom, the rule of the heavenly Father in the hearts of mankind.

The idea of battle, contention, and slaughter was repugnant to Jesus; he would have none of it. He would appear on earth as the Prince of Peace to reveal a God of love. Before his baptism he had again refused the offer of the Zealots to lead them in rebellion against the Roman oppressors. And now he made his final decision regarding those Scriptures which his mother had taught him, such as: "The Lord has said to me, 'You are my Son; this day have I begotten you. Ask of me, and I will give you the heathen for your inheritance and the uttermost parts of the earth for your possession. You shall break them with a rod of iron; you shall dash them in pieces like a potter's vessel.'"

Jesus of Nazareth reached the conclusion that such utterances did not refer to him. At last, and finally, the human mind of the Son of Man made a clean sweep of all these Messianic difficulties and contradictions—Hebrew scriptures, parental training, chazan teaching, Jewish expectations, and human ambitious longings; once and for all he decided upon his course. He would return to Galilee and quietly begin the proclamation of the kingdom and trust his Father (the Personalized Adjuster) to work out the details of procedure day by day.

By these decisions Jesus set a worthy example for every person on every world throughout a vast universe when he refused to apply material tests to prove spiritual problems, when he refused presumptuously to defy natural laws. And he set an inspiring example of universe loyalty and moral nobility when he refused to grasp temporal power as the prelude to spiritual glory.

If the Son of Man had any doubts about his mission and its nature when he went up in the hills after his baptism, he had none when he came back to his fellows following the forty days of isolation and decisions.

Jesus has formulated a program for the establishment of the Father's kingdom. He will not cater to the physical gratification of the people. He will not deal out bread to the multitudes as he has so recently seen it being done in Rome. He will not attract attention to himself by wonder-working, even though the Jews are expecting just that sort of a deliverer. Neither will he seek to win acceptance of a spiritual message by a show of political authority or temporal power.

In rejecting these methods of enhancing the coming kingdom in the eyes of the expectant Jews, Jesus made sure that these same Jews would certainly and finally reject all of his claims to authority and divinity. Knowing all this, Jesus long sought to prevent his early followers alluding to him as the Messiah.

Throughout his public ministry he was confronted with the necessity of dealing with three constantly recurring situations: the clamor to be fed, the insistence on miracles, and the final request that he allow his followers to make him king. But Jesus never departed from the decisions which he made during these days of his isolation in the Perean hills.

10. THE SIXTH DECISION

On the last day of this memorable isolation, before starting down the mountain to join John and his disciples, the Son of Man made his final decision. And this decision he communicated to the Personalized Adjuster in these words, "And in all other matters, as in these now of decision-record, I pledge you I will be subject to the will of my Father." And when he had thus spoken, he journeyed down the mountain. And his face shone with the glory of spiritual victory and moral achievement.

PAPER 137

TARRYING TIME IN GALILEE

EARLY on Saturday morning, February 23, A.D. 26, Jesus came down from the hills to rejoin John's company encamped at Pella. All that day Jesus mingled with the multitude. He ministered to a lad who had injured himself in a fall and journeyed to the near-by village of Pella to deliver the boy safely into the hands of his parents.

1. CHOOSING THE FIRST FOUR APOSTLES

During this Sabbath two of John's leading disciples spent much time with Jesus. Of all John's followers one named Andrew was the most profoundly impressed with Jesus; he accompanied him on the trip to Pella with the injured boy. On the way back to John's rendezvous he asked Jesus many questions, and just before reaching their destination, the two paused for a short talk, during which Andrew said: "I have observed you ever since you came to Capernaum, and I believe you are the new Teacher, and though I do not understand all your teaching, I have fully made up my mind to follow you; I would sit at your feet and learn the whole truth about the new kingdom." And Jesus, with hearty assurance, welcomed Andrew as the first of his apostles, that group of twelve who were to labor with him in the work of establishing the new kingdom of God in the hearts of men.

Andrew was a silent observer of, and sincere believer in, John's work, and he had a very able and enthusiastic brother, named Simon, who was one of John's foremost disciples. It would not be amiss to say that Simon was one of John's chief supporters.

Soon after Jesus and Andrew returned to the camp, Andrew sought out his brother, Simon, and taking him aside, informed him that he had settled in his own mind that Jesus was the great Teacher, and that he had pledged himself as a disciple. He went on to say that Jesus had accepted his proffer of service and suggested that he (Simon) likewise go to Jesus and offer himself for fellowship in the service of the new kingdom. Said Simon: "Ever since this man came to work in Zebedee's shop, I have believed he was sent by God, but what about John? Are we to forsake him? Is this the right thing to do?" Whereupon they agreed to go at once to consult John. John was saddened by the thought of losing two of his able advisers and most promising disciples, but he bravely answered their inquiries, saying: "This is but the beginning; presently will my work end, and we shall all become his disciples." Then Andrew beckoned to Jesus to draw aside while he announced that his brother desired to join himself to the service of the new kingdom. And in welcoming Simon as his second apostle, Jesus said: "Simon, your enthusiasm is commendable, but it is dangerous to the work of the kingdom.

I admonish you to become more thoughtful in your speech. I would change your name to Peter."

The parents of the injured lad who lived at Pella had besought Jesus to spend the night with them, to make their house his home, and he had promised. Before leaving Andrew and his brother, Jesus said, "Early on the morrow we go into Galilee."

After Jesus had returned to Pella for the night, and while Andrew and Simon were yet discussing the nature of their service in the establishment of the forthcoming kingdom, James and John the sons of Zebedee arrived upon the scene, having just returned from their long and futile searching in the hills for Jesus. When they heard Simon Peter tell how he and his brother, Andrew, had become the first accepted counselors of the new kingdom, and that they were to leave with their new Master on the morrow for Galilee, both James and John were sad. They had known Jesus for some time, and they loved him. They had searched for him many days in the hills, and now they returned to learn that others had been preferred before them. They inquired where Jesus had gone and made haste to find him.

Jesus was asleep when they reached his abode, but they awakened him, saying: "How is it that, while we who have so long lived with you are searching in the hills for you, you prefer others before us and choose Andrew and Simon as your first associates in the new kingdom?" Jesus answered them, "Be calm in your hearts and ask yourselves, 'who directed that you should search for the Son of Man when he was about his Father's business?'" After they had recited the details of their long search in the hills, Jesus further instructed them: "You should learn to search for the secret of the new kingdom in your hearts and not in the hills. That which you sought was already present in your souls. You are indeed my brethren—you needed not to be received by me—already were you of the kingdom, and you should be of good cheer, making ready also to go with us tomorrow into Galilee." John then made bold to ask, "But, Master, will James and I be associates with you in the new kingdom, even as Andrew and Simon?" And Jesus, laying a hand on the shoulder of each of them, said: "My brethren, you were already with me in the spirit of the kingdom, even before these others made request to be received. You, my brethren, have no need to make request for entrance into the kingdom; you have been with me in the kingdom from the beginning. Before men, others may take precedence over you, but in my heart did I also number you in the councils of the kingdom, even before you thought to make this request of me. And even so might you have been first before men had you not been absent engaged in a well-intentioned but self-appointed task of seeking for one who was not lost. In the coming kingdom, be not mindful of those things which foster your anxiety but rather at all times concern yourselves only with doing the will of the Father who is in heaven."

James and John received the rebuke in good grace; never more were they envious of Andrew and Simon. And they made ready, with their two associate apostles, to depart for Galilee the next morning. From this day on the term apostle was employed to distinguish the chosen family of Jesus' advisers from the vast multitude of believing disciples who subsequently followed him.

Late that evening, James, John, Andrew, and Simon held converse with John the Baptist, and with tearful eye but steady voice the stalwart Judean prophet surrendered two of his leading disciples to become the apostles of the Galilean Prince of the coming kingdom.

2. CHOOSING PHILIP AND NATHANIEL

Sunday morning, February 24, A.D. 26, Jesus took leave of John the Baptist by the river near Pella, never again to see him in the flesh.

That day, as Jesus and his four disciple-apostles departed for Galilee, there was a great tumult in the camp of John's followers. The first great division was about to take place. The day before, John had made his positive pronouncement to Andrew and Ezra that Jesus was the Deliverer. Andrew decided to follow Jesus, but Ezra rejected the mild-mannered carpenter of Nazareth, proclaiming to his associates: "The Prophet Daniel declares that the Son of Man will come with the clouds of heaven, in power and great glory. This Galilean carpenter, this Capernaum boatbuilder, cannot be the Deliverer. Can such a gift of God come out of Nazareth? This Jesus is a relative of John, and through much kindness of heart has our teacher been deceived. Let us remain aloof from this false Messiah." When John rebuked Ezra for these utterances, he drew away with many disciples and hastened south. And this group continued to baptize in John's name and eventually founded a sect of those who believed in John but refused to accept Jesus. A remnant of this group persists in Mesopotamia even to this day.

While this trouble was brewing among John's followers, Jesus and his four disciple-apostles were well on their way toward Galilee. Before they crossed the Jordan, to go by way of Nain to Nazareth, Jesus, looking ahead and up the road, saw one Philip of Bethsaida with a friend coming toward them. Jesus had known Philip aforetime, and he was also well known to all four of the new apostles. He was on his way with his friend Nathaniel to visit John at Pella to learn more about the reported coming of the kingdom of God, and he was delighted to greet Jesus. Philip had been an admirer of Jesus ever since he first came to Capernaum. But Nathaniel, who lived at Cana of Galilee, did not know Jesus. Philip went forward to greet his friends while Nathaniel rested under the shade of a tree by the roadside.

Peter took Philip to one side and proceeded to explain that they, referring to himself, Andrew, James, and John, had all become associates of Jesus in the new kingdom and strongly urged Philip to volunteer for service. Philip was in a quandary. What should he do? Here, without a moment's warning—on the roadside near the Jordan—there had come up for immediate decision the most momentous question of a lifetime. By this time he was in earnest converse with Peter, Andrew, and John while Jesus was outlining to James the trip through Galilee and on to Capernaum. Finally, Andrew suggested to Philip, "Why not ask the Teacher?"

It suddenly dawned on Philip that Jesus was a really great man, possibly the Messiah, and he decided to abide by Jesus' decision in this matter; and he went straight to him, asking, "Teacher, shall I go down to John or shall I join my friends who follow you?" And Jesus answered, "Follow me." Philip was thrilled with the assurance that he had found the Deliverer.

Philip now motioned to the group to remain where they were while he hurried back to break the news of his decision to his friend Nathaniel, who still tarried behind under the mulberry tree, turning over in his mind the many things which he had heard concerning John the Baptist, the coming kingdom, and the expected Messiah. Philip broke in upon these meditations, exclaiming, "I have found the Deliverer, him of whom Moses and the prophets wrote and whom John has proclaimed." Nathaniel, looking up, inquired, "Whence comes this teacher?" And Philip replied, "He is Jesus of Nazareth, the son of Joseph, the carpenter, more recently residing at Capernaum." And then, somewhat shocked, Nathaniel asked, "Can any such good thing come out of Nazareth?" But Philip, taking him by the arm, said, "Come and see."

Philip led Nathaniel to Jesus, who, looking benignly into the face of the sincere doubter, said: "Behold a genuine Israelite, in whom there is no deceit. Follow me." And Nathaniel, turning to Philip, said: "You are right. He is indeed a master of men. I will also follow, if I am worthy." And Jesus nodded to Nathaniel, again saying, "Follow me."

Jesus had now assembled one half of his future corps of intimate associates, five who had for some time known him and one stranger, Nathaniel. Without further delay they crossed the Jordan and, going by the village of Nain, reached Nazareth late that evening.

They all remained overnight with Joseph in Jesus' boyhood home. The associates of Jesus little understood why their new-found teacher was so concerned with completely destroying every vestige of his writing which remained about the home in the form of the ten commandments and other mottoes and sayings. But this proceeding, together with the fact that they never saw him subsequently write—except upon the dust or in the sand—made a deep impression upon their minds.

3. THE VISIT TO CAPERNAUM

The next day Jesus sent his apostles on to Cana, since all of them were invited to the wedding of a prominent young woman of that town, while he prepared to pay a hurried visit to his mother at Capernaum, stopping at Magdala to see his brother Jude.

Before leaving Nazareth, the new associates of Jesus told Joseph and other members of Jesus' family about the wonderful events of the then recent past and gave free expression to their belief that Jesus was the long-expected deliverer. And these members of Jesus' family talked all this over, and Joseph said: "Maybe, after all, Mother was right—maybe our strange brother is the coming king."

Jude was present at Jesus' baptism and, with his brother James, had become a firm believer in Jesus' mission on earth. Although both James and Jude were much perplexed as to the nature of their brother's mission, their mother had resurrected all her early hopes of Jesus as the Messiah, the son of David, and she encouraged her sons to have faith in their brother as the deliverer of Israel.

Jesus arrived in Capernaum Monday night, but he did not go to his own home, where lived James and his mother; he went directly to the home of Zebedee. All his friends at Capernaum saw a great and pleasant change in him. Once more he seemed to be comparatively cheerful and more like himself as he was during the earlier years at Nazareth. For years previous to his baptism and the isolation periods just before and just after, he had grown increasingly serious and self-contained. Now he seemed quite like his old self to all of them. There was about him something of majestic import and exalted aspect, but he was once again lighthearted and joyful.

Mary was thrilled with expectation. She anticipated that the promise of Gabriel was nearing fulfillment. She expected all Palestine soon to be startled and stunned by the miraculous revelation of her son as the supernatural king of the Jews. But to all of the many questions which his mother, James, Jude, and Zebedee asked, Jesus only smilingly replied: "It is better that I tarry here for a while; I must do the will of my Father who is in heaven."

On the next day, Tuesday, they all journeyed over to Cana for the wedding of Naomi, which was to take place on the following day. And in spite of Jesus' repeated warnings that they tell no man about him "until the Father's hour shall come," they insisted on quietly spreading the news abroad that they had found the Deliverer. They each confidently expected that Jesus would inaugurate his assumption of Messianic authority at the forthcoming wedding at Cana, and that he would do so with great power and sublime grandeur. They remembered what had been told them about the phenomena attendant upon his baptism, and they believed that his future course on earth would be marked by increasing manifestations of supernatural wonders and miraculous demonstrations. Accordingly, the entire countryside was preparing to gather together at Cana for the wedding feast of Naomi and Johab the son of Nathan.

Mary had not been so joyous in years. She journeyed to Cana in the spirit of the queen mother on the way to witness the coronation of her son. Not since he was thirteen years old had Jesus' family and friends seen him so carefree and happy, so thoughtful and understanding of the wishes and desires of his associates, so touchingly sympathetic. And so they all whispered among themselves, in small groups, wondering what was going to happen. What would this strange person do next? How would he usher in the glory of the coming kingdom? And they were all thrilled with the thought that they were to be present to see the revelation of the might and power of Israel's God.

4. THE WEDDING AT CANA

By noon on Wednesday almost a thousand guests had arrived in Cana, more than four times the number bidden to the wedding feast. It was a Jewish custom to celebrate weddings on Wednesday, and the invitations had been sent abroad for the wedding one month previously. In the forenoon and early afternoon it appeared more like a public reception for Jesus than a wedding. Everybody wanted to greet this near-famous Galilean, and he was most cordial to all, young and old, Jew and gentile. And everybody rejoiced when Jesus consented to lead the preliminary wedding procession.

Jesus was now thoroughly self-conscious regarding his human existence, his divine pre-existence, and the status of his combined, or fused, human and divine natures. With perfect poise he could at one moment enact the human role or immediately assume the personality prerogatives of the divine nature.

As the day wore on, Jesus became increasingly conscious that the people were expecting him to perform some wonder; more especially he recognized that his family and his six disciple-apostles were looking for him appropriately to announce his forthcoming kingdom by some startling and supernatural manifestation.

Early in the afternoon Mary summoned James, and together they made bold to approach Jesus to inquire if he would admit them to his confidence to the extent of informing them at what hour and at what point in connection with the wedding ceremonies he had planned to manifest himself as the "supernatural one." No sooner had they spoken of these matters to Jesus than they saw they had aroused his characteristic indignation. He said only: "If you love me, then be willing to tarry with me while I wait upon the will of my Father who is in heaven." But the eloquence of his rebuke lay in the expression of his face.

This move of his mother was a great disappointment to the human Jesus, and he was much sobered by his reaction to her suggestive proposal that he permit himself to indulge in some outward demonstration of his divinity. That was one of the very things he had decided not to do when so recently isolated in the hills. For several hours Mary was much depressed. She said to James: "I cannot understand him; what can it all mean? Is there no end to his strange conduct?" James and Jude tried to comfort their mother, while Jesus withdrew for an hour's solitude. But he returned to the gathering and was once more lighthearted and joyous.

The wedding proceeded with a hush of expectancy, but the entire ceremony was finished and not a move, not a word, from the honored guest. Then it was whispered about that the carpenter and boatbuilder, announced by John as "the Deliverer," would show his hand during the evening festivities, perhaps at the wedding supper. But all expectance of such a demonstration was effectually removed from the minds of his six disciple-apostles when he called them together just before the wedding supper and, in great earnestness, said: "Think not that I have come to this place to work some wonder for the gratification of the curious or for the conviction of those who doubt. Rather are we here to wait upon the will of our Father who is in heaven." But when Mary and the others saw him in consultation with his associates, they were fully persuaded in their own minds that something extraordinary was about to happen. And they all sat down to enjoy the wedding supper and the evening of festive good fellowship.

The father of the bridegroom had provided plenty of wine for all the guests bidden to the marriage feast, but how was he to know that the marriage of his son was to become an event so closely associated with the expected manifestation of Jesus as the Messianic deliverer? He was delighted to have the honor of numbering the celebrated Galilean among his guests, but before the wedding supper was over, the servants brought him the disconcerting news that the wine was running short. By the time the formal supper had ended and the guests were strolling about in the garden, the mother of the bridegroom confided to Mary that the supply of wine was exhausted. And Mary confidently said: "Have no worry—I will speak to my son. He will help us." And thus did she presume to speak, notwithstanding the rebuke of but a few hours before.

Throughout a period of many years, Mary had always turned to Jesus for help in every crisis of their home life at Nazareth so that it was only natural for her to think of him at this time. But this ambitious mother had still other motives for appealing to her eldest son on this occasion. As Jesus was standing alone in a corner of the garden, his mother approached him, saying, "My son, they have no wine." And Jesus answered, "My good woman, what have I to do with that?" Said Mary, "But I believe your hour has come; cannot you help us?" Jesus replied: "Again I declare that I have not come to do things in this wise. Why do you trouble me again with these matters?" And then, breaking down in tears, Mary entreated him, "But, my son, I promised them that you would help us; won't you please do something for me?" And then spoke Jesus: "Woman, what have you to do with making such promises? See that you do it not again. We must in all things wait upon the will of the Father in heaven."

Mary the mother of Jesus was crushed; she was stunned! As she stood there before him motionless, with the tears streaming down her face, the human heart of Jesus was overcome with compassion for the woman who had borne him in the flesh; and bending forward, he laid his hand tenderly upon her head, saying: "Now, now, Mother Mary, grieve not over my apparently hard sayings, for have I not many times told you that I have come only to do the will of my heavenly Father? Most gladly would I do what you ask of me if it were a part of the Father's will—" and Jesus stopped short, he hesitated. Mary seemed to sense that something was happening. Leaping up, she threw her arms around Jesus' neck, kissed him, and rushed off to the servants' quarters, saying, "Whatever my son says, that do." But Jesus said nothing. He now realized that he had already said—or rather desirefully thought—too much.

Mary was dancing with glee. She did not know how the wine would be produced, but she confidently believed that she had finally persuaded her first-born son to assert his authority, to dare to step forth and claim his position and exhibit his Messianic power. And, because of the presence and association of certain universe powers and personalities, of which all those present were wholly ignorant, she was not to be disappointed. The wine Mary desired and which Jesus, the God-man, humanly and sympathetically wished for, was forthcoming.

Near at hand stood six waterpots of stone, filled with water, holding about twenty gallons apiece. This water was intended for subsequent use in the final purification ceremonies of the wedding celebration. The commotion of the servants about these huge stone vessels, under the busy direction of his mother, attracted Jesus' attention, and going over, he observed that they were drawing wine out of them by the pitcherful.

It was gradually dawning upon Jesus what had happened. Of all persons present at the marriage feast of Cana, Jesus was the most surprised. Others had expected him to work a wonder, but that was just what he had purposed not to do. And then the Son of Man recalled the admonition of his Personalized Thought Adjuster in the hills. He recounted how the Adjuster had warned him about the inability of any power or personality to deprive him of the creator prerogative of independence of time. On this occasion power transformers, midwayers, and all other required personalities were assembled near the water and other necessary elements, and in the face of the expressed wish of the Universe Creator Sovereign, there was no escaping the instantaneous appearance of *wine*. And this occurrence was made doubly certain since the Personalized Adjuster had signified that the execution of the Son's desire was in no way a contravention of the Father's will.

But this was in no sense a miracle. No law of nature was modified, abrogated, or even transcended. Nothing happened but the abrogation of *time* in association with the celestial assembly of the chemical elements requisite for the elaboration of the wine. At Cana on this occasion the agents of the Creator made wine just as they do by the ordinary natural processes *except* that they did it independently of time and with the intervention of superhuman agencies in the matter of the space assembly of the necessary chemical ingredients.

Furthermore it was evident that the enactment of this so-called miracle was not contrary to the will of the Paradise Father, else it would not have transpired, since Jesus had already subjected himself in all things to the Father's will.

When the servants drew this new wine and carried it to the best man, the "ruler of the feast," and when he had tasted it, he called to the bridegroom, saying: "It is the custom to set out first the good wine and, when the guests have well drunk, to bring forth the inferior fruit of the vine; but you have kept the best of the wine until the last of the feast."

Mary and the disciples of Jesus were greatly rejoiced at the supposed miracle which they thought Jesus had intentionally performed, but Jesus withdrew to a sheltered nook of the garden and engaged in serious thought for a few brief moments. He finally decided that the episode was beyond his personal control under the circumstances and, not being adverse to his Father's will, was inevitable. When he returned to the people, they regarded him with awe; they all believed in him as the Messiah. But Jesus was sorely perplexed, knowing that they believed in him only because of the unusual occurrence which they had just inadvertently beheld. Again Jesus retired for a season to the housetop that he might think it all over.

Jesus now fully comprehended that he must constantly be on guard lest his indulgence of sympathy and pity become responsible for repeated episodes of this sort. Nevertheless, many similar events occurred before the Son of Man took final leave of his mortal life in the flesh.

5. BACK IN CAPERNAUM

Though many of the guests remained for the full week of wedding festivities, Jesus, with his newly chosen disciple-apostles—James, John, Andrew, Peter, Philip, and Nathaniel—departed very early the next morning for Capernaum, going away without taking leave of anyone. Jesus' family and all his friends in Cana were much distressed because he so suddenly left them, and Jude, Jesus' youngest brother, set out in search of him. Jesus and his apostles went directly to the home of Zebedee at Bethsaida. On this journey Jesus talked over many things of importance to the coming kingdom with his newly chosen associates and especially warned them to make no mention of the turning of the water into wine. He also advised them to avoid the cities of Sepphoris and Tiberias in their future work.

After supper that evening, in this home of Zebedee and Salome, there was held one of the most important conferences of all Jesus' earthly career. Only the six apostles were present at this meeting; Jude arrived as they were about to separate. These six chosen men had journeyed from Cana to Bethsaida with Jesus, walking, as it were, on air. They were alive with expectancy and thrilled with the thought of having been selected as close associates of the Son of Man. But when Jesus set out to make clear to them who he was and what was to be his mission on earth and how it might possibly end, they were stunned. They could not grasp what he was telling them. They were speechless; even Peter was crushed beyond expression. Only the deep-thinking Andrew dared to make reply to Jesus' words of counsel. When Jesus perceived that they did not comprehend his message, when he saw that their ideas of the Jewish Messiah were so completely crystallized, he sent them to their rest while he walked and talked with his brother Jude. And before Jude took leave of Jesus, he said with much feeling: "My father-brother, I never have understood you. I do not know of a certainty whether you are what my mother has taught us, and I do not fully comprehend the coming kingdom, but I do know you are a mighty man of God. I heard the voice at the Jordan, and I am a believer in you, no matter who you are." And when he had spoken, he departed, going to his own home at Magdala.

That night Jesus did not sleep. Donning his evening wraps, he sat out on the lake shore thinking, thinking until the dawn of the next day. In the long hours of that night of meditation Jesus came clearly to comprehend that he never would be able to make his followers see him in any other light than as the long-expected Messiah. At last he recognized that there was no way to launch his message of the kingdom except as the fulfillment of John's prediction and as the one for whom the Jews were looking. After all, though he was not the Davidic type of Messiah, he was truly the fulfillment of the prophetic utterances of the more spiritually minded of the olden seers. Never again did he wholly deny that he was the Messiah. He decided to leave the final untangling of this complicated situation to the outworking of the Father's will.

The next morning Jesus joined his friends at breakfast, but they were a cheerless group. He visited with them and at the end of the meal gathered them about him, saying: "It is my Father's will that we tarry hereabouts for a season. You have heard John say that he came to prepare the way for the kingdom; therefore it behooves us to await the completion of John's preaching. When the forerunner of the Son of Man shall have finished his work, we will begin the proclamation of the good tidings of the kingdom." He directed his apostles to return to their nets while he made ready to go with Zebedee to the boatshop, promising to see them the next day at the synagogue, where he was to speak, and appointing a conference with them that Sabbath afternoon.

6. THE EVENTS OF A SABBATH DAY

Jesus' first public appearance following his baptism was in the Capernaum synagogue on Sabbath, March 2, A.D. 26. The synagogue was crowded to overflowing. The story of the baptism in the Jordan was now augmented by the fresh news from Cana about the water and the wine. Jesus gave seats of honor to his six apostles, and seated with them were his brothers in the flesh James and Jude. His mother, having returned to Capernaum with James the evening before, was also present, being seated in the women's section of the synagogue. The entire audience was on edge; they expected to behold some extraordinary manifestation of supernatural power which would be a fitting testimony to the nature and authority of him who was that day to speak to them. But they were destined to disappointment.

When Jesus stood up, the ruler of the synagogue handed him the Scripture roll, and he read from the Prophet Isaiah: "Thus says the Lord: 'The heaven is my throne, and the earth is my footstool. Where is the house that you built for me? And where is the place of my dwelling? All these things have my hands made,' says the Lord. 'But to this man will I look, even to him who is poor and of a contrite spirit, and who trembles at my word.' Hear the word of the Lord, you who tremble and fear: 'Your brethren hated you and cast you out for my name's sake.' But let the Lord be glorified. He shall appear to you in joy, and all others shall be ashamed. A voice from the city, a voice from the temple, a voice from the Lord says: 'Before she travailed, she brought forth; before her pain came, she was delivered of a man child.' Who has heard such a thing? Shall the earth be made to bring forth in one day? Or can a nation be born at once? But thus says the Lord: 'Behold I will extend peace like a river, and the glory of even the gentiles shall be like a flowing stream. As one whom his mother comforts, so will I comfort you. And you shall be comforted even in Jerusalem. And when you see these things, your heart shall rejoice.'"

When he had finished this reading, Jesus handed the roll back to its keeper. Before sitting down, he simply said: "Be patient and you shall see the glory of God; even so shall it be with all those who tarry with me and thus learn to do the will of my Father who is in heaven." And the people went to their homes, wondering what was the meaning of all this.

That afternoon Jesus and his apostles, with James and Jude, entered a boat and pulled down the shore a little way, where they anchored while he talked to them about the coming kingdom. And they understood more than they had on Thursday night.

Jesus instructed them to take up their regular duties until "the hour of the kingdom comes." And to encourage them, he set an example by going back regularly to work in the boatshop. In explaining that they should spend three hours every evening in study and preparation for their future work, Jesus further said: "We will all remain hereabout until the Father bids me call you. Each of you must now return to his accustomed work just as if nothing had happened. Tell no man about me and remember that my kingdom is not to come with noise and glamor, but rather must it come through the great change which my Father will have wrought in your hearts and in the hearts of those who shall be called to join you in the councils of the kingdom. You are now my friends; I trust you and I love you; you are soon to become my personal associates. Be patient, be gentle. Be ever obedient to the Father's will. Make yourselves ready for the call of the kingdom. While you will experience great joy in the service of my Father, you should also be prepared for trouble, for I warn you that it will be only through much tribulation that many will enter the kingdom. But those who have found the kingdom, their joy will be full, and they shall be called the blest of all the earth. But do not entertain false hope; the world will stumble at my words. Even you, my friends, do not fully perceive what I am unfolding to your confused minds. Make no mistake; we go forth to labor for a generation of sign seekers. They will demand wonder-working as the proof that I am sent by my Father, and they will be slow to recognize in the revelation of my Father's *love* the credentials of my mission."

That evening, when they had returned to the land, before they went their way, Jesus, standing by the water's edge, prayed: "My Father, I thank you for these little ones who, in spite of their doubts, even now believe. And for their sakes have I set myself apart to do your will. And now may they learn to be one, even as we are one."

7. FOUR MONTHS OF TRAINING

For four long months—March, April, May, and June—this tarrying time continued; Jesus held over one hundred long and earnest, though cheerful and joyous, sessions with these six associates and his own brother James. Owing to sickness in his family, Jude seldom was able to attend these classes. James, Jesus' brother, did not lose faith in him, but during these months of delay and inaction Mary nearly despaired of her son. Her faith, raised to such heights at Cana, now sank to new low levels. She could only fall back on her so oft-repeated exclamation: "I cannot understand him. I cannot figure out what it all means." But James's wife did much to bolster Mary's courage.

Throughout these four months these seven believers, one his own brother in the flesh, were getting acquainted with Jesus; they were getting used to the idea of living with this God-man. Though they called him Rabbi, they were learning not to be afraid of him. Jesus possessed that matchless grace of personality which enabled him so to live among them that they were not dismayed by his divinity. They found it really easy to be "friends with God," God incarnate in the likeness of mortal flesh. This time of waiting severely tested the entire group of believers. Nothing, absolutely nothing, miraculous happened. Day by day they went about their ordinary work, while night after night they sat at Jesus' feet. And they were held together by his matchless personality and by the gracious words which he spoke to them evening upon evening.

This period of waiting and teaching was especially hard on Simon Peter. He repeatedly sought to persuade Jesus to launch forth with the preaching of the kingdom in Galilee while John continued to preach in Judea. But Jesus' reply to Peter ever was: "Be patient, Simon. Make progress. We shall be none too ready when the Father calls." And Andrew would calm Peter now and then with his more seasoned and philosophic counsel. Andrew was tremendously impressed with the human naturalness of Jesus. He never grew weary of contemplating how one who could live so near God could be so friendly and considerate of men.

Throughout this entire period Jesus spoke in the synagogue but twice. By the end of these many weeks of waiting the reports about his baptism and the wine of Cana had begun to quiet down. And Jesus saw to it that no more apparent miracles happened during this time. But even though they lived so quietly at Bethsaida, reports of the strange doings of Jesus had been carried to Herod Antipas, who in turn sent spies to ascertain what he was about. But Herod was more concerned about the preaching of John. He decided not to molest Jesus, whose work continued along so quietly at Capernaum.

In this time of waiting Jesus endeavored to teach his associates what their attitude should be toward the various religious groups and the political parties of Palestine. Jesus' words always were, "We are seeking to win all of them, but we are not *of* any of them."

The scribes and rabbis, taken together, were called Pharisees. They referred to themselves as the "associates." In many ways they were the progressive group among the Jews, having adopted many teachings not clearly found in the Hebrew scriptures, such as belief in the resurrection of the dead, a doctrine only mentioned by a later prophet, Daniel.

The Sadducees consisted of the priesthood and certain wealthy Jews. They were not such sticklers for the details of law enforcement. The Pharisees and Sadducees were really religious parties, rather than sects.

The Essenes were a true religious sect, originating during the Maccabean revolt, whose requirements were in some respects more exacting than those of the Pharisees. They had adopted many Persian beliefs and practices, lived as a brotherhood in monasteries, refrained from marriage, and had all things in common. They specialized in teachings about angels.

The Zealots were a group of intense Jewish patriots. They advocated that any and all methods were justified in the struggle to escape the bondage of the Roman yoke.

The Herodians were a purely political party that advocated emancipation from the direct Roman rule by a restoration of the Herodian dynasty.

In the very midst of Palestine there lived the Samaritans, with whom "the Jews had no dealings," notwithstanding that they held many views similar to the Jewish teachings.

All of these parties and sects, including the smaller Nazarite brotherhood, believed in the sometime coming of the Messiah. They all looked for a national deliverer. But Jesus was very positive in making it clear that he and his disciples would not become allied to any of these schools of thought or practice. The Son of Man was to be neither a Nazarite nor an Essene.

While Jesus later directed that the apostles should go forth, as John had, preaching the gospel and instructing believers, he laid emphasis on the proclamation of the "good tidings of the kingdom of heaven." He unfailingly impressed upon his associates that they must "show forth love, compassion, and sympathy." He early taught his followers that the kingdom of heaven was a spiritual experience having to do with the enthronement of God in the hearts of men.

As they thus tarried before embarking on their active public preaching, Jesus and the seven spent two evenings each week at the synagogue in the study of the Hebrew scriptures. In later years after seasons of intense public work, the apostles looked back upon these four months as the most precious and profitable of all their association with the Master. Jesus taught these men all they could assimilate. He did not make the mistake of overteaching them. He did not precipitate confusion by the presentation of truth too far beyond their capacity to comprehend.

8. SERMON ON THE KINGDOM

On Sabbath, June 22, shortly before they went out on their first preaching tour and about ten days after John's imprisonment, Jesus occupied the synagogue pulpit for the second time since bringing his apostles to Capernaum.

A few days before the preaching of this sermon on "The Kingdom," as Jesus was at work in the boatshop, Peter brought him the news of John's arrest. Jesus laid down his tools once more, removed his apron, and said to Peter: "The Father's hour has come. Let us make ready to proclaim the gospel of the kingdom."

Jesus did his last work at the carpenter bench on this Tuesday, June 18, A.D. 26. Peter rushed out of the shop and by midafternoon had rounded up all of his associates, and leaving them in a grove by the shore, he went in quest of Jesus. But he could not find him, for the Master had gone to a different grove to pray. And they did not see him until late that evening when he returned to Zebedee's house and asked for food. The next day he sent his brother James to ask for the privilege of speaking in the synagogue the coming Sabbath day. And the ruler of the synagogue was much pleased that Jesus was again willing to conduct the service.

Before Jesus preached this memorable sermon on the kingdom of God, the first pretentious effort of his public career, he read from the Scriptures these passages: "You shall be to me a kingdom of priests, a holy people. Yahweh is our judge, Yahweh is our lawgiver, Yahweh is our king; he will save us. Yahweh is my king and my God. He is a great king over all the earth. Loving-kindness is upon Israel in this kingdom. Blessed be the glory of the Lord for he is our King."

When he had finished reading, Jesus said:

"I have come to proclaim the establishment of the Father's kingdom. And this kingdom shall include the worshiping souls of Jew and gentile, rich and poor, free and bond, for my Father is no respecter of persons; his love and his mercy are over all.

"The Father in heaven sends his spirit to indwell the minds of men, and when I shall have finished my work on earth, likewise shall the Spirit of Truth be poured out upon all flesh. And the spirit of my Father and the Spirit of Truth shall establish you in the coming kingdom of spiritual understanding and divine righteousness. My kingdom is not of this world. The Son of Man will not lead forth armies in battle for the establishment of a throne of power or a kingdom of worldly glory. When my kingdom shall have come, you shall know the Son of Man as the Prince of Peace, the revelation of the everlasting Father. The children of this world fight for the establishment and enlargement of the kingdoms of this world, but my disciples shall enter the kingdom of heaven by their moral decisions and by their spirit victories; and when they once enter therein, they shall find joy, righteousness, and eternal life.

"Those who first seek to enter the kingdom, thus beginning to strive for a nobility of character like that of my Father, shall presently possess all else that is needful. But I say to you in all sincerity: Unless you seek entrance into the kingdom with the faith and trusting dependence of a little child, you shall in no wise gain admission.

"Be not deceived by those who come saying here is the kingdom or there is the kingdom, for my Father's kingdom concerns not things visible and material. And this kingdom is even now among you, for where the spirit of God teaches and leads the soul of man, there in reality is the kingdom of heaven. And this kingdom of God is righteousness, peace, and joy in the Holy Spirit.

"John did indeed baptize you in token of repentance and for the remission of your sins, but when you enter the heavenly kingdom, you will be baptized with the Holy Spirit.

"In my Father's kingdom there shall be neither Jew nor gentile, only those who seek perfection through service, for I declare that he who would be great in my Father's kingdom must first become server of all. If you are willing to serve your fellows, you shall sit down with me in my kingdom, even as, by serving in the similitude of the creature, I shall presently sit down with my Father in his kingdom.

"This new kingdom is like a seed growing in the good soil of a field. It does not attain full fruit quickly. There is an interval of time between the establishment of the kingdom in the soul of man and that hour when the kingdom ripens into the full fruit of everlasting righteousness and eternal salvation.

"And this kingdom which I declare to you is not a reign of power and plenty. The kingdom of heaven is not a matter of meat and drink but rather a life of progressive righteousness and increasing joy in the perfecting service of my

Father who is in heaven. For has not the Father said of his children of the world, ‘It is my will that they should eventually be perfect, even as I am perfect.’

“I have come to preach the glad tidings of the kingdom. I have not come to add to the heavy burdens of those who would enter this kingdom. I proclaim the new and better way, and those who are able to enter the coming kingdom shall enjoy the divine rest. And whatever it shall cost you in the things of the world, no matter what price you may pay to enter the kingdom of heaven, you shall receive manyfold more of joy and spiritual progress in this world, and in the age to come eternal life.

“Entrance into the Father’s kingdom waits not upon marching armies, upon overturned kingdoms of this world, nor upon the breaking of captive yokes. The kingdom of heaven is at hand, and all who enter therein shall find abundant liberty and joyous salvation.

“This kingdom is an everlasting dominion. Those who enter the kingdom shall ascend to my Father; they will certainly attain the right hand of his glory in Paradise. And all who enter the kingdom of heaven shall become the sons of God, and in the age to come so shall they ascend to the Father. And I have not come to call the would-be righteous but sinners and all who hunger and thirst for the righteousness of divine perfection.

“John came preaching repentance to prepare you for the kingdom; now have I come proclaiming faith, the gift of God, as the price of entrance into the kingdom of heaven. If you would but believe that my Father loves you with an infinite love, then you are in the kingdom of God.”

When he had thus spoken, he sat down. All who heard him were astonished at his words. His disciples marveled. But the people were not prepared to receive the good news from the lips of this God-man. About one third who heard him believed the message even though they could not fully comprehend it; about one third prepared in their hearts to reject such a purely spiritual concept of the expected kingdom, while the remaining one third could not grasp his teaching, many truly believing that he “was beside himself.”

PAPER 138

TRAINING THE KINGDOM'S MESSENGERS

AFTER preaching the sermon on "The Kingdom," Jesus called the six apostles together that afternoon and began to disclose his plans for visiting the cities around and about the Sea of Galilee. His brothers James and Jude were very much hurt because they were not called to this conference. Up to this time they had regarded themselves as belonging to Jesus' inner circle of associates. But Jesus planned to have no close relatives as members of this corps of apostolic directors of the kingdom. This failure to include James and Jude among the chosen few, together with his apparent aloofness from his mother ever since the experience at Cana, was the starting point of an ever-widening gulf between Jesus and his family. This situation continued throughout his public ministry—they very nearly rejected him—and these differences were not fully removed until after his death and resurrection. His mother constantly wavered between attitudes of fluctuating faith and hope, and increasing emotions of disappointment, humiliation, and despair. Only Ruth, the youngest, remained unswervingly loyal to her father-brother.

Until after the resurrection, Jesus' entire family had very little to do with his ministry. If a prophet is not without honor save in his own country, he is not without understanding appreciation save in his own family.

1. FINAL INSTRUCTIONS

The next day, Sunday, June 23, A.D. 26, Jesus imparted his final instructions to the six. He directed them to go forth, two and two, to teach the glad tidings of the kingdom. He forbade them to baptize and advised against public preaching. He went on to explain that later he would permit them to preach in public, but that for a season, and for many reasons, he desired them to acquire practical experience in dealing personally with their fellow men. Jesus purposed to make their first tour entirely one of *personal work.* Although this announcement was something of a disappointment to the apostles, still they saw, at least in part, Jesus' reason for thus beginning the proclamation of the kingdom, and they started out in good heart and with confident enthusiasm. He sent them forth by twos, James and John going to Kheresa, Andrew and Peter to Capernaum, while Philip and Nathaniel went to Tarichea.

Before they began this first two weeks of service, Jesus announced to them that he desired to ordain twelve apostles to continue the work of the kingdom after his departure and authorized each of them to choose one man from among his early converts for membership in the projected corps of apostles. John spoke up, asking: "But, Master, will these six men come into our midst and share all things equally with us who have been with you since the Jordan and have heard all your teaching in preparation for this, our first labor for the kingdom?" And Jesus replied: "Yes, John, the men you choose shall become one with us, and you will teach them all that pertains to the kingdom, even as I have taught you." After thus speaking, Jesus left them.

The six did not separate to go to their work until they had exchanged many words in discussion of Jesus' instruction that each of them should choose a new apostle. Andrew's counsel finally prevailed, and they went forth to their labors. In substance Andrew said: "The Master is right; we are too few to encompass this work. There is need for more teachers, and the Master has manifested great confidence in us inasmuch as he has intrusted us with the choosing of these six new apostles." This morning, as they separated to go to their work, there was a bit of concealed depression in each heart. They knew they were going to miss Jesus, and besides their fear and timidity, this was not the way they had pictured the kingdom of heaven being inaugurated.

It had been arranged that the six were to labor for two weeks, after which they were to return to the home of Zebedee for a conference. Meantime Jesus went over to Nazareth to visit with Joseph and Simon and other members of his family living in that vicinity. Jesus did everything humanly possible, consistent with his dedication to the doing of his Father's will, to retain the confidence and affection of his family. In this matter he did his full duty and more.

While the apostles were out on this mission, Jesus thought much about John, now in prison. It was a great temptation to use his potential powers to release him, but once more he resigned himself to "wait upon the Father's will."

2. CHOOSING THE SIX

This first missionary tour of the six was eminently successful. They all discovered the great value of direct and personal contact with men. They returned to Jesus more fully realizing that, after all, religion is purely and wholly a matter of *personal experience.* They began to sense how hungry were the common people to hear words of religious comfort and spiritual good cheer. When they assembled about Jesus, they all wanted to talk at once, but Andrew assumed charge, and as he called upon them one by one, they made their formal reports to the Master and presented their nominations for the six new apostles.

Jesus, after each man had presented his selection for the new apostleships, asked all the others to vote upon the nomination; thus all six of the new apostles were formally accepted by all of the older six. Then Jesus announced that they would all visit these candidates and give them the call to service.

The newly selected apostles were:

1. *Matthew Levi,* the customs collector of Capernaum, who had his office just to the east of the city, near the borders of Batanea. He was selected by Andrew.

2. *Thomas Didymus,* a fisherman of Tarichea and onetime carpenter and stone mason of Gadara. He was selected by Philip.

3. *James Alpheus,* a fisherman and farmer of Kheresa, was selected by James Zebedee.

4. *Judas Alpheus,* the twin brother of James Alpheus, also a fisherman, was selected by John Zebedee.

5. *Simon Zelotes* was a high officer in the patriotic organization of the Zealots, a position which he gave up to join Jesus' apostles. Before joining the Zealots, Simon had been a merchant. He was selected by Peter.

6. *Judas Iscariot* was an only son of wealthy Jewish parents living in Jericho. He had become attached to John the Baptist, and his Sadducee parents had disowned him. He was looking for employment in these regions when Jesus' apostles found him, and chiefly because of his experience with finances, Nathaniel invited him to join their ranks. Judas Iscariot was the only Judean among the twelve apostles.

Jesus spent a full day with the six, answering their questions and listening to the details of their reports, for they had many interesting and profitable experiences to relate. They now saw the wisdom of the Master's plan of sending them out to labor in a quiet and personal manner before the launching of their more pretentious public efforts.

3. THE CALL OF MATTHEW AND SIMON

The next day Jesus and the six went to call upon Matthew, the customs collector. Matthew was awaiting them, having balanced his books and made ready to turn the affairs of his office over to his brother. As they approached the toll house, Andrew stepped forward with Jesus, who, looking into Matthew's face, said, "Follow me." And he arose and went to his house with Jesus and the apostles.

Matthew told Jesus of the banquet he had arranged for that evening, at least that he wished to give such a dinner to his family and friends if Jesus would approve and consent to be the guest of honor. And Jesus nodded his consent. Peter then took Matthew aside and explained that he had invited one Simon to join the apostles and secured his consent that Simon be also bidden to this feast.

After a noontide luncheon at Matthew's house they all went with Peter to call upon Simon the Zealot, whom they found at his old place of business, which was now being conducted by his nephew. When Peter led Jesus up to Simon, the Master greeted the fiery patriot and only said, "Follow me."

They all returned to Matthew's home, where they talked much about politics and religion until the hour of the evening meal. The Levi family had long been engaged in business and tax gathering; therefore many of the guests bidden to this banquet by Matthew would have been denominated "publicans and sinners" by the Pharisees.

In those days, when a reception-banquet of this sort was tendered a prominent individual, it was the custom for all interested persons to linger about the banquet room to observe the guests at meat and to listen to the conversation and speeches of the men of honor. Accordingly, most of the Capernaum Pharisees were present on this occasion to observe Jesus' conduct at this unusual social gathering.

As the dinner progressed, the joy of the diners mounted to heights of good cheer, and everybody was having such a splendid time that the onlooking Pharisees began, in their hearts, to criticize Jesus for his participation in such a lighthearted and carefree affair. Later in the evening, when they were making speeches, one of the more malignant of the Pharisees went so far as to criticize

Jesus' conduct to Peter, saying: "How dare you to teach that this man is righteous when he eats with publicans and sinners and thus lends his presence to such scenes of careless pleasure making." Peter whispered this criticism to Jesus before he spoke the parting blessing upon those assembled. When Jesus began to speak, he said: "In coming here tonight to welcome Matthew and Simon to our fellowship, I am glad to witness your lightheartedness and social good cheer, but you should rejoice still more because many of you will find entrance into the coming kingdom of the spirit, wherein you shall more abundantly enjoy the good things of the kingdom of heaven. And to you who stand about criticizing me in your hearts because I have come here to make merry with these friends, let me say that I have come to proclaim joy to the socially downtrodden and spiritual liberty to the moral captives. Need I remind you that they who are whole need not a physician, but rather those who are sick? I have come, not to call the righteous, but sinners."

And truly this was a strange sight in all Jewry: to see a man of righteous character and noble sentiments mingling freely and joyously with the common people, even with an irreligious and pleasure-seeking throng of publicans and reputed sinners. Simon Zelotes desired to make a speech at this gathering in Matthew's house, but Andrew, knowing that Jesus did not want the coming kingdom to become confused with the Zealots' movement, prevailed upon him to refrain from making any public remarks.

Jesus and the apostles remained that night in Matthew's house, and as the people went to their homes, they spoke of but one thing: the goodness and friendliness of Jesus.

4. THE CALL OF THE TWINS

On the morrow all nine of them went by boat over to Kheresa to execute the formal calling of the next two apostles, James and Judas the twin sons of Alpheus, the nominees of James and John Zebedee. The fisherman twins were expecting Jesus and his apostles and were therefore awaiting them on the shore. James Zebedee presented the Master to the Kheresa fishermen, and Jesus, gazing on them, nodded and said, "Follow me."

That afternoon, which they spent together, Jesus fully instructed them concerning attendance upon festive gatherings, concluding his remarks by saying: "All men are my brothers. My Father in heaven does not despise any creature of our making. The kingdom of heaven is open to all men and women. No man may close the door of mercy in the face of any hungry soul who may seek to gain an entrance thereto. We will sit at meat with all who desire to hear of the kingdom. As our Father in heaven looks down upon men, they are all alike. Refuse not therefore to break bread with Pharisee or sinner, Sadducee or publican, Roman or Jew, rich or poor, free or bond. The door of the kingdom is wide open for all who desire to know the truth and to find God."

That night at a simple supper at the Alpheus home, the twin brothers were received into the apostolic family. Later in the evening Jesus gave his apostles their first lesson dealing with the origin, nature, and destiny of unclean spirits, but they could not comprehend the import of what he told them. They found it very easy to love and admire Jesus but very difficult to understand many of his teachings.

After a night of rest the entire party, now numbering eleven, went by boat over to Tarichea.

5. THE CALL OF THOMAS AND JUDAS

Thomas the fisherman and Judas the wanderer met Jesus and the apostles at the fisher-boat landing at Tarichea, and Thomas led the party to his near-by home. Philip now presented Thomas as his nominee for apostleship and Nathaniel presented Judas Iscariot, the Judean, for similar honors. Jesus looked upon Thomas and said: "Thomas, you lack faith; nevertheless, I receive you. Follow me." To Judas Iscariot the Master said: "Judas, we are all of one flesh, and as I receive you into our midst, I pray that you will always be loyal to your Galilean brethren. Follow me."

When they had refreshed themselves, Jesus took the twelve apart for a season to pray with them and to instruct them in the nature and work of the Holy Spirit, but again did they largely fail to comprehend the meaning of those wonderful truths which he endeavored to teach them. One would grasp one point and one would comprehend another, but none of them could encompass the whole of his teaching. Always would they make the mistake of trying to fit Jesus' new gospel into their old forms of religious belief. They could not grasp the idea that Jesus had come to proclaim a new gospel of salvation and to establish a new way of finding God; they did not perceive that he *was* a new revelation of the Father in heaven.

The next day Jesus left his twelve apostles quite alone; he wanted them to become acquainted and desired that they be alone to talk over what he had taught them. The Master returned for the evening meal, and during the after-supper hours he talked to them about the ministry of seraphim, and some of the apostles comprehended his teaching. They rested for a night and the next day departed by boat for Capernaum.

Zebedee and Salome had gone to live with their son David so that their large home could be turned over to Jesus and his twelve apostles. Here Jesus spent a quiet Sabbath with his chosen messengers; he carefully outlined the plans for proclaiming the kingdom and fully explained the importance of avoiding any clash with the civil authorities, saying: "If the civil rulers are to be rebuked, leave that task to me. See that you make no denunciations of Caesar or his servants." It was this same evening that Judas Iscariot took Jesus aside to inquire why nothing was done to get John out of prison. And Judas was not wholly satisfied with Jesus' attitude.

6. THE WEEK OF INTENSIVE TRAINING

The next week was devoted to a program of intense training. Each day the six new apostles were put in the hands of their respective nominators for a thoroughgoing review of all they had learned and experienced in preparation for the work of the kingdom. The older apostles carefully reviewed, for the benefit of the younger six, Jesus' teachings up to that hour. Evenings they all assembled in Zebedee's garden to receive Jesus' instruction.

It was at this time that Jesus established the mid-week holiday for rest and recreation. And they pursued this plan of relaxation for one day each week throughout the remainder of his material life. As a general rule, they never prosecuted their regular activities on Wednesday. On this weekly holiday Jesus would usually take himself away from them, saying: "My children, go for a day of play. Rest yourselves from the arduous labors of the kingdom and enjoy the refreshment that comes from reverting to your former vocations or from discovering new sorts of recreational activity." While Jesus, at this period of his earth life, did not actually require this day of rest, he conformed to this plan because he knew it was best for his human associates. Jesus was the teacher—the Master; his associates were his pupils—disciples.

Jesus endeavored to make clear to his apostles the difference between his teachings and his *life among them* and the teachings which might subsequently spring up *about* him. Said Jesus: "My kingdom and the gospel related thereto shall be the burden of your message. Be not sidetracked into preaching *about* me and *about* my teachings. Proclaim the gospel of the kingdom and portray my revelation of the Father in heaven but do not be misled into the bypaths of creating legends and building up a cult having to do with beliefs and teachings *about* my beliefs and teachings." But again they did not understand why he thus spoke, and no man dared to ask why he so taught them.

In these early teachings Jesus sought to avoid controversies with his apostles as far as possible excepting those involving wrong concepts of his Father in heaven. In all such matters he never hesitated to correct erroneous beliefs. There was just *one* motive in Jesus' postbaptismal life on Urantia, and that was a better and truer revelation of his Paradise Father; he was the pioneer of the new and better way to God, the way of faith and love. Ever his exhortation to the apostles was: "Go seek for the sinners; find the downhearted and comfort the anxious."

Jesus had a perfect grasp of the situation; he possessed unlimited power, which might have been utilized in the furtherance of his mission, but he was wholly content with means and personalities which most people would have regarded as inadequate and would have looked upon as insignificant. He was engaged in a mission of enormous dramatic possibilities, but he insisted on going about his Father's business in the most quiet and undramatic manner; he studiously avoided all display of power. And he now planned to work quietly, at least for several months, with his twelve apostles around about the Sea of Galilee.

7. ANOTHER DISAPPOINTMENT

Jesus had planned for a quiet missionary campaign of five months' personal work. He did not tell the apostles how long this was to last; they worked from week to week. And early on this first day of the week, just as he was about to announce this to his twelve apostles, Simon Peter, James Zebedee, and Judas Iscariot came to have private converse with him. Taking Jesus aside, Peter made bold to say: "Master, we come at the behest of our associates to inquire whether the time is not now ripe to enter into the kingdom. And will you proclaim the kingdom at Capernaum, or are we to move on to Jerusalem? And when shall we learn, each of us, the positions we are to occupy with you in the establishment of the kingdom—" and Peter would have gone on asking further questions, but Jesus raised an admonitory hand and stopped him. And beckoning the other apostles standing near by to join them, Jesus said: "My little children, how long shall I bear with you! Have I not made it plain to you that my kingdom is not of this world? I have told you many times that I have not come to sit on David's throne, and now how is it that you are inquiring which place each of you will occupy in the Father's kingdom? Can you not perceive that I have called you as ambassadors of a spiritual kingdom? Do you not understand that soon, very soon, you are to represent me in the world and in the proclamation of the kingdom, even as I now represent my Father who is in heaven? Can it be that I have chosen you and instructed you as messengers of the kingdom, and yet you do not comprehend the nature and significance of this coming kingdom of divine pre-eminence in the hearts of men? My friends, hear me once more. Banish from your minds this idea that my kingdom is a rule of power or a reign of glory. Indeed, all power in heaven and on earth will presently be given into my hands, but it is not the Father's will that we use this divine endowment to glorify ourselves during this age. In another age you shall indeed sit with me in power and glory, but it behooves us now to submit to the will of the Father and to go forth in humble obedience to execute his bidding on earth."

Once more were his associates shocked, stunned. Jesus sent them away two and two to pray, asking them to return to him at noontime. On this crucial forenoon they each sought to find God, and each endeavored to cheer and strengthen the other, and they returned to Jesus as he had bidden them.

Jesus now recounted for them the coming of John, the baptism in the Jordan, the marriage feast at Cana, the recent choosing of the six, and the withdrawal from them of his own brothers in the flesh, and warned them that the enemy of the kingdom would seek also to draw them away. After this short but earnest talk the apostles all arose, under Peter's leadership, to declare their undying devotion to their Master and to pledge their unswerving loyalty to the kingdom, as Thomas expressed it, "To this coming kingdom, no matter what it is and even if I do not fully understand it." They all truly *believed in Jesus,* even though they did not fully comprehend his teaching.

Jesus now asked them how much money they had among them; he also inquired as to what provision had been made for their families. When it developed that they had hardly sufficient funds to maintain themselves for two weeks, he said: "It is not the will of my Father that we begin our work in this way. We will remain here by the sea two weeks and fish or do whatever our hands find to do; and in the meantime, under the guidance of Andrew, the first chosen apostle, you shall so organize yourselves as to provide for everything needful in your future work, both for the present personal ministry and also when I shall subsequently ordain you to preach the gospel and instruct believers." They were all greatly cheered by these words; this was their first clear-cut and positive intimation that Jesus designed later on to enter upon more aggressive and pretentious public efforts.

The apostles spent the remainder of the day perfecting their organization and completing arrangements for boats and nets for embarking on the morrow's fishing as they had all decided to devote themselves to fishing; most of them had been fishermen, even Jesus was an experienced boatman and fisherman. Many of the boats which they used the next few years had been built by Jesus' own hands. And they were good and trustworthy boats.

Jesus enjoined them to devote themselves to fishing for two weeks, adding, "And then will you go forth to become fishers of men." They fished in three groups, Jesus going out with a different group each night. And they all so much enjoyed Jesus! He was a good fisherman, a cheerful companion, and an inspiring friend; the more they worked with him, the more they loved him. Said Matthew one day: "The more you understand some people, the less you admire them, but of this man, even the less I comprehend him, the more I love him."

This plan of fishing two weeks and going out to do personal work in behalf of the kingdom for two weeks was followed for more than five months, even to the end of this year of A.D. 26, until after the cessation of those special persecutions which had been directed against John's disciples subsequent to his imprisonment.

8. FIRST WORK OF THE TWELVE

After disposing of the fish catches of two weeks, Judas Iscariot, the one chosen to act as treasurer of the twelve, divided the apostolic funds into six equal portions, funds for the care of dependent families having been already provided. And then near the middle of August, in the year A.D. 26, they went forth two and two to the fields of work assigned by Andrew. The first two weeks Jesus went out with Andrew and Peter, the second two weeks with James and John, and so on with the other couples in the order of their choosing. In this way he was able to go out at least once with each couple before he called them together for the beginning of their public ministry.

Jesus taught them to preach the forgiveness of sin through *faith in God* without penance or sacrifice, and that the Father in heaven loves all his children with the same eternal love. He enjoined his apostles to refrain from discussing:

1. The work and imprisonment of John the Baptist.
2. The voice at the baptism. Said Jesus: "Only those who heard the voice may refer to it. Speak only that which you have heard from me; speak not hearsay."
3. The turning of the water into wine at Cana. Jesus seriously charged them, saying, "Tell no man about the water and the wine."

They had wonderful times throughout these five or six months during which they worked as fishermen every alternate two weeks, thereby earning enough money to support themselves in the field for each succeeding two weeks of missionary work for the kingdom.

The common people marveled at the teaching and ministry of Jesus and his apostles. The rabbis had long taught the Jews that the ignorant could not be pious or righteous. But Jesus' apostles were both pious and righteous; yet they were cheerfully ignorant of much of the learning of the rabbis and the wisdom of the world.

Jesus made plain to his apostles the difference between the repentance of so-called good works as taught by the Jews and the change of mind by faith—the new birth—which he required as the price of admission to the kingdom. He taught his apostles that *faith* was the only requisite to entering the Father's kingdom. John had taught them "repentance—to flee from the wrath to come." Jesus taught, "Faith is the open door for entering into the present, perfect, and eternal love of God." Jesus did not speak like a prophet, one who comes to declare the word of God. He seemed to speak of himself as one having authority. Jesus sought to divert their minds from miracle seeking to the finding of a real and personal experience in the satisfaction and assurance of the indwelling of God's spirit of love and saving grace.

The disciples early learned that the Master had a profound respect and sympathetic regard for *every* human being he met, and they were tremendously impressed by this uniform and unvarying consideration which he so consistently gave to all sorts of men, women, and children. He would pause in the midst of a profound discourse that he might go out in the road to speak good cheer to a passing woman laden with her burden of body and soul. He would interrupt a serious conference with his apostles to fraternize with an intruding child. Nothing ever seemed so important to Jesus as the *individual human* who chanced to be in his immediate presence. He was master and teacher, but he was more—he was also a friend and neighbor, an understanding comrade.

Though Jesus' public teaching mainly consisted in parables and short discourses, he invariably taught his apostles by questions and answers. He would always pause to answer sincere questions during his later public discourses.

The apostles were at first shocked by, but early became accustomed to, Jesus' treatment of women; he made it very clear to them that women were to be accorded equal rights with men in the kingdom.

9. FIVE MONTHS OF TESTING

This somewhat monotonous period of alternate fishing and personal work proved to be a grueling experience for the twelve apostles, but they endured the test. With all of their grumblings, doubts, and transient dissatisfactions they remained true to their vows of devotion and loyalty to the Master. It was their personal association with Jesus during these months of testing that so endeared him to them that they all (save Judas Iscariot) remained loyal and true to him even in the dark hours of the trial and crucifixion. Real men simply could not actually desert a revered teacher who had lived so close to them and had been so devoted to them as had Jesus. Through the dark hours of the Master's death, in the hearts of these apostles all reason, judgment, and logic were set aside in deference to just one extraordinary human emotion—the supreme sentiment of friendship-loyalty. These five months of work with Jesus led these apostles, each one of them, to regard him as the best *friend* he had in all the world. And it was this human sentiment, and not his superb teachings or marvelous doings, that held them together until after the resurrection and the renewal of the proclamation of the gospel of the kingdom.

Not only were these months of quiet work a great test to the apostles, a test which they survived, but this season of public inactivity was a great trial to Jesus' family. By the time Jesus was prepared to launch forth on his public work, his entire family (except Ruth) had practically deserted him. On only a few occasions did they attempt to make subsequent contact with him, and then it was to persuade him to return home with them, for they came near to believing that he was beside himself. They simply could not fathom his philosophy nor grasp his teaching; it was all too much for those of his own flesh and blood.

The apostles carried on their personal work in Capernaum, Bethsaida-Julias, Chorazin, Gerasa, Hippos, Magdala, Cana, Bethlehem of Galilee, Jotapata, Ramah, Safed, Gischala, Gadara, and Abila. Besides these towns they labored in many villages as well as in the countryside. By the end of this period the twelve had worked out fairly satisfactory plans for the care of their respective families. Most of the apostles were married, some had several children, but they had made such arrangements for the support of their home folks that, with some little assistance from the apostolic funds, they could devote their entire energies to the

Master's work without having to worry about the financial welfare of their families.

10. ORGANIZATION OF THE TWELVE

The apostles early organized themselves in the following manner:

1. Andrew, the first chosen apostle, was designated chairman and director general of the twelve.

2. Peter, James, and John were appointed personal companions of Jesus. They were to attend him day and night, to minister to his physical and sundry needs, and to accompany him on those night vigils of prayer and mysterious communion with the Father in heaven.

3. Philip was made steward of the group. It was his duty to provide food and to see that visitors, and even the multitude of listeners at times, had something to eat.

4. Nathaniel watched over the needs of the families of the twelve. He received regular reports as to the requirements of each apostle's family and, making requisition on Judas, the treasurer, would send funds each week to those in need.

5. Matthew was the fiscal agent of the apostolic corps. It was his duty to see that the budget was balanced, the treasury replenished. If the funds for mutual support were not forthcoming, if donations sufficient to maintain the party were not received, Matthew was empowered to order the twelve back to their nets for a season. But this was never necessary after they began their public work; he always had sufficient funds in the treasurer's hands to finance their activities.

6. Thomas was manager of the itinerary. It devolved upon him to arrange lodgings and in a general way select places for teaching and preaching, thereby insuring a smooth and expeditious travel schedule.

7. James and Judas the twin sons of Alpheus were assigned to the management of the multitudes. It was their task to deputize a sufficient number of assistant ushers to enable them to maintain order among the crowds during the preaching.

8. Simon Zelotes was given charge of recreation and play. He managed the Wednesday programs and also sought to provide for a few hours of relaxation and diversion each day.

9. Judas Iscariot was appointed treasurer. He carried the bag. He paid all expenses and kept the books. He made budget estimates for Matthew from week to week and also made weekly reports to Andrew. Judas paid out funds on Andrew's authorization.

In this way the twelve functioned from their early organization up to the time of the reorganization made necessary by the desertion of Judas, the betrayer. The Master and his disciple-apostles went on in this simple manner until Sunday, January 12, A.D. 27, when he called them together and formally ordained them as ambassadors of the kingdom and preachers of its glad tidings. And soon thereafter they prepared to start for Jerusalem and Judea on their first public preaching tour.

PAPER 139

THE TWELVE APOSTLES

IT IS an eloquent testimony to the charm and righteousness of Jesus' earth life that, although he repeatedly dashed to pieces the hopes of his apostles and tore to shreds their every ambition for personal exaltation, only one deserted him.

The apostles learned from Jesus about the kingdom of heaven, and Jesus learned much from them about the kingdom of men, human nature as it lives on Urantia and on the other evolutionary worlds of time and space. These twelve men represented many different types of human temperament, and they had not been made *alike* by schooling. Many of these Galilean fishermen carried heavy strains of gentile blood as a result of the forcible conversion of the gentile population of Galilee one hundred years previously.

Do not make the mistake of regarding the apostles as being altogether ignorant and unlearned. All of them, except the Alpheus twins, were graduates of the synagogue schools, having been thoroughly trained in the Hebrew scriptures and in much of the current knowledge of that day. Seven were graduates of the Capernaum synagogue schools, and there were no better Jewish schools in all Galilee.

When your records refer to these messengers of the kingdom as being "ignorant and unlearned," it was intended to convey the idea that they were laymen, unlearned in the lore of the rabbis and untrained in the methods of rabbinical interpretation of the Scriptures. They were lacking in so-called higher education. In modern times they would certainly be considered uneducated, and in some circles of society even uncultured. One thing is certain: They had not all been put through the same rigid and stereotyped educational curriculum. From adolescence on they had enjoyed separate experiences of learning how to live.

1. ANDREW, THE FIRST CHOSEN

Andrew, chairman of the apostolic corps of the kingdom, was born in Capernaum. He was the oldest child in a family of five—himself, his brother Simon, and three sisters. His father, now dead, had been a partner of Zebedee in the fish-drying business at Bethsaida, the fishing harbor of Capernaum. When he became an apostle, Andrew was unmarried but made his home with his married brother, Simon Peter. Both were fishermen and partners of James and John the sons of Zebedee.

In A.D. 26, the year he was chosen as an apostle, Andrew was 33, a full year older than Jesus and the oldest of the apostles. He sprang from an excellent line of ancestors and was the ablest man of the twelve. Excepting oratory, he was the peer of his associates in almost every imaginable ability. Jesus never gave Andrew a nickname, a fraternal designation. But even as the apostles soon began to call Jesus Master, so they also designated Andrew by a term the equivalent of Chief.

Andrew was a good organizer but a better administrator. He was one of the inner circle of four apostles, but his appointment by Jesus as the head of the apostolic group made it necessary for him to remain on duty with his brethren while the other three enjoyed very close communion with the Master. To the very end Andrew remained dean of the apostolic corps.

Although Andrew was never an effective preacher, he was an efficient personal worker, being the pioneer missionary of the kingdom in that, as the first chosen apostle, he immediately brought to Jesus his brother, Simon, who subsequently became one of the greatest preachers of the kingdom. Andrew was the chief supporter of Jesus' policy of utilizing the program of personal work as a means of training the twelve as messengers of the kingdom.

Whether Jesus privately taught the apostles or preached to the multitude, Andrew was usually conversant with what was going on; he was an understanding executive and an efficient administrator. He rendered a prompt decision on every matter brought to his notice unless he deemed the problem one beyond the domain of his authority, in which event he would take it straight to Jesus.

Andrew and Peter were very unlike in character and temperament, but it must be recorded everlastingly to their credit that they got along together splendidly. Andrew was never jealous of Peter's oratorical ability. Not often will an older man of Andrew's type be observed exerting such a profound influence over a younger and talented brother. Andrew and Peter never seemed to be in the least jealous of each other's abilities or achievements. Late on the evening of the day of Pentecost, when, largely through the energetic and inspiring preaching of Peter, two thousand souls were added to the kingdom, Andrew said to his brother: "I could not do that, but I am glad I have a brother who could." To which Peter replied: "And but for your bringing me to the Master and by your steadfastness *keeping* me with him, I should not have been here to do this." Andrew and Peter were the exceptions to the rule, proving that even brothers can live together peaceably and work together effectively.

After Pentecost Peter was famous, but it never irritated the older Andrew to spend the rest of his life being introduced as "Simon Peter's brother."

Of all the apostles, Andrew was the best judge of men. He knew that trouble was brewing in the heart of Judas Iscariot even when none of the others suspected that anything was wrong with their treasurer; but he told none of them his fears. Andrew's great service to the kingdom was in advising Peter, James, and John concerning the choice of the first missionaries who were sent out to proclaim the gospel, and also in counseling these early leaders about the organization of the administrative affairs of the kingdom. Andrew had a great gift for discovering the hidden resources and latent talents of young people.

Very soon after Jesus' ascension on high, Andrew began the writing of a personal record of many of the sayings and doings of his departed Master. After Andrew's death other copies of this private record were made and circulated freely among the early teachers of the Christian church. These informal notes of Andrew's were subsequently edited, amended, altered, and added to until they made up a fairly consecutive narrative of the Master's life on earth. The last of these few altered and amended copies was destroyed by fire at Alexandria about one hundred years after the original was written by the first chosen of the twelve apostles.

Andrew was a man of clear insight, logical thought, and firm decision, whose great strength of character consisted in his superb stability. His temperamental handicap was his lack of enthusiasm; he many times failed to encourage his associates by judicious commendation. And this reticence to praise the worthy accomplishments of his friends grew out of his abhorrence of flattery and insincerity. Andrew was one of those all-round, even-tempered, self-made, and successful men of modest affairs.

Every one of the apostles loved Jesus, but it remains true that each of the twelve was drawn toward him because of some certain trait of personality which made a special appeal to the individual apostle. Andrew admired Jesus because of his consistent sincerity, his unaffected dignity. When men once knew Jesus, they were possessed with the urge to share him with their friends; they really wanted all the world to know him.

When the later persecutions finally scattered the apostles from Jerusalem, Andrew journeyed through Armenia, Asia Minor, and Macedonia and, after bringing many thousands into the kingdom, was finally apprehended and crucified in Patrae in Achaia. It was two full days before this robust man expired on the cross, and throughout these tragic hours he continued effectively to proclaim the glad tidings of the salvation of the kingdom of heaven.

2. SIMON PETER

When Simon joined the apostles, he was thirty years of age. He was married, had three children, and lived at Bethsaida, near Capernaum. His brother, Andrew, and his wife's mother lived with him. Both Peter and Andrew were fisher partners of the sons of Zebedee.

The Master had known Simon for some time before Andrew presented him as the second of the apostles. When Jesus gave Simon the name Peter, he did it with a smile; it was to be a sort of nickname. Simon was well known to all his friends as an erratic and impulsive fellow. True, later on, Jesus did attach a new and significant import to this lightly bestowed nickname.

Simon Peter was a man of impulse, an optimist. He had grown up permitting himself freely to indulge strong feelings; he was constantly getting into difficulties because he persisted in speaking without thinking. This sort of thoughtlessness also made incessant trouble for all of his friends and associates and was the cause of his receiving many mild rebukes from his Master. The only reason Peter did not get into more trouble because of his thoughtless speaking was that he very early learned to talk over many of his plans and schemes with his brother, Andrew, before he ventured to make public proposals.

Peter was a fluent speaker, eloquent and dramatic. He was also a natural and inspirational leader of men, a quick thinker but not a deep reasoner. He asked many questions, more than all the apostles put together, and while the majority of these questions were good and relevant, many of them were thoughtless and foolish. Peter did not have a deep mind, but he knew his mind fairly well. He was therefore a man of quick decision and sudden action. While others talked in their astonishment at seeing Jesus on the beach, Peter jumped in and swam ashore to meet the Master.

The one trait which Peter most admired in Jesus was his supernal tenderness. Peter never grew weary of contemplating Jesus' forbearance. He never forgot the lesson about forgiving the wrongdoer, not only seven times but seventy times and seven. He thought much about these impressions of the Master's forgiving character during those dark and dismal days immediately following his thoughtless and unintended denial of Jesus in the high priest's courtyard.

Simon Peter was distressingly vacillating; he would suddenly swing from one extreme to the other. First he refused to let Jesus wash his feet and then, on hearing the Master's reply, begged to be washed all over. But, after all, Jesus knew that Peter's faults were of the head and not of the heart. He was one of the most inexplicable combinations of courage and cowardice that ever lived on earth. His great strength of character was loyalty, friendship. Peter really and truly loved Jesus. And yet despite this towering strength of devotion he was so unstable and inconstant that he permitted a servant girl to tease him into denying his Lord and Master. Peter could withstand persecution and any other form of direct assault, but he withered and shrank before ridicule. He was a brave soldier when facing a frontal attack, but he was a fear-cringing coward when surprised with an assault from the rear.

Peter was the first of Jesus' apostles to come forward to defend the work of Philip among the Samaritans and Paul among the gentiles; yet later on at Antioch he reversed himself when confronted by ridiculing Judaizers, temporarily withdrawing from the gentiles only to bring down upon his head the fearless denunciation of Paul.

He was the first one of the apostles to make wholehearted confession of Jesus' combined humanity and divinity and the first—save Judas—to deny him. Peter was not so much of a dreamer, but he disliked to descend from the clouds of ecstasy and the enthusiasm of dramatic indulgence to the plain and matter-of-fact world of reality.

In following Jesus, literally and figuratively, he was either leading the procession or else trailing behind—"following afar off." But he was the outstanding preacher of the twelve; he did more than any other one man, aside from Paul, to establish the kingdom and send its messengers to the four corners of the earth in one generation.

After his rash denials of the Master he found himself, and with Andrew's sympathetic and understanding guidance he again led the way back to the fish nets while the apostles tarried to find out what was to happen after the crucifixion. When he was fully assured that Jesus had forgiven him and knew he had been received back into the Master's fold, the fires of the kingdom burned so brightly within his soul that he became a great and saving light to thousands who sat in darkness.

After leaving Jerusalem and before Paul became the leading spirit among the gentile Christian churches, Peter traveled extensively, visiting all the churches from Babylon to Corinth. He even visited and ministered to many of the churches which had been raised up by Paul. Although Peter and Paul differed much in temperament and education, even in theology, they worked together harmoniously for the upbuilding of the churches during their later years.

Something of Peter's style and teaching is shown in the sermons partially recorded by Luke and in the Gospel of Mark. His vigorous style was better shown in his letter known as the First Epistle of Peter; at least this was true before it was subsequently altered by a disciple of Paul.

But Peter persisted in making the mistake of trying to convince the Jews that Jesus was, after all, really and truly the Jewish Messiah. Right up to the day of his death, Simon Peter continued to suffer confusion in his mind between the concepts of Jesus as the Jewish Messiah, Christ as the world's redeemer, and the Son of Man as the revelation of God, the loving Father of all mankind.

Peter's wife was a very able woman. For years she labored acceptably as a member of the women's corps, and when Peter was driven out of Jerusalem, she accompanied him upon all his journeys to the churches as well as on all his missionary excursions. And the day her illustrious husband yielded up his life, she was thrown to the wild beasts in the arena at Rome.

And so this man Peter, an intimate of Jesus, one of the inner circle, went forth from Jerusalem proclaiming the glad tidings of the kingdom with power and glory until the fullness of his ministry had been accomplished; and he regarded himself as the recipient of high honors when his captors informed him that he must die as his Master had died—on the cross. And thus was Simon Peter crucified in Rome.

3. JAMES ZEBEDEE

James, the older of the two apostle sons of Zebedee, whom Jesus nicknamed "sons of thunder," was thirty years old when he became an apostle. He was married, had four children, and lived near his parents in the outskirts of Capernaum, Bethsaida. He was a fisherman, plying his calling in company with his younger brother John and in association with Andrew and Simon. James and his brother John enjoyed the advantage of having known Jesus longer than any of the other apostles.

This able apostle was a temperamental contradiction; he seemed really to possess two natures, both of which were actuated by strong feelings. He was particularly vehement when his indignation was once fully aroused. He had a fiery temper when once it was adequately provoked, and when the storm was over, he was always wont to justify and excuse his anger under the pretense that it was wholly a manifestation of righteous indignation. Except for these periodic upheavals of wrath, James's personality was much like that of Andrew. He did not have Andrew's discretion or insight into human nature, but he was a much better public speaker. Next to Peter, unless it was Matthew, James was the best public orator among the twelve.

Though James was in no sense moody, he could be quiet and taciturn one day and a very good talker and storyteller the next. He usually talked freely with Jesus, but among the twelve, for days at a time he was the silent man. His one great weakness was these spells of unaccountable silence.

The outstanding feature of James's personality was his ability to see all sides of a proposition. Of all the twelve, he came the nearest to grasping the real import and significance of Jesus' teaching. He, too, was slow at first to comprehend the Master's meaning, but ere they had finished their training, he had acquired a superior concept of Jesus' message. James was able to understand a wide range of human nature; he got along well with the versatile Andrew, the impetuous Peter, and his self-contained brother John.

Though James and John had their troubles trying to work together, it was inspiring to observe how well they got along. They did not succeed quite so well as Andrew and Peter, but they did much better than would ordinarily be expected of two brothers, especially such headstrong and determined brothers. But, strange as it may seem, these two sons of Zebedee were much more tolerant of each other than they were of strangers. They had great affection for one another; they had always been happy playmates. It was these "sons of thunder" who wanted to call fire down from heaven to destroy the Samaritans who presumed to show disrespect for their Master. But the untimely death of James greatly modified the vehement temperament of his younger brother John.

That characteristic of Jesus which James most admired was the Master's sympathetic affection. Jesus' understanding interest in the small and the great, the rich and the poor, made a great appeal to him.

James Zebedee was a well-balanced thinker and planner. Along with Andrew, he was one of the more level-headed of the apostolic group. He was a vigorous individual but was never in a hurry. He was an excellent balance wheel for Peter.

He was modest and undramatic, a daily server, an unpretentious worker, seeking no special reward when he once grasped something of the real meaning of the kingdom. And even in the story about the mother of James and John, who asked that her sons be granted places on the right hand and the left hand of Jesus, it should be remembered that it was the mother who made this request. And when they signified that they were ready to assume such responsibilities, it should be recognized that they were cognizant of the dangers accompanying the Master's supposed revolt against the Roman power, and that they were also willing to pay the price. When Jesus asked if they were ready to drink the cup, they replied that they were. And as concerns James, it was literally true—he did drink the cup with the Master, seeing that he was the first of the apostles to experience martyrdom, being early put to death with the sword by Herod Agrippa. James was thus the first of the twelve to sacrifice his life upon the new battle line of the kingdom. Herod Agrippa feared James above all the other apostles. He was indeed often quiet and silent, but he was brave and determined when his convictions were aroused and challenged.

James lived his life to the full, and when the end came, he bore himself with such grace and fortitude that even his accuser and informer, who attended his trial and execution, was so touched that he rushed away from the scene of James's death to join himself to the disciples of Jesus.

4. JOHN ZEBEDEE

When he became an apostle, John was twenty-four years old and was the youngest of the twelve. He was unmarried and lived with his parents at Bethsaida; he was a fisherman and worked with his brother James in partnership with Andrew and Peter. Both before and after becoming an apostle, John functioned as the personal agent of Jesus in dealing with the Master's family, and he continued to bear this responsibility as long as Mary the mother of Jesus lived.

Since John was the youngest of the twelve and so closely associated with Jesus in his family affairs, he was very dear to the Master, but it cannot be truthfully said that he was "the disciple whom Jesus loved." You would hardly suspect such a magnanimous personality as Jesus to be guilty of showing favoritism, of loving one of his apostles more than the others. The fact that John was one of the three personal aides of Jesus lent further color to this mistaken idea, not to mention that John, along with his brother James, had known Jesus longer than the others.

Peter, James, and John were assigned as personal aides to Jesus soon after they became apostles. Shortly after the selection of the twelve and at the time Jesus appointed Andrew to act as director of the group, he said to him: "And now I desire that you assign two or three of your associates to be with me and to remain by my side, to comfort me and to minister to my daily needs." And Andrew thought best to select for this special duty the next three first-chosen apostles. He would have liked to volunteer for such a blessed service himself, but the Master had already given him his commission; so he immediately directed that Peter, James, and John attach themselves to Jesus.

John Zebedee had many lovely traits of character, but one which was not so lovely was his inordinate but usually well-concealed conceit. His long association with Jesus made many and great changes in his character. This conceit was greatly lessened, but after growing old and becoming more or less childish, this self-esteem reappeared to a certain extent, so that, when engaged in directing Nathan in the writing of the Gospel which now bears his name, the aged apostle did not hesitate repeatedly to refer to himself as the "disciple whom Jesus loved." In view of the fact that John came nearer to being the chum of Jesus than any other earth mortal, that he was his chosen personal representative in so many matters, it is not strange that he should have come to regard himself as the "disciple whom Jesus loved" since he most certainly knew he was the disciple whom Jesus so frequently trusted.

The strongest trait in John's character was his dependability; he was prompt and courageous, faithful and devoted. His greatest weakness was this characteristic conceit. He was the youngest member of his father's family and the youngest of the apostolic group. Perhaps he was just a bit spoiled; maybe he had been humored slightly too much. But the John of after years was a very different type of person than the self-admiring and arbitrary young man who joined the ranks of Jesus' apostles when he was twenty-four.

Those characteristics of Jesus which John most appreciated were the Master's love and unselfishness; these traits made such an impression on him that his whole subsequent life became dominated by the sentiment of love and brotherly devotion. He talked about love and wrote about love. This "son of thunder" became the "apostle of love"; and at Ephesus, when the aged bishop was no longer able to stand in the pulpit and preach but had to be carried to church in a chair, and when at the close of the service he was asked to say a few words to the believers, for years his only utterance was, "My little children, love one another."

John was a man of few words except when his temper was aroused. He thought much but said little. As he grew older, his temper became more subdued, better controlled, but he never overcame his disinclination to talk; he never fully mastered this reticence. But he was gifted with a remarkable and creative imagination.

There was another side to John that one would not expect to find in this quiet and introspective type. He was somewhat bigoted and inordinately intolerant. In this respect he and James were much alike—they both wanted to call down fire from heaven on the heads of the disrespectful Samaritans. When John encountered some strangers teaching in Jesus' name, he promptly forbade them. But he was not the only one of the twelve who was tainted with this kind of self-esteem and superiority consciousness.

John's life was tremendously influenced by the sight of Jesus' going about without a home as he knew how faithfully he had made provision for the care of his mother and family. John also deeply sympathized with Jesus because of his family's failure to understand him, being aware that they were gradually withdrawing from him. This entire situation, together with Jesus' ever deferring his slightest wish to the will of the Father in heaven and his daily life of implicit trust, made such a profound impression on John that it produced marked and permanent changes in his character, changes which manifested themselves throughout his entire subsequent life.

John had a cool and daring courage which few of the other apostles possessed. He was the one apostle who followed right along with Jesus the night of his arrest and dared to accompany his Master into the very jaws of death. He was present and near at hand right up to the last earthly hour and was found faithfully carrying out his trust with regard to Jesus' mother and ready to receive such additional instructions as might be given during the last moments of the Master's mortal existence. One thing is certain, John was thoroughly dependable. John usually sat on Jesus' right hand when the twelve were at meat. He was the first of the twelve really and fully to believe in the resurrection, and he was the first to recognize the Master when he came to them on the seashore after his resurrection.

This son of Zebedee was very closely associated with Peter in the early activities of the Christian movement, becoming one of the chief supporters of the Jerusalem church. He was the right-hand support of Peter on the day of Pentecost.

Several years after the martyrdom of James, John married his brother's widow. The last twenty years of his life he was cared for by a loving granddaughter.

John was in prison several times and was banished to the Isle of Patmos for a period of four years until another emperor came to power in Rome. Had not John been tactful and sagacious, he would undoubtedly have been killed as was his more outspoken brother James. As the years passed, John, together with James the Lord's brother, learned to practice wise conciliation when they appeared before the civil magistrates. They found that a "soft answer turns away wrath." They also learned to represent the church as a "spiritual brotherhood devoted to the social service of mankind" rather than as "the kingdom of heaven." They taught loving service rather than ruling power—kingdom and king.

When in temporary exile on Patmos, John wrote the Book of Revelation, which you now have in greatly abridged and distorted form. This Book of Revelation contains the surviving fragments of a great revelation, large portions of which were lost, other portions of which were removed, subsequent to John's writing. It is preserved in only fragmentary and adulterated form.

John traveled much, labored incessantly, and after becoming bishop of the Asia churches, settled down at Ephesus. He directed his associate, Nathan, in the writing of the so-called "Gospel according to John," at Ephesus, when he was ninety-nine years old. Of all the twelve apostles, John Zebedee eventually became the outstanding theologian. He died a natural death at Ephesus in A.D. 103 when he was one hundred and one years of age.

5. PHILIP THE CURIOUS

Philip was the fifth apostle to be chosen, being called when Jesus and his first four apostles were on their way from John's rendezvous on the Jordan to Cana of Galilee. Since he lived at Bethsaida, Philip had for some time known of Jesus, but it had not occurred to him that Jesus was a really great man until that day in the Jordan valley when he said, "Follow me." Philip was also somewhat influenced by the fact that Andrew, Peter, James, and John had accepted Jesus as the Deliverer.

Philip was twenty-seven years of age when he joined the apostles; he had recently been married, but he had no children at this time. The nickname which the apostles gave him signified "curiosity." Philip was always wanting to be shown. He never seemed to see very far into any proposition. He was not necessarily dull, but he lacked imagination. This lack of imagination was the great weakness of his character. He was a commonplace and matter-of-fact individual.

When the apostles were organized for service, Philip was made steward; it was his duty to see that they were at all times supplied with provisions. And he was a good steward. His strongest characteristic was his methodical thoroughness; he was both mathematical and systematic.

Philip came from a family of seven, three boys and four girls. He was next to the oldest, and after the resurrection he baptized his entire family into the kingdom. Philip's people were fisherfolk. His father was a very able man, a deep thinker, but his mother was of a very mediocre family. Philip was not a man who could be expected to do big things, but he was a man who could do little things in a big way, do them well and acceptably. Only a few times in four years did he fail to have food on hand to satisfy the needs of all. Even the many emergency demands attendant upon the life they lived seldom found him unprepared. The commissary department of the apostolic family was intelligently and efficiently managed.

The strong point about Philip was his methodical reliability; the weak point in his make-up was his utter lack of imagination, the absence of the ability to put two and two together to obtain four. He was mathematical in the abstract but not constructive in his imagination. He was almost entirely lacking in certain types of imagination. He was the typical everyday and commonplace average man. There were a great many such men and women among the multitudes who came to hear Jesus teach and preach, and they derived great comfort from observing one like themselves elevated to an honored position in the councils of the Master; they derived courage from the fact that one like themselves had already found a high place in the affairs of the kingdom. And Jesus learned much about the way some human minds function as he so patiently listened to Philip's foolish questions and so many times complied with his steward's request to "be shown."

The one quality about Jesus which Philip so continuously admired was the Master's unfailing generosity. Never could Philip find anything in Jesus which was small, niggardly, or stingy, and he worshiped this ever-present and unfailing liberality.

There was little about Philip's personality that was impressive. He was often spoken of as "Philip of Bethsaida, the town where Andrew and Peter live." He was almost without discerning vision; he was unable to grasp the dramatic possibilities of a given situation. He was not pessimistic; he was simply prosaic. He was also greatly lacking in spiritual insight. He would not hesitate to interrupt Jesus in the midst of one of the Master's most profound discourses to ask an apparently foolish question. But Jesus never reprimanded him for such thoughtlessness; he was patient with him and considerate of his inability to grasp the deeper meanings of the teaching. Jesus well knew that, if he once rebuked Philip for asking these annoying questions, he would not only wound this honest soul, but such a reprimand would so hurt Philip that he would never again feel free to ask questions. Jesus knew that on his worlds of space there were untold billions of similar slow-thinking mortals, and he wanted to encourage them all to look to him and always to feel free to come to him with their questions and problems. After all, Jesus was really more interested in Philip's foolish questions than in the sermon he might be preaching. Jesus was supremely interested in *men,* all kinds of men.

The apostolic steward was not a good public speaker, but he was a very persuasive and successful personal worker. He was not easily discouraged; he was a plodder and very tenacious in anything he undertook. He had that great and rare gift of saying, "Come." When his first convert, Nathaniel, wanted to argue about the merits and demerits of Jesus and Nazareth, Philip's effective reply was, "Come and see." He was not a dogmatic preacher who exhorted his hearers to "Go"—do this and do that. He met all situations as they arose in his work with "Come"—"come with me; I will show you the way." And that is always the effective technique in all forms and phases of teaching. Even parents may learn from Philip the better way of saying to their children *not* "Go do this and go do that," but rather, "Come with us while we show and share with you the better way."

The inability of Philip to adapt himself to a new situation was well shown when the Greeks came to him at Jerusalem, saying: "Sir, we desire to see Jesus." Now Philip would have said to any Jew asking such a question, "Come." But these men were foreigners, and Philip could remember no instructions from his superiors regarding such matters; so the only thing he could think to do was to consult the chief, Andrew, and then they both escorted the inquiring Greeks to Jesus. Likewise, when he went into Samaria preaching and baptizing believers, as he had been instructed by his Master, he refrained from laying hands on his converts in token of their having received the Spirit of Truth. This was done by Peter and John, who presently came down from Jerusalem to observe his work in behalf of the mother church.

Philip went on through the trying times of the Master's death, participated in the reorganization of the twelve, and was the first to go forth to win souls for the kingdom outside of the immediate Jewish ranks, being most successful in his work for the Samaritans and in all his subsequent labors in behalf of the gospel.

Philip's wife, who was an efficient member of the women's corps, became actively associated with her husband in his evangelistic work after their flight from the Jerusalem persecutions. His wife was a fearless woman. She stood at the foot of Philip's cross encouraging him to proclaim the glad tidings even to his murderers, and when his strength failed, she began the recital of the story of salvation by faith in Jesus and was silenced only when the irate Jews rushed upon her and stoned her to death. Their eldest daughter, Leah, continued their work, later on becoming the renowned prophetess of Hierapolis.

Philip, the onetime steward of the twelve, was a mighty man in the kingdom, winning souls wherever he went; and he was finally crucified for his faith and buried at Hierapolis.

6. HONEST NATHANIEL

Nathaniel, the sixth and last of the apostles to be chosen by the Master himself, was brought to Jesus by his friend Philip. He had been associated in several business enterprises with Philip and, with him, was on the way down to see John the Baptist when they encountered Jesus.

When Nathaniel joined the apostles, he was twenty-five years old and was the next to the youngest of the group. He was the youngest of a family of seven, was unmarried, and the only support of aged and infirm parents, with whom he lived at Cana; his brothers and sister were either married or deceased, and none lived there. Nathaniel and Judas Iscariot were the two best educated men among the twelve. Nathaniel had thought to become a merchant.

Jesus did not himself give Nathaniel a nickname, but the twelve soon began to speak of him in terms that signified honesty, sincerity. He was "without guile." And this was his great virtue; he was both honest and sincere. The weakness of his character was his pride; he was very proud of his family, his city, his reputation, and his nation, all of which is commendable if it is not carried too far. But Nathaniel was inclined to go to extremes with his personal prejudices. He was disposed to prejudge individuals in accordance with his personal opinions. He was not slow to ask the question, even before he had met Jesus, "Can any good thing come out of Nazareth?" But Nathaniel was not obstinate, even if he was proud. He was quick to reverse himself when he once looked into Jesus' face.

In many respects Nathaniel was the odd genius of the twelve. He was the apostolic philosopher and dreamer, but he was a very practical sort of dreamer. He alternated between seasons of profound philosophy and periods of rare and droll humor; when in the proper mood, he was probably the best storyteller among the twelve. Jesus greatly enjoyed hearing Nathaniel discourse on things both serious and frivolous. Nathaniel progressively took Jesus and the kingdom more seriously, but never did he take himself seriously.

The apostles all loved and respected Nathaniel, and he got along with them splendidly, excepting Judas Iscariot. Judas did not think Nathaniel took his apostleship sufficiently seriously and once had the temerity to go secretly to Jesus and lodge complaint against him. Said Jesus: "Judas, watch carefully your steps; do not overmagnify your office. Who of us is competent to judge his brother? It is not the Father's will that his children should partake only of the serious things of life. Let me repeat: I have come that my brethren in the flesh may have joy, gladness, and life more abundantly. Go then, Judas, and do well that which has been intrusted to you but leave Nathaniel, your brother, to give account of himself to God." And the memory of this, with that of many similar experiences, long lived in the self-deceiving heart of Judas Iscariot.

Many times, when Jesus was away on the mountain with Peter, James, and John, and things were becoming tense and tangled among the apostles, when even Andrew was in doubt about what to say to his disconsolate brethren, Nathaniel would relieve the tension by a bit of philosophy or a flash of humor; good humor, too.

Nathaniel's duty was to look after the families of the twelve. He was often absent from the apostolic councils, for when he heard that sickness or anything out of the ordinary had happened to one of his charges, he lost no time in getting to that home. The twelve rested securely in the knowledge that their families' welfare was safe in the hands of Nathaniel.

Nathaniel most revered Jesus for his tolerance. He never grew weary of contemplating the broadmindedness and generous sympathy of the Son of Man.

Nathaniel's father (Bartholomew) died shortly after Pentecost, after which this apostle went into Mesopotamia and India proclaiming the glad tidings of the kingdom and baptizing believers. His brethren never knew what became of their onetime philosopher, poet, and humorist. But he also was a great man in the kingdom and did much to spread his Master's teachings, even though he did not participate in the organization of the subsequent Christian church. Nathaniel died in India.

7. MATTHEW LEVI

Matthew, the seventh apostle, was chosen by Andrew. Matthew belonged to a family of tax gatherers, or publicans, but was himself a customs collector in Capernaum, where he lived. He was thirty-one years old and married and had four children. He was a man of moderate wealth, the only one of any means belonging to the apostolic corps. He was a good business man, a good social mixer, and was gifted with the ability to make friends and to get along smoothly with a great variety of people.

Andrew appointed Matthew the financial representative of the apostles. In a way he was the fiscal agent and publicity spokesman for the apostolic organization. He was a keen judge of human nature and a very efficient propagandist. His is a personality difficult to visualize, but he was a very earnest disciple and an increasing believer in the mission of Jesus and in the certainty of the kingdom. Jesus never gave Levi a nickname, but his fellow apostles commonly referred to him as the "money-getter."

Levi's strong point was his wholehearted devotion to the cause. That he, a publican, had been taken in by Jesus and his apostles was the cause for overwhelming gratitude on the part of the former revenue collector. However, it required some little time for the rest of the apostles, especially Simon Zelotes and Judas Iscariot, to become reconciled to the publican's presence in their midst. Matthew's weakness was his shortsighted and materialistic viewpoint of life. But in all these matters he made great progress as the months went by. He, of course, had to be absent from many of the most precious seasons of instruction as it was his duty to keep the treasury replenished.

It was the Master's forgiving disposition which Matthew most appreciated. He would never cease to recount that faith only was necessary in the business of finding God. He always liked to speak of the kingdom as "this business of finding God."

Though Matthew was a man with a past, he gave an excellent account of himself, and as time went on, his associates became proud of the publican's performances. He was one of the apostles who made extensive notes on the sayings of Jesus, and these notes were used as the basis of Isador's subsequent narrative of the sayings and doings of Jesus, which has become known as the Gospel according to Matthew.

The great and useful life of Matthew, the business man and customs collector of Capernaum, has been the means of leading thousands upon thousands of other business men, public officials, and politicians, down through the subsequent ages, also to hear that engaging voice of the Master saying, "Follow me." Matthew really was a shrewd politician, but he was intensely loyal to Jesus and supremely devoted to the task of seeing that the messengers of the coming kingdom were adequately financed.

The presence of Matthew among the twelve was the means of keeping the doors of the kingdom wide open to hosts of downhearted and outcast souls who had regarded themselves as long since without the bounds of religious consolation. Outcast and despairing men and women flocked to hear Jesus, and he never turned one away.

Matthew received freely tendered offerings from believing disciples and the immediate auditors of the Master's teachings, but he never openly solicited funds from the multitudes. He did all his financial work in a quiet and personal way and raised most of the money among the more substantial class of interested believers. He gave practically the whole of his modest fortune to the work of the Master and his apostles, but they never knew of this generosity, save Jesus, who knew all about it. Matthew hesitated openly to contribute to the apostolic funds for fear that Jesus and his associates might regard his money as being tainted; so he gave much in the names of other believers. During the earlier months, when Matthew knew his presence among them was more or less of a trial, he was strongly tempted to let them know that his funds often supplied them with their daily bread, but he did not yield. When evidence of the disdain of the publican would become manifest, Levi would burn to reveal to them his generosity, but always he managed to keep still.

When the funds for the week were short of the estimated requirements, Levi would often draw heavily upon his own personal resources. Also, sometimes when he became greatly interested in Jesus' teaching, he preferred to remain and hear the instruction, even though he knew he must personally make up for his failure to solicit the necessary funds. But Levi did so wish that Jesus might know that much of the money came from his pocket! He little realized that the Master knew all about it. The apostles all died without knowing that Matthew was their benefactor to such an extent that, when he went forth to proclaim the gospel of the kingdom after the beginning of the persecutions, he was practically penniless.

When these persecutions caused the believers to forsake Jerusalem, Matthew journeyed north, preaching the gospel of the kingdom and baptizing believers. He was lost to the knowledge of his former apostolic associates, but on he went, preaching and baptizing, through Syria, Cappadocia, Galatia, Bithynia, and Thrace. And it was in Thrace, at Lysimachia, that certain unbelieving Jews conspired with the Roman soldiers to encompass his death. And this regenerated publican died triumphant in the faith of a salvation he had so surely learned from the teachings of the Master during his recent sojourn on earth.

8. THOMAS DIDYMUS

Thomas was the eighth apostle, and he was chosen by Philip. In later times he has become known as "doubting Thomas," but his fellow apostles hardly looked upon him as a chronic doubter. True, his was a logical, skeptical type of mind, but he had a form of courageous loyalty which forbade those who knew him intimately to regard him as a trifling skeptic.

When Thomas joined the apostles, he was twenty-nine years old, was married, and had four children. Formerly he had been a carpenter and stone mason, but latterly he had become a fisherman and resided at Tarichea, situated on the west bank of the Jordan where it flows out of the Sea of Galilee, and he was regarded as the leading citizen of this little village. He had little education, but he possessed a keen, reasoning mind and was the son of excellent parents, who lived at Tiberias. Thomas had the one truly analytical mind of the twelve; he was the real scientist of the apostolic group.

The early home life of Thomas had been unfortunate; his parents were not altogether happy in their married life, and this was reflected in Thomas's adult experience. He grew up having a very disagreeable and quarrelsome disposition. Even his wife was glad to see him join the apostles; she was relieved by the thought that her pessimistic husband would be away from home most of the time. Thomas also had a streak of suspicion which made it very difficult to get along peaceably with him. Peter was very much upset by Thomas at first, complaining to his brother, Andrew, that Thomas was "mean, ugly, and always suspicious." But the better his associates knew Thomas, the more they liked him. They found he was superbly honest and unflinchingly loyal. He was perfectly sincere and unquestionably truthful, but he was a natural-born faultfinder and had grown up to become a real pessimist. His analytical mind had become cursed with suspicion. He was rapidly losing faith in his fellow men when he became associated with the twelve and thus came in contact with the noble character of Jesus. This association with the Master began at once to transform Thomas's whole disposition and to effect great changes in his mental reactions to his fellow men.

Thomas's great strength was his superb analytical mind coupled with his unflinching courage—when he had once made up his mind. His great weakness was his suspicious doubting, which he never fully overcame throughout his whole lifetime in the flesh.

In the organization of the twelve Thomas was assigned to arrange and manage the itinerary, and he was an able director of the work and movements of the apostolic corps. He was a good executive, an excellent businessman, but he was handicapped by his many moods; he was one man one day and another man the next. He was inclined toward melancholic brooding when he joined the apostles, but contact with Jesus and the apostles largely cured him of this morbid introspection.

Jesus enjoyed Thomas very much and had many long, personal talks with him. His presence among the apostles was a great comfort to all honest doubters and encouraged many troubled minds to come into the kingdom, even if they could not wholly understand everything about the spiritual and philosophic phases of the teachings of Jesus. Thomas's membership in the twelve was a standing declaration that Jesus loved even honest doubters.

The other apostles held Jesus in reverence because of some special and outstanding trait of his replete personality, but Thomas revered his Master because of his superbly balanced character. Increasingly Thomas admired and honored one who was so lovingly merciful yet so inflexibly just and fair; so firm but never obstinate; so calm but never indifferent; so helpful and so sympathetic but never meddlesome or dictatorial; so strong but at the same time so gentle; so positive but never rough or rude; so tender but never vacillating; so pure and innocent but at the same time so virile, aggressive, and forceful; so truly courageous but never rash or foolhardy; such a lover of nature but so free from all tendency to revere nature; so humorous and so playful, but so free from levity and frivolity. It was this matchless symmetry of personality that so charmed Thomas. He probably enjoyed the highest intellectual understanding and personality appreciation of Jesus of any of the twelve.

In the councils of the twelve Thomas was always cautious, advocating a policy of safety first, but if his conservatism was voted down or overruled, he was always the first fearlessly to move out in execution of the program decided upon. Again and again would he stand out against some project as being foolhardy and presumptuous; he would debate to the bitter end, but when Andrew would put the proposition to a vote, and after the twelve would elect to do that which he had so strenuously opposed, Thomas was the first to say, "Let's go!" He was a good loser. He did not hold grudges nor nurse wounded feelings. Time and again did he oppose letting Jesus expose himself to danger, but when the Master would decide to take such risks, always was it Thomas who rallied the apostles with his courageous words, "Come on, comrades, let's go and die with him."

Thomas was in some respects like Philip; he also wanted "to be shown," but his outward expressions of doubt were based on entirely different intellectual operations. Thomas was analytical, not merely skeptical. As far as personal physical courage was concerned, he was one of the bravest among the twelve.

Thomas had some very bad days; he was blue and downcast at times. The loss of his twin sister when he was nine years old had occasioned him much youthful sorrow and had added to his temperamental problems of later life. When Thomas would become despondent, sometimes it was Nathaniel who helped him to recover, sometimes Peter, and not infrequently one of the Alpheus twins. When he was most depressed, unfortunately he always tried to avoid coming in direct contact with Jesus. But the Master knew all about this and had an understanding sympathy for his apostle when he was thus afflicted with depression and harassed by doubts.

Sometimes Thomas would get permission from Andrew to go off by himself for a day or two. But he soon learned that such a course was not wise; he early found that it was best, when he was downhearted, to stick close to his work and to remain near his associates. But no matter what happened in his emotional life, he kept right on being an apostle. When the time actually came to move forward, it was always Thomas who said, "Let's go!"

Thomas is the great example of a human being who has doubts, faces them, and wins. He had a great mind; he was no carping critic. He was a logical thinker; he was the acid test of Jesus and his fellow apostles. If Jesus and his work had not been genuine, it could not have held a man like Thomas from the start to the finish. He had a keen and sure sense of *fact.* At the first appearance of fraud or deception Thomas would have forsaken them all. Scientists may not fully understand all about Jesus and his work on earth, but there lived and worked with the Master and his human associates a man whose mind was that of a true scientist—Thomas Didymus—and he believed in Jesus of Nazareth.

Thomas had a trying time during the days of the trial and crucifixion. He was for a season in the depths of despair, but he rallied his courage, stuck to the apostles, and was present with them to welcome Jesus on the Sea of Galilee. For a while he succumbed to his doubting depression but eventually rallied his faith and courage. He gave wise counsel to the apostles after Pentecost and, when persecution scattered the believers, went to Cyprus, Crete, the North African coast, and Sicily, preaching the glad tidings of the kingdom and baptizing believers. And Thomas continued preaching and baptizing until he was apprehended by the agents of the Roman government and was put to death in Malta. Just a few weeks before his death he had begun the writing of the life and teachings of Jesus.

9. and 10. JAMES AND JUDAS ALPHEUS

James and Judas the sons of Alpheus, the twin fishermen living near Kheresa, were the ninth and tenth apostles and were chosen by James and John Zebedee. They were twenty-six years old and married, James having three children, Judas two.

There is not much to be said about these two commonplace fisherfolk. They loved their Master and Jesus loved them, but they never interrupted his discourses with questions. They understood very little about the philosophical discussions or the theological debates of their fellow apostles, but they rejoiced to find themselves numbered among such a group of mighty men. These two men were almost identical in personal appearance, mental characteristics, and extent of spiritual perception. What may be said of one should be recorded of the other.

Andrew assigned them to the work of policing the multitudes. They were the chief ushers of the preaching hours and, in fact, the general servants and errand boys of the twelve. They helped Philip with the supplies, they carried money to the families for Nathaniel, and always were they ready to lend a helping hand to any one of the apostles.

The multitudes of the common people were greatly encouraged to find two like themselves honored with places among the apostles. By their very acceptance as apostles these mediocre twins were the means of bringing a host of fainthearted believers into the kingdom. And, too, the common people took more kindly to the idea of being directed and managed by official ushers who were very much like themselves.

James and Judas, who were also called Thaddeus and Lebbeus, had neither strong points nor weak points. The nicknames given them by the disciples were good-natured designations of mediocrity. They were "the least of all the apostles"; they knew it and felt cheerful about it.

James Alpheus especially loved Jesus because of the Master's simplicity. These twins could not comprehend the mind of Jesus, but they did grasp the sympathetic bond between themselves and the heart of their Master. Their minds were not of a high order; they might even reverently be called stupid, but they had a real experience in their spiritual natures. They believed in Jesus; they were sons of God and fellows of the kingdom.

Judas Alpheus was drawn toward Jesus because of the Master's unostentatious humility. Such humility linked with such personal dignity made a great appeal to Judas. The fact that Jesus would always enjoin silence regarding his unusual acts made a great impression on this simple child of nature.

The twins were good-natured, simple-minded helpers, and everybody loved them. Jesus welcomed these young men of one talent to positions of honor on his personal staff in the kingdom because there are untold millions of other such simple and fear-ridden souls on the worlds of space whom he likewise wishes to welcome into active and believing fellowship with himself and his outpoured Spirit of Truth. Jesus does not look down upon littleness, only upon evil and sin. James and Judas were *little,* but they were also *faithful.* They were simple and ignorant, but they were also big-hearted, kind, and generous.

And how gratefully proud were these humble men on that day when the Master refused to accept a certain rich man as an evangelist unless he would sell his goods and help the poor. When the people heard this and beheld the twins among his counselors, they knew of a certainty that Jesus was no respecter of persons. But only a divine institution—the kingdom of heaven—could ever have been built upon such a mediocre human foundation!

Only once or twice in all their association with Jesus did the twins venture to ask questions in public. Judas was once intrigued into asking Jesus a question when the Master had talked about revealing himself openly to the world. He felt a little disappointed that there were to be no more secrets among the twelve, and he made bold to ask: "But, Master, when you do thus declare yourself to the world, how will you favor us with special manifestations of your goodness?"

The twins served faithfully until the end, until the dark days of trial, crucifixion, and despair. They never lost their heart faith in Jesus, and (save John) they were the first to believe in his resurrection. But they could not comprehend the establishment of the kingdom. Soon after their Master was crucified, they returned to their families and nets; their work was done. They had not the ability to go on in the more complex battles of the kingdom. But they lived and died conscious of having been honored and blessed with four years of close and personal association with a Son of God, the sovereign maker of a universe.

11. SIMON THE ZEALOT

Simon Zelotes, the eleventh apostle, was chosen by Simon Peter. He was an able man of good ancestry and lived with his family at Capernaum. He was twenty-eight years old when he became attached to the apostles. He was a fiery agitator and was also a man who spoke much without thinking. He had been a merchant in Capernaum before he turned his entire attention to the patriotic organization of the Zealots.

Simon Zelotes was given charge of the diversions and relaxation of the apostolic group, and he was a very efficient organizer of the play life and recreational activities of the twelve.

Simon's strength was his inspirational loyalty. When the apostles found a man or woman who floundered in indecision about entering the kingdom, they would send for Simon. It usually required only about fifteen minutes for this enthusiastic advocate of salvation through faith in God to settle all doubts and remove all indecision, to see a new soul born into the "liberty of faith and the joy of salvation."

Simon's great weakness was his material-mindedness. He could not quickly change himself from a Jewish nationalist to a spiritually minded internationalist. Four years was too short a time in which to make such an intellectual and emotional transformation, but Jesus was always patient with him.

The one thing about Jesus which Simon so much admired was the Master's calmness, his assurance, poise, and inexplicable composure.

Although Simon was a rabid revolutionist, a fearless firebrand of agitation, he gradually subdued his fiery nature until he became a powerful and effective preacher of "Peace on earth and good will among men." Simon was a great debater; he did like to argue. And when it came to dealing with the legalistic minds of the educated Jews or the intellectual quibblings of the Greeks, the task was always assigned to Simon.

He was a rebel by nature and an iconoclast by training, but Jesus won him for the higher concepts of the kingdom of heaven. He had always identified himself with the party of protest, but he now joined the party of progress, unlimited and eternal progression of spirit and truth. Simon was a man of intense loyalties and warm personal devotions, and he did profoundly love Jesus.

Jesus was not afraid to identify himself with business men, laboring men, optimists, pessimists, philosophers, skeptics, publicans, politicians, and patriots.

The Master had many talks with Simon, but he never fully succeeded in making an internationalist out of this ardent Jewish nationalist. Jesus often told Simon that it was proper to want to see the social, economic, and political orders improved, but he would always add: "That is not the business of the kingdom of heaven. We must be dedicated to the doing of the Father's will. Our business is to be ambassadors of a spiritual government on high, and we must not immediately concern ourselves with aught but the representation of the will and character of the divine Father who stands at the head of the government whose credentials we bear." It was all difficult for Simon to comprehend, but gradually he began to grasp something of the meaning of the Master's teaching.

After the dispersion because of the Jerusalem persecutions, Simon went into temporary retirement. He was literally crushed. As a nationalist patriot he had surrendered in deference to Jesus' teachings; now all was lost. He was in despair, but in a few years he rallied his hopes and went forth to proclaim the gospel of the kingdom.

He went to Alexandria and, after working up the Nile, penetrated into the heart of Africa, everywhere preaching the gospel of Jesus and baptizing believers. Thus he labored until he was an old man and feeble. And he died and was buried in the heart of Africa.

12. JUDAS ISCARIOT

Judas Iscariot, the twelfth apostle, was chosen by Nathaniel. He was born in Kerioth, a small town in southern Judea. When he was a lad, his parents moved to Jericho, where he lived and had been employed in his father's various business enterprises until he became interested in the preaching and work of

John the Baptist. Judas's parents were Sadducees, and when their son joined John's disciples, they disowned him.

When Nathaniel met Judas at Tarichea, he was seeking employment with a fish-drying enterprise at the lower end of the Sea of Galilee. He was thirty years of age and unmarried when he joined the apostles. He was probably the best-educated man among the twelve and the only Judean in the Master's apostolic family. Judas had no outstanding trait of personal strength, though he had many outwardly appearing traits of culture and habits of training. He was a good thinker but not always a truly *honest* thinker. Judas did not really understand himself; he was not really sincere in dealing with himself.

Andrew appointed Judas treasurer of the twelve, a position which he was eminently fitted to hold, and up to the time of the betrayal of his Master he discharged the responsibilities of his office honestly, faithfully, and most efficiently.

There was no special trait about Jesus which Judas admired above the generally attractive and exquisitely charming personality of the Master. Judas was never able to rise above his Judean prejudices against his Galilean associates; he would even criticize in his mind many things about Jesus. Him whom eleven of the apostles looked upon as the perfect man, as the "one altogether lovely and the chiefest among ten thousand," this self-satisfied Judean often dared to criticize in his own heart. He really entertained the notion that Jesus was timid and somewhat afraid to assert his own power and authority.

Judas was a good business man. It required tact, ability, and patience, as well as painstaking devotion, to manage the financial affairs of such an idealist as Jesus, to say nothing of wrestling with the helter-skelter business methods of some of his apostles. Judas really was a great executive, a farseeing and able financier. And he was a stickler for organization. None of the twelve ever criticized Judas. As far as they could see, Judas Iscariot was a matchless treasurer, a learned man, a loyal (though sometimes critical) apostle, and in every sense of the word a great success. The apostles loved Judas; he was really one of them. He must have *believed* in Jesus, but we doubt whether he really *loved* the Master with a whole heart. The case of Judas illustrates the truthfulness of that saying: "There is a way that seems right to a man, but the end thereof is death." It is altogether possible to fall victim to the peaceful deception of pleasant adjustment to the paths of sin and death. Be assured that Judas was always financially loyal to his Master and his fellow apostles. Money could never have been the motive for his betrayal of the Master.

Judas was an only son of unwise parents. When very young, he was pampered and petted; he was a spoiled child. As he grew up, he had exaggerated ideas about his self-importance. He was a poor loser. He had loose and distorted ideas about fairness; he was given to the indulgence of hate and suspicion. He was an expert at misinterpretation of the words and acts of his friends. All through his life Judas had cultivated the habit of getting even with those whom he fancied had mistreated him. His sense of values and loyalties was defective.

To Jesus, Judas was a faith adventure. From the beginning the Master fully understood the weakness of this apostle and well knew the dangers of admitting him to fellowship. But it is the nature of the Sons of God to give every created being a full and equal chance for salvation and survival. Jesus wanted not only the mortals of this world but the onlookers of innumerable other worlds to know that, when doubts exist as to the sincerity and wholeheartedness of a creature's devotion to the kingdom, it is the invariable practice of the Judges of men fully to receive the doubtful candidate. The door of eternal life is wide open to all; "whosoever will may come"; there are no restrictions or qualifications save the *faith* of the one who comes.

This is just the reason why Jesus permitted Judas to go on to the very end, always doing everything possible to transform and save this weak and confused apostle. But when light is not honestly received and lived up to, it tends to become darkness within the soul. Judas grew intellectually regarding Jesus' teachings about the kingdom, but he did not make progress in the acquirement of spiritual character as did the other apostles. He failed to make satisfactory personal progress in spiritual experience.

Judas became increasingly a brooder over personal disappointment, and finally he became a victim of resentment. His feelings had been many times hurt, and he grew abnormally suspicious of his best friends, even of the Master. Presently he became obsessed with the idea of getting even, anything to avenge himself, yes, even betrayal of his associates and his Master.

But these wicked and dangerous ideas did not take definite shape until the day when a grateful woman broke an expensive box of incense at Jesus' feet. This seemed wasteful to Judas, and when his public protest was so sweepingly disallowed by Jesus right there in the hearing of all, it was too much. That event determined the mobilization of all the accumulated hate, hurt, malice, prejudice, jealousy, and revenge of a lifetime, and he made up his mind to get even with he knew not whom; but he crystallized all the evil of his nature upon the *one* innocent person in all the sordid drama of his unfortunate life just because Jesus happened to be the chief actor in the episode which marked his passing from the progressive kingdom of light into that self-chosen domain of darkness.

The Master many times, both privately and publicly, had warned Judas that he was slipping, but divine warnings are usually useless in dealing with embittered human nature. Jesus did everything possible, consistent with man's moral freedom, to prevent Judas's choosing to go the wrong way. The great test finally came. The son of resentment failed; he yielded to the sour and sordid dictates of a proud and vengeful mind of exaggerated self-importance and swiftly plunged on down into confusion, despair, and depravity.

Judas then entered into the base and shameful intrigue to betray his Lord and Master and quickly carried the nefarious scheme into effect. During the outworking of his anger-conceived plans of traitorous betrayal, he experienced moments of regret and shame, and in these lucid intervals he faintheartedly conceived, as a defense in his own mind, the idea that Jesus might possibly exert his power and deliver himself at the last moment.

When the sordid and sinful business was all over, this renegade mortal, who thought lightly of selling his friend for thirty pieces of silver to satisfy his long-nursed craving for revenge, rushed out and committed the final act in the drama of fleeing from the realities of mortal existence—suicide.

The eleven apostles were horrified, stunned. Jesus regarded the betrayer only with pity. The worlds have found it difficult to forgive Judas, and his name has become eschewed throughout a far-flung universe.

PAPER 140

THE ORDINATION OF THE TWELVE

JUST before noon on Sunday, January 12, A.D. 27, Jesus called the apostles together for their ordination as public preachers of the gospel of the kingdom. The twelve were expecting to be called almost any day; so this morning they did not go out far from the shore to fish. Several of them were lingering near the shore repairing their nets and tinkering with their fishing paraphernalia.

As Jesus started down the seashore calling the apostles, he first hailed Andrew and Peter, who were fishing near the shore; next he signaled to James and John, who were in a boat near by, visiting with their father, Zebedee, and mending their nets. Two by two he gathered up the other apostles, and when he had assembled all twelve, he journeyed with them to the highlands north of Capernaum, where he proceeded to instruct them in preparation for their formal ordination.

For once all twelve of the apostles were silent; even Peter was in a reflective mood. At last the long-waited-for hour had come! They were going apart with the Master to participate in some sort of solemn ceremony of personal consecration and collective dedication to the sacred work of representing their Master in the proclamation of the coming of his Father's kingdom.

1. PRELIMINARY INSTRUCTION

Before the formal ordination service Jesus spoke to the twelve as they were seated about him: "My brethren, this hour of the kingdom has come. I have brought you apart here with me to present you to the Father as ambassadors of the kingdom. Some of you heard me speak of this kingdom in the synagogue when you first were called. Each of you has learned more about the Father's kingdom since you have been with me working in the cities around about the Sea of Galilee. But just now I have something more to tell you concerning this kingdom.

"The new kingdom which my Father is about to set up in the hearts of his earth children is to be an everlasting dominion. There shall be no end of this rule of my Father in the hearts of those who desire to do his divine will. I declare to you that my Father is not the God of Jew or gentile. Many shall come from the east and from the west to sit down with us in the Father's kingdom, while many of the children of Abraham will refuse to enter this new brotherhood of the rule of the Father's spirit in the hearts of the children of men.

"The power of this kingdom shall consist, not in the strength of armies nor in the might of riches, but rather in the glory of the divine spirit that shall come to teach the minds and rule the hearts of the reborn citizens of this heavenly kingdom, the sons of God. This is the brotherhood of love wherein righteousness reigns, and whose battle cry shall be: Peace on earth and good will to all men. This kingdom, which you are so soon to go forth proclaiming, is the desire of the good men of all ages, the hope of all the earth, and the fulfillment of the wise promises of all the prophets.

"But for you, my children, and for all others who would follow you into this kingdom, there is set a severe test. Faith alone will pass you through its portals, but you must bring forth the fruits of my Father's spirit if you would continue to ascend in the progressive life of the divine fellowship. Verily, verily, I say to you, not every one who says, 'Lord, Lord,' shall enter the kingdom of heaven; but rather he who does the will of my Father who is in heaven.

"Your message to the world shall be: Seek first the kingdom of God and his righteousness, and in finding these, all other things essential to eternal survival shall be secured therewith. And now would I make it plain to you that this kingdom of my Father will not come with an outward show of power or with unseemly demonstration. You are not to go hence in the proclamation of the kingdom, saying, 'it is here' or 'it is there,' for this kingdom of which you preach is God within you.

"Whosoever would become great in my Father's kingdom shall become a minister to all; and whosoever would be first among you, let him become the server of his brethren. But when you are once truly received as citizens in the heavenly kingdom, you are no longer servants but sons, sons of the living God. And so shall this kingdom progress in the world until it shall break down every barrier and bring all men to know my Father and believe in the saving truth which I have come to declare. Even now is the kingdom at hand, and some of you will not die until you have seen the reign of God come in great power.

"And this which your eyes now behold, this small beginning of twelve commonplace men, shall multiply and grow until eventually the whole earth shall be filled with the praise of my Father. And it will not be so much by the words you speak as by the lives you live that men will know you have been with me and have learned of the realities of the kingdom. And while I would lay no grievous burdens upon your minds, I am about to put upon your souls the solemn responsibility of representing me in the world when I shall presently leave you as I now represent my Father in this life which I am living in the flesh." And when he had finished speaking, he stood up.

2. THE ORDINATION

Jesus now instructed the twelve mortals who had just listened to his declaration concerning the kingdom to kneel in a circle about him. Then the Master placed his hands upon the head of each apostle, beginning with Judas Iscariot and ending with Andrew. When he had blessed them, he extended his hands and prayed:

"My Father, I now bring to you these men, my messengers. From among our children on earth I have chosen these twelve to go forth to represent me as I came forth to represent you. Love them and be with them as you have loved and been with me. And now, my Father, give these men wisdom as I place all the affairs of the coming kingdom in their hands. And I would, if it is your will, tarry on earth a time to help them in their labors for the kingdom. And again, my Father, I thank you for these men, and I commit them to your keeping while I go on to finish the work you have given me to do."

When Jesus had finished praying, the apostles remained each man bowed in his place. And it was many minutes before even Peter dared lift up his eyes to look upon the Master. One by one they embraced Jesus, but no man said aught. A great silence pervaded the place while a host of celestial beings looked down upon this solemn and sacred scene—the Creator of a universe placing the affairs of the divine brotherhood of man under the direction of human minds.

3. THE ORDINATION SERMON

Then Jesus spoke, saying: "Now that you are ambassadors of my Father's kingdom, you have thereby become a class of men separate and distinct from all other men on earth. You are not now as men among men but as the enlightened citizens of another and heavenly country among the ignorant creatures of this dark world. It is not enough that you live as you were before this hour, but henceforth must you live as those who have tasted the glories of a better life and have been sent back to earth as ambassadors of the Sovereign of that new and better world. Of the teacher more is expected than of the pupil; of the master more is exacted than of the servant. Of the citizens of the heavenly kingdom more is required than of the citizens of the earthly rule. Some of the things which I am about to say to you may seem hard, but you have elected to represent me in the world even as I now represent the Father; and as my agents on earth you will be obligated to abide by those teachings and practices which are reflective of my ideals of mortal living on the worlds of space, and which I exemplify in my earth life of revealing the Father who is in heaven.

"I send you forth to proclaim liberty to the spiritual captives, joy to those in the bondage of fear, and to heal the sick in accordance with the will of my Father in heaven. When you find my children in distress, speak encouragingly to them, saying:

"Happy are the poor in spirit, the humble, for theirs are the treasures of the kingdom of heaven.

"Happy are they who hunger and thirst for righteousness, for they shall be filled.

"Happy are the meek, for they shall inherit the earth.

"Happy are the pure in heart, for they shall see God.

"And even so speak to my children these further words of spiritual comfort and promise:

"Happy are they who mourn, for they shall be comforted. Happy are they who weep, for they shall receive the spirit of rejoicing.

"Happy are the merciful, for they shall obtain mercy.

"Happy are the peacemakers, for they shall be called the sons of God.

"Happy are they who are persecuted for righteousness' sake, for theirs is the kingdom of heaven. Happy are you when men shall revile you and persecute you and shall say all manner of evil against you falsely. Rejoice and be exceedingly glad, for great is your reward in heaven.

"My brethren, as I send you forth, you are the salt of the earth, salt with a saving savor. But if this salt has lost its savor, wherewith shall it be salted? It is henceforth good for nothing but to be cast out and trodden under foot of men.

"You are the light of the world. A city set upon a hill cannot be hid. Neither do men light a candle and put it under a bushel, but on a candlestick; and it gives light to all who are in the house. Let your light so shine before men that they may see your good works and be led to glorify your Father who is in heaven.

"I am sending you out into the world to represent me and to act as ambassadors of my Father's kingdom, and as you go forth to proclaim the glad tidings, put your trust in the Father whose messengers you are. Do not forcibly resist injustice; put not your trust in the arm of the flesh. If your neighbor smites you on the right cheek, turn to him the other also. Be willing to suffer injustice rather than to go to law among yourselves. In kindness and with mercy minister to all who are in distress and in need.

"I say to you: Love your enemies, do good to those who hate you, bless those who curse you, and pray for those who despitefully use you. And whatsoever you believe that I would do to men, do you also to them.

"Your Father in heaven makes the sun to shine on the evil as well as upon the good; likewise he sends rain on the just and the unjust. You are the sons of God; even more, you are now the ambassadors of my Father's kingdom. Be merciful, even as God is merciful, and in the eternal future of the kingdom you shall be perfect, even as your heavenly Father is perfect.

"You are commissioned to save men, not to judge them. At the end of your earth life you will all expect mercy; therefore do I require of you during your mortal life that you show mercy to all of your brethren in the flesh. Make not the mistake of trying to pluck a mote out of your brother's eye when there is a beam in your own eye. Having first cast the beam out of your own eye, you can the better see to cast the mote out of your brother's eye.

"Discern the truth clearly; live the righteous life fearlessly; and so shall you be my apostles and my Father's ambassadors. You have heard it said: 'If the blind lead the blind, they both shall fall into the pit.' If you would guide others into the kingdom, you must yourselves walk in the clear light of living truth. In all the business of the kingdom I exhort you to show just judgment and keen wisdom. Present not that which is holy to dogs, neither cast your pearls before swine, lest they trample your gems under foot and turn to rend you.

"I warn you against false prophets who will come to you in sheep's clothing, while on the inside they are as ravening wolves. By their fruits you shall know them. Do men gather grapes from thorns or figs from thistles? Even so, every good tree brings forth good fruit, but the corrupt tree bears evil fruit. A good tree cannot yield evil fruit, neither can a corrupt tree produce good fruit. Every tree that does not bring forth good fruit is presently hewn down and cast into the fire. In gaining an entrance into the kingdom of heaven, it is the motive that counts. My Father looks into the hearts of men and judges by their inner longings and their sincere intentions.

"In the great day of the kingdom judgment, many will say to me, 'Did we not prophesy in your name and by your name do many wonderful works?' But I will be compelled to say to them, 'I never knew you; depart from me you who are false teachers.' But every one who hears this charge and sincerely executes his commission to represent me before men even as I have represented my Father to you, shall find an abundant entrance into my service and into the kingdom of the heavenly Father."

Never before had the apostles heard Jesus speak in this way, for he had talked to them as one having supreme authority. They came down from the mountain about sundown, but no man asked Jesus a question.

4. YOU ARE THE SALT OF THE EARTH

The so-called "Sermon on the Mount" is not the gospel of Jesus. It does contain much helpful instruction, but it was Jesus' ordination charge to the twelve apostles. It was the Master's personal commission to those who were to go on preaching the gospel and aspiring to represent him in the world of men even as he was so eloquently and perfectly representative of his Father.

"You are the salt of the earth, salt with a saving savor. But if this salt has lost its savor, wherewith shall it be salted? It is henceforth good for nothing but to be cast out and trodden under foot of men."

In Jesus' time salt was precious. It was even used for money. The modern word "salary" is derived from salt. Salt not only flavors food, but it is also a preservative. It makes other things more tasty, and thus it serves by being spent.

"You are the light of the world. A city set on a hill cannot be hid. Neither do men light a candle and put it under a bushel, but on a candlestick; and it gives light to all who are in the house. Let your light so shine before men that they may see your good works and be led to glorify your Father who is in heaven."

While light dispels darkness, it can also be so "blinding" as to confuse and frustrate. We are admonished to let our light *so* shine that our fellows will be guided into new and godly paths of enhanced living. Our light should so shine as not to attract attention to self. Even one's vocation can be utilized as an effective "reflector" for the dissemination of this light of life.

Strong characters are not derived from *not* doing wrong but rather from actually doing right. Unselfishness is the badge of human greatness. The highest levels of self-realization are attained by worship and service. The happy and effective person is motivated, not by fear of wrongdoing, but by love of right doing.

"By their fruits you shall know them." Personality is basically changeless; that which changes—grows—is the moral character. The major error of modern religions is negativism. The tree which bears no fruit is "hewn down and cast into the fire." Moral worth cannot be derived from mere repression—obeying the injunction "Thou shalt not." Fear and shame are unworthy motivations for religious living. Religion is valid only when it reveals the fatherhood of God and enhances the brotherhood of men.

An effective philosophy of living is formed by a combination of cosmic insight and the total of one's emotional reactions to the social and economic environment. Remember: While inherited urges cannot be fundamentally modified, emotional responses to such urges can be changed; therefore the moral nature can be modified, character can be improved. In the strong character emotional responses are integrated and co-ordinated, and thus is produced a unified personality. Deficient unification weakens the moral nature and engenders unhappiness.

Without a worthy goal, life becomes aimless and unprofitable, and much unhappiness results. Jesus' discourse at the ordination of the twelve constitutes a master philosophy of life. Jesus exhorted his followers to exercise experiential faith. He admonished them not to depend on mere intellectual assent, credulity, and established authority.

Education should be a technique of learning (discovering) the better methods of gratifying our natural and inherited urges, and happiness is the resulting total of these enhanced techniques of emotional satisfactions. Happiness is little dependent on environment, though pleasing surroundings may greatly contribute thereto.

Every mortal really craves to be a complete person, to be perfect even as the Father in heaven is perfect, and such attainment is possible because in the last analysis the "universe is truly fatherly."

5. FATHERLY AND BROTHERLY LOVE

From the Sermon on the Mount to the discourse of the Last Supper, Jesus taught his followers to manifest *fatherly* love rather than *brotherly* love. Brotherly love would love your neighbor as you love yourself, and that would be adequate fulfillment of the "golden rule." But fatherly affection would require that you should love your fellow mortals as Jesus loves you.

Jesus loves mankind with a dual affection. He lived on earth as a twofold personality—human and divine. As the Son of God he loves man with a fatherly love—he is man's Creator, his universe Father. As the Son of Man, Jesus loves mortals as a brother—he was truly a man among men.

Jesus did not expect his followers to achieve an impossible manifestation of brotherly love, but he did expect them to so strive to be like God—to be perfect even as the Father in heaven is perfect—that they could begin to look upon man as God looks upon his creatures and therefore could begin to love men as God loves them—to show forth the beginnings of a fatherly affection. In the course of these exhortations to the twelve apostles, Jesus sought to reveal this new concept of *fatherly love* as it is related to certain emotional attitudes concerned in making numerous environmental social adjustments.

The Master introduced this momentous discourse by calling attention to four *faith* attitudes as the prelude to the subsequent portrayal of his four transcendent and supreme reactions of fatherly love in contrast to the limitations of mere brotherly love.

He first talked about those who were poor in spirit, hungered after righteousness, endured meekness, and who were pure in heart. Such spirit-discerning mortals could be expected to attain such levels of divine selflessness as to be able to attempt the amazing exercise of *fatherly* affection; that even as mourners they would be empowered to show mercy, promote peace, and endure persecutions, and throughout all of these trying situations to love even unlovely mankind with a fatherly love. A father's affection can attain levels of devotion that immeasurably transcend a brother's affection.

The faith and the love of these beatitudes strengthen moral character and create happiness. Fear and anger weaken character and destroy happiness. This momentous sermon started out upon the note of happiness.

1. *"Happy are the poor in spirit—the humble."* To a child, happiness is the satisfaction of immediate pleasure craving. The adult is willing to sow seeds of self-denial in order to reap subsequent harvests of augmented happiness. In Jesus' times and since, happiness has all too often been associated with the idea of the possession of wealth. In the story of the Pharisee and the publican praying in the temple, the one felt rich in spirit—egotistical; the other felt "poor in spirit"—

humble. One was self-sufficient; the other was teachable and truth-seeking. The poor in spirit seek for goals of spiritual wealth—for God. And such seekers after truth do not have to wait for rewards in a distant future; they are rewarded *now.* They find the kingdom of heaven within their own hearts, and they experience such happiness *now.*

2. *"Happy are they who hunger and thirst for righteousness, for they shall be filled."* Only those who feel poor in spirit will ever hunger for righteousness. Only the humble seek for divine strength and crave spiritual power. But it is most dangerous to knowingly engage in spiritual fasting in order to improve one's appetite for spiritual endowments. Physical fasting becomes dangerous after four or five days; one is apt to lose all desire for food. Prolonged fasting, either physical or spiritual, tends to destroy hunger.

Experiential righteousness is a pleasure, not a duty. Jesus' righteousness is a dynamic love—fatherly-brotherly affection. It is not the negative or thou-shalt-not type of righteousness. How could one ever hunger for something negative—something "not to do"?

It is not so easy to teach a child mind these first two of the beatitudes, but the mature mind should grasp their significance.

3. *"Happy are the meek, for they shall inherit the earth."* Genuine meekness has no relation to fear. It is rather an attitude of man co-operating with God—"Your will be done." It embraces patience and forbearance and is motivated by an unshakable faith in a lawful and friendly universe. It masters all temptations to rebel against the divine leading. Jesus was the ideal meek man of Urantia, and he inherited a vast universe.

4. *"Happy are the pure in heart, for they shall see God."* Spiritual purity is not a negative quality, except that it does lack suspicion and revenge. In discussing purity, Jesus did not intend to deal exclusively with human sex attitudes. He referred more to that faith which man should have in his fellow man; that faith which a parent has in his child, and which enables him to love his fellows even as a father would love them. A father's love need not pamper, and it does not condone evil, but it is always anticynical. Fatherly love has singleness of purpose, and it always looks for the best in man; that is the attitude of a true parent.

To see God—by faith—means to acquire true spiritual insight. And spiritual insight enhances Adjuster guidance, and these in the end augment God-consciousness. And when you know the Father, you are confirmed in the assurance of divine sonship, and you can increasingly love each of your brothers in the flesh, not only as a brother—with brotherly love—but also as a father—with fatherly affection.

It is easy to teach this admonition even to a child. Children are naturally trustful, and parents should see to it that they do not lose that simple faith. In dealing with children, avoid all deception and refrain from suggesting suspicion. Wisely help them to choose their heroes and select their lifework.

And then Jesus went on to instruct his followers in the realization of the chief purpose of all human struggling—perfection—even divine attainment. Always he admonished them: "Be you perfect, even as your Father in heaven is perfect." He did not exhort the twelve to love their neighbors as they loved themselves. That would have been a worthy achievement; it would have indicated the achievement of brotherly love. He rather admonished his apostles to love men as he had loved them—to love with a *fatherly* as well as a brotherly affection. And he illustrated this by pointing out four supreme reactions of fatherly love:

1. *"Happy are they who mourn, for they shall be comforted."* So-called common sense or the best of logic would never suggest that happiness could be derived from mourning. But Jesus did not refer to outward or ostentatious mourning. He alluded to an emotional attitude of tenderheartedness. It is a great error to teach boys and young men that it is unmanly to show tenderness or otherwise to give evidence of emotional feeling or physical suffering. Sympathy is a worthy attribute of the male as well as the female. It is not necessary to be calloused in order to be manly. This is the wrong way to create courageous men. The world's great men have not been afraid to mourn. Moses, the mourner, was a greater man than either Samson or Goliath. Moses was a superb leader, but he was also a man of meekness. Being sensitive and responsive to human need creates genuine and lasting happiness, while such kindly attitudes safeguard the soul from the destructive influences of anger, hate, and suspicion.

2. *"Happy are the merciful, for they shall obtain mercy."* Mercy here denotes the height and depth and breadth of the truest friendship—loving-kindness. Mercy sometimes may be passive, but here it is active and dynamic—supreme fatherliness. A loving parent experiences little difficulty in forgiving his child, even many times. And in an unspoiled child the urge to relieve suffering is natural. Children are normally kind and sympathetic when old enough to appreciate actual conditions.

3. *"Happy are the peacemakers, for they shall be called the sons of God."* Jesus' hearers were longing for military deliverance, not for peacemakers. But Jesus' peace is not of the pacific and negative kind. In the face of trials and persecutions he said, "My peace I leave with you." "Let not your heart be troubled, neither let it be afraid." This is the peace that prevents ruinous conflicts. Personal peace integrates personality. Social peace prevents fear, greed, and anger. Political peace prevents race antagonisms, national suspicions, and war. Peacemaking is the cure of distrust and suspicion.

Children can easily be taught to function as peacemakers. They enjoy team activities; they like to play together. Said the Master at another time: "Whosoever will save his life shall lose it, but whosoever will lose his life shall find it."

4. *"Happy are they who are persecuted for righteousness' sake, for theirs is the kingdom of heaven. Happy are you when men shall revile you and persecute you and shall say all manner of evil against you falsely. Rejoice and be exceedingly glad, for great is your reward in heaven."*

So often persecution does follow peace. But young people and brave adults never shun difficulty or danger. "Greater love has no man than to lay down his life for his friends." And a fatherly love can freely do all these things—things which brotherly love can hardly encompass. And progress has always been the final harvest of persecution.

Children always respond to the challenge of courage. Youth is ever willing to "take a dare." And every child should early learn to sacrifice.

And so it is revealed that the beatitudes of the Sermon on the Mount are based on faith and love and not on law—ethics and duty.

Fatherly love delights in returning good for evil—doing good in retaliation for injustice.

6. THE EVENING OF THE ORDINATION

Sunday evening, on reaching the home of Zebedee from the highlands north of Capernaum, Jesus and the twelve partook of a simple meal. Afterward, while Jesus went for a walk along the beach, the twelve talked among themselves. After a brief conference, while the twins built a small fire to give them warmth and more light, Andrew went out to find Jesus, and when he had overtaken him, he said: "Master, my brethren are unable to comprehend what you have said about the kingdom. We do not feel able to begin this work until you have given us further instruction. I have come to ask you to join us in the garden and help us to understand the meaning of your words." And Jesus went with Andrew to meet with the apostles.

When he had entered the garden, he gathered the apostles around him and taught them further, saying: "You find it difficult to receive my message because you would build the new teaching directly upon the old, but I declare that you must be reborn. You must start out afresh as little children and be willing to trust my teaching and believe in God. The new gospel of the kingdom cannot be made to conform to that which is. You have wrong ideas of the Son of Man and his mission on earth. But do not make the mistake of thinking that I have come to set aside the law and the prophets; I have not come to destroy but to fulfill, to enlarge and illuminate. I come not to transgress the law but rather to write these new commandments on the tablets of your hearts.

"I demand of you a righteousness that shall exceed the righteousness of those who seek to obtain the Father's favor by almsgiving, prayer, and fasting. If you would enter the kingdom, you must have a righteousness that consists in love, mercy, and truth—the sincere desire to do the will of my Father in heaven."

Then said Simon Peter: "Master, if you have a new commandment, we would hear it. Reveal the new way to us." Jesus answered Peter: "You have heard it said by those who teach the law: 'You shall not kill; that whosoever kills shall be subject to judgment.' But I look beyond the act to uncover the motive. I declare to you that every one who is angry with his brother is in danger of condemnation. He who nurses hatred in his heart and plans vengeance in his mind stands in danger of judgment. You must judge your fellows by their deeds; the Father in heaven judges by the intent.

"You have heard the teachers of the law say, 'You shall not commit adultery.' But I say to you that every man who looks upon a woman with intent to lust after her has already committed adultery with her in his heart. You can only judge men by their acts, but my Father looks into the hearts of his children and in mercy adjudges them in accordance with their intents and real desires."

Jesus was minded to go on discussing the other commandments when James Zebedee interrupted him, asking: "Master, what shall we teach the people regarding divorcement? Shall we allow a man to divorce his wife as Moses has directed?" And when Jesus heard this question, he said: "I have not come to legislate but to enlighten. I have come not to reform the kingdoms of this world but rather to establish the kingdom of heaven. It is not the will of the Father that I should yield to the temptation to teach you rules of government, trade, or social behavior, which, while they might be good for today, would be far from suitable for the society of another age. I am on earth solely to comfort the minds, liberate the spirits, and save the souls of men. But I will say, concerning this question of divorcement, that, while Moses looked with favor upon such things, it was not so in the days of Adam and in the Garden."

After the apostles had talked among themselves for a short time, Jesus went on to say: "Always must you recognize the two viewpoints of all mortal conduct—the human and the divine; the ways of the flesh and the way of the spirit; the estimate of time and the viewpoint of eternity." And though the twelve could not comprehend all that he taught them, they were truly helped by this instruction.

And then said Jesus: "But you will stumble over my teaching because you are wont to interpret my message literally; you are slow to discern the spirit of my teaching. Again must you remember that you are my messengers; you are beholden to live your lives as I have in spirit lived mine. You are my personal representatives; but do not err in expecting all men to live as you do in every particular. Also must you remember that I have sheep not of this flock, and that I am beholden to them also, to the end that I must provide for them the pattern of doing the will of God while living the life of the mortal nature."

Then asked Nathaniel: "Master, shall we give no place to justice? The law of Moses says, 'An eye for an eye, and a tooth for a tooth.' What shall we say?" And Jesus answered: "You shall return good for evil. My messengers must not strive with men, but be gentle toward all. Measure for measure shall not be your rule. The rulers of men may have such laws, but not so in the kingdom; mercy always shall determine your judgments and love your conduct. And if these are hard sayings, you can even now turn back. If you find the requirements of apostleship too hard, you may return to the less rigorous pathway of discipleship."

On hearing these startling words, the apostles drew apart by themselves for a while, but they soon returned, and Peter said: "Master, we would go on with you; not one of us would turn back. We are fully prepared to pay the extra price; we will drink the cup. We would be apostles, not merely disciples."

When Jesus heard this, he said: "Be willing, then, to take up your responsibilities and follow me. Do your good deeds in secret; when you give alms, let not the left hand know what the right hand does. And when you pray, go apart by yourselves and use not vain repetitions and meaningless phrases. Always remember that the Father knows what you need even before you ask him. And be not given to fasting with a sad countenance to be seen by men. As my chosen apostles, now set apart for the service of the kingdom, lay not up for yourselves treasures on earth, but by your unselfish service lay up for yourselves treasures in heaven, for where your treasures are, there will your hearts be also.

"The lamp of the body is the eye; if, therefore, your eye is generous, your whole body will be full of light. But if your eye is selfish, the whole body will be filled with darkness. If the very light which is in you is turned to darkness, how great is that darkness!"

And then Thomas asked Jesus if they should "continue having everything in common." Said the Master: "Yes, my brethren, I would that we should live together as one understanding family. You are intrusted with a great work, and I crave your undivided service. You know that it has been well said: 'No man can serve two masters.' You cannot sincerely worship God and at the same time wholeheartedly serve mammon. Having now enlisted unreservedly in the work of the kingdom, be not anxious for your lives; much less be concerned with what you shall eat or what you shall drink; nor yet for your bodies, what clothing you shall wear. Already have you learned that willing hands and earnest hearts shall not go hungry. And now, when you prepare to devote all of your energies to the work of the kingdom, be assured that the Father will not be unmindful of your needs. Seek first the kingdom of God, and when you have found entrance thereto, all things needful shall be added to you. Be not, therefore, unduly anxious for the morrow. Sufficient for the day is the trouble thereof."

When Jesus saw they were disposed to stay up all night to ask questions, he said to them: "My brethren, you are earthen vessels; it is best for you to go to your rest so as to be ready for the morrow's work." But sleep had departed from their eyes. Peter ventured to request of his Master that "I have just a little private talk with you. Not that I would have secrets from my brethren, but I have a troubled spirit, and if, perchance, I should deserve a rebuke from my Master, I could the better endure it alone with you." And Jesus said, "Come with me, Peter"—leading the way into the house. When Peter returned from the presence of his Master much cheered and greatly encouraged, James decided to go in to talk with Jesus. And so on through the early hours of the morning, the other apostles went in one by one to talk with the Master. When they had all held personal conferences with him save the twins, who had fallen asleep, Andrew went in to Jesus and said: "Master, the twins have fallen asleep in the garden by the fire; shall I arouse them to inquire if they would also talk with you?" And Jesus smilingly said to Andrew, "They do well—trouble them not." And now the night was passing; the light of another day was dawning.

7. THE WEEK FOLLOWING THE ORDINATION

After a few hours' sleep, when the twelve were assembled for a late breakfast with Jesus, he said: "Now must you begin your work of preaching the glad tidings and instructing believers. Make ready to go to Jerusalem." After Jesus had spoken, Thomas mustered up courage to say: "I know, Master, that we should now be ready to enter upon the work, but I fear we are not yet able to accomplish this great undertaking. Would you consent for us to stay hereabouts for just a few days more before we begin the work of the kingdom?" And when Jesus saw that all of his apostles were possessed by this same fear, he said: "It shall be as you have requested; we will remain here over the Sabbath day."

For weeks and weeks small groups of earnest truth seekers, together with curious spectators, had been coming to Bethsaida to see Jesus. Already word about him had spread over the countryside; inquiring groups had come from cities as far away as Tyre, Sidon, Damascus, Caesarea, and Jerusalem. Heretofore, Jesus had greeted these people and taught them concerning the kingdom, but the Master now turned this work over to the twelve. Andrew would select one of the apostles and assign him to a group of visitors, and sometimes all twelve of them were so engaged.

For two days they worked, teaching by day and holding private conferences late into the night. On the third day Jesus visited with Zebedee and Salome while he sent his apostles off to "go fishing, seek carefree change, or perchance visit your families." On Thursday they returned for three more days of teaching.

During this week of rehearsing, Jesus many times repeated to his apostles the two great motives of his postbaptismal mission on earth:

1. To reveal the Father to man.

2. To lead men to become son-conscious—to faith-realize that they are the children of the Most High.

One week of this varied experience did much for the twelve; some even became over self-confident. At the last conference, the night after the Sabbath, Peter and James came to Jesus, saying, "We are ready—let us now go forth to take the kingdom." To which Jesus replied, "May your wisdom equal your zeal and your courage atone for your ignorance."

Though the apostles failed to comprehend much of his teaching, they did not fail to grasp the significance of the charmingly beautiful life he lived with them.

8. THURSDAY AFTERNOON ON THE LAKE

Jesus well knew that his apostles were not fully assimilating his teachings. He decided to give some special instruction to Peter, James, and John, hoping they would be able to clarify the ideas of their associates. He saw that, while some features of the idea of a spiritual kingdom were being grasped by the twelve, they steadfastly persisted in attaching these new spiritual teachings directly onto their old and entrenched literal concepts of the kingdom of heaven as a restoration of David's throne and the re-establishment of Israel as a temporal power on earth. Accordingly, on Thursday afternoon Jesus went out from the shore in a boat with Peter, James, and John to talk over the affairs of the kingdom. This was a four hours' teaching conference, embracing scores of questions and answers, and may most profitably be put in this record by reorganizing the summary of this momentous afternoon as it was given by Simon Peter to his brother, Andrew, the following morning:

1. *Doing the Father's will.* Jesus' teaching to trust in the overcare of the heavenly Father was not a blind and passive fatalism. He quoted with approval, on this afternoon, an old Hebrew saying: "He who will not work shall not eat." He pointed to his own experience as sufficient commentary on his teachings. His precepts about trusting the Father must not be adjudged by the social or economic conditions of modern times or any other age. His instruction embraces the ideal principles of living near God in all ages and on all worlds.

Jesus made clear to the three the difference between the requirements of apostleship and discipleship. And even then he did not forbid the exercise of prudence and foresight by the twelve. What he preached against was not forethought but anxiety, worry. He taught the active and alert submission to God's will. In answer to many of their questions regarding frugality and thriftiness, he simply called attention to his life as carpenter, boatmaker, and fisherman, and to his careful organization of the twelve. He sought to make it clear that the world is not to be regarded as an enemy; that the circumstances of life constitute a divine dispensation working along with the children of God.

Jesus had great difficulty in getting them to understand his personal practice of nonresistance. He absolutely refused to defend himself, and it appeared to the apostles that he would be pleased if they would pursue the same policy. He taught them not to resist evil, not to combat injustice or injury, but he did not teach passive tolerance of wrongdoing. And he made it plain on this afternoon that he approved of the social punishment of evildoers and criminals, and that the civil government must sometimes employ force for the maintenance of social order and in the execution of justice.

He never ceased to warn his disciples against the evil practice of *retaliation*; he made no allowance for revenge, the idea of getting even. He deplored the holding of grudges. He disallowed the idea of an eye for an eye and a tooth for a tooth. He discountenanced the whole concept of private and personal revenge, assigning these matters to civil government, on the one hand, and to the judgment of God, on the other. He made it clear to the three that his teachings applied to the *individual,* not the state. He summarized his instructions up to that time regarding these matters, as:

Love your enemies—remember the moral claims of human brotherhood.

The futility of evil: A wrong is not righted by vengeance. Do not make the mistake of fighting evil with its own weapons.

Have faith—confidence in the eventual triumph of divine justice and eternal goodness.

2. *Political attitude.* He cautioned his apostles to be discreet in their remarks concerning the strained relations then existing between the Jewish people and the Roman government; he forbade them to become in any way embroiled in these difficulties. He was always careful to avoid the political snares of his enemies, ever making reply, "Render to Caesar the things which are Caesar's and to God the things which are God's." He refused to have his attention diverted from his mission of establishing a new way of salvation; he would not permit himself to be concerned about anything else. In his personal life he was always duly observant of all civil laws and regulations; in all his public teachings he ignored the civic, social, and economic realms. He told the three apostles that he was concerned only with the principles of man's inner and personal spiritual life.

Jesus was not, therefore, a political reformer. He did not come to reorganize the world; even if he had done this, it would have been applicable only to that day and generation. Nevertheless, he did show man the best way of living, and no generation is exempt from the labor of discovering how best to adapt Jesus' life to its own problems. But never make the mistake of identifying Jesus' teachings with any political or economic theory, with any social or industrial system.

3. *Social attitude.* The Jewish rabbis had long debated the question: Who is my neighbor? Jesus came presenting the idea of active and spontaneous kindness, a love of one's fellow men so genuine that it expanded the neighborhood to include the whole world, thereby making all men one's neighbors. But with all this, Jesus was interested only in the individual, not the mass. Jesus was not a sociologist, but he did labor to break down all forms of selfish isolation. He taught pure sympathy, compassion. Michael of Nebadon is a mercy-dominated Son; compassion is his very nature.

The Master did not say that men should never entertain their friends at meat, but he did say that his followers should make feasts for the poor and the unfortunate. Jesus had a firm sense of justice, but it was always tempered with mercy. He did not teach his apostles that they were to be imposed upon by social parasites or professional alms-seekers. The nearest he came to making sociological pronouncements was to say, "Judge not, that you be not judged."

He made it clear that indiscriminate kindness may be blamed for many social evils. The following day Jesus definitely instructed Judas that no apostolic funds were to be given out as alms except upon his request or upon the joint petition of two of the apostles. In all these matters it was the practice of Jesus always to say, "Be as wise as serpents but as harmless as doves." It seemed to be his purpose in all social situations to teach patience, tolerance, and forgiveness.

The family occupied the very center of Jesus' philosophy of life—here and hereafter. He based his teachings about God on the family, while he sought to correct the Jewish tendency to overhonor ancestors. He exalted family life as the highest human duty but made it plain that family relationships must not interfere with religious obligations. He called attention to the fact that the family is a temporal institution; that it does not survive death. Jesus did not hesitate to give up his family when the family ran counter to the Father's will. He taught the new and larger brotherhood of man—the sons of God. In Jesus' time divorce practices were lax in Palestine and throughout the Roman Empire. He repeatedly refused to lay down laws regarding marriage and divorce, but many of Jesus' early followers had strong opinions on divorce and did not hesitate to attribute them to him. All of the New Testament writers held to these more stringent and advanced ideas about divorce except John Mark.

4. *Economic attitude.* Jesus worked, lived, and traded in the world as he found it. He was not an economic reformer, although he did frequently call attention to the injustice of the unequal distribution of wealth. But he did not offer any suggestions by way of remedy. He made it plain to the three that, while his apostles were not to hold property, he was not preaching against wealth and property, merely its unequal and unfair distribution. He recognized the need for social justice and industrial fairness, but he offered no rules for their attainment.

He never taught his followers to avoid earthly possessions, only his twelve apostles. Luke, the physician, was a strong believer in social equality, and he did much to interpret Jesus' sayings in harmony with his personal beliefs. Jesus never personally directed his followers to adopt a communal mode of life; he made no pronouncement of any sort regarding such matters.

Jesus frequently warned his listeners against covetousness, declaring that "a man's happiness consists not in the abundance of his material possessions." He constantly reiterated, "What shall it profit a man if he gain the whole world and lose his own soul?" He made no direct attack on the possession of property, but he did insist that it is eternally essential that spiritual values come first. In his later teachings he sought to correct many erroneous Urantia views of life by narrating numerous parables which he presented in the course of his public ministry. Jesus never intended to formulate economic theories; he well knew that each age must evolve its own remedies for existing troubles. And if Jesus were on earth today, living his life in the flesh, he would be a great disappointment to the majority of good men and women for the simple reason that he would not take sides in present-day political, social, or economic disputes. He would remain grandly aloof while teaching you how to perfect your inner spiritual life so as to render you manyfold more competent to attack the solution of your purely human problems.

Jesus would make all men Godlike and then stand by sympathetically while these sons of God solve their own political, social, and economic problems. It was not wealth that he denounced, but what wealth does to the majority of its devotees. On this Thursday afternoon Jesus first told his associates that "it is more blessed to give than to receive."

5. *Personal religion.* You, as did his apostles, should the better understand Jesus' teachings by his life. He lived a perfected life on Urantia, and his unique

teachings can only be understood when that life is visualized in its immediate background. It is his life, and not his lessons to the twelve or his sermons to the multitudes, that will assist most in revealing the Father's divine character and loving personality.

Jesus did not attack the teachings of the Hebrew prophets or the Greek moralists. The Master recognized the many good things which these great teachers stood for, but he had come down to earth to teach something *additional,* "the voluntary conformity of man's will to God's will." Jesus did not want simply to produce a *religious man,* a mortal wholly occupied with religious feelings and actuated only by spiritual impulses. Could you have had but one look at him, you would have known that Jesus was a real man of great experience in the things of this world. The teachings of Jesus in this respect have been grossly perverted and much misrepresented all down through the centuries of the Christian era; you have also held perverted ideas about the Master's meekness and humility. What he aimed at in his life appears to have been a *superb self-respect.* He only advised man to humble himself that he might become truly exalted; what he really aimed at was true humility toward God. He placed great value upon sincerity—a pure heart. Fidelity was a cardinal virtue in his estimate of character, while *courage* was the very heart of his teachings. "Fear not" was his watchword, and patient endurance his ideal of strength of character. The teachings of Jesus constitute a religion of valor, courage, and heroism. And this is just why he chose as his personal representatives twelve commonplace men, the majority of whom were rugged, virile, and manly fishermen.

Jesus had little to say about the social vices of his day; seldom did he make reference to moral delinquency. He was a positive teacher of true virtue. He studiously avoided the negative method of imparting instruction; he refused to advertise evil. He was not even a moral reformer. He well knew, and so taught his apostles, that the sensual urges of mankind are not suppressed by either religious rebuke or legal prohibitions. His few denunciations were largely directed against pride, cruelty, oppression, and hypocrisy.

Jesus did not vehemently denounce even the Pharisees, as did John. He knew many of the scribes and Pharisees were honest of heart; he understood their enslaving bondage to religious traditions. Jesus laid great emphasis on "first making the tree good." He impressed the three that he valued the whole life, not just a certain few special virtues.

The one thing which John gained from this day's teaching was that the heart of Jesus' religion consisted in the acquirement of a compassionate character coupled with a personality motivated to do the will of the Father in heaven.

Peter grasped the idea that the gospel they were about to proclaim was really a fresh beginning for the whole human race. He conveyed this impression subsequently to Paul, who formulated therefrom his doctrine of Christ as "the second Adam."

James grasped the thrilling truth that Jesus wanted his children on earth to live as though they were already citizens of the completed heavenly kingdom.

Jesus knew men were different, and he so taught his apostles. He constantly exhorted them to refrain from trying to mold the disciples and believers according to some set pattern. He sought to allow each soul to develop in its own way, a perfecting and separate individual before God. In answer to one of Peter's many questions, the Master said: "I want to set men free so that they can start out afresh as little children upon the new and better life." Jesus always insisted that true goodness must be unconscious, in bestowing charity not allowing the left hand to know what the right hand does.

The three apostles were shocked this afternoon when they realized that their Master's religion made no provision for spiritual self-examination. All religions before and after the times of Jesus, even Christianity, carefully provide for conscientious self-examination. But not so with the religion of Jesus of Nazareth. Jesus' philosophy of life is without religious introspection. The carpenter's son never taught character *building;* he taught character *growth,* declaring that the kingdom of heaven is like a mustard seed. But Jesus said nothing which would proscribe self-analysis as a prevention of conceited egotism.

The right to enter the kingdom is conditioned by faith, personal belief. The cost of remaining in the progressive ascent of the kingdom is the pearl of great price, in order to possess which a man sells all that he has.

The teaching of Jesus is a religion for everybody, not alone for weaklings and slaves. His religion never became crystallized (during his day) into creeds and theological laws; he left not a line of writing behind him. His life and teachings were bequeathed the universe as an inspirational and idealistic inheritance suitable for the spiritual guidance and moral instruction of all ages on all worlds. And even today, Jesus' teaching stands apart from all religions, as such, albeit it is the living hope of every one of them.

Jesus did not teach his apostles that religion is man's only earthly pursuit; that was the Jewish idea of serving God. But he did insist that religion was the exclusive business of the twelve. Jesus taught nothing to deter his believers from the pursuit of genuine culture; he only detracted from the tradition-bound religious schools of Jerusalem. He was liberal, big-hearted, learned, and tolerant. Self-conscious piety had no place in his philosophy of righteous living.

The Master offered no solutions for the nonreligious problems of his own age nor for any subsequent age. Jesus wished to develop spiritual insight into eternal realities and to stimulate initiative in the originality of living; he concerned himself exclusively with the underlying and permanent spiritual needs of the human race. He revealed a goodness equal to God. He exalted love—truth, beauty, and goodness—as the divine ideal and the eternal reality.

The Master came to create in man a new spirit, a new will—to impart a new capacity for knowing the truth, experiencing compassion, and choosing goodness—the will to be in harmony with God's will, coupled with the eternal urge to become perfect, even as the Father in heaven is perfect.

9. THE DAY OF CONSECRATION

The next Sabbath day Jesus devoted to his apostles, journeying back to the highland where he had ordained them; and there, after a long and beautifully touching personal message of encouragement, he engaged in the solemn act of the consecration of the twelve. This Sabbath afternoon Jesus assembled the apostles around him on the hillside and gave them into the hands of his heavenly Father in preparation for the day when he would be compelled to leave them alone in the world. There was no new teaching on this occasion, just visiting and communion.

Jesus reviewed many features of the ordination sermon, delivered on this same spot, and then, calling them before him one by one, he commissioned them to go forth in the world as his representatives. The Master's consecration charge was: "Go into all the world and preach the glad tidings of the kingdom. Liberate spiritual captives, comfort the oppressed, and minister to the afflicted. Freely you have received, freely give."

Jesus advised them to take neither money nor extra clothing, saying, "The laborer is worthy of his hire." And finally he said: "Behold I send you forth as sheep in the midst of wolves; be you therefore as wise as serpents and as harmless as doves. But take heed, for your enemies will bring you up before their councils, while in their synagogues they will castigate you. Before governors and rulers you will be brought because you believe this gospel, and your very testimony shall be a witness for me to them. And when they lead you to judgment, be not anxious about what you shall say, for the spirit of my Father indwells you and will at such a time speak through you. Some of you will be put to death, and before you establish the kingdom on earth, you will be hated by many peoples because of this gospel; but fear not; I will be with you, and my spirit shall go before you into all the world. And my Father's presence will abide with you while you go first to the Jews, then to the gentiles."

And when they came down from the mountain, they journeyed back to their home in Zebedee's house.

10. THE EVENING AFTER THE CONSECRATION

That evening while teaching in the house, for it had begun to rain, Jesus talked at great length, trying to show the twelve what they must *be,* not what they must *do.* They knew only a religion that imposed the *doing* of certain things as the means of attaining righteousness—salvation. But Jesus would reiterate, "In the kingdom you must *be* righteous in order to do the work." Many times did he repeat, "*Be* you therefore perfect, even as your Father in heaven is perfect." All the while was the Master explaining to his bewildered apostles that the salvation which he had come to bring to the world was to be had only by *believing,* by simple and sincere faith. Said Jesus: "John preached a baptism of repentance, sorrow for the old way of living. You are to proclaim the baptism of fellowship with God. Preach repentance to those who stand in need of such teaching, but to those already seeking sincere entrance to the kingdom, open the doors wide and bid them enter into the joyous fellowship of the sons of God." But it was a difficult task to persuade these Galilean fishermen that, in the kingdom, *being* righteous, by faith, must precede *doing* righteousness in the daily life of the mortals of earth.

Another great handicap in this work of teaching the twelve was their tendency to take highly idealistic and spiritual principles of religious truth and remake them into concrete rules of personal conduct. Jesus would present to them the beautiful spirit of the soul's attitude, but they insisted on translating such teachings into rules of personal behavior. Many times, when they did make sure to remember what the Master said, they were almost certain to forget what he did *not* say. But they slowly assimilated his teaching because Jesus *was* all that he taught. What they could not gain from his verbal instruction, they gradually acquired by living with him.

It was not apparent to the apostles that their Master was engaged in living a life of spiritual inspiration for every person of every age on every world of a far-flung universe. Notwithstanding what Jesus told them from time to time, the apostles did not grasp the idea that he was doing a work *on* this world but *for* all other worlds in his vast creation. Jesus lived his earth life on Urantia, not to set a personal example of mortal living for the men and women of this world, but rather to create a *high spiritual and inspirational ideal* for all mortal beings on all worlds.

This same evening Thomas asked Jesus: "Master, you say that we must become as little children before we can gain entrance to the Father's kingdom, and yet you have warned us not to be deceived by false prophets nor to become guilty of casting our pearls before swine. Now, I am honestly puzzled. I cannot understand your teaching." Jesus replied to Thomas: "How long shall I bear with you! Ever you insist on making literal all that I teach. When I asked you to become as little children as the price of entering the kingdom, I referred not to ease of deception, mere willingness to believe, nor to quickness to trust pleasing strangers. What I did desire that you should gather from the illustration was the child-father relationship. You are the child, and it is *your* Father's kingdom you seek to enter. There is present that natural affection between every normal child and its father which insures an understanding and loving relationship, and which forever precludes all disposition to bargain for the Father's love and mercy. And the gospel you are going forth to preach has to do with a salvation growing out of the faith-realization of this very and eternal child-father relationship."

The one characteristic of Jesus' teaching was that the *morality* of his philosophy originated in the personal relation of the individual to God—this very child-father relationship. Jesus placed emphasis on the *individual,* not on the race or nation. While eating supper, Jesus had the talk with Matthew in which he explained that the morality of any act is determined by the individual's motive. Jesus' morality was always positive. The golden rule as restated by Jesus demands active social contact; the older negative rule could be obeyed in isolation. Jesus stripped morality of all rules and ceremonies and elevated it to majestic levels of spiritual thinking and truly righteous living.

This new religion of Jesus was not without its practical implications, but whatever of practical political, social, or economic value there is to be found in his teaching is the natural outworking of this inner experience of the soul as it manifests the fruits of the spirit in the spontaneous daily ministry of genuine personal religious experience.

After Jesus and Matthew had finished talking, Simon Zelotes asked, "But, Master, are *all* men the sons of God?" And Jesus answered: "Yes, Simon, all men are the sons of God, and that is the good news you are going to proclaim." But the apostles could not grasp such a doctrine; it was a new, strange, and startling announcement. And it was because of his desire to impress this truth upon them that Jesus taught his followers to treat all men as their brothers.

In response to a question asked by Andrew, the Master made it clear that the morality of his teaching was inseparable from the religion of his living. He taught morality, not from the *nature* of man, but from the *relation* of man to God.

John asked Jesus, "Master, what is the kingdom of heaven?" And Jesus answered: "The kingdom of heaven consists in these three essentials: first, recognition of the fact of the sovereignty of God; second, belief in the truth of sonship with God; and third, faith in the effectiveness of the supreme human desire to do the will of God—to be like God. And this is the good news of the gospel: that by faith every mortal may have all these essentials of salvation."

And now the week of waiting was over, and they prepared to depart on the morrow for Jerusalem.

PAPER 141

BEGINNING THE PUBLIC WORK

ON THE first day of the week, January 19, A.D. 27, Jesus and the twelve apostles made ready to depart from their headquarters in Bethsaida. The twelve knew nothing of their Master's plans except that they were going up to Jerusalem to attend the Passover feast in April, and that it was the intention to journey by way of the Jordan valley. They did not get away from Zebedee's house until near noon because the families of the apostles and others of the disciples had come to say good-bye and wish them well in the new work they were about to begin.

Just before leaving, the apostles missed the Master, and Andrew went out to find him. After a brief search he found Jesus sitting in a boat down the beach, and he was weeping. The twelve had often seen their Master when he seemed to grieve, and they had beheld his brief seasons of serious preoccupation of mind, but none of them had ever seen him weep. Andrew was somewhat startled to see the Master thus affected on the eve of their departure for Jerusalem, and he ventured to approach Jesus and ask: "On this great day, Master, when we are to depart for Jerusalem to proclaim the Father's kingdom, why is it that you weep? Which of us has offended you?" And Jesus, going back with Andrew to join the twelve, answered him: "No one of you has grieved me. I am saddened only because none of my father Joseph's family have remembered to come over to bid us Godspeed." At this time Ruth was on a visit to her brother Joseph at Nazareth. Other members of his family were kept away by pride, disappointment, misunderstanding, and petty resentment indulged as a result of hurt feelings.

1. LEAVING GALILEE

Capernaum was not far from Tiberias, and the fame of Jesus had begun to spread well over all of Galilee and even to parts beyond. Jesus knew that Herod would soon begin to take notice of his work; so he thought best to journey south and into Judea with his apostles. A company of over one hundred believers desired to go with them, but Jesus spoke to them and besought them not to accompany the apostolic group on their way down the Jordan. Though they consented to remain behind, many of them followed after the Master within a few days.

The first day Jesus and the apostles only journeyed as far as Tarichea, where they rested for the night. The next day they traveled to a point on the Jordan near Pella where John had preached about one year before, and where Jesus had received baptism. Here they tarried for more than two weeks, teaching and preaching. By the end of the first week several hundred people had assembled in a camp near where Jesus and the twelve dwelt, and they had come from Galilee, Phoenicia, Syria, the Decapolis, Perea, and Judea.

Jesus did no public preaching. Andrew divided the multitude and assigned the preachers for the forenoon and afternoon assemblies; after the evening meal Jesus talked with the twelve. He taught them nothing new but reviewed his former teaching and answered their many questions. On one of these evenings he told the twelve something about the forty days which he spent in the hills near this place.

Many of those who came from Perea and Judea had been baptized by John and were interested in finding out more about Jesus' teachings. The apostles made much progress in teaching the disciples of John inasmuch as they did not in any way detract from John's preaching, and since they did not at this time even baptize their new disciples. But it was always a stumbling stone to John's followers that Jesus, if he were all that John had announced, did nothing to get him out of prison. John's disciples never could understand why Jesus did not prevent the cruel death of their beloved leader.

From night to night Andrew carefully instructed his fellow apostles in the delicate and difficult task of getting along smoothly with the followers of John the Baptist. During this first year of Jesus' public ministry more than three fourths of his followers had previously followed John and had received his baptism. This entire year of A.D. 27 was spent in quietly taking over John's work in Perea and Judea.

2. GOD'S LAW AND THE FATHER'S WILL

The night before they left Pella, Jesus gave the apostles some further instruction with regard to the new kingdom. Said the Master: "You have been taught to look for the coming of the kingdom of God, and now I come announcing that this long-looked-for kingdom is near at hand, even that it is already here and in our midst. In every kingdom there must be a king seated upon his throne and decreeing the laws of the realm. And so have you developed a concept of the kingdom of heaven as a glorified rule of the Jewish people over all the peoples of the earth with Messiah sitting on David's throne and from this place of miraculous power promulgating the laws of all the world. But, my children, you see not with the eye of faith, and you hear not with the understanding of the spirit. I declare that the kingdom of heaven is the realization and acknowledgment of God's rule within the hearts of men. True, there is a King in this kingdom, and that King is my Father and your Father. We are indeed his loyal subjects, but far transcending that fact is the transforming truth that we are his *sons*. In my life this truth is to become manifest to all. Our Father also sits upon a throne, but not one made with hands. The throne of the Infinite is the eternal dwelling place of the Father in the heaven of heavens; he fills all things and proclaims his laws to universes upon universes. And the Father also rules within the hearts of his children on earth by the spirit which he has sent to live within the souls of mortal men.

"When you are the subjects of this kingdom, you indeed are made to hear the law of the Universe Ruler; but when, because of the gospel of the kingdom which I have come to declare, you faith-discover yourselves as sons, you henceforth look not upon yourselves as law-subject creatures of an all-powerful king but as privileged sons of a loving and divine Father. Verily, verily, I say to you, when the Father's will is your *law,* you are hardly in the kingdom. But when the Father's will becomes truly your *will,* then are you in very truth in the kingdom because the kingdom has thereby become an established experience in you. When God's will is your law, you are noble slave subjects; but when you believe in this new gospel of divine sonship, my Father's will becomes your will, and you are elevated to the high position of the free children of God, liberated sons of the kingdom."

Some of the apostles grasped something of this teaching, but none of them comprehended the full significance of this tremendous announcement, unless it was James Zebedee. But these words sank into their hearts and came forth to gladden their ministry during later years of service.

3. THE SOJOURN AT AMATHUS

The Master and his apostles remained near Amathus for almost three weeks. The apostles continued to preach twice daily to the multitude, and Jesus preached each Sabbath afternoon. It became impossible to continue the Wednesday playtime; so Andrew arranged that two apostles should rest each day of the six days in the week, while all were on duty during the Sabbath services.

Peter, James, and John did most of the public preaching. Philip, Nathaniel, Thomas, and Simon did much of the personal work and conducted classes for special groups of inquirers; the twins continued their general police supervision, while Andrew, Matthew, and Judas developed into a general managerial committee of three, although each of these three also did considerable religious work.

Andrew was much occupied with the task of adjusting the constantly recurring misunderstandings and disagreements between the disciples of John and the newer disciples of Jesus. Serious situations would arise every few days, but Andrew, with the assistance of his apostolic associates, managed to induce the contending parties to come to some sort of agreement, at least temporarily. Jesus refused to participate in any of these conferences; neither would he give any advice about the proper adjustment of these difficulties. He never once offered a suggestion as to how the apostles should solve these perplexing problems. When Andrew came to Jesus with these questions, he would always say: "It is not wise for the host to participate in the family troubles of his guests; a wise parent never takes sides in the petty quarrels of his own children."

The Master displayed great wisdom and manifested perfect fairness in all of his dealings with his apostles and with all of his disciples. Jesus was truly a master of men; he exercised great influence over his fellow men because of the combined charm and force of his personality. There was a subtle commanding influence in his rugged, nomadic, and homeless life. There was intellectual attractiveness and spiritual drawing power in his authoritative manner of teaching, in his lucid logic, his strength of reasoning, his sagacious insight, his alertness of mind, his matchless poise, and his sublime tolerance. He was simple, manly, honest, and fearless. With all of this physical and intellectual influence manifest in the Master's presence, there were also all those spiritual charms of being which have become associated with his personality—patience, tenderness, meekness, gentleness, and humility.

Jesus of Nazareth was indeed a strong and forceful personality; he was an intellectual power and a spiritual stronghold. His personality not only appealed to the spiritually minded women among his followers, but also to the educated and intellectual Nicodemus and to the hardy Roman soldier, the captain stationed on guard at the cross, who, when he had finished watching the Master die, said, "Truly, this was a Son of God." And red-blooded, rugged Galilean fishermen called him Master.

The pictures of Jesus have been most unfortunate. These paintings of the Christ have exerted a deleterious influence on youth; the temple merchants would hardly have fled before Jesus if he had been such a man as your artists usually have depicted. His was a dignified manhood; he was good, but natural. Jesus did not pose as a mild, sweet, gentle, and kindly mystic. His teaching was thrillingly dynamic. He not only *meant well,* but he went about actually *doing good.*

The Master never said, "Come to me all you who are indolent and all who are dreamers." But he did many times say, "Come to me all you who *labor,* and I will give you rest—spiritual strength." The Master's yoke is, indeed, easy, but even so, he never imposes it; every individual must take this yoke of his own free will.

Jesus portrayed conquest by sacrifice, the sacrifice of pride and selfishness. By showing mercy, he meant to portray spiritual deliverance from all grudges, grievances, anger, and the lust for selfish power and revenge. And when he said, "Resist not evil," he later explained that he did not mean to condone sin or to counsel fraternity with iniquity. He intended the more to teach forgiveness, to "resist not evil treatment of one's personality, evil injury to one's feelings of personal dignity."

4. TEACHING ABOUT THE FATHER

While sojourning at Amathus, Jesus spent much time with the apostles instructing them in the new concept of God; again and again did he impress upon them that *God is a Father,* not a great and supreme bookkeeper who is chiefly engaged in making damaging entries against his erring children on earth, recordings of sin and evil to be used against them when he subsequently sits in judgment upon them as the just Judge of all creation. The Jews had long conceived of God as a king over all, even as a Father of the nation, but never before had large numbers of mortal men held the idea of God as a loving Father of the *individual.*

In answer to Thomas's question, "Who is this God of the kingdom?" Jesus replied: "God is *your* Father, and religion—my gospel—is nothing more nor less than the believing recognition of the truth that you are his son. And I am here among you in the flesh to make clear both of these ideas in my life and teachings."

Jesus also sought to free the minds of his apostles from the idea of offering animal sacrifices as a religious duty. But these men, trained in the religion of the daily sacrifice, were slow to comprehend what he meant. Nevertheless, the Master did not grow weary in his teaching. When he failed to reach the minds of all of the apostles by means of one illustration, he would restate his message and employ another type of parable for purposes of illumination.

At this same time Jesus began to teach the twelve more fully concerning their mission "to comfort the afflicted and minister to the sick." The Master taught them much about the whole man—the union of body, mind, and spirit to form the individual man or woman. Jesus told his associates about the three forms of affliction they would meet and went on to explain how they should minister to all who suffer the sorrows of human sickness. He taught them to recognize:

1. Diseases of the flesh—those afflictions commonly regarded as physical sickness.

2. Troubled minds—those nonphysical afflictions which were subsequently looked upon as emotional and mental difficulties and disturbances.

3. The possession of evil spirits.

Jesus explained to his apostles on several occasions the nature, and something concerning the origin, of these evil spirits, in that day often also called unclean spirits. The Master well knew the difference between the possession of evil spirits and insanity, but the apostles did not. Neither was it possible, in view of their limited knowledge of the early history of Urantia, for Jesus to undertake to make this matter fully understandable. But he many times said to them, alluding to these evil spirits: "They shall no more molest men when I shall have ascended to my Father in heaven, and after I shall have poured out my spirit upon all flesh in those times when the kingdom will come in great power and spiritual glory."

From week to week and from month to month, throughout this entire year, the apostles paid more and more attention to the healing ministry of the sick.

5. SPIRITUAL UNITY

One of the most eventful of all the evening conferences at Amathus was the session having to do with the discussion of spiritual unity. James Zebedee had asked, "Master, how shall we learn to see alike and thereby enjoy more harmony among ourselves?" When Jesus heard this question, he was stirred within his spirit, so much so that he replied: "James, James, when did I teach you that you should all see alike? I have come into the world to proclaim spiritual liberty to the end that mortals may be empowered to live individual lives of originality and freedom before God. I do not desire that social harmony and fraternal peace shall be purchased by the sacrifice of free personality and spiritual originality. What I require of you, my apostles, is *spirit unity*—and that you can experience in the joy of your united dedication to the wholehearted doing of the will of my Father in heaven. You do not have to see alike or feel alike or even think alike in order spiritually to *be alike.* Spiritual unity is derived from the consciousness that each of you is indwelt, and increasingly dominated, by the spirit gift of the heavenly Father. Your apostolic harmony must grow out of the fact that the spirit hope of each of you is identical in origin, nature, and destiny.

"In this way you may experience a perfected unity of spirit purpose and spirit understanding growing out of the mutual consciousness of the identity of each of your indwelling Paradise spirits; and you may enjoy all of this profound spiritual unity in the very face of the utmost diversity of your individual attitudes of intellectual thinking, temperamental feeling, and social conduct. Your personalities may be refreshingly diverse and markedly different, while your spiritual natures and spirit fruits of divine worship and brotherly love may be so unified that all who behold your lives will of a surety take cognizance of this spirit identity and soul unity; they will recognize that you have been with me and have thereby learned, and acceptably, how to do the will of the Father in heaven. You can achieve the unity of the service of God even while you render such service in accordance with the technique of your own original endowments of mind, body, and soul.

"Your spirit unity implies two things, which always will be found to harmonize in the lives of individual believers: First, you are possessed with a common motive for life service; you all desire above everything to do the will of the Father in heaven. Second, you all have a common goal of existence; you all purpose to find the Father in heaven, thereby proving to the universe that you have become like him."

Many times during the training of the twelve Jesus reverted to this theme. Repeatedly he told them it was not his desire that those who believed in him should become dogmatized and standardized in accordance with the religious interpretations of even good men. Again and again he warned his apostles against the formulation of creeds and the establishment of traditions as a means of guiding and controlling believers in the gospel of the kingdom.

6. LAST WEEK AT AMATHUS

Near the end of the last week at Amathus, Simon Zelotes brought to Jesus one Teherma, a Persian doing business at Damascus. Teherma had heard of Jesus and had come to Capernaum to see him, and there learning that Jesus had gone with his apostles down the Jordan on the way to Jerusalem, he set out to find him. Andrew had presented Teherma to Simon for instruction. Simon looked upon the Persian as a "fire worshiper," although Teherma took great pains to explain that fire was only the visible symbol of the Pure and Holy One. After talking with Jesus, the Persian signified his intention of remaining for several days to hear the teaching and listen to the preaching.

When Simon Zelotes and Jesus were alone, Simon asked the Master: "Why is it that I could not persuade him? Why did he so resist me and so readily lend an ear to you?" Jesus answered: "Simon, Simon, how many times have I instructed you to refrain from all efforts to take something *out* of the hearts of those who seek salvation? How often have I told you to labor only to put something *into* these hungry souls? Lead men into the kingdom, and the great and living truths of the kingdom will presently drive out all serious error. When you have presented to mortal man the good news that God is his Father, you can the easier persuade him that he is in reality a son of God. And having done that, you have brought the light of salvation to the one who sits in darkness. Simon, when the Son of Man came first to you, did he come denouncing Moses and the prophets and proclaiming a new and better way of life? No. I came not to take away that which you had from your forefathers but to show you the perfected vision of that which your fathers saw only in part. Go then, Simon, teaching and preaching the kingdom, and when you have a man safely and securely within the kingdom, then is the time, when such a one shall come to you with inquiries, to impart instruction having to do with the progressive advancement of the soul within the divine kingdom."

Simon was astonished at these words, but he did as Jesus had instructed him, and Teherma, the Persian, was numbered among those who entered the kingdom.

That night Jesus discoursed to the apostles on the new life in the kingdom. He said in part: "When you enter the kingdom, you are reborn. You cannot teach the deep things of the spirit to those who have been born only of the flesh; first see that men are born of the spirit before you seek to instruct them in the advanced ways of the spirit. Do not undertake to show men the beauties of the temple until you have first taken them into the temple. Introduce men to God and *as* the sons of God before you discourse on the doctrines of the fatherhood of God and the sonship of men. Do not strive with men—always be patient. It is not your kingdom; you are only ambassadors. Simply go forth proclaiming: This is the kingdom of heaven—God is your Father and you are his sons, and this good news, if you wholeheartedly believe it, *is* your eternal salvation."

The apostles made great progress during the sojourn at Amathus. But they were very much disappointed that Jesus would give them no suggestions about dealing with John's disciples. Even in the important matter of baptism, all that Jesus said was: "John did indeed baptize with water, but when you enter the kingdom of heaven, you shall be baptized with the Spirit."

7. AT BETHANY BEYOND JORDAN

On February 26, Jesus, his apostles, and a large group of followers journeyed down the Jordan to the ford near Bethany in Perea, the place where John first made proclamation of the coming kingdom. Jesus with his apostles remained here, teaching and preaching, for four weeks before they went on up to Jerusalem.

The second week of the sojourn at Bethany beyond Jordan, Jesus took Peter, James, and John into the hills across the river and south of Jericho for a three days' rest. The Master taught these three many new and advanced truths about the kingdom of heaven. For the purpose of this record we will reorganize and classify these teachings as follows:

Jesus endeavored to make clear that he desired his disciples, having tasted of the good spirit realities of the kingdom, so to live in the world that men, by *seeing* their lives, would become kingdom conscious and hence be led to inquire of believers concerning the ways of the kingdom. All such sincere seekers for the truth are always glad to *hear* the glad tidings of the faith gift which insures admission to the kingdom with its eternal and divine spirit realities.

The Master sought to impress upon all teachers of the gospel of the kingdom that their only business was to reveal God to the individual man as his Father—to lead this individual man to become son-conscious; then to present this same man to God as his faith son. Both of these essential revelations are accomplished in Jesus. He became, indeed, "the way, the truth, and the life." The religion of Jesus was wholly based on the living of his bestowal life on earth. When Jesus departed from this world, he left behind no books, laws, or other forms of human organization affecting the religious life of the individual.

Jesus made it plain that he had come to establish personal and eternal relations with men which should forever take precedence over all other human relationships. And he emphasized that this intimate spiritual fellowship was to be extended to all men of all ages and of all social conditions among all peoples. The only reward which he held out for his children was: in this world—spiritual joy and divine communion; in the next world—eternal life in the progress of the divine spirit realities of the Paradise Father.

Jesus laid great emphasis upon what he called the two truths of first import in the teachings of the kingdom, and they are: the attainment of salvation by faith, and faith alone, associated with the revolutionary teaching of the attainment of human liberty through the sincere recognition of truth, "You shall know the truth, and the truth shall make you free." Jesus was the truth made manifest in the flesh, and he promised to send his Spirit of Truth into the hearts of all his children after his return to the Father in heaven.

The Master was teaching these apostles the essentials of truth for an entire age on earth. They often listened to his teachings when in reality what he said was intended for the inspiration and edification of other worlds. He exemplified a new and original plan of life. From the human standpoint he was indeed a Jew, but he lived his life for all the world as a mortal of the realm.

To insure the recognition of his Father in the unfolding of the plan of the kingdom, Jesus explained that he had purposely ignored the "great men of earth." He began his work with the poor, the very class which had been so neglected by most of the evolutionary religions of preceding times. He despised no man; his plan was world-wide, even universal. He was so bold and emphatic in these announcements that even Peter, James, and John were tempted to think he might possibly be beside himself.

He sought mildly to impart to these apostles the truth that he had come on this bestowal mission, not to set an example for a few earth creatures, but to establish and demonstrate a standard of human life for all peoples upon all worlds throughout his entire universe. And this standard approached the highest perfection, even the final goodness of the Universal Father. But the apostles could not grasp the meaning of his words.

He announced that he had come to function as a teacher, a teacher sent from heaven to present spiritual truth to the material mind. And this is exactly what he did; he was a teacher, not a preacher. From the human viewpoint Peter was a much more effective preacher than Jesus. Jesus' preaching was so effective because of his unique personality, not so much because of compelling oratory or emotional appeal. Jesus spoke directly to men's souls. He was a teacher of man's spirit, but through the mind. He lived with men.

It was on this occasion that Jesus intimated to Peter, James, and John that his work on earth was in some respects to be limited by the commission of his "associate on high," referring to the prebestowal instructions of his Paradise brother, Immanuel. He told them that he had come to do his Father's will and only his Father's will. Being thus motivated by a wholehearted singleness of purpose, he was not anxiously bothered by the evil in the world.

The apostles were beginning to recognize the unaffected friendliness of Jesus. Though the Master was easy of approach, he always lived independent of, and above, all human beings. Not for one moment was he ever dominated by any purely mortal influence or subject to frail human judgment. He paid no attention to public opinion, and he was uninfluenced by praise. He seldom paused to correct misunderstandings or to resent misrepresentation. He never asked any man for advice; he never made requests for prayers.

James was astonished at how Jesus seemed to see the end from the beginning. The Master rarely appeared to be surprised. He was never excited, vexed, or disconcerted. He never apologized to any man. He was at times saddened, but never discouraged.

More clearly John recognized that, notwithstanding all of his divine endowments, after all, he was human. Jesus lived as a man among men and understood, loved, and knew how to manage men. In his personal life he was so human, and yet so faultless. And he was always unselfish.

Although Peter, James, and John could not understand very much of what Jesus said on this occasion, his gracious words lingered in their hearts, and after the crucifixion and resurrection they came forth greatly to enrich and gladden their subsequent ministry. No wonder these apostles did not fully comprehend the Master's words, for he was projecting to them the plan of a new age.

8. WORKING IN JERICHO

Throughout the four weeks' sojourn at Bethany beyond Jordan, several times each week Andrew would assign apostolic couples to go up to Jericho for a day or two. John had many believers in Jericho, and the majority of them welcomed the more advanced teachings of Jesus and his apostles. On these Jericho visits the apostles began more specifically to carry out Jesus' instructions to minister to the sick; they visited every house in the city and sought to comfort every afflicted person.

The apostles did some public work in Jericho, but their efforts were chiefly of a more quiet and personal nature. They now made the discovery that the good news of the kingdom was very comforting to the sick; that their message carried healing for the afflicted. And it was in Jericho that Jesus' commission to the twelve to preach the glad tidings of the kingdom and minister to the afflicted was first fully carried into effect.

They stopped in Jericho on the way up to Jerusalem and were overtaken by a delegation from Mesopotamia that had come to confer with Jesus. The apostles had planned to spend but a day here, but when these truth seekers from the East arrived, Jesus spent three days with them, and they returned to their various homes along the Euphrates happy in the knowledge of the new truths of the kingdom of heaven.

9. DEPARTING FOR JERUSALEM

On Monday, the last day of March, Jesus and the apostles began their journey up the hills toward Jerusalem. Lazarus of Bethany had been down to the Jordan twice to see Jesus, and every arrangement had been made for the Master and his apostles to make their headquarters with Lazarus and his sisters at Bethany as long as they might desire to stay in Jerusalem.

The disciples of John remained at Bethany beyond the Jordan, teaching and baptizing the multitudes, so that Jesus was accompanied only by the twelve when he arrived at Lazarus's home. Here Jesus and the apostles tarried for five days, resting and refreshing themselves before going on to Jerusalem for the Passover. It was a great event in the lives of Martha and Mary to have the Master and his apostles in the home of their brother, where they could minister to their needs.

On Sunday morning, April 6, Jesus and the apostles went down to Jerusalem; and this was the first time the Master and all of the twelve had been there together.

PAPER 142

THE PASSOVER AT JERUSALEM

THE month of April Jesus and the apostles worked in Jerusalem, going out of the city each evening to spend the night at Bethany. Jesus himself spent one or two nights each week in Jerusalem at the home of Flavius, a Greek Jew, where many prominent Jews came in secret to interview him.

The first day in Jerusalem Jesus called upon his friend of former years, Annas, the onetime high priest and relative of Salome, Zebedee's wife. Annas had been hearing about Jesus and his teachings, and when Jesus called at the high priest's home, he was received with much reserve. When Jesus perceived Annas's coldness, he took immediate leave, saying as he departed: "Fear is man's chief enslaver and pride his great weakness; will you betray yourself into bondage to both of these destroyers of joy and liberty?" But Annas made no reply. The Master did not again see Annas until the time when he sat with his son-in-law in judgment on the Son of Man.

1. TEACHING IN THE TEMPLE

Throughout this month Jesus or one of the apostles taught daily in the temple. When the Passover crowds were too great to find entrance to the temple teaching, the apostles conducted many teaching groups outside the sacred precincts. The burden of their message was:

1. The kingdom of heaven is at hand.

2. By faith in the fatherhood of God you may enter the kingdom of heaven, thus becoming the sons of God.

3. Love is the rule of living within the kingdom—supreme devotion to God while loving your neighbor as yourself.

4. Obedience to the will of the Father, yielding the fruits of the spirit in one's personal life, is the law of the kingdom.

The multitudes who came to celebrate the Passover heard this teaching of Jesus, and hundreds of them rejoiced in the good news. The chief priests and rulers of the Jews became much concerned about Jesus and his apostles and debated among themselves as to what should be done with them.

Besides teaching in and about the temple, the apostles and other believers were engaged in doing much personal work among the Passover throngs. These interested men and women carried the news of Jesus' message from this Passover celebration to the uttermost parts of the Roman Empire and also to the East. This was the beginning of the spread of the gospel of the kingdom to the outside world. No longer was the work of Jesus to be confined to Palestine.

2. GOD'S WRATH

There was in Jerusalem in attendance upon the Passover festivities one Jacob, a wealthy Jewish trader from Crete, and he came to Andrew making request to see Jesus privately. Andrew arranged this secret meeting with Jesus at Flavius's home the evening of the next day. This man could not comprehend the Master's teachings, and he came because he desired to inquire more fully about the kingdom of God. Said Jacob to Jesus: "But, Rabbi, Moses and the olden prophets tell us that Yahweh is a jealous God, a God of great wrath and fierce anger. The prophets say he hates evildoers and takes vengeance on those who obey not his law. You and your disciples teach us that God is a kind and compassionate Father who so loves all men that he would welcome them into this new kingdom of heaven, which you proclaim is so near at hand."

When Jacob finished speaking, Jesus replied: "Jacob, you have well stated the teachings of the olden prophets who taught the children of their generation in accordance with the light of their day. Our Father in Paradise is changeless. But the concept of his nature has enlarged and grown from the days of Moses down through the times of Amos and even to the generation of the prophet Isaiah. And now have I come in the flesh to reveal the Father in new glory and to show forth his love and mercy to all men on all worlds. As the gospel of this kingdom shall spread over the world with its message of good cheer and good will to all men, there will grow up improved and better relations among the families of all nations. As time passes, fathers and their children will love each other more, and thus will be brought about a better understanding of the love of the Father in heaven for his children on earth. Remember, Jacob, that a good and true father not only loves his family as a whole—as a family—but he also truly loves and affectionately cares for each *individual* member."

After considerable discussion of the heavenly Father's character, Jesus paused to say: "You, Jacob, being a father of many, know well the truth of my words." And Jacob said: "But, Master, who told you I was the father of six children? How did you know this about me?" And the Master replied: "Suffice it to say that the Father and the Son know all things, for indeed they see all. Loving your children as a father on earth, you must now accept as a reality the love of the heavenly Father for *you*—not just for all the children of Abraham, but for you, your individual soul."

Then Jesus went on to say: "When your children are very young and immature, and when you must chastise them, they may reflect that their father is angry and filled with resentful wrath. Their immaturity cannot penetrate beyond the punishment to discern the father's farseeing and corrective affection. But when these same children become grown-up men and women, would it not be folly for them to cling to these earlier and misconceived notions regarding their father? As men and women they should now discern their father's love in all these early disciplines. And should not mankind, as the centuries pass, come the better to understand the true nature and loving character of the Father in heaven? What profit have you from successive generations of spiritual illumination if you persist in viewing God as Moses and the prophets saw him? I say to you, Jacob, under the bright light of this hour you should see the Father as none of those who have gone before ever beheld him. And thus seeing him, you should rejoice to enter the kingdom wherein such a merciful Father rules, and you should seek to have his will of love dominate your life henceforth."

And Jacob answered: "Rabbi, I believe; I desire that you lead me into the Father's kingdom."

3. THE CONCEPT OF GOD

The twelve apostles, most of whom had listened to this discussion of the character of God, that night asked Jesus many questions about the Father in heaven. The Master's answers to these questions can best be presented by the following summary in modern phraseology:

Jesus mildly upbraided the twelve, in substance saying: Do you not know the traditions of Israel relating to the growth of the idea of Yahweh, and are you ignorant of the teaching of the Scriptures concerning the doctrine of God? And then did the Master proceed to instruct the apostles about the evolution of the concept of Deity throughout the course of the development of the Jewish people. He called attention to the following phases of the growth of the God idea:

1. *Yahweh*—the god of the Sinai clans. This was the primitive concept of Deity which Moses exalted to the higher level of the Lord God of Israel. The Father in heaven never fails to accept the sincere worship of his children on earth, no matter how crude their concept of Deity or by what name they symbolize his divine nature.

2. *The Most High.* This concept of the Father in heaven was proclaimed by Melchizedek to Abraham and was carried far from Salem by those who subsequently believed in this enlarged and expanded idea of Deity. Abraham and his brother left Ur because of the establishment of sun worship, and they became believers in Melchizedek's teaching of El Elyon—the Most High God. Theirs was a composite concept of God, consisting in a blending of their older Mesopotamian ideas and the Most High doctrine.

3. *El Shaddai.* During these early days many of the Hebrews worshiped El Shaddai, the Egyptian concept of the God of heaven, which they learned about during their captivity in the land of the Nile. Long after the times of Melchizedek all three of these concepts of God became joined together to form the doctrine of the creator Deity, the Lord God of Israel.

4. *Elohim.* From the times of Adam the teaching of the Paradise Trinity has persisted. Do you not recall how the Scriptures begin by asserting that "In the beginning the Gods created the heavens and the earth"? This indicates that when that record was made the Trinity concept of three Gods in one had found lodgment in the religion of our forebears.

5. *The Supreme Yahweh.* By the times of Isaiah these beliefs about God had expanded into the concept of a Universal Creator who was simultaneously all-powerful and all-merciful. And this evolving and enlarging concept of God virtually supplanted all previous ideas of Deity in our fathers' religion.

6. *The Father in heaven.* And now do we know God as our Father in heaven. Our teaching provides a religion wherein the believer *is* a son of God. That is the good news of the gospel of the kingdom of heaven. Coexistent with the Father are the Son and the Spirit, and the revelation of the nature and ministry

of these Paradise Deities will continue to enlarge and brighten throughout the endless ages of the eternal spiritual progression of the ascending sons of God. At all times and during all ages the true worship of any human being—as concerns individual spiritual progress—is recognized by the indwelling spirit as homage rendered to the Father in heaven.

Never before had the apostles been so shocked as they were upon hearing this recounting of the growth of the concept of God in the Jewish minds of previous generations; they were too bewildered to ask questions. As they sat before Jesus in silence, the Master continued: "And you would have known these truths had you read the Scriptures. Have you not read in Samuel where it says: 'And the anger of the Lord was kindled against Israel, so much so that he moved David against them, saying, go number Israel and Judah'? And this was not strange because in the days of Samuel the children of Abraham really believed that Yahweh created both good and evil. But when a later writer narrated these events, subsequent to the enlargement of the Jewish concept of the nature of God, he did not dare attribute evil to Yahweh; therefore he said: 'And Satan stood up against Israel and provoked David to number Israel.' Cannot you discern that such records in the Scriptures clearly show how the concept of the nature of God continued to grow from one generation to another?

"Again should you have discerned the growth of the understanding of divine law in perfect keeping with these enlarging concepts of divinity. When the children of Israel came out of Egypt in the days before the enlarged revelation of Yahweh, they had ten commandments which served as their law right up to the times when they were encamped before Sinai. And these ten commandments were:

"1. You shall worship no other god, for the Lord is a jealous God.

"2. You shall not make molten gods.

"3. You shall not neglect to keep the feast of unleavened bread.

"4. Of all the males of men or cattle, the first-born are mine, says the Lord.

"5. Six days you may work, but on the seventh day you shall rest.

"6. You shall not fail to observe the feast of the first fruits and the feast of the ingathering at the end of the year.

"7. You shall not offer the blood of any sacrifice with leavened bread.

"8. The sacrifice of the feast of the Passover shall not be left until morning.

"9. The first of the first fruits of the ground you shall bring to the house of the Lord your God.

"10. You shall not seethe a kid in its mother's milk.

"And then, amidst the thunders and lightnings of Sinai, Moses gave them the new ten commandments, which you will all allow are more worthy utterances to accompany the enlarging Yahweh concepts of Deity. And did you never take notice of these commandments as twice recorded in the Scriptures, that in the first case deliverance from Egypt is assigned as the reason for Sabbath keeping, while in a later record the advancing religious beliefs of our forefathers demanded that this be changed to the recognition of the fact of creation as the reason for Sabbath observance?

"And then will you remember that once again—in the greater spiritual enlightenment of Isaiah's day—these ten negative commandments were changed into the great and positive law of love, the injunction to love God supremely and your neighbor as yourself. And it is this supreme law of love for God and for man that I also declare to you as constituting the whole duty of man."

And when he had finished speaking, no man asked him a question. They went, each one to his sleep.

4. FLAVIUS AND GREEK CULTURE

Flavius, the Greek Jew, was a proselyte of the gate, having been neither circumcised nor baptized; and since he was a great lover of the beautiful in art and sculpture, the house which he occupied when sojourning in Jerusalem was a beautiful edifice. This home was exquisitely adorned with priceless treasures which he had gathered up here and there on his world travels. When he first thought of inviting Jesus to his home, he feared that the Master might take offense at the sight of these so-called images. But Flavius was agreeably surprised when Jesus entered the home that, instead of rebuking him for having these supposedly idolatrous objects scattered about the house, he manifested great interest in the entire collection and asked many appreciative questions about each object as Flavius escorted him from room to room, showing him all of his favorite statues.

The Master saw that his host was bewildered at his friendly attitude toward art; therefore, when they had finished the survey of the entire collection, Jesus said: "Because you appreciate the beauty of things created by my Father and fashioned by the artistic hands of man, why should you expect to be rebuked? Because Moses onetime sought to combat idolatry and the worship of false gods, why should all men frown upon the reproduction of grace and beauty? I say to you, Flavius, Moses' children have misunderstood him, and now do they make false gods of even his prohibitions of images and the likeness of things in heaven and on earth. But even if Moses taught such restrictions to the darkened minds of those days, what has that to do with this day when the Father in heaven is revealed as the universal Spirit Ruler over all? And, Flavius, I declare that in the coming kingdom they shall no longer teach, 'Do not worship this and do not worship that'; no longer shall they concern themselves with commands to refrain from this and take care not to do that, but rather shall all be concerned with one supreme duty. And this duty of man is expressed in two great privileges: sincere worship of the infinite Creator, the Paradise Father, and loving service bestowed upon one's fellow men. If you love your neighbor as you love yourself, you really know that you are a son of God.

"In an age when my Father was not well understood, Moses was justified in his attempts to withstand idolatry, but in the coming age the Father will have been revealed in the life of the Son; and this new revelation of God will make it forever unnecessary to confuse the Creator Father with idols of stone or images of gold and silver. Henceforth, intelligent men may enjoy the treasures of art without confusing such material appreciation of beauty with the worship and service of the Father in Paradise, the God of all things and all beings."

Flavius believed all that Jesus taught him. The next day he went to Bethany beyond the Jordan and was baptized by the disciples of John. And this he did because the apostles of Jesus did not yet baptize believers. When Flavius returned to Jerusalem, he made a great feast for Jesus and invited sixty of his friends. And many of these guests also became believers in the message of the coming kingdom.

5. THE DISCOURSE ON ASSURANCE

One of the great sermons which Jesus preached in the temple this Passover week was in answer to a question asked by one of his hearers, a man from Damascus. This man asked Jesus: "But, Rabbi, how shall we know of a certainty that you are sent by God, and that we may truly enter into this kingdom which you and your disciples declare is near at hand?" And Jesus answered:

"As to my message and the teaching of my disciples, you should judge them by their fruits. If we proclaim to you the truths of the spirit, the spirit will witness in your hearts that our message is genuine. Concerning the kingdom and your assurance of acceptance by the heavenly Father, let me ask what father among you who is a worthy and kindhearted father would keep his son in anxiety or suspense regarding his status in the family or his place of security in the affections of his father's heart? Do you earth fathers take pleasure in torturing your children with uncertainty about their place of abiding love in your human hearts? Neither does your Father in heaven leave his faith children of the spirit in doubtful uncertainty as to their position in the kingdom. If you receive God as your Father, then indeed and in truth are you the sons of God. And if you are sons, then are you secure in the position and standing of all that concerns eternal and divine sonship. If you believe my words, you thereby believe in Him who sent me, and by thus believing in the Father, you have made your status in heavenly citizenship sure. If you do the will of the Father in heaven, you shall never fail in the attainment of the eternal life of progress in the divine kingdom.

"The Supreme Spirit shall bear witness with your spirits that you are truly the children of God. And if you are the sons of God, then have you been born of the spirit of God; and whosoever has been born of the spirit has in himself the power to overcome all doubt, and this is the victory that overcomes all uncertainty, even your faith.

"Said the Prophet Isaiah, speaking of these times: 'When the spirit is poured upon us from on high, then shall the work of righteousness become peace, quietness, and assurance forever.' And for all who truly believe this gospel, I will become surety for their reception into the eternal mercies and the everlasting life of my Father's kingdom. You, then, who hear this message and believe this gospel of the kingdom are the sons of God, and you have life everlasting; and the evidence to all the world that you have been born of the spirit is that you sincerely love one another."

The throng of listeners remained many hours with Jesus, asking him questions and listening attentively to his comforting answers. Even the apostles were emboldened by Jesus' teaching to preach the gospel of the kingdom with more power and assurance. This experience at Jerusalem was a great inspiration to the twelve. It was their first contact with such enormous crowds, and they learned many valuable lessons which proved of great assistance in their later work.

6. THE VISIT WITH NICODEMUS

One evening at the home of Flavius there came to see Jesus one Nicodemus, a wealthy and elderly member of the Jewish Sanhedrin. He had heard much about the teachings of this Galilean, and so he went one afternoon to hear him as he taught in the temple courts. He would have gone often to hear Jesus teach, but he feared to be seen by the people in attendance upon his teaching, for already were the rulers of the Jews so at variance with Jesus that no member of the Sanhedrin would want to be identified in any open manner with him. Accordingly, Nicodemus had arranged with Andrew to see Jesus privately and after nightfall on this particular evening. Peter, James, and John were in Flavius's garden when the interview began, but later they all went into the house where the discourse continued.

In receiving Nicodemus, Jesus showed no particular deference; in talking with him, there was no compromise or undue persuasiveness. The Master made no attempt to repulse his secretive caller, nor did he employ sarcasm. In all his dealings with the distinguished visitor, Jesus was calm, earnest, and dignified. Nicodemus was not an official delegate of the Sanhedrin; he came to see Jesus wholly because of his personal and sincere interest in the Master's teachings.

Upon being presented by Flavius, Nicodemus said: "Rabbi, we know that you are a teacher sent by God, for no mere man could so teach unless God were with him. And I am desirous of knowing more about your teachings regarding the coming kingdom."

Jesus answered Nicodemus: "Verily, verily, I say to you, Nicodemus, except a man be born from above, he cannot see the kingdom of God." Then replied Nicodemus: "But how can a man be born again when he is old? He cannot enter a second time into his mother's womb to be born."

Jesus said: "Nevertheless, I declare to you, except a man be born of the spirit, he cannot enter into the kingdom of God. That which is born of the flesh is flesh, and that which is born of the spirit is spirit. But you should not marvel that I said you must be born from above. When the wind blows, you hear the rustle of the leaves, but you do not see the wind—whence it comes or whither it goes—and so it is with everyone born of the spirit. With the eyes of the flesh you can behold the manifestations of the spirit, but you cannot actually discern the spirit."

Nicodemus replied: "But I do not understand—how can that be?" Said Jesus: "Can it be that you are a teacher in Israel and yet ignorant of all this? It becomes, then, the duty of those who know about the realities of the spirit to reveal these things to those who discern only the manifestations of the material world. But will you believe us if we tell you of the heavenly truths? Do you have the courage, Nicodemus, to believe in one who has descended from heaven, even the Son of Man?"

And Nicodemus said: "But how can I begin to lay hold upon this spirit which is to remake me in preparation for entering into the kingdom?" Jesus answered: "Already does the spirit of the Father in heaven indwell you. If you would be led by this spirit from above, very soon would you begin to see with the eyes of the spirit, and then by the wholehearted choice of spirit guidance would you be born of the spirit since your only purpose in living would be to do the will of your Father who is in heaven. And so finding yourself born of the spirit and happily in the kingdom of God, you would begin to bear in your daily life the abundant fruits of the spirit."

Nicodemus was thoroughly sincere. He was deeply impressed but went away bewildered. Nicodemus was accomplished in self-development, in self-restraint, and even in high moral qualities. He was refined, egoistic, and altruistic; but he did not know how to *submit* his will to the will of the divine Father as a little child is willing to submit to the guidance and leading of a wise and loving earthly father, thereby becoming in reality a son of God, a progressive heir of the eternal kingdom.

But Nicodemus did summon faith enough to lay hold of the kingdom. He faintly protested when his colleagues of the Sanhedrin sought to condemn Jesus without a hearing; and with Joseph of Arimathea, he later boldly acknowledged his faith and claimed the body of Jesus, even when most of the disciples had fled in fear from the scenes of their Master's final suffering and death.

7. THE LESSON ON THE FAMILY

After the busy period of teaching and personal work of Passover week in Jerusalem, Jesus spent the next Wednesday at Bethany with his apostles, resting. That afternoon, Thomas asked a question which elicited a long and instructive answer. Said Thomas: "Master, on the day we were set apart as ambassadors of the kingdom, you told us many things, instructed us regarding our personal mode of life, but what shall we teach the multitude? How are these people to live after the kingdom more fully comes? Shall your disciples own slaves? Shall your believers court poverty and shun property? Shall mercy alone prevail so that we shall have no more law and justice?" Jesus and the twelve spent all afternoon and all that evening, after supper, discussing Thomas's questions. For the purposes of this record we present the following summary of the Master's instruction:

Jesus sought first to make plain to his apostles that he himself was on earth living a unique life in the flesh, and that they, the twelve, had been called to participate in this bestowal experience of the Son of Man; and as such coworkers, they, too, must share in many of the special restrictions and obligations of the entire bestowal experience. There was a veiled intimation that the Son of Man was the only person who had ever lived on earth who could simultaneously see into the very heart of God and into the very depths of man's soul.

Very plainly Jesus explained that the kingdom of heaven was an evolutionary experience, beginning here on earth and progressing up through successive life stations to Paradise. In the course of the evening he definitely stated that at some future stage of kingdom development he would revisit this world in spiritual power and divine glory.

He next explained that the "kingdom idea" was not the best way to illustrate man's relation to God; that he employed such figures of speech because the Jewish people were expecting the kingdom, and because John had preached in terms of the coming kingdom. Jesus said: "The people of another age will better understand the gospel of the kingdom when it is presented in terms expressive of the family relationship—when man understands religion as the teaching of the fatherhood of God and the brotherhood of man, sonship with God." Then the Master discoursed at some length on the earthly family as an illustration of the heavenly family, restating the two fundamental laws of living: the first commandment of love for the father, the head of the family, and the second commandment of mutual love among the children, to love your brother as yourself. And then he explained that such a quality of brotherly affection would invariably manifest itself in unselfish and loving social service.

Following that, came the memorable discussion of the fundamental characteristics of family life and their application to the relationship existing between

God and man. Jesus stated that a true family is founded on the following seven facts:

1. *The fact of existence.* The relationships of nature and the phenomena of mortal likenesses are bound up in the family: Children inherit certain parental traits. The children take origin in the parents; personality existence depends on the act of the parent. The relationship of father and child is inherent in all nature and pervades all living existences.

2. *Security and pleasure.* True fathers take great pleasure in providing for the needs of their children. Many fathers are not content with supplying the mere wants of their children but enjoy making provision for their pleasures also.

3. *Education and training.* Wise fathers carefully plan for the education and adequate training of their sons and daughters. When young they are prepared for the greater responsibilities of later life.

4. *Discipline and restraint.* Farseeing fathers also make provision for the necessary discipline, guidance, correction, and sometimes restraint of their young and immature offspring.

5. *Companionship and loyalty.* The affectionate father holds intimate and loving intercourse with his children. Always is his ear open to their petitions; he is ever ready to share their hardships and assist them over their difficulties. The father is supremely interested in the progressive welfare of his progeny.

6. *Love and mercy.* A compassionate father is freely forgiving; fathers do not hold vengeful memories against their children. Fathers are not like judges, enemies, or creditors. Real families are built upon tolerance, patience, and forgiveness.

7. *Provision for the future.* Temporal fathers like to leave an inheritance for their sons. The family continues from one generation to another. Death only ends one generation to mark the beginning of another. Death terminates an individual life but not necessarily the family.

For hours the Master discussed the application of these features of family life to the relations of man, the earth child, to God, the Paradise Father. And this was his conclusion: "This entire relationship of a son to the Father, I know in perfection, for all that you must attain of sonship in the eternal future I have now already attained. The Son of Man is prepared to ascend to the right hand of the Father, so that in me is the way now open still wider for all of you to see God and, ere you have finished the glorious progression, to become perfect, even as your Father in heaven is perfect."

When the apostles heard these startling words, they recalled the pronouncements which John made at the time of Jesus' baptism, and they also vividly recalled this experience in connection with their preaching and teaching subsequent to the Master's death and resurrection.

Jesus is a divine Son, one in the Universal Father's full confidence. He had been with the Father and comprehended him fully. He had now lived his earth life to the full satisfaction of the Father, and this incarnation in the flesh had enabled him fully to comprehend man. Jesus was the perfection of man; he had attained just such perfection as all true believers are destined to attain in him and through him. Jesus revealed a God of perfection to man and presented in himself the perfected son of the realms to God.

Although Jesus discoursed for several hours, Thomas was not yet satisfied, for he said: "But, Master, we do not find that the Father in heaven always deals kindly and mercifully with us. Many times we grievously suffer on earth, and not always are our prayers answered. Where do we fail to grasp the meaning of your teaching?"

Jesus replied: "Thomas, Thomas, how long before you will acquire the ability to listen with the ear of the spirit? How long will it be before you discern that this kingdom is a spiritual kingdom, and that my Father is also a spiritual being? Do you not understand that I am teaching you as spiritual children in the spirit family of heaven, of which the fatherhead is an infinite and eternal spirit? Will you not allow me to use the earth family as an illustration of divine relationships without so literally applying my teaching to material affairs? In your minds cannot you separate the spiritual realities of the kingdom from the material, social, economic, and political problems of the age? When I speak the language of the spirit, why do you insist on translating my meaning into the language of the flesh just because I presume to employ commonplace and literal relationships for purposes of illustration? My children, I implore that you cease to apply the teaching of the kingdom of the spirit to the sordid affairs of slavery, poverty, houses, and lands, and to the material problems of human equity and justice. These temporal matters are the concern of the men of this world, and while in a way they affect all men, you have been called to represent me in the world, even as I represent my Father. You are spiritual ambassadors of a spiritual kingdom, special representatives of the spirit Father. By this time it should be possible for me to instruct you as full-grown men of the spirit kingdom. Must I ever address you only as children? Will you never grow up in spirit perception? Nevertheless, I love you and will bear with you, even to the very end of our association in the flesh. And even then shall my spirit go before you into all the world."

8. IN SOUTHERN JUDEA

By the end of April the opposition to Jesus among the Pharisees and Sadducees had become so pronounced that the Master and his apostles decided to leave Jerusalem for a while, going south to work in Bethlehem and Hebron. The entire month of May was spent in doing personal work in these cities and among the people of the surrounding villages. No public preaching was done on this trip, only house-to-house visitation. A part of this time, while the apostles taught the gospel and ministered to the sick, Jesus and Abner spent at Engedi, visiting the Nazarite colony. John the Baptist had gone forth from this place, and Abner had been head of this group. Many of the Nazarite brotherhood became believers in Jesus, but the majority of these ascetic and eccentric men refused to accept him as a teacher sent from heaven because he did not teach fasting and other forms of self-denial.

The people living in this region did not know that Jesus had been born in Bethlehem. They always supposed the Master had been born at Nazareth, as did the vast majority of his disciples, but the twelve knew the facts.

This sojourn in the south of Judea was a restful and fruitful season of labor; many souls were added to the kingdom. By the first days of June the agitation against Jesus had so quieted down in Jerusalem that the Master and the apostles returned to instruct and comfort believers.

Although Jesus and the apostles spent the entire month of June in or near Jerusalem, they did no public teaching during this period. They lived for the most part in tents, which they pitched in a shaded park, or garden, known in that day as Gethsemane. This park was situated on the western slope of the Mount of Olives not far from the brook Kidron. The Sabbath weekends they usually spent with Lazarus and his sisters at Bethany. Jesus entered within the walls of Jerusalem only a few times, but a large number of interested inquirers came out to Gethsemane to visit with him. One Friday evening Nicodemus and one Joseph of Arimathea ventured out to see Jesus but turned back through fear even after they were standing before the entrance to the Master's tent. And, of course, they did not perceive that Jesus knew all about their doings.

When the rulers of the Jews learned that Jesus had returned to Jerusalem, they prepared to arrest him; but when they observed that he did no public preaching, they concluded that he had become frightened by their previous agitation and decided to allow him to carry on his teaching in this private manner without further molestation. And thus affairs moved along quietly until the last days of June, when one Simon, a member of the Sanhedrin, publicly espoused the teachings of Jesus, after so declaring himself before the rulers of the Jews. Immediately a new agitation for Jesus' apprehension sprang up and grew so strong that the Master decided to retire into the cities of Samaria and the Decapolis.

PAPER 143
GOING THROUGH SAMARIA

AT THE end of June, A.D. 27, because of the increasing opposition of the Jewish religious rulers, Jesus and the twelve departed from Jerusalem, after sending their tents and meager personal effects to be stored at the home of Lazarus at Bethany. Going north into Samaria, they tarried over the Sabbath at Bethel. Here they preached for several days to the people who came from Gophna and Ephraim. A group of citizens from Arimathea and Thamna came over to invite Jesus to visit their villages. The Master and his apostles spent more than two weeks teaching the Jews and Samaritans of this region, many of whom came from as far as Antipatris to hear the good news of the kingdom.

The people of southern Samaria heard Jesus gladly, and the apostles, with the exception of Judas Iscariot, succeeded in overcoming much of their prejudice against the Samaritans. It was very difficult for Judas to love these Samaritans. The last week of July Jesus and his associates made ready to depart for the new Greek cities of Phasaelis and Archelais near the Jordan.

1. PREACHING AT ARCHELAIS

The first half of the month of August the apostolic party made its headquarters at the Greek cities of Archelais and Phasaelis, where they had their first experience preaching to well-nigh exclusive gatherings of gentiles—Greeks, Romans, and Syrians—for few Jews dwelt in these two Greek towns. In contacting with these Roman citizens, the apostles encountered new difficulties in the proclamation of the message of the coming kingdom, and they met with new objections to the teachings of Jesus. At one of the many evening conferences with his apostles, Jesus listened attentively to these objections to the gospel of the kingdom as the twelve repeated their experiences with the subjects of their personal labors.

A question asked by Philip was typical of their difficulties. Said Philip: "Master, these Greeks and Romans make light of our message, saying that such teachings are fit for only weaklings and slaves. They assert that the religion of the heathen is superior to our teaching because it inspires to the acquirement of a strong, robust, and aggressive character. They affirm that we would convert all men into enfeebled specimens of passive nonresisters who would soon perish from the face of the earth. They like you, Master, and freely admit that your teaching is heavenly and ideal, but they will not take us seriously. They assert that your religion is not for this world; that men cannot live as you teach. And now, Master, what shall we say to these gentiles?"

After Jesus had heard similar objections to the gospel of the kingdom presented by Thomas, Nathaniel, Simon Zelotes, and Matthew, he said to the twelve:

"I have come into this world to do the will of my Father and to reveal his loving character to all mankind. That, my brethren, is my mission. And this one thing I will do, regardless of the misunderstanding of my teachings by Jews or gentiles of this day or of another generation. But you should not overlook the fact that even divine love has its severe disciplines. A father's love for his son oftentimes impels the father to restrain the unwise acts of his thoughtless offspring. The child does not always comprehend the wise and loving motives of the father's restraining discipline. But I declare to you that my Father in Paradise does rule a universe of universes by the compelling power of his love. Love is the greatest of all spirit realities. Truth is a liberating revelation, but love is the supreme relationship. And no matter what blunders your fellow men make in their world management of today, in an age to come the gospel which I declare to you will rule this very world. The ultimate goal of human progress is the reverent recognition of the fatherhood of God and the loving materialization of the brotherhood of man.

"But who told you that my gospel was intended only for slaves and weaklings? Do you, my chosen apostles, resemble weaklings? Did John look like a weakling? Do you observe that I am enslaved by fear? True, the poor and oppressed of this generation have the gospel preached to them. The religions of this world have neglected the poor, but my Father is no respecter of persons. Besides, the poor of this day are the first to heed the call to repentance and acceptance of sonship. The gospel of the kingdom is to be preached to all men—Jew and gentile, Greek and Roman, rich and poor, free and bond—and equally to young and old, male and female.

"Because my Father is a God of love and delights in the practice of mercy, do not imbibe the idea that the service of the kingdom is to be one of monotonous ease. The Paradise ascent is the supreme adventure of all time, the rugged achievement of eternity. The service of the kingdom on earth will call for all the courageous manhood that you and your coworkers can muster. Many of you will be put to death for your loyalty to the gospel of this kingdom. It is easy to die in the line of physical battle when your courage is strengthened by the presence of your fighting comrades, but it requires a higher and more profound form of human courage and devotion calmly and all alone to lay down your life for the love of a truth enshrined in your mortal heart.

"Today, the unbelievers may taunt you with preaching a gospel of nonresistance and with living lives of nonviolence, but you are the first volunteers of a long line of sincere believers in the gospel of this kingdom who will astonish all mankind by their heroic devotion to these teachings. No armies of the world have ever displayed more courage and bravery than will be portrayed by you and your loyal successors who shall go forth to all the world proclaiming the good news—the fatherhood of God and the brotherhood of men. The courage of the flesh is the lowest form of bravery. Mind bravery is a higher type of human courage, but the highest and supreme is uncompromising loyalty to the enlightened convictions of profound spiritual realities. And such courage constitutes the heroism of the God-knowing man. And you are all God-knowing men; you are in very truth the personal associates of the Son of Man."

This was not all that Jesus said on that occasion, but it is the introduction of his address, and he went on at great length in amplification and in illustration of this pronouncement. This was one of the most impassioned addresses which

Jesus ever delivered to the twelve. Seldom did the Master speak to his apostles with evident strong feeling, but this was one of those few occasions when he spoke with manifest earnestness, accompanied by marked emotion.

The result upon the public preaching and personal ministry of the apostles was immediate; from that very day their message took on a new note of courageous dominance. The twelve continued to acquire the spirit of positive aggression in the new gospel of the kingdom. From this day forward they did not occupy themselves so much with the preaching of the negative virtues and the passive injunctions of their Master's many-sided teaching.

2. Lesson on Self-Mastery

The Master was a perfected specimen of human self-control. When he was reviled, he reviled not; when he suffered, he uttered no threats against his tormentors; when he was denounced by his enemies, he simply committed himself to the righteous judgment of the Father in heaven.

At one of the evening conferences, Andrew asked Jesus: "Master, are we to practice self-denial as John taught us, or are we to strive for the self-control of your teaching? Wherein does your teaching differ from that of John?" Jesus answered: "John indeed taught you the way of righteousness in accordance with the light and laws of his fathers, and that was the religion of self-examination and self-denial. But I come with a new message of self-forgetfulness and self-control. I show to you the way of life as revealed to me by my Father in heaven.

"Verily, verily, I say to you, he who rules his own self is greater than he who captures a city. Self-mastery is the measure of man's moral nature and the indicator of his spiritual development. In the old order you fasted and prayed; as the new creature of the rebirth of the spirit, you are taught to believe and rejoice. In the Father's kingdom you are to become new creatures; old things are to pass away; behold I show you how all things are to become new. And by your love for one another you are to convince the world that you have passed from bondage to liberty, from death into life everlasting.

"By the old way you seek to suppress, obey, and conform to the rules of living; by the new way you are first *transformed* by the Spirit of Truth and thereby strengthened in your inner soul by the constant spiritual renewing of your mind, and so are you endowed with the power of the certain and joyous performance of the gracious, acceptable, and perfect will of God. Forget not—it is your personal faith in the exceedingly great and precious promises of God that ensures your becoming partakers of the divine nature. Thus by your faith and the spirit's transformation, you become in reality the temples of God, and his spirit actually dwells within you. If, then, the spirit dwells within you, you are no longer bondslaves of the flesh but free and liberated sons of the spirit. The new law of the spirit endows you with the liberty of self-mastery in place of the old law of the fear of self-bondage and the slavery of self-denial.

"Many times, when you have done evil, you have thought to charge up your acts to the influence of the evil one when in reality you have but been led astray by your own natural tendencies. Did not the Prophet Jeremiah long ago tell you that the human heart is deceitful above all things and sometimes even desperately wicked? How easy for you to become self-deceived and thereby fall into foolish fears, divers lusts, enslaving pleasures, malice, envy, and even vengeful hatred!

"Salvation is by the regeneration of the spirit and not by the self-righteous deeds of the flesh. You are justified by faith and fellowshipped by grace, not by fear and the self-denial of the flesh, albeit the Father's children who have been born of the spirit are ever and always *masters* of the self and all that pertains to the desires of the flesh. When you know that you are saved by faith, you have real peace with God. And all who follow in the way of this heavenly peace are destined to be sanctified to the eternal service of the ever-advancing sons of the eternal God. Henceforth, it is not a duty but rather your exalted privilege to cleanse yourselves from all evils of mind and body while you seek for perfection in the love of God.

"Your sonship is grounded in faith, and you are to remain unmoved by fear. Your joy is born of trust in the divine word, and you shall not therefore be led to doubt the reality of the Father's love and mercy. It is the very goodness of God that leads men into true and genuine repentance. Your secret of the mastery of self is bound up with your faith in the indwelling spirit, which ever works by love. Even this saving faith you have not of yourselves; it also is the gift of God. And if you are the children of this living faith, you are no longer the bondslaves of self but rather the triumphant masters of yourselves, the liberated sons of God.

"If, then, my children, you are born of the spirit, you are forever delivered from the self-conscious bondage of a life of self-denial and watchcare over the desires of the flesh, and you are translated into the joyous kingdom of the spirit, whence you spontaneously show forth the fruits of the spirit in your daily lives; and the fruits of the spirit are the essence of the highest type of enjoyable and ennobling self-control, even the heights of terrestrial mortal attainment—true self-mastery."

3. DIVERSION AND RELAXATION

About this time a state of great nervous and emotional tension developed among the apostles and their immediate disciple associates. They had hardly become accustomed to living and working together. They were experiencing increasing difficulties in maintaining harmonious relations with John's disciples. The contact with the gentiles and the Samaritans was a great trial to these Jews. And besides all this, the recent utterances of Jesus had augmented their disturbed state of mind. Andrew was almost beside himself; he did not know what next to do, and so he went to the Master with his problems and perplexities. When Jesus had listened to the apostolic chief relate his troubles, he said: "Andrew, you cannot talk men out of their perplexities when they reach such a stage of involvement, and when so many persons with strong feelings are concerned. I cannot do what you ask of me—I will not participate in these personal social difficulties—but I will join you in the enjoyment of a three-day period of rest and relaxation. Go to your brethren and announce that all of you are to go with me up on Mount Sartaba, where I desire to rest for a day or two.

"Now you should go to each of your eleven brethren and talk with him privately, saying: 'The Master desires that we go apart with him for a season to rest and relax. Since we all have recently experienced much vexation of spirit and stress of mind, I suggest that no mention be made of our trials and troubles while on this holiday. Can I depend upon you to co-operate with me in this matter?' In this way privately and personally approach each of your brethren." And Andrew did as the Master had instructed him.

This was a marvelous occasion in the experience of each of them; they never forgot the day going up the mountain. Throughout the entire trip hardly a word was said about their troubles. Upon reaching the top of the mountain, Jesus seated them about him while he said: "My brethren, you must all learn the value of rest and the efficacy of relaxation. You must realize that the best method of solving some entangled problems is to forsake them for a time. Then when you go back fresh from your rest or worship, you are able to attack your troubles with a clearer head and a steadier hand, not to mention a more resolute heart. Again, many times your problem is found to have shrunk in size and proportions while you have been resting your mind and body."

The next day Jesus assigned to each of the twelve a topic for discussion. The whole day was devoted to reminiscences and to talking over matters not related to their religious work. They were momentarily shocked when Jesus even neglected to give thanks—verbally—when he broke bread for their noontide lunch. This was the first time they had ever observed him to neglect such formalities.

When they went up the mountain, Andrew's head was full of problems. John was inordinately perplexed in his heart. James was grievously troubled in his soul. Matthew was hard pressed for funds inasmuch as they had been sojourning among the gentiles. Peter was overwrought and had recently been more temperamental than usual. Judas was suffering from a periodic attack of sensitiveness and selfishness. Simon was unusually upset in his efforts to reconcile his patriotism with the love of the brotherhood of man. Philip was more and more nonplused by the way things were going. Nathaniel had been less humorous since they had come in contact with the gentile populations, and Thomas was in the midst of a severe season of depression. Only the twins were normal and unperturbed. All of them were exceedingly perplexed about how to get along peaceably with John's disciples.

The third day when they started down the mountain and back to their camp, a great change had come over them. They had made the important discovery that many human perplexities are in reality nonexistent, that many pressing troubles are the creations of exaggerated fear and the offspring of augmented apprehension. They had learned that all such perplexities are best handled by being forsaken; by going off they had left such problems to solve themselves.

Their return from this holiday marked the beginning of a period of greatly improved relations with the followers of John. Many of the twelve really gave way to mirth when they noted the changed state of everybody's mind and observed the freedom from nervous irritability which had come to them as a result of their three days' vacation from the routine duties of life. There is always danger that monotony of human contact will greatly multiply perplexities and magnify difficulties.

Not many of the gentiles in the two Greek cities of Archelais and Phasaelis believed in the gospel, but the twelve apostles gained a valuable experience in this their first extensive work with exclusively gentile populations. On a Monday morning, about the middle of the month, Jesus said to Andrew: "We go into Samaria." And they set out at once for the city of Sychar, near Jacob's well.

4. THE JEWS AND THE SAMARITANS

For more than six hundred years the Jews of Judea, and later on those of Galilee also, had been at enmity with the Samaritans. This ill feeling between the Jews and the Samaritans came about in this way: About seven hundred years B.C., Sargon, king of Assyria, in subduing a revolt in central Palestine, carried away and into captivity over twenty-five thousand Jews of the northern kingdom of Israel and installed in their place an almost equal number of the descendants of the Cuthites, Sepharvites, and the Hamathites. Later on, Ashurbanipal sent still other colonies to dwell in Samaria.

The religious enmity between the Jews and the Samaritans dated from the return of the former from the Babylonian captivity, when the Samaritans worked to prevent the rebuilding of Jerusalem. Later they offended the Jews by extending friendly assistance to the armies of Alexander. In return for their friendship Alexander gave the Samaritans permission to build a temple on Mount Gerizim, where they worshiped Yahweh and their tribal gods and offered sacrifices much after the order of the temple services at Jerusalem. At least they continued this worship up to the time of the Maccabees, when John Hyrcanus destroyed their temple on Mount Gerizim. The Apostle Philip, in his labors for the Samaritans after the death of Jesus, held many meetings on the site of this old Samaritan temple.

The antagonisms between the Jews and the Samaritans were time-honored and historic; increasingly since the days of Alexander they had had no dealings with each other. The twelve apostles were not averse to preaching in the Greek and other gentile cities of the Decapolis and Syria, but it was a severe test of their loyalty to the Master when he said, "Let us go into Samaria." But in the year and more they had been with Jesus, they had developed a form of personal loyalty which transcended even their faith in his teachings and their prejudices against the Samaritans.

5. THE WOMAN OF SYCHAR

When the Master and the twelve arrived at Jacob's well, Jesus, being weary from the journey, tarried by the well while Philip took the apostles with him to assist in bringing food and tents from Sychar, for they were disposed to stay in this vicinity for a while. Peter and the Zebedee sons would have remained with Jesus, but he requested that they go with their brethren, saying: "Have no fear for me; these Samaritans will be friendly; only our brethren, the Jews, seek to harm us." And it was almost six o'clock on this summer's evening when Jesus sat down by the well to await the return of the apostles.

The water of Jacob's well was less mineral than that from the wells of Sychar and was therefore much valued for drinking purposes. Jesus was thirsty, but there was no way of getting water from the well. When, therefore, a woman of Sychar came up with her water pitcher and prepared to draw from the well, Jesus said to her, "Give me a drink." This woman of Samaria knew Jesus was a Jew by his appearance and dress, and she surmised that he was a Galilean Jew from his accent. Her name was Nalda and she was a comely creature. She was much surprised to have a Jewish man thus speak to her at the well and ask for water, for it was not deemed proper in those days for a self-respecting man to speak to a woman in public, much less for a Jew to converse with a Samaritan. Therefore Nalda asked Jesus, "How is it that you, being a Jew, ask for a drink of me, a Samaritan woman?" Jesus answered: "I have indeed asked you for a drink, but if you could only understand, you would ask me for a draught of the living water." Then said Nalda: "But, Sir, you have nothing to draw with, and the well is deep; whence, then, have you this living water? Are you greater than our father Jacob who gave us this well, and who drank thereof himself and his sons and his cattle also?"

Jesus replied: "Everyone who drinks of this water will thirst again, but whosoever drinks of the water of the living spirit shall never thirst. And this living water shall become in him a well of refreshment springing up even to eternal life." Nalda then said: "Give me this water that I thirst not, neither come all the way hither to draw. Besides, anything which a Samaritan woman could receive from such a commendable Jew would be a pleasure."

Nalda did not know how to take Jesus' willingness to talk with her. She beheld in the Master's face the countenance of an upright and holy man, but she mistook friendliness for commonplace familiarity, and she misinterpreted his figure of speech as a form of making advances to her. And being a woman of lax morals, she was minded openly to become flirtatious, when Jesus, looking straight into her eyes, with a commanding voice said, "Woman, go get your husband and bring him hither." This command brought Nalda to her senses. She saw that she had misjudged the Master's kindness; she perceived that she had misconstrued his manner of speech. She was frightened; she began to realize that she stood in the presence of an unusual person, and groping about in her mind for a suitable reply, in great confusion, she said, "But, Sir, I cannot call my husband, for I have no husband." Then said Jesus: "You have spoken the truth, for, while you may have once had a husband, he with whom you are now living is not your husband. Better it would be if you would cease to trifle with my words and seek for the living water which I have this day offered you."

By this time Nalda was sobered, and her better self was awakened. She was not an immoral woman wholly by choice. She had been ruthlessly and unjustly cast aside by her husband and in dire straits had consented to live with a certain Greek as his wife, but without marriage. Nalda now felt greatly ashamed that she had so unthinkingly spoken to Jesus, and she most penitently addressed the Master, saying: "My Lord, I repent of my manner of speaking to you, for I perceive that you are a holy man or maybe a prophet." And she was just about to seek direct and personal help from the Master when she did what so many have done before and since—dodged the issue of personal salvation by turning to the discussion of theology and philosophy. She quickly turned the conversation from her own needs to a theological controversy. Pointing over to Mount Gerizim, she continued: "Our fathers worshiped on this mountain, and yet *you* would say that in Jerusalem is the place where men ought to worship; which, then, is the right place to worship God?"

Jesus perceived the attempt of the woman's soul to avoid direct and searching contact with its Maker, but he also saw that there was present in her soul a desire to know the better way of life. After all, there was in Nalda's heart a true thirst for the living water; therefore he dealt patiently with her, saying: "Woman, let me say to you that the day is soon coming when neither on this mountain nor in Jerusalem will you worship the Father. But now you worship that which you know not, a mixture of the religion of many pagan gods and gentile philosophies. The Jews at least know whom they worship; they have removed all confusion by concentrating their worship upon one God, Yahweh. But you should believe me when I say that the hour will soon come—even now is—when all sincere worshipers will worship the Father in spirit and in truth, for it is just such worshipers the Father seeks. God is spirit, and they who worship him must worship him in spirit and in truth. Your salvation comes not from knowing how others should worship or where but by receiving into your own heart this living water which I am offering you even now."

But Nalda would make one more effort to avoid the discussion of the embarrassing question of her personal life on earth and the status of her soul before God. Once more she resorted to questions of general religion, saying: "Yes, I know, Sir, that John has preached about the coming of the Converter, he who will be called the Deliverer, and that, when he shall come, he will declare to us all things"—and Jesus, interrupting Nalda, said with startling assurance, "I who speak to you am he."

This was the first direct, positive, and undisguised pronouncement of his divine nature and sonship which Jesus had made on earth; and it was made to a woman, a Samaritan woman, and a woman of questionable character in the eyes of men up to this moment, but a woman whom the divine eye beheld as having been sinned against more than as sinning of her own desire and as *now* being a human soul who desired salvation, desired it sincerely and wholeheartedly, and that was enough.

As Nalda was about to voice her real and personal longing for better things and a more noble way of living, just as she was ready to speak the real desire of her heart, the twelve apostles returned from Sychar, and coming upon this scene of Jesus' talking so intimately with this woman—this Samaritan woman, and alone—they were more than astonished. They quickly deposited their supplies and drew aside, no man daring to reprove him, while Jesus said to Nalda: "Woman, go your way; God has forgiven you. Henceforth you will live a new life. You have received the living water, and a new joy will spring up within your soul, and you shall become a daughter of the Most High." And the woman, perceiving the disapproval of the apostles, left her waterpot and fled to the city.

As she entered the city, she proclaimed to everyone she met: "Go out to Jacob's well and go quickly, for there you will see a man who told me all I ever did. Can this be the Converter?" And ere the sun went down, a great crowd had assembled at Jacob's well to hear Jesus. And the Master talked to them more about the water of life, the gift of the indwelling spirit.

The apostles never ceased to be shocked by Jesus' willingness to talk with women, women of questionable character, even immoral women. It was very difficult for Jesus to teach his apostles that women, even so-called immoral women, have souls which can choose God as their Father, thereby becoming daughters of God and candidates for life everlasting. Even nineteen centuries later many show the same unwillingness to grasp the Master's teachings. Even the Christian religion has been persistently built up around the fact of the death of Christ instead of around the truth of his life. The world should be more concerned with his happy and God-revealing life than with his tragic and sorrowful death.

Nalda told this entire story to the Apostle John the next day, but he never revealed it fully to the other apostles, and Jesus did not speak of it in detail to the twelve.

Nalda told John that Jesus had told her "all I ever did." John many times wanted to ask Jesus about this visit with Nalda, but he never did. Jesus told her only one thing about herself, but his look into her eyes and the manner of his dealing with her had so brought all of her checkered life in panoramic review before her mind in a moment of time that she associated all of this self-revelation of her past life with the look and the word of the Master. Jesus never told her she had had five husbands. She had lived with four different men since her husband cast her aside, and this, with all her past, came up so vividly in her mind at the moment when she realized Jesus was a man of God that she subsequently repeated to John that Jesus had really told her all about herself.

6. THE SAMARITAN REVIVAL

On the evening that Nalda drew the crowd out from Sychar to see Jesus, the twelve had just returned with food, and they besought Jesus to eat with them instead of talking to the people, for they had been without food all day and were hungry. But Jesus knew that darkness would soon be upon them; so he persisted in his determination to talk to the people before he sent them away. When Andrew sought to persuade him to eat a bite before speaking to the crowd, Jesus said, "I have meat to eat that you do not know about." When the apostles heard this, they said among themselves: "Has any man brought him aught to eat? Can it be that the woman gave him food as well as drink?" When Jesus heard them talking among themselves, before he spoke to the people, he turned aside and said to the twelve: "My meat is to do the will of Him who sent me and to accomplish His work. You should no longer say it is such and such a time until the harvest. Behold these people coming out from a Samaritan city to hear us; I tell you the fields are already white for the harvest. He who reaps receives wages and gathers this fruit to eternal life; consequently the sowers and the reapers rejoice together. For herein is the saying true: 'One sows and another reaps.' I am now sending you to reap that whereon you have not labored; others have labored, and you are about to enter into their labor." This he said in reference to the preaching of John the Baptist.

Jesus and the apostles went into Sychar and preached two days before they established their camp on Mount Gerizim. And many of the dwellers in Sychar believed the gospel and made request for baptism, but the apostles of Jesus did not yet baptize.

The first night of the camp on Mount Gerizim the apostles expected that Jesus would rebuke them for their attitude toward the woman at Jacob's well, but he made no reference to the matter. Instead he gave them that memorable talk on "The realities which are central in the kingdom of God." In any religion it is very easy to allow values to become disproportionate and to permit facts to occupy the place of truth in one's theology. The fact of the cross became the very center of subsequent Christianity; but it is not the central truth of the religion which may be derived from the life and teachings of Jesus of Nazareth.

The theme of Jesus' teaching on Mount Gerizim was: That he wants all men to see God as a Father-friend just as he (Jesus) is a brother-friend. And again and again he impressed upon them that love is the greatest relationship in the world—in the universe—just as truth is the greatest pronouncement of the observation of these divine relationships.

Jesus declared himself so fully to the Samaritans because he could safely do so, and because he knew that he would not again visit the heart of Samaria to preach the gospel of the kingdom.

Jesus and the twelve camped on Mount Gerizim until the end of August. They preached the good news of the kingdom—the fatherhood of God—to the Samaritans in the cities by day and spent the nights at the camp. The work which Jesus and the twelve did in these Samaritan cities yielded many souls for the kingdom and did much to prepare the way for the marvelous work of Philip in these regions after Jesus' death and resurrection, subsequent to the dispersion of the apostles to the ends of the earth by the bitter persecution of believers at Jerusalem.

7. TEACHINGS ABOUT PRAYER AND WORSHIP

At the evening conferences on Mount Gerizim, Jesus taught many great truths, and in particular he laid emphasis on the following:

True religion is the act of an individual soul in its self-conscious relations with the Creator; organized religion is man's attempt to *socialize* the worship of individual religionists.

Worship—contemplation of the spiritual—must alternate with service, contact with material reality. Work should alternate with play; religion should be balanced by humor. Profound philosophy should be relieved by rhythmic poetry. The strain of living—the time tension of personality—should be relaxed by the restfulness of worship. The feelings of insecurity arising from the fear of personality isolation in the universe should be antidoted by the faith contemplation of the Father and by the attempted realization of the Supreme.

Prayer is designed to make man less thinking but more *realizing;* it is not designed to increase knowledge but rather to expand insight.

Worship is intended to anticipate the better life ahead and then to reflect these new spiritual significances back onto the life which now is. Prayer is spiritually sustaining, but worship is divinely creative.

Worship is the technique of looking to the *One* for the inspiration of service to the *many.* Worship is the yardstick which measures the extent of the soul's detachment from the material universe and its simultaneous and secure attachment to the spiritual realities of all creation.

Prayer is self-reminding—sublime thinking; worship is self-forgetting—superthinking. Worship is effortless attention, true and ideal soul rest, a form of restful spiritual exertion.

Worship is the act of a part identifying itself with the Whole; the finite with the Infinite; the son with the Father; time in the act of striking step with eternity. Worship is the act of the son's personal communion with the divine Father, the assumption of refreshing, creative, fraternal, and romantic attitudes by the human soul-spirit.

Although the apostles grasped only a few of his teachings at the camp, other worlds did, and other generations on earth will.

PAPER 144

AT GILBOA AND IN THE DECAPOLIS

SEPTEMBER and October were spent in retirement at a secluded camp upon the slopes of Mount Gilboa. The month of September Jesus spent here alone with his apostles, teaching and instructing them in the truths of the kingdom.

There were a number of reasons why Jesus and his apostles were in retirement at this time on the borders of Samaria and the Decapolis. The Jerusalem religious rulers were very antagonistic; Herod Antipas still held John in prison, fearing either to release or execute him, while he continued to entertain suspicions that John and Jesus were in some way associated. These conditions made it unwise to plan for aggressive work in either Judea or Galilee. There was a third reason: the slowly augmenting tension between the leaders of John's disciples and the apostles of Jesus, which grew worse with the increasing number of believers.

Jesus knew that the days of the preliminary work of teaching and preaching were about over, that the next move involved the beginning of the full and final effort of his life on earth, and he did not wish the launching of this undertaking to be in any manner either trying or embarrassing to John the Baptist. Jesus had therefore decided to spend some time in retirement rehearsing his apostles and then to do some quiet work in the cities of the Decapolis until John should be either executed or released to join them in a united effort.

1. THE GILBOA ENCAMPMENT

As time passed, the twelve became more devoted to Jesus and increasingly committed to the work of the kingdom. Their devotion was in large part a matter of personal loyalty. They did not grasp his many-sided teaching; they did not fully comprehend the nature of Jesus or the significance of his bestowal on earth.

Jesus made it plain to his apostles that they were in retirement for three reasons:

1. To confirm their understanding of, and faith in, the gospel of the kingdom.

2. To allow opposition to their work in both Judea and Galilee to quiet down.

3. To await the fate of John the Baptist.

While tarrying on Gilboa, Jesus told the twelve much about his early life and his experiences on Mount Hermon; he also revealed something of what happened in the hills during the forty days immediately after his baptism. And he directly charged them that they should tell no man about these experiences until after he had returned to the Father.

During these September weeks they rested, visited, recounted their experiences since Jesus first called them to service, and engaged in an earnest effort to co-ordinate what the Master had so far taught them. In a measure they all sensed that this would be their last opportunity for prolonged rest. They realized that their next public effort in either Judea or Galilee would mark the beginning of the final proclamation of the coming kingdom, but they had little or no settled idea as to what the kingdom would be when it came. John and Andrew thought the kingdom had already come; Peter and James believed that it was yet to come; Nathaniel and Thomas frankly confessed they were puzzled; Matthew, Philip, and Simon Zelotes were uncertain and confused; the twins were blissfully ignorant of the controversy; and Judas Iscariot was silent, noncommittal.

Much of this time Jesus was alone on the mountain near the camp. Occasionally he took with him Peter, James, or John, but more often he went off to pray or commune alone. Subsequent to the baptism of Jesus and the forty days in the Perean hills, it is hardly proper to speak of these seasons of communion with his Father as prayer, nor is it consistent to speak of Jesus as worshiping, but it is altogether correct to allude to these seasons as personal communion with his Father.

The central theme of the discussions throughout the entire month of September was prayer and worship. After they had discussed worship for some days, Jesus finally delivered his memorable discourse on prayer in answer to Thomas's request: "Master, teach us how to pray."

John had taught his disciples a prayer, a prayer for salvation in the coming kingdom. Although Jesus never forbade his followers to use John's form of prayer, the apostles very early perceived that their Master did not fully approve of the practice of uttering set and formal prayers. Nevertheless, believers constantly requested to be taught how to pray. The twelve longed to know what form of petition Jesus would approve. And it was chiefly because of this need for some simple petition for the common people that Jesus at this time consented, in answer to Thomas's request, to teach them a suggestive form of prayer. Jesus gave this lesson one afternoon in the third week of their sojourn on Mount Gilboa.

2. THE DISCOURSE ON PRAYER

"John indeed taught you a simple form of prayer: 'O Father, cleanse us from sin, show us your glory, reveal your love, and let your spirit sanctify our hearts forevermore, Amen!' He taught this prayer that you might have something to teach the multitude. He did not intend that you should use such a set and formal petition as the expression of your own souls in prayer.

"Prayer is entirely a personal and spontaneous expression of the attitude of the soul toward the spirit; prayer should be the communion of sonship and the expression of fellowship. Prayer, when indited by the spirit, leads to co-operative spiritual progress. The ideal prayer is a form of spiritual communion which leads to intelligent worship. True praying is the sincere attitude of reaching heavenward for the attainment of your ideals.

"Prayer is the breath of the soul and should lead you to be persistent in your attempt to ascertain the Father's will. If any one of you has a neighbor, and you go to him at midnight and say: 'Friend, lend me three loaves, for a friend of mine on a journey has come to see me, and I have nothing to set before him'; and if your neighbor answers, 'Trouble me not, for the door is now shut and the children and I are in bed; therefore I cannot rise and give you bread,' you will persist, explaining that your friend hungers, and that you have no food to offer him. I say to you, though your neighbor will not rise and give you bread because he is your friend, yet because of your importunity he will get up and give you as many loaves as you need. If, then, persistence will win favors even from mortal man, how much more will your persistence in the spirit win the bread of life for you from the willing hands of the Father in heaven. Again I say to you: Ask and it shall be given you; seek and you shall find; knock and it shall be opened to you. For every one who asks receives; he who seeks finds; and to him who knocks the door of salvation will be opened.

"Which of you who is a father, if his son asks unwisely, would hesitate to give in accordance with parental wisdom rather than in the terms of the son's faulty petition? If the child needs a loaf, will you give him a stone just because he unwisely asks for it? If your son needs a fish, will you give him a watersnake just because it may chance to come up in the net with the fish and the child foolishly asks for the serpent? If you, then, being mortal and finite, know how to answer prayer and give good and appropriate gifts to your children, how much more shall your heavenly Father give the spirit and many additional blessings to those who ask him? Men ought always to pray and not become discouraged.

"Let me tell you the story of a certain judge who lived in a wicked city. This judge feared not God nor had respect for man. Now there was a needy widow in that city who came repeatedly to this unjust judge, saying, 'Protect me from my adversary.' For some time he would not give ear to her, but presently he said to himself: 'Though I fear not God nor have regard for man, yet because this widow ceases not to trouble me, I will vindicate her lest she wear me out by her continual coming.' These stories I tell you to encourage you to persist in praying and not to intimate that your petitions will change the just and righteous Father above. Your persistence, however, is not to win favor with God but to change your earth attitude and to enlarge your soul's capacity for spirit receptivity.

"But when you pray, you exercise so little faith. Genuine faith will remove mountains of material difficulty which may chance to lie in the path of soul expansion and spiritual progress."

3. THE BELIEVER'S PRAYER

But the apostles were not yet satisfied; they desired Jesus to give them a model prayer which they could teach the new disciples. After listening to this discourse on prayer, James Zebedee said: "Very good, Master, but we do not desire a form of prayer for ourselves so much as for the newer believers who so frequently beseech us, 'Teach us how acceptably to pray to the Father in heaven.'"

When James had finished speaking, Jesus said: "If, then, you still desire such a prayer, I would present the one which I taught my brothers and sisters in Nazareth":

Our Father who is in heaven,
Hallowed be your name.
Your kingdom come; your will be done
On earth as it is in heaven.
Give us this day our bread for tomorrow;
Refresh our souls with the water of life.
And forgive us every one our debts
As we also have forgiven our debtors.
Save us in temptation, deliver us from evil,
And increasingly make us perfect like yourself.

It is not strange that the apostles desired Jesus to teach them a model prayer for believers. John the Baptist had taught his followers several prayers; all great teachers had formulated prayers for their pupils. The religious teachers of the Jews had some twenty-five or thirty set prayers which they recited in the synagogues and even on the street corners. Jesus was particularly averse to praying in public. Up to this time the twelve had heard him pray only a few times. They observed him spending entire nights at prayer or worship, and they were very curious to know the manner or form of his petitions. They were really hard pressed to know what to answer the multitudes when they asked to be taught how to pray as John had taught his disciples.

Jesus taught the twelve always to pray in secret; to go off by themselves amidst the quiet surroundings of nature or to go in their rooms and shut the doors when they engaged in prayer.

After Jesus' death and ascension to the Father it became the practice of many believers to finish this so-called Lord's prayer by the addition of—"In the name of the Lord Jesus Christ." Still later on, two lines were lost in copying, and there was added to this prayer an extra clause, reading: "For yours is the kingdom and the power and the glory, forevermore."

Jesus gave the apostles the prayer in collective form as they had prayed it in the Nazareth home. He never taught a formal personal prayer, only group, family, or social petitions. And he never volunteered to do that.

Jesus taught that effective prayer must be:

1. Unselfish—not alone for oneself.
2. Believing—according to faith.
3. Sincere—honest of heart.
4. Intelligent—according to light.
5. Trustful—in submission to the Father's all-wise will.

When Jesus spent whole nights on the mountain in prayer, it was mainly for his disciples, particularly for the twelve. The Master prayed very little for himself, although he engaged in much worship of the nature of understanding communion with his Paradise Father.

4. MORE ABOUT PRAYER

For days after the discourse on prayer the apostles continued to ask the Master questions regarding this all-important and worshipful practice. Jesus' instruction to the apostles during these days, regarding prayer and worship, may be summarized and restated in modern phraseology as follows:

The earnest and longing repetition of any petition, when such a prayer is the sincere expression of a child of God and is uttered in faith, no matter how ill-advised or impossible of direct answer, never fails to expand the soul's capacity for spiritual receptivity.

In all praying, remember that sonship is a *gift.* No child has aught to do with *earning* the status of son or daughter. The earth child comes into being by the will of its parents. Even so, the child of God comes into grace and the new life of the spirit by the will of the Father in heaven. Therefore must the kingdom of heaven—divine sonship—be *received* as by a little child. You earn righteousness—progressive character development—but you receive sonship by grace and through faith.

Prayer led Jesus up to the supercommunion of his soul with the Supreme Rulers of the universe of universes. Prayer will lead the mortals of earth up to the communion of true worship. The soul's spiritual capacity for receptivity determines the quantity of heavenly blessings which can be personally appropriated and consciously realized as an answer to prayer.

Prayer and its associated worship is a technique of detachment from the daily routine of life, from the monotonous grind of material existence. It is an avenue of approach to spiritualized self-realization and individuality of intellectual and religious attainment.

Prayer is an antidote for harmful introspection. At least, prayer as the Master taught it is such a beneficent ministry to the soul. Jesus consistently employed the beneficial influence of praying for one's fellows. The Master usually prayed in the plural, not in the singular. Only in the great crises of his earth life did Jesus ever pray for himself.

Prayer is the breath of the spirit life in the midst of the material civilization of the races of mankind. Worship is salvation for the pleasure-seeking generations of mortals.

As prayer may be likened to recharging the spiritual batteries of the soul, so worship may be compared to the act of tuning in the soul to catch the universe broadcasts of the infinite spirit of the Universal Father.

Prayer is the sincere and longing look of the child to its spirit Father; it is a psychologic process of exchanging the human will for the divine will. Prayer is a part of the divine plan for making over that which is into that which ought to be.

One of the reasons why Peter, James, and John, who so often accompanied Jesus on his long night vigils, never heard Jesus pray, was because their Master so rarely uttered his prayers as spoken words. Practically all of Jesus' praying was done in the spirit and in the heart—silently.

Of all the apostles, Peter and James came the nearest to comprehending the Master's teaching about prayer and worship.

5. OTHER FORMS OF PRAYER

From time to time, during the remainder of Jesus' sojourn on earth, he brought to the notice of the apostles several additional forms of prayer, but he did this only in illustration of other matters, and he enjoined that these "parable prayers" should not be taught to the multitudes. Many of them were from other inhabited planets, but this fact Jesus did not reveal to the twelve. Among these prayers were the following:

Our Father in whom consist the universe realms,
Uplifted be your name and all-glorious your character.
Your presence encompasses us, and your glory is manifested
Imperfectly through us as it is in perfection shown on high.
Give us this day the vivifying forces of light,
And let us not stray into the evil bypaths of our imagination,
For yours is the glorious indwelling, the everlasting power,
And to us, the eternal gift of the infinite love of your Son.
Even so, and everlastingly true.

***

Our creative Parent, who is in the center of the universe,
Bestow upon us your nature and give to us your character.
Make us sons and daughters of yours by grace
And glorify your name through our eternal achievement.
Your adjusting and controlling spirit give to live and dwell within us
That we may do your will on this sphere as angels do your bidding in light.
Sustain us this day in our progress along the path of truth.
Deliver us from inertia, evil, and all sinful transgression.
Be patient with us as we show loving-kindness to our fellows.
Shed abroad the spirit of your mercy in our creature hearts.
Lead us by your own hand, step by step, through the uncertain maze of life,
And when our end shall come, receive into your own bosom our faithful spirits.
Even so, not our desires but your will be done.

***

Our perfect and righteous heavenly Father,
This day guide and direct our journey.
Sanctify our steps and co-ordinate our thoughts.
Ever lead us in the ways of eternal progress.
Fill us with wisdom to the fullness of power
And vitalize us with your infinite energy.
Inspire us with the divine consciousness of
The presence and guidance of the seraphic hosts.
Guide us ever upward in the pathway of light;
Justify us fully in the day of the great judgment.
Make us like yourself in eternal glory
And receive us into your endless service on high.

***

Our Father who is in the mystery,
Reveal to us your holy character.
Give your children on earth this day
To see the way, the light, and the truth.
Show us the pathway of eternal progress
And give us the will to walk therein.
Establish within us your divine kingship
And thereby bestow upon us the full mastery of self.
Let us not stray into paths of darkness and death;
Lead us everlastingly beside the waters of life.
Hear these our prayers for your own sake;
Be pleased to make us more and more like yourself.

At the end, for the sake of the divine Son,
    Receive us into the eternal arms.
Even so, not our will but yours be done.

***

Glorious Father and Mother, in one parent combined,
    Loyal would we be to your divine nature.
Your own self to live again in and through us
    By the gift and bestowal of your divine spirit,
Thus reproducing you imperfectly in this sphere
    As you are perfectly and majestically shown on high.
Give us day by day your sweet ministry of brotherhood
    And lead us moment by moment in the pathway of loving service.
Be you ever and unfailingly patient with us
    Even as we show forth your patience to our children.
Give us the divine wisdom that does all things well
    And the infinite love that is gracious to every creature.
Bestow upon us your patience and loving-kindness
    That our charity may enfold the weak of the realm.
And when our career is finished, make it an honor to your name,
    A pleasure to your good spirit, and a satisfaction to our soul helpers.
Not as we wish, our loving Father, but as you desire the eternal good of your mortal children,
Even so may it be.

***

Our all-faithful Source and all-powerful Center,
    Reverent and holy be the name of your all-gracious Son.
Your bounties and your blessings have descended upon us,
    Thus empowering us to perform your will and execute your bidding.
Give us moment by moment the sustenance of the tree of life;
    Refresh us day by day with the living waters of the river thereof.
Step by step lead us out of darkness and into the divine light.
    Renew our minds by the transformations of the indwelling spirit,
And when the mortal end shall finally come upon us,
    Receive us to yourself and send us forth in eternity.
Crown us with celestial diadems of fruitful service,
    And we shall glorify the Father, the Son, and the Holy Influence.
Even so, throughout a universe without end.

***

Our Father who dwells in the secret places of the universe,
    Honored be your name, reverenced your mercy, and respected your judgment.
Let the sun of righteousness shine upon us at noontime,
    While we beseech you to guide our wayward steps in the twilight.
Lead us by the hand in the ways of your own choosing
    And forsake us not when the path is hard and the hours are dark.
Forget us not as we so often neglect and forget you.
    But be you merciful and love us as we desire to love you.
Look down upon us in kindness and forgive us in mercy
    As we in justice forgive those who distress and injure us.

May the love, devotion, and bestowal of the majestic Son
    Make available life everlasting with your endless mercy and love.
May the God of universes bestow upon us the full measure of his spirit;
    Give us grace to yield to the leading of this spirit.
By the loving ministry of devoted seraphic hosts
    May the Son guide and lead us to the end of the age.
Make us ever and increasingly like yourself
    And at our end receive us into the eternal Paradise embrace.
Even so, in the name of the bestowal Son
    And for the honor and glory of the Supreme Father.

Though the apostles were not at liberty to present these prayer lessons in their public teachings, they profited much from all of these revelations in their personal religious experiences. Jesus utilized these and other prayer models as illustrations in connection with the intimate instruction of the twelve, and specific permission has been granted for transcribing these seven specimen prayers into this record.

6. CONFERENCE WITH JOHN'S APOSTLES

Around the first of October, Philip and some of his fellow apostles were in a near-by village buying food when they met some of the apostles of John the Baptist. As a result of this chance meeting in the market place there came about a three weeks' conference at the Gilboa camp between the apostles of Jesus and the apostles of John, for John had recently appointed twelve of his leaders to be apostles, following the precedent of Jesus. John had done this in response to the urging of Abner, the chief of his loyal supporters. Jesus was present at the Gilboa camp throughout the first week of this joint conference but absented himself the last two weeks.

By the beginning of the second week of this month, Abner had assembled all of his associates at the Gilboa camp and was prepared to go into council with the apostles of Jesus. For three weeks these twenty-four men were in session three times a day and for six days each week. The first week Jesus mingled with them between their forenoon, afternoon, and evening sessions. They wanted the Master to meet with them and preside over their joint deliberations, but he steadfastly refused to participate in their discussions, though he did consent to speak to them on three occasions. These talks by Jesus to the twenty-four were on sympathy, co-operation, and tolerance.

Andrew and Abner alternated in presiding over these joint meetings of the two apostolic groups. These men had many difficulties to discuss and numerous problems to solve. Again and again would they take their troubles to Jesus, only to hear him say: "I am concerned only with your personal and purely religious problems. I am the representative of the Father to the *individual,* not to the group. If you are in personal difficulty in your relations with God, come to me, and I will hear you and counsel you in the solution of your problem. But when you enter upon the co-ordination of divergent human interpretations of religious questions and upon the socialization of religion, you are destined to solve all such problems by your own decisions. Albeit, I am ever sympathetic and always interested, and when you arrive at your conclusions touching these matters of non-spiritual import, provided you are all agreed, then I pledge in advance my full approval and hearty co-operation. And now, in order to leave you unhampered in your deliberations, I am leaving you for two weeks. Be not anxious about me, for I will return to you. I will be about my Father's business, for we have other realms besides this one."

After thus speaking, Jesus went down the mountainside, and they saw him no more for two full weeks. And they never knew where he went or what he did during these days. It was some time before the twenty-four could settle down to the serious consideration of their problems, they were so disconcerted by the absence of the Master. However, within a week they were again in the heart of their discussions, and they could not go to Jesus for help.

The first item the group agreed upon was the adoption of the prayer which Jesus had so recently taught them. It was unanimously voted to accept this prayer as the one to be taught believers by both groups of apostles.

They next decided that, as long as John lived, whether in prison or out, both groups of twelve apostles would go on with their work, and that joint meetings for one week would be held every three months at places to be agreed upon from time to time.

But the most serious of all their problems was the question of baptism. Their difficulties were all the more aggravated because Jesus had refused to make any pronouncement upon the subject. They finally agreed: As long as John lived, or until they might jointly modify this decision, only the apostles of John would baptize believers, and only the apostles of Jesus would finally instruct the new disciples. Accordingly, from that time until after the death of John, two of the apostles of John accompanied Jesus and his apostles to baptize believers, for the joint council had unanimously voted that baptism was to become the initial step in the outward alliance with the affairs of the kingdom.

It was next agreed, in case of the death of John, that the apostles of John would present themselves to Jesus and become subject to his direction, and that they would baptize no more unless authorized by Jesus or his apostles.

And then was it voted that, in case of John's death, the apostles of Jesus would begin to baptize with water as the emblem of the baptism of the divine Spirit. As to whether or not *repentance* should be attached to the preaching of baptism was left optional; no decision was made binding upon the group. John's apostles preached, "Repent and be baptized." Jesus' apostles proclaimed, "Believe and be baptized."

And this is the story of the first attempt of Jesus' followers to co-ordinate divergent efforts, compose differences of opinion, organize group undertakings, legislate on outward observances, and socialize personal religious practices.

Many other minor matters were considered and their solutions unanimously agreed upon. These twenty-four men had a truly remarkable experience these two weeks when they were compelled to face problems and compose difficulties without Jesus. They learned to differ, to debate, to contend, to pray, and to compromise, and throughout it all to remain sympathetic with the other person's viewpoint and to maintain at least some degree of tolerance for his honest opinions.

On the afternoon of their final discussion of financial questions, Jesus returned, heard of their deliberations, listened to their decisions, and said: "These, then, are your conclusions, and I shall help you each to carry out the spirit of your united decisions."

Two months and a half from this time John was executed, and throughout this period the apostles of John remained with Jesus and the twelve. They all worked together and baptized believers during this season of labor in the cities of the Decapolis. The Gilboa camp was broken up on November 2, A.D. 27.

7. IN THE DECAPOLIS CITIES

Throughout the months of November and December, Jesus and the twenty-four worked quietly in the Greek cities of the Decapolis, chiefly in Scythopolis, Gerasa, Abila, and Gadara. This was really the end of that preliminary period of taking over John's work and organization. Always does the socialized religion of a new revelation pay the price of compromise with the established forms and usages of the preceding religion which it seeks to salvage. Baptism was the price which the followers of Jesus paid in order to carry with them, as a socialized religious group, the followers of John the Baptist. John's followers, in joining Jesus' followers, gave up just about everything except water baptism.

Jesus did little public teaching on this mission to the cities of the Decapolis. He spent considerable time teaching the twenty-four and had many special sessions with John's twelve apostles. In time they became more understanding as to why Jesus did not go to visit John in prison, and why he made no effort to secure his release. But they never could understand why Jesus did no marvelous works, why he refused to produce outward signs of his divine authority. Before coming to the Gilboa camp, they had believed in Jesus mostly because of John's testimony, but soon they were beginning to believe as a result of their own contact with the Master and his teachings.

For these two months the group worked most of the time in pairs, one of Jesus' apostles going out with one of John's. The apostle of John baptized, the apostle of Jesus instructed, while they both preached the gospel of the kingdom as they understood it. And they won many souls among these gentiles and apostate Jews.

Abner, the chief of John's apostles, became a devout believer in Jesus and was later on made the head of a group of seventy teachers whom the Master commissioned to preach the gospel.

8. IN CAMP NEAR PELLA

The latter part of December they all went over near the Jordan, close by Pella, where they again began to teach and preach. Both Jews and gentiles came to this camp to hear the gospel. It was while Jesus was teaching the multitude one afternoon that some of John's special friends brought the Master the last message which he ever had from the Baptist.

John had now been in prison a year and a half, and most of this time Jesus had labored very quietly; so it was not strange that John should be led to wonder about the kingdom. John's friends interrupted Jesus' teaching to say to him: "John the Baptist has sent us to ask—are you truly the Deliverer, or shall we look for another?"

Jesus paused to say to John's friends: "Go back and tell John that he is not forgotten. Tell him what you have seen and heard, that the poor have good tidings preached to them." And when Jesus had spoken further to the messengers of John, he turned again to the multitude and said: "Do not think that John doubts the gospel of the kingdom. He makes inquiry only to assure his disciples who are also my disciples. John is no weakling. Let me ask you who heard John preach before Herod put him in prison: What did you behold in John—a reed shaken with the wind? A man of changeable moods and clothed in soft raiment? As a rule they who are gorgeously appareled and who live delicately are in kings' courts and in the mansions of the rich. But what did you see when you beheld John? A prophet? Yes, I say to you, and much more than a prophet. Of John it was written: 'Behold, I send my messenger before your face; he shall prepare the way before you.'

"Verily, verily, I say to you, among those born of women there has not arisen a greater than John the Baptist; yet he who is but small in the kingdom of heaven is greater because he has been born of the spirit and knows that he has become a son of God."

Many who heard Jesus that day submitted themselves to John's baptism, thereby publicly professing entrance into the kingdom. And the apostles of John were firmly knit to Jesus from that day forward. This occurrence marked the real union of John's and Jesus' followers.

After the messengers had conversed with Abner, they departed for Machaerus to tell all this to John. He was greatly comforted, and his faith was strengthened by the words of Jesus and the message of Abner.

On this afternoon Jesus continued to teach, saying: "But to what shall I liken this generation? Many of you will receive neither John's message nor my teaching. You are like the children playing in the market place who call to their fellows and say: 'We piped for you and you did not dance; we wailed and you did not mourn.' And so with some of you. John came neither eating nor drinking, and they said he had a devil. The Son of Man comes eating and drinking, and these same people say: 'Behold, a gluttonous man and a winebibber, a friend of publicans and sinners!' Truly, wisdom is justified by her children.

"It would appear that the Father in heaven has hidden some of these truths from the wise and haughty, while he has revealed them to babes. But the Father does all things well; the Father reveals himself to the universe by the methods of his own choosing. Come, therefore, all you who labor and are heavy laden, and you shall find rest for your souls. Take upon you the divine yoke, and you will experience the peace of God, which passes all understanding."

9. DEATH OF JOHN THE BAPTIST

John the Baptist was executed by order of Herod Antipas on the evening of January 10, A.D. 28. The next day a few of John's disciples who had gone to Machaerus heard of his execution and, going to Herod, made request for his body, which they put in a tomb, later giving it burial at Sebaste, the home of Abner. The following day, January 12, they started north to the camp of John's and Jesus' apostles near Pella, and they told Jesus about the death of John. When Jesus heard their report, he dismissed the multitude and, calling the twenty-four together, said: "John is dead. Herod has beheaded him. Tonight go into joint council and arrange your affairs accordingly. There shall be delay no longer. The hour has come to proclaim the kingdom openly and with power. Tomorrow we go into Galilee."

Accordingly, early on the morning of January 13, A.D. 28, Jesus and the apostles, accompanied by some twenty-five disciples, made their way to Capernaum and lodged that night in Zebedee's house.

PAPER 145

FOUR EVENTFUL DAYS AT CAPERNAUM

JESUS and the apostles arrived in Capernaum the evening of Tuesday, January 13. As usual, they made their headquarters at the home of Zebedee in Bethsaida. Now that John the Baptist had been sent to his death, Jesus prepared to launch out in the first open and public preaching tour of Galilee. The news that Jesus had returned rapidly spread throughout the city, and early the next day, Mary the mother of Jesus hastened away, going over to Nazareth to visit her son Joseph.

Wednesday, Thursday, and Friday Jesus spent at the Zebedee house instructing his apostles preparatory to their first extensive public preaching tour. He also received and taught many earnest inquirers, both singly and in groups. Through Andrew, he arranged to speak in the synagogue on the coming Sabbath day.

Late on Friday evening Jesus' baby sister, Ruth, secretly paid him a visit. They spent almost an hour together in a boat anchored a short distance from the shore. No human being, save John Zebedee, ever knew of this visit, and he was admonished to tell no man. Ruth was the only member of Jesus' family who consistently and unwaveringly believed in the divinity of his earth mission from the times of her earliest spiritual consciousness right on down through his eventful ministry, death, resurrection, and ascension; and she finally passed on to the worlds beyond never having doubted the supernatural character of her father-brother's mission in the flesh. Baby Ruth was the chief comfort of Jesus, as regards his earth family, throughout the trying ordeal of his trial, rejection, and crucifixion.

1. THE DRAUGHT OF FISHES

On Friday morning of this same week, when Jesus was teaching by the seaside, the people crowded him so near the water's edge that he signaled to some fishermen occupying a near-by boat to come to his rescue. Entering the boat, he continued to teach the assembled multitude for more than two hours. This boat was named "Simon"; it was the former fishing vessel of Simon Peter and had been built by Jesus' own hands. On this particular morning the boat was being used by David Zebedee and two associates, who had just come in near shore from a fruitless night of fishing on the lake. They were cleaning and mending their nets when Jesus requested them to come to his assistance.

After Jesus had finished teaching the people, he said to David: "As you were delayed by coming to my help, now let me work with you. Let us go fishing; put out into yonder deep and let down your nets for a draught." But Simon, one of David's assistants, answered: "Master, it is useless. We toiled all night and took nothing; however, at your bidding we will put out and let down the nets." And Simon consented to follow Jesus' directions because of a gesture made by his master, David. When they had proceeded to the place designated by Jesus, they let down their nets and enclosed such a multitude of fish that they feared the nets would break, so much so that they signaled to their associates on the shore to come to their assistance. When they had filled all three boats with fish, almost to sinking, this Simon fell down at Jesus' knees, saying, "Depart from me, Master, for I am a sinful man." Simon and all who were concerned in this episode were amazed at the draught of fishes. From that day David Zebedee, this Simon, and their associates forsook their nets and followed Jesus.

But this was in no sense a miraculous draught of fishes. Jesus was a close student of nature; he was an experienced fisherman and knew the habits of the fish in the Sea of Galilee. On this occasion he merely directed these men to the place where the fish were usually to be found at this time of day. But Jesus' followers always regarded this as a miracle.

2. AFTERNOON AT THE SYNAGOGUE

The next Sabbath, at the afternoon service in the synagogue, Jesus preached his sermon on "The Will of the Father in Heaven." In the morning Simon Peter had preached on "The Kingdom." At the Thursday evening meeting of the synagogue Andrew had taught, his subject being "The New Way." At this particular time more people believed in Jesus in Capernaum than in any other one city on earth.

As Jesus taught in the synagogue this Sabbath afternoon, according to custom he took the first text from the law, reading from the Book of Exodus: "And you shall serve the Lord, your God, and he shall bless your bread and your water, and all sickness shall be taken away from you." He chose the second text from the Prophets, reading from Isaiah: "Arise and shine, for your light has come, and the glory of the Lord has risen upon you. Darkness may cover the earth and gross darkness the people, but the spirit of the Lord shall arise upon you, and the divine glory shall be seen with you. Even the gentiles shall come to this light, and many great minds shall surrender to the brightness of this light."

This sermon was an effort on Jesus' part to make clear the fact that religion is a *personal experience.* Among other things, the Master said:

"You well know that, while a kindhearted father loves his family as a whole, he so regards them as a group because of his strong affection for each individual member of that family. No longer must you approach the Father in heaven as a child of Israel but as a *child of God.* As a group, you are indeed the children of Israel, but as individuals, each one of you is a child of God. I have come, not to reveal the Father to the children of Israel, but rather to bring this knowledge of God and the revelation of his love and mercy to the individual believer as a genuine personal experience. The prophets have all taught you that Yahweh cares for his people, that God loves Israel. But I have come among you to proclaim a greater truth, one which many of the later prophets also grasped, that God loves *you*—every one of you—as individuals. All these generations have you had a national or racial religion; now have I come to give you a personal religion.

"But even this is not a new idea. Many of the spiritually minded among you have known this truth, inasmuch as some of the prophets have so instructed you. Have you not read in the Scriptures where the Prophet Jeremiah says: 'In those days they shall no more say, the fathers have eaten sour grapes and the children's teeth are set on edge. Every man shall die for his own iniquity; every man who eats sour grapes, his teeth shall be set on edge. Behold, the days shall come when I will make a new covenant with my people, not according to the covenant which I made with their fathers when I brought them out of the land of Egypt, but according to the new way. I will even write my law in their hearts. I will be their God, and they shall be my people. In that day they shall not say, one man to his neighbor, do you know the Lord? Nay! For they shall all know me personally, from the least to the greatest.'

"Have you not read these promises? Do you not believe the Scriptures? Do you not understand that the prophet's words are fulfilled in what you behold this very day? And did not Jeremiah exhort you to make religion an affair of the heart, to relate yourselves to God as individuals? Did not the prophet tell you that the God of heaven would search your individual hearts? And were you not warned that the natural human heart is deceitful above all things and oftentimes desperately wicked?

"Have you not read also where Ezekiel taught even your fathers that religion must become a reality in your individual experiences? No more shall you use the proverb which says, 'The fathers have eaten sour grapes and the children's teeth are set on edge.' 'As I live,' says the Lord God, 'behold all souls are mine; as the soul of the father, so also the soul of the son. Only the soul that sins shall die.' And then Ezekiel foresaw even this day when he spoke in behalf of God, saying: 'A new heart also will I give you, and a new spirit will I put within you.'

"No more should you fear that God will punish a nation for the sin of an individual; neither will the Father in heaven punish one of his believing children for the sins of a nation, albeit the individual member of any family must often suffer the material consequences of family mistakes and group transgressions. Do you not realize that the hope of a better nation—or a better world—is bound up in the progress and enlightenment of the individual?"

Then the Master portrayed that the Father in heaven, after man discerns this spiritual freedom, wills that his children on earth should begin that eternal ascent of the Paradise career which consists in the creature's conscious response to the divine urge of the indwelling spirit to find the Creator, to know God and to seek to become like him.

The apostles were greatly helped by this sermon. All of them realized more fully that the gospel of the kingdom is a message directed to the individual, not to the nation.

Even though the people of Capernaum were familiar with Jesus' teaching, they were astonished at his sermon on this Sabbath day. He taught, indeed, as one having authority and not as the scribes.

Just as Jesus finished speaking, a young man in the congregation who had been much agitated by his words was seized with a violent epileptic attack and loudly cried out. At the end of the seizure, when recovering consciousness, he spoke in a dreamy state, saying: "What have we to do with you, Jesus of Nazareth? You are the holy one of God; have you come to destroy us?" Jesus bade the people be quiet and, taking the young man by the hand, said, "Come out of it"—and he was immediately awakened.

This young man was not possessed of an unclean spirit or demon; he was a victim of ordinary epilepsy. But he had been taught that his affliction was due to possession by an evil spirit. He believed this teaching and behaved accordingly in all that he thought or said concerning his ailment. The people all believed that such phenomena were directly caused by the presence of unclean spirits. Accordingly they believed that Jesus had cast a demon out of this man. But Jesus did not at that time cure his epilepsy. Not until later on that day, after sundown, was this man really healed. Long after the day of Pentecost the Apostle John, who was the last to write of Jesus' doings, avoided all reference to these so-called acts of "casting out devils," and this he did in view of the fact that such cases of demon possession never occurred after Pentecost.

As a result of this commonplace incident the report was rapidly spread through Capernaum that Jesus had cast a demon out of a man and miraculously healed him in the synagogue at the conclusion of his afternoon sermon. The Sabbath was just the time for the rapid and effective spreading of such a startling rumor. This report was also carried to all the smaller settlements around Capernaum, and many of the people believed it.

The cooking and the housework at the large Zebedee home, where Jesus and the twelve made their headquarters, was for the most part done by Simon Peter's wife and her mother. Peter's home was near that of Zebedee; and Jesus and his friends stopped there on the way from the synagogue because Peter's wife's mother had for several days been sick with chills and fever. Now it chanced that, at about the time Jesus stood over this sick woman, holding her hand, smoothing her brow, and speaking words of comfort and encouragement, the fever left her. Jesus had not yet had time to explain to his apostles that no miracle had been wrought at the synagogue; and with this incident so fresh and vivid in their minds, and recalling the water and the wine at Cana, they seized upon this coincidence as another miracle, and some of them rushed out to spread the news abroad throughout the city.

Amatha, Peter's mother-in-law, was suffering from malarial fever. She was not miraculously healed by Jesus at this time. Not until several hours later, after sundown, was her cure effected in connection with the extraordinary event which occurred in the front yard of the Zebedee home.

And these cases are typical of the manner in which a wonder-seeking generation and a miracle-minded people unfailingly seized upon all such coincidences as the pretext for proclaiming that another miracle had been wrought by Jesus.

3. THE HEALING AT SUNDOWN

By the time Jesus and his apostles had made ready to partake of their evening meal near the end of this eventful Sabbath day, all Capernaum and its environs were agog over these reputed miracles of healing; and all who were sick or afflicted began preparations to go to Jesus or to have themselves carried there by their friends just as soon as the sun went down. According to Jewish teaching it was not permissible even to go in quest of health during the sacred hours of the Sabbath.

Therefore, as soon as the sun sank beneath the horizon, scores of afflicted men, women, and children began to make their way toward the Zebedee home in Bethsaida. One man started out with his paralyzed daughter just as soon as the sun sank behind his neighbor's house.

The whole day's events had set the stage for this extraordinary sundown scene. Even the text Jesus had used for his afternoon sermon had intimated that sickness should be banished; and he had spoken with such unprecedented power and authority! His message was so compelling! While he made no appeal to human authority, he did speak directly to the consciences and souls of men. Though he did not resort to logic, legal quibbles, or clever sayings, he did make a powerful, direct, clear, and personal appeal to the hearts of his hearers.

That Sabbath was a great day in the earth life of Jesus, yes, in the life of a universe. To all local universe intents and purposes the little Jewish city of Capernaum was the real capital of Nebadon. The handful of Jews in the Capernaum synagogue were not the only beings to hear that momentous closing statement of Jesus' sermon: "Hate is the shadow of fear; revenge the mask of cowardice." Neither could his hearers forget his blessed words, declaring, "Man is the son of God, not a child of the devil."

Soon after the setting of the sun, as Jesus and the apostles still lingered about the supper table, Peter's wife heard voices in the front yard and, on going to the door, saw a large company of sick folks assembling, and that the road from Capernaum was crowded by those who were on their way to seek healing at Jesus' hands. On seeing this sight, she went at once and informed her husband, who told Jesus.

When the Master stepped out of the front entrance of Zebedee's house, his eyes met an array of stricken and afflicted humanity. He gazed upon almost one thousand sick and ailing human beings; at least that was the number of persons gathered together before him. Not all present were afflicted; some had come assisting their loved ones in this effort to secure healing.

The sight of these afflicted mortals, men, women, and children, suffering in large measure as a result of the mistakes and misdeeds of his own trusted Sons of universe administration, peculiarly touched the human heart of Jesus and challenged the divine mercy of this benevolent Creator Son. But Jesus well knew he could never build an enduring spiritual movement upon the foundation of purely material wonders. It had been his consistent policy to refrain from exhibiting his creator prerogatives. Not since Cana had the supernatural or miraculous attended his teaching; still, this afflicted multitude touched his sympathetic heart and mightily appealed to his understanding affection.

A voice from the front yard exclaimed: "Master, speak the word, restore our health, heal our diseases, and save our souls." No sooner had these words been uttered than a vast retinue of seraphim, physical controllers, Life Carriers, and midwayers, such as always attended this incarnated Creator of a universe, made themselves ready to act with creative power should their Sovereign give the signal. This was one of those moments in the earth career of Jesus in which divine wisdom and human compassion were so interlocked in the judgment of the Son of Man that he sought refuge in appeal to his Father's will.

When Peter implored the Master to heed their cry for help, Jesus, looking down upon the afflicted throng, answered: "I have come into the world to reveal the Father and establish his kingdom. For this purpose have I lived my life to this hour. If, therefore, it should be the will of Him who sent me and not inconsistent with my dedication to the proclamation of the gospel of the kingdom of heaven, I would desire to see my children made whole—and —" but the further words of Jesus were lost in the tumult.

Jesus had passed the responsibility of this healing decision to the ruling of his Father. Evidently the Father's will interposed no objection, for the words of the Master had scarcely been uttered when the assembly of celestial personalities serving under the command of Jesus' Personalized Thought Adjuster was mightily astir. The vast retinue descended into the midst of this motley throng of afflicted mortals, and in a moment of time 683 men, women, and children were made whole, were perfectly healed of all their physical diseases and other material disorders. Such a scene was never witnessed on earth before that day, nor since. And for those of us who were present to behold this creative wave of healing, it was indeed a thrilling spectacle.

But of all the beings who were astonished at this sudden and unexpected outbreak of supernatural healing, Jesus was the most surprised. In a moment when his human interests and sympathies were focused upon the scene of suffering and affliction there spread out before him, he neglected to bear in his human mind the admonitory warnings of his Personalized Adjuster regarding the impossibility of limiting the time element of the creator prerogatives of a Creator Son under certain conditions and in certain circumstances. Jesus desired to see these suffering mortals made whole if his Father's will would not thereby be violated. The Personalized Adjuster of Jesus instantly ruled that such an act of creative energy at that time would not transgress the will of the Paradise Father, and by such a decision—in view of Jesus' preceding expression of healing desire—the creative act *was*. What a *Creator Son* desires and his Father *wills* IS. Not in all of Jesus' subsequent earth life did another such en masse physical healing of mortals take place.

As might have been expected, the fame of this sundown healing at Bethsaida in Capernaum spread throughout all Galilee and Judea and to the regions beyond. Once more were the fears of Herod aroused, and he sent watchers to report on the work and teachings of Jesus and to ascertain if he was the former carpenter of Nazareth or John the Baptist risen from the dead.

Chiefly because of this unintended demonstration of physical healing, henceforth, throughout the remainder of his earth career, Jesus became as much a physician as a preacher. True, he continued his teaching, but his personal work consisted mostly in ministering to the sick and the distressed, while his apostles did the work of public preaching and baptizing believers.

But the majority of those who were recipients of supernatural or creative physical healing at this sundown demonstration of divine energy were not permanently spiritually benefited by this extraordinary manifestation of mercy. A small number were truly edified by this physical ministry, but the spiritual kingdom was not advanced in the hearts of men by this amazing eruption of timeless creative healing.

The healing wonders which every now and then attended Jesus' mission on earth were not a part of his plan of proclaiming the kingdom. They were incidentally inherent in having on earth a divine being of well-nigh unlimited creator prerogatives in association with an unprecedented combination of divine mercy and human sympathy. But such so-called miracles gave Jesus much trouble in that they provided prejudice-raising publicity and afforded much unsought notoriety.

4. THE EVENING AFTER

Throughout the evening following this great outburst of healing, the rejoicing and happy throng overran Zebedee's home, and the apostles of Jesus were keyed up to the highest pitch of emotional enthusiasm. From a human standpoint, this was probably the greatest day of all the great days of their association with Jesus. At no time before or after did their hopes surge to such heights of confident expectation. Jesus had told them only a few days before, and when they were yet within the borders of Samaria, that the hour had come when the kingdom was to be proclaimed in *power,* and now their eyes had seen what they supposed was the fulfillment of that promise. They were thrilled by the vision of what was to come if this amazing manifestation of healing power was just the beginning. Their lingering doubts of Jesus' divinity were banished. They were literally intoxicated with the ecstasy of their bewildered enchantment.

But when they sought for Jesus, they could not find him. The Master was much perturbed by what had happened. These men, women, and children who had been healed of diverse diseases lingered late into the evening, hoping for Jesus' return that they might thank him. The apostles could not understand the Master's conduct as the hours passed and he remained in seclusion; their joy would have been full and perfect but for his continued absence. When Jesus did return to their midst, the hour was late, and practically all of the beneficiaries of the healing episode had gone to their homes. Jesus refused the congratulations and adoration of the twelve and the others who had lingered to greet him, only saying: "Rejoice not that my Father is powerful to heal the body, but rather that he is mighty to save the soul. Let us go to our rest, for tomorrow we must be about the Father's business."

And again did twelve disappointed, perplexed, and heart-sorrowing men go to their rest; few of them, except the twins, slept much that night. No sooner would the Master do something to cheer the souls and gladden the hearts of his apostles, than he seemed immediately to dash their hopes in pieces and utterly to demolish the foundations of their courage and enthusiasm. As these bewildered fishermen looked into each other's eyes, there was but one thought: "We cannot understand him. What does all this mean?"

5. EARLY SUNDAY MORNING

Neither did Jesus sleep much that Saturday night. He realized that the world was filled with physical distress and overrun with material difficulties, and he contemplated the great danger of being compelled to devote so much of his time to the care of the sick and afflicted that his mission of establishing the spiritual kingdom in the hearts of men would be interfered with or at least subordinated to the ministry of things physical. Because of these and similar thoughts which occupied the mortal mind of Jesus during the night, he arose that Sunday morning long before daybreak and went all alone to one of his favorite places for communion with the Father. The theme of Jesus' prayer on this early morning was for wisdom and judgment that he might not allow his human sympathy, joined with his divine mercy, to make such an appeal to him in the presence of mortal suffering that all of his time would be occupied with physical ministry to the neglect of the spiritual. Though he did not wish altogether to avoid ministering to the sick, he knew that he must also do the more important work of spiritual teaching and religious training.

Jesus went out in the hills to pray so many times because there were no private rooms suitable for his personal devotions.

Peter could not sleep that night; so, very early, shortly after Jesus had gone out to pray, he aroused James and John, and the three went to find their Master. After more than an hour's search they found Jesus and besought him to tell them the reason for his strange conduct. They desired to know why he appeared to be troubled by the mighty outpouring of the spirit of healing when all the people were overjoyed and his apostles so much rejoiced.

For more than four hours Jesus endeavored to explain to these three apostles what had happened. He taught them about what had transpired and explained the dangers of such manifestations. Jesus confided to them the reason for his coming forth to pray. He sought to make plain to his personal associates the real reasons why the kingdom of the Father could not be built upon wonder-working and physical healing. But they could not comprehend his teaching.

Meanwhile, early Sunday morning, other crowds of afflicted souls and many curiosity seekers began to gather about the house of Zebedee. They clamored to see Jesus. Andrew and the apostles were so perplexed that, while Simon Zelotes talked to the assembly, Andrew, with several of his associates, went to find Jesus. When Andrew had located Jesus in company with the three, he said: "Master, why do you leave us alone with the multitude? Behold, all men seek you; never before have so many sought after your teaching. Even now the house is surrounded by those who have come from near and far because of your mighty works. Will you not return with us to minister to them?"

When Jesus heard this, he answered: "Andrew, have I not taught you and these others that my mission on earth is the revelation of the Father, and my message the proclamation of the kingdom of heaven? How is it, then, that you would have me turn aside from my work for the gratification of the curious and for the satisfaction of those who seek for signs and wonders? Have we not been among these people all these months, and have they flocked in multitudes to hear the good news of the kingdom? Why have they now come to besiege us? Is it not because of the healing of their physical bodies rather than as a result of the reception of spiritual truth for the salvation of their souls? When men are attracted to us because of extraordinary manifestations, many of them come seeking not for truth and salvation but rather in quest of healing for their physical ailments and to secure deliverance from their material difficulties.

"All this time I have been in Capernaum, and both in the synagogue and by the seaside have I proclaimed the good news of the kingdom to all who had ears to hear and hearts to receive the truth. It is not the will of my Father that I should return with you to cater to these curious ones and to become occupied with the ministry of things physical to the exclusion of the spiritual. I have ordained you to preach the gospel and minister to the sick, but I must not become engrossed in healing to the exclusion of my teaching. No, Andrew, I will not return with you. Go and tell the people to believe in that which we have taught them and to rejoice in the liberty of the sons of God, and make ready for our departure for the other cities of Galilee, where the way has already been prepared for the preaching of the good tidings of the kingdom. It was for this purpose that I came forth from the Father. Go, then, and prepare for our immediate departure while I here await your return."

When Jesus had spoken, Andrew and his fellow apostles sorrowfully made their way back to Zebedee's house, dismissed the assembled multitude, and quickly made ready for the journey as Jesus had directed. And so, on the afternoon of Sunday, January 18, A.D. 28, Jesus and the apostles started out upon their first really public and open preaching tour of the cities of Galilee. On this first tour they preached the gospel of the kingdom in many cities, but they did not visit Nazareth.

That Sunday afternoon, shortly after Jesus and his apostles had left for Rimmon, his brothers James and Jude came to see him, calling at Zebedee's house. About noon of that day Jude had sought out his brother James and insisted that they go to Jesus. By the time James consented to go with Jude, Jesus had already departed.

The apostles were loath to leave the great interest which had been aroused at Capernaum. Peter calculated that no less than one thousand believers could have been baptized into the kingdom. Jesus listened to them patiently, but he would not consent to return. Silence prevailed for a season, and then Thomas addressed his fellow apostles, saying: "Let's go! The Master has spoken. No matter if we cannot fully comprehend the mysteries of the kingdom of heaven, of one thing we are certain: We follow a teacher who seeks no glory for himself." And reluctantly they went forth to preach the good tidings in the cities of Galilee.

PAPER 146

FIRST PREACHING TOUR OF GALILEE

THE first public preaching tour of Galilee began on Sunday, January 18, A.D. 28, and continued for about two months, ending with the return to Capernaum on March 17. On this tour Jesus and the twelve apostles, assisted by the former apostles of John, preached the gospel and baptized believers in Rimmon, Jotapata, Ramah, Zebulun, Iron, Gischala, Chorazin, Madon, Cana, Nain, and Endor. In these cities they tarried and taught, while in many other smaller towns they proclaimed the gospel of the kingdom as they passed through.

This was the first time Jesus permitted his associates to preach without restraint. On this tour he cautioned them on only three occasions; he admonished them to remain away from Nazareth and to be discreet when passing through Capernaum and Tiberias. It was a source of great satisfaction to the apostles at last to feel they were at liberty to preach and teach without restriction, and they threw themselves into the work of preaching the gospel, ministering to the sick, and baptizing believers, with great earnestness and joy.

1. PREACHING AT RIMMON

The small city of Rimmon had once been dedicated to the worship of a Babylonian god of the air, Ramman. Many of the earlier Babylonian and later Zoroastrian teachings were still embraced in the beliefs of the Rimmonites; therefore did Jesus and the twenty-four devote much of their time to the task of making plain the difference between these older beliefs and the new gospel of the kingdom. Peter here preached one of the great sermons of his early career on "Aaron and the Golden Calf."

Although many of the citizens of Rimmon became believers in Jesus' teachings, they made great trouble for their brethren in later years. It is difficult to convert nature worshipers to the full fellowship of the adoration of a spiritual ideal during the short space of a single lifetime.

Many of the better of the Babylonian and Persian ideas of light and darkness, good and evil, time and eternity, were later incorporated in the doctrines of so-called Christianity, and their inclusion rendered the Christian teachings more immediately acceptable to the peoples of the Near East. In like manner, the inclusion of many of Plato's theories of the ideal spirit or invisible patterns of all things visible and material, as later adapted by Philo to the Hebrew theology, made Paul's Christian teachings more easy of acceptance by the western Greeks.

It was at Rimmon that Todan first heard the gospel of the kingdom, and he later carried this message into Mesopotamia and far beyond. He was among the first to preach the good news to those who dwelt beyond the Euphrates.

2. AT JOTAPATA

While the common people of Jotapata heard Jesus and his apostles gladly and many accepted the gospel of the kingdom, it was the discourse of Jesus to the twenty-four on the second evening of their sojourn in this small town that distinguishes the Jotapata mission. Nathaniel was confused in his mind about the Master's teachings concerning prayer, thanksgiving, and worship, and in response to his question Jesus spoke at great length in further explanation of his teaching. Summarized in modern phraseology, this discourse may be presented as emphasizing the following points:

1. The conscious and persistent regard for iniquity in the heart of man gradually destroys the prayer connection of the human soul with the spirit circuits of communication between man and his Maker. Naturally God hears the petition of his child, but when the human heart deliberately and persistently harbors the concepts of iniquity, there gradually ensues the loss of personal communion between the earth child and his heavenly Father.

2. That prayer which is inconsistent with the known and established laws of God is an abomination to the Paradise Deities. If man will not listen to the Gods as they speak to their creation in the laws of spirit, mind, and matter, the very act of such deliberate and conscious disdain by the creature turns the ears of spirit personalities away from hearing the personal petitions of such lawless and disobedient mortals. Jesus quoted to his apostles from the Prophet Zechariah: "But they refused to hearken and pulled away the shoulder and stopped their ears that they should not hear. Yes, they made their hearts adamant like a stone, lest they should hear my law and the words which I sent by my spirit through the prophets; therefore did the results of their evil thinking come as a great wrath upon their guilty heads. And so it came to pass that they cried for mercy, but there was no ear open to hear." And then Jesus quoted the proverb of the wise man who said: "He who turns away his ear from hearing the divine law, even his prayer shall be an abomination."

3. By opening the human end of the channel of the God-man communication, mortals make immediately available the ever-flowing stream of divine ministry to the creatures of the worlds. When man hears God's spirit speak within the human heart, inherent in such an experience is the fact that God simultaneously hears that man's prayer. Even the forgiveness of sin operates in this same unerring fashion. The Father in heaven has forgiven you even before you have thought to ask him, but such forgiveness is not available in your personal religious experience until such a time as you forgive your fellow men. God's forgiveness in *fact* is not conditioned upon your forgiving your fellows, but in *experience* it is exactly so conditioned. And this fact of the synchrony of divine and human forgiveness was thus recognized and linked together in the prayer which Jesus taught the apostles.

4. There is a basic law of justice in the universe which mercy is powerless to circumvent. The unselfish glories of Paradise are not possible of reception by a thoroughly selfish creature of the realms of time and space. Even the infinite love of God cannot force the salvation of eternal survival upon any mortal creature who does not choose to survive. Mercy has great latitude of bestowal,

but, after all, there are mandates of justice which even love combined with mercy cannot effectively abrogate. Again Jesus quoted from the Hebrew scriptures: "I have called and you refused to hear; I stretched out my hand, but no man regarded. You have set at naught all my counsel, and you have rejected my reproof, and because of this rebellious attitude it becomes inevitable that you shall call upon me and fail to receive an answer. Having rejected the way of life, you may seek me diligently in your times of suffering, but you will not find me."

5. They who would receive mercy must show mercy; judge not that you be not judged. With the spirit with which you judge others you also shall be judged. Mercy does not wholly abrogate universe fairness. In the end it will prove true: "Whoso stops his ears to the cry of the poor, he also shall some day cry for help, and no one will hear him." The sincerity of any prayer is the assurance of its being heard; the spiritual wisdom and universe consistency of any petition is the determiner of the time, manner, and degree of the answer. A wise father does not *literally* answer the foolish prayers of his ignorant and inexperienced children, albeit the children may derive much pleasure and real soul satisfaction from the making of such absurd petitions.

6. When you have become wholly dedicated to the doing of the will of the Father in heaven, the answer to all your petitions will be forthcoming because your prayers will be in full accordance with the Father's will, and the Father's will is ever manifest throughout his vast universe. What the true son desires and the infinite Father wills IS. Such a prayer cannot remain unanswered, and no other sort of petition can possibly be fully answered.

7. The cry of the righteous is the faith act of the child of God which opens the door of the Father's storehouse of goodness, truth, and mercy, and these good gifts have long been in waiting for the son's approach and personal appropriation. Prayer does not change the divine attitude toward man, but it does change man's attitude toward the changeless Father. The *motive* of the prayer gives it right of way to the divine ear, not the social, economic, or outward religious status of the one who prays.

8. Prayer may not be employed to avoid the delays of time or to transcend the handicaps of space. Prayer is not designed as a technique for aggrandizing self or for gaining unfair advantage over one's fellows. A thoroughly selfish soul cannot pray in the true sense of the word. Said Jesus: "Let your supreme delight be in the character of God, and he shall surely give you the sincere desires of your heart." "Commit your way to the Lord; trust in him, and he will act." "For the Lord hears the cry of the needy, and he will regard the prayer of the destitute."

9. "I have come forth from the Father; if, therefore, you are ever in doubt as to what you would ask of the Father, ask in my name, and I will present your petition in accordance with your real needs and desires and in accordance with my Father's will." Guard against the great danger of becoming self-centered in your prayers. Avoid praying much for yourself; pray more for the spiritual progress of your brethren. Avoid materialistic praying; pray in the spirit and for the abundance of the gifts of the spirit.

10. When you pray for the sick and afflicted, do not expect that your petitions will take the place of loving and intelligent ministry to the necessities of these afflicted ones. Pray for the welfare of your families, friends, and fellows,

but especially pray for those who curse you, and make loving petitions for those who persecute you. "But when to pray, I will not say. Only the spirit that dwells within you may move you to the utterance of those petitions which are expressive of your inner relationship with the Father of spirits."

11. Many resort to prayer only when in trouble. Such a practice is thoughtless and misleading. True, you do well to pray when harassed, but you should also be mindful to speak as a son to your Father even when all goes well with your soul. Let your real petitions always be in secret. Do not let men hear your personal prayers. Prayers of thanksgiving are appropriate for groups of worshipers, but the prayer of the soul is a personal matter. There is but one form of prayer which is appropriate for all God's children, and that is: "Nevertheless, your will be done."

12. All believers in this gospel should pray sincerely for the extension of the kingdom of heaven. Of all the prayers of the Hebrew scriptures he commented most approvingly on the petition of the Psalmist: "Create in me a clean heart, O God, and renew a right spirit within me. Purge me from secret sins and keep back your servant from presumptuous transgression." Jesus commented at great length on the relation of prayer to careless and offending speech, quoting: "Set a watch, O Lord, before my mouth; keep the door of my lips." "The human tongue," said Jesus, "is a member which few men can tame, but the spirit within can transform this unruly member into a kindly voice of tolerance and an inspiring minister of mercy."

13. Jesus taught that the prayer for divine guidance over the pathway of earthly life was next in importance to the petition for a knowledge of the Father's will. In reality this means a prayer for divine wisdom. Jesus never taught that human knowledge and special skill could be gained by prayer. But he did teach that prayer is a factor in the enlargement of one's capacity to receive the presence of the divine spirit. When Jesus taught his associates to pray in the spirit and in truth, he explained that he referred to praying sincerely and in accordance with one's enlightenment, to praying wholeheartedly and intelligently, earnestly and steadfastly.

14. Jesus warned his followers against thinking that their prayers would be rendered more efficacious by ornate repetitions, eloquent phraseology, fasting, penance, or sacrifices. But he did exhort his believers to employ prayer as a means of leading up through thanksgiving to true worship. Jesus deplored that so little of the spirit of thanksgiving was to be found in the prayers and worship of his followers. He quoted from the Scriptures on this occasion, saying: "It is a good thing to give thanks to the Lord and to sing praises to the name of the Most High, to acknowledge his loving-kindness every morning and his faithfulness every night, for God has made me glad through his work. In everything I will give thanks according to the will of God."

15. And then Jesus said: "Be not constantly overanxious about your common needs. Be not apprehensive concerning the problems of your earthly existence, but in all these things by prayer and supplication, with the spirit of sincere thanksgiving, let your needs be spread out before your Father who is in heaven." Then he quoted from the Scriptures: "I will praise the name of God with a song and will magnify him with thanksgiving. And this will please the Lord better than the sacrifice of an ox or bullock with horns and hoofs."

16. Jesus taught his followers that, when they had made their prayers to the Father, they should remain for a time in silent receptivity to afford the indwelling spirit the better opportunity to speak to the listening soul. The spirit of the Father speaks best to man when the human mind is in an attitude of true worship. We worship God by the aid of the Father's indwelling spirit and by the illumination of the human mind through the ministry of truth. Worship, taught Jesus, makes one increasingly like the being who is worshiped. Worship is a transforming experience whereby the finite gradually approaches and ultimately attains the presence of the Infinite.

And many other truths did Jesus tell his apostles about man's communion with God, but not many of them could fully encompass his teaching.

3. THE STOP AT RAMAH

At Ramah Jesus had the memorable discussion with the aged Greek philosopher who taught that science and philosophy were sufficient to satisfy the needs of human experience. Jesus listened with patience and sympathy to this Greek teacher, allowing the truth of many things he said but pointing out that, when he was through, he had failed in his discussion of human existence to explain "whence, why, and whither," and added: "Where you leave off, we begin. Religion is a revelation to man's soul dealing with spiritual realities which the mind alone could never discover or fully fathom. Intellectual strivings may reveal the facts of life, but the gospel of the kingdom unfolds the *truths* of being. You have discussed the material shadows of truth; will you now listen while I tell you about the eternal and spiritual realities which cast these transient time shadows of the material facts of mortal existence?" For more than an hour Jesus taught this Greek the saving truths of the gospel of the kingdom. The old philosopher was susceptible to the Master's mode of approach, and being sincerely honest of heart, he quickly believed this gospel of salvation.

The apostles were a bit disconcerted by the open manner of Jesus' assent to many of the Greek's propositions, but Jesus afterward privately said to them: "My children, marvel not that I was tolerant of the Greek's philosophy. True and genuine inward certainty does not in the least fear outward analysis, nor does truth resent honest criticism. You should never forget that intolerance is the mask covering up the entertainment of secret doubts as to the trueness of one's belief. No man is at any time disturbed by his neighbor's attitude when he has perfect confidence in the truth of that which he wholeheartedly believes. Courage is the confidence of thoroughgoing honesty about those things which one professes to believe. Sincere men are unafraid of the critical examination of their true convictions and noble ideals."

On the second evening at Ramah, Thomas asked Jesus this question: "Master, how can a new believer in your teaching really know, really be certain, about the truth of this gospel of the kingdom?"

And Jesus said to Thomas: "Your assurance that you have entered into the kingdom family of the Father, and that you will eternally survive with the children of the kingdom, is wholly a matter of personal experience—faith in the word of truth. Spiritual assurance is the equivalent of your personal religious experience in the eternal realities of divine truth and is otherwise equal to your intelligent understanding of truth realities plus your spiritual faith and minus your honest doubts.

"The Son is naturally endowed with the life of the Father. Having been endowed with the living spirit of the Father, you are therefore sons of God. You survive your life in the material world of the flesh because you are identified with the Father's living spirit, the gift of eternal life. Many, indeed, had this life before I came forth from the Father, and many more have received this spirit because they believed my word; but I declare that, when I return to the Father, he will send his spirit into the hearts of all men.

"While you cannot observe the divine spirit at work in your minds, there is a practical method of discovering the degree to which you have yielded the control of your soul powers to the teaching and guidance of this indwelling spirit of the heavenly Father, and that is the degree of your love for your fellow men. This spirit of the Father partakes of the love of the Father, and as it dominates man, it unfailingly leads in the directions of divine worship and loving regard for one's fellows. At first you believe that you are sons of God because my teaching has made you more conscious of the inner leadings of our Father's indwelling presence; but presently the Spirit of Truth shall be poured out upon all flesh, and it will live among men and teach all men, even as I now live among you and speak to you the words of truth. And this Spirit of Truth, speaking for the spiritual endowments of your souls, will help you to know that you are the sons of God. It will unfailingly bear witness with the Father's indwelling presence, your spirit, then dwelling in all men as it now dwells in some, telling you that you are in reality the sons of God.

"Every earth child who follows the leading of this spirit shall eventually know the will of God, and he who surrenders to the will of my Father shall abide forever. The way from the earth life to the eternal estate has not been made plain to you, but there is a way, there always has been, and I have come to make that way new and living. He who enters the kingdom has eternal life already—he shall never perish. But much of this you will the better understand when I shall have returned to the Father and you are able to view your present experiences in retrospect."

And all who heard these blessed words were greatly cheered. The Jewish teachings had been confused and uncertain regarding the survival of the righteous, and it was refreshing and inspiring for Jesus' followers to hear these very definite and positive words of assurance about the eternal survival of all true believers.

The apostles continued to preach and baptize believers, while they kept up the practice of visiting from house to house, comforting the downcast and ministering to the sick and afflicted. The apostolic organization was expanded in that each of Jesus' apostles now had one of John's as an associate; Abner was the associate of Andrew; and this plan prevailed until they went down to Jerusalem for the next Passover.

The special instruction given by Jesus during their stay at Zebulun had chiefly to do with further discussions of the mutual obligations of the kingdom and embraced teaching designed to make clear the differences between personal religious experience and the amities of social religious obligations. This was one of the few times the Master ever discussed the social aspects of religion. Throughout his entire earth life Jesus gave his followers very little instruction regarding the socialization of religion.

In Zebulun the people were of a mixed race, hardly Jew or gentile, and few of them really believed in Jesus, notwithstanding they had heard of the healing of the sick at Capernaum.

4. THE GOSPEL AT IRON

At Iron, as in many of even the smaller cities of Galilee and Judea, there was a synagogue, and during the earlier times of Jesus' ministry it was his custom to speak in these synagogues on the Sabbath day. Sometimes he would speak at the morning service, and Peter or one of the other apostles would preach at the afternoon hour. Jesus and the apostles would also often teach and preach at the weekday evening assemblies at the synagogue. Although the religious leaders at Jerusalem became increasingly antagonistic toward Jesus, they exercised no direct control over the synagogues outside of that city. It was not until later in Jesus' public ministry that they were able to create such a widespread sentiment against him as to bring about the almost universal closing of the synagogues to his teaching. At this time all the synagogues of Galilee and Judea were open to him.

Iron was the site of extensive mineral mines for those days, and since Jesus had never shared the life of the miner, he spent most of his time, while sojourning at Iron, in the mines. While the apostles visited the homes and preached in the public places, Jesus worked in the mines with these underground laborers. The fame of Jesus as a healer had spread even to this remote village, and many sick and afflicted sought help at his hands, and many were greatly benefited by his healing ministry. But in none of these cases did the Master perform a so-called miracle of healing save in that of the leper.

Late on the afternoon of the third day at Iron, as Jesus was returning from the mines, he chanced to pass through a narrow side street on his way to his lodging place. As he drew near the squalid hovel of a certain leprous man, the afflicted one, having heard of his fame as a healer, made bold to accost him as he passed his door, saying as he knelt before him: "Lord, if only you would, you could make me clean. I have heard the message of your teachers, and I would enter the kingdom if I could be made clean." And the leper spoke in this way because among the Jews lepers were forbidden even to attend the synagogue or otherwise engage in public worship. This man really believed that he could not be received into the coming kingdom unless he could find a cure for his leprosy. And when Jesus saw him in his affliction and heard his words of clinging faith, his human heart was touched, and the divine mind was moved with compassion. As Jesus looked upon him, the man fell upon his face and worshiped. Then the Master stretched forth his hand and, touching him, said: "I will—be clean." And immediately he was healed; the leprosy no longer afflicted him.

When Jesus had lifted the man upon his feet, he charged him: "See that you tell no man about your healing but rather go quietly about your business, showing yourself to the priest and offering those sacrifices commanded by Moses in testimony of your cleansing." But this man did not do as Jesus had instructed him. Instead, he began to publish abroad throughout the town that Jesus had cured his leprosy, and since he was known to all the village, the people could plainly see that he had been cleansed of his disease. He did not go to the priests as Jesus had admonished him. As a result of his spreading abroad the news that Jesus had healed him, the Master was so thronged by the sick that he was forced to rise early the next day and leave the village. Although Jesus did not again enter the town, he remained two days in the outskirts near the mines, continuing to instruct the believing miners further regarding the gospel of the kingdom.

This cleansing of the leper was the first so-called miracle which Jesus had intentionally and deliberately performed up to this time. And this was a case of real leprosy.

From Iron they went to Gischala, spending two days proclaiming the gospel, and then departed for Chorazin, where they spent almost a week preaching the good news; but they were unable to win many believers for the kingdom in Chorazin. In no place where Jesus had taught had he met with such a general rejection of his message. The sojourn at Chorazin was very depressing to most of the apostles, and Andrew and Abner had much difficulty in upholding the courage of their associates. And so, passing quietly through Capernaum, they went on to the village of Madon, where they fared little better. There prevailed in the minds of most of the apostles the idea that their failure to meet with success in these towns so recently visited was due to Jesus' insistence that they refrain, in their teaching and preaching, from referring to him as a healer. How they wished he would cleanse another leper or in some other manner so manifest his power as to attract the attention of the people! But the Master was unmoved by their earnest urging.

5. BACK IN CANA

The apostolic party was greatly cheered when Jesus announced, "Tomorrow we go to Cana." They knew they would have a sympathetic hearing at Cana, for Jesus was well known there. They were doing well with their work of bringing people into the kingdom when, on the third day, there arrived in Cana a certain prominent citizen of Capernaum, Titus, who was a partial believer, and whose son was critically ill. He heard that Jesus was at Cana; so he hastened over to see him. The believers at Capernaum thought Jesus could heal any sickness.

When this nobleman had located Jesus in Cana, he besought him to hurry over to Capernaum and heal his afflicted son. While the apostles stood by in breathless expectancy, Jesus, looking at the father of the sick boy, said: "How long shall I bear with you? The power of God is in your midst, but except you see signs and behold wonders, you refuse to believe." But the nobleman pleaded with Jesus, saying: "My Lord, I do believe, but come ere my child perishes, for when I left him he was even then at the point of death." And when Jesus had bowed his head a moment in silent meditation, he suddenly spoke, "Return to your home; your son will live." Titus believed the word of Jesus and hastened back to Capernaum. And as he was returning, his servants came out to meet him, saying, "Rejoice, for your son is improved—he lives." Then Titus inquired of them at what hour the boy began to mend, and when the servants answered "yesterday about the seventh hour the fever left him," the father recalled that it was about that hour when Jesus had said, "Your son will live." And Titus henceforth believed with a whole heart, and all his family also believed. This son became a mighty minister of the kingdom and later yielded up his life with those who suffered in Rome. Though the entire household of Titus, their friends, and even the apostles regarded this episode as a miracle, it was not. At least this was not a miracle of curing physical disease. It was merely a case of preknowledge concerning the course of natural law, just such knowledge as Jesus frequently resorted to subsequent to his baptism.

Again was Jesus compelled to hasten away from Cana because of the undue attention attracted by the second episode of this sort to attend his ministry in this village. The townspeople remembered the water and the wine, and now that he was supposed to have healed the nobleman's son at so great a distance, they came to him, not only bringing the sick and afflicted but also sending messengers requesting that he heal sufferers at a distance. And when Jesus saw that the whole countryside was aroused, he said, "Let us go to Nain."

6. NAIN AND THE WIDOW'S SON

These people believed in signs; they were a wonder-seeking generation. By this time the people of central and southern Galilee had become miracle minded regarding Jesus and his personal ministry. Scores, hundreds, of honest persons suffering from purely nervous disorders and afflicted with emotional disturbances came into Jesus' presence and then returned home to their friends announcing that Jesus had healed them. And such cases of mental healing these ignorant and simple-minded people regarded as physical healing, miraculous cures.

When Jesus sought to leave Cana and go to Nain, a great multitude of believers and many curious people followed after him. They were bent on beholding miracles and wonders, and they were not to be disappointed. As Jesus and his apostles drew near the gate of the city, they met a funeral procession on its way to the near-by cemetery, carrying the only son of a widowed mother of Nain. This woman was much respected, and half of the village followed the bearers of the bier of this supposedly dead boy. When the funeral procession had come up to Jesus and his followers, the widow and her friends recognized the Master and besought him to bring the son back to life. Their miracle expectancy was aroused to such a high pitch they thought Jesus could cure any human disease, and why could not such a healer even raise the dead? Jesus, while being thus importuned, stepped forward and, raising the covering of the bier, examined the boy. Discovering that the young man was not really dead, he perceived the tragedy which his presence could avert; so, turning to the mother, he said: "Weep not. Your son is not dead; he sleeps. He will be restored to you." And then, taking the young man by the hand, he said, "Awake and arise." And the youth who was supposed to be dead presently sat up and began to speak, and Jesus sent them back to their homes.

Jesus endeavored to calm the multitude and vainly tried to explain that the lad was not really dead, that he had not brought him back from the grave, but it was useless. The multitude which followed him, and the whole village of Nain, were aroused to the highest pitch of emotional frenzy. Fear seized many, panic others, while still others fell to praying and wailing over their sins. And it was not until long after nightfall that the clamoring multitude could be dispersed. And, of course, notwithstanding Jesus' statement that the boy was not dead, everyone insisted that a miracle had been wrought, even the dead raised. Although Jesus told them the boy was merely in a deep sleep, they explained that that was the manner of his speaking and called attention to the fact that he always in great modesty tried to hide his miracles.

So the word went abroad throughout Galilee and into Judea that Jesus had raised the widow's son from the dead, and many who heard this report believed it. Never was Jesus able to make even all his apostles fully understand that the widow's son was not really dead when he bade him awake and arise. But he did impress them sufficiently to keep it out of all subsequent records except that of Luke, who recorded it as the episode had been related to him. And again was Jesus so besieged as a physician that he departed early the next day for Endor.

7. AT ENDOR

At Endor Jesus escaped for a few days from the clamoring multitudes in quest of physical healing. During their sojourn at this place the Master recounted for the instruction of the apostles the story of King Saul and the witch of Endor. Jesus plainly told his apostles that the stray and rebellious midwayers who had oftentimes impersonated the supposed spirits of the dead would soon be brought under control so that they could no more do these strange things. He told his followers that, after he returned to the Father, and after they had poured out their spirit upon all flesh, no more could such semispirit beings—so-called unclean spirits—possess the feeble- and evil-minded among mortals.

Jesus further explained to his apostles that the spirits of departed human beings do not come back to the world of their origin to communicate with their living fellows. Only after the passing of a dispensational age would it be possible for the advancing spirit of mortal man to return to earth and then only in exceptional cases and as a part of the spiritual administration of the planet.

When they had rested two days, Jesus said to his apostles: "On the morrow let us return to Capernaum to tarry and teach while the countryside quiets down. At home they will have by this time partly recovered from this sort of excitement."

PAPER 147

THE INTERLUDE VISIT TO JERUSALEM

JESUS and the apostles arrived in Capernaum on Wednesday, March 17, and spent two weeks at the Bethsaida headquarters before they departed for Jerusalem. These two weeks the apostles taught the people by the seaside while Jesus spent much time alone in the hills about his Father's business. During this period Jesus, accompanied by James and John Zebedee, made two secret trips to Tiberias, where they met with the believers and instructed them in the gospel of the kingdom.

Many of the household of Herod believed in Jesus and attended these meetings. It was the influence of these believers among Herod's official family that had helped to lessen that ruler's enmity toward Jesus. These believers at Tiberias had fully explained to Herod that the "kingdom" which Jesus proclaimed was spiritual in nature and not a political venture. Herod rather believed these members of his own household and therefore did not permit himself to become unduly alarmed by the spreading abroad of the reports concerning Jesus' teaching and healing. He had no objections to Jesus' work as a healer or religious teacher. Notwithstanding the favorable attitude of many of Herod's advisers, and even of Herod himself, there existed a group of his subordinates who were so influenced by the religious leaders at Jerusalem that they remained bitter and threatening enemies of Jesus and the apostles and, later on, did much to hamper their public activities. The greatest danger to Jesus lay in the Jerusalem religious leaders and not in Herod. And it was for this very reason that Jesus and the apostles spent so much time and did most of their public preaching in Galilee rather than at Jerusalem and in Judea.

1. THE CENTURION'S SERVANT

On the day before they made ready to go to Jerusalem for the feast of the Passover, Mangus, a centurion, or captain, of the Roman guard stationed at Capernaum, came to the rulers of the synagogue, saying: "My faithful orderly is sick and at the point of death. Would you, therefore, go to Jesus in my behalf and beseech him to heal my servant?" The Roman captain did this because he thought the Jewish leaders would have more influence with Jesus. So the elders went to see Jesus and their spokesman said: "Teacher, we earnestly request you to go over to Capernaum and save the favorite servant of the Roman centurion, who is worthy of your notice because he loves our nation and even built us the very synagogue wherein you have so many times spoken."

And when Jesus had heard them, he said, "I will go with you." And as he went with them over to the centurion's house, and before they had entered his yard, the Roman soldier sent his friends out to greet Jesus, instructing them to say: "Lord, trouble not yourself to enter my house, for I am not worthy that you should come under my roof. Neither did I think myself worthy to come to you; wherefore I sent the elders of your own people. But I know that you can speak the word where you stand and my servant will be healed. For I am myself under the orders of others, and I have soldiers under me, and I say to this one go, and he goes; to another come, and he comes, and to my servants do this or do that, and they do it."

And when Jesus heard these words, he turned and said to his apostles and those who were with them: "I marvel at the belief of the gentile. Verily, verily, I say to you, I have not found so great faith, no, not in Israel." Jesus, turning from the house, said, "Let us go hence." And the friends of the centurion went into the house and told Mangus what Jesus had said. And from that hour the servant began to mend and was eventually restored to his normal health and usefulness.

But we never knew just what happened on this occasion. This is simply the record, and as to whether or not invisible beings ministered healing to the centurion's servant, was not revealed to those who accompanied Jesus. We only know of the fact of the servant's complete recovery.

2. THE JOURNEY TO JERUSALEM

Early on the morning of Tuesday, March 30, Jesus and the apostolic party started on their journey to Jerusalem for the Passover, going by the route of the Jordan valley. They arrived on the afternoon of Friday, April 2, and established their headquarters, as usual, at Bethany. Passing through Jericho, they paused to rest while Judas made a deposit of some of their common funds in the bank of a friend of his family. This was the first time Judas had carried a surplus of money, and this deposit was left undisturbed until they passed through Jericho again when on that last and eventful journey to Jerusalem just before the trial and death of Jesus.

The party had an uneventful trip to Jerusalem, but they had hardly got themselves settled at Bethany when from near and far those seeking healing for their bodies, comfort for troubled minds, and salvation for their souls, began to congregate, so much so that Jesus had little time for rest. Therefore they pitched tents at Gethsemane, and the Master would go back and forth from Bethany to Gethsemane to avoid the crowds which so constantly thronged him. The apostolic party spent almost three weeks at Jerusalem, but Jesus enjoined them to do no public preaching, only private teaching and personal work.

At Bethany they quietly celebrated the Passover. And this was the first time that Jesus and all of the twelve partook of the bloodless Passover feast. The apostles of John did not eat the Passover with Jesus and his apostles; they celebrated the feast with Abner and many of the early believers in John's preaching. This was the second Passover Jesus had observed with his apostles in Jerusalem.

When Jesus and the twelve departed for Capernaum, the apostles of John did not return with them. Under the direction of Abner they remained in Jerusalem and the surrounding country, quietly laboring for the extension of the kingdom, while Jesus and the twelve returned to work in Galilee. Never again were the twenty-four all together until a short time before the commissioning and sending forth of the seventy evangelists. But the two groups were cooperative, and notwithstanding their differences of opinion, the best of feelings prevailed.

3. AT THE POOL OF BETHESDA

The afternoon of the second Sabbath in Jerusalem, as the Master and the apostles were about to participate in the temple services, John said to Jesus, "Come with me, I would show you something." John conducted Jesus out through one of the Jerusalem gates to a pool of water called Bethesda. Surrounding this pool was a structure of five porches under which a large group of sufferers lingered in quest of healing. This was a hot spring whose reddish-tinged water would bubble up at irregular intervals because of gas accumulations in the rock caverns underneath the pool. This periodic disturbance of the warm waters was believed by many to be due to supernatural influences, and it was a popular belief that the first person who entered the water after such a disturbance would be healed of whatever infirmity he had.

The apostles were somewhat restless under the restrictions imposed by Jesus, and John, the youngest of the twelve, was especially restive under this restraint. He had brought Jesus to the pool thinking that the sight of the assembled sufferers would make such an appeal to the Master's compassion that he would be moved to perform a miracle of healing, and thereby would all Jerusalem be astounded and presently be won to believe in the gospel of the kingdom. Said John to Jesus: "Master, see all of these suffering ones; is there nothing we can do for them?" And Jesus replied: "John, why would you tempt me to turn aside from the way I have chosen? Why do you go on desiring to substitute the working of wonders and the healing of the sick for the proclamation of the gospel of eternal truth? My son, I may not do that which you desire, but gather together these sick and afflicted that I may speak words of good cheer and eternal comfort to them."

In speaking to those assembled, Jesus said: "Many of you are here, sick and afflicted, because of your many years of wrong living. Some suffer from the accidents of time, others as a result of the mistakes of their forebears, while some of you struggle under the handicaps of the imperfect conditions of your temporal existence. But my Father works, and I would work, to improve your earthly state but more especially to insure your eternal estate. None of us can do much to change the difficulties of life unless we discover the Father in heaven so wills. After all, we are all beholden to do the will of the Eternal. If you could all be healed of your physical afflictions, you would indeed marvel, but it is even greater that you should be cleansed of all spiritual disease and find yourselves healed of all moral infirmities. You are all God's children; you are the sons of the heavenly Father. The bonds of time may seem to afflict you, but the God of eternity loves you. And when the time of judgment shall come, fear not, you shall all find, not only justice, but an abundance of mercy. Verily, verily, I say to you: He who hears the gospel of the kingdom and believes in this teaching of sonship with God, has eternal life; already are such believers passing from judgment and death to light and life. And the hour is coming in which even those who are in the tombs shall hear the voice of the resurrection."

And many of those who heard believed the gospel of the kingdom. Some of the afflicted were so inspired and spiritually revivified that they went about proclaiming that they had also been cured of their physical ailments.

One man who had been many years downcast and grievously afflicted by the infirmities of his troubled mind, rejoiced at Jesus' words and, picking up his bed, went forth to his home, even though it was the Sabbath day. This afflicted man had waited all these years for *somebody* to help him; he was such a victim of the feeling of his own helplessness that he had never once entertained the idea of helping himself which proved to be the one thing he had to do in order to effect recovery—take up his bed and walk.

Then said Jesus to John: "Let us depart ere the chief priests and the scribes come upon us and take offense that we spoke words of life to these afflicted ones." And they returned to the temple to join their companions, and presently all of them departed to spend the night at Bethany. But John never told the other apostles of this visit of himself and Jesus to the pool of Bethesda on this Sabbath afternoon.

4. THE RULE OF LIVING

On the evening of this same Sabbath day, at Bethany, while Jesus, the twelve, and a group of believers were assembled about the fire in Lazarus's garden, Nathaniel asked Jesus this question: "Master, although you have taught us the positive version of the old rule of life, instructing us that we should do to others as we wish them to do to us, I do not fully discern how we can always abide by such an injunction. Let me illustrate my contention by citing the example of a lustful man who thus wickedly looks upon his intended consort in sin. How can we teach that this evil-intending man should do to others as he would they should do to him?"

When Jesus heard Nathaniel's question, he immediately stood upon his feet and, pointing his finger at the apostle, said: "Nathaniel, Nathaniel! What manner of thinking is going on in your heart? Do you not receive my teachings as one who has been born of the spirit? Do you not hear the truth as men of wisdom and spiritual understanding? When I admonished you to do to others as you would have them do to you, I spoke to men of high ideals, not to those who would be tempted to distort my teaching into a license for the encouragement of evil-doing."

When the Master had spoken, Nathaniel stood up and said: "But, Master, you should not think that I approve of such an interpretation of your teaching. I asked the question because I conjectured that many such men might thus misjudge your admonition, and I hoped you would give us further instruction regarding these matters." And then when Nathaniel had sat down, Jesus continued speaking: "I well know, Nathaniel, that no such idea of evil is approved in your mind, but I am disappointed in that you all so often fail to put a genuinely spiritual interpretation upon my commonplace teachings, instruction which must be given you in human language and as men must speak. Let me now teach you concerning the differing levels of meaning attached to the interpretation of this rule of living, this admonition to 'do to others that which you desire others to do to you':

"1. *The level of the flesh.* Such a purely selfish and lustful interpretation would be well exemplified by the supposition of your question.

"2. *The level of the feelings.* This plane is one level higher than that of the flesh and implies that sympathy and pity would enhance one's interpretation of this rule of living.

"3. *The level of mind.* Now come into action the reason of mind and the intelligence of experience. Good judgment dictates that such a rule of living should be interpreted in consonance with the highest idealism embodied in the nobility of profound self-respect.

"4. *The level of brotherly love.* Still higher is discovered the level of unselfish devotion to the welfare of one's fellows. On this higher plane of wholehearted social service growing out of the consciousness of the fatherhood of God and the consequent recognition of the brotherhood of man, there is discovered a new and far more beautiful interpretation of this basic rule of life.

"5. *The moral level.* And then when you attain true philosophic levels of interpretation, when you have real insight into the *rightness* and *wrongness* of things, when you perceive the eternal fitness of human relationships, you will begin to view such a problem of interpretation as you would imagine a high-minded, idealistic, wise, and impartial third person would so view and interpret such an injunction as applied to your personal problems of adjustment to your life situations.

"6. *The spiritual level.* And then last, but greatest of all, we attain the level of spirit insight and spiritual interpretation which impels us to recognize in this rule of life the divine command to treat all men as we conceive God would treat them. That is the universe ideal of human relationships. And this is your attitude toward all such problems when your supreme desire is ever to do the Father's will. I would, therefore, that you should do to all men that which you know I would do to them in like circumstances."

Nothing Jesus had said to the apostles up to this time had ever more astonished them. They continued to discuss the Master's words long after he had retired. While Nathaniel was slow to recover from his supposition that Jesus had misunderstood the spirit of his question, the others were more than thankful that their philosophic fellow apostle had had the courage to ask such a thought-provoking question.

5. VISITING SIMON THE PHARISEE

Though Simon was not a member of the Jewish Sanhedrin, he was an influential Pharisee of Jerusalem. He was a halfhearted believer, and notwithstanding that he might be severely criticized therefor, he dared to invite Jesus and his personal associates, Peter, James, and John, to his home for a social meal. Simon had long observed the Master and was much impressed with his teachings and even more so with his personality.

The wealthy Pharisees were devoted to almsgiving, and they did not shun publicity regarding their philanthropy. Sometimes they would even blow a trumpet as they were about to bestow charity upon some beggar. It was the custom of these Pharisees, when they provided a banquet for distinguished guests, to leave the doors of the house open so that even the street beggars might come in and, standing around the walls of the room behind the couches of the diners, be in position to receive portions of food which might be tossed to them by the banqueters.

On this particular occasion at Simon's house, among those who came in off the street was a woman of unsavory reputation who had recently become a believer in the good news of the gospel of the kingdom. This woman was well known throughout all Jerusalem as the former keeper of one of the so-called high-class brothels located hard by the temple court of the gentiles. She had, on accepting the teachings of Jesus, closed up her nefarious place of business and had induced the majority of the women associated with her to accept the gospel and change their mode of living; notwithstanding this, she was still held in great disdain by the Pharisees and was compelled to wear her hair down —the badge of harlotry. This unnamed woman had brought with her a large flask of perfumed anointing lotion and, standing behind Jesus as he reclined at meat, began to anoint his feet while she also wet his feet with her tears of gratitude, wiping them with the hair of her head. And when she had finished this anointing, she continued weeping and kissing his feet.

When Simon saw all this, he said to himself: "This man, if he were a prophet, would have perceived who and what manner of woman this is who thus touches him; that she is a notorious sinner." And Jesus, knowing what was going on in Simon's mind, spoke up, saying: "Simon, I have something which I would like to say to you." Simon answered, "Teacher, say on." Then said Jesus: "A certain wealthy moneylender had two debtors. The one owed him five hundred denarii and the other fifty. Now, when neither of them had wherewith to pay, he forgave them both. Which of them do you think, Simon, would love him most?" Simon answered, "He, I suppose, whom he forgave the most." And Jesus said, "You have rightly judged," and pointing to the woman, he continued: "Simon, take a good look at this woman. I entered your house as an invited guest, yet you gave me no water for my feet. This grateful woman has washed my feet with tears and wiped them with the hair of her head. You gave me no kiss of friendly greeting, but this woman, ever since she came in, has not ceased to kiss my feet. My head with oil you neglected to anoint, but she has anointed my feet with precious lotions. And what is the meaning of all this? Simply that her many sins have been forgiven, and this has led her to love much. But those who have received but little forgiveness sometimes love but little." And turning around toward the woman, he took her by the hand and, lifting her up, said: "You have indeed repented of your sins, and they are forgiven. Be not discouraged by the thoughtless and unkind attitude of your fellows; go on in the joy and liberty of the kingdom of heaven."

When Simon and his friends who sat at meat with him heard these words, they were the more astonished, and they began to whisper among themselves, "Who is this man that he even dares to forgive sins?" And when Jesus heard them thus murmuring, he turned to dismiss the woman, saying, "Woman, go in peace; your faith has saved you."

As Jesus arose with his friends to leave, he turned to Simon and said: "I know your heart, Simon, how you are torn betwixt faith and doubts, how you are distraught by fear and troubled by pride; but I pray for you that you may yield to the light and may experience in your station in life just such mighty transformations of mind and spirit as may be comparable to the tremendous changes which the gospel of the kingdom has already wrought in the heart of your unbidden and unwelcome guest. And I declare to all of you that the Father has opened the doors of the heavenly kingdom to all who have the faith to enter, and no man or association of men can close those doors even to the most humble soul or supposedly most flagrant sinner on earth if such sincerely seek an entrance." And Jesus, with Peter, James, and John, took leave of their host and went to join the rest of the apostles at the camp in the garden of Gethsemane.

That same evening Jesus made the long-to-be-remembered address to the apostles regarding the relative value of status with God and progress in the eternal ascent to Paradise. Said Jesus: "My children, if there exists a true and living connection between the child and the Father, the child is certain to progress continuously toward the Father's ideals. True, the child may at first make slow progress, but the progress is none the less sure. The important thing is not the rapidity of your progress but rather its certainty. Your actual achievement is not so important as the fact that the *direction* of your progress is Godward. What you are becoming day by day is of infinitely more importance than what you are today.

"This transformed woman whom some of you saw at Simon's house today is, at this moment, living on a level which is vastly below that of Simon and his well-meaning associates; but while these Pharisees are occupied with the false progress of the illusion of traversing deceptive circles of meaningless ceremonial services, this woman has, in dead earnest, started out on the long and eventful search for God, and her path toward heaven is not blocked by spiritual pride and moral self-satisfaction. The woman is, humanly speaking, much farther away from God than Simon, but her soul is in progressive motion; she is on the way toward an eternal goal. There are present in this woman tremendous spiritual possibilities for the future. Some of you may not stand high in actual levels of soul and spirit, but you are making daily progress on the living way opened up, through faith, to God. There are tremendous possibilities in each of you for the future. Better by far to have a small but living and growing faith than to be possessed of a great intellect with its dead stores of worldly wisdom and spiritual unbelief."

But Jesus earnestly warned his apostles against the foolishness of the child of God who presumes upon the Father's love. He declared that the heavenly Father is not a lax, loose, or foolishly indulgent parent who is ever ready to condone sin and forgive recklessness. He cautioned his hearers not mistakenly to apply his illustrations of father and son so as to make it appear that God is like some overindulgent and unwise parents who conspire with the foolish of earth to encompass the moral undoing of their thoughtless children, and who are thereby certainly and directly contributing to the delinquency and early demoralization of their own offspring. Said Jesus: "My Father does not indulgently condone those acts and practices of his children which are self-destructive and suicidal to all moral growth and spiritual progress. Such sinful practices are an abomination in the sight of God."

Many other semiprivate meetings and banquets did Jesus attend with the high and the low, the rich and the poor, of Jerusalem before he and his apostles finally departed for Capernaum. And many, indeed, became believers in the gospel of the kingdom and were subsequently baptized by Abner and his associates, who remained behind to foster the interests of the kingdom in Jerusalem and thereabouts.

6. RETURNING TO CAPERNAUM

The last week of April, Jesus and the twelve departed from their Bethany headquarters near Jerusalem and began their journey back to Capernaum by way of Jericho and the Jordan.

The chief priests and the religious leaders of the Jews held many secret meetings for the purpose of deciding what to do with Jesus. They were all agreed that something should be done to put a stop to his teaching, but they could not agree on the method. They had hoped that the civil authorities would dispose of him as Herod had put an end to John, but they discovered that Jesus was so conducting his work that the Roman officials were not much alarmed by his preaching. Accordingly, at a meeting which was held the day before Jesus' departure for Capernaum, it was decided that he would have to be apprehended on a religious charge and be tried by the Sanhedrin. Therefore a commission of six secret spies was appointed to follow Jesus, to observe his words and acts, and when they had amassed sufficient evidence of lawbreaking and blasphemy, to return to Jerusalem with their report. These six Jews caught up with the apostolic party, numbering about thirty, at Jericho and, under the pretense of desiring to become disciples, attached themselves to Jesus' family of followers, remaining with the group up to the time of the beginning of the second preaching tour in Galilee; whereupon three of them returned to Jerusalem to submit their report to the chief priests and the Sanhedrin.

Peter preached to the assembled multitude at the crossing of the Jordan, and the following morning they moved up the river toward Amathus. They wanted to proceed straight on to Capernaum, but such a crowd gathered here they remained three days, preaching, teaching, and baptizing. They did not move toward home until early Sabbath morning, the first day of May. The Jerusalem spies were sure they would now secure their first charge against Jesus—that of Sabbath breaking—since he had presumed to start his journey on the Sabbath day. But they were doomed to disappointment because, just before their departure, Jesus called Andrew into his presence and before them all instructed him to proceed for a distance of only one thousand yards, the legal Jewish Sabbath day's journey.

But the spies did not have long to wait for their opportunity to accuse Jesus and his associates of Sabbath breaking. As the company passed along the narrow road, the waving wheat, which was just then ripening, was near at hand on either side, and some of the apostles, being hungry, plucked the ripe grain and ate it. It was customary for travelers to help themselves to grain as they passed along the road, and therefore no thought of wrongdoing was attached to such conduct. But the spies seized upon this as a pretext for assailing Jesus. When they saw Andrew rub the grain in his hand, they went up to him and said: "Do you not know that it is unlawful to pluck and rub the grain on the Sabbath day?" And Andrew answered: "But we are hungry and rub only sufficient for our needs; and since when did it become sinful to eat grain on the Sabbath day?" But the Pharisees answered: "You do no wrong in eating, but you do break the law in plucking and rubbing out the grain between your hands; surely your Master would not approve of such acts." Then said Andrew: "But if it is not wrong to eat the grain, surely the rubbing out between our hands is hardly more work than the chewing of the grain, which you allow; wherefore do you quibble over such trifles?" When Andrew intimated that they were quibblers, they were indignant, and rushing back to where Jesus walked along, talking to Matthew, they protested, saying: "Behold, Teacher, your apostles do that which is unlawful on the Sabbath day; they pluck, rub, and eat the grain. We are sure you will command them to cease." And then said Jesus to the accusers: "You are indeed zealous for the law, and you do well to remember the Sabbath day to keep it holy; but did you never read in the Scripture that, one day when David was hungry, he and they who were with him entered the house of God and ate the showbread, which it was not lawful for anyone to eat save the priests? and David also gave this bread to those who were with him. And have you not read in our law that it is lawful to do many needful things on the Sabbath day? And shall I not, before the day is finished, see you eat that which you have brought along for the needs of this day? My good men, you do well to be zealous for the Sabbath, but you would do better to guard the health and well-being of your fellows. I declare that the Sabbath was made for man and not man for the Sabbath. And if you are here present with us to watch my words, then will I openly proclaim that the Son of Man is lord even of the Sabbath."

The Pharisees were astonished and confounded by his words of discernment and wisdom. For the remainder of the day they kept by themselves and dared not ask any more questions.

Jesus' antagonism to the Jewish traditions and slavish ceremonials was always *positive.* It consisted in what he did and in what he affirmed. The Master spent little time in negative denunciations. He taught that those who know God can enjoy the liberty of living without deceiving themselves by the licenses of sinning. Said Jesus to the apostles: "Men, if you are enlightened by the truth and really know what you are doing, you are blessed; but if you know not the divine way, you are unfortunate and already breakers of the law."

7. BACK IN CAPERNAUM

It was around noon on Monday, May 3, when Jesus and the twelve came to Bethsaida by boat from Tarichea. They traveled by boat in order to escape those who journeyed with them. But by the next day the others, including the official spies from Jerusalem, had again found Jesus.

On Tuesday evening Jesus was conducting one of his customary classes of questions and answers when the leader of the six spies said to him: "I was today talking with one of John's disciples who is here attending upon your teaching, and we were at a loss to understand why you never command your disciples to fast and pray as we Pharisees fast and as John bade his followers." And Jesus, referring to a statement by John, answered this questioner: "Do the sons of the bridechamber fast while the bridegroom is with them? As long as the bridegroom remains with them, they can hardly fast. But the time is coming when the bridegroom shall be taken away, and during those times the children of the bridechamber undoubtedly will fast and pray. To pray is natural for the children of light, but fasting is not a part of the gospel of the kingdom of heaven. Be reminded that a wise tailor does not sew a piece of new and unshrunk cloth upon an old garment, lest, when it is wet, it shrink and produce a worse rent. Neither do men put new wine into old wine skins, lest the new wine burst the skins so that both the wine and the skins perish. The wise man puts the new wine into fresh wine skins. Therefore do my disciples show wisdom in that they do not bring too much of the old order over into the new teaching of the gospel of the kingdom. You who have lost your teacher may be justified in fasting for a time. Fasting may be an appropriate part of the law of Moses, but in the coming kingdom the sons of God shall experience freedom from fear and joy in the divine spirit."

And when they heard these words, the disciples of John were comforted while the Pharisees themselves were the more confounded.

Then the Master proceeded to warn his hearers against entertaining the notion that all olden teaching should be replaced entirely by new doctrines. Said Jesus: "That which is old and also *true* must abide. Likewise, that which is new but false must be rejected. But that which is new and also true, have the faith and courage to accept. Remember it is written: 'Forsake not an old friend, for the new is not comparable to him. As new wine, so is a new friend; if it becomes old, you shall drink it with gladness.'"

8. THE FEAST OF SPIRITUAL GOODNESS

That night, long after the usual listeners had retired, Jesus continued to teach his apostles. He began this special instruction by quoting from the Prophet Isaiah:

"'Why have you fasted? For what reason do you afflict your souls while you continue to find pleasure in oppression and to take delight in injustice? Behold, you fast for the sake of strife and contention and to smite with the fist of wickedness. But you shall not fast in this way to make your voices heard on high.

"'Is it such a fast that I have chosen—a day for a man to afflict his soul? Is it to bow down his head like a bulrush, to grovel in sackcloth and ashes? Will you dare to call this a fast and an acceptable day in the sight of the Lord? Is not this the fast I should choose: to loose the bonds of wickedness, to undo the knots of heavy burdens, to let the oppressed go free, and to break every yoke? Is it not to share my bread with the hungry and to bring those who are homeless and poor to my house? And when I see those who are naked, I will clothe them.

"'Then shall your light break forth as the morning while your health springs forth speedily. Your righteousness shall go before you while the glory of the Lord shall be your rear guard. Then will you call upon the Lord, and he shall answer; you will cry out, and he shall say—Here am I. And all this he will do if you refrain from oppression, condemnation, and vanity. The Father rather desires that you draw out your heart to the hungry, and that you minister to the afflicted souls; then shall your light shine in obscurity, and even your darkness shall be as the noonday. Then shall the Lord guide you continually, satisfying your soul and renewing your strength. You shall become like a watered garden, like a spring whose waters fail not. And they who do these things shall restore the wasted glories; they shall raise up the foundations of many generations; they shall be called the rebuilders of broken walls, the restorers of safe paths in which to dwell.'"

And then long into the night Jesus propounded to his apostles the truth that it was their faith that made them secure in the kingdom of the present and the future, and not their affliction of soul nor fasting of body. He exhorted the apostles at least to live up to the ideas of the prophet of old and expressed the hope that they would progress far beyond even the ideals of Isaiah and the older prophets. His last words that night were: "Grow in grace by means of that living faith which grasps the fact that you are the sons of God while at the same time it recognizes every man as a brother."

It was after two o'clock in the morning when Jesus ceased speaking and every man went to his place for sleep.

PAPER 148

TRAINING EVANGELISTS AT BETHSAIDA

FROM May 3 to October 3, A.D. 28, Jesus and the apostolic party were in residence at the Zebedee home at Bethsaida. Throughout this five months' period of the dry season an enormous camp was maintained by the seaside near the Zebedee residence, which had been greatly enlarged to accommodate the growing family of Jesus. This seaside camp, occupied by an ever-changing population of truth seekers, healing candidates, and curiosity devotees, numbered from five hundred to fifteen hundred. This tented city was under the general supervision of David Zebedee, assisted by the Alpheus twins. The encampment was a model in order and sanitation as well as in its general administration. The sick of different types were segregated and were under the supervision of a believer physician, a Syrian named Elman.

Throughout this period the apostles would go fishing at least one day a week, selling their catch to David for consumption by the seaside encampment. The funds thus received were turned over to the group treasury. The twelve were permitted to spend one week out of each month with their families or friends.

While Andrew continued in general charge of the apostolic activities, Peter was in full charge of the school of the evangelists. The apostles all did their share in teaching groups of evangelists each forenoon, and both teachers and pupils taught the people during the afternoons. After the evening meal, five nights a week, the apostles conducted question classes for the benefit of the evangelists. Once a week Jesus presided at this question hour, answering the holdover questions from previous sessions.

In five months several thousand came and went at this encampment. Interested persons from every part of the Roman Empire and from the lands east of the Euphrates were in frequent attendance. This was the longest settled and well-organized period of the Master's teaching. Jesus' immediate family spent most of this time at either Nazareth or Cana.

The encampment was not conducted as a community of common interests, as was the apostolic family. David Zebedee managed this large tent city so that it became a self-sustaining enterprise, notwithstanding that no one was ever turned away. This ever-changing camp was an indispensable feature of Peter's evangelistic training school.

1. A NEW SCHOOL OF THE PROPHETS

Peter, James, and Andrew were the committee designated by Jesus to pass upon applicants for admission to the school of evangelists. All the races and nationalities of the Roman world and the East, as far as India, were represented among the students in this new school of the prophets. This school was conducted on the plan of learning and doing. What the students learned during the forenoon they taught to the assembly by the seaside during the afternoon. After supper they informally discussed both the learning of the forenoon and the teaching of the afternoon.

Each of the apostolic teachers taught his own view of the gospel of the kingdom. They made no effort to teach just alike; there was no standardized or dogmatic formulation of theologic doctrines. Though they all taught the *same truth,* each apostle presented his own personal interpretation of the Master's teaching. And Jesus upheld this presentation of the diversity of personal experience in the things of the kingdom, unfailingly harmonizing and co-ordinating these many and divergent views of the gospel at his weekly question hours. Notwithstanding this great degree of personal liberty in matters of teaching, Simon Peter tended to dominate the theology of the school of evangelists. Next to Peter, James Zebedee exerted the greatest personal influence.

The one hundred and more evangelists trained during this five months by the seaside represented the material from which (excepting Abner and John's apostles) the later seventy gospel teachers and preachers were drawn. The school of evangelists did not have everything in common to the same degree as did the twelve.

These evangelists, though they taught and preached the gospel, did not baptize believers until after they were later ordained and commissioned by Jesus as the seventy messengers of the kingdom. Only seven of the large number healed at the sundown scene at this place were to be found among these evangelistic students. The nobleman's son of Capernaum was one of those trained for gospel service in Peter's school.

2. THE BETHSAIDA HOSPITAL

In connection with the seaside encampment, Elman, the Syrian physician, with the assistance of a corps of twenty-five young women and twelve men, organized and conducted for four months what should be regarded as the kingdom's first hospital. At this infirmary, located a short distance to the south of the main tented city, they treated the sick in accordance with all known material methods as well as by the spiritual practices of prayer and faith encouragement. Jesus visited the sick of this encampment not less than three times a week and made personal contact with each sufferer. As far as we know, no so-called miracles of supernatural healing occurred among the one thousand afflicted and ailing persons who went away from this infirmary improved or cured. However, the vast majority of these benefited individuals ceased not to proclaim that Jesus had healed them.

Many of the cures effected by Jesus in connection with his ministry in behalf of Elman's patients did, indeed, appear to resemble the working of miracles, but we were instructed that they were only just such transformations of mind and spirit as may occur in the experience of expectant and faith-dominated persons who are under the immediate and inspirational influence of a strong, positive, and beneficent personality whose ministry banishes fear and destroys anxiety.

Elman and his associates endeavored to teach the truth to these sick ones concerning the "possession of evil spirits," but they met with little success. The belief that physical sickness and mental derangement could be caused by the dwelling of a so-called unclean spirit in the mind or body of the afflicted person was well-nigh universal.

In all his contact with the sick and afflicted, when it came to the technique of treatment or the revelation of the unknown causes of disease, Jesus did not disregard the instructions of his Paradise brother, Immanuel, given ere he embarked upon the venture of the Urantia incarnation. Notwithstanding this, those who ministered to the sick learned many helpful lessons by observing the manner in which Jesus inspired the faith and confidence of the sick and suffering.

The camp disbanded a short time before the season for the increase in chills and fever drew on.

3. THE FATHER'S BUSINESS

Throughout this period Jesus conducted public services at the encampment less than a dozen times and spoke only once in the Capernaum synagogue, the second Sabbath before their departure with the newly trained evangelists upon their second public preaching tour of Galilee.

Not since his baptism had the Master been so much alone as during this period of the evangelists' training encampment at Bethsaida. Whenever any one of the apostles ventured to ask Jesus why he was absent so much from their midst, he would invariably answer that he was "about the Father's business."

During these periods of absence, Jesus was accompanied by only two of the apostles. He had released Peter, James, and John temporarily from their assignment as his personal companions that they might also participate in the work of training the new evangelistic candidates, numbering more than one hundred. When the Master desired to go to the hills about the Father's business, he would summon to accompany him any two of the apostles who might be at liberty. In this way each of the twelve enjoyed an opportunity for close association and intimate contact with Jesus.

It has not been revealed for the purposes of this record, but we have been led to infer that the Master, during many of these solitary seasons in the hills, was in direct and executive association with many of his chief directors of universe affairs. Ever since about the time of his baptism this incarnated Sovereign of our universe had become increasingly and consciously active in the direction of certain phases of universe administration. And we have always held the opinion that, in some way not revealed to his immediate associates, during these weeks of decreased participation in the affairs of earth he was engaged in the direction of those high spirit intelligences who were charged with the running of a vast universe, and that the human Jesus chose to designate such activities on his part as being "about his Father's business."

Many times, when Jesus was alone for hours, but when two of his apostles were near by, they observed his features undergo rapid and multitudinous changes, although they heard him speak no words. Neither did they observe any visible manifestation of celestial beings who might have been in communication with their Master, such as some of them did witness on a subsequent occasion.

4. EVIL, SIN, AND INIQUITY

It was the habit of Jesus two evenings each week to hold special converse with individuals who desired to talk with him, in a certain secluded and sheltered corner of the Zebedee garden. At one of these evening conversations in private Thomas asked the Master this question: "Why is it necessary for men to be born of the spirit in order to enter the kingdom? Is rebirth necessary to escape the control of the evil one? Master, what is evil?" When Jesus heard these questions, he said to Thomas:

"Do not make the mistake of confusing *evil* with the *evil one,* more correctly the *iniquitous one.* He whom you call the evil one is the son of self-love, the high administrator who knowingly went into deliberate rebellion against the rule of my Father and his loyal Sons. But I have already vanquished these sinful rebels. Make clear in your mind these different attitudes toward the Father and his universe. Never forget these laws of relation to the Father's will:

"Evil is the unconscious or unintended transgression of the divine law, the Father's will. Evil is likewise the measure of the imperfectness of obedience to the Father's will.

"Sin is the conscious, knowing, and deliberate transgression of the divine law, the Father's will. Sin is the measure of unwillingness to be divinely led and spiritually directed.

"Iniquity is the willful, determined, and persistent transgression of the divine law, the Father's will. Iniquity is the measure of the continued rejection of the Father's loving plan of personality survival and the Sons' merciful ministry of salvation.

"By nature, before the rebirth of the spirit, mortal man is subject to inherent evil tendencies, but such natural imperfections of behavior are neither sin nor iniquity. Mortal man is just beginning his long ascent to the perfection of the Father in Paradise. To be imperfect or partial in natural endowment is not sinful. Man is indeed subject to evil, but he is in no sense the child of the evil one unless he has knowingly and deliberately chosen the paths of sin and the life of iniquity. Evil is inherent in the natural order of this world, but sin is an attitude of conscious rebellion which was brought to this world by those who fell from spiritual light into gross darkness.

"You are confused, Thomas, by the doctrines of the Greeks and the errors of the Persians. You do not understand the relationships of evil and sin because you view mankind as beginning on earth with a perfect Adam and rapidly degenerating, through sin, to man's present deplorable estate. But why do you refuse to comprehend the meaning of the record which discloses how Cain, the son of Adam, went over into the land of Nod and there got himself a wife? And why do you refuse to interpret the meaning of the record which portrays the sons of God finding wives for themselves among the daughters of men?

"Men are, indeed, by nature evil, but not necessarily sinful. The new birth—the baptism of the spirit—is essential to deliverance from evil and necessary for entrance into the kingdom of heaven, but none of this detracts from the fact that man is the son of God. Neither does this inherent presence of potential evil mean that man is in some mysterious way estranged from the Father in heaven so that, as an alien, foreigner, or stepchild, he must in some manner seek for legal adoption by the Father. All such notions are born, first, of your misunderstanding of the Father and, second, of your ignorance of the origin, nature, and destiny of man.

"The Greeks and others have taught you that man is descending from godly perfection steadily down toward oblivion or destruction; I have come to show that man, by entrance into the kingdom, is ascending certainly and surely up to God and divine perfection. Any being who in any manner falls short of the divine and spiritual ideals of the eternal Father's will is potentially evil, but such beings are in no sense sinful, much less iniquitous.

"Thomas, have you not read about this in the Scriptures, where it is written: 'You are the children of the Lord your God.' 'I will be his Father and he shall be my son.' 'I have chosen him to be my son—I will be his Father.' 'Bring my sons from far and my daughters from the ends of the earth; even every one who is called by my name, for I have created them for my glory.' 'You are the sons of the living God.' 'They who have the spirit of God are indeed the sons of God.' While there is a material part of the human father in the natural child, there is a spiritual part of the heavenly Father in every faith son of the kingdom."

All this and much more Jesus said to Thomas, and much of it the apostle comprehended, although Jesus admonished him to "speak not to the others concerning these matters until after I shall have returned to the Father." And Thomas did not mention this interview until after the Master had departed from this world.

5. THE PURPOSE OF AFFLICTION

At another of these private interviews in the garden Nathaniel asked Jesus: "Master, though I am beginning to understand why you refuse to practice healing indiscriminately, I am still at a loss to understand why the loving Father in heaven permits so many of his children on earth to suffer so many afflictions." The Master answered Nathaniel, saying:

"Nathaniel, you and many others are thus perplexed because you do not comprehend how the natural order of this world has been so many times upset by the sinful adventures of certain rebellious traitors to the Father's will. And I have come to make a beginning of setting these things in order. But many ages will be required to restore this part of the universe to former paths and thus release the children of men from the extra burdens of sin and rebellion. The presence of evil alone is sufficient test for the ascension of man—sin is not essential to survival.

"But, my son, you should know that the Father does not purposely afflict his children. Man brings down upon himself unnecessary affliction as a result of his persistent refusal to walk in the better ways of the divine will. Affliction is potential in evil, but much of it has been produced by sin and iniquity. Many unusual events have transpired on this world, and it is not strange that all thinking men should be perplexed by the scenes of suffering and affliction which they witness. But of one thing you may be sure: The Father does not send affliction as an arbitrary punishment for wrongdoing. The imperfections and handicaps of evil are inherent; the penalties of sin are inevitable; the destroying consequences of iniquity are inexorable. Man should not blame God for those afflictions which are the natural result of the life which he chooses to live; neither should man complain of those experiences which are a part of life as it is lived on this world. It is the Father's will that mortal man should work persistently and consistently toward the betterment of his estate on earth. Intelligent application would enable man to overcome much of his earthly misery.

"Nathaniel, it is our mission to help men solve their spiritual problems and in this way to quicken their minds so that they may be the better prepared and inspired to go about solving their manifold material problems. I know of your confusion as you have read the Scriptures. All too often there has prevailed a tendency to ascribe to God the responsibility for everything which ignorant man fails to understand. The Father is not personally responsible for all you may fail to comprehend. Do not doubt the love of the Father just because some just and wise law of his ordaining chances to afflict you because you have innocently or deliberately transgressed such a divine ordinance.

"But, Nathaniel, there is much in the Scriptures which would have instructed you if you had only read with discernment. Do you not remember that it is written: 'My son, despise not the chastening of the Lord; neither be weary of his correction, for whom the Lord loves he corrects, even as the father corrects the son in whom he takes delight.' 'The Lord does not afflict willingly.' 'Before I was afflicted, I went astray, but now do I keep the law. Affliction was good for me that I might thereby learn the divine statutes.' 'I know your sorrows. The eternal God is your refuge, while underneath are the everlasting arms.' 'The Lord also is a refuge for the oppressed, a haven of rest in times of trouble.' 'The Lord will strengthen him upon the bed of affliction; the Lord will not forget the sick.' 'As a father shows compassion for his children, so is the Lord compassionate to those who fear him. He knows your body; he remembers that you are dust.' 'He heals the brokenhearted and binds up their wounds.' 'He is the hope of the poor, the strength of the needy in his distress, a refuge from the storm, and a shadow from the devastating heat.' 'He gives power to the faint, and to them who have no might he increases strength.' 'A bruised reed shall he not break, and the smoking flax he will not quench.' 'When you pass through the waters of affliction, I will be with you, and when the rivers of adversity overflow you, I will not forsake you.' 'He has sent me to bind up the brokenhearted, to proclaim liberty to the captives, and to comfort all who mourn.' 'There is correction in suffering; affliction does not spring forth from the dust.'"

6. THE MISUNDERSTANDING OF SUFFERING—DISCOURSE ON JOB

It was this same evening at Bethsaida that John also asked Jesus why so many apparently innocent people suffered from so many diseases and experienced so many afflictions. In answering John's questions, among many other things, the Master said:

"My son, you do not comprehend the meaning of adversity or the mission of suffering. Have you not read that masterpiece of Semitic literature—the Scripture story of the afflictions of Job? Do you not recall how this wonderful parable begins with the recital of the material prosperity of the Lord's servant? You well remember that Job was blessed with children, wealth, dignity, position, health, and everything else which men value in this temporal life. According to the time-honored teachings of the children of Abraham such material prosperity was all-sufficient evidence of divine favor. But such material possessions and such temporal prosperity do not indicate God's favor. My Father in heaven loves the poor just as much as the rich; he is no respecter of persons.

"Although transgression of divine law is sooner or later followed by the harvest of punishment, while men certainly eventually do reap what they sow, still you should know that human suffering is not always a punishment for antecedent sin. Both Job and his friends failed to find the true answer for their perplexities. And with the light you now enjoy you would hardly assign to either Satan or God the parts they play in this unique parable. While Job did not, through suffering, find the resolution of his intellectual troubles or the solution of his philosophical difficulties, he did achieve great victories; even in the very face of the breakdown of his theological defenses he ascended to those spiritual heights where he could sincerely say, 'I abhor myself'; then was there granted him the salvation of a *vision of God.* So even through misunderstood suffering, Job ascended to the superhuman plane of moral understanding and spiritual insight. When the suffering servant obtains a vision of God, there follows a soul peace which passes all human understanding.

"The first of Job's friends, Eliphaz, exhorted the sufferer to exhibit in his afflictions the same fortitude he had prescribed for others during the days of his prosperity. Said this false comforter: 'Trust in your religion, Job; remember that it is the wicked and not the righteous who suffer. You must deserve this punishment, else you would not be afflicted. You well know that no man can be righteous in God's sight. You know that the wicked never really prosper. Anyway, man seems predestined to trouble, and perhaps the Lord is only chastising you for your own good.' No wonder poor Job failed to get much comfort from such an interpretation of the problem of human suffering.

"But the counsel of his second friend, Bildad, was even more depressing, notwithstanding its soundness from the standpoint of the then accepted theology. Said Bildad: 'God cannot be unjust. Your children must have been sinners since they perished; you must be in error, else you would not be so afflicted. And if you are really righteous, God will certainly deliver you from your afflictions. You should learn from the history of God's dealings with man that the Almighty destroys only the wicked.'

"And then you remember how Job replied to his friends, saying: 'I well know that God does not hear my cry for help. How can God be just and at the same time so utterly disregard my innocence? I am learning that I can get no satisfaction from appealing to the Almighty. Cannot you discern that God tolerates the persecution of the good by the wicked? And since man is so weak, what chance has he for consideration at the hands of an omnipotent God? God has made me as I am, and when he thus turns upon me, I am defenseless. And why did God ever create me just to suffer in this miserable fashion?'

"And who can challenge the attitude of Job in view of the counsel of his friends and the erroneous ideas of God which occupied his own mind? Do you not see that Job longed for a *human* God, that he hungered to commune with a divine Being who knows man's mortal estate and understands that the just must often suffer in innocence as a part of this first life of the long Paradise ascent? Wherefore has the Son of Man come forth from the Father to live such a life in the flesh that he will be able to comfort and succor all those who must henceforth be called upon to endure the afflictions of Job.

"Job's third friend, Zophar, then spoke still less comforting words when he said: 'You are foolish to claim to be righteous, seeing that you are thus afflicted. But I admit that it is impossible to comprehend God's ways. Perhaps there is some hidden purpose in all your miseries.' And when Job had listened to all three of his friends, he appealed directly to God for help, pleading the fact that 'man, born of woman, is few of days and full of trouble.'

"Then began the second session with his friends. Eliphaz grew more stern, accusing, and sarcastic. Bildad became indignant at Job's contempt for his friends. Zophar reiterated his melancholy advice. Job by this time had become disgusted with his friends and appealed again to God, and now he appealed to a just God against the God of injustice embodied in the philosophy of his friends and enshrined even in his own religious attitude. Next Job took refuge in the consolation of a future life in which the inequities of mortal existence may be more justly rectified. Failure to receive help from man drives Job to God. Then ensues the great struggle in his heart between faith and doubt. Finally, the human sufferer begins to see the light of life; his tortured soul ascends to new heights of hope and courage; he may suffer on and even die, but his enlightened soul now utters that cry of triumph, 'My Vindicator lives!'

"Job was altogether right when he challenged the doctrine that God afflicts children in order to punish their parents. Job was ever ready to admit that God is righteous, but he longed for some soul-satisfying revelation of the personal character of the Eternal. And that is our mission on earth. No more shall suffering mortals be denied the comfort of knowing the love of God and understanding the mercy of the Father in heaven. While the speech of God spoken from the whirlwind was a majestic concept for the day of its utterance, you have already learned that the Father does not thus reveal himself, but rather that he speaks within the human heart as a still, small voice, saying, 'This is the way; walk therein.' Do you not comprehend that God dwells within you, that he has become what you are that he may make you what he is!"

Then Jesus made this final statement: "The Father in heaven does not willingly afflict the children of men. Man suffers, first, from the accidents of time and the imperfections of the evil of an immature physical existence. Next, he suffers the inexorable consequences of sin—the transgression of the laws of life and light. And finally, man reaps the harvest of his own iniquitous persistence in rebellion against the righteous rule of heaven on earth. But man's miseries are not a *personal* visitation of divine judgment. Man can, and will, do much to lessen his temporal sufferings. But once and for all be delivered from the superstition that God afflicts man at the behest of the evil one. Study the Book of Job just to discover how many wrong ideas of God even good men may honestly entertain; and then note how even the painfully afflicted Job found the God of comfort and salvation in spite of such erroneous teachings. At last his faith pierced the clouds of suffering to discern the light of life pouring forth from the Father as healing mercy and everlasting righteousness."

John pondered these sayings in his heart for many days. His entire afterlife was markedly changed as a result of this conversation with the Master in the garden, and he did much, in later times, to cause the other apostles to change their viewpoints regarding the source, nature, and purpose of commonplace human afflictions. But John never spoke of this conference until after the Master had departed.

7. THE MAN WITH THE WITHERED HAND

The second Sabbath before the departure of the apostles and the new corps of evangelists on the second preaching tour of Galilee, Jesus spoke in the

Capernaum synagogue on the "Joys of Righteous Living." When Jesus had finished speaking, a large group of those who were maimed, halt, sick, and afflicted crowded up around him, seeking healing. Also in this group were the apostles, many of the new evangelists, and the Pharisaic spies from Jerusalem. Everywhere that Jesus went (except when in the hills about the Father's business) the six Jerusalem spies were sure to follow.

The leader of the spying Pharisees, as Jesus stood talking to the people, induced a man with a withered hand to approach him and ask if it would be lawful to be healed on the Sabbath day or should he seek help on another day. When Jesus saw the man, heard his words, and perceived that he had been sent by the Pharisees, he said: "Come forward while I ask you a question. If you had a sheep and it should fall into a pit on the Sabbath day, would you reach down, lay hold on it, and lift it out? Is it lawful to do such things on the Sabbath day?" And the man answered: "Yes, Master, it would be lawful thus to do well on the Sabbath day." Then said Jesus, speaking to all of them: "I know wherefore you have sent this man into my presence. You would find cause for offense in me if you could tempt me to show mercy on the Sabbath day. In silence you all agreed that it was lawful to lift the unfortunate sheep out of the pit, even on the Sabbath, and I call you to witness that it is lawful to exhibit loving-kindness on the Sabbath day not only to animals but also to men. How much more valuable is a man than a sheep! I proclaim that it is lawful to do good to men on the Sabbath day." And as they all stood before him in silence, Jesus, addressing the man with the withered hand, said: "Stand up here by my side that all may see you. And now that you may know that it is my Father's will that you do good on the Sabbath day, if you have the faith to be healed, I bid you stretch out your hand."

And as this man stretched forth his withered hand, it was made whole. The people were minded to turn upon the Pharisees, but Jesus bade them be calm, saying: "I have just told you that it is lawful to do good on the Sabbath, to save life, but I did not instruct you to do harm and give way to the desire to kill." The angered Pharisees went away, and notwithstanding it was the Sabbath day, they hastened forthwith to Tiberias and took counsel with Herod, doing everything in their power to arouse his prejudice in order to secure the Herodians as allies against Jesus. But Herod refused to take action against Jesus, advising that they carry their complaints to Jerusalem.

This is the first case of a miracle to be wrought by Jesus in response to the challenge of his enemies. And the Master performed this so-called miracle, not as a demonstration of his healing power, but as an effective protest against making the Sabbath rest of religion a veritable bondage of meaningless restrictions upon all mankind. This man returned to his work as a stone mason, proving to be one of those whose healing was followed by a life of thanksgiving and righteousness.

8. LAST WEEK AT BETHSAIDA

The last week of the sojourn at Bethsaida the Jerusalem spies became much divided in their attitude toward Jesus and his teachings. Three of these Pharisees were tremendously impressed by what they had seen and heard. Meanwhile, at Jerusalem, Abraham, a young and influential member of the Sanhedrin, publicly espoused the teachings of Jesus and was baptized in the pool of Siloam by Abner. All Jerusalem was agog over this event, and messengers were immediately dispatched to Bethsaida recalling the six spying Pharisees.

The Greek philosopher who had been won for the kingdom on the previous tour of Galilee returned with certain wealthy Jews of Alexandria, and once more they invited Jesus to come to their city for the purpose of establishing a joint school of philosophy and religion as well as an infirmary for the sick. But Jesus courteously declined the invitation.

About this time there arrived at the Bethsaida encampment a trance prophet from Bagdad, one Kirmeth. This supposed prophet had peculiar visions when in trance and dreamed fantastic dreams when his sleep was disturbed. He created a considerable disturbance at the camp, and Simon Zelotes was in favor of dealing rather roughly with the self-deceived pretender, but Jesus intervened and allowed him entire freedom of action for a few days. All who heard his preaching soon recognized that his teaching was not sound as judged by the gospel of the kingdom. He shortly returned to Bagdad, taking with him only a half dozen unstable and erratic souls. But before Jesus interceded for the Bagdad prophet, David Zebedee, with the assistance of a self-appointed committee, had taken Kirmeth out into the lake and, after repeatedly plunging him into the water, had advised him to depart hence—to organize and build a camp of his own.

On this same day, Beth-Marion, a Phoenician woman, became so fanatical that she went out of her head and, after almost drowning from trying to walk on the water, was sent away by her friends.

The new Jerusalem convert, Abraham the Pharisee, gave all of his worldly goods to the apostolic treasury, and this contribution did much to make possible the immediate sending forth of the one hundred newly trained evangelists. Andrew had already announced the closing of the encampment, and everybody prepared either to go home or else to follow the evangelists into Galilee.

9. HEALING THE PARALYTIC

On Friday afternoon, October 1, when Jesus was holding his last meeting with the apostles, evangelists, and other leaders of the disbanding encampment, and with the six Pharisees from Jerusalem seated in the front row of this assembly in the spacious and enlarged front room of the Zebedee home, there occurred one of the strangest and most unique episodes of all Jesus' earth life. The Master was, at this time, speaking as he stood in this large room, which had been built to accommodate these gatherings during the rainy season. The house was entirely surrounded by a vast concourse of people who were straining their ears to catch some part of Jesus' discourse.

While the house was thus thronged with people and entirely surrounded by eager listeners, a man long afflicted with paralysis was carried down from Capernaum on a small couch by his friends. This paralytic had heard that Jesus was about to leave Bethsaida, and having talked with Aaron the stone mason, who had been so recently made whole, he resolved to be carried into Jesus' presence, where he could seek healing. His friends tried to gain entrance to Zebedee's house by both the front and back doors, but too many people were crowded together. But the paralytic refused to accept defeat; he directed his friends to procure ladders by which they ascended to the roof of the room in which Jesus was speaking, and after loosening the tiles, they boldly lowered the sick man on his couch by ropes until the afflicted one rested on the floor immediately in front of the Master. When Jesus saw what they had done, he ceased speaking, while those who were with him in the room marveled at the perseverance of the sick man and his friends. Said the paralytic: "Master, I would not disturb your teaching, but I am determined to be made whole. I am not like those who received healing and immediately forgot your teaching. I would be made whole that I might serve in the kingdom of heaven." Now, notwithstanding that this man's affliction had been brought upon him by his own misspent life, Jesus, seeing his faith, said to the paralytic: "Son, fear not; your sins are forgiven. Your faith shall save you."

When the Pharisees from Jerusalem, together with other scribes and lawyers who sat with them, heard this pronouncement by Jesus, they began to say to themselves: "How dare this man thus speak? Does he not understand that such words are blasphemy? Who can forgive sin but God?" Jesus, perceiving in his spirit that they thus reasoned within their own minds and among themselves, spoke to them, saying: "Why do you so reason in your hearts? Who are you that you sit in judgment over me? What is the difference whether I say to this paralytic, your sins are forgiven, or arise, take up your bed, and walk? But that you who witness all this may finally know that the Son of Man has authority and power on earth to forgive sins, I will say to this afflicted man, Arise, take up your bed, and go to your own house." And when Jesus had thus spoken, the paralytic arose, and as they made way for him, he walked out before them all. And those who saw these things were amazed. Peter dismissed the assemblage, while many prayed and glorified God, confessing that they had never before seen such strange happenings.

And it was about this time that the messengers of the Sanhedrin arrived to bid the six spies return to Jerusalem. When they heard this message, they fell to earnest debate among themselves; and after they had finished their discussions, the leader and two of his associates returned with the messengers to Jerusalem, while three of the spying Pharisees confessed faith in Jesus and, going immediately to the lake, were baptized by Peter and fellowshipped by the apostles as children of the kingdom.

PAPER 149

THE SECOND PREACHING TOUR

THE second public preaching tour of Galilee began on Sunday, October 3, A.D. 28, and continued for almost three months, ending on December 30. Participating in this effort were Jesus and his twelve apostles, assisted by the newly recruited corps of 117 evangelists and by numerous other interested persons. On this tour they visited Gadara, Ptolemais, Japhia, Dabaritta, Megiddo, Jezreel, Scythopolis, Tarichea, Hippos, Gamala, Bethsaida-Julias, and many other cities and villages.

Before the departure on this Sunday morning Andrew and Peter asked Jesus to give the final charge to the new evangelists, but the Master declined, saying that it was not his province to do those things which others could acceptably perform. After due deliberation it was decided that James Zebedee should administer the charge. At the conclusion of James's remarks Jesus said to the evangelists: "Go now forth to do the work as you have been charged, and later on, when you have shown yourselves competent and faithful, I will ordain you to preach the gospel of the kingdom."

On this tour only James and John traveled with Jesus. Peter and the other apostles each took with them about one dozen of the evangelists and maintained close contact with them while they carried on their work of preaching and teaching. As fast as believers were ready to enter the kingdom, the apostles would administer baptism. Jesus and his two companions traveled extensively during these three months, often visiting two cities in one day to observe the work of the evangelists and to encourage them in their efforts to establish the kingdom. This entire second preaching tour was principally an effort to afford practical experience for this corps of 117 newly trained evangelists.

Throughout this period and subsequently, up to the time of the final departure of Jesus and the twelve for Jerusalem, David Zebedee maintained a permanent headquarters for the work of the kingdom in his father's house at Bethsaida. This was the clearinghouse for Jesus' work on earth and the relay station for the messenger service which David carried on between the workers in various parts of Palestine and adjacent regions. He did all of this on his own initiative but with the approval of Andrew. David employed forty to fifty messengers in this intelligence division of the rapidly enlarging and extending work of the kingdom. While thus employed, he partially supported himself by spending some of his time at his old work of fishing.

1. THE WIDESPREAD FAME OF JESUS

By the time the camp at Bethsaida had been broken up, the fame of Jesus, particularly as a healer, had spread to all parts of Palestine and through all of

Syria and the surrounding countries. For weeks after they left Bethsaida, the sick continued to arrive, and when they did not find the Master, on learning from David where he was, they would go in search of him. On this tour Jesus did not deliberately perform any so-called miracles of healing. Nevertheless, scores of afflicted found restoration of health and happiness as a result of the reconstructive power of the intense faith which impelled them to seek for healing.

There began to appear about the time of this mission—and continued throughout the remainder of Jesus' life on earth—a peculiar and unexplained series of healing phenomena. In the course of this three months' tour more than one hundred men, women, and children from Judea, Idumea, Galilee, Syria, Tyre, and Sidon, and from beyond the Jordan were beneficiaries of this unconscious healing by Jesus and, returning to their homes, added to the enlargement of Jesus' fame. And they did this notwithstanding that Jesus would, every time he observed one of these cases of spontaneous healing, directly charge the beneficiary to "tell no man."

It was never revealed to us just what occurred in these cases of spontaneous or unconscious healing. The Master never explained to his apostles how these healings were effected, other than that on several occasions he merely said, "I perceive that power has gone forth from me." On one occasion he remarked when touched by an ailing child, "I perceive that life has gone forth from me."

In the absence of direct word from the Master regarding the nature of these cases of spontaneous healing, it would be presuming on our part to undertake to explain how they were accomplished, but it will be permissible to record our opinion of all such healing phenomena. We believe that many of these apparent miracles of healing, as they occurred in the course of Jesus' earth ministry, were the result of the coexistence of the following three powerful, potent, and associated influences:

1. The presence of strong, dominant, and living faith in the heart of the human being who persistently sought healing, together with the fact that such healing was desired for its spiritual benefits rather than for purely physical restoration.

2. The existence, concomitant with such human faith, of the great sympathy and compassion of the incarnated and mercy-dominated Creator Son of God, who actually possessed in his person almost unlimited and timeless creative healing powers and prerogatives.

3. Along with the faith of the creature and the life of the Creator it should also be noted that this God-man was the personified expression of the Father's will. If, in the contact of the human need and the divine power to meet it, the Father did not will otherwise, the two became one, and the healing occurred unconsciously to the human Jesus but was immediately recognized by his divine nature. The explanation, then, of many of these cases of healing must be found in a great law which has long been known to us, namely, What the Creator Son desires and the eternal Father wills IS.

It is, then, our opinion that, in the personal presence of Jesus, certain forms of profound human faith were literally and truly *compelling* in the manifestation of healing by certain creative forces and personalities of the universe who were at that time so intimately associated with the Son of Man. It therefore becomes a fact of record that Jesus did frequently suffer men to heal themselves in his presence by their powerful, personal faith.

Many others sought healing for wholly selfish purposes. A rich widow of Tyre, with her retinue, came seeking to be healed of her infirmities, which were many; and as she followed Jesus about through Galilee, she continued to offer more and more money, as if the power of God were something to be purchased by the highest bidder. But never would she become interested in the gospel of the kingdom; it was only the cure of her physical ailments that she sought.

2. ATTITUDE OF THE PEOPLE

Jesus understood the minds of men. He knew what was in the heart of man, and had his teachings been left as he presented them, the only commentary being the inspired interpretation afforded by his earth life, all nations and all religions of the world would speedily have embraced the gospel of the kingdom. The well-meant efforts of Jesus' early followers to restate his teachings so as to make them the more acceptable to certain nations, races, and religions, only resulted in making such teachings the less acceptable to all other nations, races, and religions.

The Apostle Paul, in his efforts to bring the teachings of Jesus to the favorable notice of certain groups in his day, wrote many letters of instruction and admonition. Other teachers of Jesus' gospel did likewise, but none of them realized that some of these writings would subsequently be brought together by those who would set them forth as the embodiment of the teachings of Jesus. And so, while so-called Christianity does contain more of the Master's gospel than any other religion, it does also contain much that Jesus did not teach. Aside from the incorporation of many teachings from the Persian mysteries and much of the Greek philosophy into early Christianity, two great mistakes were made:

1. The effort to connect the gospel teaching directly onto the Jewish theology, as illustrated by the Christian doctrines of the atonement—the teaching that Jesus was the sacrificed Son who would satisfy the Father's stern justice and appease the divine wrath. These teachings originated in a praiseworthy effort to make the gospel of the kingdom more acceptable to disbelieving Jews. Though these efforts failed as far as winning the Jews was concerned, they did not fail to confuse and alienate many honest souls in all subsequent generations.

2. The second great blunder of the Master's early followers, and one which all subsequent generations have persisted in perpetuating, was to organize the Christian teaching so completely about the *person* of Jesus. This overemphasis of the personality of Jesus in the theology of Christianity has worked to obscure his teachings, and all of this has made it increasingly difficult for Jews, Mohammedans, Hindus, and other Eastern religionists to accept the teachings of Jesus. We would not belittle the place of the person of Jesus in a religion which might bear his name, but we would not permit such consideration to eclipse his inspired life or to supplant his saving message: the fatherhood of God and the brotherhood of man.

The teachers of the religion of Jesus should approach other religions with the recognition of the truths which are held in common (many of which come directly or indirectly from Jesus' message) while they refrain from placing so much emphasis on the differences.

While, at that particular time, the fame of Jesus rested chiefly upon his reputation as a healer, it does not follow that it continued so to rest. As time passed, more and more he was sought for spiritual help. But it was the physical cures that made the most direct and immediate appeal to the common people. Jesus was increasingly sought by the victims of moral enslavement and mental harassments, and he invariably taught them the way of deliverance. Fathers sought his advice regarding the management of their sons, and mothers came for help in the guidance of their daughters. Those who sat in darkness came to him, and he revealed to them the light of life. His ear was ever open to the sorrows of mankind, and he always helped those who sought his ministry.

When the Creator himself was on earth, incarnated in the likeness of mortal flesh, it was inevitable that some extraordinary things should happen. But you should never approach Jesus through these so-called miraculous occurrences. Learn to approach the miracle through Jesus, but do not make the mistake of approaching Jesus through the miracle. And this admonition is warranted, notwithstanding that Jesus of Nazareth is the only founder of a religion who performed supermaterial acts on earth.

The most astonishing and the most revolutionary feature of Michael's mission on earth was his attitude toward women. In a day and generation when a man was not supposed to salute even his own wife in a public place, Jesus dared to take women along as teachers of the gospel in connection with his third tour of Galilee. And he had the consummate courage to do this in the face of the rabbinic teaching which declared that it was "better that the words of the law should be burned than delivered to women."

In one generation Jesus lifted women out of the disrespectful oblivion and the slavish drudgery of the ages. And it is the one shameful thing about the religion that presumed to take Jesus' name that it lacked the moral courage to follow this noble example in its subsequent attitude toward women.

As Jesus mingled with the people, they found him entirely free from the superstitions of that day. He was free from religious prejudices; he was never intolerant. He had nothing in his heart resembling social antagonism. While he complied with the good in the religion of his fathers, he did not hesitate to disregard man-made traditions of superstition and bondage. He dared to teach that catastrophes of nature, accidents of time, and other calamitous happenings are not visitations of divine judgments or mysterious dispensations of Providence. He denounced slavish devotion to meaningless ceremonials and exposed the fallacy of materialistic worship. He boldly proclaimed man's spiritual freedom and dared to teach that mortals of the flesh are indeed and in truth sons of the living God.

Jesus transcended all the teachings of his forebears when he boldly substituted clean hearts for clean hands as the mark of true religion. He put reality in the place of tradition and swept aside all pretensions of vanity and hypocrisy. And yet this fearless man of God did not give vent to destructive criticism or manifest an utter disregard of the religious, social, economic, and political usages of his day. He was not a militant revolutionist; he was a progressive evolutionist. He engaged in the destruction of that which *was* only when he simultaneously offered his fellows the superior thing which *ought to be.*

Jesus received the obedience of his followers without exacting it. Only three men who received his personal call refused to accept the invitation to discipleship. He exercised a peculiar drawing power over men, but he was not dictatorial. He commanded confidence, and no man ever resented his giving a command. He assumed absolute authority over his disciples, but no one ever objected. He permitted his followers to call him Master.

The Master was admired by all who met him except by those who entertained deep-seated religious prejudices or those who thought they discerned political dangers in his teachings. Men were astonished at the originality and authoritativeness of his teaching. They marveled at his patience in dealing with backward and troublesome inquirers. He inspired hope and confidence in the hearts of all who came under his ministry. Only those who had not met him feared him, and he was hated only by those who regarded him as the champion of that truth which was destined to overthrow the evil and error which they had determined to hold in their hearts at all cost.

On both friends and foes he exercised a strong and peculiarly fascinating influence. Multitudes would follow him for weeks, just to hear his gracious words and behold his simple life. Devoted men and women loved Jesus with a well-nigh superhuman affection. And the better they knew him the more they loved him. And all this is still true; even today and in all future ages, the more man comes to know this God-man, the more he will love and follow after him.

3. HOSTILITY OF THE RELIGIOUS LEADERS

Notwithstanding the favorable reception of Jesus and his teachings by the common people, the religious leaders at Jerusalem became increasingly alarmed and antagonistic. The Pharisees had formulated a systematic and dogmatic theology. Jesus was a teacher who taught as the occasion served; he was not a systematic teacher. Jesus taught not so much from the law as from life, by parables. (And when he employed a parable for illustrating his message, he designed to utilize just *one* feature of the story for that purpose. Many wrong ideas concerning the teachings of Jesus may be secured by attempting to make allegories out of his parables.)

The religious leaders at Jerusalem were becoming well-nigh frantic as a result of the recent conversion of young Abraham and by the desertion of the three spies who had been baptized by Peter, and who were now out with the evangelists on this second preaching tour of Galilee. The Jewish leaders were increasingly blinded by fear and prejudice, while their hearts were hardened by the continued rejection of the appealing truths of the gospel of the kingdom. When men shut off the appeal to the spirit that dwells within them, there is little that can be done to modify their attitude.

When Jesus first met with the evangelists at the Bethsaida camp, in concluding his address, he said: "You should remember that in body and mind—emotionally—men react individually. The only *uniform* thing about men is the indwelling spirit. Though divine spirits may vary somewhat in the nature and extent of their experience, they react uniformly to all spiritual appeals. Only through, and by appeal to, this spirit can mankind ever attain unity and brotherhood." But many of the leaders of the Jews had closed the doors of their hearts to the spiritual appeal of the gospel. From this day on they ceased not to plan and plot for the Master's destruction. They were convinced that Jesus must be apprehended, convicted, and executed as a religious offender, a violator of the cardinal teachings of the Jewish sacred law.

4. PROGRESS OF THE PREACHING TOUR

Jesus did very little public work on this preaching tour, but he conducted many evening classes with the believers in most of the cities and villages where he chanced to sojourn with James and John. At one of these evening sessions one of the younger evangelists asked Jesus a question about anger, and the Master, among other things, said in reply:

"Anger is a material manifestation which represents, in a general way, the measure of the failure of the spiritual nature to gain control of the combined intellectual and physical natures. Anger indicates your lack of tolerant brotherly love plus your lack of self-respect and self-control. Anger depletes the health, debases the mind, and handicaps the spirit teacher of man's soul. Have you not read in the Scriptures that 'wrath kills the foolish man,' and that man 'tears himself in his anger'? That 'he who is slow of wrath is of great understanding,' while 'he who is hasty of temper exalts folly'? You all know that 'a soft answer turns away wrath,' and how 'grievous words stir up anger.' 'Discretion defers anger,' while 'he who has no control over his own self is like a defenseless city without walls.' 'Wrath is cruel and anger is outrageous.' 'Angry men stir up strife, while the furious multiply their transgressions.' 'Be not hasty in spirit, for anger rests in the bosom of fools.'" Before Jesus ceased speaking, he said further: "Let your hearts be so dominated by love that your spirit guide will have little trouble in delivering you from the tendency to give vent to those outbursts of animal anger which are inconsistent with the status of divine sonship."

On this same occasion the Master talked to the group about the desirability of possessing well-balanced characters. He recognized that it was necessary for most men to devote themselves to the mastery of some vocation, but he deplored all tendency toward overspecialization, toward becoming narrow-minded and circumscribed in life's activities. He called attention to the fact that any virtue, if carried to extremes, may become a vice. Jesus always preached temperance and taught consistency—proportionate adjustment of life problems. He pointed out that overmuch sympathy and pity may degenerate into serious emotional instability; that enthusiasm may drive on into fanaticism. He discussed one of their former associates whose imagination had led him off into visionary and impractical undertakings. At the same time he warned them against the dangers of the dullness of overconservative mediocrity.

And then Jesus discoursed on the dangers of courage and faith, how they sometimes lead unthinking souls on to recklessness and presumption. He also showed how prudence and discretion, when carried too far, lead to cowardice and failure. He exhorted his hearers to strive for originality while they shunned all tendency toward eccentricity. He pleaded for sympathy without sentimentality, piety without sanctimoniousness. He taught reverence free from fear and superstition.

It was not so much what Jesus taught about the balanced character that impressed his associates as the fact that his own life was such an eloquent exemplification of his teaching. He lived in the midst of stress and storm, but he never wavered. His enemies continually laid snares for him, but they never entrapped him. The wise and learned endeavored to trip him, but he did not stumble. They sought to embroil him in debate, but his answers were always enlightening, dignified, and final. When he was interrupted in his discourses with multitudinous questions, his answers were always significant and conclusive. Never did he resort to ignoble tactics in meeting the continuous pressure of his enemies, who did not hesitate to employ every sort of false, unfair, and unrighteous mode of attack upon him.

While it is true that many men and women must assiduously apply themselves to some definite pursuit as a livelihood vocation, it is nevertheless wholly desirable that human beings should cultivate a wide range of cultural familiarity with life as it is lived on earth. Truly educated persons are not satisfied with remaining in ignorance of the lives and doings of their fellows.

5. LESSON REGARDING CONTENTMENT

When Jesus was visiting the group of evangelists working under the supervision of Simon Zelotes, during their evening conference Simon asked the Master: "Why are some persons so much more happy and contented than others? Is contentment a matter of religious experience?" Among other things, Jesus said in answer to Simon's question:

"Simon, some persons are naturally more happy than others. Much, very much, depends upon the willingness of man to be led and directed by the Father's spirit which lives within him. Have you not read in the Scriptures the words of the wise man, 'The spirit of man is the candle of the Lord, searching all the inward parts'? And also that such spirit-led mortals say: 'The lines are fallen to me in pleasant places; yes, I have a goodly heritage.' 'A little that a righteous man has is better than the riches of many wicked,' for 'a good man shall be satisfied from within himself.' 'A merry heart makes a cheerful countenance and is a continual feast. Better is a little with the reverence of the Lord than great treasure and trouble therewith. Better is a dinner of herbs where love is than a fatted ox and hatred therewith. Better is a little with righteousness than great revenues without rectitude.' 'A merry heart does good like a medicine.' 'Better is a handful with composure than a superabundance with sorrow and vexation of spirit.'

"Much of man's sorrow is born of the disappointment of his ambitions and the wounding of his pride. Although men owe a duty to themselves to make the best of their lives on earth, having thus sincerely exerted themselves, they should cheerfully accept their lot and exercise ingenuity in making the most of that which has fallen to their hands. All too many of man's troubles take origin in the fear soil of his own natural heart. 'The wicked flee when no man pursues.' 'The wicked are like the troubled sea, for it cannot rest, but its waters cast up mire and dirt; there is no peace, says God, for the wicked.'

"Seek not, then, for false peace and transient joy but rather for the assurance of faith and the sureties of divine sonship which yield composure, contentment, and supreme joy in the spirit."

Jesus hardly regarded this world as a "vale of tears." He rather looked upon it as the birth sphere of the eternal and immortal spirits of Paradise ascension, the "vale of soul making."

6. THE "FEAR OF THE LORD"

It was at Gamala, during the evening conference, that Philip said to Jesus: "Master, why is it that the Scriptures instruct us to 'fear the Lord,' while you would have us look to the Father in heaven without fear? How are we to harmonize these teachings?" And Jesus replied to Philip, saying:

"My children, I am not surprised that you ask such questions. In the beginning it was only through fear that man could learn reverence, but I have come to reveal the Father's love so that you will be attracted to the worship of the Eternal by the drawing of a son's affectionate recognition and reciprocation of the Father's profound and perfect love. I would deliver you from the bondage of driving yourselves through slavish fear to the irksome service of a jealous and wrathful King-God. I would instruct you in the Father-son relationship of God and man so that you may be joyfully led into that sublime and supernal free worship of a loving, just, and merciful Father-God.

"The 'fear of the Lord' has had different meanings in the successive ages, coming up from fear, through anguish and dread, to awe and reverence. And now from reverence I would lead you up, through recognition, realization, and appreciation, to *love.* When man recognizes only the works of God, he is led to fear the Supreme; but when man begins to understand and experience the personality and character of the living God, he is led increasingly to love such a good and perfect, universal and eternal Father. And it is just this changing of the relation of man to God that constitutes the mission of the Son of Man on earth.

"Intelligent children do not fear their father in order that they may receive good gifts from his hand; but having already received the abundance of good things bestowed by the dictates of the father's affection for his sons and daughters, these much loved children are led to love their father in responsive recognition and appreciation of such munificent beneficence. The goodness of God leads to repentance; the beneficence of God leads to service; the mercy of God leads to salvation; while the love of God leads to intelligent and free-hearted worship.

"Your forebears feared God because he was mighty and mysterious. You shall adore him because he is magnificent in love, plenteous in mercy, and glorious in truth. The power of God engenders fear in the heart of man, but the nobility and righteousness of his personality beget reverence, love, and willing worship. A dutiful and affectionate son does not fear or dread even a mighty and noble father. I have come into the world to put love in the place of fear, joy in the place of sorrow, confidence in the place of dread, loving service and appreciative worship in the place of slavish bondage and meaningless ceremonies. But it is still true of those who sit in darkness that 'the fear of the Lord is the beginning of wisdom.' But when the light has more fully come, the sons of God are led to praise the Infinite for what he *is* rather than to fear him for what he *does.*

"When children are young and unthinking, they must necessarily be admonished to honor their parents; but when they grow older and become somewhat more appreciative of the benefits of the parental ministry and protection, they are led up, through understanding respect and increasing affection, to that level of experience where they actually love their parents for what they are more than for what they have done. The father naturally loves his child, but the child must develop his love for the father from the fear of what the father can do, through awe, dread, dependence, and reverence, to the appreciative and affectionate regard of love.

"You have been taught that you should 'fear God and keep his commandments, for that is the whole duty of man.' But I have come to give you a new and higher commandment. I would teach you to 'love God and learn to do his will, for that is the highest privilege of the liberated sons of God.' Your fathers were taught to 'fear God—the Almighty King.' I teach you, 'Love God—the all-merciful Father.'

"In the kingdom of heaven, which I have come to declare, there is no high and mighty king; this kingdom is a divine family. The universally recognized and unreservedly worshiped center and head of this far-flung brotherhood of intelligent beings is my Father and your Father. I am his Son, and you are also his sons. Therefore it is eternally true that you and I are brethren in the heavenly estate, and all the more so since we have become brethren in the flesh of the earthly life. Cease, then, to fear God as a king or serve him as a master; learn to reverence him as the Creator; honor him as the Father of your spirit youth; love him as a merciful defender; and ultimately worship him as the loving and all-wise Father of your more mature spiritual realization and appreciation.

"Out of your wrong concepts of the Father in heaven grow your false ideas of humility and springs much of your hypocrisy. Man may be a worm of the dust by nature and origin, but when he becomes indwelt by my Father's spirit, that man becomes divine in his destiny. The bestowal spirit of my Father will surely return to the divine source and universe level of origin, and the human soul of mortal man which shall have become the reborn child of this indwelling spirit shall certainly ascend with the divine spirit to the very presence of the eternal Father.

"Humility, indeed, becomes mortal man who receives all these gifts from the Father in heaven, albeit there is a divine dignity attached to all such faith candidates for the eternal ascent of the heavenly kingdom. The meaningless and menial practices of an ostentatious and false humility are incompatible with the appreciation of the source of your salvation and the recognition of the destiny of your spirit-born souls. Humility before God is altogether appropriate in the depths of your hearts; meekness before men is commendable; but the hypocrisy of self-conscious and attention-craving humility is childish and unworthy of the enlightened sons of the kingdom.

"You do well to be meek before God and self-controlled before men, but let your meekness be of spiritual origin and not the self-deceptive display of a self-conscious sense of self-righteous superiority. The prophet spoke advisedly when he said, 'Walk humbly with God,' for, while the Father in heaven is the Infinite and the Eternal, he also dwells 'with him who is of a contrite mind and a humble spirit.' My Father disdains pride, loathes hypocrisy, and abhors iniquity. And it was to emphasize the value of sincerity and perfect trust in the loving support and faithful guidance of the heavenly Father that I have so often referred to the little child as illustrative of the attitude of mind and the response of spirit which are so essential to the entrance of mortal man into the spirit realities of the kingdom of heaven.

"Well did the Prophet Jeremiah describe many mortals when he said: 'You are near God in the mouth but far from him in the heart.' And have you not also read that direful warning of the prophet who said: 'The priests thereof teach for hire, and the prophets thereof divine for money. At the same time they profess piety and proclaim that the Lord is with them.' Have you not been well warned against those who 'speak peace to their neighbors when mischief is in their hearts,' those who 'flatter with the lips while the heart is given to double-dealing'? Of all the sorrows of a trusting man, none are so terrible as to be 'wounded in the house of a trusted friend.'"

7. RETURNING TO BETHSAIDA

Andrew, in consultation with Simon Peter and with the approval of Jesus, had instructed David at Bethsaida to dispatch messengers to the various preaching groups with instructions to terminate the tour and return to Bethsaida sometime on Thursday, December 30. By supper time on that rainy day all of the apostolic party and the teaching evangelists had arrived at the Zebedee home.

The group remained together over the Sabbath day, being accommodated in the homes of Bethsaida and near-by Capernaum, after which the entire party was granted a two weeks' recess to go home to their families, visit their friends, or go fishing. The two or three days they were together in Bethsaida were, indeed, exhilarating and inspiring; even the older teachers were edified by the young preachers as they narrated their experiences.

Of the 117 evangelists who participated in this second preaching tour of Galilee, only about seventy-five survived the test of actual experience and were on hand to be assigned to service at the end of the two weeks' recess. Jesus, with Andrew, Peter, James, and John, remained at the Zebedee home and spent much time in conference regarding the welfare and extension of the kingdom.

PAPER 150

THE THIRD PREACHING TOUR

On SUNDAY evening, January 16, A.D. 29, Abner, with the apostles of John, reached Bethsaida and went into joint conference with Andrew and the apostles of Jesus the next day. Abner and his associates made their headquarters at Hebron and were in the habit of coming up to Bethsaida periodically for these conferences.

Among the many matters considered by this joint conference was the practice of anointing the sick with certain forms of oil in connection with prayers for healing. Again did Jesus decline to participate in their discussions or to express himself regarding their conclusions. The apostles of John had always used the anointing oil in their ministry to the sick and afflicted, and they sought to establish this as a uniform practice for both groups, but the apostles of Jesus refused to bind themselves by such a regulation.

On Tuesday, January 18, the twenty-four were joined by the tested evangelists, about seventy-five in number, at the Zebedee house in Bethsaida preparatory to being sent forth on the third preaching tour of Galilee. This third mission continued for a period of seven weeks.

The evangelists were sent out in groups of five, while Jesus and the twelve traveled together most of the time, the apostles going out two and two to baptize believers as occasion required. For a period of almost three weeks Abner and his associates also worked with the evangelistic groups, advising them and baptizing believers. They visited Magdala, Tiberias, Nazareth, and all the principal cities and villages of central and southern Galilee, all the places previously visited and many others. This was their last message to Galilee, except to the northern portions.

1. THE WOMEN'S EVANGELISTIC CORPS

Of all the daring things which Jesus did in connection with his earth career, the most amazing was his sudden announcement on the evening of January 16: "On the morrow we will set apart ten women for the ministering work of the kingdom." At the beginning of the two weeks' period during which the apostles and the evangelists were to be absent from Bethsaida on their furlough, Jesus requested David to summon his parents back to their home and to dispatch messengers calling to Bethsaida ten devout women who had served in the administration of the former encampment and the tented infirmary. These women had all listened to the instruction given the young evangelists, but it had never occurred to either themselves or their teachers that Jesus would dare to commission women to teach the gospel of the kingdom and minister to the sick. These ten women selected and commissioned by Jesus were: Susanna, the daughter of the former chazan of the Nazareth synagogue; Joanna, the wife of Chuza, the steward of Herod Antipas; Elizabeth, the daughter of a wealthy Jew of Tiberias and Sepphoris; Martha, the elder sister of Andrew and Peter; Rachel, the sister-in-law of Jude, the Master's brother in the flesh; Nasanta, the daughter of Elman, the Syrian physician; Milcha, a cousin of the Apostle Thomas; Ruth, the eldest daughter of Matthew Levi; Celta, the daughter of a Roman centurion; and Agaman, a widow of Damascus. Subsequently, Jesus added two other women to this group—Mary Magdalene and Rebecca, the daughter of Joseph of Arimathea.

Jesus authorized these women to effect their own organization and directed Judas to provide funds for their equipment and for pack animals. The ten elected Susanna as their chief and Joanna as their treasurer. From this time on they furnished their own funds; never again did they draw upon Judas for support.

It was most astounding in that day, when women were not even allowed on the main floor of the synagogue (being confined to the women's gallery), to behold them being recognized as authorized teachers of the new gospel of the kingdom. The charge which Jesus gave these ten women as he set them apart for gospel teaching and ministry was the emancipation proclamation which set free all women and for all time; no more was man to look upon woman as his spiritual inferior. This was a decided shock to even the twelve apostles. Notwithstanding they had many times heard the Master say that "in the kingdom of heaven there is neither rich nor poor, free nor bond, male nor female, all are equally the sons and daughters of God," they were literally stunned when he proposed formally to commission these ten women as religious teachers and even to permit their traveling about with them. The whole country was stirred up by this proceeding, the enemies of Jesus making great capital out of this move, but everywhere the women believers in the good news stood stanchly behind their chosen sisters and voiced no uncertain approval of this tardy acknowledgment of woman's place in religious work. And this liberation of women, giving them due recognition, was practiced by the apostles immediately after the Master's departure, albeit they fell back to the olden customs in subsequent generations. Throughout the early days of the Christian church women teachers and ministers were called *deaconesses* and were accorded general recognition. But Paul, despite the fact that he conceded all this in theory, never really incorporated it into his own attitude and personally found it difficult to carry out in practice.

2. THE STOP AT MAGDALA

As the apostolic party journeyed from Bethsaida, the women traveled in the rear. During the conference time they always sat in a group in front and to the right of the speaker. Increasingly, women had become believers in the gospel of the kingdom, and it had been a source of much difficulty and no end of embarrassment when they had desired to hold personal converse with Jesus or one of the apostles. Now all this was changed. When any of the women believers desired to see the Master or confer with the apostles, they went to Susanna, and in company with one of the twelve women evangelists, they would go at once into the presence of the Master or one of his apostles.

It was at Magdala that the women first demonstrated their usefulness and vindicated the wisdom of their choosing. Andrew had imposed rather strict rules upon his associates about doing personal work with women, especially with those of questionable character. When the party entered Magdala, these ten women evangelists were free to enter the evil resorts and preach the glad tidings directly to all their inmates. And when visiting the sick, these women were able to draw very close in their ministry to their afflicted sisters. As the result of the ministry of these ten women (afterward known as the twelve women) at this place, Mary Magdalene was won for the kingdom. Through a succession of misfortunes and in consequence of the attitude of reputable society toward women who commit such errors of judgment, this woman had found herself in one of the nefarious resorts of Magdala. It was Martha and Rachel who made plain to Mary that the doors of the kingdom were open to even such as she. Mary believed the good news and was baptized by Peter the next day.

Mary Magdalene became the most effective teacher of the gospel among this group of twelve women evangelists. She was set apart for such service, together with Rebecca, at Jotapata about four weeks subsequent to her conversion. Mary and Rebecca, with the others of this group, went on through the remainder of Jesus' life on earth, laboring faithfully and effectively for the enlightenment and uplifting of their downtrodden sisters; and when the last and tragic episode in the drama of Jesus' life was being enacted, notwithstanding the apostles all fled but one, these women were all present, and not one either denied or betrayed him.

3. SABBATH AT TIBERIAS

The Sabbath services of the apostolic party had been put in the hands of the women by Andrew, upon instructions from Jesus. This meant, of course, that they could not be held in the new synagogue. The women selected Joanna to have charge of this occasion, and the meeting was held in the banquet room of Herod's new palace, Herod being away in residence at Julias in Perea. Joanna read from the Scriptures concerning woman's work in the religious life of Israel, making reference to Miriam, Deborah, Esther, and others.

Late that evening Jesus gave the united group a memorable talk on "Magic and Superstition." In those days the appearance of a bright and supposedly new star was regarded as a token indicating that a great man had been born on earth. Such a star having then recently been observed, Andrew asked Jesus if these beliefs were well founded. In the long answer to Andrew's question the Master entered upon a thoroughgoing discussion of the whole subject of human superstition. The statement which Jesus made at this time may be summarized in modern phraseology as follows:

1. The courses of the stars in the heavens have nothing whatever to do with the events of human life on earth. Astronomy is a proper pursuit of science, but astrology is a mass of superstitious error which has no place in the gospel of the kingdom.

2. The examination of the internal organs of an animal recently killed can reveal nothing about weather, future events, or the outcome of human affairs.

3. The spirits of the dead do not come back to communicate with their families or their onetime friends among the living.

4. Charms and relics are impotent to heal disease, ward off disaster, or influence evil spirits; the belief in all such material means of influencing the spiritual world is nothing but gross superstition.

5. Casting lots, while it may be a convenient way of settling many minor difficulties, is not a method designed to disclose the divine will. Such outcomes are purely matters of material chance. The only means of communion with the spiritual world is embraced in the spirit endowment of mankind, the indwelling spirit of the Father, together with the outpoured spirit of the Son and the omnipresent influence of the Infinite Spirit.

6. Divination, sorcery, and witchcraft are superstitions of ignorant minds, as also are the delusions of magic. The belief in magic numbers, omens of good luck, and harbingers of bad luck, is pure and unfounded superstition.

7. The interpretation of dreams is largely a superstitious and groundless system of ignorant and fantastic speculation. The gospel of the kingdom must have nothing in common with the soothsayer priests of primitive religion.

8. The spirits of good or evil cannot dwell within material symbols of clay, wood, or metal; idols are nothing more than the material of which they are made.

9. The practices of the enchanters, the wizards, the magicians, and the sorcerers, were derived from the superstitions of the Egyptians, the Assyrians, the Babylonians, and the ancient Canaanites. Amulets and all sorts of incantations are futile either to win the protection of good spirits or to ward off supposed evil spirits.

10. He exposed and denounced their belief in spells, ordeals, bewitching, cursing, signs, mandrakes, knotted cords, and all other forms of ignorant and enslaving superstition.

4. SENDING THE APOSTLES OUT TWO AND TWO

The next evening, having gathered together the twelve apostles, the apostles of John, and the newly commissioned women's group, Jesus said: "You see for yourselves that the harvest is plenteous, but the laborers are few. Let us all, therefore, pray the Lord of the harvest that he send forth still more laborers into his fields. While I remain to comfort and instruct the younger teachers, I would send out the older ones two and two that they may pass quickly over all Galilee preaching the gospel of the kingdom while it is yet convenient and peaceful." Then he designated the pairs of apostles as he desired them to go forth, and they were: Andrew and Peter, James and John Zebedee, Philip and Nathaniel, Thomas and Matthew, James and Judas Alpheus, Simon Zelotes and Judas Iscariot.

Jesus arranged the date for meeting the twelve at Nazareth, and in parting, he said: "On this mission go not to any city of the gentiles, neither go into Samaria, but go instead to the lost sheep of the house of Israel. Preach the gospel of the kingdom and proclaim the saving truth that man is a son of God. Remember that the disciple is hardly above his master nor a servant greater than his lord. It is enough for the disciple to be equal with his master and the servant to become like his lord. If some people have dared to call the master of the house an associate of Beelzebub, how much more shall they so regard those of his household! But you should not fear these unbelieving enemies. I declare to you that there is nothing covered up that is not going to be revealed; there is nothing hidden that shall not be known. What I have taught you privately, that preach with wisdom in the open. What I have revealed to you in the inner chamber, that you are to proclaim in due season from the housetops. And I say to you, my friends and disciples, be not afraid of those who can kill the body, but who are not able to destroy the soul; rather put your trust in Him who is able to sustain the body and save the soul.

"Are not two sparrows sold for a penny? And yet I declare that not one of them is forgotten in God's sight. Know you not that the very hairs of your head are all numbered? Fear not, therefore; you are of more value than a great many sparrows. Be not ashamed of my teaching; go forth proclaiming peace and good will, but be not deceived—peace will not always attend your preaching. I came to bring peace on earth, but when men reject my gift, division and turmoil result. When all of a family receive the gospel of the kingdom, truly peace abides in that house; but when some of the family enter the kingdom and others reject the gospel, such division can produce only sorrow and sadness. Labor earnestly to save the whole family lest a man's foes become those of his own household. But, when you have done your utmost for all of every family, I declare to you that he who loves father or mother more than this gospel is not worthy of the kingdom."

When the twelve had heard these words, they made ready to depart. And they did not again come together until the time of their assembling at Nazareth to meet with Jesus and the other disciples as the Master had arranged.

5. WHAT MUST I DO TO BE SAVED?

One evening at Shunem, after John's apostles had returned to Hebron, and after Jesus' apostles had been sent out two and two, when the Master was engaged in teaching a group of twelve of the younger evangelists who were laboring under the direction of Jacob, together with the twelve women, Rachel asked Jesus this question: "Master, what shall we answer when women ask us, What shall I do to be saved?" When Jesus heard this question, he answered:

"When men and women ask what shall we do to be saved, you shall answer, Believe this gospel of the kingdom; accept divine forgiveness. By faith recognize the indwelling spirit of God, whose acceptance makes you a son of God. Have you not read in the Scriptures where it says, 'In the Lord have I righteousness and strength.' Also where the Father says, 'My righteousness is near; my salvation has gone forth, and my arms shall enfold my people.' 'My soul shall be joyful in the love of my God, for he has clothed me with the garments of salvation and has covered me with the robe of his righteousness.' Have you not also read of the Father that his name 'shall be called the Lord our righteousness.' 'Take away the filthy rags of self-righteousness and clothe my son with the robe of divine righteousness and eternal salvation.' It is forever true, 'the just shall live by faith.' Entrance into the Father's kingdom is wholly free, but progress—growth in grace—is essential to continuance therein.

"Salvation is the gift of the Father and is revealed by his Sons. Acceptance by faith on your part makes you a partaker of the divine nature, a son or a daughter of God. By faith you are justified; by faith are you saved; and by this same faith are you eternally advanced in the way of progressive and divine perfection. By faith was Abraham justified and made aware of salvation by the teachings of Melchizedek. All down through the ages has this same faith saved the sons of men, but now has a Son come forth from the Father to make salvation more real and acceptable."

When Jesus had left off speaking, there was great rejoicing among those who had heard these gracious words, and they all went on in the days that followed proclaiming the gospel of the kingdom with new power and with renewed energy and enthusiasm. And the women rejoiced all the more to know they were included in these plans for the establishment of the kingdom on earth.

In summing up his final statement, Jesus said: "You cannot buy salvation; you cannot earn righteousness. Salvation is the gift of God, and righteousness is the natural fruit of the spirit-born life of sonship in the kingdom. You are not to be saved because you live a righteous life; rather is it that you live a righteous life because you have already been saved, have recognized sonship as the gift of God and service in the kingdom as the supreme delight of life on earth. When men believe this gospel, which is a revelation of the goodness of God, they will be led to voluntary repentance of all known sin. Realization of sonship is incompatible with the desire to sin. Kingdom believers hunger for righteousness and thirst for divine perfection."

6. THE EVENING LESSONS

At the evening discussions Jesus talked upon many subjects. During the remainder of this tour—before they all reunited at Nazareth—he discussed "The Love of God," "Dreams and Visions," "Malice," "Humility and Meekness," "Courage and Loyalty," "Music and Worship," "Service and Obedience," "Pride and Presumption," "Forgiveness in Relation to Repentance," "Peace and Perfection," "Evil Speaking and Envy," "Evil, Sin, and Temptation," "Doubts and Unbelief," "Wisdom and Worship." With the older apostles away, these younger groups of both men and women more freely entered into these discussions with the Master.

After spending two or three days with one group of twelve evangelists, Jesus would move on to join another group, being informed as to the whereabouts and movements of all these workers by David's messengers. This being their first tour, the women remained much of the time with Jesus. Through the messenger service each of these groups was kept fully informed concerning the progress of the tour, and the receipt of news from other groups was always a source of encouragement to these scattered and separated workers.

Before their separation it had been arranged that the twelve apostles, together with the evangelists and the women's corps, should assemble at Nazareth to meet the Master on Friday, March 4. Accordingly, about this time, from all parts of central and southern Galilee these various groups of apostles and evangelists began moving toward Nazareth. By midafternoon, Andrew and Peter, the last to arrive, had reached the encampment prepared by the early arrivals and situated on the highlands to the north of the city. And this was the first time Jesus had visited Nazareth since the beginning of his public ministry.

7. THE SOJOURN AT NAZARETH

This Friday afternoon Jesus walked about Nazareth quite unobserved and wholly unrecognized. He passed by the home of his childhood and the carpenter shop and spent a half hour on the hill which he so much enjoyed when a lad. Not since the day of his baptism by John in the Jordan had the Son of Man had such a flood of human emotion stirred up within his soul. While coming down from the mount, he heard the familiar sounds of the trumpet blast announcing the going down of the sun, just as he had so many, many times heard it when a boy growing up in Nazareth. Before returning to the encampment, he walked down by the synagogue where he had gone to school and indulged his mind in many reminiscences of his childhood days. Earlier in the day Jesus had sent Thomas to arrange with the ruler of the synagogue for his preaching at the Sabbath morning service.

The people of Nazareth were never reputed for piety and righteous living. As the years passed, this village became increasingly contaminated by the low moral standards of near-by Sepphoris. Throughout Jesus' youth and young manhood there had been a division of opinion in Nazareth regarding him; there was much resentment when he moved to Capernaum. While the inhabitants of Nazareth had heard much about the doings of their former carpenter, they were offended that he had never included his native village in any of his earlier preaching tours. They had indeed heard of Jesus' fame, but the majority of the citizens were angry because he had done none of his great works in the city of his youth. For months the people of Nazareth had discussed Jesus much, but their opinions were, on the whole, unfavorable to him.

Thus did the Master find himself in the midst of, not a welcome homecoming, but a decidedly hostile and hypercritical atmosphere. But this was not all. His enemies, knowing that he was to spend this Sabbath day in Nazareth and supposing that he would speak in the synagogue, had hired numerous rough and uncouth men to harass him and in every way possible make trouble.

Most of the older of Jesus' friends, including the doting chazan teacher of his youth, were dead or had left Nazareth, and the younger generation was prone to resent his fame with strong jealousy. They failed to remember his early devotion to his father's family, and they were bitter in their criticism of his neglect to visit his brother and his married sisters living in Nazareth. The attitude of Jesus' family toward him had also tended to increase this unkind feeling of the citizenry. The orthodox among the Jews even presumed to criticize Jesus because he walked too fast on the way to the synagogue this Sabbath morning.

8. THE SABBATH SERVICE

This Sabbath was a beautiful day, and all Nazareth, friends and foes, turned out to hear this former citizen of their town discourse in the synagogue. Many of the apostolic retinue had to remain without the synagogue; there was not room for all who had come to hear him. As a young man Jesus had often spoken in this place of worship, and this morning, when the ruler of the synagogue handed him the roll of sacred writings from which to read the Scripture lesson, none present seemed to recall that this was the very manuscript which he had presented to this synagogue.

The services on this day were conducted just as when Jesus had attended them as a boy. He ascended the speaking platform with the ruler of the synagogue, and the service was begun by the recital of two prayers: "Blessed is the Lord, King of the world, who forms the light and creates the darkness, who makes peace and creates everything; who, in mercy, gives light to the earth and to those who dwell upon it and in goodness, day by day and every day, renews the works of creation. Blessed is the Lord our God for the glory of his handiworks and for the light-giving lights which he has made for his praise. Selah. Blessed is the Lord our God, who has formed the lights."

After a moment's pause they again prayed: "With great love has the Lord our God loved us, and with much overflowing pity has he pitied us, our Father and our King, for the sake of our fathers who trusted in him. You taught them the statutes of life; have mercy upon us and teach us. Enlighten our eyes in the law; cause our hearts to cleave to your commandments; unite our hearts to love and fear your name, and we shall not be put to shame, world without end. For you are a God who prepares salvation, and us have you chosen from among all nations and tongues, and in truth have you brought us near your great name—selah—that we may lovingly praise your unity. Blessed is the Lord, who in love chose his people Israel."

The congregation then recited the Shema, the Jewish creed of faith. This ritual consisted in repeating numerous passages from the law and indicated that the worshipers took upon themselves the yoke of the kingdom of heaven, also the yoke of the commandments as applied to the day and the night.

And then followed the third prayer: "True it is that you are Yahweh, our God and the God of our fathers; our King and the King of our fathers; our Savior and the Savior of our fathers; our Creator and the rock of our salvation; our help and our deliverer. Your name is from everlasting, and there is no God beside you. A new song did they that were delivered sing to your name by the seashore; together did all praise and own you King and say, Yahweh shall reign, world without end. Blessed is the Lord who saves Israel."

The ruler of the synagogue then took his place before the ark, or chest, containing the sacred writings and began the recitation of the nineteen prayer eulogies, or benedictions. But on this occasion it was desirable to shorten the service in order that the distinguished guest might have more time for his discourse; accordingly, only the first and last of the benedictions were recited. The first was: "Blessed is the Lord our God, and the God of our fathers, the God of Abraham, and the God of Isaac, and the God of Jacob; the great, the mighty, and the terrible God, who shows mercy and kindness, who creates all things, who remembers the gracious promises to the fathers and brings a savior to their children's children for his own name's sake, in love. O King, helper, savior, and shield! Blessed are you, O Yahweh, the shield of Abraham."

Then followed the last benediction: "O bestow on your people Israel great peace forever, for you are King and the Lord of all peace. And it is good in your eyes to bless Israel at all times and at every hour with peace. Blessed are you, Yahweh, who blesses his people Israel with peace." The congregation looked not at the ruler as he recited the benedictions. Following the benedictions he offered an informal prayer suitable for the occasion, and when this was concluded, all the congregation joined in saying amen.

Then the chazan went over to the ark and brought out a roll, which he presented to Jesus that he might read the Scripture lesson. It was customary to call upon seven persons to read not less than three verses of the law, but this practice was waived on this occasion that the visitor might read the lesson of his own selection. Jesus, taking the roll, stood up and began to read from Deuteronomy: "For this commandment which I give you this day is not hidden from you, neither is it far off. It is not in heaven, that you should say, who shall go up for us to heaven and bring it down to us that we may hear and do it? Neither is it beyond the sea, that you should say, who will go over the sea for us to bring the commandment to us that we may hear and do it? No, the word of life is very near to you, even in your presence and in your heart, that you may know and obey it."

And when he had ceased reading from the law, he turned to Isaiah and began to read: "The spirit of the Lord is upon me because he has anointed me to preach good tidings to the poor. He has sent me to proclaim release to the captives and the recovering of sight to the blind, to set at liberty those who are bruised and to proclaim the acceptable year of the Lord."

Jesus closed the book and, after handing it back to the ruler of the synagogue, sat down and began to discourse to the people. He began by saying: "Today are these Scriptures fulfilled." And then Jesus spoke for almost fifteen minutes on "The Sons and Daughters of God." Many of the people were pleased with the discourse, and they marveled at his graciousness and wisdom.

It was customary in the synagogue, after the conclusion of the formal service, for the speaker to remain so that those who might be interested could ask him questions. Accordingly, on this Sabbath morning Jesus stepped down into the crowd which pressed forward to ask questions. In this group were many turbulent individuals whose minds were bent on mischief, while about the fringe of this crowd there circulated those debased men who had been hired to make trouble for Jesus. Many of the disciples and evangelists who had remained without now pressed into the synagogue and were not slow to recognize that trouble was brewing. They sought to lead the Master away, but he would not go with them.

9. THE NAZARETH REJECTION

Jesus found himself surrounded in the synagogue by a great throng of his enemies and a sprinkling of his own followers, and in reply to their rude questions and sinister banterings he half humorously remarked: "Yes, I am Joseph's son; I am the carpenter, and I am not surprised that you remind me of the proverb, 'Physician heal yourself,' and that you challenge me to do in Nazareth what you have heard I did at Capernaum; but I call you to witness that even the Scriptures declare that 'a prophet is not without honor save in his own country and among his own people.'"

But they jostled him and, pointing accusing fingers at him, said: "You think you are better than the people of Nazareth; you moved away from us, but your brother is a common workman, and your sisters still live among us. We know your mother, Mary. Where are they today? We hear big things about you, but we notice that you do no wonders when you come back." Jesus answered them: "I love the people who dwell in the city where I grew up, and I would rejoice to see you all enter the kingdom of heaven, but the doing of the works of God is not for me to determine. The transformations of grace are wrought in response to the living faith of those who are the beneficiaries."

Jesus would have good-naturedly managed the crowd and effectively disarmed even his violent enemies had it not been for the tactical blunder of one of his own apostles, Simon Zelotes, who, with the help of Nahor, one of the younger evangelists, had meanwhile gathered together a group of Jesus' friends from among the crowd and, assuming a belligerent attitude, had served notice on the enemies of the Master to go hence. Jesus had long taught the apostles that a soft answer turns away wrath, but his followers were not accustomed to seeing their beloved teacher, whom they so willingly called Master, treated with such discourtesy and disdain. It was too much for them, and they found themselves giving expression to passionate and vehement resentment, all of which only tended to arouse the mob spirit in this ungodly and uncouth assembly. And so, under the leadership of hirelings, these ruffians laid hold upon Jesus and rushed him out of the synagogue to the brow of a near-by precipitous hill, where they were minded to shove him over the edge to his death below. But just as they were about to push him over the edge of the cliff, Jesus turned suddenly upon his captors and, facing them, quietly folded his arms. He said nothing, but his friends were more than astonished when, as he started to walk forward, the mob parted and permitted him to pass on unmolested.

Jesus, followed by his disciples, proceeded to their encampment, where all this was recounted. And they made ready that evening to go back to Capernaum early the next day, as Jesus had directed. This turbulent ending of the third public preaching tour had a sobering effect upon all of Jesus' followers. They were beginning to realize the meaning of some of the Master's teachings; they were awaking to the fact that the kingdom would come only through much sorrow and bitter disappointment.

They left Nazareth this Sunday morning, and traveling by different routes, they all finally assembled at Bethsaida by noon on Thursday, March 10. They came together as a sober and serious group of disillusioned preachers of the gospel of truth and not as an enthusiastic and all-conquering band of triumphant crusaders.

PAPER 151

TARRYING AND TEACHING BY THE SEASIDE

BY MARCH 10 all of the preaching and teaching groups had forgathered at Bethsaida. Thursday night and Friday many of them went out to fish, while on the Sabbath day they attended the synagogue to hear an aged Jew of Damascus discourse on the glory of father Abraham. Jesus spent most of this Sabbath day alone in the hills. That Saturday night the Master talked for more than an hour to the assembled groups on "The mission of adversity and the spiritual value of disappointment." This was a memorable occasion, and his hearers never forgot the lesson he imparted.

Jesus had not fully recovered from the sorrow of his recent rejection at Nazareth; the apostles were aware of a peculiar sadness mingled with his usual cheerful demeanor. James and John were with him much of the time, Peter being more than occupied with the many responsibilities having to do with the welfare and direction of the new corps of evangelists. This time of waiting before starting for the Passover at Jerusalem, the women spent in visiting from house to house, teaching the gospel, and ministering to the sick in Capernaum and the surrounding cities and villages.

1. THE PARABLE OF THE SOWER

About this time Jesus first began to employ the parable method of teaching the multitudes that so frequently gathered about him. Since Jesus had talked with the apostles and others long into the night, on this Sunday morning very few of the group were up for breakfast; so he went out by the seaside and sat alone in the boat, the old fishing boat of Andrew and Peter, which was always kept at his disposal, and meditated on the next move to be made in the work of extending the kingdom. But the Master was not to be alone for long. Very soon the people from Capernaum and near-by villages began to arrive, and by ten o'clock that morning almost one thousand were assembled on shore near Jesus' boat and were clamoring for attention. Peter was now up and, making his way to the boat, said to Jesus, "Master, shall I talk to them?" But Jesus answered, "No, Peter, I will tell them a story." And then Jesus began the recital of the parable of the sower, one of the first of a long series of such parables which he taught the throngs that followed after him. This boat had an elevated seat on which he sat (for it was the custom to sit when teaching) while he talked to the crowd assembled along the shore. After Peter had spoken a few words, Jesus said:

"A sower went forth to sow, and it came to pass as he sowed that some seed fell by the wayside to be trodden underfoot and devoured by the birds of heaven. Other seed fell upon the rocky places where there was little earth, and immediately it sprang up because there was no depth to the soil, but as soon as the sun shone, it withered because it had no root whereby to secure moisture. Other seed fell among the thorns, and as the thorns grew up, it was choked so that it yielded no grain. Still other seed fell upon good ground and, growing, yielded, some thirtyfold, some sixtyfold, and some a hundredfold." And when he had finished speaking this parable, he said to the multitude, "He who has ears to hear, let him hear."

The apostles and those who were with them, when they heard Jesus teach the people in this manner, were greatly perplexed; and after much talking among themselves, that evening in the Zebedee garden Matthew said to Jesus: "Master, what is the meaning of the dark sayings which you present to the multitude? Why do you speak in parables to those who seek the truth?" And Jesus answered:

"In patience have I instructed you all this time. To you it is given to know the mysteries of the kingdom of heaven, but to the undiscerning multitudes and to those who seek our destruction, from now on, the mysteries of the kingdom shall be presented in parables. And this we will do so that those who really desire to enter the kingdom may discern the meaning of the teaching and thus find salvation, while those who listen only to ensnare us may be the more confounded in that they will see without seeing and will hear without hearing. My children, do you not perceive the law of the spirit which decrees that to him who has shall be given so that he shall have an abundance; but from him who has not shall be taken away even that which he has. Therefore will I henceforth speak to the people much in parables to the end that our friends and those who desire to know the truth may find that which they seek, while our enemies and those who love not the truth may hear without understanding. Many of these people follow not in the way of the truth. The prophet did, indeed, describe all such undiscerning souls when he said: 'For this people's heart has waxed gross, and their ears are dull of hearing, and their eyes they have closed lest they should discern the truth and understand it in their hearts.'"

The apostles did not fully comprehend the significance of the Master's words. As Andrew and Thomas talked further with Jesus, Peter and the other apostles withdrew to another portion of the garden where they engaged in earnest and prolonged discussion.

2. INTERPRETATION OF THE PARABLE

Peter and the group about him came to the conclusion that the parable of the sower was an allegory, that each feature had some hidden meaning, and so they decided to go to Jesus and ask for an explanation. Accordingly, Peter approached the Master, saying: "We are not able to penetrate the meaning of this parable, and we desire that you explain it to us since you say it is given us to know the mysteries of the kingdom." And when Jesus heard this, he said to Peter: "My son, I desire to withhold nothing from you, but first suppose you tell me what you have been talking about; what is your interpretation of the parable?"

After a moment of silence, Peter said: "Master, we have talked much concerning the parable, and this is the interpretation I have decided upon: The sower is the gospel preacher; the seed is the word of God. The seed which fell by the wayside represents those who do not understand the gospel teaching. The birds which snatched away the seed that fell upon the hardened ground represent Satan, or the evil one, who steals away that which has been sown in the hearts of these ignorant ones. The seed which fell upon the rocky places, and which sprang up so suddenly, represents those superficial and unthinking persons who, when they hear the glad tidings, receive the message with joy; but because the truth has no real root in their deeper understanding, their devotion is short-lived in the face of tribulation and persecution. When trouble comes, these believers stumble; they fall away when tempted. The seed which fell among thorns represents those who hear the word willingly, but who allow the cares of the world and the deceitfulness of riches to choke the word of truth so that it becomes unfruitful. Now the seed which fell on good ground and sprang up to bear, some thirty, some sixty, and some a hundredfold, represents those who, when they have heard the truth, receive it with varying degrees of appreciation—owing to their differing intellectual endowments—and hence manifest these varying degrees of religious experience."

Jesus, after listening to Peter's interpretation of the parable, asked the other apostles if they did not also have suggestions to offer. To this invitation only Nathaniel responded. Said he: "Master, while I recognize many good things about Simon Peter's interpretation of the parable, I do not fully agree with him. My idea of this parable would be: The seed represents the gospel of the kingdom, while the sower stands for the messengers of the kingdom. The seed which fell by the wayside on hardened ground represents those who have heard but little of the gospel, along with those who are indifferent to the message, and who have hardened their hearts. The birds of the sky that snatched away the seed which fell by the wayside represent one's habits of life, the temptation of evil, and the desires of the flesh. The seed which fell among the rocks stands for those emotional souls who are quick to receive new teaching and equally quick to give up the truth when confronted with the difficulties and realities of living up to this truth; they lack spiritual perception. The seed which fell among the thorns represents those who are attracted to the truths of the gospel; they are minded to follow its teachings, but they are prevented by the pride of life, jealousy, envy, and the anxieties of human existence. The seed which fell on good soil, springing up to bear, some thirty, some sixty, and some a hundredfold, represents the natural and varying degrees of ability to comprehend truth and respond to its spiritual teachings by men and women who possess diverse endowments of spirit illumination."

When Nathaniel had finished speaking, the apostles and their associates fell into serious discussion and engaged in earnest debate, some contending for the correctness of Peter's interpretation, while almost an equal number sought to defend Nathaniel's explanation of the parable. Meanwhile Peter and Nathaniel had withdrawn to the house, where they were involved in a vigorous and determined effort the one to convince and change the mind of the other.

The Master permitted this confusion to pass the point of most intense expression; then he clapped his hands and called them about him. When they had all gathered around him once more, he said, "Before I tell you about this parable, do any of you have aught to say?" Following a moment of silence, Thomas spoke up: "Yes, Master, I wish to say a few words. I remember that you once told us to beware of this very thing. You instructed us that, when using illustrations for our preaching, we should employ true stories, not fables, and that we should select a story best suited to the illustration of the one central and vital truth which we wished to teach the people, and that, having so used the story, we should not attempt to make a spiritual application of all the minor details involved in the telling of the story. I hold that Peter and Nathaniel are both wrong in their attempts to interpret this parable. I admire their ability to do these things, but I am equally sure that all such attempts to make a natural parable yield spiritual analogies in all its features can only result in confusion and serious misconception of the true purpose of such a parable. That I am right is fully proved by the fact that, whereas we were all of one mind an hour ago, now are we divided into two separate groups who hold different opinions concerning this parable and hold such opinions so earnestly as to interfere, in my opinion, with our ability fully to grasp the great truth which you had in mind when you presented this parable to the multitude and subsequently asked us to make comment upon it."

The words which Thomas spoke had a quieting effect on all of them. He caused them to recall what Jesus had taught them on former occasions, and before Jesus resumed speaking, Andrew arose, saying: "I am persuaded that Thomas is right, and I would like to have him tell us what meaning he attaches to the parable of the sower." After Jesus had beckoned Thomas to speak, he said: "My brethren, I did not wish to prolong this discussion, but if you so desire, I will say that I think this parable was spoken to teach us one great truth. And that is that our teaching of the gospel of the kingdom, no matter how faithfully and efficiently we execute our divine commissions, is going to be attended by varying degrees of success; and that all such differences in results are directly due to conditions inherent in the circumstances of our ministry, conditions over which we have little or no control."

When Thomas had finished speaking, the majority of his fellow preachers were about ready to agree with him, even Peter and Nathaniel were on their way over to speak with him, when Jesus arose and said: "Well done, Thomas; you have discerned the true meaning of parables; but both Peter and Nathaniel have done you all equal good in that they have so fully shown the danger of undertaking to make an allegory out of my parables. In your own hearts you may often profitably engage in such flights of the speculative imagination, but you make a mistake when you seek to offer such conclusions as a part of your public teaching."

Now that the tension was over, Peter and Nathaniel congratulated each other on their interpretations, and with the exception of the Alpheus twins, each of the apostles ventured to make an interpretation of the parable of the sower before they retired for the night. Even Judas Iscariot offered a very plausible interpretation. The twelve would often, among themselves, attempt to figure out the Master's parables as they would an allegory, but never again did they regard such speculations seriously. This was a very profitable session for the apostles and their associates, especially so since from this time on Jesus more and more employed parables in connection with his public teaching.

3. MORE ABOUT PARABLES

The apostles were parable-minded, so much so that the whole of the next evening was devoted to the further discussion of parables. Jesus introduced the evening's conference by saying: "My beloved, you must always make a difference in teaching so as to suit your presentation of truth to the minds and hearts before you. When you stand before a multitude of varying intellects and temperaments, you cannot speak different words for each class of hearers, but you can tell a story to convey your teaching; and each group, even each individual, will be able to make his own interpretation of your parable in accordance with his own intellectual and spiritual endowments. You are to let your light shine but do so with wisdom and discretion. No man, when he lights a lamp, covers it up with a vessel or puts it under the bed; he puts his lamp on a stand where all can behold the light. Let me tell you that nothing is hid in the kingdom of heaven which shall not be made manifest; neither are there any secrets which shall not ultimately be made known. Eventually, all these things shall come to light. Think not only of the multitudes and how they hear the truth; take heed also to yourselves how you hear. Remember that I have many times told you: To him who has shall be given more, while from him who has not shall be taken away even that which he thinks he has."

The continued discussion of parables and further instruction as to their interpretation may be summarized and expressed in modern phraseology as follows:

1. Jesus advised against the use of either fables or allegories in teaching the truths of the gospel. He did recommend the free use of parables, especially nature parables. He emphasized the value of utilizing the *analogy* existing between the natural and the spiritual worlds as a means of teaching truth. He frequently alluded to the natural as "the unreal and fleeting shadow of spirit realities."

2. Jesus narrated three or four parables from the Hebrew scriptures, calling attention to the fact that this method of teaching was not wholly new. However, it became almost a new method of teaching as he employed it from this time onward.

3. In teaching the apostles the value of parables, Jesus called attention to the following points:

The parable provides for a simultaneous appeal to vastly different levels of mind and spirit. The parable stimulates the imagination, challenges the discrimination, and provokes critical thinking; it promotes sympathy without arousing antagonism.

The parable proceeds from the things which are known to the discernment of the unknown. The parable utilizes the material and natural as a means of introducing the spiritual and the supermaterial.

Parables favor the making of impartial moral decisions. The parable evades much prejudice and puts new truth gracefully into the mind and does all this with the arousal of a minimum of the self-defense of personal resentment.

To reject the truth contained in parabolical analogy requires conscious intellectual action which is directly in contempt of one's honest judgment and fair decision. The parable conduces to the forcing of thought through the sense of hearing.

The use of the parable form of teaching enables the teacher to present new and even startling truths while at the same time he largely avoids all controversy and outward clashing with tradition and established authority.

The parable also possesses the advantage of stimulating the memory of the truth taught when the same familiar scenes are subsequently encountered.

In this way Jesus sought to acquaint his followers with many of the reasons underlying his practice of increasingly using parables in his public teaching.

Toward the close of the evening's lesson Jesus made his first comment on the parable of the sower. He said the parable referred to two things: First, it was a review of his own ministry up to that time and a forecast of what lay ahead of him for the remainder of his life on earth. And second, it was also a hint as to what the apostles and other messengers of the kingdom might expect in their ministry from generation to generation as time passed.

Jesus also resorted to the use of parables as the best possible refutation of the studied effort of the religious leaders at Jerusalem to teach that all of his work was done by the assistance of demons and the prince of devils. The appeal to nature was in contravention of such teaching since the people of that day looked upon all natural phenomena as the product of the direct act of spiritual beings and supernatural forces. He also determined upon this method of teaching because it enabled him to proclaim vital truths to those who desired to know the better way while at the same time affording his enemies less opportunity to find cause for offense and for accusations against him.

Before he dismissed the group for the night, Jesus said: "Now will I tell you the last of the parable of the sower. I would test you to know how you will receive this: The kingdom of heaven is also like a man who cast good seed upon the earth; and while he slept by night and went about his business by day, the seed sprang up and grew, and although he knew not how it came about, the plant came to fruit. First there was the blade, then the ear, then the full grain in the ear. And then when the grain was ripe, he put forth the sickle, and the harvest was finished. He who has an ear to hear, let him hear."

Many times did the apostles turn this saying over in their minds, but the Master never made further mention of this addition to the parable of the sower.

4. MORE PARABLES BY THE SEA

The next day Jesus again taught the people from the boat, saying: "The kingdom of heaven is like a man who sowed good seed in his field; but while he slept, his enemy came and sowed weeds among the wheat and hastened away. And so when the young blades sprang up and later were about to bring forth fruit, there appeared also the weeds. Then the servants of this householder came and said to him: 'Sir, did you not sow good seed in your field? Whence then come these weeds?' And he replied to his servants, 'An enemy has done this.' The servants then asked their master, 'Would you have us go out and pluck up these weeds?' But he answered them and said: 'No, lest while you are gathering them up, you uproot the wheat also. Rather let them both grow together until the time of the harvest, when I will say to the reapers, Gather up first the weeds and bind them in bundles to burn and then gather up the wheat to be stored in my barn.'"

After the people had asked a few questions, Jesus spoke another parable: "The kingdom of heaven is like a grain of mustard seed which a man sowed in his field. Now a mustard seed is the least of seeds, but when it is full grown, it becomes the greatest of all herbs and is like a tree so that the birds of heaven are able to come and rest in the branches thereof."

"The kingdom of heaven is also like leaven which a woman took and hid in three measures of meal, and in this way it came about that all of the meal was leavened."

"The kingdom of heaven is also like a treasure hidden in a field, which a man discovered. In his joy he went forth to sell all he had that he might have the money to buy the field."

"The kingdom of heaven is also like a merchant seeking goodly pearls; and having found one pearl of great price, he went out and sold everything he possessed that he might be able to buy the extraordinary pearl."

"Again, the kingdom of heaven is like a sweep net which was cast into the sea, and it gathered up every kind of fish. Now, when the net was filled, the fishermen drew it up on the beach, where they sat down and sorted out the fish, gathering the good into vessels while the bad they threw away."

Many other parables spoke Jesus to the multitudes. In fact, from this time forward he seldom taught the masses except by this means. After speaking to a public audience in parables, he would, during the evening classes, more fully and explicitly expound his teachings to the apostles and the evangelists.

5. THE VISIT TO KHERESA

The multitude continued to increase throughout the week. On Sabbath Jesus hastened away to the hills, but when Sunday morning came, the crowds returned. Jesus spoke to them in the early afternoon after the preaching of Peter, and when he had finished, he said to his apostles: "I am weary of the throngs; let us cross over to the other side that we may rest for a day."

On the way across the lake they encountered one of those violent and sudden windstorms which are characteristic of the Sea of Galilee, especially at this season of the year. This body of water is almost seven hundred feet below the level of the sea and is surrounded by high banks, especially on the west. There are steep gorges leading up from the lake into the hills, and as the heated air rises in a pocket over the lake during the day, there is a tendency after sunset for the cooling air of the gorges to rush down upon the lake. These gales come on quickly and sometimes go away just as suddenly.

It was just such an evening gale that caught the boat carrying Jesus over to the other side on this Sunday evening. Three other boats containing some of the younger evangelists were trailing after. This tempest was severe, notwithstanding that it was confined to this region of the lake, there being no evidence of a storm on the western shore. The wind was so strong that the waves began to wash over the boat. The high wind had torn the sail away before the apostles could furl it, and they were now entirely dependent on their oars as they laboriously pulled for the shore, a little more than a mile and a half distant.

Meanwhile Jesus lay asleep in the stern of the boat under a small overhead shelter. The Master was weary when they left Bethsaida, and it was to secure rest that he had directed them to sail him across to the other side. These ex-fishermen were strong and experienced oarsmen, but this was one of the worst gales they had ever encountered. Although the wind and the waves tossed their boat about as though it were a toy ship, Jesus slumbered on undisturbed. Peter was at the right-hand oar near the stern. When the boat began to fill with water, he dropped his oar and, rushing over to Jesus, shook him vigorously in order to awaken him, and when he was aroused, Peter said: "Master, don't you know we are in a violent storm? If you do not save us, we will all perish."

As Jesus came out in the rain, he looked first at Peter, and then peering into the darkness at the struggling oarsmen, he turned his glance back upon Simon Peter, who, in his agitation, had not yet returned to his oar, and said: "Why are all of you so filled with fear? Where is your faith? Peace, be quiet." Jesus had hardly uttered this rebuke to Peter and the other apostles, he had hardly bidden Peter seek peace wherewith to quiet his troubled soul, when the disturbed atmosphere, having established its equilibrium, settled down into a great calm. The angry waves almost immediately subsided, while the dark clouds, having spent themselves in a short shower, vanished, and the stars of heaven shone overhead. All this was purely coincidental as far as we can judge; but the apostles, particularly Simon Peter, never ceased to regard the episode as a nature miracle. It was especially easy for the men of that day to believe in nature miracles inasmuch as they firmly believed that all nature was a phenomenon directly under the control of spirit forces and supernatural beings.

Jesus plainly explained to the twelve that he had spoken to their troubled spirits and had addressed himself to their fear-tossed minds, that he had not commanded the elements to obey his word, but it was of no avail. The Master's followers always persisted in placing their own interpretation on all such coincidental occurrences. From this day on they insisted on regarding the Master as having absolute power over the natural elements. Peter never grew weary of reciting how "even the winds and the waves obey him."

It was late in the evening when Jesus and his associates reached the shore, and since it was a calm and beautiful night, they all rested in the boats, not going ashore until shortly after sunrise the next morning. When they were gathered together, about forty in all, Jesus said: "Let us go up into yonder hills and tarry for a few days while we ponder over the problems of the Father's kingdom."

6. THE KHERESA LUNATIC

Although most of the near-by eastern shore of the lake sloped up gently to the highlands beyond, at this particular spot there was a steep hillside, the shore in some places dropping sheer down into the lake. Pointing up to the side of the near-by hill, Jesus said: "Let us go up on this hillside for our breakfast and under some of the shelters rest and talk."

This entire hillside was covered with caverns which had been hewn out of the rock. Many of these niches were ancient sepulchres. About halfway up the hillside on a small, relatively level spot was the cemetery of the little village of Kheresa. As Jesus and his associates passed near this burial ground, a lunatic who lived in these hillside caverns rushed up to them. This demented man was well known about these parts, having onetime been bound with fetters and chains and confined in one of the grottoes. Long since he had broken his shackles and now roamed at will among the tombs and abandoned sepulchres.

This man, whose name was Amos, was afflicted with a periodic form of insanity. There were considerable spells when he would find some clothing and deport himself fairly well among his fellows. During one of these lucid intervals he had gone over to Bethsaida, where he heard the preaching of Jesus and the apostles, and at that time had become a halfhearted believer in the gospel of the kingdom. But soon a stormy phase of his trouble appeared, and he fled to the tombs, where he moaned, cried out aloud, and so conducted himself as to terrorize all who chanced to meet him.

When Amos recognized Jesus, he fell down at his feet and exclaimed: "I know you, Jesus, but I am possessed of many devils, and I beseech that you will not torment me." This man truly believed that his periodic mental affliction was due to the fact that, at such times, evil or unclean spirits entered into him and dominated his mind and body. His troubles were mostly emotional—his brain was not grossly diseased.

Jesus, looking down upon the man crouching like an animal at his feet, reached down and, taking him by the hand, stood him up and said to him: "Amos, you are not possessed of a devil; you have already heard the good news that you are a son of God. I command you to come out of this spell." And when Amos heard Jesus speak these words, there occurred such a transformation in his intellect that he was immediately restored to his right mind and the normal control of his emotions. By this time a considerable crowd had assembled from the near-by village, and these people, augmented by the swine herders from the highland above them, were astonished to see the lunatic sitting with Jesus and his followers, in possession of his right mind and freely conversing with them.

As the swine herders rushed into the village to spread the news of the taming of the lunatic, the dogs charged upon a small and untended herd of about thirty swine and drove most of them over a precipice into the sea. And it was this incidental occurrence, in connection with the presence of Jesus and the supposed miraculous curing of the lunatic, that gave origin to the legend that Jesus had cured Amos by casting a legion of devils out of him, and that these devils had entered into the herd of swine, causing them forthwith to rush headlong to their destruction in the sea below. Before the day was over, this episode was published abroad by the swine tenders, and the whole village believed it. Amos most certainly believed this story; he saw the swine tumbling over the brow of the hill shortly after his troubled mind had quieted down, and he always believed that they carried with them the very evil spirits which had so long tormented and afflicted him. And this had a good deal to do with the permanency of his cure. It is equally true that all of Jesus' apostles (save Thomas) believed that the episode of the swine was directly connected with the cure of Amos.

Jesus did not obtain the rest he was looking for. Most of that day he was thronged by those who came in response to the word that Amos had been cured, and who were attracted by the story that the demons had gone out of the lunatic into the herd of swine. And so, after only one night of rest, early Tuesday morning Jesus and his friends were awakened by a delegation of these swine-raising gentiles who had come to urge that he depart from their midst. Said their spokesman to Peter and Andrew: "Fishermen of Galilee, depart from us and take your prophet with you. We know he is a holy man, but the gods of our country do not know him, and we stand in danger of losing many swine. The fear of you has descended upon us, so that we pray you to go hence." And when Jesus heard them, he said to Andrew, "Let us return to our place."

As they were about to depart, Amos besought Jesus to permit him to go back with them, but the Master would not consent. Said Jesus to Amos: "Forget not that you are a son of God. Return to your own people and show them what great things God has done for you." And Amos went about publishing that Jesus had cast a legion of devils out of his troubled soul, and that these evil spirits had entered into a herd of swine, driving them to quick destruction. And he did not stop until he had gone into all the cities of the Decapolis, declaring what great things Jesus had done for him.

PAPER 152

EVENTS LEADING UP TO THE CAPERNAUM CRISIS

THE story of the cure of Amos, the Kheresa lunatic, had already reached Bethsaida and Capernaum, so that a great crowd was waiting for Jesus when his boat landed that Tuesday forenoon. Among this throng were the new observers from the Jerusalem Sanhedrin who had come down to Capernaum to find cause for the Master's apprehension and conviction. As Jesus spoke with those who had assembled to greet him, Jairus, one of the rulers of the synagogue, made his way through the crowd and, falling down at his feet, took him by the hand and besought that he would hasten away with him, saying: "Master, my little daughter, an only child, lies in my home at the point of death. I pray that you will come and heal her." When Jesus heard the request of this father, he said: "I will go with you."

As Jesus went along with Jairus, the large crowd which had heard the father's request followed on to see what would happen. Shortly before they reached the ruler's house, as they hastened through a narrow street and as the throng jostled him, Jesus suddenly stopped, exclaiming, "Someone touched me." And when those who were near him denied that they had touched him, Peter spoke up: "Master, you can see that this crowd presses you, threatening to crush us, and yet you say 'someone has touched me.' What do you mean?" Then Jesus said: "I asked who touched me, for I perceived that living energy had gone forth from me." As Jesus looked about him, his eyes fell upon a near-by woman, who, coming forward, knelt at his feet and said: "For years I have been afflicted with a scourging hemorrhage. I have suffered many things from many physicians; I have spent all my substance, but none could cure me. Then I heard of you, and I thought if I may but touch the hem of his garment, I shall certainly be made whole. And so I pressed forward with the crowd as it moved along until, standing near you, Master, I touched the border of your garment, and I was made whole; I know that I have been healed of my affliction."

When Jesus heard this, he took the woman by the hand and, lifting her up, said: "Daughter, your faith has made you whole; go in peace." It was her *faith* and not her *touch* that made her whole. And this case is a good illustration of many apparently miraculous cures which attended upon Jesus' earth career, but which he in no sense consciously willed. The passing of time demonstrated that this woman was really cured of her malady. Her faith was of the sort that laid direct hold upon the creative power resident in the Master's person. With the faith she had, it was only necessary to approach the Master's person. It was not at all necessary to touch his garment; that was merely the superstitious part of her belief. Jesus called this woman, Veronica of Caesarea-Philippi, into his presence to correct two errors which might have lingered in her mind, or which might have persisted in the minds of those who witnessed this healing: He did not want Veronica to go away thinking that her fear in attempting to steal her cure had been honored, or that her superstition in associating the touch of his garment with her healing had been effective. He desired all to know that it was her pure and living *faith* that had wrought the cure.

1. AT JAIRUS'S HOUSE

Jairus was, of course, terribly impatient of this delay in reaching his home; so they now hastened on at quickened pace. Even before they entered the ruler's yard, one of his servants came out, saying: "Trouble not the Master; your daughter is dead." But Jesus seemed not to heed the servant's words, for, taking with him Peter, James, and John, he turned and said to the grief-stricken father: "Fear not; only believe." When he entered the house, he found the flute-players already there with the mourners, who were making an unseemly tumult; already were the relatives engaged in weeping and wailing. And when he had put all the mourners out of the room, he went in with the father and mother and his three apostles. He had told the mourners that the damsel was not dead, but they laughed him to scorn. Jesus now turned to the mother, saying: "Your daughter is not dead; she is only asleep." And when the house had quieted down, Jesus, going up to where the child lay, took her by the hand and said, "Daughter, I say to you, awake and arise!" And when the girl heard these words, she immediately rose up and walked across the room. And presently, after she had recovered from her daze, Jesus directed that they should give her something to eat, for she had been a long time without food.

Since there was much agitation in Capernaum against Jesus, he called the family together and explained that the maiden had been in a state of coma following a long fever, and that he had merely aroused her, that he had not raised her from the dead. He likewise explained all this to his apostles, but it was futile; they all believed he had raised the little girl from the dead. What Jesus said in explanation of many of these apparent miracles had little effect on his followers. They were miracle-minded and lost no opportunity to ascribe another wonder to Jesus. Jesus and the apostles returned to Bethsaida after he had specifically charged all of them that they should tell no man.

When he came out of Jairus's house, two blind men led by a dumb boy followed him and cried out for healing. About this time Jesus' reputation as a healer was at its very height. Everywhere he went the sick and the afflicted were waiting for him. The Master now looked much worn, and all of his friends were becoming concerned lest he continue his work of teaching and healing to the point of actual collapse.

Jesus' apostles, let alone the common people, could not understand the nature and attributes of this God-man. Neither has any subsequent generation been able to evaluate what took place on earth in the person of Jesus of Nazareth. And there can never occur an opportunity for either science or religion to check up on these remarkable events for the simple reason that such an extraordinary situation can never again occur, either on this world or on any other world in Nebadon. Never again, on any world in this entire universe, will a being appear in the likeness of mortal flesh, at the same time embodying all the attributes of creative energy combined with spiritual endowments which transcend time and most other material limitations.

Never before Jesus was on earth, nor since, has it been possible so directly and graphically to secure the results attendant upon the strong and living faith of mortal men and women. To repeat these phenomena, we would have to go into the immediate presence of Michael, the Creator, and find him as he was in those days—the Son of Man. Likewise, today, while his absence prevents such material manifestations, you should refrain from placing any sort of limitation on the possible exhibition of his *spiritual power.* Though the Master is absent as a material being, he is present as a spiritual influence in the hearts of men. By going away from the world, Jesus made it possible for his spirit to live alongside that of his Father which indwells the minds of all mankind.

2. FEEDING THE FIVE THOUSAND

Jesus continued to teach the people by day while he instructed the apostles and evangelists at night. On Friday he declared a furlough of one week that all his followers might go home or to their friends for a few days before preparing to go up to Jerusalem for the Passover. But more than one half of his disciples refused to leave him, and the multitude was daily increasing in size, so much so that David Zebedee desired to establish a new encampment, but Jesus refused consent. The Master had so little rest over the Sabbath that on Sunday morning, March 27, he sought to get away from the people. Some of the evangelists were left to talk to the multitude while Jesus and the twelve planned to escape, unnoticed, to the opposite shore of the lake, where they proposed to obtain much needed rest in a beautiful park south of Bethsaida-Julias. This region was a favorite resorting place for Capernaum folks; they were all familiar with these parks on the eastern shore.

But the people would not have it so. They saw the direction taken by Jesus' boat, and hiring every craft available, they started out in pursuit. Those who could not obtain boats fared forth on foot to walk around the upper end of the lake.

By late afternoon more than a thousand persons had located the Master in one of the parks, and he spoke to them briefly, being followed by Peter. Many of these people had brought food with them, and after eating the evening meal, they gathered about in small groups while Jesus' apostles and disciples taught them.

Monday afternoon the multitude had increased to more than three thousand. And still—way into the evening—the people continued to flock in, bringing all manner of sick folks with them. Hundreds of interested persons had made their plans to stop over at Capernaum to see and hear Jesus on their way to the Passover, and they simply refused to be disappointed. By Wednesday noon about five thousand men, women, and children were assembled here in this park to the south of Bethsaida-Julias. The weather was pleasant, it being near the end of the rainy season in this locality.

Philip had provided a three days' supply of food for Jesus and the twelve, which was in the custody of the Mark lad, their boy of all chores. By afternoon of this, the third day for almost half of this multitude, the food the people had brought with them was nearly exhausted. David Zebedee had no tented city here to feed and accommodate the crowds. Neither had Philip made food provision for such a multitude. But the people, even though they were hungry, would not go away. It was being quietly whispered about that Jesus, desiring to avoid trouble with both Herod and the Jerusalem leaders, had chosen this quiet spot outside the jurisdiction of all his enemies as the proper place to be crowned king. The enthusiasm of the people was rising every hour. Not a word was said to Jesus, though, of course, he knew all that was going on. Even the twelve apostles were still tainted with such notions, and especially the younger evangelists. The apostles who favored this attempt to proclaim Jesus king were Peter, John, Simon Zelotes, and Judas Iscariot. Those opposing the plan were Andrew, James, Nathaniel, and Thomas. Matthew, Philip, and the Alpheus twins were noncommittal. The ringleader of this plot to make him king was Joab, one of the young evangelists.

This was the stage setting about five o'clock on Wednesday afternoon, when Jesus asked James Alpheus to summon Andrew and Philip. Said Jesus: "What shall we do with the multitude? They have been with us now three days, and many of them are hungry. They have no food." Philip and Andrew exchanged glances, and then Philip answered: "Master, you should send these people away so that they may go to the villages around about and buy themselves food." And Andrew, fearing the materialization of the king plot, quickly joined with Philip, saying: "Yes, Master, I think it best that you dismiss the multitude so that they may go their way and buy food while you secure rest for a season." By this time others of the twelve had joined the conference. Then said Jesus: "But I do not desire to send them away hungry; can you not feed them?" This was too much for Philip, and he spoke right up: "Master, in this country place where can we buy bread for this multitude? Two hundred denarii worth would not be enough for lunch."

Before the apostles had an opportunity to express themselves, Jesus turned to Andrew and Philip, saying: "I do not want to send these people away. Here they are, like sheep without a shepherd. I would like to feed them. What food have we with us?" While Philip was conversing with Matthew and Judas, Andrew sought out the Mark lad to ascertain how much was left of their store of provisions. He returned to Jesus, saying: "The lad has left only five barley loaves and two dried fishes"—and Peter promptly added, "We have yet to eat this evening."

For a moment Jesus stood in silence. There was a faraway look in his eyes. The apostles said nothing. Jesus turned suddenly to Andrew and said, "Bring me the loaves and fishes." And when Andrew had brought the basket to Jesus, the Master said: "Direct the people to sit down on the grass in companies of one hundred and appoint a leader over each group while you bring all of the evangelists here with us."

Jesus took up the loaves in his hands, and after he had given thanks, he broke the bread and gave to his apostles, who passed it on to their associates, who in turn carried it to the multitude. Jesus in like manner broke and distributed the fishes. And this multitude did eat and were filled. And when they had finished eating, Jesus said to the disciples: "Gather up the broken pieces that remain over so that nothing will be lost." And when they had finished gathering up the fragments, they had twelve basketfuls. They who ate of this extraordinary feast numbered about five thousand men, women, and children.

And this is the first and only nature miracle which Jesus performed as a result of his conscious preplanning. It is true that his disciples were disposed to call many things miracles which were not, but this was a genuine supernatural ministration. In this case, so we were taught, Michael multiplied food elements as he always does except for the elimination of the time factor and the visible life channel.

3. THE KING-MAKING EPISODE

The feeding of the five thousand by supernatural energy was another of those cases where human pity plus creative power equaled that which happened. Now that the multitude had been fed to the full, and since Jesus' fame was then and there augmented by this stupendous wonder, the project to seize the Master and proclaim him king required no further personal direction. The idea seemed to spread through the crowd like a contagion. The reaction of the multitude to this sudden and spectacular supplying of their physical needs was profound and overwhelming. For a long time the Jews had been taught that the Messiah, the son of David, when he should come, would cause the land again to flow with milk and honey, and that the bread of life would be bestowed upon them as manna from heaven was supposed to have fallen upon their forefathers in the wilderness. And was not all of this expectation now fulfilled right before their eyes? When this hungry, undernourished multitude had finished gorging itself with the wonder-food, there was but one unanimous reaction: "Here is our king." The wonder-working deliverer of Israel had come. In the eyes of these simple-minded people the power to feed carried with it the right to rule. No wonder, then, that the multitude, when it had finished feasting, rose as one man and shouted, "Make him king!"

This mighty shout enthused Peter and those of the apostles who still retained the hope of seeing Jesus assert his right to rule. But these false hopes were not to live for long. This mighty shout of the multitude had hardly ceased to reverberate from the near-by rocks when Jesus stepped upon a huge stone and, lifting up his right hand to command their attention, said: "My children, you mean well, but you are shortsighted and material-minded." There was a brief pause; this stalwart Galilean was there majestically posed in the enchanting glow of that eastern twilight. Every inch he looked a king as he continued to speak to this breathless multitude: "You would make me king, not because your souls have been lighted with a great truth, but because your stomachs have been filled with bread. How many times have I told you that my kingdom is not of this world? This kingdom of heaven which we proclaim is a spiritual brotherhood, and no man rules over it seated upon a material throne. My Father in heaven is the all-wise and the all-powerful Ruler over this spiritual brotherhood of the sons of God on earth. Have I so failed in revealing to you the Father of spirits that you would make a king of his Son in the flesh! Now all of you go hence to your own homes. If you must have a king, let the Father of lights be enthroned in the heart of each of you as the spirit Ruler of all things."

These words of Jesus sent the multitude away stunned and disheartened. Many who had believed in him turned back and followed him no more from that day. The apostles were speechless; they stood in silence gathered about the twelve baskets of the fragments of food; only the chore boy, the Mark lad, spoke, "And he refused to be our king." Jesus, before going off to be alone in the hills, turned to Andrew and said: "Take your brethren back to Zebedee's house and pray with them, especially for your brother, Simon Peter."

4. SIMON PETER'S NIGHT VISION

The apostles, without their Master—sent off by themselves—entered the boat and in silence began to row toward Bethsaida on the western shore of the lake. None of the twelve was so crushed and downcast as Simon Peter. Hardly a word was spoken; they were all thinking of the Master alone in the hills. Had he forsaken them? He had never before sent them all away and refused to go with them. What could all this mean?

Darkness descended upon them, for there had arisen a strong and contrary wind which made progress almost impossible. As the hours of darkness and hard rowing passed, Peter grew weary and fell into a deep sleep of exhaustion. Andrew and James put him to rest on the cushioned seat in the stern of the boat. While the other apostles toiled against the wind and the waves, Peter dreamed a dream; he saw a vision of Jesus coming to them walking on the sea. When the Master seemed to walk on by the boat, Peter cried out, "Save us, Master, save us." And those who were in the rear of the boat heard him say some of these words. As this apparition of the night season continued in Peter's mind, he dreamed that he heard Jesus say: "Be of good cheer; it is I; be not afraid." This was like the balm of Gilead to Peter's disturbed soul; it soothed his troubled spirit, so that (in his dream) he cried out to the Master: "Lord, if it really is you, bid me come and walk with you on the water." And when Peter started to walk upon the water, the boisterous waves frightened him, and as he was about to sink, he cried out, "Lord, save me!" And many of the twelve heard him utter this cry. Then Peter dreamed that Jesus came to the rescue and, stretching forth his hand, took hold and lifted him up, saying: "O, you of little faith, wherefore did you doubt?"

In connection with the latter part of his dream Peter arose from the seat whereon he slept and actually stepped overboard and into the water. And he awakened from his dream as Andrew, James, and John reached down and pulled him out of the sea.

To Peter this experience was always real. He sincerely believed that Jesus came to them that night. He only partially convinced John Mark, which explains why Mark left a portion of the story out of his narrative. Luke, the physician, who made careful search into these matters, concluded that the episode was a vision of Peter's and therefore refused to give place to this story in the preparation of his narrative.

5. BACK IN BETHSAIDA

Thursday morning, before daylight, they anchored their boat offshore near Zebedee's house and sought sleep until about noontime. Andrew was first up and, going for a walk by the sea, found Jesus, in company with their chore boy, sitting on a stone by the water's edge. Notwithstanding that many of the multitude and the young evangelists searched all night and much of the next day about the eastern hills for Jesus, shortly after midnight he and the Mark lad had started to walk around the lake and across the river, back to Bethsaida.

Of the five thousand who were miraculously fed, and who, when their stomachs were full and their hearts empty, would have made him king, only about five hundred persisted in following after him. But before these received word that he was back in Bethsaida, Jesus asked Andrew to assemble the twelve apostles and their associates, including the women, saying, "I desire to speak with them." And when all were ready, Jesus said:

"How long shall I bear with you? Are you all slow of spiritual comprehension and deficient in living faith? All these months have I taught you the truths of the kingdom, and yet are you dominated by material motives instead of spiritual considerations. Have you not even read in the Scriptures where Moses exhorted the unbelieving children of Israel, saying: 'Fear not, stand still and see the salvation of the Lord'? Said the singer: 'Put your trust in the Lord.' 'Be patient, wait upon the Lord and be of good courage. He shall strengthen your heart.' 'Cast your burden on the Lord, and he shall sustain you. Trust him at all times and pour out your heart to him, for God is your refuge.' 'He who dwells in the secret place of the Most High shall abide under the shadow of the Almighty.' 'It is better to trust the Lord than to put confidence in human princes.'

"And now do you all see that the working of miracles and the performance of material wonders will not win souls for the spiritual kingdom? We fed the multitude, but it did not lead them to hunger for the bread of life neither to thirst for the waters of spiritual righteousness. When their hunger was satisfied, they sought not entrance into the kingdom of heaven but rather sought to proclaim the Son of Man king after the manner of the kings of this world, only that they might continue to eat bread without having to toil therefor. And all this, in which many of you did more or less participate, does nothing to reveal the heavenly Father or to advance his kingdom on earth. Have we not sufficient enemies among the religious leaders of the land without doing that which is likely to estrange also the civil rulers? I pray that the Father will anoint your eyes that you may see and open your ears that you may hear, to the end that you may have full faith in the gospel which I have taught you."

Jesus then announced that he wished to withdraw for a few days of rest with his apostles before they made ready to go up to Jerusalem for the Passover, and he forbade any of the disciples or the multitude to follow him. Accordingly they went by boat to the region of Gennesaret for two or three days of rest and sleep. Jesus was preparing for a great crisis of his life on earth, and he therefore spent much time in communion with the Father in heaven.

The news of the feeding of the five thousand and the attempt to make Jesus king aroused widespread curiosity and stirred up the fears of both the religious leaders and the civil rulers throughout all Galilee and Judea. While this great miracle did nothing to further the gospel of the kingdom in the souls of material-minded and halfhearted believers, it did serve the purpose of bringing to a head the miracle-seeking and king-craving proclivities of Jesus' immediate family of apostles and close disciples. This spectacular episode brought an end to the early era of teaching, training, and healing, thereby preparing the way for the inauguration of this last year of proclaiming the higher and more spiritual phases of the new gospel of the kingdom—divine sonship, spiritual liberty, and eternal salvation.

6. AT GENNESARET

While resting at the home of a wealthy believer in the Gennesaret region, Jesus held informal conferences with the twelve every afternoon. The ambassadors of the kingdom were a serious, sober, and chastened group of disillusioned men. But even after all that had happened, and as subsequent events disclosed, these twelve men were not yet fully delivered from their inbred and long-cherished notions about the coming of the Jewish Messiah. Events of the preceding few weeks had moved too swiftly for these astonished fishermen to grasp their full significance. It requires time for men and women to effect radical and extensive changes in their basic and fundamental concepts of social conduct, philosophic attitudes, and religious convictions.

While Jesus and the twelve were resting at Gennesaret, the multitudes dispersed, some going to their homes, others going on up to Jerusalem for the Passover. In less than one month's time the enthusiastic and open followers of Jesus, who numbered more than fifty thousand in Galilee alone, shrank to less than five hundred. Jesus desired to give his apostles such an experience with the fickleness of popular acclaim that they would not be tempted to rely on such manifestations of transient religious hysteria after he should leave them alone in the work of the kingdom, but he was only partially successful in this effort.

The second night of their sojourn at Gennesaret the Master again told the apostles the parable of the sower and added these words: "You see, my children, the appeal to human feelings is transitory and utterly disappointing; the exclusive appeal to the intellect of man is likewise empty and barren; it is only by making your appeal to the spirit which lives within the human mind that you can hope to achieve lasting success and accomplish those marvelous transformations of human character that are presently shown in the abundant yielding of the genuine fruits of the spirit in the daily lives of all who are thus delivered from the darkness of doubt by the birth of the spirit into the light of faith—the kingdom of heaven."

Jesus taught the appeal to the emotions as the technique of arresting and focusing the intellectual attention. He designated the mind thus aroused and quickened as the gateway to the soul, where there resides that spiritual nature of man which must recognize truth and respond to the spiritual appeal of the gospel in order to afford the permanent results of true character transformations.

Jesus thus endeavored to prepare the apostles for the impending shock—the crisis in the public attitude toward him which was only a few days distant. He explained to the twelve that the religious rulers of Jerusalem would conspire with Herod Antipas to effect their destruction. The twelve began to realize more fully (though not finally) that Jesus was not going to sit on David's throne. They saw more fully that spiritual truth was not to be advanced by material wonders. They began to realize that the feeding of the five thousand and the popular movement to make Jesus king was the apex of the miracle-seeking, wonder-working expectance of the people and the height of Jesus' acclaim by the populace. They vaguely discerned and dimly foresaw the approaching times of spiritual sifting and cruel adversity. These twelve men were slowly awaking to the realization of the real nature of their task as ambassadors of the kingdom, and they began to gird themselves for the trying and testing ordeals of the last year of the Master's ministry on earth.

Before they left Gennesaret, Jesus instructed them regarding the miraculous feeding of the five thousand, telling them just why he engaged in this extraordinary manifestation of creative power and also assuring them that he did not thus yield to his sympathy for the multitude until he had ascertained that it was "according to the Father's will."

7. AT JERUSALEM

Sunday, April 3, Jesus, accompanied only by the twelve apostles, started from Bethsaida on the journey to Jerusalem. To avoid the multitudes and to attract as little attention as possible, they journeyed by way of Gerasa and Philadelphia. He forbade them to do any public teaching on this trip; neither did he permit them to teach or preach while sojourning in Jerusalem. They arrived at Bethany, near Jerusalem, late on Wednesday evening, April 6. For this one night they stopped at the home of Lazarus, Martha, and Mary, but the next day they separated. Jesus, with John, stayed at the home of a believer named Simon, near the house of Lazarus in Bethany. Judas Iscariot and Simon Zelotes stopped with friends in Jerusalem, while the rest of the apostles sojourned, two and two, in different homes.

Jesus entered Jerusalem only once during this Passover, and that was on the great day of the feast. Many of the Jerusalem believers were brought out by Abner to meet Jesus at Bethany. During this sojourn at Jerusalem the twelve learned how bitter the feeling was becoming toward their Master. They departed from Jerusalem all believing that a crisis was impending.

On Sunday, April 24, Jesus and the apostles left Jerusalem for Bethsaida, going by way of the coast cities of Joppa, Caesarea, and Ptolemais. Thence, overland they went by Ramah and Chorazin to Bethsaida, arriving on Friday, April 29. Immediately on reaching home, Jesus dispatched Andrew to ask of the ruler of the synagogue permission to speak the next day, that being the Sabbath, at the afternoon service. And Jesus well knew that that would be the last time he would ever be permitted to speak in the Capernaum synagogue.

PAPER 153
THE CRISIS AT CAPERNAUM

ON FRIDAY evening, the day of their arrival at Bethsaida, and on Sabbath morning, the apostles noticed that Jesus was seriously occupied with some momentous problem; they were cognizant that the Master was giving unusual thought to some important matter. He ate no breakfast and but little at noontide. All of Sabbath morning and the evening before, the twelve and their associates were gathered together in small groups about the house, in the garden, and along the seashore. There was a tension of uncertainty and a suspense of apprehension resting upon all of them. Jesus had said little to them since they left Jerusalem.

Not in months had they seen the Master so preoccupied and uncommunicative. Even Simon Peter was depressed, if not downcast. Andrew was at a loss to know what to do for his dejected associates. Nathaniel said they were in the midst of the "lull before the storm." Thomas expressed the opinion that "something out of the ordinary is about to happen." Philip advised David Zebedee to "forget about plans for feeding and lodging the multitude until we know what the Master is thinking about." Matthew was putting forth renewed efforts to replenish the treasury. James and John talked over the forthcoming sermon in the synagogue and speculated much as to its probable nature and scope. Simon Zelotes expressed the belief, in reality a hope, that "the Father in heaven may be about to intervene in some unexpected manner for the vindication and support of his Son," while Judas Iscariot dared to indulge the thought that possibly Jesus was oppressed with regrets that "he did not have the courage and daring to permit the five thousand to proclaim him king of the Jews."

It was from among such a group of depressed and disconsolate followers that Jesus went forth on this beautiful Sabbath afternoon to preach his epoch-making sermon in the Capernaum synagogue. The only word of cheerful greeting or well-wishing from any of his immediate followers came from one of the unsuspecting Alpheus twins, who, as Jesus left the house on his way to the synagogue, saluted him cheerily and said: "We pray the Father will help you, and that we may have bigger multitudes than ever."

1. THE SETTING OF THE STAGE

A distinguished congregation greeted Jesus at three o'clock on this exquisite Sabbath afternoon in the new Capernaum synagogue. Jairus presided and handed Jesus the Scriptures to read. The day before, fifty-three Pharisees and Sadducees had arrived from Jerusalem; more than thirty of the leaders and rulers of the neighboring synagogues were also present. These Jewish religious leaders were acting directly under orders from the Sanhedrin at Jerusalem, and they constituted the orthodox vanguard which had come to inaugurate open warfare on Jesus and his disciples. Sitting by the side of these Jewish leaders, in the synagogue seats of honor, were the official observers of Herod Antipas, who had been directed to ascertain the truth concerning the disturbing reports that an attempt had been made by the populace to proclaim Jesus the king of the Jews, over in the domains of his brother Philip.

Jesus comprehended that he faced the immediate declaration of avowed and open warfare by his increasing enemies, and he elected boldly to assume the offensive. At the feeding of the five thousand he had challenged their ideas of the material Messiah; now he chose again openly to attack their concept of the Jewish deliverer. This crisis, which began with the feeding of the five thousand, and which terminated with this Sabbath afternoon sermon, was the outward turning of the tide of popular fame and acclaim. Henceforth, the work of the kingdom was to be increasingly concerned with the more important task of winning lasting spiritual converts for the truly religious brotherhood of mankind. This sermon marks the crisis in the transition from the period of discussion, controversy, and decision to that of open warfare and final acceptance or final rejection.

The Master well knew that many of his followers were slowly but surely preparing their minds finally to reject him. He likewise knew that many of his disciples were slowly but certainly passing through that training of mind and that discipline of soul which would enable them to triumph over doubt and courageously to assert their full-fledged faith in the gospel of the kingdom. Jesus fully understood how men prepare themselves for the decisions of a crisis and the performance of sudden deeds of courageous choosing by the slow process of the reiterated choosing between the recurring situations of good and evil. He subjected his chosen messengers to repeated rehearsals in disappointment and provided them with frequent and testing opportunities for choosing between the right and the wrong way of meeting spiritual trials. He knew he could depend on his followers, when they met the final test, to make their vital decisions in accordance with prior and habitual mental attitudes and spirit reactions.

This crisis in Jesus' earth life began with the feeding of the five thousand and ended with this sermon in the synagogue; the crisis in the lives of the apostles began with this sermon in the synagogue and continued for a whole year, ending only with the Master's trial and crucifixion.

As they sat there in the synagogue that afternoon before Jesus began to speak, there was just one great mystery, just one supreme question, in the minds of all. Both his friends and his foes pondered just one thought, and that was: "Why did he himself so deliberately and effectively turn back the tide of popular enthusiasm?" And it was immediately before and immediately after this sermon that the doubts and disappointments of his disgruntled adherents grew into unconscious opposition and eventually turned into actual hatred. It was after this sermon in the synagogue that Judas Iscariot entertained his first conscious thought of deserting. But he did, for the time being, effectively master all such inclinations.

Everyone was in a state of perplexity. Jesus had left them dumfounded and confounded. He had recently engaged in the greatest demonstration of supernatural power to characterize his whole career. The feeding of the five thousand was the one event of his earth life which made the greatest appeal to the Jewish concept of the expected Messiah. But this extraordinary advantage was immediately and unexplainedly offset by his prompt and unequivocal refusal to be made king.

On Friday evening, and again on Sabbath morning, the Jerusalem leaders had labored long and earnestly with Jairus to prevent Jesus' speaking in the synagogue, but it was of no avail. Jairus's only reply to all this pleading was: "I have granted this request, and I will not violate my word."

2. THE EPOCHAL SERMON

Jesus introduced this sermon by reading from the law as found in Deuteronomy: "But it shall come to pass, if this people will not hearken to the voice of God, that the curses of transgression shall surely overtake them. The Lord shall cause you to be smitten by your enemies; you shall be removed into all the kingdoms of the earth. And the Lord shall bring you and the king you have set up over you into the hands of a strange nation. You shall become an astonishment, a proverb, and a byword among all nations. Your sons and your daughters shall go into captivity. The strangers among you shall rise high in authority while you are brought very low. And these things shall be upon you and your seed forever because you would not hearken to the word of the Lord. Therefore shall you serve your enemies who shall come against you. You shall endure hunger and thirst and wear this alien yoke of iron. The Lord shall bring against you a nation from afar, from the end of the earth, a nation whose tongue you shall not understand, a nation of fierce countenance, a nation which will have little regard for you. And they shall besiege you in all your towns until the high fortified walls wherein you have trusted come down; and all the land shall fall into their hands. And it shall come to pass that you will be driven to eat the fruit of your own bodies, the flesh of your sons and daughters, during this time of siege, because of the straitness wherewith your enemies shall press you."

And when Jesus had finished this reading, he turned to the Prophets and read from Jeremiah: "'If you will not hearken to the words of my servants the prophets whom I have sent you, then will I make this house like Shiloh, and I will make this city a curse to all the nations of the earth.' And the priests and the teachers heard Jeremiah speak these words in the house of the Lord. And it came to pass that, when Jeremiah had made an end of speaking all that the Lord had commanded him to speak to all the people, the priests and teachers laid hold of him, saying, 'You shall surely die.' And all the people crowded around Jeremiah in the house of the Lord. And when the princes of Judah heard these things, they sat in judgment on Jeremiah. Then spoke the priests and the teachers to the princes and to all the people, saying: 'This man is worthy to die, for he has prophesied against our city, and you have heard him with your own ears.' Then spoke Jeremiah to all the princes and to all the people: 'The Lord sent me to prophesy against this house and against this city all the words which you have heard. Now, therefore, amend your ways and reform your doings and obey the voice of the Lord your God that you may escape the evil which has been pronounced against you. As for me, behold I am in your hands. Do with me as seems good and right in your eyes. But know you for certain that, if you put me to death, you shall bring innocent blood upon yourselves and upon this people, for of a truth the Lord has sent me to speak all these words in your ears.'

"The priests and teachers of that day sought to kill Jeremiah, but the judges would not consent, albeit, for his words of warning, they did let him down by cords in a filthy dungeon until he sank in mire up to his armpits. That is what this people did to the Prophet Jeremiah when he obeyed the Lord's command to warn his brethren of their impending political downfall. Today, I desire to ask you: What will the chief priests and religious leaders of this people do with the man who dares to warn them of the day of their spiritual doom? Will you also seek to put to death the teacher who dares to proclaim the word of the Lord, and who fears not to point out wherein you refuse to walk in the way of light which leads to the entrance to the kingdom of heaven?

"What is it you seek as evidence of my mission on earth? We have left you undisturbed in your positions of influence and power while we preached glad tidings to the poor and the outcast. We have made no hostile attack upon that which you hold in reverence but have rather proclaimed new liberty for man's fear-ridden soul. I came into the world to reveal my Father and to establish on earth the spiritual brotherhood of the sons of God, the kingdom of heaven. And notwithstanding that I have so many times reminded you that my kingdom is not of this world, still has my Father granted you many manifestations of material wonders in addition to more evidential spiritual transformations and regenerations.

"What new sign is it that you seek at my hands? I declare that you already have sufficient evidence to enable you to make your decision. Verily, verily, I say to many who sit before me this day, you are confronted with the necessity of choosing which way you will go; and I say to you, as Joshua said to your forefathers, 'choose you this day whom you will serve.' Today, many of you stand at the parting of the ways.

"Some of you, when you could not find me after the feasting of the multitude on the other side, hired the Tiberias fishing fleet, which a week before had taken shelter near by during a storm, to go in pursuit of me, and what for? Not for truth and righteousness or that you might the better know how to serve and minister to your fellow men! No, but rather that you might have more bread for which you had not labored. It was not to fill your souls with the word of life, but only that you might fill the belly with the bread of ease. And long have you been taught that the Messiah, when he should come, would work those wonders which would make life pleasant and easy for all the chosen people. It is not strange, then, that you who have been thus taught should long for the loaves and the fishes. But I declare to you that such is not the mission of the Son of Man. I have come to proclaim spiritual liberty, teach eternal truth, and foster living faith.

"My brethren, hanker not after the meat which perishes but rather seek for the spiritual food that nourishes even to eternal life; and this is the bread of life which the Son gives to all who will take it and eat, for the Father has given the Son this life without measure. And when you asked me, 'What must we do to perform the works of God?' I plainly told you: 'This is the work of God, that you believe him whom he has sent.'"

And then said Jesus, pointing up to the device of a pot of manna which decorated the lintel of this new synagogue, and which was embellished with grape clusters: "You have thought that your forefathers in the wilderness ate manna—the bread of heaven—but I say to you that this was the bread of earth. While Moses did not give your fathers bread from heaven, my Father now stands ready to give you the true bread of life. The bread of heaven is that which comes down from God and gives eternal life to the men of the world. And when you say to me, Give us this living bread, I will answer: I am this bread of life. He who comes to me shall not hunger, while he who believes me shall never thirst. You have seen me, lived with me, and beheld my works, yet you believe not that I came forth from the Father. But to those who do believe—fear not. All those led of the Father shall come to me, and he who comes to me shall in nowise be cast out.

"And now let me declare to you, once and for all time, that I have come down upon the earth, not to do my own will, but the will of Him who sent me. And this is the final will of Him who sent me, that of all those he has given me I should not lose one. And this is the will of the Father: That every one who beholds the Son and who believes him shall have eternal life. Only yesterday did I feed you with bread for your bodies; today I offer you the bread of life for your hungry souls. Will you now take the bread of the spirit as you then so willingly ate the bread of this world?"

As Jesus paused for a moment to look over the congregation, one of the teachers from Jerusalem (a member of the Sanhedrin) rose up and asked: "Do I understand you to say that you are the bread which comes down from heaven, and that the manna which Moses gave to our fathers in the wilderness did not?" And Jesus answered the Pharisee, "You understood aright." Then said the Pharisee: "But are you not Jesus of Nazareth, the son of Joseph, the carpenter? Are not your father and mother, as well as your brothers and sisters, well known to many of us? How then is it that you appear here in God's house and declare that you have come down from heaven?"

By this time there was much murmuring in the synagogue, and such a tumult was threatened that Jesus stood up and said: "Let us be patient; the truth never suffers from honest examination. I am all that you say but more. The Father and I are one; the Son does only that which the Father teaches him, while all those who are given to the Son by the Father, the Son will receive to himself. You have read where it is written in the Prophets, 'You shall all be taught by God,' and that 'Those whom the Father teaches will hear also his Son.' Every one who yields to the teaching of the Father's indwelling spirit will eventually come to me. Not that any man has seen the Father, but the Father's spirit does live within man. And the Son who came down from heaven, he has surely seen the Father. And those who truly believe this Son already have eternal life.

"I am this bread of life. Your fathers ate manna in the wilderness and are dead. But this bread which comes down from God, if a man eats thereof, he shall never die in spirit. I repeat, I am this living bread, and every soul who attains the realization of this united nature of God and man shall live forever. And this bread of life which I give to all who will receive is my own living and combined nature. The Father in the Son and the Son one with the Father—that is my life-giving revelation to the world and my saving gift to all nations."

When Jesus had finished speaking, the ruler of the synagogue dismissed the congregation, but they would not depart. They crowded up around Jesus to ask more questions while others murmured and disputed among themselves. And this state of affairs continued for more than three hours. It was well past seven o'clock before the audience finally dispersed.

3. THE AFTER MEETING

Many were the questions asked Jesus during this after meeting. Some were asked by his perplexed disciples, but more were asked by caviling unbelievers who sought only to embarrass and entrap him.

One of the visiting Pharisees, mounting a lampstand, shouted out this question: "You tell us that you are the bread of life. How can you give us your flesh to eat or your blood to drink? What avail is your teaching if it cannot be carried out?" And Jesus answered this question, saying: "I did not teach you that my flesh is the bread of life nor that my blood is the water thereof. But I did say that my life in the flesh is a bestowal of the bread of heaven. The fact of the Word of God bestowed in the flesh and the phenomenon of the Son of Man subject to the will of God, constitute a reality of experience which is equivalent to the divine sustenance. You cannot eat my flesh nor can you drink my blood, but you can become one in spirit with me even as I am one in spirit with the Father. You can be nourished by the eternal word of God, which is indeed the bread of life, and which has been bestowed in the likeness of mortal flesh; and you can be watered in soul by the divine spirit, which is truly the water of life. The Father has sent me into the world to show how he desires to indwell and direct all men; and I have so lived this life in the flesh as to inspire all men likewise ever to seek to know and do the will of the indwelling heavenly Father."

Then one of the Jerusalem spies who had been observing Jesus and his apostles, said: "We notice that neither you nor your apostles wash your hands properly before you eat bread. You must well know that such a practice as eating with defiled and unwashed hands is a transgression of the law of the elders. Neither do you properly wash your drinking cups and eating vessels. Why is it that you show such disrespect for the traditions of the fathers and the laws of our elders?" And when Jesus heard him speak, he answered: "Why is it that you transgress the commandments of God by the laws of your tradition? The commandment says, 'Honor your father and your mother,' and directs that you share with them your substance if necessary; but you enact a law of tradition which permits undutiful children to say that the money wherewith the parents might have been assisted has been 'given to God.' The law of the elders thus relieves such crafty children of their responsibility, notwithstanding that the children subsequently use all such monies for their own comfort. Why is it that you in this way make void the commandment by your own tradition? Well did Isaiah prophesy of you hypocrites, saying: 'This people honors me with their lips, but their heart is far from me. In vain do they worship me, teaching as their doctrines the precepts of men.'

"You can see how it is that you desert the commandment while you hold fast to the tradition of men. Altogether willing are you to reject the word of God while you maintain your own traditions. And in many other ways do you dare to set up your own teachings above the law and the prophets."

Jesus then directed his remarks to all present. He said: "But hearken to me, all of you. It is not that which enters into the mouth that spiritually defiles the man, but rather that which proceeds out of the mouth and from the heart." But even the apostles failed fully to grasp the meaning of his words, for Simon Peter also asked him: "Lest some of your hearers be unnecessarily offended, would you explain to us the meaning of these words?" And then said Jesus to Peter:

"Are you also hard of understanding? Know you not that every plant which my heavenly Father has not planted shall be rooted up? Turn now your attention to those who would know the truth. You cannot compel men to love the truth. Many of these teachers are blind guides. And you know that, if the blind lead the blind, both shall fall into the pit. But hearken while I tell you the truth concerning those things which morally defile and spiritually contaminate men. I declare it is not that which enters the body by the mouth or gains access to the mind through the eyes and ears, that defiles the man. Man is only defiled by that evil which may originate within the heart, and which finds expression in the words and deeds of such unholy persons. Do you not know it is from the heart that there come forth evil thoughts, wicked projects of murder, theft, and adulteries, together with jealousy, pride, anger, revenge, railings, and false witness? And it is just such things that defile men, and not that they eat bread with ceremonially unclean hands."

The Pharisaic commissioners of the Jerusalem Sanhedrin were now almost convinced that Jesus must be apprehended on a charge of blasphemy or on one of flouting the sacred law of the Jews; wherefore their efforts to involve him in the discussion of, and possible attack upon, some of the traditions of the elders, or so-called oral laws of the nation. No matter how scarce water might be, these traditionally enslaved Jews would never fail to go through with the required ceremonial washing of the hands before every meal. It was their belief that "it is better to die than to transgress the commandments of the elders." The spies asked this question because it had been reported that Jesus had said, "Salvation is a matter of clean hearts rather than of clean hands." But such beliefs, when they once become a part of one's religion, are hard to get away from. Even many years after this day the Apostle Peter was still held in the bondage of fear to many of these traditions about things clean and unclean, only being finally delivered by experiencing an extraordinary and vivid dream. All of this can the better be understood when it is recalled that these Jews looked upon eating with unwashed hands in the same light as commerce with a harlot, and both were equally punishable by excommunication.

Thus did the Master elect to discuss and expose the folly of the whole rabbinic system of rules and regulations which was represented by the oral law—the traditions of the elders, all of which were regarded as more sacred and more binding upon the Jews than even the teachings of the Scriptures. And Jesus spoke out with less reserve because he knew the hour had come when he could do nothing more to prevent an open rupture of relations with these religious leaders.

4. LAST WORDS IN THE SYNAGOGUE

In the midst of the discussions of this after meeting, one of the Pharisees from Jerusalem brought to Jesus a distraught youth who was possessed of an unruly and rebellious spirit. Leading this demented lad up to Jesus, he said: "What can you do for such affliction as this? Can you cast out devils?" And when the Master looked upon the youth, he was moved with compassion and, beckoning for the lad to come to him, took him by the hand and said: "You know who I am; come out of him; and I charge one of your loyal fellows to see that you do not return." And immediately the lad was normal and in his right mind. And this is the first case where Jesus really cast an "evil spirit" out of a human being. All of the previous cases were only supposed possession of the devil; but this was a genuine case of demoniac possession, even such as sometimes occurred in those days and right up to the day of Pentecost, when the Master's spirit was poured out upon all flesh, making it forever impossible for these few celestial rebels to take such advantage of certain unstable types of human beings.

When the people marveled, one of the Pharisees stood up and charged that Jesus could do these things because he was in league with devils; that he admitted in the language which he employed in casting out this devil that they were known to each other; and he went on to state that the religious teachers and leaders at Jerusalem had decided that Jesus did all his so-called miracles by the power of Beelzebub, the prince of devils. Said the Pharisee: "Have nothing to do with this man; he is in partnership with Satan."

Then said Jesus: "How can Satan cast out Satan? A kingdom divided against itself cannot stand; if a house be divided against itself, it is soon brought to desolation. Can a city withstand a siege if it is not united? If Satan casts out Satan, he is divided against himself; how then shall his kingdom stand? But you should know that no one can enter into the house of a strong man and despoil his goods except he first overpower and bind that strong man. And so, if I by the power of Beelzebub cast out devils, by whom do your sons cast them out? Therefore shall they be your judges. But if I, by the spirit of God, cast out devils, then has the kingdom of God truly come upon you. If you were not blinded by prejudice and misled by fear and pride, you would easily perceive that one who is greater than devils stands in your midst. You compel me to declare that he who is not with me is against me, while he who gathers not with me scatters abroad. Let me utter a solemn warning to you who would presume, with your eyes open and with premeditated malice, knowingly to ascribe the works of God to the doings of devils! Verily, verily, I say to you, all your sins shall be forgiven, even all of your blasphemies, but whosoever shall blaspheme against God with deliberation and wicked intention shall never obtain forgiveness. Since such persistent workers of iniquity will never seek nor receive forgiveness, they are guilty of the sin of eternally rejecting divine forgiveness.

"Many of you have this day come to the parting of the ways; you have come to a beginning of the making of the inevitable choice between the will of the Father and the self-chosen ways of darkness. And as you now choose, so shall you eventually be. You must either make the tree good and its fruit good, or else will the tree become corrupt and its fruit corrupt. I declare that in my Father's eternal kingdom the tree is known by its fruits. But some of you who are as vipers, how can you, having already chosen evil, bring forth good fruits? After all, out of the abundance of the evil in your hearts your mouths speak."

Then stood up another Pharisee, who said: "Teacher, we would have you give us a predetermined sign which we will agree upon as establishing your authority and right to teach. Will you agree to such an arrangement?" And when Jesus heard this, he said: "This faithless and sign-seeking generation seeks a token, but no sign shall be given you other than that which you already have, and that which you shall see when the Son of Man departs from among you."

And when he had finished speaking, his apostles surrounded him and led him from the synagogue. In silence they journeyed home with him to Bethsaida. They were all amazed and somewhat terror-stricken by the sudden change in the

Master's teaching tactics. They were wholly unaccustomed to seeing him perform in such a militant manner.

5. THE SATURDAY EVENING

Time and again had Jesus dashed to pieces the hopes of his apostles, repeatedly had he crushed their fondest expectations, but no time of disappointment or season of sorrow had ever equaled that which now overtook them. And, too, there was now admixed with their depression a real fear for their safety. They were all surprisingly startled by the suddenness and completeness of the desertion of the populace. They were also somewhat frightened and disconcerted by the unexpected boldness and assertive determination exhibited by the Pharisees who had come down from Jerusalem. But most of all they were bewildered by Jesus' sudden change of tactics. Under ordinary circumstances they would have welcomed the appearance of this more militant attitude, but coming as it did, along with so much that was unexpected, it startled them.

And now, on top of all of these worries, when they reached home, Jesus refused to eat. For hours he isolated himself in one of the upper rooms. It was almost midnight when Joab, the leader of the evangelists, returned and reported that about one third of his associates had deserted the cause. All through the evening loyal disciples had come and gone, reporting that the revulsion of feeling toward the Master was general in Capernaum. The leaders from Jerusalem were not slow to feed this feeling of disaffection and in every way possible to seek to promote the movement away from Jesus and his teachings. During these trying hours the twelve women were in session over at Peter's house. They were tremendously upset, but none of them deserted.

It was a little after midnight when Jesus came down from the upper chamber and stood among the twelve and their associates, numbering about thirty in all. He said: "I recognize that this sifting of the kingdom distresses you, but it is unavoidable. Still, after all the training you have had, was there any good reason why you should stumble at my words? Why is it that you are filled with fear and consternation when you see the kingdom being divested of these lukewarm multitudes and these halfhearted disciples? Why do you grieve when the new day is dawning for the shining forth in new glory of the spiritual teachings of the kingdom of heaven? If you find it difficult to endure this test, what, then, will you do when the Son of Man must return to the Father? When and how will you prepare yourselves for the time when I ascend to the place whence I came to this world?

"My beloved, you must remember that it is the spirit that quickens; the flesh and all that pertains thereto is of little profit. The words which I have spoken to you are spirit and life. Be of good cheer! I have not deserted you. Many shall be offended by the plain speaking of these days. Already you have heard that many of my disciples have turned back; they walk no more with me. From the beginning I knew that these halfhearted believers would fall out by the way. Did I not choose you twelve men and set you apart as ambassadors of the kingdom? And now at such a time as this would you also desert? Let each of you look to his own faith, for one of you stands in grave danger." And when Jesus had finished speaking, Simon Peter said: "Yes, Lord, we are sad and perplexed, but we will never forsake you. You have taught us the words of eternal life. We have believed in you and followed with you all this time. We will not turn back, for we know that you are sent by God." And as Peter ceased speaking, they all with one accord nodded their approval of his pledge of loyalty.

Then said Jesus: "Go to your rest, for busy times are upon us; active days are just ahead."

PAPER 154

LAST DAYS AT CAPERNAUM

ON THE eventful Saturday night of April 30, as Jesus was speaking words of comfort and courage to his downcast and bewildered disciples, at Tiberias a council was being held between Herod Antipas and a group of special commissioners representing the Jerusalem Sanhedrin. These scribes and Pharisees urged Herod to arrest Jesus; they did their best to convince him that Jesus was stirring up the populace to dissension and even to rebellion. But Herod refused to take action against him as a political offender. Herod's advisers had correctly reported the episode across the lake when the people sought to proclaim Jesus king and how he rejected the proposal.

One of Herod's official family, Chuza, whose wife belonged to the women's ministering corps, had informed him that Jesus did not propose to meddle with the affairs of earthly rule; that he was only concerned with the establishment of the spiritual brotherhood of his believers, which brotherhood he called the kingdom of heaven. Herod had confidence in Chuza's reports, so much so that he refused to interfere with Jesus' activities. Herod was also influenced at this time, in his attitude toward Jesus, by his superstitious fear of John the Baptist. Herod was one of those apostate Jews who, while he believed nothing, feared everything. He had a bad conscience for having put John to death, and he did not want to become entangled in these intrigues against Jesus. He knew of many cases of sickness which had been apparently healed by Jesus, and he regarded him as either a prophet or a relatively harmless religious fanatic.

When the Jews threatened to report to Caesar that he was shielding a traitorous subject, Herod ordered them out of his council chamber. Thus matters rested for one week, during which time Jesus prepared his followers for the impending dispersion.

1. A WEEK OF COUNSEL

From May 1 to May 7 Jesus held intimate counsel with his followers at the Zebedee house. Only the tried and trusted disciples were admitted to these conferences. At this time there were only about one hundred disciples who had the moral courage to brave the opposition of the Pharisees and openly declare their adherence to Jesus. With this group he held sessions morning, afternoon, and evening. Small companies of inquirers assembled each afternoon by the seaside, where some of the evangelists or apostles discoursed to them. These groups seldom numbered more than fifty.

On Friday of this week official action was taken by the rulers of the Capernaum synagogue closing the house of God to Jesus and all his followers. This action was taken at the instigation of the Jerusalem Pharisees. Jairus resigned as chief ruler and openly aligned himself with Jesus.

The last of the seaside meetings was held on Sabbath afternoon, May 7. Jesus talked to less than one hundred and fifty who had assembled at that time. This Saturday night marked the time of the lowest ebb in the tide of popular regard for Jesus and his teachings. From then on there was a steady, slow, but more healthful and dependable growth in favorable sentiment; a new following was built up which was better grounded in spiritual faith and true religious experience. The more or less composite and compromising transition stage between the materialistic concepts of the kingdom held by the Master's followers and those more idealistic and spiritual concepts taught by Jesus, had now definitely ended. From now on there was a more open proclamation of the gospel of the kingdom in its larger scope and in its far-flung spiritual implications.

2. A WEEK OF REST

Sunday, May 8, A.D. 29, at Jerusalem, the Sanhedrin passed a decree closing all the synagogues of Palestine to Jesus and his followers. This was a new and unprecedented usurpation of authority by the Jerusalem Sanhedrin. Theretofore each synagogue had existed and functioned as an independent congregation of worshipers and was under the rule and direction of its own board of governors. Only the synagogues of Jerusalem had been subject to the authority of the Sanhedrin. This summary action of the Sanhedrin was followed by the resignation of five of its members. One hundred messengers were immediately dispatched to convey and enforce this decree. Within the short space of two weeks every synagogue in Palestine had bowed to this manifesto of the Sanhedrin except the synagogue at Hebron. The rulers of the Hebron synagogue refused to acknowledge the right of the Sanhedrin to exercise such jurisdiction over their assembly. This refusal to accede to the Jerusalem decree was based on their contention of congregational autonomy rather than on sympathy with Jesus' cause. Shortly thereafter the Hebron synagogue was destroyed by fire.

This same Sunday morning, Jesus declared a week's holiday, urging all of his disciples to return to their homes or friends to rest their troubled souls and speak words of encouragement to their loved ones. He said: "Go to your several places to play or fish while you pray for the extension of the kingdom."

This week of rest enabled Jesus to visit many families and groups about the seaside. He also went fishing with David Zebedee on several occasions, and while he went about alone much of the time, there always lurked near by two or three of David's most trusted messengers, who had no uncertain orders from their chief respecting the safeguarding of Jesus. There was no public teaching of any sort during this week of rest.

This was the week that Nathaniel and James Zebedee suffered from more than a slight illness. For three days and nights they were acutely afflicted with a painful digestive disturbance. On the third night Jesus sent Salome, James's mother, to her rest, while he ministered to his suffering apostles. Of course Jesus could have instantly healed these two men, but that is not the method of either the Son or the Father in dealing with these commonplace difficulties and afflictions of the children of men on the evolutionary worlds of time and space. Never once, throughout all of his eventful life in the flesh, did Jesus engage in any sort of supernatural ministration to any member of his earth family or in behalf of any one of his immediate followers.

Universe difficulties must be met and planetary obstacles must be encountered as a part of the experience training provided for the growth and development, the progressive perfection, of the evolving souls of mortal creatures. The spiritualization of the human soul requires intimate experience with the educational solving of a wide range of real universe problems. The animal nature and the lower forms of will creatures do not progress favorably in environmental ease. Problematic situations, coupled with exertion stimuli, conspire to produce those activities of mind, soul, and spirit which contribute mightily to the achievement of worthy goals of mortal progression and to the attainment of higher levels of spirit destiny.

3. THE SECOND TIBERIAS CONFERENCE

On May 16 the second conference at Tiberias between the authorities at Jerusalem and Herod Antipas was convened. Both the religious and the political leaders from Jerusalem were in attendance. The Jewish leaders were able to report to Herod that practically all the synagogues in both Galilee and Judea were closed to Jesus' teachings. A new effort was made to have Herod place Jesus under arrest, but he refused to do their bidding. On May 18, however, Herod did agree to the plan of permitting the Sanhedrin authorities to seize Jesus and carry him to Jerusalem to be tried on religious charges, provided the Roman ruler of Judea concurred in such an arrangement. Meanwhile, Jesus' enemies were industriously spreading the rumor throughout Galilee that Herod had become hostile to Jesus, and that he meant to exterminate all who believed in his teachings.

On Saturday night, May 21, word reached Tiberias that the civil authorities at Jerusalem had no objection to the agreement between Herod and the Pharisees that Jesus be seized and carried to Jerusalem for trial before the Sanhedrin on charges of flouting the sacred laws of the Jewish nation. Accordingly, just before midnight of this day, Herod signed the decree which authorized the officers of the Sanhedrin to seize Jesus within Herod's domains and forcibly to carry him to Jerusalem for trial. Strong pressure from many sides was brought to bear upon Herod before he consented to grant this permission, and he well knew that Jesus could not expect a fair trial before his bitter enemies at Jerusalem.

4. SATURDAY NIGHT IN CAPERNAUM

On this same Saturday night, in Capernaum a group of fifty leading citizens met at the synagogue to discuss the momentous question: "What shall we do with Jesus?" They talked and debated until after midnight, but they could not find any common ground for agreement. Aside from a few persons who inclined to the belief that Jesus might be the Messiah, at least a holy man, or perhaps a prophet, the meeting was divided into four nearly equal groups who held, respectively, the following views of Jesus:

1. That he was a deluded and harmless religious fanatic.
2. That he was a dangerous and designing agitator who might stir up rebellion.

3. That he was in league with devils, that he might even be a prince of devils.

4. That he was beside himself, that he was mad, mentally unbalanced.

There was much talk about Jesus' preaching doctrines which were upsetting for the common people; his enemies maintained that his teachings were impractical, that everything would go to pieces if everybody made an honest effort to live in accordance with his ideas. And the men of many subsequent generations have said the same things. Many intelligent and well-meaning men, even in the more enlightened age of these revelations, maintain that modern civilization could not have been built upon the teachings of Jesus—and they are partially right. But all such doubters forget that a much better civilization could have been built upon his teachings, and sometime will be. This world has never seriously tried to carry out the teachings of Jesus on a large scale, notwithstanding that halfhearted attempts have often been made to follow the doctrines of so-called Christianity.

5. THE EVENTFUL SUNDAY MORNING

May 22 was an eventful day in the life of Jesus. On this Sunday morning, before daybreak, one of David's messengers arrived in great haste from Tiberias, bringing the word that Herod had authorized, or was about to authorize, the arrest of Jesus by the officers of the Sanhedrin. The receipt of the news of this impending danger caused David Zebedee to arouse his messengers and send them out to all the local groups of disciples, summoning them for an emergency council at seven o'clock that morning. When the sister-in-law of Jude (Jesus' brother) heard this alarming report, she hastened word to all of Jesus' family who dwelt near by, summoning them forthwith to assemble at Zebedee's house. And in response to this hasty call, presently there were assembled Mary, James, Joseph, Jude, and Ruth.

At this early morning meeting Jesus imparted his farewell instructions to the assembled disciples; that is, he bade them farewell for the time being, knowing well that they would soon be dispersed from Capernaum. He directed them all to seek God for guidance and to carry on the work of the kingdom regardless of consequences. The evangelists were to labor as they saw fit until such time as they might be called. He selected twelve of the evangelists to accompany him; the twelve apostles he directed to remain with him no matter what happened. The twelve women he instructed to remain at the Zebedee house and at Peter's house until he should send for them.

Jesus consented to David Zebedee's continuing his countrywide messenger service, and in bidding the Master farewell presently, David said: "Go forth to your work, Master. Don't let the bigots catch you, and never doubt that the messengers will follow after you. My men will never lose contact with you, and through them you shall know of the kingdom in other parts, and by them we will all know about you. Nothing that might happen to me will interfere with this service, for I have appointed first and second leaders, even a third. I am neither a teacher nor a preacher, but it is in my heart to do this, and none can stop me."

About 7:30 this morning Jesus began his parting address to almost one hundred believers who had crowded indoors to hear him. This was a solemn occasion for all present, but Jesus seemed unusually cheerful; he was once more like his normal self. The seriousness of weeks had gone, and he inspired all of them with his words of faith, hope, and courage.

6. JESUS' FAMILY ARRIVES

It was about eight o'clock on this Sunday morning when five members of Jesus' earth family arrived on the scene in response to the urgent summons of Jude's sister-in-law. Of all his family in the flesh, only one, Ruth, believed wholeheartedly and continuously in the divinity of his mission on earth. Jude and James, and even Joseph, still retained much of their faith in Jesus, but they had permitted pride to interfere with their better judgment and real spiritual inclinations. Mary was likewise torn between love and fear, between mother love and family pride. Though she was harassed by doubts, she could never quite forget the visit of Gabriel ere Jesus was born. The Pharisees had been laboring to persuade Mary that Jesus was beside himself, demented. They urged her to go with her sons and seek to dissuade him from further efforts at public teaching. They assured Mary that soon Jesus' health would break, and that only dishonor and disgrace could come upon the entire family as a result of allowing him to go on. And so, when the word came from Jude's sister-in-law, all five of them started at once for Zebedee's house, having been together at Mary's home, where they had met with the Pharisees the evening before. They had talked with the Jerusalem leaders long into the night, and all were more or less convinced that Jesus was acting strangely, that he had acted strangely for some time. While Ruth could not explain all of his conduct, she insisted that he had always treated his family fairly and refused to agree to the program of trying to dissuade him from further work.

On the way to Zebedee's house they talked these things over and agreed among themselves to try to persuade Jesus to come home with them, for, said Mary: "I know I could influence my son if he would only come home and listen to me." James and Jude had heard rumors concerning the plans to arrest Jesus and take him to Jerusalem for trial. They also feared for their own safety. As long as Jesus was a popular figure in the public eye, his family allowed matters to drift along, but now that the people of Capernaum and the leaders at Jerusalem had suddenly turned against him, they began keenly to feel the pressure of the supposed disgrace of their embarrassing position.

They had expected to meet Jesus, take him aside, and urge him to go home with them. They had thought to assure him that they would forget his neglect of them—they would forgive and forget—if he would only give up the foolishness of trying to preach a new religion which could bring only trouble to himself and dishonor upon his family. To all of this Ruth would say only: "I will tell my brother that I think he is a man of God, and that I hope he would be willing to die before he would allow these wicked Pharisees to stop his preaching." Joseph promised to keep Ruth quiet while the others labored with Jesus.

When they reached the Zebedee house, Jesus was in the very midst of delivering his parting address to the disciples. They sought to gain entrance to the house, but it was crowded to overflowing. Finally they established themselves on the back porch and had word passed in to Jesus, from person to person, so that it finally was whispered to him by Simon Peter, who interrupted his talking for the purpose, and who said: "Behold, your mother and your brothers are outside, and they are very anxious to speak with you." Now it did not occur to his mother how important was the giving of this parting message to his followers, neither did she know that his address was likely to be terminated any moment by the arrival of his apprehenders. She really thought, after so long an apparent estrangement, in view of the fact that she and his brothers had shown the grace actually to come to him, that Jesus would cease speaking and come to them the moment he received word they were waiting.

It was just another of those instances in which his earth family could not comprehend that he must be about his Father's business. And so Mary and his brothers were deeply hurt when, notwithstanding that he paused in his speaking to receive the message, instead of his rushing out to greet them, they heard his musical voice speak with increased volume: "Say to my mother and my brothers that they should have no fear for me. The Father who sent me into the world will not forsake me; neither shall any harm come upon my family. Bid them be of good courage and put their trust in the Father of the kingdom. But, after all, who is my mother and who are my brothers?" And stretching forth his hands toward all of his disciples assembled in the room, he said: "I have no mother; I have no brothers. Behold my mother and behold my brethren! For whosoever does the will of my Father who is in heaven, the same is my mother, my brother, and my sister."

And when Mary heard these words, she collapsed in Jude's arms. They carried her out in the garden to revive her while Jesus spoke the concluding words of his parting message. He would then have gone out to confer with his mother and his brothers, but a messenger arrived in haste from Tiberias bringing word that the officers of the Sanhedrin were on their way with authority to arrest Jesus and carry him to Jerusalem. Andrew received this message and, interrupting Jesus, told it to him.

Andrew did not recall that David had posted some twenty-five sentinels about the Zebedee house, and that no one could take them by surprise; so he asked Jesus what should be done. The Master stood there in silence while his mother, having heard the words, "I have no mother," was recovering from the shock in the garden. It was at just this time that a woman in the room stood up and exclaimed, "Blessed is the womb that bore you and blessed are the breasts that nursed you." Jesus turned aside a moment from his conversation with Andrew to answer this woman by saying, "No, rather is the one blessed who hears the word of God and dares to obey it."

Mary and Jesus' brothers thought that Jesus did not understand them, that he had lost interest in them, little realizing that it was they who failed to understand Jesus. Jesus fully understood how difficult it is for men to break with their past. He knew how human beings are swayed by the preacher's eloquence, and how the conscience responds to emotional appeal as the mind does to logic and reason, but he also knew how far more difficult it is to persuade men to *disown the past.*

It is forever true that all who may think they are misunderstood or not appreciated have in Jesus a sympathizing friend and an understanding counselor. He had warned his apostles that a man's foes may be they of his own household, but he had hardly realized how near this prediction would come to apply to his own experience. Jesus did not forsake his earth family to do his Father's work—they forsook him. Later on, after the Master's death and resurrection, when James became connected with the early Christian movement, he suffered immeasurably as a result of his failure to enjoy this earlier association with Jesus and his disciples.

In passing through these events, Jesus chose to be guided by the limited knowledge of his human mind. He desired to undergo the experience with his associates as a mere man. And it was in the human mind of Jesus to see his family before he left. He did not wish to stop in the midst of his discourse and thus render their first meeting after so long a separation such a public affair. He had intended to finish his address and then have a visit with them before leaving, but this plan was thwarted by the conspiracy of events which immediately followed.

The haste of their flight was augmented by the arrival of a party of David's messengers at the rear entrance of the Zebedee home. The commotion produced by these men frightened the apostles into thinking that these new arrivals might be their apprehenders, and in fear of immediate arrest, they hastened through the front entrance to the waiting boat. And all of this explains why Jesus did not see his family waiting on the back porch.

But he did say to David Zebedee as he entered the boat in hasty flight: "Tell my mother and my brothers that I appreciate their coming, and that I intended to see them. Admonish them to find no offense in me but rather to seek for a knowledge of the will of God and for grace and courage to do that will."

7. THE HASTY FLIGHT

And so it was on this Sunday morning, the twenty-second of May, in the year A.D. 29, that Jesus, with his twelve apostles and the twelve evangelists, engaged in this hasty flight from the Sanhedrin officers who were on their way to Bethsaida with authority from Herod Antipas to arrest him and take him to Jerusalem for trial on charges of blasphemy and other violations of the sacred laws of the Jews. It was almost half past eight this beautiful morning when this company of twenty-five manned the oars and pulled for the eastern shore of the Sea of Galilee.

Following the Master's boat was another and smaller craft, containing six of David's messengers, who had instructions to maintain contact with Jesus and his associates and to see that information of their whereabouts and safety was regularly transmitted to the home of Zebedee in Bethsaida, which had served as headquarters for the work of the kingdom for some time. But Jesus was never again to make his home at the house of Zebedee. From now on, throughout the remainder of his earth life, the Master truly "had not where to lay his head." No more did he have even the semblance of a settled abode.

They rowed over to near the village of Kheresa, put their boat in the custody of friends, and began the wanderings of this eventful last year of the Master's life on earth. For a time they remained in the domains of Philip, going from Kheresa up to Caesarea-Philippi, thence making their way over to the coast of Phoenicia.

The crowd lingered about the home of Zebedee watching these two boats make their way over the lake toward the eastern shore, and they were well started when the Jerusalem officers hurried up and began their search for Jesus. They refused to believe he had escaped them, and while Jesus and his party were journeying northward through Batanea, the Pharisees and their assistants spent almost a full week vainly searching for him in the neighborhood of Capernaum.

Jesus' family returned to their home in Capernaum and spent almost a week in talking, debating, and praying. They were filled with confusion and consternation. They enjoyed no peace of mind until Thursday afternoon, when Ruth returned from a visit to the Zebedee house, where she learned from David that her father-brother was safe and in good health and making his way toward the Phoenician coast.

PAPER 155

FLEEING THROUGH NORTHERN GALILEE

SOON after landing near Kheresa on this eventful Sunday, Jesus and the twenty-four went a little way to the north, where they spent the night in a beautiful park south of Bethsaida-Julias. They were familiar with this camping place, having stopped there in days gone by. Before retiring for the night, the Master called his followers around him and discussed with them the plans for their projected tour through Batanea and northern Galilee to the Phoenician coast.

1. WHY DO THE HEATHEN RAGE?

Said Jesus: "You should all recall how the Psalmist spoke of these times, saying, 'Why do the heathen rage and the peoples plot in vain? The kings of the earth set themselves, and the rulers of the people take counsel together, against the Lord and against his anointed, saying, Let us break the bonds of mercy asunder and let us cast away the cords of love.'

"Today you see this fulfilled before your eyes. But you shall not see the remainder of the Psalmist's prophecy fulfilled, for he entertained erroneous ideas about the Son of Man and his mission on earth. My kingdom is founded on love, proclaimed in mercy, and established by unselfish service. My Father does not sit in heaven laughing in derision at the heathen. He is not wrathful in his great displeasure. True is the promise that the Son shall have these so-called heathen (in reality his ignorant and untaught brethren) for an inheritance. And I will receive these gentiles with open arms of mercy and affection. All this loving-kindness shall be shown the so-called heathen, notwithstanding the unfortunate declaration of the record which intimates that the triumphant Son 'shall break them with a rod of iron and dash them to pieces like a potter's vessel.' The Psalmist exhorted you to 'serve the Lord with fear'—I bid you enter into the exalted privileges of divine sonship by faith; he commands you to rejoice with trembling; I bid you rejoice with assurance. He says, 'Kiss the Son, lest he be angry, and you perish when his wrath is kindled.' But you who have lived with me well know that anger and wrath are not a part of the establishment of the kingdom of heaven in the hearts of men. But the Psalmist did glimpse the true light when, in finishing this exhortation, he said: 'Blessed are they who put their trust in this Son.'"

Jesus continued to teach the twenty-four, saying: "The heathen are not without excuse when they rage at us. Because their outlook is small and narrow, they are able to concentrate their energies enthusiastically. Their goal is near and more or less visible; wherefore do they strive with valiant and effective execution. You who have professed entrance into the kingdom of heaven are altogether too vacillating and indefinite in your teaching conduct. The heathen strike directly for their objectives; you are guilty of too much chronic yearning. If you desire to enter the kingdom, why do you not take it by spiritual assault even as the heathen take a city they lay siege to? You are hardly worthy of the kingdom when your service consists so largely in an attitude of regretting the past, whining over the present, and vainly hoping for the future. Why do the heathen rage? Because they know not the truth. Why do you languish in futile yearning? Because you *obey* not the truth. Cease your useless yearning and go forth bravely doing that which concerns the establishment of the kingdom.

"In all that you do, become not one-sided and overspecialized. The Pharisees who seek our destruction verily think they are doing God's service. They have become so narrowed by tradition that they are blinded by prejudice and hardened by fear. Consider the Greeks, who have a science without religion, while the Jews have a religion without science. And when men become thus misled into accepting a narrow and confused disintegration of truth, their only hope of salvation is to become truth-co-ordinated—converted.

"Let me emphatically state this eternal truth: If you, by truth co-ordination, learn to exemplify in your lives this beautiful wholeness of righteousness, your fellow men will then seek after you that they may gain what you have so acquired. The measure wherewith truth seekers are drawn to you represents the measure of your truth endowment, your righteousness. The extent to which you have to go with your message to the people is, in a way, the measure of your failure to live the whole or righteous life, the truth-co-ordinated life."

And many other things the Master taught his apostles and the evangelists before they bade him good night and sought rest upon their pillows.

2. THE EVANGELISTS IN CHORAZIN

On Monday morning, May 23, Jesus directed Peter to go over to Chorazin with the twelve evangelists while he, with the eleven, departed for Caesarea-Philippi, going by way of the Jordan to the Damascus-Capernaum road, thence northeast to the junction with the road to Caesarea-Philippi, and then on into that city, where they tarried and taught for two weeks. They arrived during the afternoon of Tuesday, May 24.

Peter and the evangelists sojourned in Chorazin for two weeks, preaching the gospel of the kingdom to a small but earnest company of believers. But they were not able to win many new converts. No city of all Galilee yielded so few souls for the kingdom as Chorazin. In accordance with Peter's instructions the twelve evangelists had less to say about healing—things physical—while they preached and taught with increased vigor the spiritual truths of the heavenly kingdom. These two weeks at Chorazin constituted a veritable baptism of adversity for the twelve evangelists in that it was the most difficult and unproductive period in their careers up to this time. Being thus deprived of the satisfaction of winning souls for the kingdom, each of them the more earnestly and honestly took stock of his own soul and its progress in the spiritual paths of the new life.

When it appeared that no more people were minded to seek entrance into the kingdom, Peter, on Tuesday, June 7, called his associates together and departed for Caesarea-Philippi to join Jesus and the apostles. They arrived about noontime on Wednesday and spent the entire evening in rehearsing their experiences among the unbelievers of Chorazin. During the discussions of this evening Jesus made further reference to the parable of the sower and taught them much about the meaning of the apparent failure of life undertakings.

3. AT CAESAREA-PHILIPPI

Although Jesus did no public work during this two weeks' sojourn near Caesarea-Philippi, the apostles held numerous quiet evening meetings in the city, and many of the believers came out to the camp to talk with the Master. Very few were added to the group of believers as a result of this visit. Jesus talked with the apostles each day, and they more clearly discerned that a new phase of the work of preaching the kingdom of heaven was now beginning. They were commencing to comprehend that the "kingdom of heaven is not meat and drink but the realization of the spiritual joy of the acceptance of divine sonship."

The sojourn at Caesarea-Philippi was a real test to the eleven apostles; it was a difficult two weeks for them to live through. They were well-nigh depressed, and they missed the periodic stimulation of Peter's enthusiastic personality. In these times it was truly a great and testing adventure to believe in Jesus and go forth to follow after him. Though they made few converts during these two weeks, they did learn much that was highly profitable from their daily conferences with the Master.

The apostles learned that the Jews were spiritually stagnant and dying because they had crystallized truth into a creed; that when truth becomes formulated as a boundary line of self-righteous exclusiveness instead of serving as signposts of spiritual guidance and progress, such teachings lose their creative and life-giving power and ultimately become merely preservative and fossilizing.

Increasingly they learned from Jesus to look upon human personalities in terms of their possibilities in time and in eternity. They learned that many souls can best be led to love the unseen God by being first taught to love their brethren whom they can see. And it was in this connection that new meaning became attached to the Master's pronouncement concerning unselfish service for one's fellows: "Inasmuch as you did it to one of the least of my brethren, you did it to me."

One of the great lessons of this sojourn at Caesarea had to do with the origin of religious traditions, with the grave danger of allowing a sense of sacredness to become attached to nonsacred things, common ideas, or everyday events. From one conference they emerged with the teaching that true religion was man's heartfelt loyalty to his highest and truest convictions.

Jesus warned his believers that, if their religious longings were only material, increasing knowledge of nature would, by progressive displacement of the supposed supernatural origin of things, ultimately deprive them of their faith in God. But that, if their religion were spiritual, never could the progress of physical science disturb their faith in eternal realities and divine values.

They learned that, when religion is wholly spiritual in motive, it makes all life more worth while, filling it with high purposes, dignifying it with transcendent values, inspiring it with superb motives, all the while comforting the human soul with a sublime and sustaining hope. True religion is designed to lessen the strain of existence; it releases faith and courage for daily living and unselfish serving. Faith promotes spiritual vitality and righteous fruitfulness.

Jesus repeatedly taught his apostles that no civilization could long survive the loss of the best in its religion. And he never grew weary of pointing out to the twelve the great danger of accepting religious symbols and ceremonies in the place of religious experience. His whole earth life was consistently devoted to the mission of thawing out the frozen forms of religion into the liquid liberties of enlightened sonship.

4. ON THE WAY TO PHOENICIA

On Thursday morning, June 9, after receiving word regarding the progress of the kingdom brought by the messengers of David from Bethsaida, this group of twenty-five teachers of truth left Caesarea-Philippi to begin their journey to the Phoenician coast. They passed around the marsh country, by way of Luz, to the point of junction with the Magdala-Mount Lebanon trail road, thence to the crossing with the road leading to Sidon, arriving there Friday afternoon.

While pausing for lunch under the shadow of an overhanging ledge of rock, near Luz, Jesus delivered one of the most remarkable addresses which his apostles ever listened to throughout all their years of association with him. No sooner had they seated themselves to break bread than Simon Peter asked Jesus: "Master, since the Father in heaven knows all things, and since his spirit is our support in the establishment of the kingdom of heaven on earth, why is it that we flee from the threats of our enemies? Why do we refuse to confront the foes of truth?" But before Jesus had begun to answer Peter's question, Thomas broke in, asking: "Master, I should really like to know just what is wrong with the religion of our enemies at Jerusalem. What is the real difference between their religion and ours? Why is it we are at such diversity of belief when we all profess to serve the same God?" And when Thomas had finished, Jesus said: "While I would not ignore Peter's question, knowing full well how easy it would be to misunderstand my reasons for avoiding an open clash with the rulers of the Jews at just this time, still it will prove more helpful to all of you if I choose rather to answer Thomas's question. And that I will proceed to do when you have finished your lunch."

5. THE DISCOURSE ON TRUE RELIGION

This memorable discourse on religion, summarized and restated in modern phraseology, gave expression to the following truths:

While the religions of the world have a double origin—natural and revelatory—at any one time and among any one people there are to be found three distinct forms of religious devotion. And these three manifestations of the religious urge are:

1. *Primitive religion.* The seminatural and instinctive urge to fear mysterious energies and worship superior forces, chiefly a religion of the physical nature, the religion of fear.

2. *The religion of civilization.* The advancing religious concepts and practices of the civilizing races—the religion of the mind—the intellectual theology of the authority of established religious tradition.

3. *True religion—the religion of revelation.* The revelation of supernatural values, a partial insight into eternal realities, a glimpse of the goodness and beauty of the infinite character of the Father in heaven—the religion of the spirit as demonstrated in human experience.

The religion of the physical senses and the superstitious fears of natural man, the Master refused to belittle, though he deplored the fact that so much of this primitive form of worship should persist in the religious forms of the more intelligent races of mankind. Jesus made it clear that the great difference between the religion of the mind and the religion of the spirit is that, while the former is upheld by ecclesiastical authority, the latter is wholly based on human experience.

And then the Master, in his hour of teaching, went on to make clear these truths:

Until the races become highly intelligent and more fully civilized, there will persist many of those childlike and superstitious ceremonies which are so characteristic of the evolutionary religious practices of primitive and backward peoples. Until the human race progresses to the level of a higher and more general recognition of the realities of spiritual experience, large numbers of men and women will continue to show a personal preference for those religions of authority which require only intellectual assent, in contrast to the religion of the spirit, which entails active participation of mind and soul in the faith adventure of grappling with the rigorous realities of progressive human experience.

The acceptance of the traditional religions of authority presents the easy way out for man's urge to seek satisfaction for the longings of his spiritual nature. The settled, crystallized, and established religions of authority afford a ready refuge to which the distracted and distraught soul of man may flee when harassed by fear and tormented by uncertainty. Such a religion requires of its devotees, as the price to be paid for its satisfactions and assurances, only a passive and purely intellectual assent.

And for a long time there will live on earth those timid, fearful, and hesitant individuals who will prefer thus to secure their religious consolations, even though, in so casting their lot with the religions of authority, they compromise the sovereignty of personality, debase the dignity of self-respect, and utterly surrender the right to participate in that most thrilling and inspiring of all possible human experiences: the personal quest for truth, the exhilaration of facing the perils of intellectual discovery, the determination to explore the realities of personal religious experience, the supreme satisfaction of experiencing the personal triumph of the actual realization of the victory of spiritual faith over intellectual doubt as it is honestly won in the supreme adventure of all human existence—man seeking God, for himself and as himself, and finding him.

The religion of the spirit means effort, struggle, conflict, faith, determination, love, loyalty, and progress. The religion of the mind—the theology of authority—requires little or none of these exertions from its formal believers. Tradition is a safe refuge and an easy path for those fearful and halfhearted souls who instinctively shun the spirit struggles and mental uncertainties associated with those faith voyages of daring adventure out upon the high seas of unexplored truth in search for the farther shores of spiritual realities as they may be discovered by the progressive human mind and experienced by the evolving human soul.

And Jesus went on to say: "At Jerusalem the religious leaders have formulated the various doctrines of their traditional teachers and the prophets of other days into an established system of intellectual beliefs, a religion of authority.

The appeal of all such religions is largely to the mind. And now are we about to enter upon a deadly conflict with such a religion since we will so shortly begin the bold proclamation of a new religion—a religion which is not a religion in the present-day meaning of that word, a religion that makes its chief appeal to the divine spirit of my Father which resides in the mind of man; a religion which shall derive its authority from the fruits of its acceptance that will so certainly appear in the personal experience of all who really and truly become believers in the truths of this higher spiritual communion."

Pointing out each of the twenty-four and calling them by name, Jesus said: "And now, which one of you would prefer to take this easy path of conformity to an established and fossilized religion, as defended by the Pharisees at Jerusalem, rather than to suffer the difficulties and persecutions attendant upon the mission of proclaiming a better way of salvation to men while you realize the satisfaction of discovering for yourselves the beauties of the realities of a living and personal experience in the eternal truths and supreme grandeurs of the kingdom of heaven? Are you fearful, soft, and ease-seeking? Are you afraid to trust your future in the hands of the God of truth, whose sons you are? Are you distrustful of the Father, whose children you are? Will you go back to the easy path of the certainty and intellectual settledness of the religion of traditional authority, or will you gird yourselves to go forward with me into that uncertain and troublous future of proclaiming the new truths of the religion of the spirit, the kingdom of heaven in the hearts of men?"

All twenty-four of his hearers rose to their feet, intending to signify their united and loyal response to this, one of the few emotional appeals which Jesus ever made to them, but he raised his hand and stopped them, saying: "Go now apart by yourselves, each man alone with the Father, and there find the unemotional answer to my question, and having found such a true and sincere attitude of soul, speak that answer freely and boldly to my Father and your Father, whose infinite life of love is the very spirit of the religion we proclaim."

The evangelists and apostles went apart by themselves for a short time. Their spirits were uplifted, their minds were inspired, and their emotions mightily stirred by what Jesus had said. But when Andrew called them together, the Master said only: "Let us resume our journey. We go into Phoenicia to tarry for a season, and all of you should pray the Father to transform your emotions of mind and body into the higher loyalties of mind and the more satisfying experiences of the spirit."

As they journeyed on down the road, the twenty-four were silent, but presently they began to talk one with another, and by three o'clock that afternoon they could not go farther; they came to a halt, and Peter, going up to Jesus, said: "Master, you have spoken to us the words of life and truth. We would hear more; we beseech you to speak to us further concerning these matters."

6. THE SECOND DISCOURSE ON RELIGION

And so, while they paused in the shade of the hillside, Jesus continued to teach them regarding the religion of the spirit, in substance saying:

You have come out from among those of your fellows who choose to remain satisfied with a religion of mind, who crave security and prefer conformity. You have elected to exchange your feelings of authoritative certainty for the assurances of the spirit of adventurous and progressive faith. You have dared to protest against the grueling bondage of institutional religion and to reject the authority of the traditions of record which are now regarded as the word of God. Our Father did indeed speak through Moses, Elijah, Isaiah, Amos, and Hosea, but he did not cease to minister words of truth to the world when these prophets of old made an end of their utterances. My Father is no respecter of races or generations in that the word of truth is vouchsafed one age and withheld from another. Commit not the folly of calling that divine which is wholly human, and fail not to discern the words of truth which come not through the traditional oracles of supposed inspiration.

I have called upon you to be born again, to be born of the spirit. I have called you out of the darkness of authority and the lethargy of tradition into the transcendent light of the realization of the possibility of making for yourselves the greatest discovery possible for the human soul to make—the supernal experience of finding God for yourself, in yourself, and of yourself, and of doing all this as a fact in your own personal experience. And so may you pass from death to life, from the authority of tradition to the experience of knowing God; thus will you pass from darkness to light, from a racial faith inherited to a personal faith achieved by actual experience; and thereby will you progress from a theology of mind handed down by your ancestors to a true religion of spirit which shall be built up in your souls as an eternal endowment.

Your religion shall change from the mere intellectual belief in traditional authority to the actual experience of that living faith which is able to grasp the reality of God and all that relates to the divine spirit of the Father. The religion of the mind ties you hopelessly to the past; the religion of the spirit consists in progressive revelation and ever beckons you on toward higher and holier achievements in spiritual ideals and eternal realities.

While the religion of authority may impart a present feeling of settled security, you pay for such a transient satisfaction the price of the loss of your spiritual freedom and religious liberty. My Father does not require of you as the price of entering the kingdom of heaven that you should force yourself to subscribe to a belief in things which are spiritually repugnant, unholy, and untruthful. It is not required of you that your own sense of mercy, justice, and truth should be outraged by submission to an outworn system of religious forms and ceremonies. The religion of the spirit leaves you forever free to follow the truth wherever the leadings of the spirit may take you. And who can judge—perhaps this spirit may have something to impart to this generation which other generations have refused to hear?

Shame on those false religious teachers who would drag hungry souls back into the dim and distant past and there leave them! And so are these unfortunate persons doomed to become frightened by every new discovery, while they are discomfited by every new revelation of truth. The prophet who said, "He will be kept in perfect peace whose mind is stayed on God," was not a mere intellectual believer in authoritative theology. This truth-knowing human had discovered God; he was not merely talking about God.

I admonish you to give up the practice of always quoting the prophets of old and praising the heroes of Israel, and instead aspire to become living prophets of the Most High and spiritual heroes of the coming kingdom. To honor the God-knowing leaders of the past may indeed be worth while, but why, in so doing, should you sacrifice the supreme experience of human existence: finding God for yourselves and knowing him in your own souls?

Every race of mankind has its own mental outlook upon human existence; therefore must the religion of the mind ever run true to these various racial viewpoints. Never can the religions of authority come to unification. Human unity and mortal brotherhood can be achieved only by and through the superendowment of the religion of the spirit. Racial minds may differ, but all mankind is indwelt by the same divine and eternal spirit. The hope of human brotherhood can only be realized when, and as, the divergent mind religions of authority become impregnated with, and overshadowed by, the unifying and ennobling religion of the spirit—the religion of personal spiritual experience.

The religions of authority can only divide men and set them in conscientious array against each other; the religion of the spirit will progressively draw men together and cause them to become understandingly sympathetic with one another. The religions of authority require of men uniformity in belief, but this is impossible of realization in the present state of the world. The religion of the spirit requires only unity of experience—uniformity of destiny—making full allowance for diversity of belief. The religion of the spirit requires only uniformity of insight, not uniformity of viewpoint and outlook. The religion of the spirit does not demand uniformity of intellectual views, only unity of spirit feeling. The religions of authority crystallize into lifeless creeds; the religion of the spirit grows into the increasing joy and liberty of ennobling deeds of loving service and merciful ministration.

But watch, lest any of you look with disdain upon the children of Abraham because they have fallen on these evil days of traditional barrenness. Our forefathers gave themselves up to the persistent and passionate search for God, and they found him as no other whole race of men have ever known him since the times of Adam, who knew much of this as he was himself a Son of God. My Father has not failed to mark the long and untiring struggle of Israel, ever since the days of Moses, to find God and to know God. For weary generations the Jews have not ceased to toil, sweat, groan, travail, and endure the sufferings and experience the sorrows of a misunderstood and despised people, all in order that they might come a little nearer the discovery of the truth about God. And, notwithstanding all the failures and falterings of Israel, our fathers progressively, from Moses to the times of Amos and Hosea, did reveal increasingly to the whole world an ever clearer and more truthful picture of the eternal God. And so was the way prepared for the still greater revelation of the Father which you have been called to share.

Never forget there is only one adventure which is more satisfying and thrilling than the attempt to discover the will of the living God, and that is the supreme experience of honestly trying to do that divine will. And fail not to remember that the will of God can be done in any earthly occupation. Some callings are not holy and others secular. All things are sacred in the lives of those who are spirit led; that is, subordinated to truth, ennobled by love, dominated by mercy, and restrained by fairness—justice. The spirit which my Father and I shall send into the world is not only the Spirit of Truth but also the spirit of idealistic beauty.

You must cease to seek for the word of God only on the pages of the olden records of theologic authority. Those who are born of the spirit of God shall henceforth discern the word of God regardless of whence it appears to take origin. Divine truth must not be discounted because the channel of its bestowal is apparently human. Many of your brethren have minds which accept the theory of God while they spiritually fail to realize the presence of God. And that is just the reason why I have so often taught you that the kingdom of heaven can best be realized by acquiring the spiritual attitude of a sincere child. It is not the mental immaturity of the child that I commend to you but rather the *spiritual simplicity* of such an easy-believing and fully-trusting little one. It is not so important that you should know about the fact of God as that you should increasingly grow in the ability to *feel the presence of God.*

When you once begin to find God in your soul, presently you will begin to discover him in other men's souls and eventually in all the creatures and creations of a mighty universe. But what chance does the Father have to appear as a God of supreme loyalties and divine ideals in the souls of men who give little or no time to the thoughtful contemplation of such eternal realities? While the mind is not the seat of the spiritual nature, it is indeed the gateway thereto.

But do not make the mistake of trying to prove to other men that you have found God; you cannot consciously produce such valid proof, albeit there are two positive and powerful demonstrations of the fact that you are God-knowing, and they are:

1. The fruits of the spirit of God showing forth in your daily routine life.

2. The fact that your entire life plan furnishes positive proof that you have unreservedly risked everything you are and have on the adventure of survival after death in the pursuit of the hope of finding the God of eternity, whose presence you have foretasted in time.

Now, mistake not, my Father will ever respond to the faintest flicker of faith. He takes note of the physical and superstitious emotions of the primitive man. And with those honest but fearful souls whose faith is so weak that it amounts to little more than an intellectual conformity to a passive attitude of assent to religions of authority, the Father is ever alert to honor and foster even all such feeble attempts to reach out for him. But you who have been called out of darkness into the light are expected to believe with a whole heart; your faith shall dominate the combined attitudes of body, mind, and spirit.

You are my apostles, and to you religion shall not become a theologic shelter to which you may flee in fear of facing the rugged realities of spiritual progress and idealistic adventure; but rather shall your religion become the fact of real experience which testifies that God has found you, idealized, ennobled, and spiritualized you, and that you have enlisted in the eternal adventure of finding the God who has thus found and sonshipped you.

And when Jesus had finished speaking, he beckoned to Andrew and, pointing to the west toward Phoenicia, said: "Let us be on our way."

PAPER 156

THE SOJOURN AT TYRE AND SIDON

ON FRIDAY afternoon, June 10, Jesus and his associates arrived in the environs of Sidon, where they stopped at the home of a well-to-do woman who had been a patient in the Bethsaida hospital during the times when Jesus was at the height of his popular favor. The evangelists and the apostles were lodged with her friends in the immediate neighborhood, and they rested over the Sabbath day amid these refreshing surroundings. They spent almost two and one-half weeks in Sidon and vicinity before they prepared to visit the coast cities to the north.

This June Sabbath day was one of great quiet. The evangelists and apostles were altogether absorbed in their meditations regarding the discourses of the Master on religion to which they had listened en route to Sidon. They were all able to appreciate something of what he had told them, but none of them fully grasped the import of his teaching.

1. THE SYRIAN WOMAN

There lived near the home of Karuska, where the Master lodged, a Syrian woman who had heard much of Jesus as a great healer and teacher, and on this Sabbath afternoon she came over, bringing her little daughter. The child, about twelve years old, was afflicted with a grievous nervous disorder characterized by convulsions and other distressing manifestations.

Jesus had charged his associates to tell no one of his presence at the home of Karuska, explaining that he desired to have a rest. While they had obeyed their Master's instructions, the servant of Karuska had gone over to the house of this Syrian woman, Norana, to inform her that Jesus lodged at the home of her mistress and had urged this anxious mother to bring her afflicted daughter for healing. This mother, of course, believed that her child was possessed by a demon, an unclean spirit.

When Norana arrived with her daughter, the Alpheus twins explained through an interpreter that the Master was resting and could not be disturbed; whereupon Norana replied that she and the child would remain right there until the Master had finished his rest. Peter also endeavored to reason with her and to persuade her to go home. He explained that Jesus was weary with much teaching and healing, and that he had come to Phoenicia for a period of quiet and rest. But it was futile; Norana would not leave. To Peter's entreaties she replied only: "I will not depart until I have seen your Master. I know he can cast the demon out of my child, and I will not go until the healer has looked upon my daughter."

Then Thomas sought to send the woman away but met only with failure. To him she said: "I have faith that your Master can cast out this demon which torments my child. I have heard of his mighty works in Galilee, and I believe in him. What has happened to you, his disciples, that you would send away those who come seeking your Master's help?" And when she had thus spoken, Thomas withdrew.

Then came forward Simon Zelotes to remonstrate with Norana. Said Simon: "Woman, you are a Greek-speaking gentile. It is not right that you should expect the Master to take the bread intended for the children of the favored household and cast it to the dogs." But Norana refused to take offense at Simon's thrust. She replied only: "Yes, teacher, I understand your words. I am only a dog in the eyes of the Jews, but as concerns your Master, I am a believing dog. I am determined that he shall see my daughter, for I am persuaded that, if he shall but look upon her, he will heal her. And even you, my good man, would not dare to deprive the dogs of the privilege of obtaining the crumbs which chance to fall from the children's table."

At just this time the little girl was seized with a violent convulsion before them all, and the mother cried out: "There, you can see that my child is possessed by an evil spirit. If our need does not impress you, it would appeal to your Master, who I have been told loves all men and dares even to heal the gentiles when they believe. You are not worthy to be his disciples. I will not go until my child has been cured."

Jesus, who had heard all of this conversation through an open window, now came outside, much to their surprise, and said: "O woman, great is your faith, so great that I cannot withhold that which you desire; go your way in peace. Your daughter already has been made whole." And the little girl was well from that hour. As Norana and the child took leave, Jesus entreated them to tell no one of this occurrence; and while his associates did comply with this request, the mother and the child ceased not to proclaim the fact of the little girl's healing throughout all the countryside and even in Sidon, so much so that Jesus found it advisable to change his lodgings within a few days.

The next day, as Jesus taught his apostles, commenting on the cure of the daughter of the Syrian woman, he said: "And so it has been all the way along; you see for yourselves how the gentiles are able to exercise saving faith in the teachings of the gospel of the kingdom of heaven. Verily, verily, I tell you that the Father's kingdom shall be taken by the gentiles if the children of Abraham are not minded to show faith enough to enter therein."

2. TEACHING IN SIDON

In entering Sidon, Jesus and his associates passed over a bridge, the first one many of them had ever seen. As they walked over this bridge, Jesus, among other things, said: "This world is only a bridge; you may pass over it, but you should not think to build a dwelling place upon it."

As the twenty-four began their labors in Sidon, Jesus went to stay in a home just north of the city, the house of Justa and her mother, Bernice. Jesus taught the twenty-four each morning at the home of Justa, and they went abroad in Sidon to teach and preach during the afternoons and evenings.

The apostles and the evangelists were greatly cheered by the manner in which the gentiles of Sidon received their message; during their short sojourn many were added to the kingdom. This period of about six weeks in Phoenicia was a very fruitful time in the work of winning souls, but the later Jewish writers of the Gospels were wont lightly to pass over the record of this warm reception of Jesus' teachings by these gentiles at this very time when such a large number of his own people were in hostile array against him.

In many ways these gentile believers appreciated Jesus' teachings more fully than the Jews. Many of these Greek-speaking Syrophoenicians came to know not only that Jesus was like God but also that God was like Jesus. These so-called heathen achieved a good understanding of the Master's teachings about the uniformity of the laws of this world and the entire universe. They grasped the teaching that God is no respecter of persons, races, or nations; that there is no favoritism with the Universal Father; that the universe is wholly and ever law-abiding and unfailingly dependable. These gentiles were not afraid of Jesus; they dared to accept his message. All down through the ages men have not been unable to comprehend Jesus; they have been afraid to.

Jesus made it clear to the twenty-four that he had not fled from Galilee because he lacked courage to confront his enemies. They comprehended that he was not yet ready for an open clash with established religion, and that he did not seek to become a martyr. It was during one of these conferences at the home of Justa that the Master first told his disciples that "even though heaven and earth shall pass away, my words of truth shall not."

The theme of Jesus' instructions during the sojourn at Sidon was spiritual progression. He told them they could not stand still; they must go forward in righteousness or retrogress into evil and sin. He admonished them to "forget those things which are in the past while you push forward to embrace the greater realities of the kingdom." He besought them not to be content with their childhood in the gospel but to strive for the attainment of the full stature of divine sonship in the communion of the spirit and in the fellowship of believers.

Said Jesus: "My disciples must not only cease to do evil but learn to do well; you must not only be cleansed from all conscious sin, but you must refuse to harbor even the feelings of guilt. If you confess your sins, they are forgiven; therefore must you maintain a conscience void of offense."

Jesus greatly enjoyed the keen sense of humor which these gentiles exhibited. It was the sense of humor displayed by Norana, the Syrian woman, as well as her great and persistent faith, that so touched the Master's heart and appealed to his mercy. Jesus greatly regretted that his people—the Jews—were so lacking in humor. He once said to Thomas: "My people take themselves too seriously; they are just about devoid of an appreciation of humor. The burdensome religion of the Pharisees could never have had origin among a people with a sense of humor. They also lack consistency; they strain at gnats and swallow camels."

3. THE JOURNEY UP THE COAST

On Tuesday, June 28, the Master and his associates left Sidon, going up the coast to Porphyreon and Heldua. They were well received by the gentiles, and many were added to the kingdom during this week of teaching and preaching. The apostles preached in Porphyreon and the evangelists taught in Heldua.

While the twenty-four were thus engaged in their work, Jesus left them for a period of three or four days, paying a visit to the coast city of Beirut, where he visited with a Syrian named Malach, who was a believer, and who had been at Bethsaida the year before.

On Wednesday, July 6, they all returned to Sidon and tarried at the home of Justa until Sunday morning, when they departed for Tyre, going south along the coast by way of Sarepta, arriving at Tyre on Monday, July 11. By this time the apostles and the evangelists were becoming accustomed to working among these so-called gentiles, who were in reality mainly descended from the earlier Canaanite tribes of still earlier Semitic origin. All of these peoples spoke the Greek language. It was a great surprise to the apostles and evangelists to observe the eagerness of these gentiles to hear the gospel and to note the readiness with which many of them believed.

4. AT TYRE

From July 11 to July 24 they taught in Tyre. Each of the apostles took with him one of the evangelists, and thus two and two they taught and preached in all parts of Tyre and its environs. The polyglot population of this busy seaport heard them gladly, and many were baptized into the outward fellowship of the kingdom. Jesus maintained his headquarters at the home of a Jew named Joseph, a believer, who lived three or four miles south of Tyre, not far from the tomb of Hiram who had been king of the city-state of Tyre during the times of David and Solomon.

Daily, for this period of two weeks, the apostles and evangelists entered Tyre by way of Alexander's mole to conduct small meetings, and each night most of them would return to the encampment at Joseph's house south of the city. Every day believers came out from the city to talk with Jesus at his resting place. The Master spoke in Tyre only once, on the afternoon of July 20, when he taught the believers concerning the Father's love for all mankind and about the mission of the Son to reveal the Father to all races of men. There was such an interest in the gospel of the kingdom among these gentiles that, on this occasion, the doors of the Melkarth temple were opened to him, and it is interesting to record that in subsequent years a Christian church was built on the very site of this ancient temple.

Many of the leaders in the manufacture of Tyrian purple, the dye that made Tyre and Sidon famous the world over, and which contributed so much to their world-wide commerce and consequent enrichment, believed in the kingdom. When, shortly thereafter, the supply of the sea animals which were the source of this dye began to diminish, these dye makers went forth in search of new habitats of these shellfish. And thus migrating to the ends of the earth, they carried with them the message of the fatherhood of God and the brotherhood of man—the gospel of the kingdom.

5. JESUS' TEACHING AT TYRE

On this Wednesday afternoon, in the course of his address, Jesus first told his followers the story of the white lily which rears its pure and snowy head high into the sunshine while its roots are grounded in the slime and muck of the darkened soil beneath. "Likewise," said he, "mortal man, while he has his roots of origin and being in the animal soil of human nature, can by faith raise his spiritual nature up into the sunlight of heavenly truth and actually bear the noble fruits of the spirit."

It was during this same sermon that Jesus made use of his first and only parable having to do with his own trade—carpentry. In the course of his admonition to "Build well the foundations for the growth of a noble character of spiritual endowments," he said: "In order to yield the fruits of the spirit, you must be born of the spirit. You must be taught by the spirit and be led by the spirit if you would live the spirit-filled life among your fellows. But do not make the mistake of the foolish carpenter who wastes valuable time squaring, measuring, and smoothing his worm-eaten and inwardly rotting timber and then, when he has thus bestowed all of his labor upon the unsound beam, must reject it as unfit to enter into the foundations of the building which he would construct to withstand the assaults of time and storm. Let every man make sure that the intellectual and moral foundations of character are such as will adequately support the superstructure of the enlarging and ennobling spiritual nature, which is thus to transform the mortal mind and then, in association with that re-created mind, is to achieve the evolvement of the soul of immortal destiny. Your spirit nature—the jointly created soul—is a living growth, but the mind and morals of the individual are the soil from which these higher manifestations of human development and divine destiny must spring. The soil of the evolving soul is human and material, but the destiny of this combined creature of mind and spirit is spiritual and divine."

On the evening of this same day Nathaniel asked Jesus: "Master, why do we pray that God will lead us not into temptation when we well know from your revelation of the Father that he never does such things?" Jesus answered Nathaniel:

"It is not strange that you ask such questions seeing that you are beginning to know the Father as I know him, and not as the early Hebrew prophets so dimly saw him. You well know how our forefathers were disposed to see God in almost everything that happened. They looked for the hand of God in all natural occurrences and in every unusual episode of human experience. They connected God with both good and evil. They thought he softened the heart of Moses and hardened the heart of Pharaoh. When man had a strong urge to do something, good or evil, he was in the habit of accounting for these unusual emotions by remarking: 'The Lord spoke to me saying, do thus and so, or go here and there.' Accordingly, since men so often and so violently ran into temptation, it became the habit of our forefathers to believe that God led them thither for testing, punishing, or strengthening. But you, indeed, now know better. You know that men are all too often led into temptation by the urge of their own selfishness and by the impulses of their animal natures. When you are in this way tempted, I admonish you that, while you recognize temptation honestly and sincerely for just what it is, you intelligently redirect the energies of spirit, mind, and body, which are seeking expression, into higher channels and toward more idealistic goals. In this way may you transform your temptations into the highest types of uplifting mortal ministry while you almost wholly avoid these wasteful and weakening conflicts between the animal and spiritual natures.

"But let me warn you against the folly of undertaking to surmount temptation by the effort of supplanting one desire by another and supposedly superior desire through the mere force of the human will. If you would be truly triumphant over the temptations of the lesser and lower nature, you must come to that place of spiritual advantage where you have really and truly developed an actual interest in, and love for, those higher and more idealistic forms of conduct which your mind is desirous of substituting for these lower and less idealistic habits of behavior that you recognize as temptation. You will in this way be delivered through spiritual transformation rather than be increasingly overburdened with the deceptive suppression of mortal desires. The old and the inferior will be forgotten in the love for the new and the superior. Beauty is always triumphant over ugliness in the hearts of all who are illuminated by the love of truth. There is mighty power in the expulsive energy of a new and sincere spiritual affection. And again I say to you, be not overcome by evil but rather overcome evil with good."

Long into the night the apostles and evangelists continued to ask questions, and from the many answers we would present the following thoughts, restated in modern phraseology:

Forceful ambition, intelligent judgment, and seasoned wisdom are the essentials of material success. Leadership is dependent on natural ability, discretion, will power, and determination. Spiritual destiny is dependent on faith, love, and devotion to truth—hunger and thirst for righteousness—the wholehearted desire to find God and to be like him.

Do not become discouraged by the discovery that you are human. Human nature may tend toward evil, but it is not inherently sinful. Be not downcast by your failure wholly to forget some of your regrettable experiences. The mistakes which you fail to forget in time will be forgotten in eternity. Lighten your burdens of soul by speedily acquiring a long-distance view of your destiny, a universe expansion of your career.

Make not the mistake of estimating the soul's worth by the imperfections of the mind or by the appetites of the body. Judge not the soul nor evaluate its destiny by the standard of a single unfortunate human episode. Your spiritual destiny is conditioned only by your spiritual longings and purposes.

Religion is the exclusively spiritual experience of the evolving immortal soul of the God-knowing man, but moral power and spiritual energy are mighty forces which may be utilized in dealing with difficult social situations and in solving intricate economic problems. These moral and spiritual endowments make all levels of human living richer and more meaningful.

You are destined to live a narrow and mean life if you learn to love only those who love you. Human love may indeed be reciprocal, but divine love is outgoing in all its satisfaction-seeking. The less of love in any creature's nature, the greater the love need, and the more does divine love seek to satisfy such need. Love is never self-seeking, and it cannot be self-bestowed. Divine love cannot be self-contained; it must be unselfishly bestowed.

Kingdom believers should possess an implicit faith, a whole-souled belief, in the certain triumph of righteousness. Kingdom builders must be undoubting of the truth of the gospel of eternal salvation. Believers must increasingly learn how to step aside from the rush of life—escape the harassments of material existence—while they refresh the soul, inspire the mind, and renew the spirit by worshipful communion.

God-knowing individuals are not discouraged by misfortune or downcast by disappointment. Believers are immune to the depression consequent upon purely material upheavals; spirit livers are not perturbed by the episodes of the material world. Candidates for eternal life are practitioners of an invigorating and constructive technique for meeting all of the vicissitudes and harassments of mortal living. Every day a true believer lives, he finds it *easier* to do the right thing.

Spiritual living mightily increases true self-respect. But self-respect is not self-admiration. Self-respect is always co-ordinate with the love and service of one's fellows. It is not possible to respect yourself more than you love your neighbor; the one is the measure of the capacity for the other.

As the days pass, every true believer becomes more skillful in alluring his fellows into the love of eternal truth. Are you more resourceful in revealing goodness to humanity today than you were yesterday? Are you a better righteousness recommender this year than you were last year? Are you becoming increasingly artistic in your technique of leading hungry souls into the spiritual kingdom?

Are your ideals sufficiently high to insure your eternal salvation while your ideas are so practical as to render you a useful citizen to function on earth in association with your mortal fellows? In the spirit, your citizenship is in heaven; in the flesh, you are still citizens of the earth kingdoms. Render to the Caesars the things which are material and to God those which are spiritual.

The measure of the spiritual capacity of the evolving soul is your faith in truth and your love for man, but the measure of your human strength of character is your ability to resist the holding of grudges and your capacity to withstand brooding in the face of deep sorrow. Defeat is the true mirror in which you may honestly view your real self.

As you grow older in years and more experienced in the affairs of the kingdom, are you becoming more tactful in dealing with troublesome mortals and more tolerant in living with stubborn associates? Tact is the fulcrum of social leverage, and tolerance is the earmark of a great soul. If you possess these rare and charming gifts, as the days pass you will become more alert and expert in your worthy efforts to avoid all unnecessary social misunderstandings. Such wise souls are able to avoid much of the trouble which is certain to be the portion of all who suffer from lack of emotional adjustment, those who refuse to grow up, and those who refuse to grow old gracefully.

Avoid dishonesty and unfairness in all your efforts to preach truth and proclaim the gospel. Seek no unearned recognition and crave no undeserved sympathy. Love, freely receive from both divine and human sources regardless of your deserts, and love freely in return. But in all other things related to honor and adulation seek only that which honestly belongs to you.

The God-conscious mortal is certain of salvation; he is unafraid of life; he is honest and consistent. He knows how bravely to endure unavoidable suffering; he is uncomplaining when faced by inescapable hardship.

The true believer does not grow weary in well-doing just because he is thwarted. Difficulty whets the ardor of the truth lover, while obstacles only challenge the exertions of the undaunted kingdom builder.

And many other things Jesus taught them before they made ready to depart from Tyre.

The day before Jesus left Tyre for the return to the region of the Sea of Galilee, he called his associates together and directed the twelve evangelists to go back by a route different from that which he and the twelve apostles were to take. And after the evangelists here left Jesus, they were never again so intimately associated with him.

6. THE RETURN FROM PHOENICIA

About noon on Sunday, July 24, Jesus and the twelve left the home of Joseph, south of Tyre, going down the coast to Ptolemais. Here they tarried for a day, speaking words of comfort to the company of believers resident there. Peter preached to them on the evening of July 25.

On Tuesday they left Ptolemais, going east inland to near Jotapata by way of the Tiberias road. Wednesday they stopped at Jotapata and instructed the believers further in the things of the kingdom. Thursday they left Jotapata, going north on the Nazareth-Mount Lebanon trail to the village of Zebulun, by way of Ramah. They held meetings at Ramah on Friday and remained over the Sabbath. They reached Zebulun on Sunday, the 31st, holding a meeting that evening and departing the next morning.

Leaving Zebulun, they journeyed over to the junction with the Magdala-Sidon road near Gischala, and thence they made their way to Gennesaret on the western shores of the lake of Galilee, south of Capernaum, where they had appointed to meet with David Zebedee, and where they intended to take counsel as to the next move to be made in the work of preaching the gospel of the kingdom.

During a brief conference with David they learned that many leaders were then gathered together on the opposite side of the lake near Kheresa, and accordingly, that very evening a boat took them across. For one day they rested quietly in the hills, going on the next day to the park, near by, where the Master once fed the five thousand. Here they rested for three days and held daily conferences, which were attended by about fifty men and women, the remnants of the once numerous company of believers resident in Capernaum and its environs.

While Jesus was absent from Capernaum and Galilee, the period of the Phoenician sojourn, his enemies reckoned that the whole movement had been broken up and concluded that Jesus' haste in withdrawing indicated he was so thoroughly frightened that he would not likely ever return to bother them. All active opposition to his teachings had about subsided. The believers were beginning to hold public meetings once more, and there was occurring a gradual but effective consolidation of the tried and true survivors of the great sifting through which the gospel believers had just passed.

Philip, the brother of Herod, had become a halfhearted believer in Jesus and sent word that the Master was free to live and work in his domains.

The mandate to close the synagogues of all Jewry to the teachings of Jesus and all his followers had worked adversely upon the scribes and Pharisees. Immediately upon Jesus' removing himself as an object of controversy, there occurred a reaction among the entire Jewish people; there was general resentment against the Pharisees and the Sanhedrin leaders at Jerusalem. Many of the rulers of the synagogues began surreptitiously to open their synagogues to Abner and his associates, claiming that these teachers were followers of John and not disciples of Jesus.

Even Herod Antipas experienced a change of heart and, on learning that Jesus was sojourning across the lake in the territory of his brother Philip, sent word to him that, while he had signed warrants for his arrest in Galilee, he had not so authorized his apprehension in Perea, thus indicating that Jesus would not be molested if he remained outside of Galilee; and he communicated this same ruling to the Jews at Jerusalem.

And that was the situation about the first of August, A.D. 29, when the Master returned from the Phoenician mission and began the reorganization of his scattered, tested, and depleted forces for this last and eventful year of his mission on earth.

The issues of battle are clearly drawn as the Master and his associates prepare to begin the proclamation of a new religion, the religion of the spirit of the living God who dwells in the minds of men.

PAPER 157

AT CAESAREA-PHILIPPI

BEFORE Jesus took the twelve for a short sojourn in the vicinity of Caesarea-Philippi, he arranged through the messengers of David to go over to Capernaum on Sunday, August 7, for the purpose of meeting his family. By prearrangement this visit was to occur at the Zebedee boatshop. David Zebedee had arranged with Jude, Jesus' brother, for the presence of the entire Nazareth family—Mary and all of Jesus' brothers and sisters—and Jesus went with Andrew and Peter to keep this appointment. It was certainly the intention of Mary and the children to keep this engagement, but it so happened that a group of the Pharisees, knowing that Jesus was on the opposite side of the lake in Philip's domains, decided to call upon Mary to learn what they could of his whereabouts. The arrival of these Jerusalem emissaries greatly perturbed Mary, and noting the tension and nervousness of the entire family, they concluded that Jesus must have been expected to pay them a visit. Accordingly they installed themselves in Mary's home and, after summoning reinforcements, waited patiently for Jesus' arrival. And this, of course, effectively prevented any of the family from attempting to keep their appointment with Jesus. Several times during the day both Jude and Ruth endeavored to elude the vigilance of the Pharisees in their efforts to send word to Jesus, but it was of no avail.

Early in the afternoon David's messengers brought Jesus word that the Pharisees were encamped on the doorstep of his mother's house, and therefore he made no attempt to visit his family. And so again, through no fault of either, Jesus and his earth family failed to make contact.

1. THE TEMPLE-TAX COLLECTOR

As Jesus, with Andrew and Peter, tarried by the lake near the boatshop, a temple-tax collector came upon them and, recognizing Jesus, called Peter to one side and said: "Does not your Master pay the temple tax?" Peter was inclined to show indignation at the suggestion that Jesus should be expected to contribute to the maintenance of the religious activities of his sworn enemies, but, noting a peculiar expression on the face of the tax collector, he rightly surmised that it was the purpose to entrap them in the act of refusing to pay the customary half shekel for the support of the temple services at Jerusalem. Accordingly, Peter replied: "Why of course the Master pays the temple tax. You wait by the gate, and I will presently return with the tax."

Now Peter had spoken hastily. Judas carried their funds, and he was across the lake. Neither he, his brother, nor Jesus had brought along any money. And knowing that the Pharisees were looking for them, they could not well go to Bethsaida to obtain money. When Peter told Jesus about the collector and that he had promised him the money, Jesus said: "If you have promised, then should you pay. But wherewith will you redeem your promise? Will you again become a fisherman that you may honor your word? Nevertheless, Peter, it is well in the circumstances that we pay the tax. Let us give these men no occasion for offense at our attitude. We will wait here while you go with the boat and cast for the fish, and when you have sold them at yonder market, pay the collector for all three of us."

All of this had been overheard by the secret messenger of David who stood near by, and who then signaled to an associate, fishing near the shore, to come in quickly. When Peter made ready to go out in the boat for a catch, this messenger and his fisherman friend presented him with several large baskets of fish and assisted him in carrying them to the fish merchant near by, who purchased the catch, paying sufficient, with what was added by the messenger of David, to meet the temple tax for the three. The collector accepted the tax, forgoing the penalty for tardy payment because they had been for some time absent from Galilee.

It is not strange that you have a record of Peter's catching a fish with a shekel in its mouth. In those days there were current many stories about finding treasures in the mouths of fishes; such tales of near miracles were commonplace. So, as Peter left them to go toward the boat, Jesus remarked, half-humorously: "Strange that the sons of the king must pay tribute; usually it is the stranger who is taxed for the upkeep of the court, but it behooves us to afford no stumbling block for the authorities. Go hence! maybe you will catch the fish with the shekel in its mouth." Jesus having thus spoken, and Peter so soon appearing with the temple tax, it is not surprising that the episode became later expanded into a miracle as recorded by the writer of Matthew's Gospel.

Jesus, with Andrew and Peter, waited by the seashore until nearly sundown. Messengers brought them word that Mary's house was still under surveillance; therefore, when it grew dark, the three waiting men entered their boat and slowly rowed away toward the eastern shore of the Sea of Galilee.

2. AT BETHSAIDA-JULIAS

On Monday, August 8, while Jesus and the twelve apostles were encamped in Magadan Park, near Bethsaida-Julias, more than one hundred believers, the evangelists, the women's corps, and others interested in the establishment of the kingdom, came over from Capernaum for a conference. And many of the Pharisees, learning that Jesus was here, came also. By this time some of the Sadducees were united with the Pharisees in their effort to entrap Jesus. Before going into the closed conference with the believers, Jesus held a public meeting at which the Pharisees were present, and they heckled the Master and otherwise sought to disturb the assembly. Said the leader of the disturbers: "Teacher, we would like you to give us a sign of your authority to teach, and then, when the same shall come to pass, all men will know that you have been sent by God." And Jesus answered them: "When it is evening, you say it will be fair weather, for the heaven is red; in the morning it will be foul weather, for the heaven is red and lowering. When you see a cloud rising in the west, you say showers will come; when the wind blows from the south, you say scorching heat will come.

How is it that you so well know how to discern the face of the heavens but are so utterly unable to discern the signs of the times? To those who would know the truth, already has a sign been given; but to an evil-minded and hypocritical generation no sign shall be given."

When Jesus had thus spoken, he withdrew and prepared for the evening conference with his followers. At this conference it was decided to undertake a united mission throughout all the cities and villages of the Decapolis as soon as Jesus and the twelve should return from their proposed visit to Caesarea-Philippi. The Master participated in planning for the Decapolis mission and, in dismissing the company, said: "I say to you, beware of the leaven of the Pharisees and the Sadducees. Be not deceived by their show of much learning and by their profound loyalty to the forms of religion. Be only concerned with the spirit of living truth and the power of true religion. It is not the fear of a dead religion that will save you but rather your faith in a living experience in the spiritual realities of the kingdom. Do not allow yourselves to become blinded by prejudice and paralyzed by fear. Neither permit reverence for the traditions so to pervert your understanding that your eyes see not and your ears hear not. It is not the purpose of true religion merely to bring peace but rather to insure progress. And there can be no peace in the heart or progress in the mind unless you fall wholeheartedly in love with truth, the ideals of eternal realities. The issues of life and death are being set before you—the sinful pleasures of time against the righteous realities of eternity. Even now you should begin to find deliverance from the bondage of fear and doubt as you enter upon the living of the new life of faith and hope. And when the feelings of service for your fellow men arise within your soul, do not stifle them; when the emotions of love for your neighbor well up within your heart, give expression to such urges of affection in intelligent ministry to the real needs of your fellows."

3. PETER'S CONFESSION

Early Tuesday morning Jesus and the twelve apostles left Magadan Park for Caesarea-Philippi, the capital of the Tetrarch Philip's domain. Caesarea-Philippi was situated in a region of wondrous beauty. It nestled in a charming valley between scenic hills where the Jordan poured forth from an underground cave. The heights of Mount Hermon were in full view to the north, while from the hills just to the south a magnificent view was had of the upper Jordan and the Sea of Galilee.

Jesus had gone to Mount Hermon in his early experience with the affairs of the kingdom, and now that he was entering upon the final epoch of his work, he desired to return to this mount of trial and triumph, where he hoped the apostles might gain a new vision of their responsibilities and acquire new strength for the trying times just ahead. As they journeyed along the way, about the time of passing south of the Waters of Merom, the apostles fell to talking among themselves about their recent experiences in Phoenicia and elsewhere and to recounting how their message had been received, and how the different peoples regarded their Master.

As they paused for lunch, Jesus suddenly confronted the twelve with the first question he had ever addressed to them concerning himself. He asked this surprising question, "Who do men say that I am?"

Jesus had spent long months in training these apostles as to the nature and character of the kingdom of heaven, and he well knew the time had come when he must begin to teach them more about his own nature and his personal relationship to the kingdom. And now, as they were seated under the mulberry trees, the Master made ready to hold one of the most momentous sessions of his long association with the chosen apostles.

More than half the apostles participated in answering Jesus' question. They told him that he was regarded as a prophet or as an extraordinary man by all who knew him; that even his enemies greatly feared him, accounting for his powers by the indictment that he was in league with the prince of devils. They told him that some in Judea and Samaria who had not met him personally believed he was John the Baptist risen from the dead. Peter explained that he had been, at sundry times and by various persons, compared with Moses, Elijah, Isaiah, and Jeremiah. When Jesus had listened to this report, he drew himself upon his feet, and looking down upon the twelve sitting about him in a semicircle, with startling emphasis he pointed to them with a sweeping gesture of his hand and asked, "But who say you that I am?" There was a moment of tense silence. The twelve never took their eyes off the Master, and then Simon Peter, springing to his feet, exclaimed: "You are the Deliverer, the Son of the living God." And the eleven sitting apostles arose to their feet with one accord, thereby indicating that Peter had spoken for all of them.

When Jesus had beckoned them again to be seated, and while still standing before them, he said: "This has been revealed to you by my Father. The hour has come when you should know the truth about me. But for the time being I charge you that you tell this to no man. Let us go hence."

And so they resumed their journey to Caesarea-Philippi, arriving late that evening and stopping at the home of Celsus, who was expecting them. The apostles slept little that night; they seemed to sense that a great event in their lives and in the work of the kingdom had transpired.

4. THE TALK ABOUT THE KINGDOM

Since the occasions of Jesus' baptism by John and the turning of the water into wine at Cana, the apostles had, at various times, virtually accepted him as the Messiah. For short periods some of them had truly believed that he was the expected Deliverer. But hardly would such hopes spring up in their hearts than the Master would dash them to pieces by some crushing word or disappointing deed. They had long been in a state of turmoil due to conflict between the concepts of the expected Messiah which they held in their minds and the experience of their extraordinary association with this extraordinary man which they held in their hearts.

It was late forenoon on this Wednesday when the apostles assembled in Celsus' garden for their noontime meal. During most of the night and since they had arisen that morning, Simon Peter and Simon Zelotes had been earnestly laboring with their brethren to bring them all to the point of the wholehearted acceptance of the Master, not merely as the Messiah, but also as the divine Son of the living God. The two Simons were well-nigh agreed in their estimate of Jesus, and they labored diligently to bring their brethren around to the full acceptance of their views. While Andrew continued as the director-general of the apostolic corps, his brother, Simon Peter, was becoming, increasingly and by common consent, the spokesman for the twelve.

They were all seated in the garden at just about noon when the Master appeared. They wore expressions of dignified solemnity, and all arose to their feet as he approached them. Jesus relieved the tension by that friendly and fraternal smile which was so characteristic of him when his followers took themselves, or some happening related to themselves, too seriously. With a commanding gesture he indicated that they should be seated. Never again did the twelve greet their Master by arising when he came into their presence. They saw that he did not approve of such an outward show of respect.

After they had partaken of their meal and were engaged in discussing plans for the forthcoming tour of the Decapolis, Jesus suddenly looked up into their faces and said: "Now that a full day has passed since you assented to Simon Peter's declaration regarding the identity of the Son of Man, I would ask if you still hold to your decision?" On hearing this, the twelve stood upon their feet, and Simon Peter, stepping a few paces forward toward Jesus, said: "Yes, Master, we do. We believe that you are the Son of the living God." And Peter sat down with his brethren.

Jesus, still standing, then said to the twelve: "You are my chosen ambassadors, but I know that, in the circumstances, you could not entertain this belief as a result of mere human knowledge. This is a revelation of the spirit of my Father to your inmost souls. And when, therefore, you make this confession by the insight of the spirit of my Father which dwells within you, I am led to declare that upon this foundation will I build the brotherhood of the kingdom of heaven. Upon this rock of spiritual reality will I build the living temple of spiritual fellowship in the eternal realities of my Father's kingdom. All the forces of evil and the hosts of sin shall not prevail against this human fraternity of the divine spirit. And while my Father's spirit shall ever be the divine guide and mentor of all who enter the bonds of this spirit fellowship, to you and your successors I now deliver the keys of the outward kingdom—the authority over things temporal—the social and economic features of this association of men and women as fellows of the kingdom." And again he charged them, for the time being, that they should tell no man that he was the Son of God.

Jesus was beginning to have faith in the loyalty and integrity of his apostles. The Master conceived that a faith which could stand what his chosen representatives had recently passed through would undoubtedly endure the fiery trials which were just ahead and emerge from the apparent wreckage of all their hopes into the new light of a new dispensation and thereby be able to go forth to enlighten a world sitting in darkness. On this day the Master began to believe in the faith of his apostles, save one.

And ever since that day this same Jesus has been building that living temple upon that same eternal foundation of his divine sonship, and those who thereby become self-conscious sons of God are the human stones which constitute this living temple of sonship erecting to the glory and honor of the wisdom and love of the eternal Father of spirits.

And when Jesus had thus spoken, he directed the twelve to go apart by themselves in the hills to seek wisdom, strength, and spiritual guidance until the time of the evening meal. And they did as the Master admonished them.

5. THE NEW CONCEPT

The new and vital feature of Peter's confession was the clear-cut recognition that Jesus was the Son of God, of his unquestioned divinity. Ever since his baptism and the wedding at Cana these apostles had variously regarded him as the Messiah, but it was not a part of the Jewish concept of the national deliverer that he should be *divine.* The Jews had not taught that the Messiah would spring from divinity; he was to be the "anointed one," but hardly had they contemplated him as being "the Son of God." In the second confession more emphasis was placed upon the *combined nature,* the supernal fact that he was the Son of Man *and* the Son of God, and it was upon this great truth of the union of the human nature with the divine nature that Jesus declared he would build the kingdom of heaven.

Jesus had sought to live his life on earth and complete his bestowal mission as the Son of Man. His followers were disposed to regard him as the expected Messiah. Knowing that he could never fulfill their Messianic expectations, he endeavored to effect such a modification of their concept of the Messiah as would enable him partially to meet their expectations. But he now recognized that such a plan could hardly be carried through successfully. He therefore elected boldly to disclose the third plan—openly to announce his divinity, acknowledge the truthfulness of Peter's confession, and directly proclaim to the twelve that he was a Son of God.

For three years Jesus had been proclaiming that he was the "Son of Man," while for these same three years the apostles had been increasingly insistent that he was the expected Jewish Messiah. He now disclosed that he was the Son of God, and upon the concept of the *combined nature* of the Son of Man and the Son of God, he determined to build the kingdom of heaven. He had decided to refrain from further efforts to convince them that he was not the Messiah. He now proposed boldly to reveal to them what he *is,* and then to ignore their determination to persist in regarding him as the Messiah.

6. THE NEXT AFTERNOON

Jesus and the apostles remained another day at the home of Celsus, waiting for messengers to arrive from David Zebedee with funds. Following the collapse of the popularity of Jesus with the masses there occurred a great falling off in revenue. When they reached Caesarea-Philippi, the treasury was empty. Matthew was loath to leave Jesus and his brethren at such a time, and he had no ready funds of his own to hand over to Judas as he had so many times done in the past. However, David Zebedee had foreseen this probable diminution of revenue and had accordingly instructed his messengers that, as they made their way through Judea, Samaria, and Galilee, they should act as collectors of money to be forwarded to the exiled apostles and their Master. And so, by evening of this day, these messengers arrived from Bethsaida bringing funds sufficient to sustain the apostles until their return to embark upon the Decapolis tour. Matthew expected to have money from the sale of his last piece of property in Capernaum by that time, having arranged that these funds should be anonymously turned over to Judas.

Neither Peter nor the other apostles had a very adequate conception of Jesus' divinity. They little realized that this was the beginning of a new epoch in their Master's career on earth, the time when the teacher-healer was becoming the newly conceived Messiah—the Son of God. From this time on a new note appeared in the Master's message. Henceforth his one ideal of living was the revelation of the Father, while his one idea in teaching was to present to his universe the personification of that supreme wisdom which can only be comprehended by living it. He came that we all might have life and have it more abundantly.

Jesus now entered upon the fourth and last stage of his human life in the flesh. The first stage was that of his childhood, the years when he was only dimly conscious of his origin, nature, and destiny as a human being. The second stage was the increasingly self-conscious years of youth and advancing manhood, during which he came more clearly to comprehend his divine nature and human mission. This second stage ended with the experiences and revelations associated with his baptism. The third stage of the Master's earth experience extended from the baptism through the years of his ministry as teacher and healer and up to this momentous hour of Peter's confession at Caesarea-Philippi. This third period of his earth life embraced the times when his apostles and his immediate followers knew him as the Son of Man and regarded him as the Messiah. The fourth and last period of his earth career began here at Caesarea-Philippi and extended on to the crucifixion. This stage of his ministry was characterized by his acknowledgment of divinity and embraced the labors of his last year in the flesh. During the fourth period, while the majority of his followers still regarded him as the Messiah, he became known to the apostles as the Son of God. Peter's confession marked the beginning of the new period of the more complete realization of the truth of his supreme ministry as a bestowal Son on Urantia and for an entire universe, and the recognition of that fact, at least hazily, by his chosen ambassadors.

Thus did Jesus exemplify in his life what he taught in his religion: the growth of the spiritual nature by the technique of living progress. He did not place emphasis, as did his later followers, upon the incessant struggle between the soul and the body. He rather taught that the spirit was easy victor over both and effective in the profitable reconciliation of much of this intellectual and instinctual warfare.

A new significance attaches to all of Jesus' teachings from this point on. Before Caesarea-Philippi he presented the gospel of the kingdom as its master teacher. After Caesarea-Philippi he appeared not merely as a teacher but as the divine representative of the eternal Father, who is the center and circumference of this spiritual kingdom, and it was required that he do all this as a human being, the Son of Man.

Jesus had sincerely endeavored to lead his followers into the spiritual kingdom as a teacher, then as a teacher-healer, but they would not have it so. He well knew that his earth mission could not possibly fulfill the Messianic expectations of the Jewish people; the olden prophets had portrayed a Messiah which he could never be. He sought to establish the Father's kingdom as the Son of Man, but his followers would not go forward in the adventure. Jesus, seeing this, then elected to meet his believers part way and in so doing prepared openly to assume the role of the bestowal Son of God.

Accordingly, the apostles heard much that was new as Jesus talked to them this day in the garden. And some of these pronouncements sounded strange even to them. Among other startling announcements they listened to such as the following:

"From this time on, if any man would have fellowship with us, let him assume the obligations of sonship and follow me. And when I am no more with you, think not that the world will treat you better than it did your Master. If you love me, prepare to prove this affection by your willingness to make the supreme sacrifice."

"And mark well my words: I have not come to call the righteous, but sinners. The Son of Man came not to be ministered to, but to minister and to bestow his life as the gift for all. I declare to you that I have come to seek and to save those who are lost."

"No man in this world now sees the Father except the Son who came forth from the Father. But if the Son be lifted up, he will draw all men to himself, and whosoever believes this truth of the combined nature of the Son shall be endowed with life that is more than age-abiding."

"We may not yet proclaim openly that the Son of Man is the Son of God, but it has been revealed to you; wherefore do I speak boldly to you concerning these mysteries. Though I stand before you in this physical presence, I came forth from God the Father. Before Abraham was, I am. I did come forth from the Father into this world as you have known me, and I declare to you that I must presently leave this world and return to the work of my Father."

"And now can your faith comprehend the truth of these declarations in the face of my warning you that the Son of Man will not meet the expectations of your fathers as they conceived the Messiah? My kingdom is not of this world. Can you believe the truth about me in the face of the fact that, though the foxes have holes and the birds of heaven have nests, I have not where to lay my head?"

"Nevertheless, I tell you that the Father and I are one. He who has seen me has seen the Father. My Father is working with me in all these things, and he will never leave me alone in my mission, even as I will never forsake you when you presently go forth to proclaim this gospel throughout the world.

"And now have I brought you apart with me and by yourselves for a little while that you may comprehend the glory, and grasp the grandeur, of the life to which I have called you: the faith-adventure of the establishment of my Father's kingdom in the hearts of mankind, the building of my fellowship of living association with the souls of all who believe this gospel."

The apostles listened to these bold and startling statements in silence; they were stunned. And they dispersed in small groups to discuss and ponder the Master's words. They had confessed that he was the Son of God, but they could not grasp the full meaning of what they had been led to do.

7. ANDREW'S CONFERENCE

That evening Andrew took it upon himself to hold a personal and searching conference with each of his brethren, and he had profitable and heartening talks with all of his associates except Judas Iscariot. Andrew had never enjoyed such intimate personal association with Judas as with the other apostles and therefore had not thought it of serious account that Judas never had freely and confidentially related himself to the head of the apostolic corps. But Andrew was now so worried by Judas's attitude that, later on that night, after all the apostles were fast asleep, he sought out Jesus and presented his cause for anxiety to the Master. Said Jesus: "It is not amiss, Andrew, that you have come to me with this matter, but there is nothing more that we can do; only go on placing the utmost confidence in this apostle. And say nothing to his brethren concerning this talk with me."

And that was all Andrew could elicit from Jesus. Always had there been some strangeness between this Judean and his Galilean brethren. Judas had been shocked by the death of John the Baptist, severely hurt by the Master's rebukes on several occasions, disappointed when Jesus refused to be made king, humiliated when he fled from the Pharisees, chagrined when he refused to accept the challenge of the Pharisees for a sign, bewildered by the refusal of his Master to resort to manifestations of power, and now, more recently, depressed and sometimes dejected by an empty treasury. And Judas missed the stimulus of the multitudes.

Each of the other apostles was, in some and varying measure, likewise affected by these selfsame trials and tribulations, but they loved Jesus. At least they must have loved the Master more than did Judas, for they went through with him to the bitter end.

Being from Judea, Judas took personal offense at Jesus' recent warning to the apostles to "beware the leaven of the Pharisees"; he was disposed to regard this statement as a veiled reference to himself. But the great mistake of Judas was: Time and again, when Jesus would send his apostles off by themselves to pray, Judas, instead of engaging in sincere communion with the spiritual forces of the universe, indulged in thoughts of human fear while he persisted in the entertainment of subtle doubts about the mission of Jesus as well as giving in to his unfortunate tendency to harbor feelings of revenge.

And now Jesus would take his apostles along with him to Mount Hermon, where he had appointed to inaugurate his fourth phase of earth ministry as the Son of God. Some of them were present at his baptism in the Jordan and had witnessed the beginning of his career as the Son of Man, and he desired that some of them should also be present to hear his authority for the assumption of the new and public role of a Son of God. Accordingly, on the morning of Friday, August 12, Jesus said to the twelve: "Lay in provisions and prepare yourselves for a journey to yonder mountain, where the spirit bids me go to be endowed for the finish of my work on earth. And I would take my brethren along that they may also be strengthened for the trying times of going with me through this experience."

PAPER 158

THE MOUNT OF TRANSFIGURATION

IT WAS near sundown on Friday afternoon, August 12, A.D. 29, when Jesus and his associates reached the foot of Mount Hermon, near the very place where the lad Tiglath once waited while the Master ascended the mountain alone to settle the spiritual destinies of Urantia and technically to terminate the Lucifer rebellion. And here they sojourned for two days in spiritual preparation for the events so soon to follow.

In a general way, Jesus knew beforehand what was to transpire on the mountain, and he much desired that all his apostles might share this experience. It was to fit them for this revelation of himself that he tarried with them at the foot of the mountain. But they could not attain those spiritual levels which would justify their exposure to the full experience of the visitation of the celestial beings so soon to appear on earth. And since he could not take all of his associates with him, he decided to take only the three who were in the habit of accompanying him on such special vigils. Accordingly, only Peter, James, and John shared even a part of this unique experience with the Master.

1. THE TRANSFIGURATION

Early on the morning of Monday, August 15, Jesus and the three apostles began the ascent of Mount Hermon, and this was six days after the memorable noontide confession of Peter by the roadside under the mulberry trees.

Jesus had been summoned to go up on the mountain, apart by himself, for the transaction of important matters having to do with the progress of his bestowal in the flesh as this experience was related to the universe of his own creation. It is significant that this extraordinary event was timed to occur while Jesus and the apostles were in the lands of the gentiles, and that it actually transpired on a mountain of the gentiles.

They reached their destination, about halfway up the mountain, shortly before noon, and while eating lunch, Jesus told the three apostles something of his experience in the hills to the east of Jordan shortly after his baptism and also some more of his experience on Mount Hermon in connection with his former visit to this lonely retreat.

When a boy, Jesus used to ascend the hill near his home and dream of the battles which had been fought by the armies of empires on the plain of Esdraelon; now he ascended Mount Hermon to receive the endowment which was to prepare him to descend upon the plains of the Jordan to enact the closing scenes of the drama of his bestowal on Urantia. The Master could have relinquished the struggle this day on Mount Hermon and returned to his rule of the universe domains, but he not only chose to meet the requirements of his order of divine sonship embraced in the mandate of the Eternal Son on Paradise, but he also elected to meet the last and full measure of the present will of his Paradise Father. On this day in August three of his apostles saw him decline to be invested with full universe authority. They looked on in amazement as the celestial messengers departed, leaving him alone to finish out his earth life as the Son of Man and the Son of God.

The faith of the apostles was at a high point at the time of the feeding of the five thousand, and then it rapidly fell almost to zero. Now, as a result of the Master's admission of his divinity, the lagging faith of the twelve arose in the next few weeks to its highest pitch, only to undergo a progressive decline. The third revival of their faith did not occur until after the Master's resurrection.

It was about three o'clock on this beautiful afternoon that Jesus took leave of the three apostles, saying: "I go apart by myself for a season to commune with the Father and his messengers; I bid you tarry here and, while awaiting my return, pray that the Father's will may be done in all your experience in connection with the further bestowal mission of the Son of Man." And after saying this to them, Jesus withdrew for a long conference with Gabriel and the Father Melchizedek, not returning until about six o'clock. When Jesus saw their anxiety over his prolonged absence, he said: "Why were you afraid? You well know I must be about my Father's business; wherefore do you doubt when I am not with you? I now declare that the Son of Man has chosen to go through his full life in your midst and as one of you. Be of good cheer; I will not leave you until my work is finished."

As they partook of their meager evening meal, Peter asked the Master, "How long do we remain on this mountain away from our brethren?" And Jesus answered: "Until you shall see the glory of the Son of Man and know that whatsoever I have declared to you is true." And they talked over the affairs of the Lucifer rebellion while seated about the glowing embers of their fire until darkness drew on and the apostles' eyes grew heavy, for they had begun their journey very early that morning.

When the three had been fast asleep for about half an hour, they were suddenly awakened by a near-by crackling sound, and much to their amazement and consternation, on looking about them, they beheld Jesus in intimate converse with two brilliant beings clothed in the habiliments of the light of the celestial world. And Jesus' face and form shone with the luminosity of a heavenly light. These three conversed in a strange language, but from certain things said, Peter erroneously conjectured that the beings with Jesus were Moses and Elijah; in reality, they were Gabriel and the Father Melchizedek. The physical controllers had arranged for the apostles to witness this scene because of Jesus' request.

The three apostles were so badly frightened that they were slow in collecting their wits, but Peter, who was first to recover himself, said, as the dazzling vision faded from before them and they observed Jesus standing alone: "Jesus, Master, it is good to have been here. We rejoice to see this glory. We are loath to go back down to the inglorious world. If you are willing, let us abide here, and we will erect three tents, one for you, one for Moses, and one for Elijah." And Peter said this because of his confusion, and because nothing else came into his mind at just that moment.

While Peter was yet speaking, a silvery cloud drew near and overshadowed the four of them. The apostles now became greatly frightened, and as they fell down on their faces to worship, they heard a voice, the same that had spoken on the occasion of Jesus' baptism, say: "This is my beloved Son; give heed to him." And when the cloud vanished, again was Jesus alone with the three, and he reached down and touched them, saying: "Arise and be not afraid; you shall see greater things than this." But the apostles were truly afraid; they were a silent and thoughtful trio as they made ready to descend the mountain shortly before midnight.

2. COMING DOWN THE MOUNTAIN

For about half the distance down the mountain not a word was spoken. Jesus then began the conversation by remarking: "Make certain that you tell no man, not even your brethren, what you have seen and heard on this mountain until the Son of Man has risen from the dead." The three apostles were shocked and bewildered by the Master's words, "until the Son of Man has risen from the dead." They had so recently reaffirmed their faith in him as the Deliverer, the Son of God, and they had just beheld him transfigured in glory before their very eyes, and now he began to talk about "rising from the dead"!

Peter shuddered at the thought of the Master's dying—it was too disagreeable an idea to entertain—and fearing that James or John might ask some question relative to this statement, he thought best to start up a diverting conversation and, not knowing what else to talk about, gave expression to the first thought coming into his mind, which was: "Master, why is it that the scribes say that Elijah must first come before the Messiah shall appear?" And Jesus, knowing that Peter sought to avoid reference to his death and resurrection, answered: "Elijah indeed comes first to prepare the way for the Son of Man, who must suffer many things and finally be rejected. But I tell you that Elijah has already come, and they received him not but did to him whatsoever they willed." And then did the three apostles perceive that he referred to John the Baptist as Elijah. Jesus knew that, if they insisted on regarding him as the Messiah, then must John be the Elijah of the prophecy.

Jesus enjoined silence about their observation of the foretaste of his post-resurrection glory because he did not want to foster the notion that, being now received as the Messiah, he would in any degree fulfill their erroneous concepts of a wonder-working deliverer. Although Peter, James, and John pondered all this in their minds, they spoke not of it to any man until after the Master's resurrection.

As they continued to descend the mountain, Jesus said to them: "You would not receive me as the Son of Man; therefore have I consented to be received in accordance with your settled determination, but, mistake not, the will of my Father must prevail. If you thus choose to follow the inclination of your own wills, you must prepare to suffer many disappointments and experience many trials, but the training which I have given you should suffice to bring you triumphantly through even these sorrows of your own choosing."

Jesus did not take Peter, James, and John with him up to the mount of the transfiguration because they were in any sense better prepared than the other apostles to witness what happened, or because they were spiritually more fit to enjoy such a rare privilege. Not at all. He well knew that none of the twelve were spiritually qualified for this experience; therefore did he take with him only the three apostles who were assigned to accompany him at those times when he desired to be alone to enjoy solitary communion.

3. MEANING OF THE TRANSFIGURATION

That which Peter, James, and John witnessed on the mount of transfiguration was a fleeting glimpse of a celestial pageant which transpired that eventful day on Mount Hermon. The transfiguration was the occasion of:

1. The acceptance of the fullness of the bestowal of the incarnated life of Michael on Urantia by the Eternal Mother-Son of Paradise. As far as concerned the requirements of the Eternal Son, Jesus had now received assurance of their fulfillment. And Gabriel brought Jesus that assurance.

2. The testimony of the satisfaction of the Infinite Spirit as to the fullness of the Urantia bestowal in the likeness of mortal flesh. The universe representative of the Infinite Spirit, the immediate associate of Michael on Salvington and his ever-present coworker, on this occasion spoke through the Father Melchizedek.

Jesus welcomed this testimony regarding the success of his earth mission presented by the messengers of the Eternal Son and the Infinite Spirit, but he noted that his Father did not indicate that the Urantia bestowal was finished; only did the unseen presence of the Father bear witness through Jesus' Personalized Adjuster, saying, "This is my beloved Son; give heed to him." And this was spoken in words to be heard also by the three apostles.

After this celestial visitation Jesus sought to know his Father's will and decided to pursue the mortal bestowal to its natural end. This was the significance of the transfiguration to Jesus. To the three apostles it was an event marking the entrance of the Master upon the final phase of his earth career as the Son of God and the Son of Man.

After the formal visitation of Gabriel and the Father Melchizedek, Jesus held informal converse with these, his Sons of ministry, and communed with them concerning the affairs of the universe.

4. THE EPILEPTIC BOY

It was shortly before breakfast time on this Tuesday morning when Jesus and his companions arrived at the apostolic camp. As they drew near, they discerned a considerable crowd gathered around the apostles and soon began to hear the loud words of argument and disputation of this group of about fifty persons, embracing the nine apostles and a gathering equally divided between Jerusalem scribes and believing disciples who had tracked Jesus and his associates in their journey from Magadan.

Although the crowd engaged in numerous arguments, the chief controversy was about a certain citizen of Tiberias who had arrived the preceding day in quest of Jesus. This man, James of Safed, had a son about fourteen years old, an only child, who was severely afflicted with epilepsy. In addition to this nervous malady this lad had become possessed by one of those wandering, mischievous, and rebellious midwayers who were then present on earth and uncontrolled, so that the youth was both epileptic and demon-possessed.

For almost two weeks this anxious father, a minor official of Herod Antipas, had wandered about through the western borders of Philip's domains, seeking Jesus that he might entreat him to cure this afflicted son. And he did not catch up with the apostolic party until about noon of this day when Jesus was up on the mountain with the three apostles.

The nine apostles were much surprised and considerably perturbed when this man, accompanied by almost forty other persons who were looking for Jesus, suddenly came upon them. At the time of the arrival of this group the nine apostles, at least the majority of them, had succumbed to their old temptation—that of discussing who should be greatest in the coming kingdom; they were busily arguing about the probable positions which would be assigned the individual apostles. They simply could not free themselves entirely from the long-cherished idea of the material mission of the Messiah. And now that Jesus himself had accepted their confession that he was indeed the Deliverer—at least he had admitted the fact of his divinity—what was more natural than that, during this period of separation from the Master, they should fall to talking about those hopes and ambitions which were uppermost in their hearts. And they were engaged in these discussions when James of Safed and his fellow seekers after Jesus came upon them.

Andrew stepped up to greet this father and his son, saying, "Whom do you seek?" Said James: "My good man, I search for your Master. I seek healing for my afflicted son. I would have Jesus cast out this devil that possesses my child." And then the father proceeded to relate to the apostles how his son was so afflicted that he had many times almost lost his life as a result of these malignant seizures.

As the apostles listened, Simon Zelotes and Judas Iscariot stepped into the presence of the father, saying: "We can heal him; you need not wait for the Master's return. We are ambassadors of the kingdom; no longer do we hold these things in secret. Jesus is the Deliverer, and the keys of the kingdom have been delivered to us." By this time Andrew and Thomas were in consultation at one side. Nathaniel and the others looked on in amazement; they were all aghast at the sudden boldness, if not presumption, of Simon and Judas. Then said the father: "If it has been given you to do these works, I pray that you will speak those words which will deliver my child from this bondage." Then Simon stepped forward and, placing his hand on the head of the child, looked directly into his eyes and commanded: "Come out of him, you unclean spirit; in the name of Jesus obey me." But the lad had only a more violent fit, while the scribes mocked the apostles in derision, and the disappointed believers suffered the taunts of these unfriendly critics.

Andrew was deeply chagrined at this ill-advised effort and its dismal failure. He called the apostles aside for conference and prayer. After this season of meditation, feeling keenly the sting of their defeat and sensing the humiliation resting upon all of them, Andrew sought, in a second attempt, to cast out the demon, but only failure crowned his efforts. Andrew frankly confessed defeat and requested the father to remain with them overnight or until Jesus' return, saying: "Perhaps this sort goes not out except by the Master's personal command."

And so, while Jesus was descending the mountain with the exuberant and ecstatic Peter, James, and John, their nine brethren likewise were sleepless in their confusion and downcast humiliation. They were a dejected and chastened group. But James of Safed would not give up. Although they could give him no idea as to when Jesus might return, he decided to stay on until the Master came back.

5. JESUS HEALS THE BOY

As Jesus drew near, the nine apostles were more than relieved to welcome him, and they were greatly encouraged to behold the good cheer and unusual enthusiasm which marked the countenances of Peter, James, and John. They all rushed forward to greet Jesus and their three brethren. As they exchanged greetings, the crowd came up, and Jesus asked, "What were you disputing about as we drew near?" But before the disconcerted and humiliated apostles could reply to the Master's question, the anxious father of the afflicted lad stepped forward and, kneeling at Jesus' feet, said: "Master, I have a son, an only child, who is possessed by an evil spirit. Not only does he cry out in terror, foam at the mouth, and fall like a dead person at the time of seizure, but oftentimes this evil spirit which possesses him rends him in convulsions and sometimes has cast him into the water and even into the fire. With much grinding of teeth and as a result of many bruises, my child wastes away. His life is worse than death; his mother and I are of a sad heart and a broken spirit. About noon yesterday, seeking for you, I caught up with your disciples, and while we were waiting, your apostles sought to cast out this demon, but they could not do it. And now, Master, will you do this for us, will you heal my son?"

When Jesus had listened to this recital, he touched the kneeling father and bade him rise while he gave the near-by apostles a searching survey. Then said Jesus to all those who stood before him: "O faithless and perverse generation, how long shall I bear with you? How long shall I be with you? How long ere you learn that the works of faith come not forth at the bidding of doubting unbelief?" And then, pointing to the bewildered father, Jesus said, "Bring hither your son." And when James had brought the lad before Jesus, he asked, "How long has the boy been afflicted in this way?" The father answered, "Since he was a very young child." And as they talked, the youth was seized with a violent attack and fell in their midst, gnashing his teeth and foaming at the mouth. After a succession of violent convulsions he lay there before them as one dead. Now did the father again kneel at Jesus' feet while he implored the Master, saying: "If you can cure him, I beseech you to have compassion on us and deliver us from this affliction." And when Jesus heard these words, he looked down into the father's anxious face, saying: "Question not my Father's power of love, only the sincerity and reach of your faith. All things are possible to him who really believes." And then James of Safed spoke those long-to-be-remembered words of commingled faith and doubt, "Lord, I believe. I pray you help my unbelief."

When Jesus heard these words, he stepped forward and, taking the lad by the hand, said: "I will do this in accordance with my Father's will and in honor of living faith. My son, arise! Come out of him, disobedient spirit, and go not back into him." And placing the hand of the lad in the hand of the father, Jesus said: "Go your way. The Father has granted the desire of your soul." And all who were present, even the enemies of Jesus, were astonished at what they saw.

It was indeed a disillusionment for the three apostles who had so recently enjoyed the spiritual ecstasy of the scenes and experiences of the transfiguration, so soon to return to this scene of the defeat and discomfiture of their fellow apostles. But it was ever so with these twelve ambassadors of the kingdom.

They never failed to alternate between exaltation and humiliation in their life experiences.

This was a true healing of a double affliction, a physical ailment and a spirit malady. And the lad was permanently cured from that hour. When James had departed with his restored son, Jesus said: "We go now to Caesarea-Philippi; make ready at once." And they were a quiet group as they journeyed southward while the crowd followed on behind.

6. IN CELSUS' GARDEN

They remained overnight with Celsus, and that evening in the garden, after they had eaten and rested, the twelve gathered about Jesus, and Thomas said: "Master, while we who tarried behind still remain ignorant of what transpired up on the mountain, and which so greatly cheered our brethren who were with you, we crave to have you talk with us concerning our defeat and instruct us in these matters, seeing that those things which happened on the mountain cannot be disclosed at this time."

And Jesus answered Thomas, saying: "Everything which your brethren heard on the mountain shall be revealed to you in due season. But I will now show you the cause of your defeat in that which you so unwisely attempted. While your Master and his companions, your brethren, ascended yonder mountain yesterday to seek for a larger knowledge of the Father's will and to ask for a richer endowment of wisdom effectively to do that divine will, you who remained on watch here with instructions to strive to acquire the mind of spiritual insight and to pray with us for a fuller revelation of the Father's will, failed to exercise the faith at your command but, instead, yielded to the temptation and fell into your old evil tendencies to seek for yourselves preferred places in the kingdom of heaven—the material and temporal kingdom which you persist in contemplating. And you cling to these erroneous concepts in spite of the reiterated declaration that my kingdom is not of this world.

"No sooner does your faith grasp the identity of the Son of Man than your selfish desire for worldly preferment creeps back upon you, and you fall to discussing among yourselves as to who should be greatest in the kingdom of heaven, a kingdom which, as you persist in conceiving it, does not exist, nor ever shall. Have not I told you that he who would be greatest in the kingdom of my Father's spiritual brotherhood must become little in his own eyes and thus become the server of his brethren? Spiritual greatness consists in an understanding love that is Godlike and not in an enjoyment of the exercise of material power for the exaltation of self. In what you attempted, in which you so completely failed, your purpose was not pure. Your motive was not divine. Your ideal was not spiritual. Your ambition was not altruistic. Your procedure was not based on love, and your goal of attainment was not the will of the Father in heaven.

"How long will it take you to learn that you cannot time-shorten the course of established natural phenomena except when such things are in accordance with the Father's will? nor can you do spiritual work in the absence of spiritual power. And you can do neither of these, even when their potential is present, without the existence of that third and essential human factor, the personal experience of the possession of living faith. Must you always have material manifestations as an attraction for the spiritual realities of the kingdom? Can you not grasp the spirit significance of my mission without the visible exhibition of unusual works? When can you be depended upon to adhere to the higher and spiritual realities of the kingdom regardless of the outward appearance of all material manifestations?"

When Jesus had thus spoken to the twelve, he added: "And now go to your rest, for on the morrow we return to Magadan and there take counsel concerning our mission to the cities and villages of the Decapolis. And in the conclusion of this day's experience, let me declare to each of you that which I spoke to your brethren on the mountain, and let these words find a deep lodgment in your hearts: The Son of Man now enters upon the last phase of the bestowal. We are about to begin those labors which shall presently lead to the great and final testing of your faith and devotion when I shall be delivered into the hands of the men who seek my destruction. And remember what I am saying to you: The Son of Man will be put to death, but he shall rise again."

They retired for the night, sorrowful. They were bewildered; they could not comprehend these words. And while they were afraid to ask aught concerning what he had said, they did recall all of it subsequent to his resurrection.

7. PETER'S PROTEST

Early this Wednesday morning Jesus and the twelve departed from Caesarea-Philippi for Magadan Park near Bethsaida-Julias. The apostles had slept very little that night, so they were up early and ready to go. Even the stolid Alpheus twins had been shocked by this talk about the death of Jesus. As they journeyed south, just beyond the Waters of Merom they came to the Damascus road, and desiring to avoid the scribes and others whom Jesus knew would presently be coming along after them, he directed that they go on to Capernaum by the Damascus road which passes through Galilee. And he did this because he knew that those who followed after him would go on down over the east Jordan road since they reckoned that Jesus and the apostles would fear to pass through the territory of Herod Antipas. Jesus sought to elude his critics and the crowd which followed him that he might be alone with his apostles this day.

They traveled on through Galilee until well past the time for their lunch, when they stopped in the shade to refresh themselves. And after they had partaken of food, Andrew, speaking to Jesus, said: "Master, my brethren do not comprehend your deep sayings. We have come fully to believe that you are the Son of God, and now we hear these strange words about leaving us, about dying. We do not understand your teaching. Are you speaking to us in parables? We pray you to speak to us directly and in undisguised form."

In answer to Andrew, Jesus said: "My brethren, it is because you have confessed that I am the Son of God that I am constrained to begin to unfold to you the truth about the end of the bestowal of the Son of Man on earth. You insist on clinging to the belief that I am the Messiah, and you will not abandon the idea that the Messiah must sit upon a throne in Jerusalem; wherefore do I persist in telling you that the Son of Man must presently go to Jerusalem, suffer many things, be rejected by the scribes, the elders, and the chief priests, and after all this be killed and raised from the dead. And I speak not a parable to you; I speak the truth to you that you may be prepared for these events when they suddenly come upon us." And while he was yet speaking, Simon Peter, rushing impetuously toward him, laid his hand upon the Master's shoulder and said: "Master, be it far from us to contend with you, but I declare that these things shall never happen to you."

Peter spoke thus because he loved Jesus; but the Master's human nature recognized in these words of well-meant affection the subtle suggestion of temptation that he change his policy of pursuing to the end his earth bestowal in accordance with the will of his Paradise Father. And it was because he detected the danger of permitting the suggestions of even his affectionate and loyal friends to dissuade him, that he turned upon Peter and the other apostles, saying: "Get you behind me. You savor of the spirit of the adversary, the tempter. When you talk in this manner, you are not on my side but rather on the side of our enemy. In this way do you make your love for me a stumbling block to my doing the Father's will. Mind not the ways of men but rather the will of God."

After they had recovered from the first shock of Jesus' stinging rebuke, and before they resumed their journey, the Master spoke further: "If any man would come after me, let him disregard himself, take up his responsibilities daily, and follow me. For whosoever would save his life selfishly, shall lose it, but whosoever loses his life for my sake and the gospel's, shall save it. What does it profit a man to gain the whole world and lose his own soul? What would a man give in exchange for eternal life? Be not ashamed of me and my words in this sinful and hypocritical generation, even as I will not be ashamed to acknowledge you when in glory I appear before my Father in the presence of all the celestial hosts. Nevertheless, many of you now standing before me shall not taste death till you see this kingdom of God come with power."

And thus did Jesus make plain to the twelve the painful and conflicting path which they must tread if they would follow him. What a shock these words were to these Galilean fishermen who persisted in dreaming of an earthly kingdom with positions of honor for themselves! But their loyal hearts were stirred by this courageous appeal, and not one of them was minded to forsake him. Jesus was not sending them alone into the conflict; he was leading them. He asked only that they bravely follow.

Slowly the twelve were grasping the idea that Jesus was telling them something about the possibility of his dying. They only vaguely comprehended what he said about his death, while his statement about rising from the dead utterly failed to register in their minds. As the days passed, Peter, James, and John, recalling their experience upon the mount of the transfiguration, arrived at a fuller understanding of certain of these matters.

In all the association of the twelve with their Master, only a few times did they see that flashing eye and hear such swift words of rebuke as were administered to Peter and the rest of them on this occasion. Jesus had always been patient with their human shortcomings, but not so when faced by an impending threat against the program of implicitly carrying out his Father's will regarding the remainder of his earth career. The apostles were literally stunned; they were amazed and horrified. They could not find words to express their sorrow. Slowly they began to realize what the Master must endure, and that they must go through these experiences with him, but they did not awaken to the reality of these coming events until long after these early hints of the impending tragedy of his latter days.

In silence Jesus and the twelve started for their camp at Magadan Park, going by way of Capernaum. As the afternoon wore on, though they did not converse with Jesus, they talked much among themselves while Andrew talked with the Master.

8. AT PETER'S HOUSE

Entering Capernaum at twilight, they went by unfrequented thoroughfares directly to the home of Simon Peter for their evening meal. While David Zebedee made ready to take them across the lake, they lingered at Simon's house, and Jesus, looking up at Peter and the other apostles, asked: "As you walked along together this afternoon, what was it that you talked about so earnestly among yourselves?" The apostles held their peace because many of them had continued the discussion begun at Mount Hermon as to what positions they were to have in the coming kingdom; who should be the greatest, and so on. Jesus, knowing what it was that occupied their thoughts that day, beckoned to one of Peter's little ones and, setting the child down among them, said: "Verily, verily, I say to you, except you turn about and become more like this child, you will make little progress in the kingdom of heaven. Whosoever shall humble himself and become as this little one, the same shall become greatest in the kingdom of heaven. And whoso receives such a little one receives me. And they who receive me receive also Him who sent me. If you would be first in the kingdom, seek to minister these good truths to your brethren in the flesh. But whosoever causes one of these little ones to stumble, it would be better for him if a millstone were hanged about his neck and he were cast into the sea. If the things you do with your hands, or the things you see with your eyes give offense in the progress of the kingdom, sacrifice these cherished idols, for it is better to enter the kingdom minus many of the beloved things of life rather than to cling to these idols and find yourself shut out of the kingdom. But most of all, see that you despise not one of these little ones, for their angels do always behold the faces of the heavenly hosts."

When Jesus had finished speaking, they entered the boat and sailed across to Magadan.

PAPER 159

THE DECAPOLIS TOUR

WHEN Jesus and the twelve arrived at Magadan Park, they found awaiting them a group of almost one hundred evangelists and disciples, including the women's corps, and they were ready immediately to begin the teaching and preaching tour of the cities of the Decapolis.

On this Thursday morning, August 18, the Master called his followers together and directed that each of the apostles should associate himself with one of the twelve evangelists, and that with others of the evangelists they should go out in twelve groups to labor in the cities and villages of the Decapolis. The women's corps and others of the disciples he directed to remain with him. Jesus allotted four weeks to this tour, instructing his followers to return to Magadan not later than Friday, September 16. He promised to visit them often during this time. In the course of this month these twelve groups labored in Gerasa, Gamala, Hippos, Zaphon, Gadara, Abila, Edrei, Philadelphia, Heshbon, Dium, Scythopolis, and many other cities. Throughout this tour no miracles of healing or other extraordinary events occurred.

1. THE SERMON ON FORGIVENESS

One evening at Hippos, in answer to a disciple's question, Jesus taught the lesson on forgiveness. Said the Master:

"If a kindhearted man has a hundred sheep and one of them goes astray, does he not immediately leave the ninety and nine and go out in search of the one that has gone astray? And if he is a good shepherd, will he not keep up his quest for the lost sheep until he finds it? And then, when the shepherd has found his lost sheep, he lays it over his shoulder and, going home rejoicing, calls to his friends and neighbors, 'Rejoice with me, for I have found my sheep that was lost.' I declare that there is more joy in heaven over one sinner who repents than over ninety and nine righteous persons who need no repentance. Even so, it is not the will of my Father in heaven that one of these little ones should go astray, much less that they should perish. In your religion God may receive repentant sinners; in the gospel of the kingdom the Father goes forth to find them even before they have seriously thought of repentance.

"The Father in heaven loves his children, and therefore should you learn to love one another; the Father in heaven forgives you your sins; therefore should you learn to forgive one another. If your brother sins against you, go to him and with tact and patience show him his fault. And do all this between you and him alone. If he will listen to you, then have you won your brother. But if your brother will not hear you, if he persists in the error of his way, go again to him, taking with you one or two mutual friends that you may thus have two or even three witnesses to confirm your testimony and establish the fact that you have dealt justly and mercifully with your offending brother. Now if he refuses to hear your brethren, you may tell the whole story to the congregation, and then, if he refuses to hear the brotherhood, let them take such action as they deem wise; let such an unruly member become an outcast from the kingdom. While you cannot pretend to sit in judgment on the souls of your fellows, and while you may not forgive sins or otherwise presume to usurp the prerogatives of the supervisors of the heavenly hosts, at the same time, it has been committed to your hands that you should maintain temporal order in the kingdom on earth. While you may not meddle with the divine decrees concerning eternal life, you shall determine the issues of conduct as they concern the temporal welfare of the brotherhood on earth. And so, in all these matters connected with the discipline of the brotherhood, whatsoever you shall decree on earth, shall be recognized in heaven. Although you cannot determine the eternal fate of the individual, you may legislate regarding the conduct of the group, for, where two or three of you agree concerning any of these things and ask of me, it shall be done for you if your petition is not inconsistent with the will of my Father in heaven. And all this is ever true, for, where two or three believers are gathered together, there am I in the midst of them."

Simon Peter was the apostle in charge of the workers at Hippos, and when he heard Jesus thus speak, he asked: "Lord, how often shall my brother sin against me, and I forgive him? Until seven times?" And Jesus answered Peter: "Not only seven times but even to seventy times and seven. Therefore may the kingdom of heaven be likened to a certain king who ordered a financial reckoning with his stewards. And when they had begun to conduct this examination of accounts, one of his chief retainers was brought before him confessing that he owed his king ten thousand talents. Now this officer of the king's court pleaded that hard times had come upon him, and that he did not have wherewith to pay this obligation. And so the king commanded that his property be confiscated, and that his children be sold to pay his debt. When this chief steward heard this stern decree, he fell down on his face before the king and implored him to have mercy and grant him more time, saying, 'Lord, have a little more patience with me, and I will pay you all.' And when the king looked upon this negligent servant and his family, he was moved with compassion. He ordered that he should be released, and that the loan should be wholly forgiven.

"And this chief steward, having thus received mercy and forgiveness at the hands of the king, went about his business, and finding one of his subordinate stewards who owed him a mere hundred denarii, he laid hold upon him and, taking him by the throat, said, 'Pay me all you owe.' And then did this fellow steward fall down before the chief steward and, beseeching him, said: 'Only have patience with me, and I will presently be able to pay you.' But the chief steward would not show mercy to his fellow steward but rather had him cast in prison until he should pay his debt. When his fellow servants saw what had happened, they were so distressed that they went and told their lord and master, the king. When the king heard of the doings of his chief steward, he called this ungrateful and unforgiving man before him and said: 'You are a wicked and unworthy steward. When you sought for compassion, I freely forgave you your entire debt. Why did you not also show mercy to your fellow steward, even as I showed mercy to you?' And the king was so very angry that he delivered his ungrateful chief steward to the jailers that they might hold him until he had paid all that was due. And even so shall my heavenly Father show the more abundant mercy to those who freely show mercy to their fellows. How can you come to God asking consideration for your shortcomings when you are wont to chastise your brethren for being guilty of these same human frailties? I say to all of you: Freely you have received the good things of the kingdom; therefore freely give to your fellows on earth."

Thus did Jesus teach the dangers and illustrate the unfairness of sitting in personal judgment upon one's fellows. Discipline must be maintained, justice must be administered, but in all these matters the wisdom of the brotherhood should prevail. Jesus invested legislative and judicial authority in the *group,* not in the *individual.* Even this investment of authority in the group must not be exercised as personal authority. There is always danger that the verdict of an individual may be warped by prejudice or distorted by passion. Group judgment is more likely to remove the dangers and eliminate the unfairness of personal bias. Jesus sought always to minimize the elements of unfairness, retaliation, and vengeance.

[The use of the term seventy-seven as an illustration of mercy and forbearance was derived from the Scriptures referring to Lamech's exultation because of the metal weapons of his son Tubal-Cain, who, comparing these superior instruments with those of his enemies, exclaimed: "If Cain, with no weapon in his hand, was avenged seven times, I shall now be avenged seventy-seven."]

2. THE STRANGE PREACHER

Jesus went over to Gamala to visit John and those who worked with him at that place. That evening, after the session of questions and answers, John said to Jesus: "Master, yesterday I went over to Ashtaroth to see a man who was teaching in your name and even claiming to be able to cast out devils. Now this fellow had never been with us, neither does he follow after us; therefore I forbade him to do such things." Then said Jesus: "Forbid him not. Do you not perceive that this gospel of the kingdom shall presently be proclaimed in all the world? How can you expect that all who will believe the gospel shall be subject to your direction? Rejoice that already our teaching has begun to manifest itself beyond the bounds of our personal influence. Do you not see, John, that those who profess to do great works in my name must eventually support our cause? They certainly will not be quick to speak evil of me. My son, in matters of this sort it would be better for you to reckon that he who is not against us is for us. In the generations to come many who are not wholly worthy will do many strange things in my name, but I will not forbid them. I tell you that, even when a cup of cold water is given to a thirsty soul, the Father's messengers shall ever make record of such a service of love."

This instruction greatly perplexed John. Had he not heard the Master say, "He who is not with me is against me"? And he did not perceive that in this case Jesus was referring to man's personal relation to the spiritual teachings of the kingdom, while in the other case reference was made to the outward and far-flung social relations of believers regarding the questions of administrative control and the jurisdiction of one group of believers over the work of other groups which would eventually compose the forthcoming world-wide brotherhood.

But John oftentimes recounted this experience in connection with his subsequent labors in behalf of the kingdom. Nevertheless, many times did the apostles take offense at those who made bold to teach in the Master's name. To them it always seemed inappropriate that those who had never sat at Jesus' feet should dare to teach in his name.

This man whom John forbade to teach and work in Jesus' name did not heed the apostle's injunction. He went right on with his efforts and raised up a considerable company of believers at Kanata before going on into Mesopotamia. This man, Aden, had been led to believe in Jesus through the testimony of the demented man whom Jesus healed near Kheresa, and who so confidently believed that the supposed evil spirits which the Master cast out of him entered the herd of swine and rushed them headlong over the cliff to their destruction.

3. INSTRUCTION FOR TEACHERS AND BELIEVERS

At Edrei, where Thomas and his associates labored, Jesus spent a day and a night and, in the course of the evening's discussion, gave expression to the principles which should guide those who preach truth, and which should activate all who teach the gospel of the kingdom. Summarized and restated in modern phraseology, Jesus taught:

Always respect the personality of man. Never should a righteous cause be promoted by force; spiritual victories can be won only by spiritual power. This injunction against the employment of material influences refers to psychic force as well as to physical force. Overpowering arguments and mental superiority are not to be employed to coerce men and women into the kingdom. Man's mind is not to be crushed by the mere weight of logic or overawed by shrewd eloquence. While emotion as a factor in human decisions cannot be wholly eliminated, it should not be directly appealed to in the teachings of those who would advance the cause of the kingdom. Make your appeals directly to the divine spirit that dwells within the minds of men. Do not appeal to fear, pity, or mere sentiment. In appealing to men, be fair; exercise self-control and exhibit due restraint; show proper respect for the personalities of your pupils. Remember that I have said: "Behold, I stand at the door and knock, and if any man will open, I will come in."

In bringing men into the kingdom, do not lessen or destroy their self-respect. While overmuch self-respect may destroy proper humility and end in pride, conceit, and arrogance, the loss of self-respect often ends in paralysis of the will. It is the purpose of this gospel to restore self-respect to those who have lost it and to restrain it in those who have it. Make not the mistake of only condemning the wrongs in the lives of your pupils; remember also to accord generous recognition for the most praiseworthy things in their lives. Forget not that I will stop at nothing to restore self-respect to those who have lost it, and who really desire to regain it.

Take care that you do not wound the self-respect of timid and fearful souls. Do not indulge in sarcasm at the expense of my simple-minded brethren. Be not cynical with my fear-ridden children. Idleness is destructive of self-respect; therefore, admonish your brethren ever to keep busy at their chosen tasks, and put forth every effort to secure work for those who find themselves without employment.

Never be guilty of such unworthy tactics as endeavoring to frighten men and women into the kingdom. A loving father does not frighten his children into yielding obedience to his just requirements.

Sometime the children of the kingdom will realize that strong feelings of emotion are not equivalent to the leadings of the divine spirit. To be strongly and strangely impressed to do something or to go to a certain place, does not necessarily mean that such impulses are the leadings of the indwelling spirit.

Forewarn all believers regarding the fringe of conflict which must be traversed by all who pass from the life as it is lived in the flesh to the higher life as it is lived in the spirit. To those who live quite wholly within either realm, there is little conflict or confusion, but all are doomed to experience more or less uncertainty during the times of transition between the two levels of living. In entering the kingdom, you cannot escape its responsibilities or avoid its obligations, but remember: The gospel yoke is easy and the burden of truth is light.

The world is filled with hungry souls who famish in the very presence of the bread of life; men die searching for the very God who lives within them. Men seek for the treasures of the kingdom with yearning hearts and weary feet when they are all within the immediate grasp of living faith. Faith is to religion what sails are to a ship; it is an addition of power, not an added burden of life. There is but one struggle for those who enter the kingdom, and that is to fight the good fight of faith. The believer has only one battle, and that is against doubt—unbelief.

In preaching the gospel of the kingdom, you are simply teaching friendship with God. And this fellowship will appeal alike to men and women in that both will find that which most truly satisfies their characteristic longings and ideals. Tell my children that I am not only tender of their feelings and patient with their frailties, but that I am also ruthless with sin and intolerant of iniquity. I am indeed meek and humble in the presence of my Father, but I am equally and relentlessly inexorable where there is deliberate evil-doing and sinful rebellion against the will of my Father in heaven.

You shall not portray your teacher as a man of sorrows. Future generations shall know also the radiance of our joy, the buoyance of our good will, and the inspiration of our good humor. We proclaim a message of good news which is infectious in its transforming power. Our religion is throbbing with new life and new meanings. Those who accept this teaching are filled with joy and in their hearts are constrained to rejoice evermore. Increasing happiness is always the experience of all who are certain about God.

Teach all believers to avoid leaning upon the insecure props of false sympathy. You cannot develop strong characters out of the indulgence of self-pity; honestly endeavor to avoid the deceptive influence of mere fellowship in misery. Extend sympathy to the brave and courageous while you withhold overmuch pity from those cowardly souls who only halfheartedly stand up before the trials of living. Offer not consolation to those who lie down before their troubles without a struggle. Sympathize not with your fellows merely that they may sympathize with you in return.

When my children once become self-conscious of the assurance of the divine presence, such a faith will expand the mind, ennoble the soul, reinforce the personality, augment the happiness, deepen the spirit perception, and enhance the power to love and be loved.

Teach all believers that those who enter the kingdom are not thereby rendered immune to the accidents of time or to the ordinary catastrophes of nature. Believing the gospel will not prevent getting into trouble, but it will insure that you shall be *unafraid* when trouble does overtake you. If you dare to believe in me and wholeheartedly proceed to follow after me, you shall most certainly by so doing enter upon the sure pathway to trouble. I do not promise to deliver you from the waters of adversity, but I do promise to go with you through all of them.

And much more did Jesus teach this group of believers before they made ready for the night's sleep. And they who heard these sayings treasured them in their hearts and did often recite them for the edification of the apostles and disciples who were not present when they were spoken.

4. THE TALK WITH NATHANIEL

And then went Jesus over to Abila, where Nathaniel and his associates labored. Nathaniel was much bothered by some of Jesus' pronouncements which seemed to detract from the authority of the recognized Hebrew scriptures. Accordingly, on this night, after the usual period of questions and answers, Nathaniel took Jesus away from the others and asked: "Master, could you trust me to know the truth about the Scriptures? I observe that you teach us only a portion of the sacred writings—the best as I view it—and I infer that you reject the teachings of the rabbis to the effect that the words of the law are the very words of God, having been with God in heaven even before the times of Abraham and Moses. What is the truth about the Scriptures?" When Jesus heard the question of his bewildered apostle, he answered:

"Nathaniel, you have rightly judged; I do not regard the Scriptures as do the rabbis. I will talk with you about this matter on condition that you do not relate these things to your brethren, who are not all prepared to receive this teaching. The words of the law of Moses and the teachings of the Scriptures were not in existence before Abraham. Only in recent times have the Scriptures been gathered together as we now have them. While they contain the best of the higher thoughts and longings of the Jewish people, they also contain much that is far from being representative of the character and teachings of the Father in heaven; wherefore must I choose from among the better teachings those truths which are to be gleaned for the gospel of the kingdom.

"These writings are the work of men, some of them holy men, others not so holy. The teachings of these books represent the views and extent of enlightenment of the times in which they had their origin. As a revelation of truth, the last are more dependable than the first. The Scriptures are faulty and altogether human in origin, but mistake not, they do constitute the best collection of religious wisdom and spiritual truth to be found in all the world at this time.

"Many of these books were not written by the persons whose names they bear, but that in no way detracts from the value of the truths which they contain. If the story of Jonah should not be a fact, even if Jonah had never lived, still would the profound truth of this narrative, the love of God for Nineveh and the so-called heathen, be none the less precious in the eyes of all those who love their fellow men. The Scriptures are sacred because they present the thoughts and acts of men who were searching for God, and who in these writings left on record their highest concepts of righteousness, truth, and holiness. The Scriptures contain much that is true, very much, but in the light of your present teaching, you know that these writings also contain much that is misrepresentative of the Father in heaven, the loving God I have come to reveal to all the worlds.

"Nathaniel, never permit yourself for one moment to believe the Scripture records which tell you that the God of love directed your forefathers to go forth in battle to slay all their enemies—men, women, and children. Such records are the words of men, not very holy men, and they are not the word of God. The Scriptures always have, and always will, reflect the intellectual, moral, and spiritual status of those who create them. Have you not noted that the concepts of Yahweh grow in beauty and glory as the prophets make their records from Samuel to Isaiah? And you should remember that the Scriptures are intended for religious instruction and spiritual guidance. They are not the works of either historians or philosophers.

"The thing most deplorable is not merely this erroneous idea of the absolute perfection of the Scripture record and the infallibility of its teachings, but rather the confusing misinterpretation of these sacred writings by the tradition-enslaved scribes and Pharisees at Jerusalem. And now will they employ both the doctrine of the inspiration of the Scriptures and their misinterpretations thereof in their determined effort to withstand these newer teachings of the gospel of the kingdom. Nathaniel, never forget, the Father does not limit the revelation of truth to any one generation or to any one people. Many earnest seekers after the truth have been, and will continue to be, confused and disheartened by these doctrines of the perfection of the Scriptures.

"The authority of truth is the very spirit that indwells its living manifestations, and not the dead words of the less illuminated and supposedly inspired men of another generation. And even if these holy men of old lived inspired and spirit-filled lives, that does not mean that their *words* were similarly spiritually inspired. Today we make no record of the teachings of this gospel of the kingdom lest, when I have gone, you speedily become divided up into sundry groups of truth contenders as a result of the diversity of your interpretation of my teachings. For this generation it is best that we *live* these truths while we shun the making of records.

"Mark you well my words, Nathaniel, nothing which human nature has touched can be regarded as infallible. Through the mind of man divine truth may indeed shine forth, but always of relative purity and partial divinity. The creature may crave infallibility, but only the Creators possess it.

"But the greatest error of the teaching about the Scriptures is the doctrine of their being sealed books of mystery and wisdom which only the wise minds of the nation dare to interpret. The revelations of divine truth are not sealed except by human ignorance, bigotry, and narrow-minded intolerance. The light of the Scriptures is only dimmed by prejudice and darkened by superstition. A false fear of sacredness has prevented religion from being safeguarded by common sense. The fear of the authority of the sacred writings of the past effectively prevents the honest souls of today from accepting the new light of the gospel, the light which these very God-knowing men of another generation so intensely longed to see.

"But the saddest feature of all is the fact that some of the teachers of the sanctity of this traditionalism know this very truth. They more or less fully understand these limitations of Scripture, but they are moral cowards, intellectually dishonest. They know the truth regarding the sacred writings, but they prefer to withhold such disturbing facts from the people. And thus do they pervert and distort the Scriptures, making them the guide to slavish details of the daily life and an authority in things nonspiritual instead of appealing to the sacred writings as the repository of the moral wisdom, religious inspiration, and the spiritual teaching of the God-knowing men of other generations."

Nathaniel was enlightened, and shocked, by the Master's pronouncement. He long pondered this talk in the depths of his soul, but he told no man concerning this conference until after Jesus' ascension; and even then he feared to impart the full story of the Master's instruction.

5. THE POSITIVE NATURE OF JESUS' RELIGION

At Philadelphia, where James was working, Jesus taught the disciples about the positive nature of the gospel of the kingdom. When, in the course of his remarks, he intimated that some parts of the Scripture were more truth-containing than others and admonished his hearers to feed their souls upon the best of the spiritual food, James interrupted the Master, asking: "Would you be good enough, Master, to suggest to us how we may choose the better passages from the Scriptures for our personal edification?" And Jesus replied: "Yes, James, when you read the Scriptures look for those eternally true and divinely beautiful teachings, such as:

"Create in me a clean heart, O Lord.

"The Lord is my shepherd; I shall not want.

"You should love your neighbor as yourself.

"For I, the Lord your God, will hold your right hand, saying, fear not; I will help you.

"Neither shall the nations learn war any more."

And this is illustrative of the way Jesus, day by day, appropriated the cream of the Hebrew scriptures for the instruction of his followers and for inclusion in the teachings of the new gospel of the kingdom. Other religions had suggested the thought of the nearness of God to man, but Jesus made the care of God for man like the solicitude of a loving father for the welfare of his dependent children and then made this teaching the cornerstone of his religion. And thus did the doctrine of the fatherhood of God make imperative the practice of the brotherhood of man. The worship of God and the service of man became the sum and substance of his religion. Jesus took the best of the Jewish religion and translated it to a worthy setting in the new teachings of the gospel of the kingdom.

Jesus put the spirit of positive action into the passive doctrines of the Jewish religion. In the place of negative compliance with ceremonial requirements, Jesus enjoined the positive doing of that which his new religion required of those who accepted it. Jesus' religion consisted not merely in *believing,* but in actually *doing,* those things which the gospel required. He did not teach that the essence of his religion consisted in social service, but rather that social service was one of the certain effects of the possession of the spirit of true religion.

Jesus did not hesitate to appropriate the better half of a Scripture while he repudiated the lesser portion. His great exhortation, "Love your neighbor as yourself," he took from the Scripture which reads: "You shall not take vengeance against the children of your people, but you shall love your neighbor as yourself." Jesus appropriated the positive portion of this Scripture while rejecting the negative part. He even opposed negative or purely passive nonresistance. Said he: "When an enemy smites you on one cheek, do not stand there dumb and passive but in positive attitude turn the other; that is, do the best thing possible actively to lead your brother in error away from the evil paths into the better ways of righteous living." Jesus required his followers to react positively and aggressively to every life situation. The turning of the other cheek, or whatever act that may typify, demands initiative, necessitates vigorous, active, and courageous expression of the believer's personality.

Jesus did not advocate the practice of negative submission to the indignities of those who might purposely seek to impose upon the practitioners of nonresistance to evil, but rather that his followers should be wise and alert in the quick and positive reaction of good to evil to the end that they might effectively overcome evil with good. Forget not, the truly good is invariably more powerful than the most malignant evil. The Master taught a positive standard of righteousness: "Whosoever wishes to be my disciple, let him disregard himself and take up the full measure of his responsibilities daily to follow me." And he so lived himself in that "he went about doing good." And this aspect of the gospel was well illustrated by many parables which he later spoke to his followers. He never exhorted his followers patiently to bear their obligations but rather with energy and enthusiasm to live up to the full measure of their human responsibilities and divine privileges in the kingdom of God.

When Jesus instructed his apostles that they should, when one unjustly took away the coat, offer the other garment, he referred not so much to a literal second coat as to the idea of doing something *positive* to save the wrongdoer in the place of the olden advice to retaliate—"an eye for an eye" and so on. Jesus abhorred the idea either of retaliation or of becoming just a passive sufferer or victim of injustice. On this occasion he taught them the three ways of contending with, and resisting, evil:

1. To return evil for evil—the positive but unrighteous method.

2. To suffer evil without complaint and without resistance—the purely negative method.

3. To return good for evil, to assert the will so as to become master of the situation, to overcome evil with good—the positive and righteous method.

One of the apostles once asked: "Master, what should I do if a stranger forced me to carry his pack for a mile?" Jesus answered: "Do not sit down and sigh for relief while you berate the stranger under your breath. Righteousness comes not from such passive attitudes. If you can think of nothing more effectively positive to do, you can at least carry the pack a second mile. That will of a certainty challenge the unrighteous and ungodly stranger."

The Jews had heard of a God who would forgive repentant sinners and try to forget their misdeeds, but not until Jesus came, did men hear about a God who went in search of lost sheep, who took the initiative in looking for sinners, and who rejoiced when he found them willing to return to the Father's house. This positive note in religion Jesus extended even to his prayers. And he converted the negative golden rule into a positive admonition of human fairness.

In all his teaching Jesus unfailingly avoided distracting details. He shunned flowery language and avoided the mere poetic imagery of a play upon words. He habitually put large meanings into small expressions. For purposes of illustration Jesus reversed the current meanings of many terms, such as salt, leaven, fishing, and little children. He most effectively employed the antithesis, comparing the minute to the infinite and so on. His pictures were striking, such as, "The blind leading the blind." But the greatest strength to be found in his illustrative teaching was its naturalness. Jesus brought the philosophy of religion from heaven down to earth. He portrayed the elemental needs of the soul with a new insight and a new bestowal of affection.

6. THE RETURN TO MAGADAN

The mission of four weeks in the Decapolis was moderately successful. Hundreds of souls were received into the kingdom, and the apostles and evangelists had a valuable experience in carrying on their work without the inspiration of the immediate personal presence of Jesus.

On Friday, September 16, the entire corps of workers assembled by prearrangement at Magadan Park. On the Sabbath day a council of more than one hundred believers was held at which the future plans for extending the work of the kingdom were fully considered. The messengers of David were present and made reports concerning the welfare of the believers throughout Judea, Samaria, Galilee, and adjoining districts.

Few of Jesus' followers at this time fully appreciated the great value of the services of the messenger corps. Not only did the messengers keep the believers throughout Palestine in touch with each other and with Jesus and the apostles, but during these dark days they also served as collectors of funds, not only for the sustenance of Jesus and his associates, but also for the support of the families of the twelve apostles and the twelve evangelists.

About this time Abner moved his base of operations from Hebron to Bethlehem, and this latter place was also the headquarters in Judea for David's messengers. David maintained an overnight relay messenger service between Jerusalem and Bethsaida. These runners left Jerusalem each evening, relaying at Sychar and Scythopolis, arriving in Bethsaida by breakfast time the next morning.

Jesus and his associates now prepared to take a week's rest before they made ready to start upon the last epoch of their labors in behalf of the kingdom. This was their last rest, for the Perean mission developed into a campaign of preaching and teaching which extended right on down to the time of their arrival at Jerusalem and of the enactment of the closing episodes of Jesus' earth career.

PAPER 160
RODAN OF ALEXANDRIA

ON SUNDAY morning, September 18, Andrew announced that no work would be planned for the coming week. All of the apostles, except Nathaniel and Thomas, went home to visit their families or to sojourn with friends. This week Jesus enjoyed a period of almost complete rest, but Nathaniel and Thomas were very busy with their discussions with a certain Greek philosopher from Alexandria named Rodan. This Greek had recently become a disciple of Jesus through the teaching of one of Abner's associates who had conducted a mission at Alexandria. Rodan was now earnestly engaged in the task of harmonizing his philosophy of life with Jesus' new religious teachings, and he had come to Magadan hoping that the Master would talk these problems over with him. He also desired to secure a firsthand and authoritative version of the gospel from either Jesus or one of his apostles. Though the Master declined to enter into such a conference with Rodan, he did receive him graciously and immediately directed that Nathaniel and Thomas should listen to all he had to say and tell him about the gospel in return.

1. RODAN'S GREEK PHILOSOPHY

Early Monday morning, Rodan began a series of ten addresses to Nathaniel, Thomas, and a group of some two dozen believers who chanced to be at Magadan. These talks, condensed, combined, and restated in modern phraseology, present the following thoughts for consideration:

Human life consists in three great drives—urges, desires, and lures. Strong character, commanding personality, is only acquired by converting the natural urge of life into the social art of living, by transforming present desires into those higher longings which are capable of lasting attainment, while the commonplace lure of existence must be transferred from one's conventional and established ideas to the higher realms of unexplored ideas and undiscovered ideals.

The more complex civilization becomes, the more difficult will become the art of living. The more rapid the changes in social usage, the more complicated will become the task of character development. Every ten generations mankind must learn anew the art of living if progress is to continue. And if man becomes so ingenious that he more rapidly adds to the complexities of society, the art of living will need to be remastered in less time, perhaps every single generation. If the evolution of the art of living fails to keep pace with the technique of existence, humanity will quickly revert to the simple urge of living—the attainment of the satisfaction of present desires. Thus will humanity remain immature; society will fail in growing up to full maturity.

Social maturity is equivalent to the degree to which man is willing to surrender the gratification of mere transient and present desires for the entertainment of those superior longings the striving for whose attainment affords the more abundant satisfactions of progressive advancement toward permanent goals. But the true badge of social maturity is the willingness of a people to surrender the right to live peaceably and contentedly under the ease-promoting standards of the lure of established beliefs and conventional ideas for the disquieting and energy-requiring lure of the pursuit of the unexplored possibilities of the attainment of undiscovered goals of idealistic spiritual realities.

Animals respond nobly to the urge of life, but only man can attain the art of living, albeit the majority of mankind only experience the animal urge to live. Animals know only this blind and instinctive urge; man is capable of transcending this urge to natural function. Man may elect to live upon the high plane of intelligent art, even that of celestial joy and spiritual ecstasy. Animals make no inquiry into the purposes of life; therefore they never worry, neither do they commit suicide. Suicide among men testifies that such beings have emerged from the purely animal stage of existence, and to the further fact that the exploratory efforts of such human beings have failed to attain the artistic levels of mortal experience. Animals know not the meaning of life; man not only possesses capacity for the recognition of values and the comprehension of meanings, but he also is conscious of the meaning of meanings—he is self-conscious of insight.

When men dare to forsake a life of natural craving for one of adventurous art and uncertain logic, they must expect to suffer the consequent hazards of emotional casualties—conflicts, unhappiness, and uncertainties—at least until the time of their attainment of some degree of intellectual and emotional maturity. Discouragement, worry, and indolence are positive evidence of moral immaturity. Human society is confronted with two problems: attainment of the maturity of the individual and attainment of the maturity of the race. The mature human being soon begins to look upon all other mortals with feelings of tenderness and with emotions of tolerance. Mature men view immature folks with the love and consideration that parents bear their children.

Successful living is nothing more or less than the art of the mastery of dependable techniques for solving common problems. The first step in the solution of any problem is to locate the difficulty, to isolate the problem, and frankly to recognize its nature and gravity. The great mistake is that, when life problems excite our profound fears, we refuse to recognize them. Likewise, when the acknowledgment of our difficulties entails the reduction of our long-cherished conceit, the admission of envy, or the abandonment of deep-seated prejudices, the average person prefers to cling to the old illusions of safety and to the long-cherished false feelings of security. Only a brave person is willing honestly to admit, and fearlessly to face, what a sincere and logical mind discovers.

The wise and effective solution of any problem demands that the mind shall be free from bias, passion, and all other purely personal prejudices which might interfere with the disinterested survey of the actual factors that go to make up the problem presenting itself for solution. The solution of life problems requires courage and sincerity. Only honest and brave individuals are able to follow valiantly through the perplexing and confusing maze of living to where the logic of a fearless mind may lead. And this emancipation of the mind and soul can never be effected without the driving power of an intelligent enthusiasm which borders on religious zeal. It requires the lure of a great ideal to drive man on in the pursuit of a goal which is beset with difficult material problems and manifold intellectual hazards.

Even though you are effectively armed to meet the difficult situations of life, you can hardly expect success unless you are equipped with that wisdom of mind and charm of personality which enable you to win the hearty support and co-operation of your fellows. You cannot hope for a large measure of success in either secular or religious work unless you can learn how to persuade your fellows, to prevail with men. You simply must have tact and tolerance.

But the greatest of all methods of problem solving I have learned from Jesus, your Master. I refer to that which he so consistently practices, and which he has so faithfully taught you, the isolation of worshipful meditation. In this habit of Jesus' going off so frequently by himself to commune with the Father in heaven is to be found the technique, not only of gathering strength and wisdom for the ordinary conflicts of living, but also of appropriating the energy for the solution of the higher problems of a moral and spiritual nature. But even correct methods of solving problems will not compensate for inherent defects of personality or atone for the absence of the hunger and thirst for true righteousness.

I am deeply impressed with the custom of Jesus in going apart by himself to engage in these seasons of solitary survey of the problems of living; to seek for new stores of wisdom and energy for meeting the manifold demands of social service; to quicken and deepen the supreme purpose of living by actually subjecting the total personality to the consciousness of contacting with divinity; to grasp for possession of new and better methods of adjusting oneself to the ever-changing situations of living existence; to effect those vital reconstructions and readjustments of one's personal attitudes which are so essential to enhanced insight into everything worth while and real; and to do all of this with an eye single to the glory of God—to breathe in sincerity your Master's favorite prayer, "Not my will, but yours, be done."

This worshipful practice of your Master brings that relaxation which renews the mind; that illumination which inspires the soul; that courage which enables one bravely to face one's problems; that self-understanding which obliterates debilitating fear; and that consciousness of union with divinity which equips man with the assurance that enables him to dare to be Godlike. The relaxation of worship, or spiritual communion as practiced by the Master, relieves tension, removes conflicts, and mightily augments the total resources of the personality. And all this philosophy, plus the gospel of the kingdom, constitutes the new religion as I understand it.

Prejudice blinds the soul to the recognition of truth, and prejudice can be removed only by the sincere devotion of the soul to the adoration of a cause that is all-embracing and all-inclusive of one's fellow men. Prejudice is inseparably linked to selfishness. Prejudice can be eliminated only by the abandonment of self-seeking and by substituting therefor the quest of the satisfaction of the service of a cause that is not only greater than self, but one that is even greater than all humanity—the search for God, the attainment of divinity. The evidence of maturity of personality consists in the transformation of human desire so that it constantly seeks for the realization of those values which are highest and most divinely real.

In a continually changing world, in the midst of an evolving social order, it is impossible to maintain settled and established goals of destiny. Stability of personality can be experienced only by those who have discovered and embraced the living God as the eternal goal of infinite attainment. And thus to transfer one's goal from time to eternity, from earth to Paradise, from the human to the divine, requires that man shall become regenerated, converted, be born again; that he shall become the re-created child of the divine spirit; that he shall gain entrance into the brotherhood of the kingdom of heaven. All philosophies and religions which fall short of these ideals are immature. The philosophy which I teach, linked with the gospel which you preach, represents the new religion of maturity, the ideal of all future generations. And this is true because our ideal is final, infallible, eternal, universal, absolute, and infinite.

My philosophy gave me the urge to search for the realities of true attainment, the goal of maturity. But my urge was impotent; my search lacked driving power; my quest suffered from the absence of certainty of directionization. And these deficiencies have been abundantly supplied by this new gospel of Jesus, with its enhancement of insights, elevation of ideals, and settledness of goals. Without doubts and misgivings I can now wholeheartedly enter upon the eternal venture.

2. THE ART OF LIVING

There are just two ways in which mortals may live together: the material or animal way and the spiritual or human way. By the use of signals and sounds animals are able to communicate with each other in a limited way. But such forms of communication do not convey meanings, values, or ideas. The one distinction between man and the animal is that man can communicate with his fellows by means of *symbols* which most certainly designate and identify meanings, values, ideas, and even ideals.

Since animals cannot communicate ideas to each other, they cannot develop personality. Man develops personality because he can thus communicate with his fellows concerning both ideas and ideals.

It is this ability to communicate and share meanings that constitutes human culture and enables man, through social associations, to build civilizations. Knowledge and wisdom become cumulative because of man's ability to communicate these possessions to succeeding generations. And thereby arise the cultural activities of the race: art, science, religion, and philosophy.

Symbolic communication between human beings predetermines the bringing into existence of social groups. The most effective of all social groups is the family, more particularly the *two parents*. Personal affection is the spiritual bond which holds together these material associations. Such an effective relationship is also possible between two persons of the same sex, as is so abundantly illustrated in the devotions of genuine friendships.

These associations of friendship and mutual affection are socializing and ennobling because they encourage and facilitate the following essential factors of the higher levels of the art of living:

1. *Mutual self-expression and self-understanding.* Many noble human impulses die because there is no one to hear their expression. Truly, it is not good for man to be alone. Some degree of recognition and a certain amount of appreciation are essential to the development of human character. Without the genuine love of a home, no child can achieve the full development of normal

character. Character is something more than mere mind and morals. Of all social relations calculated to develop character, the most effective and ideal is the affectionate and understanding friendship of man and woman in the mutual embrace of intelligent wedlock. Marriage, with its manifold relations, is best designed to draw forth those precious impulses and those higher motives which are indispensable to the development of a strong character. I do not hesitate thus to glorify family life, for your Master has wisely chosen the father-child relationship as the very cornerstone of this new gospel of the kingdom. And such a matchless community of relationship, man and woman in the fond embrace of the highest ideals of time, is so valuable and satisfying an experience that it is worth any price, any sacrifice, requisite for its possession.

2. *Union of souls—the mobilization of wisdom.* Every human being sooner or later acquires a certain concept of this world and a certain vision of the next. Now it is possible, through personality association, to unite these views of temporal existence and eternal prospects. Thus does the mind of one augment its spiritual values by gaining much of the insight of the other. In this way men enrich the soul by pooling their respective spiritual possessions. Likewise, in this same way, man is enabled to avoid that ever-present tendency to fall victim to distortion of vision, prejudice of viewpoint, and narrowness of judgment. Fear, envy, and conceit can be prevented only by intimate contact with other minds. I call your attention to the fact that the Master never sends you out alone to labor for the extension of the kingdom; he always sends you out two and two. And since wisdom is superknowledge, it follows that, in the union of wisdom, the social group, small or large, mutually shares all knowledge.

3. *The enthusiasm for living.* Isolation tends to exhaust the energy charge of the soul. Association with one's fellows is essential to the renewal of the zest for life and is indispensable to the maintenance of the courage to fight those battles consequent upon the ascent to the higher levels of human living. Friendship enhances the joys and glorifies the triumphs of life. Loving and intimate human associations tend to rob suffering of its sorrow and hardship of much of its bitterness. The presence of a friend enhances all beauty and exalts every goodness. By intelligent symbols man is able to quicken and enlarge the appreciative capacities of his friends. One of the crowning glories of human friendship is this power and possibility of the mutual stimulation of the imagination. Great spiritual power is inherent in the consciousness of wholehearted devotion to a common cause, mutual loyalty to a cosmic Deity.

4. *The enhanced defense against all evil.* Personality association and mutual affection is an efficient insurance against evil. Difficulties, sorrow, disappointment, and defeat are more painful and disheartening when borne alone. Association does not transmute evil into righteousness, but it does aid in greatly lessening the sting. Said your Master, "Happy are they who mourn"—if a friend is at hand to comfort. There is positive strength in the knowledge that you live for the welfare of others, and that these others likewise live for your welfare and advancement. Man languishes in isolation. Human beings unfailingly become discouraged when they view only the transitory transactions of time. The present, when divorced from the past and the future, becomes exasperatingly trivial. Only a glimpse of the circle of eternity can inspire man to do his best and

can challenge the best in him to do its utmost. And when man is thus at his best, he lives most unselfishly for the good of others, his fellow sojourners in time and eternity.

I repeat, such inspiring and ennobling association finds its ideal possibilities in the human marriage relation. True, much is attained out of marriage, and many, many marriages utterly fail to produce these moral and spiritual fruits. Too many times marriage is entered by those who seek other values which are lower than these superior accompaniments of human maturity. Ideal marriage must be founded on something more stable than the fluctuations of sentiment and the fickleness of mere sex attraction; it must be based on genuine and mutual personal devotion. And thus, if you can build up such trustworthy and effective small units of human association, when these are assembled in the aggregate, the world will behold a great and glorified social structure, the civilization of mortal maturity. Such a race might begin to realize something of your Master's ideal of "peace on earth and good will among men." While such a society would not be perfect or entirely free from evil, it would at least approach the stabilization of maturity.

3. THE LURES OF MATURITY

The effort toward maturity necessitates work, and work requires energy. Whence the power to accomplish all this? The physical things can be taken for granted, but the Master has well said, "Man cannot live by bread alone." Granted the possession of a normal body and reasonably good health, we must next look for those lures which will act as a stimulus to call forth man's slumbering spiritual forces. Jesus has taught us that God lives in man; then how can we induce man to release these soul-bound powers of divinity and infinity? How shall we induce men to let go of God that he may spring forth to the refreshment of our own souls while in transit outward and then to serve the purpose of enlightening, uplifting, and blessing countless other souls? How best can I awaken these latent powers for good which lie dormant in your souls? One thing I am sure of: Emotional excitement is not the ideal spiritual stimulus. Excitement does not augment energy; it rather exhausts the powers of both mind and body. Whence then comes the energy to do these great things? Look to your Master. Even now he is out in the hills taking in power while we are here giving out energy. The secret of all this problem is wrapped up in spiritual communion, in worship. From the human standpoint it is a question of combined meditation and relaxation. Meditation makes the contact of mind with spirit; relaxation determines the capacity for spiritual receptivity. And this interchange of strength for weakness, courage for fear, the will of God for the mind of self, constitutes worship. At least, that is the way the philosopher views it.

When these experiences are frequently repeated, they crystallize into habits, strength-giving and worshipful habits, and such habits eventually formulate themselves into a spiritual character, and such a character is finally recognized by one's fellows as a *mature personality.* These practices are difficult and time-consuming at first, but when they become habitual, they are at once restful and timesaving. The more complex society becomes, and the more the lures of civilization multiply, the more urgent will become the necessity for God-knowing individuals to form such protective habitual practices designed to conserve and augment their spiritual energies.

Another requirement for the attainment of maturity is the co-operative adjustment of social groups to an ever-changing environment. The immature individual arouses the antagonisms of his fellows; the mature man wins the hearty co-operation of his associates, thereby many times multiplying the fruits of his life efforts.

My philosophy tells me that there are times when I must fight, if need be, for the defense of my concept of righteousness, but I doubt not that the Master, with a more mature type of personality, would easily and gracefully gain an equal victory by his superior and winsome technique of tact and tolerance. All too often, when we battle for the right, it turns out that both the victor and the vanquished have sustained defeat. I heard the Master say only yesterday that the "wise man, when seeking entrance through the locked door, would not destroy the door but rather would seek for the key wherewith to unlock it." Too often we engage in a fight merely to convince ourselves that we are not afraid.

This new gospel of the kingdom renders a great service to the art of living in that it supplies a new and richer incentive for higher living. It presents a new and exalted goal of destiny, a supreme life purpose. And these new concepts of the eternal and divine goal of existence are in themselves transcendent stimuli, calling forth the reaction of the very best that is resident in man's higher nature. On every mountaintop of intellectual thought are to be found relaxation for the mind, strength for the soul, and communion for the spirit. From such vantage points of high living, man is able to transcend the material irritations of the lower levels of thinking—worry, jealousy, envy, revenge, and the pride of immature personality. These high-climbing souls deliver themselves from a multitude of the crosscurrent conflicts of the trifles of living, thus becoming free to attain consciousness of the higher currents of spirit concept and celestial communication. But the life purpose must be jealously guarded from the temptation to seek for easy and transient attainment; likewise must it be so fostered as to become immune to the disastrous threats of fanaticism.

4. THE BALANCE OF MATURITY

While you have an eye single to the attainment of eternal realities, you must also make provision for the necessities of temporal living. While the spirit is our goal, the flesh is a fact. Occasionally the necessities of living may fall into our hands by accident, but in general, we must intelligently work for them. The two major problems of life are: making a temporal living and the achievement of eternal survival. And even the problem of making a living requires religion for its ideal solution. These are both highly personal problems. True religion, in fact, does not function apart from the individual.

The essentials of the temporal life, as I see them, are:

1. Good physical health.
2. Clear and clean thinking.
3. Ability and skill.
4. Wealth—the goods of life.
5. Ability to withstand defeat.
6. Culture—education and wisdom.

Even the physical problems of bodily health and efficiency are best solved when they are viewed from the religious standpoint of our Master's teaching: That the body and mind of man are the dwelling place of the gift of the Gods, the spirit of God becoming the spirit of man. The mind of man thus becomes the mediator between material things and spiritual realities.

It requires intelligence to secure one's share of the desirable things of life. It is wholly erroneous to suppose that faithfulness in doing one's daily work will insure the rewards of wealth. Barring the occasional and accidental acquirement of wealth, the material rewards of the temporal life are found to flow in certain well-organized channels, and only those who have access to these channels may expect to be well rewarded for their temporal efforts. Poverty must ever be the lot of all men who seek for wealth in isolated and individual channels. Wise planning, therefore, becomes the one thing essential to worldly prosperity. Success requires not only devotion to one's work but also that one should function as a part of some one of the channels of material wealth. If you are unwise, you can bestow a devoted life upon your generation without material reward; if you are an accidental beneficiary of the flow of wealth, you may roll in luxury even though you have done nothing worth while for your fellow men.

Ability is that which you inherit, while skill is what you acquire. Life is not real to one who cannot do some one thing well, expertly. Skill is one of the real sources of the satisfaction of living. Ability implies the gift of foresight, farseeing vision. Be not deceived by the tempting rewards of dishonest achievement; be willing to toil for the later returns inherent in honest endeavor. The wise man is able to distinguish between means and ends; otherwise, sometimes overplanning for the future defeats its own high purpose. As a pleasure seeker you should aim always to be a producer as well as a consumer.

Train your memory to hold in sacred trust the strength-giving and worthwhile episodes of life, which you can recall at will for your pleasure and edification. Thus build up for yourself and in yourself reserve galleries of beauty, goodness, and artistic grandeur. But the noblest of all memories are the treasured recollections of the great moments of a superb friendship. And all of these memory treasures radiate their most precious and exalting influences under the releasing touch of spiritual worship.

But life will become a burden of existence unless you learn how to fail gracefully. There is an art in defeat which noble souls always acquire; you must know how to lose cheerfully; you must be fearless of disappointment. Never hesitate to admit failure. Make no attempt to hide failure under deceptive smiles and beaming optimism. It sounds well always to claim success, but the end results are appalling. Such a technique leads directly to the creation of a world of unreality and to the inevitable crash of ultimate disillusionment.

Success may generate courage and promote confidence, but wisdom comes only from the experiences of adjustment to the results of one's failures. Men who prefer optimistic illusions to reality can never become wise. Only those who face facts and adjust them to ideals can achieve wisdom. Wisdom embraces both the fact and the ideal and therefore saves its devotees from both of those barren extremes of philosophy—the man whose idealism excludes facts and the materialist who is devoid of spiritual outlook. Those timid souls who can only keep up the struggle of life by the aid of continuous false illusions of success are doomed to suffer failure and experience defeat as they ultimately awaken from the dream world of their own imaginations.

And it is in this business of facing failure and adjusting to defeat that the far-reaching vision of religion exerts its supreme influence. Failure is simply an educational episode—a cultural experiment in the acquirement of wisdom—in the experience of the God-seeking man who has embarked on the eternal adventure of the exploration of a universe. To such men defeat is but a new tool for the achievement of higher levels of universe reality.

The career of a God-seeking man may prove to be a great success in the light of eternity, even though the whole temporal-life enterprise may appear as an overwhelming failure, provided each life failure yielded the culture of wisdom and spirit achievement. Do not make the mistake of confusing knowledge, culture, and wisdom. They are related in life, but they represent vastly differing spirit values; wisdom ever dominates knowledge and always glorifies culture.

5. THE RELIGION OF THE IDEAL

You have told me that your Master regards genuine human religion as the individual's experience with spiritual realities. I have regarded religion as man's experience of reacting to something which he regards as being worthy of the homage and devotion of all mankind. In this sense, religion symbolizes our supreme devotion to that which represents our highest concept of the ideals of reality and the farthest reach of our minds toward eternal possibilities of spiritual attainment.

When men react to religion in the tribal, national, or racial sense, it is because they look upon those without their group as not being truly human. We always look upon the object of our religious loyalty as being worthy of the reverence of all men. Religion can never be a matter of mere intellectual belief or philosophic reasoning; religion is always and forever a mode of reacting to the situations of life; it is a species of conduct. Religion embraces thinking, feeling, and acting reverently toward some reality which we deem worthy of universal adoration.

If something has become a religion in your experience, it is self-evident that you already have become an active evangel of that religion since you deem the supreme concept of your religion as being worthy of the worship of all mankind, all universe intelligences. If you are not a positive and missionary evangel of your religion, you are self-deceived in that what you call a religion is only a traditional belief or a mere system of intellectual philosophy. If your religion is a spiritual experience, your object of worship must be the universal spirit reality and ideal of all your spiritualized concepts. All religions based on fear, emotion, tradition, and philosophy I term the intellectual religions, while those based on true spirit experience I would term the true religions. The object of religious devotion may be material or spiritual, true or false, real or unreal, human or divine. Religions can therefore be either good or evil.

Morality and religion are not necessarily the same. A system of morals, by grasping an object of worship, may become a religion. A religion, by losing its universal appeal to loyalty and supreme devotion, may evolve into a system of philosophy or a code of morals. This thing, being, state, or order of existence, or possibility of attainment which constitutes the supreme ideal of religious loyalty, and which is the recipient of the religious devotion of those who worship, is God. Regardless of the name applied to this ideal of spirit reality, it is God.

The social characteristics of a true religion consist in the fact that it invariably seeks to convert the individual and to transform the world. Religion implies the existence of undiscovered ideals which far transcend the known standards of ethics and morality embodied in even the highest social usages of the most mature institutions of civilization. Religion reaches out for undiscovered ideals, unexplored realities, superhuman values, divine wisdom, and true spirit attainment. True religion does all of this; all other beliefs are not worthy of the name. You cannot have a genuine spiritual religion without the supreme and supernal ideal of an eternal God. A religion without this God is an invention of man, a human institution of lifeless intellectual beliefs and meaningless emotional ceremonies. A religion might claim as the object of its devotion a great ideal. But such ideals of unreality are not attainable; such a concept is illusionary. The only ideals susceptible of human attainment are the divine realities of the infinite values resident in the spiritual fact of the eternal God.

The word God, the *idea* of God as contrasted with the *ideal* of God, can become a part of any religion, no matter how puerile or false that religion may chance to be. And this idea of God can become anything which those who entertain it may choose to make it. The lower religions shape their ideas of God to meet the natural state of the human heart; the higher religions demand that the human heart shall be changed to meet the demands of the ideals of true religion.

The religion of Jesus transcends all our former concepts of the idea of worship in that he not only portrays his Father as the ideal of infinite reality but positively declares that this divine source of values and the eternal center of the universe is truly and personally attainable by every mortal creature who chooses to enter the kingdom of heaven on earth, thereby acknowledging the acceptance of sonship with God and brotherhood with man. That, I submit, is the highest concept of religion the world has ever known, and I pronounce that there can never be a higher since this gospel embraces the infinity of realities, the divinity of values, and the eternity of universal attainments. Such a concept constitutes the achievement of the experience of the idealism of the supreme and the ultimate.

I am not only intrigued by the consummate ideals of this religion of your Master, but I am mightily moved to profess my belief in his announcement that these ideals of spirit realities are attainable; that you and I can enter upon this long and eternal adventure with his assurance of the certainty of our ultimate arrival at the portals of Paradise. My brethren, I am a believer, I have embarked; I am on my way with you in this eternal venture. The Master says he came from the Father, and that he will show us the way. I am fully persuaded he speaks the truth. I am finally convinced that there are no attainable ideals of reality or values of perfection apart from the eternal and Universal Father.

I come, then, to worship, not merely the God of existences, but the God of the possibility of all future existences. Therefore must your devotion to a supreme ideal, if that ideal is real, be devotion to this God of past, present, and future universes of things and beings. And there is no other God, for there cannot possibly be any other God. All other gods are figments of the imagination, illusions of mortal mind, distortions of false logic, and the self-deceptive idols of those who create them. Yes, you can have a religion without this God, but it does not mean anything. And if you seek to substitute the word God for the reality of this ideal of the living God, you have only deluded yourself by putting an idea in the place of an ideal, a divine reality. Such beliefs are merely religions of wishful fancy.

I see in the teachings of Jesus, religion at its best. This gospel enables us to seek for the true God and to find him. But are we willing to pay the price of this entrance into the kingdom of heaven? Are we willing to be born again? to be remade? Are we willing to be subject to this terrible and testing process of self-destruction and soul reconstruction? Has not the Master said: "Whoso would save his life must lose it. Think not that I have come to bring peace but rather a soul struggle"? True, after we pay the price of dedication to the Father's will, we do experience great peace provided we continue to walk in these spiritual paths of consecrated living.

Now are we truly forsaking the lures of the known order of existence while we unreservedly dedicate our quest to the lures of the unknown and unexplored order of the existence of a future life of adventure in the spirit worlds of the higher idealism of divine reality. And we seek for those symbols of meaning wherewith to convey to our fellow men these concepts of the reality of the idealism of the religion of Jesus, and we will not cease to pray for that day when all mankind shall be thrilled by the communal vision of this supreme truth. Just now, our focalized concept of the Father, as held in our hearts, is that God is spirit; as conveyed to our fellows, that God is love.

The religion of Jesus demands living and spiritual experience. Other religions may consist in traditional beliefs, emotional feelings, philosophic consciousness, and all of that, but the teaching of the Master requires the attainment of actual levels of real spirit progression.

The consciousness of the impulse to be like God is not true religion. The feelings of the emotion to worship God are not true religion. The knowledge of the conviction to forsake self and serve God is not true religion. The wisdom of the reasoning that this religion is the best of all is not religion as a personal and spiritual experience. True religion has reference to destiny and reality of attainment as well as to the reality and idealism of that which is wholeheartedly faith-accepted. And all of this must be made personal to us by the revelation of the Spirit of Truth.

And thus ended the dissertations of the Greek philosopher, one of the greatest of his race, who had become a believer in the gospel of Jesus.

PAPER 161

FURTHER DISCUSSIONS WITH RODAN

ON SUNDAY, September 25, A.D. 29, the apostles and the evangelists assembled at Magadan. After a long conference that evening with his associates, Jesus surprised all by announcing that early the next day he and the twelve apostles would start for Jerusalem to attend the feast of tabernacles. He directed that the evangelists visit the believers in Galilee, and that the women's corps return for a while to Bethsaida.

When the hour came to leave for Jerusalem, Nathaniel and Thomas were still in the midst of their discussions with Rodan of Alexandria, and they secured the Master's permission to remain at Magadan for a few days. And so, while Jesus and the ten were on their way to Jerusalem, Nathaniel and Thomas were engaged in earnest debate with Rodan. The week prior, in which Rodan had expounded his philosophy, Thomas and Nathaniel had alternated in presenting the gospel of the kingdom to the Greek philosopher. Rodan discovered that he had been well instructed in Jesus' teachings by one of the former apostles of John the Baptist who had been his teacher at Alexandria.

1. THE PERSONALITY OF GOD

There was one matter on which Rodan and the two apostles did not see alike, and that was the personality of God. Rodan readily accepted all that was presented to him regarding the attributes of God, but he contended that the Father in heaven is not, cannot be, a person as man conceives personality. While the apostles found themselves in difficulty trying to prove that God is a person, Rodan found it still more difficult to prove he is not a person.

Rodan contended that the fact of personality consists in the coexistent fact of full and mutual communication between beings of equality, beings who are capable of sympathetic understanding. Said Rodan: "In order to be a person, God must have symbols of spirit communication which would enable him to become fully understood by those who make contact with him. But since God is infinite and eternal, the Creator of all other beings, it follows that, as regards beings of equality, God is alone in the universe. There are none equal to him; there are none with whom he can communicate as an equal. God indeed may be the source of all personality, but as such he is transcendent to personality, even as the Creator is above and beyond the creature."

This contention greatly troubled Thomas and Nathaniel, and they had asked Jesus to come to their rescue, but the Master refused to enter into their discussions. He did say to Thomas: "It matters little what *idea* of the Father you may entertain as long as you are spiritually acquainted with the *ideal* of his infinite and eternal nature."

Thomas contended that God does communicate with man, and therefore that the Father is a person, even within the definition of Rodan. This the Greek rejected on the ground that God does not reveal himself personally; that he is still a mystery. Then Nathaniel appealed to his own personal experience with God, and that Rodan allowed, affirming that he had recently had similar experiences, but these experiences, he contended, proved only the *reality* of God, not his *personality*.

By Monday night Thomas gave up. But by Tuesday night Nathaniel had won Rodan to believe in the personality of the Father, and he effected this change in the Greek's views by the following steps of reasoning:

1. The Father in Paradise does enjoy equality of communication with at least two other beings who are fully equal to himself and wholly like himself—the Eternal Son and the Infinite Spirit. In view of the doctrine of the Trinity, the Greek was compelled to concede the personality possibility of the Universal Father. (It was the later consideration of these discussions which led to the enlarged conception of the Trinity in the minds of the twelve apostles. Of course, it was the general belief that Jesus was the Eternal Son.)

2. Since Jesus was equal with the Father, and since this Son had achieved the manifestation of personality to his earth children, such a phenomenon constituted proof of the fact, and demonstration of the possibility, of the possession of personality by all three of the Godheads and forever settled the question regarding the ability of God to communicate with man and the possibility of man's communicating with God.

3. That Jesus was on terms of mutual association and perfect communication with man; that Jesus was the Son of God. That the relation of Son and Father presupposes equality of communication and mutuality of sympathetic understanding; that Jesus and the Father were one. That Jesus maintained at one and the same time understanding communication with both God and man, and that, since both God and man comprehended the meaning of the symbols of Jesus' communication, both God and man possessed the attributes of personality in so far as the requirements of the ability of intercommunication were concerned. That the personality of Jesus demonstrated the personality of God, while it proved conclusively the presence of God in man. That two things which are related to the same thing are related to each other.

4. That personality represents man's highest concept of human reality and divine values; that God also represents man's highest concept of divine reality and infinite values; therefore, that God must be a divine and infinite personality, a personality in reality although infinitely and eternally transcending man's concept and definition of personality, but nevertheless always and universally a personality.

5. That God must be a personality since he is the Creator of all personality and the destiny of all personality. Rodan had been tremendously influenced by the teaching of Jesus, "Be you therefore perfect, even as your Father in heaven is perfect."

When Rodan heard these arguments, he said: "I am convinced. I will confess God as a person if you will permit me to qualify my confession of such a belief by attaching to the meaning of personality a group of extended values, such as superhuman, transcendent, supreme, infinite, eternal, final, and universal. I am now convinced that, while God must be infinitely more than a personality, he cannot be anything less. I am satisfied to end the argument and to accept Jesus as the personal revelation of the Father and the satisfaction of all unsatisfied factors in logic, reason, and philosophy."

2. THE DIVINE NATURE OF JESUS

Since Nathaniel and Thomas had so fully approved Rodan's views of the gospel of the kingdom, there remained only one more point to consider, the teaching dealing with the divine nature of Jesus, a doctrine only so recently publicly announced. Nathaniel and Thomas jointly presented their views of the divine nature of the Master, and the following narrative is a condensed, rearranged, and restated presentation of their teaching:

1. Jesus has admitted his divinity, and we believe him. Many remarkable things have happened in connection with his ministry which we can understand only by believing that he is the Son of God as well as the Son of Man.

2. His life association with us exemplifies the ideal of human friendship; only a divine being could possibly be such a human friend. He is the most truly unselfish person we have ever known. He is the friend even of sinners; he dares to love his enemies. He is very loyal to us. While he does not hesitate to reprove us, it is plain to all that he truly loves us. The better you know him, the more you will love him. You will be charmed by his unswerving devotion. Through all these years of our failure to comprehend his mission, he has been a faithful friend. While he makes no use of flattery, he does treat us all with equal kindness; he is invariably tender and compassionate. He has shared his life and everything else with us. We are a happy community; we share all things in common. We do not believe that a mere human could live such a blameless life under such trying circumstances.

3. We think Jesus is divine because he never does wrong; he makes no mistakes. His wisdom is extraordinary; his piety superb. He lives day by day in perfect accord with the Father's will. He never repents of misdeeds because he transgresses none of the Father's laws. He prays for us and with us, but he never asks us to pray for him. We believe that he is consistently sinless. We do not think that one who is only human ever professed to live such a life. He claims to live a perfect life, and we acknowledge that he does. Our piety springs from repentance, but his piety springs from righteousness. He even professes to forgive sins and does heal diseases. No mere man would sanely profess to forgive sin; that is a divine prerogative. And he has seemed to be thus perfect in his righteousness from the times of our first contact with him. We grow in grace and in the knowledge of the truth, but our Master exhibits maturity of righteousness to start with. All men, good and evil, recognize these elements of goodness in Jesus. And yet never is his piety obtrusive or ostentatious. He is both meek and fearless. He seems to approve of our belief in his divinity. He is either what he professes to be, or else he is the greatest hypocrite and fraud the world has ever known. We are persuaded that he is just what he claims to be.

4. The uniqueness of his character and the perfection of his emotional control convince us that he is a combination of humanity and divinity. He

unfailingly responds to the spectacle of human need; suffering never fails to appeal to him. His compassion is moved alike by physical suffering, mental anguish, or spiritual sorrow. He is quick to recognize and generous to acknowledge the presence of faith or any other grace in his fellow men. He is so just and fair and at the same time so merciful and considerate. He grieves over the spiritual obstinacy of the people and rejoices when they consent to see the light of truth.

5. He seems to know the thoughts of men's minds and to understand the longings of their hearts. And he is always sympathetic with our troubled spirits. He seems to possess all our human emotions, but they are magnificently glorified. He strongly loves goodness and equally hates sin. He possesses a superhuman consciousness of the presence of Deity. He prays like a man but performs like a God. He seems to foreknow things; he even now dares to speak about his death, some mystic reference to his future glorification. While he is kind, he is also brave and courageous. He never falters in doing his duty.

6. We are constantly impressed by the phenomenon of his superhuman knowledge. Hardly does a day pass but something transpires to disclose that the Master knows what is going on away from his immediate presence. He also seems to know about the thoughts of his associates. He undoubtedly has communion with celestial personalities; he unquestionably lives on a spiritual plane far above the rest of us. Everything seems to be open to his unique understanding. He asks us questions to draw us out, not to gain information.

7. Recently the Master does not hesitate to assert his superhumanity. From the day of our ordination as apostles right on down to recent times, he has never denied that he came from the Father above. He speaks with the authority of a divine teacher. The Master does not hesitate to refute the religious teachings of today and to declare the new gospel with positive authority. He is assertive, positive, and authoritative. Even John the Baptist, when he heard Jesus speak, declared that he was the Son of God. He seems to be so sufficient within himself. He craves not the support of the multitude; he is indifferent to the opinions of men. He is brave and yet so free from pride.

8. He constantly talks about God as an ever-present associate in all that he does. He goes about doing good, for God seems to be in him. He makes the most astounding assertions about himself and his mission on earth, statements which would be absurd if he were not divine. He once declared, "Before Abraham was, I am." He has definitely claimed divinity; he professes to be in partnership with God. He well-nigh exhausts the possibilities of language in the reiteration of his claims of intimate association with the heavenly Father. He even dares to assert that he and the Father are one. He says that anyone who has seen him has seen the Father. And he says and does all these tremendous things with such childlike naturalness. He alludes to his association with the Father in the same manner that he refers to his association with us. He seems to be so sure about God and speaks of these relations in such a matter-of-fact way.

9. In his prayer life he appears to communicate directly with his Father. We have heard few of his prayers, but these few would indicate that he talks with God, as it were, face to face. He seems to know the future as well as the past. He simply could not be all of this and do all of these extraordinary things

unless he were something more than human. We know he is human, we are sure of that, but we are almost equally sure that he is also divine. We believe that he is divine. We are convinced that he is the Son of Man and the Son of God.

When Nathaniel and Thomas had concluded their conferences with Rodan, they hurried on toward Jerusalem to join their fellow apostles, arriving on Friday of that week. This had been a great experience in the lives of all three of these believers, and the other apostles learned much from the recounting of these experiences by Nathaniel and Thomas.

Rodan made his way back to Alexandria, where he long taught his philosophy in the school of Meganta. He became a mighty man in the later affairs of the kingdom of heaven; he was a faithful believer to the end of his earth days, yielding up his life in Greece with others when the persecutions were at their height.

3. Jesus' Human and Divine Minds

Consciousness of divinity was a gradual growth in the mind of Jesus up to the occasion of his baptism. After he became fully self-conscious of his divine nature, prehuman existence, and universe prerogatives, he seems to have possessed the power of variously limiting his human consciousness of his divinity. It appears to us that from his baptism until the crucifixion it was entirely optional with Jesus whether to depend only on the human mind or to utilize the knowledge of both the human and the divine minds. At times he appeared to avail himself of only that information which was resident in the human intellect. On other occasions he appeared to act with such fullness of knowledge and wisdom as could be afforded only by the utilization of the superhuman content of his divine consciousness.

We can understand his unique performances only by accepting the theory that he could, at will, self-limit his divinity consciousness. We are fully cognizant that he frequently withheld from his associates his foreknowledge of events, and that he was aware of the nature of their thinking and planning. We understand that he did not wish his followers to know too fully that he was able to discern their thoughts and to penetrate their plans. He did not desire too far to transcend the concept of the human as it was held in the minds of his apostles and disciples.

We are utterly at a loss to differentiate between his practice of self-limiting his divine consciousness and his technique of concealing his preknowledge and thought discernment from his human associates. We are convinced that he used both of these techniques, but we are not always able, in a given instance, to specify which method he may have employed. We frequently observed him acting with only the human content of consciousness; then would we behold him in conference with the directors of the celestial hosts of the universe and discern the undoubted functioning of the divine mind. And then on almost numberless occasions did we witness the working of this combined personality of man and God as it was activated by the apparent perfect union of the human and the divine minds. This is the limit of our knowledge of such phenomena; we really do not actually know the full truth about this mystery.

PAPER 162

AT THE FEAST OF TABERNACLES

WHEN Jesus started up to Jerusalem with the ten apostles, he planned to go through Samaria, that being the shorter route. Accordingly, they passed down the eastern shore of the lake and, by way of Scythopolis, entered the borders of Samaria. Near nightfall Jesus sent Philip and Matthew over to a village on the eastern slopes of Mount Gilboa to secure lodging for the company. It so happened that these villagers were greatly prejudiced against the Jews, even more so than the average Samaritans, and these feelings were heightened at this particular time as so many were on their way to the feast of tabernacles. These people knew very little about Jesus, and they refused him lodging because he and his associates were Jews. When Matthew and Philip manifested indignation and informed these Samaritans that they were declining to entertain the Holy One of Israel, the infuriated villagers chased them out of the little town with sticks and stones.

After Philip and Matthew had returned to their fellows and reported how they had been driven out of the village, James and John stepped up to Jesus and said: "Master, we pray you to give us permission to bid fire come down from heaven to devour these insolent and impenitent Samaritans." But when Jesus heard these words of vengeance, he turned upon the sons of Zebedee and severely rebuked them: "You know not what manner of attitude you manifest. Vengeance savors not of the outlook of the kingdom of heaven. Rather than dispute, let us journey over to the little village by the Jordan ford." Thus because of sectarian prejudice these Samaritans denied themselves the honor of showing hospitality to the Creator Son of a universe.

Jesus and the ten stopped for the night at the village near the Jordan ford. Early the next day they crossed the river and continued on to Jerusalem by way of the east Jordan highway, arriving at Bethany late Wednesday evening. Thomas and Nathaniel arrived on Friday, having been delayed by their conferences with Rodan.

Jesus and the twelve remained in the vicinity of Jerusalem until the end of the following month (October), about four and one-half weeks. Jesus himself went into the city only a few times, and these brief visits were made during the days of the feast of tabernacles. He spent a considerable portion of October with Abner and his associates at Bethlehem.

1. THE DANGERS OF THE VISIT TO JERUSALEM

Long before they fled from Galilee, the followers of Jesus had implored him to go to Jerusalem to proclaim the gospel of the kingdom in order that his message might have the prestige of having been preached at the center of Jewish culture and learning; but now that he had actually come to Jerusalem to teach, they were afraid for his life. Knowing that the Sanhedrin had sought to bring Jesus to Jerusalem for trial and recalling the Master's recently reiterated declarations that he must be subject to death, the apostles had been literally stunned by his sudden decision to attend the feast of tabernacles. To all their previous entreaties that he go to Jerusalem he had replied, "The hour has not yet come." Now, to their protests of fear he answered only, "But the hour has come."

During the feast of tabernacles Jesus went boldly into Jerusalem on several occasions and publicly taught in the temple. This he did in spite of the efforts of his apostles to dissuade him. Though they had long urged him to proclaim his message in Jerusalem, they now feared to see him enter the city at this time, knowing full well that the scribes and Pharisees were bent on bringing about his death.

Jesus' bold appearance in Jerusalem more than ever confused his followers. Many of his disciples, and even Judas Iscariot, the apostle, had dared to think that Jesus had fled in haste into Phoenicia because he feared the Jewish leaders and Herod Antipas. They failed to comprehend the significance of the Master's movements. His presence in Jerusalem at the feast of tabernacles, even in opposition to the advice of his followers, sufficed forever to put an end to all whisperings about fear and cowardice.

During the feast of tabernacles, thousands of believers from all parts of the Roman Empire saw Jesus, heard him teach, and many even journeyed out to Bethany to confer with him regarding the progress of the kingdom in their home districts.

There were many reasons why Jesus was able publicly to preach in the temple courts throughout the days of the feast, and chief of these was the fear that had come over the officers of the Sanhedrin as a result of the secret division of sentiment in their own ranks. It was a fact that many of the members of the Sanhedrin either secretly believed in Jesus or else were decidedly averse to arresting him during the feast, when such large numbers of people were present in Jerusalem, many of whom either believed in him or were at least friendly to the spiritual movement which he sponsored.

The efforts of Abner and his associates throughout Judea had also done much to consolidate sentiment favorable to the kingdom, so much so that the enemies of Jesus dared not be too outspoken in their opposition. This was one of the reasons why Jesus could publicly visit Jerusalem and live to go away. One or two months before this he would certainly have been put to death.

But the audacious boldness of Jesus in publicly appearing in Jerusalem overawed his enemies; they were not prepared for such a daring challenge. Several times during this month the Sanhedrin made feeble attempts to place the Master under arrest, but nothing came of these efforts. His enemies were so taken aback by Jesus' unexpected public appearance in Jerusalem that they conjectured he must have been promised protection by the Roman authorities. Knowing that Philip (Herod Antipas's brother) was almost a follower of Jesus, the members of the Sanhedrin speculated that Philip had secured for Jesus promises of protection against his enemies. Jesus had departed from their jurisdiction before they awakened to the realization that they had been mistaken in the belief that his sudden and bold appearance in Jerusalem had been due to a secret understanding with the Roman officials.

Only the twelve apostles had known that Jesus intended to attend the feast of tabernacles when they had departed from Magadan. The other followers of the Master were greatly astonished when he appeared in the temple courts and began publicly to teach, and the Jewish authorities were surprised beyond expression when it was reported that he was teaching in the temple.

Although his disciples had not expected Jesus to attend the feast, the vast majority of the pilgrims from afar who had heard of him entertained the hope that they might see him at Jerusalem. And they were not disappointed, for on several occasions he taught in Solomon's Porch and elsewhere in the temple courts. These teachings were really the official or formal announcement of the divinity of Jesus to the Jewish people and to the whole world.

The multitudes who listened to the Master's teachings were divided in their opinions. Some said he was a good man; some a prophet; some that he was truly the Messiah; others said he was a mischievous meddler, that he was leading the people astray with his strange doctrines. His enemies hesitated to denounce him openly for fear of his friendly believers, while his friends feared to acknowledge him openly for fear of the Jewish leaders, knowing that the Sanhedrin was determined to put him to death. But even his enemies marveled at his teaching, knowing that he had not been instructed in the schools of the rabbis.

Every time Jesus went to Jerusalem, his apostles were filled with terror. They were the more afraid as, from day to day, they listened to his increasingly bold pronouncements regarding the nature of his mission on earth. They were unaccustomed to hearing Jesus make such positive claims and such amazing assertions even when preaching among his friends.

2. THE FIRST TEMPLE TALK

The first afternoon that Jesus taught in the temple, a considerable company sat listening to his words depicting the liberty of the new gospel and the joy of those who believe the good news, when a curious listener interrupted him to ask: "Teacher, how is it you can quote the Scriptures and teach the people so fluently when I am told that you are untaught in the learning of the rabbis?" Jesus replied: "No man has taught me the truths which I declare to you. And this teaching is not mine but His who sent me. If any man really desires to do my Father's will, he shall certainly know about my teaching, whether it be God's or whether I speak for myself. He who speaks for himself seeks his own glory, but when I declare the words of the Father, I thereby seek the glory of him who sent me. But before you try to enter into the new light, should you not rather follow the light you already have? Moses gave you the law, yet how many of you honestly seek to fulfill its demands? Moses in this law enjoins you, saying, 'You shall not kill'; notwithstanding this command some of you seek to kill the Son of Man."

When the crowd heard these words, they fell to wrangling among themselves. Some said he was mad; some that he had a devil. Others said this was indeed the prophet of Galilee whom the scribes and Pharisees had long sought to kill. Some said the religious authorities were afraid to molest him; others thought that they laid not hands upon him because they had become believers in him. After considerable debate one of the crowd stepped forward and asked Jesus, "Why do the rulers seek to kill you?" And he replied: "The rulers seek to kill me because they resent my teaching about the good news of the kingdom, a gospel that sets men free from the burdensome traditions of a formal religion of ceremonies which these teachers are determined to uphold at any cost. They circumcise in accordance with the law on the Sabbath day, but they would kill me because I once on the Sabbath day set free a man held in the bondage of affliction. They follow after me on the Sabbath to spy on me but would kill me because on another occasion I chose to make a grievously stricken man completely whole on the Sabbath day. They seek to kill me because they well know that, if you honestly believe and dare to accept my teaching, their system of traditional religion will be overthrown, forever destroyed. Thus will they be deprived of authority over that to which they have devoted their lives since they steadfastly refuse to accept this new and more glorious gospel of the kingdom of God. And now do I appeal to every one of you: Judge not according to outward appearances but rather judge by the true spirit of these teachings; judge righteously."

Then said another inquirer: "Yes, Teacher, we do look for the Messiah, but when he comes, we know that his appearance will be in mystery. We know whence you are. You have been among your brethren from the beginning. The deliverer will come in power to restore the throne of David's kingdom. Do you really claim to be the Messiah?" And Jesus replied: "You claim to know me and to know whence I am. I wish your claims were true, for indeed then would you find abundant life in that knowledge. But I declare that I have not come to you for myself; I have been sent by the Father, and he who sent me is true and faithful. By refusing to hear me, you are refusing to receive Him who sends me. You, if you will receive this gospel, shall come to know Him who sent me. I know the Father, for I have come from the Father to declare and reveal him to you."

The agents of the scribes wanted to lay hands upon him, but they feared the multitude, for many believed in him. Jesus' work since his baptism had become well known to all Jewry, and as many of these people recounted these things, they said among themselves: "Even though this teacher is from Galilee, and even though he does not meet all of our expectations of the Messiah, we wonder if the deliverer, when he does come, will really do anything more wonderful than this Jesus of Nazareth has already done."

When the Pharisees and their agents heard the people talking this way, they took counsel with their leaders and decided that something should be done forthwith to put a stop to these public appearances of Jesus in the temple courts. The leaders of the Jews, in general, were disposed to avoid a clash with Jesus, believing that the Roman authorities had promised him immunity. They could not otherwise account for his boldness in coming at this time to Jerusalem; but the officers of the Sanhedrin did not wholly believe this rumor. They reasoned that the Roman rulers would not do such a thing secretly and without the knowledge of the highest governing body of the Jewish nation.

Accordingly, Eber, the proper officer of the Sanhedrin, with two assistants was dispatched to arrest Jesus. As Eber made his way toward Jesus, the Master said: "Fear not to approach me. Draw near while you listen to my teaching. I know you have been sent to apprehend me, but you should understand that nothing will befall the Son of Man until his hour comes. You are not arrayed against me; you come only to do the bidding of your masters, and even these rulers of the Jews verily think they are doing God's service when they secretly seek my destruction.

"I bear none of you ill will. The Father loves you, and therefore do I long for your deliverance from the bondage of prejudice and the darkness of tradition. I offer you the liberty of life and the joy of salvation. I proclaim the new and living way, the deliverance from evil and the breaking of the bondage of sin. I have come that you might have life, and have it eternally. You seek to be rid of me and my disquieting teachings. If you could only realize that I am to be with you only a little while! In just a short time I go to Him who sent me into this world. And then will many of you diligently seek me, but you shall not discover my presence, for where I am about to go you cannot come. But all who truly seek to find me shall sometime attain the life that leads to my Father's presence."

Some of the scoffers said among themselves: "Where will this man go that we cannot find him? Will he go to live among the Greeks? Will he destroy himself? What can he mean when he declares that soon he will depart from us, and that we cannot go where he goes?"

Eber and his assistants refused to arrest Jesus; they returned to their meeting place without him. When, therefore, the chief priests and the Pharisees upbraided Eber and his assistants because they had not brought Jesus with them, Eber only replied: "We feared to arrest him in the midst of the multitude because many believe in him. Besides, we never heard a man speak like this man. There is something out of the ordinary about this teacher. You would all do well to go over to hear him." And when the chief rulers heard these words, they were astonished and spoke tauntingly to Eber: "Are you also led astray? Are you about to believe in this deceiver? Have you heard that any of our learned men or any of the rulers have believed in him? Have any of the scribes or the Pharisees been deceived by his clever teachings? How does it come that you are influenced by the behavior of this ignorant multitude who know not the law or the prophets? Do you not know that such untaught people are accursed?" And then answered Eber: "Even so, my masters, but this man speaks to the multitude words of mercy and hope. He cheers the downhearted, and his words were comforting even to our souls. What can there be wrong in these teachings even though he may not be the Messiah of the Scriptures? And even then does not our law require fairness? Do we condemn a man before we hear him?" And the chief of the Sanhedrin was wroth with Eber and, turning upon him, said: "Have you gone mad? Are you by any chance also from Galilee? Search the Scriptures, and you will discover that out of Galilee arises no prophet, much less the Messiah."

The Sanhedrin disbanded in confusion, and Jesus withdrew to Bethany for the night.

3. THE WOMAN TAKEN IN ADULTERY

It was during this visit to Jerusalem that Jesus dealt with a certain woman of evil repute who was brought into his presence by her accusers and his enemies. The distorted record you have of this episode would suggest that this woman had been brought before Jesus by the scribes and Pharisees, and that Jesus so dealt with them as to indicate that these religious leaders of the Jews might themselves have been guilty of immorality. Jesus well knew that, while these scribes and Pharisees were spiritually blind and intellectually prejudiced by their loyalty to tradition, they were to be numbered among the most thoroughly moral men of that day and generation.

What really happened was this: Early the third morning of the feast, as Jesus approached the temple, he was met by a group of the hired agents of the Sanhedrin who were dragging a woman along with them. As they came near, the spokesman said: "Master, this woman was taken in adultery—in the very act. Now, the law of Moses commands that we should stone such a woman. What do you say should be done with her?"

It was the plan of Jesus' enemies, if he upheld the law of Moses requiring that the self-confessed transgressor be stoned, to involve him in difficulty with the Roman rulers, who had denied the Jews the right to inflict the death penalty without the approval of a Roman tribunal. If he forbade stoning the woman, they would accuse him before the Sanhedrin of setting himself up above Moses and the Jewish law. If he remained silent, they would accuse him of cowardice. But the Master so managed the situation that the whole plot fell to pieces of its own sordid weight.

This woman, once comely, was the wife of an inferior citizen of Nazareth, a man who had been a troublemaker for Jesus throughout his youthful days. The man, having married this woman, did most shamefully force her to earn their living by making commerce of her body. He had come up to the feast at Jerusalem that his wife might thus prostitute her physical charms for financial gain. He had entered into a bargain with the hirelings of the Jewish rulers thus to betray his own wife in her commercialized vice. And so they came with the woman and her companion in transgression for the purpose of ensnaring Jesus into making some statement which could be used against him in case of his arrest.

Jesus, looking over the crowd, saw her husband standing behind the others. He knew what sort of man he was and perceived that he was a party to the despicable transaction. Jesus first walked around to near where this degenerate husband stood and wrote upon the sand a few words which caused him to depart in haste. Then he came back before the woman and wrote again upon the ground for the benefit of her would-be accusers; and when they read his words, they, too, went away, one by one. And when the Master had written in the sand the third time, the woman's companion in evil took his departure, so that, when the Master raised himself up from this writing, he beheld the woman standing alone before him. Jesus said: "Woman, where are your accusers? did no man remain to stone you?" And the woman, lifting up her eyes, answered, "No man, Lord." And then said Jesus: "I know about you; neither do I condemn you. Go your way in peace." And this woman, Hildana, forsook her wicked husband and joined herself to the disciples of the kingdom.

4. THE FEAST OF TABERNACLES

The presence of people from all of the known world, from Spain to India, made the feast of tabernacles an ideal occasion for Jesus for the first time publicly to proclaim his full gospel in Jerusalem. At this feast the people lived much in the open air, in leafy booths. It was the feast of the harvest ingathering, and coming, as it did, in the cool of the autumn months, it was more generally attended by the Jews of the world than was the Passover at the end of the winter or Pentecost at the beginning of summer. The apostles at last beheld their Master making the bold announcement of his mission on earth before all the world, as it were.

This was the feast of feasts, since any sacrifice not made at the other festivals could be made at this time. This was the occasion of the reception of the temple offerings; it was a combination of vacation pleasures with the solemn rites of religious worship. Here was a time of racial rejoicing, mingled with sacrifices, Levitical chants, and the solemn blasts of the silvery trumpets of the priests. At night the impressive spectacle of the temple and its pilgrim throngs was brilliantly illuminated by the great candelabras which burned brightly in the court of the women as well as by the glare of scores of torches standing about the temple courts. The entire city was gaily decorated except the Roman castle of Antonia, which looked down in grim contrast upon this festive and worshipful scene. And how the Jews did hate this ever-present reminder of the Roman yoke!

Seventy bullocks were sacrificed during the feast, the symbol of the seventy nations of heathendom. The ceremony of the outpouring of the water symbolized the outpouring of the divine spirit. This ceremony of the water followed the sunrise procession of the priests and Levites. The worshipers passed down the steps leading from the court of Israel to the court of the women while successive blasts were blown upon the silvery trumpets. And then the faithful marched on toward the Beautiful Gate, which opened upon the court of the gentiles. Here they turned about to face westward, to repeat their chants, and to continue their march for the symbolic water.

On the last day of the feast almost four hundred and fifty priests with a corresponding number of Levites officiated. At daybreak the pilgrims assembled from all parts of the city, each carrying in the right hand a sheaf of myrtle, willow, and palm branches, while in the left hand each one carried a branch of the paradise apple—the citron, or the "forbidden fruit." These pilgrims divided into three groups for this early morning ceremony. One band remained at the temple to attend the morning sacrifices; another group marched down below Jerusalem to near Maza to cut the willow branches for the adornment of the sacrificial altar, while the third group formed a procession to march from the temple behind the water priest, who, to the sound of the silvery trumpets, bore the golden pitcher which was to contain the symbolic water, out through Ophel to near Siloam, where was located the fountain gate. After the golden pitcher had been filled at the pool of Siloam, the procession marched back to the temple, entering by way of the water gate and going directly to the court of the priests, where the priest bearing the water pitcher was joined by the priest bearing the wine for the drink offering. These two priests then repaired to the silver funnels leading to the base of the altar and poured the contents of the pitchers therein. The execution of this rite of pouring the wine and the water was the signal for the assembled pilgrims to begin the chanting of the Psalms from 113 to 118 inclusive, in alternation with the Levites. And as they repeated these lines, they would wave their sheaves at the altar. Then followed the sacrifices for the day, associated with the repeating of the Psalm for the day, the Psalm for the last day of the feast being the eighty-second, beginning with the fifth verse.

5. SERMON ON THE LIGHT OF THE WORLD

On the evening of the next to the last day of the feast, when the scene was brilliantly illuminated by the lights of the candelabras and the torches, Jesus stood up in the midst of the assembled throng and said:

"I am the light of the world. He who follows me shall not walk in darkness but shall have the light of life. Presuming to place me on trial and assuming to sit as my judges, you declare that, if I bear witness of myself, my witness cannot be true. But never can the creature sit in judgment on the Creator. Even if I do bear witness about myself, my witness is everlastingly true, for I know whence I came, who I am, and whither I go. You who would kill the Son of Man know not whence I came, who I am, or whither I go. You only judge by the appearances of the flesh; you do not perceive the realities of the spirit. I judge no man, not even my archenemy. But if I should choose to judge, my judgment would be true and righteous, for I would judge not alone but in association with my Father, who sent me into the world, and who is the source of all true judgment. You even allow that the witness of two reliable persons may be accepted—well, then, I bear witness of these truths; so also does my Father in heaven. And when I told you this yesterday, in your darkness you asked me, 'Where is your Father?' Truly, you know neither me nor my Father, for if you had known me, you would also have known the Father.

"I have already told you that I am going away, and that you will seek me and not find me, for where I am going you cannot come. You who would reject this light are from beneath; I am from above. You who prefer to sit in darkness are of this world; I am not of this world, and I live in the eternal light of the Father of lights. You all have had abundant opportunity to learn who I am, but you shall have still other evidence confirming the identity of the Son of Man. I am the light of life, and every one who deliberately and with understanding rejects this saving light shall die in his sins. Much I have to tell you, but you are unable to receive my words. However, he who sent me is true and faithful; my Father loves even his erring children. And all that my Father has spoken I also proclaim to the world.

"When the Son of Man is lifted up, then shall you all know that I am he, and that I have done nothing of myself but only as the Father has taught me. I speak these words to you and to your children. And he who sent me is even now with me; he has not left me alone, for I do always that which is pleasing in his sight."

As Jesus thus taught the pilgrims in the temple courts, many believed. And no man dared to lay hands upon him.

6. DISCOURSE ON THE WATER OF LIFE

On the last day, the great day of the feast, as the procession from the pool of Siloam passed through the temple courts, and just after the water and the wine had been poured down upon the altar by the priests, Jesus, standing among the pilgrims, said: "If any man thirst, let him come to me and drink. From the Father above I bring to this world the water of life. He who believes me shall be filled with the spirit which this water represents, for even the Scriptures have said, 'Out of him shall flow rivers of living waters.' When the Son of Man has finished his work on earth, there shall be poured out upon all flesh the living Spirit of Truth. Those who receive this spirit shall never know spiritual thirst."

Jesus did not interrupt the service to speak these words. He addressed the worshipers immediately after the chanting of the Hallel, the responsive reading of the Psalms accompanied by waving of the branches before the altar. Just here was a pause while the sacrifices were being prepared, and it was at this time that the pilgrims heard the fascinating voice of the Master declare that he was the giver of living water to every spirit-thirsting soul.

At the conclusion of this early morning service Jesus continued to teach the multitude, saying: "Have you not read in the Scripture: 'Behold, as the waters are poured out upon the dry ground and spread over the parched soil, so will I give the spirit of holiness to be poured out upon your children for a blessing even to your children's children'? Why will you thirst for the ministry of the spirit while you seek to water your souls with the traditions of men, poured from the broken pitchers of ceremonial service? That which you see going on about this temple is the way in which your fathers sought to symbolize the bestowal of the divine spirit upon the children of faith, and you have done well to perpetuate these symbols, even down to this day. But now has come to this generation the revelation of the Father of spirits through the bestowal of his Son, and all of this will certainly be followed by the bestowal of the spirit of the Father and the Son upon the children of men. To every one who has faith shall this bestowal of the spirit become the true teacher of the way which leads to life everlasting, to the true waters of life in the kingdom of heaven on earth and in the Father's Paradise over there."

And Jesus continued to answer the questions of both the multitude and the Pharisees. Some thought he was a prophet; some believed him to be the Messiah; others said he could not be the Christ, seeing that he came from Galilee, and that the Messiah must restore David's throne. Still they dared not arrest him.

7. THE DISCOURSE ON SPIRITUAL FREEDOM

On the afternoon of the last day of the feast and after the apostles had failed in their efforts to persuade him to flee from Jerusalem, Jesus again went into the temple to teach. Finding a large company of believers assembled in Solomon's Porch, he spoke to them, saying:

"If my words abide in you and you are minded to do the will of my Father, then are you truly my disciples. You shall know the truth, and the truth shall make you free. I know how you will answer me: We are the children of Abraham, and we are in bondage to none; how then shall we be made free? Even so, I do not speak of outward subjection to another's rule; I refer to the liberties of the soul. Verily, verily, I say to you, everyone who commits sin is the bond servant of sin. And you know that the bond servant is not likely to abide forever in the master's house. You also know that the son does remain in his father's house. If, therefore, the Son shall make you free, shall make you sons, you shall be free indeed.

"I know that you are Abraham's seed, yet your leaders seek to kill me because my word has not been allowed to have its transforming influence in their hearts. Their souls are sealed by prejudice and blinded by the pride of revenge. I declare to you the truth which the eternal Father shows me, while these deluded teachers seek to do the things which they have learned only from their temporal fathers. And when you reply that Abraham is your father, then do I tell you that, if you were the children of Abraham, you would do the works of Abraham. Some of you believe my teaching, but others seek to destroy me because I have told you the truth which I received from God. But Abraham did not so treat the truth of God. I perceive that some among you are determined to do the works of the evil one. If God were your Father, you would know me and love the truth which I reveal. Will you not see that I come forth from the Father, that I am sent by God, that I am not doing this work of myself? Why do you not understand my words? Is it because you have chosen to become the children of evil? If you are the children of darkness, you will hardly walk in the light of the truth which I reveal. The children of evil follow only in the ways of their father, who was a deceiver and stood not for the truth because there came to be no truth in him. But now comes the Son of Man speaking and living the truth, and many of you refuse to believe.

"Which of you convicts me of sin? If I, then, proclaim and live the truth shown me by the Father, why do you not believe? He who is of God hears gladly the words of God; for this cause many of you hear not my words, because you are not of God. Your teachers have even presumed to say that I do my works by the power of the prince of devils. One near by has just said that I have a devil, that I am a child of the devil. But all of you who deal honestly with your own souls know full well that I am not a devil. You know that I honor the Father even while you would dishonor me. I seek not my own glory, only the glory of my Paradise Father. And I do not judge you, for there is one who judges for me.

"Verily, verily, I say to you who believe the gospel that, if a man will keep this word of truth alive in his heart, he shall never taste death. And now just at my side a scribe says this statement proves that I have a devil, seeing that Abraham is dead, also the prophets. And he asks: 'Are you so much greater than Abraham and the prophets that you dare to stand here and say that whoso keeps your word shall not taste death? Who do you claim to be that you dare to utter such blasphemies?' And I say to all such that, if I glorify myself, my glory is as nothing. But it is the Father who shall glorify me, even the same Father whom you call God. But you have failed to know this your God and my Father, and I have come to bring you together; to show you how to become truly the sons of God. Though you know not the Father, I truly know him. Even Abraham rejoiced to see my day, and by faith he saw it and was glad."

When the unbelieving Jews and the agents of the Sanhedrin who had gathered about by this time heard these words, they raised a tumult, shouting: "You are not fifty years of age, and yet you talk about seeing Abraham; you are a child of the devil!" Jesus was unable to continue the discourse. He only said as he departed, "Verily, verily, I say to you, before Abraham was, I am." Many of the unbelievers rushed forth for stones to cast at him, and the agents of the Sanhedrin sought to place him under arrest, but the Master quickly made his way through the temple corridors and escaped to a secret meeting place near Bethany where Martha, Mary, and Lazarus awaited him.

8. THE VISIT WITH MARTHA AND MARY

It had been arranged that Jesus should lodge with Lazarus and his sisters at a friend's house, while the apostles were scattered here and there in small groups, these precautions being taken because the Jewish authorities were again becoming bold with their plans to arrest him.

For years it had been the custom for these three to drop everything and listen to Jesus' teaching whenever he chanced to visit them. With the loss of their parents, Martha had assumed the responsibilities of the home life, and so on this occasion, while Lazarus and Mary sat at Jesus' feet drinking in his refreshing teaching, Martha made ready to serve the evening meal. It should be explained that Martha was unnecessarily distracted by numerous needless tasks, and that she was cumbered by many trivial cares; that was her disposition.

As Martha busied herself with all these supposed duties, she was perturbed because Mary did nothing to help. Therefore she went to Jesus and said: "Master, do you not care that my sister has left me alone to do all of the serving? Will you not bid her to come and help me?" Jesus answered: "Martha, Martha, why are you always anxious about so many things and troubled by so many trifles? Only one thing is really worth while, and since Mary has chosen this good and needful part, I shall not take it away from her. But when will both of you learn to live as I have taught you: both serving in co-operation and both refreshing your souls in unison? Can you not learn that there is a time for everything—that the lesser matters of life should give way before the greater things of the heavenly kingdom?"

9. AT BETHLEHEM WITH ABNER

Throughout the week that followed the feast of tabernacles, scores of believers forgathered at Bethany and received instruction from the twelve apostles. The Sanhedrin made no effort to molest these gatherings since Jesus was not present; he was throughout this time working with Abner and his associates in Bethlehem. The day following the close of the feast, Jesus had departed for Bethany, and he did not again teach in the temple during this visit to Jerusalem.

At this time, Abner was making his headquarters at Bethlehem, and from that center many workers had been sent to the cities of Judea and southern Samaria and even to Alexandria. Within a few days of his arrival, Jesus and Abner completed the arrangements for the consolidation of the work of the two groups of apostles.

Throughout his visit to the feast of tabernacles, Jesus had divided his time about equally between Bethany and Bethlehem. At Bethany he spent considerable time with his apostles; at Bethlehem he gave much instruction to Abner and the other former apostles of John. And it was this intimate contact that finally led them to believe in him. These former apostles of John the Baptist were influenced by the courage he displayed in his public teaching in Jerusalem as well as by the sympathetic understanding they experienced in his private teaching at Bethlehem. These influences finally and fully won over each of Abner's associates to a wholehearted acceptance of the kingdom and all that such a step implied.

Before leaving Bethlehem for the last time, the Master made arrangements for them all to join him in the united effort which was to precede the ending of his earth career in the flesh. It was agreed that Abner and his associates were to join Jesus and the twelve in the near future at Magadan Park.

In accordance with this understanding, early in November Abner and his eleven fellows cast their lot with Jesus and the twelve and labored with them as one organization right on down to the crucifixion.

In the latter part of October Jesus and the twelve withdrew from the immediate vicinity of Jerusalem. On Sunday, October 30, Jesus and his associates left the city of Ephraim, where he had been resting in seclusion for a few days, and, going by the west Jordan highway directly to Magadan Park, arrived late on the afternoon of Wednesday, November 2.

The apostles were greatly relieved to have the Master back on friendly soil; no more did they urge him to go up to Jerusalem to proclaim the gospel of the kingdom.

PAPER 163

ORDINATION OF THE SEVENTY AT MAGADAN

A FEW days after the return of Jesus and the twelve to Magadan from Jerusalem, Abner and a group of some fifty disciples arrived from Bethlehem. At this time there were also assembled at Magadan Camp the evangelistic corps, the women's corps, and about one hundred and fifty other true and tried disciples from all parts of Palestine. After devoting a few days to visiting and the reorganization of the camp, Jesus and the twelve began a course of intensive training for this special group of believers, and from this well-trained and experienced aggregation of disciples the Master subsequently chose the seventy teachers and sent them forth to proclaim the gospel of the kingdom. This regular instruction began on Friday, November 4, and continued until Sabbath, November 19.

Jesus gave a talk to this company each morning. Peter taught methods of public preaching; Nathaniel instructed them in the art of teaching; Thomas explained how to answer questions; while Matthew directed the organization of their group finances. The other apostles also participated in this training in accordance with their special experience and natural talents.

1. ORDINATION OF THE SEVENTY

The seventy were ordained by Jesus on Sabbath afternoon, November 19, at the Magadan Camp, and Abner was placed at the head of these gospel preachers and teachers. This corps of seventy consisted of Abner and ten of the former apostles of John, fifty-one of the earlier evangelists, and eight other disciples who had distinguished themselves in the service of the kingdom.

About two o'clock on this Sabbath afternoon, between showers of rain, a company of believers, augmented by the arrival of David and the majority of his messenger corps and numbering over four hundred, assembled on the shore of the lake of Galilee to witness the ordination of the seventy.

Before Jesus laid his hands upon the heads of the seventy to set them apart as gospel messengers, addressing them, he said: "The harvest is indeed plenteous, but the laborers are few; therefore I exhort all of you to pray that the Lord of the harvest will send still other laborers into his harvest. I am about to set you apart as messengers of the kingdom; I am about to send you to Jew and gentile as lambs among wolves. As you go your ways, two and two, I instruct you to carry neither purse nor extra clothing, for you go forth on this first mission for only a short season. Salute no man by the way, attend only to your work. Whenever you go to stay at a home, first say: Peace be to this household. If those who love peace live therein, you shall abide there; if not, then shall you depart. And having selected this home, remain there for your stay in that city, eating and drinking whatever is set before you. And you do this because the laborer is worthy of his sustenance. Move not from house to house because a better lodging may be offered. Remember, as you go forth proclaiming peace on earth and good will among men, you must contend with bitter and self-deceived enemies; therefore be as wise as serpents while you are also as harmless as doves.

"And everywhere you go, preach, saying, 'The kingdom of heaven is at hand,' and minister to all who may be sick in either mind or body. Freely you have received of the good things of the kingdom; freely give. If the people of any city receive you, they shall find an abundant entrance into the Father's kingdom; but if the people of any city refuse to receive this gospel, still shall you proclaim your message as you depart from that unbelieving community, saying, even as you leave, to those who reject your teaching: 'Notwithstanding you reject the truth, it remains that the kingdom of God has come near you.' He who hears you hears me. And he who hears me hears Him who sent me. He who rejects your gospel message rejects me. And he who rejects me rejects Him who sent me."

When Jesus had thus spoken to the seventy, he began with Abner and, as they knelt in a circle about him, laid his hands upon the head of every man.

Early the next morning Abner sent the seventy messengers into all the cities of Galilee, Samaria, and Judea. And these thirty-five couples went forth preaching and teaching for about six weeks, all of them returning to the new camp near Pella, in Perea, on Friday, December 30.

2. THE RICH YOUNG MAN AND OTHERS

Over fifty disciples who sought ordination and appointment to membership in the seventy were rejected by the committee appointed by Jesus to select these candidates. This committee consisted of Andrew, Abner, and the acting head of the evangelistic corps. In all cases where this committee of three were not unanimous in agreement, they brought the candidate to Jesus, and while the Master never rejected a single person who craved ordination as a gospel messenger, there were more than a dozen who, when they had talked with Jesus, no more desired to become gospel messengers.

One earnest disciple came to Jesus, saying: "Master, I would be one of your new apostles, but my father is very old and near death; could I be permitted to return home to bury him?" To this man Jesus said: "My son, the foxes have holes, and the birds of heaven have nests, but the Son of Man has nowhere to lay his head. You are a faithful disciple, and you can remain such while you return home to minister to your loved ones, but not so with my gospel messengers. They have forsaken all to follow me and proclaim the kingdom. If you would be an ordained teacher, you must let others bury the dead while you go forth to publish the good news." And this man went away in great disappointment.

Another disciple came to the Master and said: "I would become an ordained messenger, but I would like to go to my home for a short while to comfort my family." And Jesus replied: "If you would be ordained, you must be willing to forsake all. The gospel messengers cannot have divided affections. No man, having put his hand to the plough, if he turns back, is worthy to become a messenger of the kingdom."

Then Andrew brought to Jesus a certain rich young man who was a devout believer, and who desired to receive ordination. This young man, Matadormus, was a member of the Jerusalem Sanhedrin; he had heard Jesus teach and had been subsequently instructed in the gospel of the kingdom by Peter and the other apostles. Jesus talked with Matadormus concerning the requirements of ordination and requested that he defer decision until after he had thought more fully about the matter. Early the next morning, as Jesus was going for a walk, this young man accosted him and said: "Master, I would know from you the assurances of eternal life. Seeing that I have observed all the commandments from my youth, I would like to know what more I must do to gain eternal life?" In answer to this question Jesus said: "If you keep all the commandments—do not commit adultery, do not kill, do not steal, do not bear false witness, do not defraud, honor your parents—you do well, but salvation is the reward of faith, not merely of works. Do you believe this gospel of the kingdom?" And Matadormus answered: "Yes, Master, I do believe everything you and your apostles have taught me." And Jesus said, "Then are you indeed my disciple and a child of the kingdom."

Then said the young man: "But, Master, I am not content to be your disciple; I would be one of your new messengers." When Jesus heard this, he looked down upon him with a great love and said: "I will have you to be one of my messengers if you are willing to pay the price, if you will supply the one thing which you lack." Matadormus replied: "Master, I will do anything if I may be allowed to follow you." Jesus, kissing the kneeling young man on the forehead, said: "If you would be my messenger, go and sell all that you have and, when you have bestowed the proceeds upon the poor or upon your brethren, come and follow me, and you shall have treasure in the kingdom of heaven."

When Matadormus heard this, his countenance fell. He arose and went away sorrowful, for he had great possessions. This wealthy young Pharisee had been raised to believe that wealth was the token of God's favor. Jesus knew that he was not free from the love of himself and his riches. The Master wanted to deliver him from the *love* of wealth, not necessarily from the wealth. While the disciples of Jesus did not part with all their worldly goods, the apostles and the seventy did. Matadormus desired to be one of the seventy new messengers, and that was the reason for Jesus' requiring him to part with all of his temporal possessions.

Almost every human being has some one thing which is held on to as a pet evil, and which the entrance into the kingdom of heaven requires as a part of the price of admission. If Matadormus had parted with his wealth, it probably would have been put right back into his hands for administration as treasurer of the seventy. For later on, after the establishment of the church at Jerusalem, he did obey the Master's injunction, although it was then too late to enjoy membership in the seventy, and he became the treasurer of the Jerusalem church, of which James the Lord's brother in the flesh was the head.

Thus always it was and forever will be: Men must arrive at their own decisions. There is a certain range of the freedom of choice which mortals may exercise. The forces of the spiritual world will not coerce man; they allow him to go the way of his own choosing.

Jesus foresaw that Matadormus, with his riches, could not possibly become an ordained associate of men who had forsaken all for the gospel; at the same time, he saw that, without his riches, he would become the ultimate leader of all of them. But, like Jesus' own brethren, he never became great in the kingdom because he deprived himself of that intimate and personal association with the Master which might have been his experience had he been willing to do at this time the very thing which Jesus asked, and which, several years subsequently, he actually did.

Riches have nothing directly to do with entrance into the kingdom of heaven, but the *love of wealth does.* The spiritual loyalties of the kingdom are incompatible with servility to materialistic mammon. Man may not share his supreme loyalty to a spiritual ideal with a material devotion.

Jesus never taught that it was wrong to have wealth. He required only the twelve and the seventy to dedicate all of their worldly possessions to the common cause. Even then, he provided for the profitable liquidation of their property, as in the case of the Apostle Matthew. Jesus many times advised his well-to-do disciples as he taught the rich man of Rome. The Master regarded the wise investment of excess earnings as a legitimate form of insurance against future and unavoidable adversity. When the apostolic treasury was overflowing, Judas put funds on deposit to be used subsequently when they might suffer greatly from a diminution of income. This Judas did after consultation with Andrew. Jesus never personally had anything to do with the apostolic finances except in the disbursement of alms. But there was one economic abuse which he many times condemned, and that was the unfair exploitation of the weak, unlearned, and less fortunate of men by their strong, keen, and more intelligent fellows. Jesus declared that such inhuman treatment of men, women, and children was incompatible with the ideals of the brotherhood of the kingdom of heaven.

3. THE DISCUSSION ABOUT WEALTH

By the time Jesus had finished talking with Matadormus, Peter and a number of the apostles had gathered about him, and as the rich young man was departing, Jesus turned around to face the apostles and said: "You see how difficult it is for those who have riches to enter fully into the kingdom of God! Spiritual worship cannot be shared with material devotions; no man can serve two masters. You have a saying that it is 'easier for a camel to go through the eye of a needle than for the heathen to inherit eternal life.' And I declare that it is as easy for this camel to go through the needle's eye as for these self-satisfied rich ones to enter the kingdom of heaven."

When Peter and the apostles heard these words, they were astonished exceedingly, so much so that Peter said: "Who then, Lord, can be saved? Shall all who have riches be kept out of the kingdom?" And Jesus replied: "No, Peter, but all who put their trust in riches shall hardly enter into the spiritual life that leads to eternal progress. But even then, much which is impossible to man is not beyond the reach of the Father in heaven; rather should we recognize that with God all things are possible."

As they went off by themselves, Jesus was grieved that Matadormus did not remain with them, for he greatly loved him. And when they had walked down by the lake, they sat there beside the water, and Peter, speaking for the twelve (who were all present by this time), said: "We are troubled by your words to the rich young man. Shall we require those who would follow you to give up all their worldly goods?" And Jesus said: "No, Peter, only those who would become apostles, and who desire to live with me as you do and as one family. But the Father requires that the affections of his children be pure and undivided.

Whatever thing or person comes between you and the love of the truths of the kingdom, must be surrendered. If one's wealth does not invade the precincts of the soul, it is of no consequence in the spiritual life of those who would enter the kingdom."

And then said Peter, "But, Master, we have left everything to follow you, what then shall we have?" And Jesus spoke to all of the twelve: "Verily, verily, I say to you, there is no man who has left wealth, home, wife, brethren, parents, or children for my sake and for the sake of the kingdom of heaven who shall not receive manifold more in this world, perhaps with some persecutions, and in the world to come eternal life. But many who are first shall be last, while the last shall often be first. The Father deals with his creatures in accordance with their needs and in obedience to his just laws of merciful and loving consideration for the welfare of a universe.

"The kingdom of heaven is like a householder who was a large employer of men, and who went out early in the morning to hire laborers to work in his vineyard. When he had agreed with the laborers to pay them a denarius a day, he sent them into the vineyard. Then he went out about nine o'clock, and seeing others standing in the market place idle, he said to them: 'Go you also to work in my vineyard, and whatsoever is right I will pay you.' And they went at once to work. Again he went out about twelve and about three and did likewise. And going to the market place about five in the afternoon, he found still others standing idle, and he inquired of them, 'Why do you stand here idle all the day?' And the men answered, 'Because nobody has hired us.' Then said the householder: 'Go you also to work in my vineyard, and whatever is right I will pay you.'

"When evening came, this owner of the vineyard said to his steward: 'Call the laborers and pay them their wages, beginning with the last hired and ending with the first.' When those who were hired about five o'clock came, they received a denarius each, and so it was with each of the other laborers. When the men who were hired at the beginning of the day saw how the later comers were paid, they expected to receive more than the amount agreed upon. But like the others every man received only a denarius. And when each had received his pay, they complained to the householder, saying: 'These men who were hired last worked only one hour, and yet you have paid them the same as us who have borne the burden of the day in the scorching sun.'

"Then answered the householder: 'My friends, I do you no wrong. Did not each of you agree to work for a denarius a day? Take now that which is yours and go your way, for it is my desire to give to those who came last as much as I have given to you. Is it not lawful for me to do what I will with my own? or do you begrudge my generosity because I desire to be good and to show mercy?'"

4. FAREWELL TO THE SEVENTY

It was a stirring time about the Magadan Camp the day the seventy went forth on their first mission. Early that morning, in his last talk with the seventy, Jesus placed emphasis on the following:

1. The gospel of the kingdom must be proclaimed to all the world, to gentile as well as to Jew.

2. While ministering to the sick, refrain from teaching the expectation of miracles.

3. Proclaim a spiritual brotherhood of the sons of God, not an outward kingdom of worldly power and material glory.

4. Avoid loss of time through overmuch social visiting and other trivialities which might detract from wholehearted devotion to preaching the gospel.

5. If the first house to be selected for a headquarters proves to be a worthy home, abide there throughout the sojourn in that city.

6. Make clear to all faithful believers that the time for an open break with the religious leaders of the Jews at Jerusalem has now come.

7. Teach that man's whole duty is summed up in this one commandment: Love the Lord your God with all your mind and soul and your neighbor as yourself. (This they were to teach as man's whole duty in place of the 613 rules of living expounded by the Pharisees.)

When Jesus had talked thus to the seventy in the presence of all the apostles and disciples, Simon Peter took them off by themselves and preached to them their ordination sermon, which was an elaboration of the Master's charge given at the time he laid his hands upon them and set them apart as messengers of the kingdom. Peter exhorted the seventy to cherish in their experience the following virtues:

1. *Consecrated devotion.* To pray always for more laborers to be sent forth into the gospel harvest. He explained that, when one so prays, he will the more likely say, "Here am I; send me." He admonished them to neglect not their daily worship.

2. *True courage.* He warned them that they would encounter hostility and be certain to meet with persecution. Peter told them their mission was no undertaking for cowards and advised those who were afraid to step out before they started. But none withdrew.

3. *Faith and trust.* They must go forth on this short mission wholly unprovided for; they must trust the Father for food and shelter and all other things needful.

4. *Zeal and initiative.* They must be possessed with zeal and intelligent enthusiasm; they must attend strictly to their Master's business. Oriental salutation was a lengthy and elaborate ceremony; therefore had they been instructed to "salute no man by the way," which was a common method of exhorting one to go about his business without the waste of time. It had nothing to do with the matter of friendly greeting.

5. *Kindness and courtesy.* The Master had instructed them to avoid unnecessary waste of time in social ceremonies, but he enjoined courtesy toward all with whom they should come in contact. They were to show every kindness to those who might entertain them in their homes. They were strictly warned against leaving a modest home to be entertained in a more comfortable or influential one.

6. *Ministry to the sick.* The seventy were charged by Peter to search out the sick in mind and body and to do everything in their power to bring about the alleviation or cure of their maladies.

And when they had been thus charged and instructed, they started out, two and two, on their mission in Galilee, Samaria, and Judea.

Although the Jews had a peculiar regard for the number seventy, sometimes considering the nations of heathendom as being seventy in number, and although these seventy messengers were to go with the gospel to all peoples, still as far as we can discern, it was only coincidental that this group happened to number just seventy. Certain it was that Jesus would have accepted no less than half a dozen others, but they were unwilling to pay the price of forsaking wealth and families.

5. MOVING THE CAMP TO PELLA

Jesus and the twelve now prepared to establish their last headquarters in Perea, near Pella, where the Master was baptized in the Jordan. The last ten days of November were spent in council at Magadan, and on Tuesday, December 6, the entire company of almost three hundred started out at daybreak with all their effects to lodge that night near Pella by the river. This was the same site, by the spring, that John the Baptist had occupied with his camp several years before.

After the breaking up of the Magadan Camp, David Zebedee returned to Bethsaida and began immediately to curtail the messenger service. The kingdom was taking on a new phase. Daily, pilgrims arrived from all parts of Palestine and even from remote regions of the Roman Empire. Believers occasionally came from Mesopotamia and from the lands east of the Tigris. Accordingly, on Sunday, December 18, David, with the help of his messenger corps, loaded on to the pack animals the camp equipage, then stored in his father's house, with which he had formerly conducted the camp of Bethsaida by the lake. Bidding farewell to Bethsaida for the time being, he proceeded down the lake shore and along the Jordan to a point about one-half mile north of the apostolic camp; and in less than a week he was prepared to offer hospitality to almost fifteen hundred pilgrim visitors. The apostolic camp could accommodate about five hundred. This was the rainy season in Palestine, and these accommodations were required to take care of the ever-increasing number of inquirers, mostly earnest, who came into Perea to see Jesus and to hear his teaching.

David did all this on his own initiative, though he had taken counsel with Philip and Matthew at Magadan. He employed the larger part of his former messenger corps as his helpers in conducting this camp; he now used less than twenty men on regular messenger duty. Near the end of December and before the return of the seventy, almost eight hundred visitors were gathered about the Master, and they found lodging in David's camp.

6. THE RETURN OF THE SEVENTY

On Friday, December 30, while Jesus was away in the near-by hills with Peter, James, and John, the seventy messengers were arriving by couples, accompanied by numerous believers, at the Pella headquarters. All seventy were assembled at the teaching site about five o'clock when Jesus returned to the camp. The evening meal was delayed for more than an hour while these enthusiasts for the gospel of the kingdom related their experiences. David's messengers had brought much of this news to the apostles during previous weeks, but it was truly inspiring to hear these newly ordained teachers of the gospel personally tell how their message had been received by hungry Jews and gentiles. At last Jesus was able to see men going out to spread the good news without his personal presence. The Master now knew that he could leave this world without seriously hindering the progress of the kingdom.

When the seventy related how "even the devils were subject" to them, they referred to the wonderful cures they had wrought in the cases of victims of nervous disorders. Nevertheless, there had been a few cases of real spirit possession relieved by these ministers, and referring to these, Jesus said: "It is not strange that these disobedient minor spirits should be subject to you, seeing that I beheld Satan falling as lightning from heaven. But rejoice not so much over this, for I declare to you that, as soon as I return to my Father, we will send forth our spirits into the very minds of men so that no more can these few lost spirits enter the minds of unfortunate mortals. I rejoice with you that you have power with men, but be not lifted up because of this experience but the rather rejoice that your names are written on the rolls of heaven, and that you are thus to go forward in an endless career of spiritual conquest."

And it was at this time, just before partaking of the evening meal, that Jesus experienced one of those rare moments of emotional ecstasy which his followers had occasionally witnessed. He said: "I thank you, my Father, Lord of heaven and earth, that, while this wonderful gospel was hidden from the wise and self-righteous, the spirit has revealed these spiritual glories to these children of the kingdom. Yes, my Father, it must have been pleasing in your sight to do this, and I rejoice to know that the good news will spread to all the world even after I shall have returned to you and the work which you have given me to perform. I am mightily moved as I realize you are about to deliver all authority into my hands, that only you really know who I am, and that only I really know you, and those to whom I have revealed you. And when I have finished this revelation to my brethren in the flesh, I will continue the revelation to your creatures on high."

When Jesus had thus spoken to the Father, he turned aside to speak to his apostles and ministers: "Blessed are the eyes which see and the ears which hear these things. Let me say to you that many prophets and many of the great men of the past ages have desired to behold what you now see, but it was not granted them. And many generations of the children of light yet to come will, when they hear of these things, envy you who have heard and seen them."

Then, speaking to all the disciples, he said: "You have heard how many cities and villages have received the good news of the kingdom, and how my ministers and teachers have been received by both the Jew and the gentile. And blessed indeed are these communities which have elected to believe the gospel of the kingdom. But woe upon the light-rejecting inhabitants of Chorazin, Bethsaida-Julias, and Capernaum, the cities which did not well receive these messengers. I declare that, if the mighty works done in these places had been done in Tyre and Sidon, the people of these so-called heathen cities would have long since repented in sackcloth and ashes. It shall indeed be more tolerable for Tyre and Sidon in the day of judgment."

The next day being the Sabbath, Jesus went apart with the seventy and said to them: "I did indeed rejoice with you when you came back bearing the good tidings of the reception of the gospel of the kingdom by so many people scattered throughout Galilee, Samaria, and Judea. But why were you so surprisingly elated? Did you not expect that your message would manifest power in its delivery? Did you go forth with so little faith in this gospel that you come back in surprise at its effectiveness? And now, while I would not quench your spirit of rejoicing, I would sternly warn you against the subtleties of pride, spiritual pride. If you could understand the downfall of Lucifer, the iniquitous one, you would solemnly shun all forms of spiritual pride.

"You have entered upon this great work of teaching mortal man that he is a son of God. I have shown you the way; go forth to do your duty and be not weary in well doing. To you and to all who shall follow in your steps down through the ages, let me say: I always stand near, and my invitation-call is, and ever shall be, Come to me all you who labor and are heavy laden, and I will give you rest. Take my yoke upon you and learn of me, for I am true and loyal, and you shall find spiritual rest for your souls."

And they found the Master's words to be true when they put his promises to the test. And since that day countless thousands also have tested and proved the surety of these same promises.

7. PREPARATION FOR THE LAST MISSION

The next few days were busy times in the Pella camp; preparations for the Perean mission were being completed. Jesus and his associates were about to enter upon their last mission, the three months' tour of all Perea, which terminated only upon the Master's entering Jerusalem for his final labors on earth. Throughout this period the headquarters of Jesus and the twelve apostles was maintained here at the Pella camp.

It was no longer necessary for Jesus to go abroad to teach the people. They now came to him in increasing numbers each week and from all parts, not only from Palestine but from the whole Roman world and from the Near East. Although the Master participated with the seventy in the tour of Perea, he spent much of his time at the Pella camp, teaching the multitude and instructing the twelve. Throughout this three months' period at least ten of the apostles remained with Jesus.

The women's corps also prepared to go out, two and two, with the seventy to labor in the larger cities of Perea. This original group of twelve women had recently trained a larger corps of fifty women in the work of home visitation and in the art of ministering to the sick and the afflicted. Perpetua, Simon Peter's wife, became a member of this new division of the women's corps and was intrusted with the leadership of the enlarged women's work under Abner. After Pentecost she remained with her illustrious husband, accompanying him on all of his missionary tours; and on the day Peter was crucified in Rome, she was fed to the wild beasts in the arena. This new women's corps also had as members the wives of Philip and Matthew and the mother of James and John.

The work of the kingdom now prepared to enter upon its terminal phase under the personal leadership of Jesus. And this present phase was one of spiritual depth in contrast with the miracle-minded and wonder-seeking multitudes who followed after the Master during the former days of popularity in Galilee. However, there were still any number of his followers who were material-minded, and who failed to grasp the truth that the kingdom of heaven is the spiritual brotherhood of man founded on the eternal fact of the universal fatherhood of God.

PAPER 164

AT THE FEAST OF DEDICATION

AS THE camp at Pella was being established, Jesus, taking with him Nathaniel and Thomas, secretly went up to Jerusalem to attend the feast of the dedication. Not until they passed over the Jordan at the Bethany ford, did the two apostles become aware that their Master was going on to Jerusalem. When they perceived that he really intended to be present at the feast of dedication, they remonstrated with him most earnestly, and using every sort of argument, they sought to dissuade him. But their efforts were of no avail; Jesus was determined to visit Jerusalem. To all their entreaties and to all their warnings emphasizing the folly and danger of placing himself in the hands of the Sanhedrin, he would reply only, "I would give these teachers in Israel another opportunity to see the light, before my hour comes."

On they went toward Jerusalem, the two apostles continuing to express their feelings of fear and to voice their doubts about the wisdom of such an apparently presumptuous undertaking. They reached Jericho about half past four and prepared to lodge there for the night.

1. STORY OF THE GOOD SAMARITAN

That evening a considerable company gathered about Jesus and the two apostles to ask questions, many of which the apostles answered, while others the Master discussed. In the course of the evening a certain lawyer, seeking to entangle Jesus in a compromising disputation, said: "Teacher, I would like to ask you just what I should do to inherit eternal life?" Jesus answered, "What is written in the law and the prophets; how do you read the Scriptures?" The lawyer, knowing the teachings of both Jesus and the Pharisees, answered: "To love the Lord God with all your heart, soul, mind, and strength, and your neighbor as yourself." Then said Jesus: "You have answered right; this, if you really do, will lead to life everlasting."

But the lawyer was not wholly sincere in asking this question, and desiring to justify himself while also hoping to embarrass Jesus, he ventured to ask still another question. Drawing a little closer to the Master, he said, "But, Teacher, I should like you to tell me just who is my neighbor?" The lawyer asked this question hoping to entrap Jesus into making some statement that would contravene the Jewish law which defined one's neighbor as "the children of one's people." The Jews looked upon all others as "gentile dogs." This lawyer was somewhat familiar with Jesus' teachings and therefore well knew that the Master thought differently; thus he hoped to lead him into saying something which could be construed as an attack upon the sacred law.

But Jesus discerned the lawyer's motive, and instead of falling into the trap, he proceeded to tell his hearers a story, a story which would be fully appreciated by any Jericho audience. Said Jesus: "A certain man was going down from Jerusalem to Jericho, and he fell into the hands of cruel brigands, who robbed him, stripped him and beat him, and departing, left him half dead. Very soon, by chance, a certain priest was going down that way, and when he came upon the wounded man, seeing his sorry plight, he passed by on the other side of the road. And in like manner a Levite also, when he came along and saw the man, passed by on the other side. Now, about this time, a certain Samaritan, as he journeyed down to Jericho, came across this wounded man; and when he saw how he had been robbed and beaten, he was moved with compassion, and going over to him, he bound up his wounds, pouring on oil and wine, and setting the man upon his own beast, brought him here to the inn and took care of him. And on the morrow he took out some money and, giving it to the host, said: 'Take good care of my friend, and if the expense is more, when I come back again, I will repay you.' Now let me ask you: Which of these three turned out to be the neighbor of him who fell among the robbers?" And when the lawyer perceived that he had fallen into his own snare, he answered, "He who showed mercy on him." And Jesus said, "Go and do likewise."

The lawyer answered, "He who showed mercy," that he might refrain from even speaking that odious word, Samaritan. The lawyer was forced to give the very answer to the question, "Who is my neighbor?" which Jesus wished given, and which, if Jesus had so stated, would have directly involved him in the charge of heresy. Jesus not only confounded the dishonest lawyer, but he told his hearers a story which was at the same time a beautiful admonition to all his followers and a stunning rebuke to all Jews regarding their attitude toward the Samaritans. And this story has continued to promote brotherly love among all who have subsequently believed the gospel of Jesus.

2. AT JERUSALEM

Jesus had attended the feast of tabernacles that he might proclaim the gospel to the pilgrims from all parts of the empire; he now went up to the feast of the dedication for just one purpose: to give the Sanhedrin and the Jewish leaders another chance to see the light. The principal event of these few days in Jerusalem occurred on Friday night at the home of Nicodemus. Here were gathered together some twenty-five Jewish leaders who believed Jesus' teaching. Among this group were fourteen men who were then, or had recently been, members of the Sanhedrin. This meeting was attended by Eber, Matadormus, and Joseph of Arimathea.

On this occasion Jesus' hearers were all learned men, and both they and his two apostles were amazed at the breadth and depth of the remarks which the Master made to this distinguished group. Not since the times when he had taught in Alexandria, Rome, and in the islands of the Mediterranean, had he exhibited such learning and shown such a grasp of the affairs of men, both secular and religious.

When this little meeting broke up, all went away mystified by the Master's personality, charmed by his gracious manner, and in love with the man. They had sought to advise Jesus concerning his desire to win the remaining members of the Sanhedrin. The Master listened attentively, but silently, to all their proposals. He well knew none of their plans would work. He surmised that the majority of the Jewish leaders never would accept the gospel of the kingdom; nevertheless, he gave them all this one more chance to choose. But when he went forth that night, with Nathaniel and Thomas, to lodge on the Mount of Olives, he had not yet decided upon the method he would pursue in bringing his work once more to the notice of the Sanhedrin.

That night Nathaniel and Thomas slept little; they were too much amazed by what they had heard at Nicodemus's house. They thought much over the final remark of Jesus regarding the offer of the former and present members of the Sanhedrin to go with him before the seventy. The Master said: "No, my brethren, it would be to no purpose. You would multiply the wrath to be visited upon your own heads, but you would not in the least mitigate the hatred which they bear me. Go, each of you, about the Father's business as the spirit leads you while I once more bring the kingdom to their notice in the manner which my Father may direct."

3. HEALING THE BLIND BEGGAR

The next morning the three went over to Martha's home at Bethany for breakfast and then went immediately into Jerusalem. This Sabbath morning, as Jesus and his two apostles drew near the temple, they encountered a well-known beggar, a man who had been born blind, sitting at his usual place. Although these mendicants did not solicit or receive alms on the Sabbath day, they were permitted thus to sit in their usual places. Jesus paused and looked upon the beggar. As he gazed upon this man who had been born blind, the idea came into his mind as to how he would once more bring his mission on earth to the notice of the Sanhedrin and the other Jewish leaders and religious teachers.

As the Master stood there before the blind man, engrossed in deep thought, Nathaniel, pondering the possible cause of this man's blindness, asked: "Master, who did sin, this man or his parents, that he should be born blind?"

The rabbis taught that all such cases of blindness from birth were caused by sin. Not only were children conceived and born in sin, but a child could be born blind as a punishment for some specific sin committed by its father. They even taught that a child itself might sin before it was born into the world. They also taught that such defects could be caused by some sin or other indulgence of the mother while carrying the child.

There was, throughout all these regions, a lingering belief in reincarnation. The older Jewish teachers, together with Plato, Philo, and many of the Essenes, tolerated the theory that men may reap in one incarnation what they have sown in a previous existence; thus in one life they were believed to be expiating the sins committed in preceding lives. The Master found it difficult to make men believe that their souls had not had previous existences.

However, inconsistent as it seems, while such blindness was supposed to be the result of sin, the Jews held that it was meritorious in a high degree to give alms to these blind beggars. It was the custom of these blind men constantly to chant to the passers-by, "O tenderhearted, gain merit by assisting the blind."

Jesus entered into the discussion of this case with Nathaniel and Thomas, not only because he had already decided to use this blind man as the means of that day bringing his mission once more prominently to the notice of the Jewish leaders, but also because he always encouraged his apostles to seek for the true causes of all phenomena, natural or spiritual. He had often warned them to avoid the common tendency to assign spiritual causes to commonplace physical events.

Jesus decided to use this beggar in his plans for that day's work, but before doing anything for the blind man, Josiah by name, he proceeded to answer Nathaniel's question. Said the Master: "Neither did this man sin nor his parents that the works of God might be manifest in him. This blindness has come upon him in the natural course of events, but we must now do the works of Him who sent me, while it is still day, for the night will certainly come when it will be impossible to do the work we are about to perform. When I am in the world, I am the light of the world, but in only a little while I will not be with you."

When Jesus had spoken, he said to Nathaniel and Thomas: "Let us create the sight of this blind man on this Sabbath day that the scribes and Pharisees may have the full occasion which they seek for accusing the Son of Man." Then, stooping over, he spat on the ground and mixed the clay with the spittle, and speaking of all this so that the blind man could hear, he went up to Josiah and put the clay over his sightless eyes, saying: "Go, my son, wash away this clay in the pool of Siloam, and immediately you shall receive your sight." And when Josiah had so washed in the pool of Siloam, he returned to his friends and family, seeing.

Having always been a beggar, he knew nothing else; so, when the first excitement of the creation of his sight had passed, he returned to his usual place of alms-seeking. His friends, neighbors, and all who had known him aforetime, when they observed that he could see, all said, "Is this not Josiah the blind beggar?" Some said it was he, while others said, "No, it is one like him, but this man can see." But when they asked the man himself, he answered, "I am he."

When they began to inquire of him how he was able to see, he answered them: "A man called Jesus came by this way, and when talking about me with his friends, he made clay with spittle, anointed my eyes, and directed that I should go and wash in the pool of Siloam. I did what this man told me, and immediately I received my sight. And that is only a few hours ago. I do not yet know the meaning of much that I see." And when the people who began to gather about him asked where they could find the strange man who had healed him, Josiah could answer only that he did not know.

This is one of the strangest of all the Master's miracles. This man did not ask for healing. He did not know that the Jesus who had directed him to wash at Siloam, and who had promised him vision, was the prophet of Galilee who had preached in Jerusalem during the feast of tabernacles. This man had little faith that he would receive his sight, but the people of that day had great faith in the efficacy of the spittle of a great or holy man; and from Jesus' conversation with Nathaniel and Thomas, Josiah had concluded that his would-be benefactor was a great man, a learned teacher or a holy prophet; accordingly he did as Jesus directed him.

Jesus made use of the clay and the spittle and directed him to wash in the symbolic pool of Siloam for three reasons:

1. This was not a miracle response to the individual's faith. This was a wonder which Jesus chose to perform for a purpose of his own, but which he so arranged that this man might derive lasting benefit therefrom.

2. As the blind man had not asked for healing, and since the faith he had was slight, these material acts were suggested for the purpose of encouraging him. He did believe in the superstition of the efficacy of spittle, and he knew the pool of Siloam was a semisacred place. But he would hardly have gone there had it not been necessary to wash away the clay of his anointing. There was just enough ceremony about the transaction to induce him to act.

3. But Jesus had a third reason for resorting to these material means in connection with this unique transaction: This was a miracle wrought purely in obedience to his own choosing, and thereby he desired to teach his followers of that day and all subsequent ages to refrain from despising or neglecting material means in the healing of the sick. He wanted to teach them that they must cease to regard miracles as the only method of curing human diseases.

Jesus gave this man his sight by miraculous working, on this Sabbath morning and in Jerusalem near the temple, for the prime purpose of making this act an open challenge to the Sanhedrin and all the Jewish teachers and religious leaders. This was his way of proclaiming an open break with the Pharisees. He was always positive in everything he did. And it was for the purpose of bringing these matters before the Sanhedrin that Jesus brought his two apostles to this man early in the afternoon of this Sabbath day and deliberately provoked those discussions which compelled the Pharisees to take notice of the miracle.

4. JOSIAH BEFORE THE SANHEDRIN

By midafternoon the healing of Josiah had raised such a discussion around the temple that the leaders of the Sanhedrin decided to convene the council in its usual temple meeting place. And they did this in violation of a standing rule which forbade the meeting of the Sanhedrin on the Sabbath day. Jesus knew that Sabbath breaking would be one of the chief charges to be brought against him when the final test came, and he desired to be brought before the Sanhedrin for adjudication of the charge of having healed a blind man on the Sabbath day, when the very session of the high Jewish court sitting in judgment on him for this act of mercy would be deliberating on these matters on the Sabbath day and in direct violation of their own self-imposed laws.

But they did not call Jesus before them; they feared to. Instead, they sent forthwith for Josiah. After some preliminary questioning, the spokesman for the Sanhedrin (about fifty members being present) directed Josiah to tell them what had happened to him. Since his healing that morning Josiah had learned from Thomas, Nathaniel, and others that the Pharisees were angry about his healing on the Sabbath, and that they were likely to make trouble for all concerned; but Josiah did not yet perceive that Jesus was he who was called the Deliverer. So, when the Pharisees questioned him, he said: "This man came along, put clay upon my eyes, told me to go wash in Siloam, and I do now see."

One of the older Pharisees, after making a lengthy speech, said: "This man cannot be from God because you can see that he does not observe the Sabbath. He violates the law, first, in making the clay, then, in sending this beggar to wash in Siloam on the Sabbath day. Such a man cannot be a teacher sent from God."

Then one of the younger men who secretly believed in Jesus, said: "If this man is not sent by God, how can he do these things? We know that one who is a common sinner cannot perform such miracles. We all know this beggar and that he was born blind; now he sees. Will you still say that this prophet does all these wonders by the power of the prince of devils?" And for every Pharisee who dared to accuse and denounce Jesus one would arise to ask entangling and embarrassing questions, so that a serious division arose among them. The presiding officer saw whither they were drifting, and in order to allay the discussion, he prepared further to question the man himself. Turning to Josiah, he said: "What do you have to say about this man, this Jesus, whom you claim opened your eyes?" And Josiah answered, "I think he is a prophet."

The leaders were greatly troubled and, knowing not what else to do, decided to send for Josiah's parents to learn whether he had actually been born blind. They were loath to believe that the beggar had been healed.

It was well known about Jerusalem, not only that Jesus was denied entrance into all synagogues, but that all who believed in his teaching were likewise cast out of the synagogue, excommunicated from the congregation of Israel; and this meant denial of all rights and privileges of every sort throughout all Jewry except the right to buy the necessaries of life.

When, therefore, Josiah's parents, poor and fear-burdened souls, appeared before the august Sanhedrin, they were afraid to speak freely. Said the spokesman of the court: "Is this your son? and do we understand aright that he was born blind? If this is true, how is it that he can now see?" And then Josiah's father, seconded by his mother, answered: "We know that this is our son, and that he was born blind, but how it is that he has come to see, or who it was that opened his eyes, we know not. Ask him; he is of age; let him speak for himself."

They now called Josiah up before them a second time. They were not getting along well with their scheme of holding a formal trial, and some were beginning to feel strange about doing this on the Sabbath; accordingly, when they recalled Josiah, they attempted to ensnare him by a different mode of attack. The officer of the court spoke to the former blind man, saying: "Why do you not give God the glory for this? why do you not tell us the whole truth about what happened? We all know that this man is a sinner. Why do you refuse to discern the truth? You know that both you and this man stand convicted of Sabbath breaking. Will you not atone for your sin by acknowledging God as your healer, if you still claim that your eyes have this day been opened?"

But Josiah was neither dumb nor lacking in humor; so he replied to the officer of the court: "Whether this man is a sinner, I know not; but one thing I do know—that, whereas I was blind, now I see." And since they could not entrap Josiah, they sought further to question him, asking: "Just how did he open your eyes? what did he actually do to you? what did he say to you? did he ask you to believe in him?"

Josiah replied, somewhat impatiently: "I have told you exactly how it all happened, and if you did not believe my testimony, why would you hear it again? Would you by any chance also become his disciples?" When Josiah had thus spoken, the Sanhedrin broke up in confusion, almost violence, for the leaders rushed upon Josiah, angrily exclaiming: "You may talk about being this man's disciple, but we are disciples of Moses, and we are the teachers of the laws of God. We know that God spoke through Moses, but as for this man Jesus, we know not whence he is."

Then Josiah, standing upon a stool, shouted abroad to all who could hear, saying: "Hearken, you who claim to be the teachers of all Israel, while I declare to you that herein is a great marvel since you confess that you know not whence this man is, and yet you know of a certainty, from the testimony which you have heard, that he opened my eyes. We all know that God does not perform such works for the ungodly; that God would do such a thing only at the request of a true worshiper—for one who is holy and righteous. You know that not since the beginning of the world have you ever heard of the opening of the eyes of one who was born blind. Look, then, all of you, upon me and realize what has been done this day in Jerusalem! I tell you, if this man were not from God, he could not do this." And as the Sanhedrists departed in anger and confusion, they shouted to him: "You were altogether born in sin, and do you now presume to teach us? Maybe you were not really born blind, and even if your eyes were opened on the Sabbath day, this was done by the power of the prince of devils." And they went at once to the synagogue to cast out Josiah.

Josiah entered this trial with meager ideas about Jesus and the nature of his healing. Most of the daring testimony which he so cleverly and courageously bore before this supreme tribunal of all Israel developed in his mind as the trial proceeded along such unfair and unjust lines.

5. TEACHING IN SOLOMON'S PORCH

All of the time this Sabbath-breaking session of the Sanhedrin was in progress in one of the temple chambers, Jesus was walking about near at hand, teaching the people in Solomon's Porch, hoping that he would be summoned before the Sanhedrin where he could tell them the good news of the liberty and joy of divine sonship in the kingdom of God. But they were afraid to send for him. They were always disconcerted by these sudden and public appearances of Jesus in Jerusalem. The very occasion they had so ardently sought, Jesus now gave them, but they feared to bring him before the Sanhedrin even as a witness, and even more they feared to arrest him.

This was midwinter in Jerusalem, and the people sought the partial shelter of Solomon's Porch; and as Jesus lingered, the crowds asked him many questions, and he taught them for more than two hours. Some of the Jewish teachers sought to entrap him by publicly asking him: "How long will you hold us in suspense? If you are the Messiah, why do you not plainly tell us?" Said Jesus: "I have told you about myself and my Father many times, but you will not believe me. Can you not see that the works I do in my Father's name bear witness for me? But many of you believe not because you belong not to my fold. The teacher of truth attracts only those who hunger for the truth and who thirst for righteousness. My sheep hear my voice and I know them and they follow me. And to all who follow my teaching I give eternal life; they shall never perish, and no one shall snatch them out of my hand. My Father, who has given me these children, is greater than all, so that no one is able to pluck them out of my Father's hand. The Father and I are one." Some of the unbelieving Jews rushed over to where they were still building the temple to pick up stones to cast at Jesus, but the believers restrained them.

Jesus continued his teaching: "Many loving works have I shown you from the Father, so that now would I inquire for which one of these good works do you think to stone me?" And then answered one of the Pharisees: "For no good work would we stone you but for blasphemy, inasmuch as you, being a man, dare to make yourself equal with God." And Jesus answered: "You charge the

Son of Man with blasphemy because you refused to believe me when I declared to you that I was sent by God. If I do not the works of God, believe me not, but if I do the works of God, even though you believe not in me, I should think you would believe the works. But that you may be certain of what I proclaim, let me again assert that the Father is in me and I in the Father, and that, as the Father dwells in me, so will I dwell in every one who believes this gospel." And when the people heard these words, many of them rushed out to lay hands upon the stones to cast at him, but he passed out through the temple precincts; and meeting Nathaniel and Thomas, who had been in attendance upon the session of the Sanhedrin, he waited with them near the temple until Josiah came from the council chamber.

Jesus and the two apostles did not go in search of Josiah at his home until they heard he had been cast out of the synagogue. When they came to his house, Thomas called him out in the yard, and Jesus, speaking to him, said: "Josiah, do you believe in the Son of God?" And Josiah answered, "Tell me who he is that I may believe in him." And Jesus said: "You have both seen and heard him, and it is he who now speaks to you." And Josiah said, "Lord, I believe," and falling down, he worshiped.

When Josiah learned that he had been cast out of the synagogue, he was at first greatly downcast, but he was much encouraged when Jesus directed that he should immediately prepare to go with them to the camp at Pella. This simple-minded man of Jerusalem had indeed been cast out of a Jewish synagogue, but behold the Creator of a universe leading him forth to become associated with the spiritual nobility of that day and generation.

And now Jesus left Jerusalem, not again to return until near the time when he prepared to leave this world. With the two apostles and Josiah the Master went back to Pella. And Josiah proved to be one of the recipients of the Master's miraculous ministry who turned out fruitfully, for he became a lifelong preacher of the gospel of the kingdom.

PAPER 165

THE PEREAN MISSION BEGINS

ON TUESDAY, January 3, A.D. 30, Abner, the former chief of the twelve apostles of John the Baptist, a Nazarite and onetime head of the Nazarite school at Engedi, now chief of the seventy messengers of the kingdom, called his associates together and gave them final instructions before sending them on a mission to all of the cities and villages of Perea. This Perean mission continued for almost three months and was the last ministry of the Master. From these labors Jesus went directly to Jerusalem to pass through his final experiences in the flesh. The seventy, supplemented by the periodic labors of Jesus and the twelve apostles, worked in the following cities and towns and some fifty additional villages: Zaphon, Gadara, Macad, Arbela, Ramath, Edrei, Bosora, Caspin, Mispeh, Gerasa, Ragaba, Succoth, Amathus, Adam, Penuel, Capitolias, Dion, Hatita, Gadda, Philadelphia, Jogbehah, Gilead, Beth-Nimrah, Tyrus, Elealah, Livias, Heshbon, Callirrhoe, Beth-Peor, Shittim, Sibmah, Medeba, Beth-Meon, Areopolis, and Aroer.

Throughout this tour of Perea the women's corps, now numbering sixty-two, took over most of the work of ministration to the sick. This was the final period of the development of the higher spiritual aspects of the gospel of the kingdom, and there was, accordingly, an absence of miracle working. No other part of Palestine was so thoroughly worked by the apostles and disciples of Jesus, and in no other region did the better classes of citizens so generally accept the Master's teaching.

Perea at this time was about equally gentile and Jewish, the Jews having been generally removed from these regions during the times of Judas Maccabee. Perea was the most beautiful and picturesque province of all Palestine. It was generally referred to by the Jews as "the land beyond the Jordan."

Throughout this period Jesus divided his time between the camp at Pella and trips with the twelve to assist the seventy in the various cities where they taught and preached. Under Abner's instructions the seventy baptized all believers, although Jesus had not so charged them.

1. AT THE PELLA CAMP

By the middle of January more than twelve hundred persons were gathered together at Pella, and Jesus taught this multitude at least once each day when he was in residence at the camp, usually speaking at nine o'clock in the morning if not prevented by rain. Peter and the other apostles taught each afternoon. The evenings Jesus reserved for the usual sessions of questions and answers with the twelve and other advanced disciples. The evening groups averaged about fifty.

By the middle of March, the time when Jesus began his journey toward Jerusalem, over four thousand persons composed the large audience which heard

Jesus or Peter preach each morning. The Master chose to terminate his work on earth when the interest in his message had reached a high point, the highest point attained under this second or nonmiraculous phase of the progress of the kingdom. While three quarters of the multitude were truth seekers, there were also present a large number of Pharisees from Jerusalem and elsewhere, together with many doubters and cavilers.

Jesus and the twelve apostles devoted much of their time to the multitude assembled at the Pella camp. The twelve paid little or no attention to the field work, only going out with Jesus to visit Abner's associates from time to time. Abner was very familiar with the Perean district since this was the field in which his former master, John the Baptist, had done most of his work. After beginning the Perean mission, Abner and the seventy never returned to the Pella camp.

2. SERMON ON THE GOOD SHEPHERD

A company of over three hundred Jerusalemites, Pharisees and others, followed Jesus north to Pella when he hastened away from the jurisdiction of the Jewish rulers at the ending of the feast of the dedication; and it was in the presence of these Jewish teachers and leaders, as well as in the hearing of the twelve apostles, that Jesus preached the sermon on the "Good Shepherd." After half an hour of informal discussion, speaking to a group of about one hundred, Jesus said:

"On this night I have much to tell you, and since many of you are my disciples and some of you my bitter enemies, I will present my teaching in a parable, so that you may each take for yourself that which finds a reception in your heart.

"Tonight, here before me are men who would be willing to die for me and for this gospel of the kingdom, and some of them will so offer themselves in the years to come; and here also are some of you, slaves of tradition, who have followed me down from Jerusalem, and who, with your darkened and deluded leaders, seek to kill the Son of Man. The life which I now live in the flesh shall judge both of you, the true shepherds and the false shepherds. If the false shepherd were blind, he would have no sin, but you claim that you see; you profess to be teachers in Israel; therefore does your sin remain upon you.

"The true shepherd gathers his flock into the fold for the night in times of danger. And when the morning has come, he enters into the fold by the door, and when he calls, the sheep know his voice. Every shepherd who gains entrance to the sheepfold by any other means than by the door is a thief and a robber. The true shepherd enters the fold after the porter has opened the door for him, and his sheep, knowing his voice, come out at his word; and when they that are his are thus brought forth, the true shepherd goes before them; he leads the way and the sheep follow him. His sheep follow him because they know his voice; they will not follow a stranger. They will flee from the stranger because they know not his voice. This multitude which is gathered about us here are like sheep without a shepherd, but when we speak to them, they know the shepherd's voice, and they follow after us; at least, those who hunger for truth and thirst for righteousness do. Some of you are not of my fold; you know not my voice, and you do not follow me. And because you are false shepherds, the sheep know not your voice and will not follow you."

And when Jesus had spoken this parable, no one asked him a question. After a time he began again to speak and went on to discuss the parable:

"You who would be the undershepherds of my Father's flocks must not only be worthy leaders, but you must also *feed* the flock with good food; you are not true shepherds unless you lead your flocks into green pastures and beside still waters.

"And now, lest some of you too easily comprehend this parable, I will declare that I am both the door to the Father's sheepfold and at the same time the true shepherd of my Father's flocks. Every shepherd who seeks to enter the fold without me shall fail, and the sheep will not hear his voice. I, with those who minister with me, am the door. Every soul who enters upon the eternal way by the means I have created and ordained shall be saved and will be able to go on to the attainment of the eternal pastures of Paradise.

"But I also am the true shepherd who is willing even to lay down his life for the sheep. The thief breaks into the fold only to steal, and to kill, and to destroy; but I have come that you all may have life and have it more abundantly. He who is a hireling, when danger arises, will flee and allow the sheep to be scattered and destroyed; but the true shepherd will not flee when the wolf comes; he will protect his flock and, if necessary, lay down his life for his sheep. Verily, verily, I say to you, friends and enemies, I am the true shepherd; I know my own and my own know me. I will not flee in the face of danger. I will finish this service of the completion of my Father's will, and I will not forsake the flock which the Father has intrusted to my keeping.

"But I have many other sheep not of this fold, and these words are true not only of this world. These other sheep also hear and know my voice, and I have promised the Father that they shall all be brought into one fold, one brotherhood of the sons of God. And then shall you all know the voice of one shepherd, the true shepherd, and shall all acknowledge the fatherhood of God.

"And so shall you know why the Father loves me and has put all of his flocks in this domain in my hands for keeping; it is because the Father knows that I will not falter in the safeguarding of the sheepfold, that I will not desert my sheep, and that, if it shall be required, I will not hesitate to lay down my life in the service of his manifold flocks. But, mind you, if I lay down my life, I will take it up again. No man nor any other creature can take away my life. I have the right and the power to lay down my life, and I have the same power and right to take it up again. You cannot understand this, but I received such authority from my Father even before this world was."

When they heard these words, his apostles were confused, his disciples were amazed, while the Pharisees from Jerusalem and around about went out into the night, saying, "He is either mad or has a devil." But even some of the Jerusalem teachers said: "He speaks like one having authority; besides, who ever saw one having a devil open the eyes of a man born blind and do all of the wonderful things which this man has done?"

On the morrow about half of these Jewish teachers professed belief in Jesus, and the other half in dismay returned to Jerusalem and their homes.

3. SABBATH SERMON AT PELLA

By the end of January the Sabbath-afternoon multitudes numbered almost three thousand. On Saturday, January 28, Jesus preached the memorable sermon on "Trust and Spiritual Preparedness." After preliminary remarks by Simon Peter, the Master said:

"What I have many times said to my apostles and to my disciples, I now declare to this multitude: Beware of the leaven of the Pharisees which is hypocrisy, born of prejudice and nurtured in traditional bondage, albeit many of these Pharisees are honest of heart and some of them abide here as my disciples. Presently all of you shall understand my teaching, for there is nothing now covered that shall not be revealed. That which is now hid from you shall all be made known when the Son of Man has completed his mission on earth and in the flesh.

"Soon, very soon, will the things which our enemies now plan in secrecy and in darkness be brought out into the light and be proclaimed from the housetops. But I say to you, my friends, when they seek to destroy the Son of Man, be not afraid of them. Fear not those who, although they may be able to kill the body, after that have no more power over you. I admonish you to fear none, in heaven or on earth, but to rejoice in the knowledge of Him who has power to deliver you from all unrighteousness and to present you blameless before the judgment seat of a universe.

"Are not five sparrows sold for two pennies? And yet, when these birds flit about in quest of their sustenance, not one of them exists without the knowledge of the Father, the source of all life. To the seraphic guardians the very hairs of your head are numbered. And if all of this is true, why should you live in fear of the many trifles which come up in your daily lives? I say to you: Fear not; you are of much more value than many sparrows.

"All of you who have had the courage to confess faith in my gospel before men I will presently acknowledge before the angels of heaven; but he who shall knowingly deny the truth of my teachings before men shall be denied by his guardian of destiny even before the angels of heaven.

"Say what you will about the Son of Man, and it shall be forgiven you; but he who presumes to blaspheme against God shall hardly find forgiveness. When men go so far as knowingly to ascribe the doings of God to the forces of evil, such deliberate rebels will hardly seek forgiveness for their sins.

"And when our enemies bring you before the rulers of the synagogues and before other high authorities, be not concerned about what you should say and be not anxious as to how you should answer their questions, for the spirit that dwells within you shall certainly teach you in that very hour what you should say in honor of the gospel of the kingdom.

"How long will you tarry in the valley of decision? Why do you halt between two opinions? Why should Jew or gentile hesitate to accept the good news that he is a son of the eternal God? How long will it take us to persuade you to enter joyfully into your spiritual inheritance? I came into this world to reveal the Father to you and to lead you to the Father. The first I have done, but the last I may not do without your consent; the Father never compels any man to enter the kingdom. The invitation ever has been and always will be: Whosoever will, let him come and freely partake of the water of life."

When Jesus had finished speaking, many went forth to be baptized by the apostles in the Jordan while he listened to the questions of those who remained.

4. DIVIDING THE INHERITANCE

As the apostles baptized believers, the Master talked with those who tarried. And a certain young man said to him: "Master, my father died leaving much property to me and my brother, but my brother refuses to give me that which is my own. Will you, then, bid my brother divide this inheritance with me?" Jesus was mildly indignant that this material-minded youth should bring up for discussion such a question of business; but he proceeded to use the occasion for the impartation of further instruction. Said Jesus: "Man, who made me a divider over you? Where did you get the idea that I give attention to the material affairs of this world?" And then, turning to all who were about him, he said: "Take heed and keep yourselves free from covetousness; a man's life consists not in the abundance of the things which he may possess. Happiness comes not from the power of wealth, and joy springs not from riches. Wealth, in itself, is not a curse, but the love of riches many times leads to such devotion to the things of this world that the soul becomes blinded to the beautiful attractions of the spiritual realities of the kingdom of God on earth and to the joys of eternal life in heaven.

"Let me tell you a story of a certain rich man whose ground brought forth plentifully; and when he had become very rich, he began to reason with himself, saying: 'What shall I do with all my riches? I now have so much that I have no place to store my wealth.' And when he had meditated on his problem, he said: 'This I will do; I will pull down my barns and build greater ones, and thus will I have abundant room in which to store my fruits and my goods. Then can I say to my soul, soul, you have much wealth laid up for many years; take now your ease; eat, drink, and be merry, for you are rich and increased in goods.'

"But this rich man was also foolish. In providing for the material requirements of his mind and body, he had failed to lay up treasures in heaven for the satisfaction of the spirit and for the salvation of the soul. And even then he was not to enjoy the pleasure of consuming his hoarded wealth, for that very night was his soul required of him. That night there came the brigands who broke into his house to kill him, and after they had plundered his barns, they burned that which remained. And for the property which escaped the robbers his heirs fell to fighting among themselves. This man laid up treasures for himself on earth, but he was not rich toward God."

Jesus thus dealt with the young man and his inheritance because he knew that his trouble was covetousness. Even if this had not been the case, the Master would not have interfered, for he never meddled with the temporal affairs of even his apostles, much less his disciples.

When Jesus had finished his story, another man rose up and asked him: "Master, I know that your apostles have sold all their earthly possessions to follow you, and that they have all things in common as do the Essenes, but would you have all of us who are your disciples do likewise? Is it a sin to possess honest wealth?" And Jesus replied to this question: "My friend, it is not a sin to have honorable wealth; but it is a sin if you convert the wealth of material possessions into *treasures* which may absorb your interests and divert your affections from devotion to the spiritual pursuits of the kingdom. There is no sin in having honest possessions on earth provided your *treasure* is in heaven, for where your treasure is there will your heart be also. There is a great difference between wealth which leads to covetousness and selfishness and that which is held and dispensed in the spirit of stewardship by those who have an abundance of this world's goods, and who so bountifully contribute to the support of those who devote all their energies to the work of the kingdom. Many of you who are here and without money are fed and lodged in yonder tented city because liberal men and women of means have given funds to your host, David Zebedee, for such purposes.

"But never forget that, after all, wealth is unenduring. The love of riches all too often obscures and even destroys the spiritual vision. Fail not to recognize the danger of wealth's becoming, not your servant, but your master."

Jesus did not teach nor countenance improvidence, idleness, indifference to providing the physical necessities for one's family, or dependence upon alms. But he did teach that the material and temporal must be subordinated to the welfare of the soul and the progress of the spiritual nature in the kingdom of heaven.

Then, as the people went down by the river to witness the baptizing, the first man came privately to Jesus about his inheritance inasmuch as he thought Jesus had dealt harshly with him; and when the Master had again heard him, he replied: "My son, why do you miss the opportunity to feed upon the bread of life on a day like this in order to indulge your covetous disposition? Do you not know that the Jewish laws of inheritance will be justly administered if you will go with your complaint to the court of the synagogue? Can you not see that my work has to do with making sure that you know about your heavenly inheritance? Have you not read the Scripture: 'There is he who waxes rich by his wariness and much pinching, and this is the portion of his reward: Whereas he says, I have found rest and now shall be able to eat continually of my goods, yet he knows not what time shall bring upon him, and also that he must leave all these things to others when he dies.' Have you not read the commandment: 'You shall not covet.' And again, 'They have eaten and filled themselves and waxed fat, and then did they turn to other gods.' Have you read in the Psalms that 'the Lord abhors the covetous,' and that 'the little a righteous man has is better than the riches of many wicked.' 'If riches increase, set not your heart upon them.' Have you read where Jeremiah said, 'Let not the rich man glory in his riches'; and Ezekiel spoke truth when he said, 'With their mouths they make a show of love, but their hearts are set upon their own selfish gain.'"

Jesus sent the young man away, saying to him, "My son, what shall it profit you if you gain the whole world and lose your own soul?"

To another standing near by who asked Jesus how the wealthy would stand in the day of judgment, he replied: "I have come to judge neither the rich nor the poor, but the lives men live will sit in judgment on all. Whatever else may concern the wealthy in the judgment, at least three questions must be answered by all who acquire great wealth, and these questions are:

"1. How much wealth did you accumulate?

"2. How did you get this wealth?

"3. How did you use your wealth?"

Then Jesus went into his tent to rest for a while before the evening meal. When the apostles had finished with the baptizing, they came also and would have talked with him about wealth on earth and treasure in heaven, but he was asleep.

5. TALKS TO THE APOSTLES ON WEALTH

That evening after supper, when Jesus and the twelve gathered together for their daily conference, Andrew asked: "Master, while we were baptizing the believers, you spoke many words to the lingering multitude which we did not hear. Would you be willing to repeat these words for our benefit?" And in response to Andrew's request, Jesus said:

"Yes, Andrew, I will speak to you about these matters of wealth and self-support, but my words to you, the apostles, must be somewhat different from those spoken to the disciples and the multitude since you have forsaken everything, not only to follow me, but to be ordained as ambassadors of the kingdom. Already have you had several years' experience, and you know that the Father whose kingdom you proclaim will not forsake you. You have dedicated your lives to the ministry of the kingdom; therefore be not anxious or worried about the things of the temporal life, what you shall eat, nor yet for your body, what you shall wear. The welfare of the soul is more than food and drink; the progress in the spirit is far above the need of raiment. When you are tempted to doubt the sureness of your bread, consider the ravens; they sow not neither reap, they have no storehouses or barns, and yet the Father provides food for every one of them that seeks it. And of how much more value are you than many birds! Besides, all of your anxiety or fretting doubts can do nothing to supply your material needs. Which of you by anxiety can add a handbreadth to your stature or a day to your life? Since such matters are not in your hands, why do you give anxious thought to any of these problems?

"Consider the lilies, how they grow; they toil not, neither do they spin; yet I say to you, even Solomon in all his glory was not arrayed like one of these. If God so clothes the grass of the field, which is alive today and tomorrow is cut down and cast into the fire, how much more shall he clothe you, the ambassadors of the heavenly kingdom. O you of little faith! When you wholeheartedly devote yourselves to the proclamation of the gospel of the kingdom, you should not be of doubtful minds concerning the support of yourselves or the families you have forsaken. If you give your lives truly to the gospel, you shall live by the gospel. If you are only believing disciples, you must earn your own bread and contribute to the sustenance of all who teach and preach and heal. If you are anxious about your bread and water, wherein are you different from the nations of the world who so diligently seek such necessities? Devote yourselves to your work, believing that both the Father and I know that you have need of all these things. Let me assure you, once and for all, that, if you dedicate your lives to the work of the kingdom, all your real needs shall be supplied. Seek the greater thing, and the lesser will be found therein; ask for the heavenly, and the earthly shall be included. The shadow is certain to follow the substance.

"You are only a small group, but if you have faith, if you will not stumble in fear, I declare that it is my Father's good pleasure to give you this kingdom. You have laid up your treasures where the purse waxes not old, where no thief can despoil, and where no moth can destroy. And as I told the people, where your treasure is, there will your heart be also.

"But in the work which is just ahead of us, and in that which remains for you after I go to the Father, you will be grievously tried. You must all be on your watch against fear and doubts. Every one of you, gird up the loins of your minds and let your lamps be kept burning. Keep yourselves like men who are watching for their master to return from the marriage feast so that, when he comes and knocks, you may quickly open to him. Such watchful servants are blessed by the master who finds them faithful at such a great moment. Then will the master make his servants sit down while he himself serves them. Verily, verily, I say to you that a crisis is just ahead in your lives, and it behooves you to watch and be ready.

"You well understand that no man would suffer his house to be broken into if he knew what hour the thief was to come. Be you also on watch for yourselves, for in an hour that you least suspect and in a manner you think not, shall the Son of Man depart."

For some minutes the twelve sat in silence. Some of these warnings they had heard before but not in the setting presented to them at this time.

6. ANSWER TO PETER'S QUESTION

As they sat thinking, Simon Peter asked: "Do you speak this parable to us, your apostles, or is it for all the disciples?" And Jesus answered:

"In the time of testing, a man's soul is revealed; trial discloses what really is in the heart. When the servant is tested and proved, then may the lord of the house set such a servant over his household and safely trust this faithful steward to see that his children are fed and nurtured. Likewise, will I soon know who can be trusted with the welfare of my children when I shall have returned to the Father. As the lord of the household shall set the true and tried servant over the affairs of his family, so will I exalt those who endure the trials of this hour in the affairs of my kingdom.

"But if the servant is slothful and begins to say in his heart, 'My master delays his coming,' and begins to mistreat his fellow servants and to eat and drink with the drunken, then the lord of that servant will come at a time when he looks not for him and, finding him unfaithful, will cast him out in disgrace. Therefore you do well to prepare yourselves for that day when you will be visited suddenly and in an unexpected manner. Remember, much has been given to you; therefore will much be required of you. Fiery trials are drawing near you. I have a baptism to be baptized with, and I am on watch until this is accomplished. You preach peace on earth, but my mission will not bring peace in the material affairs of men—not for a time, at least. Division can only be the result where two members of a family believe in me and three members reject this gospel. Friends, relatives, and loved ones are destined to be set against each other by the gospel you preach. True, each of these believers shall have great and lasting peace in his own heart, but peace on earth will not come until all are willing to believe and enter into their glorious inheritance of sonship with God. Nevertheless, go into all the world proclaiming this gospel to all nations, to every man, woman, and child."

And this was the end of a full and busy Sabbath day. On the morrow Jesus and the twelve went into the cities of northern Perea to visit with the seventy, who were working in these regions under Abner's supervision.

PAPER 166

LAST VISIT TO NORTHERN PEREA

FROM February 11 to 20, Jesus and the twelve made a tour of all the cities and villages of northern Perea where the associates of Abner and the members of the women's corps were working. They found these messengers of the gospel meeting with success, and Jesus repeatedly called the attention of his apostles to the fact that the gospel of the kingdom could spread without the accompaniment of miracles and wonders.

This entire mission of three months in Perea was successfully carried on with little help from the twelve apostles, and the gospel from this time on reflected, not so much Jesus' personality, as his *teachings.* But his followers did not long follow his instructions, for soon after Jesus' death and resurrection they departed from his teachings and began to build the early church around the miraculous concepts and the glorified memories of his divine-human personality.

1. THE PHARISEES AT RAGABA

On Sabbath, February 18, Jesus was at Ragaba, where there lived a wealthy Pharisee named Nathaniel; and since quite a number of his fellow Pharisees were following Jesus and the twelve around the country, he made a breakfast on this Sabbath morning for all of them, about twenty in number, and invited Jesus as the guest of honor.

By the time Jesus arrived at this breakfast, most of the Pharisees, with two or three lawyers, were already there and seated at the table. The Master immediately took his seat at the left of Nathaniel without going to the water basins to wash his hands. Many of the Pharisees, especially those favorable to Jesus' teachings, knew that he washed his hands only for purposes of cleanliness, that he abhorred these purely ceremonial performances; so they were not surprised at his coming directly to the table without having twice washed his hands. But Nathaniel was shocked by this failure of the Master to comply with the strict requirements of Pharisaic practice. Neither did Jesus wash his hands, as did the Pharisees, after each course of food nor at the end of the meal.

After considerable whispering between Nathaniel and an unfriendly Pharisee on his right and after much lifting of eyebrows and sneering curling of lips by those who sat opposite the Master, Jesus finally said: "I had thought that you invited me to this house to break bread with you and perchance to inquire of me concerning the proclamation of the new gospel of the kingdom of God; but I perceive that you have brought me here to witness an exhibition of ceremonial devotion to your own self-righteousness. That service you have now done me; what next will you honor me with as your guest on this occasion?"

When the Master had thus spoken, they cast their eyes upon the table and remained silent. And since no one spoke, Jesus continued: "Many of you Pharisees are here with me as friends, some are even my disciples, but the majority of the Pharisees are persistent in their refusal to see the light and acknowledge the truth, even when the work of the gospel is brought before them in great power. How carefully you cleanse the outside of the cups and the platters while the spiritual-food vessels are filthy and polluted! You make sure to present a pious and holy appearance to the people, but your inner souls are filled with self-righteousness, covetousness, extortion, and all manner of spiritual wickedness. Your leaders even dare to plot and plan the murder of the Son of Man. Do not you foolish men understand that the God of heaven looks at the inner motives of the soul as well as on your outer pretenses and your pious professions? Think not that the giving of alms and the paying of tithes will cleanse you from unrighteousness and enable you to stand clean in the presence of the Judge of all men. Woe upon you Pharisees who have persisted in rejecting the light of life! You are meticulous in tithing and ostentatious in almsgiving, but you knowingly spurn the visitation of God and reject the revelation of his love. Though it is all right for you to give attention to these minor duties, you should not have left these weightier requirements undone. Woe upon all who shun justice, spurn mercy, and reject truth! Woe upon all those who despise the revelation of the Father while they seek the chief seats in the synagogue and crave flattering salutations in the market places!"

When Jesus would have risen to depart, one of the lawyers who was at the table, addressing him, said: "But, Master, in some of your statements you reproach us also. Is there nothing good in the scribes, the Pharisees, or the lawyers?" And Jesus, standing, replied to the lawyer: "You, like the Pharisees, delight in the first places at the feasts and in wearing long robes while you put heavy burdens, grievous to be borne, on men's shoulders. And when the souls of men stagger under these heavy burdens, you will not so much as lift with one of your fingers. Woe upon you who take your greatest delight in building tombs for the prophets your fathers killed! And that you consent to what your fathers did is made manifest when you now plan to kill those who come in this day doing what the prophets did in their day—proclaiming the righteousness of God and revealing the mercy of the heavenly Father. But of all the generations that are past, the blood of the prophets and the apostles shall be required of this perverse and self-righteous generation. Woe upon all of you lawyers who have taken away the key of knowledge from the common people! You yourselves refuse to enter into the way of truth, and at the same time you would hinder all others who seek to enter therein. But you cannot thus shut up the doors of the kingdom of heaven; these we have opened to all who have the faith to enter, and these portals of mercy shall not be closed by the prejudice and arrogance of false teachers and untrue shepherds who are like whited sepulchres which, while outwardly they appear beautiful, are inwardly full of dead men's bones and all manner of spiritual uncleanness."

And when Jesus had finished speaking at Nathaniel's table, he went out of the house without partaking of food. And of the Pharisees who heard these words, some became believers in his teaching and entered into the kingdom, but the larger number persisted in the way of darkness, becoming all the more determined to lie in wait for him that they might catch some of his words which could be used to bring him to trial and judgment before the Sanhedrin at Jerusalem.

There were just three things to which the Pharisees paid particular attention:

1. The practice of strict tithing.
2. Scrupulous observance of the laws of purification.
3. Avoidance of association with all non-Pharisees.

At this time Jesus sought to expose the spiritual barrenness of the first two practices, while he reserved his remarks designed to rebuke the Pharisees' refusal to engage in social intercourse with non-Pharisees for another and subsequent occasion when he would again be dining with many of these same men.

2. THE TEN LEPERS

The next day Jesus went with the twelve over to Amathus, near the border of Samaria, and as they approached the city, they encountered a group of ten lepers who sojourned near this place. Nine of this group were Jews, one a Samaritan. Ordinarily these Jews would have refrained from all association or contact with this Samaritan, but their common affliction was more than enough to overcome all religious prejudice. They had heard much of Jesus and his earlier miracles of healing, and since the seventy made a practice of announcing the time of Jesus' expected arrival when the Master was out with the twelve on these tours, the ten lepers had been made aware that he was expected to appear in this vicinity at about this time; and they were, accordingly, posted here on the outskirts of the city where they hoped to attract his attention and ask for healing. When the lepers saw Jesus drawing near them, not daring to approach him, they stood afar off and cried to him: "Master, have mercy on us; cleanse us from our affliction. Heal us as you have healed others."

Jesus had just been explaining to the twelve why the gentiles of Perea, together with the less orthodox Jews, were more willing to believe the gospel preached by the seventy than were the more orthodox and tradition-bound Jews of Judea. He had called their attention to the fact that their message had likewise been more readily received by the Galileans, and even by the Samaritans. But the twelve apostles were hardly yet willing to entertain kind feelings for the long-despised Samaritans.

Accordingly, when Simon Zelotes observed the Samaritan among the lepers, he sought to induce the Master to pass on into the city without even hesitating to exchange greetings with them. Said Jesus to Simon: "But what if the Samaritan loves God as well as the Jews? Should we sit in judgment on our fellow men? Who can tell? if we make these ten men whole, perhaps the Samaritan will prove more grateful even than the Jews. Do you feel certain about your opinions, Simon?" And Simon quickly replied, "If you cleanse them, you will soon find out." And Jesus replied: "So shall it be, Simon, and you will soon know the truth regarding the gratitude of men and the loving mercy of God."

Jesus, going near the lepers, said: "If you would be made whole, go forthwith and show yourselves to the priests as required by the law of Moses." And as they went, they were made whole. But when the Samaritan saw that he was being healed, he turned back and, going in quest of Jesus, began to glorify God with a loud voice. And when he had found the Master, he fell on his knees at his feet and gave thanks for his cleansing. The nine others, the Jews, had also discovered their healing, and while they also were grateful for their cleansing, they continued on their way to show themselves to the priests.

As the Samaritan remained kneeling at Jesus' feet, the Master, looking about at the twelve, especially at Simon Zelotes, said: "Were not ten cleansed? Where, then, are the other nine, the Jews? Only one, this alien, has returned to give glory to God." And then he said to the Samaritan, "Arise and go your way; your faith has made you whole."

Jesus looked again at his apostles as the stranger departed. And the apostles all looked at Jesus, save Simon Zelotes, whose eyes were downcast. The twelve said not a word. Neither did Jesus speak; it was not necessary that he should.

Though all ten of these men really believed they had leprosy, only four were thus afflicted. The other six were cured of a skin disease which had been mistaken for leprosy. But the Samaritan really had leprosy.

Jesus enjoined the twelve to say nothing about the cleansing of the lepers, and as they went on into Amathus, he remarked: "You see how it is that the children of the house, even when they are insubordinate to their Father's will, take their blessings for granted. They think it a small matter if they neglect to give thanks when the Father bestows healing upon them, but the strangers, when they receive gifts from the head of the house, are filled with wonder and are constrained to give thanks in recognition of the good things bestowed upon them." And still the apostles said nothing in reply to the Master's words.

3. THE SERMON AT GERASA

As Jesus and the twelve visited with the messengers of the kingdom at Gerasa, one of the Pharisees who believed in him asked this question: "Lord, will there be few or many really saved?" And Jesus, answering, said:

"You have been taught that only the children of Abraham will be saved; that only the gentiles of adoption can hope for salvation. Some of you have reasoned that, since the Scriptures record that only Caleb and Joshua from among all the hosts that went out of Egypt lived to enter the promised land, only a comparatively few of those who seek the kingdom of heaven shall find entrance thereto.

"You also have another saying among you, and one that contains much truth: That the way which leads to eternal life is straight and narrow, that the door which leads thereto is likewise narrow so that, of those who seek salvation, few can find entrance through this door. You also have a teaching that the way which leads to destruction is broad, that the entrance thereto is wide, and that there are many who choose to go this way. And this proverb is not without its meaning. But I declare that salvation is first a matter of your personal choosing. Even if the door to the way of life is narrow, it is wide enough to admit all who sincerely seek to enter, for I am that door. And the Son will never refuse entrance to any child of the universe who, by faith, seeks to find the Father through the Son.

"But herein is the danger to all who would postpone their entrance into the kingdom while they continue to pursue the pleasures of immaturity and indulge the satisfactions of selfishness: Having refused to enter the kingdom as a spiritual experience, they may subsequently seek entrance thereto when the glory of the better way becomes revealed in the age to come. And when, therefore, those who spurned the kingdom when I came in the likeness of humanity seek to find an entrance when it is revealed in the likeness of divinity, then will I say to all such selfish ones: I know not whence you are. You had your chance to prepare for this heavenly citizenship, but you refused all such proffers of mercy; you rejected all invitations to come while the door was open. Now, to you who have refused salvation, the door is shut. This door is not open to those who would enter the kingdom for selfish glory. Salvation is not for those who are unwilling to pay the price of wholehearted dedication to doing my Father's will. When in spirit and soul you have turned your backs upon the Father's kingdom, it is useless in mind and body to stand before this door and knock, saying, 'Lord, open to us; we would also be great in the kingdom.' Then will I declare that you are not of my fold. I will not receive you to be among those who have fought the good fight of faith and won the reward of unselfish service in the kingdom on earth. And when you say, 'Did we not eat and drink with you, and did you not teach in our streets?' then shall I again declare that you are spiritual strangers; that we were not fellow servants in the Father's ministry of mercy on earth; that I do not know you; and then shall the Judge of all the earth say to you: 'Depart from us, all you who have taken delight in the works of iniquity.'

"But fear not; every one who sincerely desires to find eternal life by entrance into the kingdom of God shall certainly find such everlasting salvation. But you who refuse this salvation will some day see the prophets of the seed of Abraham sit down with the believers of the gentile nations in this glorified kingdom to partake of the bread of life and to refresh themselves with the water thereof. And they who shall thus take the kingdom in spiritual power and by the persistent assaults of living faith will come from the north and the south and from the east and the west. And, behold, many who are first will be last, and those who are last will many times be first."

This was indeed a new and strange version of the old and familiar proverb of the straight and narrow way.

Slowly the apostles and many of the disciples were learning the meaning of Jesus' early declaration: "Unless you are born again, born of the spirit, you cannot enter the kingdom of God." Nevertheless, to all who are honest of heart and sincere in faith, it remains eternally true: "Behold, I stand at the doors of men's hearts and knock, and if any man will open to me, I will come in and sup with him and will feed him with the bread of life; we shall be one in spirit and purpose, and so shall we ever be brethren in the long and fruitful service of the search for the Paradise Father." And so, whether few or many are to be saved altogether depends on whether few or many will heed the invitation: "I am the door, I am the new and living way, and whosoever wills may enter to embark upon the endless truth-search for eternal life."

Even the apostles were unable fully to comprehend his teaching as to the necessity for using spiritual force for the purpose of breaking through all material resistance and for surmounting every earthly obstacle which might chance to stand in the way of grasping the all-important spiritual values of the new life in the spirit as the liberated sons of God.

4. TEACHING ABOUT ACCIDENTS

While most Palestinians ate only two meals a day, it was the custom of Jesus and the apostles, when on a journey, to pause at midday for rest and refreshment. And it was at such a noontide stop on the way to Philadelphia that Thomas asked Jesus: "Master, from hearing your remarks as we journeyed this morning, I would like to inquire whether spiritual beings are concerned in the production of strange and extraordinary events in the material world and, further, to ask whether the angels and other spirit beings are able to prevent accidents."

In answer to Thomas's inquiry, Jesus said: "Have I been so long with you, and yet you continue to ask me such questions? Have you failed to observe how the Son of Man lives as one with you and consistently refuses to employ the forces of heaven for his personal sustenance? Do we not all live by the same means whereby all men exist? Do you see the power of the spiritual world manifested in the material life of this world, save for the revelation of the Father and the sometime healing of his afflicted children?

"All too long have your fathers believed that prosperity was the token of divine approval; that adversity was the proof of God's displeasure. I declare that such beliefs are superstitions. Do you not observe that far greater numbers of the poor joyfully receive the gospel and immediately enter the kingdom? If riches evidence divine favor, why do the rich so many times refuse to believe this good news from heaven?

"The Father causes his rain to fall on the just and the unjust; the sun likewise shines on the righteous and the unrighteous. You know about those Galileans whose blood Pilate mingled with the sacrifices, but I tell you these Galileans were not in any manner sinners above all their fellows just because this happened to them. You also know about the eighteen men upon whom the tower of Siloam fell, killing them. Think not that these men who were thus destroyed were offenders above all their brethren in Jerusalem. These folks were simply innocent victims of one of the accidents of time.

"There are three groups of events which may occur in your lives:

"1. You may share in those normal happenings which are a part of the life you and your fellows live on the face of the earth.

"2. You may chance to fall victim to one of the accidents of nature, one of the mischances of men, knowing full well that such occurrences are in no way prearranged or otherwise produced by the spiritual forces of the realm.

"3. You may reap the harvest of your direct efforts to comply with the natural laws governing the world.

"There was a certain man who planted a fig tree in his yard, and when he had many times sought fruit thereon and found none, he called the vinedressers before him and said: 'Here have I come these three seasons looking for fruit on this fig tree and have found none. Cut down this barren tree; why should it encumber the ground?' But the head gardener answered his master: 'Let it alone for one more year so that I may dig around it and put on fertilizer, and then, next year, if it bears no fruit, it shall be cut down.' And when they had thus complied with the laws of fruitfulness, since the tree was living and good, they were rewarded with an abundant yield.

"In the matter of sickness and health, you should know that these bodily states are the result of material causes; health is not the smile of heaven, neither is affliction the frown of God.

"The Father's human children have equal capacity for the reception of material blessings; therefore does he bestow things physical upon the children of men without discrimination. When it comes to the bestowal of spiritual gifts, the Father is limited by man's capacity for receiving these divine endowments. Although the Father is no respecter of persons, in the bestowal of spiritual gifts he is limited by man's faith and by his willingness always to abide by the Father's will."

As they journeyed on toward Philadelphia, Jesus continued to teach them and to answer their questions having to do with accidents, sickness, and miracles, but they were not able fully to comprehend this instruction. One hour of teaching will not wholly change the beliefs of a lifetime, and so Jesus found it necessary to reiterate his message, to tell again and again that which he wished them to understand; and even then they failed to grasp the meaning of his earth mission until after his death and resurrection.

5. THE CONGREGATION AT PHILADELPHIA

Jesus and the twelve were on their way to visit Abner and his associates, who were preaching and teaching in Philadelphia. Of all the cities of Perea, in Philadelphia the largest group of Jews and gentiles, rich and poor, learned and unlearned, embraced the teachings of the seventy, thereby entering into the kingdom of heaven. The synagogue of Philadelphia had never been subject to the supervision of the Sanhedrin at Jerusalem and therefore had never been closed to the teachings of Jesus and his associates. At this very time, Abner was teaching three times a day in the Philadelphia synagogue.

This very synagogue later on became a Christian church and was the missionary headquarters for the promulgation of the gospel through the regions to the east. It was long a stronghold of the Master's teachings and stood alone in this region as a center of Christian learning for centuries.

The Jews at Jerusalem had always had trouble with the Jews of Philadelphia. And after the death and resurrection of Jesus the Jerusalem church, of which James the Lord's brother was head, began to have serious difficulties with the Philadelphia congregation of believers. Abner became the head of the Philadelphia church, continuing as such until his death. And this estrangement with Jerusalem explains why nothing is heard of Abner and his work in the Gospel records of the New Testament. This feud between Jerusalem and Philadelphia lasted throughout the lifetimes of James and Abner and continued for some time after the destruction of Jerusalem. Philadelphia was really the headquarters of the early church in the south and east as Antioch was in the north and west.

It was the apparent misfortune of Abner to be at variance with all of the leaders of the early Christian church. He fell out with Peter and James (Jesus' brother) over questions of administration and the jurisdiction of the Jerusalem church; he parted company with Paul over differences of philosophy and theology. Abner was more Babylonian than Hellenic in his philosophy, and he stubbornly resisted all attempts of Paul to remake the teachings of Jesus so as to present less that was objectionable, first to the Jews, then to the Greco-Roman believers in the mysteries.

Thus was Abner compelled to live a life of isolation. He was head of a church which was without standing at Jerusalem. He had dared to defy James the Lord's brother, who was subsequently supported by Peter. Such conduct effectively separated him from all his former associates. Then he dared to withstand Paul. Although he was wholly sympathetic with Paul in his mission to the gentiles, and though he supported him in his contentions with the church at Jerusalem, he bitterly opposed the version of Jesus' teachings which Paul elected to preach. In his last years Abner denounced Paul as the "clever corrupter of the life teachings of Jesus of Nazareth, the Son of the living God."

During the later years of Abner and for some time thereafter, the believers at Philadelphia held more strictly to the religion of Jesus, as he lived and taught, than any other group on earth.

Abner lived to be 89 years old, dying at Philadelphia on the 21st day of November, A.D. 74. And to the very end he was a faithful believer in, and teacher of, the gospel of the heavenly kingdom.

PAPER 167

THE VISIT TO PHILADELPHIA

THROUGHOUT this period of the Perean ministry, when mention is made of Jesus and the apostles visiting the various localities where the seventy were at work, it should be recalled that, as a rule, only ten were with him since it was the practice to leave at least two of the apostles at Pella to instruct the multitude. As Jesus prepared to go on to Philadelphia, Simon Peter and his brother, Andrew, returned to the Pella encampment to teach the crowds there assembled. When the Master left the camp at Pella to visit about Perea, it was not uncommon for from three to five hundred of the campers to follow him. When he arrived at Philadelphia, he was accompanied by over six hundred followers.

No miracles had attended the recent preaching tour through the Decapolis, and, excepting the cleansing of the ten lepers, thus far there had been no miracles on this Perean mission. This was a period when the gospel was proclaimed with power, without miracles, and most of the time without the personal presence of Jesus or even of his apostles.

Jesus and the ten apostles arrived at Philadelphia on Wednesday, February 22, and spent Thursday and Friday resting from their recent travels and labors. That Friday night James spoke in the synagogue, and a general council was called for the following evening. They were much rejoiced over the progress of the gospel at Philadelphia and among the near-by villages. The messengers of David also brought word of the further advancement of the kingdom throughout Palestine, as well as good news from Alexandria and Damascus.

1. BREAKFAST WITH THE PHARISEES

There lived in Philadelphia a very wealthy and influential Pharisee who had accepted the teachings of Abner, and who invited Jesus to his house Sabbath morning for breakfast. It was known that Jesus was expected in Philadelphia at this time; so a large number of visitors, among them many Pharisees, had come over from Jerusalem and from elsewhere. Accordingly, about forty of these leading men and a few lawyers were bidden to this breakfast, which had been arranged in honor of the Master.

As Jesus lingered by the door, speaking with Abner, and after the host had seated himself, there came into the room one of the leading Pharisees of Jerusalem, a member of the Sanhedrin, and as was his habit, he made straight for the seat of honor at the left of the host. But since this place had been reserved for the Master and that on the right for Abner, the host beckoned the Jerusalem Pharisee to sit four seats to the left, and this dignitary was much offended because he did not receive the seat of honor.

Soon they were all seated and enjoying the visiting among themselves since the majority of those present were disciples of Jesus or else were friendly to the gospel. Only his enemies took notice of the fact that he did not observe the ceremonial washing of his hands before he sat down to eat. Abner washed his hands at the beginning of the meal but not during the serving.

Near the end of the meal there came in from the street a man long afflicted with a chronic disease and now in a dropsical condition. This man was a believer, having recently been baptized by Abner's associates. He made no request of Jesus for healing, but the Master knew full well that this afflicted man came to this breakfast hoping thereby to escape the crowds which thronged him and thus be more likely to engage his attention. This man knew that few miracles were then being performed; however, he had reasoned in his heart that his sorry plight might possibly appeal to the Master's compassion. And he was not mistaken, for, when he entered the room, both Jesus and the self-righteous Pharisee from Jerusalem took notice of him. The Pharisee was not slow to voice his resentment that such a one should be permitted to enter the room. But Jesus looked upon the sick man and smiled so benignly that he drew near and sat down upon the floor. As the meal was ending, the Master looked over his fellow guests and then, after glancing significantly at the man with dropsy, said: "My friends, teachers in Israel and learned lawyers, I would like to ask you a question: Is it lawful to heal the sick and afflicted on the Sabbath day, or not?" But those who were there present knew Jesus too well; they held their peace; they answered not his question.

Then went Jesus over to where the sick man sat and, taking him by the hand, said: "Arise and go your way. You have not asked to be healed, but I know the desire of your heart and the faith of your soul." Before the man left the room, Jesus returned to his seat and, addressing those at the table, said: "Such works my Father does, not to tempt you into the kingdom, but to reveal himself to those who are already in the kingdom. You can perceive that it would be like the Father to do just such things because which one of you, having a favorite animal that fell in the well on the Sabbath day, would not go right out and draw him up?" And since no one would answer him, and inasmuch as his host evidently approved of what was going on, Jesus stood up and spoke to all present: "My brethren, when you are bidden to a marriage feast, sit not down in the chief seat, lest, perchance, a more honored man than you has been invited, and the host will have to come to you and request that you give your place to this other and honored guest. In this event, with shame you will be required to take a lower place at the table. When you are bidden to a feast, it would be the part of wisdom, on arriving at the festive table, to seek for the lowest place and take your seat therein, so that, when the host looks over the guests, he may say to you: 'My friend, why sit in the seat of the least? come up higher'; and thus will such a one have glory in the presence of his fellow guests. Forget not, every one who exalts himself shall be humbled, while he who truly humbles himself shall be exalted. Therefore, when you entertain at dinner or give a supper, invite not always your friends, your brethren, your kinsmen, or your rich neighbors that they in return may bid you to their feasts, and thus will you be recompensed. When you give a banquet, sometimes bid the poor, the maimed, and the blind. In this way you shall be blessed in your heart, for you well know that the lame and the halt cannot repay you for your loving ministry."

2. PARABLE OF THE GREAT SUPPER

As Jesus finished speaking at the breakfast table of the Pharisee, one of the lawyers present, desiring to relieve the silence, thoughtlessly said: "Blessed is he who shall eat bread in the kingdom of God"—that being a common saying of those days. And then Jesus spoke a parable, which even his friendly host was compelled to take to heart. He said:

"A certain ruler gave a great supper, and having bidden many guests, he dispatched his servants at suppertime to say to those who were invited, 'Come, for everything is now ready.' And they all with one accord began to make excuses. The first said, 'I have just bought a farm, and I must needs go to prove it; I pray you have me excused.' Another said, 'I have bought five yoke of oxen, and I must go to receive them; I pray you have me excused.' And another said, 'I have just married a wife, and therefore I cannot come.' So the servants went back and reported this to their master. When the master of the house heard this, he was very angry, and turning to his servants, he said: 'I have made ready this marriage feast; the fatlings are killed, and all is in readiness for my guests, but they have spurned my invitation; they have gone every man after his lands and his merchandise, and they even show disrespect to my servants who bid them come to my feast. Go out quickly, therefore, into the streets and lanes of the city, out into the highways and the byways, and bring hither the poor and the outcast, the blind and the lame, that the marriage feast may have guests.' And the servants did as their lord commanded, and even then there was room for more guests. Then said the lord to his servants: 'Go now out into the roads and the countryside and constrain those who are there to come in that my house may be filled. I declare that none of those who were first bidden shall taste of my supper.' And the servants did as their master commanded, and the house was filled."

And when they heard these words, they departed; every man went to his own place. At least one of the sneering Pharisees present that morning comprehended the meaning of this parable, for he was baptized that day and made public confession of his faith in the gospel of the kingdom. Abner preached on this parable that night at the general council of believers.

The next day all of the apostles engaged in the philosophic exercise of endeavoring to interpret the meaning of this parable of the great supper. Though Jesus listened with interest to all of these differing interpretations, he steadfastly refused to offer them further help in understanding the parable. He would only say, "Let every man find out the meaning for himself and in his own soul."

3. THE WOMAN WITH THE SPIRIT OF INFIRMITY

Abner had arranged for the Master to teach in the synagogue on this Sabbath day, the first time Jesus had appeared in a synagogue since they had all been closed to his teachings by order of the Sanhedrin. At the conclusion of the service Jesus looked down before him upon an elderly woman who wore a downcast expression, and who was much bent in form. This woman had long been fear-ridden, and all joy had passed out of her life. As Jesus stepped down from the pulpit, he went over to her and, touching her bowed-over form on the shoulder, said: "Woman, if you would only believe, you could be wholly loosed from your spirit of infirmity." And this woman, who had been bowed down and bound up by the depressions of fear for more than eighteen years, believed the words of the Master and by faith straightened up immediately. When this woman saw that she had been made straight, she lifted up her voice and glorified God.

Notwithstanding that this woman's affliction was wholly mental, her bowed-over form being the result of her depressed mind, the people thought that Jesus had healed a real physical disorder. Although the congregation of the synagogue at Philadelphia was friendly toward the teachings of Jesus, the chief ruler of the synagogue was an unfriendly Pharisee. And as he shared the opinion of the congregation that Jesus had healed a physical disorder, and being indignant because Jesus had presumed to do such a thing on the Sabbath, he stood up before the congregation and said: "Are there not six days in which men should do all their work? In these working days come, therefore, and be healed, but not on the Sabbath day."

When the unfriendly ruler had thus spoken, Jesus returned to the speaker's platform and said: "Why play the part of hypocrites? Does not every one of you, on the Sabbath, loose his ox from the stall and lead him forth for watering? If such a service is permissible on the Sabbath day, should not this woman, a daughter of Abraham who has been bound down by evil these eighteen years, be loosed from this bondage and led forth to partake of the waters of liberty and life, even on this Sabbath day?" And as the woman continued to glorify God, his critic was put to shame, and the congregation rejoiced with her that she had been healed.

As a result of his public criticism of Jesus on this Sabbath the chief ruler of the synagogue was deposed, and a follower of Jesus was put in his place.

Jesus frequently delivered such victims of fear from their spirit of infirmity, from their depression of mind, and from their bondage of fear. But the people thought that all such afflictions were either physical disorders or possession of evil spirits.

Jesus taught again in the synagogue on Sunday, and many were baptized by Abner at noon on that day in the river which flowed south of the city. On the morrow Jesus and the ten apostles would have started back to the Pella encampment but for the arrival of one of David's messengers, who brought an urgent message to Jesus from his friends at Bethany, near Jerusalem.

4. THE MESSAGE FROM BETHANY

Very late on Sunday night, February 26, a runner from Bethany arrived at Philadelphia, bringing a message from Martha and Mary which said, "Lord, he whom you love is very sick." This message reached Jesus at the close of the evening conference and just as he was taking leave of the apostles for the night. At first Jesus made no reply. There occurred one of those strange interludes, a time when he appeared to be in communication with something outside of, and beyond, himself. And then, looking up, he addressed the messenger in the hearing of the apostles, saying: "This sickness is really not to the death. Doubt not that it may be used to glorify God and exalt the Son."

Jesus was very fond of Martha, Mary, and their brother, Lazarus; he loved them with a fervent affection. His first and human thought was to go to their assistance at once, but another idea came into his combined mind. He had almost given up hope that the Jewish leaders at Jerusalem would ever accept the kingdom, but he still loved his people, and there now occurred to him a plan whereby the scribes and Pharisees of Jerusalem might have one more chance to accept his teachings; and he decided, his Father willing, to make this last appeal to Jerusalem the most profound and stupendous outward working of his entire earth career. The Jews clung to the idea of a wonder-working deliverer. And though he refused to stoop to the performance of material wonders or to the enactment of temporal exhibitions of political power, he did now ask the Father's consent for the manifestation of his hitherto unexhibited power over life and death.

The Jews were in the habit of burying their dead on the day of their demise; this was a necessary practice in such a warm climate. It often happened that they put in the tomb one who was merely comatose, so that on the second or even the third day, such a one would come forth from the tomb. But it was the belief of the Jews that, while the spirit or soul might linger near the body for two or three days, it never tarried after the third day; that decay was well advanced by the fourth day, and that no one ever returned from the tomb after the lapse of such a period. And it was for these reasons that Jesus tarried yet two full days in Philadelphia before he made ready to start for Bethany.

Accordingly, early on Wednesday morning he said to his apostles: "Let us prepare at once to go into Judea again." And when the apostles heard their Master say this, they drew off by themselves for a time to take counsel of one another. James assumed the direction of the conference, and they all agreed that it was only folly to allow Jesus to go again into Judea, and they came back as one man and so informed him. Said James: "Master, you were in Jerusalem a few weeks back, and the leaders sought your death, while the people were minded to stone you. At that time you gave these men their chance to receive the truth, and we will not permit you to go again into Judea."

Then said Jesus: "But do you not understand that there are twelve hours of the day in which work may safely be done? If a man walks in the day, he does not stumble inasmuch as he has light. If a man walks in the night, he is liable to stumble since he is without light. As long as my day lasts, I fear not to enter Judea. I would do one more mighty work for these Jews; I would give them one more chance to believe, even on their own terms—conditions of outward glory and the visible manifestation of the power of the Father and the love of the Son. Besides, do you not realize that our friend Lazarus has fallen asleep, and I would go to awake him out of this sleep!"

Then said one of the apostles: "Master, if Lazarus has fallen asleep, then will he the more surely recover." It was the custom of the Jews at that time to speak of death as a form of sleep, but as the apostles did not understand that Jesus meant that Lazarus had departed from this world, he now said plainly: "Lazarus is dead. And I am glad for your sakes, even if the others are not thereby saved, that I was not there, to the end that you shall now have new cause to believe in me; and by that which you will witness, you should all be strengthened in preparation for that day when I shall take leave of you and go to the Father."

When they could not persuade him to refrain from going into Judea, and when some of the apostles were loath even to accompany him, Thomas addressed his fellows, saying: "We have told the Master our fears, but he is determined to go to Bethany. I am satisfied it means the end; they will surely kill him, but if that is the Master's choice, then let us acquit ourselves like men of courage; let us go also that we may die with him." And it was ever so; in matters requiring deliberate and sustained courage, Thomas was always the mainstay of the twelve apostles.

5. ON THE WAY TO BETHANY

On the way to Judea Jesus was followed by a company of almost fifty of his friends and enemies. At their noon lunchtime, on Wednesday, he talked to his apostles and this group of followers on the "Terms of Salvation," and at the end of this lesson told the parable of the Pharisee and the publican (a tax collector). Said Jesus: "You see, then, that the Father gives salvation to the children of men, and this salvation is a free gift to all who have the faith to receive sonship in the divine family. There is nothing man can do to earn this salvation. Works of self-righteousness cannot buy the favor of God, and much praying in public will not atone for lack of living faith in the heart. Men you may deceive by your outward service, but God looks into your souls. What I am telling you is well illustrated by two men who went into the temple to pray, the one a Pharisee and the other a publican. The Pharisee stood and prayed to himself: 'O God, I thank you that I am not like the rest of men, extortioners, unlearned, unjust, adulterers, or even like this publican. I fast twice a week; I give tithes of all that I get.' But the publican, standing afar off, would not so much as lift his eyes to heaven but smote his breast, saying, 'God be merciful to me a sinner.' I tell you that the publican went home with God's approval rather than the Pharisee, for every one who exalts himself shall be humbled, but he who humbles himself shall be exalted."

That night, in Jericho, the unfriendly Pharisees sought to entrap the Master by inducing him to discuss marriage and divorce, as did their fellows one time in Galilee, but Jesus artfully avoided their efforts to bring him into conflict with their laws concerning divorce. As the publican and the Pharisee illustrated good and bad religion, their divorce practices served to contrast the better marriage laws of the Jewish code with the disgraceful laxity of the Pharisaic interpretations of these Mosaic divorce statutes. The Pharisee judged himself by the lowest standard; the publican squared himself by the highest ideal. Devotion, to the Pharisee, was a means of inducing self-righteous inactivity and the assurance of false spiritual security; devotion, to the publican, was a means of stirring up his soul to the realization of the need for repentance, confession, and the acceptance, by faith, of merciful forgiveness. The Pharisee sought justice; the publican sought mercy. The law of the universe is: Ask and you shall receive; seek and you shall find.

Though Jesus refused to be drawn into a controversy with the Pharisees concerning divorce, he did proclaim a positive teaching of the highest ideals regarding marriage. He exalted marriage as the most ideal and highest of all human relationships. Likewise, he intimated strong disapproval of the lax and unfair divorce practices of the Jerusalem Jews, who at that time permitted a man to divorce his wife for the most trifling of reasons, such as being a poor cook, a faulty housekeeper, or for no better reason than that he had become enamored of a better-looking woman.

The Pharisees had even gone so far as to teach that divorce of this easy variety was a special dispensation granted the Jewish people, particularly the Pharisees. And so, while Jesus refused to make pronouncements dealing with marriage and divorce, he did most bitterly denounce these shameful floutings of the marriage relationship and pointed out their injustice to women and children. He never sanctioned any divorce practice which gave man any advantage over woman; the Master countenanced only those teachings which accorded women equality with men.

Although Jesus did not offer new mandates governing marriage and divorce, he did urge the Jews to live up to their own laws and higher teachings. He constantly appealed to the written Scriptures in his effort to improve their practices along these social lines. While thus upholding the high and ideal concepts of marriage, Jesus skillfully avoided clashing with his questioners about the social practices represented by either their written laws or their much-cherished divorce privileges.

It was very difficult for the apostles to understand the Master's reluctance to make positive pronouncements relative to scientific, social, economic, and political problems. They did not fully realize that his earth mission was exclusively concerned with revelations of spiritual and religious truths.

After Jesus had talked about marriage and divorce, later on that evening his apostles privately asked many additional questions, and his answers to these inquiries relieved their minds of many misconceptions. At the conclusion of this conference Jesus said: "Marriage is honorable and is to be desired by all men. The fact that the Son of Man pursues his earth mission alone is in no way a reflection on the desirability of marriage. That I should so work is the Father's will, but this same Father has directed the creation of male and female, and it is the divine will that men and women should find their highest service and consequent joy in the establishment of homes for the reception and training of children, in the creation of whom these parents become copartners with the Makers of heaven and earth. And for this cause shall a man leave his father and mother and shall cleave to his wife, and they two shall become as one."

And in this way Jesus relieved the minds of the apostles of many worries about marriage and cleared up many misunderstandings regarding divorce; at the same time he did much to exalt their ideals of social union and to augment their respect for women and children and for the home.

6. BLESSING THE LITTLE CHILDREN

That evening Jesus' message regarding marriage and the blessedness of children spread all over Jericho, so that the next morning, long before Jesus and the apostles prepared to leave, even before breakfast time, scores of mothers came to where Jesus lodged, bringing their children in their arms and leading them by their hands, and desired that he bless the little ones. When the apostles went out to view this assemblage of mothers with their children, they endeavored to send them away, but these women refused to depart until the Master laid his hands on their children and blessed them. And when the apostles loudly rebuked these mothers, Jesus, hearing the tumult, came out and indignantly reproved them, saying: "Suffer little children to come to me; forbid them not, for of such is the kingdom of heaven. Verily, verily, I say to you, whosoever receives not the kingdom of God as a little child shall hardly enter therein to grow up to the full stature of spiritual manhood."

And when the Master had spoken to his apostles, he received all of the children, laying his hands on them, while he spoke words of courage and hope to their mothers.

Jesus often talked to his apostles about the celestial mansions and taught that the advancing children of God must there grow up spiritually as children grow up physically on this world. And so does the sacred oftentimes appear to be the common, as on this day these children and their mothers little realized that the onlooking intelligences of Nebadon beheld the children of Jericho playing with the Creator of a universe.

Woman's status in Palestine was much improved by Jesus' teaching; and so it would have been throughout the world if his followers had not departed so far from that which he painstakingly taught them.

It was also at Jericho, in connection with the discussion of the early religious training of children in habits of divine worship, that Jesus impressed upon his apostles the great value of beauty as an influence leading to the urge to worship, especially with children. The Master by precept and example taught the value of worshiping the Creator in the midst of the natural surroundings of creation. He preferred to commune with the heavenly Father amidst the trees and among the lowly creatures of the natural world. He rejoiced to contemplate the Father through the inspiring spectacle of the starry realms of the Creator Sons.

When it is not possible to worship God in the tabernacles of nature, men should do their best to provide houses of beauty, sanctuaries of appealing simplicity and artistic embellishment, so that the highest of human emotions may be aroused in association with the intellectual approach to spiritual communion with God. Truth, beauty, and holiness are powerful and effective aids to true worship. But spirit communion is not promoted by mere massive ornateness and overmuch embellishment with man's elaborate and ostentatious art. Beauty is most religious when it is most simple and naturelike. How unfortunate that little children should have their first introduction to concepts of public worship in cold and barren rooms so devoid of the beauty appeal and so empty of all suggestion of good cheer and inspiring holiness! The child should be introduced to worship in nature's outdoors and later accompany his parents to public houses of religious assembly which are at least as materially attractive and artistically beautiful as the home in which he is daily domiciled.

7. THE TALK ABOUT ANGELS

As they journeyed up the hills from Jericho to Bethany, Nathaniel walked most of the way by the side of Jesus, and their discussion of children in relation to the kingdom of heaven led indirectly to the consideration of the ministry of angels. Nathaniel finally asked the Master this question: "Seeing that the high priest is a Sadducee, and since the Sadducees do not believe in angels, what shall we teach the people regarding the heavenly ministers?" Then, among other things, Jesus said:

"The angelic hosts are a separate order of created beings; they are entirely different from the material order of mortal creatures, and they function as a distinct group of universe intelligences. Angels are not of that group of creatures called 'the Sons of God' in the Scriptures; neither are they the glorified spirits of mortal men who have gone on to progress through the mansions on high. Angels are a direct creation, and they do not reproduce themselves. The angelic hosts have only a spiritual kinship with the human race. As man progresses in the journey to the Father in Paradise, he does traverse a state of being at one time analogous to the state of the angels, but mortal man never becomes an angel.

"The angels never die, as man does. The angels are immortal unless, perchance, they become involved in sin as did some of them with the deceptions of Lucifer. The angels are the spirit servants in heaven, and they are neither all-wise nor all-powerful. But all of the loyal angels are truly pure and holy.

"And do you not remember that I said to you once before that, if you had your spiritual eyes anointed, you would then see the heavens opened and behold the angels of God ascending and descending? It is by the ministry of the angels that one world may be kept in touch with other worlds, for have I not repeatedly told you that I have other sheep not of this fold? And these angels are not the spies of the spirit world who watch upon you and then go forth to tell the Father the thoughts of your heart and to report on the deeds of the flesh. The Father has no need of such service inasmuch as his own spirit lives within you. But these angelic spirits do function to keep one part of the heavenly creation informed concerning the doings of other and remote parts of the universe. And many of the angels, while functioning in the government of the Father and the universes of the Sons, are assigned to the service of the human races. When I taught you that many of these seraphim are ministering spirits, I spoke not in figurative language nor in poetic strains. And all this is true, regardless of your difficulty in comprehending such matters.

"Many of these angels are engaged in the work of saving men, for have I not told you of the seraphic joy when one soul elects to forsake sin and begin the search for God? I did even tell you of the joy in the *presence of the angels* of heaven over one sinner who repents, thereby indicating the existence of other and higher orders of celestial beings who are likewise concerned in the spiritual welfare and with the divine progress of mortal man.

"Also are these angels very much concerned with the means whereby man's spirit is released from the tabernacles of the flesh and his soul escorted to the mansions in heaven. Angels are the sure and heavenly guides of the soul of man during that uncharted and indefinite period of time which intervenes between the death of the flesh and the new life in the spirit abodes."

And he would have spoken further with Nathaniel regarding the ministry of angels, but he was interrupted by the approach of Martha, who had been informed that the Master was drawing near to Bethany by friends who had observed him ascending the hills to the east. And she now hastened to greet him.

PAPER 168

THE RESURRECTION OF LAZARUS

IT WAS shortly after noon when Martha started out to meet Jesus as he came over the brow of the hill near Bethany. Her brother, Lazarus, had been dead four days and had been laid away in their private tomb at the far end of the garden late on Sunday afternoon. The stone at the entrance of the tomb had been rolled in place on the morning of this day, Thursday.

When Martha and Mary sent word to Jesus concerning Lazarus's illness, they were confident the Master would do something about it. They knew that their brother was desperately sick, and though they hardly dared hope that Jesus would leave his work of teaching and preaching to come to their assistance, they had such confidence in his power to heal disease that they thought he would just speak the curative words, and Lazarus would immediately be made whole. And when Lazarus died a few hours after the messenger left Bethany for Philadelphia, they reasoned that it was because the Master did not learn of their brother's illness until it was too late, until he had already been dead for several hours.

But they, with all of their believing friends, were greatly puzzled by the message which the runner brought back Tuesday forenoon when he reached Bethany. The messenger insisted that he heard Jesus say, ". . . this sickness is really not to the death." Neither could they understand why he sent no word to them nor otherwise proffered assistance.

Many friends from near-by hamlets and others from Jerusalem came over to comfort the sorrow-stricken sisters. Lazarus and his sisters were the children of a well-to-do and honorable Jew, one who had been the leading resident of the little village of Bethany. And notwithstanding that all three had long been ardent followers of Jesus, they were highly respected by all who knew them. They had inherited extensive vineyards and olive orchards in this vicinity, and that they were wealthy was further attested by the fact that they could afford a private burial tomb on their own premises. Both of their parents had already been laid away in this tomb.

Mary had given up the thought of Jesus' coming and was abandoned to her grief, but Martha clung to the hope that Jesus would come, even up to the time on that very morning when they rolled the stone in front of the tomb and sealed the entrance. Even then she instructed a neighbor lad to keep watch down the Jericho road from the brow of the hill to the east of Bethany; and it was this lad who brought tidings to Martha that Jesus and his friends were approaching.

When Martha met Jesus, she fell at his feet, exclaiming, "Master, if you had been here, my brother would not have died!" Many fears were passing through Martha's mind, but she gave expression to no doubt, nor did she venture to criticize or question the Master's conduct as related to Lazarus's death. When she had spoken, Jesus reached down and, lifting her upon her feet, said, "Only have faith, Martha, and your brother shall rise again." Then answered Martha: "I know that he will rise again in the resurrection of the last day; and even now I believe that whatever you shall ask of God, our Father will give you."

Then said Jesus, looking straight into the eyes of Martha: "I am the resurrection and the life; he who believes in me, though he dies, yet shall he live. In truth, whosoever lives and believes in me shall never really die. Martha, do you believe this?" And Martha answered the Master: "Yes, I have long believed that you are the Deliverer, the Son of the living God, even he who should come to this world."

Jesus having inquired for Mary, Martha went at once into the house and, whispering to her sister, said, "The Master is here and has asked for you." And when Mary heard this, she rose up quickly and hastened out to meet Jesus, who still tarried at the place, some distance from the house, where Martha had first met him. The friends who were with Mary, seeking to comfort her, when they saw that she rose up quickly and went out, followed her, supposing that she was going to the tomb to weep.

Many of those present were Jesus' bitter enemies. That is why Martha had come out to meet him alone, and also why she went in secretly to inform Mary that he had asked for her. Martha, while craving to see Jesus, desired to avoid any possible unpleasantness which might be caused by his coming suddenly into the midst of a large group of his Jerusalem enemies. It had been Martha's intention to remain in the house with their friends while Mary went to greet Jesus, but in this she failed, for they all followed Mary and so found themselves unexpectedly in the presence of the Master.

Martha led Mary to Jesus, and when she saw him, she fell at his feet, exclaiming, "If you had only been here, my brother would not have died!" And when Jesus saw how they all grieved over the death of Lazarus, his soul was moved with compassion.

When the mourners saw that Mary had gone to greet Jesus, they withdrew for a short distance while both Martha and Mary talked with the Master and received further words of comfort and exhortation to maintain strong faith in the Father and complete resignation to the divine will.

The human mind of Jesus was mightily moved by the contention between his love for Lazarus and the bereaved sisters and his disdain and contempt for the outward show of affection manifested by some of these unbelieving and murderously intentioned Jews. Jesus indignantly resented the show of forced and outward mourning for Lazarus by some of these professed friends inasmuch as such false sorrow was associated in their hearts with so much bitter enmity toward himself. Some of these Jews, however, were sincere in their mourning, for they were real friends of the family.

1. AT THE TOMB OF LAZARUS

After Jesus had spent a few moments in comforting Martha and Mary, apart from the mourners, he asked them, "Where have you laid him?" Then Martha said, "Come and see." And as the Master followed on in silence with the two sorrowing sisters, he wept. When the friendly Jews who followed after them saw his tears, one of them said: "Behold how he loved him. Could not he who opened the eyes of the blind have kept this man from dying?" By this time they were standing before the family tomb, a small natural cave, or declivity, in the ledge of rock which rose up some thirty feet at the far end of the garden plot.

It is difficult to explain to human minds just why Jesus wept. While we have access to the registration of the combined human emotions and divine thoughts, as of record in the mind of the Personalized Adjuster, we are not altogether certain about the real cause of these emotional manifestations. We are inclined to believe that Jesus wept because of a number of thoughts and feelings which were going through his mind at this time, such as:

1. He felt a genuine and sorrowful sympathy for Martha and Mary; he had a real and deep human affection for these sisters who had lost their brother.

2. He was perturbed in his mind by the presence of the crowd of mourners, some sincere and some merely pretenders. He always resented these outward exhibitions of mourning. He knew the sisters loved their brother and had faith in the survival of believers. These conflicting emotions may possibly explain why he groaned as they came near the tomb.

3. He truly hesitated about bringing Lazarus back to the mortal life. His sisters really needed him, but Jesus regretted having to summon his friend back to experience the bitter persecution which he well knew Lazarus would have to endure as a result of being the subject of the greatest of all demonstrations of the divine power of the Son of Man.

And now we may relate an interesting and instructive fact: Although this narrative unfolds as an apparently natural and normal event in human affairs, it has some very interesting side lights. While the messenger went to Jesus on Sunday, telling him of Lazarus's illness, and while Jesus sent word that it was "not to the death," at the same time he went in person up to Bethany and even asked the sisters, "Where have you laid him?" Even though all of this seems to indicate that the Master was proceeding after the manner of this life and in accordance with the limited knowledge of the human mind, nevertheless, the records of the universe reveal that Jesus' Personalized Adjuster issued orders for the indefinite detention of Lazarus's Thought Adjuster on the planet subsequent to Lazarus's death, and that this order was made of record just fifteen minutes before Lazarus breathed his last.

Did the divine mind of Jesus know, even before Lazarus died, that he would raise him from the dead? We do not know. We know only what we are herewith placing on record.

Many of Jesus' enemies were inclined to sneer at his manifestations of affection, and they said among themselves: "If he thought so much of this man, why did he tarry so long before coming to Bethany? If he is what they claim, why did he not save his dear friend? What is the good of healing strangers in Galilee if he cannot save those whom he loves?" And in many other ways they mocked and made light of the teachings and works of Jesus.

And so, on this Thursday afternoon at about half past two o'clock, was the stage all set in this little hamlet of Bethany for the enactment of the greatest of all works connected with the earth ministry of Michael of Nebadon, the greatest manifestation of divine power during his incarnation in the flesh, since his own resurrection occurred after he had been liberated from the bonds of mortal habitation.

The small group assembled before Lazarus's tomb little realized the presence near at hand of a vast concourse of all orders of celestial beings assembled under the leadership of Gabriel and now in waiting, by direction of the Personalized Adjuster of Jesus, vibrating with expectancy and ready to execute the bidding of their beloved Sovereign.

When Jesus spoke those words of command, "Take away the stone," the assembled celestial hosts made ready to enact the drama of the resurrection of Lazarus in the likeness of his mortal flesh. Such a form of resurrection involves difficulties of execution which far transcend the usual technique of the resurrection of mortal creatures in morontia form and requires far more celestial personalities and a far greater organization of universe facilities.

When Martha and Mary heard this command of Jesus directing that the stone in front of the tomb be rolled away, they were filled with conflicting emotions. Mary hoped that Lazarus was to be raised from the dead, but Martha, while to some extent sharing her sister's faith, was more exercised by the fear that Lazarus would not be presentable, in his appearance, to Jesus, the apostles, and their friends. Said Martha: "Must we roll away the stone? My brother has now been dead four days, so that by this time decay of the body has begun." Martha also said this because she was not certain as to why the Master had requested that the stone be removed; she thought maybe Jesus wanted only to take one last look at Lazarus. She was not settled and constant in her attitude. As they hesitated to roll away the stone, Jesus said: "Did I not tell you at the first that this sickness was not to the death? Have I not come to fulfill my promise? And after I came to you, did I not say that, if you would only believe, you should see the glory of God? Wherefore do you doubt? How long before you will believe and obey?"

When Jesus had finished speaking, his apostles, with the assistance of willing neighbors, laid hold upon the stone and rolled it away from the entrance to the tomb.

It was the common belief of the Jews that the drop of gall on the point of the sword of the angel of death began to work by the end of the third day, so that it was taking full effect on the fourth day. They allowed that the soul of man might linger about the tomb until the end of the third day, seeking to reanimate the dead body; but they firmly believed that such a soul had gone on to the abode of departed spirits ere the fourth day had dawned.

These beliefs and opinions regarding the dead and the departure of the spirits of the dead served to make sure, in the minds of all who were now present at Lazarus's tomb and subsequently to all who might hear of what was about to occur, that this was really and truly a case of the raising of the dead by the personal working of one who declared he was "the resurrection and the life."

2. THE RESURRECTION OF LAZARUS

As this company of some forty-five mortals stood before the tomb, they could dimly see the form of Lazarus, wrapped in linen bandages, resting on the right lower niche of the burial cave. While these earth creatures stood there in almost breathless silence, a vast host of celestial beings had swung into their places preparatory to answering the signal for action when it should be given by Gabriel, their commander.

Jesus lifted up his eyes and said: "Father, I am thankful that you heard and granted my request. I know that you always hear me, but because of those who stand here with me, I thus speak with you, that they may believe that you have sent me into the world, and that they may know that you are working with me in that which we are about to do." And when he had prayed, he cried with a loud voice, "Lazarus, come forth!"

Though these human observers remained motionless, the vast celestial host was all astir in unified action in obedience to the Creator's word. In just twelve seconds of earth time the hitherto lifeless form of Lazarus began to move and presently sat up on the edge of the stone shelf whereon it had rested. His body was bound about with grave cloths, and his face was covered with a napkin. And as he stood up before them—alive—Jesus said, "Loose him and let him go."

All, save the apostles, with Martha and Mary, fled to the house. They were pale with fright and overcome with astonishment. While some tarried, many hastened to their homes.

Lazarus greeted Jesus and the apostles and asked the meaning of the grave cloths and why he had awakened in the garden. Jesus and the apostles drew to one side while Martha told Lazarus of his death, burial, and resurrection. She had to explain to him that he had died on Sunday and was now brought back to life on Thursday, inasmuch as he had had no consciousness of time since falling asleep in death.

As Lazarus came out of the tomb, the Personalized Adjuster of Jesus, now chief of his kind in this local universe, gave command to the former Adjuster of Lazarus, now in waiting, to resume abode in the mind and soul of the resurrected man.

Then went Lazarus over to Jesus and, with his sisters, knelt at the Master's feet to give thanks and offer praise to God. Jesus, taking Lazarus by the hand, lifted him up, saying: "My son, what has happened to you will also be experienced by all who believe this gospel except that they shall be resurrected in a more glorious form. You shall be a living witness of the truth which I spoke—I am the resurrection and the life. But let us all now go into the house and partake of nourishment for these physical bodies."

As they walked toward the house, Gabriel dismissed the extra groups of the assembled heavenly host while he made record of the first instance on Urantia, and the last, where a mortal creature had been resurrected in the likeness of the physical body of death.

Lazarus could hardly comprehend what had occurred. He knew he had been very sick, but he could recall only that he had fallen asleep and been awakened. He was never able to tell anything about these four days in the tomb because he was wholly unconscious. Time is nonexistent to those who sleep the sleep of death.

Though many believed in Jesus as a result of this mighty work, others only hardened their hearts the more to reject him. By noon the next day this story had spread over all Jerusalem. Scores of men and women went to Bethany to look upon Lazarus and talk with him, and the alarmed and disconcerted Pharisees hastily called a meeting of the Sanhedrin that they might determine what should be done about these new developments.

3. MEETING OF THE SANHEDRIN

Even though the testimony of this man raised from the dead did much to consolidate the faith of the mass of believers in the gospel of the kingdom, it had little or no influence on the attitude of the religious leaders and rulers at Jerusalem except to hasten their decision to destroy Jesus and stop his work.

At one o'clock the next day, Friday, the Sanhedrin met to deliberate further on the question, "What shall we do with Jesus of Nazareth?" After more than two hours of discussion and acrimonious debate, a certain Pharisee presented a resolution calling for Jesus' immediate death, proclaiming that he was a menace to all Israel and formally committing the Sanhedrin to the decision of death, without trial and in defiance of all precedent.

Time and again had this august body of Jewish leaders decreed that Jesus be apprehended and brought to trial on charges of blasphemy and numerous other accusations of flouting the Jewish sacred law. They had once before even gone so far as to declare he should die, but this was the first time the Sanhedrin had gone on record as desiring to decree his death in advance of a trial. But this resolution did not come to a vote since fourteen members of the Sanhedrin resigned in a body when such an unheard-of action was proposed. While these resignations were not formally acted upon for almost two weeks, this group of fourteen withdrew from the Sanhedrin on that day, never again to sit in the council. When these resignations were subsequently acted upon, five other members were thrown out because their associates believed they entertained friendly feelings toward Jesus. With the ejection of these nineteen men the Sanhedrin was in a position to try and to condemn Jesus with a solidarity bordering on unanimity.

The following week Lazarus and his sisters were summoned to appear before the Sanhedrin. When their testimony had been heard, no doubt could be entertained that Lazarus had been raised from the dead. Though the transactions of the Sanhedrin virtually admitted the resurrection of Lazarus, the record carried a resolution attributing this and all other wonders worked by Jesus to the power of the prince of devils, with whom Jesus was declared to be in league.

No matter what the source of his wonder-working power, these Jewish leaders were persuaded that, if he were not immediately stopped, very soon all the common people would believe in him; and further, that serious complications with the Roman authorities would arise since so many of his believers regarded him as the Messiah, Israel's deliverer.

It was at this same meeting of the Sanhedrin that Caiaphas the high priest first gave expression to that old Jewish adage, which he so many times repeated: "It is better that one man die, than that the community perish."

Although Jesus had received warning of the doings of the Sanhedrin on this dark Friday afternoon, he was not in the least perturbed and continued resting over the Sabbath with friends in Bethpage, a hamlet near Bethany. Early Sunday morning Jesus and the apostles assembled, by prearrangement, at the home of Lazarus, and taking leave of the Bethany family, they started on their journey back to the Pella encampment.

4. THE ANSWER TO PRAYER

On the way from Bethany to Pella the apostles asked Jesus many questions, all of which the Master freely answered except those involving the details of the resurrection of the dead. Such problems were beyond the comprehension capacity of his apostles; therefore did the Master decline to discuss these questions with them. Since they had departed from Bethany in secret, they were alone. Jesus therefore embraced the opportunity to say many things to the ten which he thought would prepare them for the trying days just ahead.

The apostles were much stirred up in their minds and spent considerable time discussing their recent experiences as they were related to prayer and its answering. They all recalled Jesus' statement to the Bethany messenger at Philadelphia, when he said plainly, "This sickness is not really to the death." And yet, in spite of this promise, Lazarus actually died. All that day, again and again, they reverted to the discussion of this question of the answer to prayer.

Jesus' answers to their many questions may be summarized as follows:

1. Prayer is an expression of the finite mind in an effort to approach the Infinite. The making of a prayer must, therefore, be limited by the knowledge, wisdom, and attributes of the finite; likewise must the answer be conditioned by the vision, aims, ideals, and prerogatives of the Infinite. There never can be observed an unbroken continuity of material phenomena between the making of a prayer and the reception of the full spiritual answer thereto.

2. When a prayer is apparently unanswered, the delay often betokens a better answer, although one which is for some good reason greatly delayed. When Jesus said that Lazarus's sickness was really not to the death, he had already been dead eleven hours. No sincere prayer is denied an answer except when the superior viewpoint of the spiritual world has devised a better answer, an answer which meets the petition of the spirit of man as contrasted with the prayer of the mere mind of man.

3. The prayers of time, when indited by the spirit and expressed in faith, are often so vast and all-encompassing that they can be answered only in eternity; the finite petition is sometimes so fraught with the grasp of the Infinite that the answer must long be postponed to await the creation of adequate capacity for receptivity; the prayer of faith may be so all-embracing that the answer can be received only on Paradise.

4. The answers to the prayer of the mortal mind are often of such a nature that they can be received and recognized only after that same praying mind has attained the immortal state. The prayer of the material being can many times be answered only when such an individual has progressed to the spirit level.

5. The prayer of a God-knowing person may be so distorted by ignorance and so deformed by superstition that the answer thereto would be highly undesirable. Then must the intervening spirit beings so translate such a prayer that, when the answer arrives, the petitioner wholly fails to recognize it as the answer to his prayer.

6. All true prayers are addressed to spiritual beings, and all such petitions must be answered in spiritual terms, and all such answers must consist in spiritual realities. Spirit beings cannot bestow material answers to the spirit

petitions of even material beings. Material beings can pray effectively only when they "pray in the spirit."

7. No prayer can hope for an answer unless it is born of the spirit and nurtured by faith. Your sincere faith implies that you have in advance virtually granted your prayer hearers the full right to answer your petitions in accordance with that supreme wisdom and that divine love which your faith depicts as always actuating those beings to whom you pray.

8. The child is always within his rights when he presumes to petition the parent; and the parent is always within his parental obligations to the immature child when his superior wisdom dictates that the answer to the child's prayer be delayed, modified, segregated, transcended, or postponed to another stage of spiritual ascension.

9. Do not hesitate to pray the prayers of spirit longing; doubt not that you shall receive the answer to your petitions. These answers will be on deposit, awaiting your achievement of those future spiritual levels of actual cosmic attainment, on this world or on others, whereon it will become possible for you to recognize and appropriate the long-waiting answers to your earlier but ill-timed petitions.

10. All genuine spirit-born petitions are certain of an answer. Ask and you shall receive. But you should remember that you are progressive creatures of time and space; therefore must you constantly reckon with the time-space factor in the experience of your personal reception of the full answers to your manifold prayers and petitions.

5. WHAT BECAME OF LAZARUS

Lazarus remained at the Bethany home, being the center of great interest to many sincere believers and to numerous curious individuals, until the days of the crucifixion of Jesus, when he received warning that the Sanhedrin had decreed his death. The rulers of the Jews were determined to put a stop to the further spread of the teachings of Jesus, and they well judged that it would be useless to put Jesus to death if they permitted Lazarus, who represented the very peak of his wonder-working, to live and bear testimony to the fact that Jesus had raised him from the dead. Already had Lazarus suffered bitter persecution from them.

And so Lazarus took hasty leave of his sisters at Bethany, fleeing down through Jericho and across the Jordan, never permitting himself to rest long until he had reached Philadelphia. Lazarus knew Abner well, and here he felt safe from the murderous intrigues of the wicked Sanhedrin.

Soon after this Martha and Mary disposed of their lands at Bethany and joined their brother in Perea. Meantime, Lazarus had become the treasurer of the church at Philadelphia. He became a strong supporter of Abner in his controversy with Paul and the Jerusalem church and ultimately died, when 67 years old, of the same sickness that carried him off when he was a younger man at Bethany.

PAPER 169

LAST TEACHING AT PELLA

LATE on Monday evening, March 6, Jesus and the ten apostles arrived at the Pella camp. This was the last week of Jesus' sojourn there, and he was very active in teaching the multitude and instructing the apostles. He preached every afternoon to the crowds and each night answered questions for the apostles and certain of the more advanced disciples residing at the camp.

Word regarding the resurrection of Lazarus had reached the encampment two days before the Master's arrival, and the entire assembly was agog. Not since the feeding of the five thousand had anything occurred which so aroused the imagination of the people. And thus it was at the very height of the second phase of the public ministry of the kingdom that Jesus planned to teach this one short week at Pella and then to begin the tour of southern Perea which led right up to the final and tragic experiences of the last week in Jerusalem.

The Pharisees and the chief priests had begun to formulate their charges and to crystallize their accusations. They objected to the Master's teachings on these grounds:

1. He is a friend of publicans and sinners; he receives the ungodly and even eats with them.

2. He is a blasphemer; he talks about God as being his Father and thinks he is equal with God.

3. He is a lawbreaker. He heals disease on the Sabbath and in many other ways flouts the sacred law of Israel.

4. He is in league with devils. He works wonders and does seeming miracles by the power of Beelzebub, the prince of devils.

1. PARABLE OF THE LOST SON

On Thursday afternoon Jesus talked to the multitude about the "Grace of Salvation." In the course of this sermon he retold the story of the lost sheep and the lost coin and then added his favorite parable of the prodigal son. Said Jesus:

"You have been admonished by the prophets from Samuel to John that you should seek for God—search for truth. Always have they said, 'Seek the Lord while he may be found.' And all such teaching should be taken to heart. But I have come to show you that, while you are seeking to find God, God is likewise seeking to find you. Many times have I told you the story of the good shepherd who left the ninety and nine sheep in the fold while he went forth searching for the one that was lost, and how, when he had found the straying sheep, he laid it over his shoulder and tenderly carried it back to the fold. And when the lost sheep had been restored to the fold, you remember that the good shepherd called in his friends and bade them rejoice with him over the finding of the sheep that had been lost. Again I say there is more joy in heaven over one sinner who repents than over the ninety and nine just persons who need no repentance. The fact that souls are *lost* only increases the interest of the heavenly Father. I have come to this world to do my Father's bidding, and it has truly been said of the Son of Man that he is a friend of publicans and sinners.

"You have been taught that divine acceptance comes after your repentance and as a result of all your works of sacrifice and penitence, but I assure you that the Father accepts you even before you have repented and sends the Son and his associates to find you and bring you, with rejoicing, back to the fold, the kingdom of sonship and spiritual progress. You are all like sheep which have gone astray, and I have come to seek and to save those who are lost.

"And you should also remember the story of the woman who, having had ten pieces of silver made into a necklace of adornment, lost one piece, and how she lit the lamp and diligently swept the house and kept up the search until she found the lost piece of silver. And as soon as she found the coin that was lost, she called together her friends and neighbors, saying, 'Rejoice with me, for I have found the piece that was lost.' So again I say, there is always joy in the presence of the angels of heaven over one sinner who repents and returns to the Father's fold. And I tell you this story to impress upon you that the Father and his Son go forth to *search* for those who are lost, and in this search we employ all influences capable of rendering assistance in our diligent efforts to find those who are lost, those who stand in need of salvation. And so, while the Son of Man goes out in the wilderness to seek for the sheep gone astray, he also searches for the coin which is lost in the house. The sheep wanders away, unintentionally; the coin is covered by the dust of time and obscured by the accumulation of the things of men.

"And now I would like to tell you the story of a thoughtless son of a well-to-do farmer who *deliberately* left his father's house and went off into a foreign land, where he fell into much tribulation. You recall that the sheep strayed away without intention, but this youth left his home with premeditation. It was like this:

"A certain man had two sons; one, the younger, was lighthearted and carefree, always seeking for a good time and shirking responsibility, while his older brother was serious, sober, hard-working, and willing to bear responsibility. Now these two brothers did not get along well together; they were always quarreling and bickering. The younger lad was cheerful and vivacious, but indolent and unreliable; the older son was steady and industrious, at the same time self-centered, surly, and conceited. The younger son enjoyed play but shunned work; the older devoted himself to work but seldom played. This association became so disagreeable that the younger son came to his father and said: 'Father, give me the third portion of your possessions which would fall to me and allow me to go out into the world to seek my own fortune.' And when the father heard this request, knowing how unhappy the young man was at home and with his older brother, he divided his property, giving the youth his share.

"Within a few weeks the young man gathered together all his funds and set out upon a journey to a far country, and finding nothing profitable to do which was also pleasurable, he soon wasted all his inheritance in riotous living. And when he had spent all, there arose a prolonged famine in that country, and he found himself in want. And so, when he suffered hunger and his distress was great, he found employment with one of the citizens of that country, who sent him into the fields to feed swine. And the young man would fain have filled himself with the husks which the swine ate, but no one would give him anything.

"One day, when he was very hungry, he came to himself and said: 'How many hired servants of my father have bread enough and to spare while I perish with hunger, feeding swine off here in a foreign country! I will arise and go to my father, and I will say to him: Father, I have sinned against heaven and against you. I am no more worthy to be called your son; only be willing to make me one of your hired servants.' And when the young man had reached this decision, he arose and started out for his father's house.

"Now this father had grieved much for his son; he had missed the cheerful, though thoughtless, lad. This father loved this son and was always on the lookout for his return, so that on the day he approached his home, even while he was yet afar off, the father saw him and, being moved with loving compassion, ran out to meet him, and with affectionate greeting he embraced and kissed him. And after they had thus met, the son looked up into his father's tearful face and said: 'Father, I have sinned against heaven and in your sight; I am no more worthy to be called a son'—but the lad did not find opportunity to complete his confession because the overjoyed father said to the servants who had by this time come running up: 'Bring quickly his best robe, the one I have saved, and put it on him and put the son's ring on his hand and fetch sandals for his feet.'

"And then, after the happy father had led the footsore and weary lad into the house, he called to his servants: 'Bring on the fatted calf and kill it, and let us eat and make merry, for this my son was dead and is alive again; he was lost and is found.' And they all gathered about the father to rejoice with him over the restoration of his son.

"About this time, while they were celebrating, the elder son came in from his day's work in the field, and as he drew near the house, he heard the music and the dancing. And when he came up to the back door, he called out one of the servants and inquired as to the meaning of all this festivity. And then said the servant: 'Your long-lost brother has come home, and your father has killed the fatted calf to rejoice over his son's safe return. Come in that you also may greet your brother and receive him back into your father's house.'

"But when the older brother heard this, he was so hurt and angry he would not go into the house. When his father heard of his resentment of the welcome of his younger brother, he went out to entreat him. But the older son would not yield to his father's persuasion. He answered his father, saying: 'Here these many years have I served you, never transgressing the least of your commands, and yet you never gave me even a kid that I might make merry with my friends. I have remained here to care for you all these years, and you never made rejoicing over my faithful service, but when this your son returns, having squandered your substance with harlots, you make haste to kill the fatted calf and make merry over him.'

"Since this father truly loved both of his sons, he tried to reason with this older one: 'But, my son, you have all the while been with me, and all this which I have is yours. You could have had a kid at any time you had made friends to share your merriment. But it is only proper that you should now join with me in being glad and merry because of your brother's return. Think of it, my son, your brother was lost and is found; he has returned alive to us!'"

This was one of the most touching and effective of all the parables which Jesus ever presented to impress upon his hearers the Father's willingness to receive all who seek entrance into the kingdom of heaven.

Jesus was very partial to telling these three stories at the same time. He presented the story of the lost sheep to show that, when men unintentionally stray away from the path of life, the Father is mindful of such *lost* ones and goes out, with his Sons, the true shepherds of the flock, to seek the lost sheep. He then would recite the story of the coin lost in the house to illustrate how thorough is the divine *searching* for all who are confused, confounded, or otherwise spiritually blinded by the material cares and accumulations of life. And then he would launch forth into the telling of this parable of the lost son, the reception of the returning prodigal, to show how complete is the *restoration* of the lost son into his Father's house and heart.

Many, many times during his years of teaching, Jesus told and retold this story of the prodigal son. This parable and the story of the good Samaritan were his favorite means of teaching the love of the Father and the neighborliness of man.

2. PARABLE OF THE SHREWD STEWARD

One evening Simon Zelotes, commenting on one of Jesus' statements, said: "Master, what did you mean when you said today that many of the children of the world are wiser in their generation than are the children of the kingdom since they are skillful in making friends with the mammon of unrighteousness?" Jesus answered:

"Some of you, before you entered the kingdom, were very shrewd in dealing with your business associates. If you were unjust and often unfair, you were nonetheless prudent and farseeing in that you transacted your business with an eye single to your present profit and future safety. Likewise should you now so order your lives in the kingdom as to provide for your present joy while you also make certain of your future enjoyment of treasures laid up in heaven. If you were so diligent in making gains for yourselves when in the service of self, why should you show less diligence in gaining souls for the kingdom since you are now servants of the brotherhood of man and stewards of God?

"You may all learn a lesson from the story of a certain rich man who had a shrewd but unjust steward. This steward had not only oppressed his master's clients for his own selfish gain, but he had also directly wasted and squandered his master's funds. When all this finally came to the ears of his master, he called the steward before him and asked the meaning of these rumors and required that he should give immediate accounting of his stewardship and prepare to turn his master's affairs over to another.

"Now this unfaithful steward began to say to himself: 'What shall I do since I am about to lose this stewardship? I have not the strength to dig; to beg I am ashamed. I know what I will do to make certain that, when I am put out of this stewardship, I will be welcomed into the houses of all who do business with my master.' And then, calling in each of his lord's debtors, he said to the first, 'How much do you owe my master?' He answered, 'A hundred measures of oil.' Then said the steward, 'Take your wax board bond, sit down quickly, and change it to fifty.' Then he said to another debtor, 'How much do you owe?' And he replied, 'A hundred measures of wheat.' Then said the steward, 'Take your bond and write fourscore.' And this he did with numerous other debtors. And so did this dishonest steward seek to make friends for himself after he would be discharged from his stewardship. Even his lord and master, when he subsequently found out about this, was compelled to admit that his unfaithful steward had at least shown sagacity in the manner in which he had sought to provide for future days of want and adversity.

"And it is in this way that the sons of this world sometimes show more wisdom in their preparation for the future than do the children of light. I say to you who profess to be acquiring treasure in heaven: Take lessons from those who make friends with the mammon of unrighteousness, and likewise so conduct your lives that you make eternal friendship with the forces of righteousness in order that, when all things earthly fail, you shall be joyfully received into the eternal habitations.

"I affirm that he who is faithful in little will also be faithful in much, while he who is unrighteous in little will also be unrighteous in much. If you have not shown foresight and integrity in the affairs of this world, how can you hope to be faithful and prudent when you are trusted with the stewardship of the true riches of the heavenly kingdom? If you are not good stewards and faithful bankers, if you have not been faithful in that which is another's, who will be foolish enough to give you great treasure in your own name?

"And again I assert that no man can serve two masters; either he will hate the one and love the other, or else he will hold to one while he despises the other. You cannot serve God and mammon."

When the Pharisees who were present heard this, they began to sneer and scoff since they were much given to the acquirement of riches. These unfriendly hearers sought to engage Jesus in unprofitable argumentation, but he refused to debate with his enemies. When the Pharisees fell to wrangling among themselves, their loud speaking attracted large numbers of the multitude encamped thereabouts; and when they began to dispute with each other, Jesus withdrew, going to his tent for the night.

3. THE RICH MAN AND THE BEGGAR

When the meeting became too noisy, Simon Peter, standing up, took charge, saying: "Men and brethren, it is not seemly thus to dispute among yourselves. The Master has spoken, and you do well to ponder his words. And this is no new doctrine which he proclaimed to you. Have you not also heard the allegory of the Nazarites concerning the rich man and the beggar? Some of us heard John the Baptist thunder this parable of warning to those who love riches and covet dishonest wealth. And while this olden parable is not according to the gospel we preach, you would all do well to heed its lessons until such a time as you comprehend the new light of the kingdom of heaven. The story as John told it was like this:

"There was a certain rich man named Dives, who, being clothed in purple and fine linen, lived in mirth and splendor every day. And there was a certain beggar named Lazarus, who was laid at this rich man's gate, covered with sores and desiring to be fed with the crumbs which fell from the rich man's table; yes, even the dogs came and licked his sores. And it came to pass that the beggar died and was carried away by the angels to rest in Abraham's bosom. And then, presently, this rich man also died and was buried with great pomp and regal splendor. When the rich man departed from this world, he waked up in Hades, and finding himself in torment, he lifted up his eyes and beheld Abraham afar off and Lazarus in his bosom. And then Dives cried aloud: 'Father Abraham, have mercy on me and send over Lazarus that he may dip the tip of his finger in water to cool my tongue, for I am in great anguish because of my punishment.' And then Abraham replied: 'My son, you should remember that in your lifetime you enjoyed the good things while Lazarus in like manner suffered the evil. But now all this is changed, seeing that Lazarus is comforted while you are tormented. And besides, between us and you there is a great gulf so that we cannot go to you, neither can you come over to us.' Then said Dives to Abraham: 'I pray you send Lazarus back to my father's house, inasmuch as I have five brothers, that he may so testify as to prevent my brothers from coming to this place of torment.' But Abraham said: 'My son, they have Moses and the prophets; let them hear them.' And then answered Dives: 'No, No, Father Abraham! but if one go to them from the dead, they will repent.' And then said Abraham: 'If they hear not Moses and the prophets, neither will they be persuaded even if one were to rise from the dead.'"

After Peter had recited this ancient parable of the Nazarite brotherhood, and since the crowd had quieted down, Andrew arose and dismissed them for the night. Although both the apostles and his disciples frequently asked Jesus questions about the parable of Dives and Lazarus, he never consented to make comment thereon.

4. THE FATHER AND HIS KINGDOM

Jesus always had trouble trying to explain to the apostles that, while they proclaimed the establishment of the kingdom of God, the Father in heaven *was not a king.* At the time Jesus lived on earth and taught in the flesh, the people of Urantia knew mostly of kings and emperors in the governments of the nations, and the Jews had long contemplated the coming of the kingdom of God. For these and other reasons, the Master thought best to designate the spiritual brotherhood of man as the kingdom of heaven and the spirit head of this brotherhood as the *Father in heaven.* Never did Jesus refer to his Father as a king. In his intimate talks with the apostles he always referred to himself as the Son of Man and as their elder brother. He depicted all his followers as servants of mankind and messengers of the gospel of the kingdom.

Jesus never gave his apostles a systematic lesson concerning the personality and attributes of the Father in heaven. He never asked men to believe in his Father; he took it for granted they did. Jesus never belittled himself by offering arguments in proof of the reality of the Father. His teaching regarding the Father all centered in the declaration that he and the Father are one; that he who has seen the Son has seen the Father; that the Father, like the Son, knows all things; that only the Son really knows the Father, and he to whom the Son will reveal him; that he who knows the Son knows also the Father; and that the Father sent him into the world to reveal their combined natures and to show forth their conjoint work. He never made other pronouncements about his Father except to the woman of Samaria at Jacob's well, when he declared, "God is spirit."

You learn about God from Jesus by observing the divinity of his life, not by depending on his teachings. From the life of the Master you may each assimilate that concept of God which represents the measure of your capacity to perceive realities spiritual and divine, truths real and eternal. The finite can never hope to comprehend the Infinite except as the Infinite was focalized in the time-space personality of the finite experience of the human life of Jesus of Nazareth.

Jesus well knew that God can be known only by the realities of experience; never can he be understood by the mere teaching of the mind. Jesus taught his apostles that, while they never could fully understand God, they could most certainly *know* him, even as they had known the Son of Man. You can know God, not by understanding what Jesus said, but by knowing what Jesus was. Jesus *was* a revelation of God.

Except when quoting the Hebrew scriptures, Jesus referred to Deity by only two names: God and Father. And when the Master made reference to his Father as God, he usually employed the Hebrew word signifying the plural God (the Trinity) and not the word Yahweh, which stood for the progressive conception of the tribal God of the Jews.

Jesus never called the Father a king, and he very much regretted that the Jewish hope for a restored kingdom and John's proclamation of a coming kingdom made it necessary for him to denominate his proposed spiritual brotherhood the kingdom of heaven. With the one exception—the declaration that "God is spirit"—Jesus never referred to Deity in any manner other than in terms descriptive of his own personal relationship with the First Source and Center of Paradise.

Jesus employed the word God to designate the *idea* of Deity and the word Father to designate the *experience* of knowing God. When the word Father is employed to denote God, it should be understood in its largest possible meaning. The word God cannot be defined and therefore stands for the infinite concept of the Father, while the term Father, being capable of partial definition, may be employed to represent the human concept of the divine Father as he is associated with man during the course of mortal existence.

To the Jews, Elohim was the God of gods, while Yahweh was the God of Israel. Jesus accepted the concept of Elohim and called this supreme group of beings God. In the place of the concept of Yahweh, the racial deity, he introduced the idea of the fatherhood of God and the world-wide brotherhood of man. He exalted the Yahweh concept of a deified racial Father to the idea of a Father of all the children of men, a divine Father of the individual believer. And he further taught that this God of universes and this Father of all men were one and the same Paradise Deity.

Jesus never claimed to be the manifestation of Elohim (God) in the flesh. He never declared that he was a revelation of Elohim (God) to the worlds. He never taught that he who had seen him had seen Elohim (God). But he did proclaim himself as the revelation of the Father in the flesh, and he did say that whoso had seen him had seen the Father. As the divine Son he claimed to represent only the Father.

He was, indeed, the Son of even the Elohim God; but in the likeness of mortal flesh and to the mortal sons of God, he chose to limit his life revelation to the portrayal of his Father's character in so far as such a revelation might be comprehensible to mortal man. As regards the character of the other persons of the Paradise Trinity, we shall have to be content with the teaching that they are altogether like the Father, who has been revealed in personal portraiture in the life of his incarnated Son, Jesus of Nazareth.

Although Jesus revealed the true nature of the heavenly Father in his earth life, he taught little about him. In fact, he taught only two things: that God in himself is spirit, and that, in all matters of relationship with his creatures, he is a Father. On this evening Jesus made the final pronouncement of his relationship with God when he declared: "I have come out from the Father, and I have come into the world; again, I will leave the world and go to the Father."

But mark you! never did Jesus say, "Whoso has heard me has heard God." But he did say, "He who has *seen* me has seen the Father." To hear Jesus' teaching is not equivalent to knowing God, but to *see* Jesus is an experience which in itself is a revelation of the Father to the soul. The God of universes rules the far-flung creation, but it is the Father in heaven who sends forth his spirit to dwell within your minds.

Jesus is the spiritual lens in human likeness which makes visible to the material creature Him who is invisible. He is your elder brother who, in the flesh, makes *known* to you a Being of infinite attributes whom not even the celestial hosts can presume fully to understand. But all of this must consist in the personal experience of the *individual believer.* God who is spirit can be known only as a spiritual experience. God can be revealed to the finite sons of the material worlds, by the divine Son of the spiritual realms, only as a *Father.* You can know the Eternal as a Father; you can worship him as the God of universes, the infinite Creator of all existences.

PAPER 170

THE KINGDOM OF HEAVEN

SATURDAY afternoon, March 11, Jesus preached his last sermon at Pella. This was among the notable addresses of his public ministry, embracing a full and complete discussion of the kingdom of heaven. He was aware of the confusion which existed in the minds of his apostles and disciples regarding the meaning and significance of the terms "kingdom of heaven" and "kingdom of God," which he used as interchangeable designations of his bestowal mission. Although the very term kingdom of *heaven* should have been enough to separate what it stood for from all connection with *earthly* kingdoms and temporal governments, it was not. The idea of a temporal king was too deep-rooted in the Jewish mind thus to be dislodged in a single generation. Therefore Jesus did not at first openly oppose this long-nourished concept of the kingdom.

This Sabbath afternoon the Master sought to clarify the teaching about the kingdom of heaven; he discussed the subject from every viewpoint and endeavored to make clear the many different senses in which the term had been used. In this narrative we will amplify the address by adding numerous statements made by Jesus on previous occasions and by including some remarks made only to the apostles during the evening discussions of this same day. We will also make certain comments dealing with the subsequent outworking of the kingdom idea as it is related to the later Christian church.

1. CONCEPTS OF THE KINGDOM OF HEAVEN

In connection with the recital of Jesus' sermon it should be noted that throughout the Hebrew scriptures there was a dual concept of the kingdom of heaven. The prophets presented the kingdom of God as:

1. A present reality; and as

2. A future hope—when the kingdom would be realized in fullness upon the appearance of the Messiah. This is the kingdom concept which John the Baptist taught.

From the very first Jesus and the apostles taught both of these concepts. There were two other ideas of the kingdom which should be borne in mind:

3. The later Jewish concept of a world-wide and transcendental kingdom of supernatural origin and miraculous inauguration.

4. The Persian teachings portraying the establishment of a divine kingdom as the achievement of the triumph of good over evil at the end of the world.

Just before the advent of Jesus on earth, the Jews combined and confused all of these ideas of the kingdom into their apocalyptic concept of the Messiah's coming to establish the age of the Jewish triumph, the eternal age of God's supreme rule on earth, the new world, the era in which all mankind would worship Yahweh. In choosing to utilize this concept of the kingdom of heaven, Jesus elected to appropriate the most vital and culminating heritage of both the Jewish and Persian religions.

The kingdom of heaven, as it has been understood and misunderstood down through the centuries of the Christian era, embraced four distinct groups of ideas:

1. The concept of the Jews.

2. The concept of the Persians.

3. The personal-experience concept of Jesus—"the kingdom of heaven within you."

4. The composite and confused concepts which the founders and promulgators of Christianity have sought to impress upon the world.

At different times and in varying circumstances it appears that Jesus may have presented numerous concepts of the "kingdom" in his public teachings, but to his apostles he always taught the kingdom as embracing man's personal experience in relation to his fellows on earth and to the Father in heaven. Concerning the kingdom, his last word always was, "The kingdom is within you."

Centuries of confusion regarding the meaning of the term "kingdom of heaven" have been due to three factors:

1. The confusion occasioned by observing the idea of the "kingdom" as it passed through the various progressive phases of its recasting by Jesus and his apostles.

2. The confusion which was inevitably associated with the transplantation of early Christianity from a Jewish to a gentile soil.

3. The confusion which was inherent in the fact that Christianity became a religion which was organized about the central idea of Jesus' person; the gospel of the kingdom became more and more a religion *about* him.

2. JESUS' CONCEPT OF THE KINGDOM

The Master made it clear that the kingdom of heaven must begin with, and be centered in, the dual concept of the truth of the fatherhood of God and the correlated fact of the brotherhood of man. The acceptance of such a teaching, Jesus declared, would liberate man from the age-long bondage of animal fear and at the same time enrich human living with the following endowments of the new life of spiritual liberty:

1. The possession of new courage and augmented spiritual power. The gospel of the kingdom was to set man free and inspire him to dare to hope for eternal life.

2. The gospel carried a message of new confidence and true consolation for all men, even for the poor.

3. It was in itself a new standard of moral values, a new ethical yardstick wherewith to measure human conduct. It portrayed the ideal of a resultant new order of human society.

4. It taught the pre-eminence of the spiritual compared with the material; it glorified spiritual realities and exalted superhuman ideals.

5. This new gospel held up spiritual attainment as the true goal of living. Human life received a new endowment of moral value and divine dignity.

6. Jesus taught that eternal realities were the result (reward) of righteous earthly striving. Man's mortal sojourn on earth acquired new meanings consequent upon the recognition of a noble destiny.

7. The new gospel affirmed that human salvation is the revelation of a far-reaching divine purpose to be fulfilled and realized in the future destiny of the endless service of the salvaged sons of God.

These teachings cover the expanded idea of the kingdom which was taught by Jesus. This great concept was hardly embraced in the elementary and confused kingdom teachings of John the Baptist.

The apostles were unable to grasp the real meaning of the Master's utterances regarding the kingdom. The subsequent distortion of Jesus' teachings, as they are recorded in the New Testament, is because the concept of the gospel writers was colored by the belief that Jesus was then absent from the world for only a short time; that he would soon return to establish the kingdom in power and glory—just such an idea as they held while he was with them in the flesh. But Jesus did not connect the establishment of the kingdom with the idea of his return to this world. That centuries have passed with no signs of the appearance of the "New Age" is in no way out of harmony with Jesus' teaching.

The great effort embodied in this sermon was the attempt to translate the concept of the kingdom of heaven into the ideal of the idea of doing the will of God. Long had the Master taught his followers to pray: "Your kingdom come; your will be done"; and at this time he earnestly sought to induce them to abandon the use of the term *kingdom of God* in favor of the more practical equivalent, *the will of God.* But he did not succeed.

Jesus desired to substitute for the idea of the kingdom, king, and subjects, the concept of the heavenly family, the heavenly Father, and the liberated sons of God engaged in joyful and voluntary service for their fellow men and in the sublime and intelligent worship of God the Father.

Up to this time the apostles had acquired a double viewpoint of the kingdom; they regarded it as:

1. A matter of personal experience then present in the hearts of true believers, and

2. A question of racial or world phenomena; that the kingdom was in the future, something to look forward to.

They looked upon the coming of the kingdom in the hearts of men as a gradual development, like the leaven in the dough or like the growing of the mustard seed. They believed that the coming of the kingdom in the racial or world sense would be both sudden and spectacular. Jesus never tired of telling them that the kingdom of heaven was their personal experience of realizing the higher qualities of spiritual living; that these realities of the spirit experience are progressively translated to new and higher levels of divine certainty and eternal grandeur.

On this afternoon the Master distinctly taught a new concept of the double nature of the kingdom in that he portrayed the following two phases:

"First. The kingdom of God in this world, the supreme desire to do the will of God, the unselfish love of man which yields the good fruits of improved ethical and moral conduct.

"Second. The kingdom of God in heaven, the goal of mortal believers, the estate wherein the love for God is perfected, and wherein the will of God is done more divinely."

Jesus taught that, by faith, the believer enters the kingdom *now.* In the various discourses he taught that two things are essential to faith-entrance into the kingdom:

1. *Faith, sincerity.* To come as a little child, to receive the bestowal of sonship as a gift; to submit to the doing of the Father's will without questioning and in the full confidence and genuine trustfulness of the Father's wisdom; to come into the kingdom free from prejudice and preconception; to be open-minded and teachable like an unspoiled child.

2. *Truth hunger.* The thirst for righteousness, a change of mind, the acquirement of the motive to be like God and to find God.

Jesus taught that sin is not the child of a defective nature but rather the offspring of a knowing mind dominated by an unsubmissive will. Regarding sin, he taught that God *has* forgiven; that we make such forgiveness personally available by the act of forgiving our fellows. When you forgive your brother in the flesh, you thereby create the capacity in your own soul for the reception of the reality of God's forgiveness of your own misdeeds.

By the time the Apostle John began to write the story of Jesus' life and teachings, the early Christians had experienced so much trouble with the kingdom-of-God idea as a breeder of persecution that they had largely abandoned the use of the term. John talks much about the "eternal life." Jesus often spoke of it as the "kingdom of life." He also frequently referred to "the kingdom of God within you." He once spoke of such an experience as "family fellowship with God the Father." Jesus sought to substitute many terms for the kingdom but always without success. Among others, he used: the family of God, the Father's will, the friends of God, the fellowship of believers, the brotherhood of man, the Father's fold, the children of God, the fellowship of the faithful, the Father's service, and the liberated sons of God.

But he could not escape the use of the kingdom idea. It was more than fifty years later, not until after the destruction of Jerusalem by the Roman armies, that this concept of the kingdom began to change into the cult of eternal life as its social and institutional aspects were taken over by the rapidly expanding and crystallizing Christian church.

3. IN RELATION TO RIGHTEOUSNESS

Jesus was always trying to impress upon his apostles and disciples that they must acquire, by faith, a righteousness which would exceed the righteousness of slavish works which some of the scribes and Pharisees paraded so vaingloriously before the world.

Though Jesus taught that faith, simple childlike belief, is the key to the door of the kingdom, he also taught that, having entered the door, there are the progressive steps of righteousness which every believing child must ascend in order to grow up to the full stature of the robust sons of God.

It is in the consideration of the technique of *receiving* God's forgiveness that the attainment of the righteousness of the kingdom is revealed. Faith is the price you pay for entrance into the family of God; but forgiveness is the act of God which accepts your faith as the price of admission. And the reception of the forgiveness of God by a kingdom believer involves a definite and actual experience and consists in the following four steps, the kingdom steps of inner righteousness:

1. God's forgiveness is made actually available and is personally experienced by man just in so far as he forgives his fellows.

2. Man will not truly forgive his fellows unless he loves them as himself.

3. To thus love your neighbor as yourself *is* the highest ethics.

4. Moral conduct, true righteousness, becomes, then, the natural result of such love.

It therefore is evident that the true and inner religion of the kingdom unfailingly and increasingly tends to manifest itself in practical avenues of social service. Jesus taught a living religion that impelled its believers to engage in the doing of loving service. But Jesus did not put ethics in the place of religion. He taught religion as a cause and ethics as a result.

The righteousness of any act must be measured by the motive; the highest forms of good are therefore unconscious. Jesus was never concerned with morals or ethics as such. He was wholly concerned with that inward and spiritual fellowship with God the Father which so certainly and directly manifests itself as outward and loving service for man. He taught that the religion of the kingdom is a genuine personal experience which no man can contain within himself; that the consciousness of being a member of the family of believers leads inevitably to the practice of the precepts of the family conduct, the service of one's brothers and sisters in the effort to enhance and enlarge the brotherhood.

The religion of the kingdom is personal, individual; the fruits, the results, are familial, social. Jesus never failed to exalt the sacredness of the individual as contrasted with the community. But he also recognized that man develops his character by unselfish service; that he unfolds his moral nature in loving relations with his fellows.

By teaching that the kingdom is within, by exalting the individual, Jesus struck the deathblow of the old society in that he ushered in the new dispensation of true social righteousness. This new order of society the world has little known because it has refused to practice the principles of the gospel of the kingdom of heaven. And when this kingdom of spiritual pre-eminence does come upon the earth, it will not be manifested in mere improved social and material conditions, but rather in the glories of those enhanced and enriched spiritual values which are characteristic of the approaching age of improved human relations and advancing spiritual attainments.

4. JESUS' TEACHING ABOUT THE KINGDOM

Jesus never gave a precise definition of the kingdom. At one time he would discourse on one phase of the kingdom, and at another time he would discuss a different aspect of the brotherhood of God's reign in the hearts of men. In the course of this Sabbath afternoon's sermon Jesus noted no less than five phases, or epochs, of the kingdom, and they were:

1. The personal and inward experience of the spiritual life of the fellowship of the individual believer with God the Father.

2. The enlarging brotherhood of gospel believers, the social aspects of the enhanced morals and quickened ethics resulting from the reign of God's spirit in the hearts of individual believers.

3. The supermortal brotherhood of invisible spiritual beings which prevails on earth and in heaven, the superhuman kingdom of God.

4. The prospect of the more perfect fulfillment of the will of God, the advance toward the dawn of a new social order in connection with improved spiritual living—the next age of man.

5. The kingdom in its fullness, the future spiritual age of light and life on earth.

Wherefore must we always examine the Master's teaching to ascertain which of these five phases he may have reference to when he makes use of the term kingdom of heaven. By this process of gradually changing man's will and thus affecting human decisions, Michael and his associates are likewise gradually but certainly changing the entire course of human evolution, social and otherwise.

The Master on this occasion placed emphasis on the following five points as representing the cardinal features of the gospel of the kingdom:

1. The pre-eminence of the individual.

2. The will as the determining factor in man's experience.

3. Spiritual fellowship with God the Father.

4. The supreme satisfactions of the loving service of man.

5. The transcendency of the spiritual over the material in human personality.

This world has never seriously or sincerely or honestly tried out these dynamic ideas and divine ideals of Jesus' doctrine of the kingdom of heaven. But you should not become discouraged by the apparently slow progress of the kingdom idea on Urantia. Remember that the order of progressive evolution is subjected to sudden and unexpected periodical changes in both the material and the spiritual worlds. The bestowal of Jesus as an incarnated Son was just such a strange and unexpected event in the spiritual life of the world. Neither make the fatal mistake, in looking for the age manifestation of the kingdom, of failing to effect its establishment within your own souls.

Although Jesus referred one phase of the kingdom to the future and did, on numerous occasions, intimate that such an event might appear as a part of a world crisis; and though he did likewise most certainly, on several occasions, definitely promise sometime to return to Urantia, it should be recorded that he never positively linked these two ideas together. He promised a new revelation of the kingdom on earth and at some future time; he also promised sometime to come back to this world in person; but he did not say that these two events were synonymous. From all we know these promises may, or may not, refer to the same event.

His apostles and disciples most certainly linked these two teachings together. When the kingdom failed to materialize as they had expected, recalling the Master's teaching concerning a future kingdom and remembering his promise to come again, they jumped to the conclusion that these promises referred to an identical event; and therefore they lived in hope of his immediate second coming to establish the kingdom in its fullness and with power and glory. And so have successive believing generations lived on earth entertaining the same inspiring but disappointing hope.

5. LATER IDEAS OF THE KINGDOM

Having summarized the teachings of Jesus about the kingdom of heaven, we are permitted to narrate certain later ideas which became attached to the concept of the kingdom and to engage in a prophetic forecast of the kingdom as it may evolve in the age to come.

Throughout the first centuries of the Christian propaganda, the idea of the kingdom of heaven was tremendously influenced by the then rapidly spreading notions of Greek idealism, the idea of the natural as the shadow of the spiritual —the temporal as the time shadow of the eternal.

But the great step which marked the transplantation of the teachings of Jesus from a Jewish to a gentile soil was taken when the Messiah of the kingdom became the Redeemer of the church, a religious and social organization growing out of the activities of Paul and his successors and based on the teachings of Jesus as they were supplemented by the ideas of Philo and the Persian doctrines of good and evil.

The ideas and ideals of Jesus, embodied in the teaching of the gospel of the kingdom, nearly failed of realization as his followers progressively distorted his pronouncements. The Master's concept of the kingdom was notably modified by two great tendencies:

1. The Jewish believers persisted in regarding him as the *Messiah.* They believed that Jesus would very soon return actually to establish the world-wide and more or less material kingdom.

2. The gentile Christians began very early to accept the doctrines of Paul, which led increasingly to the general belief that Jesus was the *Redeemer* of the children of the church, the new and institutional successor of the earlier concept of the purely spiritual brotherhood of the kingdom.

The church, as a social outgrowth of the kingdom, would have been wholly natural and even desirable. The evil of the church was not its existence, but rather that it almost completely supplanted the Jesus concept of the kingdom. Paul's institutionalized church became a virtual substitute for the kingdom of heaven which Jesus had proclaimed.

But doubt not, this same kingdom of heaven which the Master taught exists within the heart of the believer, will yet be proclaimed to this Christian church, even as to all other religions, races, and nations on earth—even to every individual.

The kingdom of Jesus' teaching, the spiritual ideal of individual righteousness and the concept of man's divine fellowship with God, became gradually submerged into the mystic conception of the person of Jesus as the Redeemer-Creator and spiritual head of a socialized religious community. In this way a formal and institutional church became the substitute for the individually spirit-led brotherhood of the kingdom.

The church was an inevitable and useful *social* result of Jesus' life and teachings; the tragedy consisted in the fact that this social reaction to the teachings of the kingdom so fully displaced the spiritual concept of the real kingdom as Jesus taught and lived it.

The kingdom, to the Jews, was the Israelite *community;* to the gentiles it became the Christian *church.* To Jesus the kingdom was the sum of those *individuals* who had confessed their faith in the fatherhood of God, thereby declaring their wholehearted dedication to the doing of the will of God, thus becoming members of the spiritual brotherhood of man.

The Master fully realized that certain social results would appear in the world as a consequence of the spread of the gospel of the kingdom; but he intended that all such desirable social manifestations should appear as unconscious and inevitable outgrowths, or natural fruits, of this inner personal experience of individual believers, this purely spiritual fellowship and communion with the divine spirit which indwells and activates all such believers.

Jesus foresaw that a social organization, or church, would follow the progress of the true spiritual kingdom, and that is why he never opposed the apostles' practicing the rite of John's baptism. He taught that the truth-loving soul, the one who hungers and thirsts for righteousness, for God, is admitted by faith to the spiritual kingdom; at the same time the apostles taught that such a believer is admitted to the social organization of disciples by the outward rite of baptism.

When Jesus' immediate followers recognized their partial failure to realize his ideal of the establishment of the kingdom in the hearts of men by the spirit's domination and guidance of the individual believer, they set about to save his teaching from being wholly lost by substituting for the Master's ideal of the kingdom the gradual creation of a visible social organization, the Christian church. And when they had accomplished this program of substitution, in order to maintain consistency and to provide for the recognition of the Master's teaching regarding the fact of the kingdom, they proceeded to set the kingdom off into the future. The church, just as soon as it was well established, began to teach that the kingdom was in reality to appear at the culmination of the Christian age, at the second coming of Christ.

In this manner the kingdom became the concept of an age, the idea of a future visitation, and the ideal of the final redemption of the saints of the Most High. The early Christians (and all too many of the later ones) generally lost sight of the Father-and-son idea embodied in Jesus' teaching of the kingdom, while they substituted therefor the well-organized social fellowship of the church. The church thus became in the main a *social* brotherhood which effectively displaced Jesus' concept and ideal of a *spiritual* brotherhood.

Jesus' ideal concept largely failed, but upon the foundation of the Master's personal life and teachings, supplemented by the Greek and Persian concepts of eternal life and augmented by Philo's doctrine of the temporal contrasted with the spiritual, Paul went forth to build up one of the most progressive human societies which has ever existed on Urantia.

The concept of Jesus is still alive in the advanced religions of the world. Paul's Christian church is the socialized and humanized shadow of what Jesus intended the kingdom of heaven to be—and what it most certainly will yet become. Paul and his successors partly transferred the issues of eternal life from the individual to the church. Christ thus became the head of the church rather than the elder brother of each individual believer in the Father's family of the kingdom. Paul and his contemporaries applied all of Jesus' spiritual implications regarding himself and the individual believer to the *church* as a group of believers; and in doing this, they struck a deathblow to Jesus' concept of the divine kingdom in the heart of the individual believer.

And so, for centuries, the Christian church has labored under great embarrassment because it dared to lay claim to those mysterious powers and privileges of the kingdom, powers and privileges which can be exercised and experienced only between Jesus and his spiritual believer brothers. And thus it becomes apparent that membership in the church does not necessarily mean fellowship in the kingdom; one is spiritual, the other mainly social.

Sooner or later another and greater John the Baptist is due to arise proclaiming "the kingdom of God is at hand"—meaning a return to the high spiritual concept of Jesus, who proclaimed that the kingdom is the will of his heavenly Father dominant and transcendent in the heart of the believer—and doing all this without in any way referring either to the visible church on earth or to the anticipated second coming of Christ. There must come a revival of the *actual* teachings of Jesus, such a restatement as will undo the work of his early followers who went about to create a sociophilosophical system of belief regarding the *fact* of Michael's sojourn on earth. In a short time the teaching of this story *about* Jesus nearly supplanted the preaching of Jesus' gospel of the kingdom. In this way a historical religion displaced that teaching in which Jesus had blended man's highest moral ideas and spiritual ideals with man's most sublime hope for the future—eternal life. And that was the gospel of the kingdom.

It is just because the gospel of Jesus was so many-sided that within a few centuries students of the records of his teachings became divided up into so many cults and sects. This pitiful subdivision of Christian believers results from failure to discern in the Master's manifold teachings the divine oneness of his matchless life. But someday the true believers in Jesus will not be thus spiritually divided in their attitude before unbelievers. Always we may have diversity of intellectual comprehension and interpretation, even varying degrees of socialization, but lack of spiritual brotherhood is both inexcusable and reprehensible.

Mistake not! there is in the teachings of Jesus an eternal nature which will not permit them forever to remain unfruitful in the hearts of thinking men. The kingdom as Jesus conceived it has to a large extent failed on earth; for the time being, an outward church has taken its place; but you should comprehend that this church is only the larval stage of the thwarted spiritual kingdom, which will carry it through this material age and over into a more spiritual dispensation where the Master's teachings may enjoy a fuller opportunity for development. Thus does the so-called Christian church become the cocoon in which the kingdom of Jesus' concept now slumbers. The kingdom of the divine brotherhood is still alive and will eventually and certainly come forth from this long submergence, just as surely as the butterfly eventually emerges as the beautiful unfolding of its less attractive creature of metamorphic development.

PAPER 171

ON THE WAY TO JERUSALEM

THE day after the memorable sermon on "The Kingdom of Heaven," Jesus announced that on the following day he and the apostles would depart for the Passover at Jerusalem, visiting numerous cities in southern Perea on the way.

The address on the kingdom and the announcement that he was going to the Passover set all his followers to thinking that he was going up to Jerusalem to inaugurate the temporal kingdom of Jewish supremacy. No matter what Jesus said about the nonmaterial character of the kingdom, he could not wholly remove from the minds of his Jewish hearers the idea that the Messiah was to establish some kind of nationalistic government with headquarters at Jerusalem.

What Jesus said in his Sabbath sermon only tended to confuse the majority of his followers; very few were enlightened by the Master's discourse. The leaders understood something of his teachings regarding the inner kingdom, "the kingdom of heaven within you," but they also knew that he had spoken about another and future kingdom, and it was this kingdom they believed he was now going up to Jerusalem to establish. When they were disappointed in this expectation, when he was rejected by the Jews, and later on, when Jerusalem was literally destroyed, they still clung to this hope, sincerely believing that the Master would soon return to the world in great power and majestic glory to establish the promised kingdom.

It was on this Sunday afternoon that Salome the mother of James and John Zebedee came to Jesus with her two apostle sons and, in the manner of approaching an Oriental potentate, sought to have Jesus promise in advance to grant whatever request she might make. But the Master would not promise; instead, he asked her, "What do you want me to do for you?" Then answered Salome: "Master, now that you are going up to Jerusalem to establish the kingdom, I would ask you in advance to promise me that these my sons shall have honor with you, the one to sit on your right hand and the other to sit on your left hand in your kingdom."

When Jesus heard Salome's request, he said: "Woman, you know not what you ask." And then, looking straight into the eyes of the two honor-seeking apostles, he said: "Because I have long known and loved you; because I have even lived in your mother's house; because Andrew has assigned you to be with me at all times; therefore do you permit your mother to come to me secretly, making this unseemly request. But let me ask you: Are you able to drink the cup I am about to drink?" And without a moment for thought, James and John answered, "Yes, Master, we are able." Said Jesus: "I am saddened that you know not why we go up to Jerusalem; I am grieved that you understand not the nature of my kingdom; I am disappointed that you bring your mother to make this request of me; but I know you love me in your hearts; therefore I declare that you shall indeed drink of my cup of bitterness and share in my humiliation, but to sit on my right hand and on my left hand is not mine to give. Such honors are reserved for those who have been designated by my Father."

By this time someone had carried word of this conference to Peter and the other apostles, and they were highly indignant that James and John would seek to be preferred before them, and that they would secretly go with their mother to make such a request. When they fell to arguing among themselves, Jesus called them all together and said: "You well understand how the rulers of the gentiles lord it over their subjects, and how those who are great exercise authority. But it shall not be so in the kingdom of heaven. Whosoever would be great among you, let him first become your servant. He who would be first in the kingdom, let him become your minister. I declare to you that the Son of Man came not to be ministered to but to minister; and I now go up to Jerusalem to lay down my life in the doing of the Father's will and in the service of my brethren." When the apostles heard these words, they withdrew by themselves to pray. That evening, in response to the labors of Peter, James and John made suitable apologies to the ten and were restored to the good graces of their brethren.

In asking for places on the right hand and on the left hand of Jesus at Jerusalem, the sons of Zebedee little realized that in less than one month their beloved teacher would be hanging on a Roman cross with a dying thief on one side and another transgressor on the other side. And their mother, who was present at the crucifixion, well remembered the foolish request she had made of Jesus at Pella regarding the honors she so unwisely sought for her apostle sons.

1. THE DEPARTURE FROM PELLA

On the forenoon of Monday, March 13, Jesus and his twelve apostles took final leave of the Pella encampment, starting south on their tour of the cities of southern Perea, where Abner's associates were at work. They spent more than two weeks visiting among the seventy and then went directly to Jerusalem for the Passover.

When the Master left Pella, the disciples encamped with the apostles, about one thousand in number, followed after him. About one half of this group left him at the Jordan ford on the road to Jericho when they learned he was going over to Heshbon, and after he had preached the sermon on "Counting the Cost." They went on up to Jerusalem, while the other half followed him for two weeks, visiting the towns in southern Perea.

In a general way, most of Jesus' immediate followers understood that the camp at Pella had been abandoned, but they really thought this indicated that their Master at last intended to go to Jerusalem and lay claim to David's throne. A large majority of his followers never were able to grasp any other concept of the kingdom of heaven; no matter what he taught them, they would not give up this Jewish idea of the kingdom.

Acting on the instructions of the Apostle Andrew, David Zebedee closed the visitors' camp at Pella on Wednesday, March 15. At this time almost four thousand visitors were in residence, and this does not include the one thousand and more persons who sojourned with the apostles at what was known as the teachers' camp, and who went south with Jesus and the twelve. Much as David disliked to do it, he sold the entire equipment to numerous buyers and proceeded with the funds to Jerusalem, subsequently turning the money over to Judas Iscariot.

David was present in Jerusalem during the tragic last week, taking his mother back with him to Bethsaida after the crucifixion. While awaiting Jesus and the apostles, David stopped with Lazarus at Bethany and became tremendously agitated by the manner in which the Pharisees had begun to persecute and harass him since his resurrection. Andrew had directed David to discontinue the messenger service; and this was construed by all as an indication of the early establishment of the kingdom at Jerusalem. David found himself without a job, and he had about decided to become the self-appointed defender of Lazarus when presently the object of his indignant solicitude fled in haste to Philadelphia. Accordingly, sometime after the resurrection and also after the death of his mother, David betook himself to Philadelphia, having first assisted Martha and Mary in disposing of their real estate; and there, in association with Abner and Lazarus, he spent the remainder of his life, becoming the financial overseer of all those large interests of the kingdom which had their center at Philadelphia during the lifetime of Abner.

Within a short time after the destruction of Jerusalem, Antioch became the headquarters of *Pauline Christianity,* while Philadelphia remained the center of the *Abnerian kingdom of heaven.* From Antioch the Pauline version of the teachings of Jesus and about Jesus spread to all the Western world; from Philadelphia the missionaries of the Abnerian version of the kingdom of heaven spread throughout Mesopotamia and Arabia until the later times when these uncompromising emissaries of the teachings of Jesus were overwhelmed by the sudden rise of Islam.

2. ON COUNTING THE COST

When Jesus and the company of almost one thousand followers arrived at the Bethany ford of the Jordan sometimes called Bethabara, his disciples began to realize that he was not going directly to Jerusalem. While they hesitated and debated among themselves, Jesus climbed upon a huge stone and delivered that discourse which has become known as "Counting the Cost." The Master said:

"You who would follow after me from this time on, must be willing to pay the price of wholehearted dedication to the doing of my Father's will. If you would be my disciples, you must be willing to forsake father, mother, wife, children, brothers, and sisters. If any one of you would now be my disciple, you must be willing to give up even your life just as the Son of Man is about to offer up his life for the completion of the mission of doing the Father's will on earth and in the flesh.

"If you are not willing to pay the full price, you can hardly be my disciple. Before you go further, you should each sit down and count the cost of being my disciple. Which one of you would undertake to build a watchtower on your lands without first sitting down to count up the cost to see whether you had money enough to complete it? If you fail thus to reckon the cost, after you have laid the foundation, you may discover that you are unable to finish that which you have begun, and therefore will all your neighbors mock you, saying, 'Behold, this man began to build but was unable to finish his work.' Again, what king, when he prepares to make war upon another king, does not first sit down and take counsel as to whether he will be able, with ten thousand men, to meet him who comes against him with twenty thousand? If the king cannot afford to meet his enemy because he is unprepared, he sends an embassy to this other king, even when he is yet a great way off, asking for terms of peace.

"Now, then, must each of you sit down and count the cost of being my disciple. From now on you will not be able to follow after us, listening to the teaching and beholding the works; you will be required to face bitter persecutions and to bear witness for this gospel in the face of crushing disappointment. If you are unwilling to renounce all that you are and to dedicate all that you have, then are you unworthy to be my disciple. If you have already conquered yourself within your own heart, you need have no fear of that outward victory which you must presently gain when the Son of Man is rejected by the chief priests and the Sadducees and is given into the hands of mocking unbelievers.

"Now should you examine yourself to find out your motive for being my disciple. If you seek honor and glory, if you are worldly minded, you are like the salt when it has lost its savor. And when that which is valued for its saltiness has lost its savor, wherewith shall it be seasoned? Such a condiment is useless; it is fit only to be cast out among the refuse. Now have I warned you to turn back to your homes in peace if you are not willing to drink with me the cup which is being prepared. Again and again have I told you that my kingdom is not of this world, but you will not believe me. He who has ears to hear let him hear what I say."

Immediately after speaking these words, Jesus, leading the twelve, started off on the way to Heshbon, followed by about five hundred. After a brief delay the other half of the multitude went on up to Jerusalem. His apostles, together with the leading disciples, thought much about these words, but still they clung to the belief that, after this brief period of adversity and trial, the kingdom would certainly be set up somewhat in accordance with their long-cherished hopes.

3. THE PEREAN TOUR

For more than two weeks Jesus and the twelve, followed by a crowd of several hundred disciples, journeyed about in southern Perea, visiting all of the towns wherein the seventy labored. Many gentiles lived in this region, and since few were going up to the Passover feast at Jerusalem, the messengers of the kingdom went right on with their work of teaching and preaching.

Jesus met Abner at Heshbon, and Andrew directed that the labors of the seventy should not be interrupted by the Passover feast; Jesus advised that the messengers should go forward with their work in complete disregard of what was about to happen at Jerusalem. He also counseled Abner to permit the women's corps, at least such as desired, to go to Jerusalem for the Passover. And this was the last time Abner ever saw Jesus in the flesh. His farewell to Abner was: "My son, I know you will be true to the kingdom, and I pray the Father to grant you wisdom that you may love and understand your brethren."

As they traveled from city to city, large numbers of their followers deserted to go on to Jerusalem so that, by the time Jesus started for the Passover, the number of those who followed along with him day by day had dwindled to less than two hundred.

The apostles understood that Jesus was going to Jerusalem for the Passover. They knew that the Sanhedrin had broadcast a message to all Israel that he had been condemned to die and directing that anyone knowing his whereabouts should inform the Sanhedrin; and yet, despite all this, they were not so alarmed as they had been when he had announced to them in Philadelphia that he was going to Bethany to see Lazarus. This change of attitude from that of intense fear to a state of hushed expectancy was mostly because of Lazarus's resurrection. They had reached the conclusion that Jesus might, in an emergency, assert his divine power and put to shame his enemies. This hope, coupled with their more profound and mature faith in the spiritual supremacy of their Master, accounted for the outward courage displayed by his immediate followers, who now made ready to follow him into Jerusalem in the very face of the open declaration of the Sanhedrin that he must die.

The majority of the apostles and many of his inner disciples did not believe it possible for Jesus to die; they, believing that he was "the resurrection and the life," regarded him as immortal and already triumphant over death.

4. TEACHING AT LIVIAS

On Wednesday evening, March 29, Jesus and his followers encamped at Livias on their way to Jerusalem, after having completed their tour of the cities of southern Perea. It was during this night at Livias that Simon Zelotes and Simon Peter, having conspired to have delivered into their hands at this place more than one hundred swords, received and distributed these arms to all who would accept them and wear them concealed beneath their cloaks. Simon Peter was still wearing his sword on the night of the Master's betrayal in the garden.

Early on Thursday morning before the others were awake, Jesus called Andrew and said: "Awaken your brethren! I have something to say to them." Jesus knew about the swords and which of his apostles had received and were wearing these weapons, but he never disclosed to them that he knew such things. When Andrew had aroused his associates, and they had assembled off by themselves, Jesus said: "My children, you have been with me a long while, and I have taught you much that is needful for this time, but I would now warn you not to put your trust in the uncertainties of the flesh nor in the frailties of man's defense against the trials and testing which lie ahead of us. I have called you apart here by yourselves that I may once more plainly tell you that we are going up to Jerusalem, where you know the Son of Man has already been condemned to death. Again am I telling you that the Son of Man will be delivered into the hands of the chief priests and the religious rulers; that they will condemn him and then deliver him into the hands of the gentiles. And so will they mock the Son of Man, even spit upon him and scourge him, and they will deliver him up to death. And when they kill the Son of Man, be not dismayed, for I declare that on the third day he shall rise. Take heed to yourselves and remember that I have forewarned you."

Again were the apostles amazed, stunned; but they could not bring themselves to regard his words as literal; they could not comprehend that the Master meant just what he said. They were so blinded by their persistent belief in the temporal kingdom on earth, with headquarters at Jerusalem, that they simply could not—would not—permit themselves to accept Jesus' words as literal. They pondered all that day as to what the Master could mean by such strange pronouncements. But none of them dared to ask him a question concerning these statements. Not until after his death did these bewildered apostles wake up to the realization that the Master had spoken to them plainly and directly in anticipation of his crucifixion.

It was here at Livias, just after breakfast, that certain friendly Pharisees came to Jesus and said: "Flee in haste from these parts, for Herod, just as he sought John, now seeks to kill you. He fears an uprising of the people and has decided to kill you. We bring you this warning that you may escape."

And this was partly true. The resurrection of Lazarus frightened and alarmed Herod, and knowing that the Sanhedrin had dared to condemn Jesus, even in advance of a trial, Herod made up his mind either to kill Jesus or to drive him out of his domains. He really desired to do the latter since he so feared him that he hoped he would not be compelled to execute him.

When Jesus heard what the Pharisees had to say, he replied: "I well know about Herod and his fear of this gospel of the kingdom. But, mistake not, he would much prefer that the Son of Man go up to Jerusalem to suffer and die at the hands of the chief priests; he is not anxious, having stained his hands with the blood of John, to become responsible for the death of the Son of Man. Go you and tell that fox that the Son of Man preaches in Perea today, tomorrow goes into Judea, and after a few days, will be perfected in his mission on earth and prepared to ascend to the Father."

Then turning to his apostles, Jesus said: "From olden times the prophets have perished in Jerusalem, and it is only befitting that the Son of Man should go up to the city of the Father's house to be offered up as the price of human bigotry and as the result of religious prejudice and spiritual blindness. O Jerusalem, Jerusalem, which kills the prophets and stones the teachers of truth! How often would I have gathered your children together even as a hen gathers her own brood under her wings, but you would not let me do it! Behold, your house is about to be left to you desolate! You will many times desire to see me, but you shall not. You will then seek but not find me." And when he had spoken, he turned to those around him and said: "Nevertheless, let us go up to Jerusalem to attend the Passover and do that which becomes us in fulfilling the will of the Father in heaven."

It was a confused and bewildered group of believers who this day followed Jesus into Jericho. The apostles could discern only the certain note of final triumph in Jesus' declarations regarding the kingdom; they just could not bring themselves to that place where they were willing to grasp the warnings of the impending setback. When Jesus spoke of "rising on the third day," they seized upon this statement as signifying a sure triumph of the kingdom immediately following an unpleasant preliminary skirmish with the Jewish religious leaders. The "third day" was a common Jewish expression signifying "presently" or "soon thereafter." When Jesus spoke of "rising," they thought he referred to the "rising of the kingdom."

Jesus had been accepted by these believers as the Messiah, and the Jews knew little or nothing about a suffering Messiah. They did not understand that Jesus was to accomplish many things by his death which could never have been achieved by his life. While it was the resurrection of Lazarus that nerved the apostles to enter Jerusalem, it was the memory of the transfiguration that sustained the Master at this trying period of his bestowal.

5. THE BLIND MAN AT JERICHO

Late on the afternoon of Thursday, March 30, Jesus and his apostles, at the head of a band of about two hundred followers, approached the walls of Jericho. As they came near the gate of the city, they encountered a throng of beggars, among them one Bartimeus, an elderly man who had been blind from his youth. This blind beggar had heard much about Jesus and knew all about his healing of the blind Josiah at Jerusalem. He had not known of Jesus' last visit to Jericho until he had gone on to Bethany. Bartimeus had resolved that he would never again allow Jesus to visit Jericho without appealing to him for the restoration of his sight.

News of Jesus' approach had been heralded throughout Jericho, and hundreds of the inhabitants flocked forth to meet him. When this great crowd came back escorting the Master into the city, Bartimeus, hearing the heavy tramping of the multitude, knew that something unusual was happening, and so he asked those standing near him what was going on. And one of the beggars replied, "Jesus of Nazareth is passing by." When Bartimeus heard that Jesus was near, he lifted up his voice and began to cry aloud, "Jesus, Jesus, have mercy upon me!" And as he continued to cry louder and louder, some of those near to Jesus went over and rebuked him, requesting him to hold his peace; but it was of no avail; he cried only the more and the louder.

When Jesus heard the blind man crying out, he stood still. And when he saw him, he said to his friends, "Bring the man to me." And then they went over to Bartimeus, saying: "Be of good cheer; come with us, for the Master calls for you." When Bartimeus heard these words, he threw aside his cloak, springing forward toward the center of the road, while those near by guided him to Jesus. Addressing Bartimeus, Jesus said: "What do you want me to do for you?" Then answered the blind man, "I would have my sight restored." And when Jesus heard this request and saw his faith, he said: "You shall receive your sight; go your way; your faith has made you whole." Immediately he received his sight, and he remained near Jesus, glorifying God, until the Master started on the next day for Jerusalem, and then he went before the multitude declaring to all how his sight had been restored in Jericho.

6. THE VISIT TO ZACCHEUS

When the Master's procession entered Jericho, it was nearing sundown, and he was minded to abide there for the night. As Jesus passed by the customs house, Zaccheus the chief publican, or tax collector, happened to be present, and he much desired to see Jesus. This chief publican was very rich and had heard much about this prophet of Galilee. He had resolved that he would see what sort of a man Jesus was the next time he chanced to visit Jericho; accordingly, Zaccheus sought to press through the crowd, but it was too great, and being short of stature, he could not see over their heads. And so the chief publican followed on with the crowd until they came near the center of the city and not far from where he lived. When he saw that he would be unable to penetrate the crowd, and thinking that Jesus might be going right on through the city without stopping, he ran on ahead and climbed up into a sycamore tree whose spreading branches overhung the roadway. He knew that in this way he could obtain a good view of the Master as he passed by. And he was not disappointed, for, as Jesus passed by, he stopped and, looking up at Zaccheus, said: "Make haste, Zaccheus, and come down, for tonight I must abide at your house." And when Zaccheus heard these astonishing words, he almost fell out of the tree in his haste to get down, and going up to Jesus, he expressed great joy that the Master should be willing to stop at his house.

They went at once to the home of Zaccheus, and those who lived in Jericho were much surprised that Jesus would consent to abide with the chief publican. Even while the Master and his apostles lingered with Zaccheus before the door of his house, one of the Jericho Pharisees, standing near by, said: "You see how this man has gone to lodge with a sinner, an apostate son of Abraham who is an extortioner and a robber of his own people." And when Jesus heard this, he looked down at Zaccheus and smiled. Then Zaccheus stood upon a stool and said: "Men of Jericho, hear me! I may be a publican and a sinner, but the great Teacher has come to abide in my house; and before he goes in, I tell you that I am going to bestow one half of all my goods upon the poor, and beginning tomorrow, if I have wrongfully exacted aught from any man, I will restore fourfold. I am going to seek salvation with all my heart and learn to do righteousness in the sight of God."

When Zaccheus had ceased speaking, Jesus said: "Today has salvation come to this home, and you have become indeed a son of Abraham." And turning to the crowd assembled about them, Jesus said: "And marvel not at what I say nor take offense at what we do, for I have all along declared that the Son of Man has come to seek and to save that which is lost."

They lodged with Zaccheus for the night. On the morrow they arose and made their way up the "road of robbers" to Bethany on their way to the Passover at Jerusalem.

7. "AS JESUS PASSED BY"

Jesus spread good cheer everywhere he went. He was full of grace and truth. His associates never ceased to wonder at the gracious words that proceeded out of his mouth. You can cultivate gracefulness, but graciousness is the aroma of friendliness which emanates from a love-saturated soul.

Goodness always compels respect, but when it is devoid of grace, it often repels affection. Goodness is universally attractive only when it is gracious. Goodness is effective only when it is attractive.

Jesus really understood men; therefore could he manifest genuine sympathy and show sincere compassion. But he seldom indulged in pity. While his compassion was boundless, his sympathy was practical, personal, and constructive. Never did his familiarity with suffering breed indifference, and he was able to minister to distressed souls without increasing their self-pity.

Jesus could help men so much because he loved them so sincerely. He truly loved each man, each woman, and each child. He could be such a true friend because of his remarkable insight—he knew so fully what was in the heart and in the mind of man. He was an interested and keen observer. He was an expert in the comprehension of human need, clever in detecting human longings.

Jesus was never in a hurry. He had time to comfort his fellow men "as he passed by." And he always made his friends feel at ease. He was a charming listener. He never engaged in the meddlesome probing of the souls of his associates. As he comforted hungry minds and ministered to thirsty souls, the recipients of his mercy did not so much feel that they were confessing *to* him as that they were conferring *with* him. They had unbounded confidence in him because they saw he had so much faith in them.

He never seemed to be curious about people, and he never manifested a desire to direct, manage, or follow them up. He inspired profound self-confidence and robust courage in all who enjoyed his association. When he smiled on a man, that mortal experienced increased capacity for solving his manifold problems.

Jesus loved men so much and so wisely that he never hesitated to be severe with them when the occasion demanded such discipline. He frequently set out to help a person by asking for help. In this way he elicited interest, appealed to the better things in human nature.

The Master could discern saving faith in the gross superstition of the woman who sought healing by touching the hem of his garment. He was always ready and willing to stop a sermon or detain a multitude while he ministered to the needs of a single person, even to a little child. Great things happened not only because people had faith in Jesus, but also because Jesus had so much faith in them.

Most of the really important things which Jesus said or did seemed to happen casually, "as he passed by." There was so little of the professional, the well-planned, or the premeditated in the Master's earthly ministry. He dispensed health and scattered happiness naturally and gracefully as he journeyed through life. It was literally true, "He went about doing good."

And it behooves the Master's followers in all ages to learn to minister as "they pass by"—to do unselfish good as they go about their daily duties.

8. PARABLE OF THE POUNDS

They did not start from Jericho until near noon since they sat up late the night before while Jesus taught Zaccheus and his family the gospel of the kingdom. About halfway up the ascending road to Bethany the party paused for lunch while the multitude passed on to Jerusalem, not knowing that Jesus and the apostles were going to abide that night on the Mount of Olives.

The parable of the pounds, unlike the parable of the talents, which was intended for all the disciples, was spoken more exclusively to the apostles and was largely based on the experience of Archelaus and his futile attempt to gain the rule of the kingdom of Judea. This is one of the few parables of the Master to be founded on an actual historic character. It was not strange that they should have had Archelaus in mind inasmuch as the house of Zaccheus in Jericho was very near the ornate palace of Archelaus, and his aqueduct ran along the road by which they had departed from Jericho.

Said Jesus: "You think that the Son of Man goes up to Jerusalem to receive a kingdom, but I declare that you are doomed to disappointment. Do you not remember about a certain prince who went into a far country to receive for himself a kingdom, but even before he could return, the citizens of his province, who in their hearts had already rejected him, sent an embassy after him, saying, 'We will not have this man to reign over us'? As this king was rejected in the temporal rule, so is the Son of Man to be rejected in the spiritual rule. Again I declare that my kingdom is not of this world; but if the Son of Man had been accorded the spiritual rule of his people, he would have accepted such a kingdom of men's souls and would have reigned over such a dominion of human hearts. Notwithstanding that they reject my spiritual rule over them, I will return again to receive from others such a kingdom of spirit as is now denied me. You will see the Son of Man rejected now, but in another age that which the children of Abraham now reject will be received and exalted.

"And now, as the rejected nobleman of this parable, I would call before me my twelve servants, special stewards, and giving into each of your hands the sum of one pound, I would admonish each to heed well my instructions that you trade diligently with your trust fund while I am away that you may have wherewith to justify your stewardship when I return, when a reckoning shall be required of you.

"And even if this rejected Son should not return, another Son will be sent to receive this kingdom, and this Son will then send for all of you to receive your report of stewardship and to be made glad by your gains.

"And when these stewards were subsequently called together for an accounting, the first came forward, saying, 'Lord, with your pound I have made ten pounds more.' And his master said to him: 'Well done; you are a good servant; because you have proved faithful in this matter, I will give you authority over ten cities.' And the second came, saying, 'Your pound left with me, Lord, has made five pounds.' And the master said, 'I will accordingly make you ruler over five cities.' And so on down through the others until the last of the servants, on being called to account, reported: 'Lord, behold, here is your pound, which I have kept safely done up in this napkin. And this I did because I feared you; I believed that you were unreasonable, seeing that you take up where you have not laid down, and that you seek to reap where you have not sown.' Then said his lord: 'You negligent and unfaithful servant, I will judge you out of your own mouth. You knew that I reap where I have apparently not sown; therefore you knew this reckoning would be required of you. Knowing this, you should have at least given my money to the banker that at my coming I might have had it with proper interest.'

"And then said this ruler to those who stood by: 'Take the money from this slothful servant and give it to him who has ten pounds.' And when they reminded the master that such a one already had ten pounds, he said: 'To every one who has shall be given more, but from him who has not, even that which he has shall be taken away from him.'"

And then the apostles sought to know the difference between the meaning of this parable and that of the former parable of the talents, but Jesus would only say, in answer to their many questions: "Ponder well these words in your hearts while each of you finds out their true meaning."

It was Nathaniel who so well taught the meaning of these two parables in the after years, summing up his teachings in these conclusions:

1. Ability is the practical measure of life's opportunities. You will never be held responsible for the accomplishment of that which is beyond your abilities.

2. Faithfulness is the unerring measure of human trustworthiness. He who is faithful in little things is also likely to exhibit faithfulness in everything consistent with his endowments.

3. The Master grants the lesser reward for lesser faithfulness when there is like opportunity.

4. He grants a like reward for like faithfulness when there is lesser opportunity.

When they had finished their lunch, and after the multitude of followers had gone on toward Jerusalem, Jesus, standing there before the apostles in the shade of an overhanging rock by the roadside, with cheerful dignity and a gracious majesty pointed his finger westward, saying: "Come, my brethren, let us go on into Jerusalem, there to receive that which awaits us; thus shall we fulfill the will of the heavenly Father in all things."

And so Jesus and his apostles resumed this, the Master's last journey to Jerusalem in the likeness of the flesh of mortal man.

PAPER 172

GOING INTO JERUSALEM

JESUS and the apostles arrived at Bethany shortly after four o'clock on Friday afternoon, March 31, A.D. 30. Lazarus, his sisters, and their friends were expecting them; and since so many people came every day to talk with Lazarus about his resurrection, Jesus was informed that arrangements had been made for him to stay with a neighboring believer, one Simon, the leading citizen of the little village since the death of Lazarus's father.

That evening, Jesus received many visitors, and the common folks of Bethany and Bethpage did their best to make him feel welcome. Although many thought Jesus was now going into Jerusalem, in utter defiance of the Sanhedrin's decree of death, to proclaim himself king of the Jews, the Bethany family—Lazarus, Martha, and Mary—more fully realized that the Master was not that kind of a king; they dimly felt that this might be his last visit to Jerusalem and Bethany.

The chief priests were informed that Jesus lodged at Bethany, but they thought best not to attempt to seize him among his friends; they decided to await his coming on into Jerusalem. Jesus knew about all this, but he was majestically calm; his friends had never seen him more composed and congenial; even the apostles were astounded that he should be so unconcerned when the Sanhedrin had called upon all Jewry to deliver him into their hands. While the Master slept that night, the apostles watched over him by twos, and many of them were girded with swords. Early the next morning they were awakened by hundreds of pilgrims who came out from Jerusalem, even on the Sabbath day, to see Jesus and Lazarus, whom he had raised from the dead.

1. SABBATH AT BETHANY

Pilgrims from outside of Judea, as well as the Jewish authorities, had all been asking: "What do you think? will Jesus come up to the feast?" Therefore, when the people heard that Jesus was at Bethany, they were glad, but the chief priests and Pharisees were somewhat perplexed. They were pleased to have him under their jurisdiction, but they were a trifle disconcerted by his boldness; they remembered that on his previous visit to Bethany, Lazarus had been raised from the dead, and Lazarus was becoming a big problem to the enemies of Jesus.

Six days before the Passover, on the evening after the Sabbath, all Bethany and Bethpage joined in celebrating the arrival of Jesus by a public banquet at the home of Simon. This supper was in honor of both Jesus and Lazarus; it was tendered in defiance of the Sanhedrin. Martha directed the serving of the food; her sister Mary was among the women onlookers as it was against the custom of the Jews for a woman to sit at a public banquet. The agents of the Sanhedrin were present, but they feared to apprehend Jesus in the midst of his friends.

Jesus talked with Simon about Joshua of old, whose namesake he was, and recited how Joshua and the Israelites had come up to Jerusalem through Jericho. In commenting on the legend of the walls of Jericho falling down, Jesus said: "I am not concerned with such walls of brick and stone; but I would cause the walls of prejudice, self-righteousness, and hate to crumble before this preaching of the Father's love for all men."

The banquet went along in a very cheerful and normal manner except that all the apostles were unusually sober. Jesus was exceptionally cheerful and had been playing with the children up to the time of coming to the table.

Nothing out of the ordinary happened until near the close of the feasting when Mary the sister of Lazarus stepped forward from among the group of women onlookers and, going up to where Jesus reclined as the guest of honor, proceeded to open a large alabaster cruse of very rare and costly ointment; and after anointing the Master's head, she began to pour it upon his feet as she took down her hair and wiped them with it. The whole house became filled with the odor of the ointment, and everybody present was amazed at what Mary had done. Lazarus said nothing, but when some of the people murmured, showing indignation that so costly an ointment should be thus used, Judas Iscariot stepped over to where Andrew reclined and said: "Why was this ointment not sold and the money bestowed to feed the poor? You should speak to the Master that he rebuke such waste."

Jesus, knowing what they thought and hearing what they said, put his hand upon Mary's head as she knelt by his side and, with a kindly expression upon his face, said: "Let her alone, every one of you. Why do you trouble her about this, seeing that she has done a good thing in her heart? To you who murmur and say that this ointment should have been sold and the money given to the poor, let me say that you have the poor always with you so that you may minister to them at any time it seems good to you; but I shall not always be with you; I go soon to my Father. This woman has long saved this ointment for my body at its burial, and now that it has seemed good to her to make this anointing in anticipation of my death, she shall not be denied such satisfaction. In the doing of this, Mary has reproved all of you in that by this act she evinces faith in what I have said about my death and ascension to my Father in heaven. This woman shall not be reproved for that which she has this night done; rather do I say to you that in the ages to come, wherever this gospel shall be preached throughout the whole world, what she has done will be spoken of in memory of her."

It was because of this rebuke, which he took as a personal reproof, that Judas Iscariot finally made up his mind to seek revenge for his hurt feelings. Many times had he entertained such ideas subconsciously, but now he dared to think such wicked thoughts in his open and conscious mind. And many others encouraged him in this attitude since the cost of this ointment was a sum equal to the earnings of one man for one year—enough to provide bread for five thousand persons. But Mary loved Jesus; she had provided this precious ointment with which to embalm his body in death, for she believed his words when he forewarned them that he must die, and it was not to be denied her if she changed her mind and chose to bestow this offering upon the Master while he yet lived.

Both Lazarus and Martha knew that Mary had long saved the money wherewith to buy this cruse of spikenard, and they heartily approved of her doing as her heart desired in such a matter, for they were well-to-do and could easily afford to make such an offering.

When the chief priests heard of this dinner in Bethany for Jesus and Lazarus, they began to take counsel among themselves as to what should be done with Lazarus. And presently they decided that Lazarus must also die. They rightly concluded that it would be useless to put Jesus to death if they permitted Lazarus, whom he had raised from the dead, to live.

2. SUNDAY MORNING WITH THE APOSTLES

On this Sunday morning, in Simon's beautiful garden, the Master called his twelve apostles around him and gave them their final instructions preparatory to entering Jerusalem. He told them that he would probably deliver many addresses and teach many lessons before returning to the Father but advised the apostles to refrain from doing any public work during this Passover sojourn in Jerusalem. He instructed them to remain near him and to "watch and pray." Jesus knew that many of his apostles and immediate followers even then carried swords concealed on their persons, but he made no reference to this fact.

This morning's instructions embraced a brief review of their ministry from the day of their ordination near Capernaum down to this day when they were preparing to enter Jerusalem. The apostles listened in silence; they asked no questions.

Early that morning David Zebedee had turned over to Judas the funds realized from the sale of the equipment of the Pella encampment, and Judas, in turn, had placed the greater part of this money in the hands of Simon, their host, for safekeeping in anticipation of the exigencies of their entry into Jerusalem.

After the conference with the apostles Jesus held converse with Lazarus and instructed him to avoid the sacrifice of his life to the vengefulness of the Sanhedrin. It was in obedience to this admonition that Lazarus, a few days later, fled to Philadelphia when the officers of the Sanhedrin sent men to arrest him.

In a way, all of Jesus' followers sensed the impending crisis, but they were prevented from fully realizing its seriousness by the unusual cheerfulness and exceptional good humor of the Master.

3. THE START FOR JERUSALEM

Bethany was about two miles from the temple, and it was half past one that Sunday afternoon when Jesus made ready to start for Jerusalem. He had feelings of profound affection for Bethany and its simple people. Nazareth, Capernaum, and Jerusalem had rejected him, but Bethany had accepted him, had believed in him. And it was in this small village, where almost every man, woman, and child were believers, that he chose to perform the mightiest work of his earth bestowal, the resurrection of Lazarus. He did not raise Lazarus that the villagers might believe, but rather because they already believed.

All morning Jesus had thought about his entry into Jerusalem. Heretofore he had always endeavored to suppress all public acclaim of him as the Messiah, but it was different now; he was nearing the end of his career in the flesh, his death had been decreed by the Sanhedrin, and no harm could come from allowing his disciples to give free expression to their feelings, just as might occur if he elected to make a formal and public entry into the city.

Jesus did not decide to make this public entrance into Jerusalem as a last bid for popular favor nor as a final grasp for power. Neither did he do it altogether to satisfy the human longings of his disciples and apostles. Jesus entertained none of the illusions of a fantastic dreamer; he well knew what was to be the outcome of this visit.

Having decided upon making a public entrance into Jerusalem, the Master was confronted with the necessity of choosing a proper method of executing such a resolve. Jesus thought over all of the many more or less contradictory so-called Messianic prophecies, but there seemed to be only one which was at all appropriate for him to follow. Most of these prophetic utterances depicted a king, the son and successor of David, a bold and aggressive temporal deliverer of all Israel from the yoke of foreign domination. But there was one Scripture that had sometimes been associated with the Messiah by those who held more to the spiritual concept of his mission, which Jesus thought might consistently be taken as a guide for his projected entry into Jerusalem. This Scripture was found in Zechariah, and it said: "Rejoice greatly, O daughter of Zion; shout, O daughter of Jerusalem. Behold, your king comes to you. He is just and he brings salvation. He comes as the lowly one, riding upon an ass, upon a colt, the foal of an ass."

A warrior king always entered a city riding upon a horse; a king on a mission of peace and friendship always entered riding upon an ass. Jesus would not enter Jerusalem as a man on horseback, but he was willing to enter peacefully and with good will as the Son of Man on a donkey.

Jesus had long tried by direct teaching to impress upon his apostles and his disciples that his kingdom was not of this world, that it was a purely spiritual matter; but he had not succeeded in this effort. Now, what he had failed to do by plain and personal teaching, he would attempt to accomplish by a symbolic appeal. Accordingly, right after the noon lunch, Jesus called Peter and John, and after directing them to go over to Bethpage, a neighboring village a little off the main road and a short distance northwest of Bethany, he further said: "Go to Bethpage, and when you come to the junction of the roads, you will find the colt of an ass tied there. Loose the colt and bring it back with you. If any one asks you why you do this, merely say, 'The Master has need of him.'" And when the two apostles had gone into Bethpage as the Master had directed, they found the colt tied near his mother in the open street and close to a house on the corner. As Peter began to untie the colt, the owner came over and asked why they did this, and when Peter answered him as Jesus had directed, the man said: "If your Master is Jesus from Galilee, let him have the colt." And so they returned bringing the colt with them.

By this time several hundred pilgrims had gathered around Jesus and his apostles. Since midforenoon the visitors passing by on their way to the Passover had tarried. Meanwhile, David Zebedee and some of his former messenger associates took it upon themselves to hasten on down to Jerusalem, where they effectively spread the report among the throngs of visiting pilgrims about the temple that Jesus of Nazareth was making a triumphal entry into the city. Accordingly, several thousand of these visitors flocked forth to greet this much-talked-of prophet and wonder-worker, whom some believed to be the Messiah. This multitude, coming out from Jerusalem, met Jesus and the crowd going into the city just after they had passed over the brow of Olivet and had begun the descent into the city.

As the procession started out from Bethany, there was great enthusiasm among the festive crowd of disciples, believers, and visiting pilgrims, many hailing from Galilee and Perea. Just before they started, the twelve women of the original women's corps, accompanied by some of their associates, arrived on the scene and joined this unique procession as it moved on joyously toward the city.

Before they started, the Alpheus twins put their cloaks on the donkey and held him while the Master got on. As the procession moved toward the summit of Olivet, the festive crowd threw their garments on the ground and brought branches from the near-by trees in order to make a carpet of honor for the donkey bearing the royal Son, the promised Messiah. As the merry crowd moved on toward Jerusalem, they began to sing, or rather to shout in unison, the Psalm, "Hosanna to the son of David; blessed is he who comes in the name of the Lord. Hosanna in the highest. Blessed be the kingdom that comes down from heaven."

Jesus was lighthearted and cheerful as they moved along until he came to the brow of Olivet, where the city and the temple towers came into full view; there the Master stopped the procession, and a great silence came upon all as they beheld him weeping. Looking down upon the vast multitude coming forth from the city to greet him, the Master, with much emotion and with tearful voice, said: "O Jerusalem, if you had only known, even you, at least in this your day, the things which belong to your peace, and which you could so freely have had! But now are these glories about to be hid from your eyes. You are about to reject the Son of Peace and turn your backs upon the gospel of salvation. The days will soon come upon you wherein your enemies will cast a trench around about you and lay siege to you on every side; they shall utterly destroy you, insomuch that not one stone shall be left upon another. And all this shall befall you because you knew not the time of your divine visitation. You are about to reject the gift of God, and all men will reject you."

When he had finished speaking, they began the descent of Olivet and presently were joined by the multitude of visitors who had come from Jerusalem waving palm branches, shouting hosannas, and otherwise expressing gleefulness and good fellowship. The Master had not planned that these crowds should come out from Jerusalem to meet them; that was the work of others. He never premeditated anything which was dramatic.

Along with the multitude which poured out to welcome the Master, there came also many of the Pharisees and his other enemies. They were so much perturbed by this sudden and unexpected outburst of popular acclaim that they feared to arrest him lest such action precipitate an open revolt of the populace. They greatly feared the attitude of the large numbers of visitors, who had heard much of Jesus, and who, many of them, believed in him.

As they neared Jerusalem, the crowd became more demonstrative, so much so that some of the Pharisees made their way up alongside Jesus and said: "Teacher, you should rebuke your disciples and exhort them to behave more seemly." Jesus answered: "It is only fitting that these children should welcome the Son of Peace, whom the chief priests have rejected. It would be useless to stop them lest in their stead these stones by the roadside cry out."

The Pharisees hastened on ahead of the procession to rejoin the Sanhedrin, which was then in session at the temple, and they reported to their associates: "Behold, all that we do is of no avail; we are confounded by this Galilean. The people have gone mad over him; if we do not stop these ignorant ones, all the world will go after him."

There really was no deep significance to be attached to this superficial and spontaneous outburst of popular enthusiasm. This welcome, although it was joyous and sincere, did not betoken any real or deep-seated conviction in the hearts of this festive multitude. These same crowds were equally as willing quickly to reject Jesus later on this week when the Sanhedrin once took a firm and decided stand against him, and when they became disillusioned—when they realized that Jesus was not going to establish the kingdom in accordance with their long-cherished expectations.

But the whole city was mightily stirred up, insomuch that everyone asked, "Who is this man?" And the multitude answered, "This is the prophet of Galilee, Jesus of Nazareth."

4. VISITING ABOUT THE TEMPLE

While the Alpheus twins returned the donkey to its owner, Jesus and the ten apostles detached themselves from their immediate associates and strolled about the temple, viewing the preparations for the Passover. No attempt was made to molest Jesus as the Sanhedrin greatly feared the people, and that was, after all, one of the reasons Jesus had for allowing the multitude thus to acclaim him. The apostles little understood that this was the only human procedure which could have been effective in preventing Jesus' immediate arrest upon entering the city. The Master desired to give the inhabitants of Jerusalem, high and low, as well as the tens of thousands of Passover visitors, this one more and last chance to hear the gospel and receive, if they would, the Son of Peace.

And now, as the evening drew on and the crowds went in quest of nourishment, Jesus and his immediate followers were left alone. What a strange day it had been! The apostles were thoughtful, but speechless. Never, in their years of association with Jesus, had they seen such a day. For a moment they sat down by the treasury, watching the people drop in their contributions: the rich putting much in the receiving box and all giving something in accordance with the extent of their possessions. At last there came along a poor widow, scantily attired, and they observed as she cast two mites (small coppers) into the trumpet. And then said Jesus, calling the attention of the apostles to the widow: "Heed well what you have just seen. This poor widow cast in more than all the others, for all these others, from their superfluity, cast in some trifle as a gift, but this poor woman, even though she is in want, gave all that she had, even her living."

As the evening drew on, they walked about the temple courts in silence, and after Jesus had surveyed these familiar scenes once more, recalling his emotions in connection with previous visits, not excepting the earlier ones, he said, "Let us go up to Bethany for our rest." Jesus, with Peter and John, went to the home of Simon, while the other apostles lodged among their friends in Bethany and Bethpage.

5. THE APOSTLES' ATTITUDE

This Sunday evening as they returned to Bethany, Jesus walked in front of the apostles. Not a word was spoken until they separated after arriving at Simon's house. No twelve human beings ever experienced such diverse and inexplicable emotions as now surged through the minds and souls of these ambassadors of the kingdom. These sturdy Galileans were confused and disconcerted; they did not know what to expect next; they were too surprised to be much afraid. They knew nothing of the Master's plans for the next day, and they asked no questions. They went to their lodgings, though they did not sleep much, save the twins. But they did not keep armed watch over Jesus at Simon's house.

Andrew was thoroughly bewildered, well-nigh confused. He was the one apostle who did not seriously undertake to evaluate the popular outburst of acclaim. He was too preoccupied with the thought of his responsibility as chief of the apostolic corps to give serious consideration to the meaning or significance of the loud hosannas of the multitude. Andrew was busy watching some of his associates who he feared might be led away by their emotions during the excitement, particularly Peter, James, John, and Simon Zelotes. Throughout this day and those which immediately followed, Andrew was troubled with serious doubts, but he never expressed any of these misgivings to his apostolic associates. He was concerned about the attitude of some of the twelve who he knew were armed with swords; but he did not know that his own brother, Peter, was carrying such a weapon. And so the procession into Jerusalem made a comparatively superficial impression upon Andrew; he was too busy with the responsibilities of his office to be otherwise affected.

Simon Peter was at first almost swept off his feet by this popular manifestation of enthusiasm; but he was considerably sobered by the time they returned to Bethany that night. Peter simply could not figure out what the Master was about. He was terribly disappointed that Jesus did not follow up this wave of popular favor with some kind of a pronouncement. Peter could not understand why Jesus did not speak to the multitude when they arrived at the temple, or at least permit one of the apostles to address the crowd. Peter was a great preacher, and he disliked to see such a large, receptive, and enthusiastic audience go to waste. He would so much have liked to preach the gospel of the kingdom to that throng right there in the temple; but the Master had specifically charged them that they were to do no teaching or preaching while in Jerusalem this Passover week. The reaction from the spectacular procession into the city was disastrous to Simon Peter; by night he was sobered and inexpressibly saddened.

To James Zebedee, this Sunday was a day of perplexity and profound confusion; he could not grasp the purport of what was going on; he could not comprehend the Master's purpose in permitting this wild acclaim and then in refusing to say a word to the people when they arrived at the temple. As the procession moved down Olivet toward Jerusalem, more especially when they were met by the thousands of pilgrims who poured forth to welcome the Master, James was cruelly torn by his conflicting emotions of elation and gratification at what he saw and by his profound feeling of fear as to what would happen when they reached the temple. And then was he downcast and overcome by disappointment when Jesus climbed off the donkey and proceeded to walk leisurely about the temple courts. James could not understand the reason for throwing away such a magnificent opportunity to proclaim the kingdom. By night, his mind was held firmly in the grip of a distressing and dreadful uncertainty.

John Zebedee came somewhere near understanding why Jesus did this; at least he grasped in part the spiritual significance of this so-called triumphal entry into Jerusalem. As the multitude moved on toward the temple, and as John beheld his Master sitting there astride the colt, he recalled hearing Jesus onetime quote the passage of Scripture, the utterance of Zechariah, which described the coming of the Messiah as a man of peace and riding into Jerusalem on an ass.

As John turned this Scripture over in his mind, he began to comprehend the symbolic significance of this Sunday-afternoon pageant. At least, he grasped enough of the meaning of this Scripture to enable him somewhat to enjoy the episode and to prevent his becoming overmuch depressed by the apparent purposeless ending of the triumphal procession. John had a type of mind which naturally tended to think and feel in symbols.

Philip was entirely unsettled by the suddenness and spontaneity of the outburst. He could not collect his thoughts sufficiently while on the way down Olivet to arrive at any settled notion as to what all the demonstration was about. In a way, he enjoyed the performance because his Master was being honored. By the time they reached the temple, he was perturbed by the thought that Jesus might possibly ask him to feed the multitude, so that the conduct of Jesus in turning leisurely away from the crowds, which so sorely disappointed the majority of the apostles, was a great relief to Philip. Multitudes had sometimes been a great trial to the steward of the twelve. After he was relieved of these personal fears regarding the material needs of the crowds, Philip joined with Peter in the expression of disappointment that nothing was done to teach the multitude. That night Philip got to thinking over these experiences and was tempted to doubt the whole idea of the kingdom; he honestly wondered what all these things could mean, but he expressed his doubts to no one; he loved Jesus too much. He had great personal faith in the Master.

Nathaniel, aside from the symbolic and prophetic aspects, came the nearest to understanding the Master's reason for enlisting the popular support of the Passover pilgrims. He reasoned it out, before they reached the temple, that without such a demonstrative entry into Jerusalem Jesus would have been arrested by the Sanhedrin officials and cast into prison the moment he presumed to enter the city. He was not, therefore, in the least surprised that the Master made no further use of the cheering crowds when he had once got inside the walls of the city and had thus so forcibly impressed the Jewish leaders that they would refrain from placing him under immediate arrest. Understanding the real reason for the Master's entering the city in this manner, Nathaniel naturally followed along with more poise and was less perturbed and disappointed by Jesus' subsequent conduct than were the other apostles. Nathaniel had great confidence in Jesus' understanding of men as well as in his sagacity and cleverness in handling difficult situations.

Matthew was at first nonplused by this pageant performance. He did not grasp the meaning of what his eyes were seeing until he also recalled the Scripture in Zechariah where the prophet had alluded to the rejoicing of Jerusalem because her king had come bringing salvation and riding upon the colt of an ass. As the procession moved in the direction of the city and then drew on toward the temple, Matthew became ecstatic; he was certain that something extraordinary would happen when the Master arrived at the temple at the head of this shouting multitude. When one of the Pharisees mocked Jesus, saying, "Look, everybody, see who comes here, the king of the Jews riding on an ass!" Matthew kept his hands off of him only by exercising great restraint. None of the twelve was more depressed on the way back to Bethany that evening. Next to Simon Peter and Simon Zelotes, he experienced the highest nervous tension and was in a state of exhaustion by night. But by morning Matthew was much cheered; he was, after all, a cheerful loser.

Thomas was the most bewildered and puzzled man of all the twelve. Most of the time he just followed along, gazing at the spectacle and honestly wondering what could be the Master's motive for participating in such a peculiar demonstration. Down deep in his heart he regarded the whole performance as a little childish, if not downright foolish. He had never seen Jesus do anything like this and was at a loss to account for his strange conduct on this Sunday afternoon. By the time they reached the temple, Thomas had deduced that the purpose of this popular demonstration was so to frighten the Sanhedrin that they would not dare immediately to arrest the Master. On the way back to Bethany Thomas thought much but said nothing. By bedtime the Master's cleverness in staging the tumultuous entry into Jerusalem had begun to make a somewhat humorous appeal, and he was much cheered up by this reaction.

This Sunday started off as a great day for Simon Zelotes. He saw visions of wonderful doings in Jerusalem the next few days, and in that he was right, but Simon dreamed of the establishment of the new national rule of the Jews, with Jesus on the throne of David. Simon saw the nationalists springing into action as soon as the kingdom was announced, and himself in supreme command of the assembling military forces of the new kingdom. On the way down Olivet he even envisaged the Sanhedrin and all of their sympathizers dead before sunset of that day. He really believed something great was going to happen. He was the noisiest man in the whole multitude. By five o'clock that afternoon he was a silent, crushed, and disillusioned apostle. He never fully recovered from the depression which settled down on him as a result of this day's shock; at least not until long after the Master's resurrection.

To the Alpheus twins this was a perfect day. They really enjoyed it all the way through, and not being present during the time of quiet visitation about the temple, they escaped much of the anticlimax of the popular upheaval. They could not possibly understand the downcast behavior of the apostles when they came back to Bethany that evening. In the memory of the twins this was always their day of being nearest heaven on earth. This day was the satisfying climax of their whole career as apostles. And the memory of the elation of this Sunday afternoon carried them on through all of the tragedy of this eventful week, right up to the hour of the crucifixion. It was the most befitting entry of the king the twins could conceive; they enjoyed every moment of the whole pageant. They fully approved of all they saw and long cherished the memory.

Of all the apostles, Judas Iscariot was the most adversely affected by this processional entry into Jerusalem. His mind was in a disagreeable ferment because of the Master's rebuke the preceding day in connection with Mary's anointing at the feast in Simon's house. Judas was disgusted with the whole spectacle. To him it seemed childish, if not indeed ridiculous. As this vengeful apostle looked upon the proceedings of this Sunday afternoon, Jesus seemed to him more to resemble a clown than a king. He heartily resented the whole performance. He shared the views of the Greeks and Romans, who looked down upon anyone who would consent to ride upon an ass or the colt of an ass. By the time the triumphal procession had entered the city, Judas had about made up his mind to abandon the whole idea of such a kingdom; he was almost resolved to forsake all such farcical attempts to establish the kingdom of heaven. And then he thought of the resurrection of Lazarus, and many other things, and decided to stay on with the twelve, at least for another day. Besides, he carried the bag, and he would not desert with the apostolic funds in his possession. On the way back to Bethany that night his conduct did not seem strange since all of the apostles were equally downcast and silent.

Judas was tremendously influenced by the ridicule of his Sadducean friends. No other single factor exerted such a powerful influence on him, in his final determination to forsake Jesus and his fellow apostles, as a certain episode which occurred just as Jesus reached the gate of the city: A prominent Sadducee (a friend of Judas's family) rushed up to him in a spirit of gleeful ridicule and, slapping him on the back, said: "Why so troubled of countenance, my good friend; cheer up and join us all while we acclaim this Jesus of Nazareth the king of the Jews as he rides through the gates of Jerusalem seated on an ass." Judas had never shrunk from persecution, but he could not stand this sort of ridicule. With the long-nourished emotion of revenge there was now blended this fatal fear of ridicule, that terrible and fearful feeling of being ashamed of his Master and his fellow apostles. At heart, this ordained ambassador of the kingdom was already a deserter; it only remained for him to find some plausible excuse for an open break with the Master.

PAPER 173

MONDAY IN JERUSALEM

EARLY on this Monday morning, by prearrangement, Jesus and the apostles assembled at the home of Simon in Bethany, and after a brief conference they set out for Jerusalem. The twelve were strangely silent as they journeyed on toward the temple; they had not recovered from the experience of the preceding day. They were expectant, fearful, and profoundly affected by a certain feeling of detachment growing out of the Master's sudden change of tactics, coupled with his instruction that they were to engage in no public teaching throughout this Passover week.

As this group journeyed down Mount Olivet, Jesus led the way, the apostles following closely behind in meditative silence. There was just one thought uppermost in the minds of all save Judas Iscariot, and that was: What will the Master do today? The one absorbing thought of Judas was: What shall I do? Shall I go on with Jesus and my associates, or shall I withdraw? And if I am going to quit, how shall I break off?

It was about nine o'clock on this beautiful morning when these men arrived at the temple. They went at once to the large court where Jesus so often taught, and after greeting the believers who were awaiting him, Jesus mounted one of the teaching platforms and began to address the gathering crowd. The apostles withdrew for a short distance and awaited developments.

1. CLEANSING THE TEMPLE

A huge commercial traffic had grown up in association with the services and ceremonies of the temple worship. There was the business of providing suitable animals for the various sacrifices. Though it was permissible for a worshiper to provide his own sacrifice, the fact remained that this animal must be free from all "blemish" in the meaning of the Levitical law and as interpreted by official inspectors of the temple. Many a worshiper had experienced the humiliation of having his supposedly perfect animal rejected by the temple examiners. It therefore became the more general practice to purchase sacrificial animals at the temple, and although there were several stations on near-by Olivet where they could be bought, it had become the vogue to buy these animals directly from the temple pens. Gradually there had grown up this custom of selling all kinds of sacrificial animals in the temple courts. An extensive business, in which enormous profits were made, had thus been brought into existence. Part of these gains was reserved for the temple treasury, but the larger part went indirectly into the hands of the ruling high-priestly families.

This sale of animals in the temple prospered because, when the worshiper purchased such an animal, although the price might be somewhat high, no more fees had to be paid, and he could be sure the intended sacrifice would not be rejected on the ground of possessing real or technical blemishes. At one time or another systems of exorbitant overcharge were practiced upon the common people, especially during the great national feasts. At one time the greedy priests went so far as to demand the equivalent of the value of a week's labor for a pair of doves which should have been sold to the poor for a few pennies. The "sons of Annas" had already begun to establish their bazaars in the temple precincts, those very merchandise marts which persisted to the time of their final overthrow by a mob three years before the destruction of the temple itself.

But traffic in sacrificial animals and sundry merchandise was not the only way in which the courts of the temple were profaned. At this time there was fostered an extensive system of banking and commercial exchange which was carried on right within the temple precincts. And this all came about in the following manner: During the Asmonean dynasty the Jews coined their own silver money, and it had become the practice to require the temple dues of one-half shekel and all other temple fees to be paid with this Jewish coin. This regulation necessitated that money-changers be licensed to exchange the many sorts of currency in circulation throughout Palestine and other provinces of the Roman Empire for this orthodox shekel of Jewish coining. The temple head tax, payable by all except women, slaves, and minors, was one-half shekel, a coin about the size of a ten-cent piece but twice as thick. By the times of Jesus the priests had also been exempted from the payment of temple dues. Accordingly, from the 15th to the 25th of the month preceding the Passover, accredited money-changers erected their booths in the principal cities of Palestine for the purpose of providing the Jewish people with proper money to meet the temple dues after they had reached Jerusalem. After this ten-day period these money-changers moved on to Jerusalem and proceeded to set up their exchange tables in the courts of the temple. They were permitted to charge the equivalent of from three to four cents commission for the exchange of a coin valued at about ten cents, and in case a coin of larger value was offered for exchange, they were allowed to collect double. Likewise did these temple bankers profit from the exchange of all money intended for the purchase of sacrificial animals and for the payment of vows and the making of offerings.

These temple money-changers not only conducted a regular banking business for profit in the exchange of more than twenty sorts of money which the visiting pilgrims would periodically bring to Jerusalem, but they also engaged in all other kinds of transactions pertaining to the banking business. Both the temple treasury and the temple rulers profited tremendously from these commercial activities. It was not uncommon for the temple treasury to hold upwards of ten million dollars while the common people languished in poverty and continued to pay these unjust levies.

In the midst of this noisy aggregation of money-changers, merchandisers, and cattle sellers, Jesus, on this Monday morning, attempted to teach the gospel of the heavenly kingdom. He was not alone in resenting this profanation of the temple; the common people, especially the Jewish visitors from foreign provinces, also heartily resented this profiteering desecration of their national house of worship. At this time the Sanhedrin itself held its regular meetings in a chamber surrounded by all this babble and confusion of trade and barter.

As Jesus was about to begin his address, two things happened to arrest his attention. At the money table of a near-by exchanger a violent and heated argument had arisen over the alleged overcharging of a Jew from Alexandria, while at the same moment the air was rent by the bellowing of a drove of some one hundred bullocks which was being driven from one section of the animal pens to another. As Jesus paused, silently but thoughtfully contemplating this scene of commerce and confusion, close by he beheld a simple-minded Galilean, a man he had once talked with in Iron, being ridiculed and jostled about by supercilious and would-be superior Judeans; and all of this combined to produce one of those strange and periodic uprisings of indignant emotion in the soul of Jesus.

To the amazement of his apostles, standing near at hand, who refrained from participation in what so soon followed, Jesus stepped down from the teaching platform and, going over to the lad who was driving the cattle through the court, took from him his whip of cords and swiftly drove the animals from the temple. But that was not all; he strode majestically before the wondering gaze of the thousands assembled in the temple court to the farthest cattle pen and proceeded to open the gates of every stall and to drive out the imprisoned animals. By this time the assembled pilgrims were electrified, and with uproarious shouting they moved toward the bazaars and began to overturn the tables of the money-changers. In less than five minutes all commerce had been swept from the temple. By the time the near-by Roman guards had appeared on the scene, all was quiet, and the crowds had become orderly; Jesus, returning to the speaker's stand, spoke to the multitude: "You have this day witnessed that which is written in the Scriptures: 'My house shall be called a house of prayer for all nations, but you have made it a den of robbers.'"

But before he could utter other words, the great assembly broke out in hosannas of praise, and presently a throng of youths stepped out from the crowd to sing grateful hymns of appreciation that the profane and profiteering merchandisers had been ejected from the sacred temple. By this time certain of the priests had arrived on the scene, and one of them said to Jesus, "Do you not hear what the children of the Levites say?" And the Master replied, "Have you never read, 'Out of the mouths of babes and sucklings has praise been perfected'?" And all the rest of that day while Jesus taught, guards set by the people stood watch at every archway, and they would not permit anyone to carry even an empty vessel across the temple courts.

When the chief priests and the scribes heard about these happenings, they were dumfounded. All the more they feared the Master, and all the more they determined to destroy him. But they were nonplused. They did not know how to accomplish his death, for they greatly feared the multitudes, who were now so outspoken in their approval of his overthrow of the profane profiteers. And all this day, a day of quiet and peace in the temple courts, the people heard Jesus' teaching and literally hung on his words.

This surprising act of Jesus was beyond the comprehension of his apostles. They were so taken aback by this sudden and unexpected move of their Master that they remained throughout the whole episode huddled together near the speaker's stand; they never lifted a hand to further this cleansing of the temple. If this spectacular event had occurred the day before, at the time of Jesus' triumphal arrival at the temple at the termination of his tumultuous procession through the gates of the city, all the while loudly acclaimed by the multitude, they would have been ready for it, but coming as it did, they were wholly unprepared to participate.

This cleansing of the temple discloses the Master's attitude toward commercializing the practices of religion as well as his detestation of all forms of unfairness and profiteering at the expense of the poor and the unlearned. This episode also demonstrates that Jesus did not look with approval upon the refusal to employ force to protect the majority of any given human group against the unfair and enslaving practices of unjust minorities who may be able to entrench themselves behind political, financial, or ecclesiastical power. Shrewd, wicked, and designing men are not to be permitted to organize themselves for the exploitation and oppression of those who, because of their idealism, are not disposed to resort to force for self-protection or for the furtherance of their laudable life projects.

2. CHALLENGING THE MASTER'S AUTHORITY

On Sunday the triumphal entry into Jerusalem so overawed the Jewish leaders that they refrained from placing Jesus under arrest. Today, this spectacular cleansing of the temple likewise effectively postponed the Master's apprehension. Day by day the rulers of the Jews were becoming more and more determined to destroy him, but they were distraught by two fears, which conspired to delay the hour of striking. The chief priests and the scribes were unwilling to arrest Jesus in public for fear the multitude might turn upon them in a fury of resentment; they also dreaded the possibility of the Roman guards being called upon to quell a popular uprising.

At the noon session of the Sanhedrin it was unanimously agreed that Jesus must be speedily destroyed, inasmuch as no friend of the Master attended this meeting. But they could not agree as to when and how he should be taken into custody. Finally they agreed upon appointing five groups to go out among the people and seek to entangle him in his teaching or otherwise to discredit him in the sight of those who listened to his instruction. Accordingly, about two o'clock, when Jesus had just begun his discourse on "The Liberty of Sonship," a group of these elders of Israel made their way up near Jesus and, interrupting him in the customary manner, asked this question: "By what authority do you do these things? Who gave you this authority?"

It was altogether proper that the temple rulers and the officers of the Jewish Sanhedrin should ask this question of anyone who presumed to teach and perform in the extraordinary manner which had been characteristic of Jesus, especially as concerned his recent conduct in clearing the temple of all commerce. These traders and money-changers all operated by direct license from the highest rulers, and a percentage of their gains was supposed to go directly into the temple treasury. Do not forget that *authority* was the watchword of all Jewry. The prophets were always stirring up trouble because they so boldly presumed to teach without authority, without having been duly instructed in the rabbinic academies and subsequently regularly ordained by the Sanhedrin. Lack of this authority in pretentious public teaching was looked upon as indicating either ignorant presumption or open rebellion. At this time only the Sanhedrin could ordain an elder or teacher, and such a ceremony had to take place in the presence of at least three persons who had previously been so ordained. Such an ordination conferred the title of "rabbi" upon the teacher and also qualified him to act as a judge, "binding and loosing such matters as might be brought to him for adjudication."

The rulers of the temple came before Jesus at this afternoon hour challenging not only his teaching but his acts. Jesus well knew that these very men had long publicly taught that his authority for teaching was Satanic, and that all his mighty works had been wrought by the power of the prince of devils. Therefore did the Master begin his answer to their question by asking them a counter-question. Said Jesus: "I would also like to ask you one question which, if you will answer me, I likewise will tell you by what authority I do these works. The baptism of John, whence was it? Did John get his authority from heaven or from men?"

And when his questioners heard this, they withdrew to one side to take counsel among themselves as to what answer they might give. They had thought to embarrass Jesus before the multitude, but now they found themselves much confused before all who were assembled at that time in the temple court. And their discomfiture was all the more apparent when they returned to Jesus, saying: "Concerning the baptism of John, we cannot answer; we do not know." And they so answered the Master because they had reasoned among themselves: If we shall say from heaven, then will he say, Why did you not believe him, and perchance will add that he received his authority from John; and if we shall say from men, then might the multitude turn upon us, for most of them hold that John was a prophet; and so they were compelled to come before Jesus and the people confessing that they, the religious teachers and leaders of Israel, could not (or would not) express an opinion about John's mission. And when they had spoken, Jesus, looking down upon them, said, "Neither will I tell you by what authority I do these things."

Jesus never intended to appeal to John for his authority; John had never been ordained by the Sanhedrin. Jesus' authority was in himself and in his Father's eternal supremacy.

In employing this method of dealing with his adversaries, Jesus did not mean to dodge the question. At first it may seem that he was guilty of a masterly evasion, but it was not so. Jesus was never disposed to take unfair advantage of even his enemies. In this apparent evasion he really supplied all his hearers with the answer to the Pharisees' question as to the authority behind his mission. They had asserted that he performed by authority of the prince of devils. Jesus had repeatedly asserted that all his teaching and works were by the power and authority of his Father in heaven. This the Jewish leaders refused to accept and were seeking to corner him into admitting that he was an irregular teacher since he had never been sanctioned by the Sanhedrin. In answering them as he did, while not claiming authority from John, he so satisfied the people with the inference that the effort of his enemies to ensnare him was effectively turned upon themselves and was much to their discredit in the eyes of all present.

And it was this genius of the Master for dealing with his adversaries that made them so afraid of him. They attempted no more questions that day; they retired to take further counsel among themselves. But the people were not slow to discern the dishonesty and insincerity in these questions asked by the Jewish rulers. Even the common folk could not fail to distinguish between the moral majesty of the Master and the designing hypocrisy of his enemies. But the cleansing of the temple had brought the Sadducees over to the side of the Pharisees in perfecting the plan to destroy Jesus. And the Sadducees now represented a majority of the Sanhedrin.

3. PARABLE OF THE TWO SONS

As the caviling Pharisees stood there in silence before Jesus, he looked down on them and said: "Since you are in doubt about John's mission and arrayed in enmity against the teaching and the works of the Son of Man, give ear while I tell you a parable: A certain great and respected landholder had two sons, and desiring the help of his sons in the management of his large estates, he came to one of them, saying, 'Son, go work today in my vineyard.' And this unthinking son answered his father, saying, 'I will not go'; but afterward he repented and went. When he had found his older son, likewise he said to him, 'Son, go work in my vineyard.' And this hypocritical and unfaithful son answered, 'Yes, my father, I will go.' But when his father had departed, he went not. Let me ask you, which of these sons really did his father's will?"

And the people spoke with one accord, saying, "The first son." And then said Jesus: "Even so; and now do I declare that the publicans and harlots, even though they appear to refuse the call to repentance, shall see the error of their way and go on into the kingdom of God before you, who make great pretensions of serving the Father in heaven while you refuse to do the works of the Father. It was not you, the Pharisees and scribes, who believed John, but rather the publicans and sinners; neither do you believe my teaching, but the common people hear my words gladly."

Jesus did not despise the Pharisees and Sadducees personally. It was their systems of teaching and practice which he sought to discredit. He was hostile to no man, but here was occurring the inevitable clash between a new and living religion of the spirit and the older religion of ceremony, tradition, and authority.

All this time the twelve apostles stood near the Master, but they did not in any manner participate in these transactions. Each one of the twelve was reacting in his own peculiar way to the events of these closing days of Jesus' ministry in the flesh, and each one likewise remained obedient to the Master's injunction to refrain from all public teaching and preaching during this Passover week.

4. PARABLE OF THE ABSENT LANDLORD

When the chief Pharisees and the scribes who had sought to entangle Jesus with their questions had finished listening to the story of the two sons, they withdrew to take further counsel, and the Master, turning his attention to the listening multitude, told another parable:

"There was a good man who was a householder, and he planted a vineyard. He set a hedge about it, dug a pit for the wine press, and built a watchtower for the guards. Then he let this vineyard out to tenants while he went on a long journey into another country. And when the season of the fruits drew near, he sent servants to the tenants to receive his rental. But they took counsel among themselves and refused to give these servants the fruits due their master; instead, they fell upon his servants, beating one, stoning another, and sending the others away empty-handed. And when the householder heard about all this, he sent other and more trusted servants to deal with these wicked tenants, and these they wounded and also treated shamefully. And then the householder sent his favorite servant, his steward, and him they killed. And still, in patience and with forbearance, he dispatched many other servants, but none would they receive. Some they beat, others they killed, and when the householder had been so dealt with, he decided to send his son to deal with these ungrateful tenants, saying to himself, 'They may mistreat my servants, but they will surely show respect for my beloved son.' But when these unrepentant and wicked tenants saw the son, they reasoned among themselves: 'This is the heir; come, let us kill him and then the inheritance will be ours.' So they laid hold on him, and after casting him out of the vineyard, they killed him. When the lord of that vineyard shall hear how they have rejected and killed his son, what will he do to those ungrateful and wicked tenants?"

And when the people heard this parable and the question Jesus asked, they answered, "He will destroy those miserable men and let out his vineyard to other and honest farmers who will render to him the fruits in their season." And when some of them who heard perceived that this parable referred to the Jewish nation and its treatment of the prophets and to the impending rejection of Jesus and the gospel of the kingdom, they said in sorrow, "God forbid that we should go on doing these things."

Jesus saw a group of the Sadducees and Pharisees making their way through the crowd, and he paused for a moment until they drew near him, when he said: "You know how your fathers rejected the prophets, and you well know that you are set in your hearts to reject the Son of Man." And then, looking with searching gaze upon those priests and elders who were standing near him, Jesus said: "Did you never read in the Scripture about the stone which the builders rejected, and which, when the people had discovered it, was made into the cornerstone? And so once more do I warn you that, if you continue to reject this gospel, presently will the kingdom of God be taken away from you and be given to a people willing to receive the good news and to bring forth the fruits of the spirit. And there is a mystery about this stone, seeing that whoso falls upon it, while he is thereby broken in pieces, shall be saved; but on whomsoever this stone falls, he will be ground to dust and his ashes scattered to the four winds."

When the Pharisees heard these words, they understood that Jesus referred to themselves and the other Jewish leaders. They greatly desired to lay hold on him then and there, but they feared the multitude. However, they were so angered by the Master's words that they withdrew and held further counsel among themselves as to how they might bring about his death. And that night both the Sadducees and the Pharisees joined hands in the plan to entrap him the next day.

5. PARABLE OF THE MARRIAGE FEAST

After the scribes and rulers had withdrawn, Jesus addressed himself again to the assembled crowd and spoke the parable of the wedding feast. He said:

"The kingdom of heaven may be likened to a certain king who made a marriage feast for his son and dispatched messengers to call those who had previously been invited to the feast to come, saying, 'Everything is ready for the marriage supper at the king's palace.' Now, many of those who had once promised to attend, at this time refused to come. When the king heard of these rejections of his invitation, he sent other servants and messengers, saying: 'Tell all those who were bidden, to come, for, behold, my dinner is ready. My oxen and my fatlings are killed, and all is in readiness for the celebration of the forthcoming marriage of my son.' But again did the thoughtless make light of this call of their king, and they went their ways, one to the farm, another to the pottery, and others to their merchandise. Still others were not content thus to slight the king's call, but in open rebellion they laid hands on the king's messengers and shamefully mistreated them, even killing some of them. And when the king perceived that his chosen guests, even those who had accepted his preliminary invitation and had promised to attend the wedding feast, had finally rejected his call and in rebellion had assaulted and slain his chosen messengers, he was exceedingly wroth. And then this insulted king ordered out his armies and the armies of his allies and instructed them to destroy these rebellious murderers and to burn down their city.

"And when he had punished those who spurned his invitation, he appointed yet another day for the wedding feast and said to his messengers: 'They who were first bidden to the wedding were not worthy; so go now into the parting of the ways and into the highways and even beyond the borders of the city, and as many as you shall find, bid even these strangers to come in and attend this wedding feast.' And then these servants went out into the highways and the out-of-the-way places, and they gathered together as many as they found, good and bad, rich and poor, so that at last the wedding chamber was filled with willing guests. When all was ready, the king came in to view his guests, and much to his surprise he saw there a man without a wedding garment. The king, since he had freely provided wedding garments for all his guests, addressing this man, said: 'Friend, how is it that you come into my guest chamber on this occasion without a wedding garment?' And this unprepared man was speechless. Then said the king to his servants: 'Cast out this thoughtless guest from my house to share the lot of all the others who have spurned my hospitality and rejected my call. I will have none here except those who delight to accept my invitation, and who do me the honor to wear those guest garments so freely provided for all.'"

After speaking this parable, Jesus was about to dismiss the multitude when a sympathetic believer, making his way through the crowds toward him, asked: "But, Master, how shall we know about these things? how shall we be ready for the king's invitation? what sign will you give us whereby we shall know that you are the Son of God?" And when the Master heard this, he said, "Only one sign shall be given you." And then, pointing to his own body, he continued, "Destroy this temple, and in three days I will raise it up." But they did not understand him, and as they dispersed, they talked among themselves, saying, "Almost fifty years has this temple been in building, and yet he says he will destroy it and raise it up in three days." Even his own apostles did not comprehend the significance of this utterance, but subsequently, after his resurrection, they recalled what he had said.

About four o'clock this afternoon Jesus beckoned to his apostles and indicated that he desired to leave the temple and to go to Bethany for their evening meal and a night of rest. On the way up Olivet Jesus instructed Andrew, Philip, and Thomas that, on the morrow, they should establish a camp nearer the city which they could occupy during the remainder of the Passover week. In compliance with this instruction the following morning they pitched their tents in the hillside ravine overlooking the public camping park of Gethsemane, on a plot of ground belonging to Simon of Bethany.

Again it was a silent group of Jews who made their way up the western slope of Olivet on this Monday night. These twelve men, as never before, were beginning to sense that something tragic was about to happen. While the dramatic cleansing of the temple during the early morning had aroused their hopes of seeing the Master assert himself and manifest his mighty powers, the events of the entire afternoon only operated as an anticlimax in that they all pointed to the certain rejection of Jesus' teaching by the Jewish authorities. The apostles were gripped by suspense and were held in the firm grasp of a terrible uncertainty. They realized that only a few short days could intervene between the events of the day just passed and the crash of an impending doom. They all felt that something tremendous was about to happen, but they knew not what to expect. They went to their various places for rest, but they slept very little. Even the Alpheus twins were at last aroused to the realization that the events of the Master's life were moving swiftly toward their final culmination.

PAPER 174
TUESDAY MORNING IN THE TEMPLE

ABOUT seven o'clock on this Tuesday morning Jesus met the apostles, the women's corps, and some two dozen other prominent disciples at the home of Simon. At this meeting he said farewell to Lazarus, giving him that instruction which led him so soon to flee to Philadelphia in Perea, where he later became connected with the missionary movement having its headquarters in that city. Jesus also said good-bye to the aged Simon, and gave his parting advice to the women's corps, as he never again formally addressed them.

This morning he greeted each of the twelve with a personal salutation. To Andrew he said: "Be not dismayed by the events just ahead. Keep a firm hold on your brethren and see that they do not find you downcast." To Peter he said: "Put not your trust in the arm of flesh nor in weapons of steel. Establish yourself on the spiritual foundations of the eternal rocks." To James he said: "Falter not because of outward appearances. Remain firm in your faith, and you shall soon know of the reality of that which you believe." To John he said: "Be gentle; love even your enemies; be tolerant. And remember that I have trusted you with many things." To Nathaniel he said: "Judge not by appearances; remain firm in your faith when all appears to vanish; be true to your commission as an ambassador of the kingdom." To Philip he said: "Be unmoved by the events now impending. Remain unshaken, even when you cannot see the way. Be loyal to your oath of consecration." To Matthew he said: "Forget not the mercy that received you into the kingdom. Let no man cheat you of your eternal reward. As you have withstood the inclinations of the mortal nature, be willing to be steadfast." To Thomas he said: "No matter how difficult it may be, just now you must walk by faith and not by sight. Doubt not that I am able to finish the work I have begun, and that I shall eventually see all of my faithful ambassadors in the kingdom beyond." To the Alpheus twins he said: "Do not allow the things which you cannot understand to crush you. Be true to the affections of your hearts and put not your trust in either great men or the changing attitude of the people. Stand by your brethren." And to Simon Zelotes he said: "Simon, you may be crushed by disappointment, but your spirit shall rise above all that may come upon you. What you have failed to learn from me, my spirit will teach you. Seek the true realities of the spirit and cease to be attracted by unreal and material shadows." And to Judas Iscariot he said: "Judas, I have loved you and have prayed that you would love your brethren. Be not weary in well doing; and I would warn you to beware the slippery paths of flattery and the poison darts of ridicule."

And when he had concluded these greetings, he departed for Jerusalem with Andrew, Peter, James, and John as the other apostles set about the establishment of the Gethsemane camp, where they were to go that night, and where they made their headquarters for the remainder of the Master's life in the flesh. About halfway down the slope of Olivet Jesus paused and visited more than an hour with the four apostles.

1. DIVINE FORGIVENESS

For several days Peter and James had been engaged in discussing their differences of opinion about the Master's teaching regarding the forgiveness of sin. They had both agreed to lay the matter before Jesus, and Peter embraced this occasion as a fitting opportunity for securing the Master's counsel. Accordingly, Simon Peter broke in on the conversation dealing with the differences between praise and worship, by asking: "Master, James and I are not in accord regarding your teachings having to do with the forgiveness of sin. James claims you teach that the Father forgives us even before we ask him, and I maintain that repentance and confession must precede the forgiveness. Which of us is right? what do you say?"

After a short silence Jesus looked significantly at all four and answered: "My brethren, you err in your opinions because you do not comprehend the nature of those intimate and loving relations between the creature and the Creator, between man and God. You fail to grasp that understanding sympathy which the wise parent entertains for his immature and sometimes erring child. It is indeed doubtful whether intelligent and affectionate parents are ever called upon to forgive an average and normal child. Understanding relationships associated with attitudes of love effectively prevent all those estrangements which later necessitate the readjustment of repentance by the child with forgiveness by the parent.

"A part of every father lives in the child. The father enjoys priority and superiority of understanding in all matters connected with the child-parent relationship. The parent is able to view the immaturity of the child in the light of the more advanced parental maturity, the riper experience of the older partner. With the earthly child and the heavenly Father, the divine parent possesses infinity and divinity of sympathy and capacity for loving understanding. Divine forgiveness is inevitable; it is inherent and inalienable in God's infinite understanding, in his perfect knowledge of all that concerns the mistaken judgment and erroneous choosing of the child. Divine justice is so eternally fair that it unfailingly embodies understanding mercy.

"When a wise man understands the inner impulses of his fellows, he will love them. And when you love your brother, you have already forgiven him. This capacity to understand man's nature and forgive his apparent wrongdoing is Godlike. If you are wise parents, this is the way you will love and understand your children, even forgive them when transient misunderstanding has apparently separated you. The child, being immature and lacking in the fuller understanding of the depth of the child-father relationship, must frequently feel a sense of guilty separation from a father's full approval, but the true father is never conscious of any such separation. Sin is an experience of creature consciousness; it is not a part of God's consciousness.

"Your inability or unwillingness to forgive your fellows is the measure of your immaturity, your failure to attain adult sympathy, understanding, and love. You hold grudges and nurse vengefulness in direct proportion to your ignorance of the inner nature and true longings of your children and your fellow beings. Love is the outworking of the divine and inner urge of life. It is founded on understanding, nurtured by unselfish service, and perfected in wisdom."

2. QUESTIONS BY THE JEWISH RULERS

On Monday evening there had been held a council between the Sanhedrin and some fifty additional leaders selected from among the scribes, Pharisees, and the Sadducees. It was the consensus of this meeting that it would be dangerous to arrest Jesus in public because of his hold upon the affections of the common people. It was also the opinion of the majority that a determined effort should be made to discredit him in the eyes of the multitude before he should be arrested and brought to trial. Accordingly, several groups of learned men were designated to be on hand the next morning in the temple to undertake to entrap him with difficult questions and otherwise to seek to embarrass him before the people. At last, the Pharisees, Sadducees, and even the Herodians were all united in this effort to discredit Jesus in the eyes of the Passover multitudes.

Tuesday morning, when Jesus arrived in the temple court and began to teach, he had uttered but few words when a group of the younger students from the academies, who had been rehearsed for this purpose, came forward and by their spokesman addressed Jesus: "Master, we know you are a righteous teacher, and we know that you proclaim the ways of truth, and that you serve only God, for you fear no man, and that you are no respecter of persons. We are only students, and we would know the truth about a matter which troubles us; our difficulty is this: Is it lawful for us to give tribute to Caesar? Shall we give or shall we not give?" Jesus, perceiving their hypocrisy and craftiness, said to them: "Why do you thus come to tempt me? Show me the tribute money, and I will answer you." And when they handed him a denarius, he looked at it and said, "Whose image and superscription does this coin bear?" And when they answered him, "Caesar's," Jesus said, "Render to Caesar the things that are Caesar's and render to God the things that are God's."

When he had thus answered these young scribes and their Herodian accomplices, they withdrew from his presence, and the people, even the Sadducees, enjoyed their discomfiture. Even the youths who had endeavored to entrap him marveled greatly at the unexpected sagacity of the Master's answer.

The previous day the rulers had sought to trip him before the multitude on matters of ecclesiastical authority, and having failed, they now sought to involve him in a damaging discussion of civil authority. Both Pilate and Herod were in Jerusalem at this time, and Jesus' enemies conjectured that, if he would dare to advise against the payment of tribute to Caesar, they could go at once before the Roman authorities and charge him with sedition. On the other hand, if he should advise the payment of tribute in so many words, they rightly calculated that such a pronouncement would greatly wound the national pride of his Jewish hearers, thereby alienating the good will and affection of the multitude.

In all this the enemies of Jesus were defeated since it was a well-known ruling of the Sanhedrin, made for the guidance of the Jews dispersed among the gentile nations, that the "right of coinage carried with it the right to levy taxes." In this manner Jesus avoided their trap. To have answered "No" to their question would have been equivalent to inciting rebellion; to have answered "Yes" would have shocked the deep-rooted nationalist sentiments of that day. The Master did not evade the question; he merely employed the wisdom of making a double reply. Jesus was never evasive, but he was always wise in his dealings with those who sought to harass and destroy him.

3. THE SADDUCEES AND THE RESURRECTION

Before Jesus could get started with his teaching, another group came forward to question him, this time a company of the learned and crafty Sadducees. Their spokesman, drawing near to him, said: "Master, Moses said that if a married man should die, leaving no children, his brother should take the wife and raise up seed for the deceased brother. Now there occurred a case where a certain man who had six brothers died childless; his next brother took his wife but also soon died, leaving no children. Likewise did the second brother take the wife, but he also died leaving no offspring. And so on until all six of the brothers had had her, and all six of them passed on without leaving children. And then, after them all, the woman herself died. Now, what we would like to ask you is this: In the resurrection whose wife will she be since all seven of these brothers had her?"

Jesus knew, and so did the people, that these Sadducees were not sincere in asking this question because it was not likely that such a case would really occur; and besides, this practice of the brothers of a dead man seeking to beget children for him was practically a dead letter at this time among the Jews. Nevertheless, Jesus condescended to reply to their mischievous question. He said: "You all do err in asking such questions because you know neither the Scriptures nor the living power of God. You know that the sons of this world can marry and are given in marriage, but you do not seem to understand that they who are accounted worthy to attain the worlds to come, through the resurrection of the righteous, neither marry nor are given in marriage. Those who experience the resurrection from the dead are more like the angels of heaven, and they never die. These resurrected ones are eternally the sons of God; they are the children of light resurrected into the progress of eternal life. And even your Father Moses understood this, for, in connection with his experiences at the burning bush, he heard the Father say, 'I *am* the God of Abraham, the God of Isaac, and the God of Jacob.' And so, along with Moses, do I declare that my Father is not the God of the dead but of the living. In him you all do live, reproduce, and possess your mortal existence."

When Jesus had finished answering these questions, the Sadducees withdrew, and some of the Pharisees so far forgot themselves as to exclaim, "True, true, Master, you have well answered these unbelieving Sadducees." The Sadducees dared not ask him any more questions, and the common people marveled at the wisdom of his teaching.

Jesus appealed only to Moses in his encounter with the Sadducees because this religio-political sect acknowledged the validity of only the five so-called Books of Moses; they did not allow that the teachings of the prophets were admissible as a basis of doctrinal dogmas. The Master in his answer, though positively affirming the fact of the survival of mortal creatures by the technique of the resurrection, did not in any sense speak approvingly of the Pharisaic beliefs in the resurrection of the literal human body. The point Jesus wished to emphasize was: That the Father had said, "I *am* the God of Abraham, Isaac, and Jacob," not I *was* their God.

The Sadducees had thought to subject Jesus to the withering influence of *ridicule,* knowing full well that persecution in public would most certainly create further sympathy for him in the minds of the multitude.

4. THE GREAT COMMANDMENT

Another group of Sadducees had been instructed to ask Jesus entangling questions about angels, but when they beheld the fate of their comrades who had sought to entrap him with questions concerning the resurrection, they very wisely decided to hold their peace; they retired without asking a question. It was the prearranged plan of the confederated Pharisees, scribes, Sadducees, and Herodians to fill up the entire day with these entangling questions, hoping thereby to discredit Jesus before the people and at the same time effectively to prevent his having any time for the proclamation of his disturbing teachings.

Then came forward one of the groups of the Pharisees to ask harassing questions, and the spokesman, signaling to Jesus, said: "Master, I am a lawyer, and I would like to ask you which, in your opinion, is the greatest commandment?" Jesus answered: "There is but one commandment, and that one is the greatest of all, and that commandment is: 'Hear O Israel, the Lord our God, the Lord is one; and you shall love the Lord your God with all your heart and with all your soul, with all your mind and with all your strength.' This is the first and great commandment. And the second commandment is like this first; indeed, it springs directly therefrom, and it is: 'You shall love your neighbor as yourself.' There is no other commandment greater than these; on these two commandments hang all the law and the prophets."

When the lawyer perceived that Jesus had answered not only in accordance with the highest concept of Jewish religion, but that he had also answered wisely in the sight of the assembled multitude, he thought it the better part of valor openly to commend the Master's reply. Accordingly, he said: "Of a truth, Master, you have well said that God is one and there is none beside him; and that to love him with all the heart, understanding, and strength, and also to love one's neighbor as one's self, is the first and great commandment; and we are agreed that this great commandment is much more to be regarded than all the burnt offerings and sacrifices." When the lawyer answered thus discreetly, Jesus looked down upon him and said, "My friend, I perceive that you are not far from the kingdom of God."

Jesus spoke the truth when he referred to this lawyer as being "not far from the kingdom," for that very night he went out to the Master's camp near Gethsemane, professed faith in the gospel of the kingdom, and was baptized by Josiah, one of the disciples of Abner.

Two or three other groups of the scribes and Pharisees were present and had intended to ask questions, but they were either disarmed by Jesus' answer to the lawyer, or they were deterred by the discomfiture of all who had undertaken to ensnare him. After this no man dared to ask him another question in public.

When no more questions were forthcoming, and as the noon hour was near, Jesus did not resume his teaching but was content merely to ask the Pharisees and their associates a question. Said Jesus: "Since you ask no more questions, I would like to ask you one. What do you think of the Deliverer? That is, whose son is he?" After a brief pause one of the scribes answered, "The Messiah is the son of David." And since Jesus knew that there had been much debate, even among his own disciples, as to whether or not he was the son of David, he asked this further question: "If the Deliverer is indeed the son of David, how is it that, in the Psalm which you accredit to David, he himself, speaking in the spirit, says, 'The Lord said to my lord, sit on my right hand until I make your enemies the footstool of your feet.' If David calls him Lord, how then can he be his son?" Although the rulers, the scribes, and the chief priests made no reply to this question, they likewise refrained from asking him any more questions in an effort to entangle him. They never answered this question which Jesus put to them, but after the Master's death they attempted to escape the difficulty by changing the interpretation of this Psalm so as to make it refer to Abraham instead of the Messiah. Others sought to escape the dilemma by disallowing that David was the author of this so-called Messianic Psalm.

A short time back the Pharisees had enjoyed the manner in which the Sadducees had been silenced by the Master; now the Sadducees were delighted by the failure of the Pharisees; but such rivalry was only momentary; they speedily forgot their time-honored differences in the united effort to stop Jesus' teachings and doings. But throughout all of these experiences the common people heard him gladly.

5. THE INQUIRING GREEKS

About noontime, as Philip was purchasing supplies for the new camp which was that day being established near Gethsemane, he was accosted by a delegation of strangers, a group of believing Greeks from Alexandria, Athens, and Rome, whose spokesman said to the apostle: "You have been pointed out to us by those who know you; so we come to you, Sir, with the request to see Jesus, your Master." Philip was taken by surprise thus to meet these prominent and inquiring Greek gentiles in the market place, and, since Jesus had so explicitly charged all of the twelve not to engage in any public teaching during the Passover week, he was a bit perplexed as to the right way to handle this matter. He was also disconcerted because these men were foreign gentiles. If they had been Jews or near-by and familiar gentiles, he would not have hesitated so markedly. What he did was this: He asked these Greeks to remain right where they were. As he hastened away, they supposed that he went in search of Jesus, but in reality he hurried off to the home of Joseph, where he knew Andrew and the other apostles were at lunch; and calling Andrew out, he explained the purpose of his coming, and then, accompanied by Andrew, he returned to the waiting Greeks.

Since Philip had about finished the purchasing of supplies, he and Andrew returned with the Greeks to the home of Joseph, where Jesus received them; and they sat near while he spoke to his apostles and a number of leading disciples assembled at this luncheon. Said Jesus:

"My Father sent me to this world to reveal his loving-kindness to the children of men, but those to whom I first came have refused to receive me. True, indeed, many of you have believed my gospel for yourselves, but the children of Abraham and their leaders are about to reject me, and in so doing they will reject Him who sent me. I have freely proclaimed the gospel of salvation to this people; I have told them of sonship with joy, liberty, and life more abundant in the spirit. My Father has done many wonderful works among these fear-ridden sons of men. But truly did the Prophet Isaiah refer to this people when he wrote: 'Lord, who has believed our teachings? And to whom has the Lord been revealed?' Truly have the leaders of my people deliberately blinded their eyes that they see not, and hardened their hearts lest they believe and be saved. All these years have I sought to heal them of their unbelief that they might be recipients of the Father's eternal salvation. I know that not all have failed me; some of you have indeed believed my message. In this room now are a full score of men who were once members of the Sanhedrin, or who were high in the councils of the nation, albeit even some of you still shrink from open confession of the truth lest they cast you out of the synagogue. Some of you are tempted to love the glory of men more than the glory of God. But I am constrained to show forbearance since I fear for the safety and loyalty of even some of those who have been so long near me, and who have lived so close by my side.

"In this banquet chamber I perceive there are assembled Jews and gentiles in about equal numbers, and I would address you as the first and last of such a group that I may instruct in the affairs of the kingdom before I go to my Father."

These Greeks had been in faithful attendance upon Jesus' teaching in the temple. On Monday evening they had held a conference at the home of Nicodemus, which lasted until the dawn of day, and thirty of them had elected to enter the kingdom.

As Jesus stood before them at this time, he perceived the end of one dispensation and the beginning of another. Turning his attention to the Greeks, the Master said:

"He who believes this gospel, believes not merely in me but in Him who sent me. When you look upon me, you see not only the Son of Man but also Him who sent me. I am the light of the world, and whosoever will believe my teaching shall no longer abide in darkness. If you gentiles will hear me, you shall receive the words of life and shall enter forthwith into the joyous liberty of the truth of sonship with God. If my fellow countrymen, the Jews, choose to reject me and to refuse my teachings, I will not sit in judgment on them, for I came not to judge the world but to offer it salvation. Nevertheless, they who reject me and refuse to receive my teaching shall be brought to judgment in due season by my Father and those whom he has appointed to sit in judgment on such as reject the gift of mercy and the truths of salvation. Remember, all of you, that I speak not of myself, but that I have faithfully declared to you that which the Father commanded I should reveal to the children of men. And these words which the Father directed me to speak to the world are words of divine truth, everlasting mercy, and eternal life.

"But to both Jew and gentile I declare the hour has about come when the Son of Man will be glorified. You well know that, except a grain of wheat falls into the earth and dies, it abides alone; but if it dies in good soil, it springs up again to life and bears much fruit. He who selfishly loves his life stands in danger of losing it; but he who is willing to lay down his life for my sake and the gospel's shall enjoy a more abundant existence on earth and in heaven, life eternal. If you will truly follow me, even after I have gone to my Father, then shall you become my disciples and the sincere servants of your fellow mortals.

"I know my hour is approaching, and I am troubled. I perceive that my people are determined to spurn the kingdom, but I am rejoiced to receive these truth-seeking gentiles who come here today inquiring for the way of light. Nevertheless, my heart aches for my people, and my soul is distraught by that which lies just before me. What shall I say as I look ahead and discern what is about to befall me? Shall I say, Father save me from this awful hour? No! For this very purpose have I come into the world and even to this hour. Rather will I say, and pray that you will join me: Father, glorify your name; your will be done."

When Jesus had thus spoken, the Personalized Adjuster of his indwelling during prebaptismal times appeared before him, and as he paused noticeably, this now mighty spirit of the Father's representation spoke to Jesus of Nazareth, saying: "I have glorified my name in your bestowals many times, and I will glorify it once more."

While the Jews and gentiles here assembled heard no voice, they could not fail to discern that the Master had paused in his speaking while a message came to him from some superhuman source. They all said, every man to the one who was by him, "An angel has spoken to him."

Then Jesus continued to speak: "All this has not happened for my sake but for yours. I know of a certainty that the Father will receive me and accept my mission in your behalf, but it is needful that you be encouraged and be made ready for the fiery trial which is just ahead. Let me assure you that victory shall eventually crown our united efforts to enlighten the world and liberate mankind. The old order is bringing itself to judgment; the Prince of this world I have cast down; and all men shall become free by the light of the spirit which I will pour out upon all flesh after I have ascended to my Father in heaven.

"And now I declare to you that I, if I be lifted up on earth and in your lives, will draw all men to myself and into the fellowship of my Father. You have believed that the Deliverer would abide on earth forever, but I declare that the Son of Man will be rejected by men, and that he will go back to the Father. Only a little while will I be with you; only a little time will the living light be among this darkened generation. Walk while you have this light so that the oncoming darkness and confusion may not overtake you. He who walks in the darkness knows not where he goes; but if you will choose to walk in the light, you shall all indeed become liberated sons of God. And now, all of you, come with me while we go back to the temple and I speak farewell words to the chief priests, the scribes, the Pharisees, the Sadducees, the Herodians, and the benighted rulers of Israel."

Having thus spoken, Jesus led the way over the narrow streets of Jerusalem back to the temple. They had just heard the Master say that this was to be his farewell discourse in the temple, and they followed him in silence and in deep meditation.

PAPER 175

THE LAST TEMPLE DISCOURSE

SHORTLY after two o'clock on this Tuesday afternoon, Jesus, accompanied by eleven apostles, Joseph of Arimathea, the thirty Greeks, and certain other disciples, arrived at the temple and began the delivery of his last address in the courts of the sacred edifice. This discourse was intended to be his last appeal to the Jewish people and the final indictment of his vehement enemies and would-be destroyers—the scribes, Pharisees, Sadducees, and the chief rulers of Israel. Throughout the forenoon the various groups had had an opportunity to question Jesus; this afternoon no one asked him a question.

As the Master began to speak, the temple court was quiet and orderly. The money-changers and the merchandisers had not dared again to enter the temple since Jesus and the aroused multitude had driven them out the previous day. Before beginning the discourse, Jesus tenderly looked down upon this audience which was so soon to hear his farewell public address of mercy to mankind coupled with his last denunciation of the false teachers and the bigoted rulers of the Jews.

1. THE DISCOURSE

"This long time have I been with you, going up and down in the land proclaiming the Father's love for the children of men, and many have seen the light and, by faith, have entered into the kingdom of heaven. In connection with this teaching and preaching the Father has done many wonderful works, even to the resurrection of the dead. Many sick and afflicted have been made whole because they believed; but all of this proclamation of truth and healing of disease has not opened the eyes of those who refuse to see light, those who are determined to reject this gospel of the kingdom.

"In every manner consistent with doing my Father's will, I and my apostles have done our utmost to live in peace with our brethren, to conform with the reasonable requirements of the laws of Moses and the traditions of Israel. We have persistently sought peace, but the leaders of Israel will not have it. By rejecting the truth of God and the light of heaven, they are aligning themselves on the side of error and darkness. There cannot be peace between light and darkness, between life and death, between truth and error.

"Many of you have dared to believe my teachings and have already entered into the joy and liberty of the consciousness of sonship with God. And you will bear me witness that I have offered this same sonship with God to all the Jewish nation, even to these very men who now seek my destruction. And even now would my Father receive these blinded teachers and these hypocritical leaders if they would only turn to him and accept his mercy. Even now it is not too late for this people to receive the word of heaven and to welcome the Son of Man.

"My Father has long dealt in mercy with this people. Generation after generation have we sent our prophets to teach and warn them, and generation after generation have they killed these heaven-sent teachers. And now do your willful high priests and stubborn rulers go right on doing this same thing. As Herod brought about the death of John, you likewise now make ready to destroy the Son of Man.

"As long as there is a chance that the Jews will turn to my Father and seek salvation, the God of Abraham, Isaac, and Jacob will keep his hands of mercy outstretched toward you; but when you have once filled up your cup of impenitence, and when once you have finally rejected my Father's mercy, this nation will be left to its own counsels, and it shall speedily come to an inglorious end. This people was called to become the light of the world, to show forth the spiritual glory of a God-knowing race, but you have so far departed from the fulfillment of your divine privileges that your leaders are about to commit the supreme folly of all the ages in that they are on the verge of finally rejecting the gift of God to all men and for all ages—the revelation of the love of the Father in heaven for all his creatures on earth.

"And when you do once reject this revelation of God to man, the kingdom of heaven shall be given to other peoples, to those who will receive it with joy and gladness. In the name of the Father who sent me, I solemnly warn you that you are about to lose your position in the world as the standard-bearers of eternal truth and the custodians of the divine law. I am just now offering you your last chance to come forward and repent, to signify your intention to seek God with all your hearts and to enter, like little children and by sincere faith, into the security and salvation of the kingdom of heaven.

"My Father has long worked for your salvation, and I came down to live among you and personally show you the way. Many of both the Jews and the Samaritans, and even the gentiles, have believed the gospel of the kingdom, but those who should be first to come forward and accept the light of heaven have steadfastly refused to believe the revelation of the truth of God—God revealed in man and man uplifted to God.

"This afternoon my apostles stand here before you in silence, but you shall soon hear their voices ringing out with the call to salvation and with the urge to unite with the heavenly kingdom as the sons of the living God. And now I call to witness these, my disciples and believers in the gospel of the kingdom, as well as the unseen messengers by their sides, that I have once more offered Israel and her rulers deliverance and salvation. But you all behold how the Father's mercy is slighted and how the messengers of truth are rejected. Nevertheless, I admonish you that these scribes and Pharisees still sit in Moses' seat, and therefore, until the Most Highs who rule in the kingdoms of men shall finally overthrow this nation and destroy the place of these rulers, I bid you co-operate with these elders in Israel. You are not required to unite with them in their plans to destroy the Son of Man, but in everything related to the peace of Israel you are to be subject to them. In all these matters do whatsoever they bid you and observe the essentials of the law but do not pattern after their evil works. Remember, this is the sin of these rulers: They say that which is good, but they do it not. You well know how these leaders bind heavy burdens on your shoulders, burdens grievous to bear, and that they will not lift as much as one finger to help you bear these weighty burdens. They have oppressed you with ceremonies and enslaved you by traditions.

"Furthermore, these self-centered rulers delight in doing their good works so that they will be seen by men. They make broad their phylacteries and enlarge the borders of their official robes. They crave the chief places at the feasts and demand the chief seats in the synagogues. They covet laudatory salutations in the market places and desire to be called rabbi by all men. And even while they seek all this honor from men, they secretly lay hold of widows' houses and take profit from the services of the sacred temple. For a pretense these hypocrites make long prayers in public and give alms to attract the notice of their fellows.

"While you should honor your rulers and reverence your teachers, you should call no man Father in the spiritual sense, for there is one who is your Father, even God. Neither should you seek to lord it over your brethren in the kingdom. Remember, I have taught you that he who would be greatest among you should become the server of all. If you presume to exalt yourselves before God, you will certainly be humbled; but whoso truly humbles himself will surely be exalted. Seek in your daily lives, not self-glorification, but the glory of God. Intelligently subordinate your own wills to the will of the Father in heaven.

"Mistake not my words. I bear no malice toward these chief priests and rulers who even now seek my destruction; I have no ill will for these scribes and Pharisees who reject my teachings. I know that many of you believe in secret, and I know you will openly profess your allegiance to the kingdom when my hour comes. But how will your rabbis justify themselves since they profess to talk with God and then presume to reject and destroy him who comes to reveal the Father to the worlds?

"Woe upon you, scribes and Pharisees, hypocrites! You would shut the doors of the kingdom of heaven against sincere men because they happen to be unlearned in the ways of your teaching. You refuse to enter the kingdom and at the same time do everything within your power to prevent all others from entering. You stand with your backs to the doors of salvation and fight with all who would enter therein.

"Woe upon you, scribes and Pharisees, hypocrites that you are! for you do indeed encompass land and sea to make one proselyte, and when you have succeeded, you are not content until you have made him twofold worse than he was as a child of the heathen.

"Woe upon you, chief priests and rulers who lay hold of the property of the poor and demand heavy dues of those who would serve God as they think Moses ordained! You who refuse to show mercy, can you hope for mercy in the worlds to come?

"Woe upon you, false teachers, blind guides! What can be expected of a nation when the blind lead the blind? They both shall stumble into the pit of destruction.

"Woe upon you who dissimulate when you take an oath! You are tricksters since you teach that a man may swear by the temple and break his oath, but that whoso swears by the gold in the temple must remain bound. You are all fools and blind. You are not even consistent in your dishonesty, for which is the greater, the gold or the temple which has supposedly sanctified the gold? You also teach that, if a man swears by the altar, it is nothing; but that, if one swears by the gift that is upon the altar, then shall he be held as a debtor. Again are you blind to the truth, for which is the greater, the gift or the altar which sanctifies the gift? How can you justify such hypocrisy and dishonesty in the sight of the God of heaven?

"Woe upon you, scribes and Pharisees and all other hypocrites who make sure that they tithe mint, anise, and cumin and at the same time disregard the weightier matters of the law—faith, mercy, and judgment! Within reason, the one you ought to have done but not to have left the other undone. You are truly blind guides and dumb teachers; you strain out the gnat and swallow the camel.

"Woe upon you, scribes, Pharisees, and hypocrites! for you are scrupulous to cleanse the outside of the cup and the platter, but within there remains the filth of extortion, excesses, and deception. You are spiritually blind. Do you not recognize how much better it would be first to cleanse the inside of the cup, and then that which spills over would of itself cleanse the outside? You wicked reprobates! you make the outward performances of your religion to conform with the letter of your interpretation of Moses' law while your souls are steeped in iniquity and filled with murder.

"Woe upon all of you who reject truth and spurn mercy! Many of you are like whited sepulchres, which outwardly appear beautiful but within are full of dead men's bones and all sorts of uncleanness. Even so do you who knowingly reject the counsel of God appear outwardly to men as holy and righteous, but inwardly your hearts are filled with hypocrisy and iniquity.

"Woe upon you, false guides of a nation! Over yonder have you built a monument to the martyred prophets of old, while you plot to destroy Him of whom they spoke. You garnish the tombs of the righteous and flatter yourselves that, had you lived in the days of your fathers, you would not have killed the prophets; and then in the face of such self-righteous thinking you make ready to slay him of whom the prophets spoke, the Son of Man. Inasmuch as you do these things, are you witness to yourselves that you are the wicked sons of them who slew the prophets. Go on, then, and fill up the cup of your condemnation to the full!

"Woe upon you, children of evil! John did truly call you the offspring of vipers, and I ask how can you escape the judgment that John pronounced upon you?

"But even now I offer you in my Father's name mercy and forgiveness; even now I proffer the loving hand of eternal fellowship. My Father has sent you the wise men and the prophets; some you have persecuted and others you have killed. Then appeared John proclaiming the coming of the Son of Man, and him you destroyed after many had believed his teaching. And now you make ready to shed more innocent blood. Do you not comprehend that a terrible day of reckoning will come when the Judge of all the earth shall require of this people an accounting for the way they have rejected, persecuted, and destroyed these messengers of heaven? Do you not understand that you must account for all of this righteous blood, from the first prophet killed down to the times of Zechariah, who was slain between the sanctuary and the altar? And if you go on in your evil ways, this accounting may be required of this very generation.

"O Jerusalem and the children of Abraham, you who have stoned the prophets and killed the teachers that were sent to you, even now would I gather your children together as a hen gathers her chickens under her wings, but you will not!

"And now I take leave of you. You have heard my message and have made your decision. Those who have believed my gospel are even now safe within the kingdom of God. To you who have chosen to reject the gift of God, I say that you will no more see me teaching in the temple. My work for you is done. Behold, I now go forth with my children, and your house is left to you desolate!"

And then the Master beckoned his followers to depart from the temple.

2. STATUS OF INDIVIDUAL JEWS

The fact that the spiritual leaders and the religious teachers of the Jewish nation onetime rejected the teachings of Jesus and conspired to bring about his cruel death, does not in any manner affect the status of any individual Jew in his standing before God. And it should not cause those who profess to be followers of the Christ to be prejudiced against the Jew as a fellow mortal. The Jews, as a nation, as a sociopolitical group, paid in full the terrible price of rejecting the Prince of Peace. Long since they ceased to be the spiritual torchbearers of divine truth to the races of mankind, but this constitutes no valid reason why the individual descendants of these long-ago Jews should be made to suffer the persecutions which have been visited upon them by intolerant, unworthy, and bigoted professed followers of Jesus of Nazareth, who was, himself, a Jew by natural birth.

Many times has this unreasoning and un-Christlike hatred and persecution of modern Jews terminated in the suffering and death of some innocent and unoffending Jewish individual whose very ancestors, in the times of Jesus, heartily accepted his gospel and presently died unflinchingly for that truth which they so wholeheartedly believed. What a shudder of horror passes over the onlooking celestial beings as they behold the professed followers of Jesus indulge themselves in persecuting, harassing, and even murdering the later-day descendants of Peter, Philip, Matthew, and others of the Palestinian Jews who so gloriously yielded up their lives as the first martyrs of the gospel of the heavenly kingdom!

How cruel and unreasoning to compel innocent children to suffer for the sins of their progenitors, misdeeds of which they are wholly ignorant, and for which they could in no way be responsible! And to do such wicked deeds in the name of one who taught his disciples to love even their enemies! It has become necessary, in this recital of the life of Jesus, to portray the manner in which certain of his fellow Jews rejected him and conspired to bring about his ignominious death; but we would warn all who read this narrative that the presentation of such a historical recital in no way justifies the unjust hatred, nor condones the unfair attitude of mind, which so many professed Christians have maintained toward individual Jews for many centuries. Kingdom believers, those who follow the teachings of Jesus, must cease to mistreat the individual Jew as one who is guilty of the rejection and crucifixion of Jesus. The Father and his Creator Son have never ceased to love the Jews. God is no respecter of persons, and salvation is for the Jew as well as for the gentile.

3. THE FATEFUL SANHEDRIN MEETING

At eight o'clock on this Tuesday evening the fateful meeting of the Sanhedrin was called to order. On many previous occasions had this supreme court of the Jewish nation informally decreed the death of Jesus. Many times had this august ruling body determined to put a stop to his work, but never before had they resolved to place him under arrest and to bring about his death at any and all costs. It was just before midnight on this Tuesday, April 4, A.D. 30, that the Sanhedrin, as then constituted, officially and *unanimously* voted to impose the death sentence upon both Jesus and Lazarus. This was the answer to the Master's last appeal to the rulers of the Jews which he had made in the temple only a few hours before, and it represented their reaction of bitter resentment toward Jesus' last and vigorous indictment of these same chief priests and impenitent Sadducees and Pharisees. The passing of death sentence (even before his trial) upon the Son of God was the Sanhedrin's reply to the last offer of heavenly mercy ever to be extended to the Jewish nation, as such.

From this time on the Jews were left to finish their brief and short lease of national life wholly in accordance with their purely human status among the nations of Urantia. Israel had repudiated the Son of the God who made a covenant with Abraham, and the plan to make the children of Abraham the light-bearers of truth to the world had been shattered. The divine covenant had been abrogated, and the end of the Hebrew nation drew on apace.

The officers of the Sanhedrin were given the orders for Jesus' arrest early the next morning, but with instructions that he must not be apprehended in public. They were told to plan to take him in secret, preferably suddenly and at night. Understanding that he might not return that day (Wednesday) to teach in the temple, they instructed these officers of the Sanhedrin to "bring him before the high Jewish court sometime before midnight on Thursday."

4. THE SITUATION IN JERUSALEM

At the conclusion of Jesus' last discourse in the temple, the apostles once more were left in confusion and consternation. Before the Master began his terrible denunciation of the Jewish rulers, Judas had returned to the temple, so that all twelve heard this latter half of Jesus' last discourse in the temple. It is unfortunate that Judas Iscariot could not have heard the first and mercy-proffering half of this farewell address. He did not hear this last offer of mercy to the Jewish rulers because he was still in conference with a certain group of Sadducean relatives and friends with whom he had lunched, and with whom he was conferring as to the most fitting manner of dissociating himself from Jesus and his fellow apostles. It was while listening to the Master's final indictment of the Jewish leaders and rulers that Judas finally and fully made up his mind to forsake the gospel movement and wash his hands of the whole enterprise. Nevertheless, he left the temple in company with the twelve, went with them to Mount Olivet, where, with his fellow apostles, he listened to that fateful discourse on the destruction of Jerusalem and the end of the Jewish nation, and remained with them that Tuesday night at the new camp near Gethsemane.

The multitude who heard Jesus swing from his merciful appeal to the Jewish leaders into that sudden and scathing rebuke which bordered on ruthless denunciation, were stunned and bewildered. That night, while the Sanhedrin sat in death judgment upon Jesus, and while the Master sat with his apostles and certain of his disciples out on the Mount of Olives foretelling the death of the Jewish nation, all Jerusalem was given over to the serious and suppressed discussion of just one question: "What will they do with Jesus?"

At the home of Nicodemus more than thirty prominent Jews who were secret believers in the kingdom met and debated what course they would pursue in case an open break with the Sanhedrin should come. All present agreed that they would make open acknowledgment of their allegiance to the Master in the very hour they should hear of his arrest. And that is just what they did.

The Sadducees, who now controlled and dominated the Sanhedrin, were desirous of making away with Jesus for the following reasons:

1. They feared that the increased popular favor with which the multitude regarded him threatened to endanger the existence of the Jewish nation by possible involvement with the Roman authorities.

2. His zeal for temple reform struck directly at their revenues; the cleansing of the temple affected their pocketbooks.

3. They felt themselves responsible for the preservation of social order, and they feared the consequences of the further spread of Jesus' strange and new doctrine of the brotherhood of man.

The Pharisees had different motives for wanting to see Jesus put to death. They feared him because:

1. He was arrayed in telling opposition to their traditional hold upon the people. The Pharisees were ultraconservative, and they bitterly resented these supposedly radical attacks upon their vested prestige as religious teachers.

2. They held that Jesus was a lawbreaker; that he had shown utter disregard for the Sabbath and numerous other legal and ceremonial requirements.

3. They charged him with blasphemy because he alluded to God as his Father.

4. And now were they thoroughly angry with him because of his last discourse of bitter denunciation which he had this day delivered in the temple as the concluding portion of his farewell address.

The Sanhedrin, having formally decreed the death of Jesus and having issued orders for his arrest, adjourned on this Tuesday near midnight, after appointing to meet at ten o'clock the next morning at the home of Caiaphas the high priest for the purpose of formulating the charges on which Jesus should be brought to trial.

A small group of the Sadducees had actually proposed to dispose of Jesus by assassination, but the Pharisees utterly refused to countenance such a procedure.

And this was the situation in Jerusalem and among men on this eventful day while a vast concourse of celestial beings hovered over this momentous scene on earth, anxious to do something to assist their beloved Sovereign but powerless to act because they were effectively restrained by their commanding superiors.

PAPER 176

TUESDAY EVENING ON MOUNT OLIVET

THIS Tuesday afternoon, as Jesus and the apostles passed out of the temple on their way to the Gethsemane camp, Matthew, calling attention to the temple construction, said: "Master, observe what manner of buildings these are. See the massive stones and the beautiful adornment; can it be that these buildings are to be destroyed?" As they went on toward Olivet, Jesus said: "You see these stones and this massive temple; verily, verily, I say to you: In the days soon to come there shall not be left one stone upon another. They shall all be thrown down." These remarks depicting the destruction of the sacred temple aroused the curiosity of the apostles as they walked along behind the Master; they could conceive of no event short of the end of the world which would occasion the destruction of the temple.

In order to avoid the crowds passing along the Kidron valley toward Gethsemane, Jesus and his associates were minded to climb up the western slope of Olivet for a short distance and then follow a trail over to their private camp near Gethsemane located a short distance above the public camping ground. As they turned to leave the road leading on to Bethany, they observed the temple, glorified by the rays of the setting sun; and while they tarried on the mount, they saw the lights of the city appear and beheld the beauty of the illuminated temple; and there, under the mellow light of the full moon, Jesus and the twelve sat down. The Master talked with them, and presently Nathaniel asked this question: "Tell us, Master, how shall we know when these events are about to come to pass?"

1. THE DESTRUCTION OF JERUSALEM

In answering Nathaniel's question, Jesus said: "Yes, I will tell you about the times when this people shall have filled up the cup of their iniquity; when justice shall swiftly descend upon this city of our fathers. I am about to leave you; I go to the Father. After I leave you, take heed that no man deceive you, for many will come as deliverers and will lead many astray. When you hear of wars and rumors of wars, be not troubled, for though all these things will happen, the end of Jerusalem is not yet at hand. You should not be perturbed by famines or earthquakes; neither should you be concerned when you are delivered up to the civil authorities and are persecuted for the sake of the gospel. You will be thrown out of the synagogue and put in prison for my sake, and some of you will be killed. When you are brought up before governors and rulers, it shall be for a testimony of your faith and to show your steadfastness in the gospel of the kingdom. And when you stand before judges, be not anxious beforehand as to what you should say, for the spirit will teach you in that very hour what you should answer your adversaries. In these days of travail, even your own kinsfolk, under the leadership of those who have rejected the Son of Man, will deliver you up to prison and death. For a time you may be hated by all men for my sake, but even in these persecutions I will not forsake you; my spirit will not desert you. Be patient! doubt not that this gospel of the kingdom will triumph over all enemies and, eventually, be proclaimed to all nations."

Jesus paused while he looked down upon the city. The Master realized that the rejection of the spiritual concept of the Messiah, the determination to cling persistently and blindly to the material mission of the expected deliverer, would presently bring the Jews in direct conflict with the powerful Roman armies, and that such a contest could only result in the final and complete overthrow of the Jewish nation. When his people rejected his spiritual bestowal and refused to receive the light of heaven as it so mercifully shone upon them, they thereby sealed their doom as an independent people with a special spiritual mission on earth. Even the Jewish leaders subsequently recognized that it was this secular idea of the Messiah which directly led to the turbulence which eventually brought about their destruction.

Since Jerusalem was to become the cradle of the early gospel movement, Jesus did not want its teachers and preachers to perish in the terrible overthrow of the Jewish people in connection with the destruction of Jerusalem; wherefore did he give these instructions to his followers. Jesus was much concerned lest some of his disciples become involved in these soon-coming revolts and so perish in the downfall of Jerusalem.

Then Andrew inquired: "But, Master, if the Holy City and the temple are to be destroyed, and if you are not here to direct us, when should we forsake Jerusalem?" Said Jesus: "You may remain in the city after I have gone, even through these times of travail and bitter persecution, but when you finally see Jerusalem being encompassed by the Roman armies after the revolt of the false prophets, then will you know that her desolation is at hand; then must you flee to the mountains. Let none who are in the city and around about tarry to save aught, neither let those who are outside dare to enter therein. There will be great tribulation, for these will be the days of gentile vengeance. And after you have deserted the city, this disobedient people will fall by the edge of the sword and will be led captive into all nations; and so shall Jerusalem be trodden down by the gentiles. In the meantime, I warn you, be not deceived. If any man comes to you, saying, 'Behold, here is the Deliverer,' or 'Behold, there is he,' believe it not, for many false teachers will arise and many will be led astray; but you should not be deceived, for I have told you all this beforehand."

The apostles sat in silence in the moonlight for a considerable time while these astounding predictions of the Master sank into their bewildered minds. And it was in conformity with this very warning that practically the entire group of believers and disciples fled from Jerusalem upon the first appearance of the Roman troops, finding a safe shelter in Pella to the north.

Even after this explicit warning, many of Jesus' followers interpreted these predictions as referring to the changes which would obviously occur in Jerusalem when the reappearing of the Messiah would result in the establishment of the New Jerusalem and in the enlargement of the city to become the world's capital. In their minds these Jews were determined to connect the destruction of the temple with the "end of the world." They believed this New Jerusalem would fill all Palestine; that the end of the world would be followed by the immediate appearance of the "new heavens and the new earth." And so it was not strange that Peter should say: "Master, we know that all things will pass away when the new heavens and the new earth appear, but how shall we know when you will return to bring all this about?"

When Jesus heard this, he was thoughtful for some time and then said: "You ever err since you always try to attach the new teaching to the old; you are determined to misunderstand all my teaching; you insist on interpreting the gospel in accordance with your established beliefs. Nevertheless, I will try to enlighten you."

2. THE MASTER'S SECOND COMING

On several occasions Jesus had made statements which led his hearers to infer that, while he intended presently to leave this world, he would most certainly return to consummate the work of the heavenly kingdom. As the conviction grew on his followers that he was going to leave them, and after he had departed from this world, it was only natural for all believers to lay fast hold upon these promises to return. The doctrine of the second coming of Christ thus became early incorporated into the teachings of the Christians, and almost every subsequent generation of disciples has devoutly believed this truth and has confidently looked forward to his sometime coming.

If they were to part with their Master and Teacher, how much more did these first disciples and the apostles grasp at this promise to return, and they lost no time in associating the predicted destruction of Jerusalem with this promised second coming. And they continued thus to interpret his words notwithstanding that, throughout this evening of instruction on Mount Olivet, the Master took particular pains to prevent just such a mistake.

In further answer to Peter's question, Jesus said: "Why do you still look for the Son of Man to sit upon the throne of David and expect that the material dreams of the Jews will be fulfilled? Have I not told you all these years that my kingdom is not of this world? The things which you now look down upon are coming to an end, but this will be a new beginning out of which the gospel of the kingdom will go to all the world and this salvation will spread to all peoples. And when the kingdom shall have come to its full fruition, be assured that the Father in heaven will not fail to visit you with an enlarged revelation of truth and an enhanced demonstration of righteousness, even as he has already bestowed upon this world him who became the prince of darkness, and then Adam, who was followed by Melchizedek, and in these days, the Son of Man. And so will my Father continue to manifest his mercy and show forth his love, even to this dark and evil world. So also will I, after my Father has invested me with all power and authority, continue to follow your fortunes and to guide in the affairs of the kingdom by the presence of my spirit, who shall shortly be poured out upon all flesh. Even though I shall thus be present with you in spirit, I also promise that I will sometime return to this world, where I have lived this life in the flesh and achieved the experience of simultaneously revealing God to man and leading man to God. Very soon must I leave you and take up the work the Father has intrusted to my hands, but be of good courage, for I will sometime return. In the meantime, my Spirit of the Truth of a universe shall comfort and guide you.

"You behold me now in weakness and in the flesh, but when I return, it shall be with power and in the spirit. The eye of flesh beholds the Son of Man in the flesh, but only the eye of the spirit will behold the Son of Man glorified by the Father and appearing on earth in his own name.

"But the times of the reappearing of the Son of Man are known only in the councils of Paradise; not even the angels of heaven know when this will occur. However, you should understand that, when this gospel of the kingdom shall have been proclaimed to all the world for the salvation of all peoples, and when the fullness of the age has come to pass, the Father will send you another dispensational bestowal, or else the Son of Man will return to adjudge the age.

"And now concerning the travail of Jerusalem, about which I have spoken to you, even this generation will not pass away until my words are fulfilled; but concerning the times of the coming again of the Son of Man, no one in heaven or on earth may presume to speak. But you should be wise regarding the ripening of an age; you should be alert to discern the signs of the times. You know when the fig tree shows its tender branches and puts forth its leaves that summer is near. Likewise, when the world has passed through the long winter of material-mindedness and you discern the coming of the spiritual springtime of a new dispensation, should you know that the summertime of a new visitation draws near.

"But what is the significance of this teaching having to do with the coming of the Sons of God? Do you not perceive that, when each of you is called to lay down his life struggle and pass through the portal of death, you stand in the immediate presence of judgment, and that you are face to face with the facts of a new dispensation of service in the eternal plan of the infinite Father? What the whole world must face as a literal fact at the end of an age, you, as individuals, must each most certainly face as a personal experience when you reach the end of your natural life and thereby pass on to be confronted with the conditions and demands inherent in the next revelation of the eternal progression of the Father's kingdom."

Of all the discourses which the Master gave his apostles, none ever became so confused in their minds as this one, given this Tuesday evening on the Mount of Olives, regarding the twofold subject of the destruction of Jerusalem and his own second coming. There was, therefore, little agreement between the subsequent written accounts based on the memories of what the Master said on this extraordinary occasion. Consequently, when the records were left blank concerning much that was said that Tuesday evening, there grew up many traditions; and very early in the second century a Jewish apocalyptic about the Messiah written by one Selta, who was attached to the court of the Emperor Caligula, was bodily copied into the Matthew Gospel and subsequently added (in part) to the Mark and Luke records. It was in these writings of Selta that the parable of the ten virgins appeared. No part of the gospel record ever suffered such confusing misconstruction as this evening's teaching. But the Apostle John never became thus confused.

As these thirteen men resumed their journey toward the camp, they were speechless and under great emotional tension. Judas had finally confirmed his decision to abandon his associates. It was a late hour when David Zebedee, John Mark, and a number of the leading disciples welcomed Jesus and the twelve to the new camp, but the apostles did not want to sleep; they wanted to know more about the destruction of Jerusalem, the Master's departure, and the end of the world.

3. LATER DISCUSSION AT THE CAMP

As they gathered about the campfire, some twenty of them, Thomas asked: "Since you are to return to finish the work of the kingdom, what should be our attitude while you are away on the Father's business?" As Jesus looked them over by the firelight, he answered:

"And even you, Thomas, fail to comprehend what I have been saying. Have I not all this time taught you that your connection with the kingdom is spiritual and individual, wholly a matter of personal experience in the spirit by the faith-realization that you are a son of God? What more shall I say? The downfall of nations, the crash of empires, the destruction of the unbelieving Jews, the end of an age, even the end of the world, what have these things to do with one who believes this gospel, and who has hid his life in the surety of the eternal kingdom? You who are God-knowing and gospel-believing have already received the assurances of eternal life. Since your lives have been lived in the spirit and for the Father, nothing can be of serious concern to you. Kingdom builders, the accredited citizens of the heavenly worlds, are not to be disturbed by temporal upheavals or perturbed by terrestrial cataclysms. What does it matter to you who believe this gospel of the kingdom if nations overturn, the age ends, or all things visible crash, since you know that your life is the gift of the Son, and that it is eternally secure in the Father? Having lived the temporal life by faith and having yielded the fruits of the spirit as the righteousness of loving service for your fellows, you can confidently look forward to the next step in the eternal career with the same survival faith that has carried you through your first and earthly adventure in sonship with God.

"Each generation of believers should carry on their work, in view of the possible return of the Son of Man, exactly as each individual believer carries forward his lifework in view of inevitable and ever-impending natural death. When you have by faith once established yourself as a son of God, nothing else matters as regards the surety of survival. But make no mistake! this survival faith is a living faith, and it increasingly manifests the fruits of that divine spirit which first inspired it in the human heart. That you have once accepted sonship in the heavenly kingdom will not save you in the face of the knowing and persistent rejection of those truths which have to do with the progressive spiritual fruit-bearing of the sons of God in the flesh. You who have been with me in the Father's business on earth can even now desert the kingdom if you find that you love not the way of the Father's service for mankind.

"As individuals, and as a generation of believers, hear me while I speak a parable: There was a certain great man who, before starting out on a long journey to another country, called all his trusted servants before him and delivered into their hands all his goods. To one he gave five talents, to another two, and to another one. And so on down through the entire group of honored stewards, to each he intrusted his goods according to their several abilities; and then he set out on his journey. When their lord had departed, his servants set themselves at work to gain profits from the wealth intrusted to them. Immediately he who had received five talents began to trade with them and very soon had made a profit of another five talents. In like manner he who had received two talents soon had gained two more. And so did all of these servants make gains for their master except him who received but one talent. He went away by himself and dug a hole in the earth where he hid his lord's money. Presently the lord of those servants unexpectedly returned and called upon his stewards for a reckoning. And when they had all been called before their master, he who had received the five talents came forward with the money which had been intrusted to him and brought five additional talents, saying, 'Lord, you gave me five talents to invest, and I am glad to present five other talents as my gain.' And then his lord said to him: 'Well done, good and faithful servant, you have been faithful over a few things; I will now set you as steward over many; enter forthwith into the joy of your lord.' And then he who had received the two talents came forward, saying: 'Lord, you delivered into my hands two talents; behold, I have gained these other two talents.' And his lord then said to him: 'Well done, good and faithful steward; you also have been faithful over a few things, and I will now set you over many; enter you into the joy of your lord.' And then there came to the accounting he who had received the one talent. This servant came forward, saying, 'Lord, I knew you and realized that you were a shrewd man in that you expected gains where you had not personally labored; therefore was I afraid to risk aught of that which was intrusted to me. I safely hid your talent in the earth; here it is; you now have what belongs to you.' But his lord answered: 'You are an indolent and slothful steward. By your own words you confess that you knew I would require of you an accounting with reasonable profit, such as your diligent fellow servants have this day rendered. Knowing this, you ought, therefore, to have at least put my money into the hands of the bankers that on my return I might have received my own with interest.' And then to the chief steward this lord said: 'Take away this one talent from this unprofitable servant and give it to him who has the ten talents.'

"To every one who has, more shall be given, and he shall have abundance; but from him who has not, even that which he has shall be taken away. You cannot stand still in the affairs of the eternal kingdom. My Father requires all his children to grow in grace and in a knowledge of the truth. You who know these truths must yield the increase of the fruits of the spirit and manifest a growing devotion to the unselfish service of your fellow servants. And remember that, inasmuch as you minister to one of the least of my brethren, you have done this service to me.

"And so should you go about the work of the Father's business, now and henceforth, even forevermore. Carry on until I come. In faithfulness do that which is intrusted to you, and thereby shall you be ready for the reckoning call of death. And having thus lived for the glory of the Father and the satisfaction of the Son, you shall enter with joy and exceedingly great pleasure into the eternal service of the everlasting kingdom."

Truth is living; the Spirit of Truth is ever leading the children of light into new realms of spiritual reality and divine service. You are not given truth to crystallize into settled, safe, and honored forms. Your revelation of truth must be so enhanced by passing through your personal experience that new beauty and actual spiritual gains will be disclosed to all who behold your spiritual fruits and in consequence thereof are led to glorify the Father who is in heaven. Only those faithful servants who thus grow in the knowledge of the truth, and who thereby develop the capacity for divine appreciation of spiritual realities, can ever hope to "enter fully into the joy of their Lord." What a sorry sight for successive generations of the professed followers of Jesus to say, regarding their stewardship of divine truth: "Here, Master, is the truth you committed to us a hundred or a thousand years ago. We have lost nothing; we have faithfully preserved all you gave us; we have allowed no changes to be made in that which you taught us; here is the truth you gave us." But such a plea concerning spiritual indolence will not justify the barren steward of truth in the presence of the Master. In accordance with the truth committed to your hands will the Master of truth require a reckoning.

In the next world you will be asked to give an account of the endowments and stewardships of this world. Whether inherent talents are few or many, a just and merciful reckoning must be faced. If endowments are used only in selfish pursuits and no thought is bestowed upon the higher duty of obtaining increased yield of the fruits of the spirit, as they are manifested in the ever-expanding service of men and the worship of God, such selfish stewards must accept the consequences of their deliberate choosing.

And how much like all selfish mortals was this unfaithful servant with the one talent in that he blamed his slothfulness directly upon his lord. How prone is man, when he is confronted with the failures of his own making, to put the blame upon others, oftentimes upon those who least deserve it!

Said Jesus that night as they went to their rest: "Freely have you received; therefore freely should you give of the truth of heaven, and in the giving will this truth multiply and show forth the increasing light of saving grace, even as you minister it."

4. THE RETURN OF MICHAEL

Of all the Master's teachings no one phase has been so misunderstood as his promise sometime to come back in person to this world. It is not strange that Michael should be interested in sometime returning to the planet whereon he experienced his seventh and last bestowal, as a mortal of the realm. It is only natural to believe that Jesus of Nazareth, now sovereign ruler of a vast universe, would be interested in coming back, not only once but even many times, to the world whereon he lived such a unique life and finally won for himself the Father's unlimited bestowal of universe power and authority. Urantia will eternally be one of the seven nativity spheres of Michael in the winning of universe sovereignty.

Jesus did, on numerous occasions and to many individuals, declare his intention of returning to this world. As his followers awakened to the fact that their Master was not going to function as a temporal deliverer, and as they listened to his predictions of the overthrow of Jerusalem and the downfall of the Jewish nation, they most naturally began to associate his promised return with these catastrophic events. But when the Roman armies leveled the walls of Jerusalem, destroyed the temple, and dispersed the Judean Jews, and still the Master did not reveal himself in power and glory, his followers began the formulation of that belief which eventually associated the second coming of Christ with the end of the age, even with the end of the world.

Jesus promised to do two things after he had ascended to the Father, and after all power in heaven and on earth had been placed in his hands. He promised, first, to send into the world, and in his stead, another teacher, the Spirit of Truth; and this he did on the day of Pentecost. Second, he most certainly promised his followers that he would sometime personally return to this world. But he did not say how, where, or when he would revisit this planet of his bestowal experience in the flesh. On one occasion he intimated that, whereas the eye of flesh had beheld him when he lived here in the flesh, on his return (at least on one of his possible visits) he would be discerned only by the eye of spiritual faith.

Many of us are inclined to believe that Jesus will return to Urantia many times during the ages to come. We do not have his specific promise to make these plural visits, but it seems most probable that he who carries among his universe titles that of Planetary Prince of Urantia will many times visit the world whose conquest conferred such a unique title upon him.

We most positively believe that Michael will again come in person to Urantia, but we have not the slightest idea as to when or in what manner he may choose to come. Will his second advent on earth be timed to occur in connection with the terminal judgment of this present age, either with or without the associated appearance of a Magisterial Son? Will he come in connection with the termination of some subsequent Urantian age? Will he come unannounced and as an isolated event? We do not know. Only one thing we are certain of, that is, when he does return, all the world will likely know about it, for he must come as the supreme ruler of a universe and not as the obscure babe of Bethlehem. But if every eye is to behold him, and if only spiritual eyes are to discern his presence, then must his advent be long deferred.

You would do well, therefore, to disassociate the Master's personal return to earth from any and all set events or settled epochs. We are sure of only one thing: He has promised to come back. We have no idea as to when he will fulfill this promise or in what connection. As far as we know, he may appear on earth any day, and he may not come until age after age has passed and been duly adjudicated by his associated Sons of the Paradise corps.

The second advent of Michael on earth is an event of tremendous sentimental value to both midwayers and humans; but otherwise it is of no immediate moment to midwayers and of no more practical importance to human beings than the common event of natural death, which so suddenly precipitates mortal man into the immediate grasp of that succession of universe events which leads directly to the presence of this same Jesus, the sovereign ruler of our universe. The children of light are all destined to see him, and it is of no serious concern whether we go to him or whether he should chance first to come to us. Be you therefore ever ready to welcome him on earth as he stands ready to welcome you in heaven. We confidently look for his glorious appearing, even for repeated comings, but we are wholly ignorant as to how, when, or in what connection he is destined to appear.

PAPER 177

WEDNESDAY, THE REST DAY

WHEN the work of teaching the people did not press them, it was the custom of Jesus and his apostles to rest from their labors each Wednesday. On this particular Wednesday they ate breakfast somewhat later than usual, and the camp was pervaded by an ominous silence; little was said during the first half of this morning meal. At last Jesus spoke: "I desire that you rest today. Take time to think over all that has happened since we came to Jerusalem and meditate on what is just ahead, of which I have plainly told you. Make sure that the truth abides in your lives, and that you daily grow in grace."

After breakfast the Master informed Andrew that he intended to be absent for the day and suggested that the apostles be permitted to spend the time in accordance with their own choosing, except that under no circumstances should they go within the gates of Jerusalem.

When Jesus made ready to go into the hills alone, David Zebedee accosted him, saying: "You well know, Master, that the Pharisees and rulers seek to destroy you, and yet you make ready to go alone into the hills. To do this is folly; I will therefore send three men with you well prepared to see that no harm befalls you." Jesus looked over the three well-armed and stalwart Galileans and said to David: "You mean well, but you err in that you fail to understand that the Son of Man needs no one to defend him. No man will lay hands on me until that hour when I am ready to lay down my life in conformity to my Father's will. These men may not accompany me. I desire to go alone, that I may commune with the Father."

Upon hearing these words, David and his armed guards withdrew; but as Jesus started off alone, John Mark came forward with a small basket containing food and water and suggested that, if he intended to be away all day, he might find himself hungry. The Master smiled on John and reached down to take the basket.

1. ONE DAY ALONE WITH GOD

As Jesus was about to take the lunch basket from John's hand, the young man ventured to say: "But, Master, you may set the basket down while you turn aside to pray and go on without it. Besides, if I should go along to carry the lunch, you would be more free to worship, and I will surely be silent. I will ask no questions and will stay by the basket when you go apart by yourself to pray."

While making this speech, the temerity of which astonished some of the near-by listeners, John had made bold to hold on to the basket. There they stood, both John and Jesus holding the basket. Presently the Master let go and, looking down on the lad, said: "Since with all your heart you crave to go with me, it shall not be denied you. We will go off by ourselves and have a good visit. You may ask me any question that arises in your heart, and we will comfort and console each other. You may start out carrying the lunch, and when you grow weary, I will help you. Follow on with me."

Jesus did not return to the camp that evening until after sunset. The Master spent this last day of quiet on earth visiting with this truth-hungry youth and talking with his Paradise Father. This event has become known on high as "the day which a young man spent with God in the hills." Forever this occasion exemplifies the willingness of the Creator to fellowship the creature. Even a youth, if the desire of the heart is really supreme, can command the attention and enjoy the loving companionship of the God of a universe, actually experience the unforgettable ecstasy of being alone with God in the hills, and for a whole day. And such was the unique experience of John Mark on this Wednesday in the hills of Judea.

Jesus visited much with John, talking freely about the affairs of this world and the next. John told Jesus how much he regretted that he had not been old enough to be one of the apostles and expressed his great appreciation that he had been permitted to follow on with them since their first preaching at the Jordan ford near Jericho, except for the trip to Phoenicia. Jesus warned the lad not to become discouraged by impending events and assured him he would live to become a mighty messenger of the kingdom.

John Mark was thrilled by the memory of this day with Jesus in the hills, but he never forgot the Master's final admonition, spoken just as they were about to return to the Gethsemane camp, when he said: "Well, John, we have had a good visit, a real day of rest, but see to it that you tell no man the things which I told you." And John Mark never did reveal anything that transpired on this day which he spent with Jesus in the hills.

Throughout the few remaining hours of Jesus' earth life John Mark never permitted the Master for long to get out of his sight. Always was the lad in hiding near by; he slept only when Jesus slept.

2. EARLY HOME LIFE

In the course of this day's visiting with John Mark, Jesus spent considerable time comparing their early childhood and later boyhood experiences. Although John's parents possessed more of this world's goods than had Jesus' parents, there was much experience in their boyhood which was very similar. Jesus said many things which helped John better to understand his parents and other members of his family. When the lad asked the Master how he could know that he would turn out to be a "mighty messenger of the kingdom," Jesus said:

"I know you will prove loyal to the gospel of the kingdom because I can depend upon your present faith and love when these qualities are grounded upon such an early training as has been your portion at home. You are the product of a home where the parents bear each other a sincere affection, and therefore you have not been overloved so as injuriously to exalt your concept of self-importance. Neither has your personality suffered distortion in consequence of your parents' loveless maneuvering for your confidence and loyalty, the one against the other. You have enjoyed that parental love which insures laudable self-confidence and which fosters normal feelings of security. But you have also been fortunate in that your parents possessed wisdom as well as love; and it was wisdom which led them to withhold most forms of indulgence and many luxuries which wealth can buy while they sent you to the synagogue school along with your neighborhood playfellows, and they also encouraged you to learn how to live in this world by permitting you to have original experience. You came over to the Jordan, where we preached and John's disciples baptized, with your young friend Amos. Both of you desired to go with us. When you returned to Jerusalem, your parents consented; Amos's parents refused; they loved their son so much that they denied him the blessed experience which you have had, even such as you this day enjoy. By running away from home, Amos could have joined us, but in so doing he would have wounded love and sacrificed loyalty. Even if such a course had been wise, it would have been a terrible price to pay for experience, independence, and liberty. Wise parents, such as yours, see to it that their children do not have to wound love or stifle loyalty in order to develop independence and enjoy invigorating liberty when they have grown up to your age.

"Love, John, is the supreme reality of the universe when bestowed by all-wise beings, but it is a dangerous and oftentimes semiselfish trait as it is manifested in the experience of mortal parents. When you get married and have children of your own to rear, make sure that your love is admonished by wisdom and guided by intelligence.

"Your young friend Amos believes this gospel of the kingdom just as much as you, but I cannot fully depend upon him; I am not certain about what he will do in the years to come. His early home life was not such as would produce a wholly dependable person. Amos is too much like one of the apostles who failed to enjoy a normal, loving, and wise home training. Your whole afterlife will be more happy and dependable because you spent your first eight years in a normal and well-regulated home. You possess a strong and well-knit character because you grew up in a home where love prevailed and wisdom reigned. Such a childhood training produces a type of loyalty which assures me that you will go through with the course you have begun."

For more than an hour Jesus and John continued this discussion of home life. The Master went on to explain to John how a child is wholly dependent on his parents and the associated home life for all his early concepts of everything intellectual, social, moral, and even spiritual since the family represents to the young child all that he can first know of either human or divine relationships. The child must derive his first impressions of the universe from the mother's care; he is wholly dependent on the earthly father for his first ideas of the heavenly Father. The child's subsequent life is made happy or unhappy, easy or difficult, in accordance with his early mental and emotional life, conditioned by these social and spiritual relationships of the home. A human being's entire afterlife is enormously influenced by what happens during the first few years of existence.

It is our sincere belief that the gospel of Jesus' teaching, founded as it is on the father-child relationship, can hardly enjoy a world-wide acceptance until such a time as the home life of the modern civilized peoples embraces more of love and more of wisdom. Notwithstanding that parents of the twentieth century possess great knowledge and increased truth for improving the home and ennobling the home life, it remains a fact that very few modern homes are such good places in which to nurture boys and girls as Jesus' home in Galilee and John Mark's home in Judea, albeit the acceptance of Jesus' gospel will result in the immediate improvement of home life. The love life of a wise home and the loyal devotion of true religion exert a profound reciprocal influence upon each other. Such a home life enhances religion, and genuine religion always glorifies the home.

It is true that many of the objectionable stunting influences and other cramping features of these olden Jewish homes have been virtually eliminated from many of the better-regulated modern homes. There is, indeed, more spontaneous freedom and far more personal liberty, but this liberty is not restrained by love, motivated by loyalty, nor directed by the intelligent discipline of wisdom. As long as we teach the child to pray, "Our Father who is in heaven," a tremendous responsibility rests upon all earthly fathers so to live and order their homes that the word *father* becomes worthily enshrined in the minds and hearts of all growing children.

3. THE DAY AT CAMP

The apostles spent most of this day walking about on Mount Olivet and visiting with the disciples who were encamped with them, but early in the afternoon they became very desirous of seeing Jesus return. As the day wore on, they grew increasingly anxious about his safety; they felt inexpressibly lonely without him. There was much debating throughout the day as to whether the Master should have been allowed to go off by himself in the hills, accompanied only by an errand boy. Though no man openly so expressed his thoughts, there was not one of them, save Judas Iscariot, who did not wish himself in John Mark's place.

It was about midafternoon when Nathaniel made his speech on "Supreme Desire" to about half a dozen of the apostles and as many disciples, the ending of which was: "What is wrong with most of us is that we are only halfhearted. We fail to love the Master as he loves us. If we had all wanted to go with him as much as John Mark did, he would surely have taken us all. We stood by while the lad approached the Master and offered him the basket, but when the Master took hold of it, the lad would not let go. And so the Master left us here while he went off to the hills with basket, boy, and all."

About four o'clock, runners came to David Zebedee bringing him word from his mother at Bethsaida and from Jesus' mother. Several days previously David had made up his mind that the chief priests and rulers were going to kill Jesus. David knew they were determined to destroy the Master, and he was about convinced that Jesus would neither exert his divine power to save himself nor permit his followers to employ force in his defense. Having reached these conclusions, he lost no time in dispatching a messenger to his mother, urging her to come at once to Jerusalem and to bring Mary the mother of Jesus and every member of his family.

David's mother did as her son requested, and now the runners came back to David bringing the word that his mother and Jesus' entire family were on the way to Jerusalem and should arrive sometime late on the following day or very early the next morning. Since David did this on his own initiative, he thought it wise to keep the matter to himself. He told no one, therefore, that Jesus' family was on the way to Jerusalem.

Shortly after noon, more than twenty of the Greeks who had met with Jesus and the twelve at the home of Joseph of Arimathea arrived at the camp, and Peter and John spent several hours in conference with them. These Greeks, at least some of them, were well advanced in the knowledge of the kingdom, having been instructed by Rodan at Alexandria.

That evening, after returning to the camp, Jesus visited with the Greeks, and had it not been that such a course would have greatly disturbed his apostles and many of his leading disciples, he would have ordained these twenty Greeks, even as he had the seventy.

While all of this was going on at the camp, in Jerusalem the chief priests and elders were amazed that Jesus did not return to address the multitudes. True, the day before, when he left the temple, he had said, "I leave your house to you desolate." But they could not understand why he would be willing to forgo the great advantage which he had built up in the friendly attitude of the crowds. While they feared he would stir up a tumult among the people, the Master's last words to the multitude had been an exhortation to conform in every reasonable manner with the authority of those "who sit in Moses' seat." But it was a busy day in the city as they simultaneously prepared for the Passover and perfected their plans for destroying Jesus.

Not many people came to the camp, for its establishment had been kept a well-guarded secret by all who knew that Jesus was expecting to stay there in place of going out to Bethany every night.

4. JUDAS AND THE CHIEF PRIESTS

Shortly after Jesus and John Mark left the camp, Judas Iscariot disappeared from among his brethren, not returning until late in the afternoon. This confused and discontented apostle, notwithstanding his Master's specific request to refrain from entering Jerusalem, went in haste to keep his appointment with Jesus' enemies at the home of Caiaphas the high priest. This was an informal meeting of the Sanhedrin and had been appointed for shortly after ten o'clock that morning. This meeting was called to discuss the nature of the charges which should be lodged against Jesus and to decide upon the procedure to be employed in bringing him before the Roman authorities for the purpose of securing the necessary civil confirmation of the death sentence which they had already passed upon him.

On the preceding day Judas had disclosed to some of his relatives and to certain Sadducean friends of his father's family that he had reached the conclusion that, while Jesus was a well-meaning dreamer and idealist, he was not the expected deliverer of Israel. Judas stated that he would very much like to find some way of withdrawing gracefully from the whole movement. His friends flatteringly assured him that his withdrawal would be hailed by the Jewish rulers as a great event, and that nothing would be too good for him. They led him to believe that he would forthwith receive high honors from the Sanhedrin, and that he would at last be in a position to erase the stigma of his well-meant but "unfortunate association with untaught Galileans."

Judas could not quite believe that the mighty works of the Master had been wrought by the power of the prince of devils, but he was now fully convinced that Jesus would not exert his power in self-aggrandizement; he was at last convinced that Jesus would allow himself to be destroyed by the Jewish rulers, and he could not endure the humiliating thought of being identified with a movement of defeat. He refused to entertain the idea of apparent failure. He thoroughly understood the sturdy character of his Master and the keenness of that majestic and merciful mind, yet he derived pleasure from even the partial entertainment of the suggestion of one of his relatives that Jesus, while he was a well-meaning fanatic, was probably not really sound of mind; that he had always appeared to be a strange and misunderstood person.

And now, as never before, Judas found himself becoming strangely resentful that Jesus had never assigned him a position of greater honor. All along he had appreciated the honor of being the apostolic treasurer, but now he began to feel that he was not appreciated; that his abilities were unrecognized. He was suddenly overcome with indignation that Peter, James, and John should have been honored with close association with Jesus, and at this time, when he was on the way to the high priest's home, he was bent on getting even with Peter, James, and John more than he was concerned with any thought of betraying Jesus. But over and above all, just then, a new and dominating thought began to occupy the forefront of his conscious mind: He had set out to get honor for himself, and if this could be secured simultaneously with getting even with those who had contributed to the greatest disappointment of his life, all the better. He was seized with a terrible conspiracy of confusion, pride, desperation, and determination. And so it must be plain that it was not for money that Judas was then on his way to the home of Caiaphas to arrange for the betrayal of Jesus.

As Judas approached the home of Caiaphas, he arrived at the final decision to abandon Jesus and his fellow apostles; and having thus made up his mind to desert the cause of the kingdom of heaven, he was determined to secure for himself as much as possible of that honor and glory which he had thought would sometime be his when he first identified himself with Jesus and the new gospel of the kingdom. All of the apostles once shared this ambition with Judas, but as time passed they learned to admire truth and to love Jesus, at least more than did Judas.

The traitor was presented to Caiaphas and the Jewish rulers by his cousin, who explained that Judas, having discovered his mistake in allowing himself to be misled by the subtle teaching of Jesus, had arrived at the place where he wished to make public and formal renunciation of his association with the Galilean and at the same time to ask for reinstatement in the confidence and fellowship of his Judean brethren. This spokesman for Judas went on to explain that Judas recognized it would be best for the peace of Israel if Jesus should be taken into custody, and that, as evidence of his sorrow in having participated in such a movement of error and as proof of his sincerity in now returning to the teachings of Moses, he had come to offer himself to the Sanhedrin as one who could so arrange with the captain holding the orders for Jesus' arrest that he could be taken into custody quietly, thus avoiding any danger of stirring up the multitudes or the necessity of postponing his arrest until after the Passover.

When his cousin had finished speaking, he presented Judas, who, stepping forward near the high priest, said: "All that my cousin has promised, I will do, but what are you willing to give me for this service?" Judas did not seem to discern the look of disdain and even disgust that came over the face of the hardhearted and vainglorious Caiaphas; his heart was too much set on self-glory and the craving for the satisfaction of self-exaltation.

And then Caiaphas looked down upon the betrayer while he said: "Judas, you go to the captain of the guard and arrange with that officer to bring your Master to us either tonight or tomorrow night, and when he has been delivered by you into our hands, you shall receive your reward for this service." When Judas heard this, he went forth from the presence of the chief priests and rulers and took counsel with the captain of the temple guards as to the manner in which Jesus was to be apprehended. Judas knew that Jesus was then absent from the camp and had no idea when he would return that evening, and so they agreed among themselves to arrest Jesus the next evening (Thursday) after the people of Jerusalem and all of the visiting pilgrims had retired for the night.

Judas returned to his associates at the camp intoxicated with thoughts of grandeur and glory such as he had not had for many a day. He had enlisted with Jesus hoping some day to become a great man in the new kingdom. He at last realized that there was to be no new kingdom such as he had anticipated. But he rejoiced in being so sagacious as to trade off his disappointment in failing to achieve glory in an anticipated new kingdom for the immediate realization of honor and reward in the old order, which he now believed would survive, and which he was certain would destroy Jesus and all that he stood for. In its last motive of conscious intention, Judas's betrayal of Jesus was the cowardly act of a selfish deserter whose only thought was his own safety and glorification, no matter what might be the results of his conduct upon his Master and upon his former associates.

But it was ever just that way. Judas had long been engaged in this deliberate, persistent, selfish, and vengeful consciousness of progressively building up in his mind, and entertaining in his heart, these hateful and evil desires of revenge and disloyalty. Jesus loved and trusted Judas even as he loved and trusted the other apostles, but Judas failed to develop loyal trust and to experience whole-hearted love in return. And how dangerous ambition can become when it is once wholly wedded to self-seeking and supremely motivated by sullen and long-suppressed vengeance! What a crushing thing is disappointment in the lives of those foolish persons who, in fastening their gaze on the shadowy and evanescent allurements of time, become blinded to the higher and more real achievements of the everlasting attainments of the eternal worlds of divine values and true spiritual realities. Judas craved worldly honor in his mind and grew to love this desire with his whole heart; the other apostles likewise craved this same worldly honor in their minds, but with their hearts they loved Jesus and were doing their best to learn to love the truths which he taught them.

Judas did not realize it at this time, but he had been a subconscious critic of Jesus ever since John the Baptist was beheaded by Herod. Deep down in his heart Judas always resented the fact that Jesus did not save John. You should not forget that Judas had been a disciple of John before he became a follower of Jesus. And all these accumulations of human resentment and bitter disappointment which Judas had laid by in his soul in habiliments of hate were now well organized in his subconscious mind and ready to spring up to engulf him when he once dared to separate himself from the supporting influence of his brethren while at the same time exposing himself to the clever insinuations and subtle ridicule of the enemies of Jesus. Every time Judas allowed his hopes to soar high and Jesus would do or say something to dash them to pieces, there was always left in Judas's heart a scar of bitter resentment; and as these scars multiplied, presently that heart, so often wounded, lost all real affection for the one who had inflicted this distasteful experience upon a well-intentioned but cowardly and self-centered personality. Judas did not realize it, but he was a coward. Accordingly was he always inclined to assign to Jesus cowardice as the motive which led him so often to refuse to grasp for power or glory when they were apparently within his easy reach. And every mortal man knows full well how love, even when once genuine, can, through disappointment, jealousy, and long-continued resentment, be eventually turned into actual hate.

At last the chief priests and elders could breathe easily for a few hours. They would not have to arrest Jesus in public, and the securing of Judas as a traitorous ally insured that Jesus would not escape from their jurisdiction as he had so many times in the past.

5. THE LAST SOCIAL HOUR

Since it was Wednesday, this evening at the camp was a social hour. The Master endeavored to cheer his downcast apostles, but that was well-nigh impossible. They were all beginning to realize that disconcerting and crushing events were impending. They could not be cheerful, even when the Master recounted their years of eventful and loving association. Jesus made careful inquiry about the families of all of the apostles and, looking over toward David Zebedee, asked if anyone had heard recently from his mother, his youngest sister, or other members of his family. David looked down at his feet; he was afraid to answer.

This was the occasion of Jesus' warning his followers to beware of the support of the multitude. He recounted their experiences in Galilee when time and again great throngs of people enthusiastically followed them around and then just as ardently turned against them and returned to their former ways of believing and living. And then he said: "And so you must not allow yourselves to be deceived by the great crowds who heard us in the temple, and who seemed to believe our teachings. These multitudes listen to the truth and believe it superficially with their minds, but few of them permit the word of truth to strike down into the heart with living roots. Those who know the gospel only in the mind, and who have not experienced it in the heart, cannot be depended upon for support when real trouble comes. When the rulers of the Jews reach an agreement to destroy the Son of Man, and when they strike with one accord, you will see the multitude either flee in dismay or else stand by in silent amazement while these maddened and blinded rulers lead the teachers of the gospel truth to their death. And then, when adversity and persecution descend upon you, still others who you think love the truth will be scattered, and some will renounce the gospel and desert you. Some who have been very close to us have already made up their minds to desert. You have rested today in preparation for those times which are now upon us. Watch, therefore, and pray that on the morrow you may be strengthened for the days that are just ahead."

The atmosphere of the camp was charged with an inexplicable tension. Silent messengers came and went, communicating with only David Zebedee. Before the evening had passed, certain ones knew that Lazarus had taken hasty flight from Bethany. John Mark was ominously silent after returning to camp, notwithstanding he had spent the whole day in the Master's company. Every effort to persuade him to talk only indicated clearly that Jesus had told him not to talk.

Even the Master's good cheer and his unusual sociability frightened them. They all felt the certain drawing upon them of the terrible isolation which they realized was about to descend with crashing suddenness and inescapable terror. They vaguely sensed what was coming, and none felt prepared to face the test. The Master had been away all day; they had missed him tremendously.

This Wednesday evening was the low-tide mark of their spiritual status up to the actual hour of the Master's death. Although the next day was one more day nearer the tragic Friday, still, he was with them, and they passed through its anxious hours more gracefully.

It was just before midnight when Jesus, knowing this would be the last night he would ever sleep through with his chosen family on earth, said, as he dispersed them for the night: "Go to your sleep, my brethren, and peace be upon you till we rise on the morrow, one more day to do the Father's will and experience the joy of knowing that we are his sons."

PAPER 178

LAST DAY AT THE CAMP

JESUS planned to spend this Thursday, his last free day on earth as a divine Son incarnated in the flesh, with his apostles and a few loyal and devoted disciples. Soon after the breakfast hour on this beautiful morning, the Master led them to a secluded spot a short distance above their camp and there taught them many new truths. Although Jesus delivered other discourses to the apostles during the early evening hours of the day, this talk of Thursday forenoon was his farewell address to the combined camp group of apostles and chosen disciples, both Jews and gentiles. The twelve were all present save Judas. Peter and several of the apostles remarked about his absence, and some of them thought Jesus had sent him into the city to attend to some matter, probably to arrange the details of their forthcoming celebration of the Passover. Judas did not return to the camp until midafternoon, a short time before Jesus led the twelve into Jerusalem to partake of the Last Supper.

1. DISCOURSE ON SONSHIP AND CITIZENSHIP

Jesus talked to about fifty of his trusted followers for almost two hours and answered a score of questions regarding the relation of the kingdom of heaven to the kingdoms of this world, concerning the relation of sonship with God to citizenship in earthly governments. This discourse, together with his answers to questions, may be summarized and restated in modern language as follows:

The kingdoms of this world, being material, may often find it necessary to employ physical force in the execution of their laws and for the maintenance of order. In the kingdom of heaven true believers will not resort to the employment of physical force. The kingdom of heaven, being a spiritual brotherhood of the spirit-born sons of God, may be promulgated only by the power of the spirit. This distinction of procedure refers to the relations of the kingdom of believers to the kingdoms of secular government and does not nullify the right of social groups of believers to maintain order in their ranks and administer discipline upon unruly and unworthy members.

There is nothing incompatible between sonship in the spiritual kingdom and citizenship in the secular or civil government. It is the believer's duty to render to Caesar the things which are Caesar's and to God the things which are God's. There cannot be any disagreement between these two requirements, the one being material and the other spiritual, unless it should develop that a Caesar presumes to usurp the prerogatives of God and demand that spiritual homage and supreme worship be rendered to him. In such a case you shall worship only God while you seek to enlighten such misguided earthly rulers and in this way lead them also to the recognition of the Father in heaven. You shall not render spiritual worship to earthly rulers; neither should you employ the physical forces of earthly governments, whose rulers may sometime become believers, in the work of furthering the mission of the spiritual kingdom.

Sonship in the kingdom, from the standpoint of advancing civilization, should assist you in becoming the ideal citizens of the kingdoms of this world since brotherhood and service are the cornerstones of the gospel of the kingdom. The love call of the spiritual kingdom should prove to be the effective destroyer of the hate urge of the unbelieving and war-minded citizens of the earthly kingdoms. But these material-minded sons in darkness will never know of your spiritual light of truth unless you draw very near them with that unselfish social service which is the natural outgrowth of the bearing of the fruits of the spirit in the life experience of each individual believer.

As mortal and material men, you are indeed citizens of the earthly kingdoms, and you should be good citizens, all the better for having become reborn spirit sons of the heavenly kingdom. As faith-enlightened and spirit-liberated sons of the kingdom of heaven, you face a double responsibility of duty to man and duty to God while you voluntarily assume a third and sacred obligation: service to the brotherhood of God-knowing believers.

You may not worship your temporal rulers, and you should not employ temporal power in the furtherance of the spiritual kingdom; but you should manifest the righteous ministry of loving service to believers and unbelievers alike. In the gospel of the kingdom there resides the mighty Spirit of Truth, and presently I will pour out this same spirit upon all flesh. The fruits of the spirit, your sincere and loving service, are the mighty social lever to uplift the races of darkness, and this Spirit of Truth will become your power-multiplying fulcrum.

Display wisdom and exhibit sagacity in your dealings with unbelieving civil rulers. By discretion show yourselves to be expert in ironing out minor disagreements and in adjusting trifling misunderstandings. In every possible way—in everything short of your spiritual allegiance to the rulers of the universe—seek to live peaceably with all men. Be you always as wise as serpents but as harmless as doves.

You should be made all the better citizens of the secular government as a result of becoming enlightened sons of the kingdom; so should the rulers of earthly governments become all the better rulers in civil affairs as a result of believing this gospel of the heavenly kingdom. The attitude of unselfish service of man and intelligent worship of God should make all kingdom believers better world citizens, while the attitude of honest citizenship and sincere devotion to one's temporal duty should help to make such a citizen the more easily reached by the spirit call to sonship in the heavenly kingdom.

So long as the rulers of earthly governments seek to exercise the authority of religious dictators, you who believe this gospel can expect only trouble, persecution, and even death. But the very light which you bear to the world, and even the very manner in which you will suffer and die for this gospel of the kingdom, will, in themselves, eventually enlighten the whole world and result in the gradual divorcement of politics and religion. The persistent preaching of this gospel of the kingdom will some day bring to all nations a new and unbelievable liberation, intellectual freedom, and religious liberty.

Under the soon-coming persecutions by those who hate this gospel of joy and liberty, you will thrive and the kingdom will prosper. But you will stand in grave danger in subsequent times when most men will speak well of kingdom believers and many in high places nominally accept the gospel of the heavenly kingdom. Learn to be faithful to the kingdom even in times of peace and prosperity. Tempt not the angels of your supervision to lead you in troublous ways as a loving discipline designed to save your ease-drifting souls.

Remember that you are commissioned to preach this gospel of the kingdom—the supreme desire to do the Father's will coupled with the supreme joy of the faith realization of sonship with God—and you must not allow anything to divert your devotion to this one duty. Let all mankind benefit from the overflow of your loving spiritual ministry, enlightening intellectual communion, and uplifting social service; but none of these humanitarian labors, nor all of them, should be permitted to take the place of proclaiming the gospel. These mighty ministrations are the social by-products of the still more mighty and sublime ministrations and transformations wrought in the heart of the kingdom believer by the living Spirit of Truth and by the personal realization that the faith of a spirit-born man confers the assurance of living fellowship with the eternal God.

You must not seek to promulgate truth nor to establish righteousness by the power of civil governments or by the enaction of secular laws. You may always labor to persuade men's minds, but you must never dare to compel them. You must not forget the great law of human fairness which I have taught you in positive form: Whatsoever you would that men should do to you, do even so to them.

When a kingdom believer is called upon to serve the civil government, let him render such service as a temporal citizen of such a government, albeit such a believer should display in his civil service all of the ordinary traits of citizenship as these have been enhanced by the spiritual enlightenment of the ennobling association of the mind of mortal man with the indwelling spirit of the eternal God. If the unbeliever can qualify as a superior civil servant, you should seriously question whether the roots of truth in your heart have not died from the lack of the living waters of combined spiritual communion and social service. The consciousness of sonship with God should quicken the entire life service of every man, woman, and child who has become the possessor of such a mighty stimulus to all the inherent powers of a human personality.

You are not to be passive mystics or colorless ascetics; you should not become dreamers and drifters, supinely trusting in a fictitious Providence to provide even the necessities of life. You are indeed to be gentle in your dealings with erring mortals, patient in your intercourse with ignorant men, and forbearing under provocation; but you are also to be valiant in defense of righteousness, mighty in the promulgation of truth, and aggressive in the preaching of this gospel of the kingdom, even to the ends of the earth.

This gospel of the kingdom is a living truth. I have told you it is like the leaven in the dough, like the grain of mustard seed; and now I declare that it is like the seed of the living being, which, from generation to generation, while it remains the same living seed, unfailingly unfolds itself in new manifestations and grows acceptably in channels of new adaptation to the peculiar needs and conditions of each successive generation. The revelation I have made to you is a *living revelation,* and I desire that it shall bear appropriate fruits in each individual and in each generation in accordance with the laws of spiritual growth, increase, and adaptative development. From generation to generation this gospel must show increasing vitality and exhibit greater depth of spiritual power. It must not be permitted to become merely a sacred memory, a mere tradition about me and the times in which we now live.

And forget not: We have made no direct attack upon the persons or upon the authority of those who sit in Moses' seat; we only offered them the new light, which they have so vigorously rejected. We have assailed them only by the denunciation of their spiritual disloyalty to the very truths which they profess to teach and safeguard. We clashed with these established leaders and recognized rulers only when they threw themselves directly in the way of the preaching of the gospel of the kingdom to the sons of men. And even now, it is not we who assail them, but they who seek our destruction. Do not forget that you are commissioned to go forth preaching only the good news. You are not to attack the old ways; you are skillfully to put the leaven of new truth in the midst of the old beliefs. Let the Spirit of Truth do his own work. Let controversy come only when they who despise the truth force it upon you. But when the willful unbeliever attacks you, do not hesitate to stand in vigorous defense of the truth which has saved and sanctified you.

Throughout the vicissitudes of life, remember always to love one another. Do not strive with men, even with unbelievers. Show mercy even to those who despitefully abuse you. Show yourselves to be loyal citizens, upright artisans, praiseworthy neighbors, devoted kinsmen, understanding parents, and sincere believers in the brotherhood of the Father's kingdom. And my spirit shall be upon you, now and even to the end of the world.

When Jesus had concluded his teaching, it was almost one o'clock, and they immediately went back to the camp, where David and his associates had lunch ready for them.

2. AFTER THE NOONTIME MEAL

Not many of the Master's hearers were able to take in even a part of his forenoon address. Of all who heard him, the Greeks comprehended most. Even the eleven apostles were bewildered by his allusions to future political kingdoms and to successive generations of kingdom believers. Jesus' most devoted followers could not reconcile the impending end of his earthly ministry with these references to an extended future of gospel activities. Some of these Jewish believers were beginning to sense that earth's greatest tragedy was about to take place, but they could not reconcile such an impending disaster with either the Master's cheerfully indifferent personal attitude or his forenoon discourse, wherein he repeatedly alluded to the future transactions of the heavenly kingdom, extending over vast stretches of time and embracing relations with many and successive temporal kingdoms on earth.

By noon of this day all the apostles and disciples had learned about the hasty flight of Lazarus from Bethany. They began to sense the grim determination of the Jewish rulers to exterminate Jesus and his teachings.

David Zebedee, through the work of his secret agents in Jerusalem, was fully advised concerning the progress of the plan to arrest and kill Jesus. He knew all about the part of Judas in this plot, but he never disclosed this knowledge to the other apostles nor to any of the disciples. Shortly after lunch he did lead Jesus aside and, making bold, asked him whether he knew—but he never got further with his question. The Master, holding up his hand, stopped him, saying: "Yes, David, I know all about it, and I know that you know, but see to it that you tell no man. Only doubt not in your own heart that the will of God will prevail in the end."

This conversation with David was interrupted by the arrival of a messenger from Philadelphia bringing word that Abner had heard of the plot to kill Jesus and asking if he should depart for Jerusalem. This runner hastened off for Philadelphia with this word for Abner: "Go on with your work. If I depart from you in the flesh, it is only that I may return in the spirit. I will not forsake you. I will be with you to the end."

About this time Philip came to the Master and asked: "Master, seeing that the time of the Passover draws near, where would you have us prepare to eat it?" And when Jesus heard Philip's question, he answered: "Go and bring Peter and John, and I will give you directions concerning the supper we will eat together this night. As for the Passover, that you will have to consider after we have first done this."

When Judas heard the Master speaking with Philip about these matters, he drew closer that he might overhear their conversation. But David Zebedee, who was standing near, stepped up and engaged Judas in conversation while Philip, Peter, and John went to one side to talk with the Master.

Said Jesus to the three: "Go immediately into Jerusalem, and as you enter the gate, you will meet a man bearing a water pitcher. He will speak to you, and then shall you follow him. When he leads you to a certain house, go in after him and ask of the good man of that house, 'Where is the guest chamber wherein the Master is to eat supper with his apostles?' And when you have thus inquired, this householder will show you a large upper room all furnished and ready for us."

When the apostles reached the city, they met the man with the water pitcher near the gate and followed on after him to the home of John Mark, where the lad's father met them and showed them the upper room in readiness for the evening meal.

And all of this came to pass as the result of an understanding arrived at between the Master and John Mark during the afternoon of the preceding day when they were alone in the hills. Jesus wanted to be sure he would have this one last meal undisturbed with his apostles, and believing if Judas knew beforehand of their place of meeting he might arrange with his enemies to take him, he made this secret arrangement with John Mark. In this way Judas did not learn of their place of meeting until later on when he arrived there in company with Jesus and the other apostles.

David Zebedee had much business to transact with Judas so that he was easily prevented from following Peter, John, and Philip, as he so much desired to do. When Judas gave David a certain sum of money for provisions, David said to him: "Judas, might it not be well, under the circumstances, to provide me with a little money in advance of my actual needs?" And after Judas had reflected for a moment, he answered: "Yes, David, I think it would be wise. In fact, in view of the disturbed conditions in Jerusalem, I think it would be best for me to turn over all the money to you. They plot against the Master, and in case anything should happen to me, you would not be hampered."

And so David received all the apostolic cash funds and receipts for all money on deposit. Not until the evening of the next day did the apostles learn of this transaction.

It was about half past four o'clock when the three apostles returned and informed Jesus that everything was in readiness for the supper. The Master immediately prepared to lead his twelve apostles over the trail to the Bethany road and on into Jerusalem. And this was the last journey he ever made with all twelve of them.

3. ON THE WAY TO THE SUPPER

Seeking again to avoid the crowds passing through the Kidron valley back and forth between Gethsemane Park and Jerusalem, Jesus and the twelve walked over the western brow of Mount Olivet to meet the road leading from Bethany down to the city. As they drew near the place where Jesus had tarried the previous evening to discourse on the destruction of Jerusalem, they unconsciously paused while they stood and looked down in silence upon the city. As they were a little early, and since Jesus did not wish to pass through the city until after sunset, he said to his associates:

"Sit down and rest yourselves while I talk with you about what must shortly come to pass. All these years have I lived with you as brethren, and I have taught you the truth concerning the kingdom of heaven and have revealed to you the mysteries thereof. And my Father has indeed done many wonderful works in connection with my mission on earth. You have been witnesses of all this and partakers in the experience of being laborers together with God. And you will bear me witness that I have for some time warned you that I must presently return to the work the Father has given me to do; I have plainly told you that I must leave you in the world to carry on the work of the kingdom. It was for this purpose that I set you apart, in the hills of Capernaum. The experience you have had with me, you must now make ready to share with others. As the Father sent me into this world, so am I about to send you forth to represent me and finish the work I have begun.

"You look down on yonder city in sorrow, for you have heard my words telling of the end of Jerusalem. I have forewarned you lest you should perish in her destruction and so delay the proclamation of the gospel of the kingdom. Likewise do I warn you to take heed lest you needlessly expose yourselves to peril when they come to take the Son of Man. I must go, but you are to remain to witness to this gospel when I have gone, even as I directed that Lazarus flee from the wrath of man that he might live to make known the glory of God. If it is the Father's will that I depart, nothing you may do can frustrate the divine plan. Take heed to yourselves lest they kill you also. Let your souls be valiant in defense of the gospel by spirit power but be not misled into any foolish attempt to defend the Son of Man. I need no defense by the hand of man; the armies of heaven are even now near at hand; but I am determined to do the will of my Father in heaven, and therefore must we submit to that which is so soon to come upon us.

"When you see this city destroyed, forget not that you have entered already upon the eternal life of endless service in the ever-advancing kingdom of heaven, even of the heaven of heavens. You should know that in my Father's universe and in mine are many abodes, and that there awaits the children of light the revelation of cities whose builder is God and worlds whose habit of life is righteousness and joy in the truth. I have brought the kingdom of heaven to you here on earth, but I declare that all of you who by faith enter therein and remain therein by the living service of truth, shall surely ascend to the worlds on high and sit with me in the spirit kingdom of our Father. But first must you gird yourselves and complete the work which you have begun with me. You must first pass through much tribulation and endure many sorrows—and these trials are even now upon us—and when you have finished your work on earth, you shall come to my joy, even as I have finished my Father's work on earth and am about to return to his embrace."

When the Master had spoken, he arose, and they all followed him down Olivet and into the city. None of the apostles, save three, knew where they were going as they made their way along the narrow streets in the approaching darkness. The crowds jostled them, but no one recognized them nor knew that the Son of God was passing by on his way to the last mortal rendezvous with his chosen ambassadors of the kingdom. And neither did the apostles know that one of their own number had already entered into a conspiracy to betray the Master into the hands of his enemies.

John Mark had followed them all the way into the city, and after they had entered the gate, he hurried on by another street so that he was waiting to welcome them to his father's home when they arrived.

PAPER 179

THE LAST SUPPER

DURING the afternoon of this Thursday, when Philip reminded the Master about the approaching Passover and inquired concerning his plans for its celebration, he had in mind the Passover supper which was due to be eaten on the evening of the next day, Friday. It was the custom to begin the preparations for the celebration of the Passover not later than noon of the preceding day. And since the Jews reckoned the day as beginning at sunset, this meant that Saturday's Passover supper would be eaten on Friday night, sometime before the midnight hour.

The apostles were, therefore, entirely at a loss to understand the Master's announcement that they would celebrate the Passover one day early. They thought, at least some of them did, that he knew he would be placed under arrest before the time of the Passover supper on Friday night and was therefore calling them together for a special supper on this Thursday evening. Others thought that this was merely a special occasion which was to precede the regular Passover celebration.

The apostles knew that Jesus had celebrated other Passovers without the lamb; they knew that he did not personally participate in any sacrificial service of the Jewish system. He had many times partaken of the paschal lamb as a guest, but always, when he was the host, no lamb was served. It would not have been a great surprise to the apostles to have seen the lamb omitted even on Passover night, and since this supper was given one day earlier, they thought nothing of its absence.

After receiving the greetings of welcome extended by the father and mother of John Mark, the apostles went immediately to the upper chamber while Jesus lingered behind to talk with the Mark family.

It had been understood beforehand that the Master was to celebrate this occasion alone with his twelve apostles; therefore no servants were provided to wait upon them.

1. THE DESIRE FOR PREFERENCE

When the apostles had been shown upstairs by John Mark, they beheld a large and commodious chamber, which was completely furnished for the supper, and observed that the bread, wine, water, and herbs were all in readiness on one end of the table. Except for the end on which rested the bread and wine, this long table was surrounded by thirteen reclining couches, just such as would be provided for the celebration of the Passover in a well-to-do Jewish household.

As the twelve entered this upper chamber, they noticed, just inside the door, the pitchers of water, the basins, and towels for laving their dusty feet; and since no servant had been provided to render this service, the apostles began to look at one another as soon as John Mark had left them, and each began to think within himself, Who shall wash our feet? And each likewise thought that it would not be he who would thus seem to act as the servant of the others.

As they stood there, debating in their hearts, they surveyed the seating arrangement of the table, taking note of the higher divan of the host with one couch on the right and eleven arranged around the table on up to opposite this second seat of honor on the host's right.

They expected the Master to arrive any moment, but they were in a quandary as to whether they should seat themselves or await his coming and depend on him to assign them their places. While they hesitated, Judas stepped over to the seat of honor, at the left of the host, and signified that he intended there to recline as the preferred guest. This act of Judas immediately stirred up a heated dispute among the other apostles. Judas had no sooner seized the seat of honor than John Zebedee laid claim to the next preferred seat, the one on the right of the host. Simon Peter was so enraged at this assumption of choice positions by Judas and John that, as the other angry apostles looked on, he marched clear around the table and took his place on the lowest couch, the end of the seating order and just opposite to that chosen by John Zebedee. Since others had seized the high seats, Peter thought to choose the lowest, and he did this, not merely in protest against the unseemly pride of his brethren, but with the hope that Jesus, when he should come and see him in the place of least honor, would call him up to a higher one, thus displacing one who had presumed to honor himself.

With the highest and the lowest positions thus occupied, the rest of the apostles chose places, some near Judas and some near Peter, until all were located. They were seated about the U-shaped table on these reclining divans in the following order: on the right of the Master, John; on the left, Judas, Simon Zelotes, Matthew, James Zebedee, Andrew, the Alpheus twins, Philip, Nathaniel, Thomas, and Simon Peter.

They are gathered together to celebrate, at least in spirit, an institution which antedated even Moses and referred to the times when their fathers were slaves in Egypt. This supper is their last rendezvous with Jesus, and even in such a solemn setting, under the leadership of Judas the apostles are led once more to give way to their old predilection for honor, preference, and personal exaltation.

They were still engaged in voicing angry recriminations when the Master appeared in the doorway, where he hesitated a moment as a look of disappointment slowly crept over his face. Without comment he went to his place, and he did not disturb their seating arrangement.

They were now ready to begin the supper, except that their feet were still unwashed, and they were in anything but a pleasant frame of mind. When the Master arrived, they were still engaged in making uncomplimentary remarks about one another, to say nothing of the thoughts of some who had sufficient emotional control to refrain from publicly expressing their feelings.

2. BEGINNING THE SUPPER

For a few moments after the Master had gone to his place, not a word was spoken. Jesus looked them all over and, relieving the tension with a smile, said: "I have greatly desired to eat this Passover with you. I wanted to eat with you once more before I suffered, and realizing that my hour has come, I arranged to have this supper with you tonight, for, as concerns the morrow, we are all in the hands of the Father, whose will I have come to execute. I shall not again eat with you until you sit down with me in the kingdom which my Father will give me when I have finished that for which he sent me into this world."

After the wine and the water had been mixed, they brought the cup to Jesus, who, when he had received it from the hand of Thaddeus, held it while he offered thanks. And when he had finished offering thanks, he said: "Take this cup and divide it among yourselves and, when you partake of it, realize that I shall not again drink with you the fruit of the vine since this is our last supper. When we sit down again in this manner, it will be in the kingdom to come."

Jesus began thus to talk to his apostles because he knew that his hour had come. He understood that the time had come when he was to return to the Father, and that his work on earth was almost finished. The Master knew he had revealed the Father's love on earth and had shown forth his mercy to mankind, and that he had completed that for which he came into the world, even to the receiving of all power and authority in heaven and on earth. Likewise, he knew Judas Iscariot had fully made up his mind to deliver him that night into the hands of his enemies. He fully realized that this traitorous betrayal was the work of Judas, but that it also pleased Lucifer, Satan, and Caligastia the prince of darkness. But he feared none of those who sought his spiritual overthrow any more than he feared those who sought to accomplish his physical death. The Master had but one anxiety, and that was for the safety and salvation of his chosen followers. And so, with the full knowledge that the Father had put all things under his authority, the Master now prepared to enact the parable of brotherly love.

3. WASHING THE APOSTLES' FEET

After drinking the first cup of the Passover, it was the Jewish custom for the host to arise from the table and wash his hands. Later on in the meal and after the second cup, all of the guests likewise rose up and washed their hands. Since the apostles knew that their Master never observed these rites of ceremonial hand washing, they were very curious to know what he intended to do when, after they had partaken of this first cup, he arose from the table and silently made his way over to near the door, where the water pitchers, basins, and towels had been placed. And their curiosity grew into astonishment as they saw the Master remove his outer garment, gird himself with a towel, and begin to pour water into one of the foot basins. Imagine the amazement of these twelve men, who had so recently refused to wash one another's feet, and who had engaged in such unseemly disputes about positions of honor at the table, when they saw him make his way around the unoccupied end of the table to the lowest seat of the feast, where Simon Peter reclined, and, kneeling down in the attitude of a servant, make ready to wash Simon's feet. As the Master knelt, all twelve arose as one man to their feet; even the traitorous Judas so far forgot his infamy for a moment as to arise with his fellow apostles in this expression of surprise, respect, and utter amazement.

There stood Simon Peter, looking down into the upturned face of his Master. Jesus said nothing; it was not necessary that he should speak. His attitude plainly revealed that he was minded to wash Simon Peter's feet. Notwithstanding his frailties of the flesh, Peter loved the Master. This Galilean fisherman was the first human being wholeheartedly to believe in the divinity of Jesus *and* to make full and public confession of that belief. And Peter had never since really doubted the divine nature of the Master. Since Peter so revered and honored Jesus in his heart, it was not strange that his soul resented the thought of Jesus' kneeling there before him in the attitude of a menial servant and proposing to wash his feet as would a slave. When Peter presently collected his wits sufficiently to address the Master, he spoke the heart feelings of all his fellow apostles.

After a few moments of this great embarrassment, Peter said, "Master, do you really mean to wash my feet?" And then, looking up into Peter's face, Jesus said: "You may not fully understand what I am about to do, but hereafter you will know the meaning of all these things." Then Simon Peter, drawing a long breath, said, "Master, you shall never wash my feet!" And each of the apostles nodded their approval of Peter's firm declaration of refusal to allow Jesus thus to humble himself before them.

The dramatic appeal of this unusual scene at first touched the heart of even Judas Iscariot; but when his vainglorious intellect passed judgment upon the spectacle, he concluded that this gesture of humility was just one more episode which conclusively proved that Jesus would never qualify as Israel's deliverer, and that he had made no mistake in the decision to desert the Master's cause.

As they all stood there in breathless amazement, Jesus said: "Peter, I declare that, if I do not wash your feet, you will have no part with me in that which I am about to perform." When Peter heard this declaration, coupled with the fact that Jesus continued kneeling there at his feet, he made one of those decisions of blind acquiescence in compliance with the wish of one whom he respected and loved. As it began to dawn on Simon Peter that there was attached to this proposed enactment of service some signification that determined one's future connection with the Master's work, he not only became reconciled to the thought of allowing Jesus to wash his feet but, in his characteristic and impetuous manner, said: "Then, Master, wash not my feet only but also my hands and my head."

As the Master made ready to begin washing Peter's feet, he said: "He who is already clean needs only to have his feet washed. You who sit with me tonight are clean—but not all. But the dust of your feet should have been washed away before you sat down at meat with me. And besides, I would perform this service for you as a parable to illustrate the meaning of a new commandment which I will presently give you."

In like manner the Master went around the table, in silence, washing the feet of his twelve apostles, not even passing by Judas. When Jesus had finished washing the feet of the twelve, he donned his cloak, returned to his place as host, and after looking over his bewildered apostles, said:

"Do you really understand what I have done to you? You call me Master, and you say well, for so I am. If, then, the Master has washed your feet, why was it that you were unwilling to wash one another's feet? What lesson should you learn from this parable in which the Master so willingly does that service which his brethren were unwilling to do for one another? Verily, verily, I say to you: A servant is not greater than his master; neither is one who is sent greater than he who sends him. You have seen the way of service in my life among you, and blessed are you who will have the gracious courage so to serve. But why are you so slow to learn that the secret of greatness in the spiritual kingdom is not like the methods of power in the material world?

"When I came into this chamber tonight, you were not content proudly to refuse to wash one another's feet, but you must also fall to disputing among yourselves as to who should have the places of honor at my table. Such honors the Pharisees and the children of this world seek, but it should not be so among the ambassadors of the heavenly kingdom. Do you not know that there can be no place of preferment at my table? Do you not understand that I love each of you as I do the others? Do you not know that the place nearest me, as men regard such honors, can mean nothing concerning your standing in the kingdom of heaven? You know that the kings of the gentiles have lordship over their subjects, while those who exercise this authority are sometimes called benefactors. But it shall not be so in the kingdom of heaven. He who would be great among you, let him become as the younger; while he who would be chief, let him become as one who serves. Who is the greater, he who sits at meat, or he who serves? Is it not commonly regarded that he who sits at meat is the greater? But you will observe that I am among you as one who serves. If you are willing to become fellow servants with me in doing the Father's will, in the kingdom to come you shall sit with me in power, still doing the Father's will in future glory."

When Jesus had finished speaking, the Alpheus twins brought on the bread and wine, with the bitter herbs and the paste of dried fruits, for the next course of the Last Supper.

4. LAST WORDS TO THE BETRAYER

For some minutes the apostles ate in silence, but under the influence of the Master's cheerful demeanor they were soon drawn into conversation, and ere long the meal was proceeding as if nothing out of the ordinary had occurred to interfere with the good cheer and social accord of this extraordinary occasion. After some time had elapsed, in about the middle of this second course of the meal, Jesus, looking them over, said: "I have told you how much I desired to have this supper with you, and knowing how the evil forces of darkness have conspired to bring about the death of the Son of Man, I determined to eat this supper with you in this secret chamber and a day in advance of the Passover since I will not be with you by this time tomorrow night. I have repeatedly told you that I must return to the Father. Now has my hour come, but it was not required that one of you should betray me into the hands of my enemies."

When the twelve heard this, having already been robbed of much of their self-assertiveness and self-confidence by the parable of the feet washing and the Master's subsequent discourse, they began to look at one another while in disconcerted tones they hesitatingly inquired, "Is it I?" And when they had all so inquired, Jesus said: "While it is necessary that I go to the Father, it was not required that one of you should become a traitor to fulfill the Father's will. This is the coming to fruit of the concealed evil in the heart of one who failed to love the truth with his whole soul. How deceitful is the intellectual pride that precedes the spiritual downfall! My friend of many years, who even now eats my bread, will be willing to betray me, even as he now dips his hand with me in the dish."

And when Jesus had thus spoken, they all began again to ask, "Is it I?" And as Judas, sitting on the left of his Master, again asked, "Is it I?" Jesus, dipping the bread in the dish of herbs, handed it to Judas, saying, "You have said." But the others did not hear Jesus speak to Judas. John, who reclined on Jesus' right hand, leaned over and asked the Master: "Who is it? We should know who it is that has proved untrue to his trust." Jesus answered: "Already have I told you, even he to whom I gave the sop." But it was so natural for the host to give a sop to the one who sat next to him on the left that none of them took notice of this, even though the Master had so plainly spoken. But Judas was painfully conscious of the meaning of the Master's words associated with his act, and he became fearful lest his brethren were likewise now aware that he was the betrayer.

Peter was highly excited by what had been said, and leaning forward over the table, he addressed John, "Ask him who it is, or if he has told you, tell me who is the betrayer."

Jesus brought their whisperings to an end by saying: "I sorrow that this evil should have come to pass and hoped even up to this hour that the power of truth might triumph over the deceptions of evil, but such victories are not won without the faith of the sincere love of truth. I would not have told you these things at this, our last supper, but I desire to warn you of these sorrows and so prepare you for what is now upon us. I have told you of this because I desire that you should recall, after I have gone, that I knew about all these evil plottings, and that I forewarned you of my betrayal. And I do all this only that you may be strengthened for the temptations and trials which are just ahead."

When Jesus had thus spoken, leaning over toward Judas, he said: "What you have decided to do, do quickly." And when Judas heard these words, he arose from the table and hastily left the room, going out into the night to do what he had set his mind to accomplish. When the other apostles saw Judas hasten off after Jesus had spoken to him, they thought he had gone to procure something additional for the supper or to do some other errand for the Master since they supposed he still carried the bag.

Jesus now knew that nothing could be done to keep Judas from turning traitor. He started with twelve—now he had eleven. He chose six of these apostles, and though Judas was among those nominated by his first-chosen apostles, still the Master accepted him and had, up to this very hour, done everything possible to sanctify and save him, even as he had wrought for the peace and salvation of the others.

This supper, with its tender episodes and softening touches, was Jesus' last appeal to the deserting Judas, but it was of no avail. Warning, even when administered in the most tactful manner and conveyed in the most kindly spirit, as a rule, only intensifies hatred and fires the evil determination to carry out to the full one's own selfish projects, when love is once really dead.

5. ESTABLISHING THE REMEMBRANCE SUPPER

As they brought Jesus the third cup of wine, the "cup of blessing," he arose from the couch and, taking the cup in his hands, blessed it, saying: "Take this cup, all of you, and drink of it. This shall be the cup of my remembrance. This is the cup of the blessing of a new dispensation of grace and truth. This shall be to you the emblem of the bestowal and ministry of the divine Spirit of Truth. And I will not again drink this cup with you until I drink in new form with you in the Father's eternal kingdom."

The apostles all sensed that something out of the ordinary was transpiring as they drank of this cup of blessing in profound reverence and perfect silence. The old Passover commemorated the emergence of their fathers from a state of racial slavery into individual freedom; now the Master was instituting a new remembrance supper as a symbol of the new dispensation wherein the enslaved individual emerges from the bondage of ceremonialism and selfishness into the spiritual joy of the brotherhood and fellowship of the liberated faith sons of the living God.

When they had finished drinking this new cup of remembrance, the Master took up the bread and, after giving thanks, broke it in pieces and, directing them to pass it around, said: "Take this bread of remembrance and eat it. I have told you that I am the bread of life. And this bread of life is the united life of the Father and the Son in one gift. The word of the Father, as revealed in the Son, is indeed the bread of life." When they had partaken of the bread of remembrance, the symbol of the living word of truth incarnated in the likeness of mortal flesh, they all sat down.

In instituting this remembrance supper, the Master, as was always his habit, resorted to parables and symbols. He employed symbols because he wanted to teach certain great spiritual truths in such a manner as to make it difficult for his successors to attach precise interpretations and definite meanings to his words. In this way he sought to prevent successive generations from crystallizing his teaching and binding down his spiritual meanings by the dead chains of tradition and dogma. In the establishment of the only ceremony or sacrament associated with his whole life mission, Jesus took great pains to *suggest* his meanings rather than to commit himself to *precise definitions.* He did not wish to destroy the individual's concept of divine communion by establishing a precise form; neither did he desire to limit the believer's spiritual imagination by formally cramping it. He rather sought to set man's reborn soul free upon the joyous wings of a new and living spiritual liberty.

Notwithstanding the Master's effort thus to establish this new sacrament of the remembrance, those who followed after him in the intervening centuries saw to it that his express desire was effectively thwarted in that his simple spiritual symbolism of that last night in the flesh has been reduced to precise interpretations and subjected to the almost mathematical precision of a set formula. Of all Jesus' teachings none have become more tradition-standardized.

This supper of remembrance, when it is partaken of by those who are Son-believing and God-knowing, does not need to have associated with its symbolism any of man's puerile misinterpretations regarding the meaning of the divine presence, for upon all such occasions the Master is *really present.* The remembrance supper is the believer's symbolic rendezvous with Michael. When you become thus spirit-conscious, the Son is actually present, and his spirit fraternizes with the indwelling fragment of his Father.

After they had engaged in meditation for a few moments, Jesus continued speaking: "When you do these things, recall the life I have lived on earth among you and rejoice that I am to continue to live on earth with you and to serve through you. As individuals, contend not among yourselves as to who shall be greatest. Be you all as brethren. And when the kingdom grows to embrace large groups of believers, likewise should you refrain from contending for greatness or seeking preferment between such groups."

And this mighty occasion took place in the upper chamber of a friend. There was nothing of sacred form or of ceremonial consecration about either the supper or the building. The remembrance supper was established without ecclesiastical sanction.

When Jesus had thus established the supper of the remembrance, he said to the eleven: "And as often as you do this, do it in remembrance of me. And when you do remember me, first look back upon my life in the flesh, recall that I was once with you, and then, by faith, discern that you shall all sometime sup with me in the Father's eternal kingdom. This is the new Passover which I leave with you, even the memory of my bestowal life, the word of eternal truth; and of my love for you, the outpouring of my Spirit of Truth upon all flesh."

And they ended this celebration of the old but bloodless Passover in connection with the inauguration of the new supper of the remembrance, by singing, all together, the one hundred and eighteenth Psalm.

PAPER 180

THE FAREWELL DISCOURSE

AFTER singing the Psalm at the conclusion of the Last Supper, the apostles thought that Jesus intended to return immediately to the camp, but he indicated that they should sit down. Said the Master:

"You well remember when I sent you forth without purse or wallet and even advised that you take with you no extra clothes. And you will all recall that you lacked nothing. But now have you come upon troublous times. No longer can you depend upon the good will of the multitudes. Henceforth, he who has a purse, let him take it with him. When you go out into the world to proclaim this gospel, make such provision for your support as seems best. I have come to bring peace, but it will not appear for a time.

"The time has now come for the Son of Man to be glorified, and the Father shall be glorified in me. My friends, I am to be with you only a little longer. Soon you will seek for me, but you will not find me, for I am going to a place to which you cannot, at this time, come. But when you have finished your work on earth as I have now finished mine, you shall then come to me even as I now prepare to go to my Father. In just a short time I am going to leave you, you will see me no more on earth, but you shall all see me in the age to come when you ascend to the kingdom which my Father has given to me."

1. THE NEW COMMANDMENT

After a few moments of informal conversation, Jesus stood up and said: "When I enacted for you a parable indicating how you should be willing to serve one another, I said that I desired to give you a new commandment; and I would do this now as I am about to leave you. You well know the commandment which directs that you love one another; that you love your neighbor even as yourself. But I am not wholly satisfied with even that sincere devotion on the part of my children. I would have you perform still greater acts of love in the kingdom of the believing brotherhood. And so I give you this new commandment: That you love one another even as I have loved you. And by this will all men know that you are my disciples if you thus love one another.

"When I give you this new commandment, I do not place any new burden upon your souls; rather do I bring you new joy and make it possible for you to experience new pleasure in knowing the delights of the bestowal of your heart's affection upon your fellow men. I am about to experience the supreme joy, even though enduring outward sorrow, in the bestowal of my affection upon you and your fellow mortals.

"When I invite you to love one another, even as I have loved you, I hold up before you the supreme measure of true affection, for greater love can no man have than this: that he will lay down his life for his friends. And you are my friends; you will continue to be my friends if you are but willing to do what I have taught you. You have called me Master, but I do not call you servants. If you will only love one another as I am loving you, you shall be my friends, and I will ever speak to you of that which the Father reveals to me.

"You have not merely chosen me, but I have also chosen you, and I have ordained you to go forth into the world to yield the fruit of loving service to your fellows even as I have lived among you and revealed the Father to you. The Father and I will both work with you, and you shall experience the divine fullness of joy if you will only obey my command to love one another, even as I have loved you."

If you would share the Master's joy, you must share his love. And to share his love means that you have shared his service. Such an experience of love does not deliver you from the difficulties of this world; it does not create a new world, but it most certainly does make the old world new.

Keep in mind: It is loyalty, not sacrifice, that Jesus demands. The consciousness of sacrifice implies the absence of that wholehearted affection which would have made such a loving service a supreme joy. The idea of *duty* signifies that you are servant-minded and hence are missing the mighty thrill of doing your service as a friend and for a friend. The impulse of friendship transcends all convictions of duty, and the service of a friend for a friend can never be called a sacrifice. The Master has taught the apostles that they are the sons of God. He has called them brethren, and now, before he leaves, he calls them his friends.

2. THE VINE AND THE BRANCHES

Then Jesus stood up again and continued teaching his apostles: "I am the true vine, and my Father is the husbandman. I am the vine, and you are the branches. And the Father requires of me only that you shall bear much fruit. The vine is pruned only to increase the fruitfulness of its branches. Every branch coming out of me which bears no fruit, the Father will take away. Every branch which bears fruit, the Father will cleanse that it may bear more fruit. Already are you clean through the word I have spoken, but you must continue to be clean. You must abide in me, and I in you; the branch will die if it is separated from the vine. As the branch cannot bear fruit except it abides in the vine, so neither can you yield the fruits of loving service except you abide in me. Remember: I am the real vine, and you are the living branches. He who lives in me, and I in him, will bear much fruit of the spirit and experience the supreme joy of yielding this spiritual harvest. If you will maintain this living spiritual connection with me, you will bear abundant fruit. If you abide in me and my words live in you, you will be able to commune freely with me, and then can my living spirit so infuse you that you may ask whatsoever my spirit wills and do all this with the assurance that the Father will grant us our petition. Herein is the Father glorified: that the vine has many living branches, and that every branch bears much fruit. And when the world sees these fruit-bearing branches—my friends who love one another, even as I have loved them—all men will know that you are truly my disciples.

"As the Father has loved me, so have I loved you. Live in my love even as I live in the Father's love. If you do as I have taught you, you shall abide in my love even as I have kept the Father's word and evermore abide in his love."

The Jews had long taught that the Messiah would be "a stem arising out of the vine" of David's ancestors, and in commemoration of this olden teaching a large emblem of the grape and its attached vine decorated the entrance to Herod's temple. The apostles all recalled these things while the Master talked to them this night in the upper chamber.

But great sorrow later attended the misinterpretation of the Master's inferences regarding prayer. There would have been little difficulty about these teachings if his exact words had been remembered and subsequently truthfully recorded. But as the record was made, believers eventually regarded prayer in Jesus' name as a sort of supreme magic, thinking that they would receive from the Father anything they asked for. For centuries honest souls have continued to wreck their faith against this stumbling block. How long will it take the world of believers to understand that prayer is not a process of getting your way but rather a program of taking God's way, an experience of learning how to recognize and execute the Father's will? It is entirely true that, when your will has been truly aligned with his, you can ask anything conceived by that will-union, and it will be granted. And such a will-union is effected by and through Jesus even as the life of the vine flows into and through the living branches.

When there exists this living connection between divinity and humanity, if humanity should thoughtlessly and ignorantly pray for selfish ease and vainglorious accomplishments, there could be only one divine answer: more and increased bearing of the fruits of the spirit on the stems of the living branches. When the branch of the vine is alive, there can be only one answer to all its petitions: increased grape bearing. In fact, the branch exists only for, and can do nothing except, fruit bearing, yielding grapes. So does the true believer exist only for the purpose of bearing the fruits of the spirit: to love man as he himself has been loved by God—that we should love one another, even as Jesus has loved us.

And when the Father's hand of discipline is laid upon the vine, it is done in love, in order that the branches may bear much fruit. And a wise husbandman cuts away only the dead and fruitless branches.

Jesus had great difficulty in leading even his apostles to recognize that prayer is a function of spirit-born believers in the spirit-dominated kingdom.

3. ENMITY OF THE WORLD

The eleven had scarcely ceased their discussions of the discourse on the vine and the branches when the Master, indicating that he was desirous of speaking to them further and knowing that his time was short, said: "When I have left you, be not discouraged by the enmity of the world. Be not downcast even when fainthearted believers turn against you and join hands with the enemies of the kingdom. If the world shall hate you, you should recall that it hated me even before it hated you. If you were of this world, then would the world love its own, but because you are not, the world refuses to love you. You are in this world, but your lives are not to be worldlike. I have chosen you out of the world to represent the spirit of another world even to this world from which you have been chosen. But always remember the words I have spoken to you: The servant is not greater than his master. If they dare to persecute me, they will also persecute you. If my words offend the unbelievers, so also will your words offend the ungodly. And all of this will they do to you because they believe not in me nor in Him who sent me; so will you suffer many things for the sake of my gospel. But when you endure these tribulations, you should recall that I also suffered before you for the sake of this gospel of the heavenly kingdom.

"Many of those who will assail you are ignorant of the light of heaven, but this is not true of some who now persecute us. If we had not taught them the truth, they might do many strange things without falling under condemnation, but now, since they have known the light and presumed to reject it, they have no excuse for their attitude. He who hates me hates my Father. It cannot be otherwise; the light which would save you if accepted can only condemn you if it is knowingly rejected. And what have I done to these men that they should hate me with such a terrible hatred? Nothing, save to offer them fellowship on earth and salvation in heaven. But have you not read in the Scripture the saying: 'And they hated me without a cause'?

"But I will not leave you alone in the world. Very soon, after I have gone, I will send you a spirit helper. You shall have with you one who will take my place among you, one who will continue to teach you the way of truth, who will even comfort you.

"Let not your hearts be troubled. You believe in God; continue to believe also in me. Even though I must leave you, I will not be far from you. I have already told you that in my Father's universe there are many tarrying-places. If this were not true, I would not have repeatedly told you about them. I am going to return to these worlds of light, stations in the Father's heaven to which you shall sometime ascend. From these places I came into this world, and the hour is now at hand when I must return to my Father's work in the spheres on high.

"If I thus go before you into the Father's heavenly kingdom, so will I surely send for you that you may be with me in the places that were prepared for the mortal sons of God before this world was. Even though I must leave you, I will be present with you in spirit, and eventually you shall be with me in person when you have ascended to me in my universe even as I am about to ascend to my Father in his greater universe. And what I have told you is true and everlasting, even though you may not fully comprehend it. I go to the Father, and though you cannot now follow me, you shall certainly follow me in the ages to come."

When Jesus sat down, Thomas arose and said: "Master, we do not know where you are going; so of course we do not know the way. But we will follow you this very night if you will show us the way."

When Jesus heard Thomas, he answered: "Thomas, I am the way, the truth, and the life. No man goes to the Father except through me. All who find the Father, first find me. If you know me, you know the way to the Father. And you do know me, for you have lived with me and you now see me."

But this teaching was too deep for many of the apostles, especially for Philip, who, after speaking a few words with Nathaniel, arose and said: "Master, show us the Father, and everything you have said will be made plain."

And when Philip had spoken, Jesus said: "Philip, have I been so long with you and yet you do not even now know me? Again do I declare: He who has seen me has seen the Father. How can you then say, Show us the Father? Do you not believe that I am in the Father and the Father in me? Have I not taught you that the words which I speak are not my words but the words of the Father? I speak for the Father and not of myself. I am in this world to do the

Father's will, and that I have done. My Father abides in me and works through me. Believe me when I say that the Father is in me, and that I am in the Father, or else believe me for the sake of the very life I have lived—for the work's sake."

As the Master went aside to refresh himself with water, the eleven engaged in a spirited discussion of these teachings, and Peter was beginning to deliver himself of an extended speech when Jesus returned and beckoned them to be seated.

4. THE PROMISED HELPER

Jesus continued to teach, saying: "When I have gone to the Father, and after he has fully accepted the work I have done for you on earth, and after I have received the final sovereignty of my own domain, I shall say to my Father: Having left my children alone on earth, it is in accordance with my promise to send them another teacher. And when the Father shall approve, I will pour out the Spirit of Truth upon all flesh. Already is my Father's spirit in your hearts, and when this day shall come, you will also have me with you even as you now have the Father. This new gift is the spirit of living truth. The unbelievers will not at first listen to the teachings of this spirit, but the sons of light will all receive him gladly and with a whole heart. And you shall know this spirit when he comes even as you have known me, and you will receive this gift in your hearts, and he will abide with you. You thus perceive that I am not going to leave you without help and guidance. I will not leave you desolate. Today I can be with you only in person. In the times to come I will be with you and all other men who desire my presence, wherever you may be, and with each of you at the same time. Do you not discern that it is better for me to go away; that I leave you in the flesh so that I may the better and the more fully be with you in the spirit?

"In just a few hours the world will see me no more; but you will continue to know me in your hearts even until I send you this new teacher, the Spirit of Truth. As I have lived with you in person, then shall I live in you; I shall be one with your personal experience in the spirit kingdom. And when this has come to pass, you shall surely know that I am in the Father, and that, while your life is hid with the Father in me, I am also in you. I have loved the Father and have kept his word; you have loved me, and you will keep my word. As my Father has given me of his spirit, so will I give you of my spirit. And this Spirit of Truth which I will bestow upon you shall guide and comfort you and shall eventually lead you into all truth.

"I am telling you these things while I am still with you that you may be the better prepared to endure those trials which are even now right upon us. And when this new day comes, you will be indwelt by the Son as well as by the Father. And these gifts of heaven will ever work the one with the other even as the Father and I have wrought on earth and before your very eyes as one person, the Son of Man. And this spirit friend will bring to your remembrance everything I have taught you."

As the Master paused for a moment, Judas Alpheus made bold to ask one of the few questions which either he or his brother ever addressed to Jesus in public. Said Judas: "Master, you have always lived among us as a friend; how shall we know you when you no longer manifest yourself to us save by this spirit? If the world sees you not, how shall we be certain about you? How will you show yourself to us?"

Jesus looked down upon them all, smiled, and said: "My little children, I am going away, going back to my Father. In a little while you will not see me as you do here, as flesh and blood. In a very short time I am going to send you my spirit, just like me except for this material body. This new teacher is the Spirit of Truth who will live with each one of you, in your hearts, and so will all the children of light be made one and be drawn toward one another. And in this very manner will my Father and I be able to live in the souls of each one of you and also in the hearts of all other men who love us and make that love real in their experiences by loving one another, even as I am now loving you."

Judas Alpheus did not fully understand what the Master said, but he grasped the promise of the new teacher, and from the expression on Andrew's face, he perceived that his question had been satisfactorily answered.

5. THE SPIRIT OF TRUTH

The new helper which Jesus promised to send into the hearts of believers, to pour out upon all flesh, is the *Spirit of Truth.* This divine endowment is not the letter or law of truth, neither is it to function as the form or expression of truth. The new teacher is the *conviction of truth,* the consciousness and assurance of true meanings on real spirit levels. And this new teacher is the spirit of living and growing truth, expanding, unfolding, and adaptative truth.

Divine truth is a spirit-discerned and living reality. Truth exists only on high spiritual levels of the realization of divinity and the consciousness of communion with God. You can know the truth, and you can live the truth; you can experience the growth of truth in the soul and enjoy the liberty of its enlightenment in the mind, but you cannot imprison truth in formulas, codes, creeds, or intellectual patterns of human conduct. When you undertake the human formulation of divine truth, it speedily dies. The post-mortem salvage of imprisoned truth, even at best, can eventuate only in the realization of a peculiar form of intellectualized glorified wisdom. Static truth is dead truth, and only dead truth can be held as a theory. Living truth is dynamic and can enjoy only an experiential existence in the human mind.

Intelligence grows out of a material existence which is illuminated by the presence of the cosmic mind. Wisdom comprises the consciousness of knowledge elevated to new levels of meaning and activated by the presence of the universe endowment of the adjutant of wisdom. Truth is a spiritual reality value experienced only by spirit-endowed beings who function upon supermaterial levels of universe consciousness, and who, after the realization of truth, permit its spirit of activation to live and reign within their souls.

The true child of universe insight looks for the living Spirit of Truth in every wise saying. The God-knowing individual is constantly elevating wisdom to the living-truth levels of divine attainment; the spiritually unprogressive soul is all the while dragging the living truth down to the dead levels of wisdom and to the domain of mere exalted knowledge.

The golden rule, when divested of the superhuman insight of the Spirit of Truth, becomes nothing more than a rule of high ethical conduct. The golden rule, when literally interpreted, may become the instrument of great offense to one's fellows. Without a spiritual discernment of the golden rule of wisdom you might reason that, since you are desirous that all men speak the full and frank truth of their minds to you, you should therefore fully and frankly speak the full thought of your mind to your fellow beings. Such an unspiritual interpretation of the golden rule might result in untold unhappiness and no end of sorrow.

Some persons discern and interpret the golden rule as a purely intellectual affirmation of human fraternity. Others experience this expression of human relationship as an emotional gratification of the tender feelings of the human personality. Another mortal recognizes this same golden rule as the yardstick for measuring all social relations, the standard of social conduct. Still others look upon it as being the positive injunction of a great moral teacher who embodied in this statement the highest concept of moral obligation as regards all fraternal relationships. In the lives of such moral beings the golden rule becomes the wise center and circumference of all their philosophy.

In the kingdom of the believing brotherhood of God-knowing truth lovers, this golden rule takes on living qualities of spiritual realization on those higher levels of interpretation which cause the mortal sons of God to view this injunction of the Master as requiring them so to relate themselves to their fellows that they will receive the highest possible good as a result of the believer's contact with them. This is the essence of true religion: that you love your neighbor as yourself.

But the highest realization and the truest interpretation of the golden rule consists in the consciousness of the spirit of the truth of the enduring and living reality of such a divine declaration. The true cosmic meaning of this rule of universal relationship is revealed only in its spiritual realization, in the interpretation of the law of conduct by the spirit of the Son to the spirit of the Father that indwells the soul of mortal man. And when such spirit-led mortals realize the true meaning of this golden rule, they are filled to overflowing with the assurance of citizenship in a friendly universe, and their ideals of spirit reality are satisfied only when they love their fellows as Jesus loved us all, and that is the reality of the realization of the love of God.

This same philosophy of the living flexibility and cosmic adaptability of divine truth to the individual requirements and capacity of every son of God, must be perceived before you can hope adequately to understand the Master's teaching and practice of nonresistance to evil. The Master's teaching is basically a spiritual pronouncement. Even the material implications of his philosophy cannot be helpfully considered apart from their spiritual correlations. The spirit of the Master's injunction consists in the nonresistance of all selfish reaction to the universe, coupled with the aggressive and progressive attainment of righteous levels of true spirit values: divine beauty, infinite goodness, and eternal truth—to know God and to become increasingly like him.

Love, unselfishness, must undergo a constant and living readaptative interpretation of relationships in accordance with the leading of the Spirit of Truth. Love must thereby grasp the ever-changing and enlarging concepts of the highest cosmic good of the individual who is loved. And then love goes on to strike this same attitude concerning all other individuals who could possibly be influenced by the growing and living relationship of one spirit-led mortal's love for other citizens of the universe. And this entire living adaptation of love must be effected in the light of both the environment of present evil and the eternal goal of the perfection of divine destiny.

And so must we clearly recognize that neither the golden rule nor the teaching of nonresistance can ever be properly understood as dogmas or precepts. They can only be comprehended by living them, by realizing their meanings in the living interpretation of the Spirit of Truth, who directs the loving contact of one human being with another.

And all this clearly indicates the difference between the old religion and the new. The old religion taught self-sacrifice; the new religion teaches only self-forgetfulness, enhanced self-realization in conjoined social service and universe comprehension. The old religion was motivated by fear-consciousness; the new gospel of the kingdom is dominated by truth-conviction, the spirit of eternal and universal truth. And no amount of piety or creedal loyalty can compensate for the absence in the life experience of kingdom believers of that spontaneous, generous, and sincere friendliness which characterizes the spirit-born sons of the living God. Neither tradition nor a ceremonial system of formal worship can atone for the lack of genuine compassion for one's fellows.

6. THE NECESSITY FOR LEAVING

After Peter, James, John, and Matthew had asked the Master numerous questions, he continued his farewell discourse by saying: "And I am telling you about all this before I leave you in order that you may be so prepared for what is coming upon you that you will not stumble into serious error. The authorities will not be content with merely putting you out of the synagogues; I warn you the hour draws near when they who kill you will think they are doing a service to God. And all of these things they will do to you and to those whom you lead into the kingdom of heaven because they do not know the Father. They have refused to know the Father by refusing to receive me; and they refuse to receive me when they reject you, provided you have kept my new commandment that you love one another even as I have loved you. I am telling you in advance about these things so that, when your hour comes, as mine now has, you may be strengthened in the knowledge that all was known to me, and that my spirit shall be with you in all your sufferings for my sake and the gospel's. It was for this purpose that I have been talking so plainly to you from the very beginning. I have even warned you that a man's foes may be those of his own household. Although this gospel of the kingdom never fails to bring great peace to the soul of the individual believer, it will not bring peace on earth until man is willing to believe my teaching wholeheartedly and to establish the practice of doing the Father's will as the chief purpose in living the mortal life.

"Now that I am leaving you, seeing that the hour has come when I am about to go to the Father, I am surprised that none of you have asked me, Why do you leave us? Nevertheless, I know that you ask such questions in your hearts. I will speak to you plainly, as one friend to another. It is really profitable for you that I go away. If I go not away, the new teacher cannot come into your hearts. I must be divested of this mortal body and be restored to my place on high before I can send this spirit teacher to live in your souls and lead your spirits into the truth. And when my spirit comes to indwell you, he will illuminate the difference between sin and righteousness and will enable you to judge wisely in your hearts concerning them.

"I have yet much to say to you, but you cannot stand any more just now. Albeit, when he, the Spirit of Truth, comes, he shall eventually guide you into all truth as you pass through the many abodes in my Father's universe.

"This spirit will not speak of himself, but he will declare to you that which the Father has revealed to the Son, and he will even show you things to come;

he will glorify me even as I have glorified my Father. This spirit comes forth from me, and he will reveal my truth to you. Everything which the Father has in this domain is now mine; wherefore did I say that this new teacher would take of that which is mine and reveal it to you.

"In just a little while I will leave you for a short time. Afterward, when you again see me, I shall already be on my way to the Father so that even then you will not see me for long."

While he paused for a moment, the apostles began to talk with each other: "What is this that he tells us? 'In just a little while I will leave you,' and 'When you see me again it will not be for long, for I will be on my way to the Father.' What can he mean by this 'little while' and 'not for long'? We cannot understand what he is telling us."

And since Jesus knew they asked these questions, he said: "Do you inquire among yourselves about what I meant when I said that in a little while I would not be with you, and that, when you would see me again, I would be on my way to the Father? I have plainly told you that the Son of Man must die, but that he will rise again. Can you not then discern the meaning of my words? You will first be made sorrowful, but later on will you rejoice with many who will understand these things after they have come to pass. A woman is indeed sorrowful in the hour of her travail, but when she is once delivered of her child, she immediately forgets her anguish in the joy of the knowledge that a man has been born into the world. And so are you about to sorrow over my departure, but I will soon see you again, and then will your sorrow be turned into rejoicing, and there shall come to you a new revelation of the salvation of God which no man can ever take away from you. And all the worlds will be blessed in this same revelation of life in effecting the overthrow of death. Hitherto have you made all your requests in my Father's name. After you see me again, you may also ask in my name, and I will hear you.

"Down here I have taught you in proverbs and spoken to you in parables. I did so because you were only children in the spirit; but the time is coming when I will talk to you plainly concerning the Father and his kingdom. And I shall do this because the Father himself loves you and desires to be more fully revealed to you. Mortal man cannot see the spirit Father; therefore have I come into the world to show the Father to your creature eyes. But when you have become perfected in spirit growth, you shall then see the Father himself."

When the eleven had heard him speak, they said to each other: "Behold, he does speak plainly to us. Surely the Master did come forth from God. But why does he say he must return to the Father?" And Jesus saw that they did not even yet comprehend him. These eleven men could not get away from their long-nourished ideas of the Jewish concept of the Messiah. The more fully they believed in Jesus as the Messiah, the more troublesome became these deep-rooted notions regarding the glorious material triumph of the kingdom on earth.

PAPER 181

FINAL ADMONITIONS AND WARNINGS

AFTER the conclusion of the farewell discourse to the eleven, Jesus visited informally with them and recounted many experiences which concerned them as a group and as individuals. At last it was beginning to dawn upon these Galileans that their friend and teacher was going to leave them, and their hope grasped at the promise that, after a little while, he would again be with them, but they were prone to forget that this return visit was also for a little while. Many of the apostles and the leading disciples really thought that this promise to return for a short season (the short interval between the resurrection and the ascension) indicated that Jesus was just going away for a brief visit with his Father, after which he would return to establish the kingdom. And such an interpretation of his teaching conformed both with their preconceived beliefs and with their ardent hopes. Since their lifelong beliefs and hopes of wish fulfillment were thus agreed, it was not difficult for them to find an interpretation of the Master's words which would justify their intense longings.

After the farewell discourse had been discussed and had begun to settle down in their minds, Jesus again called the apostles to order and began the impartation of his final admonitions and warnings.

1. LAST WORDS OF COMFORT

When the eleven had taken their seats, Jesus stood and addressed them: "As long as I am with you in the flesh, I can be but one individual in your midst or in the entire world. But when I have been delivered from this investment of mortal nature, I will be able to return as a spirit indweller of each of you and of all other believers in this gospel of the kingdom. In this way the Son of Man will become a spiritual incarnation in the souls of all true believers.

"When I have returned to live in you and work through you, I can the better lead you on through this life and guide you through the many abodes in the future life in the heaven of heavens. Life in the Father's eternal creation is not an endless rest of idleness and selfish ease but rather a ceaseless progression in grace, truth, and glory. Each of the many, many stations in my Father's house is a stopping place, a life designed to prepare you for the next one ahead. And so will the children of light go on from glory to glory until they attain the divine estate wherein they are spiritually perfected even as the Father is perfect in all things.

"If you would follow after me when I leave you, put forth your earnest efforts to live in accordance with the spirit of my teachings and with the ideal of my life—the doing of my Father's will. This do instead of trying to imitate my natural life in the flesh as I have, perforce, been required to live it on this world.

"The Father sent me into this world, but only a few of you have chosen fully to receive me. I will pour out my spirit upon all flesh, but all men will not choose to receive this new teacher as the guide and counselor of the soul. But as many as do receive him shall be enlightened, cleansed, and comforted. And this Spirit of Truth will become in them a well of living water springing up into eternal life.

"And now, as I am about to leave you, I would speak words of comfort. Peace I leave with you; my peace I give to you. I make these gifts not as the world gives—by measure—I give each of you all you will receive. Let not your heart be troubled, neither let it be fearful. I have overcome the world, and in me you shall all triumph through faith. I have warned you that the Son of Man will be killed, but I assure you I will come back before I go to the Father, even though it be for only a little while. And after I have ascended to the Father, I will surely send the new teacher to be with you and to abide in your very hearts. And when you see all this come to pass, be not dismayed, but rather believe, inasmuch as you knew it all beforehand. I have loved you with a great affection, and I would not leave you, but it is the Father's will. My hour has come.

"Doubt not any of these truths even after you are scattered abroad by persecution and are downcast by many sorrows. When you feel that you are alone in the world, I will know of your isolation even as, when you are scattered every man to his own place, leaving the Son of Man in the hands of his enemies, you will know of mine. But I am never alone; always is the Father with me. Even at such a time I will pray for you. And all of these things have I told you that you might have peace and have it more abundantly. In this world you will have tribulation, but be of good cheer; I have triumphed in the world and shown you the way to eternal joy and everlasting service."

Jesus gives peace to his fellow doers of the will of God but not on the order of the joys and satisfactions of this material world. Unbelieving materialists and fatalists can hope to enjoy only two kinds of peace and soul comfort: Either they must be stoics, with steadfast resolution determined to face the inevitable and to endure the worst; or they must be optimists, ever indulging that hope which springs eternal in the human breast, vainly longing for a peace which never really comes.

A certain amount of both stoicism and optimism are serviceable in living a life on earth, but neither has aught to do with that superb peace which the Son of God bestows upon his brethren in the flesh. The peace which Michael gives his children on earth is that very peace which filled his own soul when he himself lived the mortal life in the flesh and on this very world. The peace of Jesus is the joy and satisfaction of a God-knowing individual who has achieved the triumph of learning fully how to do the will of God while living the mortal life in the flesh. The peace of Jesus' mind was founded on an absolute human faith in the actuality of the divine Father's wise and sympathetic overcare. Jesus had trouble on earth, he has even been falsely called the "man of sorrows," but in and through all of these experiences he enjoyed the comfort of that confidence which ever empowered him to proceed with his life purpose in the full assurance that he was achieving the Father's will.

Jesus was determined, persistent, and thoroughly devoted to the accomplishment of his mission, but he was not an unfeeling and calloused stoic; he ever sought for the cheerful aspects of his life experiences, but he was not a blind and self-deceived optimist. The Master knew all that was to befall him, and he was unafraid. After he had bestowed this peace upon each of his followers, he could consistently say, "Let not your heart be troubled, neither let it be afraid."

The peace of Jesus is, then, the peace and assurance of a son who fully believes that his career for time and eternity is safely and wholly in the care and keeping of an all-wise, all-loving, and all-powerful spirit Father. And this is, indeed, a peace which passes the understanding of mortal mind, but which can be enjoyed to the full by the believing human heart.

2. FAREWELL PERSONAL ADMONITIONS

The Master had finished giving his farewell instructions and imparting his final admonitions to the apostles as a group. He then addressed himself to saying good-bye individually and to giving each a word of personal advice, together with his parting blessing. The apostles were still seated about the table as when they first sat down to partake of the Last Supper, and as the Master went around the table talking to them, each man rose to his feet when Jesus addressed him.

To John, Jesus said: "You, John, are the youngest of my brethren. You have been very near me, and while I love you all with the same love which a father bestows upon his sons, you were designated by Andrew as one of the three who should always be near me. Besides this, you have acted for me and must continue so to act in many matters concerning my earthly family. And I go to the Father, John, having full confidence that you will continue to watch over those who are mine in the flesh. See to it that their present confusion regarding my mission does not in any way prevent your extending to them all sympathy, counsel, and help even as you know I would if I were to remain in the flesh. And when they all come to see the light and enter fully into the kingdom, while you all will welcome them joyously, I depend upon you, John, to welcome them for me.

"And now, as I enter upon the closing hours of my earthly career, remain near at hand that I may leave any message with you regarding my family. As concerns the work put in my hands by the Father, it is now finished except for my death in the flesh, and I am ready to drink this last cup. But as for the responsibilities left to me by my earthly father, Joseph, while I have attended to these during my life, I must now depend upon you to act in my stead in all these matters. And I have chosen you to do this for me, John, because you are the youngest and will therefore very likely outlive these other apostles.

"Once we called you and your brother sons of thunder. You started out with us strong-minded and intolerant, but you have changed much since you wanted me to call fire down upon the heads of ignorant and thoughtless unbelievers. And you must change yet more. You should become the apostle of the new commandment which I have this night given you. Dedicate your life to teaching your brethren how to love one another, even as I have loved you."

As John Zebedee stood there in the upper chamber, the tears rolling down his cheeks, he looked into the Master's face and said: "And so I will, my Master, but how can I learn to love my brethren more?" And then answered Jesus: "You will learn to love your brethren more when you first learn to love their Father in heaven more, and after you have become truly more interested in their welfare in time and in eternity. And all such human interest is fostered by understanding sympathy, unselfish service, and unstinted forgiveness. No man should despise your youth, but I exhort you always to give due consideration to the fact that age oftentimes represents experience, and that nothing in human affairs can take the place of actual experience. Strive to live peaceably with all men, especially your friends in the brotherhood of the heavenly kingdom. And, John, always remember, strive not with the souls you would win for the kingdom."

And then the Master, passing around his own seat, paused a moment by the side of the place of Judas Iscariot. The apostles were rather surprised that Judas had not returned before this, and they were very curious to know the significance of Jesus' sad countenance as he stood by the betrayer's vacant seat. But none of them, except possibly Andrew, entertained even the slightest thought that their treasurer had gone out to betray his Master, as Jesus had intimated to them earlier in the evening and during the supper. So much had been going on that, for the time being, they had quite forgotten about the Master's announcement that one of them would betray him.

Jesus now went over to Simon Zelotes, who stood up and listened to this admonition: "You are a true son of Abraham, but what a time I have had trying to make you a son of this heavenly kingdom. I love you and so do all of your brethren. I know that you love me, Simon, and that you also love the kingdom, but you are still set on making this kingdom come according to your liking. I know full well that you will eventually grasp the spiritual nature and meaning of my gospel, and that you will do valiant work in its proclamation, but I am distressed about what may happen to you when I depart. I would rejoice to know that you would not falter; I would be made happy if I could know that, after I go to the Father, you would not cease to be my apostle, and that you would acceptably deport yourself as an ambassador of the heavenly kingdom."

Jesus had hardly ceased speaking to Simon Zelotes when the fiery patriot, drying his eyes, replied: "Master, have no fears for my loyalty. I have turned my back upon everything that I might dedicate my life to the establishment of your kingdom on earth, and I will not falter. I have survived every disappointment so far, and I will not forsake you."

And then, laying his hand on Simon's shoulder, Jesus said: "It is indeed refreshing to hear you talk like that, especially at such a time as this, but, my good friend, you still do not know what you are talking about. Not for one moment would I doubt your loyalty, your devotion; I know you would not hesitate to go forth in battle and die for me, as all these others would" (and they all nodded a vigorous approval), "but that will not be required of you. I have repeatedly told you that my kingdom is not of this world, and that my disciples will not fight to effect its establishment. I have told you this many times, Simon, but you refuse to face the truth. I am not concerned with your loyalty to me and to the kingdom, but what will you do when I go away and you at last wake up to the realization that you have failed to grasp the meaning of my teaching, and that you must adjust your misconceptions to the reality of another and spiritual order of affairs in the kingdom?"

Simon wanted to speak further, but Jesus raised his hand and, stopping him, went on to say: "None of my apostles are more sincere and honest at heart than you, but not one of them will be so upset and disheartened as you, after my departure. In all of your discouragement my spirit shall abide with you, and these, your brethren, will not forsake you. Do not forget what I have taught you regarding the relation of citizenship on earth to sonship in the Father's spiritual kingdom. Ponder well all that I have said to you about rendering to Caesar the things which are Caesar's and to God that which is God's. Dedicate your life, Simon, to showing how acceptably mortal man may fulfill my injunction concerning the simultaneous recognition of temporal duty to civil powers and spiritual service in the brotherhood of the kingdom. If you will be taught by the Spirit of Truth, never will there be conflict between the requirements of citizenship on earth and sonship in heaven unless the temporal rulers presume to require of you the homage and worship which belong only to God.

"And now, Simon, when you do finally see all of this, and after you have shaken off your depression and have gone forth proclaiming this gospel in great power, never forget that I was with you even through all of your season of discouragement, and that I will go on with you to the very end. You shall always be my apostle, and after you become willing to see by the eye of the spirit and more fully to yield your will to the will of the Father in heaven, then will you return to labor as my ambassador, and no one shall take away from you the authority which I have conferred upon you, because of your slowness of comprehending the truths I have taught you. And so, Simon, once more I warn you that they who fight with the sword perish with the sword, while they who labor in the spirit achieve life everlasting in the kingdom to come with joy and peace in the kingdom which now is. And when the work given into your hands is finished on earth, you, Simon, shall sit down with me in my kingdom over there. You shall really see the kingdom you have longed for, but not in this life. Continue to believe in me and in that which I have revealed to you, and you shall receive the gift of eternal life."

When Jesus had finished speaking to Simon Zelotes, he stepped over to Matthew Levi and said: "No longer will it devolve upon you to provide for the treasury of the apostolic group. Soon, very soon, you will all be scattered; you will not be permitted to enjoy the comforting and sustaining association of even one of your brethren. As you go onward preaching this gospel of the kingdom, you will have to find for yourselves new associates. I have sent you forth two and two during the times of your training, but now that I am leaving you, after you have recovered from the shock, you will go out alone, and to the ends of the earth, proclaiming this good news: That faith-quickened mortals are the sons of God."

Then spoke Matthew: "But, Master, who will send us, and how shall we know where to go? Will Andrew show us the way?" And Jesus answered: "No, Levi, Andrew will no longer direct you in the proclamation of the gospel. He will, indeed, continue as your friend and counselor until that day whereon the new teacher comes, and then shall the Spirit of Truth lead each of you abroad to labor for the extension of the kingdom. Many changes have come over you since that day at the customhouse when you first set out to follow me; but many more must come before you will be able to see the vision of a brotherhood in which gentile sits alongside Jew in fraternal association. But go on with your urge to win your Jewish brethren until you are fully satisfied and then turn with power to the gentiles. One thing you may be certain of, Levi: You have won the confidence and affection of your brethren; they all love you." (And all ten of them signified their acquiescence in the Master's words.)

"Levi, I know much about your anxieties, sacrifices, and labors to keep the treasury replenished which your brethren do not know, and I am rejoiced that, though he who carried the bag is absent, the publican ambassador is here at my farewell gathering with the messengers of the kingdom. I pray that you may discern the meaning of my teaching with the eyes of the spirit. And when the new teacher comes into your heart, follow on as he will lead you and let your brethren see—even all the world—what the Father can do for a hated tax-gatherer who dared to follow the Son of Man and to believe the gospel of the kingdom. Even from the first, Levi, I loved you as I did these other Galileans. Knowing then so well that neither the Father nor the Son has respect of persons, see to it that you make no such distinctions among those who become believers in the gospel through your ministry. And so, Matthew, dedicate your whole future life service to showing all men that God is no respecter of persons; that, in the sight of God and in the fellowship of the kingdom, all men are equal, all believers are the sons of God."

Jesus then stepped over to James Zebedee, who stood in silence as the Master addressed him, saying: "James, when you and your younger brother once came to me seeking preferment in the honors of the kingdom, and I told you such honors were for the Father to bestow, I asked if you were able to drink my cup, and both of you answered that you were. Even if you were not then able, and if you are not now able, you will soon be prepared for such a service by the experience you are about to pass through. By such behavior you angered your brethren at that time. If they have not already fully forgiven you, they will when they see you drink my cup. Whether your ministry be long or short, possess your soul in patience. When the new teacher comes, let him teach you the poise of compassion and that sympathetic tolerance which is born of sublime confidence in me and of perfect submission to the Father's will. Dedicate your life to the demonstration of that combined human affection and divine dignity of the God-knowing and Son-believing disciple. And all who thus live will reveal the gospel even in the manner of their death. You and your brother John will go different ways, and one of you may sit down with me in the eternal kingdom long before the other. It would help you much if you would learn that true wisdom embraces discretion as well as courage. You should learn sagacity to go along with your aggressiveness. There will come those supreme moments wherein my disciples will not hesitate to lay down their lives for this gospel, but in all ordinary circumstances it would be far better to placate the wrath of unbelievers that you might live and continue to preach the glad tidings. As far as lies in your power, live long on the earth that your life of many years may be fruitful in souls won for the heavenly kingdom."

When the Master had finished speaking to James Zebedee, he stepped around to the end of the table where Andrew sat and, looking his faithful helper in the eyes, said: "Andrew, you have faithfully represented me as acting head of the ambassadors of the heavenly kingdom. Although you have sometimes doubted and at other times manifested dangerous timidity, still, you have always been sincerely just and eminently fair in dealing with your associates. Ever since the ordination of you and your brethren as messengers of the kingdom, you have been self-governing in all group administrative affairs except that I designated you as the acting head of these chosen ones. In no other temporal matter have I acted to direct or to influence your decisions. And this I did in order to provide for leadership in the direction of all your subsequent group deliberations. In my universe and in my Father's universe of universes, our brethren-sons are dealt with as individuals in all their spiritual relations, but in all group relationships we unfailingly provide for definite leadership. Our kingdom is a realm of order, and where two or more will creatures act in co-operation, there is always provided the authority of leadership.

"And now, Andrew, since you are the chief of your brethren by authority of my appointment, and since you have thus served as my personal representative, and as I am about to leave you and go to my Father, I release you from all responsibility as regards these temporal and administrative affairs. From now on you may exercise no jurisdiction over your brethren except that which you have earned in your capacity as spiritual leader, and which your brethren therefore freely recognize. From this hour you may exercise no authority over your brethren unless they restore such jurisdiction to you by their definite legislative action after I shall have gone to the Father. But this release from responsibility as the administrative head of this group does not in any manner lessen your moral responsibility to do everything in your power to hold your brethren together with a firm and loving hand during the trying time just ahead, those days which must intervene between my departure in the flesh and the sending of the new teacher who will live in your hearts, and who ultimately will lead you into all truth. As I prepare to leave you, I would liberate you from all administrative responsibility which had its inception and authority in my presence as one among you. Henceforth I shall exercise only spiritual authority over you and among you.

"If your brethren desire to retain you as their counselor, I direct that you should, in all matters temporal and spiritual, do your utmost to promote peace and harmony among the various groups of sincere gospel believers. Dedicate the remainder of your life to promoting the practical aspects of brotherly love among your brethren. Be kind to my brothers in the flesh when they come fully to believe this gospel; manifest loving and impartial devotion to the Greeks in the West and to Abner in the East. Although these, my apostles, are soon going to be scattered to the four corners of the earth, there to proclaim the good news of the salvation of sonship with God, you are to hold them together during the trying time just ahead, that season of intense testing during which you must learn to believe this gospel without my personal presence while you patiently await the arrival of the new teacher, the Spirit of Truth. And so, Andrew, though it may not fall to you to do the great works as seen by men, be content to be the teacher and counselor of those who do such things. Go on with your work on earth to the end, and then shall you continue this ministry in the eternal kingdom, for have I not many times told you that I have other sheep not of this flock?"

Jesus then went over to the Alpheus twins and, standing between them, said: "My little children, you are one of the three groups of brothers who chose to follow after me. All six of you have done well to work in peace with your own flesh and blood, but none have done better than you. Hard times are just ahead of us. You may not understand all that will befall you and your brethren, but never doubt that you were once called to the work of the kingdom. For some time there will be no multitudes to manage, but do not become discouraged; when your lifework is finished, I will receive you on high, where in glory you shall tell of your salvation to seraphic hosts and to multitudes of the high Sons of God. Dedicate your lives to the enhancement of commonplace toil. Show all men on earth and the angels of heaven how cheerfully and courageously mortal man can, after having been called to work for a season in the special service of God, return to the labors of former days. If, for the time being, your work in the outward affairs of the kingdom should be completed, you should go back to your former labors with the new enlightenment of the experience of sonship with God and with the exalted realization that, to him who is God-knowing, there is no such thing as common labor or secular toil. To you who have worked with me, all things have become sacred, and all earthly labor has become a service even to God the Father. And when you hear the news of the doings of your former apostolic associates, rejoice with them and continue your daily work as those who wait upon God and serve while they wait. You have been my apostles, and you always shall be, and I will remember you in the kingdom to come."

And then Jesus went over to Philip, who, standing up, heard this message from his Master: "Philip, you have asked me many foolish questions, but I have done my utmost to answer every one, and now would I answer the last of such questionings which have arisen in your most honest but unspiritual mind. All the time I have been coming around toward you, have you been saying to yourself, 'What shall I ever do if the Master goes away and leaves us alone in the world?' O, you of little faith! And yet you have almost as much as many of your brethren. You have been a good steward, Philip. You failed us only a few times, and one of those failures we utilized to manifest the Father's glory. Your office of stewardship is about over. You must soon more fully do the work you were called to do—the preaching of this gospel of the kingdom. Philip, you have always wanted to be shown, and very soon shall you see great things. Far better that you should have seen all this by faith, but since you were sincere even in your material sightedness, you will live to see my words fulfilled. And then, when you are blessed with spiritual vision, go forth to your work, dedicating your life to the cause of leading mankind to search for God and to seek eternal realities with the eye of spiritual faith and not with the eyes of the material mind. Remember, Philip, you have a great mission on earth, for the world is filled with those who look at life just as you have tended to. You have a great work to do, and when it is finished in faith, you shall come to me in my kingdom, and I will take great pleasure in showing you that which eye has not seen, ear heard, nor the mortal mind conceived. In the meantime, become as a little child in the kingdom of the spirit and permit me, as the spirit of the new teacher, to lead you forward in the spiritual kingdom. And in this way will I be able to do much for you which I was not able to accomplish when I sojourned with you as a mortal of the realm. And always remember, Philip, he who has seen me has seen the Father."

Then went the Master over to Nathaniel. As Nathaniel stood up, Jesus bade him be seated and, sitting down by his side, said: "Nathaniel, you have learned to live above prejudice and to practice increased tolerance since you became my apostle. But there is much more for you to learn. You have been a blessing to your fellows in that they have always been admonished by your consistent sincerity. When I have gone, it may be that your frankness will interfere with your getting along well with your brethren, both old and new. You should learn that the expression of even a good thought must be modulated in accordance with the intellectual status and spiritual development of the hearer. Sincerity is most serviceable in the work of the kingdom when it is wedded to discretion.

"If you would learn to work with your brethren, you might accomplish more permanent things, but if you find yourself going off in quest of those who think as you do, in that event dedicate your life to proving that the God-knowing disciple can become a kingdom builder even when alone in the world and wholly isolated from his fellow believers. I know you will be faithful to the end, and I will some day welcome you to the enlarged service of my kingdom on high."

Then Nathaniel spoke, asking Jesus this question: "I have listened to your teaching ever since you first called me to the service of this kingdom, but I honestly cannot understand the full meaning of all you tell us. I do not know what to expect next, and I think most of my brethren are likewise perplexed, but they hesitate to confess their confusion. Can you help me?" Jesus, putting his hand on Nathaniel's shoulder, said: "My friend, it is not strange that you should encounter perplexity in your attempt to grasp the meaning of my spiritual teachings since you are so handicapped by your preconceptions of Jewish tradition and so confused by your persistent tendency to interpret my gospel in accordance with the teachings of the scribes and Pharisees.

"I have taught you much by word of mouth, and I have lived my life among you. I have done all that can be done to enlighten your minds and liberate your souls, and what you have not been able to get from my teachings and my life, you must now prepare to acquire at the hand of that master of all teachers—actual experience. And in all of this new experience which now awaits you, I will go before you and the Spirit of Truth shall be with you. Fear not; that which you now fail to comprehend, the new teacher, when he has come, will reveal to you throughout the remainder of your life on earth and on through your training in the eternal ages."

And then the Master, turning to all of them, said: "Be not dismayed that you fail to grasp the full meaning of the gospel. You are but finite, mortal men, and that which I have taught you is infinite, divine, and eternal. Be patient and of good courage since you have the eternal ages before you in which to continue your progressive attainment of the experience of becoming perfect, even as your Father in Paradise is perfect."

And then Jesus went over to Thomas, who, standing up, heard him say: "Thomas, you have often lacked faith; however, when you have had your seasons with doubt, you have never lacked courage. I know well that the false prophets and spurious teachers will not deceive you. After I have gone, your brethren will the more appreciate your critical way of viewing new teachings. And when you all are scattered to the ends of the earth in the times to come, remember that you are still my ambassador. Dedicate your life to the great work of showing how the critical material mind of man can triumph over the inertia of intellectual doubting when faced by the demonstration of the manifestation of living truth as it operates in the experience of spirit-born men and women who yield the fruits of the spirit in their lives, and who love one another, even as I have loved you. Thomas, I am glad you joined us, and I know, after a short period of perplexity, you will go on in the service of the kingdom. Your doubts have perplexed your brethren, but they have never troubled me. I have confidence in you, and I will go before you even to the uttermost parts of the earth."

Then the Master went over to Simon Peter, who stood up as Jesus addressed him: "Peter, I know you love me, and that you will dedicate your life to the public proclamation of this gospel of the kingdom to Jew and gentile, but I am distressed that your years of such close association with me have not done more to help you think before you speak. What experience must you pass through before you will learn to set a guard upon your lips? How much trouble have you made for us by your thoughtless speaking, by your presumptuous self-confidence! And you are destined to make much more trouble for yourself if you do not master this frailty. You know that your brethren love you in spite of this weakness, and you should also understand that this shortcoming in no way impairs my affection for you, but it lessens your usefulness and never ceases to make trouble for you. But you will undoubtedly receive great help from the experience you will pass through this very night. And what I now say to you, Simon Peter, I likewise say to all your brethren here assembled: This night you will all be in great danger of stumbling over me. You know it is written, 'The shepherd will be smitten and the sheep will be scattered abroad.' When I am absent, there is great danger that some of you will succumb to doubts and stumble because of what befalls me. But I promise you now that I will come back to you for a little while, and that I will then go before you into Galilee."

Then said Peter, placing his hand on Jesus' shoulder: "No matter if all my brethren should succumb to doubts because of you, I promise that I will not stumble over anything you may do. I will go with you and, if need be, die for you."

As Peter stood there before his Master, all atremble with intense emotion and overflowing with genuine love for him, Jesus looked straight into his moistened eyes as he said: "Peter, verily, verily, I say to you, this night the cock will not crow until you have denied me three or four times. And thus what you have failed to learn from peaceful association with me, you will learn through much trouble and many sorrows. And after you have really learned this needful lesson, you should strengthen your brethren and go on living a life dedicated to preaching this gospel, though you may fall into prison and, perhaps, follow me in paying the supreme price of loving service in the building of the Father's kingdom.

"But remember my promise: When I am raised up, I will tarry with you for a season before I go to the Father. And even this night will I make supplication to the Father that he strengthen each of you for that which you must now so soon pass through. I love you all with the love wherewith the Father loves me, and therefore should you henceforth love one another, even as I have loved you."

And then, when they had sung a hymn, they departed for the camp on the Mount of Olives.

PAPER 182
IN GETHSEMANE

IT WAS about ten o'clock this Thursday night when Jesus led the eleven apostles from the home of Elijah and Mary Mark on their way back to the Gethsemane camp. Ever since that day in the hills, John Mark had made it his business to keep a watchful eye on Jesus. John, being in need of sleep, had obtained several hours of rest while the Master had been with his apostles in the upper room, but on hearing them coming downstairs, he arose and, quickly throwing a linen coat about himself, followed them through the city, over the brook Kidron, and on to their private encampment adjacent to Gethsemane Park. And John Mark remained so near the Master throughout this night and the next day that he witnessed everything and overheard much of what the Master said from this time on to the hour of the crucifixion.

As Jesus and the eleven made their way back to camp, the apostles began to wonder about the meaning of Judas's prolonged absence, and they spoke to one another concerning the Master's prediction that one of them would betray him, and for the first time they suspected that all was not well with Judas Iscariot. But they did not engage in open comment about Judas until they reached the camp and observed that he was not there, waiting to receive them. When they all besieged Andrew to know what had become of Judas, their chief remarked only, "I do not know where Judas is, but I fear he has deserted us."

1. THE LAST GROUP PRAYER

A few moments after arriving at camp, Jesus said to them: "My friends and brethren, my time with you is now very short, and I desire that we draw apart by ourselves while we pray to our Father in heaven for strength to sustain us in this hour and henceforth in all the work we must do in his name."

When Jesus had thus spoken, he led the way a short distance up on Olivet, and in full view of Jerusalem he bade them kneel on a large flat rock in a circle about him as they had done on the day of their ordination; and then, as he stood there in the midst of them glorified in the mellow moonlight, he lifted up his eyes toward heaven and prayed:

"Father, my hour has come; now glorify your Son that the Son may glorify you. I know that you have given me full authority over all living creatures in my realm, and I will give eternal life to all who will become faith sons of God. And this is eternal life, that my creatures should know you as the only true God and Father of all, and that they should believe in him whom you sent into the world. Father, I have exalted you on earth and have accomplished the work which you gave me to do. I have almost finished my bestowal upon the children of our own creation; there remains only for me to lay down my life in the flesh. And now,

O my Father, glorify me with the glory which I had with you before this world was and receive me once more at your right hand.

"I have manifested you to the men whom you chose from the world and gave to me. They are yours—as all life is in your hands—you gave them to me, and I have lived among them, teaching them the way of life, and they have believed. These men are learning that all I have comes from you, and that the life I live in the flesh is to make known my Father to the worlds. The truth which you have given to me I have revealed to them. These, my friends and ambassadors, have sincerely willed to receive your word. I have told them that I came forth from you, that you sent me into this world, and that I am about to return to you. Father, I do pray for these chosen men. And I pray for them not as I would pray for the world, but as for those whom I have chosen out of the world to represent me to the world after I have returned to your work, even as I have represented you in this world during my sojourn in the flesh. These men are mine; you gave them to me; but all things which are mine are ever yours, and all that which was yours you have now caused to be mine. You have been exalted in me, and I now pray that I may be honored in these men. I can no longer be in this world; I am about to return to the work you have given me to do. I must leave these men behind to represent us and our kingdom among men. Father, keep these men faithful as I prepare to yield up my life in the flesh. Help these, my friends, to be one in spirit, even as we are one. As long as I could be with them, I could watch over them and guide them, but now am I about to go away. Be near them, Father, until we can send the new teacher to comfort and strengthen them.

"You gave me twelve men, and I have kept them all save one, the son of revenge, who would not have further fellowship with us. These men are weak and frail, but I know we can trust them; I have proved them; they love me, even as they reverence you. While they must suffer much for my sake, I desire that they should also be filled with the joy of the assurance of sonship in the heavenly kingdom. I have given these men your word and have taught them the truth. The world may hate them, even as it has hated me, but I do not ask that you take them out of the world, only that you keep them from the evil in the world. Sanctify them in the truth; your word is truth. And as you sent me into this world, even so am I about to send these men into the world. For their sakes I have lived among men and have consecrated my life to your service that I might inspire them to be purified through the truth I have taught them and the love I have revealed to them. I well know, my Father, that there is no need for me to ask you to watch over these brethren after I have gone; I know you love them even as I, but I do this that they may the better realize the Father loves mortal men even as does the Son.

"And now, my Father, I would pray not only for these eleven men but also for all others who now believe, or who may hereafter believe the gospel of the kingdom through the word of their future ministry. I want them all to be one, even as you and I are one. You are in me and I am in you, and I desire that these believers likewise be in us; that both of our spirits indwell them. If my children are one as we are one, and if they love one another as I have loved them, all men will then believe that I came forth from you and be willing to receive the revelation of truth and glory which I have made. The glory which you gave me I have revealed to these believers. As you have lived with me in spirit, so have I lived with them in the flesh. As you have been one with me, so have I been one with them, and so will the new teacher ever be one with them and in them. And all this have I done that my brethren in the flesh may know that the Father loves them even as does the Son, and that you love them even as you love me. Father, work with me to save these believers that they may presently come to be with me in glory and then go on to join you in the Paradise embrace. Those who serve with me in humiliation, I would have with me in glory so that they may see all you have given into my hands as the eternal harvest of the seed sowing of time in the likeness of mortal flesh. I long to show my earthly brethren the glory I had with you before the founding of this world. This world knows very little of you, righteous Father, but I know you, and I have made you known to these believers, and they will make known your name to other generations. And now I promise them that you will be with them in the world even as you have been with me—even so."

The eleven remained kneeling in this circle about Jesus for several minutes before they arose and in silence made their way back to the near-by camp.

Jesus prayed for *unity* among his followers, but he did not desire uniformity. Sin creates a dead level of evil inertia, but righteousness nourishes the creative spirit of individual experience in the living realities of eternal truth and in the progressive communion of the divine spirits of the Father and the Son. In the spiritual fellowship of the believer-son with the divine Father there can never be doctrinal finality and sectarian superiority of group consciousness.

The Master, during the course of this final prayer with his apostles, alluded to the fact that he had manifested the Father's *name* to the world. And that is truly what he did by the revelation of God through his perfected life in the flesh. The Father in heaven had sought to reveal himself to Moses, but he could proceed no further than to cause it to be said, "I AM." And when pressed for further revelation of himself, it was only disclosed, "I AM that I AM." But when Jesus had finished his earth life, this name of the Father had been so revealed that the Master, who was the Father incarnate, could truly say:

I am the bread of life.
I am the living water.
I am the light of the world.
I am the desire of all ages.
I am the open door to eternal salvation.
I am the reality of endless life.
I am the good shepherd.
I am the pathway of infinite perfection.
I am the resurrection and the life.
I am the secret of eternal survival.
I am the way, the truth, and the life.
I am the infinite Father of my finite children.
I am the true vine; you are the branches.
I am the hope of all who know the living truth.
I am the living bridge from one world to another.
I am the living link between time and eternity.

Thus did Jesus enlarge the living revelation of the name of God to all generations. As divine love reveals the nature of God, eternal truth discloses his name in ever-enlarging proportions.

2. LAST HOUR BEFORE THE BETRAYAL

The apostles were greatly shocked when they returned to their camp and found Judas absent. While the eleven were engaged in a heated discussion of their traitorous fellow apostle, David Zebedee and John Mark took Jesus to one side and revealed that they had kept Judas under observation for several days, and that they knew he intended to betray him into the hands of his enemies. Jesus listened to them but only said: "My friends, nothing can happen to the Son of Man unless the Father in heaven so wills. Let not your hearts be troubled; all things will work together for the glory of God and the salvation of men."

The cheerful attitude of Jesus was waning. As the hour passed, he grew more and more serious, even sorrowful. The apostles, being much agitated, were loath to return to their tents even when requested to do so by the Master himself. Returning from his talk with David and John, he addressed his last words to all eleven, saying: "My friends, go to your rest. Prepare yourselves for the work of tomorrow. Remember, we should all submit ourselves to the will of the Father in heaven. My peace I leave with you." And having thus spoken, he motioned them to their tents, but as they went, he called to Peter, James, and John, saying, "I desire that you remain with me for a little while."

The apostles fell asleep only because they were literally exhausted; they had been running short on sleep ever since their arrival in Jerusalem. Before they went to their separate sleeping quarters, Simon Zelotes led them all over to his tent, where were stored the swords and other arms, and supplied each of them with this fighting equipment. All of them received these arms and girded themselves therewith except Nathaniel. Nathaniel, in refusing to arm himself, said: "My brethren, the Master has repeatedly told us that his kingdom is not of this world, and that his disciples should not fight with the sword to bring about its establishment. I believe this; I do not think the Master needs to have us employ the sword in his defense. We have all seen his mighty power and know that he could defend himself against his enemies if he so desired. If he will not resist his enemies, it must be that such a course represents his attempt to fulfill his Father's will. I will pray, but I will not wield the sword." When Andrew heard Nathaniel's speech, he handed his sword back to Simon Zelotes. And so nine of them were armed as they separated for the night.

Resentment of Judas's being a traitor for the moment eclipsed everything else in the apostles' minds. The Master's comment in reference to Judas, spoken in the course of the last prayer, opened their eyes to the fact that he had forsaken them.

After the eight apostles had finally gone to their tents, and while Peter, James, and John were standing by to receive the Master's orders, Jesus called to David Zebedee, "Send to me your most fleet and trustworthy messenger." When David brought to the Master one Jacob, once a runner on the overnight messenger service between Jerusalem and Bethsaida, Jesus, addressing him, said: "In all haste, go to Abner at Philadelphia and say: 'The Master sends greetings of peace to you and says that the hour has come when he will be delivered into the hands of his enemies, who will put him to death, but that he will rise from the dead and appear to you shortly, before he goes to the Father, and that he will then give you guidance to the time when the new teacher shall come to live in your hearts.'" And when Jacob had rehearsed this message to the

Master's satisfaction, Jesus sent him on his way, saying: "Fear not what any man may do to you, Jacob, for this night an unseen messenger will run by your side."

Then Jesus turned to the chief of the visiting Greeks who were encamped with them, and said: "My brother, be not disturbed by what is about to take place since I have already forewarned you. The Son of Man will be put to death at the instigation of his enemies, the chief priests and the rulers of the Jews, but I will rise to be with you a short time before I go to the Father. And when you have seen all this come to pass, glorify God and strengthen your brethren."

In ordinary circumstances the apostles would have bidden the Master a personal good night, but this evening they were so preoccupied with the sudden realization of Judas's desertion and so overcome by the unusual nature of the Master's farewell prayer that they listened to his good-bye salutation and went away in silence.

Jesus did say this to Andrew as he left his side that night: "Andrew, do what you can to keep your brethren together until I come again to you after I have drunk this cup. Strengthen your brethren, seeing that I have already told you all. Peace be with you."

None of the apostles expected anything out of the ordinary to happen that night since it was already so late. They sought sleep that they might rise up early in the morning and be prepared for the worst. They thought that the chief priests would seek to apprehend their Master early in the morning as no secular work was ever done after noon on the preparation day for the Passover. Only David Zebedee and John Mark understood that the enemies of Jesus were coming with Judas that very night.

David had arranged to stand guard that night on the upper trail which led to the Bethany-Jerusalem road, while John Mark was to watch along the road coming up by the Kidron to Gethsemane. Before David went to his self-imposed task of outpost duty, he bade farewell to Jesus, saying: "Master, I have had great joy in my service with you. My brothers are your apostles, but I have delighted to do the lesser things as they should be done, and I shall miss you with all my heart when you are gone." And then said Jesus to David: "David, my son, others have done that which they were directed to do, but this service have you done of your own heart, and I have not been unmindful of your devotion. You, too, shall some day serve with me in the eternal kingdom."

And then, as he prepared to go on watch by the upper trail, David said to Jesus: "You know, Master, I sent for your family, and I have word by a messenger that they are tonight in Jericho. They will be here early tomorrow forenoon since it would be dangerous for them to come up the bloody way by night." And Jesus, looking down upon David, only said: "Let it be so, David."

When David had gone up Olivet, John Mark took up his vigil near the road which ran by the brook down to Jerusalem. And John would have remained at this post but for his great desire to be near Jesus and to know what was going on. Shortly after David left him, and when John Mark observed Jesus withdraw, with Peter, James, and John, into a near-by ravine, he was so overcome with combined devotion and curiosity that he forsook his sentinel post and followed after them, hiding himself in the bushes, from which place he saw and overheard all that transpired during those last moments in the garden and just before Judas and the armed guards appeared to arrest Jesus.

While all this was in progress at the Master's camp, Judas Iscariot was in conference with the captain of the temple guards, who had assembled his men preparatory to setting out, under the leadership of the betrayer, to arrest Jesus.

3. ALONE IN GETHSEMANE

After all was still and quiet about the camp, Jesus, taking Peter, James, and John, went a short way up a near-by ravine where he had often before gone to pray and commune. The three apostles could not help recognizing that he was grievously oppressed; never before had they observed their Master to be so heavy-laden and sorrowful. When they arrived at the place of his devotions, he bade the three sit down and watch with him while he went off about a stone's throw to pray. And when he had fallen down on his face, he prayed: "My Father, I came into this world to do your will, and so have I. I know that the hour has come to lay down this life in the flesh, and I do not shrink therefrom, but I would know that it is your will that I drink this cup. Send me the assurance that I will please you in my death even as I have in my life."

The Master remained in a prayerful attitude for a few moments, and then, going over to the three apostles, he found them sound asleep, for their eyes were heavy and they could not remain awake. As Jesus awoke them, he said: "What! can you not watch with me even for one hour? Cannot you see that my soul is exceedingly sorrowful, even to death, and that I crave your companionship?" After the three had aroused from their slumber, the Master again went apart by himself and, falling down on the ground, again prayed: "Father, I know it is possible to avoid this cup—all things are possible with you—but I have come to do your will, and while this is a bitter cup, I would drink it if it is your will." And when he had thus prayed, a mighty angel came down by his side and, speaking to him, touched him and strengthened him.

When Jesus returned to speak with the three apostles, he again found them fast asleep. He awakened them, saying: "In such an hour I need that you should watch and pray with me—all the more do you need to pray that you enter not into temptation—wherefore do you fall asleep when I leave you?"

And then, for a third time, the Master withdrew and prayed: "Father, you see my sleeping apostles; have mercy upon them. The spirit is indeed willing, but the flesh is weak. And now, O Father, if this cup may not pass, then would I drink it. Not my will, but yours, be done." And when he had finished praying, he lay for a moment prostrate on the ground. When he arose and went back to his apostles, once more he found them asleep. He surveyed them and, with a pitying gesture, tenderly said: "Sleep on now and take your rest; the time of decision is past. The hour is now upon us wherein the Son of Man will be betrayed into the hands of his enemies." As he reached down to shake them that he might awaken them, he said: "Arise, let us be going back to the camp, for, behold, he who betrays me is at hand, and the hour has come when my flock shall be scattered. But I have already told you about these things."

During the years that Jesus lived among his followers, they did, indeed, have much proof of his divine nature, but just now are they about to witness new evidences of his humanity. Just before the greatest of all the revelations of his divinity, his resurrection, must now come the greatest proofs of his mortal nature, his humiliation and crucifixion.

Each time he prayed in the garden, his humanity laid a firmer faith-hold upon his divinity; his human will more completely became one with the divine will of his Father. Among other words spoken to him by the mighty angel was the message that the Father desired his Son to finish his earth bestowal by passing through the creature experience of death just as all mortal creatures must experience material dissolution in passing from the existence of time into the progression of eternity.

Earlier in the evening it had not seemed so difficult to drink the cup, but as the human Jesus bade farewell to his apostles and sent them to their rest, the trial grew more appalling. Jesus experienced that natural ebb and flow of feeling which is common to all human experience, and just now he was weary from work, exhausted from the long hours of strenuous labor and painful anxiety concerning the safety of his apostles. While no mortal can presume to understand the thoughts and feelings of the incarnate Son of God at such a time as this, we know that he endured great anguish and suffered untold sorrow, for the perspiration rolled off his face in great drops. He was at last convinced that the Father intended to allow natural events to take their course; he was fully determined to employ none of his sovereign power as the supreme head of a universe to save himself.

The assembled hosts of a vast creation are now hovered over this scene under the transient joint command of Gabriel and the Personalized Adjuster of Jesus. The division commanders of these armies of heaven have repeatedly been warned not to interfere with these transactions on earth unless Jesus himself should order them to intervene.

The experience of parting with the apostles was a great strain on the human heart of Jesus; this sorrow of love bore down on him and made it more difficult to face such a death as he well knew awaited him. He realized how weak and how ignorant his apostles were, and he dreaded to leave them. He well knew that the time of his departure had come, but his human heart longed to find out whether there might not possibly be some legitimate avenue of escape from this terrible plight of suffering and sorrow. And when it had thus sought escape, and failed, it was willing to drink the cup. The divine mind of Michael knew he had done his best for the twelve apostles; but the human heart of Jesus wished that more might have been done for them before they should be left alone in the world. Jesus' heart was being crushed; he truly loved his brethren. He was isolated from his family in the flesh; one of his chosen associates was betraying him. His father Joseph's people had rejected him and thereby sealed their doom as a people with a special mission on earth. His soul was tortured by baffled love and rejected mercy. It was just one of those awful human moments when everything seems to bear down with crushing cruelty and terrible agony.

Jesus' humanity was not insensible to this situation of private loneliness, public shame, and the appearance of the failure of his cause. All these sentiments bore down on him with indescribable heaviness. In this great sorrow his mind went back to the days of his childhood in Nazareth and to his early work in Galilee. At the time of this great trial there came up in his mind many of those pleasant scenes of his earthly ministry. And it was from these old memories of Nazareth, Capernaum, Mount Hermon, and of the sunrise and sunset on the shimmering Sea of Galilee, that he soothed himself as he made his human heart strong and ready to encounter the traitor who should so soon betray him.

Before Judas and the soldiers arrived, the Master had fully regained his customary poise; the spirit had triumphed over the flesh; faith had asserted itself over all human tendencies to fear or entertain doubt. The supreme test of the full realization of the human nature had been met and acceptably passed. Once more the Son of Man was prepared to face his enemies with equanimity and in the full assurance of his invincibility as a mortal man unreservedly dedicated to the doing of his Father's will.

PAPER 183

THE BETRAYAL AND ARREST OF JESUS

AFTER Jesus had finally awakened Peter, James, and John, he suggested that they go to their tents and seek sleep in preparation for the duties of the morrow. But by this time the three apostles were wide awake; they had been refreshed by their short naps, and besides, they were stimulated and aroused by the arrival on the scene of two excited messengers who inquired for David Zebedee and quickly went in quest of him when Peter informed them where he kept watch.

Although eight of the apostles were sound asleep, the Greeks who were encamped alongside them were more fearful of trouble, so much so that they had posted a sentinel to give the alarm in case danger should arise. When these two messengers hurried into camp, the Greek sentinel proceeded to arouse all of his fellow countrymen, who streamed forth from their tents, fully dressed and fully armed. All the camp was now aroused except the eight apostles. Peter desired to call his associates, but Jesus definitely forbade him. The Master mildly admonished them all to return to their tents, but they were reluctant to comply with his suggestion.

Failing to disperse his followers, the Master left them and walked down toward the olive press near the entrance to Gethsemane Park. Although the three apostles, the Greeks, and the other members of the camp hesitated immediately to follow him, John Mark hastened around through the olive trees and secreted himself in a small shed near the olive press. Jesus withdrew from the camp and from his friends in order that his apprehenders, when they arrived, might arrest him without disturbing his apostles. The Master feared to have his apostles awake and present at the time of his arrest lest the spectacle of Judas's betraying him should so arouse their animosity that they would offer resistance to the soldiers and would be taken into custody with him. He feared that, if they should be arrested with him, they might also perish with him.

Though Jesus knew that the plan for his death had its origin in the councils of the rulers of the Jews, he was also aware that all such nefarious schemes had the full approval of Lucifer, Satan, and Caligastia. And he well knew that these rebels of the realms would also be pleased to see all of the apostles destroyed with him.

Jesus sat down, alone, on the olive press, where he awaited the coming of the betrayer, and he was seen at this time only by John Mark and an innumerable host of celestial observers.

1. THE FATHER'S WILL

There is great danger of misunderstanding the meaning of numerous sayings and many events associated with the termination of the Master's career in the flesh. The cruel treatment of Jesus by the ignorant servants and the calloused soldiers, the unfair conduct of his trials, and the unfeeling attitude of the professed religious leaders, must not be confused with the fact that Jesus, in patiently submitting to all this suffering and humiliation, was truly doing the will of the Father in Paradise. It was, indeed and in truth, the will of the Father that his Son should drink to the full the cup of mortal experience, from birth to death, but the Father in heaven had nothing whatever to do with instigating the barbarous behavior of those supposedly civilized human beings who so brutally tortured the Master and so horribly heaped successive indignities upon his nonresisting person. These inhuman and shocking experiences which Jesus was called upon to endure in the final hours of his mortal life were not in any sense a part of the divine will of the Father, which his human nature had so triumphantly pledged to carry out at the time of the final surrender of man to God as signified in the threefold prayer which he indited in the garden while his weary apostles slept the sleep of physical exhaustion.

The Father in heaven desired the bestowal Son to finish his earth career *naturally,* just as all mortals must finish up their lives on earth and in the flesh. Ordinary men and women cannot expect to have their last hours on earth and the supervening episode of death made easy by a special dispensation. Accordingly, Jesus elected to lay down his life in the flesh in the manner which was in keeping with the outworking of natural events, and he steadfastly refused to extricate himself from the cruel clutches of a wicked conspiracy of inhuman events which swept on with horrible certainty toward his unbelievable humiliation and ignominious death. And every bit of all this astounding manifestation of hatred and this unprecedented demonstration of cruelty was the work of evil men and wicked mortals. God in heaven did not will it, neither did the archenemies of Jesus dictate it, though they did much to insure that unthinking and evil mortals would thus reject the bestowal Son. Even the father of sin turned his face away from the excruciating horror of the scene of the crucifixion.

2. JUDAS IN THE CITY

After Judas so abruptly left the table while eating the Last Supper, he went directly to the home of his cousin, and then did the two go straight to the captain of the temple guards. Judas requested the captain to assemble the guards and informed him that he was ready to lead them to Jesus. Judas having appeared on the scene a little before he was expected, there was some delay in getting started for the Mark home, where Judas expected to find Jesus still visiting with the apostles. The Master and the eleven left the home of Elijah Mark fully fifteen minutes before the betrayer and the guards arrived. By the time the apprehenders reached the Mark home, Jesus and the eleven were well outside the walls of the city and on their way to the Olivet camp.

Judas was much perturbed by this failure to find Jesus at the Mark residence and in the company of eleven men, only two of whom were armed for resistance. He happened to know that, in the afternoon when they had left camp, only Simon Peter and Simon Zelotes were girded with swords; Judas had hoped to take Jesus when the city was quiet, and when there was little chance of resistance. The betrayer feared that, if he waited for them to return to their camp, more than threescore of devoted disciples would be encountered, and he also knew that Simon Zelotes had an ample store of arms in his possession. Judas was becoming increasingly nervous as he meditated how the eleven loyal apostles would detest him, and he feared they would all seek to destroy him. He was not only disloyal, but he was a real coward at heart.

When they failed to find Jesus in the upper chamber, Judas asked the captain of the guard to return to the temple. By this time the rulers had begun to assemble at the high priest's home preparatory to receiving Jesus, seeing that their bargain with the traitor called for Jesus' arrest by midnight of that day. Judas explained to his associates that they had missed Jesus at the Mark home, and that it would be necessary to go to Gethsemane to arrest him. The betrayer then went on to state that more than threescore devoted followers were encamped with him, and that they were all well armed. The rulers of the Jews reminded Judas that Jesus had always preached nonresistance, but Judas replied that they could not depend upon all Jesus' followers obeying such teaching. He really feared for himself and therefore made bold to ask for a company of forty armed soldiers. Since the Jewish authorities had no such force of armed men under their jurisdiction, they went at once to the fortress of Antonia and requested the Roman commander to give them this guard; but when he learned that they intended to arrest Jesus, he promptly refused to accede to their request and referred them to his superior officer. In this way more than an hour was consumed in going from one authority to another until they finally were compelled to go to Pilate himself in order to obtain permission to employ the armed Roman guards. It was late when they arrived at Pilate's house, and he had retired to his private chambers with his wife. He hesitated to have anything to do with the enterprise, all the more so since his wife had asked him not to grant the request. But inasmuch as the presiding officer of the Jewish Sanhedrin was present and making personal request for this assistance, the governor thought it wise to grant the petition, thinking he could later on right any wrong they might be disposed to commit.

Accordingly, when Judas Iscariot started out from the temple, about half after eleven o'clock, he was accompanied by more than sixty persons—temple guards, Roman soldiers, and curious servants of the chief priests and rulers.

3. THE MASTER'S ARREST

As this company of armed soldiers and guards, carrying torches and lanterns, approached the garden, Judas stepped well out in front of the band that he might be ready quickly to identify Jesus so that the apprehenders could easily lay hands on him before his associates could rally to his defense. And there was yet another reason why Judas chose to be ahead of the Master's enemies: He thought it would appear that he had arrived on the scene ahead of the soldiers so that the apostles and others gathered about Jesus might not directly connect him with the armed guards following so closely upon his heels. Judas had even thought to pose as having hastened out to warn them of the coming of the apprehenders, but this plan was thwarted by Jesus' blighting greeting of the betrayer. Though the Master spoke to Judas kindly, he greeted him as a traitor.

As soon as Peter, James, and John, with some thirty of their fellow campers, saw the armed band with torches swing around the brow of the hill, they knew that these soldiers were coming to arrest Jesus, and they all rushed down to near the olive press where the Master was sitting in moonlit solitude. As the company of soldiers approached on one side, the three apostles and their associates approached on the other. As Judas strode forward to accost the Master, there the two groups stood, motionless, with the Master between them and Judas making ready to impress the traitorous kiss upon his brow.

It had been the hope of the betrayer that he could, after leading the guards to Gethsemane, simply point Jesus out to the soldiers, or at most carry out the promise to greet him with a kiss, and then quickly retire from the scene. Judas greatly feared that the apostles would all be present, and that they would concentrate their attack upon him in retribution for his daring to betray their beloved teacher. But when the Master greeted him as a betrayer, he was so confused that he made no attempt to flee.

Jesus made one last effort to save Judas from actually betraying him in that, before the traitor could reach him, he stepped to one side and, addressing the foremost soldier on the left, the captain of the Romans, said, "Whom do you seek?" The captain answered, "Jesus of Nazareth." Then Jesus stepped up immediately in front of the officer and, standing there in the calm majesty of the God of all this creation, said, "I am he." Many of this armed band had heard Jesus teach in the temple, others had learned about his mighty works, and when they heard him thus boldly announce his identity, those in the front ranks fell suddenly backward. They were overcome with surprise at his calm and majestic announcement of identity. There was, therefore, no need for Judas to go on with his plan of betrayal. The Master had boldly revealed himself to his enemies, and they could have taken him without Judas's assistance. But the traitor had to do something to account for his presence with this armed band, and besides, he wanted to make a show of carrying out his part of the betrayal bargain with the rulers of the Jews in order to be eligible for the great reward and honors which he believed would be heaped upon him in compensation for his promise to deliver Jesus into their hands.

As the guards rallied from their first faltering at the sight of Jesus and at the sound of his unusual voice, and as the apostles and disciples drew nearer, Judas stepped up to Jesus and, placing a kiss upon his brow, said, "Hail, Master and Teacher." And as Judas thus embraced his Master, Jesus said, "Friend, is it not enough to do this! Would you even betray the Son of Man with a kiss?"

The apostles and disciples were literally stunned by what they saw. For a moment no one moved. Then Jesus, disengaging himself from the traitorous embrace of Judas, stepped up to the guards and soldiers and again asked, "Whom do you seek?" And again the captain said, "Jesus of Nazareth." And again answered Jesus: "I have told you that I am he. If, therefore, you seek me, let these others go their way. I am ready to go with you."

Jesus was ready to go back to Jerusalem with the guards, and the captain of the soldiers was altogether willing to allow the three apostles and their associates to go their way in peace. But before they were able to get started, as Jesus stood there awaiting the captain's orders, one Malchus, the Syrian body-guard of the high priest, stepped up to Jesus and made ready to bind his hands behind his back, although the Roman captain had not directed that Jesus should be thus bound. When Peter and his associates saw their Master being subjected to this indignity, they were no longer able to restrain themselves. Peter drew his sword and with the others rushed forward to smite Malchus. But before the soldiers could come to the defense of the high priest's servant, Jesus raised a forbidding hand to Peter and, speaking sternly, said: "Peter, put up your sword. They who take the sword shall perish by the sword. Do you not understand that it is the Father's will that I drink this cup? And do you not further know that I could even now command more than twelve legions of angels and their associates, who would deliver me from the hands of these few men?"

While Jesus thus effectively put a stop to this show of physical resistance by his followers, it was enough to arouse the fear of the captain of the guards, who now, with the help of his soldiers, laid heavy hands on Jesus and quickly bound him. And as they tied his hands with heavy cords, Jesus said to them: "Why do you come out against me with swords and with staves as if to seize a robber? I was daily with you in the temple, publicly teaching the people, and you made no effort to take me."

When Jesus had been bound, the captain, fearing that the followers of the Master might attempt to rescue him, gave orders that they be seized; but the soldiers were not quick enough since, having overheard the captain's orders to arrest them, Jesus' followers fled in haste back into the ravine. All this time John Mark had remained secluded in the near-by shed. When the guards started back to Jerusalem with Jesus, John Mark attempted to steal out of the shed in order to catch up with the fleeing apostles and disciples; but just as he emerged, one of the last of the returning soldiers who had pursued the fleeing disciples was passing near and, seeing this young man in his linen coat, gave chase, almost overtaking him. In fact, the soldier got near enough to John to lay hold upon his coat, but the young man freed himself from the garment, escaping naked while the soldier held the empty coat. John Mark made his way in all haste to David Zebedee on the upper trail. When he had told David what had happened, they both hastened back to the tents of the sleeping apostles and informed all eight of the Master's betrayal and arrest.

At about the time the eight apostles were being awakened, those who had fled up the ravine were returning, and they all gathered together near the olive press to debate what should be done. In the meantime, Simon Peter and John Zebedee, who had hidden among the olive trees, had already gone on after the mob of soldiers, guards, and servants, who were now leading Jesus back to Jerusalem as they would have led a desperate criminal. John followed close behind the mob, but Peter followed afar off. After John Mark's escape from the clutch of the soldier, he provided himself with a cloak which he found in the tent of Simon Peter and John Zebedee. He suspected the guards were going to take Jesus to the home of Annas, the high priest emeritus; so he skirted around through the olive orchards and was there ahead of the mob, hiding near the entrance to the gate of the high priest's palace.

4. DISCUSSION AT THE OLIVE PRESS

James Zebedee found himself separated from Simon Peter and his brother John, and so he now joined the other apostles and their fellow campers at the olive press to deliberate on what should be done in view of the Master's arrest.

Andrew had been released from all responsibility in the group management of his fellow apostles; accordingly, in this greatest of all crises in their lives, he was silent. After a short informal discussion, Simon Zelotes stood up on the stone wall of the olive press and, making an impassioned plea for loyalty to the Master and the cause of the kingdom, exhorted his fellow apostles and the other disciples to hasten on after the mob and effect the rescue of Jesus. The majority of the company would have been disposed to follow his aggressive leadership had it not been for the advice of Nathaniel, who stood up the moment Simon had finished speaking and called their attention to Jesus' oft-repeated teachings regarding nonresistance. He further reminded them that Jesus had that very night instructed them that they should preserve their lives for the time when they should go forth into the world proclaiming the good news of the gospel of the heavenly kingdom. And Nathaniel was encouraged in this stand by James Zebedee, who now told how Peter and others drew their swords to defend the Master against arrest, and that Jesus bade Simon Peter and his fellow swordsmen sheathe their blades. Matthew and Philip also made speeches, but nothing definite came of this discussion until Thomas, calling their attention to the fact that Jesus had counseled Lazarus against exposing himself to death, pointed out that they could do nothing to save their Master inasmuch as he refused to allow his friends to defend him, and since he persisted in refraining from the use of his divine powers to frustrate his human enemies. Thomas persuaded them to scatter, every man for himself, with the understanding that David Zebedee would remain at the camp to maintain a clearinghouse and messenger headquarters for the group. By half past two o'clock that morning the camp was deserted; only David remained on hand with three or four messengers, the others having been dispatched to secure information as to where Jesus had been taken, and what was going to be done with him.

Five of the apostles, Nathaniel, Matthew, Philip, and the twins, went into hiding at Bethpage and Bethany. Thomas, Andrew, James, and Simon Zelotes were hiding in the city. Simon Peter and John Zebedee followed along to the home of Annas.

Shortly after daybreak, Simon Peter wandered back to the Gethsemane camp, a dejected picture of deep despair. David sent him in charge of a messenger to join his brother, Andrew, who was at the home of Nicodemus in Jerusalem.

Until the very end of the crucifixion, John Zebedee remained, as Jesus had directed him, always near at hand, and it was he who supplied David's messengers with information from hour to hour which they carried to David at the garden camp, and which was then relayed to the hiding apostles and to Jesus' family.

Surely, the shepherd is smitten and the sheep are scattered! While they all vaguely realize that Jesus has forewarned them of this very situation, they are too severely shocked by the Master's sudden disappearance to be able to use their minds normally.

It was shortly after daylight and just after Peter had been sent to join his brother, that Jude, Jesus' brother in the flesh, arrived in the camp, almost breathless and in advance of the rest of Jesus' family, only to learn that the Master had already been placed under arrest; and he hastened back down the Jericho road to carry this information to his mother and to his brothers and sisters. David Zebedee sent word to Jesus' family, by Jude, to forgather at the house of Martha and Mary in Bethany and there await news which his messengers would regularly bring them.

This was the situation during the last half of Thursday night and the early morning hours of Friday as regards the apostles, the chief disciples, and the earthly family of Jesus. And all these groups and individuals were kept in touch with each other by the messenger service which David Zebedee continued to operate from his headquarters at the Gethsemane camp.

5. ON THE WAY TO THE HIGH PRIEST'S PALACE

Before they started away from the garden with Jesus, a dispute arose between the Jewish captain of the temple guards and the Roman captain of the company of soldiers as to where they were to take Jesus. The captain of the temple guards gave orders that he should be taken to Caiaphas, the acting high priest. The captain of the Roman soldiers directed that Jesus be taken to the palace of Annas, the former high priest and father-in-law of Caiaphas. And this he did because the Romans were in the habit of dealing directly with Annas in all matters having to do with the enforcement of the Jewish ecclesiastical laws. And the orders of the Roman captain were obeyed; they took Jesus to the home of Annas for his preliminary examination.

Judas marched along near the captains, overhearing all that was said, but took no part in the dispute, for neither the Jewish captain nor the Roman officer would so much as speak to the betrayer—they held him in such contempt.

About this time John Zebedee, remembering his Master's instructions to remain always near at hand, hurried up near Jesus as he marched along between the two captains. The commander of the temple guards, seeing John come up alongside, said to his assistant: "Take this man and bind him. He is one of this fellow's followers." But when the Roman captain heard this and, looking around, saw John, he gave orders that the apostle should come over by him, and that no man should molest him. Then the Roman captain said to the Jewish captain: "This man is neither a traitor nor a coward. I saw him in the garden, and he did not draw a sword to resist us. He has the courage to come forward to be with his Master, and no man shall lay hands on him. The Roman law allows that any prisoner may have at least one friend to stand with him before the judgment bar, and this man shall not be prevented from standing by the side of his Master, the prisoner." And when Judas heard this, he was so ashamed and humiliated that he dropped back behind the marchers, coming up to the palace of Annas alone.

And this explains why John Zebedee was permitted to remain near Jesus all the way through his trying experiences this night and the next day. The Jews feared to say aught to John or to molest him in any way because he had something of the status of a Roman counselor designated to act as observer of the transactions of the Jewish ecclesiastical court. John's position of privilege was made all the more secure when, in turning Jesus over to the captain of the temple guards at the gate of Annas's palace, the Roman, addressing his assistant, said: "Go along with this prisoner and see that these Jews do not kill him without Pilate's consent. Watch that they do not assassinate him, and see that his friend, the Galilean, is permitted to stand by and observe all that goes on." And thus was John able to be near Jesus right on up to the time of his death on the cross, though the other ten apostles were compelled to remain in hiding. John was acting under Roman protection, and the Jews dared not molest him until after the Master's death.

And all the way to the palace of Annas, Jesus opened not his mouth. From the time of his arrest to the time of his appearance before Annas, the Son of Man spoke no word.

PAPER 184

BEFORE THE SANHEDRIN COURT

REPRESENTATIVES of Annas had secretly instructed the captain of the Roman soldiers to bring Jesus immediately to the palace of Annas after he had been arrested. The former high priest desired to maintain his prestige as the chief ecclesiastical authority of the Jews. He also had another purpose in detaining Jesus at his house for several hours, and that was to allow time for legally calling together the court of the Sanhedrin. It was not lawful to convene the Sanhedrin court before the time of the offering of the morning sacrifice in the temple, and this sacrifice was offered about three o'clock in the morning.

Annas knew that a court of Sanhedrists was in waiting at the palace of his son-in-law, Caiaphas. Some thirty members of the Sanhedrin had gathered at the home of the high priest by midnight so that they would be ready to sit in judgment on Jesus when he might be brought before them. Only those members were assembled who were strongly and openly opposed to Jesus and his teaching since it required only twenty-three to constitute a trial court.

Jesus spent about three hours at the palace of Annas on Mount Olivet, not far from the garden of Gethsemane, where they arrested him. John Zebedee was free and safe in the palace of Annas not only because of the word of the Roman captain, but also because he and his brother James were well known to the older servants, having many times been guests at the palace as the former high priest was a distant relative of their mother, Salome.

1. EXAMINATION BY ANNAS

Annas, enriched by the temple revenues, his son-in-law the acting high priest, and with his relations to the Roman authorities, was indeed the most powerful single individual in all Jewry. He was a suave and politic planner and plotter. He desired to direct the matter of disposing of Jesus; he feared to trust such an important undertaking wholly to his brusque and aggressive son-in-law. Annas wanted to make sure that the Master's trial was kept in the hands of the Sadducees; he feared the possible sympathy of some of the Pharisees, seeing that practically all of those members of the Sanhedrin who had espoused the cause of Jesus were Pharisees.

Annas had not seen Jesus for several years, not since the time when the Master called at his house and immediately left upon observing his coldness and reserve in receiving him. Annas had thought to presume on this early acquaintance and thereby attempt to persuade Jesus to abandon his claims and leave Palestine. He was reluctant to participate in the murder of a good man and had reasoned that Jesus might choose to leave the country rather than to suffer death. But when Annas stood before the stalwart and determined Galilean, he knew at once that it would be useless to make such proposals. Jesus was even more majestic and well poised than Annas remembered him.

When Jesus was young, Annas had taken a great interest in him, but now his revenues were threatened by what Jesus had so recently done in driving the money-changers and other commercial traders out of the temple. This act had aroused the enmity of the former high priest far more than had Jesus' teachings.

Annas entered his spacious audience chamber, seated himself in a large chair, and commanded that Jesus be brought before him. After a few moments spent in silently surveying the Master, he said: "You realize that something must be done about your teaching since you are disturbing the peace and order of our country." As Annas looked inquiringly at Jesus, the Master looked full into his eyes but made no reply. Again Annas spoke, "What are the names of your disciples, besides Simon Zelotes, the agitator?" Again Jesus looked down upon him, but he did not answer.

Annas was considerably disturbed by Jesus' refusal to answer his questions, so much so that he said to him: "Do you have no care as to whether I am friendly to you or not? Do you have no regard for the power I have in determining the issues of your coming trial?" When Jesus heard this, he said: "Annas, you know that you could have no power over me unless it were permitted by my Father. Some would destroy the Son of Man because they are ignorant; they know no better, but you, friend, know what you are doing. How can you, therefore, reject the light of God?"

The kindly manner in which Jesus spoke to Annas almost bewildered him. But he had already determined in his mind that Jesus must either leave Palestine or die; so he summoned up his courage and asked: "Just what is it you are trying to teach the people? What do you claim to be?" Jesus answered: "You know full well that I have spoken openly to the world. I have taught in the synagogues and many times in the temple, where all the Jews and many of the gentiles have heard me. In secret I have spoken nothing; why, then, do you ask me about my teaching? Why do you not summon those who have heard me and inquire of them? Behold, all Jerusalem has heard that which I have spoken even if you have not yourself heard these teachings." But before Annas could make reply, the chief steward of the palace, who was standing near, struck Jesus in the face with his hand, saying, "How dare you answer the high priest with such words?" Annas spoke no words of rebuke to his steward, but Jesus addressed him, saying, "My friend, if I have spoken evil, bear witness against the evil; but if I have spoken the truth, why, then, should you smite me?"

Although Annas regretted that his steward had struck Jesus, he was too proud to take notice of the matter. In his confusion he went into another room, leaving Jesus alone with the household attendants and the temple guards for almost an hour.

When he returned, going up to the Master's side, he said, "Do you claim to be the Messiah, the deliverer of Israel?" Said Jesus: "Annas, you have known me from the times of my youth. You know that I claim to be nothing except that which my Father has appointed, and that I have been sent to all men, gentile as well as Jew." Then said Annas: "I have been told that you have claimed to be the Messiah; is that true?" Jesus looked upon Annas but only replied, "So you have said."

About this time messengers arrived from the palace of Caiaphas to inquire what time Jesus would be brought before the court of the Sanhedrin, and since it was nearing the break of day, Annas thought best to send Jesus bound and in the custody of the temple guards to Caiaphas. He himself followed after them shortly.

2. PETER IN THE COURTYARD

As the band of guards and soldiers approached the entrance to the palace of Annas, John Zebedee was marching by the side of the captain of the Roman soldiers. Judas had dropped some distance behind, and Simon Peter followed afar off. After John had entered the palace courtyard with Jesus and the guards, Judas came up to the gate but, seeing Jesus and John, went on over to the home of Caiaphas, where he knew the real trial of the Master would later take place. Soon after Judas had left, Simon Peter arrived, and as he stood before the gate, John saw him just as they were about to take Jesus into the palace. The portress who kept the gate knew John, and when he spoke to her, requesting that she let Peter in, she gladly assented.

Peter, upon entering the courtyard, went over to the charcoal fire and sought to warm himself, for the night was chilly. He felt very much out of place here among the enemies of Jesus, and indeed he was out of place. The Master had not instructed him to keep near at hand as he had admonished John. Peter belonged with the other apostles, who had been specifically warned not to endanger their lives during these times of the trial and crucifixion of their Master.

Peter threw away his sword shortly before he came up to the palace gate so that he entered the courtyard of Annas unarmed. His mind was in a whirl of confusion; he could scarcely realize that Jesus had been arrested. He could not grasp the reality of the situation—that he was here in the courtyard of Annas, warming himself beside the servants of the high priest. He wondered what the other apostles were doing and, in turning over in his mind as to how John came to be admitted to the palace, concluded that it was because he was known to the servants, since he had bidden the gate-keeper admit him.

Shortly after the portress let Peter in, and while he was warming himself by the fire, she went over to him and mischievously said, "Are you not also one of this man's disciples?" Now Peter should not have been surprised at this recognition, for it was John who had requested that the girl let him pass through the palace gates; but he was in such a tense nervous state that this identification as a disciple threw him off his balance, and with only one thought uppermost in his mind—the thought of escaping with his life—he promptly answered the maid's question by saying, "I am not."

Very soon another servant came up to Peter and asked: "Did I not see you in the garden when they arrested this fellow? Are you not also one of his followers?" Peter was now thoroughly alarmed; he saw no way of safely escaping from these accusers; so he vehemently denied all connection with Jesus, saying, "I know not this man, neither am I one of his followers."

About this time the portress of the gate drew Peter to one side and said: "I am sure you are a disciple of this Jesus, not only because one of his followers bade me let you in the courtyard, but my sister here has seen you in the temple with this man. Why do you deny this?" When Peter heard the maid accuse him, he denied all knowledge of Jesus with much cursing and swearing, again saying,

"I am not this man's follower; I do not even know him; I never heard of him before."

Peter left the fireside for a time while he walked about the courtyard. He would have liked to have escaped, but he feared to attract attention to himself. Getting cold, he returned to the fireside, and one of the men standing near him said: "Surely you are one of this man's disciples. This Jesus is a Galilean, and your speech betrays you, for you also speak as a Galilean." And again Peter denied all connection with his Master.

Peter was so perturbed that he sought to escape contact with his accusers by going away from the fire and remaining by himself on the porch. After more than an hour of this isolation, the gate-keeper and her sister chanced to meet him, and both of them again teasingly charged him with being a follower of Jesus. And again he denied the accusation. Just as he had once more denied all connection with Jesus, the cock crowed, and Peter remembered the words of warning spoken to him by his Master earlier that same night. As he stood there, heavy of heart and crushed with the sense of guilt, the palace doors opened, and the guards led Jesus past on the way to Caiaphas. As the Master passed Peter, he saw, by the light of the torches, the look of despair on the face of his former self-confident and superficially brave apostle, and he turned and looked upon Peter. Peter never forgot that look as long as he lived. It was such a glance of commingled pity and love as mortal man had never beheld in the face of the Master.

After Jesus and the guards passed out of the palace gates, Peter followed them, but only for a short distance. He could not go farther. He sat down by the side of the road and wept bitterly. And when he had shed these tears of agony, he turned his steps back toward the camp, hoping to find his brother, Andrew. On arriving at the camp, he found only David Zebedee, who sent a messenger to direct him to where his brother had gone to hide in Jerusalem.

Peter's entire experience occurred in the courtyard of the palace of Annas on Mount Olivet. He did not follow Jesus to the palace of the high priest, Caiaphas. That Peter was brought to the realization that he had repeatedly denied his Master by the crowing of a cock indicates that this all occurred outside of Jerusalem since it was against the law to keep poultry within the city proper.

Until the crowing of the cock brought Peter to his better senses, he had only thought, as he walked up and down the porch to keep warm, how cleverly he had eluded the accusations of the servants, and how he had frustrated their purpose to identify him with Jesus. For the time being, he had only considered that these servants had no moral or legal right thus to question him, and he really congratulated himself over the manner in which he thought he had avoided being identified and possibly subjected to arrest and imprisonment. Not until the cock crowed did it occur to Peter that he had denied his Master. Not until Jesus looked upon him, did he realize that he had failed to live up to his privileges as an ambassador of the kingdom.

Having taken the first step along the path of compromise and least resistance, there was nothing apparent to Peter but to go on with the course of conduct decided upon. It requires a great and noble character, having started out wrong, to turn about and go right. All too often one's own mind tends to justify continuance in the path of error when once it is entered upon.

Peter never fully believed that he could be forgiven until he met his Master after the resurrection and saw that he was received just as before the experiences of this tragic night of the denials.

3. BEFORE THE COURT OF SANHEDRISTS

It was about half past three o'clock this Friday morning when the chief priest, Caiaphas, called the Sanhedrist court of inquiry to order and asked that Jesus be brought before them for his formal trial. On three previous occasions the Sanhedrin, by a large majority vote, had decreed the death of Jesus, had decided that he was worthy of death on informal charges of lawbreaking, blasphemy, and flouting the traditions of the fathers of Israel.

This was not a regularly called meeting of the Sanhedrin and was not held in the usual place, the chamber of hewn stone in the temple. This was a special trial court of some thirty Sanhedrists and was convened in the palace of the high priest. John Zebedee was present with Jesus throughout this so-called trial.

How these chief priests, scribes, Sadducees, and some of the Pharisees flattered themselves that Jesus, the disturber of their position and the challenger of their authority, was now securely in their hands! And they were resolved that he should never live to escape their vengeful clutches.

Ordinarily, the Jews, when trying a man on a capital charge, proceeded with great caution and provided every safeguard of fairness in the selection of witnesses and the entire conduct of the trial. But on this occasion, Caiaphas was more of a prosecutor than an unbiased judge.

Jesus appeared before this court clothed in his usual garments and with his hands bound together behind his back. The entire court was startled and somewhat confused by his majestic appearance. Never had they gazed upon such a prisoner nor witnessed such composure in a man on trial for his life.

The Jewish law required that at least two witnesses must agree upon any point before a charge could be laid against the prisoner. Judas could not be used as a witness against Jesus because the Jewish law specifically forbade the testimony of a traitor. More than a score of false witnesses were on hand to testify against Jesus, but their testimony was so contradictory and so evidently trumped up that the Sanhedrists themselves were very much ashamed of the performance. Jesus stood there, looking down benignly upon these perjurers, and his very countenance disconcerted the lying witnesses. Throughout all this false testimony the Master never said a word; he made no reply to their many false accusations.

The first time any two of their witnesses approached even the semblance of an agreement was when two men testified that they had heard Jesus say in the course of one of his temple discourses that he would "destroy this temple made with hands and in three days make another temple without hands." That was not exactly what Jesus said, regardless of the fact that he pointed to his own body when he made the remark referred to.

Although the high priest shouted at Jesus, "Do you not answer any of these charges?" Jesus opened not his mouth. He stood there in silence while all of these false witnesses gave their testimony. Hatred, fanaticism, and unscrupulous exaggeration so characterized the words of these perjurers that their testimony fell in its own entanglements. The very best refutation of their false accusations was the Master's calm and majestic silence.

Shortly after the beginning of the testimony of the false witnesses, Annas arrived and took his seat beside Caiaphas. Annas now arose and argued that this threat of Jesus to destroy the temple was sufficient to warrant three charges against him:

1. That he was a dangerous traducer of the people. That he taught them impossible things and otherwise deceived them.

2. That he was a fanatical revolutionist in that he advocated laying violent hands on the sacred temple, else how could he destroy it?

3. That he taught magic inasmuch as he promised to build a new temple, and that without hands.

Already had the full Sanhedrin agreed that Jesus was guilty of death-deserving transgressions of the Jewish laws, but they were now more concerned with developing charges regarding his conduct and teachings which would justify Pilate in pronouncing the death sentence upon their prisoner. They knew that they must secure the consent of the Roman governor before Jesus could legally be put to death. And Annas was minded to proceed along the line of making it appear that Jesus was a dangerous teacher to be abroad among the people.

But Caiaphas could not longer endure the sight of the Master standing there in perfect composure and unbroken silence. He thought he knew at least one way in which the prisoner might be induced to speak. Accordingly, he rushed over to the side of Jesus and, shaking his accusing finger in the Master's face, said: "I adjure you, in the name of the living God, that you tell us whether you are the Deliverer, the Son of God." Jesus answered Caiaphas: "I am. Soon I go to the Father, and presently shall the Son of Man be clothed with power and once more reign over the hosts of heaven."

When the high priest heard Jesus utter these words, he was exceedingly angry, and rending his outer garments, he exclaimed: "What further need have we of witnesses? Behold, now have you all heard this man's blasphemy. What do you now think should be done with this lawbreaker and blasphemer?" And they all answered in unison, "He is worthy of death; let him be crucified."

Jesus manifested no interest in any question asked him when before Annas or the Sanhedrists except the one question relative to his bestowal mission. When asked if he were the Son of God, he instantly and unequivocally answered in the affirmative.

Annas desired that the trial proceed further, and that charges of a definite nature regarding Jesus' relation to the Roman law and Roman institutions be formulated for subsequent presentation to Pilate. The councilors were anxious to carry these matters to a speedy termination, not only because it was the preparation day for the Passover and no secular work should be done after noon, but also because they feared Pilate might any time return to the Roman capital of Judea, Caesarea, since he was in Jerusalem only for the Passover celebration.

But Annas did not succeed in keeping control of the court. After Jesus had so unexpectedly answered Caiaphas, the high priest stepped forward and smote him in the face with his hand. Annas was truly shocked as the other members of the court, in passing out of the room, spit in Jesus' face, and many of them mockingly slapped him with the palms of their hands. And thus in disorder and with such unheard-of confusion this first session of the Sanhedrist trial of Jesus ended at half past four o'clock.

Thirty prejudiced and tradition-blinded false judges, with their false witnesses, are presuming to sit in judgment on the righteous Creator of a universe. And these impassioned accusers are exasperated by the majestic silence and superb bearing of this God-man. His silence is terrible to endure; his speech is fearlessly defiant. He is unmoved by their threats and undaunted by their assaults. Man sits in judgment on God, but even then he loves them and would save them if he could.

4. THE HOUR OF HUMILIATION

The Jewish law required that, in the matter of passing the death sentence, there should be two sessions of the court. This second session was to be held on the day following the first, and the intervening time was to be spent in fasting and mourning by the members of the court. But these men could not await the next day for the confirmation of their decision that Jesus must die. They waited only one hour. In the meantime Jesus was left in the audience chamber in the custody of the temple guards, who, with the servants of the high priest, amused themselves by heaping every sort of indignity upon the Son of Man. They mocked him, spit upon him, and cruelly buffeted him. They would strike him in the face with a rod and then say, "Prophesy to us, you the Deliverer, who it was that struck you." And thus they went on for one full hour, reviling and mistreating this unresisting man of Galilee.

During this tragic hour of suffering and mock trials before the ignorant and unfeeling guards and servants, John Zebedee waited in lonely terror in an adjoining room. When these abuses first started, Jesus indicated to John, by a nod of his head, that he should retire. The Master well knew that, if he permitted his apostle to remain in the room to witness these indignities, John's resentment would be so aroused as to produce such an outbreak of protesting indignation as would probably result in his death.

Throughout this awful hour Jesus uttered no word. To this gentle and sensitive soul of humankind, joined in personality relationship with the God of all this universe, there was no more bitter portion of his cup of humiliation than this terrible hour at the mercy of these ignorant and cruel guards and servants, who had been stimulated to abuse him by the example of the members of this so-called Sanhedrist court.

The human heart cannot possibly conceive of the shudder of indignation that swept out over a vast universe as the celestial intelligences witnessed this sight of their beloved Sovereign submitting himself to the will of his ignorant and misguided creatures on the sin-darkened sphere of unfortunate Urantia.

What is this trait of the animal in man which leads him to want to insult and physically assault that which he cannot spiritually attain or intellectually achieve? In the half-civilized man there still lurks an evil brutality which seeks to vent itself upon those who are superior in wisdom and spiritual attainment. Witness the evil coarseness and the brutal ferocity of these supposedly civilized men as they derived a certain form of animal pleasure from this physical attack upon the unresisting Son of Man. As these insults, taunts, and blows fell upon

Jesus, he was undefending but not defenseless. Jesus was not vanquished, merely uncontending in the material sense.

These are the moments of the Master's greatest victories in all his long and eventful career as maker, upholder, and savior of a vast and far-flung universe. Having lived to the full a life of revealing God to man, Jesus is now engaged in making a new and unprecedented revelation of man to God. Jesus is now revealing to the worlds the final triumph over all fears of creature personality isolation. The Son of Man has finally achieved the realization of identity as the Son of God. Jesus does not hesitate to assert that he and the Father are one; and on the basis of the fact and truth of that supreme and supernal experience, he admonishes every kingdom believer to become one with him even as he and his Father are one. The living experience in the religion of Jesus thus becomes the sure and certain technique whereby the spiritually isolated and cosmically lonely mortals of earth are enabled to escape personality isolation, with all its consequences of fear and associated feelings of helplessness. In the fraternal realities of the kingdom of heaven the faith sons of God find final deliverance from the isolation of the self, both personal and planetary. The God-knowing believer increasingly experiences the ecstasy and grandeur of spiritual socialization on a universe scale—citizenship on high in association with the eternal realization of the divine destiny of perfection attainment.

5. THE SECOND MEETING OF THE COURT

At five-thirty o'clock the court reassembled, and Jesus was led into the adjoining room, where John was waiting. Here the Roman soldier and the temple guards watched over Jesus while the court began the formulation of the charges which were to be presented to Pilate. Annas made it clear to his associates that the charge of blasphemy would carry no weight with Pilate. Judas was present during this second meeting of the court, but he gave no testimony.

This session of the court lasted only a half hour, and when they adjourned to go before Pilate, they had drawn up the indictment of Jesus, as being worthy of death, under three heads:

1. That he was a perverter of the Jewish nation; he deceived the people and incited them to rebellion.

2. That he taught the people to refuse to pay tribute to Caesar.

3. That, by claiming to be a king and the founder of a new sort of kingdom, he incited treason against the emperor.

This entire procedure was irregular and wholly contrary to the Jewish laws. No two witnesses had agreed on any matter except those who testified regarding Jesus' statement about destroying the temple and raising it again in three days. And even concerning that point, no witnesses spoke for the defense, and neither was Jesus asked to explain his intended meaning.

The only point the court could have consistently judged him on was that of blasphemy, and that would have rested entirely on his own testimony. Even concerning blasphemy, they failed to cast a formal ballot for the death sentence.

And now they presumed to formulate three charges, with which to go before Pilate, on which no witnesses had been heard, and which were agreed upon while the accused prisoner was absent. When this was done, three of the Pharisees took their leave; they wanted to see Jesus destroyed, but they would not formulate charges against him without witnesses and in his absence.

Jesus did not again appear before the Sanhedrist court. They did not want again to look upon his face as they sat in judgment upon his innocent life. Jesus did not know (as a man) of their formal charges until he heard them recited by Pilate.

While Jesus was in the room with John and the guards, and while the court was in its second session, some of the women about the high priest's palace, together with their friends, came to look upon the strange prisoner, and one of them asked him, "Are you the Messiah, the Son of God?" And Jesus answered: "If I tell you, you will not believe me; and if I ask you, you will not answer."

At six o'clock that morning Jesus was led forth from the home of Caiaphas to appear before Pilate for confirmation of the sentence of death which this Sanhedrist court had so unjustly and irregularly decreed.

PAPER 185

THE TRIAL BEFORE PILATE

SHORTLY after six o'clock on this Friday morning, April 7, A.D. 30, Jesus was brought before Pilate, the Roman procurator who governed Judea, Samaria, and Idumea under the immediate supervision of the legatus of Syria. The Master was taken into the presence of the Roman governor by the temple guards, bound, and was accompanied by about fifty of his accusers, including the Sanhedrist court (principally Sadduceans), Judas Iscariot, and the high priest, Caiaphas, and by the Apostle John. Annas did not appear before Pilate.

Pilate was up and ready to receive this group of early morning callers, having been informed by those who had secured his consent, the previous evening, to employ the Roman soldiers in arresting the Son of Man, that Jesus would be early brought before him. This trial was arranged to take place in front of the praetorium, an addition to the fortress of Antonia, where Pilate and his wife made their headquarters when stopping in Jerusalem.

Though Pilate conducted much of Jesus' examination within the praetorium halls, the public trial was held outside on the steps leading up to the main entrance. This was a concession to the Jews, who refused to enter any gentile building where leaven might be used on this day of preparation for the Passover. Such conduct would not only render them ceremonially unclean and thereby debar them from partaking of the afternoon feast of thanksgiving but would also necessitate their subjection to purification ceremonies after sundown, before they would be eligible to partake of the Passover supper.

Although these Jews were not at all bothered in conscience as they intrigued to effect the judicial murder of Jesus, they were nonetheless scrupulous regarding all these matters of ceremonial cleanness and traditional regularity. And these Jews have not been the only ones to fail in the recognition of high and holy obligations of a divine nature while giving meticulous attention to things of trifling importance to human welfare in both time and eternity.

1. PONTIUS PILATE

If Pontius Pilate had not been a reasonably good governor of the minor provinces, Tiberius would hardly have suffered him to remain as procurator of Judea for ten years. Although he was a fairly good administrator, he was a moral coward. He was not a big enough man to comprehend the nature of his task as governor of the Jews. He failed to grasp the fact that these Hebrews had a *real* religion, a faith for which they were willing to die, and that millions upon millions of them, scattered here and there throughout the empire, looked to Jerusalem as the shrine of their faith and held the Sanhedrin in respect as the highest tribunal on earth.

Pilate did not love the Jews, and this deep-seated hatred early began to manifest itself. Of all the Roman provinces, none was more difficult to govern than Judea. Pilate never really understood the problems involved in the management of the Jews and, therefore, very early in his experience as governor, made a series of almost fatal and well-nigh suicidal blunders. And it was these blunders that gave the Jews such power over him. When they wanted to influence his decisions, all they had to do was to threaten an uprising, and Pilate would speedily capitulate. And this apparent vacillation, or lack of moral courage, of the procurator was chiefly due to the memory of a number of controversies he had had with the Jews and because in each instance they had worsted him. The Jews knew that Pilate was afraid of them, that he feared for his position before Tiberius, and they employed this knowledge to the great disadvantage of the governor on numerous occasions.

Pilate's disfavor with the Jews came about as a result of a number of unfortunate encounters. First, he failed to take seriously their deep-seated prejudice against all images as symbols of idol worship. Therefore he permitted his soldiers to enter Jerusalem without removing the images of Caesar from their banners, as had been the practice of the Roman soldiers under his predecessor. A large deputation of Jews waited upon Pilate for five days, imploring him to have these images removed from the military standards. He flatly refused to grant their petition and threatened them with instant death. Pilate, himself being a skeptic, did not understand that men of strong religious feelings will not hesitate to die for their religious convictions; and therefore was he dismayed when these Jews drew themselves up defiantly before his palace, bowed their faces to the ground, and sent word that they were ready to die. Pilate then realized that he had made a threat which he was unwilling to carry out. He surrendered, ordered the images removed from the standards of his soldiers in Jerusalem, and found himself from that day on to a large extent subject to the whims of the Jewish leaders, who had in this way discovered his weakness in making threats which he feared to execute.

Pilate subsequently determined to regain this lost prestige and accordingly had the shields of the emperor, such as were commonly used in Caesar worship, put up on the walls of Herod's palace in Jerusalem. When the Jews protested, he was adamant. When he refused to listen to their protests, they promptly appealed to Rome, and the emperor as promptly ordered the offending shields removed. And then was Pilate held in even lower esteem than before.

Another thing which brought him into great disfavor with the Jews was that he dared to take money from the temple treasury to pay for the construction of a new aqueduct to provide increased water supply for the millions of visitors to Jerusalem at the times of the great religious feasts. The Jews held that only the Sanhedrin could disburse the temple funds, and they never ceased to inveigh against Pilate for this presumptuous ruling. No less than a score of riots and much bloodshed resulted from this decision. The last of these serious outbreaks had to do with the slaughter of a large company of Galileans even as they worshiped at the altar.

It is significant that, while this vacillating Roman ruler sacrificed Jesus to his fear of the Jews and to safeguard his personal position, he finally was deposed as a result of the needless slaughter of Samaritans in connection with the pretensions of a false Messiah who led troops to Mount Gerizim, where he claimed the temple vessels were buried; and fierce riots broke out when he failed to reveal the hiding place of the sacred vessels, as he had promised. As a result of this episode, the legatus of Syria ordered Pilate to Rome. Tiberius died while Pilate was on the way to Rome, and he was not reappointed as procurator of Judea. He never fully recovered from the regretful condemnation of having consented to the crucifixion of Jesus. Finding no favor in the eyes of the new emperor, he retired to the province of Lausanne, where he subsequently committed suicide.

Claudia Procula, Pilate's wife, had heard much of Jesus through the word of her maid-in-waiting, who was a Phoenician believer in the gospel of the kingdom. After the death of Pilate, Claudia became prominently identified with the spread of the good news.

And all this explains much that transpired on this tragic Friday forenoon. It is easy to understand why the Jews presumed to dictate to Pilate—to get him up at six o'clock to try Jesus—and also why they did not hesitate to threaten to charge him with treason before the emperor if he dared to refuse their demands for Jesus' death.

A worthy Roman governor who had not become disadvantageously involved with the rulers of the Jews would never have permitted these bloodthirsty religious fanatics to bring about the death of a man whom he himself had declared to be innocent of their false charges and without fault. Rome made a great blunder, a far-reaching error in earthly affairs, when she sent the second-rate Pilate to govern Palestine. Tiberius had better have sent to the Jews the best provincial administrator in the empire.

2. JESUS APPEARS BEFORE PILATE

When Jesus and his accusers had gathered in front of Pilate's judgment hall, the Roman governor came out and, addressing the company assembled, asked, "What accusation do you bring against this fellow?" The Sadducees and councilors who had taken it upon themselves to put Jesus out of the way had determined to go before Pilate and ask for confirmation of the death sentence pronounced upon Jesus, without volunteering any definite charge. Therefore did the spokesman for the Sanhedrist court answer Pilate: "If this man were not an evildoer, we should not have delivered him up to you."

When Pilate observed that they were reluctant to state their charges against Jesus, although he knew they had been all night engaged in deliberations regarding his guilt, he answered them: "Since you have not agreed on any definite charges, why do you not take this man and pass judgment on him in accordance with your own laws?"

Then spoke the clerk of the Sanhedrin court to Pilate: "It is not lawful for us to put any man to death, and this disturber of our nation is worthy to die for the things which he has said and done. Therefore have we come before you for confirmation of this decree."

To come before the Roman governor with this attempt at evasion discloses both the ill-will and the ill-humor of the Sanhedrists toward Jesus as well as their lack of respect for the fairness, honor, and dignity of Pilate. What effrontery for these subject citizens to appear before their provincial governor asking for a decree of execution against a man before affording him a fair trial and without even preferring definite criminal charges against him!

Pilate knew something of Jesus' work among the Jews, and he surmised that the charges which might be brought against him had to do with infringements of the Jewish ecclesiastical laws; therefore he sought to refer the case back to their own tribunal. Again, Pilate took delight in making them publicly confess that they were powerless to pronounce and execute the death sentence upon even one of their own race whom they had come to despise with a bitter and envious hatred.

It was a few hours previously, shortly before midnight and after he had granted permission to use Roman soldiers in effecting the secret arrest of Jesus, that Pilate had heard further concerning Jesus and his teaching from his wife, Claudia, who was a partial convert to Judaism, and who later on became a full-fledged believer in Jesus' gospel.

Pilate would have liked to postpone this hearing, but he saw the Jewish leaders were determined to proceed with the case. He knew that this was not only the forenoon of preparation for the Passover, but that this day, being Friday, was also the preparation day for the Jewish Sabbath of rest and worship.

Pilate, being keenly sensitive to the disrespectful manner of the approach of these Jews, was not willing to comply with their demands that Jesus be sentenced to death without a trial. When, therefore, he had waited a few moments for them to present their charges against the prisoner, he turned to them and said: "I will not sentence this man to death without a trial; neither will I consent to examine him until you have presented your charges against him in writing."

When the high priest and the others heard Pilate say this, they signaled to the clerk of the court, who then handed to Pilate the written charges against Jesus. And these charges were:

"We find in the Sanhedrist tribunal that this man is an evildoer and a disturber of our nation in that he is guilty of:

"1. Perverting our nation and stirring up our people to rebellion.

"2. Forbidding the people to pay tribute to Caesar.

"3. Calling himself the king of the Jews and teaching the founding of a new kingdom."

Jesus had not been regularly tried nor legally convicted on any of these charges. He did not even hear these charges when first stated, but Pilate had him brought from the praetorium, where he was in the keeping of the guards, and he insisted that these charges be repeated in Jesus' hearing.

When Jesus heard these accusations, he well knew that he had not been heard on these matters before the Jewish court, and so did John Zebedee and his accusers, but he made no reply to their false charges. Even when Pilate bade him answer his accusers, he opened not his mouth. Pilate was so astonished at the unfairness of the whole proceeding and so impressed by Jesus' silent and masterly bearing that he decided to take the prisoner inside the hall and examine him privately.

Pilate was confused in mind, fearful of the Jews in his heart, and mightily stirred in his spirit by the spectacle of Jesus' standing there in majesty before his bloodthirsty accusers and gazing down on them, not in silent contempt, but with an expression of genuine pity and sorrowful affection.

3. THE PRIVATE EXAMINATION BY PILATE

Pilate took Jesus and John Zebedee into a private chamber, leaving the guards outside in the hall, and requesting the prisoner to sit down, he sat down by his side and asked several questions. Pilate began his talk with Jesus by assuring him that he did not believe the first count against him: that he was a perverter of the nation and an inciter to rebellion. Then he asked, "Did you ever teach that tribute should be refused Caesar?" Jesus, pointing to John, said, "Ask him or any other man who has heard my teaching." Then Pilate questioned John about this matter of tribute, and John testified concerning his Master's teaching and explained that Jesus and his apostles paid taxes both to Caesar and to the temple. When Pilate had questioned John, he said, "See that you tell no man that I talked with you." And John never did reveal this matter.

Pilate then turned around to question Jesus further, saying: "And now about the third accusation against you, are you the king of the Jews?" Since there was a tone of possibly sincere inquiry in Pilate's voice, Jesus smiled on the procurator and said: "Pilate, do you ask this for yourself, or do you take this question from these others, my accusers?" Whereupon, in a tone of partial indignation, the governor answered: "Am I a Jew? Your own people and the chief priests delivered you up and asked me to sentence you to death. I question the validity of their charges and am only trying to find out for myself what you have done. Tell me, have you said that you are the king of the Jews, and have you sought to found a new kingdom?"

Then said Jesus to Pilate: "Do you not perceive that my kingdom is not of this world? If my kingdom were of this world, surely would my disciples fight that I should not be delivered into the hands of the Jews. My presence here before you in these bonds is sufficient to show all men that my kingdom is a spiritual dominion, even the brotherhood of men who, through faith and by love, have become the sons of God. And this salvation is for the gentile as well as for the Jew."

"Then you are a king after all?" said Pilate. And Jesus answered: "Yes, I am such a king, and my kingdom is the family of the faith sons of my Father who is in heaven. For this purpose was I born into this world, even that I should show my Father to all men and bear witness to the truth of God. And even now do I declare to you that every one who loves the truth hears my voice."

Then said Pilate, half in ridicule and half in sincerity, "Truth, what is truth—who knows?"

Pilate was not able to fathom Jesus' words, nor was he able to understand the nature of his spiritual kingdom, but he was now certain that the prisoner had done nothing worthy of death. One look at Jesus, face to face, was enough to convince even Pilate that this gentle and weary, but majestic and upright, man was no wild and dangerous revolutionary who aspired to establish himself on the temporal throne of Israel. Pilate thought he understood something of what Jesus meant when he called himself a king, for he was familiar with the teachings of the Stoics, who declared that "the wise man is king." Pilate was thoroughly convinced that, instead of being a dangerous seditionmonger, Jesus was nothing more or less than a harmless visionary, an innocent fanatic.

After questioning the Master, Pilate went back to the chief priests and the accusers of Jesus and said: "I have examined this man, and I find no fault in him. I do not think he is guilty of the charges you have made against him; I think he ought to be set free." And when the Jews heard this, they were moved with great anger, so much so that they wildly shouted that Jesus should die; and one of the Sanhedrists boldly stepped up by the side of Pilate, saying: "This man stirs up the people, beginning in Galilee and continuing throughout all Judea. He is a mischief-maker and an evildoer. You will long regret it if you let this wicked man go free."

Pilate was hard pressed to know what to do with Jesus; therefore, when he heard them say that he began his work in Galilee, he thought to avoid the responsibility of deciding the case, at least to gain time for thought, by sending Jesus to appear before Herod, who was then in the city attending the Passover. Pilate also thought that this gesture would help to antidote some of the bitter feeling which had existed for some time between himself and Herod, due to numerous misunderstandings over matters of jurisdiction.

Pilate, calling the guards, said: "This man is a Galilean. Take him forthwith to Herod, and when he has examined him, report his findings to me." And they took Jesus to Herod.

4. JESUS BEFORE HEROD

When Herod Antipas stopped in Jerusalem, he dwelt in the old Maccabean palace of Herod the Great, and it was to this home of the former king that Jesus was now taken by the temple guards, and he was followed by his accusers and an increasing multitude. Herod had long heard of Jesus, and he was very curious about him. When the Son of Man stood before him, on this Friday morning, the wicked Idumean never for one moment recalled the lad of former years who had appeared before him in Sepphoris pleading for a just decision regarding the money due his father, who had been accidentally killed while at work on one of the public buildings. As far as Herod knew, he had never seen Jesus, although he had worried a great deal about him when his work had been centered in Galilee. Now that he was in custody of Pilate and the Judeans, Herod was desirous of seeing him, feeling secure against any trouble from him in the future. Herod had heard much about the miracles wrought by Jesus, and he really hoped to see him do some wonder.

When they brought Jesus before Herod, the tetrarch was startled by his stately appearance and the calm composure of his countenance. For some fifteen minutes Herod asked Jesus questions, but the Master would not answer. Herod taunted and dared him to perform a miracle, but Jesus would not reply to his many inquiries or respond to his taunts.

Then Herod turned to the chief priests and the Sadducees and, giving ear to their accusations, heard all and more than Pilate had listened to regarding the alleged evil doings of the Son of Man. Finally, being convinced that Jesus would neither talk nor perform a wonder for him, Herod, after making fun of him for a time, arrayed him in an old purple royal robe and sent him back to Pilate. Herod knew he had no jurisdiction over Jesus in Judea. Though he was glad to believe that he was finally to be rid of Jesus in Galilee, he was thankful that it was Pilate who had the responsibility of putting him to death. Herod never had fully recovered from the fear that cursed him as a result of killing John the Baptist. Herod had at certain times even feared that Jesus was John risen from the dead. Now he was relieved of that fear since he observed that Jesus was a very different sort of person from the outspoken and fiery prophet who dared to expose and denounce his private life.

5. JESUS RETURNS TO PILATE

When the guards had brought Jesus back to Pilate, he went out on the front steps of the praetorium, where his judgment seat had been placed, and calling together the chief priests and Sanhedrists, said to them: "You brought this man before me with charges that he perverts the people, forbids the payment of taxes, and claims to be king of the Jews. I have examined him and fail to find him guilty of these charges. In fact, I find no fault in him. Then I sent him to Herod, and the tetrarch must have reached the same conclusion since he has sent him back to us. Certainly, nothing worthy of death has been done by this man. If you still think he needs to be disciplined, I am willing to chastise him before I release him."

Just as the Jews were about to engage in shouting their protests against the release of Jesus, a vast crowd came marching up to the praetorium for the purpose of asking Pilate for the release of a prisoner in honor of the Passover feast. For some time it had been the custom of the Roman governors to allow the populace to choose some imprisoned or condemned man for pardon at the time of the Passover. And now that this crowd had come before him to ask for the release of a prisoner, and since Jesus had so recently been in great favor with the multitudes, it occurred to Pilate that he might possibly extricate himself from his predicament by proposing to this group that, since Jesus was now a prisoner before his judgment seat, he release to them this man of Galilee as the token of Passover good will.

As the crowd surged up on the steps of the building, Pilate heard them calling out the name of one Barabbas. Barabbas was a noted political agitator and murderous robber, the son of a priest, who had recently been apprehended in the act of robbery and murder on the Jericho road. This man was under sentence to die as soon as the Passover festivities were over.

Pilate stood up and explained to the crowd that Jesus had been brought to him by the chief priests, who sought to have him put to death on certain charges, and that he did not think the man was worthy of death. Said Pilate: "Which, therefore, would you prefer that I release to you, this Barabbas, the murderer, or this Jesus of Galilee?" And when Pilate had thus spoken, the chief priests and the Sanhedrin councilors all shouted at the top of their voices, "Barabbas, Barabbas!" And when the people saw that the chief priests were minded to have Jesus put to death, they quickly joined in the clamor for his life while they loudly shouted for the release of Barabbas.

A few days before this the multitude had stood in awe of Jesus, but the mob did not look up to one who, having claimed to be the Son of God, now found himself in the custody of the chief priests and the rulers and on trial before Pilate for his life. Jesus could be a hero in the eyes of the populace when he was driving the money-changers and the traders out of the temple, but not when he was a nonresisting prisoner in the hands of his enemies and on trial for his life.

Pilate was angered at the sight of the chief priests clamoring for the pardon of a notorious murderer while they shouted for the blood of Jesus. He saw their malice and hatred and perceived their prejudice and envy. Therefore he said to them: "How could you choose the life of a murderer in preference to this man's whose worst crime is that he figuratively calls himself the king of the Jews?" But this was not a wise statement for Pilate to make. The Jews were a proud people, now subject to the Roman political yoke but hoping for the coming of a Messiah who would deliver them from gentile bondage with a great show of power and glory. They resented, more than Pilate could know, the intimation that this meek-mannered teacher of strange doctrines, now under arrest and charged with crimes worthy of death, should be referred to as "the king of the Jews." They looked upon such a remark as an insult to everything which they held sacred and honorable in their national existence, and therefore did they all let loose their mighty shouts for Barabbas's release and Jesus' death.

Pilate knew Jesus was innocent of the charges brought against him, and had he been a just and courageous judge, he would have acquitted him and turned him loose. But he was afraid to defy these angry Jews, and while he hesitated to do his duty, a messenger came up and presented him with a sealed message from his wife, Claudia.

Pilate indicated to those assembled before him that he wished to read the communication which he had just received before he proceeded further with the matter before him. When Pilate opened this letter from his wife, he read: "I pray you have nothing to do with this innocent and just man whom they call Jesus. I have suffered many things in a dream this night because of him." This note from Claudia not only greatly upset Pilate and thereby delayed the adjudication of this matter, but it unfortunately also provided considerable time in which the Jewish rulers freely circulated among the crowd and urged the people to call for the release of Barabbas and to clamor for the crucifixion of Jesus.

Finally, Pilate addressed himself once more to the solution of the problem which confronted him, by asking the mixed assembly of Jewish rulers and the pardon-seeking crowd, "What shall I do with him who is called the king of the Jews?" And they all shouted with one accord, "Crucify him! Crucify him!" The unanimity of this demand from the mixed multitude startled and alarmed Pilate, the unjust and fear-ridden judge.

Then once more Pilate said: "Why would you crucify this man? What evil has he done? Who will come forward to testify against him?" But when they heard Pilate speak in defense of Jesus, they only cried out all the more, "Crucify him! Crucify him!"

Then again Pilate appealed to them regarding the release of the Passover prisoner, saying: "Once more I ask you, which of these prisoners shall I release to you at this, your Passover time?" And again the crowd shouted, "Give us Barabbas!"

Then said Pilate: "If I release the murderer, Barabbas, what shall I do with Jesus?" And once more the multitude shouted in unison, "Crucify him! Crucify him!"

Pilate was terrorized by the insistent clamor of the mob, acting under the direct leadership of the chief priests and the councilors of the Sanhedrin; nevertheless, he decided upon at least one more attempt to appease the crowd and save Jesus.

6. PILATE'S LAST APPEAL

In all that is transpiring early this Friday morning before Pilate, only the enemies of Jesus are participating. His many friends either do not yet know of his night arrest and early morning trial or are in hiding lest they also be apprehended and adjudged worthy of death because they believe Jesus' teachings. In the multitude which now clamors for the Master's death are to be found only his sworn enemies and the easily led and unthinking populace.

Pilate would make one last appeal to their pity. Being afraid to defy the clamor of this misled mob who cried for the blood of Jesus, he ordered the Jewish guards and the Roman soldiers to take Jesus and scourge him. This was in itself an unjust and illegal procedure since the Roman law provided that only those condemned to die by crucifixion should be thus subjected to scourging. The guards took Jesus into the open courtyard of the praetorium for this ordeal. Though his enemies did not witness this scourging, Pilate did, and before they had finished this wicked abuse, he directed the scourgers to desist and indicated that Jesus should be brought to him. Before the scourgers laid their knotted whips upon Jesus as he was bound to the whipping post, they again put upon him the purple robe, and plaiting a crown of thorns, they placed it upon his brow. And when they had put a reed in his hand as a mock scepter, they knelt before him and mocked him, saying, "Hail, king of the Jews!" And they spit upon him and struck him in the face with their hands. And one of them, before they returned him to Pilate, took the reed from his hand and struck him upon the head.

Then Pilate led forth this bleeding and lacerated prisoner and, presenting him before the mixed multitude, said: "Behold the man! Again I declare to you that I find no crime in him, and having scourged him, I would release him."

There stood Jesus of Nazareth, clothed in an old purple royal robe with a crown of thorns piercing his kindly brow. His face was bloodstained and his form bowed down with suffering and grief. But nothing can appeal to the unfeeling hearts of those who are victims of intense emotional hatred and slaves to religious prejudice. This sight sent a mighty shudder through the realms of a vast universe, but it did not touch the hearts of those who had set their minds to effect the destruction of Jesus.

When they had recovered from the first shock of seeing the Master's plight, they only shouted the louder and the longer, "Crucify him! Crucify him! Crucify him!"

And now did Pilate comprehend that it was futile to appeal to their supposed feelings of pity. He stepped forward and said: "I perceive that you are determined this man shall die, but what has he done to deserve death? Who will declare his crime?"

Then the high priest himself stepped forward and, going up to Pilate, angrily declared: "We have a sacred law, and by that law this man ought to die because he made himself out to be the Son of God." When Pilate heard this, he was all the more afraid, not only of the Jews, but recalling his wife's note and the Greek mythology of the gods coming down on earth, he now trembled at the thought of Jesus possibly being a divine personage. He waved to the crowd to hold its peace while he took Jesus by the arm and again led him inside the building that he might further examine him. Pilate was now confused by fear, bewildered by superstition, and harassed by the stubborn attitude of the mob.

7. Pilate's Last Interview

As Pilate, trembling with fearful emotion, sat down by the side of Jesus, he inquired: "Where do you come from? Really, who are you? What is this they say, that you are the Son of God?"

But Jesus could hardly answer such questions when asked by a man-fearing, weak, and vacillating judge who was so unjust as to subject him to flogging even when he had declared him innocent of all crime, and before he had been duly sentenced to die. Jesus looked Pilate straight in the face, but he did not answer him. Then said Pilate: "Do you refuse to speak to me? Do you not realize that I still have power to release you or to crucify you?" Then said Jesus: "You could have no power over me except it were permitted from above. You could exercise no authority over the Son of Man unless the Father in heaven allowed it. But you are not so guilty since you are ignorant of the gospel. He who betrayed me and he who delivered me to you, they have the greater sin."

This last talk with Jesus thoroughly frightened Pilate. This moral coward and judicial weakling now labored under the double weight of the superstitious fear of Jesus and mortal dread of the Jewish leaders.

Again Pilate appeared before the crowd, saying: "I am certain this man is only a religious offender. You should take him and judge him by your law. Why should you expect that I would consent to his death because he has clashed with your traditions?"

Pilate was just about ready to release Jesus when Caiaphas, the high priest, approached the cowardly Roman judge and, shaking an avenging finger in Pilate's face, said with angry words which the entire multitude could hear: "If you release this man, you are not Caesar's friend, and I will see that the emperor knows all." This public threat was too much for Pilate. Fear for his personal fortunes now eclipsed all other considerations, and the cowardly governor ordered Jesus brought out before the judgment seat. As the Master stood there before them, he pointed to him and tauntingly said, "Behold your king." And the Jews answered, "Away with him. Crucify him!" And then Pilate said, with much irony and sarcasm, "Shall I crucify your king?" And the Jews answered, "Yes, crucify him! We have no king but Caesar." And then did Pilate realize that there was no hope of saving Jesus since he was unwilling to defy the Jews.

8. PILATE'S TRAGIC SURRENDER

Here stood the Son of God incarnate as the Son of Man. He was arrested without indictment; accused without evidence; adjudged without witnesses; punished without a verdict; and now was soon to be condemned to die by an unjust judge who confessed that he could find no fault in him. If Pilate had thought to appeal to their patriotism by referring to Jesus as the "king of the Jews," he utterly failed. The Jews were not expecting any such a king. The declaration of the chief priests and the Sadducees, "We have no king but Caesar," was a shock even to the unthinking populace, but it was too late now to save Jesus even had the mob dared to espouse the Master's cause.

Pilate was afraid of a tumult or a riot. He dared not risk having such a disturbance during Passover time in Jerusalem. He had recently received a reprimand from Caesar, and he would not risk another. The mob cheered when he ordered the release of Barabbas. Then he ordered a basin and some water, and there before the multitude he washed his hands, saying: "I am innocent of the blood of this man. You are determined that he shall die, but I have found no guilt in him. See you to it. The soldiers will lead him forth." And then the mob cheered and replied, "His blood be on us and on our children."

PAPER 186

JUST BEFORE THE CRUCIFIXION

AS JESUS and his accusers started off to see Herod, the Master turned to the Apostle John and said: "John, you can do no more for me. Go to my mother and bring her to see me ere I die." When John heard his Master's request, although reluctant to leave him alone among his enemies, he hastened off to Bethany, where the entire family of Jesus was assembled in waiting at the home of Martha and Mary, the sisters of Lazarus whom Jesus raised from the dead.

Several times during the morning, messengers had brought news to Martha and Mary concerning the progress of Jesus' trial. But the family of Jesus did not reach Bethany until just a few minutes before John arrived bearing the request of Jesus to see his mother before he was put to death. After John Zebedee had told them all that had happened since the midnight arrest of Jesus, Mary his mother went at once in the company of John to see her eldest son. By the time Mary and John reached the city, Jesus, accompanied by the Roman soldiers who were to crucify him, had already arrived at Golgotha.

When Mary the mother of Jesus started out with John to go to her son, his sister Ruth refused to remain behind with the rest of the family. Since she was determined to accompany her mother, her brother Jude went with her. The rest of the Master's family remained in Bethany under the direction of James, and almost every hour the messengers of David Zebedee brought them reports concerning the progress of that terrible business of putting to death their eldest brother, Jesus of Nazareth.

1. THE END OF JUDAS ISCARIOT

It was about half past eight o'clock this Friday morning when the hearing of Jesus before Pilate was ended and the Master was placed in the custody of the Roman soldiers who were to crucify him. As soon as the Romans took possession of Jesus, the captain of the Jewish guards marched with his men back to their temple headquarters. The chief priest and his Sanhedrist associates followed close behind the guards, going directly to their usual meeting place in the hall of hewn stone in the temple. Here they found many other members of the Sanhedrin waiting to learn what had been done with Jesus. As Caiaphas was engaged in making his report to the Sanhedrin regarding the trial and condemnation of Jesus, Judas appeared before them to claim his reward for the part he had played in his Master's arrest and sentence of death.

All of these Jews loathed Judas; they looked upon the betrayer with only feelings of utter contempt. Throughout the trial of Jesus before Caiaphas and during his appearance before Pilate, Judas was pricked in his conscience about his traitorous conduct. And he was also beginning to become somewhat disillusioned regarding the reward he was to receive as payment for his services as Jesus' betrayer. He did not like the coolness and aloofness of the Jewish authorities; nevertheless, he expected to be liberally rewarded for his cowardly conduct. He anticipated being called before the full meeting of the Sanhedrin and there hearing himself eulogized while they conferred upon him suitable honors in token of the great service which he flattered himself he had rendered his nation. Imagine, therefore, the great surprise of this egotistic traitor when a servant of the high priest, tapping him on the shoulder, called him just outside the hall and said: "Judas, I have been appointed to pay you for the betrayal of Jesus. Here is your reward." And thus speaking, the servant of Caiaphas handed Judas a bag containing thirty pieces of silver—the current price of a good, healthy slave.

Judas was stunned, dumfounded. He rushed back to enter the hall but was debarred by the doorkeeper. He wanted to appeal to the Sanhedrin, but they would not admit him. Judas could not believe that these rulers of the Jews would allow him to betray his friends and his Master and then offer him as a reward thirty pieces of silver. He was humiliated, disillusioned, and utterly crushed. He walked away from the temple, as it were, in a trance. He automatically dropped the money bag in his deep pocket, that same pocket wherein he had so long carried the bag containing the apostolic funds. And he wandered out through the city after the crowds who were on their way to witness the crucifixions.

From a distance Judas saw them raise the cross piece with Jesus nailed thereon, and upon sight of this he rushed back to the temple and, forcing his way past the doorkeeper, found himself standing in the presence of the Sanhedrin, which was still in session. The betrayer was well-nigh breathless and highly distraught, but he managed to stammer out these words: "I have sinned in that I have betrayed innocent blood. You have insulted me. You have offered me as a reward for my service, money—the price of a slave. I repent that I have done this; here is your money. I want to escape the guilt of this deed."

When the rulers of the Jews heard Judas, they scoffed at him. One of them sitting near where Judas stood, motioned that he should leave the hall and said: "Your Master has already been put to death by the Romans, and as for your guilt, what is that to us? See you to that—and begone!"

As Judas left the Sanhedrin chamber, he removed the thirty pieces of silver from the bag and threw them broadcast over the temple floor. When the betrayer left the temple, he was almost beside himself. Judas was now passing through the experience of the realization of the true nature of sin. All the glamor, fascination, and intoxication of wrongdoing had vanished. Now the evildoer stood alone and face to face with the judgment verdict of his disillusioned and disappointed soul. Sin was bewitching and adventurous in the committing, but now must the harvest of the naked and unromantic facts be faced.

This onetime ambassador of the kingdom of heaven on earth now walked through the streets of Jerusalem, forsaken and alone. His despair was desperate and well-nigh absolute. On he journeyed through the city and outside the walls, on down into the terrible solitude of the valley of Hinnom, where he climbed up the steep rocks and, taking the girdle of his cloak, fastened one end to a small tree, tied the other about his neck, and cast himself over the precipice. Ere he was dead, the knot which his nervous hands had tied gave way, and the betrayer's body was dashed to pieces as it fell on the jagged rocks below.

2. THE MASTER'S ATTITUDE

When Jesus was arrested, he knew that his work on earth, in the likeness of mortal flesh, was finished. He fully understood the sort of death he would die, and he was little concerned with the details of his so-called trials.

Before the Sanhedrist court Jesus declined to make replies to the testimony of perjured witnesses. There was but one question which would always elicit an answer, whether asked by friend or foe, and that was the one concerning the nature and divinity of his mission on earth. When asked if he were the Son of God, he unfailingly made reply. He steadfastly refused to speak when in the presence of the curious and wicked Herod. Before Pilate he spoke only when he thought that Pilate or some other sincere person might be helped to a better knowledge of the truth by what he said. Jesus had taught his apostles the uselessness of casting their pearls before swine, and he now dared to practice what he had taught. His conduct at this time exemplified the patient submission of the human nature coupled with the majestic silence and solemn dignity of the divine nature. He was altogether willing to discuss with Pilate any question related to the political charges brought against him—any question which he recognized as belonging to the governor's jurisdiction.

Jesus was convinced that it was the will of the Father that he submit himself to the natural and ordinary course of human events just as every other mortal creature must, and therefore he refused to employ even his purely human powers of persuasive eloquence to influence the outcome of the machinations of his socially nearsighted and spiritually blinded fellow mortals. Although Jesus lived and died on Urantia, his whole human career, from first to last, was a spectacle designed to influence and instruct the entire universe of his creation and unceasing upholding.

These shortsighted Jews clamored unseemlily for the Master's death while he stood there in awful silence looking upon the death scene of a nation—his earthly father's own people.

Jesus had acquired that type of human character which could preserve its composure and assert its dignity in the face of continued and gratuitous insult. He could not be intimidated. When first assaulted by the servant of Annas, he had only suggested the propriety of calling witnesses who might duly testify against him.

From first to last, in his so-called trial before Pilate, the onlooking celestial hosts could not refrain from broadcasting to the universe the depiction of the scene of "Pilate on trial before Jesus."

When before Caiaphas, and when all the perjured testimony had broken down, Jesus did not hesitate to answer the question of the chief priest, thereby providing in his own testimony that which they desired as a basis for convicting him of blasphemy.

The Master never displayed the least interest in Pilate's well-meant but halfhearted efforts to effect his release. He really pitied Pilate and sincerely endeavored to enlighten his darkened mind. He was wholly passive to all the Roman governor's appeals to the Jews to withdraw their criminal charges against him. Throughout the whole sorrowful ordeal he bore himself with simple dignity and unostentatious majesty. He would not so much as cast reflections of insincerity upon his would-be murderers when they asked if he were "king of the Jews." With but little qualifying explanation he accepted the designation, knowing that, while they had chosen to reject him, he would be the last to afford them real national leadership, even in a spiritual sense.

Jesus said little during these trials, but he said enough to show all mortals the kind of human character man can perfect in partnership with God and to reveal to all the universe the manner in which God can become manifest in the life of the creature when such a creature truly chooses to do the will of the Father, thus becoming an active son of the living God.

His love for ignorant mortals is fully disclosed by his patience and great self-possession in the face of the jeers, blows, and buffetings of the coarse soldiers and the unthinking servants. He was not even angry when they blindfolded him and, derisively striking him in the face, exclaimed: "Prophesy to us who it was that struck you."

Pilate spoke more truly than he knew when, after Jesus had been scourged, he presented him before the multitude, exclaiming, "Behold the man!" Indeed, the fear-ridden Roman governor little dreamed that at just that moment the universe stood at attention, gazing upon this unique scene of its beloved Sovereign thus subjected in humiliation to the taunts and blows of his darkened and degraded mortal subjects. And as Pilate spoke, there echoed throughout all Nebadon, "Behold God and man!" Throughout a universe, untold millions have ever since that day continued to behold that man, while the God of Havona, the supreme ruler of the universe of universes, accepts the man of Nazareth as the satisfaction of the ideal of the mortal creatures of this local universe of time and space. In his matchless life he never failed to reveal God to man. Now, in these final episodes of his mortal career and in his subsequent death, he made a new and touching revelation of man to God.

3. THE DEPENDABLE DAVID ZEBEDEE

Shortly after Jesus was turned over to the Roman soldiers at the conclusion of the hearing before Pilate, a detachment of the temple guards hastened out to Gethsemane to disperse or arrest the followers of the Master. But long before their arrival these followers had scattered. The apostles had retired to designated hiding places; the Greeks had separated and gone to various homes in Jerusalem; the other disciples had likewise disappeared. David Zebedee believed that Jesus' enemies would return; so he early removed some five or six tents up the ravine near where the Master so often retired to pray and worship. Here he proposed to hide and at the same time maintain a center, or co-ordinating station, for his messenger service. David had hardly left the camp when the temple guards arrived. Finding no one there, they contented themselves with burning the camp and then hastened back to the temple. On hearing their report, the Sanhedrin was satisfied that the followers of Jesus were so thoroughly frightened and subdued that there would be no danger of an uprising or any attempt to rescue Jesus from the hands of his executioners. They were at last able to breathe easily, and so they adjourned, every man going his way to prepare for the Passover.

As soon as Jesus was turned over to the Roman soldiers by Pilate for crucifixion, a messenger hastened away to Gethsemane to inform David, and within five minutes runners were on their way to Bethsaida, Pella, Philadelphia, Sidon,

Shechem, Hebron, Damascus, and Alexandria. And these messengers carried the news that Jesus was about to be crucified by the Romans at the insistent behest of the rulers of the Jews.

Throughout this tragic day, until the message finally went forth that the Master had been laid in the tomb, David sent messengers about every half hour with reports to the apostles, the Greeks, and Jesus' earthly family, assembled at the home of Lazarus in Bethany. When the messengers departed with the word that Jesus had been buried, David dismissed his corps of local runners for the Passover celebration and for the coming Sabbath of rest, instructing them to report to him quietly on Sunday morning at the home of Nicodemus, where he proposed to go in hiding for a few days with Andrew and Simon Peter.

This peculiar-minded David Zebedee was the only one of the leading disciples of Jesus who was inclined to take a literal and plain matter-of-fact view of the Master's assertion that he would die and "rise again on the third day." David had once heard him make this prediction and, being of a literal turn of mind, now proposed to assemble his messengers early Sunday morning at the home of Nicodemus so that they would be on hand to spread the news in case Jesus rose from the dead. David soon discovered that none of Jesus' followers were looking for him to return so soon from the grave; therefore did he say little about his belief and nothing about the mobilization of all his messenger force on early Sunday morning except to the runners who had been dispatched on Friday forenoon to distant cities and believer centers.

And so these followers of Jesus, scattered throughout Jerusalem and its environs, that night partook of the Passover and the following day remained in seclusion.

4. PREPARATION FOR THE CRUCIFIXION

After Pilate had washed his hands before the multitude, thus seeking to escape the guilt of delivering up an innocent man to be crucified just because he feared to resist the clamor of the rulers of the Jews, he ordered the Master turned over to the Roman soldiers and gave the word to their captain that he was to be crucified immediately. Upon taking charge of Jesus, the soldiers led him back into the courtyard of the praetorium, and after removing the robe which Herod had put on him, they dressed him in his own garments. These soldiers mocked and derided him, but they did not inflict further physical punishment. Jesus was now alone with these Roman soldiers. His friends were in hiding; his enemies had gone their way; even John Zebedee was no longer by his side.

It was a little after eight o'clock when Pilate turned Jesus over to the soldiers and a little before nine o'clock when they started for the scene of the crucifixion. During this period of more than half an hour Jesus never spoke a word. The executive business of a great universe was practically at a standstill. Gabriel and the chief rulers of Nebadon were either assembled here on Urantia, or else they were closely attending upon the space reports of the archangels in an effort to keep advised as to what was happening to the Son of Man on Urantia.

By the time the soldiers were ready to depart with Jesus for Golgotha, they had begun to be impressed by his unusual composure and extraordinary dignity, by his uncomplaining silence.

Much of the delay in starting off with Jesus for the site of the crucifixion was due to the last-minute decision of the captain to take along two thieves who had been condemned to die; since Jesus was to be crucified that morning, the Roman captain thought these two might just as well die with him as wait for the end of the Passover festivities.

As soon as the thieves could be made ready, they were led into the courtyard, where they gazed upon Jesus, one of them for the first time, but the other had often heard him speak, both in the temple and many months before at the Pella camp.

5. JESUS' DEATH IN RELATION TO THE PASSOVER

There is no direct relation between the death of Jesus and the Jewish Passover. True, the Master did lay down his life in the flesh on this day, the day of the preparation for the Jewish Passover, and at about the time of the sacrificing of the Passover lambs in the temple. But this coincidental occurrence does not in any manner indicate that the death of the Son of Man on earth has any connection with the Jewish sacrificial system. Jesus was a Jew, but as the Son of Man he was a mortal of the realms. The events already narrated and leading up to this hour of the Master's impending crucifixion are sufficient to indicate that his death at about this time was a purely natural and man-managed affair.

It was man and not God who planned and executed the death of Jesus on the cross. True, the Father refused to interfere with the march of human events on Urantia, but the Father in Paradise did not decree, demand, or require the death of his Son as it was carried out on earth. It is a fact that in some manner, sooner or later, Jesus would have had to divest himself of his mortal body, his incarnation in the flesh, but he could have executed such a task in countless ways without dying on a cross between two thieves. All of this was man's doing, not God's.

At the time of the Master's baptism he had already completed the technique of the required experience on earth and in the flesh which was necessary for the completion of his seventh and last universe bestowal. At this very time Jesus' duty on earth was done. All the life he lived thereafter, and even the manner of his death, was a purely personal ministry on his part for the welfare and uplifting of his mortal creatures on this world and on other worlds.

The gospel of the good news that mortal man may, by faith, become spirit-conscious that he is a son of God, is not dependent on the death of Jesus. True, indeed, all this gospel of the kingdom has been tremendously illuminated by the Master's death, but even more so by his life.

All that the Son of Man said or did on earth greatly embellished the doctrines of sonship with God and of the brotherhood of men, but these essential relationships of God and men are inherent in the universe facts of God's love for his creatures and the innate mercy of the divine Sons. These touching and divinely beautiful relations between man and his Maker, on this world and on all others throughout the universe of universes, have existed from eternity; and they are not in any sense dependent on these periodic bestowal enactments of the Creator Sons of God, who thus assume the nature and likeness of their created intelligences as a part of the price which they must pay for the final acquirement of unlimited sovereignty over their respective local universes.

The Father in heaven loved mortal man on earth just as much before the life and death of Jesus on Urantia as he did after this transcendent exhibition of the copartnership of man and God. This mighty transaction of the incarnation of the God of Nebadon as a man on Urantia could not augment the attributes of the eternal, infinite, and universal Father, but it did enrich and enlighten all other administrators and creatures of the universe of Nebadon. While the Father in heaven loves us no more because of this bestowal of Michael, all other celestial intelligences do. And this is because Jesus not only made a revelation of God to man, but he also likewise made a new revelation of man to the Gods and to the celestial intelligences of the universe of universes.

Jesus is not about to die as a sacrifice for sin. He is not going to atone for the inborn moral guilt of the human race. Mankind has no such racial guilt before God. Guilt is purely a matter of personal sin and knowing, deliberate rebellion against the will of the Father and the administration of his Sons.

Sin and rebellion have nothing to do with the fundamental bestowal plan of the Paradise Sons of God, albeit it does appear to us that the salvage plan is a provisional feature of the bestowal plan.

The salvation of God for the mortals of Urantia would have been just as effective and unerringly certain if Jesus had not been put to death by the cruel hands of ignorant mortals. If the Master had been favorably received by the mortals of earth and had departed from Urantia by the voluntary relinquishment of his life in the flesh, the fact of the love of God and the mercy of the Son—the fact of sonship with God—would have in no wise been affected. You mortals are the sons of God, and only one thing is required to make such a truth factual in your personal experience, and that is your spirit-born faith.

PAPER 187
THE CRUCIFIXION

AFTER the two brigands had been made ready, the soldiers, under the direction of a centurion, started for the scene of the crucifixion. The centurion in charge of these twelve soldiers was the same captain who had led forth the Roman soldiers the previous night to arrest Jesus in Gethsemane. It was the Roman custom to assign four soldiers for each person to be crucified. The two brigands were properly scourged before they were taken out to be crucified, but Jesus was given no further physical punishment; the captain undoubtedly thought he had already been sufficiently scourged, even before his condemnation.

The two thieves crucified with Jesus were associates of Barabbas and would later have been put to death with their leader if he had not been released as the Passover pardon of Pilate. Jesus was thus crucified in the place of Barabbas.

What Jesus is now about to do, submit to death on the cross, he does of his own free will. In foretelling this experience, he said: "The Father loves and sustains me because I am willing to lay down my life. But I will take it up again. No one takes my life away from me—I lay it down of myself. I have authority to lay it down, and I have authority to take it up. I have received such a commandment from my Father."

It was just before nine o'clock this morning when the soldiers led Jesus from the praetorium on the way to Golgotha. They were followed by many who secretly sympathized with Jesus, but most of this group of two hundred or more were either his enemies or curious idlers who merely desired to enjoy the shock of witnessing the crucifixions. Only a few of the Jewish leaders went out to see Jesus die on the cross. Knowing that he had been turned over to the Roman soldiers by Pilate, and that he was condemned to die, they busied themselves with their meeting in the temple, whereat they discussed what should be done with his followers.

1. ON THE WAY TO GOLGOTHA

Before leaving the courtyard of the praetorium, the soldiers placed the crossbeam on Jesus' shoulders. It was the custom to compel the condemned man to carry the crossbeam to the site of the crucifixion. Such a condemned man did not carry the whole cross, only this shorter timber. The longer and upright pieces of timber for the three crosses had already been transported to Golgotha and, by the time of the arrival of the soldiers and their prisoners, had been firmly implanted in the ground.

According to custom the captain led the procession, carrying small white boards on which had been written with charcoal the names of the criminals and the nature of the crimes for which they had been condemned. For the two thieves the centurion had notices which gave their names, underneath which was written the one word, "Brigand." It was the custom, after the victim had been nailed to the crossbeam and hoisted to his place on the upright timber, to nail this notice to the top of the cross, just above the head of the criminal, that all witnesses might know for what crime the condemned man was being crucified. The legend which the centurion carried to put on the cross of Jesus had been written by Pilate himself in Latin, Greek, and Aramaic, and it read: "Jesus of Nazareth—the King of the Jews."

Some of the Jewish authorities who were yet present when Pilate wrote this legend made vigorous protest against calling Jesus the "king of the Jews." But Pilate reminded them that such an accusation was part of the charge which led to his condemnation. When the Jews saw they could not prevail upon Pilate to change his mind, they pleaded that at least it be modified to read, "He said, 'I am the king of the Jews.'" But Pilate was adamant; he would not alter the writing. To all further supplication he only replied, "What I have written, I have written."

Ordinarily, it was the custom to journey to Golgotha by the longest road in order that a large number of persons might view the condemned criminal, but on this day they went by the most direct route to the Damascus gate, which led out of the city to the north, and following this road, they soon arrived at Golgotha, the official crucifixion site of Jerusalem. Beyond Golgotha were the villas of the wealthy, and on the other side of the road were the tombs of many well-to-do Jews.

Crucifixion was not a Jewish mode of punishment. Both the Greeks and the Romans learned this method of execution from the Phoenicians. Even Herod, with all his cruelty, did not resort to crucifixion. The Romans never crucified a Roman citizen; only slaves and subject peoples were subjected to this dishonorable mode of death. During the siege of Jerusalem, just forty years after the crucifixion of Jesus, all of Golgotha was covered by thousands upon thousands of crosses upon which, from day to day, there perished the flower of the Jewish race. A terrible harvest, indeed, of the seed-sowing of this day.

As the death procession passed along the narrow streets of Jerusalem, many of the tenderhearted Jewish women who had heard Jesus' words of good cheer and compassion, and who knew of his life of loving ministry, could not refrain from weeping when they saw him being led forth to such an ignoble death. As he passed by, many of these women bewailed and lamented. And when some of them even dared to follow along by his side, the Master turned his head toward them and said: "Daughters of Jerusalem, weep not for me, but rather weep for yourselves and for your children. My work is about done—soon I go to my Father—but the times of terrible trouble for Jerusalem are just beginning. Behold, the days are coming in which you shall say: Blessed are the barren and those whose breasts have never suckled their young. In those days will you pray the rocks of the hills to fall on you in order that you may be delivered from the terrors of your troubles."

These women of Jerusalem were indeed courageous to manifest sympathy for Jesus, for it was strictly against the law to show friendly feelings for one who was being led forth to crucifixion. It was permitted the rabble to jeer, mock, and ridicule the condemned, but it was not allowed that any sympathy should be expressed. Though Jesus appreciated the manifestation of sympathy in this dark hour when his friends were in hiding, he did not want these kindhearted women to incur the displeasure of the authorities by daring to show compassion in his behalf. Even at such a time as this Jesus thought little about himself, only of the terrible days of tragedy ahead for Jerusalem and the whole Jewish nation.

As the Master trudged along on the way to the crucifixion, he was very weary; he was nearly exhausted. He had had neither food nor water since the Last Supper at the home of Elijah Mark; neither had he been permitted to enjoy one moment of sleep. In addition, there had been one hearing right after another up to the hour of his condemnation, not to mention the abusive scourgings with their accompanying physical suffering and loss of blood. Superimposed upon all this was his extreme mental anguish, his acute spiritual tension, and a terrible feeling of human loneliness.

Shortly after passing through the gate on the way out of the city, as Jesus staggered on bearing the crossbeam, his physical strength momentarily gave way, and he fell beneath the weight of his heavy burden. The soldiers shouted at him and kicked him, but he could not arise. When the captain saw this, knowing what Jesus had already endured, he commanded the soldiers to desist. Then he ordered a passerby, one Simon from Cyrene, to take the crossbeam from Jesus' shoulders and compelled him to carry it the rest of the way to Golgotha.

This man Simon had come all the way from Cyrene, in northern Africa, to attend the Passover. He was stopping with other Cyrenians just outside the city walls and was on his way to the temple services in the city when the Roman captain commanded him to carry Jesus' crossbeam. Simon lingered all through the hours of the Master's death on the cross, talking with many of his friends and with his enemies. After the resurrection and before leaving Jerusalem, he became a valiant believer in the gospel of the kingdom, and when he returned home, he led his family into the heavenly kingdom. His two sons, Alexander and Rufus, became very effective teachers of the new gospel in Africa. But Simon never knew that Jesus, whose burden he bore, and the Jewish tutor who once befriended his injured son, were the same person.

It was shortly after nine o'clock when this procession of death arrived at Golgotha, and the Roman soldiers set themselves about the task of nailing the two brigands and the Son of Man to their respective crosses.

2. THE CRUCIFIXION

The soldiers first bound the Master's arms with cords to the crossbeam, and then they nailed his hands to the wood. When they had hoisted this crossbeam up on the post, and after they had nailed it securely to the upright timber of the cross, they bound and nailed his feet to the wood, using one long nail to penetrate both feet. The upright timber had a large peg, inserted at the proper height, which served as a sort of saddle for supporting the body weight. The cross was not high, the Master's feet being only about three feet from the ground. He was therefore able to hear all that was said of him in derision and could plainly see the expression on the faces of all those who so thoughtlessly mocked him. And also could those present easily hear all that Jesus said during these hours of lingering torture and slow death.

It was the custom to remove all clothes from those who were to be crucified, but since the Jews greatly objected to the public exposure of the naked human form, the Romans always provided a suitable loin cloth for all persons crucified at Jerusalem. Accordingly, after Jesus' clothes had been removed, he was thus garbed before he was put upon the cross.

Crucifixion was resorted to in order to provide a cruel and lingering punishment, the victim sometimes not dying for several days. There was considerable sentiment against crucifixion in Jerusalem, and there existed a society of Jewish women who always sent a representative to crucifixions for the purpose of offering drugged wine to the victim in order to lessen his suffering. But when Jesus tasted this narcotized wine, as thirsty as he was, he refused to drink it. The Master chose to retain his human consciousness until the very end. He desired to meet death, even in this cruel and inhuman form, and conquer it by voluntary submission to the full human experience.

Before Jesus was put on his cross, the two brigands had already been placed on their crosses, all the while cursing and spitting upon their executioners. Jesus' only words, as they nailed him to the crossbeam, were, "Father, forgive them, for they know not what they do." He could not have so mercifully and lovingly interceded for his executioners if such thoughts of affectionate devotion had not been the mainspring of all his life of unselfish service. The ideas, motives, and longings of a lifetime are openly revealed in a crisis.

After the Master was hoisted on the cross, the captain nailed the title up above his head, and it read in three languages, "Jesus of Nazareth—the King of the Jews." The Jews were infuriated by this believed insult. But Pilate was chafed by their disrespectful manner; he felt he had been intimidated and humiliated, and he took this method of obtaining petty revenge. He could have written "Jesus, a rebel." But he well knew how these Jerusalem Jews detested the very name of Nazareth, and he was determined thus to humiliate them. He knew that they would also be cut to the very quick by seeing this executed Galilean called "The King of the Jews."

Many of the Jewish leaders, when they learned how Pilate had sought to deride them by placing this inscription on the cross of Jesus, hastened out to Golgotha, but they dared not attempt to remove it since the Roman soldiers were standing on guard. Not being able to remove the title, these leaders mingled with the crowd and did their utmost to incite derision and ridicule, lest any give serious regard to the inscription.

The Apostle John, with Mary the mother of Jesus, Ruth, and Jude, arrived on the scene just after Jesus had been hoisted to his position on the cross, and just as the captain was nailing the title above the Master's head. John was the only one of the eleven apostles to witness the crucifixion, and even he was not present all of the time since he ran into Jerusalem to bring back his mother and her friends soon after he had brought Jesus' mother to the scene.

As Jesus saw his mother, with John and his brother and sister, he smiled but said nothing. Meanwhile the four soldiers assigned to the Master's crucifixion, as was the custom, had divided his clothes among them, one taking the sandals, one the turban, one the girdle, and the fourth the cloak. This left the tunic, or seamless vestment reaching down to near the knees, to be cut up into four pieces, but when the soldiers saw what an unusual garment it was, they decided to cast lots for it. Jesus looked down on them while they divided his garments, and the thoughtless crowd jeered at him.

It was well that the Roman soldiers took possession of the Master's clothing. Otherwise, if his followers had gained possession of these garments, they would have been tempted to resort to superstitious relic worship. The Master desired that his followers should have nothing material to associate with his life on earth. He wanted to leave mankind only the memory of a human life dedicated to the high spiritual ideal of being consecrated to doing the Father's will.

3. THOSE WHO SAW THE CRUCIFIXION

At about half past nine o'clock this Friday morning, Jesus was hung upon the cross. Before eleven o'clock, upward of one thousand persons had assembled to witness this spectacle of the crucifixion of the Son of Man. Throughout these dreadful hours the unseen hosts of a universe stood in silence while they gazed upon this extraordinary phenomenon of the Creator as he was dying the death of the creature, even the most ignoble death of a condemned criminal.

Standing near the cross at one time or another during the crucifixion were Mary, Ruth, Jude, John, Salome (John's mother), and a group of earnest women believers including Mary the wife of Clopas and sister of Jesus' mother, Mary Magdalene, and Rebecca, onetime of Sepphoris. These and other friends of Jesus held their peace while they witnessed his great patience and fortitude and gazed upon his intense sufferings.

Many who passed by wagged their heads and, railing at him, said: "You who would destroy the temple and build it again in three days, save yourself. If you are the Son of God, why do you not come down from your cross?" In like manner some of the rulers of the Jews mocked him, saying, "He saved others, but himself he cannot save." Others said, "If you are the king of the Jews, come down from the cross, and we will believe in you." And later on they mocked him the more, saying: "He trusted in God to deliver him. He even claimed to be the Son of God—look at him now—crucified between two thieves." Even the two thieves also railed at him and cast reproach upon him.

Inasmuch as Jesus would make no reply to their taunts, and since it was nearing noontime of this special preparation day, by half past eleven o'clock most of the jesting and jeering crowd had gone its way; less than fifty persons remained on the scene. The soldiers now prepared to eat lunch and drink their cheap, sour wine as they settled down for the long deathwatch. As they partook of their wine, they derisively offered a toast to Jesus, saying, "Hail and good fortune! to the king of the Jews." And they were astonished at the Master's tolerant regard of their ridicule and mocking.

When Jesus saw them eat and drink, he looked down upon them and said, "I thirst." When the captain of the guard heard Jesus say, "I thirst," he took some of the wine from his bottle and, putting the saturated sponge stopper upon the end of a javelin, raised it to Jesus so that he could moisten his parched lips.

Jesus had purposed to live without resort to his supernatural power, and he likewise elected to die as an ordinary mortal upon the cross. He had lived as a man, and he would die as a man—doing the Father's will.

4. THE THIEF ON THE CROSS

One of the brigands railed at Jesus, saying, "If you are the Son of God, why do you not save yourself and us?" But when he had reproached Jesus, the other thief, who had many times heard the Master teach, said: "Do you have no fear even of God? Do you not see that we are suffering justly for our deeds, but that this man suffers unjustly? Better that we should seek forgiveness for our sins and salvation for our souls." When Jesus heard the thief say this, he turned his face toward him and smiled approvingly. When the malefactor saw the face of Jesus turned toward him, he mustered up his courage, fanned the flickering flame of his faith, and said, "Lord, remember me when you come into your kingdom." And then Jesus said, "Verily, verily, I say to you today, you shall sometime be with me in Paradise."

The Master had time amidst the pangs of mortal death to listen to the faith confession of the believing brigand. When this thief reached out for salvation, he found deliverance. Many times before this he had been constrained to believe in Jesus, but only in these last hours of consciousness did he turn with a whole heart toward the Master's teaching. When he saw the manner in which Jesus faced death upon the cross, this thief could no longer resist the conviction that this Son of Man was indeed the Son of God.

During this episode of the conversion and reception of the thief into the kingdom by Jesus, the Apostle John was absent, having gone into the city to bring his mother and her friends to the scene of the crucifixion. Luke subsequently heard this story from the converted Roman captain of the guard.

The Apostle John told about the crucifixion as he remembered the event two thirds of a century after its occurrence. The other records were based upon the recital of the Roman centurion on duty who, because of what he saw and heard, subsequently believed in Jesus and entered into the full fellowship of the kingdom of heaven on earth.

This young man, the penitent brigand, had been led into a life of violence and wrongdoing by those who extolled such a career of robbery as an effective patriotic protest against political oppression and social injustice. And this sort of teaching, plus the urge for adventure, led many otherwise well-meaning youths to enlist in these daring expeditions of robbery. This young man had looked upon Barabbas as a hero. Now he saw that he had been mistaken. Here on the cross beside him he saw a really great man, a true hero. Here was a hero who fired his zeal and inspired his highest ideas of moral self-respect and quickened all his ideals of courage, manhood, and bravery. In beholding Jesus, there sprang up in his heart an overwhelming sense of love, loyalty, and genuine greatness.

And if any other person among the jeering crowd had experienced the birth of faith within his soul and had appealed to the mercy of Jesus, he would have been received with the same loving consideration that was displayed toward the believing brigand.

Just after the repentant thief heard the Master's promise that they should sometime meet in Paradise, John returned from the city, bringing with him his mother and a company of almost a dozen women believers. John took up his position near Mary the mother of Jesus, supporting her. Her son Jude stood on the other side. As Jesus looked down upon this scene, it was noontide, and he said to his mother, "Woman, behold your son!" And speaking to John, he said, "My son, behold your mother!" And then he addressed them both, saying, "I desire that you depart from this place." And so John and Jude led Mary away from Golgotha. John took the mother of Jesus to the place where he tarried in Jerusalem and then hastened back to the scene of the crucifixion. After the Passover Mary returned to Bethsaida, where she lived at John's home for the rest of her natural life. Mary did not live quite one year after the death of Jesus.

After Mary left, the other women withdrew for a short distance and remained in attendance upon Jesus until he expired on the cross, and they were yet standing by when the body of the Master was taken down for burial.

5. LAST HOUR ON THE CROSS

Although it was early in the season for such a phenomenon, shortly after twelve o'clock the sky darkened by reason of the fine sand in the air. The people of Jerusalem knew that this meant the coming of one of those hot-wind sandstorms from the Arabian Desert. Before one o'clock the sky was so dark the sun was hid, and the remainder of the crowd hastened back to the city. When the Master gave up his life shortly after this hour, less than thirty people were present, only the thirteen Roman soldiers and a group of about fifteen believers. These believers were all women except two, Jude, Jesus' brother, and John Zebedee, who returned to the scene just before the Master expired.

Shortly after one o'clock, amidst the increasing darkness of the fierce sandstorm, Jesus began to fail in human consciousness. His last words of mercy, forgiveness, and admonition had been spoken. His last wish—concerning the care of his mother—had been expressed. During this hour of approaching death the human mind of Jesus resorted to the repetition of many passages in the Hebrew scriptures, particularly the Psalms. The last conscious thought of the human Jesus was concerned with the repetition in his mind of a portion of the Book of Psalms now known as the twentieth, twenty-first, and twenty-second Psalms. While his lips would often move, he was too weak to utter the words as these passages, which he so well knew by heart, would pass through his mind. Only a few times did those standing by catch some utterance, such as, "I know the Lord will save his anointed," "Your hand shall find out all my enemies," and "My God, my God, why have you forsaken me?" Jesus did not for one moment entertain the slightest doubt that he had lived in accordance with the Father's will; and he never doubted that he was now laying down his life in the flesh in accordance with his Father's will. He did not feel that the Father had forsaken him; he was merely reciting in his vanishing consciousness many Scriptures, among them this twenty-second Psalm, which begins with "My God, my God, why have you forsaken me?" And this happened to be one of the three passages which were spoken with sufficient clearness to be heard by those standing by.

The last request which the mortal Jesus made of his fellows was about half past one o'clock when, a second time, he said, "I thirst," and the same captain of the guard again moistened his lips with the same sponge wet in the sour wine, in those days commonly called vinegar.

The sandstorm grew in intensity and the heavens increasingly darkened. Still the soldiers and the small group of believers stood by. The soldiers crouched near the cross, huddled together to protect themselves from the cutting sand. The mother of John and others watched from a distance where they were somewhat sheltered by an overhanging rock. When the Master finally breathed his last, there were present at the foot of his cross John Zebedee, his brother Jude, his sister Ruth, Mary Magdalene, and Rebecca, onetime of Sepphoris.

It was just before three o'clock when Jesus, with a loud voice, cried out, "It is finished! Father, into your hands I commend my spirit." And when he had thus spoken, he bowed his head and gave up the life struggle. When the Roman centurion saw how Jesus died, he smote his breast and said: "This was indeed a righteous man; truly he must have been a Son of God." And from that hour he began to believe in Jesus.

Jesus died royally—as he had lived. He freely admitted his kingship and remained master of the situation throughout the tragic day. He went willingly to his ignominious death, after he had provided for the safety of his chosen apostles. He wisely restrained Peter's trouble-making violence and provided that John might be near him right up to the end of his mortal existence. He revealed his true nature to the murderous Sanhedrin and reminded Pilate of the source of his sovereign authority as a Son of God. He started out to Golgotha bearing his own crossbeam and finished up his loving bestowal by handing over his spirit of mortal acquirement to the Paradise Father. After such a life—and at such a death—the Master could truly say, "It is finished."

Because this was the preparation day for both the Passover and the Sabbath, the Jews did not want these bodies to be exposed on Golgotha. Therefore they went before Pilate asking that the legs of these three men be broken, that they be dispatched, so that they could be taken down from their crosses and cast into the criminal burial pits before sundown. When Pilate heard this request, he forthwith sent three soldiers to break the legs and dispatch Jesus and the two brigands.

When these soldiers arrived at Golgotha, they did accordingly to the two thieves, but they found Jesus already dead, much to their surprise. However, in order to make sure of his death, one of the soldiers pierced his left side with his spear. Though it was common for the victims of crucifixion to linger alive upon the cross for even two or three days, the overwhelming emotional agony and the acute spiritual anguish of Jesus brought an end to his mortal life in the flesh in a little less than five and one-half hours.

6. AFTER THE CRUCIFIXION

In the midst of the darkness of the sandstorm, about half past three o'clock, David Zebedee sent out the last of the messengers carrying the news of the Master's death. The last of his runners he dispatched to the home of Martha and Mary in Bethany, where he supposed the mother of Jesus stopped with the rest of her family.

After the death of the Master, John sent the women, in charge of Jude, to the home of Elijah Mark, where they tarried over the Sabbath day. John himself, being well known by this time to the Roman centurion, remained at Golgotha until Joseph and Nicodemus arrived on the scene with an order from Pilate authorizing them to take possession of the body of Jesus.

Thus ended a day of tragedy and sorrow for a vast universe whose myriads of intelligences had shuddered at the shocking spectacle of the crucifixion of the human incarnation of their beloved Sovereign; they were stunned by this exhibition of mortal callousness and human perversity.

PAPER 188

THE TIME OF THE TOMB

THE day and a half that Jesus' mortal body lay in the tomb of Joseph, the period between his death on the cross and his resurrection, is a chapter in the earth career of Michael which is little known to us. We can narrate the burial of the Son of Man and put in this record the events associated with his resurrection, but we cannot supply much information of an authentic nature about what really transpired during this epoch of about thirty-six hours, from three o'clock Friday afternoon to three o'clock Sunday morning. This period in the Master's career began shortly before he was taken down from the cross by the Roman soldiers. He hung upon the cross about one hour after his death. He would have been taken down sooner but for the delay in dispatching the two brigands.

The rulers of the Jews had planned to have Jesus' body thrown in the open burial pits of Gehenna, south of the city; it was the custom thus to dispose of the victims of crucifixion. If this plan had been followed, the body of the Master would have been exposed to the wild beasts.

In the meantime, Joseph of Arimathea, accompanied by Nicodemus, had gone to Pilate and asked that the body of Jesus be turned over to them for proper burial. It was not uncommon for friends of crucified persons to offer bribes to the Roman authorities for the privilege of gaining possession of such bodies. Joseph went before Pilate with a large sum of money, in case it became necessary to pay for permission to remove Jesus' body to a private burial tomb. But Pilate would not take money for this. When he heard the request, he quickly signed the order which authorized Joseph to proceed to Golgotha and take immediate and full possession of the Master's body. In the meantime, the sandstorm having considerably abated, a group of Jews representing the Sanhedrin had gone out to Golgotha for the purpose of making sure that Jesus' body accompanied those of the brigands to the open public burial pits.

1. THE BURIAL OF JESUS

When Joseph and Nicodemus arrived at Golgotha, they found the soldiers taking Jesus down from the cross and the representatives of the Sanhedrin standing by to see that none of Jesus' followers prevented his body from going to the criminal burial pits. When Joseph presented Pilate's order for the Master's body to the centurion, the Jews raised a tumult and clamored for its possession. In their raving they sought violently to take possession of the body, and when they did this, the centurion ordered four of his soldiers to his side, and with drawn swords they stood astride the Master's body as it lay there on the ground.

The centurion ordered the other soldiers to leave the two thieves while they drove back this angry mob of infuriated Jews. When order had been restored, the centurion read the permit from Pilate to the Jews and, stepping aside, said to Joseph: "This body is yours to do with as you see fit. I and my soldiers will stand by to see that no man interferes."

A crucified person could not be buried in a Jewish cemetery; there was a strict law against such a procedure. Joseph and Nicodemus knew this law, and on the way out to Golgotha they had decided to bury Jesus in Joseph's new family tomb, hewn out of solid rock, located a short distance north of Golgotha and across the road leading to Samaria. No one had ever lain in this tomb, and they thought it appropriate that the Master should rest there. Joseph really believed that Jesus would rise from the dead, but Nicodemus was very doubtful. These former members of the Sanhedrin had kept their faith in Jesus more or less of a secret, although their fellow Sanhedrists had long suspected them, even before they withdrew from the council. From now on they were the most outspoken disciples of Jesus in all Jerusalem.

At about half past four o'clock the burial procession of Jesus of Nazareth started from Golgotha for Joseph's tomb across the way. The body was wrapped in a linen sheet as the four men carried it, followed by the faithful women watchers from Galilee. The mortals who bore the material body of Jesus to the tomb were: Joseph, Nicodemus, John, and the Roman centurion.

They carried the body into the tomb, a chamber about ten feet square, where they hurriedly prepared it for burial. The Jews did not really bury their dead; they actually embalmed them. Joseph and Nicodemus had brought with them large quantities of myrrh and aloes, and they now wrapped the body with bandages saturated with these solutions. When the embalming was completed, they tied a napkin about the face, wrapped the body in a linen sheet, and reverently placed it on a shelf in the tomb.

After placing the body in the tomb, the centurion signaled for his soldiers to help roll the doorstone up before the entrance to the tomb. The soldiers then departed for Gehenna with the bodies of the thieves while the others returned to Jerusalem, in sorrow, to observe the Passover feast according to the laws of Moses.

There was considerable hurry and haste about the burial of Jesus because this was preparation day and the Sabbath was drawing on apace. The men hurried back to the city, but the women lingered near the tomb until it was very dark.

While all this was going on, the women were hiding near at hand so that they saw it all and observed where the Master had been laid. They thus secreted themselves because it was not permissible for women to associate with men at such a time. These women did not think Jesus had been properly prepared for burial, and they agreed among themselves to go back to the home of Joseph, rest over the Sabbath, make ready spices and ointments, and return on Sunday morning properly to prepare the Master's body for the death rest. The women who thus tarried by the tomb on this Friday evening were: Mary Magdalene, Mary the wife of Clopas, Martha another sister of Jesus' mother, and Rebecca of Sepphoris.

Aside from David Zebedee and Joseph of Arimathea, very few of Jesus' disciples really believed or understood that he was due to arise from the tomb on the third day.

2. SAFEGUARDING THE TOMB

If Jesus' followers were unmindful of his promise to rise from the grave on the third day, his enemies were not. The chief priests, Pharisees, and Sadducees recalled that they had received reports of his saying he would rise from the dead.

This Friday night, after the Passover supper, about midnight a group of the Jewish leaders gathered at the home of Caiaphas, where they discussed their fears concerning the Master's assertions that he would rise from the dead on the third day. This meeting ended with the appointment of a committee of Sanhedrists who were to visit Pilate early the next day, bearing the official request of the Sanhedrin that a Roman guard be stationed before Jesus' tomb to prevent his friends from tampering with it. Said the spokesman of this committee to Pilate: "Sir, we remember that this deceiver, Jesus of Nazareth, said, while he was yet alive, 'After three days I will rise again.' We have, therefore, come before you to request that you issue such orders as will make the sepulchre secure against his followers, at least until after the third day. We greatly fear lest his disciples come and steal him away by night and then proclaim to the people that he has risen from the dead. If we should permit this to happen, this mistake would be far worse than to have allowed him to live."

When Pilate heard this request of the Sanhedrists, he said: "I will give you a guard of ten soldiers. Go your way and make the tomb secure." They went back to the temple, secured ten of their own guards, and then marched out to Joseph's tomb with these ten Jewish guards and ten Roman soldiers, even on this Sabbath morning, to set them as watchmen before the tomb. These men rolled yet another stone before the tomb and set the seal of Pilate on and around these stones, lest they be disturbed without their knowledge. And these twenty men remained on watch up to the hour of the resurrection, the Jews carrying them their food and drink.

3. DURING THE SABBATH DAY

Throughout this Sabbath day the disciples and the apostles remained in hiding, while all Jerusalem discussed the death of Jesus on the cross. There were almost one and one-half million Jews present in Jerusalem at this time, hailing from all parts of the Roman Empire and from Mesopotamia. This was the beginning of the Passover week, and all these pilgrims would be in the city to learn of the resurrection of Jesus and to carry the report back to their homes.

Late Saturday night, John Mark summoned the eleven apostles secretly to come to the home of his father, where, just before midnight, they all assembled in the same upper chamber where they had partaken of the Last Supper with their Master two nights previously.

Mary the mother of Jesus, with Ruth and Jude, returned to Bethany to join their family this Saturday evening just before sunset. David Zebedee remained at the home of Nicodemus, where he had arranged for his messengers to assemble early Sunday morning. The women of Galilee, who prepared spices for the further embalming of Jesus' body, tarried at the home of Joseph of Arimathea.

We are not able fully to explain just what happened to Jesus of Nazareth during this period of a day and a half when he was supposed to be resting in

Joseph's new tomb. Apparently he died the same natural death on the cross as would any other mortal in the same circumstances. We heard him say, "Father, into your hands I commend my spirit." We do not fully understand the meaning of such a statement inasmuch as his Thought Adjuster had long since been personalized and so maintained an existence apart from Jesus' mortal being. The Master's Personalized Adjuster could in no sense be affected by his physical death on the cross. That which Jesus put in the Father's hands for the time being must have been the spirit counterpart of the Adjuster's early work in spiritizing the mortal mind so as to provide for the transfer of the transcript of the human experience to the mansion worlds. There must have been some spiritual reality in the experience of Jesus which was analogous to the spirit nature, or soul, of the faith-growing mortals of the spheres. But this is merely our opinion—we do not really know what Jesus commended to his Father.

We know that the physical form of the Master rested there in Joseph's tomb until about three o'clock Sunday morning, but we are wholly uncertain regarding the status of the personality of Jesus during that period of thirty-six hours. We have sometimes dared to explain these things to ourselves somewhat as follows:

1. The Creator consciousness of Michael must have been at large and wholly free from its associated mortal mind of the physical incarnation.

2. The former Thought Adjuster of Jesus we know to have been present on earth during this period and in personal command of the assembled celestial hosts.

3. The acquired spirit identity of the man of Nazareth which was built up during his lifetime in the flesh, first, by the direct efforts of his Thought Adjuster, and later, by his own perfect adjustment between the physical necessities and the spiritual requirements of the ideal mortal existence, as it was effected by his never-ceasing choice of the Father's will, must have been consigned to the custody of the Paradise Father. Whether or not this spirit reality returned to become a part of the resurrected personality, we do not know, but we believe it did. But there are those in the universe who hold that this soul-identity of Jesus now reposes in the "bosom of the Father," to be subsequently released for leadership of the Nebadon Corps of the Finality in their undisclosed destiny in connection with the uncreated universes of the unorganized realms of outer space.

4. We think the human or mortal consciousness of Jesus slept during these thirty-six hours. We have reason to believe that the human Jesus knew nothing of what transpired in the universe during this period. To the mortal consciousness there appeared no lapse of time; the resurrection of life followed the sleep of death as of the same instant.

And this is about all we can place on record regarding the status of Jesus during this period of the tomb. There are a number of correlated facts to which we can allude, although we are hardly competent to undertake their interpretation.

In the vast court of the resurrection halls of the first mansion world of Satania, there may now be observed a magnificent material-morontia structure known as the "Michael Memorial," now bearing the seal of Gabriel. This memorial was created shortly after Michael departed from this world, and it bears this inscription: "In commemoration of the mortal transit of Jesus of Nazareth on Urantia."

There are records extant which show that during this period the supreme council of Salvington, numbering one hundred, held an executive meeting on Urantia under the presidency of Gabriel. There are also records showing that the Ancients of Days of Uversa communicated with Michael regarding the status of the universe of Nebadon during this time.

We know that at least one message passed between Michael and Immanuel on Salvington while the Master's body lay in the tomb.

There is good reason for believing that some personality sat in the seat of Caligastia in the system council of the Planetary Princes on Jerusem which convened while the body of Jesus rested in the tomb.

The records of Edentia indicate that the Constellation Father of Norlatiadek was on Urantia, and that he received instructions from Michael during this time of the tomb.

And there is much other evidence which suggests that not all of the personality of Jesus was asleep and unconscious during this time of apparent physical death.

4. MEANING OF THE DEATH ON THE CROSS

Although Jesus did not die this death on the cross to atone for the racial guilt of mortal man nor to provide some sort of effective approach to an otherwise offended and unforgiving God; even though the Son of Man did not offer himself as a sacrifice to appease the wrath of God and to open the way for sinful man to obtain salvation; notwithstanding that these ideas of atonement and propitiation are erroneous, nonetheless, there are significances attached to this death of Jesus on the cross which should not be overlooked. It is a fact that Urantia has become known among other neighboring inhabited planets as the "World of the Cross."

Jesus desired to live a full mortal life in the flesh on Urantia. Death is, ordinarily, a part of life. Death is the last act in the mortal drama. In your well-meant efforts to escape the superstitious errors of the false interpretation of the meaning of the death on the cross, you should be careful not to make the great mistake of failing to perceive the true significance and the genuine import of the Master's death.

Mortal man was never the property of the archdeceivers. Jesus did not die to ransom man from the clutch of the apostate rulers and fallen princes of the spheres. The Father in heaven never conceived of such crass injustice as damning a mortal soul because of the evil-doing of his ancestors. Neither was the Master's death on the cross a sacrifice which consisted in an effort to pay God a debt which the race of mankind had come to owe him.

Before Jesus lived on earth, you might possibly have been justified in believing in such a God, but not since the Master lived and died among your fellow mortals. Moses taught the dignity and justice of a Creator God; but Jesus portrayed the love and mercy of a heavenly Father.

The animal nature—the tendency toward evil-doing—may be hereditary, but sin is not transmitted from parent to child. Sin is the act of conscious and deliberate rebellion against the Father's will and the Sons' laws by an individual will creature.

Jesus lived and died for a whole universe, not just for the races of this one world. While the mortals of the realms had salvation even before Jesus lived and died on Urantia, it is nevertheless a fact that his bestowal on this world greatly illuminated the way of salvation; his death did much to make forever plain the certainty of mortal survival after death in the flesh.

Though it is hardly proper to speak of Jesus as a sacrificer, a ransomer, or a redeemer, it is wholly correct to refer to him as a *savior.* He forever made the way of salvation (survival) more clear and certain; he did better and more surely show the way of salvation for all the mortals of all the worlds of the universe of Nebadon.

When once you grasp the idea of God as a true and loving Father, the only concept which Jesus ever taught, you must forthwith, in all consistency, utterly abandon all those primitive notions about God as an offended monarch, a stern and all-powerful ruler whose chief delight is to detect his subjects in wrongdoing and to see that they are adequately punished, unless some being almost equal to himself should volunteer to suffer for them, to die as a substitute and in their stead. The whole idea of ransom and atonement is incompatible with the concept of God as it was taught and exemplified by Jesus of Nazareth. The infinite love of God is not secondary to anything in the divine nature.

All this concept of atonement and sacrificial salvation is rooted and grounded in selfishness. Jesus taught that *service* to one's fellows is the highest concept of the brotherhood of spirit believers. Salvation should be taken for granted by those who believe in the fatherhood of God. The believer's chief concern should not be the selfish desire for personal salvation but rather the unselfish urge to love and, therefore, serve one's fellows even as Jesus loved and served mortal men.

Neither do genuine believers trouble themselves so much about the future punishment of sin. The real believer is only concerned about present separation from God. True, wise fathers may chasten their sons, but they do all this in love and for corrective purposes. They do not punish in anger, neither do they chastise in retribution.

Even if God were the stern and legal monarch of a universe in which justice ruled supreme, he certainly would not be satisfied with the childish scheme of substituting an innocent sufferer for a guilty offender.

The great thing about the death of Jesus, as it is related to the enrichment of human experience and the enlargement of the way of salvation, is not the *fact* of his death but rather the superb manner and the matchless spirit in which he met death.

This entire idea of the ransom of the atonement places salvation upon a plane of unreality; such a concept is purely philosophic. Human salvation is *real;* it is based on two realities which may be grasped by the creature's faith and thereby become incorporated into individual human experience: the fact of the fatherhood of God and its correlated truth, the brotherhood of man. It is true, after all, that you are to be "forgiven your debts, even as you forgive your debtors."

5. LESSONS FROM THE CROSS

The cross of Jesus portrays the full measure of the supreme devotion of the true shepherd for even the unworthy members of his flock. It forever places all relations between God and man upon the family basis. God is the Father; man is his son. Love, the love of a father for his son, becomes the central truth in the universe relations of Creator and creature—not the justice of a king which seeks satisfaction in the sufferings and punishment of the evil-doing subject.

The cross forever shows that the attitude of Jesus toward sinners was neither condemnation nor condonation, but rather eternal and loving salvation. Jesus is truly a savior in the sense that his life and death do win men over to goodness and righteous survival. Jesus loves men so much that his love awakens the response of love in the human heart. Love is truly contagious and eternally creative. Jesus' death on the cross exemplifies a love which is sufficiently strong and divine to forgive sin and swallow up all evil-doing. Jesus disclosed to this world a higher quality of righteousness than justice—mere technical right and wrong. Divine love does not merely forgive wrongs; it absorbs and actually destroys them. The forgiveness of love utterly transcends the forgiveness of mercy. Mercy sets the guilt of evil-doing to one side; but love destroys forever the sin and all weakness resulting therefrom. Jesus brought a new method of living to Urantia. He taught us not to resist evil but to find through him a goodness which effectually destroys evil. The forgiveness of Jesus is not condonation; it is salvation from condemnation. Salvation does not slight wrongs; it *makes them right.* True love does not compromise nor condone hate; it destroys it. The love of Jesus is never satisfied with mere forgiveness. The Master's love implies rehabilitation, eternal survival. It is altogether proper to speak of salvation as redemption if you mean this eternal rehabilitation.

Jesus, by the power of his personal love for men, could break the hold of sin and evil. He thereby set men free to choose better ways of living. Jesus portrayed a deliverance from the past which in itself promised a triumph for the future. Forgiveness thus provided salvation. The beauty of divine love, once fully admitted to the human heart, forever destroys the charm of sin and the power of evil.

The sufferings of Jesus were not confined to the crucifixion. In reality, Jesus of Nazareth spent upward of twenty-five years on the cross of a real and intense mortal existence. The real value of the cross consists in the fact that it was the supreme and final expression of his love, the completed revelation of his mercy.

On millions of inhabited worlds, tens of trillions of evolving creatures who may have been tempted to give up the moral struggle and abandon the good fight of faith, have taken one more look at Jesus on the cross and then have forged on ahead, inspired by the sight of God's laying down his incarnate life in devotion to the unselfish service of man.

The triumph of the death on the cross is all summed up in the spirit of Jesus' attitude toward those who assailed him. He made the cross an eternal symbol of the triumph of love over hate and the victory of truth over evil when he prayed, "Father, forgive them, for they know not what they do." That devotion of love was contagious throughout a vast universe; the disciples caught it from their Master. The very first teacher of his gospel who was called upon to lay down his life in this service, said, as they stoned him to death, "Lay not this sin to their charge."

The cross makes a supreme appeal to the best in man because it discloses one who was willing to lay down his life in the service of his fellow men. Greater love no man can have than this: that he would be willing to lay down his life for his friends—and Jesus had such a love that he was willing to lay down his life for his enemies, a love greater than any which had hitherto been known on earth.

On other worlds, as well as on Urantia, this sublime spectacle of the death of the human Jesus on the cross of Golgotha has stirred the emotions of mortals, while it has aroused the highest devotion of the angels.

The cross is that high symbol of sacred service, the devotion of one's life to the welfare and salvation of one's fellows. The cross is not the symbol of the sacrifice of the innocent Son of God in the place of guilty sinners and in order to appease the wrath of an offended God, but it does stand forever, on earth and throughout a vast universe, as a sacred symbol of the good bestowing themselves upon the evil and thereby saving them by this very devotion of love. The cross does stand as the token of the highest form of unselfish service, the supreme devotion of the full bestowal of a righteous life in the service of wholehearted ministry, even in death, the death of the cross. And the very sight of this great symbol of the bestowal life of Jesus truly inspires all of us to want to go and do likewise.

When thinking men and women look upon Jesus as he offers up his life on the cross, they will hardly again permit themselves to complain at even the severest hardships of life, much less at petty harassments and their many purely fictitious grievances. His life was so glorious and his death so triumphant that we are all enticed to a willingness to share both. There is true drawing power in the whole bestowal of Michael, from the days of his youth to this overwhelming spectacle of his death on the cross.

Make sure, then, that when you view the cross as a revelation of God, you do not look with the eyes of the primitive man nor with the viewpoint of the later barbarian, both of whom regarded God as a relentless Sovereign of stern justice and rigid law-enforcement. Rather, make sure that you see in the cross the final manifestation of the love and devotion of Jesus to his life mission of bestowal upon the mortal races of his vast universe. See in the death of the Son of Man the climax of the unfolding of the Father's divine love for his sons of the mortal spheres. The cross thus portrays the devotion of willing affection and the bestowal of voluntary salvation upon those who are willing to receive such gifts and devotion. There was nothing in the cross which the Father required—only that which Jesus so willingly gave, and which he refused to avoid.

If man cannot otherwise appreciate Jesus and understand the meaning of his bestowal on earth, he can at least comprehend the fellowship of his mortal sufferings. No man can ever fear that the Creator does not know the nature or extent of his temporal afflictions.

We know that the death on the cross was not to effect man's reconciliation to God but to stimulate man's *realization* of the Father's eternal love and his Son's unending mercy, and to broadcast these universal truths to a whole universe.

PAPER 189
THE RESURRECTION

SOON after the burial of Jesus on Friday afternoon, the chief of the archangels of Nebadon, then present on Urantia, summoned his council of the resurrection of sleeping will creatures and entered upon the consideration of a possible technique for the restoration of Jesus. These assembled sons of the local universe, the creatures of Michael, did this on their own responsibility; Gabriel had not assembled them. By midnight they had arrived at the conclusion that the creature could do nothing to facilitate the resurrection of the Creator. They were disposed to accept the advice of Gabriel, who instructed them that, since Michael had "laid down his life of his own free will, he also had power to take it up again in accordance with his own determination." Shortly after the adjournment of this council of the archangels, the Life Carriers, and their various associates in the work of creature rehabilitation and morontia creation, the Personalized Adjuster of Jesus, being in personal command of the assembled celestial hosts then on Urantia, spoke these words to the anxious waiting watchers:

"Not one of you can do aught to assist your Creator-father in the return to life. As a mortal of the realm he has experienced mortal death; as the Sovereign of a universe he still lives. That which you observe is the mortal transit of Jesus of Nazareth from life in the flesh to life in the morontia. The spirit transit of this Jesus was completed at the time I separated myself from his personality and became your temporary director. Your Creator-father has elected to pass through the whole of the experience of his mortal creatures, from birth on the material worlds, on through natural death and the resurrection of the morontia, into the status of true spirit existence. A certain phase of this experience you are about to observe, but you may not participate in it. Those things which you ordinarily do for the creature, you may not do for the Creator. A Creator Son has within himself the power to bestow himself in the likeness of any of his created sons; he has within himself the power to lay down his observable life and to take it up again; and he has this power because of the direct command of the Paradise Father, and I know whereof I speak."

When they heard the Personalized Adjuster so speak, they all assumed the attitude of anxious expectancy, from Gabriel down to the most humble cherubim. They saw the mortal body of Jesus in the tomb; they detected evidences of the universe activity of their beloved Sovereign; and not understanding such phenomena, they waited patiently for developments.

1. THE MORONTIA TRANSIT

At two forty-five Sunday morning, the Paradise incarnation commission, consisting of seven unidentified Paradise personalities, arrived on the scene and immediately deployed themselves about the tomb. At ten minutes before three, intense vibrations of commingled material and morontia activities began to issue from Joseph's new tomb, and at two minutes past three o'clock, this Sunday morning, April 9, A.D. 30, the resurrected morontia form and personality of Jesus of Nazareth came forth from the tomb.

After the resurrected Jesus emerged from his burial tomb, the body of flesh in which he had lived and wrought on earth for almost thirty-six years was still lying there in the sepulchre niche, undisturbed and wrapped in the linen sheet, just as it had been laid to rest by Joseph and his associates on Friday afternoon. Neither was the stone before the entrance of the tomb in any way disturbed; the seal of Pilate was still unbroken; the soldiers were still on guard. The temple guards had been on continuous duty; the Roman guard had been changed at midnight. None of these watchers suspected that the object of their vigil had risen to a new and higher form of existence, and that the body which they were guarding was now a discarded outer covering which had no further connection with the delivered and resurrected morontia personality of Jesus.

Mankind is slow to perceive that, in all that is personal, matter is the skeleton of morontia, and that both are the reflected shadow of enduring spirit reality. How long before you will regard time as the moving image of eternity and space as the fleeting shadow of Paradise realities?

As far as we can judge, no creature of this universe nor any personality from another universe had anything to do with this morontia resurrection of Jesus of Nazareth. On Friday he laid down his life as a mortal of the realm; on Sunday morning he took it up again as a morontia being of the system of Satania in Norlatiadek. There is much about the resurrection of Jesus which we do not understand. But we know that it occurred as we have stated and at about the time indicated. We can also record that all known phenomena associated with this mortal transit, or morontia resurrection, occurred right there in Joseph's new tomb, where the mortal material remains of Jesus lay wrapped in burial cloths.

We know that no creature of the local universe participated in this morontia awakening. We perceived the seven personalities of Paradise surround the tomb, but we did not see them do anything in connection with the Master's awakening. Just as soon as Jesus appeared beside Gabriel, just above the tomb, the seven personalities from Paradise signalized their intention of immediate departure for Uversa.

Let us forever clarify the concept of the resurrection of Jesus by making the following statements:

1. His material or physical body was not a part of the resurrected personality. When Jesus came forth from the tomb, his body of flesh remained undisturbed in the sepulchre. He emerged from the burial tomb without moving the stones before the entrance and without disturbing the seals of Pilate.

2. He did not emerge from the tomb as a spirit nor as Michael of Nebadon; he did not appear in the form of the Creator Sovereign, such as he had had before his incarnation in the likeness of mortal flesh on Urantia.

3. He did come forth from this tomb of Joseph in the very likeness of the morontia personalities of those who, as resurrected morontia ascendant beings, emerge from the resurrection halls of the first mansion world of this local system

of Satania. And the presence of the Michael memorial in the center of the vast court of the resurrection halls of mansonia number one leads us to conjecture that the Master's resurrection on Urantia was in some way fostered on this, the first of the system mansion worlds.

The first act of Jesus on arising from the tomb was to greet Gabriel and instruct him to continue in executive charge of universe affairs under Immanuel, and then he directed the chief of the Melchizedeks to convey his brotherly greetings to Immanuel. He thereupon asked the Most High of Edentia for the certification of the Ancients of Days as to his mortal transit; and turning to the assembled morontia groups of the seven mansion worlds, here gathered together to greet and welcome their Creator as a creature of their order, Jesus spoke the first words of the postmortal career. Said the morontia Jesus: "Having finished my life in the flesh, I would tarry here for a short time in transition form that I may more fully know the life of my ascendant creatures and further reveal the will of my Father in Paradise."

After Jesus had spoken, he signaled to the Personalized Adjuster, and all universe intelligences who had been assembled on Urantia to witness the resurrection were immediately dispatched to their respective universe assignments.

Jesus now began the contacts of the morontia level, being introduced, as a creature, to the requirements of the life he had chosen to live for a short time on Urantia. This initiation into the morontia world required more than an hour of earth time and was twice interrupted by his desire to communicate with his former associates in the flesh as they came out from Jerusalem wonderingly to peer into the empty tomb to discover what they considered evidence of his resurrection.

Now is the mortal transit of Jesus—the morontia resurrection of the Son of Man—completed. The transitory experience of the Master as a personality midway between the material and the spiritual has begun. And he has done all this through power inherent within himself; no personality has rendered him any assistance. He now lives as Jesus of morontia, and as he begins this morontia life, the material body of his flesh lies there undisturbed in the tomb. The soldiers are still on guard, and the seal of the governor about the rocks has not yet been broken.

2. THE MATERIAL BODY OF JESUS

At ten minutes past three o'clock, as the resurrected Jesus fraternized with the assembled morontia personalities from the seven mansion worlds of Satania, the chief of archangels—the angels of the resurrection—approached Gabriel and asked for the mortal body of Jesus. Said the chief of the archangels: "We may not participate in the morontia resurrection of the bestowal experience of Michael our sovereign, but we would have his mortal remains put in our custody for immediate dissolution. We do not propose to employ our technique of dematerialization; we merely wish to invoke the process of accelerated time. It is enough that we have seen the Sovereign live and die on Urantia; the hosts of heaven would be spared the memory of enduring the sight of the slow decay of the human form of the Creator and Upholder of a universe. In the name of the celestial intelligences of all Nebadon, I ask for a mandate giving me the custody of the mortal body of Jesus of Nazareth and empowering us to proceed with its immediate dissolution."

And when Gabriel had conferred with the senior Most High of Edentia, the archangel spokesman for the celestial hosts was given permission to make such disposition of the physical remains of Jesus as he might determine.

After the chief of archangels had been granted this request, he summoned to his assistance many of his fellows, together with a numerous host of the representatives of all orders of celestial personalities, and then, with the aid of the Urantia midwayers, proceeded to take possession of Jesus' physical body. This body of death was a purely material creation; it was physical and literal; it could not be removed from the tomb as the morontia form of the resurrection had been able to escape the sealed sepulchre. By the aid of certain morontia auxiliary personalities, the morontia form can be made at one time as of the spirit so that it can become indifferent to ordinary matter, while at another time it can become discernible and contactable to material beings, such as the mortals of the realm.

As they made ready to remove the body of Jesus from the tomb preparatory to according it the dignified and reverent disposal of near-instantaneous dissolution, it was assigned the secondary Urantia midwayers to roll away the stones from the entrance of the tomb. The larger of these two stones was a huge circular affair, much like a millstone, and it moved in a groove chiseled out of the rock, so that it could be rolled back and forth to open or close the tomb. When the watching Jewish guards and the Roman soldiers, in the dim light of the morning, saw this huge stone begin to roll away from the entrance of the tomb, apparently of its own accord—without any visible means to account for such motion—they were seized with fear and panic, and they fled in haste from the scene. The Jews fled to their homes, afterward going back to report these doings to their captain at the temple. The Romans fled to the fortress of Antonia and reported what they had seen to the centurion as soon as he arrived on duty.

The Jewish leaders began the sordid business of supposedly getting rid of Jesus by offering bribes to the traitorous Judas, and now, when confronted with this embarrassing situation, instead of thinking of punishing the guards who deserted their post, they resorted to bribing these guards and the Roman soldiers. They paid each of these twenty men a sum of money and instructed them to say to all: "While we slept during the nighttime, his disciples came upon us and took away the body." And the Jewish leaders made solemn promises to the soldiers to defend them before Pilate in case it should ever come to the governor's knowledge that they had accepted a bribe.

The Christian belief in the resurrection of Jesus has been based on the fact of the "empty tomb." It was indeed a *fact* that the tomb was empty, but this is not the *truth* of the resurrection. The tomb was truly empty when the first believers arrived, and this fact, associated with that of the undoubted resurrection of the Master, led to the formulation of a belief which was not true: the teaching that the material and mortal body of Jesus was raised from the grave. Truth having to do with spiritual realities and eternal values cannot always be built up by a combination of apparent facts. Although individual facts may be materially true, it does not follow that the association of a group of facts must necessarily lead to truthful spiritual conclusions.

The tomb of Joseph was empty, not because the body of Jesus had been rehabilitated or resurrected, but because the celestial hosts had been granted their request to afford it a special and unique dissolution, a return of the "dust to dust," without the intervention of the delays of time and without the operation of the ordinary and visible processes of mortal decay and material corruption.

The mortal remains of Jesus underwent the same natural process of elemental disintegration as characterizes all human bodies on earth except that, in point of time, this natural mode of dissolution was greatly accelerated, hastened to that point where it became well-nigh instantaneous.

The true evidences of the resurrection of Michael are spiritual in nature, albeit this teaching is corroborated by the testimony of many mortals of the realm who met, recognized, and communed with the resurrected morontia Master. He became a part of the personal experience of almost one thousand human beings before he finally took leave of Urantia.

3. THE DISPENSATIONAL RESURRECTION

A little after half past four o'clock this Sunday morning, Gabriel summoned the archangels to his side and made ready to inaugurate the general resurrection of the termination of the Adamic dispensation on Urantia. When the vast host of the seraphim and the cherubim concerned in this great event had been marshaled in proper formation, the morontia Michael appeared before Gabriel, saying: "As my Father has life in himself, so has he given it to the Son to have life in himself. Although I have not yet fully resumed the exercise of universe jurisdiction, this self-imposed limitation does not in any manner restrict the bestowal of life upon my sleeping sons; let the roll call of the planetary resurrection begin."

The circuit of the archangels then operated for the first time from Urantia. Gabriel and the archangel hosts moved to the place of the spiritual polarity of the planet; and when Gabriel gave the signal, there flashed to the first of the system mansion worlds the voice of Gabriel, saying: "By the mandate of Michael, let the dead of a Urantia dispensation rise!" Then all the survivors of the human races of Urantia who had fallen asleep since the days of Adam, and who had not already gone on to judgment, appeared in the resurrection halls of mansonia in readiness for morontia investiture. And in an instant of time the seraphim and their associates made ready to depart for the mansion worlds. Ordinarily these seraphic guardians, onetime assigned to the group custody of these surviving mortals, would have been present at the moment of their awaking in the resurrection halls of mansonia, but they were on this world itself at this time because of the necessity of Gabriel's presence here in connection with the morontia resurrection of Jesus.

Notwithstanding that countless individuals having personal seraphic guardians and those achieving the requisite attainment of spiritual personality progress had gone on to mansonia during the ages subsequent to the times of Adam and Eve, and though there had been many special and millennial resurrections of Urantia sons, this was the third of the planetary roll calls, or complete dispensational resurrections. The first occurred at the time of the arrival of the Planetary Prince, the second during the time of Adam, and this, the third, signalized the morontia resurrection, the mortal transit, of Jesus of Nazareth.

When the signal of the planetary resurrection had been received by the chief of archangels, the Personalized Adjuster of the Son of Man relinquished his authority over the celestial hosts assembled on Urantia, turning all these sons of the local universe back to the jurisdiction of their respective commanders. And when he had done this, he departed for Salvington to register with Immanuel the completion of the mortal transit of Michael. And he was immediately followed by all the celestial host not required for duty on Urantia. But Gabriel remained on Urantia with the morontia Jesus.

And this is the recital of the events of the resurrection of Jesus as viewed by those who saw them as they really occurred, free from the limitations of partial and restricted human vision.

4. DISCOVERY OF THE EMPTY TOMB

As we approach the time of the resurrection of Jesus on this early Sunday morning, it should be recalled that the ten apostles were sojourning at the home of Elijah and Mary Mark, where they were asleep in the upper chamber, resting on the very couches whereon they reclined during the last supper with their Master. This Sunday morning they were all there assembled except Thomas. Thomas was with them for a few minutes late Saturday night when they first got together, but the sight of the apostles, coupled with the thought of what had happened to Jesus, was too much for him. He looked his associates over and immediately left the room, going to the home of Simon in Bethpage, where he thought to grieve over his troubles in solitude. The apostles all suffered, not so much from doubt and despair as from fear, grief, and shame.

At the home of Nicodemus there were gathered together, with David Zebedee and Joseph of Arimathea, some twelve or fifteen of the more prominent of the Jerusalem disciples of Jesus. At the home of Joseph of Arimathea there were some fifteen or twenty of the leading women believers. Only these women abode in Joseph's house, and they had kept close within during the hours of the Sabbath day and the evening after the Sabbath, so that they were ignorant of the military guard on watch at the tomb; neither did they know that a second stone had been rolled in front of the tomb, and that both of these stones had been placed under the seal of Pilate.

A little before three o'clock this Sunday morning, when the first signs of day began to appear in the east, five of the women started out for the tomb of Jesus. They had prepared an abundance of special embalming lotions, and they carried many linen bandages with them. It was their purpose more thoroughly to give the body of Jesus its death anointing and more carefully to wrap it up with the new bandages.

The women who went on this mission of anointing Jesus' body were: Mary Magdalene, Mary the mother of the Alpheus twins, Salome the mother of the Zebedee brothers, Joanna the wife of Chuza, and Susanna the daughter of Ezra of Alexandria.

It was about half past three o'clock when the five women, laden with their ointments, arrived before the empty tomb. As they passed out of the Damascus gate, they encountered a number of soldiers fleeing into the city more or less panic-stricken, and this caused them to pause for a few minutes; but when nothing more developed, they resumed their journey.

They were greatly surprised to see the stone rolled away from the entrance to the tomb, inasmuch as they had said among themselves on the way out, "Who will help us roll away the stone?" They set down their burdens and began to look upon one another in fear and with great amazement. While they stood there, atremble with fear, Mary Magdalene ventured around the smaller stone and dared to enter the open sepulchre. This tomb of Joseph was in his garden on the hillside on the eastern side of the road, and it also faced toward the east. By this hour there was just enough of the dawn of a new day to enable Mary to look back to the place where the Master's body had lain and to discern that it was gone. In the recess of stone where they had laid Jesus, Mary saw only the folded napkin where his head had rested and the bandages wherewith he had been wrapped lying intact and as they had rested on the stone before the celestial hosts removed the body. The covering sheet lay at the foot of the burial niche.

After Mary had tarried in the doorway of the tomb for a few moments (she did not see distinctly when she first entered the tomb), she saw that Jesus' body was gone and in its place only these grave cloths, and she uttered a cry of alarm and anguish. All the women were exceedingly nervous; they had been on edge ever since meeting the panicky soldiers at the city gate, and when Mary uttered this scream of anguish, they were terror-stricken and fled in great haste. And they did not stop until they had run all the way to the Damascus gate. By this time Joanna was conscience-stricken that they had deserted Mary; she rallied her companions, and they started back for the tomb.

As they drew near the sepulchre, the frightened Magdalene, who was even more terrorized when she failed to find her sisters waiting when she came out of the tomb, now rushed up to them, excitedly exclaiming: "He is not there—they have taken him away!" And she led them back to the tomb, and they all entered and saw that it was empty.

All five of the women then sat down on the stone near the entrance and talked over the situation. It had not yet occurred to them that Jesus had been resurrected. They had been by themselves over the Sabbath, and they conjectured that the body had been moved to another resting place. But when they pondered such a solution of their dilemma, they were at a loss to account for the orderly arrangement of the grave cloths; how could the body have been removed since the very bandages in which it was wrapped were left in position and apparently intact on the burial shelf?

As these women sat there in the early hours of the dawn of this new day, they looked to one side and observed a silent and motionless stranger. For a moment they were again frightened, but Mary Magdalene, rushing toward him and addressing him as if she thought he might be the caretaker of the garden, said, "Where have you taken the Master? Where have they laid him? Tell us that we may go and get him." When the stranger did not answer Mary, she began to weep. Then spoke Jesus to them, saying, "Whom do you seek?" Mary said: "We seek for Jesus who was laid to rest in Joseph's tomb, but he is gone. Do you know where they have taken him?" Then said Jesus: "Did not this Jesus tell you, even in Galilee, that he would die, but that he would rise again?" These words startled the women, but the Master was so changed that they did not yet recognize him with his back turned to the dim light. And as they pondered his words, he addressed the Magdalene with a familiar voice, saying, "Mary." And when she heard that word of well-known sympathy and affectionate greeting, she knew it was the voice of the Master, and she rushed to kneel at his feet while she exclaimed, "My Lord, and my Master!" And all of the other women recognized that it was the Master who stood before them in glorified form, and they quickly knelt before him.

These human eyes were enabled to see the morontia form of Jesus because of the special ministry of the transformers and the midwayers in association with certain of the morontia personalities then accompanying Jesus.

As Mary sought to embrace his feet, Jesus said: "Touch me not, Mary, for I am not as you knew me in the flesh. In this form will I tarry with you for a season before I ascend to the Father. But go, all of you, now and tell my apostles—and Peter—that I have risen, and that you have talked with me."

After these women had recovered from the shock of their amazement, they hastened back to the city and to the home of Elijah Mark, where they related to the ten apostles all that had happened to them; but the apostles were not inclined to believe them. They thought at first that the women had seen a vision, but when Mary Magdalene repeated the words which Jesus had spoken to them, and when Peter heard his name, he rushed out of the upper chamber, followed closely by John, in great haste to reach the tomb and see these things for himself.

The women repeated the story of talking with Jesus to the other apostles, but they would not believe; and they would not go to find out for themselves as had Peter and John.

5. PETER AND JOHN AT THE TOMB

As the two apostles raced for Golgotha and the tomb of Joseph, Peter's thoughts alternated between fear and hope; he feared to meet the Master, but his hope was aroused by the story that Jesus had sent special word to him. He was half persuaded that Jesus was really alive; he recalled the promise to rise on the third day. Strange to relate, this promise had not occurred to him since the crucifixion until this moment as he hurried north through Jerusalem. As John hastened out of the city, a strange ecstasy of joy and hope welled up in his soul. He was half convinced that the women really had seen the risen Master.

John, being younger than Peter, outran him and arrived first at the tomb. John tarried at the door, viewing the tomb, and it was just as Mary had described it. Very soon Simon Peter rushed up and, entering, saw the same empty tomb with the grave cloths so peculiarly arranged. And when Peter had come out, John also went in and saw it all for himself, and then they sat down on the stone to ponder the meaning of what they had seen and heard. And while they sat there, they turned over in their minds all that had been told them about Jesus, but they could not clearly perceive what had happened.

Peter at first suggested that the grave had been rifled, that enemies had stolen the body, perhaps bribed the guards. But John reasoned that the grave would hardly have been left so orderly if the body had been stolen, and he also raised the question as to how the bandages happened to be left behind, and so apparently intact. And again they both went back into the tomb more closely to examine the grave cloths. As they came out of the tomb the second time, they found Mary Magdalene returned and weeping before the entrance. Mary had gone to the apostles believing that Jesus had risen from the grave, but when they all refused to believe her report, she became downcast and despairing. She longed to go back near the tomb, where she thought she had heard the familiar voice of Jesus.

As Mary lingered after Peter and John had gone, the Master again appeared to her, saying: "Be not doubting; have the courage to believe what you have seen and heard. Go back to my apostles and again tell them that I have risen, that I will appear to them, and that presently I will go before them into Galilee as I promised."

Mary hurried back to the Mark home and told the apostles she had again talked with Jesus, but they would not believe her. But when Peter and John returned, they ceased to ridicule and became filled with fear and apprehension.

PAPER 190

MORONTIA APPEARANCES OF JESUS

THE resurrected Jesus now prepares to spend a short period on Urantia for the purpose of experiencing the ascending morontia career of a mortal of the realms. Although this time of the morontia life is to be spent on the world of his mortal incarnation, it will, however, be in all respects the counterpart of the experience of Satania mortals who pass through the progressive morontia life of the seven mansion worlds of Jerusem.

All this power which is inherent in Jesus—the endowment of life—and which enabled him to rise from the dead, is the very gift of eternal life which he bestows upon kingdom believers, and which even now makes certain their resurrection from the bonds of natural death.

The mortals of the realms will arise in the morning of the resurrection with the same type of transition or morontia body that Jesus had when he arose from the tomb on this Sunday morning. These bodies do not have circulating blood, and such beings do not partake of ordinary material food; nevertheless, these morontia forms are *real.* When the various believers saw Jesus after his resurrection, they really saw him; they were not the self-deceived victims of visions or hallucinations.

Abiding faith in the resurrection of Jesus was the cardinal feature of the faith of all branches of the early gospel teaching. In Jerusalem, Alexandria, Antioch, and Philadelphia all the gospel teachers united in this implicit faith in the Master's resurrection.

In viewing the prominent part which Mary Magdalene took in proclaiming the Master's resurrection, it should be recorded that Mary was the chief spokesman for the women's corps, as was Peter for the apostles. Mary was not chief of the women workers, but she was their chief teacher and public spokesman. Mary had become a woman of great circumspection, so that her boldness in speaking to a man whom she considered to be the caretaker of Joseph's garden only indicates how horrified she was to find the tomb empty. It was the depth and agony of her love, the fullness of her devotion, that caused her to forget, for a moment, the conventional restraints of a Jewish woman's approach to a strange man.

1. HERALDS OF THE RESURRECTION

The apostles did not want Jesus to leave them; therefore had they slighted all his statements about dying, along with his promises to rise again. They were not expecting the resurrection as it came, and they refused to believe until they were confronted with the compulsion of unimpeachable evidence and the absolute proof of their own experiences.

When the apostles refused to believe the report of the five women who represented that they had seen Jesus and talked with him, Mary Magdalene returned to the tomb, and the others went back to Joseph's house, where they related their experiences to his daughter and the other women. And the women believed their report. Shortly after six o'clock the daughter of Joseph of Arimathea and the four women who had seen Jesus went over to the home of Nicodemus, where they related all these happenings to Joseph, Nicodemus, David Zebedee, and the other men there assembled. Nicodemus and the others doubted their story, doubted that Jesus had risen from the dead; they conjectured that the Jews had removed the body. Joseph and David were disposed to believe the report, so much so that they hurried out to inspect the tomb, and they found everything just as the women had described. And they were the last to so view the sepulchre, for the high priest sent the captain of the temple guards to the tomb at half past seven o'clock to remove the grave cloths. The captain wrapped them all up in the linen sheet and threw them over a near-by cliff.

From the tomb David and Joseph went immediately to the home of Elijah Mark, where they held a conference with the ten apostles in the upper chamber. Only John Zebedee was disposed to believe, even faintly, that Jesus had risen from the dead. Peter had believed at first but, when he failed to find the Master, fell into grave doubting. They were all disposed to believe that the Jews had removed the body. David would not argue with them, but when he left, he said: "You are the apostles, and you ought to understand these things. I will not contend with you; nevertheless, I now go back to the home of Nicodemus, where I have appointed with the messengers to assemble this morning, and when they have gathered together, I will send them forth on their last mission, as heralds of the Master's resurrection. I heard the Master say that, after he should die, he would rise on the third day, and I believe him." And thus speaking to the dejected and forlorn ambassadors of the kingdom, this self-appointed chief of communication and intelligence took leave of the apostles. On his way from the upper chamber he dropped the bag of Judas, containing all the apostolic funds, in the lap of Matthew Levi.

It was about half past nine o'clock when the last of David's twenty-six messengers arrived at the home of Nicodemus. David promptly assembled them in the spacious courtyard and addressed them:

"Men and brethren, all this time you have served me in accordance with your oath to me and to one another, and I call you to witness that I have never yet sent out false information at your hands. I am about to send you on your last mission as volunteer messengers of the kingdom, and in so doing I release you from your oaths and thereby disband the messenger corps. Men, I declare to you that we have finished our work. No more does the Master have need of mortal messengers; he has risen from the dead. He told us before they arrested him that he would die and rise again on the third day. I have seen the tomb—it is empty. I have talked with Mary Magdalene and four other women, who have talked with Jesus. I now disband you, bid you farewell, and send you on your respective assignments, and the message which you shall bear to the believers is: 'Jesus has risen from the dead; the tomb is empty.'"

The majority of those present endeavored to persuade David not to do this. But they could not influence him. They then sought to dissuade the messengers, but they would not heed the words of doubt. And so, shortly before ten o'clock this Sunday morning, these twenty-six runners went forth as the first heralds of the mighty truth-fact of the resurrected Jesus. And they started out on this mission as they had on so many others, in fulfillment of their oath to David Zebedee and to one another. These men had great confidence in David. They departed on this assignment without even tarrying to talk with those who had seen Jesus; they took David at his word. The majority of them believed what David had told them, and even those who somewhat doubted, carried the message just as certainly and just as swiftly.

The apostles, the spiritual corps of the kingdom, are this day assembled in the upper chamber, where they manifest fear and express doubts, while these laymen, representing the first attempt at the socialization of the Master's gospel of the brotherhood of man, under the orders of their fearless and efficient leader, go forth to proclaim the risen Savior of a world and a universe. And they engage in this eventful service ere his chosen representatives are willing to believe his word or to accept the evidence of eyewitnesses.

These twenty-six were dispatched to the home of Lazarus in Bethany and to all of the believer centers, from Beersheba in the south to Damascus and Sidon in the north; and from Philadelphia in the east to Alexandria in the west.

When David had taken leave of his brethren, he went over to the home of Joseph for his mother, and they then went out to Bethany to join the waiting family of Jesus. David abode there in Bethany with Martha and Mary until after they had disposed of their earthly possessions, and he accompanied them on their journey to join their brother, Lazarus, at Philadelphia.

In about one week from this time John Zebedee took Mary the mother of Jesus to his home in Bethsaida. James, Jesus' eldest brother, remained with his family in Jerusalem. Ruth remained at Bethany with Lazarus's sisters. The rest of Jesus' family returned to Galilee. David Zebedee left Bethany with Martha and Mary, for Philadelphia, early in June, the day after his marriage to Ruth, Jesus' youngest sister.

2. JESUS' APPEARANCE AT BETHANY

From the time of the morontia resurrection until the hour of his spirit ascension on high, Jesus made nineteen separate appearances in visible form to his believers on earth. He did not appear to his enemies nor to those who could not make spiritual use of his manifestation in visible form. His first appearance was to the five women at the tomb; his second, to Mary Magdalene, also at the tomb.

The third appearance occurred about noon of this Sunday at Bethany. Shortly after noontide, Jesus' oldest brother, James, was standing in the garden of Lazarus before the empty tomb of the resurrected brother of Martha and Mary, turning over in his mind the news brought to them about one hour previously by the messenger of David. James had always inclined to believe in his eldest brother's mission on earth, but he had long since lost contact with Jesus' work and had drifted into grave doubting regarding the later claims of the apostles that Jesus was the Messiah. The whole family was startled and well-nigh confounded by the news brought by the messenger. Even as James stood before Lazarus's empty tomb, Mary Magdalene arrived on the scene and was excitedly relating to the family her experiences of the early morning hours at the tomb of Joseph. Before she had finished, David Zebedee and his mother arrived. Ruth, of course, believed the report, and so did Jude after he had talked with David and Salome.

In the meantime, as they looked for James and before they found him, while he stood there in the garden near the tomb, he became aware of a near-by presence, as if someone had touched him on the shoulder; and when he turned to look, he beheld the gradual appearance of a strange form by his side. He was too much amazed to speak and too frightened to flee. And then the strange form spoke, saying: "James, I come to call you to the service of the kingdom. Join earnest hands with your brethren and follow after me." When James heard his name spoken, he knew that it was his eldest brother, Jesus, who had addressed him. They all had more or less difficulty in recognizing the morontia form of the Master, but few of them had any trouble recognizing his voice or otherwise identifying his charming personality when he once began to communicate with them.

When James perceived that Jesus was addressing him, he started to fall to his knees, exclaiming, "My father and my brother," but Jesus bade him stand while he spoke with him. And they walked through the garden and talked for almost three minutes; talked over experiences of former days and forecast the events of the near future. As they neared the house, Jesus said, "Farewell, James, until I greet you all together."

James rushed into the house, even while they looked for him at Bethpage, exclaiming: "I have just seen Jesus and talked with him, visited with him. He is not dead; he has risen! He vanished before me, saying, 'Farewell until I greet you all together.'" He had scarcely finished speaking when Jude returned, and he retold the experience of meeting Jesus in the garden for the benefit of Jude. And they all began to believe in the resurrection of Jesus. James now announced that he would not return to Galilee, and David exclaimed: "He is seen not only by excited women; even stronghearted men have begun to see him. I expect to see him myself."

And David did not long wait, for the fourth appearance of Jesus to mortal recognition occurred shortly before two o'clock in this very home of Martha and Mary, when he appeared visibly before his earthly family and their friends, twenty in all. The Master appeared in the open back door, saying: "Peace be upon you. Greetings to those once near me in the flesh and fellowship for my brothers and sisters in the kingdom of heaven. How could you doubt? Why have you lingered so long before choosing to follow the light of truth with a whole heart? Come, therefore, all of you into the fellowship of the Spirit of Truth in the Father's kingdom." As they began to recover from the first shock of their amazement and to move toward him as if to embrace him, he vanished from their sight.

They all wanted to rush off to the city to tell the doubting apostles about what had happened, but James restrained them. Mary Magdalene, only, was permitted to return to Joseph's house. James forbade their publishing abroad the fact of this morontia visit because of certain things which Jesus had said to him as they conversed in the garden. But James never revealed more of his visit with the risen Master on this day at the Lazarus home in Bethany.

3. AT THE HOME OF JOSEPH

The fifth morontia manifestation of Jesus to the recognition of mortal eyes occurred in the presence of some twenty-five women believers assembled at the home of Joseph of Arimathea, at about fifteen minutes past four o'clock on this same Sunday afternoon. Mary Magdalene had returned to Joseph's house just a few minutes before this appearance. James, Jesus' brother, had requested that nothing be said to the apostles concerning the Master's appearance at Bethany. He had not asked Mary to refrain from reporting the occurrence to her sister believers. Accordingly, after Mary had pledged all the women to secrecy, she proceeded to relate what had so recently happened while she was with Jesus' family at Bethany. And she was in the very midst of this thrilling recital when a sudden and solemn hush fell over them; they beheld in their very midst the fully visible form of the risen Jesus. He greeted them, saying: "Peace be upon you. In the fellowship of the kingdom there shall be neither Jew nor gentile, rich nor poor, free nor bond, man nor woman. You also are called to publish the good news of the liberty of mankind through the gospel of sonship with God in the kingdom of heaven. Go to all the world proclaiming this gospel and confirming believers in the faith thereof. And while you do this, forget not to minister to the sick and strengthen those who are fainthearted and fear-ridden. And I will be with you always, even to the ends of the earth." And when he had thus spoken, he vanished from their sight, while the women fell on their faces and worshiped in silence.

Of the five morontia appearances of Jesus occurring up to this time, Mary Magdalene had witnessed four.

As a result of sending out the messengers during the midforenoon and from the unconscious leakage of intimations concerning this appearance of Jesus at Joseph's house, word began to come to the rulers of the Jews during the early evening that it was being reported about the city that Jesus had risen, and that many persons were claiming to have seen him. The Sanhedrists were thoroughly aroused by these rumors. After a hasty consultation with Annas, Caiaphas called a meeting of the Sanhedrin to convene at eight o'clock that evening. It was at this meeting that action was taken to throw out of the synagogues any person who made mention of Jesus' resurrection. It was even suggested that anyone claiming to have seen him should be put to death; this proposal, however, did not come to a vote since the meeting broke up in confusion bordering on actual panic. They had dared to think they were through with Jesus. They were about to discover that their real trouble with the man of Nazareth had just begun.

4. APPEARANCE TO THE GREEKS

About half past four o'clock, at the home of one Flavius, the Master made his sixth morontia appearance to some forty Greek believers there assembled. While they were engaged in discussing the reports of the Master's resurrection, he manifested himself in their midst, notwithstanding that the doors were securely fastened, and speaking to them, said: "Peace be upon you. While the Son of Man appeared on earth among the Jews, he came to minister to all men.

In the kingdom of my Father there shall be neither Jew nor gentile; you will all be brethren—the sons of God. Go you, therefore, to all the world, proclaiming this gospel of salvation as you have received it from the ambassadors of the kingdom, and I will fellowship you in the brotherhood of the Father's sons of faith and truth." And when he had thus charged them, he took leave, and they saw him no more. They remained within the house all evening; they were too much overcome with awe and fear to venture forth. Neither did any of these Greeks sleep that night; they stayed awake discussing these things and hoping that the Master might again visit them. Among this group were many of the Greeks who were at Gethsemane when the soldiers arrested Jesus and Judas betrayed him with a kiss.

Rumors of Jesus' resurrection and reports concerning the many appearances to his followers are spreading rapidly, and the whole city is being wrought up to a high pitch of excitement. Already the Master has appeared to his family, to the women, and to the Greeks, and presently he manifests himself in the midst of the apostles. The Sanhedrin is soon to begin the consideration of these new problems which have been so suddenly thrust upon the Jewish rulers. Jesus thinks much about his apostles but desires that they be left alone for a few more hours of solemn reflection and thoughtful consideration before he visits them.

5. THE WALK WITH TWO BROTHERS

At Emmaus, about seven miles west of Jerusalem, there lived two brothers, shepherds, who had spent the Passover week in Jerusalem attending upon the sacrifices, ceremonials, and feasts. Cleopas, the elder, was a partial believer in Jesus; at least he had been cast out of the synagogue. His brother, Jacob, was not a believer, although he was much intrigued by what he had heard about the Master's teachings and works.

On this Sunday afternoon, about three miles out of Jerusalem and a few minutes before five o'clock, as these two brothers trudged along the road to Emmaus, they talked in great earnestness about Jesus, his teachings, work, and more especially concerning the rumors that his tomb was empty, and that certain of the women had talked with him. Cleopas was half a mind to believe these reports, but Jacob was insistent that the whole affair was probably a fraud. While they thus argued and debated as they made their way toward home, the morontia manifestation of Jesus, his seventh appearance, came alongside them as they journeyed on. Cleopas had often heard Jesus teach and had eaten with him at the homes of Jerusalem believers on several occasions. But he did not recognize the Master even when he spoke freely with them.

After walking a short way with them, Jesus said: "What were the words you exchanged so earnestly as I came upon you?" And when Jesus had spoken, they stood still and viewed him with sad surprise. Said Cleopas: "Can it be that you sojourn in Jerusalem and know not the things which have recently happened?" Then asked the Master, "What things?" Cleopas replied: "If you do not know about these matters, you are the only one in Jerusalem who has not heard these rumors concerning Jesus of Nazareth, who was a prophet mighty in word and in deed before God and all the people. The chief priests and our rulers delivered him up to the Romans and demanded that they crucify him. Now many of us had hoped that it was he who would deliver Israel from the yoke of the gentiles. But that is not all. It is now the third day since he was crucified, and certain women have this day amazed us by declaring that very early this morning they went to his tomb and found it empty. And these same women insist that they talked with this man; they maintain that he has risen from the dead. And when the women reported this to the men, two of his apostles ran to the tomb and likewise found it empty"—and here Jacob interrupted his brother to say, "but they did not see Jesus."

As they walked along, Jesus said to them: "How slow you are to comprehend the truth! When you tell me that it is about the teachings and work of this man that you have your discussions, then may I enlighten you since I am more than familiar with these teachings. Do you not remember that this Jesus always taught that his kingdom was not of this world, and that all men, being the sons of God, should find liberty and freedom in the spiritual joy of the fellowship of the brotherhood of loving service in this new kingdom of the truth of the heavenly Father's love? Do you not recall how this Son of Man proclaimed the salvation of God for all men, ministering to the sick and afflicted and setting free those who were bound by fear and enslaved by evil? Do you not know that this man of Nazareth told his disciples that he must go to Jerusalem, be delivered up to his enemies, who would put him to death, and that he would arise on the third day? Have you not been told all this? And have you never read in the Scriptures concerning this day of salvation for Jew and gentile, where it says that in him shall all the families of the earth be blessed; that he will hear the cry of the needy and save the souls of the poor who seek him; that all nations shall call him blessed? That such a Deliverer shall be as the shadow of a great rock in a weary land. That he will feed the flock like a true shepherd, gathering the lambs in his arms and tenderly carrying them in his bosom. That he will open the eyes of the spiritually blind and bring the prisoners of despair out into full liberty and light; that all who sit in darkness shall see the great light of eternal salvation. That he will bind up the brokenhearted, proclaim liberty to the captives of sin, and open up the prison to those who are enslaved by fear and bound by evil. That he will comfort those who mourn and bestow upon them the joy of salvation in the place of sorrow and heaviness. That he shall be the desire of all nations and the everlasting joy of those who seek righteousness. That this Son of truth and righteousness shall rise upon the world with healing light and saving power; even that he will save his people from their sins; that he will really seek and save those who are lost. That he will not destroy the weak but minister salvation to all who hunger and thirst for righteousness. That those who believe in him shall have eternal life. That he will pour out his spirit upon all flesh, and that this Spirit of Truth shall be in each believer a well of water, springing up into everlasting life. Did you not understand how great was the gospel of the kingdom which this man delivered to you? Do you not perceive how great a salvation has come upon you?"

By this time they had come near to the village where these brothers dwelt. Not a word had these two men spoken since Jesus began to teach them as they walked along the way. Soon they drew up in front of their humble dwelling place, and Jesus was about to take leave of them, going on down the road, but they constrained him to come in and abide with them. They insisted that it was near nightfall, and that he tarry with them. Finally Jesus consented, and very soon after they went into the house, they sat down to eat. They gave him the bread to bless, and as he began to break and hand to them, their eyes were opened, and

Cleopas recognized that their guest was the Master himself. And when he said, "It is the Master —," the morontia Jesus vanished from their sight.

And then they said, the one to the other, "No wonder our hearts burned within us as he spoke to us while we walked along the road! and while he opened up to our understanding the teachings of the Scriptures!"

They would not stop to eat. They had seen the morontia Master, and they rushed from the house, hastening back to Jerusalem to spread the good news of the risen Savior.

About nine o'clock that evening and just before the Master appeared to the ten, these two excited brothers broke in upon the apostles in the upper chamber, declaring that they had seen Jesus and talked with him. And they told all that Jesus had said to them and how they had not discerned who he was until the time of the breaking of the bread.

PAPER 191

APPEARANCES TO THE APOSTLES AND OTHER LEADERS

RESURRECTION Sunday was a terrible day in the lives of the apostles; ten of them spent the larger part of the day in the upper chamber behind barred doors. They might have fled from Jerusalem, but they were afraid of being arrested by the agents of the Sanhedrin if they were found abroad. Thomas was brooding over his troubles alone at Bethpage. He would have fared better had he remained with his fellow apostles, and he would have aided them to direct their discussions along more helpful lines.

All day long John upheld the idea that Jesus had risen from the dead. He recounted no less than five different times when the Master had affirmed he would rise again and at least three times when he alluded to the third day. John's attitude had considerable influence on them, especially on his brother James and on Nathaniel. John would have influenced them more if he had not been the youngest member of the group.

Their isolation had much to do with their troubles. John Mark kept them in touch with developments about the temple and informed them as to the many rumors gaining headway in the city, but it did not occur to him to gather up news from the different groups of believers to whom Jesus had already appeared. That was the kind of service which had heretofore been rendered by the messengers of David, but they were all absent on their last assignment as heralds of the resurrection to those groups of believers who dwelt remote from Jerusalem. For the first time in all these years the apostles realized how much they had been dependent on David's messengers for their daily information regarding the affairs of the kingdom.

All this day Peter characteristically vacillated emotionally between faith and doubt concerning the Master's resurrection. Peter could not get away from the sight of the grave cloths resting there in the tomb as if the body of Jesus had just evaporated from within. "But," reasoned Peter, "if he has risen and can show himself to the women, why does he not show himself to us, his apostles?" Peter would grow sorrowful when he thought that maybe Jesus did not come to them on account of his presence among the apostles, because he had denied him that night in Annas's courtyard. And then would he cheer himself with the word brought by the women, "Go tell my apostles—and Peter." But to derive encouragement from this message implied that he must believe that the women had really seen and heard the risen Master. Thus Peter alternated between faith and doubt throughout the whole day, until a little after eight o'clock, when he ventured out into the courtyard. Peter thought to remove himself from among the apostles so that he might not prevent Jesus' coming to them because of his denial of the Master.

James Zebedee at first advocated that they all go to the tomb; he was strongly in favor of doing something to get to the bottom of the mystery. It was Nathaniel who prevented them from going out in public in response to James's urging, and he did this by reminding them of Jesus' warning against unduly jeopardizing their lives at this time. By noontime James had settled down with the others to watchful waiting. He said little; he was tremendously disappointed because Jesus did not appear to them, and he did not know of the Master's many appearances to other groups and individuals.

Andrew did much listening this day. He was exceedingly perplexed by the situation and had more than his share of doubts, but he at least enjoyed a certain sense of freedom from responsibility for the guidance of his fellow apostles. He was indeed grateful that the Master had released him from the burdens of leadership before they fell upon these distracting times.

More than once during the long and weary hours of this tragic day, the only sustaining influence of the group was the frequent contribution of Nathaniel's characteristic philosophic counsel. He was really the controlling influence among the ten throughout the entire day. Never once did he express himself concerning either belief or disbelief in the Master's resurrection. But as the day wore on, he became increasingly inclined toward believing that Jesus had fulfilled his promise to rise again.

Simon Zelotes was too much crushed to participate in the discussions. Most of the time he reclined on a couch in a corner of the room with his face to the wall; he did not speak half a dozen times throughout the whole day. His concept of the kingdom had crashed, and he could not discern that the Master's resurrection could materially change the situation. His disappointment was very personal and altogether too keen to be recovered from on short notice, even in the face of such a stupendous fact as the resurrection.

Strange to record, the usually inexpressive Philip did much talking throughout the afternoon of this day. During the forenoon he had little to say, but all afternoon he asked questions of the other apostles. Peter was often annoyed by Philip's questions, but the others took his inquiries good-naturedly. Philip was particularly desirous of knowing, provided Jesus had really risen from the grave, whether his body would bear the physical marks of the crucifixion.

Matthew was highly confused; he listened to the discussions of his fellows but spent most of the time turning over in his mind the problem of their future finances. Regardless of Jesus' supposed resurrection, Judas was gone, David had unceremoniously turned the funds over to him, and they were without an authoritative leader. Before Matthew got around to giving serious consideration to their arguments about the resurrection, he had already seen the Master face to face.

The Alpheus twins took little part in these serious discussions; they were fairly busy with their customary ministrations. One of them expressed the attitude of both when he said, in reply to a question asked by Philip: "We do not understand about the resurrection, but our mother says she talked with the Master, and we believe her."

Thomas was in the midst of one of his typical spells of despairing depression. He slept a portion of the day and walked over the hills the rest of the time. He felt the urge to rejoin his fellow apostles, but the desire to be by himself was the stronger.

The Master put off the first morontia appearance to the apostles for a number of reasons. First, he wanted them to have time, after they heard of his resurrection, to think well over what he had told them about his death and resurrection when he was still with them in the flesh. The Master wanted Peter to wrestle through with some of his peculiar difficulties before he manifested himself to them all. In the second place, he desired that Thomas should be with them at the time of his first appearance. John Mark located Thomas at the home of Simon in Bethpage early this Sunday morning, bringing word to that effect to the apostles about eleven o'clock. Any time during this day Thomas would have gone back to them if Nathaniel or any two of the other apostles had gone for him. He really wanted to return, but having left as he did the evening before, he was too proud to go back of his own accord so soon. By the next day he was so depressed that it required almost a week for him to make up his mind to return. The apostles waited for him, and he waited for his brethren to seek him out and ask him to come back to them. Thomas thus remained away from his associates until the next Saturday evening, when, after darkness had come on, Peter and John went over to Bethpage and brought him back with them. And this is also the reason why they did not go at once to Galilee after Jesus first appeared to them; they would not go without Thomas.

1. THE APPEARANCE TO PETER

It was near half past eight o'clock this Sunday evening when Jesus appeared to Simon Peter in the garden of the Mark home. This was his eighth morontia manifestation. Peter had lived under a heavy burden of doubt and guilt ever since his denial of the Master. All day Saturday and this Sunday he had fought the fear that, perhaps, he was no longer an apostle. He had shuddered at the fate of Judas and even thought that he, too, had betrayed his Master. All this afternoon he thought that it might be his presence with the apostles that prevented Jesus' appearing to them, provided, of course, he had really risen from the dead. And it was to Peter, in such a frame of mind and in such a state of soul, that Jesus appeared as the dejected apostle strolled among the flowers and shrubs.

When Peter thought of the loving look of the Master as he passed by on Annas's porch, and as he turned over in his mind that wonderful message brought him early that morning by the women who came from the empty tomb, "Go tell my apostles—and Peter"—as he contemplated these tokens of mercy, his faith began to surmount his doubts, and he stood still, clenching his fists, while he spoke aloud: "I believe he has risen from the dead; I will go and tell my brethren." And as he said this, there suddenly appeared in front of him the form of a man, who spoke to him in familiar tones, saying: "Peter, the enemy desired to have you, but I would not give you up. I knew it was not from the heart that you disowned me; therefore I forgave you even before you asked; but now must you cease to think about yourself and the troubles of the hour while you prepare to carry the good news of the gospel to those who sit in darkness. No longer should you be concerned with what you may obtain from the kingdom but rather be exercised about what you can give to those who live in dire spiritual poverty. Gird yourself, Simon, for the battle of a new day, the struggle with spiritual darkness and the evil doubtings of the natural minds of men."

Peter and the morontia Jesus walked through the garden and talked of things past, present, and future for almost five minutes. Then the Master vanished from his gaze, saying, "Farewell, Peter, until I see you with your brethren."

For a moment, Peter was overcome by the realization that he had talked with the risen Master, and that he could be sure he was still an ambassador of the kingdom. He had just heard the glorified Master exhort him to go on preaching the gospel. And with all this welling up within his heart, he rushed to the upper chamber and into the presence of his fellow apostles, exclaiming in breathless excitement: "I have seen the Master; he was in the garden. I talked with him, and he has forgiven me."

Peter's declaration that he had seen Jesus in the garden made a profound impression upon his fellow apostles, and they were about ready to surrender their doubts when Andrew got up and warned them not to be too much influenced by his brother's report. Andrew intimated that Peter had seen things which were not real before. Although Andrew did not directly allude to the vision of the night on the Sea of Galilee wherein Peter claimed to have seen the Master coming to them walking on the water, he said enough to betray to all present that he had this incident in mind. Simon Peter was very much hurt by his brother's insinuations and immediately lapsed into crestfallen silence. The twins felt very sorry for Peter, and they both went over to express their sympathy and to say that they believed him and to reassert that their own mother had also seen the Master.

2. FIRST APPEARANCE TO THE APOSTLES

Shortly after nine o'clock that evening, after the departure of Cleopas and Jacob, while the Alpheus twins comforted Peter, and while Nathaniel remonstrated with Andrew, and as the ten apostles were there assembled in the upper chamber with all the doors bolted for fear of arrest, the Master, in morontia form, suddenly appeared in the midst of them, saying: "Peace be upon you. Why are you so frightened when I appear, as though you had seen a spirit? Did I not tell you about these things when I was present with you in the flesh? Did I not say to you that the chief priests and the rulers would deliver me up to be killed, that one of your own number would betray me, and that on the third day I would rise? Wherefore all your doubtings and all this discussion about the reports of the women, Cleopas and Jacob, and even Peter? How long will you doubt my words and refuse to believe my promises? And now that you actually see me, will you believe? Even now one of you is absent. When you are gathered together once more, and after all of you know of a certainty that the Son of Man has risen from the grave, go hence into Galilee. Have faith in God; have faith in one another; and so shall you enter into the new service of the kingdom of heaven. I will tarry in Jerusalem with you until you are ready to go into Galilee. My peace I leave with you."

When the morontia Jesus had spoken to them, he vanished in an instant from their sight. And they all fell on their faces, praising God and venerating their vanished Master. This was the Master's ninth morontia appearance.

3. WITH THE MORONTIA CREATURES

The next day, Monday, was spent wholly with the morontia creatures then present on Urantia. As participants in the Master's morontia-transition experience, there had come to Urantia more than one million morontia directors and associates, together with transition mortals of various orders from the seven mansion worlds of Satania. The morontia Jesus sojourned with these splendid intelligences for forty days. He instructed them and learned from their directors the life of morontia transition as it is traversed by the mortals of the inhabited worlds of Satania as they pass through the system morontia spheres.

About midnight of this Monday the Master's morontia form was adjusted for transition to the second stage of morontia progression. When he next appeared to his mortal children on earth, it was as a second-stage morontia being. As the Master progressed in the morontia career, it became, technically, more and more difficult for the morontia intelligences and their transforming associates to visualize the Master to mortal and material eyes.

Jesus made the transit to the third stage of morontia on Friday, April 14; to the fourth stage on Monday, the 17th; to the fifth stage on Saturday, the 22nd; to the sixth stage on Thursday, the 27th; to the seventh stage on Tuesday, May 2; to Jerusem citizenship on Sunday, the 7th; and he entered the embrace of the Most Highs of Edentia on Sunday, the 14th.

In this manner did Michael of Nebadon complete his service of universe experience since he had already, in connection with his previous bestowals, experienced to the full the life of the ascendant mortals of time and space from the sojourn on the headquarters of the constellation even on to, and through, the service of the headquarters of the superuniverse. And it was by these very morontia experiences that the Creator Son of Nebadon really finished and acceptably terminated his seventh and final universe bestowal.

4. THE TENTH APPEARANCE (AT PHILADELPHIA)

The tenth morontia manifestation of Jesus to mortal recognition occurred a short time after eight o'clock on Tuesday, April 11, at Philadelphia, where he showed himself to Abner and Lazarus and some one hundred and fifty of their associates, including more than fifty of the evangelistic corps of the seventy. This appearance occurred just after the opening of a special meeting in the synagogue which had been called by Abner to discuss the crucifixion of Jesus and the more recent report of the resurrection which had been brought by David's messenger. Inasmuch as the resurrected Lazarus was now a member of this group of believers, it was not difficult for them to believe the report that Jesus had risen from the dead.

The meeting in the synagogue was just being opened by Abner and Lazarus, who were standing together in the pulpit, when the entire audience of believers saw the form of the Master appear suddenly. He stepped forward from where he had appeared between Abner and Lazarus, neither of whom had observed him, and saluting the company, said:

"Peace be upon you. You all know that we have one Father in heaven, and that there is but one gospel of the kingdom—the good news of the gift of eternal life which men receive by faith. As you rejoice in your loyalty to the gospel, pray the Father of truth to shed abroad in your hearts a new and greater love for your brethren. You are to love all men as I have loved you; you are to serve all men as I have served you. With understanding sympathy and brotherly affection, fellowship all your brethren who are dedicated to the proclamation of the good news, whether they be Jew or gentile, Greek or Roman, Persian or Ethiopian. John proclaimed the kingdom in advance; you have preached the gospel in power; the Greeks already teach the good news; and I am soon to send forth the Spirit of Truth into the souls of all these, my brethren, who have so unselfishly dedicated their lives to the enlightenment of their fellows who sit in spiritual darkness. You are all the children of light; therefore stumble not into the misunderstanding entanglements of mortal suspicion and human intolerance. If you are ennobled, by the grace of faith, to love unbelievers, should you not also equally love those who are your fellow believers in the far-spreading household of faith? Remember, as you love one another, all men will know that you are my disciples.

"Go, then, into all the world proclaiming this gospel of the fatherhood of God and the brotherhood of men to all nations and races and ever be wise in your choice of methods for presenting the good news to the different races and tribes of mankind. Freely you have received this gospel of the kingdom, and you will freely give the good news to all nations. Fear not the resistance of evil, for I am with you always, even to the end of the ages. And my peace I leave with you."

When he had said, "My peace I leave with you," he vanished from their sight. With the exception of one of his appearances in Galilee, where upward of five hundred believers saw him at one time, this group in Philadelphia embraced the largest number of mortals who saw him on any single occasion.

Early the next morning, even while the apostles tarried in Jerusalem awaiting the emotional recovery of Thomas, these believers at Philadelphia went forth proclaiming that Jesus of Nazareth had risen from the dead.

The next day, Wednesday, Jesus spent without interruption in the society of his morontia associates, and during the midafternoon hours he received visiting morontia delegates from the mansion worlds of every local system of inhabited spheres throughout the constellation of Norlatiadek. And they all rejoiced to know their Creator as one of their own order of universe intelligence.

5. SECOND APPEARANCE TO THE APOSTLES

Thomas spent a lonesome week alone with himself in the hills around about Olivet. During this time he saw only those at Simon's house and John Mark. It was about nine o'clock on Saturday, April 15, when the two apostles found him and took him back with them to their rendezvous at the Mark home. The next day Thomas listened to the telling of the stories of the Master's various appearances, but he steadfastly refused to believe. He maintained that Peter had enthused them into thinking they had seen the Master. Nathaniel reasoned with him, but it did no good. There was an emotional stubbornness associated with his customary doubtfulness, and this state of mind, coupled with his chagrin at having run away from them, conspired to create a situation of isolation which even Thomas himself did not fully understand. He had withdrawn from his fellows, he had gone his own way, and now, even when he was back among them, he unconsciously tended to assume an attitude of disagreement. He was slow to surrender; he disliked to give in. Without intending it, he really enjoyed the attention paid him; he derived unconscious satisfaction from the efforts of all his fellows to convince and convert him. He had missed them for a full week, and he obtained considerable pleasure from their persistent attentions.

They were having their evening meal a little after six o'clock, with Peter sitting on one side of Thomas and Nathaniel on the other, when the doubting apostle said: "I will not believe unless I see the Master with my own eyes and put my finger in the mark of the nails." As they thus sat at supper, and while the doors were securely shut and barred, the morontia Master suddenly appeared inside the curvature of the table and, standing directly in front of Thomas, said:

"Peace be upon you. For a full week have I tarried that I might appear again when you were all present to hear once more the commission to go into all the world and preach this gospel of the kingdom. Again I tell you: As the Father sent me into the world, so send I you. As I have revealed the Father, so shall you reveal the divine love, not merely with words, but in your daily living. I send you forth, not to love the souls of men, but rather to *love men.* You are not merely to proclaim the joys of heaven but also to exhibit in your daily experience these spirit realities of the divine life since you already have eternal life, as the gift of God, through faith. When you have faith, when power from on high, the Spirit of Truth, has come upon you, you will not hide your light here behind closed doors; you will make known the love and the mercy of God to all mankind. Through fear you now flee from the facts of a disagreeable experience, but when you shall have been baptized with the Spirit of Truth, you will bravely and joyously go forth to meet the new experiences of proclaiming the good news of eternal life in the kingdom of God. You may tarry here and in Galilee for a short season while you recover from the shock of the transition from the false security of the authority of traditionalism to the new order of the authority of facts, truth, and faith in the supreme realities of living experience. Your mission to the world is founded on the fact that I lived a God-revealing life among you; on the truth that you and all other men are the sons of God; and it shall consist in the life which you will live among men—the actual and living experience of loving men and serving them, even as I have loved and served you. Let faith reveal your light to the world; let the revelation of truth open the eyes blinded by tradition; let your loving service effectually destroy the prejudice engendered by ignorance. By so drawing close to your fellow men in understanding sympathy and with unselfish devotion, you will lead them into a saving knowledge of the Father's love. The Jews have extolled goodness; the Greeks have exalted beauty; the Hindus preach devotion; the faraway ascetics teach reverence; the Romans demand loyalty; but I require of my disciples life, even a life of loving service for your brothers in the flesh."

When the Master had so spoken, he looked down into the face of Thomas and said: "And you, Thomas, who said you would not believe unless you could see me and put your finger in the nail marks of my hands, have now beheld me and heard my words; and though you see no nail marks on my hands, since I am raised in the form that you also shall have when you depart from this world, what will you say to your brethren? You will acknowledge the truth, for already in your heart you had begun to believe even when you so stoutly asserted your unbelief. Your doubts, Thomas, always most stubbornly assert themselves just as they are about to crumble. Thomas, I bid you be not faithless but believing—and I know you will believe, even with a whole heart."

When Thomas heard these words, he fell on his knees before the morontia Master and exclaimed, "I believe! My Lord and my Master!" Then said Jesus to Thomas: "You have believed, Thomas, because you have really seen and heard me. Blessed are those in the ages to come who will believe even though they have not seen with the eye of flesh nor heard with the mortal ear."

And then, as the Master's form moved over near the head of the table, he addressed them all, saying: "And now go all of you to Galilee, where I will presently appear to you." After he said this, he vanished from their sight.

The eleven apostles were now fully convinced that Jesus had risen from the dead, and very early the next morning, before the break of day, they started out for Galilee.

6. THE ALEXANDRIAN APPEARANCE

While the eleven apostles were on the way to Galilee, drawing near their journey's end, on Tuesday evening, April 18, at about half past eight o'clock, Jesus appeared to Rodan and some eighty other believers, in Alexandria. This was the Master's twelfth appearance in morontia form. Jesus appeared before these Greeks and Jews at the conclusion of the report of David's messenger regarding the crucifixion. This messenger, being the fifth in the Jerusalem-Alexandria relay of runners, had arrived in Alexandria late that afternoon, and when he had delivered his message to Rodan, it was decided to call the believers together to receive this tragic word from the messenger himself. At about eight o'clock, the messenger, Nathan of Busiris, came before this group and told them in detail all that had been told him by the preceding runner. Nathan ended his touching recital with these words: "But David, who sends us this word, reports that the Master, in foretelling his death, declared that he would rise again." Even as Nathan spoke, the morontia Master appeared there in full view of all. And when Nathan sat down, Jesus said:

"Peace be upon you. That which my Father sent me into the world to establish belongs not to a race, a nation, nor to a special group of teachers or preachers. This gospel of the kingdom belongs to both Jew and gentile, to rich and poor, to free and bond, to male and female, even to the little children. And you are all to proclaim this gospel of love and truth by the lives which you live in the flesh. You shall love one another with a new and startling affection, even as I have loved you. You will serve mankind with a new and amazing devotion, even as I have served you. And when men see you so love them, and when they behold how fervently you serve them, they will perceive that you have become faith-fellows of the kingdom of heaven, and they will follow after the Spirit of Truth which they see in your lives, to the finding of eternal salvation.

"As the Father sent me into this world, even so now send I you. You are all called to carry the good news to those who sit in darkness. This gospel of the kingdom belongs to all who believe it; it shall not be committed to the custody of mere priests. Soon will the Spirit of Truth come upon you, and he shall lead you into all truth. Go you, therefore, into all the world preaching this gospel, and lo, I am with you always, even to the end of the ages."

When the Master had so spoken, he vanished from their sight. All that night these believers remained there together recounting their experiences as kingdom believers and listening to the many words of Rodan and his associates. And they all believed that Jesus had risen from the dead. Imagine the surprise of David's herald of the resurrection, who arrived the second day after this, when they replied to his announcement, saying: "Yes, we know, for we have seen him. He appeared to us day before yesterday."

PAPER 192

APPEARANCES IN GALILEE

BY THE time the apostles left Jerusalem for Galilee, the Jewish leaders had quieted down considerably. Since Jesus appeared only to his family of kingdom believers, and since the apostles were in hiding and did no public preaching, the rulers of the Jews concluded that the gospel movement was, after all, effectually crushed. They were, of course, disconcerted by the increasing spread of rumors that Jesus had risen from the dead, but they depended upon the bribed guards effectively to counteract all such reports by their reiteration of the story that a band of his followers had removed the body.

From this time on, until the apostles were dispersed by the rising tide of persecution, Peter was the generally recognized head of the apostolic corps. Jesus never gave him any such authority, and his fellow apostles never formally elected him to such a position of responsibility; he naturally assumed it and held it by common consent and also because he was their chief preacher. From now on public preaching became the main business of the apostles. After their return from Galilee, Matthias, whom they chose to take the place of Judas, became their treasurer.

During the week they tarried in Jerusalem, Mary the mother of Jesus spent much of the time with the women believers who were stopping at the home of Joseph of Arimathea.

Early this Monday morning when the apostles departed for Galilee, John Mark went along. He followed them out of the city, and when they had passed well beyond Bethany, he boldly came up among them, feeling confident they would not send him back.

The apostles paused several times on the way to Galilee to tell the story of their risen Master and therefore did not arrive at Bethsaida until very late on Wednesday night. It was noontime on Thursday before they were all awake and ready to partake of breakfast.

1. APPEARANCE BY THE LAKE

About six o'clock Friday morning, April 21, the morontia Master made his thirteenth appearance, the first in Galilee, to the ten apostles as their boat drew near the shore close to the usual landing place at Bethsaida.

After the apostles had spent the afternoon and early evening of Thursday in waiting at the Zebedee home, Simon Peter suggested that they go fishing. When Peter proposed the fishing trip, all of the apostles decided to go along. All night they toiled with the nets but caught no fish. They did not much mind the failure to make a catch, for they had many interesting experiences to talk over, things which had so recently happened to them at Jerusalem. But when daylight came, they decided to return to Bethsaida. As they neared the shore, they saw someone on the beach, near the boat landing, standing by a fire. At first they thought it was John Mark, who had come down to welcome them back with their catch, but as they drew nearer the shore, they saw they were mistaken—the man was too tall for John. It had occurred to none of them that the person on the shore was the Master. They did not altogether understand why Jesus wanted to meet with them amidst the scenes of their earlier associations and out in the open in contact with nature, far away from the shut-in environment of Jerusalem with its tragic associations of fear, betrayal, and death. He had told them that, if they would go into Galilee, he would meet them there, and he was about to fulfill that promise.

As they dropped anchor and prepared to enter the small boat for going ashore, the man on the beach called to them, "Lads, have you caught anything?" And when they answered, "No," he spoke again. "Cast the net on the right side of the boat, and you will find fish." While they did not know it was Jesus who had directed them, with one accord they cast in the net as they had been instructed, and immediately it was filled, so much so that they were hardly able to draw it up. Now, John Zebedee was quick of perception, and when he saw the heavy-laden net, he perceived that it was the Master who had spoken to them. When this thought came into his mind, he leaned over and whispered to Peter, "It is the Master." Peter was ever a man of thoughtless action and impetuous devotion; so when John whispered this in his ear, he quickly arose and cast himself into the water that he might the sooner reach the Master's side. His brethren came up close behind him, having come ashore in the small boat, hauling the net of fishes after them.

By this time John Mark was up and, seeing the apostles coming ashore with the heavy-laden net, ran down the beach to greet them; and when he saw eleven men instead of ten, he surmised that the unrecognized one was the risen Jesus, and as the astonished ten stood by in silence, the youth rushed up to the Master and, kneeling at his feet, said, "My Lord and my Master." And then Jesus spoke, not as he had in Jerusalem, when he greeted them with "Peace be upon you," but in commonplace tones he addressed John Mark: "Well, John, I am glad to see you again and in carefree Galilee, where we can have a good visit. Stay with us, John, and have breakfast."

As Jesus talked with the young man, the ten were so astonished and surprised that they neglected to haul the net of fish in upon the beach. Now spoke Jesus: "Bring in your fish and prepare some for breakfast. Already we have the fire and much bread."

While John Mark had paid homage to the Master, Peter had for a moment been shocked at the sight of the coals of fire glowing there on the beach; the scene reminded him so vividly of the midnight fire of charcoal in the courtyard of Annas, where he had disowned the Master, but he shook himself and, kneeling at the Master's feet, exclaimed, "My Lord and my Master!"

Peter then joined his comrades as they hauled in the net. When they had landed their catch, they counted the fish, and there were 153 large ones. And again was the mistake made of calling this another miraculous catch of fish. There was no miracle connected with this episode. It was merely an exercise of the Master's preknowledge. He knew the fish were there and accordingly directed the apostles where to cast the net.

Jesus spoke to them, saying: "Come now, all of you, to breakfast. Even the twins should sit down while I visit with you; John Mark will dress the fish." John Mark brought seven good-sized fish, which the Master put on the fire, and when they were cooked, the lad served them to the ten. Then Jesus broke the bread and handed it to John, who in turn served it to the hungry apostles. When they had all been served, Jesus bade John Mark sit down while he himself served the fish and the bread to the lad. And as they ate, Jesus visited with them and recounted their many experiences in Galilee and by this very lake.

This was the third time Jesus had manifested himself to the apostles as a group. When Jesus first addressed them, asking if they had any fish, they did not suspect who he was because it was a common experience for these fishermen on the Sea of Galilee, when they came ashore, to be thus accosted by the fish merchants of Tarichea, who were usually on hand to buy the fresh catches for the drying establishments.

Jesus visited with the ten apostles and John Mark for more than an hour, and then he walked up and down the beach, talking with them two and two—but not the same couples he had at first sent out together to teach. All eleven of the apostles had come down from Jerusalem together, but Simon Zelotes grew more and more despondent as they drew near Galilee, so that, when they reached Bethsaida, he forsook his brethren and returned to his home.

Before taking leave of them this morning, Jesus directed that two of the apostles should volunteer to go to Simon Zelotes and bring him back that very day. And Peter and Andrew did so.

2. VISITING WITH THE APOSTLES TWO AND TWO

When they had finished breakfast, and while the others sat by the fire, Jesus beckoned to Peter and to John that they should come with him for a stroll on the beach. As they walked along, Jesus said to John, "John, do you love me?" And when John answered, "Yes, Master, with all my heart," the Master said: "Then, John, give up your intolerance and learn to love men as I have loved you. Devote your life to proving that love is the greatest thing in the world. It is the love of God that impels men to seek salvation. Love is the ancestor of all spiritual goodness, the essence of the true and the beautiful."

Jesus then turned toward Peter and asked, "Peter, do you love me?" Peter answered, "Lord, you know I love you with all my soul." Then said Jesus: "If you love me, Peter, feed my lambs. Do not neglect to minister to the weak, the poor, and the young. Preach the gospel without fear or favor; remember always that God is no respecter of persons. Serve your fellow men even as I have served you; forgive your fellow mortals even as I have forgiven you. Let experience teach you the value of meditation and the power of intelligent reflection."

After they had walked along a little farther, the Master turned to Peter and asked, "Peter, do you really love me?" And then said Simon, "Yes, Lord, you know that I love you." And again said Jesus: "Then take good care of my sheep. Be a good and a true shepherd to the flock. Betray not their confidence in you. Be not taken by surprise at the enemy's hand. Be on guard at all times—watch and pray."

When they had gone a few steps farther, Jesus turned to Peter and, for the third time, asked, "Peter, do you truly love me?" And then Peter, being slightly grieved at the Master's seeming distrust of him, said with considerable feeling, "Lord, you know all things, and therefore do you know that I really and truly love you." Then said Jesus: "Feed my sheep. Do not forsake the flock. Be an example and an inspiration to all your fellow shepherds. Love the flock as I have loved you and devote yourself to their welfare even as I have devoted my life to your welfare. And follow after me even to the end."

Peter took this last statement literally—that he should continue to follow after him—and turning to Jesus, he pointed to John, asking, "If I follow on after you, what shall this man do?" And then, perceiving that Peter had misunderstood his words, Jesus said: "Peter, be not concerned about what your brethren shall do. If I will that John should tarry after you are gone, even until I come back, what is that to you? Only make sure that you follow me."

This remark spread among the brethren and was received as a statement by Jesus to the effect that John would not die before the Master returned, as many thought and hoped, to establish the kingdom in power and glory. It was this interpretation of what Jesus said that had much to do with getting Simon Zelotes back into service, and keeping him at work.

When they returned to the others, Jesus went for a walk and talk with Andrew and James. When they had gone a short distance, Jesus said to Andrew, "Andrew, do you trust me?" And when the former chief of the apostles heard Jesus ask such a question, he stood still and answered, "Yes, Master, of a certainty I trust you, and you know that I do." Then said Jesus: "Andrew, if you trust me, trust your brethren more—even Peter. I once trusted you with the leadership of your brethren. Now must you trust others as I leave you to go to the Father. When your brethren begin to scatter abroad because of bitter persecutions, be a considerate and wise counselor to James my brother in the flesh when they put heavy burdens upon him which he is not qualified by experience to bear. And then go on trusting, for I will not fail you. When you are through on earth, you shall come to me."

Then Jesus turned to James, asking, "James, do you trust me?" And of course James replied, "Yes, Master, I trust you with all my heart." Then said Jesus: "James, if you trust me more, you will be less impatient with your brethren. If you will trust me, it will help you to be kind to the brotherhood of believers. Learn to weigh the consequences of your sayings and your doings. Remember that the reaping is in accordance with the sowing. Pray for tranquillity of spirit and cultivate patience. These graces, with living faith, shall sustain you when the hour comes to drink the cup of sacrifice. But never be dismayed; when you are through on earth, you shall also come to be with me."

Jesus next talked with Thomas and Nathaniel. Said he to Thomas, "Thomas, do you serve me?" Thomas replied, "Yes, Lord, I serve you now and always." Then said Jesus: "If you would serve me, serve my brethren in the flesh even as I have served you. And be not weary in this well-doing but persevere as one who has been ordained by God for this service of love. When you have finished your service with me on earth, you shall serve with me in glory. Thomas, you must cease doubting; you must grow in faith and the knowledge of truth. Believe in God like a child but cease to act so childishly. Have courage; be strong in faith and mighty in the kingdom of God."

Then said the Master to Nathaniel, "Nathaniel, do you serve me?" And the apostle answered, "Yes, Master, and with an undivided affection." Then said Jesus: "If, therefore, you serve me with a whole heart, make sure that you are devoted to the welfare of my brethren on earth with tireless affection. Admix friendship with your counsel and add love to your philosophy. Serve your fellow men even as I have served you. Be faithful to men as I have watched over you. Be less critical; expect less of some men and thereby lessen the extent of your disappointment. And when the work down here is over, you shall serve with me on high."

After this the Master talked with Matthew and Philip. To Philip he said, "Philip, do you obey me?" Philip answered, "Yes, Lord, I will obey you even with my life." Then said Jesus: "If you would obey me, go then into the lands of the gentiles and proclaim this gospel. The prophets have told you that to obey is better than to sacrifice. By faith have you become a God-knowing kingdom son. There is but one law to obey—that is the command to go forth proclaiming the gospel of the kingdom. Cease to fear men; be unafraid to preach the good news of eternal life to your fellows who languish in darkness and hunger for the light of truth. No more, Philip, shall you busy yourself with money and goods. You now are free to preach the glad tidings just as are your brethren. And I will go before you and be with you even to the end."

And then, speaking to Matthew, the Master asked, "Matthew, do you have it in your heart to obey me?" Matthew answered, "Yes, Lord, I am fully dedicated to doing your will." Then said the Master: "Matthew, if you would obey me, go forth to teach all peoples this gospel of the kingdom. No longer will you serve your brethren the material things of life; henceforth you are also to proclaim the good news of spiritual salvation. From now on have an eye single only to obeying your commission to preach this gospel of the Father's kingdom. As I have done the Father's will on earth, so shall you fulfill the divine commission. Remember, both Jew and gentile are your brethren. Fear no man when you proclaim the saving truths of the gospel of the kingdom of heaven. And where I go, you shall presently come."

Then he walked and talked with the Alpheus twins, James and Judas, and speaking to both of them, he asked, "James and Judas, do you believe in me?" And when they both answered, "Yes, Master, we do believe," he said: "I will soon leave you. You see that I have already left you in the flesh. I tarry only a short time in this form before I go to my Father. You believe in me—you are my apostles, and you always will be. Go on believing and remembering your association with me, when I am gone, and after you have, perchance, returned to the work you used to do before you came to live with me. Never allow a change in your outward work to influence your allegiance. Have faith in God to the end of your days on earth. Never forget that, when you are a faith son of God, all upright work of the realm is sacred. Nothing which a son of God does can be common. Do your work, therefore, from this time on, as for God. And when you are through on this world, I have other and better worlds where you shall likewise work for me. And in all of this work, on this world and on other worlds, I will work with you, and my spirit shall dwell within you."

It was almost ten o'clock when Jesus returned from his visit with the Alpheus twins, and as he left the apostles, he said: "Farewell, until I meet you all on the mount of your ordination tomorrow at noontime." When he had thus spoken, he vanished from their sight.

3. ON THE MOUNT OF ORDINATION

At noon on Saturday, April 22, the eleven apostles assembled by appointment on the hill near Capernaum, and Jesus appeared among them. This meeting occurred on the very mount where the Master had set them apart as his apostles and as ambassadors of the Father's kingdom on earth. And this was the Master's fourteenth morontia manifestation.

At this time the eleven apostles knelt in a circle about the Master and heard him repeat the charges and saw him re-enact the ordination scene even as when they were first set apart for the special work of the kingdom. And all of this was to them as a memory of their former consecration to the Father's service, except the Master's prayer. When the Master—the morontia Jesus—now prayed, it was in tones of majesty and with words of power such as the apostles had never before heard. Their Master now spoke with the rulers of the universes as one who, in his own universe, had had all power and authority committed to his hand. And these eleven men never forgot this experience of the morontia rededication to the former pledges of ambassadorship. The Master spent just one hour on this mount with his ambassadors, and when he had taken an affectionate farewell of them, he vanished from their sight.

And no one saw Jesus for a full week. The apostles really had no idea what to do, not knowing whether the Master had gone to the Father. In this state of uncertainty they tarried at Bethsaida. They were afraid to go fishing lest he come to visit them and they miss seeing him. During this entire week Jesus was occupied with the morontia creatures on earth and with the affairs of the morontia transition which he was experiencing on this world.

4. THE LAKESIDE GATHERING

Word of the appearances of Jesus was spreading throughout Galilee, and every day increasing numbers of believers arrived at the Zebedee home to inquire about the Master's resurrection and to find out the truth about these reputed appearances. Peter, early in the week, sent out word that a public meeting would be held by the seaside the next Sabbath at three o'clock in the afternoon.

Accordingly, on Saturday, April 29, at three o'clock, more than five hundred believers from the environs of Capernaum assembled at Bethsaida to hear Peter preach his first public sermon since the resurrection. The apostle was at his best, and after he had finished his appealing discourse, few of his hearers doubted that the Master had risen from the dead.

Peter ended his sermon, saying: "We affirm that Jesus of Nazareth is not dead; we declare that he has risen from the tomb; we proclaim that we have seen him and talked with him." Just as he finished making this declaration of faith, there by his side, in full view of all these people, the Master appeared in morontia form and, speaking to them in familiar accents, said, "Peace be upon you, and my peace I leave with you." When he had thus appeared and had so spoken to them, he vanished from their sight. This was the fifteenth morontia manifestation of the risen Jesus.

Because of certain things said to the eleven while they were in conference with the Master on the mount of ordination, the apostles received the impression that their Master would presently make a public appearance before a group of the Galilean believers, and that, after he had done so, they were to return to Jerusalem. Accordingly, early the next day, Sunday, April 30, the eleven left Bethsaida for Jerusalem. They did considerable teaching and preaching on the way down the Jordan, so that they did not arrive at the home of the Marks in Jerusalem until late on Wednesday, May 3.

This was a sad home-coming for John Mark. Just a few hours before he reached home, his father, Elijah Mark, suddenly died from a hemorrhage in the brain. Although the thought of the certainty of the resurrection of the dead did much to comfort the apostles in their grief, at the same time they truly mourned the loss of their good friend, who had been their stanch supporter even in the times of great trouble and disappointment. John Mark did all he could to comfort his mother and, speaking for her, invited the apostles to continue to make their home at her house. And the eleven made this upper chamber their headquarters until after the day of Pentecost.

The apostles had purposely entered Jerusalem after nightfall that they might not be seen by the Jewish authorities. Neither did they publicly appear in connection with the funeral of Elijah Mark. All the next day they remained in quiet seclusion in this eventful upper chamber.

On Thursday night the apostles had a wonderful meeting in this upper chamber and all pledged themselves to go forth in the public preaching of the new gospel of the risen Lord except Thomas, Simon Zelotes, and the Alpheus twins. Already had begun the first steps of changing the gospel of the kingdom—sonship with God and brotherhood with man—into the proclamation of the resurrection of Jesus. Nathaniel opposed this shift in the burden of their public message, but he could not withstand Peter's eloquence, neither could he overcome the enthusiasm of the disciples, especially the women believers.

And so, under the vigorous leadership of Peter and ere the Master ascended to the Father, his well-meaning representatives began that subtle process of gradually and certainly changing the religion *of* Jesus into a new and modified form of religion *about* Jesus.

PAPER 193

FINAL APPEARANCES AND ASCENSION

THE sixteenth morontia manifestation of Jesus occurred on Friday, May 5, in the courtyard of Nicodemus, about nine o'clock at night. On this evening the Jerusalem believers had made their first attempt to get together since the resurrection. Assembled here at this time were the eleven apostles, the women's corps and their associates, and about fifty other leading disciples of the Master, including a number of the Greeks. This company of believers had been visiting informally for more than half an hour when, suddenly, the morontia Master appeared in full view and immediately began to instruct them. Said Jesus:

"Peace be upon you. This is the most representative group of believers—apostles and disciples, both men and women—to which I have appeared since the time of my deliverance from the flesh. I now call you to witness that I told you beforehand that my sojourn among you must come to an end; I told you that presently I must return to the Father. And then I plainly told you how the chief priests and the rulers of the Jews would deliver me up to be put to death, and that I would rise from the grave. Why, then, did you allow yourselves to become so disconcerted by all this when it came to pass? and why were you so surprised when I rose from the tomb on the third day? You failed to believe me because you heard my words without comprehending the meaning thereof.

"And now you should give ear to my words lest you again make the mistake of hearing my teaching with the mind while in your hearts you fail to comprehend the meaning. From the beginning of my sojourn as one of you, I taught you that my one purpose was to reveal my Father in heaven to his children on earth. I have lived the God-revealing bestowal that you might experience the God-knowing career. I have revealed God as your Father in heaven; I have revealed you as the sons of God on earth. It is a fact that God loves you, his sons. By faith in my word this fact becomes an eternal and living truth in your hearts. When, by living faith, you become divinely God-conscious, you are then born of the spirit as children of light and life, even the eternal life wherewith you shall ascend the universe of universes and attain the experience of finding God the Father on Paradise.

"I admonish you ever to remember that your mission among men is to proclaim the gospel of the kingdom—the reality of the fatherhood of God and the truth of the sonship of man. Proclaim the whole truth of the good news, not just a part of the saving gospel. Your message is not changed by my resurrection experience. Sonship with God, by faith, is still the saving truth of the gospel of the kingdom. You are to go forth preaching the love of God and the service of man. That which the world needs most to know is: Men are the sons of God, and through faith they can actually realize, and daily experience, this ennobling truth.

My bestowal should help all men to know that they are the children of God, but such knowledge will not suffice if they fail personally to faith-grasp the saving truth that they are the living spirit sons of the eternal Father. The gospel of the kingdom is concerned with the love of the Father and the service of his children on earth.

"Among yourselves, here, you share the knowledge that I have risen from the dead, but that is not strange. I have the power to lay down my life and to take it up again; the Father gives such power to his Paradise Sons. You should the rather be stirred in your hearts by the knowledge that the dead of an age entered upon the eternal ascent soon after I left Joseph's new tomb. I lived my life in the flesh to show how you can, through loving service, become God-revealing to your fellow men even as, by loving you and serving you, I have become God-revealing to you. I have lived among you as the Son of Man that you, and all other men, might know that you are all indeed the sons of God. Therefore, go you now into all the world preaching this gospel of the kingdom of heaven to all men. Love all men as I have loved you; serve your fellow mortals as I have served you. Freely you have received, freely give. Only tarry here in Jerusalem while I go to the Father, and until I send you the Spirit of Truth. He shall lead you into the enlarged truth, and I will go with you into all the world. I am with you always, and my peace I leave with you."

When the Master had spoken to them, he vanished from their sight. It was near daybreak before these believers dispersed; all night they remained together, earnestly discussing the Master's admonitions and contemplating all that had befallen them. James Zebedee and others of the apostles also told them of their experiences with the morontia Master in Galilee and recited how he had three times appeared to them.

1. THE APPEARANCE AT SYCHAR

About four o'clock on Sabbath afternoon, May 13, the Master appeared to Nalda and about seventy-five Samaritan believers near Jacob's well, at Sychar. The believers were in the habit of meeting at this place, near where Jesus had spoken to Nalda concerning the water of life. On this day, just as they had finished their discussions of the reported resurrection, Jesus suddenly appeared before them, saying:

"Peace be upon you. You rejoice to know that I am the resurrection and the life, but this will avail you nothing unless you are first born of the eternal spirit, thereby coming to possess, by faith, the gift of eternal life. If you are the faith sons of my Father, you shall never die; you shall not perish. The gospel of the kingdom has taught you that all men are the sons of God. And this good news concerning the love of the heavenly Father for his children on earth must be carried to all the world. The time has come when you worship God neither on Gerizim nor at Jerusalem, but where you are, as you are, in spirit and in truth. It is your faith that saves your souls. Salvation is the gift of God to all who believe they are his sons. But be not deceived; while salvation is the free gift of God and is bestowed upon all who accept it by faith, there follows the experience of bearing the fruits of this spirit life as it is lived in the flesh. The acceptance of the doctrine of the fatherhood of God implies that you also freely accept the associated truth of the brotherhood of man. And if man is your brother, he is even more than your neighbor, whom the Father requires you to love as yourself. Your brother, being of your own family, you will not only love with a family affection, but you will also serve as you would serve yourself. And you will thus love and serve your brother because you, being my brethren, have been thus loved and served by me. Go, then, into all the world telling this good news to all creatures of every race, tribe, and nation. My spirit shall go before you, and I will be with you always."

These Samaritans were greatly astonished at this appearance of the Master, and they hastened off to the near-by towns and villages, where they published abroad the news that they had seen Jesus, and that he had talked to them. And this was the seventeenth morontia appearance of the Master.

2. THE PHOENICIAN APPEARANCE

The Master's eighteenth morontia appearance was at Tyre, on Tuesday, May 16, at a little before nine o'clock in the evening. Again he appeared at the close of a meeting of believers, as they were about to disperse, saying:

"Peace be upon you. You rejoice to know that the Son of Man has risen from the dead because you thereby know that you and your brethren shall also survive mortal death. But such survival is dependent on your having been previously born of the spirit of truth-seeking and God-finding. The bread of life and the water thereof are given only to those who hunger for truth and thirst for righteousness—for God. The fact that the dead rise is not the gospel of the kingdom. These great truths and these universe facts are all related to this gospel in that they are a part of the result of believing the good news and are embraced in the subsequent experience of those who, by faith, become, in deed and in truth, the everlasting sons of the eternal God. My Father sent me into the world to proclaim this salvation of sonship to all men. And so send I you abroad to preach this salvation of sonship. Salvation is the free gift of God, but those who are born of the spirit will immediately begin to show forth the fruits of the spirit in loving service to their fellow creatures. And the fruits of the divine spirit which are yielded in the lives of spirit-born and God-knowing mortals are: loving service, unselfish devotion, courageous loyalty, sincere fairness, enlightened honesty, undying hope, confiding trust, merciful ministry, unfailing goodness, forgiving tolerance, and enduring peace. If professed believers bear not these fruits of the divine spirit in their lives, they are dead; the Spirit of Truth is not in them; they are useless branches on the living vine, and they soon will be taken away. My Father requires of the children of faith that they bear much spirit fruit. If, therefore, you are not fruitful, he will dig about your roots and cut away your unfruitful branches. Increasingly, must you yield the fruits of the spirit as you progress heavenward in the kingdom of God. You may enter the kingdom as a child, but the Father requires that you grow up, by grace, to the full stature of spiritual adulthood. And when you go abroad to tell all nations the good news of this gospel, I will go before you, and my Spirit of Truth shall abide in your hearts. My peace I leave with you."

And then the Master disappeared from their sight. The next day there went out from Tyre those who carried this story to Sidon and even to Antioch and Damascus. Jesus had been with these believers when he was in the flesh, and they were quick to recognize him when he began to teach them. While his friends could not readily recognize his morontia form when made visible, they were never slow to identify his personality when he spoke to them.

3. LAST APPEARANCE IN JERUSALEM

Early Thursday morning, May 18, Jesus made his last appearance on earth as a morontia personality. As the eleven apostles were about to sit down to breakfast in the upper chamber of Mary Mark's home, Jesus appeared to them and said:

"Peace be upon you. I have asked you to tarry here in Jerusalem until I ascend to the Father, even until I send you the Spirit of Truth, who shall soon be poured out upon all flesh, and who shall endow you with power from on high." Simon Zelotes interrupted Jesus, asking, "Then, Master, will you restore the kingdom, and will we see the glory of God manifested on earth?" When Jesus had listened to Simon's question, he answered: "Simon, you still cling to your old ideas about the Jewish Messiah and the material kingdom. But you will receive spiritual power after the spirit has descended upon you, and you will presently go into all the world preaching this gospel of the kingdom. As the Father sent me into the world, so do I send you. And I wish that you would love and trust one another. Judas is no more with you because his love grew cold, and because he refused to trust you, his loyal brethren. Have you not read in the Scripture where it is written: 'It is not good for man to be alone. No man lives to himself'? And also where it says: 'He who would have friends must show himself friendly'? And did I not even send you out to teach, two and two, that you might not become lonely and fall into the mischief and miseries of isolation? You also well know that, when I was in the flesh, I did not permit myself to be alone for long periods. From the very beginning of our associations I always had two or three of you constantly by my side or else very near at hand even when I communed with the Father. Trust, therefore, and confide in one another. And this is all the more needful since I am this day going to leave you alone in the world. The hour has come; I am about to go to the Father."

When he had spoken, he beckoned for them to come with him, and he led them out on the Mount of Olives, where he bade them farewell preparatory to departing from Urantia. This was a solemn journey to Olivet. Not a word was spoken by any of them from the time they left the upper chamber until Jesus paused with them on the Mount of Olives.

4. CAUSES OF JUDAS'S DOWNFALL

It was in the first part of the Master's farewell message to his apostles that he alluded to the loss of Judas and held up the tragic fate of their traitorous fellow worker as a solemn warning against the dangers of social and fraternal isolation. It may be helpful to believers, in this and in future ages, briefly to review the causes of Judas's downfall in the light of the Master's remarks and in view of the accumulated enlightenment of succeeding centuries.

As we look back upon this tragedy, we conceive that Judas went wrong, primarily, because he was very markedly an isolated personality, a personality shut in and away from ordinary social contacts. He persistently refused to confide in, or freely fraternize with, his fellow apostles. But his being an isolated type of personality would not, in and of itself, have wrought such mischief for Judas had it not been that he also failed to increase in love and grow in spiritual grace. And then, as if to make a bad matter worse, he persistently harbored grudges and fostered such psychologic enemies as revenge and the generalized craving to "get even" with somebody for all his disappointments.

This unfortunate combination of individual peculiarities and mental tendencies conspired to destroy a well-intentioned man who failed to subdue these evils by love, faith, and trust. That Judas need not have gone wrong is well proved by the cases of Thomas and Nathaniel, both of whom were cursed with this same sort of suspicion and overdevelopment of the individualistic tendency. Even Andrew and Matthew had many leanings in this direction; but all these men grew to love Jesus and their fellow apostles more, and not less, as time passed. They grew in grace and in a knowledge of the truth. They became increasingly more trustful of their brethren and slowly developed the ability to confide in their fellows. Judas persistently refused to confide in his brethren. When he was impelled, by the accumulation of his emotional conflicts, to seek relief in self-expression, he invariably sought the advice and received the unwise consolation of his unspiritual relatives or those chance acquaintances who were either indifferent, or actually hostile, to the welfare and progress of the spiritual realities of the heavenly kingdom, of which he was one of the twelve consecrated ambassadors on earth.

Judas met defeat in his battles of the earth struggle because of the following factors of personal tendencies and character weakness:

1. He was an isolated type of human being. He was highly individualistic and chose to grow into a confirmed "shut-in" and unsociable sort of person.

2. As a child, life had been made too easy for him. He bitterly resented thwarting. He always expected to win; he was a very poor loser.

3. He never acquired a philosophic technique for meeting disappointment. Instead of accepting disappointments as a regular and commonplace feature of human existence, he unfailingly resorted to the practice of blaming someone in particular, or his associates as a group, for all his personal difficulties and disappointments.

4. He was given to holding grudges; he was always entertaining the idea of revenge.

5. He did not like to face facts frankly; he was dishonest in his attitude toward life situations.

6. He disliked to discuss his personal problems with his immediate associates; he refused to talk over his difficulties with his real friends and those who truly loved him. In all the years of their association he never once went to the Master with a purely personal problem.

7. He never learned that the real rewards for noble living are, after all, spiritual prizes, which are not always distributed during this one short life in the flesh.

As a result of his persistent isolation of personality, his griefs multiplied, his sorrows increased, his anxieties augmented, and his despair deepened almost beyond endurance.

While this self-centered and ultraindividualistic apostle had many psychic, emotional, and spiritual troubles, his main difficulties were: In personality, he was isolated. In mind, he was suspicious and vengeful. In temperament, he was surly and vindictive. Emotionally, he was loveless and unforgiving. Socially, he was unconfiding and almost wholly self-contained. In spirit, he became arrogant and selfishly ambitious. In life, he ignored those who loved him, and in death, he was friendless.

These, then, are the factors of mind and influences of evil which, taken altogether, explain why a well-meaning and otherwise onetime sincere believer in Jesus, even after several years of intimate association with his transforming personality, forsook his fellows, repudiated a sacred cause, renounced his holy calling, and betrayed his divine Master.

5. THE MASTER'S ASCENSION

It was almost half past seven o'clock this Thursday morning, May 18, when Jesus arrived on the western slope of Mount Olivet with his eleven silent and somewhat bewildered apostles. From this location, about two thirds the way up the mountain, they could look out over Jerusalem and down upon Gethsemane. Jesus now prepared to say his last farewell to the apostles before he took leave of Urantia. As he stood there before them, without being directed they knelt about him in a circle, and the Master said:

"I bade you tarry in Jerusalem until you were endowed with power from on high. I am now about to take leave of you; I am about to ascend to my Father, and soon, very soon, will we send into this world of my sojourn the Spirit of Truth; and when he has come, you shall begin the new proclamation of the gospel of the kingdom, first in Jerusalem and then to the uttermost parts of the world. Love men with the love wherewith I have loved you and serve your fellow mortals even as I have served you. By the spirit fruits of your lives impel souls to believe the truth that man is a son of God, and that all men are brethren. Remember all I have taught you and the life I have lived among you. My love overshadows you, my spirit will dwell with you, and my peace shall abide upon you. Farewell."

When the morontia Master had thus spoken, he vanished from their sight. This so-called ascension of Jesus was in no way different from his other disappearances from mortal vision during the forty days of his morontia career on Urantia.

The Master went to Edentia by way of Jerusem, where the Most Highs, under the observation of the Paradise Son, released Jesus of Nazareth from the morontia state and, through the spirit channels of ascension, returned him to the status of Paradise sonship and supreme sovereignty on Salvington.

It was about seven forty-five this morning when the morontia Jesus disappeared from the observation of his eleven apostles to begin the ascent to the right hand of his Father, there to receive formal confirmation of his completed sovereignty of the universe of Nebadon.

6. PETER CALLS A MEETING

Acting upon the instruction of Peter, John Mark and others went forth to call the leading disciples together at the home of Mary Mark. By ten thirty, one hundred and twenty of the foremost disciples of Jesus living in Jerusalem had forgathered to hear the report of the farewell message of the Master and to learn of his ascension. Among this company was Mary the mother of Jesus. She had returned to Jerusalem with John Zebedee when the apostles came back from their recent sojourn in Galilee. Soon after Pentecost she returned to the home of Salome at Bethsaida. James the brother of Jesus was also present at this meeting, the first conference of the Master's disciples to be called after the termination of his planetary career.

Simon Peter took it upon himself to speak for his fellow apostles and made a thrilling report of the last meeting of the eleven with their Master and most touchingly portrayed the Master's final farewell and his ascension disappearance. It was a meeting the like of which had never before occurred on this world. This part of the meeting lasted not quite one hour. Peter then explained that they had decided to choose a successor to Judas Iscariot, and that a recess would be granted to enable the apostles to decide between the two men who had been suggested for this position, Matthias and Justus.

The eleven apostles then went downstairs, where they agreed to cast lots in order to determine which of these men should become an apostle to serve in Judas's place. The lot fell on Matthias, and he was declared to be the new apostle. He was duly inducted into his office and then appointed treasurer. But Matthias had little part in the subsequent activities of the apostles.

Soon after Pentecost the twins returned to their homes in Galilee. Simon Zelotes was in retirement for some time before he went forth preaching the gospel. Thomas worried for a shorter period and then resumed his teaching. Nathaniel differed increasingly with Peter regarding preaching about Jesus in the place of proclaiming the former gospel of the kingdom. This disagreement became so acute by the middle of the following month that Nathaniel withdrew, going to Philadelphia to visit Abner and Lazarus; and after tarrying there for more than a year, he went on into the lands beyond Mesopotamia preaching the gospel as he understood it.

This left but six of the original twelve apostles to become actors on the stage of the early proclamation of the gospel in Jerusalem: Peter, Andrew, James, John, Philip, and Matthew.

Just about noon the apostles returned to their brethren in the upper chamber and announced that Matthias had been chosen as the new apostle. And then Peter called all of the believers to engage in prayer, prayer that they might be prepared to receive the gift of the spirit which the Master had promised to send.

PAPER 194

BESTOWAL OF THE SPIRIT OF TRUTH

ABOUT one o'clock, as the one hundred and twenty believers were engaged in prayer, they all became aware of a strange presence in the room. At the same time these disciples all became conscious of a new and profound sense of spiritual joy, security, and confidence. This new consciousness of spiritual strength was immediately followed by a strong urge to go out and publicly proclaim the gospel of the kingdom and the good news that Jesus had risen from the dead.

Peter stood up and declared that this must be the coming of the Spirit of Truth which the Master had promised them and proposed that they go to the temple and begin the proclamation of the good news committed to their hands. And they did just what Peter suggested.

These men had been trained and instructed that the gospel which they should preach was the fatherhood of God and the sonship of man, but at just this moment of spiritual ecstasy and personal triumph, the best tidings, the greatest news, these men could think of was the *fact* of the risen Master. And so they went forth, endowed with power from on high, preaching glad tidings to the people—even salvation through Jesus—but they unintentionally stumbled into the error of substituting some of the facts associated with the gospel for the gospel message itself. Peter unwittingly led off in this mistake, and others followed after him on down to Paul, who created a new religion out of the new version of the good news.

The gospel of the kingdom is: the fact of the fatherhood of God, coupled with the resultant truth of the sonship-brotherhood of men. Christianity, as it developed from that day, is: the fact of God as the Father of the Lord Jesus Christ, in association with the experience of believer-fellowship with the risen and glorified Christ.

It is not strange that these spirit-infused men should have seized upon this opportunity to express their feelings of triumph over the forces which had sought to destroy their Master and end the influence of his teachings. At such a time as this it was easier to remember their personal association with Jesus and to be thrilled with the assurance that the Master still lived, that their friendship had not ended, and that the spirit had indeed come upon them even as he had promised.

These believers felt themselves suddenly translated into another world, a new existence of joy, power, and glory. The Master had told them the kingdom would come with power, and some of them thought they were beginning to discern what he meant.

And when all of this is taken into consideration, it is not difficult to understand how these men came to preach a *new gospel about Jesus* in the place of their former message of the fatherhood of God and the brotherhood of men.

1. THE PENTECOST SERMON

The apostles had been in hiding for forty days. This day happened to be the Jewish festival of Pentecost, and thousands of visitors from all parts of the world were in Jerusalem. Many arrived for this feast, but a majority had tarried in the city since the Passover. Now these frightened apostles emerged from their weeks of seclusion to appear boldly in the temple, where they began to preach the new message of a risen Messiah. And all the disciples were likewise conscious of having received some new spiritual endowment of insight and power.

It was about two o'clock when Peter stood up in that very place where his Master had last taught in this temple, and delivered that impassioned appeal which resulted in the winning of more than two thousand souls. The Master had gone, but they suddenly discovered that this story about him had great power with the people. No wonder they were led on into the further proclamation of that which vindicated their former devotion to Jesus and at the same time so constrained men to believe in him. Six of the apostles participated in this meeting: Peter, Andrew, James, John, Philip, and Matthew. They talked for more than an hour and a half and delivered messages in Greek, Hebrew, and Aramaic, as well as a few words in even other tongues with which they had a speaking acquaintance.

The leaders of the Jews were astounded at the boldness of the apostles, but they feared to molest them because of the large numbers who believed their story.

By half past four o'clock more than two thousand new believers followed the apostles down to the pool of Siloam, where Peter, Andrew, James, and John baptized them in the Master's name. And it was dark when they had finished with baptizing this multitude.

Pentecost was the great festival of baptism, the time for fellowshipping the proselytes of the gate, those gentiles who desired to serve Yahweh. It was, therefore, the more easy for large numbers of both the Jews and believing gentiles to submit to baptism on this day. In doing this, they were in no way disconnecting themselves from the Jewish faith. Even for some time after this the believers in Jesus were a sect within Judaism. All of them, including the apostles, were still loyal to the essential requirements of the Jewish ceremonial system.

2. THE SIGNIFICANCE OF PENTECOST

Jesus lived on earth and taught a gospel which redeemed man from the superstition that he was a child of the devil and elevated him to the dignity of a faith son of God. Jesus' message, as he preached it and lived it in his day, was an effective solvent for man's spiritual difficulties in that day of its statement. And now that he has personally left the world, he sends in his place his Spirit of Truth, who is designed to live in man and, for each new generation, to restate the Jesus message so that every new group of mortals to appear upon the face of the earth shall have a new and up-to-date version of the gospel, just such personal enlightenment and group guidance as will prove to be an effective solvent for man's ever-new and varied spiritual difficulties.

The first mission of this spirit is, of course, to foster and personalize truth, for it is the comprehension of truth that constitutes the highest form of human liberty. Next, it is the purpose of this spirit to destroy the believer's feeling of orphanhood. Jesus having been among men, all believers would experience a sense of loneliness had not the Spirit of Truth come to dwell in men's hearts.

This bestowal of the Son's spirit effectively prepared all normal men's minds for the subsequent universal bestowal of the Father's spirit (the Adjuster) upon all mankind. In a certain sense, this Spirit of Truth is the spirit of both the Universal Father and the Creator Son.

Do not make the mistake of expecting to become strongly intellectually conscious of the outpoured Spirit of Truth. The spirit never creates a consciousness of himself, only a consciousness of Michael, the Son. From the beginning Jesus taught that the spirit would not speak of himself. The proof, therefore, of your fellowship with the Spirit of Truth is not to be found in your consciousness of this spirit but rather in your experience of enhanced fellowship with Michael.

The spirit also came to help men recall and understand the words of the Master as well as to illuminate and reinterpret his life on earth.

Next, the Spirit of Truth came to help the believer to witness to the realities of Jesus' teachings and his life as he lived it in the flesh, and as he now again lives it anew and afresh in the individual believer of each passing generation of the spirit-filled sons of God.

Thus it appears that the Spirit of Truth comes really to lead all believers into all truth, into the expanding knowledge of the experience of the living and growing spiritual consciousness of the reality of eternal and ascending sonship with God.

Jesus lived a life which is a revelation of man submitted to the Father's will, not an example for any man literally to attempt to follow. This life in the flesh, together with his death on the cross and subsequent resurrection, presently became a new gospel of the ransom which had thus been paid in order to purchase man back from the clutch of the evil one—from the condemnation of an offended God. Nevertheless, even though the gospel did become greatly distorted, it remains a fact that this new message about Jesus carried along with it many of the fundamental truths and teachings of his earlier gospel of the kingdom. And, sooner or later, these concealed truths of the fatherhood of God and the brotherhood of men will emerge to effectually transform the civilization of all mankind.

But these mistakes of the intellect in no way interfered with the believer's great progress in growth in spirit. In less than a month after the bestowal of the Spirit of Truth, the apostles made more individual spiritual progress than during their almost four years of personal and loving association with the Master. Neither did this substitution of the *fact* of the resurrection of Jesus for the saving gospel *truth* of sonship with God in any way interfere with the rapid spread of their teachings; on the contrary, this overshadowing of Jesus' message by the new teachings about his person and resurrection seemed greatly to facilitate the preaching of the good news.

The term "baptism of the spirit," which came into such general use about this time, merely signified the conscious reception of this gift of the Spirit of Truth and the personal acknowledgment of this new spiritual power as an augmentation of all spiritual influences previously experienced by God-knowing souls.

Since the bestowal of the Spirit of Truth, man is subject to the teaching and guidance of a threefold spirit endowment: the spirit of the Father, the Thought

Adjuster; the spirit of the Son, the Spirit of Truth; the spirit of the Spirit, the Holy Spirit.

In a way, mankind is subject to the double influence of the sevenfold appeal of the universe spirit influences. The early evolutionary races of mortals are subject to the progressive contact of the seven adjutant mind-spirits of the local universe Mother Spirit. As man progresses upward in the scale of intelligence and spiritual perception, there eventually come to hover over him and dwell within him the seven higher spirit influences. And these seven spirits of the advancing worlds are:

1. The bestowed spirit of the Universal Father—the Thought Adjusters.

2. The spirit presence of the Eternal Son—the spirit gravity of the universe of universes and the certain channel of all spirit communion.

3. The spirit presence of the Infinite Spirit—the universal spirit-mind of all creation, the spiritual source of the intellectual kinship of all progressive intelligences.

4. The spirit of the Universal Father and the Creator Son—the Spirit of Truth, generally regarded as the spirit of the Universe Son.

5. The spirit of the Infinite Spirit and the Universe Mother Spirit—the Holy Spirit, generally regarded as the spirit of the Universe Spirit.

6. The mind-spirit of the Universe Mother Spirit—the seven adjutant mind-spirits of the local universe.

7. The spirit of the Father, Sons, and Spirits—the new-name spirit of the ascending mortals of the realms after the fusion of the mortal spirit-born soul with the Paradise Thought Adjuster and after the subsequent attainment of the divinity and glorification of the status of the Paradise Corps of the Finality.

And so did the bestowal of the Spirit of Truth bring to the world and its peoples the last of the spirit endowment designed to aid in the ascending search for God.

3. WHAT HAPPENED AT PENTECOST

Many queer and strange teachings became associated with the early narratives of the day of Pentecost. In subsequent times the events of this day, on which the Spirit of Truth, the new teacher, came to dwell with mankind, have become confused with the foolish outbreaks of rampant emotionalism. The chief mission of this outpoured spirit of the Father and the Son is to teach men about the truths of the Father's love and the Son's mercy. These are the truths of divinity which men can comprehend more fully than all the other divine traits of character. The Spirit of Truth is concerned primarily with the revelation of the Father's spirit nature and the Son's moral character. The Creator Son, in the flesh, revealed God to men; the Spirit of Truth, in the heart, reveals the Creator Son to men. When man yields the "fruits of the spirit" in his life, he is simply showing forth the traits which the Master manifested in his own earthly life. When Jesus was on earth, he lived his life as one personality—Jesus of Nazareth. As the indwelling spirit of the "new teacher," the Master has, since Pentecost, been able to live his life anew in the experience of every truth-taught believer.

Many things which happen in the course of a human life are hard to understand, difficult to reconcile with the idea that this is a universe in which truth prevails and in which righteousness triumphs. It so often appears that slander, lies, dishonesty, and unrighteousness—sin—prevail. Does faith, after all, triumph over evil, sin, and iniquity? It does. And the life and death of Jesus are the eternal proof that the truth of goodness and the faith of the spirit-led creature will always be vindicated. They taunted Jesus on the cross, saying, "Let us see if God will come and deliver him." It looked dark on that day of the crucifixion, but it was gloriously bright on the resurrection morning; it was still brighter and more joyous on the day of Pentecost. The religions of pessimistic despair seek to obtain release from the burdens of life; they crave extinction in endless slumber and rest. These are the religions of primitive fear and dread. The religion of Jesus is a new gospel of faith to be proclaimed to struggling humanity. This new religion is founded on faith, hope, and love.

To Jesus, mortal life had dealt its hardest, cruelest, and bitterest blows; and this man met these ministrations of despair with faith, courage, and the unswerving determination to do his Father's will. Jesus met life in all its terrible reality and mastered it—even in death. He did not use religion as a release from life. The religion of Jesus does not seek to escape this life in order to enjoy the waiting bliss of another existence. The religion of Jesus provides the joy and peace of another and spiritual existence to enhance and ennoble the life which men now live in the flesh.

If religion is an opiate to the people, it is not the religion of Jesus. On the cross he refused to drink the deadening drug, and his spirit, poured out upon all flesh, is a mighty world influence which leads man upward and urges him onward. The spiritual forward urge is the most powerful driving force present in this world; the truth-learning believer is the one progressive and aggressive soul on earth.

On the day of Pentecost the religion of Jesus broke all national restrictions and racial fetters. It is forever true, "Where the spirit of the Lord is, there is liberty." On this day the Spirit of Truth became the personal gift from the Master to every mortal. This spirit was bestowed for the purpose of qualifying believers more effectively to preach the gospel of the kingdom, but they mistook the experience of receiving the outpoured spirit for a part of the new gospel which they were unconsciously formulating.

Do not overlook the fact that the Spirit of Truth was bestowed upon all sincere believers; this gift of the spirit did not come only to the apostles. The one hundred and twenty men and women assembled in the upper chamber all received the new teacher, as did all the honest of heart throughout the whole world. This new teacher was bestowed upon mankind, and every soul received him in accordance with the love for truth and the capacity to grasp and comprehend spiritual realities. At last, true religion is delivered from the custody of priests and all sacred classes and finds its real manifestation in the individual souls of men.

The religion of Jesus fosters the highest type of human civilization in that it creates the highest type of spiritual personality and proclaims the sacredness of that person.

The coming of the Spirit of Truth on Pentecost made possible a religion which is neither radical nor conservative; it is neither the old nor the new; it is to be dominated neither by the old nor the young. The fact of Jesus' earthly life provides a fixed point for the anchor of time, while the bestowal of the Spirit of

Truth provides for the everlasting expansion and endless growth of the religion which he lived and the gospel which he proclaimed. The spirit guides into *all* truth; he is the teacher of an expanding and always-growing religion of endless progress and divine unfolding. This new teacher will be forever unfolding to the truth-seeking believer that which was so divinely folded up in the person and nature of the Son of Man.

The manifestations associated with the bestowal of the "new teacher," and the reception of the apostles' preaching by the men of various races and nations gathered together at Jerusalem, indicate the universality of the religion of Jesus. The gospel of the kingdom was to be identified with no particular race, culture, or language. This day of Pentecost witnessed the great effort of the spirit to liberate the religion of Jesus from its inherited Jewish fetters. Even after this demonstration of pouring out the spirit upon all flesh, the apostles at first endeavored to impose the requirements of Judaism upon their converts. Even Paul had trouble with his Jerusalem brethren because he refused to subject the gentiles to these Jewish practices. No revealed religion can spread to all the world when it makes the serious mistake of becoming permeated with some national culture or associated with established racial, social, or economic practices.

The bestowal of the Spirit of Truth was independent of all forms, ceremonies, sacred places, and special behavior by those who received the fullness of its manifestation. When the spirit came upon those assembled in the upper chamber, they were simply sitting there, having just been engaged in silent prayer. The spirit was bestowed in the country as well as in the city. It was not necessary for the apostles to go apart to a lonely place for years of solitary meditation in order to receive the spirit. For all time, Pentecost disassociates the idea of spiritual experience from the notion of especially favorable environments.

Pentecost, with its spiritual endowment, was designed forever to loose the religion of the Master from all dependence upon physical force; the teachers of this new religion are now equipped with spiritual weapons. They are to go out to conquer the world with unfailing forgiveness, matchless good will, and abounding love. They are equipped to overcome evil with good, to vanquish hate by love, to destroy fear with a courageous and living faith in truth. Jesus had already taught his followers that his religion was never passive; always were his disciples to be active and positive in their ministry of mercy and in their manifestations of love. No longer did these believers look upon Yahweh as "the Lord of Hosts." They now regarded the eternal Deity as the "God and Father of the Lord Jesus Christ." They made that progress, at least, even if they did in some measure fail fully to grasp the truth that God is also the spiritual Father of every individual.

Pentecost endowed mortal man with the power to forgive personal injuries, to keep sweet in the midst of the gravest injustice, to remain unmoved in the face of appalling danger, and to challenge the evils of hate and anger by the fearless acts of love and forbearance. Urantia has passed through the ravages of great and destructive wars in its history. All participants in these terrible struggles met with defeat. There was but one victor; there was only one who came out of these embittered struggles with an enhanced reputation—that was Jesus of Nazareth and his gospel of overcoming evil with good. The secret of a better civilization is bound up in the Master's teachings of the brotherhood of man, the good will of love and mutual trust.

Up to Pentecost, religion had revealed only man seeking for God; since Pentecost, man is still searching for God, but there shines out over the world the spectacle of God also seeking for man and sending his spirit to dwell within him when he has found him.

Before the teachings of Jesus which culminated in Pentecost, women had little or no spiritual standing in the tenets of the older religions. After Pentecost, in the brotherhood of the kingdom woman stood before God on an equality with man. Among the one hundred and twenty who received this special visitation of the spirit were many of the women disciples, and they shared these blessings equally with the men believers. No longer can man presume to monopolize the ministry of religious service. The Pharisee might go on thanking God that he was "not born a woman, a leper, or a gentile," but among the followers of Jesus woman has been forever set free from all religious discriminations based on sex. Pentecost obliterated all religious discrimination founded on racial distinction, cultural differences, social caste, or sex prejudice. No wonder these believers in the new religion would cry out, "Where the spirit of the Lord is, there is liberty."

Both the mother and brother of Jesus were present among the one hundred and twenty believers, and as members of this common group of disciples, they also received the outpoured spirit. They received no more of the good gift than did their fellows. No special gift was bestowed upon the members of Jesus' earthly family. Pentecost marked the end of special priesthoods and all belief in sacred families.

Before Pentecost the apostles had given up much for Jesus. They had sacrificed their homes, families, friends, worldly goods, and positions. At Pentecost they gave themselves to God, and the Father and the Son responded by giving themselves to man—sending their spirits to live within men. This experience of losing self and finding the spirit was not one of emotion; it was an act of intelligent self-surrender and unreserved consecration.

Pentecost was the call to spiritual unity among gospel believers. When the spirit descended on the disciples at Jerusalem, the same thing happened in Philadelphia, Alexandria, and at all other places where true believers dwelt. It was literally true that "there was but one heart and soul among the multitude of the believers." The religion of Jesus is the most powerful unifying influence the world has ever known.

Pentecost was designed to lessen the self-assertiveness of individuals, groups, nations, and races. It is this spirit of self-assertiveness which so increases in tension that it periodically breaks loose in destructive wars. Mankind can be unified only by the spiritual approach, and the Spirit of Truth is a world influence which is universal.

The coming of the Spirit of Truth purifies the human heart and leads the recipient to formulate a life purpose single to the will of God and the welfare of men. The material spirit of selfishness has been swallowed up in this new spiritual bestowal of selflessness. Pentecost, then and now, signifies that the Jesus of history has become the divine Son of living experience. The joy of this outpoured spirit, when it is consciously experienced in human life, is a tonic for health, a stimulus for mind, and an unfailing energy for the soul.

Prayer did not bring the spirit on the day of Pentecost, but it did have much to do with determining the capacity of receptivity which characterized the individual believers. Prayer does not move the divine heart to liberality of bestowal, but it does so often dig out larger and deeper channels wherein the divine bestowals may flow to the hearts and souls of those who thus remember to maintain unbroken communion with their Maker through sincere prayer and true worship.

4. BEGINNINGS OF THE CHRISTIAN CHURCH

When Jesus was so suddenly seized by his enemies and so quickly crucified between two thieves, his apostles and disciples were completely demoralized. The thought of the Master, arrested, bound, scourged, and crucified, was too much for even the apostles. They forgot his teachings and his warnings. He might, indeed, have been "a prophet mighty in deed and word before God and all the people," but he could hardly be the Messiah they had hoped would restore the kingdom of Israel.

Then comes the resurrection, with its deliverance from despair and the return of their faith in the Master's divinity. Again and again they see him and talk with him, and he takes them out on Olivet, where he bids them farewell and tells them he is going back to the Father. He has told them to tarry in Jerusalem until they are endowed with power—until the Spirit of Truth shall come. And on the day of Pentecost this new teacher comes, and they go out at once to preach their gospel with new power. They are the bold and courageous followers of a living Lord, not a dead and defeated leader. The Master lives in the hearts of these evangelists; God is not a doctrine in their minds; he has become a living presence in their souls.

"Day by day they continued steadfastly and with one accord in the temple and breaking bread at home. They took their food with gladness and singleness of heart, praising God and having favor with all the people. They were all filled with the spirit, and they spoke the word of God with boldness. And the multitudes of those who believed were of one heart and soul; and not one of them said that aught of the things which he possessed was his own, and they had all things in common."

What has happened to these men whom Jesus had ordained to go forth preaching the gospel of the kingdom, the fatherhood of God and the brotherhood of man? They have a new gospel; they are on fire with a new experience; they are filled with a new spiritual energy. Their message has suddenly shifted to the proclamation of the risen Christ: "Jesus of Nazareth, a man God approved by mighty works and wonders; him, being delivered up by the determinate counsel and foreknowledge of God, you did crucify and slay. The things which God foreshadowed by the mouth of all the prophets, he thus fulfilled. This Jesus did God raise up. God has made him both Lord and Christ. Being, by the right hand of God, exalted and having received from the Father the promise of the spirit, he has poured forth this which you see and hear. Repent, that your sins may be blotted out; that the Father may send the Christ, who has been appointed for you, even Jesus, whom the heaven must receive until the times of the restoration of all things."

The gospel of the kingdom, the message of Jesus, had been suddenly changed into the gospel of the Lord Jesus Christ. They now proclaimed the facts of his life, death, and resurrection and preached the hope of his speedy return to this world to finish the work he began. Thus the message of the early believers had to do with preaching about the facts of his first coming and with teaching the hope of his second coming, an event which they deemed to be very near at hand.

Christ was about to become the creed of the rapidly forming church. Jesus lives; he died for men; he gave the spirit; he is coming again. Jesus filled all their thoughts and determined all their new concepts of God and everything else. They were too much enthused over the new doctrine that "God is the Father of the Lord Jesus" to be concerned with the old message that "God is the loving Father of all men," even of every single individual. True, a marvelous manifestation of brotherly love and unexampled good will did spring up in these early communities of believers. But it was a fellowship of believers in Jesus, not a fellowship of brothers in the family kingdom of the Father in heaven. Their good will arose from the love born of the concept of Jesus' bestowal and not from the recognition of the brotherhood of mortal man. Nevertheless, they were filled with joy, and they lived such new and unique lives that all men were attracted to their teachings about Jesus. They made the great mistake of using the living and illustrative commentary on the gospel of the kingdom for that gospel, but even that represented the greatest religion mankind had ever known.

Unmistakably, a new fellowship was arising in the world. "The multitude who believed continued steadfastly in the apostles' teaching and fellowship, in the breaking of bread, and in prayers." They called each other brother and sister; they greeted one another with a holy kiss; they ministered to the poor. It was a fellowship of living as well as of worship. They were not communal by decree but by the desire to share their goods with their fellow believers. They confidently expected that Jesus would return to complete the establishment of the Father's kingdom during their generation. This spontaneous sharing of earthly possessions was not a direct feature of Jesus' teaching; it came about because these men and women so sincerely and so confidently believed that he was to return any day to finish his work and to consummate the kingdom. But the final results of this well-meant experiment in thoughtless brotherly love were disastrous and sorrow-breeding. Thousands of earnest believers sold their property and disposed of all their capital goods and other productive assets. With the passing of time, the dwindling resources of Christian "equal-sharing" came to an *end*—but the world did not. Very soon the believers at Antioch were taking up a collection to keep their fellow believers at Jerusalem from starving.

In these days they celebrated the Lord's Supper after the manner of its establishment; that is, they assembled for a social meal of good fellowship and partook of the sacrament at the end of the meal.

At first they baptized in the name of Jesus; it was almost twenty years before they began to baptize in "the name of the Father, the Son, and the Holy Spirit." Baptism was all that was required for admission into the fellowship of believers. They had no organization as yet; it was simply the Jesus brotherhood.

This Jesus sect was growing rapidly, and once more the Sadducees took notice of them. The Pharisees were little bothered about the situation, seeing that none of the teachings in any way interfered with the observance of the Jewish laws. But the Sadducees began to put the leaders of the Jesus sect in jail until they were prevailed upon to accept the counsel of one of the leading rabbis, Gamaliel, who advised them: "Refrain from these men and let them alone, for if this counsel or this work is of men, it will be overthrown; but if it is of God, you will not be able to overthrow them, lest haply you be found even to be fighting against God." They decided to follow Gamaliel's counsel, and there ensued a time of peace and quiet in Jerusalem, during which the new gospel about Jesus spread rapidly.

And so all went well in Jerusalem until the time of the coming of the Greeks in large numbers from Alexandria. Two of the pupils of Rodan arrived in Jerusalem and made many converts from among the Hellenists. Among their early converts were Stephen and Barnabas. These able Greeks did not so much have the Jewish viewpoint, and they did not so well conform to the Jewish mode of worship and other ceremonial practices. And it was the doings of these Greek believers that terminated the peaceful relations between the Jesus brotherhood and the Pharisees and Sadducees. Stephen and his Greek associate began to preach more as Jesus taught, and this brought them into immediate conflict with the Jewish rulers. In one of Stephen's public sermons, when he reached the objectionable part of the discourse, they dispensed with all formalities of trial and proceeded to stone him to death on the spot.

Stephen, the leader of the Greek colony of Jesus' believers in Jerusalem, thus became the first martyr to the new faith and the specific cause for the formal organization of the early Christian church. This new crisis was met by the recognition that believers could not longer go on as a sect within the Jewish faith. They all agreed that they must separate themselves from unbelievers; and within one month from the death of Stephen the church at Jerusalem had been organized under the leadership of Peter, and James the brother of Jesus had been installed as its titular head.

And then broke out the new and relentless persecutions by the Jews, so that the active teachers of the new religion about Jesus, which subsequently at Antioch was called Christianity, went forth to the ends of the empire proclaiming Jesus. In carrying this message, before the time of Paul the leadership was in Greek hands; and these first missionaries, as also the later ones, followed the path of Alexander's march of former days, going by way of Gaza and Tyre to Antioch and then over Asia Minor to Macedonia, then on to Rome and to the uttermost parts of the empire.

PAPER 195

AFTER PENTECOST

THE results of Peter's preaching on the day of Pentecost were such as to decide the future policies, and to determine the plans, of the majority of the apostles in their efforts to proclaim the gospel of the kingdom. Peter was the real founder of the Christian church; Paul carried the Christian message to the gentiles, and the Greek believers carried it to the whole Roman Empire.

Although the tradition-bound and priest-ridden Hebrews, as a people, refused to accept either Jesus' gospel of the fatherhood of God and the brotherhood of man or Peter's and Paul's proclamation of the resurrection and ascension of Christ (subsequent Christianity), the rest of the Roman Empire was found to be receptive to the evolving Christian teachings. Western civilization was at this time intellectual, war weary, and thoroughly skeptical of all existing religions and universe philosophies. The peoples of the Western world, the beneficiaries of Greek culture, had a revered tradition of a great past. They could contemplate the inheritance of great accomplishments in philosophy, art, literature, and political progress. But with all these achievements they had no soul-satisfying religion. Their spiritual longings remained unsatisfied.

Upon such a stage of human society the teachings of Jesus, embraced in the Christian message, were suddenly thrust. A new order of living was thus presented to the hungry hearts of these Western peoples. This situation meant immediate conflict between the older religious practices and the new Christianized version of Jesus' message to the world. Such a conflict must result in either decided victory for the new or for the old or in some degree of *compromise.* History shows that the struggle ended in compromise. Christianity presumed to embrace too much for any one people to assimilate in one or two generations. It was not a simple spiritual appeal, such as Jesus had presented to the souls of men; it early struck a decided attitude on religious rituals, education, magic, medicine, art, literature, law, government, morals, sex regulation, polygamy, and, in limited degree, even slavery. Christianity came not merely as a new religion—something all the Roman Empire and all the Orient were waiting for—but as a *new order of human society.* And as such a pretension it quickly precipitated the social-moral clash of the ages. The ideals of Jesus, as they were reinterpreted by Greek philosophy and socialized in Christianity, now boldly challenged the traditions of the human race embodied in the ethics, morality, and religions of Western civilization.

At first, Christianity won as converts only the lower social and economic strata. But by the beginning of the second century the very best of Greco-Roman culture was increasingly turning to this new order of Christian belief, this new concept of the purpose of living and the goal of existence.

How did this new message of Jewish origin, which had almost failed in the land of its birth, so quickly and effectively capture the very best minds of the Roman Empire? The triumph of Christianity over the philosophic religions and the mystery cults was due to:

1. Organization. Paul was a great organizer and his successors kept up the pace he set.

2. Christianity was thoroughly Hellenized. It embraced the best in Greek philosophy as well as the cream of Hebrew theology.

3. But best of all, it contained a new and great *ideal,* the echo of the life bestowal of Jesus and the reflection of his message of salvation for all mankind.

4. The Christian leaders were willing to make such compromises with Mithraism that the better half of its adherents were won over to the Antioch cult.

5. Likewise did the next and later generations of Christian leaders make such further compromises with paganism that even the Roman emperor Constantine was won to the new religion.

But the Christians made a shrewd bargain with the pagans in that they adopted the ritualistic pageantry of the pagan while compelling the pagan to accept the Hellenized version of Pauline Christianity. They made a better bargain with the pagans than they did with the Mithraic cult, but even in that earlier compromise they came off more than conquerors in that they succeeded in eliminating the gross immoralities and also numerous other reprehensible practices of the Persian mystery.

Wisely or unwisely, these early leaders of Christianity deliberately compromised the *ideals* of Jesus in an effort to save and further many of his *ideas.* And they were eminently successful. But mistake not! these compromised ideals of the Master are still latent in his gospel, and they will eventually assert their full power upon the world.

By this paganization of Christianity the old order won many minor victories of a ritualistic nature, but the Christians gained the ascendancy in that:

1. A new and enormously higher note in human morals was struck.

2. A new and greatly enlarged concept of God was given to the world.

3. The hope of immortality became a part of the assurance of a recognized religion.

4. Jesus of Nazareth was given to man's hungry soul.

Many of the great truths taught by Jesus were almost lost in these early compromises, but they yet slumber in this religion of paganized Christianity, which was in turn the Pauline version of the life and teachings of the Son of Man. And Christianity, even before it was paganized, was first thoroughly Hellenized. Christianity owes much, very much, to the Greeks. It was a Greek, from Egypt, who so bravely stood up at Nicaea and so fearlessly challenged this assembly that it dared not so obscure the concept of the nature of Jesus that the real truth of his bestowal might have been in danger of being lost to the world. This Greek's name was Athanasius, and but for the eloquence and the logic of this believer, the persuasions of Arius would have triumphed.

1. INFLUENCE OF THE GREEKS

The Hellenization of Christianity started in earnest on that eventful day when the Apostle Paul stood before the council of the Areopagus in Athens and told the Athenians about "the Unknown God." There, under the shadow of the Acropolis, this Roman citizen proclaimed to these Greeks his version of the new religion which had taken origin in the Jewish land of Galilee. And there was something strangely alike in Greek philosophy and many of the teachings of Jesus. They had a common goal—both aimed at the *emergence of the individual.* The Greek, at social and political emergence; Jesus, at moral and spiritual emergence. The Greek taught intellectual liberalism leading to political freedom; Jesus taught spiritual liberalism leading to religious liberty. These two ideas put together constituted a new and mighty charter for human freedom; they presaged man's social, political, and spiritual liberty.

Christianity came into existence and triumphed over all contending religions primarily because of two things:

1. The Greek mind was willing to borrow new and good ideas even from the Jews.

2. Paul and his successors were willing but shrewd and sagacious compromisers; they were keen theologic traders.

At the time Paul stood up in Athens preaching "Christ and Him Crucified," the Greeks were spiritually hungry; they were inquiring, interested, and actually looking for spiritual truth. Never forget that at first the Romans fought Christianity, while the Greeks embraced it, and that it was the Greeks who literally forced the Romans subsequently to accept this new religion, as then modified, as a part of Greek culture.

The Greek revered beauty, the Jew holiness, but both peoples loved truth. For centuries the Greek had seriously thought and earnestly debated about all human problems—social, economic, political, and philosophic—except religion. Few Greeks had paid much attention to religion; they did not take even their own religion very seriously. For centuries the Jews had neglected these other fields of thought while they devoted their minds to religion. They took their religion very seriously, too seriously. As illuminated by the content of Jesus' message, the united product of the centuries of the thought of these two peoples now became the driving power of a new order of human society and, to a certain extent, of a new order of human religious belief and practice.

The influence of Greek culture had already penetrated the lands of the western Mediterranean when Alexander spread Hellenistic civilization over the near-Eastern world. The Greeks did very well with their religion and their politics as long as they lived in small city-states, but when the Macedonian king dared to expand Greece into an empire, stretching from the Adriatic to the Indus, trouble began. The art and philosophy of Greece were fully equal to the task of imperial expansion, but not so with Greek political administration or religion. After the city-states of Greece had expanded into empire, their rather parochial gods seemed a little queer. The Greeks were really searching for *one God,* a greater and better God, when the Christianized version of the older Jewish religion came to them.

The Hellenistic Empire, as such, could not endure. Its cultural sway continued on, but it endured only after securing from the West the Roman political genius for empire administration and after obtaining from the East a religion whose one God possessed empire dignity.

In the first century after Christ, Hellenistic culture had already attained its highest levels; its retrogression had begun; learning was advancing but genius was declining. It was at this very time that the ideas and ideals of Jesus, which were partially embodied in Christianity, became a part of the salvage of Greek culture and learning.

Alexander had charged on the East with the cultural gift of the civilization of Greece; Paul assaulted the West with the Christian version of the gospel of Jesus. And wherever the Greek culture prevailed throughout the West, there Hellenized Christianity took root.

The Eastern version of the message of Jesus, notwithstanding that it remained more true to his teachings, continued to follow the uncompromising attitude of Abner. It never progressed as did the Hellenized version and was eventually lost in the Islamic movement.

2. THE ROMAN INFLUENCE

The Romans bodily took over Greek culture, putting representative government in the place of government by lot. And presently this change favored Christianity in that Rome brought into the whole Western world a new tolerance for strange languages, peoples, and even religions.

Much of the early persecution of Christians in Rome was due solely to their unfortunate use of the term "kingdom" in their preaching. The Romans were tolerant of any and all religions but very resentful of anything that savored of political rivalry. And so, when these early persecutions, due so largely to misunderstanding, died out, the field for religious propaganda was wide open. The Roman was interested in political administration; he cared little for either art or religion, but he was unusually tolerant of both.

Oriental law was stern and arbitrary; Greek law was fluid and artistic; Roman law was dignified and respect-breeding. Roman education bred an unheard-of and stolid loyalty. The early Romans were politically devoted and sublimely consecrated individuals. They were honest, zealous, and dedicated to their ideals, but without a religion worthy of the name. Small wonder that their Greek teachers were able to persuade them to accept Paul's Christianity.

And these Romans were a great people. They could govern the Occident because they did govern themselves. Such unparalleled honesty, devotion, and stalwart self-control was ideal soil for the reception and growth of Christianity.

It was easy for these Greco-Romans to become just as spiritually devoted to an institutional church as they were politically devoted to the state. The Romans fought the church only when they feared it as a competitor of the state. Rome, having little national philosophy or native culture, took over Greek culture for its own and boldly adopted Christ as its moral philosophy. Christianity became the moral culture of Rome but hardly its religion in the sense of being the individual experience in spiritual growth of those who embraced the new religion in such a wholesale manner. True, indeed, many individuals did penetrate beneath the surface of all this state religion and found for the nourishment of their souls the real values of the hidden meanings held within the latent truths of Hellenized and paganized Christianity.

The Stoic and his sturdy appeal to "nature and conscience" had only the better prepared all Rome to receive Christ, at least in an intellectual sense. The Roman was by nature and training a lawyer; he revered even the laws of nature. And now, in Christianity, he discerned in the laws of nature the laws of God. A people that could produce Cicero and Vergil were ripe for Paul's Hellenized Christianity.

And so did these Romanized Greeks force both Jews and Christians to philosophize their religion, to co-ordinate its ideas and systematize its ideals, to adapt religious practices to the existing current of life. And all this was enormously helped by translation of the Hebrew scriptures into Greek and by the later recording of the New Testament in the Greek tongue.

The Greeks, in contrast with the Jews and many other peoples, had long provisionally believed in immortality, some sort of survival after death, and since this was the very heart of Jesus' teaching, it was certain that Christianity would make a strong appeal to them.

A succession of Greek-cultural and Roman-political victories had consolidated the Mediterranean lands into one empire, with one language and one culture, and had made the Western world ready for one God. Judaism provided this God, but Judaism was not acceptable as a religion to these Romanized Greeks. Philo helped some to mitigate their objections, but Christianity revealed to them an even better concept of one God, and they embraced it readily.

3. UNDER THE ROMAN EMPIRE

After the consolidation of Roman political rule and after the dissemination of Christianity, the Christians found themselves with one God, a great religious concept, but without empire. The Greco-Romans found themselves with a great empire but without a God to serve as the suitable religious concept for empire worship and spiritual unification. The Christians accepted the empire; the empire adopted Christianity. The Roman provided a unity of political rule; the Greek, a unity of culture and learning; Christianity, a unity of religious thought and practice.

Rome overcame the tradition of nationalism by imperial universalism and for the first time in history made it possible for different races and nations at least nominally to accept one religion.

Christianity came into favor in Rome at a time when there was great contention between the vigorous teachings of the Stoics and the salvation promises of the mystery cults. Christianity came with refreshing comfort and liberating power to a spiritually hungry people whose language had no word for "unselfishness."

That which gave greatest power to Christianity was the way its believers lived lives of service and even the way they died for their faith during the earlier times of drastic persecution.

The teaching regarding Christ's love for children soon put an end to the widespread practice of exposing children to death when they were not wanted, particularly girl babies.

The early plan of Christian worship was largely taken over from the Jewish synagogue, modified by the Mithraic ritual; later on, much pagan pageantry was added. The backbone of the early Christian church consisted of Christianized Greek proselytes to Judaism.

The second century after Christ was the best time in all the world's history for a good religion to make progress in the Western world. During the first century Christianity had prepared itself, by struggle and compromise, to take root and rapidly spread. Christianity adopted the emperor; later, he adopted Christianity. This was a great age for the spread of a new religion. There was religious liberty; travel was universal and thought was untrammeled.

The spiritual impetus of nominally accepting Hellenized Christianity came to Rome too late to prevent the well-started moral decline or to compensate for the already well-established and increasing racial deterioration. This new religion was a cultural necessity for imperial Rome, and it is exceedingly unfortunate that it did not become a means of spiritual salvation in a larger sense.

Even a good religion could not save a great empire from the sure results of lack of individual participation in the affairs of government, from overmuch paternalism, overtaxation and gross collection abuses, unbalanced trade with the Levant which drained away the gold, amusement madness, Roman standardization, the degradation of woman, slavery and race decadence, physical plagues, and a state church which became institutionalized nearly to the point of spiritual barrenness.

Conditions, however, were not so bad at Alexandria. The early schools continued to hold much of Jesus' teachings free from compromise. Pantaenus taught Clement and then went on to follow Nathaniel in proclaiming Christ in India. While some of the ideals of Jesus were sacrificed in the building of Christianity, it should in all fairness be recorded that, by the end of the second century, practically all the great minds of the Greco-Roman world had become Christian. The triumph was approaching completion.

And this Roman Empire lasted sufficiently long to insure the survival of Christianity even after the empire collapsed. But we have often conjectured what would have happened in Rome and in the world if it had been the gospel of the kingdom which had been accepted in the place of Greek Christianity.

4. THE EUROPEAN DARK AGES

The church, being an adjunct to society and the ally of politics, was doomed to share in the intellectual and spiritual decline of the so-called European "dark ages." During this time, religion became more and more monasticized, asceticized, and legalized. In a spiritual sense, Christianity was hibernating. Throughout this period there existed, alongside this slumbering and secularized religion, a continuous stream of mysticism, a fantastic spiritual experience bordering on unreality and philosophically akin to pantheism.

During these dark and despairing centuries, religion became virtually secondhanded again. The individual was almost lost before the overshadowing authority, tradition, and dictation of the church. A new spiritual menace arose in the creation of a galaxy of "saints" who were assumed to have special influence at the divine courts, and who, therefore, if effectively appealed to, would be able to intercede in man's behalf before the Gods.

But Christianity was sufficiently socialized and paganized that, while it was impotent to stay the oncoming dark ages, it was the better prepared to survive this long period of moral darkness and spiritual stagnation. And it did persist on through the long night of Western civilization and was still functioning as a moral influence in the world when the renaissance dawned. The rehabilitation of Christianity, following the passing of the dark ages, resulted in bringing into existence numerous sects of the Christian teachings, beliefs suited to special intellectual, emotional, and spiritual types of human personality. And many of these special Christian groups, or religious families, still persist at the time of the making of this presentation.

Christianity exhibits a history of having originated out of the unintended transformation of the religion of Jesus into a religion about Jesus. It further presents the history of having experienced Hellenization, paganization, secularization, institutionalization, intellectual deterioration, spiritual decadence, moral hibernation, threatened extinction, later rejuvenation, fragmentation, and more recent relative rehabilitation. Such a pedigree is indicative of inherent vitality and the possession of vast recuperative resources. And this same Christianity is now present in the civilized world of Occidental peoples and stands face to face with a struggle for existence which is even more ominous than those eventful crises which have characterized its past battles for dominance.

Religion is now confronted by the challenge of a new age of scientific minds and materialistic tendencies. In this gigantic struggle between the secular and the spiritual, the religion of Jesus will eventually triumph.

5. THE MODERN PROBLEM

The twentieth century has brought new problems for Christianity and all other religions to solve. The higher a civilization climbs, the more necessitous becomes the duty to "seek first the realities of heaven" in all of man's efforts to stabilize society and facilitate the solution of its material problems.

Truth often becomes confusing and even misleading when it is dismembered, segregated, isolated, and too much analyzed. Living truth teaches the truth seeker aright only when it is embraced in wholeness and as a living spiritual reality, not as a fact of material science or an inspiration of intervening art.

Religion is the revelation to man of his divine and eternal destiny. Religion is a purely personal and spiritual experience and must forever be distinguished from man's other high forms of thought, such as:

1. Man's logical attitude toward the things of material reality.
2. Man's aesthetic appreciation of beauty contrasted with ugliness.
3. Man's ethical recognition of social obligations and political duty.
4. Even man's sense of human morality is not, in and of itself, religious.

Religion is designed to find those values in the universe which call forth faith, trust, and assurance; religion culminates in worship. Religion discovers for the soul those supreme values which are in contrast with the relative values discovered by the mind. Such superhuman insight can be had only through genuine religious experience.

A lasting social system without a morality predicated on spiritual realities can no more be maintained than could the solar system without gravity.

Do not try to satisfy the curiosity or gratify all the latent adventure surging within the soul in one short life in the flesh. Be patient! be not tempted to indulge in a lawless plunge into cheap and sordid adventure. Harness your energies and bridle your passions; be calm while you await the majestic unfolding of an endless career of progressive adventure and thrilling discovery.

In confusion over man's origin, do not lose sight of his eternal destiny. Forget not that Jesus loved even little children, and that he forever made clear the great worth of human personality.

As you view the world, remember that the black patches of evil which you see are shown against a white background of ultimate good. You do not view merely white patches of good which show up miserably against a black background of evil.

When there is so much good truth to publish and proclaim, why should men dwell so much upon the evil in the world just because it appears to be a fact? The beauties of the spiritual values of truth are more pleasurable and uplifting than is the phenomenon of evil.

In religion, Jesus advocated and followed the method of experience, even as modern science pursues the technique of experiment. We find God through the leadings of spiritual insight, but we approach this insight of the soul through the love of the beautiful, the pursuit of truth, loyalty to duty, and the worship of divine goodness. But of all these values, love is the true guide to real insight.

6. MATERIALISM

Scientists have unintentionally precipitated mankind into a materialistic panic; they have started an unthinking run on the moral bank of the ages, but this bank of human experience has vast spiritual resources; it can stand the demands being made upon it. Only unthinking men become panicky about the spiritual assets of the human race. When the materialistic-secular panic is over, the religion of Jesus will not be found bankrupt. The spiritual bank of the kingdom of heaven will be paying out faith, hope, and moral security to all who draw upon it "in His name."

No matter what the apparent conflict between materialism and the teachings of Jesus may be, you can rest assured that, in the ages to come, the teachings of the Master will fully triumph. In reality, true religion cannot become involved in any controversy with science; it is in no way concerned with material things. Religion is simply indifferent to, but sympathetic with, science, while it supremely concerns itself with the *scientist.*

The pursuit of mere knowledge, without the attendant interpretation of wisdom and the spiritual insight of religious experience, eventually leads to pessimism and human despair. A little knowledge is truly disconcerting.

At the time of this writing the worst of the materialistic age is over; the day of a better understanding is already beginning to dawn. The higher minds of the scientific world are no longer wholly materialistic in their philosophy, but the rank and file of the people still lean in that direction as a result of former teachings. But this age of physical realism is only a passing episode in man's life on earth. Modern science has left true religion—the teachings of Jesus as translated in the lives of his believers—untouched. All science has done is to destroy the childlike illusions of the misinterpretations of life.

Science is a quantitative experience, religion a qualitative experience, as regards man's life on earth. Science deals with phenomena; religion, with origins, values, and goals. To assign *causes* as an explanation of physical phenomena is to confess ignorance of ultimates and in the end only leads the scientist straight back to the first great cause—the Universal Father of Paradise.

The violent swing from an age of miracles to an age of machines has proved altogether upsetting to man. The cleverness and dexterity of the false philosophies of mechanism belie their very mechanistic contentions. The fatalistic agility of the mind of a materialist forever disproves his assertions that the universe is a blind and purposeless energy phenomenon.

The mechanistic naturalism of some supposedly educated men and the thoughtless secularism of the man in the street are both exclusively concerned with *things;* they are barren of all real values, sanctions, and satisfactions of a spiritual nature, as well as being devoid of faith, hope, and eternal assurances. One of the great troubles with modern life is that man thinks he is too busy to find time for spiritual meditation and religious devotion.

Materialism reduces man to a soulless automaton and constitutes him merely an arithmetical symbol finding a helpless place in the mathematical formula of an unromantic and mechanistic universe. But whence comes all this vast universe of mathematics without a Master Mathematician? Science may expatiate on the conservation of matter, but religion validates the conservation of men's souls—it concerns their experience with spiritual realities and eternal values.

The materialistic sociologist of today surveys a community, makes a report thereon, and leaves the people as he found them. Nineteen hundred years ago, unlearned Galileans surveyed Jesus giving his life as a spiritual contribution to man's inner experience and then went out and turned the whole Roman Empire upside down.

But religious leaders are making a great mistake when they try to call modern man to spiritual battle with the trumpet blasts of the Middle Ages. Religion must provide itself with new and up-to-date slogans. Neither democracy nor any other political panacea will take the place of spiritual progress. False religions may represent an evasion of reality, but Jesus in his gospel introduced mortal man to the very entrance upon an eternal reality of spiritual progression.

To say that mind "emerged" from matter explains nothing. If the universe were merely a mechanism and mind were unapart from matter, we would never have two differing interpretations of any observed phenomenon. The concepts of truth, beauty, and goodness are not inherent in either physics or chemistry. A machine cannot *know,* much less know truth, hunger for righteousness, and cherish goodness.

Science may be physical, but the mind of the truth-discerning scientist is at once supermaterial. Matter knows not truth, neither can it love mercy nor delight in spiritual realities. Moral convictions based on spiritual enlightenment and rooted in human experience are just as real and certain as mathematical deductions based on physical observations, but on another and higher level.

If men were only machines, they would react more or less uniformly to a material universe. Individuality, much less personality, would be nonexistent.

The fact of the absolute mechanism of Paradise at the center of the universe of universes, in the presence of the unqualified volition of the Second Source and Center, makes forever certain that determiners are not the exclusive law of the cosmos. Materialism is there, but it is not exclusive; mechanism is there, but it is not unqualified; determinism is there, but it is not alone.

The finite universe of matter would eventually become uniform and deterministic but for the combined presence of mind and spirit. The influence of the cosmic mind constantly injects spontaneity into even the material worlds.

Freedom or initiative in any realm of existence is directly proportional to the degree of spiritual influence and cosmic-mind control; that is, in human experience, the degree of the actuality of doing "the Father's will." And so, when you once start out to find God, that is the conclusive proof that God has already found you.

The sincere pursuit of goodness, beauty, and truth leads to God. And every scientific discovery demonstrates the existence of both freedom and uniformity in the universe. The discoverer was free to make the discovery. The thing discovered is real and apparently uniform, or else it could not have become known as a *thing.*

7. THE VULNERABILITY OF MATERIALISM

How foolish it is for material-minded man to allow such vulnerable theories as those of a mechanistic universe to deprive him of the vast spiritual resources of the personal experience of true religion. Facts never quarrel with real spiritual faith; theories may. Better that science should be devoted to the destruction of superstition rather than attempting the overthrow of religious faith—human belief in spiritual realities and divine values.

Science should do for man materially what religion does for him spiritually: extend the horizon of life and enlarge his personality. True science can have no lasting quarrel with true religion. The "scientific method" is merely an intellectual yardstick wherewith to measure material adventures and physical achievements. But being material and wholly intellectual, it is utterly useless in the evaluation of spiritual realities and religious experiences.

The inconsistency of the modern mechanist is: If this were merely a material universe and man only a machine, such a man would be wholly unable to recognize himself as such a machine, and likewise would such a machine-man be wholly unconscious of the fact of the existence of such a material universe. The materialistic dismay and despair of a mechanistic science has failed to recognize the fact of the spirit-indwelt mind of the scientist whose very supermaterial insight formulates these mistaken and self-contradictory *concepts* of a materialistic universe.

Paradise values of eternity and infinity, of truth, beauty, and goodness, are concealed within the facts of the phenomena of the universes of time and space. But it requires the eye of faith in a spirit-born mortal to detect and discern these spiritual values.

The realities and values of spiritual progress are not a "psychologic projection"—a mere glorified daydream of the material mind. Such things are the spiritual forecasts of the indwelling Adjuster, the spirit of God living in the mind of man. And let not your dabblings with the faintly glimpsed findings of "relativity" disturb your concepts of the eternity and infinity of God. And in all your solicitation concerning the necessity for *self-expression* do not make the mistake of failing to provide for *Adjuster-expression,* the manifestation of your real and better self.

If this were only a material universe, material man would never be able to arrive at the concept of the mechanistic character of such an exclusively material existence. This very *mechanistic concept* of the universe is in itself a nonmaterial phenomenon of mind, and all mind is of nonmaterial origin, no matter how thoroughly it may appear to be materially conditioned and mechanistically controlled.

The partially evolved mental mechanism of mortal man is not overendowed with consistency and wisdom. Man's conceit often outruns his reason and eludes his logic.

The very pessimism of the most pessimistic materialist is, in and of itself, sufficient proof that the universe of the pessimist is not wholly material. Both optimism and pessimism are concept reactions in a mind conscious of *values* as well as of *facts.* If the universe were truly what the materialist regards it to be, man as a human machine would then be devoid of all conscious recognition of that very *fact.* Without the consciousness of the concept of *values* within the spirit-born mind, the fact of universe materialism and the mechanistic phenomena of universe operation would be wholly unrecognized by man. One machine cannot be conscious of the nature or value of another machine.

A mechanistic philosophy of life and the universe cannot be scientific because science recognizes and deals only with materials and facts. Philosophy is inevitably superscientific. Man is a material fact of nature, but his *life* is a phenomenon which transcends the material levels of nature in that it exhibits the control attributes of mind and the creative qualities of spirit.

The sincere effort of man to become a mechanist represents the tragic phenomenon of that man's futile effort to commit intellectual and moral suicide. But he cannot do it.

If the universe were only material and man only a machine, there would be no science to embolden the scientist to postulate this mechanization of the universe. Machines cannot measure, classify, nor evaluate themselves. Such a scientific piece of work could be executed only by some entity of supermachine status.

If universe reality is only one vast machine, then man must be outside of the universe and apart from it in order to recognize such a *fact* and become conscious of the *insight* of such an *evaluation.*

If man is only a machine, by what technique does this man come to *believe* or claim to *know* that he is only a machine? The experience of self-conscious evaluation of one's self is never an attribute of a mere machine. A self-conscious and avowed mechanist is the best possible answer to mechanism. If materialism were a fact, there could be no self-conscious mechanist. It is also true that one must first be a moral person before one can perform immoral acts.

The very claim of materialism implies a supermaterial consciousness of the mind which presumes to assert such dogmas. A mechanism might deteriorate, but it could never progress. Machines do not think, create, dream, aspire, idealize, hunger for truth, or thirst for righteousness. They do not motivate their lives with the passion to serve other machines and to choose as their goal of eternal progression the sublime task of finding God and striving to be like him. Machines are never intellectual, emotional, aesthetic, ethical, moral, or spiritual.

Art proves that man is not mechanistic, but it does not prove that he is spiritually immortal. Art is mortal morontia, the intervening field between man, the material, and man, the spiritual. Poetry is an effort to escape from material realities to spiritual values.

In a high civilization, art humanizes science, while in turn it is spiritualized by true religion—insight into spiritual and eternal values. Art represents the human and time-space evaluation of reality. Religion *is* the divine embrace of cosmic values and connotes eternal progression in spiritual ascension and expansion. The art of time is dangerous only when it becomes blind to the spirit standards of the divine patterns which eternity reflects as the reality shadows of time. True art is the effective manipulation of the material things of life; religion is the ennobling transformation of the material facts of life, and it never ceases in its spiritual evaluation of art.

How foolish to presume that an automaton could conceive a philosophy of automatism, and how ridiculous that it should presume to form such a concept of other and fellow automatons!

Any scientific interpretation of the material universe is valueless unless it provides due recognition for the *scientist.* No appreciation of art is genuine unless it accords recognition to the *artist.* No evaluation of morals is worth while unless it includes the *moralist.* No recognition of philosophy is edifying if it ignores the *philosopher,* and religion cannot exist without the real experience of the *religionist* who, in and through this very experience, is seeking to find God and to know him. Likewise is the universe of universes without significance apart from the I AM, the infinite God who made it and unceasingly manages it.

Mechanists—humanists—tend to drift with the material currents. Idealists and spiritists *dare* to use their oars with intelligence and vigor in order to modify the apparently purely material course of the energy streams.

Science lives by the mathematics of the mind; music expresses the tempo of the emotions. Religion is the spiritual rhythm of the soul in time-space harmony with the higher and eternal melody measurements of Infinity. Religious experience is something in human life which is truly supermathematical.

In language, an alphabet represents the mechanism of materialism, while the words expressive of the meaning of a thousand thoughts, grand ideas, and noble ideals—of love and hate, of cowardice and courage—represent the performances of mind within the scope defined by both material and spiritual law, directed by the assertion of the will of personality, and limited by the inherent situational endowment.

The universe is not like the laws, mechanisms, and the uniformities which the scientist discovers, and which he comes to regard as science, but rather like the curious, thinking, choosing, creative, combining, and discriminating *scientist* who thus observes universe phenomena and classifies the mathematical facts inherent in the mechanistic phases of the material side of creation. Neither is the universe like the art of the artist, but rather like the striving, dreaming, aspiring, and advancing *artist* who seeks to transcend the world of material things in an effort to achieve a spiritual goal.

The scientist, not science, perceives the reality of an evolving and advancing universe of energy and matter. The artist, not art, demonstrates the existence of the transient morontia world intervening between material existence and spiritual liberty. The religionist, not religion, proves the existence of the spirit realities and divine values which are to be encountered in the progress of eternity.

8. SECULAR TOTALITARIANISM

But even after materialism and mechanism have been more or less vanquished, the devastating influence of twentieth-century secularism will still blight the spiritual experience of millions of unsuspecting souls.

Modern secularism has been fostered by two world-wide influences. The father of secularism was the narrow-minded and godless attitude of nineteenth- and twentieth-century so-called science—atheistic science. The mother of modern secularism was the totalitarian medieval Christian church. Secularism had its inception as a rising protest against the almost complete domination of Western civilization by the institutionalized Christian church.

At the time of this revelation, the prevailing intellectual and philosophical climate of both European and American life is decidedly secular—humanistic. For three hundred years Western thinking has been progressively secularized. Religion has become more and more a nominal influence, largely a ritualistic exercise. The majority of professed Christians of Western civilization are unwittingly actual secularists.

It required a great power, a mighty influence, to free the thinking and living of the Western peoples from the withering grasp of a totalitarian ecclesiastical domination. Secularism did break the bonds of church control, and now in turn it threatens to establish a new and godless type of mastery over the hearts and minds of modern man. The tyrannical and dictatorial political state is the direct offspring of scientific materialism and philosophic secularism. Secularism no sooner frees man from the domination of the institutionalized church than it sells him into slavish bondage to the totalitarian state. Secularism frees man from ecclesiastical slavery only to betray him into the tyranny of political and economic slavery.

Materialism denies God, secularism simply ignores him; at least that was the earlier attitude. More recently, secularism has assumed a more militant attitude, assuming to take the place of the religion whose totalitarian bondage it onetime resisted. Twentieth-century secularism tends to affirm that man does not need God. But beware! this godless philosophy of human society will lead only to unrest, animosity, unhappiness, war, and world-wide disaster.

Secularism can never bring peace to mankind. Nothing can take the place of God in human society. But mark you well! do not be quick to surrender the beneficent gains of the secular revolt from ecclesiastical totalitarianism. Western civilization today enjoys many liberties and satisfactions as a result of the secular revolt. The great mistake of secularism was this: In revolting against the almost total control of life by religious authority, and after attaining the liberation from such ecclesiastical tyranny, the secularists went on to institute a revolt against God himself, sometimes tacitly and sometimes openly.

To the secularistic revolt you owe the amazing creativity of American industrialism and the unprecedented material progress of Western civilization. And because the secularistic revolt went too far and lost sight of God and *true* religion, there also followed the unlooked-for harvest of world wars and international unsettledness.

It is not necessary to sacrifice faith in God in order to enjoy the blessings of the modern secularistic revolt: tolerance, social service, democratic government, and civil liberties. It was not necessary for the secularists to antagonize true religion in order to promote science and to advance education.

But secularism is not the sole parent of all these recent gains in the enlargement of living. Behind the gains of the twentieth century are not only science and secularism but also the unrecognized and unacknowledged spiritual workings of the life and teaching of Jesus of Nazareth.

Without God, without religion, scientific secularism can never co-ordinate its forces, harmonize its divergent and rivalrous interests, races, and nationalisms. This secularistic human society, notwithstanding its unparalleled materialistic achievement, is slowly disintegrating. The chief cohesive force resisting this disintegration of antagonism is nationalism. And nationalism is the chief barrier to world peace.

The inherent weakness of secularism is that it discards ethics and religion for politics and power. You simply cannot establish the brotherhood of men while ignoring or denying the fatherhood of God.

Secular social and political optimism is an illusion. Without God, neither freedom and liberty, nor property and wealth will lead to peace.

The complete secularization of science, education, industry, and society can lead only to disaster. During the first third of the twentieth century Urantians killed more human beings than were killed during the whole of the Christian dispensation up to that time. And this is only the beginning of the dire harvest of materialism and secularism; still more terrible destruction is yet to come.

9. CHRISTIANITY'S PROBLEM

Do not overlook the value of your spiritual heritage, the river of truth running down through the centuries, even to the barren times of a materialistic and secular age. In all your worthy efforts to rid yourselves of the superstitious creeds of past ages, make sure that you hold fast the eternal truth. But be patient! when the present superstition revolt is over, the truths of Jesus' gospel will persist gloriously to illuminate a new and better way.

But paganized and socialized Christianity stands in need of new contact with the uncompromised teachings of Jesus; it languishes for lack of a new vision of the Master's life on earth. A new and fuller revelation of the religion of Jesus is destined to conquer an empire of materialistic secularism and to overthrow a world sway of mechanistic naturalism. Urantia is now quivering on the very brink of one of its most amazing and enthralling epochs of social readjustment, moral quickening, and spiritual enlightenment.

The teachings of Jesus, even though greatly modified, survived the mystery cults of their birthtime, the ignorance and superstition of the dark ages, and are even now slowly triumphing over the materialism, mechanism, and secularism of the twentieth century. And such times of great testing and threatened defeat are always times of great revelation.

Religion does need new leaders, spiritual men and women who will dare to depend solely on Jesus and his incomparable teachings. If Christianity persists in neglecting its spiritual mission while it continues to busy itself with social and material problems, the spiritual renaissance must await the coming of these new teachers of Jesus' religion who will be exclusively devoted to the spiritual regeneration of men. And then will these spirit-born souls quickly supply the leadership and inspiration requisite for the social, moral, economic, and political reorganization of the world.

The modern age will refuse to accept a religion which is inconsistent with facts and out of harmony with its highest conceptions of truth, beauty, and goodness. The hour is striking for a rediscovery of the true and original foundations of present-day distorted and compromised Christianity—the real life and teachings of Jesus.

Primitive man lived a life of superstitious bondage to religious fear. Modern, civilized men dread the thought of falling under the dominance of strong religious convictions. Thinking man has always feared to be *held* by a religion. When a strong and moving religion threatens to dominate him, he invariably tries to rationalize, traditionalize, and institutionalize it, thereby hoping to gain control of it. By such procedure, even a revealed religion becomes man-made and man-dominated. Modern men and women of intelligence evade the religion of Jesus because of their fears of what it will do *to* them—and *with* them. And all such fears are well founded. The religion of Jesus does, indeed, dominate and transform its believers, demanding that men dedicate their lives to seeking for a knowledge of the will of the Father in heaven and requiring that the energies of living be consecrated to the unselfish service of the brotherhood of man.

Selfish men and women simply will not pay such a price for even the greatest spiritual treasure ever offered mortal man. Only when man has become sufficiently disillusioned by the sorrowful disappointments attendant upon the foolish and deceptive pursuits of selfishness, and subsequent to the discovery of the barrenness of formalized religion, will he be disposed to turn wholeheartedly to the gospel of the kingdom, the religion of Jesus of Nazareth.

The world needs more firsthand religion. Even Christianity—the best of the religions of the twentieth century—is not only a religion *about* Jesus, but it is so largely one which men experience secondhand. They take their religion wholly as handed down by their accepted religious teachers. What an awakening the world would experience if it could only see Jesus as he really lived on earth and know, firsthand, his life-giving teachings! Descriptive words of things beautiful cannot thrill like the sight thereof, neither can creedal words inspire men's souls like the experience of knowing the presence of God. But expectant faith will ever keep the hope-door of man's soul open for the entrance of the eternal spiritual realities of the divine values of the worlds beyond.

Christianity has dared to lower its ideals before the challenge of human greed, war-madness, and the lust for power; but the religion of Jesus stands as the unsullied and transcendent spiritual summons, calling to the best there is in man to rise above all these legacies of animal evolution and, by grace, attain the moral heights of true human destiny.

Christianity is threatened by slow death from formalism, overorganization, intellectualism, and other nonspiritual trends. The modern Christian church is not such a brotherhood of dynamic believers as Jesus commissioned continuously to effect the spiritual transformation of successive generations of mankind.

So-called Christianity has become a social and cultural movement as well as a religious belief and practice. The stream of modern Christianity drains many an ancient pagan swamp and many a barbarian morass; many olden cultural watersheds drain into this present-day cultural stream as well as the high Galilean tablelands which are supposed to be its exclusive source.

10. THE FUTURE

Christianity has indeed done a great service for this world, but what is now most needed is Jesus. The world needs to see Jesus living again on earth in the experience of spirit-born mortals who effectively reveal the Master to all men. It is futile to talk about a revival of primitive Christianity; you must go forward from where you find yourselves. Modern culture must become spiritually baptized with a new revelation of Jesus' life and illuminated with a new understanding of his gospel of eternal salvation. And when Jesus becomes thus lifted up, he will draw all men to himself. Jesus' disciples should be more than conquerors, even overflowing sources of inspiration and enhanced living to all men. Religion is only an exalted humanism until it is made divine by the discovery of the reality of the presence of God in personal experience.

The beauty and sublimity, the humanity and divinity, the simplicity and uniqueness, of Jesus' life on earth present such a striking and appealing picture of man-saving and God-revealing that the theologians and philosophers of all time should be effectively restrained from daring to form creeds or create theological systems of spiritual bondage out of such a transcendental bestowal of God in the form of man. In Jesus the universe produced a mortal man in whom the spirit of love triumphed over the material handicaps of time and overcame the fact of physical origin.

Ever bear in mind—God and men need each other. They are mutually necessary to the full and final attainment of eternal personality experience in the divine destiny of universe finality.

"The kingdom of God is within you" was probably the greatest pronouncement Jesus ever made, next to the declaration that his Father is a living and loving spirit.

In winning souls for the Master, it is not the first mile of compulsion, duty, or convention that will transform man and his world, but rather the *second* mile of free service and liberty-loving devotion that betokens the Jesusonian reaching forth to grasp his brother in love and sweep him on under spiritual guidance toward the higher and divine goal of mortal existence. Christianity even now willingly goes the *first* mile, but mankind languishes and stumbles along in moral darkness because there are so few genuine second-milers—so few professed followers of Jesus who really live and love as he taught his disciples to live and love and serve.

The call to the adventure of building a new and transformed human society by means of the spiritual rebirth of Jesus' brotherhood of the kingdom should thrill all who believe in him as men have not been stirred since the days when they walked about on earth as his companions in the flesh.

No social system or political regime which denies the reality of God can contribute in any constructive and lasting manner to the advancement of human civilization. But Christianity, as it is subdivided and secularized today, presents the greatest single obstacle to its further advancement; especially is this true concerning the Orient.

Ecclesiasticism is at once and forever incompatible with that living faith, growing spirit, and firsthand experience of the faith-comrades of Jesus in the brotherhood of man in the spiritual association of the kingdom of heaven. The praiseworthy desire to preserve traditions of past achievement often leads to the defense of outgrown systems of worship. The well-meant desire to foster ancient thought systems effectually prevents the sponsoring of new and adequate means and methods designed to satisfy the spiritual longings of the expanding and advancing minds of modern men. Likewise, the Christian churches of the twentieth century stand as great, but wholly unconscious, obstacles to the immediate advance of the real gospel—the teachings of Jesus of Nazareth.

Many earnest persons who would gladly yield loyalty to the Christ of the gospel find it very difficult enthusiastically to support a church which exhibits so little of the spirit of his life and teachings, and which they have been erroneously taught he founded. Jesus did not found the so-called Christian church, but he has, in every manner consistent with his nature, *fostered* it as the best existent exponent of his lifework on earth.

If the Christian church would only dare to espouse the Master's program, thousands of apparently indifferent youths would rush forward to enlist in such a spiritual undertaking, and they would not hesitate to go all the way through with this great adventure.

Christianity is seriously confronted with the doom embodied in one of its own slogans: "A house divided against itself cannot stand." The non-Christian world will hardly capitulate to a sect-divided Christendom. The living Jesus is the only hope of a possible unification of Christianity. The true church—the Jesus brotherhood—is invisible, spiritual, and is characterized by *unity,* not necessarily by *uniformity.* Uniformity is the earmark of the physical world of mechanistic nature. Spiritual unity is the fruit of faith union with the living Jesus. The visible church should refuse longer to handicap the progress of the invisible and spiritual brotherhood of the kingdom of God. And this brotherhood is destined to become a *living organism* in contrast to an institutionalized social organization. It may well utilize such social organizations, but it must not be supplanted by them.

But the Christianity of even the twentieth century must not be despised. It is the product of the combined moral genius of the God-knowing men of many races during many ages, and it has truly been one of the greatest powers for good on earth, and therefore no man should lightly regard it, notwithstanding its inherent and acquired defects. Christianity still contrives to move the minds of reflective men with mighty moral emotions.

But there is no excuse for the involvement of the church in commerce and politics; such unholy alliances are a flagrant betrayal of the Master. And the genuine lovers of truth will be slow to forget that this powerful institutionalized church has often dared to smother newborn faith and persecute truth bearers who chanced to appear in unorthodox raiment.

It is all too true that such a church would not have survived unless there had been men in the world who preferred such a style of worship. Many spiritually indolent souls crave an ancient and authoritative religion of ritual and sacred traditions. Human evolution and spiritual progress are hardly sufficient to enable all men to dispense with religious authority. And the invisible brotherhood of the kingdom may well include these family groups of various social and temperamental classes if they are only willing to become truly spirit-led sons of God. But in this brotherhood of Jesus there is no place for sectarian rivalry, group bitterness, nor assertions of moral superiority and spiritual infallibility.

These various groupings of Christians may serve to accommodate numerous different types of would-be believers among the various peoples of Western civilization, but such division of Christendom presents a grave weakness when it attempts to carry the gospel of Jesus to Oriental peoples. These races do not yet understand that there is a *religion of Jesus* separate, and somewhat apart, from Christianity, which has more and more become a *religion about Jesus.*

The great hope of Urantia lies in the possibility of a new revelation of Jesus with a new and enlarged presentation of his saving message which would spiritually unite in loving service the numerous families of his present-day professed followers.

Even secular education could help in this great spiritual renaissance if it would pay more attention to the work of teaching youth how to engage in life planning and character progression. The purpose of all education should be to foster and further the supreme purpose of life, the development of a majestic and well-balanced personality. There is great need for the teaching of moral discipline in the place of so much self-gratification. Upon such a foundation religion may contribute its spiritual incentive to the enlargement and enrichment of mortal life, even to the security and enhancement of life eternal.

Christianity is an extemporized religion, and therefore must it operate in low gear. High-gear spiritual performances must await the new revelation and the more general acceptance of the real religion of Jesus. But Christianity is a mighty religion, seeing that the commonplace disciples of a crucified carpenter set in motion those teachings which conquered the Roman world in three hundred years and then went on to triumph over the barbarians who overthrew Rome. This same Christianity conquered—absorbed and exalted—the whole stream of Hebrew theology and Greek philosophy. And then, when this Christian religion became comatose for more than a thousand years as a result of an overdose of mysteries and paganism, it resurrected itself and virtually reconquered the whole Western world. Christianity contains enough of Jesus' teachings to immortalize it.

If Christianity could only grasp more of Jesus' teachings, it could do so much more in helping modern man to solve his new and increasingly complex problems.

Christianity suffers under a great handicap because it has become identified in the minds of all the world as a part of the social system, the industrial life, and the moral standards of Western civilization; and thus has Christianity unwittingly seemed to sponsor a society which staggers under the guilt of tolerating science without idealism, politics without principles, wealth without work, pleasure without restraint, knowledge without character, power without conscience, and industry without morality.

The hope of modern Christianity is that it should cease to sponsor the social systems and industrial policies of Western civilization while it humbly bows itself before the cross it so valiantly extols, there to learn anew from Jesus of Nazareth the greatest truths mortal man can ever hear—the living gospel of the fatherhood of God and the brotherhood of man.

PAPER 196

THE FAITH OF JESUS

JESUS enjoyed a sublime and wholehearted faith in God. He experienced the ordinary ups and downs of mortal existence, but he never religiously doubted the certainty of God's watchcare and guidance. His faith was the outgrowth of the insight born of the activity of the divine presence, his indwelling Adjuster. His faith was neither traditional nor merely intellectual; it was wholly personal and purely spiritual.

The human Jesus saw God as being holy, just, and great, as well as being true, beautiful, and good. All these attributes of divinity he focused in his mind as the "will of the Father in heaven." Jesus' God was at one and the same time "The Holy One of Israel" and "The living and loving Father in heaven." The concept of God as a Father was not original with Jesus, but he exalted and elevated the idea into a sublime experience by achieving a new revelation of God and by proclaiming that every mortal creature is a child of this Father of love, a son of God.

Jesus did not cling to faith in God as would a struggling soul at war with the universe and at death grips with a hostile and sinful world; he did not resort to faith merely as a consolation in the midst of difficulties or as a comfort in threatened despair; faith was not just an illusory compensation for the unpleasant realities and the sorrows of living. In the very face of all the natural difficulties and the temporal contradictions of mortal existence, he experienced the tranquillity of supreme and unquestioned trust in God and felt the tremendous thrill of living, by faith, in the very presence of the heavenly Father. And this triumphant faith was a living experience of actual spirit attainment. Jesus' great contribution to the values of human experience was not that he revealed so many new ideas about the Father in heaven, but rather that he so magnificently and humanly demonstrated a new and higher type of *living faith in God.* Never on all the worlds of this universe, in the life of any one mortal, did God ever become such a *living reality* as in the human experience of Jesus of Nazareth.

In the Master's life on Urantia, this and all other worlds of the local creation discover a new and higher type of religion, religion based on personal spiritual relations with the Universal Father and wholly validated by the supreme authority of genuine personal experience. This living faith of Jesus was more than an intellectual reflection, and it was not a mystic meditation.

Theology may fix, formulate, define, and dogmatize faith, but in the human life of Jesus faith was personal, living, original, spontaneous, and purely spiritual. This faith was not reverence for tradition nor a mere intellectual belief which he held as a sacred creed, but rather a sublime experience and a profound conviction which *securely held him.* His faith was so real and all-encompassing that it absolutely swept away any spiritual doubts and effectively destroyed every conflicting desire. Nothing was able to tear him away from the spiritual anchorage of this fervent, sublime, and undaunted faith. Even in the face of apparent defeat or in the throes of disappointment and threatening despair, he calmly stood in the divine presence free from fear and fully conscious of spiritual invincibility. Jesus enjoyed the invigorating assurance of the possession of unflinching faith, and in each of life's trying situations he unfailingly exhibited an unquestioning loyalty to the Father's will. And this superb faith was undaunted even by the cruel and crushing threat of an ignominious death.

In a religious genius, strong spiritual faith so many times leads directly to disastrous fanaticism, to exaggeration of the religious ego, but it was not so with Jesus. He was not unfavorably affected in his practical life by his extraordinary faith and spirit attainment because this spiritual exaltation was a wholly unconscious and spontaneous soul expression of his personal experience with God.

The all-consuming and indomitable spiritual faith of Jesus never became fanatical, for it never attempted to run away with his well-balanced intellectual judgments concerning the proportional values of practical and commonplace social, economic, and moral life situations. The Son of Man was a splendidly unified human personality; he was a perfectly endowed divine being; he was also magnificently co-ordinated as a combined human and divine being functioning on earth as a single personality. Always did the Master co-ordinate the faith of the soul with the wisdom-appraisals of seasoned experience. Personal faith, spiritual hope, and moral devotion were always correlated in a matchless religious unity of harmonious association with the keen realization of the reality and sacredness of all human loyalties—personal honor, family love, religious obligation, social duty, and economic necessity.

The faith of Jesus visualized all spirit values as being found in the kingdom of God; therefore he said, "Seek first the kingdom of heaven." Jesus saw in the advanced and ideal fellowship of the kingdom the achievement and fulfillment of the "will of God." The very heart of the prayer which he taught his disciples was, "Your kingdom come; your will be done." Having thus conceived of the kingdom as comprising the will of God, he devoted himself to the cause of its realization with amazing self-forgetfulness and unbounded enthusiasm. But in all his intense mission and throughout his extraordinary life there never appeared the fury of the fanatic nor the superficial frothiness of the religious egotist.

The Master's entire life was consistently conditioned by this living faith, this sublime religious experience. This spiritual attitude wholly dominated his thinking and feeling, his believing and praying, his teaching and preaching. This personal faith of a son in the certainty and security of the guidance and protection of the heavenly Father imparted to his unique life a profound endowment of spiritual reality. And yet, despite this very deep consciousness of close relationship with divinity, this Galilean, God's Galilean, when addressed as Good Teacher, instantly replied, "Why do you call me good?" When we stand confronted by such splendid self-forgetfulness, we begin to understand how the Universal Father found it possible so fully to manifest himself to him and reveal himself through him to the mortals of the realms.

Jesus brought to God, as a man of the realm, the greatest of all offerings: the consecration and dedication of his own will to the majestic service of doing the divine will. Jesus always and consistently interpreted religion wholly in terms of the Father's will. When you study the career of the Master, as concerns prayer or any other feature of the religious life, look not so much for what he taught as for what he did. Jesus never prayed as a religious duty. To him prayer was a sincere expression of spiritual attitude, a declaration of soul loyalty, a recital of personal devotion, an expression of thanksgiving, an avoidance of emotional tension, a prevention of conflict, an exaltation of intellection, an ennoblement of desire, a vindication of moral decision, an enrichment of thought, an invigoration of higher inclinations, a consecration of impulse, a clarification of viewpoint, a declaration of faith, a transcendental surrender of will, a sublime assertion of confidence, a revelation of courage, the proclamation of discovery, a confession of supreme devotion, the validation of consecration, a technique for the adjustment of difficulties, and the mighty mobilization of the combined soul powers to withstand all human tendencies toward selfishness, evil, and sin. He lived just such a life of prayerful consecration to the doing of his Father's will and ended his life triumphantly with just such a prayer. The secret of his unparalleled religious life was this consciousness of the presence of God; and he attained it by intelligent prayer and sincere worship—unbroken communion with God—and not by leadings, voices, visions, or extraordinary religious practices.

In the earthly life of Jesus, religion was a living experience, a direct and personal movement from spiritual reverence to practical righteousness. The faith of Jesus bore the transcendent fruits of the divine spirit. His faith was not immature and credulous like that of a child, but in many ways it did resemble the unsuspecting trust of the child mind. Jesus trusted God much as the child trusts a parent. He had a profound confidence in the universe—just such a trust as the child has in its parental environment. Jesus' wholehearted faith in the fundamental goodness of the universe very much resembled the child's trust in the security of its earthly surroundings. He depended on the heavenly Father as a child leans upon its earthly parent, and his fervent faith never for one moment doubted the certainty of the heavenly Father's overcare. He was not disturbed seriously by fears, doubts, and skepticism. Unbelief did not inhibit the free and original expression of his life. He combined the stalwart and intelligent courage of a full-grown man with the sincere and trusting optimism of a believing child. His faith grew to such heights of trust that it was devoid of fear.

The faith of Jesus attained the purity of a child's trust. His faith was so absolute and undoubting that it responded to the charm of the contact of fellow beings and to the wonders of the universe. His sense of dependence on the divine was so complete and so confident that it yielded the joy and the assurance of absolute personal security. There was no hesitating pretense in his religious experience. In this giant intellect of the full-grown man the faith of the child reigned supreme in all matters relating to the religious consciousness. It is not strange that he once said, "Except you become as a little child, you shall not enter the kingdom." Notwithstanding that Jesus' faith was *childlike,* it was in no sense *childish.*

Jesus does not require his disciples to believe in him but rather to believe *with* him, believe in the reality of the love of God and in full confidence accept the security of the assurance of sonship with the heavenly Father. The Master desires that all his followers should fully share his transcendent faith. Jesus most touchingly challenged his followers, not only to believe *what* he believed, but also to believe *as* he believed. This is the full significance of his one supreme requirement, "Follow me."

Jesus' earthly life was devoted to one great purpose—doing the Father's will, living the human life religiously and by faith. The faith of Jesus was trusting, like that of a child, but it was wholly free from presumption. He made robust and manly decisions, courageously faced manifold disappointments, resolutely surmounted extraordinary difficulties, and unflinchingly confronted the stern requirements of duty. It required a strong will and an unfailing confidence to believe what Jesus believed and *as* he believed.

1. JESUS—THE MAN

Jesus' devotion to the Father's will and the service of man was even more than mortal decision and human determination; it was a wholehearted consecration of himself to such an unreserved bestowal of love. No matter how great the fact of the sovereignty of Michael, you must not take the human Jesus away from men. The Master has ascended on high as a man, as well as God; he belongs to men; men belong to him. How unfortunate that religion itself should be so misinterpreted as to take the human Jesus away from struggling mortals! Let not the discussions of the humanity or the divinity of the Christ obscure the saving truth that Jesus of Nazareth was a religious man who, by faith, achieved the knowing and the doing of the will of God; he was the most truly religious man who has ever lived on Urantia.

The time is ripe to witness the figurative resurrection of the human Jesus from his burial tomb amidst the theological traditions and the religious dogmas of nineteen centuries. Jesus of Nazareth must not be longer sacrificed to even the splendid concept of the glorified Christ. What a transcendent service if, through this revelation, the Son of Man should be recovered from the tomb of traditional theology and be presented as the living Jesus to the church that bears his name, and to all other religions! Surely the Christian fellowship of believers will not hesitate to make such adjustments of faith and of practices of living as will enable it to "follow after" the Master in the demonstration of his real life of religious devotion to the doing of his Father's will and of consecration to the unselfish service of man. Do professed Christians fear the exposure of a self-sufficient and unconsecrated fellowship of social respectability and selfish economic maladjustment? Does institutional Christianity fear the possible jeopardy, or even the overthrow, of traditional ecclesiastical authority if the Jesus of Galilee is reinstated in the minds and souls of mortal men as the ideal of personal religious living? Indeed, the social readjustments, the economic transformations, the moral rejuvenations, and the religious revisions of Christian civilization would be drastic and revolutionary if the living religion of Jesus should suddenly supplant the theologic religion about Jesus.

To "follow Jesus" means to personally share his religious faith and to enter into the spirit of the Master's life of unselfish service for man. One of the most important things in human living is to find out what Jesus believed, to discover his ideals, and to strive for the achievement of his exalted life purpose. Of all human knowledge, that which is of greatest value is to know the religious life of Jesus and how he lived it.

The common people heard Jesus gladly, and they will again respond to the presentation of his sincere human life of consecrated religious motivation if such truths shall again be proclaimed to the world. The people heard him gladly because he was one of them, an unpretentious layman; the world's greatest religious teacher was indeed a layman.

It should not be the aim of kingdom believers literally to imitate the outward life of Jesus in the flesh but rather to share his faith; to trust God as he trusted God and to believe in men as he believed in men. Jesus never argued about either the fatherhood of God or the brotherhood of men; he was a living illustration of the one and a profound demonstration of the other.

Just as men must progress from the consciousness of the human to the realization of the divine, so did Jesus ascend from the nature of man to the consciousness of the nature of God. And the Master made this great ascent from the human to the divine by the conjoint achievement of the faith of his mortal intellect and the acts of his indwelling Adjuster. The fact-realization of the attainment of totality of divinity (all the while fully conscious of the reality of humanity) was attended by seven stages of faith consciousness of progressive divinization. These stages of progressive self-realization were marked off by the following extraordinary events in the Master's bestowal experience:

1. The arrival of the Thought Adjuster.
2. The messenger of Immanuel who appeared to him at Jerusalem when he was about twelve years old.
3. The manifestations attendant upon his baptism.
4. The experiences on the Mount of Transfiguration.
5. The morontia resurrection.
6. The spirit ascension.
7. The final embrace of the Paradise Father, conferring unlimited sovereignty of his universe.

2. THE RELIGION OF JESUS

Some day a reformation in the Christian church may strike deep enough to get back to the unadulterated religious teachings of Jesus, the author and finisher of our faith. You may *preach* a religion *about* Jesus, but, perforce, you must *live* the religion *of* Jesus. In the enthusiasm of Pentecost, Peter unintentionally inaugurated a new religion, the religion of the risen and glorified Christ. The Apostle Paul later on transformed this new gospel into Christianity, a religion embodying his own theologic views and portraying his own *personal experience* with the Jesus of the Damascus road. The gospel of the kingdom is founded on the personal religious experience of the Jesus of Galilee; Christianity is founded almost exclusively on the personal religious experience of the Apostle Paul. Almost the whole of the New Testament is devoted, not to the portrayal of the significant and inspiring religious life of Jesus, but to a discussion of Paul's religious experience and to a portrayal of his personal religious convictions. The only notable exceptions to this statement, aside from certain parts of Matthew, Mark, and Luke, are the Book of Hebrews and the Epistle of James. Even Peter, in his writing, only once reverted to the personal religious life of his Master. The New Testament is a superb Christian document, but it is only meagerly Jesusonian.

Jesus' life in the flesh portrays a transcendent religious growth from the early ideas of primitive awe and human reverence up through years of personal spiritual communion until he finally arrived at that advanced and exalted status of the consciousness of his oneness with the Father. And thus, in one short life, did Jesus traverse that experience of religious spiritual progression which man begins on earth and ordinarily achieves only at the conclusion of his long sojourn in the spirit training schools of the successive levels of the pre-Paradise career. Jesus progressed from a purely human consciousness of the faith certainties of personal religious experience to the sublime spiritual heights of the positive realization of his divine nature and to the consciousness of his close association with the Universal Father in the management of a universe. He progressed from the humble status of mortal dependence which prompted him spontaneously to say to the one who called him Good Teacher, "Why do you call me good? None is good but God," to that sublime consciousness of achieved divinity which led him to exclaim, "Which one of you convicts me of sin?" And this progressing ascent from the human to the divine was an exclusively mortal achievement. And when he had thus attained divinity, he was still the same human Jesus, the Son of Man as well as the Son of God.

Mark, Matthew, and Luke retain something of the picture of the human Jesus as he engaged in the superb struggle to ascertain the divine will and to do that will. John presents a picture of the triumphant Jesus as he walked on earth in the full consciousness of divinity. The great mistake that has been made by those who have studied the Master's life is that some have conceived of him as entirely human, while others have thought of him as only divine. Throughout his entire experience he was truly both human and divine, even as he yet is.

But the greatest mistake was made in that, while the human Jesus was recognized as *having* a religion, the divine Jesus (Christ) almost overnight became a religion. Paul's Christianity made sure of the adoration of the divine Christ, but it almost wholly lost sight of the struggling and valiant human Jesus of Galilee, who, by the valor of his personal religious faith and the heroism of his indwelling Adjuster, ascended from the lowly levels of humanity to become one with divinity, thus becoming the new and living way whereby all mortals may so ascend from humanity to divinity. Mortals in all stages of spirituality and on all worlds may find in the personal life of Jesus that which will strengthen and inspire them as they progress from the lowest spirit levels up to the highest divine values, from the beginning to the end of all personal religious experience.

At the time of the writing of the New Testament, the authors not only most profoundly believed in the divinity of the risen Christ, but they also devotedly and sincerely believed in his immediate return to earth to consummate the heavenly kingdom. This strong faith in the Lord's immediate return had much to do with the tendency to omit from the record those references which portrayed the purely human experiences and attributes of the Master. The whole Christian movement tended away from the human picture of Jesus of Nazareth toward the exaltation of the risen Christ, the glorified and soon-returning Lord Jesus Christ.

Jesus founded the religion of personal experience in doing the will of God and serving the human brotherhood; Paul founded a religion in which the glorified Jesus became the object of worship and the brotherhood consisted of fellow believers in the divine Christ. In the bestowal of Jesus these two concepts were potential in his divine-human life, and it is indeed a pity that his followers failed to create a unified religion which might have given proper recognition to both the human and the divine natures of the Master as they were inseparably bound up in his earth life and so gloriously set forth in the original gospel of the kingdom.

You would be neither shocked nor disturbed by some of Jesus' strong pronouncements if you would only remember that he was the world's most wholehearted and devoted religionist. He was a wholly consecrated mortal, unreservedly dedicated to doing his Father's will. Many of his apparently hard sayings were more of a personal confession of faith and a pledge of devotion than commands to his followers. And it was this very singleness of purpose and unselfish devotion that enabled him to effect such extraordinary progress in the conquest of the human mind in one short life. Many of his declarations should be considered as a confession of what he demanded of himself rather than what he required of all his followers. In his devotion to the cause of the kingdom, Jesus burned all bridges behind him; he sacrificed all hindrances to the doing of his Father's will.

Jesus blessed the poor because they were usually sincere and pious; he condemned the rich because they were usually wanton and irreligious. He would equally condemn the irreligious pauper and commend the consecrated and worshipful man of wealth.

Jesus led men to feel at home in the world; he delivered them from the slavery of taboo and taught them that the world was not fundamentally evil. He did not long to escape from his earthly life; he mastered a technique of acceptably doing the Father's will while in the flesh. He attained an idealistic religious life in the very midst of a realistic world. Jesus did not share Paul's pessimistic view of humankind. The Master looked upon men as the sons of God and foresaw a magnificent and eternal future for those who chose survival. He was not a moral skeptic; he viewed man positively, not negatively. He saw most men as weak rather than wicked, more distraught than depraved. But no matter what their status, they were all God's children and his brethren.

He taught men to place a high value upon themselves in time and in eternity. Because of this high estimate which Jesus placed upon men, he was willing to spend himself in the unremitting service of humankind. And it was this infinite worth of the finite that made the golden rule a vital factor in his religion. What mortal can fail to be uplifted by the extraordinary faith Jesus has in him?

Jesus offered no rules for social advancement; his was a religious mission, and religion is an exclusively individual experience. The ultimate goal of society's most advanced achievement can never hope to transcend Jesus' brotherhood of men based on the recognition of the fatherhood of God. The ideal of all social attainment can be realized only in the coming of this divine kingdom.

3. THE SUPREMACY OF RELIGION

Personal, spiritual religious experience is an efficient solvent for most mortal difficulties; it is an effective sorter, evaluator, and adjuster of all human problems. Religion does not remove or destroy human troubles, but it does dissolve, absorb, illuminate, and transcend them. True religion unifies the personality for effective adjustment to all mortal requirements. Religious faith—the positive leading of the indwelling divine presence—unfailingly enables the God-knowing man to bridge that gulf existing between the intellectual logic which recognizes the Universal First Cause as *It* and those positive affirmations of the soul which aver this First Cause is *He,* the heavenly Father of Jesus' gospel, the personal God of human salvation.

There are just three elements in universal reality: fact, idea, and relation. The religious consciousness identifies these realities as science, philosophy, and truth. Philosophy would be inclined to view these activities as reason, wisdom, and faith—physical reality, intellectual reality, and spiritual reality. We are in the habit of designating these realities as thing, meaning, and value.

The progressive comprehension of reality is the equivalent of approaching God. The finding of God, the consciousness of identity with reality, is the equivalent of the experiencing of self-completion—self-entirety, self-totality. The experiencing of total reality is the full realization of God, the finality of the God-knowing experience.

The full summation of human life is the knowledge that man is educated by fact, ennobled by wisdom, and saved—justified—by religious faith.

Physical certainty consists in the logic of science; moral certainty, in the wisdom of philosophy; spiritual certainty, in the truth of genuine religious experience.

The mind of man can attain high levels of spiritual insight and corresponding spheres of divinity of values because it is not wholly material. There is a spirit nucleus in the mind of man—the Adjuster of the divine presence. There are three separate evidences of this spirit indwelling of the human mind:

1. Humanitarian fellowship—love. The purely animal mind may be gregarious for self-protection, but only the spirit-indwelt intellect is unselfishly altruistic and unconditionally loving.

2. Interpretation of the universe—wisdom. Only the spirit-indwelt mind can comprehend that the universe is friendly to the individual.

3. Spiritual evaluation of life—worship. Only the spirit-indwelt man can realize the divine presence and seek to attain a fuller experience in and with this foretaste of divinity.

The human mind does not create real values; human experience does not yield universe insight. Concerning insight, the recognition of moral values and the discernment of spiritual meanings, all that the human mind can do is to discover, recognize, interpret, and *choose.*

The moral values of the universe become intellectual possessions by the exercise of the three basic judgments, or choices, of the mortal mind:

1. Self-judgment—moral choice.

2. Social-judgment—ethical choice.

3. God-judgment—religious choice.

Thus it appears that all human progress is effected by a technique of conjoint *revelational evolution.*

Unless a divine lover lived in man, he could not unselfishly and spiritually love. Unless an interpreter lived in the mind, man could not truly realize the unity of the universe. Unless an evaluator dwelt with man, he could not possibly appraise moral values and recognize spiritual meanings. And this lover hails from the very source of infinite love; this interpreter is a part of Universal Unity; this evaluator is the child of the Center and Source of all absolute values of divine and eternal reality.

Moral evaluation with a religious meaning—spiritual insight—connotes the individual's choice between good and evil, truth and error, material and spiritual, human and divine, time and eternity. Human survival is in great measure dependent on consecrating the human will to the choosing of those values selected by this spirit-value sorter—the indwelling interpreter and unifier. Personal religious experience consists in two phases: discovery in the human mind and revelation by the indwelling divine spirit. Through oversophistication or as a result of the irreligious conduct of professed religionists, a man, or even a generation of men, may elect to suspend their efforts to discover the God who indwells them; they may fail to progress in and attain the divine revelation. But such attitudes of spiritual nonprogression cannot long persist because of the presence and influence of the indwelling Thought Adjusters.

This profound experience of the reality of the divine indwelling forever transcends the crude materialistic technique of the physical sciences. You cannot put spiritual joy under a microscope; you cannot weigh love in a balance; you cannot measure moral values; neither can you estimate the quality of spiritual worship.

The Hebrews had a religion of moral sublimity; the Greeks evolved a religion of beauty; Paul and his conferees founded a religion of faith, hope, and charity. Jesus revealed and exemplified a religion of love: security in the Father's love, with joy and satisfaction consequent upon sharing this love in the service of the human brotherhood.

Every time man makes a reflective moral choice, he immediately experiences a new divine invasion of his soul. Moral choosing constitutes religion as the motive of inner response to outer conditions. But such a real religion is not a purely subjective experience. It signifies the whole of the subjectivity of the individual engaged in a meaningful and intelligent response to total objectivity—the universe and its Maker.

The exquisite and transcendent experience of loving and being loved is not just a psychic illusion because it is so purely subjective. The one truly divine and objective reality that is associated with mortal beings, the Thought Adjuster, functions to human observation apparently as an exclusively subjective phenomenon. Man's contact with the highest objective reality, God, is only through the purely subjective experience of knowing him, of worshiping him, of realizing sonship with him.

True religious worship is not a futile monologue of self-deception. Worship is a personal communion with that which is divinely real, with that which is the very source of reality. Man aspires by worship to be better and thereby eventually attains the *best.*

The idealization and attempted service of truth, beauty, and goodness is not a substitute for genuine religious experience—spiritual reality. Psychology and idealism are not the equivalent of religious reality. The projections of the human intellect may indeed originate false gods—gods in man's image—but the true God-consciousness does not have such an origin. The God-consciousness is resident in the indwelling spirit. Many of the religious systems of man come from the formulations of the human intellect, but the God-consciousness is not necessarily a part of these grotesque systems of religious slavery.

God is not the mere invention of man's idealism; he is the very source of all such superanimal insights and values. God is not a hypothesis formulated to unify the human concepts of truth, beauty, and goodness; he is the personality of love from whom all of these universe manifestations are derived. The truth, beauty, and goodness of man's world are unified by the increasing spirituality of the experience of mortals ascending toward Paradise realities. The unity of truth, beauty, and goodness can only be realized in the spiritual experience of the God-knowing personality.

Morality is the essential pre-existent soil of personal God-consciousness, the personal realization of the Adjuster's inner presence, but such morality is not the source of religious experience and the resultant spiritual insight. The moral nature is superanimal but subspiritual. Morality is equivalent to the recognition of duty, the realization of the existence of right and wrong. The moral zone intervenes between the animal and the human types of mind as morontia functions between the material and the spiritual spheres of personality attainment.

The evolutionary mind is able to discover law, morals, and ethics; but the bestowed spirit, the indwelling Adjuster, reveals to the evolving human mind the lawgiver, the Father-source of all that is true, beautiful, and good; and such an illuminated man has a religion and is spiritually equipped to begin the long and adventurous search for God.

Morality is not necessarily spiritual; it may be wholly and purely human, albeit real religion enhances all moral values, makes them more meaningful. Morality without religion fails to reveal ultimate goodness, and it also fails to provide for the survival of even its own moral values. Religion provides for the enhancement, glorification, and assured survival of everything morality recognizes and approves.

Religion stands above science, art, philosophy, ethics, and morals, but not independent of them. They are all indissolubly interrelated in human experience, personal and social. Religion is man's supreme experience in the mortal nature, but finite language makes it forever impossible for theology ever adequately to depict real religious experience.

Religious insight possesses the power of turning defeat into higher desires and new determinations. Love is the highest motivation which man may utilize in his universe ascent. But love, divested of truth, beauty, and goodness, is only a sentiment, a philosophic distortion, a psychic illusion, a spiritual deception. Love must always be redefined on successive levels of morontia and spirit progression.

Art results from man's attempt to escape from the lack of beauty in his material environment; it is a gesture toward the morontia level. Science is man's effort to solve the apparent riddles of the material universe. Philosophy is man's attempt at the unification of human experience. Religion is man's supreme gesture, his magnificent reach for final reality, his determination to find God and to be like him.

In the realm of religious experience, spiritual possibility is potential reality. Man's forward spiritual urge is not a psychic illusion. All of man's universe romancing may not be fact, but much, very much, is truth.

Some men's lives are too great and noble to descend to the low level of being merely successful. The animal must adapt itself to the environment, but the religious man transcends his environment and in this way escapes the limitations of the present material world through this insight of divine love. This concept of love generates in the soul of man that superanimal effort to find truth, beauty, and goodness; and when he does find them, he is glorified in their embrace; he is consumed with the desire to live them, to do righteousness.

Be not discouraged; human evolution is still in progress, and the revelation of God to the world, in and through Jesus, shall not fail.

The great challenge to modern man is to achieve better communication with the divine Monitor that dwells within the human mind. Man's greatest adventure in the flesh consists in the well-balanced and sane effort to advance the borders of self-consciousness out through the dim realms of embryonic soul-consciousness in a wholehearted effort to reach the borderland of spirit-consciousness—contact with the divine presence. Such an experience constitutes God-consciousness, an experience mightily confirmative of the pre-existent truth of the religious experience of knowing God. Such spirit-consciousness is the equivalent of the knowledge of the actuality of sonship with God. Otherwise, the assurance of sonship is the experience of faith.

And God-consciousness is equivalent to the integration of the self with the universe, and on its highest levels of spiritual reality. Only the spirit content of any value is imperishable. Even that which is true, beautiful, and good may not perish in human experience. If man does not choose to survive, then does the surviving Adjuster conserve those realities born of love and nurtured in service. And all these things are a part of the Universal Father. The Father is living love, and this life of the Father is in his Sons. And the spirit of the Father is in his Sons' sons—mortal men. When all is said and done, the Father idea is still the highest human concept of God.